UNIVERSITY CASEBOOK SERIES®

STATUTORY INTERPRETATION

SECOND EDITION

CALEB NELSON
Emerson G. Spies Distinguished Professor of Law
and Edward F. Howrey Professor of Law
University of Virginia School of Law

860 Blue Gentian Road, Suite 350
Eagan, MN 55121
1-877-888-1330

Published in the United States of America

ISBN: 978-1-68561-283-2

For my parents, Mary and David Nelson—
my first, best, and much-loved teachers

For my parents, Mary and David Nelson—
my first, best, and most-loved teachers

AUTHOR'S NOTE FOR THE FIRST EDITION

This book grows out of lecture notes and materials that I have assembled over the years for the course on statutory interpretation that I teach at the University of Virginia School of Law. When I first started teaching that course, I used the pathbreaking casebook by Professors William N. Eskridge, Jr., and Philip P. Frickey (and, later, Elizabeth Garrett). I have also taught the course from the foundational materials prepared in the 1950s by Henry M. Hart, Jr., and Albert M. Sacks, which Professors Eskridge and Frickey generously shepherded into print in 1994. The imprint of both those books is stamped on this one.

Of course, *all* current casebooks in this field owe a great debt both to Professors Hart and Sacks (whose materials provided a lasting structure for academic inquiry into the interpretation and application of statutes) and to Professors Eskridge and Frickey (whose casebook revived a largely moribund field and showed the richness and subtlety of the issues that statutory interpretation raises). But my debt is larger than most. For one thing, some of the materials in this book began as companions to or commentary upon either Eskridge, Frickey, and Garrett or Hart and Sacks. More generally, those books set the mold for my conception of a course on statutory interpretation. While I have tried to cite and credit both books throughout these materials, I am sure that they have informed and influenced my thinking in ways that I cannot adequately acknowledge.

I am also indebted to the academic culture of the University of Virginia School of Law, which is nurtured by the entire faculty and student body. John Harrison deserves special thanks for his patience in educating me for the last twelve years. Fred Schauer generously volunteered to read the manuscript and offered helpful comments. Other colleagues—including Ann Woolhandler, Michael Collins, Barry Cushman, Rachel Harmon, Paul Mahoney, and George Rutherglen—have shared both their friendship and their expertise on various questions that crop up in this book. Reference librarians Xinh Luu, Amy Wharton, and Alison White cheerfully helped track down details about *Riggs v. Palmer*. In addition, many talented and engaged students over the years contributed ideas that have corrected and shaped both this book's analysis and its presentation.

Some passages in [what is now Chapter 6.B] reflect correspondence with Judge Stephen F. Williams (without whom I would not be a law professor at all). Of course, neither he nor any of the people mentioned in the previous paragraph should be blamed for the views that I express or for the mistakes that I have undoubtedly made.

As with all writing projects that I undertake, this one has generated its share of mood swings. I am grateful to Liz (my wife of nearly twenty years) and Max and Katy (our two wonderful children) for putting up with them, and with me.

My father died just as this book was going to press. He was a man of unfailing grace and wisdom, and I wish that I could offer him a better memorial than the pages that follow.

Charlottesville, Virginia
October 2010

EDITING CONVENTIONS AND DISCLAIMERS

In presenting excerpts from cases in this book, I have omitted many of the courts' footnotes and some citations, without indicating each omission. I have also changed the formatting of some citations, again without indicating the changes.

Nothing in this book constitutes legal or other professional advice. If you have legal questions or require legal advice, do not rely on this book; instead, seek the services of a competent attorney.

SUMMARY OF CONTENTS

TABLE OF CONTENTS

TABLE OF CASES

The principal cases are in bold type.

TABLE OF AUTHORITIES

Protections, 80 Brooklyn L. Rev. 1309 (2015), 762
Stewart, Constitutionality of the Legislative Veto, 13 Harv. J. Legis. 593 (1976), 416
Stewart, Reformation of American Administrative Law, 88 Harv. L. Rev. 1667 (1975), 414
Stone, Katherine Van Wezel, Rustic Justice: Community and Coercion Under the Federal Arbitration Act, 77 N.C. L. Rev. 931 (1999), 764
Story, Joseph, Commentaries on the Conflict of Laws 19 (1834), 233
Strauss, Peter L., One Hundred Fifty Cases Per Year: Some Implications of the Supreme Court's Limited Resources for Judicial Review of Agency Action, 87 Colum. L. Rev. 1093 (1987), 877
Strauss, Peter L., When the Judge Is Not the Primary Official with Responsibility to Read: Agency Interpretation and the Problem of Legislative History, 66 Chi.-Kent L. Rev. 321 (1990), 874, 986
Sullivan, John V., How Our Laws Are Made, H.R. Doc. No. 110–49 (2007), 349, 404
Sullivan, Kathleen M., The Supreme Court, 1991 Term—Foreword: The Justices of Rules and Standards, 106 Harv. L. Rev. 22 (1992), 92, 318
Summers, "Good Faith" in General Contract Law and the Sales Provisions of the Uniform Commercial Code, 54 Va. L. Rev. 195 (1968), 1112
Sumner, Charles, Opinion in the Case of the Impeachment of Andrew Johnson (1868), in 12 The Works of Charles Sumner 318, 361 (1877), 352
Sunstein & Vermeule, The Unbearable Rightness of Auer, 84 U. Chi. L. Rev. 297 (2017), 1012
Sunstein, Cass R. & Adrian Vermeule, Interpretation and Institutions, 101 Mich. L. Rev. 885 (2003), 935
Sunstein, Cass R., Chevron Step Zero, 92 Va. L. Rev. 187 (2006), 869, 893, 972
Sunstein, Cass R., Interpreting Statutes in the Regulatory State, 103 Harv. L. Rev. 405 (1989), 108, 211, 872
Sunstein, Cass R., Law and Administration After Chevron, 90 Colum. L. Rev. 2071 (1990), 937, 971
Sunstein, Cass R., Nondelegation Canons, 67 U. Chi. L. Rev. 315 (2000), 164, 892
Sunstein, Cass R., Problems with Rules, 83 Cal. L. Rev. 953 (1995), 92
Sunstein, Cass R., There Are Two "Major Questions" Doctrines, 73 Admin. L. Rev. 475 (2021), 892
Sutherland, J., Statutes and Statutory Construction (4th ed. C. Sands 1972), 724
Sutherland, J., Statutory Construction (3d ed. 1943), 1289, 1294
Sutherland, J.G. & John Lewis, Statutes and Statutory Construction (2d ed. 1904), 355, 1303, 1306
Sykes, The Economics of Vicarious Liability, 93 Yale L.J. 1231 (1984), 1216
Symeonides, Symeon C., Choice of Law 123 (2016), 236
Symposium, The Case of the Speluncean Explorers: Revisited, 112 Harv. L. Rev. 1876 (1999), 85
Taft, W., The Presidency: Its Duties, Its Powers, Its Opportunities and Its Limitations 11 (1916), 818
Thumma, Samuel A. & Jeffrey L. Kirchmeier, The Lexicon Has Become a Fortress: The United States Supreme Court's Use of Dictionaries, 47 Buff. L. Rev. 227 (1999), 112
Tiefer, Charles, The Reconceptualization of Legislative History in the Supreme Court, 2000 Wisc. L. Rev. 205, 446
Tribe, L., American Constitutional Law 480 (2d ed. 1988), 1069
Tribe, Laurence H., American Constitutional Law (3d ed. 2000), 780, 944
Vaas, Title VII: Legislative History, 7 B.C. Ind. & Com. L. Rev. 431 (1966), 378
Verdier, Pierre-Hugues, The New Financial Extraterritoriality, 87 Geo. Wash. L. Rev. 239 (2019), 271
Vermeule, Adrian, Interpretation, Empiricism, and the Closure Problem, 66 U. Chi. L. Rev. 698 (1999), 359
Vermeule, Adrian, Judging Under Uncertainty: An Institutional Theory of Legal Interpretation (2006), 456, 468, 875, 940, 986
Vermeule, Adrian, Legislative History and the Limits of Judicial Competence: The Untold Story of

UNIVERSITY CASEBOOK SERIES®

STATUTORY INTERPRETATION

SECOND EDITION

CHAPTER 1

AN INTRODUCTION TO THE INTERPLAY BETWEEN PURPOSE AND TEXT

Techniques of statutory interpretation are partly about how language works and partly about how law and government work. Those topics are each extraordinarily complex in their own right, and their interaction has occupied thinkers since at least the time of Aristotle.

To say that people have spent millennia thinking about the interpretation of written laws is not to say that they have sorted everything out. In present-day America, there is considerable common ground among different schools of statutory interpretation. But there are also some sharp disagreements, including disagreements about the goals that interpretive techniques should be designed to achieve and the methods that are most likely to promote those goals.

To get you thinking about some of the central issues, this chapter begins with a brief note about the criteria by which interpretive principles might be evaluated. It then presents a few canonical cases raising themes that will run throughout this course.

PRELIMINARY NOTE ON THE GOALS OF STATUTORY INTERPRETATION (WITH PARTICULAR ATTENTION TO THE RELATION BETWEEN MEANING AND LEGISLATIVE INTENT)

Imagine, for a moment, that the principles of statutory interpretation were comprehensive and uncontroversial, and that they could be applied without substantial disagreement. We could then confidently speak of the "meaning" of statutory language as emerging from the application of those settled principles to the data that the principles make relevant (including the statutory text and whatever other information interpreters are supposed to consult).

In fact, of course, the principles of statutory interpretation are not quite so well settled and easily applicable. What is more, their details have changed in some respects over time. To the extent that legislators draft and enact statutes against the backdrop of the interpretive practices in vogue at the time of enactment, it is possible that present-day interpreters should take a different approach to old statutes than they take to more recent statutes. It is also possible that what we think of as interpretation entails some judgment calls that are made by the interpreters themselves and that are not dictated by pre-existing principles. But subject to qualifications and complications, it is still useful to think of a statute's "meaning" as the output that interpreters should get when they apply the appropriate interpretive principles to the statutory text and the other information that the principles tell them to take into account. *Cf.* Nicholas Quinn Rosenkranz, *Federal Rules of Statutory Interpretation*, 115 HARV. L. REV. 2085, 2142 (2002) ("[M]eaning derives from the interaction of a text and an interpretive regime.").

This way of thinking about statutory meaning highlights two important facts. First, statutes are not entirely self-contained; the meaning that interpreters should attribute to a statute depends not simply on the statute's own words but also on the applicable principles of interpretation (and, perhaps, on other sources of information that those principles make relevant). Second, statutes can have meanings that members of the enacting legislature did not fully appreciate. Indeed, even if legislators were to enact a statute without reading it, and without forming any impression of its contents at all, the statute would still have meaning.

To be sure, responsible legislators and their staffs do not behave that way. If legislators do not personally read every line of every bill on which they vote, they at least rely on the representations of people who are familiar with the bill's terms (and who are also familiar with the general principles that legal interpreters use to determine the meaning of such terms). When a legislature enacts a statute, then, its members typically cast their votes with some understanding of the legal directives that the statute establishes. Where legislators have indeed formed such understandings, moreover, it is possible that courts and administrative agencies should take those understandings into account when interpreting the resulting statute. As we shall see in Chapter 3, for instance, many modern lawyers and judges maintain that if the publicly available "legislative history" of a statute sheds light on what members of the enacting legislature understood the statute to mean, that information can affect what the statute *does* mean. On this view, the principles of interpretation that help determine the "meaning" of a statute instruct interpreters to consider committee reports, transcripts of floor debates, and other publicly available information about the internal legislative process that might reveal the understandings upon which members of the enacting legislature acted.

Still, no one thinks that the principles of statutory interpretation should be geared *entirely* toward capturing the subjective understandings of members of the enacting legislature. Whatever weight one puts on that goal, everyone agrees that other goals also matter. For instance, the interpretive principles that courts and administrative agencies use to ascribe meaning to statutes reflect the need for people in the private sector to have fair notice of the law's content. Statutes are not secret messages from one branch of government to another; they have important consequences for many people outside the legislatures that enact them, and those people (or the lawyers who advise them) need some way of predicting what the statutes will be understood to mean. As a general rule, then, courts and administrative agencies shy away from interpretive techniques that would require reference to after-the-fact testimony or documents that are not publicly available—even if those techniques might help interpreters figure out what members of the enacting legislature really intended. By the same token, courts and administrative agencies also resist interpretive methods that would be too expensive or time-consuming to apply. Even if a particular technique would marginally advance one of the other goals of statutory interpretation, the resulting benefits might not be sufficient to justify the resources that application of the technique requires. To the extent that the principles of statutory interpretation are designed to keep the costs of litigation and decision within reasonable bounds, they can again lead to gaps between statutory meaning and legislative intent.

For these and other reasons,[1] everyone acknowledges that even when members of the enacting legislature had some collective understanding of the bill that they were enacting, the "meaning" generated by proper application of the principles of statutory interpretation may differ from that understanding. But one should not leap to the conclusion that the interpretive principles used to generate "meaning" have no relationship to "legislative intent" at all. Just as the principles of statutory interpretation that courts and administrative agencies apply should be designed to help the citizenry have fair notice of the law's content and to keep the process of interpretation from being

---

[1] As we shall see later in this book, some of the reasons for the gap between "meaning" and "intent" are less about the competing goals of statutory interpretation than about the practical methods by which an interpreter interested in unearthing intent might proceed. Even insofar as the principles of interpretation are designed to produce the maximum possible overlap between the meaning that interpreters ascribe to statutory language and the meaning that members of the enacting legislature intended to convey, perfection is too much to expect. With respect to certain issues, moreover, the best way for interpreters to identify the likely intended meaning of statutory language might be to follow blanket rules that are designed to play the odds but that will produce mismatches between "meaning" and "intent" in some fraction of cases.

For an example that is artificial in various ways but that illustrates the point, suppose we could somehow know the following empirical facts: (1) in 95% of the statutes that use a certain word in a certain context, members of the enacting legislature collectively intended to use that word in its most common sense; (2) in the remaining 5% of the relevant statutes, members of the enacting legislature were using the word more idiosyncratically; (3) courts cannot reliably tell which statutes are which; and (4) courts tend to err on the side of diagnosing idiosyncratic usages. Under these circumstances, if we wanted to maximize the overlap between the meaning that courts ascribe to statutes and the meaning that members of the enacting legislature intended to convey, we might well instruct courts simply to assume, whenever they encounter the word in this context, that members of the enacting legislature were using the word in its most common sense. *Cf.* Frederick Schauer, *The Practice and Problems of Plain Meaning: A Response to Aleinikoff and Shaw*, 45 VAND. L. REV. 715, 729–30 (1992) (discussing the conditions under which we might want to give courts this sort of instruction). For one in every twenty statutes, though, the "meaning" that results from the application of this interpretive principle will diverge from the meaning that members of the enacting legislature actually intended to convey—even though the applicable principle of interpretation was designed entirely for the purpose of minimizing such gaps, and even though the courts are applying that principle exactly as they are supposed to.

too costly, it is entirely possible that they should also be designed to effectuate legislative intent (subject to the constraints imposed by the other goals of interpretation).

One way of putting this point is that gaps between the meaning that courts ascribe to a statute and the meaning that members of the enacting legislature intended to convey are necessary evils—things to be tolerated but not celebrated. In a system of government that allocates primary policymaking authority to legislatures, it is surely desirable for the legal directives that interpreters ascribe to statutes to correlate in some way with the legal directives that members of the enacting legislatures understood themselves to be establishing. At the very least, the interpretive principles that courts and administrative agencies use to ascribe meaning to statutes should not make it unnecessarily difficult for the legislature to enact statutes that really do mean something along the lines of what legislators understood them to mean. If our chosen methods of statutory interpretation consistently produced big gaps between the meaning that interpreters ascribe to statutes and the meaning that legislators intended to convey, and if some alternative set of interpretive principles would reliably produce smaller gaps without sacrificing any of the other important goals of statutory interpretation (such as ensuring adequate notice and avoiding excessive decision costs), we probably would want to rethink our chosen methods. Thus, one of the criteria by which many people evaluate proposed techniques of statutory interpretation is whether, across the universe of cases, use of the techniques will help avoid mismatches between the *intended* meaning and the *interpreted* meaning of statutory language.

This line of thought invites a variety of questions that we are not yet ready to discuss in detail, but that you should begin to consider. Is it even coherent to refer to the meaning that a collective entity like a legislature "intended" a statute to have? To impute intentions to the legislature as a whole, we presumably have to come up with some way of aggregating the intentions of individual legislators (and perhaps other people who are involved in the legislative process). But those intentions are sure to be incomplete, and they may also conflict with each other in various ways. Given that fact, can the notion of collective intent be robust enough to be of any practical use in statutory interpretation? If we do embrace a robust notion of collective intent, should the interpretive techniques that are influenced by that notion operate entirely through rule-like canons and presumptions, or should we ask interpreters to gather particularized information about legislative intent on a case-by-case basis? If the latter, what sources of information should courts or administrative agencies consider, and what sources should be off limits to them? To the extent that interpreters are supposed to investigate the mindsets of particular individuals involved in the legislative process, what aspects of legislative procedure should affect how interpreters combine those potentially conflicting mindsets into intentions that can plausibly be imputed to the legislature as a whole? For that matter, what *kinds* of intentions should factor into the "meaning" of a statutory directive? Are intentions relevant only to the extent that they bear on how the legislature collectively intended to use particular words, or can the enacting legislature's collective expectations about the consequences that a particular directive would produce ever affect how interpreters should understand the directive itself? Do intentions have to be conscious in at least one person's mind to count, or should interpreters ever try to imagine what members of the enacting legislature *would have* thought about issues that they did not consciously consider? What role should background principles gleaned from other aspects of law, or from our legal traditions in general, play in the construction of intentions that can properly be imputed to the legislature?

To introduce some of these questions (and to show their longevity), we will begin with the classic case of *Riggs v. Palmer*, decided by New York's highest court in 1889. Over the years, the majority opinion in *Riggs* has been alternately attacked and praised by an extraordinary number of high-powered scholars and judges, including Roscoe Pound, Benjamin Cardozo, Ronald Dworkin, Richard Posner, and Frank Easterbrook. Its prominence stems in part from the hugely influential teaching materials that Henry Hart and Albert Sacks used at Harvard Law School in the 1950s, which spread in mimeographed form to law schools around the country and which used the majority opinion in *Riggs* as an introductory problem.[2] But Cardozo described it as a "famous case" long before then. BENJAMIN N. CARDOZO, THE NATURE OF THE JUDICIAL PROCESS 40 (1921).

The facts of the case are relatively simple. On August 13, 1880, Francis B. Palmer of New York made his last will and testament. After giving small legacies to his two daughters (Cecilia and Lorette), the will specified that the remainder of his estate should go to his grandson Elmer (the child of Francis's deceased son Byron). At the time, Elmer was 15 years old and was living with his mother (Byron's widow) on Francis's farm. Aside from a provision for the support of Elmer's mother (who died in 1881 and thus turned out not to need support), the only relevant condition stated by the will was that if Elmer survived Francis but subsequently died without wife or children of his own before coming of age, then the property that had gone to him would pass to Francis's daughters.

---

[2] In 1994, Professors William Eskridge and Philip Frickey performed the enormous public service of shepherding into print the 1958 edition of Hart and Sacks's teaching materials. *See* HENRY M. HART, JR. & ALBERT M. SACKS, THE LEGAL PROCESS: BASIC PROBLEMS IN THE MAKING AND APPLICATION OF LAW (tent. ed. 1958) (William N. Eskridge, Jr. & Philip P. Frickey eds. 1994). The case study that Hart and Sacks built around *Riggs v. Palmer* is "Problem No. 2" in these materials. *See id.* at 68–102.

On April 25, 1882, Francis suddenly died. A few weeks later, the state indicted Elmer for murder. According to newspaper accounts, evidence at trial indicated that in the period leading up to his death, Francis had been displeased with Elmer's conduct and had threatened "that unless [Elmer] did better, [Francis] would make a new will and would not leave him a cent." *The Palmer Will Case*, COURIER & FREEMAN, July 22, 1885, p. 5. To prevent his grandfather from making good on this threat, Elmer apparently had poisoned Francis.

In the fall of 1882, Elmer was convicted of second-degree murder and was sentenced to the state reformatory. Soon thereafter, Francis's will was admitted to probate. Francis's daughters then raised the question of what should happen to Francis's property. Eventually, they filed suit against Elmer and the administrator of Francis's estate (among others), arguing that Elmer "is estopped from claiming benefits from a death which he himself murderously caused" and "cannot take [Francis's property] under the will." *Shall a Man Who Murdered for Money Be Estopped from Enjoying It?*, N.Y. TIMES, Aug. 4, 1885, p. 3. Their position implicated two separate sets of provisions in the Revised Statutes of the State of New York.[3]

The first set of provisions addressed wills. The relevant title of New York's Revised Statutes allowed all competent adults to make written wills that would control the distribution of both their real estate and their personal property after death. *See* N.Y. Rev. Stat. pt. 2, ch. 6, tit. 1, art. 1, § 1, *in* 3 N.Y. Rev. Stat. 2283 (7th ed. 1882) ("All persons, except idiots, persons of unsound mind and infants, may devise their real estate, by a last will and testament, duly executed according to the provisions of this title."); *id.* art. 2, § 21, *in* 3 N.Y. Rev. Stat. 2285 (7th ed. 1882) ("Every male person of the age of eighteen years or upwards, and every female of the age of sixteen years or upwards, of sound mind and memory, and no others, may give and bequeath his or her personal estate, by will in

[3] The Revised Statutes of New York were a landmark in American legal history. In 1825, the state legislature had appointed three lawyers to collect the various statutes that were then in force in New York and that were "general and permanent in their nature," to work on revising and consolidating them, and to propose a more organized version that the legislature could then enact if it chose. *See* An Act for Revising and Publishing the Laws of this State, ch. 324, 1825 N.Y. Laws 446; *see also* CHARLES M. COOK, THE AMERICAN CODIFICATION MOVEMENT: A STUDY OF ANTEBELLUM LEGAL REFORM 141–42 (1981) (noting that the revisors' mandate to take "the whole body of New York statute law, which had been a century and a half in the making," and to rework it into a more coherent and systematic code, "was totally without precedent in Anglo-American legal history"). This project became the Revised Statutes, which the state legislature enacted in chunks in 1827 and 1828. As amended over the years, it was still in force at the time of *Riggs v. Palmer*.

The success of New York's project helped lead to similar efforts in some other states. *See id.* at 167. Indeed, Congress itself eventually authorized a similar effort with respect to federal statutes. *See* Act of June 27, 1866, ch. 140, 14 Stat. 74 (authorizing the appointment of three commissioners "to revise, simplify, arrange, and consolidate all statutes of the United States, general and permanent in their nature," and to submit their arrangement to Congress for possible enactment); Act of Mar. 3, 1873, ch. 241, 17 Stat. 579 (authorizing further work on this project). That effort produced the *Revised Statutes of the United States*, a mammoth federal statute that Congress enacted on June 22, 1874. *See* 18 Stat. 1–1092 (1874). Portions of the *Revised Statutes of the United States* remain in effect to this day.

writing."). To make a valid will, people had to observe some formalities; for instance, the testator had to sign the will at the end, and there also had to be at least two attesting witnesses. *See* N.Y. Rev. Stat. pt. 2, ch. 6, tit. 1, art. 3, § 40, *in* 3 N.Y. Rev. Stat. 2285 (7th ed. 1882). Likewise, once a will had been made, the testator had to go through some formalities to revoke or alter it. Section 42 of the relevant title of New York's Revised Statutes read as follows:

> "No will in writing, except in the cases hereinafter mentioned, nor any part thereof, shall be revoked, or altered, otherwise than by some other will in writing, or some other writing of the testator, declaring such revocation or alteration and executed with the same formalities with which the will itself was required by law to be executed; or unless such will be burnt, torn, cancelled, obliterated or destroyed, with the intent and for the purpose of revoking the same, by the testator himself, or by another person in his presence, by his direction and consent; and when so done by another person, the direction and consent of the testator, and the fact of such injury or destruction, shall be proved by at least two witnesses."

N.Y. Rev. Stat. pt. 2, ch. 6, tit. 1, art. 3, § 42, *in* 3 N.Y. Rev. Stat. 2286 (7th ed. 1882).

Sections 43 through 53 of the same title set out a few exceptions to section 42—a few situations in which a will would be deemed to be revoked or altered by operation of law, without the testator having gone through any formalities to change it.[4] Those situations were what section 42 called "the cases hereinafter mentioned." Sections 43 through 53, however, did not address cases in which one of the beneficiaries named in a will murdered the testator. By its terms, moreover, section 42 seemed to say that the cases mentioned in sections 43 through 53 were the *only* situations in which wills would be deemed to be revoked or altered by operation of law, without the testators themselves having gone through the formal requirements for revocation or alteration.

Apart from the provisions about wills, the Revised Statutes also included provisions about the descent of property belonging to people who die intestate or whose wills cover only part of their estates. In general, New York law provided that "the real estate of every person, who shall

---

[4] *See, e.g.*, N.Y. Rev. Stat. pt. 2, ch. 6, tit. 1, art. 3, § 43, *in* 3 N.Y. Rev. Stat. 2286 (7th ed. 1882) (providing that a will "shall be deemed revoked" in certain cases where, after making it, the testator "shall marry, and have issue of such marriage, born either in his life-time or after his death, and the wife or the issue of such marriage shall be living at the death of the testator"); *id.* § 44, *in* 3 N.Y. Rev. Stat. 2286 (7th ed. 1882) ("A will executed by an unmarried woman, shall be deemed revoked by her subsequent marriage."); *id.* § 49, *in* 3 N.Y. Rev. Stat. 2287 (7th ed. 1882) ("Whenever a testator shall have a child born after the making of a last will, either in the life-time or after the death of such testator, and shall die leaving such child, so after born, unprovided for by any settlement, and neither provided for, nor in any way mentioned in such will, every such child shall succeed to the same portion of such parent's real and personal estate as would have descended or been distributed to such child, if such parent had died intestate, and shall be entitled to recover the same portion from the devisees and legatees, in proportion to and out of the parts devised and bequeathed to them by such will.").

die without devising the same, shall descend . . . [t]o his lineal descendants" if they were alive at the time of his death. N.Y. Rev. Stat. pt. 2, ch. 2, § 1, *in* 3 N.Y. Rev. Stat. 2210 (7th ed. 1882). The statutes went on to provide the following details:

- "If the intestate shall leave several descendants in the direct line of lineal descent, and all of equal degree of consanguinity to such intestate, the inheritance shall descend to such persons in equal parts . . . ." *Id.* § 2, *in* 3 N.Y. Rev. Stat. 2210 (7th ed. 1882).
- "If any of the children of such intestate be living, and any be dead, the inheritance shall descend to the children who are living, and to the descendants of such children as shall have died; so that each child who shall be living, shall inherit such share as would have descended to him, if all the children of the intestate who shall have died leaving issue, had been living; and so that the descendants of each child who shall be dead, shall inherit the share, which their parent would have received if living." *Id.* § 3, *in* 3 N.Y. Rev. Stat. 2210–11 (7th ed. 1882).

The Revised Statutes made somewhat similar provisions for the descent of personal property not bequeathed by will. *See* N.Y. Rev. Stat. pt. 2, ch. 6, tit. 1, art. 3, § 75, *in* 3 N.Y. Rev. Stat. 2303–05 (7th ed. 1882).

Both the statutes about wills and the statutes about intestate succession posed challenges for Francis's daughters. Unless a court was willing to engage in creative reading of Francis's will itself, the will seemed to make Elmer the principal beneficiary of Francis's estate. And while Francis, in the waning moments of his life, may perhaps have formed a definite intention to revoke or alter that provision, he had not gone through the statutorily required formalities for doing so. The statutes about wills might therefore seem to require a court to give effect to the provision in the will conveying Francis's property to Elmer. Even if a court were willing to disregard that aspect of the will, moreover, Elmer might still be entitled to claim a one-third share of Francis's estate under the statutes about intestate succession.

At the trial level, the suit that Francis's daughters brought against Elmer was heard by a referee. Based on the evidence, the referee found that Elmer had poisoned Francis for the purpose of coming into immediate possession of Francis's estate, and that "Francis . . . presumably would have altered his will . . . had he known or suspected Elmer's murderous intent." As a matter of law, however, the referee concluded that New York's statutes about wills made no exception for cases of this sort—with the result that "Elmer E. Palmer, though having wickedly and maliciously compassed the death of the testator, is still entitled under the statutes of this State to take under [Francis's] will and enjoy the fruits of his crime." Judgment accordingly was entered in Elmer's favor, and a three-judge panel affirmed that judgment. On appeal, though, New York's highest court reversed, issuing the opinions that follow.

Riggs v. Palmer

22 N.E. 188 (N.Y. 1889)

■ *JUDGE EARL delivered the opinion of the Court:*

. . . . The defendants say that the testator is dead; that his will was made in due form, and has been admitted to probate; and that therefore it must have effect according to the letter of the law. It is quite true that statutes regulating the making, proof, and effect of wills and the devolution of property, if literally construed, and if their force and effect can in no way and under no circumstances be controlled or modified, give this property to the murderer.

The purpose of those statutes was to enable testators to dispose of their estates to the objects of their bounty at death, and to carry into effect their final wishes legally expressed; and in considering and giving effect to them this purpose must be kept in view. It was the intention of the law-makers that the donees in a will should have the property given to them. But it never could have been their intention that a donee who murdered the testator to make the will operative should have any benefit under it. If such a case had been present to their minds, and it had been supposed necessary to make some provision of law to meet it, it cannot be doubted that they would have provided for it. It is a familiar canon of construction that a thing which is within the intention of the makers of a statute is as much within the statute as if it were within the letter; and a thing which is within the letter of the statute is not within the statute unless it be within the intention of the makers. The writers of laws do not always express their intention perfectly, but either exceed it or fall short of it, so that judges are to collect it from probable or rational conjectures only, and this is called "rational interpretation"; and Rutherford, in his *Institutes,* says: "Where we make use of rational interpretation, sometimes we restrain the meaning of the writer so as to take in less, and sometimes we extend or enlarge his meaning so as to take in more, than his words express."

Such a construction ought to be put upon a statute as will best answer the intention which the makers had in view, for *qui haeret in litera, haeret in cortice* ["he who considers merely the letter of an instrument goes but skin deep into its meaning"—*Black's Law Dictionary*]. In *Bacon's Abridgment* [and other sources] . . . many cases are mentioned where it was held that matters embraced in the general words of statutes nevertheless were not within the statutes, because it could not have been the intention of the law-makers that they should be included. They were taken out of the statutes by an equitable construction; and it is said in Bacon:

> "By an equitable construction a case not within the letter of a statute is sometimes holden to be within the meaning, because it is within the mischief for which a remedy is provided. The reason for such construction is that the law-makers could not set down every case in

> express terms. In order to form a right judgment whether a case be within the equity of a statute, it is a good way to suppose the law-maker present, and that you have asked him this question: Did you intend to comprehend this case? Then you must give yourself such answer as you imagine he, being an upright and reasonable man, would have given. If this be that he did mean to comprehend it, you may safely hold the case to be within the equity of the statute; for while you do no more than he would have done, you do not act contrary to the statute, but in conformity thereto."

9 Bac. Abr. 248. In some cases the letter of a legislative act is restrained by an equitable construction; in others, it is enlarged; in others, the construction is contrary to the letter. The equitable construction which restrains the letter of a statute is defined by Aristotle as frequently quoted in this manner: *Aequitas est correctio legis generaliter latae qua parte deficit* ["equity is the correction of that wherein the law, by reason of its generality, is deficient"—*Black's Law Dictionary*]. If the law-makers could, as to this case, be consulted, would they say that they intended by their general language that the property of a testator or of an ancestor should pass to one who had taken his life for the express purpose of getting his property? In 1 *Blackstone's Commentaries* 91, the learned author, speaking of the construction of statutes, says:

> "If there arise out of them collaterally any absurd consequences manifestly contradictory to common reason, they are with regard to those collateral consequences void. . . . Where some collateral matter arises out of the general words, and happens to be unreasonable, there the judges are in decency to conclude that this consequence was not foreseen by the parliament, and therefore they are at liberty to expound the statute by equity, and only *quoad hoc* disregard it";

and he gives as an illustration, if an act of parliament gives a man power to try all causes that arise within his manor of Dale, yet, if a cause should arise in which he himself is party, the act is construed not to extend to that, because it is unreasonable that any man should determine his own quarrel.

There was a statute in Bologna that whoever drew blood in the streets should be severely punished, and yet it was held not to apply to the case of a barber who opened a vein in the street.[*] It is commanded

[*] *Editor's note*: Judge Earl probably drew this illustration too from Blackstone, who in turn got it from Samuel Pufendorf's *De Jure Naturae et Gentium Libri Octo* (1688), which credited it to Nicolaus Everardi's *Loci Argumentorum Legales* (1567). But while this example is a classic in statutory-interpretation circles, Judge Earl's summary is apt to mislead students. The "barber" to whom Judge Earl referred would have been one of the "barber-surgeons" of Bologna, who were licensed to perform a variety of medical procedures. *See* GIANNA POMATA, CONTRACTING A CURE: PATIENTS, HEALERS, AND THE LAW IN EARLY MODERN BOLOGNA 64–65 (1998). In the case in question, a Bolognese tribunal apparently had to decide whether to punish a barber-surgeon who had "bled" a patient in the streets under exigent circumstances. *Cf.* 1 WILLIAM BLACKSTONE, COMMENTARIES ON THE LAWS OF ENGLAND 60 (1765) ("[T]he Bolognian law, mentioned by Puffendorf, which enacted 'that whoever drew blood in the streets should be

in the decalogue that no work shall be done upon the Sabbath, and yet giving the command a rational interpretation founded upon its design the Infallible Judge held that it did not prohibit works of necessity, charity, or benevolence on that day.

What could be more unreasonable than to suppose that it was the legislative intention in the general laws passed for the orderly, peaceable, and just devolution of property that they should have operation in favor of one who murdered his ancestor that he might speedily come into the possession of his estate? Such an intention is inconceivable. We need not, therefore, be much troubled by the general language contained in the laws.

Besides, all laws, as well as all contracts, may be controlled in their operation and effect by general, fundamental maxims of the common law. No one shall be permitted to profit by his own fraud, or to take advantage of his own wrong, or to found any claim upon his own iniquity, or to acquire property by his own crime. These maxims are dictated by public policy, have their foundation in universal law administered in all civilized countries, and have nowhere been superseded by statutes. They were applied in the decision of the case of [*New York Mutual Life Insurance Co. v. Armstrong*, 117 U. S. 591 (1886)]. There it was held that the person who procured a policy upon the life of another, payable at his death, and then murdered the assured to make the policy payable, could not recover thereon. Mr. Justice Field, writing the opinion, said: "[I]ndependently of any proof of the motives of Hunter in obtaining the policy, and even assuming that they were just and proper, he forfeited all rights under it when, to secure its immediate payment, he murdered the assured. It would be a reproach to the jurisprudence of the country, if one could recover insurance money payable on the death of a party whose life he had feloniously taken. As well might he recover insurance money upon a building that he had wilfully fired."

These maxims, without any statute giving them force or operation, frequently control the effect and nullify the language of wills. A will procured by fraud and deception, like any other instrument, may be decreed void, and set aside; and so a particular portion of a will may be excluded from probate, or held inoperative, if induced by the fraud or undue influence of the person in whose favor it is. *Allen v. McPherson*, 1 H. L. Cas. 191; *Harrison's Appeal*, 48 Conn. 202. So a will may contain provisions which are immoral, irreligious, or against public policy, and they will be held void.

Here there was no certainty that this murderer would survive the testator, or that the testator would not change his will, and there was no certainty that he would get this property if nature was allowed to take its course. He therefore murdered the testator expressly to vest himself

---

punished with the utmost severity,' was held after long debate not to extend to the surgeon, who opened the vein of a person that fell down in the street with a fit.").

with an estate. Under such circumstances, what law, human or divine, will allow him to take the estate and enjoy the fruits of his crime? The will spoke and became operative at the death of the testator. He caused that death, and thus by his crime made it speak and have operation. Shall it speak and operate in his favor? If he had met the testator, and taken his property by force, he would have had no title to it. Shall he acquire title by murdering him? If he had gone to the testator's house, and by force compelled him, or by fraud or undue influence had induced him, to will him his property, the law would not allow him to hold it. But can he give effect and operation to a will by murder, and yet take the property? To answer these questions in the affirmative it seems to me would be a reproach to the jurisprudence of our state, and an offense against public policy.

Under the civil law, evolved from the general principles of natural law and justice by many generations of jurisconsults, philosophers, and statesmen, one cannot take property by inheritance or will from an ancestor or benefactor whom he has murdered. Dom. Civil Law, pt. 2, bk. 1, tit. 1, § 3; Code Nap. § 727; Mack. Rom. Law, 530, 550. In the Civil Code of Lower Canada the provisions on the subject in the Code Napoleon have been substantially copied. But, so far as I can find, in no country where the common law prevails has it been deemed important to enact a law to provide for such a case. Our revisers and law-makers were familiar with the civil law, and they did not deem it important to incorporate into our statutes its provisions upon this subject. This is not a *casus omissus*. It was evidently supposed that the maxims of the common law were sufficient to regulate such a case, and that a specific enactment for that purpose was not needed.

For the same reasons the defendant Palmer cannot take any of this property as heir [under the statutory provisions dealing with intestate succession]. Just before the murder he was not an heir, and it was not certain that he ever would be. He might have died before his grandfather, or might have been disinherited by him. He made himself an heir by the murder, and he seeks to take property as the fruit of his crime. What has before been said as to him as legatee applies to him with equal force as an heir. He cannot vest himself with title by crime.

My view of this case does not inflict upon Elmer any greater or other punishment for his crime than the law specifies. It takes from him no property, but simply holds that he shall not acquire property by his crime, and thus be rewarded for its commission.

Our attention is called to *Owens v. Owens*, 100 N.C. 240 (1888), as a case quite like this. There a wife had been convicted of being an accessory before the fact to the murder of her husband, and it was held that she was nevertheless entitled to dower. I am unwilling to assent to the doctrine of that case. The statutes provide dower for a wife who has the misfortune to survive her husband, and thus lose his support and protection. It is clear beyond their purpose to make provision for a wife who by her own crime makes herself a widow, and willfully and intentionally deprives herself of the support and protection of her husband. As she might have died before him, and thus never have been his widow, she cannot by her crime vest herself with an estate. The principle which lies at the bottom of the maxim *volenti non fit injuria* [defeating recovery in tort for people who voluntarily assumed the risk that led to their losses] should be applied to such a case, and a widow should not, for the purpose of acquiring, as such, property rights, be permitted to allege a widowhood which she has wickedly and intentionally created.

.... The judgment ... should therefore be reversed, and judgment should be entered as follows: That Elmer E. Palmer and the administrator be enjoined from using any of the personalty or real estate left by the testator for Elmer's benefit; that the devise and bequest in the will to Elmer be declared ineffective to pass the title to him; that by reason of the crime of murder committed upon the grandfather he is deprived of any interest in the estate left by him; [and] that the plaintiffs are the true owners of the real and personal estate left by the testator ....

■ *JUDGE GRAY, joined by JUDGE DANFORTH, dissenting:*

... [I]f I believed that the decision of the question could be effected by considerations of an equitable nature, I should not hesitate to assent to views which commend themselves to the conscience. But the matter does not lie within the domain of conscience. We are bound by the rigid rules of law, which have been established by the legislature, and within the limits of which the determination of this question is confined. The question we are dealing with is whether a testamentary disposition can be altered, or a will revoked, after the testator's death, through an appeal to the courts, when the legislature has by its enactments prescribed exactly when and how wills may be made, altered, and revoked, and apparently, as it seems to me, when they have been fully complied with, has left no room for the exercise of an equitable jurisdiction by courts over such matters. Modern jurisprudence, in recognizing the right of the individual, under more or less restrictions, to dispose of his property after his death, subjects it to legislative control, both as to extent and as to mode of exercise. Complete freedom of testamentary disposition of one's property has not been and is not the universal rule, as we see from the provisions of the Napoleonic Code, from the systems of jurisprudence in countries which are modeled upon the Roman law, and from the statutes of many of our states. To the statutory restraints which are imposed upon the disposition of one's property by will are added strict and systematic statutory rules for the execution, alteration, and revocation of the will, which must be, at least substantially, if not exactly, followed to insure validity and performance. The reason for the establishment of such rules, we may naturally assume, consists in the purpose to create those safeguards about these grave and important acts which experience has demonstrated to be the wisest and surest. That freedom which is permitted to be exercised in the testamentary disposition of one's estate by the laws of the state is subject to its being exercised in conformity with the regulations of the statutes. The capacity and the power of the individual to dispose of his property after death, and the mode by which that power can be exercised, are matters of which the legislature has assumed the entire control, and has undertaken to regulate with comprehensive particularity.

The appellants' argument is not helped by reference to those rules of the civil law, or to those laws of other governments, by which the heir, or legatee, is excluded from benefit under the testament if he has been convicted of killing, or attempting to kill, the testator. In the absence of such legislation here, the courts are not empowered to institute such a system of remedial justice. The deprivation of the heir of his testamentary succession by the Roman law, when guilty of such a crime, plainly was intended to be in the nature of a punishment imposed upon him. The succession, in such a case of guilt, escheated to the exchequer. See Dom. Civil Law, pt. 2, bk. 1, tit. 1, § 3.

I concede that rules of law which annul testamentary provisions made for the benefit of those who have become unworthy of them may be based on principles of equity and of natural justice. It is quite reasonable to suppose that a testator would revoke or alter his will, where his mind has been so angered and changed as to make him unwilling to have his will executed as it stood. But these principles only suggest sufficient reasons for the enactment of laws to meet such cases.

The statutes of this state have prescribed various ways in which a will may be altered or revoked; but the very provision defining the modes of alteration and revocation implies a prohibition of alteration or revocation in any other way. The words of the section of the statute are: "No will in writing, except in the cases hereinafter mentioned, nor any part thereof, shall be revoked or altered otherwise," *etc.* Where, therefore, none of the cases mentioned are met by the facts, and the revocation is not in the way described in the section, the will of the testator is unalterable. I think that a valid will must continue as a will always, unless revoked in the manner provided by the statutes. Mere intention to revoke a will does not have the effect of revocation. The intention to revoke is necessary to constitute the effective revocation of a will, but it must be demonstrated by one of the acts contemplated by the statute. . . .

The finding of fact of the referee that presumably the testator would have altered his will had he known of his grantor's murderous intent cannot affect the question. We may concede it to the fullest extent; but still the cardinal objection is undisposed of—that the making and the revocation of a will are purely matters of statutory regulation, by which the court is bound in the determination of questions relating to these acts. Two cases—in this state and in Kentucky—at an early day, seem to me to be much in point. *Gains v. Gains*, 2 A. K. Marsh. 190, was decided by the Kentucky court of appeals in 1820. It was there urged that the testator intended to have destroyed his will, and that he was forcibly prevented from doing so by the defendant in error or devisee; and it was insisted that the will, though not expressly, was thereby virtually, revoked. The court held [that], as the [statute] concerning wills prescribed the manner in which a will might be revoked, [and] as none of the acts evidencing revocation were done, the intention could not be substituted for the act. In that case the will was snatched away, and forcibly retained. In 1854, Surrogate Bradford, whose opinions are entitled to the highest consideration, decided the case of *Leaycraft v. Simmons*, 3 Bradf. Sur. 35. In that case the testator, a man of 89 years of age, desired to make a codicil to his will, in order to enlarge the provisions for his daughter. His son, having the custody of the instrument, and the one to be prejudiced by the change, refused to produce the will at testator's request, for the purpose of alteration. The learned surrogate refers to the provisions of the civil law for such and other cases of unworthy conduct in the heir or legatee, and says: "Our statute has undertaken to prescribe the mode in which wills can be revoked [citing the statutory provision]. This is the law by which I am governed in passing upon questions touching the revocation of wills. The whole of this subject is now regulated by statute; and a mere intention to revoke, however well authenticated, or however defeated, is not sufficient." And he held that the will must be admitted to probate. I may refer also to a case in the Pennsylvania courts. In that state the statute prescribed the mode for repealing or altering a will, and in *Clingan v. Micheltree*, 31 Pa. St. 25, the supreme court of the state held, where a will was kept from destruction by the fraud and misrepresentation of the devisee, that to declare it canceled as against the fraudulent party would be to enlarge the statute.

I cannot find any support for the argument that the respondent's succession to the property should be avoided because of his criminal act, when the laws are silent. Public policy does not demand it; for the demands of public policy are satisfied by the proper execution of the laws and the punishment of the crime. . . . The appellants' argument practically amounts to this: that, as the legatee has been guilty of a crime, by the commission of which he is placed in a position to sooner receive the benefits of the testamentary provision, his rights to the property should be forfeited, and he should be divested of his estate. To allow their argument to prevail, would involve the diversion by the court of the testator's estate into the hands of persons whom, possibly enough, for all we know, the testator might not have chosen or desired as its recipients. Practically the court is asked to make another will for the testator. The laws do not warrant this judicial action, and mere presumption would not be strong enough to sustain it.

But, more than this, to concede the appellants' views would involve the imposition of an additional punishment or penalty upon the respondent. What power or warrant have the courts to add to the respondent's penalties by depriving him of property? The law has punished him for his crime, and we may not say that it was an insufficient punishment. In the trial and punishment of the respondent the law has vindicated itself for the outrage which he committed, and further judicial utterance upon the subject of punishment or deprivation of rights is barred. We may not, in the language of the court in *People v. Thornton*, 25 Hun 456, "enhance the pains, penalties, and forfeitures provided by law for the punishment of crime." The judgment should be affirmed . . . .

NOTES AND QUESTIONS

1. Judge Earl's majority opinion referred to "the intention of the law-makers" who enacted New York's statutes of wills. For the most part, though, he did not seem to be claiming that those law-makers had foreseen the problem raised by *Riggs v. Palmer* and had formed a specific intention about how to handle it. Instead, his opinion used the rhetoric of what is sometimes called "imaginative reconstruction"—an approach that calls upon interpreters to "imagine how [members of the enacting legislature] would have wanted the statute applied to the case at bar." *See* Richard Posner, *Statutory Interpretation—In the Classroom and in the Courtroom*, 50 U. CHI. L. REV. 800, 817 (1983).

Of course, both the federal Constitution and its state counterparts separate the legislative and judicial branches precisely because it is thought to be a bad idea for the same body both to write the laws and to apply them in particular cases. Does imaginative reconstruction undercut this separation between the branches? Was Judge Earl effectively asking how the enacting legislature would have decided this case if the legislature were the judge—that is, if the New York constitution did not provide for the separation of powers?

Sophisticated advocates of imaginative reconstruction have an answer to that criticism. The interpretive principles that they advocate do not ask interpreters to imagine how the legislature would have decided the case at hand if there were no separation of powers and the legislators were acting as judges in each individual case. Rather than imagining a unitary government with no separation between the legislature and the judiciary, interpreters are simply supposed to consider how members of the enacting legislature might have worded their general instructions to the courts—their statute—if they had specifically contemplated this sort of case. Is that answer adequate? Even if it is, might the project of imaginative reconstruction raise other separation-of-powers concerns?

Could advocates of imaginative reconstruction respond that our separation of powers requires courts to take a sympathetic approach to the legislatures' statutes? Might they plausibly contend that the real separation-of-powers concerns would arise if courts *refused* to engage in any imaginative reconstruction (with the result that they insisted on enforcing policies that the legislature did not understand itself to have set)? *Cf.* Felix Frankfurter, *Some Reflections on the Reading of Statutes*, 47 COLUM. L. REV. 527, 533 (1947) ("[Laws] are expressions of policy arising out of specific situations and addressed to the attainment of particular ends. The difficulty is that the legislative ideas which laws embody are both explicit and immanent. And so the bottom problem is: What is below the surface of the words and yet fairly a part of them?").

2. Shortly after the New York Court of Appeals issued its decision in *Riggs v. Palmer*, the Supreme Court of Nebraska heard a similar case involving a father who had murdered his daughter to obtain property by intestate succession. Initially, the Nebraska court followed Judge Earl's approach and used imaginative reconstruction to justify inferring an unstated exception to Nebraska's statute of descent. *See* Shellenberger v. Ransom, 47 N.W. 700, 704 (Neb. 1891) ("[H]ad it been in the mind of the framers of our statute of descent that a case like this would arise under it, they would have so framed the law that its letter would have left no hope for the obtaining of an inheritance by such means."). On rehearing, however, the Nebraska court changed its mind and emphatically condemned this technique:

> "In our statute of descent there is neither ambiguity, nor room for construction. The intention of the legislature is free from doubt. The question is not what the framers of our statute of descent would have done, had it been in their minds that a case like this would arise, but what in fact they did, without perhaps anticipating the possibility of its existence. This is determined, not by hypothetical resort to conjecture as to their meaning, but by a construction of the language used.
>
> "The majority opinion in *Riggs v. Palmer*, as well as the opinion already filed in this case, seems to have been prompted largely by the horror and repulsion with which it may justly be supposed the framers of our statute would have viewed the crime and its consequences. This is no justification to this court for assuming to supply legislation, the necessity for which has been suggested by subsequent events, but which did not occur to the minds of those legislators by whom our statute of descent was framed. Neither the limitations of the civil law nor the promptings of humanity can be read into a statute from which, without question, they are absent, no matter how desirable the result to be attained may be. . . . The facts of the case at bar may impress upon some future legislature the necessity of an amendment of our law of descent; from that source alone can such an amendment come."

Shellenberger v. Ransom, 59 N.W. 935, 939 (Neb. 1894).

Was the Nebraska court's response to Judge Earl conclusive? Or might Judge Earl have been able to recast his rhetoric in terms acceptable to the Nebraska court? Instead of talking about what the enacting legislature *would have* decided *if* it had confronted some question that it did not actually consider, could he not have said that he too was trying to understand what the legislature really did decide? Wasn't his point that if one reads the general language of New York's statute of wills (or Nebraska's statute of descent) in its proper context, that language does not reflect a deliberate decision to let murderous beneficiaries like Elmer Palmer (or murderous heirs like Leander Shellenberger) profit from their crimes? Must that conclusion be phrased in hypothetical terms, or can it be cast as a claim about the meaning of the words that the legislature really did enact?

3. Was Judge Earl correct that it is simply "inconceivable" that the New York legislature could have intended its statutes of wills and descent to operate "in favor of one who murdered his ancestor that he might speedily come into the possession of his estate"? Judge Gray's dissent suggested that while murder is bad, the New York legislature did not use the statutes of wills and descent to specify the punishments for it; that was the function of other statutes (such as the statute under which Elmer was convicted in the criminal case against him). Could a legislature sensibly decide to specify the legal consequences of murder entirely in the criminal law, and to lump murderers together with other beneficiaries for purposes of the statutes of wills and descent?

At the time relevant to *Riggs v. Palmer*, New York's criminal law recognized two degrees of murder (along with four degrees of manslaughter). Murder in the first degree included killings that were "perpetrated from a deliberate and premeditated design to effect the death of the person killed." N.Y. Rev. Stat. pt. 4, ch. 1, tit. 1, § 5, 3 N.Y. Rev. Stat. 2470–71 (7th ed. 1882). Murder in the second degree included most killings that were "perpetrated intentionally, but without deliberation or premeditation." *Id.* Judges had little discretion about the punishments for murder; New York law specified that "[e]very person who shall . . . be convicted . . . [o]f murder in the first degree . . . shall suffer death for the same," and "[e]very person who shall be convicted of murder in the second degree . . . shall be punishable by imprisonment in a state prison during the period of his natural life." *Id.* §§ 1, __,[5] 3 N.Y. Rev. Stat. 2470, 2472 (7th ed. 1882). Admittedly, a separate statute allowed certain offenders "between the ages of sixteen and thirty" to be sentenced to the state reformatory for an indefinite duration rather than to a state prison for life, and the judge who sentenced Elmer chose that option—so Elmer himself did have some prospect of regaining his freedom. *See* An Act in Relation to the State Reformatory, ch. 427, §§ 9–10, 1870 N.Y. Acts 973, 975–76; *see also* William B. Meyer, *The Background to* Riggs v. Palmer, 60 AM. J. LEGAL HIST. 48, 57 (2020) (reporting that Elmer had already been released by the time of Judge

[5] The quoted language about the punishment for second-degree murder was added to the relevant title in the Revised Statutes in 1873, but the legislature did not give this provision a section number.

Earl's opinion). But in many cases, people convicted of murder in New York were in no position to enjoy their property.[6] As a result, the practical consequences of a legal rule disinheriting known murderers might have fallen less on the murderers themselves than on their heirs or creditors. Could a legislature sensibly conclude that the bad consequences of the murderer's crime should not radiate outward to strip these innocent people of property that they would otherwise have been able to claim? Could the legislature act upon that conclusion by allowing property to descend to known murderers (including even murderers who had committed their crimes for the purpose of inheriting property) on the same terms that property descends to other people? *Cf.* Deem v. Millikin, 3 Ohio Cir. Dec. 491 (1892) (raising some question about whether the Ohio legislature would even have the *power* to carve convicted murderers and their heirs out of Ohio's statute of descents, because the state constitution specified that "[n]o conviction shall work corruption of blood"), *aff'd*, 53 Ohio St. 668 (1895).

This line of questions suggests that Judge Earl could not be absolutely sure that the enacting legislature would really have endorsed the exceptions that he read into its statutes of wills and descent. If you had to bet, though, you might well think it more likely than not that members of the enacting legislature would indeed have agreed with Judge Earl's bottom line. Is that enough to justify his approach, or should courts insist upon a higher level of confidence before being willing to infer exceptions to a generally worded statute on the theory that the enacting legislature would have embraced those exceptions if it had thought about

---

[6] For much of the nineteenth century, one might have thought that people who were convicted of second-degree murder in New York, and who were sentenced to prison for life as a result, were not even in a position to *own* property. In 1799, the New York legislature had declared that a person convicted of a felony and sentenced to the state prison for life "shall be deemed and taken to be civilly dead, to all intents and purposes in the law." Act of March 29, 1799, *reprinted in* 4 LAWS OF THE STATE OF NEW YORK, PASSED AT THE SESSIONS OF THE LEGISLATURE HELD IN THE YEARS 1797, 1798, 1799 AND 1800, INCLUSIVE 372–73 (Albany 1887). Several New York judges discussing this statute assumed that for purposes of property ownership, "civil death" had the same consequences as actual death—so that when people were sentenced to life imprisonment in New York, their estates immediately descended to their heirs or were distributed according to their wills. *See, e.g.*, Platner v. Sherwood, 6 Johns. Ch. 118 (N.Y. Ch. 1822) (dictum); In re Deming, 10 Johns. 232 (N.Y. Sup. Ct. 1813) (dictum). A few years later, language derived from the 1799 statute was re-enacted as part of New York's Revised Statutes. *See* N.Y. Rev. Stat., pt. 4, ch. 1, tit. 7, § 20, 2 N.Y. Rev. Stat. 701 (1829) ("A person sentenced to imprisonment in a state prison for life, shall thereafter be deemed civilly dead."); *accord id.*, 3 N.Y. Rev. Stat. 2538 (7th ed. 1882). As late as 1887, New York lawyers could therefore argue that when a person was sentenced to a state prison for life, "his estate descends to his heirs, or is administered upon according to law as if he were actually dead." *Avery v. Everett*, 110 N.Y. 317, 319 (1888) (argument of counsel).

One year before its decision in *Riggs v. Palmer*, however, New York's highest court rejected that understanding of "civil death." *See Avery*, 110 N.Y. at 332 (majority opinion) (observing that "no case in this state can be found where the will of a person imprisoned on a life sentence has been admitted to probate during his natural life, or where administration has been granted on his estate . . . as if he was dead," and concluding that "the doctrine that civil death . . . divests the criminal of his estate, has no foundation in our law"). *But see id.* at 334–36 (Earl, J., dissenting). *See generally* Kim Lane Scheppele, *Facing Facts in Legal Interpretation*, *in* LAW AND THE ORDER OF CULTURE 42 (Robert Post ed., 1991) (calling attention to the doctrine of "civil death" and discussing its potential intersection with *Riggs v. Palmer*).

them? If a 51/49 level of confidence is not enough, how about 70/30? Or is there some reason for courts to insist upon almost complete certainty before reading unstated exceptions into statutes on this basis?

4. Suppose one thinks that interpreters should be willing to infer exceptions to generally worded statutory language whenever they are sufficiently confident that (1) the language chosen by the enacting legislature does not reflect a deliberate decision to reject those exceptions and (2) the enacting legislature would in fact have embraced the exceptions (and reformulated the statutory language accordingly) if the issues raised by the exceptions had occurred to its members. One might still think that this test will only rarely be satisfied. Given the vicissitudes of the legislative process, no one can be very confident about how particular proposals would have fared in a legislature that did not actually consider them. Even if it seems likely that some legislators would have supported a particular exception had it occurred to them, perhaps some other legislators would have opposed that exception or would have preferred to pursue other priorities. There is no obvious formula that people outside the legislative process should use to determine how the potentially competing views of individual legislators might coalesce into a collective position that can properly be imputed to the legislature as a whole.

Does this line of reasoning suggest that imaginative reconstruction might be more appropriate when courts are interpreting a will (which is the product of a single individual) than when they are interpreting a statute (which is the product of a group)? If you are skeptical of Judge Earl's decision to read implicit exceptions into New York's statutes of wills and descent, might he have been on sounder footing if he had instead read the same sort of exception into Francis Palmer's will? At the time that he wrote his will, Francis Palmer probably did not contemplate the possibility that Elmer would poison him in order to get Francis's estate. But if testators routinely were asked about that possibility, the vast majority of them probably would say that they do not want their property to go to someone who murders them to get it. To give effect to this likely intention, could Judge Earl have read the seemingly general words of Francis's will (which gave Elmer the bulk of Francis's estate) as coming with an implied qualification ("but not if he murders me")? This sort of imaginative reconstruction of the meaning of Francis's will would have permitted Judge Earl to reach essentially the same bottom line in *Riggs v. Palmer*[7] without having to confront any problems of collective

[7] One potential difference between the legal rules articulated by Judge Earl in *Riggs v. Palmer* and a legal rule that depends instead on the meaning of the testator's will is that a testator could opt out of the latter rule; if Francis Palmer's will had said that "these bequests and devises shall be effective even if Elmer murders me in order to receive them," then the will itself could not plausibly be read to cut Elmer out of Francis's estate. Of course, even if an idiosyncratic testator wants to give effect to bequests or devises that would encourage someone to murder him, perhaps the law should not do so. Just as courts will not enforce murder-for-hire contracts, so too one might think that courts should not enforce testamentary provisions that amount to invitations for other people to kill the testator. To build this public-policy exception

intent. Instead of having to reconstruct and aggregate the potentially competing preferences of a large number of legislators, Judge Earl would simply have had to reconstruct the likely preferences of a single testator.

In other fields of interpretation, our legal system is at least somewhat receptive to this sort of imaginative reconstruction. Even when interpreting contracts (which, unlike wills, require some aggregation of the potentially competing intentions of different parties), courts apply default rules that are supposed to reflect what most contracting parties would have wanted at the time of contracting if they had specifically considered issues that they did not actually address. Shouldn't this style of interpretation be even more appropriate in the case of wills?

If you are drawn to this argument, though, should you really refuse to extend it to the interpretation of statutes? In *Riggs v. Palmer*, we have little specific information about how Francis Palmer would have reacted had he known of Elmer's murderous bent. If we nonetheless read an implied exception into Francis's will, we are relying primarily on our belief that the vast majority of people in Francis's position would not want their estates to pass to grandsons who poison them. If we are willing to impute that intention to Francis Palmer (and to every other testator, in the absence of some clear statement to the contrary), why wouldn't we be willing to impute a similar intention to individual legislators (and to every other legislator, in the absence of some clear statement to the contrary)? Is the problem of collective intent really very troubling in this sort of situation?

A second argument against basing the result in *Riggs v. Palmer* on clever interpretation of Francis Palmer's will, while resisting similarly clever interpretation of New York's statutes, is that rules about how to interpret wills kick in only when someone has a will. If courts are prepared to read exceptions into the will of every testator who does not explicitly address the issue, so that the estates of those testators do not go to beneficiaries who murder them, should courts really refuse to read a similar exception into the statute of descent that governs the distribution of property belonging to people who die intestate? Why should the law create this disparity between the treatment of property

---

into the enforcement of wills, though, we presumably would need to get into questions of statutory interpretation of the sort confronted by Judge Earl.

Cases of voluntary euthanasia raise additional issues along these lines. People who want to die, but who need a relative's help to do so, probably would not want the relative to be disqualified from receiving property out of their estates. Perhaps for that reason, at least one state that has enacted a "slayer statute" codifying the rule of *Riggs v. Palmer* explicitly allows testators to opt out of that rule. *See* Wis. Stat. § 854.14(6)(b) ("This section does not apply if . . . [t]he decedent provided in his or her will, by specific reference to this section, that this section does not apply."); *see also* Adam D. Hansen, *Arizona's Slayer Statute: The Killer of Testator Intent*, 7 ARIZ. SUMMIT L. REV. 755, 780 (2014) (arguing that Arizona should amend its own slayer statute to include a similar exception); Jeffrey G. Sherman, *Mercy Killing and the Right to Inherit*, 61 U. CIN. L. REV. 803, 808, 866 (1993) (supporting such an exception and arguing more broadly that "the slayer rule should not be applied in cases of mercy killing or assisted suicide, even if the criminal law continues to regard such actions as unlawful" (footnote omitted)).

belonging to people like Francis Palmer (who have wills) and the treatment of property belonging to people like Maggie Shellenberger (who do not)?

5. If one accepts Judge Earl's imaginative reconstruction of the intended meaning of New York's statutes of wills and descent, how should one handle the various questions of detail that will then arise? First, which kinds of homicide (or offenses that involve aiding and abetting homicide) should disqualify beneficiaries from taking property under a will or heirs from taking property by intestate succession? In cases of murder, does the motive for the murder matter, or should the rule of *Riggs v. Palmer* prevent the victim's property from passing to the murderer even if the murderer killed the victim for reasons unrelated to the acquisition of property? *Cf.* RESTATEMENT (THIRD) OF PROPERTY: WILLS AND OTHER DONATIVE TRANSFERS § 8.4 cmt. b (AM. L. INST. 2003) ("The slayer's motive in committing the wrong is irrelevant."). If motive is irrelevant, so that all murderers are categorically disqualified from inheriting their victims' property, should certain grades of manslaughter trigger the same disqualification? *Cf. id.* cmt. f (indicating that "reckless, accidental, or negligent" killings do not trigger the disqualification). How should the statutes of wills and descent be understood to treat purported beneficiaries or heirs who do not themselves kill anyone, but who are accessories before the fact? What if they are merely accessories *after* the fact? *Cf. id.* § 8.4(a) (applying the disqualification to anyone "who, without legal excuse or justification, is responsible for the felonious and intentional killing of another"); *id.* cmt. g (clarifying that "[a]n accomplice, co-conspirator, or accessory before the fact can share responsibility for the felonious and intentional killing of another" in the sense that triggers the disqualification).

Whichever crimes trigger the disqualification, a second set of questions concerns the mechanism for proving that a purported beneficiary or heir committed one of those crimes. To avoid having to hold what amounts to a murder trial as part of probate proceedings or other civil lawsuits, should courts enforce the bar contemplated by Judge Earl only against people who have already been tried for and convicted of a disqualifying crime (as Elmer Palmer had been)? Or should the parties in probate or other civil proceedings be allowed to introduce evidence that a purported heir or beneficiary who has not yet been convicted in a criminal case is nonetheless guilty of the sort of crime that disqualifies him from acquiring his victim's property by will or intestate succession? If courts will indeed investigate this issue in the context of probate or other noncriminal proceedings, what standard of proof should they apply? Is it enough to establish by a preponderance of the evidence that the purported heir or beneficiary intentionally killed his benefactor without legal excuse or justification? Or must each element of the disqualifying crime be proved beyond a reasonable doubt (as would be necessary to support a criminal conviction)?

Whatever the applicable standard of proof, a third set of questions concerns the proper disposition of the property that the killer is disqualified from receiving. Should the disqualification extend to anyone who claims property through the killer? Or should the law simply treat the killer as if he had died before his victim (with the result that the victim's property will typically skip the killer but go to the killer's heirs)? In the latter case, should the fiction that the killer pre-deceased his victim persist with respect to future dispositions of the property? For instance, suppose that a man kills his mother-in-law, whose estate passes to the man's wife, who herself then dies for other reasons. Should the law disqualify the murderer from receiving any portion of his wife's estate that can be traced to the estate of his victim? Would it matter if the wife died so soon after the victim that the victim's estate had not yet been distributed (so that tracing the assets does not raise any practical problem)? *See* In re Edwards, 991 N.Y.S.2d 431, 435 (App. Div. 2014) (extending *Riggs* to this situation); *cf.* In re Estate of Vallerius, 629 N.E.2d 1185, 1188 (Ill. App. 1994) (interpreting the Illinois slayer statute to reach the same result).

Even if one is fairly confident about how the enacting legislature would have handled the basic question addressed by Judge Earl, one cannot be nearly so confident about how any particular legislature would have handled all these further questions of detail. In the absence of statutes addressing them, should courts be willing to supply answers on a case-by-case basis, drawing upon judicial precedents and their own sense of sound policy? Or is the prospect of having to supply all these details a reason for courts not to go down Judge Earl's road in the first place?

6. Less than a decade after *Riggs v. Palmer*, the New York Court of Appeals recharacterized what Judge Earl had held. According to *Ellerson v. Westcott*, 42 N.E. 540 (N.Y. 1896), the legal title to property can indeed pass by will or intestate succession to murderous beneficiaries or heirs like Elmer Palmer, but courts of equity can grant relief depriving them of the use of the property. *Cf.* James Barr Ames, *Can a Murderer Acquire Title by His Crime and Keep It?*, 45 AM. L. REG. & REV. 225, 227 (1897) (endorsing the idea that in cases of this sort, "[t]he legal title passes to the murderer, but equity will treat him as a constructive trustee of the title because of the unconscionable mode of its acquisition, and compel him to convey it to the heirs of the deceased, exclusive of the murderer").

If you disagree with Judge Earl's approach in *Riggs v. Palmer*, are you any more comfortable with *Ellerson*? If New York's statutes of wills and descent should be understood to cause legal title to vest in a murderous beneficiary or heir, should courts nonetheless be able to transcend the unjust consequences of those statutes by invoking equity jurisprudence to impose constructive trusts on the property?

7. What is the relevance, if any, of other sorts of background legal principles? In addition to speculating about how members of the enacting legislature would have handled the issue raised by *Riggs v. Palmer* if they had thought about it, Judge Earl also advanced a second argument: seemingly general statutory language should be construed to accommodate "fundamental maxims of the common law." One of those maxims is that the law will not let anyone take advantage of his own legal wrong. *See, e.g.*, HERBERT BROOM, A SELECTION OF LEGAL MAXIMS, CLASSIFIED AND ILLUSTRATED 279–99 (8th American ed. 1882) (discussing the maxim *nullus commodum capere potest de injuria sua propria*). Should courts normally read statutes to conform to such time-honored principles unless the statutes specifically indicate that the legislature intended to establish a different policy? In the absence of any reason to think that the New York legislature wanted its statutes of wills and descent to depart from these longstanding maxims, shouldn't the existence of the maxims shed light on the true meaning of the statutes?

If your answer to this question is "no" (that is, if you would read New York's statutes of wills and descent to trump the common-law maxim), are there *ever* occasions on which courts should invoke our common-law traditions to justify reading implicit exceptions into seemingly unqualified statutory texts? For instance, when a federal statute creates a private cause of action in seemingly broad terms, can courts recognize defenses that the statute does not itself recite but that are supported by general principles of common law?

For a concrete setting in which to consider the latter question, consider the federal Electronic Fund Transfer Act. Subject to certain exceptions, one of the provisions in that Act establishes the following rule: "[A] financial institution shall be liable to a consumer for all damages proximately caused by—(1) the financial institution's failure to make an electronic fund transfer, in accordance with the terms and conditions of an account, in the correct amount or in a timely manner when properly instructed to do so by the consumer . . . ." Act of Nov. 10, 1978, Pub. L. 95–630, sec. 2001, § 910(a), 92 Stat. 3641, 3735–36 (codified at 15 U.S.C. § 1693h(a)). Imagine that Plaintiff notifies Bank of a claim under this provision; Plaintiff and Bank enter into a contract purporting to settle this claim for $10,000; Bank duly pays Plaintiff $10,000; and Plaintiff then regrets settling his claim for so little. Ultimately, Plaintiff sues Bank for an additional $5,000 on the theory that Plaintiff suffered a total of $15,000 in actual damages. When Bank raises the settlement contract in defense, Plaintiff argues that the statute does not recognize the defense of accord and satisfaction; Congress provided that the financial institution "shall" be liable "for all damages proximately caused," and Congress did not add any qualifying phrases like "unless the consumer has already settled his claim for some lesser amount." Should Plaintiff be able to get out from under the settlement agreement on the strength of this argument? Or should the statute be understood to accommodate the common-law defense of accord and satisfaction (on the theory, perhaps, that Congress was not trying to supersede the ordinary principle that claims can be settled out of court, and the statute therefore leaves room for the application of this defense)? Is there a difference between reading statutory causes of action to leave room for the application of traditional common-law defenses (unless the statute either expressly or implicitly overrides them) and reading the language of New York's statutes of wills and descent to accommodate the traditional principle that the law does not reward people for their own legal wrongs?

8. Along the same lines, what do you make of the passage that Judge Earl quoted from Blackstone on p. 10? Blackstone opined that if the English Parliament had enacted a statute giving the lord of a manor "power to try all causes that arise within his manor," the statute would not properly have been understood to cover cases "in which he himself is party." 1 WILLIAM BLACKSTONE, COMMENTARIES ON THE LAWS OF ENGLAND 91 (1765). Is that because there was then a collective understanding that people should not be judges in their own cases, and this collective understanding formed the backdrop for statutes that did not clearly reject it? Is there any difference in meaning between a statute saying simply that "the lord of the manor shall be the judge of all cases that arise within the manor" and a statute saying that "the lord of the manor shall be the judge of all cases that arise within the manor, *including even cases in which he himself is a party*"?

9. Was Judge Earl correct to see the federal Supreme Court's decision in *New York Mutual Life Insurance Co. v. Armstrong*, 117 U.S. 591 (1886), as a relevant precedent? That case indicated that under the general common law, the beneficiary of a life-insurance policy forfeits his rights under the policy if he murders the insured for the purpose of getting the insurance proceeds. How much did this precedent about the content of the common law support Judge Earl's interpretation of New York's statutes of wills and descent?

The dissenting judges seemed to believe that the answer is "not very much." Whatever they would have said about the common-law rule applicable in cases involving insurance contracts, they took the statute of wills to have occupied the field that it addressed and to leave no room for the sort of exception articulated in *Armstrong*. But if the policymakers for a state were addressing whether property should pass to a murderer who killed his victim in order to get it, would we expect their answer to vary according to whether the property passed by virtue of a will, a life-insurance policy, or a statute of descent? If the answer to that question is "no" (or at least "probably not"), should courts read unstated exceptions into New York's statutes of wills and descent in order to make the policies reflected in those statutes more consistent (in the judges' view) with the common-law rule that would govern life-insurance cases in New York? In the alternative, should the apparent breadth of New York's statutes of wills and descent spill over to affect the courts' understanding of the common-law rule that would govern life-insurance cases in New York?

Or can courts apply the common law of contracts and the state's statutes of wills and descent in splendid isolation from each other?

For a dramatic illustration of this issue, consider *Murchison v. Murchison*, 203 S.W. 423 (Tex. Civ. App. 1918). Margurite Murchison was alleged to have murdered her husband for the purpose of securing payment under a life-insurance policy naming her as the beneficiary. The Texas Court of Civil Appeals agreed with the general rule that "it would be against sound public policy to permit any beneficiary in a life insurance policy, who should feloniously take the life of the insured, to recover money due under the terms of the policy." *Id.* at 425. As a result, "if the right of Margurite Murchison to the proceeds of the policy in question depended upon the provisions of the policy itself, as a contract," and if she had indeed murdered her husband for the purpose of getting the policy proceeds, then the policy proceeds would go to Mr. Murchison's estate rather than to her. *See id.* But the distribution of Mr. Murchison's estate was controlled by statute rather than by common law. Texas's statute of descent, moreover, specified that when an intestate decedent died without children (as Mr. Murchison had), " 'the surviving . . . wife shall be entitled to all the personal estate.' " *Id.* at 426 (quoting the then-existing version of the statute of descent). According to the court, this statutory language "is plain and positive, and leaves nothing for construction by the courts . . . ." *Id.* As a result, even though "the public policy of this state" militated against letting a murderess collect upon the victim's life-insurance contract in her capacity as the beneficiary of that contract, the proceeds of the insurance contract still passed to Mrs. Murchison in her capacity as statutory heir. *Id.* at 425–26.

10. At least where statutes of descent came into play, the majority opinion in *Riggs v. Palmer* turned out to be unusual for its time. In most states where the question arose, courts of the day interpreted generally worded statutes of descent as allowing property to pass to people who had committed murder to get it. Under the majority rule, moreover, courts did not assert authority to impose constructive trusts on this property. *See, e.g.*, Wall v. Pfanschmidt, 106 N.E. 785 (Ill. 1914); McAllister v. Fair, 84 P. 112 (Kan. 1906); In re Carpenter's Estate, 32 A. 637 (Pa. 1895); *see also* Hagan v. Cone, 94 S.E. 602, 603 (Ga. App. 1917) ("While in some of the states it has been held that one who kills another cannot inherit from the deceased, yet the strong current of authority is against this opinion . . . .").[8]

---

[8] In keeping with the logic of the *Murchison* case discussed in the previous note, courts tended to distinguish these inheritance cases (governed by statutes of descent) from insurance cases (governed by the common law of contract). "The courts [were] in agreement that a beneficiary cannot maintain an action for insurance proceeds after having murdered the insured." But "the majority ruling" in cases governed by a generally worded statute of descent was that "complete ownership of the property will pass to the slayer in spite of his wrong." John W. Wade, *Acquisition of Property by Wilfully Killing Another—A Statutory Solution*, 49 HARV. L. REV. 715, 717 & n.8 (1936).

Cases involving wills were rarer, and they were potentially distinguishable from cases involving intestate succession under a statute of descent. *See supra* pp. 20–21 (raising the

Legislatures reacted to these decisions. Beginning in the early twentieth century, various states enacted some sort of "slayer statute" to handle the cases of murderous heirs and beneficiaries. Almost all American states now have some such statute, although their details vary. *See, e.g.*, Karen J. Sneddon, *Should Cain's Children Inherit Abel's Property?: Wading into the Extended Slayer Rule Quagmire*, 76 UMKC L. REV. 101, 109 (2007) (citing and categorizing such statutes in 45 states and the District of Columbia).

Here, for instance, is West Virginia's statute:

> "A person who has been convicted of feloniously killing another, or of conspiracy in the killing of another, may not take or acquire any money or property, real or personal, or interest in the money or property, from the one killed or conspired against, either by descent and distribution, or by will, or by any policy or certificate of insurance, or otherwise; but the money or the property to which the convicted person would otherwise have been entitled shall go to the person or persons who would have taken the money or property if the convicted person had been dead at the date of the death of the one killed or conspired against, unless by some rule of law or equity the money or the property would pass to some other person or persons."

W. VA. CODE § 42–4–2(a). Does this language deal with all of the different factual contexts that cases of murderous heirs or beneficiaries might present? (For instance, does it mean that murderous heirs are disqualified only if they are criminally prosecuted and convicted, and that those who are beyond the reach of criminal process—or who are acquitted at trial because the admissible evidence does not establish their guilt beyond a reasonable doubt—are entitled to collect their inheritances? Or does the statute simply not address murderous heirs who have not been convicted, leaving courts to handle those cases without specific statutory guidance? *See* Plumley v. Bledsoe, 613 S.E.2d 102, 104 (W. Va. 2005) ("[I]t is settled law that the 'slayer rule' is a common-law principle in West Virginia, and that [the statute] . . . is designed to authorize the application of the slayer rule 'automatically' in the instance of a felony conviction—but not to otherwise limit the application of the common-law rule.").) With respect to the factual contexts that the statute addresses, does the statute introduce any new uncertainties? (With respect to conspiracy offenses, for instance, does the statute apply only when the conspiracy was successful, or does it prevent

---

possibility that courts might engage in more creative interpretation of wills than of statutes); *see also* In re Wilkins' Estate, 211 N.W. 652 (Wis. 1927) (following *Riggs v. Palmer* in a will case, and emphasizing that the murderer had "deprived the testatrix of th[e] sacred right to revoke her will, thus producing a changed situation not contemplated by the testatrix"); *cf.* In re Carpenter's Estate, 32 A. 637, 638 (Pa. 1895) ("While we do not agree to the conclusion reached [in *Riggs v. Palmer*], the case only involved the operation of a private grant [in a will], and therein differs widely from a case in which the statutory law of descent is in question."). Still, courts that enforced the surface meaning of their state's statutes of descent often indicated that they would disagree with *Riggs v. Palmer* even in a case under a will.

even unsuccessful conspirators from later receiving property under the will of the person against whom they had once conspired?)

Virginia has a much more elaborate slayer statute, which includes the following provisions (among others):

§ 64.2–2500. Definitions

As used in this chapter:

"Decedent" means any person whose life has been taken as a result of murder or voluntary manslaughter.

"Property" includes any real and personal property and any right or interest therein.

"Slayer" means any person (i) who is convicted of the murder or voluntary manslaughter of the decedent or, (ii) in the absence of such conviction, who is determined, whether before or after his death, by a court of appropriate jurisdiction by a preponderance of the evidence to have committed one of the offenses listed in clause (i) resulting in the death of the decedent. For the purposes of clause (ii), the party seeking to establish that a decedent was slain by such person shall have the burden of proof.

§ 64.2–2501. Slayer not to acquire property as result of slaying

A slayer, or any transferee, assignee, or other person claiming through the slayer, shall not in any way acquire any property or receive any benefits as the result of the death of the decedent, but such property or benefits shall pass as provided in this chapter.

§ 64.2–2502. Property passing by will or intestate succession; surviving spouse

A. The slayer shall be deemed to have predeceased the decedent as to property that would have passed from the estate of the decedent to the slayer by intestate succession or that the slayer would have acquired by statutory right as the decedent's surviving spouse. An heir or distributee who establishes his kinship to the decedent by way of his kinship to a slayer shall be deemed to be claiming from the decedent and not through the slayer.

B. The slayer shall be deemed to have predeceased the decedent as to property that would have passed to the slayer by the will of the decedent . . . .

. . . .

§ 64.2–2508. Proceeds of insurance; bona fide payment by insurance company or obligor

A. Insurance proceeds payable to the slayer as the beneficiary or assignee of any policy or certificate of insurance or bond or other contractual agreement on the life of the decedent or as the survivor of a joint life policy shall be paid to the estate of the decedent, unless the policy or certificate designates some person as an alternative beneficiary to the slayer.

B. If the decedent is the beneficiary or assignee of any policy or certificate of insurance on the life of the slayer, the proceeds shall be paid to the estate of the decedent upon the death of the slayer, unless the policy names some person other than the slayer or his estate as an alternative beneficiary, or unless the slayer, by naming a new beneficiary or by assigning the policy, performs an act that would have deprived the decedent of his interest in the policy if he had been living.

C. No insurance company shall be subject to liability on a policy insuring the life of the decedent if (i) as a part of the slayer's plan to murder the decedent, such policy was procured and maintained by the slayer or as a result of actions taken or participated in by the slayer whether directly or indirectly and (ii) the decedent's death resulted from the slayer's act committed within two years from the date such policy was issued by the insurance company.

D. Any insurer making payment according to the terms of its policy or contract or any bank or other person performing an obligation for the slayer as one of several joint obligees shall not be subjected to additional liability by the terms of this section if such payment or performance is made without notice of circumstances bringing it within the provisions of this section.

§ 64.2–2509. Persons acquiring from slayer protected

The provisions of this chapter shall not affect the right of any person who, before the interests of the slayer have been adjudicated, acquires from the slayer for adequate consideration property or an interest therein that the slayer would have received except for the terms of this chapter, provided that such property or interest is acquired without notice of circumstances tending to bring it within the provisions of this chapter. All consideration received by the slayer shall be held by him in trust for the persons entitled to the property under the provisions of this chapter, and the slayer shall be liable for any portion of such consideration that he may have dissipated and for any difference between the actual value of the property and the amount of such consideration.

§ 64.2–2510. Admissibility of judicial record determining slayer

The record of the judicial proceeding in which a person is determined to be a slayer shall be admissible in evidence for or against a claimant of property in any civil action arising under this chapter. A conviction shall be conclusive evidence of the guilt of the slayer.

§ 64.2–2511. Construction

A. This chapter shall not be considered penal in nature, but shall be construed broadly in order to effect the policy of the Commonwealth that no person shall be allowed to profit by his own wrong, wherever committed. In furtherance of this policy, the provisions of this chapter are not intended to be exclusive and all common law rights and remedies that prevent one who has participated in the willful and unlawful killing of another from profiting by his wrong shall continue to exist in the Commonwealth.

. . . .

No matter how much detail a statute provides, though, cases may present issues that the statute does not specifically address. Consider *Osman v. Osman*, 737 S.E.2d 876 (Va. 2013). A man with "a very long history of mental illness" had killed his mother. *Id.* at 878. The state charged him with first-degree murder, but prosecutors agreed that he had been insane at the time of the killing, and he was found not guilty by reason of insanity. In later civil proceedings about the disposition of his mother's estate, judges had to decide whether he met the definition of a "slayer" in what is now VA. CODE § 64.2–2500. Clause (i) in that definition did not apply, because he had not been convicted in the criminal case against him. But the Virginia Supreme Court concluded that he still had "committed . . . the offense[ ]" of murder within the meaning of clause (ii), and Virginia's slayer statute therefore disqualified him from sharing in his mother's estate.

Was the Virginia Supreme Court correct about what clause (ii) means? On the one hand, a person who is not guilty (even by reason of insanity) might be said not to have committed any "offense" at all. In addition, some forms of insanity might prevent a person from satisfying the *mens rea* element of murder, and a person who does not satisfy one of the basic elements of murder presumably has not committed that offense.

On the other hand, the particular type of insanity that afflicted the killer in *Osman* might not have negated the *mens rea* element of murder; even though the killer was motivated by delusions, he apparently had known what he was doing. Unlike self-defense, moreover, insanity is an "excuse" rather than a "justification." Perhaps Virginia law could be said to take the following position: the killer in *Osman* had indeed committed the offense of murder, but he was excused from criminal punishment because he was insane at the time of the offense. Indeed, some of Virginia's statutes about the insanity defense arguably speak in these terms. *See, e.g.*, VA. CODE § 19.2–182.2 ("When the defense is insanity of the defendant at the time the offense was committed, the jurors shall be instructed, if they acquit him on that ground, to state the fact with their verdict.").

Osman appears to be an outlier. *See* Estate of Armstrong v. Armstrong, 170 So. 3d 510, 515–16 (Miss. 2015) (citing cases on both sides, but concluding that "the majority of states" that have faced the question have interpreted their states' slayer statutes not to disinherit killers who are not guilty by reason of insanity); *see also id.* (emphasizing the word "wilfully" in Mississippi's slayer statute and following the majority rule).

11. What do you make of the fact that in states whose courts disagreed with *Riggs v. Palmer* and understood then-existing state laws to let murderous heirs or beneficiaries receive property by will or intestate succession, state legislatures almost universally reacted by enacting a slayer statute? Does that fact tend to vindicate Judge Earl's position in *Riggs v. Palmer*? Or does the fact that New York remains one of the few states without a slayer statute (except in a few special areas) actually suggest an argument for Judge Gray's dissent? If Judge Earl had not leaped into the breach, the New York legislature might have felt more pressure to enact legislation spelling out the state's policy on at least some of the questions of detail flagged above. On the other hand, isn't it perverse for courts to try to goad legislatures into action by articulating rules of law that the legislatures are almost certain to hate?

To bring these questions up to the present day, imagine a state that does not have a slayer statute, but whose courts have not yet had to decide how to handle questions of the sort presented in *Riggs v. Palmer*. If a case like *Riggs v. Palmer* arose today in such a state, should the fact that virtually every other state has embraced the general policy reflected in Judge Earl's opinion lead the state's courts to agree with Judge Earl? Or should the fact that most states adopted that policy by statute, and that the state in which the question has arisen lacks any such statute, reinforce the arguments advanced by Judge Gray's dissent?

---

23 STAT. 332 (1885)

The next case that we will consider, *Church of the Holy Trinity v. United States*, is almost as old as *Riggs v. Palmer*, and remains just as prominent. It involved the meaning of the following federal statute, which Congress enacted on February 26, 1885:

Chap. 164.—An act to prohibit the importation and migration of foreigners and aliens under contract or agreement to perform labor in the United States, its Territories, and the District of Columbia.

Be it enacted by the Senate and House of Representatives of the United States of America in Congress assembled, That from and after the passage of this act it shall be unlawful for any person, company, partnership, or corporation, in any manner whatsoever, to prepay the transportation, or in any way assist or encourage the importation or migration of any alien or aliens, any foreigner or foreigners, into the United States, its Territories, or the District of Columbia, under contract or agreement, parol or special, express or implied, made previous to the importation or migration of such alien or aliens, foreigner or foreigners, to perform labor or service of any kind in the United States, its Territories, or the District of Columbia.

SEC. 2. That all contracts or agreements, express or implied, parol or special, which may hereafter be made by and between any person, company, partnership, or corporation, and any foreigner or foreigners, alien or aliens, to perform labor or service or having reference to the performance of labor or service by any person in the United States, its Territories, or the District of Columbia previous to the migration or importation of the person or persons whose labor or service is contracted for into the United States, shall be utterly void and of no effect.

SEC. 3. That for every violation of any of the provisions of section one of this act the person, partnership, company, or corporation violating the same, by knowingly assisting, encouraging or soliciting the migration or importation of any alien or aliens, foreigner or foreigners, into the United States, its Territories, or the District of Columbia, to perform labor or service of any kind under contract or agreement, express or implied, parol or special, with such alien or aliens, foreigner or foreigners, previous to becoming residents or citizens of the United States, shall forfeit and pay for every such offence the sum of one thousand dollars, which may be sued for and recovered by the United States or by any person who shall first bring his action therefor including any such alien or foreigner who may be a party to any such contract or agreement, as debts of like amount are now recovered in the circuit courts of the United States; the proceeds to be paid into the Treasury of the United States; and separate suits may be brought for each alien or foreigner being a party to such contract or agreement aforesaid. And it shall be the duty of the district attorney of the proper district to prosecute every such suit at the expense of the United States.

SEC. 4. That the master of any vessel who shall knowingly bring within the United States on any such vessel, and land, or permit to be landed, from any foreign port or place, any alien laborer, mechanic, or artisan who, previous to embarkation on such vessel, had entered into contract or agreement, parol or special, express or implied, to perform labor or service in the United States, shall be deemed guilty of a misdemeanor, and on conviction thereof, shall be punished by a fine of not more than five hundred dollars for each and every such alien laborer, mechanic or artisan so brought as aforesaid, and may also be imprisoned for a term not exceeding six months.

SEC. 5. That nothing in this act shall be so construed as to prevent any citizen or subject of any foreign country temporarily residing in the United States, either in private or official capacity, from engaging, under contract or otherwise, persons not residents or citizens of the United States to act as private secretaries, servants, or domestics for such foreigner temporarily residing in the United States as aforesaid; nor shall this act be so construed as to prevent any person, or persons, partnership, or corporation from engaging, under contract or agreement, skilled workman in foreign countries to perform labor in the United States in or upon any new industry not at present established in the United States: *Provided,* That skilled labor for that purpose cannot be otherwise obtained; nor shall the provisions of this act apply to professional actors, artists, lecturers, or singers, nor to persons employed strictly as personal or domestic servants: *Provided,* That nothing in this act shall be construed as prohibiting any individual from assisting any member of his family or any relative or personal friend, to migrate from any foreign country to the United States, for the purpose of settlement here.

SEC. 6. That all laws or parts of laws conflicting herewith be, and the same are hereby, repealed.

Church of the Holy Trinity v. United States

143 U.S. 457 (1892)

■ *JUSTICE BREWER delivered the opinion of the Court:*

Plaintiff in error is a corporation duly organized and incorporated as a religious society under the laws of the state of New York. E. Walpole Warren was, prior to September 1887, an alien residing in England. In that month the plaintiff in error made a contract with him, by which he was to remove to the city of New York, and enter into its service as rector and pastor; and, in pursuance of such contract, Warren did so remove and enter upon such service. It is claimed by the United States that this contract on the part of the plaintiff in error was forbidden by chapter 164, 23 Stat. 332; and an action was commenced to recover the penalty prescribed by that act. The circuit court held that the contract was within the prohibition of the statute, and rendered judgment accordingly, and the single question presented for our determination is whether it erred in that conclusion.

The first section describes the act forbidden, and is in these words:

"*Be it enacted by the Senate and House of Representatives of the United States of America, in Congress assembled*, That from and after the passage of this act it shall be unlawful for any person, company, partnership, or corporation, in any manner whatsoever, to prepay the transportation, or in any way assist or encourage the importation or migration of any alien or aliens, any foreigner or foreigners, into the United States, its Territories, or the District of Columbia, under contract or agreement, parol or special, express or implied, made previous to the importation or migration of such alien or aliens, foreigner or foreigners, to perform labor or service of any kind in the United States, its Territories, or the District of Columbia."

It must be conceded that the act of the corporation is within the letter of this section, for the relation of rector to his church is one of service, and implies labor on the one side with compensation on the other. Not only are the general words "labor" and "service" both used, but also, as it were to guard against any narrow interpretation and emphasize a breadth of meaning, to them is added "of any kind"; and, further, as noticed by the Circuit Judge in his opinion, the fifth section, which makes specific exceptions, among them professional actors, artists, lecturers, singers, and domestic servants, strengthens the idea that every other kind of labor and service was intended to be reached by the first section. While there is great force to this reasoning, we cannot think Congress intended to denounce with penalties a transaction like that in the present case. It is a familiar rule that a thing may be within the letter of the statute and yet not within the statute, because not within its spirit nor within the intention of its makers. This has been often asserted, and the Reports are full of cases illustrating its application. This is not the substitution of the will of the judge for that of the legislator; for frequently words of general meaning are used in a statute, words broad enough to include an act in question, and yet a consideration of the whole legislation, or of the circumstances surrounding its enactment, or of the absurd results which follow from giving such broad meaning to the words, makes it unreasonable to believe that the legislator intended to include the particular act. . . .

In *Margate Pier Co. v. Hannam*, 3 B. & Ald. 266, 270, Abbott, C. J. quotes from Lord Coke as follows: "Acts of parliament are to be so construed as no man that is innocent or free from injury or wrong be, by a literal construction, punished or endangered." In the case of *State v. Clark*, 29 N. J. Law (5 Dutcher) 96, 98, 99, it appeared that an act had been passed, making it a misdemeanor to willfully break down a fence in the possession of another person. Clark was indicted under that statute. The defense was that the act of breaking down the fence, though willful, was in the exercise of a legal right to go upon his own lands. The trial court rejected the testimony offered to sustain the defense, and the supreme court held that this ruling was error. In its opinion the court used this language:

> "The act of 1855, in terms, makes the willful opening, breaking down, or injuring of any fences belonging to or in the possession of any other person a misdemeanor. In what sense is the term 'willful' used? In common parlance, 'willful' is used in the sense of 'intentional,' as distinguished from 'accidental' or 'involuntary.' Whatever one does intentionally, he does willfully. Is it used in that sense in this act? Did the legislature intend to make the intentional opening of a fence for the purpose of going upon the land of another indictable, if done by permission or for a lawful purpose? . . . We cannot suppose such to have been the actual intent. To adopt such a construction would put a stop to the ordinary business of life. The language of the act, if construed literally, evidently leads to an absurd result. If a literal construction of the words of a statute be absurd, the act must be so construed as to avoid the absurdity. The court must restrain the words. The object designed to be reached by the act must limit and control the literal import of the terms and phrases employed."

In *United States v. Kirby*, [74 U.S. (7 Wall.) 482 (1869)], the defendants were indicted for the violation of an act of Congress providing "that if any person shall knowingly and willfully obstruct or retard the passage of the mail, or of any driver or carrier, or of any horse or carriage carrying the same, he shall, upon conviction, for every such offence pay a fine not exceeding one hundred dollars." [Act of Mar. 3, 1825, ch. 64, § 9, 4 Stat. 102, 104.] The specific charge was that the defendants knowingly and willfully retarded the passage of one Farris, a carrier of the mail, while engaged in the performance of his duty, and also in like manner retarded the steam-boat Gen. Buell, at that time engaged in carrying the mail. To this indictment the defendants pleaded specially that Farris had been indicted for murder by a court of competent authority in Kentucky; that a bench-warrant had been issued and placed in the hands of the defendant Kirby, the sheriff of the county, commanding him to arrest Farris, and bring him before the court to answer to the indictment; and that, in obedience to this warrant, he and the other defendants, as his posse, entered upon the steamboat Gen. Buell and arrested Farris, and used only such force as was necessary to accomplish that arrest. The question as to the sufficiency of this plea was certified to this court, and it was held that the arrest of Farris upon the warrant from the state court was not an obstruction of the mail, or the retarding of the passage of a carrier of the mail, within the meaning of the act. In its opinion the court says:

> "All laws should receive a sensible construction. General terms should be so limited in their application as not to lead to injustice, oppression, or an absurd consequence. It will always, therefore, be presumed that the legislature intended exceptions to its language which would avoid results of this character. The reason of the law in

such cases should prevail over its letter. The common sense of man approves the judgment mentioned by Puffendorf, that the Bolognian law which enacted 'that whoever drew blood in the streets should be punished with the utmost severity,' did not extend to the surgeon who opened the vein of a person that fell down in the street in a fit. The same common sense accepts the ruling, cited by Plowden, that the statute of 1st Edward II., which enacts that a prisoner who breaks prison shall be guilty of felony, does not extend to a prisoner who breaks out when the prison is on fire, 'for he is not to be hanged because he would not stay to be burnt.' And we think that a like common sense will sanction the ruling we make, that the act of Congress which punishes the obstruction or retarding of the passage of the mail, or of its carrier, does not apply to a case of temporary detention of the mail caused by the arrest of the carrier upon an indictment for murder."

[*Id.* at 486.] . . .[*]

---

[*] *Editor's note*: After reading this passage, you may be wondering why the federal government chose to prosecute Sheriff Kirby in the first place. For a fuller picture of the facts, see David Achtenberg, *With Malice Toward Some:* United States v. Kirby, *Malicious Prosecution, and the Fourteenth Amendment*, 26 RUTGERS L.J. 273, 275 (1995).

During the Civil War, Cyrus Farris (the mail carrier) had been the Union Army's deputy provost marshal for Gallatin County, Kentucky. *Id.* at 279. Although Kentucky remained in the Union, Gallatin County was "a hotbed of pro-Confederate sympathy," and pro-Confederate "guerrillas" were very active there. *Id.* at 282. One such guerrilla, John Morrow, threatened to kill Farris, and Farris eventually caused a detachment of Union soldiers to search for Morrow. *See id.* at 288–93. When they found him, the soldiers shot and killed Morrow and a man who had been helping him. *Id.* at 293–95.

After the war ended, Farris could not safely remain in Gallatin County, so he moved to Cincinnati, Ohio. *See id.* at 303–06. The federal government soon hired him as the "mail agent" on a steamboat that carried the mail along the Ohio River. *Id.* at 310.

Meanwhile, back in Gallatin County, former Confederates and Confederate sympathizers dominated the local government. *See id.* at 303. The sheriff, John Kirby, was John Morrow's brother-in-law, and Kirby's deputy was Morrow's brother. *Id.* at 282, 309. Likewise, eleven of the sixteen members of the grand jury that convened in 1866 "were returned Confederates or Southern sympathizers." *Id.* at 306. This was the grand jury that indicted Farris on the murder charges, which were about the shootings of John Morrow and his helper by the Union Army during the war. *See id.* at 306–07; *see also id.* at 298–302, 337–42 (noting that the prosecution of Farris and other former Union soldiers was part of a pattern not only in Kentucky but also "in other states where former Confederates gained control of the local judicial system").

After the grand jury indicted Farris and a local court issued a warrant for his arrest, Sheriff Kirby immediately sent his deputy and three other men (all of whom had been Confederate soldiers) to seize Farris on the mail steamboat. *See id.* at 308–11. Those four men ended up having a violent confrontation with the crew of the steamboat; according to a military board of investigation, they would have murdered Farris, but the crew rescued him. *See id.* at 311–13. The four men then "found Sheriff Kirby and, with his help, gathered a mob to stop the ship." *Id.* at 313 (footnotes omitted). Ultimately, Kirby and the mob caught up with the steamboat, tied it to a landing, searched it, and seized Farris. *See id.* at 313–18. By this time, though, people who supported Farris had also arrived—which may be why Farris was simply arrested and not murdered. *See id.* at 318–19.

This background helps explain why the federal government chose to prosecute Sheriff Kirby, but the Supreme Court may not have known about it. *See id.* at 330–36 (explaining that the case reached the Court after the prosecution demurred to Kirby's pleas in defense, with the result that the Court considered the case on the facts as pleaded by the defendant). If the Court had known the facts reported by Professor Achtenberg, should it have adopted a different interpretation of the statute about obstructing the mails, or are those facts relevant only to whether Sheriff Kirby really qualified for the exception or defense that the Court recognized?

Among other things which may be considered in determining the intent of the legislature is the title of the act. We do not mean that it may be used to add to or take from the body of the statute, *Hadden v. The Collector*, [72 U.S. (5 Wall.) 107 (1867)], but it may help to interpret its meaning. In the case of *United States v. Fisher*, [6 U.S. (2 Cranch) 358, 386 (1805)], Chief Justice Marshall said: "On the influence which the title ought to have in construing the enacting clauses, much has been said, and yet it is not easy to discern the point of difference between the opposing counsel in this respect. Neither party contends that the title of an act can control plain words in the body of the statute; and neither denies that, taken with other parts, it may assist in removing ambiguities. Where the intent is plain, nothing is left to construction. Where the mind labors to discover the design of the legislature, it seizes everything from which aid can be derived; and in such case the title claims a degree of notice, and will have its due share of consideration." And in the case of *United States v. Palmer*, [16 U.S. (3 Wheat.) 610 (1818)], the same judge applied the doctrine in this way:

> "The words of the section [providing that 'if any person or persons shall commit, upon the high seas, . . . murder or robbery, . . . every such offender shall be deemed, taken, and adjudged to be a pirate and felon, and being thereof convicted, shall suffer death'] are in terms of unlimited extent. The words 'any person or persons' are broad enough to comprehend every human being. But general words must not only be limited to cases within the jurisdiction of the state, but also to those objects to which the legislature intended to apply them. Did the legislature intend to apply these words to the subjects of a foreign power, who in a foreign ship may commit murder or robbery on the high seas [against other subjects of a foreign power on board a ship that does not belong even in part to the United States or to any citizen thereof]?
>
> "The title of an act cannot control its words, but may furnish some aid in showing what was in the mind of the legislature. The title of this act is, 'an act for the punishment of certain crimes against the United States.' It would seem that offences against the United States, not offences against the human race, were the crimes which the legislature intended by this law to punish."

[*Id.* at 631.]

. . . . [In the case at hand], the title of this act is, "An act to prohibit the importation and migration of foreigners and aliens under contract or agreement to perform labor in the United States, its Territories, and the District of Columbia." Obviously the thought expressed in this reaches only to the work of the manual laborer, as distinguished from that of the professional man. No one reading such a title would suppose that Congress had in its mind any purpose of staying the coming into this country of ministers of the gospel, or, indeed, of any class whose toil is that of the brain. The common understanding of the terms "labor" and "laborers" does not include preaching and preachers, and it is to be assumed that words and phrases are used in their ordinary meaning. So whatever of light is thrown upon the statute by the language of the title indicates an exclusion from its penal provisions of all contracts for the employment of ministers, rectors, and pastors.

Again, another guide to the meaning of a statute is found in the evil which it is designed to remedy; and for this the court properly looks at contemporaneous events, the situation as it existed, and as it was pressed upon the attention of the legislative body. *United States v. Union Pacific Railroad*, 91 U. S. 72, 79 [(1875)]. The situation which called for this statute was briefly but fully stated by Mr. Justice Brown when, as district judge, he decided the case of *United States v. Craig*, 28 F. 795, 798 [(C.C.E.D. Mich. 1886)]:

> "The motives and history of the act are matters of common knowledge. It had become the practice for large capitalists in this country to contract with their agents abroad for the shipment of great numbers of an ignorant and servile class of foreign laborers, under contracts by which the employer agreed, upon the one hand, to prepay their passage, while, upon the other hand, the laborers agreed to work after their arrival for a certain time at a low rate of wages. The effect of this was to break down the labor market, and to reduce other laborers engaged in like occupations to the level of the assisted immigrant. The evil finally became so flagrant that an appeal was made to Congress for relief by the passage of the act in question, the design of which was to raise the standard of foreign immigrants, and to discountenance the migration of those who had not sufficient means in their own hands, or those of their friends, to pay their passage."

It appears, also, from the petitions, and in the testimony presented before the committees of Congress, that it was this cheap, unskilled labor which was making the trouble, and the influx of which Congress sought to prevent. It was never suggested that we had in this country a surplus of brain toilers, and, least of all, that the market for the services of Christian ministers was depressed by foreign competition. Those were matters to which the attention of Congress, or of the people, was not directed. So far, then, as the evil which was sought to be remedied interprets the statute, it also guides to an exclusion of this contract from the penalties of the act.

A singular circumstance, throwing light upon the intent of Congress, is found in this extract from the report of the Senate Committee on Education and Labor, recommending the passage of the bill:

> "The general facts and considerations which induce the committee to recommend the passage of this bill are set forth in the Report of the Committee of the House. The committee report the bill back without amendment, although there are certain features thereof which might well be changed or modified, in the hope that the bill

> may not fail of passage during the present session. Especially would the committee have otherwise recommended amendments, substituting for the expression 'labor and service,' whenever it occurs in the body of the bill, the words 'manual labor' or 'manual service,' as sufficiently broad to accomplish the purposes of the bill, and that such amendments would remove objections which a sharp and perhaps unfriendly criticism may urge to the proposed legislation. The committee, however, believing that the bill in its present form will be construed as including only those whose labor or service is manual in character, and being very desirous that the bill become a law before the adjournment, have reported the bill without change." Congressional Record, 48th Cong., p. 6059.

And, referring back to the report of the Committee of the House, there appears this language:

> "It seeks to restrain and prohibit the immigration or importation of laborers who would have never seen our shores but for the inducements and allurements of men whose only object is to obtain labor at the lowest possible rate, regardless of the social and material well-being of our own citizens, and regardless of the evil consequences which result to American laborers from such immigration. This class of immigrants care nothing about our institutions, and in many instances never even heard of them. They are men whose passage is paid by the importers. They come here under contract to labor for a certain number of years. They are ignorant of our social condition, and, that they may remain so, they are isolated and prevented from coming into contact with Americans. They are generally from the lowest social stratum, and live upon the coarsest food, and in hovels of a character before unknown to American workmen. They, as a rule, do not become citizens, and are certainly not a desirable acquisition to the body politic. The inevitable tendency of their presence among us is to degrade American labor, and to reduce it to the level of the imported pauper labor." Congressional Record, 48th Cong., p. 5359.

We find, therefore, that the title of the act, the evil which was intended to be remedied, the circumstances surrounding the appeal to Congress, the reports of the committee of each house, all concur in affirming that the intent of Congress was simply to stay the influx of this cheap, unskilled labor.

But, beyond all these matters, no purpose of action against religion can be imputed to any legislation, state or national, because this is a religious people. This is historically true. From the discovery of this continent to the present hour, there is a single voice making this affirmation. The commission to Christopher Columbus, prior to his sail westward, is from "Ferdinand and Isabella, by the grace of God, king and queen of Castile," etc., and recites that "it is hoped that by God's assistance some of the continents and islands in the ocean will be discovered," etc. The first colonial grant, that made to Sir Walter Raleigh in 1584, was from "Elizabeth, by the grace of God, of England, Fraunce and Ireland, queene, defender of the faith," etc.; and the grant authorizing him to enact statutes of the government of the proposed colony provided that "they be not against the true Christian faith nowe professed in the Church of England." The first charter of Virginia, granted by King James I in 1606, after reciting the application of certain parties for a charter, commenced the grant in these words: "We, greatly commending, and graciously accepting of, their Desires for the Furtherance of so noble a Work, which may, by the Providence of Almighty God, hereafter tend to the Glory of his Divine Majesty, in propagating of Christian Religion to such People, as yet live in Darkness and miserable Ignorance of the true Knowledge and Worship of God, and may in time bring the Infidels and Savages, living in those parts, to human Civility, and to a settled and quiet Government; DO, by these our Letters-Patents, graciously accept of, and agree to, their humble and well-intended Desires."

Language of similar import may be found in . . . the various charters granted to the other colonies. . . .

Coming nearer to the present time, the Declaration of Independence recognizes the presence of the Divine in human affairs in these words: "We hold these truths to be self-evident, that all men are created equal, that they are endowed by their Creator with certain unalienable Rights, that among these are Life, Liberty, and the pursuit of Happiness." "We, therefore, the Representatives of the united States of America, in General Congress, Assembled, appealing to the Supreme Judge of the world for the rectitude of our intentions, do, in the Name and by Authority of the good People of these Colonies, solemnly publish and declare," etc.; "And for the support of this Declaration, with a firm reliance on the Protection of Divine Providence, we mutually pledge to each other our Lives, our Fortunes, and our sacred Honor."

If we examine the constitutions of the various States, we find in them a constant recognition of religious obligations. Every constitution of every one of the forty-four States contains language which, either directly or by clear implication, recognizes a profound reverence for religion, and an assumption that its influence in all human affairs is essential to the well-being of the community. [Many quotations omitted.] . . .

Even the Constitution of the United States, which is supposed to have little touch upon the private life of the individual, contains in the First Amendment a declaration common to the constitutions of all the states, as follows: "Congress shall make no law respecting an establishment of religion, or prohibiting the free exercise thereof," etc. And also provides in Article 1, § 7, (a provision common to many constitutions,) that the executive shall have ten days (Sundays excepted) within which to determine whether he will approve or veto a bill.

There is no dissonance in these declarations. There is a universal language pervading them all, having one meaning; they affirm and reaffirm that this is a religious nation. . . .

If we pass beyond these matters to a view of American life, as expressed by its laws, its business, its customs, and its society, we find everywhere a clear recognition of the same truth. Among other matters note the following: The form of oath universally prevailing, concluding with an appeal to the Almighty; the custom of opening sessions of all deliberative bodies and most conventions with prayer; the prefatory words of all wills, "In the name of God, amen"; the laws respecting the observance of the Sabbath, with the general cessation of all secular business, and the closing of courts, legislatures, and other similar public assemblies on that day; the churches and church organizations which abound in every city, town, and hamlet; the multitude of charitable organizations existing every where under Christian auspices; the gigantic missionary associations, with general support, and aiming to establish Christian missions in every quarter of the globe. These, and many other matters which might be noticed, add a volume of unofficial declarations to the mass of organic utterances that this is a Christian nation. In the face of all these, shall it be believed that a Congress of the United States intended to make it a misdemeanor for a church of this country to contract for the services of a Christian minister residing in another nation?

Suppose in the Congress that passed this act some member had offered a bill which in terms declared that, if any Roman Catholic church in this country should contract with Cardinal Manning to come to this country and enter into its service as pastor and priest; or any Episcopal church should enter into a like contract with Canon Farrar; or any Baptist church should make similar arrangements with Rev. Mr. Spurgeon; or any Jewish synagogue with some eminent Rabbi, such contract should be adjudged unlawful and void, and the church making it be subject to prosecution and punishment[.] Can it be believed that it would have received a minute of approving thought or a single vote? Yet it is contended that such was, in effect, the meaning of this statute. The construction invoked cannot be accepted as correct. It is a case where there was presented a definite evil, in view of which the legislature used general terms with the purpose of reaching all phases of that evil; and thereafter, unexpectedly, it is developed that the general language thus employed is broad enough to reach cases and acts which the whole history and life of the country affirm could not have been intentionally legislated against. It is the duty of the courts, under those circumstances, to say that, however broad the language of the statute may be, the act, although within the letter, is not within the intention of the legislature, and therefore cannot be within the statute. . . .

NOTES AND QUESTIONS

1. In the Tanner Lectures that he delivered at Princeton in 1994–1995 and that were subsequently published in essay form, Justice Scalia called *Church of the Holy Trinity* "the prototypical case involving the triumph of supposed 'legislative intent' (a handy cover for judicial intent) over the text of the law." He indicated that he would have approached the case quite differently than Justice Brewer: "I think that the [church's conduct] was within the letter of the statute, and was therefore within the statute: end of case." To this day, Justice Scalia complained, "*Church of the Holy Trinity* is cited to us whenever counsel wants us to ignore the narrow, deadening text of the statute, and pay attention to the life-giving legislative intent. It is nothing but an invitation to judicial lawmaking." Antonin Scalia, *Common-Law Courts in a Civil-Law System: The Role of United States Federal Courts in Interpreting the Constitution and Laws*, *in* A MATTER OF INTERPRETATION: FEDERAL COURTS AND THE LAW 3, 18–21 (Amy Gutmann ed., 1997).

Despite their disagreement about the proper outcome, Justice Scalia and Justice Brewer both started from the same premise: the letter of section 1 of the statute prohibits what the church did. Is the statutory language really as clear as they suggested? At least in other contexts, couldn't one plausibly read the word "labor" to cover only work of the sort performed by "laborers" (a word that typically connotes manual employment) and "service" to cover only work of the sort performed by "servants" (a word that has many different shades of meaning, but that can certainly be used to refer only to people who perform duties relating to their employer's house or person)? To be sure, section 1 of the relevant statute referred to "labor or service *of any kind*." But does the italicized phrase unambiguously mean that the statutory language covers anything that could conceivably be called "labor" or "service" (including the work performed by ministers and other "brain toilers")? Or can we first interpret the words "labor" or "service," figure out what categories of work they cover, and then apply the phrase "of any kind" to mean simply that the words cover everything within those categories?

Read in isolation, the phrase "labor or service of any kind" might well be ambiguous. But the exceptions set forth in section 5 of the statute suggest that Congress was using it fairly broadly in the context of this particular statute. For instance, section 5 makes an exception for "skilled workm[e]n" hired to "perform labor in the United States in or upon any new industry," *if* "skilled labor for that purpose cannot be otherwise obtained." This exception suggests that section 1 was not thought to be confined to unskilled manual labor, but also included at least *skilled* labor. Section 5 also makes an exception for "professional actors, artists, lecturers, or singers," which again suggests that the phrase "labor or service" in section 1 is not restricted to the work done by manual laborers and low-level servants. After all, if people brought to America to work as artists, singers, and the like were not covered by section 1 in the first place, then the special exception in section 5 might seem unnecessary.[9]

The latter argument may well be the basis for Justice Scalia's view that the church violated the letter of section 1. But is that argument really independent of any sort of legislative intent? To the extent that the exceptions in section 5 affect the meaning that courts should ascribe to the phrase "labor or service of any kind" in section 1, exactly why are those exceptions relevant? Isn't the point that they shed light on what the enacting Congress understood section 1 to mean—on the scope of the legal directive that Congress intended to establish? *Cf.* Brown v. Maryland, 25 U.S. (12 Wheat.) 419, 438 (1827) ("[T]he exception of a particular thing from general words, proves that, *in the opinion of the lawgiver*, the thing excepted would be within the general clause had the exception not been made." (emphasis added)).

One might respond, as Justice Scalia did, that the kind of legislative intent properly sought by courts is not purely "subjective" and need not always match what members of the enacting legislature actually had in mind. Instead, "[w]e look for a sort of 'objectified' intent—the intent that a reasonable person would gather from the text of the law, placed alongside the remainder of the *corpus juris*." Scalia, *supra*, at 17. But even if we filter our approach to statutory interpretation through a hypothetical reasonable reader (who is familiar with the relevant principles of interpretation and who knows whatever information those principles make relevant), aren't we imagining that our hypothetical reader will go through the logic that I just described? When we try to explain why section 5 bears on the meaning that a reasonable reader would assign to section 1, won't we gravitate toward saying that section 5 tells the reader something about the *intended* meaning of section 1—about the message that section 1 apparently was intended to communicate? At a minimum, is it not clear (as Justice Scalia himself acknowledged) that the concept of "what the text would reasonably be understood to mean" and the concept of "what it was intended to mean" will "chase one another back and forth to some extent"? *See* Antonin Scalia, *Response*, *in* A MATTER OF INTERPRETATION, *supra*, at 129, 144.

If that is so, then what exactly did Justice Scalia mean when he inveighed against Justice Brewer's opinion in *Church of the Holy Trinity* for elevating legislative intent over statutory text? Might the problem (according to Justice Scalia) be that Justice Brewer focused on the wrong *kind* of legislative intent—that he went beyond the intended meaning of the words and phrases in the statute and ended up following purported intentions that Congress had not actually enacted into law? Or is the problem that Justice Brewer constructed his vision of legislative intent not simply from sources of the sort that Justice Scalia considered

[9] Similarly, if the word "service" in section 1 were read narrowly to refer only to work of the sort done by "servants," then the explicit exception in section 5 for "persons employed strictly as personal or domestic servants" might leave the word with no real function in the statute.

acceptable (like the public history of the times and the language of other provisions in the same statute) but also from sources of the sort that Justice Scalia generally considered off limits (like the committee reports that Justice Brewer quoted)?

2. Whatever the answer to the last set of questions, there is no doubt that Justice Scalia did not want courts to ascribe meaning to statutes on the basis of the reports that congressional committees prepared during the process of enactment (or, for that matter, on the basis of speeches made during the process by individual legislators). Chapter 3 considers that issue in detail. For now, you should just note that Justice Brewer's opinion in *Church of the Holy Trinity* is a relatively early example of the use of internal legislative history in statutory interpretation, and that in this respect it differs from Judge Earl's opinion in *Riggs v. Palmer* (which conducted imaginative reconstruction without the benefit of any internal legislative history).

In recent years, scholars have debated whether Justice Brewer drew the correct conclusions from the committee reports that he considered (assuming that he was right to consider those reports at all). *Compare* Adrian Vermeule, *Legislative History and the Limits of Judicial Competence: The Untold Story of* Holy Trinity Church, 50 STAN. L. REV. 1833 (1998) (arguing that the legislative history actually cut against Justice Brewer's conclusions), *with* Carol Chomsky, *Unlocking the Mysteries of* Holy Trinity*: Spirit, Letter, and History in Statutory Interpretation*, 100 COLUM. L. REV. 901 (2000) (acknowledging that Justice Brewer's research was insufficiently thorough, but arguing that his bottom line was correct). It is true, as the Court said, that the report of the Senate's Committee on Education and Labor (1) expressed the committee's belief that the bill would be interpreted to cover "only those whose labor or service is manual in character," (2) also expressed the committee's preference for making this limitation explicit by inserting the word "manual" before the words "labor" and "service" wherever they appeared in the bill, and (3) explained that the committee was reporting the bill back to the full Senate without this or any other change "in the hope that the bill may not fail of passage during the present session." As Professor Vermeule's research revealed, though, that session was the first session of the 48th Congress, which ended on July 7, 1884. At the behest of a member of the committee, the full Senate did consider the bill in the waning days of that session, but the Senate ultimately voted to put the bill off until the next session.

When the Senate took up the bill again in the second session, it adopted several amendments proposed by Senator Blair (a member of the committee). But Blair did not propose the insertion of the word "manual" before "labor" or "service," and the Senate did not make this change. One possible explanation, of course, is that Sen. Blair and his colleagues simply considered the change unnecessary, because they thought that the bill would be understood to be limited to manual laborers even without any such amendment. But Professor Vermeule reads some of the floor debates in the second session to cut against this explanation, and to indicate that members of Congress expected the statute to cover the importation of lawyers, journalists, and other professional people under contract to perform work in the United States. In any event, contrary to the implication of the Supreme Court's opinion, the Senate did not actually rush the bill through the first session (as the committee had hoped). How much does this information undermine the conclusion that the Court drew from the committee's report?

3. At the end of the day, what exactly did Justice Brewer's opinion in *Church of the Holy Trinity* read section 1 to cover? When Justice Brewer argued that "this is a religious people" and that Congress presumably had not intended "to make it a misdemeanor for a church of this country to contract for the services of a Christian minister residing in another nation," was he suggesting that a special religious exception should be read into section 1—so that the statute did not reach "contracts for the employment of ministers, rectors, and pastors" even though it did reach contracts for the importation of other professional people? Or were his comments about religion part of a broader argument to the effect that section 1 covered only the importation of "cheap, unskilled labor" and did not reach any "brain toilers" at all (notwithstanding the contrary clues provided by section 5)? Would one of these interpretations of section 1 be more defensible than the other? Did Justice Brewer's opinion end up choosing between them?

4. On one way of thinking, Justice Brewer's opinion in *Church of the Holy Trinity* read an unstated exception into a broadly worded statute so as to prevent the statute from applying in a situation where the Court thought that its application would be absurd as a policy matter. Arguably, that is also what Judge Earl did in *Riggs v. Palmer* (at least to the extent that his opinion rested on *ad hoc* imaginative reconstruction rather than an applicable rule of common law).

In modern times, this version of the presumption against absurd results has fallen out of favor. Some "textualists" have entirely rejected it; in their view, judges have no warrant to second-guess a statute's breadth and to infer *ad hoc* exceptions on policy grounds. *See, e.g.*, John F. Manning, *The Absurdity Doctrine*, 116 HARV. L. REV. 2387 (2003); *see also* Jaskolski v. Daniels, 427 F.3d 456, 462 (7th Cir. 2005) (Easterbrook, J.) [*infra* p. 97] ("Today the anti-absurdity canon is linguistic rather than substantive. It deals with texts that don't scan as written . . . rather than with statutes that seem poor fits for the task at hand."). Other modern jurists do not go that far, but they set a very high threshold for identifying the sort of "absurdity" that would persuade them to read an unstated exception into seemingly general statutory language. *See, e.g.*, Public Citizen v. United States Dep't of Justice, 491 U.S. 440, 470–71 (1989) (Kennedy, J., concurring in the judgment) (arguing that a result is "absurd" in the relevant sense only "where it is quite impossible that

Congress could have intended the result . . . and where the alleged absurdity is so clear as to be obvious to most anyone"). Why might one set such a high threshold? *Cf. infra* p. 70 (discussing the level of confidence that judges should have before diagnosing a drafting error in a statute).

Of course, even if judges should not lightly read an unstated exception into seemingly general statutory language so as to avoid an application that they consider "absurd," the fact that one interpretation of a statute would produce absurd results can still affect how judges resolve *ambiguities* in the statute. In the words of the United States Court of Appeals for the Tenth Circuit, "When statutory language reasonably admits of alternative constructions, there is nothing remarkable about resolving the textual ambiguity against the alternative meaning that produces a result the framers are highly unlikely to have intended. We choose the reasonable result over the 'absurd' one." *Robbins v. Chronister*, 435 F.3d 1238, 1241 (10th Cri. 2006) (en banc).

5. Does the penal nature of the statute in *Church of the Holy Trinity* help to justify Justice Brewer's style of analysis? Should courts read penal statutes more stingily than other statutes, and be more willing to infer unstated exceptions for morally blameless conduct that the legislature may not have intended to reach? (Return to this question after you have read the materials in Chapter 2 about the rule of lenity.)

6. The opinion issued by the trial court in *Church of the Holy Trinity* reached a different result than Justice Brewer. The trial court acknowledged that "[e]xcept [for] the language of the statute[,] there is no reason to suppose a contract like the present to be within the evils which the law was designed to suppress; and, indeed, it would not be indulging a violent supposition to assume that no legislative body in this country would have advisedly enacted a law framed so as to cover a case like the present." But the trial court insisted that "[n]evertheless, where the terms of a statute are plain, unambiguous, and explicit, the courts are not at liberty to go outside of the language to search for a meaning which it does not reasonably bear in the effort to ascertain and give effect to what may be imagined to have been or not to have been the intention of Congress." Informed by the exceptions in section 5 of the statute, the trial court held that the church had violated section 1 and was liable for the fine prescribed by section 3. *United States v. Church of the Holy Trinity*, 36 F. 303, 304 (C.C.S.D.N.Y. 1888).

As Professor Chomsky has noted (*see* Chomsky, *supra*, 100 COLUM. L. REV. at 935–38), Congress reacted to the trial court's decision by adding exemptions to section 5 of the statute for "ministers of any religious denomination, . . . persons belonging to any recognized profession, [and] professors for colleges and seminaries." *See* An Act in Amendment to the Various Acts Relative to Immigration and the Importation of Aliens Under Contract or Agreement to Perform Labor, ch. 551, § 5, 26 Stat. 1084, 1085 (1891). But although Congress made this change while the church's appeal was pending before the Supreme Court, the amending statute (which addressed a multitude of other issues too) specified that "nothing contained in this act shall be construed to affect any prosecution or other proceeding, criminal or civil, begun under any existing act or any acts hereby amended, but such prosecution or other proceedings . . . shall proceed as if this act had not been passed." *Id.* § 12, 26 Stat. at 1086. Should the passage of the amendment nonetheless have colored the Supreme Court's interpretation of the statute that was at issue in *Church of the Holy Trinity*? If so, which side would it tend to support?

NOTE ON THE *STATUTES AT LARGE* AND THE *UNITED STATES CODE*

Pages 32–33 of this book provide the text of a federal statute as printed in the *United States Statutes at Large*. You will also see cases that cite statutory provisions as presented in the *United States Code*. This Note describes the difference between those two sources and why the difference sometimes matters.

After Congress enacts a statute, the complete text of the statute as enacted by Congress will eventually be reprinted in the *United States Statutes at Large*—a multi-volume set of books that contains all the statutes enacted by Congress going back to 1789, as well as some other materials. The set is organized chronologically; volume 1 contains statutes enacted by Congress between 1789 and 1799, volume 2 contains statutes enacted between 1799 and 1813, and so on. In more recent times, each volume of the *Statutes at Large* has contained the laws enacted during a single regular session of Congress (plus any extra session preceding the regular session). *See* 1 U.S.C. § 112. Every statute that Congress enacts is reprinted in the *Statutes at Large* in the form that Congress enacted it, although the editors often add cross-references in the margins.

Because the *Statutes at Large* is simply a chronological presentation of the complete text of every statute that Congress has enacted, it can be unwieldy. For instance, suppose you wanted to use the *Statutes at Large* to figure out the current wording of section 302(b) of the Small Business Investment Act of 1958 as it has been amended over the years. The version of the statute that Congress enacted in 1958 appears in volume 72 of the *Statutes at Large*, and section 302(b) read as follows:

> "Shares of stock in small business investment companies shall be eligible for purchase by national banks, and shall be eligible for purchase by other member banks of the Federal Reserve System and nonmember insured banks to the extent permitted under applicable State law; except that in no event shall any such bank hold shares

in small business investment companies in an amount aggregating more than 1 percent of its capital and surplus."

Small Business Investment Act of 1958, Pub. L. 85–699, § 302(b), 72 Stat. 689, 692 (1958). In 1960, Congress enacted a statute that added a new phrase at the beginning of this provision. *See* Small Business Investment Act Amendments of 1960, Pub. L. 86–502, § 5, 74 Stat. 196, 196 ("Subsection 302(b) of the Act is amended by deleting the first word and inserting in lieu thereof the following: 'Notwithstanding the provisions of section 6(a)(1) of the Bank Holding Company Act of 1956, shares'."). The following year, another statute made an additional change. *See* Small Business Investment Act Amendments of 1961, Pub. L. 87–341, § 3(b), 75 Stat. 752, 752 ("Section 302(b) of such Act is amended by striking out '1 percent of its capital and surplus' and inserting in lieu thereof '2 percent of its capital and surplus'."). Further changes have followed. *See, e.g.*, Act of Oct. 11, 1967, Pub. L. 90–104, § 204, 81 Stat. 268, 270; Act of June 4, 1976, Pub. L. 94–305, § 107, 90 Stat. 663, 666; Act of Aug. 4, 1977, Pub. L. 95–89, § 210, 91 Stat. 553, 558; Act of Dec. 2, 1997, Pub. L. 105–135, § 215(a), 111 Stat. 2592, 2601; Act of Dec. 21, 2000, Pub. L. 106–554, App. I, § 403, 114 Stat. 2763, 2763A–690. To use the *Statutes at Large* to determine the law as it currently stands, you would need to find all of these statutes. Starting with the original version of section 302(b) as enacted in 1958, you would follow the instructions of each successive statute to figure out what Congress has added and subtracted over the years.

For quick-and-dirty purposes, though, lawyers can avoid a lot of that work by using a different set of books—not the *Statutes at Large* but the *United States Code*. The *United States Code* is based on the statutes that Congress has enacted, but it does not contain the raw statutes themselves. Instead, it is an editorial compilation and consolidation of provisions found in those statutes. It is published by an office within the United States House of Representatives called the Office of the Law Revision Counsel (OLRC). *See* 2 U.S.C. § 285 (establishing this office). Every six years, the OLRC publishes a new edition of the *United States Code*. In between, the OLRC publishes annual supplements, and it also helps to maintain a website with the current version of the Code.

Unlike the *Statutes at Large* (which contains the complete text of every statute that Congress has enacted), the *United States Code* does not reflect every single provision of every single statute, or even every single statute that is currently in force. Instead, the Code is supposed to contain only "the general and permanent laws of the United States." 2 U.S.C. § 285b.[10] As a result, some statutory provisions do not appear

[10] The section designation "285b," in which a letter appears without parentheses, does not refer to subsection (b) of section 285. (That would be cited as "§ 285(b).") Instead, 2 U.S.C. § 285b is an entire section, which follows sections 285 and 285a but precedes section 285c. Letters might be used this way in section designations when some newly enacted sections belong between two pre-existing sections of the Code, but the pre-existing section numbers do not leave

anywhere in the *United States Code. See* OLRC, *Frequently Asked Questions and Glossary*, uscode.house.gov/faq.xhtml (last visited Dec. 28, 2022) ("Temporary laws, such as appropriations acts, and special laws, such as one naming a post office, are not included in the Code."). Other enacted provisions, including some provisions that can play important roles in statutory interpretation, might appear only in the Code's "notes"—meaning that instead of being designated as sections of the Code in their own right, they appear in the fine print beneath some other section. *See* Jarrod Shobe, *Codification and the Hidden Work of Congress*, 67 UCLA L. REV. 640, 643 (2020) (observing that "important enacted provisions like findings, purposes, and rules of construction" might be "hidden away in notes of the Code"). Of course, even statutory provisions that do not appear in the Code or that are presented only in notes have still been enacted by Congress and still have legal effect. To find them, though, you might need to look in the *Statutes at Large*.

The rest of this Note describes the *United States Code*. As explained below, some of the titles in the *United States Code* have been enacted by Congress as such, with the structure that appears in the *United States Code*. But other titles in the *United States Code* have simply been put together by the OLRC or its predecessors on the basis of the statutes that Congress has enacted. That is not a mechanical process. Unlike the *Statutes at Large* (which simply presents entire statutes in chronological order), the *United States Code* is organized according to the subject matter of the provisions that it contains. A single statute might contain some provisions that belong in one title of the *United States Code*, other provisions that belong in a different title, and still other provisions that the OLRC decides not to include in the *United States Code* at all.

The *United States Code* is currently divided into the following fifty-four titles. (The names of most of the first fifty titles date back to 1926, when the first edition of the *United States Code* was published, and they reflect the language of that era. For now, ignore the asterisks that appear in front of some of the titles.)

*Title 1: General Provisions
Title 2: The Congress
*Title 3: The President
*Title 4: Flag and Seal, Seat of Government, and the States
*Title 5: Government Organization and Employees; and Appendix
Title 6: Domestic Security
Title 7: Agriculture
Title 8: Aliens and Nationality

enough room for each of the new sections to have a purely numerical designation. Indeed, you will sometimes see even more complex section designations. *See, e.g.*, 42 U.S.C. § 2000bb–1.

*Title 9: Arbitration
*Title 10: Armed Forces
*Title 11: Bankruptcy; and Appendix
Title 12: Banks and Banking
*Title 13: Census
*Title 14: Coast Guard
Title 15: Commerce and Trade
Title 16: Conservation
*Title 17: Copyrights
*Title 18: Crimes and Criminal Procedure; and Appendix
Title 19: Customs Duties
Title 20: Education
Title 21: Food and Drugs
Title 22: Foreign Relations and Intercourse
*Title 23: Highways
Title 24: Hospitals and Asylums
Title 25: Indians
Title 26: Internal Revenue Code
Title 27: Intoxicating Liquors
*Title 28: Judiciary and Judicial Procedure; and Appendix
Title 29: Labor
Title 30: Mineral Lands and Mining
*Title 31: Money and Finance
*Title 32: National Guard
Title 33: Navigation and Navigable Waters
Title 34: Crime Control and Law Enforcement
*Title 35: Patents
*Title 36: Patriotic and National Observances, Ceremonies, and Organizations
*Title 37: Pay and Allowances of the Uniformed Services
*Title 38: Veterans' Benefits
*Title 39: Postal Service
*Title 40: Public Buildings, Property, and Works
*Title 41: Public Contracts
Title 42: The Public Health and Welfare
Title 43: Public Lands

*Title 44: Public Printing and Documents
Title 45: Railroads
*Title 46: Shipping
Title 47: Telecommunications
Title 48: Territories and Insular Possessions
*Title 49: Transportation
Title 50: War and National Defense
*Title 51: National and Commercial Space Programs
Title 52: Voting and Elections
Title 53: [reserved]
*Title 54: National Park Service and Related Programs

The OLRC keeps the provisions in all of these titles up to date (albeit with some lag time), so the current edition of the *United States Code* reflects amendments that Congress has made over time to the underlying statutes. Again, consider the Small Business Investment Act of 1958. After Congress enacted the original Act, the predecessor of the OLRC chose to put many of the Act's provisions in Title 15 of the *United States Code*. For instance, section 302 of the Act was codified at 15 U.S.C. § 682. Each time Congress has amended section 302 since then, the OLRC or its predecessor has revised the language of 15 U.S.C. § 682 to reflect those changes. Thus, the version of 15 U.S.C. § 682 in the 2018 edition of the *United States Code* reflects the net result of amendments that Congress enacted in 1960, 1961, 1964, 1967, 1976, 1977, 1978, 1992, 1996, 1997, and 2000. Looking up the current version of 15 U.S.C. § 682 in the *United States Code* (and checking the online version to pick up more recent changes) is much quicker than using the *Statutes at Large* to track all the amendments yourself.[11]

Title 15 is one of the titles in the *United States Code* that Congress has *not* enacted as such. The provisions that appear in those titles all derive from statutes that Congress has enacted, like the Small Business Investment Act of 1958 and its amendments. But which provisions appear in which titles has not been decreed by Congress. With respect to the titles of the *United States Code* that Congress has not enacted as such, lawyers within the OLRC make decisions about how to "classify" all of the various statutory provisions that Congress enacts—that is, which statutory provisions to put into which titles of the *United States Code*, and where to put them within those titles. *See* OLRC, *About*

[11] Even so, it is often worthwhile to use the *Statutes at Large* to piece together all the changes for yourself. Seeing how the text of a provision has evolved may suggest arguments about how the current version of the provision should be interpreted. Likewise, lawyers can benefit from seeing what else Congress did in a statute that enacted or amended the provision.

Classification of Laws to the United States Code, uscode.house.gov/about_classification.xhtml (last visited Dec. 28, 2022).

One consequence of this fact is that the section numbers in those titles of the *United States Code* usually do not correspond to the section numbers in the statutes that Congress actually enacted. (As noted above, for instance, section 302 of the Small Business Investment Act of 1958 is found at section 682 of Title 15 of the *United States Code*.) That is not surprising. The section numbers in each statute that Congress enacts reflect the structure of that particular statute, and they would not fit the structure of a title of the *United States Code* that consists of provisions from many unconnected statutes.

Some other differences between the *United States Code* and the statutes that Congress actually enacted are more important (and may be more surprising). For the convenience of readers, individual sections and subsections in the *United States Code* have headings that describe their topics. In the titles of the *United States Code* that Congress has not enacted as such, however, many of those headings are not actually part of the law; while some of the section or subsection headings were part of the underlying statutes as enacted by Congress, others have simply been inserted by the OLRC or its predecessors after the fact. The only way to tell which are which is to check the *Statutes at Large*. But the difference can matter. If a section or subsection heading is part of the underlying statute that Congress itself enacted, interpreters might sometimes let the heading that Congress chose affect their interpretation of the section or subsection that the heading describes. By contrast, interpreters probably should not put any weight on headings that were simply added by the OLRC after the fact.

The differences between the *United States Code* and the statutes that Congress actually enacted can extend even to the operative words of a provision. In the titles of the *United States Code* that have simply been compiled by the OLRC without being enacted by Congress as such, the OLRC routinely makes a few kinds of changes when the OLRC puts a provision into the *United States Code*. As the OLRC explains, "the text of a Code section [in these titles] is based on the text of a section of an act as enacted by Congress, but certain editorial changes are made to integrate the section into the Code." OLRC, *Detailed Guide to the United States Code Content and Features*, uscode.house.gov/detailed_guide.xhtml (last visited Dec. 28, 2022). For instance, if a statute uses a phrase like "the date of enactment of this Act," the OLRC will replace that phrase with the actual date. *Id.* Likewise, if a statute includes a cross-reference, the OLRC will modify the cross-reference so that it refers to the relevant section or unit in the *United States Code* rather than the underlying statute. *Id.*

Those differences usually do not matter. Very occasionally, however, they can be significant. For instance, consider the following timeline:

- In 1952, Congress enacted the Immigration and Nationality Act, ch. 477, 66 Stat. 163. As enacted by Congress, the Act was divided into Title I (consisting of sections 101 through 105), Title II (sections 201 through 292), Title III (sections 301 through 360), and Title IV (sections 401 through 407). The predecessor of the OLRC put most of the Act's provisions in Title 8 of the *United States Code.*
- In 1966, Congress enacted a separate statute giving the Attorney General discretion to adjust the immigration status of certain people from Cuba. *See* Act of Nov. 2, 1966, Pub. L. 89–732, 80 Stat. 1161. This provision was not an amendment to the Immigration and Nationality Act; instead, it was a freestanding statutory provision. Presumably because it was not "general," the OLRC's predecessor decided not to include it in the main text of the *United States Code,* but the 1966 statute is reprinted in small type in the notes underneath 8 U.S.C. § 1255 (the codified version of section 245 of the Immigration and Nationality Act).
- In 1996, Congress amended section 242 of the Immigration and Nationality Act to include the following language: "Notwithstanding any other provision of law, no court shall have jurisdiction to review . . . any . . . decision or action of the Attorney General the authority for which is specified under this title to be in the discretion of the Attorney General . . . ." Act of Sept. 30, 1996, Pub. L. 104–208, § 306, 110 Stat. 3009, 3009–607. In the *United States Code,* the current version of this language appears at 8 U.S.C. § 1252(a)(2)(B), except that the OLRC replaced the phrase "this title" (which referred to Title II of the Immigration and Nationality Act) with the phrase "this subchapter" (referring to subchapter II of chapter 12 of Title 8 of the Code, where the provisions that correspond to Title II of the Immigration and Nationality Act appear).

Some courts have wrestled with whether 8 U.S.C. § 1252(a)(2)(B) deprives them of jurisdiction to review decisions made by the Attorney General under the discretionary authority conferred by the 1966 statute. *See, e.g.,* Baez v. United States, 715 F. Supp. 2d 1165, 1175–78 (D. Or. 2010) (calling this "a close question"). In the view of those courts, the issue boils down to the proper interpretation of the phrase "this subchapter" in 8 U.S.C. § 1252(a)(2)(B): Does that phrase include only the provisions that are designated as separate sections in subchapter II of chapter 12 of Title 8 of the *United States Code* (that is, 8 U.S.C. §§ 1151–1382), or does it also include provisions set forth in the notes underneath those sections? But that is the wrong question. The actual phrase that Congress enacted in 1996 was not "this subchapter" but "this title," and the 1966 statute definitely is *not* part of Title II of the Immigration and Nationality Act, as amended.[12]

With respect to the titles of the *United States Code* that Congress has not enacted as such, federal law provides that the current edition of the *United States Code* and its current supplement "establish prima facie the laws of the United States, general and permanent in their nature." 1 U.S.C. § 204(a). But the *Statutes at Large* are more powerful: Congress has specified that the *Statutes at Large* are "legal evidence" of the laws that they contain, 1 U.S.C. § 112, and "legal" evidence is understood to be better than "prima facie" evidence. Thus, in the event of differences between the *Statutes at Large* and the unenacted titles of the *United States Code*, courts are supposed to rely on the *Statutes at Large*.

Because the *United States Code* is easier to work with than the *Statutes at Large*, though, Congress has sporadically enacted entire titles of the *United States Code* as statutes. That project began in earnest in the 1940s, when Congress enacted Titles 1, 3, 4, 9, 14, 17, 18, and 28. The pace has slowed since then, but the project continues; for instance, Congress enacted Title 54 in 2014. As of this writing, Congress has enacted roughly half of the titles in the United States Code as such. The enacted titles are the ones designated with asterisks in the list on pp. 49–51 above.[13] (The statutes enacting those titles do not encompass the appendices, if any.)

To understand what it means for Congress to enact a title of the *United States Code* as a statute, you need an example. Take Title 18. On June 25, 1948, Congress enacted "An Act to Revise, Codify, and Enact into Positive Law, Title 18 of the United States Code, Entitled 'Crimes and Criminal Procedure.' " Ch. 645, 62 Stat. 683 (1948). Section 1 of that Act began as follows: "*Be it enacted by the Senate and House of Representatives of the United States of America in Congress assembled*, That Title 18 of the United States Code, entitled 'Crimes and Criminal Procedure,' is hereby revised, codified, and enacted into positive law, . . . as follows . . . ." The rest of section 1, which went on for the next 175 pages of the *Statutes at Large*, presented Title 18 exactly as Congress was enacting it. *Id.* at 683–858; *see also id.* § 21, 62 Stat. at 862–68 (repealing the corresponding provisions in prior statutes).

The fact that Congress has enacted Title 18 as a statute affects how Congress legislates going forward. If the current Congress wants to eliminate or change a provision found in Title 18, or if Congress wants to add a new provision to Title 18, Congress will enact a statute that

---

[12] Of course, there might be other obstacles to judicial review of the Attorney General's decisions about whether to exercise the discretion that the 1966 statute confers. *See* 5 U.S.C. § 701(a)(2) (indicating that the Administrative Procedure Act's chapter about judicial review does not apply "to the extent that . . . agency action is committed to agency discretion by law"); Garriga v. Hackbarth, 548 F. App'x 559, 561 (11th Cir. 2013) (invoking this provision to foreclose judicial review of decisions under the 1966 statute).

[13] In addition, Congress has enacted the Internal Revenue Code with the same structure that is found in Title 26. *See* Internal Revenue Code of 1954, ch. 736, 68A Stat. 3.

amends Title 18 directly. *See, e.g.*, Act of June 18, 2008, Pub. L. 110–246, § 14207(b), 122 Stat. 1651, 2224 ("Section 49 of title 18, United States Code, is amended by striking '3 years' and inserting '5 years'."). Congress should not (and usually does not) proceed this way with respect to the titles of the *United States Code* that have not been enacted as such. To change provisions found in those unenacted titles, Congress will amend the underlying statutes.

When the OLRC puts together each new edition of the *United States Code*, it incorporates the changes that Congress has made since the last edition. With respect to the titles that Congress has enacted as such, though, the OLRC does not have to do any work to integrate provisions into the style and structure of the Code. Thus, the OLRC does not make "editorial changes" in the titles that Congress has enacted as such. *Cf. supra* p. 52 (describing the kinds of changes that the OLRC makes with respect to provisions in titles of the *United States Code* that Congress has not enacted as such).

Partly for that reason, the *United States Code* is more authoritative with respect to the titles that Congress has enacted as such than with respect to the other titles. Although the unenacted titles are only "prima facie" evidence of the laws, Congress has provided that the text of the enacted titles is "legal evidence" of the laws that they contain. 1 U.S.C. § 204. With respect to the enacted titles, then, the *United States Code* is on a par with the *Statutes at Large*. But even with respect to those titles, lawyers who are carefully investigating the meaning of a provision should use the *Statutes at Large* to track the evolution of the statutory language. *See supra* p. 51, n.11. Lawyers should also be aware that some of the statutes by which Congress has enacted entire titles of the *United States Code* contain rules of construction or other special instructions that Congress did not make part of those titles, but that nonetheless can bear on questions of interpretation. *See, e.g., infra* p. 159 (noting that many such statutes instruct interpreters not to draw inferences about legislative intent from the section headings that appear in the titles of the *United States Code* that the statutes are enacting).

United States v. Locke

471 U.S. 84 (1985)

■ *JUSTICE MARSHALL delivered the opinion of the Court:*

. . . .

I

From the enactment of the general mining laws in the 19th century until 1976, those who sought to make their living by locating and developing minerals on federal lands were virtually unconstrained by the fetters of federal control. The general mining laws, 30 U.S.C. § 22 *et seq.*, still in effect today, allow United States citizens to go onto unappropriated, unreserved public land to prospect for and develop certain minerals. "Discovery" of a mineral deposit, followed by the minimal procedures required to formally "locate" the deposit, gives an individual the right of exclusive possession of the land for mining purposes, 30 U.S.C. § 26; as long as $100 of assessment work is performed annually, the individual may continue to extract and sell minerals from the claim without paying any royalty to the United States, 30 U.S.C. § 28. For a nominal sum, and after certain statutory conditions are fulfilled, an individual may patent the claim, thereby purchasing from the Federal Government the land and minerals and obtaining ultimate title to them. Patenting, however, is not required, and an unpatented mining claim remains a fully recognized possessory interest . . . .

By the 1960's, it had become clear that this 19th-century laissez-faire regime had created virtual chaos with respect to the public lands. . . . [I]n the absence of a federal recording system, no simple way existed for determining which public lands were subject to mining locations, and whether those locations were valid or invalid. As a result, federal land managers had to proceed slowly and cautiously in taking any action affecting federal land lest the federal property rights of claimants be unlawfully disturbed. . . .

After more than a decade of studying this problem in the context of a broader inquiry into the proper management of the public lands in the modern era, Congress in 1976 enacted [the Federal Land Policy and Management Act (FLPMA)], Pub. L. 94–579, 90 Stat. 2743 (codified at 43 U.S.C. § 1701 *et seq.*). Section 314 of the Act establishes a federal recording system that is designed both to rid federal lands of stale mining claims and to provide federal land managers with up-to-date information that allows them to make informed land management decisions.[2] For

---

[2] The text of 43 U.S.C. § 1744 provides, in relevant part, as follows:

"Recordation of Mining Claims

"(a) Filing requirements

"The owner of an unpatented lode or placer mining claim located prior to October 21, 1976, shall, within the three-year period following October 21, 1976 and prior to December 31 of each year thereafter, file the instruments required by paragraphs (1) and (2) of this subsection. . . .

"(1) File for record in the office where the location notice or certificate is recorded either a notice of intention to hold the mining claim (including but not limited to such notices as are provided by law to be filed when there has been a suspension or deferment of annual assessment work), an affidavit of assessment work performed thereon, on a detailed report provided by section 28–1 of title 30, relating thereto.

"(2) File in the office of the Bureau designated by the Secretary a copy of the official record of the instrument filed or recorded pursuant to paragraph (1) of this subsection, including a description of the location of the mining claim sufficient to locate the claimed lands on the ground.

"(b) Additional filing requirements

"The owner of an unpatented lode or placer mining claim or mill or tunnel site located prior to October 21, 1976 shall, within the three-year period following October 21, 1976, file in the office of the Bureau designated by the Secretary a copy of the official record of the notice of location or certificate of location, including a description of the location of the mining claim or mill or tunnel site sufficient to locate the claimed lands on the ground. The owner

claims located before FLPMA's enactment, the federal recording system imposes two general requirements. First, the claims must initially be registered with the [Bureau of Land Management (BLM)] by filing, within three years of FLPMA's enactment, a copy of the official record of the notice or certificate of location. 90 Stat. 2743, § 314(b), 43 U.S.C. § 1744(b). Second, in the year of the initial recording, and "prior to December 31" of every year after that, the claimant must file with state officials and with BLM a notice of intention to hold the claim, an affidavit of assessment work performed on the claim, or a detailed reporting form. 90 Stat. 2743, § 314(a), 43 U.S.C. § 1744(a). Section 314(c) of the Act provides that failure to comply with either of these requirements "shall be deemed conclusively to constitute an abandonment of the mining claim . . . by the owner." 43 U.S.C. § 1744(c).

The second of these requirements—the annual filing obligation—has created the dispute underlying this appeal. Appellees, four individuals engaged "in the business of operating mining properties in Nevada," purchased in 1960 and 1966 ten unpatented mining claims on public lands near Ely, Nevada. These claims were major sources of gravel and building material: the claims are valued at several million dollars, and, in the 1979–1980 assessment year alone, appellees' gross income totaled more than $1 million. Throughout the period during which they owned the claims, appellees complied with annual state-law filing and assessment work requirements. In addition, appellees satisfied FLPMA's initial recording requirement by properly filing with BLM a notice of location, thereby putting their claims on record for purposes of FLPMA.

At the end of 1980, however, appellees failed to meet on time their first annual obligation to file with the Federal Government. After allegedly receiving misleading information from a BLM employee,[7]

---

of an unpatented lode or placer mining claim or mill or tunnel site located after October 21, 1976 shall, within ninety days after the date of location of such claim, file in the office of the Bureau designated by the Secretary a copy of the official record of the notice of location or certificate of location, including a description of the location of the mining claim or mill or tunnel site sufficient to locate the claimed lands on the ground.

"(c) Failure to file as constituting abandonment; defective or untimely filing

"The failure to file such instruments as required by subsections (a) and (b) of this subsection shall be deemed conclusively to constitute an abandonment of the mining claim or mill or tunnel site by the owner; but it shall not be considered a failure to file if the instrument is defective or not timely filed for record under other Federal laws permitting filing or recording thereof, or if the instrument is filed for record by or on behalf of some but not all of the owners of the mining claim or mill or tunnel site."

[7] An affidavit submitted to the District Court by one of appellees' employees stated that BLM officials in Ely had told the employee that the filing could be made at the BLM Reno office "on or before December 31, 1980." Affidavit of Laura C. Locke ¶ 3. The 1978 version of a BLM question and answer pamphlet erroneously stated that the annual filings had to be made "on or before December 31" of each year. Staking a Mining Claim on Federal Lands 9–10 (1978). Later versions have corrected this error to bring the pamphlet into accord with the BLM regulations that require the filings to be made "on or before December 30."

[The dissenters] seek to make much of this pamphlet and of the uncontroverted evidence that appellees were told a December 31 filing would comply with the statute. However, at the time appellees filed in 1980, BLM regulations and the then-current pamphlets made clear that the filing was required "on or before December 30." Thus, the dissenters' reliance on this pamphlet would seem better directed to the claim that the United States was equitably estopped

appellees waited until December 31 to submit to BLM the annual notice of intent to hold or proof of assessment work performed required under § 314(a) of FLPMA, 43 U.S.C. § 1744(a). As noted above, that section requires these documents to be filed annually "prior to December 31." Had appellees checked, they further would have discovered that BLM regulations made quite clear that claimants were required to make the annual filings in the proper BLM office "on or before December 30 of each calendar year." 43 CFR § 3833.2–1(a) (1980) (current version at 43 CFR § 3833.2–1(b)(1) (1984)). Thus, appellees' filing was one day too late.

This fact was brought painfully home to appellees when they received a letter from the BLM Nevada State Office informing them that their claims had been declared abandoned and void due to their tardy filing. In many cases, loss of a claim in this way would have minimal practical effect; the claimant could simply locate the same claim again and then rerecord it with BLM. In this case, however, relocation of appellees' claims, which were initially located by appellees' predecessors in 1952 and 1954, was prohibited by the Common Varieties Act of 1955, 30 U.S.C. § 611; that Act prospectively barred location of the sort of minerals yielded by appellees' claims. Appellees' mineral deposits thus escheated to the Government.

After losing an administrative appeal, appellees filed the present action in the United States District Court for the District of Nevada. Their complaint alleged, *inter alia,* that § 314(c) effected an unconstitutional taking of their property without just compensation and denied them due process. On summary judgment, the District Court held that § 314(c) did indeed deprive appellees of the process to which they were constitutionally due. 573 F. Supp. 472 (1983). . . . Alternatively, the District Court held that the 1-day late filing "substantially complied" with the Act and regulations.

. . . . We now reverse.

. . . .

III

A

Before the District Court, appellees asserted that the § 314(a) requirement of a filing "prior to December 31 of each year" should be construed to require a filing "on or before December 31." Thus, appellees argued, their December 31 filing had in fact complied with the statute, and the BLM had acted ultra vires in voiding their claims.

Although the District Court did not address this argument, the argument raises a question sufficiently legal in nature that we choose to

---

from forfeiting appellees' claims, given the advice of the BLM agent and the objective basis the 1978 pamphlet provides for crediting the claim that such advice was given. The District Court did not consider this estoppel claim. Without expressing any view as to whether, as a matter of law, appellees could prevail on such a theory, . . . we leave any further treatment of this issue, including fuller development of the record, to the District Court on remand.

address it even in the absence of lower court analysis. . . . [T]he plain language of the statute simply cannot sustain the gloss appellees would put on it. As even counsel for appellees conceded at oral argument, § 314(a) "is a statement that Congress wanted it filed by December 30th. I think that is a clear statement . . . ." Tr. of Oral Arg. 27; see also id. at 37 ("A literal reading of the statute would require a December 30th filing . . . ."). While we will not allow a literal reading of a statute to produce a result "demonstrably at odds with the intentions of its drafters," *Griffin v. Oceanic Contractors, Inc.*, 458 U.S. 564, 571 (1982), with respect to filing deadlines a literal reading of Congress' words is generally the only proper reading of those words. To attempt to decide whether some date other than the one set out in the statute is the date actually "intended" by Congress is to set sail on an aimless journey, for the purpose of a filing deadline would be just as well served by nearly any date a court might choose as by the date Congress has in fact set out in the statute. "Actual purpose is sometimes unknown," *United States Railroad Retirement Board v. Fritz*, 449 U.S. 166, 180 (1980) (Stevens, J., concurring), and such is the case with filing deadlines; as might be expected, nothing in the legislative history suggests why Congress chose December 30 over December 31, or over September 1 (the end of the assessment year for mining claims, 30 U.S.C. § 28), as the last day on which the required filings could be made. But "[d]eadlines are inherently arbitrary," while fixed dates "are often essential to accomplish necessary results." *United States v. Boyle*, 469 U.S. 241, 249 (1985). Faced with the inherent arbitrariness of filing deadlines, we must, at least in a civil case, apply by its terms the date fixed by the statute. . . .

Moreover, BLM regulations have made absolutely clear since the enactment of FLPMA that "prior to December 31" means what it says. As the current version of the filing regulations states:

> "The owner of an unpatented mining claim located on Federal lands . . . shall have filed or caused to have been filed *on or before December 30* of each calendar year . . . evidence of annual assessment work performed during the previous assessment year or a notice of intention to hold the mining claim." 43 CFR § 3833.2–1(b)(1) (1984) (emphasis added).

. . . . Leading mining treatises similarly inform claimants that "[i]t is important to note that the filing of a notice of intention or evidence of assessment work must be done *prior* to December 31 of each year, i.e., on or before December 30." 2 American Law of Mining § 7.23D, p. 150.2 (Supp. 1983) (emphasis in original); see also 23 Rocky Mountain Mineral Law Institute 25 (1977) (same). If appellees, who were businessmen involved in the running of a major mining operation for more than 20 years, had any questions about whether a December 31 filing complied with the statute, it was incumbent upon them, as it is upon other businessmen, see *United States v. Boyle*, *supra*, to have checked the regulations or to have consulted an attorney for legal advice. Pursuit of either of these courses, rather than the submission of a last-minute filing, would surely have led appellees to the conclusion that December 30 was the last day on which they could file safely.

In so saying, we are not insensitive to the problems posed by congressional reliance on the words "prior to December 31." . . . But the fact that Congress might have acted with greater clarity or foresight does not give courts a *carte blanche* to redraft statutes in an effort to achieve that which Congress is perceived to have failed to do. "There is a basic difference between filling a gap left by Congress' silence and rewriting rules that Congress has affirmatively and specifically enacted." *Mobil Oil Corp. v. Higginbotham*, 436 U.S. 618, 625 (1978). Nor is the Judiciary licensed to attempt to soften the clear import of Congress' chosen words whenever a court believes those words lead to a harsh result. See *Northwest Airlines, Inc. v. Transport Workers*, 451 U.S. 77, 98 (1981). On the contrary, deference to the supremacy of the Legislature, as well as recognition that Congressmen typically vote on the language of a bill, generally requires us to assume that "the legislative purpose is expressed by the ordinary meaning of the words used." *Richards v. United States*, 369 U.S. 1, 9 (1962). "Going behind the plain language of a statute in search of a possibly contrary congressional intent is 'a step to be taken cautiously' even under the best of circumstances." *American Tobacco Co. v. Patterson*, 456 U.S. 63, 75 (1982) (quoting *Piper v. Chris-Craft Industries, Inc.*, 430 U.S. 1, 26 (1977)). When even after taking this step nothing in the legislative history remotely suggests a congressional intent contrary to Congress' chosen words, and neither appellees nor the dissenters have pointed to anything that so suggests, any further steps take the courts out of the realm of interpretation and place them in the domain of legislation. The phrase "prior to" may be clumsy, but its meaning is clear. Under these circumstances, we are obligated to apply the "prior to December 31" language by its terms. . . .

The agency's regulations clarify and confirm the import of the statutory language by making clear that the annual filings must be made on or before December 30. These regulations provide a conclusive answer to appellees' claim, for where the language of a filing deadline is plain and the agency's construction completely consistent with that language, the agency's construction simply cannot be found "sufficiently unreasonable" as to be unacceptable. *FEC v. Democratic Senatorial Campaign Committee*, 454 U.S. 27, 39 (1981).

We cannot press statutory construction "to the point of disingenuous evasion" even to avoid a constitutional question. *Moore Ice Cream Co. v. Rose*, 289 U.S. 373, 379 (1933) (Cardozo, J.).[12] We therefore hold that

[12] We note that the United States Code is sprinkled with provisions that require action "prior to" some date, including at least 14 provisions that contemplate action "prior to December 31." [Citations omitted.] Dozens of state statutes and local ordinances undoubtedly incorporate similar "prior to December 31" deadlines. . . .

It is unclear whether the arguments advanced by the dissenters are meant to apply to all of these provisions, or only to some of them; if the latter, we are given little guidance as to how

BLM did not act ultra vires in concluding that appellees' filing was untimely.

. . . . [The majority went on to conclude that the statute, as construed by the majority, did not violate the Constitution.]

▪ *[A concurring opinion by JUSTICE O'CONNOR and a dissenting opinion by JUSTICE POWELL are omitted.]*

▪ *JUSTICE STEVENS, with whom JUSTICE BRENNAN joins, dissenting:*

The Court's opinion is contrary to the intent of Congress, engages in unnecessary constitutional adjudication, and unjustly creates a trap for unwary property owners. First, the choice of the language "prior to December 31" when read in context in 43 U.S.C. § 1744(a) is, at least, ambiguous, and, at best, "the consequence of a legislative *accident*, perhaps caused by nothing more than the unfortunate fact that Congress is too busy to do all of its work as carefully as it should." [*Delaware Tribal Business Committee v. Weeks*, 430 U.S. 73, 97 (1977) (Stevens, J., dissenting).] In my view, Congress actually intended to authorize an annual filing at any time prior to the close of business on December 31st, that is, prior to the end of the calendar year to which the filing pertains. Second, even if Congress irrationally intended that the applicable deadline for a calendar year should end *one day before* the end of the calendar year that has been recognized since the amendment of the Julian Calendar in 8 B.C., it is clear that appellees have substantially complied with the requirements of the statute, in large part because the Bureau of Land Management has issued interpreting regulations that recognize substantial compliance. Further, the Court today violates not only the long-followed principle that a court should "not pass on the constitutionality of an Act of Congress if a construction of the statute is fairly possible by which the question may be avoided," [*United States v. Clark*, 445 U.S. 23, 27 (1980),] but also the principle that a court should "not decide a constitutional question if there is some other ground upon which to dispose of the case." [*Escambia County v. McMillan*, 466 U.S. 48, 51 (1984) (per curiam).]

I

Congress enacted § 314 of the Federal Land Policy and Management Act to establish for federal land planners and managers a federal recording system designed to cope with the problem of stale claims, and to provide "an easy way of discovering which Federal lands are subject to either valid or invalid mining claim locations."[6] I submit that the

---

a court is to go about the rather eclectic task of choosing which "prior to December 31" deadlines it can interpret "flexibly." . . .

[6] S. Rep. No. 94–583, p. 65 (1975). The Court agrees regarding the first purpose, but inexplicably and without citation concludes that another purpose of § 314 is "to provide federal land managers with up-to-date information that allows them to make informed management decisions." *Ante* at 87. This latter statutory "purpose" is not mentioned in the legislative history; rather, it is a variation of a "purpose," equally without citation, offered by appellants. See Brief for Appellants 45, 47.

appellees' actions in this case did not diminish the importance of these congressional purposes; to the contrary, their actions were entirely consistent with the statutory purposes, despite the confusion created by the "inartful draftsmanship" of the statutory language.

A careful reading of § 314 discloses at least three respects in which its text cannot possibly reflect the actual intent of Congress. First, the description of what must be filed in the initial filing and subsequent annual filings is quite obviously garbled. Read literally, § 314(a)(2) seems to require that a notice of intent to hold the claim and an affidavit of assessment work performed on the claim must be filed "on a detailed report provided by § 28–1 of Title 30." One must substitute the word "or" for the word "on" to make any sense at all out of this provision. This error should cause us to pause before concluding that Congress commanded blind allegiance to the remainder of the literal text of § 314.

Second, the express language of the statute is unambiguous in describing the place where the second annual filing shall be made. If the statute is read inflexibly, the owner must "file in the office of the Bureau" the required documents. [See 43 U.S.C. § 1744(a)(2).] Yet the regulations that the Bureau itself has drafted, quite reasonably, construe the statute to allow filing in a mailbox, provided that the document is actually received by the Bureau prior to the close of business on January 19 of the year following the year in which the statute requires the filing to be made. A notice mailed on December 30, 1982, and received by the Bureau on January 19, 1983, was filed "in the office of the Bureau" during 1982 within the meaning of the statute, but one that is hand-delivered to the office on December 31, 1982, cannot be accepted as a 1982 "filing."

The Court finds comfort in the fact that the implementing regulations have eliminated the risk of injustice. But if one must rely on those regulations, it should be apparent that the meaning of the statute itself is not all that obvious. To begin with, the regulations do not use the language "prior to December 31"; instead, they use "on or before December 30 of each year." The Bureau's drafting of the regulations using this latter phrase indicates that the meaning of the statute itself is not quite as "plain" as the Court assumes; if the language were plain, it is doubtful that the Bureau would have found it necessary to change the language at all. Moreover, the Bureau, under the aegis of the Department of the Interior, once issued a pamphlet entitled "Staking a Mining Claim on Federal Lands" that contained the following information:

> "Owners of claims or sites located on or before Oct. 21, 1976, have until Oct. 22, 1979, to file evidence of assessment work performed the preceding year or to file a notice of intent to hold the claim or site. Once the claim or site is recorded with BLM, *these documents must be filed on or before December 31 of each subsequent year.*" *Id.* at 9–10 (1978) (emphasis added).

"Plain language," indeed.

There is a more important reason why the implementing regulations cannot be supportive of the result the Court reaches today: the Bureau's own deviation from the statutory language in its mail-filing regulation. If the Bureau had issued regulations expressly stating that a December 31 filing would be considered timely—just as it has stated that a mail filing received on January 19 is timely—it is inconceivable that anyone would question the validity of its regulation. It appears, however, that the Bureau has more power to interpret an awkwardly drafted statute in an enlightened manner consistent with Congress' intent than does this Court.

In light of the foregoing, I cannot believe that Congress intended the words "prior to December 31 of each year" to be given the literal reading the Court adopts today. The statutory scheme requires periodic filings on a calendar-year basis. The end of the calendar year is, of course, correctly described either as "prior to the close of business on December 31," or "on or before December 31," but it is surely understandable that the author of § 314 might inadvertently use the words "prior to December 31" when he meant to refer to the end of the calendar year. As the facts of this case demonstrate, the scrivener's error is one that can be made in good faith. The risk of such an error is, of course, the greatest when the reference is to the end of the calendar year. That it was in fact an error seems rather clear to me because no one has suggested any rational basis for omitting just one day from the period in which an annual filing may be made, and I would not presume that Congress deliberately created a trap for the unwary by such an omission.

It would be fully consistent with the intent of Congress to treat any filing received during the 1980 calendar year as a timely filing for that year. Such an interpretation certainly does not interfere with Congress' intent to establish a federal recording system designed to cope with the problem of stale mining claims on federal lands. . . .[12] . . . .

Additionally, a sensible construction of the statute does not interfere with Congress' intention to provide "an easy way of discovering which Federal lands are subject to either valid or invalid mining claim locations." [S. Rep. No. 94–583, p. 65 (1975).] The Bureau in this case was well aware of the existence and production of appellees' mining claims; only by blinking reality could the Bureau reach the decision that it did. It is undisputed that the appellees made the first 1980 filing on August 29, 1980, and made the second required filing on December 31, 1980; the Bureau did not declare the mining claims "abandoned and void" until

[12] Several *amici* have filed materials listing numerous cases in which it is asserted that the Bureau is using every technical construction of the statute to suck up active mining claims much as a vacuum cleaner, if not watched closely, will suck up jewelry or loose money. . . . According to the Bureau's own calculations, thousands of active mining claims have been terminated because filings made on December 31 were considered untimely. These representations confirm the picture painted by *amici* of a federal bureaucracy virtually running amok, and surely operating contrary to the intent of Congress, by terminating the valuable property rights of hardworking, productive citizens of our country.

April 4, 1981. Thus, appellees lost their entire livelihood for no practical reason, contrary to the intent of Congress, and because of the hypertechnical construction of a poorly drafted statute, which an agency interprets to allow "filings" far beyond December 30 in some circumstances, but then interprets inflexibly in others. Appellants acknowledge that "[i]t may well be that Congress wished to require filing by the end of the calendar year and that the earlier deadline resulted from careless draftmanship." Brief for Appellants 42, n. 31. I have no doubt that Congress would have chosen to adopt a construction of the statute that filing take place by the end of the calendar year if its attention had been focused on this precise issue. . . .

NOTES AND QUESTIONS

1. Is it fair to say that Justice Marshall's opinion in *Locke* reflects a different approach to statutory interpretation than Justice Brewer's opinion in *Church of the Holy Trinity*? Or might one say that the question presented in *Locke* ("what is the deadline for filing these papers?") is precisely the question that Congress apparently wrote § 314(a) of the FLPMA to answer, and that courts should hew especially close to the letter of the statute when that condition is satisfied? Do we know that this condition was *not* satisfied in *Church of the Holy Trinity*?

Unlike in *Church of the Holy Trinity*, the Court in *Locke* was not being asked to infer an unstated exception to a general rule. Instead, the Court had to determine the content of the general rule itself: what filing deadline did the statute establish? Even if modern courts will not depart from the "plain language" of a statute just because it has a few strange applications, should they be more concerned about reading a statute to establish a strange general rule?

2. In *Locke*, the majority surely is correct that the phrase "prior to" normally means "before" rather than "on or before." But is this point about ordinary meaning equally applicable to the phrase "prior to December 31"? In the context of a statute establishing an annual filing deadline, might "prior to December 31" simply mean "prior to the end of the calendar year"—with the result that the Lockes' filing was timely?

If you are sympathetic to that idea, here is a follow-up question. In late March 2020, Congress enacted the CARES Act, a mammoth statute designed to provide relief in connection with the COVID-19 epidemic. As part of a provision appropriating funds for payments to state, local, and tribal governments, the statute specified that those governments could use the funds only to cover costs that "were incurred during the period that begins on March 1, 2020, and ends on December 30, 2020." CARES Act, Pub. L. 116–136, sec. 5001(a), § 601(d)(3), 134 Stat. 281, 503 (2020). Can that language be understood to encompass December 31?[14]

[14] I am indebted to James Y. Stern for this example.

3. Suppose you agree with the majority about "the plain language of the statute" in *Locke*. Even so, Justice Stevens argued that this language was a mistake—what he called a "scrivener's error."

Technically, the word "scrivener" refers to a copyist or scribe. Although the advent of photocopying machines and computers has reduced demand for scriveners, lawyers still use the phrase "scrivener's error" to refer to the kinds of mistakes that someone might make when transcribing a bill or when preparing a clean version of the bill during the legislative process. Typographical errors, inappropriate punctuation marks, and mistaken cross-references are all paradigmatic "scrivener's errors." *See, e.g.*, United States v. Massey, 2022 WL 79870 at *1 n.1 (N.D. Ill. Jan. 7, 2022) ("The reference to 'subparagraph (A), (B), (C), or (D)' in [18 U.S.C. § 2101(a)], which do not exist, is a scrivener's error. The Act should instead be read as referring to paragraphs (1) through (4) of subsection (a)."). The Supreme Court has also used the phrase "scrivener's error" to encompass certain other kinds of drafting mistakes, such as referring to an agency by the wrong name. *See* Graham Cty. Soil & Water Conservation Dist. v. United States ex rel. Wilson, 559 U.S. 280, 287 n.6 (2010) (discussing a federal statute that used the phrase "Government Accounting Office" in apparent reference to what was then the General Accounting Office); *see also* Ryan D. Doerfler, *The Scrivener's Error*, 110 NW. U. L. REV. 811, 820–21 (2016) (noting the difference between erroneous references of this sort and statutes that use different words than members of the enacting Congress intended to use, but treating both as "scrivener's errors").

Section 314(a)(1) of the FLPMA definitely contained at least one "scrivener's error." As enacted, the statute said that people who want to preserve their mining claims must file "either a notice of intention to hold the mining claim . . . , an affidavit of assessment work performed thereon, ***on*** a detailed report provided by section 28–1 of title 30." The word "on" in this sentence obviously should be "or"; the sentence would not parse otherwise, and no reader would think that Congress really intended to require a notice or affidavit to be filed "on" some other type of report. When statutes contain obvious typos of this sort, even committed "textualists" are willing to correct the errors through interpretation—so that § 314(a)(1) of the FLPMA means the same thing that it would mean if the word "or" appeared where a reasonable reader knows that it was supposed to appear. *See, e.g.*, Antonin Scalia, *Common-Law Courts in a Civil-Law System: The Role of United States Federal Courts in Interpreting the Constitution and Laws*, *in* A MATTER OF INTERPRETATION 3, 20–21 (Amy Gutmann ed., 1997) (explaining that in such cases, interpreters can properly "give the totality of context precedence over a single word").

Because textualists often speak as if statutory interpreters should not concern themselves with legislative intent, some critics see the textualists' willingness to correct scrivener's errors as "an escape from their own theory." Jonathan R. Siegel, *What Statutory Drafting Errors Teach Us About Statutory Interpretation*, 69 GEO. WASH. L. REV. 309, 310 (2001). After all, the very concept of a scrivener's error requires "a baseline of legislative intent," because it entails identifying the content of the legal directive that members of the enacting legislature intended to establish (or, perhaps, the legal directive that a reasonable reader would think they intended to establish on the basis of the text and the other information that the reader is allowed to consider). *See* Larry Alexander & Saikrishna Prakash, *Is That English You're Speaking? Why Intention Free Interpretation is an Impossibility*, 41 SAN DIEGO L. REV. 967, 979–80 (2004). But the same can be said of other interpretive principles used by textualists. *See id.* at 982 ("[A]lthough textualists often claim that authorial intentions do not matter, operationally they act as if authorial intentions *do* matter."); *see also supra* pp. 42–43 (linking the presumption against superfluity to some concept of intended meaning and discussing Justice Scalia's concept of " 'objectified' intent"). We will return to the textualists' rhetoric against "legislative intent" in Chapter 3.C.2, when we consider debates about the use of internal legislative history in statutory interpretation. As Professors Alexander and Prakash observe, however, the fact that many textualists want interpreters to ignore certain extratextual evidence of a statute's intended meaning does not mean that they must also disregard *textual* evidence of the intended meaning of a statute. *See* Alexander & Prakash, *supra*, at 969–70 (noting possible policy reasons for ignoring legislative history). In any event, most textualists—like most other interpreters—are willing to let interpreters mentally correct obvious "scrivener's errors" when determining what a statute means.

In *Locke*, though, Congress presumably intended to use the phrase "prior to December 31"; that phrase is not a typo. If Justice Stevens is correct that the ordinary meaning of the phrase does not really capture what members of Congress intended, the problem either is that their phrasing was sloppy or that they idiosyncratically used "prior to" to mean "on or before." Should either of those problems be called a "scrivener's error"? *Compare* Doerfler, *supra*, 110 NW. U. L. REV. at 816–23 (using "scrivener's error" to encompass a broad category of "linguistic mistakes," including mistakes about "the conventional meaning of words"), *with* Niz-Chavez v. Garland, 141 S. Ct. 1474, 1480 n.1 (2021) (asserting that "the 'scrivener's error' doctrine . . . applies only in exceptional circumstances to obvious technical drafting errors").

Even if idiosyncratic usage is not exactly a "scrivener's error," is it still something that interpreters should correct through interpretation when they can reliably identify it? If the FLPMA had explicitly defined the phrase "prior to" to mean "on or before" throughout the Act, interpreters surely would accept and apply that definition even though it is idiosyncratic. Even in the absence of an explicit definition of this sort, can't context sometimes supply an *implicit* definition—so that if interpreters are sufficiently confident that Congress was using "prior to" to mean "on or before," they should interpret the statute accordingly?

If you are tempted to argue that courts should always give statutory language its ordinary meaning, even when they are positive that members of the enacting legislature really intended something else, recall the West Virginia slayer statute quoted on p. 27. Here is the basic language of that statute: "A person who has been convicted of feloniously killing another . . . may not take or acquire any money or property, real or personal, or interest in the money or property, from the one killed . . . , either by descent and distribution, or by will, or by any policy or certificate of insurance, or otherwise . . . ." W. VA. CODE § 42–4–2(a). How does this language interact with the typical life-insurance policy (a contract providing that upon the death of the person whose life is insured, the insurance company will pay a specified amount of money to the beneficiary named in the contract)? Strictly as a matter of ordinary meaning, a murderer who acquires money from an insurance company by virtue of the victim's death probably would not be said to be acquiring money "from the one killed." Still, shouldn't courts interpret the language of the slayer statute to prevent convicted killers from collecting upon their victims' life-insurance policies? Is there anything wrong with reading a statute to establish the legal directive that every reasonable reader would understand that the statute was intended to establish?

4. In *Locke*, Justice Stevens emphasized one contextual clue that Congress might have been using the phrase "prior to December 31" to mean "prior to the end of the calendar year": it seems odd for Congress to establish an annual deadline that ends on December 30 rather than December 31. Still, how confident can we be about Congress's intentions? Is it conceivable that members of Congress had some reason for wanting to establish a December 30 deadline? For instance, might members of Congress have thought that a lot of BLM employees would want to leave work early on New Year's Eve? *Cf.* Mark Seidenfeld, *A Process Failure Theory of Statutory Interpretation*, 56 WM. & MARY L. REV. 467, 517 n.185 (2014) (discussing this possibility but calling it "far-fetched").

Along the same lines, think about the nature of the property interests that the 1976 statute jeopardized. Those interests were generated by federal statutes, dating back to the nineteenth century, that allowed American citizens to go onto land owned by the federal government, look for deposits of hardrock minerals, lay claims to those deposits, extract the minerals from the ground by mining, and keep the profits for themselves. By 1976, many people saw these statutes as an enormous and unwarranted give-away of public property. Does this background suggest that some members of Congress might conceivably have *wanted* to set a trap for the unwary?

Even if these questions suggest that a rational Congress could have chosen to make the deadline December 30 rather than December 31, isn't Justice Stevens correct to doubt that members of the enacting Congress really made that choice? If one agrees with Justice Stevens that when courts detect a drafting error in a statute, they can legitimately read the statute to mean what they think that Congress was trying to say, what level of confidence should courts insist upon before they apply this principle? Can courts deviate from what appears to be the letter of statutory language whenever courts think it more likely than not that Congress made some sort of mistake, or are there reasons to require more certainty?

5. *Locke* concerned the meaning of the phrase "prior to December 31" in the first sentence of § 314(a) of the FLPMA. But the second sentence, which the Court did not quote, may shed some light on that topic. Here are the first two sentences of § 314(a) as enacted by Congress:

> "The owner of an unpatented lode or placer mining claim located prior to the date of this Act shall, within the three-year period following the date of the approval of this Act and prior to December 31 of each year thereafter, file the instruments required by paragraphs (1) and (2) of this subsection. The owner of an unpatented lode or placer mining claim located after the date of this Act shall, prior to December 31 of each year following the calendar year in which the said claim was located, file the instruments required by paragraphs (1) and (2) of this subsection."[15]

This language establishes filing requirements for claims located "prior to the date of this Act" and for claims located "after the date of this Act." Judge Posner has raised a good question: What does this language mean for claims that were located *on* the date of the Act—which turned out to be October 21, 1976 (the date President Ford signed the FLPMA into law)? It seems odd for Congress not to require any filings for claims located on that one date. But if § 314(a) covers those claims, it must be using either "prior to" or "after" idiosyncratically. (The same point applies to § 314(b), which again speaks of claims "located prior to the date of approval of this Act" and claims "located after the date of approval of this Act" without specifically addressing claims located *on* that date.)

Assuming that Congress used the phrase "prior to" in the same way throughout § 314, doesn't this additional context provide a strong argument against the majority's position in *Locke*? In conjunction with the statutory requirement that papers be filed "prior to December 31," does it suggest that Congress was using the phrase "prior to [a particular

[15] After Congress enacted the FLPMA, the Office of the Law Revision Counsel (OLRC) codified its provisions at 43 U.S.C. § 1701 *et seq.* Footnote 2 of the majority opinion in *Locke* quotes 43 U.S.C. § 1744, which is the codified version of § 314 of the FLPMA. If you compare 43 U.S.C. § 1744 to the language that Congress actually enacted, you will see two differences. First, the OLRC inserted headings for each subsection in 43 U.S.C. § 1744; those subsection headings were not actually enacted by Congress. Second, for the convenience of readers, the OLRC replaced the phrases "the date of this Act" and "the date of the approval of this Act" with "October 21, 1976." As noted above, the OLRC routinely makes changes of this sort when it integrates statutory provisions into the unenacted titles of the *United States Code*. *See* Note on the *Statutes at Large* and the *United States Code*, *supra* p. 52.

date]" to mean "no later than [that date]" throughout § 314? *See* RICHARD A. POSNER, THE PROBLEMS OF JURISPRUDENCE 267–68 (1990).

In 1977, when the Bureau of Land Management promulgated regulations to implement § 314, those regulations indicated that claims located on the date of the Act were subject to the filing requirements for claims located "prior to" the date of the Act. *See* Recordation of Mining Claims and Filing Evidence of Annual Assessment Work or Notice of Intention to Hold Mining Claims, 42 Fed. Reg. 5298, 5301 (Jan. 27, 1977) (promulgating 43 C.F.R. § 3833.1–2) (distinguishing between the filing requirements for claims located "on or before October 21, 1976," and the requirements for claims located "after October 21, 1976"). In effect, then, the agency read the phrase "prior to the date of this Act" in § 314 to mean "on or before the date of this Act." By contrast, the agency ultimately interpreted the phrase "prior to December 31" in § 314 to mean *before* December 31, not on or before December 31. As amended in 1979, the relevant regulation specified that annual filings had to be made "on or before December 30" of each year. *See* Recordation of Unpatented Mining Claims, 44 Fed. Reg. 9720, 9723 (Feb. 14, 1979). Are those two different aspects of the agency's interpretation consistent? If the agency was willing to read "prior to" as meaning "on or before" in one place in § 314(a), should the agency have assumed that Congress was using "prior to" the same way in the part of § 314(a) that required annual filings to be made "prior to December 31"?

6. We should not necessarily assume that the Supreme Court would have reached the same result in *Locke* had members of the majority focused on the argument noted by Judge Posner. After all, neither Justice Marshall's majority opinion nor Justice Stevens's dissent raised that argument. Like the Court, then, let us simply ignore that argument and assume that the rest of § 314 sheds no light on the meaning of the phrase "prior to December 31."

Even absent any specific contextual clues of the sort noted by Judge Posner, might it be permissible for courts to articulate a "clear-statement rule" designed to handle questions like the one presented in *Locke*? For instance, courts could apply the following rule: "Statutory texts should be interpreted to conform to what an objective outside reader, who is familiar with how things normally work, would think Congress probably intended. Accordingly, if Congress really wants to establish a legal directive that an objective reader would be likely to chalk up to a mistake, Congress needs to make that intention clear. Otherwise, courts should mentally correct that apparent mistake when they interpret the statute." That sort of background rule would leave it within Congress's power to set a December 30 deadline if Congress wanted to do so. Here, for instance, if the statute had said that papers had to be filed on or before December 30 and would be late if filed on or after December 31, courts would know that Congress really meant to make December 30 the deadline. But in the absence of such clarity, courts might assume that

Congress intended to establish a normal calendar-year deadline, and they might read the statute to do so. Should a background rule of this sort be among the interpretive principles that courts use to identify the meaning of statutory language? What are its pros and cons?

Professor Schauer has sketched out one possible argument for a strong or even conclusive presumption against second-guessing what statutory texts seem to say on the ground that they produce absurdity and that the enacting legislature must have meant something else. As Professor Schauer notes, any test for identifying such absurdity risks mistakes of two different sorts—"false positives" (in which the decisionmaker applying the test concludes that the test is triggered even though an omniscient observer would say that no absurdity or drafting error is present) and "false negatives" (in which the decisionmaker applying the test concludes that the test is *not* triggered even though an omniscient observer would know that a drafting error did occur and that the results produced by literal application of the statute are indeed absurd). A relatively conservative test—for instance, a test that allows courts to diagnose a drafting error only when it is obvious from the face of the statute that Congress misspoke—risks generating many false negatives. But a test that is easier to satisfy will reduce false negatives only at the cost of increasing false positives. Even if one has no principled objection to letting courts deviate from the conventional meaning of statutory language in pursuit of the enacting legislature's true intentions, there will come a point at which this tradeoff is not worth making: further liberalization of the test for drafting errors will produce more than one false positive for each false negative that it eliminates.[16] The more one distrusts the ad hoc judgments that tests for "absurdity" and "drafting errors" necessitate, the sooner one will expect that point to be reached, and the more conservative one's favored test will be. At the extreme, one might advocate eliminating the absurdity doctrine altogether, "on the controversial but not implausible supposition that interpreters empowered to set aside plain language in the service of intent-negating absurdity would be so over-inclined to place cases in this category as to outweigh in expected harm the harm that would come from prohibiting them from placing *any* cases in this category." *See* Frederick Schauer, *The Practice and Problems of Plain Meaning: A Response to Aleinikoff and Shaw*, 45 VAND. L. REV. 715, 729–32 (1992).[17]

7. Suppose that after considering these issues, one settles upon the following position with respect to "drafting errors." When the sources of information that our theory of statutory interpretation allows courts to

[16] I am simplifying Schauer's analysis by assuming that "false positives" and "false negatives" have the same costs. If that assumption is wrong—for instance, if "false positives" (which lead courts to depart from the conventional meaning of statutory language) tend to cause more harm than "false negatives" (which lead courts to follow the conventional meaning of statutory language under circumstances where the legislature actually meant something else)—then analysis of the tradeoff would need to include appropriate weightings.

[17] This paragraph is a slightly reworded version of the summary of Professor Schauer's argument that appears in Caleb Nelson, *What Is Textualism?*, 91 VA. L. REV. 347, 381 (2005).

consult for this purpose lead courts to conclude that a statute's text reflects a "drafting error," courts can legitimately interpret the statute to have the same meaning that they would have ascribed to a properly drafted statute. But courts should do so only when they have a very high level of confidence that the statutory text does indeed reflect a "drafting error"; if there is any plausible reason to think that Congress might really have intended to establish the legal directive that the statutory text seems (on its face) to establish, courts should not diagnose a "drafting error."

Many modern courts seem to take something like this approach. But exactly which sorts of questions trigger it? In many cases of statutory interpretation, courts are asked to read into a statute some qualification or embellishment that is not stated anywhere in the statutory text, but that might be thought to be implicit in it. Should all such cases be thought of as asking the courts to diagnose "drafting errors" (which, by hypothesis, courts should do only if they can satisfy the extraordinarily high threshold described in the previous paragraph)? The answer is surely "no": courts can sometimes draw inferences or read unstated qualifications into statutory texts without purporting to be diagnosing "drafting errors." But how would you articulate the distinction that this statement assumes?

For example, consider the question raised on p. 24 about the Electronic Fund Transfer Act. Most people have no objection to reading federal statutes in light of the idea that private causes of action can be settled out of court, and hence that the typical statutory cause of action is subject to the defense of accord and satisfaction. Given the language of the Electronic Fund Transfer Act, though, does that approach take liberties with the statutory text? Did Congress make a "drafting error" in the Electronic Fund Transfer Act? Before courts read the statute to accommodate an accord-and-satisfaction defense (or other common-law defenses), should they demand an extraordinarily high level of confidence about Congress's intentions?

8. In *Locke*, the Supreme Court was not the only entity that interpreted the statute to establish a December 30 deadline; the Bureau of Land Management had promulgated regulations that reflected the same interpretation. Once you have read the materials on *Chevron* deference in Chapter 5, return to *Locke* and ask yourself the following question: even if you are inclined to agree with Justice Stevens's dissent about the best interpretation of the phrase "prior to December 31" in § 314(a) of the statute, was the BLM's more literal reading at least permissible under the *Chevron* framework? Or did the administrative agency that Congress had entrusted with implementation of the statute have no power to read the statute to mean what its literal language seemed to say?

NOTE ON JUDICIAL INTERPRETATIONS OF 28 U.S.C. § 1453(c)(1)

If you are sympathetic to the majority's position in *Locke*, how far would you take your approach? The Class Action Fairness Act of 2005 (CAFA) presented a concrete setting in which to consider that question.

CAFA sought to rein in what Congress described as "abuses of the class action device," especially in state and local courts. *See* CAFA, Pub. L. 109–2, § 2(a), 119 Stat. 4, 4–5 (2005). To that end, Congress gave federal district courts jurisdiction over many big-dollar class actions that would not previously have triggered federal jurisdiction. *See id.* § 4, 119 Stat. at 9–12 (enacting 28 U.S.C. § 1332(d)). Congress further specified that when plaintiffs file a class action covered by CAFA in state court, any defendant can remove the suit to federal court, without regard to some of the usual statutory restrictions on removal. *Id.* § 5, 119 Stat. at 12–13 (enacting 28 U.S.C. § 1453).

A pre-existing federal statute, 28 U.S.C. § 1447, tells federal courts how to proceed in cases that have been removed from state court. Among other things, § 1447 raises the possibility that the federal court will remand such a case back to state court, either because the federal court determines that it does not actually have jurisdiction over the case or because one of the parties has properly objected to some other defect with the removal. *See* 28 U.S.C. § 1447(c). Ordinarily, § 1447(d) forecloses appellate review of orders remanding a case for one of these reasons. *See* 28 U.S.C. § 1447(d) (establishing the general rule that "[a]n order remanding a case to the State court from which it was removed is not reviewable on appeal or otherwise"); *cf.* Thermtron Products, Inc. v. Hermansdorfer, 423 U.S. 336 (1976) (reading § 1447(d) narrowly, but still giving it considerable effect).[18]

As part of CAFA, however, Congress made a special exception to § 1447(d). The new § 1453—the provision addressing the removal of class actions covered by CAFA from state to federal court—included the following subsection:

> **(c) Review of remand orders.**—
>
> **(1) In general.**—Section 1447 shall apply to any removal of a case under this section, except that notwithstanding section 1447(d), a court of appeals may accept an appeal from an order of a district court granting or denying a motion to remand a class action to the State court from which it was removed if application is made to the court of appeals not less than 7 days after entry of the order.

---

[18] If a case has been removed from state to federal court and the federal district court *refuses* to remand it, that refusal may eventually be subject to appellate review—but usually only after the district court decides the case and enters final judgment. *See* 28 U.S.C. § 1291 (authorizing appeals from "final decisions" of federal district courts); *cf.* 28 U.S.C. § 1292(b) (creating a mechanism for immediate appeal of many interlocutory orders that are not "final decisions," but only if both the district court and the court of appeals exercise discretion in favor of allowing an immediate appeal).

(2) **Time period for judgment.**—If the court of appeals accepts an appeal under paragraph (1), the court shall complete all action on such appeal, including rendering judgment, not later than 60 days after the date on which such appeal was filed, unless an extension is granted under paragraph (3).

(3) **Extension of time period.**—The court of appeals may grant an extension of the 60-day period described in paragraph (2) if—

(A) all parties to the proceeding agree to such extension, for any period of time; or

(B) such extension is for good cause shown and in the interests of justice, for a period not to exceed 10 days.

(4) **Denial of appeal.**—If a final judgment on the appeal under paragraph (1) is not issued before the end of the period described in paragraph (2), including any extension under paragraph (3), the appeal shall be denied.

119 Stat. at 12–13.

Suppose that a class action is filed in state court, that a defendant removes it to federal court, and that the plaintiff class asks the federal district court to remand the case back to state court. Whether the district court grants this motion or denies it, § 1453(c) allows the disappointed side to apply to the appropriate federal circuit court for leave to appeal the district court's order on an interlocutory basis. According to the version of § 1453(c)(1) that Congress enacted as part of CAFA, the circuit court has discretion to entertain such an appeal if such an application is made to it "not less than 7 days after entry of the order."

If you have not yet noticed what is weird about this provision, read it again. Ordinarily, provisions about the timing of appeals establish *deadlines*. Read literally, though, § 1453(c)(1) seemed to establish a *waiting period*. That would be very strange. So far as I know, no other federal statute about the timing of appeals from federal district courts to federal circuit courts establishes a waiting period rather than a deadline. Given the emphasis on speed in § 1453(c)(2), moreover, a waiting period would seem particularly bizarre here.

The first federal circuit court to confront § 1453(c)(1) initially failed to notice this issue. *See* Pritchett v. Office Depot, Inc., 404 F.3d 1232, 1234 (10th Cir. 2005) (describing § 1453(c) as having "expressly give[n] the United States courts of appeals discretionary jurisdiction to consider appeals of remand orders in certain class action cases . . . , provided that the appeal is taken within seven days of the remand order"). After law professor Georgene M. Vairo wrote a column pointing out its oversight, however, the court issued a revised opinion. The court noted that internal legislative history—a report prepared by the Senate Judiciary Committee—suggested that Congress had intended to establish a deadline rather than a waiting period. *See* S. REP. NO. 109–14, at 49 (2005) ("New subsection 1453(c) provides discretionary appellate review of remand orders under this legislation but also imposes time limits. Specifically, parties must file a notice of appeal within seven days after entry of a remand order."). As a matter of policy, moreover, the court "[could] think of no plausible reason why the . . . Act would . . . impose a seven-day waiting period followed by a limitless window for appeal." The court concluded that the text of § 1453(c)(1) reflected a "typographical error" and that "[t]he statute should read that an appeal is permissible if filed 'not more than' seven days after entry of the remand order." *Pritchett v. Office Depot, Inc.*, 420 F.3d 1090, 1093 n.2 (10th Cir. 2005). In the case before it, the court observed, "the petition for leave to appeal was filed well within the seven-day time limit, and jurisdiction vested in the Tenth Circuit Court of Appeals at that time." *Id.* at 1093.

A number of other courts reached the same conclusion. In the words of the Ninth Circuit, "the statute should . . . be read to require that an application to appeal under § 1453(c)(1) must be filed . . . not *more* than 7 days after the district court's order." *Amalgamated Transit Union Local 1309 v. Laidlaw Transit Services, Inc.*, 435 F.3d 1140, 1146 (9th Cir. 2006); *accord* Estate of Pew v. Cardarelli, 527 F.3d 25, 28 (2d Cir. 2008) ("We join our sister circuits in interpreting the statute to mean 'not *more* than 7 days.' "); Morgan v. Gay, 466 F.3d 276, 277 (3d Cir. 2006); Miedema v. Maytag Corp., 450 F.3d 1322, 1326 (11th Cir. 2006).

The Ninth Circuit's decision, however, led one of the court's judges to propose rehearing the case *en banc*. When the court rejected that suggestion, moreover, Judge Jay Bybee wrote a strongly worded dissent for himself and five of his colleagues. According to Judge Bybee's dissent, "The text of 28 U.S.C. § 1453(c)(1) is unmistakably clear, and the panel should have applied the statute as written." *Amalgamated Transit Union Local 1309 v. Laidlaw Transit Services, Inc.*, 448 F.3d 1092, 1095 (9th Cir. 2006) (Bybee, J., dissenting from the denial of rehearing en banc).

Judge Bybee was unwilling to conclude that Congress had really intended to establish a deadline rather than a waiting period. As he noted, the statutory text as enacted was "fully grammatical" and could be applied as written. *Id.* at 1098. And while the rule that those words established might seem illogical as a matter of policy, Judge Bybee denied that courts could properly diagnose and correct a drafting error on that basis. *See id.* at 1097 ("We cannot declare Congress's choice of the statutory language in 28 U.S.C. § 1453(c)(1) a clerical error simply because we disagree with the logic of the terms that Congress used."); *see also id.* at 1096 ("[I]t is not the courts' role to assess whether a statute is wise or logical."); *id.* at 1098–99 ("The panel cannot declare with any certainty that Congress would never have intended to impose a waiting period before which filing a petition for permission to appeal is too early.").

Nor was Judge Bybee swayed by the internal legislative history that the panel had invoked. To begin with, he characterized the enacted statutory text as "unambiguous," and he suggested that legislative history should never be allowed to "trump" statutory language of this sort. *See id.* at 1096 ("Once it recognized that the statute is unambiguous, the panel should have stopped . . . ."). Separate and apart from this point, Judge Bybee argued that the report of the Senate Judiciary Committee was particularly irrelevant, because it apparently was not issued until after the Senate had acted. *See id.* (noting that the report was dated February 28, 2005—"eighteen days after the Senate had passed the bill, eleven days after the House had passed the bill, and ten days after the President signed the bill into law").

One of Judge Bybee's main themes was that courts could not be absolutely, positively, 100% *certain* that Congress had really intended § 1453(c)(1) to establish a deadline rather than a waiting period. *See, e.g.*, *id.* at 1100 ("What if the legislative history is inaccurate? What if some member of Congress made the change deliberately at the last moment?"). But apart from arguments about legislative intent, Judge Bybee also made a point about notice. On the panel's reading, the true meaning of § 1453(c)(1) was almost the opposite of the surface meaning of the text: instead of being *forbidden* to act until seven days after the entry of the district court's order, parties were *required* to act within that period. Judge Bybee objected that "the panel's decision strips citizens of the ability to rely on the laws as written." *Id.* In the next case, Judge Frank Easterbrook—who is a leader of the interpretive approach that goes by the name of "textualism"—put that concern at the center of his analysis.

Spivey v. Vertrue, Inc.

528 F.3d 982 (7th Cir. 2008)

■ *JUDGE EASTERBROOK delivered the panel's opinion:*

Quinten Spivey filed suit [against Vertrue] in state court, seeking to represent a class . . . . Vertrue removed the proceeding to federal court under 28 U.S.C. § 1453. . . . Spivey moved to remand [on the ground that the case did not meet CAFA's requirements for jurisdiction]. . . . The district judge agreed and remanded the case [on April 8, 2008]. . . . Vertrue's lawyer mailed [a] petition [for leave to appeal] on the seventh day after the district court's remand order[.] . . . [T]he petition reached this court, and so was "filed," see Fed. Rule App. Proc. 25(a)(2), on April 18, 2008, the tenth day after the district court's order. Spivey contends that this is too late and that we lack jurisdiction.

Spivey's argument rests not on the statutory text but on the proposition that the law cannot mean what it says. Someone must have set out to write "not more than 7 days" or "not later than 7 days" or "within 7 days" . . . but came up with "not less than 7 days" instead. No one noticed the gaffe (or the misuse of the word "less" when correct diction requires "fewer") before the statute was enacted. . . .

[Published opinions from the 2nd, 3rd, 9th, 10th, and 11th Circuits] all say that "less" should be read as "more," because the latter word best fits with the norm in appellate deadlines and the likely goal of the legislature—to compel prompt action that will resolve with dispatch the question which court will conduct the litigation. Section 1453(c)(2) requires the court of appeals to make its decision (if it accepts the appeal) "not later than 60 days after the date on which such appeal was filed" unless an extension is granted under another subsection. . . . There's not much point in directing the court of appeals to make a swift decision, if the aggrieved party can take forever to appeal . . . . Congress sometimes enacts cooling-off periods, but § 1453(c)(1) lacks the deadline that usually accompanies such a period. . . .

That Congress has written a deadline imprecisely, or even perversely, is not a sufficient reason to disregard the enacted language. So the Supreme Court held in . . . *United States v. Locke*, 471 U.S. 84 (1985). . . . Turning "less" into "more" would be a feat more closely associated with the mutating commandments on the barn's wall in *Animal Farm* than with sincere interpretation. . . .

To the extent that our colleagues in other circuits hold that a petition filed within seven days of the district court's order should be accepted, rather than thrown out with instructions to submit another once a week has passed, we concur. Whether a petition filed within a week after the remand is timely was the question actually presented in those appeals. An affirmative answer tracks Fed. Rule App. Proc. 4(a)(2), which says that a premature notice of appeal remains on file and springs into effect when the decision becomes appealable.[*] It makes sense to use the same approach for a premature pe[tition] for leave to appeal.

But to the extent that language in other circuits' opinions implies that they would deem a petition filed on the eighth day (or, here, the tenth) jurisdictionally and thus irreparably late, we do not concur. Even judges who, like the dissenters in *Locke*, think that a statute should be construed to prevent litigants from being sandbagged by misleading language, would not pull the rug out from under a litigant who relied on the enacted text. None of the other circuits whose opinions we have cited dismissed a petition as untimely. Doubtless many Members of Congress

[*] *Editor's note*: Federal Rule of Appellate Procedure 4 addresses appeals as of right—appeals that a litigant can take without any special permission from either the district court or the court of appeals. Congress has authorized appeals as of right from a district court's "final decisions" and from a few categories of interlocutory orders. *See* 28 U.S.C. §§ 1291, 1292(a). To take such an appeal, a litigant must file a "notice of appeal" in the district court. *See* FED. R. APP. P. 3. The time for filing a notice of appeal begins to run upon "entry of the judgment or order appealed from." FED. R. APP. P. 4(a)(1); *see also* 28 U.S.C. § 2107. The current version of Rule 4(a)(2) addresses premature notices of appeal as follows: "A notice of appeal filed after the court announces a decision or order—but before the entry of the judgment or order—is treated as filed on the date of and after the entry." FED. R. APP. P. 4(a)(2). Rule 5, which addresses appeals by permission rather than appeals as of right, does not contain a similar provision.

wanted a short deadline for appeals, but legislative history can not justify reading a statute to mean the opposite of what it says. . . . Legislative history may help disambiguate a cloudy text by showing how words work in context; it does not permit a judge to turn a clear text on its head.

. . . [I]t would be foolish, as well as countertextual, to throw out of court a petition that is timely under the statute actually enacted. Whatever scope courts may have to accept petitions or appeals that meet the legislative objective of prompt filing (and could be re-filed in a few days agreeably to the statute's text), there is none for rejecting a petition or appeal that is timely under the enacted law. Litigants and lawyers always should be safe in relying on a statute's actual language.

To the possibility that this gives litigants forever to appeal, and thus interferes with the objective of ascertaining the correct forum as quickly as possible, we say: No way. The open-ended "not less than 7 days" means that there is no terminal date for appeal. And the Federal Rules of Appellate Procedure cover the possibility that some laws or rules allowing interlocutory appeals omit deadlines. Rule 5(a)(2) says that, when there is no other limit, a petition for permission to appeal must be filed "within the time provided by Rule 4(a) for filing a notice of appeal." That time is 30 days [from the entry of the judgment or order being appealed]. . . . Reading § 1453(c)(1) to mean what it says thus does not authorize indefinite delay. Although it may allow a party 23 days more than the authors anticipated, our reading avoids nasty surprises for litigants who believe—and are entitled to believe—that courts will honor the language in the enrolled bill that the President signs. Vertrue's petition is timely. . . .

NOTES AND QUESTIONS

1. Unlike Judge Bybee, Judge Easterbrook seemed prepared to concede that the drafter(s) of § 1453(c)(1) made a mistake. But Easterbrook still read § 1453(c)(1) to "mean what it says." Rather than taking liberties with the text, he indicated that circuit courts lacked jurisdiction to entertain appeals under § 1453(c)(1) until seven days had elapsed from the entry of the district court's order. If we are overwhelmingly confident that members of Congress did not actually mean to establish this waiting period, is there any way to justify Judge Easterbrook's position? Is there any reason why the interpretive principles that courts use to ascribe meaning to statutes should emphasize the surface meaning of the text even in situations like this one, where an objective outside reader would almost certainly diagnose a drafting error? *Cf.* Antonin Scalia, *Common-Law Courts in a Civil-Law System: The Role of United States Federal Courts in Interpreting the Constitution and Laws*, *in* A MATTER OF INTERPRETATION: FEDERAL COURTS AND THE LAW 3, 24 (Amy Gutmann ed., 1997) ("[T]he good textualist is not a literalist . . . .").

Even if courts can indeed diagnose a drafting error in CAFA's version of § 1453(c)(1), they might not be able to tell exactly what the error was. Perhaps the problem is the word "not": the drafter upon whom Congress was relying meant to establish a deadline of "less than 7 days." Or perhaps the problem is the word "less": the drafter meant to establish a deadline of "not more than 7 days." The choice between those two possibilities would matter if a prospective appellant sought permission to appeal on the seventh day itself. If you believe that courts should read § 1453(c)(1) to mean what they think Congress meant to say, how do you want courts to treat such an appellant? If no permissible sources of information shed any light on whether Congress meant to establish a deadline of "less than 7 days" or a deadline of "not more than 7 days," can courts simply make their own choice between those possibilities? For instance, can a court adopt the latter reading on the theory that it is kinder to would-be appellants (since it gives them one more day to seek leave to appeal)? Or does the uncertainty about what Congress really meant provide an argument for not going down this road at all?

Judge Easterbrook himself relied upon a different sort of argument. Even if the principles of statutory interpretation that we tell courts to use should be designed to promote successful communication between the legislature and the judiciary (so that the legal directives that courts read statutes to establish have some relationship to the legal directives that members of the enacting legislature understood themselves to be establishing), those principles should also be designed to give the citizenry fair notice of the law's requirements. According to Judge Easterbrook, that goal cuts against taking a provision that is cast as a waiting period and reading it to establish a deadline instead. In Judge Easterbrook's words, "Litigants and lawyers always should be safe in relying on a statute's actual language."

To dramatize this concern, Judge Easterbrook invited us to imagine an innocent litigant who relied upon the surface meaning of § 1453(c)(1) and who therefore did not seek leave to appeal until eight days after entry of the district court's order. In the Second, Third, Ninth, Tenth, and Eleventh Circuits, such a litigant might be out of luck. According to those courts, after all, § 1453(c)(1) was properly interpreted to apply only when "application is made to the court of appeals not [more] than 7 days after entry of the order." On that interpretation of § 1453(c)(1), the general rule of nonreviewability established by § 1447(d) presumably would continue to govern all other cases—with the result that the circuit court would lack authority to entertain our hypothetical litigant's (untimely) request for leave to appeal.

Is that result really unthinkable? Is it any more troubling than other situations in which litigants fail to anticipate the principles of statutory interpretation that courts will apply? Should litigants always be able to rely upon the surface meaning of statutory language, without regard to any technical canons of construction?[19]

Judge Easterbrook emphasized that "[n]one of the other circuits whose opinions we have cited dismissed a petition as untimely." Most of those other circuits had been facing the opposite sort of case, where a petition for leave to appeal arguably had been filed *too early* (on the literal reading of the statute). None of the circuits had confronted a case like Judge Easterbrook's hypothetical, in which a litigant relied on the literal language of the statute and therefore did not seek leave to appeal until seven days had passed. As a result, we do not know how the other circuits would have handled such a case. Still, what do you make of the fact that none of the reported cases presented a clear case of "reliance interests" generated by the statutory language?

2. To what extent are the principles of interpretation advocated by Judge Easterbrook driven by concerns about notice, and to what extent are they driven by other concerns? Consider how Judge Easterbrook might have voted in *Locke*. To judge from his references to that case, he seems to agree with the majority's position. In *Locke*, however, the problem of notice did not loom very large: if the Supreme Court had interpreted the phrase "prior to December 31" in the flexible manner that the dissenters proposed, so that the filing deadline was December 31 rather than December 30, it would not necessarily have been dashing the expectations of anyone who was subject to the deadline. To the extent that his interpretive approach is driven by concerns about notice, should Judge Easterbrook be willing to tolerate more flexible interpretation in cases like *Locke* than in cases like *Spivey*?

3. In *Spivey*, Judge Easterbrook acknowledged that his literal interpretation of § 1453(c)(1) might be thought to produce two practical problems. First, if § 1453(c)(1) established a waiting period rather than a deadline for the appeals that it covered, one might worry that those appeals would be subject to no deadline at all. As Judge Easterbrook noted, though, Federal Rule of Appellate Procedure 5 took care of that potential problem: Rule 5 establishes a fallback deadline (usually 30 days) for situations in which Congress has authorized discretionary appeals but has failed to set any other deadline. *See* FED. R. APP. P. 5(a)(2); *see also* Adam N. Steinman, *"Less" is "More"? Textualism, Intentionalism, and a Better Solution to the Class Action Fairness Act's Appellate Deadline Riddle*, 92 IOWA L. REV. 1183 (2007) (proposing this analysis). Second, one might also worry that Judge Easterbrook's literal reading of § 1453(c)(1) would create a trap for litigants who filed "premature" applications for leave to appeal—that is, litigants who presented their applications to the court of appeals during the waiting period that Judge Easterbrook read § 1453(c)(1) to establish. Again,

[19] *Cf.* Jesse M. Cross, *The Fair Notice Fiction*, 75 ALA. L. REV. (forthcoming 2023) (arguing that because of the length and "non-transparent interconnectivity" of federal statutory law, ordinary people cannot grasp the law's content for themselves by reading statutory texts).

though, Judge Easterbrook argued that there was a way around this problem. Drawing an analogy to Federal Rule of Appellate Procedure 4(a)(2), he maintained that a "premature" application could spring into effect on the seventh day after entry of the district court's order, without any need for the would-be appellant to present a new application.

If these ways to limit the practical damage caused by a literal reading of § 1453(c)(1) had not been available, might Judge Easterbrook have taken a less literal approach to § 1453(c)(1)?

4. Although the strange wording of § 1453(c)(1) persisted for four years, Congress then eliminated this anomaly. *See* Statutory Time-Periods Technical Amendments Act of 2009, Pub. L. 111–16, § 6(2), 123 Stat. 1607, 1608 (2009) (amending § 1453(c)(1) by replacing "not less than 7 days" with "not more than 10 days"). Some people see Congress's ability to enact such amendments as a point in favor of Judge Easterbrook's interpretive approach. On that view, the fact that Congress can fix its own mistakes should deter courts from trying to do so through interpretation.

Does that argument work? Imagine that Congress has enacted a statutory provision that seems garbled in some way. It is certainly true that if courts enforce the statutory language as written, and if members of the current Congress do not like the rule that the courts are enforcing, Congress can amend the statute to fix the problem going forward. But the same would be true if courts take the opposite approach and interpret the garbled provision to mean what they think members of the enacting Congress really intended. After all, if members of the current Congress decide that they prefer the garbled version, Congress can enact a second statute reiterating the earlier language and telling courts not to take liberties with it. Does the simple fact that Congress can respond to judicial decisions tell us much about the interpretive approach that those decisions should use?

The idea that courts should let Congress correct its own mistakes resonates with what Professors Hart and Sacks called "the flagellant theory of statutory interpretation," which instructs courts "to discipline the legislature by taking it literally whenever it forgets to deal with special cases or otherwise fails to speak clearly." Henry M. Hart, Jr. & Albert M. Sacks, The Legal Process: Basic Problems in the Making and Application of Law 91 (tent. ed. 1958) (William N. Eskridge, Jr. & Philip P. Frickey eds., 1994). As described by Hart and Sacks, this approach does not assume that statutes are currently drafted with exquisite care or that giving effect to their surface meaning is the best way of getting at what the enacting legislature probably intended. Instead, Hart and Sacks opined, the approach is designed to affect how legislatures behave in the future: if courts consistently refuse to rescue legislatures from their own mistakes, perhaps legislatures will adopt more careful drafting practices, so that the statutes that they adopt say exactly what members of the enacting legislature really mean. *See id.*

According to Hart and Sacks, "[a]lmost every law student finds himself attracted to this view at some stage in his education," and "[s]ome . . . never get over the attraction." But Hart and Sacks themselves criticized the approach on various grounds. *See id.* at 91–92 (raising concerns about the costs that mindlessly literal readings can visit upon society, the futility of trying to draft statutes with complete specificity, and the undesirability of allowing important policy questions to be settled by accident). Do these criticisms cut against Judge Easterbrook's approach in *Spivey*? If it is not appropriate for courts to read statutes literally as a means of encouraging legislatures to be more careful in the future, might there nonetheless be other reasons why courts should apply a heavy presumption in favor of enforcing the surface meaning of statutory language?

5. You should not assume that all textualists would side with Judge Easterbrook in *Spivey*. Justice Scalia, for one, appeared to agree with the courts that had understood "less" to mean "more." *See* ANTONIN SCALIA & BRYAN A. GARNER, READING LAW: THE INTERPRETATION OF LEGAL TEXTS 235 & n.5 (2012) (citing those cases approvingly). In a book co-authored with Bryan Garner, he also offered a hypothetical example that pointed in the same direction:

> "Consider . . . a provision in a statute creating a new claim by saying that 'the winning party must pay the other side's reasonable attorney's fees.' That is entirely absurd, and it is virtually certain that *winning party* was meant to be *losing party*. May the court read it that way, in defiance of the plain text?
>
> "We agree with those authorities who say that it may. . . . [W]e are not revising the apparent meaning of the text but are giving it the meaning that it would convey to a reasonable person, who would understand that misprints had occurred. . . . [A] text that assesses attorneys' fees against the winning party does not make sense unless *winning* is understood to be a drafter's error for *losing*."

Id. at 235.

NOTE ON THE CASE OF THE SPELUNCEAN EXPLORERS

The next case that we will consider is not a real case at all. Harvard professor Lon Fuller wrote it in the 1940s to illustrate "certain divergent philosophies of law and government." *See* Lon L. Fuller, *The Case of the Speluncean Explorers*, 62 HARV. L. REV. 616, 645 (1949).[20] Still, the case

[20] Fuller's hypothetical case was loosely inspired by a real-life English case that students continue to read in many Criminal Law courses. *See* Regina v. Dudley & Stephens, 14 Q.B.D. 273 (1884) (finding two seamen guilty of murder for killing and eating a weakened teenager in a lifeboat after a shipwreck); *cf.* United States v. Holmes, 26 F. Cas. 360 (C.C.E.D. Pa. 1842) (No. 15,383) (convicting a sailor of manslaughter for having thrown passengers off a lifeboat in order to lighten it).

has become a common reference point for students of both jurisprudence and statutory interpretation. *See generally* David L. Shapiro, *Foreword: A Cave Drawing for the Ages*, 112 HARV. L. REV. 1834 (1999) (discussing Fuller's achievement).

To emphasize the enduring nature of the underlying issues, Professor Fuller reported the case as if it had reached the highest court of the fictional jurisdiction of Newgarth in the year 4300. According to Fuller's hypothetical facts, five amateur spelunkers had set off in May 4299 to explore a cave. While they were underground, a landslide completely blocked their exit. The trapped explorers had not brought much food with them, and there was none in the cave. Rescue crews established radio contact with the five men on the twentieth day of their ordeal, and the men were told that they could not possibly be released for at least ten more days. The men asked to speak with medical experts, who advised them that they were unlikely to be alive at the end of that period if they did not eat in the meantime. On the thirty-second day after the explorers entered the cave, rescue crews finally freed them. Now, however, there were only four explorers. On the twenty-third day of their ordeal, they had killed and eaten the fifth explorer.

One of Newgarth's criminal statutes provided that "[w]hoever shall willfully take the life of another shall be punished by death," and Newgarth authorities prosecuted the four survivors for violating this statute. Evidence at trial provided details about the death of the fifth explorer, Roger Whetmore. Apparently, the idea of saving four explorers by eating one had originated with Whetmore himself. Whetmore had further suggested that the victim be selected at random through the use of some dice that he had brought into the cave. After considerable discussion, the five explorers had agreed upon this plan and settled on a method of selection. Before they rolled the dice, though, Whetmore had tried to back out; he said that they should wait one more week. But the others rolled for him, and Whetmore was selected for death by the process upon which he had originally agreed.

The applicable trial procedure called upon the jury to find the facts by special verdict and to leave application of the law to the judge. After the jury found the facts recited above, the trial judge held the defendants guilty and sentenced them to be hanged. The judge and jurors, however, sent letters urging the Chief Executive of Newgarth to grant clemency and commute this sentence to a short term of imprisonment.

The defendants appealed their convictions to the Supreme Court of Newgarth. Professor Fuller presented five *seriatim* opinions—one by each of the fictional members of the Court. Justice Keen (who would today be called a textualist) and Chief Justice Truepenny (who did not articulate a particular theoretical approach but who thought that executive clemency would be the best way to achieve justice "without impairing either the letter or spirit of our statutes") both voted to affirm the defendants' convictions. Justice Foster (who would today be called a purposivist) and Justice Handy (a legal realist) voted to reverse. The fifth member of the Court, Justice Tatting, criticized Justice Foster's reasoning but ultimately could not reach a conclusion and therefore recused himself—with the result that the defendants' convictions were affirmed by an equally divided Court.

For our purposes, the three most relevant opinions are those of Justice Foster (the purposivist), Justice Tatting (the indecisive critic of purposivism), and Justice Keen (the textualist). Justice Foster's first argument was purposivism writ large. In his words, "If we look to the purposes of law and government, and to the premises underlying our positive law, these men when they made their fateful decision were as remote from our legal order as if they had been a thousand miles beyond our boundaries." Fuller, *supra*, 62 HARV. L. REV. at 621. Rather than being covered by the law of Newgarth after the landslide, the men had effectively been in the state of nature, and Foster thought it appropriate to judge their conduct according to either the law of nature or the "new charter of government" that they had made for themselves in the cave. *Id.* at 620–22. In Justice Foster's view, moreover, the defendants' conduct had conformed to those sources of law.

Foster's second argument was more conventional, and he saw it as being independent of his first argument. Assuming that the defendants had been covered by the positive law of Newgarth, Foster conceded that they had violated the statute's literal language. *Id.* at 623–24. But he insisted that "[e]very proposition of positive law, whether contained in a statute or a judicial precedent, is to be interpreted reasonably, in the light of its evident purpose." *Id.* at 624. Foster invoked various precedents in which the Supreme Court of Newgarth had applied this principle. In one case, the Court had detected a drafting error in a statute (involving the misplacement of the word "not"), and the Court had read the statute to mean what the Court thought the legislature had intended to say. In another case, a statute had forbidden people to park a car in specified areas for more than two hours, but the Court had inferred an exception for a defendant who had been unable to move his car because an unexpected political demonstration had blocked the streets. Foster also observed that the very statute at issue in this case had been understood not to cover killings in self-defense. Although people had tried to square the courts' treatment of self-defense with the statutory language, *see id.* at 629 (opinion of Tatting, J.) (reciting the "familiar explanation" that someone who kills in self-defense is not acting "willfully" within the meaning of the statute), Foster was not impressed with that explanation: "The truth is that the exception in favor of self-defense cannot be reconciled with the *words* of the statute, but only with its *purpose*." *Id.* at 624 (opinion of Foster, J.).

Foster elaborated upon the logic that, in his view, justified the established exception for self-defense. As he noted, one of the main purposes of the criminal law is deterrence. But no one could think that a rule against killing people in self-defense would serve that purpose, because someone whose life is in danger will defend himself even if the law tells him not to. According to Foster, that was the real justification for concluding that the statute did not apply in cases of self-defense. In Foster's view, moreover, similar logic applied to the case of the speluncean explorers. *See id.* at 625 ("If in the future any group of men ever find themselves in the tragic predicament of these defendants, we may be sure that their decision whether to live or die will not be controlled by the contents of our criminal code."). While Foster did not claim that the explorers had acted in self-defense, he believed that courts should infer an exception for this sort of case just as they allegedly had inferred an exception for self-defense.

Foster denied that this reasoning went beyond the proper role of the courts. To be sure, some people objected "whenever a court, after analyzing the purpose of a statute, gives to its words a meaning that is not at once apparent to the casual reader who has not studied the statute closely or examined the objectives it seeks to attain." *Id.* But Foster insisted that this objection was misplaced. Rather than denying the need for "fidelity to enacted law," he saw himself simply as advocating "intelligent" fidelity. *Id.* In support of that point, he suggested that although courts are supposed to be faithful servants of the legislature, the legislature itself would want its servants to exercise good judgment about what a statute really commands. In Foster's (dated) words, "The stupidest housemaid knows . . . that when her master tells her to 'drop everything and come running' he has overlooked the possibility that she is . . . in the act of rescuing the baby from the rain barrel." *Id.* By the same token, Foster argued that Newgarth's murder statute should be understood to be more qualified than a mindless literalist would think, and that the defendants' convictions should be set aside.

Foster may well have been articulating Professor Fuller's own approach. *See* Shapiro, *supra*, 112 HARV. L. REV. at 1839. Still, the opinions that Professor Fuller wrote for Justices Tatting and Keen voiced sharp criticisms of that approach. *See id.* (praising Fuller for exhibiting "a hallmark of true scholarship").

Justice Tatting worried about Justice Foster's effort to interpret the murder statute in light of a single purpose (deterrence). As Tatting noted, the criminal law had also been said to serve other purposes, including retribution and rehabilitation. *See* Fuller, *supra*, 62 HARV. L. REV. at 628 (opinion of Tatting, J.); *cf. id.* at 635 (opinion of Keen, J.) (suggesting that the murder statute might not be designed to serve instrumental goals at all). The diversity of possible purposes posed an obvious problem for Justice Foster's approach. *See id.* at 628–29 (opinion of Tatting, J.). But even if one focused exclusively on deterrence, Justice Tatting observed that applying the murder statute to the speluncean explorers could have *some* deterrent effect. *See id.* at 630 (positing that knowledge of the legal consequences of their act could have caused the explorers to wait a little longer before killing Whetmore).[21]

As for the precedents that Justice Foster had invoked, Justice Tatting noted a different line of cases that cut against Justice Foster's point. In one famous case, the Newgarth courts had refused to treat the defendant's extreme hunger (verging on starvation) as a legal excuse for stealing a loaf of bread.

But while Justice Tatting did not agree with Justice Foster's arguments, he could not bring himself to vote to affirm the defendants' convictions. Not knowing how to decide the case, he chose not to participate further.

Justice Keen, the textualist, showed no such indecision. He thought that the "natural meaning" of the statute's words clearly covered what the defendants had done. *See id.* at 632 (opinion of Keen, J.). To the extent that his colleagues resisted affirming the judgment below, he accused them of failing to keep their personal moral judgments separate from their interpretation and application of the written law. *See id.* at 633. In particular, he argued that Justice Foster's purposivist approach was a way to reach exactly the results that Justice Foster himself thought sensible in each case. According to Keen, Foster did so in three steps. First, Foster sought "to divine some single 'purpose' which the statute serves" (a project that Keen regarded as artificial). Second, Foster concluded that "a mythical being called 'the legislator,' in the pursuit of this imagined 'purpose,' overlooked something or left some gap or imperfection in his work." Third, Foster "fill[ed] in the blank thus created." *Id.* at 634.

Keen argued that the text of the murder statute left no room for judges to "legislate" in this way. Indeed, he suggested that the courts had erred in the past when they had recognized an exception for self-defense.[22] But in any event, Keen noted that the self-defense exception, as recognized by the courts, applied only when someone "resist[ed] an aggressive threat." *Id.* at 636. Because the explorers' case did not fit that template, the established exception for self-defense was inapplicable, and Keen would not extrapolate from it to create an unjustified new exception to the statute.

* * * * *

To celebrate the fiftieth anniversary of the publication of Professor Fuller's case, the *Harvard Law Review* asked various scholars and judges to write their own opinions. *See* Symposium, *The Case of the Spelunean*

---

[21] Justice Tatting could perhaps have added that applying the murder statute in cases of this sort might also have a marginal impact on people's decisions about whether to engage in risky activities like spelunking in the first place.

[22] Keen opined that if the courts had refused to infer an exception for self-defense, the legislature would have amended the statute to create one. According to Keen, moreover, the legislature would have been better able to determine the proper scope of such an exception. *See id.* at 637.

Explorers: Revisited, 112 HARV. L. REV. 1876–1923 (1999). Interestingly, the two prominent "textualist" judges who participated in the symposium—Alex Kozinski of the United States Court of Appeals for the Ninth Circuit and Frank Easterbrook of the United States Court of Appeals for the Seventh Circuit—reached different conclusions.

Judge Kozinski voted to affirm the defendants' convictions, for essentially Justice Keen's reasons. While conceding that there may be "good arguments" that executing the defendants would be unjust, Kozinski insisted that those arguments were being "presented to the wrong people"; as far as "judges in an age of statutes" are concerned, "justice consists of applying the laws passed by the legislature, precisely as written by the legislature." *Id.* at 1876–77. According to Kozinski, the relevant statute is not "unclear or ambiguous," and it leaves "no room for interpretation" or for the "exercise of judgment." *Id.* at 1876.

Kozinski conceded that "[w]hether the deliberate killing of a human being under these circumstances should be criminal is a difficult question." *Id.* at 1877. But Kozinski asserted that this question was not for the courts to resolve: "It must be answered by the conscience of the community, and that conscience is better gauged by the 535 members of the Newgarth legislature than by six unelected, effectively unremovable judges." *Id.* Although one might doubt that the Newgarth legislature really had expressed a considered view on that question (because the question may not have been in anyone's mind when the legislature enacted the relevant statute), Kozinski refused to assume that the statute's broad language was an oversight. *See id.* at 1877–78 ("Unfortunate incidents like these do happen from time to time, and we must presume the legislature was aware of them . . . ."). In any event, Kozinski maintained that "even if this were a case of legislative oversight, it would make no difference"; whether or not the enacting legislature had imagined the case of trapped spelunkers who cannibalize one of their companions, courts still would not be "free to ignore or augment the legislature's words just because we think it would have said something else, had it but thought of it." *Id.* at 1878. If the current legislature sympathized with the defendants, of course, it could enact a statute retroactively decriminalizing their conduct. But given what Kozinski took to be the plain meaning of the existing statute, any recourse for the defendants lay in "the political arena" rather than the courts. *Id.*

By contrast, Judge Easterbrook called for the convictions to be reversed. "Were the language of the statute the end of matters," he wrote, "the right judgment would be straightforward, as Justices Keen and Kozinski conclude. . . . Then when the hangman had finished implementing the judgment, he too would be doomed, for the executioner takes life willfully . . . ." *Id.* at 1913. As this opening dig suggests, Easterbrook accused Keen and Kozinski of reading the statute's bare language without regard to the "historical and governmental contexts" that informed its meaning. *Id.* When one took proper account of those contexts, Easterbrook argued, the legal rule established by the statute was not as unqualified as it seemed on its face.

Easterbrook's analysis relied upon what he described as longstanding practice. For many years, he asserted, "criminal statutes have been understood to operate only when the acts were unjustified." *Id.* What is more, "[a]ll three branches of government historically have been entitled to assess claims of justification—the legislature by specifying the prohibition and allowing exceptions, the executive by declining to prosecute (or by pardon after conviction), and the judiciary by developing defenses." *Id.* at 1913–14. Under the ordinary operation of this system, "criminal punishment is meted out only when all three branches (plus a jury representing private citizens) concur that public force may be used against the individual." *Id.* at 1914. Easterbrook took this allegedly longstanding practice to supply a background principle for interpreting criminal statutes: generally worded prohibitions like the one at hand should be understood to leave room for courts to consider justification-based defenses, including the defense of "necessity."[23]

Easterbrook conceded that this background principle was merely a default rule. If the legislature so chose, it could bar the judiciary from developing defenses like "necessity"; for instance, the legislature could enact a list of valid defenses and specify that the judiciary cannot supplement this list. But Easterbrook did not understand the statute at issue in the Case of the Speluncean Explorers to alter the normal default rule in this way. To the contrary, he argued that "[o]ur legislature could write a law as simple as [this one] precisely because it knew that courts entertain claims of justification." *Id.* Given the facts found by the jury (and relying upon a waiver or two by the prosecution), Easterbrook proceeded to conclude that the defendants' acts had in fact been justified. *See id.* at 1914–17.

* * * * *

Judge Easterbrook did not explicitly cast his point in terms of the relationship between statutes and the common law. But that may be the best way to understand his position (and it may also be the best way to analyze the case).

We have already touched on one aspect of the interaction between statutes and the common law. When Congress enacts a generally worded statute that creates a civil cause of action for damages, Congress normally does not say anything one way or the other about the possibility of out-of-court settlement. Absent some specific indication to the contrary, though, courts normally assume that disputes can indeed be settled, and that a valid settlement contract between the parties will defeat additional recovery on the statutory cause of action. In other

[23] Although Judge Easterbrook spoke of "justification" defenses, he presumably would also have recognized "excuse" defenses (like duress or insanity).

words, the typical statute creating a private cause of action for damages is presumed to accommodate the common-law defense of "accord and satisfaction." *See supra* pp. 24–25 (raising this issue in the context of the federal Electronic Fund Transfer Act).

As Judge Easterbrook suggested, the same has traditionally been true of criminal statutes. Start with *state* criminal statutes. At the time that Professor Fuller was writing, the American Law Institute had not yet started work on the Model Penal Code, and many states had old-fashioned criminal statutes like Newgarth's. Even with respect to the definition of offenses, those statutes often referred to common-law concepts (like "murder") without specifying their content. *See* Herbert Wechsler, *The Challenge of a Model Penal Code*, 65 HARV. L. REV. 1097, 1100 (1952). Defenses often were not codified at all. *Id.* Still, courts assumed that crimes specified by statute were subject to generic defenses supplied by the common law. That assumption rested partly on statutory interpretation, in that the statutes specifying particular crimes were understood to leave room for the application of common-law defenses. But the courts would not necessarily have said that they were reading each criminal statute to *incorporate* the generic defenses that were recognized at common law. Instead, the common law could be seen as operating of its own force to supply defenses that cut across criminal statutes except to the extent that particular statutes superseded them.

On that way of thinking, the Newgarth courts were correct to recognize the defense of self-defense—and they would have been correct to do so even if Newgarth's murder statute had used the word "knowingly" rather than "willfully." If we read Newgarth's murder statute to define an offense (and to specify the punishment for that offense) but to leave room for generic defenses to operate as a matter of common law, then the content of the relevant defenses would not have to be linked to the text of the statute. Instead, courts would simply have to decide whether the common law recognizes the defense of self-defense—and the answer to that question is "yes."

The same idea would explain why, as Judge Easterbrook argued, the executioners who carry out death sentences on behalf of Newgarth are not themselves violating the murder statute. Just as the common law has long recognized self-defense as a generic defense to criminal liability, so too the common law has recognized "execution of a public duty" as another generic defense. *Cf.* Paul H. Robinson et al., *The American Criminal Code: General Defenses*, 7 J. LEGAL ANALYSIS 37, 46 (2015) (noting that "[t]here is wide consensus among American jurisdictions concerning both the existence and general contours of the defense for execution of a public duty," and "not all jurisdictions that apply this defense in practice bother to codify it").[24]

[24] Indeed, if the execution of a state public duty can supply a defense to a federal criminal statute, the U.S. Supreme Court could perhaps have invoked this common-law defense in *United States v. Kirby*, 74 U.S. (7 Wall.) 482 (1869). *See supra* pp. 35–36.

Of course, the speluncean explorers were not executing a public duty, nor did they have a standard self-defense argument. Their defense rested instead on "necessity" (or "choice of evils"). The status and contours of that defense at common law are not clear. While conceding that "the point has not been entirely free from controversy," the revised comments to the Model Penal Code assert that "necessity seems clearly to have standing as a common law defense"—but the comments acknowledge longstanding debates about the "definition and extent" of that defense. MODEL PENAL CODE § 3.02 cmt. 1 (AM. L. INST. 1985). As a modern critic has observed, moreover, the "vast majority" of judicial opinions that speak of a necessity defense proceed to hold that "the defense does not apply" in the cases that they are deciding. Michael H. Hoffheimer, *Codifying Necessity: Legislative Resistance to Enacting Choice-of-Evils Defenses to Criminal Liability*, 82 TUL. L. REV. 191, 195 n.12 (2007).

Still, questions about whether and under what circumstances the common law recognizes a necessity defense are not central to this course. For our purposes, the most important point—brought out by Judge Easterbrook's opinion—is that old-fashioned criminal statutes like Newgarth's might be understood as leaving room for the common law to supply defenses. If we interpret the statutes that way, moreover, the ensuing questions about the content of those defenses are questions about the content of the common law, not questions of statutory interpretation.

In many states, criminal statutes now have a somewhat different relationship to the common law. In the 1950s, the American Law Institute began work on its Model Penal Code, which it finalized in 1962. Part II of the Model Penal Code defines a long list of specific crimes, but Part I includes "general provisions" of various sorts, including codified versions of many generic defenses recognized at common law. Many state legislatures have followed suit. To be sure, state legislatures have not enacted all of the formulations found in the Model Penal Code, and they may have been especially resistant to the Model Penal Code's broad version of the "choice of evils" defense. *See* Hoffheimer, *supra*, 82 TUL. L. REV. at 232–43 (noting that only nineteen states have codified the necessity defense at all, and only two of those states have adopted the Model Penal Code's version). But it is now very common for state criminal codes to identify a set of defenses that cut across specific crimes. *See* Robinson et al., *supra*, 7 J. LEGAL ANALYSIS at 127–49 (providing a fifty-state survey of various justification and excuse defenses); *cf.* Paul H. Robinson, Michael T. Cahill & Usman Mohammad, *The Five Worst (and Five Best) American Criminal Codes*, 95 NW. U. L. REV. 1, 50 nn.184–85 (2000) (noting that fourteen states and the District of Columbia have not codified any such defenses).

The fact that a state has codified some generic defenses does not necessarily prevent the state's courts from continuing to recognize other defenses as a matter of common law. *See* Caleb Nelson, *State and Federal*

Models of the Interaction Between Statutes and Unwritten Law, 80 U. CHI. L. REV. 657, 760 n.454 (2013) (contrasting statutes in two states that explicitly abolish common-law defenses to crimes with statutes in four other states that explicitly preserve some common-law defenses). But at least in states that have codified a particular version of the necessity defense, the scope of that defense will be a matter of statutory interpretation rather than common law.

What about *federal* criminal statutes? Many of those statutes are found in Title 18 of the United States Code, which is one of the titles that Congress has enacted as such. But Congress enacted Title 18 in 1948, before the American Law Institute began work on the Model Penal Code, and its structure is old-fashioned. *See* Paul H. Robinson & Markus D. Dubber, *The American Model Penal Code: A Brief Overview*, 10 NEW CRIM. L. REV. 319, 327 (2007) ("The present federal criminal code is not significantly different in form from the alphabetical listing of offenses that was typical of American codes in the 1800s."). In particular, Congress has not enacted anything like the "general part" of the Model Penal Code, with its set of generic defenses (and general principles of liability). *See* Eric A. Johnson, *Dynamic Incorporation of the General Part: Criminal Law's Missing (Hyper)Link*, 48 U.C. DAVIS L. REV. 1831, 1846 (2015).

It does not follow, as Justice Keen and Judge Kozinski might think, that there are no generic defenses to federal criminal statutes. To be sure, the modern Supreme Court has said that "it is an open question whether federal courts ever have authority to recognize a necessity defense not provided by statute." *United States v. Oakland Cannabis Buyers' Cooperative*, 532 U.S. 483, 490 (2001). But the Justices' doubts on that point may have been at least partly specific to the necessity defense. *Cf. id.* ("Even at common law, the defense of necessity was somewhat controversial. And under our constitutional system, in which federal crimes are defined by statute rather than common law, it is especially so." (citations omitted)). In other cases, moreover, the Court has seemed less doubtful about the relevance of common-law defenses in federal criminal prosecutions. *See, e.g.*, Dixon v. United States, 548 U.S. 1, 13–17 (2006) (assuming without deciding that duress can be a defense in prosecutions under 18 U.S.C. § 922(a)(6) and (n), and proceeding to resolve details about the burden of proof with respect to that defense); United States v. Bailey, 444 U.S. 394, 415–16 n.11 (1980) ("We . . . recognize that Congress in enacting criminal statutes legislates against a background of Anglo-Saxon common law, and that therefore a defense of duress or coercion may well have been contemplated when it enacted [18 U.S.C. § 751(a), which criminalizes escapes from federal custody]. . . . Our principal difference with the dissent . . . is not as to the existence of such a defense but as to the importance of surrender as an element of it." (citation omitted)).

Perhaps because of concerns about the status of the common law at the federal level, the modern Supreme Court has tended to speak as if the common law does not operate of its own force in this context; instead, whatever substantive defenses courts recognize in federal criminal prosecutions must be read into the particular criminal statute in question. *See* Nelson, *supra*, 80 U. CHI. L. REV. at 751–58 (citing examples of opinions that use this locution); *see also id.* at 755 n.438 (noting that different judges have suggested different ideas about whether each federal criminal statute should be presumed to incorporate common-law doctrines as they were understood when the statute was enacted, with the result that even generic defenses might vary from statute to statute). But the idea that each federal criminal statute should be presumed to incorporate all of the generic defenses supplied by the common law is obviously artificial. A better approach might be to presume that each federal criminal statute *accommodates* those defenses, in the sense that it leaves room for them to continue operating as a matter of common law. *See* Stephen E. Sachs, *Constitutional Backdrops*, 80 GEO. WASH. L. REV. 1813, 1846 (2012) ("The best justification for adhering to the common law rule is not that Congress wanted it, but that *it's part of the law*, and that it hasn't yet been repealed."); *cf.* Caleb Nelson, *The Legitimacy of (Some) Federal Common Law*, 101 VA. L. REV. 1, 63 (2015) ("Because unwritten law can operate of its own force at the federal level [on questions not governed by state law], it is not necessary to pretend that written federal law encompasses all issues on which courts need federal rules of decision.").[25]

NOTE ON THE CONCEPT OF "RULES" AND "STANDARDS"[26]

A number of the cases that you have read so far refer to the "purposes" of a statute, and they allow the purposes that they identify to influence the content of the legal directives that they ascribe to the statute. As you think about the concept of statutory "purpose," though, you should recognize that statutes can reflect many different kinds of purposes. For instance, in addition to being designed to achieve certain substantive goals in the real world, statutes also reflect judgments about *how* to achieve those goals. In other words, the purposes that should be ascribed to statutes are not exclusively substantive; they can address questions of implementation too.

Ever since Hart and Sacks, scholars have used the terminology of "rules" and "standards" to describe some of those questions. Although different scholars provide somewhat different definitions of those terms (and although modern scholars tend to speak of a continuum of "ruleness"

[25] Chapter 6.C of this book considers various aspects of the relationship between federal statutes and the common law.

[26] Some of the material in this note originally appeared (in somewhat different form) in Caleb Nelson, *What Is Textualism?*, 91 VA. L. REV. 347 (2005).

rather than a binary opposition), the basic distinction relates to the character of the judgments that implementing officials must make in order to apply a legal principle or directive to particular cases. Most legal principles or directives are designed to serve certain goals, but they can do so in different ways. A "standard" might simply state those goals and leave implementing officials in charge of deciding how best to promote them under each set of facts that might arise. A more "rule-like" principle or directive will itself incorporate some advance judgments on that score—generalizations that the implementing officials might think unfounded in a particular case, but that they are nonetheless supposed to accept. *See* FREDERICK SCHAUER, PLAYING BY THE RULES: A PHILOSOPHICAL EXAMINATION OF RULE-BASED DECISION-MAKING IN LAW AND IN LIFE 51–52 (1991). Thus, a rule might tell implementing officials to ignore some circumstances that they otherwise would have thought relevant to the goal behind the rule and to focus exclusively on a narrower set of issues identified by the rule. *Id.* at 53. Or it might permit implementing officials to consider all the circumstances they like, but still make some binding generalizations about how those circumstances usually play out or about the proper weight of various factors. According to Professor Schauer's helpful formulation, a legal principle or directive is "rule-like" to the extent that it "entrenches" such generalizations, so that implementing officials follow them even when some other course might seem more likely to promote the rule's underlying justifications in the case at hand. *Id.* at 51; *cf.* Kathleen M. Sullivan, *The Supreme Court, 1991 Term—Foreword: The Justices of Rules and Standards*, 106 HARV. L. REV. 22, 58 (1992) ("A legal directive is 'standard'-like when it tends to collapse decisionmaking back into the direct application of the background . . . policy to a fact situation.").

Every time legislators and their staffs draft a statute, they have to consider not only the mix of objectives that they are trying to achieve, but also whether those objectives will be best accomplished by directives that are more or less rule-like. Thanks to the work of diverse scholars, the principal costs and benefits of formulating legal directives as rules are now familiar.[27] On the "cost" side of the ledger, rules inevitably draw arbitrary lines; they can magnify small differences and overlook big ones. Almost all rules, moreover, are simultaneously over- and under-inclusive: they apply in some situations not warranted by their underlying purposes, and they fail to reach other situations that those purposes would seem to cover. The fact that the drafters of a rule cannot foresee everything that may happen in the future exacerbates this

---

[27] For a small sampling of the rich literature on this topic, see SCHAUER, *supra*; Colin S. Diver, *The Optimal Precision of Administrative Rules*, 93 YALE L.J. 65 (1983); Isaac Ehrlich & Richard A. Posner, *An Economic Analysis of Legal Rulemaking*, 3 J. LEGAL STUD. 257 (1974); Louis Kaplow, *Rules Versus Standards: An Economic Analysis*, 42 DUKE L.J. 557 (1992); Duncan Kennedy, *Form and Substance in Private Law Adjudication*, 89 HARV. L. REV. 1685 (1976); Pierre Schlag, *Rules and Standards*, 33 UCLA L. REV. 379 (1985); and Cass R. Sunstein, *Problems with Rules*, 83 CAL. L. REV. 953 (1995).

drawback; rules that seem justified now run the risk of being too inflexible later.

But formulating directives in relatively rule-like terms has familiar benefits too. When legislators suspect that their outlook on the world differs from that of the officials who will implement the directive, they may want to leave fewer contestable decisions up to the implementing officials. The results that the directive produces might come closer to the legislators' preferences if the legislators formulate the directive as a rule (incorporating the generalizations that they themselves think appropriate) than if they formulate it as a standard (leaving more room for whatever generalizations the implementing officials would draw on their own). Even if legislators do not fear that implementing officials will *systematically* promote an agenda that the current legislature opposes, legislators might simply fear that different implementing officials will have divergent outlooks and that the development of a standard through case-by-case adjudication will therefore yield unduly varied results. In some situations, moreover, relatively rule-like directives might do a better job of giving citizens advance notice of the legal requirements to which they will be held, and legislators might value the advance notice provided by rules more than they value the promise of retrospective reasonableness held out by standards. *See* SCHAUER, *supra*, at 137–45 (discussing the conditions under which this argument applies).

This quick summary of the costs and benefits of rules is not exhaustive. But the basic point is simple: the ideal degree of ruleness that a legislature should choose in a particular policy area is itself a difficult policy question that rarely has a canonical answer. Most of the time, some considerations will cut in favor of rules and others will cut against them.

In the first instance, the choice between rules and standards is obviously up to the legislature. But the background principles that courts use to interpret the legislature's words help determine how rule-like statutory directives are in practice. As we saw in both *Riggs v. Palmer* and *Church of the Holy Trinity*, litigants often ask interpreters to infer exceptions to a statutory provision when, in the interpreters' judgment, application of the provision would not serve the enacting legislature's apparent goals. Conversely, litigants sometimes ask interpreters to pay attention to the provision (as a matter of either statutory interpretation or "federal common law") in situations that are not covered by its explicit terms but that, in their judgment, implicate the policy behind it. As Judge Easterbrook has explained, interpreters who accede to such requests are understanding the provision to be less "rule-like" than it seems at first glance; rather than staying entirely within the categories identified on the face of the statute, the interpreters are asserting authority to make their own determinations about how the enacting legislature's underlying purposes play out in the case at hand. *See* Frank

H. Easterbrook, *Text, History, and Structure in Statutory Interpretation,* 17 HARV. J.L. & PUB. POL'Y 61, 68 (1994).

* * * * *

Judge Easterbrook made further comments about "rule-ness" in the next case, which involved Federal Rule of Criminal Procedure 6. At the time relevant to the case, Rule 6(e) included the following provisions:

Rule 6. The Grand Jury

. . . .

(e) Recording and Disclosing the Proceedings.

. . . .

(2) Secrecy.

(A) No obligation of secrecy may be imposed on any person except in accordance with Rule 6(e)(2)(B).

(B) Unless these rules provide otherwise, the following persons must not disclose a matter occurring before the grand jury:

(i) a grand juror;

(ii) an interpreter;

(iii) a court reporter;

(iv) an operator of a recording device;

(v) a person who transcribes recorded testimony;

(vi) an attorney for the government; or

(vii) a person to whom disclosure is made under Rule 6(e)(3)(A)(ii) or (iii).

(3) Exceptions.

(A) Disclosure of a grand-jury matter—other than the grand jury's deliberations or any grand juror's vote—may be made to:

(i) an attorney for the government for use in performing that attorney's duty;

(ii) any government personnel—including those of a state, state subdivision, Indian tribe, or foreign government—that an attorney for the government considers necessary to assist in performing that attorney's duty to enforce federal criminal law; or

(iii) a person authorized by 18 U.S.C. § 3322.

(B) A person to whom information is disclosed under Rule 6(e)(3)(A)(ii) may use that information only to assist an attorney for the government in performing that attorney's duty to enforce federal criminal law. An attorney for the government must promptly provide the court that impaneled the grand jury with the names of all persons to whom a disclosure has been made, and must certify that the attorney has advised those persons of their obligation of secrecy under this rule. . . .

(E) The court may authorize disclosure—at a time, in a manner, and subject to any other conditions that it directs—of a grand-jury matter:

(i) preliminarily to or in connection with a judicial proceeding . . . .

(F) A petition to disclose a grand-jury matter under Rule 6(e)(3)(E)(i) must be filed in the district where the grand jury convened. . . .

Jaskolski v. Daniels

427 F.3d 456 (7th Cir. 2005)

■ *JUDGE EASTERBROOK delivered the opinion of the court:*

Joseph Jaskolski assisted federal prosecutors in an investigation that led to the indictment of Rick Daniels and three of his relatives for insurance fraud. After the defendants (collectively "Daniels") were acquitted, they sued Jaskolski and his employer, the National Insurance Crime Bureau, in state court, charging them with the tort of malicious prosecution. During discovery Daniels sought documents that Jaskolski deemed to be grand jury materials protected from disclosure by Fed. Rule Crim. Proc. 6(e). When the state judge sided with Daniels and ordered Jaskolski to hand over everything plaintiffs wanted, Jaskolski and the Bureau filed this suit in federal court seeking an injunction. District Judge Lozano obliged and enjoined Daniels from pursuing discovery in state court; instead they must turn to District Judge Moody, who supervised the federal grand jury and under the injunction has exclusive authority to decide which materials in Jaskolski's (and the Bureau's) files will be released to the plaintiffs in the tort litigation.

In this court the parties have devoted their energies to debating whether Jaskolski played the role of "government personnel" in the criminal prosecution—for, if he did, then he "must not disclose a matter occurring before the grand jury." Fed. Rule Crim. Proc. 6(e)(2)(B). Many persons who learn information about a criminal investigation are free to disclose what they know, and "[n]o obligation of secrecy may be imposed except in accordance with Rule 6(e)(2)(B)." That subsection covers, among others, any "person to whom disclosure is made under Rule 6(e)(3)(A)(ii) or (iii)." Rule 6(e)(2)(B)(vii). Rule 6(e)(3)(A)(ii) in turn refers to "any government personnel—including those of a state, state subdivision, Indian tribe, or foreign government—that an attorney for the government considers necessary to assist in performing that attorney's duty to enforce federal criminal law."

During the criminal investigation, an Assistant United States Attorney concluded that Jaskolski's assistance was "necessary" and informed Judge Moody that Jaskolski would be allowed access to some grand jury materials. If Jaskolski served the investigation as "government personnel" then he is forbidden to disclose what he learned, without the federal court's approval. One appellate decision holds, however, that investigators who work for the Insurance Crime Bureau are not "government personnel" even if a federal prosecutor supervises their activities. See *United States v. Tager*, 638 F.2d 167 (10th Cir. 1980). Other decisions are more favorable to the idea that private employees detailed to assist federal prosecutors are "government personnel" for that prosecution. See *United States v. Lartey*, 716 F.2d 955 (2d Cir. 1983); *United States v. Benjamin*, 852 F.2d 413 (9th Cir. 1988). The parties (and the United States, appearing as *amicus curiae*) want us to determine the proper classification of private insurance investigators under Rule 6(e)(3)(A)(ii).

[Before getting there, the panel concluded that the district court had enjoyed subject-matter jurisdiction under 18 U.S.C. § 3231. The panel also concluded that by failing to invoke either issue preclusion or the Anti-Injunction Act (which restricts the power of federal courts to enjoin proceedings in state courts), Daniels had forfeited the possible benefit of those doctrines.]

. . . . A reader who expects us to turn at last to the question whether Jaskolski acted as "government personnel" in the investigation will be disappointed, for that issue turns out to be non-dispositive. An affirmative answer would resolve the dispute in Jaskolski's favor—but a negative answer does not lead to victory for Daniels, so we leave the question for another case in which the resolution matters. Recall the language of Rule 6(e)(2)(B): "[T]he following persons must not disclose a matter occurring before the grand jury: . . . (vii) a person to whom disclosure is made under Rule 6(e)(3)(A)(ii)." Disclosure was made to Jaskolski under Rule 6(e)(3)(A)(ii). Whether the disclosure was made "properly" or "correctly" is neither here nor there. Rule 6(e)(2)(B) asks whether disclosure has been "made under" a particular subsection, not whether the subsection was applied correctly. This protects the prosecutor's (and the witnesses') reliance interests and prevents a blunder from opening the investigatory files.

Daniels contends that it would be "absurd" to read Rule 6(e)(2)(B) to bypass the question whether a given person should have received the grand jury materials now in his possession. He invokes the doctrine that judges avoid giving statutes absurd readings, but he misunderstands its scope. This doctrine does not license courts to improve statutes (or rules) substantively, so that their outcomes accord more closely with judicial beliefs about how matters ought to be resolved. The Supreme Court made this point recently. "It is beyond our province to rescue Congress from its drafting errors, and to provide for what we might think . . . is the preferred result." *Lamie v. United States Trustee*, 540 U.S. 526, 542 (2004), quoting from *United States v. Granderson*, 511 U.S. 39, 68 (1994) (concurring opinion).

In deciding how to address a subject, the legislature—Rule 6(e) is the work of Congress rather than the Supreme Court under the Rules Enabling Act—must choose between a rule and a standard. Rules such as "determine how the holder came by the information" are easy to administer but are inevitably both too narrow in some situations (all rules have loopholes) and overbroad in others. Standards such as "determine whether the prosecutor acted in good faith in providing the information, or some other error occurred" could in principle match the outcome more closely to the legislative objective, but standards are difficult to administer and create errors of their own. Courts cannot ascertain intent or good faith without hearings; the principal evidence would be oral and correspondingly difficult to evaluate. Rules have lower administrative costs and will be preferable unless they increase the error costs (the sum of false positives and false negatives) by more than the savings in administrative costs. Whether to choose a rule or a standard is a legislative decision. Judges ought not turn a rule into a standard; that amounts to little more than disagreement with a legislative choice. Boosting the level of generality by attempting to discern and enforce legislative "purposes" or "goals" instead of the enacted language is just a means to turn rules into standards. Cf. *Rodriguez v. United States*, 480 U.S. 522 (1987). Rule 6(e)(2)(B) creates a bright line, and we must enforce it that way.

What Daniels labels "absurd" results are nothing but the rough cuts inevitable with decision by rule. To observe that error costs exist is not to justify use of a standard—first because the choice is for political actors, and second because we cannot be sure that Rule 6(e)(2)(B) as written produces more costs than would a judicial attempt to assess the prosecutor's good faith and the assistant's "government personnel" status one case at a time.

When an opinion says that courts interpret statutes to avoid absurd results, it is not inviting judges to convert rules into standards. *Church of the Holy Trinity v. United States*, 143 U.S. 457 (1892), which invoked the norm against absurd outcomes to make the law more in line with the Justices' substantive preferences, has no modern traction. Today the anti-absurdity canon is linguistic rather than substantive. It deals with texts that don't scan as written and thus need repair work, rather than with statutes that seem poor fits for the task at hand. In other words, the modern decisions draw a line between poor exposition and benighted substantive choice; the latter is left alone, because what judges deem a "correction" or "fix" is from another perspective a deliberate interference with the legislative power to choose what makes for a good rule. Admit the propriety of "fixing mistakes" and you allow a general power to *identify* "mistakes," which means a privilege to make the real substantive decision. Even when the statute *invites* modification, as the "context clause" in some definitions does, judges are limited to considering the linguistic context rather than trying to "improve" the statute's substantive effect. See *Rowland v. California Men's Colony, Unit II Men's Advisory Council*, 506 U.S. 194 (1993).

The only recent decision in which the anti-absurdity canon played an important role, *Green v. Bock Laundry Machine Co.*, 490 U.S. 504 (1989), dealt with an incomplete and baffling rule. Other decisions that cite the doctrine, such as *Public Citizen v. Department of Justice*, 491 U.S. 440 (1989), and *United States v. X-Citement Video, Inc.*, 513 U.S. 64 (1994), use it to avoid an unconstitutional reading. The dearth of modern "substantive absurdity" decisions is readily understandable. Scholars as well as judges have recognized that a power to fix statutes substantively would give the Judicial Branch too much leeway to prefer its views about what makes for "good" laws over those of the Legislative Branch. See, e.g., John Manning, *The Absurdity Doctrine*, 116 Harv. L. Rev. 2387 (2003); Adrian Vermeule, *Legislative History and the Limits of Judicial Competence: The Untold Story of Holy Trinity Church*, 50 Stan. L. Rev. 1833 (1998). The Supreme Court has been willing to enforce even statutes that seem to set traps for the unwary or unfortunate. *Dodd v. United States*, 545 U.S. 353 (2005), is a good example: The Court held that the statute of limitations for collateral attacks on criminal convictions may expire before the decision supporting the challenge becomes applicable, and it rejected an argument that this linguistically sound reading should be rejected as substantively absurd.

Another good example is *United States v. Locke*, 471 U.S. 84 (1985), which dealt with a statute that required certain documents to be filed "before December 31." Unwary readers might read this as equivalent to "before the end of the year," and inevitably some did. The Court held that a person who filed *on* December 31 had filed too late. The statute was complete as written, and though the use of "before December 31" rather than "on or before December 31" may have been a blunder there was no linguistic defect, and hence no role for the anti-absurdity canon. The unfortunate outcome for the late filers, the Court held, was just a normal effect of any rule; no matter where the line may be placed, someone always files one day too late. . . .

Guidry v. Sheet Metal Workers National Pension Fund, 493 U.S. 365 (1990), supplies another example. Curtis Guidry pleaded guilty to embezzling funds from a pension plan of which he had been a trustee. Guidry was himself entitled to a pension from the plan, and the remaining trustees confiscated the value of his pension in partial fulfilment of Guidry's obligation to repay what he stole. Guidry filed suit, contending that this offset violated ERISA's anti-alienation clause. He lost in the court of appeals, which said that an anti-alienation clause is designed to protect pensioners from their own improvident spending, not to enable them to retain ill-got gains. If the enacting Congress had been asked: "Would you make an exception to the anti-alienation clause for persons who steal from the pension fund?", it likely would have answered yes. This is the method of *Riggs v. Palmer*, 115 N.Y. 506, 22 N.E. 188 (1889), the famous decision holding that to avoid (substantive) absurdity murdering heirs cannot inherit despite the Statute of Wills. Yet the Supreme Court ruled in Guidry's favor. ERISA's anti-alienation clause is coherent as written and contains no exceptions. Whatever Congress *might* have done, it had not done. To the extent that the Justices referred to purposes at all, they conceived them concretely rather than abstractly. What is the purpose of an anti-alienation clause? It is to prevent appeals to the equities case by case. In other words the Justices did not ask, "What is the value served by this particular rule?" Instead they asked "What is the value served by *rules*, in general?" This led the Court to enforce the rule and to rebuff efforts at reconstruction. *Guidry* represents today's interpretive norm.

Our final example is *Lamie*, to which we have referred already. Until 1994 the Bankruptcy Code provided that courts could authorize compensation to the debtor's attorney in Chapter 7 proceedings. In 1994 the vital language—"or to the debtor's attorney"—vanished from 11 U.S.C. § 330(a). There was some reason to think that the deletion had been an accidental byproduct of other changes made to this section; the phrase (or an equivalent) probably should have been moved but not eliminated. But it *was* eliminated, the statute as revised could be parsed, and the Court therefore held that the judicial authority to award fees to counsel in Chapter 7 cases had lapsed. The Justices allowed that the change might be unfortunate for some debtors, even counterproductive for the bankruptcy system as a whole, but concluded that such observations must be addressed to the legislature; bad consequences do not allow creative "interpretation" to avoid them. 540 U.S. at 536–37. "Our unwillingness to soften the import of Congress' chosen words even if we believe the words lead to a harsh outcome is longstanding. It results from 'deference to the supremacy of the legislature,'" *id.* at 538, quoting from *Locke*, 471 U.S. at 95.

Rule 6(e)(2)(B) makes sense as written. It parses without the assistance of a red pencil, and judges are not authorized to add words (such as "properly") that would change the Rule's substantive effect. . . .

NOTES AND QUESTIONS

1. As Judge Easterbrook suggested, the distinction between "rules" and "standards" provides a useful way to think about *Riggs v. Palmer* and *Church of the Holy Trinity v. United States*. But how much light does it actually shed on the question that Judge Easterbrook was addressing in *Jaskolski* itself? Compare two possible readings of Federal Rule of Criminal Procedure 6(e)(2)(B)(vii). On Judge Easterbrook's reading, Rule

6(e)(2)(B)(vii) imposes an obligation of secrecy on any person to whom disclosure of grand-jury materials was made under the purported authority of Rule 6(e)(3)(A)(ii), whether or not that disclosure was proper. On the competing reading, Rule 6(e)(2)(B)(vii) imposes an obligation of secrecy only upon people to whom disclosures were *properly* made under Rule 6(e)(3)(A)(ii)—that is, people who really are "government personnel" within the meaning of Rule 6(e)(3)(A)(ii). Is that reading really less rule-like than Judge Easterbrook's reading?

2. Whatever your answer to that question, is the key phrase "a person to whom disclosure is made under Rule 6(e)(3)(A)(ii)" as unambiguous on its face as Judge Easterbrook suggested? If one thinks about these words in isolation, without thinking about the apparent purposes behind Rule 6(e), is it clear that "a person to whom disclosure is made under Rule 6(e)(3)(A)(ii)" means any person to whom disclosure is made under the *purported* authority of Rule 6(e)(3)(A)(ii), whether or not Rule 6(e)(3)(A)(ii) actually authorized the disclosure? Or could one plausibly say that if Mr. Jaskolski wasn't "government personnel" within the meaning of Rule 6(e)(3)(A)(ii), then he couldn't be "a person to whom disclosure is made under Rule 6(e)(3)(A)(ii)"—even if federal prosecutors invoked that rule when disclosing the grand-jury materials to him?

If these two readings both seem equally natural when we think only about the text, how should a court decide which reading to adopt? At least to the extent that the court confronts a genuine ambiguity in the text, is it not natural for the court to try to resolve the ambiguity by thinking about the purposes that Congress seems to have been trying to balance? Would Judge Easterbrook himself have any objection to that way of resolving a genuine ambiguity? Wasn't his argument primarily about the inappropriateness of taking statutory language that seems relatively clear on its face and converting it into something more standard-like than it appears to be?

3. If one agrees that the language of Rule 6(e)(2)(B)(vii) is genuinely ambiguous, and if one also agrees that courts can properly think about Congress's apparent purposes when trying to resolve the ambiguity, what are those purposes? On the one hand, Congress did not want government attorneys to publicize information that comes out before the grand jury. To the extent that government attorneys bring other government personnel into an investigation, Congress plainly wanted to impose a secrecy obligation on them too. But Rule 6(e)(2)(A) says that "[n]o obligation of secrecy may be imposed on any person except in accordance with Rule 6(e)(2)(B)." That provision suggests that Congress did not want excessively broad gag rules. Can we tell from the provisions that Congress enacted whether Judge Easterbrook's reading or the competing reading fits better with Congress's apparent purposes?

If the disclosure to Mr. Jaskolski was proper, then Jaskolski plainly would have been subject to the gag rule. On the other hand, if Mr. Jaskolski didn't count as "government personnel" within the meaning of

Rule 6(e)(3)(A)(ii), then the prosecutor wasn't supposed to disclose grand-jury materials to him in the first place. It seems, then, that Congress did not want grand-jury information to get disseminated to the public through the prosecutor. Should we infer that if the prosecutor makes a mistake about whom Rule 6(e)(3)(A)(ii) covers, the person to whom the prosecutor discloses the information is subject to the same secrecy obligations that plainly would have applied if the disclosure had been proper? Or might one respond that Congress's *way* of making sure that private-sector investigators like Mr. Jaskolski didn't publicize grand-jury materials was not to impose a gag rule on them, but just to forbid prosecutors from showing them grand-jury materials in the first place?

Does Rule 6(e)(3)(B) help us choose between these two possibilities? It requires prosecutors to give the supervising judge "the names of *all persons* to whom a disclosure has been made," and to certify that the prosecutor has advised all of those people "of their obligation of secrecy under this rule." Does that language suggest that everyone who gets grand-jury material from the prosecutor does have an obligation of secrecy, and hence that Judge Easterbrook's reading of Rule 6(e)(2)(B)(vii) is better than the competing reading? Would Judge Easterbrook have any objection to this style of argument?

4. Compare Judge Easterbrook's comments in *Jaskolski* to Judge Easterbrook's logic in the Case of the Speluncean Explorers. In the latter case, he understood Newgarth's murder statute to be substantially less rule-like than the surface meaning of its words might suggest. In particular, background principles about the operation of criminal statutes led him to presume that courts could consider justification-based defenses, including the defense of "necessity." Is Judge Easterbrook's position simply that while courts should interpret statutes in light of the applicable background principles, and while those principles might make statutes less rule-like than they seem on their face, courts should not otherwise second-guess the level of rule-ness apparently chosen by the legislature? Is the point of such a distinction that the principles of interpretation used by courts should themselves be relatively rule-like?

Assuming that background principles can indeed qualify the surface meaning of statutory language, would there be anything wrong with a general background principle that encouraged courts to push seemingly rule-like directives in the direction of standards? Think, for instance, of Judge Earl's opinion in *Riggs v. Palmer*, which referred to the "familiar canon of construction that . . . a thing which is within the letter of the statute is not within the statute unless it be within the intention of the makers" in the sense that Judge Earl proceeded to describe. Or recall the passage that Justice Brewer quoted from *United States v. Kirby* in *Church of the Holy Trinity*:

> "All laws should receive a sensible construction. General terms should be so limited in their application as not to lead to injustice, oppression, or an absurd consequence. It will always, therefore, be

presumed that the legislature intended exceptions to its language which would avoid results of this character. The reason of the law in such cases should prevail over its letter."

To the extent that Judge Easterbrook criticizes the logic of *Riggs v. Palmer* and *Church of the Holy Trinity*, he must see some flaw in these general background principles. What flaw do you think that he sees? Is the problem (from Judge Easterbrook's perspective) simply that the background principles invoked by Judge Earl and Justice Brewer rest on an assumption that he considers empirically unfounded—the assumption that legislatures usually do not mean statutory language to be quite as rule-like as it seems? Is there some other reason why the background principles invoked by Judge Earl and Justice Brewer are less defensible than the background principle that Judge Easterbrook relied upon in the Case of the Speluncean Explorers?

NOTE ON AMBIGUITY VS. VAGUENESS IN STATUTORY LANGUAGE

Many of the judicial opinions that you will read in the ensuing chapters refer to some sort of "ambiguity" in statutory language. Unfortunately, lawyers and judges use that term to cover myriad distinct phenomena. Not surprisingly, philosophers of language have developed a more precise vocabulary. In particular, they have developed a distinction between what they call "ambiguity" and what they call "vagueness." That distinction is potentially relevant to various doctrines of statutory interpretation, so this introductory chapter closes with a brief summary.

In philosophical jargon, "ambiguity" is not an umbrella term for all linguistic indeterminacies. Instead, it refers only to one *type* of indeterminacy. Specifically, an expression is said to be "ambiguous" if it might be understood in two or more distinct senses.[28] For instance, if someone told you to collect all of the "light" notebooks in a room, you would not know (without further information) whether you were supposed to focus on weight or color. *See, e.g.*, WILLARD VAN ORMAN QUINE, WORD AND OBJECT 129–32 (1960).

By contrast, an expression is said to be "vague" if it refers to a range with fuzzy borders, so that its application to particular circumstances requires lines to be drawn in places whose specific location is not dictated by the expression itself. Suppose, for instance, that the surrounding context eliminates all ambiguity in the directive about collecting "light" notebooks and makes clear that the directive is about physical weight. Even so, the tipping points on the spectrum from "light" to "normal" to "heavy" are indistinct, and you might draw the necessary lines in a different place than I would. In this context, the word "light" is vague but

---

[28] Linguistic philosophers often go on to distinguish "semantic" ambiguity from "syntactic" ambiguity.

not ambiguous. *See id.* at 125–29; *see also* TIMOTHY A.O. ENDICOTT, VAGUENESS IN LAW 31 (2000) ("An expression is vague if there are borderline cases for its application."); Jeremy Waldron, *Vagueness in Law and Language: Some Philosophical Issues*, 82 CAL. L. REV. 509, 513 (1994) (providing a more formal definition).

In statutory language, "ambiguity" and "vagueness" frequently have very different sources. Vagueness often reflects a deliberate decision by members of the enacting legislature to transfer various important decisions to the courts or agencies that must apply the statute. When legislators use a vague word like "reasonable," they are not embedding all the answers in the statute itself. Instead, they are trusting those who will apply the statute to draw the necessary lines on a case-by-case basis. Often, the legislators' decision to take this approach is well considered and is designed to serve important policy goals of the sort associated with the choice between rules and standards. *Cf.* FREDERICK SCHAUER, THINKING LIKE A LAWYER: A NEW INTRODUCTION TO LEGAL REASONING 188–94 (2009) (identifying the spectrum from precision to vagueness with the spectrum from rules to standards). As a result, "vagueness in statutory language is never, in itself, evidence of a mistake." W. David Slawson, *Legislative History and the Need to Bring Statutory Interpretation Under the Rule of Law*, 44 STAN. L. REV. 383, 423 (1992).

On the other hand, what philosophers call "ambiguity" in statutory language is less likely to be deliberate. *Cf. id.* (asserting that "ambiguities are almost always mistakes"). To appreciate this point, we need to think more carefully about the various sources of ambiguity in statutes.

Some ambiguities inhere in the conventional meanings of the words that the legislature chose or the way in which the legislature put those words together. Simply as a matter of ordinary usage, statutory language sometimes lends itself to two or more different readings. Other ambiguities stem instead from principles specific to our system of statutory interpretation, which can generate multiple possible readings of language that seems unambiguous as a matter of ordinary usage. In some cases, for instance, interpreters will not know whether to read a particular statute against the backdrop of concepts drawn from the common law, or how the statute that they are trying to interpret interacts with another statute. For at least some interpreters, ambiguity can also be generated by doubts about whether members of the enacting legislature really intended to establish the policy that their chosen language seems to state. For instance, if one accepts the interpretive method of *Riggs v. Palmer* and *Church of the Holy Trinity v. United States*, one sometimes will be unsure whether a statutory directive is just as general as it seems on its face or instead accommodates implicit exceptions for situations that members of the enacting legislature did not foresee. Likewise, interpreters who are open to the possibility of correcting "scrivener's errors" will occasionally encounter cases that lie on the margins of their tests for identifying such errors.

Each of these sources of ambiguity is different. But they share a common feature: with respect to each of these sources of ambiguity, it is possible that members of the enacting legislature did not recognize the ambiguity and did not intend to entrust interpreters with the choice between the two possible readings. Perhaps members of the enacting legislature collectively intended to establish Directive *A* rather than Directive *A′*, but inadvertently drafted statutory language that is open to both interpretations. (This problem might be called a *failure of communication.*) Or perhaps members of the enacting legislature never focused on the issue that separates the two possible versions of their directive and failed to make any collective choice between them. (This sort of oversight might be called a *failure of conception.*)

To the extent that statutory ambiguity is inadvertent, interpreters often can resolve it. If an ambiguity simply reflects a failure of communication, interpreters may well be able to gather clues to the intended meaning of the relevant provision from other aspects of the same statute, or its legislative history, or information about the statute's overall purposes, or information about legislative habits more generally (of the sort embedded in many canons of construction). Even if the ambiguity reflects a failure of conception, the same sources might help interpreters identify the interpretation that members of the enacting legislature probably *would have* preferred *if* they had squarely confronted the choice. Thus, when statutory interpreters identify an apparent ambiguity in statutory language, the solution is typically to engage in more interpretation. Judicial opinions often reflect this fact: they refer to something as an "ambiguity," but further interpretive efforts enable them to identify a single determinate meaning that they portray as having been established by the legislature itself. (As you read opinions in the ensuing chapters, do not get confused by this locution. There is a difference between *superficial* ambiguities, which trigger the need for further interpretation but which ultimately can be resolved in line with legislatively created meaning, and *residual* or *end-stage* ambiguities, the resolution of which cannot confidently be attributed to the enacting legislature.)

By contrast, "vagueness" cannot be eliminated through further interpretation. In a sense, indeed, vagueness is not really an *interpretive* problem at all. When a statute uses vague words like "reasonable," interpreters may well have no doubt about the content of the directive that the legislature established. The hard questions are less about *interpreting* the directive (that is, identifying what the word "reasonable" means) than about *applying* the directive to particular circumstances (that is, deciding what *is* reasonable under the circumstances). The judgment calls that go into answering those questions, moreover, often require a very different type of analysis than the interpretive techniques that courts and agencies use to resolve ambiguity.

Notwithstanding this fact, lawyers and judges are not in the habit of distinguishing between "ambiguity" and "vagueness." As a result, the judicial opinions and other quoted material in this book tend to use the word "ambiguity" to cover both types of indeterminacy. In the materials that follow, though, we will occasionally want to ask whether particular doctrines and practices are better suited to handling one type of indeterminacy than the other. *See, e.g., infra* p. 441 (noting Professor Slawson's argument that courts and administrative agencies should use legislative history to resolve "ambiguity" but not "vagueness"). To preserve the vocabulary for considering these issues, the note material in this book (as opposed to the excerpts from judicial opinions) often uses the word "ambiguity" in contrast to vagueness. *Cf.* REED DICKERSON, THE INTERPRETATION AND APPLICATION OF STATUTES 48 (1975) ("It is unfortunate that many lawyers persist in using the word 'ambiguity' to include vagueness.").

CHAPTER 2

CANONS OF CONSTRUCTION

A. INTRODUCTION

The opening chapter was more evocative than systematic. Its goal was to get you thinking about various questions that all theories of statutory interpretation must confront. In what ways can the meaning of statutory language go beyond or even contradict what members of the enacting legislature consciously intended? Under what circumstances (and for what reasons) should courts read unstated exceptions or qualifications into statutory language that seems, on its face, to be quite general? Are there any parallel situations in which courts should read statutory language to be *broader* than it seems on its face? When should courts feel free to make their own judgments about whether a particular application of a statute would advance the substantive purposes that the enacting legislature apparently was trying to achieve? Should the attitude with which courts approach statutes vary according to the kind of statutes that they are approaching and the legal consequences that are at stake? What efforts should courts make to reconcile the legal directives that they ascribe to particular statutes with the courts' own sense of good policy, or with the legal directives that the courts associate with other sources of law (such as other statutes, or the common law, or the Constitution itself)? In our system of government, what are the general roles and responsibilities of the legislatures that enact statutes and the courts or administrative agencies that subsequently apply them? What are the tradeoffs between the demands of democracy (which might seem to cut against judicial creativity) and the difficulty of crafting sensible rules in advance for cases whose details cannot be foreseen at the time of enactment (which might seem to favor background rules that let courts pour considerable content into statutes during the course of application)?

With all these questions on the table, this chapter takes a step back. To show you the relevance of certain kinds of background principles to the proper interpretation of statutes, this chapter introduces some longstanding canons of construction and discusses the famous attack on those canons launched by Professor Karl Llewellyn.

Modern judges disagree with each other about how much weight to give the canons. Judges also disagree about how fine-grained the canons should get: is it more useful to have rough but simple canons (which might overlook many nuances) or to have highly reticulated canons (which might be harder to apply in a consistent way)? Even with these disagreements, though, canons play an important role in many cases about statutory interpretation, and lawyers frequently make arguments about how particular canons apply to particular statutes. Familiarity with the canons is one of the most useful things that you can take away from this course.

Of course, referring to "the canons" as a group overlooks many important distinctions; different canons serve different purposes and operate in different ways. When you are trying to understand any given canon, keep the following questions in mind:

- What is the justification for this particular canon? Professor Cass Sunstein has distinguished among canons that reflect widely shared principles of communication, canons that are specific to legislation and that reflect the legislature's own instructions (actual or presumed) about how statutes should be interpreted, canons that are designed "to improve lawmaking processes and the deliberation and accountability that are supposed to accompany them," and canons that promote particular substantive policies (perhaps derived from the Constitution or other aspects of our legal traditions, but not necessarily embraced by members of the enacting legislature). *See* Cass R. Sunstein, *Interpreting Statutes in the Regulatory State*, 103 HARV. L. REV. 405, 454–60 (1989). Professor Stephen Ross has proposed a simpler distinction between "descriptive" canons (which provide guidance about "what the legislature . . . probably meant") and "normative" canons (which "do not purport to describe accurately what Congress actually intended" but instead "direct courts to construe any ambiguity in a particular way in order to further some policy objective"). Stephen F. Ross, *Where Have You Gone, Karl Llewellyn? Should Congress Turn Its Lonely Eyes to You?*, 45 VAND. L. REV. 561, 563 (1992).

  Even within the category of "descriptive" or intent-oriented canons, different canons can relate to legislative intent in different ways. Some canons are designed to shed light on how members of the enacting legislature probably were using particular words or phrases. Other canons address a different species of legislative intent; they reflect policy decisions that members of the enacting legislature probably favored (or would have favored if they had thought about questions that they did not actually consider), and they encourage interpreters to interpret statutes accordingly. Still other canons might not accurately capture legislative intent when they are first announced, but they establish a framework that legislators can then use to communicate their intentions more effectively.[1]

---

[1] Supporters of canons often suggest that canons have "feedback effects" on legislative drafting: legislators will learn about the canons that interpreters use, and legislators will draft bills accordingly. If that were true, then even a seemingly artificial canon might be a reliable guide to the intended meaning of statutes enacted after the canon became prominent. Surveys suggest, however, that congressional staffers involved in the drafting process do not know as much about the canons as this argument assumes. *See* Abbe R. Gluck & Lisa Schultz Bressman,

- What is the trigger for the canon? Some canons come into play only if a statutory provision is superficially *ambiguous* or *vague*; on its face, a word or phrase in the provision could be understood or applied in different ways, and the canon helps interpreters choose among the possible understandings or applications. (As we shall see, the presumption against superfluity is an example.) Other canons are triggered by *generally worded* provisions; if a statute does not specifically address the issue on which the canon focuses, and there are not other indications that members of the enacting legislature thought about that issue, the canon might encourage interpreters to read an implied limitation into the statute so as to handle the issue in the way that the canon favors. (The presumptions against retroactivity and extraterritoriality are examples.)
- How much weight does the canon deserve, and what type of information will overcome the canon? Most canons are rebuttable presumptions rather than ironclad rules; interpreters might be persuaded that a particular statute means something different than the canon would suggest. Still, some canons establish stronger presumptions than others. For instance, the presumption that the legislature was using words in their ordinary sense tends to be strong, while the *expressio unius* canon tends to be weaker or more contestable.
- At what stage of the interpretive process does the canon come into play? Many canons are relevant throughout the interpretive process. But some canons are tools of last resort; they operate only as tie-breakers when a court's other interpretive tools leave the court pretty much in equipoise between two possible readings.

This chapter surveys some of the most prominent canons of statutory interpretation. It begins with canons that formalize common principles of English usage. It then considers several different types of canons that formalize principles specific to the interpretation of statutes. It also discusses the hierarchy of canons and their place in the broader project of statutory interpretation.

There are many canons, and this chapter does not aspire to be comprehensive. Some very important canons dovetail with the material in later chapters, and we will consider them there. Other canons that you

---

Statutory Interpretation from the Inside—An Empirical Study of Congressional Drafting, Delegation, and the Canons: Part I, 65 STAN. L. REV. 901 (2013); Lisa Schultz Bressman & Abbe R. Gluck, *Statutory Interpretation from the Inside—An Empirical Study of Congressional Drafting, Delegation, and the Canons: Part II*, 66 STAN. L. REV. 725 (2014). Of course, that does not mean that there is no such thing as a "descriptive" canon; a canon that accurately captures common patterns of linguistic usage or common policy preferences can be a reliable guide to intended meaning even if members of Congress do not know that courts use it. But if the only justification for a canon rests on its "feedback effects," the canon might not have much justification.

might encounter in your legal career are not discussed anywhere in this book, or are mentioned only in a footnote.[2] For a book proceeding canon-by-canon through more than fifty canons, see ANTONIN SCALIA & BRYAN A. GARNER, READING LAW: THE INTERPRETATION OF LEGAL TEXTS (2012). For a wider-ranging list of interpretive principles that appeared in the Supreme Court's opinions from 1986 to 2016, see WILLIAM N. ESKRIDGE, JR., INTERPRETING LAW: A PRIMER ON HOW TO READ STATUTES AND THE CONSTITUTION app. at 407–45 (2016).

Although there are many canons, you should beware of imitations. Sometimes, treatises or even judicial opinions recite principles of interpretation that do not actually have much support and that are not widely used by interpreters. *See, e.g.*, 2B NORMAN J. SINGER & J.D. SHAMBIE SINGER, SUTHERLAND STATUTES AND STATUTORY CONSTRUCTION § 50:4 (7th ed. 2012) (asserting that "courts interpret federal statutes in light of the common law existing before the Declaration of Independence"). In addition, even some canons that do have support in the case law might not really be justified. *Cf.* SCALIA & GARNER, *supra*, at 9 (describing their book as an "attempt . . . to collect and arrange only the valid canons (perhaps a third of the possible candidates)").

B. CANONS THAT FORMALIZE COMMON PRINCIPLES OF TEXTUAL INTERPRETATION

Some canons have their roots in principles that are part of our everyday communicative practices—principles that we might use to interpret just about any utterance or document (though we might not emphasize them quite as much as some judges emphasize the canons). For the most part, moreover, those principles are part of our everyday communicative practices because they help to promote successful communication; they increase the chances that listeners or readers will understand a statement to mean what the speaker or author intended it to convey. In Professor Ross's terminology, the canons based on these principles are "descriptive." *See supra* p. 108.

Those canons are important; courts invoke them frequently, and you need to learn how they are used. Precisely because they come up so often, though, no single case is the paradigmatic example of how they work. Rather than providing a full-length case for each canon, this section of the book therefore proceeds more in the manner of a treatise; it summarizes some of the standard text-based descriptive canons and cites illustrative cases without providing long excerpts.

---

[2] For example, courts sometimes say that statutes making grants of land (or other things that the government is giving away) should be construed strictly, that federal statutes granting benefits to veterans should be construed liberally in favor of the veterans, and that federal statutes addressing matters related to Native Americans should be construed liberally in favor of the Native Americans.

1. THE "ORDINARY MEANING" PRINCIPLE

Courts and administrative agencies interpreting statutes typically start with the principle that "words used in a statute are to be given their ordinary meaning in the absence of persuasive reasons to the contrary." *Burns v. Alcala*, 420 U.S. 575, 581–82 (1975). The Supreme Court has repeatedly referred to this principle as a "fundamental canon of statutory construction." *Perrin v. United States*, 444 U.S. 37, 42 (1979); *see also, e.g.*, WILLIAM N. ESKRIDGE JR., INTERPRETING LAW: A PRIMER ON HOW TO READ STATUTES AND THE CONSTITUTION 34–35 (2016) (noting that "for hard cases as well as easy ones, the *ordinary meaning* . . . of the relevant statutory text is the anchor for statutory interpretation," and observing that "[t]here are excellent reasons for the primacy of the ordinary meaning rule"). When courts are using this canon to understand a particular term in a statute, moreover, what matters is "the ordinary meaning of the term . . . at the time Congress enacted the statute." *Perrin*, 444 U.S. at 42; *accord, e.g.*, New Prime Inc. v. Oliveira, 139 S. Ct. 532, 539 (2019).

Of course, when a statute specifically defines one of the terms that it uses, courts apply the stated definition in preference to the ordinary meaning of that term. *See, e.g.*, Tanzin v. Tanvir, 141 S. Ct. 486, 490 (2020) (citing cases). Even then, though, ordinary understandings of the term can color the courts' interpretation of the definition that the legislature has provided. *See* Bond v. United States, 572 U.S. 844, 861 (2014) ("In settling on a fair reading of a statute, it is not unusual to consider the ordinary meaning of a defined term, particularly where there is dissonance between that ordinary meaning and the reach of the definition."); *see also, e.g.*, Sackett v. EPA, 143 S. Ct. 1322, 1336–37 (2023) (noting that the term "navigable waters" had "a well-established meaning at the time of the [Clean Water Act's] enactment," and reading the Act's definition of the term to "align" with that meaning). *But see* Babbitt v. Sweet Home Chapter of Communities for a Great Oregon, 515 U.S. 687, 697 n.10 (1995) (rejecting the dissent's inquiry into the historical concept of "taking" wildlife, and observing that "Congress explicitly defined the operative term 'take' in the [Endangered Species Act], . . . thereby obviating the need for us to probe its meaning").

The "ordinary meaning" principle has some specific applications that crop up in many cases. As one would expect, for instance, whether a statute uses the word "may" or the word "shall" often matters; in many contexts, courts understand "may" to confer discretion and "shall" to convey a requirement. *See, e.g.*, Kingdomware Techs., Inc. v. United States, 579 U.S. 162, 171–72 (2016). Similarly, the difference between "and" and "or" is often significant. For instance, requiring someone to do A *and* B differs from requiring someone to do only A *or* B.

Professor Lawrence Solan, who has a Ph.D. in linguistics in addition to being a law professor, cautions that the "ordinary meaning" of statutory language can differ from what he calls "definitional meaning" (identified by looking up a word in a dictionary and plugging in the definition "without regard to the circumstances in which the word is used in a particular instance"). LAWRENCE M. SOLAN, THE LANGUAGE OF STATUTES: LAWS AND THEIR INTERPRETATION 53 (2010). In practice, though, judges often do use dictionaries to help identify ordinary meaning. *See, e.g.*, Samuel A. Thumma & Jeffrey L. Kirchmeier, *The Lexicon Has Become a Fortress: The United States Supreme Court's Use of Dictionaries*, 47 BUFF. L. REV. 227, 244–60 (1999) (chronicling the history and growing use of dictionaries in Supreme Court opinions); *cf.* John Calhoun, Note, *Measuring the Fortress: Explaining Trends in Supreme Court and Circuit Court Dictionary Use*, 124 YALE L.J. 484, 497–502 (2014) (finding that "the Supreme Court dramatically increased its dictionary usage" in the period from 1985 to 2010, but circuit courts increased their usage of dictionaries only "slightly" during that period).

There is nothing inherently wrong with using dictionaries as a tool in statutory interpretation, as long as lawyers and judges understand what dictionaries are and are not. A good dictionary can provide "a decent two-line approximation" of the sense(s) in which the members of particular linguistic communities have been in the habit of using particular words. *See* Lawrence Solan, *When Judges Use the Dictionary*, 68 AM. SPEECH 50, 54 (1993). But such approximations "are only starting points" for understanding how the word is actually being used in a particular setting. *See* Note, *Looking It Up: Dictionaries and Statutory Interpretation*, 107 HARV. L. REV. 1437, 1450 (1994). For one thing, some words refer to categories that cannot be captured perfectly by a single set of criteria of the sort commonly found in dictionary definitions. *See, e.g.*, LUDWIG WITTGENSTEIN, PHILOSOPHICAL INVESTIGATIONS §§ 65–77 (G.E.M. Anscombe trans., 2d ed. 1958) (introducing the concept of "family resemblance" to describe how some words are used); Solan, *supra*, 68 AM. SPEECH at 53 (invoking Wittgenstein in discussing the complexity of identifying "the necessary and sufficient conditions for membership in a category denoted by a word"). In any event, the meaning of any individual word depends partly on context, and dictionaries obviously cannot anticipate and analyze each context in which the word might be used. *See* HENRY M. HART, JR. & ALBERT M. SACKS, THE LEGAL PROCESS: BASIC PROBLEMS IN THE MAKING AND APPLICATION OF LAW 1190 (tent. ed. 1958) (William N. Eskridge, Jr. & Philip P. Frickey eds., 1994) (referring to "the one-word, one-meaning fallacy," and noting that "[t]he editors of dictionaries" do not themselves subscribe to that fallacy).

Because dictionary definitions are brief and acontextual approximations of concepts that are nuanced and context-dependent, the dictionary definition of a word in common usage cannot possibly "capture all that we, as native speakers of English, know about the word." Solan, *supra*, 68 AM. SPEECH at 54. That is not to say that judges should never look up any commonly used word. The dictionary definition of a word may help judges organize their thoughts about the word, check that those thoughts are not idiosyncratic, and even recognize ambiguities that they would otherwise have overlooked. But dictionaries may well be most useful when judges want information about linguistic communities to which they themselves do not belong—for instance, when judges are trying to understand a statute enacted in the distant past or a statute that uses technical terms. Judges also need to remember that the "ordinary meaning" of a phrase as used in a particular context is not necessarily the sum of the dictionary definitions of its component words. *See* Craig Hoffman, *Parse the Sentence First: Curbing the Urge to Resort to the Dictionary When Interpreting Legal Texts*, 6 N.Y.U. J. LEGIS. & PUB. POL'Y 401, 438 (2003) ("Although dictionaries are useful for divining the derivations and denotations of individual lexical items, dictionaries are not so useful when interpreting complex phrases in legal texts.").

To the extent that judges do look up words in dictionaries, they should be aware that different dictionaries might offer somewhat different definitions of the same word. Some scholars have expressed concern about "dictionary shopping" either in litigants' briefs or in judges' opinions. *See* Ellen P. Aprill, *The Law of the Word: Dictionary Shopping in the Supreme Court*, 30 ARIZ. ST. L.J. 275, 300 (1998) (noting that Supreme Court opinions "often cite or rely on only one definition in only one dictionary" but "fail to explain or justify the basis for their choice"). Justice Scalia, who invoked dictionaries frequently, agreed that "a comparative weighing of dictionaries is often necessary." ANTONIN SCALIA & BRYAN A. GARNER, READING LAW: THE INTERPRETATION OF LEGAL TEXTS app. A at 417 (2012); *see also id.* at 419–24 (providing a list of preferred dictionaries).

Judges also need to understand the details of each dictionary that they use. In some dictionaries, the editors arrange their definitions of a word according to the frequency of current usage, so that the first definitions are the senses that the editors believe to be most common. *See* Stephen C. Mouritsen, Note, *The Dictionary is Not a Fortress: Definitional Fallacies and a Corpus-Based Approach to Plain Meaning*, 2010 BYU L. REV. 1915, 1935 (referring to the *Random House Dictionary of the English Language*). In other dictionaries, however, definitions are arranged chronologically; within a given grouping of senses, the first definition is the *oldest* known usage of the word, not the usage that is most common today. *See id.* at 1929–35 (discussing the *Oxford English Dictionary* and *Webster's Third New International Dictionary*). To understand the information that any particular dictionary is trying to convey, you should read the explanatory material at the front of that particular dictionary. Unfortunately, even members of the Supreme Court sometimes fail to do so. *See infra* p. 179.

Recently, some scholars have argued that instead of consulting dictionaries, judges who are trying to identify the ordinary meaning of a word in a given context would do better to make their own use of tools from the field of "corpus linguistics." A "corpus" is a large body of writings that can be searched by computer. In our age of big data, a number of on-line corpora now exist. For instance, the Corpus of Contemporary American English (COCA)—created by Professor Mark Davies of Brigham Young University—is currently available at www.english-corpora.org/coca. COCA contains more than a billion words of text balanced across thirty years (1990–2019) and eight different "genres" (newspapers, popular magazines, academic journals, transcripts from television and radio news and talk shows, subtitles from other television programs and movies, fiction, web pages, and blogs). Through appropriate searches, users can get randomized samples of actual usages of a word or phrase, learn which other words or phrases most often appear nearby, and gather other information that can shed light on how often particular words are used in particular senses.[3]

Corpus analysis was being used by people in linguistics well before most lawyers had heard of it. In 2005, Professor Solan briefly alluded to its possibilities for statutory interpretation. *See* Lawrence M. Solan, *The New Textualists' New Text*, 38 LOY. L.A. L. REV. 2027, 2059–60 (2005). But the first law-review article that really explained corpus analysis and emphasized its potential utility was a student note published by Stephen Mouritsen in 2010. Mouritsen's note suggested that corpus analysis could help judges ground decisions about the "ordinary meaning" of statutory language in something more solid than their own intuitions and more fine-grained than the information available in conventional dictionaries. *See* Mouritsen, *supra*, 2010 BYU L. REV. at 1919–25, 1951–70.

Mouritsen published this note while he was clerking for Justice Thomas R. Lee of the Utah Supreme Court, and Justice Lee saw the possibilities of corpus analysis. In 2011, he used data from COCA in a concurring opinion about the meaning of a statute. *See* In re Adoption of Baby E.Z., 266 P.3d 702, 723–31 (Utah 2011) (Lee, J., concurring in part and concurring in the judgment). More recently, Lee and Mouritsen have published extensive scholarly articles about the promise and practice of corpus analysis in legal interpretation. *See* Thomas R. Lee & Stephen C. Mouritsen, *Judging Ordinary Meaning*, 127 YALE L.J. 788 (2018); *see also* Thomas R. Lee & Stephen C. Mouritsen, *The Corpus and the Critics*, 88 U. CHI. L. REV. 275 (2021) (responding to criticisms). By now, however, corpus analysis has spread well beyond them. *See id.* at 278 & nn.10–14 (citing examples).

Of course, professional lexicographers use corpora when they compile dictionaries, and they are likely to draw more accurate conclusions from the data than individual lawyers and judges would. But when a judge wants tailored information about the usage of particular

[3] COCA draws its texts from 1990 to 2019, but users interested in older usages of words can turn to the Corpus of Historical American English (which draws upon texts from the 1820s on and is available at www.english-corpora.org/coha). Scholars at BYU are also continuing to develop a Corpus of Founding Era American English.

combinations of words in particular contexts, searches in large on-line corpora will supply more information than conventional dictionaries can. Although judges who try to "become their own lexicographers" (Solan, *supra*, 38 LOY. L.A. L. REV. at 2060) surely will make mistakes, so too will judges who base arguments about ordinary meaning on the dictionary definitions of individual words.

According to Lee and Mouritsen, discussions of corpus linguistics can also contribute to statutory interpretation at a more abstract level, by highlighting questions about exactly what "ordinary meaning" is and how judges should identify it. In Lee and Mouritsen's words, "Are we looking for the most common sense of a given term or phrase in a given linguistic setting? Or is it enough that a given sense is . . . somewhat frequent?" Lee & Mouritsen, *supra*, 88 U. CHI. L. REV. at 298. In practice, the answer might be that the "ordinary meaning" principle operates on a sliding scale. Absent any contrary indications, courts might presume that the legislature was using the term or phrase in the sense that is "most common" in the relevant context. But litigants might find it easier to overcome this presumption when they argue that the legislature was using the term or phrase in a sense that is at least "somewhat frequent" than when they argue that the legislature was using the term or phrase in a highly unusual way.

2. THE POSSIBLE RELEVANCE OF TERMS OF ART

a. TERMS WITH TECHNICAL MEANINGS IN PARTICULAR FIELDS

Some statutory terms have no meaning in ordinary parlance; they are used exclusively by experts in a particular field. In the absence of contrary indications, courts typically read such terms in accordance with their technical meaning. *See* Louisiana Pub. Serv. Comm'n v. FCC, 476 U.S. 355, 372 (1986) (referring to "the rule of construction that technical terms of art should be interpreted by reference to the trade or industry to which they apply").

Matters get more complicated when a word is commonly used to mean one thing in ordinary parlance and something more specialized in a technical field. When a statute uses such a word, interpreters have to decide whether to treat the word as a technical term of art or instead to understand the word as a layman would. Contextual clues often point in one direction or another. For instance, if the statute has nothing to do with the field in which the word has a specialized meaning, interpreters naturally will gravitate toward the nontechnical interpretation. Conversely, if the statute does implicate the relevant technical field, the surrounding context may well lead interpreters to adopt the specialized interpretation. *Cf.* Utah v. Evans, 536 U.S. 452, 467 (2002) (interpreting a statute that referred to "the statistical method known as 'sampling,' " and concluding that "the words 'known as' and the quotation marks that surround 'sampling' " both suggest that Congress was using "sampling" as a term of art).

For an example of a statute that presented a difficult version of this problem, consider the federal Equal Pay Act of 1963, Pub L. 88–38, 77 Stat. 56. That statute amended a section of the Fair Labor Standards Act to include the following language:

> "No employer having employees subject to any provisions of this section shall discriminate, within any establishment in which such employees are employed, between employees on the basis of sex by paying wages to employees in such establishment at a rate less than the rate at which he pays wages to employees of the opposite sex in such establishment for equal work on jobs the performance of which requires equal skill, effort, and responsibility, **and which are performed under similar working conditions**, except where such payment is made pursuant to (i) a seniority system; (ii) a merit system; (iii) a system which measures earnings by quantity or quality of production; or (iv) a differential based on any other factor other than sex: *Provided*, That an employer who is paying a wage rate differential in violation of this subsection shall not, in order to comply with the provisions of this subsection, reduce the wage rate of any employee."

Id. § 3, 77 Stat. at 56–57 (emphasis added) (codified at 29 U.S.C. § 206(d)(1)). In *Corning Glass Works v. Brennan*, 417 U.S. 188 (1974), the Supreme Court had to decide whether the difference between working on the night shift and working during the day was a difference in "working conditions" within the meaning of this statute. The Court concluded that "[w]hile a layman might well assume that time of day worked reflects one aspect of a job's 'working conditions,' the term has a different and much more specific meaning in the language of industrial relations." According to the Court, in the language of industrial relations, the term "working conditions" refers only to "surroundings" and "hazards." Thus, the term takes into account "the elements, such as toxic chemicals and fumes, regularly encountered by a worker, their intensity, and their frequency," and it also takes into account "the physical hazards regularly encountered, their frequency, and the severity of injury they can cause." But "the concept of 'working conditions,' as used in the specialized language of job evaluation systems, simply does not encompass shift differentials." *Id.* at 202. The Court understood the Equal Pay Act to be using the term "working conditions" in this technical sense rather than in the sense that ordinary people might use it.

b. TERMS THAT HAVE ACQUIRED PRIOR MEANING IN THE LAW

In addition to using terms that have specialized meanings in particular trades or industries, legislatures sometimes use words or phrases that have acquired prior meaning in the law. Interpreters then confront the same sort of question: should the words be understood as *legal* terms of art, or should courts instead read them in a lay sense?

Consider the federal Jones Act of 1920. In *The Osceola*, 189 U.S. 158 (1903), the Supreme Court had held that under general maritime law, seamen aboard a vessel cannot recover damages from the vessel's owner for injuries that they sustained through the negligence of the vessel's master or another member of the crew. According to *The Osceola*, seamen in this position were entitled only to the expense of their maintenance and cure. The Jones Act changed this result by providing a cause of action for "any seaman" who was injured by negligence in the course of his employment. *See* ch. 250, § 33, 41 Stat. 988, 1007 (1920). But the Jones Act did not define the term "seaman." In *McDermott International, Inc. v. Wilander*, 498 U.S. 337 (1991), the Supreme Court declared that this word was "a maritime term of art." The Court added that "[i]n the absence of contrary indication, we assume that when a statute uses such a term, Congress intended it to have its established meaning." Accordingly, the Court set itself the task of "determin[ing] who was a seaman under the general maritime law when Congress passed the Jones Act." *Id.* at 342.

Some of the canons covered later in this chapter (especially in Sections D and E) raise the same general issue. Instead of being based on common principles of communication, those canons are specific to the interpretation of laws, and nonlawyers do not necessarily know about them. Such canons encourage interpreters to attribute different meanings to statutory language than ordinary people might.

3. *NOSCITUR A SOCIIS*

Like other legal principles, canons of statutory interpretation sound fancier and more rule-like when they are expressed in Latin. Accordingly, statutory interpreters often use the phrase *noscitur a sociis* to express the idea that a word is known (*noscitur*) by its companions (*sociis*)—the words that appear around it.

Noscitur a sociis reflects the basic idea that we read words in context, so the meaning that we ascribe to one word is influenced by the accompanying words. That idea obviously applies very broadly. But the label *noscitur a sociis* is most often used to refer to one particular application of that idea, involving the interpretation of items in a series—a list of words or phrases with a parallel structure, like A, B, C, and D. Suppose that words A, C, and D all share some feature, while word B could be read either to share the same feature or to be talking about something else. Often, the fact that word B appears in parallel with words A, C, and D will affect how interpreters resolve this superficial ambiguity: invoking *noscitur a sociis*, interpreters will read word B in the way that makes it share the same feature as words A, C, and D. *See, e.g.*, Beecham v. United States, 511 U.S. 368, 371 (1994) ("That several items in a list share an attribute counsels in favor of interpreting the other items as possessing that attribute as well.").

For a concrete illustration, consider *Dolan v. United States Postal Service*, 546 U.S. 481 (2006). The Federal Tort Claims Act waives the sovereign immunity of the United States for certain torts committed by federal employees acting within the scope of their employment. Under 28 U.S.C. § 2680(b), however, this waiver does not apply to "[a]ny claim arising out of the loss, miscarriage, or negligent transmission of letters or postal matter." In *Dolan*, a woman had tripped over mail that her postal carrier had left on her porch. Seeking compensation for the injuries that ensued, she sued the United States under the Federal Tort Claims Act. The government argued that § 2680(b) defeated her claim; according to the government, the woman's claim arose out of the "negligent transmission" of mail. But the Supreme Court disagreed. The other terms in the statutory list—"loss" and "miscarriage"—referred to "failings in the postal obligation to deliver mail in a timely manner to the right address," and the Court understood the phrase "negligent transmission" to be similarly limited. In particular, the Court held that the phrase "negligent transmission" (read in light of the accompanying words) "does not go beyond negligence causing mail to be lost or to arrive late, in damaged condition, or at the wrong address." *Dolan*, 546 U.S. at 486–87.

Over the years, the Supreme Court has applied *noscitur a sociis* in many other cases too. For instance:

- The federal bribery statute defines the term "official act" to mean "any decision or action on any question, matter, cause, suit, proceeding, or controversy, which may at any time be pending, or which may by law be brought before any public official, in such official's official capacity, or in such official's place of trust or profit." 18 U.S.C. § 201(a)(3). Invoking *noscitur a sociis*, the Supreme Court has read the words "question" and "matter" relatively narrowly in this context. *See* McDonnell v. United States, 579 U.S. 550, 569 (2016) ("Because a typical meeting, call, or event arranged by a public official is not of the same stripe as a lawsuit before a court, a determination before an agency, or a hearing before a committee, it does not qualify as a 'question' or 'matter' under § 201(a)(3).").
- Section 2(10) of the Securities Act of 1933, as amended, says that "unless the context otherwise requires" (and subject to a few other specified exceptions), "[t]he term 'prospectus' means any prospectus, notice, circular, advertisement, letter, or communication, written or by radio or television, which offers any security for sale or confirms the sale of any security . . . ." 15 U.S.C. § 77b(a)(10). By a vote of 5–4, Justice Kennedy's majority opinion in *Gustafson v. Alloyd Co.*, 513 U.S. 561 (1995), held that this definition does not encompass "every written

communication" but only "communications held out to the public at large," such as "documents of wide dissemination." *Id.* at 574–76.

- For a time, a provision in the Internal Revenue Code gave special treatment to "[i]ncome resulting from exploration, discovery, or prospecting, or any combination of the foregoing, extending over a period of more than 12 months." 26 U.S.C. § 456(a)(2)(B) (1952). In *Jarecki v. G.D. Searle & Co.*, 367 U.S. 303 (1961), the Supreme Court held that the word "discovery" in this provision "means only the discovery of mineral resources," not inventions or other types of discoveries. *Id.* at 307.

To apply *noscitur a sociis*, interpreters need to identify the pattern or common theme that runs throughout the series that they are interpreting. Sometimes, that requires interpreters to make contestable judgment calls; there might be more than one possible theme, and lawyers will disagree about which theme is relevant. Likewise, interpreters sometimes will disagree about whether a series has a common theme at all, or instead consists of disparate items that do not color each other's meaning. *Compare* Graham County Soil & Water Conservation Dist. v. United States ex rel. Wilson, 559 U.S. 280, 288–89 & n.7 (2010) (finding *noscitur a sociis* "less helpful in this case" than in *Jarecki* because the three items at issue were "too few and too disparate" to establish much of a pattern), *with id.* at 305–06 (Sotomayor, J., dissenting) (disagreeing with this assessment).

Arguments based on *noscitur a sociis* are strongest when the particular word or item that the court is trying to interpret is superficially ambiguous or vague on its own: as a matter of ordinary usage, the word has a sense that fits the pattern established by the other items, even though the word also is sometimes used more broadly. Indeed, courts sometimes suggest that *noscitur a sociis* is relevant *only* where "the meaning of the words considered severally is . . . in doubt" (in which case "the associated words" might "remove the obscurity"). *Russell Motor Car Co. v. United States*, 261 U.S. 514, 520 (1923); *see also id.* at 519 ("That a word may be known by the company it keeps is . . . not an invariable rule, for the word may have a character of its own not to be submerged by its association."); United States v. Stevens, 559 U.S. 460, 474 (2010) (describing *noscitur a sociis* as a tool for interpreting "an ambiguous term," and concluding that two terms in a list carried their "ordinary meaning" even though the other three terms shared a limiting feature). But this purportedly categorical limitation on *noscitur a sociis* is less solid than it might seem, because all interpretation (including the identification of ambiguity) is contextual. Take the word "discovery." Considered in isolation, that word might not seem to be limited to the discovery of any one thing—but in the context of the statute at issue in *Jarecki*, the Supreme Court understood it to refer only to "the discovery of mineral resources." *Jarecki*, 367 U.S. at 307.

Students sometimes make the mistake of assuming that *noscitur a sociis* is a technical principle of statutory interpretation and that its proper use therefore depends on artificial rules known only to lawyers and judges. As with the other canons covered in this section of the book, though, the principle that lies behind *noscitur a sociis* is not limited to statutes, or even to contracts and other kinds of legal documents. Instead, it is part of ordinary communication. If you were reading a story in a newspaper that referred to "letters, e-mails, and text messages," you would know that the word "letters" referred to correspondence rather than letters of the alphabet. That is how judges should use *noscitur a sociis* too. Normally, arguments based on *noscitur a sociis* can be assessed according to whether they seem likely to capture the intended meaning of the words in question—which is more a question of contextual interpretation than of the mechanical application of artificial rules. *Cf. Beecham*, 511 U.S. at 371 (acknowledging that "this canon of construction is by no means a hard and fast rule").

4. *EJUSDEM GENERIS*

The principle of *ejusdem generis* is closely related to *noscitur a sociis*. As with *noscitur a sociis*, courts invoke *ejusdem generis* to interpret words in a series, and both principles tell interpreters to consider whether the items in the series fit a pattern. But while *noscitur a sociis* is about how to interpret a specific item in the series, *ejusdem generis* is about how to interpret a residual or catchall phrase (often at the end of the series). In *Hall Street Associates, L.L.C. v. Mattel, Inc.*, 552 U.S. 576 (2008), the Supreme Court stated the idea of *ejusdem generis* this way: "when a statute sets out a series of specific items ending with a general term, that general term is confined to covering subjects comparable to the specifics it follows." *Id.* at 586. (Literally, *ejusdem generis* means "of the same kind.")

For a concrete example, consider Section 1 of the Federal Arbitration Act. That Act, which dates back to 1925, establishes a general rule in favor of the enforceability of written arbitration clauses in contracts evidencing transactions that involve interstate or foreign commerce. *See* 9 U.S.C. § 2. But Section 1 states an exception: the Act does not apply to "contracts of employment of seamen, railroad employees, or any other class of workers engaged in foreign or interstate commerce." *Id.* § 1. This exception takes the form of a list with two specific items ("seamen" and "railroad employees") followed by a residual phrase ("any other class of workers engaged in foreign or interstate commerce"). In *Circuit City Stores, Inc. v. Adams*, 532 U.S. 105 (2001), a closely divided Supreme Court adopted a narrow reading of the residual phrase, partly on the strength of *ejusdem generis*. According to the majority, the reference to "any other class of workers engaged in foreign or interstate commerce" covers only workers who, like seamen and railroad employees, are engaged in transportation. *See id.* at 114–15; *see also* Sw. Airlines Co. v.

Saxon, 142 S. Ct. 1783, 1790 (2022) (discussing what *Circuit City* meant by transportation workers); Wallace v. Grubhub Holdings, Inc., 970 F.3d 798, 801–03 (7th Cir. 2020) (concluding that Grubhub drivers do not count).

Or consider *Washington State Department of Social and Health Services v. Guardianship Estate of Keffeler*, 537 U.S. 371 (2003). Title II of the federal Social Security Act provides that "none of the moneys paid or payable . . . under this title shall be subject to execution, levy, attachment, garnishment, or other legal process . . . ." Act of Aug. 14, 1935, ch. 531, § 208, 49 Stat. 620, 625 (codified at 42 U.S.C. § 407(a)). In *Keffeler*, the Supreme Court had to interpret the phrase "other legal process." Invoking *noscitur a sociis* and *ejusdem generis*, the Court unanimously held that this phrase should be understood to be limited to "process much like the processes of execution, levy, attachment, and garnishment"—with the result, "at a minimum," that the phrase referred only to process that uses "some judicial or quasi-judicial mechanism . . . by which control over property passes from one person to another in order to discharge or secure discharge of an allegedly existing or anticipated liability." *Keffeler*, 537 U.S. at 385.

Like *noscitur a sociis*, *ejusdem generis* reflects ordinary principles of contextual interpretation, and those principles cabin its proper application. The canon is helpful because it reminds judges of a recurring situation in which attention to context can promote successful communication. Again, though, judges should not use the canon to narrow catchall phrases artificially, without regard to common-sensical judgments about what the words in question were probably intended to mean. *Cf.* Ali v. Fed. Bureau of Prisons, 552 U.S. 214, 227 (2008) ("[W]e do not woodenly apply limiting principles every time Congress includes a specific example along with a general phrase.").

As with *noscitur a sociis*, courts sometimes say that *ejusdem generis* comes into play "only when there is uncertainty" about the meaning of the residual phrase—suggesting, perhaps, that the canon is relevant only if the residual phrase is superficially ambiguous or vague. *See* Harrison v. PPG Indus., Inc., 446 U.S. 578, 588–89 (1980) (quoting United States v. Powell, 423 U.S. 87, 91 (1975), in turn quoting Gooch v. United States, 297 U.S. 124, 128 (1936)). That may indeed be the paradigmatic case for applying *ejusdem generis*: if a statutory list itemizes things that all belong to a particular class, but also includes a residual term that could be read either narrowly (so that it covers only other things in that same class) or broadly (so that it covers many things in other classes too), the narrower reading will often be best. Again, though, one cannot really determine whether a phrase is ambiguous on its own, because interpretation is contextual. The very fact that a statute carefully lists specific items may sometimes be enough to create uncertainty about the proper interpretation of a catchall term, even if that term would not seem ambiguous in other contexts. After all, if the specific items in a list all fit into one cohesive category, but the catchall term at the end of the list is read to encompass not only other things in that category but also everything in many other categories too, one might wonder why the legislature listed the specific items at all. *See, e.g.*, Yates v. United States, 574 U.S. 528, 545–46 (2015) (using this argument to support the application of *ejusdem generis* to a broad term that would not otherwise seem ambiguous).

Of course, when "a list of specific items" is followed by a "catchall phrase," the catchall phrase usually should be understood to pick up some things that the list of specific items does not already cover. *See* Christopher v. SmithKline Beecham Corp., 567 U.S. 142, 163 & n.20 (2012) (arguing that the dissent's proposed interpretation of the catchall phrase failed this test and therefore "would render the general statutory language meaningless"). Courts hesitate to apply *ejusdem generis* in a way that would conflict with the presumption against superfluity. Thus, courts normally will prefer interpretations that preserve a role both for the specific items (which help identify the relevant category) and for the catchall phrase (which encompasses some additional things in the same category).

There is some debate about whether *ejusdem generis* operates only where a catchall phrase appears *after* a list of specific items, or whether the canon also applies where a catchall phrase appears *before* a list of specific examples. For instance, if a statute refers to "all pants, skirts, shirts, and other articles of clothing," *ejusdem generis* might suggest that the catchall phrase "articles of clothing" does not include parkas. Is the same argument available if the statute instead refers to "all articles of clothing, including pants, skirts, and shirts," and is that argument also called *ejusdem generis*? Various authorities say "yes." In the words of one prominent treatise,

> "*Ejusdem generis* instructs that, where general words follow specific words in an enumeration describing a statute's legal subject, the general words are construed to embrace only objects similar in nature to those objects enumerated by the preceding specific words. The doctrine applies equally to the opposite sequence, *i.e.*, specific words following general ones, to restrict application of the general terms to things that are similar to those enumerated."

2A NORMAN J. SINGER & SHAMBIE SINGER, SUTHERLAND STATUTES AND STATUTORY CONSTRUCTION § 47:17 (7th ed. 2014) (footnotes omitted); *accord, e.g.*, Flye v. Spotts, 94 So. 3d 240, 245 (Miss. 2012); Peterson v. Haw. Elec. Light Co., 944 P.2d 1265, 1271–72 (Haw. 1997); McClellan v. Health Maintenance Org. of Pa., 686 A.2d 801, 806 (Pa. 1996); *see also* State v. Bagnes, 322 P.3d 719, 724 (Utah 2014) ("In essence, [*ejusdem generis*] posits that general catchall terms appearing at the beginning or the end of an exemplary statutory list are understood to be informed by the content of the terms of the list."). According to Justice Scalia and Bryan Garner, however, the traditional principle of *ejusdem generis* applied only to "the specific-general sequence" and not to "a general-specific sequence." ANTONIN SCALIA & BRYAN A. GARNER, READING LAW: THE INTERPRETATION OF LEGAL TEXTS 203 (2012). Scalia and Garner endorsed that limitation, *id.* at 204–05, and some modern judges apparently do too. *See, e.g.*, Pfizer, Inc. v. U.S. Dep't of Health & Human Servs., 42 F.4th 67, 76 (2d Cir. 2022); Starnes v. Wallace, 849 F.3d 627, 636 n.9 (5th Cir. 2017); *see also* United States v. Marston, 694 F.3d 131, 136 (1st Cir. 2012) ("[T]he canon is weakest, and only dubiously applicable, where as here the general term comes first."). Still, Scalia and Garner acknowledged that a general-specific sequence could trigger what they called the "associated-words canon" (a broad version of *noscitur a sociis*), *see* SCALIA & GARNER, *supra*, at 205, so the disagreement may be of little consequence.

* * * * *

Just as the nature of the specific items in a series can sometimes affect the proper interpretation of a residual term, so too the scope of the residual term can sometimes affect the proper interpretation of one or more of the specific items—a principle that Judge Stephen F. Williams aptly called "a sort of reverse ejusdem generis." *United States v. Williams-Davis*, 90 F.3d 490, 508–09 (D.C. Cir. 1996); *see also* Jay Wexler, *Fun with Reverse* Ejusdem Generis, 105 MINN. L. REV. 1 (2020) (providing illustrations of this canon and discussing when it should apply). Take 5 U.S.C. § 552(f), which defines "agency" to include "any executive department, military department, Government corporation, Government controlled corporation, or other establishment in the executive branch of the Government (including the Executive Office of the President), or any independent regulatory agency." In this context, the U.S. Court of Appeals for the D.C. Circuit held that the specific items "Government corporation" and "Government controlled corporation" were limited to corporations in the executive branch of the Government. *Dong v. Smithsonian Institution*, 125 F.3d 877, 879–80 (D.C. Cir. 1997) (emphasizing the word "other" in the residual phrase in § 552(f)). As Judge Williams explained, "the phrase 'A, B, or any other C' indicates that A is a subset of C." *Id.* (quoting *Williams-Davis*, 90 F.3d at 509).

5. THE PRESUMPTION OF CONSISTENT USAGE

Both *noscitur a sociis* and *ejusdem generis* encourage interpreters to read statutory terms in light of other words that appear in the same provision. But it is also common for interpreters to seek guidance about the meaning of a word by examining how other parts of the statute use the same word.

Suppose that as enacted by Congress, a bill uses the same word in two different places—section 5 and section 11. The immediate context of section 5 does not make clear how the legislature was using the word, but the context of section 11 provides more clues. Unless there is some reason to think that the legislature was using the word differently in section 5 than in section 11, courts often will presume that the word has the same meaning throughout the statute. Thus, the context that surrounds the word in section 11 may influence how courts read the same word in section 5 too. According to many opinions of the Supreme Court, "it is a normal rule of statutory construction that identical words used in different parts of the same statute are generally presumed to have the same meaning." *Pereira v. Sessions*, 138 S. Ct. 2105, 2115 (2018) (quoting Taniguchi v. Kan Pacific Saipan, Ltd., 566 U.S. 560, 571 (2012) (internal quotation marks omitted)); *see also* Fourth Estate Pub. Benefit Corp. v. Wall-Street.com, LLC, 139 S. Ct. 881, 889 (2019) (suggesting that when a word is repeated "in consecutive, related sentences within a single statutory provision," there is an especially strong presumption that the word has the same meaning in both sentences).

At first, this principle did not have a shorthand label. Eventually, though, a pathbreaking casebook began referring to it as "the presumption of consistent usage." WILLIAM N. ESKRIDGE, JR. & PHILIP P. FRICKEY, CASES AND MATERIALS ON LEGISLATION: STATUTES AND THE CREATION OF PUBLIC POLICY 645 (2d ed. 1995). After some delay, that label started to appear in federal judicial opinions, and it is now common.

In any particular context, of course, other clues about the intended meaning of a provision may be stronger than the presumption of consistent usage—so the presumption can certainly be overcome. Long ago, the Supreme Court put the point this way:

> "Undoubtedly, there is a natural presumption that identical words used in different parts of the same act are intended to have the same meaning. But the presumption is not rigid and readily yields whenever there is such variation in the connection in which the words are used as reasonably to warrant the conclusion that they were employed in different parts of the act with different intent. Where the subject matter to which the words refer is not the same in the several places where they are used, or the conditions are different, or the scope of the legislative power exercised in one case is broader than that exercised in another, the meaning well may vary to meet the purposes of the law, to be arrived at by a consideration of the language in which those purposes are expressed, and of the circumstances under which the language was employed.
>
> "It is not unusual for the same word to be used with different meanings in the same act, and there is no rule of statutory construction which precludes the courts from giving to the word the meaning which the legislature intended it should have in each instance."

Atlantic Cleaners & Dyers, Inc. v. United States, 286 U.S. 427, 433 (1932) (citations omitted). To this day, there are plenty of cases in which courts conclude that the presumption of consistent usage has been rebutted. *See, e.g.*, Roberts v. Sea-Land Servs., Inc., 566 U.S. 93, 107–11 (2012);

General Dynamics Land Systems, Inc. v. Cline, 540 U.S. 581, 595–97 (2004); Robinson v. Shell Oil Co., 519 U.S. 337, 343 (1997); *see also* SCALIA & GARNER, *supra*, at 170–71 ("Though one might wish it were otherwise, drafters more than rarely use the same word to denote different concepts . . . . Because it is so often disregarded, this canon is particularly defeasible by context."). The presumption is especially weak when the word in question "has several commonly understood meanings among which a speaker can alternate in the course of an ordinary conversation, without being confused or getting confusing." *General Dynamics*, 540 U.S. at 595–96.

Often, though, if a word is used in a similar context in two different places in the same enactment, judges will start with the assumption that the enacting legislature was using the word in the same sense in both places, and many judges will stick with that assumption unless there are pretty good reasons to think otherwise. *See, e.g.*, Henson v. Santander Consumer USA Inc., 582 U.S. 79, 85 (2017) ("[P]etitioners offer us no persuasive reason . . . why we should abandon our usual presumption that 'identical words used in different parts of the same statute' carry 'the same meaning.' " (quoting IBP, Inc. v. Alvarez, 546 U.S. 21, 34 (2005))). As a result, lawyers who are developing arguments about what a word or phrase means in one provision of a statute should examine the whole statute (as printed in the *United States Statutes at Large* for federal statutes or the equivalent for state statutes) to see whether the same word or phrase appears in other provisions, and they should look for clues about what the word or phrase means in those other provisions too.

In addition to basing arguments on the fact that the legislature used the same word or phrase in multiple places within a statute, interpreters occasionally base arguments on the fact that the legislature chose to use *different* words in different places. Indeed, some authorities have articulated a canon that is the converse of the presumption of consistent usage: "where [a] document has used one term in one place, and a materially different term in another, the presumption is that the different term denotes a different idea." SCALIA & GARNER, *supra*, at 170; *see also* WILLIAM N. ESKRIDGE, JR., PHILIP P. FRICKEY & ELIZABETH GARRETT, CASES AND MATERIALS ON LEGISLATION: STATUTES AND THE CREATION OF PUBLIC POLICY 833 (3d ed. 2001) (referring to this idea as the presumption of "meaningful variation," though indicating that the presumption is weak); Sw. Airlines Co. v. Saxon, 142 S. Ct. 1783, 1789 (2022) (mentioning "the meaningful-variation canon"). One can imagine cases in which this conclusion makes sense; for instance, if one provision appears to be modeled on another, variations in terminology may indeed be significant. Still, the English language has plenty of synonyms. A general "presumption of meaningful variation" may be too broad to be a reliable guide to the intended meaning of statutory language, and it has less support in the case law than the presumption of consistent usage.

6. THE PRESUMPTION AGAINST SUPERFLUITY

Suppose that when read in isolation, a statutory provision might be understood in either of two different ways. Courts often say that if one of those interpretations would make either the provision itself or something else in the statute superfluous, that is a reason to favor the other interpretation (assuming that it would not create superfluity of its own). *See, e.g.*, Nat'l Ass'n of Home Builders v. Defenders of Wildlife, 551 U.S. 644, 669 (2007) ("[W]e have cautioned against reading a text in a way that makes part of it redundant."); Mackey v. Lanier Collection Agency & Serv., Inc., 486 U.S. 825, 837 (1988) ("As our cases have noted in the past, we are hesitant to adopt an interpretation of a congressional enactment which renders superfluous another portion of that same law." (citing cases)); *cf. supra* pp. 42–43 (explaining why the exception for "professional actors, artists, lecturers, or singers" in § 5 of the statute at issue in *Church of the Holy Trinity v. United States* might cut against a narrow interpretation of the phrase "labor or service of any kind" in § 1).

Interpreters have been invoking versions of this idea for centuries. For instance, here is what the Supreme Court said in *Washington Market Co. v. Hoffman*, 101 U.S. 112 (1879):

> "We are not at liberty to construe any statute so as to deny effect to any part of its language. It is a cardinal rule of statutory construction that significance and effect shall, if possible, be accorded to every word. As early as in Bacon's Abridgment, sect. 2, it was said that 'a statute ought, upon the whole, to be so construed that, if it can be prevented, no clause, sentence, or word shall be superfluous, void, or insignificant.' This rule has been repeated innumerable times."

Id. at 115–16.

As this statement indicates, the presumption against superfluity can be invoked at the level of individual words, not just at the level of clauses or provisions. Thus, the Supreme Court has spoken of "the presumption that each word Congress uses is there for a reason" and has said that "[o]ur practice . . . is to 'give effect, if possible, to every clause and word of a statute.' " *Advocate Health Care Network v. Stapleton*, 581 U.S. 468, 477–78 (2017) (quoting *Williams v. Taylor*, 529 U.S. 362, 404 (2000), which in turn was quoting *United States v. Menasche*, 348 U.S. 528, 538–39 (1955), which in turn was quoting *Inhabitants of Montclair Twp. v. Ramsdell*, 107 U.S. 147, 152 (1883)). For instance:

- The Tax Injunction Act in title 28 of the United States Code provides that federal district courts "shall not enjoin, suspend or restrain the assessment, levy or collection of any tax under State law where a plain, speedy and efficient remedy may be had in the courts of such State." 28 U.S.C. § 1341. In *Hibbs v. Winn*, 542 U.S. 88 (2004), the Supreme Court resisted a broad interpretation of the word "assessment" partly because it would make the words "levy" and "collection" unnecessary. *See id.* at 101.

- In *Bailey v. United States*, 516 U.S. 137 (1995), the Supreme Court had to interpret a federal statute imposing special criminal penalties on anyone who "uses or carries a firearm" during and in relation to certain other federal crimes. *See* 18 U.S.C. § 924(c)(1) (1994). In an opinion joined by all nine Justices, the Court resisted reading the word "uses" so broadly as to leave no role for the word "carries." *See Bailey*, 516 U.S. at 146.

To some extent, the presumption against superfluity reflects ordinary principles of communication. If someone who has a spouse, two children, and a brother speaks of "my family and my brother," you probably would understand the word "family" as referring to the speaker's spouse and children rather than all of the speaker's relatives; otherwise, the speaker would not have added a separate reference to "my brother." In other respects, though, we accept and expect some amount of superfluity in communication. *See, e.g.*, John M. Golden, *Redundancy: When Law Repeats Itself*, 94 TEX. L. REV. 629, 631 (2016) (observing that "standard human communication tends to be full of redundancy" and that redundancy often improves the success of communication); *cf.* Anya Bernstein, *Legal Corpus Linguistics and the Half-Empirical Attitude*, 106 CORNELL L. REV. 1397, 1450–51 (2021) (suggesting the need for corpus analysis of "whether [or in what contexts] the rule against surplusage governs everyday conversation or published writing").

Of course, statutory provisions may be formulated with more care than extemporaneous speech. But that care is not necessarily directed toward eliminating any and all superfluity. To the contrary, many of the congressional staff members surveyed by Professors Gluck and Bressman reported that people who draft statutes "intentionally err on the side of redundancy" in order to avoid unintended gaps in coverage. Abbe R. Gluck & Lisa Schultz Bressman, *Statutory Interpretation from the Inside—An Empirical Study of Congressional Drafting, Delegation, and the Canons: Part I*, 65 STAN. L. REV. 901, 934 (2013). Perhaps that approach is more likely with respect to some kinds of provisions or formulations than others. *Cf.* Babbitt v. Sweet Home Chapter of Communities for a Great Oregon, 515 U.S. 687, 721 (1995) (Scalia, J., dissenting) (questioning the assumption that each word in "long lawyers' listings" will add something that none of the other words covers). Sometimes, however, statutes include potentially superfluous language out of "an abundance of caution," to guard against the potential misunderstanding of other language. *See* Ethan J. Leib & James J. Brudney, *The Belt-and-Suspenders Canon*, 105 IOWA L. REV. 735, 742 (2020). Likewise, staff members report that language might be inserted in bills to satisfy political constituencies that want certain words to appear whether or not those words are strictly necessary. Gluck &

Bressman, *supra*, 65 STAN. L. REV. at 934–35. Superfluity can also be inadvertent, as when two complex bills are combined into one during the legislative process. *See, e.g.*, Seila Law LLC v. Consumer Fin. Prot. Bureau, 140 S. Ct. 2183, 2210 (2020) (opinion of Roberts, C.J.).

In keeping with these points, the Supreme Court does not treat the presumption against superfluity as an ironclad rule. *See, e.g.*, United States v. Atlantic Research Corp., 551 U.S. 128, 137 (2007) ("[O]ur hesitancy to construe statutes to render language superfluous does not require us to avoid surplusage at all costs."); Gutierrez v. Ada, 528 U.S. 250, 258 (2000) ("[A]s one rule of construction among many, albeit an important one, the rule against redundancy does not necessarily have the strength to turn a tide of good cause to come out the other way."). In the Court's words, canons like the presumption against superfluity "are tools designed to help courts better determine what Congress intended, not to lead courts to interpret the law contrary to that intent"—which may suggest that judges should determine the persuasive force of the presumption against superfluity in any given context by thinking about whether the presumption is likely to be accurate in that context. *See* Scheidler v. Nat'l Org. for Women, Inc., 547 U.S. 9, 23 (2006).

Still, different opinions of the Supreme Court have expressed the presumption against superfluity with different levels of force. The Court has called the presumption against superfluity "one of the most basic interpretive canons," *Corley v. United States*, 556 U.S. 303, 314 (2009), and a "cardinal principle of interpretation," *Loughrin v. United States*, 573 U.S. 351, 358 (2014) (internal quotation marks omitted). On the other hand, the Court has also observed that "redundancies are common in statutory drafting—sometimes in a congressional effort to be doubly sure, sometimes because of congressional inadvertence or lack of foresight, or sometimes simply because of the shortcomings of human communication." *Barton v. Barr*, 140 S. Ct. 1442, 1453 (2020). In the words of one recent opinion,

> "If one possible interpretation of a statute would cause some redundancy and another interpretation would avoid redundancy, that difference in the two interpretations can supply a clue as to the better interpretation of a statute. But only a clue. Sometimes the better overall reading of the statute contains some redundancy."

Rimini Street, Inc. v. Oracle USA, Inc., 139 S. Ct. 873, 881 (2019).

As this formulation suggests, the presumption against superfluity normally comes into play only when statutory language lends itself to two possible interpretations. *See, e.g.*, Marx v. General Revenue Corp., 668 F.3d 1174, 1183 (10th Cir. 2011) ("A court should not apply the superfluity canon unless it first determines that the term being construed is ambiguous."), *aff'd*, 568 U.S. 371 (2013); *see also* Artola v. Garland, 996 F.3d 840, 844 (8th Cir. 2021) ("As the Supreme Court has explained, when confronted with a choice between an interpretation that honors a statute's plain meaning but produces surplusage, and an interpretation that ignores the plain meaning but avoids surplusage, there is no choice at all—the plain meaning must control." (citing Lamie v. U.S. Trustee, 540 U.S. 526, 536 (2004))); *cf.* SCALIA & GARNER, *supra*, at 176 ("[A] court may well prefer ordinary meaning to an unusual meaning that will avoid surplusage."). And even if a provision does have two possible interpretations, the presumption against superfluity normally will not help courts choose between them if *both* interpretations would produce superfluity. *See, e.g.*, Marx v. General Revenue Corp., 568 U.S. 371, 385 (2013); Freeman v. Quicken Loans, 566 U.S. 624, 635 (2012); Microsoft Corp. v. i4i Ltd. Partnership, 564 U.S. 91, 106–07 (2011); Bruesewitz v. Wyeth LLC, 562 U.S. 223, 236 (2011).

Courts have not been very precise about exactly what counts as superfluity, of the sort that statutes should be presumed to avoid. On occasion, the Supreme Court has invoked the canon when one of the possible interpretations would make a provision "largely superfluous," even though the provision would still have work to do in unusual situations. *City of Chicago v. Fulton*, 141 S. Ct. 585, 591 (2021). In such cases, however, the persuasiveness of the canon presumably depends on whether there are reasons to believe that the provision was intended to do more work than that. *See id.* (identifying such reasons with respect to the particular provision in question).

The Supreme Court has also observed that "a phrase is not superfluous if used to 'remove . . . doubt' about an issue," even if judges would have ended up resolving the doubt the same way absent the phrase. *Marx*, 568 U.S. at 383 (quoting Ali v. Fed. Bureau of Prisons, 552 U.S. 214, 226 (2008)). That is a valuable reminder of the different functions that statutory language might serve, and a caution against using the presumption against superfluity in overly mechanical ways that would distort the intended meaning of statutes. *Cf.* Leib & Brudney, *supra*, 105 IOWA L. REV. at 769 (suggesting that courts currently put too much weight on the presumption against superfluity and that "more attention to the belt-and-suspenders drafting techniques" used by Congress would help correct this problem).

7. *EXPRESSIO UNIUS EST EXCLUSIO ALTERIUS*

The final canon covered in this section of the book is *expressio unius est exclusio alterius* (or *expressio unius* for short). Literally, that Latin phrase means "the expression of one thing is the exclusion of another." As used by interpreters, though, the canon is less clearcut than this literal translation might suggest. Basically, the *expressio unius* canon simply tells courts to be alert to the possibility of negative implications.

Imagine, for instance, that a statute establishes a general rule and then itemizes one or more exceptions. Courts facing such a statute may wonder whether they can recognize additional exceptions. Litigants who argue that the answer is "no" are likely to invoke *expressio unius*: they will say that the statute specifies the exceptions that the legislature wanted courts to recognize, and the expression of those exceptions implicitly instructs the courts not to recognize others (or at least not to recognize other exceptions of the same type as the specified ones). *See, e.g.*, Andrus v. Glover Constr. Co., 446 U.S. 608, 616–17 (1980) ("Where Congress explicitly enumerates certain exceptions to a general prohibition, additional exceptions are not to be implied, in the absence of evidence of a contrary legislative intent.").

You might think that the presence of the specified exceptions does no real work in this example: if a case falls within the general rule that the statute establishes, and if the statute does not establish any relevant exception, courts should apply the statute to the case *whether or not* the statute establishes any exceptions for other cases. But recall the hypothetical statute at issue in the Case of the Speluncean Explorers: "Whoever shall willfully take the life of another shall be punished by death." As we saw in Chapter 1, Judge Easterbrook would interpret this general language to leave room for courts to recognize common-law defenses that sound in justification. *See supra* pp. 86–87. Wouldn't his position be weaker if the statute itself set forth a detailed list of such defenses? Suppose, for instance, that the statute had explicitly recognized most of the justification-based defenses known to the common law and reflected in the Model Penal Code (such as self-defense, defense of others, and execution of public duty), but had not recognized the necessity defense. Couldn't the prosecution plausibly argue that the statute listed the only justification-based defenses that the legislature had wanted courts to entertain in homicide cases and that the statute implicitly foreclosed other such defenses—even though courts arguably *could* have recognized other such defenses if the statute had simply stated a general prohibition without listing any defenses at all?[4]

The Supreme Court accepted this sort of argument in *TRW Inc. v. Andrews*, 534 U.S. 19 (2001). A federal statute called the Fair Credit Reporting Act imposes various duties on credit reporting agencies, and it creates a private cause of action allowing people to bring suit to recover damages caused by breaches of those duties. But the statute also contains a limitations period. Until 2003, when Congress revised the relevant provision in order to override the decision that I am about to describe, § 618 of the Act indicated that an action to enforce any liability created by the Act must be brought "within two years from the date on which the liability arises, except that where a defendant has materially and willfully misrepresented any information required under [the Act] to be disclosed to an individual and the information so misrepresented is

[4] If you were representing the defendants, how would you respond to this argument? Is it possible that members of the enacting legislature reached a collective agreement to codify the defenses that the statute lists, but did not reach an agreement either to codify the necessity defense or to foreclose it—which is why the statute said nothing on that topic one way or the other? More generally, might the statute have been meant to ensure that courts would recognize certain defenses (the ones listed in the statute), but not to occupy the field and to prevent courts from considering other defenses as a matter of common law?

material to the establishment of the defendant's liability to that individual under [the Act], the action may be brought at any time within two years after discovery by the individual of the misrepresentation." 15 U.S.C. § 1681p (2000 ed.).

In October 1996, Adelaide Andrews sued TRW for allegedly violating the Fair Credit Reporting Act on four different occasions, two of which had occurred more than two years earlier. On the strength of the statute of limitations, the district court granted summary judgment to TRW with respect to those two alleged violations. On appeal, however, the Ninth Circuit concluded that Andrews's claims were not time-barred. The Ninth Circuit thought that in the absence of express statutory language to the contrary, federal statutes of limitations should not be interpreted to start running until the would-be plaintiff "knows or has reason to know" of her injury. Because Andrews apparently had not discovered TRW's alleged violations until 1995, the Ninth Circuit did not think that the limitations period barred any of her claims.

The Supreme Court agreed with the district court and reversed the Ninth Circuit. Whatever the merits of the Ninth Circuit's general presumption that a "discovery rule" should be read into federal statutes of limitations,[5] the Supreme Court held that the wording of § 618 overcame any such presumption. The Supreme Court relied in part on the *expressio unius* idea. According to the Court, the exception that Congress had expressly provided in § 618 was itself a sort of discovery rule (although one that was too demanding for Andrews to satisfy). "The most natural reading of [§ 618]," Justice Ginsburg wrote for the Court, "is that Congress implicitly excluded a general discovery rule by explicitly including a more limited one." *TRW*, 534 U.S. at 28.[6]

For another illustration of the *expressio unius* principle in action, consider *Leatherman v. Tarrant County Narcotics Intelligence and Coordination Unit*, 507 U.S. 163 (1993). Federal Rule of Civil Procedure 8(a) requires complaints and other pleadings that set forth claims for relief to include "a short and plain statement of the claim showing that the pleader is entitled to relief." Federal Rule of Civil Procedure 9(b) establishes a heightened pleading standard for two specific kinds of allegations: when a pleading alleges "fraud" or "mistake," the

---

[5] The Supreme Court has subsequently criticized this idea. *See* Rotkiske v. Klemm, 140 S. Ct. 355, 360–61 (2019) (agreeing with Justice Scalia's view that the Ninth Circuit's position "is a 'bad wine of recent vintage' " (quoting *TRW*, 534 U.S. at 37 (Scalia, J., concurring in the judgment))); *cf. id.* at 361 (acknowledging the possibility of a special discovery rule that operates as an equitable doctrine in fraud cases and that supplements "the traditional equitable tolling doctrine"); Boechler, P.C. v. Comm'r, 142 S. Ct. 1493, 1500 (2022) (noting that "nonjurisdictional limitations periods [in federal statutes] are presumptively subject to equitable tolling" because "[e]quitable tolling is a traditional feature of American jurisprudence and a background principle against which Congress drafts limitations periods").

[6] The Supreme Court also invoked the presumption against superfluity, which it found "[a]t least equally telling" as the *expressio unius* idea. *See id.* at 29 ("[I]ncorporating a general discovery rule into [§ 618] would not merely supplement the explicit exception contrary to Congress' apparent intent; it would in practical effect render that exception entirely superfluous in all but the most unusual circumstances.").

circumstances constituting fraud or mistake must be stated "with particularity." Before *Leatherman*, some federal courts had asserted authority to require other sorts of claims too to be pleaded with more specificity than usual; for instance, the Fifth Circuit required complaints to include more detail than usual when they alleged that a municipality was liable to the plaintiff under 42 U.S.C. § 1983. In *Leatherman*, however, the Supreme Court held that this practice was inconsistent with the Federal Rules of Civil Procedure. As the Supreme Court interpreted the Rules, federal courts lack authority to supplement Rule 8(a) by imposing heightened pleading standards on complaints asserting municipal liability under § 1983. The Court supported this interpretation of the Rules by pointing to the heightened pleading standard that Rule 9(b) expressly created for allegations of fraud and mistake. *See Leatherman*, 507 U.S. at 168 ("[T]he Federal Rules do address in Rule 9(b) the question of the need for greater particularity in pleading certain actions, but do not include among the enumerated actions any reference to complaints alleging municipal liability under § 1983. *Expressio unius est exclusio alterius.*").

Litigants try to invoke the *expressio unius* idea in many different situations, so it is hard to generalize about exactly when the idea might be relevant. Still, the gist of many *expressio unius* arguments is that certain statutory provisions not only establish the rules of decision that they explicitly establish, but also implicitly occupy the field that they address to the exclusion of other sources of law (such as doctrines that would otherwise operate as a matter of common law, or qualifications that purposivist judges might otherwise be inclined to read into the statute itself). Courts evaluating such arguments need to consider two basic interpretive questions: (1) Should the statutory provisions in question really be understood to occupy the field in this sense, and (2) if so, what is the scope of that field—that is, how far does the implied exclusivity of these provisions reach?

There cannot possibly be an across-the-board presumption in favor of drawing negative inferences or in favor of reading statutory provisions to occupy whatever fields they address. In the Supreme Court's words,

> "The force of any negative implication . . . depends on context. We have long held that the *expressio unius* canon does not apply 'unless it is fair to suppose that Congress considered the unnamed possibility and meant to say no to it,' *Barnhart v. Peabody Coal Co.*, 537 U.S. 149, 168 (2003), and [we have also long held] that the canon can be overcome by 'contrary indications that adopting a particular rule or statute was probably not meant to signal any exclusion,' *United States v. Vonn*, 535 U.S. 55, 65 (2002)."

Marx v. General Revenue Corp., 568 U.S. 371, 381 (2013); *see also* NLRB v. SW General, Inc., 580 U.S. 288, 302–04 (2017) (expressing similar caution about the *expressio unius* canon).

Indeed, *expressio unius* may not really be a canon at all, at least in the same sense as the other principles discussed in this section. When used properly, the maxim may simply highlight a recurring interpretive question without establishing a presumption about how to answer it. Here is what a panel of the U.S. Court of Appeals for the D.C. Circuit recently said about *expressio unius*:

> "As courts and commentators have noted, this canon (if it can be called a canon) is entirely dependent upon context. . . . When context indicates a list is meant to be exclusive, the 'canon' applies; when context does not so indicate, the 'canon' does not apply. There is thus much truth to the observation that 'this maxim is at best a description, after the fact, of what the court has discovered from context.' "

Doe v. Securities & Exchange Comm'n, 28 F.4th 1306, 1314 (D.C. Cir. 2022) (quoting REED DICKERSON, THE INTERPRETATION AND APPLICATION OF STATUTES 235 (1975)).

In any given context, even if a court concludes that certain statutory provisions were indeed meant to be exclusive (and to prevent other sources of law from supplying missing items), the court may still face hard questions about the scope of the exclusivity. Normally, *expressio unius* arguments will be strongest when the items or exceptions that a statute explicitly lists are of the same type as the item or exception that *expressio unius* is being invoked to rule out. Thus, the Supreme Court has said that "the canon *expressio unius est exclusio alterius* does not apply to every statutory listing or grouping; it has force only when the items expressed are members of an 'associated group or series,' justifying the inference that items not mentioned were excluded by deliberate choice, not inadvertence." *Barnhart v. Peabody Coal Co.*, 537 U.S. 149, 168 (2003) (quoting United States v. Vonn, 535 U.S. 55, 65 (2002)); *see also* Chevron U.S.A. Inc. v. Echazabal, 536 U.S. 73, 81 (2002) ("The canon depends on identifying a series of two or more terms or things that should be understood to go hand in hand, which is abridged in circumstances supporting a sensible inference that the term left out must have been meant to be excluded.").

Even when this condition is satisfied, though, *expressio unius* arguments will often be contestable. The mere fact that a statute contains some specific provisions does not necessarily support negative inferences on related topics. Perhaps the legislature enacted the specific provisions simply because legislators were able to reach a collective agreement on those topics but not others—in which case a court that interpreted the statute as implicitly establishing the opposite rule on the other topics would be going beyond the legislative bargain. *See, e.g.*, Landgraf v. USI Film Products, 511 U.S. 244, 261 & n.12 (1994) (offering this sort of response to an *expressio unius* argument). Or perhaps there are other reasons why the legislature enacted the specific provisions, and those reasons do not support any negative inferences. For one of many possible illustrations, consider the following case.

Mission Product Holdings, Inc. v. Tempnology, LLC

139 S. Ct. 1652 (2019)

■ *JUSTICE KAGAN delivered the opinion of the Court:*

. . . .

I

. . . . Tempnology, LLC, manufactured clothing and accessories designed to stay cool when used in exercise. It marketed those products under the brand name "Coolcore," using trademarks (*e.g.*, logos and labels) to distinguish the gear from other athletic apparel. In 2012, Tempnology entered into a contract with petitioner Mission Product Holdings, Inc. . . . The agreement gave Mission an exclusive license to distribute certain Coolcore products in the United States. And more important here, it granted Mission a non-exclusive license to use the Coolcore trademarks, both in the United States and around the world. The agreement was set to expire in July 2016. But in September 2015, Tempnology filed a petition for Chapter 11 bankruptcy. And it soon afterward asked the Bankruptcy Court to allow it to "reject" the licensing agreement. [11 U.S.C.] § 365(a).

Chapter 11 of the Bankruptcy Code sets out a framework for reorganizing a bankrupt business. See §§ 1101–1174. The filing of a petition creates a bankruptcy estate consisting of all the debtor's assets and rights. See § 541. The estate is the pot out of which creditors' claims are paid. It is administered by either a trustee or, as in this case, the debtor itself. See §§ 1101, 1107.

Section 365(a) of the Code provides that a "trustee [or debtor], subject to the court's approval, may assume or reject any executory contract." § 365(a). A contract is executory if "performance remains due to some extent on both sides." *NLRB v. Bildisco & Bildisco*, 465 U.S. 513, 522, n. 6 (1984) (internal quotation marks omitted). Such an agreement represents both an asset (the debtor's right to the counterparty's future performance) and a liability (the debtor's own obligations to perform). Section 365(a) enables the debtor (or its trustee), upon entering bankruptcy, to decide whether the contract is a good deal for the estate going forward. If so, the debtor will want to assume the contract, fulfilling its obligations while benefiting from the counterparty's performance. But if not, the debtor will want to reject the contract, repudiating any further performance of its duties. The bankruptcy court will generally approve that choice, under the deferential "business judgment" rule. *Id.* at 523.

According to Section 365(g), "the rejection of an executory contract[ ] constitutes a breach of such contract." As both parties here agree, the counterparty thus has a claim against the estate for damages resulting from the debtor's nonperformance. . . . But such a claim is unlikely to ever be paid in full. That is because the debtor's breach is deemed to occur "immediately before the date of the filing of the [bankruptcy] petition," rather than on the actual post-petition rejection date. § 365(g)(1). By thus giving the counterparty a pre-petition claim, Section 365(g) places that party in the same boat as the debtor's unsecured creditors, who in a typical bankruptcy may receive only cents on the dollar. See *Bildisco*, 465 U.S. at 531–532 (noting the higher priority of post-petition claims).

In this case, the Bankruptcy Court (per usual) approved Tempnology's proposed rejection of its executory licensing agreement with Mission. . . . That meant, as laid out above, two things on which the parties agree. First, Tempnology could stop performing under the contract. And second, Mission could assert (for whatever it might be worth) a pre-petition claim in the bankruptcy proceeding for damages resulting from Tempnology's nonperformance.

But Tempnology thought still another consequence ensued, and it returned to the Bankruptcy Court for a declaratory judgment confirming its view. According to Tempnology, its rejection of the contract also terminated the rights it had granted Mission to use the Coolcore trademarks. Tempnology based its argument on a negative inference. . . . Several provisions in Section 365 state that a counterparty to specific kinds of agreements may keep exercising contractual rights after a debtor's rejection. For example, Section 365(h) provides that if a bankrupt landlord rejects a lease, the tenant need not move out; instead, she may stay and pay rent (just as she did before) until the lease term expires. And still closer to home, Section 365(n) sets out a similar rule for some types of intellectual property licenses: If the debtor-licensor rejects the agreement, the licensee can continue to use the property (typically, a patent), so long as it makes whatever payments the contract demands. But Tempnology pointed out that neither Section 365(n) nor any similar provision covers trademark licenses. So, it reasoned, in that sort of contract a different rule must apply: The debtor's rejection must extinguish the rights that the agreement had conferred on the trademark licensee. The Bankruptcy Court agreed. See *In re Tempnology, LLC*, 541 B.R. 1 (Bkrtcy. Ct. NH 2015). It held, relying on the same "negative inference," that Tempnology's rejection of the licensing agreement revoked Mission's right to use the Coolcore marks. *Id.* at 7.

The Bankruptcy Appellate Panel reversed, relying heavily on a decision of the Court of Appeals for the Seventh Circuit about the effects of rejection on trademark licensing agreements. See *In re Tempnology, LLC*, 559 B.R. 809, 820–823 (Bkrtcy. App. Panel CA1 2016); *Sunbeam Products, Inc. v. Chicago Am. Mfg., LLC*, 686 F.3d 372, 376–377 (CA7 2012). . . .

But the Court of Appeals for the First Circuit rejected the Panel's and Seventh Circuit's view, and reinstated the Bankruptcy Court decision terminating Mission's license. See *In re Tempnology, LLC*, 879 F.3d 389 (2018). . . .

We granted certiorari to resolve the division between the First and Seventh Circuits. . . . We now affirm the Seventh's reasoning and reverse the decision below. . . .

III

. . . .

A

We start with the text of the Code's principal provisions on rejection—and find that it does much of the work. As noted earlier, Section 365(a) gives a debtor the option, subject to court approval, to "assume or reject any executory contract." And Section 365(g) describes what rejection means. Rejection "constitutes a breach of [an executory] contract," deemed to occur "immediately before the date of the filing of the petition." . . . . And "breach" is neither a defined nor a specialized bankruptcy term. It means in the Code what it means in contract law outside bankruptcy. See *Field v. Mans*, 516 U.S. 59, 69 (1995) (Congress generally meant for the Bankruptcy Code to "incorporate the established meaning" of "terms that have accumulated settled meaning" (internal quotation marks omitted)). So the first place to go in divining the effects of rejection is to non-bankruptcy contract law, which can tell us the effects of breach.

Consider a made-up executory contract to see how the law of breach works outside bankruptcy. A dealer leases a photocopier to a law firm, while agreeing to service it every month; in exchange, the firm commits to pay a monthly fee. During the lease term, the dealer decides to stop servicing the machine, thus breaching the agreement in a material way. The law firm now has a choice (assuming no special contract term or state law). The firm can keep up its side of the bargain, continuing to pay for use of the copier, while suing the dealer for damages from the service breach. Or the firm can call the whole deal off, halting its own payments and returning the copier, while suing for any damages incurred. See 13 R. Lord, Williston on Contracts § 39:32, pp. 701–702 (4th ed. 2013) ("[W]hen a contract is breached in the course of performance, the injured party may elect to continue the contract or refuse to perform further"). But to repeat: The choice to terminate the agreement and send back the copier is for the *law firm*. By contrast, the *dealer* has no ability, based on its own breach, to terminate the agreement. Or otherwise said, the dealer cannot get back the copier just by refusing to show up for a service appointment. The contract gave the law firm continuing rights in the copier, which the dealer cannot unilaterally revoke.

And now to return to bankruptcy: If the rejection of the photocopier contract "constitutes a breach," as the Code says, then the same results should follow (save for one twist as to timing). Assume here that the dealer files a Chapter 11 petition and decides to reject its agreement with the law firm. That means, as above, that the dealer will stop servicing the copier. It means, too, that the law firm has an option about how to respond—continue the contract or walk away, while suing for whatever damages go with its choice. (Here is where the twist comes in: Because the rejection is deemed to occur "immediately before" bankruptcy, the firm's damages suit is treated as a pre-petition claim on the estate, which will likely receive only cents on the dollar. . . .) And most important, it means that assuming the law firm wants to keep using the copier, the dealer cannot take it back. A rejection does not terminate the contract. When it occurs, the debtor and counterparty do not go back to their pre-contract positions. Instead, the counterparty retains the rights it has received under the agreement. As after a breach, so too after a rejection, those rights survive.

. . . . Sections 365(a) and (g) speak broadly, to "any executory contract[s]." Many licensing agreements involving trademarks or other property are of that kind (including, all agree, the Tempnology-Mission contract). The licensor not only grants a license, but provides associated goods or services during its term; the licensee pays continuing royalties or fees. If the licensor breaches the agreement outside bankruptcy (again, barring any special contract term or state law), everything said above goes. In particular, the breach does not revoke the license or stop the licensee from doing what it allows. . . . And because rejection "constitutes a breach," § 365(g), the same consequences follow in bankruptcy. The debtor can stop performing its remaining obligations under the agreement. But the debtor cannot rescind the license already conveyed. So the licensee can continue to do whatever the license authorizes.

In preserving those rights, Section 365 reflects a general bankruptcy rule: The estate cannot possess anything more than the debtor itself did outside bankruptcy. See *Board of Trade of Chicago v. Johnson*, 264 U.S. 1, 15 (1924) (establishing that principle); § 541(a)(1) (defining the estate to include the "interests *of the debtor* in property" (emphasis added)). . . . So if the not-yet debtor was subject to a counterparty's contractual right (say, to retain a copier or use a trademark), so too is the trustee or debtor once the bankruptcy petition has been filed. . . .

. . . .

B

Tempnology's main argument to the contrary . . . rests on a negative inference. . . . Several provisions of Section 365, Tempnology notes, "identif[y] categories of contracts under which a counterparty" may retain specified contract rights "notwithstanding rejection." Brief for Respondent 34. Sections 365(h) and (i) make clear that certain purchasers and lessees of real property and timeshare interests can continue to exercise rights after a debtor has rejected the lease or sales contract. See § 365(h)(1) (real-property leases); § 365(i) (real-property sales contracts); §§ 365(h)(2), (i) (timeshare interests). And Section 365(n) similarly provides that licensees of some intellectual property—

but not trademarks—retain contractual rights after rejection. See § 365(n); § 101(35A) . . . . Tempnology argues from those provisions that the ordinary consequence of rejection must be something different—*i.e.*, the termination, rather than survival, of contractual rights previously granted. Otherwise, Tempnology concludes, the statute's "general rule" would "swallow the exceptions." Brief for Respondent 19.

But that argument pays too little heed to the main provisions governing rejection and too much to subsidiary ones. On the one hand, it offers no account of how to read Section 365(g) (recall, rejection "constitutes a breach") to say essentially its opposite (*i.e.*, that rejection and breach have divergent consequences). On the other hand, it treats as a neat, reticulated scheme of "narrowly tailored exception[s]," *id.* at 36 (emphasis deleted), what history reveals to be anything but. Each of the provisions Tempnology highlights emerged at a different time, over a span of half a century. See, *e.g.*, 52 Stat. 881 (1938) (real-property leases); § 1(b), 102 Stat. 2538 (1988) (intellectual property). And each responded to a discrete problem—as often as not, correcting a judicial ruling of just the kind Tempnology urges. See Andrew, Executory Contracts in Bankruptcy, 59 U. Colo. L. Rev. 845, 911–912, 916–919 (1988) (identifying judicial decisions that the provisions overturned); compare, *e.g.*, *In re Sombrero Reef Club, Inc.*, 18 B.R. 612, 618–619 (Bkrtcy. Ct. SD Fla. 1982), with, *e.g.*, §§ 365(h)(2), (i). Read as generously as possible to Tempnology, this mash-up of legislative interventions says nothing much of anything about the content of Section 365(g)'s general rule. Read less generously, it affirmatively refutes Tempnology's rendition. As one bankruptcy scholar noted after an exhaustive review of the history: "What the legislative record [reflects] is that whenever Congress has been confronted with the consequences of the [view that rejection terminates all contractual rights], it has expressed its disapproval." Andrew, 59 U. Colo. L. Rev. at 928. On that account, Congress enacted the provisions, as and when needed, to reinforce or clarify the general rule that contractual rights survive rejection.[2]

Consider more closely, for example, Congress's enactment of Section 365(n), which addresses certain intellectual property licensing agreements. No one disputes how that provision came about. In *Lubrizol Enterprises v. Richmond Metal Finishers*, the Fourth Circuit held that a debtor's rejection of an executory contract worked to revoke its grant of a patent license. See 756 F.2d 1043, 1045–1048 (1985). In other words, *Lubrizol* adopted the same rule for patent licenses that the First Circuit announced for trademark licenses here. Congress sprang into action,

[2] At the same time, Congress took the opportunity when drafting those provisions to fill in certain details, generally left to state law, about the post-rejection relationship between the debtor and counterparty. See, *e.g.*, Andrew, Executory Contracts in Bankruptcy, 59 U. Colo. L. Rev. 845, 903, n. 200 (1988) (describing Congress's addition of subsidiary rules for real property leases in Section 365(h)); Brief for United States as *Amicus Curiae* 29 (noting that Congress similarly set out detailed rules for patent licenses in Section 365(n)). The provisions are therefore not redundant of Section 365(g): Each sets out a remedial scheme embellishing on or tweaking the general rejection-as-breach rule.

drafting Section 365(n) to reverse *Lubrizol* and ensure the continuation of patent (and some other intellectual property) licensees' rights. See 102 Stat. 2538 (1988); S. Rep. No. 100–505, pp. 2–4 (1988) (explaining that Section 365(n) "corrects [*Lubrizol*'s] perception" that "Section 365 was ever intended to be a mechanism for stripping innocent licensee[s] of rights"). As Tempnology highlights, that provision does not cover trademark licensing agreements, which continue to fall, along with most other contracts, within Section 365(g)'s general rule. See Brief for Respondent 38. But what of that? Even put aside the claim that Section 365(n) is part of a pattern—that Congress whacked Tempnology's view of rejection wherever it raised its head. . . . Still, Congress's repudiation of *Lubrizol* for patent contracts does not show any intent to *ratify* that decision's approach for almost all others. Which is to say that no negative inference arises. Congress did nothing in adding Section 365(n) to alter the natural reading of Section 365(g)—that rejection and breach have the same results.

. . . .

■ *JUSTICE SOTOMAYOR, concurring:*

. . . .

. . . . The Court rightly rejects Tempnology's argument that the presence of § 365(n) changes what § 365(g) says. As the Senate Report accompanying § 365(n) explained, the bill did not "address or intend any inference to be drawn concerning the treatment of executory contracts" under § 365's general rule. S. Rep. No. 100–505, p. 5 (1988). To the extent trademark licensees are treated differently from licensees of other forms of intellectual property, that outcome leaves Congress with the option to tailor a provision for trademark licenses, as it has repeatedly in other contexts. . . .

■ *[JUSTICE GORSUCH dissented. Without reaching the merits, he argued that the case may have become moot, and he would have dismissed the petition for certiorari as improvidently granted.]*

NOTE

Although the opinions in *Mission Product Holdings* do not use the phrase "*expressio unius*," that is one way to describe Tempnology's main argument. A few provisions in the Bankruptcy Code addressed specific categories of contracts, such as contracts to sell or lease real estate and contracts to license patents. Congress had specified that if a party to one of those kinds of contracts declared bankruptcy and rejected the contract, the other party could continue to exercise certain rights under the contract. Tempnology wanted courts to draw the negative inference that the rejection of *other* kinds of contracts must end all rights under the contract.

According to the Supreme Court, however, the provisions cited by Tempnology did not really justify this negative inference. As Justice

Kagan explained, Congress had enacted each of those provisions in response to previous judicial opinions that had misinterpreted the statute; when courts had erroneously held that the rejection of a real-estate contract or a patent-licensing contract completely nullified the contract, Congress had stepped in and said that it didn't. Admittedly, Congress had limited those provisions to the specific situations that the courts had been addressing. But the fact that Congress had repudiated the courts' misinterpretations of the statute only in the specific contexts that the courts had addressed surely does not mean that Congress had implicitly ratified those misinterpretations in all other areas. When one looks at the history of the specific provisions in question, one can see why Congress enacted each of them, and those reasons do not support the negative inference that Tempnology wanted to draw.

This analysis suggests a useful lesson for practicing lawyers: if a statute has taken its current shape in stages, by means of amendments enacted at different times, you should try to trace how and why the language evolved as it did. Sometimes, the current version of a statute as presented in the *United States Code* might seem to support an *expressio unius* argument. But if you go back and investigate why Congress enacted each of the amendments in question, you might be able to identify reasons that weaken or eliminate any negative inference.

So far, this section of the book has discussed one canon at a time. In practice, though, a particular question of statutory interpretation can implicate multiple canons (as well as other interpretive principles). In the following case, the majority and the dissent debated and deployed a number of the canons covered above.

Yates v. United States

574 U.S. 528 (2015)

■ *JUSTICE GINSBURG announced the judgment of the Court and delivered an opinion, in which CHIEF JUSTICE ROBERTS and JUSTICES BREYER and SOTOMAYOR join:*

John Yates, a commercial fisherman, caught undersized red grouper in federal waters in the Gulf of Mexico. To prevent federal authorities from confirming that he had harvested undersized fish, Yates ordered a crew member to toss the suspect catch into the sea. For this offense, he was charged with, and convicted of, violating 18 U.S.C. § 1519, which provides:

> "Whoever knowingly alters, destroys, mutilates, conceals, covers up, falsifies, or makes a false entry in any record, document, or tangible object with the intent to impede, obstruct, or influence the investigation or proper administration of any matter within the jurisdiction of any department or agency of the United States or any

> case filed under title 11, or in relation to or contemplation of any such matter or case, shall be fined under this title, imprisoned not more than 20 years, or both."

Yates was also indicted and convicted under [18 U.S.C.] § 2232(a), which provides:

> "DESTRUCTION OR REMOVAL OF PROPERTY TO PREVENT SEIZURE.—Whoever, before, during, or after any search for or seizure of property by any person authorized to make such search or seizure, knowingly destroys, damages, wastes, disposes of, transfers, or otherwise takes any action, or knowingly attempts to destroy, damage, waste, dispose of, transfer, or otherwise take any action, for the purpose of preventing or impairing the Government's lawful authority to take such property into its custody or control or to continue holding such property under its lawful custody and control, shall be fined under this title or imprisoned not more than 5 years, or both."

Yates does not contest his conviction for violating § 2232(a), but he maintains that fish are not trapped within the term "tangible object," as that term is used in § 1519.

Section 1519 was enacted as part of the Sarbanes-Oxley Act of 2002, 116 Stat. 745, legislation designed to protect investors and restore trust in financial markets following the collapse of Enron Corporation. . . . [I]t would cut § 1519 loose from its financial-fraud mooring to hold that it encompasses any and all objects, whatever their size or significance, destroyed with obstructive intent. Mindful that in Sarbanes-Oxley, Congress trained its attention on corporate and accounting deception and coverups, we conclude that a matching construction of § 1519 is in order: A tangible object captured by § 1519, we hold, must be one used to record or preserve information.

I

On August 23, 2007, the *Miss Katie*, a commercial fishing boat, was six days into an expedition in the Gulf of Mexico. Her crew numbered three, including Yates, the captain. Engaged in a routine offshore patrol . . . , Officer John Jones of the Florida Fish and Wildlife Conservation Commission decided to board the *Miss Katie* to check on the vessel's compliance with fishing rules. . . . Because he had been deputized as a federal agent by the National Marine Fisheries Service, Officer Jones had authority to enforce federal, as well as state, fishing laws.

Upon boarding the *Miss Katie*, Officer Jones noticed three red grouper that appeared to be undersized hanging from a hook on the deck. At the time, federal conservation regulations required immediate release of red grouper less than 20 inches long. 50 C.F.R. § 622.37(d)(2)(ii) (effective April 2, 2007). Violation of those regulations is a civil offense punishable by a fine or fishing license suspension. See 16 U.S.C. §§ 1857(1)(A), (G), 1858(a), (g).

Suspecting that other undersized fish might be on board, Officer Jones proceeded to inspect the ship's catch, setting aside and measuring only fish that appeared to him to be shorter than 20 inches. Officer Jones ultimately determined that 72 fish fell short of the 20-inch mark. A fellow officer recorded the length of each of the undersized fish on a catch measurement verification form. . . . After separating the fish measuring below 20 inches from the rest of the catch by placing them in wooden crates, Officer Jones directed Yates to leave the fish, thus segregated, in the crates until the *Miss Katie* returned to port. Before departing, Officer Jones issued Yates a citation for possession of undersized fish.

Four days later, after the *Miss Katie* had docked in Cortez, Florida, Officer Jones measured the fish contained in the wooden crates. This time, . . . the measured fish, although still less than 20 inches, slightly exceeded the lengths recorded on board. Jones surmised that the fish brought to port were not the same as those he had detected during his initial inspection. Under questioning, one of the crew members admitted that, at Yates's direction, he had thrown overboard the fish Officer Jones had measured at sea, and that he and Yates had replaced the tossed grouper with fish from the rest of the catch.

. . . . On May 5, 2010, [Yates] was indicted for destroying property to prevent a federal seizure, in violation of § 2232(a), and for destroying, concealing, and covering up undersized fish to impede a federal investigation, in violation of § 1519. By the time of the indictment, the minimum legal length for Gulf red grouper had been lowered from 20 inches to 18 inches. See 50 C.F.R. § 622.37(d)(2)(iv) (effective May 18, 2009). No measured fish in Yates's catch fell below that limit. . . .

Yates was tried on the criminal charges in August 2011. . . .

. . . . The trial judge expressed misgivings about reading "tangible object" as broadly as the Government urged: "Isn't there a Latin phrase [about] construction of a statute[?] . . . . The gist of it is . . . you take a look at [a] line of words, and you interpret the words consistently. So if you're talking about documents[ ] and records, tangible objects are tangible objects in the nature of a document or a record, as opposed to a fish." The . . . judge nonetheless followed controlling Eleventh Circuit precedent [which favored the broad reading]. . . . For violating § 1519 and § 2232(a), the court sentenced Yates to imprisonment for 30 days, followed by supervised release for three years. For life, he will bear the stigma of having a federal felony conviction.

On appeal, the Eleventh Circuit [affirmed] . . . .

II

The Sarbanes-Oxley Act, all agree, was prompted by the exposure of Enron's massive accounting fraud and revelations that the company's outside auditor, Arthur Andersen LLP, had systematically destroyed potentially incriminating documents. The Government acknowledges that § 1519 was intended to prohibit, in particular, corporate document-shredding to hide evidence of financial wrongdoing. Brief for United States 46. Prior law made it an offense to "intimidat[e], threate[n], or corruptly persuad[e] *another person*" to shred documents. § 1512(b) (emphasis added). Section 1519 cured a conspicuous omission by imposing liability on a person who destroys records himself. . . . The new section also expanded prior law by including within the provision's reach "any matter within the jurisdiction of any department or agency of the United States."

In the Government's view, § 1519 extends beyond the principal evil motivating its passage. The words of § 1519, the Government argues, support reading the provision as a general ban on the spoliation of evidence, covering all physical items that might be relevant to any matter under federal investigation.

Yates urges a contextual reading of § 1519, tying "tangible object" to the surrounding words, the placement of the provision within the Sarbanes-Oxley Act, and related provisions enacted at the same time, in particular § 1520 and § 1512(c)(1) . . . . Section 1519, he maintains, targets not all manner of evidence, but records, documents, and tangible objects used to preserve them, *e.g.*, computers, servers, and other media on which information is stored.

We agree with Yates . . . . "Tangible object" in § 1519, we conclude, is better read to cover only objects one can use to record or preserve information, not all objects in the physical world.

A

The ordinary meaning of an "object" that is "tangible," as stated in dictionary definitions, is "a discrete . . . thing," Webster's Third New International Dictionary 1555 (2002), that "possess[es] physical form," Black's Law Dictionary 1683 (10th ed. 2014). . . .

Whether a statutory term is unambiguous, however, does not turn solely on dictionary definitions of its component words. Rather, "[t]he plainness or ambiguity of statutory language is determined [not only] by reference to the language itself, [but as well by] the specific context in which that language is used, and the broader context of the statute as a whole." *Robinson v. Shell Oil Co.*, 519 U.S. 337, 341 (1997). . . . Ordinarily, a word's usage accords with its dictionary definition. In law as in life, however, the same words, placed in different contexts, sometimes mean different things.

We have several times affirmed that identical language may convey varying content when used in different statutes, sometimes even in different provisions of the same statute. See, *e.g.*, *FAA v. Cooper*, 566 U.S. 284, 292–293 (2012) ("actual damages" has different meanings in different statutes); *Wachovia Bank, N.A. v. Schmidt*, 546 U.S. 303, 313–314 (2006) ("located" has different meanings in different provisions of the

National Bank Act); *General Dynamics Land Systems, Inc. v. Cline*, 540 U.S. 581, 595–597 (2004) ("age" has different meanings in different provisions of the Age Discrimination in Employment Act of 1967); [other citations omitted]. . . .

. . . [T]he Government points to . . . Federal Rule of Criminal Procedure 16[,] . . . [which] requires the prosecution to grant a defendant's request to inspect "tangible objects" within the Government's control that have utility for the defense. See Fed. Rule Crim. Proc. 16(a)(1)(E).

Rule 16's reference to "tangible objects" has been interpreted to include any physical evidence. . . . [But] Rule 16 is a discovery rule designed to protect defendants by compelling the prosecution to turn over to the defense evidence material to the charges at issue. In that context, a comprehensive construction of "tangible objects" is fitting. In contrast, § 1519 is a penal provision that refers to "tangible object" not in relation to a request for information relevant to a specific court proceeding, but rather in relation to federal investigations or proceedings of every kind, including those not yet begun. . . . Just as the context of Rule 16 supports giving "tangible object" a meaning as broad as its dictionary definition, the context of § 1519 tugs strongly in favor of a narrower reading.

B

Familiar interpretive guides aid our construction of the words "tangible object" as they appear in § 1519.

We note first § 1519's caption: "Destruction, alteration, or falsification of records in Federal investigations and bankruptcy." That heading conveys no suggestion that the section prohibits spoliation of any and all physical evidence, however remote from records. Neither does the title of the section of the Sarbanes-Oxley Act in which § 1519 was placed, § 802: "Criminal penalties for altering documents." 116 Stat. 800. Furthermore, § 1520, the only other provision passed as part of § 802, is titled "Destruction of corporate audit records" and addresses only that specific subset of records and documents. While these headings are not commanding, they supply cues that Congress did not intend "tangible object" in § 1519 to sweep within its reach physical objects of every kind, including things no one would describe as records, documents, or devices closely associated with them. See *Almendarez-Torres v. United States*, 523 U.S. 224, 234 (1998) ("[T]he title of a statute and the heading of a section are tools available for the resolution of a doubt about the meaning of a statute." (internal quotation marks omitted)). . . .

Section 1519's position within Chapter 73 of Title 18 further signals that § 1519 was not intended to serve as a cross-the-board ban on the destruction of physical evidence of every kind. Congress placed § 1519 (and its companion provision § 1520) at the end of the chapter, following immediately after the pre-existing § 1516, § 1517, and § 1518, each of them prohibiting obstructive acts in specific contexts. See § 1516 (audits of recipients of federal funds); § 1517 (federal examinations of financial institutions); § 1518 (criminal investigations of federal health care offenses). . . .

But Congress did not direct codification of the Sarbanes-Oxley Act's other additions to Chapter 73 adjacent to these specialized provisions. Instead, Congress directed placement of those additions within or alongside retained provisions that address obstructive acts relating broadly to official proceedings and criminal trials[.] Section 806, "Civil Action to protect against retaliation in fraud cases," was codified as § 1514A and inserted between the pre-existing § 1514, which addresses civil actions to restrain harassment of victims and witnesses in criminal cases, and § 1515, which defines terms used in § 1512 and § 1513. Section 1102, "Tampering with a record or otherwise impeding an official proceeding," was codified as § 1512(c) and inserted within the pre-existing § 1512, which addresses tampering with a victim, witness, or informant to impede any official proceeding. Section 1107, "Retaliation against informants," was codified as § 1513(e) and inserted within the pre-existing § 1513, which addresses retaliation against a victim, witness, or informant in any official proceeding. Congress thus ranked § 1519, not among the broad proscriptions, but together with specialized provisions expressly aimed at corporate fraud and financial audits. This placement accords with the view that Congress' conception of § 1519's coverage was considerably more limited than the Government's.[4]

The contemporaneous passage of § 1512(c)(1), which was contained in a section of the Sarbanes-Oxley Act discrete from the section embracing § 1519 and § 1520, is also instructive. Section 1512(c)(1) provides:

> "(c) Whoever corruptly—
>
> > "(1) alters, destroys, mutilates, or conceals a record, document, or other object, or attempts to do so, with the intent to impair the object's integrity or availability for use in an official proceeding
> >
> > ". . .
> >
> > "shall be fined under this title or imprisoned not more than 20 years, or both."

The legislative history reveals that § 1512(c)(1) was drafted and proposed after § 1519. . . . The Government argues, and Yates does not dispute, that § 1512(c)(1)'s reference to "other object" includes any and every physical object. But if § 1519's reference to "tangible object" already

---

[4] The dissent contends that nothing can be drawn from the placement of § 1519 because, before and after Sarbanes-Oxley, "all of Chapter 73 was ordered chronologically." *Post* at 560. The argument might have some force if the factual premise were correct. In Sarbanes-Oxley, Congress directed insertion of § 1514A *before* § 1518, then the last section in Chapter 73. If, as the dissent argues, Congress adopted § 1519 to fill out § 1512, *post* at 557–558, it would have made more sense for Congress to codify the substance of § 1519 within § 1512 or in a new § 1512A, rather than placing § 1519 among specialized provisions. . . .

included all physical objects, as the Government and the dissent contend, then Congress had no reason to enact § 1512(c)(1): Virtually any act that would violate § 1512(c)(1) no doubt would violate § 1519 as well . . . .[5]

The Government acknowledges that, under its reading, § 1519 and § 1512(c)(1) "significantly overlap." Brief for United States 49. Nowhere does the Government explain what independent function § 1512(c)(1) would serve if the Government is right about the sweeping scope of § 1519. We resist a reading of § 1519 that would render superfluous an entire provision passed in proximity as part of the same Act. See *Marx v. General Revenue Corp.*, 568 U.S. 371, 386 (2013) ("[T]he canon against surplusage is strongest when an interpretation would render superfluous another part of the same statutory scheme.").

The words immediately surrounding "tangible object" in § 1519—"falsifies, or makes a false entry in any record [or] document"—also cabin the contextual meaning of that term. As explained in *Gustafson v. Alloyd Co.*, 513 U.S. 561, 575 (1995), we rely on the principle of *noscitur a sociis*—a word is known by the company it keeps—to "avoid ascribing to one word a meaning so broad that it is inconsistent with its accompanying words, thus giving unintended breadth to the Acts of Congress." (internal quotation marks omitted). . . . In *Gustafson*, we interpreted the word "communication" in § 2(10) of the Securities Act of 1933 to refer to a public communication, rather than any communication, because the word appeared in a list with other words, notably "notice, circular, [and] advertisement," making it "apparent that the list refer[red] to documents of wide dissemination." 513 U.S. at 575–576. And we did so even though the list began with the word "any."

The *noscitur a sociis* canon operates in a similar manner here. "Tangible object" is the last in a list of terms that begins "any record [or] document." The term is therefore appropriately read to refer, not to any tangible object, but specifically to the subset of tangible objects involving records and documents, *i.e.*, objects used to record or preserve information. . . .

This moderate interpretation of "tangible object" accords with the list of actions § 1519 proscribes. The section applies to anyone who "alters, destroys, mutilates, conceals, covers up, *falsifies*, or *makes a false entry in* any record, document, or tangible object" with the requisite

[5] [Section 1519 covers "the investigation or proper administration of any matter within the jurisdiction of any department or agency of the United States . . . or in relation to or contemplation of any such matter."] . . . [T]he dissent remarkably suggests that § 1519 does not "ordinarily operate in th[e] context [of] federal court[s]," for those courts are not "department[s] or agenc[ies]." *Post* at 561. That suggestion . . . does not withstand examination. The Senate Committee Report on § 1519, on which the dissent elsewhere relies, . . . explained that . . . § 1519 "is . . . meant to do away with the distinctions, which some courts have read into obstruction statutes, between court proceedings, investigations, regulatory or administrative proceedings (whether formal or not), and less formal government inquiries, regardless of their title." [S. Rep. 107–146] at 15 [(2002)]. . . . [T]he Report added, "[t]he intent of the provision is simple; people should not be destroying, altering, or falsifying documents to obstruct any government function." *Ibid.*

obstructive intent. (Emphasis added.) The last two verbs, "falsif[y]" and "mak[e] a false entry in," typically take as grammatical objects records, documents, or things used to record or preserve information, such as logbooks or hard drives. . . . It would be unnatural, for example, to describe a killer's act of wiping his fingerprints from a gun as "falsifying" the murder weapon. But it would not be strange to refer to "falsifying" data stored on a hard drive as simply "falsifying" a hard drive. Furthermore, Congress did not include on § 1512(c)(1)'s list of prohibited actions "falsifies" or "makes a false entry in." See § 1512(c)(1) (making it unlawful to "alte[r], destro[y], mutilat[e], or concea[l] a record, document, or other object" with the requisite obstructive intent). That contemporaneous omission also suggests that Congress intended "tangible object" in § 1519 to have a narrower scope than "other object" in § 1512(c)(1).[7]

A canon related to *noscitur a sociis, ejusdem generis,* counsels: "Where general words follow specific words in a statutory enumeration, the general words are [usually] construed to embrace only objects similar in nature to those objects enumerated by the preceding specific words." *Washington State Dept. of Social and Health Servs. v. Guardianship Estate of Keffeler,* 537 U.S. 371, 384 (2003) (internal quotation marks omitted). In *Begay v. United States,* 553 U.S. 137, 142–143 (2008), for example, we relied on this principle to determine what crimes were covered by the statutory phrase "any crime . . . that . . . is burglary, arson, or extortion, involves use of explosives, or otherwise involves conduct that presents a serious potential risk of physical injury to another," 18 U.S.C. § 924(e)(2)(B)(ii). The enumeration of specific crimes, we explained, indicates that the "otherwise involves" provision covers "only *similar* crimes, rather than *every* crime that 'presents a serious potential risk of physical injury to another.' " 553 U.S. at 142. Had Congress intended the latter "all encompassing" meaning, we observed, "it is hard to see why it would have needed to include the examples at all." *Ibid.* . . . Just so here. Had Congress intended "tangible object" in § 1519 to be interpreted so generically as to capture physical objects as dissimilar as documents and fish, Congress would have had no reason to refer specifically to "record" or "document." The Government's unbounded reading of "tangible object" would render those words misleading surplusage.

. . . [W]e are persuaded that an aggressive interpretation of "tangible object" must be rejected. It is highly improbable that Congress would

---

[7] . . . . When Congress passed Sarbanes-Oxley in 2002, courts had already interpreted the phrase "alter, destroy, mutilate, or conceal an object" in § 1512(b)(2)(B) to apply to all types of physical evidence. See, *e.g., United States v. Applewhaite,* 195 F.3d 679, 688 (CA3 1999) (affirming conviction under § 1512(b)(2)(B) for persuading another person to paint over blood spatter). Congress' use of a formulation in § 1519 that did not track the one used in § 1512(b)(2)(B) (and repeated in § 1512(c)(1)) suggests that Congress designed § 1519 to be interpreted apart from § 1512, not in lockstep with it.

have buried a general spoliation statute covering objects of any and every kind in a provision targeting fraud in financial record-keeping.

The Government argues, however, that . . . we [should] . . . consider the origins of the phrase "record, document, or tangible object." Congress drew that phrase, the Government says, from a 1962 Model Penal Code (MPC) provision, and reform proposals based on that provision. The MPC provision and proposals prompted by it would have imposed liability on anyone who "alters, destroys, mutilates, conceals, or removes a record, document or thing." See ALI, MPC § 241.7(1), p. 175 (1962). Those prescriptions were understood to refer to all physical evidence. See MPC § 241.7, Comment 3, at 179 (1980) (provision "applies to any physical object"). Accordingly, the Government reasons, and the dissent exuberantly agrees, Congress must have intended § 1519 to apply to the universe of physical evidence.

This inference is unwarranted. True, the 1962 MPC provision prohibited tampering with any kind of physical evidence. But unlike § 1519, the MPC provision did not prohibit actions that specifically relate to records, documents, and objects used to record or preserve information. The MPC provision also ranked the offense as a misdemeanor and limited liability to instances in which the actor "believe[s] that an official proceeding or investigation is pending or about to be instituted." MPC § 241.7(1), at 175. . . .

Section 1519 conspicuously lacks the limits built into the MPC provision . . . . It describes not a misdemeanor, but a felony punishable by up to 20 years in prison. And the section covers conduct intended to impede any federal investigation or proceeding, including one not even on the verge of commencement. Given these significant differences, the meaning of "record, document, or thing" in the MPC provision and a kindred proposal is not a reliable indicator of the meaning Congress assigned to "record, document, or tangible object" in § 1519. . . .

C

Finally, if our recourse to traditional tools of statutory construction leaves any doubt about the meaning of "tangible object," as that term is used in § 1519, we would invoke the rule that "ambiguity concerning the ambit of criminal statutes should be resolved in favor of lenity." *Cleveland v. United States*, 531 U.S. 12, 25 (2000) (quoting *Rewis v. United States*, 401 U.S. 808, 812 (1971)). That interpretative principle is relevant here, where the Government urges a reading of § 1519 that exposes individuals to 20-year prison sentences for tampering with *any* physical object that *might* have evidentiary value in *any* federal investigation into *any* offense, no matter whether the investigation is pending or merely contemplated, or whether the offense subject to investigation is criminal or civil. . . .

* * *

For the reasons stated, we resist reading § 1519 expansively to create a coverall spoliation of evidence statute, advisable as such a measure might be. Leaving that important decision to Congress, we hold that a "tangible object" within § 1519's compass is one used to record or preserve information. . . .

■ *JUSTICE ALITO, concurring in the judgment:*

. . . . [T]hough the question is close, traditional tools of statutory construction confirm that John Yates has the better of the argument. Three features of 18 U.S.C. § 1519 stand out to me: the statute's list of nouns, its list of verbs, and its title. Although perhaps none of these features by itself would tip the case in favor of Yates, the three combined do so.

Start with the nouns. Section 1519 refers to "any record, document, or tangible object." . . . Applying [*noscitur a sociis* and *ejusdem generis*] to § 1519's list of nouns, the term "tangible object" should refer to something similar to records or documents. A fish does not spring to mind—nor does an antelope, a colonial farmhouse, a hydrofoil, or an oil derrick. All are "objects" that are "tangible." But who wouldn't raise an eyebrow if a neighbor, when asked to identify something similar to a "record" or "document," said "crocodile"?

This reading, of course, has its shortcomings. For instance, this is an imperfect *ejusdem generis* case because "record" and "document" are themselves quite general. And there is a risk that "tangible object" may be made superfluous—what is similar to a "record" or "document" but yet is not one? An e-mail, however, could be such a thing. . . . A hard drive . . . is tangible and can contain files that are precisely akin to [a "document" or "record" even on a narrow understanding of those words]. . . . [A]dding "tangible object" to § 1519 would ensure beyond question that electronic files are included. To be sure, "tangible object" presumably can capture more than just e-mails; Congress enacts "catchall[s]" for "known unknowns." . . . But where *noscitur a sociis* and *ejusdem generis* apply, "known unknowns" should be similar to known knowns, *i.e.*, here, records and documents. This is especially true because reading "tangible object" too broadly could render "record" and "document" superfluous.

Next, consider § 1519's list of verbs: "alters, destroys, mutilates, conceals, covers up, falsifies, or makes a false entry in." Although many of those verbs could apply to nouns as far-flung as salamanders, satellites, or sand dunes, the last phrase in the list—"makes a false entry in"—makes no sense outside of filekeeping. How does one make a false entry in a fish? "Alters" and especially "falsifies" are also closely associated with filekeeping. Not one of the verbs, moreover, *cannot* be applied to filekeeping—certainly not in the way that "makes a false entry in" is always inconsistent with the aquatic.

. . . . One can imagine Congress trying to write a law so broadly that not every verb lines up with every noun. But failure to "line up" may suggest that something has gone awry in one's interpretation of a text. Where, as here, each of a statute's verbs applies to a certain category of nouns, there is some reason to think that Congress had that category in mind. . . . Here, focusing on the verbs, the category of nouns appears to be filekeeping. This observation is not dispositive, but neither is it nothing. . . .

Finally, my analysis is influenced by § 1519's title: "Destruction, alteration, or falsification of *records* in Federal investigations and bankruptcy." (Emphasis added.) This too points toward filekeeping, not fish. Titles can be useful devices to resolve " 'doubt about the meaning of a statute.' " *Porter v. Nussle,* 534 U.S. 516, 527–528 (2002) (quoting *Almendarez-Torres v. United States,* 523 U.S. 224, 234 (1998)) . . . . The title is especially valuable here because it reinforces what the text's nouns and verbs independently suggest—that no matter how other statutes might be read, this particular one does not cover every noun in the universe with tangible form.

Titles, of course, are also not dispositive. Here, if the list of nouns did not already suggest that "tangible object" should mean something similar to records or documents, especially when read in conjunction with § 1519's peculiar list of verbs with their focus on filekeeping, then the title would not be enough on its own. In conjunction with those other two textual features, however, the Government's argument, though colorable, becomes too implausible to accept. . . .

■ *JUSTICE KAGAN, with whom JUSTICES SCALIA, KENNEDY, and THOMAS join, dissenting:*

A criminal law, 18 U.S.C. § 1519, prohibits tampering with "any record, document, or tangible object" in an attempt to obstruct a federal investigation. This case raises the question whether the term "tangible object" means the same thing in § 1519 as it means in everyday language—any object capable of being touched. The answer should be easy: Yes. The term "tangible object" is broad, but clear. Throughout the U.S. Code and many States' laws, it invariably covers physical objects of all kinds. And in § 1519, context confirms what bare text says: All the words surrounding "tangible object" show that Congress meant the term to have a wide range. That fits with Congress's evident purpose in enacting § 1519: to punish those who alter or destroy physical evidence—*any* physical evidence—with the intent of thwarting federal law enforcement.

The plurality instead interprets "tangible object" to cover "only objects one can use to record or preserve information." The concurring opinion similarly, if more vaguely, contends that "tangible object" should refer to "something similar to records or documents"—and shouldn't include colonial farmhouses, crocodiles, or fish. In my view, conventional tools of statutory construction all lead to a more conventional result: A "tangible object" is an object that's tangible. I would apply the statute that Congress enacted and affirm the judgment below.

I

While the plurality starts its analysis with § 1519's heading, see *ante* at 539 ("We note first § 1519's caption"), I would begin with § 1519's text. When Congress has not supplied a definition, we generally give a statutory term its ordinary meaning. See, *e.g.*, *Schindler Elevator Corp. v. United States ex rel. Kirk*, 563 U.S. 401, 407 (2011). As the plurality . . . acknowledge[s], the ordinary meaning of "tangible object" is "a discrete thing that possesses physical form." *Ante* at 537 (punctuation and citation omitted). A fish is, of course, a discrete thing that possesses physical form. See generally Dr. Seuss, One Fish Two Fish Red Fish Blue Fish (1960). So the ordinary meaning of the term "tangible object" in § 1519, as no one here disputes, covers fish . . . .

That interpretation accords with endless uses of the term in statute and rule books as construed by courts. Dozens of federal laws and rules of procedure (and hundreds of state enactments) include the term "tangible object" or its first cousin "tangible thing"—some in association with documents, others not. [Many citations omitted.] To my knowledge, no court has ever read any such provision to exclude things that don't record or preserve data; rather, all courts have adhered to the statutory language's ordinary (*i.e.*, expansive) meaning. For example, courts have understood the phrases "tangible objects" and "tangible things" in the Federal Rules of Criminal and Civil Procedure to cover everything from guns to drugs to machinery to . . . animals. [Many more citations omitted.] No surprise, then, that—until today—courts have uniformly applied the term "tangible object" in § 1519 in the same way. See, *e.g.*, *United States v. McRae*, 702 F.3d 806, 834–838 (CA5 2012) (corpse); *United States v. Maury*, 695 F.3d 227, 243–244 (CA3 2012) (cement mixer).

That is not necessarily the end of the matter; I agree with the plurality (really, who doesn't?) that context matters in interpreting statutes. . . . [S]ometimes that means, as the plurality says, that the dictionary definition of a disputed term cannot control. See, *e.g.*, *Bloate v. United States*, 559 U.S. 196, 205 n. 9 (2010). But this is not such an occasion, for here the text and its context point the same way. . . .

Begin with the way the surrounding words in § 1519 reinforce the breadth of the term at issue. Section 1519 refers to "any" tangible object, thus indicating (in line with *that* word's plain meaning) a tangible object "of whatever kind." Webster's Third New International Dictionary 97 (2002). This Court has time and again recognized that "any" has "an expansive meaning," bringing within a statute's reach *all* types of the item (here, "tangible object") to which the law refers. [Citations omitted.] And the adjacent laundry list of verbs in § 1519 ("alters, destroys, mutilates, conceals, covers up, falsifies, or makes a false entry") further shows that Congress wrote a statute with a wide scope. Those words are supposed to ensure—just as "tangible object" is meant to—that § 1519 covers the whole world of evidence-tampering, in all its prodigious variety. . . .

Still more, "tangible object" appears as part of a three-noun phrase (including also "records" and "documents") common to evidence-tampering laws and always understood to embrace things of all kinds. The Model Penal Code's evidence-tampering section, drafted more than 50 years ago, similarly prohibits a person from "alter[ing], destroy[ing], conceal[ing] or remov[ing] any *record, document or thing*" in an effort to thwart an official investigation or proceeding. ALI, Model Penal Code § 241.7(1), p. 175 (1962) (emphasis added). The Code's commentary emphasizes that the offense described in that provision is "not limited to conduct that [alters] a written instrument." *Id.* § 241.7, Comment 3, at 179. Rather, the language extends to "any physical object." *Ibid.* Consistent with that statement—and, of course, with ordinary meaning—courts in the more than 15 States that have laws based on the Model Code's tampering provision apply them to all tangible objects, including drugs, guns, vehicles and . . . yes, animals. [Citations omitted.] Not a one has limited the phrase's scope to objects that record or preserve information.

The words "record, document, or tangible object" in § 1519 also track language in 18 U.S.C. § 1512, the federal witness-tampering law covering (as even the plurality accepts) physical evidence in all its forms. Section 1512, both in its original version (preceding § 1519) and today, repeatedly uses the phrase "record, document, or other object"—most notably, in a provision prohibiting the use of force or threat to induce another person to withhold any of those materials from an official proceeding. § 4(a) of the Victim and Witness Protection Act of 1982, 96 Stat. 1249, as amended, 18 U.S.C. § 1512(b)(2). That language, which itself likely derived from the Model Penal Code, encompasses no less the bloody knife than the incriminating letter, as all courts have for decades agreed. [Citations omitted.] And typically "only the most compelling evidence" will persuade this Court that Congress intended "nearly identical language" in provisions dealing with related subjects to bear different meanings. *Communications Workers v. Beck*, 487 U.S. 735, 754 (1988); see A. Scalia & B. Garner, Reading Law: The Interpretation of Legal Texts 252 (2012). Context thus again confirms what text indicates.

And legislative history, for those who care about it, puts extra icing on a cake already frosted. Section 1519, as the plurality notes, was enacted after the Enron Corporation's collapse, as part of the Sarbanes-Oxley Act of 2002, 116 Stat. 745. But the provision began its life in a separate bill, and the drafters emphasized that Enron was "only a case study exposing the shortcomings in our current laws" relating to both "corporate and criminal" fraud. S. Rep. No. 107–146, pp. 2, 11 (2002). The primary "loophole[ ]" Congress identified, see *id.* at 14, arose from limits in the part of § 1512 just described: That provision, as uniformly construed, prohibited a person from inducing another to destroy "record[s], document[s], or other object[s]"—of every type—but not from doing so himself. § 1512(b)(2) . . . . Congress (as even the plurality agrees) enacted § 1519 to close that yawning gap. But § 1519 could fully achieve that goal only if it covered all the records, documents, and objects § 1512 did, as well as all the means of tampering with them. And so § 1519 was written to do exactly that—"to apply broadly to any acts to destroy or fabricate physical evidence," as long as performed with the requisite intent. S. Rep. No. 107–146, at 14. "When a person destroys evidence," the drafters explained, "overly technical legal distinctions should neither hinder nor prevent prosecution." *Id.* at 7. Ah well: Congress, meet today's Court, which here invents just such a distinction with just such an effect. See *United States v. Philadelphia Nat. Bank*, 374 U.S. 321, 343 (1963) ("[C]reat[ing] a large loophole in a statute designed to close a loophole" is "illogical and disrespectful of . . . congressional purpose").

As Congress recognized in using a broad term, giving immunity to those who destroy non-documentary evidence has no sensible basis in penal policy. A person who hides a murder victim's body is no less culpable than one who burns the victim's diary. A fisherman, like John Yates, who dumps undersized fish to avoid a fine is no less blameworthy than one who shreds his vessel's catch log for the same reason. Congress thus treated both offenders in the same way. It understood, in enacting § 1519, that destroying evidence is destroying evidence, whether or not that evidence takes documentary form.

II

A

The plurality searches far and wide for anything—*anything*—to support its interpretation of § 1519. But its fishing expedition comes up empty.

The plurality's analysis starts with § 1519's title: "Destruction, alteration, or falsification of records in Federal investigations and bankruptcy." . . . That's already a sign something is amiss. I know of no other case in which we have *begun* our interpretation of a statute with the title, or relied on a title to override the law's clear terms. Instead, we have followed "the wise rule that the title of a statute and the heading of a section cannot limit the plain meaning of the text." *Trainmen v. Baltimore & Ohio R. Co.*, 331 U.S. 519, 528–529 (1947).

The reason for that "wise rule" is easy to see: A title is, almost necessarily, an abridgment. Attempting to mention every term in a statute "would often be ungainly as well as useless"; accordingly, "matters in the text . . . are frequently unreflected in the headings." *Id.* at 528. Just last year, this Court observed that two titles in a nearby section of Sarbanes-Oxley serve as "but a short-hand reference to the general subject matter" of the provision at issue, "not meant to take the place of the detailed provisions of the text." *Lawson v. FMR LLC*, 571

U.S. 429, 446 (2014) (quoting *Trainmen*, 331 U.S. at 528). The "under-inclusiveness" of the headings, we stated, was "apparent." *Lawson*, 571 U.S. at 446. So too for § 1519's title, which refers to "destruction, alteration, or falsification" but *not* to mutilation, concealment, or covering up, and likewise mentions "records" but *not* other documents or objects. . . .

The plurality next tries to divine meaning from § 1519's "position within Chapter 73 of Title 18." *Ante* at 540. But that move is yet odder than the last. As far as I can tell, this Court has never once suggested that the section number assigned to a law bears upon its meaning. . . . And even on its own terms, the plurality's argument is hard to fathom. The plurality claims that if § 1519 applied to objects generally, Congress would not have placed it "after the pre-existing § 1516, § 1517, and § 1518" because those are "specialized provisions." *Ante* at 540. But search me if I can find a better place for a broad ban on evidence-tampering. The plurality seems to agree that the law properly goes in Chapter 73—the criminal code's chapter on "obstruction of justice." But the provision does not logically fit into any of that chapter's pre-existing sections. And with the first 18 numbers of the chapter already taken (starting with § 1501 and continuing through § 1518), the law naturally took the 19th place. That is standard operating procedure. Prior to the Sarbanes-Oxley Act of 2002, all of Chapter 73 was ordered chronologically: Section 1518 was later enacted than § 1517, which was later enacted than § 1516, which was . . . well, you get the idea. And after Sarbanes-Oxley, Congress has continued in the same vein. Section 1519 is thus right where you would expect it (as is the contemporaneously passed § 1520)—between § 1518 (added in 1996) and § 1521 (added in 2008).[2]

The plurality's third argument, relying on the surplusage canon, at least invokes a known tool of statutory construction—but it too comes to nothing. Says the plurality: If read naturally, § 1519 "would render superfluous" § 1512(c)(1), which Congress passed "as part of the same act." *Ante* at 543. But that is not so: Although the two provisions significantly overlap, each applies to conduct the other does not. The key difference between the two is that § 1519 protects the integrity of "matter[s] within the jurisdiction of any [federal] department or agency" whereas § 1512(c)(1) safeguards "official proceeding[s]" as defined in § 1515(a)(1)(A). Section 1519's language often applies more broadly than § 1512(c)(1)'s, as the plurality notes. For example, an FBI investigation

[2] The lonesome exception to Chapter 73's chronological order is § 1514A, added in Sarbanes-Oxley to create a civil action to protect whistleblowers. Congress decided to place that provision right after the only other section in Chapter 73 to authorize a civil action (that one to protect victims and witnesses). The plurality, seizing on the § 1514 example, says it likewise "would have made more sense for Congress to codify the substance of § 1519 within § 1512 or in a new § 1512A." *Ante* at 541, n. 4. But § 1512 is titled "Tampering with a witness, victim, or an informant," and its provisions almost all protect witnesses from intimidation and harassment. It makes perfect sense that Congress wanted a broad ban on evidence-spoliation to stand on its own rather than as part of—or an appendage to—a witness-tampering provision.

counts as a matter within a federal department's jurisdiction, but falls outside the statutory definition of "official proceeding" as construed by courts. See, *e.g.*, *United States v. Gabriel*, 125 F.3d 89, 105, n. 13 (CA2 1997). But conversely, § 1512(c)(1) sometimes reaches more widely than § 1519. For example, because an "official proceeding" includes any "proceeding before a judge or court of the United States," § 1512(c)(1) prohibits tampering with evidence in federal litigation between private parties. See § 1515(a)(1)(A) . . . . By contrast, § 1519 wouldn't ordinarily operate in that context because a federal court isn't a "department or agency." See *Hubbard v. United States*, 514 U.S. 695, 715 (1995).[3] So the surplusage canon doesn't come into play. Overlap—even significant overlap—abounds in the criminal law. See *Loughrin v. United States*, 571 U.S. 351, 358 n.4 (2014). . . .

And the legislative history to which the plurality appeals, see *ante* at 536, only cuts against it because those materials show that lawmakers knew that § 1519 and § 1512(c)(1) share much common ground. Minority Leader Lott introduced the amendment that included § 1512(c)(1) (along with other criminal and corporate fraud provisions) late in the legislative process, explaining that he did so at the specific request of the President. See 148 Cong. Rec. 12509, 12512 (2002) (remarks of Sen. Lott). Not only Lott but several other Senators noted the overlap between the President's package and provisions already in the bill, most notably § 1519. See *id.* at 12512 (remarks of Sen. Lott); *id.* at 12513 (remarks of Sen. Biden); *id.* at 12517 (remarks of Sens. Hatch and Gramm). The presence of both § 1519 and § 1512(c)(1) in the final Act may have reflected belt-and-suspenders caution: If § 1519 contained some flaw, § 1512(c)(1) would serve as a backstop. Or the addition of § 1512(c)(1) may have derived solely from legislators' wish "to satisfy audiences other than courts"—that is, the President and his Justice Department. Gluck & Bressman, Statutory Interpretation from the Inside, 65 Stan. L. Rev. 901, 935 (2013) (emphasis deleted). Whichever the case, Congress's consciousness of overlap between the two provisions removes any conceivable reason to cast aside § 1519's ordinary meaning in service of preventing some statutory repetition.

Indeed, the inclusion of § 1512(c)(1) in Sarbanes-Oxley creates a far worse problem for the plurality's construction of § 1519 than for mine.

---

[3] The plurality's objection to this statement is difficult to understand. . . . [*Hubbard* held] that "a federal court is neither a 'department' nor an 'agency' " in a statute referring, just as § 1519 does, to "any matter within the jurisdiction of any department or agency of the United States." 514 U.S. at 698, 715. . . . [T]he federal government, as far as I can tell, has never once brought a prosecution under § 1519 for evidence-tampering in litigation between private parties. It instead uses § 1512(c)(1) for that purpose.

[*Ed.*: In *Hubbard*, the Court was interpreting 18 U.S.C. § 1001 (1988 ed.). Although § 1001 has since been amended, the version at issue in *Hubbard* read as follows: "Whoever, in any matter within the jurisdiction of any department or agency of the United States knowingly and willfully falsifies, conceals or covers up by any trick, scheme, or device a material fact, or makes any false, fictitious or fraudulent statements or representations, or makes or uses any false writing or document knowing the same to contain any false, fictitious or fraudulent statement or entry, shall be fined not more than $10,000 or imprisoned not more than five years, or both."]

Section 1512(c)(1) criminalizes the destruction of any "record, document, or other object"; § 1519 of any "record, document, or tangible object." On the plurality's view, one "object" is really an object, whereas the other is only an object that preserves or stores information. But "[t]he normal rule of statutory construction assumes that identical words used in different parts of the same act," passed at the same time, "are intended to have the same meaning." *Sorenson v. Secretary of Treasury*, 475 U.S. 851, 860 (1986) (internal quotation marks omitted). And that is especially true when the different provisions pertain to the same subject. The plurality doesn't—really, can't—explain why it instead interprets the same words used in two provisions of the same Act addressing the same basic problem to mean fundamentally different things.

Getting nowhere with surplusage, the plurality switches canons, hoping that *noscitur a sociis* and *ejusdem generis* will save it. . . .

As an initial matter, this Court uses *noscitur a sociis* and *ejusdem generis* to resolve ambiguity, not create it. Those principles are "useful rule[s] of construction where words are of obscure or doubtful meaning." *Russell Motor Car Co. v. United States*, 261 U.S. 514, 520 (1923). But when words have a clear definition, and all other contextual clues support that meaning, the canons cannot properly defeat Congress's decision to draft broad legislation. . . .

Anyway, assigning "tangible object" its ordinary meaning comports with *noscitur a sociis* and *ejusdem generis* when applied, as they should be, with attention to § 1519's subject and purpose. Those canons require identifying a common trait that links all the words in a statutory phrase. . . . [T]he plurality characterizes records and documents as things that preserve information—and so they are. But just as much, they are things that provide information, and thus potentially serve as evidence relevant to matters under review. And in a statute pertaining to obstruction of federal investigations, that evidentiary function comes to the fore. The destruction of records and documents prevents law enforcement agents from gathering facts relevant to official inquiries. And so too does the destruction of tangible objects—of whatever kind. Whether the item is a fisherman's ledger or an undersized fish, throwing it overboard has the identical effect on the administration of justice. For purposes of § 1519, records, documents, and (all) tangible objects are therefore alike.

Indeed, even the plurality can't fully credit its *noscitur/ejusdem* argument. The same reasoning would apply to *every* law placing the word "object" (or "thing") after "record" and "document." But as noted earlier, such statutes are common: The phrase appears (among other places) in many state laws based on the Model Penal Code, as well as in multiple provisions of § 1512. The plurality accepts that in those laws "object" means object; its argument about superfluity positively *depends* on giving § 1512(c)(1) that broader reading. What, then, is the difference here? The plurality proposes that some of those statutes describe less serious offenses than § 1519. How and why that distinction affects application of the *noscitur a sociis* and *ejusdem generis* canons is left obscure: Count it as one more of the plurality's never-before-propounded, not-readily-explained interpretive theories. But in any event, that rationale cannot support the plurality's willingness to give "object" its natural meaning in § 1512, which (like § 1519) sets out felonies with penalties of up to 20 years. See §§ 1512(a)(3)(C), (b), (c). The canons, in the plurality's interpretive world, apparently switch on and off whenever convenient.

And the plurality's invocation of § 1519's verbs does nothing to buttress its canon-based argument. . . . The plurality observes that § 1519 prohibits "falsif[ying]" or "mak[ing] a false entry in" a tangible object, and no one can do those things to, say, a murder weapon (or a fish). But of course someone can alter, destroy, mutilate, conceal, or cover up such a tangible object, and § 1519 prohibits those actions too. The Court has never before suggested that all the verbs in a statute need to match up with all the nouns. See *Robers v. United States*, 572 U.S. 639, 643–644 (2014) ("[T]he law does not require legislators to write extra language specifically exempting, phrase by phrase, applications in respect to which a portion of a phrase is not needed"). And for good reason. It is exactly when Congress sets out to draft a statute broadly—to include every imaginable variation on a theme—that such mismatches will arise. To respond by narrowing the law, as the plurality does, is thus to flout both what Congress wrote and what Congress wanted.

Finally, when all else fails, the plurality invokes the rule of lenity. But even in its most robust form, that rule only kicks in when, "after all legitimate tools of interpretation have been exhausted, 'a reasonable doubt persists' regarding whether Congress has made the defendant's conduct a federal crime." *Abramski v. United States*, 573 U.S. 169, 204 (2014) (Scalia, J., dissenting) (quoting *Moskal v. United States*, 498 U.S. 103, 108 (1990)). No such doubt lingers here. The plurality points to the breadth of § 1519, as though breadth were equivalent to ambiguity. It is not. Section 1519 *is* very broad. It is also very clear. Every traditional tool of statutory interpretation points in the same direction, toward "object" meaning object. Lenity offers no proper refuge from that straightforward (even though capacious) construction.

. . . .

III

If none of the traditional tools of statutory interpretation can produce today's result, then what accounts for it? The plurality offers a clue when it emphasizes the disproportionate penalties § 1519 imposes if the law is read broadly. Section 1519, the plurality objects, would then "expose[ ] individuals to 20-year prison sentences for tampering with *any* physical object that *might* have evidentiary value in *any* federal investigation into *any* offense." *Ante* at 548. That brings to the surface the real issue: overcriminalization and excessive punishment in the U.S. Code.

Now as to this statute, I think the plurality somewhat—though only somewhat—exaggerates the matter. The plurality omits from its description of § 1519 the requirement that a person act "knowingly" and with "the intent to impede, obstruct, or influence" federal law enforcement. And in highlighting § 1519's maximum penalty, the plurality glosses over the absence of any prescribed minimum. (Let's not forget that Yates's sentence was not 20 years, but 30 days.) Congress presumably enacts laws with high maximums and no minimums when it thinks the prohibited conduct may run the gamut from major to minor. . . . Still and all, I tend to think, for the reasons the plurality gives, that § 1519 is a bad law—too broad and undifferentiated, with too-high maximum penalties, which give prosecutors too much leverage and sentencers too much discretion. And I'd go further: In those ways, § 1519 is unfortunately not an outlier, but an emblem of a deeper pathology in the federal criminal code.

But whatever the wisdom or folly of § 1519, this Court does not get to rewrite the law. . . . If judges disagree with Congress's choice, we are perfectly entitled to say so—in lectures, in law review articles, and even in dicta. But we are not entitled to replace the statute Congress enacted with an alternative of our own design. . . .

NOTES AND QUESTIONS

1. Together, the various opinions in *Yates* invoked many different canons, including *noscitur a sociis*, *ejusdem generis*, the presumption against superfluity, the presumption of consistent usage, and the rule of lenity. The plurality's position, however, appeared to be driven more by the plurality's sense of the overall purpose behind the Sarbanes-Oxley Act. In the plurality's words, when Congress enacted the Sarbanes-Oxley Act, "Congress trained its attention on corporate and accounting deception and cover-ups"—and 18 U.S.C. § 1519, in particular, grew out of some highly publicized incidents of document-shredding. Does the fact that Congress enacted § 1519 as part of the Sarbanes-Oxley Act, combined with the rule of lenity and the plurality's other arguments, justify the plurality's relatively narrow reading of the phrase "any record, document, or tangible object" in § 1519?

2. The opinions in *Yates* paid considerable attention to the caption (or "catchline") of 18 U.S.C. § 1519: "Destruction, alteration, or falsification of records in Federal investigations and bankruptcy." With respect to provisions in Title 18 of the United States Code, though, courts should think carefully before basing arguments on captions.

To be sure, all the captions in Title 18 have been enacted by Congress (rather than simply having been inserted during the codification process by the Office of the Law Revision Counsel or its predecessors), because

Title 18 is one of the titles of the United States Code that Congress has enacted as such. *See supra* pp. 54–55. Congress enacted Title 18 in 1948. As is the practice for such enactments, Section 1 of the 1948 statute set forth the entire Title that Congress was enacting, divided into chapters and complete with section headings. *See* An Act to Revise, Codify, and Enact into Positive Law, Title 18 of the United States Code, Entitled "Crimes and Criminal Procedure," ch. 645, § 1, 62 Stat. 683, 683–858 (1948).

Nonetheless, Section 19 of the same 1948 statute read as follows: "No inference of a legislative construction is to be drawn by reason of the chapter in Title 18, Crimes and Criminal Procedure, as set out in section 1 of this Act, in which any particular section is placed, nor by reason of the catchlines used in such title." *Id.* § 19, 62 Stat. at 862 (emphasis added); *see also* Tobias A. Dorsey, *Some Reflections on* Yates *and the Statutes We Threw Away*, 18 GREEN BAG 2d 377, 379–81 (2015) (discussing the history of such provisions and noting that similar provisions appear in the statutes enacting Titles 5, 13, 14, 28, 31, 36, 39, 40, 44, 46, and 49, as well as the Uniform Code of Military Justice). At least with respect to the captions in Title 18 that date back to 1948, then, Congress instructed courts not to use those captions as the basis for inferences about the intended meaning of the provisions that the captions accompanied.

This instruction in the 1948 statute does not necessarily apply to the captions in Title 18 that Congress has enacted since 1948, like the caption of 18 U.S.C. § 1519 (which Congress enacted as part of the Sarbanes-Oxley Act in 2002). As discussed in Chapter 4.B.4 of this book, there are limits on one Congress's ability to control the interpretation of statutes enacted by later Congresses. But the Congress that enacted Section 19 in 1948 might not even have been *trying* to forbid courts to pay attention to whatever captions Congress might add to Title 18 in the future. By its terms, Section 19 can be read to address only the catchlines in Title 18 "as set out in section 1 of this Act"—that is, the version that Congress was enacting in 1948. The fact that Congress did not make Section 19 part of Title 18 itself may also suggest that the enacting Congress did not intend Section 19 to reach provisions that later Congresses might add to Title 18. As a policy matter, moreover, there are reasons why the Congress that enacted Section 19 might have decided to treat the captions that were part of Title 18 in 1948 differently than the captions that would be enacted in the future. In 1948, when Congress was enacting all of Title 18 as such, Congress apparently did not want to take a position about the accuracy of each and every caption in the version of Title 18 that Congress was enacting; some of those captions had originally been drafted by the people who compiled the United States Code rather than by Congress itself, and Congress might have wanted to carry these captions forward for the sake of convenience without having to vouch for them all. By contrast, when later Congresses add new provisions to Title 18, Congress can give individualized attention to the relevant captions—with the result, perhaps, that Congress is willing to let interpreters consider those captions when interpreting the meaning of the new provisions.

Given these arguments, do you agree that the captions of provisions like 18 U.S.C. § 1519, which Congress added to Title 18 *after* 1948, are potentially relevant to the proper interpretation of those provisions? Even if you do *not* think it appropriate to consult the caption of 18 U.S.C. § 1519, how about the caption of Section 802 of the Sarbanes-Oxley Act—the section that amended Title 18 to include § 1519 and § 1520? As the plurality noted, the caption of Section 802 was "Criminal penalties for altering documents." *See* Sarbanes-Oxley Act § 802, 116 Stat. 745, 800 (2002). The instruction in Section 19 of the 1948 statute plainly does not reach *that* caption.

Does the fact that these captions refer only to "records" or "documents" support a narrow reading of the phrase "tangible object" in the operative language of § 1519? Or is that argument only as strong as the plurality's claims about *noscitur a sociis* and *ejusdem generis*—so that the captions do not refute Justice Kagan's view that § 1519 is about "things that provide information" rather than simply "things that preserve information"?

C. THE RULE OF LENITY

The canons that we have considered so far all reflect familiar principles—principles that have long been used to interpret many different sorts of documents. Some other canons, though, draw upon principles that apply specifically to the interpretation of statutes. This section takes up one of those canons, now called the "rule of lenity."

The rule of lenity addresses how interpreters should approach vagueness and ambiguity in so-called "penal" statutes (or in "penal" provisions of statutes that contain other sorts of provisions too). The rule of lenity crops up most frequently when courts are construing statutes that authorize criminal punishment. But the category of "penal" provisions that can trigger the rule of lenity extends somewhat farther. For instance, provisions authorizing fines or forfeitures are sometimes classified as "penal" for this purpose even though they are enforced through civil rather than criminal process.

The traditional rule of lenity, which told courts to construe penal statutes "strictly," sometimes applied even when modern courts would not detect any indeterminacy, or at least would think it easy to figure out what the enacting legislature had meant to prohibit. In modern times, the rule of lenity has a more modest scope. It tells courts that when they encounter vagueness or ambiguity in a "penal" statute (or a "penal" provision in a statute that contains both penal and nonpenal provisions), *and when they cannot resolve the indeterminacy by applying various other interpretive tools*, they should adopt the least harsh of the permissible interpretations. Thus, if a criminal statute is genuinely unclear about how broadly its prohibitions sweep, courts are supposed to assume that the statute prohibits less conduct rather than more. Similarly, if there is genuine doubt about the severity of the punishments that a statute authorizes, courts are again supposed to resolve their doubts in the direction of lenity. *See, e.g.*, Bifulco v. United States, 447 U.S. 381, 387 (1980) (noting that the rule of lenity "applies not only to interpretations of the substantive ambit of criminal prohibitions, but also to the penalties they impose").

At the state level, quite a few legislatures have purported to turn off the traditional rule of lenity, and perhaps even its more modest modern descendant. *See, e.g.*, Cal. Penal Code § 4 ("The rule of the common law, that penal statutes are to be strictly construed, has no application to this Code. All its provisions are to be construed according to the fair import of their terms, with a view to effect its objects and to promote justice."); *cf.* People v. Avery, 27 Cal. 4th 49, 57–58 (2002) (recognizing a limited role for the rule of lenity notwithstanding this provision, but confining that role to situations in which the rival interpretations " 'stand in relative equipoise' " (quoting People v. Jones, 46 Cal. 3d 585, 599 (1988))). *See generally* Zachary Price, *The Rule of Lenity as a Rule of Structure*, 72 FORDHAM L. REV. 885, 902–04 (2004) (canvassing provisions of this sort in other states and noting the varied judicial responses to them); Livingston Hall, *Strict or Liberal Construction of Penal Statutes*, 48 HARV. L. REV. 748, 752–56 (1935) (tracing the history of such provisions, which date back to the nineteenth century). Assume for now that American-style separation of powers does not prevent legislatures from giving courts general instructions about how to interpret statutes, as long as the content of those instructions does not offend any other constitutional doctrines. (Chapter 4.B.4 will consider that topic in detail.) Are there any reasons why it might be unconstitutional for a legislature to turn off the rule of lenity?

The rule of lenity is often said to reflect "constitutional values." *See, e.g.*, William N. Eskridge, Jr. & Philip P. Frickey, *Quasi-Constitutional Law: Clear Statement Rules as Constitutional Lawmaking*, 45 VAND. L. REV. 593, 597, 600 (1992) (associating the rule of lenity with some of the same concerns as the Due Process Clauses). But while the rule of lenity does indeed reflect some of the same values as various provisions in both the federal Constitution and its state counterparts, the rule of lenity arguably takes those values farther than the constitutional provisions do. One certainly should not assume that if the rule of lenity did not exist, all statutes that currently trigger it would have to be held "void for vagueness" as a matter of constitutional law (or, equivalently, that the legislature cannot constitutionally delegate to the judiciary the range of interpretive choices that those statutes would present). To say that a statute triggers the rule of lenity is not necessarily to say that the Constitution itself requires the court to construe it narrowly.

Still, even if it is permissible for legislatures to turn off the rule of lenity, Congress has not done so. Courts therefore continue to apply the rule of lenity to federal penal statutes. The rule of lenity also retains some force in most states.

In practice, different judges may put different amounts of weight on the rule of lenity. For instance, Justices Scalia and Ginsburg often seemed to apply the rule of lenity more forcefully than some of their colleagues. *See, e.g.*, Elliot Greenfield, *A Lenity Exception to* Chevron *Deference*, 58 BAYLOR L. REV. 1, 6 (2006) (observing that Justices Scalia and Ginsburg "both assert a strong version of the rule of lenity"). But most judges speak as if the rule of lenity has force at least as a tie-breaker—a means of responding to close questions. Why should it have weight even in those cases? What are the justifications for giving the rule of lenity whatever force it has?

There is widespread agreement that the rule of lenity is *not* a tool for identifying what members of the enacting legislature probably intended penal statutes to mean. Instead of helping to *resolve* superficial indeterminacy about a statute's intended meaning, it tells courts how to *respond to* indeterminacy that remains after they have used their ordinary interpretive techniques. In the terminology introduced at the start of this chapter, the rule of lenity is not a "descriptive" canon. Indeed, it is probably the most purely "normative" of the canons that we will study in this course.

One traditional justification for the rule of lenity has to do with concepts of notice or "fair warning." Justice Holmes provided a classic statement of this justification in *McBoyle v. United States*, 283 U.S. 25, 27 (1931):

> "Although it is not likely that a criminal will carefully consider the text of the law before he murders or steals, it is reasonable that a fair warning should be given to the world[,] in language that the common world will understand, of what the law intends to do if a certain line is passed. To make the warning fair, so far as possible the line should be clear."

In *McBoyle* itself, Justice Holmes used this argument to explain why courts should not use imaginative reconstruction to extend a penal statute beyond its apparent terms, so as to reach conduct that members of the enacting legislature might well have wanted to prohibit if they had thought about it. *See id.* (holding that the National Motor Vehicle Theft Act of 1919 did not prohibit interstate transportation of a stolen airplane, because an airplane did not fit the statutory definition of a "motor vehicle"). But Justice Holmes's observation about "fair warning" has also been seen as a reason for courts to read the terms of penal statutes relatively narrowly, so that they do not reach conduct that they might or might not be understood to prohibit. *See, e.g.*, United States v. Bass, 404 U.S. 336, 347–48 (1971).

This argument might be pitched either from the standpoint of potential defendants (the individuals whom society proposes to punish for violating statutory obligations) or from the standpoint of society itself. From the individual standpoint, one might say that it is fair to punish defendants for acting in particular ways only if the laws gave them sufficiently clear warning, in advance, that those actions were forbidden and were causes for punishment. How persuasive is this argument about notice? Does it justify applying the rule of lenity to statutes that prohibit *mala in se* (acts like murder and rape, which people with a conventional sense of morality expect to be illegal), or does the "notice" argument apply only to the subset of penal statutes that address *mala prohibita* (regulatory offenses that would not offend society's general sense of morality if they had not been prohibited by statute)? *Cf.* REED DICKERSON, THE INTERPRETATION AND APPLICATION OF STATUTES 209–11 (1975) (taking the latter position). Whatever the scope of the argument, what exactly is the connection between notice and the text of penal statutes? Wasn't Justice Holmes right to concede that would-be criminals do not really get their notice of what the law prohibits by going to the library and reading statutes for themselves? But if the mechanisms by which people get notice of the law's requirements are more complex than that, couldn't those mechanisms continue to provide adequate notice of the law's requirements even if courts did not apply the rule of lenity? For instance, if courts consistently applied a "rule of harshness" (that is, if they consistently resolved residual indeterminacy in penal statutes *against* criminal defendants), wouldn't people have just as much advance notice of what courts will understand the law to prohibit as the rule of lenity currently gives them? More modestly, why can't people be said to be on notice that if conduct fits within one of the plausible interpretations of a penal statute, it *might* be held to be a crime, and anyone who engages in that conduct is therefore running some risk of criminal punishment?

This line of questions might make one doubt that concerns about notice or "fair warning" to potential defendants are sufficient to justify the rule of lenity. But perhaps Justice Holmes's point was less about individualized notice than about the rule of law in our society. Even if we do not rely upon the "naïve assumption 'that offenders against the law carefully read the penal code before they embark on crime,' " perhaps the rule of lenity reflects our "instinctive distaste against men languishing in prison unless the lawmaker has clearly said they should." HENRY J. FRIENDLY, *Mr. Justice Frankfurter and the Reading of Statutes, in* BENCHMARKS 196, 209 (1967) (quoting Bell v. United States, 349 U.S. 81, 83–84 (1955)). Along the same lines, the federal Supreme Court often says that "because of the seriousness of criminal penalties, and because criminal punishment usually represents the moral condemnation of the community, legislatures and not courts should define criminal activity." *Bass*, 404 U.S. at 348; *see also* Cass R. Sunstein, *Nondelegation Canons*, 67 U. CHI. L. REV. 315, 332 (2000) ("One function of the lenity principle is to ensure against delegations. Criminal law must be a product of a clear judgment on Congress's part.").

This argument sounds in the separation of powers. But does it really justify the rule of lenity? Conventional ideas about the separation of powers put the legislature in charge of policymaking not just with respect to crimes, but with respect to other things too. Outside of the penal context, though, people often say that if statutes are ambiguous or otherwise partially indeterminate, the courts or agencies that administer the statutes have some interpretive freedom; they get to pick from among the permissible interpretations, perhaps on the basis of considerations that are not fully embedded in the statutes. If we are comfortable with that allocation of authority for other important statutes (including zoning statutes that keep people from using their property as they please, economic regulations that restrict people's ability to pursue their chosen callings, and immigration statutes that keep people from even entering the country), is there any reason to distinguish penal statutes? Should the rule of lenity at least be confined to penal statutes that call for imprisoning or executing someone, as opposed to penal statutes that simply trigger fines?

Aside from having to explain why separation-of-powers principles should lead courts to treat penal statutes differently than nonpenal statutes, arguments based on the principle of legislative supremacy must also cope with the fact that legislatures themselves do not necessarily want courts to apply the rule of lenity. At the state level, many more state legislatures have abrogated the rule of lenity (or at least the traditional rule of "strict construction" of penal statutes) than have codified it. *See* Price, *supra*, 72 FORDHAM L. REV. at 902–03. At the federal level, a famous study of instances between 1967 and 1990 in which Congress passed a new statute to override the meaning that the Supreme Court had ascribed to an earlier statute found that such statutory overrides were more common in criminal law than in any other field and that the decisions being overridden almost always had gone in favor of the criminal defendant. *See* William N. Eskridge, Jr., *Overriding Supreme Court Statutory Interpretation Decisions*, 101 YALE L.J. 331 (1991). Does this pattern suggest that application of the rule of lenity is contrary to Congress's likely desires? If so, should we care?

In modern times, there have been strong political incentives for legislators at both the state and the federal level to seem tough on crime, or at least on many kinds of crime. Given those incentives, it is not surprising that Congress has proved much more likely to override judicial decisions that resolve interpretive doubt in the direction of lenity than to override judicial decisions that side with the prosecution. Some commentators have suggested that this asymmetry actually provides an argument in favor of the rule of lenity—not simply to counterbalance political incentives that might be considered bad, but to help courts get more accurate information about what Congress really wants. *See, e.g.*, EINER ELHAUGE, STATUTORY DEFAULT RULES: HOW TO INTERPRET UNCLEAR LEGISLATION 169 (2008).

The argument can be put this way. When a statute criminalizes something but is unclear about exactly how far the prohibition goes or exactly how harsh the punishment should be, courts need some way to handle the indeterminacy. To encourage consistency in those determinations, we might prefer courts to apply a formal canon rather than just flipping a coin or responding to the indeterminacy in some other *ad hoc* way. But we need to decide which way the canon should run: should it favor lenity, harshness, or something in between? The asymmetry in legislators' political incentives might bear on that question. If a penal statute is genuinely ambiguous but the judiciary resolves the ambiguity *against* criminal defendants, the judiciary is unlikely to elicit any new information from the legislature. By contrast, if the judiciary applies the rule of lenity, and if people in the political branches do not like the resulting understanding of the law, those people have ample resources to fix the perceived problem by enacting a new statute. In Justice Scalia's words, the rule of lenity arguably "places the weight of inertia upon the party that can best induce Congress to speak more clearly." *United States v. Santos*, 553 U.S. 507, 514 (2008) (plurality opinion). Thus, it can be seen as what Professor Elhauge calls a "preference-eliciting default rule"—a rule that operates within the zone of indeterminacy left by conventional interpretive techniques, but that works to "elicit a more nuanced or precise statute that satisfies enactable preferences more exactly than any plausible interpretation [of the old statute] could." ELHAUGE, *supra*, at 153.

Whatever the best justification for the rule of lenity is, many modern cases treat the rule as a last resort. At least with respect to federal statutes, the Supreme Court has said that "[t]he rule of lenity applies only if, after seizing everything from which aid can be derived, . . . we can make no more than a guess as to what Congress intended." *United States v. Wells*, 519 U.S. 482, 499 (1997) (internal quotation marks omitted). On this view, courts should apply all their tools for figuring out what the legislature probably meant, including all relevant "descriptive" canons, before they even think about applying the rule of lenity. If the ordinary tools of statutory interpretation provide a clear enough answer to the interpretive question that the courts are confronting, the rule of lenity will not come into play. Only if the statute remains intractably ambiguous or vague should courts proceed to apply the rule of lenity—and even then, they should use the rule simply to choose among the options that their other interpretive tools have identified as all being pretty much equally plausible.

Opinions vary as to how often courts face such intractable ambiguities. But if the rule of lenity is indeed limited to situations near equipoise, it might be relatively unimportant. According to Justice Kavanaugh, "because a court must exhaust all the tools of statutory interpretation before resorting to the rule of lenity, and because a court that does so often determines the best reading of a statute, the rule of lenity rarely if ever comes into play." *Wooden v. United States*, 142 S. Ct. 1063, 1075 (2022) (Kavanaugh, J., concurring).

On the other hand, some Justices have advocated a more powerful version of the rule of lenity. In his book with Bryan Garner, Justice Scalia suggested that courts ought to apply the rule of lenity whenever "the matter is not beyond reasonable doubt." ANTONIN SCALIA & BRYAN A. GARNER, READING LAW: THE INTERPRETATION OF LEGAL TEXTS 299 (2012); *see also* Abramski v. United States, 573 U.S. 169, 204 (2014) (Scalia, J., dissenting) ("Contrary to the majority's miserly approach, the rule of lenity applies whenever, after all legitimate tools of interpretation have been exhausted, 'a reasonable doubt persists' about whether Congress has made the defendant's conduct a federal crime, *Moskal* v. *United States*, 498 U.S. 103, 108 (1990)—in other words, whenever those tools do not decisively dispel the statute's ambiguity."). On the current Supreme Court, Justice Gorsuch has echoed that formulation (in an opinion joined on this point by Justice Sotomayor). *See Wooden*, 142 S. Ct. at 1084–85 (Gorsuch, J., concurring in the judgment).

As Justice Gorsuch noted, the "reasonable doubt" formulation has some historical support. For instance, here is a passage from an opinion that Justice Brockholst Livingston delivered while riding circuit in 1810:

> "It should be a principle of every criminal code, and certainly belongs to ours, that no person be adjudged guilty of an offence unless it be created and promulgated in terms which leave no reasonable doubt of their meaning. If it be the duty of a jury to acquit where such doubts exist concerning a fact, it is equally incumbent on a judge not to apply the law to a case where he labours under the same uncertainty as to the meaning of the legislature."

The Enterprise, 8 F. Cas. 732, 734 (C.C.D.N.Y. 1810) (No. 4,499); *see also* Shon Hopwood, *Restoring the Historical Rule of Lenity as a Canon*, 95 N.Y.U. L. REV. 918, 927–28 & nn. 50–51 (2020) (citing other examples of this formulation in nineteenth-century cases and treatises).

The "reasonable doubt" formulation favored by Justices Scalia and Gorsuch gets rhetorical punch from the standard of proof that applies to certain *factual* questions in criminal cases. (In every criminal case, the prosecution is required to prove each element of the crime beyond a reasonable doubt.[7]) But does the standard of proof that courts use for

[7] *See* In re Winship, 397 U.S. 358, 364 (1970); *cf.* Patterson v. New York, 432 U.S. 197, 210 (1977) (distinguishing between facts relevant to the elements of an offense and facts relevant to an affirmative defense).

factual questions about whether the defendant did something have any logical relationship to the canons of interpretation that courts use to decide what a criminal statute means? If one reading of a statute seems better than another, should courts be obliged to pick the worse reading just because that reading is more lenient and the courts are not *sure* what the enacting legislature meant? To the extent that the rule of lenity is associated with the separation of powers and the idea that legislatures should be in charge of defining crimes, wouldn't it be paradoxical if this judge-made canon systematically caused courts to depart from the most likely intended meaning of statutes?

In the case that follows, the majority opinion articulated the conventional view that the rule of lenity is a mere tie-breaker. But the case has some other interesting features—including the use of a rudimentary type of corpus analysis.

Muscarello v. United States

524 U.S. 125 (1998)

■ *JUSTICE BREYER delivered the opinion of the Court:*

A provision in . . . the federal criminal code imposes a 5-year mandatory prison term upon a person who "uses or carries a firearm" "during and in relation to" a "drug trafficking crime." 18 U.S.C. § 924(c)(1). The question before us is whether the phrase "carries a firearm" is limited to the carrying of firearms on the person. We hold that it is not so limited. Rather, it also applies to a person who knowingly possesses and conveys firearms in a vehicle, including in the locked glove compartment or trunk of a car, which the person accompanies.

I

The question arises in two cases, which we have consolidated for argument. Petitioner in the first case, Frank J. Muscarello, unlawfully sold marijuana, which he carried in his truck to the place of sale. Police officers found a handgun locked in the truck's glove compartment. During plea proceedings, Muscarello admitted that he had "carried" the gun "for protection in relation" to the drug offense, though he later claimed to the contrary, and added that, in any event, his "carr[ying]" of the gun in the glove compartment did not fall within the scope of the statutory word "carries."

Petitioners in the second case, Donald Cleveland and Enrique Gray-Santana, placed several guns in a bag, put the bag in the trunk of a car, and then traveled by car to a proposed drug-sale point, where they intended to steal drugs from the sellers. Federal agents at the scene stopped them, searched the cars, found the guns and drugs, and arrested them. . . .

II

A

We begin with the statute's language. The parties vigorously contest the ordinary English meaning of the phrase "carries a firearm." Because they essentially agree that Congress intended the phrase to convey its ordinary, and not some special legal, meaning, and because they argue the linguistic point at length, we too have looked into the matter in more than usual depth. Although the word "carry" has many different meanings, only two are relevant here. When one uses the word in the first, or primary, meaning, one can, as a matter of ordinary English, "carry firearms" in a wagon, car, truck, or other vehicle that one accompanies. When one uses the word in a different, rather special, way, to mean, for example, "bearing" or (in slang) "packing" (as in "packing a gun"), the matter is less clear. But, for reasons we shall set out below, we believe Congress intended to use the word in its primary sense and not in this latter, special way.

Consider first the word's primary meaning. The Oxford English Dictionary gives as its *first* definition "convey, originally by cart or wagon, hence in any vehicle, by ship, on horseback, etc." 2 Oxford English Dictionary 919 (2d ed. 1989); see also Webster's Third New International Dictionary 343 (1986) (*first* definition: "move while supporting (*as in a vehicle* or in one's hands or arms)"); The Random House Dictionary of the English Language Unabridged 319 (2d ed. 1987) (*first* definition: "to take or support from one place to another; convey; transport").

The origin of the word "carries" explains why the first, or basic, meaning of the word "carry" includes conveyance in a vehicle. See The Barnhart Dictionary of Etymology 146 (1988) (tracing the word from Latin "carum," which means "car" or "cart"); 2 Oxford English Dictionary, *supra,* at 919 (tracing the word from Old French "carier" and the late Latin "carricare," which meant to "convey in a car"); The Oxford Dictionary of English Etymology 148 (C. Onions ed. 1966) (same); The Barnhart Dictionary of Etymology, *supra,* at 143 (explaining that the term "car" has been used to refer to the automobile since 1896).

The greatest of writers have used the word with this meaning. See, e.g., the King James Bible, 2 Kings 9:28 ("[H]is servants carried him in a chariot to Jerusalem"); *id.,* Isaiah 30:6 ("[T]hey will carry their riches upon the shoulders of young asses"). Robinson Crusoe says, "[w]ith my boat, I carry'd away every Thing." D. Defoe, Robinson Crusoe 174 (J. Crowley ed. 1972). And the owners of Queequeg's ship, Melville writes, "had lent him a [wheelbarrow], in which to carry his heavy chest to his boarding-house." H. Melville, Moby Dick 43 (U. Chicago 1952). This Court, too, has spoken of the "carrying" of drugs in a car or in its "trunk." *California v. Acevedo,* 500 U.S. 565, 572–573 (1991) . . . .

These examples do not speak directly about carrying guns. But there is nothing linguistically special about the fact that weapons, rather than drugs, are being carried. . . . And, to make certain that there is no special ordinary English restriction (unmentioned in dictionaries) upon the use of "carry" in respect to guns, we have surveyed modern press usage, albeit crudely, by searching computerized newspaper databases—both the New York Times database in Lexis/Nexis[ ] and the "US News" database in Westlaw. We looked for sentences in which the words "carry," "vehicle," and "weapon" (or variations thereof) all appear. We found thousands of such sentences, and random sampling suggests that many, perhaps more than one third, are sentences used to convey the meaning at issue here, i.e., the carrying of guns in a car.

. . . .

Now consider a different, somewhat special meaning of the word "carry"—a meaning upon which the linguistic arguments of petitioners and the dissent must rest. The Oxford English Dictionary's *twenty-sixth* definition of "carry" is "bear, wear, hold up, or sustain, as one moves about; habitually to bear about with one." 2 Oxford English Dictionary at 921. Webster's defines "carry" as "to move while supporting," not just in a vehicle, but also "in one's hands or arms." Webster's Third New International Dictionary, *supra*, at 343. And Black's Law Dictionary defines the entire phrase "carry arms or weapons" as

> "To wear, bear or carry them upon the person or in the clothing or in a pocket, for the purpose of use, or for the purpose of being armed and ready for offensive or defensive action in case of a conflict with another person." Black's Law Dictionary 214 (6th ed. 1990).

These special definitions, however, do not purport to *limit* the "carrying of arms" to the circumstances they describe. No one doubts that one who bears arms on his person "carries a weapon." But to say that is not to deny that one may *also* "carry a weapon" tied to the saddle of a horse or placed in a bag in a car.

Nor is there any linguistic reason to think that Congress intended to limit the word "carries" in the statute to any of these special definitions. To the contrary, all these special definitions embody a form of an important, but secondary, meaning of "carry," a meaning that suggests support rather than movement or transportation, as when, for example, a column "carries" the weight of an arch. 2 Oxford English Dictionary at 919, 921. In this sense a gangster might "carry" a gun (in colloquial language, he might "pack a gun") even though he does not move from his chair. It is difficult to believe, however, that Congress intended to limit the statutory word to this definition—imposing special punishment upon the comatose gangster while ignoring drug lords who drive to a sale carrying an arsenal of weapons in their van.

We recognize, as the dissent emphasizes, that the word "carry" has other meanings as well. But those other meanings (e.g., "carry all he knew," "carries no colours") . . . are not relevant here. . . . The relevant linguistic facts are that the word "carry" in its ordinary sense includes carrying in a car and that the word, used in its ordinary sense, keeps the same meaning whether one carries a gun, a suitcase, or a banana.

Given the ordinary meaning of the word "carry," it is not surprising to find that the Federal Circuit Courts of Appeals have unanimously concluded that "carry" is not limited to the carrying of weapons directly on the person but can include their carriage in a car. . . .

B

We now explore more deeply the purely legal question of whether Congress intended to use the word "carry" in its ordinary sense, or whether it intended to limit the scope of the phrase to instances in which a gun is carried "on the person." We conclude that neither the statute's basic purpose nor its legislative history support circumscribing the scope of the word "carry" by applying an "on the person" limitation.

This Court has described the statute's basic purpose broadly, as an effort to combat the "dangerous combination" of "drugs and guns." *Smith v. United States*, 508 U.S. 223, 240 (1993). And the provision's chief legislative sponsor has said that the provision seeks "to persuade the man who is tempted to commit a Federal felony to leave his gun at home." 114 Cong. Rec. 22231 (1968) (Rep. Poff); see *Busic v. United States*, 446 U.S. 398, 405 (1980) (describing Poff's comments as "crucial material" in interpreting the purpose of § 924(c)); *Simpson v. United States*, 435 U.S. 6, 13–14 (1978) (concluding that Poff's comments are "clearly probative" and "certainly entitled to weight"); see also . . . [114 Cong. Rec.] at 22244 ("Of course, what we are trying to do by these penalties is to persuade the criminal to leave his gun at home") (Rep. Randall); *id.* at 22236 ("We are concerned . . . with having the criminal leave his gun at home") (Rep. Meskill).

From the perspective of any such purpose (persuading a criminal "to leave his gun at home") what sense would it make for this statute to penalize one who walks with a gun in a bag to the site of a drug sale, but to ignore a similar individual who, like defendant Gray-Santana, travels to a similar site with a similar gun in a similar bag, but instead of walking, drives there with the gun in his car? How persuasive is a punishment that is without effect until a drug dealer who has brought his gun to a sale (indeed has it available for use) actually takes it from the trunk (or unlocks the glove compartment) of his car? It is difficult to say that, considered as a class, those who prepare, say, to sell drugs by placing guns in their cars are less dangerous, or less deserving of punishment, than those who carry handguns on their person.

We have found no significant indication elsewhere in the legislative history of any more narrowly focused relevant purpose. We have found an instance in which a legislator referred to the statute as applicable when an individual "has a firearm on his person," *ibid.* (Rep. Meskill); an instance in which a legislator speaks of "a criminal who takes a gun in his hand," *id.* at 22239 (Rep. Pucinski); and a reference in the Senate

Report to a "gun carried in a pocket." S. Rep. No. 98–225, p. 314, n. 10 (1983) . . . . But in these instances no one purports to define the scope of the term "carries": and the examples of guns carried on the person are not used to illustrate the reach of the term "carries" but to illustrate, or to criticize, a different aspect of the statute. . . .

C

We are not convinced by petitioners' remaining arguments to the contrary. First, they say that our definition of "carry" makes it the equivalent of "transport." Yet, Congress elsewhere in related statutes used the word "transport" deliberately to signify a different, and broader, statutory coverage. The immediately preceding statutory subsection, for example, imposes a different set of penalties on one who, with an intent to commit a crime, "ships, transports, or receives a firearm" in interstate commerce. 18 U.S.C. § 924(b). Moreover, § 926A specifically "entitle[s]" a person "not otherwise prohibited . . . from transporting, shipping, or receiving a firearm" to "transport a firearm . . . from any place where he may lawfully possess and carry" it to "any other place" where he may do so. Why, petitioners ask, would Congress have used the word "transport," or used both "carry" and "transport" in the same provision, if it had intended to obliterate the distinction between the two?

The short answer is that our definition does not equate "carry" and "transport." "Carry" implies personal agency and some degree of possession, whereas "transport" does not have such a limited connotation and, in addition, implies the movement of goods in bulk over great distances. See Webster's Third New International Dictionary at 343 (noting that "carry" means "moving to a location some distance away while supporting or maintaining off the ground" and "is a natural word to use in ref. to cargoes and loads on trucks, wagons, planes, ships, or even beasts of burden," while "transport refers to carriage in bulk or number over an appreciable distance and, typically, by a customary or usual carrier agency") . . . . "[T]ransport" is a broader category that includes "carry" but also encompasses other activity.

. . . .

As we interpret the statutory scheme, it makes sense. Congress has imposed a variable penalty with no mandatory minimum sentence upon a person who "transports" (or "ships" or "receives") a firearm knowing it will be used to commit any "offense punishable by imprisonment for [more than] . . . one year," § 924(b), and it has imposed a 5-year mandatory minimum sentence upon one who "carries" a firearm "during and in relation to" a "drug trafficking crime," § 924(c). The first subsection imposes a less strict sentencing regime upon one who, say, ships firearms by mail for use in a crime elsewhere; the latter subsection imposes a mandatory sentence upon one who, say, brings a weapon with him (on his person or in his car) to the site of a drug sale.

Second, petitioners point out that, in *Bailey v. United States*, 516 U.S. 137 (1995), we considered the related phrase "uses . . . a firearm" found in the same statutory provision now before us. See 18 U.S.C. § 924(c)(1) ("uses or carries a firearm"). We construed the term "use" narrowly, limiting its application to the "active employment" of a firearm. *Bailey*, 516 U.S. at 144. Petitioners argue that it would be anomalous to construe broadly the word "carries," its statutory next-door neighbor.

In *Bailey*, however, we limited "use" of a firearm to "active employment" in part because we assumed "that Congress . . . intended each term to have a particular, non-superfluous meaning." *Id.* at 146. A broader interpretation of "use," we said, would have swallowed up the term "carry." *Ibid.* But "carry" as we interpret that word does not swallow up the term "use." "Use" retains the same independent meaning we found for it in *Bailey*, where we provided examples involving the displaying or the bartering of a gun. *Ibid.* "Carry" also retains an independent meaning, for, under Bailey, carrying a gun in a car does not necessarily involve the gun's "active employment." More importantly, having construed "use" narrowly in *Bailey*, we cannot also construe "carry" narrowly without undercutting the statute's basic objective. For the narrow interpretation would remove the act of carrying a gun in a car entirely from the statute's reach, leaving a gap in coverage that we do not believe Congress intended.

Third, petitioners say that our reading of the statute would extend its coverage to passengers on buses, trains, or ships, who have placed a firearm, say, in checked luggage. To extend this statute so far, they argue, is unfair, going well beyond what Congress likely would have thought possible. . . .

In our view, this argument does not take adequate account of other limiting words in the statute—words that make the statute applicable only where a defendant "carries" a gun *both* "during *and* in relation to" a drug crime. § 924(c)(1) (emphasis added). Congress added these words in part to prevent prosecution where guns "played" no part in the crime. See S. Rep. No. 98–225, at 314, n. 10; *cf. United States v. Stewart*, 779 F.2d 538, 539 (CA9 1985) (Kennedy, J.) (observing that " 'in relation to' " was "added to allay explicitly the concern that a person could be prosecuted . . . for committing an entirely unrelated crime while in possession of a firearm"), overruled in part on other grounds, *United States v. Hernandez*, 80 F.3d 1253, 1257 (CA9 1996).

Once one takes account of the words "during" and "in relation to," it no longer seems beyond Congress' likely intent, or otherwise unfair, to interpret the statute as we have done. If one carries a gun in a car "during" and "in relation to" a drug sale, for example, the fact that the gun is carried in the car's trunk or locked glove compartment seems . . . beside the point.

At the same time, the narrow interpretation creates its own anomalies. The statute, for example, defines "firearm" to include a "bomb," "grenade," "rocket having a propellant charge of more than four ounces," or "missile having an explosive or incendiary charge of more than one-quarter ounce," where such device is "explosive," "incendiary," or delivers "poison gas." 18 U.S.C. § 921(a)(4)(A). On petitioners' reading, the "carry" provision would not apply to instances where drug lords, engaged in a major transaction, took with them "firearms" such as these, which most likely could not be carried on the person.

Fourth, petitioners argue that we should construe the word "carry" to [be limited to instances in which the gun is immediately accessible, thereby most likely excluding from coverage a gun carried in a car's trunk or locked glove compartment]. . . . [T]hey point out that several Circuit Courts of Appeals have limited the statute's scope in this way. [Two citations omitted.] That interpretation, however, is difficult to square with the statute's language, for one "carries" a gun in the glove compartment whether or not that glove compartment is locked. Nothing in the statute's history suggests that Congress intended that limitation. . . .

Finally, petitioners and the dissent invoke the "rule of lenity." The simple existence of some statutory ambiguity, however, is not sufficient to warrant application of that rule, for most statutes are ambiguous to some degree. *Cf. Smith*, 508 U.S. at 239 ("The mere possibility of articulating a narrower construction . . . does not by itself make the rule of lenity applicable"). "The rule of lenity applies only if, after seizing everything from which aid can be derived, . . . we can make no more than a guess as to what Congress intended." *United States v. Wells*, 519 U.S. 482, 499 (1997) [internal quotation marks omitted]. To invoke the rule, we must conclude that there is a " 'grievous ambiguity or uncertainty' in the statute." *Staples v. United States*, 511 U.S. 600, 619, n. 17 (1994) (quoting *Chapman v. United States*, 500 U.S. 453, 463 (1991)). Certainly, our decision today is based on much more than a "guess as to what Congress intended," and there is no "grievous ambiguity" here. The problem of statutory interpretation in this case is indeed no different from that in many of the criminal cases that confront us. Yet, this Court has never held that the rule of lenity automatically permits a defendant to win. . . .

■ *JUSTICE GINSBURG, with whom CHIEF JUSTICE REHNQUIST and JUSTICES SCALIA and SOUTER join, dissenting:*

. . . .

It is uncontested that § 924(c)(1) applies when the defendant bears a firearm, *i.e.*, carries the weapon on or about his person "for the purpose of being armed and ready for offensive or defensive action in case of a conflict." Black's Law Dictionary 214 (6th ed. 1990) (defining the phrase "carry arms or weapons") . . . . The Court holds that, in addition, "carries a firearm," in the context of § 924(c)(1), means personally transporting, possessing, or keeping a firearm in a vehicle, anyplace in a vehicle.

Without doubt, "carries" is a word of many meanings, definable to mean or include carting about in a vehicle. But that encompassing definition is not a ubiquitously necessary one. Nor, in my judgment, is it a proper construction of "carries" as the term appears in § 924(c)(1). In line with *Bailey* and the principle of lenity the Court has long followed, I would confine "carries a firearm," for § 924(c)(1) purposes, to the undoubted meaning of that expression in the relevant context. I would read the words to indicate not merely keeping arms on one's premises or in one's vehicle, but bearing them in such manner as to be ready for use as a weapon.

I

A

I note first what is at stake for petitioners. The question before the Court "is not *whether* possession of a gun [on the drug offender's premises or in his car, during and in relation to commission of the offense,] means a longer sentence for a convicted drug dealer. It most certainly does .... Rather, the question concerns *which sentencing statute* governs the precise length of the extra term of punishment"[—]§ 924(c)(1)'s "blunt 'mandatory minimum' " five-year sentence, or the more finely tuned "sentencing guideline statutes, under which extra punishment for drug-related gun possession varies with the seriousness of the drug crime." *United States v. McFadden*, 13 F.3d 463, 466 (CA1 1994) (Breyer, C.J., dissenting). [The Sentencing Guidelines, promulgated by the U.S. Sentencing Commission pursuant to authority delegated by Congress, "provide for a two-level (i.e., a 30% to 40%) sentence enhancement where a 'firearm . . . was possessed' by a drug offender, U.S.S.G. § 2D1.1(b)(1), unless the possession clearly was not 'connected with the [drug] offense.' " *Id.* at 467.]

Accordingly, there would be no "gap," see *ante* at 137, no relevant conduct "ignore[d]," see *ante* at 133, were the Court to reject the Government's broad reading of § 924(c)(1). . . . In Muscarello's case, for example, the . . . Guidelines regime would have added four months to Muscarello's prison time . . . .[1]

---

[1] The Sentencing Guidelines carry out "a major congressional effort to create a fairly sophisticated . . . system that distinguishes among different kinds of criminal behavior and punishes accordingly." *United States v. McFadden*, 13 F.3d at 467–468 (Breyer, C.J., dissenting). A "mandatory minimum" statute deviates from the general regime Congress installed. "Given the importance (to Congress) of the Guidelines system, . . . courts should take care not to interpret [with unnecessary breadth] . . . deviations from the basic congressionally-directed effort to rationalize sentencing." *Id.* at 468.

[*Ed.*: At the time of this case, the Sentencing Guidelines were thought to be binding. For reasons relating to the constitutional right to trial by jury, however, the Supreme Court later held that the Guidelines could not validly operate as Congress had intended. As a means of solving the constitutional problem that the Court had identified, the Court held that "the provision of the federal sentencing statute that makes the Guidelines mandatory . . . must be severed and excised," with the result that judges should treat the Guidelines as advisory rather than obligatory. *See* United States v. Booker, 543 U.S. 220, 245 (2005).]

In sum, drug traffickers will receive significantly longer sentences if they are caught travelling in vehicles in which they have placed firearms. The question that divides the Court concerns the proper reference for enhancement in the cases at hand, the Guidelines or § 924(c)(1).

B

Unlike the Court, I do not think dictionaries, surveys of press reports, or the Bible tell us, dispositively, what "carries" means embedded in § 924(c)(1). On definitions, "carry" in legal formulations could mean, *inter alia*, transport, possess, have in stock, prolong (carry over), be infectious, or wear or bear on one's person.[5] At issue here is not "carries" at large but "carries a firearm." The Court's computer search of newspapers is revealing in this light. Carrying guns in a car showed up as the meaning "perhaps more than one third" of the time. *Ante* at 129. One is left to wonder what meaning showed up some two thirds of the time. Surely a most familiar meaning is, as the Constitution's Second Amendment ("keep and *bear* Arms") (emphasis added) and Black's Law Dictionary . . . indicate: "wear, bear, or carry . . . upon the person or in the clothing or in a pocket, for the purpose . . . of being armed and ready for offensive or defensive action in a case of conflict with another person."

On lessons from literature, a scan of Bartlett's and other quotation collections shows how highly selective the Court's choices are. . . . If "[t]he greatest of writers" have used "carry" to mean convey or transport in a vehicle, so have they used the hydra-headed word to mean, *inter alia*, carry in one's hand, arms, head, heart, or soul, sans vehicle. Consider, among countless examples:

> "[H]e shall gather the lambs with his arm, and carry them in his bosom." The King James Bible, Isaiah 40:11.
>
> "And still they gaz'd, and still the wonder grew,
> That one small head could carry all he knew." O. Goldsmith, *The Deserted Village*, ll. 215–216, in The Poetical Works of Oliver Goldsmith 30 (A. Dobson ed. 1949).
>
> "There's a Legion that never was 'listed,
> That carries no colours or crest." R. Kipling, *The Lost Legion*, st. 1, in Rudyard Kipling's Verse, 1885–1918, p. 222 (1920).
>
> "There is a homely adage which runs, 'Speak softly and carry a big stick; you will go far.' " T. Roosevelt, Speech at Minnesota State Fair, Sept. 2, 1901, in J. Bartlett, Familiar Quotations 575:16 (J. Kaplan ed. 1992).

These and the Court's lexicological sources demonstrate vividly that "carry" is a word commonly used to convey various messages. Such

---

[5] The dictionary to which this Court referred in *Bailey v. United States*, 516 U.S. 137, 145 (1995), contains 32 discrete definitions of "carry," including "[t]o make good or valid," "to bear the aspect of," and even "[t]o bear (a hawk) on the fist." See Webster's New International Dictionary of English Language 412 (2d ed. 1949).

references, given their variety, are not reliable indicators of what Congress meant, in § 924(c)(1), by "carries a firearm."

C

Noting the paradoxical statement, " 'I *use* a gun to protect my house, but I've never had to *use* it,' " the Court in *Bailey*, 516 U.S. at 143, emphasized the importance of context—the statutory context. Just as "uses" was read to mean not simply "possession," but "active employment," so "carries," correspondingly, is properly read to signal the most dangerous cases—the gun at hand, ready for use as a weapon.[7] It is reasonable to comprehend Congress as having provided mandatory minimums for the most life-jeopardizing gun-connection cases (guns in or at the defendant's hand when committing an offense), leaving other, less imminently threatening, situations for the more flexible guidelines regime. As the Ninth Circuit suggested, it is not apparent why possession of a gun in a drug dealer's moving vehicle would be thought more dangerous than gun possession on premises where drugs are sold: "A drug dealer who packs heat is more likely to hurt someone or provoke someone else to violence. A gun in a bag under a tarp in a truck bed [or in a bedroom closet] poses substantially less risk." *United States v. Foster*, 133 F.3d 704, 707 (CA9 1998) (en banc).[9]

For indicators from Congress itself, it is appropriate to consider word usage in other provisions of Title 18's chapter on "Firearms." See *Bailey*, 516 U.S. at 143, 146 (interpreting § 924(c)(1) in light of 18 U.S.C. §§ 922(g), 922(j), 922(k), 922(*o*)(1), 924(d)(1), 930(a), 930(b)). . . . [On the basis of the other provisions that she had in mind, Justice Ginsburg argued that Congress had used forms of the word "transport," rather than "carry," to refer to the conveyance of firearms in one's vehicle.]

Section 925(a)(2)(B), for example, provides that no criminal sanction shall attend "the transportation of [a] firearm or ammunition carried out to enable a person, who lawfully received such firearm or ammunition from the Secretary of the Army, to engage in military training or in competitions." The full text of § 926A . . . is also telling:

> "Notwithstanding any other provision of any law or any rule or regulation of a State or any political subdivision thereof, any person who is not otherwise prohibited by this chapter from transporting, shipping, or receiving a firearm shall be entitled to transport a firearm for any lawful purpose from any place where he may lawfully possess and carry such firearm to any other place where he may lawfully possess and carry such firearm if, during such

---

[7] In my view, the Government would carry its burden by proving a firearm was kept so close to the person as to approximate placement in a pocket or holster, *e.g.*, guns carried at one's side in a briefcase or handbag, or strapped to the saddle of a horse. See *ante* at 130.

[9] The "Firearms" statutes indicate that Congress, unlike the Court, recognizes that a gun in the hand is indeed more dangerous than a gun in the trunk. See, *e.g.*, 18 U.S.C. § 926A (permitting the transportation of firearms in a vehicle, but only if "neither the firearm nor any ammunition being transported is readily accessible or is directly accessible from the passenger compartment of such transporting vehicle").

transportation the firearm is unloaded, and neither the firearm nor any ammunition being transported is readily accessible or is directly accessible from the passenger compartment of such transporting vehicle: Provided, That in the case of a vehicle without a compartment separate from the driver's compartment the firearm or ammunition shall be contained in a locked container other than the glove compartment or console."

In describing when and how a person may travel in a vehicle that contains his firearm without violating the law, §§ 925(a)(2)(B) and 926A use "transport," not "carry" . . . .[10]

Reading "carries" in § 924(c)(1) to mean "on or about [one's] person" is fully compatible with these and other "Firearms" statutes.[11] For example, under § 925(a)(2)(B), one could carry his gun to a car, transport it to the shooting competition, and use it to shoot targets. Under the conditions of § 926A, one could transport her gun in a car, but under no circumstances could the gun be readily accessible while she travels in the car. "[C]ourts normally try to read language in different, but related, statutes, so as best to reconcile those statutes, in light of their purposes and of common sense." *McFadden*, 13 F.3d at 467 (Breyer, C.J., dissenting). So reading the "Firearms" statutes, I would not extend the word "carries" in § 924(c)(1) to mean transports out of hand's reach in a vehicle.[12]

---

[10] The Court asserts that " 'transport' is a broader category that includes 'carry' but encompasses other activity." *Ante* at 135. "Carry," however, is not merely a subset of "transport." A person seated at a desk with a gun in hand or pocket is carrying the gun, but is not transporting it. Yes, the words "carry" and "transport" often can be employed interchangeably, as can the words "carry" and "use." But in *Bailey*, this Court settled on constructions that gave "carry" and "use" independent meanings. See 516 U.S. at 145–146. Without doubt, Congress is alert to the discrete meanings of "transport" and "carry" in the context of vehicles, as the Legislature's placement of each word in § 926A illustrates. The narrower reading of "carry" preserves discrete meanings for the two words, while in the context of vehicles the Court's interpretation of "carry" is altogether synonymous with "transport." Tellingly, when referring to firearms traveling in vehicles, the "Firearms" statutes routinely use a form of "transport"; they never use a form of "carry."

[11] . . . . The Government points to numerous federal statutes that authorize law enforcement officers to "carry firearms" and notes that, in those authorizing provisions, "carry" of course means "both on the person and in a vehicle." Brief for United States 31–32, and n. 18. Quite right. But as viewers of "Sesame Street" will quickly recognize, "one of these things [a statute *authorizing* conduct] is not like the other [a statute *criminalizing* conduct]." The authorizing statutes in question are properly accorded a construction compatible with the clear purpose of the legislation to aid federal law enforcers in the performance of their official duties. It is fundamental, however, that a penal statute is not to be construed generously in the Government's favor. . . .

[12] The Court places undue reliance on Representative Poff's statement that § 924(c)(1) seeks " 'to persuade the man who is tempted to commit a Federal felony to leave his gun at home.' " *Ante* at 132 (quoting 114 Cong. Rec. 22231 (1968)). As the Government argued in its brief to this Court in *Bailey*:

> "In making that statement, Representative Poff was not referring to the 'carries' prong of the original Section 924(c). As originally enacted, the 'carries' prong of the statute prohibited only the 'unlawful' carrying of a firearm while committing an offense. The statute would thus not have applied to an individual who, for instance, had a permit for carrying a gun and carried it with him when committing an offense, and it would have had no force in 'persuading' such an individual 'to leave his gun at home.' Instead,

II

Section 924(c)(1), as the foregoing discussion details, is not decisively clear one way or another. The sharp division in the Court on the proper reading of the measure confirms, "[a]t the very least, . . . that the issue is subject to some doubt. Under these circumstances, we adhere to the familiar rule that, 'where there is ambiguity in a criminal statute, doubts are resolved in favor of the defendant.' " *Adamo Wrecking Co. v. United States*, 434 U.S. 275, 284–285 (1978) (citation omitted); see *United States v. Granderson*, 511 U.S. 39, 54 (1994) ("[W]here text, structure, and history fail to establish that the Government's position is unambiguously correct—we apply the rule of lenity and resolve the ambiguity in [the defendant's] favor."). "Carry" bears many meanings, as the Court and the "Firearms" statutes demonstrate. The narrower "on or about [one's] person" interpretation is hardly implausible nor at odds with an accepted meaning of "carries a firearm."

Overlooking that there will be an enhanced sentence for the gun-possessing drug dealer in any event, the Court asks rhetorically: "How persuasive is a punishment that is without effect until a drug dealer who has brought his gun to a sale (indeed has it available for use) actually takes it from the trunk (or unlocks the glove compartment) of his car?" . . . . [T]he Court's inquiry pays scant attention to a core reason for the rule of lenity: "[B]ecause of the seriousness of criminal penalties, and because criminal punishment usually represents the moral condemnation of the community, legislatures and not courts should define criminal activity. This policy embodies 'the instinctive distaste against men languishing in prison unless the lawmaker has clearly said they should.' " *United States v. Bass*, 404 U.S. 336, 348 (1971) (quoting H. Friendly, Mr. Justice Frankfurter and the Reading of Statutes, in Benchmarks 196, 209 (1967)).

* * *

The narrower "on or about [one's] person" construction of "carries a firearm" is consistent with the Court's construction of "uses" in *Bailey* to entail an immediacy element. It respects the Guidelines system by resisting overbroad readings of statutes that deviate from that system. See *McFadden*, 13 F.3d at 468 (Breyer, C.J., dissenting). It fits plausibly with other provisions of the "Firearms" chapter, and it adheres to the principle that, given two readings of a penal provision, both consistent with the statutory text, we do not choose the harsher construction. The Court, in my view, should leave it to Congress to speak " 'in language that is clear and definite' " if the Legislature wishes to impose the sterner penalty. *Bass*, 404 U.S. at 347. . . .

Representative Poff was referring to the 'uses' prong of the original Section 924(c)." Brief for United States in *Bailey v. United States*, O.T. 1995, Nos. 94–7448 and 94–7492, p. 28.

Representative Poff's next sentence confirms that he was speaking of "uses," not "carries": "Any person should understand that if he *uses* his gun and is caught and convicted, he is going to jail." 114 Cong. Rec. at 22231 (emphasis added).

NOTES AND QUESTIONS

1. At the outset of his opinion, Justice Breyer talked about what he called the "primary meaning" of the word "carry." To identify the "primary meaning," he looked at various dictionaries. Embarrassingly, though, he assumed that all dictionaries sequence their definitions in the same way, and that they all start with the meaning that their editors believe to be the most common in current usage. Thus, he emphasized that the sense of the word "carry" that he adopted is the very *first* definition of the word in the Oxford English Dictionary, whereas the sense of the word that seemed most helpful to the dissent is only the *twenty-sixth* definition.

In fact, within each group of senses, the editors of the Oxford English Dictionary sequence their definitions in chronological order, so that the first definition reflects the *oldest* known sense of the word—not necessarily the sense that is most common today. *See* 1 OXFORD ENGLISH DICTIONARY xxix (2d ed. 1989) ("[T]hat sense is placed first which was actually the earliest in the language: the others follow in the order in which they appear to have arisen."). The same is true of Webster's Third New International Dictionary, which Justice Breyer also cited. *See* WEBSTER'S THIRD NEW INTERNATIONAL DICTIONARY OF THE ENGLISH LANGUAGE UNABRIDGED 17a (1986) ("The order of senses is historical: the one known to have been first used in English is entered first."). It is no surprise, then, that the etymology recited by Justice Breyer (tracing the word "carry" to the Latin word for "cart") matches the first definition in the O.E.D. But when we are interpreting a modern federal statute—rather than, say, *Beowulf*—we should not put too much emphasis on the fact that a definition comes first in the O.E.D. *See* Caleb Nelson, *Originalism and Interpretive Conventions*, 70 U. CHI. L. REV. 519, 519 & n.1 (2003) (noting Justice Breyer's mistake in *Muscarello*); Stephen C. Mouritsen, Note, *The Dictionary is Not a Fortress: Definitional Fallacies and a Corpus-Based Approach to Plain Meaning*, 2010 BYU L. REV. 1915, 1931–35 (discussing the mistake).

The other dictionary that Justice Breyer quoted, the Random House Dictionary of the English Language, does use the order of its definitions to convey a sense of the frequency of current use. *See* THE RANDOM HOUSE DICTIONARY OF THE ENGLISH LANGUAGE UNABRIDGED xxxii (2d ed. 1987) ("In each part of speech group, the most frequently encountered meanings generally come before less common ones."). But the first definition in the Random House dictionary is not particularly helpful to Justice Breyer's argument. Unlike the first definitions in the O.E.D. and Webster's, which indicate that one is "carrying" something if one conveys it by cart or wagon, the first definition in the Random House dictionary does not specifically address that issue. It says only that to carry something is "to take or support [it] from one place to another; convey; transport." This definition indicates that if I drive along with a gun in the trunk of my car, the car can be said to be carrying the gun as well as me. But it does not necessarily follow that *I* am carrying the gun throughout my drive. The Random House dictionary's definition seems too general to answer that question. And the examples that the Random House dictionary offers for its first definition of "carry"—"He carried her for a mile in his arms" and "This elevator cannot carry more than ten people"—are compatible with the dissent's position.

2. Aside from invoking dictionaries, Justice Breyer also conducted a species of corpus analysis, "searching computerized newspaper databases . . . for sentences in which the words 'carry,' 'vehicle,' and 'weapon' (or variations thereof) all appear." *Muscarello*, 524 U.S. at 129. On the basis of random sampling, he reported that many of those sentences ("perhaps more than one third") were referring to "the carrying of guns in a car"—a fact that he took to support his interpretation of the statute. *Id.*

Of course, by limiting the universe to sentences that included the word "vehicle," Justice Breyer stacked the deck in favor of his conclusion. In his pathbreaking student note about corpus analysis, *see supra* p. 114, Stephen Mouritsen argued that less skewed analysis of uses of the verb "carry" in the Corpus of Contemporary American English strongly favored the dissenters' position. *See* Mouritsen, *supra*, 2010 BYU L. REV. at 1947, 1954–66. More recently, Mouritsen and Justice Thomas R. Lee reached a similar conclusion using the "News on the Web" corpus, which has billions of words from news articles appearing on the Internet from 2010 on. *See* Thomas R. Lee & Stephen C. Mouritsen, *Judging Ordinary Meaning*, 127 YALE L.J. 788, 833–34, 845–48 (2018) (studying 271 lines "in which *carry* co-occurred with *firearm(s), gun(s), pistol(s), handgun(s)*, and *rifle(s)*," and finding that "104 instances indicated a sense of *carries a firearm on one's person*, while only five instances suggested a *carry a firearm in a car* sense").

Still, data about the usage of words in a corpus of news articles might reflect not only linguistic facts (about what words mean in ordinary usage) but also *nonlinguistic* facts (about the frequency with which different things occur in the real world and the newsworthiness of those events). Take the word "carries" in connection with firearms. Even if someone who has a gun in the glove compartment or trunk of his car could be described as "carrying" the gun, reporters might be more likely to write an article about an event in which someone carried a gun in his hand. If so, then the fact that a corpus of news articles contains more usages of the word "carries" in reference to people who have guns in their hands than in reference to people who simply have guns in their cars might tell us more about what is newsworthy than about the ordinary meaning of the word "carries."

That is not to say that corpus analysis has no value for statutory interpreters. To the contrary, big-data tools surely can provide finer-grained information about actual usage than conventional dictionaries can. Still, random judges might not be very sophisticated users of corpora, and they might not draw the correct inferences from any giving sampling of usages in a corpus. Of course, judges also are not very sophisticated users of dictionaries, and unsophisticated corpus analysis will not necessarily produce worse results than unsophisticated use of dictionaries. But might the typical judge's own knowledge of English be more nuanced and more powerful than how the typical judge would use *either* an on-line corpus *or* a traditional dictionary?

3. How would your own sense of ordinary usage have guided you in *Muscarello*? When someone drives around town with a gun in the trunk of his car, would you say that he is "carrying" the gun? Or would that mean that the driver has the gun on his own person?

If you are inclined to say that the driver *is* "carrying" the gun, what if he has some passengers in his car too? Are they *all* "carrying" the gun that is in the trunk? Or is only the driver carrying the gun, because he is the one who is causing the car to move? Does it matter who put the gun in the trunk, thereby causing the car to carry it when the car moved? Does it matter who knows that the gun is in the trunk? If one of the passengers has a gun in his pocket, is the driver "carrying" that gun too?

Along the same lines, imagine that you buy groceries and drive them back to your apartment in your car. Later, someone who saw you at the store asks how you managed to get all those groceries back to your apartment. You probably would not say, "I carried them."[8] Perhaps you would say, "I carried them in my car"—but without the additional phrase "in my car," the statement "I carried them" would suggest lugging the groceries home without the aid of a vehicle. (In ordinary usage, then, the statement "I carried the groceries in my car" is not simply a subset of the statement "I carried the groceries.")

At least as applied to groceries, experts in corpus analysis have tended to confirm this point. Using the Corpus of Contemporary American English, Neal Goldfarb found reason to believe that "phrases following the pattern *[human] carry [object]* are not used to express the meaning HUMAN CARRY OBJECT IN VEHICLE unless the IN VEHICLE part is explicitly encoded or otherwise supported by something in the context." Neal Goldfarb, *A Lawyer's Introduction to Meaning in the Framework of Corpus Linguistics*, 2017 BYU L. REV. 1359, 1405. But while this conclusion held true for most objects, Goldfarb expressed more uncertainty about how "carry" is used in conjunction with firearms. In his view, a significant number of lines that fit the pattern HUMAN CARRY FIREARM did not rule out the idea of carriage by vehicle. *See id.* at 1405, 1411–12.

4. Although Justice Breyer discussed the word "carries" at length, his conclusion may have been motivated by what he saw as "the statute's basic purpose." *Muscarello*, 524 U.S. at 132. Recall that § 924(c), as it stood at the time of *Muscarello*, imposed special criminal penalties on anyone who "uses or carries a firearm" during and in relation to a federal

[8] I owe this example to John Harrison.

drug-trafficking offense. Quoting "the provision's chief legislative sponsor," Justice Breyer indicated that the purpose of § 924(c) was " 'to persuade the man who is tempted to commit a Federal felony to leave his gun at home.' " *Id.* (quoting 114 CONG. REC. 22231 (1968) (remarks of Rep. Poff)).

As Justice Ginsburg noted in footnote 12 of her dissent, this statement might have related more to the word "uses" than to the word "carries." But in *Bailey v. United States*, 516 U.S. 137 (1995), the Supreme Court interpreted the word "uses" relatively narrowly, so that it covered only "active employment." *Id.* at 144. According to *Bailey*, a person who brought a gun to the scene of a drug-trafficking crime (to be available if needed), but who kept the gun hidden and did not end up disclosing it or even mentioning it, had not "us[ed]" the gun in the sense that the statute covered. *See id.* at 149.

In *Muscarello*, Justice Breyer argued that "having construed 'use' narrowly in *Bailey*, we cannot also construe 'carry' narrowly without undercutting the statute's basic objective." *Muscarello*, 524 U.S. at 136. Justice Breyer explained that if the Court read *both* "uses" *and* "carries" narrowly, so that the statute did not reach people who put guns in their cars in order to have weapons available at a drug buy if needed, then the statute would not serve the purpose that its sponsor had identified; the statute would not cause people to leave their guns at home. *See id.* at 136–37.

Given his focus on the overall purpose of the statute, Justice Breyer might not have cared how much of the work is done by "carries" as opposed to "uses." Because *Bailey* had read "uses" narrowly, though, he thought that "carries" needed to pick up the slack in order to avoid "a gap in coverage that we do not believe Congress intended." *Id.* at 137. If you would otherwise consider Justice Breyer's interpretation of "carries" implausibly broad, does this argument change your mind? Or, given the doctrine of *stare decisis*, should the Court simply have accepted *Bailey*'s narrow interpretation of "uses" and not looked for an offsetting interpretation of "carries"? Does the rule of lenity bear on these questions?

If Justice Breyer's main point was that the statute covers people who bring guns to drug buys in order to have weapons available if needed, and if Justice Breyer did not really care whether the work is done by the word "uses" or the word "carries," can linguistic analysis of the word "carries" defeat his point? But if Justice Breyer was correct about the statute's basic purpose, why did Congress use the phrase "uses or carries" rather than, say, "possesses"?[9]

---

[9] Less than six months after *Muscarello*, Congress amended § 924(c). *See* Act of Nov. 13, 1998, Pub. L. 105–386, 112 Stat. 3469. The current version of the statute establishes a mandatory sentence of at least five years in prison not only for anyone who "uses or carries a firearm" during and in relation to a federal drug-trafficking crime but also for anyone "who, in furtherance of any such crime, possesses a firearm." The minimum sentence rises to seven years

NOTE ON "HYBRID CIVIL/CRIMINAL STATUTE[S]"

It is not unusual for Congress to enact "a hybrid civil/criminal statute," which not only authorizes civil enforcement of the duties that it creates but also criminalizes certain violations of the same duties. *See* Epstein v. Epstein, 966 F. Supp. 260, 261 (S.D.N.Y. 1997) (discussing the Racketeer Influenced and Corrupt Organizations Act); *see also* Margaret V. Sachs, *Harmonizing Civil and Criminal Enforcement of Federal Regulatory Statutes: The Case of the Securities Exchange Act of 1934*, 2001 U. ILL. L. REV. 1025, 1026–27 (noting that "[m]any federal regulatory statutes are hybrid statutes" in this sense). As described in a student note by Jonathan Marx, such a statute might take the following form: "Section One requires or prohibits certain conduct, Section Two creates a private cause of action for damages caused by violations of Section One, and Section Three makes willful or knowing violation of Section One a crime." Jonathan Marx, Note, *How to Construe a Hybrid Statute*, 93 VA. L. REV. 235, 235 (2007).

When confronting a statute of this sort, how should courts resolve indeterminacies in Section One? If the statute did not contain Section Two (so that the statute was purely penal), a court presumably would apply the rule of lenity and construe Section One narrowly. On the other hand, if the statute did not contain Section Three (so that the statute was purely compensatory), the rule of lenity would not apply; to the extent that the scope of Section One remained unclear after the court had applied other interpretive techniques, the court would not feel obliged to adopt the narrowest possible reading. This dichotomy presents courts with a difficult question: given that the statute contains *both* Section Two *and* Section Three, how should the rule of lenity affect the courts' understanding of Section One?

Conceivably, courts might try to toggle between two different readings of Section One; to the extent that Section One is ambiguous, perhaps courts could read it to mean something different (and narrower) in criminal cases brought under Section Three than in civil cases brought under Section Two. But that approach would be unconventional, and the Supreme Court has appeared to reject it. *See, e.g.*, Leocal v. Ashcroft, 543 U.S. 1, 11 n.8 (2004) ("[W]e must interpret the statute consistently, whether we encounter its application in a criminal or noncriminal context . . . ."); *see also* Sessions v. Dimaya, 138 S. Ct. 1204, 1217 (2018) (plurality opinion of Kagan, J.) (quoting *Leocal* and treating its statement as obviously correct); Clark v. Martinez, 543 U.S. 371, 380 (2005) (citing additional cases). *Compare* Sachs, *supra*, 2001 U. ILL. L. REV. at 1029–33 (agreeing that "prohibitions in hybrid statutes should be limited to one interpretation apiece"), *and* Marx, *supra*, 93 VA. L. REV. at 266–76 (similarly opposing "dual construction" of a single provision), *with* Justin

"if the firearm is brandished" and to ten years "if the firearm is discharged." 18 U.S.C. § 924(c)(1)(A).

Levine, Note, *A Clash of Canons: Lenity,* Chevron, *and the One-Statute, One-Interpretation Rule*, 107 GEO. L.J. 1423, 1438–40 (2019) (arguing that dual construction should not be off limits).

Assuming that Section One has the same meaning in suits brought under Section Two as in prosecutions brought under Section Three, we must still consider the relevance of the rule of lenity in identifying what that meaning is. There are at least three possibilities:

(1) Courts should apply the rule of lenity to Section One in exactly the same way that they would if the statute were purely penal. On this view, courts would use the rule of lenity to resolve all residual indeterminacy in any statutory provision (such as Section One) that is subject to penal enforcement, even if the provision is also subject to nonpenal enforcement.

(2) Courts should not apply the rule of lenity to Section One at all. On this view, the rule of lenity would affect the interpretation of Section Three, but not Section One.

(3) Courts should decide whether to apply the rule of lenity to Section One (and how much force to give it) on the basis of considerations specific to the particular hybrid statute in question.

Marx advocated a version of the third approach. For some provisions in some hybrid statutes, he suggested, the nonpenal forms of enforcement dominate the penal forms of enforcement so completely that the rule of lenity is entirely inapplicable. For instance, consider provisions in the Bankruptcy Code that are common both to bankruptcy crimes and to ordinary bankruptcy filings. Marx suggested that the rule of lenity should have no effect on judicial interpretations of these provisions, because the number of ordinary bankruptcy proceedings exceeds the number of bankruptcy prosecutions by many orders of magnitude. *See* Marx, *supra*, 93 VA. L. REV. at 282 n.138. Along the same lines, he posited that "many hybrid statutes arise when Congress is passing civil legislation and adds criminal penalties as an afterthought, thinking that doing so will create additional deterrence, but most likely not realizing that these criminal penalties may result in narrowing civil constructions . . . ." *Id.* at 282. According to Marx, a court attempting to resolve indeterminacy in such statutes might sensibly conclude that "the 'push' of the penal applications (cutting in favor of narrow construction) is so outweighed by the 'pull' of remedial applications (cutting in favor of broader construction) that, for practical purposes, [the court] can interpret the statute as if it were purely civil." *Id.* at 281.

By contrast, the balance might be exactly the opposite for provisions in some other hybrid statutes: penal forms of enforcement might dominate nonpenal forms of enforcement so completely as to make the rule of lenity applicable in full force. In Marx's words, "if a court knows that a hybrid statute is overwhelmingly enforced criminally, it might decide that lenity is an appropriate rule for construing all of the statute's ambiguities." *Id.* at 282.

Of course, many statutory provisions that are subject to both penal and nonpenal forms of enforcement lie somewhere in between these two extremes. Marx suggested that when courts confront indeterminacies in such provisions, they should give the rule of lenity *some* weight, but probably not the *full* weight that the rule receives with respect to purely penal provisions. Marx elaborated as follows:

> "[W]hen a hybrid statute is sufficiently ambiguous that a court would apply lenity were the statute purely criminal, and the court concludes (based on the 'pull' of any other relevant interpretive rules) that the statute should be read more broadly in the remedial context than lenity would permit, the presumption [that the applicable provision means the same thing whether it is being enforced criminally or civilly] should almost always lead [the court] to apply a broader reading in the penal context than lenity would permit. However, the court should not necessarily construe the statute as broadly as it would if the only interpretive rules were those favoring broad construction. The presence of penal applications militates against that."

Id. at 281. (As this analysis suggests, Marx argued that when courts construe language in hybrid statutes, they should not focus on the happenstance of whether the particular case before them involves a penal or nonpenal application of that language. Instead, they should "remain mindful" of the fact that the relevant statutory language is susceptible to both sorts of applications, and they should construe it accordingly.)

Is the statute-by-statute, sliding-scale approach advocated by Marx consistent with the idea behind having canons of construction in the first place? Or should the rule be less fine-grained?

How, exactly, would Marx's sliding-scale approach work in practice? Even when interpreting purely penal statutes, many judges apply the rule of lenity only at the end of the interpretive process, and only if their normal interpretive tools have left them pretty much in equipoise between two possible readings. When these judges confront a "hybrid" statute instead, is there any way for them to give the rule of lenity *less* weight while still giving it *some* weight?

D. STATUTES AND THE CONSTITUTION

The rule of lenity is said to be inspired by values that are also found in the Constitution, including ideas about the proper roles of legislatures and courts and the need for people to have "fair warning" of the content of penal laws. Still, the connection between the rule of lenity and the Constitution is loose, and the rule of lenity probably would exist even if the Constitution did not. This section of the book considers several canons of interpretation that focus more specifically on the interaction between statutes and the Constitution.

By and large, the cases covered in this section address the interaction between *federal* statutes and the *federal* Constitution. Of course, the federal Constitution also limits what state statutes can validly do, and each state's statutes are subject to limitations imposed by the state constitution too.[10] But this section is concerned with principles of statutory interpretation, not with constitutional limitations per se, and the canons that govern the interpretation of state statutes can vary from state to state. That does not mean that state courts can apply state statutes in violation of the federal Constitution; both the federal Constitution and "the Laws of the United States which shall be made in Pursuance thereof" are part of "the supreme Law of the Land," and "the Judges in every State shall be bound thereby, any Thing in the Constitution or Laws of any State to the Contrary notwithstanding." U.S. CONST. art. VI, cl. 2. Before courts can decide whether a state statute is constitutional, though, they have to decide what the statute means—and where state statutes are concerned, that is regarded as a question of state law. As a matter of state law, most states do have canons advising courts to interpret state statutes in light of constitutional limitations on the state legislature's powers, and in many states those canons resemble the principles that this section of the book discusses with respect to federal statutes. Rather than canvass each state's canons about how to interpret state statutes, though, this section focuses on the interpretation of *federal* statutes (which is regarded as a matter of federal law, as to which canons embraced by the U.S. Supreme Court provide authoritative guidance).

Broadly speaking, the federal Constitution limits the federal government's legislative powers in two different ways. First, the Constitution establishes the principle of enumerated powers: Congress has only the powers that the Constitution gives it. *See* U.S. CONST. art. I, § 1 ("All legislative powers *herein granted* shall be vested in a Congress of the United States . . . ." (emphasis added)); *see also, e.g., id.* § 8 (listing various powers of Congress, such as the power "[t]o regulate Commerce with foreign Nations, and among the several States, and with the Indian tribes"). Second, provisions like the First Amendment restrict how the federal government can use even its enumerated powers.[11]

If you have taken a course on Constitutional Law, you have already studied an important respect in which constitutional limitations on legislative power can come up in court. Whenever courts are deciding a case within their jurisdiction, they need to do so according to the

[10] State constitutions do not limit federal statutes. Under the American system of federalism, the people of a single state cannot restrict the powers of the nation as a whole.

[11] Insofar as the federal Constitution limits the powers of *state* governments, those limitations take only the second form. State governments do not get their powers from the federal Constitution, so the federal Constitution does not establish a principle of enumerated powers as to them.

applicable law. Often, some of the applicable rules of decision will come from statutes. But statutes rank beneath the federal Constitution in the hierarchy of American law—meaning that insofar as statutes conflict with the Constitution, the Constitution wins. *See* Marbury v. Madison, 5 U.S. (1 Cranch) 137, 177 (1803) (describing the Constitution as "a superior, paramount law"). More precisely, when courts are deciding cases within their jurisdiction, courts are not supposed to apply statutory provisions to the extent that those provisions are unconstitutional (assuming that the courts can detect the constitutional problem and that the parties have not forfeited the relevant arguments). *See id.* at 177–78. That is the idea of "judicial review": even if a statute is crystal clear, courts will not apply it to the extent that it is unconstitutional.

The idea of judicial review is not itself a matter of statutory interpretation. But it gives rise to various questions that *are* matters of statutory interpretation. This section of the book considers several of those questions.

The section begins with the topic of "separability" (also known as "severability").[12] Suppose that a statute is unconstitutional in some of its aspects or applications. We know that courts will not apply the statute to the extent that it is unconstitutional. But does the statute provide rules of decision for cases in which its application would be constitutional? As we shall see, that depends on whether and to what extent the constitutional aspects or applications of the statute are "separable" from the unconstitutional aspects or applications of the statute. Under current doctrine, separability is largely a question of statutory interpretation, and modern courts have articulated a canon that addresses it: by and large, there is a presumption in favor of separability.

Questions of separability come into play if a statute is partially unconstitutional. Where possible, though, the Supreme Court encourages courts to interpret federal statutes so as to steer clear of constitutional difficulties in the first place. That is another important canon. We will cover both its traditional form (which favored interpretations that preserve a statute's constitutionality over interpretations that would make the statute unconstitutional) and its more aggressive modern form (which encourages courts to interpret statutes so as to avoid even serious *questions* about whether the statutes are unconstitutional).

---

[12] In using the term "separability," I am following in distinguished footsteps. *See, e.g.*, HENRY M. HART, JR. & HERBERT WECHSLER, THE FEDERAL COURTS AND THE FEDERAL SYSTEM 177–80 (1953). Admittedly, modern courts are more apt to use the term "severability," and you might want to follow their locution when writing briefs. But when you are trying to understand the relevant principles, I think that "separability" is a more helpful term. *Cf.* John Copeland Nagle, *Severability*, 72 N.C. L. REV. 203, 228–29 (1993) (criticizing "the misleading metaphor of 'severance' " for conjuring up images of a court changing the content of a statute by "physically remov[ing]" an unconstitutional provision).

1. SEPARABILITY

Courts obviously should not apply a statute to the extent that it is unconstitutional (assuming that litigants point out the constitutional problem). The basic question of separability concerns the legal effect of *other* aspects or applications of the statute. If the constitutional problem with the statute is limited to a certain provision or to certain applications of a provision, is the statute still operative in other respects? Or should courts disregard not only the aspects or applications of the statute that are unconstitutional, but also some or all of the rest of the statute, on the theory that those other aspects or applications of the statute are "inseparable" from the unconstitutional aspects or applications?

This question can arise in at least two different situations. First, a statute might contain one provision (or one set of words within a provision) that is unconstitutional in all of its applications, but other provisions that are constitutional. For instance, perhaps Section 1 of the statute purports to establish a legal rule that the legislature has no power to establish for any cases, but Section 2 establishes a different legal rule that the legislature does have the power to establish. *See* Robert L. Stern, *Separability and Separability Clauses in the Supreme Court*, 51 HARV. L. REV. 76, 79 (1937) (describing this situation as "the problem of separable language"). Second, a single provision (or set of words within a provision) might have some applications that are unconstitutional, but other applications that are constitutional. For instance, perhaps Section 3 of the statute is unconstitutional as applied to some fact patterns but constitutional as applied to others. *See id.* (describing this situation as "the problem of separable applications").

In important respects, the problem of separable applications is more complex than the problem of separable language. *See id.* at 106; *see also* Richard H. Fallon, Jr., *Facial Challenges, Saving Constructions, and Statutory Severability*, 99 TEX. L. REV. 215, 259 (2020) ("Successfully theorizing the process of severing invalid from valid statutory applications poses conceptual mysteries as well as practical challenges.").[13] Without always recognizing those complexities, though,

---

[13] The extra complexity arises because some constitutional limitations on legislative power (and some of the doctrinal tests that modern courts have articulated to implement such limitations) operate at the level of rules rather than at the level of particular applications of a rule. *See* Fallon, *supra*, 99 TEX. L. REV. at 218 (pointing, for example, to tiers of scrutiny that evaluate the fit between a rule and legitimate governmental interests); *see also* John Harrison, *Power, Duty, and Facial Invalidity*, 16 U. PA. J. CONST'L L. 501, 505–06 (2013) (contrasting constitutional provisions that generate "[r]ule-level invalidity" with provisions that simply prevent certain applications of a rule). In Professor Fallon's telling, when a court concludes that the rule purportedly established by a statutory provision is unconstitutional, the court might proceed to consider whether the provision can be understood to consist of multiple "subrules" that the provision does not explicitly identify as such but that are included in the rule that the provision states. If some of those subrules are constitutional and are separable from the rest of the provision, courts often can apply them—generating what look like separable applications of the rule that the provision explicitly states. *See* Fallon, *supra*, 99 TEX. L. REV. at 259–61.

If Professor Fallon is correct, cases of this sort might best be described as raising a third type of separability problem. They do not involve the separability of two discrete provisions ("the problem of separable language"), but they also do not really involve the separability of valid

modern courts tend to recite the same basic test for separability in both contexts. *See* John Copeland Nagle, *Severability*, 72 N.C. L. REV. 203, 208 n.24 (1993).

Before I describe the evolution of that test, it is worth thinking about the *nature* of separability. In recent years, the Supreme Court has sometimes spoken as if separability is a branch of the law of remedies. *See* John Harrison, *Severability, Remedies, and Constitutional Adjudication*, 83 GEO. WASH. L. REV. 56, 59–80 (2014) (citing examples of this locution, though criticizing it). According to one proponent of this way of thinking, when a litigant challenges the constitutionality of a statute and a court agrees that the statute is partially unconstitutional, the court has to decide "the scope of the relief": should the court "invalidate the statute as a whole," or should the court instead "revise the statute by eliminating the offending clause or application"? David H. Gans, *Severability as Judicial Lawmaking*, 76 GEO. WASH. L. REV. 639, 643 (2008).

If one thinks that judicial determinations of separability entail revising or "rewriting" a statute, *id.*, one might wonder where courts get that power. Indeed, this line of thinking led Tom Campbell (a law professor turned Member of Congress turned law-school dean) to "call for the complete abolition of the severability doctrine." Tom Campbell, *Severability of Statutes*, 62 HASTINGS L.J. 1495, 1497 (2011). In Dean Campbell's view, if a court concludes that one aspect or application of a

---

applications of a rule from invalid applications of the same rule (the image suggested by "the problem of separable applications"). In the situations that Professor Fallon discusses, the rule purportedly stated by a statute is invalid on its face, because it conflicts with a constitutional limitation that operates at the level of rules. To salvage any applications of the rule, the court must first find an appropriate subrule that can properly be attributed to the statute, and then decide whether that subrule is separable from the broader rule that the statute actually states.

Courts cannot always do that. Indeed, the Constitution itself has been understood to impose some limits on the courts' ability to find and enforce valid subrules within a broader statutory provision. A classic example is First Amendment "overbreadth" doctrine: if Congress were to enact a statute purporting to criminalize all speech, the First Amendment would prevent courts from holding that the statute supplies valid rules of decision for all cases involving speech that Congress can constitutionally criminalize. Overbreadth doctrine is often regarded as a constitutionally inspired principle of inseparability. *See* Henry Paul Monaghan, *Overbreadth*, 1981 SUP. CT. REV. 1, 14–23 (discussing this view). But if Congress had itself broken the overbroad statute into valid and invalid subrules, the First Amendment might not prevent courts from treating the valid subrules as separable from the invalid subrules. The constitutional problem is less about the separability of subrules than about the need for the courts to identify subrules in the first place.

One should not assume that all constitutional doctrines that operate at the level of rules work the same way as First Amendment overbreadth doctrine. In Professor Fallon's words, the relevant principles "are aspects of the particular constitutional tests developed by the Supreme Court to enforce specific constitutional provisions," and First Amendment overbreadth doctrine reflects special concerns about the risk of "chill[ing]" protected speech. *See* Richard H. Fallon, Jr., *As-Applied and Facial Challenges and Third-Party Standing*, 113 HARV. L. REV. 1321, 1351–52 (2000). Still, the modern Supreme Court has said relatively little about constitutional limits on the courts' ability to find valid subrules within statutory provisions that are unconstitutional "on their face" (because they conflict with constitutional doctrines that operate at the level of rules). Because the key questions may involve constitutional law as much as they involve statutory interpretation, and also because I do not know the answers, I will not dwell on them. But it seems likely that different constitutional doctrines intersect with "the problem of separable applications" in different ways.

statute is unconstitutional and therefore unenforceable, but that other aspects or applications of the statute are separable and therefore enforceable, the court is creating a new statute—one that Congress did not enact in the form that the court is enforcing. *See id.* at 1498–99. Because courts cannot "amend" statutes, *id.* at 1499, Dean Campbell argued that courts must treat every statute as an inseparable unit—so that if any single aspect or application of the statute is unconstitutional, the statute would be wholly void. *See id.* at 1496.

This argument, however, rests on a dubious premise. Both the idea that "severability is a remedial doctrine," Gans, *supra*, 76 GEO. WASH. L. REV. at 660, and the idea that it "permits a judicial amendment" of a statute, *id.* at 658, are contrary to conventional understandings. *See* Harrison, *supra*, 83 GEO. WASH. L. REV. at 81–90 (explaining why separability analysis is not part of the law of remedies and does not entail a power to change the law); *cf.* Fallon, *supra*, 99 TEX. L. REV. at 258 ("[R]eferring to severance as a remedy invites confusion.").

To understand this point, you must start by remembering the traditional account of judicial review. In *Marbury v. Madison*, Chief Justice Marshall explained that when litigants bring a case to court and the court is trying to decide it, the court must do so according to the applicable law. As the court is identifying the content of the applicable law, moreover, the court must keep in mind that the Constitution is a higher type of law than statutes. If a statute purports to govern a question that the case presents, but the legislature lacks the constitutional power to provide the answer that the statute purports to supply, then that answer is not actually the applicable rule of decision and the court should not apply it. The court's refusal to apply an unconstitutional rule purportedly supplied by the legislature is what we think of as judicial review, but it is not a matter of the law of "remedies" as lawyers normally use that term. Instead, it is simply an outgrowth of the court's obligation to decide cases according to the applicable legal rules (with due regard for the hierarchy of those rules). *See* Harrison, *supra*, 83 GEO. WASH. L. REV. at 85–86 (discussing *Marbury*).[14]

By the same token, standard separability analysis does not entail "rewriting" statutes. Again, take *Marbury* (and ensuing cases). Section

[14] In many cases, of course, litigants ask courts to do more than simply disregard a statute. For instance, if a government official is threatening to enforce a statute against you, but you think that the statute is unconstitutional, you might be able to initiate a lawsuit for injunctive relief against the official, seeking to enjoin the official from enforcing the statute against you. The availability of such relief *is* a matter of law of remedies. Under conventional understandings, though, the relief will not entail an order erasing the statute from the books or otherwise changing its content. *See* Harrison, *supra*, 83 GEO. WASH. L. REV. at 82 ("Injunctions against enforcement . . . can make statutory provisions virtually inoperative, but they do not purport to make any law actually inoperative the way its repeal would.").

Judicial review, moreover, does not hinge on the availability of any sort of injunctive relief. If the government prosecutes you for violating the statute, you can argue in defense that the statute does not really supply a rule of decision for your case because the rule of decision that the statute purports to supply is unconstitutional. Such arguments are about the content of the applicable law, not about "remedies" in the usual sense.

13 of the Judiciary Act of 1789 said that "[t]he Supreme Court . . . shall have power to issue . . . writs of *mandamus*, in cases warranted by the principles and usages of law, to any courts appointed, or persons holding office, under the authority of the United States." Judiciary Act of 1789, ch. 20, § 13, 1 Stat. 73, 81. To the extent that this provision purported to give the Supreme Court original jurisdiction over William Marbury's suit for mandamus against Secretary of State Madison, the Supreme Court held that it was unconstitutional; according to Chief Justice Marshall's opinion for the Court, the Original Jurisdiction Clause of Article III of the Constitution identifies the only kinds of cases over which the Supreme Court can exercise original jurisdiction, and William Marbury's suit for mandamus against an executive official was not among those cases. But while the Supreme Court could not apply § 13 in *Marbury* itself, the Court could still issue writs of mandamus pursuant to § 13 in cases over which the Court validly had jurisdiction, such as cases in which the Supreme Court was being asked to exercise *appellate* jurisdiction by issuing mandamus against a lower court. *See, e.g.*, Ex parte Crane, 30 U.S. (5 Pet.) 190, 193–94 (1831) (asserting jurisdiction, though ultimately denying the request on the merits). When the Supreme Court applied § 13 in cases where it could constitutionally be applied but not in cases like *Marbury*, the Court was not "rewriting" or "amending" § 13 in the way that a legislature might. Instead, the Court was identifying the legal rules produced by the combination of the statute that Congress had enacted and the Constitution. *See, e.g.*, Nagle, *supra*, 72 N.C. L. REV. at 228–29 (explaining this point); *see also* Harrison, *supra*, 83 GEO. WASH. L. REV. at 84 ("When a court determines that it may lawfully apply a provision of a statute because it is severable from another unconstitutional provision, the court does not revise the statute the way a legislature would, taking a juridical act that purports to eliminate one part while retaining another part."); Lindenbaum v. Realgy, LLC, 13 F.4th 524, 528 (6th Cir. 2021) ("Courts do not change statutes.").[15]

[15] The complexity mentioned in footnote 13 above might seem to change this analysis, but in my view it does not. As Professor Fallon notes, when a statutory provision conflicts with a constitutional doctrine that operates at the level of rules, and when courts think about whether they can properly find any valid subrules within the provision, courts sometimes must exercise "judicial judgment and even creativity." *See* Fallon, *supra*, 99 TEX. L. REV. at 236 (observing that in this situation, "a court—even though prescribing no applications that Congress had not previously enacted—must nevertheless articulate a line of severance that effectively formulates a rule of law, not previously articulated by Congress, that itself can survive applicable tests of constitutional validity"). But while courts sometimes must make nonobvious judgments about how to articulate the relevant subrules, this process should remain grounded in the combination of the statute that Congress enacted and the Constitution. Indeed, if the combination of the statute and the Constitution provides too little guidance about the content of the subrules that the statute contains, then the courts presumably should not undertake this process. *Cf.* United States v. Davis, 139 S. Ct. 2319, 2323 (2019) ("When Congress passes a vague law, the role of courts under our Constitution is not to fashion a new, clearer law to take its place, but to treat the law as a nullity and invite Congress to try again."). Thus, Professor Fallon agrees that "[w]hen the Supreme Court severs either invalid statutory applications or invalid statutory provisions, complaints that the Court has 'rewritten' the statute are typically misplaced." Fallon, *supra*, 99 TEX. L. REV. at 255.

As a historical matter, scholars agree that the courts' approach to separability has gone through different phases. Until the mid-nineteenth century, courts may not even have perceived the possibility of inseparability. At any rate, without analyzing that possibility, courts typically acted as if the statutes that they encountered were fully separable. *See* Nagle, *supra,* 72 N.C. L. REV. at 212 (observing that in the first half of the nineteenth century, "the severability of statutory provisions was usually assumed"); Stern, *supra,* 51 HARV. L. REV. at 79 ("The problem of separability, as we know it today, was not recognized in the first cases in which the Supreme Court held parts of statutes unconstitutional. In the few opinions before 1870 in which any mention was made of the fact that only some of the provisions of a statute were being held invalid, the Court assumed as obvious that 'full effect will be given to such as are not repugnant to the Constitution.' " (quoting Bank of Hamilton v. Dudley, 27 U.S. (2 Pet.) 492, 526 (1829))); *see also* Kevin C. Walsh, *Partial Unconstitutionality,* 85 N.Y.U. L. REV. 738, 768–69 (2010) (describing the early Supreme Court as taking a "displacement-based approach," under which a statutory rule was displaced only to the extent that it was unconstitutional).

Had legislatures so desired, of course, they could have explicitly told courts to treat some portions of a statute as indivisible units. For instance, a statute could have included an "inseparability clause" specifying that some aspects or applications of the statute were contingent upon the constitutionality of others—and that if the latter were unconstitutional, then the former did not have legal effect either. But that possibility may not have occurred to legislators any more than it occurred to judges.

Even in the absence of an explicit inseparability clause, though, courts eventually started to *infer* that some provisions in a statute were inseparable from others. The first decision of this sort may have been *Warren v. Mayor of Charlestown,* 68 Mass. (2 Gray) 84 (1854). *See* Stern, *supra,* 51 HARV. L. REV. at 79–80. There, Chief Justice Lemuel Shaw of the Massachusetts Supreme Judicial Court noted that "the same act of legislation may be unconstitutional in some of its provisions, and yet constitutional in others." *Warren,* 68 Mass. (2 Gray) at 98. He acknowledged, too, that the constitutional parts could "have the full force of law" notwithstanding the unconstitutional parts. *Id.* at 99. According to Shaw, however, this principle was subject to a limitation. Sometimes, the constitutional and unconstitutional parts of a statute "are so mutually connected with and dependent on each other, as conditions, considerations or compensations for each other, as to warrant a belief that the legislature intended them as a whole, and that, if all could not be carried into effect, the legislature would not pass the residue independently." *Id.* In situations of this sort, Shaw suggested, courts should not give effect even to the constitutional parts of the statute.

Other state courts soon articulated similar doctrines. *See* Stern, *supra*, 51 HARV. L. REV. at 80; Nagel, *supra*, 72 N.C. L. REV. at 213–14. By the early 1880s, the U.S. Supreme Court did too. *See id.* at 214 (citing Allen v. Louisiana, 103 U.S. 80, 84 (1881)).

Shaw's formulation of the doctrine used the rhetoric of imaginative reconstruction. To decide whether the constitutional parts of a statute were separable from the unconstitutional parts, courts were to ask something like the following question: if members of the enacting legislature had known that the unconstitutional parts of the statute were unconstitutional and would have no legal effect, how much of the rest of the statute would the legislature have enacted? Other state courts used similar rhetoric. For many years, so did the U.S. Supreme Court. *See* Carter v. Carter Coal Co., 298 U.S. 238, 313 (1936) ("[I]n order to hold one part of a statute unconstitutional and uphold another part as separable, they must not be mutually dependent upon one another. Perhaps a fair approach . . . is to suppose that while the bill was pending in Congress a motion to strike out the [unconstitutional] provisions had prevailed, and to inquire whether, in that event, the statute should be so construed as to justify the conclusion that Congress . . . probably would not have passed the [other] provisions . . . ."); *cf.* Alaska Airlines, Inc. v. Brock, 480 U.S. 678, 685 (1987) ("The final test . . . is the traditional one: the unconstitutional provision must be severed unless the statute created in its absence is legislation that Congress would not have enacted.").

This way of framing the question puts substantial constraints on the courts' imagination. If the enacting legislature had known that some parts of its statute would have no effect, it might have decided to take a completely different approach to the topic that it was addressing, and it might therefore have redrafted the entire statute. Neither Shaw's formulation nor subsequent versions of separability doctrine invited courts to canvass all the different possibilities that the enacting legislature could have considered. Instead, courts simply imagined an up-or-down vote on the existing statute minus the unconstitutional provisions.

Because the courts' imagination was constrained in this way, the rhetoric of imaginative reconstruction was not really necessary. Shaw could have cast his approach entirely in terms of the meaning of the provisions that the legislature had actually enacted. The key question, he could have said, is whether some of those provisions should be understood to come with an implied condition, so that they had legal effect only if other provisions did too. *See* Harrison, *supra*, 83 GEO. WASH. L. REV. at 57–58 n.3 ("[S]everability is about implicit conditionality: a provision that is inseverable from another is implicitly conditional on the other."); *accord* Eric S. Fish, *Severability as Conditionality*, 64 EMORY L.J. 1293, 1298 (2015) ("[I]nseverability is the product of a legislative decision to make one part of a statute conditional on another part of a statute.").

Simply as a matter of logic and policy, interpreters might sometimes have good reason to infer that one provision is predicated on another. For instance, one provision might impose a tax, the revenue from which is earmarked to fund a program established by another provision—but if the program is unconstitutional, the tax would not be necessary. Likewise, one provision might create special procedures or safeguards that ameliorate the effects of another provision—but if either provision is unconstitutional, perhaps the other should be understood to be inseparable from it. The same might be true if a statute is designed to achieve a particular object through a series of steps; if all of those steps are necessary to effectuate the statute's purpose, but one of the steps is unconstitutional and cannot take effect, perhaps the other steps should not take effect either.[16]

Still, whether courts speak in terms of imaginative reconstruction or in terms of implied conditions, there will be plenty of murky cases—situations in which two provisions are not "wholly independent of each other," *Warren*, 68 Mass. (2 Gray) at 99, but also are not so obviously interconnected that one makes sense only if the other is also in effect. The murkiness expands when we move beyond questions about the separability of distinct provisions (the problem that Shaw was addressing) and consider the separability of different applications of a single provision. Wherever it operated, Shaw's approach required courts to make judgment calls.

Especially in the late nineteenth and early twentieth centuries, the courts making those judgment calls did not always favor separability. To the contrary, some state courts apparently approached statutes with a presumption *against* separability. *See* Nagel, *supra*, 72 N.C. L. REV. at 218 (citing Iowa Life Ins. Co. v. Eastern Mut. Life Ins. Co., 45 A. 762, 764 (N.J. 1900), and Skagit County v. Stiles, 39 P. 116, 116 (Wash. 1894), among other cases). For a time, the U.S. Supreme Court similarly suggested that federal statutes should be considered separable "only where it is plain that Congress would have enacted the legislation with the unconstitutional provisions eliminated." *The Employers' Liability Cases*, 207 U.S. 463, 501 (1908); *accord* El Paso & N.E. Ry. Co. v. Gutierrez, 215 U.S. 87, 97 (1909) (finding this test satisfied, but agreeing that doubts should be resolved against separability); *see also, e.g.*, Carter v. Carter Coal Co., 298 U.S. 238, 312 (1936) (asserting in dicta that unless a statute contains a separability clause, there is a "presumption in favor

[16] At the time that Chief Justice Shaw wrote *Warren*, courts did not tend to interpret statutes in light of what modern lawyers call "internal legislative history," such as records of legislative debates on the relevant bill or reports prepared by the responsible legislative committees during the process of enactment. *See infra* Chapter 3 (discussing shifts over time in the use of such information in statutory interpretation). Now that many judges do consult internal legislative history, though, it sometimes may provide additional reasons to think that one provision was predicated on another. Even if two provisions are not logically interdependent, records of the legislative process may suggest that they were enacted as part of a package deal between different segments of the legislature. After you have read the materials about legislative history in Chapter 3, ask yourself whether courts should infer inseparability on this basis.

of inseparability," and "the burden is upon the supporter of the legislation to show the separability of the provisions involved"). As a result, quite a few statutes were held inseparable. *See* Nagel, *supra*, 72 N.C. L. REV. at 218–19 (referring to "[t]he large number of Supreme Court decisions holding statutes nonseverable during the last quarter of the nineteenth century and the first decades of the twentieth century"); *see also* Stern, *supra*, 51 HARV. L. REV. at 90 (analyzing Supreme Court opinions from the 1870s to the 1930s, and concluding that "[t]en of the fifteen cases dealing with federal statutes, in which the problem of separable applications has been raised, have treated the laws as inseparable");[17] *id.* at 107 & n.138 (tabulating cases that instead involved the problem of separable language, and concluding that in those cases the Court had found "11 federal laws separable . . . and 6 federal laws inseparable").

To guard against the risk of inseparability, legislatures eventually came up with the idea of including "separability clauses" in particular statutes, explicitly declaring that those statutes were separable. State legislatures appear to have introduced such clauses in the first decade of the twentieth century,[18] and Congress followed suit in the following decade. Thus, the federal Shipping Act of 1916 included the following separability clause:

> "[I]f any provision of this Act, or the application of such provision to certain circumstances, is held unconstitutional, the remainder of the Act, and the application of such provision to circumstances other than those as to which it is held unconstitutional, shall not be affected thereby."

Act of Sept. 7, 1916, ch. 451, § 34, 39 Stat. 728, 738. Over the years, Congress has included similar language in many other federal statutes.

---

[17] Some of these cases may relate to the complexity flagged in footnote 13 above, about the extent to which courts can read statutory provisions that are unconstitutional on their face as containing narrower subrules that are valid. For instance, in *United States v. Reese*, 92 U.S. 214 (1876), the Supreme Court held that two penal provisions in the Enforcement Act of 1870 were too broadly worded to qualify as "appropriate legislation" to enforce the Fifteenth Amendment, and the Court also declined to find more limited provisions within the ambit of the broader ones. *See id.* at 221 ("It would certainly be dangerous if the legislature could set a net large enough to catch all possible offenders, and leave it to the courts to step inside and say who could be rightfully detained, and who should be set at large. . . . To limit this statute in the manner now asked for would be to make a new law, not to enforce an old one."). The Court reached similar conclusions in some later cases, but with varying explanations. *Compare, e.g.*, The Trade-Mark Cases, 100 U.S. 82, 99 (1879) (expressing doubt that Congress would have enacted the subrule that the Court had in mind), *with, e.g.*, Hill v. Wallace, 259 U.S. 44, 70 (1922) (declining "to dissect an unconstitutional measure and reframe a valid one out of it by inserting limitations it does not contain," and asserting that "[t]his is legislative work beyond the power and function of the court"). *See also* Stern, *supra*, 51 HARV. L. REV. at 97 (discussing this line of cases and noting "the hazards which necessarily accompany any attempt to read the Court's collective mind in a field of conflicting decisions where the opinions are not clear"). As above, I will bracket questions about the outer limits of the courts' ability to find valid subrules within statutory language that is unconstitutional as formulated.

[18] *See, e.g.*, Act of Mar. 16, 1901, ch. 76, § 27, 1901 Wash. Laws 137, 149; Act of May 26, 1905, ch. 646, § 21, 1905 N.Y. Laws 1621, 1639; Act of Apr. 13, 1907, ch. 71, art. XIV, § 45, 1907 Tex. Local & Spec. Laws 568, 658; Act of June 4, 1911, ch. 189, § 5, 1911 Colo. Laws 548, 550; Act of May 3, 1911, ch. 50, sec. 1, § 2394–32, 1911 Wis. Laws 43, 57–58; Act of Dec. 23, 1911, ch. 14, § 84, 1911 Cal. Stat. 18, 63 (Extra Sess.).

See, e.g., Dodd-Frank Wall Street Reform and Consumer Protection Act, Pub. L. 111–203, § 3, 124 Stat. 1376, 1390 (2010) (codified at 12 U.S.C. § 5302); Federal Election Campaign Act of 1971, Pub. L. 92–225, § 404, 86 Stat. 3, 20 (1972) (codified at 52 U.S.C. § 30144); Internal Revenue Code of 1954, ch. 736, § 7852(a), 68A Stat. 1, 922–23 (codified at 26 U.S.C. § 7852(a)); Social Security Act, ch. 531, § 1103, 49 Stat. 620, 648 (1935) (codified at 42 U.S.C. § 1303); Tariff Act of 1930, ch. 497, § 652, 46 Stat. 590, 763 (codified at 19 U.S.C. § 1652); Packers and Stockyards Act of 1921, ch. 64, § 408, 42 Stat. 159, 169 (1921) (codified at 7 U.S.C. § 229c). Likewise, when Congress has enacted particular titles of the United States Code as such, Congress has sometimes included a separability clause in the enacting statute (albeit not in the relevant title of the Code itself). *See, e.g.*, Act of June 25, 1948, ch. 645, § 18, 62 Stat. 683, 862 ("If any part of Title 18, Crimes and Criminal Procedure, as set out in section 1 of this Act, shall be held invalid the remainder shall not be affected thereby.").

Early on, the Supreme Court asserted that although separability clauses "may sometimes aid in determining [the legislature's] intent," they were not conclusive on that topic. *Dorchy v. Kansas*, 264 U.S. 286, 290 (1924) (describing a separability clause in a state statute as "an aid" but "not an inexorable command"). With respect to both state and federal statutes, the Court said that such clauses supported a "presumption" that the enacting legislature had intended the provisions covered by the clause to be separable, but this presumption could "be overcome by considerations which establish . . . 'the clear probability that the legislature would not have been satisfied with the statute unless it had included the invalid part.' " *Carter v. Carter Coal Co.*, 298 U.S. 238, 312–13 (1936) (quoting Utah Power & Light Co. v. Pfost, 286 U.S. 165, 184–85 (1932)); *see also id.* at 313–16 (applying this doctrine to a separability clause in a federal statute and concluding, notwithstanding the clause, that Congress would not have passed certain provisions of the statute in the absence of the unconstitutional provisions); Williams v. Standard Oil Co., 278 U.S. 235, 242 (1929) (applying the same doctrine to a separability clause in a state statute and again finding that the presumption established by the clause was overcome).

It might seem strange that explicit statutory provisions about separability were said merely to create a "presumption" about the legislature's desires, or that courts would ever second guess such clauses in the name of legislative intent. Still, the typical separability clause may have seemed too sweeping to be taken literally. Writing in 1937, Robert Stern explained:

> "When legislatures declared that 'The invalidity of any part of this statute shall not affect the remainder', they did not mean it. They doubtless did intend that if unimportant parts of a law were invalidated the remainder should not be affected. They probably also meant that if important provisions in a statute or important

> applications were unconstitutional, other important provisions or applications which might succeed in at least partly achieving the policy of the legislation should not be nullified. But the Court, with considerable justification, did not believe that it was intended that subsidiary or auxiliary features of a general statutory plan were to remain effective if none of the basic objects of the law could constitutionally be achieved."

Stern, *supra*, 51 HARV. L. REV. at 122–23.

For many years, the Supreme Court continued to say that explicit separability clauses in federal statutes merely created a "presumption" that operated "unless there is strong evidence that Congress intended otherwise." *Alaska Airlines, Inc. v. Brock*, 480 U.S. 678, 686 (1987). With the rise of textualism, though, this position came under increasing criticism. *See, e.g.*, Nagel, *supra*, 72 N.C. L. REV. at 234–46 (considering "[t]he justifications for not reading a severability clause according to its plain meaning," but rejecting them as "unconvincing"); Michael D. Shumsky, *Severability, Inseverability, and the Rule of Law*, 41 HARV. J. LEGIS. 227, 245 (2004) (similarly advocating "a textualist approach to severability and inseverability clauses"). Recently, a plurality of the Supreme Court repudiated the idea that a separability clause creates only a presumption and that Congress might actually have intended something else. In Justice Kavanaugh's words, "That kind of argument may have carried some force back when courts paid less attention to statutory text as the definitive expression of Congress's will. But courts today zero in on the precise statutory text and, as a result, courts hew closely to the text of severability or nonseverability clauses." *Barr v. Am. Ass'n of Political Consultants*, 140 S. Ct. 2335, 2349 (2020) (plurality opinion of Kavanaugh, J.).[19]

---

[19] As the name suggests, a "nonseverability clause" (or what I would call an inseparability clause) is the opposite of a separability clause: it instructs courts to treat some or all of a statute's provisions as being inseparable. Inseparability clauses are much less common than separability clauses, presumably because legislatures normally prefer separability. Still, they are not unknown. For instance, the original version of the National Childhood Vaccine Injury Act of 1986 included the following inseparability clause: "If any provision of this title or the application of any provision of this title to any person or circumstance is held invalid by reason of a violation of the Constitution, the entire title shall be considered invalid." Act of Nov. 14, 1986, Pub. L. 99–660, § 344, 100 Stat. 3743, 3783 (amended by Act of Dec. 19, 1989, Pub. L. 101–239, § 6602, 103 Stat. 2106, 2293, and Act of Nov. 3, 1990, Pub. L. 101–502, § 5(g), 104 Stat. 1285, 1288).

Apart from the standard separability or inseparability clause, legislatures might also get more creative. In modern times, a small number of federal statutes have included elaborate "fallback provisions" that operate only if other provisions in the statute are unconstitutional and that depart from the terms of those other provisions. *See* Michael C. Dorf, *Fallback Law*, 107 COLUM. L. REV. 303, 305, 313–14 (2007) (providing examples from the Gramm-Rudman-Hollings Act and the NAFTA Implementation Act). Indeed, Professor Dorf describes the standard separability clause as itself being a "fallback provision." *See id.* at 305 (characterizing separability clauses as "provid[ing] that in the event that the original law is held partly invalid, a fallback of the original law minus the invalid provision or application will take effect"); *cf.* John Harrison, *Power, Duty, and Facial Invalidity*, 16 U. PA. J. CONST'L L. 501, 540–41 (2013) (observing that "[s]tandard severability clauses do not address the situation in which a provision is wholly invalid, and the question is whether some similar provision is available as a fallback," but arguing that the idea of an implied "fallback arrangement" explains why some statutory

In addition to including separability clauses in individual statutes, many *state* legislatures have enacted generic instructions that favor separability with respect to all of the state's statutes. *See* Jacob Scott, *Codified Canons and the Common Law of Interpretation*, 98 GEO. L.J. 341, 385–87 (2010) (reporting that thirty-four states and the District of Columbia have codified a generic principle in favor of separability, and no states have codified a contrary generic principle). In many states, the generic instruction favoring separability is cast as a default rule that can be overcome by contrary indications of legislative intent. *See, e.g.*, WIS. STAT. § 990.001 (including the pro-separability principle in a list of rules that operate unless they "would produce a result inconsistent with the manifest intent of the legislature"). Some states have purported to cast their generic instruction more strongly, so that all subsequently enacted state statutes are separable unless they otherwise provide. *See, e.g.*, ARK. CODE ANN. § 1–2–205; 5 ILL. COMP. STAT. § 70/1.31. Indeed, some states have purported to state the generic instruction without any exceptions at all. *See, e.g.*, CONN. GEN. STAT. § 1–3 ("If any provision of any act passed by the General Assembly or its application to any person or circumstances is held invalid, such invalidity shall not affect other provisions or applications of such act.").

The legal effect of these generic instructions about the separability of state statutes is a matter of state law. Still, no matter what instructions a state legislature purports to establish for the interpretation of future statutes, a future legislature presumably can opt out. If there are strong enough indications that the enacting legislature intends a particular statute to be inseparable, moreover, courts might conclude that the statute is inseparable even if it does not *explicitly* opt out of or repeal the generic instructions provided by a previous legislature. As applied to future statutes, then, generic instructions favoring separability may not really be capable of establishing more than a presumption in favor of separability, even if they are worded in absolute terms. *See infra* Chapter 4.B.4 (discussing the legal effect of statutory instructions about the interpretation of future statutes); *see also* State v. Menillo, 368 A.2d 136, 138 (Conn. 1976) (treating Conn. Gen. Stat. § 1–3 as supporting "a presumption of separability," but one that can be overcome). In this respect, generic instructions about the separability of future statutes may differ from separability clauses contained in a particular statute.

Be that as it may, Congress has not enacted generic instructions favoring the separability of *federal* statutes. Instead, Congress has contented itself with including separability clauses in some individual statutes. If a federal statute does contain a separability clause (or an inseparability clause), the plurality opinion in *Barr v. American Association of Political Consultants* advises courts not to second-guess

---

rules that are unconstitutional as formulated can be taken to establish narrower rules that are valid).

the clause's instructions: "At least absent extraordinary circumstances, the Court should adhere to the text of the severability or nonseverability clause." *Am. Ass'n of Political Consultants*, 140 S. Ct. at 2349 (plurality opinion of Kavanaugh, J.).[20]

What about federal statutes that do not include any explicit instructions about separability? At least until recently, courts continued to determine the separability of such statutes by asking the question that Chief Justice Shaw had suggested long ago: if members of the enacting legislature had known that some aspects or applications of the statute could not be given effect, would the legislature have enacted the rest of the statute? *See, e.g., Alaska Airlines*, 480 U.S. at 691 (concluding that "Congress would have enacted [the statutory provisions at issue in *Alaska Airlines*] even without [the provision that was unconstitutional]"). Indeed, separability doctrine seemed to be one of the last redoubts of imaginative reconstruction in statutory interpretation. But members of the Supreme Court began to criticize imaginative reconstruction in this context as in others, *see, e.g.*, Murphy v. NCAA, 138 S. Ct. 1461, 1486–87 (2018) (Thomas, J., concurring), and the plurality in *Barr v. American Association of Political Consultants* agreed. In the plurality's words,

> "[C]ourts are not well equipped to imaginatively reconstruct a prior Congress's hypothetical intent.... [A]bsent a severability or nonseverability clause, a court often cannot really know what the two Houses of Congress and the President from the time of original enactment of a law would have wanted if one provision of a law were later declared unconstitutional."

140 S. Ct. at 2350 (plurality opinion of Kavanaugh, J.).

Rather than trusting *ad hoc* imaginative reconstruction, the plurality asserted that "[t]he Court's cases have instead developed a strong presumption of severability." *Id.*[21] By casting this presumption as a response to uncertainty about hypothetical legislative intent, the plurality left room for the possibility that the presumption could be overcome by clear signs that one aspect or application of a statute was

---

[20] Of course, to the extent that the Constitution imposes limits on separability, courts will not apply separability clauses in violation of those limits. *See, e.g.*, Harrison, *supra*, 16 U. PA. J. CONST'L L. at 545 ("[A] legislature cannot solve [First Amendment overbreadth problems] simply by including an ordinary severability clause."); *cf. supra* p. 189 n.13 (mentioning overbreadth doctrine and other possible constitutional limits on separability).

[21] As noted above, in the early decades of the twentieth century, the Supreme Court sometimes articulated the opposite presumption. *See, e.g.*, Carter v. Carter Coal Co., 298 U.S. 238, 312 (1936) ("In the absence of [a separability clause], the presumption is that the legislature intends an act to be effective as an entirety—that is to say, the rule is against the mutilation of a statute; and if any provision be unconstitutional, the presumption is that the remaining provisions fall with it."). Later, however, the Court repudiated that idea. *See Alaska Airlines*, 480 U.S. at 686 ("In the absence of a severability clause, . . . Congress' silence is just that—silence—and does not raise a presumption against severability."). In 1984, indeed, a plurality of the Court said that "the presumption is in favor of severability." *Regan v. Time, Inc.*, 468 U.S. 641, 653 (1984) (plurality opinion of White, J.); *cf.* Nagel, *supra*, 72 N.C. L. REV. at 220–21 (noting that "[r]ecent years have witnessed a trend toward finding statutes severable," but adding that as of 1993, "a majority of the Supreme Court has not acknowledged a general presumption of severability, despite opportunities to endorse the *Regan* plurality's view").

conditioned on another. But at least in the absence of any clear signs either way, the plurality indicated that federal statutes should normally be regarded as fully separable. *See id.* at 2351; *cf. id.* at 2352 (recognizing an exception for the "fairly unusual" situation in which the constitutional parts of a statute are not " 'capable of functioning independently' " (quoting Seila Law LLC v. Consumer Fin. Prot. Bureau, 140 S. Ct. 2183, 2209 (2020) (plurality opinion of Roberts, C.J.) (internal quotation marks omitted))).

Although the plurality described the presumption in favor of separability as an alternative to free-floating speculations about congressional intent, even advocates of imaginative reconstruction might support the same starting presumption. The available evidence suggests that as a general rule, legislatures prefer separability to inseparability. At the state level, a large majority of state legislatures have enacted generic instructions in favor of separability, and no state legislature has done the opposite. *See* Scott, *supra*, 98 GEO. L.J. at 385. At the federal level, separability clauses in individual federal statutes are common, and inseparability clauses are rare.

In any event, current doctrine about the separability of federal statutes probably is pretty close to what the plurality in *Barr v. American Association of Political Consultants* said. If Congress provides explicit instructions about separability (by enacting a separability clause, an inseparability clause, or a more elaborate fallback provision), courts normally will follow those instructions. In the absence of such instructions, courts will start with a presumption in favor of separability, but that presumption might be overcome by specific reasons to believe that some aspects or applications of a statute should be understood to be conditioned on others.

2. THE TRADITIONAL SAVING CANON

If some aspects or applications of a statute are unconstitutional, courts will face questions about the separability of other aspects or applications of the statute. Where possible, though, courts often try to interpret statutes so that the statutes are not even partially unconstitutional. Thus, the modern Supreme Court has referred to "our established practice of interpreting statutes to avoid constitutional difficulties." *Office of Senator Mark Dayton v. Hanson*, 550 U.S. 511, 514 (2007).

As the Court itself has acknowledged, however, "[t]here are at least two different canons of construction that sometimes go by the name 'constitutional avoidance.' " *United States v. Davis*, 139 S. Ct. 2319, 2332 n.6 (2019). One canon tells courts to prefer readings of a statute that preserve the statute's constitutionality over readings that would make the statute unconstitutional (in whole or in part). The other canon, which is more controversial and in my view less justified, tells courts to try to read statutes so as to avoid even serious *questions* about their constitutionality. Because judicial opinions often conflate these two canons, commentators have had to come up with their own distinct labels. *See, e.g.*, Lisa A. Kloppenberg, *Avoiding Serious Constitutional Doubts: The Supreme Court's Construction of Statutes Raising Free Speech Concerns*, 30 U.C. DAVIS L. REV. 1, 10–11 (calling the former idea the "narrow approach" to the avoidance canon and the latter idea the "broad approach"); John Copeland Nagle, Delaware & Hudson *Revisited*, 72 NOTRE DAME L. REV. 1495, 1496 (1997) (calling the former idea the "unconstitutionality" canon and the latter idea the "doubts" canon); Adrian Vermeule, *Saving Constructions*, 85 GEO. L.J. 1945, 1949 (1997) (calling the former idea "classical avoidance" and the latter "modern avoidance"). In this book, I will refer to the canon about avoiding actual unconstitutionality as the "saving" canon and the other idea as the canon that favors avoiding "constitutional doubts." I will discuss the saving canon in this section and the canon that favors avoiding constitutional doubts in the next section.

The saving canon dates far back. *See, e.g.*, *United States v. Coombs*, 37 U.S. (12 Pet.) 72, 76 (1838) ("[I]f the section admits of two interpretations, one of which brings it within, and the other presses it beyond the constitutional authority of congress, it will become our duty to adopt the former construction; because a presumption ought never to be indulged, that congress meant to exercise or usurp any unconstitutional authority, unless that conclusion is forced upon the Court by language altogether unambiguous."); *see also* Bloodgood v. Mohawk & Hudson R.R. Co., 18 Wend. 9, 19 (N.Y. 1837) (opinion of Walworth, C.) ("It is a primary rule in the construction of statutes in those countries where the limits of the legislative power are restricted by the provisions of a written constitution, to endeavor if possible to interpret the language of the legislature in such a manner as to make it consistent with the constitution or fundamental law."); Auditor of Public Accounts v. Graham, 5 Va. (1 Call) 475, 476 (Va. 1798) (opinion of Roane, J.) ("[W]e ought not, where another reasonable construction can be adopted, to resort to one which makes the Legislature infringe the spirit of the constitution.").

In many of the cases in which courts apply the saving canon, it can plausibly be justified as a "descriptive" canon—a useful guide to the intended meaning of statutory language. If a statutory provision could be read to establish either of two different legal directives, and if one of those directives would be considered unconstitutional for reasons that members of the enacting legislature could have been expected to know, that very fact may suggest that members of the enacting legislature understood themselves to be establishing the other directive.

Admittedly, this generalization might be more accurate in some circumstances than others. Low-profile constitutional doctrines might not be at the forefront of legislators' minds even if legislators should know about them. Even when an aspect of constitutional doctrine is well known, moreover, there are some circumstances in which legislatures might deliberately enact a statute that conflicts with it. Perhaps legislators disagree with the doctrine and are trying to give the courts an opportunity to change it, or perhaps legislators are simply trying to appeal to voters and do not care whether courts actually apply the statute.

To date, scholars have conducted only limited empirical research into the relationship between legislative drafting choices and the Constitution (or the courts' constitutional doctrines). At a guess, though, the saving canon does deserve some weight as a guide to likely legislative intent in the mine run of circumstances where legislators have reason to know about some aspect of constitutional doctrine and have no apparent desire to challenge it. Consistent with that idea, at least eight state legislatures have codified the saving canon, and seven of them have explicitly cast it as a presumption about their likely intent. *See* TEX. GOV'T CODE ANN. § 311.021(1) ("In enacting a statute, it is presumed that . . . compliance with the constitutions of this state and the United States is intended . . . ."); COLO. REV. STAT. § 2–4–201(1)(a) (same); IOWA CODE § 4.4(1) (same); N.D. CENT. CODE § 1–02–38(1) (same); OHIO REV. CODE ANN. § 1.47(A) (same); 1 PA. CONS. STAT. § 1922(3) ("In ascertaining the intention of the General Assembly in the enactment of a statute the following presumptions, among others, may be used: . . . (3) That the General Assembly does not intend to violate the Constitution of the United States or of this Commonwealth."); MINN. STAT. § 645.17(3) (similar); *see also* N.M. STAT. ANN. § 12–2A–18(A)(3) ("A statute or rule is construed, if possible, to . . . avoid an unconstitutional, absurd or unachievable result."); EINER ELHAUGE, STATUTORY DEFAULT RULES: HOW TO INTERPRET UNCLEAR LEGISLATION 354 n.37 (2008) (collecting these citations).

Apart from the straightforward "descriptive" argument for the saving canon (which maintains that the canon is a plausible guide to the intended meaning of particular statutes), commentators also sometimes link the saving canon to a different kind of legislative intent. When a statute lends itself to two possible interpretations and courts do not know which was intended, perhaps members of the enacting legislature themselves would want courts to adopt whichever interpretation preserves the statute's constitutionality. According to Professor Einer Elhauge, "[a]ny enacting legislative polity would normally want such a default rule," because the enacting legislature "usually would want to preserve as much of its statute as possible." *Id.* at 133.

Even in situations where the saving canon would not otherwise have "descriptive" force, this argument may justify using the canon as a tie-breaker when two interpretations of a statute otherwise seem about equally good. But what if it seems somewhat more likely than not that members of the enacting legislature intended to establish the directive that courts consider unconstitutional? If members of the enacting legislature probably intended to establish Directive #1, but that interpretation would make the statute unconstitutional (in whole or in part) and the statute could be read to establish Directive #2 instead, is it safe to assume that members of the enacting legislature would want courts to adopt the latter interpretation? Or would members of the enacting legislature want courts to give effect to the legislature's likely intent by reading the statute to establish Directive #1 and then invoking the presumption of separability to salvage as many applications of the statute as possible? *Cf. id.* (surmising that legislatures want courts to use both the saving canon and the presumption of separability, but not considering the possibility that the existence of the presumption of separability might weaken this rationale for the saving canon).

In some circumstances, legislators might not care whether courts apply the saving canon or instead rely on the presumption of separability, because those approaches will produce a similar bottom line. Consider the following example. Suppose that a particular statute could be given either a broad interpretation or a narrower interpretation. The narrower interpretation coincides with constitutional limits on the legislature's power, in the following sense: the rule established by this interpretation of the statute would cover all of the conduct that the legislature has the power to regulate and no more. The broad interpretation encompasses all of that conduct, but also purports to cover additional conduct that the legislature does not have the constitutional power to regulate. In this situation, the saving canon would encourage courts to adopt the narrower interpretation if that interpretation is fairly possible. But even if courts find that the saving canon is overcome and adopt the broad interpretation, the Constitution would prevent courts from applying the statute to the conduct that the legislature does not have the power to regulate. Assuming that the constitutional applications of the broad interpretation are separable from the unconstitutional applications, the courts would end up applying the statute in exactly the same cases that the narrower interpretation would have covered, and no more.

Presumably because of examples of this sort, Professor Vermeule has asserted that the saving canon "is in effect identical to severance conducted after a constitutional ruling." Vermeule, *supra*, 85 GEO. L.J. at 1957 n.69. But that is not always correct. Again, imagine a statute that could be interpreted either broadly or more narrowly, but this time suppose that the narrower interpretation does not go as far as the Constitution would permit; while the broad interpretation goes somewhat farther than the Constitution allows, the narrower interpretation stops well short of the constitutional line. In that situation, a court that adopted the broad interpretation of the statute and applied it where constitutional (on the theory that the statute's constitutional applications are separable from its unconstitutional applications) would end up in a different place than a court that adopted the narrower interpretation of the statute. The same is true whenever the possible interpretations of a statute differ in kind rather than simply in degree. For instance, imagine that a statute could be understood to cover either all conduct of Type A or all conduct of Type B, and imagine that the legislature does not have the constitutional power to regulate some of the Type B conduct. If members of the enacting legislature really intended to regulate the Type B conduct, is there any reason to assume that they nonetheless would want courts to invoke the saving canon and read the statute as covering the Type A conduct? Isn't it more likely that members of the enacting legislature would want courts to give the statute its intended meaning (so that it regulates the Type B conduct) and then invoke the presumption of separability (with the result that the statute will govern as much of the Type B conduct as the courts decide the legislature has the constitutional authority to regulate)?[22]

Aside from justifications that are grounded in legislative intent, the saving canon may also have some normative justifications. When a court refuses to apply a statute (in whole or in part) on the ground that the statute is unconstitutional, the court is sometimes said to be creating "friction" between the legislature and the judiciary. That harm might be more serious in some cases than in others, but the saving canon can be seen as a rule-like way of guarding against it: when a statute can plausibly be read in such a way as to preserve its constitutionality (thereby avoiding whatever friction might follow from a declaration of invalidity), perhaps courts ordinarily should take that route. *See, e.g.*, William N. Eskridge, Jr., *Public Values in Statutory Interpretation*, 137 U. PA. L. REV. 1007, 1020 (1989) (observing that the saving canon is often explained on the ground that "[t]he Court should avoid constitutional confrontations with Congress"); *cf. id.* at 1020–21 (noting other possible normative arguments for the canon).

Of course, "[s]potting a constitutional issue does not give a court the authority to rewrite a statute as it pleases." *Jennings v. Rodriguez*, 138 S. Ct. 830, 843 (2018). In the Supreme Court's words, "the canon of constitutional avoidance" (which encompasses both the saving canon and the canon that favors avoiding constitutional doubts) " 'comes into play only when, after the application of ordinary textual analysis, the statute is found to be susceptible of more than one construction.' " *Id.* at 842 (quoting Clark v. Martinez, 543 U.S. 371, 385 (2005)). "In the absence of more than one plausible construction, the canon ' "simply has no application." ' " *Id.* (quoting Warger v. Shauers, 574 U.S. 40, 50 (2014), which in turn was quoting United States v. Oakland Cannabis Buyers' Cooperative, 532 U.S. 483, 494 (2001)); *accord, e.g.*, United States v.

[22] Writing during the New Deal, Robert Stern observed that "[i]n recent years it has become the custom [for Congress] to attach separability clauses to almost all statutes regarded as of possibly doubtful constitutionality." Robert L. Stern, *Separability and Separability Clauses in the Supreme Court*, 51 HARV. L. REV. 76, 121 (1937). This experience suggests that at least during eras when Congress does not see eye to eye with the Supreme Court about the meaning of the Constitution, Congress might want courts to adopt the most natural reading of a statute's language and to rely on separability more than the saving canon.

Palomar-Santiago, 141 S. Ct. 1615, 1622 (2021); McFadden v. United States, 576 U.S. 186, 197 (2015). Still, different interpreters may have somewhat different views about exactly what it takes for an interpretation to be "plausible" in the relevant sense.

Different people may also have different views about how the saving canon should work when prevailing understandings of the Constitution have changed between the time a statute was enacted and the time it is being interpreted. Should courts apply the saving canon with reference to understandings of the Constitution as they stood at the time of enactment, as they stand at the time of interpretation, or both? *See* WILLIAM N. ESKRIDGE, JR., PHILIP P. FRICKEY & ELIZABETH GARRETT, CASES AND MATERIALS ON LEGISLATION: STATUTES AND THE CREATION OF PUBLIC POLICY 884–86 (3d ed. 2001) (raising this issue); *see also* Robert W. Scheef, *Temporal Dynamics in Statutory Interpretation: Courts, Congress, and the Canon of Constitutional Avoidance*, 64 U. PITT. L. REV. 529 (2003).

For example, certain aspects of constitutional doctrine have become less restrictive over time (with the result that legislatures are now understood to have more power). Imagine that a statute is superficially ambiguous; it could plausibly be given either Interpretation #1 or Interpretation #2. Suppose that by the time courts are interpreting it, they would consider both readings of the statute perfectly constitutional. But suppose that prevailing constitutional doctrines were different when the statute was enacted; back then, courts would have held that Interpretation #1 is unconstitutional, and there is no evidence that members of the enacting legislature were trying to challenge or subvert that understanding of the Constitution. In this situation, your views about whether modern courts should apply the saving canon probably depend on which of the justifications for the canon you accept. If you accept the straightforward "descriptive" justification for the canon, you probably think that courts should apply the saving canon with reference to the understandings of the Constitution that were common at the time of enactment—the understandings that members of the enacting legislature might be expected to know about. On that analysis, the saving canon would support adopting Interpretation #2. By contrast, if you see the saving canon as purely "normative," you might think that the canon does not apply at all in this situation; because the courts would now say that both interpretations are constitutional, neither interpretation would lead to a confrontation between the courts and Congress.

Now consider the opposite sort of change, in which constitutional doctrine becomes *more* restrictive over time (with the result that legislatures are now understood to have less power). Again, imagine a superficially ambiguous statute. This time, suppose that both of the possible interpretations would have been considered perfectly constitutional under the doctrines that prevailed at the time of enactment, but prevailing understandings of the Constitution have shifted, and Interpretation #1 would now be considered unconstitutional. In this situation, the straightforward "descriptive" argument for the saving canon does not work; the fact that modern courts would consider Interpretation #1 unconstitutional does not suggest that members of the enacting legislature intended Interpretation #2 instead, because members of the enacting legislature would not have perceived the constitutional defect that courts have now identified. In situations of this sort, should the saving canon be restricted to a tie-breaking role, so that it would come into play only if courts are otherwise in equipoise between the two possible interpretations?[23]

This line of questions suggests that courts should not take a one-size-fits-all approach to the saving canon; they should give the canon more force in situations where it could be a reliable guide to legislative intent. But even if one accepts the premise that the justifications for the saving canon are stronger in some situations than in others, might one resist the conclusion that courts should try to draw those distinctions? If we try to make the saving canon (or any other canon) so fine-grained that the results it supports in each case accord with our intuitions about how that case should be decided in the canon's absence, have we effectively eliminated the canon and replaced it with a holistic, totality-of-the-circumstances approach? To the extent that canons are rule-like methods of advancing the goals of statutory interpretation (including the goal of producing matches between the intended meaning and the interpreted meaning of statutory language), they might have to be somewhat over- or under-inclusive. *Cf.* Jaskolski v. Daniels, *supra* p. 97 (referring to "the rough cuts inevitable with decision by rule"). Can courts entirely eliminate this cost of canons without also eliminating their benefits? If not, is there a principled way of figuring out how fine-grained any particular canon should be—of identifying the point at which the costs of additional "ruleness" begin to exceed the benefits?

3. THE CANON THAT FAVORS AVOIDING CONSTITUTIONAL DOUBTS

In the early twentieth century, the Supreme Court started to say that "[a] statute must be construed, if fairly possible, so as to avoid not only the conclusion that it is unconstitutional, but also grave doubts on that score." *United States v. Jin Fuey Moy*, 241 U.S. 394, 401 (1916); *see also* United States ex rel. Att'y Gen. v. Delaware & Hudson Co., 213 U.S. 366, 408 (1909) ("[W]here a statute is susceptible of two constructions, by

[23] Suppose you think that the saving canon should have force even in this situation, so that modern courts should favor Interpretation #2. Would your answer change if, shortly after the statute's enactment, appellate courts had authoritatively adopted Interpretation #1 (the interpretation that courts would now consider unconstitutional)? After constitutional doctrine changes, if the same courts are asked to hold the statute unconstitutional, should they do so? Or should they instead overrule their past decisions and re-interpret the statute to adopt Interpretation #2? In other words, how should the justifications behind the saving canon interact with the justifications behind the doctrine of *stare decisis*? (Return to these questions after you have read the materials about *stare decisis* in Chapter 4.)

one of which grave and doubtful constitutional questions arise and by the other of which such questions are avoided, our duty is to adopt the latter."); John Copeland Nagle, Delaware & Hudson *Revisited*, 72 NOTRE DAME L. REV. 1495, 1496–97, 1510–12 (1997) (finding hints of this canon in a few earlier cases, but treating *Delaware & Hudson* as its source). The modern Supreme Court continues to recite this idea. *See* United States v. Palomar-Santiago, 141 S. Ct. 1615, 1622 (2021) (quoting *Jin Fuey Moy*, though finding the canon inapplicable because "the text of [the statute] unambiguously forecloses Palomar-Santiago's interpretation"); *see also, e.g.*, Gomez v. United States, 490 U.S. 858, 864 (1989) ("It is our settled policy to avoid an interpretation of a federal statute that engenders constitutional issues if a reasonable alternative interpretation poses no constitutional question.").

The Supreme Court has sometimes conflated the canon that favors avoiding constitutional doubts with the traditional saving canon. *See, e.g.*, Edward J. DeBartolo Corp. v. Fla. Gulf Coast Bldg. & Constr. Trades Council, 485 U.S. 568, 575 (1988). But the two are not the same. The canon that favors avoiding constitutional doubts applies no matter how courts would end up answering the constitutional questions that the canon encourages them to avoid. If a federal statute lends itself to two possible interpretations, one of which is plainly constitutional but the other of which might not be, the canon that favors avoiding constitutional doubts will support the former interpretation—even if, had the court adopted the other interpretation and confronted the ensuing constitutional questions, the court ultimately would have answered those questions in favor of the statute's constitutionality.

Admittedly, now that the canon that favors avoiding constitutional doubts exists, it does not leave much independent room for the saving canon. *See, e.g.*, Neal Kumar Katyal & Thomas P. Schmidt, *Active Avoidance: The Modern Supreme Court and Legal Change*, 128 HARV. L. REV. 2109, 2117 (2015) (asserting that the traditional saving canon "has been mostly superseded by 'modern' avoidance"). If one reading of a statute would raise serious questions about whether the statute is constitutional and another plausible reading of the statute would not, the canon that favors avoiding constitutional doubts encourages the courts to adopt the reading that easily preserves the statute's constitutionality. If the courts do so, they will not have to decide whether the other reading would actually be unconstitutional, so they will not have occasion to apply the saving canon. That may be why the modern Supreme Court has sometimes conflated the two canons: if the Court favors interpretations that avoid even constitutional doubts, there is rarely much reason for the Court to articulate a separate canon about avoiding actual unconstitutionality. *But see* United States v. Davis, 139 S. Ct. 2319, 2332 n.6 (2019) (noting that the traditional saving canon "is distinct from the more modern (and more debated) constitutional doubt canon"); *see also* Edmond v. United States, 520 U.S. 651, 658 (1997) (addressing an unusual situation in which interpreting one statutory provision so as to preserve its constitutionality entailed interpreting a different statutory provision in a manner that raised a substantial question about its constitutionality, and prioritizing the saving canon over the canon that favors avoiding constitutional doubts).

As both commentators and distinguished circuit judges have observed, however, the canon that favors avoiding constitutional doubts is harder to justify than the traditional saving canon. *See, e.g.*, HENRY J. FRIENDLY, *Mr. Justice Frankfurter and the Reading of Statutes, in* BENCHMARKS 196, 210–12 (1967) (referring to the saving canon as "[a] . . . principle of unquestionable validity," but expressing grave qualms about the doubts canon); *see also* Caleb Nelson, *Avoiding Constitutional Questions Versus Avoiding Unconstitutionality*, 128 HARV. L. REV. F. 331, 331 nn.3–5 (2015) (citing additional critics of the doubts canon). Especially where constitutional doctrine has been stable over time, the saving canon may well help interpreters identify the meaning that members of the enacting legislature probably intended a statute to convey; if the statute could fairly be interpreted to establish either of two different directives, but lawyers would consider one of those directives unconstitutional (in whole or in part) for reasons that members of the enacting legislature probably would have known about and probably were not trying to challenge, that very fact is some evidence that members of the enacting legislature were trying to establish the other directive. In my view, though, this straightforward "descriptive" argument cannot readily be extended to the canon that favors avoiding constitutional doubts.

Here is one way of formulating the key question. Imagine that members of Congress are considering a policy proposal that they know will be attacked on constitutional grounds and that courts might not uphold. But imagine that under existing constitutional doctrine, members of Congress think there is a 60 percent chance that the courts will uphold the statute; although there are serious questions about the statute's constitutionality, members of Congress expect that the courts are likely to resolve those questions in favor of constitutionality. Would members of Congress see the very existence of those questions as a reason not to enact this proposal?

Writing in 1995, Professor Frederick Schauer observed that "there is no evidence whatsoever that members of Congress are risk-averse about the possibility that legislation they believe to be wise policy will be invalidated by the courts." Frederick Schauer, *Ashwander Revisited*, 1995 SUP. CT. REV. 71, 92. To the contrary, Schauer hypothesized that because of legislators' political incentives, "one would expect members of Congress . . . to err on the side of assuming constitutionality under conditions of uncertainty about what the courts are likely to do." *Id.* at 92–93.

Perhaps Professor Schauer's hypothesis is not universally true. Maybe some members of Congress have an ethic of steering well clear of some constitutional boundaries. *But cf.* Edward O. Correia, *A Legislative Conception of Legislative Supremacy*, 42 CASE W. RES. L. REV. 1129, 1178 & n.169 (1992) (suggesting that Congress often "intend[s] to exercise the full reach of its authority, thus pressing against the 'limits' of the Constitution"). Even if members of Congress are simply trying to advance their views of wise policy, moreover, they might sometimes have policy reasons to favor a proposal that will not be subject to constitutional attack over a proposal that will be. In my view, though, the generalization that legislatures try to avoid enacting statutes whose constitutionality might be questioned is not true often enough to justify having an across-the-board canon to that effect. I would expect courts to reach more accurate assessments of the intended meaning of statutes if they proceeded "doubt by doubt and statute by statute." Nelson, *supra*, 128 HARV. L. REV. F. at 335–36.

There may be some tension between my intuition that the saving canon has a solid "descriptive" justification and my intuition that the canon about avoiding constitutional doubts does not. Suppose, as Professor Schauer suspects, that "Congress is rarely concerned with the fact of unconstitutionality independent of the likelihood that an Act of Congress will be overturned by the courts." Schauer, *supra*, 1995 SUP. CT. REV. at 92. If so, then the "descriptive" justification for the saving canon should itself be phrased in terms of probabilities; it posits that legislators normally do not intend to enact statutes that they think courts are very likely to hold unconstitutional. The descriptive justification for the canon about avoiding constitutional doubts simply goes farther down the same spectrum; it posits that legislators normally do not intend to enact statutes that they think courts *might possibly* hold unconstitutional. Yet even if the descriptive justifications for these two canons exist on the same spectrum, one stopping point might be more accurate than the other. In my view, the saving canon is likely to be a better guide to the intended meaning of statutes than the canon about avoiding even constitutional doubts.

Consistent with that view, there is little evidence that legislatures themselves want courts to apply the canon that favors avoiding constitutional doubts. Professor Elhauge reports that although some state legislatures have codified the *saving* canon, "no state legislature directs courts to avoid constitutional doubts that do not result in actual invalidity." EINER ELHAUGE, STATUTORY DEFAULT RULES: HOW TO INTERPRET UNCLEAR LEGISLATION 237 (2008). That would have come as no surprise to Judge Henry Friendly, who pioneered criticisms of the canon about avoiding constitutional doubts. As he wrote in the 1960s,

> "It does not seem in any way obvious . . . that the legislature would prefer a narrow construction which does not raise constitutional doubts to a broader one which does raise them. For there is always

> the chance, usually a good one, that the doubts will be settled favorably, and if they are not, the conceded rule of construing to avoid unconstitutionality will come into operation and save the day. People in such a heads-I-win, tails-you-lose position do not readily sacrifice it. . . ."

FRIENDLY, *supra*, at 210.

Despite these arguments, the Supreme Court sometimes portrays the canon about avoiding constitutional doubts as a standard "descriptive" canon. In the words of one such opinion, "It is a tool for choosing between competing plausible interpretations of a statutory text, resting on the reasonable presumption that Congress did not intend the alternative which raises serious constitutional doubts. The canon is thus a means of giving effect to congressional intent . . . ." *Clark v. Martinez*, 543 U.S. 371, 381 (2005) (citations omitted). In his famous concurring opinion in *Ashwander v. TVA*, 297 U.S. 288 (1936), however, Justice Brandeis listed a version of the canon as a rule that the Supreme Court had developed "for its own governance." *Id.* at 346, 348 (Brandeis, J., concurring). More recent cases likewise refer to "the policy of construing a statute to avoid constitutional questions where possible." *Verizon Communications, Inc. v. FCC*, 535 U.S. 467, 525 (2002). That way of talking suggests that the canon is more normative than descriptive.

Many distinguished scholars have indeed characterized the canon as "normative" and have defended it in those terms. *See, e.g.*, Philip P. Frickey, *Getting from Joe to Gene (McCarthy): The Avoidance Canon, Legal Process Theory, and Narrowing Statutory Interpretation in the Early Warren Court*, 93 CAL. L. REV. 397, 450 (2005); Ernest A. Young, *Constitutional Avoidance, Resistance Norms, and the Preservation of Judicial Review*, 78 TEX. L. REV. 1549, 1551 (2000). On one view, the Constitution identifies certain values that legislatures might not share, and that legislatures can override when they really want to, but that statutes should not be understood to override unless the statutes speak with special clarity. In effect, those values would enjoy an intermediate level of protection against the legislature—not the robust protection that comes from firm constitutional limitations (which flatly prevent legislatures from doing certain things), but still some insulation against ill-considered overrides. *See id.* at 1585–99 (characterizing the canon that favors avoiding constitutional doubts as a "resistance norm" that imposes a "soft limit" on the legislature).

But if the Constitution does indeed give Congress the power to establish particular legal directives, and if ordinary principles of interpretation suggest that Congress intended to use that power, is it really appropriate for courts to read the statute to mean something else just because Congress was not crystal clear? Does that approach give supposed "constitutional values" more protection than the Constitution itself truly gives them?

Some advocates of the canon have responded to this concern by invoking the concept of "underenforced constitutional norms."[24] Suppose that a particular interpretation of a statute would raise serious constitutional doubts. Even if courts would ultimately resolve those doubts in favor of constitutionality, that outcome might simply reflect limitations on the courts' institutional capacities and role; the doctrinal tests that courts have developed to implement the Constitution will not catch all constitutional defects in all statutes. According to some scholars, a canon that encourages courts to look for a different interpretation of the statute (thereby avoiding policies that might *be* unconstitutional even though courts cannot *hold* them unconstitutional) is an appropriate way to strengthen otherwise underenforced constitutional norms. *See* Cass Sunstein, *Interpreting Statutes in the Regulatory State*, 103 HARV. L. REV. 405, 468–69 (1989); *accord* WILLIAM N. ESKRIDGE, JR., DYNAMIC STATUTORY INTERPRETATION 286–87 (1994); Frickey, *supra*, 93 CAL. L. REV. at 455; Katyal & Schmidt, *supra*, 128 HARV. L. REV. at 2159–60; Young, *supra*, 78 TEX. L. REV. at 1603–04, 1609–13.

If the canon about avoiding constitutional doubts rests on this argument, though, should the canon operate only with respect to aspects of the Constitution that are "underenforced" in the relevant sense? Can courts reliably distinguish those aspects of the Constitution from others? *Cf.* Sunstein, *supra*, 103 HARV. L. REV. at 468 n.229 (noting "the highly controversial nature of particular views about which constitutional norms are underenforced").

Even if courts can indeed tell which constitutional norms are underenforced, and even if institutional constraints prevent the courts from beefing up direct enforcement of those norms, might the courts' efforts to achieve *indirect* enforcement (via a normative canon of statutory interpretation) end up doing more harm than good? Imagine that a statute is not crystal clear, but the ordinary techniques that courts use for identifying the intended meaning of statutory language favor Interpretation #1. Imagine, however, that this reading would trench on an "underenforced constitutional norm" (meaning that although Interpretation #1 satisfies the doctrinal tests that courts use to implement the Constitution, there is still some chance that it is unconstitutional). Even though standard "descriptive" analysis persuades courts that members of the enacting legislature probably intended Interpretation #1, and even though Interpretation #1 satisfies the best doctrinal tests that courts have been able to develop to enforce the Constitution, should courts adopt a different interpretation so as to reduce the risk of enforcing an unconstitutional directive? Wouldn't that approach predictably create more mismatches between the meanings that courts ascribe to statutes and the meanings that members of the

---

[24] That phrase comes from Lawrence Gene Sager, *Fair Measure: The Legal Status of Underenforced Constitutional Norms*, 91 HARV. L. REV. 1212 (1978), although Dean Sager was not himself discussing the canon that favors avoiding constitutional doubts.

enacting legislature collectively intended, and don't such mismatches create risks of their own—such as potentially throwing wrenches into complicated statutory schemes, or blocking policies that are both constitutional and (in Congress's judgment) good for society?[25]

Of course, if the canon that favors avoiding constitutional doubts causes courts to depart from the intended meaning of a statute, Congress could respond by reiterating its preferred directives in clearer language. *Cf.* ESKRIDGE, *supra*, at 286 (arguing for this reason that the canon "is not seriously undemocratic"). According to Judge Richard Posner, however, that possibility does not reduce the costs of the canon as much as one might think. In his words,

> "Congress's practical ability to overrule a judicial decision misconstruing one of its statutes, given all the other matters pressing for its attention, is less today than ever before, and probably was never very great. The practical effect of interpreting statutes to avoid raising constitutional questions is therefore to enlarge the already vast reach of constitutional prohibition beyond even the most extravagant modern interpretation of the Constitution—to create a judge-made constitutional 'penumbra' that has much the same prohibitory effect as the judge-made (or at least judge-amplified) Constitution itself. And we do not need that."

Richard A. Posner, *Statutory Interpretation—in the Classroom and in the Courtroom*, 50 U. CHI. L. REV. 800, 816 (1983).

Judge Easterbrook, whose textualist approach to interpretation is very different than Judge Posner's pragmatism, shares Judge Posner's distaste for the canon about avoiding constitutional doubts. *See* Frank H. Easterbrook, *Do Liberals and Conservatives Differ in Judicial Activism?*, 73 U. COLO. L. REV. 1401, 1405–06 (2002) (calling the canon "wholly illegitimate" and "a misuse of judicial power"). Among other things, Judge Easterbrook notes that the canon lends itself to manipulation:

> "Because the many hundreds of constitutional decisions over the years represent coalitions of Justices with very different approaches to constitutional law, doubt is everywhere; a large stock of precedents containing incompatible decisions enables almost anything to be 'proved' in a semi-logical manner, which greatly increases the domain of constitutional doubts. Thus this canon acts as a roving commission to rewrite statutes to taste. Because doubt is pervasive, Justices can seize on that uncertainty to disregard the actual legislative resolution—yet without finding the law unconstitutional."

[25] This paragraph distills arguments from Nelson, *supra*, 128 HARV. L. REV. F. at 344–45. *Cf. id.* at 345 ("I am skeptical that courts should *ever* adopt an interpretive attitude of deliberate resistance to the directives that Congress probably intended to establish. . . . I would prefer courts simply to do the best job they can both in conducting judicial review and in interpreting statutes, without trying to compensate for their imperfections in one realm by magnifying their imperfections in the other.").

Id. at 1405 (footnote omitted).

Are these arguments best understood as wholesale repudiations of the canon about avoiding constitutional doubts? Or are they instead arguments for applying the canon only when a statute is genuinely indeterminate on some point—that is, only when the court is otherwise in equipoise between two interpretations of the statute, neither of which seems more likely than the other to reflect what the enacting legislature really meant but one of which would force the court to address a difficult question of constitutional law? *Cf.* Schauer, *supra*, 1995 SUP. CT. REV. at 83, 98 (finding it "hard to imagine" a case of true equipoise, and proceeding to contemplate "abandoning [the canon] entirely").

The following case is one of the most frequently cited precedents that relies on the canon about avoiding constitutional doubts. As you read it, ask yourself whether the majority used the canon too aggressively.

NLRB v. Catholic Bishop of Chicago

440 U.S. 490 (1979)

■ *CHIEF JUSTICE BURGER delivered the opinion of the Court:*

This case arises out of the National Labor Relations Board's exercise of jurisdiction over lay faculty members at two groups of Catholic high schools. We granted certiorari to consider two questions: (a) Whether teachers in schools operated by a church to teach both religious and secular subjects are within the jurisdiction granted by the National Labor Relations Act; and (b) if the Act authorizes such jurisdiction, does its exercise violate the guarantees of the Religion Clauses of the First Amendment?

I

One group of schools is operated by the Catholic Bishop of Chicago, a corporation sole .... [It] consists of two schools, Quigley North and Quigley South. Those schools are termed "minor seminaries" because of their role in educating high school students who may become priests.... The schools ... provide special religious instruction not offered in other Catholic secondary schools. The[y] ... also offer essentially the same college-preparatory curriculum as public secondary schools....

[The other group of schools, operated by the Diocese of Fort Wayne-South Bend, consists of five high schools.] Unlike the Quigley schools, the special recommendation of a priest is not a prerequisite for admission. Like the Quigley schools, however, these high schools seek to provide a traditional secular education but oriented to the tenets of the Roman Catholic faith; religious training is also mandatory....

[In 1974 and 1975, labor unions filed representation petitions with respect to lay teachers at these schools. In proceedings before the National Labor Relations Board, the schools challenged the Board's assertion of jurisdiction on both statutory and constitutional grounds.

The Board rejected the schools' arguments and ordered representation elections to be held. The Board relied upon a prior decision in which it had distinguished organizations that were "completely religious" from organizations that were merely "religiously associated"; while the Board declined to exercise jurisdiction over organizations that were "completely religious," it held that the schools here did not fit into that category.]

In the Board-supervised election at the Quigley schools, the Quigley Education Alliance, a union affiliated with the Illinois Education Association, prevailed and was certified as the exclusive bargaining representative for 46 lay teachers. In the Diocese of Fort Wayne-South Bend, the Community Alliance for Teachers of Catholic High Schools, a similar union organization, prevailed and was certified as the representative for the approximately 180 lay teachers. Notwithstanding the Board's order, the schools declined to recognize the unions or to bargain. The unions filed unfair labor practice complaints with the Board under §§ 8(a)(1) and (5) of the National Labor Relations Act, 49 Stat. 452, as amended, 29 U.S.C. §§ 158(a)(1) and (5). The schools . . . again challeng[ed] the Board's exercise of jurisdiction over religious schools on both statutory and constitutional grounds.

. . . . The Board concluded that the schools had violated the Act and ordered that they cease their unfair labor practices and that they bargain collectively with the unions. . . .

II

The schools challenged the Board's orders in petitions to the Court of Appeals for the Seventh Circuit. That court denied enforcement of the Board's orders. 559 F.2d 1112 (1977). . . . It concluded that . . . the Board's distinction between "completely religious" and "merely religiously associated" failed to provide a workable guide for the exercise of discretion. . . .

The Court of Appeals recognized that the rejection of [this distinction] . . . meant that the Board would extend its jurisdiction to all church-operated schools. The court therefore turned to the question of whether the Board could exercise that jurisdiction, consistent with constitutional limitations. It concluded that both the Free Exercise Clause and the Establishment Clause of the First Amendment foreclosed the Board's jurisdiction. It reasoned that from the initial act of certifying a union as the bargaining agent for lay teachers the Board's action would impinge upon the freedom of church authorities to shape and direct teaching in accord with the requirements of their religion. . . .

The court distinguished local regulations which required fire inspections or state laws mandating attendance, reasoning that they did not "have the clear inhibiting potential upon the relationship between teachers and employers with which the present Board order is directly concerned." *Id.* at 1124. The court held that interference with management prerogatives, found acceptable in an ordinary commercial setting, was not acceptable in an area protected by the First Amendment. "The real difficulty is found in the chilling aspect that the requirement of bargaining will impose on the exercise of the bishops' control of the religious mission of the schools." *Ibid.* . . .

IV

. . . .

Although the respondents press their claims under the Religion Clauses, the question we consider first is whether Congress intended the Board to have jurisdiction over teachers in church-operated schools. In a number of cases the Court has heeded the essence of Mr. Chief Justice Marshall's admonition in *Murray v. The Charming Betsy*, 2 Cranch 64, 118 (1804), by holding that an Act of Congress ought not be construed to violate the Constitution if any other possible construction remains available. Moreover, the Court has followed this policy in the interpretation of the Act now before us and related statutes.

In *Machinists v. Street*, 367 U.S. 740 (1961), for example, the Court considered claims that serious First Amendment questions would arise if the Railway Labor Act were construed to allow compulsory union dues to be used to support political candidates or causes not approved by some members. The Court looked to the language of the Act and the legislative history and concluded that they did not permit union dues to be used for such political purposes, thus avoiding "serious doubt of [the Act's] constitutionality." *Id.* at 749.

Similarly in *McCulloch v. Sociedad Nacional de Marineros de Honduras*, 372 U.S. 10 (1963), a case involving the Board's assertion of jurisdiction over foreign seamen, the Court declined to read the National Labor Relations Act so as to give rise to a serious question of separation of powers which in turn would have implicated sensitive issues of the authority of the Executive over relations with foreign nations. The international implications of the case led the Court to describe it as involving "public questions particularly high in the scale of our national interest." *Id.* at 17. Because of those questions the Court held that before sanctioning the Board's exercise of jurisdiction " 'there must be present the affirmative intention of the Congress clearly expressed.' " *Id.* at 21–22 (quoting *Benz v. Compania Naviera Hidalgo*, 353 U.S. 138, 147 (1957)).

The values enshrined in the First Amendment plainly rank high "in the scale of our national values." In keeping with the Court's prudential policy it is incumbent on us to determine whether the Board's exercise of its jurisdiction here would give rise to serious constitutional questions. If so, we must first identify "the affirmative intention of the Congress clearly expressed" before concluding that the Act grants jurisdiction.

V

In recent decisions involving aid to parochial schools we have recognized the critical and unique role of the teacher in fulfilling the mission of a church-operated school. What was said of the schools in *Lemon v. Kurtzman*, 403 U.S. 602, 617 (1971), is true of the schools in this case: "Religious authority necessarily pervades the school system." The key role played by teachers in such a school system has been the predicate for our conclusions that governmental aid channeled through teachers creates an impermissible risk of excessive governmental entanglement in the affairs of the church-operated schools. For example, in *Lemon* we wrote:

> "In terms of potential for involving some aspect of faith or morals *in secular subjects*, a textbook's content is ascertainable, but a teacher's handling of a subject is not. We cannot ignore the danger that a teacher under religious control and discipline poses to the separation of the religious from the purely secular aspects of pre-college education. The conflict of functions inheres in the situation." (Emphasis added.)

Only recently we again noted the importance of the teacher's function in a church school: "Whether the subject is 'remedial reading,' 'advanced reading,' or simply 'reading,' a teacher remains a teacher, and the danger that religious doctrine will become intertwined with secular instruction persists." *Meek v. Pittenger*, 421 U.S. 349, 370 (1975). . . . Good intentions by government—or third parties—can surely no more avoid entanglement with the religious mission of the school in the setting of mandatory collective bargaining than in the well-motivated legislative efforts consented to by the church-operated schools which we found unacceptable in *Lemon*, *Meek*, and *Wolman v. Walter*, 433 U.S. 229 (1977).

The Board argues that it can avoid excessive entanglement since it will resolve only factual issues such as whether an anti-union animus motivated an employer's action. But at this stage of our consideration we are not compelled to determine whether the entanglement is excessive as we would were we considering the constitutional issue. Rather, we make a narrow inquiry whether the exercise of the Board's jurisdiction presents a significant risk that the First Amendment will be infringed.

Moreover, it is already clear that the Board's actions will go beyond resolving factual issues. The Court of Appeals' opinion refers to charges of unfair labor practices filed against religious schools. 559 F.2d at 1125, 1126. The court observed that in those cases the schools had responded that their challenged actions were mandated by their religious creeds. The resolution of such charges by the Board, in many instances, will necessarily involve inquiry into the good faith of the position asserted by the clergy-administrators and its relationship to the school's religious mission. It is not only the conclusions that may be reached by the Board which may impinge on rights guaranteed by the Religion Clauses, but also the very process of inquiry leading to findings and conclusions.

The Board's exercise of jurisdiction will have at least one other impact on church-operated schools. The Board will be called upon to decide what are "terms and conditions of employment" and therefore mandatory subjects of bargaining. See 29 U.S.C. § 158(d). Although the Board has not interpreted that phrase as it relates to educational institutions, similar state provisions provide insight into the effect of mandatory bargaining. The Oregon Court of Appeals noted that "nearly everything that goes on in the schools affects teachers and is therefore arguably a 'condition of employment.'" *Springfield Education Assn. v. Springfield School Dist. No. 19*, 547 P.2d 647, 650 (Or. App. 1976).

The Pennsylvania Supreme Court aptly summarized the effect of mandatory bargaining when it observed that the "introduction of a concept of mandatory collective bargaining, regardless of how narrowly the scope of negotiation is defined, necessarily represents an encroachment upon the former autonomous position of management." *Pennsylvania Labor Relations Board v. State College Area School Dist.*, 337 A.2d 262, 267 (Pa. 1975). . . . Inevitably the Board's inquiry will implicate sensitive issues that open the door to conflicts between clergy-administrators and the Board, or conflicts with negotiators for unions. What we said in *Lemon* applies as well here: "[P]arochial schools involve substantial religious activity and purpose. The substantial religious character of these church-related schools gives rise to entangling church-state relationships of the kind the Religion Clauses sought to avoid." [403 U.S. at 616 (footnote omitted).] Mr. Justice Douglas emphasized this in his concurring opinion in *Lemon*, noting "the admitted and obvious fact that the *raison d'être* of parochial schools is the propagation of a religious faith." [*Id.*] at 628.

The church-teacher relationship in a church-operated school differs from the employment relationship in a public or other nonreligious school. We see no escape from conflicts flowing from the Board's exercise of jurisdiction over teachers in church-operated schools and the consequent serious First Amendment questions that would follow. We therefore turn to an examination of the National Labor Relations Act to decide whether it must be read to confer jurisdiction that would in turn require a decision on the constitutional claims raised by respondents.

VI

There is no clear expression of an affirmative intention of Congress that teachers in church-operated schools should be covered by the Act. Admittedly, Congress defined the Board's jurisdiction in very broad terms; we must therefore examine the legislative history of the Act to determine whether Congress contemplated that the grant of jurisdiction would include teachers in such schools.

In enacting the National Labor Relations Act in 1935, Congress sought to protect the right of American workers to bargain collectively. The concern that was repeated throughout the debates was the need to assure workers the right to organize to counterbalance the collective activities of employers which had been authorized by the National Industrial Recovery Act. But congressional attention focused on employment in private industry and on industrial recovery. See, *e.g.*, 79 Cong. Rec. 7573 (1935) (remarks of Sen. Wagner), 2 National Labor Relations Board, Legislative History of the National Labor Relations Act, 1935, pp. 2341–2343 (1949).

Our examination of the statute and its legislative history indicates that Congress simply gave no consideration to church-operated schools. It is not without significance, however, that the Senate Committee on Education and Labor chose a college professor's dispute with the college as an example of employer-employee relations *not* covered by the Act. S. Rep. No. 573, 74th Cong., 1st Sess., 7 (1935), 2 Legislative History, *supra*, at 2307.

Congress' next major consideration of the jurisdiction of the Board came during the passage of the Labor Management Relations Act of 1947—the Taft-Hartley Act. In that Act Congress amended the definition of "employer" in § 2 of the original Act to exclude nonprofit hospitals. 61 Stat. 137, 29 U.S.C. § 152(2) (1970 ed.). There was some discussion of the scope of the Board's jurisdiction but the consensus was that nonprofit institutions in general did not fall within the Board's jurisdiction because they did not affect commerce. . . .

The most recent significant amendment to the Act was passed in 1974, removing the exemption of nonprofit hospitals. Pub. L. 93–360, 88 Stat. 395. The Board relies upon that amendment as showing that Congress approved the Board's exercise of jurisdiction over church-operated schools. A close examination of that legislative history, however, reveals nothing to indicate an affirmative intention that such schools be within the Board's jurisdiction. Since the Board did not assert jurisdiction over teachers in a church-operated school until after the 1974 amendment, nothing in the history of the amendment can be read as reflecting Congress' tacit approval of the Board's action.

During the debate there were expressions of concern about the effect of the bill on employees of religious hospitals whose religious beliefs would not permit them to join a union. 120 Cong. Rec. 12946, 16914 (1974), Legislative History of the Coverage of Nonprofit Hospitals under the National Labor Relations Act, 1974, 93d Cong., 2d Sess., 118, 331–332 (1974) (remarks of Sen. Ervin and Rep. Erlenborn). The result of those concerns was an amendment which reflects congressional sensitivity to First Amendment guarantees:

> "Any employee of a health care institution who is a member of and adheres to established and traditional tenets or teachings of a bona fide religion, body, or sect which has historically held conscientious objections to joining or financially supporting labor organizations shall not be required to join or financially support any labor organization as a condition of employment; except that such employee may be required, in lieu of periodic dues and initiation fees, to pay sums equal to such dues and initiation fees to a nonreligious charitable fund exempt from taxation under section 501(c)(3) of title

> 26, chosen by such employee from a list of at least three such funds, designated in a contract between such institution and a labor organization, or if the contract fails to designate such funds, then to any such fund chosen by the employee." 29 U.S.C. § 169.

The absence of an "affirmative intention of the Congress clearly expressed" fortifies our conclusion that Congress did not contemplate that the Board would require church-operated schools to grant recognition to unions as bargaining agents for their teachers.

The Board relies heavily upon *Associated Press v. NLRB*, 301 U.S. 103 (1937). There the Court held that the First Amendment was no bar to the application of the Act to the Associated Press, an organization engaged in collecting information and news throughout the world and distributing it to its members. Perceiving nothing to suggest that application of the Act would infringe First Amendment guarantees of press freedoms, the Court sustained Board jurisdiction. Here, on the contrary, the record affords abundant evidence that the Board's exercise of jurisdiction over teachers in church-operated schools would implicate the guarantees of the Religion Clauses.

Accordingly, in the absence of a clear expression of Congress' intent to bring teachers in church-operated schools within the jurisdiction of the Board, we decline to construe the Act in a manner that could in turn call upon the Court to resolve difficult and sensitive questions arising out of the guarantees of the First Amendment Religion Clauses. . . .

■ *JUSTICE BRENNAN, with whom JUSTICES WHITE, MARSHALL, and BLACKMUN join, dissenting:*

The Court today holds that coverage of the National Labor Relations Act does not extend to lay teachers employed by church-operated schools. That construction is plainly wrong in light of the Act's language, its legislative history, and this Court's precedents. It is justified solely on the basis of a canon of statutory construction seemingly invented by the Court for the purpose of deciding this case. I dissent.

I

The general principle of construing statutes to avoid unnecessary constitutional decisions is a well-settled and salutary one. The governing canon, however, is *not* that expressed by the Court today. The Court requires that there be a "clear expression of an affirmative intention of Congress" before it will bring within the coverage of a broadly worded regulatory statute certain persons whose coverage might raise constitutional questions. But those familiar with the legislative process know that explicit expressions of congressional intent in such broadly inclusive statutes are not commonplace. Thus, by strictly or loosely applying its requirement, the Court can virtually remake congressional enactments. This flouts Mr. Chief Justice Taft's admonition "that amendment may not be substituted for construction, and that a court may not exercise legislative functions to save [a] law from conflict with constitutional limitation." *Yu Cong Eng v. Trinidad*, 271 U.S. 500, 518 (1926). . . .

The settled canon for construing statutes wherein constitutional questions may lurk was stated in *Machinists v. Street*, 367 U.S. 740 (1961) . . . :

> " 'When the validity of an act of the Congress is drawn in question, and even if a serious doubt of constitutionality is raised, it is a cardinal principle that this Court will first ascertain whether a construction of the statute is *fairly possible* by which the question may be avoided.' *Crowell v. Benson*, 285 U.S. 22, 62." *Id.* at 749–750 (emphasis added).

. . . . This limitation to constructions that are "fairly possible," and "reasonable," see *Yu Cong Eng v. Trinidad*, 271 U.S. at 518, acts as a brake against wholesale judicial dismemberment of congressional enactments. It confines the judiciary to its proper role in construing statutes, which is to interpret them so as to give effect to congressional intention. The Court's new "affirmative expression" rule releases that brake.

II

The interpretation of the National Labor Relations Act announced by the Court today is not "fairly possible." The Act's wording, its legislative history, and the Court's own precedents leave "the intention of the Congress . . . revealed too distinctly to permit us to ignore it because of mere misgivings as to power." *Moore Ice Cream Co. v. Rose*, [289 U.S. 373, 379 (1933)]. Section 2(2) of the Act, 29 U.S.C. § 152(2), [says that the term] "employer" [includes] . . .

> ". . . any person acting as an agent of an employer, directly or indirectly, *but shall not include* the United States or any wholly owned Government corporation, or any Federal Reserve Bank, or any State or political subdivision thereof, or any person subject to the Railway Labor Act, as amended from time to time, or any labor organization (other than when acting as an employer), or anyone acting in the capacity of officer or agent of such labor organization." (Emphasis added.)

Thus, the Act covers all employers not within the eight express exceptions. The Court today substitutes amendment for construction to insert one more exception—for church-operated schools. This is a particularly transparent violation of the judicial role: The legislative history reveals that Congress itself considered and rejected a very similar amendment.

The pertinent legislative history of the NLRA begins with the Wagner Act of 1935, 49 Stat. 449. Section 2(2) of that Act, identical in all relevant respects to the current section, excluded from its coverage neither church-operated schools nor any other private nonprofit organization. Accordingly, in applying that Act, the National Labor

Relations Board did not recognize an exception for nonprofit employers, even when religiously associated. An argument for an implied nonprofit exemption was rejected because the design of the Act was as clear then as it is now: "[N]either charitable institutions nor their employees are exempted from operation of the Act by its terms, although certain other employers and employees are exempted." *Central Dispensary & Emergency Hospital*, 44 N.L.R.B. 533, 540 (1942) (footnotes omitted), enf'd, 79 U.S. App. D.C. 274, 145 F.2d 852 (1944). Both the lower courts and this Court concurred in the Board's construction. See *Polish National Alliance v. NLRB*, 322 U.S. 643 (1944), aff'g 136 F.2d 175 (CA7 1943); *Associated Press v. NLRB*, 301 U.S. 103 (1937), aff'g 85 F.2d 56 (CA2 1936) . . . .

The Hartley bill, which passed the House of Representatives in 1947, would have provided the exception the Court today writes into the statute:

> "The term 'employer' . . . shall not include . . . any corporation, community chest, fund, or foundation organized and operated exclusively for *religious*, charitable, scientific, literary, or *educational* purposes, . . . no part of the net earnings of which inures to the benefit of any private shareholder or individual . . . ." (Emphasis added.) H.R. 3020, 80th Cong., 1st Sess., § 2(2) (Apr. 18, 1947), reprinted in National Labor Relations Board, Legislative History of the Labor Management Relations Act, 1947, pp. 160–161 (hereafter, 1947 Leg. Hist.).

But the proposed exception was not enacted.[5] The bill reported by the Senate Committee on Labor and Public Welfare did not contain the Hartley exception. . . . Instead, the Senate proposed an exception limited to nonprofit hospitals, and passed the bill in that form. . . . The Senate version was accepted by the House in conference, thus limiting the exception for nonprofit employers to nonprofit hospitals. Ch. 120, 61 Stat. 136.[6]

---

[5] A number of reasons were offered for the rejection of the Hartley bill's exception. Some Congressmen strongly opposed the exception, see 93 Cong. Rec. 3446 (1947) (remarks of Rep. Klein); some were opposed to additional exceptions to the Board's jurisdiction, see *id.* at 4997 (remarks of Sen. Taft); and some thought it unnecessary, see H.R. Conf. Rep. No. 510, 80th Cong., 1st Sess., 32 (1947), 1947 Leg. Hist. 536. See generally *NLRB v. Wentworth Institute*, 515 F.2d 550, 555 (CA1 1975) ("[P]erhaps the most obvious[ ] interpretation of the rejection of the House exclusion would be that Congress meant to include nonprofit organizations [within the scope of the Act]"); Sherman & Black, The Labor Board and the Private Nonprofit Employer: A Critical Examination of the Board's Worthy Cause Exemption, 83 Harv. L. Rev. 1323, 1331–1337 (1970). But whatever the reasons, it is clear that an amendment similar to that made by the Court today was proposed and rejected in 1947.

[6] The Board's contemporaneous construction of the 1947 amendment was that only nonprofit hospitals were intended to be exempt. In 1950, for example, in asserting jurisdiction over a nonprofit religious organization, the Board stated:

> "The Employer asserts that, as it is a nonprofit organization which is engaged in purely religious activities, it is not engaged in commerce within the meaning of the Act. We find no merit in this contention. . . . As this Board and the courts have held, it is immaterial that the Employer may be a nonprofit organization, or that its activities may be motivated by considerations other than those applicable to enterprises which are, in the generally

Even that limited exemption was ultimately repealed in 1974. Pub. L. 93–360, 88 Stat. 395. In doing so, Congress confirmed the view of the Act expressed here: that it was intended to cover all employers—including nonprofit employers—unless expressly excluded, and that the 1947 amendment excluded only nonprofit hospitals. See H.R. Rep. No. 93–1051, p. 4 (1974), reprinted in Senate Committee on Labor and Public Welfare, Legislative History of the Coverage of Nonprofit Hospitals under the National Labor Relations Act, 1974, p. 272 (Comm. Print 1974) (hereafter 1974 Leg. Hist.) . . . .[7] Moreover, it is significant that in considering the 1974 amendments, the Senate expressly rejected an amendment proposed by Senator Ervin that was analogous to the one the Court today creates—an amendment to exempt nonprofit hospitals operated by religious groups. . . . Senator Cranston, floor manager of the Senate Committee bill and primary opponent of the proposed religious exception, explained:

> "[S]uch an exception for religiously affiliated hospitals would seriously erode *the existing national policy which holds religiously affiliated institutions generally such as* proprietary nursing homes, residential communities, and *educational facilities to the same standards as their nonsectarian counterparts*." 120 Cong. Rec. 12957 (1974), 1974 Leg. Hist. 137 (emphasis added).

See also *ibid.* (Sen. Javits); 120 Cong. Rec. 12957 (1974), 1974 Leg. Hist. 138 (Sen. Williams).

In construing the Board's jurisdiction to exclude church-operated schools, therefore, the Court today is faithful to neither the statute's

---

accepted sense, commercial." *Sunday School Board of the Southern Baptist Convention*, 92 N.L.R.B. 801, 802.

It is true that in *Trustees of Columbia University*, 97 N.L.R.B. 424 (1951), the Board indicated that it would not exercise jurisdiction over nonprofit, educational institutions; but it expressly did so as a matter of discretion, affirming that the activities of the University did come within the Act and the Board's jurisdiction. *Id.* at 425. That 1951 discretionary decision does not undermine the validity of the Board's determination in *Cornell University*, 183 N.L.R.B. 329 (1970), that changing conditions—particularly the increasing impact of such institutions on interstate commerce—now required a change in policy leading to the renewed exercise of Board jurisdiction. As we emphasized in *NLRB v. J. Weingarten, Inc.*, 420 U.S. 251, 265–266 (1975):

> "To hold that the Board's earlier decisions froze the development of this important aspect of the national labor law would misconceive the nature of administrative decisionmaking. ' "Cumulative experience" begets understanding and insight by which judgments . . . are validated or qualified or invalidated. The constant process of trial and error, on a wider and fuller scale than a single adversary litigation permits, differentiates perhaps more than anything else the administrative from the judicial process.' *NLRB v. Seven-Up Co.*, 344 U.S. 344, 349 (1953)."

[7] The House Report stated: "Currently, the only broad area of charitable, eleemosynary, educational institutions wherein the Board does not now exercise jurisdiction concerns the nonprofit hospitals, explicitly excluded by section 2(2) of the Act. . . . [T]he bill removes the existing Taft-Hartley exemption in section 2(2) of the Act. It restores to the employees of nonprofit hospitals the same rights and protections enjoyed by the employees of proprietary hospitals and most all other employees." H.R. Rep. No. 93–1051, p. 4 (1974). Similarly, Senator Williams, Chairman of the Senate Committee on Labor and Public Welfare, criticized the nonprofit-hospital exemption as "not only inconsistent with the protection enjoyed by proprietary hospitals and other types of health care institutions, but . . . also inconsistent with the coverage of other nonprofit activities." 120 Cong. Rec. 12938 (1974), 1974 Leg. Hist. 95. See also 120 Cong. Rec. 16900 (1974), 1974 Leg. Hist. 291 (Rep. Ashbrook).

language nor its history. Moreover, it is also untrue to its own precedents. . . . Indeed, *Associated Press v. NLRB*, 301 U.S. 103 (1937), construed the Act to cover editorial employees of a nonprofit news-gathering organization despite a claim—precisely parallel to that made here—that their inclusion rendered the Act in violation of the First Amendment. Today's opinion is simply unable to explain the grounds that distinguish that case from this one.

Thus, the available authority indicates that Congress intended to include—not exclude—lay teachers of church-operated schools. The Court does not counter this with evidence that Congress *did* intend an exception it never stated. Instead, despite the legislative history to the contrary, it construes the Act as excluding lay teachers only because Congress did not state explicitly that they were covered. In Mr. Justice Cardozo's words, this presses "avoidance of a difficulty . . . to the point of disingenuous evasion." *Moore Ice Cream Co. v. Rose*, 289 U.S. at 379.[11]

III

Under my view that the NLRA includes within its coverage lay teachers employed by church-operated schools, the constitutional questions presented would have to be reached. I do not now do so only because the Court does not. See *Sierra Club v. Morton*, 405 U.S. 727, 755 (1972) (Brennan, J., dissenting). I repeat for emphasis, however, that while the resolution of the constitutional question is not without difficulty, it is irresponsible to avoid it by a cavalier exercise in statutory interpretation which succeeds only in defying congressional intent. A statute is not "a nose of wax to be changed from that which the plain language imports . . . ." *Yu Cong Eng v. Trinidad*, 271 U.S. at 518.

NOTES AND QUESTIONS

1. Whatever the justifications for the canon that favors avoiding constitutional doubts, the Supreme Court has said that "[s]tatutes should be interpreted to avoid *serious* constitutional doubts, . . . not to eliminate all possible contentions that the statute *might* be unconstitutional." *Reno v. Flores*, 507 U.S. 292, 314 n.9 (1993). In the Court's words, "those who invoke the doctrine must believe that the alternative is a serious likelihood that the statute will be held unconstitutional." *Almendarez-*

[11] Not even the Court's redrafting of the statute causes all First Amendment problems to disappear. The Court's opinion implies limitation of its exception to church-operated schools. That limitation is doubtless necessary since this Court has already rejected a more general exception for nonprofit organizations. See *Polish National Alliance v. NLRB*, 322 U.S. 643 (1944). But such an exemption, available only to church-operated schools, generates a possible Establishment Clause *question* of its own. *Walz v. Tax Comm'n*, 397 U.S. 664 (1970), does not put that question to rest, for in upholding the property tax exemption for churches there at issue, we emphasized that New York had "not singled out . . . churches as such; rather, it has granted exemption to all houses of religious worship within a broad class of property owned by nonprofit, quasi-public corporations . . . ." *Id.* at 673. Like the Court, "at this stage of [my] consideration [I am] not compelled to determine whether the [Establishment Clause problem] is [as significant] as [I] would were [I] considering the constitutional issue." *Ante* at 502. It is enough to observe that no matter which way the Court turns in interpreting the Act, it cannot avoid constitutional questions.

Torres v. United States, 523 U.S. 224, 238 (1998); *see also, e.g.*, Gonzalez v. United States, 553 U.S. 242, 251 (2008) ("The canon . . . does not apply unless there are 'serious concerns about the statute's constitutionality.' " (quoting Harris v. United States, 536 U.S. 545, 555 (2002))); United States ex rel. Att'y Gen. v. Delaware & Hudson Co., 213 U.S. 366, 408 (1909) (referring to "grave and doubtful constitutional questions").

In the 1970s, when the Court heard the *Catholic Bishop* case, judicial doctrine was quite receptive to claims that the Constitution prevented a generally applicable statute from operating against someone whose religious practices it would burden. *See, e.g.*, Wisconsin v. Yoder, 406 U.S. 205 (1972) (Burger, C.J.) (holding that the Free Exercise Clause, as incorporated against the states by the Fourteenth Amendment, prevented Wisconsin from applying its general laws about school attendance to the Old Order Amish). In 1990, the Court changed its doctrine on this point. *See* Emp't Div. v. Smith, 494 U.S. 872, 879 (1990) ("[T]he right of free exercise does not relieve an individual of the obligation to comply with a 'valid and neutral law of general applicability on the ground that the law proscribes (or prescribes) conduct that his religion prescribes (or proscribes).' " (quoting United States v. Lee, 455 U.S. 252, 263 n.3 (1982) (Stevens, J., concurring in judgment))). Notwithstanding that change, though, the current Supreme Court might still have serious doubts about the constitutionality of applying the National Labor Relations Act with respect to at least some lay teachers in church-operated schools. *See* Our Lady of Guadalupe School v. Morrissey-Berru, 140 S. Ct. 2049 (2020) (holding that the Religion Clauses of the First Amendment prevent the Age Discrimination in Employment Act and the Americans with Disabilities Act from regulating relations between Catholic schools and lay teachers whose duties include teaching religion); *see also* Tandon v. Newsom, 141 S. Ct. 1294, 1296 (2021) (per curiam) (indicating that if government regulations exempt any secular activities from their coverage, the failure to exempt comparable religious activities is suspect).

2. In his dissenting opinion in *Catholic Bishop*, Justice Brennan did not deny that the constitutional question flagged by Chief Justice Burger was serious, but he did deny that the statute could fairly be read in a way that would avoid it. That argument relates to a second condition for application of the canon that favors avoiding constitutional doubts: "the statutory construction that avoids the constitutional question [must be] a 'fair' one," meaning that "the statute must be genuinely susceptible to two constructions [even] after . . . its complexities are unraveled." *Almendarez-Torres*, 523 U.S. at 238; *see also, e.g.*, Iancu v. Brunetti, 139 S. Ct. 2294, 2301 (2019) ("[T]hat canon of construction applies only when ambiguity exists."); Nielsen v. Preap, 139 S. Ct. 954, 972 (2019) ("Here the text of [the statute] cuts clearly against respondents' position, . . . making constitutional avoidance irrelevant."); Whitman v. Am. Trucking Ass'ns, 531 U.S. 457, 471 (2001) ("No matter how severe the constitutional doubt, courts may choose only between reasonably available interpretations of a text."); Miller v. French, 530 U.S. 327, 341 (2000) (concluding that the dissent's "flexible" interpretation of the relevant statute was not good enough to satisfy this standard); United States v. Locke, 471 U.S. 84, 96 (1985) ("We cannot press statutory construction 'to the point of disingenuous evasion' even to avoid a constitutional question.").

Did the statute that the Court was interpreting in *Catholic Bishop* satisfy this condition? Section 10 of the National Labor Relations Act empowered the National Labor Relations Board "to prevent any person from engaging in any unfair labor practice . . . affecting commerce." Section 8 defined the term "unfair labor practice" in terms of conduct by an "employer," while section 2 defined the word "commerce" to mean interstate or foreign commerce and the phrase "affecting commerce" to mean "in commerce, or burdening or obstructing commerce or the free flow of commerce, or having led or tending to lead to a labor dispute burdening or obstructing commerce or the free flow of commerce." The statutory-interpretation question in *Catholic Bishop* apparently boiled down to whether church-operated schools are "employers" whose unfair labor practices with respect to teachers "affect[ ] commerce." Did Chief Justice Burger's majority opinion interpret any of these terms? Or did it simply infer an unstated exception for teachers in church-operated schools, without identifying any particular textual hook?

If it did the latter, wasn't Justice Brennan right to object that the canon that favors avoiding constitutional doubts should operate only when statutory language is genuinely ambiguous or otherwise indeterminate? *Cf.* United States v. Albertini, 472 U.S. 675, 680 (1985) ("Statutes should be construed to avoid constitutional questions, but this interpretative canon is not a license for the judiciary to rewrite language enacted by the legislature."); *accord, e.g., Iancu*, 139 S. Ct. at 2301; Jennings v. Rodriguez, 138 S. Ct. 830, 842–43 (2018); Salinas v. United States, 522 U.S. 52, 59–60 (1997). Or can courts legitimately read unstated exceptions into seemingly general statutory language to avoid applications of the statute that would raise serious constitutional questions and that members of the enacting legislature did not seem to be thinking about? Does the fact that the legislature probably did not specifically contemplate these applications of its general rule itself create enough of an ambiguity to trigger the canon that favors avoiding constitutional doubts? *Compare* Zadvydas v. Davis, 533 U.S. 678, 688–99 (2001) (invoking the canon to support reading an "implicit limitation" into statutory language), *with id.* at 707 (Kennedy, J., dissenting) (protesting that the canon is not a license for the Court to "amend[ ] the statute"); *cf. Jennings*, 138 S. Ct. at 843 (calling *Zadvydas* "a notably generous application of the constitutional-avoidance canon").

3. If the majority in *Catholic Bishop* had been looking for a textual hook, where should it have turned? Justice Brennan was surely correct, was he not, that church-operated schools qualify as "employers" within the meaning of the Act? Insofar as they employ people, they fit the ordinary meaning of that term. Without making any exception for church-operated schools, moreover, § 2 of the statute expressly excepted eight other kinds of entities that might otherwise have qualified as "employers." The *expressio unius* canon thus reinforces Justice Brennan's view that courts lack authority to recognize further exceptions of the courts' own choosing.

But is it so clear that the activities of the typical church-operated school "affect[ ] commerce" within the meaning of the National Labor Relations Act of 1935? At least in 1935, many people would have doubted that the Commerce Clause, even in conjunction with the Necessary and Proper Clause, gave Congress the power to regulate labor relations at nonprofit local schools. Even in 1947, when Congress explicitly exempted nonprofit hospitals from the NLRA's definition of "employer," conferees for the House of Representatives assured their colleagues that the failure to include an explicit exemption for nonprofit schools, nonprofit religious corporations, and other nonprofit entities did not much matter: "only in exceptional circumstances and in connection with purely commercial activities of such organizations have any of the activities of such organizations or of their employees been considered as affecting commerce so as to bring them within the scope of the National Labor Relations Act." Statement of the Managers on the Part of the House, H.R. CONF. REP. NO. 510, 80th Cong., 1st Sess., at 32 (1947). *But see* Fredrick E. Sherman & Dennis B. Black, *The Labor Board and the Private Nonprofit Employer: A Critical Examination of the Board's Worthy Cause Exemption*, 83 HARV. L. REV. 1323, 1331 (1970) (questioning the "credibility" of this statement by the House conferees and arguing that its assurances "must be viewed with some skepticism").

By 1979, when the Supreme Court decided *Catholic Bishop*, "no one doubt[ed]" that Congress could use its commerce powers to regulate labor relations at nonprofit schools as well as at other businesses. *Catholic Bishop*, 440 U.S. at 516 (Brennan, J., dissenting). But when the NLRA was enacted in 1935, questions about the constitutionality of such a regulation would probably have centered on the scope of Congress's commerce powers rather than the possibility that application of the statute to teachers in church-operated schools would violate the Free Exercise Clause. Does it follow that Chief Justice Burger's opinion focused on the wrong constitutional doubt? If the canon about avoiding constitutional doubts is purely a "normative" canon designed to help courts avoid constitutional questions that they currently perceive as difficult, then the constitutional doubts that should guide its application are presumably those that exist at the time of interpretation rather than those that existed at the time of enactment. But Justices who see the canon as having more "descriptive" force may take the opposite position. *Cf.* WILLIAM N. ESKRIDGE, JR., PHILIP P. FRICKEY & ELIZABETH GARRETT,

CASES AND MATERIALS ON LEGISLATION: STATUTES AND THE CREATION OF PUBLIC POLICY 884 (3d ed. 2001) (observing that "when constitutional law has changed since the enactment of the statute," the canon that favors avoiding constitutional questions has an "artificial character"); Robert W. Scheef, *Temporal Dynamics in Statutory Interpretation: Courts, Congress, and the Canon of Constitutional Avoidance*, 64 U. PITT. L. REV. 529, 531 (2003) (arguing that the Supreme Court should apply the canon "in light of [constitutional doctrine] as it stood at the time Congress enacted the statute").

An interesting version of this question came up in *Harris v. United States*, 536 U.S. 545 (2002). As you saw in *Muscarello v. United States* (*supra* p. 167), 18 U.S.C. § 924(c)(1) made it a distinct federal crime for anyone to "use[ ]" or "carr[y]" a firearm "during and in relation to any . . . [federal] drug trafficking crime." In 1998, in reaction to the Supreme Court's narrow interpretation of the word "uses" in *Bailey v. United States*, 516 U.S. 137 (1995), Congress amended § 924(c)(1) so that it also covers anyone who "possesses" a firearm in furtherance of a drug trafficking crime. Congress set the base level of punishment for this crime at a minimum of five years in prison, but required offenders to be sentenced to at least seven years "if the firearm is brandished" and at least ten years "if the firearm is discharged." 18 U.S.C. § 924(c)(1)(A). In *Harris*, the Supreme Court had to decide whether the statute made "brandishing" a mere sentencing factor (to be applied by the judge at sentencing) or an element of the crime (to be proved to the jury beyond a reasonable doubt at trial). At the time that Congress had enacted the 1998 amendment, the governing precedent—*McMillan v. Pennsylvania*, 477 U.S. 79 (1986)—indicated that both of these options were within Congress's power. But the Supreme Court's subsequent decision in *Apprendi v. New Jersey*, 530 U.S. 466 (2000), called *McMillan* into question. In *Harris*, a defendant argued that in order to avoid having to confront the constitutional questions that *Apprendi* had identified, the Court should interpret the 1998 amendment to make "brandish[ing]" an element of the crime. But the Court rejected this invocation of the canon about avoiding constitutional doubts. Writing for a majority of the Court, Justice Kennedy observed:

> "The statute at issue in this case was passed when *McMillan* provided the controlling instruction, and Congress would have had no reason to believe that it was approaching the constitutional line by following that instruction. We would not further the canon's goal of eliminating friction with our coordinate branch, moreover, if we alleviated our doubt about a constitutional premise we had supplied by adopting a strained reading of a statute that Congress had enacted in reliance on the premise. And if we stretched the text to avoid the question of *McMillan*'s continuing vitality, the canon would embrace a dynamic view of statutory interpretation, under which the text might mean one thing when enacted yet another if

the prevailing view of the Constitution later changed. We decline to adopt that approach."

Harris, 536 U.S. at 556.[26]

Chapter 7 of this book will consider the concept of "dynamic" statutory interpretation in more detail. But was Justice Kennedy's position consistent with what the majority did in *Catholic Bishop*?

4. Even if one thinks that Chief Justice Burger's opinion in *Catholic Bishop* was correct to focus on the constitutional questions that were unsettled *in 1979* (which involved the Free Exercise Clause rather than the Commerce Clause), would it have been legitimate for the Court to avoid those questions by adopting a narrow interpretation of the statutory phrase "affecting commerce"? Or do the constitutional questions that trigger the canon have to match up more closely with the statutory language that the Court construes in such a way as to avoid them?

If this sort of matching up is not required, could a *secular* nonprofit school have taken advantage of the canon that favors avoiding constitutional doubts? Imagine that instead of accusing a church-operated school of unfair labor practices, the NLRB had launched similar proceedings against a nonreligious private school. Imagine further that the school had submitted the following argument to the Supreme Court: "If you interpret the statute to cover us (because our activities with our teachers 'affect[ ] commerce' within the meaning of the NLRA), then the statute would also cover church-operated schools; courts can't possibly say that our activities affect commerce but theirs do not. Interpreting the statute to cover church-operated schools, though, would raise serious questions under the Free Exercise Clause. To avoid having to face those questions later on, you should read the phrase 'affecting commerce' more narrowly, so that it does not reach local nonprofit schools." This sort of argument would be perfectly legitimate, wouldn't it? *See, e.g.*, Clark v. Martinez, 543 U.S. 371, 380 (2005) ("[W]hen deciding which of two plausible statutory constructions to adopt, a court must consider the necessary consequences of its choice. If one of them would raise a multitude of constitutional problems, the other should prevail—whether

---

[26] Although a majority of the Court joined the part of Justice Kennedy's opinion in *Harris* that included this passage, only a plurality joined the part in which Justice Kennedy answered the constitutional question that the Court had declined to avoid. *See id.* at 556–68 (plurality opinion of Kennedy, J.) (reaffirming *McMillan* and upholding the statute). The Supreme Court later overruled his answer. *See* Alleyne v. United States, 570 U.S. 99 (2013).

In retrospect, does the fate of Justice Kennedy's opinion in *Harris* suggest that it would have been desirable for him to have avoided the constitutional question after all? When courts confront and decide hard questions of constitutional law, they are likely to get some fraction of the answers wrong. Does that fact suggest a normative argument for the canon about avoiding constitutional doubts? If so, how would that argument interact with standard "descriptive" principles? Should courts ever deliberately read a statute to mean something other than what the enacting legislature probably intended so as to avoid having to face a hard constitutional question that the courts might get wrong?

or not those constitutional problems pertain to the particular litigant before the Court.").[27]

5. What exactly did the majority opinion in *Catholic Bishop* interpret the National Labor Relations Act to mean? Justice Brennan's dissent portrayed the majority as holding that church-operated schools are not "employers" within the meaning of the Act. *Catholic Bishop*, 440 U.S. at 511 (Brennan, J., dissenting). If that were true, though, then the Act would not govern the schools' relations with *any* of their employees. Is that what the majority said, or did it leave the scope of its holding unclear? *Compare* NLRB v. Hanna Boys Center, 940 F.2d 1295, 1300–02 (9th Cir. 1991) (noting that the constitutional question identified by the majority in *Catholic Bishop* involved teachers rather than other employees, and interpreting the Act to protect various "non-teaching employees" at a church-operated school), *with* Duquesne Univ. of the Holy Spirit v. NLRB, 947 F.3d 824, 837 (D.C. Cir. 2020) ("[W]e need not resolve the extent of the Board's jurisdiction under the NLRA in cases involving religious schools and their non-faculty employees . . . .").

E. CLEAR-STATEMENT AND IMPLIED-LIMITATION RULES

Most of the canons covered so far in this chapter can operate with respect to many different questions of statutory interpretation. But some canons are more targeted: they focus on a particular policy issue, and they tell courts to handle that issue in a certain way unless there are sufficiently clear indications that the enacting legislature meant to handle it differently. *See, e.g.*, Reno v. Catholic Social Servs., Inc., 509 U.S. 43, 63–64 (1993) (indicating that a federal statute should not be interpreted as foreclosing judicial review of the legality of administrative action unless there is "clear and convincing evidence" that Congress intended to do so).

---

[27] Justice Thomas dissented in *Clark v. Martinez*. He argued that "[a] litigant ordinarily cannot attack statutes as constitutionally invalid based on constitutional doubts concerning other litigants or factual circumstances," and he suggested that courts applying either the traditional saving canon or the canon that favors avoiding constitutional doubts should follow what he called "the usual rules of constitutional adjudication." *Id.* at 395–97 (Thomas, J., dissenting). But wasn't the majority correct to reject this argument? *See id.* at 381–82 (majority opinion) (noting that canons are about statutory interpretation, and the meaning of a statute does not vary "depending on the presence or absence of constitutional concerns in each individual case").

Justice Thomas's concerns sounded in doctrines about standing. But if you are concerned about a secular school's standing to point out the possible unconstitutionality of applying the NLRA against church-operated schools, think about exactly what the secular school would be arguing. The secular school would be arguing that the NLRA does not reach its own conduct—that the activities of local schools like it should not be understood to "affect commerce" within the meaning of the statute. Admittedly, the logic behind that argument would require reference to the fact that some other schools are operated by churches, and that an interpretation of the NLRA that reaches the secular school would also reach those other schools. But would the secular school really be trying to invoke the rights of those third parties in a way that standing doctrine prohibits? Wouldn't the secular school simply be explaining why the NLRA should not be interpreted to reach its own conduct—a position that it surely has standing to take?

Issue-specific canons of this sort sometimes are called "clear-statement rules," but that label may carry confusing overtones, and different people use it in different ways.[28] Whatever the proper label, though, issue-specific canons do exist.

Different issue-specific canons work in different ways. Some are simply tools for resolving conventional linguistic indeterminacy in statutes; they come into play when the ordinary meaning of statutory language is ambiguous or vague, and they help courts choose among the possible readings.[29] But other issue-specific canons target a different sort of uncertainty, generated by the special role of statutes in communicating policy decisions. Even in the absence of any conventional linguistic indeterminacy, interpreters might resist reading a generally worded statute to chart an unusual course on a sensitive policy question that the statute does not specifically address. Some canons formalize that hesitancy: they single out a particular issue and tell interpreters to handle it in a certain way *unless* there are sufficient indications that the legislature specifically confronted that issue and decided to handle it differently. In practice, canons of this sort encourage courts to read implied limitations into seemingly general statutory language—language that is broad enough as a matter of ordinary usage to encompass the issue in question, but that does not specifically address that issue or show that members of the enacting legislature thought about it.

The next two canons that we will cover—the presumption against extraterritoriality and the presumption against retroactivity—are good examples. When Congress drafts a statute, Congress often uses seemingly universal terms: the statute might regulate "any person" who engages in "any" conduct of a certain sort, and the statute says that "all" such conduct is unlawful. Often, though, there is no reason to think that Congress intended to regulate all people and all conduct throughout the whole world. Unless there is a clear indication that Congress intended the statute to operate "extraterritorially," courts will read implied geographic limitations into the statute. Similarly, there often is no reason

[28] For instance, Justice Thurgood Marshall's dissenting opinion in *EEOC v. Arabian American Oil Co.*, 499 U.S. 244 (1991), used the term "clear-statement rules" more narrowly than some other people do. In Justice Marshall's usage, a "clear-statement rule" is a normative canon that is designed "to shield important values" from legislative incursions and that can be overcome only by a clear statement in the text of the statute itself. *See id.* at 261–66 (Marshall, J., dissenting) (distinguishing "clear-statement rules" from less powerful canons that can be overcome by "all available indicia of Congress' intent," including legislative history and statutory structure). At least for judges who believe in the use of legislative history in statutory interpretation, relatively few canons are "clear-statement rules" in Justice Marshall's sense.

[29] Following Timothy Endicott, I am using the phrase "linguistic indeterminacy" as a catch-all for indeterminacy associated with general linguistic conventions (including conventions of vocabulary, punctuation, and grammar). I mean to contrast this sort of indeterminacy in statutes with indeterminacy that arises from concerns specific to the law. *See* Timothy A.O. Endicott, *Linguistic Indeterminacy*, 16 OXFORD J. LEGAL STUD. 667, 669 (1996) (using the phrase "linguistic indeterminacy" to refer to "unclarity in the meaning of linguistic expressions" that happen to appear in statutes, and distinguishing it from indeterminacy that is more specifically "legal").

to think that Congress intended a regulatory statute to supply rules of decision for cases involving conduct that occurred before the statute was enacted, under circumstances where application of the statute would be "retroactive." Even if the statute is cast in general terms and lacks any explicit temporal limitation, courts often will infer such a limitation.

Following Justice Kennedy's lead, I will refer to canons of this sort as "implied-limitation rules." (That label is not in widespread use, but it usefully captures how these canons work.) In his plurality opinion in *Spector v. Norwegian Cruise Lines Ltd.*, 545 U.S. 119 (2005), Justice Kennedy offered the following description:

> "Implied limitation rules avoid applications of otherwise unambiguous statutes that would intrude on sensitive domains in a way that Congress is unlikely to have intended had it considered the matter. In these instances, the absence of a clear congressional statement is, in effect, equivalent to a statutory qualification saying, for example, 'Notwithstanding any general language of this statute, this statute shall not apply extraterritorially'; or '. . . this statute shall not abrogate the sovereign immunity of nonconsenting States'; or '. . . this statute does not regulate the internal affairs of foreign-flag vessels.' These clear statement rules ensure Congress does not, by broad or general language, legislate on a sensitive topic inadvertently or without due deliberation."

Id. at 139 (plurality opinion).

Note the two different types of justifications that Justice Kennedy suggested in this passage. In defending the use of appropriate "implied-limitation rules," he advanced both a descriptive justification (about a version of legislative intent) and a normative justification (about trying to affect the legislative process and to promote "due deliberation" before the legislature wields power in certain sensitive areas). Both types of justifications are common. Many implied-limitation rules purport to identify policies that legislators ordinarily accept and that generally worded statutes normally are not intended to override. Rules of this sort can be seen as "descriptive" principles that help interpreters capture the legal directives that members of the enacting legislature intended to establish (or, in Justice Kennedy's telling, the legal directives that members of the enacting legislature probably would have wanted to establish if they had considered the specific issues on which the rules focus). Still, many implied-limitation rules also have "normative" aspirations; they are designed in part to push the law in the direction of good policy.

Once you know about the concept of "implied-limitation rules," you can use that concept to describe some of the debates that you have already studied. For instance, recall the disagreement between Chief Justice Burger and Justice Brennan in *NLRB v. Catholic Bishop of Chicago*, 440 U.S. 490 (1979). Justice Brennan's dissent suggested that the canon about avoiding constitutional doubts is simply a tool for resolving conventional ambiguity or vagueness in statutes. *See Catholic Bishop*, 440 U.S. at 510–11 (Brennan, J., dissenting) (arguing that the canon comes into play only if a reading that avoids the constitutional doubts is "fairly possible," and complaining that the majority's interpretation failed that test (quoting *Crowell v. Benson*, 285 U.S. 22, 62 (1932))). By contrast, Chief Justice Burger's majority opinion assumed that the canon about avoiding constitutional doubts is also an implied-limitation rule. According to the majority opinion, because applying the general language of the National Labor Relations Act to teachers in church-operated schools would raise serious constitutional questions, and because Congress may not have contemplated this specific application of the Act, the canon about avoiding constitutional doubts supported inferring a special exception for teachers in church-operated schools. *See id.* at 504–07 (majority opinion).

Even if you agree with Justice Brennan that the canon about avoiding constitutional doubts should not operate as an implied-limitation rule, you should not lightly conclude that *all* implied-limitation rules are illegitimate. Can't statutory interpreters, like other sorts of interpreters, assume that certain things go without saying unless the speaker wants to say the opposite? But you also should not embrace implied-limitation rules too casually. For one thing, how should courts identify the issues that those rules single out for special treatment?

1. THE PRESUMPTION AGAINST EXTRATERRITORIALITY

Up to this point in the book, most of the canons that we have covered are commonly applied when courts are interpreting state statutes no less than when courts are interpreting federal statutes. Of course, state courts do not *have* to use the same canons to interpret state statutes that the U.S. Supreme Court uses to interpret federal statutes; the proper interpretation of state statutes is a matter of state law, and different states can take different approaches to statutory interpretation. *See* Abbe R. Gluck, *The States as Laboratories of Statutory Interpretation: Methodological Consensus and the New Modified Textualism*, 119 YALE L.J. 1750 (2010). In many states, though, the canons that we have covered so far are commonly applied to state statutes in much the same way that courts would apply them to federal statutes.

That is not so true of the presumption against extraterritoriality. To be sure, even if a state legislature enacts a statute that purports to regulate "all" transactions of a certain sort and that does not have any explicit geographic limitations, the state's courts will not necessarily apply the statute to transactions that take place outside the state. Usually, though, they will think about that issue under the rubric of the state's ordinary choice-of-law doctrines.[30] In other words, rather than

[30] "Choice-of-law doctrines" tell courts which sovereign's law governs which issues in a case. For instance, imagine that a person in Virginia enters into an agreement over the telephone with a person in California, and performance of the agreement will require some acts

assuming that each of their state's statutes defines its own geographic reach and that any geographic limitations on the statute's applicability need to be found in the statute itself, the state's courts are likely to determine the typical statute's applicability according to choice-of-law doctrines that operate outside the statute. *See* Caleb Nelson, *State and Federal Models of the Interaction Between Statutes and Unwritten Law*, 80 U. CHI. L. REV. 657, 665–70 (2013).

Of course, if a particular statute enacted by the state legislature provides special instructions on this topic, or otherwise implies that the state's courts should *not* use the state's normal choice-of-law doctrines to identify the cases for which the statute supplies rules of decision, then the state's courts are bound to do what their state's legislature has told them to do (within constitutional limits). Still, state courts appear to apply a rebuttable presumption that the typical statute enacted by their state's legislature does not give them such instructions and therefore does not supplant the state's ordinary choice-of-law doctrines. *See id.* Because of the nature of modern choice-of-law doctrines, that is not exactly a presumption against extraterritoriality, but it addresses the same basic questions of applicability. As a result, references to a freestanding presumption against extraterritoriality are less common with respect to state statutes than with respect to federal statutes (although the prominence of that presumption with respect to federal statutes may spill over and affect how some state courts talk about state statutes).[31]

A hundred years ago, this difference did not exist, or at least was less stark; courts relied heavily on choice-of-law ideas when determining the applicability of federal statutes as well as state statutes. As elaborated from the nineteenth century through the first third of the twentieth century, though, prevailing choice-of-law ideas emphasized each sovereign's control over particular territory. Thus, Joseph Story—who did more than anyone else to systematize choice-of-law analysis—asserted that "all reasonings on the subject" rested on a few foundational propositions, of which "[t]he first . . . is . . . that every nation possesses an exclusive sovereignty and jurisdiction within its territory." JOSEPH STORY, COMMENTARIES ON THE CONFLICT OF LAWS 19 (1834). For Story and his successors, this proposition meant that legal questions about

in Michigan. If one party eventually sues the other in a Virginia state court for breach of contract, the Virginia court will use Virginia's choice-of-law doctrines to figure out which issues are governed by Virginia law and which are governed instead by California or Michigan law.

In theory, state legislatures could enact choice-of-law rules by statute for their state's courts to use, and some state legislatures have done so. But in most states, choice-of-law doctrines are largely unwritten; they are regarded as being part of the state's common law. (In the old days, courts across the United States understood themselves to be applying the same basic choice-of-law principles, which were thought of as being a matter of "general" common law. Nowadays, though, lawyers think of each state as having its own choice-of-law doctrines.)

[31] For very crude support of this point, run the following search in Westlaw: <"presumption against extra-territorial!">. As of September 1, 2023, this search produced only 36 cases in Westlaw's database of state judicial opinions and more than 1,100 cases in Westlaw's database of federal judicial opinions.

particular transactions should generally be answered according to the law of the place where those transactions had occurred.

That principle was easy enough to apply when all of the steps in a transaction occurred in the same place. But what if a transaction consisted of multiple events that occurred in different jurisdictions? For instance, if a person in New York reached an agreement by telegraph with a person in Ohio, which state's law would determine whether the agreement was a valid contract?

Roughly speaking, traditional choice-of-law doctrine told courts to approach questions of this sort as follows. First, courts would classify each legal issue that they had to decide: was this a question about the validity of a contract, or about the law of real property, or about the existence of a cause of action in tort, or what? For each category of questions, choice-of-law doctrine supplied a set of rules about where to look for answers. Typically, those rules homed in on a single aspect of the transaction or fact pattern that the court was facing, treated the whole transaction as having its "situs" or location at the place where that aspect had occurred, and told the court to apply the law of that place. *See* Nelson, *supra*, 80 U. CHI. L. REV. at 672 (citing sources).

The first Restatement of the Law of Conflict of Laws, published by the American Law Institute in 1934, reflected that approach. In tort cases, various questions were to be answered according to the law of "the place of wrong," which the first Restatement defined as "the state where the last event necessary to make an actor liable for an alleged tort takes place"—often, the place where the direct injury occurred. *See* RESTATEMENT OF THE LAW OF CONFLICT OF LAWS § 377 (AM. L. INST. 1934). Likewise, many questions about the legal effect of a purported contract were supposed to be handled according to the law of "the place of contracting," which the first Restatement identified as "the place of the principal event, if any, which, under the general law of Contracts, would result in a contract." *Id.* § 311 cmt. d. In effect, these rules assigned cross-border transactions to a particular place.

The territorial emphasis of traditional choice-of-law doctrine dovetailed with how people talked about the applicability of statutes. In *American Banana Co. v. United Fruit Co.*, 213 U.S. 347 (1909), in the course of holding that the Sherman Act did not reach "what the defendant did in Panama or Costa Rica," the Supreme Court quoted an English jurist's observation that " '[a]ll legislation is prima facie territorial.' " *Id.* at 357 (quoting *Ex parte Blain*, 12 Ch. D. 522 (C.A. 1879)). State courts similarly spoke of "the general presumption that statutes are not intended to have any extra-territorial effect." *Merrill v. Boston & Lowell R.R.*, 63 N.H. 259, 265 (1884). As commentators noted, however, such statements simply expressed "[t]he presumption that statutes are not intended to alter principles of conflict of laws"—so that ordinary choice-of-law doctrines would determine the applicability of any statute that did not implicitly or explicitly opt out of them. *See* Note, *Preserving the*

Inviolability of Rules of Conflict of Laws by Statutory Construction, 49 HARV. L. REV. 319, 319 (1935); *see also* JOEL PRENTISS BISHOP, COMMENTARIES ON THE WRITTEN LAWS AND THEIR INTERPRETATION 129 (1882) (casting the presumption that generally worded statutes did not have "[e]xtra-territorial force" as a manifestation of the idea that statutes should be "construed harmoniously with the Common Law"); Larry Kramer, *Vestiges of Beale: Extraterritorial Application of American Law*, 1991 SUP. CT. REV. 179, 186 (observing that Justice Holmes, who wrote the Supreme Court's opinion in *American Banana*, "saw [the case] as a conventional conflict of laws problem").

In the nineteenth and early twentieth centuries, prevailing choice-of-law doctrines not only led courts to presume that generally worded statutes did not have "extraterritorial" applications, but also gave practical content to the concept of "extraterritoriality." For a simple example, consider how the Supreme Court analyzed *New York Central Railroad Co. v. Chisholm*, 268 U.S. 29 (1925). As enacted by Congress in 1908, the Federal Employer's Liability Act (FELA) created the following right of action in favor of railroad employees:

> "[E]very common carrier by railroad while engaging in commerce between any of the several States or Territories, or between . . . any of the States or Territories and any foreign nation or nations, shall be liable in damages to any person suffering injury while he is employed by such carrier in such commerce, or, in the case of the death of such employee, to his or her personal representative, . . . for such injury or death resulting in whole or in part from the negligence of any of the officers, agents, or employees of such carrier . . . ."

FELA, ch. 149, § 1, 35 Stat. 65, 65 (1908) (codified as amended at 45 U.S.C. § 51). In *Chisholm*, an employee had suffered fatal injuries aboard a train from New York to Canada; at a stop in Canada, a car had been coupled to the train with such force that a heavy object had fallen on the employee, causing his death. Ultimately, the Supreme Court held that the FELA did not provide a right of action to the administrator of the employee's estate. The Court began its analysis by classifying the legal claim that the FELA created: in the Court's words, "demands under [the FELA] are based wholly upon tort." *Chisholm*, 268 U.S. at 31. Consistent with the idea that torts occur at the place of wrong, the Court took for granted that the tort at issue in *Chisholm* had occurred in Canada. For the Court, it followed that applying the FELA to these facts would be giving the statute "extraterritorial effect"—which would not be appropriate, because the FELA "contains no words which definitely disclose an intention to give it extraterritorial effect, nor do the circumstances require an inference of such purpose." *Id.*

Neither *Chisholm* nor other cases from the same era made clear the precise relationship between federal statutes and common-law doctrines about the choice of law. *See* Nelson, *supra*, 80 U. CHI. L. REV. at 696–701 (noting imprecision about whether general choice-of-law doctrines operated of their own force to determine the applicability of U.S. law, or whether such doctrines instead operated via implicit incorporation into each individual federal statute). One way or another, though, early twentieth-century decisions like *American Banana* and *Chisholm* reflected the choice-of-law doctrines of that era.

Around the middle of the century, two things changed. First, perhaps because of pressures created by the Supreme Court's decisions in *Erie Railroad Co. v. Tompkins*, 304 U.S. 64 (1938), and *Klaxon Co. v. Stentor Electric Manufacturing Co.*, 313 U.S. 487 (1941), courts began to analyze the applicability of federal statutes entirely under the rubric of statutory interpretation; general choice-of-law doctrines came into play only to the extent that courts read them into individual federal statutes. *See* Nelson, *supra*, 80 U. CHI. L. REV. at 701–11 (tracing this development to the 1940s). Second, choice-of-law doctrines themselves began to change. As early as 1945, but starting in earnest in the 1960s, an increasing number of state courts stopped using the first Restatement's approach in contract and tort cases. *See* SYMEON C. SYMEONIDES, CHOICE OF LAW 123–43 (2016) (providing state-by-state information). In the late 1950s, indeed, Professor Brainerd Currie began urging courts to scrap traditional choice-of-law analysis altogether; in his view, courts attempting to determine the reach of any of their jurisdiction's laws should analyze the interests served by that particular law and use something like imaginative reconstruction to determine its applicability in any given case. *See* Nelson, *supra*, 80 U. CHI. L. REV. at 681–88. Although American courts did not fully embrace that position, the situs-ascribing rules of the first Restatement did give way to more flexible, multifactor analyses (such as the approach advocated by the second Restatement, which the American Law Institute began working on in 1952 and adopted in 1969).

From the 1940s through the 1980s, federal courts charted an uncertain path with respect to the geographic reach of federal statutes. In *Foley Bros. v. Filardo*, 336 U.S. 281 (1949), the Supreme Court articulated and applied "[t]he canon of construction which teaches that legislation of Congress, unless a contrary intent appears, is meant to apply only within the territorial jurisdiction of the United States." *Id.* at 285. But in *Steele v. Bulova Watch Co.*, 344 U.S. 280 (1952), the Court interpreted the Lanham Act to reach a U.S. citizen's use of the "Bulova" trademark on watches that he assembled and sold in Mexico without the permission of the trademark's owner. Although that conclusion arguably rested on specific language in the Lanham Act (which said that "[t]he intent of this Act is to regulate commerce within the control of Congress" and defined "commerce" to mean "all commerce which may lawfully be regulated by Congress," ch. 540, § 45, 60 Stat. 427, 443–44 (1946) (codified as amended at 15 U.S.C. § 1127)), courts also applied other federal statutes expansively. *See, e.g.*, Bersch v. Drexel Firestone, Inc., 519 F.2d 974, 993 (2d Cir. 1975) (summarizing the Second Circuit's precedents about the applicability of anti-fraud provisions in federal securities laws); United States v. Aluminum Co. of America, 148 F.2d 416, 443–44 (2d Cir. 1945) (discussing the reach of the Sherman Act); *see also* Hartford Fire Ins. Co. v. California, 509 U.S. 764, 795–96 (1993) ("Although the proposition was perhaps not always free from doubt, see *American Banana Co.* v. *United Fruit Co.*, 213 U.S. 347 (1909), it is well established by now that the Sherman Act applies to foreign conduct that was meant to produce and did in fact produce some substantial effect in the United States."); Envtl. Def. Fund, Inc. v. Massey, 986 F.2d 528, 531 (D.C. Cir. 1993) (asserting that "the presumption [against extraterritoriality] is generally not applied where the failure to extend the scope of the statute to a foreign setting will result in adverse effects within the United States").

Under current doctrine, however, courts approach federal statutes with a much stronger presumption against extraterritoriality than some of these cases suggest. *See, e.g.*, Morrison v. Nat'l Australia Bank Ltd., 561 U.S. 247, 255–61 (2010) (rejecting the Second Circuit's approach to the securities laws); *cf.* Abitron Austria GmbH v. Hetronic Int'l, Inc., 143 S. Ct. 2522, 2529–31 (2023) (casting *Steele* as a "narrow and factbound" decision and denying that the Lanham Act's broad definition of "commerce" is enough to rebut the presumption against extraterritoriality).

This development started with *EEOC v. Arabian American Oil Co.*, 499 U.S. 244 (1991) ("*Aramco*"), which involved Title VII of the Civil Rights Act of 1964. Section 703(a) of that landmark federal statute makes it unlawful "for an employer . . . to fail or refuse to hire or to discharge any individual, or otherwise to discriminate against any individual with respect to his compensation, terms, conditions, or privileges of employment, because of such individual's race, color, religion, sex, or national origin." Civil Rights Act of 1964, Pub. L. 88–352, § 703(a), 78 Stat. 241, 255 (codified as amended at 42 U.S.C. § 2000e–2(a)). Ali Boureslan, a United States citizen who had worked in Saudi Arabia for a company that was incorporated in the United States but had its principal place of business in Saudi Arabia, alleged that he had been harassed on the job (and ultimately discharged) because of his race, religion, and national origin. The Supreme Court understood his case to present the question "whether Title VII applies extraterritorially to regulate the employment practices of United States employers who employ United States citizens abroad." *Aramco*, 499 U.S. at 246; *see also id.* at 248 ("It is our task to determine whether Congress intended the protections of Title VII to apply to United States citizens employed by American employers outside of the United States.").[32] Chief Justice Rehnquist's

[32] This way of framing the question focuses attention on the place where the employee works—Saudi Arabia, in Mr. Boureslan's case. Judging from lower-court opinions in the case, that was also the site of the acts and decisions that Mr. Boureslan was complaining about. *See* Boureslan v. Aramco, 653 F. Supp. 629, 629 (S.D. Tex. 1987), *aff'd*, 857 F.2d 1014, 1016 (5th Cir. 1988) (indicating that Mr. Boureslan's allegations centered on the conduct of his supervisor

majority opinion answered that question "no." According to the majority, courts were supposed to interpret federal statutes against the backdrop of a general presumption against extraterritoriality, which could be overcome only by clear evidence that Congress had specifically intended a particular statute to operate extraterritorially. *See id.* at 248. With respect to Title VII, moreover, the majority concluded that the evidence was too inconclusive to rebut the presumption. *See id.* at 249 ("[P]etitioners' evidence, while not totally lacking in probative value, falls short of demonstrating the affirmative congressional intent required to extend the protections of Title VII beyond our territorial borders.").

Writing in dissent, Justice Marshall acknowledged the existence of a general presumption against extraterritoriality, but he thought that the text and legislative history of Title VII were sufficient to overcome it. He pointed, in particular, to § 702, which specified that "[t]his title shall not apply to an employer with respect to the employment of aliens outside any State . . . ." 78 Stat. at 255 (codified as amended at 42 U.S.C. § 2000e–1(a)); *see also id.* § 701(i) (defining "State" broadly to include "a State of the United States, the District of Columbia, Puerto Rico, the Virgin Islands, American Samoa, Guam, Wake Island, the Canal Zone, and Outer Continental Shelf lands defined in the Outer Continental Shelf Lands Act") (codified at 42 U.S.C. § 2000e(i)). Justice Marshall drew the negative inference that Congress had intended Title VII to apply with respect to the employment of *U.S. citizens* in foreign countries, at least by American employers. *See Aramco*, 499 U.S. at 267–71 (Marshall, J., dissenting).[33]

Justice Marshall also accused the majority of giving more weight to the presumption against extraterritoriality than the Court's precedents warranted. According to Justice Marshall, some of the cases cited by the Court were really about a different canon—the long-standing principle that "an act of Congress ought never to be construed to violate the law of nations if any other possible construction remains." *Murray v. Schooner Charming Betsy*, 6 U.S. (2 Cranch) 64, 118 (1804). (By the "law of nations," early lawyers and judges meant a transnational body of legal principles about the rights and duties of each nation vis à vis other

---

in Saudi Arabia), *reaff'd en banc*, 892 F.2d 1271 (5th Cir. 1990). But one can imagine a case in which a company makes a discriminatory decision in the United States to fire an employee who works overseas. Would the application of Title VII to such a case be "extraterritorial"?

[33] The majority did not have a good explanation for why Congress would have enacted § 702 unless members of Congress had expected Title VII to operate with respect to some employment in foreign countries. *Compare Aramco*, 499 U.S. at 254–55 (summarizing the defendants' arguments about § 702), *with id.* at 269–71 (Marshall, J., dissenting) (explaining why those arguments were unpersuasive and citing legislative history that undermined them). Still, the majority suggested that other aspects of Title VII supported the opposite inference. *See id.* at 256 (majority opinion) (suggesting that if Congress had expected Title VII to operate with respect to foreign workplaces, the statute's venue provisions would have been worded differently, and Congress also would have said something about cases in which foreign law requires practices that Title VII prohibits).

nations—the ancestor of what is today called international law.[34]) Justice Marshall argued that the *Charming Betsy* canon is more powerful than the simple presumption against extraterritoriality, and the majority was falling into error by conflating them.

Admittedly, the *Charming Betsy* canon can bear on questions about the geographic reach of federal statutes, because international law recognizes limits on each nation's legitimate "prescriptive jurisdiction" (that is, its authority to prescribe legal rules). *See* RESTATEMENT (FOURTH) OF THE FOREIGN RELATIONS LAW OF THE UNITED STATES §§ 407–13 (AM. L. INST. 2018) (describing customary international law on this topic); *see also id.* § 404, Reporters' Note 1 (saying that "[t]he presumption against extraterritoriality has its roots in the [*Charming Betsy*] canon"). Under current understandings of customary international law, though, each nation has legitimate authority to regulate not only conduct within its own territory, *id.* § 408, but also certain categories of conduct outside its territory. *See, e.g.*, *id.* § 409 ("conduct that has a substantial effect within its territory"); *id.* § 411 ("certain conduct outside its territory that harms its nationals"); *id.* § 412 ("certain conduct . . . that is directed against the security of the state or against a limited class of other fundamental state interests"). Significantly, customary international law recognizes each nation's jurisdiction to regulate how its own nationals behave anywhere in the world. *See id.* § 410; *see also id.* cmt. b (noting that the term "nationals" can include not only the nation's citizens but also corporations that it has chartered). Because reading Title VII to regulate the employment practices of American corporations throughout the world would not violate the limits on prescriptive jurisdiction recognized by customary international law, Justice Marshall argued that the *Aramco* case did not implicate the *Charming Betsy* canon. *See Aramco*, 499 U.S. at 264–66 (Marshall, J., dissenting); *cf. id.* at 274–75 (suggesting that the *Charming Betsy* canon might cut against reading Title VII to regulate *foreign* corporations that employ U.S. citizens in foreign territory).

Of course, even if the *Charming Betsy* canon was inapplicable, Justice Marshall conceded that the plaintiff was seeking an "extraterritorial" application of Title VII. According to Justice Marshall, though, the ordinary presumption against extraterritoriality could be overcome with something less than "the affirmative intention of the Congress clearly expressed." *See id.* at 264–65 (quoting *Benz v. Compania Naviera Hidalgo, S.A.*, 353 U.S. 138, 147 (1957), and *McCulloch v. Sociedad Nacional de Marineros de Honduras*, 372 U.S. 10, 21–22 (1963), but arguing that those cases addressed what is necessary to overcome the *Charming Betsy* canon rather than the ordinary presumption against extraterritoriality). With respect to Title VII, Justice Marshall thought that the negative implications of § 702 (along with legislative history and

[34] "International law" is not associated with a single sovereign. By contrast, lawyers use the phrase "foreign law" to refer to the laws of particular foreign countries.

administrative interpretations) were strong enough to overcome the presumption against extraterritoriality, even though they might not be enough to overcome the *Charming Betsy* canon in cases where it applied. *See id.* at 265–66, 278; *see also* John H. Knox, *A Presumption Against Extrajurisdictionality*, 104 AM. J. INT'L L. 351, 353 (2010) (advocating tiered canons of this sort).

Roughly eight months after the Supreme Court decided *Aramco*, Congress amended Title VII so as to produce something like Justice Marshall's bottom line. *See* Civil Rights Act of 1991, Pub. L. 102–166, § 109(a), 105 Stat. 1071, 1077 (amending Title VII's definition of "employee" to include U.S. citizens who are employed in foreign countries); *id.* § 109(b), 105 Stat. at 1077 (amending § 702 in Title VII to exempt "the foreign operations of an employer that is a foreign person not controlled by an American employer"); *cf. id.* (adding an exemption, "with respect to an employee in a workplace in a foreign country," when Title VII would otherwise require an employer "to violate the law of the foreign country in which such workplace is located").[35] Does this congressional response cast doubt on the strength of the presumption against extraterritoriality that the majority applied in *Aramco*, or does it simply show that a later Congress changed the reach of Title VII going forward? *Cf. id.* § 109(c), 105 Stat. at 1078 ("The amendments made by this section shall not apply with respect to conduct occurring before the date of the enactment of this Act.")

The Supreme Court continues to approach federal statutes with a strong presumption against extraterritoriality. The next case both illustrates that point and, importantly, addresses how to decide whether a particular application of a statute would be "extraterritorial" in the sense that the presumption disfavors.

Morrison v. National Australia Bank Ltd.

561 U.S. 247 (2010)

■ *JUSTICE SCALIA delivered the opinion of the Court:*

We decide whether § 10(b) of the Securities Exchange Act of 1934 provides a cause of action to foreign plaintiffs suing foreign and American defendants for misconduct in connection with securities traded on foreign exchanges.

I

Respondent National Australia Bank Limited (National) was, during the relevant time, the largest bank in Australia. Its Ordinary Shares—what in America would be called "common stock"—are traded on the Australian Stock Exchange Limited and on other foreign securities

[35] In 1984, Congress had added similar provisions to the Age Discrimination in Employment Act of 1967. *See* Act of Oct. 9, 1984, Pub. L. 98–459, § 802, 98 Stat. 1767, 1792; *see also Aramco*, 499 U.S. at 273 n.7 (Marshall, J., dissenting) (discussing the genesis and legislative history of this amendment).

exchanges, but not on any exchange in the United States. There are listed on the New York Stock Exchange, however, National's American Depositary Receipts (ADRs), which represent the right to receive a specified number of National's Ordinary Shares. . . .

The complaint alleges the following facts, which we accept as true. In February 1998, National bought respondent HomeSide Lending, Inc., a mortgage-servicing company headquartered in Florida. HomeSide's business was to receive fees for servicing mortgages (essentially the administrative tasks associated with collecting mortgage payments . . .). . . .

From 1998 until 2001, National's annual reports and other public documents touted the success of HomeSide's business, and respondents Frank Cicutto (National's managing director and chief executive officer), Kevin Race (HomeSide's chief operating officer), and Hugh Harris (HomeSide's chief executive officer) did the same in public statements. But on July 5, 2001, National announced that it was writing down the value of HomeSide's assets by $450 million; and then again on September 3, by another $1.75 billion. The prices of both Ordinary Shares and ADRs slumped. . . . According to the complaint, . . . HomeSide, Race, Harris, and another HomeSide senior executive who is also a respondent here had manipulated HomeSide's financial models . . . to cause the mortgage-servicing rights to appear more valuable than they really were. The complaint also alleges that National and Cicutto were aware of this deception by July 2000, but did nothing about it.

As relevant here, petitioners Russell Leslie Owen and Brian and Geraldine Silverlock, all Australians, purchased National's Ordinary Shares in 2000 and 2001, before the writedowns.[1] They sued National, HomeSide, Cicutto, and the three HomeSide executives in the United States District Court for the Southern District of New York for alleged violations of [§]10(b) . . . of the Securities Exchange Act of 1934, 48 Stat. 891, 15 U.S.C. [§]78j(b) . . . , and Securities and Exchange Commission (SEC) Rule 10b–5, 17 CFR § 240.10b–5 (2009), promulgated pursuant to § 10(b). They sought to represent a class of foreign purchasers of National's Ordinary Shares during a specified period up to the September writedown. . . .

Respondents moved to dismiss for lack of subject-matter jurisdiction under Federal Rule of Civil Procedure 12(b)(1) and for failure to state a claim under Rule 12(b)(6). The District Court granted the motion on the former ground, finding no jurisdiction because the acts in this country were, "at most, a link in the chain of an alleged overall securities fraud scheme that culminated abroad." *In re National Australia Bank Securities Litigation*, No. 03 Civ. 6537(BSJ), 2006 WL 3844465, *8 (SDNY, Oct. 25, 2006). The Court of Appeals for the Second Circuit

[1] Robert Morrison, an American investor in National's ADRs, also brought suit, but his claims were dismissed by the District Court because he failed to allege damages. . . . Petitioners did not appeal that decision, . . . and it is not before us. . . .

affirmed on similar grounds. [547 F.3d 167 (CA2 2008).] . . . We granted certiorari . . . .

II

Before addressing the question presented, we must correct a threshold error in the Second Circuit's analysis. It considered the extraterritorial reach of § 10(b) to raise a question of subject-matter jurisdiction . . . . In this regard it was following Circuit precedent, see *Schoenbaum v. Firstbrook*, 405 F.2d 200, 208, modified on other grounds en banc, 405 F.2d 215 (1968). The Second Circuit is hardly alone in taking this position, see, *e.g.*, *In re CP Ships Ltd. Securities Litigation*, 578 F.3d 1306, 1313 (CA11 2009); *Continental Grain (Australia) Pty. Ltd. v. Pacific Oilseeds, Inc.*, 592 F.2d 409, 421 (CA8 1979).

But to ask what conduct § 10(b) reaches is to ask what conduct § 10(b) prohibits, which is a merits question. . . . The District Court here had jurisdiction under 15 U.S.C. § 78aa[3] to adjudicate the question whether § 10(b) applies to National's conduct.

In view of this error, which the parties do not dispute, petitioners ask us to remand. We think that unnecessary. Since nothing in the analysis of the courts below turned on the mistake, a remand would only require a new Rule 12(b)(6) label for the same Rule 12(b)(1) conclusion. As we have done before in situations like this, . . . we proceed to address whether petitioners' allegations state a claim.

III

A

It is a "longstanding principle of American law 'that legislation of Congress, unless a contrary intent appears, is meant to apply only within the territorial jurisdiction of the United States.'" *EEOC v. Arabian American Oil Co.*, 499 U.S. 244, 248 (1991) *(Aramco)* (quoting *Foley Bros., Inc. v. Filardo*, 336 U.S. 281, 285 (1949)). This principle represents a canon of construction, or a presumption about a statute's meaning, rather than a limit upon Congress's power to legislate, see *Blackmer v. United States*, 284 U.S. 421, 437 (1932). It rests on the perception that Congress ordinarily legislates with respect to domestic, not foreign, matters. . . . Thus, "unless there is the affirmative intention of the Congress clearly expressed" to give a statute extraterritorial effect, "we must presume it is primarily concerned with domestic conditions." *Aramco*, *supra*, at 248 (internal quotation marks omitted). The canon or presumption applies regardless of whether there is a risk of conflict between the American statute and a foreign law, see *Sale v. Haitian Centers Council, Inc.*, 509

[3] Section 78aa provides:

"The district courts of the United States . . . shall have exclusive jurisdiction of violations of [the Exchange Act] or the rules and regulations thereunder, and of all suits in equity and actions at law brought to enforce any liability or duty created by [the Exchange Act] or the rules and regulations thereunder."

U.S. 155, 173–174 (1993). When a statute gives no clear indication of an extraterritorial application, it has none.

Despite this principle of interpretation, long and often recited in our opinions, the Second Circuit believed that, because the Exchange Act is silent as to the extraterritorial application of § 10(b), it was left to the court to "discern" whether Congress would have wanted the statute to apply. See 547 F.3d at 170 (internal quotation marks omitted). This disregard of the presumption against extraterritoriality did not originate with the Court of Appeals panel in this case. It has been repeated over many decades by various courts of appeals in determining the application of the Exchange Act, and § 10(b) in particular, to fraudulent schemes that involve conduct and effects abroad. That has produced a collection of tests for divining what Congress would have wanted, complex in formulation and unpredictable in application.

As of 1967, district courts at least in the Southern District of New York had consistently concluded that, by reason of the presumption against extraterritoriality, § 10(b) did not apply when the stock transactions underlying the violation occurred abroad. See *Schoenbaum v. Firstbrook*, 268 F. Supp. 385, 392 (1967) . . . . *Schoenbaum* involved the sale in Canada of the treasury shares of a Canadian corporation whose publicly traded shares (but not, of course, its treasury shares) were listed on both the American Stock Exchange and the Toronto Stock Exchange. Invoking the presumption against extraterritoriality, the [district] court held that § 10(b) was inapplicable[, but the Second Circuit reversed. *Schoenbaum v. Firstbrook*, 405 F.2d 200 (2d Cir. 1968).] . . . [The Second Circuit reasoned] that, although the transactions in treasury shares took place in Canada, they affected the value of the common shares publicly traded in the United States. See *id.* at 208–209. Application of § 10(b), the Second Circuit found, was "necessary to protect American investors," *id.* at 206.

The Second Circuit took another step with *Leasco Data Processing Equip. Corp. v. Maxwell*, 468 F.2d 1326 (1972), which involved an American company that had been fraudulently induced to buy securities in England. There, unlike in *Schoenbaum*, some of the deceptive conduct had occurred in the United States but the corporation whose securities were traded (abroad) was not listed on any domestic exchange. *Leasco* said that the presumption against extraterritoriality applies only to matters over which the United States would not have prescriptive jurisdiction . . . . Congress had prescriptive jurisdiction to regulate the deceptive conduct in this country, the language of the Act could be read to cover that conduct, and the court concluded that "if Congress had thought about the point," it would have wanted § 10(b) to apply. *Id.* at 1334–1337.

With *Schoenbaum* and *Leasco* on the books, the Second Circuit had excised the presumption against extraterritoriality from the jurisprudence of § 10(b) and replaced it with the inquiry whether it would be reasonable (and hence what Congress would have wanted) to apply the statute to a given situation. As long as there was prescriptive jurisdiction to regulate, the Second Circuit explained, whether to apply § 10(b) even to "predominantly foreign" transactions became a matter of whether a court thought Congress "wished the precious resources of United States courts and law enforcement agencies to be devoted to them rather than leave the problem to foreign countries." *Bersch v. Drexel Firestone, Inc.*, 519 F.2d 974, 985 (CA2 1975) . . . .

The Second Circuit had thus established that application of § 10(b) could be premised upon either some effect on American securities markets or investors (*Schoenbaum*) or significant conduct in the United States (*Leasco*). It later formalized these two applications into (1) an "effects test," "whether the wrongful conduct had a substantial effect in the United States or upon United States citizens," and (2) a "conduct test," "whether the wrongful conduct occurred in the United States." *SEC v. Berger*, 322 F.3d 187, 192–193 (CA2 2003). These became the north star of the Second Circuit's § 10(b) jurisprudence, pointing the way to what Congress would have wished. . . . The Second Circuit never put forward a textual or even extratextual basis for these tests. As early as *Bersch*, it confessed that "if we were asked to point to language in the statutes, or even in the legislative history, that compelled these conclusions, we would be unable to respond," 519 F.2d at 993.

As they developed, these tests were not easy to administer. The conduct test was held to apply differently depending on whether the harmed investors were Americans or foreigners: When the alleged damages consisted of losses to American investors abroad, it was enough that acts "of material importance" performed in the United States "significantly contributed" to that result; whereas those acts must have "directly caused" the result when losses to foreigners abroad were at issue. See *ibid.* And "merely preparatory activities in the United States" did not suffice "to trigger application of the securities laws for injury to foreigners located abroad." *Id.* at 992. This required the court to distinguish between mere preparation and using the United States as a "base" for fraudulent activities in other countries. [*IIT v. Vencap, Ltd.*, 519 F.2d 1001, 1017–1018 (CA2 1975)]. But merely satisfying the conduct test was sometimes insufficient without " 'some additional factor tipping the scales' " in favor of the application of American law. *Interbrew v. Edperbrascan Corp.*, 23 F. Supp. 2d 425, 432 (SDNY 1998) (quoting *Europe & Overseas Commodity Traders, S.A. v. Banque Paribas London*, 147 F.3d 118, 129 (CA2 1998)). District Courts have noted the difficulty of applying such vague formulations. See, *e.g.*, *In re Alstom SA*, 406 F. Supp. 2d 346, 366–385 (SDNY 2005). . . .

Other Circuits embraced the Second Circuit's approach, though not its precise application. . . . While applying the same fundamental methodology of balancing interests and arriving at what seemed the best policy, they produced a proliferation of vaguely related variations on the "conduct" and "effects" tests. . . .

. . . .

Commentators have criticized the unpredictable and inconsistent application of § 10(b) to transnational cases. . . .

The criticisms seem to us justified. The results of judicial-speculation-made-law—divining what Congress would have wanted if it had thought of the situation before the court—demonstrate the wisdom of the presumption against extraterritoriality. Rather than guess anew in each case, we apply the presumption in all cases, preserving a stable background against which Congress can legislate with predictable effects.[5]

B

Rule 10b–5, the regulation under which petitioners have brought suit, was promulgated under § 10(b), and "does not extend beyond conduct encompassed by § 10(b)'s prohibition." *United States v. O'Hagan*, 521 U.S. 642, 651 (1997). Therefore, if § 10(b) is not extraterritorial, neither is Rule 10b–5.

On its face, § 10(b) contains nothing to suggest it applies abroad:

> "It shall be unlawful for any person, directly or indirectly, by the use of any means or instrumentality of interstate commerce or of the mails, or of any facility of any national securities exchange—
>
> ". . . .
>
> "[t]o use or employ, in connection with the purchase or sale of any security registered on a national securities exchange or any security not so registered, . . . any manipulative or deceptive device or contrivance in contravention of such rules and regulations as the [Securities and Exchange] Commission may prescribe . . . ." 15 U.S.C. 78j(b).

Petitioners and the Solicitor General contend, however, that [other aspects of the statute suggest] that § 10(b) or the Exchange Act in general has at least some extraterritorial application.

First, they point to the definition of "interstate commerce," a term used in § 10(b), which includes "trade, commerce, transportation, or communication . . . between any foreign country and any State." 15 U.S.C. § 78c(a)(17). But "we have repeatedly held that even statutes

[5] The concurrence urges us to cast aside our inhibitions and join in the judicial lawmaking, because "[t]his entire area of law is replete with judge-made rules," *post* at 276. It is doubtless true that, because the implied private cause of action under § 10(b) and Rule 10b–5 is a thing of our own creation, we have also defined its contours. . . . But when it comes to "the scope of [the] conduct prohibited by [Rule 10b–5 and] § 10(b), the text of the statute controls our decision." *Central Bank of Denver, N.A. v. First Interstate Bank of Denver, N.A.*, 511 U.S. 164, 173 (1994). It is only with respect to the additional "elements of the 10b–5 private liability scheme" that we "have had 'to infer how the 1934 Congress would have addressed the issue[s] had the 10b–5 action been included as an express provision in the 1934 Act.' " *Ibid.* (quoting *Musick, Peeler & Garrett v. Employers Ins. of Wausau*, 508 U.S. 286, 294 (1993)).

that contain broad language in their definitions of 'commerce' that expressly refer to '*foreign* commerce' do not apply abroad." *Aramco*, 499 U.S. at 251; see *id.* at 251–252 (discussing cases). The general reference to foreign commerce in the definition of "interstate commerce" does not defeat the presumption against extraterritoriality.[7]

. . . .

Finally, there is § 30(b) of the Exchange Act, 15 U.S.C. § 78dd(b), which *does* mention the Act's extraterritorial application: "The provisions of [the Exchange Act] or of any rule or regulation thereunder shall not apply to any person insofar as he transacts a business in securities without the jurisdiction of the United States," unless he does so in violation of regulations promulgated by the Securities and Exchange Commission "to prevent . . . evasion of [the Act]." (The parties have pointed us to no regulation promulgated pursuant to § 30(b).) The Solicitor General argues that "[this] exemption would have no function if the Act did not apply in the first instance to securities transactions that occur abroad." Brief for United States as *Amicus Curiae* 14.

We are not convinced. . . . [I]f the whole Act applied abroad, why would the Commission's enabling regulations be limited to those preventing "evasion" of the Act, rather than all those preventing "violation"? The provision seems to us directed at actions abroad that might conceal a domestic violation, or might cause what would otherwise be a domestic violation to escape on a technicality. At most, the Solicitor General's proposed inference is possible; but possible interpretations of statutory language do not override the presumption against extraterritoriality. See *Aramco, supra*, at 253.

The Solicitor General also fails to account for § 30(a), which reads in relevant part as follows:

> "It shall be unlawful for any broker or dealer . . . to make use of the mails or of any means or instrumentality of interstate commerce for the purpose of effecting on an exchange not within or subject to the jurisdiction of the United States, any transaction in any security the issuer of which is a resident of, or is organized under the laws of, or has its principal place of business in, a place within or subject to the jurisdiction of the United States, in contravention of such rules and regulations as the Commission may prescribe . . . ." 15 U.S.C. § 78dd(a).

[This provision] contains what § 10(b) lacks: a clear statement of extraterritorial effect. Its explicit provision for a specific extraterritorial

---

[7] This conclusion does not render meaningless the inclusion of "trade, commerce, transportation, or communication . . . between any foreign country and any State" in the definition of "interstate commerce." 15 U.S.C. § 78c(a)(17). For example, an issuer based abroad, whose executives approve the publication in the United States of misleading information affecting the price of the issuer's securities traded on the New York Stock Exchange, probably will make use of some instrumentality of "communication . . . between [a] foreign country and [a] State."

application would be quite superfluous if the rest of the Exchange Act already applied to transactions on foreign exchanges—and its limitation of that application to securities of domestic issuers would be inoperative. . . .

The concurrence claims we have impermissibly narrowed the inquiry in evaluating whether a statute applies abroad, citing for that point the dissent in *Aramco* . . . . But we do not say, as the concurrence seems to think, that the presumption against extraterritoriality is a "clear statement rule," *post* at 278, if by that is meant a requirement that a statute say "this law applies abroad." Assuredly context can be consulted as well. But whatever sources of statutory meaning one consults to give "the most faithful reading" of the text, *post* at 280, there is no clear indication of extraterritoriality here. The concurrence does not even try to refute that conclusion, but merely puts forward the same (at best) uncertain indications relied upon by petitioners and the Solicitor General. As the opinion *for the Court* in *Aramco* (which we prefer to the dissent) shows, those uncertain indications do not suffice.[8]

In short, there is no affirmative indication in the Exchange Act that § 10(b) applies extraterritorially, and we therefore conclude that it does not.

IV

A

Petitioners argue that the conclusion that § 10(b) does not apply extraterritorially does not resolve this case. They contend that they seek no more than domestic application anyway, since Florida is where HomeSide and its senior executives engaged in the deceptive conduct of manipulating HomeSide's financial models; their complaint also alleged that Race and Hughes made misleading public statements there. This is less an answer to the presumption against extraterritorial application than it is an assertion—a quite valid assertion—that that presumption here (as often) is not self-evidently dispositive . . . . [Still,] the presumption against extraterritorial application would be a craven watchdog indeed if it retreated to its kennel whenever *some* domestic activity is involved in the case. . . . In *Aramco*, for example, the Title VII plaintiff had been hired in Houston, and was an American citizen. See 499 U.S. at 247. The Court concluded, however, that neither that territorial event nor that relationship was the "focus" of congressional concern, *id.* at 255, but rather domestic employment. . . .

Applying the same mode of analysis here, we think that the focus of the Exchange Act is not upon the place where the deception originated, but upon purchases and sales of securities in the United States. Section

[8] The concurrence notes that, post-*Aramco*, Congress provided explicitly for extraterritorial application of Title VII, the statute at issue in *Aramco*. *Post* at 279, n. 6. All this shows is that Congress knows how to give a statute explicit extraterritorial effect—and how to limit that effect to particular applications, which is what the cited amendment did. See Civil Rights Act of 1991, § 109, 105 Stat. 1077.

10(b) does not punish deceptive conduct, but only deceptive conduct "in connection with the purchase or sale of any security registered on a national securities exchange or any security not so registered." 15 U.S.C. § 78j(b). . . . Those purchase-and-sale transactions are the objects of the statute's solicitude. It is those transactions that the statute seeks to "regulate," see *Superintendent of Ins. of N.Y. v. Bankers Life & Casualty Co.*, 404 U.S. 6, 12 (1971); it is parties or prospective parties to those transactions that the statute seeks to "protec[t]," *id.* at 10. . . . And it is in our view only transactions in securities listed on domestic exchanges, and domestic transactions in other securities, to which § 10(b) applies.[9]

The primacy of the domestic exchange is suggested by the very prologue of the Exchange Act, which sets forth as its object "[t]o provide for the regulation of securities exchanges . . . operating in interstate and foreign commerce and through the mails, to prevent inequitable and unfair practices on such exchanges . . . ." 48 Stat. 881. We know of no one who thought that the Act was intended to "regulat[e]" *foreign* securities exchanges—or indeed who even believed that under established principles of international law Congress had the power to do so. The Act's registration requirements apply only to securities listed on national securities exchanges. 15 U.S.C. § 78*l*(a).

With regard to securities *not* registered on domestic exchanges, the exclusive focus on *domestic* purchases and sales[10] is strongly confirmed by § 30(a) and (b), discussed earlier. The former extends the normal scope of the Exchange Act's prohibitions to acts effecting, in violation of rules prescribed by the Commission, a "transaction" in a United States security "on an exchange not within or subject to the jurisdiction of the United States." § 78dd(a). And the latter specifies that the Act does not apply to "any person insofar as he transacts a business in securities without the jurisdiction of the United States," unless he does so in violation of regulations promulgated by the Commission "to prevent the evasion [of the Act]." § 78dd(b). Under both provisions it is the foreign location of the

---

[9] The concurrence seems to think this test has little to do with our conclusion in Part III . . . that § 10(b) does not apply extraterritorially. See *post* at 284–285. That is not so. If § 10(b) did apply abroad, we would not need to determine which transnational frauds it applied to; it would apply to all of them (barring some other limitation). Thus, although it is true, as we have said, that our threshold conclusion that § 10(b) has no extraterritorial effect does not resolve this case, it is a necessary first step in the analysis.

The concurrence also makes the curious criticism that our evaluation of where a putative violation occurs is based on the text of § 10(b) rather than the doctrine in the Courts of Appeals. *Post* at 274–275. Although it concedes that our test is textually plausible, *post* at 274, it does not (and cannot) make the same claim for the Court-of-Appeals doctrine it endorses. That is enough to make our test the better one.

[10] That is in our view the meaning which the presumption against extraterritorial application requires for the words "purchase or sale of . . . any security not so registered" in § 10(b)'s phrase "in connection with the purchase or sale of any security registered on a national securities exchange *or any security not so registered*." (Emphasis added.) Even without the presumption against extraterritorial application, the only alternative to that reading makes nonsense of the phrase, causing it to cover all purchases and sales of registered securities, and all purchases and sales of nonregistered securities—a thought which, if intended, would surely have been expressed by the simpler phrase "all purchases and sales of securities."

transaction that establishes (or reflects the presumption of) the Act's inapplicability, absent regulations by the Commission.

The same focus on domestic transactions is evident in the Securities Act of 1933, 48 Stat. 74, enacted by the same Congress as the Exchange Act, and forming part of the same comprehensive regulation of securities trading. See *Central Bank of Denver, N.A. v. First Interstate Bank of Denver, N. A.*, 511 U.S. 164, 170–171 (1994). That legislation makes it unlawful to sell a security, through a prospectus or otherwise, making use of "any means or instruments of transportation or communication in interstate commerce or of the mails," unless a registration statement is in effect. 15 U.S.C. § 77e(a)(1). The Commission has interpreted that requirement "not to include . . . sales that occur outside the United States." 17 CFR § 230.901 (2009).

Finally, we reject the notion that the Exchange Act reaches conduct in this country affecting exchanges or transactions abroad for the same reason that *Aramco* rejected overseas application of Title VII to all domestically concluded employment contracts or all employment contracts with American employers: The probability of incompatibility with the applicable laws of other countries is so obvious that if Congress intended such foreign application "it would have addressed the subject of conflicts with foreign laws and procedures." 499 U.S. at 256. Like the United States, foreign countries regulate their domestic securities exchanges and securities transactions occurring within their territorial jurisdiction. And the regulation of other countries often differs from ours as to what constitutes fraud, what disclosures must be made, what damages are recoverable, what discovery is available in litigation, what individual actions may be joined in a single suit, what attorney's fees are recoverable, and many other matters. . . . [Amicus briefs filed in this case by various foreign countries and international and foreign organizations] complain of the interference with foreign securities regulation that application of § 10(b) abroad would produce, and urge the adoption of a clear test that will avoid that consequence. The transactional test we have adopted—whether the purchase or sale is made in the United States, or involves a security listed on a domestic exchange—meets that requirement.

B

The Solicitor General suggests a different test, which petitioners also endorse: "[A] transnational securities fraud violates [§]10(b) when the fraud involves significant conduct in the United States that is material to the fraud's success." Brief for United States as *Amicus Curiae* 16; see Brief for Petitioners 26. Neither the Solicitor General nor petitioners provide any textual support for this test. The Solicitor General sets forth a number of purposes such a test would serve: achieving a high standard of business ethics in the securities industry, ensuring honest securities markets and thereby promoting investor confidence, and preventing the United States from becoming a "Barbary Coast" for malefactors perpetrating frauds in foreign markets. Brief for United States as *Amicus Curiae* 16–17. But it provides no textual support for the last of these purposes, or for the first two as applied to the foreign securities industry and securities markets abroad. It is our function to give the statute the effect its language suggests, however modest that may be; not to extend it to admirable purposes it might be used to achieve.

If, moreover, one is to be attracted by the desirable consequences of the "significant and material conduct" test, one should also be repulsed by its adverse consequences. While there is no reason to believe that the United States has become the Barbary Coast for those perpetrating frauds on foreign securities markets, some fear that it has become the Shangri-La of class-action litigation for lawyers representing those allegedly cheated in foreign securities markets. . . .

. . . .

. . . [T]he Solicitor General argues that the Commission has adopted an interpretation similar to the "significant and material conduct" test, and that we should defer to that. In the two adjudications the Solicitor General cites, however, the Commission did not purport to be providing its own interpretation of the statute, but relied on decisions of federal courts—mainly Court of Appeals decisions that in turn relied on the *Schoenbaum* and *Leasco* decisions of the Second Circuit that we discussed earlier. . . . We need "accept only those agency interpretations that are reasonable in light of the principles of construction courts normally employ." *Aramco*, 499 U.S. at 260 (Scalia, J., concurring in part and concurring in judgment). Since the Commission's interpretations relied on cases we disapprove, which ignored or discarded the presumption against extraterritoriality, we owe them no deference.

* * *

Section 10(b) reaches the use of a manipulative or deceptive device or contrivance only in connection with the purchase or sale of a security listed on an American stock exchange, and the purchase or sale of any other security in the United States. This case involves no securities listed on a domestic exchange, and all aspects of the purchases complained of by those petitioners who still have live claims occurred outside the United States. Petitioners have therefore failed to state a claim on which relief can be granted. We affirm the dismissal of petitioners' complaint on this ground.

■ *JUSTICE SOTOMAYOR took no part in the consideration or decision of this case.*

■ [*JUSTICE BREYER wrote a brief opinion, omitted here, concurring in part and concurring in the judgment.*]

■ *JUSTICE STEVENS, with whom JUSTICE GINSBURG joins, concurring in the judgment:*

While I agree that petitioners have failed to state a claim on which relief can be granted, my reasoning differs from the Court's. I would adhere to the general approach that has been the law in the Second Circuit, and most of the rest of the country, for nearly four decades.

I

Today the Court announces a new "transactional test," *ante* at 269, for defining the reach of § 10(b) of the Securities Exchange Act of 1934 (Exchange Act), 15 U.S.C. § 78j(b), and SEC Rule 10b–5, 17 CFR § 240.10b–5(b) (2009): Henceforth, those provisions will extend only to "transactions in securities listed on domestic exchange[s] and domestic transactions in other securities," *ante* at 267. If one confines one's gaze to the statutory text, the Court's conclusion is a plausible one. But the federal courts have been construing § 10(b) in a different manner for a long time, and the Court's textual analysis is not nearly so compelling, in my view, as to warrant the abandonment of their doctrine.

The text and history of § 10(b) are famously opaque on the question of when, exactly, transnational securities frauds fall within the statute's compass. As those types of frauds became more common in the latter half of the 20th century, the federal courts were increasingly called upon to wrestle with that question. The Court of Appeals for the Second Circuit, located in the Nation's financial center, led the effort. Beginning in earnest with *Schoenbaum v. Firstbrook*, 405 F.2d 200, rev'd on rehearing on other grounds, 405 F.2d 215 (1968) (en banc), that court strove, over an extended series of cases, to "discern" under what circumstances "Congress would have wished the precious resources of the United States courts and law enforcement agencies to be devoted to [transnational] transactions," 547 F.3d 167, 170 (2008) [case below] (internal quotation marks omitted). Relying on opinions by Judge Henry Friendly, the Second Circuit eventually settled on a conduct-and-effects test. This test asks "(1) whether the wrongful conduct occurred in the United States, and (2) whether the wrongful conduct had a substantial effect in the United States or upon United States citizens." *Id.* at 171. Numerous cases flesh out the proper application of each prong.

The Second Circuit's test became the "north star" of § 10(b) jurisprudence, *ante* at 257, not just regionally but nationally as well. With minor variations, other courts converged on the same basic approach. See Brief for United States as *Amicus Curiae* 15 ("The courts have uniformly agreed that Section 10(b) can apply to a transnational securities fraud either when fraudulent conduct has effects in the United States or when sufficient conduct relevant to the fraud occurs in the United States"); see also 1 Restatement (Third) of Foreign Relations Law of the United States § 416 (1986) (setting forth conduct-and-effects test). Neither Congress nor the Securities Exchange Commission acted to change the law. To the contrary, the Commission largely adopted the Second Circuit's position in its own adjudications. See *ante* at 272.

In light of this history, the Court's critique of the decision below for applying "judge-made rules" is quite misplaced. *Ante* at 261. This entire area of law is replete with judge-made rules, which give concrete meaning to Congress' general commands.[3] . . .

The development of § 10(b) law was hardly an instance of judicial usurpation. Congress invited an expansive role for judicial elaboration when it crafted such an open-ended statute in 1934. And both Congress and the Commission subsequently affirmed that role when they left intact the relevant statutory and regulatory language, respectively, throughout all the years that followed. . . .

. . . .

Thus, while the Court devotes a considerable amount of attention to the development of the case law, *ante* at 255–260, it draws the wrong conclusions. The Second Circuit refined its test over several decades and dozens of cases, with the tacit approval of Congress and the Commission and with the general assent of its sister Circuits. That history is a reason we should give additional weight to the Second Circuit's "judge-made" doctrine, not a reason to denigrate it. "The longstanding acceptance by the courts, coupled with Congress' failure to reject [its] reasonable interpretation of the wording of § 10(b), . . . argues significantly in favor of acceptance of the [Second Circuit] rule by this Court." [*Blue Chip Stamps* v. *Manor Drug Stores*, 421 U.S. 723, 733 (1975).]

II

The Court's other main critique of the Second Circuit's approach—apart from what the Court views as its excessive reliance on functional considerations and reconstructed congressional intent—is that the Second Circuit has "disregard[ed]" the presumption against extraterritoriality. *Ante* at 255. It is the Court, however, that misapplies the presumption, in two main respects.

First, the Court seeks to transform the presumption from a flexible rule of thumb into something more like a clear statement rule. We have been here before. In the case on which the Court primarily relies, *EEOC v. Arabian American Oil Co.*, 499 U.S. 244 (1991) *(Aramco)*, Chief Justice Rehnquist's majority opinion included a sentence that appeared to make the same move. See *id.* at 258 ("Congress' awareness of the need to make a clear statement that a statute applies overseas is amply demonstrated by the numerous occasions on which it has expressly legislated the extraterritorial application of a statute"). Justice Marshall, in dissent,

[3] It is true that "when it comes to 'the scope of [the] conduct prohibited by [Rule 10b–5 and] § 10(b), the text of the statute [has] control[led] our decision[s].' " *Ante* at 261, n. 5 (quoting *Central Bank of Denver, N.A. v. First Interstate Bank of Denver, N.A.*, 511 U.S. 164, 173 (1994); some brackets in original). The problem, when it comes to transnational securities frauds, is that the text of the statute does not provide a great deal of control. As with any broadly phrased, longstanding statute, courts have had to fill in the gaps.

vigorously objected. See *id.* at 261 ("[C]ontrary to what one would conclude from the majority's analysis, this canon is *not* a 'clear statement' rule, the application of which relieves a court of the duty to give effect to all available indicia of the legislative will").

Yet even *Aramco*—surely the most extreme application of the presumption against extraterritoriality in my time on the Court[6]—contained numerous passages suggesting that the presumption may be overcome without a clear directive. See *id.* at 248–255 (majority opinion) (repeatedly identifying congressional "intent" as the touchstone of the presumption). And our cases both before and after *Aramco* make perfectly clear that the Court continues to give effect to "*all available evidence* about the meaning" of a provision when considering its extraterritorial application, lest we defy Congress' will. *Sale v. Haitian Centers Council, Inc.*, 509 U.S. 155, 177 (1993) (emphasis added). Contrary to Justice Scalia's personal view of statutory interpretation, that evidence legitimately encompasses more than the enacted text. Hence, while the Court's dictum that "[w]hen a statute gives no clear indication of an extraterritorial application, it has none," *ante* at 255, makes for a nice catchphrase, the point is overstated. The presumption against extraterritoriality can be useful as a theory of congressional purpose, a tool for managing international conflict, a background norm, a tiebreaker. It does not relieve courts of their duty to give statutes the most faithful reading possible.

Second, and more fundamentally, the Court errs in suggesting that the presumption against extraterritoriality is fatal to the Second Circuit's test. For even if the presumption really were a clear statement (or "clear indication," *ante* at 255, 265) rule, it would have only marginal relevance to this case.

It is true, of course, that "this Court ordinarily construes ambiguous statutes to avoid unreasonable interference with the sovereign authority of other nations," *F. Hoffmann-La Roche Ltd. v. Empagran S. A.*, 542 U.S. 155, 164 (2004), and that, absent contrary evidence, we presume "Congress is primarily concerned with domestic conditions," *Foley Bros., Inc. v. Filardo*, 336 U.S. 281, 285 (1949). Accordingly, the presumption against extraterritoriality "provides a sound basis for concluding that Section 10(b) does not apply when a securities fraud with no effects in the United States is hatched and executed entirely outside this country." Brief for United States as *Amicus Curiae* 22. But that is just about all it provides a sound basis for concluding. And the conclusion is not very illuminating, because no party to the litigation disputes it. No one contends that § 10(b) applies to wholly foreign frauds.

Rather, the real question in this case is how much, and what kinds of, *domestic* contacts are sufficient to trigger application of § 10(b). In

[6] And also one of the most short lived. See Civil Rights Act of 1991, § 109, 105 Stat. 1077 (repudiating *Aramco*).

developing its conduct-and-effects test, the Second Circuit endeavored to derive a solution from the Exchange Act's text, structure, history, and purpose. Judge Friendly and his colleagues were well aware that United States courts "cannot and should not expend [their] resources resolving cases that do not affect Americans or involve fraud emanating from America." 547 F.3d at 175; see also *id.* at 171 (overriding concern is " 'whether there is sufficient United States involvement' " (quoting *Itoba Ltd. v. Lep Group PLC*, 54 F.3d 118, 122 (CA2 1995))).

The question just stated does not admit of an easy answer. The text of the Exchange Act indicates that § 10(b) extends to at least some activities with an international component, but, again, it is not pellucid as to which ones.[9] The Second Circuit draws the line as follows: Section 10(b) extends to transnational frauds "only when substantial acts in furtherance of the fraud were committed within the United States," *SEC v. Berger*, 322 F.3d 187, 193 (CA2 2003) (internal quotation marks omitted), or when the fraud was " 'intended to produce' " and did produce " 'detrimental effects within' " the United States, *Schoenbaum*, 405 F.2d at 206.[10]

This approach is consistent with the understanding shared by most scholars that Congress, in passing the Exchange Act, "expected U.S. securities laws to apply to certain international transactions or conduct." Buxbaum, Multinational Class Actions Under Federal Securities Law: Managing Jurisdictional Conflict, 46 Colum. J. Transnat'l L. 14, 19 (2007); see also *Leasco Data Processing Equip. Corp. v. Maxwell*, 468 F.2d 1326, 1336 (CA2 1972) (Friendly, J.) (detailing evidence that Congress "meant § 10(b) to protect against fraud in the sale or purchase of securities whether or not these were traded on organized United States markets"). It is also consistent with the traditional understanding, regnant in the 1930's as it is now, that the presumption against extraterritoriality does not apply "when the conduct [at issue] occurs

[9] By its terms, § 10(b) regulates "interstate commerce," 15 U.S.C. § 78j, which the Exchange Act defines to include "trade, commerce, transportation, or communication . . . between any foreign country and any State, or between any State and any place or ship outside thereof." § 78c(a)(17). Other provisions of the Exchange Act make clear that Congress contemplated some amount of transnational application. See, *e.g.*, § 78b(2) (stating, in explaining necessity for regulation, that "[t]he prices established and offered in [securities] transactions are generally disseminated and quoted throughout the United States and foreign countries and constitute a basis for determining and establishing the prices at which securities are bought and sold"); § 78dd(b) (exempting from regulation foreign parties "*unless*" they transact business in securities "in contravention of such rules and regulations as the Commission may prescribe as necessary or appropriate to prevent the evasion of this chapter" (emphasis added)); see also *Schoenbaum*, 405 F.2d at 206–208 (reviewing statutory text and legislative history). The Court finds these textual references insufficient to overcome the presumption against extraterritoriality, . . . but as explained in the main text, that finding rests upon the Court's misapplication of the presumption.

[10] The Government submits that a "transnational securities fraud violates Section 10(b) if significant conduct material to the fraud's success occurs in the United States." Brief for United States as *Amicus Curiae* 6. I understand the Government's submission to be largely a repackaging of the "conduct" prong of the Second Circuit's test. The Government expresses no view on that test's "effects" prong, as the decision below considered only respondents' conduct. See *id.* at 15, n. 2; 547 F.3d 167, 171 (CA2 2008).

within the United States," and has lesser force when "the failure to extend the scope of the statute to a foreign setting will result in adverse effects within the United States." *Environmental Defense Fund, Inc. v. Massey*, 986 F.2d 528, 531 (CADC 1993); accord, Restatement (Second) of Foreign Relations Law of the United States § 38 (1964–1965) . . . . And it strikes a reasonable balance between the goals of "preventing the export of fraud from America," protecting shareholders, enhancing investor confidence, and deterring corporate misconduct, on the one hand, and conserving United States resources and limiting conflict with foreign law, on the other.[11] 547 F.3d at 175.

Thus, while § 10(b) may not give any "clear indication" on its face as to how it should apply to transnational securities frauds, *ante* at 255, 265, it does give strong clues that it should cover at least some of them, see n. 9, *supra*. And in my view, the Second Circuit has done the best job of discerning what sorts of transnational frauds Congress meant in 1934—and still means today—to regulate. . . .

Repudiating the Second Circuit's approach in its entirety, the Court establishes a novel rule that will foreclose private parties from bringing § 10(b) actions whenever the relevant securities were purchased or sold abroad and are not listed on a domestic exchange.[12] . . . [W]hile the clarity and simplicity of the Court's test may have some salutary consequences, like all bright-line rules it also has drawbacks.

Imagine, for example, an American investor who buys shares in a company listed only on an overseas exchange. That company has a major American subsidiary with executives based in New York City; and it was in New York City that the executives masterminded and implemented a massive deception which artificially inflated the stock price—and which will, upon its disclosure, cause the price to plummet. Or, imagine that those same executives go knocking on doors in Manhattan and convince an unsophisticated retiree, on the basis of material misrepresentations, to invest her life savings in the company's doomed securities. Both of these investors would, under the Court's new test, be barred from seeking relief under § 10(b).

. . . . [I]n walling off such individuals from § 10(b), the Court narrows the provision's reach to a degree that would surprise and alarm

[11] . . . I expect that virtually all " 'foreign-cubed' " actions—actions in which "(1) *foreign* plaintiffs [are] suing (2) a *foreign* issuer in an American court for violations of American securities laws based on securities transactions in (3) *foreign* countries," 547 F.3d at 172—would fail the Second Circuit's test. . . . Under these circumstances, the odds of the fraud having a substantial connection to the United States are low. In recognition of the Exchange Act's focus on American investors and the novelty of foreign-cubed lawsuits, and in the interest of promoting clarity, it might have been appropriate to incorporate one bright line into the Second Circuit's test, by categorically excluding such lawsuits from § 10(b)'s ambit.

[12] The Court's opinion does not, however, foreclose the Commission from bringing enforcement actions in additional circumstances, as no issue concerning the Commission's authority is presented by this case. The Commission's enforcement proceedings not only differ from private § 10(b) actions in numerous potentially relevant respects, . . . but they also pose a lesser threat to international comity . . . .

generations of American investors—and, I am convinced, the Congress that passed the Exchange Act. . . .

III

In my judgment, if petitioners' allegations of fraudulent misconduct that took place in Florida are true, then respondents may have violated § 10(b), and could potentially be held accountable in an enforcement proceeding brought by the Commission. But it does not follow that shareholders who have failed to allege that the bulk or the heart of the fraud occurred in the United States, or that the fraud had an adverse impact on American investors or markets, may maintain a private action to recover damages they suffered abroad. Some cases involving foreign securities transactions have extensive links to, and ramifications for, this country; this case has Australia written all over it. Accordingly, for essentially the reasons stated in the Court of Appeals' opinion, I would affirm its judgment. . . .

NOTES AND QUESTIONS

1. Less than a month after the Supreme Court decided *Morrison*, Congress enacted the Dodd-Frank Wall Street Reform and Consumer Protection Act, Pub. L. 111–203, 124 Stat. 1376 (2010), a massive statute that Congress had been working on for some time. Section 929P(b)(2) of the Dodd-Frank Act amended § 27 of the Securities Exchange Act (the jurisdictional provision quoted in footnote 3 of the majority opinion in *Morrison*) to include the following new subsection:

> "(b) EXTRATERRITORIAL JURISDICTION.—The district courts of the United States . . . shall have jurisdiction of an action or proceeding brought or instituted by the [Securities and Exchange] Commission or the United States alleging a violation of the antifraud provisions of this title involving—
>
> "(1) conduct within the United States that constitutes significant steps in furtherance of the violation, even if the securities transaction occurs outside the United States and involves only foreign investors; or
>
> "(2) conduct occurring outside the United States that has a foreseeable substantial effect within the United States."

Id. § 929P(b)(2), 124 Stat. at 1865; *see also id.* § 929P(b)(1), (b)(3), 124 Stat. at 1864–65 (making similar changes to the jurisdictional provisions of the Securities Act of 1933 and the Investment Advisers Act of 1940). This language seemed designed to codify something like the Second Circuit's "conduct" and "effects" tests for use in civil and criminal cases brought by the SEC or the United States, but not in suits by private plaintiffs. *Cf. id.* § 929Y, 124 Stat. at 1871 (directing the SEC to "conduct a study to determine the extent to which private rights of action under the antifraud provisions of the Securities and [sic] Exchange Act of 1934 . . . should be extended to cover" conduct of this sort).

Confusingly, however, Congress cast the new language simply as a grant of subject-matter jurisdiction, not as altering the substantive rules of decision that courts apply in cases that they have jurisdiction to adjudicate. That reflects how some lawyers and judges had talked before *Morrison*; people often had cast questions about the extraterritorial reach of statutes like the Securities Exchange Act in terms of the courts' jurisdiction to adjudicate cases involving overseas conduct. In *Morrison*, though, Part II of the majority opinion rejected this way of talking. *See Morrison*, 561 U.S. at 253–54 (explaining that the extraterritorial reach of § 10(b) is "a merits question" about the scope of the rule of decision created by § 10(b), not "a question of subject-matter jurisdiction"). In *Morrison* itself, § 27 of the Securities Exchange Act had given the district court subject-matter jurisdiction, but the plaintiffs lost on the merits because (according to the majority) the duties created by § 10(b) did not reach overseas transactions in securities not listed on American stock exchanges.

After *Morrison*, the best way for Congress to codify the "conduct" and "effects" tests with respect to the Securities Exchange Act would have been to expand the substantive duties created by § 10(b), not to amend the grant of jurisdiction in § 27. But although the Dodd-Frank Act was enacted after the Supreme Court decided *Morrison*, the language added by § 929P(b) had been drafted before then, and Congress did not recast that language in light of *Morrison*. *See* SEC v. Traffic Monsoon, LLC, 245 F. Supp. 3d 1275, 1290–92 (D. Utah 2017) (summarizing the legislative history), *aff'd sub nom.* SEC v. Scoville, 913 F.3d 1204 (10th Cir. 2019).

In a memorandum released on the day that the Dodd-Frank Act became law, George Conway (who had argued *Morrison* on behalf of National Australia Bank) suggested that the language added by § 929P(b) did not actually change anything, even in suits brought by the SEC; that language simply addressed subject-matter jurisdiction (which had already existed), and it "does not expand the geographic scope of any substantive regulatory provision." George T. Conway III, Extraterritoriality of the Federal Securities Laws After Dodd-Frank: Partly Because of a Drafting Error, the Status Quo Should Remain Unchanged (July 21, 2010), https://www.wlrk.com/webdocs/wlrknew/ClientMemos/WLRK/WLRK.17763.10.pdf. Courts have given this argument a respectful hearing. *See, e.g.*, SEC v. A Chicago Convention Center, LLC, 961 F. Supp. 2d 905, 909–17 (N.D. Ill. 2013) (calling the issue "complex" and canvassing the arguments on both sides). As of this writing, however, the few judges who have resolved the issue have ruled against Mr. Conway's position. *See Scoville*, 913 F.3d at 1218 (concluding that "Congress has 'affirmatively and unmistakably' indicated that the antifraud provisions of the federal securities acts apply extraterritorially [in cases brought by the SEC] when the statutory conduct-and-effects test is met"). Aren't those judges correct to read the language added by the Dodd-Frank Act to establish the legal rule that Congress obviously intended to communicate (assuming that this intended meaning is apparent from the text and other permissible sources of information)?

2. The Supreme Court has continued to follow the approach that Justice Scalia laid out in *Morrison*. Although the Court's understanding of that approach arguably has evolved in some respects, here is how the Court described it in *RJR Nabisco, Inc. v. European Community*, 579 U.S. 325 (2016).

In the Court's words, "*Morrison* and [*Kiobel v. Royal Dutch Petroleum Co.*, 569 U.S. 108 (2013),] reflect a two-step framework for analyzing extraterritoriality issues." *Id.* at 337. The first step is to "ask whether the presumption against extraterritoriality has been rebutted—that is, whether the statute gives a clear, affirmative indication that it applies extraterritorially." *Id.*[36] To the extent that the answer is "yes," the court should apply the statute according to its terms (assuming that Congress has the constitutional authority to reach whatever foreign conduct the statute reaches). But if the answer is "no," then the statute does not have any extraterritorial applications. In that scenario, the court must move on to the second step, and ask whether applying the statute in the case at hand would be causing the statute to operate "extraterritorially."

This second step itself has two components. To begin with, the court must interpret the statute to identify its "focus" (or, more precisely, the "focus" that is relevant to the provision or set of provisions that the court is being asked to apply).[37] At least with respect to regulatory statutes, the "focus" of the statute may well be some category of activity, such as the type of conduct that the statute regulates or acts upon. Once the court has identified the statute's "focus," the court must think about the facts of the case at hand: in this case, where did "the conduct relevant to the statute's focus" occur? *See RJR Nabisco*, 579 U.S. at 337. "If the conduct relevant to the statute's focus occurred in the United States, then the case involves a permissible domestic application [of the statute] even if other conduct occurred abroad," and the court can go ahead and apply the statute. *Id.* By contrast, "if the conduct relevant to the [statute's] focus occurred in a foreign country," then the court should *not* apply the statute in this case; under the circumstances, this application of the statute would be "extraterritorial," and the court has already decided (at the first step of the analysis) that the statute has no extraterritorial applications. *Id.*

---

[36] Although *RJR Nabisco* "refer[red] to whether the 'statute' applies extraterritorially," the Supreme Court has clarified that "the two-step analysis applies at the level of the particular provision implicated." *Abitron Austria GmbH v. Hetronic Int'l, Inc.*, 143 S. Ct. 2522, 2529 n.3 (2023). Thus, it is possible for a statute to rebut the presumption against extraterritoriality with respect to some provisions but not others. Indeed, that happened in *RJR Nabisco* itself.

[37] *See supra* note 36; *cf. WesternGeco LLC v. ION Geophysical Corp.*, 138 S. Ct. 2129, 2137 (2018) ("When determining the focus of a statute, we do not analyze the provision at issue in a vacuum. If the statutory provision at issue works in tandem with other provisions, it must be assessed in concert with those other provisions." (citation omitted)).

This analysis tries to give practical content to the concept of "extraterritoriality" on a statute-by-statute basis, without having to rely on the situs-ascribing rules of traditional choice-of-law doctrines. *Cf. supra* pp. 234–235 (explaining how courts of the early twentieth century would have used those doctrines to decide whether any particular application of a statute would be "extraterritorial"). But the typical statute may not really provide the tools to accomplish this task. Critics have charged that *Morrison*'s concept of the "focus" of a statute is indeterminate and therefore unpredictable. *See, e.g.*, Natascha Born, *The Presumption Against Extraterritoriality: Reconciling Canons of Statutory Interpretation with Textualism*, 41 U. PA. J. INT'L L. 541, 572 (2020) (calling the concept "undefined and ambiguous"); Kyle A. Mason, *The "Presumption Against Extra(subjective)territoriality":* Morrison*'s Confounding "Focus" Test*, 38 REV. LITIG. 385, 407 (2019) (noting that lower courts have reached "a wide variety of results" when trying to apply *Morrison* to particular statutes); Julie Rose O'Sullivan, *The Extraterritorial Application of Federal Criminal Statutes: Analytical Roadmap, Normative Conclusions, and a Plea to Congress for Direction*, 106 GEO. L.J. 1021, 1060 (2018) ("The test is difficult to apply because Congress does not normally identify a statutory focus.").[38]

In *Morrison* itself, for instance, one might have assumed that the "focus" of § 10(b) of the Securities Exchange Act is deceptive conduct. If so, the plaintiffs in *Morrison* might have had a claim for relief even under Justice Scalia's approach; some (though not all) of the deceptive conduct that they were alleging had taken place in the United States. According to Justice Scalia, though, the "focus" of the statute is really "purchases and sales of securities." Justice Scalia based this conclusion partly on the language of § 10(b), *see Morrison*, 561 U.S. at 266 (observing that instead of covering all deceptive conduct, § 10(b) covers "only deceptive conduct 'in connection with the purchase or sale of any security registered on a national securities exchange or any security not so registered' "), and partly on what he took to be the thrust of the statute as a whole, *see id.* at 267 ("Those purchase-and-sale transactions are the objects of the statute's solicitude. It is those transactions that the statute seeks to 'regulate'; it is parties or prospective parties to those transactions that the statute seeks to 'protec[t].' " (citations omitted)).[39]

---

[38] Although *Morrison* attributed the idea of a statute's "focus" to the Court's earlier decision in *Aramco*, commentators agree that *Morrison* was articulating a new approach. *See* O'Sullivan, *supra*, 106 GEO. L.J. at 1059 ("[T]he *Morrison* Court chose to create its own 'focus' test, which had no precedential support."); *see also* Franklin A. Gevurtz, *Determining Extraterritoriality*, 56 WM. & MARY L. REV. 341, 371 (2014) (explaining that *Aramco* had spoken of Title VII's "domestic focus" only when addressing whether the presumption against extraterritoriality had been overcome, not as part of a test for deciding which applications of the statute would be extraterritorial).

[39] In a footnote, Justice Scalia argued that his conclusion helped resolve a textual puzzle: why does § 10(b) refer to "the purchase or sale of any security registered on a national securities exchange or any security not so registered," rather than simply "the purchase or sale of any security"? *See Morrison*, 561 U.S. at 268 n.10. Justice Scalia suggested that § 10(b) uses this phrasing because it treats the purchase of sale of securities listed on American exchanges

The latter argument might seem to invoke the purpose of the statute—whom was Congress trying to protect against what? In a parallel context involving the presumption against retroactivity, though, Justice Scalia suggested that what matters is the conduct that the statute directly acts upon—what it regulates, rather than the reason behind the regulation. *See infra* p. 307 (discussing Justice Scalia's dissenting opinion in *Vartelas v. Holder*, 566 U.S. 257 (2012)). If one associates the "focus" of a statute with the category of behavior that the statute directly acts upon, which one discerns by reading the statutory text, does Justice Scalia's approach amount to looking for phrases in the relevant provision (like "purchase or sale" in § 10(b)) that could be read to come with the implied adjective "domestic"? Is that what Justice Scalia meant when he suggested that his position was grounded in the text of § 10(b)? *See Morrison*, 561 U.S. at 267 n.9.

However one identifies the "focus" of a statute, how promising is this method of giving practical content to the concept of extraterritoriality? Traditionally, that function was served by choice-of-law doctrines. Could courts go back to that approach, and would that be better than reading each individual federal statute to determine its own reach (even when it does not seem to address that topic)? Admittedly, modern federal courts have not been eager to try to articulate an overarching set of federal choice-of-law doctrines; when federal district courts have to decide which sovereign's law to apply to issues that are not governed by substantive federal law, they usually piggyback on the choice-of-law doctrines of the particular state in which they sit. *See* Klaxon Co. v. Stentor Electric Mfg. Co., 313 U.S. 487 (1941). For the last half century or so, moreover, state courts have taken more diverse approaches to choice-of-law questions than they once did. Even today, though, the choice-of-law doctrines recognized by most states fall into some patterns, so we might still be able to speak of ordinary American choice-of-law jurisprudence on many topics. *Cf.* Caleb Nelson, *The Persistence of General Law*, 106 COLUM. L. REV. 503, 539–43 (2006). If so, could courts use that jurisprudence to help define the expected geographic reach of federal statutes? Might one say that a federal statute is being given "extraterritorial" effect whenever a court applies it to an issue that ordinary American choice-of-law principles would suggest should be governed by the law of a foreign country instead? Equivalently, but without casting the key point in terms of "extraterritoriality," should courts simply presume that the typical federal statute has the reach suggested by general American choice-of-

---

differently than the purchase or sale of other securities. In particular, Justice Scalia indicated that even if § 10(b) covers the purchase or sale anywhere in the world of securities that are registered on an American stock exchange, it should be understood to cover only the *domestic* purchase or sale of other securities. *See id.* at 273. Is that a plausible explanation for the phrasing of § 10(b)? Isn't it more likely that Congress simply wanted to make clear that unlike § 10(a), which applies only with respect to "any security registered on a national securities exchange," the antifraud provisions in § 10(b) apply with respect to other securities too (including but perhaps not limited to securities that are exempt from the statute's registration requirements)? *See* Securities Exchange Act § 10, 48 Stat. at 891.

law principles (absent a sufficiently clear indication that Congress intended the statute to have a different reach)?[40] *Cf.* Yegiazaryan v. Smagin, 143 S. Ct. 1900, 1911 (2023) ("Petitioners . . . do not clearly explain why choice-of-law principles are germane here . . . . While legal fictions regarding the situs of economic injuries and intangible property have their justifications in other areas of law, those justifications do not necessarily translate to the presumption against extraterritoriality, with its distinctive concerns for comity and discerning congressional meaning.").

3. The *RJR Nabisco* case is worth considering in its own right. The case involved a title of the Organized Crime Control Act of 1970 known as the Racketeer Influenced and Corrupt Organizations Act (RICO), which enacted the provisions found at 18 U.S.C. §§ 1961–1968.

The first of those provisions, 18 U.S.C. § 1961, defines some key phrases by referring to other laws. As used in RICO, the phrase "racketeering activity" includes various categories of behavior that amount to felonies under state law, as well as acts that are indictable under a long list of federal statutory provisions. Likewise, the phrase "pattern of racketeering activity" refers to two or more of those predicate offenses committed within ten years of each other.

Section 1962 then uses those phrases to prohibit certain conduct. In the words of Justice Alito's opinion for the Supreme Court in *RJR Nabisco*,

> "RICO's § 1962 sets forth four specific prohibitions aimed at different ways in which a pattern of racketeering activity may be used to infiltrate, control, or operate 'a[n] enterprise which is engaged in, or the activities of which affect, interstate or foreign commerce.' These prohibitions can be summarized as follows. Section 1962(a) makes it unlawful to invest income derived from a pattern of racketeering activity in an enterprise. Section 1962(b) makes it unlawful to acquire or maintain an interest in an enterprise through a pattern of racketeering activity. Section 1962(c) makes it unlawful for a person employed by or associated with an enterprise to conduct the enterprise's affairs through a pattern of racketeering activity. Finally, § 1962(d) makes it unlawful to conspire to violate any of the other three prohibitions."

579 U.S. at 330.

Sections 1963 and 1964 address the consequences of violating § 1962. Section 1963 establishes stiff criminal penalties, and § 1964 addresses civil remedies. Specifically, § 1964(a) gives the federal district courts "jurisdiction to prevent and restrain violations of § 1962 . . . by issuing appropriate orders," and § 1964(b) provides that "[t]he Attorney

---

[40] Return to these questions after you have read the materials in Chapter 6.C about the interaction between federal statutes and "general law."

General may institute proceedings under this section."[41] Section 1964(c) creates a private right of action in the following terms: "Any person injured in his business or property by reason of a violation of section 1962 . . . may sue therefor in any appropriate United States district court and recover threefold the damages he sustains and the cost of the suit, including a reasonable attorney's fee . . . ."

In *RJR Nabisco*, the European Community and twenty-six of its member nations were suing RJR Nabisco and related companies under the private cause of action created by § 1964(c), on the theory that the defendants had violated § 1962 and the plaintiffs had been injured in their business or property as a result. Some of the defendants' alleged violations of § 1962 involved foreign conduct, and the plaintiffs had suffered their damages overseas. According to the Supreme Court, the case therefore presented two questions: "First, do RICO's substantive prohibitions, contained in § 1962, apply to conduct that occurs in foreign countries? Second, does RICO's private right of action, contained in § 1964(c), apply to injuries that are suffered in foreign countries?" *RJR Nabisco*, 579 U.S. at 335.

All seven of the Justices who participated in deciding the case answered the first question "yes" (to some extent).[42] As the Court explained, the definition of "racketeering activity" in § 1961 covers a long list of predicate offenses defined by other statutory provisions, and some of those other statutory provisions explicitly reach conduct in foreign countries. *See RJR Nabisco*, 579 U.S. at 338 (providing examples). As a result, it is possible for certain conduct in foreign countries to come within RICO's definition of "racketeering activity." The same point applies to RICO's definition of a *pattern* of racketeering activity. In Justice Alito's words, "a pattern of racketeering activity [as defined in RICO] may include or consist of offenses committed abroad in violation of a predicate statute for which the presumption against extraterritoriality has been overcome." *Id.* at 339.

Because § 1962 is keyed to these definitions, the Supreme Court had no difficulty concluding that § 1962 has some extraterritorial applications. *See id.* at 340. In particular, all seven Justices agreed that foreign conduct can violate both § 1962(b) ("It shall be unlawful for any person through a pattern of racketeering activity . . . to acquire or maintain . . . any interest in or control of any enterprise which is engaged in, or the activities of which affect, interstate or foreign commerce") and § 1962(c) ("It shall be unlawful for any person employed by or associated with any enterprise engaged in, or the activities of which affect,

[41] There is a circuit split as to whether § 1964 allows *only* the government to bring civil suits seeking injunctive relief or whether private plaintiffs can do so too. *See* Hengle v. Treppa, 19 F.4th 324, 353 (4th Cir. 2021) (citing cases); *see also RJR Nabisco*, 579 U.S. at 354–55 n.13 (expressing no opinion on this question).

[42] The Court decided *RJR Nabisco* after Justice Scalia's death, but before he was replaced, so it was short one Justice. In addition, Justice Sotomayor did not participate in the case.

interstate or foreign commerce, to conduct . . . such enterprise's affairs through a pattern of racketeering activity . . . ."). As the Court explained:

> "A violation of § 1962 may be based on a pattern of racketeering that includes predicate offenses committed abroad, provided that each of those offenses violates a predicate statute that is itself extraterritorial. This fact is determinative as to § 1962(b) and § 1962(c), both of which prohibit the employment of a pattern of racketeering."

RJR Nabisco, 579 U.S. at 340.[43] Because the presumption against extraterritoriality had been overcome with respect to these provisions, moreover, there was no need to identify RICO's "focus" and to infer a corresponding geographic limitation. *See id.* at 341–44 (rejecting the defendants' argument that RICO should be presumed to operate only with respect to *domestic* enterprises).

In the case at hand, Justice Alito assumed for the sake of argument that the complaint adequately alleged that the defendants had violated § 1962(b) and (c). Among other things, he assumed that all of the predicate offenses that were part of the defendants' alleged pattern of racketeering activity "were either committed in the United States or committed in a foreign country in violation of a predicate statute that applies extraterritorially." *Id.* at 345.

By a vote of four to three, though, the Court concluded that the plaintiffs still lost. While the presumption against extraterritoriality had been overcome with respect to the substantive prohibitions in § 1962(b) and (c), Justice Alito's majority opinion applied the presumption separately to § 1964(c)—the provision creating a private right of action in favor of "[a]ny person injured in his business or property by reason of a violation of section 1962." According to the majority, nothing in the statute overcame the presumption against extraterritoriality with respect to § 1964(c). *See id.* at 346–50. For the majority, it followed that when § 1964(c) refers to a person "injured in his business or property," it should be presumed to mean only a person who has suffered a *domestic* injury—an injury suffered in the United States. *Id.* at 354.[44] In *RJR*

[43] Justice Alito reserved judgment about the proper interpretation of § 1962(a), which restricts the use of income derived from a pattern of racketeering activity. *See id.* at 341 ("While we have no difficulty concluding that this prohibition applies to income derived from foreign patterns of racketeering (within the limits we have discussed), arguably § 1962(a) extends only to domestic uses of the income."). He also did not address the reach of § 1962(d)'s prohibition on conspiracies to violate the other provisions of § 1962. *Id.*

[44] Despite reciting *Morrison*'s framework earlier in the opinion, the majority reached this conclusion without talking about the "focus" of RICO in general or § 1964(c) in particular. Still, the majority apparently thought that the location of the plaintiffs' injury was critical to the proper application of § 1964(c)—suggesting, perhaps, that the majority viewed "injury" as the relevant focus.

More recently, the Court has clarified that "§ 1964(c)'s focus is on the injury, not in isolation, but as the product of racketeering activity." *Yegiazaryan v. Smagin*, 143 S. Ct. 1900, 1910 (2023). While adhering to *RJR Nabisco*'s holding that § 1964(c) provides a right of action only for "domestic injury" to the plaintiff's business or property, the Court has suggested that the location of the racketeering activity that caused an injury can bear on whether the injury itself

Nabisco, the plaintiffs had waived any claims for damages suffered in the United States; the damages claims that the plaintiffs were pursuing "rest[ed] entirely on injury suffered abroad." *Id.* The majority therefore concluded that the plaintiffs did not have a right of action under § 1964(c).

Does that make any sense? Even if the presumption against extraterritoriality should apply not only to statutory provisions that regulate people's conduct but also to statutory provisions creating remedial rights for violations of those regulations, why wouldn't the same considerations that overcame the presumption with respect to § 1962 also overcome it with respect to § 1964(c)? If Congress creates substantive duties that operate extraterritorially (as § 1962 does), and if Congress creates remedial rights in favor of people who are injured by violation of those duties, would you normally expect that right of action to be limited to people who are injured in the United States? Or when Congress prohibits certain conduct throughout the world, and when Congress allows "[a]ny person injured in his business or property by reason of a violation" of that prohibition to "sue therefor . . . and . . . recover threefold the damages he sustains," would you assume that injuries are compensable even if they occur in the same place as the prohibited conduct? *See RJR Nabisco*, 579 U.S. at 358 (Ginsburg, J., dissenting) ("I would not distinguish, as the Court does, between the extraterritorial compass of a private right of action and that of the underlying proscribed conduct.").

4. In *RJR Nabisco*, the majority asserted that *Morrison*'s two-step framework operates "regardless of whether the statute in question regulates conduct, affords relief, or merely confers jurisdiction." *Id.* at 337. No matter what the type of statute or statutory provision, then, lawyers apparently should think about (1) "whether the presumption against extraterritoriality has been rebutted" and (2) if not, whether application of the statute in the case at hand would be "extraterritorial." *See id.*

Still, what would it mean for a provision authorizing the award of damages to operate "extraterritorially"? Imagine that a federal statute both prohibits certain conduct and gives people who are harmed by such conduct a private right of action for damages. Imagine further that the statute says nothing to overcome any presumption against extraterritoriality. Acting entirely within the United States, a defendant violates the statute, and a plaintiff sues for damages. Would it be "extraterritorial" for the measure of damages to include harms that the

is "domestic." *See id.* (noting that in the case at hand, "[m]uch of the alleged racketeering activity that caused the injury occurred in the United States," though adding that "the injurious effects of the racketeering activity [also] largely manifested in California"); *see also id.* ("[I]n assessing whether there is a domestic injury, courts should engage in a case-specific analysis that looks to the circumstances surrounding the injury. If those circumstances sufficiently ground the injury in the United States, such that it is clear that the injury arose domestically, then the plaintiff has alleged a domestic injury.").

plaintiff suffered elsewhere in the world as a proximate result of the defendant's unlawful conduct in the United States? Should the answer vary from statute to statute, depending on whether courts think that the "focus" of the statute is the defendant's conduct (which occurred in the United States) or the harm to the plaintiff (some of which occurred overseas)? Or should courts apply a general presumption that when Congress backs up a statutory duty with a private right of action for damages, Congress normally wants defendants to have to make plaintiffs whole—with the result that the measure of damages normally should take account of losses that plaintiffs suffer anywhere as a proximate result of the defendants' unlawful conduct in the United States?

The Supreme Court faced a version of this question in *WesternGeco LLC v. ION Geophysical Corp.*, 138 S. Ct. 2129 (2018). That case involved the measure of damages for patent infringement.

Subject to some conditions and requirements, the federal Patent Act enables anyone who invents or discovers something new and useful to obtain a patent from the federal government. *See* 35 U.S.C. § 101 (defining patentability); *id.* § 154 (describing the rights conferred by a patent). Section 271 of the Act addresses what counts as "infringement" of a patent. By the time relevant to the *WesternGeco* case, § 271 included the following provisions:

§ 271. Infringement of patent

(a) Except as otherwise provided in this title, whoever without authority makes, uses, offers to sell, or sells any patented invention, within the United States or imports into the United States any patented invention during the term of the patent therefor, infringes the patent.

. . . .

(f)(1) Whoever without authority supplies or causes to be supplied in or from the United States all or a substantial portion of the components of a patented invention, where such components are uncombined in whole or in part, in such manner as to actively induce the combination of such components outside of the United States in a manner that would infringe the patent if such combination occurred within the United States, shall be liable as an infringer.

(2) Whoever without authority supplies or causes to be supplied in or from the United States any component of a patented invention that is especially made or especially adapted for use in the invention and not a staple article or commodity of commerce suitable for substantial noninfringing use, where such component is uncombined in whole or in part, knowing that such component is so made or adapted and intending that such component will be combined outside of the United States in a manner that would infringe the patent if such combination occurred within the United States, shall be liable as an infringer.

. . . .

Id. § 271.[45] Section 281 provides that "[a] patentee shall have remedy by civil action for infringement of his patent." *Id.* § 281. After § 283 addresses injunctive relief, § 284 addresses damages as follows: "Upon finding for the claimant the court shall award the claimant damages adequate to compensate for the infringement, but in no event less than a reasonable royalty for the use made of the invention by the infringer . . . ." *Id.* § 284.

The plaintiff in *WesternGeco* owned patents relating to a system that it used for surveying the ocean floor to find deposits of oil and gas. For a time, the plaintiff was the only company in the world that used this system, and petroleum companies hired the plaintiff to conduct surveys in various places around the world. In 2007, though, the defendant started making the components for a similar system. The defendant made those components in the United States and shipped them to foreign customers, who assembled the components into a finished system and used that system to compete with the plaintiff. At trial, the plaintiff proved that the defendant's conduct had caused the plaintiff to lose business around the world. The jury concluded that the defendant's actions amounted to infringement under § 271(f), and the jury awarded the plaintiff $93.4 million in lost profits. The defendant protested that the plaintiff would have earned those profits by conducting surveys outside of the United States, and the defendant argued that the measure of damages under § 284 should not include lost *foreign* profits. But the Supreme Court rejected that argument. According to the Court, what § 284 calls "damages adequate to compensate for the infringement" are supposed to make the plaintiff whole—and when the defendant's conduct in the United States amounts to infringement under § 271(f)(2), the damages authorized by § 284 can include lost profits no matter where the plaintiff would have earned those profits. *See WesternGeco*, 138 S. Ct. at 2139.[46]

---

[45] Congress had added subsection (f) to § 271 in 1984, in response to *Deepsouth Packing Co. v. Laitram Corp.*, 406 U.S. 518 (1972). Laitram Corp. owned so-called "combination patents" with respect to some machinery. (A "combination patent" protects a way of arranging parts in relation to each other, but does not claim intellectual-property rights in the parts themselves.) After extensive litigation, courts concluded that a machine that the Deepsouth Packing Co. was then making and selling in the United States infringed Laitram's patents. Still, Deepsouth argued that § 271(a) did not prevent Deepsouth from making the *parts* for this machine in the United States and shipping those parts to foreign purchasers, who could then quickly assemble the complete machine outside the United States. By a vote of 5 to 4, the Supreme Court agreed that this conduct would not constitute infringement. Congress eventually enacted § 271(f) to override that result. *See* Patent Law Amendments Act of 1984, Pub. L. 98–622, § 101(a), 98 Stat. 3383, 3383 (enacting § 271(f)); Microsoft Corp. v. AT&T Corp., 550 U.S. 437, 442–45 (2007) (describing § 271(f) as a response to *Deepsouth*).

[46] This paragraph recites the posture of the case as considered by the Supreme Court. During the pendency of the case, however, an administrative tribunal held that various aspects of the plaintiff's patents were invalid. *See* WesternGeco LLC v. ION Geophysical Corp., 889 F.3d 1308 (Fed. Cir. 2018) (affirming the administrative tribunal's decisions). After the Supreme Court issued its opinion, the Federal Circuit remanded the case to the district court for further proceedings "[i]n light of the Supreme Court's decision and the intervening invalidation of four

Although Justices Gorsuch and Breyer dissented on other grounds, all nine Justices agreed that this interpretation did not cause § 284 to have "extraterritorial" effect. Writing for the majority, Justice Thomas cast that conclusion in *Morrison*'s terms. In his view, the "focus" of § 284 is "the infringement"—and if the infringement occurs in the United States, there is nothing "extraterritorial" about making the plaintiff whole for the losses that the plaintiff has suffered worldwide. *See WesternGeco*, 138 S. Ct. at 2137; *see also id.* at 2138 ("[T]he focus of § 284, in a case involving infringement under § 271(f)(2), is on the act of exporting components from the United States.").

Although the majority cast its analysis as being specific to the Patent Act, its conclusion is consistent with how damages work under many private rights of action. For instance, suppose that while a Japanese surgeon is on vacation in the United States, she is injured in a car accident that is caused by the other driver's negligence. If she brings a tort suit against the other driver, wouldn't her measure of damages normally include the income that she loses as a result of the accident—even though she would have earned that income in Japan? Likewise, suppose that a European company enters into a contract in the United States for materials of a certain quality to be supplied to its agent in New York, who will then ship the materials to Europe to be incorporated in the products that the company makes there. If the materials that the supplier sends to the agent in New York do not satisfy the quality standards specified in the contract, and if the company suffers foreseeable harm in Europe as a result, wouldn't the company's measure of damages for breach of contract normally include that harm?

Would ordinary remedial principles of this sort have offered a sounder basis for the majority's conclusion than what the majority said about the "focus" of § 284? In *WesternGeco*, the defendant argued that the "focus" of § 284 was not the defendant's acts of infringement, but rather the award of damages—and awarding damages for lost foreign profits would therefore be "an impermissible extraterritorial application of Section 284." Brief for the Respondent 24, *WesternGeco*, 138 S. Ct. 2129 (No. 16–1011). Is there any objective way to decide whether the "focus" of a provision like § 284 is the defendant's conduct or the plaintiff's losses?

Is *WesternGeco* consistent with *RJR Nabisco*? In *RJR Nabisco*, the Court held that the presumption against extraterritoriality had been overcome with respect to some of RICO's substantive provisions, including at least certain aspects of 18 U.S.C. § 1962; those provisions do regulate some overseas conduct. But Justice Alito's majority opinion said that the presumption against extraterritoriality applied separately to 18 U.S.C. § 1964(c), the provision that creates a private right of action for treble damages in favor of "[a]ny person injured in his business or property by reason of a violation of section 1962." As interpreted by the

of the five asserted patent claims that could support the lost profits award." *WesternGeco LLC v. ION Geophysical Corp.*, 913 F.3d 1067, 1069 (Fed. Cir. 2019).

majority, § 1964(c) did not authorize recovery for foreign injuries; the phrase "[a]ny person injured in his business or property" referred only to people who suffered "a *domestic* injury to [their] business or property." *See RJR Nabisco*, 579 U.S. at 346. If that is correct (and it might not be), should *WesternGeco* have come out differently?

In *WesternGeco*, the Court asserted that the majority opinion in *RJR Nabisco* had not said anything about damages; instead, "*RJR Nabisco* was applying the presumption against extraterritoriality to interpret the scope of § 1964(c)'s injury requirement." *WesternGeco*, 138 S. Ct. at 2138. Should we infer that the Court would have reached a different conclusion in *WesternGeco* if § 284 of the Patent Act had used the word "injury"? For instance, suppose that § 284 had said: "Upon finding for the claimant, the court shall award the claimant damages adequate to compensate for the injury caused by the infringement." Would the Court then have said that the plaintiff was *not* entitled to compensation for lost foreign profits?

5. In the recent case of *Abitron Austria GmbH v. Hetronic International, Inc.*, 143 S. Ct. 2522 (2023), Justice Alito's majority opinion suggested that the presumption against extraterritoriality is centrally concerned with the location of *conduct*. Specifically, what the Court calls the presumption against extraterritoriality "refers to a 'presumption against application [of federal statutes] to conduct in the territory of another sovereign.' " *Id.* at 2528 (quoting Kiobel v. Royal Dutch Petroleum Co., 569 U.S. 108, 119 (2013)). In Justice Alito's telling, the "focus" analysis that operates at Step Two of the *Morrison* framework is a way to handle "claims that involve both domestic and foreign activity"; by identifying the type of conduct that is relevant to the statute's focus, the court can home in on "the activity that matters" and ask where it occurred. *See id.* at 2529.

With respect to statutes that regulate how people behave, this analysis may dovetail with your intuitions about extraterritoriality. The "focus" of many such statutes will be a particular type of conduct—the kind of behavior that the statute regulates. Under the *Morrison* framework, unless the statute contains sufficient indications to rebut the presumption against extraterritoriality, the statute will apply only to the extent that the relevant conduct occurs in the United States. That is what you might expect: roughly speaking, regulatory statutes will be presumed to regulate behavior in the United States but not elsewhere.

But what if the "focus" of a particular statute is something other than conduct? That is possible. *Cf. WesternGeco*, 138 S. Ct. at 2137 ("The focus of a statute is 'the objec[t] of [its] solicitude,' which can include the conduct it 'seeks to "regulate," ' as well as the parties and interests it 'seeks to "protec[t]" ' or vindicate." (quoting *Morrison*, 561 U.S. at 267)). In *Abitron*, Justice Alito's majority opinion suggested that even if the focus of a statute is not itself conduct, Step Two of the *Morrison* framework still requires judges to " 'as[k] whether the *conduct relevant to that focus* occurred in United States territory.' " *Abitron*, 143 S. Ct. at

2528 (quoting *WesternGeco*, 138 S. Ct. at 2136 (emphasis added in *Abitron*)); *cf. id.* at 2540 (Sotomayor, J., concurring in the judgment) ("[I]nstead of discerning the statute's focus and assessing whether that focus is found domestically, as the Court's precedents command, the majority now requires a third step: an assessment of whether the 'conduct relevant to the focus' occurred domestically, even when the focus of the statute is not conduct.").

Sometimes, it might be possible to apply this analysis in a non-arbitrary way. For instance, imagine a statute whose "focus" is the *effects* of conduct (rather than the conduct itself). The "conduct relevant to that focus" presumably is the conduct that causes those effects. Under Justice Alito's understanding of the *Morrison* framework, if that conduct occurs only outside the United States, then applying the statute would be "extraterritorial" even if the effects of the conduct are felt inside the United States. But will this analysis always work so neatly? When a statute "focuses" on something other than conduct, will it always be apparent what conduct is "relevant to" the statute's focus?

If one accepts Justice Alito's analysis in *Abitron*, would one need to modify the Court's holding in *RJR Nabisco*? Even if the "focus" of 18 U.S.C. § 1964(c) is some sort of injury to the plaintiff's business or property, the "conduct relevant to that focus" presumably would be the racketeering activity that caused the injury. If this racketeering activity occurred in foreign territory (albeit in violation of § 1962), does § 1964(c) create a right of action in favor of plaintiffs who have suffered injury to their business or property in the United States, or would Justice Alito now have to describe that as an "extraterritorial" application of § 1964(c)?

Conversely, imagine that a defendant's purely domestic violations of § 1962 in the United States cause harm to a plaintiff's business or property in Europe. Justice Alito's majority opinion in *RJR Nabisco* suggested that § 1964(c) would not give the plaintiff a right of action with respect to those injuries. *See RJR Nabisco*, 579 U.S. at 354 ("Section 1964(c) requires a civil RICO plaintiff to allege and prove a domestic injury to business or property and does not allow recovery for foreign injuries."). After *Abitron*, though, would this application of § 1964(c) still be considered "extraterritorial"? *Cf. Abitron*, 143 S. Ct. at 2529 (describing *WesternGeco* as having held that the plaintiffs' claim for lost foreign profits "was a domestic application of the Patent Act because the infringing acts—the conduct relevant to the focus of the provisions at issue—were committed in the United States").

6. Modern cases about the presumption against extraterritoriality might be thought to undermine the Supreme Court's holding in *United States v. Bowman*, 260 U.S. 94 (1922). That case concerned the geographic scope of the following provision in the then-existing Criminal Code of the United States:

> "[W]hoever shall enter into any agreement, combination, or conspiracy to defraud the Government of the United States, or any

department or officer thereof, or any corporation in which the United States of America is a stockholder, by obtaining or aiding to obtain the payment or allowance of any false or fraudulent claim[,] . . . shall be fined not more than $10,000 or imprisoned not more than ten years, or both."

Act of Oct. 23, 1918, ch. 194, 40 Stat. 1015, 1016 (1918) (amending § 35 of the Criminal Code).

In *Bowman*, the Supreme Court indicated that when a federal criminal statute did not specifically address its territorial scope, judges should consider both (1) "the purpose of Congress as evinced by the description and nature of the crime" and (2) background norms supplied by the law of nations. *Bowman*, 260 U.S. at 97–98. According to Chief Justice Taft's opinion for the Court, this analysis supported applying a presumption against extraterritoriality to many types of criminal statutes, but not all:

> "Crimes against private individuals or their property, like assaults, murder, burglary, larceny, robbery, arson, embezzlement and frauds of all kinds, which affect the peace and good order of the community, must of course be committed within the territorial jurisdiction of the government where it may properly exercise it. If punishment of them is to be extended to include those committed outside of the strict territorial jurisdiction, it is natural for Congress to say so in the statute, and failure to do so will negative the purpose of Congress in this regard. . . .
>
> "But the same rule of interpretation should not be applied to criminal statutes which are, as a class, not logically dependent on their locality for the Government's jurisdiction, but are enacted because of the right of the Government to defend itself against obstruction, or fraud wherever perpetrated, especially if committed by its own citizens, officers or agents. Some such offenses . . . are such that to limit their *locus* to the strictly territorial jurisdiction would be greatly to curtail the scope and usefulness of the statute and leave open a large immunity for frauds as easily committed by citizens on the high seas and in foreign countries as at home."

Id. at 98. On the basis of this analysis, the Court concluded that the statute at issue in *Bowman* made it a crime for American citizens to conspire anywhere in the world to defraud the United States government or a federally owned corporation. *Id.* at 100–02; *cf. id.* at 102–03 (reserving judgment about the statute's extraterritorial applicability to citizens or subjects of other countries).

Although *Bowman*'s analysis "sits uneasily with" the modern Supreme Court's opinions about the presumption against extraterritoriality, the Supreme Court has not overruled it, so "*Bowman* remains binding on the lower courts." *United States v. Al-Imam*, 373 F. Supp. 3d 247, 257 (D.D.C. 2019); *cf.* United States v. Leija-Sanchez, 820

F.3d 899, 900–01 (7th Cir. 2016) (taking *Bowman* to mean that "extraterritorial application of criminal laws" calls for a different analysis than "extraterritorial application of civil laws"). Indeed, some lower courts have applied *Bowman* expansively; partly because of circuit precedents that took root before *Aramco* and have not been cut back, they have identified numerous federal criminal statutes that allegedly fit into *Bowman*'s second category and that therefore reach conduct outside the United States. *See* Pierre-Hugues Verdier, *The New Financial Extraterritoriality*, 87 GEO. WASH. L. REV. 239, 268–69 (2019) (citing cases and commentary); *see also id.* at 270 (concluding that some of these precedents "appear fundamentally incompatible with the [Supreme] Court's post-*Morrison* line of cases" and "may be revisited").

7. The general federal conspiracy statute, 18 U.S.C. § 371, provides that "[i]f two or more persons conspire either to commit any offense against the United States, or to defraud the United States, or any agency thereof in any manner or for any purpose, and one or more of such persons do any act to effect the object of the conspiracy, each shall be fined under this title or imprisoned not more than five years, or both" (except that the statute establishes lesser penalties for conspiracies to commit a misdemeanor). To the extent that courts continue to follow *Bowman*, the portion of this statute about conspiracies "to defraud the United States" might operate on a worldwide basis (at least where the conspirators are American citizens). *See, e.g., United States v. Cotten*, 471 F.2d 744, 750 (9th Cir. 1973) (reading § 371 to cover a conspiracy formed in Vietnam by American citizens who acted in Vietnam and Japan). Should the same be true of the portion of the statute that addresses conspiracies "to commit any offense against the United States" (that is, any other federal crime)?

If you were using *Bowman*'s categories, might this part of § 371 be one of those "criminal statutes which are . . . not logically dependent on . . . locality for the Government's jurisdiction"? *See Bowman*, 260 U.S. at 98. Start by thinking about whether this part of § 371 should be understood to reach people who conspire in foreign countries or on the high seas to commit federal crimes within the borders of the United States. Wouldn't it be natural for Congress to want to punish conspirators who target United States territory in this way? Should a generally worded statute like § 371 be understood to do so, or should courts require a more specific indication from Congress?

Now consider people who conspire in foreign countries or on the high seas to commit federal crimes that would themselves take place abroad. For this scenario to make sense, Congress must have called for "extraterritorial" application of the underlying criminal statutes (that is, the statutes outlawing the conduct that the conspirators are planning). Given the anti-conspiracy policy reflected in § 371, and given Congress's decision to criminalize the underlying conduct even when it occurs overseas, is there any reason to suppose that Congress would *not* have wanted to criminalize overseas conspiracies to commit that conduct? *Cf.* United States v. Belfast, 611 F.3d 783, 813 (11th Cir. 2010) (recognizing a general presumption that "extraterritorial jurisdiction over a conspiracy charge exists whenever the underlying substantive crime applies to extraterritorial conduct").

How, if at all, should *Morrison* affect the courts' analysis of these issues? After *Morrison*, courts might not start by asking whether § 371 is the sort of statute that triggers the presumption against extraterritoriality. (Although the modern Supreme Court has not specifically discussed whether *Bowman*'s framework survives, *Morrison* does not itself suggest that there are any categorical exemptions from the presumption against extraterritoriality.) Instead, the first step of the *Morrison* framework is simply to ask whether the presumption has been rebutted. Even though § 371 does not itself say anything on this topic, the presumption against extraterritoriality might conceivably be rebutted with respect to some applications of § 371, involving conspiracies to violate federal statutes that themselves operate extraterritorially. *Cf. RJR Nabisco*, 579 U.S. at 340 (concluding that RICO's "unique structure"—specifically, the fact that RICO piggybacks upon predicate statutes, including some that operate extraterritorially—"makes RICO the rare statute that clearly evidences extraterritorial effect despite lacking an express statement of extraterritoriality"). But other applications of § 371, involving conspiracies to violate federal criminal statutes that do not themselves operate extraterritorially, would not implicate this argument. With respect to those conspiracies, at least, courts presumably would need to move on to the second step of the *Morrison* framework.

At that step, courts would start by trying to identify the "focus" of § 371 (or, perhaps, the "focus" of the combination of § 371 and the underlying statute that the defendants allegedly conspired to violate). What should they conclude? Is the "focus" the conspiracy, or is it the underlying offense that the defendants allegedly were planning? If the focus is the conspiracy, does that mean the *whole* conspiracy—not just its formation but also its continued existence and development? Are any overt acts in furtherance of the conspiracy also part of the "focus" of the statute? How can we tell?

Once courts have identified the "focus" of the statute, they would need to examine the facts of the case at hand to decide where "the conduct relevant to the statute's focus" occurred. *RJR Nabisco*, 579 U.S. at 337. In theory, that determines whether applying § 371 to this case would entail "a permissible domestic application" or "an impermissible extraterritorial application." *Id.* The broader the statute's "focus" is said to be, however, the more conduct is potentially relevant, and the greater the chances that some of it will have occurred in the United States. If courts think that the "focus" of § 371 is the whole conspiracy, how should they decide whether § 371 applies to a conspiracy was formed outside the

United States but that continued while some of the co-conspirators were inside the United States? Do courts need to identify the *primary* location of the conspiracy, and how would they do so? What if the conspiracy was formed and maintained overseas, but one or more of the overt acts was committed in the United States, or the ultimate object of the conspiracy would have involved conduct in the United States?

8. Suppose that Congress has authorized a federal agency or officer to take actions in foreign territory on behalf of the United States. How should courts determine the applicability of other federal statutes that regulate agencies' decisionmaking processes, require record-keeping, or otherwise constrain agencies? Is there any reason to read implied geographic limits into such statutes? *Compare* Envtl. Def. Fund, Inc. v. Massey, 986 F.2d 528, 529 (D.C. Cir. 1993) (interpreting a generally worded provision in the National Environmental Policy Act as requiring a federal agency to prepare an environmental impact statement before taking certain actions in Antarctica), *with* Lujan v. Defenders of Wildlife, 504 U.S. 555, 585–89 (1992) (Stevens, J., concurring in the judgment) (applying the presumption against extraterritoriality to conclude that a consultation requirement in the Endangered Species Act applies only with respect to agency actions in the United States, not in foreign countries).

Assuming that *Morrison*'s framework applies not only to statutes that regulate private conduct but also to statutes that regulate how the federal government works, how would *Morrison* operate in this context? For instance, what is the "focus" of the typical statute that regulates agencies' decisionmaking processes? If the focus is decisionmaking, the statute might govern all decisions made within the United States (even if those decisions are about actions abroad) but would not govern any decisions that agency personnel make elsewhere. By contrast, if the "focus" of the statute is the actions that the agency ultimately takes or does not take, the location of those actions would matter. How would you choose between these possibilities?

9. So far, this section has cast the presumption against extraterritoriality entirely as an implied-limitation rule—a canon that encourages courts to read implicit qualifications into generally worded statutes that do not specifically address their geographic reach. But in *Microsoft Corp. v. AT&T Corp.*, 550 U.S. 437 (2007), the Supreme Court suggested that the presumption against extraterritoriality is *also* a tool for resolving conventional linguistic indeterminacy in statutes that *do* specifically address their geographic reach. According to the Court, even if a statute specifically makes an exception to the normal rule against extraterritorial application, the presumption against extraterritoriality "remains instructive in determining the *extent* of the statutory exception." *Id.* at 456.

For instance, imagine that a federal statute includes an explicit "extraterritoriality clause" calling for the statute to operate extraterritorially, but the clause is ambiguously worded. *Microsoft* suggests that courts should resolve those ambiguities in whichever way minimizes the statute's extraterritorial application; in other words, courts should read the extraterritoriality clause to be as narrow as possible.[47] Can this principle of interpretation be defended in "descriptive" terms (as a reliable guide to the clause's likely intended meaning), or does it simply reflect the courts' own aversion to extraterritorial applications of federal statutes?

The implied-limitation version of the presumption against extraterritoriality has both descriptive and normative justifications. Descriptively, it arguably reflects Congress's own habits: when a federal statute regulates conduct without specifically addressing the statute's geographic reach, maybe Congress normally intends to regulate conduct within the United States but not conduct throughout the world. Normatively, that might also seem like a good idea: even apart from any arguments about legislative intent, minimizing the extraterritorial application of federal statutes might be a desirable way to respect the sovereignty of other countries, reduce the risks of conflict between U.S. and foreign law, and avoid unnecessary tensions in foreign relations.

At first glance, you might assume that the same mix of descriptive and normative justifications must also apply to the version of the presumption that *Microsoft* suggested—the one that operates not as an implied-limitation rule (triggered by generally worded statutes that say nothing about extraterritoriality) but instead as a tool for resolving conventional linguistic indeterminacy (triggered by statutory provisions that do specifically address extraterritoriality but are unclear in some respect). In fact, however, the principle that the Court articulated in *Microsoft* may not really have much "descriptive" force. When Congress has specifically addressed the geographic reach of a statute and has enacted a provision calling for the statute to have some extraterritorial applications, Congress presumably chose words that would convey the amount of extraterritoriality that Congress intended. If the provision is ambiguous, a narrow interpretation of those words may be no more likely to capture Congress's true intent than a normal interpretation. *Cf. infra* pp. 1097–1100 (discussing a similar issue involving the interpretation of express "preemption clauses" in federal statutes).

---

2. THE PRESUMPTION AGAINST RETROACTIVITY

The presumption against retroactivity is another prominent implied-limitation rule. It works in much the same way as the presumption against extraterritoriality: just as courts often read geographic limitations into seemingly general statutory language so that federal

---

[47] This is not the situation that the Court was actually confronting in *Microsoft*, so perhaps what *Microsoft* said is merely dictum on this point.

statutes do not operate "extraterritorially," so too courts often read temporal limitations into seemingly general statutory language so that statutes do not operate "retroactively."[48] As we shall see, moreover, just as the Supreme Court has had difficulty defining the sort of "extraterritoriality" that triggers the presumption against extraterritoriality, so too there are questions about how to define the sort of "retroactivity" that triggers the presumption against retroactivity.

Of course, even apart from any principles of statutory interpretation, the federal Constitution and its state counterparts impose some limits on retroactive legislation. Because of those constitutional limits, there are some things that American legislatures cannot do retroactively, no matter how clearly they write their statutes.

For instance, Article I of the Constitution says that neither Congress nor the states can pass any "ex post facto Law." U.S. CONST. art. I, §§ 9–10. That limitation is not as broad as you might think, because the Supreme Court has long interpreted the phrase "ex post facto Law" in the Constitution as a term of art that refers only to *penal* laws. *See, e.g.*, *Calder v. Bull*, 3 U.S. (3 Dall.) 386 (1798). A statute is a prohibited "ex post facto Law" if it criminalizes an act that was not subject to punishment when committed, or even if it just adds to the punishment for an act that was subject to less severe punishment under the law that was in effect when the act was committed. Indeed, statutes can be "penal" within the meaning of Ex Post Facto jurisprudence even if they do not technically involve the criminal law; if the statute takes away certain kinds of private rights for the purpose of punishment, it might trigger the restrictions of the Ex Post Facto Clauses. But current doctrine is quite clear that those Clauses apply only to "penal" statutes. As a result, they do not prevent either Congress or the state legislatures from retroactively changing the law applicable to civil cases for reasons unconnected with punishing past behavior.

Some other constitutional provisions do impose a few restrictions on retroactive statutes that are not "penal." For instance, the Contracts Clause of Article I, Section 10, forbids states to pass laws impairing the obligation of contracts. In modern times, that Clause is not as much of a safeguard against retroactive legislation as it once was; longstanding doctrine holds that people enter into contracts subject to the possibility that state governments may exercise their police powers in ways that

[48] I have deliberately referred to "federal statutes" in the portion of this sentence that discusses the presumption against extraterritoriality and to "statutes" in the portion that discusses the presumption against retroactivity. As noted above, the presumption against extraterritoriality comes up more frequently with respect to federal statutes than with respect to state statutes. (To decide whether any particular state statute reaches a cross-border transaction, state courts often simply use their state's normal choice-of-law doctrines, which their state's statutes are presumed to accommodate. *See supra* pp. 232–233.) By contrast, some version of a presumption against retroactivity is commonly applied to state as well as federal statutes. For ease in exposition, this section of the book focuses on the version of the presumption against retroactivity that the Supreme Court has articulated for federal statutes, but many state courts apply a similar canon to their state's statutes.

affect the performance of those contracts, and twentieth-century cases dramatically expanded the scope of the powers that state governments can use in this way. But the Contracts Clause remains a restraint on at least some extreme forms of retroactive state and local legislation. And while the Contracts Clause applies only against state and local governments, the Due Process Clause of the Fifth Amendment is thought to subject the federal government to some of the same sorts of restrictions.

Even when no contracts are in the picture, the Due Process Clauses of the Fifth and Fourteenth Amendments were long understood to impose some additional constitutional restraints on the ability of legislatures to act retroactively. *See, e.g.*, Ann Woolhandler, *Public Rights, Private Rights, and Statutory Retroactivity*, 94 GEO. L.J. 1015, 1023–27 (2006). In the nineteenth century, it was commonly said that neither the federal Congress nor state legislatures could validly divest people of certain types of private rights that had vested in them under the existing law. Indeed, this notion of "vested rights" was absolutely crucial to American constitutional jurisprudence for a substantial part of the nineteenth century. *See* Edward S. Corwin, *The Basic Doctrine of American Constitutional Law*, 12 MICH. L. REV. 247 (1914). But the notion of "vested rights" has faded today. While the Due Process Clauses are still understood to provide *some* protection against retroactive legislation, and while the same is true of the Takings Clause, modern doctrine assumes that both Congress and the state legislatures do have considerable power to enact retroactive statutes. *Cf.* Woolhandler, *supra*, at 1056–63 (defending the older, more categorical approach).

The precise limits on this power are not clear. But let us assume that Congress or a state legislature could make a particular statute retroactive if it wanted to do so. When that is true, questions about whether the statute is indeed retroactive will boil down to questions of statutory interpretation rather than constitutional law. In the following seminal case, the Supreme Court both articulated a strong presumption against reading federal statutes to apply "retroactively" and attempted to describe what counts as "retroactivity" for this purpose.

Landgraf v. USI Film Products

511 U.S. 244 (1994)

■ *JUSTICE STEVENS delivered the opinion of the Court:*

[Section 102(a) of] the Civil Rights Act of 1991 (1991 Act or Act) creates a right to recover compensatory and punitive damages for certain violations of Title VII of the Civil Rights Act of 1964 [which prohibits various forms of discrimination in employment but, as interpreted before the 1991 Act, authorized only equitable remedies]. . . . [Section 102(c) of the 1991 Act] further provides that any party may demand a trial by jury if such damages are sought. We granted certiorari to decide whether these provisions apply to a Title VII case that was pending on appeal when the statute was enacted. We hold that they do not.

I

From September 4, 1984, through January 17, 1986, petitioner Barbara Landgraf was employed in the USI Film Products (USI) plant in Tyler, Texas. . . . A fellow employee named John Williams repeatedly harassed her with inappropriate remarks and physical contact. Petitioner's complaints to her immediate supervisor brought her no relief, but when she reported the incidents to the personnel manager, he conducted an investigation, reprimanded Williams, and transferred him to another department. Four days later petitioner quit her job.

. . . .

On July 21, 1989, [after proceedings before the Equal Employment Opportunity Commission,] petitioner commenced this action against USI, its corporate owner, and that company's successor in interest. After a bench trial, the District Court found that Williams had sexually harassed petitioner causing her to suffer mental anguish. However, the court concluded that she had not been constructively discharged. . . . Because the court found that petitioner's employment was not terminated in violation of Title VII, she was not entitled to equitable relief, and because Title VII did not then authorize any other form of relief, the court dismissed her complaint.

On November 21, 1991, while petitioner's appeal was pending, the President signed into law the Civil Rights Act of 1991. The Court of Appeals rejected petitioner's argument that her case should be remanded for a jury trial on damages pursuant to the 1991 Act. . . . [T]he Court of Appeals affirmed the judgment for respondents.

We granted certiorari . . . . Our order limited argument to the question whether § 102 of the 1991 Act applies to cases pending when it became law. . . . Accordingly, for purposes of our decision, we assume that the District Court and the Court of Appeals properly applied the law in effect at the time of the discriminatory conduct and that the relevant findings of fact were correct. We therefore assume that petitioner was the victim of sexual harassment violative of Title VII, but that the law did not then authorize any recovery of damages even though she was injured. We also assume, *arguendo*, that if the same conduct were to occur today, petitioner would be entitled to a jury trial and that the jury might find that she was constructively discharged, or that her mental anguish or other injuries would support an award of damages against her former employer. Thus, the controlling question is whether the Court of Appeals should have applied the law in effect at the time the discriminatory conduct occurred, or at the time of its decision in July 1992.

II

Petitioner's primary submission is that the text of the 1991 Act requires that it be applied to cases pending on its enactment. Her argument, if accepted, would make the entire Act (with two narrow exceptions) applicable to conduct that occurred, and to cases that were filed, before the Act's effective date. Although only § 102 is at issue in this case, we preface our analysis with a brief description of the scope of the 1991 Act.

The 1991 Act is in large part a response to a series of decisions of this Court interpreting the Civil Rights Acts of 1866 and 1964. Section 3(4) . . . expressly identifies as one of the Act's purposes "to respond to recent decisions of the Supreme Court by expanding the scope of relevant civil rights statutes in order to provide adequate protection to victims of discrimination." That section, as well as a specific finding in § 2(2), identifies *Wards Cove Packing Co. v. Atonio*, 490 U.S. 642 (1989), as a decision that gave rise to special concerns. Section 105 of the Act, entitled "Burden of Proof in Disparate Impact Cases," is a direct response to *Wards Cove*.

Other sections of the Act were obviously drafted with "recent decisions of the Supreme Court" in mind. Thus, § 101 . . . amended the 1866 Civil Rights Act's prohibition of racial discrimination in the "mak[ing] and enforce[ment] [of] contracts," 42 U.S.C. § 1981, in response to *Patterson v. McLean Credit Union*, 491 U.S. 164 (1989); § 107 responds to *Price Waterhouse v. Hopkins*, 490 U.S. 228 (1989), by setting forth standards applicable in "mixed motive" cases; § 108 responds to *Martin v. Wilks*, 490 U.S. 755 (1989), by prohibiting certain challenges to employment practices implementing consent decrees; § 109 responds to *EEOC v. Arabian American Oil Co.*, 499 U.S. 244 (1991), by redefining the term "employee" as used in Title VII to include certain United States citizens working in foreign countries for United States employers; § 112 responds to *Lorance v. AT&T Technologies, Inc.*, 490 U.S. 900 (1989), by expanding employees' rights to challenge discriminatory seniority systems; § 113 responds to *West Virginia Univ. Hospitals, Inc. v. Casey*, 499 U.S. 83 (1991), by providing that an award of attorney's fees may include expert fees; and § 114 responds to *Library of Congress v. Shaw*, 478 U.S. 310 (1986), by allowing interest on judgments against the United States.

A number of important provisions in the Act, however, were not responses to Supreme Court decisions. For example, § 106 enacts a new prohibition against adjusting test scores "on the basis of race, color, religion, sex, or national origin"; § 117 extends the coverage of Title VII to include the House of Representatives and certain employees of the Legislative Branch; and §§ 301–325 establish special procedures to protect Senate employees from discrimination. Among the provisions that did not directly respond to any Supreme Court decision is the one at issue in this case, § 102.

Entitled "Damages in Cases of Intentional Discrimination," § 102 provides in relevant part:

"(a) Right of Recovery.—

"(1) Civil Rights.—In an action brought by a complaining party under section 706 or 717 of the Civil Rights Act of 1964 (42 U.S.C. 2000e–5) against a respondent who engaged in unlawful intentional discrimination (not an employment practice that is unlawful because of its disparate impact) prohibited under section 703, 704, or 717 of the Act (42 U.S.C. 2000e–2 or 2000e–3), and provided that the complaining party cannot recover under section 1977 of the Revised Statutes (42 U.S.C. 1981), the complaining party may recover compensatory and punitive damages . . . in addition to any relief authorized by section 706(g) of the Civil Rights Act of 1964, from the respondent.

. . . . .

"(c) Jury Trial.—If a complaining party seeks compensatory or punitive damages under this section—

"(1) any party may demand a trial by jury."

Before the enactment of the 1991 Act, Title VII afforded only "equitable" remedies. The primary form of monetary relief available was backpay. . . .

Section 102 significantly expands the monetary relief potentially available to plaintiffs who would have been entitled to backpay under prior law. Before 1991, for example, monetary relief for a discriminatorily discharged employee generally included "only an amount equal to the wages the employee would have earned from the date of discharge to the date of reinstatement, along with lost fringe benefits such as vacation pay and pension benefits." *United States v. Burke*, 504 U.S. 229, 239 (1992). Under § 102, however, a Title VII plaintiff who wins a backpay award may also seek compensatory damages for "future pecuniary losses, emotional pain, suffering, inconvenience, mental anguish, loss of enjoyment of life, and other nonpecuniary losses." § 102(b)(3). In addition, when it is shown that the employer acted "with malice or with reckless indifference to the [plaintiff's] federally protected rights," § 102(b)(1), a plaintiff may recover punitive damages.[6]

Section 102 also allows monetary relief for some forms of workplace discrimination that would not previously have justified *any* relief under Title VII. As this case illustrates, even if unlawful discrimination was proved, under prior law a Title VII plaintiff could not recover monetary relief unless the discrimination was also found to have some concrete effect on the plaintiff's employment status, such as a denied promotion, a differential in compensation, or termination. . . . Section 102, however,

[6] Section 102(b)(3) imposes limits, varying with the size of the employer, on the amount of compensatory and punitive damages that may be awarded to an individual plaintiff. Thus, the sum of such damages awarded a plaintiff may not exceed $50,000 for employers with between 14 and 100 employees; $100,000 for employers with between 101 and 200 employees; $200,000 for employers with between 200 and 500 employees; and $300,000 for employers with more than 500 employees.

allows a plaintiff to recover in circumstances in which there has been unlawful discrimination in the "terms, conditions, or privileges of employment," 42 U.S.C. § 2000e–2(a)(1), even though the discrimination did not involve a discharge or a loss of pay. In short, to further Title VII's "central statutory purposes of eradicating discrimination throughout the economy and making persons whole for injuries suffered through past discrimination," *Albemarle Paper Co. v. Moody*, 422 U.S. 405, 421 (1975), § 102 of the 1991 Act effects a major expansion in the relief available to victims of employment discrimination.

In 1990, a comprehensive civil rights bill passed both Houses of Congress. Although similar to the 1991 Act in many other respects, the 1990 bill differed in that it contained language expressly calling for application of many of its provisions, including the section providing for damages in cases of intentional employment discrimination, to cases arising before its (expected) enactment.[8] The President vetoed the 1990 legislation, however, citing the bill's "unfair retroactivity rules" as one reason for his disapproval.[9] Congress narrowly failed to override the veto.

---

[8] The relevant section of the Civil Rights Act of 1990, S. 2104, 101st Cong., 1st Sess. (1990), provided:

"SEC. 15. APPLICATION OF AMENDMENTS AND TRANSITION RULES.

"(a) APPLICATION OF AMENDMENTS.—The amendments made by—

"(1) section 4 shall apply to all proceedings pending on or commenced after June 5, 1989 [the date of *Wards Cove Packing Co.* v. *Atonio*, 490 U.S. 642];

"(2) section 5 shall apply to all proceedings pending on or commenced after May 1, 1989 [the date of *Price Waterhouse* v. *Hopkins*, 490 U.S. 228];

"(3) section 6 shall apply to all proceedings pending on or commenced after June 12, 1989 [the date of *Martin* v. *Wilks*, 490 U.S. 755];

"(4) sections 7(a)(1), 7(a)(3) and 7(a)(4), 7(b), 8 [providing for compensatory and punitive damages for intentional discrimination], 9, 10, and 11 shall apply to all proceedings pending on or commenced after the date of enactment of this Act;

"(5) section 7(a)(2) shall apply to all proceedings pending on or after June 12, 1989 [the date of *Lorance* v. *AT&T Technologies, Inc.*, 490 U.S. 900]; and

"(6) section 12 shall apply to all proceedings pending on or commenced after June 15, 1989 [the date of *Patterson* v. *McLean Credit Union*, 491 U.S. 164].

"(b) TRANSITION RULES.—

"(1) IN GENERAL.—Any orders entered by a court between the effective dates described in subsection (a) and the date of enactment of this Act that are inconsistent with the amendments made by sections 4, 5, 7(a)(2), or 12, shall be vacated if, not later than 1 year after such date of enactment, a request for such relief is made.

. . . . .

"(3) FINAL JUDGMENTS.—Pursuant to paragraphs (1) and (2), any final judgment entered prior to the date of the enactment of this Act as to which the rights of any of the parties thereto have become fixed and vested, where the time for seeking further judicial review of such judgment has otherwise expired pursuant to title 28 of the United States Code, the Federal Rules of Civil Procedure, and the Federal Rules of Appellate Procedure, shall be vacated in whole or in part if justice requires pursuant to rule 60(b)(6) of the Federal Rules of Civil Procedure or other appropriate authority, and consistent with the constitutional requirements of due process of law."

[9] See President's Message to the Senate Returning Without Approval the Civil Rights Act of 1990, 26 Weekly Comp. Pres. Doc. 1632–1634 (Oct. 22, 1990), reprinted in 136 Cong. Rec. S16418, S16419 (Oct. 22, 1990). The President's veto message referred to the bill's "retroactivity" only briefly . . . .

See 136 Cong. Rec. S16589 (Oct. 24, 1990) (66 to 34 Senate vote in favor of override).

The absence of comparable language in the 1991 Act cannot realistically be attributed to oversight or to unawareness of the retroactivity issue. Rather, it seems likely that one of the compromises that made it possible to enact the 1991 version was an agreement *not* to include the kind of explicit retroactivity command found in the 1990 bill.

The omission of the elaborate retroactivity provision of the 1990 bill—which was by no means the only source of political controversy over that legislation—is not dispositive because it does not tell us precisely where the compromise was struck in the 1991 Act. The Legislature might, for example, have settled in 1991 on a less expansive form of retroactivity that, unlike the 1990 bill, did not reach cases already finally decided. See n. 8, *supra*. A decision to reach only cases still pending might explain Congress' failure to provide in the 1991 Act, as it had in 1990, that certain sections would apply to proceedings pending on specific preenactment dates. Our first question, then, is whether the statutory text on which petitioner relies manifests an intent that the 1991 Act should be applied to cases that arose and went to trial before its enactment.

III

Petitioner's textual argument relies on three provisions of the 1991 Act: §§ 402(a), 402(b), and 109(c). Section 402(a), the only provision of the Act that speaks directly to the question before us, states:

> "Except as otherwise specifically provided, this Act and the amendments made by this Act shall take effect upon enactment."

That language does not, by itself, resolve the question before us. A statement that a statute will become effective on a certain date does not even arguably suggest that it has any application to conduct that occurred at an earlier date.[10] Petitioner does not argue otherwise. Rather,

---

[10] The history of prior amendments to Title VII suggests that the "effective-upon-enactment" formula would have been an especially inapt way to reach pending cases. When it amended Title VII in the Equal Employment Opportunity Act of 1972, Congress explicitly provided:

> "The amendments made by this Act to section 706 of the Civil Rights Act of 1964 shall be applicable with respect to charges pending with the Commission on the date of enactment of this Act and all charges filed thereafter." Pub. L. 92–261, § 14, 86 Stat. 113.

In contrast, in amending Title VII to bar discrimination on the basis of pregnancy in 1978, Congress provided:

> "Except as provided in subsection (b), the amendment made by this Act shall be effective on the date of enactment." § 2(a), 92 Stat. 2076.

The only Courts of Appeals to consider whether the 1978 amendments applied to pending cases concluded that they did not. See *Schwabenbauer v. Board of Ed. of School Dist. of Olean*, 667 F.2d 305, 310 n. 7 (CA2 1981); *Condit v. United Air Lines, Inc.*, 631 F.2d 1136, 1139–1140 (CA4 1980). See also *Jensen v. Gulf Oil Refining & Marketing Co.*, 623 F.2d 406, 410 (CA5 1980) (Age Discrimination in Employment Act amendments designated to "take effect on the date of enactment of this Act" inapplicable to case arising before enactment); *Sikora v. American Can Co.*, 622 F.2d 1116, 1119–1124 (CA3 1980) (same). If we assume that Congress was familiar

she contends that the introductory clause of § 402(a) would be superfluous unless it refers to §§ 402(b) and 109(c), which provide for prospective application in limited contexts.

The parties agree that § 402(b) was intended to exempt a single disparate impact lawsuit against the Wards Cove Packing Company. Section 402(b) provides:

> "(b) CERTAIN DISPARATE IMPACT CASES.—Notwithstanding any other provision of this Act, nothing in this Act shall apply to any disparate impact case for which a complaint was filed before March 1, 1975, and for which an initial decision was rendered after October 30, 1983."

Section 109(c), part of the section extending Title VII to overseas employers, states:

> "(c) APPLICATION OF AMENDMENTS.—The amendments made by this section shall not apply with respect to conduct occurring before the date of the enactment of this Act."

According to petitioner, these two subsections are the "other provisions" contemplated in the first clause of § 402(a), and together create a strong negative inference that all sections of the Act not specifically declared prospective apply to pending cases that arose before November 21, 1991.

Before addressing the particulars of petitioner's argument, we observe that she places extraordinary weight on two comparatively minor and narrow provisions in a long and complex statute. Applying the entire Act to cases arising from preenactment conduct would have important consequences, including the possibility that trials completed before its enactment would need to be retried and the possibility that employers would be liable for punitive damages for conduct antedating the Act's enactment. Purely prospective application, on the other hand, would prolong the life of a remedial scheme, and of judicial constructions of civil rights statutes, that Congress obviously found wanting. Given the high stakes of the retroactivity question, the broad coverage of the statute, and the prominent and specific retroactivity provisions in the 1990 bill, it would be surprising for Congress to have chosen to resolve that question through negative inferences drawn from two provisions of quite limited effect.

Petitioner, however, invokes the canon that a court should give effect to every provision of a statute and thus avoid redundancy among different provisions. Unless the word "otherwise" in § 402(a) refers to either § 402(b) or § 109(c), she contends, the first five words in § 402(a) are entirely superfluous. Moreover, relying on the canon "*[e]xpressio unius est exclusio alterius,*" petitioner argues that because Congress provided specifically for prospectivity in two places (§§ 109(c) and 402(b)),

with those decisions, cf. *Cannon v. University of Chicago*, 441 U.S. 677, 698–699 (1979), its choice of language in § 402(a) would imply nonretroactivity.

we should infer that it intended the opposite for the remainder of the statute.

Petitioner emphasizes that § 402(a) begins: "Except as otherwise specifically provided." A scan of the statute for other "specific provisions" concerning effective dates reveals that §§ 402(b) and 109(c) are the most likely candidates. Since those provisions decree prospectivity, and since § 402(a) tells us that the specific provisions are *exceptions*, § 402[(a)] should be considered as prescribing a general rule of retroactivity. Petitioner's argument has some force, but we find it most unlikely that Congress intended the introductory clause to carry the critically important meaning petitioner assigns it. Had Congress wished § 402(a) to have such a determinate meaning, it surely would have used language comparable to its reference to the predecessor Title VII damages provisions in the 1990 legislation: that the new provisions "shall apply to all proceedings pending on or commenced after the date of enactment of this Act." S. 2104, 101st Cong., 1st Sess. § 15(a)(4) (1990).

It is entirely possible that Congress inserted the "otherwise specifically provided" language not because it understood the "takes effect" clause to establish a rule of retroactivity to which only two "other specific provisions" would be exceptions, but instead to assure that any specific timing provisions in the Act would prevail over the general "take effect on enactment" command. The drafters of a complicated piece of legislation containing more than 50 separate sections may well have inserted the "except as otherwise provided" language merely to avoid the risk of an inadvertent conflict in the statute.[11] If the introductory clause of § 402(a) was intended to refer specifically to §§ 402(b), 109(c), or both, it is difficult to understand why the drafters chose the word "otherwise" rather than either or both of the appropriate section numbers.

We are also unpersuaded by petitioner's argument that both §§ 402(b) and 109(c) merely duplicate the "take effect upon enactment" command of § 402(a) unless all other provisions, including the damages provisions of § 102, apply to pending cases. That argument depends on the assumption that all those other provisions must be treated uniformly for purposes of their application to pending cases based on preenactment conduct. That thesis, however, is by no means an inevitable one. It is entirely possible—indeed, highly probable—that, because it was unable to resolve the retroactivity issue with the clarity of the 1990 legislation, Congress viewed the matter as an open issue to be resolved by the courts. Our precedents on retroactivity left doubts about what default rule would apply in the absence of congressional guidance, and suggested that some provisions might apply to cases arising before enactment while others

[11] There is some evidence that the drafters of the 1991 Act did not devote particular attention to the interplay of the Act's "effective date" provisions. Section 110, which directs the EEOC to establish a "Technical Assistance Training Institute" to assist employers in complying with antidiscrimination laws and regulations, contains a subsection providing that it "shall take effect on the date of the enactment of this Act." § 110(b). That provision and § 402(a) are unavoidably redundant.

might not.[12] Compare *Bowen v. Georgetown Univ. Hospital*, 488 U.S. 204 (1988), with *Bradley v. School Bd. of Richmond*, 416 U.S. 696 (1974).... The only matters Congress did *not* leave to the courts were set out with specificity in §§ 109(c) and 402(b). Congressional doubt concerning judicial retroactivity doctrine, coupled with the likelihood that the routine "take effect upon enactment" language would require courts to fall back upon that doctrine, provide a plausible explanation for both §§ 402(b) and 109(c) that makes neither provision redundant.

Turning to the text of § 402(b), it seems unlikely that the introductory phrase ("Notwithstanding any other provision of this Act") was meant to refer to the immediately preceding subsection. Since petitioner does not contend that any *other* provision speaks to the general effective date issue, the logic of her argument requires us to interpret that phrase to mean nothing more than "Notwithstanding § 402(a)." Petitioner's textual argument assumes that the drafters selected the indefinite word "otherwise" in § 402(a) to identify two specific subsections and the even more indefinite term "any other provision" in § 402(b) to refer to nothing more than § 402(b)'s next-door neighbor—§ 402(a). Here again, petitioner's statutory argument would require us to assume that Congress chose a surprisingly indirect route to convey an important and easily expressed message concerning the Act's effect on pending cases.

The relevant legislative history of the 1991 Act reinforces our conclusion that §§ 402(a), 109(c), and 402(b) cannot bear the weight petitioner places upon them. The 1991 bill as originally introduced in the House contained explicit retroactivity provisions similar to those found in the 1990 bill.[13] However, the Senate substitute that was agreed upon omitted those explicit retroactivity provisions.[14] The legislative history discloses some frankly partisan statements about the meaning of the final effective date language, but those statements cannot plausibly be read as reflecting any general agreement.[15] The history reveals no

[12] This point also diminishes the force of petitioner's "*expressio unius*" argument. Once one abandons the unsupported assumption that Congress expected that all of the Act's provisions would be treated alike, and takes account of uncertainty about the applicable default rule, §§ 109(c) and 402(b) do not carry the negative implication petitioner draws from them. We do not read either provision as doing anything more than definitively rejecting retroactivity with respect to the specific matters covered by its plain language.

[13] See, *e.g.*, H.R. 1, 102d Cong., 1st Sess. § 113 (1991), reprinted in 137 Cong. Rec. H3924–H3925 (Jan. 3, 1991). The prospectivity proviso to the section extending Title VII to overseas employers was first added to legislation that generally was to apply to pending cases. See H.R. 1, 102d Cong., 1st Sess. § 119(c) (1991), reprinted in 137 Cong. Rec. H3925–H3926 (June 5, 1991). Thus, at the time its language was introduced, the provision that became § 109(c) was surely not redundant.

[14] On the other hand, two proposals that would have provided explicitly for prospectivity also foundered. See 137 Cong. Rec. S3021, S3023 (Mar. 12, 1991); *id.* at 13255, 13265–13266.

[15] For example, in an "interpretive memorandum" introduced on behalf of seven Republican sponsors of S. 1745, the bill that became the 1991 Act, Senator Danforth stated that "[t]he bill provides that, unless otherwise specified, the provisions of this legislation shall take effect upon enactment *and shall not apply retroactively*." *Id.* at 29047 (emphasis added). Senator Kennedy responded that it "will be up to the courts to determine the extent to which the bill will apply to cases and claims that were pending on the date of enactment." *Ibid.* (citing *Bradley v. School Bd. of Richmond*, 416 U.S. 696 (1974)). The legislative history reveals other partisan

evidence that Members believed that an agreement had been tacitly struck on the controversial retroactivity issue, and little to suggest that *Congress* understood or intended the interplay of §§ 402(a), 402(b), and 109(c) to have the decisive effect petitioner assigns them. Instead, the history of the 1991 Act conveys the impression that legislators agreed to disagree about whether and to what extent the Act would apply to preenactment conduct.

Although the passage of the 1990 bill may indicate that a majority of the 1991 Congress also favored retroactive application, even the will of the majority does not become law unless it follows the path charted in Article I, § 7, cl. 2, of the Constitution. See *INS v. Chadha*, 462 U.S. 919, 946–951 (1983). In the absence of the kind of unambiguous directive found in § 15 of the 1990 bill, we must look elsewhere for guidance on whether § 102 applies to this case.

IV

It is not uncommon to find "apparent tension" between different canons of statutory construction. As Professor Llewellyn famously illustrated, many of the traditional canons have equal opposites. In order to resolve the question left open by the 1991 Act, federal courts have labored to reconcile two seemingly contradictory statements found in our decisions concerning the effect of intervening changes in the law. Each statement is framed as a generally applicable rule for interpreting statutes that do not specify their temporal reach. The first is the rule that "a court is to apply the law in effect at the time it renders its decision," *Bradley*, 416 U.S. at 711. The second is the axiom that "[r]etroactivity is not favored in the law," and its interpretive corollary that "congressional enactments and administrative rules will not be construed to have retroactive effect unless their language requires this result." *Bowen*, 488 U.S. at 208. . . .

A

. . . [T]he presumption against retroactive legislation is deeply rooted in our jurisprudence, and embodies a legal doctrine centuries older than our Republic. Elementary considerations of fairness dictate that individuals should have an opportunity to know what the law is and to conform their conduct accordingly; settled expectations should not be lightly disrupted. For that reason, the "principle that the legal effect of conduct should ordinarily be assessed under the law that existed when the conduct took place has timeless and universal appeal." [*Kaiser Aluminum & Chemical Corp. v. Bonjorno*, 494 U.S. 827, 855 (1990) (Scalia, J., concurring).] In a free, dynamic society, creativity in both

---

statements on the proper meaning of the Act's "effective date" provisions. Senator Danforth observed that such statements carry little weight as legislative history. As he put it: "[A] court would be well advised to take with a large grain of salt floor debate and statements placed in the Congressional Record which purport to create an interpretation for the legislation that is before us." 137 Cong. Rec. S15325 (Oct. 29, 1991).

commercial and artistic endeavors is fostered by a rule of law that gives people confidence about the legal consequences of their actions.

It is therefore not surprising that the antiretroactivity principle finds expression in several provisions of our Constitution. The *Ex Post Facto* Clause flatly prohibits retroactive application of penal legislation. Article I, § 10, cl. 1, prohibits States from passing another type of retroactive legislation, laws "impairing the Obligation of Contracts." The Fifth Amendment's Takings Clause prevents the Legislature (and other government actors) from depriving private persons of vested property rights except for a "public use" and upon payment of "just compensation." The prohibitions on "Bills of Attainder" in Art. I, §§ 9–10, prohibit legislatures from singling out disfavored persons and meting out summary punishment for past conduct. See, *e.g.*, *United States v. Brown*, 381 U.S. 437, 456–462 (1965). The Due Process Clause also protects the interests in fair notice and repose that may be compromised by retroactive legislation; a justification sufficient to validate a statute's prospective application under the Clause "may not suffice" to warrant its retroactive application. *Usery v. Turner Elkhorn Mining Co.*, 428 U.S. 1, 17 (1976).

These provisions demonstrate that retroactive statutes raise particular concerns. The Legislature's unmatched powers allow it to sweep away settled expectations suddenly and without individualized consideration. Its responsivity to political pressures poses a risk that it may be tempted to use retroactive legislation as a means of retribution against unpopular groups or individuals. As Justice Marshall observed in his opinion for the Court in *Weaver v. Graham*, 450 U.S. 24 (1981), the *Ex Post Facto* Clause not only ensures that individuals have "fair warning" about the effect of criminal statutes, but also "restricts governmental power by restraining arbitrary and potentially vindictive legislation." *Id.* at 28–29 (citations omitted).

The Constitution's restrictions, of course, are of limited scope. Absent a violation of one of those specific provisions, the potential unfairness of retroactive civil legislation is not a sufficient reason for a court to fail to give a statute its intended scope.[21] Retroactivity provisions often serve entirely benign and legitimate purposes, whether to respond to emergencies, to correct mistakes, to prevent circumvention of a new statute in the interval immediately preceding its passage, or simply to give comprehensive effect to a new law Congress considers salutary. However, a requirement that Congress first make its intention clear

[21] In some cases, however, the interest in avoiding the adjudication of constitutional questions will counsel against a retroactive application. For if a challenged statute is to be given retroactive effect, the regulatory interest that supports prospective application will not necessarily also sustain its application to past events. See *Pension Benefit Guaranty Corporation v. R. A. Gray & Co.*, 467 U.S. 717, 730 (1984); *Usery v. Turner Elkhorn Mining Co.*, 428 U.S. 1, 17 (1976). In this case the punitive damages provision may raise a question, but for present purposes we assume that Congress has ample power to provide for retroactive application of § 102.

helps ensure that Congress itself has determined that the benefits of retroactivity outweigh the potential for disruption or unfairness.

While statutory retroactivity has long been disfavored, deciding when a statute operates "retroactively" is not always a simple or mechanical task. Sitting on Circuit, Justice Story offered an influential definition in *Society for Propagation of the Gospel v. Wheeler*, 22 F. Cas. 756 (No. 13,156) (CCNH 1814), a case construing a provision of the New Hampshire Constitution that broadly prohibits "retrospective" laws both criminal and civil. Justice Story first rejected the notion that the provision bars only explicitly retroactive legislation, *i.e.*, "statutes . . . enacted to take effect from a time anterior to their passage." *Id.* at 767. Such a construction, he concluded, would be "utterly subversive of all the objects" of the prohibition. *Ibid.* Instead, the ban on retrospective legislation embraced "all statutes, which, though operating only from their passage, affect vested rights and past transactions." *Ibid.* "Upon principle," Justice Story elaborated,

> "every statute, which takes away or impairs vested rights acquired under existing laws, or creates a new obligation, imposes a new duty, or attaches a new disability, in respect to transactions or considerations already past, must be deemed retrospective . . . ." *Ibid.* (citing *Calder v. Bull*, 3 Dall. 386 (1798), and *Dash v. Van Kleeck*, 7 Johns. *477 (N.Y. 1811)).

Though the formulas have varied, similar functional conceptions of legislative "retroactivity" have found voice in this Court's decisions and elsewhere.

A statute does not operate "retrospectively" merely because it is applied in a case arising from conduct antedating the statute's enactment, see *Republic Nat. Bank of Miami v. United States*, 506 U.S. 80, 100 (1992) (Thomas, J., concurring in part and concurring in judgment), or upsets expectations based in prior law.[24] Rather, the court must ask whether the new provision attaches new legal consequences to events completed before its enactment. The conclusion that a particular rule operates "retroactively" comes at the end of a process of judgment concerning the nature and extent of the change in the law and the degree of connection between the operation of the new rule and a relevant past event. Any test of retroactivity will leave room for disagreement in hard cases, and is unlikely to classify the enormous variety of legal changes with perfect philosophical clarity. However, retroactivity is a matter on which judges tend to have "sound . . . instinct[s]," see *Danforth v. Groton Water Co.*, 178 Mass. 472, 476 (1901) (Holmes, J.), and familiar

[24] Even uncontroversially prospective statutes may unsettle expectations and impose burdens on past conduct: a new property tax or zoning regulation may upset the reasonable expectations that prompted those affected to acquire property; a new law banning gambling harms the person who had begun to construct a casino before the law's enactment or spent his life learning to count cards. . . . Moreover, a statute "is not made retroactive merely because it draws upon antecedent facts for its operation." *Cox v. Hart*, 260 U.S. 427, 435 (1922).

considerations of fair notice, reasonable reliance, and settled expectations offer sound guidance.

Since the early days of this Court, we have declined to give retroactive effect to statutes burdening private rights unless Congress had made clear its intent.... The presumption against statutory retroactivity has consistently been explained by reference to the unfairness of imposing new burdens on persons after the fact. Indeed, at common law a contrary rule applied to statutes that merely *removed* a burden on private rights by repealing a penal provision (whether criminal or civil); such repeals were understood to preclude punishment for acts antedating the repeal. See, *e.g.*, *United States v. Chambers*, 291 U.S. 217, 223–224 (1934); . . . *Yeaton v. United States*, 5 Cranch 281, 284 (1809). But see 1 U.S.C. § 109 (repealing common-law rule).

The largest category of cases in which we have applied the presumption against statutory retroactivity has involved new provisions affecting contractual or property rights, matters in which predictability and stability are of prime importance. The presumption has not, however, been limited to such cases. At issue in *Chew Heong v. United States*, 112 U.S. 536 (1884), for example, was a provision of the "Chinese Restriction Act" of 1882 barring Chinese laborers from reentering the United States without a certificate prepared when they exited this country. We held that the statute did not bar the reentry of a laborer who had left the United States before the certification requirement was promulgated. Justice Harlan's opinion for the Court observed that the law in effect before the 1882 enactment had accorded laborers a right to reenter without a certificate, and invoked the "uniformly" accepted rule against "giv[ing] to statutes a retrospective operation, whereby rights previously vested are injuriously affected, unless compelled to do so by language so clear and positive as to leave no room to doubt that such was the intention of the legislature." *Id.* at 559.

Our statement in *Bowen* that "congressional enactments and administrative rules will not be construed to have retroactive effect unless their language requires this result," 488 U.S. at 208, was in step with this long line of cases. *Bowen* itself was a paradigmatic case of retroactivity in which a federal agency sought to recoup, under cost limit regulations issued in 1984, funds that had been paid to hospitals for services rendered earlier, see *id.* at 207; our search for clear congressional intent authorizing retroactivity was consistent with the approach taken in decisions spanning two centuries.

The presumption against statutory retroactivity had special force in the era in which courts tended to view legislative interference with property and contract rights circumspectly. In this century, legislation has come to supply the dominant means of legal ordering, and circumspection has given way to greater deference to legislative judgments. See *Usery v. Turner Elkhorn Mining Co.*, 428 U.S. at 15–16; *Home Building & Loan Assn. v. Blaisdell*, 290 U.S. 398, 436–444 (1934).

But while the *constitutional* impediments to retroactive civil legislation are now modest, prospectivity remains the appropriate default rule. Because it accords with widely held intuitions about how statutes ordinarily operate, a presumption against retroactivity will generally coincide with legislative and public expectations. Requiring clear intent assures that Congress itself has affirmatively considered the potential unfairness of retroactive application and determined that it is an acceptable price to pay for the countervailing benefits. Such a requirement allocates to Congress responsibility for fundamental policy judgments concerning the proper temporal reach of statutes, and has the additional virtue of giving legislators a predictable background rule against which to legislate.

B

Although we have long embraced a presumption against statutory retroactivity, for just as long we have recognized that, in many situations, a court should "apply the law in effect at the time it renders its decision," *Bradley*, 416 U.S. at 711, even though that law was enacted after the events that gave rise to the suit. There is, of course, no conflict between that principle and a *presumption* against retroactivity when the statute in question is unambiguous. Chief Justice Marshall's opinion in *United States v. Schooner Peggy*, 1 Cranch 103 (1801), illustrates this point. Because a treaty signed on September 30, 1800, while the case was pending on appeal, unambiguously provided for the restoration of captured property "not yet *definitively* condemned," *id.* at 107 (emphasis in original), we reversed a decree entered on September 23, 1800, condemning a French vessel that had been seized in American waters. Our application of "the law in effect" at the time of our decision in *Schooner Peggy* was simply a response to the language of the statute. *Id.* at 109.

Even absent specific legislative authorization, application of new statutes passed after the events in suit is unquestionably proper in many situations. When the intervening statute authorizes or affects the propriety of prospective relief, application of the new provision is not retroactive. Thus, in *American Steel Foundries v. Tri-City Central Trades Council*, 257 U.S. 184 (1921), we held that § 20 of the Clayton Act, enacted while the case was pending on appeal, governed the propriety of injunctive relief against labor picketing. In remanding the suit for application of the intervening statute, we observed that "relief by injunction operates *in futuro*," and that the plaintiff had no "vested right" in the decree entered by the trial court. *Id.* at 201.

We have regularly applied intervening statutes conferring or ousting jurisdiction, whether or not jurisdiction lay when the underlying conduct occurred or when the suit was filed. Thus, in *Bruner v. United States*, 343 U.S. 112, 116–117 (1952), . . . we ordered an action dismissed because the jurisdictional statute under which it had been (properly) filed was subsequently repealed. Conversely, in *Andrus v. Charlestone Stone*

Products Co., 436 U.S. 604, 607–608, n. 6 (1978), we held that, because a statute passed while the case was pending on appeal had eliminated the amount-in-controversy requirement for federal-question cases, the fact that respondent had failed to allege $10,000 in controversy at the commencement of the action was "now of no moment." Application of a new jurisdictional rule usually "takes away no substantive right but simply changes the tribunal that is to hear the case." *Hallowell v. Commons*, 239 U.S. 506, 508 (1916). Present law normally governs in such situations because jurisdictional statutes "speak to the power of the court rather than to the rights or obligations of the parties," *Republic Nat. Bank of Miami*, 506 U.S. at 100 (Thomas, J., concurring).

Changes in procedural rules may often be applied in suits arising before their enactment without raising concerns about retroactivity. For example, in *Ex parte Collett*, 337 U.S. 55, 71 (1949), we held that 28 U.S.C. § 1404(a) governed the transfer of an action instituted prior to that statute's enactment. We noted the diminished reliance interests in matters of procedure. 337 U.S. at 71. Because rules of procedure regulate secondary rather than primary conduct, the fact that a new procedural rule was instituted after the conduct giving rise to the suit does not make application of the rule at trial retroactive.[29]

Petitioner relies principally upon *Bradley v. School Bd. of Richmond*, 416 U.S. 696 (1974), and *Thorpe v. Housing Authority of Durham*, 393 U.S. 268 (1969), in support of her argument that our ordinary interpretive rules support application of § 102 to her case. In *Thorpe*, we held that an agency circular requiring a local housing authority to give notice of reasons and opportunity to respond before evicting a tenant was applicable to an eviction proceeding commenced before the regulation issued. *Thorpe* shares much with both the "procedural" and "prospective-relief" cases. Thus, we noted in *Thorpe* that new hearing procedures did not affect either party's obligations under the lease agreement between the housing authority and the petitioner, 393 U.S. at 279, and, because the tenant had "not yet vacated," we saw no significance in the fact that the housing authority had "decided to evict her before the circular was issued," *id.* at 283. The Court in *Thorpe* viewed the new eviction procedures as "essential to remove a serious impediment to the successful

[29] Of course, the mere fact that a new rule is procedural does not mean that it applies to every pending case. A new rule concerning the filing of complaints would not govern an action in which the complaint had already been properly filed under the old regime, and the promulgation of a new rule of evidence would not require an appellate remand for a new trial. Our orders approving amendments to federal procedural rules reflect the commonsense notion that the applicability of such provisions ordinarily depends on the posture of the particular case. See, *e.g.*, Order Amending Federal Rules of Criminal Procedure, 495 U.S. 969 (1990) (amendments applicable to pending cases "insofar as just and practicable") . . . . Contrary to Justice Scalia's suggestion [in the concurring opinion that follows], . . . we do not restrict the presumption against statutory retroactivity to cases involving "vested rights." (Neither is Justice Story's definition of retroactivity, quoted *supra*, so restricted.) Nor do we suggest that concerns about retroactivity have no application to procedural rules.

protection of constitutional rights." *Ibid.*[30] Cf. *Youakim v. Miller*, 425 U.S. 231, 237 (1976) (*per curiam*) (citing *Thorpe* for propriety of applying new law to avoid[ ] necessity of deciding constitutionality of old one).

Our holding in *Bradley* is similarly compatible with the line of decisions disfavoring "retroactive" application of statutes. In *Bradley*, the District Court had awarded attorney's fees and costs, upon general equitable principles, to parents who had prevailed in an action seeking to desegregate the public schools of Richmond, Virginia. While the case was pending before the Court of Appeals, Congress enacted § 718 of the Education Amendments of 1972, which authorized federal courts to award the prevailing parties in school desegregation cases a reasonable attorney's fee. The Court of Appeals held that the new fee provision did not authorize the award of fees for services rendered before the effective date of the amendments. This Court reversed. We concluded that the private parties could rely on § 718 to support their claim for attorney's fees, resting our decision "on the principle that a court is to apply the law in effect at the time it renders its decision, unless doing so would result in manifest injustice or there is statutory direction or legislative history to the contrary." 416 U.S. at 711.

Although that language suggests a categorical presumption in favor of application of *all* new rules of law, we now make it clear that *Bradley* did not alter the well-settled presumption against application of the class of new statutes that would have genuinely "retroactive" effect. Like the new hearing requirement in *Thorpe*, the attorney's fee provision at issue in *Bradley* did not resemble the cases in which we have invoked the presumption against statutory retroactivity. Attorney's fee determinations, we have observed, are "collateral to the main cause of action" and "uniquely separable from the cause of action to be proved at trial." *White v. New Hampshire Dept. of Employment Security*, 455 U.S. 445, 451–452 (1982). Moreover, even before the enactment of § 718, federal courts had authority (which the District Court in *Bradley* had exercised) to award fees based upon equitable principles. As our opinion in *Bradley* made clear, it would be difficult to imagine a stronger equitable case for an attorney's fee award than a lawsuit in which the plaintiff parents would otherwise have to bear the costs of desegregating their children's public schools. See 416 U.S. at 718 (noting that the plaintiffs had brought the school board "into compliance with its constitutional mandate") (citing *Brown v. Board of Education*, 347 U.S. 483, 494 (1954)). In light of the prior availability of a fee award, and the likelihood that fees would be assessed under pre-existing theories, we concluded that the new fee statute simply "d[id] not impose an additional or unforeseeable obligation" upon the school board. *Bradley*, 416 U.S. at 721.

---

[30] *Thorpe* is consistent with the principle, analogous to that at work in the common-law presumption about repeals of criminal statutes, that the government should accord grace to private parties disadvantaged by an old rule when it adopts a new and more generous one. . . .

In approving application of the new fee provision, *Bradley* did not take issue with the long line of decisions applying the presumption against retroactivity. Our opinion distinguished, but did not criticize, prior cases that had applied the antiretroactivity canon. . . .

When a case implicates a federal statute enacted after the events in suit, the court's first task is to determine whether Congress has expressly prescribed the statute's proper reach. If Congress has done so, of course, there is no need to resort to judicial default rules. When, however, the statute contains no such express command, the court must determine whether the new statute would have retroactive effect [if applied to the case at hand], *i.e.*, whether it would impair rights a party possessed when he acted, increase a party's liability for past conduct, or impose new duties with respect to transactions already completed. If the statute would operate retroactively, our traditional presumption teaches that it does not govern absent clear congressional intent favoring such a result.

V

We now ask whether, given the absence of guiding instructions from Congress, § 102 of the Civil Rights Act of 1991 is the type of provision that should govern cases arising before its enactment. As we observed *supra*, . . . there is no special reason to think that all the diverse provisions of the Act must be treated uniformly for such purposes. To the contrary, we understand the instruction that the provisions are to "take effect upon enactment" to mean that courts should evaluate each provision of the Act in light of ordinary judicial principles concerning the application of new rules to pending cases and preenactment conduct.

Two provisions of § 102 may be readily classified according to these principles. The jury trial right set out in § 102(c)(1) is plainly a procedural change of the sort that would ordinarily govern in trials conducted after its effective date. If § 102 did no more than introduce a right to jury trial in Title VII cases, the provision would presumably apply to cases tried after November 21, 1991, regardless of when the underlying conduct occurred.[34] However, because § 102(c) makes a jury trial available only "[i]f a complaining party seeks compensatory or punitive damages," the jury trial option must stand or fall with the attached damages provisions.

Section 102(b)(1) is clearly on the other side of the line. That subsection authorizes punitive damages if the plaintiff shows that the defendant "engaged in a discriminatory practice or discriminatory practices with malice or with reckless indifference to the federally protected rights of an aggrieved individual." The very labels given "punitive" or "exemplary" damages, as well as the rationales that support them, demonstrate that they share key characteristics of criminal sanctions. Retroactive imposition of punitive damages would raise a

[34] As the Court of Appeals recognized, however, the promulgation of a new jury trial rule would ordinarily not warrant retrial of cases that had previously been tried to a judge. See n. 29, *supra*. Thus, customary practice would not support remand for a jury trial in this case.

serious constitutional question. See *Turner Elkhorn*, 428 U.S. at 17 (Court would "hesitate to approve the retrospective imposition of liability on any theory of deterrence . . . or blameworthiness"); *De Veau v. Braisted*, 363 U.S. 144, 160 (1960) ("The mark of an *ex post facto* law is the imposition of what can fairly be designated punishment for past acts"). . . . Before we entertained that question, we would have to be confronted with a statute that explicitly authorized punitive damages for preenactment conduct. The Civil Rights Act of 1991 contains no such explicit command.

The provision of § 102(a)(1) authorizing the recovery of compensatory damages is not easily classified. It does not make unlawful conduct that was lawful when it occurred; . . . § 102 only reaches discriminatory conduct already prohibited by Title VII. Concerns about a lack of fair notice are further muted by the fact that such discrimination was in many cases (although not this one) already subject to monetary liability in the form of backpay. Nor could anyone seriously contend that the compensatory damages provisions smack of a "retributive" or other suspect legislative purpose. Section 102 reflects Congress' desire to afford victims of discrimination more complete redress for violations of rules established more than a generation ago in the Civil Rights Act of 1964. At least with respect to its compensatory damages provisions, then, § 102 is not in a category in which objections to retroactive application on grounds of fairness have their greatest force.

Nonetheless, the new compensatory damages provision would operate "retrospectively" if it were applied to conduct occurring before November 21, 1991. Unlike certain other forms of relief, compensatory damages are quintessentially backward looking. Compensatory damages may be *intended* less to sanction wrongdoers than to make victims whole, but they do so by a mechanism that affects the liabilities of defendants. They do not "compensate" by distributing funds from the public coffers, but by requiring particular employers to pay for harms they caused. The introduction of a right to compensatory damages is also the type of legal change that would have an impact on private parties' planning. In this case, the event to which the new damages provision relates is the discriminatory conduct of respondents' agent John Williams; if applied here, that provision would attach an important new legal burden to that conduct. The new damages remedy in § 102, we conclude, is the kind of provision that does not apply to events antedating its enactment in the absence of clear congressional intent.

In cases like this one, in which prior law afforded no relief, § 102 can be seen as creating a new cause of action, and its impact on parties' rights is especially pronounced. Section 102 confers a new right to monetary relief on persons like petitioner who were victims of a hostile work environment but were not constructively discharged, and the novel prospect of damages liability for their employers. Because Title VII previously authorized recovery of backpay in some cases, and because compensatory damages under § 102(a) are in addition to any backpay recoverable, the new provision also resembles a statute increasing the amount of damages available under a preestablished cause of action. Even under that view, however, the provision would, if applied in cases arising before the Act's effective date, undoubtedly impose on employers found liable a "new disability" in respect to past events. See *Society for Propagation of the Gospel*, 22 F. Cas. at 767. The *extent* of a party's liability, in the civil context as well as the criminal, is an important legal consequence that cannot be ignored. Neither in *Bradley* itself, nor in any case before or since in which Congress had not clearly spoken, have we read a statute substantially increasing the monetary liability of a private party to apply to conduct occurring before the statute's enactment. See *Winfree v. Northern Pacific R. Co.*, 227 U.S. 296, 301 (1913) (statute creating new federal cause of action for wrongful death inapplicable to case arising before enactment in absence of "explicit words" or "clear implication") . . . .[37]

It will frequently be true, as petitioner and *amici* forcefully argue here, that retroactive application of a new statute would vindicate its purpose more fully. That consideration, however, is not sufficient to rebut the presumption against retroactivity. Statutes are seldom crafted to pursue a single goal, and compromises necessary to their enactment may require adopting means other than those that would most effectively pursue the main goal. A legislator who supported a prospective statute might reasonably oppose retroactive application of the same statute. Indeed, there is reason to believe that the omission of the 1990 version's express retroactivity provisions was a factor in the passage of the 1991 bill. Section 102 is plainly not the sort of provision that *must* be understood to operate retroactively because a contrary reading would render it ineffective.

The presumption against statutory retroactivity is founded upon sound considerations of general policy and practice, and accords with long held and widely shared expectations about the usual operation of legislation. We are satisfied that it applies to § 102. Because we have found no clear evidence of congressional intent that § 102 of the Civil Rights Act of 1991 should apply to cases arising before its enactment, we conclude that the judgment of the Court of Appeals must be affirmed.

---

[37] We have sometimes said that new "remedial" statutes, like new "procedural" ones, should presumptively apply to pending cases. See, *e.g.*, *Ex parte Collett*, 337 U.S. at 71, and n. 38 ("Clearly, § 1404(a) is a remedial provision applicable to pending actions"); *Beazell*, 269 U.S. at 171 (*Ex Post Facto* Clause does not limit "legislative control of remedies and modes of procedure which do not affect matters of substance"). While that statement holds true for some kinds of remedies, see *supra* (discussing prospective relief), we have not classified a statute introducing damages liability as the sort of "remedial" change that should presumptively apply in pending cases. "Retroactive modification" of damages remedies may "normally harbo[r] much less potential for mischief than retroactive changes in the principles of liability," *Hastings v. Earth Satellite Corp.*, 628 F.2d 85, 93 (CADC 1980), but that potential is nevertheless still significant.

■ *JUSTICE SCALIA, with whom JUSTICES KENNEDY and THOMAS join, concurring in the judgment:*

I

I of course agree with the Court that there exists a judicial presumption, of great antiquity, that a legislative enactment affecting substantive rights does not apply retroactively absent *clear statement* to the contrary. See generally *Kaiser Aluminum & Chemical Corp. v. Bonjorno*, 494 U.S. 827, 840 (1990) (Scalia, J., concurring). The Court, however, is willing to let that clear statement be supplied, not by the text of the law in question, but by individual legislators who participated in the enactment of the law, and even legislators in an earlier Congress which tried and failed to enact a similar law. For the Court not only combs the floor debate and Committee Reports of the statute at issue, the Civil Rights Act of 1991, but also reviews the procedural history of an earlier, unsuccessful, attempt by a *different* Congress to enact similar legislation, the Civil Rights Act of 1990.

This effectively converts the "clear statement" rule into a "discernible legislative intent" rule—and even that understates the difference. The Court's rejection of the floor statements of certain Senators because they are "frankly partisan" and "cannot plausibly be read as reflecting any general agreement," *ante* at 262, reads like any other exercise in the soft science of legislative historicizing, undisciplined by any distinctive "clear statement" requirement. If it is a "clear statement" we are seeking, surely it is not enough to insist that the statement can "plausibly be read as reflecting general agreement"; the statement must *clearly* reflect general agreement. No legislative history can do that, . . . but only the text of the statute itself. That has been the meaning of the "clear statement" retroactivity rule from the earliest times. . . . I do not deem that clear rule to be changed by the Court's dicta regarding legislative history in the present case.

. . . .

II

The Court's opinion begins with an evaluation of petitioner's argument that the text of the statute dictates its retroactive application. The Court's rejection of that argument cannot be as forceful as it ought, so long as it insists upon compromising the clarity of the ancient and constant assumption that legislation is prospective, by attributing a comparable pedigree to the nouveau *Bradley* presumption in favor of applying the law in effect at the time of decision. See *Bradley v. School Bd. of Richmond*, 416 U.S. 696, 711–716 (1974). As I have demonstrated elsewhere and need not repeat here, *Bradley* and *Thorpe v. Housing Authority of Durham*, 393 U.S. 268 (1969), simply misread our precedents and invented an utterly new and erroneous rule. See generally *Bonjorno*, 494 U.S. at 840 (Scalia, J., concurring).

Besides embellishing the pedigree of the *Bradley-Thorpe* presumption, the Court goes out of its way to reaffirm the holdings of those cases. I see nothing to be gained by overruling them, but neither do I think the indefensible should needlessly be defended. And *Thorpe*, at least, is really indefensible. The regulation at issue there required that "before *instituting an eviction proceeding* local housing authorities . . . should inform the tenant . . . of the reasons for the eviction . . . ." *Thorpe*, [393 U.S.] at 272, and n. 8 (emphasis added). The Court imposed that requirement on an eviction proceeding *instituted 18 months before the regulation issued*. That application was plainly retroactive and was wrong. The result in *Bradley* presents a closer question; application of an attorney's fees provision to ongoing litigation is arguably not retroactive. If it *were* retroactive, however, it would surely not be saved (as the Court suggests) by the existence of another theory under which attorney's fees might have been discretionarily awarded. . . .

III

My last, and most significant, disagreement with the Court's analysis of this case pertains to the meaning of retroactivity. The Court adopts as its own the definition crafted by Justice Story in a case involving a provision of the New Hampshire Constitution that prohibited "retrospective" laws: a law is retroactive only if it "takes away or impairs vested rights acquired under existing laws, or creates a new obligation, imposes a new duty, or attaches a new disability, in respect to transactions or considerations already past." *Society for Propagation of the Gospel* v. *Wheeler*, 22 F. Cas. 756, 767 (No. 13,1516) (CCNH 1814) (Story, J.).

One might expect from this "vested rights" focus that the Court would hold all changes in rules of procedure (as opposed to matters of substance) to apply retroactively. And one would draw the same conclusion from the Court's formulation of the test as being "whether the new provision attaches new legal consequences to events completed before its enactment"—a test borrowed directly from our *Ex Post Facto* Clause jurisprudence, see, *e.g.*, *Miller v. Florida*, 482 U.S. 423, 430 (1987), where we have adopted a substantive-procedural line, see *id.* at 433 ("[N]o *ex post facto* violation occurs if the change in the law is merely procedural"). In fact, however, the Court shrinks from faithfully applying the test that it has announced. It first seemingly defends the procedural-substantive distinction that a "vested rights" theory entails . . . . But it soon acknowledges a broad and ill-defined (indeed, utterly undefined) exception: "[T]he mere fact that a new rule is procedural does not mean that it applies to every pending case." *Ante* at 275, n. 29. Under this exception, "a new rule concerning the filing of complaints would not govern an action in which the complaint had already been properly filed," *ibid.*, and "the promulgation of a new jury trial rule would ordinarily not warrant retrial of cases that had previously been tried to a judge," *ante* at 281, n. 34. It is hard to see how either of these refusals to allow retroactive application preserves any "vested right." " 'No one has a vested right in any given mode of procedure.' " *Ex parte Collett*, 337 U.S. 55, 71 (1949), quoting *Crane v. Hahlo*, 258 U.S. 142, 147 (1922).

The seemingly random exceptions to the Court's "vested rights" (substance-*vs.*-procedure) criterion must be made, I suggest, because that criterion is fundamentally wrong. It may well be that the upsetting of "vested substantive rights" was the proper touchstone for interpretation of New Hampshire's constitutional prohibition, as it is for interpretation of the United States Constitution's *Ex Post Facto* Clauses . . . . But I doubt that it has anything to do with the more mundane question before us here: absent clear statement to the contrary, what is the presumed temporal application of a statute? For purposes of *that* question, a *procedural* change should no more be presumed to be retroactive than a *substantive* one. The critical issue, I think, is not whether the rule affects "vested rights," or governs substance or procedure, but rather what is the relevant activity that the rule regulates. Absent clear statement otherwise, only such relevant activity which occurs *after* the effective date of the statute is covered. Most statutes are meant to regulate primary conduct, and hence will not be applied in trials involving conduct that occurred before their effective date. But other statutes have a different purpose and therefore a different relevant retroactivity event. A new rule of evidence governing expert testimony, for example, is aimed at regulating the conduct of trial, and the event relevant to retroactivity of the rule is introduction of the testimony. Even though it is a procedural rule, it would unquestionably not be applied to *testimony already taken*—reversing a case on appeal, for example, because the new rule had not been applied at a trial which antedated the statute.

The inadequacy of the Court's "vested rights" approach becomes apparent when a change in one of the incidents of trial alters substantive entitlements. The opinion classifies attorney's fees provisions as procedural and permits "retroactive" application (in the sense of application to cases involving pre-enactment conduct). It seems to me, however, that holding a person liable for attorney's fees affects a "substantive right" no less than holding him liable for compensatory or punitive damages, which the Court treats as affecting a vested right. If attorney's fees can be awarded in a suit involving conduct that antedated the fee-authorizing statute, it is because the purpose of the fee award is not to affect that conduct, but to encourage suit for the vindication of certain rights—so that the retroactivity event is the filing of suit, whereafter encouragement is no longer needed. Or perhaps because the purpose of the fee award is to *facilitate* suit—so that the retroactivity event is the termination of suit, whereafter facilitation can no longer be achieved.

The "vested rights" test does not square with our consistent practice of giving immediate effect to statutes that alter a court's jurisdiction. . . . The Court explains this aspect of our retroactivity jurisprudence by noting that "a new jurisdictional rule" will often not involve retroactivity in Justice Story's sense because it " 'takes away no substantive right but simply changes the tribunal that is to hear the case.' " 511 U.S. at 274, quoting *Hallowell*, 239 U.S. at 508. That may be true sometimes, but surely not always. A jurisdictional rule can deny a litigant a forum for his claim entirely, see Portal-to-Portal Act of 1947, 61 Stat. 84, as amended, 29 U.S.C. §§ 251–262, or may leave him with an alternate forum that will deny relief for some collateral reason (*e.g.*, a statute of limitations bar). Our jurisdiction cases are explained, I think, by the fact that the purpose of provisions conferring or eliminating jurisdiction is to permit or forbid the exercise of judicial power—so that the relevant event for retroactivity purposes is the moment at which that power is sought to be exercised. Thus, applying a jurisdiction-eliminating statute to undo past judicial action would be applying it retroactively; but applying it to prevent any judicial action after the statute takes effect is applying it prospectively.

Finally, statutes eliminating previously available forms of prospective relief provide another challenge to the Court's approach. Courts traditionally withhold requested injunctions that are not authorized by then-current law, even if they were authorized at the time suit commenced and at the time the primary conduct sought to be enjoined was first engaged in. See, *e.g.*, *American Steel Foundries v. Tri-City Central Trades Council*, 257 U.S. 184 (1921); *Duplex Printing Press Co. v. Deering*, 254 U.S. 443, 464 (1921). The reason, which has nothing to do with whether it is possible to have a vested right to prospective relief, is that "[o]bviously, this form of relief operates only *in futuro*," *ibid.* Since the purpose of prospective relief is to affect the future rather than remedy the past, the relevant time for judging its retroactivity is the very moment at which it is ordered.[3]

I do not maintain that it will always be easy to determine, from the statute's purpose, the relevant event for assessing its retroactivity. As I have suggested, for example, a statutory provision for attorney's fees presents a difficult case. Ordinarily, however, the answer is clear . . . . [The provisions at issue in this case] are all directed at the regulation of primary conduct, and the occurrence of the primary conduct is the relevant event.

[3] A focus on the relevant retroactivity event also explains why the presumption against retroactivity is not violated by interpreting a statute to alter the future legal effect of past transactions—so-called secondary retroactivity, see *Bowen v. Georgetown Univ. Hospital*, 488 U.S. 204, 219–220 (1988) (Scalia, J., concurring) (citing McNulty, Corporations and the Intertemporal Conflict of Laws, 55 Calif. L. Rev. 12, 58–60 (1967)); cf. *Cox v. Hart*, 260 U.S. 427, 435 (1922). A new ban on gambling applies to existing casinos and casinos under construction, see 511 U.S. at 269–270, n. 24, even though it "attaches a new disability" to those past investments. The relevant retroactivity event is the primary activity of gambling, not the primary activity of constructing casinos.

■ *JUSTICE BLACKMUN, dissenting:*

. . . .

A straightforward textual analysis of the Act indicates that § 102's provision of compensatory damages and its attendant right to a jury trial apply to cases pending on appeal on the date of enactment. This analysis begins with § 402(a) of the Act: "Except as otherwise specifically provided, this Act and the amendments made by this Act shall take effect upon enactment." Under the "settled rule that a statute must, if possible, be construed in such fashion that every word has operative effect," *United States v. Nordic Village, Inc.*, 503 U.S. 30, 36 (1992), § 402(a)'s qualifying clause, "[e]xcept as otherwise specifically provided," cannot be dismissed as mere surplusage or an "insurance policy" against future judicial interpretation. Cf. *Gersman v. Group Health Assn., Inc.*, 975 F.2d 886, 890 (CADC 1992). Instead, it most logically refers to the Act's two sections "specifically provid[ing]" that the statute does not apply to cases pending on the date of enactment: (a) § 402(b), which provides, in effect, that the Act did not apply to the then-pending case of *Wards Cove Packing Co. v. Atonio*, 490 U.S. 642 (1989), and (b) § 109(c), which states that the Act's protections of overseas employment "shall not apply with respect to conduct occurring before the date of the enactment of this Act." Self-evidently, if the entire Act were inapplicable to pending cases, §§ 402(b) and 109(c) would be "entirely redundant." Thus, the clear implication is that, while §§ 402(b) and 109(c) do not apply to pending cases, other provisions—including § 102—do. . . .

Even if the language of the statute did not answer the retroactivity question, it would be appropriate under our precedents to apply § 102 to pending cases.[3] The well-established presumption against retroactive legislation, which serves to protect settled expectations, is grounded in a respect for vested rights. . . . This presumption need not be applied to remedial legislation, such as § 102, that does not proscribe any conduct that was previously legal. . . .

At no time within the last generation has an employer had a vested right to engage in or to permit sexual harassment . . . . Section 102 of the Act expands the remedies available for acts of intentional discrimination, but does not alter the scope of the employee's basic right to be free from discrimination or the employer's corresponding legal duty. There is nothing unjust about holding an employer responsible for injuries caused by conduct that has been illegal for almost 30 years. . . .

---

[3] Directly at issue in this case are compensatory damages and the right to a jury trial. While there is little unfairness in requiring an employer to compensate the victims of intentional acts of discrimination, or to have a jury determine those damages, the imposition of punitive damages for preenactment conduct represents a more difficult question, one not squarely addressed in this case and one on which I express no opinion.

NOTES AND QUESTIONS

1. Recall the distinction introduced on pp. 230–231 between tools for the resolution of linguistic indeterminacy (which help interpreters choose among the possible readings of words and phrases that have multiple meanings as a matter of conventional usage) and "implied-limitation rules" (which encourage interpreters to read certain unstated exceptions into seemingly unqualified statutory language). Which sort of interpretive principle was the majority applying in *Landgraf*? The specific provision that Ms. Landgraf was invoking, § 102 of the Civil Rights Act of 1991, enacted the following language: "In an action brought by a complaining party under section 706 or 717 of the Civil Rights Act of 1964 . . . against a respondent who engaged in unlawful intentional discrimination . . . prohibited under section 703, 704, or 717 of the Act. . . , the complaining party may recover compensatory and punitive damages . . . from the respondent." Civil Rights Act of 1991, Pub. L. 102–166, § 102, 105 Stat. 1071, 1072 (enacting Rev. Stat. § 1977A, which is codified at 42 U.S.C. § 1981a). The Court interpreted this provision to make compensatory damages available not in all actions that were pending when the statute was enacted, or even in all actions that were filed after that date, but only in actions about conduct that occurred after that date. That interpretation doesn't have any textual warrant, does it?

If you disagreed with the majority opinion in *NLRB v. Catholic Bishop of Chicago* (which read an unstated limitation into the National Labor Relations Act so as to avoid an application of the Act that would have raised a serious constitutional question), should you also disagree with the Court's opinion in *Landgraf*? Or is there some relevant difference between the appropriate trigger for the canon that favors avoiding constitutional doubts and the appropriate trigger for the presumption against retroactivity? Might one plausibly argue that the canon about avoiding constitutional doubts should apply only when there is linguistic indeterminacy in a statute, while the presumption against retroactivity should apply unless Congress has provided some clear indication that it really intended to alter the legal consequences of past conduct in a way that burdens private rights?

2. What is the purpose of the presumption against retroactivity? On the one hand, the presumption seems to reflect normative judgments about the unfairness of changing legal rules after the fact. On the other hand, the typical legislator might well share those normative judgments and usually intend to honor them; as the Court asserted in *Landgraf*, the presumption "accords with long held and widely shared expectations about the usual operation of legislation" and reflects "[e]lementary considerations of fairness" that are "deeply rooted in our jurisprudence." Is it fair to say that the presumption against retroactivity is partly a "descriptive" canon designed to minimize gaps between the legal directives that interpreters understand statutes to establish and the legal directives that members of the enacting legislature understood

themselves to be establishing (or, perhaps, the legal directives that members of the enacting legislature probably would have wanted to establish if they had considered questions about the directives' temporal reach), but that the presumption gets some extra force because of its normative aspirations?

3. The majority in *Landgraf* gave an interesting response to Ms. Landgraf's argument about the negative implications of § 109 of the Civil Rights Act of 1991. Recall that in *EEOC v. Arabian American Oil Co.*, 499 U.S. 244 (1991), the Supreme Court had interpreted the then-existing version of Title VII not to operate "extraterritorially." In response, § 109 of the Civil Rights Act of 1991 amended Title VII to protect American citizens working for American employers abroad. Still, § 109(c) specified that "the amendments made by this section shall not apply with respect to conduct occurring before the date of the enactment of this Act." According to Ms. Landgraf, the absence of similar language in other provisions of the Civil Rights Act of 1991 implied that Congress had collectively decided to make those other provisions reach pre-enactment conduct. But the Supreme Court thought it more likely that while Congress had been able to reach a collective decision that the amendments made by § 109 should not apply to pre-enactment conduct, Congress had not come to any other collective agreement about the statute's temporal effect (except for the agreement reflected in § 402(b), to the effect that nothing in the Civil Rights Act of 1991 should apply to the ongoing litigation in the *Wards Cove* case).

Note the competing assumptions of these two arguments. Ms. Landgraf's argument suggested that Congress had reached a consensus about the temporal effect of each provision in the Civil Rights Act of 1991, and that close parsing of Congress's words could reveal this consensus. Thus, Ms. Landgraf spoke as if there were only two options with respect to each provision: either Congress had authoritatively indicated that the provision *did* apply in cases about pre-enactment conduct or Congress had authoritatively indicated that the provision *did not* apply in such cases. Ms. Landgraf's *expressio unius* argument was a bid to put every provision other than § 109 in the former category. But the majority noted the possibility of a third category: perhaps Congress had not itself given any special instructions about the temporal effect of some of the provisions in the Civil Rights Act of 1991, with the result that courts should determine the temporal effect of those provisions according to the courts' normal doctrines. The majority proceeded to put every provision other than § 109 in that third category. In the majority's words, the Civil Rights Act of 1991 made the temporal reach of each of those provisions "an open issue to be resolved by the courts."

Can this sort of response *always* be used to weaken the force of *expressio unius* arguments? Or do some negative inferences stand on stronger ground than the one that Ms. Landgraf wanted the Court to draw?

4. To handle the questions that Congress allegedly had left for the courts, Justice Stevens's majority opinion in *Landgraf* articulated a powerful presumption against retroactivity. Basically, *Landgraf* held that provisions in federal statutes should not lightly be understood to have any "retroactive" applications (of the sort that the presumption against retroactivity disfavors). This presumption can be overcome by clear evidence of congressional intent, but otherwise courts will read statutes to come with implied limitations that prevent the statutes from operating retroactively.

The presumption against retroactivity does not automatically come into play just because a case involves events that occurred before a statutory provision was enacted. To the contrary, "[e]ven absent specific legislative authorization, application of new statutes passed after the events in suit is unquestionably proper in many situations." *Landgraf*, 511 U.S. at 273. That is because the concept of "retroactivity" is more complicated than you might think. Depending on the nature of the legal rule that a statutory provision establishes, applying the provision even in cases that were pending when the provision was enacted might not be "retroactive" in the relevant sense.

The majority opinion in *Landgraf* did not provide a crystal-clear definition of "retroactivity." Still, it established an important test. When courts are trying to decide whether applying a statutory provision in a particular case would give the provision "retroactive" effect, *Landgraf* instructs them to ask whether this application of the provision would "attach[ ] new legal consequences to events completed before [the provision's] enactment." *Id.* at 269–70.

If the answer to this question is "no," then this application of the provision would not be "retroactive" and the presumption against retroactivity does not come into play. The majority opinion in *Landgraf* offered several examples:

- Suppose that a federal statute gives courts new authority to grant injunctive relief preventing defendants from behaving in certain ways in the future. According to the majority opinion in *Landgraf*, the presumption against retroactivity normally will not prevent courts from applying this statute even in cases that were already pending when the statute was enacted, because doing so would not attach new legal consequences to events that have already occurred. Instead of being triggered by what defendants did in the past, the relief that the statute authorizes is triggered by the threat of what defendants will do in the future. *See id.* at 273 ("When the intervening statute authorizes or affects the propriety of prospective relief, application of the new provision is not retroactive.").
- Suppose that a federal statute amends the Federal Rules of Civil Procedure, which govern how federal district courts process cases. According to the majority opinion in *Landgraf*, it

normally would not be "retroactive" for courts to apply the new procedures in cases about events that occurred before the statute was enacted, because doing so would not attach new legal consequences to those events; instead of altering the parties' underlying rights and duties, the statute would simply be changing how the adjudicative process works.

- For the same reason, the majority opinion in *Landgraf* indicated that a statute reallocating jurisdiction among courts normally is not operating "retroactively" even if it eliminates a court's jurisdiction over cases that were pending when the statute was enacted. Perhaps that depends on whether the statute leaves some other court with jurisdiction over those cases. Normally, though, statutes changing which courts have jurisdiction over which cases do not attach new legal consequences to past events, and so their application to pending cases is not "retroactive" in *Landgraf*'s sense.

What if the answer to *Landgraf*'s question is "yes": applying a statutory provision in a particular case *would* attach new legal consequences to events completed before the provision's enactment? I am not sure whether Justice Stevens thought that *every* such application of a statutory provision would necessarily be "retroactive" in the sense that the presumption against retroactivity disfavors, or whether his position was a little less categorical. Justice Stevens did not crave bright lines as much as some of his colleagues did, and his majority opinion in *Landgraf* suggested that the test for retroactivity is not mechanical. In his words, "The conclusion that a particular rule operates 'retroactively' comes at the end of a process of judgment concerning the nature and extent of the change in the law and the degree of connection between the operation of the new rule and a relevant past event." *Id.* at 270. Thus, even if applying a statute in a particular case would attach new legal consequences to events that were completed before the statute's enactment, perhaps there are some new consequences that Justice Stevens would not have considered "retroactive."

More importantly, Justice Stevens did not define exactly what he meant by "attach[ing] new legal consequences to events completed before [a provision's] enactment." He drew a distinction between "attach[ing] new legal consequences" to past events (which was part of his test for retroactivity) and simply "upset[ting] expectations based in prior law" (which was not). *Id.* at 269–70. Rather than offering a precise explanation of that difference, though, Justice Stevens contented himself with examples. For instance, imagine that I buy land and start to build a casino, but the legislature then bans gambling. According to Justice Stevens, applying the statute to prevent all future gambling on my land would not be "retroactive"; while this application of the statute upsets the *expectations* that I formed based on the prior law, it does not attach any *new legal consequences* to pre-enactment events. *Id.* at 269 n.24.

This example seems intuitively correct, but it relies on unstated assumptions about the rights that I acquired when I bought the land. In the nineteenth century, lawyers would have expressed those assumptions in terms of "vested rights." Under then-existing understandings of constitutional law, statutes could not validly "divest" people of certain kinds of legal interests that had "vested" in them under pre-existing law. Even during the heyday of the Doctrine of Vested Rights, though, those interests would not have included my ability to operate a casino on my land. Even if gambling was legal when I bought the land, and even if I expected it to remain legal, nineteenth-century lawyers would have agreed that the legislature could change the law going forward; land-owners did not have a "vested right" to be free from all future regulation of the uses to which they put their land.

Modern lawyers no longer apply a robust Doctrine of Vested Rights as a matter of constitutional law. Instead, the presumption against retroactivity discussed in *Landgraf* is just a principle of statutory interpretation. Still, Justice Stevens's understanding of the trigger for that presumption—that is, his concept of "retroactivity"—arguably incorporated some notion of "vested rights." Without such a notion, indeed, it might not be possible to distinguish a statute that merely disrupts people's "expectations" (of the sort that do not raise concerns about retroactivity) from a statute that attaches new legal consequences to past events; in a sense, to call something a mere "expectation" is to say that it is not yet "vested." While Justice Stevens presumably would not have drawn the line between "vested rights" and mere "expectations" in exactly the same place as nineteenth-century lawyers, some such line might have been built into his test for retroactivity.

Relatedly, the majority opinion in *Landgraf* was also unclear about the scope of the presumption against retroactivity. Although some passages in the opinion spoke as if all retroactivity is disfavored, other passages referred to a presumption against "giv[ing] retroactive effect to statutes burdening private rights." *Id.* at 270.[49] The difference between those two formulations could affect the temporal effect of a statute that burdens only *public* rights (such as interests belonging to the government or to the public as a whole). If application of a statute would attach new legal consequences to pre-enactment events, but those consequences would operate only against the government itself, does the presumption against retroactivity come into play? *Compare id.* at 271 n.25 ("While the great majority of our decisions relying upon the antiretroactivity presumption have involved intervening statutes burdening private parties, we have applied the presumption in cases involving new monetary obligations that fell only on the government."), *with* Republic

---

[49] In this context, the phrase "private rights" would encompass interests belonging to any private individual or entity, including not only Ms. Landgraf but also the company that employed her. To the extent that Section 102 of the Civil Rights Act of 1991 imposed liability on private employers, it counted as a "statute[ ] burdening private rights," and the Court interpreted it not to have "retroactive" applications.

of Austria v. Altmann, 541 U.S. 677, 696 (2004) (Stevens, J.) ("In our view, . . . *Landgraf*'s antiretroactivity presumption, while not strictly confined to cases involving private rights, is most helpful in that context.").

5. Justice Scalia's concurring opinion in *Landgraf* agreed with the majority that there is and should be a presumption against retroactivity. But Justice Scalia disagreed with the majority about how to decide whether the application of a particular statute in a particular case would be "retroactive" in the sense that the presumption disfavors. Interestingly, Justice Scalia wanted to define "retroactivity" in much the same way that his majority opinion in *Morrison v. National Australia Bank* would later define "extraterritoriality." But while a majority of the Court has embraced Justice Scalia's approach to defining "extraterritoriality," a majority of the Court has *not* adopted Justice Scalia's proposed test for "retroactivity."

According to Justice Scalia, when a statute has established a new legal rule and a court is trying to decide whether applying the rule in a particular case would be "retroactive," the court should start by asking "what is the relevant activity that the rule regulates." (That is analogous to what *Morrison* later called the "focus" of the statute.) Once the court has identified the type of activity that the rule regulates, the court should then consider the facts of the case at hand: in this case, did that activity occur before the statute's effective date? If so, then applying the statutory rule in this case would be "retroactive," and Justice Scalia would not read the rule to apply in this case unless "the text of the statute itself" overcomes the presumption against retroactivity.[50] But if the activity that the statutory rule regulates occurred *after* the statute's effective date, then Justice Scalia's version of the presumption against retroactivity would not come into play.

6. Although Justice Scalia and the majority suggested somewhat different tests for identifying "retroactive" effects, their tests produced the same result in *Landgraf* itself. But the difference between the tests mattered in *Vartelas v. Holder*, 566 U.S. 257 (2012).

Panagis Vartelas was a Greek citizen who lived in the United States as a lawful permanent resident. In 1994, he pleaded guilty to the crime of conspiring to make or possess a counterfeit security, and he served four months in prison. Under the Supreme Court's interpretations of the federal immigration statutes as they stood in 1994, his conviction did not affect his ability to leave the United States, travel abroad for brief periods, and then re-enter the United States legally. *See* Rosenberg v. Fleuti, 374 U.S. 449, 462 (1963). But the Illegal Immigration Reform and

---

[50] That is another respect in which Justice Scalia's version of the presumption against retroactivity differed from the majority's version. According to Justice Scalia, indications of congressional intent gleaned from a bill's drafting history or from the relevant committee reports should not be sufficient to overcome the presumption against retroactivity. This position reflected Justice Scalia's more general aversion to the use of internal legislative history in statutory interpretation, a topic covered in Chapter 3 of this book.

Immigrant Responsibility Act of 1996 (IIRIRA) arguably changed federal immigration law on this topic. Under the new statutory scheme, a noncitizen who "has committed an offense identified in section 212(a)(2)" of the Immigration and Nationality Act (which arguably encompassed the offense of which Mr. Vartelas had been convicted) is regarded as seeking "admission" to the United States whenever he re-enters the country from abroad. *See* IIRIRA § 301, 110 Stat. 3009–546, 3009–575 (amending § 101(a)(13) of the Immigration and Nationality Act, 8 U.S.C. § 1101(a)(13)). That is a problem, because such convictions make noncitizens "ineligible to be admitted" (and subject to removal if they do re-enter the country). *See id.* § 308(d)(1)(B), 110 Stat. at 3009–617 (rewording § 212(a) of the Immigration and Nationality Act, 8 U.S.C. § 1182(a)).

Notwithstanding IIRIRA, Mr. Vartelas continued to make brief trips to Greece to visit his aging parents. Upon his return from one such trip in 2003, an American immigration officer identified him as a noncitizen seeking "admission," and the United States commenced proceedings to remove him from the country. Ultimately, however, the Supreme Court held that applying IIRIRA to Mr. Vartelas in this manner would be giving the statute "retroactive" effect.

Using the same test as the majority in *Landgraf*, the Court reasoned that the proposed application of IIRIRA "would . . . attach 'a new disability' " (to wit, ineligibility for re-entry after brief sojourns abroad) to conduct and events that had occurred before the provision's enactment (Mr. Vartelas's crime, guilty plea, and conviction). *See Vartelas*, 566 U.S. at 267 (quoting *Society for Propagation of Gospel v. Wheeler*, 22 F. Cas. 756, 767 (C.C.D.N.H. 1814) (No. 13,156)). Because "Congress did not expressly prescribe the temporal reach of the IIRIRA provision in question," the Court refused to give that provision any "retroactive" operation—which meant, for the Court, that "[t]he impact of Vartelas' brief travel abroad on his permanent resident status is . . . determined not by IIRIRA, but by the legal regime in force at the time of his conviction." *Id.* at 267, 261.[51]

Writing in dissent, though, Justice Scalia observed that it is possible to imagine many laws that limit people's future behavior based on past events. For instance, a statute might "prohibit[ ] those convicted of sex crimes from working in certain jobs that involve repeated contact with minors" or might "prohibit[ ] those previously committed for mental instability from purchasing guns." *Id.* at 281 (Scalia, J., dissenting).

---

[51] Although this passage refers to "the time of his conviction," other passages in the majority opinion referred to two other potentially relevant dates—"the time of Vartelas' plea," *id.* at 260, and the time of his criminal "conduct," *id.* at 267. The opinion was imprecise about which of these dates matters. In Mr. Vartelas's case, all three dates preceded IIRIRA's enactment, and so the ambiguity made no difference. But it is possible to imagine other noncitizens who were convicted after IIRIRA of offenses that they committed before IIRIRA. *See, e.g.*, Centurion v. Holder, 755 F.3d 115, 120–24 (2d Cir. 2014) (concluding that a different provision in IIRIRA does apply to such a noncitizen).

According to Justice Scalia, courts should not presume that such statutes apply only to people whose convictions or commitments postdate the statutes. For purposes of the presumption against retroactivity, he argued, a statute that regulates the future behavior of a category of people is not "retroactive" even if the category is defined by past events.

The majority agreed that the specific statutes cited by Justice Scalia could properly be applied to someone who had been convicted or committed before the statutes' enactment, and that this application of the statutes would not be "retroactive[ ]." To explain that conclusion, the majority observed that these statutes "address dangers that arise postenactment." *Id.* at 271 n.7. For instance, think about why the legislature might want to prohibit convicted child molesters from working in day-care centers. Rather than trying to impose additional punishment for past crimes, the legislature might simply be trying to regulate the qualifications of day-care workers so as to cut down on child abuse in the future. But how does that argument square with the majority's test for retroactivity? Regardless of the statute's purpose, if the statute is applied to people who were convicted before its enactment, is it not attaching a new disability to pre-enactment events?[52]

For Justice Scalia, the majority's struggles with this question suggested that the majority was using the wrong test for "retroactivity." Rather than simply asking whether a statute attaches new legal consequences to events completed before its enactment, Justice Scalia touted the alternative approach described in his separate opinion in *Landgraf*, which focused on "the activity a statute is intended to regulate." *See Vartelas*, 566 U.S. at 277 (Scalia, J., dissenting).

In his concurring opinion in *Landgraf*, Justice Scalia had suggested that courts should identify that activity in light of the "purpose" of the statute. *See Landgraf*, 511 U.S. at 291 (Scalia, J., concurring in the judgment); *see also id.* at 292 (discussing the fee-shifting statute in *Bradley v. School Board of Richmond*, 416 U.S. 696 (1974), and suggesting that the statute's temporal reach should depend on "the purpose of the fee award" that the statute authorized). In his dissenting opinion in *Vartelas*, however, Justice Scalia either clarified or adjusted that approach. He specifically disclaimed the idea that "the *reason* for a prohibition" bears on the proper application of the presumption against retroactivity. *Vartelas*, 566 U.S. at 279 (Scalia, J., dissenting). No matter what behavior a statute might be designed to affect in the real world, Justice Scalia suggested that the activity that the statute "regulates" is whatever activity the statute itself acts upon (identified by the statute's terms rather than its underlying purpose).

---

[52] In *Landgraf* itself, footnote 24 of the majority opinion asserted that "a statute 'is not made retroactive merely because it draws upon antecedent facts for its operation.' " *Landgraf*, 511 U.S. at 270 n.24 (quoting Cox v. Hart, 260 U.S. 427, 435 (1922)). Again, though, how does that statement square with the majority's test for "retroactivity"? What is the difference, if any, between a statute that simply "draws upon antecedent facts for its operation" and a statute that "attaches new legal consequences to events completed before its enactment"?

Thus, Justice Scalia thought that if a statute forbids or requires certain conduct, the proper "reference point" for determining whether application of the statute to a particular party would be retroactive is "the moment at which the party does what the statute forbids or fails to do what it requires." *Id.* at 277. According to Justice Scalia, "if a person engages in the primary regulated activity *after* the statute's effective date," then applying the statute to the party's conduct is not "retroactive" in the sense that the presumption against retroactivity discourages. *Id.* Applying this analysis to the question presented in *Vartelas*, Justice Scalia concluded that the relevant provision of IIRIRA regulated "reentry into the United States"—and because Mr. Vartelas's attempted reentry had occurred in 2003 (well after IIRIRA's effective date), Justice Scalia argued that applying the provision to Mr. Vartelas would not be "retroactive" in the sense that matters to the presumption against retroactivity. *Id.* at 277–78.

As Justice Scalia acknowledged, this approach defines "retroactivity" somewhat differently than courts do when applying the Ex Post Facto Clauses of the Constitution. *See id.* at 279. Imagine that a statute imposes new limitations on all people who have committed certain kinds of crimes; it bars them from certain types of employment, or it makes them ineligible for certain kinds of benefits. If the legislature enacted this statute for the purpose of ratcheting up the punishment for the crimes in question, then the statute might well be considered penal, and the Ex Post Facto Clause would prevent courts from applying the statute to people who committed their crimes before it was enacted. *See* Smith v. Doe, 538 U.S. 84, 92 (2003) (summarizing the doctrinal framework for deciding whether a statute "constitutes retroactive punishment forbidden by the *Ex Post Facto* Clause," and observing that "[i]f the intention of the legislature was to impose punishment, that ends the inquiry"). Even so, Justice Scalia apparently would not have classified such applications of the statute as "retroactive" in the sense relevant to the presumption against retroactivity. That seems odd: under Justice Scalia's analysis, a statute enacted for punitive reasons might be *ex post facto* in the sense that the Constitution forbids even though it is not "retroactive" in the sense that the presumption against retroactivity discourages. Is this a sign that Justice Scalia's test for retroactivity is too narrow?[53]

---

[53] Justice Blackmun's dissent in *Landgraf* invites the same criticism. In *Landgraf*, Justice Blackmun suggested that the presumption against retroactivity should apply only to statutory provisions that redefine someone's primary legal duties, and not to provisions that simply make new remedies available for existing duties. In the penal context, though, even if a statute does not change the definition of a crime (and hence does not alter anyone's primary legal duties), it is *ex post facto* if it "changes the punishment, and inflicts a greater punishment, than the law annexed to the crime, when committed." *Calder v. Bull*, 3 U.S. (3 Dall.) 386, 390 (1798). If this sort of retroactivity is unconstitutional in the penal context, is there any reason to exempt it from the presumption against retroactivity that courts apply when interpreting nonpenal statutes?

NOTE ON *RIVERS V. ROADWAY EXPRESS* AND *LINDH V. MURPHY*

As the majority observed in *Landgraf*, many provisions in the Civil Rights Act of 1991 were designed to override recent decisions of the Supreme Court. That was not true of the provision that the Court was interpreting in *Landgraf*, but it was true of the provision at issue in the companion case of *Rivers v. Roadway Express*, 511 U.S. 298 (1994). Even in *Rivers*, though, the Court applied the presumption against retroactivity.

The timeline relevant to *Rivers* is complicated. Ever since Reconstruction, section 1977 of the Revised Statutes of the United States has specified that "[a]ll persons within the jurisdiction of the United States shall have the same right in every State and Territory to make and enforce contracts . . . and to the full and equal benefit of all laws and proceedings for the security of persons and property as is enjoyed by white citizens . . . ." Rev. Stat. § 1977, 18 Stat. 348 (1874); *see also* Civil Rights Act of 1866, § 1, 14 Stat. 27, 27 (enacting the original version of this provision). Nowadays, lawyers typically refer to this provision as 42 U.S.C. § 1981, because that is where it appears in the United States Code.

In a series of cases that began with *Jones v. Alfred H. Mayer Co.*, 392 U.S. 409 (1968), and continued through *Runyon v. McCrary*, 427 U.S. 160 (1976), the Supreme Court read 42 U.S.C. § 1981 to prohibit private people from discriminating on the basis of race in contracting. Informed by this line of cases, a number of lower courts interpreted 42 U.S.C. § 1981 broadly to bar employers from firing employees on the basis of race, and hence to overlap substantially with the protections conferred by Title VII of the Civil Rights Act of 1964. In 1986, Roadway Express allegedly violated this proscription by firing Rivers. Rivers sued, asserting claims under both Title VII and 42 U.S.C. § 1981.

While this suit was pending in the district court, the Supreme Court interpreted 42 U.S.C. § 1981 more narrowly than many lower courts had. In *Patterson v. McLean Credit Union*, 491 U.S. 164 (1989), a bare majority of the Supreme Court held that 42 U.S.C. § 1981 "does not apply to conduct which occurs after the formation of a contract and which does not interfere with the right to enforce established contractual obligations." *Id.* at 171.

Meanwhile, Rivers's suit against Roadway Express was about to go to trial. On the strength of *Patterson*, the district court dismissed Rivers's claim under 42 U.S.C. § 1981. Under then-existing law, that dismissal eliminated Rivers's right to get a jury to decide the factual disputes that were common to his claims under 42 U.S.C. § 1981 and Title VII. The district court therefore held a bench trial on Rivers's Title VII claim. After making factual findings in favor of Roadway Express, the district court entered judgment for the defendant.

While the case was pending on appeal, though, Congress enacted the Civil Rights Act of 1991. In response to *Patterson*, § 101 of the Act amended section 1977 of the Revised Statutes (the provision codified at 42 U.S.C. § 1981) by adding a definition of the phrase "make and enforce contracts." Under the new definition, this phrase "includes the making, performance, modification, and termination of contracts, and the enjoyment of all benefits, privileges, terms, and conditions of the contractual relationship." *See* Civil Rights Act of 1991, Pub. L. 102–166, § 101, 105 Stat. 1071, 1071–72. When Rivers's case reached the Supreme Court, the Court had to decide whether this amendment applied to cases involving conduct that had occurred before the 1991 statute was enacted (such as Roadway Express's alleged discrimination against Rivers). Dividing in exactly the same way as in *Landgraf*, the Court held that the answer was "no": the new definition reached only conduct that occurred after Congress adopted it. According to the majority, using the 1991 amendment to determine Roadway Express's liability to Rivers would be "retroactive" in the *Landgraf* sense, and Congress had not clearly indicated that the amendment should operate in that way.

Rivers protested that the 1991 amendment was intended "to restore what [Congress] and virtually all the lower courts thought had been the reach of § 1981 before *Patterson*," and that the Court should therefore presume that the 1991 amendment operated wherever § 1981 did—with the result that the 1991 amendment reached pending as well as future cases. *See* Brief for Petitioners at 35–38, *Rivers*, 511 U.S. 298 (No. 92–938) (asserting that there is a "presumption in favor of application of restorative statutes"). But the Court rejected this argument. In the words of Justice Stevens's majority opinion, "A restorative purpose may be relevant to whether Congress specifically intended a new statute to govern past conduct, but we do not 'presume' an intent to act retroactively in such cases. We still require clear evidence of intent to impose the restorative statute 'retroactively.'" *Rivers*, 511 U.S. at 311. Such evidence was lacking with respect to the 1991 amendment. *Id.*; *cf.* United States ex rel. Int'l Bhd. of Elec. Workers v. Farfield Co., 5 F.4th 315, 329–35 (3d Cir. 2021) (finding enough evidence with respect to a different statute that overrode a different Supreme Court decision and that explicitly made the override applicable to claims pending on or after June 7, 2008—two days before the date of the decision).

As you evaluate *Rivers*, it may help to think about what the law really was at the time Roadway Express acted. One possibility is that the then-existing version of 42 U.S.C. § 1981 did indeed mean what the Supreme Court was about to say it meant in *Patterson*, and that the broader interpretation endorsed by some lower courts was wrong. If so, the 1991 Act did not simply "restore" what the Supreme Court should have understood the law to mean all along; instead, it established a new rule. In that case, one might well conclude that the presumption against retroactivity should apply to *Rivers* in the same way that it applied to *Landgraf*.

The other possibility is that *Patterson* was wrong about the meaning of the earlier version of 42 U.S.C. § 1981 and that the 1991 Act *did* simply restore what the Supreme Court should already have said was the law. Even if that were true, though, the doctrine of *stare decisis* probably would have caused the Supreme Court to adhere to *Patterson* in later cases if Congress had not enacted the 1991 Act. That is potentially relevant to the proper analysis of *Rivers*, because common arguments in favor of *stare decisis* in statutory cases are connected with concerns about retroactivity: advocates of *stare decisis* say that when the Supreme Court has settled on a particular interpretation of a statute, changes in that interpretation usually should not be made retroactive (as would happen if the Court changed its mind about what the law has always been), but instead should be purely prospective (as the legislature can accomplish by enacting a new statute). If the Supreme Court would have considered these concerns weighty enough to justify continued adherence to *Patterson* in the absence of the 1991 Act, are they not also weighty enough to justify a presumption that the 1991 Act overrides *Patterson* only prospectively (in the absence of contrary indications from Congress)?

One might respond that these questions adopt the wrong perspective: they proceed from on high rather than focusing on the likely intentions of the Congress that enacted the 1991 Act. Even if *Patterson* might have been correct about the meaning of 42 U.S.C. § 1981 as it stood before 1991, perhaps the fact that Congress enacted the 1991 Act indicates that the Congress of 1991 *thought* that the decision was wrong. When Congress thinks that a new statute is simply restoring the prior law, moreover, perhaps courts should presume that Congress ordinarily intends the statute to operate retroactively.

Still, those arguments are contestable. The fact that Congress responds to a judicial decision by codifying the losing side's position does not automatically mean that Congress disagrees with the court about the content of the prior law; members of Congress might simply decide that whatever the law meant before, they want the law going forward to reflect what the new statute says. And even if members of Congress do disapprove of the judicial decision to which they are responding, one cannot automatically infer that they want their response not simply to override the decision going forward, but also to govern conduct that predates their response. Isn't it possible that Congress values the same policy goals that the Supreme Court identifies with *stare decisis*, so that Congress typically intends statutes overriding judicial decisions to apply only prospectively?

Of course, the doctrine of *stare decisis* is premised at least in part on the reliance interests that judicial decisions can generate, and those reliance interests do not exist before the decisions have been rendered. Could one plausibly argue that when Congress acts to override a specific

Supreme Court decision, the new rule should normally be presumed to govern *both* conduct that occurs after the effective date of the new statute *and* conduct that occurred before the date of the judicial decision to which Congress is responding, but *not* conduct that occurred in between? Or is this presumption too intricate to be a plausible canon? Even if it is not too intricate, would it be too hard to apply in practice, given the difficulty of distinguishing between statutes that are designed only to restore prior understandings of the law and statutes that also tweak those understandings in some way? Would we also have to distinguish between situations in which the decision to which Congress is responding upset a genuine consensus about the pre-existing law and situations in which the decision simply adopted one of several competing positions that were all in play at the time?

If we proceed down a path that requires courts to make these fine-grained distinctions, are we sacrificing some of the potential benefits of canon-based decisionmaking? Might those benefits justify having a broad-gauged presumption against retroactivity even if (as cases like *Rivers* may suggest) it poses some risk of overinclusiveness?

* * * * *

A few years after deciding *Landgraf* and *Rivers*, the Court had to address the temporal reach of provisions in the Antiterrorism and Effective Death Penalty Act of 1996 (AEDPA), Pub. L. 104–132, 110 Stat. 1214. Among other things, that statute restricted the circumstances in which federal courts can grant writs of habeas corpus on behalf of prisoners who are in custody pursuant to the judgment of a state court. Before Congress enacted AEDPA, all habeas proceedings in federal courts had been governed by chapter 153 of title 28 of the United States Code. AEDPA amended chapter 153 in ways that were generally unfavorable to prisoners. AEDPA also added a new chapter 154 that targeted federal habeas petitions by state prisoners on death row, but that applied only as to states with satisfactory mechanisms for appointing lawyers for such prisoners in *state* proceedings for postconviction relief. (In essence, chapter 154 offered states a deal: if they established a qualifying mechanism for providing counsel to death-row inmates in state postconviction proceedings, then the state-friendly provisions in chapter 154 would apply when those inmates sought habeas from federal courts.) Section 107(c) of AEDPA specified that "Chapter 154 . . . shall apply to cases pending on or after the date of enactment of this Act." 110 Stat. at 1226.

In *Lindh v. Murphy*, 521 U.S. 320 (1997), the Supreme Court drew the negative inference that AEDPA's amendments to chapter *153* did *not* apply to cases that had been pending on the date of AEDPA's enactment. The majority suggested that § 107(c) reflected Congress's doubts about whether application of the new chapter 154 to pending cases would be "retroactive" in the *Landgraf* sense. The majority further suggested that this uncertainty on Congress's part was understandable: the new chapter

154 did not simply prescribe procedural rules for habeas cases, but also established new standards that would affect prisoners' "substantive entitlement to relief." *Lindh*, 521 U.S. at 327. To be sure, those new standards did not necessarily attach new legal consequences to the crimes for which prisoners were being held. The majority expressed no firm view about whether application of the new chapter 154 to pending cases would really trigger *Landgraf*'s presumption against retroactivity (or, if the application of certain provisions in chapter 154 to pending cases would indeed be "retroactive," whether § 107(c) was a clear enough statement to overcome that presumption). The majority's point was simply that Congress seemed to have been concerned about whether courts would apply anything in chapter 154 to pending cases in the absence of § 107(c). According to the majority, however, those same concerns would have applied equally to the amendments that AEDPA made to chapter 153. Because AEDPA did not specify that those latter amendments applied to pending cases, the Court inferred that Congress had wanted the amendments to chapter 153 to apply only to "cases . . . filed after the date of the Act." *Lindh*, 521 U.S. at 327; *see also id.* at 329 ("If . . . Congress was reasonably concerned to ensure that chapter 154 be applied to pending cases, it should have been just as concerned about chapter 153, unless it had the different intent that the latter chapter not be applied to the general run of pending cases. Nothing . . . but a different intent explains the different treatment.").

Chief Justice Rehnquist's dissent protested against this application of *expressio unius*. In his view, § 107(c) did not necessarily carry the negative implication that the majority claimed. Chief Justice Rehnquist advanced two possible reasons why Congress might have entertained more doubts about whether courts would apply the new chapter 154 in pending cases than about whether courts would apply the amendments to chapter 153 in pending cases:

> "First, because Chapter 154's applicability is conditioned upon antecedent events—namely, a State's establishing qualifying capital habeas representation procedures—Congress could have perceived a greater likelihood that, absent express provision otherwise, courts would fail to apply that chapter's provisions to pending capital cases. Second, because of the characteristically extended pendency of collateral attacks on capital convictions, and because of Congress' concern with the perceived acquiescence in capital defendants' dilatory tactics by some federal courts . . . , Congress could very well have desired to speak with exacting clarity as to the applicability of the AEDPA to pending capital cases."

Id. at 338 (Rehnquist, C.J., dissenting) (footnote omitted). Chief Justice Rehnquist also suggested that even if the Court was correct to draw some negative inference from § 107(c), the Court might be drawing the wrong one. While § 107(c) reflected a collective decision that the new chapter 154 should apply in pending cases, perhaps Congress had simply decided to leave questions about the temporal reach of the rest of AEDPA to the courts. *See id.* ("Congress could simply have assumed that the courts would sort out such questions, using our ordinary retroactivity presumptions.").[54]

Having dispatched the *expressio unius* argument to his satisfaction, Chief Justice Rehnquist proceeded to apply "our ordinary retroactivity principles." He argued that because AEDPA's commands "are addressed to courts rather than to individuals" and because the statute "prescribes or proscribes no private conduct," the application of those commands in pending cases would not be "retroactive" in the *Landgraf* sense. (The majority, as I have said, did not think that it had to take a position on that question.) Chief Justice Rehnquist concluded that in the absence of a stronger indication to the contrary than the majority's *expressio unius* argument provided, the statute's new provisions therefore should be applied to Lindh's case (which had been pending on appeal in the Seventh Circuit when Congress enacted AEDPA).

Where does the law stand after the combination of *Landgraf* and *Lindh*? Is the following summary of the majority's bottom line accurate?

- Courts should not apply provisions of federal statutes in cases where their application would be "retroactive" (in the sense described by the majority in *Landgraf*) unless Congress has provided sufficiently clear indications that Congress really did intend the provisions to apply in cases about pre-enactment conduct.
- Even if applying a particular provision in a particular case would *not* be "retroactive" in the *Landgraf* sense, the ordinary tools of statutory interpretation might still persuade courts that the provision applies only to cases filed after the statute's effective date or to cases involving post-enactment conduct.

F. CONFLICTS AMONG CANONS

To the extent that the canons purport to provide rules for interpreting statutes, interpreters need some way to handle conflicts between the canons. What should courts do when Canon #1 points in one direction and Canon #2 points in a different direction?

In one of the most famous law-review articles ever written, Professor Karl Llewellyn argued that such conflicts are ubiquitous: "there are two opposing canons on almost every point." Karl N. Llewellyn, *Remarks on the Theory of Appellate Decision and the Rules or Canons about How*

---

[54] This last idea reflects the point that the Landgraf majority made when Barbara Landgraf tried to invoke *expressio unius*. *See supra* p. 301. In *Landgraf*, however, the majority might simply have thought that the negative inference advocated by Ms. Landgraf was not powerful enough to warrant giving "retroactive" effect to § 102 of the Civil Rights Act of 1991. In *Lindh*, by contrast, accepting the *expressio unius* argument did not entail giving "retroactive" effect to AEDPA, and so the argument did not have to be so strong as to overcome the presumption against retroactivity.

Statutes Are to be Construed, 3 VAND. L. REV. 395, 401 (1950). As a result, Professor Llewellyn suggested, the canons have no real resolving power. To be sure, courts purport to rely upon them, and "[e]very lawyer must be familiar with them all" so as to invoke the right ones. But when a lawyer wants courts to purport to follow the canon that he is invoking rather than the contrary canon that his opponent will cite, he has to go outside the canons. *See id.* ("Plainly, to make any canon take hold in a particular instance, the construction contended for must be sold, essentially, by means other than the use of the canon . . . ."). In this sense, the canons amount to no more than a "diplomatic tongue"; they do not actually control the disposition of cases.

To support this view, Llewellyn presented a table pairing canons that could be used to cancel each other out. Some of Llewellyn's pairs do indeed illustrate his point. For instance, it has long been said that "remedial" statutes ought to be construed "liberally" (that is, more flexibly than usual) so as to help effectuate their remedial purposes.[55] But it has also been said that statutes in derogation of the common law should be construed "strictly," and this principle presumably would apply to "remedial" statutes imposing duties not recognized by the common law. Llewellyn properly noted the tension between these two canons. *See* Llewellyn, *supra*, 3 VAND. L. REV. at 401 (pair 2).

As various commentators have observed, though, most of Llewellyn's pairs are not so telling; they show only that certain canons are subject to exceptions, or that certain canons state rebuttable presumptions rather than absolute and unqualified commands. *See* Antonin Scalia, *Common-Law Courts in a Civil-Law System: The Role of United States Federal Courts in Interpreting the Constitution and Laws*, *in* A MATTER OF INTERPRETATION: FEDERAL COURTS AND THE LAW 3, 27 (Amy Gutmann ed., 1997); *see also* MICHAEL SINCLAIR, KARL LLEWELLYN'S DUELING CANONS IN PERSPECTIVE (2014) (analyzing each of Llewellyn's twenty-eight pairs and concluding that Llewellyn manufactured his conflicts); EINER ELHAUGE, STATUTORY DEFAULT RULES: HOW TO INTERPRET UNCLEAR LEGISLATION 188 (2008) (calling Llewellyn's critique "overstated").

Consider the following pairs of canons from Llewellyn's article. Do any of the "Parries" really contradict the "Thrusts"?

---

[55] This canon probably is less important than it once was. *See, e.g.*, Regions Bank v. Legal Outsource PA, 936 F.3d 1184, 1195–96 (11th Cir. 2019) (saying that "it is hard to imagine a more widely criticized 'canon' of interpretation" and citing various cases in which the Supreme Court has rejected arguments based on it); Contract Courier Servs., Inc. v. Research & Special Programs Admin., 924 F.2d 112, 115 (7th Cir. 1991) ("This is a useless maxim."). When litigants invoke the canon today, some judges respond either that statutes do not pursue their purposes at all costs or that the limits on remedial statutes serve purposes too. *See id.*; *see also* Bushendorf v. Freightliner Corp., 13 F.3d 1024, 1026 (7th Cir. 1993) ("Remedial statutes like other statutes are typically compromises . . . ."). For other judges, though, the canon retains force at least as a tie-breaker, and some judges may continue to give it more weight than that. *See, e.g.*, McAdory v. M.N.S. & Assocs., LLC, 952 F.3d 1089, 1092 (9th Cir. 2020) ("Because the statute is broadly remedial, we liberally construe the [Fair Debt Collection Practices Act] in favor of consumers.").

THRUST	PARRY
11. Titles [of statutes] do not control meaning	11. The title may be consulted as a guide when there is doubt or obscurity in the body . . . .
12. If [statutory] language is plain and unambiguous it must be given effect.	12. Not when literal interpretation would lead to absurd or mischievous consequences or thwart manifest purpose.
13. Words and phrases which have received judicial construction before enactment are to be understood according to that construction.	13. Not if the statute clearly requires them to have a different meaning.
14. After enactment, judicial decision upon interpretation of particular terms and phrases controls.	14. Practical construction by executive officers is strong evidence of true meaning.
15. Words are to be taken in their ordinary meaning unless they are technical terms or words of art.	15. Popular words may bear a technical meaning and technical words may have a popular signification[,] and they should be so construed as to agree with evident intention or to make the statute operative.
16. Every word and clause must be given effect.	16. If inadvertently inserted or if repugnant to the rest of the statute, they may be rejected as surplusage.
17. The same language used repeatedly in the same connection is presumed to bear the same meaning throughout the statute.	17. This presumption will be disregarded where it is necessary to assign different meanings to make the statute consistent.

Llewellyn, *supra*, 3 VAND. L. REV. at 403–04 (footnotes omitted).

Even if the canons do not come into conflict in *all* cases or even *most* cases, though, they do come into conflict in *some* cases. Consider, for instance, the longstanding principle that "an act of Congress ought never to be construed to violate the law of nations, if any other possible construction remains." *Murray v. Schooner Charming Betsy*, 6 U.S. (2 Cranch) 64, 118 (1804). If a statute lends itself to two possible interpretations, one of which would run afoul of this canon while the other would raise a substantial constitutional question, how should courts proceed? Does the *Charming Betsy* canon trump the canon that favors avoiding constitutional doubts (with the result that courts should construe the statute so as not to violate the law of nations, and proceed to answer the constitutional question that this construction of the statute raises)? Does the canon about avoiding constitutional doubts trump the *Charming Betsy* canon? Do the two canons simply negate each other, so that courts should resolve the case on the basis of other considerations?

As commentators have noted, existing doctrine often does not answer this sort of question. *See, e.g.*, ELHAUGE, *supra*, at 2 ("Not only do the legal materials fail to specify the order in which to apply most canons, they don't even provide generally accepted criteria for making case-by-case judgments about how best to prioritize the canons."). Instead of creating a detailed hierarchy that assigns each canon a unique rank or that establishes pair-wise rules about which canons trump which other canons in head-to-head conflicts, the Supreme Court prefers to negotiate such conflicts on a statute-by-statute basis. As a result, the fact that Canon #1 trumped Canon #2 when they came into conflict in one context does not prevent Canon #2 from trumping Canon #1 when they come into conflict in a different context. The Court has resisted opportunities to articulate more categorical rules. *See, e.g.*, Chickasaw Nation v. United States, 534 U.S. 84, 95 (2001) (refusing to establish any across-the-board priority between "the pro-Indian canon" and "the canon that warns us against interpreting federal statutes as providing tax exemptions unless those exemptions are clearly expressed," and explaining that past opinions on this subject "are too individualized, involving too many different kinds of legal circumstances, to warrant any such assessment about the two canons' relative strength").

My own view is that canons with good "descriptive" justifications—that is, canons that tend to guide interpreters toward the meaning that members of the enacting legislature probably intended (or, perhaps, the meaning that they probably would have intended if they had thought about the issue that the canon addresses)—should outrank purely "normative" canons. I would confine normative canons to something like a tie-breaking role, for use if indeterminacy remains after courts have applied their descriptive canons and their other accepted tools for identifying the meaning that members of the enacting legislature probably intended to communicate.[56]

That is how most judges currently use the rule of lenity, which is indeed a purely normative canon. In the Supreme Court's words, "The rule of lenity applies only if, 'after seizing everything from which aid can be derived,' . . . we can make 'no more than a guess as to what Congress

[56] To be clear, I do not classify a canon as "normative" simply because it reflects substantive values. If the legislature itself ordinarily respects those values, a canon based on them might well be a good guide to the intended meaning of statutes, and hence would be at least partly "descriptive." As we have seen, for instance, the Supreme Court has offered intent-based justifications for both the presumption against extraterritoriality and the presumption against retroactivity.

intended.' " *Reno v. Koray*, 515 U.S. 50, 65 (1995) (first quoting *Smith v. United States*, 508 U.S. 223, 239 (1993) (internal quotation marks and brackets omitted), then quoting *Ladner v. United States*, 358 U.S. 169, 178 (1958)).[57] That is also how some judges use other normative canons. *See, e.g.*, Kisor v. McDonough, 995 F.3d 1347, 1350 (Fed. Cir. 2021) (Prost, J., concurring in the denial of rehearing en banc) (discussing the pro-veteran canon). Still, it is often said that some normative canons deserve more weight than that. *See, e.g.*, Ernest A. Young, *Constitutional Avoidance, Resistance Norms, and the Preservation of Judicial Review*, 78 TEX. L. REV. 1549, 1603–14 (2000) (discussing the legitimacy of normative canons grounded in the Constitution); *cf.* Amy Coney Barrett, *Substantive Canons and Faithful Agency*, 90 B.U. L. REV. 109, 163–64 (2010) (tentatively concluding that "constitutional values" can justify what would otherwise be an inferior interpretation of a statute, but that "[c]anons promoting extraconstitutional values" should operate only as tie-breakers).

In any event, my claim that "descriptive" canons should outrank "normative" canons does not help resolve conflicts between two canons of the same sort (whether "descriptive" or "normative"). When two "descriptive" canons both bear on a question of statutory interpretation but point in different directions, courts presumably should try to decide which canon is more reliable under the circumstances. As the Supreme Court has suggested, one should not expect this question to have the same answer across all cases; the persuasiveness of any given canon varies according to context, and so a canon might be more powerful in some cases than in others.

Aside from questions about where one canon stands in relation to other canons, one might also wonder where the canons in general stand in relation to other interpretive techniques. As one might expect, judges have disagreed about that issue, and their positions often track their general attitude toward rule-based decisionmaking. *Cf.* Kathleen M. Sullivan, *The Supreme Court, 1991 Term—Foreword: The Justices of Rules and Standards*, 106 HARV. L. REV. 22 (1992) (noting that different members of the Supreme Court seem to have different tastes for "rule-ness").

---

[57] Although current doctrine does indeed treat the rule of lenity as a mere tie-breaker, people who support giving it more weight might be able to distinguish it from other normative canons. One of the normative goals that the rule of lenity is said to serve is the goal of giving people fair notice of the content of penal laws. That goal is itself fundamental to the project of statutory interpretation; as the very first section of this book suggested, principles of interpretation should be designed not only to help interpreters identify the intended meaning of statutes but also to enable people outside government to have fair notice of the content of the law, and those goals can trade off against each other to some extent. *See supra* pp. 1–5 (discussing the goals of statutory interpretation); *see also infra* pp. 347–348 (noting that concerns about notice help explain why most courts will not consider after-the-fact testimony by legislators about what they intended a statute to mean). In this respect, the notice-related goals served by the rule of lenity may differ from the goals served by some other purely normative canons.

Consider Justice Scalia. In a broad variety of contexts, he saw value in rule-based decisionmaking and mistrusted both the accuracy and the predictability of all-things-considered judgments. *See, e.g.*, Metro. Life Ins. Co. v. Glenn, 554 U.S. 105, 127 (2008) (Scalia, J., dissenting) ("Even if the choice were mine as a policy matter, I would not adopt the Court's totality-of-the-circumstances (so-called) 'test,' in which the existence of a conflict is to be put into the mix and given some (unspecified) 'weight.' This makes each case unique, and hence the outcome of each case unpredictable . . . ."); Lawrence v. Chater, 516 U.S. 163, 191 (1996) (Scalia, J., dissenting) (criticizing a totality-of-the-circumstances test as "a plastic criterion [that] is liable to produce inconsistent results in any series of decisions"); *see also* Antonin Scalia, *The Rule of Law as a Law of Rules*, 56 U. CHI. L. REV. 1175, 1187 (1989). Consistent with that attitude, canons played a prominent role in Justice Scalia's approach to statutory interpretation. *See* William N. Eskridge, Jr., *The New Textualism*, 37 UCLA L. REV. 621, 663 (1990) (noting that Scalia and other "new textualists" have led "a revival of canons that rest upon precepts of grammar and logic, proceduralism, and federalism").

By contrast, judges who see fewer benefits to rule-based decisionmaking tend to put less weight on the canons. *See, e.g.*, Koons Buick Pontiac GMC v. Nigh, 543 U.S. 50, 65–66 (2004) (Stevens, J., concurring) ("Common sense is often more reliable than rote repetition of canons of statutory construction."); Richard A. Posner, *Statutory Interpretation—in the Classroom and in the Courtroom*, 50 U. CHI. L. REV. 800, 805–17 (1983) (attacking the "unrealistic assumptions" and "mechanical" nature of the canons, and encouraging courts to make case-by-case decisions rather than applying "algorithms"). These judges do not ignore the canons entirely, but their opinions often give other considerations more prominence.

G. THE STRANGE CASE OF THE "LAST-ANTECEDENT RULE"

When sensible canons are used sensibly, they might help courts interpret statutes to mean what members of the enacting legislature collectively intended the statutes to convey. But the desirability of any given canon depends both on the content of the canon and on how courts use it. If a canon does not really reflect how legislatures normally use language, or if the canon is only a weak guide and courts give it more weight than it deserves, then use of the canon might be counterproductive.

This chapter closes with a canon that, in my view, modern courts often misuse—the "last-antecedent rule." Suppose that a statutory provision includes a phrase that modifies or limits one of the preceding words or word groups in the provision. If the provision contains several different words or word groups that this phrase could modify, the last-antecedent rule suggests that it goes with the nearest one—the "last antecedent" of the phrase. Likewise, if a statute identifies several people or things and then uses a pronoun that is ambiguous about which one it refers to, the last-antecedent rule encourages interpreters to assume that the pronoun refers to the nearest of the plausible referents. As a leading treatise states the rule, "Referential and qualifying words and phrases, where no contrary intention appears, refer solely to the last antecedent." 2A NORMAN J. SINGER & SHAMBIE SINGER, SUTHERLAND STATUTES AND STATUTORY CONSTRUCTION § 47:33 (7th ed. 2014) (footnotes omitted); *see also* Barnhart v. Thomas, 540 U.S. 20, 26 (2003) (referring to "the grammatical 'rule of the last antecedent,' according to which a limiting clause or phrase . . . should ordinarily be read as modifying only the noun or phrase that it immediately follows").

One scholar claims that Jabez Sutherland "invented" this rule in the late 1880s, when he was writing the original edition of the treatise quoted above. Terri LeClercq, *Doctrine of the Last Antecedent: The Mystifying Morass of Ambiguous Modifiers*, 2 J. LEG. WRITING INST. 81, 87 (1996). In fact, versions of the rule go back much farther than that. *See, e.g.*, WILLIAM NOY, A TREATISE OF THE PRINCIPALL GROUNDS AND MAXIMES OF THE LAWES OF THE KINGDOME 2 (London 1642) ("Ad proxium antecedens, fiat relatio nisi impediatur Sententia."); HENRY FINCH, LAW, OR A DISCOURSE THEREOF 8 (London 1678) ("Words in construction must be referred to the next antecedent, where the matter it self doth not hinder it."). In 1842, a state legislature even codified the principle as applied to the referential words "such" and "said." *See* N.H. Rev. Stat. tit. I, ch. 1, § 12 (1842) (setting forth rules for the construction of statutes, including the following: "The words 'said' and 'such' when used by way of reference to any person or thing, shall apply to the same person or thing last mentioned"); *see also* Sims' Lessee v. Irvine, 3 U.S. (3 Dall.) 425, 444 n.* (1799) (reporting the following observation by Chief Justice Ellsworth: "The rule is that 'such' applies to the last antecedent, unless the sense of the passage requires a different construction"), *cited in* Jeremy L. Ross, *A Rule of Last Resort: A History of the Doctrine of the Last Antecedent in the United States Supreme Court*, 39 SW. L. REV. 325, 327 (2009).

Still, common formulations of the last-antecedent rule may well be too broad, and courts have sometimes applied the rule without enough sensitivity to context. *See, e.g.*, LAWRENCE M. SOLAN, THE LANGUAGE OF JUDGES 29–38 (1993) (describing inconsistent usage of the rule in the California courts); *see also* LeClercq, *supra*, 2 J. LEG. WRITING INST. at 89 (arguing that, as formulated by Sutherland, the rule "contradicts other linguistic principles" and "has . . . created as much confusion and disagreement as the ambiguous modifier its drafter set out to clarify"). Indeed, the Colorado legislature has explicitly disclaimed a version of the last-antecedent rule as previously stated by the Colorado Supreme Court. *See* Colo. Rev. Stat. § 2–4–214 ("The general assembly hereby finds and declares that the rule of statutory construction expressed in the Colorado supreme court decision entitled *People v. McPherson*, 200 Colo. 429, 619

P.2d 38 (1980), which holds that '. . . relative and qualifying words and phrases, where no contrary intention appears, are construed to refer solely to the last antecedent with which they are closely connected . . .' has not been adopted by the general assembly and does not create any presumption of statutory intent."); Act of May 18, 1981, ch. 64, 1981 Colo. L. 347 (enacting this provision).

Part of the problem, in my view, is that courts have invoked the last-antecedent rule in two very different categories of situations. Sometimes, a qualifying phrase in a sentence must go *either* with one set of words *or* with a different set of words, but cannot grammatically be applied to *both*. In the absence of any other clues about intended meaning, the last-antecedent rule tells interpreters to assume that the qualifying phrase goes with the nearest of the possible antecedents. That makes sense. As applied to situations of this sort, the last-antecedent rule simply reflects ordinary principles of English syntax. In English, more than in some other languages, the placement of words matters; modifiers normally appear near the things that they modify.

Even in situations of this sort, of course, the last-antecedent rule is merely a presumption. As the modern Supreme Court has observed, "The rule of the last antecedent . . . 'is not an absolute and can assuredly be overcome by other indicia of meaning.' " *United States v. Hayes*, 555 U.S. 415, 425 (quoting *Barnhart*, 540 U.S. at 26).[58] But if a referential or qualifying phrase can go with only one antecedent, the nearest reasonable candidate is usually the best bet unless something about the context or apparent purpose of the provision suggests otherwise.

Unfortunately, courts have also applied the last-antecedent rule in a second category of situations. Sometimes, a qualifying phrase could be understood to go with more than one antecedent; it could modify *both* the nearest antecedent *and* one or more earlier antecedents. For instance, suppose that a document refers to "bananas, melons, and pears that are ripe." Should readers assume that the qualifying phrase "that are ripe" is part of the third item in the list and modifies only that item—so that the list encompasses all bananas, all melons, and ripe pears? Or should readers instead assume that the list consists of three items (bananas, melons, and pears) followed by a qualification that applies to them all—so that all three fruits are covered only if they are ripe? The general principle of English syntax that modifiers appear near what they modify does not help readers choose between these two possibilities. As a result,

[58] That is the basis of a joke in the old movie *Animal Crackers* (Paramount Pictures 1930). In the movie, a character played by Groucho Marx says: "One morning I shot an elephant in my pajamas. How he got in my pajamas, I don't know." When we hear the first sentence, we mentally override the last-antecedent rule; although the nearest antecedent of "in my pajamas" is "elephant," we know that elephants do not wear pajamas, so we assume that the phrase goes with "I" instead. The joke is that we should have applied the last-antecedent rule after all. *See* Payless Shoesource, Inc. v. Travelers Cos., Inc., 585 F.3d 1366, 1371–72 (10th Cir. 2009) (Gorsuch, J.) (citing this joke in the course of rejecting an argument based on the last-antecedent rule).

the last-antecedent rule is less justified in this type of situation than in the first type of situation.

In situations of this second sort, interpreters have to make decisions about what math teachers would call the order of operations. Specifically, interpreters must decide whether they should first group the nouns together ("bananas, melons, and pears") and then apply the qualifying phrase to them all, or whether they should first apply the qualifying phrase to the immediately preceding noun and then perform the grouping operation.

The best answer is likely to vary from context to context. Among other things, it may matter whether the nouns make a natural unit. The more they seem to go together as a matter of logic or common usage, the more we might gravitate toward grouping them first and then applying the qualifying phrase to each one. Conversely, the weaker the connection among the nouns, the less we might expect the same qualifying phrase to go with them all.

The apparent purpose of a provision is also obviously relevant. If someone told you that "in honor of St. Patrick's Day, you should look for notebooks, thermoses, and T-shirts that are green," you would interpret the qualifying phrase to go with all three items even though the items are otherwise disparate.

Punctuation matters too. If a sentence contains a list that ends in a qualifying phrase, and if the qualifying phrase is set off from the list by a comma, interpreters may well conclude that the qualifying phrase modifies the entire list and is not simply part of the final item. *See* Facebook, Inc. v. Duguid, 141 S. Ct. 1163, 1170 (2021) ("As several leading treatises explain, ' "[a] qualifying phrase separated from antecedents by a comma is evidence that the qualifier is supposed to apply to all the antecedents instead of only to the immediately preceding one." ' " (quoting WILLIAM N. ESKRIDGE, JR., INTERPRETING LAW: A PRIMER ON HOW TO READ STATUTES AND THE CONSTITUTION 67–68 (2016), in turn quoting SUTHERLAND STATUTES AND STATUTORY CONSTRUCTION, *supra*, § 47:33)).

To illustrate the importance of commas, the Second Circuit once drew the following contrast:

> "[T]he statement, 'This basketball team has a seven-foot center, a huge power forward, and two large guards, who do spectacular dunks,' differs from the statement, 'This basketball team has a seven-foot center, a huge power forward, and two large guards who do spectacular dunks.' The first statement conveys that all four players do spectacular dunks. The latter statement conveys that only the guards do so."

American Int'l Group, Inc. v. Bank of America Corp., 712 F.3d 775, 782 (2d Cir. 2013). I agree that in the first statement, the extra comma suggests that the phrase about dunks refers to all four players. Still, I am skeptical that the absence of the comma from the second statement establishes the opposite proposition. To my way of thinking, the second statement is simply ambiguous.[59]

Indeed, some authorities suggest that even without the comma, the second statement probably should be understood to mean exactly the same thing as the first statement. In their book *Reading Law*, Justice Scalia and Bryan Garner articulated what they called the "series-qualifier canon," which they stated as follows: "When there is a straightforward, parallel construction that involves all nouns and verbs in a series, a prepositive or postpositive modifier [i.e., a modifier that is positioned before or after what it modifies] normally applies to the entire series." ANTONIN SCALIA & BRYAN A. GARNER, READING LAW 147 (2012). Even before Scalia and Garner, an old opinion by Justice Brandeis had said much the same thing. *See* Porto Rico Railway, Light & Power Co. v. Mor, 253 U.S. 345 (1920) ("When several words are followed by a clause which is applicable as much to the first and other words as to the last, the natural construction of the language demands that the clause be read as applicable to all.").

These formulations, however, may assume their own conclusion. If a qualifying phrase is indeed positioned after a series, then it can readily be understood to modify each of the items in the series. But if the qualifying phrase is simply part of the last item in the series, then it modifies only that one item. The structure of the provision—that is, whether the qualifying phrase is positioned after the series or instead is part of the final item in the series—is precisely what interpreters are trying to ascertain.

According to Professor Adam Crews, moreover, courts have not historically approached this question with a presumption in favor of either answer. To the extent that they recognized a series-qualifier principle, that principle simply advised them that they *could* read a modifier to go with all of the items in a series. On Crews's account, the series-qualifier principle effectively turned off the last-antecedent rule as applied to a series that culminates in a qualifying phrase, but did not establish the opposite presumption. *See* Adam Crews, *The So-Called Series-Qualifier Canon*, 116 NW. U. L. REV. ONLINE 198, 212–21 (2021).

Even in the absence of a presumption, of course, the context or apparent purpose of a provision might help interpreters figure out whether a qualifying phrase is part of the last item in a series or instead modifies all of the items. But interpreters will not always have any real clues about what members of the enacting legislature intended

[59] The ambiguity is generated not just by the absence of a comma but also by the fact that the final item in the list refers to *two* large guards, so that the ensuing verb would be plural even if the subject is just the guards. If someone said, "This basketball team has a seven-foot center, a huge power forward, and a large guard who does spectacular dunks," we would know that the phrase "who does spectacular dunks" goes only with the guard. By contrast, if someone said, "This basketball team has a seven-foot center, a huge power forward, and a large guard who do spectacular dunks," we would know that all three players are good dunkers.

(assuming that they did indeed have a collective intent on this point). As a matter of English syntax, this structure sometimes is intractably ambiguous.

Some state legislatures' drafting manuals therefore tell the people who draft bills to avoid this structure, and to rewrite their sentences to make clear which modifiers go with which words. Consider the following provision, which several drafting manuals have used as an example: "a licensee may hunt moose, deer or ducks that are not on the endangered species list." As the manuals note, this formulation is ambiguous. If the drafter wants the qualification to go only with "ducks," the manuals encourage putting that item first: "a licensee may hunt ducks that are not on the endangered species list, moose or deer." By contrast, if the qualification is supposed to go with all three items, the manuals suggest something like this:

> "A licensee may hunt any of the following if the animal is not on the endangered species list:
>
> "1. Moose.
> "2. Deer.
> "3. Ducks."

ARIZONA LEGISLATIVE COUNCIL, THE ARIZONA LEGISLATIVE BILL DRAFTING MANUAL, 2021–2022, at 98; *see also* LeClercq, *supra*, 2 J. LEG. WRITING INST. at 101 n.44 (quoting WISCONSIN LEGISLATIVE REFERENCE BUREAU, WISCONSIN BILL DRAFTING MANUAL, 1989–1990, at 45).

Unfortunately, legislatures do not always take this advice. In the following case, the Supreme Court had to interpret a federal statute that contained a syntactical ambiguity. As you will see, Justice Sotomayor's majority opinion responded by invoking the last-antecedent rule, while Justice Kagan's dissent instead invoked the series-qualifier principle.

Lockhart v. United States

577 U.S. 347 (2016)

■ *JUSTICE SOTOMAYOR delivered the opinion of the Court:*

Defendants convicted of possessing child pornography in violation of 18 U.S.C. § 2252(a)(4) are subject to a 10-year mandatory minimum sentence and an increased maximum sentence if they have "a prior conviction . . . under the laws of any State relating to aggravated sexual abuse, sexual abuse, or abusive sexual conduct involving a minor or ward." § 2252(b)(2).

The question before us is whether the phrase "involving a minor or ward" modifies all items in the list of predicate crimes ("aggravated sexual abuse," "sexual abuse," and "abusive sexual conduct") or only the one item that immediately precedes it ("abusive sexual conduct"). . . .

I

In April 2000, Avondale Lockhart was convicted of sexual abuse in the first degree under N.Y. Penal Law Ann. § 130.65(1) (West Cum. Supp. 2015). The crime involved his then-53-year-old girlfriend.... Eleven years later, Lockhart was indicted in the Eastern District of New York for attempting to receive child pornography in violation of 18 U.S.C. § 2252(a)(2) and for possessing child pornography in violation of § 2252(a)(4)(b). Lockhart pleaded guilty to the possession offense and the Government dismissed the receipt offense.

Lockhart's presentence report ... concluded that Lockhart was subject to § 2252(b)(2)'s mandatory minimum because his prior New York abuse conviction related "to aggravated sexual abuse, sexual abuse, or abusive sexual conduct involving a minor or ward." ...

Lockhart objected, arguing that the statutory phrase "involving a minor or ward" applies to all three listed crimes: "aggravated sexual abuse," "sexual abuse," *and* "abusive sexual conduct." He therefore contended that his prior conviction for sexual abuse involving an *adult* fell outside the enhancement's ambit. The District Court rejected Lockhart's argument and applied the mandatory minimum. The Second Circuit affirmed his sentence....

II

Section 2252(b)(2) reads [as follows] ... :

> "Whoever violates, or attempts or conspires to violate [18 U.S.C. § 2252(a)(4)] shall be fined under this title or imprisoned not more than 10 years, or both, but ... if such person has a prior conviction under this chapter, chapter 71, chapter 109A, or chapter 117, or under section 920 of title 10 (article 120 of the Uniform Code of Military Justice), or under the laws of any State relating to aggravated sexual abuse, sexual abuse, or abusive sexual conduct involving a minor or ward, or the production, possession, receipt, mailing, sale, distribution, shipment, or transportation of child pornography, such person shall be fined under this title and imprisoned for not less than 10 years nor more than 20 years."

This case concerns that provision's list of state sexual-abuse offenses. The issue before us is whether the limiting phrase that appears at the end of that list—"involving a minor or ward"—applies to all three predicate crimes preceding it in the list or only the final predicate crime. We hold that "involving a minor or ward" modifies only "abusive sexual conduct," the antecedent immediately preceding it. Although § 2252(b)(2)'s list of state predicates is awkwardly phrased (to put it charitably), the provision's text and context together reveal a straightforward reading. A timeworn textual canon is confirmed by the structure and internal logic of the statutory scheme.

A

Consider the text. When this Court has interpreted statutes that include a list of terms or phrases followed by a limiting clause, we have typically applied an interpretive strategy called the "rule of the last antecedent." See *Barnhart v. Thomas*, 540 U.S. 20, 26 (2003). The rule provides that "a limiting clause or phrase . . . should ordinarily be read as modifying only the noun or phrase that it immediately follows." *Ibid.*; see also Black's Law Dictionary 1532–1533 (10th ed. 2014) ("[Q]ualifying words or phrases modify the words or phrases immediately preceding them and not words or phrases more remote, unless the extension is necessary from the context or the spirit of the entire writing"); A. Scalia & B. Garner, Reading Law: The Interpretation of Legal Texts 144 (2012).

This Court has applied the rule from our earliest decisions to our more recent. See, *e.g.*, *Sims Lessee v. Irvine*, 3 Dall. 425, 444, n. (1799); *FTC v. Mandel Brothers, Inc.*, 359 U.S. 385, 389, n. 4 (1959); *Barnhart*, 540 U.S. at 26. The rule reflects the basic intuition that when a modifier appears at the end of a list, it is easier to apply that modifier only to the item directly before it. That is particularly true where it takes more than a little mental energy to process the individual entries in the list, making it a heavy lift to carry the modifier across them all. For example, imagine you are the general manager of the Yankees and you are rounding out your 2016 roster. You tell your scouts to find a defensive catcher, a quick-footed shortstop, or a pitcher from last year's World Champion Kansas City Royals. It would be natural for your scouts to confine their search for a pitcher to last year's championship team, but to look more broadly for catchers and shortstops.

. . . .

Of course, as with any canon of statutory interpretation, the rule of the last antecedent "is not an absolute and can assuredly be overcome by other indicia of meaning." *Barnhart*, 540 U.S. at 26 . . . . For instance, take " 'the laws, the treaties, and the constitution of the United States.' " *Post* at 367, n. 2 (Kagan, J., dissenting). A reader intuitively applies "of the United States" to "the laws," "the treaties" and "the constitution" because (among other things) laws, treaties, and the constitution are often cited together, because readers are used to seeing "of the United States" modify each of them, and because the listed items are simple and parallel without unexpected internal modifiers or structure. Section 2252(b)(2), by contrast, does not contain items that readers are used to seeing listed together or a concluding modifier that readers are accustomed to applying to each of them. And the varied syntax of each item in the list makes it hard for the reader to carry the final modifying clause across all three.

More importantly, here the interpretation urged by the rule of the last antecedent is not overcome by other indicia of meaning. To the contrary, § 2252(b)(2)'s context fortifies the meaning that principle commands.

B

Our inquiry into § 2252(b)(2)'s context begins with the internal logic of that provision. Section 2252(b)(2) establishes sentencing minimums and maximums for three categories of offenders. The first third of the section imposes a 10-year maximum sentence on offenders with no prior convictions. The second third imposes a 10-year minimum and 20-year maximum on offenders who have previously violated a federal offense listed within various chapters of the Federal Criminal Code. And the last third imposes the same minimum and maximum on offenders who have previously committed state "sexual abuse, aggravated sexual abuse, or abusive sexual conduct involving a minor or ward" as well as a number of state crimes related to the possession and distribution of child pornography.

Among the chapters of the Federal Criminal Code that can trigger § 2252(b)(2)'s recidivist enhancement are crimes "under . . . chapter 109A." Chapter 109A criminalizes a range of sexual-abuse offenses involving adults *or* minors and wards.[1] And it places those federal sexual-abuse crimes under headings that use language nearly identical to the language § 2252(b)(2) uses to enumerate the three categories of state sexual-abuse predicates. The first section in Chapter 109A is titled "Aggravated sexual abuse." 18 U.S.C. § 2241. The second is titled "Sexual abuse." § 2242. And the third is titled "Sexual abuse of a minor or ward." § 2243. . . . [T]hose sections mirror precisely the order, precisely the divisions, and nearly precisely the words used to describe the three state sexual-abuse predicate crimes in § 2252(b)(2): "aggravated sexual abuse," "sexual abuse," and "abusive sexual conduct involving a minor or ward."

This similarity appears to be more than a coincidence. We cannot state with certainty that Congress used Chapter 109A as a template for the list of state predicates set out in § 2252(b)(2), but we cannot ignore the parallel, particularly because the headings in Chapter 109A were in place when Congress amended the statute to add § 2252(b)(2)'s state sexual-abuse predicates.

If Congress had intended to limit each of the state predicates to conduct "involving a minor or ward," we doubt it would have followed . . . so closely the structure and language of Chapter 109A.[3] The conclusion

---

[1] For example, § 2241(a) of Chapter 109A prohibits forced sexual acts against "another person"—not just a person under a certain age. Section 2241(c) specially criminalizes sexual acts "with another person who has not attained the age of 12 years," and § 2243(b) does the same for sexual acts with wards who are "in official detention" or "under the custodial, supervisory, or disciplinary authority of the person so engaging."

[3] The dissent points out that § 2252(b)(2) did not also borrow from the heading of the fourth section in Chapter 109A (or, we note, from the fifth, sixth, seventh, or eighth sections) in defining its categories of state sexual-abuse predicates. *Post* at 374–375 (Kagan, J. dissenting). But the significance of the similarity between the three state predicates in § 2252(b)(2) and the wording, structure, and order of the first three sections of Chapter 109A is not diminished by the fact that Congress stopped there (especially when the remaining sections largely set out derivations from, definitions of, and penalties for the first three). See, *e.g.*, § 2244 (listing offenses derived from §§ 2241, 2242, and 2243); § 2245 (creating an enhancement for offenses under Chapter 109A resulting in death); § 2246 (listing definitions).

that Congress followed the federal template is supported by the fact that Congress did nothing to indicate that offenders with prior federal sexual-abuse convictions are more culpable, harmful, or worthy of enhanced punishment than offenders with nearly identical state priors. We therefore see no reason to interpret § 2252(b)(2) so that "[s]exual abuse" that occurs in the Second Circuit courthouse triggers the sentence enhancement, but "sexual abuse" that occurs next door in the Manhattan municipal building does not.

III

A

Lockhart argues, to the contrary, that the phrase "involving a minor or ward" should be interpreted to modify all three state sexual-abuse predicates. He first contends, as does our dissenting colleague, that the so-called series-qualifier principle supports his reading. This principle, Lockhart says, requires a modifier to apply to all items in a series when such an application would represent a natural construction. . . .

This Court has long acknowledged that structural or contextual evidence may "rebut the last antecedent inference." *Jama v. Immigration and Customs Enforcement*, 543 U.S. 335, 344, n. 4. For instance, in *Porto Rico Railway, Light & Power Co. v. Mor*, 253 U.S. 345 (1920), on which Lockhart relies, this Court declined to apply the rule of the last antecedent where "[n]o reason appears why" a modifying clause is not "applicable as much to the first and other words as to the last" and where "special reasons exist for so construing the clause in question." *Id.* at 348. In *United States v. Bass*, 404 U.S. 336 (1971), this Court declined to apply the rule of the last antecedent where "there is no reason consistent with any discernable purpose of the statute to apply" the limiting phrase to the last antecedent alone. *Id.* at 341. Likewise, in *Jama*, the Court suggested that the rule would not be appropriate where the "modifying clause appear[s] . . . at the end of a single, integrated list." 543 U.S. at 344, n. 4. And, most recently, in *Paroline v. United States*, 572 U.S. 434 (2014), the Court noted that the rule need not be applied "in a mechanical way where it would require accepting 'unlikely premises.' " *Id.* at 447.

But in none of those cases did the Court describe, much less apply, a countervailing grammatical mandate that could bear the weight that either Lockhart or the dissent places on the series qualifier principle. Instead, the Court simply observed that sometimes context weighs against the application of the rule of the last antecedent. . . . Whether a modifier is "applicable as much to the first . . . as to the last" words in a list, whether a set of items form a "single, integrated list," and whether the application of the rule would require acceptance of an "unlikely premise" are fundamentally contextual questions.

Lockhart attempts to identify contextual indicia that he says rebut the rule of the last antecedent, but those indicia hurt rather than help his prospects. He points out that the final two state predicates, "sexual abuse" and "abusive sexual conduct," are "nearly synonymous as a matter of everyday speech." Brief for Petitioner 17. And, of course, anyone who commits "aggravated sexual abuse" has also necessarily committed "sexual abuse." So, he posits, the items in the list are sufficiently similar that a limiting phrase could apply equally to all three of them.

But Lockhart's effort to demonstrate some similarity among the items in the list of state predicates reveals far too much similarity. The three state predicate crimes are not just related on Lockhart's reading; they are hopelessly redundant. Any conduct that would qualify as "aggravated sexual abuse . . . involving a minor or ward" or "sexual abuse . . . involving a minor or ward" would also qualify as "abusive sexual conduct involving a minor or ward." . . .

Applying the limiting phrase "involving a minor or ward" more sparingly, by contrast, preserves some distinction between the categories of state predicates . . . . We recognize that this interpretation does not eliminate all superfluity . . . . But there is a ready explanation for the redundancy that remains: It follows the categories in Chapter 109A's federal template. . . . We see no similar explanation for Lockhart's complete collapse of the list.

The dissent offers a suggestion rooted in its impressions about how people ordinarily speak and write. *Post* at 362–365. The problem is that, as even the dissent acknowledges, § 2252(b)(2)'s list of state predicates is hardly intuitive. No one would mistake its odd repetition and inelegant phrasing for a reflection of the accumulated wisdom of everyday speech patterns. . . .

Faced with § 2252(b)(2)'s inartful drafting, then, do we interpret the provision by viewing it as a clear, commonsense list best construed as if conversational English? Or do we look around to see if there might be some provenance to its peculiarity? With Chapter 109A so readily at hand, we are unpersuaded by our dissenting colleague's invocation of basic examples from day-to-day life. Whatever the validity of the dissent's broader point, this simply is not a case in which colloquial practice is of much use. Section 2252(b)(2)'s list is hardly the way an average person, or even an average lawyer, would set about to describe the relevant conduct if they had started from scratch.

. . . .

C

Lockhart, joined by the dissent, . . . says that the provision's legislative history supports the view that Congress deliberately structured § 2252(b)(2) to treat state and federal predicates differently. They rely on two sources. The first is a reference in a Report from the Senate Judiciary Committee on the Child Pornography Prevention Act of 1996, 110 Stat. 3009–26. That Act was the first to add the language at issue here—"aggravated sexual abuse, sexual abuse, or abusive sexual conduct involving a minor or ward"—to the U.S. Code. (It was initially added to § 2252(b)(1), then added two years later to § 2252(b)(2).)

The Report noted that the enhancement applies to persons with prior convictions "under any State child abuse law or law relating to the production, receipt or distribution of child pornography." See S. Rep. No. 104–358, p. 9 (1996). But that reference incompletely describes the state pornography production and distribution predicates, which cover not only "production, receipt, or distributing of child pornography," as the Report indicates, but also "production, possession, receipt, mailing, sale, distribution, shipment, or transportation of child pornography," § 2252(b)(2). For the reasons discussed, we have no trouble concluding that the Report also incompletely describes the state sexual-abuse predicates.

Lockhart and the dissent also rely on a letter sent from the Department of Justice (DOJ) to the House of Representative's Committee on the Judiciary commenting on the proposed "Child Protection and Sexual Predator Punishment Act of 1998." H.R. Rep. No. 105–557, pp. 26–34 (1998). In the letter, DOJ provides commentary on the then-present state of §§ 2252(b)(1) and 2252(b)(2), noting that although there is a "5-year mandatory minimum sentence for individuals charged with receipt or distribution of child pornography and who have prior state convictions for child molestation" pursuant to § 2252(b)(1), there is "no enhanced provision for those individuals charged with possession of child pornography who have prior convictions for child abuse" pursuant to § 2252(b)(2). *Id.* at 31. That letter, they say, demonstrates that DOJ understood the language at issue here to impose a sentencing enhancement only for prior state convictions involving children.

We doubt that DOJ was trying to describe the full reach of the language in § 2252(b)(1), as the dissent suggests. To the contrary, there are several clues that the letter was relying on just one of the provision's many salient features. For instance, the letter's references to "child molestation" and "child abuse" do not encompass a large number of state crimes that are unambiguously covered by "abusive sexual conduct involving a minor or ward"—namely, crimes involving "wards." Wards can be minors, but they can also be adults. See, *e.g.*, § 2243(b) (defining "wards" as persons who are "in official detention" and "under . . . custodial, supervisory, or disciplinary authority"). Moreover, we doubt that DOJ intended to express a belief that the potentially broad scope of serious crimes encompassed by "aggravated sexual abuse, sexual abuse, and abusive sexual conduct" reaches no further than state crimes that would traditionally be characterized as "child molestation" or "child abuse."

. . . . Just as importantly, the terse descriptions of the provision in the Senate Report and DOJ letter do nothing to explain *why* Congress would have wanted to apply the mandatory minimum to individuals convicted in federal court of sexual abuse or aggravated sexual abuse involving an adult, but not to individuals convicted in state court of the same. . . .

The best explanation Lockhart can muster is a basic administrability concern: Congress "knew what conduct it was capturing under federal law and could be confident that all covered federal offenses were proper predicates. But Congress did not have the same familiarity with the varied and mutable sexual-abuse laws of all fifty states." Brief for Petitioner 27. Perhaps Congress worried that state laws punishing relatively minor offenses like public lewdness or indecent exposure involving an adult would be swept into § 2252(b)(2). *Id.* at 28. But the risk Lockhart identifies is minimal. Whether the terms in § 2252(b)(2) are given their "generic" meaning . . . or are defined in light of their federal counterparts—which we do not decide—they are unlikely to sweep in the bizarre or unexpected state offenses that worry Lockhart.

D

Finally, Lockhart asks us to apply the rule of lenity. We have used the lenity principle to resolve ambiguity in favor of the defendant only "at the end of the process of construing what Congress has expressed" when the ordinary canons of statutory construction have revealed no satisfactory construction. *Callanan v. United States,* 364 U.S. 587, 596 (1961). That is not the case here. To be sure, Lockhart contends that if we applied a different principle of statutory construction—namely, his "series-qualifier principle"—we would arrive at an alternative construction of § 2252(b)(2). But the arguable availability of multiple, divergent principles of statutory construction cannot automatically trigger the rule of lenity. Cf. Llewellyn, Remarks on the Theory of Appellate Decision and the Rules or Canons About How Statutes Are To Be Construed, 3 Vand. L. Rev. 395, 401 (1950) ("[T]here are two opposing canons on almost every point"). Here, the rule of the last antecedent is well supported by context and Lockhart's alternative is not. We will not apply the rule of lenity to override a sensible grammatical principle buttressed by the statute's text and structure.

* * *

We conclude that the text and structure of § 2252(b)(2) confirm that the provision applies to prior state convictions for "sexual abuse" and "aggravated sexual abuse," whether or not the convictions involved a minor or ward. We therefore hold that Lockhart's prior conviction for sexual abuse of an adult is encompassed by § 2252(b)(2). The judgment of the Court of Appeals, accordingly, is affirmed.

■ *JUSTICE KAGAN, with whom JUSTICE BREYER joins, dissenting:*

Imagine a friend told you that she hoped to meet "an actor, director, or producer involved with the new Star Wars movie." You would know immediately that she wanted to meet an actor from the Star Wars cast—not an actor in, for example, the latest Zoolander. Suppose a real estate agent promised to find a client "a house, condo, or apartment in New

York." Wouldn't the potential buyer be annoyed if the agent sent him information about condos in Maryland or California? And consider a law imposing a penalty for the "violation of any statute, rule, or regulation relating to insider trading." Surely a person would have cause to protest if punished under that provision for violating a traffic statute. The reason in all three cases is the same: Everyone understands that the modifying phrase—"involved with the new Star Wars movie," "in New York," "relating to insider trading"—applies to each term in the preceding list, not just the last.

That ordinary understanding of how English works, in speech and writing alike, should decide this case. . . .

I

Begin where the majority does—with the rule of the last antecedent. . . . This Court most fully discussed that principle in *Barnhart v. Thomas*, 540 U.S. 20 (2003), which considered a statute providing that an individual qualifies as disabled if "he is not only unable to do his previous work but cannot, considering his age, education, and work experience, engage in any other kind of substantial gainful work *which exists in the national economy*." *Id.* at 21–22 (quoting 42 U.S.C. § 423(d)(2)(A)) (emphasis added). The Court held, invoking the last-antecedent rule, that the italicized phrase modifies only the term "substantial gainful work," and not the term "previous work" occurring earlier in the sentence. Two points are of especial note. First, *Barnhart* contained a significant caveat: The last-antecedent rule "can assuredly be overcome by other indicia of meaning." 540 U.S. at 26; see, *e.g.*, *Nobelman v. American Savings Bank*, 508 U.S. 324, 330–331 (1993) (refusing to apply the rule when a contrary interpretation was "the more reasonable one"). Second, the grammatical structure of the provision in *Barnhart* is nothing like that of the statute in this case: The modifying phrase does not, as here, immediately follow a list of multiple, parallel terms. That is true as well in the other instances in which this Court has followed the rule. See, *e.g.*, *Jama v. Immigration and Customs Enforcement*, 543 U.S. 335 (2005); *Batchelor v. United States*, 156 U.S. 426 (1895); *Sims Lessee v. Irvine*, 3 Dall. 425 (1799).

Indeed, this Court has made clear that the last-antecedent rule does not generally apply to the grammatical construction present here: when "[t]he modifying clause appear[s] . . . at the end of a single, integrated list." *Jama*, 543 U.S. at 344, n. 4. Then, the exact opposite is usually true: As in the examples beginning this opinion, the modifying phrase refers alike to each of the list's terms. A leading treatise puts the point as follows: "When there is a straightforward, parallel construction that involves all nouns or verbs in a series," a modifier at the end of the list "normally applies to the entire series." A. Scalia & B. Garner, Reading Law: The Interpretation of Legal Texts 147 (2012); compare *id.* at 152 ("When the syntax involves something other than [such] a parallel series of nouns or verbs," the modifier "normally applies only to the nearest reasonable referent"). That interpretive practice of applying the modifier to the whole list boasts a fancy name—the "series-qualifier canon," see Black's Law Dictionary 1574 (10th ed. 2014)—but, as my opening examples show, it reflects the completely ordinary way that people speak and listen, write and read.[1]

Even the exception to the series-qualifier principle is intuitive, emphasizing both its common-sensical basis and its customary usage. When the nouns in a list are so disparate that the modifying clause does not make sense when applied to them all, then the last-antecedent rule takes over. Suppose your friend told you . . . that she hopes someday to meet "a President, Supreme Court Justice, or actor involved with Star Wars." Presumably, you would know that she wants to meet a President or Justice even if that person has no connection to the famed film franchise. But so long as the modifying clause "is applicable as much to the first and other words as to the last," this Court has stated, "the natural construction of the language demands that the clause be read as applicable to all." *Paroline v. United States*, 572 U.S. 434, 447 (2014) (quoting *Porto Rico Railway, Light & Power Co. v. Mor*, 253 U.S. 345, 348 (1920)). In other words, the modifier then qualifies not just the last antecedent but the whole series.

. . . . In *Paroline*, for example, this Court considered a statute requiring possessors of child pornography to pay restitution to the individuals whose abuse is recorded in those materials. The law defines such a victim's losses to include "medical services relating to physical, psychiatric, or psychological care; physical and occupational therapy or rehabilitation; necessary transportation, temporary housing, and child care expenses; lost income; attorneys' fees, as well as other costs incurred; and any other losses suffered by the victim as a proximate result of the offense." 18 U.S.C. §§ 2259(b)(3)(A)–(F) (lettering omitted). The victim bringing the lawsuit invoked the last-antecedent rule to argue that the modifier at the end of the provision—"as a proximate result of the offense"—pertained only to the last item in the preceding list, and not to any of the others. See 572 U.S. at 446–447. But the Court rejected that view: It recited the "canon[ ] of statutory construction," derived from the "natural" use of language, that "[w]hen several words are followed by a clause" that can sensibly modify them all, it should be understood to do so. *Ibid.* Thus, the Court read the proximate-cause requirement to cover each and every term in the list.

---

[1] The majority's baseball example . . . reads the other way only because its three terms are *not* parallel. The words "catcher" and "shortstop," but not "pitcher," are qualified separate and apart from the modifying clause at the end of the sentence: "Pitcher" thus calls for a modifier of its own, and the phrase "from the Kansas City Royals" answers that call. Imagine the sentence is slightly reworded to refer to a "defensive catcher, quick-footed shortstop, or hard-throwing pitcher from the Kansas City Royals." Or, alternatively, suppose the sentence referred simply to a "catcher, shortstop, or pitcher from the Kansas City Royals." Either way, all three players must come from the Royals—because the three terms (unlike in the majority's sentence) are a parallel series with a modifying clause at the end.

United States v. Bass, 404 U.S. 336 (1971), to take just one other example, followed the same rule. There, the Court confronted a statute making it a crime for a convicted felon to "receive[ ], possess[ ], or transport[ ] in commerce or affecting commerce . . . any firearm." 18 U.S.C. App. § 1202(a) (1970 ed.) (current version at 18 U.S.C. § 922(g)). The Government contended that the modifying clause—"in commerce or affecting commerce"—applied only to "transport" and not to "receive" or "possess." But the Court rebuffed that argument. "[T]he natural construction of the language," the Court recognized, "suggests that the clause 'in commerce or affecting commerce' qualifies all three antecedents in the list." 404 U.S. at 339 (some internal quotation marks omitted). Relying on longstanding precedents endorsing such a construction, the Court explained: "Since 'in commerce or affecting commerce' undeniably applies to at least one antecedent, and since it makes sense with all three, the more plausible construction here is that it in fact applies to all three." *Id.* at 339–340 . . . ; see also, *e.g.*, *Jones v. United States*, 529 U.S. 848, 853 (2000) (similarly treating the interstate commerce element in the phrase "any building, vehicle, or other real or personal property used in interstate or foreign commerce" as applying to buildings and vehicles).

That analysis holds equally for § 2252(b)(2), the sentencing provision at issue here. The relevant language—"aggravated sexual abuse, sexual abuse, or abusive sexual conduct involving a minor or ward"—contains a "single, integrated list" of parallel terms (*i.e.*, sex crimes) followed by a modifying clause. *Jama*, 543 U.S. at 344, n. 4. Given the close relation among the terms in the series, the modifier makes sense "as much to the first and other words as to the last." *Paroline*, 572 U.S. at 447. In other words, the reference to a minor or ward applies as well to sexual abuse and aggravated sexual abuse as to abusive sexual conduct. (The case would be different if, for example, the statute established a mandatory minimum for any person previously convicted of "arson, receipt of stolen property, or abusive sexual conduct involving a minor or ward.") So interpreting the modifier "as applicable to all" the preceding terms is what "the natural construction of the language" requires. *Ibid.*; *Bass*, 404 U.S. at 339.

The majority responds to all this by claiming that the "inelegant phrasing" of § 2252(b)(2) renders it somehow exempt from a grammatical rule reflecting "how people ordinarily" use the English language. *Ante* at 357. But to begin with, the majority is wrong to suggest that the series-qualifier canon is only about "colloquial" or "conversational" English. *Ibid.* In fact, it applies to both speech and writing, in both their informal and their formal varieties. Here is a way to test my point: Pick up a journal, or a book, or for that matter a Supreme Court opinion—most of which keep "everyday" colloquialisms at a far distance. *Ibid.* You'll come across many sentences having the structure of the statutory provision at issue here: a few nouns followed by a modifying clause. And you'll discover, again and yet again, that the clause modifies every noun in the series, not just the last—in other words, that even (especially?) in formal writing, the series-qualifier principle works.[2] . . .

The majority . . . seeks refuge in the idea that applying the series-qualifier canon to § 2252(b)(2) would violate the rule against superfluity. . . . Says the majority: "Any conduct that would qualify as 'aggravated sexual abuse . . . involving a minor or ward' or 'sexual abuse . . . involving a minor or ward' would also qualify as 'abusive sexual conduct involving a minor or ward.'" *Ante* at 356. But that rejoinder doesn't work. "[T]he canon against superfluity," this Court has often stated, "assists only where a competing interpretation gives effect to every clause and word of a statute." *Microsoft Corp. v. i4i Ltd. Partnership*, 564 U.S. 91, 106 (2011) (internal quotation marks omitted) . . . . And the majority's approach (as it admits, see *ante* at 356) produces superfluity too—and in equal measure. . . . [A]ny conduct that would qualify as "abusive sexual conduct involving a minor or ward" or "aggravated sexual abuse" would also qualify as "sexual abuse." In other words, on the majority's reading as well, two listed crimes become subsets of a third, so that the three could have been written as one. And indeed, the majority's superfluity has an especially odd quality, because it relates to the modifying clause itself: The majority, that is, makes the term "involving a minor or ward" wholly unnecessary. . . .

II

Legislative history confirms what the natural construction of language shows: Each of the three predicate offenses at issue here must involve a minor. . . .

The relevant language—again, providing for a mandatory minimum sentence if a person has a prior state-law conviction for "aggravated sexual abuse, sexual abuse, or abusive sexual conduct involving a minor or ward"—first made its appearance in 1996, when Congress inserted it into § 2252(b)(1). See Child Pornography Prevention Act of 1996, § 121(5), 110 Stat. 3009–30, 18 U.S.C. § 2251 note. At that time, the Senate Report on the legislation explained what the new language

[2] Too busy to carry out this homework assignment? Consider some examples (there are many more) from just the last few months of this Court's work. In *OBB Personenverkehr AG v. Sachs*, [577 U.S. 27 (2015),] this Court described a lawsuit as alleging "wrongful arrest, imprisonment, and torture *by Saudi police*." In *James v. Boise*, [577 U.S. 306 (2016) (*per curiam*)] (quoting *Martin v. Hunter's Lessee*, 1 Wheat. 304, 348 (1816)), this Court affirmed that state courts must follow its interpretations of "the laws, the treaties, and the constitution *of the United States*." In *Musacchio v. United States*, [577 U.S. 237 (2016)] (quoting *Reed Elsevier, Inc. v. Muchnick*, 559 U.S. 154, 166 (2010)), this Court noted that in interpreting statutes it looks to the "text, context, and relevant historical treatment *of the provision at issue*." In *FERC v. Electric Power Supply Assn.*, [577 U.S. 260 (2016),] this Court applied a statute addressing "any rule, regulation, practice, or contract *affecting [a wholesale] rate [or] charge*." And in *Montanile v. Board of Trustees of Nat. Elevator Industry Health Benefit Plan*, [577 U.S. 136 (2016),] this Court interpreted an employee benefits plan requiring reimbursement "for attorneys' fees, costs, expenses or damages *claimed by the covered person*." In each case, of course, the italicized modifying clause refers to every item in the preceding list. That is because the series-qualifier rule reflects how all of us use language, in writing and in speech, in formal and informal contexts, all the time.

meant: The mandatory minimum would apply to an "offender with a prior conviction under . . . any *State child abuse law*." S. Rep. No. 104–358, p. 9 (1996) (emphasis added). It is hard to imagine saying any more directly that the just-added state sexual-abuse predicates all involve minors, and minors only.

Two years later, in urging Congress to include the same predicate offenses in § 2252(b)(2), the Department of Justice (DOJ) itself read the list that way. In a formal bill comment, DOJ noted that proposed legislation on child pornography failed to fix a statutory oddity: Only § 2252(b)(1), and not § 2252(b)(2), then contained the state predicates at issue here. DOJ described that discrepancy as follows: Whereas § 2252(b)(1) provided a penalty enhancement for "individuals charged with receipt or distribution of child pornography *and who have prior state convictions for child molestation*," the adjacent § 2252(b)(2) contained no such enhancement for those "charged with possession of child pornography *who have prior convictions for child abuse*." H.R. Rep. No. 105–557, p. 31 (1998) (emphasis added). That should change, DOJ wrote: A possessor of child pornography should also be subject to a 2-year mandatory minimum if he had "a *prior conviction for sexual abuse of a minor*." *Ibid.* (emphasis added). DOJ thus made clear that the predicate offenses it recommended adding to § 2252(b)(2)—like those already in § 2252(b)(1)—related not to all sexual abuse but only to sexual abuse of children. And Congress gave DOJ just what it wanted: Soon after receiving the letter, Congress added the language at issue to § 2252(b)(2), resulting in the requested 2-year minimum sentence. See Protection of Children From Sexual Predators Act of 1998, § 202(a)(2), 112 Stat. 2977, 18 U.S.C. § 1 note. So every indication, in 1998 no less than in 1996, was that all the predicate crimes relate to children alone.

The majority's response to this history fails to blunt its force. According to the majority, the reference to "any state child abuse law" in the Senate Report is simply an "incomplete[ ] descri[ption]" of "the state sexual-abuse predicates." *Ante* at 359. And similarly, the majority ventures, the DOJ letter was merely noting "one of the provision's many salient features." *Ibid.* But suppose that you (like the Senate Report's or DOJ letter's authors) had to paraphrase or condense the statutory language at issue here, and that you (like the majority) thought it captured *all* sexual-abuse crimes. Would you then use the phrase "any state child abuse law" as a descriptor (as the Senate Report did)? And would you refer to the whole list of state predicates as involving "sexual abuse of a minor" (as the DOJ letter did)? Of course not. But you might well use such shorthand if, alternatively, you understood the statutory language (as I do) to cover only sexual offenses against children. And so the authors of the Report and letter did here. Such documents of necessity abridge statutory language; but they do not do so by conveying an utterly false impression of what that language is most centrally about—as by describing a provision that (supposedly) covers all sexual abuse as one that reaches only child molestation.[5]

Further, the majority objects that the Senate Report's (and DOJ letter's) drafters did "nothing to explain *why*" Congress would have limited § 2252(b)'s state sexual-abuse predicates to those involving children when the provision's federal sexual-abuse predicates (as all agree) are not so confined. *Ante* at 360 (emphasis in original). But Congress is under no obligation to this Court to justify its choices. (Nor is DOJ obliged to explain them to Congress itself.) Rather, the duty is on this Court to carry out those decisions, regardless of whether it understands all that lay behind them. The Senate Report (and DOJ letter too) says what it says about § 2252(b)'s meaning, confirming in no uncertain terms the most natural reading of the statutory language. Explanation or no, that is more than sufficient.

And the majority (as it concedes) cannot claim that Congress simply must have wanted § 2252(b)(2)'s federal and state predicates to be the same.... [B]oth § 2252(b)(1) and § 2252(b)(2) contain many federal predicates lacking state matches. Under § 2252(b)(1), for example, a person is subject to a mandatory minimum if he previously violated 18 U.S.C. § 1591, which prohibits "[s]ex trafficking of children or [sex trafficking] by force, fraud, or coercion." But if the prior conviction is under state law, only sex trafficking of children will trigger that minimum; trafficking of adults, even if by force, fraud, or coercion, will not. That mismatch—trafficking of both adults and children on the federal side, trafficking of children alone on the state side—precisely parallels my view of the sexual-abuse predicates at issue here. More generally, ten federal obscenity crimes trigger both § 2252(b)(1)'s and § 2252(b)(2)'s enhanced punishments; but equivalent state crimes do not

[5] The majority tries to bolster its "incomplete description" claim by highlighting another summary statement in the Senate Report, but that reference merely illustrates my point. In amending § 2252(b)(1) (and later § 2252(b)(2)), Congress added not only the child sexual-abuse predicates at issue here, but also a set of predicate state offenses relating to child pornography. Specifically, Congress provided a mandatory minimum sentence for individuals previously convicted of the "production, possession, receipt, mailing, sale, distribution, shipment, or transportation of child pornography." Child Pornography Prevention Act, § 121(5), 110 Stat. 3009–30. The Senate Report described those predicate crimes in an abbreviated fashion as "relating to the production, receipt or distribution of child pornography." S. Rep. No. 104–358, p. 9 (1996). That synopsis doubtless leaves some things out, as any synopsis does; but no reader of the Report would be terribly surprised to see the fuller statutory list. The same cannot be said of the phrase "any state child abuse law" if that in fact refers to laws prohibiting *all* rape, sexual assault, and similar behavior.

The majority makes the identical mistake in asserting that the DOJ letter merely "highlight[s]" one of § 2252(b)(1)'s many features. *Ante* at 360. To support that claim, the majority notes that the letter omits any discussion of sexual crimes against adult wards, even though the statute covers those offenses on any theory. But that elision is perfectly natural. The number of sex crimes against adult wards pales in comparison to those against children: In discussing the latter, DOJ was focused on the mine-run offense. (For the same reason, this opinion's descriptions of § 2252(b) often skip any reference to wards.... Count that as a writer's choice to avoid extraneous detail.) The majority cannot offer any similar, simple explanation of why DOJ would have repeatedly referred only to sex crimes against children if the statutory language it was explicating—and proposing to add to another provision—also covered sex crimes against all adults.

do so. And five federal prostitution offenses prompt mandatory minimums under those provisions; but no such state offenses do. . . .

III

As against the most natural construction of § 2252(b)(2)'s language, plus unusually limpid legislative history, the majority relies on a structural argument. . . . The federal sexual-abuse predicates in § 2252(b)(2), the majority begins, are described as crimes "under . . . Chapter 109A" . . . . The headings of the sections in Chapter 109A, [the majority] contends, "mirror precisely the order . . . and nearly precisely the words used to describe" the state predicate crimes at issue. . . .

But § 2252(b)(2)'s state predicates are not nearly as similar to the federal crimes in Chapter 109A as the majority claims. That chapter includes the following offenses: "Aggravated sexual abuse," § 2241, "Sexual abuse," § 2242, "Sexual abuse of a minor or ward," § 2243, and "Abusive sexual contact," § 2244. The chapter thus contains *four* crimes—one more than found in § 2252(b)(2)'s list of state offenses. If the drafters of § 2252(b)(2) meant merely to copy Chapter 109A, why would they have left out one of its crimes? The majority has no explanation.[6] And there is more. Suppose Congress, for whatever hard-to-fathom reason, wanted to replicate only Chapter 109A's first three offenses. It would then have used the same language, referring to "the laws of any State relating to aggravated sexual abuse, sexual abuse, or sexual abuse of a minor or ward." (And had Congress used that language, the phrase "of a minor or ward" would clearly have applied only to the third term, to differentiate it from the otherwise identical second.) But contra the majority, . . . that is not what § 2252(b)(2)'s drafters did. Rather than repeating the phrase "sexual abuse," they used the phrase "abusive sexual conduct" in the list's last term—which echoes, if anything, the separate crime of "abusive sexual contact" (included in Chapter 109A's *fourth* offense, as well as in other places in the federal code, see, *e.g.*, 10 U.S.C. § 920(d)). The choice of those different words indicates, yet again, that Congress did not mean, as the majority imagines, to duplicate Chapter 109A's set of offenses.

. . . .

IV

Suppose, for a moment, that this case is not as clear as I've suggested. . . .

---

[6] In a footnote, the majority intimates that Chapter 109A contains only three crimes—but that reading is unambiguously wrong. Unlike the fifth through eighth sections of that chapter (which the majority invokes to no purpose), the fourth—again, entitled "[a]busive sexual contact"—sets out an independent substantive offense, criminalizing acts not made illegal in the first three sections. §§ 2244(a)–(c); see also 42 U.S.C. § 16911 (separately listing this offense in identifying who must register as a sex offender). The majority, as noted above, gives no reason why Congress would have ignored that fourth crime had it been using Chapter 109A as a template.

This Court has a rule for how to resolve genuine ambiguity in criminal statutes: in favor of the criminal defendant. . . . [T]he rule of lenity . . . should tip the scales in Lockhart's favor, because nothing the majority has said shows that the modifying clause in § 2252(b)(2) *unambiguously* applies to only the last term in the preceding series. . . .

NOTES AND QUESTIONS

1. The first paragraph of Justice Kagan's dissent referred to (1) a friend who hopes to meet "an actor, director, or producer involved with the new Star Wars movie," (2) a real-estate agent who is looking for "a house, condo, or apartment in New York," and (3) the penalties for violating "any statute, rule, or regulation relating to insider trading." In each of the quoted phrases, the opening article ("an," "a," or "any") plainly covers all of the items in the ensuing list, in a way that knits the list together; given the syntax, no one could think that each of the three items separated by commas is completely independent of the others. What is more, readers can be quite confident that they understand the overall purpose of the phrase, and the overall purpose supports applying the final qualifying phrase to all three antecedents. Is the same true of the key phrase in 18 U.S.C. § 2252(b)(2) ("the laws of any State relating to aggravated sexual abuse, sexual abuse, or abusive sexual conduct involving a minor or ward")?

2. The majority's best argument is that the key words in § 2252(b)(2) track the headings of the first three sections in Chapter 109A of Title 18 of the United States Code: "Aggravated sexual abuse," "Sexual abuse," and "Sexual abuse of a minor or ward." Unless the people who inserted the key language in § 2252(b) were looking at those headings, it is hard to understand why they would have included both "aggravated sexual abuse" and "sexual abuse" in the same list. And if the headings in Chapter 109A did provide the template for this language in § 2252(b),[60] the reference to "a minor or ward" would seem to be part of the third item rather than a limitation on the entire list.

As the dissent noted, however, if the drafters were indeed looking at the section headings, the drafters changed the third heading: instead of referring to state laws relating to "sexual abuse of a minor or ward," § 2252(b) refers to state laws relating to "abusive sexual conduct involving a minor or ward." What is more, the drafters also left out the fourth section heading in Chapter 109A ("Abusive sexual contact"). How much do these points disrupt the parallelism between § 2252(b) and the

[60] As Justice Kagan mentioned in her dissent, the relevant language was originally added to § 2252(b)(1) in 1996. Congress then added it to § 2252(b)(2) in 1998. Technically speaking, the template for the language in § 2252(b)(2) may simply have been the language that Congress had already added to § 2252(b)(1). Still, the language presumably means the same thing in § 2252(b)(2) that it meant in § 2252(b)(1), and the headings in Chapter 109A may have provided the original template for the language in § 2252(b)(1).

section headings in Chapter 109A, and how much does that disruption weaken the majority's point?

3. In *Lockhart*, Justice Sotomayor's majority opinion acknowledged that the last-antecedent rule is merely a rebuttable presumption and that "structural or contextual evidence" can overcome it. *Lockhart*, 577 U.S. at 355; *cf.* Cyan, Inc. v. Beaver County Employees Retirement Fund, 138 S. Ct. 1061, 1077 (2018) ("We have applied [the last-antecedent rule] when the alternative reading would 'stretch[ ] the modifier too far' by asking it to qualify a remote or otherwise disconnected phrase. . . . By contrast, we have not applied the rule when the modifier directly follows a concise and 'integrated' clause." (quoting *Jama v. Immigration & Customs Enforcement*, 543 U.S. 335, 342, 344 n.4 (2005))). Still, Justice Sotomayor resisted Justice Kagan's suggestion that this exception can itself be formulated as a canon. In particular, Justice Sotomayor sounded skeptical about "the so-called series-qualifier principle." *Lockhart*, 577 U.S. at 355 (citing cases for the proposition that "sometimes context weighs against the application of the rule of the last antecedent," but insisting that "in none of those cases did the Court describe, much less apply, a countervailing grammatical mandate that could bear the weight that . . . the dissent places on the series qualifier principle").

Five years later, though, this skepticism had vanished. In *Facebook, Inc. v. Duguid*, 141 S. Ct. 1163 (2021), Justice Sotomayor's opinion for the Court treated "the series-qualifier canon" as a well-established principle.

Facebook concerned the Telephone Consumer Protection Act of 1991, Pub. L. 102–243, 105 Stat. 2394, which restricts practices that telemarketers might otherwise use. Among other things, the Act restricts the use of any "automatic telephone dialing system," which it defines as follows:

> The term "automatic telephone dialing system" means equipment which has the capacity—
>
> (A) to store or produce telephone numbers to be called, using a random or sequential number generator; and
>
> (B) to dial such numbers.

47 U.S.C. § 227(a)(1).[61] In *Facebook*, the Supreme Court had to decide what the phrase "using a random or sequential number generator" modified.

The plaintiff, Noah Duguid, argued that the phrase should be understood to go with "produce" but not with "store." On that reading, subparagraph (A) would encompass not only equipment that has the capacity "to . . . produce telephone numbers to be called, using a random or sequential number generator," but also equipment that simply has the

[61] Although both technology and communications practices have changed enormously since 1991, Congress has not amended this definition.

capacity "to store . . . telephone numbers to be called" (even if the storage does not entail use of a random or sequential number generator).

The Supreme Court rejected this reading. Although Justice Alito wrote separately, all nine Justices agreed that the phrase "using a random or sequential number generator" should be understood to go with "store" as well as "produce." In Justice Sotomayor's words, "We hold that a necessary feature of an autodialer under § 227(a)(1)(A) is the capacity to use a random or sequential number generator to either store or produce phone numbers to be called." *Facebook*, 141 S. Ct. at 1173.

Even without regard to any canons, the syntax of the statutory definition surely favored the Court's interpretation over Mr. Duguid's interpretation. In the definition, the phrase "to store or produce" is followed by a direct object ("telephone numbers to be called") that obviously goes with "store" as well as "produce." As a matter of ordinary English syntax, the ensuing phrase ("using a random or sequential number generator") cannot readily be interpreted to skip over the shared direct object and to go with "produce" but not "store."[62]

The main argument for Mr. Duguid's interpretation was simply that random or sequential number generators are more commonly used to produce numbers than to store numbers. Still, the Supreme Court pointed out that "an autodialer might use a random number generator to determine the order in which to pick phone numbers from a preproduced list," and might "then store those numbers to be dialed at a later time." *Id.* at 1172 n.7. In other words, it is technically possible to imagine equipment that uses a random or sequential number generator in connection with the storage rather than the production of telephone numbers—so applying what the majority called "the traditional tools of interpretation" did not lead to "a 'linguistically impossible' or contextually implausible outcome." *Id.* at 1171 (quoting *Encino Motorcars, LLC v. Navarro*, 138 S. Ct. 1134, 1141 (2018)). As a policy matter, moreover, the majority worried that Mr. Duguid's alternative interpretation "would produce an outcome that makes even less sense," because it would "classif[y] almost all modern cell phones as autodialers." *Id.* at 1172.

In addition to making these arguments, though, Justice Sotomayor's opinion for the Court invoked the series-qualifier principle. Indeed,

---

[62] One might wonder whether the phrase "using a random or sequential number generator" goes with the immediately preceding words ("to be called"), rather than with "store or produce." In a careful opinion for the Seventh Circuit, then-Judge Barrett noted that "[s]ome courts . . . have alluded to this possibility, though none has adopted it." *Gadelhak v. AT&T Servs., Inc.*, 950 F.3d 458, 464 (7th Cir. 2020). As Judge Barrett observed, however, the comma in subparagraph (A) weakens this reading. *See id.* at 468 ("The comma separating 'to be called' and 'using a random or sequential number generator' . . . indicates that the moderator refers to the entire clause that precedes it—a clause driven by the verbs 'store' and 'produce' . . . ."). In addition, if Congress had intended to focus on devices that use a random or sequential number generator to place calls, subparagraph (B) might have been a more natural place for the phrase.

Justice Sotomayor presented that principle as her lead argument. Here are the opening words of her analysis:

> "We begin with the text. Congress defined an autodialer in terms of what it must do ('store or produce telephone numbers to be called') and how it must do it ('using a random or sequential number generator'). The definition uses a familiar structure: a list of verbs followed by a modifying clause. Under conventional rules of grammar, '[w]hen there is a straightforward, parallel construction that involves all nouns or verbs in a series,' a modifier at the end of the list 'normally applies to the entire series.' A. Scalia & B. Garner, Reading Law: The Interpretation of Legal Texts 147 (2012) (quotation modified). The Court often applies this interpretive rule, usually referred to as the 'series-qualifier canon.' . . . This canon generally reflects the most natural reading of a sentence."

Id. at 1169.

This argument went too far for Justice Alito, who wrote separately to suggest that his colleagues were putting too much weight on canons in general and on the series-qualifier principle in particular. With respect to canons in general, Justice Alito observed:

> "To the extent that interpretive canons accurately describe how the English language is generally used, they are useful tools. But they are not inflexible rules.
>
> "Appellate judges spend virtually every waking hour speaking, listening to, reading, or writing English prose. Statutes are written in English prose, and interpretation is not a technical exercise to be carried out by mechanically applying a set of arcane rules. Canons of interpretation can help in figuring out the meaning of troublesome statutory language, but if they are treated like rigid rules, they can lead us astray. When this Court describes canons as rules or quotes canons while omitting their caveats and limitations, we only encourage the lower courts to relegate statutory interpretation to a series of if-then computations. No reasonable reader interprets texts that way."

Id. at 1175 (Alito, J., concurring in the judgment).

With respect to the series-qualifier principle in particular, Justice Alito observed that the very source that the majority invoked—*Reading Law* by Justice Scalia and Bryan Garner—"goes out of its way to emphasize the limitations of the series-qualifier canon." *Id.* at 1174. Justice Alito added the following thoughts:

> "The [majority] writes that the series-qualifier canon 'generally reflects the most natural reading of a sentence,' . . . and *maybe* that is so. . . . But it is very easy to think of sentences that clearly go against the canon:

'At the Super Bowl party, she ate, drank, and cheered raucously.'

'On Saturday, he relaxes and exercises vigorously.'

'When his owner comes home, the dog wags his tail and barks loudly.'

'It is illegal to hunt rhinos and giraffes with necks longer than three feet.'

'She likes to swim and run wearing track spikes.'

". . . .

"The strength and validity of an interpretive canon is an empirical question, and perhaps someday it will be possible to evaluate these canons by conducting what is called a corpus linguistics analysis, that is, an analysis of how particular combinations of words are used in a vast database of English prose. See generally Lee & Mouritsen, Judging Ordinary Meaning, 127 Yale L.J. 788 (2018). If the series-qualifier canon were analyzed in this way, I suspect we would find that series qualifiers sometimes modify all the nouns or verbs in a list and sometimes modify just the last noun or verb. It would be interesting to see if the percentage of sentences in the first category is high enough to justify the canon. But no matter how the sentences with the relevant structure broke down, it would be surprising if 'the sense of the matter' did not readily reveal the meaning in the great majority of cases. Reading Law 150."

Id. at 1174–75.

CHAPTER 3

LEGISLATIVE HISTORY

A. INTRODUCTION

To identify the legal directives that they will understand a particular statute to establish, interpreters should take the principles of interpretation that they are supposed to use and apply those principles to the information that they are supposed to consider. That information surely includes the text of the statute. But what else does it include? As judges try to decide what a statute means, what sources do we want them to consult, and for what purposes?

No one thinks that judges should be limited to considering *only* the statutory text and should be forbidden to use anything else to shed light on the meaning of that text. At a minimum, judges routinely consider extrinsic information about vocabulary and other linguistic conventions. Whether that information comes from dictionaries or other books, from online corpora, or simply from the judges' own knowledge, it is not part of the statute itself—yet it colors what judges understand the statute to mean. Interpreters also commonly invoke information about a statute's legal background, such as the provisions of other statutes of the day or the content of the common law as it was understood at the time of enactment. More broadly, judges regularly consider a wide range of outside sources about "the public history of the times in which [the statute] was passed." Antonin Scalia, *Common-Law Courts in a Civil-Law System: The Role of United States Federal Courts in Interpreting the Constitution and Laws, in* A MATTER OF INTERPRETATION: FEDERAL COURTS AND THE LAW 3, 30 (Amy Gutmann ed., 1997) (quoting *Aldridge v. Williams*, 44 U.S. (3 How.) 9, 24 (1844)). It is entirely uncontroversial to say that the categories of information that statutory interpreters are free to consider extend well beyond the particular statute that is being interpreted.

It is also uncontroversial to say that some categories of information are off limits. Just about everyone who favors having formal rules of evidence agrees that restrictions on the information available to decisionmakers can sometimes be justified, either for the purpose of improving the accuracy of the decisionmaking process or for other reasons. In the specific context of statutory interpretation, moreover, there are broad areas of agreement about the content of some appropriate restrictions.

To take a simple example, "courts in most jurisdictions refuse to admit voluntary in-court testimony by legislators concerning the legislative intent underlying a previously enacted statute." Adrian Vermeule, *Legislative History and the Limits of Judicial Competence: The*

Untold Story of Holy Trinity Church, 50 STAN. L. REV. 1833, 1890 (1998). Although California state courts may have an unusual practice on this point,[1] that practice has received poor reviews and remains "isolated." *Covalt v. Carey Canada Inc.*, 860 F.2d 1434, 1439 (7th Cir. 1988). Most other courts interpreting a statute either will exclude or at least will basically ignore affidavits or oral testimony from someone who was a member of the enacting legislature about what he or his colleagues intended the statute to mean. *See, e.g.*, Bread Political Action Comm. v. Fed. Election Comm'n, 455 U.S. 577, 582 n.3 (1982); *see also* GeorgiaCarry.org, Inc. v. City of Atlanta, 602 F. Supp. 2d 1281, 1286 (N.D. Ga. 2008) ("It is a well-settled rule of statutory construction that 'affidavits by drafters after enactment of legislation will not be considered by the courts.'" (quoting Friedman v. United States, 364 F. Supp. 484, 488 (S.D. Ga. 1973))), *aff'd*, 318 F. App'x 851 (11th Cir. 2009); *cf.* Lindland v. U.S. Wrestling Ass'n, 227 F.3d 1000, 1008 (7th Cir. 2000) (refusing to give any weight to a letter from Sen. Stevens to the district court in a dispute about the effect of a provision in the "Stevens Act," 36 U.S.C. § 220509). Nor are courts likely to permit testimony to the same effect from a staff person who drafted the bill or a lobbyist who helped secure its passage. *See, e.g.*, *Covalt*, 860 F.2d at 1438–39 (paying "no heed" to after-the-fact affidavits from a lobbyist and a member of the House of Representatives about the intended meaning of a federal statute); In re G-I Holdings, 369 B.R. 832, 840–41 (D.N.J. 2007) (similarly ignoring a lobbyist's affidavit).

A constellation of reasons supports the rejection of such testimony. To begin with, even if one considers it desirable (other things being equal) for our system of statutory interpretation to produce matches between the interpreted meaning of statutory language and the meaning actually intended by members of the enacting legislature at the time of enactment, one might not think that allowing courts to consider after-

---

[1] In the 1960s, one of California's intermediate appellate courts indicated that administrative and judicial interpreters could entertain after-the-fact testimony from individual legislators about the discussions that had occurred within a committee of the state legislature as it was considering the relevant bill. At the time, contemporaneous records of those discussions did not exist, and the court seemed to view after-the-fact descriptions of what had occurred in the committee as an appropriate substitute for such records. *See* Rich v. State Bd. of Optometry, 235 Cal. App. 2d 591, 603 (1965) (drawing a distinction between "the testimony of an individual legislator as to his intention . . . or opinion with regard to a particular piece of legislation," which would be inadmissible, and testimony that simply "reiterat[ed] . . . the discussion and events which transpired in the Assembly committee hearing," which allegedly should be thought of as "a report of the committee's activity with respect to this bill"). *But see* Marc R. Perman, Comment, *Statutory Interpretation in California: Individual Testimony as an Extrinsic Aid*, 15 U.S.F. L. REV. 241, 249–52 (1980–1981) (criticizing the premise "that reiteration testimony is the equivalent of recorded legislative history"). The California Supreme Court subsequently embraced the use of some such testimony. *See, e.g.*, Calif. Teachers Ass'n v. San Diego Cmty. Coll. Dist., 621 P.2d 856, 860–61 (Cal. 1981) (confirming *Rich*'s idea, though repudiating a case that had gone even farther than *Rich*); *cf.* Ross v. RagingWire Telecomms., Inc., 174 P.3d 200, 207–08 (Cal. 2008) (rejecting the position advanced in an amicus brief by "five present and former state legislators who authored the bill," because they "do not assert . . . that they shared their view of the proposed legislation with the Legislature as a whole"). Even in California, though, this practice does not appear to be very robust. *See, e.g.*, Rose v. County of San Benito, 77 Cal. App. 5th 688, 716–17 (2022) (citing cases).

the-fact testimony from people involved in the legislative process will actually advance that goal. Like some forms of hearsay, such testimony may tend to be inaccurate in ways that courts are not well positioned to detect. Not only might a legislator's current recollections of past debates be mistaken, but the legislator might also be overconfident about the extent to which his colleagues shared his own understanding of a bill. In addition, some legislators might deliberately shade their testimony in order to advance their pet policies or to help one side or another in the current controversy.

Perhaps one could combat these concerns about accuracy by inviting testimony from other legislators too, so that the court gets a broader range of views about the mood of the enacting legislature. But that approach would address the problem of unreliability only at substantial cost to another important goal of statutory interpretation—keeping the interpretive process from consuming more resources than it should. If cases about statutory interpretation routinely featured a parade of witnesses from the enacting legislature, those cases would impose extra expense on courts (which would have to set aside time to hear the witnesses), litigants (who would have to prepare to meet the witnesses' testimony), and the legislature itself (whose members would be sidetracked from their normal duties). Even if one thinks that the resulting testimony would be sufficiently reliable, on balance, to give courts a marginally better picture of the enacting legislature's collective intentions, this benefit might not be worth the costs that it necessitates.

Apart from concerns about reliability and cost, allowing interpreters to determine a statute's meaning partly on the basis of after-the-fact testimony would also raise concerns about notice. In many contexts, basing interpretations on this sort of information risks the same sort of unfairness that we associate with retroactive legislation: if a private person has acted in a particular way, and if testimony offered only later leads a court to interpret a statute as prohibiting that action, the person might legitimately complain that he had no way of knowing his legal duties in advance. Even when those concerns are muted, one might think that interested members of the public should be able to determine the content of a law without having to compile and review transcripts of the testimony offered in every case that implicates the statute's meaning.[2]

Indeed, concerns about notice may well justify the categorical exclusion of certain other sources of information that might be considered more reliable than after-the-fact oral testimony. The private messages

[2] In addition to the arguments just recited, the Speech or Debate Clause of Article I also imposes some constitutional constraints on the use of testimony from members of the federal Congress. At a minimum, it prevents members of Congress from being *compelled* to testify about their legislative activities. *See* U.S. CONST. art. I, § 6 ("[F]or any Speech or Debate in either House, [federal Senators and Representatives] shall not be questioned in any other Place."). But even in situations not reached by this Clause, most courts and commentators seem to agree that judges trying to determine a statute's meaning should not invite people who were involved in the legislative process to submit affidavits or otherwise offer after-the-fact testimony about the legislature's intent.

that legislators exchange before a vote, the ruminations that other legislators record in their diaries that evening, and the e-mails that legislative assistants send their bosses might all be accurate reflections of the mindset with which a key bloc of legislators voted for a bill. But even if these documents emerge during discovery in subsequent litigation, courts are unlikely to use them to determine the meaning of a statute, because they were not publicly available in the necessary sense at the time of enactment. *Cf.* WILLIAM N. ESKRIDGE, JR., JAMES J. BRUDNEY & JOSH CHAFETZ, LEGISLATION AND STATUTORY INTERPRETATION 332 (3d ed. 2022) (discussing the need for availability). More fancifully, if all the legislators who voted in favor of a particular bill simultaneously signed (but did not publish) a secret interpretive memorandum, which they sealed in an envelope to be opened in the event of litigation about the meaning of the statute that they had just passed, courts probably would not let legislators communicate with them in this way.

In sum, it would be novel to contend either that *every* category of information (other than the statutory text) should be off limits to interpreters or that there should be *no* categorical restrictions on the information that interpreters can legitimately consider. As one would expect, the real controversy is about which categories of information should be fair game for which purposes. The principal debate concerns one specific category of information that falls somewhere in between "the public history of the times in which [a statute] was passed" (which almost everyone treats as fair game) and after-the-fact testimony about legislative intent offered by individual legislators (which almost everyone considers out of bounds).

The shorthand label for the debated category is "legislative history," but that label is potentially misleading. There is little debate about the courts' ability to consider some aspects of the history of a statute. For instance, if Congress enacted a statute in 2001 and then enacted amendments to the statute in 2008 and 2020, the progression of amendments can sometimes bear on questions of statutory interpretation; the proper interpretation of the language that Congress added in 2020 might be informed by the language that it replaced or supplemented. Even critics of the use of "legislative history" in statutory interpretation do not object to considering this sort of information, so the phrase "legislative history" usually refers only to unenacted materials. *See, e.g.*, O'Gilvie v. United States, 519 U.S. 79, 97 (1996) (Scalia, J., dissenting) (using the label "statutory history," rather than "legislative history," to refer to "prior enactments approved by earlier Congresses and revised or amended by later ones to produce the current text"); ANTONIN SCALIA & BRYAN A. GARNER, READING LAW: THE INTERPRETATION OF LEGAL TEXTS 256 (2012) ("We oppose the use of legislative history, which consists of the hearings, committee reports, and debate leading up to the enactment in question .... But quite separate from legislative history is *statutory* history—the statutes repealed or amended by the statute under consideration."); *cf.* Anita S. Krishnakumar, *Statutory History*, 108 VA. L. REV. 263, 297–313 (2022) (categorizing different types of inferences that Justices sometimes draw from the history of enacted amendments to a statute or from the unenacted "drafting history" of a bill).

As used in modern debates, the phrase "legislative history" usually refers to records and documents that were created within the legislature during the process by which the legislature enacted a statute, and that the legislature has made available to the public, but that are distinct from the statutory text that the legislature enacted. Committee reports are a good example. Each house of Congress has many different standing committees that cover different subject areas. When a bill is introduced in either house, the bill normally will be referred to the appropriate committee of that house, which may in turn refer it to a subcommittee. If the bill is being considered seriously, the committee or subcommittee will gather information in various ways, which can include public hearings as well as private communications. Eventually, if the committee decides to recommend passage of the bill, the committee will report the bill back to the house, often with proposed amendments. At the same time, the committee's staff will prepare a written "committee report" that typically includes an overview of the bill, the reasons to enact it, and a brief summary of each section, as well as other information. If the full house passes the bill and sends it to the other chamber, a similar process will unfold there—so by the time a statute is enacted, there will typically be at least one committee report prepared for the House of Representatives under the auspices of a House committee and another committee report prepared for the Senate under the auspices of a Senate committee. These reports have become an important part of the legislative process, and they are a paradigmatic example of what courts call "legislative history." Likewise, transcripts of debates that occur on the floor of the House or the Senate (as well as transcripts of committee hearings and mark-up sessions, if publicly available) are also part of the "legislative history" that courts might consult.[3]

---

[3] Although judges who consult legislative history may consider all of these materials, judges will not give them all equal weight. As you will learn in more detail in Section D.1 of this chapter, judges tend to put more weight on committee reports than on "the passing comments of one Member" or "casual statements from the floor debates." *Garcia v. United States*, 469 U.S. 70, 76 (1984); *see also* Zuber v. Allen, 396 U.S. 168, 186 (1969) ("A committee report represents the considered and collective understanding of those Congressmen involved in drafting and studying proposed legislation. Floor debates reflect at best the understanding of individual Congressmen.").

To understand the different types of "legislative history" that courts might consult, you need at least a general sense of the different stages through which legislative proposals pass and the publicly available documents that are generated during those stages. For an overview of the federal legislative process, as described in a booklet that is periodically revised and updated by the Parliamentarian of the House of Representatives, see JOHN V. SULLIVAN, HOW OUR LAWS ARE MADE, H.R. DOC. NO. 110–49 (2007) (available at congress.gov/help/learn-about-the-legislative-process/how-our-laws-are-made).

All these materials are sometimes called "internal" legislative history, because they were generated within the legislature as part of the legislative process. But the adjective "internal" does not mean that they are secret. At the federal level, at least, the legislative materials that courts typically rely upon when construing federal statutes are all publicly available. When courts refer to what lawmakers said about a bill on the floor of Congress, they are referring to materials that are published on a daily basis in the *Congressional Record*. When courts refer to reports issued by congressional committees or to transcripts of hearings held before those committees, they are again referring to documents disseminated publicly by the Government Publishing Office. For the most part, moreover, these legislative materials are available to the public even before Congress enacts the statute to which they relate.

Of course, the mere fact that information is publicly available does not automatically mean that it should play a role in statutory interpretation. Many modern judges believe that if a statute's text is "unambiguous" on some point, interpreters should not allow legislative history to persuade them that the statute really means something other than what it seems to say. At least according to Judge Easterbrook, indeed, the Supreme Court has authoritatively embraced this position with respect to the interpretation of federal statutes:

> "Today's Supreme Court uses legislative history only to resolve ambiguities in enacted texts. Even the plainest legislative history does not justify going against an unambiguous enactment. (Nor does explicit legislative history justify the creation of a legal rule on a subject about which the statute is silent.)"

United States v. Logan, 453 F.3d 804, 805–06 (7th Cir. 2006) (citations omitted), *aff'd*, 552 U.S. 23 (2007); *see also* Bd. of Trade v. SEC, 187 F.3d 713, 720 (7th Cir. 1999) (Easterbrook, J.) (noting that legislative history "has limited utility," but leaving room for its use "when there is a genuine ambiguity in the statute").

Justice Scalia would have gone farther. In his view, courts should not use legislative history even to help resolve apparent ambiguities in statutory language. Indeed, Justice Scalia apparently acknowledged only one legitimate interpretive use for legislative history: if a court would otherwise conclude that a statute's literal language is absurd and that the legislature could not possibly have meant what the statute seems to say, the court can consult legislative history "to verify that what seems to us an unthinkable disposition . . . was indeed unthought of" (though not to determine what else the statute should be understood to mean). *Green v. Bock Laundry Machine Co.*, 490 U.S. 504, 527–28 (1989) (Scalia, J., concurring in the judgment). On this view, legislative history would enter the picture only in extraordinary cases, and it would affect the outcome of those cases only if it *supports* what the statutory text seems to say.

Justice Scalia was at one end of the spectrum on this issue. To help you figure out where the other end is, and where you think modern-day courts should fall within that range, this chapter proceeds in four stages. Section B provides historical background about American courts' use of legislative history in statutory interpretation. (For the Supreme Court, that practice began in the late nineteenth century, boomed in the mid-twentieth century, and started receding in the 1980s.) Section C introduces and evaluates the principal arguments that Justice Scalia and other modern critics of the use of legislative history have advanced. For judges who continue to use legislative history, Section D discusses the relative importance of different kinds of legislative history and the interaction between legislative history and other interpretive tools. Section E notes that even if one believes in using legislative history to discern the *intended meaning* of a statute, other types of legislative intent might be less relevant to interpreters—with the result that courts need to think hard about the type of legislative intent that any particular piece of legislative history might illuminate.

B. THE RISE OF RELIANCE ON LEGISLATIVE HISTORY IN STATUTORY INTERPRETATION

In the beginning, most American courts did not consult internal legislative history to determine the meaning of enacted statutory texts. As H. Jefferson Powell notes, "[t]he modern practice of interpreting a law by reference to its legislative history was almost wholly nonexistent" at the time of the Founding—and, indeed, for many years thereafter. *See* H. Jefferson Powell, *The Original Understanding of Original Intent*, 98 HARV. L. REV. 885, 897 (1985); *accord* Hans W. Baade, *"Original Intent" in Historical Perspective: Some Critical Glosses*, 69 TEX. L. REV. 1001, 1008, 1025 (1991) (discussing "the English common-law rule barring recourse to legislative history in aid of statutory interpretation," and noting that American courts followed this rule well into the nineteenth century). Professor Powell elaborates as follows:

> During the great debate in the fourth Congress over the House of Representatives' right of access to the executive branch's diplomatic files, Nathaniel Smith observed that proper statutory interpretation did not involve reference to anything other than the text of the act:
>
>> This was the universal practice of the Courts of Law, who, when called on to expound an act of the Legislature, never resorted to the debates which preceded it—to the opinions of members about its signification—but inspected the act itself, and decided by its own evidence.
>
> 5 ANNALS OF CONG. 462 (1796); *accord id.* at 441 (remarks of Rep. William Smith) (in construing a federal act, the Supreme Court does not "call for the Journals of the two Houses, or the report of the

> Committee of Ways and Means, in which the law originated, or the debates of the House on passing the law").

Powell, *supra*, 98 HARV. L. REV. at 897 n.60.

During oral argument in *Aldridge v. Williams*, 44 U.S. (3 How.) 9 (1845), the prominent lawyer Reverdy Johnson sought to buttress his interpretation of a federal statute by referring to records of legislative debates that allegedly explained why a particular provision had been added to the bill and why another proposed provision had been rejected. *See id.* at 23 (argument of counsel). But Chief Justice Taney's opinion for the Supreme Court firmly rebuffed this attempt:

> "In expounding this law, the judgment of the court cannot, in any degree, be influenced by the construction placed upon it by individual members of Congress in the debate which took place on its passage, nor by the motives or reasons assigned by them for supporting or opposing amendments that were offered. The law as it passed is the will of the majority of both houses, and the only mode in which that will is spoken is in the act itself; and we must gather their intention from the language there used, comparing it, when any ambiguity exists, with the laws upon the same subject, and looking, if necessary, to the public history of the times in which it was passed."

Id. at 24; *see also* Mitchell v. Great Works Milling & Mfg. Co., 17 F. Cas. 496, 498–99 (C.C.D. Me. 1843) (No. 9,662) (Story, J.) ("What passes in Congress upon the discussion of a bill can hardly become a matter of strict judicial inquiry . . . . [I]n truth, courts of justice are not at liberty to look at considerations of this sort."). *But cf.* United States v. Corrie, 25 F. Cas. 658, 663 (C.C.D.S.C. 1860) (No. 14,869) (observing that "it has been not unusual to seek for a guide in [the interpretation of a particular federal statute] to the report of the committee, which recommended these sections, of the house of representatives," though rejecting this practice on the strength of Chief Justice Taney's opinion in *Aldridge v. Williams*).

By the 1870s (if not before), many American courts seemed willing to base inferences about the meaning of statutory language on information in the enacting legislature's official journals about the drafting history of the relevant bill—that is, the changes that had been made during the legislative process to the text of the bill itself. *See, e.g.*, Blake v. Nat'l Banks, 90 U.S. (23 Wall.) 307, 319–20 (1875); United States v. Alexander, 79 U.S. 177, 180 (1871); Walter A. Wood Mowing & Reaping Mach. Co. v. Caldwell, 54 Ind. 270, 280 (1876); *see also* Baade, *supra*, 69 TEX. L. REV. at 1063 ("As early as 1842, doubts as to the meaning of an Ohio statute were resolved by tracing the original bill through the journals of the state senate." (citing State ex rel. Peters v. McCollister, 11 Ohio 46, 55 (1841))). But most courts continued to assert that "[i]n construing an act of Congress, we are not at liberty to recur to the views of individual members in debate . . . ." *United States v. Union Pac. R.R. Co.*, 91 U.S. 72, 79 (1875); *see also* Charles Sumner, *Opinion in the Case of the Impeachment of Andrew Johnson* (1868), *in* 12 THE WORKS OF CHARLES SUMNER 318, 361 (1877) (calling this "the received rule of law"). Many courts (though not all) also seem to have eschewed reliance on committee reports, at least when interpreting public laws rather than private acts.[4] *See, e.g.*, Proprietors of the Charles River Bridge v. Proprietors of the Warren Bridge, 36 U.S. (11 Pet.) 420, 469 (1837) (argument of counsel) (acknowledging "[t]he general principle that the legislative history of the passage of a statute furnishes no rule for its exposition," but arguing that this principle "applies only to the exposition of statutes as such" and did not prevent the Court from consulting a committee report in construing a private statute that amounted to a contract between the state and another party); De Groot v. United States, 1 Ct. Cl. 97, 100–01 (1864) (refusing to consider a committee report even to interpret something in the nature of a private statute); *see also* HENRY CAMPBELL BLACK, HANDBOOK ON THE CONSTRUCTION AND INTERPRETATION OF THE LAWS 226 (1896) ("It is generally agreed, by both the English and American courts, that reports or recommendations made to the legislative bodies by their respective committees in relation to a pending measure cannot be accepted as pertinent evidence of the meaning which the legislature intended to attach to the statute."). *But see* Harrison v. Hadley, 11 F. Cas. 649, 653 (C.C.E.D. Ark. 1873) (No. 6,137) (invoking statements made by "[t]he chairman of the committee of conference on the part of the house, in reporting the action of the committee to the house," and "[t]he chairman of the committee of conference on the part of the senate, in reporting the action of the committee to the senate," though emphasizing that these statements "accord with the plain text of the act" and using them simply to "show . . . that congress was not mistaken as to the legal effect of the [statutory] language"); Dubuque & Pac. R.R. Co. v. Litchfield, 64 U.S. (23 How.) 66, 87–88 (1860) (invoking a committee report to interpret a federal statute granting a particular tract of land to a specific recipient); Baade, *supra*, 69 TEX. L. REV. at 1068–79 (discussing the *Litchfield* case). As of the 1870s, in sum, the majority view in the United States seems to have been fairly close to the traditional English rule: the meaning of statutory language did not depend in any way upon the contents of committee reports and legislative debates.[5]

---

[4] As a practical matter, courts did not face this issue as often as they would today. Although congressional committees often prepared written reports on *private* bills, written reports were less common for *public* bills. Thomas F. Broden, Jr., *Congressional Committee Reports: Their Role and History*, 33 NOTRE DAME L. REV. 209, 231 (1958) (observing that until 1880, when the House of Representatives adopted a new rule requiring committees to prepare written reports, "[no] committee handling public bills ma[d]e general use of written reports," though a few committees did prepare such reports for "a substantial minority of the [public] bills they [recommended]" (emphasis omitted)).

[5] In states with roots in the French or Spanish civil law, courts appear to have been more receptive to the use of internal legislative history in statutory interpretation. *See, e.g.*, Second Municipality of New Orleans v. Morgan, 1 La. Ann. 111, 114 (1846) ("The report of the finance committee presented to the Council with the ordinance and adopted with it, is, to all intents and purposes, its preamble, and shows in the clearest light the cause and reason of it."); Maynard v. Johnson, 2 Nev. 25, 26 (1866) ("In case of doubt, and also where a statute will bear opposite

Careful commentators of the day noted one exception to the general idea that statutory interpreters should not rely upon these materials. Just as "[c]ourts properly look into legal treatises" and "sometimes give attention to opinions of learned lawyers in the various other ways expressed," so too they could "look, if they choose, into discussions by lawyers in the legislative body"—not as a special grade of authority, but simply as a source of potentially persuasive argument about the best interpretation of statutory language. In this way, the points made in the course of the legislative process might be given the same persuasive force as the points made in panel discussions among learned lawyers elsewhere. JOEL PRENTISS BISHOP, COMMENTARIES ON THE WRITTEN LAWS AND THEIR INTERPRETATION § 76 (1882); *see also* BLACK, *supra*, at 228 (noting that although views expressed by a legislator about the meaning of a bill are not "authoritative" in any way and "are entitled only to the force of an argument," the argument might still be worth considering "if [the legislator] be a man of learning and of acute and discriminating intelligence"). Records of legislative debates might also provide a convenient source of background information about the subject that a statute addressed—the same sort of information that a court might get from a specialized treatise. *See, e.g.*, Jennison v. Kirk, 98 U.S. 453, 459–60 (1879) (appearing to use a senator's floor statement in this way). Subject to those caveats, though, commentators perceived a firm rule "that the courts cannot resort to the opinions of the individual legislators, the legislative journals, the reports of committees, or the speeches made at the time an act was passed . . . ." BISHOP, *supra*, at § 77; *see also* BLACK, *supra*, at 224–29 (noting that the weight of authority allowed courts to resolve ambiguities in statutory language by consulting the drafting history of the relevant bill as reflected in the legislative journals, but otherwise agreeing with Bishop).

In the last decade or so of the nineteenth century, courts began to break from this rule. Justice Brewer's 1892 opinion in *Church of the Holy Trinity v. United States*, which we encountered in Chapter 1, was an early exemplar of this shift: in construing the federal statute at issue in that case, Brewer quoted at length from reports prepared during the legislative process by the House Committee on Labor and the Senate Committee on Education and Labor, which he treated as providing special insight into the intended meaning of the statute in question. *See supra* pp. 38–39; *see also, e.g.*, Buttfield v. Bidwell, 96 F. 328, 329 (2d Cir. 1899) (construing a statute in light of its drafting history and the report of the Senate committee that proposed a key amendment); WILLIAM N. ESKRIDGE, JR., DYNAMIC STATUTORY INTERPRETATION 208–09 (1994)

meanings, either from inaptness of phraseology or an ungrammatical collocation of its several clauses, it is very usual to resort to the discussions of the legislators on the disputed point, with a view to the ascertainment of their intention."); *cf.* Jerome Frank, *Civil Law Influences on the Common Law—Some Reflections on "Comparative" and "Contrastive" Law*, 104 U. PA. L. REV. 887, 893 (1956) ("In interpreting a statute, the civilians have long resorted to what we call its 'legislative history.' ").

(describing *Holy Trinity* as the start of a "sea change" with respect to the use of legislative history). *But cf.* Nicholas R. Parrillo, *Leviathan and Interpretive Revolution: The Administrative State, the Judiciary, and the Rise of Legislative History, 1890–1950*, 123 YALE L.J. 266, 280 (2013) (showing that in practice, the use of legislative history in statutory interpretation "remained rare for decades after *Holy Trinity*"). By the early twentieth century, the Supreme Court took its precedents to establish that where a federal statute is ambiguous, "we have a right to consider [the report of the responsible legislative committee] as a guide to its true interpretation." *Oceanic Steam Navigation Co. v. Stranahan*, 214 U.S. 320, 333 (1909).

At the time, the Court limited this principle to committee reports, and did not extend it to floor statements made by individual members of Congress (with the exception of certain statements by the chairmen of the responsible committees). *See* Binns v. United States, 194 U.S. 486, 495 (1904) (distinguishing committee reports from "debates in Congress," which "generally . . . are not appropriate sources of information from which to discover the meaning of the language of a statute passed by that body"); *see also* Baade, *supra*, 69 TEX. L. REV. at 1068 (noting support for the same distinction in 2 J.G. SUTHERLAND, STATUTES AND STATUTORY CONSTRUCTION § 470 (John Lewis 2d ed. 1904)). Over the next quarter century, the Court continued to draw this distinction. Here, for instance, is how the Court summarized its practice as of 1921:

> "By repeated decisions of this court it has come to be well established that the debates in Congress expressive of the views and motives of individual members are not a safe guide, and hence may not be resorted to, in ascertaining the meaning and purpose of the law-making body. But reports of committees of House or Senate stand upon a more solid footing, and may be regarded as an exposition of the legislative intent in a case where otherwise the meaning of a statute is obscure. And this has been extended to include explanatory statements in the nature of a supplemental report made by the committee member in charge of a bill in course of passage."

Duplex Printing Press Co. v. Deering, 254 U.S. 443, 474–75 (1921) (citations omitted).[6]

---

[6] In one case from 1911, the Court did seem to be using records of the debates on the Sherman Antitrust Act of 1890 to identify "the main cause which led to the legislation." *See* Standard Oil Co. v. United States, 221 U.S. 1, 50 (1911) (asserting that the legislative debates "conclusively show" that the statute grew out of concerns about "the economic condition of the times, that is, the vast accumulation of wealth in the hands of corporations and individuals, the enormous development of corporate organization, the facility for combination which such organizations afforded, the fact that the facility was being used, and that combinations known as trusts were being multiplied, and the widespread impression that their power had been and would be exerted to oppress individuals and injure the public generally"). But the Court acknowledged that "debates may not be used as a means for interpreting a statute," and it pretended that it was using them simply as a source of information about "the history of the period when [the Sherman Act] was adopted." *Id.*; *cf.* ESKRIDGE, *supra*, at 394 n.12 (citing *Johnson v. Southern Pacific Co.*, 196 U.S. 1, 20 (1904), where the Supreme Court referred not only to committee reports and drafting history but also to "the debates in the Senate on the

By the 1930s, though, the Court was moving away from any categorical distinction between statements of individual legislators in debate and statements made on behalf of legislative committees. As the Court noted in one case from 1931, even individual legislators' statements could sometimes be combined to show a consensus about a statute's purpose, which in turn could shed light on the intended meaning of the statute's provisions. *See* FTC v. Raladam Co., 283 U.S. 643, 650 (1931) ("It is true, at least generally, that statements made in debate cannot be used as aids to the construction of a statute. But the fact that throughout the consideration of this legislation there was common agreement in the debate as to the great purpose of the act, may properly be considered in determining what that purpose was and what were the evils sought to be remedied."). A few years later, the Court provided the following summary of its evolving views:

> "Where the meaning of legislation is doubtful or obscure, resort may be had in its interpretation to reports of Congressional committees which have considered the measure; to exposition of the bill on the floor of Congress by those in charge of or sponsoring the legislation; to comparison of successive drafts or amendments of the measure; and to the debates in general in order to show common agreement on purpose as distinguished from interpretation of particular phraseology."

Wright v. Vinton Branch of the Mountain Trust Bank of Roanoke, 300 U.S. 440, 463 n.8 (1937) (citations omitted); *see also, e.g.*, Apex Hosiery Co. v. Leader, 310 U.S. 469, 495 n.15 (1940) ("The unanimity with which foes and supporters of the bill spoke of its aims . . . permit use of the debates in interpreting the purpose of the act.").

Because the records of legislative debates and hearings often are much more voluminous than committee reports, the Court's willingness to consult them greatly expanded the occasions on which legislative history might be relevant to statutory interpretation. In the 1940s, the Court also displayed "a tendency to decrease the measure of the ambiguity which originally justified resort to legislative history." Robert H. Jackson, *The Meaning of Statutes: What Congress Says or What the Court Says*, 34 A.B.A.J. 535, 538 (1948); *see also* Harrison v. N. Trust Co., 317 U.S. 476, 479 (1943) ("[W]ords are inexact tools at best, and for that reason there is wisely no rule of law forbidding resort to explanatory legislative history no matter how clear the words may appear on superficial examination." (internal quotation marks omitted)); United States v. Am. Trucking Ass'ns, 310 U.S. 534, 543–44 (1940) (launching the Court on this path). The result of these twin developments was a "sudden efflorescence of citations of legislative materials in briefs and

---

report of its committee"); Annotation, *Resort to Constitutional or Legislative Debates, Committee Reports, Journals, Etc., as Aid in Construction of Constitution or Statute*, 70 A.L.R. 5, 26–30 (1931) (reporting "considerable conflict and inconsistency among the authorities" about whether courts construing ambiguous statutes could properly resort to the legislative debates "for some purposes at least").

opinions." HENRY M. HART, JR. & ALBERT M. SACKS, THE LEGAL PROCESS: BASIC PROBLEMS IN THE MAKING AND APPLICATION OF LAW 1237 (tent. ed. 1958) (William N. Eskridge, Jr. & Philip P. Frickey eds., 1994); *see also* Parrillo, *supra*, 123 YALE L.J. at 287–300 (presenting quantitative and qualitative evidence that "legislative history became a normal and routine interpretive source in federal statutory interpretation just around 1940").

In a 1948 speech to the American Law Institute, Justice Robert Jackson sounded an alarm about the Court's expanding reliance upon legislative history. Under current interpretive practices, he warned, the formal text of a statute "is no longer a safe basis on which a lawyer may advise his client." The lawyer also needed to consult "all of the committee reports on the bill, and on all its antecedents, and all that its supporters and opponents said in debate," and then try to "predict what part of the conflicting views will likely appeal to a majority of the Court." Jackson, *supra*, 34 A.B.A.J. at 538. Justice Jackson expressed concern that "[t]he average law office cannot afford to collect, house and index all this material," and that the Court was therefore "put[ting] knowledge of the law practically out of reach of all except the Government and a few law offices." *Id.* He also worried about the inconclusiveness of most legislative history and its potential to "introduce[ ] the policy controversies that generated the Act into the deliberations of the Court itself." *Id.* Ultimately, Justice Jackson settled on the position that "[r]esort to legislative history is only justified where the face of the Act is inescapably ambiguous," and that even then "we should not go beyond Committee reports." *Schwegmann Bros. v. Calvert Distillers Corp.*, 341 U.S. 384, 395–96 (1951) (Jackson, J., concurring) (criticizing selective reliance upon statements from floor debates and asserting that "[i]t is the business of Congress to sum up its own debates in its legislation"); *see also* United States v. Pub. Utils. Comm'n, 345 U.S. 295, 296 (1953) (Jackson, J., concurring) (criticizing the majority's use of "statements of witnesses at [legislative] hearings" to try to determine "what Congress probably had in mind," and asserting that neither the lower court nor the respondent's lawyer "had access to the material used by the Court today"); *cf.* HART & SACKS, *supra*, at 1248–52 (arguing that materials of the sort used by the Court in the *Public Utilities Commission* case were more accessible to lawyers than Justice Jackson thought).

Notwithstanding Justice Jackson's concerns, though, the federal judiciary in general and the Supreme Court in particular put ever-increasing emphasis upon legislative history in statutory interpretation. In 1960, Chief Justice Warren opined that "frequently the legislative history of a statute is the most fruitful source of instruction as to its proper interpretation . . . ." *Flora v. United States*, 362 U.S. 145, 151 (1960). Over the course of the next two decades, moreover, the fruitfulness of research into legislative history seemed to multiply. *See* ESKRIDGE, *supra*, at 218 (describing the Court's approach to legislative history before 1962 as "fairly cautious" when compared to the approach of the later 1960s and the 1970s); *see also* William N. Eskridge, Jr. & Lauren E. Baer, *The Continuum of Deference: Supreme Court Treatment of Agency Statutory Interpretations from* Chevron *to* Hamdan, 96 GEO. L.J. 1083, 1194 (2008) ("Everyone on the Burger Court relied lavishly on legislative history . . . .").

This was true in at least two different ways. First, members of the later Warren Court and the Burger Court seemed somewhat more willing than their predecessors to let legislative history persuade them that statutory language meant something other than what the face of the statute seemed to say. *See, e.g.*, Train v. Colorado Public Interest Research Group, 426 U.S. 1 (1976) (reading the term "radioactive materials" in the Federal Water Pollution Control Act to come with a detailed qualification that was identified in a committee report but did not appear in the statutory text); *see also* William N. Eskridge, Jr., *The New Textualism*, 37 UCLA L. REV. 621, 628 (1990) (citing "a significant number of cases" between 1962 and 1986 in which "the Court has pretty much admitted that it was displacing plain meaning with apparent legislative intent or purpose gleaned from legislative history"); *cf. id.* at 627 ("In almost all of the leading plain meaning cases of the Warren and Burger Courts, the Court checked the legislative history to be certain that its confidence in the clear text did not misread the legislature's intent."). Second, the Court expanded the categories of legislative history on which it was willing to rely when the face of a statute seemed unclear and the Court was choosing between alternative constructions. By the 1970s and early 1980s, the Court was drawing conclusions about Congress's collective intentions not only from committee reports, floor debates, and drafting history, but also from testimony offered by witnesses in committee hearings and even (on occasion) colloquies among legislators that occurred long after Congress had enacted the statute in question. ESKRIDGE, *supra*, at 220–21; *see also, e.g.*, N.Y. State Dep't of Soc. Servs. v. Dublino, 413 U.S. 405, 416 n.19 (1973) (asserting that two colloquies in 1972 between legislators who had participated in enacting a statute five years earlier were "[p]erhaps the most revealing legislative expressions" about the intended meaning of that statute). The fact that certain applications of statutory language had *not* been discussed in committee hearings or floor debates also mattered more often than it had in the past. *See* ESKRIDGE, *supra*, at 220–21.

In the 1980s and 1990s, so-called "textualists" strongly criticized these practices. As we shall see in Section C of this chapter, indeed, Justice Scalia called for judges not simply to become more cautious about using legislative history, but to stop considering it at all (or at least to give it no special status as an indicator of legislative intent, and to consider it on the same terms as learned commentary prepared by people outside the legislative process). Although the Court as a whole did not accept this invitation to revert to the practices described in the late nineteenth-century treatises quoted above, the Court did become more cautious both about drawing inferences from snippets of legislative history and about allowing even the most reliable-seeming legislative history to trump seemingly unambiguous statutory language. *See, e.g.*, Adrian Vermeule, *Interpretation, Empiricism, and the Closure Problem*, 66 U. CHI. L. REV. 698, 705 (1999) (noting that "the Court's use of legislative history . . . reached an apogee during the Burger Court, and declined . . . after Justice Scalia joined the Court [in 1986]"); *cf.* James J. Brudney & Corey Ditslear, *Canons of Construction and the Elusive Quest for Neutral Reasoning*, 58 VAND. L. REV. 1, 35 & n.130 (2005) (reporting an empirical study of Supreme Court decisions about workplace law, and finding that in each five-year interval from 1969 through 1988 more than 42 percent of the majority opinions relied on legislative history, while the corresponding figure for each five-year interval from 1989 through 2002 was between 22 and 25 percent).

More recently, changes in the Supreme Court's membership have continued to move the Court in a more textualist direction, but the current Justices have a range of views about the use of legislative history in statutory interpretation.[7] As for the United States Courts of Appeals, a study of all published majority opinions from 1965 to 2011 found that since 1986, circuit judges appointed by Republican presidents have been "less likely to cite statements from floor debates or committee hearings than their Democratic counterparts," and circuit judges appointed after 1980 (whether by a Republican or a Democrat) have been "less likely to cite such statements than their earlier-appointed counterparts." Stuart Minor Benjamin & Kristen M. Renberg, *The Paradoxical Impact of Scalia's Campaign Against Legislative History*, 105 CORNELL L. REV. 1023, 1028 (2020). Interestingly, however, both Republican appointees and judges appointed after 1980 have been "*more* likely than their counterparts to cite committee reports," which traditionally have been regarded as the most reliable type of legislative history. *Id.* (emphasis added). The authors of the study concluded that Justice Scalia's attacks on the use of legislative history caused many circuit judges to think about the topic and to correct some of the perceived excesses of the 1970s, but not to reject legislative history altogether. *See id.* at 1027–28, 1083–84.

PRELIMINARY NOTE FOR *UNITED STEELWORKERS V. WEBER*

In the 1960s and 1970s, relatively few people thought much about the theory of statutory interpretation. In the 1980s, by contrast, both judges and scholars paid a great deal of attention to the subject. The next

[7] Arguments based on legislative history are unlikely to appeal to either Justice Thomas or Justice Gorsuch. As of this writing (July 2023), it is too early to say whether Justice Barrett will be in the same camp. Chief Justice Roberts and Justice Alito have been described as "textualist-leaning," but they do not categorically oppose references to legislative history. *See* Anita S. Krishnakumar, *Backdoor Purposivism*, 69 DUKE L.J. 1275, 1295–1302 (2020). Justice Kavanaugh may not either. Justices Kagan and Sotomayor both use legislative history, and Justice Jackson seems likely to do so as well.

case, *United Steelworkers v. Weber*, 443 U.S. 193 (1979), has been called "the most important decision" that helped to spark this renewed attention. Philip P. Frickey, *From the Big Sleep to the Big Heat: The Revival of Theory in Statutory Interpretation*, 77 MINN. L. REV. 241, 245 (1992); *see also* Robert J. Gregory, *Overcoming Text in an Age of Textualism: A Practitioner's Guide to Arguing Cases of Statutory Interpretation*, 35 AKRON L. REV. 451, 459 (2002) (noting that many of President Reagan's appointees to the federal bench "took a direct aim at cases such as *Weber* and the interpretive method that produced them").

To the extent that *Weber* involved debates about the use of legislative history, the debates were not about whether the legislative history of a statute can properly affect what courts understand the statute to mean. In 1979, when *Weber* was decided, all of the Justices would have said that it can. In *Weber*, though, Justice Rehnquist's dissent conducted a detailed review of the relevant statute's legislative history in an effort to show that the majority opinion was mischaracterizing the legislative history that the majority cited. Later, modern textualists started treating concerns about such mischaracterization as one of the reasons why interpreters should not consider legislative history at all.

The statute at issue in *Weber* was Title VII of the Civil Rights Act of 1964, 78 Stat. 253 (codified as amended at 42 U.S.C. §§ 2000e *et seq.*). As amended in 1972, § 703 of that statute included the following provisions:

> (a) It shall be an unlawful employment practice for an employer—
>
> (1) to fail or refuse to hire or to discharge any individual, or otherwise to discriminate against any individual with respect to his compensation, terms, conditions, or privileges of employment, because of such individual's race, color, religion, sex, or national origin; or
>
> (2) to limit, segregate, or classify his employees or applicants for employment in any way which would deprive or tend to deprive any individual of employment opportunities or otherwise adversely affect his status as an employee, because of such individual's race, color, religion, sex, or national origin.
>
> (b) It shall be an unlawful employment practice for an employment agency to fail or refuse to refer for employment, or otherwise to discriminate against, any individual because of his race, color, religion, sex, or national origin, or to classify or refer for employment any individual on the basis of his race, color, religion, sex, or national origin.
>
> (c) It shall be an unlawful employment practice for a labor organization—
>
> (1) to exclude or to expel from its membership, or otherwise to discriminate against, any individual because of his race, color, religion, sex, or national origin;

(2) to limit, segregate, or classify its membership or applicants for membership, or to classify or fail or refuse to refer for employment any individual, in any way which would deprive or tend to deprive any individual of employment opportunities, or would limit such employment opportunities or otherwise adversely affect his status as an employee or as an applicant for employment, because of such individual's race, color, religion, sex, or national origin; or

(3) to cause or attempt to cause an employer to discriminate against an individual in violation of this section.

(d) It shall be an unlawful employment practice for any employer, labor organization, or joint labor-management committee controlling apprenticeship or other training or retraining, including on-the-job training programs to discriminate against any individual because of his race, color, religion, sex, or national origin in admission to, or employment in, any program established to provide apprenticeship or other training.

(e) Notwithstanding any other provision of this title, . . . it shall not be an unlawful employment practice for an employer to hire and employ employees, for an employment agency to classify, or refer for employment any individual, for a labor organization to classify its membership or to classify or refer for employment any individual, or for an employer, labor organization, or joint labor-management committee controlling apprenticeship or other training or retraining programs to admit or employ any individual in any such program, on the basis of his religion, sex, or national origin in those certain instances where religion, sex, or national origin is a bona fide occupational qualification reasonably necessary to the normal operation of that particular business or enterprise . . . .

. . . .

(h) Notwithstanding any other provision of this title, it shall not be an unlawful employment practice for an employer to apply different standards of compensation, or different terms, conditions, or privileges of employment pursuant to a bona fide seniority or merit system, or a system which measures earnings by quantity or quality of production or to employees who work in different locations, provided that such differences are not the result of an intention to discriminate because of race, color, religion, sex, or national origin, nor shall it be an unlawful employment practice for an employer to give and to act upon the results of any professionally developed ability test provided that such test, its administration or action upon the results is not designed, intended or used to discriminate because of race, color, religion, sex or national origin. . . .

(i) Nothing contained in this title shall apply to any business or enterprise on or near an Indian reservation with respect to any publicly announced employment practice of such business or enterprise under which a preferential treatment is given to any individual because he is an Indian living on or near a reservation.

(j) Nothing contained in this title shall be interpreted to require any employer, employment agency, labor organization, or joint labor-management committee subject to this subchapter to grant preferential treatment to any individual or to any group because of the race, color, religion, sex, or national origin of such individual or group on account of an imbalance which may exist with respect to the total number or percentage of persons of any race, color, religion, sex, or national origin employed by any employer, referred or classified for employment by any employment agency or labor organization, admitted to membership or classified by any labor organization, or admitted to, or employed in, any apprenticeship or other training program, in comparison with the total number or percentage of persons of such race, color, religion, sex, or national origin in any community, State, section, or other area, or in the available work force in any community, State, section, or other area.

Section 704(b) added:

> It shall be an unlawful employment practice for an employer, labor organization, employment agency, or joint labor-management committee controlling apprenticeship or other training or retraining, including on-the-job training programs, to print or publish or cause to be printed or published any notice or advertisement relating to employment by such an employer or membership in or any classification or referral for employment by such a labor organization, or relating to any classification or referral for employment by such an employment agency, or relating to admission to, or employment in, any program established to provide apprenticeship or other training by such a joint labor-management committee, indicating any preference, limitation, specification, or discrimination, based on race, color, religion, sex, or national origin, except that such a notice or advertisement may indicate a preference, limitation, specification, or discrimination based on religion, sex, or national origin when religion, sex, or national origin is a bona fide occupational qualification for employment.

Section 706 set out provisions for the prevention of these unlawful employment practices, including a provision authorizing private lawsuits under certain circumstances. Section 701 defined some of the terms used in Title VII, including "employer," "employment agency," and "labor organization."

United Steelworkers v. Weber

443 U.S. 193 (1979)

■ *JUSTICE BRENNAN delivered the opinion of the Court:*

Challenged here is the legality of an affirmative action plan—collectively bargained by an employer and a union—that reserves for black employees 50% of the openings in an in-plant craft-training program until the percentage of black craft-workers in the plant is commensurate with the percentage of blacks in the local labor force. The question for decision is whether Congress, in Title VII of the Civil Rights Act of 1964, . . . as amended, . . . left employers and unions in the private sector free to take such race-conscious steps to eliminate manifest racial imbalances in traditionally segregated job categories. We hold that Title VII does not prohibit such race-conscious affirmative action plans.

I

In 1974, petitioner United Steelworkers of America (USWA) and petitioner Kaiser Aluminum & Chemical Corp. (Kaiser) entered into a master collective-bargaining agreement covering terms and conditions of employment at 15 Kaiser plants. The agreement contained, *inter alia*, an affirmative action plan designed to eliminate conspicuous racial imbalances in Kaiser's then almost exclusively white craft-work forces. Black craft-hiring goals were set for each Kaiser plant equal to the percentage of blacks in the respective local labor forces. To enable plants to meet these goals, on-the-job training programs were established to teach unskilled production workers—black and white—the skills necessary to become craftworkers. The plan reserved for black employees 50% of the openings in these newly created in-plant training programs.

This case arose from the operation of the plan at Kaiser's plant in Gramercy, La. Until 1974, Kaiser hired as craftworkers for that plant only persons who had had prior craft experience. Because blacks had long been excluded from craft unions, few were able to present such credentials. As a consequence, prior to 1974 only 1.83% (5 out of 273) of the skilled craftworkers at the Gramercy plant were black, even though the work force in the Gramercy area was approximately 39% black.

Pursuant to the national agreement Kaiser altered its craft-hiring practice in the Gramercy plant. Rather than hiring already trained outsiders, Kaiser established a training program to train its production workers to fill craft openings. Selection of craft trainees was made on the basis of seniority, with the proviso that at least 50% of the new trainees were to be black until the percentage of black skilled craftworkers in the Gramercy plant approximated the percentage of blacks in the local labor force.

During 1974, the first year of the operation of the Kaiser-USWA affirmative action plan, 13 craft trainees were selected from Gramercy's production work force. Of these, seven were black and six white. The most senior black selected into the program had less seniority than several white production workers whose bids for admission were rejected. Thereafter one of those white production workers, respondent Brian Weber (hereafter respondent), instituted this class action in the United States District Court for the Eastern District of Louisiana.

The complaint alleged that the filling of craft trainee positions at the Gramercy plant pursuant to the affirmative action program had resulted in junior black employees' receiving training in preference to senior white employees, thus discriminating against respondent and other similarly situated white employees in violation of §§ 703(a) and (d) of Title VII. The District Court held that the plan violated Title VII, entered a judgment in favor of the plaintiff class, and granted a permanent injunction prohibiting Kaiser and the USWA "from denying plaintiffs, Brian F. Weber and all other members of the class, access to on-the-job training programs on the basis of race." A divided panel of the Court of Appeals for the Fifth Circuit affirmed, holding that all employment preferences based upon race, including those preferences incidental to bona fide affirmative action plans, violated Title VII's prohibition against racial discrimination in employment. 563 F.2d 216 (1977). . . . We reverse.

II

We emphasize at the outset the narrowness of our inquiry. Since the Kaiser-USWA plan does not involve state action, this case does not present an alleged violation of the Equal Protection Clause of the Fourteenth Amendment. Further, since the Kaiser-USWA plan was adopted voluntarily, we are not concerned with what Title VII requires or with what a court might order to remedy a past proved violation of the Act. The only question before us is the narrow statutory issue of whether Title VII *forbids* private employers and unions from voluntarily agreeing upon bona fide affirmative action plans that accord racial preferences in the manner and for the purpose provided in the Kaiser-USWA plan. That question was expressly left open in *McDonald v. Santa Fe Trail Transp. Co.*, 427 U.S. 273, 281 n. 8 (1976), which held, in a case not involving affirmative action, that Title VII protects whites as well as blacks from certain forms of racial discrimination.

Respondent argues that Congress intended in Title VII to prohibit all race-conscious affirmative action plans. Respondent's argument rests upon a literal interpretation of §§ 703(a) and (d) of the Act. Those sections make it unlawful to "discriminate . . . because of . . . race" in hiring and in the selection of apprentices for training programs. Since, the argument runs, *McDonald* settled that Title VII forbids discrimination against whites as well as blacks, and since the Kaiser-USWA affirmative action plan operates to discriminate against white employees solely because they are white, it follows that the Kaiser-USWA plan violates Title VII.

Respondent's argument is not without force. But it overlooks the significance of the fact that the Kaiser-USWA plan is an affirmative action plan voluntarily adopted by private parties to eliminate traditional patterns of racial segregation. In this context respondent's reliance upon a literal construction of §§ 703(a) and (d) and upon *McDonald* is misplaced. It is a "familiar rule that a thing may be within the letter of the statute and yet not within the statute, because not within its spirit nor within the intention of its makers." *Holy Trinity Church v. United States*, 143 U.S. 457, 459 (1892). The prohibition against racial discrimination in §§ 703(a) and (d) of Title VII must therefore be read against the background of the legislative history of Title VII and the historical context from which the Act arose. See *Train v. Colorado Public Interest Research Group*, 426 U.S. 1, 10 (1976); . . . *United States v. American Trucking Assns.*, 310 U.S. 534, 543–544 (1940). Examination of those sources makes clear that an interpretation of the sections that forbade all race-conscious affirmative action would "bring about an end completely at variance with the purpose of the statute" and must be rejected. *United States v. Public Utilities Comm'n*, 345 U.S. 295, 315 (1953). . . .

Congress' primary concern in enacting the prohibition against racial discrimination in Title VII of the Civil Rights Act of 1964 was with "the plight of the Negro in our economy." 110 Cong. Rec. 6548 (1964) (remarks of Sen. Humphrey). Before 1964, blacks were largely relegated to "unskilled and semi-skilled jobs." *Ibid.* (remarks of Sen. Humphrey); *id.* at 7204 (remarks of Sen. Clark); *id.* at 7379–7380 (remarks of Sen. Kennedy). Because of automation the number of such jobs was rapidly decreasing. See *id.* at 6548 (remarks of Sen. Humphrey); *id.* at 7204 (remarks of Sen. Clark). As a consequence, "the relative position of the Negro worker [was] steadily worsening. In 1947 the nonwhite unemployment rate was only 64 percent higher than the white rate; in 1962 it was 124 percent higher." *Id.* at 6547 (remarks of Sen. Humphrey). See also *id.* at 7204 (remarks of Sen. Clark). Congress considered this a serious social problem. As Senator Clark told the Senate:

> "The rate of Negro unemployment has gone up consistently as compared with white unemployment for the past 15 years. This is a social malaise and a social situation which we should not tolerate. That is one of the principal reasons why the bill should pass." *Id.* at 7220.

Congress feared that the goals of the Civil Rights Act—the integration of blacks into the mainstream of American society—could not be achieved unless this trend were reversed. And Congress recognized that that would not be possible unless blacks were able to secure jobs "which have a future." *Id.* at 7204 (remarks of Sen. Clark). See also *id.* at 7379–7380 (remarks of Sen. Kennedy). As Senator Humphrey explained to the Senate:

> "What good does it do a Negro to be able to eat in a fine restaurant if he cannot afford to pay the bill? What good does it do him to be accepted in a hotel that is too expensive for his modest income? How can a Negro child be motivated to take full advantage of integrated

educational facilities if he has no hope of getting a job where he can use that education?" *Id.* at 6547. . . .

These remarks echoed President Kennedy's original message to Congress upon the introduction of the Civil Rights Act in 1963.

> "There is little value in a Negro's obtaining the right to be admitted to hotels and restaurants if he has no cash in his pocket and no job." 109 Cong. Rec. 11159.

Accordingly, it was clear to Congress that "[t]he crux of the problem [was] to open employment opportunities for Negroes in occupations which have been traditionally closed to them," 10 Cong. Rec. 6548 (1964) (remarks of Sen. Humphrey), and it was to this problem that Title VII's prohibition against racial discrimination in employment was primarily addressed.

It plainly appears from the House Report accompanying the Civil Rights Act that Congress did not intend wholly to prohibit private and voluntary affirmative action efforts as one method of solving this problem. The Report provides:

> "No bill can or should lay claim to eliminating all of the causes and consequences of racial and other types of discrimination against minorities. There is reason to believe, however, that national leadership provided by the enactment of Federal legislation dealing with the most troublesome problems *will create an atmosphere conducive to voluntary or local resolution of other forms of discrimination.*" H.R. Rep. No. 914, 88th Cong., 1st Sess., pt. 1, p. 18 (1963) (emphasis supplied).

Given this legislative history, we cannot agree with respondent that Congress intended to prohibit the private sector from taking effective steps to accomplish the goal that Congress designed Title VII to achieve. The very statutory words intended as a spur or catalyst to cause "employers and unions to self-examine and to self-evaluate their employment practices and to endeavor to eliminate, so far as possible, the last vestiges of an unfortunate and ignominious page in this country's history," *Albemarle Paper Co. v. Moody*, 422 U.S. 405, 418 (1975), cannot be interpreted as an absolute prohibition against all private, voluntary, race-conscious affirmative action efforts to hasten the elimination of such vestiges.[4] It would be ironic indeed if a law triggered by a Nation's concern over centuries of racial injustice and intended to improve the lot of those who had "been excluded from the American dream for so long," 110 Cong. Rec. 6552 (1964) (remarks of Sen. Humphrey), constituted the first legislative prohibition of all voluntary, private, race-conscious efforts to abolish traditional patterns of racial segregation and hierarchy.

[4] The problem that Congress addressed in 1964 remains with us. In 1962, the nonwhite unemployment rate was 124% higher than the white rate. See 110 Cong. Rec. 6547 (1964) (remarks of Sen. Humphrey). In 1978, the black unemployment rate was 129% higher. See Monthly Labor Review, U. S. Department of Labor, Bureau of Labor Statistics 78 (Mar. 1979).

Our conclusion is further reinforced by examination of the language and legislative history of § 703(j) of Title VII. Opponents of Title VII raised two related arguments against the bill. First, they argued that the Act would be interpreted to *require* employers with racially imbalanced work forces to grant preferential treatment to racial minorities in order to integrate. Second, they argued that employers with racially imbalanced work forces would grant preferential treatment to racial minorities, even if not required to do so by the Act. See 110 Cong. Rec. 8618–8619 (1964) (remarks of Sen. Sparkman). Had Congress meant to prohibit all race-conscious affirmative action, as respondent urges, it easily could have answered both objections by providing that Title VII would not require or *permit* racially preferential integration efforts. But Congress did not choose such a course. Rather, Congress added § 703(j) which addresses only the first objection. The section provides that nothing contained in Title VII "shall be interpreted to *require* any employer . . . to grant preferential treatment . . . to any group because of the race . . . of such . . . group on account of" a *de facto* racial imbalance in the employer's work force. The section does *not* state that "nothing in Title VII shall be interpreted to *permit*" voluntary affirmative efforts to correct racial imbalances. The natural inference is that Congress chose not to forbid all voluntary race-conscious affirmative action.

The reasons for this choice are evident from the legislative record. Title VII could not have been enacted into law without substantial support from legislators in both Houses who traditionally resisted federal regulation of private business. Those legislators demanded as a price for their support that "management prerogatives[ ] and union freedoms . . . be left undisturbed to the greatest extent possible." H.R. Rep. No. 914, 88th Cong., 1st Sess., pt. 2, p. 29 (1963). Section 703(j) was proposed by Senator Dirksen to allay any fears that the Act might be interpreted in such a way as to upset this compromise. The section was designed to prevent § 703 of Title VII from being interpreted in such a way as to lead to undue "Federal Government interference with private businesses because of some Federal employee's ideas about racial balance or racial imbalance." 110 Cong. Rec. 14314 (1964) (remarks of Sen. Miller).[6] See also *id.* at 9881 (remarks of Sen. Allott); *id.* at 10520 (remarks of Sen. Carlson); *id.* at 11471 (remarks of Sen. Javits); *id.* at 12817 (remarks of Sen. Dirksen). Clearly, a prohibition against all voluntary, race-conscious, affirmative action efforts would disserve these ends. Such a prohibition would augment the powers of the Federal Government and

---

[6] Title VI of the Civil Rights Act of 1964, considered in *University of California Regents v. Bakke*, 438 U.S. 265 (1978), contains no provision comparable to § 703(j). This is because Title VI was an exercise of federal power over a matter in which the Federal Government was already directly involved: the prohibitions against race-based conduct contained in Title VI governed "program[s] or activit[ies] receiving Federal financial assistance." 42 U.S.C. § 2000d. Congress was legislating to assure federal funds would not be used in an improper manner. Title VII, by contrast, was enacted pursuant to the commerce power to regulate purely private decisionmaking and was not intended to incorporate and particularize the commands of the Fifth and Fourteenth Amendments. Title VII and Title VI, therefore, cannot be read *in pari materia*. . . .

diminish traditional management prerogatives while at the same time impeding attainment of the ultimate statutory goals. In view of this legislative history and in view of Congress' desire to avoid undue federal regulation of private businesses, use of the word "require" rather than the phrase "require or permit" in § 703(j) fortifies the conclusion that Congress did not intend to limit traditional business freedom to such a degree as to prohibit all voluntary, race-conscious affirmative action.[7]

We therefore hold that Title VII's prohibition in §§ 703(a) and (d) against racial discrimination does not condemn all private, voluntary, race-conscious affirmative action plans.

III

We need not today define in detail the line of demarcation between permissible and impermissible affirmative action plans. It suffices to hold that the challenged Kaiser-USWA affirmative action plan falls on the permissible side of the line. The purposes of the plan mirror those of the statute. Both were designed to break down old patterns of racial segregation and hierarchy. Both were structured to "open employment opportunities for Negroes in occupations which have been traditionally closed to them." 110 Cong. Rec. 6548 (1964) (remarks of Sen. Humphrey).[8]

At the same time, the plan does not unnecessarily trammel the interests of the white employees. The plan does not require the discharge of white workers and their replacement with new black hirees. Cf. *McDonald v. Santa Fe Trail Transp. Co.*, 427 U.S. 273 (1976). Nor does the plan create an absolute bar to the advancement of white employees;

---

7 Respondent argues that our construction of § 703 conflicts with various remarks in the legislative record. See, *e.g.*, 110 Cong. Rec. 7213 (1964) (Sens. Clark and Case); *id.* at 7218 (Sens. Clark and Case); *id.* at 6549 (Sen. Humphrey); *id.* at 8921 (Sen. Williams). We do not agree. In Senator Humphrey's words, these comments were intended as assurances that Title VII would not allow establishment of systems "to *maintain* racial balance in employment." *Id.* at 11848 (emphasis added). They were not addressed to temporary, voluntary, affirmative action measures undertaken to eliminate manifest racial imbalance in traditionally segregated job categories. Moreover, the comments referred to by respondent all preceded the adoption of § 703(j), 42 U.S.C. § 2000e–2(j). After § 703(j) was adopted, congressional comments were all to the effect that employers would not be *required* to institute preferential quotas to avoid Title VII liability, see, *e.g.*, 110 Cong. Rec. 12819 (1964) (remarks of Sen. Dirksen); *id.* at 13079–13080 (remarks of Sen. Clark); *id.* at 15876 (remarks of Rep. Lindsay). There was no suggestion after the adoption of § 703(j) that wholly voluntary, race-conscious, affirmative action efforts would in themselves constitute a violation of Title VII. On the contrary, as Representative MacGregor told the House shortly before the final vote on Title VII:

> "Important as the scope and extent of this bill is, it is also vitally important that all Americans understand what this bill does not cover.
>
> "Your mail and mine, your contacts and mine with our constituents, indicates a great degree of misunderstanding about this bill. People complain about . . . preferential treatment or quotas in employment. There is a mistaken belief that Congress is legislating in these areas in this bill. When we drafted this bill we excluded these issues largely because the problems raised by these controversial questions are more properly handled at a governmental level closer to the American people and by communities and individuals themselves." 110 Cong. Rec. 15893 (1964).

8 . . . . This is not to suggest that the freedom of an employer to undertake race-conscious affirmative action efforts depends on whether or not his effort is motivated by fear of liability under Title VII.

half of those trained in the program will be white. Moreover, the plan is a temporary measure; it is not intended to maintain racial balance, but simply to eliminate a manifest racial imbalance. Preferential selection of craft trainees at the Gramercy plant will end as soon as the percentage of black skilled craftworkers in the Gramercy plant approximates the percentage of blacks in the local labor force.

We conclude, therefore, that the adoption of the Kaiser-USWA plan for the Gramercy plant falls within the area of discretion left by Title VII to the private sector voluntarily to adopt affirmative action plans designed to eliminate conspicuous racial imbalance in traditionally segregated job categories. . . .

■ *JUSTICES POWELL and STEVENS took no part in the consideration or decision of these cases.*

■ *JUSTICE BLACKMUN, concurring:*

While I share some of the misgivings expressed in Mr. Justice Rehnquist's dissent concerning the extent to which the legislative history of Title VII clearly supports the result the Court reaches today, I believe that additional considerations, practical and equitable, only partially perceived, if perceived at all, by the 88th Congress, support the conclusion reached by the Court today, and I therefore join its opinion as well as its judgment.

I

In his dissent from the decision of the United States Court of Appeals for the Fifth Circuit, Judge Wisdom pointed out that this litigation arises from a practical problem in the administration of Title VII. The broad prohibition against discrimination places the employer and the union on what he accurately described as a "high tightrope without a net beneath them." 563 F.2d 216, 230. If Title VII is read literally, on the one hand they face liability for past discrimination against blacks, and on the other they face liability to whites for any voluntary preferences adopted to mitigate the effects of prior discrimination against blacks.

In this litigation, Kaiser denies prior discrimination but concedes that its past hiring practices may be subject to question. Although the labor force in the Gramercy area was approximately 39% black, Kaiser's work force was less than 15% black, and its craftwork force was less than 2% black. Kaiser had made some effort to recruit black painters, carpenters, insulators, and other craftsmen, but it continued to insist that those hired have five years' prior industrial experience, a requirement that arguably was not sufficiently job related to justify under Title VII any discriminatory impact it may have had. . . . The parties dispute the extent to which black craftsmen were available in the local labor market. They agree, however, that after critical reviews from the Office of Federal Contract Compliance, Kaiser and the Steelworkers established the training program in question here and modeled it along the lines of a Title VII consent decree later entered for the steel industry.

See *United States v. Allegheny-Ludlum Industries, Inc.*, 517 F.2d 826 (CA5 1975). Yet when they did this, respondent Weber sued, alleging that Title VII prohibited the program because it discriminated against him as a white person and it was not supported by a prior judicial finding of discrimination against blacks.

Respondent Weber's reading of Title VII, endorsed by the Court of Appeals, places voluntary compliance with Title VII in profound jeopardy. The only way for the employer and the union to keep their footing on the "tightrope" it creates would be to eschew all forms of voluntary affirmative action. Even a whisper of emphasis on minority recruiting would be forbidden. Because Congress intended to encourage private efforts to come into compliance with Title VII, see *Alexander v. Gardner-Denver Co.*, 415 U.S. 36, 44 (1974), Judge Wisdom concluded that employers and unions who had committed "arguable violations" of Title VII should be free to make reasonable responses without fear of liability to whites. 563 F.2d at 230. Preferential hiring along the lines of the Kaiser program is a reasonable response for the employer, whether or not a court, on these facts, could order the same step as a remedy. The company is able to avoid identifying victims of past discrimination, and so avoids claims for backpay that would inevitably follow a response limited to such victims. If past victims should be benefited by the program, however, the company mitigates its liability to those persons. Also, to the extent that Title VII liability is predicated on the "disparate effect" of an employer's past hiring practices, the program makes it less likely that such an effect could be demonstrated. Cf. *County of Los Angeles v. Davis*, 440 U.S. 625, 633–634 (1979) (hiring could moot a past Title VII claim). And the Court has recently held that work-force statistics resulting from private affirmative action were probative of benign intent in a "disparate treatment" case. *Furnco Construction Corp. v. Waters*, 438 U.S. 567, 579–580 (1978).

The "arguable violation" theory has a number of advantages. It responds to a practical problem in the administration of Title VII not anticipated by Congress. It draws predictability from the outline of present law and closely effectuates the purpose of the Act. Both Kaiser and the United States urge its adoption here. Because I agree that it is the soundest way to approach this case, my preference would be to resolve this litigation by applying it and holding that Kaiser's craft training program meets the requirement that voluntary affirmative action be a reasonable response to an "arguable violation" of Title VII.

II

The Court, however, declines to consider the narrow "arguable violation" approach and adheres instead to an interpretation of Title VII that permits affirmative action by an employer whenever the job category in question is "traditionally segregated." The sources cited suggest that the Court considers a job category to be "traditionally segregated" when there has been a societal history of purposeful exclusion of blacks from the job category, resulting in a persistent disparity between the proportion of blacks in the labor force and the proportion of blacks among those who hold jobs within the category.

"Traditionally segregated job categories," where they exist, sweep far more broadly than the class of "arguable violations" of Title VII. The Court's expansive approach is somewhat disturbing for me because, as Mr. Justice Rehnquist points out, the Congress that passed Title VII probably thought it was adopting a principle of nondiscrimination that would apply to blacks and whites alike. While setting aside that principle can be justified where necessary to advance statutory policy by encouraging reasonable responses as a form of voluntary compliance that mitigates "arguable violations," discarding the principle of nondiscrimination where no countervailing statutory policy exists appears to be at odds with the bargain struck when Title VII was enacted.

A closer look at the problem, however, reveals that in each of the principal ways in which the Court's "traditionally segregated job categories" approach expands on the "arguable violations" theory, still other considerations point in favor of the broad standard adopted by the Court, and make it possible for me to conclude that the Court's reading of the statute is an acceptable one.

A.

The first point at which the Court departs from the "arguable violations" approach is that it measures an individual employer's capacity for affirmative action solely in terms of a statistical disparity. The individual employer need not have engaged in discriminatory practices in the past. . . . As a practical matter, however, this difference may not be that great. While the "arguable violation" standard is conceptually satisfying, in practice the emphasis would be on "arguable" rather than on "violation." . . . To make the "arguable violation" standard work, it would have to be set low enough to permit the employer to prove it without obligating himself to pay a damages award. The inevitable tendency would be to avoid hairsplitting litigation by simply concluding that a mere disparity between the racial composition of the employer's work force and the composition of the qualified local labor force would be an "arguable violation," even though actual liability could not be established on that basis alone.

B.

The Court also departs from the "arguable violation" approach by permitting an employer to redress discrimination that lies wholly outside the bounds of Title VII. For example, Title VII provides no remedy for pre-Act discrimination, *Hazelwood School District v. United States*, 433 U.S. 299, 309–310 (1977); yet the purposeful discrimination that creates a "traditionally segregated job category" may have entirely predated the Act. More subtly, in assessing a prima facie case of Title VII liability, the composition of the employer's work force is compared to the composition of the pool of workers who meet valid job qualifications. [*Id.*] at 308 and n. 13 .... When a "job category" is traditionally segregated, however, that pool will reflect the effects of segregation, and the Court's approach goes further and permits a comparison with the composition of the labor force as a whole, in which minorities are more heavily represented.

Strong considerations of equity support an interpretation of Title VII that would permit private affirmative action to reach where Title VII itself does not. The bargain struck in 1964 with the passage of Title VII guaranteed equal opportunity for white and black alike, but where Title VII provides no remedy for blacks, it should not be construed to foreclose private affirmative action from supplying relief. It seems unfair for respondent Weber to argue, as he does, that the asserted scarcity of black craftsmen in Louisiana, the product of historic discrimination, makes Kaiser's training program illegal because it ostensibly absolves Kaiser of all Title VII liability. Absent compelling evidence of legislative intent, I would not interpret Title VII itself as a means of "locking in" the effects of segregation for which Title VII provides no remedy. Such a construction, as the Court points out, would be "ironic," given the broad remedial purposes of Title VII.

Mr. Justice Rehnquist's dissent, while it focuses more on what Title VII does not require than on what Title VII forbids, cites several passages that appear to express an intent to "lock in" minorities. In mining the legislative history anew, however, the dissent, in my view, fails to take proper account of our prior cases that have given that history a much more limited reading than that adopted by the dissent. For example, in *Griggs v. Duke Power Co.*, 401 U.S. 424, 434–436, and n. 11 (1971), the Court refused to give controlling weight to the memorandum of Senators Clark and Case which the dissent now finds so persuasive.... [T]he passages marshaled by the dissent are not so compelling as to merit the whip hand over the obvious equity of permitting employers to ameliorate the effects of past discrimination for which Title VII provides no direct relief.

III

I also think it significant that, while the Court's opinion does not foreclose other forms of affirmative action, the Kaiser program it approves is a moderate one. The opinion notes that the program does not afford an absolute preference for blacks, and that it ends when the racial composition of Kaiser's craftwork force matches the racial composition of the local population. It thus operates as a temporary tool for remedying past discrimination without attempting to "maintain" a previously achieved balance. See *University of California Regents v. Bakke*, 438 U.S. 265, 342 n. 17 (1978) (opinion of Brennan, White, Marshall, and Blackmun, JJ.). Because the duration of the program is finite, it perhaps will end even before the "stage of maturity when action along this line is no longer necessary." *Id.* at 403 (opinion of BLACKMUN, J.). And if the Court has misperceived the political will, it has the assurance that because the question is statutory Congress may set a different course if it so chooses.

■ *CHIEF JUSTICE BURGER, dissenting:*

The Court reaches a result I would be inclined to vote for were I a Member of Congress considering a proposed amendment of Title VII. I cannot join the Court's judgment, however, because it is contrary to the explicit language of the statute and arrived at by means wholly incompatible with long-established principles of separation of powers. Under the guise of statutory "construction," the Court effectively rewrites Title VII to achieve what it regards as a desirable result. It "amends" the statute to do precisely what both its sponsors and its opponents agreed the statute was *not* intended to do.

. . . . The Court blandly tells us that Congress could not really have meant what it said, for a "literal construction" would defeat the "purpose" of the statute—at least the congressional "purpose" as five Justices divine it today. But how are judges supposed to ascertain the *purpose* of a statute except through the words Congress used and the legislative history of the statute's evolution? One need not even resort to the legislative history to recognize what is apparent from the face of Title VII—that it is specious to suggest that § 703(j) contains a negative pregnant that permits employers to do what §§ 703(a) and (d) unambiguously and unequivocally *forbid* employers from doing. Moreover, as Mr. Justice Rehnquist's opinion . . . conclusively demonstrates, the legislative history makes equally clear that the supporters and opponents of Title VII reached an agreement about the statute's intended effect. That agreement, expressed so clearly in the language of the statute that no one should doubt its meaning, forecloses the reading which the Court gives the statute today. . . .

■ *JUSTICE REHNQUIST, with whom CHIEF JUSTICE BURGER joins, dissenting:*

. . . . The operative sections of Title VII prohibit racial discrimination in employment *simpliciter*. Taken in its normal meaning and as understood by all Members of Congress who spoke to the issue during the legislative debates, this language prohibits a covered employer from considering race when making an employment decision, whether the race be black or white. . . .

We have never wavered in our understanding that Title VII "prohibits *all* racial discrimination in employment, without exception for any group of particular employees." *McDonald v. Santa Fe Trail Transp. Co.*, 427 U.S. 273, 283 (1976) (emphasis in original). In *Griggs v. Duke Power Co.*, 401 U.S. 424, 431 (1971), our first occasion to interpret Title VII, a unanimous Court observed that "[d]iscriminatory preference, for any group, minority or majority, is precisely and only what Congress has proscribed." . . . .

Today, however, the Court . . . rejects "a literal construction of § 703(a)" in favor of newly discovered "legislative history," which leads it to a conclusion directly contrary to that compelled by the "uncontradicted legislative history" unearthed in *McDonald* and our other prior decisions. . . .

. . . It may be that one or more of the principal sponsors of Title VII would have preferred to see a provision allowing preferential treatment of minorities written into the bill. Such a provision, however, would have to have been expressly or impliedly excepted from Title VII's explicit prohibition on all racial discrimination in employment. There is no such exception in the Act. And a reading of the legislative debates concerning Title VII . . . demonstrates clearly that any legislator harboring an unspoken desire for such a provision could not possibly have succeeded in enacting it into law. . . .

II

Were Congress to act today specifically to prohibit the type of racial discrimination suffered by Weber, it would be hard pressed to draft language better tailored to the task than that found in § 703(d) of Title VII:

> "It shall be an unlawful employment practice for any employer, labor organization, or joint labor-management committee controlling apprenticeship or other training or retraining, including on-the-job training programs to discriminate against any individual because of his race, color, religion, sex, or national origin in admission to, or employment in, any program established to provide apprenticeship or other training." 78 Stat. 256, 42 U.S.C. § 2000e–2(d).

Equally suited to the task would be § 703(a)(2), which makes it unlawful for an employer to classify his employees "in any way which would deprive or tend to deprive any individual of employment opportunities or otherwise adversely affect his status as an employee, because of such individual's race, color, religion, sex, or national origin." 78 Stat. 255, 42 U.S.C. § 2000e–2(a)(2).

Entirely consistent with these two express prohibitions is the language of § 703(j) of Title VII, which provides that the Act is not to be interpreted "to require any employer . . . to grant preferential treatment to any individual or to any group because of the race . . . of such individual or group" to correct a racial imbalance in the employer's work force. 42 U.S.C. § 2000e–2(j). Seizing on the word "require," the Court infers that Congress must have intended to "permit" this type of racial discrimination. Not only is this reading of § 703(j) outlandish in the light of the flat prohibitions of §§ 703(a) and (d), but also, as explained in Part III, it is totally belied by the Act's legislative history.

Quite simply, Kaiser's racially discriminatory admission quota is flatly prohibited by the plain language of Title VII. This normally dispositive fact,[9] however, gives the Court only momentary pause. An "interpretation" of the statute upholding Weber's claim would, according to the Court, " 'bring about an end completely at variance with the purpose of the statute.' " *Ante* at 202, quoting *United States v. Public Utilities Comm'n*, 345 U.S. 295, 315 (1953). To support this conclusion, the Court calls upon the "spirit" of the Act, which it divines from passages in Title VII's legislative history indicating that enactment of the statute was prompted by Congress' desire " 'to open employment opportunities for Negroes in occupations which [had] been traditionally closed to them.' " *Ante* at 203, quoting 110 Cong. Rec. 6548 (1964) (remarks of Sen. Humphrey).[10] But the legislative history invoked by the Court to avoid the plain language of §§ 703(a) and (d) simply misses the point. To be sure, the reality of employment discrimination against Negroes provided the primary impetus for passage of Title VII. But this fact by no means supports the proposition that Congress intended to leave employers free to discriminate against white persons. In most cases, "[l]egislative history . . . is more vague than the statute we are called upon to interpret." *United States v. Public Utilities Comm'n*, 345 U.S. at 320 (Jackson, J., concurring). Here, however, the legislative history of Title VII is as clear as the language of §§ 703(a) and (d), and it irrefutably demonstrates that Congress meant precisely what it said in §§ 703(a) and (d)—that *no* racial discrimination in employment is permissible under Title VII, not even preferential treatment of minorities to correct racial imbalance.

III

. . . .

A

Introduced on the floor of the House of Representatives on June 20, 1963, the bill—H.R. 7152—that ultimately became the Civil Rights Act of 1964 contained no compulsory provisions directed at private discrimination in employment. The bill was promptly referred to the Committee on the Judiciary, where it was amended to include Title VII. With two exceptions, the bill reported by the House Judiciary Committee contained §§ 703(a) and (d) as they were ultimately enacted. Amendments subsequently adopted on the House floor added § 703's

[9] ". . . [W]hen words are free from doubt they must be taken as the final expression of the legislative intent, and are not to be added to or subtracted from by considerations drawn . . . from any extraneous source." *Caminetti v. United States*, 242 U.S. 470, 490 (1917).

[10] In holding that Title VII cannot be interpreted to prohibit use of Kaiser's racially discriminatory admission quota, the Court reasons that it would be "ironic" if a law inspired by the history of racial discrimination in employment against blacks forbade employers from voluntarily discriminating against whites in favor of blacks. I see no irony in a law that prohibits *all* voluntary racial discrimination, even discrimination directed at whites in favor of blacks. The evil inherent in discrimination against Negroes is that it is based on an immutable characteristic, utterly irrelevant to employment decisions. The characteristic becomes no less immutable and irrelevant, and discrimination based thereon becomes no less evil, simply because the person excluded is a member of one race rather than another. Far from ironic, I find a prohibition on all preferential treatment based on race as elementary and fundamental as the principle that "two wrongs do not make a right."

prohibition against sex discrimination and § 703(d)'s coverage of "on-the-job training."

After noting that "[t]he purpose of [Title VII] is to eliminate . . . discrimination in employment based on race, color, religion, or national origin," the Judiciary Committee's Report simply paraphrased the provisions of Title VII without elaboration. H.R. Rep., pt. 1, p. 26. In a separate Minority Report, however, opponents of the measure on the Committee advanced a line of attack which was reiterated throughout the debates in both the House and Senate and which ultimately led to passage of § 703(j). Noting that the word "discrimination" was nowhere defined in H.R. 7152, the Minority Report charged that the absence from Title VII of any reference to "racial imbalance" was a "public relations" ruse and that "the administration intends to rely upon its own construction of 'discrimination' as including the lack of racial balance . . . ." H.R. Rep., pt. 1, pp. 67–68. To demonstrate how the bill would operate in practice, the Minority Report posited a number of hypothetical employment situations, concluding in each example that the employer "*may be forced to hire according to race,* to 'racially balance' those who work for him *in every job classification* or be in violation of Federal law." *Id.* at 69 (emphasis in original).

When H.R. 7152 reached the House floor, the opening speech in support of its passage was delivered by Representative Celler, Chairman of the House Judiciary Committee and the Congressman responsible for introducing the legislation. A portion of that speech responded to criticism "seriously misrepresent[ing] what the bill would do and grossly distort[ing] its effects":

> "[T]he charge has been made that the Equal Employment Opportunity Commission to be established by title VII of the bill would have the power to prevent a business from employing and promoting the people it wished, and that a 'Federal inspector' could then order the hiring and promotion only of employees of certain races or religious groups. This description of the bill is entirely wrong. . . .
>
> . . . .
>
> "Even [a] court could not order that any preference be given to any particular race, religion or other group, but would be limited to ordering an end of discrimination. The statement that a Federal inspector could order the employment and promotion only of members of a specific racial or religious group is therefore patently erroneous.
>
> . . . .
>
> ". . . The Bill would do no more than prevent . . . employers from discriminating against *or in favor* of workers because of their race, religion, or national origin.

> "It is likewise not true that the Equal Employment Opportunity Commission would have power to rectify existing 'racial or religious imbalance' in employment by requiring the hiring of certain people without regard to their qualifications simply because they are of a given race or religion. Only actual discrimination could be stopped." 110 Cong. Rec. 1518 (1964) (emphasis added).

Representative Celler's construction of Title VII was repeated by several other supporters during the House debate.

Thus, the battle lines were drawn early in the legislative struggle over Title VII, with opponents of the measure charging that agencies of the Federal Government such as the Equal Employment Opportunity Commission (EEOC), by interpreting the word "discrimination" to mean the existence of "racial imbalance," would "require" employers to grant preferential treatment to minorities, and supporters responding that the EEOC would be granted no such power and that, indeed, Title VII prohibits discrimination "in favor of workers because of their race." Supporters of H.R. 7152 in the House ultimately prevailed by a vote of 290 to 130, and the measure was sent to the Senate to begin what became the longest debate in that body's history.

B

The Senate debate was broken into three phases: the debate on sending the bill to Committee, the general debate on the bill prior to invocation of cloture, and the debate following cloture.

1

When debate on the motion to refer the bill to Committee opened, opponents of Title VII in the Senate immediately echoed the fears expressed by their counterparts in the House, as is demonstrated by the following colloquy between Senators Hill and Ervin:

> "Mr. ERVIN. I invite attention to . . . Section [703(a)] . . . .
>
> . . . .
>
> "I ask the Senator from Alabama if the Commission could not tell an employer that he had too few employees, that he had limited his employment, and enter an order, under [Section 703(a)], requiring him to hire more persons, not because the employer thought he needed more persons, but because the Commission wanted to compel him to employ persons of a particular race.
>
> "Mr. HILL. The Senator is correct. That power is written into the bill. The employer could be forced to hire additional persons . . . ." 110 Cong. Rec. 4764 (1964).

Senator Humphrey, perhaps the primary moving force behind H.R. 7152 in the Senate, was the first to state the proponents' understanding of Title VII. Responding to a political advertisement charging that federal agencies were at liberty to interpret the word "discrimination" in Title VII to require racial balance, Senator Humphrey stated: "[T]he meaning of racial or religious discrimination is perfectly clear. . . . [I]t means a distinction in treatment given to different individuals because of their different race, religion, or national origin." *Id.* at 5423. Stressing that Title VII "does not limit the employer's freedom to hire, fire, promote or demote for any reasons—or no reasons—so long as his action is not based on race," Senator Humphrey further stated that "nothing in the bill would permit any official or court to require any employer or labor union to give preferential treatment to any minority group." *Ibid.*

After 17 days of debate, the Senate voted to take up the bill directly, without referring it to a committee. Consequently, there is no Committee Report in the Senate.

2

Formal debate on the merits of H.R. 7152 began on March 30, 1964. Supporters of the bill in the Senate had made elaborate preparations for this second round. Senator Humphrey, the majority whip, and Senator Kuchel, the minority whip, were selected as the bipartisan floor managers on the entire civil rights bill. Responsibility for explaining and defending each important title of the bill was placed on bipartisan "captains." Senators Clark and Case were selected as the bipartisan captains responsible for Title VII. Vaas, *Title VII: Legislative History*, 7 B.C. Ind. & Com. L. Rev. 431, 444–445 (1966) (hereinafter Title VII: Legislative History).

In the opening speech of the formal Senate debate on the bill, Senator Humphrey addressed the main concern of Title VII's opponents, advising that not only does Title VII not require use of racial quotas, *it does not permit* their use. "The truth," stated the floor leader of the bill, "is that this title forbids discriminating against anyone on account of race. This is the simple and complete truth about title VII." 110 Cong. Rec. 6549 (1964). Senator Humphrey continued:

> "Contrary to the allegations of some opponents of this title, there is nothing in it that will give any power to the Commission or to any court to require hiring, firing, or promotion of employees in order to meet a racial 'quota' or to achieve a certain racial balance.
>
> "That bugaboo has been brought up a dozen times; but it is nonexistent. In fact, *the very opposite is true. Title VII prohibits discrimination.* In effect, it says that race, religion and national origin are not to be used as the basis for hiring and firing. Title VII is designed to encourage hiring on the basis of ability and qualifications, not race or religion." *Ibid.* (emphasis added).

At the close of his speech, Senator Humphrey returned briefly to the subject of employment quotas: "It is claimed that the bill would require racial quotas for all hiring, when in fact it provides that race shall not be a basis for making personnel decisions." *Id.* at 6553.

Senator Kuchel delivered the second major speech in support of H.R. 7152. In addressing the concerns of the opposition, he observed that "[n]othing could be further from the truth" than the charge that "Federal inspectors" would be empowered under Title VII to dictate racial balance and preferential advancement of minorities. *Id.* at 6563. Senator Kuchel emphasized that seniority rights would in no way be affected by Title VII: "Employers and labor organizations could not discriminate *in favor of or against* a person because of his race, his religion, or his national origin. In such matters . . . the bill now before us . . . is color-blind." *Id.* at 6564 (emphasis added).

A few days later the Senate's attention focused exclusively on Title VII, as Senators Clark and Case rose to discuss the title of H.R. 7152 on which they shared floor "captain" responsibilities. In an interpretative memorandum submitted jointly to the Senate, Senators Clark and Case took pains to refute the opposition's charge that Title VII would result in preferential treatment of minorities. Their words were clear and unequivocal:

> "There is no requirement in title VII that an employer maintain a racial balance in his work force. On the contrary, any deliberate attempt to maintain a racial balance, whatever such a balance may be, would involve a violation of title VII because maintaining such a balance would require an employer to hire or to refuse to hire on the basis of race. It must be emphasized that discrimination is prohibited as to any individual." *Id.* at 7213.[18]

Of particular relevance to the instant litigation were their observations regarding seniority rights. As if directing their comments at Brian Weber, the Senators said:

> "Title VII would have no effect on established seniority rights. Its effect is prospective and not retrospective. Thus, for example, if a business has been discriminating in the past and as a result has an

---

[18] In obvious reference to the charge that the word "discrimination" in Title VII would be interpreted by federal agencies to mean the absence of racial balance, the interpretative memorandum stated:

> "[Section 703] prohibits discrimination in employment because of race, color, religion, sex, or national origin. It has been suggested that the concept of discrimination is vague. In fact it is clear and simple and has no hidden meanings. To discriminate is to make a distinction, to make a difference in treatment *or favor*, and those distinctions or differences in treatment *or favor* which are prohibited by [Section 703] are those which are based on any five of the forbidden criteria: race, color, religion, sex, and national origin." *Id.* at 7213 (emphasis added).

Earlier in his speech, Senator Clark introduced a memorandum prepared at his request by the Justice Department with the purpose of responding to criticisms of Title VII leveled by opponents of the measure, particularly Senator Hill. With regard to racial balance, the Justice Department stated:

> "Finally, it has been asserted that title VII would impose a requirement for 'racial balance.' This is incorrect. There is no provision . . . in title VII . . . that requires or authorizes any Federal agency or Federal court to require preferential treatment for any individual or any group for the purpose of achieving racial balance. . . . No employer is required to maintain any ratio of Negroes to whites . . . . On the contrary, any deliberate attempt to maintain a given balance would almost certainly run afoul of title VII because it would involve a failure or refusal to hire some individual because of his race, color, religion, sex, or national origin. What title VII seeks to accomplish, what the civil rights bill seeks to accomplish is equal treatment for all." *Id.* at 7207.

> all-white working force, when the title comes into effect the employer's obligation would be simply to fill future vacancies on a nondiscriminatory basis. He would not be obliged—*or indeed permitted*—to fire whites in order to hire Negroes, *or to prefer Negroes for future vacancies, or, once Negroes are hired, to give them special seniority rights at the expense of the white workers hired earlier.*" *Ibid.* (emphasis added).[19]

Thus, with virtual clairvoyance the Senate's leading supporters of Title VII anticipated precisely the circumstances of this case and advised their colleagues that the type of minority preference employed by Kaiser would violate Title VII's ban on racial discrimination. To further accentuate the point, Senator Clark introduced another memorandum dealing with common criticisms of the bill, including the charge that racial quotas would be imposed under Title VII. The answer was simple and to the point: "Quotas are themselves discriminatory." *Id.* at 7218.

Despite these clear statements from the bill's leading and most knowledgeable proponents, the fears of the opponents were not put to rest. Senator Robertson reiterated the view that "discrimination" could be interpreted by a federal "bureaucrat" to require hiring quotas. *Id.* at 7418–7420. Senators Smathers and Sparkman, while conceding that Title VII does not in so many words require the use of hiring quotas, repeated the opposition's view that employers would be coerced to grant preferential hiring treatment to minorities by agencies of the Federal Government. Senator Williams was quick to respond:

> "Those opposed to H.R. 7152 should realize that to hire a Negro solely because he is a Negro is racial discrimination, just as much as a 'white only' employment policy. Both forms of discrimination are prohibited by title VII of this bill. The language of that title simply states that race is not a qualification for employment. . . . Some people charge that H.R. 7152 favors the Negro, at the expense of the white majority. But how can the language of equality favor one race or one religion over another? Equality can have only one meaning,

---

[19] A Justice Department memorandum earlier introduced by Senator Clark, see n. 18, *supra*, expressed the same view regarding Title VII's impact on seniority rights of employees . . . .

The interpretation of Title VII contained in the memoranda introduced by Senator Clark totally refutes the Court's implied suggestion that Title VII would prohibit an employer from discriminating on the basis of race in order to *maintain* a racial balance in his work force, but would permit him to do so in order to *achieve* racial balance.

The maintain-achieve distinction is analytically indefensible in any event. Apparently, the Court is saying that an employer is free to *achieve* a racially balanced work force by discriminating against whites, but that once he has reached his goal, he is no longer free to discriminate in order to maintain that racial balance. . . .

Obviously, the Court is driven to this illogical position by the glaring statement, quoted in text, of Senators Clark and Case that "any deliberate attempt to *maintain* a racial balance . . . would involve a violation of title VII because *maintaining* such a balance would require an employer to hire or to refuse to hire on the basis of race." 110 Cong. Rec. 7213 (1964) (emphasis added). Achieving a certain racial balance, however, no less than maintaining such a balance, would require an employer to hire or to refuse to hire on the basis of race. . . .

and that meaning is self-evident to reasonable men. Those who say that equality means favoritism do violence to common sense." *Id.* at 8921.

Senator Williams concluded his remarks by noting that Title VII's only purpose is "the elimination of racial and religious discrimination in employment." *Ibid.* On May 25, Senator Humphrey again took the floor to defend the bill against "the well-financed drive by certain opponents to confuse and mislead the American people." *Id.* at 11846. Turning once again to the issue of preferential treatment, Senator Humphrey remained faithful to the view that he had repeatedly expressed:

> "The title does not provide that any preferential treatment in employment shall be given to Negroes or to any other persons or groups. It does not provide that any quota systems may be established to maintain racial balance in employment. In fact, *the title would prohibit preferential treatment for any particular group*, and any person, whether or not a member of any minority group, would be permitted to file a complaint of discriminatory employment practices." *Id.* at 11848 (emphasis added).

While the debate in the Senate raged, a bipartisan coalition under the leadership of Senators Dirksen, Mansfield, Humphrey, and Kuchel was working with House leaders and representatives of the Johnson administration on a number of amendments to H.R. 7152 designed to enhance its prospects of passage. The so-called "Dirksen-Mansfield" amendment was introduced on May 26 by Senator Dirksen as a substitute for the entire House-passed bill. The substitute bill, which ultimately became law, left unchanged the basic prohibitory language of §§ 703(a) and (d), as well as the remedial provisions in § 706(g). It added, however, several provisions defining and clarifying the scope of Title VII's substantive prohibitions. One of those clarifying amendments, § 703(j), was specifically directed at the opposition's concerns regarding racial balancing and preferential treatment of minorities, providing in pertinent part: "Nothing contained in [Title VII] shall be interpreted to require any employer . . . to grant preferential treatment to any individual or to any group because of the race . . . of such individual or group on account of" a racial imbalance in the employer's work force. 42 U.S.C. § 2000e–2(j).

The Court draws from the language of § 703(j) primary support for its conclusion that Title VII's blanket prohibition on racial discrimination in employment does not prohibit preferential treatment of blacks to correct racial imbalance. Alleging that opponents of Title VII had argued (1) that the Act would be interpreted to require employers with racially imbalanced work forces to grant preferential treatment to minorities and (2) that "employers with racially imbalanced work forces would grant preferential treatment to racial minorities even if not required to do so by the Act," *ante* at 205, the Court concludes that § 703(j) is responsive only to the opponents' first objection and that Congress therefore must have intended to permit voluntary, private discrimination against whites in order to correct racial imbalance.

Contrary to the Court's analysis, the language of § 703(j) is precisely tailored to the objection voiced time and again by Title VII's opponents. Not once during the 83 days of debate in the Senate did a speaker, proponent or opponent, suggest that the bill would allow employers *voluntarily* to prefer racial minorities over white persons. In light of Title VII's flat prohibition on discrimination "against any individual . . . because of such individual's race," § 703(a), 42 U.S.C. § 2000e–2(a), such a contention would have been, in any event, too preposterous to warrant response. Indeed, speakers on both sides of the issue, as the legislative history makes clear, recognized that Title VII would tolerate no *voluntary* racial preference, whether in favor of blacks or whites. The complaint consistently voiced by the opponents was that Title VII, particularly the word "discrimination," would be *interpreted* by federal agencies such as the EEOC to *require* the correction of racial imbalance through the granting of preferential treatment to minorities. Verbal assurances that Title VII would not require—indeed, would not permit—preferential treatment of blacks having failed, supporters of H.R. 7152 responded by proposing an amendment carefully worded to meet, and put to rest, the opposition's charge. Indeed, unlike §§ 703(a) and (d), which are by their terms directed at entities—*e.g.*, employers, labor unions—whose actions are restricted by Title VII's prohibitions, the language of § 703(j) is specifically directed at entities—federal agencies and courts—charged with the responsibility of interpreting Title VII's provisions.

In light of the background and purpose of § 703(j), the irony of invoking the section to justify the result in this case is obvious. The Court's frequent references to the "voluntary" nature of Kaiser's racially discriminatory admission quota bear no relationship to the facts of this case. Kaiser and the Steelworkers acted under pressure from an agency of the Federal Government, the Office of Federal Contract Compliance, which found that minorities were being "underutilized" at Kaiser's plants. That is, Kaiser's work force was racially imbalanced. Bowing to that pressure, Kaiser instituted an admissions quota preferring blacks over whites, thus confirming that the fears of Title VII's opponents were well founded. Today, § 703(j), adopted to allay those fears, is invoked by the Court to uphold imposition of a racial quota under the very circumstances that the section was intended to prevent.[25]

[25] In support of its reading of § 703(j), the Court argues that "a prohibition against all voluntary, race-conscious, affirmative action efforts would disserve" the important policy, expressed in the House Report on H.R. 7152, that Title VII leave "management prerogatives, and union freedoms . . . undisturbed to the greatest extent possible." H.R. Rep., pt. 2, p. 29, quoted *ante* at 206. The Court thus concludes that "Congress did not intend to limit traditional business freedom to such a degree as to prohibit all voluntary, race-conscious affirmative action." *Ante* at 207.

The sentences in the House Report immediately following the statement quoted by the Court, however, belie the Court's conclusion:

Section 703(j) apparently calmed the fears of most of the opponents; after its introduction, complaints concerning racial balance and preferential treatment died down considerably. Proponents of the bill, however, continued to reassure the opposition that its concerns were unfounded. . . .

Senator Saltonstall, Chairman of the Republican Conference of Senators participating in the drafting of the Dirksen-Mansfield amendment, spoke at length on the substitute bill. He advised the Senate that the Dirksen-Mansfield substitute, which included § 703(j), "provides no preferential treatment for any group of citizens. In fact, *it specifically prohibits such treatment.*" 110 Cong. Rec. 12691 (1964) (emphasis added).

. . . .

. . . [Eventually,] the Senate turned its attention to an amendment proposed by Senator Cotton to limit application of Title VII to employers of at least 100 employees. During the course of the Senate's deliberations on the amendment, Senator Cotton had a revealing discussion with Senator Curtis, also an opponent of Title VII. Both men expressed dismay that Title VII would prohibit preferential hiring of "members of a minority race in order to enhance their opportunity":

> "Mr. CURTIS. Is it not the opinion of the Senator that any individuals who provide jobs for a class of people who have perhaps not had sufficient opportunity for jobs should be commended rather than outlawed?
>
> "Mr. COTTON. Indeed it is." *Id.* at 13086.

Thus, in the only exchange on the Senate floor raising the possibility that an employer might wish to reserve jobs for minorities in order to assist them in overcoming their employment disadvantage, both speakers concluded that Title VII prohibits such, in the words of the Court, "voluntary, private, race-conscious efforts to abolish traditional patterns of racial segregation and hierarchy." *Ante* at 204. Immediately after this discussion, both Senator Dirksen and Senator Humphrey took the floor in defense of the 25-employee limit contained in the Dirksen-Mansfield substitute bill, and neither Senator disputed the conclusions of Senators Cotton and Curtis. The Cotton amendment was defeated. . . .

"Internal affairs of employers and labor organizations must not be interfered with *except to the limited extent that correction is required in discrimination practices*. Its primary task is to make certain that the channels of employment are open to persons *regardless of their race* and that jobs in companies or membership in unions are strictly filled on the basis of qualification." H.R. Rep., pt. 2, p. 29 (emphasis added).

Thus, the House Report invoked by the Court is perfectly consistent with the countless observations elsewhere in Title VII's voluminous legislative history that employers are free to make employment decisions without governmental interference, so long as those decisions are made *without regard to race*. The whole purpose of Title VII was to deprive employers of their "traditional business freedom" to discriminate on the basis of race. In this case, the "channels of employment" at Kaiser were hardly "open" to Brian Weber.

IV

Reading the language of Title VII, as the Court purports to do, "against the background of [its] legislative history . . . and the historical context from which the Act arose," *ante* at 201, one is led inescapably to the conclusion that Congress fully understood what it was saying and meant precisely what it said. Opponents of the civil rights bill did not argue that employers would be permitted under Title VII voluntarily to grant preferential treatment to minorities to correct racial imbalance. The plain language of the statute too clearly prohibited such racial discrimination to admit of any doubt. They argued, tirelessly, that Title VII would be interpreted by federal agencies and their agents to require unwilling employers to racially balance their work forces by granting preferential treatment to minorities. Supporters of H.R. 7152 responded, equally tirelessly, that the Act would not be so interpreted because not only does it not require preferential treatment of minorities, it also does not *permit* preferential treatment of any race for any reason. . . .

To put an end to the dispute, supporters of the civil rights bill drafted and introduced § 703(j). Specifically addressed to the opposition's charge, § 703(j) simply enjoins federal agencies and courts from interpreting Title VII to require an employer to prefer certain racial groups to correct imbalances in his work force. The section says nothing about voluntary preferential treatment of minorities because such racial discrimination is plainly proscribed by §§ 703(a) and (d). Indeed, had Congress intended to except voluntary, race-conscious preferential treatment from the blanket prohibition of racial discrimination in §§ 703(a) and (d), it surely could have drafted language better suited to the task than § 703(j). It knew how. Section 703(i) provides:

> "Nothing contained in [Title VII] shall apply to any business or enterprise on or near an Indian reservation with respect to any publicly announced employment practice of such business or enterprise under which a preferential treatment is given to any individual because he is an Indian living on or near a reservation." 78 Stat. 257, 42 U.S.C. § 2000e–2(i).

V

Our task in this case, like any other case involving the construction of a statute, is to give effect to the intent of Congress. To divine that intent, we traditionally look first to the words of the statute and, if they are unclear, then to the statute's legislative history. Finding the desired result hopelessly foreclosed by these conventional sources, the Court turns to a third source—the "spirit" of the Act. But close examination of what the Court proffers as the spirit of the Act reveals it as the spirit animating the present majority, not the 88th Congress. . . .

. . . In passing Title VII, Congress outlawed *all* racial discrimination, recognizing that no discrimination based on race is benign, that no action disadvantaging a person because of his color is affirmative. With today's holding, the Court introduces into Title VII a tolerance for the very evil that the law was intended to eradicate . . . .

NOTES AND QUESTIONS

1. The dissenters came close to accusing Justice Brennan of using the legislative history dishonestly. They suggested that the text of Title VII clearly prohibited racial quotas in on-the-job training programs, that the majority was using inapposite passages from the legislative history as an excuse to deviate from the text, that the majority had culled those passages less for the purpose of getting an accurate picture of the intended meaning of Title VII than for the purpose of supporting the policy result that the majority preferred, and that a fair reading of the complete legislative history reinforced what the dissenters viewed as the plain meaning of the statutory text. Some subsequent commentators have agreed that rather than genuinely using legislative history to inform its understanding of the deals that the final version of Title VII embodied, the *Weber* majority "simply . . . pull[ed] together a hodgepodge of statements . . . to rationalize its conclusions." Daniel B. Rodriguez & Barry R. Weingast, *The Positive Political Theory of Legislative History: New Perspectives on the 1964 Civil Rights Act and Its Interpretation*, 151 U. PA. L. REV. 1417, 1521 (2003). As we shall see in Section C below, this criticism feeds into one of Justice Scalia's arguments against using legislative history in statutory interpretation. *See* Antonin Scalia, *Common-Law Courts in a Civil-Law System: The Role of United States Federal Courts in Interpreting the Constitution and Laws*, *in* A MATTER OF INTERPRETATION: FEDERAL COURTS AND THE LAW 3, 35 (1997) (asserting that "[o]n balance," the judiciary's ability to invoke legislative history in support of particular outcomes "has facilitated rather than deterred decisions that are based upon the courts' policy preferences").

One cannot fairly evaluate this criticism of the majority's use of legislative history in *Weber* without carefully reviewing all of the materials that the Justices discussed.[8] But even if one ultimately concludes that the majority (or the dissent) was shading its take on the legislative history to support its own policy views, one should not automatically assume that the Court's performance in *Weber* is representative of how modern judges will always use legislative history. Even by the standards of the Supreme Court (whose docket has a much higher percentage of politically charged cases than the dockets of the lower federal courts), *Weber* was a highly charged case. Might the use of legislative history in other cases or by other courts tend to be less policy-driven? *Cf.* James J. Brudney & Corey Ditslear, *Liberal Justices' Reliance on Legislative History: Principle, Strategy, and the Scalia Effect*, 29 BERKELEY J. EMPLOYMENT & LABOR L. 117, 173 (2008) (studying majority opinions by liberal Justices of the Supreme Court in workplace-

---

[8] The daunting nature of that task is part of what led Justice Scalia to say that judges can use legislative history as a cover for their own policy judgments.

law cases from 1969 to 2006, and concluding that the use of legislative history in these opinions "appears to be far less politicized in practice than its critics have maintained").

2. Did the *Weber* majority simply read an unstated exception into Title VII, so that race-conscious affirmative-action plans of the sort in question were permissible even though they violated what the majority called "a literal construction of §§ 703(a) and (d)"? Or is there some way of reading the statutory language not to reach those plans in the first place?

With respect to the employment decisions that they cover, §§ 703(a)(1) and 703(d) both forbid employers "to discriminate against any individual . . . because of [his] race." As Justice Rehnquist emphasized, a pre-*Weber* case had unanimously held that Title VII "proscribe[s] racial discrimination in private employment against whites on the same terms as racial discrimination against nonwhites." *McDonald v. Santa Fe Trail Transportation Co.*, 427 U.S. 273, 278–80 (1976). But exactly what does that mean? If Kaiser had denied Brian Weber's application for the training program out of racial prejudice against white people, Mr. Weber would have had a good claim under Title VII. Under the facts of the actual case, though, is it equally clear that Kaiser "discriminate[d] against [Mr. Weber] . . . because of [his] race"?

Both in the context of the Equal Protection Clause of the federal Constitution and with respect to antidiscrimination law more generally, scholars have distinguished between "anticlassification" principles (which are offended whenever decisionmakers consider someone's race) and "antisubordination" principles (which reach beyond conscious racial classifications, but which do not categorically condemn all race-conscious decisionmaking and focus instead on whether a challenged practice enforces or alleviates the subordination of historically oppressed groups). *See, e.g.*, Reva B. Siegel, *Equality Talk: Antisubordination and Anticlassification Values in Constitutional Struggles Over* Brown, 117 HARV. L. REV. 1470 (2004). Justice Rehnquist's dissent in *Weber* took Title VII to establish a strong anticlassification principle that "prohibits a covered employer from considering race when making an employment decision." *Weber*, 443 U.S. at 220 (Rehnquist, J., dissenting). The majority, by contrast, took the statute to tolerate at least some race-consciousness in the service of anti-subordination goals. Does a statutory prohibition on "discriminat[ing] against any individual . . . because of [his] race" accommodate the latter view as well as the former view? *See* WILLIAM N. ESKRIDGE, JR., DYNAMIC STATUTORY INTERPRETATION 39 (1994) (acknowledging that the text can be given Justice Rehnquist's interpretation, but pointing out that "we tend to use the word ['discriminate'] only when some 'invidious' differentiation is involved," and noting that people debate whether race-conscious affirmative action is "invidious" in the relevant sense). Even if you oppose race-conscious affirmative action, and even if you call it racial "discrimination," isn't it at least a different *sort* of discrimination (both in its motivation and in its societal effect) than what that word often connotes? *See* RANDALL KENNEDY, FOR DISCRIMINATION: RACE, AFFIRMATIVE ACTION, AND THE LAW 165 (2013) (condemning "an insistence, on the part of some . . . proponents [of immediate 'color blindness'], that affirmative action is the moral and legal equivalent of Jim Crow segregation and kindred forms of racial oppression").

Of course, even if the word "discriminate" is more complicated than Justice Rehnquist thought, § 703(a) uses some other words too. For instance, § 703(a)(2) forbids employers to "limit" or "classify" their employees "in any way which would deprive or tend to deprive any individual of employment opportunities . . . because of such individual's race." Can you interpret that provision too to accommodate race-conscious affirmative action? How about the provision in § 703(b) that forbids employment agencies to "refer for employment any individual on the basis of his race"?

Likewise, what do you make of the fact that § 704(b) forbids employers to run advertisements that "indicat[e] any preference, limitation, specification, or discrimination, based on race"? Would it violate Title VII for Kaiser to run an advertisement describing its affirmative-action plan? If so, should we conclude that § 703 must prohibit the plan itself?

3. If you are inclined to accept Justice Rehnquist's anticlassification interpretation of Title VII, how far would you take that interpretation? For instance, would §§ 703(a) and 703(d) prevent companies with on-the-job-training programs from making special efforts to solicit applications from qualified Black applicants, if the companies then judged those applications under exactly the same standards that they used for white applicants? *Cf. Weber*, 443 U.S. at 210–11 (Blackmun, J., concurring) (asserting that under Mr. Weber's interpretation of the statute, "[e]ven a whisper of emphasis on minority recruiting would be forbidden"). If you think that § 703 accommodates such recruitment efforts, must you conclude that § 703 would also tolerate a racist employer's efforts to drum up more applications from qualified *white* applicants?

4. Nowadays, strict anticlassification principles are often seen as being at odds with antisubordination principles. Debates about affirmative action bring out that conflict; anticlassification principles that condemn all race-conscious decisionmaking are incompatible with antisubordination principles that condemn racial hierarchies but that encourage race-conscious decisionmaking aimed at dismantling those hierarchies and their effects. *See, e.g.*, Owen M. Fiss, *Groups and the Equal Protection Clause*, 5 PHIL. & PUB. AFFS. 107, 129–36, 147–64 (1976) (arguing that affirmative action exposes problems with a strict anticlassification approach, and giving priority to an antisubordination approach in part for that reason). The shifting political valence of calls for "color-blindness" has also contributed to the perceived conflict. "Throughout the 1950s and '60s, . . . opponents of segregation raised high the banner of color blindness to shame, challenge, and overcome state-enforced racial separateness." KENNEDY, *supra*, at 155–56. After the demise of *de jure* segregation, though, color-blindness gained some questionable adherents. *See id.* at 163 ("[W]hite supremacists long fought against any and all versions of color blindness, only to embrace eventually a version serviceable for suppressing affirmative action."); Ian F. Haney López, *"A Nation of Minorities": Race, Ethnicity, and Reactionary Colorblindness*, 59 STAN. L. REV. 985, 1004 (2007) ("By the end of the 1960s, colorblindness had become a favored argument among those attempting to protect segregation."); *cf.* Desmond S. King & Rogers M. Smith, *"Without Regard to Race": Critical Ideational Development in Modern American Politics*, 76 J. POL. 958, 962–63 (2014) (noting "the segregationists' reformulation of their views," but adding that color-blindness also has attracted support from people with "sincere beliefs that race-conscious policies promoted racial antagonisms" and people who thought that "color-blind individual rights were part of natural justice").

In 1964, when Congress enacted the Civil Rights Act, any divide between anticlassification and antisubordination values was much less stark than you might now think. *See* Siegel, *supra*, 117 HARV. L. REV. at 1500 ("In the 1960s, questions of anticlassification and questions of group status harm were not bifurcated frames of analysis, as they would later come to be."). Anticlassification ideas had long been deployed against racial subordination, and the conflicts of the day did not suggest reasons to separate them. *See* Jack M. Balkin & Reva B. Siegel, *The American Civil Rights Tradition: Anticlassification or Antisubordination?*, 58 U. MIAMI L. REV. 9, 11–12 (2003) ("[S]egregation under Jim Crow violated both the anticlassification and antisubordination principles. Cases like *Brown* and *Loving* contained language condemning the practice of classifying citizens by race as well as language condemning practices that enforced subordination or inflicted status harm." (footnotes omitted)).

Citing legislative history, Justice Brennan's majority opinion in *Weber* asserted that "Congress' primary concern in enacting the prohibition against racial discrimination in Title VII of the Civil Rights Act of 1964 was with 'the plight of the Negro in our economy.'" *Weber*, 443 U.S. at 202 (quoting 110 CONG. REC. 6548 (1964) (remarks of Sen. Humphrey)). Also citing legislative history, Justice Rehnquist asserted that members of the enacting Congress understood Title VII to prohibit employers from making decisions "'based on race.'" *Id.* at 236–37 (Rehnquist, J., dissenting) (quoting 110 CONG. REC. 5423 (remarks of Sen. Humphrey)). The legislative history does indeed reflect both these ideas, and members of Congress could have held them simultaneously: they may have wanted *both* to mandate color-blind employment decisions *and* to lift the economic position of Black Americans into line with the economic position of white Americans. *See* ESKRIDGE, *supra*, at 30. According to Professor Eskridge, indeed, "Members of Congress who supported the civil rights bill believed, or said they believed, that these purposes were the same—that color-blind hiring and promotion would naturally generate good numbers." *Id.*

If that is what members of Congress expected, it was clear by the time of *Weber* that they had miscalculated. *See id.* As the majority put it in footnote 4, "The problem that Congress addressed in 1964 remains with us"; in fact, the disproportion between Black and white unemployment rates in the United States may have been slightly *higher* in 1978 than it had been in 1962. *See Weber*, 443 U.S. at 204 n.4. In retrospect, this result might not be surprising. Even if employers had rigorously followed Title VII from the start, past discrimination in educational and economic opportunities would still have put many Black Americans at a disadvantage—with the result that a rule of pure color-blindness in employment might not do much to reduce Black unemployment or to put Black Americans in high-wage, high-skill jobs. *See* ESKRIDGE, *supra*, at 30; *see also* T. Alexander Aleinikoff, *A Case for Race-Consciousness*, 91 COLUM. L. REV. 1060, 1088 (1991) ("It is common for advocates of affirmative action to point out that a legal strategy dedicated to 'equality of opportunity' is likely to replicate deeply embedded inequalities. The familiar metaphor is of a race between two runners, one of whom starts many yards back from the starting line . . . ."); MARTIN LUTHER KING, JR., WHY WE CAN'T WAIT 134 (1964) (using such a metaphor).

If you would otherwise have agreed with Justice Rehnquist that Title VII established a strict anticlassification principle, but if the legislative history of Title VII shows that members of Congress expected this principle to generate rapid improvements in Black Americans' economic outcomes, might this legislative history support the majority's decision to interpret Title VII as allowing race-conscious affirmative action? *Cf.* ESKRIDGE, *supra*, at 30–31 (noting that in practice, different interpreters reacted in different ways to "the disaggregation of Title VII's purpose"). If one has to choose between enforcing what one believes to be the most natural reading of the words that Congress chose and achieving the real-world results that Congress wanted those words to produce, can one argue that the latter is more important? Isn't the point of most statutes to produce particular results in the real world, and might legislators themselves therefore want interpreters to make appropriate adaptations in situations of this sort?

Or does this emphasis on the legislators' desired ends overlook the importance of the legislators' chosen means, and inappropriately assume that legislators would naturally want to give courts substantial discretion to make direct application of the legislators' underlying policy goals? (Recall the discussion about "rules" and "standards" at the end of Chapter 1.) To borrow an example from Judge Easterbrook, suppose that Congress enacts a statute reducing the tax rate on capital gains, and suppose that legislative history makes crystal clear the real-world results that Congress wanted to achieve: the majority of legislators expected and intended the rate cut to stimulate the economy to such an extent that tax revenue would actually increase. Suppose, however, that the rate cut does not actually have that effect; tax revenue falls after the rate reduction. Even so, judges surely would not be justified in interpreting the law to set a different tax rate than the legislators chose, so as to achieve the real-world increase in tax revenue that the legislators intended to produce. As Judge Easterbrook puts it, "the meaning of the law would be only that rates go down, not that revenue go up." *In re Sinclair*, 870 F.2d 1340, 1344 (7th Cir. 1989). Does this analogy defeat the argument in the previous paragraph?

If you accept Judge Easterbrook's point, should interpreters simply disregard legislative history about the real-world results that members of the enacting legislature expected a rule to produce? Or can that information ever bear on the meaning of the rule itself? Can you articulate a difference between the way that the court would be using legislative history in Judge Easterbrook's hypothetical (when the court is asked to tinker with the tax rate in order to make the statute achieve the real-world results that members of the enacting legislature anticipated) and the way that the Court used legislative history in *Weber*?

5. Justice Blackmun's concurring opinion in *Weber* was driven at least in part by the Court's prior decision in *Griggs v. Duke Power Co.*, 401 U.S. 424 (1971). Apparently relying on § 703(a)(2), *Griggs* had understood Title VII as forbidding employers to use hiring or promotion criteria that had a disparate impact on Black applicants and that were not "shown to be significantly related to successful job performance," even if the employers were not deliberately using the criteria as proxies for race and were not trying to discriminate against Black people. *See id.* at 426, 432. *Griggs* was ambiguous about many things, including the nature of the labor pools that courts should use to identify disparate impacts, the standard of proof that employers would have to satisfy in order to establish job-relatedness, and whether employers that had not overtly discriminated on the basis of race in the past would have an easier time avoiding liability than the Duke Power Co. (which, before Title VII took effect, had explicitly reserved the jobs in question for white people). *See* GEORGE RUTHERGLEN, EMPLOYMENT DISCRIMINATION LAW: VISIONS OF EQUALITY IN THEORY AND DOCTRINE 76–79 (5th ed. 2021). Despite these ambiguities, though, *Griggs* meant that companies like Kaiser Aluminum faced at least the threat of liability if the craftworkers whom they hired were disproportionately white: to the extent that Kaiser's hiring criteria had a disparate impact along racial lines, Kaiser would have to show that those criteria were required by some sort of "business necessity" (*Griggs*, 401 U.S. at 431), and Kaiser might not be able to make the necessary showing. A reasonable employer might like to avoid this risk by eliminating the disparate racial impact. In practice, though, race-based affirmative action might be the most effective way for the company to do so. If such affirmative action would also violate Title VII, then the company would be in a quandary. In the words quoted by Justice Blackmun, such a company might find itself on a "high tightrope without a net"—facing the threat of liability to Black plaintiffs if its hiring criteria had a disparate impact and the threat of liability to white plaintiffs if it used affirmative action to eliminate that disparate impact. *See* ESKRIDGE, *supra*, at 24; Philip P. Frickey, *Wisdom on* Weber, 74 TUL. L. REV. 1169, 1192–96 (2000) (explaining this dilemma).

To be sure, one might question the Court's conclusion in *Griggs*. Section 703(a)(2) talked about depriving any individual of employment opportunities "because of" his race. Instead of reading this language to reach employment practices that have disparate impacts because of pre-existing societal discrimination, one might have understood Title VII to prohibit only practices that an employer itself adopted or maintained with race in mind. On this view, promotion criteria adopted without race in mind would not have violated § 703(a)(2) even if Black employees satisfied them at lower rates than white employees.

Still, that interpretation of the statute would raise an obvious problem of proof: how do courts detect the true reasons for an employment practice that is not cast in terms of race but that has a disparate impact along racial lines? If courts had interpreted Title VII to prohibit only employment practices that are adopted or maintained with race in mind, and if courts had required individualized proof of discriminatory intent in each case, then some violations of the statute would surely have gone undetected; employers who wanted to continue discriminating against Black people would have set hiring criteria that were facially neutral, but that Black people satisfied at substantially lower rates than white people, precisely in order to favor white applicants and to discriminate against Black applicants. To deal with that problem, courts might have gravitated toward the following evidentiary presumption: when an employer (or at least an employer with the Duke Power Company's history of race discrimination) adopts employment requirements that have a disparate racial impact and that are not related to job performance, courts can presume that the employer had a discriminatory purpose. In practice, that evidentiary presumption might work exactly like the rule that the Court articulated in *Griggs*.[9]

Even if one thinks that *Griggs* was wrongly decided, moreover, one might also think that the doctrine of *stare decisis* counseled against overruling it later. Cases like *Weber* would then raise a complicated

---

[9] In defense of *Griggs*, one might also argue that unless § 703 recognizes some "disparate impact" theories of liability, Congress would not have needed to include § 703(h). *See supra* p. 361.

As far as Title VII is concerned, debates over *Griggs* are now largely moot. In 1991, Congress amended Title VII in a way that explicitly recognizes disparate-impact liability. *See* Civil Rights Act of 1991, Pub. L. 102–166, § 105, 105 Stat. 1071, 1074–75 (adding § 703(k), codified at 42 U.S.C. § 2000e–2(k)).

question about the interplay between statutory text and subsequent decisions: to what extent should the Court let its past decision in *Griggs* (which might have been erroneous, but which the Court is not going to overrule) affect its resolution of cases about other aspects of Title VII? As a legal matter, of course, the issue raised by *Weber* is distinct from the issue that the Court decided in *Griggs*. But as a practical matter, Justice Blackmun was correct that the two issues are linked. Can one understand his concurring opinion as an outgrowth of *stare decisis*—as adapting what he might have understood to be the original meaning of Title VII to accommodate the practical demands created by a later decision? *Cf.* WILLIAM N. ESKRIDGE, JR., PHILIP P. FRICKEY, & ELIZABETH GARRETT, CASES AND MATERIALS ON LEGISLATION: STATUTES AND THE CREATION OF PUBLIC POLICY 103–04 (4th ed. 2007) (describing Justice Blackmun's approach in *Weber* as a species of "dynamic" interpretation). Note that for someone who takes this approach, there are some respects in which the original legislative history of a statute—even if relevant to interpretation at the outset—will have diminishing importance over time.

6. A year before *Weber*, the Supreme Court had considered the legality of race-based affirmative action in admissions to a state university's medical school. *See* Regents of the Univ. of Cal. v. Bakke, 438 U.S. 265 (1978). To select an entering class of 100 students, the medical school of the University of California at Davis ran two separate admissions procedures; the school filled 84 seats through its regular procedure, but the school filled the remaining 16 seats through a special admissions program that, in practice, was not open to white applicants. *See* Bakke v. Regents of the Univ. of Cal., 553 P.2d 1152, 1159 (Cal. 1976) ("The University does not challenge the trial court's finding that applicants who are not members of a minority are barred from participation in the special admissions program."). Allan Bakke, a white applicant who had unsuccessfully sought admission through the regular procedure, claimed that the school's admissions practices violated both the Equal Protection Clause of the federal Constitution (which forbids each state to "deny to any person within its jurisdiction the equal protection of the laws") and the Civil Rights Act of 1964. Of course, Bakke's complaint did not rely on Title VII, which deals only with employment discrimination. Instead, Bakke invoked Title VI, which establishes the following rule: "No person in the United States shall, on the ground of race, color, or national origin, be excluded from participation in, be denied the benefits of, or be subjected to discrimination under any program or activity receiving Federal financial assistance." Civil Rights Act of 1964, Pub. L. 88–352, § 601, 78 Stat. 241, 252 (codified at 42 U.S.C. § 2000d); *see also Bakke*, 438 U.S. at 412 (Stevens, J., concurring in the judgment in part and dissenting in part) ("The University . . . acknowledges that it was, and still is, receiving federal financial assistance.").

When the case reached the Supreme Court, the Justices split 4–4–1. Speaking for one group of four Justices (including both of the Justices who would go on to dissent in *Weber*), Justice Stevens would have resolved the case entirely under Title VI. In his view, "the meaning of the Title VI ban on exclusion is crystal clear: Race cannot be the basis of excluding anyone from participation in a federally funded program." *Id.* at 418. Without addressing any questions of constitutional law, and without deciding "whether race can ever be used as a factor in an admissions decision," *id.* at 411, Justice Stevens would have held that the particular admissions procedure under review amounted to "exclu[sion]" in the relevant sense. In his words, "The University's special admissions program violated Title VI of the Civil Rights Act of 1964 by excluding Bakke from the Medical School because of his race." *Id.* at 421.

Speaking for a different group of four Justices (all of whom later joined the majority in *Weber*), Justice Brennan disagreed. Largely on the basis of legislative history, he argued that Title VI should not be understood to establish its own standards for race-consciousness, separate and apart from the standards established by the Constitution. Instead, "Title VI . . . merely extends the constraints of the Fourteenth Amendment to private parties who receive federal funds," so as "to end the Federal Government's complicity in conduct . . . inconsistent with the standards to be found in the antidiscrimination provisions of the Constitution." *Id.* at 327, 331 (Brennan, J., concurring in the judgment in part and dissenting in part). On this view, "Title VI prohibits only those uses of racial criteria that would violate the Fourteenth Amendment if employed by a State or its agencies." *Id.* at 328. According to Justice Brennan, moreover, the medical school's admissions practices did not violate the applicable constitutional standards. To be sure, Justice Brennan agreed that racial classifications triggered heightened scrutiny even when used for "ostensibly benign purposes." *Id.* at 361. But as Justice Brennan understood the Supreme Court's precedents, "a state government may adopt race-conscious programs if the purpose of such programs is to remove the disparate racial impact its actions might otherwise have and if there is reason to believe that the disparate impact is itself the product of past discrimination, whether its own or that of society at large." *Id.* at 369; *see also id.* at 362 ("Davis' articulated purpose of remedying the effects of past societal discrimination is, under our cases, sufficiently important to justify the use of race-conscious admissions programs where there is a sound basis for concluding that minority underrepresentation is substantial and chronic, and that the handicap of past discrimination is impeding access of minorities to the Medical School."). Justice Brennan added that the medical school's admissions practices did not impermissibly stigmatize anyone and that the school's use of race was reasonable under the circumstances. *See id.* at 373–78. Thus, Justice Brennan would have rejected Bakke's claims.

Justice Powell cast the decisive vote. On the basis of "the voluminous legislative history of Title VI," he agreed with Justice Brennan that "Title VI must be held to proscribe only those racial classifications that would violate the Equal Protection Clause or the Fifth Amendment." *Id.* at 284–87 (opinion of Powell, J.). As for what the constitutional standards are, though, Justice Powell charted his own course. Unlike Justice Brennan, Justice Powell suggested that the applicable constitutional standards did not allow universities to use race-based admissions practices as a means of "remedying . . . the effects of 'societal discrimination.' " *See id.* at 307–10. But while Justice Powell rejected this remedial justification for race-based affirmative action, he concluded that universities could legitimately consider race (along with other factors) for the purpose of "obtaining the educational benefits that flow from an ethnically diverse student body." *Id.* at 306, 311–15. Ultimately, Justice Powell concluded that the medical school's special admissions program was too crude to achieve this objective and that the program was therefore unconstitutional. *See id.* at 315–20. Still, Justice Powell argued that under a better-designed program, universities trying to achieve the educational benefits of diversity could validly treat "race or ethnic background . . . [as] a 'plus' in a particular applicant's file." *Id.* at 317; *see also id.* at 316–17 (offering Harvard College's admissions program as an example); *cf. id.* at 320 (majority opinion) ("[T]he State has a substantial interest that legitimately may be served by a properly devised admissions program involving the competitive consideration of race and ethnic origin. For this reason, so much of the California court's judgment as enjoins petitioner from any consideration of the race of any applicant must be reversed.").

Twenty-five years later, a majority of the Supreme Court embraced much of Justice Powell's analysis. In *Grutter v. Bollinger*, 539 U.S. 306 (2003), the Court upheld the University of Michigan Law School's use of race as a factor in admissions. Like Justice Powell, Justice O'Connor's majority opinion held that "the Equal Protection Clause does not prohibit the Law School's narrowly tailored use of race in admissions decisions to further a compelling interest in obtaining the educational benefits that flow from a diverse student body." *Id.* at 343. Because the law school's policies passed constitutional muster, moreover, the Court held that they also complied with Title VI. *See id.* (citing *Bakke*, 438 U.S. at 287 (opinion of Powell, J.)).[10]

---

[10] In *Bakke*, Justice Stevens had argued that Title VI established a legal rule of its own, not one that simply piggybacked on constitutional standards. *See Bakke*, 438 U.S. at 418 (Stevens, J., concurring in the judgment in part and dissenting in part) ("We are dealing with a distinct statutory prohibition, enacted at a particular time with particular concerns in mind; neither its language nor any prior interpretation suggests that its place in the Civil Rights Act . . . is simply that of a constitutional appendage."). In the 1980s, however, Justice Stevens acknowledged that a majority of his colleagues had "unequivocally rejected" this position, and he accepted their view on the strength of *stare decisis*. *See* Guardians Ass'n v. Civil Serv. Comm'n, 463 U.S. 582, 639–42 (1983) (Stevens, J., dissenting); *accord* Johnson v. Transportation Agency, 480 U.S. 616, 643–46 (1987) (Stevens, J., concurring). Thus, Justice Stevens joined the majority opinion in *Grutter* in full.

Still, the *Grutter* majority asserted that "race-conscious admissions policies must be limited in time." *Id.* at 342; *see also id.* (stating that there can be no "permanent justification" for such policies and suggesting that universities build in "sunset provisions . . . and periodic reviews to determine whether racial preferences are still necessary to achieve student body diversity"). The majority added that as circumstances changed, so too would its constitutional analysis: "We expect that 25 years from now, the use of racial preferences will no longer be necessary to further the interest approved today." *Id.* at 343.

Change came in *Students for Fair Admissions, Inc. v. President & Fellows of Harvard College*, 143 S. Ct. 2141 (2023). There, Chief Justice Roberts's majority opinion applied a robust form of strict scrutiny to race-conscious admissions practices used by Harvard College and the University of North Carolina. According to the majority,

> "Courts may not license separating students on the basis of race without an exceedingly persuasive justification that is measurable and concrete enough to permit judicial review. As this Court has repeatedly reaffirmed, '[r]acial classifications are simply too pernicious to permit any but the most exact connection between justification and classification.' "

Id. at 2168 (quoting Gratz v. Bollinger, 539 U.S. 244, 270 (2003) (internal quotation marks omitted)). Ultimately, the majority held that "[t]he programs at issue here do not satisfy that standard." *Id.* Although the majority did not explicitly overrule either *Grutter* or any other past decision, the admissions practices at issue in *Grutter* might not have been able to survive the majority's analysis. *See, e.g., id.* at 2166–67 (concluding that the educational benefits claimed by the universities were too immeasurable to satisfy strict scrutiny); *id.* at 2167–68 (questioning the fit between the challenged practices and the universities' articulated goals).

The majority opinion in *Students for Fair Admissions* focused on the standards allegedly supplied by the Equal Protection Clause. Because none of the parties challenged the idea that Title VI piggybacks upon those standards, the majority did not revisit that issue. *See id.* at 2157 n.2. Still, the upshot of the majority opinion was that Title VI prohibits the sort of race-conscious affirmative action that Harvard had been practicing. *See id.* (assuming that Title VI applied "the standards of the Equal Protection Clause" to Harvard); *see also id.* at 2175–76 (indicating that not only Harvard but "[m]any universities" have been violating those standards).

Writing for himself and Justice Thomas, Justice Gorsuch would have gone even farther. Harking back to Justice Stevens's opinion in *Bakke*, Justice Gorsuch argued that Title VI did not simply piggyback on constitutional standards, but instead established a distinct legal rule of its own. *See id.* at 2219–20 (Gorsuch, J., joined by Thomas J., concurring); *see also id.* at 2220 (arguing that the contrary position taken by Justices

Brennan and Powell in *Bakke* had relied on selective quotations from legislative history rather than "the text of Title VI"). As interpreted by Justice Gorsuch, moreover, the rule established by Title VI is even more categorical than the constitutional standard articulated by the majority. "Under Title VI," he asserted, "it is *always* unlawful to discriminate among persons even in part because of race, color, or national origin." *Id.*

What, if anything, do these conclusions about Title VI mean for *Weber* and Title VII? In *Weber* itself, footnote 6 of the majority opinion argued that Title VII should not be interpreted in lockstep with Title VI. *See Weber*, 443 U.S. at 206 n.6. But in *Students for Fair Admissions*, Justice Gorsuch seemed to disagree; he asserted that Titles VI and VII used "essentially identical terms" and should both be understood to "codify a categorical rule of 'individual equality, without regard to race.' " *Students for Fair Admissions*, 143 S. Ct. at 2209 (Gorsuch, J., concurring) (quoting *Bakke*, 438 U.S. at 416 n.19 (Stevens, J., concurring in the judgment in part and dissenting in part)). Thus, Justice Gorsuch might stand ready to overrule *Weber*. On the other hand, some other members of the majority in *Students for Fair Admissions* might not want to take that step. *See id.* at 2221 (Kavanaugh, J., concurring) (writing separately to claim that the Court's decision "is consistent with and follows from" the Court's precedents); *see also infra* Chapter 4.A (discussing the doctrine of *stare decisis*, which is said to be especially powerful in statutory cases).

C. RECENT DEBATES ABOUT THE USE OF LEGISLATIVE HISTORY

Section B traced the rise of interpreters' reliance upon legislative history from the nineteenth century to its high-water mark in the Burger Court. Even during the Burger Court, though, the practice did not go entirely without criticism. In a 1975 book, Professor Reed Dickerson advanced a host of arguments against it, and he concluded with a call "to end or severely limit . . . judicial use" of legislative history. REED DICKERSON, THE INTERPRETATION AND APPLICATION OF STATUTES 137–97 (1975). A decade later, Antonin Scalia—then a judge on the United States Court of Appeals for the D.C. Circuit—began to take up this cause. *See* Hirschey v. FERC, 777 F.2d 1, 7–8 (D.C. Cir. 1985) (Scalia, J., concurring); *see also* Daniel A. Farber & Philip P. Frickey, *Legislative Intent and Public Choice*, 74 VA. L. REV. 423, 442–43 (1988) (quoting from the speech that Justice Scalia delivered at various law schools in 1985 and 1986). After he joined the Supreme Court in the fall of 1986, Justice Scalia developed this position further, often writing separately to criticize his colleagues' reliance upon legislative history. *See* William N. Eskridge, Jr., *The New Textualism*, 37 UCLA L. REV. 621, 650–56 (1990) (citing cases and discussing shifts over time in Justice Scalia's arguments); *see also* Thomas W. Merrill, *Textualism and the Future of the* Chevron *Doctrine*, 72 WASH. U. L.Q. 351, 363 (1994) ("Since 1987,

Justice Scalia has been conducting what amounts to a continuous seminar on the virtues of textualism and evils of legislative history.").

Justice Scalia's position won some adherents both on and off the Court. *See id.* (noting that Justices Kennedy and Thomas both seemed sympathetic to Justice Scalia's position); *see also* Alex Kozinski, *Should Reading Legislative History Be an Impeachable Offense?*, 31 SUFFOLK U. L. REV. 807, 812 (1998) ("Led by Justice Scalia, a number of federal judges—I among them—have foresworn the use of legislative history as an interpretive tool.").[11] Perhaps more important, a larger group of people agreed that judges had been too casual about using legislative history as a substitute for statutory text and about treating isolated snippets of individual legislators' remarks as an authoritative guide to the collective intent of the whole legislature. *See, e.g.*, Bradford C. Mank, *Textualism's Selective Canons of Statutory Construction: Reinvigorating Individual Liberties, Legislative Authority, and Deference to Executive Agencies*, 86 KY. L.J. 527, 539 (1998) ("To some extent, the revival of textualism during the 1980s was a healthy reaction to the misuse by many judges of legislative history."); Stephen Breyer, *On the Uses of Legislative History in Interpreting Statutes*, 65 S. CAL. L. REV. 845, 847 (1992) (agreeing that judges should be "more sensitive to problems of the abuse of legislative history," but arguing that critics "ought not to condemn its use altogether"). On the current Supreme Court, some Justices are more receptive to legislative history than others, but collectively the Court is now "cautious [about] if not hostile to its use." David S. Romantz, *In Defense of Legislative History*, 90 MISS. L.J. 683, 706 (2021).

To help you evaluate where you should stand in these debates, this Section considers the principal arguments that Justice Scalia and other modern critics have advanced against the use of legislative history in statutory interpretation.

1. CONSTITUTIONAL ARGUMENTS

Textualists sometimes suggest that one can draw inferences about the proper method of interpreting statutes (or at least *federal* statutes) from the Constitution itself, and that the Constitution affirmatively prohibits courts from treating legislative history as authoritative. To evaluate that suggestion, though, we must first lay some groundwork.

---

[11] Early on in his tenure, moreover, Justice Scalia adopted the practice of refusing to join his colleagues' opinions to the extent that they relied upon legislative history. *See, e.g.*, Jett v. Indep. School Dist., 491 U.S. 701, 738 (1989) (Scalia, J., concurring in part and concurring in the judgment) (depriving Justice O'Connor of a fifth vote for Part III of her opinion "insofar as it relies upon legislative history"); United States v. Taylor, 487 U.S. 326, 344 (1988) (Scalia, J., concurring in part) ("I join the opinion of the Court except Part II-A . . . ."). This stance ultimately had a noticeable impact on the opinion-writing practices even of Justices who did not themselves see anything wrong with consulting legislative history. *See* Merrill, *supra*, 72 WASH. U. L.Q. at 364.

Article I of the federal Constitution addresses the structure and operation of Congress. It includes the following provisions, among others:

§ 1: All legislative Powers herein granted shall be vested in a Congress of the United States, which shall consist of a Senate and House of Representatives.

§ 2: The House of Representatives shall be composed of Members chosen every second Year by the People of the several States, and the Electors in each State shall have the Qualifications requisite for Electors of the most numerous Branch of the State Legislature. . . .

§ 3: The Senate of the United States shall be composed of two Senators from each State, chosen by the Legislature thereof, for six Years; and each Senator shall have one Vote. . . .[12]

§ 5: Each House shall be the Judge of the Elections, Returns, and Qualifications of its own Members, and a Majority of each shall constitute a Quorum to do Business; but a smaller Number may adjourn from day to day, and may be authorized to compel the Attendance of absent Members, in such Manner, and under such Penalties as each House may provide.

Each House may determine the Rules of its Proceedings, punish its Members for disorderly Behaviour, and, with the Concurrence of two thirds, expel a Member.

Each House shall keep a Journal of its Proceedings, and from time to time publish the same, excepting such Parts as may in their Judgment require Secrecy; and the Yeas and Nays of the Members of either House on any question shall, at the Desire of one fifth of those Present, be entered on the Journal. . . .

§ 7: All Bills for raising Revenue shall originate in the House of Representatives; but the Senate may propose or concur with Amendments as on other Bills.

Every Bill which shall have passed the House of Representatives and the Senate, shall, before it become a Law, be presented to the President of the United States; If he approve he shall sign it, but if not he shall return it, with his Objections to that House in which it shall have originated, who shall enter the Objections at large on their Journal, and proceed to reconsider it. If after such Reconsideration two thirds of that House shall agree to pass the Bill, it shall be sent, together with the Objections, to the other House, by which it shall likewise be

[12] The first paragraph of the 17th Amendment superseded this provision. That paragraph reads as follows: "The Senate of the United States shall be composed of two Senators from each state, elected by the people thereof, for six Years; and each Senator shall have one vote. The electors in each State shall have the qualifications requisite for electors of the most numerous branch of the State legislatures."

reconsidered, and if approved by two thirds of that House, it shall become a Law. But in all such Cases the Votes of both Houses shall be determined by Yeas and Nays, and the Names of the Persons voting for and against the Bill shall be entered on the Journal of each House respectively. If any Bill shall not be returned by the President within ten Days (Sundays excepted) after it shall have been presented to him, the Same shall be a Law, in like Manner as if he had signed it, unless the Congress by their Adjournment prevent its Return, in which Case it shall not be a Law.

Every Order, Resolution, or Vote to which the Concurrence of the Senate and House of Representatives may be necessary (except on a question of Adjournment) shall be presented to the President of the United States; and before the Same shall take Effect, shall be approved by him, or being disapproved by him, shall be repassed by two thirds of the Senate and House of Representatives, according to the Rules and Limitations prescribed in the Case of a Bill.

In *Immigration and Naturalization Service v. Chadha*, 462 U.S. 919 (1983), the Supreme Court held that aside from a few instances in which the Constitution itself sets up an alternative procedure (as Article II does for the making of treaties), the process of bicameralism and presentment spelled out in Article I is the exclusive means by which the federal government can exercise "legislative" power. What is more, an ordinary statute cannot validly change this process prospectively. For instance, a federal statute purporting to authorize a single House of Congress to exercise "legislative" power in the future would be ineffective even if the authorizing statute itself had gone through the process of bicameralism and presentment.

Chief Justice Burger, who wrote the majority opinion in *Chadha*, did not have any inkling that his opinion might be turned against the use of legislative history in statutory interpretation. That was not the question presented in *Chadha*, and it was not a question on Chief Justice Burger's radar screen. As you will see, indeed, Chief Justice Burger's opinion in *Chadha* itself referred to legislative history to help decide one of the preliminary questions in the case. But when the debate over legislative history broke out a few years later, a number of critics seized on *Chadha* as providing a constitutional argument against some or all of the practices that they were condemning. For that reason, and because arguments about *Chadha* will reappear in later chapters of this book, the case is worth studying in some detail. After presenting the case and some ensuing notes and questions, we will proceed to consider its implications (if any) for the debate over legislative history.

Immigration and Naturalization Service v. Chadha

462 U.S. 919 (1983)

■ *CHIEF JUSTICE BURGER delivered the opinion of the Court:*

... [This case] presents a challenge to the constitutionality of the provision in § 244(c)(2) of the Immigration and Nationality Act, 66 Stat. 216, as amended, 8 U.S.C. § 1254(c)(2), authorizing one House of Congress ... to invalidate the decision of the Executive Branch, [made] pursuant to authority delegated by Congress to the Attorney General of the United States, to allow a particular deportable alien to remain in the United States.

I

Chadha is an East Indian who was born in Kenya and holds a British passport. He was lawfully admitted to the United States in 1966 on a nonimmigrant student visa. His visa expired on June 30, 1972. On October 11, 1973, the District Director of the Immigration and Naturalization Service ordered Chadha to show cause why he should not be deported for having "remained in the United States for a longer time than permitted." Pursuant to § 242(b) of the Immigration and Nationality Act (Act), 8 U.S.C. § 1252(b), a deportation hearing was held before an immigration judge on January 11, 1974. Chadha conceded that he was deportable for overstaying his visa and the hearing was adjourned to enable him to file an application for suspension of deportation under § 244(a)(1) of the Act, 8 U.S.C. § 1254(a)(1). Section 244(a)(1), at the time in question, provided:

> "As hereinafter prescribed in this section, the Attorney General may, in his discretion, suspend deportation and adjust the status to that of an alien lawfully admitted for permanent residence, in the case of an alien who applies to the Attorney General for suspension of deportation and—
>
> "(1) is deportable under any law of the United States except the provisions specified in paragraph (2) of this subsection; has been physically present in the United States for a continuous period of not less than seven years immediately preceding the date of such application, and proves that during all of such period he was and is a person of good moral character; and is a person whose deportation would, in the opinion of the Attorney General, result in extreme hardship to the alien or to his spouse, parent, or child, who is a citizen of the United States or an alien lawfully admitted for permanent residence."[1]

After Chadha submitted his application for suspension of deportation, the deportation hearing was resumed on February 7, 1974.

[1] Congress delegated the major responsibilities for enforcement of the Immigration and Nationality Act to the Attorney General. 8 U.S.C. § 1103(a). The Attorney General discharges his responsibilities through the Immigration and Naturalization Service, a division of the Department of Justice. *Ibid.*

On the basis of evidence adduced at the hearing, affidavits submitted with the application, and the results of a character investigation conducted by the INS, the immigration judge, on June 25, 1974, ordered that Chadha's deportation be suspended. The immigration judge found that Chadha met the requirements of § 244(a)(1): he had resided continuously in the United States for over seven years, was of good moral character, and would suffer "extreme hardship" if deported.

Pursuant to § 244(c)(1) of the Act, 8 U.S.C. § 1254(c)(1), the immigration judge suspended Chadha's deportation and a report of the suspension was transmitted to Congress. Section 244(c)(1) provides:

> "Upon application by any alien who is found by the Attorney General to meet the requirements of subsection (a) of this section the Attorney General may in his discretion suspend deportation of such alien. If the deportation of any alien is suspended under the provisions of this subsection, a complete and detailed statement of the facts and pertinent provisions of law in the case shall be reported to the Congress with the reasons for such suspension. Such reports shall be submitted on the first day of each calendar month in which Congress is in session."

Once the Attorney General's recommendation for suspension of Chadha's deportation was conveyed to Congress, Congress had the power under § 244(c)(2) of the Act, 8 U.S.C. § 1254(c)(2), to veto[2] the Attorney General's determination that Chadha should not be deported. Section 244(c)(2) provides:

> "(2) In the case of an alien specified in paragraph (1) of subsection (a) of this subsection—
>
> "if during the session of the Congress at which a case is reported, or prior to the close of the session of the Congress next following the session at which a case is reported, either the Senate or the House of Representatives passes a resolution stating in substance that it does not favor the suspension of such deportation, the Attorney General shall thereupon deport such alien or authorize the alien's voluntary departure at his own expense under the order of deportation in the manner provided by law. If, within the time above specified, neither the Senate nor the House of Representatives shall pass such a resolution, the Attorney General shall cancel deportation proceedings."

. . . . On December 12, 1975, Representative Eilberg, Chairman of the Judiciary Subcommittee on Immigration, Citizenship, and International Law, introduced a resolution opposing "the granting of

[2] In constitutional terms, "veto" is used to describe the President's power under Art. I, § 7 of the Constitution. See Black's Law Dictionary 1403 (5th ed. 1979). It appears, however, that Congressional devices of the type authorized by § 244(c)(2) have come to be commonly referred to as a "veto." . . . We refer to the Congressional "resolution" authorized by § 244(c)(2) as a "one-House veto" of the Attorney General's decision to allow a particular deportable alien to remain in the United States.

permanent residence in the United States to [six] aliens," including Chadha. . . . The resolution was referred to the House Committee on the Judiciary. On December 16, 1975, the resolution was discharged from further consideration by the House Committee on the Judiciary and submitted to the House of Representatives for a vote. . . . The resolution had not been printed and was not made available to other Members of the House prior to or at the time it was voted on. So far as the record before us shows, the House consideration of the resolution was based on Representative Eilberg's statement from the floor that

> "[i]t was the feeling of the committee, after reviewing 340 cases, that the aliens contained in the resolution [Chadha and five others] did not meet these statutory requirements, particularly as it relates to hardship; and it is the opinion of the committee that their deportation should not be suspended." [121 Cong. Rec. 40800.]

The resolution was passed without debate or recorded vote. Since the House action was pursuant to § 244(c)(2), the resolution was not treated as an Art. I legislative act; it was not submitted to the Senate or presented to the President for his action.

After the House veto of the Attorney General's decision to allow Chadha to remain in the United States, the immigration judge reopened the deportation proceedings to implement the House order deporting Chadha. Chadha moved to terminate the proceedings on the ground that § 244(c)(2) is unconstitutional. The immigration judge held that he had no authority to rule on the constitutional validity of § 244(c)(2). On November 8, 1976, Chadha was ordered deported pursuant to the House action.

Chadha appealed the deportation order to the Board of Immigration Appeals, again contending that § 244(c)(2) is unconstitutional. The Board held that it had "no power to declare unconstitutional an act of Congress" and Chadha's appeal was dismissed.

Pursuant to § 106(a) of the Act, 8 U.S.C. § 1105a(a), Chadha filed a petition for review of the deportation order in the United States Court of Appeals for the Ninth Circuit. The Immigration and Naturalization Service agreed with Chadha's position before the Court of Appeals and joined him in arguing that § 244(c)(2) is unconstitutional. In light of the importance of the question, the Court of Appeals invited both the Senate and the House of Representatives to file briefs *amici curiae*.

After full briefing and oral argument, the Court of Appeals held that the House was without constitutional authority to order Chadha's deportation; accordingly it directed the Attorney General "to cease and desist from taking any steps to deport this alien based upon the resolution enacted by the House of Representatives." [*Chadha v. INS*,] 634 F.2d 408, 436 (1980). The essence of its holding was that § 244(c)(2) violates the constitutional doctrine of separation of powers.

We . . . now affirm.

II

Before we address the important question of the constitutionality of the one-House veto provision of § 244(c)(2), we first consider several challenges to the authority of this Court to resolve the issue raised. . . .

B

Severability

[In briefs submitted by the Senate and the House of Representatives,] Congress . . . contends that the provision for the one-House veto in § 244(c)(2) cannot be severed from § 244. Congress argues that if the provision for the one-House veto is held unconstitutional, all of § 244 must fall. If § 244 in its entirety [falls] . . . , it follows that the Attorney General has no authority to suspend Chadha's deportation under § 244(a)(1) and Chadha would be deported. From this, Congress argues that Chadha lacks standing to challenge the constitutionality of the one-House veto provision because he could receive no relief even if his constitutional challenge proves successful.

. . . . Congress itself has provided the answer to the question of severability in § 406 of the Immigration and Nationality Act, . . . which provides:

> "If *any* particular provision of this Act, or the application thereof to *any* person or circumstance, is held invalid, *the remainder of the Act and the application of such provision to other persons or circumstances shall not be affected thereby.*" (Emphasis added.)

This language is unambiguous and gives rise to a presumption that Congress did not intend the validity of the Act as a whole, or of any part of the Act, to depend upon whether the veto clause of § 244(c)(2) was invalid. . . .

The presumption as to the severability of the one-House veto provision in § 244(c)(2) is supported by the legislative history of § 244. . . .

The Immigration Act of 1924 . . . required the Secretary of Labor to deport any alien who entered or remained in the United States unlawfully. The only means by which a deportable alien could lawfully remain in the United States was to have his status altered by a private bill enacted by both Houses and presented to the President pursuant to the procedures set out in Art. I, § 7, of the Constitution. These private bills were found intolerable by Congress. In the debate on a 1937 bill introduced by Representative Dies to authorize the Secretary to grant permanent residence in "meritorious" cases, Dies stated:

> "It was my original thought that the way to handle all these meritorious cases was through special bills. I am absolutely convinced as a result of what has occurred in this House that it is impossible to deal with this situation through special bills. We had a demonstration of that fact not long ago when 15 special bills were before this House. The House consumed 5½ hours considering four

bills and made no disposition of any of the bills." 81 Cong. Rec. 5542 (1937).

Representative Dies' bill passed the House, *id.* at 5574, but did not come to a vote in the Senate . . . .

Congress first authorized the Attorney General to suspend the deportation of certain aliens in the Alien Registration Act of 1940 . . . . That Act provided that an alien was to be deported, despite the Attorney General's decision to the contrary, if both Houses, by concurrent resolution,[*] disapproved the suspension.

In 1948, Congress amended the Act to broaden the category of aliens eligible for suspension of deportation. In addition, however, Congress limited the authority of the Attorney General to suspend deportations by providing that the Attorney General could not cancel a deportation unless both Houses affirmatively voted by concurrent resolution to *approve* the Attorney General's action. . . . The provision for approval by concurrent resolution in the 1948 Act proved almost as burdensome as private bills. Just four years later, the House Judiciary Committee, in support of the predecessor to § 244(c)(2), stated in a report:

> "In the light of experience of the last several months, the committee came to the conclusion that the requirements of affirmative action by both Houses of the Congress in many thousands of individual cases which are submitted by the Attorney General every year, is not workable and places upon the Congress and particularly on the Committee on the Judiciary responsibilities which it cannot assume. The new responsibilities placed upon the Committee on the Judiciary [by the concurrent resolution mechanism] are of purely administrative nature and they seriously interfere with the legislative work of the Committee on the Judiciary and would, in time, interfere with the legislative work of the House." H.R. Rep. No. 362, 81st Cong., 1st Sess. 2 (1949).

The proposal to permit one House of Congress to veto the Attorney General's suspension of an alien's deportation was incorporated in the Immigration and Nationality Act of 1952, Pub. L. 414, § 244[ ], 66 Stat. 214. Plainly, Congress' desire to retain a veto in this area cannot be considered in isolation but must be viewed in the context of Congress' irritation with the burden of private immigration bills. This legislative history is not sufficient to rebut the presumption of severability raised by

[*] *Editor's note*: Lawyers speak of three different types of congressional resolutions. A "simple" resolution is a resolution issued by a single House of Congress. A "concurrent" resolution is approved by both Houses but is not presented to the President for signature or veto. By contrast, a "joint" resolution goes through the full process of bicameralism and presentment; it not only is approved by both Houses of Congress but also is presented to the President for signature or veto. If approved, a joint resolution is equivalent to an ordinary statute. *See* JOHN V. SULLIVAN, HOW OUR LAWS ARE MADE, H.R. DOC. NO. 110–49, at 6–8 (2007); *cf. id.* at 7 (mentioning the special case of joint resolutions that propose constitutional amendments, which must be approved by supermajorities in each House but are not presented to the President).

§ 406 because there is insufficient evidence that Congress would have continued to subject itself to the onerous burdens of private bills had it known that § 244(c)(2) would be held unconstitutional. . . .

III

A

. . . . Justice White undertakes to make a case for the proposition that the one-House veto is a useful "political invention," and we need not challenge that assertion. We can even concede this utilitarian argument although the long range political wisdom of this "invention" is arguable. . . . But policy arguments supporting even useful "political inventions" are subject to the demands of the Constitution which defines powers and, with respect to this subject, sets out just how those powers are to be exercised.

Explicit and unambiguous provisions of the Constitution prescribe and define the respective functions of the Congress and of the Executive in the legislative process. Since the precise terms of those familiar provisions are critical to the resolution of this case, we set them out verbatim. Article I provides:

> "All legislative Powers herein granted shall be vested in a Congress of the United States, which shall consist of a Senate *and* House of Representatives." Art. I, § 1 (emphasis added).
>
> "Every Bill which shall have passed the House of Representatives *and* the Senate, *shall,* before it becomes a Law, be presented to the President of the United States . . . ." Art. I, § 7, cl. 2 (emphasis added).
>
> "*Every* Order, Resolution, or Vote to which the Concurrence of the Senate and House of Representatives may be necessary (except on a question of Adjournment) *shall be* presented to the President of the United States; and before the Same shall take Effect, *shall be* approved by him, or being disapproved by him, *shall be* repassed by two thirds of the Senate and House of Representatives, according to the Rules and Limitations prescribed in the Case of a Bill." Art. I, § 7, cl. 3 (emphasis added).

These provisions of Art. I are integral parts of the constitutional design for the separation of powers. . . .

B

The Presentment Clauses

The records of the Constitutional Convention reveal that the requirement that all legislation be presented to the President before becoming law was uniformly accepted by the Framers. Presentment to the President and the Presidential veto were considered so imperative that the draftsmen took special pains to assure that these requirements could not be circumvented. During the final debate on Art. I, § 7, cl. 2, James Madison expressed concern that it might easily be evaded by the simple expedient of calling a proposed law a "resolution" or "vote" rather than a "bill." [2 M. Farrand, The Records of the Federal Convention of 1787, at 301–302.] As a consequence, Art. I, § 7, cl. 3, was added. [*Id.* at] 304–305.

The decision to provide the President with a limited and qualified power to nullify proposed legislation by veto was based on the profound conviction of the Framers that the powers conferred on Congress were the powers to be most carefully circumscribed. It is beyond doubt that lawmaking was a power to be shared by both Houses and the President. In The Federalist No. 73 (H. Lodge ed. 1888), Hamilton focused on the President's role in making laws:

> "If even no propensity had ever discovered itself in the legislative body to invade the rights of the Executive, the rules of just reasoning and theoretic propriety would of themselves teach us that the one ought not to be left to the mercy of the other, but ought to possess a constitutional and effectual power of self-defense." *Id.* at 458.

. . . . In his Commentaries on the Constitution, Joseph Story makes the same point. 1 J. Story, Commentaries on the Constitution of the United States 614–615 (3d ed. 1858).

The President's role in the lawmaking process also reflects the Framers' careful efforts to check whatever propensity a particular Congress might have to enact oppressive, improvident, or ill-considered measures. The President's veto role in the legislative process was described later during public debate on ratification:

> "It establishes a salutary check upon the legislative body, calculated to guard the community against the effects of faction, precipitancy, or of any impulse unfriendly to the public good which may happen to influence a majority of that body.
>
> ". . . The primary inducement to conferring the power in question upon the Executive is to enable him to defend himself; the secondary one is to increase the chances in favor of the community against the passing of bad laws through haste, inadvertence, or design." The Federalist No. 73, *supra*, at 458 (A. Hamilton).

. . . . The Court also has observed that the Presentment Clauses serve the important purpose of assuring that a "national" perspective is grafted on the legislative process:

> "The President is a representative of the people just as the members of the Senate and of the House are, and it may be, at some times, on some subjects, that the President elected by all the people is rather more representative of them all than are the members of either body of the Legislature whose constituencies are local and not countrywide . . . ." *Myers v. United States*, [272 U.S. 52, 123 (1926)].

C

Bicameralism

The bicameral requirement of Art. I, §§ 1, 7, was of scarcely less concern to the Framers than was the Presidential veto and indeed the two concepts are interdependent. By providing that no law could take effect without the concurrence of the prescribed majority of the Members of both Houses, the Framers reemphasized their belief, already remarked upon in connection with the Presentment Clauses, that legislation should not be enacted unless it has been carefully and fully considered by the Nation's elected officials. In the Constitutional Convention debates on the need for a bicameral legislature, James Wilson, later to become a Justice of this Court, commented:

> "Despotism comes on mankind in different shapes. sometimes in an Executive, sometimes in a military, one. Is there danger of a Legislative despotism? Theory & practice both proclaim it. If the Legislative authority be not restrained, there can be neither liberty nor stability; and it can only be restrained by dividing it within itself, into distinct and independent branches. In a single house there is no check, but the inadequate one, of the virtue & good sense of those who compose it." 1 Farrand 254.

Hamilton argued that a Congress comprised of a single House was antithetical to the very purposes of the Constitution. Were the Nation to adopt a Constitution providing for only one legislative organ, he warned:

> "[W]e shall finally accumulate, in a single body, all the most important prerogatives of sovereignty, and thus entail upon our posterity one of the most execrable forms of government that human infatuation ever contrived. Thus we should create in reality that very tyranny which the adversaries of the new Constitution either are, or affect to be, solicitous to avert." The Federalist No. 22, p. 135 (H. Lodge ed. 1888).

. . . . [A]part from their fear that special interests could be favored at the expense of public needs, the Framers were also concerned, although not of one mind, over the apprehensions of the smaller states. Those states feared a commonality of interest among the larger states would work to their disadvantage; representatives of the larger states, on the other hand, were skeptical of a legislature that could pass laws favoring a minority of the people. See 1 Farrand 176–177, 484–491. It need hardly be repeated here that the Great Compromise, under which one House was viewed as representing the people and the other the states, allayed the fears of both the large and small states.

We see therefore that the Framers were acutely conscious that the bicameral requirement and the Presentment Clauses would serve essential constitutional functions. The President's participation in the legislative process was to protect the Executive Branch from Congress and to protect the whole people from improvident laws. The division of the Congress into two distinctive bodies assures that the legislative power would be exercised only after opportunity for full study and debate in separate settings. The President's unilateral veto power, in turn, was limited by the power of two thirds of both Houses of Congress to overrule a veto thereby precluding final arbitrary action of one person. See *id.* at 99–104. It emerges clearly that the prescription for legislative action in Art. I, §§ 1, 7 represents the Framers' decision that the legislative power of the Federal Government be exercised in accord with a single, finely wrought and exhaustively considered, procedure.

IV

The Constitution sought to divide the delegated powers of the new Federal Government into three defined categories, Legislative, Executive and Judicial, to assure, as nearly as possible, that each Branch of government would confine itself to its assigned responsibility. The hydraulic pressure inherent within each of the separate Branches to exceed the outer limits of its power, even to accomplish desirable objectives, must be resisted.

Although not "hermetically" sealed from one another, . . . the powers delegated to the three Branches are functionally identifiable. When any Branch acts, it is presumptively exercising the power the Constitution has delegated to it. See *J.W. Hampton & Co. v. United States*, 276 U.S. 394, 406 (1928). When the Executive acts, he presumptively acts in an executive or administrative capacity as defined in Art. II. And when, as here, one House of Congress purports to act, it is presumptively acting within its assigned sphere.

Beginning with this presumption, we must nevertheless establish that the challenged action under § 244(c)(2) is of the kind to which the procedural requirements of Art. I, § 7 apply. Not every action taken by either House is subject to the bicameralism and presentment requirements of Art. I. See *infra* at 955, and nn. 20, 21. Whether actions taken by either House are, in law and fact, an exercise of legislative power depends not on their form but upon "whether they contain matter which is properly to be regarded as legislative in its character and effect." S. Rep. No. 1335, 54th Cong., 2d Sess., 8 (1897).

Examination of the action taken here by one House pursuant to § 244(c)(2) reveals that it was essentially legislative in purpose and effect. In purporting to exercise power defined in Art. I, § 8, cl. 4 to "establish an uniform Rule of Naturalization," the House took action that had the purpose and effect of altering the legal rights, duties and relations of persons, including the Attorney General, Executive Branch officials and Chadha, all outside the Legislative Branch. Section 244(c)(2) purports to authorize one House of Congress to require the Attorney General to deport an individual alien whose deportation otherwise would be cancelled under § 244. The one-House veto operated in these cases to overrule the Attorney General and mandate Chadha's deportation;

absent the House action, Chadha would remain in the United States. Congress has *acted* and its action has altered Chadha's status.

The legislative character of the one-House veto in these cases is confirmed by the character of the Congressional action it supplants. Neither the House of Representatives nor the Senate contends that, absent the veto provision in § 244(c)(2), either of them, or both of them acting together, could effectively require the Attorney General to deport an alien once the Attorney General, in the exercise of legislatively delegated authority,[16] had determined the alien should remain in the United States. Without the challenged provision in § 244(c)(2), this could have been achieved, if at all, only by legislation requiring deportation.[17] Similarly, a veto by one House of Congress under § 244(c)(2) cannot be justified as an attempt at amending the standards set out in § 244(a)(1), or as a repeal of § 244 as applied to Chadha. Amendment and repeal of statutes, no less than enactment, must conform with Art. I.

The nature of the decision implemented by the one-House veto in these cases further manifests its legislative character. After long experience with the clumsy, time consuming private bill procedure, Congress made a deliberate choice to delegate to the Executive Branch, and specifically to the Attorney General, the authority to allow deportable aliens to remain in this country in certain specified circumstances. It is not disputed that this choice to delegate authority is precisely the kind of decision that can be implemented only in accordance with the procedures set out in Art. I. Disagreement with the Attorney General's decision on Chadha's deportation—that is, Congress' decision to deport Chadha—no less than Congress' original choice to delegate to the Attorney General the authority to make that decision, involves

[16] Congress protests that affirming the Court of Appeals in this case will sanction "lawmaking by the Attorney General. . . . Why is the Attorney General exempt from submitting his proposed changes in the law to the full bicameral process?" Brief for Petitioner in No. 80–2170, p. 40. . . . [But] [w]hen the Attorney General performs his duties pursuant to § 244, he does not exercise "legislative" power. See *Ernst & Ernst v. Hochfelder*, 425 U.S. 185, 213–214 (1976). The bicameral process is not necessary as a check on the Executive's administration of the laws because his administrative activity cannot reach beyond the limits of the statute that created it—a statute duly enacted pursuant to Art. I, §§ 1, 7. The constitutionality of the Attorney General's execution of the authority delegated to him by § 244 involves only a question of delegation doctrine. The courts, when a case or controversy arises, can always "ascertain whether the will of Congress has been obeyed," *Yakus v. United States*, 321 U.S. 414, 425 (1944), and can enforce adherence to statutory standards. . . . It is clear, therefore, that the Attorney General acts in his presumptively Art. II capacity when he administers the Immigration and Nationality Act. Executive action under legislatively delegated authority that might resemble "legislative" action in some respects is not subject to the approval of both Houses of Congress and the President for the reason that the Constitution does not so require. That kind of Executive action is always subject to check by the terms of the legislation that authorized it; and if that authority is exceeded it is open to judicial review as well as the power of Congress to modify or revoke the authority entirely. A one-House veto is clearly legislative in both character and effect and is not so checked; the need for the check provided by Art. I, §§ 1, 7, is therefore clear. Congress' authority to delegate portions of its power to administrative agencies provides no support for the argument that Congress can constitutionally control administration of the laws by way of a congressional veto.

[17] We express no opinion as to whether such legislation would violate any constitutional provision. . . .

determinations of policy that Congress can implement in only one way: bicameral passage followed by presentment to the President. Congress must abide by its delegation of authority until that delegation is legislatively altered or revoked.[19]

Finally, we see that when the Framers intended to authorize either House of Congress to act alone and outside of its prescribed bicameral legislative role, they narrowly and precisely defined the procedure for such action. There are but four provisions in the Constitution, explicit and unambiguous, by which one House may act alone with the unreviewable force of law, not subject to the President's veto:

(a) The House of Representatives alone was given the power to initiate impeachments. Art. I, § 2, cl. 5;

(b) The Senate alone was given the power to conduct trials following impeachment on charges initiated by the House and to convict following trial. Art. I, § 3, cl. 6;

(c) The Senate alone was given final unreviewable power to approve or to disapprove Presidential appointments. Art. II, § 2, cl. 2;

(d) The Senate alone was given unreviewable power to ratify treaties negotiated by the President. Art. II, § 2, cl. 2.

Clearly, when the Draftsmen sought to confer special powers on one House, independent of the other House, or of the President, they did so in explicit, unambiguous terms.[21] These carefully defined exceptions

---

[19] This does not mean that Congress is required to capitulate to "the accretion of policy control by forces outside its chambers." Javits and Klein, Congressional Oversight and the Legislative Veto: A Constitutional Analysis, 52 N.Y.U. L. Rev. 455, 462 (1977). The Constitution provides Congress with abundant means to oversee and control its administrative creatures. Beyond the obvious fact that Congress ultimately controls administrative agencies in the legislation that creates them, other means of control, such as durational limits on authorizations and formal reporting requirements, lie well within Congress' constitutional power. See *id.* at 460–461; Kaiser, Congressional Action to Overturn Agency Rules: Alternatives to the "Legislative Veto", 32 Admin. L. Rev. 667 (1980). . . .

[21] An exception from the Presentment Clauses was ratified in *Hollingsworth v. Virginia*, [3 U.S. (3 Dall.)] 378 (1798). There the Court held [that] Presidential approval was unnecessary for a proposed constitutional amendment which had passed both Houses of Congress by the requisite two-thirds majority. See U.S. Const., Art. V.

One might also include another "exception" to the rule that congressional action having the force of law be subject to the bicameral requirement and the Presentment Clauses. Each House has the power to act alone in determining specified internal matters. Art. I, § 7, cls. 2, 3, and § 5, cl. 2. However, this "exception" only empowers Congress to bind itself and is noteworthy only insofar as it further indicates the Framers' intent that Congress not act in any legally binding manner outside a closely circumscribed legislative arena, except in specific and enumerated instances.

Although the bicameral check was not provided for in any of these provisions for independent congressional action, precautionary alternative checks are evident. For example, Art. II, § 2, requires that two-thirds of the Senators present concur in the Senate's consent to a treaty, rather than the simple majority required for passage of legislation. . . . Similarly, the Framers adopted an alternative protection, in the stead of Presidential veto and bicameralism, by requiring the concurrence of two-thirds of the Senators present for a conviction of impeachment. Art. I, § 3. We also note that the Court's holding in *Hollingsworth, supra*, that a resolution proposing an amendment to the Constitution need not be presented to the President, is subject to two alternative protections. First, a constitutional amendment must command the

from presentment and bicameralism underscore the difference between the legislative functions of Congress and other unilateral but important and binding one-House acts provided for in the Constitution. These exceptions are narrow, explicit, and separately justified; none of them authorize the action challenged here. On the contrary, they provide further support for the conclusion that Congressional authority is not to be implied and for the conclusion that the veto provided for in § 244(c)(2) is not authorized by the constitutional design of the powers of the Legislative Branch.

Since it is clear that the action by the House under § 244(c)(2) was not within any of the express constitutional exceptions authorizing one House to act alone, and equally clear that it was an exercise of legislative power, that action was subject to the standards prescribed in Art. I. The bicameral requirement, the Presentment Clauses, the President's veto, and Congress' power to override a veto were intended to erect enduring checks on each Branch and to protect the people from the improvident exercise of power by mandating certain prescribed steps. To preserve those checks, and maintain the separation of powers, the carefully defined limits on the power of each Branch must not be eroded. To accomplish what has been attempted by one House of Congress in this case requires action in conformity with the express procedures of the Constitution's prescription for legislative action: passage by a majority of both Houses and presentment to the President.[23]

The veto authorized by § 244(c)(2) doubtless has been in many respects a convenient shortcut; the "sharing" with the Executive by Congress of its authority over aliens in this manner is, on its face, an appealing compromise. In purely practical terms, it is obviously easier for action to be taken by one House without submission to the President;

---

votes of two-thirds of each House. Second, three-fourths of the states must ratify any amendment.

[23] Neither can we accept the suggestion that the one-House veto provision in § 244(c)(2) either removes or modifies the bicameralism and presentation requirements for the enactment of future legislation affecting aliens. See *Atkins v. United States,* 556 F.2d 1028, 1063–1064 (Ct. Cl. 1977), cert. denied, 434 U.S. 1009 (1978); Brief for Petitioner in No. 80–2170, p. 40. The explicit prescription for legislative action contained in Art. I cannot be amended by legislation. . . .

Justice White suggests that the Attorney General's action under § 244(c)(1) suspending deportation is equivalent to a *proposal* for legislation and that because Congressional approval is indicated "by failure to veto, the one-House veto satisfies the requirement of bicameral approval." *Post* at 997. However, as the Court of Appeals noted, that approach "would analogize the effect of the one house disapproval to the failure of one house to vote affirmatively on a private bill." 634 F.2d 408, 435 (1980). Even if it were clear that Congress entertained such an arcane theory when it enacted § 244(c)(2), which Justice White does not suggest, this would amount to nothing less than an amending of Art. I. The legislative steps outlined in Art. I are not empty formalities; they were designed to assure that both Houses of Congress and the President participate in the exercise of lawmaking authority. This does not mean that legislation must always be preceded by debate; on the contrary, we have said that it is not necessary for a legislative body to "articulate its reasons for enacting a statute." *United States Railroad Retirement Board v. Fritz,* 449 U.S. 166, 179 (1980). But the steps required by Art. I, §§ 1, 7 make certain that there is an opportunity for deliberation and debate. To allow Congress to evade the strictures of the Constitution and in effect enact Executive proposals into law by mere silence cannot be squared with Art. I.

but it is crystal clear from the records of the Convention, contemporaneous writings and debates, that the Framers ranked other values higher than efficiency. The records of the Convention and debates in the states preceding ratification underscore the common desire to define and limit the exercise of the newly created federal powers affecting the states and the people. There is unmistakable expression of a determination that legislation by the national Congress be a step-by-step, deliberate and deliberative process.

The choices we discern as having been made in the Constitutional Convention impose burdens on governmental processes that often seem clumsy, inefficient, even unworkable, but those hard choices were consciously made by men who had lived under a form of government that permitted arbitrary governmental acts to go unchecked. There is no support in the Constitution or decisions of this Court for the proposition that the cumbersomeness and delays often encountered in complying with explicit constitutional standards may be avoided, either by the Congress or by the President. See *Youngstown Sheet & Tube Co. v. Sawyer*, 343 U.S. 579 (1952). With all the obvious flaws of delay, untidiness, and potential for abuse, we have not yet found a better way to preserve freedom than by making the exercise of power subject to the carefully crafted restraints spelled out in the Constitution. . . .

▪ *[A separate opinion by JUSTICE POWELL, concurring in the judgment, is omitted.]*

▪ *JUSTICE WHITE, dissenting:*

. . . . The prominence of the legislative veto mechanism in our contemporary political system and its importance to Congress can hardly be overstated. It has become a central means by which Congress secures the accountability of executive and independent agencies. Without the legislative veto, Congress is faced with a Hobson's choice: either to refrain from delegating the necessary authority, leaving itself with a hopeless task of writing laws with the requisite specificity to cover endless special circumstances across the entire policy landscape, or in the alternative, to abdicate its law-making function to the executive branch and independent agencies. To choose the former leaves major national problems unresolved; to opt for the latter risks unaccountable policymaking by those not elected to fill that role. Accordingly, over the past five decades, the legislative veto has been placed in nearly 200 statutes. The device is known in every field of governmental concern: reorganization, budgets, foreign affairs, war powers, and regulation of trade, safety, energy, the environment and the economy.

I

The legislative veto developed initially in response to the problems of reorganizing the sprawling government structure created in response to the Depression. The Reorganization Acts established the chief model for the legislative veto. When President Hoover requested authority to reorganize the government in 1929, he coupled his request that the "Congress be willing to delegate its authority over the problem (subject to defined principles) to the Executive" with a proposal for legislative review. He proposed that the Executive "should act upon approval of a joint committee of Congress or with the reservation of power of revision by Congress within some limited period adequate for its consideration." Public Papers of the Presidents, Herbert Hoover, 1929, p. 432 (1974). Congress followed President Hoover's suggestion and authorized reorganization subject to legislative review. Act of June 30, 1932, ch. 314, § 407, 47 Stat. 414. Although the reorganization authority reenacted in 1933 did not contain a legislative veto provision, the provision returned during the Roosevelt Administration and has since been renewed numerous times. . . .

. . . . World War II occasioned the need to transfer greater authority to the President in the[ ] areas [of national security and foreign affairs]. The legislative veto offered the means by which Congress could confer additional authority while preserving its own constitutional role. During World War II, Congress enacted over 30 statutes conferring powers on the Executive with legislative veto provisions. President Roosevelt accepted the veto as the necessary price for obtaining exceptional authority.

Over the quarter century following World War II, Presidents continued to accept legislative vetoes by one or both Houses as constitutional, while regularly denouncing provisions by which Congressional committees reviewed Executive activity.[5] The legislative veto balanced delegations of statutory authority in new areas of governmental involvement: the space program, international agreements on nuclear energy, tariff arrangements, and adjustment of federal pay rates.

During the 1970s the legislative veto was important in resolving a series of major constitutional disputes between the President and Congress over claims of the President to broad impoundment, war, and national emergency powers. . . .

. . . . In the educational field, it was found that fragmented and narrow grant programs "inevitably lead to Executive-Legislative confrontations" because they inaptly limited the Commissioner of Education's authority. S. Rep. No. 93–763, p. 69 (1974). The response was to grant the Commissioner of Education rulemaking authority, subject to a legislative veto. . . .

[5] Presidential objections to the veto, until the veto by President Nixon of the War Powers Resolution, principally concerned bills authorizing committee vetoes. As the Senate Subcommittee on Separation of Powers found in 1969, "an accommodation was reached years ago on legislative vetoes exercised by the entire Congress or by one House, [while] disputes have continued to arise over the committee form of the veto." S. Rep. No. 549, 91st Cong., 1st Sess., p. 14 (1969). . . .

Even this brief review suffices to demonstrate that the legislative veto is more than "efficient, convenient, and useful." *Ante* at 944. It is an important if not indispensable political invention that allows the President and Congress to resolve major constitutional and policy differences, assures the accountability of independent regulatory agencies, and preserves Congress' control over lawmaking. Perhaps there are other means of accommodation and accountability, but the increasing reliance of Congress upon the legislative veto suggests that the alternatives to which Congress must now turn are not entirely satisfactory.[10]

The history of the legislative veto also makes clear that it has not been a sword with which Congress has struck out to aggrandize itself at the expense of the other branches—the concerns of Madison and Hamilton. Rather, the veto has been a means of defense, a reservation of ultimate authority necessary if Congress is to fulfill its designated role under Art. I as the nation's lawmaker. While the President has often objected to particular legislative vetoes, generally those left in the hands of congressional committees, the Executive has more often agreed to legislative review as the price for a broad delegation of authority. To be sure, the President may have preferred unrestricted power, but that could be precisely why Congress thought it essential to retain a check on the exercise of delegated authority.

II

For all these reasons, the apparent sweep of the Court's decision today is regrettable. The Court's Art. I analysis appears to invalidate all legislative vetoes irrespective of form or subject. . . .

[10] While Congress could write certain statutes with greater specificity, it is unlikely that this is a realistic or even desirable substitute for the legislative veto. The controversial nature of many issues would prevent Congress from reaching agreement on many major problems if specificity were required in their enactments. Fuchs, Administrative Agencies and the Energy Problem, 47 Ind. L.J. 606, 608 (1972); Stewart, Reformation of American Administrative Law, 88 Harv. L. Rev. 1667, 1695–1696 (1975). For example, in the deportation context, the solution is not for Congress to create more refined categorizations of the deportable aliens whose status should be subject to change. In 1979, the Immigration and Naturalization Service proposed regulations setting forth factors to be considered in the exercise of discretion under numerous provisions of the Act, but not including § 244, to ensure "fair and uniform" adjudication "under appropriate discretionary criteria." 44 Fed. Reg. 36187 (1979). The proposed rule was canceled in 1981, because "[t]here is an inherent failure in any attempt to list those factors which should be considered in the exercise of discretion. It is impossible to list or foresee all of the adverse or favorable factors which may be present in a given set of circumstances." 46 Fed. Reg. 9119 (1981).

Oversight hearings and congressional investigations have their purpose, but unless Congress is to be rendered a think tank or debating society, they are no substitute for the exercise of actual authority. The "delaying" procedure approved in *Sibbach v. Wilson & Co.*, 312 U.S. 1, 15 (1941), while satisfactory for certain measures, has its own shortcomings. Because a new law must be passed to restrain administrative action, Congress must delegate authority without the certain ability of being able to check its exercise.

Finally, the passage of corrective legislation after agency regulations take effect or Executive Branch officials have acted entail the drawbacks endemic to a retroactive response. . . .

.... [T]he constitutional question posed today is one of immense difficulty over which the executive and legislative branches—as well as scholars and judges—have understandably disagreed. That disagreement stems from the silence of the Constitution on the precise question: The Constitution does not directly authorize or prohibit the legislative veto. Thus, our task should be to determine whether the legislative veto is consistent with the purposes of Art. I and the principles of separation of powers which are reflected in that Article and throughout the Constitution.[15] We should not find the lack of a specific constitutional authorization for the legislative veto surprising, and I would not infer disapproval of the mechanism from its absence. From the summer of 1787 to the present the government of the United States has become an endeavor far beyond the contemplation of the Framers. Only within the last half century has the complexity and size of the Federal Government's responsibilities grown so greatly that the Congress must rely on the legislative veto as the most effective if not the only means to insure its role as the Nation's lawmaker. But the wisdom of the Framers was to anticipate that the Nation would grow and new problems of governance would require different solutions. Accordingly, our Federal Government was intentionally chartered with the flexibility to respond to contemporary needs without losing sight of fundamental democratic principles....

III

The Court holds that the disapproval of a suspension of deportation by the resolution of one House of Congress is an exercise of legislative power without compliance with the prerequisites for lawmaking set forth in Art. I of the Constitution. Specifically, the Court maintains that the provisions of § 244(c)(2) are inconsistent with the requirement of bicameral approval, implicit in Art. I, § 1, and the requirement that all bills and resolutions that require the concurrence of both Houses be presented to the President, Art. I, § 7, cl. 2 and 3.

I do not dispute the Court's truismatic exposition of these clauses.... Part III of the Court's opinion[ ] is entirely unexceptionable.

It does not, however, answer the constitutional question before us. The power to exercise a legislative veto is not the power to write new law without bicameral approval or presidential consideration. The veto must be authorized by statute and may only negative what an Executive department or independent agency has proposed. On its face, the legislative veto no more allows one House of Congress to make law than does the presidential veto confer such power upon the President. Accordingly, the Court properly recognizes that it "must establish that

[15] I limit my concern here to those legislative vetoes which require either one or both Houses of Congress to pass resolutions of approval or disapproval, and leave aside the questions arising from the exercise of such powers by committees of Congress.

the challenged action under § 244(c)(2) is of the kind to which the procedural requirements of Art. I, § 7, apply" . . . . *Ante* at 952.

A

The terms of the Presentment Clauses suggest only that bills and their equivalent are subject to the requirements of bicameral passage and presentment to the President. . . .

Although the Clause does not specify the actions for which the concurrence of both Houses is "necessary," the proceedings at the Philadelphia Convention suggest its purpose was to prevent Congress from circumventing the presentation requirement in the making of new legislation. James Madison observed that if the President's veto was confined to bills, it could be evaded by calling a proposed law a "resolution" or "vote" rather than a "bill." Accordingly, he proposed that "or resolve" should be added after "bill" in what is now clause 2 of § 7. 2 M. Farrand, The Records of the Federal Convention of 1787, pp. 301–302 (1911). After a short discussion on the subject, the amendment was rejected. On the following day, however, Randolph renewed the proposal in the substantial form as it now appears, and the motion passed. *Id.* at 304–305; 5 J. Elliot, Debates on the Federal Constitution 431 (1845). The chosen language, Madison's comment, and the brevity of the Convention's consideration[ ] all suggest [that] a modest role was intended for the Clause and no broad restraint on Congressional authority was contemplated. See Stewart, Constitutionality of the Legislative Veto, 13 Harv. J. Legis. 593, 609–611 (1976). . . . There is no record that the Convention contemplated, let alone intended, that these Art. I requirements would someday be invoked to restrain the scope of congressional authority pursuant to duly enacted law.

When the Convention did turn its attention to the scope of Congress' lawmaking power, the Framers were expansive. The Necessary and Proper Clause, Art. I, § 8, cl. 18, vests Congress with the power "to make all laws which shall be necessary and proper for carrying into Execution the foregoing Powers [the enumerated powers of § 8], and all other Powers vested by this Constitution in the government of the United States, or in any Department or Officer thereof." It is long-settled that Congress may "exercise its best judgment in the selection of measures, to carry into execution the constitutional powers of the government," and "avail itself of experience, to exercise its reason, and to accommodate its legislation to circumstances." *McCulloch v. Maryland*, 4 Wheat. 316, 415–416, 420 (1819).

B

The Court heeded this counsel in approving the modern administrative state. The Court's holding today that all legislative-type action must be enacted through the lawmaking process ignores that legislative authority is routinely delegated to the Executive branch, to the independent regulatory agencies, and to private individuals and groups.

> "The rise of administrative bodies probably has been the most significant legal trend of the last century. . . . They have become a veritable fourth branch of the Government, which has deranged our three-branch legal theories . . . ." *FTC v. Ruberoid Co.*, 343 U.S. 470, 487 (1952) (Jackson, J. dissenting).

This Court's decisions sanctioning such delegations make clear that Art. I does not require all action with the effect of legislation to be passed as a law.

Theoretically, agencies and officials were asked only to "fill up the details," and the rule was that "Congress cannot delegate any part of its legislative power except under a limitation of a prescribed standard." *United States v. Chicago, M. St. P. & P. R. Co.*, 282 U.S. 311, 324 (1931). Chief Justice Taft elaborated the standard in *J.W. Hampton & Co. v. United States*, 276 U.S. 394, 409 (1928): "If Congress shall lay down by legislative act an intelligible principle to which the person or body authorized to fix such rates is directed to conform, such legislative action is not a forbidden delegation of legislative power." In practice, however, restrictions on the scope of the power that could be delegated diminished and all but disappeared. In only two instances did the Court find an unconstitutional delegation. *Panama Refining Co. v. Ryan*, 293 U.S. 388 (1935); *A.L.A. Schechter Poultry Corp. v. United States*, 295 U.S. 495 (1935). In other cases, the "intelligible principle" through which agencies have attained enormous control over the economic affairs of the country was held to include such formulations as "just and reasonable," *Tagg Bros. & Moorhead v. United States*, 280 U.S. 420 (1930), "public interest," *New York Central Securities Corp. v. United States*, 287 U.S. 12 (1932), "public convenience, interest, or necessity," *Federal Radio Comm'n v. Nelson Bros. Bond & Mortgage Co.*, 289 U.S. 266, 285 (1933), and "unfair methods of competition." *FTC v. Gratz*, 253 U.S. 421 (1920).

The wisdom and the constitutionality of these broad delegations are matters that still have not been put to rest. But for present purposes, these cases establish that by virtue of congressional delegation, legislative power can be exercised by independent agencies and Executive departments without the passage of new legislation. For some time, the sheer amount of law—the substantive rules that regulate private conduct and direct the operation of government—made by the agencies has far outnumbered the lawmaking engaged in by Congress through the traditional process. There is no question but that agency rulemaking is lawmaking in any functional or realistic sense of the term. The Administrative Procedure Act, 5 U.S.C. § 551(4), provides that a "rule" is an agency statement "designed to implement, interpret, or prescribe law or policy." When agencies are authorized to prescribe law through substantive rulemaking, the administrator's regulation is not only due deference, but is accorded "legislative effect." See, *e.g.*,

Schweiker v. Gray Panthers, 453 U.S. 34, 43–44 (1981) .... These regulations bind courts and officers of the federal government, may pre-empt state law, see, *e.g.*, *Fidelity Federal Savings & Loan Assn. v. De la Cuesta*, 458 U.S. 141 (1982), and grant rights to and impose obligations on the public. In sum, they have the force of law.

If Congress may delegate lawmaking power to independent and executive agencies, it is most difficult to understand Art. I as forbidding Congress from also reserving a check on legislative power for itself. Absent the veto, the agencies receiving delegations of legislative or quasi-legislative power may issue regulations having the force of law without bicameral approval and without the President's signature. It is thus not apparent why the reservation of a veto over the exercise of that legislative power must be subject to a more exacting test. In both cases, it is enough that the initial statutory authorizations comply with the Art. I requirements.

Nor are there strict limits on the agents that may receive such delegations of legislative authority so that it might be said that the legislature can delegate authority to others but not to itself. While most authority to issue rules and regulations is given to the executive branch and the independent regulatory agencies, statutory delegations to private persons have also passed this Court's scrutiny. In *Currin v. Wallace*, 306 U.S. 1 (1939), the statute provided that restrictions upon the production or marketing of agricultural commodities was to become effective only upon the favorable vote by a prescribed majority of the affected farmers. *United States v. Rock Royal Co-operative, Inc.*, 307 U.S. 533, 577 (1939), upheld an act which gave producers of specified commodities the right to veto marketing orders issued by the Secretary of Agriculture. Assuming *Currin* and *Rock Royal Co-operative* remain sound law, the Court's decision today suggests that Congress may place a "veto" power over suspensions of deportation in private hands or in the hands of an independent agency, but is forbidden from reserving such authority for itself. Perhaps this odd result could be justified on other constitutional grounds, such as the separation of powers, but certainly it cannot be defended as consistent with the Court's view of the Art. I presentment and bicameralism commands.

.... Under the Court's analysis, the Executive Branch and the independent agencies may make rules with the effect of law while Congress, in whom the Framers confided the legislative power, Art. I, § 1, may not exercise a veto which precludes such rules from having operative force. If the effective functioning of a complex modern government requires the delegation of vast authority which, by virtue of its breadth, is legislative or "quasi-legislative" in character, I cannot accept that Art. I—which is, after all, the source of the non-delegation doctrine—should forbid Congress from qualifying that grant with a legislative veto.

C

The Court also takes no account of perhaps the most relevant consideration: However resolutions of disapproval under § 244(c)(2) are formally characterized, in reality, a departure from the status quo occurs only upon the concurrence of opinion among the House, Senate, and President. Reservations of legislative authority to be exercised by Congress should be upheld if the exercise of such reserved authority is consistent with the distribution of and limits upon legislative power that Art. I provides.

1

As its history reveals, § 244(c)(2) withstands this analysis.... [Justice White here presented an expanded version of the history summarized in Part II of the majority's opinion, running from the Immigration Act of 1924 to the Alien Registration Act of 1940 to the Act of July 1, 1948, to the Immigration and Nationality Act of 1952. He noted that although Congress had passed the 1952 Act over President Truman's veto, Truman's objection to the Act "was not predicated on the presence of a legislative veto." He then summarized how § 244 of the 1952 Act worked: "Section 244(a)(1) authorizes the Attorney General, in his discretion, to suspend the deportation of certain aliens who are otherwise deportable .... Under § 244(c)(1) the Attorney General must report all such suspensions, with a detailed statement of facts and reasons, to the Congress. Either House may then act, in that session or the next, to block the suspension of deportation by passing a resolution of disapproval. § 244(c)(2). Upon Congressional approval of the suspension—by its silence—the alien's permanent status is adjusted to that of a lawful resident alien."]

The history of the Immigration Act makes clear that § 244(c)(2) did not alter the division of actual authority between Congress and the Executive. At all times, whether through private bills, or through affirmative concurrent resolutions, or through the present one-House veto, a permanent change in a deportable alien's status could be accomplished only with the agreement of the Attorney General, the House, and the Senate.

2

The central concern of the presentation and bicameralism requirements of Art. I is that when a departure from the legal status quo is undertaken, it is done with the approval of the President and both Houses of Congress—or, in the event of a presidential veto, a two-thirds majority in both Houses. This interest is fully satisfied by the operation of § 244(c)(2). The President's approval is found in the Attorney General's action in recommending to Congress that the deportation order for a given alien be suspended. The House and the Senate indicate their approval of the Executive's action by not passing a resolution of disapproval within the statutory period. Thus, a change in the legal status quo—the deportability of the alien—is consummated only with the approval of each of the three relevant actors. The disagreement of any one of the three maintains the alien's pre-existing status: the Executive may choose not to recommend suspension; the House and Senate may each veto the recommendation. The effect on the rights and obligations of the affected individuals and upon the legislative system is precisely the same as if a private bill were introduced but failed to receive the necessary approval. "The President and the two Houses enjoy exactly the same say in what the law is to be as would have been true for each without the presence of the one-House veto, and nothing in the law is changed absent the concurrence of the President and a majority in each House." *Atkins v. United States*, [556 F.2d 1028, 1064 (Ct. Cl. 1977)] . . . .

Thus understood, § 244(c)(2) fully effectuates the purposes of the bicameralism and presentation requirements. I now briefly consider possible objections to the analysis.

First, it may be asserted that Chadha's status before legislative disapproval is one of nondeportation and that the exercise of the veto, unlike the failure of a private bill, works a change in the status quo. This position plainly ignores the statutory language. At no place in § 244 has Congress delegated to the Attorney General any final power to determine which aliens shall be allowed to remain in the United States. Congress has retained the ultimate power to pass on such changes in deportable status. By its own terms, § 244(a) states that whatever power the Attorney General has been delegated to suspend deportation and adjust status is to be exercisable only "as hereinafter prescribed in this section." Subsection (c) is part of that section. A grant of "suspension" does not cancel the alien's deportation or adjust the alien's status to that of a permanent resident alien. A suspension order is merely a "deferment of deportation," *McGrath v. Kristensen*, 340 U.S. 162, 168 (1950), which can mature into a cancellation of deportation and adjustment of status only upon the approval of Congress—by way of silence—under § 244(c)(2). Only then does the statute authorize the Attorney General to "cancel deportation proceedings," § 244(c)(2), and "record the alien's lawful admission for permanent residence . . . ." § 244(d). . . .

Second, it may be said that this approach leads to the incongruity that the two-House veto is more suspect than its one-House brother. Although the idea may be initially counterintuitive, on close analysis, it is not at all unusual that the one-House veto is of more certain constitutionality than the two-House version. If the Attorney General's action is a proposal for legislation, then the disapproval of but a single House is all that is required to prevent its passage. Because approval is indicated by the failure to veto, the one-House veto satisfies the requirement of bicameral approval. The two-House version may present a different question. . . .

Third, it may be objected that Congress cannot indicate its approval of legislative change by inaction. In the Court of Appeals' view, inaction by Congress "could equally imply endorsement, acquiescence, passivity, indecision or indifference," 634 F.2d 408, 435 (1980), and the Court appears to echo this concern, *ante* at 958, n. 23. This objection appears more properly directed at the wisdom of the legislative veto than its constitutionality. The Constitution does not and cannot guarantee that legislators will carefully scrutinize legislation and deliberate before acting. In a democracy it is the electorate that holds the legislators accountable for the wisdom of their choices. It is hard to maintain that a private bill receives any greater individualized scrutiny than a resolution of disapproval under § 244(c)(2). Certainly the legislative veto is no more susceptible to this attack than the Court's increasingly common practice of according weight to the failure of Congress to disturb an Executive or independent agency's action. . . . Earlier this Term, the Court found it important that Congress failed to act on bills proposed to overturn the Internal Revenue Service's interpretation of the requirements for tax-exempt status under § 501(c)(3) of the tax code. *Bob Jones University v. United States*, 461 U.S. 574, 600–601 (1983). If Congress may be said to have ratified the Internal Revenue Service's interpretation without passing new legislation, Congress may also be said to approve a suspension of deportation by the Attorney General when it fails to exercise its veto authority. . . .

NOTES AND QUESTIONS

1. The majority opinion tied itself up in knots trying to define what counts as an exercise of "legislative" power. Chief Justice Burger indicated that actions taken by a single House (or, presumably, by other entities affiliated with Congress) are "legislative" if they "ha[ve] the purpose and effect of altering the legal rights, duties and relations of persons . . . outside the Legislative Branch." *Chadha*, 462 U.S. at 952. As Justice White's dissent noted, though, Congress routinely delegates authority to the executive branch to alter the legal rights and duties of private people. Indeed, § 244(a) of the Immigration and Nationality Act did precisely that when it authorized the Attorney General to suspend people's deportations. The majority responded that in the Attorney General's hands, this power is "executive" rather than "legislative": as long as a federal statute provides an "intelligible principle" to guide the exercise of the authority that it gives administrative agencies and other actors in the executive branch, modern doctrine tells us to see those actors as "executing" the statute rather than as crafting new laws out of whole cloth. *See* J.W. Hampton, Jr., & Co. v. United States, 276 U.S. 394, 409 (1928); *Chadha*, 462 U.S. at 953 n.16. But the majority's system of classification relied on its starting presumption that "[w]hen the Executive acts, he presumptively acts in an executive or administrative capacity . . . ." *Id.* at 951. If § 244(a) had purported to authorize a single House of Congress to exercise the suspension authority that the statute gave the Attorney General, the majority would have characterized that authority as "legislative" in the House's hands.

The upshot of the majority's analysis seems to be this: When an actor within the federal government takes an action that "ha[s] the purpose and effect of altering the legal rights, duties and relations of persons . . . outside the Legislative Branch," the action should ordinarily be classified as "legislative" if the actor is within Congress, but the action should ordinarily be classified as "executive" if the actor is within the executive branch and is acting pursuant to statutory authority. This taxonomy, which depends largely on the identity of the actor rather than the nature of the power, does not seem very useful. It certainly does not carry through on the majority's claim that "the powers delegated to the three Branches are functionally identifiable." *Id.*

But wasn't the majority's effort at classification unnecessary to its decision? The authority that § 244(c)(2) purported to give each House of Congress certainly seems like *some* sort of governmental power; in exercising that authority, the House would be acting on behalf of the federal government to alter the legal status of a private individual. If one characterizes this power as "legislative," then the arguments advanced by Chief Justice Burger apply: in general, Article I permits the federal government to exercise legislative power only through the process of bicameralism and presentment, and a federal statute cannot validly excuse future exercises of the legislative power from compliance with this process. But even if one instead characterizes the power as "executive," the House of Representatives still cannot validly exercise it: Congress cannot empower the House of Representatives to "execute" the Immigration and Nationality Act of 1952, because Article II vests the federal government's executive power in the President. Similarly, if one characterizes the power to review the Attorney General's decision suspending Chadha's deportation as "judicial" (which is how Justice Powell's concurring opinion saw it), then Article *III* would keep Congress from giving the power to the House. On this analysis, § 244(c)(2) was unconstitutional no matter how one classifies the power that it purported to give each House—which means that the Court did not need to wade into the classification problem at all. *See* M. Elizabeth Magill, *Beyond Powers and Branches in Separation of Powers Law*, 150 U. PA. L. REV. 603, 615–16 (2001) (discussing this sort of argument); Metro. Washington Airports Auth. v. Citizens for the Abatement of Aircraft Noise, 501 U.S. 252, 276 (1991) (embracing the argument: "If the power is executive, the Constitution does not permit an agent of Congress to exercise it. If the power is legislative, Congress must exercise it in conformity with the bicameralism and presentment requirements of Art. I, § 7.").

2. The analysis just suggested is highly formalistic. That presumably would not have bothered the majority (whose analysis was also formalistic), but it would not have persuaded Justice White. How might he have responded?

One of Justice White's key arguments (advanced in Part III.C of his dissent) was that the Court should consider all of § 244 as a package: the legislative veto authorized by § 244(c)(2) should be analyzed in tandem with the delegation of suspension authority to the Attorney General in § 244(a). Before anyone invoked any part of § 244, Chadha was a deportable noncitizen who was being deported under the 1952 Act. Under § 244, changing that legal status quo required the concurrence of the executive branch (via the Attorney General's exercise of his suspension authority under § 244(a)) and both Houses of Congress (in that either House could use its "veto" under § 244(c)(2) to override the Attorney General's suspension decision). Justice White argued that as a functional matter, this structure gives us essentially the same thing as bicameralism and presentment.

The idea that the authority conferred by § 244 was all part of a single package suggests a possible answer to the argument advanced in the prior note. In Chadha's case, there is a sense in which the federal government was not using § 244 to do anything at all: Chadha's legal status before § 244 came into play (a deportable noncitizen who was being deported) was exactly the same as his legal status after the operation of § 244 was complete.[13] To be sure, the Attorney General's action under § 244(a) gave Chadha some hope in the middle, but the House's "veto" simply canceled that action and left Chadha where he had been at the start. Could one plausibly argue that in cases like Chadha's, the federal government has not actually used any sort of governmental power at all under § 244 (whether legislative, executive, or judicial)—and hence that the argument advanced in the prior note is inapplicable?

3. One way to think about Justice White's "package" argument is to compare the arrangement that prevailed before 1940 to the arrangement established in § 244 of the 1952 Act. Under both arrangements, the government could order the deportation of noncitizens who were deportable and who did not qualify for relief. Before 1940, the only mechanism for relief was a "private act"—a statute, enacted by Congress in conformity with the constitutional requirements of bicameralism and presentment, that named particular noncitizens and gave them the right to remain in the United States. Section 244 of the 1952 Act established an additional mechanism for relief: if the Attorney General used his delegated authority under § 244(a) to suspend a noncitizen's deportation, and if each House of Congress refrained from exercising its "veto" under § 244(c)(2), then the noncitizen would be allowed to remain in the United States. Was Justice White correct to suggest that the combination of delegation-plus-legislative-veto is the functional equivalent of bicameralism and presentment?

One obvious difference between the mechanism for relief that prevailed before 1940 and the mechanism for relief established by § 244 is that a private act granting relief to the noncitizen would require the

[13] Or, rather, Chadha's legal status before § 244 came into play was exactly the same as what his legal status would have been at the end of the process if the Supreme Court had allowed § 244(c)(2) to operate as designed.

affirmative consent of both Houses of Congress. By contrast, when the Attorney General exercised his delegated authority to suspend a noncitizen's deportation under § 244(a), Justice White proposed to infer the "agreement" of the House and Senate from their *inaction*. One might use this difference to argue that § 244 gave the executive branch too much power: it allowed the executive branch to alter a noncitizen's legal status without any affirmative indication of congressional approval. But this argument runs into a serious problem: everyone agreed that § 244 would have been constitutional if it had given the executive branch *even more* power, by delegating suspension authority to the Attorney General without retaining any "veto" authority for either House of Congress. Indeed, that is exactly what § 244 did under the majority's opinion (which held that § 244(c)(2) was unconstitutional but that the rest of § 244 was separable from it). Given the constitutionality of that *unfettered* delegation to the Attorney General, can there really be a functional problem with the somewhat more fettered delegation that Congress tried to establish?

The answer might conceivably be "yes." Consider the following three-step argument, which Justice Scalia laid out in his dissent in *Mistretta v. United States*, 488 U.S. 361 (1989).

- First, Justice Scalia emphasized the importance of the aspirations behind the nondelegation doctrine. In his words, "It is difficult to imagine a principle more essential to democratic government than that upon which the doctrine of unconstitutional delegation is founded: Except in a few areas constitutionally committed to the Executive Branch, the basic policy decisions governing society are to be made by the Legislature." *Id.* at 415 (Scalia, J., dissenting).
- Second, Justice Scalia noted the practical difficulty of using retail-level judicial review to promote those aspirations. "[W]hile the doctrine of unconstitutional delegation is unquestionably a fundamental element of our constitutional system, it is not an element readily enforceable by the courts." In particular, courts "have almost never felt qualified" to second-guess the amount of substantive discretion that Congress has decided to confer upon actors in the executive branch, and to insist that Congress must give those actors more specific guidance. *Id.* at 416. *But cf.* Gundy v. United States, 139 S. Ct. 2116, 2133–42 (2019) (Gorsuch, J., dissenting) (advocating a beefed-up nondelegation doctrine).
- Third, "[p]recisely because" courts are unable to police the scope of delegations at the retail level, Justice Scalia concluded that courts should "be particularly rigorous in preserving the Constitution's structural restrictions that deter excessive delegation." *Mistretta*, 488 U.S. at 416–17 (Scalia, J., dissenting). As Justice Scalia understood the Constitution, one

> of those restrictions is that "Congress [can] delegate lawmaking authority only at the expense of increasing the power of either the President or the courts." *Id.* at 421. The natural rivalry between Congress and the executive branch, Justice Scalia suggested, will act as a brake on Congress's inclination to pass broad laws that delegate enormous substantive discretion to the executive branch. *See id.* (describing the President as "[Congress's] primary competitor for political power").

Although Justice Scalia was advancing this argument for a different purpose in *Mistretta*, it arguably bears on *Chadha* too. If Congress cannot retain the legislative veto as a check on the executive's exercise of delegated authority, perhaps Congress will not delegate quite so much power to the executive branch. On this view, one possible problem with the legislative veto is that it makes delegation too costless for Congress; it eliminates a practical brake on Congress's tendency to hand off policy decisions to the executive branch, and such practical brakes are important because the judiciary cannot realistically enforce the nondelegation doctrine more directly. *See* John F. Manning, *Textualism as a Nondelegation Doctrine*, 97 COLUM. L. REV. 673, 716–17 (1997) (associating *Chadha* with the idea that "Congress will find it too attractive to sidestep bicameralism and presentment if it can delegate power *and* retain control over the delegatee").

Is this argument persuasive? If not, can you think of any other responses to Justice White's claim that § 244 must be evaluated as a package and that it provided the functional equivalent of bicameralism and presentment? Might one response simply be that the Constitution erects a "rule" rather than a "standard" on this point, and that courts should not try to make case-by-case judgments about whether particular arrangements will carry out the purposes that the requirement of bicameralism and presentment was designed to achieve? *Cf.* New York v. United States, 505 U.S. 144, 187 (1992) ("Much of the Constitution is concerned with setting forth the form of our government, and the courts have traditionally invalidated measures deviating from that form. The result may appear 'formalistic' in a given case to partisans of the measure at issue, because such measures are typically the product of the era's perceived necessity. But the Constitution protects us from our own best intentions: It divides power among sovereigns and among branches of government precisely so that we may resist the temptation to concentrate power in one location as an expedient solution to the crises of the day."). If you agree with that response, how do you know that the Constitution *does* establish a rule rather than standard on this point?

NOTE ON *CHADHA* AND THE DEBATE OVER LEGISLATIVE HISTORY

Although *Chadha*'s invalidation of the legislative veto was controversial in some circles, people had long accepted the basic idea that Congress can exercise "legislative" power only through the process of bicameralism and presentment spelled out in Article I, § 7. *See, e.g.*, REED DICKERSON, THE INTERPRETATION AND APPLICATION OF STATUTES 9 (1975). Professor Dickerson, moreover, had observed that this idea bore on the proper use of legislative history. As he put the point, "not even the most reliable document of legislative history, such as a conference committee report, may have the force of law." If such a document could have weight in the interpretive process, it was only as "part of proper legislative context (if it can meet the applicable standards)" for a duly enacted statute. *Id.* at 10; *see also id.* at 124 (elaborating upon "the applicable standards" for treating information as part of a statute's "context," and arguing that "[p]roper context . . . consists only of the cultural aspects of the speech community concerned that, when considered in relation to the written vehicle, are (1) relevant to the written vehicle, (2) reliably revealed, (3) shared by the author and the legislative audience, and (4) relied on by both author and audience to complete the communication").

Shortly after his appointment to the Supreme Court, Justice Scalia endorsed and extended the argument that certain uses of legislative history were unconstitutional. He also linked this argument to *Chadha*. As he observed in one separate opinion, "Committee reports, floor speeches, and . . . colloquies between Congressmen . . . are frail substitutes for bicameral vote upon the text of a law and its presentment to the President. See generally *INS* v. *Chadha*, 462 U.S. 919 (1983)." *Thompson v. Thompson*, 484 U.S. 174, 191–92 (1988) (Scalia, J., concurring in the judgment). Indeed, Justice Scalia put this argument at the top of his list of reasons to avoid reliance upon legislative history: "The greatest defect of legislative history is its illegitimacy. We are governed by laws, not by the intentions of legislators." *Conroy v. Aniskoff*, 507 U.S. 511, 519 (1993) (Scalia, J., concurring in the judgment); *see also* Begier v. IRS, 496 U.S. 53, 68 (1990) (Scalia, J., concurring in the judgment) ("Congress conveys its directions in the Statutes at Large, not in excerpts from the Congressional Record, much less in excerpts from the Congressional Record that do not clarify the text of any pending legislative proposal.").

Justice Scalia's argument is plainly correct up to a point. Nearly everyone agrees that statutory interpreters should not give legal effect to what Judge Easterbrook calls the "raw intent" of members of Congress—mental states and desires that "cannot be matched to a statute." Frank H. Easterbrook, *Text, History, and Structure in Statutory Interpretation*, 17 HARV. J. L. & PUB. POL'Y 61, 65 (1994). Under the constitutional arrangements discussed in *Chadha*, members of Congress do not make law simply by formulating ideas in their heads; to change the law, those ideas must be reduced to a written bill that is passed in the same form by each House and is signed by the President (or repassed over his veto by the necessary supermajority in each House). One consequence of this fact is that even a fully informed, deliberate decision by the President and by majorities in each House of Congress to support a particular policy is not a sufficient condition for that policy to become law. *See, e.g.*, Frank H. Easterbrook, *The Role of Original Intent in Statutory Construction*, 11 HARV. J. L. & PUB. POL'Y 59, 64 (1988) ("If we took an opinion poll of Congress today on a raft of issues and found out its views, would those views become the law? Certainly not. They must run the gamut of the process—and process is the essence of legislation. . . . [I]n [*Chadha*] . . . the Court emphasized the importance of process." (footnotes omitted)).[14]

Justice Scalia, though, took this point farther. In his view, "the only language that constitutes 'a Law' within the meaning of the Bicameralism and Presentment Clause of Article I, § 7, *and hence the only language adopted in a fashion that entitles it to our attention*, is the text of the enacted statute." *Zedner v. United States*, 547 U.S. 489, 509–10 (2006) (Scalia, J., concurring in part and concurring in the judgment) (emphasis added). It follows, he suggested, that the language of committee reports and the like deserves no weight in the interpretive process. *See id.* Even if the materials of legislative history could reliably reflect the legislature's intentions, those intentions are not the "Law" to which Article I refers; legislative intentions matter only to the extent that they are "textually expressed," and then only because the text reflects them. *See* Bank One Chicago, N.A. v. Midwest Bank & Trust Co., 516 U.S. 264, 279 (1996) (Scalia, J., concurring in part and concurring in the judgment) ("In my view a law means what its text most appropriately conveys, whatever the Congress that enacted it might have 'intended.' "); *see also, e.g.*, Zuni Pub. School Dist. No. 89 v. Dep't of Education, 550 U.S. 81, 116–17 (2007) (Scalia, J., dissenting) (associating this view with "the system of lawmaking set forth in our Constitution"). This logic, Justice Scalia suggested, leads to the conclusion that the materials of legislative history are simply irrelevant to the task of statutory interpretation. *See, e.g.*, Graham County Soil & Water Conservation Dist. v. United States ex rel. Wilson, 559 U.S. 280, 302 (2010) (Scalia, J., concurring in part and concurring in the judgment) (denying that purposes gleaned from

[14] Conversely, if a proposal *does* go through the constitutionally required procedures of bicameralism and presentment, then it *does* become law—even if it lacks the fully informed, deliberate support of majorities in each House of Congress. There are various ways in which a proposal can become law without receiving that sort of support. First, legal change can occur when Congress and the President go through the requisite constitutional formalities, even if they have not thought hard about what they are doing. Second, even when individual members of Congress have acted very deliberately and know exactly what they are doing, proposals can become law without enjoying the support of legislative majorities in an absolute sense. Perhaps a key member of Congress was able to attach a proposal as an add-on to a popular bill, and the relevant procedural rules are such that no one wants to take the time to try to eliminate the add-on. Or perhaps some vote-trading or "logrolling" has occurred, so that people in Congress who do not really like the proposal have agreed to support it in exchange for a swing bloc's support for another proposal. Or perhaps the proposal was inserted in a vain attempt to kill the entire bill, and was enacted into law even though *no one* really wanted it.

No one thinks that courts can refuse to enforce a provision simply because the provision would not have been enacted if it had been presented to Congress as a freestanding proposal under different procedural rules. In this respect, the sincere support of a majority of members in each House of Congress, who understand and embrace a particular provision on its own terms, is not a necessary condition for the provision to become law.

legislative history can properly affect the meaning that interpreters ascribe to a statutory term, and explaining that "[t]he Constitution gives legal effect to the 'Laws' Congress enacts, Art. VI, cl. 2, not the objectives its Members aimed to achieve in voting for them").

It is certainly possible to maintain (as American courts did for many years in the nineteenth century) that the "meaning" of statutory language does not depend upon information in committee reports or the like. In my view, though, it is hard to maintain that the Bicameralism and Presentment Clause of Article I *compels* this position and forbids any other interpretive regime. To say that Congress can validly exercise its legislative powers only through the process of bicameralism and presentment is not to say that the materials of legislative history are necessarily irrelevant to the interpretation of the texts that do go through that process. The "raw intent" of members of Congress is indeed beside the point; in the absence of a duly enacted text, Congress has not changed the law, and there is nothing for courts to interpret. But when a statute *has* been enacted, courts have to figure out what it means. The interpretive principles that they use for that purpose, moreover, might be designed so that (in the aggregate) the meanings that courts ascribe to duly enacted statutes bear some relationship to the messages that members of the enacting legislature collectively intended those statutes to convey. The irrelevance of "raw intent" does not establish the irrelevance of this sort of "communicative intent," or what Ronald Dworkin calls "semantic intention." *See* Ronald Dworkin, *Comment, in* A MATTER OF INTERPRETATION: FEDERAL COURTS AND THE LAW 115, 116 (Amy Gutmann ed., 1997) (defining "semantic intention" as "what [legislators] intended to say in enacting the language they used" (emphasis omitted)); *see also, e.g.*, Stanley Fish, *Almost Pragmatism: Richard Posner's Jurisprudence*, 57 U. CHI. L. REV. 1447, 1456–57 (1990) (book review) (arguing that interpretation inevitably "takes communicative intent into account" and that different readings of a text simply "proceed in the light of differently assumed communicative intents"); *cf.* LAWRENCE M. SOLAN, THE LANGUAGE OF STATUTES: LAWS AND THEIR INTERPRETATION 115 (2010) ("I do not believe that any judge or commentator can consistently maintain that courts should dispense altogether with discussion of legislative intent. The concept is just too deeply embedded in the way we see the world . . . ."). Admittedly, collective communicative intentions will not exist on every question that courts may later confront. But when the materials of legislative history suggest that they *do* exist, nothing about the constitutional requirements of bicameralism and presentment necessarily requires interpreters to ignore them. After all, the very definition of "communicative" or "semantic" intent is linked to the text that goes through the process of bicameralism and presentment, and legislators presumably cast their votes for that text on the basis of what they understand the bill to say.

Justice Scalia himself did not maintain that it is unconstitutional for interpreters to care about "semantic intention." To be sure, he preferred to refer to "import" rather than "intention," so as to put the focus "upon what the text would reasonably be understood to mean, rather than upon what it was intended to mean." Antonin Scalia, *Response, in* A MATTER OF INTERPRETATION: FEDERAL COURTS AND THE LAW 129, 144 (Amy Gutmann ed., 1997). But he acknowledged that the reasonable reader whom he envisioned, when given the information about a statute's "context" that Justice Scalia would allow interpreters to consider, would use that information to try to grasp the message that the text was designed to convey. *See id.* (conceding that the concepts of import and intention "chase one another back and forth to some extent, since the import of language depends upon its context, which includes the occasion for, and hence the evident purpose of, its utterance"); *see also supra* pp. 42–43 (using this analysis to explain why the reasonable reader would prefer to read § 1 of a statute in a way that does not make something in § 5 superfluous). Thus, Justice Scalia acknowledged that "so far Professor Dworkin and I are in accord: we both follow 'semantic intention.' " Scalia, *Response*, *supra*, at 144.

With this concession in hand, one can readily argue that genuinely interpretive uses of legislative history—that is, uses designed to capture the enacting legislature's "semantic intention" rather than simply "raw intent"—are perfectly consistent with the requirement of bicameralism and presentment. The argument proceeds as follows: (1) the Bicameralism and Presentment Clause establishes the prerequisites for a statutory text to become a "Law," but it does not provide detailed instructions about how to determine the meaning of that Law; (2) even Justice Scalia agreed that it is desirable for the meaning that interpreters ascribe to a statute to correlate in some way with the meaning that members of the enacting legislature understood themselves to be conveying (to the extent that such collective understandings exist); (3) when interpreters try to determine the meaning of a statute, they should therefore use the information that they are permitted to consider for the purpose of trying to identify the message that the enacting legislature itself associated with the statutory text that went through bicameralism and presentment; and (4) just as the information that interpreters draw upon for this purpose can include "the public history of the times," *see supra* p. 345, so too it can include publicly available legislative history—not because legislative history is a proper substitute for statutory text, but because legislative history is part of the relevant background for understanding that text. *See, e.g.*, Stephen Breyer, *On the Uses of Legislative History in Interpreting Statutes*, 65 S. CAL. L. REV. 845, 863 (1992) ("No one claims that legislative history is a statute, or even that, in any strong sense, it is 'law.' Rather, legislative history is helpful in trying to understand the meaning of the words that do make up the statute or the 'law.' ").

Textualists sometimes respond to this sort of argument by complaining that it opens a door for members of Congress or their staffs to communicate with the courts (and to give the courts instructions that the courts will treat as authoritative) outside of the medium of statutory language. Admittedly, those supplementary instructions work only to the extent that Congress goes ahead and enacts a statute through the process of bicameralism and presentment. But if courts treat committee reports and the like as an official indication of the instructions that Congress meant to convey through the statutory text, perhaps they are allowing an unfortunate circumvention of the constitutionally mandated process for making law.

Professor (now Dean) John Manning, who is the legal academy's leading defender of textualism, has elaborated upon this idea. He started with a simple observation: it clearly would be unconstitutional for Congress to enact a statute that uses a particular term and that purports to define that term as meaning whatever the relevant committees of the House and Senate declare it to mean in the future. *See* John F. Manning, *Textualism as a Nondelegation Doctrine*, 97 COLUM. L. REV. 673, 714 (1997). Of course, Congress could use the term in a statute without providing any definition at all, with the result that courts or administrative agencies could later choose from among the permissible constructions; even though the content that the courts or administrative agencies pour into the term might not itself have gone through the process of bicameralism and presentment, the Constitution does not require Congress to resolve all questions of detail itself. But *Chadha* and subsequent cases make clear that "Congress cannot delegate power to its own components or to agents under its control." *Id.* at 717.

According to Professor Manning, the uses to which courts sometimes put legislative history run afoul of this idea. In particular, when courts allow statements in committee reports or the like to determine the proper application of vague statutory language, or when they treat such statements as authoritatively resolving ambiguities in language that would otherwise lend itself to multiple constructions, they are effectively "allow[ing] Congress to shift law elaboration from the full legislative process to the less cumbersome process of generating legislative history." *Id.* at 719.[15] Professor Manning conceded that Congress as a whole might

---

[15] More precisely, Professor Manning objected to uses of legislative history that give weight to "a committee's or sponsor's mere declaration of intent," *id.* at 684, or that otherwise accord statements in legislative history special status because they come from individuals or entities within Congress. He did not object when courts use arguments or information in legislative history as they would use arguments or information in a law-review article or an amicus brief. For instance, if a committee report sets forth evidence that a particular phrase in a statute has a technical meaning as a term of art in the relevant field, and if a court evaluates that evidence and confirms its accuracy, the legislative history will have helped the court identify the phrase's meaning—not because the committee has simply declared that Congress meant to use the phrase in that way, but because the committee report has persuasively pointed the court to the same sort of outside information that a brief might highlight. *See id.* at 731–37; *see also* John F. Manning, *Putting Legislative History to a Vote: A Response to Professor Siegel*, 53 VAND. L. REV. 1529, 1529 n.2 (2000) (indicating that Professor Manning's concerns arise

want to accomplish exactly that result, and might therefore want courts to give authoritative weight to legislative history in resolving interpretive questions. But Professor Manning argued that "the prohibition against legislative self-delegation" recognized in *Chadha* cuts against an interpretive regime that allows sub-units of Congress to fill in the details of legislation in this way, even if Congress as a whole wants courts to use that regime. *See id.* at 675.

Of course, as Professor Jonathan Siegel emphasized in a response to Professor Manning's article, the fact that the Constitution prevents Congress from conferring *future* lawmaking power upon one of its committees does not mean that the Constitution prevents Congress from relying upon or incorporating into a statute work that the committee *has already done* at the time that Congress acts. *See* Jonathan R. Siegel, *The Use of Legislative History in a System of Separated Powers*, 53 VAND. L. REV. 1457 (2000). In most situations, moreover, the important pieces of legislative history that courts might use to interpret a statute have already been created by the time that both Houses of Congress take their final votes on the statute.[16] According to Professor Siegel, this fact defeats Professor Manning's argument: if our interpretive regime specifies that the pre-existing materials of legislative history can provide authoritative glosses on statutory texts, then each House of Congress and the President are effectively adopting the statute with those glosses when they take their final action upon the bill. In Professor Siegel's view, what Professor Manning refers to as a delegation of authority is better thought of as "incorporation by reference." *Id.* at 1460.

I myself doubt that current interpretive practices make legislative history relevant in quite the way that the idea of "incorporation by reference" suggests. Even judges who are willing to use legislative history do not typically think of Congress as having *enacted* the legislative history via incorporation into the statutory text. Nor is it clear what that would mean; committee reports and transcripts of legislative debates do not take the form of legal directives. Instead of treating legislative history as itself having the force of law, judges typically treat it as evidence of the communicative intent associated with the words of a statute. That information, in turn, colors how judges interpret those words.

But while the idea of "incorporation by reference" does not seem quite right, Professor Siegel's basic argument might still work. As Professor Siegel suggested, the meaning of the statutory texts that go

"when courts use [legislative history] to settle meaning while simultaneously attributing its authority to the identity of its source").

[16] There are some rare situations in which one House of Congress considers a bill after the other chamber has already approved it, creates some new legislative history that might bear on the bill's meaning, but then passes the bill in exactly the form that the first chamber approved. In such situations, the bill will go straight to the President for signature, without being submitted again to the first chamber; thus, the first chamber will have no opportunity to review the legislative history that the second chamber created. Professor Siegel seemed inclined to accept Professor Manning's argument with respect to legislative history of this sort. *See* Siegel, *supra*, 53 VAND. L. REV. at 1520–24.

through bicameralism and presentment depends *both* upon the texts themselves *and* upon the applicable principles of interpretation. Thus, the Bicameralism and Presentment Clause does not prevent courts from interpreting a statute in light of the canons or other features of the interpretive regime in place at the time of the statute's enactment. One can make the same argument about the use of legislative history: if the interpretive regime in place at the time of enactment permits interpreters to resolve ambiguities in light of the publicly available legislative history (as it stood when the bill was passed by the first House of Congress that approved the final version of the bill), why would the Bicameralism and Presentment Clause stand in the way? Can't the glosses suggested by the legislative history, like the glosses suggested by canons, be regarded as part of the meaning of the text that goes through bicameralism and presentment?

In his original article, Professor Manning had anticipated this objection and sought to refute it. One of the purposes of the requirement of bicameralism and presentment, he suggested, is to help preserve legislators' accountability to the voters. But if legislators can vote for statutory texts that are vague or ambiguous, and if courts then draw upon committee reports or the like to flesh out the meaning of those texts, rank-and-file legislators may be able to duck some of the responsibility for the details that Congress has nonetheless managed to convey to the courts. *See* Manning, *supra*, 97 COLUM. L. REV. at 720–21. Indeed, because conventional approaches to legislative history put more weight on committee reports and statements by a bill's sponsors than on individual statements by other legislators, rank-and-file legislators seeking to avoid responsibility for the details that a committee report or sponsor statement conveys to the courts "can even take to the floor and make statements disavowing the committee's or sponsor's interpretation," without affecting the courts' reliance upon those details. *See id.* at 721 ("In those circumstances, committees' and sponsors' statements may have dispositive effect, but the rank-and-file legislators need not take responsibility for their contents, either through votes or public expressions of assent.").

In a subsequent response to Professor Siegel, Professor Manning expanded upon this point. Professor Manning said that his concern about responsibility would evaporate if the statutory text on which members of Congress vote explicitly pointed to particular pieces of legislative history and adopted their glosses by reference.[17] But Professor Manning saw a

---

[17] *Cf.* Daniel A. Farber & Philip P. Frickey, *Legislative Intent and Public Choice*, 74 VA. L. REV. 423, 441 n.61 (1988) (quoting a 1982 speech in which Senator Armstrong referred to "a scheme which I have long had in mind which is to offer language to a bill . . . to simply endorse or reject specifically the language of committee reports"). As Professors Siegel and Manning both noted, the leading example along these lines comes from the Civil Rights Act of 1991. As we saw in Chapter 2, the bill that became that statute was designed to respond to a number of Supreme Court decisions, including *Wards Cove Packing Co. v. Atonio*, 490 U.S. 642 (1989). In 1990, the House and Senate both had voted for a bill that would have superseded those decisions, but the President had vetoed the bill and Congress had been unable to override the

difference between this sort of explicit incorporation (which would operate on a statute-by-statute basis) and a generic presumption that *whenever* Congress enacts a statute, the statutory text implicitly adopts whatever glosses courts can glean from the legislative history. Indeed, Professor Manning suggested that even if Congress *wants* courts to apply this generic presumption, Congress cannot validly enact a framework statute telling them to do so. Such a framework statute, Professor Manning suggested, would be no more constitutional than the legislative veto or other congressional attempts to change the constitutionally mandated procedures for exercising the legislative power. In Professor Manning's words,

> "A statute instructing courts to give [legislative] history decisive effect, without insisting upon direct and specific legislative assent, allows legislators to avoid the difficulties associated with that choice. In so doing, it effectively permits Congress to generate binding statutory details through a process other than bicameralism and presentment."

John F. Manning, *Putting Legislative History to a Vote: A Response to Professor Siegel*, 53 VAND. L. REV. 1529, 1541 (2000).

One odd feature of the debate between Professor Manning and Professor Siegel is that both scholars arguably took a different approach to the interpretation of Article I than they took to the interpretation of statutes. Professor Siegel, who is not much of a formalist in statutory interpretation, relied upon a formalistic understanding of bicameralism and presentment: if an interpretive regime is in place, then it dictates the "meaning" of bills that go through the process of bicameralism and presentment, and there can be no constitutional objection to treating the bill as a mere placeholder for that meaning. Professor Manning, who *is* a formalist when it comes to statutory interpretation, took a more functional view of the Bicameralism and Presentment Clause: he suggested that the Clause should be understood to condemn certain interpretive regimes that do not contradict its terms, but that have the potential to frustrate its underlying purposes. *See* Manning, *Textualism as a Nondelegation Doctrine*, 97 COLUM. L. REV. at 739 ("[I]f the

---

veto. The next year, lawyers in the executive branch worked with congressional staffers to hammer out a deal that would be acceptable to the President. But there was a problem: the legislative debate on the new bill was both voluminous and contentious. Particularly with respect to the *Wards Cove* issue, people involved in the negotiations seem to have been concerned that if the 1991 bill was enacted into law, courts interpreting it might seize upon statements in the legislative history that were not part of the deal. To guard against this risk, they hit upon a novel solution. During the legislative process, the text of the bill was amended so that it specifically addressed the legislative history and limited the field that courts could consult. In particular, § 105(b) of the Civil Rights Act of 1991, as enacted into law, reads as follows:

> "No statements other than the interpretive memorandum appearing at Vol. 137 Congressional Record S 15276 (daily ed. Oct. 25, 1991) shall be considered legislative history of, or relied upon in any way as legislative history in construing or applying, any provision of this Act that relates to Wards Cove—Business necessity/cumulation/alternative business practice."

procedural safeguards of bicameralism and presentment are to perform their contemplated functions . . . the constitutional separation of lawmaking from law elaboration must remain intact."); Manning, *Response to Siegel*, 53 VAND. L. REV. at 1538–40 (discussing how to "[p]reserv[e] the [a]ims of [b]icameralism and [p]resentment").

One might well agree with Professor Siegel that if Congress were to enact a generic framework statute telling interpreters to use committee reports and the like to resolve ambiguities in duly enacted statutes, courts should follow this instruction (unless they understand a particular statute to opt out of it). But even if this statute would not violate the Bicameralism and Presentment Clause, Professor Manning's point might still have some force in the absence of any such statute. If one agrees with Professor Manning about the purposes behind bicameralism and presentment, and if one further agrees with him about the potential for certain uses of legislative history to undermine those purposes, perhaps those uses of legislative history are ill-advised even if they are not actually unconstitutional. After all, if Congress does not step in and prescribe a particular interpretive regime, and if courts must therefore make their own choice between two rival regimes that both have adherents in the modern judiciary, shouldn't courts pay attention to the potential impact of their choice on the practicalities of the legislative process? And if one of the interpretive regimes would better accomplish the purposes behind the Bicameralism and Presentment Clause, isn't that a point in its favor? On this way of thinking, Professor Manning's argument about the purposes behind the Bicameralism and Presentment Clause might be relevant to the courts' choices among interpretive methods (within whatever zone of freedom existing law leaves for those choices) even if Professor Manning was wrong to treat those purposes as being hard-wired into the Clause itself.

But was Professor Manning correct that conventional uses of legislative history distort the legislative process in ways that undermine the purposes behind bicameralism and presentment? The essence of Professor Manning's argument was that if courts give authoritative weight to statements of intention that appear in committee reports (or the like) but that have not been explicitly incorporated into statutory text by vote of the full Congress, the resulting interpretive regime "creates an opportunity [for rank-and-file legislators] to separate responsibility from result" and thereby risks "defeating the principle of accountability that lies at the heart of our representative government." Manning, *Textualism as a Nondelegation Doctrine*, 97 COLUM. L. REV. at 721. But suppose that an interpretive regime of this sort were in place (either because courts had adopted it on their own or because Congress had enacted a framework statute endorsing it). If a legislator votes for a statute that is ambiguous on its face, and a court later uses a pre-existing committee report to resolve the ambiguity, will the legislator really be able to duck responsibility for his vote by telling constituents that the court's reliance upon the committee report surprised him? Isn't that story plausible only to the extent that the existing interpretive regime is unsettled—so that the legislator can plausibly tell his constituents that he had expected the courts to take a textualist approach to the statute, and that he therefore had not viewed his vote for the statute as the functional equivalent of a vote for the gloss supplied by the committee report? If the existing interpretive regime had made the report's potential relevance clear, wouldn't constituents be inclined either to disbelieve the legislator's story or at least to hold the legislator accountable for incompetence?

Professor Manning and Justice Scalia were not the only people who invoked the Constitution in the debate over legislative history. Consider the following excerpt from a report issued by the Justice Department's Office of Legal Policy (OLP) at the end of the Reagan Administration.

Office of Legal Policy, U.S. Department of Justice, USING AND MISUSING LEGISLATIVE HISTORY: A RE-EVALUATION OF THE STATUS OF LEGISLATIVE HISTORY IN STATUTORY INTERPRETATION (1989)

. . . . There is a constitutional component to the problem of statutory interpretation, but the significance of the Constitution is susceptible of both under- and over-emphasis. Thus, some may argue either that the Constitution has nothing to say on the subject because it does not specifically address it, or that the Constitution explicitly mandates that interpretation be flatly limited to the four corners of the statutory text. A better argument than either of these is more modest: The Constitution and the structure of the legislative process it establishes *assume* an approach to statutory interpretation that focuses on the actual rather than the intended meaning of the statutory text. This approach is implicit in the establishment of a bicameral legislature and in the requirement that bills be presented to the President and be subject to a qualified veto. . . .

a. Bicameralism

Article I, § 1 of the Constitution vests "[a]ll legislative Powers herein granted" in "a Congress of the United States, which shall consist of a Senate and a House of Representatives." . . . The division of Congress into two dissimilar houses is one of the important "legislative balances and checks"[101] established by the Constitution. Because any bill must be passed by both houses of Congress, it is a prerequisite to the enactment of a statute that the houses agree on at least the language of the statute. . . .

---

[101] *The Federalist*, No. 9, at 72 (A. Hamilton) [(C. Rossiter ed. 1961)].

The fact that the Constitution requires agreement between the Senate and the House on the language of legislation shows that the focus of statutory interpretation must be on the ascertainment of the actual meaning of the statutory text. Typically, legislation begins with different versions of a bill on a subject introduced in the House and Senate. . . . While there are often significant differences in the two versions of the bill, that is not always the case. Frequently, the two versions are designed to achieve the same goals and are drafted in substantially similar language. Nevertheless, the Constitution does not consider Congress' legislative task to be complete until a single text is agreed upon, even though the intended meaning of the two versions is identical. Were intended meaning to control interpretation instead of the actual meaning of the text, the Constitution would not have to require agreement on a single text. . . .

The purposes served by bicameralism lend further support to the primacy of actual meaning. One of the most important purposes served by the division of the Congress into two houses is the fostering of due deliberation over proposed legislation. There is a "propensity of all single and numerous assemblies to yield to the impulse of sudden and violent passions, and to be seduced by factious leaders into intemperate and pernicious resolutions."[107] Bicameralism imposes an obstacle to rash legislation; it requires that all bills be approved by a second body, thereby permitting additional deliberation upon the legislation by a different group of legislators. While legislators invariably deliberate upon the policy goals of the legislation, bicameralism also furthers deliberation upon the statutory means of achieving those goals, that is, the statutory language. A failure to focus on the words that the two houses of Congress have agreed upon after due deliberation undermines the deliberative function of bicameralism.

A related purpose served by bicameralism is to reduce the likelihood of "schemes of usurpation or perfidy"[110] or "attempts to carry private, personal, or party objects, not connected with the common good,"[111] by requiring that a second house separately concur in those schemes.[112]

---

[107] *The Federalist*, No. 62, at 379 (J. Madison). Madison was defending the existence of the Senate, its manner of selection, its size, and its other unique characteristics. Madison's defense of the institution of the Senate makes it plain that the significance of bicameralism as a check on legislative abuses was, in his view, not merely the existence of a second legislative body *per se* but the existence of a body differing from the first in its essential characteristics. As recently articulated by one senator who had previously served in the House, " '[t]he House is a legislative assembly line and the Senate is designed to bring a more analytical view to the process. Using the automobile as an analogy, you could say the House is the gas pedal and the Senate the brake.' " Gamarekian, *From House to the Senate: Into Another World*, N.Y. Times, Apr. 11, 1988, at B6, col. 3 (quoting Senator Daschle).

[110] [*The Federalist*, No. 62, at 379 (J. Madison).]

[111] 1 J. Story, [*Commentaries on the Constitution of the United States*], § 556, at 387–88 [(2d ed. 1851)].

[112] *See id.* at 388 ("The very circumstance, that there exists another body clothed with equal power, and jealous of its own rights, and independent of the influence of the leaders, who favor a particular measure, by whom it must be scanned, and to whom it must be recommended upon

Bicameralism ensures an independent look at improper legislation. Equally important, it effectively requires improper schemes to be reduced to writing before a statute can be passed by the Congress, because the second house must ultimately pass upon a bill that is also approved by the first house. This requirement reduces the likelihood that such legislation will be enacted, because it makes it easier for the non-originating house to detect the evil and correspondingly more embarrassing for the originating house to have passed the bill, which cannot become positive law by the mere fact of its passage by the one house. Even when improper legislation makes it past the check of bicameralism, the evil of the law may be mitigated in the legislative process. An approach to statutory interpretation that looks to the intended meaning at the expense of the meaning the statutory words actually convey is more likely to draw out precisely those improper motives and desires that bicameral enactment of the statute helped to push into the background.[113]

b. Presentment and Qualified Veto

The second important check on the legislative process is the requirement of presentment and the provision for a qualified veto by the President. This second check, located in Article I, § 7 of the Constitution, also assumes the primacy of actual meaning. . . .

In this constitutional scheme, the President is presented with a bill—a written, enrolled text—that has been approved by separate vote of each house. The function of enrollment is precisely to define the language that the two houses of Congress have adopted and that will become law upon the approval of the President. In effect, enrollment is a means of authentication. It is the text of the enrolled bill that the President reads to determine whether he "approve[s]" the bill;[117] it is that text that he signs or vetoes; and it is that text that becomes "a Law" under clause 2. The actual meaning, rather than the intended meaning, of statutory language must have primacy in interpretation, because the official act that gives the statutory text its legal effect is necessarily based upon an understanding of its language reached by a non-drafter. The

---

its own merits, will have a silent tendency to discourage the efforts to carry it by surprise, or by intrigue, or by corrupt party combinations."). . . .

[113] Drawing out improper motives is precisely what occurs if statutory interpretation is viewed as a process of reconstructing the legislative deals made by legislators and private-interest groups. . . . Jonathan Macey argues that the constitutional effort to mitigate the effect of factions on legislation is assisted by traditional statutory interpretation, which takes Congress at its word and enforces the articulated public purpose of the statute. Macey argues that, by paying attention to what Congress *says*, courts increase the risk to private-interest groups and Congress that their hidden deals will not be effectuated and encourage Congress to be more explicit about these deals. The greater the explicitness of the deal, the less likely it is to be enacted into law. *See generally* Macey, *Promoting Public-Regarding Legislation through Statutory Interpretation: An Interest Group Model*, 86 Colum. L. Rev. 223 (1986) . . . .

[117] U.S. Const. art. I, § 7, cl. 2. Like many legislators, the President typically relies on a summary of a bill rather than reading the text. In doing so, he acts on the assumption that the summary accurately reflects what the statute provides. Should the summary turn out to be inaccurate, surely no one would claim that the statute must be interpreted according to the understanding of the statute contained in the summary.

President's position is analogous to that of the ratifiers of the Constitution, who acted to approve an existing text. As Joseph Story explained in that context, "[t]he people, who adopted the Constitution, could know nothing of the private intentions of the framers. They adopted it upon its own clear import, upon its own naked text. . . . [I]t must be judged of by its words and sense, and not by any private intentions of members of the legislature."[119]

The primacy of the actual meaning of statutory language is also suggested by the function served by presentment and the President's qualified veto power. . . . Presentment places the President in the position of a third legislative body, although with primarily negative legislative powers; he acts as an additional filter through which legislation must pass. This process adds to the security provided by bicameralism, because it permits nullification of bills passed as a result of cooperation of *two* houses of Congress in improper schemes, and because, even more than bicameralism, it forces legislators either to reduce those schemes to writing so that the bill can be enrolled and presented to the President or to refrain from enacting them into law. To the extent that the requirement of presentment and the potential for a veto keeps improper designs of individual legislators out of the enacted bill, a focus upon the intended meaning rather than the actual meaning of statutory language may well draw out precisely those improper designs.

NOTES AND QUESTIONS

1. Courts and other interpreters surely should care about the "actual meaning" of statutes. But identifying that meaning requires attention to the applicable principles of interpretation. To at least some extent, moreover, the content of those principles should facilitate successful communication, so that the legal directives that statutes actually establish tend to have some relationship to the legal directives that members of the legislature intended to establish.

In the service of that goal, it is at least theoretically possible for the applicable principles of interpretation to tell interpreters to construe statutes in light of the publicly available legislative history. If the applicable principles of interpretation do indeed make legislative history relevant, then that information potentially bears on a statute's "actual meaning." As a result, to say that interpreters should enforce "the actual rather than the intended meaning of the statutory text" is not necessarily to say that interpreters should ignore legislative history.

Still, the OLP report suggests that the bicameral structure of Congress and the constitutionally mandated process for enacting legislation (in which the same text must separately pass each house of Congress and be presented to the President for signature or veto) cuts

[119] 2 J. Story, *supra*, § 1268, at 151.

against having principles of interpretation that would make legislative history relevant. Is the idea that because the Constitution requires a single document—the bill that becomes a statute—to go through the process of bicameralism and presentment, courts should not interpret that document in light of other materials created within Congress? Or is the idea simply that when the House passes a bill and sends it to the Senate, the Senate might not be familiar with the legislative history that accumulated in the House, and the President might not be familiar with the legislative history that accumulated in either chamber? How much does the argument against using legislative history in statutory interpretation depend on facts about how Congress actually behaves and how the legislative process actually works? *Cf.* Abbe R. Gluck & Lisa Schultz Bressman, *Statutory Interpretation from the Inside—An Empirical Study of Congressional Drafting, Delegation, and the Canons: Part I*, 65 STAN. L. REV. 901, 965 (2013) (reporting that in a survey of congressional staffers, "legislative history was emphatically viewed by almost all of our respondents . . . as the *most important* drafting and interpretive tool apart from text").

2. One might well think that interpreters should not let legislative history supply meanings that cannot plausibly be attributed to the statutory language. But does the OLP's argument support the further idea that interpreters should not use legislative history even to help choose among permissible constructions of ambiguities in the statutory language?

Consider the following stylized view of statutory interpretation as a two-stage process. At the first stage, interpreters determine whether the text of a statute is "ambiguous." In making this determination, interpreters either do not consult the legislative history at all or at least do not treat it as having any special weight simply because it was prepared in Congress. If interpreters conclude that the statute *is* "ambiguous" on some point, though, interpreters proceed to the second stage. As part of that stage, they ask whether the legislative history that was publicly available at the time of enactment sheds light on which of the permissible interpretations better matches the legal directives that members of Congress understood themselves to be establishing. Would this use of legislative history to resolve ambiguities in statutory texts run afoul of any of the values that the OLP report identifies?

Does your answer to that question depend on the degree of the ambiguity? A provision might lend itself to two possible readings, but one might seem somewhat more natural than the other—so that in the absence of any relevant legislative history, interpreters would consider that interpretation best. (Perhaps the key word in the provision is more commonly used in one sense than in another, or perhaps one of the possible readings seems more consistent with other provisions in the statute, or perhaps a recognized canon favors that reading.) Alternatively, a provision might contain a truly intractable ambiguity—

so that in the absence of any relevant legislative history, interpreters would be at or near equipoise as between the two possible readings. Are the arguments in the OLP report relevant even to truly intractable ambiguities?

If interpreters do *not* consider legislative history at the second stage of the process, then they will need to come up with some other way of resolving whatever ambiguity they identified at the first stage. At least if the ambiguity is truly intractable, moreover, there is a sense in which the precise meaning that interpreters ascribe to the statute will not itself have gone through the process of bicameralism and presentment. One presumably should not conclude that *all* methods of ascribing a determinate meaning to statutes whose text is intractably ambiguous violate either the Bicameralism and Presentment Clause or the purposes behind that Clause. But if some such methods are permissible, why not a method that includes consultation of the publicly available legislative history that was in existence when both Houses of Congress acted on the bill? Even if one agrees with Professor Manning that Congress should not be able to use the materials of legislative history to communicate extratextual instructions to the courts, would it be impermissible for courts to have a general practice of favoring interpretations that match up with the available legislative history—not because the statute itself *compels* courts to adopt those interpretations, but because ambiguous statutes effectively leave courts with interpretive discretion and because courts themselves have decided to favor interpretations that fit the available legislative history?

3. The analysis in the preceding note suggests an additional way to reconcile some uses of legislative history with the Bicameralism and Presentment Clause. We have already considered Professor Siegel's idea of "incorporation by reference." *See supra* pp. 431–432. But even if the glosses suggested by committee reports and the like are not thought of as being stapled to the statutory texts that go through bicameralism and presentment, courts need some method of responding to indeterminacies in those texts. Within the zone of indeterminacy, courts *could* choose among the permissible interpretations of the statutory language without consulting legislative history. If a committee report suggests a particular resolution of the indeterminacy, though, courts might decide instead to defer to that resolution—not on the theory that Congress has effectively incorporated it into the statutory text, but simply on the theory that the resolution suggested by the committee report is likely to produce better results in practice than the resolution that the courts would come up with on their own. As compared to judges, after all, the people most closely involved in the legislative process may have better access to the kinds of facts that are relevant to public policy, and the assumptions reflected in the committee report may reflect that advantage.

This argument about deference is one way of defending the position that Judge Henry Friendly staked out in the 1960s. In Judge Friendly's words, "if an intent clearly expressed in committee reports is within the permissible limits of the [statutory] language and no construction manifestly more reasonable suggests itself, a court does pretty well to read the statute to mean what the few legislators having the greatest concern with it said it meant to them." HENRY J. FRIENDLY, *Mr. Justice Frankfurter and the Reading of Statutes*, *in* BENCHMARKS 196, 216 (1967). Does anything in the Constitution prohibit courts from adopting this practice of deference, where the alternative is resolving the indeterminacy on their own? Is this justification for the use of legislative history limited to cases of truly intractable ambiguities (where the legislative history might serve only as a tie-breaker), or can it support consulting the legislative history even in cases where one interpretation of the statute seems more natural than the other?

4. As you consider the use of legislative history to resolve indeterminacies in statutory language, recall the technical distinction between "ambiguity" and "vagueness." *See supra* pp. 102–105. Even if courts can properly use legislative history to resolve "ambiguity" in statutory language, might one argue that courts should not use legislative history to reduce "vagueness"? *See* W. David Slawson, *Legislative History and the Need to Bring Statutory Interpretation Under the Rule of Law*, 44 STAN. L. REV. 383, 421–24 (1992) (taking this position).

Suppose, for instance, that Congress enacts a statute requiring regulated entities to behave "reasonably" in some respect and providing for judicial enforcement of this requirement. If committee reports generated during the legislative process elaborate upon what members of the enacting Congress consider "reasonable," should judges treat this guidance as authoritative? Would legislative history of this sort shed light on the meaning of the statutory term "reasonable" (or at least on what members of the enacting legislature intended that term to communicate)? Or would it bear only on less relevant topics, such as the enforcement decisions that members of the enacting legislature would have made if the statute had delegated adjudicative responsibility to them rather than to the courts?

Even if judges are not *bound* to apply vague terms like "reasonable" in the way that the legislative history suggests, would it be unconstitutional (or otherwise inappropriate) for judges to try to bring their applications of such terms into line with the expectations that the legislative history reflects?

5. In an article that he wrote while he was a judge on the United States Court of Appeals for the First Circuit, Justice Breyer suggested that under current legislative practices, judicial use of legislative history in statutory interpretation actually *promotes* the values that critics associate with the Bicameralism and Presentment Clause. He speculated that if courts stopped using the materials of legislative history to help interpret statutes, those materials would become less important in the legislative process, and people within Congress would spend less time fussing over their details. There might then be fewer "public reports vetted by staff," and floor debates might become less detailed. In addition, legislators operating under this regime could more easily justify "amending legislation after it leaves committee, while it is on the floor of the House or Senate, or even while both Houses of Congress confer upon the bill after it passed each in different versions." According to Justice Breyer,

> "To the extent that a change weakens the publicly accessible committee system and diminishes the need for public justification, it increases the power of the 'special interests' . . . to secure legislation that is not in the 'public interest.' Thus, if judges abandon the use of legislative history, Congress will not necessarily produce better laws.
>
> "To the contrary, insofar as courts discourage Congress from using the regular committee, floor debate, and conference process, the technical quality of statutory law is likely to deteriorate significantly. The statutory language inserted by amendment on the floor of Congress produces absurd, anomalous, or unfair results."

Stephen Breyer, *On the Uses of Legislative History in Interpreting Statutes*, 65 S. CAL. L. REV. 845, 873 (1992). Might that be a reason for courts to continue using legislative history in statutory interpretation? Should courts take it upon themselves to try to shore up the committee system?

More generally, when courts are thinking about their interpretive practices, should courts be trying to influence the legislative process in a way that they consider desirable? Or are considerations of that sort off limits to the courts, because Article I puts each House of Congress in charge of "determin[ing] the Rules of its Proceedings"? *See* Art. I, § 5.[18]

---

2. NONCONSTITUTIONAL ARGUMENTS

Even if the Constitution does not forbid reliance upon legislative history in statutory interpretation, such reliance is not necessarily a good idea. To the contrary, many people who oppose the use of legislative history in statutory interpretation do so on the basis of arguments that are not grounded in the Constitution. This section surveys a number of those arguments.

---

[18] How much does this aspect of Article I, which effectively allows each House to transfer much of the substantive work of legislation to committees and subcommittees, qualify the purposes that Professor Manning imputed to the requirement of bicameralism?

a. THEORETICAL OBJECTIONS TO THE LOGIC BEHIND THE USE OF LEGISLATIVE HISTORY

We can begin with two theoretical attacks on the logic behind the use of legislative history. According to many people who support its use, legislative history can be a valuable source of information about the enacting legislature's "intent." In response, some textualists argue that the concept of legislative intent is either incoherent (because collective entities like legislatures do not really *have* intentions) or irrelevant (because interpreters should be seeking the "objective meaning" of a statute rather than the "subjective intent" of the legislators who enacted it). We will consider those objections in turn.

(i) The Alleged Incoherence of Collective Intent

Forming any sort of intent is a mental process, and groups do not have unitary minds. For some textualists, it follows that the very concept of legislative intent is incoherent. Judge Easterbrook seemed to put the point forcefully in an early article: "Because legislatures comprise many members, they do not have 'intents' or 'designs,' hidden yet discoverable. Each member may or may not have a design. The body as a whole, however, has only outcomes." Frank H. Easterbrook, *Statutes' Domains*, 50 U. CHI. L. REV. 533, 547 (1983); *accord, e.g.*, Kenneth A. Shepsle, *Congress Is a "They," Not an "It"*, 12 INT'L REV. L. & ECON. 239, 239 (1992) (asserting that the phrase "legislative intent" is "internally inconsistent" and "has no meaning").

In context, though, Judge Easterbrook's point may be more limited than it sounds. Easterbrook attributed his position to "the discoveries of public choice theory," which taught that groups do not think in the same way as individuals. *See* Easterbrook, *supra*, 50 U. CHI. L. REV. at 547. As Kenneth Arrow demonstrated, for instance, no method for aggregating votes in multimember bodies will always produce results that seem consistent when judged by standards that we would ordinarily use to assess the consistency of an individual's preferences. *See* KENNETH J. ARROW, SOCIAL CHOICE AND INDIVIDUAL VALUES (2d ed. 1963); *see also* Easterbrook, *supra*, 50 U. CHI. L. REV. at 547 n.20 (citing Arrow); Shepsle, *supra*, 12 INT'L REV. L. & ECON. at 241–49 (elaborating upon Arrow's impossibility theorem).[19] Even apart from the particular

[19] For an illustration of the sort of problem that inspired Arrow's impossibility theorem, consider the following version of Condorcet's paradox (developed by the Marquis de Condorcet, an intellectual luminary of the 18th century). Imagine that a unicameral legislature has to decide which of three programs to fund, and its procedures call for holding pair-wise votes on the competing programs until stable majority support for a decision has emerged. Imagine further that each legislator would like to spend all available money on just one of the programs, but that the legislators have different preferences: a third of them prefer Program *A* to Program *B* and Program *B* to Program *C*, another third also prefer Program *B* to Program *C* but prefer Program *C* to Program *A*, and the remaining third prefer Program *C* to Program *A* and Program *A* to Program *B*. Even though each individual legislator's preferences are perfectly consistent, no stable winner will emerge in pair-wise voting (unless legislators vote strategically, or unless voting is cut off at some arbitrary point). If voting starts by comparing Program *B* to Program *C*, two-thirds of the legislators will vote for Program *B*. If Program *B* is then compared to

pathologies on which Arrow focused, the outcomes reached in legislative bodies will depend not simply on the preferences of individual legislators, but also on the ins and outs of the legislature's procedural rules, including especially the rules that affect the legislature's agenda. As Judge Easterbrook noted, whoever controls the legislature's agenda not only can block proposals that most legislators support, but may be able to secure passage of proposals that most legislators do *not* support (at least in any absolute sense). Because of the complexities of agenda control, Easterbrook argued, even a court that knew each individual legislator's "complete table of preferences" would still find it practically impossible to make accurate assessments of "what the whole body would have done with a proposal it did not consider in fact." Easterbrook, *supra*, 50 U. CHI. L. REV. at 547–48. Judge Easterbrook concluded that the information revealed in a statute, even considered in conjunction with legislative history, gives courts no real basis for "predictions of how the legislature would have decided issues it did not in fact decide." *Id.*

These points undermine the Burger Court's occasional practice of using legislative history to justify extending a statute beyond its terms or qualifying the statute in ways that its terms do not suggest. For the reasons identified by Judge Easterbrook, even if the materials of legislative history suggest that these extensions or qualifications enjoyed majority support in the enacting legislature, it does not follow that they would actually have been enacted if they had been cast in the form of proposed statutory language. And the fact that they were *not* cast in the form of proposed statutory language (and hence were not put on the legislature's agenda) may itself be a conclusive reason not to give them legal effect. As Judge Easterbrook noted, control over the legislature's agenda is determined by the valid procedural rules of each legislative chamber, and courts have no more warrant for ignoring the consequences of those rules than for "try[ing] to decide how the legislature would have acted were there no threat of veto or no need to cater to constituents." *Id.* at 548.

But Judge Easterbrook's arguments do not necessarily undermine other, less aggressive uses of legislative history. In particular, Judge Easterbrook's arguments do not necessarily cut against using legislative history to shed light on what members of the enacting legislature understood superficially ambiguous words or phrases in a statute to mean. Even if courts should not try to guess how proposals that were not actually introduced would have fared in the legislative process, they cannot avoid the need to interpret the provisions that *were* introduced and that the legislature actually enacted into law. The complexity of the legislature's mechanisms for agenda control, moreover, does not necessarily stand in the way of using legislative history to assess the

---

Program *A*, two-thirds of the legislators will vote for Program *A*. But if Program *A* is then compared to Program *C*, two-thirds of the legislators will vote for Program *C*, and the legislature will be back where it started. *Cf.* ARROW, *supra*, at 2–3.

intended meaning of those provisions. At least at one time, indeed, Judge Easterbrook himself endorsed "[i]ntelligent, modest use" of legislative history for that purpose. Frank H. Easterbrook, *What Does Legislative History Tell Us?*, 66 CHI.-KENT L. REV. 441, 448 (1990); *cf.* Peterson v. Somers Dublin Ltd., 729 F.3d 741, 749 (7th Cir. 2013) (Easterbrook, J.) ("Ambiguity sometimes justifies resort to legislative history, but it is used to decipher the ambiguous language, not to replace it."). *But cf.* Frank H. Easterbrook, *The Absence of Method in Statutory Interpretation*, 84 U. CHI. L. REV. 81, 90 (2017) ("Like other textualists, I object to the use of legislative history . . . .").

Of course, even if Judge Easterbrook's points about agenda control do not prevent using legislative history to help assess the intended meaning of provisions that the legislature actually enacted, we are still left with the problem that legislatures are collective entities and that the concept of collective intent is a construct. But to say that something is a construct is not to say that it is always and inevitably incoherent. To take an extreme example, no one would deny the coherence of attributing intentionality to a group "when all, or virtually all, members of the group have the same specific intention, the intention is relevant to their participation together, and the members know that the intention is shared." Kent Greenawalt, *Are Mental States Relevant for Statutory and Constitutional Interpretation?*, 85 CORNELL L. REV. 1609, 1626–27 (2000). Thus, the fact that groups do not themselves have brains does not automatically prevent us from speaking of collective intent.

It may not seem very useful to note that the concept of collective intent will be uncontroversial when all legislators have exactly the same things in mind, because the chances of such consensus are "infinitesimally small." Max Radin, *Statutory Interpretation*, 43 HARV. L. REV. 863, 870 (1930) (concluding that the concept of legislative intent is a "transparent and absurd fiction"). But even when individual legislators have somewhat different understandings of the language that they are enacting, it may well be possible to aggregate those divergent understandings into a collective view that can sensibly be imputed to the legislature as a whole. In Reed Dickerson's words, just as "a set of vectors" can be combined into a single resultant, so too one can conceive of "corporate legislative intent" as "the composite thrust of many individual intents, no one of which need wholly coincide with the composite." REED DICKERSON, THE INTERPRETATION AND APPLICATION OF STATUTES 73 (1975). To be sure, putting that idea into practical operation will require some contestable judgments. *See, e.g., id.* at 71–73 (suggesting that the weight of a particular legislator's understanding might depend on his role in the legislative process, and adding that the understandings of a bill's supporters count for more than those of its opponents). But it does not follow that the concept of "intended meaning" is entirely arbitrary or disconnected from reality. *See* Caleb Nelson, *What Is Textualism?*, 91 VA. L. REV. 347, 371 (2005) (denying "that every possible method of aggregation is just as sensible as every other possible method of aggregation"); *see also id.* at 362 ("[T]he fact that collective intent is a construct does not mean that it has no relationship to anyone's actual intent, or that the . . . tools used to generate it cannot be judged in terms of that relationship."). And even where there is room for disagreement about how to combine the intentions of individual legislators into one collective understanding, the individual intentions may at least limit the range of understandings that the legislature as a group can be said to have entertained. If two-thirds of a legislature's members understood a bill to establish Rule A and the remaining one-third understood the bill to establish Rule B, we may not be able to say definitively that the legislature intended to establish Rule A, but we probably *can* say that the legislature did *not* intend to establish Rule Z.

In practice, moreover, the materials that constitute legislative history may actually increase the cohesiveness of legislators' intentions. When members of Congress consider a proposed bill, they are not confined to individual isolation chambers, so that each member must form his own understanding of ambiguous provisions without any input from anyone else. Instead, the typical member of Congress may rely to a considerable extent on the work of those legislators and staff members who are most familiar with the bill's provisions, including the bill's primary sponsors and the people who serve on or assist the relevant committees. It is at least possible, then, that the understandings of statutory language reflected in committee reports and sponsor statements form a focal point for the legislature as a whole. "[T]o the extent that . . . other legislators rely on [committee reports and sponsor statements] to explain the import of the bills on which they are voting," the problem of constructing collective intent becomes less daunting. EINER ELHAUGE, STATUTORY DEFAULT RULES: HOW TO INTERPRET UNCLEAR LEGISLATION 132 (2008).

Indeed, advocates of the use of legislative history sometimes suggest that even when members of the relevant committees have not fully communicated their understanding of a bill to Congress as a whole, it may *still* be appropriate for courts to impute that understanding to Congress. According to one common argument, the committee structure used by Congress effectively puts committees in the role of agents who make decisions that the full body is often content to endorse without any independent re-evaluation or even comprehension. *See, e.g.*, Lawrence M. Solan, *Private Language, Public Laws: The Central Role of Legislative Intent in Statutory Interpretation*, 93 GEO. L.J. 427, 444–47 (2005); Charles Tiefer, *The Reconceptualization of Legislative History in the Supreme Court*, 2000 WISC. L. REV. 205.

Justice Stevens's concurring opinion in *Bank One Chicago, N.A. v. Midwest Bank & Trust Co.*, 516 U.S. 264 (1996), stated this idea crisply. To help interpret a section in a federal statute called the Expedited Funds Availability Act, Justice Ginsburg's majority opinion relied partly on the section's "drafting history." Specifically, the majority based some inferences on changes that a conference committee had made before each House of Congress passed the final version of the bill. *Bank One Chicago*, 516 U.S. at 273. Justice Scalia wrote separately to protest the majority's use of this information. Among other things, Justice Scalia called it "a fiction of Jack-and-the-Beanstalk proportions to assume that more than a handful of those Senators and Members of the House who voted for the final version of the . . . Act, and the President who signed it, were . . . aware of the drafting evolution that the Court describes," or "that their actions in voting for or signing the final bill show that they had the same 'intent' which that evolution suggests was in the minds of the drafters." *Id.* at 279 (Scalia, J., concurring in part and concurring in the judgment). Justice Stevens agreed that "it is unlikely that more than a handful of legislators were aware of the Act's drafting history," but he concluded that the drafting history still shed light on the meaning of the text that Congress as a whole had approved. He explained:

> "Legislators, like other busy people, often depend on the judgment of trusted colleagues when discharging their official responsibilities. If a statute such as the Expedited Funds Availability Act has bipartisan support and has been carefully considered by committees familiar with the subject matter, Representatives and Senators may appropriately rely on the views of the committee members in casting their votes. In such circumstances, since most Members are content to endorse the views of the responsible committees, the intent of those involved in the drafting process is properly regarded as the intent of the entire Congress."

Id. at 276–77 (Stevens, J., concurring).[20]

More than half a century ago, a philosopher named Gerald MacCallum described this idea as "an agency model of legislative intent," which maintained "that legislatures delegate certain responsibilities (such as filling in the statutory details) to various persons (legislative draftsmen, committee chairmen, judges, administrators), and that this may justify appealing to the intentions of these persons as the intentions of the legislature . . . ." Gerald C. MacCallum, Jr., *Legislative Intent*, 75 YALE L.J. 754, 780–81 (1966). MacCallum observed, however, that this model "is extremely perilous." For one thing, the idea that the legislature as a whole intended to endorse the views of the relevant agent(s) requires

---

[20] It is not clear how far Justice Stevens would have taken this idea. In the case at hand, all members of the Court agreed that "the statutory text . . . supports [the] construction of the Act" that the Court was adopting. And while a peculiarity in the structure of the provision "len[t] some support to the . . . [contrary] interpretation" that the lower court had adopted, "[t]he drafting history . . . provides a completely satisfactory explanation for this apparent anomaly in the text." According to Justice Stevens, then, "the net result of the inquiry into drafting history is to find the answer to an otherwise puzzling aspect of the statutory text." *Id.* at 277 (Stevens, J., concurring). This situation did not require Justice Stevens to decide what to do when the understandings apparently held by members of a relevant committee, but not shared with the rest of Congress, deviated from the meaning that outside readers would most naturally ascribe to the statutory text.

a separate, non-agency model of legislative intent. *Id.* at 782. It is not clear, moreover, how explicitly the legislature should have to manifest such an intention, or what courts should rely upon in concluding that the intention really did exist. *Id.* at 783; *cf.* OFFICE OF LEGAL POLICY, U.S. DEPARTMENT OF JUSTICE, USING AND MISUSING LEGISLATIVE HISTORY: A RE-EVALUATION OF THE STATUS OF LEGISLATIVE HISTORY IN STATUTORY INTERPRETATION 14 (1989) ("[T]he agency approach has been criticized as 'at best a legal conclusion, not a factual description,' since its proponents have not shown that nonparticipating legislators 'really believe' that they are tacitly adopting the committee's interpretive views when they vote to enact a bill." (quoting William Robert Bishin, *The Law Finders: An Essay in Statutory Interpretation*, 38 S. CAL. L. REV. 1, 15 (1965))).

Still, to the extent that the relevant committees actually communicate their understandings of a bill to their colleagues in the form of a committee report, or the sponsors or floor managers of a bill do the same in a floor statement, one need not accept the "agency model" to argue that Congress as a whole often acts upon the understandings that are made manifest to it by the responsible legislators or committees. And even if there are many questions on which a statute cannot realistically be said to have an "intended meaning," there may well be other questions on which references to collective intent have more content. *Cf.* MacCallum, *supra*, 75 YALE L.J. at 770 ("[A] person who wishes to claim that there is legislative intent in this or that specific case is not bound to claim that there is always intent in every case."). At least as a theoretical matter, the collective nature of legislative bodies does not inevitably defeat the very possibility of the sort of "legislative intent" that legislative history might illuminate.

(ii) The Alleged Irrelevance of "Subjective" Intent

According to Justice Scalia, however, even if it is coherent to refer to the concept of "legislative intent" for some purposes, the sort of intent that legislative history might illuminate is not actually relevant to statutory interpretation. In Justice Scalia's view, the point of statutory interpretation is to identify "the objective indication of the words" of the statute, not the "subjective . . . intent" of the enacting legislature. *See* Antonin Scalia, *Common-Law Courts in a Civil-Law System: The Role of United States Federal Courts in Interpreting the Constitution and Laws*, *in* A MATTER OF INTERPRETATION: FEDERAL COURTS AND THE LAW 3, 17, 29 (Amy Gutmann ed., 1997). It follows, Justice Scalia suggested, that legislative history is simply irrelevant to the interpretive project. *See id.* at 29–30; *see also id.* at 31 ("I object to the use of legislative history on principle, since I reject intent of the legislature as the proper criterion of the law.").

Despite the power of this rhetoric, though, the difference between "objective" meaning and "subjective" intent does not really amount to an independent argument against the use of legislative history. It is true that legislative history is almost entirely irrelevant to what Justice Scalia viewed as the "objective" meaning of statutory language. But that is because Justice Scalia had other reasons for putting legislative history off limits to interpreters. When Justice Scalia asserted that information in a statute's publicly available legislative history does not shape the "objective" meaning of the statutory language, he was simply stating a conclusion that he reached on other grounds.

To appreciate this point, we must start by recognizing that even for Justice Scalia, the "objective" meaning of statutory language was not completely divorced from any and all arguments about legislative intent. To the contrary, Justice Scalia embraced various principles of interpretation that rest on inferences about the likely communicative intent of members of the enacting legislature—the content of the directives that they probably understood themselves to be establishing. Admittedly, Justice Scalia wanted to restrict the sources of information on which interpreters base such inferences. But within the constraints of that approach, he did not object to arguments that favor one interpretation over another because it is more likely to match what members of the enacting legislature meant.

For an example from Chapter 1, recall Justice Scalia's commentary upon *Church of the Holy Trinity v. United States*, 143 U.S. 457 (1892). *See supra* pp. 42–44. In Justice Scalia's view, the phrase "labor or service of any kind," as used in § 1 of the relevant statute, encompassed the work of ministers. But that conclusion about the objective meaning of the words in § 1 rested in part on an argument about the *intended* meaning of those words. Reasonable readers trying to determine the meaning of § 1 would see that § 5 of the same statute made a specific exception for "professional actors, artists, lecturers, or singers." Readers would infer that members of the enacting legislature must have understood § 1 to cover more than simply manual occupations; otherwise, legislators would have seen no need for the exceptions in § 5. This inference about how members of the enacting legislature probably understood § 1, moreover, would inform the meaning that readers themselves ascribe to § 1.

In this particular example, the clue that readers use to draw inferences about the intended meaning of § 1 comes from another provision in the statutory text itself. But nothing in the concept of "objective" meaning necessarily restricts interpreters to the four corners of the statute. Justice Scalia was perfectly willing to let interpreters draw upon various other sources of information too. Most obviously, he would have let interpreters consider a wide variety of uncodified information about a statute's linguistic context, including information about how words and phrases were commonly used at the time of enactment and information about any specialized canons that were then in vogue.[21]

[21] One might respond that this information bears on the "objective" meaning of statutory language not because it sheds light on the communicative intent of the enacting legislature, but

Justice Scalia also acknowledged the relevance of what Chief Justice Taney called "the public history of the times in which [the statute] was passed"—that is, information about what was going on in the relevant jurisdiction around the time of enactment. Scalia, *supra*, at 30 (quoting Aldridge v. Williams, 44 U.S. (3 How.) 9, 24 (1844)). Again, interpreters would presumably use this information to draw inferences about a species of legislative intent: by identifying the problems to which the legislature apparently was responding, an interpreter can get a better sense of what members of the enacting legislature probably were trying to say.

Justice Scalia did not deny that inferences about intent can affect what he saw as the "objective" meaning of statutory language. But the intent that matters, he insisted, is not really the *actual* intent of the enacting legislature. Instead, interpreters "look for a sort of 'objectified' intent—the intent that a reasonable person would gather from the text of the law, placed alongside the rest of the *corpus juris*." *Id.* at 17. Quoting an old treatise, Justice Scalia suggested that the quest is not for legislative intent *per se*, but rather for " 'the meaning which the [reader] is authorized to understand the legislature intended.' " *Id.* (quoting JOEL PRENTISS BISHOP, COMMENTARIES ON THE WRITTEN LAWS AND THEIR INTERPRETATION 57–58 (1882)). In other words, the type of intent that mattered to Justice Scalia is the communicative intent that a reasonable person would impute to the enacting legislature on the basis of the information that the principles of interpretation permit the interpreter to consider. That "objectified" version of intent, in turn, contributes to what Justice Scalia thought of as the "objective" meaning of the statute—the meaning that appropriately informed readers, applying the proper principles of interpretation to the data that they are allowed to consider, would ascribe to the words that the legislature enacted. *Cf.* Jeffrey Goldsworthy, *Marmor on Meaning, Interpretation, and Legislative Intention*, 1 LEGAL THEORY 439, 442 (1995) (discussing and defending a conception of meaning under which the meaning of an utterance in everyday speech is "what [the] evidence [that is] readily available to the intended audience[ ] suggests that the speaker intended to communicate in making the utterance").

One can certainly argue (as Justice Scalia did) that legislative history should not be part of the information base that interpreters consider when constructing their "objectified" version of intent, and hence that legislative history is not relevant to the identification of a statute's "objective" meaning. But the fact that interpreters are seeking

---

only because it sheds light on the likely understandings of outside readers. But as Justice Scalia acknowledged, "those two concepts chase one another back and forth to some extent," since the reasonable reader will be trying to figure out what the enacting legislature was trying to say. Antonin Scalia, *Response*, *in* A MATTER OF INTERPRETATION: FEDERAL COURTS AND THE LAW 129, 144 (Amy Gutmann ed., 1997). In any event, the fact that Justice Scalia focused on linguistic conventions *as they stood at the time of enactment* (rather than as they stand at the time of the relevant case) suggests that arguments about the enacting legislature's communicative intent were not entirely irrelevant to his view of interpretation.

an "objectified" version of intent does not itself compel that position. If the *Congressional Record* and publicly available committee reports were included in the information that a reasonable reader is expected to take into account when determining the meaning of statutory language, one could still speak of interpreters as seeking an "objectified" version of intent—a version that might not square in all respects with the actual "subjective" intent of members of the enacting legislature. Likewise, if the applicable interpretive regime permitted interpreters to consider not only the public history of the times but also any committee reports that were publicly available at the time of enactment, then the "objective" meaning of the statutory text could reflect whatever inferences the applicable principles of interpretation permitted readers to draw from those reports. What Justice Scalia called the "objective" meaning of statutory text ignores those inferences not because it is "objective" but because Justice Scalia did not include committee reports in the data that appropriately informed readers should be presumed to know. *Cf.* City of Georgetown, 8 Op. Att'y Gen. app. 546, 560 (1856) (discussing sources that interpreters can use "to aid us in fixing the meaning of a questionable word in an act," and suggesting that "if we may seek light on the subject from 'the public history of the times in which [the act] was passed,' [*Aldridge*, 44 U.S. (3 How.) at 24]," then interpreters should also be allowed to consider legislative history), *cited in* Hans W. Baade, *"Original Intent" in Historical Perspective: Some Critical Glosses*, 69 TEX. L. REV. 1001, 1033 (1991).

As we shall see in the next section, Justice Scalia may have had some good reasons for wanting to exclude even publicly available legislative history from the information base that interpreters use to identify the "objective" meaning of statutory language. But the simple fact that legislative history bears on legislative intent is not such a reason. Plenty of interpretive principles, including all the descriptive canons, can be seen as ways to guide interpreters toward the intended meaning of statutory language. That does not make those principles incompatible with the concept of "objective" meaning. By the same token, the concept of "objective" meaning does not foreclose the very possibility of an interpretive regime in which publicly available legislative history might color the meaning that interpreters ascribe to statutes.

To the extent permitted by the other goals of statutory interpretation, indeed, we presumably should *favor* interpretive principles under which the "objective" meaning ascribed to statutory language will not diverge more than necessary from the meaning that members of the enacting legislature collectively intended to convey. No one thinks that courts should affirmatively seek to frustrate the legislature's will, or that the applicable interpretive regime should be designed to impede successful communication of the legal directives that legislators want to establish. To the contrary, the typical textualist thinks that the courts' principles of interpretation should make it possible for conscientious legislators to send courts the messages that they intend to send. *See, e.g.*, John F. Manning, *Legal Realism and the Canons' Revival*, 5 GREEN BAG 2d 283, 292 (2002) (referring to the textualists' goal of "mak[ing] the canons effective for the predictable communication of legislative directions"); *see also* Cont'l Can Co. v. Chi. Truck Drivers, Helpers & Warehouse Workers Union (Indep.) Pension Fund, 916 F.2d 1154, 1157 (7th Cir. 1990) (Easterbrook, J.) ("You don't have to be Ludwig Wittgenstein or Hans-Georg Gadamer to know that successful communication depends on meanings shared by interpretive communities.").

Of course, that is not the only goal of an interpretive regime. As the very first section of this book indicated, there is widespread agreement that the principles of statutory interpretation should be designed to serve various goals, including not just (1) facilitating successful communication of the legal directives that legislators intend to establish but also (2) enabling the citizenry to have adequate notice of the law's content and (3) keeping the interpretive process from consuming too many resources. *See supra* pp. 1–5. These other goals may lead us to put certain sources of information off limits to interpreters for reasons unconnected with the search for legislative intent, and they may also lead us to favor a more "rule-like" approach to the identification of legislative intent than we might otherwise advocate. For both those reasons, Justice Scalia was unquestionably correct that interpreters in our system do not simply seek the "subjective" intent of the enacting legislature. There can indeed be differences between the meaning that our interpretive regime tells courts to ascribe to a statute and the meaning that members of the enacting legislature actually had in mind.

Still, we might not want our interpretive regime to drive *unnecessary* wedges between the directives that courts take statutory language to establish and the directives that members of the enacting legislature subjectively intended to establish. To the extent that the applicable principles of interpretation generate a gap between "objective" meaning and "subjective" intent, we might want the gap to be justified by one of our other goals (such as promoting ideals of fair notice or reducing the costs of the interpretive process).

Assuming that courts can choose which interpretive principles to use,[22] these are the terms in which the debate over the use of legislative history in statutory interpretation should proceed. As we shall see in the next section, moreover, Justice Scalia and his allies did indeed cast

[22] To some extent, the proper principles of interpretation might be settled by custom, and current courts might not have free rein to introduce different principles. At the state level, moreover, roughly ten state legislatures have enacted generic statutes authorizing courts to consider legislative history (though often only if a statute is "ambiguous"). *See* Jacob Scott, *Codified Canons and the Common Law of Interpretation*, 98 GEO. L.J. 341, 380–82 (2010); *id.* at 419 (citing, inter alia, COLO. REV. STAT. § 2–4–203(c); IOWA CODE § 4.6(2); MINN. STAT. § 645.16(7); N.M. STAT. § 12–2A–20(C)(2); N.D. CENT. CODE § 1–02–39(3); OHIO REV. CODE ANN. § 1.49(C); OR. REV. STAT. § 174.020(1)(b); 1 PA. CONS. STAT. §§ 1921(c)(7), 1939; and TEX. GOV'T CODE ANN. § 311.023(3)).

arguments in these terms; they sought to evaluate the practical impact of using legislative history on the goals of statutory interpretation, and they advanced various reasons why consulting legislative history might do more harm than good. People who find those arguments persuasive might favor principles of interpretation that exclude reference to legislative history, and they might then say that legislative history is irrelevant to the objective meaning of statutory language (as determined by their chosen principles of interpretation). But the adjective "objective" does not itself lead ineluctably to that conclusion.

b. PRACTICAL OBJECTIONS THAT THE USE OF LEGISLATIVE HISTORY WILL DO MORE HARM THAN GOOD

The practical arguments against the use of legislative history in statutory interpretation fall into three main categories, corresponding to each of the goals mentioned above. Suppose that one accepts the coherence and potential relevance of the concept of "legislative intent." Even so, one might doubt that judges who are insulated from the legislative process can reliably use fragments of the legislative record to get a better sense of the legislature's true collective intent. Perhaps judges will actually come closer to the intended meaning of statutory language, across the mine run of cases, if they simply ignore legislative history than if they try to determine how much weight each piece of legislative history deserves under the circumstances of each case. Alternatively, even if letting courts evaluate legislative history on a case-by-case basis would marginally narrow the gap between the interpreted meaning and the intended meaning of statutory language, perhaps the use of legislative history offends the goal of providing fair notice of the law's requirements to the electorate and the people whom the law regulates. Or perhaps the marginal benefit of using legislative history is too small to justify the extra costs that this practice imposes on legislators (who must monitor the legislative record more carefully), judges (who must referee disputes about legislative history), litigants and people seeking legal advice (who must pay for lawyers to plow through voluminous legislative histories), and even other people with cases in the court system (whose disputes might be resolved more slowly because of the extra time required to process legislative history in other cases). Again, this section surveys those arguments in turn.[23]

[23] In addition to the arguments surveyed in this section, there may conceivably be other institutional reasons why courts should treat the legislative process as a black box that is not open to judicial inquiry. *Cf.* Marshall Field & Co. v. Clark, 143 U.S. 649, 672–73 (1892) (refusing to examine legislative records to determine whether an enrolled bill that had been signed by the presiding officers of each House of Congress, approved by the President, and deposited in the public archives as a statute had in fact been passed in the same form by each House); Caleb Nelson, *Judicial Review of Legislative Purpose*, 83 N.Y.U. L. REV. 1784 (2008) (noting that for much of American history, courts refused to investigate the inner workings of the legislative process to determine whether a facially valid statute had been enacted for an unconstitutional purpose). The standard practical arguments against the use of legislative history, though, are the ones surveyed in this section.

(i) *Objections to the Premise That Using Legislative History Helps Courts Identify Intended Meaning*

The most common argument *for* using legislative history in statutory interpretation is that sensible use of legislative history can help courts identify the legal directives that members of the enacting legislature collectively intended to establish. As a result, many of the most prominent arguments *against* using legislative history are aimed at debunking this claim.

We can clear away one possible argument at the outset. As an empirical matter, it is possible that the information in a statute's legislative history frequently has little bearing on the interpretive questions that later arise in court, or points in such disparate directions as to be of no use. If so, then consulting legislative history will not actually help courts identify the intended meaning of statutory language in many of the cases that currently get litigated. But even if that empirical premise were correct, it would not necessarily follow that courts should refuse to consider legislative history on questions that it does address. As a logical matter, the fact that legislative history is unhelpful in many cases is not reason enough to ignore it in all cases, unless sorting the questions on which it might be useful from the other questions would be prohibitively expensive. *See* Stephen Breyer, *On the Uses of Legislative History in Interpreting Statutes*, 65 S. CAL. L. REV. 845, 861–62 (1992). In addition, even if legislative history rarely contains useful information about the questions that currently get litigated, the courts' current willingness to consult legislative history may affect the types of questions that parties choose to litigate. If courts were to stop using legislative history, a higher percentage of litigated cases might come to involve questions that the legislative history addresses, and legislative history might seem more useful again. *Cf.* Adrian Vermeule, *The Cycles of Statutory Interpretation*, 68 U. CHI. L. REV. 149 (2001).

Yet even if we focus entirely on cases in which some piece of legislative history does seem relevant, Justice Scalia maintained that letting courts consult legislative history will not tend to bring their interpretations closer to what members of the enacting legislature collectively intended. Justice Scalia advanced at least three arguments for this position.

First, Justice Scalia asserted that "with respect to 99.99 percent of the issues of construction reaching the courts, there *is* no legislative intent, so . . . any clues provided by the legislative history are bound to be false." Scalia, *supra*, at 32. This point obviously resonates with the textualists' skepticism about the very concept of collective intent. *See supra* p. 443. As cast by Justice Scalia, though, the argument is narrower and more practical. Justice Scalia did not necessarily deny either that "legislative intent" is a coherent concept or that it might sometimes exist in practice (in the sense that the intentions of individual legislators might be sufficiently determinate and cohesive on certain points as to warrant imputing a collective intent on those points to the legislature). But according to Justice Scalia, genuine legislative intent is unlikely to exist *with respect to the sorts of issues that get litigated.* In his words,

> "Those issues almost invariably involve points of relative detail, compared with the major sweep of the statute in question. That a majority of both houses of Congress (never mind the President, if he signed rather than vetoed the bill) entertained *any* view with regard to such issues is utterly beyond belief. For a virtual certainty, the majority was blissfully unaware of the *existence* of the issue, much less had any preference as to how it should be resolved."

Scalia, *supra,* at 32. Thus, even when some piece of legislative history seems to bear on such an issue, Justice Scalia doubted that it will actually help courts ascertain the legislature's collective intent, because he doubted that there will be any genuine collective intent to ascertain.

Although this argument is not quite the same as broader-gauged attacks on the very possibility of collective intent, it is subject to some of the same responses. For instance, people who accept an "agency model" of legislative intent (*see supra* p. 447) will not accept Justice Scalia's implicit premise that we can meaningfully speak of legislative intent with respect to a particular issue only when "a majority of both houses of Congress" agree on that issue. Perhaps it is sometimes sensible to impute the views of a responsible committee to Congress as a whole, simply because members of Congress were content to accept whatever it was that the committee had done. And while that theory still requires some aggregation of individual intentions (since the responsible committee is itself a collective entity), perhaps it is more likely that a majority of committee members had specific intentions on a point of detail than that a majority of each House of Congress had such intentions.

Even for people who reject the "agency model" of legislative intent, Justice Scalia's point might seem more telling with respect to some uses of legislative history than others. Notwithstanding the coordinating effects of committee reports, it often will be implausible that majorities in the enacting legislature specifically envisioned the particular set of facts that the court is now confronting and came to a consensus about how the law should handle this set of facts. But it may not be so implausible that they had some shared understanding of the meaning of the words that they were enacting. Because law works through rules, moreover, references to the "intended meaning" of the statute can be coherent even in cases that members of the enacting legislature did not specifically have in mind. *Cf.* REED DICKERSON, THE INTERPRETATION AND APPLICATION OF STATUTES 76 (1975) (offering this response to Max Radin's dismissive comments about legislative intent).

In any event, even if Justice Scalia were correct that the use of legislative history often generates "false positives" about the existence of legislative intent, that sort of error might be less troubling than mistakes about the content of collective intentions that really did exist. To the extent that we are trying to maximize the overlap between the meaning that courts ascribe to statutes and the meaning that members of the enacting legislature actually intended, how courts determine a statute's content on matters as to which the legislature did *not* form a genuine collective intent (but that nonetheless come within the statute's domain) may be less important than whether courts recognize the intended meaning of statutory language on matters as to which the legislature did form a collective intent. As a result, interpretive techniques that are too sensitive to signs of collective intent (and that therefore generate "false positives" about the existence of an intended meaning) might sometimes be preferable to interpretive techniques that are less sensitive to signs of collective intent (and that therefore generate "false negatives").

An artificial numerical example helps connect this argument to the use of legislative history. Suppose that 90 out of every 100 times a court uses legislative history to ascribe a particular meaning to statutory language, the enacting legislature did not actually have any collective intent on the point that the court is addressing. Still, even if the legislative history falsely leads the court to believe that a collective intent did exist, we might think that little harm is being done: assuming that the point in question does indeed come within the statute's scope, the court needs to ascribe some meaning to the statute, and picking a meaning that coincides with the legislative history may be no worse than picking another meaning from within the range of permissible interpretations. If using legislative history helps courts ascertain the legislature's collective intentions on the 10 questions where such intentions really did exist, and does not affirmatively frustrate the legislature's collective intentions on the other 90 questions, then people who want to maximize the overlap between interpreted meaning and intended meaning might favor using legislative history.

Justice Scalia, however, would not have conceded that using legislative history helps courts avoid "false negatives" and accurately grasp what statutes were intended to mean on points as to which the legislature really did form a collective intent. With respect to such points, critics of the use of legislative history advance a second argument: perhaps courts are so bad at assessing the reliability of legislative history that their use of legislative history *widens* the gap between the meanings that courts ascribe to statutes and what members of the enacting legislature actually intended. If judges are prone to error when using legislative history to determine legislative intent, then they might do a better job of capturing the intended meaning of statutory language if they ignore legislative history altogether than if they try to use it for whatever it is worth in each case. *See, e.g.*, ADRIAN VERMEULE, JUDGING UNDER UNCERTAINTY: AN INSTITUTIONAL THEORY OF LEGAL INTERPRETATION 107–08 (2006).

This argument might seem perverse. To the extent that we want courts to identify the intended meaning of statutory language, shouldn't we encourage them "to consider all available evidence of Congress' true intent"? *Koons Buick Pontiac GMC, Inc. v. Nigh*, 543 U.S. 50, 65 (2004) (Stevens, J., joined by Breyer, J., concurring). But rules of evidence often proceed on the premise that excluding certain categories of information can improve the accuracy of judicial decisions. *See* VERMEULE, *supra*, at 108. For instance, one might think that the categorical exclusion of certain forms of hearsay makes the courts' factfinding processes more accurate than they would be if courts tried to evaluate each piece of hearsay on a case-by-case basis. By the same token, one might conceivably think that it is counterproductive for courts to consult legislative history when trying to determine the intended meaning of statutory language—not because legislative history is necessarily irrelevant to the kind of intent that matters, but simply because courts are likely to be bad at assessing it.

Professor Vermeule has articulated various reasons why judges make poor consumers of legislative history. Because our constitutional system deliberately separates courts from legislatures, the typical judge might have little feel for the dynamics of the legislative process, and might therefore be apt "to overestimate or underestimate the weight due to a particular item of legislative history." *Id.* at 109; *see also id.* at 113 ("[P]arties and judges will often be unfamiliar, or only superficially familiar, with the roles, characteristics, and incentives of the actors who have contributed to a legislative record . . . ."). The "massive volume of legislative history" and its "heterogeneity" may magnify this problem. *Id.* at 110–14. In addition, the habits of mind that serve judges well when interpreting statutory texts may mislead them when they are interpreting committee reports or sponsor statements. *See id.* at 113 (noting that those habits "may cause judges to accord too much weight to legislative-history documents that are not themselves legally operative").

According to Justice Scalia, moreover, participants in the legislative process take advantage of the limitations on judicial capacity by salting the legislative history with misleading statements—statements that purport to clarify the intended meaning of statutory language, but that could not really survive the process of bicameralism and presentment if they were inserted into the statutory text. Scalia, *supra*, at 34. Indeed, the Reagan Administration's Office of Legal Policy asserted that this argument "is probably the most frequently raised and the most strongly held objection to the use of legislative history." OFFICE OF LEGAL POLICY, U.S. DEPARTMENT OF JUSTICE, USING AND MISUSING LEGISLATIVE HISTORY: A RE-EVALUATION OF THE STATUS OF LEGISLATIVE HISTORY IN STATUTORY INTERPRETATION 53–54 (1989). Of course, if legislators and their staffs know that the courts rely upon legislative history in interpreting statutes, then the same incentives that might lead some participants in the legislative process to plant misleading statements in the legislative record might lead other participants to monitor and respond to those statements. But perhaps it is easier to monitor the contents of actual statutory language (which is relatively confined and which comes up for votes) than to monitor the contents of debates, floor statements, and committee reports. If members of Congress and their staffs do not filter out or respond to all the misleading statements that partisans might try to insert into the legislative record, and if courts are not very good at separating misleading statements from statements that genuinely reflect the collective intent of the enacting coalition, then perhaps the use of legislative history will lead courts astray more often than it enlightens them.

There are various ways in which the use of legislative history might spirit courts away from the intended meaning of statutory language. One concerns what Judge Easterbrook calls the "domain" of a statute—the set of issues that the statute covers in one way or another. *See* Frank H. Easterbrook, *Statutes' Domains*, 50 U. CHI. L. REV. 533 (1983). As part of the give and take of the legislative process, legislators may frequently agree to address one problem but not others, or to go so far but not farther. Courts that use legislative history aggressively risk transgressing those boundaries and applying the statute beyond its intended domain. *See* Frank H. Easterbrook, *What Does Legislative History Tell Us?*, 66 CHI.-KENT L. REV. 441, 444–45 (1990) (urging courts not to use legislative history to attribute content to a statute on matters that lie beyond its domain). *But cf. id.* (suggesting that courts can properly use legislative history to try to clarify the boundaries of the domain itself).

Another way in which legislative history might lead courts away from a statute's intended meaning concerns issues that lie within the statute's domain, but on which the legislative history might provide some basis for second-guessing what the statutory text seems to say. Perhaps the statute was cast in relatively rule-like terms, but the legislative history reflects some values or purposes that will not always be served by applying the statute as written. Under the influence of such legislative history, courts sometimes infer exceptions or embellishments that make the statute less rule-like than it seems on its face. But if the legislature really meant the statute to be as rule-like as it seemed, this use of legislative history will widen the gap between the meaning that courts ascribe to statutes and the meaning that legislators collectively intended to convey. *Cf.* Frank H. Easterbrook, *Text, History, and Structure in Statutory Interpretation*, 17 HARV. J. L. & PUB. POL'Y 61, 62–63 (1994) (complaining that such uses of legislative history "den[y] to the drafters the ability to choose rules"). Likewise, legislative history sometimes leads courts to conclude that a statute is using certain words idiosyncratically. If those clues are misleading, then again the practice of consulting legislative history might lead courts away from the meaning that members of the enacting legislature actually intended.

Unfortunately, it is hard to evaluate the likelihood of such errors, or to compare it to the likelihood that using legislative history will help courts identify genuinely intended meanings that they would not otherwise have appreciated. In the end, this aspect of the debate over legislative history boils down to empirical questions, but of a sort that resist scientific study. *See* VERMEULE, *supra,* at 153 (referring to "the stalemate of empirical intuitions" on such points); *see also id.* at 162 ("[M]any of the relevant empirical questions cannot be solved in the short or medium term . . . ."). Thus, we cannot reach definitive conclusions about the danger that legislative history will mislead judges who are conscientiously trying to give effect to the intended meaning of statutory language.

In addition to emphasizing that danger, Justice Scalia also argued that the ability to invoke legislative history gives less conscientious judges cover for making decisions that are really based on their own policy preferences. This claim amounts to a <u>third</u> reason why allowing judges to use legislative history might widen the gap between interpreted and intended meaning.

To be sure, willful judges may be willful whether or not the norms of the profession allow them to cite legislative history as an ostensible justification for their decisions. But according to Justice Scalia, the volume and diversity of legislative history make it "a uniquely broad playing field"—one that contains "something for everybody," and that can therefore be used to justify a broader range of outcomes than the statutory text alone. Scalia, *supra,* at 36. In addition, evaluating the accuracy of a court's claims about the thrust of the legislative history may require more work than evaluating the accuracy of other sorts of interpretive arguments. As a result, the ability to rationalize a decision in terms of legislative history may give willful judges a better tool for concealing their willfulness than they would otherwise have, with the result that willfulness becomes less costly to them and they indulge in it more often.

Again, though, this argument relies on a variety of empirical claims that are hard to test. Does the use of legislative history tend to expand the interpretive options that are available to courts (as Justice Scalia maintained), or does it actually *restrict* judicial discretion by helping to eliminate some of the indeterminacy that would otherwise afflict the bare statutory text? *Cf.* Bedroc Ltd., LLC v. United States, 541 U.S. 176, 192 (2004) (Stevens, J., dissenting) (arguing that the judge who categorically refuses to consult legislative history "retains greater discretion than the judge who 'will seek guidance from every reliable source,'" and concluding that because textualist interpretation "is deliberately uninformed, and hence unconstrained," by legislative history, it "increases the risk that the judge's own policy preferences will affect the decisional process" (quoting AHARON BARAK, JUDICIAL DISCRETION 62 (Yadin Kaufmann trans. 1989))); Thomas W. Merrill, *Textualism and the Future of the* Chevron *Doctrine,* 72 WASH. U. L.Q. 351, 366–70 (1994) (summarizing the debate on this point and suggesting that the limited empirical evidence cuts against Justice Scalia's position). Do readers indeed have a harder time detecting judicial willfulness when it is disguised by the invocation of legislative history than when it is disguised by the invocation of other interpretive methods? *Cf.* William N. Eskridge, Jr., *Textualism, the Unknown Ideal?*, 96 MICH. L. REV. 1509, 1545–47 (1998) (book review) (suggesting that willful judges can manipulate canons and dictionaries no less effectively than legislative history). Even if the legislative history provides especially fertile opportunities for judicial willfulness, what percentage of our nation's judges will seize those opportunities? *Cf.* Bank One Chicago, N.A. v. Midwest Bank & Trust Co., 516 U.S. 264, 277–78 (1996) (Stevens, J., concurring) (taking umbrage at Justice Scalia's suggestion that judges "use [legislative] history as a makeweight after reaching a conclusion on the basis of other factors": "I have been performing this type of work for more than 25 years and have never proceeded in the manner Justice Scalia suggests").

Like the empirical questions that bear on Justice Scalia's second argument, these questions too seem intractable. As a result, no one can really be sure whether letting judges use legislative history has the net effect of increasing or decreasing gaps between the meanings that courts ascribe to statutes and the meanings that the legislature really intended. Still, legislators themselves may be in a better position than the rest of us to make informed guesses on that topic. While current legislators have no special insight into the intended meaning of *old* statutes, they ought to have some sense of the communicative intent behind *recent* statutes. As a group, moreover, they presumably have an interest in getting courts to recognize and apply the intended meaning of their statutes—and if they were worried that the courts' use of legislative history threatens that goal, they would have the power to do something about it. For instance, Congress could readily stipulate that committee reports and the like are prepared solely for internal use and should not be taken as an indication of the collective intentions of the full Congress. *See* Easterbrook, *supra*, 17 HARV. J. L. & PUB. POL'Y at 62 ("If Congress thought that reliance on legislative history threw judges off the scent too often, it would . . . tell us not to use the stuff."); *see also infra* Chapter 4.B.4 (discussing Congress's ability to regulate the courts' use of legislative history). Should we take Congress's failure to enact such a statute (or to include a boilerplate statement to this effect in each committee report) as a sign that the problem perceived by Justice Scalia is not as serious as Justice Scalia suggested? Or is any such inference negated by the countervailing fact that back when courts did *not* consult legislative history, Congress never passed a statute saying that they should? How powerful are such arguments about legislative inaction?[24]

[24] For general discussion of arguments about legislative inaction, see Chapter 4.A.2 of this book.

(ii) Objections Based on Notice

For the sake of argument, suppose that Justice Scalia was wrong about the points that we have just been considering. In other words, suppose that if we let courts consult legislative history, the meaning that courts attribute to statutory language will come somewhat closer to what the enacting legislature intended than if we tell courts to ignore legislative history. If the sole goal of statutory interpretation were to capture the intended meaning of statutory language, we therefore would want courts to consult legislative history.

Still, other goals may cut in the opposite direction. For instance, everyone acknowledges that the goal of giving people fair notice of the law's requirements can qualify the goal of giving effect to the intended meaning of statutory language. That is one reason why most courts do not rely upon after-the-fact testimony from legislators about what was in their heads when they enacted a statute. *See supra* pp. 347–348. Likewise, nearly everyone agrees that secret messages from Congress to the courts about the meaning of a statute—such as confidential communiqués signed by all members of Congress at the time of enactment and sealed in an envelope for use in the event of litigation—should ordinarily play no role in statutory interpretation, even if there is little reason to doubt their reliability and even if considering them would therefore help courts identify the statute's intended meaning. Just as notice-related goals drive these results, so too people sometimes argue that notice-related goals cut against letting legislative history influence the meaning that courts ascribe to statutes.

This argument has been around for a long time. In the 1940s and 1950s, for instance, concerns about notice figured prominently in Justice Jackson's criticism of the Supreme Court's growing reliance upon legislative history. *See supra* p. 357. Even at that time, of course, the types of legislative history that the judiciary was using were available to the public in ways that a secret communiqué would not be. But Justice Jackson believed that the materials of legislative history were not readily accessible to ordinary people or the lawyers who advise them. *See* Robert H. Jackson, *The Meaning of Statutes: What Congress Says or What the Court Says*, 34 A.B.A.J. 535, 537–38 (1948) (concluding that the courts' practice of using legislative history "poses serious practical problems for a large part of the legal profession").

Since then, legislative history has become easier to find, at least for federal statutes.[25] Nowadays, federal legislative history of the sort that

---

[25] At the state level, some state legislatures make more materials publicly available than others. Even if materials are publicly available, though, they are not always available online or in easy-to-search formats. In addition, fewer materials may be available for older state statutes. *See, e.g.*, University of Miami School of Law Library, Law Research Guides: Florida Legislative History, library.law.miami.edu/research/guides/florida-legislative-history/index.html (visited May 7, 2023) ("The state of Florida did not begin keeping legislative materials archivally until 1969. From 1969 to about the mid '70s, most documentation is . . . sparse, and available only from the State Archives of Florida in Tallahassee. . . . Documents from mid '70s to 1988 are

courts use is available to the public on essentially the same terms as statutory texts themselves, and in most cases has been publicly available ever since those texts were enacted. For modern statutes, indeed, committee reports are available free of charge on Congress's website, and the *Congressional Record* is also online. But concerns about the *practical* accessibility of the materials of legislative history persist. *See, e.g.*, Richard A. Danner, *Justice Jackson's Lament: Historical and Comparative Perspectives on the Availability of Legislative History*, 13 DUKE J. COMP. & INT'L L. 151, 194 (Summer 2003) (concluding that although the materials of legislative history are now readily available to lawyers, "using them effectively remains difficult and costly because of the large number of possibly relevant documents, because they are poorly indexed internally, and because of the difficulties of determining in advance which parts of the history may be deemed relevant to questions of interpretation").

As Professor Dickerson noted in the 1970s, moreover, the key question is not whether lawyers can research legislative history effectively after their clients have acted and a dispute has arisen about one specific issue, but whether legislative history is sufficiently accessible to people who are seeking to plan their conduct across a broad range of issues in advance of any controversy. REED DICKERSON, THE INTERPRETATION AND APPLICATION OF STATUTES 150 (1975). At least at the time that he was writing, Professor Dickerson believed that even if legislative history is sufficiently available to lawyers who find themselves in litigation about a particular issue, "[i]t is vastly harder and usually impracticable to search all aspects of the legislative history as they relate to the myriad of potentially troublesome problems that the lawyer would like to anticipate." *Id.* at 151.

The Reagan Administration's Office of Legal Policy raised this issue even more pointedly in the 1980s. "[O]ur legal system," it noted, "is premised upon the idea that citizens read and know the law." Admittedly, this premise might not be true; the idea that citizens know the law is to some extent "a legal fiction." But the Office expressed concern about extending this fiction to legislative history as well as statutory text. In the Office's words, "If the average citizen is presumed to be aware of the legislative history as well as the statute, are we then enforcing not simply

---

complete, but also available only from the State Archives."); Sean J. Kealy, *A Guide to Gathering and Using Legislative History in Massachusetts*, 97 MASS. L. REV. 46, 46 (2016) ("[G]athering legislative history in Massachusetts is difficult at best. Unlike Congress, Massachusetts does not have anything analogous to the comprehensive *Congressional Record*, informative committee reports, or a systematic archive of relevant records used to draft and justify bills."); *cf.* IND. CODE §§ 2-5-1.1-12.1, 2-5-1.1-14, 2-5-1.1-16 (authorizing audio and video coverage of sessions of the general assembly and other legislative activities, but indicating that such coverage normally "is not part of the legislative history of an act" and should not be treated as evidence of legislative intent). The library of Indiana University's Maurer School of Law maintains a helpful inventory of information about researching legislative history in each state (currently found at https://law.indiana.libguides.com/c.php?g=19813).

unknown but almost unknowable laws?" OFFICE OF LEGAL POLICY, *supra*, at 52.

The short answer to that question may be "no, we aren't." For one thing, ordinary people do not routinely consult *either* statutory text *or* legislative history. To the extent that they nonetheless acquire some actual notice of the law's requirements, they get that notice through complex mechanisms that are not very well understood. Perhaps those mechanisms are capable of transmitting some sense of what is in a statute's legislative history just as they are capable of transmitting some sense of what is in the statutory text.

In any event, modern judges often say that they will not use legislative history to contradict or qualify seemingly clear statutory text. On this view, legislative history comes into play only when the enacted statutory language is unclear in some respect. *See, e.g.*, Penobscot Nation v. Frey, 3 F.4th 484, 491 (1st Cir. 2021) (en banc) ("When the text is unambiguous and the statutory scheme is coherent and consistent, we do not look to legislative history or Congressional intent."); *see also* Adam M. Samaha, *If the Text is Clear—Lexical Ordering in Statutory Interpretation*, 94 NOTRE DAME L. REV. 155, 160, 164–66 (2018) (noting that "[t]he demotion of legislative history into a lexically inferior tier is now endorsed by many federal judges who are not self-described textualists" and concluding that "working majorities do appear committed to the lexical inferiority of legislative history," though raising questions about this approach).[26] Whether or not courts use legislative history, people will not always be able to predict with complete confidence how courts will interpret statutes that contain ambiguities or are otherwise unclear. For purposes of evaluating notice-based objections to the use of legislative history, the key questions are therefore comparative: would an interpretive regime in which courts refuse to consult legislative history give people more notice of what statutes will be understood to mean than an interpretive regime in which courts do consult legislative history?

At least in cases where a statute contains an *otherwise intractable* ambiguity, notice-based arguments probably do not cut against letting courts consult legislative history to see whether it helps resolve the ambiguity. Imagine that a statute lends itself to two possible readings, and imagine that if not for any information in the legislative history, interpreters would be in equipoise between these readings; none of the canons or other applicable principles of interpretation would tell

[26] *Cf.* Digital Realty Trust, Inc. v. Somers, 138 S. Ct. 767, 783 (2018) (Sotomayor, J., concurring) ("Legislative history can be particularly helpful when a statute is ambiguous or deals with especially complex matters. But even when, as here, a statute's meaning can clearly be discerned from its text, consulting reliable legislative history can still be useful, as it enables us to corroborate and fortify our understanding of the text."); Koons Buick Pontiac GMC Inc. v. Nigh, 543 U.S. 50, 65 (2004) (Stevens, J., concurring) (acknowledging that "[i]n recent years the Court has suggested that we should only look at legislative history for the purpose of resolving textual ambiguities or to avoid absurdities," but criticizing this limitation and indicating that "it is always appropriate" for courts to consult legislative history).

interpreters which reading to pick. If judges do not look at legislative history in cases of this sort, they will simply choose between the two readings on their own, and they might do so on the basis of considerations that are not fully available to people in advance. By contrast, if judges *do* consult legislative history (and people know about that practice), the contents of the legislative history might provide an advance signal of how courts are likely to resolve the ambiguity. Unlike the personal predilections or intuitions of whatever judges are assigned to a case, legislative history is at least written down in advance and available to those who can afford to search it. Where courts are confronting statutes that are otherwise intractably ambiguous, then, notice-based arguments might actually *favor* telling courts to use legislative history.

Still, we cannot limit our comparison to situations of this sort, because the use of legislative history probably extends beyond the set of cases in which statutes would otherwise be intractably ambiguous. Under current practices, even if most judges restrict their use of legislative history to cases in which the enacted statutory language is ambiguous in some respect, judges do not necessarily require the ambiguity to be intractable; many judges seem willing to consult legislative history whenever two readings of a statute are both possible, even if the text of the statute gives one reading an edge over the other. If the use of legislative history can cause judges to select a reading that they would consider inferior simply on the basis of the text, the use of legislative history may sometimes have the effect of making statutory interpretation less predictable.

The same might be true if the availability of legislative history causes some courts to downplay the canons that they would otherwise use to resolve superficial ambiguities in statutory language. Suppose that a statutory provision might be read to establish either of two directives, but a canon points in favor of Directive #1. If no legislative history were available, people might be pretty confident that courts would adopt that interpretation. But if there is some legislative history that points in favor of Directive #2, yet is not completely dispositive, predictions might be difficult; some judges might follow the legislative history in preference to the canon, and other judges might follow the canon in preference to the legislative history.[27] In cases of this sort, the courts' practice of consulting legislative history might make their use of the canons less predictable than it would otherwise be. (Of course, even if this is a problem, people might disagree about whether the solution is to deemphasize legislative history or to deemphasize canons.)

Ultimately, whether the courts' willingness to consult legislative history does indeed make courts' interpretations of statutes less predictable than they otherwise would be is another empirical question that our current knowledge does not permit us to answer. So too is the

[27] Section D.2 of this chapter discusses interactions between legislative history and the canons.

question whether concerns about notice could be solved simply by restricting the use of legislative history to cases in which statutes otherwise are opaque—so that instead of using legislative history to *create* indeterminacy in statutes that seem tolerably clear on their face, judges used legislative history only to help *resolve* indeterminacy that they would detect anyway.

Even if we could know that current practices with respect to legislative history are bad from the standpoint of notice, though, we could not automatically conclude that courts should not use legislative history. Providing the citizenry with notice of the law's requirements is not the sole goal of an interpretive regime. To the contrary, it seems important for our interpretive regime *both* to enable people to have adequate notice of the law's requirements *and* to produce some correlation, in the aggregate, between the meanings that courts ascribe to statutes and the meanings that members of the enacting legislature actually intended (where such collective intentions did in fact exist).

Even committed textualists are willing to make some trade-offs between these two goals. For instance, mainstream textualists resist Alexander Aleinikoff's suggestion that courts should read even old statutes according to modern-day interpretive conventions, so that every statute means what we would think it meant if exactly the same words had been enacted this morning. *Compare* T. Alexander Aleinikoff, *Updating Statutory Interpretation*, 87 MICH. L. REV. 20 (1988) (acknowledging that "present-minded interpretation" of this sort flies in the face of conventional textualism, but arguing that this approach might serve notice-related goals better than an approach that requires readers to understand each statute according to the mindset and vocabulary that prevailed at the time of its enactment), *with* Steven D. Smith, *Law Without Mind*, 88 MICH. L. REV. 104 (1989) (complaining that Dean Aleinikoff's approach would cause the law's content to fluctuate according to fortuitous changes in linguistic conventions, and arguing that it is desirable for the legal directives that courts enforce to reflect policies that someone has actually deemed to be good ideas). The fact that most textualists emphasize the *original* meaning of old statutes, rather than the meaning that the same words would have if they were enacted today, suggests that textualists sometimes allow the goal of respecting the intended meaning of statutory language to qualify the goal of respecting the meanings that the people who are currently subject to a law would most naturally associate with the text of that law. But if the latter goal is not absolute, then it does not necessarily compel the categorical exclusion of legislative history—even if textualists are correct to assume that the use of legislative history makes the true content of the law somewhat less accessible to the citizenry.

(iii) Objections Based on Cost

Another set of arguments against the use of legislative history in statutory interpretation emphasizes the time and money that research into legislative history consumes. Assume for the sake of argument that the use of legislative history would achieve some of its claimed benefits; for instance, it would bring courts marginally closer toward the intended meaning of statutory language on issues as to which the enacting legislature really did have some collective understandings. Even so, this marginal benefit might not be big enough to justify the extra costs that using legislative history imposes on the legal system. As Reed Dickerson put it, "a prospector might wonder whether it is worth the effort to pan for gold in a stream that experience has shown will probably produce only an occasional nugget." DICKERSON, *supra*, at 164; *see also* William N. Eskridge, Jr., *The New Textualism*, 37 UCLA L. REV. 621, 684–85 (1990) (raising the possibility that the modern use of legislative history in statutory interpretation has "too little payoff" to warrant the costs that it imposes upon courts, litigants, and people seeking legal advice).

Justice Scalia embraced this argument enthusiastically. In his view, "legislative history is ordinarily so inconclusive" that its use does not actually help conscientious judges resolve most cases. But the fact that judges use legislative history imposes costs not only on the judges and their law clerks, but also on litigants and potential litigants (who must pay lawyers to plow through the available materials). According to Justice Scalia, "The most immediate and tangible change the abandonment of legislative history would effect is this: Judges, lawyers, and clients will be saved an enormous amount of time and expense." Scalia, *supra*, at 36.

As Professor Thomas Merrill has explained, moreover, "recent trends in the legislative process" have made research into legislative history even more time-consuming than Justice Scalia thought. Panel, *Text Over Intent and the Demise of Legislative History*, 43 U. DAY. L. REV. 103, 109 (2018) (remarks of Prof. Merrill). In the 1970s, most federal statutes were enacted through pretty much the same process, making it relatively easy to know where relevant pieces of legislative history might be found. *See id.* Nowadays, by contrast, Congress often enacts "mega statutes," which result from combining many separate bills—each of which has progressed some way through the legislative process on its own—into one giant bill that receives formal approval from both Houses. *See id.* at 109–10 (using as an example the Dodd-Frank Financial Reform Act of 2010, which "was stitched together from 48 separate bills, the final version of which emerged after 19 different steps in the legislative process"). Professor Merrill notes that for each mega-statute, the component bills "are patched together in a highly idiosyncratic fashion," which "makes it extremely hard to do any kind of coherent legislative history research." *Id.* Professor Merrill concludes that even though Justice Scalia's *constitutional* argument is "unsound," *see id.* at 107, his practical concern about efficiency is "a sound and compelling argument for doing away with legislative history." *Id.* at 109. *But see* VICTORIA NOURSE, MISREADING LAW, MISREADING DEMOCRACY 66, 80 (2016) (arguing that judges do not need to construct the entire legislative history of the statute that they are trying to interpret, but instead should "start by looking for the last decision-making point concerning the text at issue in the case," and should proceed backwards as necessary to understand the legislative decisions—an approach that allegedly can be efficient even with respect to omnibus statutes).

Admittedly, even if courts are willing to consider arguments based on legislative history, nothing currently *requires* lawyers to make such arguments. The fact that lawyers *do* wade through the legislative history, and that fee-paying clients tolerate this sort of research, suggests that participants in the legal system perceive research into legislative history as increasing the chances of victory enough to justify the expense. But lawyers' current practices do not really provide a market-based test of whether the societal benefits of such research outweigh the societal costs. For one thing, the fact that a lawyer's research into legislative history might improve his client's chances of winning does not necessarily produce any *societal* benefit (such as increasing the chances that the court will correctly identify the intended meaning of statutory language). *Cf.* William N. Eskridge, Jr., *Should the Supreme Court Read* The Federalist *But Not Statutory Legislative History?*, 66 GEO. WASH. L. REV. 1301, 1323 (1998) (formulating the key cost/benefit question—"Are there many cases where statutory legislative history allows us to reach correct results that cannot be reached without legislative history?"—and expressing the intuition that "these cases are exceptional"). In any event, even fee-paying clients are not bearing the full costs of research into legislative history; while they pay for the time spent by their lawyers, they do not pay for the time of judges and law clerks who have to referee disputes about legislative history. Finally, the use of legislative history may raise a collective-action problem. In the typical dispute, it is possible that each side's chances of winning would be roughly similar if *both* sides research legislative history or if *neither* side does. But if one side researches legislative history while the other does not, perhaps the researching side's chances improve noticeably. Absent collusion, the two sides might both decide to research legislative history—with the result that they both spend money, but end up with no more chance of victory than they had at the start.

As far as I know, no empirical study has quantified either the resources that society would save if courts stopped using legislative history or the benefits that society gains from the courts' current practices. *See id.* (noting lack of empirical data). What is more, it is hard to imagine any study doing so in the future; again, the relevant empirical questions seem intractable. While we await answers, though, Professor Vermeule has argued that we should advise courts *not* to consult legislative history. According to Professor Vermeule, we face "severe uncertainty" about the benefits of consulting legislative history; that is, we cannot even venture an informed guess about whether the use of legislative history tends to narrow or to widen the gap between the courts' results and the intended meaning of statutory language. In Professor Vermeule's view, we should therefore assume that the predicted value of using legislative history, when one takes account of all metrics other than "the direct costs of litigation and decision," is zero: so far as we know, the possibility that the use of legislative history will promote the goals of statutory interpretation is precisely offset by the possibility that it will frustrate them. But we *know* that the use of legislative history adds to decision costs. Thus, when we factor in "the direct costs of litigation and decision," the expected value of using legislative history turns negative. *See* ADRIAN VERMEULE, JUDGING UNDER UNCERTAINTY 192–95 (2006).

The premise of this argument is contestable: perhaps the existing uncertainty about the benefits of using legislative history is less severe than Professor Vermeule assumed, and perhaps the possible benefits of the practice are not completely offset by its possible costs. But the basic point that the use of legislative history imposes costs on our legal system, and that those costs are justified only if we can be sufficiently confident that the practice has some offsetting benefits, is an argument for putting the burden of proof on those who advocate the use of legislative history rather than those who oppose it. On the other hand, the fact that most courts currently are willing to consult legislative history for purposes of resolving ambiguities in statutory language, and that Justice Scalia was therefore calling for a marked shift in current practice, is an argument for putting the burden of proof on those who want change. Thus, even the argument about the burden of proof is inconclusive.

D. THE HIERARCHY OF LEGISLATIVE HISTORY AND ITS INTERACTION WITH OTHER INTERPRETIVE TOOLS

1. THE HIERARCHY OF TYPES OF LEGISLATIVE HISTORY

For judges who are willing to use legislative history for the purpose of shedding light on indeterminacies in statutory language, the weight that any particular piece of legislative history deserves varies according to several considerations. To begin with, judges evaluating the significance of particular statements in the legislative history must pay attention to the precise wording of the relevant bill at the time that the statements were made. Sometimes statements that seem highly relevant at first glance are really all but useless to interpreters because they addressed a different version of the bill than Congress ultimately enacted.

The weight that judges put on particular statements also varies according to the apparent likelihood that the statements reflect some sort of collective understanding. The more plausibly a particular view can be imputed to the full Congress (or at least to the coalition that voted in favor of the bill), rather than simply to an individual legislator, the more attention interpreters are likely to pay it. To some extent, that correlates with the type of legislative history in question. Here is an apt summary of the relative importance that courts tend to place on different types of legislative history:

> "Traditionally—and as a general matter—committee report explanations are considered more persuasive and reliable than statements made during floor debates or during hearings on a bill. Within the category of floor debates, statements of sponsors and explanations by floor managers usually are accorded the most weight, and statements by other committee members are next in importance. Statements by Members not associated with sponsorship or committee consideration of a bill are accorded little weight and statements by bill opponents generally are discounted or considered unreliable."

George A. Costello, *Average Voting Members and Other "Benign Fictions": The Relative Reliability of Committee Reports, Floor Debates, and Other Sources of Legislative History*, 1990 DUKE L.J. 39, 41–42. Note that the weight accorded to different types of legislative history roughly tracks the order in which these materials entered the interpretive arsenal: courts became willing to consider committee reports before they became willing to consider floor debates, and they continue to give the former more weight in the interpretive process than the latter.

Professor Victoria Nourse has argued that the implicit "judgments about reliability" reflected in the "standard hierarchy" of legislative history are wrong or at least overbroad. *See* VICTORIA NOURSE, MISREADING LAW, MISREADING DEMOCRACY 88–89 (2016). As she has observed, whether any given statement in the legislative history helps interpreters understand a statute does not necessarily depend on the type of document that contains the statement. In her view, courts should evaluate legislative history less by its type and more by its connection to the legislative decisions that produced the text being interpreted. *See id.* at 89–91 (observing that although "[c]ommittee reports have for some time been considered a reliable 'type' of legislative history," some committee reports come too early in the legislative process to shed much light on the text that Congress ultimately enacts, and a few come too late); *see also id.* at 89 (alluding to the fact that Congress does somewhat less of its work in committee these days than it used to). Those points are well taken; even judges who care about legislative history should not assume that whatever appears in a committee report is reliable and relevant. Still, when judges make case-by-case judgments about the reliability of different pieces of legislative history, statements in committee reports will often fare better than statements by individual members of Congress. *Cf.* Jesse M. Cross, *Legislative History in the*

Modern Congress, 57 HARV. J. LEGIS. 91, 96–97, 151–53 (2020) (proposing a revised hierarchy based on current legislative practices, but again putting committee reports at the top).

Empirical studies reflect the relative dominance of committee reports in the cases in which the Supreme Court invokes legislative history. A study published in 1982 concluded that from 1938 to 1979, Supreme Court opinions cited committee reports almost as often as they cited all other forms of legislative history combined. *See* Jorge L. Carro & Andrew R. Brann, *Use of Legislative Histories by the United States Supreme Court: A Statistical Analysis*, 9 J. LEGIS. 282, 291 (1982). As concerns about the use of legislative history grew in the 1980s, moreover, committee reports gained even more of an edge over other types of legislative history. Professor Brudney reports that "of the forty-two Supreme Court decisions between 1996 and 2005 in tax law and labor and employment law that actually relied on legislative history [in the sense that the majority did not merely refer to legislative history but treated it as 'a probative or determining factor'], the legislative history deemed persuasive included committee reports some three-fourths of the time." James J. Brudney, *Below the Surface: Comparing Legislative History Usage by the House of Lords and the Supreme Court*, 85 WASH. U. L. REV. 1, 30, 41 (2007); *see also id.* at 41 n.197 ("By contrast, the Court relied on hearings or floor debates in roughly one-third of these decisions . . . ."); *cf.* NLRB v. SW General, Inc., 580 U.S. 288, 307 (2017) ("[F]loor statements by individual legislators rank among the least illuminating forms of legislative history."). In the circuit courts, where legislative history may play a more important role than in the current Supreme Court, committee reports have become similarly dominant. *Compare* Stuart Minor Benjamin & Kristen M. Renberg, *The Paradoxical Impact of Scalia's Campaign Against Legislative History*, 105 CORNELL L. REV. 1023, 1066 tbl. 2 (2020) (reporting that from 1965 through 1985, circuit courts published 3,455 majority opinions that cited floor debates or committee hearings and 5,280 that cited committee reports), *with id.* (reporting that from 1986 through 2011, circuit courts published 4,348 majority opinions that cited floor debates or committee hearings and 24,935 that cited committee reports).

In opposing even the use of committee reports, Justice Scalia and Bryan Garner pointed out that "they are drafted by committee staff and are not voted on . . . by the committee members, much less by the full house"—and the workings of one house would not necessarily reflect the thinking of the other house anyway. ANTONIN SCALIA & BRYAN A. GARNER, READING LAW: THE INTERPRETATION OF LEGAL TEXTS 376 (2012). Committee reports are indeed written by the committee's legislative staff, not by members of Congress or their personal staff. *See* Cross, *supra*, 57 HARV. J. LEGIS. at 126–30. Still, there are at least three reasons why judges who care about legislative history might pay particular attention to committee reports. First, at least when the majority of the work on a bill is done in committee, the staffers who write the report are likely to have spent more time with the bill than most other people within Congress, and they also are likely to have more expertise in the relevant subject area. *See id.* at 105–09, 152. Second, unlike many floor statements by individual members of Congress, committee reports are not designed for "television or social media," *id.* at 98–99, 153, and the process by which committee reports are written includes some mechanisms for quality control. *See id.* at 129–30, 155, 160 (emphasizing that many committees routinely let the minority party's committee legislative staff review a draft and negotiate for changes before the report is issued—a practice that allegedly "promot[es] accountability and accuracy"). Third, committee reports are also thought to provide a focal point for the full chamber's consideration of a bill, with the result that members of the chamber who are not on the committee may get information about the bill from the committee report.

Of course, even if a committee report should indeed bear on the proper interpretation of a bill that the committee is recommending, bills can be amended on the floor after they have emerged from committee. If a chamber adopts an amendment that was not considered in committee, the wording of the bill as approved by the chamber will not match the wording of the bill that the committee was discussing in its report. That can affect the relevance of statements in the committee report. Before invoking such statements, judges therefore should compare the language of the bill as it left the committee to the language of the statute as enacted. *See* NOURSE, *supra*, at 89 (noting the need to "trace[ ] the statutory text"); *cf. id.* at 80 (suggesting that by tracing the text of a statute backwards through the legislative process, interpreters can identify which pieces of legislative history might be most relevant to the interpretation of particular provisions).

The explanatory statements that accompany so-called "conference reports" are not subject to this complication, because they come near the very end of the legislative process. Suppose that one house of Congress passes a bill and sends it to the other house, but the receiving house makes changes before itself passing the bill. Sometimes, the two houses will end up appointing representatives to an *ad hoc* "conference committee" charged with working out the differences between the two versions of the bill and producing a compromise version that each house can then vote up or down.[28] Technically, that version is known as the "conference report." *Cf.* NOURSE, *supra*, at 90 (noting that "*[c]onference reports are proposed text*" and should not be confused with the "committee

---

[28] Conference committees are not always necessary. Sometimes, agreement on a single bill can be reached "through informal negotiations and an exchange of amendments between the two houses." ELIZABETH RYBICKI, CONG. RSCH. SERV., 96–708, CONFERENCE COMMITTEE AND RELATED PROCEDURES: AN INTRODUCTION 2 (2021). This process of negotiation has been called "preconference," but it typically avoids the need for a true conference. Scholars of the legislative process say that preconference has become "the new norm," with the result that "there are almost no conference reports." Jesse M. Cross & Abbe R. Gluck, *The Congressional Bureaucracy*, 168 U. PA. L. REV. 1541, 1643 (2020).

reports" produced by standing committees of a single house earlier in the legislative process). But in modern times, when the conferees report a bill, they or their staffs prepare a joint explanatory statement that accompanies the conference report. Those explanatory statements often are terse, and they address only a limited set of issues; the conferees are not authorized to propose changes that go beyond the scope of the differences between the two versions of the bill, so their explanatory statement will not address provisions that were the same in both versions. *See id.* at 81; *see also* RYBICKI, *supra* note 28, at 5–6 (discussing limits on the conferees' authority). As a result, even when Congress proceeds to enact the conferees' version of the bill, the explanatory statement that accompanied the conference report will not bear on many of the questions of interpretation that come up in later litigation. On the relatively rare occasions when they are relevant, however, such explanatory statements are regarded as an especially powerful form of legislative history, both because they address the final version of the bill immediately before Congress enacted it and because they are called to the attention of the members of both chambers rather than just one. *See, e.g.*, Disabled in Action of Metro. N.Y. v. Hammons, 202 F.3d 110, 125 (2d Cir. 2000) ("The conference report stage is closest to final passage and is generally thus the best indicator of legislative meaning apart from the statute itself."); NOURSE, *supra*, at 80 (calling this "the conventional and correct wisdom").

Aside from the explanatory statements that accompany conference reports, and aside from the committee reports produced by standing committees within the House or the Senate, judges also sometimes pay attention to statements by individual members of Congress, especially if those members not only supported the bill but played a significant role in getting it enacted. *See, e.g.*, Lewis v. United States, 445 U.S. 55, 63 (1980) ("Inasmuch as Senator Long was the sponsor and floor manager of the bill, his statements are entitled to weight."); Simpson v. United States, 435 U.S. 6, 13 (1978) (quoting Representative Poff's statement on the House floor "immediately following his introduction of the amendment" that became 18 U.S.C. § 924(c), and observing that "[a]lthough these remarks are of course not dispositive of the issue of § 924(c)'s reach, they are certainly entitled to weight, coming as they do from the provision's sponsor."); Garvey v. Wilkie, 972 F.3d 1333, 1339 (Fed. Cir. 2020) (quoting remarks by the "sponsor" of the bill as printed in the *Congressional Record*); *cf.* Cross, *supra*, 57 HARV. J. LEGIS. at 151–53 (arguing that within the category of statements by individual members, statements by the chair or ranking member of a responsible committee or subcommittee normally deserve more weight than statements by the member who introduced a bill or the bill's floor sponsors). As noted above, though, both the Supreme Court and federal circuit courts now cite committee reports more often than statements by individual members of Congress. *See supra* p. 470; *see also* WILLIAM N. ESKRIDGE JR., INTERPRETING LAW: A PRIMER ON HOW TO READ STATUTES

AND THE CONSTITUTION 247–48 (2016) (observing that "[i]n recent terms, the Supreme Court curtailed its reference to sponsor's statements," though criticizing this development); *cf.* Mims v. Arrow Fin. Servs., LLC, 565 U.S. 368, 385 (2012) ("[T]he views of a single legislator, even a bill's sponsor, are not controlling."); Chrysler Corp. v. Brown, 441 U.S. 281, 311 (1979) (same). Other pieces of legislative history, such as statements by witnesses at committee hearings, are usually even harder for courts to link to the intended meaning of the resulting statute and receive correspondingly less attention. *See, e.g.*, Advocate Health Care Network v. Stapleton, 581 U.S. 468, 481 (2017) (Kagan, J.) (referring to "excerpts from committee hearings and scattered floor statements by individual lawmakers" as "lowly sources"—"the sort of stuff we have called 'among the least illuminating forms of legislative history' " (quoting NLRB v. SW General, Inc., 580 U.S. 288, 307 (2017))); *cf.* Kelly v. Robinson, 479 U.S. 36, 51 n.13 (1986) ("We acknowledge that a few comments in the hearings . . . may suggest that the language bears the interpretation adopted by the Second Circuit. But none of these statements was made by a Member of Congress, nor were they included in the official Senate and House Reports. We decline to accord any significance to these statements.").

During the heyday of reliance upon legislative history, judges occasionally made reference to so-called "subsequent" or "post-enactment" legislative history—statements made in committee reports or by individual members of Congress about the meaning of *previously enacted* statutes. *See, e.g.*, County of Washington v. Gunther, 452 U.S. 161, 194 & n.6 (1981) (Rehnquist, J., dissenting) (invoking a "clarifying statement" made in 1965 by the sponsor of an amendment that Congress had enacted as part of the Civil Rights Act of 1964). More recently, however, the Supreme Court has stated flatly that "[p]ost-enactment legislative history" of this sort "is not a legitimate tool of statutory interpretation." *Bruesewitz v. Wyeth LLC*, 562 U.S. 223, 242 (2011); *see also* United States v. Woods, 571 U.S. 31, 47–48 (2013) (unanimous opinion) (refusing to give any special weight to "Blue Books . . . prepared by the staff of the Joint Committee on Taxation as commentaries on recently passed tax laws," and disapproving a 1973 opinion that had invoked a similar document). Although a few of the Justices may not take quite such a categorical position, even supporters of the use of pre-enactment legislative history put little stock in post-enactment statements. In the words of a majority opinion by Justice Souter,

> "Those of us who look to legislative history have been wary about expecting to find reliable interpretive help outside the record of the statute being construed, and we have said repeatedly that 'subsequent legislative history will rarely override a reasonable interpretation of a statute that can be gleaned from its language and legislative history prior to its enactment,' *Solid Waste Agency of Northern Cook Cty. v. Army Corps of Engineers*, 531 U.S. 159, 170,

n. 5 (2001) (quoting *Consumer Product Safety Comm'n v. GTE Sylvania, Inc.*, 447 U.S. 102, 118, n. 13 (1980))."

Doe v. Chao, 540 U.S. 614, 626–27 (2004); *see also* Barber v. Thomas, 560 U.S. 474, 486 (2010) (Breyer, J.) ("[W]hatever interpretive force one attaches to legislative history, the Court normally gives little weight to statements . . . made *after* the bill in question has become law.").

The Supreme Court is surely correct that "subsequent legislative history is a 'hazardous basis for inferring the intent of an earlier' Congress." *Pension Benefit Guar. Corp. v. LTV Corp.*, 496 U.S. 633, 650 (1990) (quoting *United States v. Price*, 361 U.S. 304, 313 (1960)). To begin with, members of a later Congress may lack any special access to the understandings of their predecessors. Especially if substantial time has passed since the statute in question was enacted, the legislators or staff members responsible for the subsequent legislative history may not have been privy to the earlier Congress's deliberations, or their memories of those deliberations may not be reliable. *See, e.g.*, United States ex rel. Long v. SCS Bus. & Tech. Inst., Inc., 173 F.3d 870, 878–79 (D.C. Cir. 1999) (concluding that statements in a 1986 Senate report about the meaning of the False Claims Act of 1863 are "of no legal significance"). But even if relatively little time has passed, and even if the legislators or staff members responsible for subsequent legislative history were central players in the enactment of the statute that they are glossing, committee reports prepared after the fact still lack some of the indicia of reliability commonly attributed to pre-enactment legislative history. For one thing, they cannot possibly have formed the basis for anyone's vote on the statute. In addition, there is no obvious way for members of the enacting legislature who had a different understanding of the statute to register their dissent from views that have not yet been expressed—and those legislators might not be in a position to register their dissent when the views *are* expressed after the fact.

Legislators who put glosses on statutes after enactment also have substantial incentives for gamesmanship. When Congress's attention is elsewhere, they might be trying to mislead courts into enforcing policies that they were unable to get through the actual legislative process. At the very least, there is a substantial risk that their comments will reflect current political dynamics rather than the dynamics that prevailed at the time of enactment (which might have been quite different even if relatively little time has passed). For all these reasons, post-enactment legislative history may shed little true light on the intended meaning of statutory language.

If the standard arguments *in favor of* considering legislative history are weaker for post-enactment legislative history than for pre-enactment legislative history, the standard arguments *against* considering legislative history are stronger. In addition to the arguments about unreliability that we have just canvassed, judicial reliance upon post-enactment legislative history raises serious concerns about notice. If courts take post-enactment legislative history to relate back to the original date of enactment and to shed light on what the statute has always meant, its use would raise some of the same concerns as other retroactive instructions from Congress. In this respect, there is no obvious difference between judicial reliance on after-the-fact committee reports or floor statements and judicial reliance on after-the-fact testimony from individual legislators. And even if courts treat post-enactment legislative history as being relevant only in cases about conduct that occurred after the post-enactment legislative history was created, the use of post-enactment legislative history would greatly multiply concerns about the practical accessibility of legislative history. The pre-enactment legislative history of a statute might be voluminous, but at least it is confined to a particular bill or set of bills. If the legislative history of every other bill might also influence the meaning that courts ascribe to the statute, then the expense and difficulty of researching legislative history might become prohibitive.

Concerns about bicameralism and presentment also seem especially powerful in this context. In theory, of course, the subsequent committee reports or floor statements are simply being used to shed light on what a previous bill meant at the time that it went through the process of bicameralism and presentment. But in practice, to the extent that subsequent legislative history changes interpreters' minds about the best interpretation of a statute, its use causes a statute that was properly read to mean one thing at the time of enactment to have a different meaning going forward—a result that might seem to circumvent the constitutionally mandated procedures for effecting legal change. This time, moreover, Professor Siegel's arguments about "incorporation by reference" are unavailable, because the relevant committee reports or floor statements did not exist at the time that the statute in question was enacted.

Do the same reasons that have caused interpreters to downplay post-enactment legislative history also justify disregarding glosses that the President puts on a bill at the time of signing it into law? Although the federal Constitution requires the President to specify his objections when he *vetoes* a bill, it does not require him to issue any sort of statement when he *signs* a bill. On occasion, though, Presidents have issued "signing statements" of various sorts. In the mid-1980s, the Reagan Administration considered (and ultimately began to follow) the relatively "novel[ ]" practice of using such statements "to address questions of interpretation." *See* Memorandum from Deputy Assistant Attorney General Samuel A. Alito, Jr., to the Litigation Strategy Working Group (Feb. 5, 1986) at 1, http://www.archives.gov/news/samuel-alito/accession-060-89-269/Acc060-89-269-box6-SG-LSWG-AlitotoLSWG-Feb1986.pdf (last visited July 23, 2022); *see also* Christopher S. Kelley, *A Matter of Direction: The Reagan Administration, the Signing Statement, and the 1986 Westlaw Decision*, 16 WM. & MARY BILL OF RIGHTS J. 283 (2007) (discussing the evolution of the Reagan administration's policy on signing statements and its successful request that the West Publishing Company begin including signing statements in the excerpted legislative histories that are printed in the *United States Code, Congressional and Administrative News*).

In a few special contexts, courts have treated signing statements of this sort as a relevant part of a bill's legislative history. *See, e.g.*, United States v. Story, 891 F.2d 988, 993–94 (2d Cir. 1989) (treating as relevant a presidential signing statement that endorsed interpretive views expressed in the Senate rather than interpretive views expressed in the House, and noting that "President Reagan's views are significant here because the Executive Branch participated in the negotiation of the compromise legislation"). But courts have not embraced such statements with much enthusiasm. *See* John M. de Figueiredo & Edward H. Stiglitz, *Signing Statements and Presidentializing Legislative History*, 69 ADMIN. L. REV. 841, 845 (2017) (reporting an empirical study of opinions issued by the U.S. Supreme Court and the federal circuit courts between 1976 and 2011, and finding that "there is only one citation to a signing statement per 7,500 non-criminal cases"); *id.* at 846 (adding that even when federal appellate courts do cite a signing statement, "they . . . balk when the president expresses a view in his signing statement that is plainly contrary to the text of the statute or to other more conventional sources of legislative history").

That is as it should be. While the Constitution does give the President an important role in the legislative process, that role is limited to approving or disapproving—not modifying—the bills that Congress presents to him. In essence, the President is supposed to take what Congress has sent him and decide whether to sign it or to veto it. Even supporters of the use of legislative history in statutory interpretation might therefore think that legislative history is relevant only to the extent that it bears on what Congress sent the President. For obvious reasons, though, statements that the President makes at the time of signing a bill may not be very reliable guides to the meaning that each house of Congress was trying to communicate at the time that it voted on the bill. Even if the President's signing statement is issued in complete good faith, the President is a step removed from Congress. In addition, because the President's signing statement did not exist when the bill went through Congress, it could not have provided a focal point for anyone's vote in Congress, and whatever glosses it suggests cannot readily be understood to have been "incorporated" in the text that went through bicameralism.

Admittedly, the executive branch often is heavily involved in the process of enacting legislation. In situations where Congress and the President have the same goals and are cooperating with each other, the views expressed in the President's signing statement may indeed reflect what each house of Congress was trying to do. Still, the very fact that the

President is issuing a signing statement that contains interpretive glosses may suggest that the President is not totally satisfied with what emerged from Congress and is trying to put the executive branch's own spin on it. In other words, the occasions on which the President issues interpretive signing statements may disproportionately be occasions on which the President's views are in some opposition to Congress's views.

Of course, even if courts do not treat presidential signing statements as powerful parts of a bill's legislative history, such statements can perform other functions. To the extent that a bill presented to the President leaves room for administrative agencies or other interpreters within the executive branch to make some interpretive choices, signing statements are a way for the President to give those actors some early guidance. Thus, the primary audience for a particular signing statement may not be *judicial* interpreters, but rather other officials within the executive branch. *See* M. Elizabeth Magill, *The First Word*, 16 WM. & MARY BILL OF RIGHTS J. 27, 53 (2007) (discussing signing statements as one tool for "White House influence over the exercise of discretion by subordinate actors"). More subtly, interpretive signing statements may also have been developed as a strategy for getting courts to re-examine their use of legislative history in general. *See* Alito Memorandum, *supra*, at 2 ("From the perspective of the Executive Branch, the issuance of interpretive signing statements would have two chief advantages. First, it would increase the power of the Executive to shape the law. Second, by forcing some rethinking by courts, scholars, and litigants, it may help to curb some of the prevalent abuses of legislative history.").

* * * * *

The materials above identify a rough hierarchy of statements about a bill that might appear in the bill's legislative history. In addition to considering statements about a bill, though, interpreters also sometimes invoke the "drafting history" of the bill itself. In other words, interpreters sometimes refer to changes that were made to the bill's text during the legislative process (or to changes that were proposed but not adopted), and they argue that those changes shed light on the intended meaning of the statute as enacted.

As with the use of other types of legislative history, Justice Scalia criticized this practice. In his view, "drafting history is no more legitimate or reliable an indicator of the objective meaning of a statute than any other form of legislative history." *Hamdan v. Rumsfeld*, 548 U.S. 557, 668 (2006) (Scalia, J., dissenting); *see also supra* p. 447 (noting the similar statement in Justice Scalia's concurrence in *Bank One Chicago, N.A. v. Midwest Bank & Trust Co.*, 516 U.S. 264, 279 (1996)).[29] But some of

[29] To be clear, Justice Scalia objected to the practice of basing inferences about statutory meaning on *unenacted* versions of the relevant bill. He agreed with everyone else that interpreters can properly consider prior *enacted* versions of the law. In particular, he did not deny that considering how a statute evolved over the years, through amendments that were

Justice Scalia's fellow textualists have put considerable weight on at least some forms of drafting history. Consider Judge Easterbrook's opinion in *South Austin Coalition Community Council v. SBC Communications Inc.*, 274 F.3d 1168 (7th Cir. 2001), which involved whether a telecommunications company qualified as a "common carrier subject to the laws to regulate commerce" within the meaning of § 7 of the Clayton Act of 1914, ch. 323, 38 Stat. 730, 732 (codified at 15 U.S.C. § 18). Judge Easterbrook conceded that other language in § 7, which referred to "the construction of branches or short lines," lent some credence to the idea that § 7 was using the phrase "common carrier" to refer only to railroads. But Judge Easterbrook rejected this argument, in part on the strength of the relevant drafting history. As he put it:

> "[T]he legislative history—the *enactment* history, not the fog of words generated by legislators—shows that 'common carrier' means *all* common carriers. The version of § 7 . . . passed by the House used the word 'railroad'; the Senate amended this to 'common carrier,' a broader designation; the House acceded to the Senate's amendment. The Senate's committee report observed that this change was made precisely to 'apply to any common carrier, thus including telephone and pipe lines.' "

South Austin, 274 F.3d at 1172.

One should not necessarily conclude that Judge Easterbrook would put similar weight on records of changes approved with little fanfare during a committee mark-up session. Judge Easterbrook may well have thought that the timing and nature of the drafting history he invoked in *South Austin* made it especially good evidence of Congress's collective understandings. At least in circumstances like the one that he confronted in *South Austin*, though, Judge Easterbrook seems to view drafting history as a more powerful form of legislative history than the "fog of words" found in floor debates and even committee reports. *See also, e.g.*, Gonzalez v. Arizona, 677 F.3d 383, 441 (9th Cir. 2012) (en banc) (Kozinski, J., concurring) (agreeing that "drafting history can offer interpretive insight," and distinguishing it from other types of legislative history on the ground that it "consists of actions taken by legislative bodies, not just words penned by staffers or lobbyists" (emphasis omitted)), *aff'd sub nom.* Arizona v. Inter Tribal Council of Arizona, Inc., 570 U.S. 1 (2013).

2. INTERACTIONS BETWEEN LEGISLATIVE HISTORY AND THE CANONS

The preceding section discussed the hierarchy among different types of legislative history. But it is also important to think about where the use of legislative history stands in relation to other interpretive tools. In

actually enacted into law, can sometimes shed light on the meaning of the current version of the statute. *See supra* pp. 348–349 (referring to "statutory history" of this sort).

particular, courts frequently face questions about how legislative history interacts with canons of the sort surveyed in Chapter 2.

To some extent, legislative history and the canons are rivals. That is true in at least two different senses.

First, the use of generic canons and the use of particularized legislative history arguably reflect rival ways of accomplishing the same basic goal—promoting successful communication from legislatures to courts. Suppose that we are trying to devise a system of interpretation that, when implemented by courts, will best promote the various goals that we want our system of interpretation to promote. Suppose further that those goals include avoiding unwarranted mismatches[30] between the legal directives that courts ascribe to statutes and the legal directives that members of the enacting legislature collectively understood themselves to be establishing. If one trusts courts to make sound case-by-case evaluations of all the relevant data, one might think that the best way to promote this goal is to encourage courts to consider the publicly available legislative history on a case-by-case basis and to use it for whatever it seems to be worth. On the other hand, if one thinks that judges who are told to make such highly contextual decisions will often go awry, one might think that the correlation between interpreted and intended meaning will actually be higher if courts generally follow the probabilities and do not comb the legislative history for signs that a particular legislature meant to break from the patterns established by past legislatures. On this latter view, fairly close adherence to the canons—most of which can be seen as generalizations about the ways in which American legislatures typically use language or the kinds of legal directives that they typically mean to establish—might be a better way of promoting successful communication from legislatures to courts than a formless inquiry into the legislative history of each individual statute. The more one gravitates toward rule-based decisionmaking in this context, the more weight one will tend to put on generic canons of construction, and the less one will want courts to rummage through the legislative history of each individual statute.

Canons and legislative history are also rivals in a second, more practical sense. To the extent that a court uses legislative history to resolve apparent indeterminacies in a statute, it is leaving less work for the canons to do. Where relevant legislative history exists on some point, using it to clarify statutory language is an alternative to relying upon the canons for that purpose. *See* Stephen Breyer, *On the Uses of Legislative History in Interpreting Statutes*, 65 S. CAL. L. REV. 845, 869 (1992) (emphasizing this rivalry between legislative history and the canons, and

---

[30] By "unwarranted" mismatches, I mean mismatches that are not justified by any of the other goals that we want our system of interpretation to promote, such as ensuring adequate notice to the citizenry and keeping the financial costs of interpretation within reasonable limits for all concerned.

suggesting that legislative history generated within Congress is a preferable means of resolving indeterminacies).

But while canons and legislative history are rivals in both these senses, they are not complete substitutes for each other. No judge categorically refuses to apply the canons, and relatively few judges follow Justice Scalia's view that legislative history is (almost) always off limits. Thus, the typical judge is willing *both* to apply canons *and* to consult legislative history. It follows that the typical judge must figure out how particular kinds of legislative history and particular canons interact with each other: When might legislative history trump the application of a canon that would otherwise control resolution of a case, and when should canons trump legislative history?

a. CAN LEGISLATIVE HISTORY OVERCOME THE RULE OF LENITY?

We can begin with the rule of lenity. When we studied the rule of lenity in Chapter 2, we saw that it is a "normative" rather than a "descriptive" canon, and that courts typically confine it to the mop-up work that remains after they have used their normal tools for determining the intended meaning of statutory language. If one sees legislative history as such a tool, then one might naturally assume that legislative history ranks higher in the interpretive hierarchy than the rule of lenity. On this view, courts should not apply the rule of lenity until after they have consulted the legislative history of the relevant statute and have concluded that it does not help to resolve the indeterminacy that they have identified.

Although the matter remains contested, various Supreme Court opinions have endorsed this view. In *Dixson v. United States*, 465 U.S. 482 (1984), the Court had to interpret the definition of "public official" in 18 U.S.C. § 201(a), a federal criminal statute about bribery. Conceding that the words of the statute "can be interpreted to support either [the defendants' relatively narrow reading] or the Government's [broader] reading," Justice Marshall's majority opinion asserted that "[w]e must turn, therefore, to the legislative history." *Dixson*, 465 U.S. at 491. The Court concluded that the legislative history supported the broader reading, *see id.* at 491–96—and because the legislative history resolved the ambiguity, "we have no need to resort to the rule of lenity in deciding this case." *Id.* at 500 n.19. On this basis, the Court affirmed the defendants' convictions. *See id.* at 501. More generally, in *Moskal v. United States*, 498 U.S. 103 (1990), the Court asserted that "we have always reserved lenity for those situations in which a reasonable doubt persists about a statute's intended scope even *after* resort to 'the language and structure, legislative history, and motivating policies' of the statute." *Id.* at 108 (quoting Bifulco v. United States, 447 U.S. 381, 387 (1980)).

In *United States v. R.L.C.*, 503 U.S. 291 (1992), Justice Souter's plurality opinion repeated this quotation from *Moskal*. *See id.* at 305–06.

But Justice Scalia wrote a separate opinion (joined by Justices Kennedy and Thomas) suggesting that even if it were appropriate for courts to consult legislative history to resolve indeterminacies in *nonpenal* statutes, it would still be inappropriate for courts to use legislative history to resolve indeterminacies in *penal* statutes.

R.L.C. concerned the meaning of a provision in the federal Juvenile Delinquency Act, which established an outer limit on the period for which juvenile offenders could be detained for acts of delinquency. Both the plurality and Justice Scalia agreed that the text of the relevant provision was ambiguous and that one possible interpretation of the provision was more lenient than the other. According to Justice Scalia, "that conclusion should end the matter"; applying the rule of lenity, the Court should give the statute "the more lenient interpretation." *Id.* at 307–08 (Scalia, J., concurring in part and concurring in the judgment). But the plurality did not proceed to the rule of lenity so quickly. Before turning to the rule of lenity, the plurality consulted the internal legislative history of the relevant statute to determine whether it helped to resolve the ambiguity.

In *R.L.C.* itself, the plurality concluded that the legislative history supported the more lenient interpretation of the statute. As a result, the plurality and Justice Scalia reached the same result. But Justice Scalia worried about what might happen in a different case, in which a committee report seemed to support the harsher interpretation of a provision that was ambiguous on its face. Notwithstanding the Court's statement in *Moskal*, Justice Scalia argued that "it is not consistent with the rule of lenity to construe a textually ambiguous penal statute against a criminal defendant on the basis of legislative history." *Id.* at 307. Here are some excerpts from Justice Scalia's separate opinion:

> "The *Moskal* formulation of the rule, in approving reliance on a statute's 'motivating policies' (an obscure phrase), seems contrary to our statement in *Hughey v. United States*, 495 U.S. 411, 422 (1990), that '[e]ven [where] the statutory language . . . [is] ambiguous, longstanding principles of lenity . . . preclude our resolution of the ambiguity against [the criminal defendant] on the basis of general declarations of policy in the statute and legislative history.' And insofar as *Moskal* requires consideration of legislative history *at all*, it compromises what we have described to be purposes of the lenity rule. '[A] fair warning,' we have said, 'should be given to the world in language that the common world will understand, of what the law intends to do if a certain line is passed. To make the warning fair, so far as possible the line should be clear.' *McBoyle v. United States*, 283 U.S. 25, 27 (1931). '[T]he rule of lenity ensures that criminal statutes will provide fair warning concerning conduct rendered illegal.' *Liparota v. United States*, 471 U.S. 419, 427 (1985). It may well be true that in most cases the proposition that the words of the United States Code or the Statutes at Large give adequate notice to the citizen is something of a fiction, see *McBoyle*, *supra*, at 27, albeit

one required in any system of law; but necessary fiction descends to needless farce when the public is charged even with knowledge of Committee Reports.

"*Moskal*'s mode of analysis also disserves the rule of lenity's other purpose: assuring that the society, through its representatives, has genuinely called for the punishment to be meted out. '[B]ecause of the seriousness of criminal penalties, and because criminal punishment usually represents the moral condemnation of the community, legislatures and not courts should define criminal activity.' *United States v. Bass*, 404 U.S. 336, 348 (1971). . . . The rule reflects, as the plurality acknowledges, ' " 'the instinctive distaste against men languishing in prison unless the lawmaker has clearly said they should.' " ' *Ante* at 305 (quoting *Bass*, *supra*, at 348, and H. Friendly, Benchmarks 209 (1967)). But legislative history can never provide assurance against that unacceptable result. . . . [N]o matter how 'authoritative' the history may be—even if it is that veritable Rosetta Stone of legislative archaeology, a crystal clear Committee Report—one can never be sure that the legislators who voted for the text of the bill were aware of it. The only thing that was authoritatively adopted *for sure* was the text of the enactment; the rest is *necessarily* speculation. Where it is doubtful whether the text includes the penalty, the penalty ought not be imposed. '[T]he moral condemnation of the community,' *Bass*, *supra*, at 348, is no more reflected in the views of a majority of a single committee of congressmen (assuming, of course, they have genuinely considered what their staff has produced) than it is reflected in the views of a majority of an appellate court; we should feel no less concerned about 'men languishing in prison' at the direction of the one than of the other.

"We have in a number of cases other than *Moskal* done what the plurality has done here: inquired into legislative history and invoked it to support or at least permit the more lenient reading. But only once, to my knowledge, have we relied on legislative history to 'clarify' a statute, explicitly found to be facially ambiguous, against the interest of a criminal defendant. In *Dixson v. United States*, 465 U.S. 482, 500–501, n. 19 (1984), the Court relied on legislative history to determine that defendants, officers of a corporation responsible for administering federal block grants, were 'public officials' within the meaning of 18 U.S.C. § 201(a). The opinion does not trouble to discuss the 'fair warning' or 'condemnation of the community' implications of its decision, and both of the cases it cites in supposed support of its holding found the statute at hand *not* to be facially ambiguous. . . . I think *Dixson* weak (indeed, utterly unreasoned) foundation for a rule of construction that permits legislative history to satisfy the ancient requirement that criminal

> statutes speak 'plainly and unmistakably,' *United States v. Gradwell*, 243 U.S. 476, 485 (1917) . . . .
>
> "In sum, I would not embrace, as the plurality does, the *Moskal* formulation of this canon of construction, lest lower courts take the dictum to heart. I would acknowledge the tension in our precedents, the absence of an examination of the consequences of the *Moskal* mode of analysis, and the consequent conclusion that *Moskal* may not be good law."

R.L.C., 503 U.S. at 308–11 (Scalia, J., concurring in part and concurring in the judgment); *cf. id.* at 306 n.6 (plurality opinion) (observing that "the Court has not in the past approached the use of lenity in the way Justice Scalia would have it," but concluding that whether the Court should do so "is an issue that is not raised and need not be reached in this case").

Was Justice Scalia correct that the level of clarity provided by legislative history can *never* be sufficient to satisfy the purposes behind the rule of lenity, and that the rule of lenity should therefore *always* trump recourse to legislative history when a judge identifies an ambiguity in a penal provision? Can the Constitution itself plausibly be understood to require the level of clarity that Justice Scalia had in mind? If not, where would the courts get authority to develop special interpretive rules that insist upon that level of clarity even in the teeth of what courts would otherwise identify as the intended meaning of a statute?

If you think that Justice Scalia was correct, how far should courts take his idea? Should the rule of lenity also trump ordinary descriptive canons? Consider, for instance, the penal statute at issue in *Church of the Holy Trinity v. United States*, which you read in Chapter 1. If the statutory phrase "labor or service of any kind" otherwise lends itself to two possible interpretations, but canons like the presumption against superfluity or the presumption of consistent usage support the broader reading, should courts apply those (descriptive) canons, or should the rule of lenity trump them too? In *R.L.C.*, Justice Thomas submitted a separate opinion agreeing with Justice Scalia that the rule of lenity trumped recourse to legislative history, but insisting that courts could use certain other canons to resolve ambiguities before resorting to the rule of lenity. As Justice Thomas put it, "we have developed innumerable rules of construction powerful enough to make clear an otherwise ambiguous penal statute," and knowledge of those canons can properly be imputed to the citizenry. *R.L.C.*, 503 U.S. at 311–12 (Thomas, J., concurring in part and concurring in the judgment). Justice Gorsuch appears to take a similar position: he too has endorsed Justice Scalia's view that courts should not consult legislative history to resolve ambiguities in penal statutes, but he has suggested that courts should apply "the traditional tools of statutory interpretation" before the rule of lenity. *See* Wooden v. United States, 142 S. Ct. 1063, 1085–86 (2022) (Gorsuch, J., concurring in the judgment) ("Where the traditional tools of statutory interpretation yield no clear answer, the judge's next step isn't to legislative history or the law's unexpressed purposes. The next step is to lenity.").

Do the positions articulated by Justices Scalia, Thomas, and Gorsuch ultimately depend on their opposition to the use of legislative history in general? Or might one plausibly conclude that the rule of lenity trumps recourse to the legislative history of penal statutes even if one thinks that courts can and should use legislative history to resolve indeterminacies in nonpenal statutes?[31]

b. CAN LEGISLATIVE HISTORY OVERCOME IMPLIED-LIMITATION RULES?

Like many canons, the rule of lenity is triggered by conventional ambiguity or vagueness in statutory language. (Indeed, for people who regard the rule of lenity as a canon of last resort, it is triggered by a special level of ambiguity or vagueness that resists clarification through other interpretive techniques.) As we saw in Chapter 2.E, though, some other canons are triggered simply by *general* statutory language—language that seems unqualified as a matter of ordinary meaning, but that might not reflect specific consideration of the issue that the canon addresses. The presumption against retroactivity and the presumption against extraterritoriality are examples. When courts confront generally worded statutes that contain no explicit temporal or geographic limitations, these canons encourage courts to *infer* limitations so that the statutes do not operate "retroactively" or "extraterritorially."

In *Landgraf v. USI Film Products*, 511 U.S. 244 (1991), Justice Stevens's majority opinion addressed not only what triggers the presumption against retroactivity, but also what might overcome it. In his view, courts should not understand a generally worded federal statute to operate retroactively "absent clear congressional intent favoring such a result." *Id.* at 280. For Justice Stevens, though, legislative history could supply the requisite evidence of congressional intent.

In *Landgraf* itself, the Court had to interpret the following language, enacted by the Civil Rights Act of 1991: "In an action brought by a complaining party under section 706 or 717 of the Civil Rights Act of 1964 . . . against a respondent who engaged in unlawful intentional discrimination . . . prohibited under section 703, 704, or 717 of the Act . . . , the complaining party may recover compensatory and punitive damages . . . from the respondent." Civil Rights Act of 1991, Pub. L. 102–166, § 102, 106 Stat. 1071, 1072. Ultimately, the Court held that this provision did not cover *all* actions brought by a complaining party under

---

[31] Perhaps Justice Sotomayor has adopted or is moving toward this position. Although she supports the use of legislative history in statutory interpretation, she joined much of Justice Gorsuch's concurring opinion in *Wooden*, including the part that prioritized the rule of lenity over legislative history.

the specified sections, but only actions about conduct that occurred after enactment of the Civil Rights Act of 1991. Before reaching this conclusion, though, Justice Stevens's majority opinion consulted the legislative history. *See, e.g., id.* at 262–63. If the legislative history had revealed a collective decision to reach cases about pre-enactment conduct, then the Court apparently would not have inferred a temporal limitation.

As you might expect, Justice Scalia criticized this aspect of the majority opinion. Joined by Justices Kennedy and Thomas (the same Justices who later joined his separate opinion in *United States v. R.L.C.*), Justice Scalia concurred only in the judgment in *Landgraf*. In his view, "a legislative enactment affecting substantive rights does not apply retroactively absent *clear statement* to the contrary," and the necessary clear statement must appear in "the text of the statute itself"—not simply the legislative history. *See id.* at 286–88 (Scalia, J., concurring in the judgment).

That position, though, probably reflected Justice Scalia's broader opposition to the use of legislative history in statutory interpretation. If one thinks that courts can properly use legislative history to help resolve ambiguities and other indeterminacy in statutory language, one is likely to think that courts can also properly use legislative history to overcome the presumption against retroactivity. To be sure, modern judges know that they should not act as if legislative history is itself a law, separate and apart from the text that Congress actually enacted. But when legislative history persuades judges that the presumption against retroactivity has been rebutted, the judges will actually be giving the statutory text its conventional meaning; the effect of the legislative history is simply to confirm the generality of the text and to establish that Congress really did intend the statute to be just as unqualified as the text suggests (so that interpreters should not read an implied limitation into it). That seems no more aggressive than using the legislative history to resolve ambiguities in the enacted language. To this day, then, judges who do not share Justice Scalia's near-categorical opposition to the use of legislative history in statutory interpretation are willing to consult legislative history when deciding whether the presumption against retroactivity has been overcome. *See, e.g.*, United States v. Miller, 911 F.3d 638, 643 (1st Cir. 2018) ("Although 'Congress's intention [must] be unmistakable, our inquiry is not limited to the statutory text but may include an examination of standard ensigns of statutory construction, such as the statute's structure and legislative history.' " (quoting Lattab v. Ashcroft, 384 F.3d 8, 14 (1st Cir. 2004))).

The same may well be true of the presumption against extraterritoriality. Although the majority opinion in the seminal case of *EEOC v. Arabian American Oil Co.*, 499 U.S. 244 (1991), did not respond to the dissent's arguments about legislative history, the Court did cast its analysis in terms of "congressional intent." *See id.* at 249; *see also id.*

at 248 ("It is our task to determine whether Congress intended the protections of Title VII to apply to United States citizens employed by American employers outside of the United States."); *id.* at 259 ("Petitioners have failed to present sufficient affirmative evidence that Congress intended Title VII to apply abroad."). Admittedly, Justice Scalia's majority opinion in *Morrison v. National Australia Bank Ltd.*, 561 U.S. 247 (2010), can be read to suggest that the relevant signs of congressional intent need to appear in the statutory text. *See, e.g.*, *id.* at 255 ("When a statute gives no clear indication of an extraterritorial application, it has none."); *id.* at 265 ("[T]here is no affirmative indication in the Exchange Act that § 10(b) applies extraterritorially, and we therefore conclude that it does not."). Again, though, any such suggestion dovetails with Justice Scalia's broader opposition to the use of legislative history in statutory interpretation. In the lower courts, judges who are more open to the use of legislative history continue to say that legislative history can help overcome the presumption against extraterritoriality. *See, e.g.*, United States v. Ojedokun, 16 F.4th 1091, 1102 (4th Cir. 2021) ("At bottom, whether a statute should be given extraterritorial effect is a question of congressional intent, and in searching for such intent, courts may consider 'all available evidence,' to include 'the text of the statute, the overall statutory scheme, and legislative history.'" (quoting In re French, 440 F.3d 145, 151 (4th Cir. 2006))).

Although judges who accept the use of legislative history in statutory interpretation are willing to let legislative history overcome both the presumption against retroactivity and the presumption against extraterritoriality, the Supreme Court has identified a few issue-specific canons that sometimes operate as implied-limitation rules but that *cannot* be overcome by legislative history. Justice Powell's majority opinion in *Atascadero State Hospital v. Scanlon*, 473 U.S. 234 (1985), is an early example. Under current doctrine, Congress has only limited authority to expose unconsenting states to private lawsuits, but certain provisions in the Constitution have been understood to let Congress abrogate state sovereign immunity in this way. *See, e.g.*, Fitzpatrick v. Bitzer, 427 U.S. 445, 456 (1976) (discussing § 5 of the 14th Amendment). Still, the Supreme Court has held that federal statutes should not lightly be understood to exercise this power. Speaking for the Court in *Atascadero*, Justice Powell asserted that "Congress may abrogate the States' constitutionally secured immunity from suit in federal court only by making its intention unmistakably clear *in the language of the statute*." 473 U.S. at 242 (emphasis added). Subsequent cases have confirmed that "in this area of law, evidence of congressional intent must be both unequivocal and textual," and "recourse to legislative history will be futile." *Dellmuth v. Muth*, 491 U.S. 223, 230 (1989).

In *United States v. Nordic Village, Inc.*, 503 U.S. 30 (1992), Justice Scalia's majority opinion extended the same principle to the *federal* government's immunity from suit: federal statutes can waive the sovereign immunity of the United States, but they will not be interpreted to do so unless the actual statutory text is "unequivocal," and "legislative history has no bearing" on whether the text is sufficiently clear. *See id.* at 37 (internal quotation marks omitted). The Court has followed this rule ever since, often in opinions by Justices who do not categorically oppose the use of legislative history on other issues. *See, e.g.*, Fed. Aviation Admin. v. Cooper, 566 U.S. 284, 290 (2012) (Alito, J.) ("We have said on many occasions that a waiver of sovereign immunity must be 'unequivocally expressed' in statutory text. Legislative history cannot supply a waiver that is not clearly evident from the language of the statute." (citations omitted)); Lane v. Peña, 518 U.S. 187, 192 (1996) (O'Connor, J.) ("A statute's legislative history cannot supply a waiver that does not appear clearly in any statutory text; 'the "unequivocal expression" of elimination of sovereign immunity that we insist upon is an expression in statutory text.' " (quoting *Nordic Village*, 503 U.S. at 37)).

If one generally supports the use of legislative history as a valuable tool for determining the meaning of statutory language, on what basis might one refuse to use this tool when deciding whether a federal statute abrogates the states' immunity from suit or waives the federal government's own immunity? Is there any logical route to the conclusion that courts should consult legislative history to help interpret most of the rules that a statute establishes, but should refuse to read the statute to establish certain rules unless the language of the statute itself—considered without regard to legislative history—leaves no room for doubt? If courts can indeed decide not to use legislative history with respect to some substantive issues, how should courts identify those issues? *Cf.* Block v. Cmty. Nutrition Inst., 467 U.S. 340, 349 (1984) (discussing the presumption against reading a statute to foreclose judicial review of administrative action, and observing that "[t]his presumption, like all presumptions used in interpreting statutes, may be overcome by specific language or by specific legislative history that is a reliable indicator of congressional intent").

In *Atascadero*, Justice Powell suggested that the Constitution itself creates a relevant difference between state sovereign immunity and other issues. He spoke of " 'the vital role of the doctrine of sovereign immunity in our federal system,' " and he characterized Congress's power to abrogate state sovereign immunity as an exception to "the usual constitutional balance between the States and the Federal Government." *Atascadero*, 473 U.S. at 242 (quoting Pennhurst State School & Hosp. v. Halderman, 465 U.S. 89, 99 (1984)). In his view, it followed that courts should not read a federal statute to abrogate state sovereign immunity unless they are "certain of Congress' intent"—and "[t]he requirement that Congress unequivocally express this intention in the statutory language ensures such certainty." *Id.* at 243. In other words, although legislative history can create enough certainty about Congress's intentions to resolve many ordinary questions of statutory interpretation, Justice Powell thought that the decision to abrogate state sovereign immunity is especially sensitive, and courts should require unusual clarity before concluding that Congress really meant to do this sensitive thing. Does that make sense? If ordinary principles of statutory interpretation (including ordinary uses of legislative history) support reading a federal statute to abrogate state sovereign immunity, can courts properly adopt a different reading of the statute on the theory that Congress must be especially clear before exercising this particular power? Does the Constitution itself create that need for clarity, or did Justice Powell simply think that it would be a good idea? What makes the decision to abrogate state sovereign immunity different than other decisions that the Constitution also authorizes Congress to make?

Justice Stevens's opinion for the Court in *Immigration & Naturalization Service v. St. Cyr*, 533 U.S. 289 (2001), may supply an additional example of a canon that cannot be overcome by legislative history. In *St. Cyr*, the Court observed that federal statutes should not lightly be understood to repeal pre-existing statutes giving federal courts jurisdiction over applications for habeas corpus. *See id.* at 298. The Court added that "[i]mplications from statutory text or legislative history are not sufficient to repeal habeas jurisdiction; instead, Congress must articulate specific and unambiguous statutory directives to effect a repeal." *Id.* at 299.

Although *Atascadero* and *St. Cyr* have different political valences, they both involved issues that arguably implicate the Constitution. But in *United States v. Kwai Fun Wong*, 575 U.S. 402 (2015), the Supreme Court addressed a more pedestrian canon—the principle that statutes imposing procedural requirements for litigation in federal court should not be understood as "jurisdictional" limitations unless "Congress has 'clearly state[d]' " that they are. *Id.* at 409 (quoting Sebelius v. Auburn Regional Med. Ctr., 568 U.S. 145, 153 (2013)).[32] In *Wong*, Justice Kagan's majority opinion expressed doubt that legislative history could supply the necessary clarity. *See Wong*, 575 U.S. at 412 ("[E]ven assuming legislative history alone could provide a clear statement (which we doubt), none does so here.").

The doubts expressed by Justice Kagan in *Wong* dovetailed with Justice Scalia's comments in an earlier case about the same canon. *See* Gonzalez v. Thaler, 565 U.S. 134, 164–65 (2012) (Scalia, J., dissenting) ("I know of no precedent for the proposition that legislative history can satisfy a clear-statement requirement imposed by this Court's opinions."). But if one believes in using legislative history to resolve

[32] Whether a requirement is "jurisdictional" has various doctrinal consequences. For instance, it can affect whether the requirement is waivable and whether courts must consider it *sua sponte*. *See* Arbaugh v. Y & H Corp., 546 U.S. 500, 514 (2006). Likewise, with respect to time deadlines for filing suit, the Supreme Court presumes that the typical federal statute of limitations is subject to equitable tolling, but the Court does not apply this presumption if the limitations period is "jurisdictional." *See Wong*, 575 U.S. at 407–09.

ambiguities or other indeterminacies in statutory language, is there any reason why *Wong*'s "clear statement" requirement could be satisfied only by clear statements in the actual statutory text, as opposed to ambiguous text combined with clarifying legislative history?

c. CAN LEGISLATIVE HISTORY OVERCOME DESCRIPTIVE CANONS FOR RESOLVING AMBIGUITY?

So far, we have seen that many judges who believe in using legislative history to help interpret statutes are willing to let legislative history overcome the rule of lenity and various implied-limitation rules (though perhaps not some "clear statement" rules). By the same token, these judges may also let legislative history overcome standard descriptive canons like *noscitur a sociis*, the presumption against superfluity, and the presumption of consistent usage. When statutory language is ambiguous, judges who support the use of legislative history will not necessarily use a canon to resolve the ambiguity if legislative history suggests a different resolution. *See, e.g.*, General Dynamics Land Systems, Inc. v. Cline, 540 U.S. 581, 594–98 (2004) (concluding that despite the presumption of consistent usage, § 4(a)(1) of the Age Discrimination in Employment Act used the word "age" differently than § 4(f), and invoking legislative history as one of several considerations in support of this conclusion); *see also* Seneca-Cayuga Tribe v. Nat'l Indian Gaming Comm'n, 327 F.3d 1019, 1035 (10th Cir. 2003) ("The persuasive evidence from IGRA's legislative history seriously undermines the government's rather bald *expressio unius* argument. . . . [T]he canon is not particularly useful where legislative history clearly evinces congressional intent, especially in this context of construing statutes governing Native American affairs.").

That position seems sensible, but is it entirely beyond dispute? Or could one argue that even if judges are open to the use of legislative history, they should use it only to resolve ambiguities that remain *after* judges have applied the standard descriptive canons?

Recall the debate about whether consulting legislative history tends to *expand* the range of a statute's indeterminacy (as Justice Scalia argued) or instead to *narrow* it (as Justice Stevens argued). *See supra* pp. 459–460. If legislative history can indeed be used to overcome canons like the presumption of consistent usage, might Justice Scalia's position in this debate gain plausibility? Suppose that a word in § 1 of a statute is ambiguous, but § 5 of the statute uses the same word in a related context that makes its meaning in § 5 clear. In the absence of any other clues about the intended meaning of § 1, courts might well think that the presumption of consistent usage eliminates the ambiguity that they had detected at first glance; the clue in § 5 tells them how Congress was using the word in § 1. But if legislative history can rebut the presumption of consistent usage, then the ability to look at legislative history has the potential to expand the number of meanings that can plausibly be attributed to the statute: courts could give the word in § 1 *either* the meaning that the word has in § 5 *or* the alternative meaning suggested by the legislative history. To reduce the risk of unpredictability or the possibly adverse consequences of judicial discretion, should one instruct courts to be cautious about letting legislative history cancel out or trump the ordinary canons of construction? For instance, should legislative history be allowed to trump the ordinary descriptive canons only when it is so strong as to take the reading suggested by the canons entirely off the table (at least for people who are willing to consult legislative history)? Or is even moderately probative legislative history a better guide to the intended meaning of statutes than generic canons, and should the canons therefore be used primarily in situations where there is no relevant legislative history?

d. LEGISLATIVE HISTORY AND THE PRESUMPTION AGAINST ABSURDITY

Justice Scalia would have opposed letting legislative history affect the operation of any of the canons mentioned so far. But even Justice Scalia reached a different conclusion with respect to the presumption against absurdity. He expressed his views on that topic in a separate concurring opinion in *Green v. Bock Laundry Machine Co.*, 490 U.S. 504 (1989).

That case involved Federal Rule of Evidence 609, which regulates the circumstances in which witnesses can be impeached with information about their prior criminal convictions. At the time of the case, Rule 609(a) read as follows:

> "For the purpose of attacking the credibility of a witness, evidence that the witness has been convicted of a crime shall be admitted if elicited from the witness or established by public record during cross-examination but only if the crime (1) was punishable by death or imprisonment in excess of one year under the law under which the witness was convicted, and the court determines that the probative value of admitting this evidence outweighs its prejudicial effect to the defendant, or (2) involved dishonesty or false statement, regardless of the punishment."

By its terms, then, the rule allowed a witness to be impeached with evidence about the witness's past conviction for a felony that did not involve dishonesty or false statement "only if . . . the court determines that the probative value of admitting this evidence outweighs its prejudicial effect to the defendant." The rule's special concern about prejudice "to the defendant" makes sense in criminal cases. But the Federal Rules of Evidence also apply in civil cases, and special protections for the defendant would be strange in that context; in civil cases, the rules generally try to establish a level playing field between the plaintiff and the defendant. In *Green v. Bock Laundry Machine Co.*, the Supreme Court found it "unfathomable" that Rule 609 "would deny a civil plaintiff the same right to impeach an adversary's testimony that it grants to a civil defendant," and the Court refused to accept such an interpretation. 490 U.S. at 510–11. After reviewing both pre-existing law and the legislative history of Rule 609, the Court concluded that the language about prejudice to the defendant operated only in favor of "the accused in a criminal case." *See id.* at 511–24.

Justice Scalia concurred in the judgment. He agreed that "if interpreted literally," Rule 609(a)(1) "produces an absurd, and perhaps unconstitutional, result." *Id.* at 527 (Scalia, J., concurring in the judgment). Like the majority, he therefore gravitated toward the conclusion that the word "defendant" in the rule should be understood to refer only to *criminal* defendants. Perhaps surprisingly, he also agreed that before drawing this conclusion, the Court could properly examine the legislative history. In his words,

> "I think it entirely appropriate to consult all public materials, including the background of Rule 609(a)(1) and the legislative history of its adoption, to verify that what seems to us an unthinkable disposition (civil defendants but not civil plaintiffs receive the benefit of weighing prejudice) was indeed unthought of, and thus to justify a departure from the ordinary meaning of the word 'defendant' in the Rule."

Id. If the legislative history had contained evidence that the idea of benefiting civil as well as criminal defendants (but not civil plaintiffs) had come up in Congress, then Justice Scalia would have interpreted Rule 609 to use the word "defendant" in the ordinary way notwithstanding the presumption against absurdity. In that sense, he believed that legislative history could trump the presumption against absurdity. Specifically, he thought that the Court could properly use legislative history to help "confirm[ ] that the word 'defendant' cannot have been meant literally" (although not to "determin[e] what, precisely, the Rule does mean"). *Id.* at 528.

How does this position square with Justice Scalia's usual view that the contents of a statute's legislative history should not affect the meaning that interpreters ascribe to the statute? Is it relevant that if legislative history were used as Justice Scalia proposed in *Green*, it would operate only *in support of* the ordinary meaning of the statutory language?

As part of his general attack on the use of legislative history, Justice Scalia often argued that even if a particular interpretation of a statute seems to be supported by a committee report or some other piece of legislative history, courts cannot assume that the full Congress shared that interpretation. But the use of legislative history that Justice Scalia proposed in *Green* did not necessarily require any such assumption. If the legislative history of a statute shows that a particular policy idea came up in Congress, perhaps that very fact is evidence that the idea is not "absurd" in the sense that might trigger the presumption against absurdity. If so, then perhaps legislative history can properly be used to overcome the presumption against absurdity even if one is not willing to impute statements in committee reports to the full Congress.

Toward the end of his life, Justice Scalia suggested exactly this explanation of his position in *Green*. Here is what he and Bryan Garner wrote on that topic in their book *Reading Law*:

> "Using legislative history to establish what the legislature 'intended' is quite different from using it for other purposes. For example, . . . legislative history can be consulted to refute attempted application of the absurdity doctrine—to establish that it is indeed thinkable that a particular word or phrase should mean precisely what it says. . . . [T]o establish thinkability . . . , one does not have to make the implausible leap of attributing the quoted statement to the entire legislature. It suffices that a single presumably rational legislator, or a single presumably rational committee, viewed the allegedly absurd result with equanimity. This use of legislative history will be very rare (your judicial author recalls encountering it only once in 29 years on the appellate bench[65]), and it is a worthwhile check on the tendency to call absurd what is merely ill-advised."

ANTONIN SCALIA & BRYAN A. GARNER, READING LAW: THE INTERPRETATION OF LEGAL TEXTS 388 (2012).

This argument does not necessarily give legislative history any special weight because it is generated in Congress. If other public materials (like op-eds or law-review articles) had taken seriously the idea of protecting civil defendants but not civil plaintiffs against the prejudice that might flow from exposing a witness's criminal conviction, would those materials have had the same influence upon Justice Scalia as statements in the legislative history? Should any serious public discussion of an idea persuade courts that the idea is not "absurd" in the sense that might trigger the presumption against absurdity?

---

3. THE USE OF LEGISLATIVE HISTORY TO IDENTIFY "SCRIVENER'S ERRORS" (OR OTHER ERRORS THAT COURTS MIGHT CORRECT THROUGH INTERPRETATION)

The materials in Chapter 1 made glancing references to the fact that legislators and their staffs sometimes make mistakes in recording the legal directives that they intend to establish. Perhaps the enacted version of a statute transposes two words, or garbles a cross-reference to some other provision, or includes a typographical error that keeps the text from scanning. Or perhaps members of the enacting legislature made some other mistake of expression. For instance, in *United States v. Locke*—the

---

[65] *See Green v. Bock Laundry Mach. Co.*, 490 U.S. 504, 527 (1989) (Scalia, J., concurring in the judgment).

case in which a federal statute spoke of filing certain papers "prior to December 31" of each year—Justice Stevens's dissent argued that a "scrivener's error" had occurred and that Congress had not really meant to establish a calendar-year deadline that ended "*one day before* the end of the calendar year that has been recognized since the amendment of the Julian Calendar in 8 B.C." 471 U.S. 84, 119 (1985) (Stevens, J., dissenting); *see supra* pp. 65–67 (discussing the term "scrivener's error").

Although different judges have different views about exactly what counts as a drafting error of the sort that judges can properly correct through interpretation (by reading the statutory language to mean what the legislature apparently would have said but for the error), nearly everyone agrees that judges do have some role along these lines. As Justice Scalia put it, "I acknowledge an interpretative doctrine of what the old writers call *lapsus linguae* (slip of the tongue), and what our modern cases call 'scrivener's error,' where on the very face of the statute it is clear to the reader that a mistake of expression (rather than of legislative wisdom) has been made." In such cases, Justice Scalia thought that "[t]he objective import of such a statute is clear enough" even though it does not coincide with the surface meaning of the passage that Congress garbled, and courts can properly read the statute that Congress enacted to mean what a non-garbled version plainly would have meant. Antonin Scalia, *Common-Law Courts in a Civil-Law System: The Role of United States Federal Courts in Interpreting the Constitution and Laws*, *in* A MATTER OF INTERPRETATION: FEDERAL COURTS AND THE LAW 3, 20–21 (Amy Gutmann ed., 1997).

In keeping with his general opposition to the use of legislative history in statutory interpretation, Justice Scalia did *not* think it appropriate for courts to use legislative history to identify drafting errors of this sort. But in the next two cases, some of his colleagues discussed the circumstances in which legislative history might properly be used to identify a drafting mistake that does not leap out from the face of the statute itself.

Lamie v. United States Trustee

540 U.S. 526 (2004)

■ *JUSTICE KENNEDY delivered the opinion of the Court:*

Section 330(a)(1) of the Bankruptcy Code, 11 U.S.C. § 330(a)(1), regulates court awards of professional fees, including fees for services rendered by attorneys in connection with bankruptcy proceedings. Petitioner, a bankruptcy attorney, sought compensation under the section for legal services he provided to a bankrupt debtor after the proceeding was converted to a Chapter 7 bankruptcy. His application for fees was denied by the Bankruptcy Court, the District Court, and the United States Court of Appeals for the Fourth Circuit. Each court held that in a Chapter 7 proceeding § 330(a)(1) does not authorize payment of attorney's fees unless the attorney has been appointed under § 327 of the Code. See 11 U.S.C. §§ 327 and 701 *et seq*. Petitioner was not so appointed, and his fee request was denied. . . . [W]e now affirm.

I

In 1994 Congress amended the Bankruptcy Code. Bankruptcy Reform Act of 1994 (Act), 108 Stat. 4106. The subject of professional fees was addressed and comprehensive changes were made. See 3 Collier on Bankruptcy ¶ 330.LH[5], pp. 330–75 to 330–76 (rev. 15th ed. 2003). Most of the changes served to clarify the standards for the award of professional fees; but various courts disagree over the proper interpretation of the portion of the statute relevant to this dispute, concerning attorney's fees.

. . . . Before the 1994 Act, § 330(a) had read as follows:

> "(a) After notice to *any* parties in interest and *to* the United States trustee and a hearing, and subject to sections 326, 328, and 329 *of this title*, the court may award to a trustee, *to* an examiner, *to* a professional person employed under section 327 or 1103 *of this title, or to the debtor's attorney*—
>
> "(1) reasonable compensation for actual, necessary services rendered by such trustee, examiner, professional person, or attorney . . . and by any paraprofessional persons employed by such trustee, professional person, or attorney . . . ; and
>
> "(2) reimbursement for actual, necessary expenses." [11 U.S.C. § 330(a) (1988 ed.)] (emphasis added to highlight text later deleted.)

Pursuant to the 1994 Act, 11 U.S.C. § 330(a)(1) now reads as follows:

> "(a)(1) After notice to the parties in interest and the United States Trustee and a hearing, and subject to sections 326, 328, and 329, the court may award to a trustee, an examiner, a professional person employed under section 327 or 1103—
>
> "(A) reasonable compensation for actual, necessary services rendered by the trustee, examiner, professional person, or attorney and by any paraprofessional person employed by any such person; and
>
> "(B) reimbursement for actual, necessary expenses."

As can be noted, the 1994 enactment's principal, substantive alteration was its deletion of the five words at the end of what was § 330(a) and is now § 330(a)(1): "or to the debtor's attorney."

The deletion created an apparent legislative drafting error. It left current § 330(a)(1) with a missing "or" that infects its grammar (*i.e.*, "an examiner, [or] a professional person . . ."). Furthermore, the Act's inclusion of the word "attorney" in § 330(a)(1)(A) defeats the neat parallelism that otherwise marks the relationship between §§ 330(a)(1) and 330(a)(1)(A) (*i.e.*, in § 330(a)(1): "trustee, . . . examiner, [or] professional person"; in § 330(a)(1)(A): "trustee, examiner, professional person, or attorney") and so casts some doubt on the proper presence of "attorney." That the pre-1994 text had no grammatical error and was parallel in its structure strengthens the sense that error exists in the new text.

The Courts of Appeals for the Fifth and Eleventh Circuits, when asked to interpret current § 330(a)(1), concluded that its language was plain irrespective of these quirks and history. Under the statutory language as written, those courts held, fees may be awarded to attorneys for services rendered only to the extent they are payments to "a professional person employed under section 327," see, *e.g.*, § 327(a) (authorizing an appointed trustee in a Chapter 7 bankruptcy action to "employ one or more attorneys . . . to represent or assist the trustee in carrying out the trustee's duties under this title"); § 327(e) (authorizing an appointed trustee in a Chapter 7 bankruptcy action to "employ, for a specified special purpose, other than to represent the trustee in conducting the case, an attorney that has represented the debtor . . ."). . . . The Courts of Appeals for the Second, Third, and Ninth Circuits, in contrast, concluded that the text's apparent errors rendered the section ambiguous, requiring consideration of the provision's legislative history. That history, those courts held, shows Congress intended § 330(a)(1) to continue to allow compensation of Chapter 7 debtors' attorneys, irrespective of qualification under § 327. . . .

This interpretive divide became relevant to petitioner in his representation of Equipment Services, Inc. (ESI). ESI retained petitioner to prepare, file, and prosecute a Chapter 11 bankruptcy proceeding on its behalf. He did so, all the while representing ESI with the approval of the court under § 327. See . . . 11 U.S.C. § 1107(a) (authorizing debtor-in-possession to exercise the statutory rights and powers of an estate trustee, including to retain counsel under § 327). Three months into the Chapter 11 reorganization, the United States Trustee (Government) filed a motion to convert the action into a Chapter 7 liquidation proceeding. The court granted the Government's motion and appointed an estate trustee pursuant to § 701, 11 U.S.C. § 701(a). This terminated ESI's status as debtor-in-possession and so terminated petitioner's service under § 327 as an attorney for the debtor-in-possession. Yet petitioner continued to provide legal services to ESI, the debtor, even though he did not have the trustee's authorization to do so. . . .

In due course petitioner filed an application seeking fees under § 330(a)(1) for the time he spent on ESI's behalf after the Chapter 7 conversion. The Government objected to the application. It argued that § 330(a)(1) makes no provision for the estate to compensate an attorney not authorized under § 327. The court agreed and denied the fees. . . . (Petitioner was paid fees for the services he provided to ESI before conversion of the proceeding to Chapter 7 and when ESI was the debtor-in-possession. The parties do not contest those fees.)

Petitioner unsuccessfully sought reversal of the Bankruptcy Court's determination, first from the District Court, . . . then from the Court of Appeals . . . .

II

Petitioner argues that the existing statutory text is ambiguous and so requires us to consult legislative history to determine whether Congress intended to allow fees for services rendered by a debtor's attorney in a Chapter 7 proceeding, where that attorney is not authorized under § 327. He makes the case for ambiguity, for the most part, by comparing the present statute with its predecessor. Thus, he says the statute is ambiguous because subsection (A)'s "attorney" is "facially irreconcilable" with the section's first part since

> "[e]ither Congress inadvertently omitted the 'debtor's attorney' from the 'payees' list, on which the court of appeals relied, or it inadvertently retained the reference to the attorney in the latter, 'payees' list." Brief for Petitioner 17.

Similarly, with respect to the missing conjunction "or" he says,

> "[t]here is no apparent reason, other than a drafting error, that Congress would have rewritten the statute to produce a grammatically incorrect provision." *Ibid.*

This is the analysis followed by the Courts of Appeals that hold the statute is ambiguous. . . . One determines ambiguity, under this contention, by relying on the grammatical soundness of the prior statute. That contention is wrong.

The starting point in discerning congressional intent is the existing statutory text, see *Hughes Aircraft Co. v. Jacobson*, 525 U.S. 432, 438 (1999), and not the predecessor statutes. It is well established that "when the statute's language is plain, the sole function of the courts—at least where the disposition required by the text is not absurd—is to enforce it according to its terms." *Hartford Underwriters Ins. Co. v. Union Planters Bank, N.A.*, 530 U.S. 1, 6 (2000) (internal quotation marks omitted) (quoting *United States v. Ron Pair Enterprises, Inc.*, 489 U.S. 235, 241 (1989), in turn quoting *Caminetti v. United States*, 242 U.S. 470, 485 (1917)). So we begin with the present statute.

A

The statute is awkward, and even ungrammatical; but that does not make it ambiguous on the point at issue. In its first part, the statute authorizes an award of compensation to one of three types of persons: trustees, examiners, and § 327 professional persons. A debtor's attorney not engaged as provided by § 327 is simply not included within the class of persons eligible for compensation. In subsection (A) the statute further defines what type of compensation may be awarded: compensation that is reasonable; and for actual, necessary services; and rendered by four types of persons (the same three plus attorneys). Unless the applicant for compensation is in one of the named classes of persons in the first part, the kind of service rendered is irrelevant.

The missing conjunction "or" does not change our conclusion. The Government points to numerous federal statutes that inadvertently lack a conjunction. They are read, nonetheless, for their plain meaning. See Brief for Respondent 17, n. 4. Here, the missing conjunction neither alters the text's substance nor obscures its meaning. This is not a case where a "not" is missing or where an "or" inadvertently substitutes for an "and." The sentence may be awkward; yet it is straightforward.

Subsection (A)'s nonparalleled fourth category of persons who can render compensable services does not cloud the statute's meaning. Petitioner reasons that since the section is a single sentence, and since it appears to strive for parallelism between those authorized to receive fees and those whose services are compensable, there is an ambiguity as to what "attorney" in § 330(a)(1)(A) refers to in § 330(a)(1). He also points to neighboring § 331, which provides for both debtors' attorneys and § 327 professional persons to receive interim compensation after an order for relief is entered but before an application for § 330 fees is filed. He argues that since § 331 contemplates debtors' attorneys' receiving interim compensation there is reason to conclude that "attorney" in § 330(a)(1)(A) refers to debtors' attorneys in § 330(a)(1), though they go unmentioned in that clause.

Subsection (A)'s "attorney," however, can be read in a straightforward fashion to refer to those attorneys whose fees are authorized by § 330(a)(1): attorneys qualified as § 327 professional persons, that is, in a Chapter 7 context, those employed by the trustee and approved by the court. . . . Likewise, § 331's reference to interim compensation for debtors' attorneys most straightforwardly refers to debtors' attorneys authorized under § 327.

It must be acknowledged that, under our reading of the text, the word "attorney" in subsection (A) may well be surplusage. Subsection (A)'s reference to § 327 professional persons undoubtedly includes attorneys, as much as does § 330(a)(1)'s reference to professional persons. That is not controlling, however. Surplusage does not always produce ambiguity and our preference for avoiding surplusage constructions is not absolute. See *Chickasaw Nation v. United States*, 534 U.S. 84, 94 (2001) (the preference "is sometimes offset by the canon that permits a court to reject words 'as surplusage' if 'inadvertently inserted or if repugnant to the rest of the statute' "). Where there are two ways to read the text—either attorney is surplusage, in which case the text is plain; or attorney is nonsurplusage (*i.e.*, it refers to an ambiguous component in § 330(a)(1)), in which case the text is ambiguous—applying the rule against surplusage is, absent other indications, inappropriate. We should prefer the plain meaning since that approach respects the words of Congress. In this manner we avoid the pitfalls that plague too quick a turn to the more controversial realm of legislative history.

B

The plain meaning that § 330(a)(1) sets forth does not lead to absurd results requiring us to treat the text as if it were ambiguous. . . .

. . . . Sections 327 and 330, taken together, allow Chapter 7 trustees to engage attorneys, including debtors' counsel, and allow courts to award them fees. See §§ 327(a) and (e). Section 327's limitation on debtors' incurring debts for professional services without the Chapter 7 trustee's approval is not absurd. In the context of a Chapter 7 liquidation it advances the trustee's responsibility for preserving the estate.

. . . . Seeming order has attended the rule's application for five years in the Fifth Circuit and for four years in the Eleventh Circuit. . . . It appears to be routine for debtors to pay reasonable fees for legal services before filing for bankruptcy to ensure compliance with statutory requirements. . . . Section 330(a)(1) does not prevent a debtor from engaging counsel before a Chapter 7 conversion and paying reasonable compensation in advance to ensure that the filing is in order. Indeed, the Code anticipates these arrangements. See, *e.g.*, § 329 (debtors' attorneys must disclose fees they receive from a debtor in the year prior to its bankruptcy filing and courts may order excessive payments returned to the estate).

C

. . . . Our unwillingness to soften the import of Congress' chosen words even if we believe the words lead to a harsh outcome is longstanding. It results from "deference to the supremacy of the Legislature, as well as recognition that Congressmen typically vote on the language of a bill." *United States* v. *Locke*, 471 U.S. 84, 95 (1985) (citing *Richards v. United States*, 369 U.S. 1, 9 (1962)).

Adhering to conventional doctrines of statutory interpretation, we hold that § 330(a)(1) does not authorize compensation awards to debtors' attorneys from estate funds, unless they are employed as authorized by § 327. If the attorney is to be paid from estate funds under § 330(a)(1) in a Chapter 7 case, he must be employed by the trustee and approved by the court.

III[*]

Though we find it unnecessary to rely on the legislative history behind the 1994 enactment of § 330(a)(1), we find it instructive that the history creates more confusion than clarity about the congressional intent. History and policy considerations lend support both to petitioner's interpretation and to the holding we reach based on the plain language of the statute.

Petitioner, for instance, cites evidence supporting the conclusion that a scrivener's error obscures what was Congress' real intent. For over 100 years debtors' attorneys have been considered by Congress and the

[*] *Editor's note*: Justice Scalia did not join this portion of the majority's opinion.

courts to be an integral part of the bankruptcy process. . . . It is fair to doubt that Congress would so rework their longstanding role without announcing the change in the congressional record. Cf. *Cohen v. de la Cruz*, 523 U.S. 213, 221 (1998) ("We . . . will not read the Bankruptcy Code to erode past bankruptcy practice absent a clear indication that Congress intended such a departure" (internal quotation marks and citation omitted)).

The legislative processes behind the change also lend some support to petitioner's claim. In 1994 the original proposed draft of new § 330(a)(1) featured two changes: stylistic changes throughout the section and the addition of a new provision giving the Government a right to object to fee applications. See S. 540, 103d Cong., 1st Sess. (1993), reprinted in S. Rep. No. 103–168 (1993). The right to object provision was added at § 330(a)(1)'s end. Thus it came immediately after the critical text "or to the debtor's attorney," which the draft edited to read "or the debtors [*sic*] attorney." *Ibid.* Before voting the Act into law, however, Congress amended the proposed draft. See 140 Cong. Rec. 8383 (1994) (setting out amendment 1645 to S. 540). Amendment 1645 made only two changes to § 330(a)(1): It deleted the Government's right to object provision and the critical words ("or the debtors [*sic*] attorney"). . . . Legislative history explains the first deletion, for the provision was installed elsewhere, as new § 330(a)(2). Nothing, however, explains the second. That the Government's right to object was deleted and reinstated (*i.e.*, reorganized), while the words at issue, which had preceded the moved provision, were deleted with no notation in the legislative history suggests the scrivener just reached too far in his deletion. These factors combined to convince a leading treatise on bankruptcy law, Collier, that the deletion was a scrivener's error and ought not have any effect. See 3 Collier on Bankruptcy ¶ 330.LH[5], at 330–75 to 330–76.

There are other aspects of the legislative record, however, that undermine this interpretation. These considerations suggest Congress may have intended the change the scrivener worked. For example, amendment 1645 was part of a reform Act designed to curtail abuses in fee awards, according to statements by the amendment's sponsor. See 140 Cong. Rec., at 28753 (statement of Sen. Metzenbaum). These abuses were not ghosts seen only by Congress. Some bankruptcy courts had reached the same conclusion. See, *e.g.*, *In re NRG Resources, Inc.*, 64 B.R. 643 (W.D. La. 1986). The deletion at issue furthered this reform by ensuring that Chapter 7 debtors' attorneys would receive no estate compensation absent the trustee's authorization of their work. . . .

Amendment 1645, viewed in its entirety, gives further reason to think Congress may have intended the change. The amendment added a new section that authorizes fee awards to debtors' attorneys in Chapter 12 and 13 bankruptcies. 140 Cong. Rec. at 8383 (setting out new 11 U.S.C. § 330(a)(4)(B)). Since the amendment's deletion of "or the debtors [*sic*] attorney" from the original proposed draft affected Chapter 12 and

13 debtors' attorneys as much as Chapter 7 debtors' attorneys, § 330(a)(4)(B) shows a special intent to authorize the formers' fee awards in the face of the new, broad exclusion.

If Congress' action does not prove the point, the House of Representatives' inaction may. The House passed the Act after having the deletion, as well as its impact, called to its attention. See Bankruptcy Reform: Hearing before the Subcommittee on Economic and Commercial Law of the House Committee on the Judiciary, 103d Cong., 2d Sess., 551 (1994). The National Association of Consumer Bankruptcy Attorneys (NACBA), which represents those lawyers most likely to be affected by § 330(a)(1)'s change, declined to object to the deletion. *Ibid.* (noting the deletion but stating that the NACBA did "not oppose" amendment 1645's passage). This alert, followed by the Legislature's nonresponse, should support a presumption of legislative awareness and intention. The Act may now contain surplusage, along with grammatical error; but that may have been the result of trying to make the substantive change with the fewest possible textual alterations or of an error by the scrivener in carrying out the change.

These competing interpretations of the legislative history make it difficult to say with assurance whether petitioner or the Government lays better historical claim to the congressional intent. The alert to the change in policy was given, to be sure, before the House passed the final version, but that particular circumstance cannot bear too much weight. The alert was not the subject of testimony from any witness at the congressional hearing. It consisted of but two sentences contained within 472 pages of written statements delivered to the legislative subcommittee for its August 17, 1994, hearing day. Those 472 pages were added to 236 pages of prepared statements and testimony transcribed from the day's testifying witnesses. Within the NACBA's filing, the two relevant sentences appear on the 18th page of the 27-page report. Nothing in the legislative history confirms that this particular point bore on the congressional deliberations or was given specific consideration.

These uncertainties illustrate the difficulty of relying on legislative history here and the advantage of our determination to rest our holding on the statutory text. . . .

If Congress enacted into law something different from what it intended, then it should amend the statute to conform it to its intent. "It is beyond our province to rescue Congress from its drafting errors, and to provide for what we might think . . . is the preferred result." *United States v. Granderson,* 511 U.S. 39, 68 (1994) (concurring opinion). This allows both of our branches to adhere to our respected, and respective, constitutional roles. In the meantime, we must determine intent from the statute before us. The judgment of the Court of Appeals is affirmed.

■ *JUSTICE STEVENS, concurring in the judgment, joined by JUSTICES SOUTER and BREYER, concurring:*

As the majority recognizes, a leading bankruptcy law treatise concluded that the 1994 amendments to § 330(a)(1) contained an unintended error. 3 Collier on Bankruptcy ¶ 330.LH[5], pp. 330–75 to 330–76 (rev. 15th ed. 2003). Whenever there is such a plausible basis for believing that a significant change in statutory law resulted from a scrivener's error, I believe we have a duty to examine legislative history. In this case, that history reveals that the National Association of Consumer Bankruptcy Attorneys (NACBA) not only called the assumed drafting error to Congress' attention in a timely fashion, but also deemed the error unworthy of objection. This evidence convinces me that the Court's reading of the text, which surely is more natural than petitioner's, is correct. I therefore concur in the judgment.

NOTE AND QUESTION

Part III of the majority opinion briefly described the drafting history of the relevant part of the Bankruptcy Reform Act of 1994—the statute that amended 11 U.S.C. § 330(a) and that dropped the phrase "or the debtor's attorney." The bill that the Senate Judiciary Committee reported to the Senate would have amended § 330(a)(1) to read as follows:

> "(a)(1) After notice to the parties in interest and the United States trustee and a hearing, and subject to sections 326, 328, and 329, the court may award to a trustee, an examiner, a professional person employed under section 327 or 1103, or the debtor's attorney, after considering comments and objections submitted by the United States Trustee in conformance with guidelines adopted by the Executive Office for United States Trustees pursuant to section 586(a)(3)(A) of title 28—
>
> > "(A) reasonable compensation for actual, necessary services rendered by the trustee, examiner, professional person, or attorney and by any paraprofessional person employed by any such person; and
> >
> > "(B) reimbursement for actual, necessary expenses."

S. 540, 103d Cong., 1st Sess. (1993), reprinted in S. Rep. No. 103–168 (1993). Ultimately, however, the Senate approved an amendment that inserted a separate paragraph about objections by the United States Trustee, removed the corresponding language from § 330(a)(1), and also omitted the phrase "or the debtor's attorney" that came immediately before that language. *See* 140 CONG. REC. 8383 (1994) (printing Amendment No. 1645). It is very possible that whoever prepared this amendment simply meant to relocate the provision about objections by the United States Trustee, but mistakenly dropped the phrase "or the debtor's attorney" too. *See Lamie*, 540 U.S. at 540 (noting the possibility that "the scrivener just reached too far in his deletion"). That would explain why the legislative history did not reflect any discussion of the policy change that the omission of this phrase produced. It also would explain why the word "or" was missing from the final version of § 330(a)(1) and why the phrase "or attorney" still appeared in subparagraph (A).

Despite the plausibility of this theory, none of the Justices was willing to diagnose a drafting error in *Lamie*. But suppose they had been. If the drafting history of the bill had clearly established that the initial omission of the phrase "or the debtor's attorney" was inadvertent, and if the rest of the legislative history had persuaded the Court that no one in either the Senate or the House noticed the omission and intended to establish the legal rule that the omission yielded, could the Court have read the amended version of § 330(a)(1) as if it still contained the phrase "or the debtor's attorney"? If you think that mere legislative history cannot justify this interpretation unless it has some basis in the text that Congress actually enacted, does the phrase "or attorney" in subparagraph (A) provide a sufficient basis?

Koons Buick Pontiac GMC, Inc. v. Nigh

543 U.S. 50 (2004)

■ *JUSTICE GINSBURG delivered the opinion of the Court:*

. . . .

I

Congress enacted [the Truth in Lending Act (TILA or Act)] in 1968, as part of the Consumer Credit Protection Act, Pub. L. 90–321, 82 Stat. 146, . . . to "assure a meaningful disclosure of credit terms so that the consumer will be able to compare more readily the various credit terms available to him and avoid the uninformed use of credit," § 102, codified in 15 U.S.C. § 1601(a). The Act requires a creditor to disclose information relating to such things as finance charges, annual percentage rates of interest, and borrowers' rights, see §§ 1631–1632, 1635, 1637–1639, and it prescribes civil liability for any creditor who fails to do so, see § 1640. As originally enacted in 1968, the Act provided for statutory damages of twice the finance charge in connection with the transaction, except that recovery could not be less than $100 or greater than $1,000. The original civil-liability provision stated:

> "(a) [A]ny creditor who fails in connection with any consumer credit transaction to disclose to any person any information required under this chapter to be disclosed to that person is liable to that person in an amount . . . of
>
> "(1) twice the amount of the finance charge in connection with the transaction, except that liability under this paragraph shall not be less than $100 nor greater than $1,000 . . . ." Pub. L. 90–321, § 130, 82 Stat. 157.

In 1974, Congress amended TILA's civil-liability provision, 15 U.S.C. § 1640(a), to allow for the recovery of actual damages in addition to statutory damages and to provide separate statutory damages for class actions. Pub. L. 93–495, § 408(a), 88 Stat. 1518. Congress reworded the original statutory damages provision to limit it to individual actions, moved the provision from § 1640(a)(1) to § 1640(a)(2)(A), and retained the $100/$1,000 brackets on recovery. In order to account for the restructuring of the statute, Congress changed the phrase "under this paragraph" to "under this subparagraph." The amended statute provided for damages in individual actions as follows:

> "(a) [A]ny creditor who fails to comply with any requirement imposed under this chapter . . . is liable to such person in an amount equal to the sum of—
>
> "(1) any actual damage sustained by such person as a result of the failure;
>
> "(2)(A) in the case of an individual action twice the amount of any finance charge in connection with the transaction, except that the liability under this subparagraph shall not be less than $100 nor greater than $1,000 . . . ." § 408(a), 88 Stat. 1518.

A further TILA amendment in 1976 applied truth-in-lending protections to consumer leases. Consumer Leasing Act of 1976, 90 Stat. 257. Congress inserted a clause into § 1640(a)(2)(A) setting statutory damages for individual actions relating to consumer leases at 25% of the total amount of monthly payments under the lease. Again, Congress retained the $100/$1,000 brackets on statutory damages. The amended § 1640(a)(2)(A) provided for statutory damages equal to

> "(2)(A)(i) in the case of an individual action twice the amount of any finance charge in connection with the transaction, or (ii) in the case of an individual action relating to a consumer lease . . . 25 per centum of the total amount of monthly payments under the lease, except that the liability under this subparagraph shall not be less than $100 nor greater than $1,000 . . . ." Pub. L. 94–240, § 4(2), 90 Stat. 260, codified in 15 U.S.C. § 1640(a) (1976 ed.).

Following the insertion of the consumer lease provision, courts consistently held that the $100/$1,000 limitation remained applicable to all consumer financing transactions, whether lease or loan. [Citations of five circuit-court decisions are omitted.]

In 1995, Congress amended TILA's statutory damages provision once more. The 1995 amendment, which gave rise to the dispute in this case, added a new clause (iii) at the end of § 1640(a)(2)(A), setting a $200 floor and $2,000 ceiling for statutory damages in an individual action relating to a closed-end credit transaction "secured by real property or a dwelling." Truth in Lending Act Amendments of 1995, Pub. L. 104–29, § 6, 109 Stat. 274. These closed-end real estate loans, formerly encompassed by clause (i), had earlier been held subject to the

$100/$1,000 limitation. See, *e.g.*, *Mayfield v. Vanguard Sav. & Loan Assn.*, 710 F. Supp. 143, 146 (E.D. Pa. 1989) (ordering "the maximum statutory award of $1,000" for each TILA violation concerning a secured real estate loan). Section 1640(a), as amended in 1995, thus provides for statutory damages equal to

> "(2)(A)(i) in the case of an individual action twice the amount of any finance charge in connection with the transaction, (ii) in the case of an individual action relating to a consumer lease . . . 25 per centum of the total amount of monthly payments under the lease, except that the liability under this subparagraph shall not be less than $100 nor greater than $1,000, or (iii) in the case of an individual action relating to a credit transaction not under an open end credit plan that is secured by real property or a dwelling, not less than $200 or greater than $2,000 . . . ."

. . . . In 1997, the Seventh Circuit, in *Strange v. Monogram Credit Card Bank of Ga.*, 129 F.3d 943, held that the meaning of clauses (i) and (ii) remained untouched by the addition of clause (iii). The Seventh Circuit observed that prior to the addition of clause (iii) in 1995, "[c]ourts uniformly interpreted the final clause, which established the $100 minimum and the $1,000 maximum, as applying to both (A)(i) and (A)(ii)." *Id.* at 947. The 1995 amendment, the Seventh Circuit reasoned, "was designed simply to establish a more generous minimum and maximum for certain secured transactions, without changing the general rule on minimum and maximum damage awards for the other two parts of § 1640(a)(2)(A)." *Ibid.* . . .

II

On February 4, 2000, respondent Bradley Nigh attempted to purchase a used 1997 Chevrolet Blazer truck from petitioner Koons Buick Pontiac GMC. [A description of the dealings between Nigh and Koons Buick is omitted.] . . . .

On October 3, 2000, Nigh filed suit against Koons Buick alleging, among other things, a violation of TILA. Nigh sought uncapped recovery of twice the finance charge, an amount equal to $24,192.80. Koons Buick urged a $1,000 limitation on statutory damages under § 1640(a)(2)(A)(i). The District Court held that damages were not capped at $1,000, and the jury awarded Nigh $24,192.80 (twice the amount of the finance charge). . . .

A divided panel of the Fourth Circuit affirmed. [319 F.3d 119, 126–129 (CA4 2003).] The Court of Appeals acknowledged that it had previously interpreted the $1,000 cap to apply to clauses (i) and (ii). *Id.* at 126; see *Mars v. Spartanburg Chrysler Plymouth, Inc.*, 713 F.2d 65, 67 (CA4 1983). But the majority held that "by striking the 'or' preceding (ii), and inserting (iii) after the 'under this subparagraph' phrase," Congress had "rendered *Mars'* interpretation defunct." 319 F.3d at 126. According to the majority: "The inclusion of the new maximum and minimum in (iii) shows that the clause previously interpreted to apply to all of (A), can no longer apply to (A), but must now apply solely to (ii), so as not to render meaningless the maximum and minimum articulated in (iii)." *Id.* at 127. The Court of Appeals therefore allowed Nigh to recover the full uncapped amount of $24,192.80 under clause (i).

Judge Gregory dissented. The new clause (iii), he stated, operates as a specific "carve-out" for real estate transactions from the general rule establishing the $100/$1,000 liability limitation.... Judge Gregory found "no evidence that Congress intended to override the Fourth Circuit's long-standing application of the $1,000 cap to both (2)(A)(i) and (2)(A)(ii)." *Id.* at 131. If the $1,000 cap applied only to clause (ii), the dissent reasoned, the phrase "under this subparagraph" in clause (ii) would be "superfluous," because "the meaning of (ii) would be unchanged by its deletion." *Id.* at 132. . . .[3]

. . . . We now reverse the judgment of the Court of Appeals for the Fourth Circuit.

III

. . . . In this case, both the conventional meaning of "subparagraph" and standard interpretive guides point to the same conclusion: The $1,000 cap applies to recoveries under clause (i).

Congress ordinarily adheres to a hierarchical scheme in subdividing statutory sections. See L. Filson, The Legislative Drafter's Desk Reference 222 (1992) (hereinafter Desk Reference). This hierarchy is set forth in drafting manuals prepared by the legislative counsel's offices in the House and the Senate. The House manual provides:

> "To the maximum extent practicable, a section should be broken into—
>
> "(A) subsections (starting with (a));
>
> "(B) paragraphs (starting with (1));
>
> "(C) subparagraphs (starting with (A));
>
> "(D) clauses (starting with (i)) . . . ."
>
> House Legislative Counsel's Manual on Drafting Style, HLC No. 104–1, p. 24 (1995).

[3] Judge Gregory [also] noted that the phrase "under this subparagraph," as it appears in § 1640(a)(2)(B), covering statutory damages in class actions, "indisputably applies to all of subparagraph (B)." 319 F.3d 119, 132 (CA4 2003). "[T]he most logical interpretation of the statute," he concluded, "is to read the phrase 'under this subparagraph' as applying generally to an entire subparagraph, either (A) or (B), and to read (2)(A)(iii) as creating a specific carve-out from that general rule for real-estate transactions." *Ibid.*

The Senate manual similarly provides:

"A section is subdivided and indented as follows:

"(a) SUBSECTION.—

"(1) PARAGRAPH.—

"(A) SUBPARAGRAPH.—

"(i) CLAUSE.—"

Senate Office of the Legislative Counsel, Legislative Drafting Manual 10 (1997).[4]

Congress followed this hierarchical scheme in drafting TILA. The word "subparagraph" is generally used to refer to a subdivision preceded by a capital letter,[5] and the word "clause" is generally used to refer to a subdivision preceded by a lower case Roman numeral.[6] Congress applied this hierarchy in § 1640(a)(2)(B), which covers statutory damages in TILA class actions and states: "[T]he total recovery *under this subparagraph* . . . shall not be more than the lesser of $500,000 or 1 per centum of the net worth of the creditor . . . ." (Emphasis added.) In 1995, Congress plainly meant "to establish a more generous minimum and maximum" for closed-end mortgages. *Strange*, 129 F.3d at 947. On that point, there is no disagreement. Had Congress simultaneously meant to repeal the longstanding $100/$1,000 limitation on § 1640(a)(2)(A)(i), thereby confining the $100/$1,000 limitation solely to clause (ii), Congress likely would have flagged that substantial change. At the very least, a Congress so minded might have stated in clause (ii): "liability under this clause."

The statutory history resolves any ambiguity whether the $100/$1,000 brackets apply to recoveries under clause (i). Before 1995, clauses (i) and (ii) set statutory damages for the entire realm of TILA-regulated consumer credit transactions. Closed-end mortgages were encompassed by clause (i). . . . As a result of the addition of clause (iii), closed-end mortgages are subject to a higher floor and ceiling. But clause (iii) contains no other measure of damages. The specification of statutory damages in clause (i) of twice the finance charge continues to apply to loans secured by real property as it does to loans secured by personal property. Clause (iii) removes closed-end mortgages from clause (i)'s governance only to the extent that clause (iii) prescribes $200/$2,000 brackets in lieu of $100/$1,000.[9]

---

[4] These congressional drafting manuals, both postdating the 1995 TILA amendment, are consistent with earlier guides. . . .

[5] *E.g.*, 15 U.S.C. § 1602(aa)(2)(A) ("under this subparagraph"); § 1602(aa)(2)(B) ("under subparagraph (A)"); § 1605(f)(2)(A) ("except as provided in subparagraph (B)"); § 1615(c)(1)(B) ("pursuant to subparagraph (A)"); § 1637(c)(4)(D) ("in subparagraphs (A) and (B)"). But see § 1637a(a)(6)(C) ("subparagraph" appears not to refer to a capital-letter subdivision).

[6] *E.g.*, § 1637(a)(6)(B)(ii) ("described in clause (i)"); § 1637a(a)(8)(B) ("described in clauses (i) and (ii) of subparagraph (A)"); § 1640(i)(1)(B)(ii) ("described in clause (i)").

[9] . . . . If Congress had not added "(iii)" when it raised the cap on recovery for closed-end mortgages, the meaning of the amended text would be beyond debate. The limitations provision

There is scant indication that Congress meant to alter the meaning of clause (i) when it added clause (iii). Cf. *Church of Scientology of Cal. v. IRS*, 484 U.S. 9, 17–18 (1987) ("All in all, we think this is a case where common sense suggests, by analogy to Sir Arthur Conan Doyle's 'dog that didn't bark,' that an amendment having the effect petitioner ascribes to it would have been differently described by its sponsor, and not nearly as readily accepted by the floor manager of the bill."). By adding clause (iii), Congress sought to provide *increased recovery* when a TILA violation occurs in the context of a loan secured by real property. See, *e.g.*, H.R. Rep. No. 104–193, p. 99 (1995) ("[T]his amendment increases the statutory damages available in closed end credit transactions secured by real property or a dwelling . . . ."). But cf. *post* at 75 (Scalia, J., dissenting) (hypothesizing that far from focusing on *raising* damages recoverable for closed-end mortgage transactions, Congress may have "focus[ed] more intently on limiting damages" for that category of loans). . . . It would be passing strange to read the statute to cap recovery in connection with a closed-end, real-property-secured loan at an amount *substantially lower* than the recovery available when a violation occurs in the context of a personal-property-secured loan or an open-end, real-property-secured loan.[10] The text does not dictate this result; the statutory history suggests otherwise; and there is scant indication Congress meant to change the well-established meaning of clause (i). . . .

▪ *JUSTICE STEVENS, joined by JUSTICE BREYER, concurring:*

If an unambiguous text describing a plausible policy decision were a sufficient basis for determining the meaning of a statute, we would have to affirm the judgment of the Court of Appeals. The ordinary reader would think that 15 U.S.C. § 1640(a)(2)(A) is a paragraph including three subparagraphs identified as (i), (ii), and (iii). There is nothing implausible about a scheme that uses a formula to measure the maximum recovery under (i) without designating a ceiling or floor. Thus we cannot escape this unambiguous statutory command by proclaiming that it would produce an absurd result.

---

would read: "except that the liability under this subparagraph shall not be less than $100 nor greater than $1,000, or in the case of an individual action relating to a credit transaction not under an open end credit plan that is secured by real property or a dwelling, not less than $200 or greater than $2,000."

[10] This reading would lead to the anomalous result of double-the-finance-charge liability, uncapped by the fixed dollar limit, under clause (i) for an open-end loan secured by real property [such as a home equity line of credit], while liability would be capped by clause (iii) at $2,000 for a closed-end loan secured by the same real property. . . .

The dissent states that fixed mortgages are more prevalent than home equity lines of credit and that the mean home equity line of credit balance is considerably smaller than the mean first mortgage balance. But even under the dissent's reading, a borrower stands to collect greater statutory damages if a TILA violation occurs in connection with a home equity line of credit than if it occurs in connection with a home mortgage acquisition loan. . . . Additionally, the dissent's observation does not address the anomaly, illustrated by the facts of this case, of providing full double-the-finance-charge liability for recoveries under clause (i), while capping recoveries under clause (iii). Nigh was awarded over $24,000 in damages for a violation involving a car loan. Had similar misconduct occurred in connection with a home mortgage, he would have received no more than $2,000 in statutory damages.

We can, however, escape by using common sense. The history of the provision makes it perfectly clear that Congress did not intend its 1995 amendment adding (iii) to repeal the pre-existing interpretation of (i) as being limited by the ceiling contained in (ii). Thus, the Court unquestionably decides this case correctly. It has demonstrated that a busy Congress is fully capable of enacting a scrivener's error into law.

In recent years the Court has suggested that we should only look at legislative history for the purpose of resolving textual ambiguities or to avoid absurdities. It would be wiser to acknowledge that it is always appropriate to consider all available evidence of Congress' true intent when interpreting its work product.[1] Common sense is often more reliable than rote repetition of canons of statutory construction. It is unfortunate that wooden reliance on those canons has led to unjust results from time to time.[3] Fortunately, today the Court has provided us with a lucid opinion that reflects the sound application of common sense.

■ *JUSTICE KENNEDY, joined by CHIEF JUSTICE REHNQUIST, concurring:*

In the case before us, there is a respectable argument that the statutory text, 15 U.S.C. § 1640(a)(2)(A)(ii), provides unambiguous instruction in resolving the issue: The word "subparagraph" directs that the $1,000 cap applies to recoveries under both clause (A)(i) and clause (A)(ii), as both fall under subparagraph (A). Were we to adopt that analysis, our holdings in cases such as *Lamie v. United States Trustee,* 540 U.S. 526, 533–535 (2004), . . . would be applicable, absent a showing that the result made little or no sense.

The Court properly chooses not to rest its holding solely on the words of the statute. That is because of a counter-argument that "subparagraph" cannot be read straightforwardly to apply to all of subparagraph (A) in light of the different recovery cap of $2,000 for recoveries under clause (A)(iii). I agree with the Court's decision to proceed on the premise that the text is not altogether clear. That means that examination of other interpretive resources, including predecessor statutes, is necessary for a full and complete understanding of the congressional intent. This approach is fully consistent with cases in which, because the statutory provision at issue had only one plausible textual reading, we did not rely on such sources. In the instant case, the Court consults extratextual sources and, in my view, looking to these materials confirms the usual interpretation of the word "subparagraph."

. . .

■ *JUSTICE THOMAS, concurring in the judgment:*

. . . . I write separately . . . because I believe that it is unnecessary to rely on inferences from silence in the legislative history or the perceived

[1] See *Wisconsin Public Intervenor v. Mortier,* 501 U.S. 597, 611, n. 4 (1991) ("[C]ommon sense suggests that inquiry benefits from reviewing additional information rather than from ignoring it") . . . .

[3] See, *e.g.,* . . . *United States v. Locke,* 471 U.S. 84 (1985).

anomalous results posed by an alternative interpretation to answer the question presented in this case. . . . Instead, in my view, the text of 15 U.S.C. § 1640(a)(2)(A) prior to Congress' 1995 amendment to it, the consistent interpretation that the Courts of Appeals had given to the statutory language prior to the amendment, and the text of the amendment itself make clear that Congress tacked on a provision addressing a very specific set of transactions otherwise covered by the Truth in Lending Act (TILA) but not materially altering the provisions at issue here.

If the text in this case were clear, resort to anything else would be unwarranted. See *Lamie v. United States Trustee*, 540 U.S. 526, 532–533 (2004). But I agree with the Court that § 1640(a)(2)(A) is ambiguous, rather than unambiguous as Justice Stevens contends, . . . because on its face it is susceptible of several plausible interpretations. Congress, as the Court points out, used " 'subparagraph' " consistently in TILA, albeit not with perfect consistency, to refer to a third-level division introduced by a capital letter. . . . This consistent usage points toward the view that "subparagraph" here refers to the whole of subdivision (A). But other textual evidence is in tension with that reading. As the Court of Appeals correctly pointed out . . . , if "subparagraph" refers to the whole of subdivision (A), the limit of $100–$1,000 for liability set forth in clause (ii) is in direct conflict with the $200–$2,000 limit on liability found in clause (iii). . . .

The statutory history of § 1640(a)(2)(A) resolves this ambiguity. Prior to the 1995 amendment, the meaning of subdivisions (A)(i) and (ii) was clear. . . . There is no doubt that under this version of the statute the phrase "under this subparagraph" extended the liability limits to subdivision (A)(i) as well as subdivision (A)(ii). As noted above, "subparagraph" is generally used in TILA to refer to a section's third-level subdivision introduced by a capital letter. By virtue of the phrase "under this subparagraph," the liability extended to the whole of subdivision (A). The placement of this clause at the end of subdivision (A) further indicated that it was meant to refer to the whole of subdivision (A). The clarity of the meaning is borne out by the Courts of Appeals' consistent application of the limit to both clauses (i) and (ii) as they stood before the 1995 amendment. . . .

Congress' 1995 amendment did not materially alter the text of § 1640(a)(2)(A)(i) or (ii). It removed "or" between clauses (i) and (ii) and placed it between clause (ii) and the new clause (iii). Pub. L. 104–29, § 6, 109 Stat. 274. Apart from this change, it neither deleted any language from clause (i) or clause (ii) nor added any language to these clauses. The only substantive change that amendment wrought was the creation of clause (iii), which established a higher $2,000 cap on damages for a very specific set of credit transactions—closed-end credit transactions secured by real property or a dwelling—that had previously been covered by § 1640(a)(2)(A)(i) and subject to the lower $1,000 cap. *Ibid.* By so structuring the amendment, Congress evinced its intent to address only the creation of a different limit for a specific set of transactions. . . .

■ *JUSTICE SCALIA, dissenting:*

The Court views this case as a dispute about the meaning of "subparagraph" in 15 U.S.C. § 1640(a)(2)(A). I think it involves more than that. For while I agree with the construction of that word adopted by the Court, . . . I disagree with the conclusion that the Court believes follows. The ultimate question here is not the meaning of "subparagraph," but the scope of the exception which contains that term. When is "liability under this subparagraph" limited by the $100/$1,000 brackets? In answering that question, I would give dispositive weight to the structure of § 1640(a)(2)(A), which indicates that the exception is part of clause (ii) and thus does not apply to clause (i).

After establishing the fact that "subparagraph" refers to a third-level subdivision within a section, denominated by a capital letter (here subparagraph (A)), see *ante* at 60–62, the Court's analysis proceeds in five steps. First, the Court presumes that this fact determines the scope of the exception. See *ante* at 62. It does not. In context, the reference to "liability under this subparagraph" is indeterminate. Since it is not a freestanding limitation, but an exception to the liability imposed by clause (ii), it is quite possible to read it as saying that, *in the consumer-lease cases covered by clause (ii)*, "the liability under this subparagraph" would be subject to the $100/$1,000 brackets. Using "subparagraph" in that way would hardly be nonsensical, since the *only* liability under subparagraph (A) that applies to consumer-lease cases is the amount of damages specified by clause (ii). In other words, if the exception is part of clause (ii), then "liability under this subparagraph" is actually synonymous with "liability under this clause," cf. *ibid.*, in the sense that either phrase would have the same effect were it to appear in clause (ii). As a result, the term "subparagraph" cannot end our inquiry.

The structure of subparagraph (A) provides the best indication of whether the exception is part of clause (ii). In simplified form, the subparagraph reads: "(i) . . . , (ii) . . . , or (iii) . . . ." Clauses (i), (ii), and (iii) are separated by commas, and an "or" appears before clause (iii). It is reasonable to conclude that the exception—which appears between "(ii)" and the comma that precedes "or (iii)"—is part of clause (ii). . . .

In its second step, the Court notes that, before 1995, the exception was generally read as applying to both clauses (i) and (ii). See *ante* at 62. But the prior meaning is insufficient to reveal the meaning of the current version. As Justice Thomas points out, the placement of the exception "at the end of subdivision (A)" used to "indicat[e] that it was meant to refer to the whole of subdivision (A)." *Ante* at 69. That inference, however, is no longer available, since Congress eliminated the "or" between clauses (i) and (ii) and added clause (iii). If the "or" were still there, it might just be possible to conceive of clauses (i) and (ii) as a sublist to which the exception attached as a whole. But one simply does not find a purportedly universal exception at the end of the second item in a three-item list.

The Court's third step addresses clause (iii), which is not directly implicated by the facts of this case. The Court concludes that the underlying measure of damages in clause (i) (twice the finance charge) "continues to apply" to actions governed by the newly created clause (iii). *Ante* at 62. That conclusion does not follow from merely reading the exception in clause (ii) to apply to clause (i), but it is necessary because, by reading "subparagraph" in the exception to have the effect of extending the exception to all of subparagraph (A), the Court has caused *that* exception to conflict with the higher limit in clause (iii). To remedy this, the Court proceeds . . . to do further violence to § 1640(a)(2)(A), simply reading out its division into clauses (i), (ii), and (iii) entirely. It is not sound statutory construction to create a conflict by ignoring one feature of a statute and then to solve the problem by ignoring yet another. My construction of the exception in clause (ii) avoids the conflict altogether.

In its fourth step, the Court returns to the application of the $100/$1,000 brackets to clause (i). The Court finds "scant indication that Congress meant to alter the meaning of clause (i)" in 1995 and compares this to " 'Sir Arthur Conan Doyle's "dog that didn't bark." ' " *Ante* at 63 (quoting *Church of Scientology of Cal. v. IRS*, 484 U.S. 9, 17–18 (1987)). I hardly think it "scant indication" of intent to alter that Congress *amended the text of the statute* by moving the exception from the end of the list to the middle, making it impossible, without doing violence to the text, to read the exception as applying to the entire list. Needless to say, I also disagree with the Court's reliance on things that the sponsors and floor managers of the 1995 amendment *failed* to say. I have often criticized the Court's use of legislative history because it lends itself to a kind of ventriloquism. The Congressional Record or committee reports are used to make words appear to come from Congress's mouth which were spoken or written by others (individual Members of Congress, congressional aides, or even enterprising lobbyists). The Canon of Canine Silence that the Court invokes today introduces a reverse—and at least equally dangerous—phenomenon, under which courts may refuse to believe Congress's *own* words unless they can see the lips of others moving in unison. See *Morales v. Trans World Airlines, Inc.*, 504 U.S. 374, 385, n. 2 (1992) ("[L]egislative history need not confirm the details of changes in the law effected by statutory language before we will interpret that language according to its natural meaning").

In its fifth and final step, the Court asserts that it would be "anomalous" for liability to be "uncapped by the [$1,000] limit" when real property secures an open-end loan but capped by the $2,000 limit when it secures a closed-end loan, and that it would be "passing strange" for damages to be "*substantially lower*" under clause (iii) than under clause (i). *Ante* at 63 and n. 10. The lack of a $1,000 limit does not, of course, make liability under clause (i) limitless. In all cases under clause (i), the damages are twice the finance charge, and the 1-year statute of limitations, 15 U.S.C. § 1640(e), naturally limits the amount of damages that can be sought.

More importantly, Congress would have expected the amounts financed (and thus the finance charges) under clause (i) to be generally much lower than those under clause (iii). In cases (like this one) where loans are not secured by real property, the amount financed can be no greater than $25,000. § 1603(3) [(stating that TILA does not apply to "[c]redit transactions . . . in which the total amount financed exceeds $25,000" unless "a security interest is or will be acquired in real property, or in personal property used or expected to be used as the principal dwelling of the consumer")]. Where loans are secured by real property, clause (iii) includes both first mortgages and second mortgages (or home equity loans), which are far more common and significantly larger than the open-end home equity lines of credit that are still covered by clause (i). . . . Because closed-end loans are many times more common, and typically much larger, than open-end ones, the finance charges would generally be much higher under clause (iii) than under clause (i), providing a reason for Congress to focus more intently on limiting damages in clause (iii). As for the difference between clause (i) and the $1,000 cap in clause (ii): Consumer leases (principally car leases) are obviously a distinctive category and a special damages cap (which differs from clause (iii) as well as from clause (i)) no more demands an explanation than does the fact that damages for those leases are tied to monthly payments rather than to finance charges. As Justice Stevens acknowledges, applying the $1,000 cap to clause (ii) but not clause (i) is a "plausible policy decision." *Ante* at 65. The Court should not fight the current structure of the statute merely to vindicate the suspicion that Congress actually made—but neglected to explain clearly—a different policy decision.

As the Court noted earlier this year: "If Congress enacted into law something different from what it intended, then it should amend the statute to conform it to its intent. It is beyond our province to rescue Congress from its drafting errors, and to provide for what we might think is the preferred result." *Lamie v. United States Trustee*, 540 U.S. 526, 542 (2004) (internal quotation marks and alteration omitted). . . .

NOTES AND QUESTIONS

1. If you simply read the final block quotation in Part I of the majority opinion, presenting the relevant subparagraph from what the majority called "Section 1640(a), as amended in 1995," you might well agree with Justice Scalia's dissent. There are three separate clauses ((i), (ii), and (iii)), and the key phrase—"except that the liability under this subparagraph shall not be less than $100 nor greater than $1,000"—appears unambiguously to be part of clause (ii). As Justice Scalia noted, moreover, it would be very odd to "find a purportedly universal exception at the end of the second item in a three-item list."

Note, however, that Congress did not enact this language in one fell swoop, in the form presented in the block quotation. Instead of quoting the exact language of the various amendments that Congress enacted over the years, as printed in the *Statutes at Large*, the majority was quoting the compilation of those amendments that appears in the *United States Code*. (The majority's reference to "Section 1640(a)" is a tip-off; the operative statutory provision is section 130(a) of the Truth in Lending Act, as amended, but that provision has been codified at 15 U.S.C. § 1640(a).) Tracing the language of Congress's actual enactments is tedious, but it might give you a slightly different perspective on the question presented in *Koons Buick*.

As the majority mentioned, Congress enacted the original version of the Truth in Lending Act in 1968. We can pick up the story in 1974, when Congress amended § 130(a) of the Act to read as follows:

> "(a) Except as otherwise provided in this section, any creditor who fails to comply with any requirement imposed under this chapter or chapter 4 of this title with respect to any person is liable to such person in an amount equal to the sum of—
>
> "(1) any actual damage sustained by such person as a result of the failure;
>
> "(2) (A) in the case of an individual action twice the amount of any finance charge in connection with the transaction, except that the liability under this subparagraph shall not be less than $100 nor greater than $1,000; or
>
> "(B) in the case of a class action, such amount as the court may allow, except that as to each member of the class no minimum recovery shall be applicable, and the total recovery in such action shall not be more than the lesser of $100,000 or 1 per centum of the net worth of the creditor; and
>
> "(3) in the case of any successful action to enforce the foregoing liability, the costs of the action, together with a reasonable attorney's fee as determined by the court. . . ."

Act of Oct. 28, 1974, Pub. L. 93–495, § 408(a), 88 Stat. 1500, 1518. In 1976, when Congress amended the Truth in Lending Act to include a new chapter about consumer leases, Congress made a few corresponding changes to section 130(a). Specifically, the 1976 statute said:

> Section 130 of the Truth in Lending Act is amended as follows:
>
> (1) In subsection (a), after "chapter 4" insert "or 5".
>
> (2) In clause (2)(A) of subsection (a), insert "(i)" after "(A)", and insert after "transaction" a comma and the following: "or (ii) in the case of an individual action relating to a consumer

> lease under chapter 5 of this title, 25 per centum of the total amount of monthly payments under the lease". . . .

Consumer Leasing Act of 1976, Pub. L. 94–240, § 4, 90 Stat. 257, 260.

After the changes made in 1976, the compiled version of § 130(a)(2)(A) of the Truth in Lending Act (as presented in the *United States Code*) read as follows:

> "(2) (A) (i) in the case of an individual action twice the amount of any finance charge in connection with the transaction, or (ii) in the case of an individual action relating to a consumer lease under part E of this subchapter, 25 per centum of the total amount of monthly payments under the lease, except that the liability under this subparagraph shall not be less than $100 nor greater than $1,000; or"

15 U.S.C. § 1640(a)(2)(A) (1976). Especially when you trace where this language came from, you are likely to draw a distinction between clause (ii), which was added in 1976, and the limiting phrase at the end ("except that the liability under this subparagraph shall not be less than $100 nor greater than $1,000"). That limiting phrase had been part of subparagraph (A) before 1976, and the 1976 amendment adding clause (ii) did not touch it. In context, moreover, the reference to "this subparagraph" clearly covered all of subparagraph (A). That fact, and the structure of the provision, made it easy for courts to read the limiting phrase at the end as modifying the whole subparagraph. As the majority opinion in *Koons Buick* tells you, that is exactly what courts did: they understood subparagraph (A) to consist of two clauses followed by a limiting phrase that applied to both. In other words, rather than reading the limiting phrase to be part of clause (ii), courts understood the limiting phrase to come after both clauses and to limit them both.

In 1995, Congress made the further changes that generated the question in *Koons Buick*. Here is the language of the statute that Congress enacted in 1995:

> Section 130(a)(2)(A) of the Truth in Lending Act . . . is amended—
>
> (1) by striking "or (ii)" and inserting "(ii)"; and
>
> (2) by inserting before the semicolon at the end the following: ", or (iii) in the case of an individual action relating to a credit transaction not under an open end credit plan that is secured by real property or a dwelling, not less than $200 or greater than $2,000".

Truth in Lending Act Amendments of 1995, Pub. L. 104–29, § 6, 109 Stat. 271, 274.

If you make the changes listed in this statute, you will end up with the language in the block quotation at the end of Part I of the majority opinion in *Koons Buick*—the compiled version of 15 U.S.C. § 1640(a)(2)(A) as it stood after the 1995 statute. In a sense, though, the enacted language that the Court really had to interpret was the language of the 1995 statute. The question for the Court was whether the 1995 statute not only added a new clause (iii), but also had the effect of taking clause (i) out from under the limiting phrase that appears before the new clause (iii). On its face, the 1995 statute did not change anything in clause (i), and it also did not change anything in the limiting phrase that previously had applied to both clause (i) and clause (ii). But did the 1995 statute alter the structure of subparagraph (A) in such a way that the limiting phrase now was just part of clause (ii) and no longer applied to clause (i)?

Phrasing the question in this way might not have changed Justice Scalia's position. The 1995 statute did add a new clause (iii) to subparagraph (A), and the consequence of doing so might well be to change the structure of the subparagraph in the way that Justice Scalia thought. Still, does tracing the progression of the enacted language make you see more ambiguity about the structure than you otherwise might? If Congress had enacted the compiled version of 15 U.S.C. § 1640(a)(2)(A) all at once, we might agree with Justice Scalia that the statutory language cannot fairly be read to consist of clause (i), clause (ii), a limiting phrase that applies to them both, and clause (iii). But once you understand the progression of the language and the limited nature of the 1995 statute, does that reading seem more legitimate than it otherwise would? Even if you are not willing to say that the enacted text is ambiguous, does the information in this note make you more likely to conclude that Congress made a drafting error in 1995? Whether you see yourself as resolving an ambiguity or diagnosing a drafting error, is it relevant that the legislative history of the 1995 statute contains no indication that anyone in Congress thought that the 1995 statute would take clause (i) out from under the damage cap that had previously applied to it?

The majority opinion in *Koons Buick* did not purport to diagnose a drafting error. Instead, Justice Ginsburg cast her analysis as an ordinary exercise in statutory interpretation. She claimed that "the conventional meaning of 'subparagraph' " gave her position a textual basis, and she added that the "statutory history" (that is, the evolution of the enacted language) "resolves any ambiguity whether the $100/$1,000 brackets apply to recoveries under clause (i)." *Koons Buick,* 543 U.S. at 60–62. Indeed, Justice Kennedy's concurring opinion pretended that even without any reference to statutory history, the majority's position was the most natural reading of the compiled version of the provision. *See id.* at 66–67 (Kennedy, J., concurring) (asserting that "there is a respectable argument" that Justice Ginsburg's interpretation reflected the "unambiguous" command of the amended provision, but agreeing with "the Court's decision to proceed on the premise that the text is not altogether clear"). By contrast, Justice Stevens thought that the text was "unambiguous" in the opposite direction; he agreed with the majority's position only because he diagnosed a drafting error of the sort that courts could correct through interpretation. *See id.* at 65 (Stevens, J., concurring) (referring to a "scrivener's error"). Do you agree with Justice Stevens that it is necessary to diagnose a drafting error to come out as the majority did?

2. *Lamie* and *Koons Buick* presented closely parallel questions. In both cases, the Court had to determine the effect of an amendment to a pre-existing statutory scheme. In both cases, what might otherwise be the most natural reading of the amendment would have worked a significant change to that scheme. And in both cases, there was good reason to doubt that Congress had really intended to make such a significant change. But the Court reached different outcomes in the two cases. What accounts for this difference?

For some members of the majority in *Koons Buick*, the key probably was that the majority's conclusion in *Koons Buick* had a textual hook, so the Court could effectuate what was probably Congress's intent without having to say that it was diagnosing and correcting a drafting error. (Getting courts to diagnose drafting errors of the sort that they might correct through interpretation is an uphill battle; most judges are very reluctant to say that they are departing from unambiguous statutory language on the ground that Congress did not really mean it.) That explanation, however, does not work for Justices Stevens and Breyer. In *Koons Buick*, those two Justices were indeed willing to conclude that Congress had made a "scrivener's error," which (in their view) justified second-guessing the "unambiguous text" of the statute in order to give effect to "Congress' true intent." *Koons Buick*, 543 U.S. at 65 (Stevens, J., concurring). Why did Justices Stevens and Breyer not say the same thing in *Lamie*?

In *Lamie*, Justice Stevens chalked up his position to the legislative history, which showed that "the National Association of Consumer Bankruptcy Attorneys (NACBA) not only called the assumed drafting error to Congress' attention in a timely fashion, but also deemed the error unworthy of objection." *Lamie*, 540 U.S. at 543 (Stevens, J., concurring in the judgment, joined by Souter and Breyer, JJ., concurring). Because Congress did not change the bill after receiving this submission, Justice Stevens was willing to assume that Congress had enacted the language advisedly, and hence that there was no error after all.

If one is trying to explain why Justice Stevens and Breyer were willing to diagnose a drafting error in *Koons Buick* but not in *Lamie*, policy considerations might also matter. In *Lamie*, the most natural reading of the statutory text was consistent with one of the policy goals behind the Bankruptcy Reform Act of 1994 (to curtail abuses in fee awards)—a fact that cuts against diagnosing a drafting error. In *Koons Buick*, by contrast, the most natural reading of the statutory text was harder to link to any known policy concerns. (It is not apparent why the

1995 Congress would have wanted to eliminate the damage cap for clause (i) while leaving that cap in place for clause (ii).)

Still, *Lamie* suggests that even Justices Stevens and Breyer did not lightly diagnose drafting errors. They required a high level of confidence before they would do so, and even relatively minor clues (like the NACBA submission in *Lamie*) could dissuade them. *Cf. Koons Buick*, 543 U.S. at 65 (Stevens, J., concurring) (finding it "perfectly clear" that Congress had not intended the 1995 statute to take clause (i) out from under the damage cap); *supra* p. 70 (discussing the level of confidence necessary for courts to diagnose a drafting error that they will correct through interpretation).

3. In *Koons Buick*, a judge who had not yet looked at any internal legislative history, but who was familiar with the "statutory history" (that is, the progression of *enacted* amendments), might well have wondered whether the 1995 statute was intended to take clause (i) out from under the damage cap. For Justice Ginsburg, internal legislative history helped to answer that question. A House committee report summarizing the 1995 amendment made no reference to the indirect effect that the amendment might have on clause (i). Neither did anything else in the legislative history of the 1995 statute. In Justice Ginsburg's words, "There is scant indication that Congress meant to alter the meaning of clause (i) when it added clause (iii)." *Koons Buick*, 543 U.S. at 63–64.

That is a different use of legislative history than one sometimes sees. When a statute is ambiguous, judges who believe in the use of legislative history often look for affirmative statements suggesting that members of Congress held one interpretation or the other. If the legislative history does not contain any statements on the topic at all, courts often conclude that it does not shed any light. In the words of a majority opinion by Justice Thomas, "Even for those Members of this Court who consider legislative history, silence in the legislative history . . . cannot defeat the better reading of the text and statutory context. If the text is clear, it needs no repetition in the legislative history; and if the text is ambiguous, silence in the legislative history cannot lend any clarity." *Encino Motorcars, LLC v. Navarro*, 138 S. Ct. 1134, 1143 (2018). In *Koons Buick*, then, Justice Thomas wrote a separate opinion agreeing with the majority's interpretation of the 1995 statute but disclaiming reliance on "inferences from silence in the legislative history." *Koons Buick*, 543 U.S. at 67 (Thomas, J., concurring in the judgment).

As Professor Anita Krishnakumar has observed, however, the particular use of silence made by the majority in *Koons Buick* is not uncommon. Suppose that a statutory provision could be read to make a significant change to pre-existing law, but it could instead be read to do something more minor. If the change that the provision could be read to make is sufficiently important that members of Congress probably would have discussed it, and if the legislative history contains no evidence of any such discussion, judges who are willing to use legislative history might gravitate toward the other interpretation of the provision—the one that would not have been expected to attract comment. *See generally* Anita S. Krishnakumar, *The Sherlock Holmes Canon*, 84 GEO. WASH. L. REV. 1 (2016) (discussing the Supreme Court's use of this argument).

As with other uses of legislative history, many judges suggest that this argument is available only if the provision is ambiguous. If the text of a statute *unambiguously* makes a significant change to pre-existing law, courts will read the statute to do so even if the publicly available legislative history makes no mention of the change. *See, e.g.*, Harrison v. PPG Indus., Inc., 446 U.S. 578, 592 (1980) ("[I]t would be a strange canon of statutory construction that would require Congress to state in committee reports or elsewhere in its deliberations that which is obvious on the face of a statute."); *see also* Whitfield v. United States, 543 U.S. 209, 216 (2005) ("Given the clarity of the text, mere silence in the legislative history cannot justify reading an overt-act requirement . . . into [18 U.S.C.] § 1956(h)."). Assuming that some degree of ambiguity is indeed necessary for this argument to come into play, what degree of ambiguity should be required? If both interpretations are conceivable, but the interpretation that would produce the significant change seems considerably more natural than the other interpretation, should silence in the legislative history matter?

4. In both *Lamie* and *Koons Buick*, Justices Stevens and Breyer suggested that even when a statute's text seems unambiguous, judges should still be willing to examine legislative history for evidence that the text reflects a drafting error of the sort that judges can correct through interpretation. Justice Breyer took the same position in a law-review article that he published while he was a judge on the First Circuit. *See* Stephen Breyer, *On the Uses of Legislative History in Interpreting Statutes*, 65 S. CAL. L. REV. 845, 850 (1992) ("A statute's language might seem fairly clear. The language might produce a result that does not seem absurd. Yet, legislative history nonetheless might clearly show that the result is wrong because of a drafting error that courts should correct.").

Of course, this position was limited in various ways. To begin with, legislative history can reveal various kinds of mistakes that interpreters should not try to correct. Congress might be wrong about facts in the real world, or about the likely effects of adopting a particular policy, or about many other things that affect its statutes. Even so, if a statute is worded in such a way as to establish the legal rules that members of Congress intended to enact, Justices Stevens and Breyer presumably would not have diagnosed and corrected a "drafting error" just because other rules would have been better. The errors that they were open to correcting through interpretation were errors of communication, not policy. Even with respect to errors of communication, moreover, Justices Stevens and Breyer seemed reluctant to diagnose a drafting error unless they were quite sure that one had occurred. *See supra* p. 517.

Even with these limitations, though, does the position suggested by Justices Stevens and Breyer go too far? Even if judges should be willing to use legislative history to help resolve conventional ambiguities in statutes, is there something wrong with using legislative history to identify uncertainty that is not apparent from the enacted language? *Cf.* BedRoc Ltd., LLC v. United States, 541 U.S. 176, 183 (2004) (plurality opinion of Rehnquist, C.J.) ("The preeminent canon of statutory interpretation requires us to 'presume that [the] legislature says in a statute what it means and means in a statute what it says there.' . . . Thus, our inquiry begins with the statutory text, and ends there as well if the text is unambiguous." (quoting Connecticut Nat'l Bank v. Germain, 503 U.S. 249, 253–54 (1992))); St. Charles Inv. Co. v. Comm'r, 232 F.3d 773, 776 (10th Cir. 2000) ("Where the language of the statute is plain, it is improper for this Court to consult legislative history in determining congressional intent. Furthermore, legislative history may not be used to create ambiguity in the statutory language." (citation omitted)).

5. Part III of the majority opinion in *Koons Buick* provides useful information about the labels for the components of a section (such as subsection, paragraph, subparagraph, and clause). The *House Legislative Counsel's Manual on Drafting Style* tells drafters that when they are referring separately to a single unit of a section, they should use the label that goes with that unit. Thus, it is appropriate to speak of "subparagraph (A) of paragraph (2) of subsection (a) of section 130." By contrast, when drafters are referring simultaneously to more than one unit, the manual tells them to use the reference for "the senior unit"—so a drafter would refer to "section 130(a)(2)(A)," not "subparagraph 130(a)(2)(A)." *See* OFFICE OF THE LEGISLATIVE COUNSEL, U.S. HOUSE OF REPRESENTATIVES, HOUSE LEGISLATIVE COUNSEL'S MANUAL ON DRAFTING STYLE § 341(f)(2) (2022).

E. WHEN MIGHT LEGISLATIVE HISTORY BEAR ONLY ON EXPECTED APPLICATIONS AND NOT ON "MEANING"?

Most judges who use legislative history in statutory interpretation see it as evidence of legislative intent. But when Congress enacts a statute, members of Congress have different kinds of intentions, and some of those intentions may be more relevant to statutory interpretation than others. As a result, interpreters who consult legislative history should not simply give effect to whatever intentions they find there. Instead, they should think carefully about whether the information that they are gleaning from the legislative history sheds light on the kind of legislative intent that matters to interpretation, or instead is just evidence of another type of legislative intent.

In discussing legal interpretation, Professor Ronald Dworkin emphasized "the crucial distinction between what some officials intended to *say* in enacting the language they used, and what they intended—or expected or hoped—would be the *consequence* of their saying it." Ronald

Dworkin, *Comment*, *in* A MATTER OF INTERPRETATION: FEDERAL COURTS AND THE LAW 115, 116 (Amy Gutmann ed., 1997). One might well think that principles of interpretation should pay attention to intentions of the former sort, about the content of the legal rules that members of the enacting legislature intended to establish. *See id.* at 117 (using the label "semantic intention" for this type of legislative intent, and observing that "[a]ny reader of anything must attend to semantic intention" for communication to work). Indeed, even people who oppose the use of legislative history in statutory interpretation do not entirely disregard this type of intent; their interpretive system still includes descriptive canons like the presumption of consistent usage and the presumption against superfluity, which operate as generic guides to the intended meaning of statutory language. Legislative history can be an additional, more specific source of information about the same type of legislative intent. To the extent that statutory language is ambiguous or otherwise indeterminate, legislative history might shed light on which meaning members of the enacting legislature intended, and that in turn might affect which meaning interpreters ascribe to the statute.

Even if interpreters care about identifying the content of the legal rules that members of the enacting legislature intended to establish, though, it does not follow that interpreters should also care about legislators' motivations for establishing those rules or the consequences that legislators were hoping to achieve as a result. For instance, remember Judge Easterbrook's example about a hypothetical statute cutting the tax rate on capital gains. *See supra* pp. 389–390. Legislative history might establish that members of Congress expected this change to generate so much economic growth that tax revenues would increase, and legislative history might also establish that Congress would not have enacted the statute but for this expectation. Nonetheless, "the meaning of the law would be only that rates go down, not that revenue go up"—and if revenue does not actually rise, the tax rate is still what the statute says it is rather than whatever would be necessary to produce the consequences that members of Congress wanted. *In re Sinclair*, 870 F.2d 1340, 1344 (7th Cir. 1989).

By the same token, many scholars distinguish between the "intended meaning" of a law and the concrete applications that members of the enacting legislature expected the law to have. *See, e.g.*, Richard S. Kay, *Original Intention and Public Meaning in Constitutional Interpretation*, 103 NW. U. L. REV. 703, 709–10 (2009) (defining the phrase "original intended meaning" to refer to "the content of the rule the enactors intended to put into effect," and distinguishing "the enactors' expectations with respect to the particular instances that would come within the scope of the rules created"); *see also* Mark D. Greenberg & Harry Litman, *The Meaning of Original Meaning*, 86 GEO. L.J. 569, 586–97 (1998) (elaborating on the distinction between "meaning" and "application," and noting that a speaker's expectations about a provision's application can reflect not only the speaker's understanding of the provision's "meaning" but also the speaker's factual premises and other beliefs). When members of Congress enact a statute, they are likely to have intentions of both sorts: they might intend the statute to have a particular meaning, and they might also expect that meaning to have a particular set of applications or to lead to certain results in specific cases. Often, they will be right; the meaning of the directive that they established (and intended to establish) will indeed have the applications that they expected it to have. But if members of Congress had faulty premises or limited foresight, those two things can diverge.

To appreciate the difference between the "meaning" of a law and the lawmaker's contemporaneous expectations about how the directive will be applied to particular fact patterns, we can start with a simple point: legal directives have meaning even in factual settings that the lawmaker did not specifically contemplate in advance. Of course, legislators who are trying to formulate a legal directive are likely to think about how the rule that they are drafting would handle various paradigm cases that come to their minds. But legislators cannot possibly envision in advance the infinite variety of factual settings in which their directive might be applied, and they will want their directive to apply in some settings that they did not specifically contemplate. At the very least, they presumably intend their directive to have meaning not only for the precise factual settings that they imagined in advance, but also for other factual settings that are not materially different even though the legislators did not specifically contemplate them. At least in that sense, a directive operates on a different level of generality than the paradigm cases that legislators have in mind when they draft it. One might say that the directive connects the dots between those paradigm cases.

In some cases, moreover, the meaning of the directive that legislators establish (and intend to establish) will actually put some of the relevant "dots" in different places than the legislators expected when they formulated the directive. That is another important aspect of the difference between "intended meaning" and "expected application." To the extent that legislators' expectations about how a directive will be applied reflect not only their understanding of the provision's "meaning" but also their beliefs about other things (such as facts), and to the extent that some of the latter beliefs are wrong, the intended meaning of a directive might not actually have some of the applications that members of the enacting legislature expected it to have. *See* Greenberg & Litman, *supra*, 86 GEO. L.J. at 585, 588–89.

Professor Dworkin offered a useful example. Suppose that a company needs to fill a new job, and the company's boss tells the hiring manager to "hire the most qualified applicant." Dworkin, *supra*, at 116. Suppose that when the boss uses that phrase, the boss has his own son in mind; the boss is sure that his son is the most qualified applicant. *Id.* Indeed, suppose that if the boss had entertained the possibility that another applicant might be more qualified, the boss would have worded his instruction differently; he might have said something more like "hire my son." Still, that is not what the boss said. The instruction that the boss gave, and intended to give, was to hire the most qualified applicant—and if some other applicant is actually more qualified than the boss's son, then that is whom the boss's instruction would tell the manager to hire. *See id.* at 116–17.

People who accept the distinction between "intended meaning" and "expected application," and who agree that interpreters should care more about the former than the latter, need to be cautious about how they use legislative history. Suppose that a statute establishes a legal directive, and legislative history provides information about how members of Congress expected the directive to be applied. Sometimes, that information might provide evidence of the directive's "intended meaning." (For instance, if the meaning of the directive is ambiguous, but one of the possible interpretations would have been expected to have the applications that members of the enacting legislature had in mind and the other would not, the information about "expected applications" might shed light on the content of the legal rule that members of the enacting legislature intended to establish.) Sometimes, however, information about how members of Congress expected a directive to be applied might simply reflect their premises about things that Congress did not put into the statute—like the boss's assumption that his son would be the most qualified applicant.

If you believe in using legislative history to identify the intended meaning of statutory language, but you do not think that courts need to accept other premises that were in the minds of members of the enacting legislature, you will need to try to draw this distinction. As the next two cases illustrate, however, that is not always easy.

PRELIMINARY NOTE FOR *BOUTILIER V. INS*

As enacted in 1952, § 212(a) of the federal Immigration and Nationality Act listed thirty-one categories of noncitizens who were supposed to be "excluded from admission into the United States." Here is a partial excerpt:

> SEC. 212. (a) Except as otherwise provided in this Act, the following classes of aliens shall be ineligible to receive visas and shall be excluded from admission into the United States:
>
> (1) Aliens who are feeble-minded;
>
> (2) Aliens who are insane;
>
> (3) Aliens who have had one or more attacks of insanity;
>
> (4) Aliens afflicted with psychopathic personality, epilepsy, or a mental defect;
>
> (5) Aliens who are narcotic drug addicts or chronic alcoholics;

(6) Aliens who are afflicted with tuberculosis in any form, or with leprosy, or any dangerous contagious disease;

(7) Aliens not comprehended within any of the foregoing classes who are certified by the examining surgeon as having a physical defect, disease, or disability, when determined by the consular or immigration officer to be of such a nature that it may affect the ability of the alien to earn a living, unless the alien affirmatively establishes that he will not have to earn a living;

(8) Aliens who are paupers, professional beggars, or vagrants;

(9) Aliens who have been convicted of a crime involving moral turpitude (other than a purely political offense), or aliens who admit having committed such a crime, or aliens who admit committing acts which constitute the essential elements of such a crime; except that aliens who have committed only one such crime while under the age of eighteen years may be granted a visa and admitted if the crime was committed more than five years prior to the date of the application for a visa or other documentation, and more than five years prior to date of application for admission to the United States, unless the crime resulted in confinement in a prison or correctional institution, in which case such alien must have been released from such confinement more than five years prior to the date of the application for a visa or other documentation, and for admission, to the United States;

(10) Aliens who have been convicted of two or more offenses (other than purely political offenses) . . . for which the aggregate sentences to confinement actually imposed were five years or more;

(11) Aliens who are polygamists or who practice polygamy or advocate the practice of polygamy;

. . . .

66 Stat. 163, 182 (1952). Section 241(a)(1) of the Act provided for the deportation of any noncitizen who was in the United States but who "at the time of entry was within one or more of the classes of aliens excludable by the law existing at the time of such entry." *Id.* at 204.

Boutilier v. Immigration and Naturalization Service

387 U.S. 118 (1967)

■ *JUSTICE CLARK delivered the opinion of the Court:*

The petitioner, an alien, has been ordered deported to Canada as one who upon entry into this country was a homosexual and therefore "afflicted with psychopathic personality" and excludable under

§ 212(a)(4) of the Immigration and Nationality Act of 1952 .... Petitioner's appeal from the finding of the Special Inquiry Officer was dismissed by the Board of Immigration Appeals, without opinion, and his petition for review in the Court of Appeals was dismissed, with one judge dissenting. 363 F.2d 488 (2d Cir. 1966). It held that the term "psychopathic personality," as used by the Congress in § 212(a)(4), was a term of art intended to exclude homosexuals from entry into the United States. It further found that the term was not void for vagueness and was, therefore, not repugnant to the Fifth Amendment's Due Process Clause. We granted certiorari . . . and now affirm.

I

Petitioner, a Canadian national, was first admitted to this country on June 22, 1955, at the age of 21. His last entry was in 1959, at which time he was returning from a short trip to Canada. . . . In 1963 he applied for citizenship and submitted to the Naturalization Examiner an affidavit in which he admitted that he was arrested in New York in October 1959, on a charge of sodomy, which was later reduced to simple assault and thereafter dismissed on default of the complainant. In 1964, petitioner, at the request of the Government, submitted another affidavit which revealed the full history of his sexual deviate behavior. It stated that his first homosexual experience occurred when he was 14 years of age, some seven years before his entry into the United States. Petitioner was evidently a passive participant in this encounter. His next episode was at age 16 and occurred in a public park in Halifax, Nova Scotia. Petitioner was the active participant in this affair. During the next five years immediately preceding his first entry into the United States petitioner had homosexual relations on an average of three or four times a year. He also stated that prior to his entry he had engaged in heterosexual relations on three or four occasions. During the eight and one-half years immediately subsequent to his entry, and up to the time of his second statement, petitioner continued to have homosexual relations on an average of three or four times a year. Since 1959 petitioner had shared an apartment with a man with whom he had had homosexual relations.

The 1964 affidavit was submitted to the Public Health Service for its opinion as to whether petitioner was excludable for any reason at the time of his entry. The Public Health Service issued a certificate in 1964 stating that in the opinion of the subscribing physicians petitioner "was afflicted with a class A condition, namely, psychopathic personality, sexual deviate" at the time of his admission. Deportation proceedings were then instituted. "No serious question," the Special Inquiry Officer found, "has been raised either by the respondent [petitioner here], his counsel or the psychiatrists [employed by petitioner] who have submitted reports on the respondent as to his sexual deviation." Indeed, the officer found that both of petitioner's psychiatrists "concede that [he] has been a homosexual for a number of years . . . ." [T]he issue before the officer was reduced to the purely legal question of whether the term "psychopathic personality" included homosexuals and if it suffered illegality because of vagueness.

II

The legislative history of the Act indicates beyond a shadow of a doubt that the Congress intended the phrase "psychopathic personality" to include homosexuals such as petitioner.

Prior to the 1952 Act the immigration law excluded "persons of constitutional psychopathic inferiority." 39 Stat. 875, as amended, 8 U.S.C. § 136(a) (1946 ed.). Beginning in 1950, a subcommittee of the Senate Committee on the Judiciary conducted a comprehensive study of the immigration laws and in its report found "that the purpose of the provision against 'persons with constitutional psychopathic inferiority' will be more adequately served by changing that term to 'persons afflicted with psychopathic personality,' and that the classes of mentally defectives should be enlarged to include homosexuals and other sex perverts." S. Rep. No. 1515, 81st Cong., 2d Sess., p. 345. The resulting legislation was first introduced as S. 3455 and used the new phrase "psychopathic personality." The bill, however, contained an additional clause providing for the exclusion of aliens "who are homosexuals or sex perverts." As the legislation progressed (now S. 2550 in the 82d Congress), however, it omitted the latter clause "who are homosexuals or sex perverts" and used only the phrase "psychopathic personality." The omission is explained by the Judiciary Committee Report on the bill:

> "The provisio[n] of S. 716 [one of the earlier bills not enacted] which specifically excluded homosexuals and sex perverts as a separate excludable class does not appear in the instant bill. The Public Health Service has advised that the provision for the exclusion of aliens afflicted with psychopathic personality or a mental defect which appears in the instant bill is sufficiently broad to provide for the exclusion of homosexuals and sex perverts. *This change of nomenclature is not to be construed in any way as modifying the intent to exclude all aliens who are sexual deviates.*" (Emphasis supplied.) S. Rep. No. 1137, 82d Cong., 2d Sess., p. 9.

Likewise a House bill, H.R. 5678, adopted the position of the Public Health Service that the phrase "psychopathic personality" excluded from entry homosexuals and sex perverts. The report that accompanied the bill shows clearly that the House Judiciary Committee adopted the recommendation of the Public Health Service that "psychopathic personality" should be used in the Act as a phrase that would exclude from admission homosexuals and sex perverts. H.R. Rep. No. 1365, 82d Cong., 2d Sess. It quoted at length, and specifically adopted, the Public Health Service report which recommended that the term "psychopathic personality" be used to "specify such types of pathologic behavior as homosexuality or sexual perversion." We, therefore, conclude that the Congress used the phrase "psychopathic personality" not in the clinical sense, but to effectuate its purpose to exclude from entry all homosexuals and other sex perverts.

.... The Government clearly established that petitioner was a homosexual at entry. Having substantial support in the record, we do not now disturb that finding, especially since petitioner admitted being a homosexual at the time of his entry. The existence of this condition over a continuous and uninterrupted period prior to and at the time of petitioner's entry clearly supports the ultimate finding upon which the order of deportation was based.

III

Petitioner says, even so, the section as construed is constitutionally defective because it did not adequately warn him that his sexual affliction at the time of entry could lead to his deportation.... But ... § 212(a)(4) ... imposes neither regulation of nor sanction for conduct. In this situation, therefore, no necessity exists for guidance so that one may avoid the applicability of the law. The petitioner is not being deported for conduct engaged in after his entry into the United States, but rather for characteristics he possessed *at the time of* his entry....

The constitutional requirement of fair warning has no applicability to standards such as are laid down in § 212(a)(4) for admission of aliens to the United States. It has long been held that the Congress has plenary power to make rules for the admission of aliens and to exclude those who possess those characteristics which Congress has forbidden. See *The Chinese Exclusion Case*, 130 U.S. 581 (1889). Here Congress commanded that homosexuals not be allowed to enter. The petitioner was found to have that characteristic and was ordered deported. The basis of the deportation order was his affliction for a long period of time *prior to entry, i.e.*, six and one-half years before his entry. It may be, as some claim, that 'psychopathic personality' is a medically ambiguous term, including several separate and distinct afflictions. Noyes, Modern Clinical Psychiatry 410 (3d ed. 1948). But the test here is what the Congress intended, not what differing psychiatrists may think. It was not laying down a clinical test, but an exclusionary standard which it declared to be inclusive of those having homosexual and perverted characteristics. It can hardly be disputed that the legislative history of § 212(a)(4) clearly shows that Congress so intended....

■ *[JUSTICE BRENNAN noted that he dissented "for the reasons stated by Judge Moore of the Court of Appeals, 2 Cir., 363 F.2d 488, 496–499." JUSTICE DOUGLAS, joined by JUSTICE FORTAS, submitted a separate dissent.]*

NOTES AND QUESTIONS

1. The policy that the Court attributed to § 212(a)(4) of the Immigration and Nationality Act is shocking, and modern judges might well consider it unconstitutional. Admittedly, lawyers debate whether classifications based on sexual orientation should trigger heightened scrutiny in equal-protection analysis, and lawyers also debate how much equal-protection analysis limits federal immigration laws. But if even rational-basis review applies, the modern Supreme Court might refuse to uphold a policy that "is 'inexplicable by anything but animus.'" *Trump v. Hawaii*, 138 S. Ct. 2392, 2420–21 (2018) (quoting Romer v. Evans, 517 U.S. 620, 632 (1996)). The majority in *Boutilier*, however, did not see any constitutional problems with the policy that the Court interpreted § 212(a)(4) to establish.

2. As a matter of statutory interpretation, the majority seemed to think that the legislative history made the case easy. The legislative history that the majority invoked did shed light on a species of legislative intent. But did it shed light on the sort of intent that should matter to interpreters?

Suppose you think that interpreters can properly use the publicly available legislative history of a statute to determine its intended meaning. Suppose, too, that the committee reports quoted by Justice Clark persuade you that when Congress enacted the Immigration and Nationality Act in 1952, members of Congress wanted the law to deny admission to "homosexuals,"[33] and members of Congress believed that § 212(a)(4) would do so. Does this information help define the phrase "afflicted with psychopathic personality" in § 212(a)(4), or does it simply reveal how members of the enacting Congress expected that phrase to be applied? How crisp is the distinction between intended meaning and expected application in this context?

As you think about that distinction, it may help to start with a hypothetical inspired by a different paragraph in § 212(a). Paragraph (6) referred to noncitizens "who are afflicted with . . . any dangerous contagious disease." Suppose that when Congress enacted this language, everyone in Congress (and even in society as a whole) thought that a particular form of cancer is contagious. Later, though, scientific studies establish that it is not. Once this information is available, courts surely should conclude that this form of cancer is not "contagious" within the meaning of paragraph (6). Even if legislative history shows that members of the enacting Congress had this form of cancer in mind and expected paragraph (6) to cover it, this legislative history would not shed light on the *meaning* of the directive that Congress established (and intended to establish). Instead, the legislative history would simply tell us how members of the enacting legislature expected that directive to be applied, given their (imperfect) understanding of the relevant facts. *Cf.* Mark D. Greenberg & Harry Litman, *The Meaning of Original Meaning*, 86 GEO.

[33] This crude term appears in the legislative history. I will leave aside questions about what members of Congress thought it meant. *See, e.g.*, Margot Canaday, *"Who Is a Homosexual?": The Consolidation of Sexual Identities in Mid-Twentieth-Century American Immigration Law*, 28 L. & SOC. INQUIRY 351 (2003).

L.J. 569, 585 (1998) (using a similar example to illustrate the difference between meaning and application).

The key to this example is that the word "contagious," as used in the 1952 statute, referred to an underlying criterion that was independent of Congress's beliefs about which diseases satisfy that criterion. Specifically, the word referred to whether a disease can in fact spread, not to whether people in 1952 *thought* that it can spread. Statements in the legislative history about whether a particular disease is "contagious" might bear only on the latter topic, in which case they would be irrelevant to the interpretation and proper application of paragraph (6).

Can one make the same argument with respect to the legislative history that Justice Clark invoked in *Boutilier*? That is, can one say that the phrases "psychopathic personality" and "mental defect" in paragraph (4) referred to some underlying characteristics distinct from the enacting Congress's beliefs about who has those characteristics? If so, and if we now know that LGBTQ people do not automatically have the characteristics to which paragraph (4) referred, then paragraph (4) would not automatically encompass LGBTQ people—even if the legislative history shows that members of the enacting Congress thought that it would.

Someone who believes in a strong form of imaginative reconstruction might resist this argument as putting too much weight on accidents of verbal formulation and too little weight on the policies that Congress wanted to establish. Imaginative reconstruction would not affect my hypothetical about paragraph (6); if members of the enacting Congress had known that the relevant form of cancer is not contagious, they would not have expanded paragraph (6) to cover it, because they had no special desire to deny admission to cancer patients per se. In 1952, however, members of Congress apparently *did* have a special desire to exclude LGBTQ noncitizens from the country. Indeed, one of the predecessor bills had contained a specific exclusion for noncitizens "who are homosexuals," and the Senate committee report quoted by Justice Clark suggested that Congress had dropped this specific exclusion only because the Public Health Service had advised Congress that paragraph (4) made it unnecessary. That may not be as clear as Justice Clark thought,[34] but assume for the sake of argument that if Congress had known that the language of paragraph (4) might *not* cover LGBTQ people, Congress

[34] On the House side, at least, Rep. Emanuel Cellar had raised concerns about the specific exclusion two months before the date of the Public Health Service's report. *See* Canaday, *supra* note 33, at 357 (quoting Rep. Cellar's remarks from a subcommittee hearing on March 15, 1951). In addition, the Public Health Service's report was less clear than either the Senate committee or Justice Clark made it sound. *See* MARC STEIN, SEXUAL INJUSTICE: SUPREME COURT DECISIONS FROM *GRISWOLD* TO *ROE* 69–71 (2010); *see also* Boutilier v. Immigration & Naturalization Serv., 363 F.2d 488, 498 (2d Cir. 1966) (Moore, J., dissenting) (advancing a narrower interpretation of the Public Health Service's report); WILLIAM N. ESKRIDGE, JR., DYNAMIC STATUTORY INTERPRETATION 63 (1994) (same).

would have retained the specific exclusion from the earlier bill. Should interpreters care?

Even at the time of *Boutilier*, few judges would have taken imaginative reconstruction so far as to pretend that the statute contained the specific exclusion for "homosexuals" that had appeared in the earlier bill but that Congress had dropped before enactment. Still, Justice Clark thought that the legislative history should affect the Court's understanding of the language that Congress did enact in paragraph (4). In Justice Clark's words, that language "was not laying down a clinical test," of the sort that might legitimately be applied in a different way than Congress expected. Instead, Justice Clark argued, Congress specifically intended the phrase "psychopathic personality" to cover "homosexuals," and this intention was built into the meaning of paragraph (4). At least where sexual orientation is concerned, then, Justice Clark suggested that the intended meaning of paragraph (4) cannot readily be separated from Congress's expectations about how paragraph (4) would be applied.

Is that correct? If Justice Clark had been asked to provide a definition of the phrase "afflicted with psychopathic personality . . . or a mental defect" in paragraph (4), what would he have said? Whom besides LGBTQ people did he understand the phrase to cover? Were there any criteria for applying the phrase to people with characteristics that Congress did not specifically contemplate in 1952? If such criteria did exist, could the phrase plausibly be read to mean "anyone who satisfies those criteria, plus LGBTQ people"?

3. The idea that gay men and lesbians were "afflicted with psychopathic personality" did not originate with Congress. Before World War II, one of the leading guides to medical nomenclature had explicitly classified homosexuality as a "symptomatic manifestation" of "psychopathic personality with pathological sexuality." STANDARD CLASSIFIED NOMENCLATURE OF DISEASE 104 (2d ed. 1935).

By the 1940s, the general label "psychopathic personality" had come under attack for lacking theoretical coherence and for meaning different things to different people. *See, e.g.*, Paul William Preu, *The Concept of Psychopathic Personality*, *in* PERSONALITY AND THE BEHAVIOR DISORDERS: A HANDBOOK BASED ON EXPERIMENTAL AND CLINICAL RESEARCH 922, 922, 936 (J. McV. Hunt ed., 1944) (calling the label "one of the vaguest terms employed in modern clinical psychiatry" and observing that "[i]t serves as a scrap-basket to which is relegated a group of otherwise unclassified personality disorders and problems"). In 1945, when the United States Army adopted a revised nomenclature for its own use, it therefore avoided the label. Instead, under the rubric of "Character and Behavior Disorders," the Army attempted to define seven distinct "pathological personality types." Those types included "antisocial personality" (which was said to "include[ ] most cases formerly classed as . . . 'psychopathic personality' " but to be "more limited as well as more specific in its application"), "asocial personality" (which "includes most cases formerly designated as 'Psychopathic personality, with asocial and amoral trends' "), and "sexual deviate" (which "includes most of the cases formerly classed as 'Psychopathic personality, with pathologic sexuality' "). War Dep't Technical Bulletin, Medical 203 (1945), *reprinted in* 2 J. CLIN. PSYCHOLOGY 289, 292–93 (1946). The Army bulletin added that the diagnosis of "sexual deviate" should "specify the . . . type of the pathologic behavior, such as homosexuality . . . ." *Id.* at 293.

The American Psychiatric Association followed suit in the first edition of its *Diagnostic and Statistical Manual* (DSM-I), which was approved in 1951 and published in 1952. Like the Army Bulletin, the DSM-I moved away from the label "psychopathic personality." *See, e.g.*, AMERICAN PSYCHIATRIC ASSOCIATION, DIAGNOSTIC AND STATISTICAL MANUAL: MENTAL DISORDERS 36–38 (1952) (defining other diagnostic labels for "cases previously classified as . . . 'psychopathic personality' " of different sorts). As part of that approach, the DSM-I followed the Army's lead in recognizing the diagnostic label "sexual deviation," which "includes most of the cases formerly classed as 'psychopathic personality with pathologic sexuality.' " *Id.* at 38–39; *see also id.* at 39 (echoing the Army's instruction that "[t]he diagnosis will specify the type of the pathologic behavior, such as homosexuality, transvestism, pedophilia, fetishism and sexual sadism"). In the DSM-I's taxonomy, "sexual deviation" was one of a number of "[s]ociopathic personality disturbance[s]"—a category that also included alcoholism, drug addiction, "antisocial reaction," and "dyssocial reaction." *Id.* at 38–39; *cf. id.* at 38 (noting that "[i]ndividuals to be placed in this category are ill primarily in terms of society and of conformity with the prevailing cultural milieu").[35]

The psychiatric profession's role in medicalizing and enforcing norms about both sexual orientation and gender identities is an important story in its own right. But does any of this information bear on the meaning of the phrase "psychopathic personality" as used in the Immigration and Nationality Act of 1952? For instance, could interpreters plausibly have treated that phrase as simply referring to everything that had been labeled "psychopathic personality" in the most

[35] The DSM-II, published in 1968, dropped references to homosexuality as a form of "pathologic behavior" and classified it as a "non-psychotic mental disorder" rather than a "personality disorder." AMERICAN PSYCHIATRIC ASSOCIATION, DIAGNOSTIC AND STATISTICAL MANUAL OF MENTAL DISORDERS 44 (2d ed. 1968). In 1973, the American Psychiatric Association eliminated that classification too. APA Document Reference No. 730008, Homosexuality and Sexual Orientation Disturbance: Proposed Change in DSM-II, Sixth Printing, Page 44 (approved 1973) (declaring that "homosexuality . . . by itself does not constitute a psychiatric disorder," but describing a new diagnostic category for "individuals whose sexual interests are directed primarily toward people of the same sex and who are either disturbed by, in conflict with, or wish to change their sexual orientation"); *cf.* Jack Drescher, *Out of DSM: Depathologizing Homosexuality*, 5 BEHAVIORAL SCIENCES 565, 571 (2015) (noting that this new category "legitimized the practice of sexual conversion therapies," but still describing the 1973 amendment as "the beginning of the end of organized medicine's official participation in the social stigmatization of homosexuality").

recently published edition of the *Standard Nomenclature of Disease* (3d ed. 1942)? Or should interpreters instead have tried to identify the underlying criteria, if any, that would have been used to construct that list—the properties that would have appeared in a general definition of "psychopathic personality"? *See, e.g.*, Harry F. Darling, *Definition of Psychopathic Personality*, 101 J. NERVOUS & MENTAL DISEASE 121, 121–25 (1945) (acknowledging that "[d]efinitions found in the literature are all incomplete and variable," but attempting to unify them). If you were trying to choose between these two possible interpretations, would the legislative history that Justice Clark recited in *Boutilier* be of any help?

Likewise, what should we make of the DSM-I's allusion to "conformity with the prevailing cultural milieu"? To the extent that the phrase "psychopathic personality" in the 1952 statute included some component along these lines, should courts applying the phrase refer (forever afterward) to the cultural milieu of 1952? Couldn't the phrase instead be understood to invite reference to the cultural milieu of the society that an immigrant would be entering—the cultural milieu at the time of the immigrant's proposed entry into the United States? Again, if you were trying to choose between those two possible interpretations of § 212(a)(4), would the legislative history recited by Justice Clark have any bearing?

4. Although Part III of Justice Clark's opinion in *Boutilier* gave short shrift to a "void for vagueness" argument, the Ninth Circuit had reached a different conclusion in *Fleuti v. Rosenberg*, 302 F.2d 652 (9th Cir. 1962), *vacated on other grounds*, 374 U.S. 449 (1963). Under the circumstances of that case, the Ninth Circuit had allowed George Fleuti to argue that the language of § 212(a)(4) did not provide constitutionally adequate notice that it encompassed homosexuality, and the Ninth Circuit had agreed that the statute was "void for vagueness, as applied in this case." *Id.* at 656, 658; *see also id.* at 654–55 & n.5 (noting that such a challenge had to be evaluated on the basis of the statutory language, without regard to "the relatively inaccessible legislative history").

In 1965, Congress responded to *Fleuti* by inserting the phrase "sexual deviation" into § 212(a)(4). *See* Act of Oct. 3, 1965, Pub. L. 89–236, § 15(b), 79 Stat. 911, 919 ("Paragraph (4) of section 212(a) of the Immigration and Nationality Act . . . is amended by deleting the word 'epilepsy' and substituting the words 'or sexual deviation'."); *see also* 8 U.S.C. § 1182(a)(4) (Supp. I 1965) (reflecting this amendment in the codified version of paragraph (4), which now referred to "[a]liens afflicted with psychopathic personality, or sexual deviation, or a mental defect"). To explain this amendment, the committee reports in both the House and the Senate invoked the intention behind the 1952 Act. *See* William N. Eskridge, Jr., *Gadamer/Statutory Interpretation*, 90 COLUM. L. REV. 609, 642 (1990) ("[T]he committee reports suggest that Congress thought it was only reasserting its 'original' intent."). Here is the relevant passage from the House Judiciary Committee's report:

> "In view of the representations made by the U.S. Public Health Service that [the] term 'psychopathic personality' would encompass homosexuals and sex perverts, the Congress in enacting the Immigration and Nationality Act omitted from the law any specific provision relating to the ineligibility of such persons (note S. Rept. 1137, 82d Cong.).
>
> "However, the U.S. Court of Appeals for the Ninth Circuit on April 17, 1962, set aside a deportation order and enjoined its enforcement holding that section 212(a)(4) was unconstitutionally vague in that homosexuality was not sufficiently encompassed within the term 'psychopathic personality.' (*Fleuti v. Rosenberg*, 302 F.2d 652.)
>
> "To resolve any doubt the committee has specifically included the term 'sexual deviation' as a ground of exclusion in this bill."

H.R. REP. No. 745, 89th Cong., 1st Sess., at 16 (1965); *accord* S. REP. No. 748, 89th Cong., 1st Sess., at 18–19 (1965).

Although Congress enacted the 1965 amendment two years before the Supreme Court decided *Boutilier*, the amendment plainly did not apply in that case. (Section 241(a)(1) of the Immigration and Nationality Act made Mr. Boutilier deportable only if, "at the time of [his] entry" into the United States, he had been "excludable by the law existing at the time of such entry," and his last entry had occurred well before 1965.) Nonetheless, the government's brief in *Boutilier* quoted the 1965 committee reports and urged the Supreme Court to take them into account in interpreting the phrase "psychopathic personality" in the original statute. Brief for Respondent at 28–29, Boutilier v. INS, 387 U.S. 118 (1967) (No. 440). The Supreme Court apparently did not do so. For purposes of interpreting the 1952 statute, the committee reports from 1965 were simply post-enactment legislative history, and the Court's opinion in *Boutilier* made no mention of them.

Still, the 1965 amendment would have loomed larger for potential visitors and immigrants who wanted to enter the country after 1965. The text of the statute was still murky; "sexual deviation" is obviously a contestable term, *see* Eskridge, *supra*, 90 COLUM. L. REV. at 640–41, and the phrase "afflicted with . . . sexual deviation" seems even murkier. For judges who use legislative history, would the committee reports about the 1965 amendment eliminate that murkiness and establish, forever afterward, that the 1965 amendment encompassed LGBTQ people? Or is the phrase "sexual deviation" subject to the same questions that the previous notes asked about "psychopathic personality"? For instance, if "sexual deviation" was a clinical term, did it automatically encompass the examples that the DSM-I had provided under that label, or did it instead refer to some underlying criteria that the DSM-I might have misapplied? Likewise, to the extent that determining "deviation" requires reference to a comparison set of some sort, would the content of the comparison set be frozen as of 1965, or would proper application of the phrase "sexual deviation" require attention to changing mores and changing understandings of mental health? Did the legislative history of the 1965 amendment answer these questions?

Because the Supreme Court's opinion in *Boutilier* had not pursued these kinds of questions with respect to "psychopathic personality," lower courts might not have asked them with respect to "sexual deviation" either. But in 1977, four years after the American Psychiatric Association revised the DSM-II to stop characterizing homosexuality as a psychiatric disorder (*see supra* n.35), "the [Public Health Service (PHS)] notified the INS that it no longer felt professionally capable of participating in the exclusion of gay people as 'psychopathic personalities' or 'sexual deviates.' " William N. Eskridge, Jr., *Challenging the Apartheid of the Closet: Establishing Conditions for Lesbian and Gay Intimacy, Nomos, and Citizenship, 1961–1981*, 25 HOFSTRA L. REV. 817, 936 (1997). Professor Eskridge reports that this message prompted two years of "bureaucratic impasse," but in 1979 "the PHS formally abandoned any role in diagnosing gay people as 'sexual deviates' or people afflicted with 'psychopathic personality.' " *Id.* at 936–37. That had important ramifications, because the Immigration and Nationality Act arguably did not allow the INS to exclude or deport a noncitizen on purportedly "medical" grounds unless the PHS had examined the noncitizen and had certified an excludable condition. *See id.* at 937; *see also id.* at 937–39 (discussing subsequent developments and litigation). Not until 1990, however, did Congress finally eliminate what had been paragraph (4) from the statute. *See id.* at 939; *see also* Shannon Minter, Note, *Sodomy and Public Morality Offenses Under U.S. Immigration Law: Penalizing Lesbian and Gay Identity*, 26 CORNELL INT'L L.J. 771, 778–83 (1993).

5. For close analysis of the opinions in *Boutilier* and an in-depth history of the litigation, see MARC STEIN, SEXUAL INJUSTICE: SUPREME COURT DECISIONS FROM *GRISWOLD* TO *ROE* 57–93, 133–203, 243–78 (2010).

Two of the leading discussions of *Boutilier* in law reviews—T. Alexander Aleinikoff, *Updating Statutory Interpretation*, 87 MICH. L. REV. 20, 47–54 (1988), and William N. Eskridge, Jr., *Gadamer/Statutory Interpretation*, 90 COLUM. L. REV. 609 (1990)—both used the case as a launching pad for theories of "dynamic" statutory interpretation, under which the very meaning of a statute can change over time. For someone who accepts such theories, the legislative history of a statute might be important when the statute is enacted, but might become less important as the statute ages.

Such theories, however, are unconventional. On the conventional account of legal interpretation, the meaning of a statute is set at the time of enactment (subject to the possibility that the meaning might contain an intractable indeterminacy that interpreters will have to resolve later). Still, because of the complexity of the concept of "meaning," statements in the legislative history that reflect how members of the enacting legislature expected the statute to be applied will not necessarily be accurate guides to the statute's meaning. Although Justice Clark's opinion did not consider this possibility, *Boutilier* is an example of a case in which the meaning of a statute might not really require all of the applications that members of the enacting legislature expected. The next case reflects the related possibility that the meaning of a statute might have some important applications that members of the enacting legislature did *not* expect.[36]

Bostock v. Clayton County

140 S. Ct. 1731 (2020)

■ *JUSTICE GORSUCH delivered the opinion of the Court:*

Sometimes small gestures can have unexpected consequences. Major initiatives practically guarantee them. In our time, few pieces of federal legislation rank in significance with the Civil Rights Act of 1964. There, in Title VII, Congress outlawed discrimination in the workplace on the basis of race, color, religion, sex, or national origin. Today, we must decide whether an employer can fire someone simply for being homosexual or transgender. The answer is clear. An employer who fires an individual for being homosexual or transgender fires that person for traits or actions it would not have questioned in members of a different sex. Sex plays a necessary and undisguisable role in the decision, exactly what Title VII forbids.

Those who adopted the Civil Rights Act might not have anticipated their work would lead to this particular result. Likely, they weren't thinking about many of the Act's consequences that have become apparent over the years, including its prohibition against discrimination on the basis of motherhood or its ban on the sexual harassment of male employees. But the limits of the drafters' imagination supply no reason to ignore the law's demands. . . .

I

. . . . Each of the three cases before us started the same way: An employer fired a long-time employee shortly after the employee revealed that he or she is homosexual or transgender—and allegedly for no reason other than the employee's homosexuality or transgender status.

Gerald Bostock worked for Clayton County, Georgia . . . . After a decade with the county, Mr. Bostock began participating in a gay recreational softball league. Not long after that, influential members of the community allegedly made disparaging comments about Mr. Bostock's sexual orientation and participation in the league. Soon, he was fired for conduct "unbecoming" a county employee.

---

[36] Chapter 7 of this book considers additional aspects of statutory interpretation that might look dynamic in some respects, but that are consistent with the conventional account.

Donald Zarda worked as a skydiving instructor at Altitude Express in New York. After several seasons with the company, Mr. Zarda mentioned that he was gay and, days later, was fired.

Aimee Stephens worked at R.G. & G.R. Harris Funeral Homes in Garden City, Michigan. When she got the job, Ms. Stephens presented as a male. But two years into her service with the company, she began treatment for despair and loneliness. Ultimately, clinicians diagnosed her with gender dysphoria and recommended that she begin living as a woman. In her sixth year with the company, Ms. Stephens wrote a letter to her employer explaining that she planned to "live and work full-time as a woman" after she returned from an upcoming vacation. The funeral home fired her before she left, telling her "this is not going to work out."

While these cases began the same way, they ended differently. Each employee brought suit under Title VII alleging unlawful discrimination on the basis of sex. 78 Stat. 255, 42 U.S.C. § 2000e–2(a)(1). In Mr. Bostock's case, the Eleventh Circuit held that the law does not prohibit employers from firing employees for being gay and so his suit could be dismissed as a matter of law. 723 Fed. Appx. 964 (2018). Meanwhile, in Mr. Zarda's case, the Second Circuit concluded that sexual orientation discrimination does violate Title VII and allowed his case to proceed. 883 F.3d 100 (2018). Ms. Stephens's case has a more complex procedural history, but in the end the Sixth Circuit reached a decision along the same lines as the Second Circuit's, holding that Title VII bars employers from firing employees because of their transgender status. 884 F.3d 560 (2018). During the course of the proceedings in these long-running disputes, both Mr. Zarda and Ms. Stephens have passed away. But their estates continue to press their causes for the benefit of their heirs. And we granted certiorari in these matters . . . .

II

This Court normally interprets a statute in accord with the ordinary public meaning of its terms at the time of its enactment. After all, only the words on the page constitute the law adopted by Congress and approved by the President. If judges could add to, remodel, update, or detract from old statutory terms inspired only by extratextual sources and our own imaginations, we would risk amending statutes outside the legislative process reserved for the people's representatives. . . .

With this in mind, our task is clear. We must determine the ordinary public meaning of Title VII's command that it is "unlawful . . . for an employer to fail or refuse to hire or to discharge any individual, or otherwise to discriminate against any individual with respect to his compensation, terms, conditions, or privileges of employment, because of such individual's race, color, religion, sex, or national origin." § 2000e–2(a)(1). To do so, we orient ourselves to the time of the statute's adoption, here 1964, and begin by examining the key statutory terms in turn before assessing their impact on the cases at hand and then confirming our work against this Court's precedents.

A

The only statutorily protected characteristic at issue in today's cases is "sex"—and that is also the primary term in Title VII whose meaning the parties dispute. Appealing to roughly contemporaneous dictionaries, the employers say that, as used here, the term "sex" in 1964 referred to "status as either male or female [as] determined by reproductive biology." The employees counter by submitting that, even in 1964, the term bore a broader scope, capturing more than anatomy and reaching at least some norms concerning gender identity and sexual orientation. But because nothing in our approach to these cases turns on the outcome of the parties' debate, and because the employees concede the point for argument's sake, we proceed on the assumption that "sex" signified what the employers suggest, referring only to biological distinctions between male and female.

Still, . . . [t]he question isn't just what "sex" meant, but what Title VII says about it. Most notably, the statute prohibits employers from taking certain actions "because of" sex. And, as this Court has previously explained, "the ordinary meaning of 'because of' is 'by reason of' or 'on account of.' " *University of Tex. Southwestern Medical Center v. Nassar*, 570 U.S. 338, 350 (2013) (citing *Gross v. FBL Financial Services, Inc.*, 557 U.S. 167, 176 (2009); quotation altered). In the language of law, this means that Title VII's "because of" test incorporates the " 'simple' " and "traditional" standard of but-for causation. *Nassar*, 570 U.S. at 346, 360. That form of causation is established whenever a particular outcome would not have happened "but for" the purported cause. See *Gross*, 557 U.S. at 176. In other words, a but-for test directs us to change one thing at a time and see if the outcome changes. If it does, we have found a but-for cause.

This can be a sweeping standard. Often, events have multiple but-for causes. . . . [T]he adoption of the traditional but-for causation standard [in Title VII] means a defendant cannot avoid liability just by citing some *other* factor that contributed to its challenged employment decision. So long as the plaintiff's sex was one but-for cause of that decision, that is enough to trigger the law. See [*Burrage v. United States*, 571 U.S. 204, 211–212 (2014)]; *Nassar*, 570 U.S. at 350.

No doubt, Congress could have taken a more parsimonious approach. As it has in other statutes, it could have added "solely" to indicate that actions taken "because of" the confluence of multiple factors do not violate the law. Cf. 11 U.S.C. § 525; 16 U.S.C. § 511. Or it could have written "primarily because of" to indicate that the prohibited factor had to be the main cause of the defendant's challenged employment decision. Cf. 22 U.S.C. § 2688. But none of this is the law we have. If anything, Congress has moved in the opposite direction, supplementing Title VII in 1991 to allow a plaintiff to prevail merely by showing that a protected trait like sex was a "motivating factor" in a defendant's challenged employment practice. Civil Rights Act of 1991, § 107, 105 Stat. 1075, codified at 42 U.S.C. § 2000e–2(m). Under this more forgiving standard, liability can sometimes follow even if sex *wasn't* a but-for cause of the employer's challenged decision. Still, because nothing in our analysis depends on the motivating factor test, we focus on the more traditional but-for causation standard that continues to afford a viable, if no longer exclusive, path to relief under Title VII. § 2000e–2(a)(1).

. . . Title VII does not concern itself with everything that happens "because of" sex. The statute imposes liability on employers only when they "fail or refuse to hire," "discharge," "or otherwise . . . discriminate against" someone because of a statutorily protected characteristic like sex. *Ibid.* The employers acknowledge that they discharged the plaintiffs in today's cases, but assert that the statute's list of verbs is qualified by the last item on it: "otherwise . . . discriminate against." By virtue of the word *otherwise*, the employers suggest, Title VII concerns itself not with every discharge, only with those discharges that involve discrimination.

Accepting this point, too, for argument's sake, the question becomes: What did "discriminate" mean in 1964? As it turns out, it meant then roughly what it means today: "To make a difference in treatment or favor (of one as compared with others)." Webster's New International Dictionary 745 (2d ed. 1954). To "discriminate against" a person, then, would seem to mean treating that individual worse than others who are similarly situated. See *Burlington N. & S. F. R. Co. v. White*, 548 U.S. 53, 59 (2006). In so-called "disparate treatment" cases like today's, this Court has also held that the difference in treatment based on sex must be intentional. See, *e.g.*, *Watson v. Fort Worth Bank & Trust*, 487 U.S. 977, 986 (1988). So, taken together, an employer who intentionally treats a person worse because of sex—such as by firing the person for actions or attributes it would tolerate in an individual of another sex—discriminates against that person in violation of Title VII.

At first glance, another interpretation might seem possible. Discrimination sometimes involves "the act, practice, or an instance of discriminating categorically rather than individually." Webster's New Collegiate Dictionary 326 (1975); see also *post* at 1768–69, n. 22 (Alito, J., dissenting). On that understanding, the statute would require us to consider the employer's treatment of groups rather than individuals, to see how a policy affects one sex as a whole versus the other as a whole. That idea holds some intuitive appeal too. Maybe the law concerns itself simply with ensuring that employers don't treat women generally less favorably than they do men. So how can we tell which sense, individual or group, "discriminate" carries in Title VII?

The statute answers that question directly. It tells us three times—including immediately after the words "discriminate against"—that our focus should be on individuals, not groups: Employers may not "fail or refuse to hire or . . . discharge any *individual*, or otherwise . . . discriminate against any *individual* with respect to his compensation, terms, conditions, or privileges of employment, because of such *individual's* . . . sex." § 2000e–2(a)(1) (emphasis added). . . .

. . . . Suppose an employer fires a woman for refusing his sexual advances. It's no defense for the employer to note that, while he treated that individual woman worse than he would have treated a man, he gives preferential treatment to female employees overall. The employer is liable for treating *this* woman worse in part because of her sex. Nor is it a defense for an employer to say it discriminates against both men and women because of sex. This statute works to protect individuals of both sexes from discrimination, and does so equally. So an employer who fires a woman, Hannah, because she is insufficiently feminine and also fires a man, Bob, for being insufficiently masculine may treat men and women as groups more or less equally. But in *both* cases the employer fires an individual in part because of sex. Instead of avoiding Title VII exposure, this employer doubles it.

B

From the ordinary public meaning of the statute's language at the time of the law's adoption, a straightforward rule emerges: An employer violates Title VII when it intentionally fires an individual employee based in part on sex. It doesn't matter if other factors besides the plaintiff's sex contributed to the decision. And it doesn't matter if the employer treated women as a group the same when compared to men as a group. If the employer intentionally relies in part on an individual employee's sex when deciding to discharge the employee—put differently, if changing the employee's sex would have yielded a different choice by the employer—a statutory violation has occurred. Title VII's message is "simple but momentous": An individual employee's sex is "not relevant to the selection, evaluation, or compensation of employees." *Price Waterhouse v. Hopkins*, 490 U.S. 228, 239 (1989) (plurality opinion).

The statute's message for our cases is equally simple and momentous: An individual's homosexuality or transgender status is not relevant to employment decisions. That's because it is impossible to discriminate against a person for being homosexual or transgender without discriminating against that individual based on sex. Consider, for example, an employer with two employees, both of whom are attracted to men. The two individuals are, to the employer's mind, materially identical in all respects, except that one is a man and the other a woman. If the employer fires the male employee for no reason other than the fact he is attracted to men, the employer discriminates against him for traits or actions it tolerates in his female colleague. Put differently, the employer intentionally singles out an employee to fire based in part on the employee's sex, and the affected employee's sex is a but-for cause of his discharge. Or take an employer who fires a transgender person who was identified as a male at birth but who now identifies as a female. If the employer retains an otherwise identical employee who was identified as female at birth, the employer intentionally penalizes a person identified as male at birth for traits or actions that it tolerates in an employee identified as female at birth. Again, the individual employee's sex plays an unmistakable and impermissible role in the discharge decision. . . .

Nor does it matter that, when an employer treats one employee worse because of that individual's sex, other factors may contribute to the decision. Consider an employer with a policy of firing any woman he discovers to be a Yankees fan. Carrying out that rule because an employee is a woman *and* a fan of the Yankees is a firing "because of sex" if the employer would have tolerated the same allegiance in a male employee. Likewise here. When an employer fires an employee because she is homosexual or transgender, two causal factors may be in play—*both* the individual's sex *and* something else (the sex to which the individual is attracted or with which the individual identifies). But Title VII doesn't care. If an employer would not have discharged an employee but for that individual's sex, the statute's causation standard is met, and liability may attach.

Reframing the additional causes in today's cases as additional intentions can do no more to insulate the employers from liability. Intentionally burning down a neighbor's house is arson, even if the perpetrator's ultimate intention (or motivation) is only to improve the view. No less, intentional discrimination based on sex violates Title VII, even if it is intended only as a means to achieving the employer's ultimate goal of discriminating against homosexual or transgender employees. There is simply no escaping the role intent plays here: Just as sex is necessarily a but-for *cause* when an employer discriminates against homosexual or transgender employees, an employer who discriminates on these grounds inescapably *intends* to rely on sex in its decisionmaking. Imagine an employer who has a policy of firing any employee known to be homosexual. The employer hosts an office holiday party and invites employees to bring their spouses. A model employee arrives and introduces a manager to Susan, the employee's wife. Will that employee be fired? If the policy works as the employer intends, the answer depends entirely on whether the model employee is a man or a woman. To be sure, that employer's ultimate goal might be to discriminate on the basis of sexual orientation. But to achieve that purpose the employer must, along the way, intentionally treat an employee worse based in part on that individual's sex.

An employer musters no better a defense by responding that it is equally happy to fire male *and* female employees who are homosexual or transgender. Title VII liability is not limited to employers who, through the sum of all of their employment actions, treat the class of men differently than the class of women. Instead, the law makes each instance of discriminating against an individual employee because of that individual's sex an independent violation of Title VII. So just as an employer who fires both Hannah and Bob for failing to fulfill traditional sex stereotypes doubles rather than eliminates Title VII liability, an employer who fires both Hannah and Bob for being gay or transgender does the same. . . .

C

If more support for our conclusion were required, . . . [c]onsider three of our leading precedents.

In *Phillips v. Martin Marietta Corp.*, 400 U.S. 542 (1971) (*per curiam*), a company allegedly refused to hire women with young children, but did hire men with children the same age. Because its discrimination depended not only on the employee's sex as a female but also on the presence of another criterion—namely, being a parent of young children—the company contended it hadn't engaged in discrimination "because of" sex. The company maintained, too, that it hadn't violated the law because, as a whole, it tended to favor hiring women over men. . . . [T]hese submissions did not sway the Court. That an employer discriminates intentionally against an individual only in part because of sex supplies no defense to Title VII. Nor does the fact an employer may happen to favor women as a class.

In *Los Angeles Dept. of Water and Power v. Manhart*, 435 U.S. 702 (1978), an employer required women to make larger pension fund contributions than men. The employer sought to justify its disparate treatment on the ground that women tend to live longer than men, and thus are likely to receive more from the pension fund over time. By everyone's admission, the employer was not guilty of animosity against women or a "purely habitual assumptio[n] about a woman's inability to perform certain kinds of work"; instead, it relied on what appeared to be a statistically accurate statement about life expectancy. *Id.* at 707–708. Even so, the Court recognized, a rule that appears evenhanded at the group level can prove discriminatory at the level of individuals. True, women as a class may live longer than men as a class. But "[t]he statute's focus on the individual is unambiguous," and any individual woman might make the larger pension contributions and still die as early as a man. *Id.* at 708. Likewise, the Court dismissed as irrelevant the employer's insistence that its actions were motivated by a wish to achieve classwide equality between the sexes: An employer's intentional discrimination on the basis of sex is no more permissible when it is prompted by some further intention (or motivation), even one as prosaic as seeking to account for actuarial tables. *Ibid.* The employer violated Title VII because, when its policy worked exactly as planned, it could not "pass the simple test" asking whether an individual female employee would have been treated the same regardless of her sex. *Id.* at 711.

In *Oncale v. Sundowner Offshore Services, Inc.*, 523 U.S. 75 (1998), a male plaintiff alleged that he was singled out by his male co-workers for sexual harassment. The Court held it was immaterial that members of the same sex as the victim committed the alleged discrimination. Nor did the Court concern itself with whether men as a group were subject to discrimination or whether something in addition to sex contributed to the discrimination, like the plaintiff's conduct or personal attributes. "[A]ssuredly," the case didn't involve "the principal evil Congress was concerned with when it enacted Title VII." *Id.* at 79. But, the Court unanimously explained, it is "the provisions of our laws rather than the principal concerns of our legislators by which we are governed." *Ibid.* Because the plaintiff alleged that the harassment would not have taken place but for his sex—that is, the plaintiff would not have suffered similar treatment if he were female—a triable Title VII claim existed. . . .

III

What do the employers have to say in reply? . . . .

A

Maybe most intuitively, the employers assert that discrimination on the basis of homosexuality and transgender status aren't referred to as sex discrimination in ordinary conversation. If asked by a friend (rather than a judge) why they were fired, even today's plaintiffs would likely respond that it was because they were gay or transgender, not because of sex. According to the employers, that conversational answer, not the statute's strict terms, should guide our thinking and suffice to defeat any suggestion that the employees now before us were fired because of sex. . . .

But this submission rests on a mistaken understanding of what kind of cause the law is looking for in a Title VII case. In conversation, a speaker is likely to focus on what seems most relevant or informative to the listener. So an employee who has just been fired is likely to identify the primary or most direct cause rather than list literally every but-for cause. . . . But these conversational conventions do not control Title VII's legal analysis, which asks simply whether sex was a but-for cause. In *Phillips*, for example, a woman who was not hired under the employer's policy might have told her friends that her application was rejected because she was a mother, or because she had young children. Given that many women could be hired under the policy, it's unlikely she would say she was not hired because she was a woman. But the Court did not hesitate to recognize that the employer in *Phillips* discriminated against the plaintiff because of her sex. Sex wasn't the only factor, or maybe even the main factor, but it was one but-for cause—and that was enough. . . .

Trying another angle, the defendants before us suggest that an employer who discriminates based on homosexuality or transgender status doesn't *intentionally* discriminate based on sex, as a disparate treatment claim requires. . . . But, as we've seen, an employer who discriminates against homosexual or transgender employees necessarily and intentionally applies sex-based rules. An employer that announces it will not employ anyone who is homosexual, for example, intends to penalize male employees for being attracted to men and female employees for being attracted to women.

What, then, do the employers mean when they insist intentional discrimination based on homosexuality or transgender status isn't intentional discrimination based on sex? Maybe the employers mean they don't intend to harm one sex or the other as a class. But . . . the statute focuses on discrimination against individuals, not groups. Alternatively, the employers may mean that they don't perceive themselves as motivated by a desire to discriminate based on sex. But nothing in Title VII turns on the employer's labels or any further intentions (or motivations) for its conduct beyond sex discrimination. In *Manhart*, the employer intentionally required women to make higher pension contributions only to fulfill the further purpose of making things more equitable between men and women as groups. . . .

Aren't these cases different, the employers ask, given that an employer could refuse to hire a gay or transgender individual without ever learning the applicant's sex? Suppose an employer asked homosexual or transgender applicants to tick a box on its application form. The employer then had someone else redact any information that could be used to discern sex. The resulting applications would disclose which individuals are homosexual or transgender without revealing whether they also happen to be men or women. Doesn't that possibility indicate that the employer's discrimination against homosexual or transgender persons cannot be sex discrimination?

No, it doesn't. Even in this example, the individual applicant's sex still weighs as a factor in the employer's decision. . . .

. . . . There is no way for an applicant to decide whether to check the homosexual or transgender box without considering sex. To see why, imagine an applicant doesn't know what the words homosexual or transgender mean. Then try writing out instructions for who should check the box without using the words man, woman, or sex (or some synonym). It can't be done. Likewise, there is no way an employer can discriminate against those who check the homosexual or transgender box without discriminating in part because of an applicant's sex. By discriminating against homosexuals, the employer intentionally penalizes men for being attracted to men and women for being attracted to women. By discriminating against transgender persons, the employer unavoidably discriminates against persons with one sex identified at birth and another today. Any way you slice it, the employer intentionally refuses to hire applicants in part because of the affected individuals' sex, even if it never learns any applicant's sex.

Next, the employers turn to Title VII's list of protected characteristics—race, color, religion, sex, and national origin. Because homosexuality and transgender status can't be found on that list and because they are conceptually distinct from sex, the employers reason, they are implicitly excluded from Title VII's reach. Put another way, if Congress had wanted to address these matters in Title VII, it would have referenced them specifically. . . .

.... We agree that homosexuality and transgender status are distinct concepts from sex. But, as we've seen, discrimination based on homosexuality or transgender status necessarily entails discrimination based on sex; the first cannot happen without the second. Nor is there any such thing as a "canon of donut holes," in which Congress's failure to speak directly to a specific case that falls within a more general statutory rule creates a tacit exception. Instead, when Congress chooses not to include any exceptions to a broad rule, courts apply the broad rule. And that is exactly how this Court has always approached Title VII. "Sexual harassment" is conceptually distinct from sex discrimination, but it can fall within Title VII's sweep. . . . As enacted, Title VII prohibits all forms of discrimination because of sex, however they may manifest themselves or whatever other labels might attach to them.

The employers try the same point another way. Since 1964, they observe, Congress has considered several proposals to add sexual orientation to Title VII's list of protected characteristics, but no such amendment has become law. Meanwhile, Congress has enacted other statutes addressing other topics that do discuss sexual orientation. This postenactment legislative history, they urge, should tell us something. . . .

But what? There's no authoritative evidence explaining why later Congresses adopted other laws referencing sexual orientation but didn't amend this one. Maybe some in the later legislatures understood the impact Title VII's broad language already promised for cases like ours and didn't think a revision needed. Maybe others knew about its impact but hoped no one else would notice. Maybe still others, occupied by other concerns, didn't consider the issue at all. All we can know for certain is that speculation about why a later Congress declined to adopt new legislation offers a "particularly dangerous" basis on which to rest an interpretation of an existing law a different and earlier Congress did adopt. *Pension Benefit Guaranty Corporation v. LTV Corp.*, 496 U.S. 633, 650 (1990); see also . . . *Sullivan v. Finkelstein*, 496 U.S. 617, 632 (1990) (Scalia, J., concurring) ("Arguments based on subsequent legislative history . . . should not be taken seriously, not even in a footnote").

That leaves the employers to seek a different sort of exception. Maybe the traditional and simple but-for causation test should apply in all other Title VII cases, but it just doesn't work when it comes to cases involving homosexual and transgender employees. . . . The employers illustrate their concern with an example. When we apply the simple test to Mr. Bostock—asking whether Mr. Bostock, a man attracted to other men, would have been fired had he been a woman—we don't just change his sex. Along the way, we change his sexual orientation too (from homosexual to heterosexual). If the aim is to isolate whether a plaintiff's sex caused the dismissal, the employers stress, we must hold sexual orientation constant—meaning we need to change both his sex and the sex to which he is attracted. So for Mr. Bostock, the question should be whether he would've been fired if he were a woman attracted to women. And because his employer would have been as quick to fire a lesbian as it was a gay man, the employers conclude, no Title VII violation has occurred.

While the explanation is new, the mistakes are the same. The employers might be onto something if Title VII only ensured equal treatment between groups of men and women or if the statute applied only when sex is the sole or primary reason for an employer's challenged adverse employment action. But both of these premises are mistaken. Title VII's plain terms and our precedents don't care if an employer treats men and women comparably as groups; an employer who fires both lesbians and gay men equally doesn't diminish but doubles its liability. Just cast a glance back to *Manhart*, where it was no defense that the employer sought to equalize pension contributions based on life expectancy. Nor does the statute care if other factors besides sex contribute to an employer's discharge decision. Mr. Bostock's employer might have decided to fire him only because of the confluence of two factors, his sex and the sex to which he is attracted. But exactly the same might have been said in *Phillips*, where motherhood was the added variable. . . .

. . . . Consider an employer eager to revive the workplace gender roles of the 1950s. He enforces a policy that he will hire only men as mechanics and only women as secretaries. When a qualified woman applies for a mechanic position and is denied, the "simple test" immediately spots the discrimination: A qualified man would have been given the job, so sex was a but-for cause of the employer's refusal to hire. But like the employers before us today, this employer would say not so fast. By comparing the woman who applied to be a mechanic to a man who applied to be a mechanic, we've quietly changed two things: the applicant's sex and her trait of failing to conform to 1950s gender roles. The "simple test" thus overlooks that it is really the applicant's bucking of 1950s gender roles, not her sex, doing the work. So we need to hold that second trait constant: Instead of comparing the disappointed female applicant to a man who applied for the same position, the employer would say, we should compare her to a man who applied to be a secretary. And because that jobseeker would be refused too, this must not be sex discrimination.

No one thinks *that*, so the employers must scramble to justify deploying a stricter causation test for use only in cases involving discrimination based on sexual orientation or transgender status. Such a rule would create a curious discontinuity in our case law, to put it mildly. Employer hires based on sexual stereotypes? Simple test. Employer sets pension contributions based on sex? Simple test. Employer fires men who do not behave in a sufficiently masculine way around the office? Simple test. But when that same employer discriminates against women who are attracted to women, or persons identified at birth as women who later identify as men, we suddenly roll out a new and more rigorous standard? Why are *these* reasons for taking sex into account different from all the rest? Title VII's text can offer no answer.

B

Ultimately, the employers are forced to abandon the statutory text and precedent altogether and appeal to assumptions and policy. Most pointedly, they contend that few in 1964 would have expected Title VII to apply to discrimination against homosexual and transgender persons. And whatever the text and our precedent indicate, they say, shouldn't this fact cause us to pause before recognizing liability?

It might be tempting to reject this argument out of hand. This Court has explained many times over many years that, when the meaning of the statute's terms is plain, our job is at an end. The people are entitled to rely on the law as written, without fearing that courts might disregard its plain terms based on some extratextual consideration. . . . Of course, some Members of this Court have consulted legislative history when interpreting *ambiguous* statutory language. Cf. *post* at 1775 (Alito, J., dissenting). But that has no bearing here. "Legislative history, for those who take it into account, is meant to clear up ambiguity, not create it." *Milner v. Department of Navy*, 562 U.S. 562, 574 (2011). And as we have seen, no ambiguity exists about how Title VII's terms apply to the facts before us. To be sure, the statute's application in these cases reaches "beyond the principal evil" legislators may have intended or expected to address. *Oncale*, 523 U.S. at 79. But " 'the fact that [a statute] has been applied in situations not expressly anticipated by Congress' " does not demonstrate ambiguity; instead, it simply " 'demonstrates [the] breadth' " of a legislative command. *Sedima, S.P.R.L.* v. *Imrex Co.*, 473 U.S. 479, 499 (1985). And "it is ultimately the provisions of" those legislative commands "rather than the principal concerns of our legislators by which we are governed." *Oncale*, 523 U.S. at 79; see also A. Scalia & B. Garner, Reading Law: The Interpretation of Legal Texts 101 (2012) (noting that unexpected applications of broad language reflect only Congress's "presumed point [to] produce general coverage—not to leave room for courts to recognize ad hoc exceptions").

Still, while legislative history can never defeat unambiguous statutory text, historical sources can be useful for a different purpose: Because the law's ordinary meaning at the time of enactment usually governs, we must be sensitive to the possibility a statutory term that means one thing today or in one context might have meant something else at the time of its adoption or might mean something different in another context. And we must be attuned to the possibility that a statutory phrase ordinarily bears a different meaning than the terms do when viewed individually or literally. To ferret out such shifts in linguistic usage or subtle distinctions between literal and ordinary meaning, this Court has sometimes consulted the understandings of the law's drafters as some (not always conclusive) evidence. . . .

The employers, however, advocate nothing like that here. They do not seek to use historical sources to illustrate that the meaning of any of Title VII's language has changed since 1964 or that the statute's terms, whether viewed individually or as a whole, ordinarily carried some message we have missed. To the contrary, as we have seen, the employers *agree* with our understanding of all the statutory language—"discriminate against any individual . . . because of such individual's . . . sex." Nor do the competing dissents offer an alternative account about what these terms mean either when viewed individually or in the aggregate. Rather than suggesting that the statutory language bears some other *meaning*, the employers and dissents merely suggest that, because few in 1964 expected today's *result*, we should not dare to admit that it follows ineluctably from the statutory text. When a new application emerges that is both unexpected and important, they would seemingly have us merely point out the question, refer the subject back to Congress, and decline to enforce the plain terms of the law in the meantime.

That is exactly the sort of reasoning this Court has long rejected. Admittedly, the employers take pains to couch their argument in terms of seeking to honor the statute's "expected applications" rather than vindicate its "legislative intent." But the concepts are closely related. One could easily contend that legislators only intended expected applications or that a statute's purpose is limited to achieving applications foreseen at the time of enactment. However framed, the employer's logic impermissibly seeks to displace the plain meaning of the law in favor of something lying beyond it.

If anything, the employers' new framing may only add new problems. The employers assert that "no one" in 1964 or for some time after would have anticipated today's result. But is that really true? Not long after the law's passage, gay and transgender employees began filing Title VII complaints, so at least *some* people foresaw this potential application. See, *e.g.*, *Smith v. Liberty Mut. Ins. Co.*, 395 F. Supp. 1098, 1099 (ND Ga. 1975) (addressing claim from 1969); *Holloway v. Arthur Andersen & Co.*, 566 F.2d 659, 661 (CA9 1977) (addressing claim from 1974). And less than a decade after Title VII's passage, during debates over the Equal Rights Amendment, others counseled that its language—which was strikingly similar to Title VII's—might also protect homosexuals from discrimination. See, *e.g.*, Note, The Legality of Homosexual Marriage, 82 Yale L.J. 573, 583–584 (1973).

Why isn't that enough to demonstrate that today's result isn't totally unexpected? How many people have to foresee the application for it to qualify as "expected"? Do we look only at the moment the statute was enacted, or do we allow some time for the implications of a new statute to be worked out? Should we consider the expectations of those who had no reason to give a particular application any thought or only those with reason to think about the question? How do we account for those who change their minds over time, after learning new facts or hearing a new argument? How specifically or generally should we frame the "application" at issue? None of these questions have obvious answers, and the employers don't propose any.

One could also reasonably fear that objections about unexpected applications will not be deployed neutrally. Often lurking just behind such objections resides a cynicism that Congress could not *possibly* have meant to protect a disfavored group. Take this Court's encounter with the Americans with Disabilities Act's directive that no " 'public entity' " can discriminate against any " 'qualified individual with a disability.' " *Pennsylvania Dept. of Corrections v. Yeskey*, 524 U.S. 206, 208 (1998). Congress, of course, didn't list every public entity the statute would apply to. And no one batted an eye at its application to, say, post offices. But when the statute was applied to *prisons*, . . . some demanded a closer look: Pennsylvania argued that "Congress did not 'envisio[n] that the ADA would be applied to state prisoners.' " *Id.* at 211–212. This Court emphatically rejected that view, explaining that, "in the context of an unambiguous statutory text," whether a specific application was anticipated by Congress "is irrelevant." *Id.* at 212. As *Yeskey* and today's cases exemplify, applying protective laws to groups that were politically unpopular at the time of the law's passage—whether prisoners in the 1990s or homosexual and transgender employees in the 1960s—often may be seen as unexpected. But to refuse enforcement just because of that, because the parties before us happened to be unpopular at the time of the law's passage, would not only require us to abandon our role as interpreters of statutes; it would tilt the scales of justice in favor of the strong or popular and neglect the promise that all persons are entitled to the benefit of the law's terms. . . .

The employer's position also proves too much. If we applied Title VII's plain text only to applications some (yet-to-be-determined) group expected in 1964, we'd have more than a little law to overturn. Start with *Oncale*. How many people in 1964 could have expected that the law would turn out to protect male employees? Let alone to protect them from harassment by other male employees? . . . .

That's just the beginning of the law we would have to unravel. . . . [M]any, maybe most, applications of Title VII's sex provision were "unanticipated" at the time of the law's adoption. In fact, many now-obvious applications met with heated opposition early on, even among those tasked with enforcing the law. In the years immediately following Title VII's passage, the EEOC officially opined that listing men's positions and women's positions separately in job postings was simply helpful rather than discriminatory. [Franklin, Inventing the "Traditional Concept" of Sex Discrimination, 125 Harv. L. Rev. 1307, 1340 (2012)] (citing Press Release, EEOC (Sept. 22, 1965)). Some courts held that Title VII did not prevent an employer from firing an employee for refusing his sexual advances. See, *e.g.*, *Barnes v. Train*, 1974 WL 10628, *1 (D DC,

Aug. 9, 1974). And courts held that a policy against hiring mothers but not fathers of young children wasn't discrimination because of sex. See *Phillips v. Martin Marietta Corp.*, 411 F.2d 1 (CA5 1969), rev'd, 400 U.S. 542 (1971) (*per curiam*).

Over time, though, the breadth of the statutory language proved too difficult to deny. By the end of the 1960s, the EEOC reversed its stance on sex-segregated job advertising. See Franklin, 125 Harv. L. Rev. at 1345. In 1971, this Court held that treating women with children differently from men with children violated Title VII. *Phillips*, 400 U.S. at 544. And by the late 1970s, courts began to recognize that sexual harassment can sometimes amount to sex discrimination. See, *e.g.*, *Barnes v. Costle*, 561 F.2d 983, 990 (CADC 1977). While to the modern eye each of these examples may seem "plainly [to] constitut[e] discrimination because of biological sex," *post* at 1774–1775 (Alito, J., dissenting), all were hotly contested for years following Title VII's enactment. And as with the discrimination we consider today, many federal judges long accepted interpretations of Title VII that excluded these situations. Cf. *post* at 1833–1834 (Kavanaugh, J., dissenting) (highlighting that certain lower courts have rejected Title VII claims based on homosexuality and transgender status). Would the employers have us undo every one of these unexpected applications too? . . .

. . . [T]he employers . . . fall back to the last line of defense for all failing statutory interpretation arguments: naked policy appeals. If we were to apply the statute's plain language, they complain, any number of undesirable policy consequences would follow. Cf. *post* at 1778–1784 (Alito, J., dissenting). Gone here is any pretense of statutory interpretation; all that's left is a suggestion we should proceed without the law's guidance to do as we think best. But that's an invitation no court should ever take up. The place to make new legislation, or address unwanted consequences of old legislation, lies in Congress. When it comes to statutory interpretation, our role is limited to applying the law's demands as faithfully as we can in the cases that come before us. As judges we possess no special expertise or authority to declare for ourselves what a self-governing people should consider just or wise. And the same judicial humility that requires us to refrain from adding to statutes requires us to refrain from diminishing them.

What are these consequences anyway? The employers worry that our decision will sweep beyond Title VII to other federal or state laws that prohibit sex discrimination. And, under Title VII itself, they say sex-segregated bathrooms, locker rooms, and dress codes will prove unsustainable after our decision today. But none of these other laws are before us; we have not had the benefit of adversarial testing about the meaning of their terms, and we do not prejudge any such question today. Under Title VII, too, we do not purport to address bathrooms, locker rooms, or anything else of the kind. The only question before us is whether an employer who fires someone simply for being homosexual or transgender has discharged or otherwise discriminated against that individual "because of such individual's sex." . . . Whether other policies and practices might or might not qualify as unlawful discrimination or find justifications under other provisions of Title VII are questions for future cases . . . .

■ *JUSTICE ALITO, with whom JUSTICE THOMAS joins, dissenting:*

There is only one word for what the Court has done today: legislation. . . .

Title VII of the Civil Rights Act of 1964 prohibits employment discrimination on any of five specified grounds: "race, color, religion, sex, [and] national origin." 42 U.S.C. § 2000e–2(a)(1). Neither "sexual orientation" nor "gender identity" appears on that list. For the past 45 years, bills have been introduced in Congress to add "sexual orientation" to the list, and in recent years, bills have included "gender identity" as well. But to date, none has passed both Houses.

Last year, the House of Representatives passed a bill that would amend Title VII by defining sex discrimination to include both "sexual orientation" and "gender identity," H.R. 5, 116th Cong., 1st Sess. (2019), but the bill has stalled in the Senate. An alternative bill, H.R. 5331, 116th Cong., 1st Sess. (2019), would add similar prohibitions but contains provisions to protect religious liberty. This bill remains before a House Subcommittee.

Because no such amendment of Title VII has been enacted in accordance with the requirements in the Constitution (passage in both Houses and presentment to the President, Art. I, § 7, cl. 2), Title VII's prohibition of discrimination because of "sex" still means what it has always meant. But the Court is not deterred by these constitutional niceties. Usurping the constitutional authority of the other branches, the Court has essentially taken H.R. 5's provision on employment discrimination and issued it under the guise of statutory interpretation. A more brazen abuse of our authority to interpret statutes is hard to recall.

The Court tries to convince readers that it is merely enforcing the terms of the statute, but that is preposterous. Even as understood today, the concept of discrimination because of "sex" is different from discrimination because of "sexual orientation" or "gender identity." And in any event, our duty is to interpret statutory terms to "mean what they conveyed to reasonable people *at the time they were written.*" A. Scalia & B. Garner, Reading Law: The Interpretation of Legal Texts 16 (2012) (emphasis added). If every single living American had been surveyed in 1964, it would have been hard to find any who thought that discrimination because of sex meant discrimination because of sexual orientation—not to mention gender identity, a concept that was essentially unknown at the time.

The Court attempts to pass off its decision as the inevitable product of the textualist school of statutory interpretation championed by our late colleague Justice Scalia, but no one should be fooled. The Court's opinion is like a pirate ship. It sails under a textualist flag, but what it actually represents is a theory of statutory interpretation that Justice Scalia excoriated—the theory that courts should "update" old statutes so that they better reflect the current values of society. See A. Scalia, A Matter of Interpretation 22 (1997). If the Court finds it appropriate to adopt this theory, it should own up to what it is doing.

Many will applaud today's decision because they agree on policy grounds with the Court's updating of Title VII. But the question in these cases is not whether discrimination because of sexual orientation or gender identity *should be* outlawed. The question is *whether Congress did that in 1964.*

It indisputably did not.

I

A

Title VII . . . prohibits discrimination "because of . . . sex," § 2000e–2(a)(1), and in 1964, it was as clear as clear could be that this meant discrimination because of the genetic and anatomical characteristics that men and women have at the time of birth. Determined searching has not found a single dictionary from that time that defined "sex" to mean sexual orientation, gender identity, or "transgender status." . . .

. . . . If "sex" in Title VII means biologically male or female, then discrimination because of sex means discrimination because the person in question is biologically male or biologically female, not because that person is sexually attracted to members of the same sex or identifies as a member of a particular gender. . . .

. . . . In cases like those before us, a plaintiff must show that sex was a "motivating factor" in the challenged employment action, 42 U.S.C. § 2000e–2(m), so the question we must decide comes down to this: if an individual employee or applicant for employment shows that his or her sexual orientation or gender identity was a "motivating factor" in a hiring or discharge decision, for example, is that enough to establish that the employer discriminated "because of . . . sex"? Or, to put the same question in different terms, if an employer takes an employment action solely because of the sexual orientation or gender identity of an employee or applicant, has that employer necessarily discriminated because of biological sex?

The answers to those questions must be no, unless discrimination because of sexual orientation or gender identity inherently constitutes discrimination because of sex. The Court attempts to prove that point, and it argues, not merely that the terms of Title VII *can* be interpreted that way but that they *cannot reasonably be interpreted any other way*. According to the Court, the text is unambiguous. . . .

The arrogance of this argument is breathtaking. As I will show, there is not a shred of evidence that any Member of Congress interpreted the statutory text that way when Title VII was enacted. See Part III-B, *infra*. But the Court apparently thinks that this was because the Members were not "smart enough to realize" what its language means. *Hively v. Ivy Tech Community College of Ind.*, 853 F.3d 339, 357 (CA7 2017) (Posner, J., concurring). The Court seemingly has the same opinion about our colleagues on the Courts of Appeals, because until 2017, every single Court of Appeals to consider the question interpreted Title VII's prohibition against sex discrimination to mean discrimination on the basis of biological sex. See Part III-C, *infra*. And for good measure, the Court's conclusion that Title VII unambiguously reaches discrimination on the basis of sexual orientation and gender identity necessarily means that the EEOC failed to see the obvious for the first 48 years after Title VII became law.[7] Day in and day out, the Commission enforced Title VII but did not grasp what discrimination "because of . . . sex" unambiguously means. . . .

The Court's argument is not only arrogant, it is wrong. . . .

Contrary to the Court's contention, discrimination because of sexual orientation or gender identity does not in and of itself entail discrimination because of sex. We can see this because it is quite possible for an employer to discriminate on those grounds without taking the sex of an individual applicant or employee into account. An employer can have a policy that says: "We do not hire gays, lesbians, or transgender individuals." And an employer can implement this policy without paying any attention to or even knowing the biological sex of gay, lesbian, and transgender applicants. In fact, at the time of the enactment of Title VII, the United States military had a blanket policy of refusing to enlist gays or lesbians, and under this policy for years thereafter, applicants for enlistment were required to complete a form that asked whether they were "homosexual." . . .

At oral argument, the attorney representing the employees, a prominent professor of constitutional law, was asked if there would be discrimination because of sex if an employer with a blanket policy against hiring gays, lesbians, and transgender individuals implemented that policy without knowing the biological sex of any job applicants. Her candid answer was that this would "not" be sex discrimination.[10] And she was right.

---

[7] The EEOC first held that "discrimination against a transgender individual because that person is transgender" violates Title VII in 2012 in *Macy* v. *Holder*, 2012 WL 1435995, *11 (Apr. 20, 2012), though it earlier advanced that position in an *amicus* brief in Federal District Court in 2011, *ibid.*, n. 16. It did not hold that discrimination on the basis of sexual orientation violated Title VII until 2015. See *Baldwin* v. *Foxx*, 2015 WL 4397641 (July 15, 2015).

[10] See Tr. of Oral Arg. in Nos. 17–1618, 17–1623, pp. 69–70 ("If there was that case, it might be the rare case in which sexual orientation discrimination is not a subset of sex"); see also *id.* at 69 ("Somebody who comes in and says I'm not going to tell you what my sex is, but, believe me, I was fired for my sexual orientation, that person will lose").

. . . [I]f an employer discriminates against individual applicants or employees without even knowing whether they are male or female, it is impossible to argue that the employer intentionally discriminated because of sex. . . . And if an employer does not violate Title VII by discriminating on the basis of sexual orientation or gender identity without knowing the sex of the affected individuals, there is no reason why the same employer could not lawfully implement the same policy even if it knows the sex of these individuals. If an employer takes an adverse employment action for a perfectly legitimate reason—for example, because an employee stole company property—that action is not converted into sex discrimination simply because the employer knows the employee's sex. . . . [T]his example shows . . . that discrimination because of sexual orientation or gender identity does not inherently or necessarily entail discrimination because of sex, and for that reason, the Court's chief argument collapses. . . .

. . . . [A]nother hypothetical case offered by the Court is telling. But what it proves is not what the Court thinks. The Court posits:

> "Imagine an employer who has a policy of firing any employee known to be homosexual. The employer hosts an office holiday party and invites employees to bring their spouses. A model employee arrives and introduces a manager to Susan, the employee's wife. Will that employee be fired? If the policy works as the employer intends, the answer depends entirely on whether the model employee is a man or a woman." *Ante* at 1742.

This example disproves the Court's argument because it is perfectly clear that the employer's motivation in firing the female employee had nothing to do with that employee's sex. The employer presumably knew that this employee was a woman before she was invited to the fateful party. Yet the employer, far from holding her biological sex against her, rated her a "model employee." At the party, the employer learned something new, her sexual orientation, and it was this new information that motivated her discharge. So this is another example showing that discrimination because of sexual orientation does not inherently involve discrimination because of sex. . . .

The Court's remaining argument is based on [another] hypothetical that the Court finds instructive. In this hypothetical, an employer has two employees who are "attracted to men," and "*to the employer's mind*" the two employees are "materially identical" except that one is a man and the other is a woman. *Ante* at 1741 (emphasis added). The Court reasons that if the employer fires the man but not the woman, the employer is necessarily motivated by the man's biological sex. . . .

The problem with this argument is that . . . in the mind of an employer who does not want to employ individuals who are attracted to members of the same sex, these two employees are not materially identical in every respect but sex. On the contrary, they differ in another way that the employer thinks is quite material. And until Title VII is amended to add sexual orientation as a prohibited ground, this is a view that an employer is permitted to implement. . . . [O]ther than prohibiting discrimination on any of five specified grounds, "race, color, religion, sex, [and] national origin," 42 U.S.C. § 2000e–2(a)(1), Title VII allows employers to decide whether two employees are "materially identical." Even idiosyncratic criteria are permitted; if an employer thinks that Scorpios make bad employees, the employer can refuse to hire Scorpios. Such a policy would be unfair and foolish, but under Title VII, it is permitted. And until Title VII is amended, so is a policy against employing gays, lesbians, or transgender individuals.

. . . [W]hat we have in the Court's hypothetical case are two employees who differ in *two* ways—sex and sexual orientation—and if the employer fires one and keeps the other, all that can be inferred is that the employer was motivated either entirely by sexual orientation, entirely by sex, or in part by both. We cannot infer with any certainty, as the hypothetical is apparently meant to suggest, that the employer was motivated even in part by sex. . . .

In an effort to prove its point, the Court carefully includes in its example just two employees, a homosexual man and a heterosexual woman, but suppose we add two more individuals, a woman who is attracted to women and a man who is attracted to women. . . . We now have the four exemplars listed below, with the discharged employees crossed out:

~~Man attracted to men~~

Woman attracted to men

~~Woman attracted to women~~

Man attracted to women

The discharged employees have one thing in common. It is not biological sex, attraction to men, or attraction to women. It is attraction to members of their own sex—in a word, sexual orientation. And that, we can infer, is the employer's real motive. . . .

B

Although the Court relies solely on the arguments discussed above, several other arguments figure prominently in the decisions of the lower courts and in briefs submitted by or in support of the employees. The Court apparently finds these arguments unpersuasive, and so do I, but for the sake of completeness, I will address them briefly.

1

One argument, which relies on our decision in *Price Waterhouse v. Hopkins*, 490 U.S. 228 (1989) (plurality opinion), is that discrimination because of sexual orientation or gender identity violates Title VII because it constitutes prohibited discrimination on the basis of sex stereotypes. . . . The argument goes like this. Title VII prohibits discrimination based on stereotypes about the way men and women should behave; the belief that a person should be attracted only to persons of the opposite sex and the belief that a person should identify with his or her biological sex are examples of such stereotypes; therefore, discrimination on either of these grounds is unlawful.

This argument fails because it is based on a faulty premise, namely, that Title VII forbids discrimination based on sex stereotypes. It does not. It prohibits discrimination because of "sex," and the two concepts are not the same. See *Price Waterhouse*, 490 U.S. at 251. That does not mean, however, that an employee or applicant for employment cannot prevail by showing that a challenged decision was based on a sex stereotype. Such evidence is relevant to prove discrimination because of sex, and it may be convincing where the trait that is inconsistent with the stereotype is one that would be tolerated and perhaps even valued in a person of the opposite sex.

Much of the plaintiff's evidence in *Price Waterhouse* was of this nature. The plaintiff was a woman who was passed over for partnership at an accounting firm, and some of the adverse comments about her work appeared to criticize her for being forceful and insufficiently "feminin[e]." *Id.* at 235–236.

The main issue in *Price Waterhouse*—the proper allocation of the burdens of proof in a so-called mixed motives Title VII case—is not relevant here, but the plurality opinion, endorsed by four Justices, commented on the issue of sex stereotypes. The plurality observed that "sex stereotypes do not inevitably prove that gender played a part in a particular employment decision" but "can certainly be *evidence* that gender played a part." *Id.* at 251. And the plurality made it clear that "[t]he plaintiff must show that the employer actually relied on her gender in making its decision." *Ibid.*

Plaintiffs who allege that they were treated unfavorably because of their sexual orientation or gender identity are not in the same position as the plaintiff in *Price Waterhouse*. In cases involving discrimination based on sexual orientation or gender identity, the grounds for the employer's decision—that individuals should be sexually attracted only to persons of the opposite biological sex or should identify with their biological sex—apply equally to men and women. "[H]eterosexuality is not a *female* stereotype; it not a *male* stereotype; it is not a *sex-specific* stereotype at all." *Hively*, 853 F.3d at 370 (Sykes, J., dissenting).

To be sure, there may be cases in which a gay, lesbian, or transgender individual can make a claim like the one in *Price Waterhouse*. That is, there may be cases where traits or behaviors that some people associate with gays, lesbians, or transgender individuals are tolerated or valued in persons of one biological sex but not the other. But that is a different matter.

2

A second prominent argument made in support of the result that the Court now reaches analogizes discrimination against gays and lesbians to discrimination against a person who is married to or has an intimate relationship with a person of a different race. Several lower court cases have held that discrimination on this ground violates Title VII. See, *e.g.*, *Holcomb v. Iona College*, 521 F.3d 130 (CA2 2008); *Parr v. Woodmen of World Life Ins. Co.*, 791 F.2d 888 (CA11 1986). And the logic of these decisions, it is argued, applies equally where an employee or applicant is treated unfavorably because he or she is married to, or has an intimate relationship with, a person of the same sex.

This argument totally ignores the historically rooted reason why discrimination on the basis of an interracial relationship constitutes race discrimination. And without taking history into account, it is not easy to see how the decisions in question fit the terms of Title VII.

Recall that Title VII makes it unlawful for an employer to discriminate against an individual "because of *such individual's race.*" 42 U.S.C. § 2000e–2(a) (emphasis added). So if an employer is happy to employ whites and blacks but will not employ any employee in an interracial relationship, how can it be said that the employer is discriminating against either whites or blacks "because of such individual's race"? This employer would be applying the same rule to all its employees regardless of their race.

The answer is that this employer is discriminating on a ground that history tells us is a core form of race discrimination. "It would require absolute blindness to the history of racial discrimination in this country not to understand what is at stake in such cases . . . . A prohibition on 'race-mixing' was . . . grounded in bigotry against a particular race and was an integral part of preserving the rigid hierarchical distinction that denominated members of the black race as inferior to whites." 883 F.3d at 158–159 (Lynch, J., dissenting).

Discrimination because of sexual orientation is different. It cannot be regarded as a form of sex discrimination on the ground that applies in race cases since discrimination because of sexual orientation is not historically tied to a project that aims to subjugate either men or women. An employer who discriminates on this ground might be called "homophobic" or "transphobic," but not sexist. . . .

II

A

So far, I have not looked beyond dictionary definitions of "sex," but textualists like Justice Scalia do not confine their inquiry to the scrutiny of dictionaries. See Manning, Textualism and the Equity of the Statute, 101 Colum. L. Rev. 1, 109 (2001). Dictionary definitions are valuable because they are evidence of what people at the time of a statute's enactment would have understood its words to mean. *Ibid.* But they are not the only source of relevant evidence, and what matters in the end is the answer to the question that the evidence is gathered to resolve: How would the terms of a statute have been understood by ordinary people at the time of enactment?

Justice Scalia was perfectly clear on this point. The words of a law, he insisted, "mean *what they conveyed to reasonable people at the time.*" Reading Law, at 16 (emphasis added).[20]

Leading proponents of Justice Scalia's school of textualism have expounded on this principle and explained that it is grounded on an understanding of the way language works. As Dean John F. Manning explains, "the meaning of language depends on the way a linguistic community uses words and phrases in context." What Divides Textualists From Purposivists?, 106 Colum. L. Rev. 70, 78 (2006). "[O]ne can make sense of others' communications only by placing them in their appropriate social and linguistic context," *id.* at 79–80, and this is no less true of statutes than any other verbal communications. "[S]tatutes convey meaning only because members of a relevant linguistic community apply shared background conventions for understanding how particular words are used in particular contexts." Manning, The Absurdity Doctrine, 116 Harv. L. Rev. 2387, 2457 (2003). Therefore, judges should ascribe to the words of a statute "what a reasonable person conversant with applicable social conventions would have understood them to be adopting." Manning, 106 Colum. L. Rev. at 77. Or, to put the point in slightly different terms, a judge interpreting a statute should ask " 'what one would ordinarily be understood as saying, given the circumstances in which one said it.' " Manning, 116 Harv. L. Rev. at 2397–2398.

Judge Frank Easterbrook has made the same points:

> "Words are arbitrary signs, having meaning only to the extent writers and readers share an understanding. . . . Language in general, and legislation in particular, is a social enterprise to which both speakers and listeners contribute, drawing on background understandings and the structure and circumstances of the utterance." *Herrmann v. Cencom Cable Assocs., Inc.*, 978 F.2d 978, 982 (CA7 1992).

Consequently, "[s]licing a statute into phrases while ignoring . . . the setting of the enactment . . . is a formula for disaster." *Ibid.*; see also *Continental Can Co. v. Chicago Truck Drivers, Helpers and Warehouse Workers Union (Independent) Pension Fund*, 916 F.2d 1154, 1157 (CA7 1990) ("You don't have to be Ludwig Wittgenstein or Hans-Georg Gadamer to know that successful communication depends on meanings shared by interpretive communities").

---

[20] See also *Chisom v. Roemer*, 501 U.S. 380, 405 (1991) (Scalia, J., dissenting) ("We are to read the words of [a statutory] text as any ordinary Member of Congress would have read them . . . and apply the meaning so determined").

Thus, when textualism is properly understood, it calls for an examination of the social context in which a statute was enacted because this may have an important bearing on what its words were understood to mean at the time of enactment. Textualists do not read statutes as if they were messages picked up by a powerful radio telescope from a distant and utterly unknown civilization. Statutes consist of communications between members of a particular linguistic community, one that existed in a particular place and at a particular time, and these communications must therefore be interpreted as they were understood by that community at that time.

For this reason, it is imperative to consider how Americans in 1964 would have understood Title VII's prohibition of discrimination because of sex. . . .

B

The answer could not be clearer. In 1964, ordinary Americans reading the text of Title VII would not have dreamed that discrimination because of sex meant discrimination because of sexual orientation, much less gender identity. . . .

1

In 1964, the concept of prohibiting discrimination "because of sex" was no novelty. It was a familiar and well-understood concept, and what it meant was equal treatment for men and women.

Long before Title VII was adopted, many pioneering state and federal laws had used language substantively indistinguishable from Title VII's critical phrase, "discrimination because of sex." For example, the California Constitution of 1879 stipulated that no one, "*on account of sex*, [could] be disqualified from entering upon or pursuing any lawful business, vocation, or profession." Art. XX, § 18 (emphasis added). It also prohibited a student's exclusion from any state university department "on account of sex." Art. IX, § 9; accord, Mont. Const., Art. XI, § 9 (1889). . . .

The most prominent example of a provision using this language was the Nineteenth Amendment, ratified in 1920, which bans the denial or abridgment of the right to vote "on account of sex." U.S. Const., Amdt. 19. Similar language appeared in the proposal of the National Woman's Party for an Equal Rights Amendment. As framed in 1921, this proposal forbade all "political, civil or legal disabilities or inequalities *on account of sex*, [o]r on account of marriage." Women Lawyers Meet: Representatives of 20 States Endorse Proposed Equal Rights Amendment, N. Y. Times, Sept. 16, 1921, p. 10. . . .

In 1952, the new Constitution for Puerto Rico, which was approved by Congress, 66 Stat. 327, prohibited all "discrimination . . . *on account of . . . sex*," Art. II, Bill of Rights § 1 (emphasis added), and in the landmark Immigration and Nationality Act of 1952, Congress outlawed discrimination in naturalization "*because of* . . . *sex*." 8 U.S.C. § 1422 (emphasis added). . . .

In 1961, President Kennedy ordered the Civil Service Commission to review and modify personnel policies "to assure that selection for any career position is hereinafter made solely on the basis of individual merit and fitness, *without regard to sex*." He concurrently established a "Commission on the Status of Women" and directed it to recommend policies "for overcoming discriminations in government and private employment *on the basis of sex*." Exec. Order No. 10980, 3 CFR 138 (1961 Supp.) (emphasis added).

In short, the concept of discrimination "because of," "on account of," or "on the basis of" sex was well understood. It was part of the campaign for equality that had been waged by women's rights advocates for more than a century, and what it meant was equal treatment for men and women.[22]

2

Discrimination "because of sex" was not understood as having anything to do with discrimination because of sexual orientation or transgender status. Any such notion would have clashed in spectacular fashion with the societal norms of the day.

For most 21st-century Americans, it is painful to be reminded of the way our society once treated gays and lesbians, but any honest effort to understand what the terms of Title VII were understood to mean when enacted must take into account the societal norms of that time. And the plain truth is that in 1964 homosexuality was thought to be a mental disorder, and homosexual conduct was regarded as morally culpable and worthy of punishment.

In its then-most recent Diagnostic and Statistical Manual of Mental Disorders (1952) (DSM-I), the American Psychiatric Association (APA) classified same-sex attraction as a "sexual deviation," a particular type of "sociopathic personality disturbance," *id.* at 38–39, and the next edition, issued in 1968, similarly classified homosexuality as a "sexual deviatio[n]," Diagnostic and Statistical Manual of Mental Disorders 44 (2d ed.) (DSM-II). It was not until the sixth printing of the DSM-II in 1973 that this was changed.

---

[22] Analysis of the way Title VII's key language was used in books and articles during the relevant time period supports this conclusion. A study searched a vast database of documents from that time to determine how the phrase "discriminate against . . . because of [some trait]" was used. Phillips, The Overlooked Evidence in the Title VII Cases: The Linguistic (and Therefore Textualist) Principle of Compositionality (manuscript at 3) (May 11, 2020) (brackets in original) . . . . The study found that the phrase was used to denote discrimination against "someone . . . motivated by prejudice, or biased ideas or attitudes . . . directed at people with that trait in particular." *Id.* at 7 (emphasis deleted). In other words, "*discriminate against*" was "associated with negative treatment directed at members of a discrete group." *Id.* at 5. Thus, as used in 1964, "discrimination because of sex" would have been understood to mean discrimination against a woman or a man based on "unfair beliefs or attitudes" about members of that particular sex. *Id.* at 7.

Society's treatment of homosexuality and homosexual conduct was consistent with this understanding. Sodomy was a crime in every State but Illinois, see W. Eskridge, Dishonorable Passions 387–407 (2008), and in the District of Columbia, a law enacted by Congress made sodomy a felony punishable by imprisonment for up to 10 years and permitted the indefinite civil commitment of "sexual psychopath[s]," Act of June 9, 1948, §§ 104, 201–207, 62 Stat. 347–349.

This view of homosexuality was reflected in the rules governing the federal work force. In 1964, federal "[a]gencies could deny homosexual men and women employment because of their sexual orientation," and this practice continued until 1975. GAO, D. Heivilin, Security Clearances: Consideration of Sexual Orientation in the Clearance Process 2 (GAO/NSIAD–95–21, 1995). See, *e.g.*, *Anonymous v. Macy*, 398 F.2d 317, 318 (CA5 1968) (affirming dismissal of postal employee for homosexual acts).

Is the argument here we should continue doing the wrong thing?

In 1964, individuals who were known to be homosexual could not obtain security clearances, and any who possessed clearances were likely to lose them if their orientation was discovered. . . . "Until about 1991, when agencies began to change their security policies and practices regarding sexual orientation, there were a number of documented cases where defense civilian or contractor employees' security clearances were denied or revoked because of their sexual orientation." GAO, Security Clearances, at 2. . . .

The picture in state employment was similar. In 1964, it was common for States to bar homosexuals from serving as teachers. An article summarizing the situation *15 years after Title VII became law* reported that "[a]ll states have statutes that permit the revocation of teaching certificates (or credentials) for immorality, moral turpitude, or unprofessionalism," and, the survey added, "[h]omosexuality is considered to fall within all three categories." [Rivera, Our Straight-Laced Judges: The Legal Position of Homosexual Persons in the United States, 30 Hastings L.J. 799, 861 (1979).] . . . .

In 1964 and for many years thereafter, homosexuals were barred from the military. See, *e.g.*, Army Reg. 635–89, § I(2) (a) (July 15, 1966) ("Personnel who voluntarily engage in homosexual acts, irrespective of sex, will not be permitted to serve in the Army in any capacity, and their prompt separation is mandatory"); Army Reg. 600–443, § I(2) (April 10, 1953) (similar). Prohibitions against homosexual conduct by members of the military were not eliminated until 2010. See Don't Ask, Don't Tell Repeal Act of 2010, 124 Stat. 3515 (repealing 10 U.S.C. § 654, which required members of the Armed Forces to be separated for engaging in homosexual conduct).

Homosexuals were also excluded from entry into the United States. The Immigration and Nationality Act of 1952 (INA) excluded aliens "afflicted with psychopathic personality." 8 U.S.C. § 1182(a)(4) (1964 ed.). In *Boutilier v. INS*, 387 U.S. 118, 120–123 (1967), this Court, relying on the INA's legislative history, interpreted that term to encompass homosexuals and upheld an alien's deportation on that ground. Three Justices disagreed with the majority's interpretation of the phrase "psychopathic personality." But it apparently did not occur to anyone to argue that the Court's interpretation was inconsistent with the INA's express prohibition of discrimination "because of sex." That was how our society—and this Court—saw things a half century ago. Discrimination because of sex and discrimination because of sexual orientation were viewed as two entirely different concepts.

To its credit, our society has now come to recognize the injustice of past practices, and this recognition provides the impetus to "update" Title VII. But that is not our job. Our duty is to understand what the terms of Title VII were understood to mean when enacted, and in doing so, we must take into account the societal norms of that time. We must therefore ask whether ordinary Americans in 1964 would have thought that discrimination because of "sex" carried some exotic meaning under which private-sector employers would be prohibited from engaging in a practice that represented the official policy of the Federal Government with respect to its own employees. We must ask whether Americans at that time would have thought that Title VII banned discrimination against an employee for engaging in conduct that Congress had made a felony and a ground for civil commitment.

The questions answer themselves. Even if discrimination based on sexual orientation or gender identity could be squeezed into some arcane understanding of sex discrimination, the context in which Title VII was enacted would tell us that this is not what the statute's terms were understood to mean at that time. . . .

C

While Americans in 1964 would have been shocked to learn that Congress had enacted a law prohibiting sexual orientation discrimination, they would have been bewildered to hear that this law also forbids discrimination on the basis of "transgender status" or "gender identity," terms that would have left people at the time scratching their heads. The term "transgender" is said to have been coined " 'in the early 1970s,' " and the term "gender identity" . . . apparently first appeared in an academic article in 1964. . . .

While it is likely true that there have always been individuals who experience what is now termed "gender dysphoria," *i.e.*, "[d]iscomfort or distress related to an incongruence between an individual's gender identity and the gender assigned at birth," the current understanding of the concept postdates the enactment of Title VII. Nothing resembling what is now called gender dysphoria appeared in either DSM-I (1952) or DSM-II (1968). . . .

It defies belief to suggest that the public meaning of discrimination because of sex in 1964 encompassed discrimination on the basis of a concept that was essentially unknown to the public at that time.

D

1

The Court's main excuse for entirely ignoring the social context in which Title VII was enacted is that the meaning of Title VII's prohibition of discrimination because of sex is clear . . . . According to the Court, an argument that looks to the societal norms of those times represents an impermissible attempt to displace the statutory language.

The Court's argument rests on a false premise. As already explained at length, the text of Title VII does not prohibit discrimination because of sexual orientation or gender identity. And what the public thought about those issues in 1964 is relevant and important, not because it provides a ground for departing from the statutory text, but because it helps to explain what the text was understood to mean when adopted.

In arguing that we must put out of our minds what we know about the time when Title VII was enacted, the Court relies on Justice Scalia's opinion for the Court in *Oncale v. Sundowner Offshore Services, Inc.*, 523 U.S. 75 (1998). But *Oncale* is nothing like these cases, and no one should be taken in by the majority's effort to enlist Justice Scalia in its updating project.

The Court's unanimous decision in *Oncale* was thoroughly unremarkable. The Court held that a male employee who alleged that he had been sexually harassed at work by other men stated a claim under Title VII. Although the impetus for Title VII's prohibition of sex discrimination was to protect women, anybody reading its terms would immediately appreciate that it applies equally to both sexes, and by the time *Oncale* reached the Court, our precedent already established that sexual harassment may constitute sex discrimination within the meaning of Title VII. See *Meritor Savings Bank, FSB v. Vinson*, 477 U.S. 57 (1986). Given these premises, syllogistic reasoning dictated the holding. . . .

. . . . To decide for the defendants in *Oncale,* it would have been necessary to carve out an exception to the statutory text. Here, no such surgery is at issue. Even if we totally disregard the societal norms of 1964, the text of Title VII does not support the Court's holding. And the reasoning of *Oncale* does not preclude or counsel against our taking those norms into account. They are relevant, not for the purpose of creating an exception to the terms of the statute, but for the purpose of better appreciating how those terms would have been understood at the time.

2

The Court argues that two other decisions—*Phillips v. Martin Marietta Corp.*, 400 U.S. 542 (1971) (*per curiam*), and *Los Angeles Dept.*

of Water and Power v. Manhart, 435 U.S. 702 (1978)—buttress its decision, but those cases merely held that Title VII prohibits employer conduct that plainly constitutes discrimination because of biological sex. In *Philips*, the employer treated women with young children less favorably than men with young children. In *Manhart*, the employer required women to make larger pension contributions than men. . . .

. . . . There is no dispute that discrimination against an individual employee based on that person's sex cannot be justified on the ground that the employer's treatment of the average employee of that sex is at least as favorable as its treatment of the average employee of the opposite sex. Nor does it matter if an employer discriminates against only a subset of men or women, where the same subset of the opposite sex is treated differently, as in *Phillips*. That is not the issue here. An employer who discriminates equally on the basis of sexual orientation or gender identity applies the same criterion to every affected *individual* regardless of sex. See Part I-A, *supra*.

III

A

Because the opinion of the Court flies a textualist flag, I have taken pains to show that it cannot be defended on textualist grounds. But even if the Court's textualist argument were stronger, that would not explain today's decision. Many Justices of this Court, both past and present, have not espoused or practiced a method of statutory interpretation that is limited to the analysis of statutory text. Instead, when there is ambiguity in the terms of a statute, they have found it appropriate to look to other evidence of "congressional intent," including legislative history.

So, why in these cases are congressional intent and the legislative history of Title VII totally ignored? Any assessment of congressional intent or legislative history seriously undermines the Court's interpretation.

B

Are you really making this argument?

. . . [T]he legislative history of Title VII's prohibition of sex discrimination is brief, but it is nevertheless revealing. The prohibition of sex discrimination was "added to Title VII at the last minute on the floor of the House of Representatives," *Meritor Savings Bank*, 477 U.S. at 63, by Representative Howard Smith, the Chairman of the Rules Committee. See 110 Cong. Rec. 2577 (1964). Representative Smith had been an ardent opponent of the civil rights bill, and it has been suggested that he added the prohibition against discrimination on the basis of "sex" as a poison pill. . . . On this theory, Representative Smith thought that prohibiting employment discrimination against women would be unacceptable to Members who might have otherwise voted in favor of the bill and that the addition of this prohibition might bring about the bill's defeat. But if Representative Smith had been looking for a poison pill, prohibiting discrimination on the basis of sexual orientation or gender identity would have been far more potent. However, neither Representative Smith nor any other Member said one word about the possibility that the prohibition of sex discrimination might have that meaning. Instead, all the debate concerned discrimination on the basis of biological sex. See 110 Cong. Rec. 2577–2584.

Representative Smith's motivations are contested, 883 F.3d at 139–140 (Lynch, J., dissenting), but whatever they were, the meaning of *the adoption of the prohibition* of sex discrimination is clear. It was no accident. It grew out of "a long history of women's rights advocacy that had increasingly been gaining mainstream recognition and acceptance," and it marked a landmark achievement in the path toward fully equal rights for women. *Id.* at 140. "Discrimination against gay women and men, by contrast, was not on the table for public debate . . . [i]n those dark, pre-Stonewall days." *Ibid.*

For those who regard congressional intent as the touchstone of statutory interpretation, the message of Title VII's legislative history cannot be missed.

C

Post-enactment events only clarify what was apparent when Title VII was enacted. As noted, bills to add "sexual orientation" to Title VII's list of prohibited grounds were introduced in every Congress beginning in 1975, and two such bills were before Congress in 1991 when it made major changes in Title VII. At that time, the three Courts of Appeals to reach the issue had held that Title VII does not prohibit discrimination because of sexual orientation, two other Circuits had endorsed that interpretation in dicta, and no Court of Appeals had held otherwise. Similarly, the three Circuits to address the application of Title VII to transgender persons had all rejected the argument that it covered discrimination on this basis. These were also the positions of the EEOC. In enacting substantial changes to Title VII, the 1991 Congress abrogated numerous judicial decisions with which it disagreed. If it also disagreed with the decisions regarding sexual orientation and transgender discrimination, it could have easily overruled those as well, but it did not do so.

After 1991, six other Courts of Appeals reached the issue of sexual orientation discrimination, and until 2017, every single Court of Appeals decision understood Title VII's prohibition of "discrimination because of sex" to mean discrimination because of biological sex. . . .

The Court observes that "[t]he people are entitled to rely on the law as written, without fearing that courts might disregard its plain terms," *ante* at 1749, but it has no qualms about disregarding over 50 years of uniform judicial interpretation of Title VII's plain text. . . .

IV

What the Court has done today—interpreting discrimination because of "sex" to encompass discrimination because of sexual orientation or gender identity—is virtually certain to have far-reaching consequences. Over 100 federal statutes prohibit discrimination because of sex. See[,] . . . *e.g.*, 20 U.S.C. § 1681(a) (Title IX); 42 U.S.C. § 3631 (Fair Housing Act); 15 U.S.C. 1691(a)(1) (Equal Credit Opportunity Act). The briefs in these cases have called to our attention the potential effects that the Court's reasoning may have under some of these laws, but the Court waves those considerations aside. As to Title VII itself, the Court dismisses questions about "bathrooms, locker rooms, or anything else of the kind." *Ante* at 1753. And it declines to say anything about other statutes whose terms mirror Title VII's.

The Court's brusque refusal to consider the consequences of its reasoning is irresponsible. If the Court had allowed the legislative process to take its course, Congress would have had the opportunity to consider competing interests and might have found a way of accommodating at least some of them. In addition, Congress might have crafted special rules for some of the relevant statutes. But by intervening and proclaiming categorically that employment discrimination based on sexual orientation or gender identity is simply a form of discrimination because of sex, the Court has greatly impeded—and perhaps effectively ended—any chance of a bargained legislative resolution. Before issuing today's radical decision, the Court should have given some thought to where its decision would lead.

As the briefing in these cases has warned, the position that the Court now adopts will threaten freedom of religion, freedom of speech, and personal privacy and safety. No one should think that the Court's decision represents an unalloyed victory for individual liberty.

I will briefly note some of the potential consequences of the Court's decision, but I do not claim to provide a comprehensive survey or to suggest how any of these issues should necessarily play out under the Court's reasoning.[43]

[Discussion omitted.] . . . .

* * *

The updating desire to which the Court succumbs no doubt arises from humane and generous impulses. Today, many Americans know individuals who are gay, lesbian, or transgender and want them to be treated with the dignity, consideration, and fairness that everyone deserves. But the authority of this Court is limited to saying what the law *is*. . . .

---

[43] Contrary to the implication in the Court's opinion, I do not label these potential consequences "undesirable." I mention them only as possible implications of the Court's reasoning.

■ *JUSTICE KAVANAUGH, dissenting:*

. . . .

I

. . . . [T]he first 10 U.S. Courts of Appeals to consider whether Title VII prohibits sexual orientation discrimination all said no. Some 30 federal judges considered the question. All 30 judges said no, based on the text of the statute. 30 out of 30.

But in the last few years, a new theory has emerged. To end-run the bedrock separation-of-powers principle that courts may not unilaterally rewrite statutes, the plaintiffs here (and, recently, two Courts of Appeals) have advanced a novel and creative argument. They contend that discrimination "because of sexual orientation" and discrimination "because of sex" are actually not separate categories of discrimination after all. Instead, the theory goes, discrimination because of sexual orientation always qualifies as discrimination because of sex: When a gay man is fired because he is gay, he is fired because he is attracted to men, even though a similarly situated woman would not be fired just because she is attracted to men. According to this theory, it follows that the man has been fired, at least as a literal matter, because of his sex.

Yes

Under this literalist approach, sexual orientation discrimination automatically qualifies as sex discrimination, and Title VII's prohibition against sex discrimination therefore also prohibits sexual orientation discrimination—and actually has done so since 1964, unbeknownst to everyone. Surprisingly, the Court today buys into this approach.

For the sake of argument, I will assume that firing someone because of their sexual orientation may, as a very literal matter, entail making a distinction based on sex. But to prevail in this case with their literalist approach, the plaintiffs must *also* establish one of two other points. The plaintiffs must establish that courts, when interpreting a statute, adhere to literal meaning rather than ordinary meaning. Or alternatively, the plaintiffs must establish that the ordinary meaning of "discriminate because of sex"—not just the literal meaning—encompasses sexual orientation discrimination. The plaintiffs fall short on both counts.

First, courts must follow ordinary meaning, not literal meaning. And courts must adhere to the ordinary meaning of phrases, not just the meaning of the words in a phrase.

There is no serious debate about the foundational interpretive principle that courts adhere to ordinary meaning, not literal meaning, when interpreting statutes. As Justice Scalia explained, "the good textualist is not a literalist." A. Scalia, A Matter of Interpretation 24 (1997). . . . Or as Professor Manning put it, proper statutory interpretation asks "how a reasonable person, conversant with the relevant social and linguistic conventions, would read the text in context. This approach recognizes that the literal or dictionary definitions of words will often fail to account for settled nuances or background conventions that qualify the literal meaning of language and, in particular, of legal language." Manning, The Absurdity Doctrine, 116 Harv. L. Rev. 2387, 2392–2393 (2003). . . . The ordinary meaning that counts is the ordinary public meaning at the time of enactment—although in this case, that temporal principle matters little because the ordinary meaning of "discriminate because of sex" was the same in 1964 as it is now.

Judges adhere to ordinary meaning for two main reasons: rule of law and democratic accountability. A society governed by the rule of law must have laws that are known and understandable to the citizenry. And judicial adherence to ordinary meaning facilitates the democratic accountability of America's elected representatives for the laws they enact. Citizens and legislators must be able to ascertain the law by reading the words of the statute. Both the rule of law and democratic accountability badly suffer when a court adopts a hidden or obscure interpretation of the law, and not its ordinary meaning. . . .

. . . . The difference between literal and ordinary meaning becomes especially important when—as in this case—judges consider *phrases* in statutes. (Recall that the shorthand version of the phrase at issue here is "discriminate because of sex.")[3] Courts must heed the ordinary meaning of the *phrase as a whole*, not just the meaning of the words in the phrase. That is because a phrase may have a more precise or confined meaning than the literal meaning of the individual words in the phrase. . . .

This Court has often emphasized the importance of sticking to the ordinary meaning *of a phrase*, rather than the meaning of words in the phrase. In *FCC v. AT&T Inc.*, 562 U.S. 397 (2011), for example, the Court explained:

> "AT&T's argument treats the term 'personal privacy' as simply the sum of its two words: the privacy of a person. . . . But two words together may assume a more particular meaning than those words in isolation. We understand a golden cup to be a cup made of or resembling gold. A golden boy, on the other hand, is one who is charming, lucky, and talented. A golden opportunity is one not to be missed. 'Personal' in the phrase 'personal privacy' conveys more than just 'of a person.' It suggests a type of privacy evocative of human concerns—not the sort usually associated with an entity like, say, AT&T." *Id.* at 406. . . .
>
> . . . .[4] . . . .

---

[3] The full phrasing of the statute is provided above [in a footnote that this excerpt omits]. This opinion uses "discriminate because of sex" as shorthand for "discriminate . . . because of . . . sex." Also, the plaintiffs do not dispute that the ordinary meaning of the statutory phrase "discriminate" because of sex is the same as the statutory phrase "to fail or refuse to hire or to discharge any individual" because of sex.

[4] Another longstanding canon of statutory interpretation—the absurdity canon—similarly reflects the law's focus on ordinary meaning rather than literal meaning. That canon tells courts to avoid construing a statute in a way that would lead to absurd consequences. The absurdity canon, properly understood, is "an implementation of (rather than . . . an exception

Second, in light of the bedrock principle that we must adhere to the ordinary meaning of a phrase, the question in this case boils down to the ordinary meaning of the phrase "discriminate because of sex." Does the ordinary meaning of that phrase encompass discrimination because of sexual orientation? The answer is plainly no.

On occasion, it can be difficult for judges to assess ordinary meaning. Not here. Both common parlance and common legal usage treat sex discrimination and sexual orientation discrimination as two distinct categories of discrimination—back in 1964 and still today.

As to common parlance, few in 1964 (or today) would describe a firing because of sexual orientation as a firing because of sex. As commonly understood, sexual orientation discrimination is distinct from, and not a form of, sex discrimination. The majority opinion acknowledges the common understanding, noting that the plaintiffs here probably did not tell their friends that they were fired because of their sex. That observation is clearly correct. In common parlance, Bostock and Zarda were fired because they were gay, not because they were men.

Contrary to the majority opinion's approach today, this Court has repeatedly emphasized that common parlance matters in assessing the ordinary meaning of a statute, because courts heed how "most people" "would have understood" the text of a statute when enacted. *New Prime Inc. v. Oliveira*, 586 U.S. ___, ___, 139 S. Ct. 532, 538–539 (2019); see *Henson v. Santander Consumer USA Inc.*, 582 U.S. 79, 84 (2017) (using a conversation between friends to demonstrate ordinary meaning); see also *Wisconsin Central Ltd. v. United States*, 585 U.S. ___, ___, 138 S. Ct. 2067, 2070–2071 (2018) (similar); *AT&T*, 562 U.S. at 403–404 (similar). . . .

Importantly, an overwhelming body of federal law reflects and reinforces the ordinary meaning . . . . Since enacting Title VII in 1964, Congress has *never* treated sexual orientation discrimination the same as, or as a form of, sex discrimination. Instead, Congress has consistently treated sex discrimination and sexual orientation discrimination as legally distinct categories of discrimination.

Many federal statutes prohibit sex discrimination, and many federal statutes also prohibit sexual orientation discrimination. But those sexual orientation statutes expressly prohibit sexual orientation discrimination in addition to expressly prohibiting sex discrimination. *Every single one.* To this day, Congress has never defined sex discrimination to encompass sexual orientation discrimination. Instead, when Congress wants to prohibit sexual orientation discrimination in addition to sex

to) the ordinary meaning rule." W. Eskridge, Interpreting Law 72 (2016). "What the rule of absurdity seeks to do is what all rules of interpretation seek to do: *make sense* of the text." A. Scalia & B. Garner, Reading Law 235 (2012).

discrimination, Congress explicitly refers to sexual orientation discrimination.[5]

That longstanding and widespread congressional practice matters. When interpreting statutes, as the Court has often said, we "usually presume differences in language" convey "differences in meaning." *Wisconsin Central*, 585 U.S. at ___, 138 S. Ct. at 2071 (internal quotation marks omitted). When Congress chooses distinct phrases to accomplish distinct purposes, and does so over and over again for decades, we may not lightly toss aside all of Congress's careful handiwork. As Justice Scalia explained for the Court, "it is not our function" to "treat alike subjects that different Congresses have chosen to treat differently." *West Virginia Univ. Hospitals, Inc. v. Casey*, 499 U.S. 83, 101 (1991) . . . .

And the Court has likewise stressed that we may not read "a specific concept into general words when precise language in other statutes reveals that Congress knew how to identify that concept." Eskridge, Interpreting Law, at 415; [case citations omitted] . . . .

So it is here. As demonstrated by all of the statutes covering sexual orientation discrimination, Congress knows how to prohibit sexual orientation discrimination. So courts should not read that specific concept into the general words "discriminate because of sex." We cannot close our eyes to the indisputable fact that Congress—for several decades in a large number of statutes—has identified sex discrimination and sexual orientation discrimination as two distinct categories.

Where possible, we also strive to interpret statutes so as not to create undue surplusage. It is not uncommon to find some scattered redundancies in statutes. But reading sex discrimination to encompass sexual orientation discrimination would cast aside as surplusage the numerous references to sexual orientation discrimination sprinkled throughout the U.S. Code in laws enacted over the last 25 years.

In short, an extensive body of federal law both reflects and reinforces the widespread understanding that sexual orientation discrimination is distinct from, and not a form of, sex discrimination.

The story is the same with bills proposed in Congress. Since the 1970s, Members of Congress have introduced many bills to prohibit

---

[5] See 18 U.S.C. § 249(a)(2)(A) (criminalizing violence because of "gender, sexual orientation"); 20 U.S.C. § 1092(f)(1)(F)(ii) (requiring funding recipients to collect statistics on crimes motivated by the victim's "gender, . . . sexual orientation"); 34 U.S.C. § 12291(b)(13)(A) (prohibiting discrimination on the basis of "sex, . . . sexual orientation"); § 30501(1) (identifying violence motivated by "gender, sexual orientation" as national problem); § 30503(a)(1)(C) (authorizing Attorney General to assist state, local, and tribal investigations of crimes motivated by the victim's "gender, sexual orientation"); §§ 41305(b)(1), (3) (requiring Attorney General to acquire data on crimes motivated by "gender . . . , sexual orientation," but disclaiming any cause of action including one "based on discrimination due to sexual orientation"); 42 U.S.C. § 294e–1(b)(2) (conditioning funding on institution's inclusion of persons of "different genders and sexual orientations"); see also United States Sentencing Commission, Guidelines Manual § 3A1.1(a) (Nov. 2018) (authorizing increased offense level if the crime was motivated by the victim's "gender . . . or sexual orientation"); 2E Guide to Judiciary Policy § 320 (2019) (prohibiting judicial discrimination because of "sex, . . . sexual orientation").

sexual orientation discrimination in the workplace. Until very recently, all of those bills would have expressly established sexual orientation as a separately proscribed category of discrimination. The bills did not define sex discrimination to encompass sexual orientation discrimination.

The proposed bills are telling not because they are relevant to congressional intent regarding Title VII. . . . Rather, the proposed bills are telling because they, like the enacted laws, further demonstrate the widespread usage of the English language in the United States: Sexual orientation discrimination is distinct from, and not a form of, sex discrimination.

Presidential Executive Orders reflect that same common understanding. In 1967, President Johnson signed an Executive Order prohibiting sex discrimination in federal employment. In 1969, President Nixon issued a new order that did the same. . . . In 1998, President Clinton charted a new path and signed an Executive Order prohibiting sexual orientation discrimination in federal employment. . . .

. . . . President Clinton's 1998 Executive Order indicates that the Executive Branch, like Congress, has long understood sexual orientation discrimination to be distinct from, and not a form of, sex discrimination.

Federal regulations likewise reflect that same understanding. The Office of Personnel Management is the federal agency that administers and enforces personnel rules across the Federal Government. OPM has issued regulations that "govern . . . the employment practices of the Federal Government generally, and of individual agencies." 5 CFR §§ 300.101, 300.102 (2019). . . . [T]hose OPM regulations separately prohibit sex discrimination and sexual orientation discrimination.

The States have proceeded in the same fashion. A majority of States prohibit sexual orientation discrimination in employment, either by legislation applying to most workers, an executive order applying to public employees, or both. Almost every state statute or executive order proscribing sexual orientation discrimination expressly prohibits sexual orientation discrimination separately from the State's ban on sex discrimination.

That common usage in the States underscores that sexual orientation discrimination is commonly understood as a legal concept distinct from sex discrimination.

And it is the common understanding in this Court as well. Since 1971, the Court has employed rigorous or heightened constitutional scrutiny of laws that classify on the basis of sex. . . . Over the last several decades, the Court has also decided many cases involving sexual orientation. But in those cases, the Court never suggested that sexual orientation discrimination is just a form of sex discrimination. All of the Court's cases from *Bowers* to *Romer* to *Lawrence* to *Windsor* to *Obergefell* would have been far easier to analyze and decide if sexual orientation discrimination were just a form of sex discrimination and therefore received the same heightened scrutiny as sex discrimination under the Equal Protection Clause. See *Bowers v. Hardwick*, 478 U.S. 186 (1986); *Romer v. Evans*, 517 U.S. 620 (1996); *Lawrence v. Texas*, 539 U.S. 558 (2003); *United States v. Windsor*, 570 U.S. 744 (2013); *Obergefell v. Hodges*, 576 U.S. 644 (2015). . . .

II

. . . . The majority opinion . . . say[s] that courts should base their interpretation of statutes on the text as written, not on the legislators' subjective intentions. *Ante* at 1764–65, 1766–70. Of course that is true. No one disagrees. It is "the provisions of our laws rather than the principal concerns of our legislators by which we are governed." *Oncale v. Sundowner Offshore Services, Inc.*, 523 U.S. 75, 79 (1998).

But in my respectful view, the majority opinion makes a fundamental mistake by confusing ordinary meaning with subjective intentions. To briefly explain: In the early years after Title VII was enacted, some may have wondered whether Title VII's prohibition on sex discrimination protected male employees. After all, covering male employees may not have been the intent of some who voted for the statute. Nonetheless, discrimination on the basis of sex against women and discrimination on the basis of sex against men are both understood as discrimination because of sex (back in 1964 and now) and are therefore encompassed within Title VII. Cf. *id.* at 78–79; see *Newport News Shipbuilding & Dry Dock Co. v. EEOC*, 462 U.S. 669, 682–685 (1983). So too, regardless of what the intentions of the drafters might have been, the ordinary meaning of the law demonstrates that harassing an employee because of her sex is discriminating against the employee because of her sex with respect to the "terms, conditions, or privileges of employment," as this Court rightly concluded. *Meritor Savings Bank, FSB v. Vinson*, 477 U.S. 57, 64 (1986) (internal quotation marks omitted).

By contrast, this case involves sexual orientation discrimination, which has long and widely been understood as distinct from, and not a form of, sex discrimination. Until now, federal law has always reflected that common usage and recognized that distinction between sex discrimination and sexual orientation discrimination. To fire one employee because she is a woman and another employee because he is gay implicates two distinct societal concerns, reveals two distinct biases, imposes two distinct harms, and falls within two distinct statutory prohibitions. . . .

* * *

In judicially rewriting Title VII, the Court today cashiers an ongoing legislative process, at a time when a new law to prohibit sexual orientation discrimination was probably close at hand. After all, even back in 2007—a veritable lifetime ago in American attitudes about sexual orientation—the House voted 235 to 184 to prohibit sexual orientation discrimination in employment. . . . In 2013, the Senate overwhelmingly approved a similar bill, 64 to 32. . . . In 2019, the House voted 236 to 173 to amend Title VII to prohibit employment discrimination on the basis of sexual orientation. . . . It was therefore easy to envision a day, likely just in the next few years, when the House and Senate took historic votes on a bill that would prohibit employment discrimination on the basis of sexual orientation. It was easy to picture a massive and celebratory Presidential signing ceremony in the East Room or on the South Lawn.

It is true that meaningful legislative action takes time—often too much time, especially in the unwieldy morass on Capitol Hill. But . . . [t]he proper role of the Judiciary in statutory interpretation cases is "to apply, not amend, the work of the People's representatives," even when the judges might think that "Congress should reenter the field and alter the judgments it made in the past." *Henson*, 582 U.S. at 90.

Instead of a hard-earned victory won through the democratic process, today's victory is brought about by judicial dictate—judges latching on to a novel form of living literalism to rewrite ordinary meaning and remake American law. Under the Constitution and laws of the United States, this Court is the wrong body to change American law in that way. . . .

NOTES AND QUESTIONS

1. Recall that scholars of antidiscrimination law have distinguished between "anticlassification" principles and "antisubordination" principles. *See supra* p. 386. In *Bostock*, Justice Gorsuch's majority opinion interpreted Title VII to establish a very strong anticlassification principle. Justice Gorsuch noted that whenever an employer fires an employee on the basis of the employee's sexual orientation or transgender status, one step of the employer's decisionmaking process includes a reference to the employee's sex. *See, e.g.*, *Bostock*, 140 S. Ct. at 1741–42; *see also id.* at 1745 (observing that "an employer who discriminates against homosexual or transgender employees necessarily and intentionally applies sex-based rules"—rules that require classifying employees according to their sex). Justice Gorsuch interpreted Title VII to prohibit such decisionmaking processes. In his view, if an employer takes an adverse action against an employee, and if any step of the decisionmaking process that led to the action relied on the employee's sex, then the decision was made "because of such individual's . . . sex" within the meaning of Title VII.

Writing in dissent, Justice Alito interpreted Title VII to be less about classification and more about the employer's motivations. Although there is a sense in which an employer who fires someone because of her sexual orientation is taking account of her sex, Justice Alito asserted that the employer is not "holding her biological sex against her." *Id.* at 1760 (Alito, J., dissenting). Assuming that the employer would be equally biased against gay men and lesbian women, Justice Alito argued that the employer is firing her *only* because of her sexual orientation and not because of her sex. Thus, Justice Alito talked about "the employer's real motive" and the information that "motivated her discharge" (rather than information that simply went into one of the steps in the employer's decision). *Id.* at 1760, 1763.

What would these positions mean for *United Steelworkers v. Weber* (*supra* p. 363)—the 1979 case about whether Title VII prohibits race-conscious affirmative action? If you agree with Justice Gorsuch's opinion in *Bostock*, would you have to agree with the dissenters in *Weber* that Title VII forbids employers to consider an employee's race at any step of a decisionmaking process (even if their decisions are not motivated by racial prejudice)? Conversely, if you agree with the majority in *Weber* that Title VII does not prohibit all race-based affirmative action, would you have to side with the dissenters in *Bostock*? *Cf.* Students for Fair Admissions, Inc. v. President & Fellows of Harvard College, 143 S. Ct. 2141, 2209 (2023) (Gorsuch, J., concurring) (appearing to read *Bostock* to cut against race-based affirmative action).

2. Suppose that you do not read Title VII to establish as strong an anticlassification principle as Justice Gorsuch thought. Rather than reading the statute to require completely sex-blind decisionmaking (so that no step in an employer's decisionmaking process can entail noticing an employee's sex), you are inclined to assess the employer's motivation more holistically, and to ask questions like Justice Alito's: did an employee's sex "motivate[ ] her discharge"? Even so, you might think that in the case of discrimination based on sexual orientation or transgender status, the answer is "yes."

As Justice Alito's dissent mentioned, one argument along these lines grew out of cases like *Price Waterhouse v. Hopkins*, 490 U.S. 228 (1989). There, the Supreme Court indicated (albeit in splintered opinions) that Title VII forbids employers to discriminate against a woman because she does not conform to stereotypes about how women should behave or present themselves—for instance, because she does not wear makeup or because she asserts herself in ways that the employer would tolerate in men. That conclusion readily fits the language of Title VII: if an employer fires someone because she is a woman who does not act like the employer's stereotype of a woman, one might well say that the employer is firing her because of her sex. In the lead-up to *Bostock*, moreover, several lower courts had argued that this is exactly what is happening when an employer fires someone on the basis of her sexual orientation. According to those courts, firing an employee because she is a woman who is attracted to other women is firing her because she does not conform to the employer's stereotype about proper female behavior, which amounts to firing her "because of [her] . . . sex" within the meaning of Title VII. *See, e.g.*, Hively v. Ivy Tech Cmty. Coll., 853 F.3d 339, 346 (7th Cir. 2017) (en banc) ("Viewed through the lens of the gender non-conformity line of cases, Hively represents the ultimate case of failure to conform to the female stereotype .... Our panel described the line between a gender nonconformity claim and one based on sexual orientation as gossamer-thin; we conclude that it does not exist at all."); *see also* EEOC v. R.G. & G.R. Harris Funeral Homes, Inc., 884 F.3d 560, 571–74 (6th Cir. 2018) (making the same point with respect to discrimination based on an employee's transgender status), *aff'd sub nom.* Bostock v. Clayton Cty., 140 S. Ct. 1731 (2020).

Justice Alito responded to this argument by rejecting what he called the "faulty premise . . . that Title VII forbids discrimination based on sex stereotypes." In his view, proof that "a challenged decision was based on a sex stereotype" is simply "evidence" that a plaintiff can use to try to prove "discrimination because of sex." *Bostock*, 140 S. Ct. at 1764 (Alito, J., dissenting).[37] Justice Alito observed that "[s]uch evidence . . . may be convincing where the trait that is inconsistent with the stereotype is one that would be tolerated and perhaps even valued in a person of the opposite sex." *See id.* (noting that this had been the situation in *Price Waterhouse*). But while discrimination against a woman for failure to conform to sex stereotypes that are unique to women can give rise to liability under Title VII, Justice Alito reached a different conclusion about discrimination against a woman for failure to conform to stereotypes that the employer applies reciprocally to men as well. According to Justice Alito, if an employer fires women for being attracted to other women, and also fires men for being attracted to other men, the employer is not discriminating against any of them because of their sex. Likewise, Justice Alito suggested, a transphobic employer who fires all transgender employees is discriminating because of transgender status and not because of sex.

As Justice Gorsuch replied, though, the fact that the employer's policy is symmetrical does not necessarily eliminate the violation of Title VII. With respect to each individual who is fired for not conforming to the expectations that the employer associates with that person's sex, the

[37] In taking this position, Justice Alito arguably wrenched out of context some language from the plurality opinion in *Price Waterhouse*. When a plaintiff has been fired or denied promotion and wants to establish that this decision was made "because of [her] . . . sex," neither the plaintiff nor the court can simply peer into the decisionmakers' heads and see why they did what they did. As a result, employment-discrimination cases of this sort often rely on circumstantial evidence, such as sexist comments made in the period leading up to the decision. Such comments do not themselves violate Title VII (because they are not themselves adverse employment decisions), but they can be evidence that a particular decision was made for a prohibited reason. The plurality in *Price Waterhouse* made that point when discussing claims based on sex stereotyping. In the plurality's words, "Remarks at work that are based on sex stereotypes do not inevitably prove that gender played a part in a particular employment decision," but "stereotyped remarks can certainly be *evidence* that gender played a part." *Price Waterhouse*, 490 U.S. at 251 (plurality opinion of Brennan, J.). In *Bostock*, Justice Alito cut the references to *remarks* out of this passage and rendered the passage as if it was instead about *decisions* based on sex stereotypes. *See Bostock*, 140 S. Ct. at 1764 (Alito, J., dissenting) ("The plurality observed that 'sex stereotypes do not inevitably prove that gender played a part in a particular employment decision' but 'can certainly be *evidence* that gender played a part.' "). As I read the plurality opinion in *Price Waterhouse*, it did not draw Justice Alito's distinction between discrimination based on sex stereotypes and discrimination because of sex, and it did not suggest that the former was simply "evidence" of the latter.

employer might be said to be discriminating "because of such individual's . . . sex." That is potentially true even if Title VII does not establish as strong an anticlassification principle as Justice Gorsuch suggested. Firing an employee for not conforming to sex-based expectations (such as the expectation that a woman will not be attracted to other women, that a man will not be attracted to other men, and that each person's gender identity will match the sex that the person was assigned at birth) seems more directly attributable to the employee's sex than many other decisions in which an employer simply notices an employee's sex at one step of a multistep decisionmaking process.

3. Was Justice Gorsuch correct that the statute is unambiguous and that he was simply articulating its "plain meaning"? Was Justice Alito correct that the statute is unambiguous in the opposite direction and that the majority's interpretation was "preposterous"? Or were both Justices wrong to be so certain of their interpretations?

4. Nothing in the legislative history of the Civil Rights Act of 1964 suggests that anyone in Congress understood Title VII to treat sexual-orientation discrimination as a type of discrimination because of sex. Nor was that a widespread view in society at large.

For the dissenters, the fact that people in 1964 would not have understood Title VII to reach discrimination based on sexual orientation or transgender status should have prevented the majority from adopting that interpretation today. As Justice Alito explained, "Statutes consist of communications between members of a particular linguistic community, one that existed at a particular place and at a particular time," and they get their meaning in part from that "social context"; they "must therefore be interpreted as they were understood by that community at that time." *Bostock*, 140 S. Ct. at 1767 (Alito, J., dissenting); *see also id.* at 1825 (Kavanaugh, J., dissenting) (emphasizing "the ordinary public meaning at the time of enactment"). Thus, "it is imperative to consider how Americans in 1964 would have understood Title VII's prohibition of discrimination because of sex." *Id.* at 1767 (Alito, J., dissenting). According to Justice Alito, "The answer could not be clearer. In 1964, ordinary Americans reading the text of Title VII would not have dreamed that discrimination because of sex meant discrimination because of sexual orientation, much less gender identity." *Id.*

Justice Gorsuch responded, in effect, that the dissenters were confusing the original *meaning* of Title VII with the *applications* that were "foreseen at the time of enactment." *Id.* at 1750 (majority opinion). Justice Gorsuch agreed that the Court's task was to "determine the ordinary public meaning of Title VII's command," and he disclaimed any attempt to "update" the statute via interpretation. *Id.* at 1738. In his view, though, the (original) meaning of Title VII did indeed prohibit the sex-based decisionmaking that discrimination on the basis of sexual orientation or transgender status entails, even if neither members of the enacting Congress nor people in society at large drew that conclusion in 1964.

It is certainly possible for everyone at the time of enactment to be wrong about how a statute will be applied. For instance, recall the hypothetical offered above (*supra* pp. 527–528) about the phrase "dangerous contagious disease" in the Immigration and Nationality Act of 1952. If the best information available in 1952 indicated that a particular form of cancer was contagious, everyone at the time of enactment might have said that the Act would keep noncitizens with that disease out of the country. But if scientists subsequently learn that this disease is *not* contagious, then courts would say that everyone had been wrong at the time of enactment: the statute does not actually have the application that people thought it did.

Of course, this particular example is driven by a change in people's understanding of the relevant facts. Both in 1952 and today, everyone might have offered the same definition of what "contagious" *means*. What has changed is just people's understanding of facts outside the statute.

Conceivably, though, something similar is true with respect to the question in *Bostock*. There are two possible reasons why people in 1964 would not have understood Title VII to prohibit employment discrimination based on sexual orientation or transgender status. One of those reasons might indeed relate to the original meaning of Title VII: when Title VII referred to "discriminat[ion] against any individual . . . because of such individual's . . . sex," maybe nobody would have understood the statute to require sex-blind decisionmaking or to establish anything like Justice Gorsuch's anticlassification principle. But a different reason why people in 1964 did not understand Title VII to prohibit discrimination based on sexual orientation or transgender status might simply be that people in 1964 had blinders on about those issues, and they reflexively assumed that *of course* Title VII did not prohibit such discrimination—not because of anything that the statute itself said or did not say, and not because people of the day necessarily rejected Justice Gorsuch's anticlassification principle as an interpretation of Title VII, but simply because their own biases made it hard to imagine applying Title VII to protect LGBTQ people.

In *Bostock*, Justice Gorsuch claimed not simply that his reading of Title VII is a possible interpretation, but that it is the *only* possible interpretation. *See, e.g.*, *Bostock*, 140 S. Ct. at 1749 ("[N]o ambiguity exists about how Title VII's terms apply to the facts before us."). Suppose that you see more ambiguity than he acknowledged. If his interpretation would produce more unexpected applications of the statute than an alternative interpretation, is that a reason for courts to adopt the alternative interpretation? Why or why not?

CHAPTER 4

INTERPRETING STATUTES IN LIGHT OF OTHER STATUTES AND PAST INTERPRETATIONS

When legal interpreters try to determine what a statute means, they pay attention not only to the text and legislative history of the statute that they are interpreting, but also to a variety of other sources of law. In Chapter 2, for instance, we saw that courts try to read statutes in such a way as to avoid conflicts (or even *possible* conflicts) with the Constitution. Likewise, Judge Earl's opinion in *Riggs v. Palmer* spoke of interpreting statutes against the backdrop supplied by "general, fundamental maxims of the common law."

Many additional sources of law can also affect the meaning that judges and other interpreters ascribe to statutory language. This chapter devotes particular attention to the doctrine of *stare decisis* and the extent to which current interpreters of a statute might be constrained by past decisions about the statute's meaning. The chapter goes on to consider various canons that encourage interpreters to resolve questions about the meaning of one statute in light of what other statutes say (or have been understood to say). Finally, the chapter examines the extent to which a statute might affect the interpretation of other statutes more directly, by prescribing interpretive principles that the enacting legislature wants courts to use.

A. INTERPRETING STATUTES IN LIGHT OF PAST JUDICIAL DECISIONS ABOUT THE SAME STATUTES

It is commonly said that the doctrine of *stare decisis* has special force in cases of statutory interpretation. But before you can understand what that might mean, you need some background about the doctrine of *stare decisis* more generally—what it is, how it works, and why it might be considered a good idea. With that background, you will be in a better position to think about the special role of *stare decisis* in cases of statutory interpretation.

INTRODUCTORY NOTE ABOUT *STARE DECISIS*

Despite its prominence in descriptions of the American judicial system, the doctrine of *stare decisis* has no canonical formulation.

There is relatively little controversy about the "vertical" effects of precedent—the idea that lower courts should accept what the relevant appellate courts in the same judicial system have authoritatively said about the content of a legal rule, even if the lower courts would have said something else were the matter one of first impression. To be sure, what counts as authoritative is not always clear: conventional doctrine accords full precedential effect only to "holdings" (as opposed to "dicta"), and legal theorists have not reached consensus about exactly how to distill the "holdings" of particular opinions. (Among other problems, identifying the proper level of generality at which a "holding" should be formulated often requires contestable judgments. *See, e.g.*, FREDERICK SCHAUER, THINKING LIKE A LAWYER: A NEW INTRODUCTION TO LEGAL REASONING 51 (2009).) In some odd contexts, there might also be lingering questions about which appellate courts set precedents for which lower courts with respect to which cases. In the federal judicial system, and in most state judicial systems too, that concept largely follows the lines of appellate jurisdiction:[1] for the most part, the United States Supreme Court sets precedents for all lower federal courts (and also for state courts on questions of federal law), and each regional United States Court of Appeals sets precedents for the federal district courts in the states that comprise its circuit (but not for state courts, even on questions of federal law).[2] But if Congress provides for certain categories of cases to be appealed from a federal district court directly to the Supreme Court, *see, e.g.*, 52 U.S.C. § 10101(g), does the district court that hears such a case remain obliged to follow the precedents of the court of appeals for its circuit? *Compare* Michael T. Morley, *Vertical Stare Decisis and Three-Judge District Courts*, 108 GEO. L.J. 699 (2020) (noting divergent views on this question but arguing that the answer is "yes"), *with* Joshua A. Douglas & Michael E. Solimine, *Precedent, Three-Judge District Courts and the Law of Democracy*, 107 GEO. L.J. 413, 438–54 (2019) (arguing that the answer should be "no"). Likewise, if Congress exercises its authority under the Exceptions Clause of Article III, § 2, to strip the

---

[1] California state courts have a broader norm of vertical precedent that is not linked to appellate jurisdiction. Each of the state's 58 counties has a trial court. Appeals from those trial courts funnel into regional courts of appeal; the state has six appellate districts, each with a court of appeal. But published opinions rendered by *any* of those courts of appeal are said to bind *all* of the state's trial courts, including trial courts that sit in the other districts. *See* Auto Equity Sales, Inc. v. Superior Court of Santa Clara County, 369 P.2d 937, 940 (Cal. 1962); *see also, e.g.*, Sarti v. Salt Creek Ltd., 167 Cal. App. 4th 1187, 1193 & n.2 (2008) (observing that "the only qualifications" on this doctrine are that "the relevant point in the appellate decision must not have been disapproved by the California Supreme Court and must not be in conflict with another appellate decision").

[2] Within the federal judicial system, Congress has established special lines of appellate jurisdiction for a few types of cases. For instance, the United States Court of Appeals for the Federal Circuit has exclusive jurisdiction over appeals from the final decisions of federal district courts "in any civil action arising under . . . any Act of Congress relating to patents." 28 U.S.C. § 1295(a)(1). Correspondingly, district courts nationwide consider themselves bound to follow Federal Circuit precedents in such cases. *See, e.g.*, Clearplay, Inc. v. Nissim Corp., 555 F. Supp. 2d 1318, 1324–25 (S.D. Fla. 2008). That principle is subject to the qualification that the Federal Circuit itself chooses to follow the precedents of the relevant regional circuit court on federal issues not related to patent law. *See, e.g.*, In re ZTE (USA), Inc., 890 F.3d 1008, 1012 (Fed. Cir. 2018); *see also* Panduit Corp. v. All States Plastic Mfg. Co., 744 F.2d 1564, 1574–75 (Fed. Cir. 1984) ("[A]s a matter of policy, . . . the Federal Circuit shall review procedural matters, that are not unique to patent issues, under the law of the particular regional circuit court where appeals from the district court would normally lie.").

federal Supreme Court of appellate jurisdiction over some category of cases, should lower federal courts adjudicating those cases consider themselves bound by Supreme Court precedent? *Cf.* Evan H. Caminker, *Why Must Inferior Courts Obey Superior Court Precedents?*, 46 STAN. L. REV. 817 (1994) (providing a theory that bears on questions of this sort).

Still, the exotic nature of these lingering questions is telling. In the main, the "vertical" effects of precedent are pretty well established.

The "horizontal" doctrine of *stare decisis*—the idea that certain kinds of courts should recognize some sort of presumption in favor of adhering to their own past holdings about the content of a legal rule—is both more contested and more complicated. But whatever the precise nature of a court's obligation to follow its own precedents, no American court thinks of that obligation as absolute. Thus, the "horizontal" effects of precedent are more qualified than the "vertical" effects.[3]

Within the federal court system, the norms of "horizontal" *stare decisis* vary from tier to tier. At least in theory, the opinions issued by federal district courts lack any formal precedential effect at all: although a federal district court's judgment in a case will bind the parties to that case and their privies in accordance with the applicable principles of *res judicata*, the doctrine of *stare decisis* does not attach to the legal propositions upon which the judgment rests. As a result, the fact that a federal district judge takes a certain view of the law in one case will not prevent even the very same judge (let alone other judges on the same federal district court) from taking a different view of the law in another case. In practice, of course, individual district judges try to maintain some consistency in their own opinions, and they may even choose to defer to the opinions expressed by their colleagues in prior cases. But they cannot really invoke the doctrine of *stare decisis* in doing so. *See* Camreta v. Greene, 563 U.S. 692, 709 n.7 (2011) (" 'A decision of a federal district judge is not binding precedent in either a different judicial district, the same judicial district, or even upon the same judge in a different case.' " (quoting 18 J. MOORE ET AL., MOORE'S FEDERAL

[3] That fact can lead to questions about the intersection of the two doctrines. Suppose, for instance, that a precedent of the United States Supreme Court bears directly on a question that a lower court is now facing, but the lower court understands some other line of decisions to undermine the precedent's logic, and the lower court expects the Supreme Court to overrule the precedent at its next opportunity. Should the lower court feel free to disregard the precedent (notwithstanding its "vertical" authority) because the lower court believes (consistent with the qualified nature of "horizontal" *stare decisis*) that the Supreme Court is poised to overrule the precedent?

At least in the federal system, the Supreme Court has answered that question "no": Lower courts are not supposed to engage in this sort of "anticipatory overruling" with respect to Supreme Court precedents. *See, e.g.*, Rodriguez de Quijas v. Shearson/American Express, Inc., 490 U.S. 477, 484 (1989) ("If a precedent of this Court has direct application in a case, yet appears to rest on reasons rejected in some other line of decisions, the Court of Appeals should follow the case which directly controls, leaving to this Court the prerogative of overruling its own decisions."). Still, lower courts may be inclined to read vulnerable precedents more narrowly than robust ones. In practice, moreover, a lower court that *correctly* anticipates that the Supreme Court is about to overrule a precedent will not be reversed for acting upon that belief.

PRACTICE § 134.02[1][d], p. 134–26 (3d ed. 2011))). *Compare* Midlock v. Apple Vacations West, Inc., 406 F.3d 453, 458 (7th Cir. 2005) (Posner, C.J.) (attributing this principle to the structure of federal district courts, which have many dispersed judges who almost always "sit by themselves rather than in panels" and who "[o]ften . . . will render inconsistent decisions"), *with* Joseph W. Mead, *Stare Decisis in the Inferior Courts of the United States*, 12 NEV. L.J. 787 (2012) (arguing, contrary to current practice, that district courts can and should adopt strong doctrines of intradistrict *stare decisis*).

Decisions rendered by the federal circuit courts of appeal, by contrast, can trigger a very powerful form of "horizontal" *stare decisis.* The federal circuit courts decide almost all cases in panels of three judges each. In general, the published opinions of any such panel are absolutely binding on future panels in the same circuit (as well as on all district courts within that circuit).[4]

To be sure, the circuit court as a whole—as opposed to individual panels—can escape that effect. After a panel renders a decision, the full court can order the case to be reheard "en banc."[5] *See* 28 U.S.C. § 46(c) (allowing "a majority of the circuit judges of the circuit who are in regular active service" to order a hearing or rehearing en banc); FED. R. APP. P. 35(a) (referring more precisely to a majority of the active judges who are not recused from the case). In all but the Ninth Circuit,[6] the en banc court includes all the circuit judges in regular active service, and it can also include any senior-status circuit judge who was on the panel that

[4] The adjective "published" in this sentence matters. When a federal court of appeals releases an opinion, it often designates the opinion as being "not for publication." Those "unpublished" opinions are available to the public on Westlaw (and, from 2001 to 2021, in bound volumes called the *Federal Appendix*), but they are not printed in F.4th and they are conventionally said to have no effect as precedents. *See, e.g.*, Patterson v. Ga. Pac., LLC, 38 F.4th 1336, 1346 (11th Cir. 2022) ("Our unpublished opinions are not precedential, so they do not bind us or district courts to any degree.").

For many years, indeed, some federal courts of appeals forbade litigants even to cite those opinions in other cases. In the wake of controversy over such restrictions, Federal Rule of Appellate Procedure 32.1 now specifies that "[a] court may not prohibit or restrict the citation of federal judicial opinions, orders, judgments, or other written dispositions that have been: (i) designated as 'unpublished,' 'not for publication,' 'non-precedential,' 'not precedent,' or the like; and (ii) issued on or after January 1, 2007." But while such opinions may now be cited in briefs, and while other courts may sometimes be persuaded by their reasoning, conventional doctrine still withholds precedential effect from them. The "unpublished" opinions of a federal court of appeals have no more formal precedential effect than the opinions of a federal district court.

[5] Circuit courts can decide to hear a case en banc without waiting for a panel to hear it first, but that is unusual.

[6] Congress has authorized "any court of appeals having more than 15 active judges" to "perform its en banc function by such number of members of its en banc courts as may be prescribed by rule of the court of appeals." Act of Oct. 20, 1978, Pub. L. 95–486, § 6, 92 Stat. 1629, 1633. Of the circuits that qualify, only the Ninth—which is by far the largest, with 29 authorized judgeships as of this writing—has exercised this authority. *See* 9th Cir. R. 35–3 (specifying that "[t]he en banc court . . . shall consist of the Chief Judge of this circuit and 10 additional judges to be drawn by lot from the active judges of the Court," but adding that "[i]n appropriate cases, the Court may order a rehearing by the full court following a hearing or rehearing en banc"); *see also* Maggie Gardner, *District Court En Bancs*, 90 FORDHAM L. REV. 1541, 1600 n.391 (2022).

originally heard the case. *See* 28 U.S.C. § 46(c). Traditionally, when a circuit court voted to rehear a case en banc, the panel's judgment and opinion were immediately vacated, to be replaced by whatever decision the court eventually rendered en banc. That is still the customary practice in most circuits, although there are now some minor regional variations.[7]

Even if a panel issues a published opinion in a case and the circuit court does not rehear the case en banc, the circuit court can still overrule the panel's opinion when sitting en banc in a later case. In practice, en banc courts sometimes overrule previous panel decisions without any discussion of *stare decisis*, perhaps on the assumption that panel decisions have no precedential force for the en banc court. *See, e.g.*, Blackstone Headwaters Coalition, Inc. v. Gallo Builders, Inc., 32 F.4th 99 (1st Cir. 2022) (en banc) (overruling N. & S. Rivers Watershed Ass'n v. Town of Scituate, 949 F.2d 552 (1st Cir. 1991)); *cf.* John Harrison, *The Power of Congress Over the Rules of Precedent*, 50 DUKE L.J. 503, 517 (2000) (flagging the question "whether a [past] panel opinion has any precedential force at all when an issue it decided is presented to the court en banc"). En banc courts that have explicitly considered this issue, however, have said that previous panel decisions do have some precedential force. *See, e.g.*, Robert Bosch, LLC v. Pylon Mfg. Corp., 719 F.3d 1305, 1316 (Fed. Cir. 2013) (en banc); Crown Coat Front Co., Inc. v. United States, 363 F.2d 407, 414 (2d Cir. 1966) (en banc) (Friendly, J., concurring), *rev'd*, 386 U.S. 503 (1967). Still, that force may be relatively weak. *See, e.g.*, Planned Parenthood of Greater Tex. Family Planning & Preventative Health Servs., Inc. v. Kauffman, 981 F.3d 347, 369 (5th Cir. 2020) (en banc) ("[T]he court sitting en banc may overrule or abrogate a panel's decision if the en banc court concludes that panel opinion's holding was indeed flawed."). Several circuits have indicated that when they are sitting en banc, "prior en banc decisions carry more stare decisis weight than prior panel decisions." *Riccio v. Sentry Credit, Inc.*, 954 F.3d 582, 591 (3d Cir. 2020) (en banc); *accord Bosch*, 719 F.3d at 1316; McKinney v. Pate, 20 F.3d 1550, 1565 n.21 (11th Cir. 1994) (en banc). Even prior en banc decisions, moreover, are not regarded as absolutely binding. *See, e.g.*, Lighting Ballast Control LLC v. Philips Elecs. N. Am. Corp., 744 F.3d 1272, 1281–86 (Fed. Cir. 2014) (en banc) (appearing to assume that an en banc precedent is subject to the same doctrines of *stare decisis* that the Supreme Court uses when deciding whether to overrule its own decisions), *vacated*, 574 U.S. 1133 (2015); *cf. Riccio*, 954 F.3d at 590–92 (noting that "we, as a lower court, 'play a different role in the federal system' " than the Supreme Court, and identifying circumstances

[7] *Compare* 4th Cir. R. 35(c) (reflecting the traditional rule) *and* 1st Cir. I.O.P. X(D) (saying that the court "[u]sually" follows this practice) *with* D.C. Cir. R. 35(d) ("If rehearing en banc is granted, the panel's judgment, but ordinarily not its opinion, will be vacated . . . .") *and* United States Court of Appeals for the Ninth Circuit, Circuit Advisory Committee Note to Rules 35–1 to 35–3 (stating that after a grant of rehearing en banc, "[t]he three-judge panel opinion shall not be cited as precedent by or to this Court or any district court of the Ninth Circuit").

that might support overruling even en banc precedents more readily than the Supreme Court overrules some of its precedents (quoting Critical Mass Energy Project v. NRC, 975 F.2d 871, 876 (D.C. Cir. 1992) (en banc))).

Different circuit judges have expressed different views about the precise weight that various types of circuit precedent deserve when the court is sitting en banc. Whatever the answer, though, circuit courts hear only a small percentage of their cases en banc. Most cases in federal circuit courts therefore trigger the more absolute rule that prevents one panel from overruling the published decisions of a prior panel of the same circuit.[8]

The doctrines of precedent followed by the United States Supreme Court are harder to describe. At least when the Court decides a case on its merits docket (as opposed to an emergency motion) and issues a majority opinion,[9] the Court is setting a precedent for itself as well as for

---

[8] I say "more absolute," rather than simply "absolute," because the principle that a panel cannot overrule circuit precedent is not totally unqualified. When the reasons for overruling circuit precedent are relatively uncontroversial, at least some circuits have developed procedures that allow them to overrule the precedent without going to the trouble of a normal "en banc" hearing. For instance, the internal procedures of the United States Court of Appeals for the D.C. Circuit permit a panel to announce the overruling of one of the court's past decisions if the panel obtains the unanimous consent of the judges who would constitute the "en banc" court—a fact that the panel will then report in a footnote. *See* Policy Statement on *En Banc* Endorsement of Panel Decisions (Jan. 17, 1996), *available at* www.cadc.uscourts.gov/internet/home.nsf/Content/VL - RPP - Irons Footnote/$FILE/IRONS.PDF (visited Sept. 2, 2023); *see also* Amy E. Sloan, *The Dog that Didn't Bark: Stealth Procedures and the Erosion of Stare Decisis in the Federal Courts of Appeals*, 78 FORDHAM L. REV. 713 (2009) (canvassing practices in other circuits).

For discussion of issues that can arise when circuit precedent has been undermined but not directly contradicted by a later Supreme Court decision, see Henry J. Dickman, Note, *Conflicts of Precedent*, 106 VA. L. REV. 1345 (2020).

[9] Especially in the days when the Court had more mandatory appellate jurisdiction than it does now, the Court sometimes summarily affirmed the judgment below without hearing oral argument and without issuing an opinion. Such summary affirmances were said to have only limited precedential effect even for lower courts, let alone for the Supreme Court itself. *See, e.g.*, Zobel v. Williams, 457 U.S. 55, 64 n.13 (1982) ("[S]ummary affirmance by this Court is not to be read as an adoption of the reasoning supporting the judgment under review."); Mandel v. Bradley, 432 U.S. 173, 176 (1977) (per curiam) (indicating that summary affirmances bind lower courts only with respect to "the precise issues presented and necessarily decided by those actions"); *see also* Comptroller of the Treasury v. Wynne, 575 U.S. 542, 559–60 (2015) (observing that from the standpoint of the Supreme Court itself, "a summary affirmance . . . has 'considerably less precedential value than an opinion on the merits' " (quoting Illinois Bd. of Elections v. Socialist Workers Party, 440 U.S. 173, 180–81 (1979))); Metromedia, Inc. v. City of San Diego, 453 U.S. 490, 500 (1981) (plurality opinion) ("[S]ummary actions . . . do not present the same justification for declining to reconsider a prior decision as do decisions rendered after argument and with full opinion."); Fusari v. Steinberg, 419 U.S. 379, 392 (1975) (Burger, C.J., concurring) ("[U]pon fuller consideration of an issue under plenary review, the Court has not hesitated to discard a rule which a line of summary affirmances may appear to have established."). More recently, similar issues have arisen with respect to the Supreme Court's disposition of emergency motions, which often do generate opinions but are heard on an expedited basis. *See* PRESIDENTIAL COMMISSION ON THE SUPREME COURT OF THE UNITED STATES, FINAL REPORT 208–09 (2021) (noting uncertainty about the precedential effect of such decisions).

A different set of questions can arise when the Court decides a case on its regular docket after plenary consideration, but issues splintered opinions. Even if none of those opinions commands a majority, the Court has said that a precedential "holding" can at least sometimes be identified. *See* Marks v. United States, 430 U.S. 188, 193 (1977) ("When a fragmented Court

lower courts. All members of the Court accept what Richard Posner once called "[t]he essence of stare decisis"—the idea that "the mere existence of certain decisions becomes a reason for adhering to their holdings in subsequent cases." *Midlock*, 406 F.3d at 457. All members of the Court also agree that this reason is not always dispositive; the Court can overrule its own precedents when warranted. But exactly when overruling is warranted is contested. Different Justices have different ideas about the conditions under which different types of precedents can and should be repudiated. Indeed, even a single Justice might reach different conclusions in different areas of law. The fact that the Court is a multimember body only adds to the difficulty of identifying crisp rules; the coalitions that form in one case will not necessarily apply the same criteria for overruling a precedent as the coalitions that form in another case.

One consideration that is obviously relevant to whether the Court should overrule a precedent is whether the current Court thinks that the precedent was wrong. According to many Justices, though, the Court should never overrule a precedent *simply* because the Court thinks that the precedent was wrong, without considering any other factors. Indeed, Justice Scalia once wrote that the doctrine of *stare decisis* "would be no doctrine at all" if it did not require overruling courts to "give reasons . . . that go beyond mere demonstration that the overruled opinion was wrong." *Hubbard v. United States*, 514 U.S. 695, 716 (1995) (Scalia, J., concurring in part and concurring in the judgment); *accord* Ramos v. Louisiana, 140 S. Ct. 1390, 1414 (2020) (Kavanaugh, J., concurring in part) (quoting this statement).

As a logical matter, Justice Scalia's statement probably rests on the assumption that all legal questions have only one correct answer. If one concedes the possibility that law can be partially indeterminate, then a doctrine of *stare decisis* could have work to do within the zone of indeterminacy even if the Court followed a strict practice of overruling all precedents that are "demonstrat[ed]" to be "wrong." For instance, suppose that a particular legal provision lends itself to two possible interpretations. If a precedent adopted one of those two interpretations, a doctrine of *stare decisis* could encourage future Courts to adhere to the precedent even if they otherwise would have chosen the other interpretation. But if the precedent instead adopted a third reading that goes beyond the zone of indeterminacy, then the same doctrine of *stare*

---

decides a case and no single rationale explaining the result enjoys the assent of five Justices, 'the holding of the Court may be viewed as that position taken by those Members who concurred in the judgments on the narrowest grounds . . . .' " (quoting Gregg v. Georgia, 428 U.S. 153, 169 n.15 (1976) (opinion of Stewart, Powell, and Stevens, JJ.))). In practice, however, efforts to cobble together a holding from the Justices' splintered opinions may be more relevant to the lower courts than to the Supreme Court itself. *See* Richard M. Re, *Beyond the* Marks *Rule*, 132 HARV. L. REV. 1942, 1945 (2019) (concluding that "the Court feels free to ignore its own *Marks* holdings at will, even as other courts struggle over them"). In any event, the formulation that the Court adopted in *Marks* has been subjected to withering criticism. *See id.* at 1945–46 (arguing that "the *Marks* rule is wrong, root and stem," and that precedent should be formed only when a majority of the Justices expressly support the same rule of decision).

decisis might allow the Court to overrule the precedent on the ground that the precedent was wrong. *Cf.* Gamble v. United States, 139 S. Ct. 1960, 1984–88 (2019) (Thomas, J., concurring) (arguing that precedent is relevant only "within th[e] range of permissible interpretations" and suggesting that the Court has an affirmative obligation to overrule precedents that are "demonstrably erroneous").[10]

Of course, the fact that such a doctrine of *stare decisis* would be coherent does not mean either that it would be desirable or that it is the doctrine that the Supreme Court follows. Even in the realm of constitutional law, where *stare decisis* is said to have the least force, most of the Justices do not seem to treat mere error as a sufficient basis for overruling a precedent. In the words of one majority opinion, "To [overrule] a decision, we demand a 'special justification,' over and above the belief 'that the precedent was wrongly decided.' " *Allen v. Cooper*, 140 S. Ct. 994, 1003 (2020) (quoting Halliburton Co. v. Erica P. John Fund, 573 U.S. 258, 266 (2014)).

In *Planned Parenthood of Southeastern Pennsylvania v. Casey*, 505 U.S. 833 (1992), the Court divided sharply over whether to overrule *Roe v. Wade*, 410 U.S. 113 (1973). Four Justices voted to do so. *See Casey*, 505 U.S. 833, 944 (Rehnquist, C.J., concurring in the judgment in part and dissenting in part, joined by White, Scalia, and Thomas, JJ.). But the joint opinion of Justices O'Connor, Kennedy, and Souter argued that *stare decisis* supported adhering to a modified version of *Roe*. In a passage that spoke for five Justices, the joint opinion introduced its analysis as follows:

> "[W]hen this Court reexamines a prior holding, its judgment is customarily informed by a series of prudential and pragmatic considerations designed to test the consistency of overruling a prior decision with the ideal of the rule of law, and to gauge the respective costs of reaffirming and overruling a prior case. Thus, for example, we may ask whether the rule [established by the prior decision] has proven to be intolerable simply in defying practical workability, *Swift & Co. v. Wickham*, 382 U.S. 111, 116 (1965); whether the rule

---

[10] In my own prior work, I suggested the possibility of a doctrine along these lines, though I cast it in terms of rebuttable presumptions (which could be overcome by reliance interests, say) rather than crisp obligations. Here is how I put it:

> "The doctrine of *stare decisis* would indeed be no doctrine at all if courts were free to overrule a past decision simply because they would have reached a different decision as an original matter. But when a court says that a past decision is demonstrably erroneous, it is saying not only that it would have reached a different decision as an original matter, but also that the prior court went beyond the range of indeterminacy created by the relevant source of law. Those are two different statements, and the doctrine of *stare decisis* could take account of this difference: One could recognize a rebuttable presumption *against* overruling decisions that are not demonstrably erroneous while simultaneously recognizing a rebuttable presumption *in favor of* overruling decisions that *are* demonstrably erroneous. If one truly believes in the concept of 'demonstrable error,' moreover, one might see no threat to the rule of law in such a doctrine."

Caleb Nelson, *Stare Decisis and Demonstrably Erroneous Precedents*, 87 VA. L. REV. 1, 8 (2001); *see also id.* at 8–52 (claiming historical support for this type of doctrine).

> is subject to a kind of reliance that would lend a special hardship to the consequences of overruling and add inequity to the cost of repudiation, *e.g.*, *United States v. Title Ins. & Trust Co.*, 265 U.S. 472, 486 (1924); whether related principles of law have so far developed as to have left the old rule no more than a remnant of abandoned doctrine, see *Patterson v. McLean Credit Union*, 491 U.S. 164, 173–174 (1989); or whether facts have so changed, or come to be seen so differently, as to have robbed the old rule of significant application or justification, *e.g.*, *Burnet* [*v. Coronado Oil & Gas Co.*, 285 U.S. 393, 412 (1932) (Brandeis, J., dissenting)]."

Casey, 505 U.S. at 854–55. This passage identifies not only some considerations that count as "special justification[s]" for overruling a precedent (such as the unworkability of the rule that the precedent established or the fact that subsequent doctrinal evolution has already made the precedent anachronistic) but also a consideration that could give some precedents extra weight (the need to protect reliance interests). Other considerations that are frequently thrown into the mix are the "harmful effects" that a precedent allegedly is causing, *see* Henry Paul Monaghan, *Stare Decisis and Constitutional Adjudication*, 88 COLUM. L. REV. 723, 760–62 (1988) (calling it "inevitabl[e]" that "the actual consequences of a prior decision will play a major part in any American theory of stare decisis," though expressing concerns about "whether this criterion can be rendered sufficiently principled"), and the "flagrancy" of the precedent's error, *see* RANDY J. KOZEL, SETTLED VERSUS RIGHT: A THEORY OF PRECEDENT 118–21 (2017) (discussing this consideration and arguing that it does not work well where Justices have different views about what makes a decision right or wrong).

In a separate opinion written in 2020, Justice Kavanaugh tried to organize these considerations into "a structured methodology . . . for determining whether to overrule an erroneous constitutional precedent." *Ramos v. Louisiana*, 140 S. Ct. 1390, 1415 (2020) (Kavanaugh, J., concurring in part). Here is what he wrote:

> "As I read the Court's cases on precedent, those varied and somewhat elastic *stare decisis* factors fold into three broad considerations that, in my view, can . . . help determine what constitutes a 'special justification' or 'strong grounds' to overrule a prior constitutional decision.
>
> "*First*, is the prior decision not just wrong, but grievously or egregiously wrong? A garden-variety error or disagreement does not suffice to overrule. In the view of the Court that is considering whether to overrule, the precedent must be egregiously wrong as a matter of law in order for the Court to overrule it. In conducting that inquiry, the Court may examine the quality of the precedent's reasoning, consistency and coherence with other decisions, changed law, changed facts, and workability, among other factors. A case may be egregiously wrong when decided, see, *e.g.*, *Korematsu v. United*

> *States*, 323 U.S. 214 (1944); *Plessy v. Ferguson*, 163 U.S. 537 (1896), or may be unmasked as egregiously wrong based on later legal or factual understandings or developments, see, *e.g.*, *Nevada v. Hall*, 440 U.S. 410 (1979), or both, *ibid*.
>
> "*Second*, has the prior decision caused significant negative jurisprudential or real-world consequences? In conducting that inquiry, the Court may consider jurisprudential consequences (some of which are also relevant to the first inquiry), such as workability, as well as consistency and coherence with other decisions, among other factors. Importantly, the Court may also scrutinize the precedent's real-world effects on the citizenry, not just its effects on the law and the legal system. See, *e.g.*, *Brown v. Board of Education*, 347 U.S. [483,] 494–95 [(1954)] . . . .
>
> "*Third*, would overruling the prior decision unduly upset reliance interests? This consideration focuses on the legitimate expectations of those who have reasonably relied on the precedent. In conducting that inquiry, the Court may examine a variety of reliance interests and the age of the precedent, among other factors."

Id. at 1414–15.

Two years later, Justice Kavanaugh reiterated this test when he joined a majority of the Court in overruling *Roe* and *Casey*. *See* Dobbs v. Jackson Women's Health Org., 142 S. Ct. 2228, 2307 (2022) (Kavanaugh, J., concurring) ("The history of *stare decisis* in this Court establishes that a constitutional precedent may be overruled only when (i) the prior decision is not just wrong, but is egregiously wrong, (ii) the prior decision has caused significant negative jurisprudential or real-world consequences, and (iii) overruling the prior decision would not unduly upset legitimate reliance interests."). Justice Alito's majority opinion did not itself say that precedents could be overruled *only* when Justice Kavanaugh's test was satisfied, but the majority indicated that *Roe* and *Casey* did indeed qualify for overruling under that test. *See id.* at 2264–77 (majority opinion). By contrast, the dissenting Justices argued that the majority was overruling *Roe* and *Casey* simply because the Justices in the majority considered those decisions " 'egregiously wrong' "—a criterion that "could equally spell the end of any precedent with which a bare majority of the present Court disagrees." *Id.* at 2335 (Breyer, Sotomayor, and Kagan, JJ., dissenting). According to the dissenters, this criterion "makes radical change too easy and too fast, based on nothing more than the new views of new judges." *Id.*

To the extent that Justices disagree with each other about the content of the doctrine of *stare decisis* (as opposed to the proper application of that doctrine with respect to a particular precedent), what is the nature of their disagreement? Is each individual Justice free to come up with a personal approach to *stare decisis*, based on that Justice's intuitions about how much force past decisions should have? Or are doctrines of *stare decisis* a type of law, growing out of the customs of the

Supreme Court (and other courts of last resort) but binding on individual Justices in the same manner as other types of customary law?

The latter view may well be correct. *See* Harrison, *supra*, 50 DUKE L.J. at 529 ("The norms of precedent as the federal courts know them consist mainly of unwritten principles that are characterized as binding law but that reflect substantial judicial input, custom, and practice."); *id.* at 531 (describing most of those principles as "general law, or in the current phrase, federal common law"). Under current circumstances, though, the content of the relevant customs and doctrines may be sufficiently unsettled that individual Justices have substantial room to try to develop an approach that they think makes sense. In addition, at least some versions of the doctrine of *stare decisis* require case-by-case evaluation of whether the arguments for overruling a particular decision overcome the arguments for usually following precedent. As a result, it is important to understand the policy arguments that might shape a doctrine of *stare decisis*. What institutional and societal benefits might courts of last resort achieve by following their own precedents, and what are the competing considerations? *See, e.g.*, KOZEL, *supra*, at 36–53 (summarizing arguments on both sides); *cf.* HENRY M. HART, JR. & ALBERT M. SACKS, THE LEGAL PROCESS: BASIC PROBLEMS IN THE MAKING AND APPLICATION OF LAW 568–69 (tent. ed. 1958) (William N. Eskridge, Jr. & Philip P. Frickey eds., 1994) (listing "considerations which may be thought to support a general practice of adherence to prior holdings" and asking whether these considerations "warrant at least a presumption in favor of refusal to reexamine past holdings, which should yield only to a strong showing of probable error").

One obvious reason for the Supreme Court to pay attention to its precedents is that they reflect the considered judgments of a majority of the Justices who heard a prior case, and those judgments are likely to be correct. *See id.* at 569 (referring to "[t]he propriety of according respect to the conclusions of predecessor judges"). Of course, everyone can make mistakes, and the idea that judges are usually right might not itself support a presumption against overruling the subset of precedents that a later Court determines to be wrong. At a minimum, though, current Justices should not be too quick to conclude that their predecessors were mistaken.

If the current Court can often follow precedents without even having to think about whether those precedents were correctly decided, moreover, the Justices can save valuable time. A century ago, Benjamin Cardozo cast this argument for *stare decisis* in strong terms: "[T]he labor of judges would be increased almost to the breaking point if every past decision could be reopened in every case, and one could not lay one's own course of bricks on the secure foundation of the courses laid by others who had gone before him." BENJAMIN N. CARDOZO, THE NATURE OF THE JUDICIAL PROCESS 149 (1921). For several reasons, this statement may be less applicable to the modern Supreme Court than it was to the New

York Court of Appeals on which Cardozo was then sitting.[11] But relatively strong doctrines of *stare decisis* can still reduce the resources that society spends on litigation. With such doctrines in place, the Court will be able to take many past holdings as given without having to reexamine them closely on the merits, and litigants will be able to base arguments on those holdings without constantly having to relitigate them. In addition, if litigants know that they will have a hard time getting the Court to overrule a precedent, they probably will try less often. By contrast, a judicial system without a general policy of *stare decisis* might face "a rush of litigation whenever there is a change of personnel on the bench." HART & SACKS, *supra*, at 568.

At least in certain areas of the law, *stare decisis* is also often justified on the ground that people in the real world rely on what precedents say and that such reliance is desirable. Admittedly, Justices have debated the kinds of reliance interests that the doctrine of *stare decisis* should protect. *See Dobbs*, 142 S. Ct. at 2277 (asserting that "our cases . . . emphasize very concrete reliance interests"); Payne v. Tennessee, 501 U.S. 808, 828 (1991) ("Considerations in favor of *stare decisis* are at their acme in cases involving property and contract rights, where reliance interests are involved . . . ."). But the need to protect some reliance interests has long been regarded as a reason to follow even precedents that are now considered erroneous. *See* Nelson, *supra* note 10, 87 VA. L. REV. at 20 (discussing nineteenth-century statements about so-called "rules of property"). The argument can be cast in economic terms: if the rules of *stare decisis* made it easy for the Supreme Court to take one view of the law at Time 1 and the opposite view at Time 2, people might not be able to plan their activities with the optimal level of confidence, and the extra uncertainty might discourage them from making investments or behaving in other ways that would benefit society as a whole. Apart from this instrumental argument, basic fairness might point in the same direction. If people make investments or take other important actions in reliance upon what the Supreme Court has said, perhaps it is simply unjust for the Court to change its mind in a way that pulls the rug out from under those people.

Another set of arguments for *stare decisis* requires more discussion. In the words of Justice Thurgood Marshall, "*stare decisis* is important not merely because individuals rely on precedent to structure their commercial activity but because fidelity to precedent is part and parcel

---

[11] Cardozo himself acknowledged that his belief may have been "accentuate[d]" by the peculiar structure of his own court, which had been sitting in panels that rotated every week or two. *See id.* at 149–50 (explaining that "[w]e have had ten judges, of whom only seven sit at a time," and "[t]he situation would . . . be intolerable if the weekly changes in the composition of the court were accompanied by changes in its rulings"); *see also* Meredith R. Miller, *A Picture of the New York Court of Appeals at the Time of* Wood v. Lucy, Lady Duff-Gordon, 28 PACE L. REV. 357, 361–62 (2008) (describing the court's structure and one of the rotation systems that it had used). In addition, the fact that the modern Supreme Court's jurisdiction is almost entirely discretionary may weaken the force of Cardozo's observation; the Court's ability to choose the questions on which it grants certiorari (and to limit its consideration to those questions) gives it considerable control over the burdens that it faces.

of a conception of 'the judiciary as a source of impersonal and reasoned judgments.'" *Payne*, 501 U.S. at 852 (Marshall, J., dissenting) (quoting Moragne v. States Marine Lines, 398 U.S. 375, 403 (1970)). Arguments about the need for "impersonal" judgment can take various forms, but they generally cast *stare decisis* as a way to promote values associated with the rule of law. *See, e.g.*, KOZEL, *supra*, at 42 ("Fidelity to precedent ensures that the law is not reduced to the preferences and personalities of a particular group of justices assembled at a particular moment in time. This is another way of saying the *rule of law* prevails over the rule of men and women.").

Still, the suggestion that *stare decisis* is necessary for the rule of law may paint with too broad a brush. Even in cases of first impression, judges do not reach decisions simply on the basis of personal whim. Instead, judges attempt to interpret and apply the underlying sources of law (such as statutes and constitutional provisions) that bear on the case. To the extent that those sources of law are determinate, they might themselves provide an adequate foundation for impersonal judgment, without the need for strong doctrines of *stare decisis*. As a means of promoting rule-of-law values, then, *stare decisis* might have more benefits on questions as to which the underlying sources of law are indeterminate than on questions as to which those sources supply a right answer. *Cf.* Nelson, *supra* note 10, 87 VA. L. REV. at 8 (arguing that as a historical matter, *stare decisis* was seen as a way "to restrain the discretion that legal indeterminacy would otherwise give judges"). In areas where the underlying sources of law are determinate, indeed, strong doctrines of *stare decisis* might actually create hazards for the rule of law. *See, e.g.*, KOZEL, *supra*, at 53 (discussing the risk that some judges who decide cases of first impression will deliberately overreach if they know that future courts are likely to follow whatever precedents they set).

Of course, these counterarguments are themselves subject to debate. In theory, the ideas in the previous paragraph might suggest that the doctrine of *stare decisis* should have more force where the law would otherwise be indeterminate than where the underlying sources of law identify right and wrong answers. In practice, though, determinacy may often be in the eye of the beholder. In a world where different judges have very different ideas about constitutional or statutory interpretation, different judges are likely to reach different conclusions about whether and in what respects various sources of law are indeterminate. A doctrine of *stare decisis* that hinges on assessments of legal indeterminacy might therefore lend itself to inconsistent application over time, which might raise its own rule-of-law concerns. *See id.* at 103–04 (seeking to "reconstruct[ ] the doctrine of stare decisis around considerations that can operate independently of interpretive philosophy," and therefore downplaying considerations such as "flagrancy of error" and "a precedent's perceived harmfulness"). *But cf.* Amy Coney Barrett,

Precedent and Jurisprudential Disagreement, 91 TEX. L. REV. 1711, 1716–24 (2013) (suggesting that the existence of "intense jurisprudential disagreement" may actually cut *against* strong doctrines of *stare decisis* in constitutional cases).

Along with the claim that *stare decisis* promotes impersonal judgment and imposes needed constraints on judicial discretion, people also note that *stare decisis* generates a certain type of equality. If the Supreme Court treated someone a certain way in Case #1, it seems undesirable for the Court to treat an identically situated person a different way in Case #2. But the less the Court feels obliged to follow precedent, the more it will depart from the ideal of treating like cases alike.

All of these arguments are often coupled with arguments about public perceptions of the judiciary. It is sometimes said that if courts overrule past decisions too often, people will attribute the courts' fluctuations to changes in the courts' personnel, and they will come to believe that the courts are simply articulating the policy preferences of the current judges rather than following the true dictates of the law. That perception, in turn, might cause the judiciary to lose some of its perceived legitimacy, with potentially dangerous consequences. *See Payne*, 501 U.S. at 853 (Marshall, J., dissenting); *see also, e.g.*, HART & SACKS, *supra*, at 569; Deborah Hellman, *The Importance of Appearing Principled*, 37 ARIZ. L. REV. 1107 (1995); *cf. Casey*, 505 U.S. at 864–69 (arguing that overruling *Roe* would raise special concerns along these lines). *But see Dobbs*, 142 S. Ct. at 2278 (calling "concern about the public's reaction to our work" an "extraneous influence[ ]" that should not affect the Court's decisions).

In addition to highlighting the costs of overruling precedents, supporters of *stare decisis* also question the benefits of doing so. The principal benefit claimed by people who advocate relatively weak versions of *stare decisis* is the prospect of getting things right: if the Court misinterpreted the law in Case #1, there is something to be said for the idea that the Court should fix its mistake in Case #2. But critics of this argument point out that even when the current Court believes that a prior Court's decision was mistaken, we cannot be sure who is right. If it is just as likely that the past Court was correct as that the current Court is correct, then a strong doctrine of *stare decisis* might make sense even if we put a high value on getting things right.

On the other hand, later courts do have some advantages over earlier courts, and so it is plausible that a strong version of *stare decisis* would perpetuate more erroneous precedents than a weaker version. *See* Nelson, *supra* note 10, 87 VA. L. REV. at 54–61. In addition, people concerned about the costs of legal uncertainty should not automatically assume that weak versions of *stare decisis* generate substantially more uncertainty than strong versions of *stare decisis*. Even if all Justices purported to apply a strong version of *stare decisis*, some of them would not be very enthusiastic about applying precedents that they consider mistaken. If the Court's norms discourage overruling such precedents forthrightly, Justices might end up drawing fine distinctions that cabin the precedents but that are hard to predict or to apply consistently. In at least some circumstances, that technique might conceivably produce *more* overall uncertainty than the prospect of a clean break from the precedent. *See id.* at 63–65 (noting that "people concerned about the costs of change should not assume that change can occur only through frank overruling, or that a single dramatic change is always more costly than a series of incremental changes").

---

1. SHOULD *STARE DECISIS* HAVE SPECIAL FORCE IN STATUTORY CASES?

Even with respect to precedents about constitutional law, many Justices believe that "a decision to overrule should rest on some special reason over and above the belief that a prior case was wrongly decided." *Casey*, 505 U.S. at 864; *accord, e.g.*, Allen v. Cooper, 140 S. Ct. 994, 1003 (2020); Arizona v. Rumsey, 467 U.S. 203, 212 (1984). But if the Supreme Court is reluctant to overrule one of its past interpretations of the federal Constitution, the Court is even more reluctant to overrule one of its past interpretations of a federal statute. Over the years, the Court has repeatedly indicated that "[c]onsiderations of *stare decisis* have special force in the area of statutory interpretation." *Patterson v. McLean Credit Union*, 491 U.S. 164, 172 (1989); *accord, e.g.*, Kimble v. Marvel Entertainment, LLC, 576 U.S. 446, 456 (2015); Halliburton Co. v. Erica P. John Fund, Inc., 573 U.S. 258, 274 (2014). That remains true today. *See, e.g.*, Ramos v. Louisiana, 140 S. Ct. 1390, 1413 (2020) (Kavanaugh, J., concurring in part) ("In statutory cases, *stare decisis* is comparatively strict . . . ."). *But see* Gamble v. United States, 139 S. Ct. 1960, 1987 (2019) (Thomas, J., concurring) ("I am not aware of any legal (as opposed to practical) basis for applying a heightened version of *stare decisis* to statutory-interpretation decisions.").

One of the standard arguments for giving *stare decisis* more weight in statutory cases than in constitutional cases has to do with the longevity of judicial errors. If the Supreme Court misinterprets the Constitution and then refuses to overrule its precedent, there sometimes is no way for other governmental institutions to work around the Court's mistake. By contrast, if the Supreme Court misinterprets a federal statute, the current Congress can override the Court's mistake simply by passing a new statute that establishes a different rule going forward. For that reason, one might expect robust doctrines of *stare decisis* to produce fewer long-term costs in statutory cases than in constitutional cases.

But while this argument is widely accepted, how much does it really bear on the choice between strong and weaker versions of *stare decisis*?

The premise of the argument is plausible: Congress's ability to respond to judicial interpretations of federal statutes may well alleviate some of the disadvantages commonly associated with strong doctrines of *stare decisis*. Yet wouldn't the same ability also alleviate some of the disadvantages commonly associated with *weak* doctrines of *stare decisis*? For instance, suppose that the Supreme Court initially interprets a statute to mean one thing, but later changes its mind and adopts a different interpretation. If the new interpretation upsets too many people's legitimate expectations or otherwise causes problems of the sort associated with weak versions of *stare decisis*, the current Congress can react with a new statute re-establishing the earlier doctrine. In other words, just as Congress can react when a judicial decision produces "inaccuracy" costs (of the sort associated with strong versions of *stare decisis*), so too Congress can react when a judicial decision produces "instability" costs (of the sort associated with weak versions of *stare decisis*). If Congress can indeed mitigate *both* sorts of costs, does Congress's ability to react to judicial decisions really give strong versions of *stare decisis* an edge over weaker versions?

Even if one agrees that strong doctrines of *stare decisis* are likely to produce fewer costs in statutory cases than in constitutional cases, moreover, that argument may have a flip side: strong doctrines of *stare decisis* might also be likely to produce fewer *benefits* in statutory cases than in constitutional cases. After all, to the extent that Congress can freely change the law going forward, the Supreme Court is not fully in charge of the predictability of legal doctrine: even if the Court adheres to all of its precedents, there is always a risk that Congress will pass new statutes that upset people's expectations. Regardless of one's version of *stare decisis*, no court can credibly guarantee doctrinal consistency in areas that Congress periodically revisits.

Perhaps, however, the argument about Congress's ability to respond to judicial decisions has a somewhat different point. One might maintain that even when it is desirable to override a precedent, it is often best (or least costly) to do so purely prospectively, by establishing a new doctrine for future transactions while preserving the old doctrine for past transactions. One might further maintain that federal courts cannot validly act in that way; when they change their minds about the meaning of a statute, they have no way to limit their new understanding of the law to cases about future transactions while applying their old understanding of the law to cases about past transactions. *See infra* pp. 611–615 (canvassing debates about whether federal courts have the power to engage in "prospective" overruling). The legislature, by contrast, can readily act purely prospectively, simply by enacting a new statute that establishes a new rule going forward. If one thinks that most precedents should be overridden only prospectively if at all, and that courts cannot limit the temporal effect of overruling decisions in this way, then one might want the legislature to take the lead in overriding precedents that lie within its power to override (such as precedents about the meaning of its past statutes).

Historically, this argument figured prominently in opinions about the force of *stare decisis* in statutory cases. *See, e.g.*, White v. Denman, 1 Ohio St. 110, 115 (1853) ("If the law, as heretofore pronounced by the court, in giving a construction to the statute, ought not to stand, it is in the power of the Legislature to amend it without impairing rights acquired under it."). But how far does the argument go? If accepted, would it mean that the Supreme Court should establish an *absolute* rule of *stare decisis* in statutory cases—a rule that categorically forbids the Court to overrule any of its past interpretations of federal statutes? One academic commentator has supported an inflexible rule of that sort, albeit for a different reason. *See* Lawrence C. Marshall, *"Let Congress Do It": The Case for an Absolute Rule of Statutory Stare Decisis*, 88 MICH. L. REV. 177 (1989) (advocating this rule in the hope that Congress would then do more to monitor the Supreme Court's interpretations of federal statutes). But the Supreme Court has never gone nearly so far. Why not? Is there some plausible response to the concern that (prospective) statutes are a better way to override statutory precedents than (retrospective) judicial decisions, and that courts should therefore adhere to such precedents unless and until the legislature responds with a new statute?

Even if that concern has force in some contexts, does it support the broad idea that *all* precedents about statutory interpretation should have special force? Or is it limited to precedents that are likely to have generated significant reliance interests or whose overruling by courts would otherwise raise substantial concerns about retroactivity? For instance, people concerned about retroactivity might well conclude that if the Supreme Court initially interprets a penal statute narrowly, so that the statute does not criminalize certain acts that it could have been read to reach, the Court should not change its mind in some later case and hold that the statute has criminalized those acts all along. In that context, a judicial decision overruling the initial interpretation would "ha[ve], to some extent, the effect of an *ex post facto* law." *Davis v. Commonwealth*, 58 Va. 617, 622 (1867). But would the same concerns about retroactivity apply if the initial decision had read the criminal statute broadly and the Court was now thinking about adopting a narrower interpretation?

The fact that Congress has the power to override judicial interpretations of federal statutes, and to establish new rules of decision going forward, is sometimes linked to another argument for giving *stare decisis* more force as to interpretations of statutes than as to interpretations of the Constitution. According to this argument, when the Supreme Court issues a decision that Congress has the power to override (such as a decision about the meaning of a federal statute), and when Congress does not in fact override that decision, Congress's acquiescence effectively adds to the decision's precedential force. As we shall see below, there are various spins on why that might be so.

The next two cases raise many of the arguments just canvassed. As you will see, the majority opinions in both cases gave substantial weight to *stare decisis* (albeit in different ways). In both cases, though, there were strong dissents.[12]

Flood v. Kuhn

407 U.S. 258 (1972)

■ *JUSTICE BLACKMUN delivered the opinion of the Court [except as to Part I, which only JUSTICES STEWART and REHNQUIST joined]:*

For the third time in 50 years the Court is asked specifically to rule that professional baseball's reserve system is within the reach of the federal antitrust laws.[1] [In particular, the petitioner argued that the

[12] Both cases come from the Supreme Court and involve the precedential effect of past Supreme Court decisions. That is the usual context in which people discuss whether *stare decisis* should have special force with respect to statutory interpretation. As Justice Barrett noted during her days as a law professor, though, circuit courts can face the same question with respect to circuit precedents. *See* Amy Coney Barrett, *Statutory Stare Decisis in the Courts of Appeals*, 73 GEO. WASH. L. REV. 317 (2005). To be sure, a three-judge panel of a circuit court normally cannot overrule circuit precedent at all. But when circuit courts sit en banc, they sometimes have to decide whether to overrule circuit precedent—and while the en banc court may not feel bound to follow precedents established by a three-judge panel, it may give more weight to precedents that were themselves established en banc. *See supra* pp. 581–582. If you believe that the Supreme Court should give special precedential force to its past decisions about the meaning of federal statutes, do you think that circuit courts sitting en banc should be equally reluctant to overrule their own past decisions about the meaning of federal statutes? *Cf.* Barrett, *supra*, 73 GEO. WASH. L. REV. at 351–52 (concluding that even if one accepts the arguments for heightened statutory *stare decisis* at the Supreme Court level, those arguments are not persuasive with respect to circuit courts).

[1] The reserve system, publicly introduced into baseball contracts in 1887, . . . centers in the uniformity of player contracts; the confinement of the player to the club that has him under the contract; the assignability of the player's contract; and the ability of the club annually to renew the contract unilaterally, subject to a stated salary minimum. Thus

A. Rule 3 of the Major League Rules provides in part:

"(a) UNIFORM CONTRACT. To preserve morale and to produce the similarity of conditions necessary to keen competition, the contracts between all clubs and their players in the Major Leagues shall be in a single form which shall be prescribed by the Major League Executive Council. No club shall make a contract different from the uniform contract or a contract containing a non-reserve clause, except with the written approval of the Commissioner. . . .

. . . .

"(g) TAMPERING. To preserve discipline and competition, and to prevent the enticement of players, coaches, managers and umpires, there shall be no negotiations or dealings respecting employment, either present or prospective, between any player, coach or manager and any club other than the club with which he is under contract or acceptance of terms, or by which he is reserved, or which has the player on its Negotiation List, or between any umpire and any league other than the league with which he is under contract or acceptance of terms, unless the club or league with which he is connected shall have, in writing, expressly authorized such negotiations or dealings prior to their commencement."

B. Rule 9 of the Major League Rules provides in part:

"(a) NOTICE. A club may assign to another club an existing contract with a player. The player, upon receipt of written notice of such assignment, is by his contract bound to serve the assignee.

concerted activity involved in maintaining the reserve system violated § 1 of the Sherman Act, which prohibits "[e]very contract, combination, . . . or conspiracy, in restraint of trade or commerce among the several States, or with foreign nations." Act of July 2, 1890, ch. 647, 26 Stat. 209 (codified at 15 U.S.C. § 1).] . . . .

I

The Game

[Part I of Justice Blackmun's opinion was a paean to baseball. (Blackmun was a fan.) One particularly remarkable passage simply listed 88 storied players, managers, and other baseball figures—"names . . . that have sparked the diamond and its environs and that have provided tinder for recaptured thrills, for reminiscence and comparisons, and for conversation and anticipation in-season and off-season." Only two of Justice Blackmun's colleagues joined this portion of his opinion, so Part I did not speak for a majority of the Court.]

II

The Petitioner

The petitioner, Curtis Charles Flood, born in 1938, began his major league career in 1956 when he signed a contract with the Cincinnati Reds

---

. . . .

"After the date of such assignment all rights and obligations of the assignor clubs thereunder shall become the rights and obligations of the assignee club . . . ."

C. Rules 3 and 9 of the Professional Baseball Rules contain provisions parallel to those just quoted.

D. The Uniform Player's Contract provides in part:

"4. (a) . . . The Player agrees that, in addition to other remedies, the Club shall be entitled to injunctive and other equitable relief to prevent a breach of this contract by the Player, including, among others, the right to enjoin the Player from playing baseball for any other person or organization during the term of this contract."

"5. (a) The Player agrees that, while under contract, and prior to expiration of the Club's right to renew this contract, he will not play baseball otherwise than for the Club, except that the Player may participate in post-season games under the conditions prescribed in the Major League Rules. . . ."

"6. (a) The Player agrees that this contract may be assigned by the Club (and reassigned by any assignee Club) to any other Club in accordance with the Major League Rules and the Professional Baseball Rules."

"10. (a) On or before January 15 (or if a Sunday, then the next preceding business day) of the year next following the last playing season covered by this contract, the Club may tender to the Player a contract for the term of that year by mailing the same to the Player at his address following his signature hereto, or if none be given, then at his last address of record with the Club. If prior to the March 1 next succeeding said January 15, the Player and the Club have not agreed upon the terms of such contract, then on or before 10 days after said March 1, the Club shall have the right by written notice to the Player at said address to renew this contract for the period of one year on the same terms, except that the amount payable to the Player shall be such as the club shall fix in said notice; provided, however, that said amount, if fixed by a Major League Club, shall be an amount payable at a rate not less than 80% of the rate stipulated for the preceding year.

"(b) The Club's right to renew this contract, as provided in subparagraph (a) of this paragraph 10, and the promise of the Player not to play otherwise than with the Club have been taken into consideration in determining the amount payable under paragraph 2 hereof."

for a salary of $4,000 for the season. He had no attorney or agent to advise him on that occasion. He was traded to the St. Louis Cardinals before the 1958 season. Flood rose to fame as a center fielder with the Cardinals during the years 1958–1969. In those 12 seasons he compiled a batting average of .293. . . . Flood has received seven Golden Glove Awards. He was co-captain of his team from 1965–1969. He ranks among the 10 major league outfielders possessing the highest lifetime fielding averages.

Flood's St. Louis compensation for the years shown was:

1961	$13,500 (including a bonus for signing)
1962	$16,000
1963	$17,500
1964	$23,000
1965	$35,000
1966	$45,000
1967	$50,000
1968	$72,500
1969	$90,000

These figures do not include any so-called fringe benefits or World Series shares.

But at the age of 31, in October 1969, Flood was traded to the Philadelphia Phillies of the National League in a multi-player transaction. He was not consulted about the trade. He was informed by telephone and received formal notice only after the deal had been consummated. In December he complained to the Commissioner of Baseball and asked that he be made a free agent and be placed at liberty to strike his own bargain with any other major league team. His request was denied.

Flood then instituted this antitrust suit in January 1970 in federal court for the Southern District of New York. The defendants . . . were the Commissioner of Baseball, the presidents of the two major leagues, and the 24 major league clubs. . . .

Flood declined to play for Philadelphia in 1970, despite a $100,000 salary offer, and he sat out the year. After the season was concluded, Philadelphia sold its rights to Flood to the Washington Senators. Washington and the petitioner were able to come to terms for 1971 at a salary of $110,000. Flood started the season but, apparently because he was dissatisfied with his performance, he left the Washington club on April 27, early in the campaign. He has not played baseball since then.

III

The Present Litigation

Judge Cooper, in a detailed opinion, first denied a preliminary injunction, 309 F. Supp. 793 (S.D.N.Y. 1970), observing on the way:

> "Baseball has been the national pastime for over one hundred years and enjoys a unique place in our American heritage. Major league professional baseball is avidly followed by millions of fans, looked upon with fervor and pride and provides a special source of inspiration and competitive team spirit especially for the young.
>
> "Baseball's status in the life of the nation is so pervasive that it would not strain credulity to say the Court can take judicial notice that baseball is everybody's business. To put it mildly and with restraint, it would be unfortunate indeed if a fine sport and profession, which brings surcease from daily travail and an escape from the ordinary to most inhabitants of this land, were to suffer in the least because of undue concentration by any one or any group on commercial and profit considerations. The game is on higher ground; it behooves every one to keep it there." [*Id.*] at 797.

Flood's application for an early trial was granted. . . .

Trial to the court took place in May and June 1970. . . . [With respect to Flood's antitrust claims, Judge Cooper] held that *Federal Baseball Club v. National League*, 259 U.S. 200 (1922), and *Toolson v. New York Yankees, Inc.*, 346 U.S. 356 (1953), were controlling . . . and that judgment was to be entered for the defendants. . . .

On appeal, the Second Circuit felt "compelled to affirm." 443 F.2d 264, 265 (1971). . . .

We granted certiorari in order to look once again at this troublesome and unusual situation. . . .

IV

The Legal Background

A. *Federal Baseball Club v. National League*, 259 U.S. 200 (1922), was a suit for treble damages instituted by a member of the Federal League (Baltimore) against the National and American Leagues and others. The plaintiff obtained a verdict in the trial court, but the Court of Appeals reversed. The main brief filed by the plaintiff with this Court discloses that it was strenuously argued, among other things, that the business in which the defendants were engaged was interstate commerce; that the interstate relationship among the several clubs, located as they were in different States, was predominant; that organized baseball represented an investment of colossal wealth; that it was an engagement in moneymaking; that gate receipts were divided by agreement between the home club and the visiting club; and that the business of baseball was to be distinguished from the mere playing of the game as a sport for physical exercise and diversion. . . .

Mr. Justice Holmes, in speaking succinctly for a unanimous Court, said:

> "The business is giving exhibitions of base ball, which are purely state affairs. . . . [T]he fact that in order to give the exhibitions the

Leagues must induce free persons to cross state lines and must arrange and pay for their doing so is not enough to change the character of the business. . . . [T]he transport is a mere incident, not the essential thing. That to which it is incident, the exhibition, although made for money would not be called trade or commerce in the commonly accepted use of those words. As it is put by the defendant, personal effort, not related to production, is not a subject of commerce. That which in its consummation is not commerce does not become commerce among the States because the transportation that we have mentioned takes place. To repeat the illustrations given by the Court below, a firm of lawyers sending out a member to argue a case, or the Chautauqua lecture bureau sending out lecturers, does not engage in such commerce because the lawyer or lecturer goes to another State.

"If we are right[,] the plaintiff's business is to be described in the same way and the restrictions by contract that prevented the plaintiff from getting players to break their bargains and the other conduct charged against the defendants were not an interference with commerce among the States." 259 U.S. at 208–209.

. . . .

B. *Federal Baseball* was cited a year later, and without disfavor, in another opinion by Mr. Justice Holmes for a unanimous Court. The complaint charged antitrust violations with respect to vaudeville bookings. It was held, however, that the claim was not frivolous and that the bill should not have been dismissed. *Hart v. B.F. Keith Vaudeville Exchange*, 262 U.S. 271 (1923).[*]

. . . .

In the years that followed, baseball continued to be subject to intermittent antitrust attack. The courts, however, rejected these challenges on the authority of *Federal Baseball*. . . . And in the 1952 Report of the Subcommittee on Study of Monopoly Power of the House Committee on the Judiciary, H.R. Rep. No. 2002, 82d Cong., 2d Sess., 229, it was said, in conclusion:

[*] *Editor's note*: Hart, who was in the business of acting as the agent for vaudeville performers and getting contracts for them to perform in theaters across the United States, had brought an antitrust suit against various corporations in the same business and the owners of many important theaters. On the strength of *Federal Baseball*, the district court dismissed Hart's suit at the pleading stage, but the Supreme Court reversed and remanded for further proceedings. Justice Holmes's opinion for the Court suggested that there might be a distinction between the business of baseball and the business of vaudeville productions (which allegedly involved the transportation in interstate commerce of "large quantities of scenery, costumes and animals" in addition to the human performers); according to Justice Holmes, Hart might be able to show that in some instances, the interstate transportation of the apparatus used in vaudeville acts should not be deemed simply incidental to the personal efforts put forth by the performers. As it turned out, however, Hart failed to do so. He lost at trial because his evidence did not bear out the possibility that Justice Holmes had had in mind. *See* Hart v. B.F. Keith Vaudeville Exchange, 12 F.2d 341 (2d Cir. 1926) (affirming judgment for defendants).

"On the other hand the overwhelming preponderance of the evidence established baseball's need for some sort of reserve clause. Baseball's history shows that chaotic conditions prevailed when there was no reserve clause. Experience points to no feasible substitute to protect the integrity of the game or to guarantee a comparatively even competitive struggle. The evidence adduced at the hearings would clearly not justify the enactment of legislation flatly condemning the reserve clause."

C. . . . [In 1953, the Court granted certiorari in three cases in which the lower courts had relied on *Federal Baseball*,] and, by a short *per curiam* [opinion], . . . affirmed the judgments of the respective courts of appeals in those three cases. *Toolson v. New York Yankees, Inc.*, 346 U.S. 356 (1953). *Federal Baseball* was cited as holding "that the business of providing public baseball games for profit between clubs of professional baseball players was not within the scope of the federal antitrust laws," 346 U.S. at 357, and:

"Congress has had the ruling under consideration but has not seen fit to bring such business under these laws by legislation having prospective effect. The business has thus been left for thirty years to develop, on the understanding that it was not subject to existing antitrust legislation. The present cases ask us to overrule the prior decision and, with retrospective effect, hold the legislation applicable. We think that if there are evils in this field which now warrant application to it of the antitrust laws it should be by legislation. Without re-examination of the underlying issues, the judgments below are affirmed on the authority of *Federal Baseball Club of Baltimore v. National League of Professional Baseball Clubs*, *supra*, so far as that decision determines that Congress had no intention of including the business of baseball within the scope of the federal antitrust laws." *Ibid.*

This quotation reveals four reasons for the Court's affirmance . . . : (a) Congressional awareness for three decades of the Court's ruling in *Federal Baseball*, coupled with congressional inaction. (b) The fact that baseball was left alone to develop for that period upon the understanding that the reserve system was not subject to existing federal antitrust laws. (c) A reluctance to overrule *Federal Baseball* with consequent retroactive effect. (d) A professed desire that any needed remedy be provided by legislation rather than by court decree. . . .

It is of interest to note that in *Toolson* the petitioner had argued flatly that *Federal Baseball* "is wrong and must be overruled," Brief for Petitioner, No. 18, O.T. 1953, p. 19 . . . .

D. *United States v. Shubert*, 348 U.S. 222 (1955), was a civil antitrust action against defendants engaged in the production of legitimate theatrical attractions throughout the United States and in operating theaters for the presentation of such attractions. The District Court had dismissed the complaint on the authority of *Federal Baseball* and *Toolson*. . . . This Court reversed. Mr. Chief Justice Warren noted the Court's broad conception of "trade or commerce" in the antitrust statutes and the types of enterprises already held to be within the reach of that phrase. He stated that *Federal Baseball* and *Toolson* afforded no basis for a conclusion that businesses built around the performance of local exhibitions are exempt from the antitrust laws. 348 U.S. at 227. He then went on to elucidate the holding in *Toolson* by meticulously spelling out the factors mentioned above . . . .

E. *United States v. International Boxing Club*, 348 U.S. 236 (1955), was a companion to *Shubert* and was decided the same day. This was a civil antitrust action against defendants engaged in the business of promoting professional championship boxing contests. Here again the District Court had dismissed the complaint in reliance upon *Federal Baseball* and *Toolson*. The Chief Justice observed that "if it were not for *Federal Baseball* and *Toolson*, we think that it would be too clear for dispute that the Government's allegations bring the defendants within the scope of the Act." 348 U.S. at 240–241. He pointed out that the defendants relied on the two baseball cases but also would have been content with a more restrictive interpretation of them than the *Shubert* defendants, for the boxing defendants argued that the cases immunized only businesses that involve exhibitions of an athletic nature. The Court accepted neither argument. It again noted . . . that "*Toolson* neither overruled *Federal Baseball* nor necessarily reaffirmed all that was said in *Federal Baseball*." It stated:

> "The controlling consideration in *Federal Baseball* and *Hart* was, instead, a very practical one—the degree of interstate activity involved in the particular business under review. It follows that *stare decisis* cannot help the defendants here; for, contrary to their argument, *Federal Baseball* did not hold that all businesses based on professional sports were outside the scope of the antitrust laws. The issue confronting us is, therefore, not whether a previously granted exemption should continue, but whether an exemption should be granted in the first instance. And that issue is for Congress to resolve, not this Court." 348 U.S. at 243.

The Court noted the presence then in Congress of various bills forbidding the application of the antitrust laws to "organized professional sports enterprises"; the holding of extensive hearings on some of these; subcommittee opposition; a postponement recommendation as to baseball; and the fact that "Congress thus left intact the then-existing coverage of the antitrust laws." [*Id.*] at 243–244.

Mr. Justice Frankfurter, joined by Mr. Justice Minton, dissented. "It would baffle the subtlest ingenuity," he said, "to find a single differentiating factor between other sporting exhibitions . . . and baseball insofar as the conduct of the sport is relevant to the criteria or considerations by which the Sherman Law becomes applicable to a 'trade or commerce.'" [*Id.*] at 248. . . .

F. The parade marched on. *Radovich v. National Football League*, 352 U.S. 445 (1957), was a civil Clayton Act case testing the application of the antitrust laws to professional football. The District Court dismissed. The Ninth Circuit affirmed in part on the basis of *Federal Baseball* and *Toolson*. The court did not hesitate to "confess that the strength of the pull" of the baseball cases and of *International Boxing* "is about equal," but then observed that "[f]ootball is a team sport" and boxing an individual one. 231 F.2d 620, 622.

This Court reversed with an opinion by Mr. Justice Clark. He said that the Court made its ruling in *Toolson* "because it was concluded that more harm would be done in overruling *Federal Baseball* than in upholding a ruling which at best was of dubious validity." 352 U.S. at 450. He noted that Congress had not acted. He then said:

> "All this, combined with the flood of litigation that would follow its repudiation, the harassment that would ensue, and the retroactive effect of such a decision, led the Court to the practical result that it should sustain the unequivocal line of authority reaching over many years.
>
> "[S]ince *Toolson* and *Federal Baseball* are still cited as controlling authority in antitrust actions involving other fields of business, we now specifically limit the rule there established to the facts there involved, *i.e.*, the business of organized professional baseball. As long as the Congress continues to acquiesce we should adhere to—but not extend—the interpretation of the Act made in those cases. . . .
>
> "If this ruling is unrealistic, inconsistent, or illogical, it is sufficient to answer, aside from the distinctions between the businesses, that were we considering the question of baseball for the first time upon a clean slate we would have no doubts. But *Federal Baseball* held the business of baseball outside the scope of the Act. No other business claiming the coverage of those cases has such an adjudication. We therefore, conclude that the orderly way to eliminate error or discrimination, if any there be, is by legislation and not by court decision. Congressional processes are more accommodative, affording the whole industry hearings and an opportunity to assist in the formulation of new legislation. The resulting product is therefore more likely to protect the industry and the public alike. The whole scope of congressional action would be known long in advance and effective dates for the legislation could be set in the future without the injustices of retroactivity and surprise which might follow court action." 352 U.S. at 450–452 (footnote omitted).

Mr. Justice Frankfurter dissented essentially for the reasons stated in his dissent in *International Boxing*. Mr. Justice Harlan, joined by Mr. Justice Brennan, also dissented because he, too, was "unable to distinguish football from baseball." [*Id.*] at 456. Here again the dissenting

Justices did not call for the overruling of the baseball decisions. They merely could not distinguish the two sports and, out of respect for *stare decisis*, voted to affirm.

G. Finally, in *Haywood v. National Basketball Assn.*, 401 U.S. 1204 (1971), Mr. Justice Douglas, in his capacity as Circuit Justice, reinstated a District Court's injunction *pendente lite* in favor of a professional basketball player and said, "Basketball . . . does not enjoy exemption from the antitrust laws." [*Id.*] at 1205.

H. This series of decisions understandably spawned extensive commentary, some of it mildly critical and much of it not; nearly all of it looked to Congress for any remedy that might be deemed essential.

I. Legislative proposals have been numerous and persistent. Since *Toolson* more than 50 bills have been introduced in Congress relative to the applicability or nonapplicability of the antitrust laws to baseball. A few of these passed one house or the other. Those that did would have expanded, not restricted, the reserve system's exemption to other professional league sports. And the Act of Sept. 30, 1961, Pub. L. 87–331, 75 Stat. 732, and the merger addition thereto effected by the Act of Nov. 8, 1966, Pub. L. 89–800, § 6(b), 80 Stat. 1515, 15 U.S.C. §§ 1291–1295, were also expansive rather than restrictive as to antitrust exemption.[18]

V

In view of all this, it seems appropriate now to say that:

1. Professional baseball is a business and it is engaged in interstate commerce.

2. With its reserve system enjoying exemption from the federal antitrust laws, baseball is, in a very distinct sense, an exception and an anomaly. *Federal Baseball* and *Toolson* have become an aberration confined to baseball.

3. Even though others might regard this as "unrealistic, inconsistent, or illogical," see *Radovich*, 352 U.S. at 452, the aberration is an established one, and one that has been recognized not only in *Federal Baseball* and *Toolson*, but in *Shubert, International Boxing*, and *Radovich*, as well, a total of five consecutive cases in this Court. It is an aberration that has been with us now for half a century, one heretofore deemed fully entitled to the benefit of *stare decisis*, and one that has survived the Court's expanding concept of interstate commerce. It rests on a recognition and an acceptance of baseball's unique characteristics and needs.

---

[18] Title 15 U.S.C. § 1294 reads: "Nothing contained in this chapter shall be deemed to change, determine, or otherwise affect the *applicability* or *nonapplicability* of the antitrust laws to any act, contract, agreement, rule, course of conduct, or other activity by, between, or among persons engaging in, conducting, or participating in the organized professional team sports of football, baseball, basketball, or hockey, except the agreements to which section 1291 of this title shall apply." (Emphasis supplied.)

4. Other professional sports operating interstate—football, boxing, basketball, and, presumably, hockey and golf—are not so exempt.

5. The advent of radio and television, with their consequent increased coverage and additional revenues, has not occasioned an overruling of *Federal Baseball* and *Toolson*.

6. The Court has emphasized that since 1922 baseball, with full and continuing congressional awareness, has been allowed to develop and to expand unhindered by federal legislative action. Remedial legislation has been introduced repeatedly in Congress but none has ever been enacted. The Court, accordingly, has concluded that Congress as yet has had no intention to subject baseball's reserve system to the reach of the antitrust statutes. This, obviously, has been deemed to be something other than mere congressional silence and passivity. Cf. *Boys Markets, Inc. v. Retail Clerk's Union*, 398 U.S. 235, 241–242 (1970).

7. The Court has expressed concern about the confusion and the retroactivity problems that inevitably would result with a judicial overturning of *Federal Baseball*. It has voiced a preference that if any change is to be made, it come by legislative action that, by its nature, is only prospective in operation.

8. The Court noted in *Radovich*, 352 U.S. at 452, that the slate with respect to baseball is not clean. Indeed, it has not been clean for half a century.

This emphasis and this concern are still with us. We continue to be loath, 50 years after *Federal Baseball* and almost two decades after *Toolson*, to overturn those cases judicially when Congress, by its positive inaction, has allowed those decisions to stand for so long and, far beyond mere inference and implication, has clearly evinced a desire not to disapprove them legislatively.

Accordingly, we adhere once again to *Federal Baseball* and *Toolson* and to their application to professional baseball. We adhere also to *International Boxing* and *Radovich* and to their respective applications to professional boxing and professional football. If there is any inconsistency or illogic in all this, it is an inconsistency and illogic of long standing that is to be remedied by the Congress and not by this Court. If we were to act otherwise, we would be withdrawing from the conclusion as to congressional intent made in *Toolson* and from the concerns as to retrospectivity therein expressed. Under these circumstances, there is merit in consistency even though some might claim that beneath that consistency is a layer of inconsistency. . . .

The judgment of the Court of Appeals is [affirmed].

■ *JUSTICE WHITE joins in the judgment of the Court, and in all but Part I of the Court's opinion.*

■ *JUSTICE POWELL took no part in the consideration or decision of this case.*

■ *CHIEF JUSTICE BURGER, concurring:*

I concur in all but Part I of the Court's opinion but, like Mr. Justice Douglas, I have grave reservations as to the correctness of *Toolson v. New York Yankees, Inc.*, 346 U.S. 356 (1953) . . . . The error, if such it be, is one on which the affairs of a great many people have rested for a long time. Courts are not the forum in which this tangled web ought to be unsnarled. I agree with Mr. Justice Douglas that congressional inaction is not a solid base, but the least undesirable course now is to let the matter rest with Congress; it is time the Congress acted to solve this problem.

■ *JUSTICE DOUGLAS, with whom JUSTICE BRENNAN concurs, dissenting:*

This Court's decision in *Federal Baseball Club* . . . is a derelict in the stream of the law that we, its creator, should remove. Only a romantic view[1] of a rather dismal business account over the last 50 years would keep that derelict in midstream.

In 1922 the Court had a narrow, parochial view of commerce. With the demise of the old landmarks of that era, . . . the whole concept of commerce has changed.

Under the modern decisions such as . . . *United States v. Darby*, 312 U.S. 100 [(1941)]; *Wickard v. Filburn*, 317 U.S. 111 [(1942)]; [and] *United States v. South-Eastern Underwriters Assn.*, 322 U.S. 533 [(1944)], the power of Congress was recognized as broad enough to reach all phases of the vast operations of our national industrial system. An industry so dependent on radio and television as is baseball and gleaning vast interstate revenues would be hard put today to say with the Court in the *Federal Baseball Club* case that baseball was only a local exhibition, not trade or commerce.

Baseball is today big business that is packaged with beer, with broadcasting, and with other industries. The beneficiaries of the *Federal Baseball Club* decision are not the Babe Ruths, Ty Cobbs, and Lou Gehrigs.

The owners, whose records many say reveal a proclivity for predatory practices, do not come to us with equities. The equities are with the victims of the reserve clause. I use the word "victims" in the Sherman Act sense, since a contract which forbids anyone to practice his calling is commonly called an unreasonable restraint of trade. . . .

If congressional inaction is our guide, we should rely upon the fact that Congress has refused to enact bills broadly exempting professional sports from antitrust regulation.[3] H.R. Rep. No. 2002, 82nd Cong., 2d

---

[1] While I joined the Court's opinion in *Toolson v. New York Yankees, Inc.*, 346 U.S. 356, I have lived to regret it; and I would now correct what I believe to be its fundamental error.

[3] The Court's reliance upon congressional inaction disregards the wisdom of *Helvering v. Hallock*, 309 U.S. 106, 119–121 [(1940)], where we said:

> "Nor does want of specific Congressional repudiations . . . serve as an implied instruction by Congress to us not to reconsider, in the light of new experience[,] . . . those decisions . . . .

Sess. (1952). The only statutory exemption granted by Congress to professional sports concerns broadcasting rights. 15 U.S.C. §§ 1291–1295. I would not ascribe a broader exemption through inaction than Congress has seen fit to grant explicitly.

There can be no doubt "that were we considering the question of baseball for the first time upon a clean slate" we would hold it to be subject to federal antitrust regulation. *Radovich v. National Football League*, 352 U.S. 445, 452. The unbroken silence of Congress should not prevent us from correcting our own mistakes.

■ *JUSTICE MARSHALL, with whom JUSTICE BRENNAN joins, dissenting:*

.... Has Congress acquiesced in our decisions in *Federal Baseball Club* and *Toolson*? I think not. Had the Court been consistent and treated all sports in the same way baseball was treated, Congress might have become concerned enough to take action. But, the Court was inconsistent, and baseball was isolated and distinguished from all other sports. In *Toolson* the Court refused to act because Congress had been silent. But the Court may have read too much into this legislative inaction.

Americans love baseball as they love all sports. Perhaps we become so enamored of athletics that we assume that they are foremost in the minds of legislators as well as fans. We must not forget, however, that there are only some 600 major league baseball players. Whatever muscle they might have been able to muster by combining forces with other athletes has been greatly impaired by the manner in which this Court has isolated them. It is this Court that has made them impotent, and this Court should correct its error.

We do not lightly overrule our prior constructions of federal statutes, but when our errors deny substantial federal rights, like the right to compete freely and effectively to the best of one's ability as guaranteed by the antitrust laws, we must admit our error and correct it. We have done so before and we should do so again here....

To the extent that there is concern over any reliance interests that club owners may assert, they can be satisfied by making our decision prospective only. Baseball should be covered by the antitrust laws beginning with this case and henceforth, unless Congress decides otherwise.

Accordingly, I would overrule *Federal Baseball Club* and *Toolson* and reverse the decision of the Court of Appeals.

This does not mean that petitioner would necessarily prevail, however. Lurking in the background is a hurdle of recent vintage that

---

It would require very persuasive circumstances enveloping Congressional silence to debar this Court from re-examining its own doctrines.... Various considerations of parliamentary tactics and strategy might be suggested as reasons for the inaction of ... Congress, but they would only be sufficient to indicate that we walk on quicksand when we try to find in the absence of corrective legislation a controlling legal principle."

....

petitioner still must overcome. In 1966, the Major League Players Association was formed. It is the collective-bargaining representative for all major league baseball players. Respondents argue that the reserve system is now part and parcel of the collective-bargaining agreement and that because it is a mandatory subject of bargaining, the federal labor statutes are applicable, not the federal antitrust laws. The lower courts did not rule on this argument, having decided the case solely on the basis of the antitrust exemption.

.... I would remand the case to the District Court for consideration of whether petitioner can state a claim under the antitrust laws despite the collective-bargaining agreement, and, if so, for a determination of whether there has been an antitrust violation in this case.

NOTES AND QUESTIONS

1. Article I of the Constitution gives Congress the power "[t]o regulate Commerce with foreign Nations, and among the several States, and with the Indian tribes." U.S. CONST. art. I, § 8, cl. 1; *see also id.* cl. 18 (adding that Congress can also "make all Laws which shall be necessary and proper for carrying into Execution the foregoing Powers"). Congress was exercising that power when it enacted the Sherman Act in 1890. Thus, Section 1 of the Sherman Act did not prohibit *all* contracts, combinations, or conspiracies in restraint of trade, but only those "in restraint of trade or commerce among the several States, or with foreign nations." Act of July 2, 1890, ch. 647, § 1, 26 Stat. 209, 209 (codified at 15 U.S.C. § 1).

In 1890, and continuing until the 1930s, the Supreme Court had a relatively narrow understanding of Congress's constitutional power to regulate interstate and foreign commerce. The Court's 1922 decision in *Federal Baseball Club* was consistent with those cases. Although the specific issue in *Federal Baseball Club* concerned the Sherman Act's reference to "trade or commerce among the several States," the Court's rationale might have been equally applicable to the parallel phrase in Article I of the Constitution. *See* Fed. Baseball Club of Baltimore, Inc. v. Nat'l League of Prof'l Baseball Clubs, 259 U.S. 200, 209 (1922) (asserting that even when done for money, "the exhibition [of baseball games] . . . would not be called trade or commerce in the commonly accepted use of those words," and explaining that "personal effort, not related to production, is not a subject of commerce"). Thus, both the Court and members of Congress might have thought that the Constitution did not allow Congress to prohibit anticompetitive conduct with respect to the business of putting on baseball games.

By the early 1940s, however, the Supreme Court had articulated a new and broader understanding of the powers conferred by the combination of the Commerce Clause and the Necessary and Proper Clause. *See* Wickard v. Filburn, 317 U.S. 111 (1942); United States v. Darby, 312 U.S. 100 (1941); NLRB v. Jones & Laughlin Steel Corp., 301 U.S. 1 (1937); *see also* BARRY CUSHMAN, RETHINKING THE NEW DEAL

COURT: THE STRUCTURE OF A CONSTITUTIONAL REVOLUTION 224 (1998) ("By the end of 1942, the Court was thinking about the federal commerce power . . . in ways that were fundamentally at odds with the ways the Court had treated such issues only five years before.").

In *United States v. South-eastern Underwriters Ass'n*, 322 U.S. 533 (1944), the Court addressed whether this shift in constitutional doctrine should affect how courts applied the Sherman Act. A federal grand jury had indicted the South-eastern Underwriters Association and other defendants for allegedly violating the Sherman Act by conspiring to fix prices and otherwise restrict competition in the sale of fire-insurance policies in six states. In 1890, when Congress enacted the Sherman Act, courts probably would have said that the Constitution does not authorize Congress to prohibit such conspiracies; nineteenth-century cases about the dormant aspects of the Commerce Clause had held that insurance policies "are not articles of commerce in any proper meaning of the word," with the apparent result that the insurance industry could be regulated by the states but not by Congress. *See* Paul v. Virginia, 75 U.S. (8 Wall.) 168, 183 (1869); *accord, e.g.*, Hooper v. California, 155 U.S. 648, 654–55 (1895); N.Y. Life Ins. Co. v. Deer Lodge Cty., 231 U.S. 495, 502–12 (1913). In *South-eastern Underwriters*, however, the Supreme Court rethought that conclusion and held that the Commerce Clause does allow Congress to regulate the interstate business of insurance. *See South-eastern Underwriters*, 322 U.S. at 543–53. As a matter of statutory interpretation, moreover, the Court held that the Sherman Act should be understood to do so: the Act prohibited contracts, combinations, and conspiracies in restraint of trade in the insurance industry no less than in other industries.[13]

That conclusion was not inevitable. As used in the Sherman Act, the phrase "commerce among the several States" could perhaps have been interpreted to refer to constitutional doctrine as it stood at the time of enactment, so that the Act would not reach industries that were not regarded as part of "commerce" in 1890. On that interpretation of the statute, even if constitutional doctrine later changed and courts came to think that Congress does have the power to prohibit anticompetitive practices in the insurance industry, the Sherman Act would not actually do so.

In *South-eastern Underwriters*, however, a closely divided Supreme Court interpreted the Act more broadly. Citing legislative history, Justice Black's majority opinion concluded that the enacting Congress "wanted to go to the utmost extent of its Constitutional power in restraining trust and monopoly agreements such as the indictment here charges." *Id.* at

[13] Congress reacted to this decision by enacting the McCarran-Ferguson Act, ch. 24, 59 Stat. 33 (1945). That Act provided that "the Sherman Act . . . shall not apply to the business of insurance" until 1948, and even then would apply only "to the extent that such business is not regulated by State law." *Id.* §§ 2(b), 3(a), 59 Stat. at 34 (codified as amended at 15 U.S.C. §§ 1012(b), 1013(a)); *cf. id.* § 3(b), 59 Stat. at 34 (codified at 15 U.S.C. § 1013(b)) (preserving the Sherman Act's applicability with respect to boycotts and acts of "coercion[ ] or intimidation").

558. In effect, the majority read the Sherman Act to prohibit such agreements to the full extent of Congress's commerce powers, whatever that extent might be—with the result that some agreements were prohibited even though people in 1890 would not have thought that Congress *could* prohibit them.[14]

How should the Court's holding in *South-eastern Underwriters* have affected the Court's decision in *Toolson v. New York Yankees*, 346 U.S. 356 (1953)? Back in 1922, *Federal Baseball Club* had held that the Sherman Act did not reach the sort of conspiracy that was being alleged in *Toolson*, involving the business of baseball. But by 1953, when *Toolson* reached the Court, all of the Justices would have agreed that Congress has the constitutional power to prohibit such conspiracies. Given *South-eastern Underwriters*, should the *Toolson* Court have overruled *Federal Baseball Club*?

Recall that the doctrine of *stare decisis* is said to give precedents about the meaning of a statute more weight than precedents about the meaning of the Constitution. For purposes of this distinction, how would you characterize *Federal Baseball Club*? Although the case technically was about the meaning of the phrase "commerce among the several States" in the Sherman Act, the Court's holding was informed by distinctions that the Court had drawn when interpreting the parallel phrase in the Constitution. Until the 1940s, moreover, members of Congress probably would not have thought that they had the constitutional power to override *Federal Baseball Club* and extend the Sherman Act to baseball. Does that fact weaken the precedential force of *Federal Baseball Club*? Does it matter that even in the 1940s, after constitutional doctrine had shifted, Congress did not enact legislation overriding *Federal Baseball Club*?

2. The contrast between the Supreme Court's 1953 decision in *Toolson* (adhering to *Federal Baseball Club* with respect to professional baseball) and the ensuing string of decisions from the 1950s (reaching a different conclusion with respect to theatrical attractions, boxing, and football) raises a question that is central to the practical application of *stare decisis*: even if the Court decides not to overrule a precedent, how does it identify the proposition for which the precedent stands? If you had been a member of the Supreme Court in the 1950s, and if you had decided to adhere to the holding of *Federal Baseball Club* on the ground of *stare decisis*, how would you have characterized that holding going forward? What would you have taken *Federal Baseball Club* to have decided in a way that should bind later courts?

---

[14] This interpretation was not necessarily contrary to the original meaning of the Sherman Act. To be sure, the Sherman Act's reference to "commerce among the several States" could have been understood to incorporate the glosses associated with that phrase in the constitutional doctrine of 1890 (effectively freezing that doctrine in place for purposes of subsequent applications of the Sherman Act). But the phrase could also be understood to refer to whatever the same phrase means in the Constitution—with the result that the proper application of the Sherman Act would be linked to the proper interpretation of the Constitution itself.

Here are some possibilities. *Federal Baseball Club* could have been understood to cover any business built around the exhibition, in a particular locality, of any sort of performances in which the personal effort of the performers is the central focus. Or *Federal Baseball Club* could at least have been understood to cover any business built around the exhibition in a particular locality of *athletic* performances in which the personal effort of the performers is the central focus. Or the case could have been said to be only about team sports, or only about baseball, or only about baseball as it stood in the 1920s (when there were just eight teams in each league, television did not exist, and the games could really be thought of as local performances in the same way that a high-school play is a local performance). How should a Justice choose among these possible statements of the relevant holding?

Does the proposition that one takes *Federal Baseball Club* to establish need to be linked to some plausible reading of the statute that the Court was interpreting? There is no apparent reading of the Sherman Act that *does not* reach the conspiracies alleged in *Federal Baseball Club* and *Toolson* (about baseball) but that *does* reach the conspiracies alleged in the other cases from the 1950s (about theatrical performances, boxing, and football). Does it follow that the Supreme Court did something wrong in the 1950s? Or is there a plausible version of *stare decisis* under which the result that a precedent reached on particular facts is sometimes more binding than any rationale for those results—so that even if baseball and football are indistinguishable from the perspective of both the statutory text and the logic behind *Federal Baseball Club*, the Court can properly limit *Federal Baseball Club* to baseball?

3. Both in *Toolson* and in *Flood v. Kuhn*, the Court emphasized that Congress had long been aware of *Federal Baseball Club*, yet had failed to override it. Because the next section of this book considers that argument in detail, we will postpone our discussion of it for now. But the series of questions just posed is relevant to the legislative-acquiescence argument too. Suppose you had been a member of the Supreme Court in the 1950s, and you accepted the notion that Congress's acquiescence in *Federal Baseball Club* was significant. In the absence of an actual statute authoritatively telling you what Congress had decided, how would you know the *scope* of Congress's acquiescence?

In the 1950s, the Court seemed to assume that Congress had acquiesced in *Federal Baseball Club* with respect to baseball but not with respect to other sports. That conclusion, though, is narrower than anything that the logic of *Federal Baseball Club* supports. Instead of saying that baseball was special, Justice Holmes's opinion in *Federal Baseball Club* suggested that the business of putting on *any* sort of local exhibitions driven by the individual efforts of the performers is not part of "trade or commerce among the several States" within the meaning of the Sherman Act. If one takes seriously the Court's idea of legislative acquiescence, how did the Court in the 1950s know that Congress had acquiesced only in the inapplicability of the Sherman Act to baseball and not in the rationale of *Federal Baseball Club* more broadly?

4. After *Toolson*, the Supreme Court sought to "limit the rule . . . established [in *Federal Baseball Club* and *Toolson*] to the facts there involved." *Radovich v. National Football League*, 352 U.S. 445, 451 (1957). Specifically, the Court limited the precedential force of those cases to the business of baseball. But the identity of the industry involved in *Federal Baseball Club* and *Toolson* surely is not the only fact that the Court could have used to limit those precedents. Imagine that in *Flood v. Kuhn*, the Court had instead said something along the following lines:

> We're not going to overrule either *Federal Baseball Club* or *Toolson*, but we also don't agree with everything that our opinions in those cases said. In particular, we disagree with how *Toolson* characterized the holding of *Federal Baseball Club*. See *Toolson*, 346 U.S. at 357 (describing *Federal Baseball Club* as having held categorically that "the business of providing public baseball games for profit between clubs of professional baseball players was not within the scope of the federal antitrust laws"); see also *United States v. Shubert*, 348 U.S. 222, 229 (1955) (describing *Federal Baseball Club* as "specifically fixing the status of the baseball business under the antitrust laws"). As we understand *Federal Baseball Club*, it addressed only the business of baseball as it stood in the 1920s, before radio had really begun to transform that business. And as we understand *Toolson*, it addressed only the business of baseball as it stood in 1953—after television had started to have an impact, but before that impact was anything like it now is. Whatever the proper rule about the *local* exhibition of baseball games, the current business of baseball is genuinely interstate in a way that it wasn't at the time of our prior cases. We do not overrule either *Federal Baseball Club* or *Toolson*, but we also do not think that they control our decision now; the facts about the business of baseball have changed in the intervening years. Specifically, the changes wrought by television have made the interstate elements of the business so prominent that agreements among major-league teams tending to restrict competition for players do indeed amount to "conspirac[ies] in restraint of trade or commerce among the several States" within the meaning of the Sherman Act.

Such an opinion would have read the Court's precedents even more narrowly than the Court did in *Flood v. Kuhn*, but it would not actually have overruled any of those precedents on their precise facts, and it would have had the added benefit of reflecting a plausible interpretation of the statutory text. Did the doctrine of *stare decisis* prevent the Court from taking this route? *Cf.* Kevin McDonald, *Antitrust and Baseball: Stealing Holmes*, 1998-2 J. SUP. CT. HIST. 89, 107–22 (emphasizing factual changes in the business of baseball, including the importance of broadcasting, and criticizing both *Toolson* and *Flood*).

5. When the Supreme Court thinks that a prior decision was wrong, it often seems inclined to try to limit the damage caused by the decision. One way to do so might be to overrule the decision entirely. But another approach is to take a narrow view of the decision's holding, so that it can be distinguished. If you think that there are good policy arguments for a fairly strong doctrine of *stare decisis*, do those policy arguments cut against the latter strategy just as much as they cut against the former strategy? For instance, should the very same ideas that made the Court reluctant to "overrule" *Federal Baseball Club* (even though the Court no longer believed in its rationale) also have kept the Court from confining the holding of that case to baseball?

To the extent that one sees *stare decisis* as a means of promoting predictability, the Court's performance in the 1950s seems hard to defend. (The case-by-case process of distinguishing baseball from other exhibitions made the law quite murky for a number of years.) The Court also did not save itself the burden of reconsidering the merits of prior cases. (To justify limiting *Federal Baseball Club*, the Court first had to decide that it disagreed with *Federal Baseball Club*.) But do reliance interests help justify what the Court did in the 1950s? Would overruling *Federal Baseball Club* have been unfair to the baseball owners who were maintaining the reserve system in reliance upon the idea that the Sherman Act did not cover the business of baseball? Is there some reason why the reliance interests of owners in the National Football League were not equally strong?

The concept of reliance interests is linked to the content of the existing doctrines of *stare decisis*. If the Court freely overruled most precedents that it considered mistaken, even baseball owners would have been on notice that the Court might overrule *Federal Baseball Club*, and there might have been fewer reliance interests for the Court to protect. On the other hand, if the doctrine of *stare decisis* encouraged the Court to adhere to *Federal Baseball Club* with respect to baseball but allowed the Court to distinguish other sports, then baseball owners might indeed have had stronger reliance interests than football owners.

To the extent that the current Court can tweak the content of the doctrine of *stare decisis*, we presumably would like the doctrine to produce the optimal level of reliance—not too much (given the competing interests that sometimes support overruling a precedent), but also not too little (given the desirability of allowing various actors to predict the legal consequences of their activities). Aside from armchair speculation, is there any way to identify the level of reliance that is optimal? Exactly how much do we want government officials and people in the private sector to rely on what the Court says about the law, and how much do we want them to anticipate the possibility that a future Court might say something else?

6. In urging the Court to overrule both *Federal Baseball Club* and *Toolson*, Justice Marshall's dissent in *Flood v. Kuhn* asserted that "any reliance interests that club owners may assert . . . can be satisfied by making our decision prospective only." What should one make of that suggestion? Could the Supreme Court legitimately have issued an opinion declaring that although baseball owners would not be held liable under the Sherman Act for anything that they had done before the date of the Court's opinion, they should henceforth assume that the Sherman Act covers baseball to the same extent that it covers professional football and basketball?

That sort of opinion is certainly unusual. When a court decides to attribute a particular legal directive to a statute (or, indeed, to any other source of law), the court ordinarily acts as if that directive has been part of the law from the outset and applies to all pending cases governed by the statute—including cases about transactions that occurred before the court announced its understanding of the statute. Around the time of *Flood v. Kuhn*, though, the federal Supreme Court did occasionally issue opinions announcing rules of decision that the Court declined to apply to pending cases but was planning to apply in the future. *See, e.g.*, Chevron Oil Co. v. Huson, 404 U.S. 97, 105–09 (1971). Under one version of that approach, the Court might have (1) announced that in cases involving future conduct it would understand the Sherman Act to cover the business of baseball, but (2) declined to apply that interpretation of the Sherman Act in Curt Flood's case and (3) instructed the lower federal courts not to apply the new interpretation to any other cases about conduct undertaken before the date of the Court's announcement.

One drawback with this sort of "pure prospectivity" is that in certain circumstances, it might eliminate the incentive for litigants to ask the Court to overrule questionable precedents. After all, if litigants can predict that getting the Supreme Court to overrule a precedent will not do them any good, they might not push for that result. To address this problem, some jurists thought it permissible to engage in so-called "selective prospectivity." Under that approach, the Court might have announced that it no longer accepted *Federal Baseball Club*'s interpretation of the Sherman Act, but instead was embracing a new interpretation; that it was planning to apply the new interpretation in cases about future conduct; that it would also apply the new interpretation in Curt Flood's case to reward him for persuading the Court to change its mind; but that the judiciary would not apply the new interpretation to any other cases about conduct that occurred before the date of the Court's opinion. In effect, the Court's new interpretation would be purely prospective *except* for the one case that prompted the Court to overrule *Federal Baseball Club*.

In the 1980s and 1990s, however, the Court rethought the propriety of prospective decisionmaking. In *James B. Beam Distilling Co. v. Georgia*, 501 U.S. 529 (1991), members of the Supreme Court divided sharply about the propriety of prospective decisionmaking in civil cases.[15] Justice Scalia opined that the Constitution did not permit federal courts to engage in either "selective prospectivity" or "pure prospectivity" (at least with respect to federal law). In his view, "[t]he judicial Power" that Article III vests in the federal courts "must be deemed to be the judicial power as understood by our common-law tradition," which did not permit either type of prospectivity. *Id.* at 549 (Scalia, J., concurring in the judgment). Despite having raised the possibility of prospective decisionmaking in his dissent in *Flood v. Kuhn*, Justice Marshall joined Justice Scalia's opinion, as did Justice Blackmun. Two other Justices (Souter and Stevens) forswore "selective prospectivity" on the grounds that "similarly situated litigants should be treated the same," but declined to "speculate as to the bounds or propriety of pure prospectivity." *See id.* at 538–44 (opinion of Souter, J.). Justice White more grudgingly accepted the idea that "selective prospectivity" was off limits, but he affirmatively embraced "pure prospectivity" and denied that its propriety required any "speculat[ion]"; in his view, the Court's prior decisions conclusively established that pure prospectivity was permissible. *See id.* at 545–46 (White, J., concurring in the judgment). The remaining three Justices maintained that the Court should be able to engage in both "pure prospectivity" and "selective prospectivity" in appropriate cases. *See id.* at 549–59 (O'Connor, J., dissenting, joined by Kennedy, J., and Rehnquist, C.J.).

All told, a majority of the Justices in *Beam* rejected "selective prospectivity" (albeit without a majority rationale). Two years later, the Court's opinion in *Harper v. Virginia Department of Taxation*, 509 U.S. 86 (1993), confirmed this holding. *See id.* at 97 (asserting, on the basis of "the position of a majority of Justices in *Beam*," that "[w]hen this Court applies a rule of federal law to the parties before it, that rule is the controlling interpretation of federal law and must be given full retroactive effect in all cases still open on direct review and as to all events, regardless of whether such events predate or postdate our announcement of the rule.").[16] But *Harper* did not take a position on

[15] The Court had previously curtailed prospective decisionmaking in criminal cases. *See* Griffith v. Kentucky, 479 U.S. 314, 328 (1987) (holding that when the Supreme Court articulates a new understanding of the Constitution's requirements for criminal procedure, both state and federal courts should apply the new understanding in "all cases . . . pending on direct review or not yet final"). *But cf.* Teague v. Lane, 489 U.S. 288, 299–310 (1989) (plurality opinion) (indicating that new understandings of the Constitution's requirements for criminal procedure typically do not provide a basis for federal habeas relief with respect to convictions that became final before the new understandings were announced).

[16] While *Harper* itself addressed the temporal effect of a decision by the federal Supreme Court, the lower federal courts probably have no more authority than the Supreme Court to restrict the temporal effect of their interpretations of federal law. Indeed, even state courts should not refrain from applying the proper understanding of federal law to pending cases. *See Harper*, 509 U.S. at 97–99 (reversing a state court's judgment); *see also* Reynoldsville Casket Co. v. Hyde, 514 U.S. 749 (1995) (rejecting an argument that would have let state courts evade *Harper*). By its terms, though, *Harper* addressed only the temporal effect of judicial decisions about the content of *federal* law. State courts may be able to articulate different principles to govern the temporal effect of their decisions about the content of *state* law. *Compare* DiCenzo v. A-Best Products Co., 897 N.E.2d 132 (Ohio 2008) (declining to follow *Harper* with respect to the

"pure prospectivity," and federal circuit courts have debated the current state of the doctrine on that topic. *Compare* Glazner v. Glazner, 347 F.3d 1212, 1216–17 (11th Cir. 2003) (en banc) ("Although prospectivity appears to have fallen into disfavor with the Supreme Court, the Court has clearly retained the possibility of pure prospectivity and, we believe, has also retained the *Chevron Oil* test, albeit in a modified form, as the governing analysis for such determinations in civil cases." (citations omitted)), *and* Nunez-Reyes v. Holder, 646 F.3d 684, 690–92 (9th Cir. 2011) (en banc) (noting uncertainty but agreeing that *Chevron Oil* remains the governing precedent), *with* Hulin v. Fibreboard Corp., 178 F.3d 316, 333 (5th Cir. 1999) ("The Court's most recent decisions substantially reject [*Chevron Oil*] . . . and return to the general rule of adjudicative retroactivity, leaving only an indistinct possibility of the application of pure prospectivity in an extremely unusual and unforeseeable case.").

This issue goes beyond the doctrine of *stare decisis*: it is possible to imagine "purely prospective" declarations even in cases of first impression. But let us focus on the prospective overruling of past decisions. For the sake of argument, suppose that the current Supreme Court would still say that it can overrule precedents purely prospectively in certain circumstances.[17] From the standpoint of the policies behind *stare decisis*, under what circumstances (if any) might prospective overruling be preferable to regular overruling? If one is concerned about treating like cases alike and protecting common notions of judicial legitimacy, prospective overruling has no clear advantage over regular overruling and in some respects may even be worse. A court that overrules a precedent prospectively also does not reduce decision costs (since the court still must decide whether the precedent was correct). Instead, as Justice Marshall suggested in *Flood*, the main reason to overrule a precedent purely prospectively involves reliance interests.

---

power of Ohio state courts to engage in prospective decisionmaking about the content of Ohio state law), *with* Deutsche Bank Nat'l Trust Co. v. Watts, 171 A.3d 392 (Vt. 2017) (following *Harper* as a matter of Vermont law).

[17] In his separate opinions in *Beam* and *Harper*, Justice Scalia suggested that the "judicial Power" conferred by Article III does not permit any sort of prospective decisionmaking, including prospective overruling. *See Beam*, 501 U.S. at 549 (Scalia, J., concurring in the judgment); *accord Harper*, 509 U.S. at 105–08 (Scalia, J., concurring). At least with respect to prospective overruling, though, that idea strikes me as implausible. I do not read Article III's reference to "judicial Power" as codifying any particular practices with respect to *stare decisis*; in my view, those practices remained matters of customary or common law even after the Constitution was ratified, and they could develop in the way that such law does. *Cf.* Frederick G. Kempin, Jr., *Precedent and Stare Decisis: The Critical Years, 1800 to 1850*, 3 AM. J. LEGAL HIST. 28, 50 (1959) ("American cases, up to the year 1800, had no firm doctrine of stare decisis. By 1825 some of the older states had come to a firmer stand on the authority of prior cases, and by 1850 this stand was solidified."). Admittedly, at least until the twentieth century, the customary law did not give the Supreme Court the option of prospective overruling, and whether the relevant principles have changed strikes me as a difficult question. If the common law now does allow prospective overruling, though, I do not think that Article III would stand in the way. *See* Caleb Nelson, *The Legitimacy of (Some) Federal Common Law*, 101 VA. L. REV. 1, 55–62 (2015) (fleshing out these claims).

What kinds of reliance interests would the practice of prospective overruling protect? The answer depends on exactly how the Court defines prospectivity. But if the overruling decision is seen as effectively changing the law (rather than simply announcing what the law has always been), perhaps the Court would draw an analogy to the test that it uses to avoid the retroactive application of new statutes. *See* Landgraf v. USI Film Products, 511 U.S. 244 (1994). On that way of thinking, to say that the overruling decision should operate purely prospectively might be to say that the change should not attach new legal consequences to transactions that occurred before the date of the decision.

That test protects some reliance interests, but not others. For instance, imagine that a company develops a particular business model and makes various long-term investments in reliance on the views expressed in a Supreme Court opinion. If the Court then overrules those views, even "purely prospectively," the Court's new understanding of the law may well scuttle the company's business model and dash the company's investment-backed expectations. *Cf. id.* at 269 ("A statute does not operate 'retrospectively' [in *Landgraf*'s sense] merely because it . . . upsets expectations based in prior law.").

Might *Flood v. Kuhn* itself illustrate this possibility? If baseball's reserve system gave owners significant benefits at the expense of players, the holdings of *Federal Baseball Club* and *Toolson* might have led would-be owners to pay more for a franchise than they otherwise would have. If the Court had then overruled those precedents (even "purely prospectively"), the value of the owners' stakes might have dropped. As a result, even prospective overruling might have undercut some nontrivial reliance interests. How much should the Court have cared about those interests? If your answer is "not much"—in particular, if you think that the Court should have been willing to upset investment-backed expectations of this sort for the sake of adopting what it had come to see as the proper interpretation of the Sherman Act—might other sorts of reliance interests deserve more respect? How should courts determine which types of reliance interests deserve the most protection?

You should not assume that federal courts routinely engage in prospective overruling. Even at the level of the Supreme Court, regular overruling is much more common. *See, e.g.*, Agostini v. Felton, 521 U.S. 203, 237 (1997) ("Our general practice is to apply the rule of law we announce in a case to the parties before us. We adhere to this practice even when we overrule a case." (citations omitted)). The Seventh Circuit, moreover, has suggested that prospective overruling should be even more unusual with respect to circuit precedent. *See* Suesz v. Med-1 Solutions, LLC, 757 F.3d 636, 649–50 (7th Cir. 2014) (en banc) ("[A] prior decision of one intermediate appellate court does not create the degree of certainty concerning an issue of federal law that would justify reliance so complete as to justify applying a decision only prospectively in order to protect settled expectations.").

7. Even if one believes that the doctrine of *stare decisis* should be especially powerful on questions of statutory interpretation, the Sherman Act is a special sort of statute: it drew the concept of contracts in restraint of trade from the common law, and Congress may have been trying to "federalize" the relevant principles of common law without foreclosing further elaboration and development. *See* Thomas W. Merrill, *The Common Law Powers of Federal Courts*, 52 U. CHI. L. REV. 1, 44–45 (1985). Contrary to the assumptions of some modern lawyers and judges who associate the common law with freewheeling judicial policymaking, that does not mean that the Sherman Act delegated unfettered lawmaking power to the courts. *See* Daniel A. Farber & Brett H. McDonnell, *"Is There a Text in This Class?" The Conflict Between Textualism and Antitrust*, 14 J. CONTEMP. LEGAL ISSUES 619 (2005) (explaining that textualists in particular should reject this view of the Sherman Act); *see also* Nelson, *supra* note 17, 101 VA. L. REV. at 45–50 (discussing the Sherman Act and agreeing that textualists should take common law more seriously). But it does mean, perhaps, that the development of doctrine under the Sherman Act should look a bit different than the articulation of the meaning of other statutes.

In *Leegin Creative Leather Products v. PSKS, Inc.*, 551 U.S. 877 (2007), the Supreme Court asserted that this point has implications for the doctrine of *stare decisis*. In the course of overruling a line of precedent that dated back nearly a century, Justice Kennedy's majority opinion asserted that "*[s]tare decisis* is not as significant in this case" as in other cases of statutory interpretation "because the issue before us is the scope of the Sherman Act" and "the Court has treated the Sherman Act as a common-law statute." *Id.* at 899; *accord* State Oil Co. v. Khan, 522 U.S. 3, 20–21 (1997). Does that idea undercut the Court's reliance on *stare decisis* in *Flood v. Kuhn*? Or is there a relevant difference between the Sherman Act's use of terms that resonate in the common law ("in restraint of trade") and the Sherman Act's use of the terms that were most central to *Federal Baseball Club* ("commerce" and "among the several States")?

8. A few years after *Flood v. Kuhn*, and notwithstanding the Supreme Court's decision, major-league baseball players gained the right to become free agents. The seeds of free agency lay in the Uniform Player's Contract quoted in the first footnote of the majority opinion in *Flood*. Paragraph 10(a) provided that if a team and a player who was under contract did not agree to a new contract at the expiration of the old one, the team had "the right . . . to renew this contract for the period of one year on the same terms" (except for the possibility of a salary adjustment). For many years, people assumed that if the same thing happened the following year, paragraph 10(a) would again give the team the right to renew the contract. *See, e.g.*, Flood v. Kuhn, 316 F. Supp. 271, 274 n.4 (S.D.N.Y. 1970) ("Any contract so renewed would itself contain this renewal clause."). But in 1975, in a grievance proceeding authorized

by the collective-bargaining agreement between the owners and the players' union, labor arbitrator Peter Seitz ruled that paragraph 10(a) conferred only a one-time renewal right. At the expiration of the one-year renewal period, players who did not agree to a new contract became free agents who could sign with any team. *See* STUART BANNER, THE BASEBALL TRUST: A HISTORY OF BASEBALL'S ANTITRUST EXEMPTION 219–35 (2013) (describing this decision and its aftermath, and providing a valuable history more generally).

Still, the advent of free agency did not end baseball's exemption from the antitrust laws. In 1998, Congress finally pared back that exemption with respect to the employment of major-league baseball players, though not with respect to other important aspects of the business of baseball. *See* Curt Flood Act of 1998, Pub. L. 105–297, 112 Stat. 2824; *see also* BANNER, *supra*, at 247 (noting that the exemption remains for "matters relating to broadcasting, to the minor leagues, to the relationship among teams, to the location and ownership of franchises, and to the employment of umpires").

The series of cases culminating in *Flood v. Kuhn* took an unusual approach to *stare decisis*: the Supreme Court did not overrule *Federal Baseball Club*, but the Court limited that precedent's legal effect to one industry. Such blatantly artificial limitations are rare. To be sure, when the Court concludes that one of its past decisions was mistaken but nonetheless should not be overruled, the Court might read the precedent narrowly and look for ways to distinguish new cases. Normally, though, the distinctions that the Court draws will have some conceivable basis either in the reasoning of the precedent or in the underlying laws. As the next case suggests, moreover, the Court sometimes gives dubious precedents their full effect.

Kimble v. Marvel Entertainment, LLC

576 U.S. 446 (2015)

■ *JUSTICE KAGAN delivered the opinion of the Court:*

In *Brulotte v. Thys Co.*, 379 U.S. 29 (1964), this Court held that a patent holder cannot charge royalties for the use of his invention after its patent term has expired. The sole question presented here is whether we should overrule *Brulotte*. Adhering to principles of *stare decisis*, we decline to do so. Critics of the *Brulotte* rule must seek relief not from this Court but from Congress.

I

In 1990, petitioner Stephen Kimble obtained a patent on a toy that allows children (and young-at-heart adults) to role-play as "a spider person" by shooting webs—really, pressurized foam string—"from the palm of [the] hand." . . . Respondent Marvel Entertainment, LLC

(Marvel) makes and markets products featuring Spider-Man, among other comic-book characters. Seeking to sell or license his patent, Kimble met with the president of Marvel's corporate predecessor to discuss his idea for web-slinging fun. Soon afterward, but without remunerating Kimble, that company began marketing the "Web Blaster"—a toy that, like Kimble's patented invention, enables would-be action heroes to mimic Spider-Man through the use of a polyester glove and a canister of foam.

Kimble sued Marvel in 1997 alleging, among other things, patent infringement. The parties ultimately settled that litigation. Their agreement provided that Marvel would purchase Kimble's patent in exchange for a lump sum (of about a half-million dollars) and a 3% royalty on Marvel's future sales of the Web Blaster and similar products. The parties set no end date for royalties, apparently contemplating that they would continue for as long as kids want to imitate Spider-Man (by doing whatever a spider can).

And then Marvel stumbled across *Brulotte*, the case at the heart of this dispute. In negotiating the settlement, neither side was aware of *Brulotte*. But Marvel must have been pleased to learn of it. *Brulotte* had read the patent laws to prevent a patentee from receiving royalties for sales made after his patent's expiration. See 379 U.S. at 32. So the decision's effect was to sunset the settlement's royalty clause.[2] On making that discovery, Marvel sought a declaratory judgment in federal district court confirming that the company could cease paying royalties come 2010—the end of Kimble's patent term. The court approved that relief, holding that *Brulotte* made "the royalty provision . . . unenforceable after the expiration of the Kimble patent." 692 F. Supp. 2d 1156, 1161 (D. Ariz. 2010). The Court of Appeals for the Ninth Circuit affirmed, though making clear that it was none too happy about doing so. "[T]he *Brulotte* rule," the court complained, "is counterintuitive and its rationale is arguably unconvincing." 727 F.3d 856, 857 (2013).

We granted certiorari to decide whether, as some courts and commentators have suggested, we should overrule *Brulotte*. For reasons of *stare decisis*, we demur.

II

. . . . In crafting the patent laws, Congress struck a balance between fostering innovation and ensuring public access to discoveries. While a patent lasts, the patentee possesses exclusive rights to the patented article—rights he may sell or license for royalty payments if he so chooses. See 35 U.S.C. § 154(a)(1). But a patent typically expires 20 years from the day the application for it was filed. See § 154(a)(2). And when the patent expires, the patentee's prerogatives expire too, and the right

[2] In *Brulotte*, the patent holder retained ownership of the patent while licensing customers to use the patented article in exchange for royalty payments. See 379 U.S. at 29–30. By contrast, Kimble sold his whole patent to obtain royalties. But no one here disputes that *Brulotte* covers a transaction structured in that alternative way.

to make or use the article, free from all restriction, passes to the public. See *Sears, Roebuck & Co. v. Stiffel Co.*, 376 U.S. 225, 230 (1964).

This Court has carefully guarded that cut-off date, just as it has the patent laws' subject-matter limits: In case after case, the Court has construed those laws to preclude measures that restrict free access to formerly patented, as well as unpatentable, inventions. In one line of cases, we have struck down state statutes with that consequence. . . . In a related line of decisions, we have deemed unenforceable private contract provisions limiting free use of such inventions. . . .

. . . . [In *Brulotte*], an inventor licensed his patented hop-picking machine to farmers in exchange for royalties from hop crops harvested both before and after his patents' expiration dates. The Court (by an 8–1 vote) held the agreement unenforceable—"unlawful *per se*"—to the extent it provided for the payment of royalties "accru[ing] after the last of the patents incorporated into the machines had expired." 379 U.S. at 30. To arrive at that conclusion, the Court began with the statutory provision setting the length of a patent term. See *id.* at 30 (quoting the then-current version of § 154). Emphasizing that a patented invention "become[s] public property once [that term] expires," the Court then quoted from [*Scott Paper Co. v. Marcalus Mfg. Co.*, 326 U.S. 249 (1945)]: Any attempt to limit a licensee's post-expiration use of the invention, "whatever the legal device employed, runs counter to the policy and purpose of the patent laws." In the *Brulotte* Court's view, contracts to pay royalties for such use continue "the patent monopoly beyond the [patent] period," even though only as to the licensee affected. 379 U.S. at 33. And in so doing, those agreements conflict with patent law's policy of establishing a "post-expiration . . . public domain" in which every person can make free use of a formerly patented product. *Ibid.*

The *Brulotte* rule, like others making contract provisions unenforceable, prevents some parties from entering into deals they desire. As compared to lump-sum fees, royalty plans both draw out payments over time and tie those payments, in each month or year covered, to a product's commercial success. And sometimes, for some parties, the longer the arrangement lasts, the better—not just up to but beyond a patent term's end. A more extended payment period, coupled (as it presumably would be) with a lower rate, may bring the price the patent holder seeks within the range of a cash-strapped licensee. . . . Or such an extended term may better allocate the risks and rewards associated with commercializing inventions—most notably, when years of development work stand between licensing a patent and bringing a product to market. . . . As to either goal, *Brulotte* may pose an obstacle.

Yet parties can often find ways around *Brulotte*, enabling them to achieve those same ends. To start, *Brulotte* allows a licensee to defer payments for pre-expiration use of a patent into the post-expiration period; all the decision bars are royalties for using an invention after it has moved into the public domain. . . . A licensee could agree, for example, to pay the licensor a sum equal to 10% of sales during the 20-year patent term, but to amortize that amount over 40 years. That arrangement would at least bring down early outlays, even if it would not do everything the parties might want to allocate risk over a long timeframe. And parties have still more options when a licensing agreement covers either multiple patents or additional non-patent rights. Under *Brulotte*, royalties may run until the latest-running patent covered in the parties' agreement expires. See 379 U.S. at 30. Too, post-expiration royalties are allowable so long as tied to a non-patent right—even when closely related to a patent. . . . That means, for example, that a license involving both a patent and a trade secret can set a 5% royalty during the patent period (as compensation for the two combined) and a 4% royalty afterward (as payment for the trade secret alone). Finally and most broadly, *Brulotte* poses no bar to business arrangements other than royalties—all kinds of joint ventures, for example—that enable parties to share the risks and rewards of commercializing an invention.

Contending that such alternatives are not enough, Kimble asks us to abandon *Brulotte* in favor of "flexible, case-by-case analysis" of post-expiration royalty clauses "under the rule of reason." Brief for Petitioners 45. Used in antitrust law, the rule of reason requires courts to evaluate a practice's effect on competition by "taking into account a variety of factors, including specific information about the relevant business, its condition before and after the [practice] was imposed, and the [practice's] history, nature, and effect." *State Oil Co. v. Khan*, 522 U.S. 3, 10 (1997). Of primary importance in this context, Kimble posits, is whether a patent holder has power in the relevant market and so might be able to curtail competition. See Brief for Petitioners 47–48; *Illinois Tool Works Inc. v. Independent Ink, Inc.*, 547 U.S. 28, 44 (2006) ("[A] patent does not necessarily confer market power"). Resolving that issue, Kimble notes, entails "a full-fledged economic inquiry into the definition of the market, barriers to entry, and the like." Brief for Petitioners 48 (quoting 1 H. Hovenkamp, M. Janis, M. Lemley, & C. Leslie, IP and Antitrust § 3.2e, p. 3–12.1 (2d ed., Supp. 2014) (Hovenkamp)).

III

Overruling precedent is never a small matter. *Stare decisis*—in English, the idea that today's Court should stand by yesterday's decisions—is "a foundation stone of the rule of law." *Michigan v. Bay Mills Indian Community*, 572 U.S. 782, 798 (2014). Application of that doctrine, although "not an inexorable command," is the "preferred course because it promotes the evenhanded, predictable, and consistent development of legal principles, fosters reliance on judicial decisions, and contributes to the actual and perceived integrity of the judicial process." *Payne v. Tennessee*, 501 U.S. 808, 827–828 (1991). It also reduces incentives for challenging settled precedents, saving parties and courts the expense of endless relitigation.

Respecting *stare decisis* means sticking to some wrong decisions. The doctrine rests on the idea, as Justice Brandeis famously wrote, that it is usually "more important that the applicable rule of law be settled than that it be settled right." *Burnet v. Coronado Oil & Gas Co.*, 285 U.S. 393, 406 (1932) (dissenting opinion). Indeed, *stare decisis* has consequence only to the extent it sustains incorrect decisions; correct judgments have no need for that principle to prop them up. Accordingly, an argument that we got something wrong—even a good argument to that effect—cannot by itself justify scrapping settled precedent. Or otherwise said, it is not alone sufficient that we would decide a case differently now than we did then. To reverse course, we require as well what we have termed a "special justification"—over and above the belief "that the precedent was wrongly decided." *Halliburton Co. v. Erica P. John Fund, Inc.*, 573 U.S. 258, 266 (2014).

What is more, *stare decisis* carries enhanced force when a decision, like *Brulotte*, interprets a statute. Then, unlike in a constitutional case, critics of our ruling can take their objections across the street [that is, from the Supreme Court's building to the Capitol, where Congress sits], and Congress can correct any mistake it sees. See, *e.g.*, *Patterson v. McLean Credit Union*, 491 U.S. 164, 172–173 (1989). That is true, contrary to the dissent's view, . . . regardless whether our decision focused only on statutory text or also relied, as *Brulotte* did, on the policies and purposes animating the law. See, *e.g.*, *Bilski v. Kappos*, 561 U.S. 593, 601–602 (2010). Indeed, we apply statutory *stare decisis* even when a decision has announced a "judicially created doctrine" designed to implement a federal statute. *Halliburton*, 573 U.S. at 274. All our interpretive decisions, in whatever way reasoned, effectively become part of the statutory scheme, subject (just like the rest) to congressional change. Absent special justification, they are balls tossed into Congress's court, for acceptance or not as that branch elects.

And Congress has spurned multiple opportunities to reverse *Brulotte*—openings as frequent and clear as this Court ever sees. *Brulotte* has governed licensing agreements for more than half a century. See *Watson v. United States*, 552 U.S. 74, 82–83 (2007) (stating that "long congressional acquiescence," there totaling just 14 years, "enhance[s] even the usual precedential force we accord to our interpretations of statutes" (internal quotation marks omitted)). During that time, Congress has repeatedly amended the patent laws, including the specific provision (35 U.S.C. § 154) on which *Brulotte* rested. See, *e.g.*, Uruguay Round Agreements Act, § 532(a), 108 Stat. 4983 (1994) (increasing the length of the patent term); Act of Nov. 19, 1988, § 201, 102 Stat. 4676 (limiting patent-misuse claims). *Brulotte* survived every such change. Indeed, Congress has rebuffed bills that would have replaced *Brulotte*'s *per se* rule with the same antitrust-style analysis Kimble now urges. See, *e.g.*, S. 1200, 100th Cong., 1st Sess., Tit. II (1987) (providing that no patent owner would be guilty of "illegal extension of the patent right by reason of his or her licensing practices . . . unless such practices . . . violate the antitrust laws"); S. 438, 100th Cong., 2d Sess., § 201(3) (1988) (same). Congress's continual reworking of the patent laws—but never of the *Brulotte* rule—further supports leaving the decision in place.

Nor yet are we done, for the subject matter of *Brulotte* adds to the case for adhering to precedent. *Brulotte* lies at the intersection of two areas of law: property (patents) and contracts (licensing agreements). And we have often recognized that in just those contexts—"cases involving property and contract rights"—considerations favoring *stare decisis* are "at their acme." *E.g., Payne*, 501 U.S. at 828; *Khan*, 522 U.S. at 20. That is because parties are especially likely to rely on such precedents when ordering their affairs. To be sure, Marvel and Kimble disagree about whether *Brulotte* has actually generated reliance. Marvel says yes: Some parties, it claims, do not specify an end date for royalties in their licensing agreements, instead relying on *Brulotte* as a default rule. Brief for Respondent 32–33; see 1 D. Epstein, Eckstrom's Licensing in Foreign and Domestic Operations § 3.13, p. 3–13, and n. 2 (2014) (noting that it is not "necessary to specify the term . . . of the license" when a decision like *Brulotte* limits it "by law"). Overturning *Brulotte* would thus upset expectations, most so when long-dormant licenses for long-expired patents spring back to life. Not true, says Kimble: Unfair surprise is unlikely, because no "meaningful number of [such] license agreements . . . actually exist." Reply Brief 18. To be honest, we do not know (nor, we suspect, do Marvel and Kimble). But even uncertainty on this score cuts in Marvel's direction. So long as we see a reasonable possibility that parties have structured their business transactions in light of *Brulotte*, we have one more reason to let it stand.

As against this superpowered form of *stare decisis*, we would need a superspecial justification to warrant reversing *Brulotte*. But the kinds of reasons we have most often held sufficient in the past do not help Kimble here. If anything, they reinforce our unwillingness to do what he asks.

First, *Brulotte*'s statutory and doctrinal underpinnings have not eroded over time. When we reverse our statutory interpretations, we most often point to subsequent legal developments—"either the growth of judicial doctrine or further action taken by Congress"—that have removed the basis for a decision. *Patterson*, 491 U.S. at 173 (calling this "the primary reason" for overruling statutory precedent). But the core feature of the patent laws on which *Brulotte* relied remains just the same: Section 154 now, as then, draws a sharp line cutting off patent rights after a set number of years. And this Court has continued to draw from that legislative choice a broad policy favoring unrestricted use of an invention after its patent's expiration. *Scott Paper*—the decision on which *Brulotte* primarily relied—remains good law. So too do this Court's other decisions refusing to enforce either state laws or private contracts constraining individuals' free use of formerly patented (or unpatentable) discoveries. . . . *Brulotte*, then, is not the kind of doctrinal dinosaur or legal last-man-standing for which we sometimes depart from *stare decisis*. . . . To the contrary, the decision's close relation to a whole web of precedents means that reversing it could threaten others. If *Brulotte* is outdated, then (for example) is *Scott Paper* too? We would prefer not to unsettle stable law.

And second, nothing about *Brulotte* has proved unworkable. See, *e.g.*, *Patterson*, 491 U.S. at 173 (identifying unworkability as another "traditional justification" for overruling precedent). The decision is simplicity itself to apply. A court need only ask whether a licensing agreement provides royalties for post-expiration use of a patent. If not, no problem; if so, no dice. *Brulotte*'s ease of use appears in still sharper relief when compared to Kimble's proposed alternative. Recall that he wants courts to employ antitrust law's rule of reason to identify and invalidate those post-expiration royalty clauses with anti-competitive consequences. But whatever its merits may be for deciding antitrust claims, that "elaborate inquiry" produces notoriously high litigation costs and unpredictable results. *Arizona v. Maricopa County Medical Soc.*, 457 U.S. 332, 343 (1982). For that reason, trading in *Brulotte* for the rule of reason would make the law less, not more, workable than it is now. Once again, then, the case for sticking with long-settled precedent grows stronger: Even the most usual reasons for abandoning *stare decisis* cut the other way here.

IV

Lacking recourse to those traditional justifications for overruling a prior decision, Kimble offers two different ones. He claims first that *Brulotte* rests on a mistaken view of the competitive effects of post-expiration royalties. He contends next that *Brulotte* suppresses technological innovation and so harms the nation's economy. (The dissent offers versions of those same arguments. See *post* at 465–468.) We consider the two claims in turn, but our answers to both are much the same: Kimble's reasoning may give Congress cause to upset *Brulotte*, but does not warrant this Court's doing so.

A

According to Kimble, we should overrule *Brulotte* because it hinged on an error about economics: It assumed that post-patent royalty "arrangements are invariably anticompetitive." Brief for Petitioners 37. That is not true, Kimble notes; indeed, such agreements more often increase than inhibit competition, both before and after the patent expires. See *id.* at 36–40. As noted earlier, a longer payment period will typically go hand-in-hand with a lower royalty rate. See *supra* at 453. During the patent term, those reduced rates may lead to lower consumer prices, making the patented technology more competitive with alternatives; too, the lesser rates may enable more companies to afford a license, fostering competition among the patent's own users. See Brief for Petitioners 38. And after the patent's expiration, Kimble continues, further benefits follow: Absent high barriers to entry (a material caveat, as even he would agree, see Tr. of Oral Arg. 12–13, 23), the licensee's continuing obligation to pay royalties encourages new companies to begin making the product, figuring that they can quickly attract customers by undercutting the licensee on price. See Brief for Petitioners 38–39. In light of those realities, Kimble concludes, "the *Brulotte per se* rule makes little sense." *Id.* at 11.

We do not join issue with Kimble's economics—only with what follows from it. A broad scholarly consensus supports Kimble's view of the competitive effects of post-expiration royalties, and we see no error in that shared analysis. See *id.* at 13–18 (citing numerous treatises and articles critiquing *Brulotte*). Still, we must decide what that means for *Brulotte.* Kimble, of course, says it means the decision must go. Positing that *Brulotte* turned on the belief that post-expiration royalties are always anticompetitive, he invokes decisions in which this Court abandoned antitrust precedents premised on similarly shaky economic reasoning. See Brief for Petitioners 55–56 (citing, *e.g.*, *Leegin Creative Leather Products, Inc. v. PSKS, Inc.*, 551 U.S. 877 (2007); *Illinois Tool Works*, 547 U.S. 28). But to agree with Kimble's conclusion, we must resolve two questions in his favor. First, even assuming Kimble accurately characterizes *Brulotte*'s basis, does the decision's economic mistake suffice to overcome *stare decisis*? Second and more fundamentally, was *Brulotte* actually founded, as Kimble contends, on an analysis of competitive effects?

If *Brulotte* were an antitrust rather than a patent case, we might answer both questions as Kimble would like. This Court has viewed *stare decisis* as having less-than-usual force in cases involving the Sherman Act. See, *e.g.*, *Khan*, 522 U.S. at 20–21. Congress, we have explained, intended that law's reference to "restraint of trade" to have "changing content," and authorized courts to oversee the term's "dynamic potential." *Business Electronics Corp. v. Sharp Electronics Corp.*, 485 U.S. 717, 731–732 (1988). We have therefore felt relatively free to revise our legal analysis as economic understanding evolves and (just as Kimble notes) to reverse antitrust precedents that misperceived a practice's competitive consequences. See *Leegin*, 551 U.S. at 899–900. Moreover, because the question in those cases was whether the challenged activity restrained trade, the Court's rulings necessarily turned on its understanding of economics. See *Business Electronics Corp.*, 485 U.S. at 731. Accordingly, to overturn the decisions in light of sounder economic reasoning was to take them "on [their] own terms." *Halliburton*, 573 U.S. at 271.

But *Brulotte* is a patent rather than an antitrust case, and our answers to both questions instead go against Kimble. To begin, even assuming that *Brulotte* relied on an economic misjudgment, Congress is the right entity to fix it. By contrast with the Sherman Act, the patent laws do not turn over exceptional law-shaping authority to the courts. Accordingly, statutory *stare decisis*—in which this Court interprets and

Congress decides whether to amend—retains its usual strong force. . . . And as we have shown, that doctrine does not ordinarily bend to "wrong on the merits"-type arguments; it instead assumes Congress will correct whatever mistakes we commit. . . . Nor does Kimble offer any reason to think his own "the Court erred" claim is special. Indeed, he does not even point to anything that has changed since *Brulotte*—no new empirical studies or advances in economic theory. Compare, *e.g.*, *Halliburton*, 573 U.S. at 270–274 (considering, though finding insufficient, recent economic research). On his argument, the *Brulotte* Court knew all it needed to know to determine that post-patent royalties are not usually anticompetitive; it just made the wrong call. See Brief for Petitioners 36–40. That claim, even if itself dead-right, fails to clear *stare decisis*'s high bar.

And in any event, *Brulotte* did not hinge on the mistake Kimble identifies. Although some of its language invoked economic concepts, the Court did not rely on the notion that post-patent royalties harm competition. Nor is that surprising. The patent laws—unlike the Sherman Act—do not aim to maximize competition (to a large extent, the opposite). And the patent term—unlike the "restraint of trade" standard—provides an all-encompassing bright-line rule, rather than calling for practice-specific analysis. So in deciding whether post-expiration royalties comport with patent law, *Brulotte* did not undertake to assess that practice's likely competitive effects. Instead, it applied a categorical principle that all patents, and all benefits from them, must end when their terms expire. See *Brulotte,* 379 U.S. at 30–32. Or more specifically put, the Court held, as it had in *Scott Paper*, that Congress had made a judgment: that the day after a patent lapses, the formerly protected invention must be available to all for free. And further: that post-expiration restraints on even a single licensee's access to the invention clash with that principle. See *Brulotte,* 379 U.S. at 31–32 (a licensee's obligation to pay post-patent royalties conflicts with the "free market visualized for the post-expiration period" and so "runs counter to the policy and purpose of the patent laws" (quoting *Scott Paper,* 326 U.S. at 256)). That patent (not antitrust) policy gave rise to the Court's conclusion that post-patent royalty contracts are unenforceable—utterly "regardless of a demonstrable effect on competition." 1 Hovenkamp § 3.2d at 3–10.

Kimble's real complaint may go to the merits of such a patent policy—what he terms its "formalis[m]," its "rigid[ity]", and its detachment from "economic reality." Brief for Petitioners 27–28. But that is just a different version of the argument that *Brulotte* is wrong. And it is, if anything, a version less capable than the last of trumping statutory *stare decisis*. For the choice of what patent policy should be lies first and foremost with Congress. So if Kimble thinks patent law's insistence on unrestricted access to formerly patented inventions leaves too little room for pro-competitive post-expiration royalties, then Congress, not this Court, is his proper audience.

B

Kimble also seeks support from the wellspring of all patent policy: the goal of promoting innovation. *Brulotte*, he contends, "discourages technological innovation and does significant damage to the American economy." Brief for Petitioners 29. Recall that would-be licensors and licensees may benefit from post-patent royalty arrangements because they allow for a longer payment period and a more precise allocation of risk. See *supra* at 453. If the parties' ideal licensing agreement is barred, Kimble reasons, they may reach no agreement at all. See Brief for Petitioners 32. And that possibility may discourage invention in the first instance. The bottom line, Kimble concludes, is that some "breakthrough technologies will never see the light of day." *Id.* at 33.

Maybe. Or, then again, maybe not. While we recognize that post-patent royalties are sometimes not anticompetitive, we just cannot say whether barring them imposes any meaningful drag on innovation. As we have explained, *Brulotte* leaves open various ways—involving both licensing and other business arrangements—to accomplish payment deferral and risk-spreading alike. See *supra* at 453–454. Those alternatives may not offer the parties the precise set of benefits and obligations they would prefer. But they might still suffice to bring patent holders and product developers together and ensure that inventions get to the public. Neither Kimble nor his *amici* have offered any empirical evidence connecting *Brulotte* to decreased innovation; they essentially ask us to take their word for the problem. And the United States, which acts as both a licensor and a licensee of patented inventions while also implementing patent policy, vigorously disputes that *Brulotte* has caused any "significant real-world economic harm." Brief for United States as *Amicus Curiae* 30. Truth be told, if forced to decide that issue, we would not know where or how to start.

Which is one good reason why that is not our job. Claims that a statutory precedent has "serious and harmful consequences" for innovation are (to repeat this opinion's refrain) "more appropriately addressed to Congress." *Halliburton*, 573 U.S. at 277. That branch, far more than this one, has the capacity to assess Kimble's charge that *Brulotte* suppresses technological progress. And if it concludes that *Brulotte* works such harm, Congress has the prerogative to determine the exact right response—choosing the policy fix, among many conceivable ones, that will optimally serve the public interest. As we have noted, Congress legislates actively with respect to patents, considering concerns of just the kind Kimble raises. See *supra* at 456–457. In adhering to our precedent as against such complaints, we promote the rule-of-law values to which courts must attend while leaving matters of public policy to Congress.

V

What we can decide, we can undecide. But *stare decisis* teaches that we should exercise that authority sparingly. Cf. S. Lee and S. Ditko, Amazing Fantasy No. 15: "Spider-Man," p. 13 (1962) ("[I]n this world, with great power there must also come—great responsibility"). Finding many reasons for staying the *stare decisis* course and no "special justification" for departing from it, we decline Kimble's invitation to overrule *Brulotte.*

For the reasons stated, the judgment of the Court of Appeals is affirmed.

■ *JUSTICE ALITO, with whom CHIEF JUSTICE ROBERTS and JUSTICE THOMAS join, dissenting:*

The Court employs *stare decisis,* normally a tool of restraint, to reaffirm a clear case of judicial overreach. Our decision in *Brulotte v. Thys Co.*, 379 U.S. 29 (1964), held that parties cannot enter into a patent licensing agreement that provides for royalty payments to continue after the term of the patent expires. That decision was not based on anything that can plausibly be regarded as an interpretation of the terms of the Patent Act. It was based instead on an economic theory—and one that has been debunked. The decision interferes with the ability of parties to negotiate licensing agreements that reflect the true value of a patent, and it disrupts contractual expectations. *Stare decisis* does not require us to retain this baseless and damaging precedent.

I

A

The Patent Act provides that a patent grants certain exclusive rights to the patentee and "his heirs or assigns" for a term of 20 years. 35 U.S.C. §§ 154(a)(1) and (2). The Act says nothing whatsoever about post-expiration royalties. In *Brulotte*, however, the Court held that such royalties are *per se* unlawful. The Court made little pretense of finding support for this holding in the language of the Act. Instead, the Court reasoned that allowing post-expiration royalties would subject "the free market visualized for the post-expiration period . . . to monopoly influences that have no proper place there." 379 U.S. at 32–33. Invoking antitrust concepts, the decision suggested that such arrangements are "an effort to enlarge the monopoly of the patent by t[y]ing the sale or use of the patented article to the purchase or use of unpatented ones." *Id.* at 33.

Whatever the merits of this economic argument, it does not represent a serious attempt to interpret the Patent Act. A licensing agreement that provides for the payment of royalties after a patent's term expires does not enlarge the patentee's monopoly or extend the term of the patent. It simply gives the licensor a contractual right. Thus, nothing in the text of the Act even arguably forbids licensing agreements that provide for post-expiration royalties.

Brulotte was thus a bald act of policymaking. It was not simply a case of incorrect statutory interpretation. It was not really statutory interpretation at all.

B

Not only was *Brulotte* based on policymaking, it was based on a policy that is difficult to defend. Indeed, in the intervening 50 years, its reasoning has been soundly refuted. . . .

Brulotte misperceived the purpose and effect of post-expiration royalties. The decision rested on the view that post-expiration royalties extend the patent term by means of an anti-competitive tying arrangement. As the Court understood such an arrangement, the patent holder leverages its monopoly power during the patent term to require payments after the term ends, when the invention would otherwise be available for free public use. But agreements to pay licensing fees after a patent expires do not "enlarge the monopoly of the patent." 379 U.S. at 33. Instead, "[o]nce the patent term expires, the power to exclude is gone," and all that is left "is a problem about optimal contract design." Easterbrook, Contract and Copyright, 42 Hous. L. Rev. 953, 955 (2005).

The economics are simple: Extending a royalty term allows the parties to spread the licensing fees over a longer period of time, which naturally has the effect of reducing the fees during the patent term. Restricting royalty payments to the patent term, as *Brulotte* requires, compresses payment into a shorter period of higher fees. The Patent Act does not prefer one approach over the other.

There are, however, good reasons why parties sometimes prefer post-expiration royalties over upfront fees, and why such arrangements have pro-competitive effects. Patent holders and licensees are often unsure whether a patented idea will yield significant economic value, and it often takes years to monetize an innovation. In those circumstances, deferred royalty agreements are economically efficient. They encourage innovators, like universities, hospitals, and other institutions, to invest in research that might not yield marketable products until decades down the line. See Brief for Memorial Sloan Kettering Cancer Center et al. as *Amici Curiae* 8–12. And they allow producers to hedge their bets and develop more products by spreading licensing fees over longer periods. See *ibid.* By prohibiting these arrangements, *Brulotte* erects an obstacle to efficient patent use. In patent law and other areas, we have abandoned *per se* rules with similarly disruptive effects. See, *e.g., Illinois Tool Works Inc. v. Independent Ink, Inc.*, 547 U.S. 28 (2006); *Leegin Creative Leather Products, Inc. v. PSKS, Inc.*, 551 U.S. 877 (2007).

The majority downplays this harm by insisting that "parties can often find ways around *Brulotte*." *Ante* at 453. But the need to avoid *Brulotte* is an economic inefficiency in itself. Parties are not always aware of the prohibition—as this case amply demonstrates. And the suggested alternatives do not provide the same benefits as post-expiration royalty agreements. . . .

C

On top of that, *Brulotte* most often functions to upset the parties' expectations.

This case illustrates the point. No one disputes that, when "negotiating the settlement, neither side was aware of *Brulotte.*" *Ante* at 450. Without knowledge of our *per se* rule, the parties agreed that Marvel would pay 3% in royalties on all of its future sales involving the Web Blaster and similar products. If the parties had been aware of *Brulotte,* they might have agreed to higher payments during the patent term. Instead, both sides expected the royalty payments to continue until Marvel stopped selling toys that fit the terms of the agreement. But that is not what happened. When Marvel discovered *Brulotte,* it used that decision to nullify a key part of the agreement. The parties' contractual expectations were shattered, and petitioners' rights were extinguished.

The Court's suggestion that some parties have come to rely on *Brulotte* is fanciful. The Court believes that there is a "reasonable possibility that parties have structured their business transactions in light of *Brulotte.*" *Ante* at 457–458. Its only support for this conclusion is Marvel's self-serving and unsupported assertion that some contracts might not specify an end date for royalties because the parties expect *Brulotte* to supply the default rule. To its credit, the Court stops short of endorsing this unlikely prediction, saying only that "uncertainty on this score cuts in Marvel's direction." *Ante* at 457.

But there is no real uncertainty. "[W]e do not know" if Marvel's assertion is correct because Marvel has provided no evidence to support it. *Ibid.* And there are reasons to believe that, if parties actually relied on *Brulotte* to supply a default rule, courts would enforce the contracts as the parties expected. See, *e.g.*, 27 R. Lord, Williston on Contracts § 70:124 (4th ed. 2003). What we know for sure, however, is that *Brulotte* has upended the parties' expectations here and in many other cases. [Citations omitted.] These confirmed problems with retaining *Brulotte* clearly outweigh Marvel's hypothetical fears.

II

In the end, *Brulotte*'s only virtue is that we decided it. But that does not render it invincible. *Stare decisis* is important to the rule of law, but so are correct judicial decisions. Adherence to prior decisions " 'promotes the evenhanded, predictable, and consistent development of legal principles, fosters reliance on judicial decisions, and contributes to the actual and perceived integrity of the judicial process.' " *Pearson v. Callahan,* 555 U.S. 223, 233 (2009) (quoting *Payne v. Tennessee,* 501 U.S. 808, 827 (1991)). But *stare decisis* is not an "inexorable command." [*Payne, supra,*] at 828 . . . . "Revisiting precedent is particularly appropriate where, as here, a departure would not upset expectations, the precedent consists of a judge-made rule . . . , and experience has pointed up the precedent's shortcomings." *Pearson, supra*, at 233.

Our traditional approach to *stare decisis* does not require us to retain *Brulotte*'s *per se* rule. *Brulotte*'s holding had no basis in the law. Its reasoning has been thoroughly disproved. It poses economic barriers that stifle innovation. And it unsettles contractual expectations.

It is not decisive that Congress could have altered *Brulotte*'s rule. In general, we are especially reluctant to overturn decisions interpreting statutes because those decisions can be undone by Congress. [Citations omitted.] The Court calls this a "superpowered form of *stare decisis*" that renders statutory interpretation decisions nearly impervious to challenge. *Ante* at 458. I think this goes a bit too far.

As an initial matter, we do not give super-duper protection to decisions that do not actually interpret a statute. When a precedent is based on a judge-made rule and is not grounded in anything that Congress has enacted, we cannot "properly place on the shoulders of Congress" the entire burden of correcting "the Court's own error." *Girouard v. United States,* 328 U.S. 61, 69–70 (1946). On the contrary, we have recognized that it is appropriate for us to correct rules of this sort. See, *e.g.*, *Leegin*, 551 U.S. at 899–900; *State Oil Co. v. Khan*, 522 U.S. 3, 20–21 (1997).

The Court says that it might agree if *Brulotte* were an antitrust precedent because *stare decisis* has "less-than-usual force in cases involving the Sherman Act." *Ante* at 461. But this distinction is unwarranted. We have been more willing to reexamine antitrust precedents because they have attributes of common-law decisions. I see no reason why the same approach should not apply where the precedent at issue, while purporting to apply a statute, is actually based on policy concerns. Indeed, we should be even more willing to reconsider such a precedent because the role implicitly assigned to the federal courts under the Sherman Act has no parallel in Patent Act cases.

Even taking the Court on its own terms, *Brulotte* was an antitrust decision masquerading as a patent case. The Court was principally concerned with patentees improperly leveraging their monopoly power. See 379 U.S. at 32–33. And it expressly characterized post-expiration royalties as anti-competitive tying arrangements. See *id.* at 33. It makes no sense to afford greater *stare decisis* protection to *Brulotte*'s thinly veiled antitrust reasoning than to our Sherman Act decisions.

The Court also places too much weight on Congress' failure to overturn *Brulotte*. We have long cautioned that "[i]t is at best treacherous to find in congressional silence alone the adoption of a controlling rule of law." *Girouard, supra*, at 69. Even where Congress has considered, but not adopted, legislation that would abrogate a judicial ruling, it cannot be inferred that Congress' failure to act shows that it approves the ruling. See *Central Bank of Denver, N.A. v. First Interstate Bank of Denver, N.A.*,

511 U.S. 164, 187 (1994). " '[S]everal equally tenable inferences may be drawn from such inaction.' " *Ibid.* (quoting *Pension Benefit Guaranty Corporation v. LTV Corp.*, 496 U.S. 633, 650 (1990)).

Passing legislation is no easy task. A federal statute must withstand the "finely wrought" procedure of bicameralism and presentment. *INS v. Chadha*, 462 U.S. 919, 951 (1983) . . . . Within that onerous process, there are additional practical hurdles. A law must be taken up for discussion and not passed over in favor of more pressing matters, and Senate rules require 60 votes to end debate on most legislation. And even if the House and Senate agree on a general policy, the details of the measure usually must be hammered out in a conference committee and repassed by both Houses.

* * *

A proper understanding of our doctrine of *stare decisis* does not prevent us from reexamining *Brulotte*. Even the Court does not defend the decision on the merits. I would reconsider and overrule our obvious mistake. For these reasons, I respectfully dissent.

NOTES AND QUESTIONS

1. In order to create incentives for innovation and to encourage the public disclosure of new discoveries, the federal Patent Act has long offered inventors a deal. If you make certain kinds of inventions or discoveries, the Patent Act lets you obtain a patent giving you the exclusive rights to make, use, and sell your patented invention within the United States during the term of the patent. *See* 35 U.S.C. §§ 101, 271(a). But that term is limited. Under current law, patents expire twenty years after the date on which the application for the patent was filed. *Id.* § 154(a)(2).[18] As part of your application, moreover, you have to disclose your invention in such a way "as to enable any person skilled in the art to which it pertains, or with which it is most nearly connected, to make and use the same." *Id.* § 112(a). Thus, when the term of your patent expires, other people will have the practical ability to exploit your invention, and the Patent Act will not prevent them from doing so.

While a patent is in force, its owner might enter into licensing agreements that allow other people to use the patented invention in exchange for the payment of royalties. In *Brulotte*, however, Justice Douglas's majority opinion articulated a limitation on the terms of those contracts: a contractual provision purporting to require the licensee to continue paying royalties for uses of the invention that occur after the patent expires "is not enforceable." *Brulotte v. Thys Co.*, 379 U.S. 29, 32 (1964). Justice Douglas reasoned that such a provision would amount to an attempt to extend the "monopoly" granted by the patent beyond the term established by the Patent Act, contrary to "the policy and purpose

[18] At the time of the *Brulotte* case, the term was seventeen years from the date on which the patent was issued.

of the patent laws." *Id.* at 31–32 (quoting Scott Paper Co. v. Marcalus Co., 326 U.S. 249, 256 (1945)).

In *Kimble,* Justice Kagan's majority opinion noted that "*stare decisis* carries enhanced force when a decision, like *Brulotte,* interprets a statute." *Kimble,* 576 U.S. at 456. Justice Alito, however, argued that *Brulotte* should not trigger this principle; in his view, *Brulotte* had not been a genuinely interpretive decision, but instead had been "a bald act of policymaking" by the Court. *Id.* at 466 (Alito, J., dissenting); *see also id.* at 471 ("[W]e do not give super-duper protection to decisions that do not actually interpret a statute."). Still, Justice Alito appeared to concede that *Brulotte* had "*purport[ed]* to apply a statute." *Id.* (emphasis added).

In fact, the relation between *Brulotte* and the Patent Act is not clear. Justice Douglas's majority opinion in *Brulotte* did not explicitly assert that the Patent Act itself prohibited enforcement of the contractual provisions in question. Rather than attribute this rule to the Patent Act, Justice Douglas could perhaps have described it as a matter of "federal common law"—a rule that was informed by the policy behind the Patent Act but was not actually part of the Act.

Here is one possible route to that conclusion. Under the common law of contracts, courts sometimes hold that contractual provisions are unenforceable on grounds of public policy, *see* RESTATEMENT (SECOND) OF CONTRACTS § 178 (AM. L. INST. 1981), and courts sometimes derive the relevant public policy from statutes, *see id.* § 179. Perhaps *Brulotte* can be understood in these terms: Justice Douglas used the Patent Act to identify a relevant public policy, but the principle that contractual provisions in violation of that policy are unenforceable might have come from the common law. One would still need to explain why the latter principle would be a matter of *federal* common law in this context, but the fact that the relevant public policy was derived from a federal statute might have been good enough for Justice Douglas.

That might not be the right way of characterizing *Brulotte.* But suppose it is. How, if at all, would this characterization of *Brulotte* affect the operation of *stare decisis*? Even if *Brulotte* rested in part on federal common law, and even if precedents about the content of federal common law do not trigger the heightened form of *stare decisis* that the Supreme Court uses for precedents about statutory interpretation, would the heightened form of *stare decisis* still protect *Brulotte*'s identification of the policy behind the Patent Act?

2. Justice Douglas "took a dim view of patents and the exclusivity rights they granted." Gregory Dolin, *Exclusivity Without Patents: The New Frontier of FDA Regulation for Genetic Materials,* 98 IOWA L. REV. 1399, 1428 n.223 (2013); *see also, e.g.,* Mark D. Janis, *Patent Law in the Age of the Invisible Supreme Court,* 2001 U. ILL. L. REV. 387, 393 (noting that Justice Douglas "took a special interest in patent law," but "this special interest appeared to be born of an unremitting hostility towards both the concept of a patent system and the reality of patent office operation"). His opinion in *Brulotte*, which sought to prevent patent owners from using "the leverage of [their] monopoly" to create royalty obligations beyond "the monopoly period," was consistent with that attitude. *Brulotte*, 379 U.S. at 32–33.

Fifty years later, Mr. Kimble argued that *Brulotte*'s rule was nowhere to be found in the Patent Act and was bad policy to boot. According to the Supreme Court, though, Mr. Kimble's policy arguments did not provide the sort of special justification that could warrant overruling a precedent about statutory interpretation. To explain this point, the majority noted that "the choice of what patent policy should be lies first and foremost with Congress." *Kimble*, 576 U.S. at 463. The majority concluded that once *Brulotte* was decided, the Court should adhere to it unless and until Congress made a change. But does the fact that Congress is in charge of patent policy support this baseline? If *Brulotte* was wrong—that is, if Justice Douglas substituted his own ideas about patent policy for the policies that Congress had enacted—might the fact that Congress is in charge of patent policy be a reason to overrule *Brulotte* rather than a reason to follow it?

2. THEORIES OF LEGISLATIVE ACQUIESCENCE AND RATIFICATION

a. SHOULD THE LEGISLATURE'S FAILURE TO OVERRIDE A PROMINENT INTERPRETATION OF A STATUTE ADD TO THE PRECEDENTIAL FORCE OF THAT INTERPRETATION?

Apart from any other arguments about the special force of *stare decisis* in statutory cases, people sometimes say that the legislature's failure to override prominent judicial interpretations of statutes should add to the precedential force of those interpretations. For many years, the federal Supreme Court has been of two minds about that idea. The majority opinions in *Flood v. Kuhn* and *Kimble v. Marvel Entertainment, LLC* were obviously sympathetic to it, and they are not alone. *See, e.g.*, Watson v. United States, 552 U.S. 74, 82–83 (2007) (Souter, J.) (noting that in the 14 years since the Court had interpreted 18 U.S.C. § 924(c) in *Smith v. United States*, 508 U.S. 223 (1993), "Congress has taken no step to modify *Smith*'s holding, and this long congressional acquiescence 'has enhanced even the usual precedential force' we accord to our interpretations of statutes" (quoting *Shepard v. United States*, 544 U.S. 13, 23 (2005) (Souter, J.))). But majority opinions have also unceremoniously rebuffed this argument. *See, e.g.*, Patterson v. McLean Credit Union, 491 U.S. 164, 175 n.1 (1989) (refusing to overrule *Runyon v. McCrary*, 427 U.S. 160 (1976), but specifically disclaiming any reliance on "the fact that Congress itself has not overturned [*Runyon*'s] interpretation of [42 U.S.C.] § 1981" and rejecting the idea "that Congress' failure to overturn a statutory precedent is reason for this Court to adhere to it"); *cf.* Zuber v. Allen, 396 U.S. 168, 185 n.21 (1969)

("The verdict of quiescent years cannot be invoked to baptize a statutory gloss that is otherwise impermissible. This Court has many times reconsidered statutory constructions that have been passively abided by Congress."). As the Court has acknowledged, "our cases have not been consistent" on this issue. *Central Bank of Denver, N.A. v. First Interstate Bank of Denver, N.A.*, 511 U.S. 164, 187 (1994). That has been true for a long time. *See* HENRY M. HART, JR. & ALBERT M. SACKS, THE LEGAL PROCESS: BASIC PROBLEMS IN THE MAKING AND APPLICATION OF LAW 1360–64 (tent. ed. 1958) (William N. Eskridge, Jr. & Philip P. Frickey eds., 1994) (juxtaposing inconsistent statements in opinions from the 1940s).

If doctrine on this point is inconsistent, what *should* the doctrine be? If the other arguments for *stare decisis* do not persuade a court to continue following one of its past decisions about the meaning of a statute, should the fact that the legislature has not itself overridden the decision ever provide an independent reason for the court to adhere to the precedent? *See, e.g.*, William N. Eskridge, Jr., *Interpreting Legislative Inaction*, 87 MICH. L. REV. 67 (1988) (thoughtfully analyzing this and related questions).

Hardly anyone contends that the legislature's failure to respond to a court's interpretation of a statute *always* gives the interpretation extra weight as precedent. For one thing, many judicial decisions (including even some decisions by the United States Supreme Court) have a low profile, and it is hard to read much into the legislature's failure to override a decision that members of the legislature did not know about. *See, e.g.*, Johnson v. Transportation Agency, 480 U.S. 616, 629 n.7 (1987) (appearing to agree that "congressional inaction cannot be regarded as acquiescence" where it can be chalked up to "inattention"). But some judicial interpretations of statutes are sufficiently prominent that legislators can safely be assumed to know about them. Likewise, internal legislative history sometimes establishes that legislators were familiar with a particular judicial decision about the meaning of a statute. Perhaps the decision came up in legislative debates about something else. Or perhaps bills to override the decision were introduced and considered (but not enacted).

To focus our discussion, imagine a stylized scenario along these lines. At Time 1, Congress enacts a statute. At Time 2, the Supreme Court decides a high-profile case in which it interprets the statute in a particular way. In the years after Time 2, Congress does not override the Court's interpretation, despite the fact that members of Congress are familiar with it. Later, at Time 3, a litigant asks the Court to overrule its past decision and to adopt a different interpretation of the statute. If the Court at Time 3 would otherwise be inclined to do so, should it be dissuaded by the fact that members of Congress have known about the Court's past interpretation and have not overridden it?

There are at least three reasons why that fact might be thought to increase the decision's weight as precedent. First, Congress's failure to override the past decision might be a sign that the past decision was right—that it interpreted the statute correctly, or at least that the meaning it ascribed to the statute was what members of the enacting Congress had collectively intended to convey. On occasion, the Supreme Court has seemed to accept that idea. *See, e.g., id.* ("Congress has not amended the statute to reject our construction, nor have any such amendments even been proposed, and we therefore may assume that our interpretation was correct.").

Justice Scalia, however, powerfully attacked this view. *See id.* at 671 (Scalia, J., dissenting). For one thing, the Congress that is deciding whether to override the Court's precedent usually is not the Congress that enacted the statute, and in other contexts the Court discounts later Congresses' views about the meaning of earlier statutes. *See, e.g.,* Mackey v. Lanier Collection Agency & Service, 486 U.S. 825, 839 (1988) ("[T]he opinion of this later Congress as to the meaning of a law enacted 10 years earlier does not control the issue."); *see also supra* pp. 473–474 (discussing concerns about the reliability of post-enactment legislative history). *But cf.* Bennett v. Kentucky Dep't of Education, 470 U.S. 656, 665 n.3 (1985) ("Although the view of a later Congress does not definitively establish the meaning of an earlier enactment, it does have some persuasive value."). In any event, when the current Congress is considering whether to override a judicial decision about the meaning of an earlier statute, Congress is not really evaluating whether the court was correct as a legal matter. Members of the current Congress are likely to be much more interested in whether, as a policy matter, they like the rule that the court has articulated. Even if a precedent correctly understood the statute that it interpreted, the current Congress might override the precedent because the current Congress does not like what the old statute said. *See* West Virginia University Hospitals v. Casey, 499 U.S. 83, 101 n.7 (1991) (rejecting the idea "that today's holding [about the meaning of a federal statute] will be proved wrong if Congress amends the law to conform with [the] dissent"). Conversely, even if the precedent misinterpreted the statute, the current Congress might let the precedent stand because the current Congress prefers the policy reflected in the precedent to the policy that the statute actually established.

Still, this line of argument suggests a second possible reason why a court might ascribe some significance to Congress's failure to override a prominent precedent about the meaning of a statute. Even if the inaction of later Congresses does not tell us much about the views of the *enacting* Congress (and hence might not bear on whether the decision was correct as an original matter), perhaps it tells us something about the views of the *later* Congresses. In particular, the fact that Congress has not overridden the decision might suggest that regardless of whether the decision was correct about the meaning of the statute at the time of enactment, the current Congress likes the rule established by the decision and does not want the Court to change it. To put this idea in its boldest possible form, perhaps the fact that Congress has allowed the decision to stand should sometimes be understood to reflect an authoritative policy judgment along the same lines as a statute codifying the decision.[19]

This idea too is subject to attack. To begin with, there are plenty of other reasons why Congress might not have responded to the decision. Perhaps Congress simply had different priorities. (Even if members of Congress dislike a particular legal rule, crafting appropriate legislation to override that rule might keep them from devoting attention to some other bill that they consider more important.) Or perhaps majorities in various Congresses would have been perfectly happy to override the Court's decision, but a determined minority was always able to keep the issue bottled up in a committee. The mere fact that Congress has not overridden a precedent certainly does not establish that a proposal to codify the precedent would have made it through Congress; our lawmaking system has a bias toward inertia, meaning that it is substantially easier for Congress to do nothing than to enact a statute either overriding *or* codifying a precedent. Because of the complex checks built into the legislative process, indeed, Justice Scalia doubted that one can ever "assert with any degree of assurance that congressional failure to act represents (1) approval of the status quo, as opposed to (2) inability to agree upon how to alter the status quo, (3) unawareness of the status quo, (4) indifference to the status quo, or even (5) political cowardice." *Johnson*, 480 U.S. at 672 (Scalia, J., dissenting).

Even if one could get past these points, the idea that Congress's failure to override a high-profile precedent amounts to an authoritative endorsement of that precedent also runs into trouble from *INS v. Chadha*, 462 U.S. 919 (1983). As you saw in Chapter 3, *Chadha* held that in order to act with legal effect upon the rights and duties of people outside the legislative branch, Congress must go through the "finely wrought . . . procedure" of bicameralism and presentment spelled out in Article I, § 7. Congress's *in*action obviously does not go through that process. One might infer that Congress's mere failure to pass a statute therefore cannot change the law in any way—as it would if it amounted to an authoritative statement putting a precedent on sounder footing than the precedent would otherwise have enjoyed.

Professors Hart and Sacks made this point long before *Chadha*. In response to the suggestion that Congress's failure to override a precedent

[19] In *Flood v. Kuhn*, Justice Blackmun seemed to have been thinking of Congress's acquiescence in these terms. He certainly did not treat Congress's inaction as evidence that *Federal Baseball Club* had correctly interpreted the Sherman Act as an original matter. But while he saw baseball's antitrust exemption as "an aberration," he described Congress's failure to override *Federal Baseball Club* and *Toolson* as "positive inaction" that "clearly evinced a desire not to disapprove [those precedents] legislatively" and that "has been deemed to be something other than mere congressional silence and passivity." *Flood*, 407 U.S. at 282–84.

effectively expressed Congress's desire to retain the precedent, and thereby put the precedent beyond the Court's power to overrule, they asked a simple question: "But how could Congress do this without complying with the constitutional prerequisites for the enactment of bills?" HART & SACKS, *supra*, at 1358.

To dramatize this concern, consider the following scenario. Suppose that at Time 1, the House and Senate both want to establish a particular policy, which they accomplish through a duly enacted statute. Later, at Time 2, the Supreme Court misinterprets the statute to establish a different policy. Imagine that the Senate still likes the original policy and wants to override the Court's decision, but the House has changed hands and prefers the policy that the Court has mistakenly attributed to the statute. Under these circumstances, the new Congress will not override the Court's decision. But if future jurists treated Congress's inaction as an authoritative endorsement of the Court's decision, they arguably would be giving legal effect to the decision of a single House of Congress, in violation of the constitutional requirement of bicameralism.

That approach would also raise a presentment problem. Suppose that when the Court announces its (mis)interpretation of the statute at Time 2, both Houses of Congress like the new policy that the Court has articulated. Suppose, however, that the President does not; the President prefers the rule that the statute had seemed to establish before the Court misinterpreted it. If Congress could codify the new policy only by passing a new statute to that effect, then the President would have the opportunity to veto the codification. But if Congress's simple acquiescence in the Court's decision counts as something along the lines of codification, then the President has nothing to veto. Contrary to the lawmaking procedure contemplated by the Constitution, the President has been cut out of the codification process.

These points strike many observers as conclusive: Congress's failure to pass a statute overriding a particular precedent should not be treated as an authoritative endorsement of the precedent. Even if Congress's inaction does indeed reflect satisfaction with the precedent, and even if the current Congress would like the Court to adhere to the precedent, Congress cannot validly convey that instruction by doing nothing. Putting the precedent on firmer footing than the Court's own doctrine of *stare decisis* gives it would require changing the law, and Congress can change the law only by going through the process of bicameralism and presentment.

But perhaps there is a third possible reason why Congress's failure to override a high-profile decision might have the effect of helping to insulate the decision from later overruling. Under the Court's own doctrine of *stare decisis*, the Court is not supposed to overrule each and every precedent that it now regrets; even if it now considers a precedent to be mistaken, the Court is supposed to think about the costs and benefits of letting the mistaken decision stand. As the Court conducts the necessary analysis, moreover, perhaps Congress's failure to override the decision should sometimes affect how the Court assesses the relevant policy landscape. For instance, if the Court's own doctrine of *stare decisis* encourages the Court to follow its statutory precedents unless they have proven unworkable or are otherwise causing practical problems, and if a high-profile precedent has been around for a while without causing much consternation in Congress, perhaps that fact is itself some evidence that the precedent is not causing problems in practice—and hence that the precedent is not a good candidate for overruling.

Does this argument avoid problems under *Chadha*? In a way, it too allows legislative inaction to have some legal effect. But the legal effect comes through the operation of the Court's own doctrine of *stare decisis.* Rather than treating Congress's inaction as the equivalent of a legally operative instruction from Congress, the argument instead treats Congress's inaction as some evidence of factual conditions in the real world. That evidence, moreover, is relevant not because Congress has made it relevant, but because the Court's own doctrine of *stare decisis* takes it into account. Are these distinctions meaningful?

* * * * *

As noted above, the Court has waffled about whether Congress's failure to override a high-profile precedent about the meaning of a statute ever gives the Court an independent reason to continue following that precedent. Some of the current Justices have categorically rejected that idea. *See, e.g.*, Gamble v. United States, 139 S. Ct. 1960, 1987–88 (2019) (Thomas, J., concurring) (rejecting "legislative inaction" as a basis for adherence to statutory precedents); Amy Coney Barrett, *Assorted Canards of Contemporary Legal Analysis: Redux*, 70 CASE W. RES. L. REV. 855, 866–69 (2020) (same); *see also* Amy Coney Barrett, *Statutory Stare Decisis in the Courts of Appeals*, 73 GEO. WASH. L. REV. 317, 330–31 (2005) (suggesting that although "the acquiescence rationale [for statutory *stare decisis*] continues to enjoy some support in the cases and literature," it has become a minority view). But to the extent that other Justices remain open to the idea, under what circumstances might they be most likely to ascribe significance to Congress's inaction?

In *Flood v. Kuhn*, Justice Blackmun seemed to think that Congress's failure to override *Federal Baseball Club* and *Toolson* was particularly significant because bills responding to those decisions had been introduced and had failed to pass. *See Flood*, 407 U.S. at 283 (emphasizing that since 1922, when the Court decided *Federal Baseball Club*, "[r]emedial legislation has been introduced repeatedly in Congress but none has ever been enacted"). For Justice Blackmun, that fact probably resonated with the second theory described above: if Congress has repeatedly considered bills that would have overridden or modified a precedent, but each time has decided against change, perhaps the consistent defeat of those bills should be taken as a species of legislative action in its own right. In other cases, however, the Court seemed to treat

Congress's inaction as especially meaningful precisely because bills to override the precedent were *not* introduced in Congress. *See, e.g., Johnson*, 480 U.S. at 629 n.7 (stressing that "not one legislator even proposed a bill" to override the precedent established by *United Steelworkers v. Weber*, 443 U.S. 193 (1979)). That consideration arguably resonates with the first and third theories described above: if a high-profile precedent did not prompt even an *attempted* override in Congress, perhaps one can infer that the precedent was correct, or at least is not causing serious problems.

At least in the past, the Court also suggested that Congress's failure to override a decision is more significant in areas of the law that Congress actively monitors, *see* Zuber v. Allen, 396 U.S. 168, 185 n.21 (1969) (asserting in dictum that congressional inaction has its greatest significance "when the area is one of traditional year-by-year supervision, like tax, where watchdog committees are considering and revising the statutory scheme"), or in areas in which Congress has established a pattern of responding to judicial decisions, *see Johnson*, 480 U.S. at 629 n.7 (ascribing significance to Congress's failure to override the Supreme Court's decision in *Weber*, and noting that "when Congress has been displeased with our interpretation of Title VII, it has not hesitated to amend the statute to tell us so"), or where there are other reasons to expect Congress to have acted if it disliked the decision, *see* Toucey v. N.Y. Life Ins. Co., 314 U.S. 118, 141 (1941) (ascribing no significance to Congress's inaction under the circumstances of the case, but emphasizing that "[t]his is not a situation where Congress has failed to act after having been requested to act or where the circumstances are such that Congress would ordinarily be expected to act"). These considerations might be relevant on any of the three theories described above.

* * * * *

If you think that there are some circumstances in which Congress's failure to override a high-profile decision of the Supreme Court should give that decision added precedential force, what about Congress's failure to override a critical mass of decisions by *lower* courts? Are there any circumstances in which subsequent courts (including even the Supreme Court) should treat that sort of legislative inaction as meaningful too?

The modern Supreme Court has said that "we have no warrant to ignore clear statutory language on the ground that other courts have done so." *Milner v. Dep't of the Navy*, 562 U.S. 562, 576 (2011); *accord* BP P.L.C. v. Mayor of Baltimore, 141 S. Ct. 1532, 1541 (2021). At least where the Supreme Court deems statutory language unambiguous, then, the Court apparently will not care that circuit courts have adopted a different interpretation and that Congress has not overridden their interpretation. But what if the statute is not so clear?

In the past, the Supreme Court sometimes invoked the existence of a consensus among lower courts, and Congress's failure to disturb that consensus, as a reason for the Court to go along. *See, e.g.*, General Dynamics Land Systems, Inc. v. Cline, 540 U.S. 581, 593–94 (2004) ("The Courts of Appeals and the District Courts have read the law the same way, and prior to this case have enjoyed virtually unanimous accord . . . . [C]ongressional silence after years of judicial interpretation supports adherence to the traditional view."); *see also* William N. Eskridge, Jr., *Interpreting Legislative Inaction*, 87 MICH. L. REV. 67, 73 n.25 (1988) (citing other cases). The Supreme Court may have been particularly receptive to this argument in cases where, after the consensus had emerged, Congress amended the statute in other respects without making any relevant changes to the provision that the lower courts had interpreted.[20] *See Milner*, 562 U.S. at 586–87 (Breyer, J., dissenting); *see also, e.g.*, Manhattan Properties, Inc. v. Irving Trust Co., 291 U.S. 320, 336 (1934) ("From 1898 to 1932 the Bankruptcy Act was amended seven times without alteration of the section [that lower federal courts had glossed]. This is persuasive that the construction adopted by the courts has been acceptable to the legislative arm of the government."). More recently, however, the Supreme Court has indicated that "isolated amendments" to other provisions of the statute, or even to the very same provision that the circuit courts had glossed, are not a proper basis for inferring approval of the circuit courts' decisions. *See* AMG Capital Mgt., LLC v. Fed. Trade Comm'n, 141 S. Ct. 1341, 1351 (2021) (quoting Alexander v. Sandoval, 532 U.S. 275, 292 (2001)); *see also BP*, 141 S. Ct. at 1541 (refusing to infer ratification of circuit-court precedents about the meaning of 28 U.S.C. § 1447(d) from the fact that Congress had amended § 1447(d) in 2011 without repudiating those precedents); SCA Hygiene Prods. Aktiebolag v. First Quality Baby Products, LLC, 580 U.S. 328, 345 (2017) (giving short shrift to a similar ratification argument). *But see BP*, 141 S. Ct. at 1545 (Sotomayor, J., dissenting) ("That Congress did not disturb the prevailing interpretation of § 1447(d) [when Congress enacted the 2011 amendment] is a compelling reason this Court should not either."); Custis v. United States, 511 U.S. 485, 500 (1994) (Souter, J., dissenting) ("Congress's failure to express legislative disagreement with the appellate courts' reading of the [Armed Career Criminal Act of 1984] cannot be disregarded, especially since Congress has acted in this area in response to other Courts of Appeals decisions that it thought revealed statutory flaws . . . .").

Even if you think that the Supreme Court should sometimes give its own precedents added force because Congress did not respond to them, some of the premises behind that position may not extend to circuit-court precedents. Congress may pay less attention to the decisions of circuit courts than to the decisions of the Supreme Court, and members of Congress may not be aware that circuit courts have reached a consensus about the proper interpretation of a statute. Indeed, even when a

[20] The effect of reenacting that very provision without any relevant change to its text is considered separately below.

committee report on some proposed bill cites circuit-court decisions with apparent approval, such citations may be unlikely either to reflect or to prompt a considered judgment by Congress as a whole. *See* James J. Brudney, *Congressional Commentary on Judicial Interpretations of Statutes: Idle Chatter or Telling Response?*, 93 MICH. L. REV. 1, 82–84 (1995).

Perhaps the theory of legislative acquiescence could be restricted to particularly prominent decisions by circuit courts. But even then, if the Supreme Court treated Congress's failure to override lower-court precedents as implicitly ratifying those precedents, there is a sense in which the lower courts would be setting precedent for the Supreme Court. Is that a problem? Or is it simply a natural and permissible consequence of ascribing significance to Congress's acquiescence in judicial decisions about the meaning of federal statutes? *Cf.* Aaron-Andrew P. Bruhl, *Following Lower-Court Precedent*, 81 U. CHI. L. REV. 851 (2014) (evaluating various possible reasons for Supreme Court deference to lower-court precedents, but concluding that legislative acquiescence in those precedents is "rarely a powerful argument").

* * * * *

If courts sometimes ascribe significance to Congress's failure to override prominent judicial decisions about the meaning of a federal statute, what about Congress's failure to override prominent *administrative* interpretations of a federal statute? Suppose that at Time 1, Congress enacts a statute and delegates various aspects of its administration to a federal agency. At Time 2, the agency takes a high-profile position about the meaning of one of the provisions that it is in charge of administering. The agency's interpretation is prominent enough that Congress surely knows about it, but Congress does nothing to override it. Later, at Time 3, the propriety of the agency's interpretation becomes an issue in a court case. Should Congress's inaction since Time 2 put the agency's interpretation on firmer footing than it would otherwise enjoy?

Analysis of this question is complicated by *Chevron USA v. Natural Resources Defense Council*, 467 U.S. 837 (1984), which ushered in a new framework for thinking about the relationship between judicial and administrative interpretations of statutory provisions that Congress has put an agency in charge of administering. We will postpone detailed consideration of the *Chevron* framework until Chapter 5, but here is one version of the basic idea: When a provision in a federal statute is ambiguous, and when Congress has empowered the agency to act with the force of law in implementing that provision, Congress should ordinarily be presumed to have given the agency the additional authority to choose among the permissible interpretations of the provision in a way that courts should respect. Thus, if the agency adopts an interpretation of the provision in a way that triggers the *Chevron* framework, and if courts agree that the agency's interpretation is "permissible," then courts are supposed to accept and follow the agency's interpretation even if they would have preferred one of the other permissible interpretations.

The *Chevron* framework does not lock agencies into the construction that they select initially. If the agency selects Permissible Interpretation #1, that interpretation binds courts unless and until the agency abandons it—but the agency itself retains authority to change its mind and adopt Permissible Interpretation #2 later. It is very rare for the modern Supreme Court to use theories of legislative acquiescence to deprive agencies of this power. In other words, Congress's failure to override the interpretation that the agency first announced usually is not treated as the equivalent of a statute freezing that interpretation into place. But should Congress's failure to override a high-profile administrative interpretation of a statute ever be taken as confirming at least the agency's authority to adopt that interpretation?

In the years leading up to and even immediately following *Chevron*, the Supreme Court did not speak with enough precision to draw this distinction. Even when the Court ascribed significance to Congress's failure to override administrative interpretations of federal statutes, the Court did not make clear whether it was taking Congress to have tacitly ratified the particular interpretation that the agency had adopted or instead the agency's authority to adopt that interpretation. (The distinction between these two possibilities would matter if the agency later wanted to change its mind.) Still, the Court sometimes did treat Congress's inaction in the face of an agency's interpretation as an extra reason for courts to defer to that interpretation. *See, e.g.*, Commodity Futures Trading Comm'n v. Schor, 478 U.S. 833, 845–46 (1986) (observing that in the ten years since the Commission had adopted a particular interpretation of its authority under the Commodity Exchange Act, "Congress has twice amended the [Act]" without repudiating the Commission's position, and "[i]t is well established that when Congress revisits a statute giving rise to a longstanding administrative interpretation without pertinent change, the 'congressional failure to revise or repeal the agency's interpretation is persuasive evidence that the interpretation is the one intended by Congress' " (quoting NLRB v. Bell Aerospace Co., 416 U.S. 267, 274–75 (1974) (footnotes omitted))); Bob Jones Univ. v. United States, 461 U.S. 574, 599–601 (1983) (conceding that "[n]onaction by Congress is not often a useful guide," but attaching significance to Congress's failure to override two very high-profile IRS rulings that had generated numerous congressional hearings and unsuccessful override bills); United States v. Rutherford, 442 U.S. 544, 554 n.10 (1979) ("[O]nce an agency's statutory construction has been 'fully brought to the attention of the public and the Congress,' and [Congress] has not sought to alter that interpretation although it has amended the statute in other respects, then presumably the legislative intent has been correctly discerned." (quoting Apex Hosiery Co. v. Leader, 310 U.S. 469, 489 (1940))); Alstate Constr. Co. v. Durkin, 345

U.S. 13, 17 (1953) ("We decline to repudiate an administrative interpretation of the Act which Congress refused to repudiate after being repeatedly urged to do so."); Costanzo v. Tillinghast, 287 U.S. 341, 345 (1932) ("The failure of Congress to alter or amend the section, notwithstanding this consistent construction by the department charged with its enforcement, creates a presumption in favor of the administrative interpretation, to which we should give great weight, even if we doubted the correctness of the ruling of the Department of Labor."); *see also* Eskridge, *supra*, 87 MICH. L. REV. at 127–28 (citing additional cases).

Suppose you think that when the Supreme Court itself has put a high-profile gloss on a federal statute, and when members of Congress have focused on that gloss but ultimately have done nothing to disturb it, Congress's apparent acquiescence sometimes provides an independent reason for the Court to continue following the gloss. Even so, might there be reasons for courts *not* to ascribe much significance to Congress's failure to override a gloss adopted by an administrative agency?

One obvious reason is that the typical administrative decision has a lower profile than the typical decision by the Supreme Court, and hence may be less likely to come to Congress's attention. But is that the only relevant difference between judicial and administrative glosses? Or does the nature of Congress's relationship with administrative agencies (or at least some administrative agencies) differ from the nature of Congress's relationship with courts in ways that reduce the significance of Congress's failure to override even high-profile administrative decisions? For instance, might Congress delegate the administration of statutes to agencies precisely when Congress does *not* want to monitor the resulting interpretations or respond to them on an ongoing basis?

Does it matter that the typical agency is probably more likely than the Supreme Court to change its own position on matters of statutory interpretation? When the federal Supreme Court has staked out an interpretation of a federal statute, observers usually expect the Court to continue following that interpretation—partly because the Court's membership turns over slowly and partly because the doctrine of *stare decisis* is fairly powerful even when current Justices disagree with their predecessors' decisions. Administrative agencies are different in both of these respects: key personnel in most agencies turn over fairly often, and most agencies have substantially weaker norms of *stare decisis* than the Supreme Court. As a result, Congress might sensibly think that agencies are more likely than courts to correct their own mistakes. At the same time, Congress might believe that agencies are better positioned than courts to make the sorts of policy calculations that departing from a past interpretation requires. Might these considerations make Congress more likely to respond to decisions it dislikes when those decisions have been rendered by the Supreme Court than when they have simply been rendered by an administrative agency? If so, might Congress's failure to respond to a decision be more likely to signal approval of the decision in the judicial context than in the administrative context?

The modern Supreme Court may not be very receptive to legislative-acquiescence arguments even in the judicial context. Still, the Court has voiced special caution about such arguments in the administrative context. *See* Solid Waste Agency of N. Cook Cty. v. U.S. Army Corps of Eng'rs, 531 U.S. 159, 169 (2001) ("Although we have recognized congressional acquiescence to administrative interpretations of a statute in some situations, we have done so with extreme care."). *But see* Sebelius v. Auburn Reg'l Med. Ctr., 568 U.S. 145, 159 (2013) (quoting a past opinion about the significance of Congress's failure to override an administrative interpretation, and not mentioning any need for caution).

b. WHEN THE LEGISLATURE REENACTS A STATUTE WITHOUT RELEVANT CHANGE, IS THE LEGISLATURE IMPLICITLY CODIFYING PROMINENT GLOSSES ON THE OLD STATUTE?

Aside from cases of simple congressional inaction (in which members of Congress know about a prominent gloss that has been put upon a statute and do nothing to override it), we should also consider cases in which Congress reenacts the text of a statutory provision after the judiciary or an administrative agency has put some prominent gloss upon it. Imagine the following timeline. At Time 1, Congress enacted a statute. At Time 2, the Supreme Court (or a critical mass of lower courts, or an agency that Congress had put in charge of administering the statute) adopted a prominent interpretation of one of the statute's provisions. At Time 3, Congress reenacted the statute without making any relevant change to that provision. Regardless of whether the gloss articulated at Time 2 was correct as an original matter, should the new statute that Congress enacted at Time 3 be understood to incorporate that gloss? To see why the answer matters, imagine that by Time 4 interpreters regret the gloss, and imagine further that the doctrine of *stare decisis* would not ordinarily prevent them from overruling it. Should the action that Congress took at Time 3 dissuade them from doing so? Even if the statute enacted by Congress at Time 1 did not really have the meaning that interpreters ascribed to it at Time 2, might one still conclude that the statute enacted by Congress at Time 3 does have that meaning?

In *Lorillard v. Pons*, 434 U.S. 575 (1978), the Supreme Court asserted broadly that "Congress is presumed to be aware of an administrative or judicial interpretation of a statute and to adopt that interpretation when it re-enacts a statute without change." *Id.* at 580. But while later courts have frequently referred to this statement, actual judicial practice is more qualified. *See* Eskridge, *supra*, 87 MICH. L. REV. at 79 ("The rule is rarely the primary basis for the Court's decision . . . ."); *id.* app. 2 at 129–31 (collecting Supreme Court cases on both sides from 1961 to 1988). To begin with, some cases suggest that the presumption articulated in *Lorillard* cannot overcome clear statutory language. *See, e.g.*, Demarest v. Manspeaker, 498 U.S. 184, 190 (1991) ("Where the law is plain, subsequent reenactment does not constitute an adoption of a previous administrative construction."); *see also* Brown v. Gardner, 513 U.S. 115, 121 (1994) (calling this principle "an obvious trump to the reenactment argument"). In addition, the presumption applies only when the judicial or administrative gloss "represented settled law when Congress reenacted the [language in question]." *Keene Corp. v. United States*, 508 U.S. 200, 212–13 (1993) (deeming this condition satisfied); *see also* Davis v. United States, 495 U.S. 472, 482 (1990) (applying the presumption where, by the time of reenactment, repeated administrative practice and judicial decisions had established a "prevailing interpretation" of the language in question); FDIC v. Philadelphia Gear Corp., 476 U.S. 426, 437 (1986) (similarly applying the presumption where, at the time of reenactment, the administrative gloss was already "longstanding"); *cf.* Jama v. Immigration & Customs Enforcement, 543 U.S. 335, 349 (2005) (refusing to infer ratification of a gloss adopted by the Second Circuit and echoed in dicta by several other circuits, and explaining that the presumption of congressional ratification applies only when "the supposed judicial consensus" at the time of reenactment was "so broad and unquestioned that we must presume Congress knew of and endorsed it"); United States v. Powell, 379 U.S. 48, 55 n.13 (1964) (similarly refusing to apply the presumption where there was not "a settled judicial construction" at the time of reenactment). At least in the past, moreover, before treating reenactment as codifying prior glosses, courts often examined the legislative history of the reenacting statute for signs that members of the reenacting Congress knew about those glosses and viewed them favorably. *See, e.g.*, United States v. Bd. of Comm'rs, 435 U.S. 110, 134–35 (1978) (emphasizing this factor); *cf. Gardner*, 513 U.S. at 121 (refusing to infer ratification of the interpretation reflected in an administrative regulation where "the record of congressional discussion preceding reenactment makes no reference to the ... regulation, and there is no other evidence to suggest that Congress was even aware of the [agency's] interpretive position"); United States v. Calamaro, 354 U.S. 351, 359 (1957) (similarly refusing to infer ratification, and emphasizing that "[t]he re-enactment of § 3290 . . . was not accompanied by any congressional discussion which throws light on its intended scope").

Of course, textualists in the mold of Justice Scalia are not likely to agree that the meaning of the reenacting statute might depend upon its legislative history. Rather than investigating legislative history, they presumably would prefer to articulate a canon that takes a more generic approach. Which way should they set that canon? In the absence of relevant clues from legislative history, should Congress ordinarily be understood to be codifying prominent glosses on statutory language that it reenacts without relevant change, or should the typical reenactment instead be understood to leave those glosses on exactly the same footing that they had before reenactment?[21]

The *Chadha* problem discussed in the previous section has no obvious bearing on this question. Although *Chadha* does cut against treating simple legislative inaction in response to a precedent as an authoritative ratification of that precedent, the reenactment scenario involves more than mere inaction. When Congress reenacts a statute, it is going through the process of bicameralism and presentment contemplated by *Chadha*. The courts are not being asked to ascribe legal effect to Congress's failure to act, but rather to interpret the reenacting statute that Congress really did adopt.

Still, one may not want to draw stark differences between the reenactment scenario and other scenarios that fall short of reenactment. A stylized example illustrates this point. Suppose that at Time 1, Congress enacts a statute consisting of two sections. At Time 2, courts interpret the first section of the statute in a particular way. At Time 3, Congress wants to modify the *second* section of the statute. Congress might use either of two different vehicles to do so. In Scenario A, Congress enacts a statute making a targeted amendment to § 2 and saying nothing at all about § 1. In Scenario B, Congress instead repeals the original statute in its entirety, reenacts § 1 without any material changes, and enacts a modified version of § 2. The statutory text that is in force at the end of the day will be the same in both of these scenarios, and one might well think that its meaning should not depend on whether it emerged from a targeted amendment or a broader reenactment. On this view, courts should ascribe the same meaning to the law that is in effect after Time 3 whether Congress followed Scenario A or Scenario B. One way to do so would be to interpret the statute enacted at Time 3 in both scenarios as effectively accepting and adopting the gloss that courts had put on § 1 at Time 2. At least as applied to Scenario A, however, that approach will strike some interpreters as unattractive: it would require courts to treat Congress's targeted amendment of § 2 as the equivalent of a statute that *both* amends § 2 *and* codifies the gloss that the courts have put on § 1, and some jurists will resist that interpretation. (In particular, many of the same people who resist the "legislative acquiescence" theories canvassed above are likely to question the idea that Congress has authoritatively ratified the courts' interpretation of § 1 just by amending § 2.) Those jurists might therefore gravitate toward the opposite conclusion: the statute enacted at Time 3 in both scenarios should be understood to say nothing one way or the other about the gloss that the courts have put on § 1. As applied to Scenario B, that approach would mean that Congress did *not* codify the courts' gloss when Congress

---

[21] *Cf.* Bartenwerfer v. Buckley, 143 S. Ct. 665, 674–75 (2023) ("'This Court generally assumes that, when Congress enacts statutes, it is aware of this Court's relevant precedents.' *Ysleta Del Sur Pueblo v. Texas*, [142 S. Ct. 1929, 1940 (2022)] . . . . So if Congress had reenacted the discharge exception for fraud without change, we would assume that it meant to incorporate Strang's interpretation.").

reenacted § 1; instead, the reenacted version of § 1 is no different than the original version of § 1, and the reenacting statute leaves the courts' gloss on exactly the same footing that the doctrine of *stare decisis* would otherwise give it.

In general, the idea of ratification-by-reenactment seems dubious as a descriptive matter (that is, as a principle about the likely intent of members of the reenacting Congress). There are plenty of reasons to reenact a statute that have nothing to do with codifying the glosses that courts have already put on the statute.[22] To the extent that Congress reenacts statutory language for one of those other reasons, members of Congress may not intend to express any view at all about the glosses that have piled up in the meantime. Indeed, if members of Congress actually wanted to codify those glosses or to instruct courts not to overrule them, simply reenacting the original version of the statute without change would be a very indirect way of doing so.

But perhaps reenactment is a natural occasion for Congress to think about the glosses that have built up on the statute, and perhaps the courts' canons of construction should encourage Congress to seize that opportunity. A canon inferring ratification from reenactment might be defended in these terms, as a way to get Congress to take a position on the courts' past glosses: when Congress wants to reenact a statute, its members will have incentives to think about the glosses that have built up around the statute's provisions, because a reenacting statute that does not explicitly reject those glosses will be understood to codify them. In other words, the idea of ratification-by-reenactment might be seen as a quasi-normative canon designed to improve the process of communication between Congress and the courts.[23]

---

[22] For instance, maybe Congress wants to change the statute in some other respects, and finds it easier to communicate those changes by reenacting a modified version of the complete statute than by casting each discrete change as an amendment to the existing language. Maybe Congress is conducting a more general codification or reorganization of the statutes in a particular field, for the sake of making the structure of its statutes easier to follow. Or maybe Congress simply wants to enact the relevant title of the United States Code into positive law. *See supra* pp. 54–55.

[23] Supporters of the canon might also claim that even if the canon lacked much descriptive force when courts first announced it, the canon will become a more accurate guide to the intended meaning of statutory language over time. If courts apply a "reenactment canon," to the effect that the reenacted version of a statute implicitly incorporates the glosses that had built up on the original version before reenactment, then Congress might take that canon into account when reenacting a statute; if members of Congress do *not* want the reenacted version to incorporate a particular gloss, they might either change the language of the relevant statutory provision or enact a clause instructing courts not to apply the reenactment canon. Supporters of the canon might infer that if Congress simply reenacts a statute without material change (and without opting out of the reenactment canon), members of Congress really did intend to codify the existing glosses.

As usual, I am skeptical of this argument about the "feedback effects" of canons. *See supra* p. 108 n.1. Even if courts applied a reenactment canon more forcefully and consistently than they do, I am not sure that members of Congress would always have the canon in mind. In general, moreover, canons that ascribe unnatural content to statutes seem less likely to promote successful communication than canons that are more natural. When Congress reenacts a statute without material change, the most natural presumption might be that Congress is making no

That argument has been around for a long time—and so have powerful counterarguments. For instance, Professors Hart and Sacks blasted the proposed canon for adding to the costs of the legislative process in counterproductive ways. As they suggested, if a set of statutes is in disarray and matters would be improved if Congress revised and reenacted the statutes in a more streamlined form, we may want to make it easy for Congress to do so without simultaneously having to take a position on more contentious policy questions; otherwise, Congress might not muster the will to perform the revision and reenactment at all. *See* HENRY M. HART, JR. & ALBERT M. SACKS, THE LEGAL PROCESS: BASIC PROBLEMS IN THE MAKING AND APPLICATION OF LAW 1367 (tent. ed. 1958) (William N. Eskridge, Jr. & Philip P. Frickey eds., 1994) (suggesting, through rhetorical questions, that the canon in question would produce a "drag upon codification" that would be "manifestly against public policy"). Likewise, when Congress wants to make a more targeted change to a particular statute, Congress presumably should be able to make its desired change without having to address other, unrelated problems that have cropped up in the administration of the statute. Again, if the courts' interpretive rules allow Congress to solve one problem in the statute only "at the cost of being considered to have committed itself upon every question which has arisen under the provision being amended," Congress might opt not to revise the statute at all, even though its members can agree that the particular change they have in mind would be beneficial. *See id.* In addition to raising these practical arguments, Hart and Sacks also questioned the courts' authority to design a canon for the purpose of forcing Congress to take a position on the courts' past interpretations. *See id.* at 1367 ("Is not the doctrine . . . a manifestly unauthorized attempt of the judiciary to tell the legislature how it shall go about discharging its functions under the Constitution?").

Do these arguments take adequate account of the fact that the canon would just be a default rule—so that Congress could opt out of it by making clear, in the text of any particular re-enacting statute, that the new statute took no position on the propriety of whatever glosses had built up around the original statute? Does putting Congress to that burden still raise the costs of the legislative process and create risks of miscommunication?

Although Professors Hart and Sacks criticized artificial canons designed to force Congress to take a position on past interpretations of the statute that Congress was reenacting, they acknowledged that there would occasionally be evidence "that the [reenacting] legislature did know about [a particular] interpretation and did approve it." *Id.* at 1368. Sometimes the very text of a reenacting statute provides tacit support for the courts' interpretation of a provision in the original statute: even if Congress does not explicitly take a position on that interpretation,

change to the statute—not amending the statute to *reject* any intervening glosses, but also not amending the statute to *incorporate* those glosses.

changes that the reenacting statute makes to some other provision might be premised on the interpretation's correctness, and courts might properly conclude that those changes put the interpretation on firmer footing than it would otherwise have enjoyed.[24] Aside from such textual indications, Hart and Sacks were also open to the possibility that the legislative history of the reenacting statute might adequately convey approval of an existing gloss. But in the absence of statute-specific evidence, Hart and Sacks suggested that the typical reenacting statute should not be understood to take any position on the propriety of past judicial or administrative interpretations of provisions that had appeared in the original statute and that Congress was reenacting without material change.

If one is seeking a canon on this point, which is more attractive—the one suggested by the Supreme Court in *Lorillard v. Pons*, or the opposite one suggested by Professors Hart and Sacks?

* * * * *

Aside from the possible implications of reenactment, we should also consider a related but distinct situation. Suppose that at Time 1, Congress enacts a statute that uses a particular phrase in a particular context. At Time 2, the Supreme Court (or a critical mass of lower courts, or the relevant administrative agency) interprets that phrase as used in this statute. Later, at Time 3, Congress enacts another statute that uses the same phrase in a similar context. Suppose there is strong reason to believe that Congress got the phrase from the first statute. (Perhaps the phrase is distinctive enough to support this inference on its own. Or perhaps the legislative history of the second statute reveals that members of Congress deliberately cut and pasted the phrase from the earlier statute.) Should courts presume that Congress (1) knew how the phrase had been interpreted in the first statute and (2) intended the phrase to have that meaning in the second statute?

The Supreme Court has sometimes spoken as if the answer is usually "yes." *See, e.g.*, Bragdon v. Abbott, 524 U.S. 624, 645 (1998) ("When administrative and judicial interpretations have settled the meaning of an existing statutory provision, repetition of the same language in a new statute indicates, as a general matter, the intent to incorporate its administrative and judicial interpretations as well.").[25] But how strong is this presumption, and what is its rationale? Is the point

---

[24] As we shall see in the next section, there are two different ways to categorize that conclusion. It could be described as an interpretation of the reenacting statute (which, on this view, would be understood as tacitly codifying the courts' past interpretation). Alternatively, the same conclusion could be described as an aspect of the doctrine of *stare decisis* (which might encourage courts to give more precedential force to glosses on which a later Congress has based other changes to the law).

[25] Similarly, state courts sometimes say that when their state legislature bases a statute on one that was previously enacted in a different state, the statute should ordinarily be presumed to come with the glosses that the other state's highest court had already put on its language. *See, e.g.*, Jack L. Landau, *Oregon Statutory Construction*, 97 OR. L. REV. 583, 632–37 (2019).

of the presumption simply that the two statutes should be treated as being *in pari materia* (in the sense discussed in Chapter 4.B.1 of this book), with the result that courts should understand the phrase to mean the same thing in both statutes—so that decisions about the meaning of the phrase in the first statute have some precedential force in the context of the second statute too? Or is the idea that when Congress enacted the second statute at Time 3, Congress understood the phrase to come with the gloss that the decisions at Time 2 had put on it, and Congress intended the phrase to have that meaning in the second statute even if courts later change their mind about what the phrase means in the first statute?

To highlight the difference between these two possibilities, suppose that at Time 4, the relevant courts overrule their past interpretation of the first statute; they now read the phrase in the first statute to mean something other than what they had understood it to mean at Time 2.[26] Should that change affect how interpreters read the phrase in the second statute? Or should interpreters still read the phrase in the second statute to mean what the decisions at Time 2 said it meant in the first statute, even though the courts no longer accept that interpretation of the phrase in the first statute itself?

How, if at all, does this situation differ from the reenactment scenario? Suppose you agree with Professors Hart and Sacks that when Congress reenacts a statute without material change, the reenactment need not be presumed to codify prominent glosses that interpreters had put on the statutory language before reenactment. In the situation that we are considering now, where Congress has pulled a particular phrase from an earlier statute, is there more reason to assume that members of Congress intended that phrase to come with the meaning that prior interpreters had identified? Even in the absence of specific clues to that effect in the text or legislative history of the newer statute, should interpreters assume that the phrase in the newer statute means what interpreters *used* to think the phrase meant in the older statute, because that interpretation was prominent when the newer statute was enacted? Or if interpreters now consider another interpretation better in this context, should they adopt that other interpretation with respect to the newer statute too?

Similar issues can arise when Congress enacts a new version of a statute, but includes language from the earlier version. Consider the so-

[26] Hardly anyone thinks that *stare decisis* is an absolute command even in statutory cases, so this scenario is not impossible. Still, does the fact that Congress incorporated the phrase without change in the second statute give the courts an extra reason to adhere to their interpretation of the phrase in the first statute? In other words, should interpreters at Time 4 treat Congress's decision to use the phrase in the *second* statute at Time 3 as adding to the precedential force of the decisions that interpreters had reached about the *first* statute at Time 2? Might Congress's decision to incorporate the phrase without change into the second statute be understood as an authoritative endorsement of the gloss that interpreters had put on the first statute, with the same effect (for some interpreters) as reenactment of the first statute itself?

called "on-sale bar" of federal patent law. For many years, 35 U.S.C. § 102 indicated that an invention was not patentable if it had been "in public use or on sale in this country, more than one year prior to the date of the application for patent in the United States." *See* 35 U.S.C. § 102(b) (1952). While this provision was in force, both the Supreme Court and the United States Court of Appeals for the Federal Circuit interpreted what "on sale" meant. In 2011, as part of a substantial revision to federal patent law, Congress enacted a new version of 35 U.S.C. § 102. *See* Leahy-Smith America Invents Act, Pub. L. 112–29, § 3(b)(1), 125 Stat. 284, 285–87 (2011). But the new version too referred to whether the claimed invention had been "on sale," and the Supreme Court unanimously presumed that the 2011 statute "adopted the earlier judicial construction of that phrase." *Helsinn Healthcare v. Teva Pharm. USA, Inc.*, 139 S. Ct. 628, 633–34 (2019); *see also, e.g.*, Lamar, Archer & Cofrin, LLP v. Appling, 138 S. Ct. 1752, 1762 (2018) (observing that some language in the Bankruptcy Code of 1978 "can be traced back to a 1926 amendment to the Bankruptcy Act of 1898," and reading that language to come with a gloss that federal circuit courts had "consistently" put on it before 1978).

c. WHAT IF SUBSEQUENT STATUTES SUGGEST APPROVAL OF A PRECEDENT WITHOUT ACTUALLY CODIFYING IT?

Suppose that the legislature enacts a statute at Time 1, and suppose that the courts put a prominent gloss upon the statute at Time 2. We have considered whether the legislature's subsequent failure to override this gloss, or its reenactment of the statute without relevant change, should put the gloss on a sounder footing than the doctrine of *stare decisis* would otherwise give it. But we have not yet considered another common scenario. Suppose that at Time 3, after the courts have announced their gloss on the original statute, the legislature enacts a complementary statute. The new statute does not cover the same ground as the first statute (which remains in force), but the new statute proceeds on the assumption that the first statute does indeed mean what the courts have said it means, and the new statute arguably signals approval of that gloss. Suppose, however, that if not for this new statute, current courts would have been willing to overrule the gloss that their predecessors had put on the first statute at Time 2. Should the existence of the new statute, which suggests legislative approval of the prior gloss even though it does not itself codify that gloss, take that option off the table?

For a concrete example of this scenario, consider Title VI of the Civil Rights Act of 1964 and Title IX of the Education Amendments of 1972. Those statutes forbid discrimination on account of race and sex, respectively, in education programs that receive federal funds. Although neither statute explicitly creates a private cause of action in favor of the victims of such discrimination, lower federal courts inferred a private cause of action to enforce Title VI in the 1960s, and the Supreme Court extended that conclusion to Title IX in *Cannon v. University of Chicago*, 441 U.S. 677 (1979). As of the 1980s, then, federal judicial doctrine recognized private causes of action to enforce both Title VI and Title IX. In 1986, without purporting to codify these causes of action, Congress enacted a provision that arguably was premised upon their existence. Specifically, the 1986 statute (1) declared that "[a] State shall not be immune under the Eleventh Amendment of the Constitution . . . from suit in Federal court for a violation of . . . title IX of the Education Amendments of 1972 [or] . . . title VI of the Civil Rights Act of 1964" and (2) made remedies available against states in such suits "to the same extent as such remedies are available for such a violation in the suit against any public or private entity other than a State." Rehabilitation Act Amendments of 1986, § 1003(a), 100 Stat. 1807, 1845 (codified at 42 U.S.C. § 2000d–7(a)).

Writing in 1992, Justice Scalia asserted that "we have abandoned the expansive rights-creating approach exemplified by *Cannon*, . . . and perhaps ought to abandon the notion of implied causes of action entirely." *Franklin v. Gwinnett County Public Schools*, 503 U.S. 60, 78 (1992) (Scalia, J., concurring in the judgment). If not for the 1986 statute, then, Justice Scalia might have advocated overruling *Cannon* and holding that Title IX did not imply a private cause of action after all. But according to both the Court and Justice Scalia himself, the 1986 statute effectively prevented the Court from doing so. *See id.* at 72 (majority opinion) (reading the 1986 statute as "a validation of *Cannon*'s holding"); *id.* at 78 (Scalia, J., concurring in the judgment) (agreeing with the majority on this point); *accord* Alexander v. Sandoval, 532 U.S. 275, 280 (2001) (Scalia, J.) (describing the 1986 statute as having "ratified *Cannon*'s holding").

This conclusion is not controversial. When Congress enacts a statute building upon glosses that the Supreme Court has put on a past statute, the presumption against subsequently overruling those glosses tends to become well-nigh conclusive. But how would you describe the legal argument that leads to that conclusion? To the extent that the 1986 statute had the effect of insulating *Cannon* against overruling, would you say that Congress itself had forbidden the Court to overrule *Cannon*? Or would you say that the rule established by Congress in 1986 simply affected the proper application of the Court's own doctrine of *stare decisis*, which forecloses overruling decisions on which Congress has built?

The latter argument seems more sensible than the former. By its terms, the 1986 statute cannot plausibly be read as broadly authorizing private claims against non-state defendants. That is not what the 1986 statute was about. The reason that the existence of the 1986 statute prevented the Court from overruling *Cannon* is not that the 1986 statute contained secret instructions that do not appear on its face, but rather that the doctrine of *stare decisis* strongly discourages the Court from overruling precedents on which subsequent statutes build.

Is the same true of other theories of legislative acquiescence? For instance, to the extent that the legislature's reenactment of a statute that has received a prominent judicial gloss might add to the gloss's precedential force, should we attribute that consequence to the intentions of the reenacting legislature? Or should we simply say that the doctrine of *stare decisis* pays attention to the fact of reenactment, and treats that fact as adding to the weight of the relevant precedent?

B. INTERPRETING STATUTES IN LIGHT OF OTHER STATUTES (AND PAST DECISIONS ABOUT THOSE OTHER STATUTES)

In the first part of this chapter, we saw that judicial decisions about a statute's meaning can affect how later courts interpret the same statute (or a subsequent reenactment of the same statute). But courts also frequently allow their interpretations of one statute to be influenced by provisions in other statutes or by glosses that courts have put on those other statutes. The following materials consider four different ways in which that is true.

1. THE CONCEPT OF STATUTES *IN PARI MATERIA*

When multiple statutes address the same subject or seem to share a common purpose, litigants often ask courts to read each statute in light of the others. Such statutes are sometimes said to be *in pari materia*. That phrase is simply Latin for "in the same matter" or "on the same subject." BLACK'S LAW DICTIONARY 944 (11th ed., Bryan A. Garner ed. 2019). But when lawyers or judges say that two statutes are *in pari materia*, they mean that the statutes are sufficiently closely related that they should be interpreted in tandem with each other.[27]

Case law does not make clear exactly what it takes for two statutes to be "related" in the necessary sense. *See, e.g.*, Anuj C. Desai, *The Dilemma of Interstatutory Interpretation*, 77 WASH. & LEE L. REV. 177, 184–85 (2020) (noting the paucity of helpful analysis). Sometimes statutes are said to be *in pari materia* simply because they address the same subject. If that is all that it takes for two statutes to be *in pari materia*, though, then saying that two statutes are *in pari materia* should not have enormous consequences for interpretation. *Cf.* United States v. Broncheau, 645 F.3d 676, 685 (4th Cir. 2011) ("[T]he principle of *in pari materia* has no force where two statutes 'superficially relat[e] to similar subjects,' but 'a finer examination reveal[s] that the purposes underlying the laws var[y].' " (quoting Firstar Bank, N.A. v. Faul, 253 F.3d 982, 990 (7th Cir. 2001))); 2B NORMAN J. SINGER & J.D. SHAMBIE SINGER,

---

[27] In some respects, of course, courts interpret statutes in tandem with each other even when the statutes are not in *pari materia*. At a minimum, courts hesitate to read two statutes enacted by the same sovereign to contradict each other unnecessarily. *See infra* Chapter 4.B.3. But when statutes are in *pari materia*, courts will interpret them in tandem with each other to a great extent than usual.

SUTHERLAND STATUTES AND STATUTORY CONSTRUCTION § 51:3 (7th ed. 2012) ("Courts routinely find that several acts treating the same subject, but having different objects, are not *in pari materia*."). The consequences for interpretation might be greater if the two statutes not only address the same subject but can be understood to have similar purposes, and the consequences should be greater still if the legislature derived one statute from the other or designed the two statutes to work together as part of a single integrated scheme.

What might those consequences be? One important consequence, considered in more detail below, involves the doctrine of *stare decisis*: the tighter the relationship between two statutes, the more force precedents about the meaning of one of the statutes are likely to have in cases about the meaning of the other statute. But even in cases of first impression, before there are any relevant precedents to consider, the fact that two statutes are *in pari materia* can sometimes affect how courts interpret them. That is especially true where one of the statutes is indeterminate in some respect, and something about the other statute supports one of the possible interpretations. *See Broncheau*, 645 F.3d at 685 ("The principle of *in pari materia* is applicable . . . only 'where the meaning of a statute is ambiguous or doubtful.' " (quoting N. Pac. Ry. Co. v. United States, 156 F.2d 346, 350 (7th Cir. 1946), *aff'd*, 330 U.S. 248 (1947))); *cf.* HAW. REV. STAT. § 1–16 ("Laws in pari materia, or upon the same subject matter, shall be construed with reference to each other. What is clear in one statute may be called in aid to explain what is doubtful in another."). *But see* Bruce v. Kelly, 514 P.3d 1007, 1012 (Kan. 2022) ("[T]he doctrine of *in pari materia* has utility beyond those instances where statutory ambiguity exists. It can be used as a tool to assess whether the statutory language is plain and unambiguous in the first instance, and it can provide substance and meaning to a court's plain language interpretation of a statute.").

There are various ways in which courts might interpret one statute in light of other statutes that are *in pari materia*. Some arguments focus on the policies behind the statutes. In the words of one leading treatise, when a legislature has already enacted statutes on a particular subject, and when the legislature enacts a new provision on the same subject without explicitly repealing or amending the earlier statutes, "the new provision is presumed to accord with the legislative policy embodied in those prior statutes." 2B SUTHERLAND STATUTES AND STATUTORY CONSTRUCTION, *supra*, § 51:2 (footnotes omitted). As far back as 1826, Chancellor Kent stated this idea strongly:

> "Several acts *in pari materia*, and relating to the same subject, are to be taken together, and compared in the construction of them, because they are considered as having one object in view, and as acting upon one system. . . . [I]t is to be inferred, that a code of statutes relating to one subject, was governed by one spirit and

policy, and was intended to be consistent and harmonious in its several parts and provisions."

1 JAMES KENT, COMMENTARIES ON AMERICAN LAW 433 (New York, O. Halsted 1826). Some state courts continue to echo those words. *See, e.g.*, State v. Huckabay, 480 P.3d 771, 773 (Idaho 2021); Onnen v. Sioux Falls Indep. School Dist. No. 49-5, 801 N.W.2d 752, 756–57 (S.D. 2011).

The presumption that statutes *in pari materia* reflect "one spirit and policy" can matter. For example, if courts know the policy behind one statute, the idea that they should attribute the same policy to another statute can sometimes affect how they resolve indeterminacies in the other statute. *See, e.g.*, Acurio v. Acurio, 224 So. 3d 935, 938 (La. 2017) (resolving a dispute about the interpretation of one statutory provision in light of the policy reflected in a provision that was *in pari materia*). Likewise, courts have also invoked the *in pari materia* doctrine to avoid reading one statute in a way that might interfere with the operation of another. *See, e.g.*, Wheeling-Pittsburgh Steel Corp. v. Mitsui & Co., 221 F.3d 924, 927–28 (6th Cir. 2000); Miller v. Bd. of County Comm'rs, 390 P.3d 504, 511 (Kan. 2017).

Apart from these policy-based arguments, some other invocations of the *in pari materia* doctrine are text-based. Recall, from Chapter 2.B.5, that courts trying to interpret a single statute commonly apply a "presumption of consistent usage"; in the absence of contrary contextual clues, courts often presume that each word used in a statute has the same meaning throughout that statute. The text-based version of the *in pari materia* idea extends that canon to all statutes that are *in pari materia*. On this view, if two statutes that are *in pari materia* both use a particular word or phrase in a similar context, courts should apply a rebuttable presumption that the legislature was using the word or phrase the same way in both statutes. As a result, if there are any special clues that shed light on what the word or phrase means in one of the statutes, or if judicial precedents have ascribed a particular meaning to the word or phrase as used in that one statute, courts might extend those clues or precedents to the other statute too.

If the word or phrase would otherwise be ambiguous in ordinary usage, and if the two statutes were enacted at two different times by two different sets of legislators, how strong is the presumption that both statutes probably use the word or phrase in the same way? As applied to statutes that are *in pari materia* only in the weak sense that they address the same subject, the Supreme Court has suggested that this presumption "makes the most sense when the statutes were enacted by the same legislative body at the same time." *Erlenbaugh v. United States*, 409 U.S. 239, 243–44 (1972). But if two statutes are *in pari materia* in a strong sense—for instance, if one served as the template for the other, or if the two statutes are interconnected parts of a single program, or if they otherwise are so tightly connected that members of the legislature surely had one in mind when they enacted the other—then the presumption of semantic consistency might be a plausible guide to legislative intent in other settings too.

That is particularly true when courts are trying to interpret a word or phrase in the *newer* of the two statutes, and the same word or phrase has an unambiguous meaning in the *older* statute. Suppose that Congress used a particular word in Statute #1, and something else in Statute #1 makes clear how Statute #1 was using that word. Some years later, Congress enacts Statute #2, which uses the same word in a similar context. If Statute #2 is *in pari materia* with Statute #1 in a strong sense, then the meaning of the word in Statute #1 may well be a good piece of evidence about how Congress probably was using the same word in Statute #2. Just as courts can tell from the rest of Statute #1 what the word was intended to mean in Statute #1, so could the people in Congress who were considering Statute #2—and if they used the same word in a similar context in Statute #2, interpreters might start with the presumption that the word carries the same meaning in Statute #2 that the word carried in Statute #1. To be sure, this presumption is rebuttable; if something else about Statute #2 suggests that Congress was using the word in a different way, courts will not close their eyes to that possibility. But in the absence of other clues, the meaning of the word in Statute #1 is probably a decent guide to its intended meaning in a later statute that is *in pari materia* with Statute #1 in a strong sense.

The presumption of semantic consistency (that is, the text-based version of the *in pari materia* doctrine) seems much less justified if courts are trying to interpret the *older* statute in light of the *newer* one. Consider a revised hypothetical. Again, the same word appears in both Statute #1 and Statute #2, but Statute #1 provides no special clues about what the word means; those clues appear only in the *later* statute. If the two statutes were enacted years apart, do clues about what Statute #2 used the word to mean have any bearing on what the word was intended to mean in Statute #1? Why would information about the later legislature's usage shed any light on what the earlier legislature meant?[28]

Even if there is no strong descriptive argument for a presumption of semantic consistency in this latter context, perhaps there is some normative argument. All else equal, assuming that the same word means the same thing in both statutes is simpler than the alternative, and it might also increase the predictability of judicial decisions (with

---

[28] As we shall see below, one can ask similar questions about whether and why the *in pari materia* idea should apply when *neither* statute contains any special clues about how the legislature was using the shared word, but judicial precedents have interpreted the word in one of the two statutes. If the courts issued the relevant decisions before the legislature enacted the second statute, then perhaps the legislature can be presumed to have known about those decisions when it enacted the second statute and to have intended the second statute to incorporate the gloss that they suggest. (That situation resembles the reenactment scenarios considered in Chapter 4.A.2.b.) But what if the legislature enacted both statutes *before* the courts put their gloss on the word or phrase that the statutes share? In that case, the *in pari materia* idea cannot be based on a "legislative ratification" theory, though it can perhaps benefit from some of the arguments that support the doctrine of *stare decisis*.

corresponding benefits for notice to people in the real world). In my view, though, those arguments have little force except as tie-breakers, in cases where courts would otherwise be pretty much in equipoise about how to interpret the word in Statute #1.

At least where Statute #1 is ambiguous, though, some judicial opinions do support resolving the ambiguity in light of later statutes. In the old case of *United States v. Freeman*, 44 U.S. (3 How.) 556 (1845), Justice Wayne put the point this way: "[I]f it can be gathered from a subsequent statute *in pari materia*, what meaning the [later] legislature attached to the words of a former statute, they will amount to a legislative declaration of its meaning, and will govern the construction of the first statute." *Id.* at 564–65 (dictum). In modern times, Justice Scalia quoted this passage favorably in support of the conclusion that "the meaning of [a statutory provision enacted in 1967] . . . sheds light upon the meaning of [a statutory provision enacted in 1941]." *Branch v. Smith*, 538 U.S. 254, 281 (2003) (plurality opinion of Scalia, J.); *see also infra* Chapter 7.D.3 (discussing a similar issue that can arise even if the relevant statutes are not *in pari materia*). State courts have divided on this topic. *Compare* Nelson v. Hanna, 413 N.Y.S.2d 62, 63 (App. Div. 1979) ("A subsequent statute *in pari materia* with an earlier one may be considered as an aid in the construction of the earlier statute." (citation omitted)), *with* People v. Mullins, 911 N.W.2d 201, 209 (Mich. App. 2017) ("When the related statute [from which guidance is being sought] was enacted . . . after the statute at issue, the [*in pari materia*] canon is generally inapplicable.").

To the extent that the *in pari materia* doctrine encourages courts to interpret statutes with an eye toward semantic consistency, policy consistency, or both, the doctrine can matter in cases of first impression—cases in which courts are interpreting the relevant statutes for the first time. But once precedents have started to accumulate, the *in pari materia* doctrine can become even more important. In general, if courts conclude that two statutes are *in pari materia*, precedents about the meaning of one of the statutes may have considerable weight with respect to similar questions that come up under the other statute.

Smith v. City of Jackson, 544 U.S. 228 (2005), illustrates this aspect of the *in pari materia* doctrine. The case involved the following timeline.

- Title VII of the Civil Rights Act of 1964 forbade various forms of employment discrimination. Section 703(a) of the 1964 statute read as follows:

  "It shall be an unlawful employment practice for an employer—

  "(1) to fail or refuse to hire or to discharge any individual, or otherwise to discriminate against any individual with respect to his compensation, terms, conditions, or privileges of employment, because of such individual's race, color, religion, sex, or national origin; or

"(2) to limit, segregate, or classify his employees in any way which would deprive or tend to deprive any individual of employment opportunities or otherwise adversely affect his status as an employee, because of such individual's race, color, religion, sex, or national origin."

- In 1967, Congress enacted the Age Discrimination in Employment Act (ADEA). Section 4(a) of the ADEA used essentially the same language as § 703(a) of Title VII, except that Congress substituted the word "age" for the phrase "race, color, religion, sex, or national origin."
- In 1971, the Supreme Court interpreted Title VII in *Griggs v. Duke Power Co.*, a case discussed on pp. 390–391 of this book. Without engaging in close textual analysis, *Griggs* held that § 703(a)(2) forbids an employer to use hiring or promotion criteria that have a disparate impact on Black employees and that are not shown to be sufficiently related to job performance. According to *Griggs*, an employer who used such criteria was violating Title VII even if the employer was not intentionally trying to discriminate against Black people.

In *Smith*, the Supreme Court had to decide whether to interpret § 4(a)(2) of the ADEA in the same way that *Griggs* and its progeny had interpreted § 703(a)(2) of Title VII.

Writing for himself and three other Justices, Justice Stevens answered that question in the affirmative. He offered three principal reasons for concluding that the ADEA did authorize disparate-impact claims.

First, he emphasized that § 4(a)(2) of the ADEA and § 703(a)(2) of Title VII were *in pari materia* (though he did not use that phrase), and that *Griggs* was therefore an important precedent about the meaning of § 4(a)(2). The key paragraph of his plurality opinion on this point read as follows:

> "In determining whether the ADEA authorizes disparate-impact claims, we begin with the premise that when Congress uses the same language in two statutes having similar purposes, particularly when one is enacted shortly after the other, it is appropriate to presume that Congress intended that text to have the same meaning in both statutes. We have consistently applied that presumption to language in the ADEA that was 'derived *in haec verba* from Title VII.' Our unanimous interpretation of § 703(a)(2) of Title VII in *Griggs* is therefore a precedent of compelling importance."

Smith, 544 U.S. at 233–34 (plurality opinion) (citations omitted).

Second, Justice Stevens suggested that *Griggs* was correct on the merits: not only did it appropriately reflect the purposes behind both Title VII and the ADEA, but "our holding represented the better reading of the statutory text as well." According to Justice Stevens, neither § 703(a)(2) of Title VII nor § 4(a)(2) of the ADEA focuses on "the motivation for the action of the employer"; instead, the text of both provisions "focuses on the *effects* of the action on the employee." *Id.* at 235.

Third, Justice Stevens argued that some special language in the ADEA presupposed the existence of disparate-impact liability under § 4(a)(2). Section 4(f)(1) of the ADEA specified that "[i]t shall not be unlawful for an employer . . . to take any action otherwise prohibited under subsections (a), (b), (c), or (e) of this section where age is a bona fide occupational qualification reasonably necessary to the normal operation of the particular business, *or where the differentiation is based on reasonable factors other than age.*" Pub. L. 90–202, § 4(f)(1), 81 Stat. 602, 603 (1967) (emphasis added). The first part of this provision, addressing circumstances in which age is "a bona fide occupational qualification," parallels what § 703(e)(1) of Title VII says about religion, sex, and national origin. But the so-called "RFOA" provision (protecting employers from liability "where the differentiation is based on reasonable factors other than age") has no counterpart in Title VII. According to Justice Stevens, that special language in the ADEA would be largely superfluous *unless* § 4(a) is understood to recognize theories of disparate-impact liability. *Smith*, 544 U.S. at 238–39 (plurality opinion). One way of putting this argument is that if § 4(a) prohibited only deliberate discrimination based on age, then § 4(f)(1) would not have spoken about employment practices that are "otherwise prohibited under [§ 4(a)]" but "based on reasonable factors other than age."[29]

Justice O'Connor, however, found none of these arguments persuasive. In a separate opinion joined by Justices Kennedy and Thomas, she argued that the phrase "because of such individual's age" in § 4(a) of the ADEA referred only to actions "*motivated by* the individual's age." *Id.* at 249 (O'Connor, J., concurring in the judgment). She added that "[t]he legislative history of the ADEA confirms what its text plainly indicates—that Congress never intended the statute to authorize disparate impact claims." *Id.* at 253. Among other things, she emphasized that "[a]t the time the ADEA was enacted, the predominant focus of antidiscrimination law was on intentional discrimination"; that "[if] Congress [had] intended to inaugurate disparate impact liability in

---

[29] Justice Stevens also advanced a fourth argument: "[B]oth the Department of Labor . . . and the [Equal Employment Opportunity Commission (EEOC)], which is the agency charged by Congress with responsibility for implementing the statute, . . . have consistently interpreted the ADEA to authorize relief on a disparate-impact theory." *Id.* at 239. This point was decisive for Justice Scalia, who wrote separately to advocate giving *Chevron* deference to the EEOC's interpretation of the statute. *See id.* at 243 (Scalia, J., concurring in part and concurring in the judgment). Still, we will postpone considering *Chevron* until Chapter 5.

the ADEA, one would expect to find some indication of that intent in . . . the legislative history"; and that "the legislative history is devoid of any discussion of disparate impact claims." *Id.* at 258.[30]

This line of argument suggests considerable skepticism about whether *Griggs* correctly interpreted Title VII. After all, if the text of § 4(a)(2) of the ADEA "plainly" focuses on the employer's motivations, then presumably the same is true of the identical text in § 703(a)(2) of Title VII. Likewise, to speak of whether Congress had meant to "inaugurate disparate impact liability in the ADEA" is to assume (contrary to *Griggs*) that Title VII had not already provided for that sort of liability. But whether *Griggs* was right or wrong about the meaning of Title VII as an original matter, Justice O'Connor still had to deal with the idea that its precedential force should extend to the ADEA. She responded to that idea as follows:

> "The plurality [argues] . . . that the relevant provision of the ADEA should be read *in pari materia* with the parallel provision of Title VII . . . . Because *Griggs* held that Title VII's § 703(a)(2) permits disparate impact claims, the plurality concludes that we should read § 4(a)(2) of the ADEA similarly. . . .
>
> "Obviously, this argument would be a great deal more convincing had *Griggs* been decided *before* the ADEA was enacted. In that case, we could safely assume that Congress had notice (and therefore intended) that the language at issue here would be read to authorize disparate impact claims. . . . But *Griggs* was decided four years *after* the ADEA's enactment, and there is no reason to suppose that Congress in 1967 could have foreseen the interpretation of Title VII that was to come. . . .
>
> "To be sure, where two statutes use similar language we generally take this as 'a strong indication that [they] should be interpreted *pari passu*.' *Northcross v. Board of Ed. of Memphis City Schools*, 412 U.S. 427, 428 (1973) (*per curiam*). But this is not a rigid or absolute rule, and it ' "readily yields" ' to other indicia of congressional intent. *General Dynamics* [*Land Systems, Inc. v. Cline*, 540 U.S. 581, 595 (2004)] (quoting *Atlantic Cleaners & Dyers, Inc. v. United States*, 286 U.S. 427, 433 (1932)). Indeed, ' "the meaning [of the same words] well may vary to meet the purposes of the law." ' *United States v. Cleveland Indians Baseball Co.*, 532 U.S. 200, 213 (2001) (quoting *Atlantic Cleaners & Dyers*, 286 U.S. at 433; alteration in original). . . .
>
> ". . . . [A]s the Congresses that adopted *both* Title VII *and* the ADEA clearly recognized, the two statutes were intended to address qualitatively different kinds of discrimination. . . . Disparate impact

[30] In response to Justice Stevens's argument about the RFOA provision, Justice O'Connor characterized the RFOA provision as a "safe harbor" that Congress might have included out of an "abundance of caution" and that did not imply the existence of disparate-impact liability elsewhere. *See id.* at 251–53.

liability may have a legitimate role in combating the types of discrimination addressed by Title VII, but the nature of aging and of age discrimination makes such liability inappropriate for the ADEA. . . .

"Finally, nothing in the Court's decision in *Griggs* itself provides any reason to extend its holding to the ADEA. As the plurality tacitly acknowledges, . . . the decision in *Griggs* was not based on any analysis of Title VII's actual language. Rather, the *ratio decidendi* was the statute's perceived *purpose*, *i.e.*,

> 'to achieve equality of employment opportunities and remove barriers that have operated in the past to favor an identifiable group of white employees over other employees. Under the Act, practices, procedures, or tests neutral on their face, and even neutral in terms of intent, cannot be maintained if they operate to "freeze" the status quo of prior discriminatory employment practices.' [*Griggs*,] 401 U.S. at 429–430.

"In other words, the Court in *Griggs* reasoned that disparate impact liability was necessary to achieve Title VII's ostensible goal of eliminating the cumulative effects of historical racial discrimination. . . . [T]hat rationale finds no parallel in the ADEA context, . . . and it therefore should not control our decision here.

"Even venerable canons of construction must bow, in an appropriate case, to compelling evidence of congressional intent. In my judgment, the significant differences between Title VII and the ADEA are more than sufficient to overcome the default presumption that similar language is to be read similarly. See *Fogerty* [*v. Fantasy, Inc.*, 510 U.S. 517, 523–24 (1994)] (concluding that the 'normal indication' that similar language should be read similarly is 'overborne' by differences between the legislative history and purposes of two statutes)."

Smith, 544 U.S. at 259–62 (O'Connor, J., concurring in the judgment).

Compare Justice O'Connor's position in *Smith* to her position in *Rose v. Rose*, 481 U.S. 619 (1987). There, the Court had to interpret a federal statute specifying that various veterans' benefits "shall be exempt from taxation, shall be exempt from the claim of creditors, and shall not be liable to attachment, levy, or seizure by or under any legal or equitable process whatever, either before or after receipt by the beneficiary." 38 U.S.C. § 3101(a) (1982 ed.). In *Ridgway v. Ridgway*, 454 U.S. 46 (1981), the Court had adopted a broad reading of identical language in a separate federal statute—the Servicemen's Group Life Insurance Act of 1965 (SGLIA), which addressed life-insurance benefits payable under veterans' policies. But the *Rose* Court read the anti-attachment provision in 38 U.S.C. § 3101(a) more narrowly than the *Ridgway* Court had read the anti-attachment provision in the SGLIA. Justice Marshall's majority opinion in *Rose* sought to distinguish the two statutory schemes, but

Justice White's dissent denied that there was any meaningful distinction. *See Rose*, 481 U.S. at 645 (White, J., dissenting) ("The Court's decision is . . . inconsistent with *Ridgway* . . . ."). Justice O'Connor responded with a concurrence arguing that *Ridgway* had been wrongly decided. While she acknowledged that "*stare decisis* concerns may counsel against overruling *Ridgway*'s interpretation of the Servicemen's Group Life Insurance Act," she saw "no reason whatsoever" to let *Ridgway*'s faulty reading of one statute control the interpretation of a different statute—especially one that had been enacted before *Ridgway*. *Id.* at 636 (O'Connor, J., concurring in part and concurring in the judgment). Justice Stevens, who had dissented in *Ridgway*, joined her concurrence.

Might the same dynamic have been going on in *Smith*? Notwithstanding the differences between race discrimination and age discrimination, and notwithstanding the concomitant differences between the purposes of Title VII and the purposes of the ADEA, § 4(a)(2) of the ADEA was modeled on § 703(a)(2) of Title VII. If one thinks that *Griggs* correctly interpreted § 703(a)(2), wouldn't one be inclined to extend that conclusion to § 4(a)(2)? If so, then Justice O'Connor's position in *Smith* may well have reflected the premise that *Griggs*, like *Ridgway*, misinterpreted the statute it addressed.

If one accepts that premise,[31] then one confronts questions about what might be called "trans-statute" *stare decisis*. Assume that because of *stare decisis* (or because of the Civil Rights Act of 1991, the relevance of which is discussed below), the Court has decided to adhere to *Griggs*'s interpretation of Title VII. If the Court is unwilling to repudiate *Griggs* in the context of Title VII, is it obliged to extend *Griggs* to the ADEA and other statutes that are *in pari materia* with Title VII? Or when members of the Court doubt the logic of a precedent, can they legitimately confine that precedent to the particular statute it interpreted—with the result that *Griggs* might control subsequent interpretations of Title VII but not subsequent interpretations of the ADEA?

In this connection, recall the questions raised earlier in this chapter about the Court's performance after *Federal Baseball Club v. National League*, 259 U.S. 200 (1922). As a matter of *stare decisis*, the Court took that case to establish that the Sherman Act did not reach the business of baseball. In later cases under the same statute, however, the Court confined *Federal Baseball Club* to its facts; the Court held that the Sherman Act *did* reach football, boxing, theatrical exhibitions, and the

---

[31] One might not, of course. *See supra* p. 391 (discussing *Griggs*). Indeed, even if one would otherwise be skeptical of *Griggs*'s interpretation of Title VII, perhaps the fact that the ADEA and Title VII are *in pari materia* can be used to defend *Griggs*. Suppose one agrees with Justice Stevens's take on the RFOA provision in § 4(f)(1) of the ADEA: that provision, one thinks, would have no point if the rest of § 4 prohibited only employment actions that were motivated by age. If one infers from the RFOA provision that § 4(a)(2) of the ADEA does recognize some sort of disparate-impact liability, and if one agrees that § 4(a)(2) of the ADEA and § 703(a)(2) of Title VII are *in pari materia*, should the RFOA provision in the ADEA lead one to accept *Griggs*'s interpretation of Title VII? How much does the fact that Title VII was enacted a few years *before* the ADEA weaken this argument?

like. Many people criticize the Court for drawing those distinctions. They are open to the possibility that the Court should have overruled *Federal Baseball Club* outright. But they think that if *stare decisis* did indeed favor adhering to *Federal Baseball Club*, then the Court should have adhered not only to the case's outcome on its particular facts but also to its rationale—with the result that the Court should have applied the logic of *Federal Baseball Club* to football, boxing, and other sports. If you share that view about the nature of *stare decisis*, do you also have to embrace the idea of "trans-statute" *stare decisis*? Or is there some reason why it is more legitimate to confine precedents to the particular statute that they interpreted (so that the *stare decisis* effect of *Griggs* matters only for Title VII) than to confine precedents to the particular facts that they addressed (so that the *stare decisis* effect of *Griggs* would matter only for cases involving power companies)?

In practice, different judges may react in different ways when they conclude that a precedent was wrong about the statute that it interpreted. Some judges may want to overrule the precedent even with respect to the statute that the precedent directly addressed. Other judges might be willing to continue following the precedent with respect to that statute, but they might refuse to extend the precedent to other statutes that are *in pari materia*. Still other judges might oppose that middle ground as too artificial; they might conclude that the precedent *should* control how the courts interpret all statutes that are *in pari materia* and that present the same question.

* * * * *

Justice Stevens's opinion in *Smith v. City of Jackson* implicated one other set of questions about trans-statute *stare decisis*. Recall that Justice Stevens expressed no qualms about *Griggs*, and he was perfectly happy to extend *Griggs*'s conclusions about disparate-impact liability from § 703(a)(2) of Title VII to § 4(a)(2) of the ADEA. *Griggs* itself, however, was an ambiguous decision, and it left many questions open for further litigation. *See* GEORGE RUTHERGLEN, EMPLOYMENT DISCRIMINATION LAW: VISIONS OF EQUALITY IN THEORY AND DOCTRINE 76–79 (5th ed. 2021). In *Wards Cove Packing Co. v. Atonio*, 490 U.S. 642 (1989), the Supreme Court resolved some of those questions in a pro-defendant direction. As Justice Stevens put it in *Smith*, "*Wards Cove* . . . narrowly construed the employer's exposure to liability on a disparate-impact theory [under Title VII]." *Smith*, 544 U.S. at 240.

With respect to Title VII, the Civil Rights Act of 1991 overrode this aspect of *Wards Cove*. Section 2 of the 1991 Act expressed Congress's view that "the decision of the Supreme Court in *Wards Cove* . . . has weakened the scope and effectiveness of Federal civil rights protections"; § 3 declared that one of the purposes of the 1991 Act was "to codify the concepts of 'business necessity' and 'job related' enunciated by the Supreme Court in *Griggs* . . . and in the other Supreme Court decisions prior to *Wards Cove*"; and § 105 amended § 703 of Title VII so that it specifically addresses what a complaining party must show in order to establish "[a]n unlawful employment practice based on disparate impact . . . under this title." Civil Rights Act of 1991, Pub. L. 102–166, 105 Stat. 1071, 1071, 1074–75. But as Justice Stevens noted in *Smith*, "[w]hile the relevant 1991 amendments expanded the coverage of Title VII, they did not amend the ADEA or speak to the subject of age discrimination." *Smith*, 544 U.S. at 240. As a result, § 4 of the ADEA continued to use the same language that *Wards Cove* had interpreted in the context of § 703 of Title VII. Writing for a majority of the Court on this point, Justice Stevens therefore concluded that "*Wards Cove*'s pre-1991 interpretation of Title VII[ ] . . . remains applicable to the ADEA." *Id.*[32]; *cf.* Meacham v. Knolls Atomic Power Lab., 554 U.S. 84, 97–102 (2008) (clarifying which aspects of *Wards Cove* are relevant in ADEA cases).

Justice Stevens himself, however, had dissented in *Wards Cove*. Assuming that he continued to disagree with its interpretation of the pre-1991 version of Title VII, should he have resisted extending that interpretation to the ADEA? Should Congress's decision to override *Wards Cove* with respect to Title VII have made Justice Stevens especially reluctant to treat *Wards Cove* as a vibrant precedent for the interpretation of other statutes? How should trans-statute *stare decisis* work when Congress has overridden a precedent with respect to the statute that the precedent itself addressed, but not with respect to other statutes that are *in pari materia*? *Cf.* Deborah A. Widiss, *Shadow Precedents and the Separation of Powers: Statutory Interpretation of Congressional Overrides*, 84 NOTRE DAME L. REV. 511 (2009) (arguing, contrary to Justice Stevens's position in *Smith*, that such "shadow precedents" normally should lose their force).

* * * * *

In *Texas Dep't of Housing & Community Affairs v. Inclusive Communities Project*, 576 U.S. 519 (2015), the Supreme Court extended the theory of disparate-impact liability from Title VII (as interpreted in *Griggs*) and the ADEA (as interpreted by the plurality in *Smith*) to the Fair Housing Act of 1968 (FHA), Pub. L. 90–284, tit. VIII, 82 Stat. 73, 81–89 (codified as amended at 42 U.S.C. §§ 3601 *et seq.*).

The plaintiff in the Texas case was relying upon two specific provisions in the FHA. Section 804(a) establishes the general rule that "[i]t shall be unlawful . . . [t]o refuse to sell or rent after the making of a bona fide offer, or to refuse to negotiate for the sale or rental of, or otherwise make unavailable or deny, a dwelling to any person because of

---

[32] In addition to the continuing effects of *Wards Cove*, the RFOA provision in § 4(f)(1) of the ADEA further reduces the scope of disparate-impact liability under the ADEA. *See id.* (noting that for both these reasons, "the scope of disparate-impact liability under [the] ADEA is narrower than under [the current version of] Title VII"). In *Smith* itself, the Court ultimately affirmed judgment for the defendant on the strength of the RFOA provision. *See id.* at 241–43 (finding it "clear from the record" that the challenged employment practice, which involved giving proportionately greater raises to employees with less seniority, "was based on reasonable factors other than age").

race, color, religion, sex, familial status, or national origin." 42 U.S.C. § 3604(a). Section 805(a) adds that "[i]t shall be unlawful for any person or other entity whose business includes engaging in residential real-estate related transactions to discriminate against any person in making available such a transaction, or in the terms or conditions of such a transaction, because of race, color, religion, sex, handicap, familial status, or national origin." *Id.* § 3605(a). Writing for a 5–4 majority, Justice Kennedy held that these provisions prohibit not only conscious discrimination but also the use of decisionmaking criteria that have a disparate impact along racial lines and that are not shown to be "necessary to achieve a valid interest."

Justice Kennedy did not say that §§ 804(a) and 805(a) of the FHA were *in pari materia* with § 703(a)(2) of Title VII and § 4(a)(2) of the ADEA. Still, he treated *Griggs* and *Smith* as highly relevant precedents. Here are some excerpts from his majority opinion:

> "Together, *Griggs* holds and the plurality in *Smith* instructs that antidiscrimination laws must be construed to encompass disparate-impact claims when their text refers to the consequences of actions and not just to the mindset of actors, and where that interpretation is consistent with statutory purpose. . . .
>
> ". . . .
>
> "Applied here, the logic of *Griggs* and *Smith* provides strong support for the conclusion that the FHA encompasses disparate-impact claims. Congress' use of the phrase 'otherwise make unavailable' [in § 804(a)] refers to the consequences of an action rather than the actor's intent. . . . This results-oriented language counsels in favor of recognizing disparate-impact liability. See *Smith, supra*, at 236. [Likewise, t]he Court has construed statutory language similar to § 805(a) to include disparate-impact liability. See, *e.g.*, *Board of Ed. of City School Dist. of New York v. Harris*, 444 U.S. 130, 140–141 (1979) (holding the term 'discriminat[e]' encompassed disparate-impact liability in the context of a statute's text, history, purpose, and structure).
>
> "A comparison to the antidiscrimination statutes examined in *Griggs* and *Smith* is useful. Title VII's and the ADEA's 'otherwise adversely affect' language is equivalent in function and purpose to the FHA's 'otherwise make unavailable' language. In these three statutes the operative text looks to results. The relevant statutory phrases, moreover, play an identical role in the structure common to all three statutes: Located at the end of lengthy sentences that begin with prohibitions on disparate treatment, they serve as catchall phrases looking to consequences, not intent. And all three statutes use the word 'otherwise' to introduce the results-oriented phrase. 'Otherwise' means 'in a different way or manner,' thus signaling a shift in emphasis from an actor's intent to the consequences of his actions. Webster's Third New International Dictionary 1598 (1971).

This similarity in text and structure is all the more compelling given that Congress passed the FHA in 1968—only four years after passing Title VII and only four months after enacting the ADEA.

"It is true that Congress did not reiterate Title VII's exact language in the FHA, but that is because to do so would have made the relevant sentence awkward and unclear. A provision making it unlawful to 'refuse to sell[,] . . . or otherwise [adversely affect], a dwelling to any person' because of a protected trait would be grammatically obtuse, difficult to interpret, and far more expansive in scope than Congress likely intended. Congress thus chose words that serve the same purpose and bear the same basic meaning but are consistent with the structure and objectives of the FHA.

"Emphasizing that the FHA uses the phrase 'because of race,' the [Texas Department of Housing & Community Affairs] argues this language forecloses disparate-impact liability since '[a]n action is not taken "because of race" unless race is a *reason* for the action.' Brief for Petitioners 26. *Griggs* and *Smith*, however, dispose of this argument. Both Title VII and the ADEA contain identical 'because of' language, see 42 U.S.C. § 2000e–2(a)(2); 29 U.S.C. § 623(a)(2), and the Court nonetheless held those statutes impose disparate-impact liability."

Tex. Dep't of Housing, 576 U.S. at 533–35.

Justice Alito wrote the principal dissent (joined by Chief Justice Roberts and Justices Scalia and Thomas). In both § 804(a) and § 805(a), he asserted, "the key phrase is 'because of.'" *Id.* at 559 (Alito, J., dissenting). Justice Alito understood that phrase to refer to the *motivation* for an action: "Congress . . . outlawed the covered actions only when they are motivated by race or one of the other protected characteristics." *Id.* at 561. More broadly, Justice Alito asserted that "[u]nder a statute like the FHA that prohibits actions taken 'because of' protected characteristics, intent makes all the difference." *Id.* at 561–62.

Justice Alito offered two responses to the majority's emphasis on the phrase "otherwise make unavailable" in § 804(a). First, he invoked *noscitur a sociis* and *ejusdem generis*: in his view, "the phrases that precede 'make unavailable' [in § 804(a)] unmistakably describe *intentional* deprivations of equal treatment, not merely actions that happen to have a disparate effect," and the phrase "otherwise make unavailable" probably should be understood the same way even if the statute had not used the phrase "because of." *Id.* at 564. But second, he observed that the statute *did* use the phrase "because of," and that phrase went with "otherwise make unavailable" just as it went with the other words in the same list. Justice Alito expanded upon that point as follows: "Sections 804(a) and 805(a) apply only when a party makes a dwelling or transaction unavailable 'because of' race or another protected characteristic. In ordinary English usage, when a person makes something unavailable 'because of' some factor, that factor must be a reason for the act." *Id.*

In response to Justice Kennedy's reliance on *Griggs* and *Smith*, Justice Alito asserted that the Court had used "text-free reasoning" in *Griggs*. *Id.* at 578. When *Smith* had finally forced the Justices to "grapple with the text of the provision at issue," moreover, the Justices had "unanimously agreed" that § 4(a)**(1)** of the ADEA does *not* authorize disparate-impact claims. *Id.* at 579. To be sure, five of the Justices in *Smith* had concluded that § 4(a)**(2)** of the ADEA is different. In Justice Alito's words, "a majority of the Justices [in *Smith*] found that the terms of § 4(a)(2) either clearly authorize disparate-impact claims (the position of the plurality) or at least are ambiguous enough to provide a basis for deferring to such an interpretation by the Equal Employment Opportunity Commission (the position of Justice Scalia)." *Id.* According to Justice Alito, though, the position of these five Justices could be attributed to a textual difference between § 4(a)(1) and § 4(a)(2). Admittedly, both § 4(a)(1) and § 4(a)(2) use the phrase "because of." But while § 4(a)(1) forbids employers "to discriminate against any individual [in certain respects] . . . because of such individual's age," § 4(a)(2) uses a different formulation: it asks whether an employer has acted "in any way which would . . . adversely affect [an individual's] status as an employee[ ] because of such individual's age." Justice Alito understood *Smith* to suggest that the language of § 4(a)(2) is more hospitable to disparate-impact claims than the language of § 4(a)(1). *See id.* at 579–81. According to Justice Alito, however, the provisions of the Fair Housing Act at issue in the Texas case resembled § 4(a)(1) more than they resembled § 4(a)(2): "These provisions of the FHA, unlike the Title VII provision in *Griggs* or § 4(a)(2) of the ADEA, do not make it unlawful to take an action that happens to adversely affect a person because of race, religion, etc." *Id.* at 582.

Although Justice Thomas joined Justice Alito's dissent, he also wrote a separate dissent that took on *Griggs* more directly. According to Justice Thomas, "We should drop the pretense that *Griggs'* interpretation of Title VII was legitimate." *Id.* at 547 (Thomas, J., dissenting). After arguing that *Griggs* "defies . . . the statutory text," *id.* at 553, Justice Thomas added:

> "Whatever deference is due *Griggs* as a matter of *stare decisis*, we should at the very least confine it to Title VII. We should not incorporate it into statutes such as the Fair Housing Act and the ADEA, which were passed years before Congress had any reason to suppose that this Court would take the position it did in *Griggs*. . . . And we should certainly not allow it to spread to statutes like the Fair Housing Act, whose operative text, unlike . . . the ADEA's, does not even mirror Title VII's."

Id. at 556.

* * * * *

Apart from disagreeing about the effects of *Griggs* and *Smith*, the majority and the dissenters in the Texas case also disagreed about the effect of a 1988 amendment to the Fair Housing Act. Again, here are some excerpts from Justice Kennedy's majority opinion:

"[I]t is of crucial importance that the existence of disparate-impact liability is supported by amendments to the FHA that Congress enacted in 1988. By that time, all nine Courts of Appeals to have addressed the question had concluded the Fair Housing Act encompassed disparate-impact claims. [Citations omitted.]

"When it amended the FHA, Congress was aware of this unanimous precedent. And with that understanding, it made a considered judgment to retain the relevant statutory text. See H.R. Rep. No. 100–711, p. 21, n. 52 (1988) (H.R. Rep.) (discussing suits premised on disparate-impact claims and related judicial precedent); 134 Cong. Rec. 23711 (1988) (statement of Sen. Kennedy) (noting unanimity of Federal Courts of Appeals concerning disparate impact); Fair Housing Amendments Act of 1987: Hearings on S. 558 before the Subcommittee on the Constitution of the Senate Committee on the Judiciary, 100th Cong., 1st Sess., 529 (1987) (testimony of Professor Robert Schwemm) (describing consensus judicial view that the FHA imposed disparate-impact liability). Indeed, Congress rejected a proposed amendment that would have eliminated disparate-impact liability for certain zoning decisions. See H.R. Rep. at 89–93.

"Against this background understanding in the legal and regulatory system, Congress' decision in 1988 to amend the FHA while still adhering to the operative language in §§ 804(a) and 805(a) is convincing support for the conclusion that Congress accepted and ratified the unanimous holdings of the Courts of Appeals finding disparate-impact liability. 'If a word or phrase has been . . . given a uniform interpretation by inferior courts . . . , a later version of that act perpetuating the wording is presumed to carry forward that interpretation.' A. Scalia & B. Garner, Reading Law: The Interpretation of Legal Texts 322 (2012); see also *Forest Grove School Dist. v. T.A.*, 557 U.S. 230, 244, n. 11 (2009) ('When Congress amended [the Act] without altering the text of [the relevant provision], it implicitly adopted [this Court's] construction of the statute'); *Manhattan Properties, Inc. v. Irving Trust Co.*, 291 U.S. 320, 336 (1934) (explaining, where the Courts of Appeals had reached a consensus interpretation of the Bankruptcy Act and Congress had amended the Act without changing the relevant provision, '[t]his is persuasive that the construction adopted by the [lower federal] courts has been acceptable to the legislative arm of the government').

"Further and convincing confirmation of Congress' understanding that disparate-impact liability exists under the FHA is revealed by the substance of the 1988 amendments. The amendments included three exemptions from liability that assume the existence of disparate-impact claims. The most logical conclusion is that the three amendments were deemed necessary because Congress presupposed disparate impact under the FHA as it had been enacted in 1968.

"The relevant 1988 amendments were as follows. First, Congress added a clarifying provision: 'Nothing in [the FHA] prohibits a person engaged in the business of furnishing appraisals of real property to take into consideration factors other than race, color, religion, national origin, sex, handicap, or familial status.' 42 U.S.C. § 3605(c). Second, Congress provided: 'Nothing in [the FHA] prohibits conduct against a person because such person has been convicted by any court of competent jurisdiction of the illegal manufacture or distribution of a controlled substance.' § 3607(b)(4). And finally, Congress specified: 'Nothing in [the FHA] limits the applicability of any reasonable ... restrictions regarding the maximum number of occupants permitted to occupy a dwelling.' § 3607(b)(1).

"The exemptions embodied in these amendments would be superfluous if Congress had assumed that disparate-impact liability did not exist under the FHA. . . . [N]one of these amendments would make sense if the FHA encompassed only disparate-treatment claims. . . . [T]he amendments ... constrain disparate-impact liability. For instance, certain criminal convictions are correlated with sex and race. See, *e.g.*, *Kimbrough v. United States*, 552 U.S. 85, 98 (2007) (discussing the racial disparity in convictions for crack cocaine offenses). By adding an exemption from liability for exclusionary practices aimed at individuals with drug convictions, Congress ensured disparate-impact liability would not lie if a landlord excluded tenants with such convictions. The same is true of the provision allowing for reasonable restrictions on occupancy. And the exemption from liability for real-estate appraisers is in the same section as § 805(a)'s prohibition of discriminatory practices in real-estate transactions, thus indicating Congress' recognition that disparate-impact liability arose under § 805(a). In short, the 1988 amendments signal that Congress ratified disparate-impact liability."

Tex. Dep't of Housing, 576 U.S. at 535–38.

Justice Alito's dissenting opinion offered various responses to this argument. To begin with, he questioned the relevance of the pre-1988 decisions of *lower* federal courts, as opposed to the Supreme Court itself:

"While we always give respectful consideration to interpretations of statutes that garner wide acceptance in other courts, this Court has 'no warrant to ignore clear statutory language on the ground that other courts have done so,' even if they have ' "consistently" ' done so for ' "30 years." ' *Milner v. Department of Navy*, 562 U.S. 562, 575–576 (2011)."

Id. at 568 (Alito, J., dissenting). In any event, Justice Alito argued that in 1988, Congress could not have regarded the lower-court decisions cited by the majority as conclusively establishing the existence of disparate-impact liability under the Fair Housing Act, because the executive branch was continuing to contest those decisions and to argue that the Fair Housing Act did not recognize disparate-impact liability. Again, here is an excerpt from Justice Alito's dissent:

> "Shortly *before* the 1988 amendments were adopted, the United States formally argued in this Court that the FHA prohibits only intentional discrimination. See Brief for United States as *Amicus Curiae* in *Huntington v. Huntington Branch, NAACP*, O.T. 1988, No. 87–1961, p. 15 ('An action taken because of some factor other than race, *i.e.*, financial means, even if it causes a discriminatory effect, is not an example of the intentional discrimination outlawed by the statute'); *id.* at 14 ('The words "because of" plainly connote a causal connection between the housing-related action and the person's race or color'). This was the same position that the United States had taken in lower courts for years. See, *e.g.*, *United States v. Birmingham*, 538 F. Supp. 819, 827, n. 9 (E.D. Mich. 1982) (noting positional change), aff'd, 727 F.2d 560, 565–566 (CA6 1984) (adopting United States' 'concession' that there must be a ' "discriminatory motive" '). It is implausible that the 1988 Congress was aware of certain lower court decisions but oblivious to the United States' considered and public view that those decisions were wrong.
>
> "This fact is fatal to any notion that Congress implicitly ratified disparate impact in 1988. The canon of interpretation on which the Court and the Solicitor General purport to rely—the so-called 'prior-construction canon'—does not apply where lawyers cannot 'justifiably regard the point as settled' or when 'other sound rules of interpretation' are implicated. A. Scalia & B. Garner, Reading Law: The Interpretation of Legal Texts 324, 325 (2012). That was the case here. Especially after the United States began repudiating disparate impact, no one could have reasonably thought that the question was settled."

Id. at 568–69 (footnote omitted).

As for the majority's point that "Congress rejected a proposed amendment that would have eliminated disparate-impact liability for certain zoning decisions," Justice Alito cited various cases in which "we have rejected *identical* arguments." *Id.* at 570. As Justice Alito noted, moreover, rejecting a proposed amendment is not the same thing as enacting the opposite of the proposed amendment. In Justice Alito's words, "To change the meaning of language in an already enacted law, Congress must pass a new law amending that language." *Id.* at 569–70.

With respect to the amendments that Congress *did* enact in 1988, Justice Alito offered a different view than the majority about both their motivation and their import. Again, here are excerpts from the relevant portion of his dissent:

"[A]lthough the Court characterizes these provisions [that Congress added in 1988] as 'exemptions,' that characterization is inaccurate. They make no reference to § 804(a) or § 805(a) or any other provision of the FHA; nor do they state that they apply to conduct that would otherwise be prohibited. Instead, they simply make clear that certain conduct is not forbidden by the Act. *E.g.*, 42 U.S.C. § 3607(b)(4) ('Nothing in this subchapter prohibits . . .'). The Court should read these amendments to mean what they say.

"In 1988, policymakers were not of one mind about disparate-impact housing suits. Some favored the theory and presumably would have been happy to have it enshrined in the FHA. See . . . 134 Cong. Rec. 23711 (1988) (statement of Sen. Kennedy). Others worried about disparate-impact liability and recognized that this Court had not decided whether disparate-impact claims were authorized under the 1968 Act. See H.R. Rep. No. 100–711, pp. 89–93 (1988). Still others disapproved of disparate-impact liability and believed that the 1968 Act did not authorize it. That was the view of President Reagan when he signed the amendments. See Remarks on Signing the Fair Housing Amendments Act of 1988, 24 Weekly Comp. of Pres. Doc. 1140, 1141 (1988) (explaining that the amendments did 'not represent any congressional or executive branch endorsement of the notion, expressed in some judicial opinions, that [FHA] violations may be established by a showing of disparate impact' because the FHA 'speaks only to intentional discrimination').

"The 1988 safe-harbor provisions have all the hallmarks of a compromise among these factions. These provisions neither authorize nor bar disparate-impact claims, but they do provide additional protection for persons and entities engaging in certain practices that Congress especially wished to shield. We 'must respect and give effect to these sorts of compromises.' *Ragsdale v. Wolverine World Wide, Inc.*, 535 U.S. 81, 93–94 (2002).

"It is not hard to see why such a compromise was attractive. For Members of Congress who supported disparate impact, the safe harbors left the favorable lower court decisions in place. And for those who hoped that this Court would ultimately agree with the position being urged by the United States, those provisions were not surplusage. In the Circuits in which disparate-impact FHA liability had been accepted, the safe-harbor provisions furnished a measure of interim protection until the question was resolved by this Court. They also provided partial protection in the event that this Court ultimately rejected the United States' argument. Neither the Court, the principal respondent, nor the Solicitor General has cited any case in which the canon against surplusage has been applied in circumstances like these.

"On the contrary, we have previously refused to interpret enactments like the 1988 safe-harbor provisions in such a way. Our decision in *O'Gilvie v. United States*, 519 U.S. 79 (1996)[,] . . . is instructive. In that case, the question was whether a provision of the Internal Revenue Code excluding a recovery for personal injury from gross income applied to punitive damages. Well after the critical provision was enacted, Congress adopted an amendment providing that punitive damages for nonphysical injuries were not excluded. Pointing to this amendment, a taxpayer argued: 'Why . . . would Congress have enacted this amendment removing punitive damages (in nonphysical injury cases) unless Congress believed that, in the amendment's absence, punitive damages did fall within the provision's coverage?' *Id.* at 89. This argument, of course, is precisely the same as the argument made in this case. . . .

"The Court rejected the argument in *O'Gilvie*. 'The short answer,' the Court wrote, is that Congress might have simply wanted to 'clarify the matter in respect to nonphysical injuries' while otherwise 'leav[ing] the law where it found it.' *Ibid.* Although other aspects of *O'Gilvie* triggered a dissent, see *id.* at 94–101 (opinion of Scalia, J.), no one quarreled with this self-evident piece of the Court's analysis. Nor was the *O'Gilvie* Court troubled that Congress' amendment regarding nonphysical injuries turned out to have been unnecessary because punitive damages for any injuries were not excluded all along."

Id. at 571–74 (footnotes omitted); *cf. supra* p. 301 (discussing Justice Stevens's similar response to an *expressio unius* argument in *Landgraf v. USI Film Products*, 511 U.S. 244 (1994)).

Justice Alito summed up this portion of his argument as follows: "[T]he 1988 amendments did not create disparate-impact liability." *Tex. Dep't of Housing*, 576 U.S. at 575 (Alito, J., dissenting). More generally, "Congress has done nothing since 1968 to change the meaning of the FHA prohibitions at issue in this case." *Id.* at 566.

In the next case, the lower court thought that two statutory provisions about national banks were *in pari materia*, but the Supreme Court disagreed. The case illustrates the lack of a clear test for whether statutes are *in pari materia*. As the notes after the case suggest, though, even if the Court had thought that the relevant statutes were indeed *in pari materia*, it is not clear what should have followed.

Wachovia Bank, N.A. v. Schmidt

546 U.S. 303 (2006)

■ *JUSTICE GINSBURG delivered the opinion of the Court:*

This case concerns the citizenship, for purposes of federal-court diversity jurisdiction, of national banks, *i.e.*, corporate entities chartered not by any State, but by the Comptroller of the Currency of the U.S. Treasury. Congress empowered federal district courts to adjudicate civil actions between "citizens of different States" where the amount in controversy exceeds $75,000. 28 U.S.C. § 1332(a)(1). A business organized as a corporation, for diversity jurisdiction purposes, is "deemed to be a citizen of any State by which it has been incorporated" and, since 1958, also "of the State where it has its principal place of business." § 1332(c)(1). State banks, usually chartered as corporate bodies by a particular State, ordinarily fit comfortably within this prescription. Federally chartered national banks do not, for they are not incorporated by "any State." For diversity jurisdiction purposes, therefore, Congress has discretely provided that national banks "shall . . . be deemed citizens of the States in which they are respectively located." § 1348.

The question presented turns on the meaning, in § 1348's context, of the word "located." . . .

. . . [W]e hold that a national bank, for § 1348 purposes, is a citizen of the State in which its main office, as set forth in its articles of association, is located. Were we to hold, as the Court of Appeals did, that a national bank is additionally a citizen of every State in which it has established a branch, the access of a federally chartered bank to a federal forum would be drastically curtailed in comparison to the access afforded state banks and other state-incorporated entities. Congress, we are satisfied, created no such anomaly. . . .

II

When Congress first authorized national banks in 1863, it specified that any "suits, actions, and proceedings by and against [them could] be had" in federal court. See Act of Feb. 25, 1863, § 59, 12 Stat. 681. National banks thus could "sue and be sued in the federal district and circuit courts solely because they were national banks, without regard to diversity, amount in controversy or the existence of a federal question in the usual sense." *Mercantile Nat. Bank at Dallas v. Langdeau*, 371 U.S. 555, 565–566 (1963). State banks, however, like other state-incorporated entities, could initiate actions in federal court only on the basis of diversity of citizenship or the existence of a federal question. See *Petri v. Commercial Nat. Bank of Chicago*, 142 U.S. 644, 648–649 (1892).

Congress ended national banks' automatic qualification for federal jurisdiction in 1882. An enactment that year provided in relevant part:

> "[T]he jurisdiction for suits hereafter brought by or against any association established under any law providing for national-

> banking associations . . . shall be the same as, and not other than, the jurisdiction for suits by or against banks not organized under any law of the United States which do or might do banking business where such national-banking associations may be doing business when such suits may be begun[.]" Act of July 12, 1882, § 4, 22 Stat. 163.

Under this measure, national banks could no longer invoke federal-court jurisdiction solely "on the ground of their Federal origin," *Petri*, 142 U.S. at 649; instead, for federal jurisdictional purposes, Congress placed national banks "on the same footing as the banks of the state where they were located," *Leather Manufacturers' Bank v. Cooper*, 120 U.S. 778, 780 (1887).

In 1887 revisions to prescriptions on federal jurisdiction, Congress replaced the 1882 provision on jurisdiction over national banks and first used the "located" language today contained in § 1348. The 1887 provision stated in relevant part:

> "[A]ll national banking associations established under the laws of the United States shall, for the purposes of all actions by or against them, real, personal or mixed, and all suits in equity, *be deemed citizens of the States in which they are respectively located*; and in such cases the circuit and district courts shall not have jurisdiction other than such as they would have in cases between individual citizens of the same State." Act of Mar. 3, 1887, § 4, 24 Stat. 554–555 (emphasis added).

Like its 1882 predecessor, the 1887 Act "sought to limit . . . the access of national banks to, and their suability in, the federal courts to the same extent to which non-national banks [were] so limited." *Langdeau*, 371 U.S. at 565–566.

In the Judicial Code of 1911, Congress combined two formerly discrete provisions on proceedings involving national banks, but retained without alteration the clause deeming national banks to be "citizens of the States in which they are respectively located." Act of Mar. 3, 1911, § 24 (Sixteenth), 36 Stat. 1091–1093. Finally, as part of the 1948 Judicial Code revision, Congress enacted § 1348 in its current form. Act of June 24, 1948, 62 Stat. 933. The provision now reads:

> "The district courts shall have original jurisdiction of any civil action commenced by the United States, or by direction of any officer thereof, against any national banking association, any civil action to wind up the affairs of any such association, and any action by a banking association established in the district for which the court is held, under chapter 2 of Title 12, to enjoin the Comptroller of the Currency, or any receiver acting under his direction, as provided by such chapter.

"All national banking associations shall, for the purpose of all other actions by or against them, be deemed citizens of the States in which they are respectively located." 28 U.S.C. § 1348.

III

The Fourth Circuit panel majority advanced three principal reasons for deciding that Wachovia is "located" in, and therefore a "citizen" of, every State in which it maintains a branch office. First, consulting dictionaries, the Court of Appeals observed that "[i]n ordinary parlance" the term "located" refers to "physical presence in a place." [388 F.3d 414, 416–417 (CA4 2004)] (internal quotation marks omitted). Banks have a physical presence, the Fourth Circuit stated, wherever they operate branches. *Id.* at 417. Next, the court noted, "Section 1348 uses two distinct terms to refer to the presence of a banking association: 'established' and 'located.' " *Id.* at 419. "To give independent meaning" to each word, the court said, "it is most reasonable to understand the place where a national bank is 'established' to refer to a bank's charter location, and to understand the place where it is 'located' to refer to the place or places where it has a physical presence." *Ibid.* Finally, the Court of Appeals stressed that in *Citizens & Southern National Bank v. Bougas*, 434 U.S. 35 (1977), this Court interpreted the term "located" in the former venue statute for national banks, see 12 U.S.C. § 94 (1976 ed.), as encompassing any county in which a bank maintains a branch office. 388 F.3d at 419–420. Reasoning that "the jurisdiction and venue statutes pertain to the same subject matter, namely the amenability of national banking associations to suit in federal court," the panel majority concluded that, "under the *in pari materia* canon[,] the two statutes should be interpreted" consistently. *Id.* at 422.

IV

None of the Court of Appeals' rationales persuade us to read § 1348 to attribute to a national bank, for diversity jurisdiction purposes, the citizenship of each State in which the bank has established branch operations. First, the term "located," as it appears in the National Bank Act, has no fixed, plain meaning. In some provisions, the word unquestionably refers to a single place: the site of the banking association's designated main office. See, *e.g.*, 12 U.S.C. § 52 (national bank's capital stock certificates must state "the name and location of the association"); § 55 (requiring notice of sale of capital stock "in a newspaper of the city or town in which the bank is located"); § 75 (bank's regular annual shareholders' meeting shall be rescheduled when it "falls on a legal holiday in the State in which the bank is located"); § 182 (requiring publication of a notice of dissolution "in the city or town in which the association is located"). In other provisions, "located" apparently refers to or includes branch offices. See, *e.g.*, § 36(j) (defining "branch" to include "any branch place of business located in any State"); § 85 (limiting interest rate charged by national bank to "rate allowed by the laws of the State, Territory, or District where the bank is located") (construed in OCC Interpretive Letter No. 822 (Feb. 17, 1998), [1997–1998 Transfer Binder] CCH Fed. Banking L. Rep. ¶ 81–265, pp. 90, 256–90, 257); 12 U.S.C. § 92 (permitting national bank to act as insurance agent in certain circumstances when bank is "located and doing business in any place the population of which does not exceed five thousand inhabitants") (construed in 12 CFR § 7.1001 (2005)). Recognizing the controlling significance of context, we stated in *Bougas*, regarding a venue provision for national banks: "There is no enduring rigidity about the word 'located.' " 434 U.S. at 44.

Second, Congress may well have comprehended the words "located" and "established," as used in § 1348, not as contrasting, but as synonymous or alternative terms. When Congress enacted § 1348's statutory predecessors and then § 1348 itself, a national bank was almost always "located" only in the State in which it was "established," under any of the proffered definitions of the two words, for, with rare exceptions, a national bank could not operate a branch outside its home State. Not until 1994 did Congress provide broad authorization for national banks to establish branches across state lines. . . . Congress' use of the two terms may be best explained as a coincidence of statutory codification. Deriving from separate provisions enacted in different years, the word "established" appearing in the first paragraph of § 1348 and the word "located" appearing in the second paragraph were placed in the same section in the 1911 revision of the Judicial Code. . . . The codifying Act explicitly stated that "so far as [its provisions were] substantially the same as existing statutes," they should "be construed as continuations thereof, and not as new enactments." Act of Mar. 3, 1911, § 294, 36 Stat. 1167 . . . .[8] . . .

Finally, *Bougas* does not control the meaning of § 1348. In that case, we construed a now-repealed venue provision, which stated that actions against national banking associations could be filed "in any State, county, or municipal court in the county or city in which said association [was] located." 434 U.S. at 35–36 (quoting 12 U.S.C. § 94 (1976 ed.)). We held that, for purposes of this provision, a national bank was located, and venue was therefore proper, in any county or city where the bank maintained a branch office. 434 U.S. at 44–45. True, under the *in pari materia* canon of statutory construction, statutes addressing the same subject matter generally should be read " 'as if they were one law.' " *Erlenbaugh v. United States*, 409 U.S. 239, 243 (1972) (quoting *United States v. Freeman*, 3 How. 556, 564 (1845)). But venue and subject-matter jurisdiction are not concepts of the same order. Venue is largely a matter of litigational convenience; accordingly, it is waived if not timely raised.

---

[8] Context also matters in assigning meaning to the word "established." . . . Given the character of the proceedings covered by the first paragraph of § 1348, . . . one might read "established" as referring to the bank's main office as set forth in its articles of association. Other readings mentioned in Court of Appeals opinions are the bank's principal place of business and the place listed in the bank's organization certificate. . . . Because this issue is not presented by the parties or necessary to today's decision, we express no opinion on it. . . .

See, *e.g.*, . . . Fed. Rule Civ. Proc. 12(h)(1). Subject-matter jurisdiction, on the other hand, concerns a court's competence to adjudicate a particular category of cases; a matter far weightier than venue, subject-matter jurisdiction must be considered by the court on its own motion, even if no party raises an objection. See, *e.g.*, . . . Fed. Rule Civ. Proc. 12(h)(3).

Cognizant that venue "is primarily a matter of choosing a convenient forum," *Leroy v. Great Western United Corp.*, 443 U.S. 173, 180 (1979), the Court in *Bougas* stressed that its "interpretation of [the former] § 94 [would] not inconvenience the bank or unfairly burden it with distant litigation," 434 U.S. at 44, n.10. Subject-matter jurisdiction, however, does not entail an assessment of convenience. It poses a "whether," not a "where" question: Has the Legislature empowered the court to hear cases of a certain genre? See *Neirbo Co. v. Bethlehem Shipbuilding Corp.*, 308 U.S. 165, 168 (1939) ("This basic difference between the court's power and the litigant's convenience is historic in the federal courts."). Thus, the considerations that account for our decision in *Bougas* are inapplicable to § 1348, a prescription governing subject-matter jurisdiction, and the Court of Appeals erred in interpreting § 1348 *in pari materia* with the former § 94.

Significantly, this Court's reading of the venue provision in *Bougas* effectively aligned the treatment of national banks for venue purposes with the treatment of state banks and corporations. For venue in suits against state banks and other state-created corporations typically lies wherever those entities have business establishments. See 19 C.J.S., Corporations § 717(d), p. 374, n. 30 (1990) (under typical state venue statutes, "[v]enue in action against domestic corporation can be laid in any county where corporation maintains branch office"). By contrast, the Court of Appeals' decision in the instant case severely constricts national banks' access to diversity jurisdiction as compared to the access available to corporations generally. For purposes of diversity, a corporation . . . is not deemed a citizen of every State in which it maintains a business establishment. . . . Rather, under 28 U.S.C. § 1332(c)(1), a corporation is "deemed to be a citizen" only of "any State by which it has been incorporated" and "of the State where it has its principal place of business." Accordingly, while corporations ordinarily rank as citizens of at most 2 States, Wachovia, under the Court of Appeals' novel citizenship rule, would be a citizen of 16 States. . . .[9] *Bougas* does not call for this anomalous result.

---

[9] To achieve complete parity with state banks and other state-incorporated entities, a national banking association would have to be deemed a citizen of both the State of its main office and the State of its principal place of business. . . . Congress has prescribed that a corporation "shall be deemed to be a citizen of any State by which it has been incorporated *and* of the State where it has its principal place of business." 28 U.S.C. § 1332(c)(1) (emphasis added). The counterpart provision for national banking associations, § 1348, however, does not refer to "principal place of business"; it simply deems such associations "citizens of the States in which they are respectively located." The absence of a "principal place of business" reference in § 1348 may be of scant practical significance for, in almost every case, as in this one, the location of a national bank's main office and of its principal place of business coincide.

V

. . . . An individual who resides in more than one State is regarded, for purposes of federal subject-matter (diversity) jurisdiction, as a citizen of but one State. See *Newman-Green, Inc. v. Alfonzo-Larrain*, 490 U.S. 826, 828 (1989) (an individual is deemed a citizen of the State of her domicil); *Williamson v. Osenton*, 232 U.S. 619, 625 (1914) (domicil is the "technically preeminent headquarters" of a person; "[i]n its nature it is one"). Similarly, a corporation's citizenship derives, for diversity jurisdiction purposes, from its State of incorporation and principal place of business. § 1332(c)(1). It is not deemed a citizen of every State in which it conducts business or is otherwise amenable to personal jurisdiction. Reading § 1348 in this context, one would sensibly "locate" a national bank for the very same purpose, *i.e.*, qualification for diversity jurisdiction, in the State designated in its articles of association as its main office.

Treating venue and subject-matter jurisdiction prescriptions as *in pari materia*, . . . the court of appeals majority overlooked the discrete offices of those concepts. . . . [Cf.] Cook, "Substance" and "Procedure" in the Conflict of Laws, 42 Yale L.J. 333, 337 (1933) ("The tendency to assume that a word which appears in two or more legal rules, and so in connection with more than one purpose, has and should have precisely the same scope in all of them, runs all through legal discussions. It has all the tenacity of original sin and must constantly be guarded against."). The resulting Fourth Circuit decision rendered national banks singularly disfavored corporate bodies with regard to their access to federal courts. The language of § 1348 does not mandate that incongruous outcome, nor does this Court's precedent. . . .

■ *JUSTICE THOMAS did not participate in the consideration or decision of this case.*

NOTES AND QUESTIONS

1. The *Wachovia Bank* case required the Supreme Court to interpret the word "located" in 28 U.S.C. § 1348, which bears on the federal courts' subject-matter jurisdiction over suits involving national banks. Congress had also used the word "located" in the venue statute that the Supreme Court eventually interpreted in *Citizens & Southern National Bank v. Bougas*, 434 U.S. 35 (1977). At least for purposes of the venue statute, the *Bougas* Court had concluded that a national bank was "located" in every place where it maintained a branch office. In *Wachovia Bank*, the Court had to decide whether 28 U.S.C. § 1348 used the word "located" in the same way.

If the venue statute and 28 U.S.C. § 1348 were *in pari materia*, the answer might have depended on whether the Court put more weight on promoting policy consistency or semantic consistency. The venue statute and 28 U.S.C. § 1348 could be understood to promote a similar policy (to wit, treating national banks pretty much like state banks for purposes of both subject-matter jurisdiction and venue). To do so, however, the Court would have had to read the word "located" in 28 U.S.C. § 1348 to mean something different than the Court had understood it to mean in the venue statute. Thus, the policy-based and text-based versions of the *in pari materia* idea seemed to point in opposite directions.

In *Wachovia Bank,* Justice Ginsburg escaped this conundrum by saying that the two statutes were not *in pari materia.* In passages that will warm the hearts of Civil Procedure professors, Justice Ginsburg emphasized the fundamental difference between venue and subject-matter jurisdiction: how could anyone think that a statute about the proper *venue* for suits against national banks was *in pari materia* with a statute about *subject-matter jurisdiction* over those suits? But her claim that the two statutes were not *in pari materia* might strike some readers as an assertion of convenience—a position that she adopted only after concluding, on other grounds, that the word "located" means something different in § 1348 than in the venue statute. The central rationale behind her opinion seemed to be twofold.

First, she found evidence that Congress had not used the word "located" in a uniform way throughout all federal statutes about national banks; in her view, some federal statutes about national banks used the word "located" to refer only to "the site of the banking association's designated main office," while others used it to include the sites of branch offices too. If she was right about this pattern of inconsistent usage, then the fact that the venue statute used the word in the broader sense would not necessarily tell us what the word means in 28 U.S.C. § 1348.

Second, Justice Ginsburg argued that reading the word "located" in § 1348 to mean what *Bougas* said it meant in the venue statute would produce a strange result. For purposes of the federal courts' diversity jurisdiction, domestic corporations (including most banks chartered by state governments) typically qualify as citizens of only one or two states. *See* 28 U.S.C. § 1332(c)(1) (providing that for purposes of § 1332, "a corporation shall be deemed to be a citizen of every State and foreign state by which it has been incorporated and of the State or foreign state where it has its principal place of business").[33] But if the word "located" has the same meaning in § 1348 that *Bougas* ascribed to it in the venue statute, then *national* banks chartered by the federal government would be deemed to be citizens of every state in which they operated branches (which, in Wachovia's case, would have made it a citizen of sixteen different states). That result, Justice Ginsburg suggested, would be "anomalous," at least partly because it would undercut what she took to be the common purpose behind both § 1348 and the venue statute. In her view, Congress meant to treat national banks in roughly the same way as state banks with respect to both subject-matter jurisdiction (under

[33] The version of § 1332(c)(1) that Justice Ginsburg quoted in *Wachovia Bank* did not include the references to "foreign state[s]"; Congress added that language in 2011.

§ 1348) and venue (under the statute construed in *Bougas*). To accomplish that common purpose, Justice Ginsburg concluded that the word "located" must mean something different in § 1348 than *Bougas* had understood it to mean in the venue statute.

Does the second consideration suggest that when statutes are indeed *in pari materia*, Justice Ginsburg would have prioritized policy consistency over semantic consistency? Or is it hard to draw conclusions on that point, because the first consideration—Congress's inconsistent use of the word "located" in other statutes about national banks—defeated the possibility of semantic consistency anyway?

2. From the inception of the National Bank Act until the 1920s, national banks normally could not have branches at all; their main office was their only office. *See* Paul E. Lund, *National Banks and Diversity Jurisdiction*, 46 U. LOUISVILLE L. REV. 73, 79 (2007) (noting, however, that "a state bank that converted to a national bank could retain any branches it operated at the time of its conversion"); Douglas H. Ginsburg, *Interstate Banking*, 9 HOFSTRA L. REV. 1133, 1152–53 (1981) (adding that a 1918 statute created a "circuitous route" by which an existing national bank could acquire branches); Christian A. Johnson & Tara Rice, *Assessing a Decade of Interstate Bank Branching*, 65 WASH. & LEE L. REV. 73, 80–81 (2008) (providing details about the legal prohibition on branch banking). In 1927, Congress allowed national banks to open branches within the same city as their main office if the law of the relevant state permitted state banks to do so. *See id.* at 81–82 (citing McFadden Act, ch. 191, § 7, 44 Stat. 1224, 1228 (1927)). In 1933, Congress extended this idea so that national banks could open branches elsewhere in the same state, if state law gave state banks that authority. *Id.* at 82 (citing Glass-Steagall Act, ch. 89, § 23, 48 Stat. 162, 189 (1933)). Throughout this period, however, national banks were generally forbidden to engage in "interstate branching"—that is, to operate branches in more than one state. Congress did not eliminate that restriction until the 1990s. *See id.* at 86 (citing Riegle-Neal Interstate Banking and Branching Efficiency Act of 1994, Pub. L. 103–328, 108 Stat. 2338); *cf.* Ginsburg, *supra*, 9 HOFSTRA L. REV. at 1137 (observing, as of 1981, that "commercial banking enterprises may not engage in 'the business of banking' . . . in more than one state").

Justice Ginsburg was aware of this history. *See Wachovia Bank*, 546 U.S. at 307 n.2. But the history arguably undermines her assertion (in the first paragraph of Part IV) that some provisions of the National Bank Act "unquestionably" speak of a national bank as being "located" wherever its main office is, without regard to the site of its branches. All four of the examples that she offered are quite old. The provisions codified at 12 U.S.C. § 55 and § 182, which require notices to be published in a newspaper of "the city or town in which the association is located," both date back to the nineteenth century, when national banks did not have branches at all. *See* Act of June 30, 1876, ch. 156, § 4, 19 Stat. 63, 64;

National Bank Act, ch. 106, § 42, 13 Stat. 99, 112 (1864). At that time, Congress could have referred to where a national bank was "located" without taking a position on the question that Justice Ginsburg had in mind. The language found in 12 U.S.C. § 75, requiring a shareholders' meeting to be rescheduled when it falls on "a legal holiday in the State in which the bank is located," is more modern; it dates to 1959. *See* Act of Sept. 8, 1959, Pub. L. 86–230, § 9, 73 Stat. 457, 457. By then, national banks did have branches, but those branches would still have been confined to a single state—so in this statute too, the fact that Congress used the word "located" need not mean that Congress was referring only to the location of the bank's main office and not to the location of the bank's branches. How about the final provision cited by Justice Ginsburg—the language codified at 12 U.S.C. § 52, which requires stock certificates for national banking associations to identify "the name and location of the association"? That language was enacted in 1935, after Congress had started to authorize some intrastate branching. *See* Banking Act of 1935, ch. 614, § 335, 49 Stat. 684, 720. Perhaps one can infer that Congress was using the word "located" in this provision to refer exclusively to the city in which the bank had its main office. But is that inference inevitable? If a national banking association operated branches in more than one city, couldn't Congress have expected its stock certificates either (1) to list each city or (2) simply to list the relevant state?

This analysis suggests that from the standpoint of the enacting Congress, the word "located" in the provisions that Justice Ginsburg cited may have harbored a latent ambiguity. In at least three of the four provisions, there was no apparent need for the enacting Congress to be precise about whether the word referred only to the location of a bank's main office or also to every place where the bank had a branch, because the branching restrictions that existed at the time of enactment made this distinction unimportant. It is possible that members of Congress used the word "located" in these provisions without forming any collective understanding on that point.

The same can be said of both the venue provision in *Bougas* and the jurisdictional provision in *Wachovia Bank*. The venue provision, which referred to "the county or city in which [a national banking] association is located," dated back to the National Bank Act of 1864 and had last been enacted in 1875. Insofar as that statute prevented national banks from opening branches at all, members of the enacting Congress could have used the word "located" without taking any position on the question that *Bougas* later raised. Similarly, the key phrase in the jurisdictional provision was first adopted in 1887, and it has not been reenacted since Congress enacted Title 28 of the United States Code into positive law in 1948. Throughout that period, both the main office and any branches of a national bank would have been located in the same state. As a result, when Congress called for national banks to "be deemed citizens of the

States in which they are respectively located," members of Congress did not need to decide whether they were referring just to the location of the main office or also to the location of branches. *See* Lund, *supra,* 46 U. LOUISVILLE L. REV. at 107 ("Authorization of interstate branch banking by national banks was still many years in the future at the time the statutory language now found in section 1348 originated or even at the time of its most recent recodification. Thus, the effect that branch banking would create on national banks' access to diversity jurisdiction could not possibly have crossed Congress's mind." (footnote omitted)).

If you consider the venue provision and 28 U.S.C. § 1348 to be *in pari materia*, what are the implications of this analysis? Once the Court in *Bougas* read the word "located" in the venue provision to refer to any place where the relevant bank has a branch, should that holding control how courts understand the word in 28 U.S.C. § 1348 too? If you think that the original meaning of the word "located" in these provisions was indeterminate about the significance of branches, and that members of the enacting Congresses did not form any collective intention on this point, there is no apparent "descriptive" reason why courts must resolve the indeterminacy the same way in both provisions. Is there any "normative" argument for doing so? Or do the normative arguments cut *against* reading the word "located" in 28 U.S.C. § 1348 to mean what *Bougas* said it meant in the venue provision, because (given current branching practices) that reading would make it unusually difficult for national banks to invoke the diversity jurisdiction of the federal courts?

3. What should we make of Justice Ginsburg's quotation from Walter Wheeler Cook at the end of her opinion? Justice Ginsburg frequently used that quotation. *See* Georgia v. Public.Resource.Org, Inc., 140 S. Ct. 1498, 1524 n.3 (2020) (Ginsburg, J., dissenting); United States v. Cleveland Indians Baseball Co., 532 U.S. 200, 213 (2001) (Ginsburg, J.); City of Chicago v. Int'l Coll. of Surgeons, 522 U.S. 156, 184 (1997) (Ginsburg, J., dissenting); Gustafson v. Alloyd Co., 513 U.S. 561, 598 (1995) (Ginsburg, J., dissenting); NationsBank of North Carolina, N.A. v. Variable Annuity Life Ins. Co., 513 U.S. 251, 262 (1995) (Ginsburg, J.); *Hearings Before the Senate Committee on the Judiciary on the Nomination of Ruth Bader Ginsburg to be an Associate Justice of the Supreme Court of the United States*, 103rd Cong., 1st Sess. 291 (1993) (testimony of Judge Ginsburg); *see also* General Dynamics Land Systems v. Cline, 540 U.S. 581, 595 n.8 (2004) (Souter, J.) (noting that this quotation "has become a staple of our opinions," and citing two opinions by Justice Ginsburg). Might Justice Ginsburg's enthusiasm for this quotation shed light on her denial that the venue statute and 28 U.S.C. § 1348 were *in pari materia* at all? Professor Cook opposed formalism in legal thought; rather than emphasizing categories, he urged close attention to the context of each new situation that the courts confronted. *See* Perry Dane, *Vested Rights, "Vestedness," and Choice of Law*, 96 YALE L.J. 1191, 1197 (1987). Might Justice Ginsburg's opinion in *Wachovia Bank* have reflected the same impulse? To the extent that she was trying to narrow the scope of the *in pari materia* idea, did she want to reduce the pressure that judges might otherwise feel to read the same word as having the same meaning in two different statutes? Is it desirable for judges to get out from under that pressure, so that they have more freedom to resolve each interpretive question in what they see as its own context? Or might a more rule-like approach to interpretation have enough benefits to offset its inevitable costs?

---

2. "STATUTORY USAGE"

The same word or phrase sometimes recurs in a wide range of statutes. Especially if the statutes are not *in pari materia*, judges will not necessarily give the word or phrase the same interpretation everywhere it appears. On occasion, though, Congress might establish a pattern of using a particular word or phrase in a consistent way, and courts might then assume that the word or phrase has the same meaning across many different statutes. In the next case, the Justices disagreed about whether that was true of the phrase "attorney's fee."

To understand the case, you need some background. When a federal district court enters judgment in a case, 28 U.S.C. § 1920 authorizes the court to include an award of "costs" in the judgment. In the typical case, the prevailing party files a "bill of costs" itemizing the qualifying expenses that it incurred during the course of the litigation, and the court then "taxes" those costs to the losing side (that is, the court makes the losing party liable to reimburse the prevailing party for those costs). *See* FED. R. CIV. P. 54(d) (setting the default rule that a judgment shall award costs to the prevailing party unless the court otherwise directs). Section 1920 lists six different categories of "costs" that qualify for this treatment. Usually, though, the items that § 1920 lists as taxable "costs" do not amount to much. They include filing fees, fees for transcripts, the attendance fee that 28 U.S.C. § 1821(b) calls for witnesses to be paid (which was $30 per day at the time relevant to the next case), and certain other small sums. But they do not include various categories of expenses that are much more substantial, such as the prevailing party's attorney's fees. Instead, the ordinary "American rule" is that each party bears its own attorney's fees.

Some specialized federal statutes, applicable in particular kinds of cases, depart from that general rule; they authorize or even require courts to let the winning side collect a reasonable attorney's fee from the losing side. *See, e.g.*, 42 U.S.C. § 2000a–3(b) (providing that in suits under Title II of the Civil Rights Act of 1964, "the court, in its discretion, may allow the prevailing party, other than the United States, a reasonable attorney's fee as part of the costs"); 15 U.S.C. § 15 (providing that "any person who shall be injured in his business or property by reason of anything forbidden in the antitrust laws may sue therefor in [a federal] district court . . . and shall recover threefold the damages by him sustained, and the cost of suit, including a reasonable attorney's fee"). Aside from these explicit statutory provisions, federal courts have also asserted authority to shift fees where the losing party "has acted in bad faith, vexatiously, wantonly, or for oppressive reasons." *F.D. Rich Co. v. United States ex rel. Industrial Lumber Co.*, 417 U.S. 116, 129 (1974) (citing cases); *cf.* Fleischmann Distilling Corp. v. Maier Brewing Co., 386 U.S. 714, 718 (1967) (citing an opinion awarding attorney's fees "in a civil contempt action occasioned by willful disobedience of a court order"). In addition, federal courts sitting in equity have long claimed some additional power "to allow counsel fees and other expenses entailed by the litigation" even though those expenses were "not included in the ordinary taxable costs recognized by statute." *Sprague v. Ticonic Nat'l Bank*, 307 U.S. 161, 164 (1939). For instance, when the prevailing party's efforts created or preserved a fund in which others could share, federal courts sitting in equity sometimes allowed the prevailing party to recover a reasonable attorney's fee either out of the fund itself or from the other beneficiaries. *See id.*; *see also* Mills v. Electric Auto-Lite Co., 396 U.S. 375, 391–96 (1970) (discussing extensions of this rationale).

As time went by, some lower federal courts asserted broader authority to order the losing side to pay the reasonable attorney's fees of so-called "private attorneys general"—litigants who brought suit on their own behalf, but whose efforts "vindicate[d] a strong public policy and provide[d] widespread public benefit." *Incarcerated Men of Allen County Jail v. Fair*, 507 F.2d 281, 284–85 (6th Cir. 1974) (asserting that this exception to the normal American rule "has recently become well established"). But in *Alyeska Pipeline Service Co. v. Wilderness Society*, 421 U.S. 240 (1975), a majority of the Supreme Court rebuffed that theory. *Alyeska* interpreted 28 U.S.C. § 1920 and related statutes as largely occupying the field of taxable costs, and as withholding from the judiciary "any roving authority . . . to allow counsel fees . . . whenever the courts might deem them warranted." *Id.* at 260. *Alyeska* acknowledged that without regard to 28 U.S.C. § 1920, federal courts had asserted authority to shift fees in a few "limited circumstances" of the sort described in the previous paragraph. *See id.* at 257–59. But while "Congress has not repudiated the[se] judicially fashioned exceptions to the general rule against allowing substantial attorneys' fees," *id.* at 260, *Alyeska* understood Congress as having otherwise "reserved for itself" determinations about the kinds of suits that should be eligible for fee-shifting. *Id.* at 269. In the absence of statutory authorization, then, federal courts could not legitimately assert authority to shift fees on the basis of their own assessment of "the importance of the public policies involved in particular cases." *Id.*

Although *Alyeska* was not itself a civil-rights case, its holding threatened the growing practice of awarding attorney's fees to the prevailing plaintiffs in certain civil-rights cases that were not covered by any fee-shifting statutes. One year after *Alyeska*, Congress responded by enacting the Civil Rights Attorney's Fee Award Act of 1976. That Act added the following language to Rev. Stat. § 722, which is codified at 42 U.S.C. § 1988: "In any action or proceeding to enforce a provision of [various civil-rights statutes, including the ones codified at 42 U.S.C. §§ 1981, 1982, 1983, 1985, and 1986], . . . the court, in its discretion, may allow the prevailing party, other than the United States, a reasonable attorney's fee as part of the costs." Pub. L. 94–559, § 2, 90 Stat. 2641, 2641.

In the next case, the Supreme Court had to decide how this language handles fees for services rendered by experts, such as consulting experts whom the prevailing party's lawyers hired to help them prepare their case or expert witnesses whom the prevailing party's lawyers hired to present testimony at trial. In the cases that 42 U.S.C. § 1988 covers, do those expenses count as part of the "reasonable attorney's fee" that the statute authorizes federal district courts to shift?

West Virginia University Hospitals, Inc. v. Casey

499 U.S. 83 (1991)

■ *JUSTICE SCALIA delivered the opinion of the Court:*

. . . .

I

Petitioner West Virginia University Hospitals, Inc. (WVUH), operates a hospital in Morgantown, W. Va., near the Pennsylvania border. The hospital is often used by Medicaid recipients living in southwestern Pennsylvania. In January 1986, Pennsylvania's Department of Public Welfare notified WVUH of new Medicaid reimbursement schedules for services provided to Pennsylvania residents by the Morgantown hospital. In administrative proceedings, WVUH unsuccessfully objected to the new reimbursement rates on both federal statutory and federal constitutional grounds. After exhausting administrative remedies, WVUH filed suit in Federal District Court under 42 U.S.C. § 1983. Named as defendants (respondents here) were Pennsylvania Governor Robert Casey and various other Pennsylvania officials.

Counsel for WVUH employed Coopers & Lybrand, a national accounting firm, and three doctors specializing in hospital finance to assist in the preparation of the lawsuit and to testify at trial. WVUH prevailed at trial in May 1988. The District Court subsequently awarded fees pursuant to 42 U.S.C. § 1988,[1] including over $100,000 in fees

[1] Title 42 U.S.C. § 1988 provides in relevant part: "In any action or proceeding to enforce a provision of sections 1981, 1982, 1983, 1985, and 1986 of this title, title IX of Public Law 92–318 . . . , or title VI of the Civil Rights Act of 1964 . . . , the court, in its discretion, may allow the prevailing party, other than the United States, a reasonable attorney's fee as part of the costs."

attributable to expert services. The District Court found these services to have been "essential" to presentation of the case—a finding not disputed by respondents.

. . . . The Court of Appeals for the Third Circuit . . . reversed as to the expert fees, disallowing them except to the extent that they fell within the $30-per-day fees for witnesses prescribed by 28 U.S.C. § 1821(b). . . .

II

Title 28 U.S.C. § 1920 provides:

> "A judge or clerk of any court of the United States may tax as costs the following:
>
> "(1) Fees of the clerk and marshal;
>
> "(2) Fees of the court reporter for all or any part of the stenographic transcript necessarily obtained for use in the case;
>
> "(3) Fees and disbursements for printing and witnesses;
>
> "(4) Fees for exemplification and copies of papers necessarily obtained for use in the case;
>
> "(5) Docket fees under section 1923 of this title;
>
> "(6) Compensation of court appointed experts, compensation of interpreters, and salaries, fees, expenses, and costs of special interpretation services under section 1828 of this title."

Title 28 U.S.C. § 1821(b) limits the witness fees authorized by § 1920(3) as follows: "A witness shall be paid an attendance fee of $30 per day for each day's attendance. A witness shall also be paid the attendance fee for the time necessarily occupied in going to and returning from the place of attendance . . . ." In *Crawford Fitting Co. v. J.T. Gibbons, Inc.*, 482 U.S. 437 (1987), we held that these provisions define the full extent of a federal court's power to shift litigation costs absent express statutory authority to go further. "[W]hen," we said, "a prevailing party seeks reimbursement for fees paid to its own expert witnesses, a federal court is bound by the limits of § 1821(b), absent contract or explicit statutory authority to the contrary." *Id.* at 439. "We will not lightly infer that Congress has repealed §§ 1920 and 1821, either through [Federal Rule of Civil Procedure] 54(d) or any other provision not referring explicitly to witness fees." *Id.* at 445.

. . . . WVUH argues . . . that some of the expert fees it incurred in this case were unrelated to expert *testimony*, and that as to those fees the § 1821(b) limits, which apply only to witnesses in attendance at trial, are of no consequence. We agree with that, but there remains applicable the limitation of § 1920. *Crawford Fitting* said that we would not lightly find an implied repeal of § 1821 *or* of § 1920, which it held to be an express limitation upon the types of costs which, absent other authority, may be shifted by federal courts. 482 U.S. at 441. None of the categories of expenses listed in § 1920 can reasonably be read to include fees for services rendered by an expert employed by a party in a nontestimonial advisory capacity. The question before us, then, is—with regard to both testimonial and nontestimonial expert fees—whether the term "attorney's fee" in § 1988 provides the "explicit statutory authority" required by *Crawford Fitting*.[3]

III

The record of statutory usage demonstrates convincingly that attorney's fees and expert fees are regarded as separate elements of litigation cost. While some fee-shifting provisions, like § 1988, refer only to "attorney's fees," see, *e.g.*, Civil Rights Act of 1964, 42 U.S.C. § 2000e–5(k), many others explicitly shift expert witness fees *as well as* attorney's fees. In 1976, just over a week prior to the enactment of § 1988, Congress passed those provisions of the Toxic Substances Control Act, 15 U.S.C. §§ 2618(d), 2619(c)(2), which provide that a prevailing party may recover "the costs of suit and reasonable fees for attorneys *and expert witnesses.*" (Emphasis added.) Also in 1976, Congress amended the Consumer Product Safety Act, 15 U.S.C. §§ 2060(c), 2072(a), 2073, which as originally enacted in 1972 shifted to the losing party "cost[s] of suit, including a reasonable attorney's fee," see 86 Stat. 1226. In the 1976 amendment, Congress altered the fee-shifting provisions to their present form by adding a phrase shifting expert witness fees *in addition to* attorney's fees. See Pub. L. 94–284, § 10, 90 Stat. 506, 507. Two other significant Acts passed in 1976 contain similar phrasing: the Resource Conservation and Recovery Act of 1976, 42 U.S.C. § 6972(e) ("costs of litigation (including reasonable attorney and expert witness fees)"), and the Natural Gas Pipeline Safety Act Amendments of 1976, 49 U.S.C. App. § 1686(e) ("costs of suit, including reasonable attorney's fees and reasonable expert witnesses fees").

Congress enacted similarly phrased fee-shifting provisions in numerous statutes both before 1976, see, *e.g.*, Endangered Species Act of 1973, 16 U.S.C. § 1540(g)(4) ("costs of litigation (including reasonable attorney and expert witness fees)"), and afterwards, see, *e.g.*, Public Utility Regulatory Policies Act of 1978, 16 U.S.C. § 2632(a)(1) ("reasonable attorneys' fees, expert witness fees, and other reasonable costs incurred in preparation and advocacy of [the litigant's] position"). These statutes encompass diverse categories of legislation, including tax, administrative procedure, environmental protection, consumer protection, admiralty and navigation, utilities regulation, and, significantly, civil rights: The Equal Access to Justice Act (EAJA), the counterpart to § 1988 for violation of federal rights by federal employees,

---

[3] Justice Stevens suggests that the expert fees requested here might be part of the "costs" allowed by § 1988 even if they are not part of the "attorney's fee." We are aware of no authority to support the counterintuitive assertion that "[t]he term 'costs' has a different and broader meaning in fee-shifting statutes than it has in the cost statutes that apply to ordinary litigation," *post* at 104. In *Crawford Fitting* we held that the word "costs" in Federal Rule of Civil Procedure 54(d) is to be read in harmony with the word "costs" in 28 U.S.C. § 1920, and we think the same is true of the word "costs" in § 1988. . . .

states that " 'fees and other expenses' [as shifted by § 2412(d)(1)(A)] includes the reasonable expenses of expert witnesses . . . and reasonable attorney fees." 28 U.S.C. § 2412(d)(2)(A). At least 34 statutes in 10 different titles of the United States Code explicitly shift attorney's fees *and* expert witness fees.[4]

The laws that refer to fees for nontestimonial expert services are less common, but they establish a similar usage both before and after 1976: Such fees are referred to *in addition to* attorney's fees when a shift is intended. A provision of the Criminal Justice Act of 1964, 18 U.S.C. § 3006A(e), directs the court to reimburse appointed counsel for expert fees necessary to the defense of indigent criminal defendants—even though the immediately preceding provision, § 3006A(d), already directs that appointed defense counsel be paid a designated hourly rate plus "expenses reasonably incurred." WVUH's position must be that expert fees billed to a client through an attorney are "attorney's fees" because they are to be treated as part of the expenses of the attorney; but if this were normal usage, they would have been reimbursable under the Criminal Justice Act as "expenses reasonably incurred"—and subsection 3006A(e) would add nothing to the recoverable amount. The very heading of that subsection, "Services *other than* counsel" (emphasis added), acknowledges a distinction between services provided by the attorney himself and those provided to the attorney (or the client) by a nonlegal expert.

To the same effect is the 1980 EAJA, which provides: " 'fees and other expenses' [as shifted by § 2412(d)(1)(A)] includes the reasonable expenses of expert witnesses, *the reasonable cost of any study, analysis, engineering report, test, or project* which is found by the court to be necessary for the preparation of the party's case, and reasonable attorney fees." 28 U.S.C. § 2412(d)(2)(A) (emphasis added). If the reasonable cost of a "study" or "analysis"—which is but another way of describing nontestimonial expert services—is by common usage already included in the "attorney fees," again a significant and highly detailed part of the statute becomes redundant. The Administrative Procedure Act, 5 U.S.C. § 504(b)(1)(A) (added 1980), and the Tax Equity and Fiscal Responsibility Act of 1982, 26 U.S.C. § 7430(c)(1), contain similar language. Also reflecting the same usage are two railroad regulation statutes, the Regional Rail Reorganization Act of 1973, 45 U.S.C. §§ 726(f)(9) ("costs and expenses (including reasonable fees of accountants, experts, and attorneys) actually incurred"), and the Railroad Revitalization and Regulatory Reform Act of 1976, 45 U.S.C. § 854(g) ("costs and expenses (including fees of accountants, experts, and attorneys) actually and reasonably incurred").[5]

---

4 [Citations and quotations omitted.]

5 WVUH cites a House Conference Committee Report from a statute passed in 1986, stating: "The conferees intend that the term 'attorneys' fees as part of the costs' include reasonable expenses and fees of expert witnesses and the reasonable costs of any test or evaluation which is found to be necessary for the preparation of the . . . case." H.R. Conf. Rep.

We think this statutory usage shows beyond question that attorney's fees and expert fees are distinct items of expense. If, as WVUH argues, the one includes the other, dozens of statutes referring to the two separately become an inexplicable exercise in redundancy.

IV

WVUH argues that at least in pre-1976 *judicial* usage the phrase "attorney's fees" included the fees of experts. . . . [W]e disagree . . . . The judicial background against which Congress enacted § 1988 mirrored the statutory background: expert fees were regarded not as a subset of attorney's fees, but as a distinct category of litigation expense.

Certainly it is true that prior to 1976 some federal courts shifted expert fees to losing parties pursuant to various equitable doctrines—sometimes in conjunction with attorney's fees. But they did not shift them *as an element of* attorney's fees. Typical of the courts' mode of analysis (though not necessarily of their results) is *Fey v. Walston & Co.*, 493 F.2d 1036, 1055–1056 (CA7 1974), a case brought under the federal securities laws. Plaintiff won and was awarded various expenses: "Included in the . . . costs awarded by the [district] court were the sum of $1,700 for plaintiff's expert witness, expenses of an accountant in the amount of $142[ ] and of an illustrator-diagrammer for $50 . . . and attorneys' fees of $15,660." The [appellate] court treated these items separately: The services of the accountant and illustrator (who did not testify at trial) were "costs" which could be fully shifted in the discretion of the District Court; the expert witness fees also could be shifted, but only as limited by § 1821; the attorney's fees were not costs and could not be shifted at all because the case did not fit any of the traditional equitable doctrines for awarding such fees. *Id.* at 1056. . . .

Even where the courts' holdings treated attorney's fees and expert fees the same (*i.e.*, granted both or denied both), their analysis discussed them as separate categories of expense. See, *e.g.*, *Wolf v. Frank*, 477 F.2d 467, 480 (CA5 1973) ("The reimbursing of plaintiffs' costs for attorney's fees *and* expert witness fees is supported . . . by well established equitable principles") (emphasis added) . . . .

Of arguably greater significance than the courts' treatment of attorney's fees *versus* expert fees at common law is their treatment of those expenses under statutes containing fee-shifting provisions similar to § 1988. WVUH contends that in some cases courts shifted expert fees as well as the statutorily authorized attorney's fees—and thus must have thought that the latter included the former. We find, however, that the practice, at least in the overwhelming majority of cases, was otherwise.

No. 99–687, p. 5 (1986) (discussing the Handicapped Children's Protection Act of 1986, 20 U.S.C. § 1415(e)(4)(B)). In our view this undercuts rather than supports WVUH's position: The specification would have been quite unnecessary if the ordinary meaning of the term included those elements. The statement is an apparent effort to *depart* from ordinary meaning and to define a term of art.

Prior to 1976, the leading fee-shifting statute was the Clayton Act, 38 Stat. 731, as amended, 15 U.S.C. § 15 (shifting "the cost of suit, including a reasonable attorney's fee"). As of 1976, four Circuits (six Circuits, if one includes summary affirmances of district court judgments) had held that this provision did not permit a shift of expert witness fees. [Citations omitted.] No court had held otherwise. Also instructive is pre-1976 practice under the federal patent laws, which provided, 35 U.S.C. § 285, that "[t]he court in exceptional cases may award reasonable attorney fees to the prevailing party." Again, every court to consider the matter as of 1976 thought that this provision conveyed no authority to shift expert fees. *Specialty Equipment & Machinery Corp. v. Zell Motor Car Co.*, 193 F.2d 515, 521 (CA4 1952) ("Congress having dealt with the subject of costs in patent cases and having authorized the taxation of reasonable attorneys fees without making any provision with respect to . . . fees of expert witnesses must presumably have intended that they be not taxed"); [four district-court citations omitted].

. . . .

In sum, we conclude that at the time this provision was enacted neither statutory nor judicial usage regarded the phrase "attorney's fees" as embracing fees for experts' services.

V

WVUH suggests that a distinctive meaning of "attorney's fees" should be adopted with respect to § 1988 because this statute was meant to overrule our decision in *Alyeska Pipeline Service Co. v. Wilderness Society*, 421 U.S. 240 (1975). As mentioned above, prior to 1975 many courts awarded expert fees and attorney's fees in certain circumstances pursuant to their equitable discretion. In *Alyeska*, we held that this discretion did not extend beyond a few exceptional circumstances long recognized by common law. Specifically, we rejected the so-called "private attorney general" doctrine recently created by some lower federal courts, see, *e.g.*, *La Raza Unida v. Volpe*, 57 F.R.D. 94, 98–102 (ND Cal. 1972), which allowed equitable fee shifting to plaintiffs in certain types of civil rights litigation. 421 U.S. at 269. WVUH argues that § 1988 was intended to restore the pre-*Alyeska* regime—and that, since expert fees were shifted then, they should be shifted now.

Both chronology and the remarks of sponsors of the bill that became § 1988 suggest that at least some members of Congress viewed it as a response to *Alyeska*. See, *e.g.*, S. Rep. No. 94–1011, pp. 4, 6 (1976). It is a considerable step, however, from this proposition to the conclusion the hospital would have us draw, namely, that § 1988 should be read as a reversal of *Alyeska* in all respects.

By its plain language and as unanimously construed in the courts, § 1988 is both broader and narrower than the pre-*Alyeska* regime. Before *Alyeska*, civil rights plaintiffs could recover fees pursuant to the private attorney general doctrine only if private enforcement was necessary to defend important rights benefiting large numbers of people, and cost barriers might otherwise preclude private suits. *La Raza Unida, supra,* at 98–101. Section 1988 contains no similar limitation—so that in the present suit there is no question as to the propriety of shifting WVUH's *attorney's* fees, even though it is highly doubtful they could have been awarded under pre-*Alyeska* equitable theories. In other respects, however, § 1988 is not as broad as the former regime. It is limited, for example, to violations of specified civil rights statutes—which means that it would not have reversed the outcome of *Alyeska* itself, which involved not a civil rights statute but the National Environmental Policy Act of 1969, 42 U.S.C. § 4321 *et seq.* Since it is clear that, in many respects, § 1988 was not meant to return us precisely to the pre-*Alyeska* regime, the objective of achieving such a return is no reason to depart from the normal import of the text.

WVUH further argues that the congressional purpose in enacting § 1988 must prevail over the ordinary meaning of the statutory terms. It quotes, for example, the House Committee Report to the effect that "the judicial remedy [must be] full and complete," H.R. Rep. No. 94–1558, p. 1 (1976), and the Senate Committee Report to the effect that "[c]itizens must have the opportunity to recover what it costs them to vindicate [civil] rights in court," S. Rep. No. 94–1011, *supra,* at 2. As we have observed before, however, the purpose of a statute includes not only what it sets out to change, but also what it resolves to leave alone. See *Rodriguez v. United States,* 480 U.S. 522, 525–526 (1987). The best evidence of that purpose is the statutory text adopted by both Houses of Congress and submitted to the President. Where that contains a phrase that is unambiguous—that has a clearly accepted meaning in both legislative and judicial practice—we do not permit it to be expanded or contracted by the statements of individual legislators or committees during the course of the enactment process. See *United States v. Ron Pair Enterprises, Inc.,* 489 U.S. 235, 241 (1989) ("[W]here, as here, the statute's language is plain, 'the sole function of the court is to enforce it according to its terms' "), quoting *Caminetti v. United States,* 242 U.S. 470, 485 (1917). Congress could easily have shifted "attorney's fees and expert witness fees," or "reasonable litigation expenses," as it did in contemporaneous statutes; it chose instead to enact more restrictive language, and we are bound by that restriction.

WVUH asserts that we have previously been guided by the "broad remedial purposes" of § 1988, rather than its text, in a context resolving an "analogous issue": In *Missouri v. Jenkins,* 491 U.S. 274, 285 (1989), we concluded that § 1988 permitted separately billed paralegal and law clerk time to be charged to the losing party. The trouble with this argument is that *Jenkins* did *not* involve an "analogous issue," insofar as the relevant considerations are concerned. The issue there was not, as WVUH contends, whether we would permit our perception of the "policy" of the statute to overcome its "plain language." It was not remotely plain in *Jenkins* that the phrase "attorney's fee" did not include charges for law clerk and paralegal services. Such services, like the services of "secretaries, messengers, librarians, janitors, and others whose labor contributes to the work product," *id.* at 285, had traditionally been included in calculation of the lawyers' hourly rates. Only recently had there arisen "the 'increasingly widespread custom of separately billing for [such] services,'" *id.* at 286 (quoting from *Ramos v. Lamm*, 713 F.2d 546, 558 (CA10 1983)). By contrast, there has never been, to our knowledge, a practice of including the cost of expert services within attorneys' hourly rates. There was also no record in *Jenkins*—as there is a lengthy record here—of statutory usage that recognizes a distinction between the charges at issue and attorney's fees. We do not know of a single statute that shifts clerk or paralegal fees separately; and even those, such as the EAJA, which comprehensively define the assessable "litigation costs" make no separate mention of clerks or paralegals. In other words, *Jenkins* involved a respect in which the term "attorney's fees" (giving the losing argument the benefit of the doubt) was genuinely ambiguous; and we resolved that ambiguity not by invoking some policy that supersedes the text of the statute, but by concluding that charges of this sort had traditionally been included in attorney's fees and that separate billing should make no difference. The term's application to expert fees is not ambiguous; and if it were the means of analysis employed in *Jenkins* would lead to the conclusion that since such fees have not traditionally been included within the attorney's hourly rate they are not attorney's fees.

WVUH's last contention is that, even if Congress plainly did not include expert fees in the fee-shifting provisions of § 1988, it would have done so had it thought about it. Most of the pre-§ 1988 statutes that explicitly shifted expert fees dealt with environmental litigation, where the necessity of expert advice was readily apparent; and when Congress later enacted the EAJA, the federal counterpart of § 1988, it explicitly included expert fees. Thus, the argument runs, the 94th Congress simply forgot; it is our duty to ask how they would have decided had they actually considered the question. See *Friedrich v. Chicago*, 888 F.2d 511, 514 (CA7 1989) (awarding expert fees under § 1988 because a court should "complete . . . the statute by reading it to bring about the end that the legislators would have specified had they thought about it more clearly").

This argument profoundly mistakes our role. Where a statutory term presented to us for the first time is ambiguous, we construe it to contain that permissible meaning which fits most logically and comfortably into the body of both previously and subsequently enacted law. See 2 J. Sutherland, Statutory Construction § 5201 (3d F. Horack ed. 1943). We do so not because that precise accommodative meaning is what the lawmakers must have had in mind (how could an earlier Congress know what a later Congress would enact?), but because it is our role to make sense rather than nonsense out of the *corpus juris*. But where, as here, the meaning of the term prevents such accommodation, it is not our function to eliminate clearly expressed inconsistency of policy and to treat alike subjects that different Congresses have chosen to treat differently. The facile attribution of congressional "forgetfulness" cannot justify such a usurpation. Where what is at issue is not a contradictory disposition within the same enactment, but merely a difference between the more parsimonious policy of an earlier enactment and the more generous policy of a later one, there is no more basis for saying that the earlier Congress forgot than for saying that the earlier Congress felt differently. In such circumstances, the attribution of forgetfulness rests in reality upon the judge's assessment that the later statute contains the *better* disposition. But that is not for judges to prescribe. We thus reject this last argument for the same reason that Justice Brandeis, writing for the Court, once rejected a similar (though less explicit) argument by the United States:

> "[The statute's] language is plain and unambiguous. What the Government asks is not a construction of a statute, but, in effect, an enlargement of it by the court, so that what was omitted, presumably by inadvertence, may be included within its scope. To supply omissions transcends the judicial function." *Iselin v. United States*, 270 U.S. 245, 250–251 (1926).[7]

* * * * *

For the foregoing reasons, we conclude that § 1988 conveys no authority to shift expert fees. When experts appear at trial, they are of course eligible for the fee provided by § 1920 and § 1821—which was allowed in the present case by the Court of Appeals.

The judgment of the Court of Appeals is affirmed.

■ *[A brief dissenting opinion by JUSTICE MARSHALL is omitted.]*

■ *JUSTICE STEVENS, with whom JUSTICES MARSHALL and BLACKMUN join, dissenting:*

Since the enactment of the Statute of Wills in 1540, careful draftsmen have authorized executors to pay the just debts of the decedent, including the fees and expenses of the attorney for the estate. Although the omission of such an express authorization in a will might indicate that the testator had thought it unnecessary, or that he had

[7] WVUH at least asks us to guess the preferences of the *enacting* Congress. Justice Stevens apparently believes our role is to guess the desires of the *present* Congress, or of Congresses yet to be. "Only time will tell," he says, "whether the Court, with its literal reading of § 1988, has correctly interpreted the will of Congress," *post* at 116. The implication is that today's holding will be proved wrong if Congress amends the law to conform with his dissent. We think not. The "will of Congress" we look to is not a will evolving from Session to Session, but a will expressed and fixed in a particular enactment. Otherwise, we would speak not of "interpreting" the law but of "intuiting" or "predicting" it. Our role is to say what the law, as hitherto enacted, *is*; not to forecast what the law, as amended, *will be*.

overlooked the point, the omission would surely not indicate a deliberate decision by the testator to forbid any compensation to his attorney.

In the early 1970's, Congress began to focus on the importance of public interest litigation, and since that time, it has enacted numerous fee-shifting statutes. In many of these statutes, which the majority cites at length, Congress has expressly authorized the recovery of expert witness fees as part of the costs of litigation. The question in this case is whether, notwithstanding the omission of such an express authorization in 42 U.S.C. § 1988, Congress intended to authorize such recovery when it provided for "a reasonable attorney's fee as part of the costs." In my view, just as the omission of express authorization in a will does not preclude compensation to an estate's attorney, the omission of express authorization for expert witness fees in a fee-shifting provision should not preclude the award of expert witness fees. We should look at the way in which the Court has interpreted the text of *this statute* in the past, as well as *this statute's* legislative history, to resolve the question before us, rather than looking at the text of the many other statutes that the majority cites in which Congress expressly recognized the need for compensating expert witnesses.

I

Under either the broad view of "costs" typically assumed in the fee-shifting context or the broad view of "a reasonable attorney's fee" articulated by this Court, expert witness fees are a proper component of an award under § 1988. Because we are not interpreting these words for the first time, they should be evaluated in the context that this and other courts have already created. . . .

. . . .

In *Jenkins*, the Court acknowledged that the use of paralegals instead of attorneys reduced the cost of litigation, and " 'by reducing the spiraling cost of civil rights litigation, further[ed] the policies underlying civil rights statutes.' " 491 U.S. at 288. If attorneys were forced to do the work that paralegals could just as easily perform under the supervision of an attorney, such as locating and interviewing witnesses or compiling statistical and financial data, then "it would not be surprising to see a greater amount of such work performed by attorneys themselves, thus increasing the overall cost of litigation." *Id.* at 288, n. 10.

This reasoning applies equally to other forms of specialized litigation support that a trial lawyer needs and that the client customarily pays for, either directly or indirectly. Although reliance on paralegals is a more recent development than the use of traditional expert witnesses, both paralegals and expert witnesses perform important tasks that save lawyers' time and enhance the quality of their work product. In this case, it is undisputed that the District Court correctly found that the expert witnesses were "essential" and "necessary" to the successful prosecution of the plaintiff's case, and that their data and analysis played a pivotal role in the attorney's trial preparation. Had the attorneys attempted to perform the tasks that the experts performed, it obviously would have taken them far longer than the experts and the entire case would have been far more costly to the parties. As Judge Posner observed in a comparable case:

> "The time so spent by the expert is a substitute for lawyer time, just as paralegal time is, for if prohibited (or deterred by the cost) from hiring an expert the lawyer would attempt to educate himself about the expert's area of expertise. To forbid the shifting of the expert's fee would encourage underspecialization and inefficient trial preparation, just as to forbid shifting the cost of paralegals would encourage lawyers to do paralegals' work. There is thus no basis for distinguishing *Jenkins* from the present case so far as time spent by these experts in educating the plaintiffs' lawyer is concerned . . . ." *Friedrich v. Chicago*, 888 F.2d 511, 514 (CA7 1989).

In *Jenkins*, we interpreted the award of "a reasonable *attorney's* fee" to cover charges for paralegals and law clerks, even though a paralegal or law clerk is not an attorney. Similarly, the federal courts routinely allow an attorney's travel expenses or long-distance telephone calls to be awarded, even though they are not literally part of an "attorney's *fee*," or part of "costs" as defined by 28 U.S.C. § 1920. To allow reimbursement of these other categories of expenses, and yet not to include expert witness fees, is both arbitrary and contrary to the broad remedial purpose that inspired the fee-shifting provision of § 1988.

II

The Senate Report on the Civil Rights Attorney's Fees Awards Act of 1976 explained that the purpose of the proposed amendment to 42 U.S.C. § 1988 was "to remedy anomalous gaps in our civil rights laws created by the United States Supreme Court's recent decision in *Alyeska Pipeline Service Co. v. Wilderness Society*, 421 U.S. 240 (1975), and to achieve consistency in our civil rights laws." S. Rep. No. 94–1011, p. 1 (1976). The Senate Committee on the Judiciary wanted to level the playing field so that private citizens, who might have little or no money, could still serve as "private attorneys general" and afford to bring actions, even against state or local bodies, to enforce the civil rights laws. The Committee acknowledged that "[i]f private citizens are to be able to assert their civil rights, and if those who violate the Nation's fundamental laws are not to proceed with impunity, then citizens must have the opportunity to recover *what it costs them* to vindicate these rights in court." *Id.* at 2 (emphasis added). According to the Committee, the bill would create "no startling new remedy," but would simply provide "the technical requirements" requested by the Supreme Court in *Alyeska*, so that courts could "continue the practice of awarding attorneys' fees which had been going on for years prior to the Court's May decision." *Id.* at 6.

To underscore its intention to return the courts to their pre-*Alyeska* practice of shifting fees in civil rights cases, the Senate Committee's Report cited with approval not only several cases in which fees had been shifted, but also all of the cases contained in Legal Fees, Hearings before the Subcommittee on Representation of Citizen Interests of the Senate Committee on the Judiciary, 93d Cong., 1st Sess., pt. 3, pp. 888–1024, 1060–1062 (1973) (hereinafter Senate Hearings). See S. Rep. No. 94–1011, at 4, n. 3. The cases collected in the 1973 Senate Hearings included many in which courts had permitted the shifting of costs, including expert witness fees. At the time when the Committee referred to these cases, though several were later reversed, it used them to make the point that prior to *Alyeska*, courts awarded attorney's fees and costs, including expert witness fees, in civil rights cases, and that they did so in order to encourage private citizens to bring such suits.[8] It was to this pre-*Alyeska* regime, in which courts could award expert witness fees along with attorney's fees, that the Senate Committee intended to return through the passage of the fee-shifting amendment to § 1988.

The House Report expressed concerns similar to those raised by the Senate Report. . . .

. . . [T]he record of House and Senate subcommittee hearings, consisting of the testimony and written submissions of public officials, scholars, practicing attorneys, and private citizens, and the questions of the legislators, makes clear that both committees were concerned with preserving access to the courts and encouraging public interest litigation.

It is fair to say that throughout the course of the hearings, a recurring theme was the desire to return to the pre-*Alyeska* practice in which courts could shift fees, including expert witness fees, and make those who acted as private attorneys general whole again, thus encouraging the enforcement of the civil rights laws.

The case before us today is precisely the type of public interest litigation that Congress intended to encourage by amending § 1988 to provide for fee shifting of a "reasonable attorney's fee as part of the costs." . . . .

This Court's determination today that petitioner must assume the cost of $104,133 in expert witness fees is at war with the congressional purpose of making the prevailing party whole. As we said in *Hensley v. Eckerhart*, 461 U.S. 424, 435 (1983), petitioner's recovery should be "fully compensatory," or, as we expressed in *Jenkins*, petitioner's recovery should be "comparable to what 'is traditional with attorneys compensated

---

[8] See, *e.g.*, . . . *Bradley v. School Board of Richmond*, 53 F.R.D. 28, 44 (ED Va. 1971) ("Fees for expert witnesses' testimony likewise will be allowed as an expense of suit. It is difficult to imagine a more necessary item of proof (and source of assistance to the Court) than the considered opinion of an educational expert"), rev'd, 472 F.2d 318 (CA4 1972), vacated, 416 U.S. 696 (1974); *La Raza Unida v. Volpe*, 57 F.R.D. 94 (ND Cal. 1972), reprinted in Senate Hearings, pt. 3, pp. 1060, 1062 (expert witness fees allowed because experts' testimony was "helpful to the court") . . . .

by a fee-paying client.' S. Rep. No. 94–1011, p. 6 (1976) . . . ." 491 U.S. at 286.

III

In recent years the Court has vacillated between a purely literal approach to the task of statutory interpretation and an approach that seeks guidance from historical context, legislative history, and prior cases identifying the purpose that motivated the legislation. Thus, for example, in *Christiansburg Garment Co. v. EEOC*, 434 U.S. 412 (1978), we rejected a "mechanical construction," *id.* at 418, of the fee-shifting provision in § 706(k) of Title VII of the Civil Rights Act of 1964 that the prevailing defendant had urged upon us. Although the text of the statute drew no distinction between different kinds of "prevailing parties," we held that awards to prevailing plaintiffs are governed by a more liberal standard than awards to prevailing defendants. That holding rested entirely on our evaluation of the relevant congressional policy and found no support within the four corners of the statutory text. Nevertheless, the holding was unanimous and, to the best of my knowledge, evoked no adverse criticism or response in Congress.[11]

On those occasions, however, when the Court has put on its thick grammarian's spectacles and ignored the available evidence of congressional purpose and the teaching of prior cases construing a statute, the congressional response has been dramatically different. It is no coincidence that the Court's literal reading of Title VII, which led to the conclusion that disparate treatment of pregnant and nonpregnant persons was not discrimination on the basis of sex, see *General Electric Co. v. Gilbert*, 429 U.S. 125 (1976), was repudiated by the 95th Congress; that its literal reading of the "continuous physical presence" requirement

[11] Other examples of cases in which the Court eschewed the literal approach include *Steelworkers v. Weber*, 443 U.S. 193 (1979), and *Johnson v. Transportation Agency, Santa Clara County*, 480 U.S. 616 (1987). Although the dissenters had the better textual argument in both cases, and urged the Court to read the words of the statute literally, the Court, in both cases, opted for a reading that took into account congressional purpose and historical context. See *Steelworkers v. Weber*, 443 U.S. at 201 (Court rejected "literal construction of §§ 703(a) and (d)" and held that the statute must "be read against the background of the legislative history of Title VII and the historical context from which the Act arose"); *Johnson v. Transportation Agency*, 480 U.S. at 627 (legality of employer's affirmative-action plan to be assessed according to criteria announced in *Weber*). Neither decision prompted an adverse congressional response.

Although there have been those who have argued that congressional inaction cannot be seen as an endorsement of this Court's interpretations, see, *e.g.*, *Johnson v. Transportation Agency*, 480 U.S. at 671–672 (Scalia, J., dissenting); *Patterson v. McLean Credit Union*, 491 U.S. 164, 175, n. 1 (1989), that charge has been answered by the observation that "when Congress has been displeased with [the Court's] interpretation . . . , it has not hesitated to amend the statute to tell us so. . . . Surely, it is appropriate to find some probative value in such radically different congressional reactions to this Court's interpretations . . . ." *Johnson v. Transportation Agency*, 480 U.S. at 629–630, n. 7; see *Patterson v. McLean Credit Union*, 491 U.S. at 200 (Brennan, J., concurring in judgment in part and dissenting in part) ("Where our prior interpretation of congressional intent was plausible, . . . we have often taken Congress' subsequent inaction as probative to varying degrees, depending upon the circumstances, of its acquiescence"). Since Congress has had an opportunity, albeit brief, to correct our broad reading of attorney's fees in *Jenkins* if it thought that we had misapprehended its purpose, the Court has no reason to change its approach to the fee-shifting provision of § 1988, as the majority does today.

in § 244(a)(1) of the Immigration and Nationality Act, which led to the view that the statute did not permit even temporary or inadvertent absences from this country, see *INS v. Phinpathya*, 464 U.S. 183 (1984), was rebuffed by the 99th Congress; that its literal reading of the word "program" in Title IX of the Education Amendments of 1972, which led to the Court's gratuitous limit on the scope of the antidiscrimination provisions of Title IX, see *Grove City College v. Bell*, 465 U.S. 555 (1984), was rejected by the 100th Congress; or that its refusal to accept the teaching of earlier decisions in *Wards Cove Packing Co. v. Atonio*, 490 U.S. 642 (1989) (reformulating order of proof and weight of parties' burdens in disparate-impact cases), and *Patterson v. McLean Credit Union*, 491 U.S. 164 (1989) (limiting scope of 42 U.S.C. § 1981 to the making and enforcement of contracts), was overwhelmingly rejected by the 101st Congress, and its refusal to accept the widely held view of lower courts about the scope of fraud, see *McNally v. United States*, 483 U.S. 350 (1987) (limiting mail fraud to protection of property), was quickly corrected by the 100th Congress.

In the domain of statutory interpretation, Congress is the master. It obviously has the power to correct our mistakes, but we do the country a disservice when we needlessly ignore persuasive evidence of Congress' actual purpose and require it "to take the time to revisit the matter"[18] and to restate its purpose in more precise English whenever its work product suffers from an omission or inadvertent error. As Judge Learned Hand explained, statutes are likely to be imprecise.

> "All [legislators] have done is to write down certain words which they mean to apply generally to situations of that kind. To apply these literally may either pervert what was plainly their general meaning, or leave undisposed of what there is every reason to suppose they meant to provide for. Thus it is not enough for the judge just to use a dictionary. If he should do no more, he might come out with a result which every sensible man would recognize to be quite the opposite of what was really intended; which would contradict or leave unfulfilled its plain purpose." L. Hand, How Far Is a Judge Free in Rendering a Decision?, in The Spirit of Liberty 103, 106 (I. Dilliard ed. 1952).

The Court concludes its opinion with the suggestion that disagreement with its textual analysis could only be based on the dissenters' preference for a "better" statute, *ante* at 101. It overlooks the possibility that a different view may be more faithful to Congress' command. The fact that Congress has consistently provided for the inclusion of expert witness fees in fee-shifting statutes when it considered the matter is a weak reed on which to rest the conclusion that the omission of such a provision represents a deliberate decision to forbid such awards. Only time will tell whether the Court, with its literal

---

[18] *Smith v. Robinson*, 468 U.S. 992, 1031 (1984) (Brennan, J., dissenting).

reading of § 1988, has correctly interpreted the will of Congress with respect to the issue it has resolved today. . . .

NOTES AND QUESTIONS

1. In the absence of clues from other statutes, how broadly should one read the phrase "a reasonable attorney's fee" in 42 U.S.C. § 1988? In *Missouri v. Jenkins*, 491 U.S. 274 (1989), most of the Justices (including Justice Scalia) thought it clear that the phrase referred to "a reasonable fee for the work product of an attorney." *Id.* at 285. As a result, the compensable services extended beyond "work performed personally by members of the bar"; in the Court's words, "the fee must take into account the work not only of attorneys, but also of secretaries, messengers, librarians, janitors, and others whose labor contributes to the work product for which an attorney bills her client," as well as "other expenses and profit." *Id.* By the same token, *Jenkins* held that the phrase also encompassed the work of paralegals and law clerks (such as summer associates). *Id.* at 284–85.

Of course, § 1988 does not necessarily require a separate accounting for the work of every employee in a law firm. According to the Court, "A reasonable attorney's fee under § 1988 is one calculated on the basis of rates and practices prevailing in the relevant market . . . ." *Id.* at 286. In most communities, lawyers do not bill clients directly for the work that secretaries and various other staff members perform; instead, lawyers simply set their own hourly rates at a level that covers these components of their overhead. The market rate for attorney time will reflect this practice. As a result, when courts use the market rate to calculate a "reasonable attorney's fee" under 42 U.S.C. § 1988, the courts will be providing reasonable compensation for the work of the staff members whose time is not customarily billed separately. For that reason, courts applying § 1988 do not need to add extra compensation to reflect the work of these staff members.

If the custom in a particular community were to treat paralegals like secretaries for billing purposes (so that lawyers did not bill clients directly for paralegals' time, but rather built that aspect of their overhead into their own hourly rates), then the same analysis would apply to paralegals: the market rate for attorney time in the relevant community would already provide compensation for the work of paralegals, and courts applying § 1988 should not account for that work separately. These days, though, the law firms in many communities do *not* bundle compensation for paralegals' work into the lawyers' own hourly rates; instead, firms keep track of the time that paralegals spend on each case and produce bills listing separate charges for lawyer time and paralegal time. In *Jenkins*, the Supreme Court held that judges calculating "a 'reasonable' fee for the attorney's work product" under § 1988 need to take account of those practices. *Jenkins*, 491 U.S. at 285–87. If the practice in a particular community is to bill clients separately for attorney time (at one hourly rate) and for paralegal time (at a different hourly rate), then a court calculating "a reasonable attorney's fee" under § 1988 should do the same. If the court awarded compensation *only* for attorney time (at the prevailing market rates for the relevant types of attorneys) and did not also award compensation for paralegal time (at the prevailing market rate for paralegals), then the award would be too low; it would not actually reflect the market rate for the attorney's complete work product. *See id.* at 287.

How should this analysis apply to expert fees? Perhaps the time that expert witnesses spend preparing and offering testimony at trial is not part of the work product of an attorney in the same way that the work of a paralegal or a summer associate is. But what about the time spent by nontestifying expert consultants—people who are part of the litigation team and who help educate the lawyers about technical aspects of the case so that the lawyers can litigate them effectively? Is there any reason to distinguish between fees for consulting experts and fees for paralegals?

More broadly, was *Jenkins* correct to focus on "the work product of an attorney," *id.* at 285, or might that phrasing actually be too narrow? If you were considering § 1988 without regard to other statutes, could you read the phrase "a reasonable attorney's fee" as including all reasonable expenses of the litigation that the attorney is conducting—including, perhaps, the fees charged by expert witnesses whom the attorney hires to present testimony at trial?

2. To justify his conclusion that the phrase "a reasonable attorney's fee" in § 1988 does not include fees for expert witnesses, Justice Scalia relied largely on how Congress used that phrase or its cognates in other fee-shifting statutes. He quoted numerous statutes that shift *both* "reasonable attorneys' fees" *and* "reasonable . . . expert witness fees." Because the phrase "attorneys' fees" obviously does not include fees for expert witnesses in the statutes that shift the two items separately, Justice Scalia concluded that the phrase also does not include such fees in § 1988. One way of phrasing his point might be that in light of what he called "[t]he record of statutory usage," the phrase "attorney's fee" in § 1988 should be understood as a term of art; whatever else it covers, it does not include fees for expert witnesses.

Although Justice Scalia found many fee-shifting statutes that refer to fees for "attorneys" and "expert witnesses" separately, he acknowledged that "[t]he laws that refer to fees for nontestimonial expert services are less common." He seemed to conclude that most fee-shifting statutes do not shift fees for consulting experts. But might one instead conclude that the typical fee-shifting statute bundles the expense of retaining litigation consultants, where appropriate, into what it means by "a reasonable attorney's fee"? Even if the record of statutory usage establishes an important distinction between "attorney's fees" and fees for expert witnesses, wasn't Justice Scalia's argument weaker as applied to consulting experts? Or would it have been slicing things too fine to conclude that § 1988 permits fee-shifting for consulting experts but not for testifying experts?

3. In reciting all of the fee-shifting statutes that refer to "attorneys" and "expert witnesses" separately, Justice Scalia seemed to put special emphasis on statutes enacted by the same Congress as the Civil Rights Attorney's Fee Award Act of 1976. For instance, he made a point of noting that Congress enacted the Toxic Substances Control Act of 1976 "just over a week prior to the enactment of § 1988." Was Justice Scalia's emphasis on that fact consistent with his professed desire to enforce the "objective" meaning of statutes rather than the "subjective" intent of their enactors?

The answer, presumably, is "yes." Although the "objective" meaning of statutory language depends on the principles that interpreters are supposed to use to construe that language, those principles should be designed to produce fairly strong correlations between the meanings that interpreters ascribe to statutes and the meanings that members of the enacting legislature intended to convey. Of course, some gaps between interpreted and intended meaning are inevitable (not least because members of the enacting legislature will not always *have* an intent on particular questions of interpretation). But to the extent that members of the enacting legislature did intend a statute to establish a particular legal directive, textualists have no reason to revel in interpretive principles that cause courts to read the statute as establishing a different directive instead. If the interpretive principles that textualists tell courts to use would routinely produce unnecessarily large gaps between interpreted and intended meaning—gaps that are not warranted by other goals, such as giving the populace fair notice of statutory requirements and reducing the costs of decision—then textualists might well rethink the content of those interpretive principles. *See supra* p. 4, pp. 451–452. Thus, it is perfectly coherent to say *both* that "meaning" and "intent" are distinct concepts *and* that our rules for determining the "meaning" of language in one statute should pay attention to how the same Congress used the same language in other statutes enacted around the same time.

To the extent that principles of interpretation are indeed designed to guide interpreters toward a statute's intended meaning, though, how much should those principles emphasize the language of other statutes? Even though the same Congress enacted both the Toxic Substances Control Act of 1976 and the Civil Rights Attorney's Fee Award Act of 1976, those statutes were not drafted by the same people or considered by the same committees, and their paths to enactment were quite different. Comparing their texts might therefore provide relatively little insight into the intended meaning of either statute. Such comparisons might be even less informative for statutes that were enacted by different Congresses (and that are not *in pari materia*). *See* William W. Buzbee, *The One-Congress Fiction in Statutory Interpretation*, 149 U. PA. L. REV.

171, 205 (2000) (criticizing judicial opinions that treat Congress "as if it were a single natural person, albeit a person of superhuman omniscience and consistency of style"); Anita S. Krishnakumar, *Cracking the Whole Code Rule*, 96 N.Y.U. L. REV. 76, 132–44 (2021) (adding to this critique).

As you think about the relevance of interstatutory comparisons, how much do you need to know about the details of the legislative process? If statutory language were drafted primarily by individual members of Congress or their personal staffs, then interpreters might put little stock in interstatutory comparisons; the linguistic patterns used by one drafter might have little in common with the linguistic patterns used by a different drafter, and the legislative process might not harmonize those patterns. In fact, though, scholars report that "members are generally *not* involved in the actual drafting of legislation." Jesse M. Cross & Abbe R. Gluck, *The Congressional Bureaucracy*, 168 U. PA. L. REV. 1541, 1566 (2020). Instead, each House of Congress has an Office of the Legislative Counsel, and the lawyers in those Offices perform a substantial amount of the drafting work within Congress. *See id.* ("Today, the House office employs fifty-six attorneys as drafters, and the Senate office thirty-four. . . . Use of the offices' drafting services is optional, but members and committees now use them with respect to nearly every bill, resolution, and amendment introduced in Congress." (footnotes omitted)); *see also* Lisa Schultz Bressman & Abbe R. Gluck, *Statutory Interpretation from the Inside—An Empirical Study of Congressional Drafting, Delegation, and the Canons: Part II*, 66 STAN. L. REV. 725, 740 (2014) (reporting survey results indicating that even committee counsel "rarely draft statutes from 'scratch' " and that most of the drafting work is done by Legislative Counsel). The role of professional drafters in the legislative process obviously strengthens the argument for assuming some consistency across statutes. Still, lawyers in the Offices of the Legislative Counsel do not play the same role with respect to every statute. *See id.* at 747 (noting that some proposed language is prepared in the first instance by lobbyists or agencies and reviewed only later by Legislative Counsel, and adding that amendments "drafted after hours . . . or under extreme time pressure" might not involve Legislative Counsel at all). In addition, different lawyers in the Offices of the Legislative Counsel are assigned to different subjects, and "coordination is lacking"—with the result that many of those lawyers themselves caution against assuming that the same word carries the same meaning "across different statutes or different committees." *Id.* at 746–47.

Of course, if a particular phrase is known to be a term of art, then it might be used fairly consistently across a range of statutes. *Cf.* Krishnakumar, *supra*, 96 N.Y.U. L. REV. at 135 (suggesting that a presumption of cross-statute consistency makes more sense for "legal terms of art" than for "generic phrases"). But how can interpreters tell whether a phrase like "attorney's fee" is a term of art? Is the fact that many fee-shifting statutes refer to *both* attorney's fees *and* expert-witness fees enough to draw conclusions about what the phrase "attorney's fee" means in other statutes that use the phrase on its own?

4. Justice Scalia cited many fee-shifting statutes that referred separately to "attorney's fees" and "expert witness fees." All of those statutes, though, shifted *both* of those categories of expenses. As Justice Stevens suggested in his dissent, those statutes might be seen as evidence of a general policy: when Congress decided to shift attorney fees, and when it thought specifically of expert-witness fees as a separate item of expense, Congress made clear that it wanted to shift expert-witness fees too. That general policy led Justice Stevens to doubt that the phrasing of § 1988 reflected a deliberate decision by Congress to decouple fees for lawyers' services from fees for expert witnesses in civil-rights cases, and to shift *only* the former sort of fees. *Cf.* T. Alexander Aleinikoff & Theodore M. Shaw, *The Costs of Incoherence: A Comment on Plain Meaning,* West Virginia University Hospitals, Inc. v. Casey, *and Due Process of Statutory Interpretation*, 45 VAND. L. REV. 687, 696 (1992) (doubting that Congress would have chosen to make fee shifting less generous in civil-rights cases than in the cases covered by the other statutes). To the extent that there was uncertainty on this point, moreover, Justice Stevens would have resolved that uncertainty so as to keep the policy expressed in Congress's fee-shifting statutes consistent—even if the only way to do so was to ascribe a different meaning to the phrase "attorney's fee" in § 1988 than the same phrase carried in the fee-shifting statutes that Justice Scalia cited. In other words, Justice Stevens opted for policy consistency rather than semantic consistency.

Justice Scalia made the opposite judgment. To be sure, where statutory language is ambiguous, he thought that courts could properly try to resolve the ambiguities in ways that promote policy coherence. For Justice Scalia, however, the assumption that Congress was using the phrase "attorney's fee" in § 1988 in the same way that Congress used the phrase in other fee-shifting statutes trumped the desire for policy coherence, because it eliminated the ambiguity that gave that desire room to operate. In his words, "where, as here, the meaning of the term prevents such accommodation, it is not our function to eliminate clearly expressed inconsistency of policy . . . ."

Who had the better of this argument?

If you are inclined to agree with Justice Stevens, what do you make of the pre-1976 cases under the Clayton Act that Justice Scalia cited in Part IV of his opinion? Section 4 of the Clayton Act allowed the prevailing plaintiff in an antitrust action to recover "the cost of suit, including a reasonable attorney's fee." Act of Oct. 15, 1914, ch. 323, § 4, 38 Stat. 730, 731 (codified as amended at 15 U.S.C. § 15(a)). From an early date, courts concluded that the singular noun "cost" in the Clayton Act did not refer to all expenses, but only to the same types of "costs" that the Sherman Act allowed prevailing parties to recover. *See* Straus v. Victor Talking Mach. Co., 297 F. 791, 806–07 (2d Cir. 1924); *see also* Illinois v. Sangamo

Constr. Co., 657 F.2d 855, 866 (7th Cir. 1981) ("Just as the *Straus* court failed to see any significan[t difference] between 'cost' and 'costs' in the antitrust statutes, so do we fail to see any significant difference between 'cost of suit' in the Clayton Act and 'costs of suit' in Rule 54(d) and 28 U.S.C. § 1920."). By 1976, a number of circuit courts had specifically held that the Clayton Act did not shift expert-witness fees as part of the "cost of suit," and courts apparently did not regard those expenses as components of "a reasonable attorney's fee" either. *See, e.g.*, Ott v. Speedwriting Publishing Co., 518 F.2d 1143, 1149 (6th Cir. 1975) ("[T]he fees of expert witnesses are not included in the recoverable costs in an antitrust action."). If you believe in legislative-acquiescence arguments, does the fact that Congress let these decisions stand undermine Justice Stevens's belief that Congress normally would not want to shift attorney's fees without shifting expert-witness fees? What about the fact that after these decisions were in place, the Civil Rights Attorney's Fee Award Act of 1976 used the phrase "a reasonable attorney's fee as part of the costs" without separately addressing expert fees?

5. In response to *West Virginia University Hospitals v. Casey*, the Civil Rights Act of 1991 amended the statute that is codified at 42 U.S.C. § 1988. Specifically, Congress added a new subsection providing that when a court awards attorney's fees to the prevailing party in a suit to enforce a provision of 42 U.S.C. § 1981 or § 1981a, "the court, in its discretion, may include expert fees as part of the attorney's fee." Pub. L. 102–166, § 113, 105 Stat. 1071, 1079 (1991) (codified at 42 U.S.C. § 1988(c)). This provision, however, applies only to suits to enforce a provision of 42 U.S.C. §§ 1981 and 1981a, and not to suits brought under the other civil-rights statutes that trigger fee-shifting under § 1988. In particular, the provision added in 1991 does not apply to suits brought under 42 U.S.C. § 1983 (such as *West Virginia University Hospitals* itself).

For the reasons suggested in footnote 7 of the majority opinion, Justice Scalia presumably did not think that the Civil Rights Act of 1991 (enacted by the 102nd Congress) sheds any light on whether he was correct about the meaning of the original statute (enacted by the 94th Congress in 1976). But Justice Stevens seemed to disagree with footnote 7. Given the difficulty of the legislative process, could Justice Stevens have taken the fact that Congress responded at all as a vindication of his dissent? Or does the limited nature of Congress's response cast doubt on Justice Stevens's assumption that when Congress considers fee-shifting legislation, it typically elects to treat expert fees in tandem with core attorney's fees?

---

3. THE PRESUMPTION AGAINST IMPLIED REPEALS

The "presumption against implied repeals" is another way in which the existence of one statute can affect the meaning that interpreters ascribe to another statute.

Subject to a few constitutional constraints, it is well accepted that Congress (or a state legislature) can repeal its own past statutes. That idea has deep roots. For instance, the first volume of William Blackstone's *Commentaries on the Laws of England*—published in 1765—recited the maxim that *leges posteriores priores contrarias abrogant* (later laws abrogate contrary prior laws). In the United States, that idea is thought to be incorporated into Article I of the federal Constitution and its counterparts in the state constitutions, which vest legislative powers in the *current* legislature. Even if a statute enacted by a past Congress purported to specify that it could never be repealed, that provision would not actually work; the current Congress could repeal that provision along with the rest of the statute. Except to the extent that a statute has generated vested private rights of the sort that the Constitution prevents the legislature from taking away, Congress always has the power to enact a new statute repealing the earlier one (in whole or in part).

When Congress wants to repeal all or part of a previously enacted federal statute, it frequently does so expressly: the new statute explicitly says that the old statute is repealed (or that particular provisions in the old statute are repealed). But the fact that later statutes abrogate contrary prior statutes also raises the possibility of *implied* repeals. Sometimes, even though a new federal statute does not expressly say that it is repealing a prior federal statute, one of the directives set out in the new statute will contradict one or more of the directives set out in the prior statute as applied to certain situations. In those situations, courts have to choose between giving effect to the directives in the newer statute and giving effect to the directives in the older statute. (As a logical matter, courts cannot give effect to both, because the directives contradict each other.) The maxim that later laws abrogate contrary prior ones tells courts what to do in this situation—which directives take priority. The maxim says that in the event of such a contradiction, courts are supposed to follow the directives established by the newer statute. In effect, the newer statute has repealed the contradictory aspects or applications of the older statute. But Congress has not used any express words of repeal, and so courts say that the new statute has repealed the relevant portion of the earlier statute *by implication*.

As a matter of statutory interpretation, however, courts and other interpreters do not lightly find repeals by implication. At a minimum, if a new federal statute lends itself to two possible readings, one of which would cause the new statute to contradict (and therefore impliedly repeal) some aspect or application of an earlier federal statute, interpreters will usually resolve the ambiguity in the way that avoids the contradiction. In fact, interpreters sometimes go farther. Instead of simply treating the presumption against implied repeals as a tool for resolving conventional linguistic indeterminacy in the newer statute, they treat it as what Chapter 2 called an "implied-limitation rule." *See supra* p. 231. Even if the face of the newer statute seems to establish a broad and unqualified directive, courts sometimes infer an exception to that directive in order to preserve the operation of an older statute that the legislature has not expressly repealed. The Supreme Court arguably did just that in the next case.

Morton v. Mancari

417 U.S. 535 (1974)

■ *JUSTICE BLACKMUN delivered the opinion of the Court:*

The Indian Reorganization Act of 1934, . . . 48 Stat. 984, 25 U.S.C. § 461 *et seq.*, accords an employment preference for qualified Indians in the Bureau of Indian Affairs (BIA or Bureau). Appellees, non-Indian BIA employees, challenged this preference as contrary to the anti-discrimination provisions of the Equal Employment Opportunity Act of 1972, 86 Stat. 103, 42 U.S.C. § 2000e *et seq.*, and as violative of the Due Process Clause of the Fifth Amendment. A three-judge Federal District Court concluded that the Indian preference under the 1934 Act was impliedly repealed by the 1972 Act. 359 F. Supp. 585 (D.N.M. 1973). We noted probable jurisdiction in order to examine the statutory and constitutional validity of this longstanding Indian preference. . . .

I

Section 12 of the Indian Reorganization Act, 48 Stat. 986, 25 U.S.C. § 472, provides:

> "The Secretary of the Interior is directed to establish standards of health, age, character, experience, knowledge, and ability for Indians who may be appointed, without regard to civil-service laws, to the various positions maintained, now or hereafter, by the Indian Office,[1] in the administration of functions or services affecting any Indian tribe. Such qualified Indians shall hereafter have the preference to appointment to vacancies in any such positions."

In June 1972, pursuant to this provision, the Commissioner of Indian Affairs, with the approval of the Secretary of the Interior, issued a directive (Personnel Management Letter No. 72–12) stating that the BIA's policy would be to grant a preference to qualified Indians not only, as before, in the initial hiring stage, but also in the situation where an Indian and a non-Indian, both already employed by the BIA, were

---

1 The Indian Health Service was transferred in 1954 from the Department of the Interior to the Department of Health, Education and Welfare. Act of Aug. 5, 1954, § 1, 68 Stat. 674, 42 U.S.C. § 2001. Presumably, despite this transfer, the reference in § 12 to the "Indian Office" has continuing application to the Indian Health Service. See 5 CFR § 213.3116(b)(8).

competing for a promotion within the Bureau. The record indicates that this policy was implemented immediately.

Shortly thereafter, appellees, who are non-Indian employees of the BIA at Albuquerque,[4] instituted this class action, on behalf of themselves and other non-Indian employees similarly situated, in the United States District Court for the District of New Mexico, claiming that the "so-called 'Indian Preference Statutes' " ... were repealed by the 1972 Equal Employment Opportunity Act and deprived them of rights to property without due process of law, in violation of the Fifth Amendment.[5] ...

A three-judge court was convened pursuant to [the then-applicable requirements of] 28 U.S.C. § 2282 because the complaint sought to enjoin, as unconstitutional, the enforcement of a federal statute. . . .

After a short trial focusing primarily on how the new policy ... has been implemented, the District Court concluded that the Indian preference was implicitly repealed by § 11 of the Equal Employment Opportunity Act of 1972, Pub. L. 92–261, 86 Stat. 111, 42 U.S.C. § 2000e–16(a), proscribing discrimination in most federal employment on the basis of race.[6] Having found that Congress repealed the preference, it was unnecessary for the District Court to pass on its constitutionality. The court permanently enjoined appellants "from implementing any policy in the Bureau of Indian Affairs which would hire, promote, or reassign any person in preference to another solely for the reason that such person is an Indian." The execution ... of the judgment of the District Court was stayed ... pending the disposition of this appeal.

II

The federal policy of according some hiring preference to Indians in the Indian service dates at least as far back as 1834.[7] Since that time, Congress repeatedly has enacted various preferences of the general type

---

[4] The appellees state that none of them is employed on or near an Indian reservation. Brief for Appellees 8. The District Court described the appellees as "teachers ... or programmers, or in computer work." 359 F. Supp. at 587.

[5] The specific question whether § 12 of the 1934 Act authorizes a preference in promotion as well as in initial hiring was not decided by the District Court and is not now before us. We express no opinion on this issue. . . .

[6] Section 2000e–16(a) reads:

"All personnel actions affecting employees or applicants for employment (except with regard to aliens employed outside the limits of the United States) in military departments as defined in section 102 of Title 5, in executive agencies (other than the General Accounting Office) as defined in section 105 of Title 5 (including employees and applicants for employment who are paid from nonappropriated funds), in the United States Postal Service and the Postal Rate Commission, in those units of the Government of the District of Columbia having positions in the competitive service, and in those units of the legislative and judicial branches of the Federal Government having positions in the competitive service, and in the Library of Congress shall be made free from any discrimination based on race, color, religion, sex, or national origin."

[7] Act of June 30, 1834, § 9, 4 Stat. 737, 25 U.S.C. § 45:

"[I]n all cases of the appointments of interpreters or other persons employed for the benefit of the Indians, a preference shall be given to persons of Indian descent, if such can be found, who are properly qualified for the execution of the duties."

here at issue.[8] The purpose of these preferences, as variously expressed in the legislative history, has been to give Indians a greater participation in their own self-government; to further the Government's trust obligation toward the Indian tribes; and to reduce the negative effect of having non-Indians administer matters that affect Indian tribal life.

The preference directly at issue here was enacted as an important part of the sweeping Indian Reorganization Act of 1934. The overriding purpose of that particular Act was to establish machinery whereby Indian tribes would be able to assume a greater degree of self-government, both politically and economically. Congress was seeking to modify the then-existing situation whereby the primarily non-Indian-staffed BIA had plenary control, for all practical purposes, over the lives and destinies of the federally recognized Indian tribes. Initial congressional proposals would have diminished substantially the role of the BIA by turning over to federally chartered self-governing Indian communities many of the functions normally performed by the Bureau. Committee sentiment, however, ran against such a radical change in the role of the BIA. The solution ultimately adopted was to strengthen tribal government while continuing the active role of the BIA, with the understanding that the Bureau would be more responsive to the interests of the people it was created to serve.

One of the primary means by which self-government would be fostered and the Bureau made more responsive was to increase the participation of tribal Indians in the BIA operations. In order to achieve this end, it was recognized that some kind of preference and exemption from otherwise prevailing civil service requirements was necessary. Congressman Howard, the House sponsor, expressed the need for the preference:

> "The Indians have not only been thus deprived of civic rights and powers, but they have been largely deprived of the opportunity to enter the more important positions in the service of the very bureau which manages their affairs. Theoretically, the Indians have the right to qualify for the Federal civil service. In actual practice there has been no adequate program of training to qualify Indians to compete in these examinations, especially for technical and higher positions; and even if there were such training, the Indians would have to compete under existing law, on equal terms with multitudes of white applicants. . . . The various services on the Indian reservations are actually local rather than Federal services and are comparable to local municipal and county services, since they are

[8] Act of May 17, 1882, § 6, 22 Stat. 88, and Act of July 4, 1884, § 6, 23 Stat. 97, 25 U.S.C. § 46 (employment of clerical, mechanical, and other help on reservations and about agencies); Act of Aug. 15, 1894, § 10, 28 Stat. 313, 25 U.S.C. § 44 (employment of herders, teamsters, and laborers, "and where practicable in all other employments" in the Indian service); Act of June 7, 1897, § 1, 30 Stat. 83, 25 U.S.C. § 274 (employment as matrons, farmers, and industrial teachers in Indian schools); Act of June 25, 1910, § 23, 36 Stat. 861, 25 U.S.C. § 47 (general preference as to Indian labor and products of Indian industry).

dealing with purely local Indian problems. It should be possible for Indians with the requisite vocational and professional training to enter the service of their own people without the necessity of competing with white applicants for these positions. This bill permits them to do so." 78 Cong. Rec. 11729 (1934).

Congress was well aware that the proposed preference would result in employment disadvantages within the BIA for non-Indians. Not only was this displacement unavoidable if room were to be made for Indians, but it was explicitly determined that gradual replacement of non-Indians with Indians within the Bureau was a desirable feature of the entire program for self-government.[18] Since 1934, the BIA has implemented the preference with a fair degree of success. The percentage of Indians employed in the Bureau rose from 34% in 1934 to 57% in 1972. This reversed the former downward trend . . . and was due, clearly, to the presence of the 1934 Act. The Commissioner's extension of the preference in 1972 to promotions within the BIA was designed to bring more Indians into positions of responsibility and, in that regard, appears to be a logical extension of the congressional intent. See *Freeman v. Morton*, 162 U.S. App. D.C. 358, 499 F.2d 494 (1974), and n. 5, *supra*.

III

It is against this background that we encounter the first issue in the present case: whether the Indian preference was repealed by the Equal Employment Opportunity Act of 1972. Title VII of the Civil Rights Act of 1964, 78 Stat. 253, was the first major piece of federal legislation prohibiting discrimination in *private* employment on the basis of "race, color, religion, sex, or national origin." 42 U.S.C. § 2000e–2(a). Significantly, §§ 701(b) and 703(i) of that Act explicitly exempted from its coverage the preferential employment of Indians by Indian tribes or by industries located on or near Indian reservations. 42 U.S.C. §§ 2000e(b) and 2000e–2(i).[19] This exemption reveals a clear congressional recognition, within the framework of Title VII, of the unique legal status of tribal and reservation-based activities. The Senate sponsor, Senator Humphrey, stated on the floor by way of explanation:

[18] "It should be possible for Indians to enter the service of their own people without running the gauntlet of competition with whites for these positions. Indian progress and ambition will be enormously strengthened as soon as we adopt the principle that the Indian Service shall gradually become, in fact as well as in name, an Indian service predominantly in the hands of education and competent Indians." *Id.* at 11731 (remarks of Cong. Howard).

[19] Section 701(b) excludes "an Indian Tribe" from the Act's definition of "employer." Section 703(i) states:

"Nothing contained in this subchapter shall apply to any business or enterprise on or near an Indian reservation with respect to any publicly announced employment practice of such business or enterprise under which a preferential treatment is given to any individual because he is an Indian living on or near a reservation."

> "This exemption is consistent with the Federal Government's policy of encouraging Indian employment and with the special legal position of Indians." 110 Cong. Rec. 12723 (1964).[20]

The 1964 Act did not specifically outlaw employment discrimination by the Federal Government.[21] Yet the mechanism for enforcing longstanding Executive Orders forbidding Government discrimination had proved ineffective for the most part. In order to remedy this, Congress, by the 1972 Act, amended the 1964 Act and proscribed discrimination in most areas of federal employment. . . .

Appellees assert, and the District Court held, that since the 1972 Act proscribed racial discrimination in Government employment, the Act necessarily, albeit *sub silentio*, repealed the provision of the 1934 Act that called for the preference in the BIA of one racial group, Indians, over non-Indians:

> "When a conflict such as in this case, is present, the most recent law or Act should apply and the conflicting Preferences passed some 39 years earlier should be impliedly repealed." Brief for Appellees 7.

We disagree. For several reasons we conclude that Congress did not intend to repeal the Indian preference and that the District Court erred in holding that it was repealed.

First: There are the above-mentioned affirmative provisions in the 1964 Act excluding coverage of tribal employment and of preferential treatment by a business or enterprise on or near a reservation. . . . See n. 19, supra. These 1964 exemptions as to private employment indicate Congress' recognition of the longstanding federal policy of providing a unique legal status to Indians in matters concerning tribal or "on or near" reservation employment. The exemptions reveal a clear congressional sentiment that an Indian preference in the narrow context of tribal or reservation-related employment did not constitute racial discrimination of the type otherwise proscribed. In extending the general anti-discrimination machinery to federal employment in 1972, Congress in no way modified these private employment preferences built into the 1964 Act, and they are still in effect. It would be anomalous to conclude that Congress intended to eliminate the longstanding statutory preferences in BIA employment, as being racially discriminatory, at the very same time it was reaffirming the right of tribal and reservation-related private employers to provide Indian preference. Appellees' assertion that

---

[20] Senator Mundt supported these exemptions on the Senate floor by claiming that they would allow Indians "to benefit from Indian preference programs now in operation or later to be instituted." 110 Cong. Rec. 13702 (1964).

[21] The 1964 Act, however, did contain a proviso, expressed in somewhat precatory language:

> "That it shall be the policy of the United States to insure equal employment opportunities for Federal employees without discrimination because of race, color, religion, sex or national origin." 78 Stat. 254.

This statement of policy was re-enacted as 5 U.S.C. § 7151, 80 Stat. 523 (1966), and the 1964 Act's proviso was repealed, *id.* at 662.

Congress implicitly repealed the preference as racially discriminatory, while retaining the 1964 preferences, attributes to Congress irrationality and arbitrariness, an attribution we do not share.

Second: Three months after Congress passed the 1972 amendments, it enacted two *new* Indian preference laws. These were part of the Education Amendments of 1972, 86 Stat. 235, 20 U.S.C. §§ 887c(a) and (d), and § 1119a. The new laws explicitly require that Indians be given preference in Government programs for training teachers of Indian children. It is improbable, to say the least, that the same Congress which affirmatively approved and enacted these additional and similar Indian preferences was, at the same time, condemning the BIA preference as racially discriminatory. In the total absence of any manifestation of supportive intent, we are loath[ ] to imply this improbable result.

Third: Indian preferences, for many years, have been treated as exceptions to Executive Orders forbidding Government employment discrimination.[23] The 1972 extension of the Civil Rights Act to Government employment is in large part merely a codification of prior anti-discrimination Executive Orders that had proved ineffective because of inadequate enforcement machinery. There certainly was no indication that the substantive proscription against discrimination was intended to be any broader than that which previously existed. By codifying the existing anti-discrimination provisions, and by providing enforcement machinery for them, there is no reason to presume that Congress affirmatively intended to erase the preferences that previously had co-existed with broad anti-discrimination provisions in Executive Orders.

Fourth: Appellees encounter head-on the "cardinal rule . . . that repeals by implication are not favored." *Posadas v. National City Bank*, 296 U.S. 497, 503 (1936); *Wood v. United States*, 16 Pet. 342–343, 363 (1842); *Universal Interpretive Shuttle Corp. v. Washington Metropolitan Area Transit Comm'n*, 393 U.S. 186, 193 (1968). They and the District Court read the congressional silence as effectuating a repeal by implication. There is nothing in the legislative history, however, that indicates affirmatively any congressional intent to repeal the 1934 preference. Indeed, as explained above, there is ample independent evidence that the legislative intent was to the contrary.

This is a prototypical case where an adjudication of repeal by implication is not appropriate. The preference is a longstanding,

---

[23] See, e.g., Exec. Order No. 7423, July 26, 1936, 1 Fed. Reg. 885–886, 3 CFR 189 (1936–1938 Comp.). When President Eisenhower issued an Order prohibiting discrimination on the basis of race in the civil service, Exec. Order No. 10577, § 4.2, Nov. 22, 1954, 19 Fed. Reg. 7521, 3 CFR 218 (1957–1958 Comp.), he left standing earlier Executive Orders containing exceptions for the Indian service. *Id.* § 301. See also 5 CFR § 213.3112(a)(7), which provides a civil service exemption for:

> "All positions in the Bureau of Indian Affairs and other positions in the Department of the Interior directly and primarily related to the providing of services to Indians when filled by the appointment of Indians who are one-fourth or more Indian blood."

See also 5 CFR § 213.3116(b)(8) (Indian Health Services).

important component of the Government's Indian program. The anti-discrimination provision, aimed at alleviating minority discrimination in employment, obviously is designed to deal with an entirely different and, indeed, opposite problem. Any perceived conflict is thus more apparent than real.

In the absence of some affirmative showing of an intention to repeal, the only permissible justification for a repeal by implication is when the earlier and later statutes are irreconcilable. *Georgia v. Pennsylvania R. Co.*, 324 U.S. 439, 456–457 (1945). Clearly, this is not the case here. A provision aimed at furthering Indian self-government by according an employment preference within the BIA for qualified members of the governed group can readily co-exist with a general rule prohibiting employment discrimination on the basis of race. Any other conclusion can be reached only by formalistic reasoning that ignores both the history and purposes of the preference and the unique legal relationship between the Federal Government and tribal Indians.

Furthermore, the Indian preference statute is a specific provision applying to a very specific situation. The 1972 Act, on the other hand, is of general application. Where there is no clear intention otherwise, a specific statute will not be controlled or nullified by a general one, regardless of the priority of enactment. See, e.g., *Bulova Watch Co. v. United States*, 365 U.S. 753, 758 (1961); *Rodgers v. United States*, 185 U.S. 83, 87–89 (1902).

The courts are not at liberty to pick and choose among congressional enactments, and when two statutes are capable of co-existence, it is the duty of the courts, absent a clearly expressed congressional intention to the contrary, to regard each as effective. "When there are two acts upon the same subject, the rule is to give effect to both if possible . . . . The intention of the legislature to repeal 'must be clear and manifest.' " *United States v. Borden Co.*, 308 U.S. 188, 198 (1939). In light of the factors indicating no repeal, we simply cannot conclude that Congress consciously abandoned its policy of furthering Indian self-government when it passed the 1972 amendments.

We therefore hold that the District Court erred in ruling that the Indian preference was repealed by the 1972 Act.

IV

We still must decide whether, as the appellees contend, the preference constitutes invidious racial discrimination in violation of the Due Process Clause of the Fifth Amendment. *Bolling v. Sharpe*, 347 U.S. 497 (1954). . . .

Resolution of the instant issue turns on the unique legal status of Indian tribes under federal law and upon the plenary power of Congress . . . to legislate on behalf of federally recognized Indian tribes. . . .

. . . .

Contrary to the characterization made by appellees, [the preference established by the Indian Reorganization Act] does not constitute "racial discrimination." Indeed, it is not even a "racial" preference.[24] Rather, it is an employment criterion reasonably designed to make the BIA more responsive to the needs of its constituent groups. It is directed to participation by the governed in the governing agency.... The preference, as applied, is granted to Indians not as a discrete racial group, but, rather, as members of quasi-sovereign tribal entities whose lives and activities are governed by the BIA in a unique fashion. See n. 24, *supra*. ... Furthermore, the preference applies only to employment in the Indian service. The preference does not cover any other Government agency or activity, and we need not consider the obviously more difficult question that would be presented by a blanket exemption for Indians from all civil service examinations. Here, the preference is reasonably and directly related to a legitimate, nonracially based goal....

On numerous occasions this Court specifically has upheld legislation that singles out Indians for particular and special treatment. [Citations omitted.] As long as the special treatment can be tied rationally to the fulfillment of Congress' unique obligation toward the Indians, such legislative judgments will not be disturbed. Here, where the preference is reasonable and rationally designed to further Indian self-government, we cannot say that Congress' classification violates due process.

The judgment of the District Court is reversed and the cases are remanded for further proceedings consistent with this opinion.

NOTES AND QUESTIONS

1. As a matter of statutory interpretation, Part III of Justice Blackmun's opinion held that the Equal Employment Opportunity Act of 1972 (which required federal executive agencies to make all personnel decisions "free from any discrimination based on race ... or national origin") did not countermand the hiring preference that § 12 of the Indian Reorganization Act of 1934 had established for qualified Native Americans within the federal government's "Indian Office." Apart from invoking the presumption against implied repeals, Justice Blackmun advanced three other arguments. Those other arguments, however, were not very strong.

Justice Blackmun's first argument drew on § 703(i) of the Civil Rights Act of 1964. Title VII of the 1964 Act established the general rule

[24] The preference is not directed towards a "racial" group consisting of "Indians"; instead, it applies only to members of "federally recognized" tribes. This operates to exclude many individuals who are racially classified as "Indians." In this sense, the preference is political rather than racial in nature. The eligibility criteria appear in 44 BIAM 335, 3.1:

> ".1 Policy—An Indian has preference in appointment in the Bureau. To be eligible for preference in appointment, promotion, and training, an individual must be one-fourth or more degree Indian blood and be a member of a Federally-recognized tribe. . . ."

that private employers cannot discriminate against any individual, with respect to the terms or conditions of his employment, because of his race or national origin. But § 703(i) made an exception for private businesses located "on or near an Indian reservation": any such business could pursue a "publicly announced employment practice . . . under which a preferential treatment is given to any individual because he is an Indian living on or near a reservation." The 1972 statute prohibiting race discrimination in federal executive agencies left this aspect of Title VII unchanged. Thus, if the 1972 statute were interpreted in the way that the plaintiffs in *Morton v. Mancari* had advocated, the Bureau of Indian Affairs would face a different rule than private businesses located near reservations: although the private businesses could give Native American applicants a categorical preference, the Bureau of Indian Affairs could not. Justice Blackmun suggested that this distinction would be "anomalous," "irrational[ ]," and "arbitrar[y]."

But would it really be so odd for federal statutes to distinguish between the federal government's own employment practices and the employment practices of private businesses? Racial preferences implemented by the federal government raise constitutional issues that racial preferences implemented by private businesses do not. Even apart from any constitutional issues, moreover, there may well be policy arguments for letting certain private businesses engage in certain forms of affirmative action while giving the federal government itself less leeway. At least according to the majority in *United Steelworkers v. Weber* (p. 363 *supra*), the Congress that enacted Title VII cared about preserving considerable flexibility for private businesses. If so, Congress might choose to restrict the government's own employment practices in ways that Congress did not restrict the practices of private businesses.

Indeed, the existence of § 703(i) arguably hurt Justice Blackmun's argument at least as much as it helped. In 1964, when Congress forbade race discrimination in private employment, Congress created a special exception authorizing certain private employers to prefer Native American applicants. But in 1972, when Congress forbade race discrimination in government employment, Congress did *not* create a parallel exception authorizing any federal agencies at all to prefer Native American applicants. Someone sympathetic to *expressio unius* arguments might find this contrast significant.

Justice Blackmun's <u>second</u> argument was also questionable. As he noted, three months after enacting the Equal Employment Opportunity Act of 1972, Congress enacted the Education Amendments of 1972, Pub. L. 92–318, 86 Stat. 235. Two of the subsections in that mammoth statute authorized federal grants for programs to help train teachers who would serve Native American children, and each of those subsections provided that "preference shall be given to the training of Indians." *See id.*

§ 421(a), 86 Stat. at 339–40; § 451(b), 86 Stat. at 344.[34] Justice Blackmun thought it "improbable, to say the least," that the same Congress that explicitly required this preference would have decided, three months earlier, to prohibit the government from preferring Native American applicants for jobs at the Bureau of Indian Affairs. But couldn't Congress have had special reasons for wanting to expand the pool of qualified Native American teachers available to schools that serve Native American children—reasons that would not necessarily extend to jobs at the Bureau of Indian Affairs? To conclude that Congress probably would not have seen any meaningful difference between these two contexts, wouldn't we need to know more about both contexts? In any event, should we be worried about determining the meaning of the Equal Employment Opportunity Act on the basis of policy choices reflected in a later-enacted statute? Did the Equal Employment Opportunity Act mean one thing for the first few months of its existence and something different after Congress enacted the Education Amendments?

Justice Blackmun's <u>third</u> argument seems even less compelling. As he noted, the Equal Employment Opportunity Act of 1972 was "in large part merely a codification of prior . . . Executive Orders" that had broadly forbidden race discrimination in employment in the federal executive branch. *See, e.g.*, Exec. Order No. 9980, 13 Fed. Reg. 4311, 4311 (1948) ("All personnel actions taken by Federal appointing officers shall be based solely on merit and fitness; and such officers are authorized and directed to take appropriate steps to insure that in all such actions there shall be no discrimination because of race, color, religion, or national origin."); *see also* Exec. Order No. 10577, § 4.2, 19 Fed. Reg. 7521, 7523 (1954) ("No discrimination shall be exercised . . . by any person in the executive branch of the Federal Government against or in favor of any employee in the competitive service, or any . . . applicant for a position in the competitive service because of his race, political affiliation, or religious beliefs, except as may be authorized or required by law."). These anti-discrimination executive orders had co-existed with an earlier executive order—issued in conformity with § 12 of the Indian Reorganization Act of 1934—exempting positions in the Bureau of Indian Affairs from competitive examination under the civil-service rules "where the applicants are of one-fourth or more Indian blood." Exec. Order No. 7423, 1 Fed. Reg. 885, 885–86 (1936); *see also, e.g.*, 5 C.F.R. § 213.3112(a)(7) (1973 ed.) (setting forth the successor of this exemption). To the extent that "Indian preferences . . . have been treated as exceptions to [the] Executive Orders forbidding Government employment discrimination," Justice Blackmun argued that they should also be

[34] Because these provisions used the passive voice, they were ambiguous about exactly who was supposed to apply the preference. Did the provisions require all teacher-training programs that received government grants to prefer Native American trainees? Or was the point simply that government grant-makers should apply the preference in deciding which programs to fund?

treated as exceptions to the 1972 statute that grew out of those executive orders.

This argument, however, suffered from at least two flaws. First, the 1972 statute was worded substantially more broadly than the Eisenhower-era executive order that Justice Blackmun most emphasized. *See* Executive Order No. 10577, § 4.2, 19 Fed. Reg. at 7523 (covering only "the competitive service," which did not include the disputed positions in the Bureau of Indian Affairs). Second, and in any event, the fact that the Indian preferences required by § 12 of the 1934 statute had survived the subsequent executive orders forbidding race discrimination in federal employment may tell us less about the proper interpretation of those executive orders than about the hierarchy of federal law. Regardless of what the relevant executive orders were understood to mean, a mere executive order cannot set aside the provisions of a duly enacted statute. As a result, it is both unsurprising and uninformative that the executive orders forbidding race discrimination in the civil service had not been thought to abolish the Indian preferences required by the 1934 statute.

2. If Justice Blackmun's first three arguments were not fully persuasive, then the outcome of *Morton v. Mancari* arguably hinged on his fourth argument, which invoked "the 'cardinal rule . . . that repeals by implication are not favored.' " Still, Justice Blackmun did not make clear how he was using that rule.

One version of the presumption against implied repeals is a tool for resolving linguistic indeterminacy in statutes, and it operates only if there is a relevant indeterminacy. For instance, suppose that one of the provisions in a new federal statute is superficially ambiguous; it could be read in a way that would contradict an earlier federal statute as applied to a particular situation or set of situations, but the provision could instead be read in a way that would be consistent with the earlier statute. The presumption against implied repeals encourages courts to pick the latter interpretation (unless that interpretation is too much of a stretch or countervailing arguments are strong enough to overcome the presumption). In general, if a new federal statute does not acknowledge that it is repealing any aspect of a pre-existing federal statute, and if there are no other signs that the enacting Congress really intended to contradict the earlier statute, interpreters will try to read the new statute to be consistent with the earlier one.

A second, more aggressive version of the presumption against implied repeals would operate as an "implied-limitation" rule. For example, suppose that a federal statute seems to state a broad and unqualified legal directive that, in some of its applications, would contradict the directive established by an earlier federal statute. Even without a conventional linguistic indeterminacy or a textual hook, the presumption against implied repeals might sometimes encourage courts to read an implied limitation into the newer statute so as to preserve the operation of the earlier statute.

Courts might be especially likely to read such an implied limitation into the newer statute in scenarios that fit the following template. Suppose that at Time 1, Congress enacts a statute that contains a fairly specific provision about some particular situation. Later, at Time 2, Congress enacts a second statute that seems, on its face, to contradict the earlier statute as applied to the situation that the earlier statute addressed. But suppose that the second statute is more general than the first statute, and neither the text nor the legislative history of the second statute provides any reason to believe that members of Congress were thinking about the specific situation that the first statute addressed when they enacted the general language of the second statute. Sometimes, courts facing this scenario will read an unstated exception into the second statute; they will infer that the more general statute does not apply to the situation that the earlier statute addressed more specifically.

That is certainly how courts proceed when a *single statute* contains two seemingly contradictory provisions, one specific and one general. In that situation, interpreters typically give the specific provision priority over the general provision; in effect, they treat the specific provision as an exception to the general rule. *See, e.g.*, RadLAX Gateway Hotel, LLC v. Amalgamated Bank, 566 U.S. 639, 645 (2012) (calling this principle "[t]he general/specific canon"); *see also id.* at 645–47 (indicating that within a single statute, this canon can operate not only when the two provisions would otherwise contradict each other, but also when the general provision would otherwise swallow up the specific provision and make its conditions superfluous). But even when the two provisions appear in different enactments, and the statute containing the general provision was enacted more recently than the statute containing the specific provision, courts sometimes read an implied limitation into the general provision so as to preserve the operation of the specific provision. *See, e.g.*, Townsend v. Little, 109 U.S. 504, 512 (1883) (referring to "the well-settled rule" that "general and specific provisions, in apparent contradiction, whether in the same or different statutes, and without regard to priority of enactment, may subsist together, the specific qualifying and supplying exceptions to the general"); ANTONIN SCALIA & BRYAN A. GARNER, READING LAW: THE INTERPRETATION OF LEGAL TEXTS 185 (2012) (agreeing that "the general/specific canon" applies not only within a single statute but also across statutes).

Which version of the presumption against implied repeals was Justice Blackmun using in *Morton v. Mancari*? Did he think that the language of the 1972 statute was ambiguous in some respect that the presumption against implied repeals could be invoked to resolve, or was he simply reading an unstated exception into the 1972 statute to preserve the longstanding hiring preference at the Bureau of Indian Affairs?

3. Does the presumption against implied repeals have any normative appeal, or is it a purely "descriptive" canon (aimed at capturing some form of legislative intent)?

As a normative matter, Burkeans might want each new legislature to build upon what has gone before rather than contradicting it. *Cf.* David L. Shapiro, *Continuity and Change in Statutory Interpretation*, 67 N.Y.U. L. REV. 921, 925, 937 (1992) (praising the courts' "tendency to favor continuity over change" and indicating that the presumption against implied repeals "recogniz[es] the value of minimal disruption of existing arrangements consistent with the language and purpose of the new law"). That idea, however, would seem to support a presumption against *all* repeals—and hence a presumption that even statutory provisions *expressly* repealing any aspects of prior laws should be construed as narrowly as possible. Likewise, the Burkean idea would also support the presumption that statutes in derogation of the common law should be strictly construed—a presumption that bygone courts invoked quite frequently, but that has become disreputable. *Cf. id.* at 936–37 (acknowledging that this presumption is "[o]ne of the . . . most maligned maxims of statutory construction," but arguing that it "should be viewed more sympathetically" and linking it to the presumption against implied repeals). If we do not narrowly construe statutes to avoid derogation of the common law, and if we also do not narrowly construe statutes that expressly repeal past statutes, is there any normative basis for recognizing a special presumption against *implied* repeals of past statutes—that is, for disfavoring repeals of past statutes more than we disfavor changes to the common law, and for disfavoring implied repeals of past statutes more than we disfavor express repeals?

The distinction between implied repeals and express repeals, at least, might be defended on the normative ground that implied repeals generate more uncertainty than express repeals. But does that defense work when the presumption against implied repeals is operating as an implied-limitation rule (encouraging courts to read unstated exceptions into one statute so as to preserve the operation of another)? If the underlying normative idea is that legislatures should not leave things to implication, why is it better to recognize implied limitations than to find implied repeals?

4. The most common justifications for the presumption against implied repeals are descriptive rather than normative; that is, they portray the presumption as a guide to likely legislative intent. But those justifications too may be more persuasive for the version of the presumption that is triggered by conventional linguistic indeterminacy than for the version that operates as an implied-limitation rule.

Start with cases of conventional linguistic indeterminacy. Suppose that Congress enacted Statute #1 at Time 1 and Statute #2 at Time 2, and suppose that Statute #2 contains no reference to Statute #1. Suppose further that Statute #2 could fairly be read to establish either of two legal directives—Directive A, which would contradict some aspects or applications of Statute #1, or Directive B, which could co-exist with Statute #1 in all respects. The fact that Statute #2 does not say anything about repealing Statute #1 *pro tanto*—that is, the fact that any repeal would be implied rather than express—might itself suggest that members of the enacting Congress intended to establish Directive B rather than Directive A. If they had understood themselves to be contradicting something in Statute #1, one might think that they would have enacted language explicitly referring to Statute #1 and saying that it was being superseded.

Admittedly, that argument rests on the potentially unrealistic assumption that at least some members of the Congress that enacted Statute #2 knew about Statute #1. But even if no one in Congress had Statute #1 in mind when Congress enacted Statute #2, interpreters who are trying to identify the intended meaning of Statute #2 might still favor at least a weak presumption that Statute #2 is consistent with Statute #1 (especially if Time 2 came relatively soon after Time 1 and there were no significant political realignments in the interim). If we have no other information about the policy preferences of the later Congress, but we know that an earlier Congress favored the policy reflected in Statute #1 enough to overcome legislative inertia and enact it into law, maybe we should assume that members of later Congresses would continue to find that policy acceptable and would not intend to contradict it.

Are there also "descriptive" justifications for the other possible version of the presumption against implied repeals—the one that would operate as an implied-limitation rule? Suppose that instead of containing a conventional linguistic indeterminacy, Statute #2 seems unambiguous on its face and appears to contradict Statute #1 as applied to the situation that Statute #1 addresses. If Statute #2 were indeed understood to contradict Statute #1, it would impliedly repeal Statute #1 *pro tanto*. *See supra* p. 705 (noting that when two statutes enacted by the same legislative body conflict, the more recently enacted one wins). Still, suppose that Statute #1 is quite specific, while Statute #2 is more general. In *Morton v. Mancari*, the Supreme Court asserted that "[w]here there is no clear intention otherwise, a specific statute will not be controlled or nullified by a general one, regardless of the priority of enactment." *Morton*, 417 U.S. at 550–51. As applied to the hypothetical situation that we are considering now, that statement might encourage courts to read an unstated exception into Statute #2 so as to preserve the operation of Statute #1 in the specific situation that Statute #1 addressed. Could a presumption along those lines be defended as a plausible guide to the intended meaning of Statute #2?

If the general language of Statute #2 is indeed unambiguous (as we are assuming in order to separate the version of the presumption against implied repeals that is triggered by conventional linguistic indeterminacy from the version that operates as an implied-limitation rule), then the presumption that Statute #2 accommodates Statute #1 probably does not reflect the *conscious* intentions of the legislators who enacted Statute #2. After all, Statute #2 states a general rule without referring to Statute #1 or explicitly exempting the situation that Statute #1 addresses. If the general rule stated in Statute #2 unambiguously covers that situation along with others, the legislators who enacted Statute #2 probably did not consciously understand themselves to be making an exception to preserve the operation of Statute #1. Instead, the best case scenario for the application of the presumption against implied repeals is that when they enacted the general language of Statute #2, they simply were not thinking about the situation that Statute #1 addresses. The "descriptive" argument for reading an unstated exception into Statute #2 rests on a claim about what they *would have* intended *if* they had considered this issue. In other words, the argument depends on a species of imaginative reconstruction.

Devotees of imaginative reconstruction might believe that the technique is justified in this situation. Suppose it is true (as all versions of the presumption against implied repeals assume) that when members of Congress are deliberately trying to override an earlier statute, they typically enact express language of repeal. If so, then the fact that Statute #2 seems on its face to contradict Statute #1, but does not contain any express language of repeal, is a sign that something has gone wrong. Perhaps members of the Congress that enacted Statute #2 did not deliberately intend to override Statute #1; perhaps they were entirely unaware of that statute, or perhaps they did not anticipate the circumstances that have brought the two statutes into conflict. In situations of this sort, interpreters might think that some type of imaginative reconstruction is justified. And even if you do not want courts to conduct imaginative reconstruction on an *ad hoc* basis, you might not object to having courts apply some rule-like canons that reflect what legislators usually would want under the circumstances that the canons address. Indeed, that is one way to explain other prominent implied-limitation rules, including the presumption against retroactivity and the presumption against extraterritoriality.

Even if you are open to this sort of argument, though, it is not clear that imaginative reconstruction really supports the implied-limitation version of the presumption against implied repeals. Suppose it is true that when Congress enacted the general language of Statute #2, members of Congress were not specifically contemplating the situation that Statute #1 addressed. Is there some reason to assume that if they had known about Statute #1 and had realized that it might come into conflict with Statute #2, they probably would have limited the operation of Statute #2 so as to preserve the operation of the older statute?

In several opinions and articles, Judge Posner suggested that the opposite assumption might be more plausible: if the Congress that enacted the newer statute had been aware of the apparent conflict between its statute and the older law, maybe it would have expressly repealed the portions of the older law that contradict its newly chosen policy. As Judge Posner asked, "If two statutes conflict, why would the legislature that enacted the second want the first . . . to take precedence?" *In re Doctors Hosp. of Hyde Park, Inc.*, 337 F.3d 951, 960 (7th Cir. 2003); *see also* Friedrich v. City of Chicago, 888 F.2d 511, 516 (7th Cir. 1989) (Posner, J.), *vacated*, 499 U.S. 933 (1991); Edwards v. United States, 814 F.2d 486, 488 (7th Cir. 1987) (Posner, J.); Richard A. Posner, *Statutory Interpretation—in the Classroom and in the Courtroom*, 50 U. CHI. L. REV. 800, 812–13 (1983).

Judge Posner's point is obviously powerful. But is it correct in all circumstances? Can you identify any categories of situations in which it might be more likely than not that if the later legislature had been thinking about the situation addressed by the earlier statute, the legislature would have wanted to preserve the operation of the earlier statute? (In other words, to the extent that the implied-limitation version of the presumption against implied repeals rests on imaginative reconstruction, when is it most plausible?)

The next case involves a statutory provision that also made an appearance in *Wachovia Bank v. Schmidt* (p. 673 above). That provision, which was in force for many years, addressed the proper venue for suits against national banking associations in both state and federal courts.

Congress originally enacted this venue provision as part of the National Bank Act of 1864, ch. 106, § 57, 13 Stat. 99, 116–17. Congress omitted the provision from the Revised Statutes of 1874 (which repealed prior laws on the subject), but Congress reenacted the provision in 1875. *See* An Act to Correct Errors and to Supply Omissions in the Revised Statutes of the United States, ch. 80, 18 Stat. 316, 320 (1875) (amending Rev. Stat. § 5198). As enacted in 1875, the provision read as follows:

> "[S]uits, actions, and proceedings against any association under this title may be had in any circuit, district, or territorial court of the United States held within the district in which such association may be established, or in any State, county, or municipal court in the county or city in which said association is located having jurisdiction in similar cases."

Id. Case law under the corresponding provision of the National Bank Act indicated that the phrase "under this title" went with "association," not "suits, actions, and proceedings." *See* Cadle v. Tracy, 4 F. Cas. 967, 970–71 (C.C.S.D.N.Y. 1873) (No. 2,279). Thus, the provision was understood to identify the proper venues for suits against "any association under this title"—that is, any national bank. In 1911, because of changes to the structure of the federal judiciary, Congress effectively eliminated the provision's reference to federal circuit courts. *See* An Act to Codify, Revise, and Amend the Laws Relating to the Judiciary, ch. 231, § 291, 36

Stat. 1087, 1167 (1911). Otherwise, though, Congress left the provision unchanged from 1875 until 1982.[35] At the time of the next case, the provision was codified at 12 U.S.C. § 94, but it still owed its legal force to its enactment in 1875.

In *Mercantile National Bank v. Langdeau*, 371 U.S. 555 (1963), the Supreme Court held that this provision not only specified certain *proper* venues for suits against national banks in state court, but also implicitly made other venues *improper*. In particular, *Langdeau* held that state law could not validly permit suits against a national bank to proceed in state courts outside the county or city in which the bank was "located" (as 12 U.S.C. § 94 used that term). By the same token, *Langdeau* arguably suggested that the special venue provision in 12 U.S.C. § 94 for suits against national banks in *federal* court was also exclusive: venue would not properly lie outside the federal judicial districts in which the banks were "established." *See Langdeau*, 371 U.S. at 562 n.13; *see also, e.g.*, Int'l Refugee Org. v. Bank of Am., 86 F. Supp. 884, 886 (S.D.N.Y. 1949) (describing 12 U.S.C. § 94 as "one of the exceptions to the general venue section, § 1391 of Title 28"). At the time of the next case, moreover, many courts were narrowly interpreting the words "located" and "established" in 12 U.S.C. § 94, with the result that 12 U.S.C. § 94 sharply restricted the proper venues for suits against national banks. *See* 14D CHARLES ALAN WRIGHT *ET AL.*, FEDERAL PRACTICE AND PROCEDURE § 3813 at 358–59 (2007) (citing cases). *But cf.* Citizens & Southern National Bank v. Bougas, 434 U.S. 35 (1977) (ultimately adopting a broader interpretation at least of the word "located" in 12 U.S.C. § 94).

In the next case, the Supreme Court had to decide how 12 U.S.C. § 94 interacted with the more recent venue provision in the Securities Exchange Act of 1934, ch. 404, tit. I, 48 Stat. 881. Without specifically addressing suits against national banks, § 27 of the Securities Exchange Act said that "[a]ny suit or action to enforce any liability or duty created by [the Securities Exchange Act] or rules and regulations thereunder . . . may be brought" in any of a potentially broad array of federal judicial districts. *Id.* § 27, 48 Stat. at 903 (codified as amended at 15 U.S.C. § 78aa). Did that provision apply to suits against national banks just as it applied to suits against other defendants? Or would venue for suits against national banks, even for alleged violations of the Securities Exchange Act, lie only in the federal judicial districts identified by 12 U.S.C. § 94?

[35] In 1982, Congress all but eliminated the provision. *See* Act of Oct. 15, 1982, Pub. L. 97–320, § 406, 96 Stat. 1469, 1512.

Radzanower v. Touche Ross & Co.

426 U.S. 148 (1976)

■ *JUSTICE STEWART delivered the opinion of the Court:*

This case requires us to determine which venue provision controls in the event a national banking association is sued in a federal court for allegedly violating the Securities Exchange Act of 1934: the broad venue provision of the Securities Exchange Act, which allows suits under that Act to be brought in any district where the defendant may be found, or the narrow venue provision of the National Bank Act, which allows national banking associations to be sued only in the district where they are established.

The petitioner, Hyman Radzanower, instituted a class action in the District Court for the Southern District of New York alleging, *inter alia*, that the respondent, First National Bank of Boston, a national banking association with its principal office in Boston, Mass., had violated the federal securities laws by failing to disclose to the Securities and Exchange Commission and the investing public its knowledge of certain adverse financial information about one of its customers, the TelePrompter Corporation, and of securities laws violations by that company. The complaint alleged that venue was proper under § 27 of the Securities Exchange Act of 1934, 48 Stat. 902, 15 U.S.C. § 78aa, which provides that "[a]ny suit or action to enforce any liability or duty created [by or under the Securities Exchange Act] . . . may be brought in any such district [wherein any act or transaction constituting the violation occurred] or in the district wherein the defendant is found or is an inhabitant or transacts business . . . ." The bank moved to dismiss the complaint as to it, asserting that venue as to it lay only under the venue provision of the National Bank Act, Rev. Stat. § 5198 (1878), 12 U.S.C. § 94. . . .[1]

Following the settled law of the Second Circuit, the District Court granted the bank's motion to dismiss. It held that "[a]bsent waiver or consent, a national bank may be sued only in the district in which it is established. 12 U.S.C. § 94." The court noted that the bank was established in Boston "because its charter specifies Boston as its principal place of business"[2] . . . . The Court of Appeals affirmed without

[1] Section 94 in its entirety reads:

"Actions and proceedings against any association under this chapter may be had in any district or Territorial court of the United States held within the district in which such association may be established, or in any State, county, or municipal court in the county or city in which said association is located having jurisdiction in similar cases." [12 U.S.C. § 94 (1970 ed.).]

[2] The petitioner does not claim that the bank is "established" anywhere else than in Boston. Federal courts have consistently ruled that the place specified in a bank's charter as its home office is determinative of the district in which the bank is "established" for purposes of § 94. See, e.g., *Buffum v. Chase Nat. Bank*, 192 F.2d 58, 60 (CA7); *Leonardi v. Chase Nat. Bank*, 81 F.2d 19, 22 (CA2).

opinion. Because of differing views in the Circuits as to the statutory venue question presented, we granted the petition for certiorari. . . .

Section 94 provides that suits against a national banking association "may be had" in the federal district court for the district where such association is established. The Court has held that this grant of venue is mandatory and exclusive: "The phrase 'suits . . . may be had' was, in every respect, appropriate language for the purpose of specifying the precise courts in which Congress consented to have national banks subject to suit and we believe Congress intended that in those courts alone could a national bank be sued against its will." *Mercantile Nat. Bank v. Langdeau*, 371 U.S. 555, 560 . . . .[6] The venue provision of the Securities Exchange Act, by contrast, allows suits under that Act to be brought anywhere that the Act is violated or a defendant does business or can otherwise be found. It is the petitioner's contention that when a national bank is named as a defendant in a suit brought under the Securities Exchange Act, it loses the protection of the venue provisions of § 94 and may be sued in any federal judicial district where that Act was violated or where it does business or can be found. For the reasons that follow, we cannot accept that contention.

It is a basic principle of statutory construction that a statute dealing with a narrow, precise, and specific subject is not submerged by a later enacted statute covering a more generalized spectrum. "Where there is no clear intention otherwise, a specific statute will not be controlled or nullified by a general one, regardless of the priority of enactment." *Morton v. Mancari*, 417 U.S. 535, 550–551.[7] "The reason and philosophy of the rule is, that when the mind of the legislator has been turned to the details of a subject, and he has acted upon it, a subsequent statute in general terms, or treating the subject in a general manner, and not expressly contradicting the original act, shall not be considered as intended to affect the more particular or positive previous provisions, unless it is absolutely necessary to give the latter act such a construction, in order that its words shall have any meaning at all." T. Sedgwick, The Interpretation and Construction of Statutory and Constitutional Law 98 (2d ed. 1874).[8]

When Congress enacted the narrow venue provisions of the National Bank Act, it was focusing on the particularized problems of national

---

6 When the *Langdeau* Court held that the words "may be had" serve to provide mandatory and exclusive venue, it was dealing with the relationship of § 94 to a state venue statute. Since the same words are used in connection with the federal-court venue provision, the same construction is virtually inescapable. "[I]t would indeed strain language to say that the same verbs were merely permissive with respect to suits in federal courts although prohibitory as to actions in state ones." *Bruns, Nordeman & Co. v. American Nat. Bank*, [394 F.2d 300, 303 (CA2)].

7 . . . . See also *Fourco Glass Co. v. Transmirra Products Corp.*, 353 U.S. 222; *Stonite Products Co. v. Melvin Lloyd Co.*, 315 U.S. 561 (specific venue statutes for patent suits prevail over general venue statutes).

8 See also 1A J. Sutherland, Statutes and Statutory Construction § 23.15 (4th ed. C. Sands 1972).

banks that might be sued in the state or federal courts. When, 70 years later, Congress enacted the Securities Exchange Act, its focus was on the objective of promoting fair dealing in the securities markets, and it enacted a general venue provision applicable to the broad universe of potential defendants subject to the prohibitions of that Act. Thus, unless a "clear intention otherwise" can be discerned, the principle of statutory construction discussed above counsels that the specific venue provisions of § 94 are applicable to the respondent bank in this case. *Fourco Glass Co. v. Transmirra Products Corp.*, 353 U.S. 222.

The issue thus boils down to whether a "clear intention otherwise" can be discovered—whether, in short, it can be fairly concluded that the venue provision of the Securities Exchange Act operated as a *pro tanto* repeal[*] of § 94. "It is, of course, a cardinal principle of statutory construction that repeals by implication are not favored." *United States v. United Continental Tuna Corp.*, 425 U.S. 164, 168. There are, however,

> "two well-settled categories of repeals by implication—(1) where provisions in the two acts are in irreconcilable conflict, the later act to the extent of the conflict constitutes an implied repeal of the earlier one; and (2) if the later act covers the whole subject of the earlier one and is clearly intended as a substitute, it will operate similarly as a repeal of the earlier act. But, in either case, the intention of the legislature to repeal must be clear and manifest. . . ." *Posadas v. National City Bank*, 296 U.S. 497, 503.

It is evident that the "two acts" in this case fall into neither of those categories.

The statutory provisions at issue here cannot be said to be in "irreconcilable conflict" in the sense that there is a positive repugnancy between them or that they cannot mutually coexist. It is not enough to show that the two statutes produce differing results when applied to the same factual situation, for that no more than states the problem. Rather, "when two statutes are capable of co-existence, it is the duty of the courts . . . to regard each as effective." *Morton v. Mancari*, 417 U.S. at 551. As the Court put the matter in discussing the interrelationship of the antitrust laws and the securities laws: "Repeal is to be regarded as implied only if necessary to make the [later enacted law] work, and even then only to the minimum extent necessary. This is the guiding principle to reconciliation of the two statutory schemes." *Silver v. New York Stock Exchange*, 373 U.S. 341, 357.

Here the basic purposes of the Securities Exchange Act can be fairly served by giving full effect to the provisions of 12 U.S.C. § 94. The primary purpose of the Securities Exchange Act was not to regulate the activities of national banks as such but "[t]o provide fair and honest

[*] *Editor's note*: The Latin phrase "*pro tanto*" means "for so much." To say that a newer statute operates as a "*pro tanto* repeal" of an older statute is to say that the newer statute repeals the older one to the extent of any conflict between them.

mechanisms for the pricing of securities [and] to assure that dealing in securities is fair and without undue preferences or advantages among investors . . . ." H.R. Rep. No. 94–229, p. 91 (1975).[11] Its venue provision, § 27, was intended to facilitate that goal by enabling suits to enforce rights created by the Act to be brought wherever a defendant could be found. The venue provision of the National Bank Act, § 94, was intended, on the other hand, "for the convenience of those [banking] institutions, and to prevent interruption in their business that might result from their books being sent to distant counties . . . ." *Charlotte Nat. Bank v. Morgan*, 132 U.S. 141, 145, quoted in *Mercantile Nat. Bank v. Langdeau*, 371 U.S. at 561–562, n. 12.

By allowing suits against national banks to be brought only pursuant to § 94, the purposes of that section will obviously be served. Yet application of § 94 will not "unduly interfere" with the operation of the Securities Exchange Act. See *Gordon v. New York Stock Exchange*, 422 U.S. 659, 686. Section 94 will have no impact whatever upon the vast majority of lawsuits brought under that Act. In the tiny fraction of litigation where its effect will be felt, it will foreclose nobody from invoking the Act's provisions. Members of the investing public will still be free to bring actions against national banks under the Act. While suits against this narrow and infrequent category of defendants will have to be brought where the defendant is established, that is hardly an insurmountable burden in this day of easy and rapid transportation. Since it is possible for the statutes to coexist in this manner, they are not so repugnant to each other as to justify a finding of an implied repeal by this Court. It is simply not "necessary" that § 94 be repealed in part in order "to make the Securities Exchange Act work." See *Silver v. New York Stock Exchange*, [373 U.S.] at 357.

Moreover, it cannot be said either that "the later act covers the whole subject of the earlier one and is clearly intended as a substitute," or that "the intention of the legislature to repeal [is] clear and manifest." [*Posadas*,] 296 U.S. at 503. The Securities Exchange Act of 1934 covers a "subject" quite different from the National Bank Act. The 1934 Act was enacted primarily to halt securities fraud, not to regulate banks. Indeed, banks were specifically exempted from many provisions of the securities laws,[13] and Congress almost contemporaneously enacted other specific legislation dealing with the problems arising from banks' involvement in the securities business. The passage of that legislation and the exemption of national banks from important provisions of the securities laws suggest, if anything, that Congress was reaffirming its view that national

[11] The legislative history of the Securities Acts does not indicate that Congress considered banks as likely defendants in actions brought under those Acts. While Congress did examine problems stemming from the relationship of banks and the securities business in the early 1930's, see S. Rep. No. 1455, 73d Cong., 2d Sess. (1934), it dealt with those problems in comprehensive legislation dealing only with banks. See Banking Act of 1933, 48 Stat. 162. See generally *Investment Co. Institute v. Camp*, 401 U.S. 617.

[13] See 15 U.S.C. §§ 77c(a)(2), 77*l*(2); cf. 15 U.S.C. § 78c(a)(6).

banks should be regulated separately by specific legislation applying only to them.[15] And there is nothing in the legislative history of the Securities Exchange Act to support the view that Congress in enacting it gave the slightest consideration to the *pro tanto* repeal of § 94, let alone to indicate "that Congress consciously abandoned its [prior] policy," *Morton v. Mancari*, 417 U.S. at 551, or that its intent to repeal § 94 *pro tanto* was " 'clear and manifest,' " *United States v. Borden Co.*, 308 U.S. 188, 198, quoting *Red Rock v. Henry*, 106 U.S. 596, 602.[16]

For these reasons it is impossible to conclude that § 94 was partially repealed by implication in 1934. It follows under the general principles of statutory construction discussed above that the narrowly drawn, specific venue provision of the National Bank Act must prevail over the broader, more generally applicable venue provision of the Securities Exchange Act. We conclude, therefore, that a national banking association is subject to suit under the Securities Exchange Act only in that district wherein it is established, and that the judgment before us must accordingly be affirmed.

■ *JUSTICE STEVENS dissented:*

In my judgment a brief reference to the history, purpose, and language of these two special venue statutes will provide a better guide to their meaning than the exposition of the doctrine of implied repeal found in the treatise on statutory construction written by Sedgwick in 1874. Indeed, if Sedgwick were to be our guide, I would heed this advice: "When acts can be harmonized by a fair and liberal construction it must be done."[1]

It is worth repeating that both of these statutes are special venue statutes. Neither party relies on the general venue provision in 28 U.S.C. § 1391. One relies on a special statute for one kind of litigant—national banks; the other relies on a special statute for one kind of litigation—cases arising under the Securities Exchange Act of 1934. The precise issue before us involves only a tiny fraction of the cases in either special category: Most litigation against national banks does not arise under the Securities Exchange Act; and most litigation arising under the Securities Exchange Act does not involve national banks. Thus, with equal logic we

---

[15] This intention was expressly stated by Congress when it exempted bank securities from the registration statements requirements of the Securities Act of 1933: "[A]dequate supervision over the issuance of securities of a national bank is exercised by the Comptroller of the Currency." H.R. Rep. No. 85, 73d Cong., 1st Sess., 14 (1933). Subsequent Congresses have continued to follow this policy. For example, while national banks are subject to the registration, reporting, and proxy requirements of the Securities Exchange Act, in 1964 Congress amended the Act so that the administration of those parts of the Act with respect to banks was transferred from the SEC to the various federal banking authorities. See § 3(e), 78 Stat. 568, 15 U.S.C. § 78*l*(i).

[16] In 1959 Congress reviewed the National Bank Act and adopted an Act designed "to repeal certain [national banking] laws which have become obsolete." See Pub. L. 86–230, 73 Stat. 457. When it did so, it did not repeal § 94.

[1] T. Sedgwick, The Interpretation and Construction of Statutory and Constitutional Law 98 n. (a) (2d ed. 1874). . . .

might describe either statute as creating an exception from the somewhat more general provisions of the other.

The rule that the legislature presumably intended to give effect to the more specific statute could therefore be applied to support the petitioner, as well as the respondent bank, in this case.[2] Similarly, without pausing to consider the reason why each statute was enacted, we might simply apply the rule that the more recent of two conflicting statutes shall prevail, rather than the rule that the special statute takes precedence over the general. But such abstract reasoning is less instructive than a consideration of the source and the need for the alleged conflict. Of special importance is an evaluation of the intent of Congress when it enacted these statutes.

The source of the special venue statute for national banks is the Act to Provide a National Currency enacted in 1863 and amended in 1864.[5] When these statutes were enacted, Congress apparently assumed that the newly authorized national banks would not be subject to suit in state courts unless Congress gave its express consent.[6] The fact that the statute was phrased in permissive language suggests that Congress' primary purpose was to give such consent. The mandatory construction given to that language a century later when the Court decided *Mercantile Nat. Bank v. Langdeau*, 371 U.S. 555, is consistent with that purpose because it is unlikely that the Civil War Congress intended to authorize the several States to subject national banks to the potential harassment of defending litigation in places other than the county or city where the bank was located. This reason for placing a mandatory limiting construction on the authorization for suit in the state courts is not applicable to the separately enacted federal venue provision; for in any event the federal courts could only entertain such litigation against national banks as Congress might authorize.

In 1934 when Congress enacted the Securities Exchange Act, there was no reason for it to assume that the language in the special jurisdictional and venue provisions of that statute would not apply to

---

[2] The rule that the more specific legislation will usually take precedence over the more general rests on the quite reasonable assumption that the legislature's attention was probably focused more directly on the subject matter of the specific than on only one aspect of a much broader subject matter. But since the venue provision of the Civil War banking legislation was a relatively inconsequential part of the entire statute, there is no reason to assume that it was given any more attention than the venue provision in the Securities Exchange Act of 1934.

[5] The federal venue provision was first enacted in 1863, 12 Stat. 681, and in the following year, the provision was amended to authorize suit in state courts. Section 57 of the 1864 Act, which is the predecessor of 12 U.S.C. § 94, reads, in pertinent part as follows:

> "Sec. 57. And be it further enacted, That suits, actions, and proceedings, against any association under this act, may be had in any circuit, district, or territorial court of the United States held within the district in which such association may be established; or in any state, county, or municipal court in the county or city in which said association is located, having jurisdiction in similar cases: Provided, however, That all proceedings to enjoin the comptroller under this act shall be had in a circuit, district, or territorial court of the United States, held in the district in which the association is located." 13 Stat. 116.

[6] See *Charlotte Nat. Bank v. Morgan*, 132 U.S. 141, 144; *First Nat. Bank v. Union Trust Co.*, 244 U.S. 416, 428.

national banks. *Langdeau* would not be decided until almost 30 years later, the language in the venue provision of the Civil War banking legislation was permissive, and there was no recognized policy reason supporting an exceptional venue privilege for national banks in federal litigation. There was no longer any doubt about the suability of national banks in either state or federal courts. Moreover, what once might have been regarded as the significant burden of requiring a fledgling bank to haul its records from one county to another within the State, would hardly justify treating banks differently from other litigants in the 20th century.

On the other hand, the special venue section included in the Securities Acts was specifically designed to implement an important legislative objective. Indeed, in construing the comparable provision in the 1933 statute, the Court held that its benefits are so crucial to the legislative purpose that they cannot be waived [at least in advance of a dispute]. [*Wilko v. Swan*, 346 U.S. 427.] In contrast, it is well settled that a national bank's special venue privilege is waivable. Manifestly, there is a difference between the importance of the policies underlying the two statutes.

But there is no necessary conflict. Since the two Acts can be harmonized by a fair and liberal construction, if we heed Sedgwick's counsel, that "must be done." As already noted, the actual wording of the earlier statute, which used the words "may be had" provides no conflict with a literal reading of the later Act. The conflict is created solely by this Court's interpretation of those words as, in effect, meaning that the trial of a case against a national bank "must be had" in the place specified by Congress rather than the place specified by a state legislature. If we so read the statute, we need only conclude that any later enacted special venue statute which, by its own terms, applies to national banks should be read to mean what it says. Preoccupation with the ancient doctrine of implied repeal should not foreclose this simple construction of the plain language of the 1934 Act.

The rule that repeals by implication are not favored, like all other canons of statutory construction, is merely one of the guidelines to observe in the search for a construction which will best reflect the real intent of the legislature. When we are dealing with a well-established and clearly defined old rule, it is usually reasonable to suppose that the legislative intent to change such a rule would be unambiguously expressed. Or if we are dealing with an old rule that is an established and important part of our national policy, we must be sure that it is not changed simply by inadvertent use of broad statutory language. Thus, if Congress intended to modify the long-settled practice of preferential hiring of Indians on Indian reservations, or to limit the coverage of a statute as important as the Sherman Act, a court would require an unambiguous expression of intent to make such a change; without such an expression it is reasonable to believe that inadvertence, rather than an intent to repeal, is the actual explanation for the broad language that arguably changes the old rule.[13] But if neither the existence of, nor the reason for, the old rule is clear at the time of the later enactment, there is no special reason for questioning the legislative intent to have the later statute mean exactly what it says. Specifically, in this case, since it is clear that Congress intended national banks to be covered by some sections of the Securities Exchange Act, but not others,[14] and since the purpose of authorizing a broader venue in this type of litigation applies with equal force to national banks and other defendants, the canon of construction strikes me as an unreliable guide for ascertaining the true intent of Congress.

Congress may well have simply overlooked the special venue provision in the Civil War statute, particularly since *Langdeau* had not yet been decided. It may therefore be accurate to describe the omission of any reference to the earlier statute in the legislative history of the later one as inadvertent. But that merely raises the question of whether it is more realistic to imply an exception to the applicable language of the 1934 Act or to conclude that if Congress had thought about this preference for national banks it nevertheless would have enacted the statute it did enact in 1934. There is no doubt in my mind that the 1934 Congress would have done exactly what it did do even if it had foreseen not only this Court's decision in *Langdeau* but also the Court's willingness to construe the federal venue provision in the same "Draconian" fashion as the state provision, to use Judge Friendly's typically appropriate adjective. I could understand a legislative decision to exempt banks entirely from the coverage of the new law on the theory that an interest in the solvency of national banks entitles them to special immunity, but it seems wholly unrealistic to assume that Congress would treat banks like all other defendants for liability purposes and yet treat them differently for venue purposes.

It is true that we are dealing with only a tiny fraction of the litigation arising under the 1934 Act or of the litigation involving national banks. But that fact merely minimizes the likelihood that a busy Congress will correct an inequitable and anachronistic situation. It is also true that holding the trial in one forum rather than another is hardly an insurmountable burden on either the plaintiff or the bank in this day of easy and rapid transportation—unlike the situation in the Civil War

[13] When Congress intends to change a well-recognized and well-established rule of law, it customarily provides us with evidence of that specific intent. But it is unrealistic to expect the Legislature to consider and expressly mention the impact of a new statute on every old rule that it may modify, particularly if the old rule is not only unimportant but not even clearly stated at the time the new statute is enacted. In such a setting the new statute should be interpreted in the light of its own history with the expectation that a certain amount of ancient underbrush will inevitably be cut away. Only to the extent that the old roots retain sufficient vitality to support some desirable and discernible purpose at the time of the later enactment is there any real justification for avoiding an implied repeal.

[14] The Securities Act of 1933 contains explicit exemptions for national banks at 15 U.S.C. §§ 77c(a)(2), 77*l*(2), as does the Securities Exchange Act at 15 U.S.C. § 78*l*(i).

period when the statute that the Court considers controlling was enacted—but the burden on the judiciary is increased by requiring multiple trials whenever national banks participate in an allegedly unlawful securities offering.

In sum, whatever canon of statutory construction is applied, I am persuaded that we are most apt to reflect the intent of Congress faithfully if we give effect to the plain meaning of the 1934 Act and thereby place banks on an equal footing with other corporations which must defend litigation of this kind. . . .

NOTES AND QUESTIONS

1. Assume, as precedent suggested, that 12 U.S.C. § 94 was impliedly exclusive: it identified the *only* federal judicial districts in which national banks could be sued. Read literally, the venue provision of the Securities Exchange Act would have superseded that restriction for one category of suits against national banks—suits brought against national banks under the Securities Exchange Act. But the majority in *Radzanower* refused to reach that conclusion. To avoid having to recognize an implied repeal *pro tanto* of 12 U.S.C. § 94, the majority instead read an implied limitation into the venue provision of the Securities Exchange Act. In effect, the majority interpreted § 27 of the Securities Exchange Act to provide that *except for suits against national banks*, suits under the Securities Exchange Act could be brought in any of the federal judicial districts that § 27 identified.

To justify this conclusion, the majority invoked the "basic principle of statutory construction that a statute dealing with a narrow, precise, and specific subject is not submerged by a later enacted statute covering a more generalized spectrum." *Radzanower*, 426 U.S. at 153. That principle is best understood as a canon about how to interpret the later statute (here, the Securities Exchange Act): notwithstanding its apparent generality, the later statute should be read to accommodate the more specific provisions of previous statutes. Again, though, it is worth thinking about the basis for that canon.

The majority did not suggest that when Congress enacted § 27 of the Securities Exchange Act in 1934, members of Congress consciously understood § 27 to distinguish between national banks and other potential defendants. To the contrary, the majority assumed that members of Congress were not thinking about national banks at all when they enacted § 27. The point of the canon, as applied to this case, seemed to be that *if* members of Congress had thought about suits against national banks when they enacted § 27, they probably would have wanted to adhere to what their predecessors had said in the National Bank Act—the last federal statute that specifically addressed venue for suits against national banks.

As applied to this case, how plausible is that exercise in imaginative reconstruction? Does it seem likely that if Congress in 1934 had specifically considered the possibility that national banks might violate the Securities Exchange Act, Congress would have wanted the venue provision in § 27 to treat them differently than all other defendants? Or was Justice Stevens right to consider that surmise "wholly unrealistic"?

2. Even if one accepts the principle that "specific" provisions are not superseded by "general" ones (even if the "general" provisions were enacted more recently), how often will there be doubt about the proper application of those labels? In *Radzanower* itself, the majority said that the venue provision in the Securities Exchange Act was "general" (because it addressed securities lawsuits against the entire universe of potential defendants), while the venue provision in the National Bank Act was "specific" (because it dealt specifically with suits against national banks). But wasn't Justice Stevens right that one could readily flip these labels? That is, couldn't one plausibly say that the venue provision in the National Bank Act was "general" (because it addressed every possible kind of suit against national banks), while the venue provision in the Securities Exchange Act was "specific" (because it dealt specifically with just one kind of suit)?

At least in this case, each of the two relevant provisions was "general" in one respect and "specific" in another: the venue provision in the National Bank Act addressed the entire universe of suits against a single category of possible defendants, while the venue provision in the Securities Exchange Act addressed a single category of suits against the entire universe of possible defendants. Was one of these provisions inherently more "specific" than the other? Or is the application of the idea that the specific trumps the general entirely indeterminate in this context?

3. As Justice Stevens observed in his dissent, "there is no necessary conflict" between the literal language of the two statutes at issue in *Radzanower*: the venue provision found at 12 U.S.C. § 94 said that suits against a national bank "may be had" in the federal judicial district where the bank is established, and the venue provision in the Securities Exchange Act of 1934 indicated that suits under the 1934 Act "may be brought" in some other federal judicial districts too. The conflict that the majority worked so hard to avoid arose only because the Court interpreted 12 U.S.C. § 94 to carry a negative implication, and to mean that suits against national banks may *not* be had in any federal judicial district other than one in which the bank is established.

The majority attributed this reading of 12 U.S.C. § 94 to its earlier decision in *Mercantile National Bank v. Langdeau*, 371 U.S. 555 (1963). There, the Court read 12 U.S.C. § 94 to carry a negative implication at least with respect to suits against national banks in *state* courts: state law could not validly allow such suits to proceed in venues other than the ones authorized by 12 U.S.C. § 94. According to Justice Stevens, though,

12 U.S.C. § 94 did not have to be understood to be similarly exclusive with respect to suits against national banks in *federal* courts. Is that correct? If so, should the presumption against implied repeals have led the Court to favor the nonexclusive reading of 12 U.S.C. § 94, so as to avoid conflict with § 27 of the Securities Exchange Act?

Normally, the presumption against implied repeals encourages courts to read a more recent statute in such a way as not to contradict an older statute. But the question just posed requires us to consider an additional possibility: might it ever be appropriate for the presumption against implied repeals to affect how courts read the *older* statute? Suppose that at Time 1, Congress enacts Statute #1, which might plausibly be read to mean either A or B. Suppose further that at Time 2, a different Congress enacts Statute #2, which quite clearly means "Not A" in at least some circumstances. Now that Statute #2 exists, should the presumption against implied repeals cause courts to read Statute #1 to mean B, so that Statute #2 does not have the effect of repealing Statute #1 in whole or in part? (To avoid complications from the doctrine of *stare decisis*, assume that the courts did not settle upon any particular interpretation of Statute #1 in the period before Congress enacted Statute #2.)

If Times 1 and 2 are separated by many years, the presumption against implied repeals has no apparent "descriptive" force in this context; what the later Congress said in Statute #2 tells us little about what the earlier Congress probably intended Statute #1 to mean. But if Statute #1 is otherwise intractably ambiguous—that is, if our ordinary tools of statutory interpretation leave us in equipoise about whether it should be understood to mean A or B—is there some "normative" reason to pick the interpretation that avoids conflict with the later statute? In other words, would it be preferable for courts to conclude that Statute #1 means B than to conclude that Statute #1 means A and has been partially repealed by Statute #2?

4. The majority in *Radzanower* twice cited *Fourco Glass Co. v. Transmirra Products Corp.*, 353 U.S. 222 (1957). That case involved the interaction between the then-existing version of 28 U.S.C. § 1391, the most general statute addressing venue in federal district courts, and 28 U.S.C. § 1400(b), which specifically addresses venue in suits for patent infringement. Then as now, § 1400(b) was phrased in permissive terms: "Any civil action for patent infringement may be brought in the judicial district where the defendant resides, or where the defendant has committed acts of infringement and has a regular and established place of business." In *Fourco*, however, the Court concluded that this language did not simply *supplement* § 1391 by providing some additional choices for venue in patent-infringement suits. Instead, § 1400(b) specifies the *only* federal judicial districts in which such suits "may be brought." *See Fourco*, 353 U.S. at 229 ("We hold that 28 U.S.C. § 1400(b) is the sole and exclusive provision controlling venue in patent infringement actions.").

The history behind § 1400(b) supports this conclusion. The precursor of § 1400(b) was Section 48 of the Judicial Code of 1911, which in turn traced back to a freestanding statute that Congress had enacted in 1897. Before 1897, there had been confusion about how Congress's general venue statutes applied to suits for patent infringement. In *Stonite Products Co. v. Melvin Lloyd Co.*, 315 U.S. 561 (1942), the Supreme Court concluded that the 1897 statute had been intended to resolve this confusion and to specify exactly where patent-infringement suits could be brought. In *Stonite*, the Court therefore understood the 1897 statute to occupy the field that it addressed: not only did the statute specify which federal judicial districts were proper venues for patent-infringement suits, but it implied that no *other* federal judicial districts were proper venues for such suits. According to the Court's opinion in *Stonite*, moreover, the language of the 1897 statute retained this meaning when Congress re-enacted it as Section 48 of the Judicial Code of 1911. In *Fourco*, the Supreme Court concluded that the same was true of 28 U.S.C. § 1400(b), which Congress had enacted in 1948 (as part of the project of enacting Title 28 into positive law) and which was a revised version of Section 48 of the Judicial Code of 1911.

The Supreme Court's opinion in *Fourco* was based largely on *Stonite*. But in concluding that general language then found in § 1391 did not apply in suits for patent infringement, the Court also mentioned the general/specific canon: "However inclusive may be the general language of a statute, it 'will not be held to apply to a matter specifically dealt with in another part of the same enactment. . . . Specific terms prevail over the general in the same or another statute which otherwise might be controlling.' " *Fourco*, 353 U.S. at 228–29 (quoting *MacEvoy Co. v. United States*, 322 U.S. 102, 107 (1944), in turn quoting *D. Ginsberg & Sons v. Popkin*, 285 U.S. 204, 208 (1932)). If one were not aware of the special history behind 28 U.S.C. § 1400(b), would this canon still support reading the specialized provision in § 1400(b) to occupy the field that it addresses to the exclusion of the more general provisions of § 1391?

My own answer to that question is "no." If a specific federal statute is ambiguous about whether it implicitly occupies the field that it addresses to the exclusion of other federal statutes, I see no reason for courts systematically to presume that the specific statute carries a negative implication and does indeed occupy the field that it addresses. In my view, it will often be possible for courts to apply both the specific statute and other federal statutes in the same field, and the general/specific canon should not be understood to disfavor this result. Instead, the general/specific canon should come into play (if at all) only after interpreters have identified some sort of apparent conflict between the two statutes.

On the contrary view, indeed, the general/specific canon would sometimes work at cross-purposes to the presumption against implied repeals. For instance, imagine the following scenario. At Time 1,

Congress enacts a general statute. At Time 2, Congress enacts a more specific statute about a particular topic that is also covered by the general statute. Suppose that the language of the specific statute could be read simply to supplement the general statute as applied to this topic, so that both statutes supply rules in this area. If courts instead read the specific statute as implicitly occupying the field that it addresses to the exclusion of the more general statute, then the courts are reading the specific statute to repeal the more general statute, by implication, insofar as the more general statute had previously governed the same field. More broadly, whenever courts read a specific federal statute as impliedly occupying the field that it addresses to the exclusion of other, pre-existing federal statutes, the courts are effectively finding an implied repeal *pro tanto* of those other statutes. While that conclusion can be appropriate in particular circumstances (as in *Stonite*), courts should not apply an artificial presumption in favor of this result. *See* Cortez Byrd Chips, Inc. v. Bill Harbert Constr. Co., 529 U.S. 193, 204 (2000) (observing that the lesson of cases like *Stonite* and *Fourco* "is not that special venue statutes are deemed to be restrictive," but simply that statute-by-statute analysis is necessary).

5. In *POM Wonderful LLC v. Coca-Cola Co.*, 573 U.S. 102 (2014), the Supreme Court confirmed that judges should not automatically read a specific federal statute as implicitly occupying the field that it addresses to the exclusion of more general federal statutes. According to the Court's opinion in *POM Wonderful*, if one federal statute deals specifically with a particular set of issues, but both its text and its purpose are compatible with the application of other more general federal statutes, the Court will assume that the specific statute complements the other statutes instead of superseding them.

The *POM Wonderful* case arose as follows. Through its Minute Maid® division, the Coca-Cola Company manufactured and sold a product that blended five different fruit juices. The product consisted almost entirely (99.4%) of apple juice and grape juice, but it also contained 0.3% pomegranate juice, 0.2% blueberry juice, and 0.1% raspberry juice. Despite those proportions, the label for the product featured the words "pomegranate" and "blueberry" much more prominently than other words. In relevant part, the text of the label looked something like this:

POMEGRANATE
BLUEBERRY
FLAVORED BLEND OF 5 JUICES

POM Wonderful LLC makes and sells pomegranate-juice products, including a pomegranate/blueberry blend. Alleging that its competitor's label was deceptive and misleading, POM Wonderful sued Coca-Cola under the private cause of action created by section 43 of the federal Lanham Act. That statute, enacted by Congress in 1946, is mostly about trademarks, but it also creates a cause of action for unfair competition.

Specifically, section 43 of the Lanham Act (as amended over the years) includes the following language:

> Any person who, on or in connection with any goods or services, . . . uses in commerce any word, term, name, symbol, or device, or any combination thereof, or any false designation of origin, false or misleading description of fact, or false or misleading representation of fact, which—
>
> . . .
>
> (B) in commercial advertising or promotion, misrepresents the nature, characteristics, qualities, or geographic origin of his or her or another person's goods, services, or commercial activities,
>
> shall be liable in a civil action by any person who believes that he or she is or is likely to be damaged by such act.

15 U.S.C. § 1125(a)(1). On the basis of the Lanham Act's explicit statement of purposes, codified at 15 U.S.C. § 1127, the Supreme Court has concluded that only someone who alleges "an injury to a commercial interest in reputation or sales" is claiming to have been "damaged" within the meaning of section 43—with the result that section 43 creates a cause of action for competitors and other commercial plaintiffs, not for consumers. *Lexmark Int'l, Inc. v. Static Control Components, Inc.*, 572 U.S. 118, 131–32 (2014). But POM Wonderful was indeed a competitor, claiming an injury to its own sales, so it seemed to fit within the terms of the cause of action created by section 43.

Coca-Cola, however, argued that a separate federal statute—the Food, Drug, and Cosmetic Act (FDCA)—effectively limited the reach of section 43 under the circumstances. Building on the Pure Food and Drug Act of 1906, Congress had enacted the original version of the FDCA in 1938 (a few years before the Lanham Act). The FDCA specifically addresses the labeling of food and beverage products, and it identifies various labeling defects that amount to "misbrand[ing]." 21 U.S.C. § 343. The FDCA also gives additional rulemaking authority to a federal administrative agency, the Food and Drug Administration (FDA). The FDA has used that authority to promulgate detailed regulations about food and beverage labeling, including a regulation that addresses the labeling of juice blends.

According to Coca-Cola, the label for its five-juice blend complied with both the FDCA and the associated regulations.[36] Of course, POM Wonderful was suing over alleged violations of the Lanham Act, not the FDCA. But Coca-Cola argued that the "specific" provisions about

[36] Although POM Wonderful denied that Coca-Cola's label really satisfied the FDCA's requirements, the FDCA does not create a private cause of action. Instead, suits to enforce the FDCA are brought primarily by the federal government itself.

beverage labeling in the FDCA effectively took precedence over the Lanham Act's "general" provision about unfair competition.

The federal district court agreed with Coca-Cola, and the United States Court of Appeals for the Ninth Circuit affirmed. But the Supreme Court reversed. Justice Kennedy wrote the Court's opinion (which was unanimous except that Justice Breyer did not participate in the case).

In setting the stage for his decision, Justice Kennedy began by noting that the parties had invoked "two competing maxims." In his words:

> "POM argues that this case concerns whether one statute, the FDCA as amended, is an 'implied repeal' in part of another statute, . . . the Lanham Act. See, *e.g.*, *Carcieri v. Salazar*, 555 U.S. 379, 395 (2009). POM contends that in such cases courts must give full effect to both statutes unless they are in 'irreconcilable conflict,' see *ibid.* . . . Coca-Cola resists this canon and its high standard. Coca-Cola argues that the case concerns whether a more specific law, the FDCA, clarifies or narrows the scope of a more general law, the Lanham Act. See, *e.g.*, *United States v. Fausto*, 484 U.S. 439, 453 (1988) . . . . The Court's task, [Coca-Cola] claims, is to 'reconcil[e]' the laws, . . . and it says the best reconciliation is that the more specific provisions of the FDCA bar certain causes of action authorized in a general manner by the Lanham Act."

573 U.S. at 112. According to Justice Kennedy, however, "[t]he Court does not need to resolve this dispute" about the applicable principles of interpretation. Even assuming for the sake of argument that Coca-Cola was framing the question correctly, Coca-Cola was wrong about "the best way to harmonize the statutes." *Id.* at 112–13.

Justice Kennedy began by noting that "neither the Lanham Act nor the FDCA, in express terms, forbids or limits Lanham Act claims challenging labels that are regulated by the FDCA." So far as appeared from the text, then, "food and beverage labels regulated by the FDCA are not, under the terms of either statute, off limits to Lanham Act claims." *Id.* at 113.

Justice Kennedy went on to emphasize that the FDCA and section 43 of the Lanham Act served different purposes and that those purposes are "complementary." *Id.* at 118. Thus, he saw no reason to read the FDCA as somehow precluding application of section 43 of the Lanham Act (or to read section 43 of the Lanham Act as containing an implicit exception for labels covered by the FDCA). Instead, *both* statutes could be given full effect without creating any unwarranted tensions. Here is an excerpt from that portion of his opinion:

> "When two statutes complement each other, it would show disregard for the congressional design to hold that Congress nonetheless intended one federal statute to preclude the operation of the other. See *J.E.M. Ag Supply, Inc. v. Pioneer Hi-Bred Int'l, Inc.*, 534 U.S. 124, 144 (2001) ('[W]e can plainly regard each statute as effective

because of its different requirements and protections') . . . . The Lanham Act and the FDCA complement each other in major respects, for each has its own scope and purpose. Although both statutes touch on food and beverage labeling, the Lanham Act protects commercial interests against unfair competition, while the FDCA protects public health and safety. . . . The two statutes impose 'different requirements and protections.' [*Id.*]

"The two statutes complement each other with respect to remedies in a more fundamental respect. Enforcement of the FDCA and the detailed prescriptions of its implementing regulations is largely committed to the FDA. The FDA, however, does not have the same perspective or expertise in assessing market dynamics that day-to-day competitors possess. Competitors who manufacture or distribute products have detailed knowledge regarding how consumers rely upon certain sales and marketing strategies. Their awareness of unfair competition practices may be far more immediate and accurate than that of agency rulemakers and regulators. Lanham Act suits draw upon this market expertise by empowering private parties to sue competitors to protect their interests on a case-by-case basis. By 'serv[ing] a distinct compensatory function that may motivate injured persons to come forward,' Lanham Act suits, to the extent they touch on the same subject matter as the FDCA, 'provide incentives' for manufacturers to behave well. See [*Wyeth v. Levine*, 555 U.S. 555, 579 (2009)]. Allowing Lanham Act suits takes advantage of synergies among multiple methods of regulation. This is quite consistent with the congressional design to enact two different statutes, each with its own mechanisms to enhance the protection of competitors and consumers.

". . . . Because the FDA acknowledges that it does not necessarily pursue enforcement measures regarding all objectionable labels, . . . if Lanham Act claims were to be precluded then commercial interests—and indirectly the public at large—could be left with less effective protection in the food and beverage labeling realm than in many other, less regulated industries. It is unlikely that Congress intended the FDCA's protection of health and safety to result in less policing of misleading food and beverage labels than in competitive markets for other products."

Id. at 115–16.

Justice Kennedy returned to the same theme later in his opinion, in response to another argument advanced by Coca-Cola:

"Coca-Cola urges that the FDCA, and particularly its implementing regulations, addresses food and beverage labeling with much more specificity than is found in the provisions of the Lanham Act. That is true. The pages of FDA rulemakings devoted only to juice-blend labeling attest to the level of detail with which the FDA has examined the subject. *E.g.*, Food Labeling; Declaration of Ingredients; Common or Usual Name for Nonstandardized Foods; Diluted Juice Beverages, 58 Fed. Reg. 2897–2926 (1993). [But b]ecause, as we have explained, the FDCA and the Lanham Act are complementary and have separate scopes and purposes, this greater specificity would matter only if the Lanham Act and the FDCA cannot be implemented in full at the same time. See *RadLAX Gateway Hotel, LLC v. Amalgamated Bank*, 566 U.S. 639, 645–646 (2012). . . . [N]either the statutory structure nor the empirical evidence of which the Court is aware indicates there will be any difficulty in fully enforcing each statute according to its terms."

Id. at 118.

6. Statutes defining federal crimes can raise similar issues. For instance, the current version of 18 U.S.C. § 1001(a) sets out the following general prohibition:

> "[W]hoever, in any matter within the jurisdiction of the executive, legislative, or judicial branch of the Government of the United States, knowingly and willfully—
>
> "(1) falsifies, conceals, or covers up by any trick, scheme, or device a material fact;
>
> "(2) makes any materially false, fictitious, or fraudulent statement or representation; or
>
> "(3) makes or uses any false writing or document knowing the same to contain any materially false, fictitious, or fraudulent statement or entry;
>
> "shall be fined under this title, imprisoned not more than 5 years . . . , or both."

A provision along these lines has appeared in § 1001 ever since Congress enacted title 18 of the United States Code into positive law in 1948.[37]

---

[37] As originally enacted in 1948, § 1001 was structured more simply than it now is. In its entirety, the original version read as follows:

> "Whoever, in any matter within the jurisdiction of any department or agency of the United States[,] knowingly and willfully falsifies, conceals or covers up by any trick, scheme, or device a material fact, or makes any false, fictitious or fraudulent statements or representations, or makes or uses any false writing or document knowing the same to contain any false, fictitious or fraudulent statement or entry, shall be fined not more than $10,000 or imprisoned not more than five years, or both."

See An Act to Revise, Codify, and Enact into Positive Law, Title 18 of the United States Code, Entitled "Crimes and Criminal Procedure," ch. 645, 62 Stat. 683, 749 (1948). In *United States v. Bramblett*, 348 U.S. 503 (1955), the Supreme Court initially interpreted the word "department" in this provision to cover the judicial and legislative branches as well as the executive branch. But in 1995 the Court overruled *Bramblett*. *See* Hubbard v. United States, 514 U.S. 695, 715 (1995) (holding that "a federal court is neither a 'department' nor an 'agency' within the meaning of § 1001"). Congress responded by enacting a revised version of § 1001, consisting of three subsections. Subsection (a), which is quoted in the text above, specifically referred to the judicial and legislative branches as well as the executive branch. Subsections (b) and (c) then carved out a few exceptions applicable to judicial and legislative proceedings, respectively. *See* Act of Oct. 11, 1996, Pub. L. 104–292, 110 Stat. 3459. At least as applied to matters within the jurisdiction

Many more recent federal statutes, however, include their own prohibitions on specific types of false statements to federal officers. Should those statutes be understood to *supersede* or to *supplement* § 1001?

Here is a concrete context in which that question might arise. At horse shows, Tennessee Walking Horses are judged partly on their gait. People have been known to "sore" horses—that is, to burn them, cut them, or put blistering agents on their legs—in order to get them to walk in the way that judges prefer. In the 1970s, Congress passed legislation to discourage this practice. *See* Horse Protection Act of 1970, Pub. L. 91–540, 84 Stat. 1404; Horse Protection Act Amendments of 1976, Pub. L. 94–360, 90 Stat. 915. Among other things, the federal Horse Protection Act now requires the management of horse shows to keep whatever records and make whatever reports the Secretary of Agriculture reasonably requires by regulation. *Id.* at 916. The Act proceeds to criminalize false statements in such reports, as follows:

> "Any person who knowingly makes, or causes to be made, a false entry or statement in any report required under this Act . . . shall be guilty of an offense against the United States, and upon conviction thereof shall be fined not more than $5,000, or imprisoned for not more than three years, or both."

Id. at 918 (codified at 15 U.S.C. § 1825(a)(2)(B)).

Suppose that federal prosecutors want to indict the manager of a horse show for making a false statement in a report to the Secretary of Agriculture about the presence of "sored" horses. Do the prosecutors have to proceed under the criminal provision in the Horse Protection Act, which sets the maximum prison term at three years? Or do they also have the option of charging the manager with violating the more general prohibition on false statements in 18 U.S.C. § 1001, which authorizes imprisonment for up to five years? To the extent that this scenario involves a conflict between the presumption against implied repeals and the rule of lenity, which should win?

Federal courts have faced this sort of question many times. In the absence of some clear indication that Congress intended a specific statutory prohibition on false statements to supersede the more general prohibition in § 1001, courts have almost always held that both prohibitions retain full force and that prosecutors have discretion to proceed under either. *See, e.g.*, United States v. Tomeny, 144 F.3d 749, 752 (11th Cir. 1998) ("[T]his court repeatedly has upheld convictions under 18 U.S.C. § 1001 even though the defendant's conduct also fell within the scope of more specific and more recently enacted false statement provisions . . . ."); *see also id.* at 753 n.6 (citing numerous cases to the same effect from other circuits); *cf.* United States v. Batchelder,

---

of the executive branch, however, the gist of the prohibition in subsection (a) has existed in much the current form since 1948.

442 U.S. 114, 121–22 (1979) (invoking the presumption against implied repeals and finding the rule of lenity inapplicable to a somewhat analogous problem). *But see* United States v. Richardson, 8 F.3d 15, 17 (9th Cir. 1993) (per curiam) (holding that "section 1001, the general federal false-statement statute, is limited by section 1920, a specific false-statement statute applicable exclusively to representations concerning federal employees' compensation benefits and claims"); *cf.* United States v. Fitzgerald, 147 F.3d 1101, 1103 (9th Cir. 1998) (discussing subsequent amendments to § 1920).

7. The Supreme Court does not always give the presumption against implied repeals as much force as *Morton v. Mancari* and *Radzanower* might suggest. Consider *Credit Suisse Securities (USA) LLC v. Billing*, 551 U.S. 264 (2007). In that case, plaintiffs who had bought shares of stock in a company's initial public offering (IPO) filed an antitrust lawsuit against ten investment banks that had participated in the IPO as underwriters. As the Court summarized the gist of their complaint, "[t]he buyers claim that the underwriters unlawfully agreed with one another that they would not sell shares of a popular new issue to a buyer unless that buyer committed (1) to buy additional shares of that security later at escalating prices . . . , (2) to pay unusually high commissions on subsequent security purchases from the underwriters, or (3) to purchase from the underwriters other less desirable securities . . . ." *Id.* at 267. Justice Breyer's majority opinion, however, held that such claims could be pursued only under the securities laws and not under the antitrust laws. In other words, the Court held that the federal securities laws impliedly repealed, *pro tanto*, the application of the federal antitrust laws to those claims.

In reaching this conclusion, the Court reasoned that joint efforts by underwriters were "central to the proper functioning of well-regulated capital markets," *id.* at 276, that federal securities law had given the Securities and Exchange Commission "authority to supervise all of the activities here in question," *id.*, that the Commission "has continuously exercised" this regulatory authority, *id.* at 277, and that allowing private antitrust suits to challenge the same activities would deter "not simply conduct that the securities law forbids (and will likely continue to forbid), but also a wide range of joint conduct that the securities law permits or encourages," *id.* at 282. With respect to the last point, the majority asserted that "there is no practical way to confine antitrust suits so that they challenge only activity . . . that is presently unlawful and will likely remain unlawful under the securities law." *Id.* To the contrary, "antitrust courts are likely to make unusually serious mistakes in this respect." *Id.* at 281–82 (noting the subtlety of the lines drawn by the securities laws, the "need for securities-related expertise" in recognizing those lines, and the fact that "antitrust plaintiffs may bring lawsuits throughout the Nation in dozens of different courts with different nonexpert judges and different nonexpert juries"). The "securities-related costs" of those mistakes, moreover, were likely to be "unusually high," because joint underwriting activity plays an important role in the marketing of IPOs, which in turn play an "important role . . . in relation to the effective functioning of capital markets." *Id.* at 282. On the other side of the ledger, the majority added that "any enforcement-related need for an antitrust lawsuit is unusually small," both because Congress had created other ways to enforce federal securities law and because Congress had required the SEC "to take account of competitive considerations" when crafting securities policy. *Id.* at 283. According to the Court, then, "the securities laws are 'clearly incompatible' with the application of the antitrust laws in this context." *Id.* at 285.

This analysis sets a different tone than one gets from reading *Morton v. Mancari*. In *Credit Suisse*, the Court was confronting the same sort of question that it had to confront in *Morton*: should the federal securities laws be interpreted as simply *supplementing* or as partially *superseding* the antitrust laws enacted by a prior Congress? But the majority did not approach that question either by applying a generic canon or by seeking clues about the specific intentions of the enacting Congress. Instead, the majority engaged in a detailed policy analysis: would the practical effects of applying the antitrust laws in this context "threaten serious harm to the efficient functioning of the securities markets," thereby getting in the way of the general purpose that the majority imputed to the federal securities laws? If so, the majority seemed to think, one could fairly interpret the federal securities laws as implicitly pushing the antitrust laws aside.

Epic Systems Corp. v. Lewis

138 S. Ct. 1612 (2018)

■ *JUSTICE GORSUCH delivered the opinion of the Court:*

Should employees and employers be allowed to agree that any disputes between them will be resolved through one-on-one arbitration? Or should employees always be permitted to bring their claims in class or collective actions, no matter what they agreed with their employers?

As a matter of policy these questions are surely debatable. But as a matter of law the answer is clear. In the Federal Arbitration Act, Congress has instructed federal courts to enforce arbitration agreements according to their terms—including terms providing for individualized proceedings. Nor can we agree with the employees' suggestion that the National Labor Relations Act (NLRA) offers a conflicting command. It is this Court's duty to interpret Congress's statutes as a harmonious whole rather than at war with one another. . . .

I

The three cases before us differ in detail but not in substance. Take *Ernst & Young LLP v. Morris*. There Ernst & Young and one of its junior accountants, Stephen Morris, entered into an agreement providing that they would arbitrate any disputes that might arise between them. The agreement stated that the employee could choose the arbitration provider and that the arbitrator could "grant any relief that could be granted by . . . a court" in the relevant jurisdiction. The agreement also specified individualized arbitration, with claims "pertaining to different [e]mployees [to] be heard in separate proceedings."

After his employment ended, and despite having agreed to arbitrate claims against the firm, Mr. Morris sued Ernst & Young in federal court. He alleged that the firm had misclassified its junior accountants as professional employees and violated the federal Fair Labor Standards Act (FLSA) and California law by paying them salaries without overtime pay. Although the arbitration agreement provided for individualized proceedings, Mr. Morris sought to litigate the federal claim on behalf of a nationwide class under the FLSA's collective action provision, 29 U.S.C. § 216(b). He sought to pursue the state law claim as a class action under Federal Rule of Civil Procedure 23.

Ernst & Young replied with a motion to compel arbitration. The district court granted the request, but the Ninth Circuit reversed this judgment. 834 F.3d 975 (2016). The Ninth Circuit recognized that the Arbitration Act generally requires courts to enforce arbitration agreements as written. But the court reasoned that the statute's "saving clause," see 9 U.S.C. § 2, removes this obligation if an arbitration agreement violates some other federal law. And the court concluded that an agreement requiring individualized arbitration proceedings violates the NLRA by barring employees from engaging in the "concerted activit[y]," 29 U.S.C. § 157, of pursuing claims as a class or collective action.

. . . . We granted certiorari . . . .

II

We begin with the Arbitration Act and the question of its saving clause.

Congress adopted the Arbitration Act in 1925 in response to a perception that courts were unduly hostile to arbitration. . . . Before 1925, English and American common law courts routinely refused to enforce agreements to arbitrate disputes. . . . Congress directed courts to . . . treat arbitration agreements as "valid, irrevocable, and enforceable." 9 U.S.C. § 2. . . .

Not only did Congress require courts to respect and enforce agreements to arbitrate; it also specifically directed them to respect and enforce the parties' chosen arbitration procedures. See § 3 (providing for a stay of litigation pending arbitration "in accordance with the terms of the agreement"); § 4 (providing for "an order directing that . . . arbitration proceed in the manner provided for in such agreement"). Indeed, we have often observed that the Arbitration Act requires courts "rigorously" to "enforce arbitration agreements according to their terms, including terms that specify *with whom* the parties choose to arbitrate their disputes and *the rules* under which that arbitration will be conducted." *American Express Co. v. Italian Colors Restaurant*, 570 U.S. 228, 233 (2013) (some emphasis added; citations, internal quotation marks, and brackets omitted).

On first blush, these emphatic directions would seem to resolve any argument under the Arbitration Act. The parties before us contracted for arbitration. They proceeded to specify the rules that would govern their arbitrations, indicating their intention to use individualized rather than class or collective action procedures. And this much the Arbitration Act seems to protect pretty absolutely. See *AT&T Mobility LLC v. Concepcion*, 563 U.S. 333 (2011); *Italian Colors, supra*; *DIRECTV, Inc. v. Imburgia*, 577 U.S. 47 (2015). You might wonder if the balance Congress struck in 1925 between arbitration and litigation should be revisited in light of more contemporary developments. You might even ask if the Act was good policy when enacted. But all the same you might find it difficult to see how to avoid the statute's application.

Still, the employees suggest the Arbitration Act's saving clause creates an exception for cases like theirs. By its terms, the saving clause allows courts to refuse to enforce arbitration agreements "upon such grounds as exist at law or in equity for the revocation of any contract." § 2. That provision applies here, the employees tell us, because the NLRA renders their particular class and collective action waivers illegal. In their view, illegality under the NLRA is a "ground" that "exists at law . . . for the revocation" of their arbitration agreements, at least to the extent those agreements prohibit class or collective action proceedings.

The problem with this line of argument is fundamental. Put to the side the question whether the saving clause was designed to save not only state law defenses but also defenses allegedly arising from federal statutes. See 834 F.3d at 991–992, 997 (Ikuta, J., dissenting). Put to the side the question of what it takes to qualify as a ground for "revocation" of a contract. See *Concepcion, supra*, at 352–355 (Thomas, J., concurring) . . . . Put to the side for the moment, too, even the question whether the NLRA actually renders class and collective action waivers illegal. Assuming (but not granting) the employees could satisfactorily answer all those questions, the saving clause still can't save their cause.

It can't because the saving clause recognizes only defenses that apply to "any" contract. In this way the clause establishes a sort of "equal-treatment" rule for arbitration contracts. *Kindred Nursing Centers L.P. v. Clark*, 581 U.S. 246, 251 (2017). The clause "permits agreements to arbitrate to be invalidated by 'generally applicable contract defenses, such as fraud, duress, or unconscionability.' " *Concepcion*, 563 U.S. at

339. At the same time, the clause offers no refuge for "defenses that apply only to arbitration or that derive their meaning from the fact that an agreement to arbitrate is at issue." *Ibid.* Under our precedent, this means the saving clause does not save defenses that target arbitration either by name or by more subtle methods, such as by "interfer[ing] with fundamental attributes of arbitration." *Id.* at 344 . . . .

This is where the employees' argument stumbles. They don't suggest that their arbitration agreements were extracted, say, by an act of fraud or duress or in some other unconscionable way that would render *any* contract unenforceable. Instead, they object to their agreements precisely because they require individualized arbitration proceedings instead of class or collective ones. And by attacking (only) the individualized nature of the arbitration proceedings, the employees' argument seeks to interfere with one of arbitration's fundamental attributes.

We know this much because of *Concepcion*. There this Court faced a state law defense that prohibited as unconscionable class action waivers in consumer contracts. The Court readily acknowledged that the defense formally applied in both the litigation and the arbitration context. 563 U.S. at 338, 341. But, the Court held, the defense failed to qualify for protection under the saving clause because it interfered with a fundamental attribute of arbitration all the same. It did so by effectively permitting any party in arbitration to demand classwide proceedings despite the traditionally individualized and informal nature of arbitration. This "fundamental" change to the traditional arbitration process, the Court said, would "sacrific[e] the principal advantage of arbitration—its informality—and mak[e] the process slower, more costly, and more likely to generate procedural morass than final judgment." *Id.* at 347, 348. Not least, *Concepcion* noted, arbitrators would have to decide whether the named class representatives are sufficiently representative and typical of the class; what kind of notice, opportunity to be heard, and right to opt out absent class members should enjoy; and how discovery should be altered in light of the classwide nature of the proceedings. *Ibid.* All of which would take much time and effort, and introduce new risks and costs for both sides. *Ibid.* In the Court's judgment, the virtues Congress originally saw in arbitration, its speed and simplicity and inexpensiveness, would be shorn away and arbitration would wind up looking like the litigation it was meant to displace.

. . . . *Concepcion*'s essential insight remains: courts may not allow a contract defense to reshape traditional individualized arbitration by mandating classwide arbitration procedures without the parties' consent. *Id.* at 344–351 . . . . Just as judicial antagonism toward arbitration before the Arbitration Act's enactment "manifested itself in a great variety of devices and formulas declaring arbitration against public policy," *Concepcion* teaches that we must be alert to new devices and formulas that would achieve much the same result today. 563 U.S. at 342 (internal quotation marks omitted). And a rule seeking to declare individualized arbitration proceedings off limits is, the Court held, just such a device.

The employees' efforts to distinguish *Concepcion* fall short. They note that their putative NLRA defense would render an agreement "illegal" as a matter of federal statutory law rather than "unconscionable" as a matter of state common law. But we don't see how that distinction makes any difference in light of *Concepcion*'s rationale and rule. Illegality, like unconscionability, may be a traditional, generally applicable contract defense in many cases, including arbitration cases. But an argument that a contract is unenforceable *just because it requires bilateral arbitration* is a different creature. A defense of that kind, *Concepcion* tells us, is one that impermissibly disfavors arbitration whether it sounds in illegality or unconscionability. The law of precedent teaches that like cases should generally be treated alike, and appropriate respect for that principle means the Arbitration Act's saving clause can no more save the defense at issue in these cases than it did the defense at issue in *Concepcion*. . . .

III

. . . . Even if the Arbitration Act normally requires us to enforce arbitration agreements like theirs, the employees reply that the NLRA overrides that guidance in these cases . . . .

This argument faces a stout uphill climb. When confronted with two Acts of Congress allegedly touching on the same topic, this Court is not at "liberty to pick and choose among congressional enactments" and must instead strive " 'to give effect to both.' " *Morton v. Mancari*, 417 U.S. 535, 551 (1974). A party seeking to suggest that two statutes cannot be harmonized, and that one displaces the other, bears the heavy burden of showing " 'a clearly expressed congressional intention' " that such a result should follow. *Vimar Seguros y Reaseguros, S.A. v. M/V Sky Reefer*, 515 U.S. 528, 533 (1995). The intention must be " 'clear and manifest.' " *Morton, supra*, at 551. And in approaching a claimed conflict, we come armed with the "stron[g] presum[ption]" that repeals by implication are "disfavored" and that "Congress will specifically address" preexisting law when it wishes to suspend its normal operations in a later statute. *United States v. Fausto*, 484 U.S. 439, 452, 453 (1988).

These rules exist for good reasons. Respect for Congress as drafter counsels against too easily finding irreconcilable conflicts in its work. More than that, respect for the separation of powers counsels restraint. Allowing judges to pick and choose between statutes risks transforming them from expounders of what the law *is* into policymakers choosing what the law *should be*. Our rules aiming for harmony over conflict in statutory interpretation grow from an appreciation that it's the job of Congress by legislation, not this Court by supposition, both to write the laws and to repeal them.

Seeking to demonstrate an irreconcilable statutory conflict even in light of these demanding standards, the employees point to Section 7 of the NLRA. That provision guarantees workers

> "the right to self-organization, to form, join, or assist labor organizations, to bargain collectively through representatives of their own choosing, and to engage in other concerted activities for the purpose of collective bargaining or other mutual aid or protection." 29 U.S.C. § 157.

From this language, the employees ask us to infer a clear and manifest congressional command to displace the Arbitration Act and outlaw agreements like theirs.

.... Section 7 focuses on the right to organize unions and bargain collectively. It may permit unions to bargain to prohibit arbitration. Cf. *14 Penn Plaza LLC v. Pyett*, 556 U.S. 247, 256–260 (2009). But it does not express approval or disapproval of arbitration. It does not mention class or collective action procedures. It does not even hint at a wish to displace the Arbitration Act—let alone accomplish that much clearly and manifestly, as our precedents demand.

.... The notion that Section 7 confers a right to class or collective actions seems pretty unlikely when you recall that procedures like that were hardly known when the NLRA was adopted in 1935. Federal Rule of Civil Procedure 23 didn't create the modern class action until 1966; class arbitration didn't emerge until later still; and even the Fair Labor Standards Act's collective action provision postdated Section 7 by years. See ... *Califano v. Yamasaki*, 442 U.S. 682, 700–701 (1979) (noting that the "usual rule" then was litigation "conducted by and on behalf of individual named parties only"). And while some forms of group litigation existed even in 1935, ... Section 7's failure to mention them only reinforces that the statute doesn't speak to such procedures.

.... The employees direct our attention to the term "other concerted activities for the purpose of ... other mutual aid or protection." This catchall term, they say, can be read to include class and collective legal actions. But the term appears at the end of a detailed list of activities speaking of "self-organization," "form[ing], join[ing], or assist[ing] labor organizations," and "bargain[ing] collectively." 29 U.S.C. § 157. And where, as here, a more general term follows more specific terms in a list, the general term is usually understood to " 'embrace only objects similar in nature to those objects enumerated by the preceding specific words.' " *Circuit City Stores, Inc. v. Adams*, 532 U.S. 105, 115 (2001) (discussing *ejusdem generis* canon) .... All of which suggests that the term "other concerted activities" should, like the terms that precede it, serve to protect things employees "just do" for themselves in the course of exercising their right to free association in the workplace, rather than "the highly regulated, courtroom-bound 'activities' of class and joint litigation." [*NLRB v. Alternative Entertainment, Inc.*, 858 F.3d 393, 414–415 (6th Cir. 2017)] (Sutton, J., concurring in part and dissenting in part) (emphasis deleted). None of the preceding and more specific terms speaks to the procedures judges or arbitrators must apply in disputes that leave the workplace and enter the courtroom or arbitral forum, and there is no textually sound reason to suppose the final catchall term should bear such a radically different object than all its predecessors.

The NLRA's broader structure underscores the point. After speaking of various "concerted activities" in Section 7, Congress proceeded to establish a regulatory regime applicable to each of them. The NLRA provides rules for the recognition of exclusive bargaining representatives, 29 U.S.C. § 159, explains employees' and employers' obligation to bargain collectively, § 158(d), and conscribes certain labor organization practices, §§ 158(a)(3), (b). The NLRA also touches on other concerted activities closely related to organization and collective bargaining, such as picketing, § 158(b)(7), and strikes, § 163. It even sets rules for adjudicatory proceedings under the NLRA itself. §§ 160, 161. Many of these provisions were part of the original NLRA in 1935, see 49 Stat. 449, while others were added later. But missing entirely from this careful regime is any hint about what rules should govern the adjudication of class or collective actions in court or arbitration. Without some comparably specific guidance, it's not at all obvious what procedures Section 7 might protect. Would opt-out class action procedures suffice? Or would opt-in procedures be necessary? What notice might be owed to absent class members? What standards would govern class certification? Should the same rules always apply or should they vary based on the nature of the suit? Nothing in the NLRA even whispers to us on any of these essential questions. And it is hard to fathom why Congress would take such care to regulate all the other matters mentioned in Section 7 yet remain mute about this matter alone—unless, of course, Section 7 doesn't speak to class and collective action procedures in the first place.

. . . .

Still another contextual clue yields the same message. The employees' underlying causes of action involve their wages and arise not under the NLRA but under an entirely different statute, the Fair Labor Standards Act. The FLSA allows employees to sue on behalf of "themselves and other employees similarly situated," 29 U.S.C. § 216(b), and it's precisely this sort of collective action the employees before us wish to pursue. Yet they do not offer the seemingly more natural suggestion that the FLSA overcomes the Arbitration Act to permit their class and collective actions. Why not? Presumably because this Court held decades ago that an identical collective action scheme (in fact, one borrowed from the FLSA) does *not* displace the Arbitration Act or prohibit individualized arbitration proceedings. *Gilmer v. Interstate/Johnson Lane Corp.*, 500 U.S. 20, 32 (1991) (discussing Age Discrimination in Employment Act). . . . "[E]very circuit to consider the question" has held that the FLSA allows agreements for individualized arbitration. *Alternative Entertainment*, 858 F.3d at 413 (opinion of Sutton, J.) (collecting cases). . . .

. . . . In many cases over many years, this Court has heard and rejected efforts to conjure conflicts between the Arbitration Act and other federal statutes. In fact, this Court has rejected *every* such effort to date (save one temporary exception since overruled), with statutes ranging from the Sherman and Clayton Acts to the Age Discrimination in Employment Act, the Credit Repair Organizations Act, the Securities Act of 1933, the Securities Exchange Act of 1934, and the Racketeer Influenced and Corrupt Organizations Act. *Italian Colors*, 570 U.S. 228; *Gilmer*, 500 U.S. 20; *CompuCredit Corp. v. Greenwood*, 565 U.S. 95 (2012); *Rodriguez de Quijas v. Shearson/American Express, Inc.*, 490 U.S. 477 (1989) (overruling *Wilko v. Swan*, 346 U.S. 427 (1953)); *Shearson/American Express Inc. v. McMahon*, 482 U.S. 220 (1987). Throughout, we have made clear that even a statute's express provision for collective legal actions does not necessarily mean that it precludes " 'individual attempts at conciliation' " through arbitration. *Gilmer, supra*, at 32. . . .

. . . .

With so much against them in the statute and our precedent, the employees end by seeking shelter in [*Chevron U.S.A. Inc. v. Natural Resources Defense Council*, 467 U.S. 837 (1984)]. Even if this Court doesn't see what they see in Section 7, the employees say we must rule for them anyway because of the deference this Court owes to an administrative agency's interpretation of the law. To be sure, the employees do not wish us to defer to the [NLRB] general counsel's judgment in 2010 that the NLRA and the Arbitration Act coexist peaceably; they wish us to defer instead to the Board's 2012 opinion suggesting the NLRA displaces the Arbitration Act. No party to these cases has asked us to reconsider *Chevron* deference. . . . But even under *Chevron*'s terms, no deference is due. To show why, it suffices to outline just a few of the most obvious reasons.

The *Chevron* Court justified deference on the premise that a statutory ambiguity represents an "implicit" delegation to an agency to interpret a "statute which it administers." 467 U.S. at 841, 844. Here, though, the Board hasn't just sought to interpret its statute, the NLRA, in isolation; it has sought to interpret this statute in a way that limits the work of a second statute, the Arbitration Act. And on no account might we agree that Congress implicitly delegated to an agency authority to address the meaning of a second statute it does not administer. One of *Chevron*'s essential premises is simply missing here.

It's easy, too, to see why the "reconciliation" of distinct statutory regimes "is a matter for the courts," not agencies. *Gordon v. New York Stock Exchange, Inc.*, 422 U.S. 659, 685–686 (1975). An agency eager to advance its statutory mission, but without any particular interest in or expertise with a second statute, might (as here) seek to diminish the second statute's scope in favor of a more expansive interpretation of its own—effectively " 'bootstrap[ping] itself into an area in which it has no jurisdiction.' " *Adams Fruit Co. v. Barrett*, 494 U.S. 638, 650 (1990). All of which threatens to undo rather than honor legislative intentions. To preserve the balance Congress struck in its statutes, courts must exercise independent interpretive judgment. See *Hoffman Plastic Compounds, Inc. v. NLRB*, 535 U.S. 137, 144 (2002) (noting that this Court has "never deferred to the Board's remedial preferences where such preferences potentially trench upon federal statutes and policies unrelated to the NLRA").

Another justification the *Chevron* Court offered for deference is that "policy choices" should be left to Executive Branch officials "directly accountable to the people." 467 U.S. at 865. But here the Executive seems of two minds, for we have received competing briefs from the Board and from the United States (through the Solicitor General) disputing the meaning of the NLRA. And whatever argument might be mustered for deferring to the Executive on grounds of political accountability, surely it becomes a garble when the Executive speaks from both sides of its mouth, articulating no single position on which it might be held accountable. . . . In these circumstances, we will not defer.

Finally, the *Chevron* Court explained that deference is not due unless a "court, employing traditional tools of statutory construction," is left with an unresolved ambiguity. 467 U.S. at 843, n. 9. And that too is missing: the canon against reading conflicts into statutes is a traditional tool of statutory construction and it, along with the other traditional canons we have discussed, is more than up to the job of solving today's interpretive puzzle. Where, as here, the canons supply an answer, "*Chevron* leaves the stage." *Alternative Entertainment*, 858 F.3d at 417 (opinion of Sutton, J.).

IV

The dissent sees things a little bit differently. In its view, today's decision ushers us back to the *Lochner* era when this Court regularly overrode legislative policy judgments. . . .

Our decision does nothing to override Congress's policy judgments. As the dissent recognizes, the legislative policy embodied in the NLRA is aimed at "safeguard[ing], first and foremost, workers' rights to join unions and to engage in collective bargaining." *Post* at 1636. Those rights stand every bit as strong today as they did yesterday. And rather than revive "yellow dog" contracts against union organizing that the NLRA outlawed back in 1935, today's decision merely declines to read into the NLRA a novel right to class action procedures that the Board's own general counsel disclaimed as recently as 2010.

. . . . The dissent spends page after page relitigating our Arbitration Act precedents, rehashing arguments this Court has heard and rejected many times in many cases that no party has asked us to revisit. . . .

.... Our precedent clearly teaches that a contract defense "conditioning the enforceability of certain arbitration agreements on the availability of classwide arbitration procedures" is inconsistent with the Arbitration Act and its saving clause. *Concepcion, supra,* at 336. . . .

Nor is the dissent's reading of the NLRA any more available to us than its reading of the Arbitration Act. The dissent imposes a vast construction on Section 7's language. *Post* at 1637. But a statute's meaning does not always "turn solely" on the broadest imaginable "definitions of its component words." *Yates v. United States,* 574 U.S. 528, 537 (2015) (plurality opinion). Linguistic and statutory context also matter. We have offered an extensive explanation why those clues support our reading today. By contrast, the dissent rests its interpretation on legislative history. . . . But legislative history is not the law. "It is the business of Congress to sum up its own debates in its legislation," and once it enacts a statute " '[w]e do not inquire what the legislature meant; we ask only what the statute means.' " *Schwegmann Brothers v. Calvert Distillers Corp.,* 341 U.S. 384, 396, 397 (1951) (Jackson, J., concurring) (quoting Justice Holmes). . . .

.... The dissent proceeds to argue that its expansive reading of the NLRA conflicts with and should prevail over the Arbitration Act. The NLRA leaves the Arbitration Act without force, the dissent says, because it provides the more "pinpointed" direction. *Post* at 1646. Even taken on its own terms, though, this argument quickly faces trouble. The dissent says the NLRA is the more specific provision because it supposedly "speaks directly to group action by employees," while the Arbitration Act doesn't speak to such actions. *Ibid.* But the question before us is whether courts must enforce particular arbitration agreements according to their terms. And it's the Arbitration Act that speaks directly to the enforceability of arbitration agreements, while the NLRA doesn't mention arbitration at all. So if forced to choose between the two, we might well say the Arbitration Act offers the more on-point instruction. Of course, there is no need to make that call because, as our precedents demand, we have sought and found a persuasive interpretation that gives effect to all of Congress's work, not just the parts we might prefer.

Ultimately, the dissent retreats to policy arguments. . . . The respective merits of class actions and private arbitration as means of enforcing the law are questions constitutionally entrusted not to the courts to decide but to the policymakers in the political branches where those questions remain hotly contested. Just recently, for example, one federal agency banned individualized arbitration agreements it blamed for underenforcement of certain laws, only to see Congress respond by immediately repealing that rule. See 82 Fed. Reg. 33210 (2017) (cited *post* at 1647, n. 15); Pub. L. 115–74, 131 Stat. 1243. This Court is not free to substitute its preferred economic policies for those chosen by the people's representatives. *That,* we had always understood, was *Lochner*'s sin.

*

The policy may be debatable but the law is clear: Congress has instructed that arbitration agreements like those before us must be enforced as written. While Congress is of course always free to amend this judgment, we see nothing suggesting it did so in the NLRA—much less that it manifested a clear intention to displace the Arbitration Act. Because we can easily read Congress's statutes to work in harmony, that is where our duty lies. . . .

■ [*A concurring opinion by JUSTICE THOMAS is omitted.*]

■ *JUSTICE GINSBURG, with whom JUSTICES BREYER, SOTOMAYOR, and KAGAN join, dissenting:*

. . . .

In the NLRA and its forerunner, the Norris-LaGuardia Act (NLGA), 29 U.S.C. § 101 *et seq.*, Congress acted on an acute awareness: For workers striving to gain from their employers decent terms and conditions of employment, there is strength in numbers. A single employee, Congress understood, is disarmed in dealing with an employer. See *NLRB v. Jones & Laughlin Steel Corp.*, 301 U.S. 1, 33–34 (1937). The Court today subordinates employee-protective labor legislation to the Arbitration Act. In so doing, the Court forgets the labor market imbalance that gave rise to the NLGA and the NLRA, and ignores the destructive consequences of diminishing the right of employees "to band together in confronting an employer." *NLRB v. City Disposal Systems, Inc.*, 465 U.S. 822, 835 (1984). Congressional correction of the Court's elevation of the FAA over workers' rights to act in concert is urgently in order.

To explain why the Court's decision is egregiously wrong, I first refer to the extreme imbalance once prevalent in our Nation's workplaces, and Congress' aim in the NLGA and the NLRA to place employers and employees on a more equal footing. I then explain why the Arbitration Act, sensibly read, does not shrink the NLRA's protective sphere.

I

. . . .

A

The end of the 19th century and beginning of the 20th was a tumultuous era in the history of our Nation's labor relations. Under economic conditions then prevailing, workers often had to accept employment on whatever terms employers dictated. See 75 Cong. Rec. 4502 (1932). Aiming to secure better pay, shorter workdays, and safer workplaces, workers increasingly sought to band together to make their demands effective. . . .

Employers, in turn, engaged in a variety of tactics to hinder workers' efforts to act in concert for their mutual benefit. See J. Seidman, The Yellow Dog Contract 11 (1932). Notable among such devices was the "yellow-dog contract." Such agreements, which employers required employees to sign as a condition of employment, typically commanded employees to abstain from joining labor unions. See *id.* at 11, 56. Many of the employer-designed agreements cast an even wider net, "proscrib[ing] all manner of concerted activities." Finkin, The Meaning and Contemporary Vitality of the Norris-LaGuardia Act, 93 Neb. L. Rev. 6, 16 (2014); see Seidman, *supra*, at 59–60, 65–66. As a prominent United States Senator observed, contracts of the yellow-dog genre rendered the "laboring man . . . absolutely helpless" by "waiv[ing] his right . . . to free association" and by requiring that he "singly present any grievance he has." 75 Cong. Rec. 4504 (remarks of Sen. Norris).

Early legislative efforts to protect workers' rights to band together were unavailing. . . . Courts, including this one, invalidated the legislation based on then-ascendant notions about employers' and employees' constitutional right to "liberty of contract." See *Coppage* [*v. Kansas*, 236 U.S. 1, 26 (1915) (invalidating state law prohibiting employers from requiring employees, as a condition of employment, to refrain or withdraw from union membership)] . . . . While stating that legislatures could curtail contractual "liberty" in the interest of public health, safety, and the general welfare, courts placed outside those bounds legislative action to redress the bargaining power imbalance workers faced. . . .

In the 1930's, legislative efforts to safeguard vulnerable workers found more receptive audiences. As the Great Depression shifted political winds further in favor of worker-protective laws, Congress passed two statutes aimed at protecting employees' associational rights. First, in 1932, Congress passed the NLGA, which regulates the employer-employee relationship indirectly. Section 2 of the Act declares:

> "Whereas . . . the individual unorganized worker is commonly helpless to exercise actual liberty of contract and to protect his freedom of labor, . . . it is necessary that he have full freedom of association, self-organization, and designation of representatives of his own choosing, . . . and that he shall be free from the interference, restraint, or coercion of employers . . . in the designation of such representatives or in self-organization or in other concerted activities for the purpose of collective bargaining or other mutual aid or protection." 29 U.S.C. § 102.

Section 3 provides that federal courts shall not enforce "any . . . undertaking or promise in conflict with the public policy declared in [§ 2]." § 103. In adopting these provisions, Congress sought to render ineffective employer-imposed contracts proscribing employees' concerted activity of any and every kind. See 75 Cong. Rec. 4504–4505 (remarks of Sen. Norris) ("[o]ne of the objects" of the NLGA was to "outlaw" yellow-dog contracts); Finkin, *supra*, at 16 (contracts prohibiting "all manner of concerted activities apart from union membership or support . . . were understood to be 'yellow dog' contracts"). While banning court enforcement of contracts proscribing concerted action by employees, the NLGA did not directly prohibit coercive employer practices.

But Congress did so three years later, in 1935, when it enacted the NLRA. Relevant here, § 7 of the NLRA guarantees employees "the right to self-organization, to form, join, or assist labor organizations, to bargain collectively through representatives of their own choosing, *and to engage in other concerted activities for the purpose of collective bargaining or other mutual aid or protection.*" 29 U.S.C. § 157 (emphasis added). Section 8(a)(1) safeguards those rights by making it an "unfair labor practice" for an employer to "interfere with, restrain, or coerce employees in the exercise of the rights guaranteed in [§ 7]." § 158(a)(1). To oversee the Act's guarantees, the Act established the National Labor Relations Board (Board or NLRB), an independent regulatory agency empowered to administer "labor policy for the Nation." *San Diego Building Trades Council v. Garmon*, 359 U.S. 236, 242 (1959); see 29 U.S.C. § 160.

. . . . When a case challenging the NLRA's constitutionality made its way here, the Court, in retreat from its *Lochner*-era contractual-"liberty" decisions, upheld the Act as a permissible exercise of legislative authority. See *Jones & Laughlin Steel*, 301 U.S. at 33–34. . . .

B

. . . .

. . . [T]he employees involved in this litigation do not urge that they must have access to a judicial forum. They argue only that the NLRA prohibits their employers from denying them the right to pursue work-related claims in concert in any forum. If they may be stopped by employer-dictated terms from pursuing collective procedures in court, they maintain, they must at least have access to similar procedures in an arbitral forum.

C

Although the NLRA safeguards, first and foremost, workers' rights to join unions and to engage in collective bargaining, the statute speaks more embracively. In addition to protecting employees' rights "to form, join, or assist labor organizations" and "to bargain collectively through representatives of their own choosing," the Act protects employees' rights "to engage in *other* concerted activities for the purpose of . . . mutual aid or protection." 29 U.S.C. § 157 (emphasis added); see, *e.g.*, *NLRB v. Washington Aluminum Co.*, 370 U.S. 9, 14–15 (1962) (§ 7 protected unorganized employees when they walked off the job to protest cold working conditions). . . .

Suits to enforce workplace rights collectively fit comfortably under the umbrella "concerted activities for the purpose of . . . mutual aid or protection." 29 U.S.C. § 157. "Concerted" means "[p]lanned or accomplished together; combined." American Heritage Dictionary 381 (5th ed. 2011). "Mutual" means "reciprocal." *Id.* at 1163. When employees meet the requirements for litigation of shared legal claims in joint, collective, and class proceedings, the litigation of their claims is undoubtedly "accomplished together." By joining hands in litigation, workers can spread the costs of litigation and reduce the risk of employer retaliation. . . .

. . . .

Since the Act's earliest days, the Board and federal courts have understood § 7's "concerted activities" clause to protect myriad ways in which employees may join together to advance their shared interests. For example, the Board and federal courts have affirmed that the Act shields employees from employer interference when they participate in concerted appeals to the media, *e.g.*, *NLRB v. Peter Cailler Kohler Swiss Chocolates Co.*, 130 F.2d 503, 505–506 (CA2 1942), legislative bodies, *e.g.*, *Bethlehem Shipbuilding Corp. v. NLRB*, 114 F.2d 930, 937 (CA1 1940), and government agencies, *e.g.*, *Moss Planing Mill Co.*, 103 N.L.R.B. 414, 418–419, enf'd, 206 F.2d 557 (CA4 1953). "The 74th Congress," this Court has noted, "knew well enough that labor's cause often is advanced on fronts other than collective bargaining and grievance settlement within the immediate employment context." *Eastex*, 437 U.S. at 565.

Crucially important here, for over 75 years, the Board has held that the NLRA safeguards employees from employer interference when they pursue joint, collective, and class suits related to the terms and conditions of their employment. See, *e.g.*, *Spandsco Oil and Royalty Co.*, 42 N.L.R.B. 942, 948–949 (1942) (three employees' joint filing of FLSA suit ranked as concerted activity protected by the NLRA); *Poultrymen's Service Corp.*, 41 N.L.R.B. 444, 460–463, and n. 28 (1942) (same with respect to employee's filing of FLSA suit on behalf of himself and others similarly situated), enf'd, 138 F.2d 204 (CA3 1943); *Sarkes Tarzian, Inc.*, 149 N.L.R.B. 147, 149, 153 (1964) (same with respect to employees' filing class libel suit); *United Parcel Service, Inc.*, 252 N.L.R.B. 1015, 1018 (1980) (same with respect to employee's filing class action regarding break times), enf'd, 677 F.2d 421 (CA6 1982); *Harco Trucking, LLC*, 344 N.L.R.B. 478, 478–479 (2005) (same with respect to employee's maintaining class action regarding wages). For decades, federal courts have endorsed the Board's view, comprehending that "the filing of a labor related civil action by a group of employees is ordinarily a concerted activity protected by § 7." *Leviton Mfg. Co. v. NLRB*, 486 F.2d 686, 689 (CA1 1973); see, *e.g.*, *Brady v. National Football League*, 644 F.3d 661, 673 (CA8 2011) (similar). The Court pays scant heed to this longstanding line of decisions.

D

. . . . None of the Court's reasons for diminishing § 7 should carry the day.

1

The Court relies principally on the *ejusdem generis* canon. See *ante* at 1625. Observing that § 7's "other concerted activities" clause "appears at the end of a detailed list of activities," the Court says the clause should be read to "embrace" only activities "similar in nature" to those set forth first in the list, *ibid.* (internal quotation marks omitted), *i.e.*, " 'self-organization,' 'form[ing], join[ing], or assist[ing] labor organizations,' and 'bargain[ing] collectively,' " *ibid.* The Court concludes that § 7 should, therefore, be read to protect "things employees 'just do' for themselves." *Ibid.* . . . It is far from apparent why joining hands in litigation would not qualify as "things employees just do for themselves." In any event, there is no sound reason to employ the *ejusdem generis* canon to narrow § 7's protections in the manner the Court suggests.

The *ejusdem generis* canon may serve as a useful guide where it is doubtful Congress intended statutory words or phrases to have the broad scope their ordinary meaning conveys. See *Russell Motor Car Co. v. United States*, 261 U.S. 514, 519 (1923). Courts must take care, however, not to deploy the canon to undermine Congress' efforts to draft encompassing legislation. See *United States v. Powell*, 423 U.S. 87, 90 (1975) ("[W]e would be justified in narrowing the statute only if such a narrow reading was supported by evidence of congressional intent over and above the language of the statute."). Nothing suggests that Congress envisioned a cramped construction of the NLRA. Quite the opposite, Congress expressed an embracive purpose in enacting the legislation, *i.e.*, to "protec[t] the exercise by workers of full freedom of association." 29 U.S.C. § 151.

2

In search of a statutory hook to support its application of the *ejusdem generis* canon, the Court turns to the NLRA's "structure." *Ante* at 1625. Citing a handful of provisions that touch upon unionization, collective bargaining, picketing, and strikes, the Court asserts that the NLRA "establish[es] a regulatory regime" governing each of the activities protected by § 7. *Ante* at 1625–1626. That regime, the Court says, offers "specific guidance" and "rules" regulating each protected activity. Observing that none of the NLRA's provisions explicitly regulates employees' resort to collective litigation, the Court insists that "it is hard to fathom why Congress would take such care to regulate all the other matters mentioned in [§ 7] yet remain mute about this matter alone—unless, of course, [§ 7] doesn't speak to class and collective action procedures in the first place." *Ibid.*

This argument is conspicuously flawed. When Congress enacted the NLRA in 1935, the only § 7 activity Congress addressed with any specificity was employees' selection of collective-bargaining representatives. See 49 Stat. 453. The Act did not offer "specific guidance" about employees' rights to "form, join, or assist labor organizations." Nor did it set forth "specific guidance" for any activity falling within § 7's "other concerted activities" clause. The only provision that touched upon an activity falling within that clause stated: "Nothing in this Act shall be construed so as to interfere with or impede or diminish in any way the right to strike." *Id.* at 457. That provision hardly offered "specific guidance" regarding employees' right to strike.

Without much in the original Act to support its "structure" argument, the Court cites several provisions that Congress added later, in response to particular concerns. Compare 49 Stat. 449–457 with 61 Stat. 142–143 (1947) (adding § 8(d) to provide guidance regarding employees' and employers' collective-bargaining obligations); 61 Stat. 141–142 (amending § 8(a) and adding § 8(b) to proscribe specified labor organization practices); 73 Stat. 544 (1959) (adding § 8(b)(7) to place restrictions on labor organizations' right to picket employers). It is difficult to comprehend why Congress' later inclusion of specific guidance regarding some of the activities protected by § 7 sheds any light on Congress' initial conception of § 7's scope.

But even if each of the provisions the Court cites had been included in the original Act, they still would provide little support for the Court's conclusion. For going on 80 years now, the Board and federal courts—including this one—have understood § 7 to protect numerous activities for which the Act provides no "specific" regulatory guidance.

3

In a related argument, the Court maintains that the NLRA does not "even whispe[r]" about the "rules [that] should govern the adjudication of class or collective actions in court or arbitration." *Ante* at 1625–26. The employees here involved, of course, do not look to the NLRA for the procedures enabling them to vindicate their employment rights in arbitral or judicial forums. They assert that the Act establishes their right to act in concert using existing, generally available procedures, . . . and to do so free from employer interference. The FLSA and the Federal Rules on joinder and class actions provide the procedures pursuant to which the employees may ally to pursue shared legal claims. Their employers cannot lawfully cut off their access to those procedures, they urge, without according them access to similar procedures in arbitral forums. See, *e.g.*, American Arbitration Assn., Supplementary Rules for Class Arbitrations (2011).

. . . .

4

Further attempting to sow doubt about § 7's scope, the Court asserts that class and collective procedures were "hardly known when the NLRA was adopted in 1935." *Ante* at 1624–1625. . . .

First, one may ask, is there any reason to suppose that Congress intended to protect employees' right to act in concert using only those procedures and forums available in 1935? Congress framed § 7 in broad terms, "entrust[ing]" the Board with "responsibility to adapt the Act to changing patterns of industrial life." *NLRB v. J. Weingarten, Inc.*, 420 U.S. 251, 266 (1975); see *Pennsylvania Dept. of Corrections v. Yeskey*, 524 U.S. 206, 212 (1998) ("[T]he fact that a statute can be applied in situations not expressly anticipated by Congress does not demonstrate ambiguity. It demonstrates breadth." (internal quotation marks omitted)). . . .

Moreover, the Court paints an ahistorical picture. . . . By 1935, permissive joinder was scarcely uncommon in courts of equity. See 7 C. Wright, A. Miller, & M. Kane, Federal Practice and Procedure § 1651 (3d ed. 2001). Nor were representative and class suits novelties. Indeed, their origins trace back to medieval times. See S. Yeazell, From Medieval Group Litigation to the Modern Class Action 38 (1987). And beyond question, "[c]lass suits long have been a part of American jurisprudence." 7A Wright, *supra*, § 1751 at 12 (3d ed. 2005); see *Supreme Tribe of Ben-Hur v. Cauble*, 255 U.S. 356, 363 (1921). . . . Early instances of joint proceedings include cases in which employees allied to sue an employer. *E.g., Gorley v. Louisville*, 23 Ky. L. Rptr. 1782, 65 S.W. 844 (1901) (suit to recover wages brought by ten members of city police force on behalf of themselves and other officers); *Guiliano v. Daniel O'Connell's Sons*, 105 Conn. 695, 136 A. 677 (1927) (suit by two employees to recover for injuries sustained while residing in housing provided by their employer). It takes no imagination, then, to comprehend that Congress, when it enacted the NLRA, likely meant to protect employees' joining together to engage in collective litigation.

E

Because I would hold that employees' § 7 rights include the right to pursue collective litigation regarding their wages and hours, I would further hold that the employer-dictated collective-litigation stoppers, *i.e.*, "waivers," are unlawful. As earlier recounted, § 8(a)(1) makes it an "unfair labor practice" for an employer to "interfere with, restrain, or coerce" employees in the exercise of their § 7 rights. 29 U.S.C. § 158(a)(1). Beyond genuine dispute, an employer "interfere[s] with" and "restrain[s]" employees in the exercise of their § 7 rights by mandating that they prospectively renounce those rights in individual employment agreements.[8] The law could hardly be otherwise: Employees' rights to band together to meet their employers' superior strength would be worth precious little if employers could condition employment on workers signing away those rights. See *National Licorice Co. v. NLRB*, 309 U.S. 350, 364 (1940). Properly assessed, then, the "waivers" rank as unfair labor practices outlawed by the NLRA, and therefore unenforceable in court. . . .

---

[8] See, *e.g., Bethany Medical Center*, 328 N.L.R.B. 1094, 1105–1106 (1999) (holding employer violated § 8(a)(1) by conditioning employees' rehiring on the surrender of their right to engage in future walkouts); *Mandel Security Bureau Inc.*, 202 N.L.R.B. 117, 119, 122 (1973) (holding employer violated § 8(a)(1) by conditioning employee's reinstatement to former position on agreement that employee would refrain from filing charges with the Board and from circulating work-related petitions, and, instead, would "mind his own business").

II

Today's decision rests largely on the Court's finding in the Arbitration Act "emphatic directions" to enforce arbitration agreements according to their terms, including collective-litigation prohibitions. *Ante* at 1621–1622. Nothing in the FAA or this Court's case law, however, requires subordination of the NLRA's protections. Before addressing the interaction between the two laws, I briefly recall the FAA's history and the domain for which that Act was designed.

A

1

. . . .

The legislative hearings and debate leading up to the FAA's passage evidence Congress' aim to enable merchants of roughly equal bargaining power to enter into binding agreements to arbitrate *commercial* disputes. See, *e.g.*, 65 Cong. Rec. 11080 (1924) (remarks of Rep. Mills) ("This bill provides that where there are commercial contracts and there is disagreement under the contract, the court can [en]force an arbitration agreement in the same way as other portions of the contract."); Joint Hearings on S. 1005 and H.R. 646 before the Subcommittees of the Committees on the Judiciary, 68th Cong., 1st Sess. (1924) (Joint Hearings) (consistently focusing on the need for binding arbitration of commercial disputes).[10]

The FAA's legislative history also shows that Congress did not intend the statute to apply to arbitration provisions in employment contracts. . . . [W]hen the legislation was introduced, organized labor voiced concern. See Hearing on S. 4213 and S. 4214 before the Subcommittee of the Senate Committee on the Judiciary, 67th Cong., 4th Sess., 9 (1923) (Hearing). Herbert Hoover, then Secretary of Commerce, suggested that if there were "objection[s]" to including "workers' contracts in the law's scheme," Congress could amend the legislation to say: "but nothing herein contained shall apply to contracts of employment of seamen, railroad employees, or any other class of workers engaged in interstate or foreign commerce." *Id.* at 14. Congress adopted Secretary Hoover's suggestion virtually verbatim in § 1 of the Act, see . . . 9 U.S.C. § 1, and labor expressed no further opposition, see H.R. Rep. No. 96, 68th Cong., 1st Sess., 1 (1924).

---

[10] American Bar Association member Julius H. Cohen, credited with drafting the legislation, wrote shortly after the FAA's passage that the law was designed to provide a means of dispute resolution "particularly adapted to the settlement of commercial disputes." Cohen & Dayton, The New Federal Arbitration Law, 12 Va. L. Rev. 265, 279 (1926). Arbitration, he and a colleague explained, is "peculiarly suited to the disposition of the ordinary disputes between merchants as to questions of fact—quantity, quality, time of delivery, compliance with terms of payment, excuses for non-performance, and the like." *Id.* at 281. "It has a place also," they noted, "in the determination of the simpler questions of law" that "arise out of th[e] daily relations between merchants, [for example,] the passage of title, [and] the existence of warranties." *Ibid.*

Congress . . . envisioned application of the Arbitration Act to voluntary, negotiated agreements. . . . Congress never endorsed a policy favoring arbitration where one party sets the terms of an agreement while the other is left to "take it or leave it." Hearing 9 (remarks of Sen. Walsh) (internal quotation marks omitted); see *Prima Paint Corp. v. Flood & Conklin Mfg. Co.*, 388 U.S. 395, 403, n. 9 (1967) ("We note that categories of contracts otherwise within the Arbitration Act but in which one of the parties characteristically has little bargaining power are expressly excluded from the reach of the Act. See § 1.").

2

In recent decades, this Court has veered away from Congress' intent simply to afford merchants a speedy and economical means of resolving commercial disputes. . . . In 1983, the Court declared, for the first time in the FAA's then 58-year history, that the FAA evinces a "liberal federal policy favoring arbitration." *Moses H. Cone Memorial Hospital v. Mercury Constr. Corp.*, 460 U.S. 1, 24 (1983) . . . . Soon thereafter, the Court ruled, in a series of cases, that the FAA requires enforcement of agreements to arbitrate not only contract claims, but statutory claims as well. *E.g., Mitsubishi Motors Corp. v. Soler Chrysler-Plymouth, Inc.*, 473 U.S. 614 (1985); *Shearson/American Express Inc. v. McMahon*, 482 U.S. 220 (1987). Further, in 1991, the Court concluded in *Gilmer v. Interstate/Johnson Lane Corp.*, 500 U.S. 20, 23 (1991), that the FAA requires enforcement of agreements to arbitrate claims arising under the Age Discrimination in Employment Act of 1967, a workplace antidiscrimination statute. Then, in 2001, the Court ruled in *Circuit City Stores, Inc. v. Adams*, 532 U.S. 105, 109 (2001), that the Arbitration Act's exemption for employment contracts should be construed narrowly, to exclude from the Act's scope only transportation workers' contracts.

Employers have availed themselves of the opportunity opened by court decisions expansively interpreting the Arbitration Act. Few employers imposed arbitration agreements on their employees in the early 1990's. After *Gilmer* and *Circuit City*, however, employers' exaction of arbitration clauses in employment contracts grew steadily. See, *e.g.*, Economic Policy Institute (EPI), A. Colvin, The Growing Use of Mandatory Arbitration 1–2, 4 (Sept. 27, 2017), available at https://www.epi.org/files/pdf/135056.pdf (All Internet materials as visited May 18, 2018) (data indicate only 2.1% of nonunionized companies imposed mandatory arbitration agreements on their employees in 1992, but 53.9% do today). Moreover, in response to subsequent decisions addressing class arbitration, employers have increasingly included in their arbitration agreements express group-action waivers. See Ruan[, What's Left to Remedy Wage Theft? How Arbitration Mandates that Bar Class Actions Impact Low-Wage Workers, 2012 Mich. St. L. Rev. 1103,] 1129; Colvin, *supra*, at 6 (estimating that 23.1% of nonunionized employees are now subject to express class-action waivers in mandatory arbitration agreements). It is, therefore, this Court's exorbitant application of the

FAA—stretching it far beyond contractual disputes between merchants—that led the NLRB to confront, for the first time in 2012, the precise question whether employers can use arbitration agreements to insulate themselves from collective employment litigation. See *D.R. Horton*, 357 N.L.R.B. 2277 (2012), enf. denied in relevant part, 737 F.3d 344 (CA5 2013). Compare *ante* at 1620–1621 (suggesting the Board broke new ground in 2012 when it concluded that the NLRA prohibits employer-imposed arbitration agreements that mandate individual arbitration) with *supra* at 1637–1638 (NLRB decisions recognizing a § 7 right to engage in collective employment litigation) . . . .

As I see it, in relatively recent years, the Court's Arbitration Act decisions have taken many wrong turns. Yet, even accepting the Court's decisions as they are, nothing compels the destructive result the Court reaches today. . . .

B

Through the Arbitration Act, Congress sought "to make arbitration agreements as enforceable as other contracts, but not more so." *Prima Paint*, 388 U.S. at 404, n. 12. Congress thus provided in § 2 of the FAA that the terms of a written arbitration agreement "shall be valid, irrevocable, and enforceable, *save upon such grounds as exist at law or in equity for the revocation of any contract.*" 9 U.S.C. § 2 (emphasis added). Pursuant to this "saving clause," arbitration agreements and terms may be invalidated based on "generally applicable contract defenses, such as fraud, duress, or unconscionability." *Doctor's Associates, Inc. v. Casarotto*, 517 U.S. 681, 687 (1996) . . . .

Illegality is a traditional, generally applicable contract defense. See 5 R. Lord, Williston on Contracts § 12.1 (4th ed. 2009). . . . For the reasons stated *supra*, I would hold that the arbitration agreements' employer-dictated collective-litigation waivers are unlawful. By declining to enforce those adhesive waivers, courts would place them on the same footing as any other contract provision incompatible with controlling federal law. The FAA's saving clause can thus achieve harmonization of the FAA and the NLRA without undermining federal labor policy.

The Court urges that our case law—most forcibly, *AT&T Mobility LLC v. Concepcion*, 563 U.S. 333 (2011)—rules out reconciliation of the NLRA and the FAA through the latter's saving clause. I disagree. True, the Court's Arbitration Act decisions establish that the saving clause "offers no refuge" for defenses that discriminate against arbitration, "either by name or by more subtle methods." *Ante* at 1622. The Court, therefore, has rejected saving clause salvage where state courts have invoked generally applicable contract defenses to discriminate "covertly" against arbitration. *Kindred Nursing Centers L.P. v. Clark*, 581 U.S. 246, 251 (2017). In *Concepcion*, the Court held that the saving clause did not spare the California Supreme Court's invocation of unconscionability doctrine to establish a rule blocking enforcement of class-action waivers in adhesive consumer contracts. 563 U.S. at 341–344, 346–352. . . .

Here, however, the Court is not asked to apply a generally applicable contract defense to generate a rule discriminating against arbitration. At issue is application of the ordinarily superseding rule that "illegal promises will not be enforced," *Kaiser Steel*, 455 U.S. at 77, to invalidate arbitration provisions at odds with the NLRA, a pathmarking federal statute. That statute neither discriminates against arbitration on its face, nor by covert operation. It requires invalidation of *all* employer-imposed contractual provisions prospectively waiving employees' § 7 rights. See *supra* at 1641 and n. 8; cf. *Kindred Nursing Centers*, 581 U.S. at 254, n. 2 (States may enforce generally applicable rules so long as they do not "single out arbitration" for disfavored treatment).

C

Even assuming that the FAA and the NLRA were inharmonious, the NLRA should control. Enacted later in time, the NLRA should qualify as "an implied repeal" of the FAA, to the extent of any genuine conflict. See *Posadas v. National City Bank*, 296 U.S. 497, 503 (1936). Moreover, the NLRA should prevail as the more pinpointed, subject-matter specific legislation, given that it speaks directly to group action by employees to improve the terms and conditions of their employment. See *Radzanower v. Touche Ross & Co.*, 426 U.S. 148, 153 (1976) ("a specific statute" generally "will not be controlled or nullified by a general one" (internal quotation marks omitted)). . . .

III

The inevitable result of today's decision will be the underenforcement of federal and state statutes designed to advance the well-being of vulnerable workers. See generally Sternlight, Disarming Employees: How American Employers Are Using Mandatory Arbitration To Deprive Workers of Legal Protections, 80 Brooklyn L. Rev. 1309 (2015).

The probable impact on wage and hours claims of the kind asserted in the cases now before the Court is all too evident. Violations of minimum-wage and overtime laws are widespread. . . . One study estimated that in Chicago, Los Angeles, and New York City alone, low-wage workers lose nearly $3 billion in legally owed wages each year. . . . The U.S. Department of Labor, state labor departments, and state attorneys general can uncover and obtain recoveries for some violations. . . . Because of their limited resources, however, government agencies must rely on private parties to take a lead role in enforcing wage and hours laws. See Brief for State of Maryland et al. as *Amici Curiae* 29–33; Glover, The Structural Role of Private Enforcement Mechanisms in Public Law, 53 Wm. & Mary L. Rev. 1137, 1150–1151 (2012) (Department of Labor investigates fewer than 1% of FLSA-covered employers each year).

If employers can stave off collective employment litigation aimed at obtaining redress for wage and hours infractions, the enforcement gap is almost certain to widen. Expenses entailed in mounting individual claims will often far outweigh potential recoveries. See *id.* at 1184–1185 (because "the FLSA systematically tends to generate low-value claims," "mechanisms that facilitate the economics of claiming are required"); *Sutherland v. Ernst & Young LLP*, 768 F. Supp. 2d 547, 552 (S.D.N.Y. 2011) (finding that an employee utilizing Ernst & Young's arbitration program would likely have to spend $200,000 to recover only $1,867.02 in overtime pay and an equivalent amount in liquidated damages); cf. Resnik, Diffusing Disputes: The Public in the Private of Arbitration, the Private in Courts, and the Erasure of Rights, 124 Yale L.J. 2804, 2904 (2015) (analyzing available data from the consumer context to conclude that "private enforcement of small-value claims depends on collective, rather than individual, action") . . . .[15]

Fear of retaliation may also deter potential claimants from seeking redress alone. . . . Further inhibiting single-file claims is the slim relief obtainable, even of the injunctive kind. See *Califano v. Yamasaki*, 442 U.S. 682, 702 (1979) ("[T]he scope of injunctive relief is dictated by the extent of the violation established."). The upshot: Employers, aware that employees will be disinclined to pursue small-value claims when confined to proceeding one-by-one, will no doubt perceive that the cost-benefit balance of underpaying workers tips heavily in favor of skirting legal obligations.

. . . .

* * *

If these untoward consequences stemmed from legislative choices, I would be obliged to accede to them. But the edict that employees with wage and hours claims may seek relief only one-by-one does not come from Congress. It is the result of take-it-or-leave-it labor contracts harking back to the type called "yellow dog," and of the readiness of this Court to enforce those unbargained-for agreements. The FAA demands no such suppression of the right of workers to take concerted action for their "mutual aid or protection." . . .

NOTES AND QUESTIONS

1. These days, many different types of contracts contain pre-dispute arbitration agreements—provisions saying that if disputes arise, the parties will not sue each other in court, but instead will submit the disputes to binding arbitration. These provisions can also specify the manner in which the arbitration will be conducted.

---

[15] Based on a 2015 study, the Bureau of Consumer Financial Protection found that "pre-dispute arbitration agreements are being widely used to prevent consumers from seeking relief from legal violations on a class basis, and that consumers rarely file individual lawsuits or arbitration cases to obtain such relief." 82 Fed. Reg. 33210 (2017).

In the nineteenth and early twentieth centuries, such agreements usually were not worth very much. As one state supreme court observed in 1917, "at common law the power of arbitrators to make a binding award is subject to revocation at any time before an award is made, unless the submission is governed by statute or made a rule of court." *Martin v. Vansant*, 168 P. 990, 991 (Wash. 1917) (noting that this rule "has been severely criticised by many courts of high authority," but nonetheless was "too well settled to admit of dispute"). By the same token, if a party filed suit in breach of an arbitration agreement, courts would entertain the suit notwithstanding the prior agreement. *See, e.g.*, 5 C.J. *Arbitration and Award* § 7 (1916). The standard explanation for these doctrines was that "parties cannot, by private agreement, oust the courts of the jurisdiction vested in them by law, nor can [parties] irrevocably debar themselves from appealing to the established tribunals of justice." *Martin*, 168 P. at 991. Rather than triggering any type of specific enforcement, breach of an arbitration agreement would at most give rise to a separate action for damages, and the measure of damages was minimal. *See* Katherine Van Wezel Stone, *Rustic Justice: Community and Coercion Under the Federal Arbitration Act*, 77 N.C. L. REV. 931, 973 (1999).

In 1920, however, the New York legislature passed a state statute making written arbitration agreements irrevocable and beefing up their enforcement. *See* Act of Apr. 19, 1920, ch. 275, 1920 N.Y. Laws 803. In 1925, Congress enacted a similar federal statute. *See* United States Arbitration Act, ch. 213, 43 Stat. 883 (1925). With only minor changes, the provisions of that statute remain in force today as part of Title 9 of the United States Code. *See* Act of July 30, 1947, ch. 392, 61 Stat. 669 (enacting Title 9 as such). Section 2 establishes the general rule that "[a] written provision in . . . a contract evidencing a transaction involving commerce to settle by arbitration a controversy thereafter arising out of such contract . . . shall be valid, irrevocable, and enforceable, save upon such grounds as exist at law or in equity for the revocation of any contract . . . ." 9 U.S.C. § 2;[38] *see also id.* § 1 (defining "commerce" to mean "commerce among the several States or with foreign nations," as well as commerce involving federal territories or the District of Columbia). Section 3 adds that if a suit is brought in any federal court upon an issue referrable to arbitration under a written arbitration agreement, the court "shall on application of one of the parties stay the trial of the action until such arbitration has been had in accordance with the terms of the agreement." *Id.* § 3.

From the 1980s on, the Supreme Court has interpreted the Federal Arbitration Act broadly. *See* Stone, *supra*, 77 N.C. L. REV. at 943–56 (canvassing cases). In *Moses H. Cone Memorial Hospital v. Mercury*

[38] In 2022, Congress made an exception for disputes involving sexual assault or sexual harassment. The new 9 U.S.C. § 402 effectively allows claimants to opt out of pre-dispute arbitration agreements and joint-action waivers with respect to cases relating to such disputes. *See* Act of Mar. 3, 2022, Pub. L. 117–90, 136 Stat. 26.

Construction Corp., 460 U.S. 1 (1983), Justice Brennan's majority opinion agreed with lower federal courts that "as a matter of federal law, any doubts concerning the scope of arbitrable issues should be resolved in favor of arbitration." *Id.* at 24–25.[39] In *Southland Corp. v. Keating*, 465 U.S. 1 (1984), Chief Justice Burger's majority opinion held that Section 2 operates in state as well as federal courts and "foreclose[s] state legislative attempts to undercut the enforceability of arbitration agreements." *Id.* at 10–16.[40] In *Allied-Bruce Terminix Cos. v. Dobson*, 513 U.S. 265 (1995), Justice Breyer's majority opinion held that the phrase "involving commerce" in Section 2 of the Act is coextensive with Congress's constitutional authority to regulate interstate and foreign commerce, and hence reaches substantially farther than members of the enacting Congress would have thought in 1925. *See id.* at 273–77; *cf. supra* pp. 607–608 (noting the Court's similar decision with respect to the Sherman Act in *United States v. South-eastern Underwriters Ass'n*, 322 U.S. 533 (1944)).

Even after these cases, one might have thought that the Federal Arbitration Act still did not reach arbitration clauses in employment contracts (including the contracts at issue in *Epic Systems*). Ever since 1925, after all, Section 1 of the Act has said that "nothing herein contained shall apply to contracts of employment of seamen, railroad employees, or any other class of workers engaged in foreign or interstate commerce." 9 U.S.C. § 1. In *Circuit City Stores, Inc. v. Adams*, 532 U.S. 105 (2001), an employee of Circuit City argued that Section 1 should be understood to exempt all employment contracts that the Act would otherwise reach. But the Supreme Court disagreed. According to Justice Kennedy's majority opinion, "Section 1 exempts from the [Federal Arbitration Act] only contracts of employment of transportation workers." *Id.* at 119; *see id.* at 114–15 (invoking *ejusdem generis*); *see also id.* at 115–19 (arguing that even if § 1 had not referred specifically to seamen and railroad employees, the phrase "engaged in . . . commerce" in § 1 would still be narrower than the phrase "involving commerce" in § 2).

---

[39] As commentators have explained, this proposition has no apparent basis in the Act. *See, e.g.*, Margaret L. Moses, *Arbitration Law: Who's in Charge?*, 40 SETON HALL L. REV. 147, 175–76 (2010).

[40] This proposition seems natural if one regards Section 2 as establishing a substantive principle of the law of contracts. As Justice O'Connor explained in dissent, however, the Act probably was designed (and originally understood) as "a procedural statute, applicable only in federal courts." *Id.* at 25 (O'Connor, J., dissenting); *accord* Allied-Bruce Terminix Cos. v. Dobson, 513 U.S. 265, 286–93 (1995) (Thomas, J., dissenting); *see also, e.g.*, Note, *State Courts and the Federalization of Arbitration Law*, 134 HARV. L. REV. 1184, 1185 (2021) ("Historical context suggests, and most scholars agree, that Congress intended the law to be purely procedural."). *But cf.* Christopher R. Drahozal, *In Defense of* Southland*: Reexamining the Legislative History of the Federal Arbitration Act*, 78 NOTRE DAME L. REV. 101, 169 (2002) (acknowledging "the conventional wisdom that the Supreme Court's decision in *Southland* . . . was an illegitimate exercise of judicial lawmaking," but arguing that legislative history provides more support to the majority's position than critics think).

Just as the Supreme Court has interpreted the Federal Arbitration Act broadly, so too the Court has interpreted other federal statutes not to cut back on it. Part III of Justice Gorsuch's opinion in *Epic Systems* cited the most relevant precedents along those lines.

Admittedly, the first case in this sequence—*Wilko v. Swan*, 346 U.S. 427 (1953)—held that the Securities Act of 1933 *did* cut back on the Federal Arbitration Act. Subject to certain limitations, § 12(2) of the Securities Act created a private cause of action against any person who sells a security by means of a prospectus or oral communication that is materially false or misleading. In the words of § 12(2), the purchaser of the security "may sue either at law or in equity in any court of competent jurisdiction" for one of the remedies that § 12(2) authorizes. Securities Act of 1933, ch. 38, § 12(2), 48 Stat. 74, 84 (codified as amended at 15 U.S.C. § 77*l*(a)(2)). Section 22 gave potential plaintiffs a wide choice of forums for suits under the Act. *See id.* § 22(a), 48 Stat. at 86–87 (codified as amended at 15 U.S.C. § 77v(a)) (conferring subject-matter jurisdiction on federal district courts without regard to the amount in controversy, making venue proper in various federal judicial districts, and authorizing nationwide service of process). On their own, these provisions did not necessarily preclude contractual agreements to arbitrate claims rather than litigating them; just as sections 12(2) and 22 surely did not prevent parties from reaching out-of-court settlements after a claim arose, so too one might think that parties could contract in advance for claims to be resolved by arbitration rather than litigation. But § 14 of the Act contained the following limitation on private contracts: "Any condition, stipulation, or provision binding any person acquiring any security to waive compliance with any provision of this title or of the rules and regulations of the Commission shall be void." *Id.* § 14, 48 Stat. at 84 (codified at 15 U.S.C. § 77n). In *Wilko*, a majority of the Supreme Court held that "the right to select the judicial forum is the kind of 'provision' that cannot be waived under § 14 of the Securities Act." *Wilko*, 346 U.S. at 435. Notwithstanding the Federal Arbitration Act, then, the Court held that § 14 of the Securities Act prevented enforcement of an advance agreement to arbitrate issues arising under the Securities Act. *See id.* at 438.

In the 1970s and 1980s, however, the Court first limited and then overruled *Wilko*. *See* Scherk v. Alberto-Culver Co., 417 U.S. 506, 515–20 (1974) (limiting *Wilko* to domestic transactions and holding that it does not prevent enforcement of arbitration clauses in "a truly international agreement"); Shearson/American Express Inc. v. McMahon, 482 U.S. 220, 227–38 (1987) (refusing to extend *Wilko* to the Securities Exchange Act of 1934, despite the fact that § 29(a) of the 1934 Act was essentially identical to § 14 of the Securities Act of 1933); *Rodriguez de Quijas v. Shearson/American Express, Inc.*, 490 U.S. 477, 485 (1989) (overruling *Wilko* even as to the Securities Act of 1933). As the cases cited in Part III of Justice Gorsuch's opinion in *Epic Systems* indicate, that trend has continued.

Of course, Congress can supersede the Federal Arbitration Act if it wants to; newer federal statutes take priority over earlier ones, so "the Arbitration Act's mandate may be overridden by a contrary congressional command." *Shearson/American Express v. McMahon*, 482 U.S. at 226. Congress sometimes does explicitly restrict the enforceability of arbitration agreements in particular fields or with respect to particular claims.[41] But the Supreme Court has not been quick to read federal statutes as having that effect.

Take the Credit Repair Organizations Act (CROA), a consumer-protection statute regulating the credit-repair industry. *See* Act of Sept. 30, 1996, Pub. L. 104–208, § 2451, 110 Stat. 3009, 3009–454 to 3009–462 (enacting the CROA as Title IV of the Consumer Credit Protection Act) (codified at 15 U.S.C. §§ 1679 *et seq.*). The CROA prohibits various practices, *see* 15 U.S.C. § 1679b, provides the text of a disclosure statement that credit-repair organizations must supply their customers, *see id.* § 1679c, and regulates the organizations' contracts with their customers, *see id.* §§ 1679d, 1679e. As a remedy for noncompliance with any of the Act's provisions, the Act creates a private cause of action for damages, including punitive damages in such amount as "the court" may allow after considering various factors. *See id.* § 1679g. To reflect the existence of this cause of action, the disclosure statement that credit-repair organizations must supply their customers includes the following sentence: "You have a right to sue a credit repair organization that violates the Credit Repair Organization Act." *Id.* § 1679c. The CROA also includes a broad nonwaiver provision, invalidating "[a]ny waiver by any consumer of any protection provided by or any right of the consumer under [the CROA]." *Id.* § 1679f. Still, the section of the CROA that addresses the terms and conditions of credit-repair organizations' contracts does not specifically prohibit arbitration clauses, and the Supreme Court has refused to read either the nonwaiver provision or the

[41] *See, e.g.*, Act of Nov. 2, 2002, Pub. L. 107–273, § 11028(a)(2), 116 Stat. 1758, 1835 ("Notwithstanding any other provision of law, whenever a motor vehicle franchise contract provides for the use of arbitration to resolve a controversy arising out of or relating to such contract, arbitration may be used to settle such controversy only if after such controversy arises all parties to such controversy consent in writing to use arbitration to settle such controversy.") (codified at 15 U.S.C. § 1226(a)(2)); Dodd-Frank Wall Street Reform and Consumer Protection Act, Pub. L. 111–203, § 748, 124 Stat. 1376, 1746 (2010) (amending the Commodity Exchange Act to include protection for whistleblowers and to specify that "[n]o predispute arbitration agreement shall be valid or enforceable, if the agreement requires arbitration of a dispute arising under this section") (codified at 7 U.S.C. § 26(n)(2)); *id.* § 922(c)(2), 124 Stat. at 1848 (adding the same language to 18 U.S.C. § 1514A); *id.* § 1414(a), 124 Stat. at 2151 (amending the Truth in Lending Act to provide that "[n]o residential mortgage loan . . . may include terms which require arbitration or any other nonjudicial procedure as the method for resolving any controversy or settling any claims arising out of the transaction") (codified at 15 U.S.C. § 1639c(e)(1)); *see also id.* § 921, 124 Stat. at 1841 (amending the Securities Exchange Act and the Investment Advisers Act to give the Securities and Exchange Commission authority to promulgate rules prohibiting or restricting the use of arbitration agreements) (codified at 15 U.S.C. §§ 78*o*(*o*), 80b–5(f)); *id.* § 1028(b), 124 Stat. at 2004 (giving similar authority to the Bureau of Consumer Financial Protection) (codified at 12 U.S.C. § 5518(b)); *supra* note 38.

rest of the CROA to do so. *See* CompuCredit Corp. v. Greenwood, 565 U.S. 95, 104 (2012) (concluding that "the CROA is silent on whether claims under the Act can proceed in an arbitral forum," and the Federal Arbitration Act therefore applies in this area as in others).

2. Justice Gorsuch's majority opinion in *Epic Systems* reflected many of the precedents surveyed in the prior note. Part II of the opinion drew on the precedents that have interpreted the Federal Arbitration Act broadly. Part III drew on the precedents that have interpreted later federal statutes to be consistent with the Act. Because the structure of the majority's argument was complicated, this note will recap each of those parts.

Part II of the majority opinion addressed the "saving clause" in § 2 of the Federal Arbitration Act. Although Section 2 makes most arbitration clauses "valid, irrevocable, and enforceable," it recognizes an exception: arbitration clauses can be avoided "upon such grounds as exist at law or in equity for the revocation of any contract." 9 U.S.C. § 2. For instance, if a company uses fraud to get you to agree to an arbitration clause, you can invoke fraud to avoid enforcement of the arbitration clause just as you could invoke fraud to avoid enforcement of any other contract. *See, e.g.*, RESTATEMENT (SECOND) OF CONTRACTS § 164(1) (AM. LAW INST. 1981) ("If a party's manifestation of assent is induced by either a fraudulent or a material misrepresentation by the other party upon which the recipient is justified in relying, the contract is voidable by the recipient."). The Supreme Court has said that the Federal Arbitration Act "was designed . . . to place arbitration agreements 'upon the same footing as other contracts' "—not any *less* enforceable, but still subject to the same general defenses that would defeat the enforcement of other contracts. *Scherk*, 417 U.S. at 511 (quoting H.R. REP. NO. 68–96, at 1 (1924)); *see also, e.g.*, Doctor's Assocs., Inc. v. Casarotto, 517 U.S. 681, 687 (1996) ("[G]enerally applicable contract defenses, such as fraud, duress, or unconscionability, may be applied to invalidate arbitration agreements without contravening § 2.").

The plaintiffs in *Epic Systems* were trying to use one of those general defenses to avoid at least one aspect of the arbitration agreements between the plaintiffs and their employers. Those agreements not only required disputes to be resolved through arbitration rather than in court, but also required the arbitration proceeding to be individualized; no other employees' claims could be heard in the same proceeding. According to the plaintiffs, however, § 7 of the National Labor Relations Act gave them a right to join together with other claimants in legal proceedings,[42] and

[42] As revised and reenacted in the Labor-Management Relations Act of 1947, § 7 says:

> "Employees shall have the right to self-organization, to form, join, or assist labor organizations, to bargain collectively through representatives of their own choosing, and to engage in other concerted activities for the purpose of collective bargaining or other mutual aid or protection . . . ."

Labor-Management Relations Act, ch. 120, sec. 101, § 7, 61 Stat. 136, 140 (1947) (codified at 29 U.S.C. § 157).

§ 8(a)(1) forbade employers to insist that would-be employees sign away rights conferred by § 7.[43] For the plaintiffs, it followed that the arbitration agreement's individualization requirement was illegal—and just as fraud is a "generally applicable contract defense," *Doctor's Assocs.*, 517 U.S. at 687, so is illegality. Given the saving clause, then, the plaintiffs argued that the Federal Arbitration Act did not even purport to make the individualization requirement enforceable.

Part II of the majority opinion in *Epic Systems* rejected this argument on the strength of *AT&T Mobility LLC v. Concepcion*, 563 U.S. 333 (2011). There, a consumer contract had included an arbitration agreement that again purported to require individualized proceedings. The California Supreme Court had previously held that under California's version of "unconscionability" doctrine, many class-action waivers of this sort were unenforceable. *See* Discover Bank v. Superior Court, 113 P.3d 1100, 1110 (Cal. 2005) (reaching this conclusion "when the waiver is found in a consumer contract of adhesion in a setting in which disputes between the contracting parties predictably involve small amounts of damages, and when it is alleged that the party with the superior bargaining power has carried out a scheme to deliberately cheat large numbers of consumers out of individually small sums of money"). In *Concepcion*, however, the U.S. Supreme Court held that the Federal Arbitration Act preempted this aspect of California law with respect to arbitration clauses in contracts evidencing transactions involving interstate or foreign commerce. Justice Scalia's majority opinion reasoned that by preventing parties from binding themselves to simple bilateral arbitration, and requiring them to remain open to more elaborate classwide arbitration that would make the resolution of disputes more expensive and time-consuming, California's version of unconscionability doctrine would "interfere[ ] with fundamental attributes of arbitration" and frustrate the Federal Arbitration Act's "overarching purpose" of "ensur[ing] the enforcement of arbitration agreements according to their terms so as to facilitate streamlined proceedings." *Concepcion*, 563 U.S. at 344; *cf. infra* Chapter 6.B.3 (discussing the "obstacle" or "frustration of purpose" branch of conflict preemption). Justice Scalia added that the saving clause in § 2 of the Federal Arbitration Act should not be understood to protect state-law doctrines of this sort. *See Concepcion*, 563 U.S. at 343 ("Although § 2's saving clause preserves generally applicable contract defenses, nothing in it suggests an intent to preserve state-law rules that stand as an obstacle to the accomplishment of the FAA's objectives.").

In *Epic Systems*, the majority took *Concepcion* to stand for the following proposition: "courts may not allow a contract defense to reshape traditional individualized arbitration by mandating classwide

---

[43] Section 8(a)(1) says: "It shall be an unlawful labor practice for an employer . . . to interfere with, restrain, or coerce employees in the exercise of the rights guaranteed in section 7 . . . ." *Id.* § 8(a)(1), 61 Stat. at 140 (codified at 29 U.S.C. § 158(a)(1)).

arbitration procedures without the parties' consent." *Epic Systems*, 138 S. Ct. at 1623. Among other things, such defenses do not qualify as "grounds . . . for the revocation of any contract" within the meaning of § 2 of the Federal Arbitration Act. *See id.* at 1622 ("Under our precedent, . . . the saving clause does not save defenses that target arbitration either by name or by more subtle methods, such as by 'interfer[ing] with fundamental attributes of arbitration.' " (quoting *Concepcion*, 563 U.S. at 344)). That is true whether the defense is unconscionability (as in *Concepcion*) or illegality (as in *Epic Systems*). Thus, even if the plaintiffs were correct that the joinder waiver in their arbitration agreements was illegal under the National Labor Relations Act, the particular type of illegality that they were alleging would not trigger the saving clause in § 2 of the Federal Arbitration Act. Part II of the majority opinion in *Epic Systems* therefore reached the following conclusion: even if the plaintiffs were interpreting the National Labor Relations Act correctly, the Federal Arbitration Act would still purport to require the enforcement of their arbitration agreements according to the terms of those agreements (including the requirement of individualized proceedings).

Still, the plaintiffs had a second argument. If the majority was correct about how to interpret the saving clause in § 2 of the Federal Arbitration Act, but the plaintiffs were correct about the meaning of §§ 7 and 8(a)(1) of the National Labor Relations Act, then there would be a conflict between those two statutes. The plaintiffs argued that to the extent of any such conflict, the National Labor Relations Act should take priority as the later-enacted statute—with the result that notwithstanding the Federal Arbitration Act, the National Labor Relations Act would defeat enforcement of the aspect of the arbitration agreement purporting to require individualized arbitration.

Ultimately, however, Part III of the majority opinion in *Epic Systems* concluded that the plaintiffs were interpreting § 7 of the National Labor Relations Act too broadly. Section 7 says that employees have the right to form labor unions, to bargain collectively through such unions, and "to engage in other concerted activities for the purpose of collective bargaining or other mutual aid or protection." 29 U.S.C. § 157. Although the plaintiffs interpreted the final phrase as giving them the right to join together in legal proceedings, the majority argued that the *ejusdem generis* canon supported a narrower interpretation. In particular, the majority suggested that as used in § 7, the phrase "other concerted activities for the purpose of . . . other mutual aid or protection" referred only to activities that occur in the real world (as the activities specifically listed in § 7 do), not in lawsuits or arbitral proceedings. *See Epic Systems*, 138 S. Ct. at 1625. On this interpretation, moreover, the National Labor Relations Act would not come into conflict with the Federal Arbitration Act. Thus, the majority argued that "the 'stron[g] presum[ption]' " against implied repeals reinforced the narrower interpretation of § 7 of the National Labor Relations Act. *See id.* at 1624 (quoting United States v. Fausto, 484 U.S. 439, 453 (1988)).

3. Suppose that the majority had accepted the plaintiffs' interpretation of § 7 of the National Labor Relations Act. Given the majority's view of the saving clause in § 2 of the Federal Arbitration Act, the two statutes would then have conflicted with each other in cases like *Epic Systems*. Normally, when two federal statutes really do conflict with each other as applied to a case, the more recently enacted statute takes priority. In *Epic Systems*, though, which statute should have been considered the more recent one?

Congress originally enacted the Federal Arbitration Act in 1925. The National Labor Relations Act definitely is more recent than that; Congress enacted the original version in 1935 and an amended version as part of the Labor-Management Relations Act in 1947. But Congress has not re-enacted either § 7 or § 8(a)(1) of the National Labor Relations Act since June 23, 1947, when the Labor-Management Relations Act became law. Five weeks later—on July 30, 1947—Congress passed the statute that enacted Title 9 of the United States Code as such. Title 9 consists mostly of the Federal Arbitration Act, so the July 1947 statute re-enacted the provisions that had been in the Federal Arbitration Act. If the majority in *Epic Systems* had thought that §§ 7 and 8(a)(1) of the National Labor Relations Act (as enacted in 1935 and re-enacted in June 1947) conflicted with the provisions of the Federal Arbitration Act (as enacted in 1925 and re-enacted in July 1947), which should have taken priority?

4. In *Epic Systems*, the majority did not question the precedents in which the Supreme Court had interpreted the Federal Arbitration Act broadly. But if some of those precedents had come out differently, then the plaintiffs' proposed interpretation of the National Labor Relations Act might not have created any conflict with the Federal Arbitration Act.

Take *Allied-Bruce Terminix Cos. v. Dobson*, 513 U.S. 265 (1995). If *Allied-Bruce* had held that the phrase "involving commerce" in Section 2 of the Federal Arbitration Act referred to Congress's commerce powers as they were understood in 1925, then the Federal Arbitration Act might not have reached the contracts at issue in *Epic Systems* at all. Or take *Circuit City Stores, Inc. v. Adams*, 532 U.S. 105 (2001). If the dissenters in that case had prevailed, so that the Federal Arbitration Act did not reach arbitration agreements in any employment contracts (rather than just the contracts of transportation workers), then there would have been much less potential for conflict between the Federal Arbitration Act and the National Labor Relations Act in *Epic Systems*. Likewise, if the Court had come out differently in *AT&T Mobility LLC v. Concepcion*, 563 U.S. 333 (2011), then the saving clause in § 2 of the Federal Arbitration Act might again have avoided any risk of conflict between the two statutes. Thus, it is possible that the presumption against implied repeals came into play in *Epic Systems* only because the Court's own precedents had given the Federal Arbitration Act a very broad scope.

To the extent that the presumption against implied repeals affected the Court's decision in *Epic Systems*, it is worth noting the ripple effects of the Court's interpretations of the Federal Arbitration Act. Given those interpretations of the Federal Arbitration Act, reading § 7 of the National Labor Relations Act to protect the right to join together in legal proceedings would have created a conflict between the two statutes, and the presumption against implied repeals discourages readings that produce such conflicts. That apparently is one reason why the majority in *Epic Systems* read § 7 of the National Labor Relations Act more narrowly, so that it protects concerted activity in the workplace but not in the courts. Now that the Supreme Court has adopted that reading of § 7, moreover, the precedent established by *Epic Systems* will matter even for employees who are not parties to any arbitration agreements; even where arbitration is not in the picture, § 7 still will protect concerted activity only in the workplace and not in legal proceedings. For instance, it apparently would not violate § 7 of the National Labor Relations Act for an employer to insist that employees sign contracts agreeing not to be part of class-action lawsuits against the employer. Thus, even though one of the Court's rationales for reading § 7 narrowly was to avoid creating unnecessary conflicts with the Federal Arbitration Act, the narrow interpretation of § 7 will operate even in situations that do not implicate the Federal Arbitration Act.

In sum, *Epic Systems* illustrates a subtle consequence of doctrines of *stare decisis*. Because of principles like the presumption against implied repeals, precedents about the meaning of one statute can sometimes have important consequences for the Court's interpretation of otherwise unrelated statutes.

When Congress enacted the National Labor Relations Act in 1935, though, Congress could not readily have anticipated how the Supreme Court would later interpret the Federal Arbitration Act. Should the presumption against implied repeals have less force under those circumstances?

---

4. STATUTORY DIRECTIONS ABOUT HOW TO INTERPRET STATUTES

Almost all the principles of statutory interpretation that this book has covered so far have been developed (or at least articulated) primarily by courts. Occasionally, though, the book has made glancing references to the legislature's ability to regulate those principles. This section considers that issue in more detail.

In theory, a legislature might try to provide various sorts of directions about the process of ascribing meaning to statutes. *See*

Nicholas Quinn Rosenkranz, *Federal Rules of Statutory Interpretation*, 115 HARV. L. REV. 2085, 2086–87, 2140 (2002) (cataloguing a wealth of possibilities, and ultimately concluding that Congress can regulate "[m]ost of the interpretive decisions courts make [with respect to federal statutes]—whether choosing a dictionary, referencing a canon, or spurning pre-enactment legislative history"). As Professor Rosenkranz notes, every time a statute includes a definitional section, there is a sense in which it is regulating interpretation; the definitional section tells readers (including courts) what meaning to ascribe to various terms that appear elsewhere in the statute. *See id.* at 2103–06. But statutes have been known to provide other sorts of interpretive directions too.

Consider the canons—the subject of Chapter 2 of this book. Many state legislatures have enacted statutes codifying (or abrogating) particular canons that courts are (or are not) supposed to use in construing the state's laws. *See id.* at 2089 n.10. Congress has enacted fewer cross-cutting principles of interpretation, but some federal statutes include rules for interpreting those specific statutes. On occasion, a federal statute articulates a new interpretive principle and directs courts to use it as they interpret the statute. *See, e.g.*, 11 U.S.C. § 1508 ("In interpreting this chapter, the court shall consider its international origin, and the need to promote an application of this chapter that is consistent with the application of similar statutes adopted by foreign jurisdictions."). Somewhat more frequently, a federal statute recites a principle along the lines of an existing canon and instructs interpreters to read the statute accordingly. *See, e.g.*, Jarrod Shobe, *Congressional Rules of Interpretation*, 63 WM. & MARY L. REV. 1997, 2023–24 & n.118 (2022) (noting provisions in the United States Code about avoiding conflicts either with treaties or with customary international law—the topic of the *Charming Betsy* canon). Conversely, Congress sometimes purports to tell interpreters *not* to apply a particular canon that they might otherwise be inclined to deploy. *See, e.g.*, 25 U.S.C. § 2206(i)(7) (effectively instructing interpreters not to apply the rule of lenity to the "slayer statute" that governs the distribution and descent of interests in property that the federal government holds in trust for Native Americans); *see also* Military Commissions Act of 2006, Pub. L. 109–366, § 6(a)(2), 120 Stat. 2600, 2632 ("No foreign or international source of law shall supply a basis for a rule of decision in the courts of the United States in interpreting the prohibitions enumerated in [18 U.S.C. § 2441(d)]."). Apart from specific canons, Congress also sometimes tries to identify the general spirit with which interpreters should approach some or all of a federal statute. *See, e.g.*, 47 U.S.C. § 271(h) ("The provisions of subsection (g) are intended to be narrowly construed."); *cf.* Organized Crime Control Act of 1970, Pub. L. 91–452, § 904(a), 84 Stat. 922, 947 ("The provisions of this title [addressing racketeer-influenced and corrupt organizations] shall be liberally construed to effectuate its remedial purposes.").

Or consider the sources of information on which courts can draw in interpreting statutes. Again, some state legislatures have addressed this topic more than Congress has. As we saw in Chapter 3, however, it is not entirely unheard of for Congress to purport to regulate the courts' use of internal legislative history. Thus, in an apparent attempt to reduce uncertainty about how courts might reconstruct the contours of a particular legislative deal, § 105(b) of the Civil Rights Act of 1991 specifically provided that "[n]o statements other than the interpretive memorandum appearing at Vol. 137 Congressional Record S 15276 (daily ed. Oct. 25, 1991) shall be considered legislative history of, or relied upon in any way as legislative history in construing or applying, any provision of this Act that relates to Wards Cove—Business necessity/cumulation/alternative business practice." *See supra* p. 432 n.17; *see also* Rosenkranz, *supra*, 115 HARV. L. REV. at 2109 (discussing this provision).

In theory, legislatures might even try to weigh in on broad-gauged theories about the interaction between text and purpose in statutory interpretation. As Professor Rosenkranz notes, one could imagine a statute that purported to "endorse or abrogate entire theories of statutory interpretation, like textualism." *Id.* at 2087 (providing, as an example, the following hypothetical provision: "This Act shall be interpreted in textualist fashion, in accordance with principles set forth in the scholarship of Frank Easterbrook").

Interpretive directions of any of these types could vary in scope. Professor Rosenkranz usefully distinguishes "statute-specific" directions (which typically address only the interpretation of the particular statute that contains them) from more general directions (which address the interpretation of more statutes than they can specify). Within the latter category, he also notes the potential difference between directions that apply only to statutes that have already been enacted and directions that purport to govern the interpretation of future statutes. *Id.* at 2110–20.

As we shall see, statutes that purport to control the interpretation of future statutes raise special issues that require separate consideration. For now, then, let us focus on the other sorts of interpretive directions—directions purporting to regulate interpretation either of the statute that contains the directions or of other statutes previously enacted by the same legislative body. Do courts that are subject to the legislature's jurisdiction have to pay attention to such directions? Or might there be some reason why the legislature does not really have authority to regulate statutory interpretation in this way?

Definitional sections. There is little controversy about definitional sections in statutes. Courts and scholars agree that legislatures have broad power to prescribe, by statute, how particular terms in the same statute should be understood. Likewise, legislatures also have broad power to specify how terms in other statutes that already exist should be understood going forward. To be sure, a statute that purports to define how all pre-existing statutes use particular terms can be thought of as amending all past statutes that use those terms, and the Constitution will occasionally limit the legislature's ability to make the new definition govern transactions that occurred before the amendment was enacted. When courts are determining a new definition's applicability, they may also apply a rebuttable presumption against retroactivity as a matter of interpretation. *See supra* pp. 309–312 (discussing *Rivers v. Roadway Express*, 511 U.S. 298 (1994)). Subject to those caveats about retroactivity, though, there is widespread agreement that legislatures can enact and revise definitional sections telling interpreters to treat specified terms in pre-existing statutes as shorthand references to the more elaborate formulations spelled out in the definitional sections.

Sources of information. Some other sorts of interpretive directives are more controversial. For instance, Professor Jellum has suggested that Congress cannot validly regulate the sources of information that courts use to determine the meaning of federal statutes. The essence of her argument is that when Congress forbids courts to consult sources that the courts would otherwise use in statutory interpretation, or requires courts to consult sources that they would not otherwise use, Congress is "impermissibly intrud[ing] on the judiciary's core function to interpret the law." Linda D. Jellum, *"Which Is To Be Master," The Judiciary or the Legislature? When Statutory Directives Violate Separation of Powers*, 56 UCLA L. REV. 837, 882–90 (2009). But a broad-gauged version of this position may not really be tenable. While it is surely true that "the purpose of [the provisions that Professor Jellum criticizes] is to tell the judiciary what evidence to consider when interpreting statutes," *id.* at 882, the Constitution gives Congress broad power to prescribe rules of evidence for the federal courts. *See* U.S. CONST. art. I, § 8, cl. 18 (authorizing Congress "[t]o make all Laws which shall be necessary and proper for carrying into Execution" not only Congress's own powers, but also "all other Powers vested by this Constitution in the Government of the United States, or in any Department or Officer thereof"—including the judicial power that Article III vests in the federal courts); *see also* Act of Jan. 2, 1975, Pub. L. 93–595, 88 Stat. 1926 (prescribing the Federal Rules of Evidence). Within the limits of its enumerated powers, moreover, Congress presumably can cast substantive regulations in the form of rules of evidence that will apply even in state courts. To the extent that Congress can prescribe such rules of evidence, does anything in the Constitution categorically prevent Congress from extending them to address the sources of information that courts consult in interpreting federal statutes? Given that the *fact-finding* aspect of the judicial power is subject to considerable congressional regulation, why would the *law-finding* aspect of the judicial power be entirely off limits?

Perhaps we should be skeptical of federal statutes that purport to restrict the sources of information that courts can consider when interpreting the Constitution itself. In practice, a plenary power to control those sources might enable Congress to dictate the substantive meaning that courts ascribe to the Constitution—which, in turn, might seem uncomfortably close to letting Congress amend the Constitution by statute. But should we be similarly skeptical of federal statutes that purport to restrict the sources of information that courts can consider when interpreting other federal statutes? To the extent that Congress can freely amend the laws that the courts are interpreting, do we need to be concerned that Congress will change the substance of those laws under the guise of regulating the law-finding process?

Even if there is some reason for such concern, can the Constitution really be understood to invalidate *all* efforts by Congress to regulate the sources of information that courts consider when interpreting federal statutes? The Constitution surely does not prohibit Congress from trying to draft statutes in such a way as to convey the legal directives that Congress wants them to convey. In pursuit of that end, won't it sometimes be useful for Congress not only to make careful choices about a statute's words, but also to provide instructions about the other inputs that readers should or should not use to understand those words? Is there really a categorical difference between these two methods of increasing the likelihood that a statute will be taken to establish the legal directives that Congress is collectively trying to establish?[44]

Section 105(b) of the Civil Rights Act of 1991 is a good illustration. As participants in the legislative process were hammering out a deal on statutory language that would get past a key sticking point, they may well have worried that the voluminous legislative history contained many statements that did not actually reflect their deal but that courts might nonetheless seize upon when attributing meaning to the statute. The solution reflected in § 105(b), which identifies a particular interpretive memorandum as the only piece of legislative history worthy of reliance on the relevant issue, is an elegant and precise response to that concern. On what possible theory might it violate the constitutional separation of powers? And even if one persists in saying that Congress cannot dictate the courts' interpretive techniques, shouldn't the

[44] To avoid unnecessary complications, you may set aside the special case of a statute that purports to require interpreters to determine its meaning according to sources of information that do not exist when each House of Congress approves the statute, but that will be generated in the future. As Professor Rosenkranz notes, such an instruction will sometimes raise serious questions about the delegation of governmental power to whichever entities will generate the information that will in turn give content to the statute. Especially when those entities are agents of Congress itself, a statute that effectively empowers them to act with the force of law on their own might offend the principles associated with *INS v. Chadha*, 462 U.S. 919 (1983). *See* Rosenkranz, *supra*, 115 HARV. L. REV. at 2133–39 (raising this objection to a hypothetical provision specifying that "[t]his Act shall be interpreted by reference to a report that the Senate Judiciary Committee shall generate tomorrow"). Even when the entities in question are in the executive branch or the courts, Congress cannot give them completely unfettered discretion to make the statute mean whatever they want. *See id.* at 2127–31 (discussing the nondelegation doctrine). But these special problems evaporate if the sources of information to which a statute refers all existed at the time that the statute went through the process of bicameralism and presentment. *See, e.g., id.* at 2137 (noting that "a statute requiring reference to pre-enactment legislative history would be constitutional").

interpretive techniques that the courts apply on their own take heed of the guidance supplied by provisions like § 105(b)? (Is there an important difference between the view that § 105(b) applies of its own force and the view that § 105(b) applies through incorporation into the interpretive techniques that courts use on their own authority?)

However one answers these questions, it seems inevitable (as a practical matter) that entities within the legislative branch will have considerable control over the content of the internal legislative history that courts consult for purposes of statutory interpretation. Under current norms of statutory interpretation, courts typically disregard aspects of a statute's internal legislative history that are not publicly available. But each House of Congress determines which aspects of its proceedings to transcribe and release to the public. If the Senate does not release records from a particular committee's mark-up session, then the Senate is effectively ensuring that state and federal courts will not rely upon those records when interpreting the resulting statute. If you think that § 105(b) of the Civil Rights Act of 1991 intrudes impermissibly on a core judicial function, do you also think that each House of Congress has a constitutional obligation to publish all conceivable sources of information that courts would like to rely upon in construing statutes?

Canons. Aside from statutes that purport to regulate the sources of information that readers should (or should not) consult, what about statutes that purport to require (or forbid) the application of certain canons of interpretation? Here, Professor Jellum has suggested that the generality of the legislature's instruction might matter: she seems inclined to accept *statute-specific* instructions that turn a canon on or off for one particular statute, but she doubts the constitutionality of more generic instructions that purport to codify or abrogate one or more canons wholesale. *See* Jellum, *supra*, 56 UCLA L. REV. at 890–97. Does that distinction make a constitutional difference?

Professor Jellum views statute-specific instructions as legitimate tools for helping the legislature convey the legal directives that it wants to convey; properly used, they can increase the chances of successful communication from legislature to courts. *See id.* at 893. But the same might also be true of more generic instructions. If the legislature believes that the use of a particular canon across the universe of cases will hinder successful communication more often than it will help, can't a statute abrogating the canon on a wholesale basis be seen as a rule-like way of increasing the chances that courts will understand statutes to convey the legal directives that the legislature wants to convey? If this argument provides a constitutional basis for statute-specific interpretive directions abrogating particular canons, can't it work at the wholesale level too?

As applied to pre-existing statutes, moreover, a generic statute codifying or abrogating a particular canon may not even need to be defended in these terms. Can't such a statute be seen as amending all of the statutes that it covers—so that it is less about what those statutes used to mean than about what they mean going forward? In that respect, is it any different than a statute that generically amends the definition of particular terms as those terms are used in all pre-existing statutes? (As indicated above, the scholarly consensus concedes that there is no categorical bar on the latter sort of statute, as long as the amendment complies with limitations on legislative retroactivity.)

Of course, even if the Constitution does not categorically prohibit either statute-specific or generic directions about how to read pre-existing statutes, the Constitution surely imposes some more fine-grained limitations on the content of those directions. For instance, a legislature cannot validly direct courts to resolve all indeterminacies in statutes in the way most harmful to a racial or religious minority; such a direction would violate the Fifth Amendment (if it appeared in a federal statute) or the Fourteenth Amendment (if it appeared in a state statute). Aside from such extreme examples, though, what other relevant limits might the Constitution impose? Consider, for instance, the legislature's power to override "normative" canons that address what would otherwise be indeterminacies in the interpretation or application of statutes and that encourage courts to resolve those indeterminacies in a consistent direction. To the extent that the content of a particular normative canon simply reflects the judiciary's own sense of good policy, the legislature presumably can override it. But is the same true of canons like the rule of lenity or the presumption against retroactivity, the contents of which are said to reflect values inferred from the Constitution itself? *Cf.* Julian R. Murphy, *Lenity and the Constitution: Could Congress Abrogate the Rule of Lenity?*, 56 HARV. J. LEGIS. 423, 425 (2019) (suggesting that because of "separation of powers and due process concerns," Congress cannot abrogate "the irreducible core of the rule [of lenity] as a tiebreaker in circumstances where all other tools of statutory interpretation are insufficient to resolve statutory ambiguity").

Whether the legislature can abrogate a particular canon may depend, to some extent, on the source of that canon. But even canons that are said to be inspired by "constitutional values" are not typically thought to be hard-wired into the Constitution itself. If most of those canons are simply rule-like ways of handling matters on which the legislature has not been clear, is there any reason to think that the legislature cannot turn them off? *Cf.* Rosenkranz, *supra,* 115 HARV. L. REV. at 2140 (acknowledging the possibility of constitutional limits on the substance of particular interpretive directions, but concluding that such limits "are the exceptions rather than the rule").

Special problems raised by directions about how to read future statutes. Thus far, we have been considering only directives that purport to control the interpretation of either the very same statute that contains the directives or other previously enacted statutes. But statutes that purport to regulate the meanings that interpreters should ascribe to *future* statutes raise an additional set of concerns.

It is one thing to say that the current Congress can prescribe artificial rules about the meanings that interpreters should ascribe, going forward, to statutes enacted by *past* Congresses. Subject to constitutional limits, Congress can always amend pre-existing laws, and a statute purporting to control the interpretation of past statutes can be regarded as an amendment of those statutes. But the current Congress has no power to amend statutes that have not yet been enacted, so this rationale does not give the current Congress the same level of control over the meanings that interpreters will ascribe to statutes enacted by future Congresses. Even if the current Congress simply wants to establish ground rules for future communication, moreover, courts that are asked to apply those rules must keep in mind "[t]he principle . . . that one legislature cannot abridge the powers of a succeeding legislature." *Fletcher v. Peck*, 10 U.S. (6 Cranch) 87, 135 (1810).

That principle dates far back. Writing in eighteenth-century England, Blackstone famously declared that "[a]cts of parliament derogatory from the power of subsequent parliaments bind not." 1 WILLIAM BLACKSTONE, COMMENTARIES ON THE LAWS OF ENGLAND 90 (1765). For Blackstone, this conclusion followed from the concept of parliamentary supremacy, which he understood to operate on an ongoing basis. In his words, "the legislature, being in truth the sovereign power, is always of equal, always of absolute authority: it acknowledges no superior upon earth, which the prior legislature must have been, if [its] ordinances could bind the present parliament." *Id.*

In the United States, the Constitution makes matters somewhat more complicated. *See* United States v. Winstar Corp., 518 U.S. 839, 872–74 (1996) (plurality opinion of Souter, J.). Rather than having "absolute authority," Congress is limited by the Constitution, and the Constitution protects certain kinds of legal interests against legislative abrogation. To the extent that statutes can generate those sorts of interests, there are some ways in which a statute enacted today will have the effect of restricting what future legislatures can do. For instance, suppose that Congress enacts a statute transferring ownership of land from the federal government to a private person. Once title to the land has vested in the recipient, a future Congress cannot unilaterally take it back simply by repealing the original statute. The Fifth Amendment protects vested property rights against the federal government, and the statute transferring title to the private recipient generated rights of the sort that the Fifth Amendment protects. The same might be said about statutes that give rise to certain other sorts of rights, such as statutes that amount to contracts between the federal government and private entities.

Arguably, though, any restrictions on a future Congress's ability to repeal such statutes stem from the Constitution itself. The current Congress probably cannot supplement those constitutional limitations by imposing additional *statutory* restrictions on the legislative powers of future Congresses.

For example, suppose the current Congress is enacting a statute that the Constitution would not prevent future Congresses from repealing, and suppose the current Congress tries to avoid that risk by including the following provision: "No future Congress can repeal or amend this statute." That will not work. For one thing, the provision probably is unconstitutional. With Blackstone's equal-authority principle in the background, the Necessary and Proper Clause need not be understood as allowing one Congress to restrict the legislative powers of future Congresses, and such restrictions might also be thought to conflict with the Vesting Clause of Article I ("All legislative Powers herein granted shall be vested in a Congress of the United States, which shall consist of a Senate and House of Representatives").[45] But even if statutory restrictions on the legislative powers of future Congresses are not technically unconstitutional from the start, a future Congress presumably could repeal them on the same terms as any other statute. *Cf.* BLACKSTONE, *supra*, at 90–91 ("Cicero, in his letters to Atticus, treats with a proper contempt those restraining clauses which endeavour to tie up the hands of succeeding legislatures. 'When you repeal the law itself,' says he, 'you at the same time repeal the prohibitory clause, which guards against such repeal.' ").

These principles suggest at least some limits on Congress's ability to control the interpretation of future statutes. To see why, suppose that the current Congress tries a more subtle way of insulating its enactments from change by future Congresses. Instead of purporting to prohibit future Congresses from repealing a particular statute, the current Congress enacts the following interpretive direction as part of the statute that it wants to insulate: "No future statute should be understood to repeal this statute unless the operative provisions of the repealing statute use the magic word 'Shazam!' five times." Suppose, though, that a future Congress refuses to play along; when it wants to repeal the statute that its predecessor was trying to insulate, it simply enacts straightforward language saying that the earlier statute is repealed. Would courts say that the later statute does not actually repeal the earlier statute, because the interpretive direction established by the earlier statute tells them not to read the later statute as a repeal?

It seems highly unlikely that courts would say any such thing. As Professors Larry Alexander and Saikrishna Prakash have explained, the key question is not how the earlier Congress wanted courts to read the later statute, but rather what the later statute means. To the extent that any Congress's intentions bear on that question, the intentions that

[45] Although the reasons vary, most scholars agree that the Constitution does not let one Congress bind its successors. *See, e.g.*, 1 LAURENCE H. TRIBE, AMERICAN CONSTITUTIONAL LAW § 2–3 n.1 (3d ed. 2000); John O. McGinnis & Michael B. Rappaport, *The Constitutionality of Legislative Supermajority Requirements: A Defense*, 105 YALE L.J. 483, 505–06 (1995); John C. Roberts & Erwin Chemerinsky, *Entrenchment of Ordinary Legislation: A Reply to Professors Posner and Vermeule*, 91 CAL. L. REV. 1773, 1775, 1782–95 (2003). For a dissenting view, see Eric A. Posner & Adrian Vermeule, *Legislative Entrenchment: A Reappraisal*, 111 YALE L.J. 1665 (2002).

matter are those of the later Congress. And while interpretive directions provided by an earlier Congress may often be a good guide to the intended meaning of a later statute, the particular interpretive direction supplied by the earlier Congress in this hypothetical is not. As a result, it should not prevent courts from adopting the most natural reading of the later statute. *See* Larry Alexander & Saikrishna Prakash, *Mother May I? Imposing Mandatory Prospective Rules of Statutory Interpretation*, 20 CONST. COMMENT. 97 (2003).

Professor Rosenkranz does not seem to accept this analysis. In his view, as long as the earlier statute prescribes some "ascertainable" and "otherwise unobjectionable" form of words that the future Congress can enact to achieve what it wants to achieve, the earlier statute does not impinge unconstitutionally upon the legislative power of the future Congress. And if the earlier statute is constitutional, then courts must give effect to it—with the result that the future Congress can accomplish a repeal only by using the form of words that the earlier statute identifies. Professor Rosenkranz expresses that point with characteristic verve:

> Even a statute providing that "laws of the United States, including this one, may be repealed only by the words 'Mother, may I?' " would be unobjectionable, because the door would remain open to exercise the full panoply of legislative power. There would still be a form of words—"Mother, may I?"—with which Congress could achieve every legislative goal, including the repeal of the "Mother, may I?" provision.

Rosenkranz, *supra*, 115 HARV. L. REV. at 2118.

Contrary to Professor Rosenkranz's position, though, the fact that future Congresses *could* comply with the "Mother, may I" provision does not prove that they *must* do so—that a future Congress can authoritatively repeal a statute *only* by using the form of words that the earlier statute prescribed. That would be true only if the "Mother, may I?" provision had the force of law—that is, only if one Congress can validly control how its successors must express themselves in order to exercise their legislative powers. In my view, Congress has no more authority to do that than to impose other restrictions on the laws that its successors can enact. *See* Alexander & Prakash, *supra*, 20 CONST. COMMENT. at 105 ("Congress may not force a future Congress to use particular language to legislate.").

Still, suppose that Congress has more power along these lines than I think, and that the "Mother, may I?" provision starts off with the force of law. Even so, a new Congress surely could exempt one or more of its statutes from that provision. Notwithstanding the edicts of the earlier Congress, moreover, each new Congress has the authority to do so *by implication* no less than expressly. A statute saying that an earlier statute is repealed, but not using the "Mother, may I?" formulation, presumably ought to be understood as repealing the earlier statute even if that entails contradicting (and therefore impliedly repealing *pro tanto*) the "Mother, may I?" provision. *See id.* at 106 ("An implicit exemption or repeal . . . is effective, even though the prior Congress essentially attempted to prevent implicit exemptions and repeals.").

The same analysis also applies to less outlandish interpretive directions. For a real-world example, Professors Alexander and Prakash highlight 1 U.S.C. § 108. Historically, Anglo-American courts held that if Statute #1 was repealed by Statute #2, which in turn was repealed by Statute #3, then Statute #1 should ordinarily be held to be back in effect, because the legislature had repealed its repeal. *See, e.g.*, 1 BLACKSTONE, *supra*, at 90 ("If a statute, that repeals another, is itself repealed afterwards, the first statute is hereby revived, without any formal words for that purpose."). This traditional rule amounted to a judicially articulated canon about how to interpret Statute #3; in the absence of other indications, courts were supposed to read Statute #3 as resuscitating Statute #1. But in 1871, Congress prescribed a different rule for federal statutes: "Whenever an act is repealed, which repealed a former act, such former act shall not thereby be revived, unless it shall be expressly so provided." Act of Feb. 25, 1871, § 3, 16 Stat. 431, 431–32. Now found at 1 U.S.C. § 108 (which Congress enacted as such in 1947), this provision instructs courts not to interpret laws like Statute #3 as reviving Statute #1 unless they do so "expressly."

As Professors Alexander and Prakash point out, however, courts should not always follow this interpretive direction (at least with respect to later-enacted statutes). For a clear example, imagine that Statutes #2 and #3 are each just one sentence long; Statute #2 says only that "Statute #1 is hereby repealed," and Statute #3 says only that "Statute #2 is hereby repealed." In this situation, should courts understand Statute #3 to revive Statute #1? If 1 U.S.C. § 108 controlled that question, the answer would be "no"; Statute #3 says nothing "express[ ]" about the revival of Statute #1. But that answer would strip Statute #3 of the only meaning that it could possibly have; if Statute #3 does not revive Statute #1, then it does nothing at all. Rather than allow an earlier law (1 U.S.C. § 108) to negate the only meaning that can plausibly be ascribed to a later-enacted law (Statute #3), Professors Alexander and Prakash would conclude that Statute #3 *does* revive Statute #1. As they put it, a court that followed 1 U.S.C. § 108 in this situation would not really be "interpret[ing]" Statute #3 at all; instead of honestly trying to identify the meaning of Statute #3, such a court would simply be letting an earlier statute trump a later one. Alexander & Prakash, *supra*, 20 CONST. COMMENT. at 99.

One could offer many other examples of the same basic point. As enacted in 1946, for instance, § 12 of the federal Administrative Procedure Act (APA) read as follows: "No subsequent legislation shall be held to supersede or modify the provisions of this Act except to the extent that such legislation shall do so expressly." 60 Stat. 237, 244 (1946); *see also* Act of Sept. 6, 1966, Pub. L. 89–554, 80 Stat. 378, 388 (enacting a modified version of this language as part of 5 U.S.C. § 559). According to the analysis of Professors Alexander and Prakash, though, this provision does not really have the conclusive effect that it purports to have. Notwithstanding the interpretive direction in the APA, there might still be cases in which courts should read a future statute as *implicitly* superseding or modifying the APA as applied to some scenario. *Cf.* Marcello v. Bonds, 349 U.S. 302, 310 (1955) (reading the Immigration and Nationality Act of 1952 to exempt deportation hearings from the APA, but saying that the Act did so "expressly" despite the absence of any explicit provision to that effect).

Likewise, § 8(a) of the federal War Powers Resolution (which was enacted through the process of bicameralism and presentment and which therefore has the status of a statute) purports to establish the following interpretive direction:

> "Authority to introduce United States Armed Forces into hostilities or into situations wherein involvement in hostilities is clearly indicated by the circumstances shall not be inferred . . . from any provision of law (whether or not in effect before the date of the enactment of this joint resolution) . . . unless such provision specifically authorizes the introduction of United States Armed Forces into hostilities or into such situations and states that it is intended to constitute specific statutory authorization within the meaning of this joint resolution . . . ."

Pub. L. 93–148, 87 Stat. 555, 558 (1973) (codified at 50 U.S.C. § 1547(a)). Again, it is easy to imagine a future statute that does not specifically refer to the War Powers Resolution, but that nonetheless is most naturally understood as providing statutory authority for the introduction of United States troops into hostilities. The analysis of Professors Alexander and Prakash suggests that such a statute should have this effect notwithstanding the rule of construction set forth in the War Powers Resolution.[46]

---

[46] Other prominent statutes raise similar issues. *See, e.g.,* Religious Freedom Restoration Act, Pub. L. 103–141, § 6(b), 107 Stat. 1488, 1489 (1993) ("Federal statutory law adopted after the date of the enactment of this Act is subject to this Act unless such law explicitly excludes such application by reference to this Act.") (codified at 42 U.S.C. § 2000bb–3(b)); Act of April 20, 1983, Pub. L. 98–21, § 335(a)(2), 97 Stat. 65, 130 (amending § 207 of the Social Security Act to add the following language in a new subsection: "No other provision of law, enacted before, on, or after the date of the enactment of this section, may be construed to limit, supersede, or otherwise modify the provisions of this section except to the extent that it does so by express reference to this section." (codified at 42 U.S.C. § 407(b))); National Emergencies Act, Pub. L. 94–412, tit. II, § 201(b), 90 Stat. 1255, 1255 (1976) ("No law enacted after the date of enactment of this Act shall supersede this title unless it does so in specific terms, referring to this title, and declaring that the new law supersedes the provisions of this title.") (codified at 50 U.S.C. § 1621(b)); *see also* McCarran-Ferguson Act, ch. 20, § 2(b), 59 Stat. 33, 34 (1945) (establishing a general rule, subject to limited exceptions, that "[n]o Act of Congress shall be construed to invalidate, impair, or supersede any law enacted by any State for the purpose of regulating the business of insurance, or which imposes a fee or tax upon such business, unless such Act specifically relates to the business of insurance") (codified at 15 U.S.C. § 1012(b)); 28 U.S.C. § 2283 (specifying, subject to two other exceptions, that a federal court "may not grant an

You should not conclude that statutory directions about the meaning of future statutes have no effect at all. While Professors Alexander and Prakash persuasively argue that such interpretive directions are not *conclusive*, they acknowledge that interpretive directions laid down by a prior Congress "might color both how future Congresses [draft] legislation and how others will view a future Congress's handiwork." Alexander & Prakash, *supra*, 20 CONST. COMMENT. at 108. Such interpretive directions might therefore have the practical effect of justifying a rebuttable presumption: in the absence of contrary indications, courts can sensibly presume that future Congresses will draft statutes in light of the general interpretive guidelines provided by existing law. For instance, take the usual situation that 1 U.S.C. § 108 addresses. If Statute #3 does not say anything one way or the other about whether it is reviving Statute #1, courts are likely to presume (absent sufficiently strong indications to the contrary) that Statute #3 was drafted in light of the norm identified by 1 U.S.C. § 108, and hence that Statute #3 does *not* revive Statute #1. Likewise, if a later-enacted statute otherwise seems ambiguous about whether it implicitly supersedes or modifies something in the Administrative Procedure Act, courts might resolve the ambiguity in light of the interpretive principle supplied by § 12 of the APA (now 5 U.S.C. § 559).

This conclusion fits naturally into any system of interpretation that is designed, among other things, to reduce the likely gap between the interpreted and the intended meaning of statutory language. In the context that we are considering, of course, the intended meaning that matters is that of the later-enacted statute. But Congress might tend to draft new statutes in light of the statutes that are already in force, including statutes that purport to prescribe interpretive directions for the future. Unless there is adequate reason to think that the later Congress deviated from those directions without explicitly saying so, courts can sensibly interpret new statutes in light of the general interpretive guidelines that Congress laid down in the past and that, as far as we know, Congress usually continues to follow.

Someone with unbridled enthusiasm for rule-like interpretive methods might conceivably be drawn to a more extreme position. While conceding that interpreters should care about the intended meaning of the statutes that they are interpreting, such a person might think that courts will reach more accurate decisions about legislative intent if they apply an inflexible rule than if they leave themselves more wiggle room. On this view, courts should presume, irrebuttably, that a later Congress *always* follows all interpretive directions enacted by prior Congresses, except to the extent that the later Congress explicitly addresses and rejects those directions. In defense of this irrebuttable presumption, a real enthusiast for rules might argue that the escape hatch built into a

injunction to stay proceedings in a State court except as expressly authorized by Act of Congress").

weaker presumption will introduce more errors than it avoids: if courts are open to claims that the later Congress intended to opt out of prior interpretive directions (even though it did not say so expressly), courts will make more mistakes about the intended meaning of later-enacted statutes than if courts simply assume that each later Congress always intends to follow any and all interpretive principles that its predecessors codified and that it has not expressly repealed.

That argument, however, goes too far for most people to accept. As the examples offered by Professors Alexander and Prakash suggest, there are some situations in which interpreters can be very confident that a later statute was *not* drafted in light of the guidance suggested by an earlier interpretive direction. At least in such situations, an irrebuttable presumption that the interpretive direction applies anyway would predictably drive interpreters away from the intended meaning of statutory language. The same may well be true even in less clearcut cases, where interpreters simply think that a new statute *probably* was not intended to mean what an interpretive direction enacted by an earlier Congress would suggest. To be sure, different people might have different views about exactly how much weight such interpretive directions deserve as guides to the meaning of later-enacted statutes. But if one wants to reduce mismatches between the meaning that interpreters ascribe to statutes and the meaning that members of the enacting legislature collectively intended to convey, one will not favor an irrebuttable presumption that interpreters should always follow whatever interpretive guidelines an earlier legislature established.

* * * * *

To sum up, there are two different reasons why interpreters might not have to apply interpretive directions to future statutes just because an earlier Congress purported to require them to do so.

- First, many kinds of interpretive directions cannot operate of their own force as applied to future statutes. For instance, even if a prior Congress purported to provide definitions of the terms that will appear in future statutes, what those terms mean in future statutes is a question that comes within the scope of those future statutes, and the prior Congress is not in charge of the answer. *See* Alexander & Prakash, *supra*, 20 CONST. COMMENT. at 99 (observing that even if Congress enacts "prospective interpretive guidelines that suggest what future Congresses might mean when they use a particular word or phrase in subsequently enacted statutes," such guidelines "cannot directly affect a subsequent statute's actual meaning").[47]

[47] This first argument applies to many kinds of interpretive directions—not only directions purporting to define how future statutes will use certain terms, but also other directions purporting to specify the meaning of future statutes. Still, some kinds of interpretive directions might be different. In particular, this first argument might not apply to statutes regulating the sources of information that interpreters can consider—such as a federal statute that purports

- Second, and independently, even if an interpretive direction would otherwise operate of its own force, a later Congress can always repeal the earlier direction or exempt a new statute from it. Again, moreover, whether Congress has done so is a question about the meaning of the later statute, and the prior Congress is not in charge of the answer.

NOTE ON THE DICTIONARY ACT, THE REVISED STATUTES, AND TITLE 1 OF THE UNITED STATES CODE

The so-called Dictionary Act is one of the most prominent federal statutes that supplies instructions about the meaning of later-enacted statutes. Now found in Title 1 of the United States Code, the Dictionary Act dates all the way back to 1871. This note briefly describes its history and raises some questions about it.

Congress enacted the original Dictionary Act on February 25, 1871, to address a few recurring issues in statutory interpretation. For instance, section 3 of the Act contained the precursor of 1 U.S.C. § 108, about the legal effect of the repeal of a statute that had itself repealed an earlier statute. *See* Act of Feb. 25, 1871, ch. 71, § 3, 16 Stat. 431, 431–32. Likewise, section 2 articulated the general rule that "in all acts hereafter passed[,] words importing the singular number may extend and be applied to several persons and things," and "words importing the plural number may include the singular." *Id.* § 2, 16 Stat. at 431. Section 2 also addressed the scope of a few words that might appear in future federal statutes, including "person," "oath," "sworn," "insane person," and "lunatic." *Id.*

Three years later, Congress enacted a slightly revised and expanded version of these provisions as part of the Revised Statutes of 1874. *See* Rev. Stat. §§ 1–6, 12–13, 18 Stat. 1, 1–2 (1874). At the same time, Congress repealed the original Dictionary Act. *See id.* § 5596, 18 Stat. at 1091 (repealing "[a]ll acts of Congress passed prior to [December 1, 1873], any portion of which is embraced in any section of said revision").

The Revised Statutes have already come up a few times in this book, *see, e.g., supra* p. 6 n.3, but it is worth knowing more about them. They were an enormous undertaking; Congress revised and reenacted in more organized form virtually all federal statutes that were "general and permanent in their nature" and that had been in force on December 1,

---

to forbid (or to require) courts to consult internal legislative history when interpreting federal statutes. As discussed above, such provisions can be characterized as rules of evidence, and the Necessary and Proper Clause gives Congress broad authority to lay down rules of evidence for the federal courts. Normally, moreover, valid rules of evidence prescribed by Congress bind federal courts unless and until a later statute repeals them.

Admittedly, Congress does not have as much power to prescribe rules of evidence for *state* courts. But where the state courts are trying to interpret federal statutes, the Necessary and Proper Clause might let Congress regulate the information that even state courts consider.

1873. *See* Rev. Stat. § 5595, 18 Stat. at 1091. The result was a single enormous statute (spread across 73 titles) that Congress enacted on June 22, 1874.[48]

The very first title in the Revised Statutes opened with a revised version of provisions that had been in the Dictionary Act of 1871. For instance, here is Rev. Stat. § 1, which closely tracked section 2 of the original Dictionary Act:

> "In determining the meaning of the revised statutes, or of any act or resolution of Congress passed subsequent to February twenty-fifth, eighteen hundred and seventy-one, words importing the singular number may extend and be applied to several persons or things; words importing the plural number may include the singular; words importing the masculine gender may be applied to females; the words 'insane person' and 'lunatic' shall include every idiot, non compos, lunatic, and insane person; the word 'person' may extend and be applied to partnerships and corporations, and the reference to any officer shall include any person authorized by law to perform the duties of such office, unless the context shows that such words were intended to be used in a more limited sense; and a requirement of an 'oath' shall be deemed complied with by making affirmation in judicial form."

Rev. Stat. § 1, 18 Stat. at 1.

When Rev. Stat. § 1 referred to "any act . . . of Congress passed subsequent to" February 25, 1871 (the date of the original Dictionary Act), it was not simply covering statutes that had been passed between 1871 and 1874. It was also reaching into the future. Like the section of the Dictionary Act on which it was based (which had addressed "all acts hereafter passed," *see* Act of Feb. 25, 1871, § 2, 16 Stat. at 431), it was understood to bear on the interpretation of statutes that Congress would enact going forward.

By its terms, Rev. Stat. § 1 arguably established two different types of instructions. Some of its provisions said flatly that particular words or references include certain things, at least unless the context shows otherwise. *See* Rev. Stat. § 1, 18 Stat. at 1 (addressing the words "insane person" and "lunatic" and the scope of "reference[s] to any officer"); *see also* Rev. Stat. §§ 2–5, 18 Stat. at 1–2 (similarly specifying things that the words "county," "vessel," "vehicle," and "company" or "association" include). As applied to future statutes, these provisions effectively established rebuttable presumptions in favor of reading the relevant words to include the things that the provisions specified. By contrast,

---

[48] To this day, some portions of the Revised Statutes are still in force (though many other portions have been repealed or reenacted in a different form). A leading example is the provision that modern lawyers know as 42 U.S.C. § 1983. Title 42 of the United States Code is just an editorial compilation of statutory provisions that Congress has enacted over the years, not a title that Congress has enacted as such. The provision that the codifiers have put at 42 U.S.C. § 1983 was enacted as part of the Revised Statutes, and Congress has not reenacted it since. *See* Rev. Stat. § 1979, 18 Stat. at 348.

some of the other provisions in Rev. Stat. § 1 simply said that certain words or formulations "may" be applied in certain ways. Even as applied to other aspects of the Revised Statutes, let alone to future statutes, those provisions may simply have declared the *possibility* of certain interpretations without establishing any preference for those interpretations. *See* First Nat'l Bank v. Missouri ex rel. Barrett, 263 U.S. 640, 657 (1924) (noting a litigant's argument that the Court should interpret Rev. Stat. § 5190 in light of "the rule [supplied by Rev. Stat. § 1] that 'words importing the singular number may extend and be applied to several persons or things,' " but responding that "obviously this rule is not one to be applied except where it is necessary to carry out the evident intent of the statute"). *But see* Monell v. Dep't of Social Servs., 436 U.S. 658, 689 n.53 (1978) (contending that in the Dictionary Act of 1871, the word "may" was intended to mean "shall").

When the Revised Statutes were first enacted, they brought real organization to federal law. As time went by, however, disorder grew. Although Congress sometimes fit new statutory provisions into the existing structure (casting them as amendments of the Revised Statutes), Congress did not always do so. Even under the best of circumstances, moreover, keeping track of all the statutes that Congress enacted from 1874 on would have been challenging. After other efforts to solve this problem met with mixed success, codifiers eventually put together the first edition of the United States Code, which was published in 1926. *See* Mary Whisner, *The United States Code, Prima Facie Evidence, and Positive Law*, 101 L. LIBR. J. 545, 549–52 (2009) (summarizing the history). At first, all of the Code was merely "prima facie" evidence of federal laws.[49] But in the 1940s, Congress began the project of enacting individual titles of the United States Code as such. *See* Whisner, *supra*, 101 L. LIBR. J. at 553. As of now, roughly half of the titles have been enacted. *See supra* pp. 49–55 (describing the United States Code).

Fittingly, title 1 of the United States Code (which contains the provisions that correspond to the opening sections of the Revised Statutes) was one of the first titles that Congress enacted as such. *See* An Act to Codify and Enact into Positive Law, Title 1 of the United States Code, Entitled "General Provisions," ch. 388, 61 Stat. 633 (1947). The statute by which Congress enacted title 1 repealed the corresponding provisions of the Revised Statutes. *See id.* § 2, 61 Stat. at 640–41. Thus, Rev. Stat. § 1 was in force from 1874 until 1947, when it was replaced by 1 U.S.C. § 1. After substantial amendments in 1948 (and two other very minor amendments in later years), 1 U.S.C. § 1 now reads as follows:

---

[49] *See* Act of June 30, 1926, ch. 712, § 2(a), 44 Stat. 1, 1 ("The matter set forth in the Code, evidenced as hereinafter in this section provided, shall establish prima facie the laws of the United States, general and permanent in their nature, in force on the 7th day of December, 1925; but nothing in this Act shall be construed as repealing or amending any such law, or as enacting as new law any matter contained in the Code. In case of any inconsistency . . . between the provisions of any section of this Code and the corresponding portion of legislation heretofore enacted[,] effect shall be given for all purposes whatsoever to such enactments.").

> "In determining the meaning of any Act of Congress, unless the context indicates otherwise—
>
> > "words importing the singular include and apply to several persons, parties, or things;
> >
> > "words importing the plural include the singular;
> >
> > "words importing the masculine gender include the feminine as well;
> >
> > "words used in the present tense include the future as well as the present;
> >
> > "the words 'insane' and 'insane person' shall include every idiot, insane person, and person non compos mentis;
> >
> > "the words 'person' and 'whoever' include corporations, companies, associations, firms, partnerships, societies, and joint stock companies, as well as individuals;
> >
> > " 'officer' includes any person authorized by law to perform the duties of the office;
> >
> > " 'signature' or 'subscription' includes a mark when the person making the same intended it as such;
> >
> > " 'oath' includes affirmation, and 'sworn' includes affirmed;
> >
> > " 'writing' includes printing and typewriting and reproductions of visual symbols by photographing, multigraphing, mimeographing, manifolding, or otherwise."

1 U.S.C. § 1; *see also* 1 U.S.C. §§ 2–5 (making the same provisions about the words "county," "vessel," "vehicle," and "company" or "association" that had appeared in Rev. Stat. §§ 2–5).[50]

When you compare 1 U.S.C. § 1 to Rev. Stat. § 1, you will note two interesting features. First, the word "may" does not appear in 1 U.S.C. § 1; instead of simply declaring the *possibility* of certain interpretations, all of the provisions in 1 U.S.C. § 1 express a *preference* for those interpretations. *See* In re Application for Cell Tower Records Under 18 U.S.C. § 2703(d), 90 F. Supp. 3d 673, 677 & n.6 (S.D. Tex. 2015) (noting that the singular/plural provisions in 1 U.S.C. § 1 establish a "default rule of interpretation," and contrasting the weaker language in Rev. Stat. § 1). But second, the rules stated in 1 U.S.C. § 1 are subject to an exception where "the context indicates otherwise."

For purposes of interpreting statutes enacted *after* the relevant definitions in 1 U.S.C. § 1, you might wonder whether this exception makes any difference. According to the analysis of Professors Alexander and Prakash (described above), definitions enacted by the 80th Congress

[50] These provisions in title 1 purport to apply to all federal statutes. A few of the other titles in the United States Code that Congress has enacted as such include definitional sections that apply throughout the particular title that contains them. *See, e.g.*, 18 U.S.C. §§ 5–27 (defining terms for purposes of title 18); 28 U.S.C. § 451 (defining a few terms as used in title 28).

in 1947 and 1948 cannot conclusively establish how future statutes must be using the terms in question. Even if 1 U.S.C. § 1 had not itself acknowledged any exceptions, then, its provisions could justify no more than a rebuttable presumption: while interpreters might expect later-enacted statutes to use words in the way that 1 U.S.C. § 1 suggests, a particular statute could always opt out of those generic definitions, either expressly or simply by supplying enough indications that it is using words differently. Still, the fact that 1 U.S.C. § 1 does acknowledge exceptions arguably makes the presumption a little weaker than it would otherwise be.

To appreciate this point, think about why courts interpreting later-enacted statutes should pay any attention at all to provisions like 1 U.S.C. § 1. Here are some possible reasons:

- The generic definitions and other interpretive rules that Congress supplied in 1 U.S.C. § 1 might be some evidence of drafting habits that continue into the future. Unless we have reason to believe that the relevant legislative vocabulary has changed, the definitions that Congress considered sensible in 1947 and 1948 might also reflect how later Congresses use the words in question.
- No matter how later Congresses would *otherwise* use the words covered by 1 U.S.C. § 1, the definitions supplied by 1 U.S.C. § 1 might have "feedback effects." If people within Congress know about 1 U.S.C. § 1 and keep it in mind, new statutes might be drafted and enacted in light of the existing definitions. Likewise, when a later Congress wants to use a word in a different sense than 1 U.S.C. § 1 tells us to expect, maybe Congress often will opt out of 1 U.S.C. § 1 explicitly.
- Apart from these two "descriptive" arguments, a presumption in favor of following 1 U.S.C. § 1 might be *normatively* attractive. The definitions supplied by 1 U.S.C. § 1 address what otherwise would be recurring sources of ambiguity in federal statutes. (For instance, without a global definition, interpreters might often be unsure whether the word "person" in a particular federal statute refers only to individuals or also encompasses corporations and other entities.) If courts are uncertain about how a new statute uses one of the words covered by 1 U.S.C. § 1, perhaps courts should break the tie in favor of following the interpretive directions supplied by 1 U.S.C. § 1, on the theory that doing so makes the law more predictable.

None of these arguments supports more than a rebuttable presumption that later-enacted statutes use words in the way that 1 U.S.C. § 1 tells us to expect. But the strength of that presumption depends to some extent on what 1 U.S.C. § 1 says. If 1 U.S.C. § 1 had been worded like portions of Rev. Stat. § 1, so that it merely said that certain words "may" extend to certain things, then it would not have established much of a presumption at all. By the same token, the fact that 1 U.S.C. § 1 acknowledges that some statutes will not follow its generic definitions may slightly reduce the force of the presumption that courts would otherwise apply.

Without discussing these issues, the Supreme Court interpreted 1 U.S.C. § 1's "context" exception in *Rowland v. California Men's Colony*, 506 U.S. 194 (1993). That case concerned the meaning of the word "person" in 28 U.S.C. § 1915(a), which authorizes federal courts to let certain litigants proceed *in forma pauperis* (and hence without having to prepay filing fees). For many years, only citizens of the United States were eligible. In 1959, however, Congress amended § 1915(a) by replacing the word "citizen" with the word "person." Act of Sept. 21, 1959, Pub. L. 86–320, 73 Stat. 590. In *Rowland*, the Court had to decide whether an unincorporated association of prison inmates qualified as a "person" that could proceed *in forma pauperis*. The Court approached that question within the framework set by 1 U.S.C. § 1: the Justices assumed that the word "person" in the 1959 amendment came with the broad definition supplied by 1 U.S.C. § 1 (which includes entities as well as individuals) "unless the context indicates otherwise." According to the majority opinion, though, the word "indicates" in 1 U.S.C. § 1 "imposes less of a burden than, say, 'requires' or 'necessitates.'" *Rowland*, 506 U.S. at 200. By a vote of five to four, the Court held that the context of the word "person" in 28 U.S.C. § 1915 was enough to indicate that only individuals could proceed *in forma pauperis*. *Compare id.* at 201 ("Four contextual features indicate that 'person' in § 1915(a) refers only to individuals . . . .") *with id.* at 217 (Thomas, J., dissenting) ("I do not believe that § 1915 contains any language indicating that an association is not a 'person' for purposes of that provision, and I do not think it is appropriate to rely upon what are at bottom policy considerations in deciding whether 'the context indicates otherwise.'").

Despite disagreeing about some other aspects of the analysis, both Justice Souter's majority opinion in *Rowland* and Justice Thomas's dissent agreed on one important point: the word "context" in 1 U.S.C. § 1 does not encompass legislative history. *See Rowland*, 506 U.S. at 199–200 ("'Context' here means the text of the Act of Congress surrounding the word at issue, or the texts of other related congressional Acts . . . . If Congress had meant to point further afield, as to legislative history, . . . it would have been natural to use a more spacious phrase, like 'evidence of congressional intent,' in place of 'context.'"); *id.* at 213 (Thomas, J., dissenting) ("I share the Court's understanding of the word 'context.'"). Thus, when the Justices were trying to decide whether the 1959 amendment to 28 U.S.C. § 1915 used the word "person" to encompass entities or just individuals, they did not base arguments on the committee reports or congressional debates from 1959.[51]

---

[51] The majority opinion did mention the legislative history briefly. *See Rowland*, 506 U.S. at 198 & n.2 (reciting reasons for the 1959 amendment as disclosed by legislative history, and

As interpreted by the Supreme Court in *Rowland*, then, the instructions established by 1 U.S.C. § 1 apparently have two different components. First, 1 U.S.C. § 1 has the effect of establishing rebuttable presumptions about how federal statutes (including later-enacted statutes) use certain words. Second, 1 U.S.C. § 1 also tells interpreters not to rely on the legislative history of those statutes when deciding whether the presumptions established by 1 U.S.C. § 1 have been overcome. *See* Hubbard v. United States, 514 U.S. 695, 701 (1995) (discussing *Rowland*'s understanding of "context" and suggesting again that legislative history is off limits).

As applied to later-enacted statutes, there may be an important legal difference between these two components. Assuming we accept the analysis of Professors Alexander and Prakash, the first component of 1 U.S.C. § 1 is inherently limited. Even if the Congress that enacted 1 U.S.C. § 1 had wanted to establish an *irrebuttable* presumption about how future statutes would use particular words, it could not really have done so. The meaning of the words used in each later statute is a question that comes within the scope of the later statute itself. Pre-existing statutes like 1 U.S.C. § 1 can shed light on that question, but the light is indirect; the Congress that enacted 1 U.S.C. § 1 cannot definitively control the vocabulary used by its successors. But the second component of the instructions in 1 U.S.C. § 1 may be different. Instead of purporting to define what later statutes will mean by a particular word or phrase, the second component addresses a separate topic—the sources of information that courts can consider in the interpretive process. That topic does not necessarily come within the scope of the later statutes; most statutes do not say anything one way or the other about whether courts can use legislative history, and they probably do not cover that topic by implication either. Perhaps, then, the instruction that 1 U.S.C. § 1 gives courts on this topic can operate of its own force unless and until Congress provides a different instruction. If so, then the second component of the instructions in 1 U.S.C. § 1 might be capable of binding the courts in a more absolute sense than the first component. *Cf. supra* p. 785 n.47.

Of course, a later Congress can always repeal the second component of the instructions in 1 U.S.C. § 1, just as it can repeal any other statute. What is more, Congress can do so by implication as well as explicitly. Precisely because the typical federal statute does not address the sources of information that courts can use when interpreting it, though, courts normally will not have much reason to conclude that a later-enacted statute has impliedly repealed the second component of the instructions in 1 U.S.C. § 1 (even just *pro tanto*).

---

noting that "[n]one of these reasons supports extension of § 1915 benefits to artificial entities, or suggests that anyone involved with drafting or evaluating this legislation was thinking of such an extension"). Still, the Court made no reference to this legislative history when listing the "contextual features" on which the Court relied. *See id.* at 201–09.

For instance, consider the following hypothetical. Suppose that a new federal statute uses the word "person," and nothing in the surrounding text indicates whether that word refers only to individuals or also includes corporations and unincorporated associations. Suppose further that the statute does not say anything that could plausibly be interpreted as letting courts use legislative history to answer this question; the statute does not explicitly address the use of legislative history one way or the other. Even if courts nonetheless examined the statute's legislative history, moreover, suppose that they would not find any statements about whether members of the enacting Congress wanted courts to be able to consult legislative history. But suppose that the legislative history does contain statements about the intended meaning of the word "person," and those statements strongly suggest that members of Congress were not following the generic definition supplied by 1 U.S.C. § 1; although the *text* of the new statute is compatible with the meaning suggested by 1 U.S.C. § 1, committee reports suggest that members of the later Congress were using the word "person" to refer only to individuals. Would that be enough for courts to find an implied repeal, *pro tanto*, of the second component of the instruction in 1 U.S.C. § 1—the instruction that tells courts not to care about legislative history when deciding whether a statute departs from the generic definition suggested by 1 U.S.C. § 1?

The answer might well be "no": the fact that the legislative history contains information about the intended meaning of the word "person" does not automatically override (or impliedly repeal *pro tanto*) the second component of the instruction in 1 U.S.C. § 1. If that component is in force, moreover, then the legislative history about the intended meaning of "person" will not be relevant—with the result that nothing rebuts the presumption that the *first* component of 1 U.S.C. § 1 effectively establishes. Thus, even judges who otherwise would be open to the use of legislative history in statutory interpretation (such as Justice Souter, the author of the majority opinion in *Rowland*) might conclude that the word "person" in the new statute includes entities as well as individuals; 1 U.S.C. § 1 effectively establishes a rebuttable presumption to that effect, and nothing in "the context" identified by 1 U.S.C. § 1 "indicates otherwise."

* * * * *

The content of the generic definitions supplied by 1 U.S.C. §§ 1–5 is relatively innocuous. At any rate, those definitions do not have an obvious political valence, so they do not look like efforts to project the enacting Congress's policy preferences into the future.

In that respect, 1 U.S.C. § 8 is quite different. Enacted in 2002 in response to what is sometimes called partial-birth abortion, 1 U.S.C. § 8 reads as follows:

"(a) In determining the meaning of any Act of Congress, or of any ruling, regulation, or interpretation of the various administrative bureaus and agencies of the United States, the words 'person', 'human being', 'child', and 'individual', shall include every infant member of the species homo sapiens who is born alive at any stage of development.

"(b) As used in this section, the term 'born alive', with respect to a member of the species homo sapiens, means the complete expulsion or extraction from his or her mother of that member, at any stage of development, who after such expulsion or extraction breathes or has a beating heart, pulsation of the umbilical cord, or definite movement of voluntary muscles, regardless of whether the umbilical cord has been cut, and regardless of whether the expulsion or extraction occurs as a result of natural or induced labor, cesarean section, or induced abortion.

"(c) Nothing in this section shall be construed to affirm, deny, expand, or contract any legal status or legal right applicable to any member of the species homo sapiens at any point prior to being 'born alive' as defined in this section."

Born-Alive Infants Protection Act of 2002, Pub. L. 107–207, 116 Stat. 926.

For the sake of argument, set aside any substantive constitutional objections that you might have to the content of 1 U.S.C. § 8. Assume, too, that most federal statutes and regulations that use the words "person," "human being," "child," and "individual" could constitutionally use those words in the way that 1 U.S.C. § 8 says. To whatever extent that is true, the Congress that was sitting in 2002 presumably could amend all pre-existing federal statutes that used those words. As far as pre-existing statutes are concerned, 1 U.S.C. § 8 effectively did so. Whatever the words "person," "human being," "child," and "individual" had meant in those statutes before 2002, those words apparently now have the meaning provided by 1 U.S.C. § 8 (unless and until Congress enacts another relevant amendment).

By the same token, the Congress that was sitting in 2002 could specify what the same words mean in regulations promulgated by federal administrative agencies—including not only *pre-existing* regulations but even *future* regulations. If a statute enacted by Congress were to conflict with another statute enacted by Congress, the more recently enacted statute would take priority. But if a statute enacted by Congress comes into conflict with a regulation promulgated by an agency, the statute takes priority even if the regulation is more recent. By and large, federal statutes are hierarchically superior to administrative regulations; most federal administrative agencies have only the powers that Congress gives them, and Congress can regulate how agencies use those powers. It follows that if Congress wants to specify how federal agencies have to use words in the future, Congress probably can do so. As a result, the definitions supplied by 1 U.S.C. § 8 probably apply to future regulations promulgated by federal administrative agencies (unless and until a new Congress provides different instructions).

But what about future federal *statutes* that use the words defined in 1 U.S.C. § 8? For the reasons discussed by Professors Alexander and Prakash, the Congress that sat in 2002 could not authoritatively dictate how later Congresses must use those words. Still, does the existence of 1 U.S.C. § 8 support a rebuttable presumption about how future Congresses probably *are* using those words? Are there reasons why any such presumption should be weaker than the presumption established by less politically fraught definitions (like the ones in 1 U.S.C. §§ 1–5)? Should we be worried that when Congress enacted 1 U.S.C. § 8 and called for it to apply to subsequently enacted statutes, Congress was not really trying to improve communication between future Congresses and interpreters, but instead was trying to project its own policy views into later-enacted statutes that do not explicitly opt out of its definitions?[52]

Instead of involving definitions, the next case concerns the background rule established by 1 U.S.C. § 109. Like 1 U.S.C. § 108 (discussed *supra* p. 782), § 109 provides instructions about the legal effect of a federal statute that repeals another federal statute. Specifically, 1 U.S.C. § 109 says:

> "The repeal of any statute shall not have the effect to release or extinguish any penalty, forfeiture, or liability incurred under such statute, unless the repealing Act shall so expressly provide, and such statute shall be treated as still remaining in force for the purpose of sustaining any proper action or prosecution for the enforcement of such penalty, forfeiture, or liability."

[52] The so-called "Defense of Marriage Act" (DOMA), Pub. L. 104–199, 110 Stat. 2419 (1996), raised similar questions. In 1996, when it appeared likely that some states would start recognizing same-sex marriages, DOMA added the following provision to title 1 of the United States Code:

> "In determining the meaning of any Act of Congress, or of any ruling, regulation, or interpretation of the various administrative bureaus and agencies of the United States, the word 'marriage' means only a legal union between one man and one woman as husband and wife, and the word 'spouse' refers only to a person of the opposite sex who is a husband or a wife."

DOMA § 3(a), 110 Stat. at 2419 (enacting 1 U.S.C. § 7). Ultimately, however, the Supreme Court held that this provision reflected animus against same-sex couples and was therefore wholly unconstitutional. *See* United States v. Windsor, 570 U.S. 744, 769–75 (2013); *see also* Obergefell v. Hodges, 576 U.S. 644, 675–76 (2015) (holding that states cannot constitutionally deny same-sex couples the fundamental right to marry). More recently, Congress has amended 1 U.S.C. § 7 to establish the following rule:

> "For the purposes of any Federal law, rule, or regulation in which marital status is a factor, an individual shall be considered married if that individual's marriage is between 2 individuals and is valid in the State where the marriage was entered into or, in the case of a marriage entered into outside any State, if the marriage is between 2 individuals and is valid in the place where entered into and the marriage could have been entered into in a State."

Respect for Marriage Act, Pub. L. 117–228, § 5, 136 Stat. 2305, 2306 (2022).

This instruction dates back to § 4 of the Dictionary Act of 1871, 16 Stat. at 432, and Congress reenacted it most recently in 1947 (when Congress enacted title 1 of the United States Code as such).

On its face, 1 U.S.C. § 109 suggests that no future repealing statute should be understood to extinguish penalties incurred under the statute that is being repealed unless the repealing statute "expressly" so provides. In the next case, all nine Justices agreed that 1 U.S.C. § 109 cannot really have such a powerful effect; instead of establishing a hard-and-fast rule, it effectively establishes a rebuttable presumption. Still, the Justices divided five to four over whether the Fair Sentencing Act of 2010 overcame that presumption.

Dorsey v. United States

567 U.S. 260 (2012)

■ *JUSTICE BREYER delivered the opinion of the Court:*

Federal statutes impose mandatory minimum prison sentences upon those convicted of federal drug crimes. These statutes typically base the length of a minimum prison term upon the kind and amount of the drug involved. Until 2010, the relevant statute imposed upon an offender who dealt in powder cocaine the same sentence it imposed upon an offender who dealt in one one-hundredth that amount of crack cocaine. It imposed, for example, the same 5-year minimum term upon (1) an offender convicted of possessing with intent to distribute *500* grams of powder cocaine as upon (2) an offender convicted of possessing with intent to distribute *5* grams of crack.

In 2010, Congress enacted a new statute reducing the crack-to-powder cocaine disparity from 100-to-1 to 18-to-1. Fair Sentencing Act, 124 Stat. 2372. The new statute took effect on August 3, 2010. The question here is whether the Act's more lenient penalty provisions apply to offenders who committed a crack cocaine crime before August 3, 2010, but were not sentenced until after August 3. We hold that the new, more lenient mandatory minimum provisions do apply to those pre-Act offenders.

I

The underlying question before us is one of congressional intent as revealed in the Fair Sentencing Act's language, structure, and basic objectives. Did Congress intend the Act's more lenient penalties to apply to pre-Act offenders sentenced after the Act took effect?

We recognize that, because of important background principles of interpretation, we must assume that Congress did *not* intend those penalties to apply unless it clearly indicated to the contrary. See *infra* at 273–276. But we find that clear indication here. We rest our conclusion primarily upon the fact that a contrary determination would seriously undermine basic Federal Sentencing Guidelines objectives such as uniformity and proportionality in sentencing. Indeed, seen from that perspective, a contrary determination would (in respect to relevant groups of drug offenders) produce sentences less uniform and more disproportionate than if Congress had not enacted the Fair Sentencing Act at all. . . .

Because our conclusion rests upon an analysis of the Guidelines-based sentencing system Congress has established, we describe that system at the outset and include an explanation of how the Guidelines interact with federal statutes setting forth specific terms of imprisonment.

A

The Guidelines originate in the Sentencing Reform Act of 1984, 98 Stat. 1987. That statute created a federal Sentencing Commission instructed to write guidelines that judges would use to determine sentences imposed upon offenders convicted of committing federal crimes. 28 U.S.C. §§ 991, 994. Congress thereby sought to increase transparency, uniformity, and proportionality in sentencing. United States Sentencing Commission (USSC or Commission), Guidelines Manual § 1A1.3, p. 2 (Nov. 2011) (USSG); see 28 U.S.C. §§ 991(b)(1), 994(f).

The Sentencing Reform Act directed the Commission to create in the Guidelines categories of offense behavior (*e.g.*, " 'bank robbery/committed with a gun/$2500 taken' ") and offender characteristics (*e.g.*, "one prior conviction"). USSG § 1A1.2 at 1; see 28 U.S.C. § 994(a)–(e). A sentencing judge determines a Guidelines range by (1) finding the applicable offense level and offender category and then (2) consulting a table that lists proportionate sentencing ranges (*e.g.*, 18 to 24 months of imprisonment) at the intersections of rows (marking offense levels) and columns (marking offender categories). USSG ch. 5, pt. A, Sentencing Table, §§ 5E1.2, 7B1.4; see also § 1A1.4(h) at 11. The Guidelines, after telling the judge how to determine the applicable offense level and offender category, instruct the judge to apply the intersection's range in an ordinary case, but they leave the judge free to depart from that range in an unusual case. See 18 U.S.C. § 3553(b); USSG §§ 1A1.2 at 1–2, 1A1.4(b) at 6–7. This Court has held that the Guidelines are now advisory. *United States v. Booker*, 543 U.S. 220, 245, 264 (2005); see *Kimbrough v. United States*, 552 U.S. 85, 91 (2007).

The Guidelines determine most drug-crime offense levels in a special way. They set forth a Drug Quantity Table (or Table) that lists amounts of various drugs and associates different amounts with different "Base Offense Levels" (to which a judge may add or subtract levels depending upon the "specific" characteristics of the offender's behavior). See USSG § 2D1.1. . . .

In 1986, Congress enacted a more specific, drug-related sentencing statute, the Anti-Drug Abuse Act (1986 Drug Act), 100 Stat. 3207. That statute sets forth mandatory minimum penalties of 5 and 10 years applicable to a drug offender depending primarily upon the kind and amount of drugs involved in the offense. See 21 U.S.C. § 841(b)(1)(A)–(C) (2006 ed. and Supp. IV). The minimum applicable to an offender convicted of possessing with intent to distribute 500 grams or more of powder cocaine is 5 years, and for 5,000 grams or more of powder the minimum is 10 years. § 841(b)(1)(A)(ii), (B)(ii). The 1986 Drug Act, however, treated crack cocaine crimes as far more serious. It applied its 5-year minimum to an offender convicted of possessing with intent to distribute only 5 grams of crack (as compared to 500 grams of powder) and its 10-year minimum to one convicted of possessing with intent to distribute only 50 grams of crack (as compared to 5,000 grams of powder), thus producing a 100-to-1 crack-to-powder ratio. § 841(b)(1)(A)(iii), (B)(iii) (2006 ed.).

. . . . Like other sentencing statutes, [the 1986 Drug Act] trumps the Guidelines. . . . [O]rdinarily no matter what the Guidelines provide, a judge cannot sentence an offender to a sentence beyond the maximum contained in the federal statute setting forth the crime of conviction. Similarly, ordinarily no matter what range the Guidelines set forth, a sentencing judge must sentence an offender to at least the minimum prison term set forth in a statutory mandatory minimum. See 28 U.S.C. § 994(a), (b)(1); USSG § 5G1.1; *Neal v. United States*, 516 U.S. 284, 289–290, 295 (1996).

Not surprisingly, the Sentencing Commission incorporated the 1986 Drug Act's mandatory minimums into the first version of the Guidelines themselves. . . . It did so by setting a base offense level for a first-time drug offender that corresponded to the lowest Guidelines range above the applicable mandatory minimum. USSC, Report to the Congress: Mandatory Minimum Penalties in the Federal Criminal Justice System 53–54 (Oct. 2011) (2011 Report). Thus, the first Guidelines Drug Quantity Table associated 500 grams of powder cocaine with an offense level of 26, which for a first-time offender meant a sentencing range of 63 to 78 months (just above the 5-year minimum), and it associated 5,000 grams of powder cocaine with an offense level of 32, which for a first-time offender meant a sentencing range of 121 to 151 months (just above the 10-year minimum). USSG § 2D1.1 (Oct. 1987). Further reflecting the 1986 Drug Act's 100-to-1 crack-to-powder ratio, the Table associated an offense level of 26 with 5 grams of crack and an offense level of 32 with 50 grams of crack. *Ibid.*

In addition, the Drug Quantity Table set offense levels for small drug amounts that did not trigger the 1986 Drug Act's mandatory minimums so that the resulting Guidelines sentences would remain proportionate to the sentences for amounts that did trigger these minimums. 2011 Report 54. Thus, the Table associated 400 grams of powder cocaine (an amount that fell just below the amount triggering the 1986 Drug Act's 5-year minimum) with an offense level of 24, which for a first-time offender meant a sentencing range of 51 to 63 months (the range just below the 5-year minimum). USSG § 2D1.1 (Oct. 1987). Following the 100-to-1 crack-to-powder ratio, the Table associated four grams of crack (an amount that also fell just below the amount triggering the 1986 Drug Act's 5-year minimum) with an offense level of 24. *Ibid.*

The Commission did this not because it necessarily thought that those levels were most in keeping with past sentencing practice or would independently have reflected a fair set of sentences, but rather because the Commission believed that doing so was the best way to keep similar drug-trafficking sentences proportional, thereby satisfying the Sentencing Reform Act's basic "proportionality" objective. . . . [T]he Commission derived the Drug Quantity Table's entire set of crack and powder cocaine offense levels by using the 1986 Drug Act's two (5- and 10-year) minimum amounts as reference points and then extrapolating from those two amounts upward and downward to set proportional offense levels for other drug amounts. . . .

B

During the next two decades, the Commission and others in the law enforcement community strongly criticized Congress' decision to set the crack-to-powder mandatory minimum ratio at 100-to-1. The Commission issued four separate reports telling Congress that the ratio was too high and unjustified . . . . The Commission also asked Congress for new legislation embodying a lower crack-to-powder ratio. . . . And the Commission recommended that the legislation "include" an "emergency amendment" allowing "the Commission to incorporate the statutory changes" in the Guidelines while "minimiz[ing] the lag between any statutory and guideline modifications for cocaine offenders." [USSC, Report to Congress: Cocaine and Federal Sentencing Policy 9 (May 2007)].

In 2010, Congress accepted the Commission's recommendations . . . and enacted the Fair Sentencing Act into law. The Act increased the drug amounts triggering mandatory minimums for crack trafficking offenses from 5 grams to 28 grams in respect to the 5-year minimum and from 50 grams to 280 grams in respect to the 10-year minimum (while leaving powder at 500 grams and 5,000 grams respectively). § 2(a), 124 Stat. 2372. The change had the effect of lowering the 100-to-1 crack-to-powder ratio to 18-to-1. . . .

Further, the Fair Sentencing Act instructed the Commission to "make such conforming amendments to the Federal sentencing guidelines as the Commission determines necessary to achieve consistency with other guideline provisions and applicable law." § 8(2), *id.* at 2374. And it directed the Commission to "promulgate the guidelines, policy statements, or amendments provided for in this Act as soon as practicable, and in any event not later than 90 days" after the new Act took effect. § 8(1), *ibid.*

The Fair Sentencing Act took effect on August 3, 2010. The Commission promulgated conforming emergency Guidelines amendments that became effective on November 1, 2010. 75 Fed. Reg. 66188 (2010). A permanent version of those Guidelines amendments took effect on November 1, 2011. See 76 *id.* at 24960 (2011).

C

With this background in mind, we turn to the relevant facts of the cases before us. Corey Hill, one of the petitioners, unlawfully sold 53 grams of crack in March 2007, before the Fair Sentencing Act became law. . . . Hill was not sentenced, however, until December 2010, after the Fair Sentencing Act became law and after the new Guidelines amendments had become effective. . . . Under the Fair Sentencing Act, an offender who sold 53 grams of crack was subject to a 5-year, not a 10-year, minimum. § 841(b)(1)(B)(iii) (2006 ed., Supp. IV). The sentencing judge stated that, if he thought that the Fair Sentencing Act applied, he would have sentenced Hill to that Act's 5-year minimum. *Id.* at 69. But he concluded that the Fair Sentencing Act's lower minimums apply only to those who committed a drug crime after August 3, 2010—the Act's effective date. *Id.* at 65, 68. That is to say, he concluded that the new Act's more lenient sentences did not apply to those who committed a crime before August 3, even if they were sentenced after that date. Hence, the judge sentenced Hill to 10 years of imprisonment. *Id.* at 78. The Court of Appeals for the Seventh Circuit affirmed. 417 Fed. Appx. 560 (2011).

[A description of petitioner Edward Dorsey's case is omitted.]

The Courts of Appeals have come to different conclusions as to whether the Fair Sentencing Act's more lenient mandatory minimums apply to offenders whose unlawful conduct took place before, but whose sentencing took place after, the date that Act took effect, namely, August 3, 2010. [Citations omitted.] In light of that disagreement, we granted Hill's and Dorsey's petitions for certiorari. Since petitioners and the Government both take the position that the Fair Sentencing Act's new minimums do apply in these circumstances, we appointed as *amicus curiae* Miguel Estrada to argue the contrary position. . . .

II

A

The timing issue before us is difficult in part because relevant language in different statutes argues in opposite directions. . . . On the one hand, a federal saving statute, Act of Feb. 25, 1871 (1871 Act), § 4, 16 Stat. 432, phrased in general terms, provides that a new criminal statute that "repeal[s]" an older criminal statute shall not change the penalties "incurred" under that older statute "unless the repealing Act shall so expressly provide." 1 U.S.C. § 109. Case law makes clear that the word "repeal" applies when a new statute simply diminishes the penalties that the older statute set forth. See *Warden v. Marrero*, 417 U.S. 653, 659–664 (1974); see also *United States v. Tynen*, 11 Wall. 88,

92 (1871). Case law also makes clear that penalties are "incurred" under the older statute when an offender becomes subject to them, *i.e.*, commits the underlying conduct that makes the offender liable. See *United States v. Reisinger*, 128 U.S. 398, 401 (1888); *Great Northern R. Co. v. United States*, 208 U.S. 452, 464–470 (1908).

On the other hand, the Sentencing Reform Act says that, regardless of when the offender's conduct occurs, the applicable Guidelines are the ones "in effect on the date the defendant is sentenced." 18 U.S.C. § 3553(a)(4)(A)(ii). And the Fair Sentencing Act requires the Commission to change the Guidelines in the wake of the Act's new minimums, making them consistent with "other guideline provisions and applicable law." § 8(2), 124 Stat. 2374.

. . . . Six considerations, taken together, convince us that Congress intended the Fair Sentencing Act's more lenient penalties to apply to those offenders whose crimes preceded August 3, 2010, but who are sentenced after that date.

First, *the 1871 saving statute permits Congress to apply a new Act's more lenient penalties to pre-Act offenders without expressly saying so in the new Act.* It is true that the 1871 Act uses the words "expressly provide." 1 U.S.C. § 109. But the Court has long recognized that this saving statute creates what is in effect a less demanding interpretive requirement. That is because statutes enacted by one Congress cannot bind a later Congress, which remains free to repeal the earlier statute, to exempt the current statute from the earlier statute, to modify the earlier statute, or to apply the earlier statute but as modified. See, *e.g.*, *Fletcher v. Peck*, 6 Cranch 87, 135 (1810); *Reichelderfer v. Quinn*, 287 U.S. 315, 318 (1932). And Congress remains free to express any such intention either expressly or by implication as it chooses.

Thus, the Court has said that the 1871 Act "cannot justify a disregard of the will of Congress as manifested either expressly or by *necessary implication* in a subsequent enactment." *Great Northern R. Co.*, *supra*, at 465 (emphasis added). And in a comparable context the Court has emphasized that the Administrative Procedure Act's use of the word "expressly" does not require Congress to use any "magical passwords" to exempt a later statute from the provision. *Marcello v. Bonds*, 349 U.S. 302, 310 (1955). Without requiring an "express" statement, the Court has described the necessary indicia of congressional intent by the terms "necessary implication," "clear implication," and "fair implication," phrases it has used interchangeably. *Great Northern R. Co.*, *supra*, at 465, 466; *Hertz v. Woodman*, 218 U.S. 205, 218 (1910); *Marrero*, *supra*, at 660, n. 10. One Member of the Court has said we should determine whether "the plain import of a later statute directly conflicts with an earlier statute," and, if so, "the later enactment governs, *regardless* of its compliance with any earlier-enacted requirement of an express reference or other 'magical password.' " *Lockhart v. United States*, 546 U.S. 142, 149 (2005) (Scalia, J., concurring).

Hence, the Court has treated the 1871 Act as setting forth an important background principle of interpretation. The Court has also assumed Congress is well aware of the background principle when it enacts new criminal statutes. *E.g., Great Northern R. Co., supra,* at 465; *Hertz, supra,* at 217; cf. *Marcello, supra,* at 310. And the principle requires courts, before interpreting a new criminal statute to apply its new penalties to a set of pre-Act offenders, to assure themselves that ordinary interpretive considerations point clearly in that direction. Words such as "plain import," "fair implication," or the like reflect the need for that assurance. And it is that assurance, which we shall assume is conveyed by the phrases "plain import" or "fair implication," that we must look for here.

Second, *the Sentencing Reform Act sets forth a special and different background principle.* That statute says that when "determining the particular sentence to be imposed" in an initial sentencing, the sentencing court "shall consider," among other things, the "sentencing range" established by the Guidelines that are "*in effect on the date the defendant is sentenced.*" 18 U.S.C. § 3553(a)(4)(A)(ii) (emphasis added). Although the Constitution's *Ex Post Facto* Clause, Art. I, § 9, cl. 3, prohibits applying a new Act's higher penalties to pre-Act conduct, it does not prohibit applying lower penalties. See *Calder v. Bull,* 3 Dall. 386, 390–391 (1798); *Collins v. Youngblood,* 497 U.S. 37, 41–44 (1990). The Sentencing Commission has consequently instructed sentencing judges to "use the Guidelines Manual in effect on the date that the defendant is sentenced," regardless of when the defendant committed the offense, unless doing so "would violate the *ex post facto* clause." USSG § 1B1.11. And therefore when the Commission adopts new, lower Guidelines amendments, those amendments become effective to offenders who committed an offense prior to the adoption of the new amendments but are sentenced thereafter. Just as we assume Congress was aware of the 1871 Act's background norm, so we assume that Congress was aware of this different background sentencing principle.

Third, *language in the Fair Sentencing Act implies that Congress intended to follow the Sentencing Reform Act background principle here.* A section of the Fair Sentencing Act entitled "Emergency Authority for United States Sentencing Commission" requires the Commission to promulgate "as soon as practicable" (and not later than 90 days after August 3, 2010) "conforming amendments" to the Guidelines that "achieve consistency with other guideline provisions and applicable law." § 8, 124 Stat. 2374. Read most naturally, "applicable law" refers to the law as changed by the Fair Sentencing Act, including the provision reducing the crack mandatory minimums. § 2(a), *id.* at 2372. As the Commission understood this provision, achieving consistency with "other guideline provisions" means reducing the base offense levels for all crack amounts proportionally (using the new 18-to-1 ratio), including the offense levels governing small amounts of crack that did not fall within the scope of the mandatory minimum provisions. 75 Fed. Reg. 66191. And consistency with "other guideline provisions" and with prior Commission practice would require application of the new Guidelines amendments to offenders who committed their offense prior to the new amendments' effective date but were sentenced thereafter. See USSG § 1B1.11(a); *e.g.*, USSG App. C, amdts. 706, 711 (Supp. Nov. 2004–Nov. 2007); see also Memorandum from G. Schmitt, L. Reed, & K. Cohen, USSC, to Chair Hinojosa et al., Subject: Analysis of the Impact of the Crack Cocaine Amendment if Made Retroactive 23 (Oct. 3, 2007). Cf. USSG App. C, amdt. 571 (amendment *increasing* restitution, which may present *ex post facto* and one-book-rule concerns, would apply only to defendants sentenced for post-amendment offenses), discussed *post* at 292 (Scalia, J., dissenting).

Fourth, *applying the 1986 Drug Act's old mandatory minimums to the post-August 3 sentencing of pre-August 3 offenders would create disparities of a kind that Congress enacted the Sentencing Reform Act and the Fair Sentencing Act to prevent.* Two individuals with the same number of prior offenses who each engaged in the same criminal conduct involving the same amount of crack and were sentenced at the same time would receive radically different sentences. For example, a first-time post-Act offender with five grams of crack, subject to a Guidelines range of 21 to 27 months, could receive two years of imprisonment, while an otherwise identical pre-Act offender would have to receive the 5-year mandatory minimum. . . .

Moreover, unlike many prechange/postchange discrepancies, the imposition of these disparate sentences involves roughly contemporaneous sentencing, . . . thereby highlighting a kind of unfairness that modern sentencing statutes typically seek to combat. See, *e.g.*, 28 U.S.C. § 991(b)(1)(B) (purposes of Guidelines-based sentencing include "avoiding unwarranted sentencing disparities among defendants with similar records who have been found guilty of similar criminal conduct"); S. Rep. No. 98–223, p. 74 (1983) (explaining rationale for using same, current Guidelines for all roughly contemporaneous sentencings). Further, it would involve imposing upon the pre-Act offender a pre-Act sentence at a time after Congress had specifically found in the Fair Sentencing Act that such a sentence was unfairly long.

Finally, one cannot treat such problems as if they were minor ones. Given the 5-year statute of limitations for federal drug offenses, the 11-month median time between indictment and sentencing for those offenses, and the approximately 5,000 federal crack offenders convicted each year, many pre-Act offenders were not (and will not be) sentenced until after August 3, 2010, when the new, more lenient mandatory minimums took effect. . . .

Fifth, *not to apply the Fair Sentencing Act would do more than preserve a disproportionate status quo; it would make matters worse.* It would create new anomalies—new sets of disproportionate sentences—

not previously present. That is because sentencing courts must apply new Guidelines (consistent with the Fair Sentencing Act's new minimums) to pre-Act offenders, . . . and the 1986 Drug Act's old minimums would trump those new Guidelines for some pre-Act offenders but not for all of them—say, pre-Act offenders who possessed crack in small amounts not directly the subject of mandatory minimums.

Consider, for example, a first-time offender convicted of possessing with intent to distribute four grams of crack. No mandatory sentence, under the 1986 Drug Act or the Fair Sentencing Act, applies to an offender possessing so small an amount. Yet under the old law, the Commission, charged with creating proportionate sentences, had created a Guidelines range of 41 to 51 months for such an offender, a sentence proportional to the 60 months that the 1986 Drug Act required for one who trafficked five grams of crack. See . . . USSG § 2D1.1(c) (Nov. 2009).

The Fair Sentencing Act, however, requires the Commission to write new Guidelines consistent with the new law. The Commission therefore wrote new Guidelines that provide a sentencing range of 21 to 27 months—about two years—for the first-time, 4-gram offender. See USSG § 2D1.1(c) (Nov. 2011). And the Sentencing Reform Act requires application of those new Guidelines to all offenders (including pre-Act offenders) who are sentenced once those new Guidelines take effect. See 18 U.S.C. § 3553(a)(4)(A)(ii). Those new Guidelines must take effect and apply to a pre-Act 4-gram offender, for such an offender was never subject to a trumping statutory 1986 Drug Act mandatory minimum. However, unless the Fair Sentencing Act's new, more lenient mandatory minimums apply to pre-Act offenders, an otherwise identical offender who possessed five grams would have to receive a 5-year sentence. See 21 U.S.C. § 841(b)(1)(B) (2006 ed., Supp. IV).

For example, imagine that on July 1, 2010, both Smith and Jones commit a crack crime identical but for the fact that Smith possesses with intent to distribute four grams of crack and Jones five grams. Both are sentenced on December 1, 2010, after the Fair Sentencing Act and the new Guidelines take effect. Smith's Guidelines sentence would be two years, but unless the Fair Sentencing Act applies, Jones's sentence would have to be five years. The difference of one gram would make a difference, not of only one year as it did before enactment of the Fair Sentencing Act, but instead of three years. Passage of the new Act, designed to have brought about fairer sentences, would here have created a new disparate sentencing "cliff."

. . . . [O]ne can find many similar examples of disproportionalities. . . . Thus, application of the 1986 Drug Act minimums to pre-Act offenders sentenced after the new Guidelines take effect would produce a crazy quilt of sentences, at odds with Congress' basic efforts to achieve more uniform, more proportionate sentences. Congress, when enacting the Fair Sentencing Act, could not have intended any such result.

Sixth, *we have found no strong countervailing consideration*. . . . [T]he dissent note[s] that to apply the new Act's minimums to the old, pre-August 3 offenders will create a new disparity—one between pre-Act offenders sentenced before August 3 and those sentenced after that date. . . . But . . . [that disparity] will exist whenever Congress enacts a new law changing sentences (unless Congress intends re-opening sentencing proceedings concluded prior to a new law's effective date). . . .

For these reasons considered as a whole, we conclude that Congress intended the Fair Sentencing Act's new, lower mandatory minimums to apply to the post-Act sentencing of pre-Act offenders. That is the Act's "plain import" or "fair implication."

B

We add one final point. Several arguments we have discussed involve the language of statutes that determine how new *Guidelines* take effect. . . . What about those who committed an offense prior to August 3 and were sentenced after August 3 but before November 1, 2010—a period *after* the new Act's effective date but *before* the new Guidelines first took effect? . . . .

In our view, the new Act's lower minimums apply to them as well. Our reason is that the statute simply instructs the Commission to promulgate new Guidelines "as soon as practicable" (but no later than 90 days after the Act took effect). § 8(1), 124 Stat. 2374. As far as Congress was concerned, the Commission might have (having prepared new Guidelines in advance) promulgated those Guidelines within a few days—perhaps on August 3 itself. At the same time, the Commission possesses ample authority to permit appropriate adjustments to be made in the Guidelines sentences of those sentenced after August 3 but prior to the new Guidelines promulgation. See 28 U.S.C. § 994(u) (power to make Guidelines reductions retroactive); 76 Fed. Reg. 41333–41334 (2011) (amended 18-to-1 Guidelines made retroactive). In any event, courts, treating the Guidelines as advisory, possess authority to sentence in accordance with the new minimums.

For these reasons, if the Fair Sentencing Act's new minimums apply to all of those sentenced after August 3, 2010 (even if the new Guidelines were not yet ready), it is possible to foresee a reasonably smooth transition. On the other hand, it is difficult to foresee such a transition if the new Act's application is keyed to a later date, thereby leaving the courts unable to take the new Act fully into account, particularly when that circumstance might create additional disparities and uncertainties that courts and the Commission may be helpless to correct. We have no reason to believe Congress would have wanted to impose an unforeseeable, potentially complex application date. . . .

■ *JUSTICE SCALIA, with whom CHIEF JUSTICE ROBERTS and JUSTICES THOMAS and ALITO join, dissenting:*

In the Fair Sentencing Act of 2010, 124 Stat. 2372, Congress increased the threshold quantities of crack cocaine required to trigger the 5- and 10-year mandatory minimum penalties associated with offenses involving the manufacture, distribution, or dispensation of the drug .... The Act is silent as to whether these changes apply to defendants who committed their offenses before, but whose sentencing proceedings occurred after, its August 3, 2010, effective date. In my view, the general saving statute, 1 U.S.C. § 109, dictates that the new, more lenient mandatory minimum provisions do not apply to such pre-enactment offenders.

I

The Court starts off on the right foot by acknowledging ... that the ameliorative amendments at issue here trigger application of the general saving statute. Enacted in 1871 to reverse the common-law rule that the repeal or amendment of a criminal statute would abate all nonfinal convictions under the repealed or amended statute, see *Warden v. Marrero*, 417 U.S. 653, 660 (1974), the saving statute provides in relevant part:

> "The repeal of any statute shall not have the effect to release or extinguish any penalty, forfeiture, or liability incurred under such statute, unless the repealing Act shall so expressly provide, and such statute shall be treated as still remaining in force for the purpose of sustaining any proper action or prosecution for the enforcement of such penalty, forfeiture, or liability." 1 U.S.C. § 109.

By reducing the statutory penalties for crack cocaine offenses, the Fair Sentencing Act "repeal[ed]" the former penalties; for defendants who committed their offenses (and hence "incurred" the penalties) while the prior law was in force, § 109 directs that the prior law "shall be treated as still remaining in force."

Although § 109 purports to require that subsequent legislation opting out of its default rule must do so "expressly," the Court correctly observes ... that express-statement requirements of this sort are ineffective. See *Lockhart v. United States*, 546 U.S. 142, 147–150 (2005) (Scalia, J., concurring). ... [T]he express-statement requirement of § 109 is itself subject to repeal on the same terms as any other statute, which is to say that a repeal may be accomplished by implication. See, *e.g.*, *Marrero*, *supra*, at 659–660, n. 10; *Great Northern R. Co. v. United States*, 208 U.S. 452, 465 (1908).

Understanding the interpretive problem posed by these cases as one of implied repeal helps to explain the Court's observation ... that what is required to override § 109's default rule is a clear demonstration of congressional intent to do so. Admittedly, our cases have not spoken with the utmost clarity on this point. In *Marrero*, for example, we suggested that a "fair implication" from a subsequently enacted statute would suffice, 417 U.S. at 660, n. 10, while in *Hertz v. Woodman*, 218 U.S. 205 (1910), we used the phrase "*clear* implication," *id.* at 218 (emphasis added); see also *ibid.* ("plain implication"). In *Great Northern R. Co.*, we split the difference, stating at one point that § 109 controls unless Congress expresses a contrary intention "either expressly or by *necessary* implication in a subsequent enactment," 208 U.S. at 465 (emphasis added), but suggesting at another point that a "fair implication," *id.* at 466, would do. In my view, the "fair implication" formulation understates the burden properly imposed on a defendant who would claim an implicit exception from § 109's terms. Because the effect of such an exception is to work a *pro tanto* repeal of § 109's application to the defendant's case, the implication from the subsequently enacted statute must be clear enough to overcome our strong presumption against implied repeals. . . . Thus, we should conclude that Congress has deviated from § 109 (or any similar statute establishing a background interpretive principle) only when the "*plain* import of a later statute directly conflicts" with it. *Lockhart, supra*, at 149 (Scalia, J., concurring) (emphasis added).

II

A

The considerations relied upon by the Court do not come close to satisfying the demanding standard for repeal by implication. As an initial matter, there is no persuasive force whatever to the Court's observation that continuing to apply the prior mandatory minimums to pre-enactment offenders would "involve imposing upon the pre-Act offender a pre-Act sentence at a time after Congress had specifically found in the Fair Sentencing Act that such a sentence was unfairly long." *Ante* at 277. That is true *whenever* Congress reduces a criminal penalty, and so is a consequence that Congress affirmatively *embraced* when it said in § 109 that ameliorative amendments to criminal statutes do not apply to pre-enactment conduct. Nor does it matter that Congress has instructed district courts, when applying the Federal Sentencing Guidelines, to apply the version in force on the date of sentencing, with the object of reducing disparities in sentences between similar defendants who are sentenced for the same conduct at the same time. See 18 U.S.C. § 3553(a)(4)(A)(ii). The presumption against implied repeals requires us to give effect, if possible, to both § 3553(a)(4)(A)(ii) and § 109. "The courts are not at liberty to pick and choose among congressional enactments, and when two statutes are capable of co-existence, it is the duty of the courts, absent a clearly expressed congressional intention to the contrary, to regard each as effective." *Morton v. Mancari*, 417 U.S. 535, 551 (1974). We may readily do so here by holding that § 3553(a)(4)(A)(ii) applies to Guidelines amendments, and § 109 to statutory ones.

The Court also stresses that the Fair Sentencing Act instructs the Sentencing Commission to promulgate "as soon as practicable" (and not later than 90 days after August 3, 2010) "such conforming amendments" to the Sentencing Guidelines "as the Commission determines necessary to achieve consistency with other guideline provisions and applicable law." § 8, 124 Stat. 2374. The argument goes that, because the Commission implemented this directive by reducing the Guidelines ranges for crack cocaine offenses to track the 18-to-1 crack-to-powder ratio reflected in the new mandatory minimums, see 75 Fed. Reg. 66191 (2010), and because the general rule is that a sentencing court should apply the version of the Guidelines in effect at the time of sentencing, see 18 U.S.C. § 3553(a)(4)(A)(ii), Congress must have understood that the new mandatory minimums would apply immediately, since otherwise there would be a mismatch between the statutory penalties and Guidelines ranges.

That conclusion simply does not follow. For one thing, the argument begs the very question presented here: What is the "applicable law" relevant to pre-enactment offenders who are sentenced after enactment? The Commission could well have answered this question by concluding that, in light of § 109, the law applicable to such offenders is the pre-Act mandatory minimums. It might therefore have retained, as to those offenders, the existing Guidelines ranges reflecting a higher crack-to-powder ratio. Although rare, it is not unheard of for the Commission to establish Guidelines whose application turns on the date of commission of the defendant's offense. See United States Sentencing Commission, Guidelines Manual § 5E1.1(g)(1) (Nov. 2011) (governing restitution for offenses committed on or after November 1, 1997, and providing that the prior version of the Guideline shall govern all other cases); *id.* § 8B1.1(f)(1) (same for restitution obligations of organizational defendants). Of course, the Commission did not interpret the Fair Sentencing Act's directive in this manner. But the possibility that it *could* (not to mention the probability that it *should*) have done so illustrates the folly of basing inferences about what Congress intended when it passed the Fair Sentencing Act on decisions the Commission would not make until several months later.[1]

Moreover, even if one takes it as given that the Commission's new crack cocaine Guidelines would apply the lower 18-to-1 ratio to all defendants sentenced after the new Guidelines were put in place, it would not follow that Congress *necessarily* expected the new mandatory minimums to apply to pre-enactment offenders. The directive to update the Guidelines on an emergency basis is equally consistent with Congress's seeking to avoid a mismatch between the Guidelines and the

---

1 Congressional reliance on future Commission action might be plausible if the Commission had a settled practice of tying reductions in statutory mandatory minimums to immediately applicable reductions in Guidelines ranges, without any distinction based on the timing of the defendant's offense. But the Court does not cite any such settled practice, and I am not aware of any. Presumably there has been no occasion for a practice to develop either way, since congressional legislation reducing criminal penalties is, in this day and age, very rare.

statutory penalties for *post-enactment* offenders sentenced shortly after the Act's effective date.

.... [W]ithout the Fair Sentencing Act's emergency directive, amendments to the Guidelines to implement the Act likely would not have been put in place until more than a year after its passage.[2] In the interim, a great many post-Act offenders might have been sentenced under the outdated Guidelines, even though they were clearly entitled to take advantage of the statutory amendments. Because the emergency authority conferred on the Commission can reasonably be understood as directed at *this* mismatch problem, it creates no clear implication that Congress expected the new statutory penalties to apply to pre-enactment offenders.

The Court's last argument is that continuing to apply the prior mandatory minimums to pre-enactment offenders would lead to anomalous, disproportionate sentencing results. It is true enough, as the Court notes, . . . that applying the prior mandatory minimums in tandem with the new Guidelines provisions—which track the new, more lenient mandatory minimums—leads to a series of "cliffs" at the mandatory minimum thresholds. But this does not establish that Congress clearly meant the new mandatory minimums to apply to pre-enactment offenders. As noted above, . . . there is no reason to take the Guidelines amendments ultimately promulgated by the Commission as a given when evaluating what Congress would have understood when the Fair Sentencing Act was enacted. The Commission could have promulgated amendments that ameliorated this problem by retaining the old Guidelines ranges for pre-enactment offenders.

.... And it is not as though the results of continuing to apply the pre-Act statutory penalties are so senseless as to establish that Congress must not have intended them. Retaining the old mandatory minimums ensures at least rough equivalence in sentences for defendants who committed their crimes at the same time, but were sentenced at different times—even as it leads to disparities for defendants who are sentenced at the same time, but committed their offenses at different times. In light of this plausible basis for continuing to apply the prior law to pre-

[2] In the ordinary course, the Commission may submit proposed Guidelines amendments to Congress "at or after the beginning of a regular session of Congress, but not later than the first day of May." 28 U.S.C. § 994(p). Unless disapproved by Congress, the proposed amendments "take effect on a date specified by the Commission, which shall be no earlier than 180 days after being so submitted and no later than the first day of November of the calendar year in which the amendment . . . is submitted." *Ibid.* As a matter of practice, the Commission has adopted November 1 as the default effective date for its proposed amendments. See United States Sentencing Commission, Rules of Practice and Procedure, Rule 4.1 (amended Aug. 2007). Because the Fair Sentencing Act was enacted on August 3, 2010—after May 1—there would have been no opportunity for the Commission to submit proposed amendments to Congress until January 2011. Given the 180-day waiting period, the amendments could not have gone into force until the very end of June 2011 at the earliest. And in all likelihood, they would not have been effective until November 1, 2011.

enactment offenders, there is no reason to conclude that Congress *necessarily* expected the new statutory penalties to apply.

B

. . . . [T]he rule of lenity has no application here, because the background principle supplied by § 109 serves to remove the ambiguity that is a necessary precondition to invocation of the rule. See *Deal v. United States*, 508 U.S. 129, 135 (1993). . . .

* * *

In the end, the mischief of the Court's opinion is not the result in these particular cases, but rather the unpredictability it injects into the law for the future. The Court's decision is based on "[s]ix considerations, taken together," *ante* at 273, and we are not told whether any one of these considerations might have justified the Court's result in isolation, or even the relative importance of the various considerations. One of them (the Commission's emergency authority to issue conforming amendments to the Guidelines) is a particular feature of the statute at issue in these cases, but another (the fact that applying the prior statutory penalties alongside the new Guidelines leads to a mismatch) is a general feature of a sentencing scheme that calibrates Guidelines ranges to the statutory mandatory minimums for a given offense. Are we to conclude that, after the Sentencing Reform Act, § 109 has no further application to criminal penalties, at least when statutory amendments lead to modification of the Guidelines? Portions of the Court's opinion could be understood to suggest that result, but the Court leaves us in suspense.

That is most unfortunate, because the whole point of § 109, as well as other provisions of the Dictionary Act, see 1 U.S.C. §§ 1–8, and the definitional provisions of the federal criminal law, see 18 U.S.C. §§ 5–27 . . . , is to provide a stable set of background principles that will promote effective communication between Congress and the courts. In this context, stability is ensured by a healthy respect for our presumption against implied repeals, which demands a clear showing before we conclude that Congress has deviated from one of these background interpretive principles. Because the Court's result cannot be reconciled with this approach, I respectfully dissent.

NOTES AND QUESTIONS

1. The defendants in *Dorsey* were convicted under § 401 of the Controlled Substances Act, which Congress originally enacted in 1970. *See* Pub. L. 91–513, tit. II, 84 Stat. 1236 (1970). Section 401(a) provides that except as authorized by the Act, "it shall be unlawful for any person knowingly or intentionally . . . to manufacture, distribute, or dispense, or possess with intent to manufacture, distribute, or dispense, a controlled substance." *Id.* § 401(a), 84 Stat. at 1260 (codified at 21 U.S.C. § 841(a)). Section 401(b) addresses the penalties for violations of § 401(a).

As originally enacted, § 401(b) simply established *maximum* prison sentences for violations of § 401(a). *See id.* § 401(b), 84 Stat. at 1261–62 (codified as amended at 21 U.S.C. § 841(b)). But in 1986, Congress amended § 401(b) to establish mandatory *minimum* sentences for certain violations. *See* Act of Oct. 27, 1986, Pub. L. 99–570, § 1002, 100 Stat. 3207, 3207–2 to 3207–4. By and large, Congress based those minimum sentences on the weight of the substances in question. With respect to crack (or "cocaine base"), the weight thresholds were remarkably low. As amended in 1986, § 401(b) required courts to impose a prison sentence of at least five years "[i]n the case of a violation of [§ 401(a)] involving . . . 5 grams or more" or a substance containing cocaine base, and at least ten years "[i]n the case of a violation . . . involving . . . 50 grams or more." *See id.* at 3207–2 to 3207–3.

The Fair Sentencing Act of 2010 amended § 401(b) again by replacing "5 grams" with "28 grams" and by replacing "50 grams" with "280 grams." Pub. L. 111–220, § 2(a), 124 Stat. 2372, 2372 (2010). Going forward, then, the 2010 statute eliminated any mandatory minimum sentence for defendants whose crimes involved less than 28 grams of crack, and it reduced the mandatory minimum from 10 years to 5 years for defendants whose crimes involved between 28 grams and 280 grams.

There was no doubt that these changes would benefit defendants who violated § 401 after August 3, 2010 (when the 2010 statute was enacted and took effect). In *Dorsey*, though, the Supreme Court held that the changes also benefited defendants who were merely being *sentenced* after that date for crimes that they had committed earlier. As interpreted by the majority, the 2010 statute operated with respect to all defendants who were sentenced after its enactment, regardless of when they had committed their crimes. On that interpretation, the 2010 statute reduced or eliminated the mandatory minimum sentences that some defendants would have faced under the version of § 401 that was in force at the time of their crimes.

Justice Breyer's majority opinion acknowledged that this interpretation of the 2010 statute ran counter to 1 U.S.C. § 109. The 2010 statute's amendment of the weight thresholds counted as a "repeal" of the prior thresholds within the meaning of 1 U.S.C. § 109, and the 2010 statute did not "expressly provide" that this change operated with respect to crimes that had already been committed. By the terms of 1 U.S.C. § 109, then, the 2010 statute should not be understood as retroactively reducing the penalties for those crimes. But as Justice Breyer explained (and as Justice Scalia's dissent also acknowledged), the Congresses that enacted 1 U.S.C. § 109 and its predecessors could not really establish an irrebuttable rule about the meaning of subsequently enacted statutes. Even in the absence of "express[ ]" language about its temporal effect, the 2010 statute could still be read to operate with respect to all sentences imposed after its enactment—and if that was indeed the best interpretation of the 2010 statute, then courts should give effect to it notwithstanding 1 U.S.C. § 109.

The question in *Dorsey* therefore boiled down to the proper interpretation of the 2010 statute. But as Justice Breyer conceded, 1 U.S.C. § 109 was not irrelevant to that question. Even though the Congress that enacted 1 U.S.C. § 109 could not authoritatively control whether a later Congress would decide to give a new statute a broader temporal effect than 1 U.S.C. § 109 suggested, or exactly how the later Congress would express that decision, 1 U.S.C. § 109 still has the practical effect of establishing a rebuttable presumption. Absent reasons to conclude otherwise, courts will assume that provisions like 1 U.S.C. § 109 continue to reflect Congress's usual intentions on the topics that those provisions address. Thus, later-enacted statutes will be interpreted as conforming to the rule stated by 1 U.S.C. § 109 unless there is sufficient reason to interpret them as departing from that rule.

Ultimately, though, Justice Breyer and the majority saw enough reason to interpret the 2010 statute as departing from the rule that 1 U.S.C. § 109 suggested. In Part II.A, Justice Breyer listed the considerations that led him to this conclusion. *See Dorsey*, 567 U.S. at 275 (noting that Congress has long instructed sentencing courts to consider the Sentencing Commission's guidelines that "are in effect on the date the defendant is sentenced," 18 U.S.C. § 3553(a)(4)(A)); *id.* at 275–76 (noting that the 2010 statute itself authorized the Commission to make conforming amendments to the guidelines on an emergency basis); *id.* at 276–80 (arguing that the general purposes behind both the 2010 statute and the Sentencing Reform Act of 1984—in particular, Congress's concerns about nonuniform and disproportionate sentencing—support reading the 2010 statute to depart from the default rule suggested by 1 U.S.C. § 109); *cf. id.* at 264 ("We rest our conclusion primarily upon the fact that a contrary determination would seriously undermine basic Federal Sentencing Guidelines objectives such as uniformity and proportionality in sentencing.").

2. Justice Scalia's dissent questioned the force of some of these considerations. *See, e.g., id.* at 290–91 (Scalia, J., dissenting) (noting that 18 U.S.C. § 3553(a)(4)(A) addresses the temporal effect of changes to the Sentencing Commission's guidelines, not changes to *statutory* mandatory minimums); *id.* at 292–94 (proposing a different possible explanation for the 2010 statute's emergency authorization). But Justice Scalia's main disagreement with the majority may have been about the strength of the presumption established by 1 U.S.C. § 109. According to Justice Scalia, the majority was applying too weak a presumption.

The majority spoke of the "fair implication" of the 2010 statute. *See id.* at 274, 281 (majority opinion) (quoting Warden v. Marrero, 417 U.S. 653, 660 n.10 (1974)). Justice Scalia, however, thought that "the 'fair implication' formulation understates the burden properly imposed on a defendant who would claim an implicit exception from § 109's terms." *Id.*

at 289–90 (Scalia, J., dissenting). In Justice Scalia's view, "we should conclude that Congress has deviated from § 109 (or any similar statute establishing a background interpretive principle) only when the '*plain* import of a later statute directly conflicts' with it." *Id.* at 290 (quoting Lockhart v. United States, 546 U.S. 142, 149 (2005) (Scalia, J., concurring) (emphasis added)). To explain this high burden, Justice Scalia invoked "our strong presumption against implied repeals." *Id.* As Justice Scalia saw the situation, a defendant who wanted the Court to interpret a later-enacted statute as departing from 1 U.S.C. § 109 was asking the Court to find "a *pro tanto* repeal of § 109's application to the defendant's case." *Id.*

Is that correct? In the ordinary situation that implicates the presumption against implied repeals, an older statute and a newer statute both address matters that are within Congress's power to regulate, and the older statute operates of its own force unless the newer statute is interpreted to contradict it. (For instance, remember *Morton v. Mancari*: the Indian Reorganization Act of 1934 created a hiring preference that remained in effect unless the Equal Employment Opportunity Act of 1972 contradicted it.) The situation that the Court faced in *Dorsey* was different. Rather than regulating matters in the real world, 1 U.S.C. § 109 purported to regulate the legal effect of future statutes, which is not something that Congress can authoritatively do. That is why not one of the Justices applied the rule that 1 U.S.C. § 109 purports to state. Although 1 U.S.C. § 109 *says* that later-enacted statutes will not have the effect of releasing or extinguishing any penalty that has already been incurred unless they "expressly" so provide, the Congress that enacted 1 U.S.C. § 109 could not establish binding rules about how later Congresses must word the legal directives that they want to establish.

In sum, 1 U.S.C. § 109 could not and did not operate of its own force in *Dorsey* (or in any other case involving the temporal scope of later-enacted statutes). Instead, 1 U.S.C. § 109 matters only in a softer sense. Whether because 1 U.S.C. § 109 is evidence of Congress's ordinary practices or for some other reason, its existence can affect the courts' interpretation of later-enacted statutes; other things being equal, later-enacted statutes will not be understood to depart from the practice suggested by 1 U.S.C. § 109. But even when courts interpret a later-enacted statute to follow that practice, the key question is the meaning of the later-enacted statute; 1 U.S.C. § 109 is not *directly* operating. By the same token, when the majority in *Dorsey* interpreted the Fair Sentencing Act of 2010 to depart from the default rule suggested by 1 U.S.C. § 109, one need not say that the majority was interpreting the 2010 statute as impliedly "repealing" 1 U.S.C. § 109 (even *pro tanto*). The language of "repeal" might suggest that 1 U.S.C. § 109 otherwise would have operated of its own force, which is not true. Maybe it is more accurate to say simply that the majority interpreted the 2010 statute not to follow the pattern suggested by 1 U.S.C. § 109.

Of course, even if Justice Scalia was wrong to use the language of "implied repeal," the majority in *Dorsey* agreed that there is a presumption against reading later-enacted statutes to depart from the pattern suggested by 1 U.S.C. § 109. Still, the majority did not necessarily think that this presumption is as strong as the presumption against implied repeals. Where do you stand on that topic? Are the justifications for a presumption that later-enacted statutes normally conform to 1 U.S.C. § 109 (or a presumption that later-enacted statutes normally use words in the way that 1 U.S.C. § 1 tells us to expect) just as strong as the justifications for the presumption against implied repeals?

3. Although Justice Breyer listed various considerations in support of his interpretation of the 2010 statute, he did not mention the rule of lenity. For his part, Justice Scalia said that the presumption against implied repeals eliminated any ambiguity in the 2010 statute, leaving no room for the rule of lenity to operate. If you disagree with Justice Scalia about the relevance of the presumption against implied repeals, and if you would apply only a weaker presumption against reading the 2010 statute to depart from the pattern suggested by 1 U.S.C. § 109, might the rule of lenity come into play after all?

At first glance, the next case might seem out of place. When you read Justice Breyer's dissent, though, you will see why it belongs in this section of the book. Although the majority opinion was cast entirely in terms of constitutional law, the dispute between the majority and the dissenters might have been at least partly about statutory interpretation. In particular, the majority and the dissenters may have had different assumptions about whether the Line Item Veto Act of 1996 should influence the courts' interpretation of subsequently enacted statutes.

Clinton v. City of New York

524 U.S. 417 (1998)

■ *JUSTICE STEVENS delivered the opinion of the Court:*

The Line Item Veto Act (Act), 110 Stat. 1200, 2 U.S.C. § 691 *et seq.* (1994 ed., Supp. II), was enacted in April 1996 and became effective on January 1, 1997. . . . [Later, in keeping with its provisions,] the President exercised his authority to cancel one provision in the Balanced Budget Act of 1997, Pub. L. 105–33, 111 Stat. 251, 515, and two provisions in the Taxpayer Relief Act of 1997, Pub. L. 105–34, 111 Stat. 788, 895–896, 990–993. Appellees, claiming that they had been injured by two of those cancellations, filed these cases in the District Court. That Court . . . held the [Line Item Veto Act] invalid . . . . [W]e agree that the cancellation procedures set forth in the Act violate the Presentment Clause, Art. I, § 7, cl. 2, of the Constitution.

I

We begin by reviewing the canceled items that are at issue in these cases.

Section 4722(c) of the Balanced Budget Act

Title XIX of the Social Security Act, 79 Stat. 343, as amended, authorizes the Federal Government to transfer huge sums of money to the States to help finance medical care for the indigent. See 42 U.S.C. § 1396d(b). In 1991, Congress directed that those federal subsidies be reduced by the amount of certain taxes levied by the States on health care providers. In 1994, the Department of Health and Human Services notified the State of New York that 15 of its taxes were covered by the 1991 Act, and that as of June 30, 1994, the statute therefore required New York to return $955 million to the United States. . . .

. . . New York turned to Congress for relief. On August 5, 1997, Congress enacted a law that resolved the issue in New York's favor. Section 4722(c) of the Balanced Budget Act of 1997 identifies the disputed taxes and provides that they "are deemed to be permissible health care related taxes and in compliance with the requirements" of the relevant provisions of the 1991 statute.

On August 11, 1997, the President sent identical notices to the Senate and to the House of Representatives canceling "one item of new direct spending," specifying § 4722(c) as that item, and stating that he had determined that "this cancellation will reduce the Federal budget deficit." . . .

Section 968 of the Taxpayer Relief Act of 1997

A person who realizes a profit from the sale of securities is generally subject to a capital gains tax. Under existing law, however, an ordinary business corporation can acquire a corporation, including a food processing or refining company, in a merger or stock-for-stock transaction in which no gain is recognized to the seller, see 26 U.S.C. §§ 354(a), 368(a); the seller's tax payment, therefore, is deferred. If, however, the purchaser is a farmers' cooperative, the parties cannot structure such a transaction because the stock of the cooperative may be held only by its members, see § 521(b)(2); thus, a seller dealing with a farmers' cooperative cannot obtain the benefits of tax deferral.

In § 968 of the Taxpayer Relief Act of 1997, Congress amended § 1042 of the Internal Revenue Code to permit owners of certain food refiners and processors to defer the recognition of gain if they sell their stock to eligible farmers' cooperatives. . . . The amendment to § 1042 was one of the 79 "limited tax benefits" authorized by the Taxpayer Relief Act of 1997 and specifically identified in Title XVII of that Act as "subject to

[the] line item veto." [Taxpayer Relief Act of 1997, Pub. L. 105–34, § 1701(30), 111 Stat. 788, 1101.]

On the same date that he canceled the "item of new direct spending" involving New York's health care programs, the President also canceled this limited tax benefit. . . .

II

Appellees filed two separate actions against the President and other federal officials challenging these two cancellations. The plaintiffs in the first case are the City of New York, two hospital associations, one hospital, and two unions representing health care employees. The plaintiffs in the second are a farmers' cooperative consisting of about 30 potato growers in Idaho and an individual farmer who is a member and officer of the cooperative. The District Court consolidated the two cases and determined that at least one of the plaintiffs in each had standing under Article III of the Constitution.

. . . . On the merits, the District Court held that the cancellations did not conform to the constitutionally mandated procedures for the enactment or repeal of laws . . . .

IV

The Line Item Veto Act gives the President the power to "cancel in whole" three types of provisions that have been signed into law: "(1) any dollar amount of discretionary budget authority; (2) any item of new direct spending; or (3) any limited tax benefit." 2 U.S.C. § 691(a) (1994 ed., Supp. II). It is undisputed that the New York case involves an "item of new direct spending" and that the [farmers' cooperative] case involves a "limited tax benefit" as those terms are defined in the Act. It is also undisputed that each of those provisions had been signed into law pursuant to Article I, § 7, of the Constitution before it was canceled.

The Act requires the President to adhere to precise procedures whenever he exercises his cancellation authority. In identifying items for cancellation he must consider the legislative history, the purposes, and other relevant information about the items. See 2 U.S.C. § 691(b) (1994 ed., Supp. II). He must determine, with respect to each cancellation, that it will "(i) reduce the Federal budget deficit; (ii) not impair any essential Government functions; and (iii) not harm the national interest." § 691(a)(3)(A). Moreover, he must transmit a special message to Congress notifying it of each cancellation within five calendar days (excluding Sundays) after the enactment of the canceled provision. See § 691(a)(3)(B). It is undisputed that the President meticulously followed these procedures in these cases.

A cancellation takes effect upon receipt by Congress of the special message from the President. See § 691b(a). If, however, a "disapproval bill" pertaining to a special message is enacted into law, the cancellations set forth in that message become "null and void." *Ibid.* The Act sets forth a detailed expedited procedure for the consideration of a "disapproval bill," see § 691d, but no such bill was passed for either of the cancellations involved in these cases.[24] A majority vote of both Houses is sufficient to enact a disapproval bill. The Act does not grant the President the authority to cancel a disapproval bill, see § 691(c), but he does, of course, retain his constitutional authority to veto such a bill.

The effect of a cancellation is plainly stated in § 691e, which defines the principal terms used in the Act. With respect to both an item of new direct spending and a limited tax benefit, the cancellation prevents the item "from having legal force or effect." 2 U.S.C. §§ 691e(4)(B)–(C) (1994 ed., Supp. II).[26] Thus, under the plain text of the statute, the two actions of the President that are challenged in these cases prevented one section of the Balanced Budget Act of 1997 and one section of the Taxpayer Relief Act of 1997 "from having legal force or effect." The remaining provisions of those statutes, with the exception of the second canceled item in the latter, continue to have the same force and effect as they had when signed into law.

In both legal and practical effect, the President has amended two Acts of Congress by repealing a portion of each. "[R]epeal of statutes, no less than enactment, must conform with Art. I." *INS v. Chadha*, 462 U.S. 919, 954 (1983). There is no provision in the Constitution that authorizes the President to enact, to amend, or to repeal statutes. Both Article I and Article II assign responsibilities to the President that directly relate to the lawmaking process, but neither addresses the issue presented by these cases. The President "shall from time to time give to the Congress Information on the State of the Union, and recommend to their Consideration such Measures as he shall judge necessary and expedient. . . ." Art. II, § 3. Thus, he may initiate and influence legislative proposals. Moreover, after a bill has passed both Houses of Congress, but "before it become[s] a Law," it must be presented to the President. If he approves it, "he shall sign it, but if not he shall return it, with his Objections to that House in which it shall have originated, who

[24] . . . [D]espite the fact that the President has canceled at least 82 items since the Act was passed, . . . Congress has enacted only one law, over a Presidential veto, disapproving any cancellation, see Pub. L. 105–159, 112 Stat. 19 (1998) (disapproving the cancellation of 38 military construction spending items).

[26] The term "cancel," used in connection with any dollar amount of discretionary budget authority, means "to rescind." 2 U.S.C. § 691e(4)(A). The entire definition reads as follows:

"The term 'cancel' or 'cancellation' means—

"(A) with respect to any dollar amount of discretionary budget authority, to rescind;

"(B) with respect to any item of new direct spending—

"(i) that is budget authority provided by law (other than an appropriation law), to prevent such budget authority from having legal force or effect;

"(ii) that is entitlement authority, to prevent the specific legal obligation of the United States from having legal force or effect; or

"(iii) through the food stamp program, to prevent the specific provision of law that results in an increase in budget authority or outlays for that program from having legal force or effect; and

"(C) with respect to a limited tax benefit, to prevent the specific provision of law that provides such benefit from having legal force or effect."

shall enter the Objections at large on their Journal, and proceed to reconsider it." Art. I, § 7, cl. 2. His "return" of a bill, which is usually described as a "veto," is subject to being overridden by a two-thirds vote in each House.

There are important differences between the President's "return" of a bill pursuant to Article I, § 7, and the exercise of the President's cancellation authority pursuant to the Line Item Veto Act. The constitutional return takes place before the bill becomes law; the statutory cancellation occurs after the bill becomes law. The constitutional return is of the entire bill; the statutory cancellation is of only a part. Although the Constitution expressly authorizes the President to play a role in the process of enacting statutes, it is silent on the subject of unilateral Presidential action that either repeals or amends parts of duly enacted statutes.

There are powerful reasons for construing constitutional silence on this profoundly important issue as equivalent to an express prohibition. The procedures governing the enactment of statutes set forth in the text of Article I were the product of the great debates and compromises that produced the Constitution itself. Familiar historical materials provide abundant support for the conclusion that the power to enact statutes may only "be exercised in accord with a single, finely wrought and exhaustively considered, procedure." *Chadha*, 462 U.S. at 951. Our first President understood the text of the Presentment Clause as requiring that he either "approve all the parts of a Bill, or reject it in toto."[30] What has emerged in these cases from the President's exercise of his statutory cancellation powers, however, are truncated versions of two bills that passed both Houses of Congress. They are not the product of the "finely wrought" procedure that the Framers designed. . . .

V

The Government advances two related arguments to support its position that despite the unambiguous provisions of the Act, cancellations do not amend or repeal properly enacted statutes in violation of the Presentment Clause. First, relying primarily on *Field v. Clark*, 143 U.S. 649 (1892), the Government contends that the cancellations were merely exercises of discretionary authority granted to the President by the Balanced Budget Act and the Taxpayer Relief Act read in light of the previously enacted Line Item Veto Act. Second, the Government submits that the substance of the authority to cancel tax and spending items "is, in practical effect, no more and no less than the power to 'decline to spend' specified sums of money, or to 'decline to

[30] 33 Writings of George Washington 96 (J. Fitzpatrick ed., 1940); see also W. Taft, The Presidency: Its Duties, Its Powers, Its Opportunities and Its Limitations 11 (1916) (stating that the President "has no power to veto part of a bill and let the rest become a law"); cf. 1 W. Blackstone, Commentaries *154 ("The crown cannot begin of itself any alterations in the present established law; but it may approve or disapprove of the alterations suggested and consented to by the two houses").

implement' specified tax measures." Brief for Appellants 40. Neither argument is persuasive.

In *Field v. Clark*, the Court upheld the constitutionality of the Tariff Act of 1890. Act of Oct. 1, 1890, 26 Stat. 567. That statute contained a "free list" of almost 300 specific articles that were exempted from import duties "unless otherwise specially provided for in this act." *Id.* at 602. Section 3 was a special provision that directed the President to suspend that exemption for sugar, molasses, coffee, tea, and hides "whenever, and so often" as he should be satisfied that any country producing and exporting those products imposed duties on the agricultural products of the United States that he deemed to be "reciprocally unequal and unreasonable. . . ." *Id.* at 612, quoted in *Field,* 143 U.S. at 680. The section then specified the duties to be imposed on those products during any such suspension. The Court provided this explanation for its conclusion that § 3 had not delegated legislative power to the President:

> "Nothing involving the expediency or the just operation of such legislation was left to the determination of the President. . . . [W]hen he ascertained the fact that duties and exactions, reciprocally unequal and unreasonable, were imposed upon the agricultural or other products of the United States by a country producing and exporting sugar, molasses, coffee, tea or hides, it became his duty to issue a proclamation declaring the suspension, as to that country, which Congress had determined should occur. He had no discretion in the premises except in respect to the duration of the suspension so ordered. But that related only to the enforcement of the policy established by Congress. As the suspension was absolutely required when the President ascertained the existence of a particular fact, it cannot be said that in ascertaining that fact and in issuing his proclamation, in obedience to the legislative will, he exercised the function of making laws. . . . It was a part of the law itself as it left the hands of Congress that the provisions, full and complete in themselves, permitting the free introduction of sugars, molasses, coffee, tea and hides, from particular countries, should be suspended, in a given contingency, and that in case of such suspensions certain duties should be imposed." *Id.* at 693.

This passage identifies three critical differences between the power to suspend the exemption from import duties and the power to cancel portions of a duly enacted statute. First, the exercise of the suspension power was contingent upon a condition that did not exist when the Tariff Act was passed: the imposition of "reciprocally unequal and unreasonable" import duties by other countries. In contrast, the exercise of the cancellation power within five days after the enactment of the Balanced Budget and Tax Reform Acts necessarily was based on the same conditions that Congress evaluated when it passed those statutes. Second, under the Tariff Act, when the President determined that the contingency had arisen, he had a duty to suspend; in contrast, while it is true that the President was required by the Act to make three determinations before he canceled a provision, see 2 U.S.C. § 691(a)(A) (1994 ed., Supp. II), those determinations did not qualify his discretion to cancel or not to cancel. Finally, whenever the President suspended an exemption under the Tariff Act, he was executing the policy that Congress had embodied in the statute. In contrast, whenever the President cancels an item of new direct spending or a limited tax benefit he is rejecting the policy judgment made by Congress and relying on his own policy judgment.[35] Thus, the conclusion in *Field v. Clark* that the suspensions mandated by the Tariff Act were not exercises of legislative power does not undermine our opinion that cancellations pursuant to the Line Item Veto Act are the functional equivalent of partial repeals of Acts of Congress that fail to satisfy Article I, § 7.

The Government's reliance upon other tariff and import statutes, discussed in *Field*, that contain provisions similar to the one challenged in *Field* is unavailing for the same reasons.[36] Some of those statutes authorized the President to "suspen[d] and discontinu[e]" statutory duties upon his determination that discriminatory duties imposed by other nations had been abolished. See 143 U.S. at 686–687 (discussing Act of Jan. 7, 1824, ch. 4, § 4, 4 Stat. 3, and Act of May 24, 1828, ch. 111, 4 Stat. 308). A slightly different statute, Act of May 31, 1830, ch. 219, § 2, 4 Stat. 425, provided that certain statutory provisions imposing duties on foreign ships "shall be repealed" upon the same no-discrimination determination by the President. See also 143 U.S. at 686 (discussing similar tariff statute, Act of Mar. 3, 1815, ch. 77, 3 Stat. 224, which provided that duties "are hereby repealed," "[s]uch repeal to take effect . . . whenever the President" makes the required determination).

The cited statutes all relate to foreign trade, and this Court has recognized that in the foreign affairs arena, the President has "a degree of discretion and freedom from statutory restriction which would not be admissible were domestic affairs alone involved." *United States v. Curtiss-Wright Export Corp.*, 299 U.S. 304, 320 (1936). . . . More important, when enacting the statutes discussed in *Field*, Congress itself made the decision to suspend or repeal the particular provisions at issue upon the occurrence of particular events subsequent to enactment, and it left only the determination of whether such events occurred up to the President.[39] The Line Item Veto Act authorizes the President himself to effect the repeal of laws, for his own policy reasons, without observing

[35] . . . Because the Line Item Veto Act requires the President to act within five days, every exercise of the cancellation power will necessarily be based on the same facts and circumstances that Congress considered, and therefore constitute a rejection of the policy choice made by Congress.

[36] The Court did not, of course, expressly consider in *Field* whether those statutes comported with the requirements of the Presentment Clause.

[39] See also *J.W. Hampton, Jr., & Co. v. United States*, 276 U.S. 394, 407 (1928) ("Congress may feel itself unable conveniently to determine exactly when its exercise of the legislative power should become effective, because dependent on future conditions, and it may leave the determination of such time to the decision of an Executive").

the procedures set out in Article I, § 7. The fact that Congress intended such a result is of no moment. Although Congress presumably anticipated that the President might cancel some of the items in the Balanced Budget Act and in the Taxpayer Relief Act, Congress cannot alter the procedures set out in Article I, § 7, without amending the Constitution.[40]

Neither are we persuaded by the Government's contention that the President's authority to cancel new direct spending and tax benefit items is no greater than his traditional authority to decline to spend appropriated funds. The Government has reviewed in some detail the series of statutes in which Congress has given the Executive broad discretion over the expenditure of appropriated funds. For example, the First Congress appropriated "sum[s] not exceeding" specified amounts to be spent on various Government operations. See, e.g., Act of Sept. 29, 1789, ch. 23, § 1, 1 Stat. 95; Act of Mar. 26, 1790, ch. 4, § 1, 1 Stat. 104; Act of Feb. 11, 1791, ch. 6, 1 Stat. 190. In those statutes, as in later years, the President was given wide discretion with respect to both the amounts to be spent and how the money would be allocated among different functions. It is argued that the Line Item Veto Act merely confers comparable discretionary authority over the expenditure of appropriated funds. The critical difference between this statute and all of its predecessors, however, is that unlike any of them, this Act gives the President the unilateral power to change the text of duly enacted statutes. None of the Act's predecessors could even arguably have been construed to authorize such a change.

VI

Although they are implicit in what we have already written, the profound importance of these cases makes it appropriate to emphasize three points.

First, we express no opinion about the wisdom of the procedures authorized by the Line Item Veto Act. . . .

Second, although appellees challenge the validity of the Act on alternative grounds, the only issue we address concerns the "finely wrought" procedure commanded by the Constitution. *Chadha*, 462 U.S. at 951. We have been favored with extensive debate about the scope of Congress' power to delegate law-making authority, or its functional equivalent, to the President. The excellent briefs filed by the parties and their *amici curiae* have provided us with valuable historical information

[40] The Government argues that the Rules Enabling Act, 28 U.S.C. § 2072(b), permits this Court to "repeal" prior laws without violating Article I, § 7. Section 2072(b) provides that this Court may promulgate rules of procedure for the lower federal courts and that "[a]ll laws in conflict with such rules shall be of no further force or effect after such rules have taken effect." . . . In enacting § 2072(b), however, Congress expressly provided that laws inconsistent with the procedural rules promulgated by this Court would automatically be repealed upon the enactment of new rules in order to create a uniform system of rules for Article III courts. As in the tariff statutes, Congress itself made the decision to repeal prior rules upon the occurrence of a particular event—here, the promulgation of procedural rules by this Court.

that illuminates the delegation issue but does not really bear on the narrow issue that is dispositive of these cases. Thus, because we conclude that the Act's cancellation provisions violate Article I, § 7, of the Constitution, we find it unnecessary to consider the District Court's alternative holding that the Act "impermissibly disrupts the balance of powers among the three branches of government." 985 F. Supp. at 179.[43]

. . .

Third, our decision rests on the narrow ground that the procedures authorized by the Line Item Veto Act are not authorized by the Constitution. The Balanced Budget Act of 1997 is a 500-page document that became "Public Law 105–33" after three procedural steps were taken: (1) a bill containing its exact text was approved by a majority of the Members of the House of Representatives; (2) the Senate approved precisely the same text; and (3) that text was signed into law by the President. The Constitution explicitly requires that each of those three steps be taken before a bill may "become a law." Art. I, § 7. If one paragraph of that text had been omitted at any one of those three stages, Public Law 105–33 would not have been validly enacted. If the Line Item Veto Act were valid, it would authorize the President to create a different law—one whose text was not voted on by either House of Congress or presented to the President for signature. Something that might be known as "Public Law 105–33 as modified by the President" may or may not be desirable, but it is surely not a document that may "become a law" pursuant to the procedures designed by the Framers of Article I, § 7, of the Constitution.

If there is to be a new procedure in which the President will play a different role in determining the final text of what may "become a law," such change must come not by legislation but through the amendment procedures set forth in Article V of the Constitution. . . .

■ *[A concurring opinion by JUSTICE KENNEDY is omitted.]*

■ *JUSTICE SCALIA, with whom JUSTICE O'CONNOR joins, and with whom JUSTICE BREYER joins as to Part III, concurring in part and dissenting in part:*

. . . .

III

. . . . Article I, § 7 of the Constitution obviously prevents the President from cancelling a law that Congress has not authorized him to cancel. Such action cannot possibly be considered part of his execution of the law, and if it is legislative action, as the Court observes, " 'repeal of statutes, no less than enactment, must conform with Art. I.' " *Ante* at 438,

[43] We also find it unnecessary to consider whether the provisions of the Act relating to discretionary budget authority are severable from the Act's tax benefit and direct spending provisions. We note, however, that the Act contains no severability clause; a severability provision that had appeared in the Senate bill was dropped in conference without explanation. H.R. Conf. Rep. No. 104–491, at 17, 41.

quoting from *INS v. Chadha*, 462 U.S. 919, 954 (1983). But that is not this case. It was certainly arguable, as an original matter, that Art. I, § 7 also prevents the President from cancelling a law which itself authorizes the President to cancel it. But as the Court acknowledges, that argument has long since been made and rejected. In 1809, Congress passed a law authorizing the President to cancel trade restrictions against Great Britain and France if either revoked edicts directed at the United States. Act of Mar. 1, 1809, § 11, 2 Stat. 528. Joseph Story regarded the conferral of that authority as entirely unremarkable in *The Orono*, 18 F. Cas. 830, No. 10,585 (CCD Mass. 1812). The Tariff Act of 1890 authorized the President to "suspend, by proclamation to that effect" certain of its provisions if he determined that other countries were imposing "reciprocally unequal and unreasonable" duties. Act of Oct. 1, 1890, § 3, 26 Stat. 612. This Court upheld the constitutionality of that Act in *Field v. Clark*, 143 U.S. 649 (1892), reciting the history since 1798 of statutes conferring upon the President the power to, *inter alia*, "discontinue the prohibitions and restraints hereby enacted and declared," "suspend the operation of the aforesaid act," and "declare the provisions of this act to be inoperative."

As much as the Court goes on about Art. I, § 7, therefore, that provision does not demand the result the Court reaches. It no more categorically prohibits the Executive reduction of congressional dispositions in the course of implementing statutes that authorize such reduction, than it categorically prohibits the Executive augmentation of congressional dispositions in the course of implementing statutes that authorize such augmentation—generally known as substantive rulemaking. There are, to be sure, limits upon the former just as there are limits upon the latter—and I am prepared to acknowledge that the limits upon the former may be much more severe. Those limits are established, however, not by some categorical prohibition of Art. I, § 7, which our cases conclusively disprove, but by what has come to be known as the doctrine of unconstitutional delegation of legislative authority: When authorized Executive reduction or augmentation is allowed to go too far, it usurps the nondelegable function of Congress and violates the separation of powers.

It is this doctrine, and not the Presentment Clause, that was discussed in the *Field* opinion, and it is this doctrine, and not the Presentment Clause, that is the issue presented by the statute before us here. That is why the Court is correct to distinguish prior authorizations of Executive cancellation, such as the one involved in *Field*, on the ground that they were contingent upon an Executive finding of fact, and on the ground that they related to the field of foreign affairs, an area where the President has a special "degree of discretion and freedom," *ante* at 445 (citation omitted). These distinctions have nothing to do with whether the details of Art. I, § 7 have been complied with, but everything to do with whether the authorizations went too far by transferring to the

Executive a degree of political, law-making power that our traditions demand be retained by the Legislative Branch.

I turn, then, to the crux of the matter: whether Congress's authorizing the President to cancel an item of spending gives him a power that our history and traditions show must reside exclusively in the Legislative Branch. . . .

Insofar as the degree of political, "law-making" power conferred upon the Executive is concerned, there is not a dime's worth of difference between Congress's authorizing the President to cancel a spending item, and Congress's authorizing money to be spent on a particular item at the President's discretion. And the latter has been done since the Founding of the Nation. From 1789–1791, the First Congress made lump-sum appropriations for the entire Government—"sum[s] not exceeding" specified amounts for broad purposes. Act of Sept. 29, 1789, ch. 23, § 1, 1 Stat. 95; Act of Mar. 26, 1790, ch. 4, § 1, 1 Stat. 104; Act of Feb. 11, 1791, ch. 6, 1 Stat. 190. From a very early date Congress also made permissive individual appropriations, leaving the decision whether to spend the money to the President's unfettered discretion. In 1803, it appropriated $50,000 for the President to build "not exceeding fifteen gun boats, to be armed, manned and fitted out, and employed for such purposes as in his opinion the public service may require," Act of Feb. 28, 1803, ch. 11, § 3, 2 Stat. 206. President Jefferson reported that "[t]he sum of fifty thousand dollars appropriated by Congress for providing gun boats remains unexpended. The favorable and peaceable turn of affairs on the Mississippi rendered an immediate execution of that law unnecessary," 13 Annals of Cong. 14 (1803). Examples of appropriations committed to the discretion of the President abound in our history. . . . The constitutionality of such appropriations has never seriously been questioned. . . .

Certain Presidents have claimed Executive authority to withhold appropriated funds even *absent* an express conferral of discretion to do so. In 1876, for example, President Grant reported to Congress that he would not spend money appropriated for certain harbor and river improvements .... President Truman ordered the impoundment of hundreds of millions of dollars that had been appropriated for military aircraft. . . . President Nixon . . . asserted at a press conference in 1973 that his "constitutional right" to impound appropriated funds was "absolutely clear." . . . Our decision two years later in *Train v. City of New York*, 420 U.S. 35 (1975), proved him wrong, but it implicitly confirmed that Congress may confer discretion upon the executive to withhold appropriated funds, even funds appropriated for a specific purpose. . . .

The short of the matter is this: Had the Line Item Veto Act authorized the President to "decline to spend" any item of spending contained in the Balanced Budget Act of 1997, there is not the slightest doubt that authorization would have been constitutional. What the Line Item Veto Act does instead—authorizing the President to "cancel" an item of spending—is technically different. But the technical difference does not relate to the technicalities of the Presentment Clause, which have been fully complied with; and the doctrine of unconstitutional delegation, which is at issue here, is preeminently not a doctrine of technicalities. The title of the Line Item Veto Act, which was perhaps designed to simplify for public comprehension, or perhaps merely to comply with the terms of a campaign pledge, has succeeded in faking out the Supreme Court. The President's action it authorizes in fact is not a line-item veto and thus does not offend Art. I, § 7; and insofar as the substance of that action is concerned, it is no different from what Congress has permitted the President to do since the formation of the Union.

IV

I would hold that the President's cancellation of § 4722(c) of the Balanced Budget Act of 1997 as an item of direct spending does not violate the Constitution. Because I find no party before us who has standing to challenge the President's cancellation of § 968 of the Taxpayer Relief Act of 1997, I do not reach the question whether that violates the Constitution. . . .

■ *JUSTICE BREYER, with whom JUSTICE O'CONNOR and JUSTICE SCALIA join as to Part III, dissenting:*

. . . .

II

. . . . When our Nation was founded, Congress could easily have provided the President with th[e] kind of power [that the Line Item Veto Act contemplates]. In that time period, our population was less than four million, . . . federal employees numbered fewer than 5,000, . . . annual federal budget outlays totaled approximately $4 million, . . . and the entire operative text of Congress's first general appropriations law read as follows:

> "Be it enacted . . . [t]hat there be appropriated for the service of the present year, to be paid out of the monies which arise, either from the requisitions heretofore made upon the several states, or from the duties on import and tonnage, the following sums, *viz.* A sum not exceeding two hundred and sixteen thousand dollars for defraying the expenses of the civil list, under the late and present government; a sum not exceeding one hundred and thirty-seven thousand dollars for defraying the expenses of the department of war; a sum not exceeding one hundred and ninety thousand dollars for discharging the warrants issued by the late board of treasury, and remaining unsatisfied; and a sum not exceeding ninety-six thousand dollars for paying the pensions to invalids." Act of Sept. 29, 1789, ch. 23, § 1, 1 Stat. 95.

At that time, a Congress, wishing to give a President the power to select among appropriations, could simply have embodied each appropriation in a separate bill, each bill subject to a separate Presidential veto.

Today, however, our population is about 250 million, . . . the Federal Government employs more than four million people, . . . the annual federal budget is $1.5 trillion, . . . and a typical budget appropriations bill may have a dozen titles, hundreds of sections, and spread across more than 500 pages of the Statutes at Large. . . . Congress cannot divide such a bill into thousands, or tens of thousands, of separate appropriations bills, each one of which the President would have to sign, or to veto, separately. Thus, the question is whether the Constitution permits Congress to choose a particular novel *means* to achieve this same, constitutionally legitimate, *end*. . . .

III

The Court believes that the Act violates the literal text of the Constitution. A simple syllogism captures its basic reasoning:

> Major Premise: The Constitution sets forth an exclusive method for enacting, repealing, or amending laws. . . .
>
> Minor Premise: The Act authorizes the President to "repea[l] or amen[d]" laws in a different way, namely by announcing a cancellation of a portion of a previously enacted law. . . .
>
> Conclusion: The Act is inconsistent with the Constitution. . . .

I find this syllogism unconvincing, however, because its Minor Premise is faulty. When the President "canceled" the two appropriation measures now before us, he did not *repeal* any law nor did he *amend* any law. He simply *followed* the law, leaving the statutes, as they are literally written, intact.

To understand why one cannot say, *literally speaking*, that the President has repealed or amended any law, imagine how the provisions of law before us might have been, but were not, written. Imagine that the canceled New York health care tax provision at issue here, [which was enacted as § 4722(c) of the Balanced Budget Act of 1997 and then "canceled" by the President,] . . . had instead said the following:

> "Section One. Taxes . . . that were collected by the State of New York from a health care provider before June 1, 1997 and for which a waiver of provisions [requiring payment] have been sought . . . are deemed to be permissible health care related taxes . . . *provided however that the President may prevent the just-mentioned provision from having legal force or effect if he determines x, y and z.*" (Assume x, y and z to be the same determinations required by the Line Item Veto Act.)

Whatever a person might say, or think, about the constitutionality of this imaginary law, there is one thing the English language would prevent one from saying. One could not say that a President who "prevent[s]" the deeming language from "having legal force or effect," see 2 U.S.C. § 691e(4)(B) (1994 ed., Supp. II), has either *repealed* or *amended* this particular hypothetical statute. Rather, the President has *followed* that law to the letter. He has exercised the power it explicitly delegates to him. He has executed the law, not repealed it.

It could make no significant difference to this linguistic point were the italicized proviso to appear, not as part of what I have called Section One, but, instead, at the bottom of the statute page, say referenced by an asterisk, with a statement that it applies to every spending provision in the act next to which a similar asterisk appears. And that being so, it could make no difference if that proviso appeared, instead, in a different, earlier-enacted law, along with legal language that makes it applicable to every future spending provision picked out according to a specified formula. See, *e.g.*, Balanced Budget and Emergency Deficit Control Act of 1985 (Gramm-Rudman-Hollings Act), Pub. L. 99–177, 99 Stat. 1063, 2 U.S.C. § 901 *et seq.* (enforcing strict spending and deficit-neutrality limits on future appropriations statutes); see also 1 U.S.C. § 1 (in "*any* Act of Congress" singular words include plural, and vice versa) (emphasis added).

But, of course, this last-mentioned possibility is this very case. The earlier law, namely, the Line Item Veto Act, says that "the President may . . . prevent such [future] budget authority from having legal force or effect." 2 U.S.C. §§ 691(a), 691e(4)(B) (1994 ed., Supp. II). Its definitional sections make clear that it applies to the 1997 New York health care provision, see 2 U.S.C. § 691e(8), just as they give a special legal meaning to the word "cancel," 2 U.S.C. § 691e(4). For that reason, one cannot dispose of this case through a purely literal analysis as the majority does. Literally speaking, the President has not "repealed" or "amended" anything. He has simply *executed* a power conferred upon him by Congress, which power is contained in laws that were enacted in compliance with the exclusive method set forth in the Constitution. See *Field v. Clark*, 143 U.S. 649, 693 (1892) (President's power to raise tariff rates "*was a part of the law itself, as it left the hands of Congress*" (emphasis added)).

Nor can one dismiss this literal compliance as some kind of formal quibble, as if it were somehow "obvious" that what the President has done "amounts to," "comes close to," or is "analogous to" the repeal or amendment of a previously enacted law. That is because the power the Act grants the President (to render designated appropriations items without "legal force or effect") also "amounts to," "comes close to," or is "analogous to" a different legal animal, the delegation of a power to choose one legal path as opposed to another . . . .

. . . .

. . . . This is not the first time that Congress has delegated to the President or to others this kind of power—a contingent power to deny effect to certain statutory language. See, e.g., Pub. L. 95–384, § 13(a), 92

Stat. 737 ("Section 620(x) of the Foreign Assistance Act of 1961 *shall be of no further force and effect* upon the President's determination and certification to the Congress that the resumption of full military cooperation with Turkey is in the national interest of the United States and [other criteria]") (emphasis added); 28 U.S.C. § 2072 (Supreme Court is authorized to promulgate rules of practice and procedure in federal courts, and "[a]ll laws in conflict with such rules *shall be of no further force and effect*") (emphasis added); 41 U.S.C. § 405b (subsection (a) requires the Office of Federal Procurement Policy to issue "[g]overnment-wide regulations" setting forth a variety of conflict of interest standards, but subsection (e) says that "if the President determine[s]" that the regulations "would have a significantly adverse effect on the accomplishment of the mission" of government agencies, "the requirement [to promulgate] the regulations . . . *shall be null and void*") (emphasis added); Gramm-Rudman-Hollings Act, § 252(a)(4), 99 Stat. 1074 (authorizing the President to issue a "final order" that has the effect of "*permanently cancell[ing]*" sequestered amounts in spending statutes in order to achieve budget compliance) (emphasis added); Pub. L. 104–208, 110 Stat. 3009–695 ("Public Law 89–732 [dealing with immigration from Cuba] *is repealed* . . . upon a determination by the President . . . that a democratically elected government in Cuba is in power") (emphasis added); Pub. L. 99–498, § 701, 100 Stat. 1532 (amending § 758 of the Higher Education Act of 1965) (Secretary of Education "may" sell common stock in an educational loan corporation; if the Secretary decides to sell stock, and "if the Student Loan Marketing Association acquires from the Secretary" over 50 percent of the voting stock, "section 754 [governing composition of the Board of Directors] *shall be of no further force or effect*") (emphasis added); Pub. L. 104–134, § 2901(c), 110 Stat. 1321–160 (President is "authorized to suspend the provisions of the [preceding] proviso"[,] which suspension may last for *entire* effective period of proviso, if he determines suspension is "appropriate based upon the public interest in sound environmental management . . . [or] the protection of national or locally-affected interests, or protection of any cultural, biological or historic resources").

All of these examples, like the Act, delegate a power to take action that will render statutory provisions "without force or effect." Every one of these examples, like the present Act, delegates the power to choose between alternatives, each of which the statute spells out in some detail. None of these examples delegates a power to "repeal" or "amend" a statute, or to "make" a new law. Nor does the Act. Rather, the delegated power to nullify statutory language was itself created and defined by Congress, and included in the statute books on an equal footing with (indeed, as a component part of) the sections that are potentially subject to nullification. As a Pennsylvania court put the matter more than a century ago: "The legislature cannot delegate its power to make a law; but it can make a law to delegate a power." *Locke's Appeal*, 72 Pa. 491, 498 (1873). . . .

NOTES AND QUESTIONS

1. The Line Item Veto Act purported to provide a framework for the operation of future statutes. In particular, the Act purported to give the President discretionary authority to "cancel" certain types of provisions that would appear in future statutes.

In *Clinton v. City of New York*, the majority held that Congress cannot validly give the President this authority. The majority cast its analysis in terms of *INS v. Chadha*, 462 U.S. 919 (1983), and the lawmaking process required by Article I of the Constitution. Just as enacting a statute in the first place requires an exercise of "legislative" power, so does repealing a statute—and, under the Constitution, all such exercises of "legislative" power must go through the process of bicameralism and presentment. *See Chadha*, 462 U.S. at 954 ("[R]epeal of statutes, no less than enactment, must conform with Art. I."). The Congress that enacted the Line Item Veto Act obviously could not change the requirements of Article I; a statute cannot validly provide that in the future, certain exercises of "legislative" power do not need to go through bicameralism and presentment. In the majority's view, though, that was exactly what the Line Item Veto Act purported to say. The majority characterized the Line Item Veto Act as purporting to authorize the President to "repeal" portions of subsequently enacted statutes, and the majority said that Congress cannot give the President this authority; only Congress can repeal a federal statute, and Congress has to go through the process of bicameralism and presentment to do so.

To the extent that the Line Item Veto Act purported to let the President negate the provisions of later-enacted statutes (contrary to the meaning of those statutes), the majority's analysis seems correct. But what if a later-enacted statute incorporates the Line Item Veto Act by reference and makes its own provisions subject to the cancellation authority that the Line Item Veto Act described? Does the Constitution prevent a statute from giving the President discretion to cancel some of the line items that the *same statute* contains?

As Justice Breyer observed in Part III of his dissent, the majority's analysis does not readily cover this situation. If a statute itself authorizes the President to cancel some of the line items that the statute contains, and if the President exercises that authority with respect to one of those items, the President need not be described as "repealing" the statute (even in part). Instead, the President is simply choosing a path that the statute itself allows; by its terms, the statute makes the relevant line item contingent, and the statute itself turns the item off when the contingency occurs. Rather than *repealing* anything in the statute, the President is *carrying out* the statute in one of the ways that the statute allows.

2. This way of thinking led the dissenters to focus on the proper interpretation of the statutes containing the line items that President

Clinton purported to cancel. One of those statutes—the Taxpayer Relief Act of 1997—explicitly indicated that the line item in question was subject to cancellation as described in the Line Item Veto Act.

Explaining that point requires some detail. In the early 1970s, President Nixon repeatedly claimed authority under existing law to "impound" (not spend) funds that Congress had appropriated for federal programs. *See* Note, *Impoundment of Funds*, 86 HARV. L. REV. 1505, 1512–29 (1973) (analyzing the Administration's arguments and rejecting most of them); *see also* Train v. City of New York, 420 U.S. 35 (1975) (ultimately ruling against the Administration's position in one such controversy). Congress responded by enacting the Congressional Budget and Impoundment Control Act of 1974, which largely denied the President this authority. *See* Pub. L. 93–344, 88 Stat. 297 (1974). In 1996, the Line Item Veto Act cast its key provisions as amendments to that Act. *See* Line Item Veto Act, Pub. L. 104–130, sec. 2(a), §§ 1021–1027, 110 Stat. 1200, 1200–11 (1996).

The Line Item Veto Act purported to give the President authority to cancel three different types of line items: "(1) any dollar amount of discretionary budget authority; (2) any item of new direct spending; or (3) any limited tax benefit." *Id.* § 1021(a), 110 Stat. at 1200. But Congress knew that identifying "limited tax benefit[s]" would not be easy. *Cf. id.* § 1026(9), 110 Stat. at 1209 (defining this term in a way that required knowing how many beneficiaries a provision would have). The Line Item Veto Act therefore specified that going forward, when a conference committee was preparing a revenue or reconciliation bill that included any amendments to the Internal Revenue Code, the Joint Committee on Taxation would review the bill and identify any "limited tax benefits" that the bill contained. *Id.* § 1027(a), 110 Stat. at 1210. The Line Item Veto Act further authorized the conference committee to add the following provision to the bill: "Section 1021(a)(3) of the Congressional Budget and Impoundment Control Act of 1974" (the provision added by the Line Item Veto Act that authorized the President to cancel any limited tax benefit) "shall only apply to" the provisions that the Joint Committee on Taxation had identified. *Id.* § 1027(b), 110 Stat. at 1210. Alternatively, if the Joint Committee on Taxation declared that the bill did not contain any limited tax benefits, the conference committee could add the following provision: "Section 1021(a)(3) of the Congressional Budget and Impoundment Control Act of 1974 shall not apply to any provision of this Act." *Id.*[53] Ultimately, Congress would consider and might enact the bill that the conference committee reported.

The following year, Congress followed this procedure with respect to the Taxpayer Relief Act of 1997, Pub. L. 105–34, 111 Stat. 788. As the

[53] These suggested provisions presumably reflected the difficulty of identifying which items in a bill were "limited tax benefit[s]" within the meaning of the Line Item Veto Act. The provisions addressed the risk that the President might take a broader view than the Joint Committee on Taxation on that topic.

relevant conference committee was working on the bill, the Joint Committee on Taxation gave it a list of 79 provisions in the bill that qualified as limited tax benefits. *See* 143 CONG. REC. 16,905–16,906 (1997) (reprinting the list). The conference committee duly inserted into the bill the language suggested by the Line Item Veto Act. As enacted by Congress, then, the final section of the Taxpayer Relief Act of 1997 (captioned "Identification of Limited Tax Benefits Subject to Line Item Veto") specified that "Section 1021(a)(3) of the Congressional Budget and Impoundment Control Act of 1974 shall only apply to [the 79 listed provisions]." Taxpayer Relief Act of 1997 § 1701, 111 Stat. at 1099–1103. One of those provisions was "section 968 (relating to nonrecognition of gain on sale of stock to certain farmers' cooperatives)," *id.* at 1101—the provision at issue in *Clinton v. City of New York*.

In this manner, the Taxpayer Relief Act of 1997 specifically indicated that § 968 was subject to the cancellation authority previously described in the Line Item Veto Act. It follows that when President Clinton exercised his authority to cancel this provision of the Taxpayer Relief Act, we need not think of him as using the authority that Congress had conferred *in 1996*. Instead, he could be seen as exercising authority that the Taxpayer Relief Act of 1997 itself gave him—authority that the enacting Congress had recognized and had explicitly made applicable to § 968.

Doesn't that way of thinking undermine the majority's analysis in *Clinton v. City of New York*? The majority surely was correct that one Congress (such as the Congress that enacted the Line Item Veto Act in 1996) cannot really authorize the President to cancel provisions in later-enacted statutes that are not properly interpreted to make their provisions contingent on the President's decisions. At least with respect to § 968 of the Taxpayer Relief Act of 1997, though, that was not the situation that the Court faced in *Clinton v. City of New York*. By explicitly providing that the Line Item Veto Act would apply to § 968, the Taxpayer Relief Act of 1997 itself gave President Clinton the cancellation authority that he tried to exercise with respect to that line item.

To be sure, even if President Clinton was simply doing what the 1997 statute itself authorized him to do, the statute still could not authorize him to exercise "legislative" power. The majority thought that President Clinton's cancellation of § 968 was indeed "legislative." But *Chadha* provides little support for that conclusion. In *Chadha*, § 244(c)(2) of the Immigration and Nationality Act had purported to grant a power to each House of Congress (acting on its own). While *Chadha* did characterize this power as "legislative" in nature (and hence subject to the requirement of bicameralism and presentment), that was only because entities within Congress cannot wield "executive" power. *Chadha* explicitly indicated that if the same power had been conferred upon the President, the Court would have started with the presumption that the power was "executive." *Chadha*, 462 U.S. at 951.

To the extent that a federal statute makes the legal effect of some of its provisions contingent on decisions by the President, *Chadha* does not tell us to characterize the President's decisions as "legislative" simply because they affect the operation of a statute. At least according to the dissenters in the Line Item Veto case, the main constitutional limit on such grants of authority is not *Chadha* but the nondelegation doctrine. *Cf. Chadha*, 462 U.S. at 953 n.16 ("When the Attorney General performs his duties pursuant to § 244, he does not exercise 'legislative' power. . . . The constitutionality of the Attorney General's execution of the authority delegated to him by § 244 involves only a question of delegation doctrine."). Under the nondelegation doctrine, if a statute purported to authorize the President to make up any legal rules that the President likes on any subject that the President chooses, the statute might be regarded as an unconstitutional attempt to give the President "legislative" power. By contrast, a statute that gives the President more limited authority to make judgment calls identified by the statute might be upheld on the theory that the relevant judgment calls amount to "executing" the statute. *Compare* Gundy v. United States, 139 S. Ct. 2116, 2129 (2019) ("[T]his Court has held that a delegation is constitutional so long as Congress has set out an 'intelligible principle' to guide the delegee's exercise of authority. . . . Those standards, the Court has made clear, are not demanding." (quoting J.W. Hampton, Jr., & Co. v. United States, 276 U.S. 394, 409 (1928))), *with id.* at 2133–42 (Gorsuch, J., dissenting) (advocating a more robust version of the nondelegation doctrine).

In a portion of his dissent in the Line Item Veto case that is not excerpted above, Justice Breyer argued that the nondelegation doctrine did not prevent Congress from giving the President discretionary authority to cancel either items of new direct spending or limited tax benefits according to the criteria and procedures that the Line Item Veto Act described. *See Clinton v. City of New York*, 524 U.S. at 484–496 (Breyer, J., dissenting). Justice Scalia agreed about the authority to cancel spending items, though he did not reach the parallel question about limited tax benefits. *See id.* at 465–69 (Scalia, J., concurring in part and dissenting in part). The majority, for its part, did not address the nondelegation doctrine one way or the other. *See id.* at 448 (majority opinion). Instead, the majority resolved the case on a different ground: Congress cannot "give[ ] the President the unilateral power to change the text of duly enacted statutes." *Id.* at 447.

Again, though, this way of framing the case assumed that President Clinton had indeed unilaterally amended or repealed the statutes containing the line items that he cancelled. At least as applied to the Taxpayer Relief Act of 1997, this assumption is questionable. Didn't the text of the Taxpayer Relief Act itself make § 968 subject to the cancellation procedure previously described in the Line Item Veto Act?

When President Clinton chose one of the paths that the text authorized, was he really "chang[ing] the text" of the statute?

3. If we think about the case in the dissenters' terms, the harder questions may concern President Clinton's effort to cancel § 4722(c) of the Balanced Budget Act of 1997. Congress passed that Act in tandem with the Taxpayer Relief Act of 1997, and President Clinton signed them into law on the same day. Members of Congress definitely had the Line Item Veto Act in mind when they enacted the Balanced Budget Act; the Joint Committee on Taxation identified one "limited tax benefit" in the bill that became the Balanced Budget Act, and the Balanced Budget Act included something like the language suggested by the Line Item Veto Act with respect to that item. *See* Balanced Budget Act of 1997, Pub. L. 105–33, § 9304, 111 Stat. 251, 677 ("Section 1021(a)(3) of the Congressional Budget Act of 1974 shall only apply to 3306(c)(21) of the Internal Revenue Code of 1986 (as added by section 5406 of this Act)."). That limited tax benefit, however, was not the item that President Clinton chose to cancel. Instead, he purported to cancel § 4722(c)—a provision that was an "item of new direct spending" rather than a "limited tax benefit." Perhaps because items of new direct spending are easier to identify than limited tax benefits, Congress was not in the habit of listing items of new direct spending as being subject to the Line Item Veto Act, and the Balanced Budget Act of 1997 did not do so.

Here, then, was the situation. The Line Item Veto Act of 1996 purported to say that when later-enacted statutes include "any item of new direct spending," the President can cancel that item if he makes the determinations and follows the procedures described in the Line Item Veto Act. The following year, the Balanced Budget Act of 1997 contained such an item (§ 4722(c)). On the surface, though, the Balanced Budget Act of 1997 did not itself say that the President could cancel this item. If the Balanced Budget Act of 1997 did *not* give the President this authority, then the majority's analysis in *Clinton v. City of New York* would work: when the President tried to cancel § 4722(c), he would be purporting to "repeal" a portion of the Balanced Budget Act of 1997, and an earlier Congress could not give him that authority. But if the Balanced Budget Act of 1997 is best interpreted as implicitly making all of its items of new direct spending subject to the Line Item Veto Act, so that the Balanced Budget Act of 1997 itself implicitly authorized the President to cancel those items, then the majority's analysis would not work (at least in my view).

If one thinks along these lines, the crucial question boils down to one of statutory interpretation. Should we read the Balanced Budget Act of 1997 as implicitly incorporating or at least accommodating the Line Item Veto Act with respect to the items of new direct spending that it contains, so that those items are more contingent than they seem on their face? Or should we read the Balanced Budget Act of 1997 to say what it says without any implied limitations, and hence to leave no room for application of the Line Item Veto Act?

As you think about this question of interpretation, does it matter that the Balanced Budget Act of 1997 followed the template suggested by the Line Item Veto Act with respect to the one "limited tax benefit" that it contained? Perhaps that fact suggests that the Balanced Budget Act of 1997 was also meant to follow the Line Item Veto Act with respect to the items of new direct spending that it contained.[54]

Even if that was the *intention* of the enacting Congress, though, did the 1997 statute say enough to accomplish that intention? It is possible that when Congress enacted the 1997 statute, Congress assumed that the Line Item Veto Act would apply of its own force to authorize the President to cancel any items of new direct spending in the 1997 statute, without any need for the 1997 statute itself to incorporate the cancellation authority that the Line Item Veto Act described. If the 1997 statute was predicated on the assumption that the Line Item Veto Act could operate of its own force (rather than via incorporation into the 1997 statute), and if that assumption is false (for the reasons that the majority identified), would you conclude that § 4722(c) of the Balanced Budget Act of 1997 was not really subject to cancellation? Or would you try to protect the enacting Congress's expectations by adjusting your interpretation of the 1997 statute, so that it implicitly incorporates the Line Item Veto Act after all?

4. Part III of Justice Breyer's dissent began by pointing out that a later-enacted statute could include a proviso making some of the statute's own provisions dependent on certain contingencies (such as whether the President makes certain determinations). "[T]hat being so," Justice Breyer added, "it could make no difference if that proviso appeared, instead, in a different, earlier-enacted law, along with legal language that makes it applicable to every future spending provision picked out according to a specified formula." *Clinton v. City of New York*, 524 U.S. at 475 (Breyer, J., dissenting).

This statement may suggest that, in Justice Breyer's view, the Line Item Veto Act could operate *of its own force* even with respect to provisions contained in later-enacted statutes. If that is what he had in mind, wasn't he incorrect? The topic that the Line Item Veto Act purported to regulate—the legal effect of line items in later-enacted statutes—is not something that the Line Item Veto Act could directly control. Whether the line items in later-enacted statutes are always binding, or instead are contingent on the President's authority to cancel them, is a question that lies squarely within the scope of the later-

[54] The *expressio unius* canon probably does not support a contrary conclusion. There were special reasons for the 1997 statute to refer to the Line Item Veto Act with respect to "limited tax benefits." *See supra* p. 830 & n.53. Under the circumstances, the fact that the 1997 statute did *not* refer to the Line Item Veto Act with respect to items of new direct spending does not warrant the inference that Congress intended those items to be exempt from the Act.

enacted statutes; it is a question about the meaning of those statutes. The Congress that was sitting in 1996 cannot conclusively dictate what later-enacted statutes will mean.

Instead of arguing that the Line Item Veto Act could operate *of its own force* with respect to later-enacted statutes, though, Justice Breyer may have been taking a more modest position. Perhaps he simply thought that when courts were interpreting later-enacted statutes, courts should not lightly understand those statutes to depart from the framework established by the Line Item Veto Act. On that view, the existence of the Line Item Veto Act might support the following background principle of interpretation: In the absence of contrary indications, any later-enacted federal statute that contains a limited tax benefit, an item of new direct spending, or any dollar amount of discretionary budget authority should be presumed to make those items subject to the cancellation mechanism described in the Line Item Veto Act. If courts used this presumption when interpreting later-enacted statutes, courts would read all such statutes as implicitly giving the President the authority described in the Line Item Veto Act except to the extent that the later-enacted statutes opt out of this arrangement. Thus, rather than requiring later-enacted statutes to *opt into* the Line Item Veto Act (if the later Congress wants it to apply), courts would interpret later-enacted statutes as implicitly adopting the Line Item Veto Act's framework unless they *opt out*.

Might the existence of the Line Item Veto Act support this presumption about the meaning of later-enacted statutes that do not refer to the Line Item Veto Act one way or the other? Would this principle of interpretation simply be an application of the traditional presumption against implied repeals, or is it weaker than that? *Cf. supra* pp. 813–814 (raising similar questions about the effect of 1 U.S.C. § 109).

5. If you believe that the existence of the Line Item Veto Act does indeed support some sort of presumption about the meaning of later-enacted statutes, are there any limits on Congress's ability to establish such presumptions? Suppose that today's Congress opposes high taxes. In an attempt to project that policy position into the future, Congress enacts the following direction: "From now on, whenever an Act of Congress imposes a new tax or prescribes new rates for an existing tax, the Act should not be understood to establish the tax rates set forth on the face of the Act. Instead, the Act should be interpreted as establishing tax rates equal to one-half of those set forth on the face of the Act." A future Congress could always opt out of this interpretive direction, either by repealing the earlier statute wholesale or by explicitly exempting particular Acts from it. But if the interpretive direction remains on the books, should courts apply it to a later-enacted tax Act that says nothing one way or the other about the earlier interpretive direction (and whose legislative history provides no relevant guidance)?

Interpretive directions of this sort purport to give a special technical meaning to language that would mean something else in ordinary usage. One drawback of such interpretive directions is that they introduce a new source of uncertainty: the language of a later-enacted statute will not always reveal whether the enacting Congress was using words in their ordinary sense or instead was following the artificial rule suggested by the prior Congress. In the tax-rate hypothetical, for instance, if a later-enacted Act says that the tax rate on something "shall be 30 percent," it is possible either that the enacting Congress meant to establish a 30% rate or that the enacting Congress remembered the prior interpretive direction and meant to establish an actual rate of 15%. Is that potential uncertainty anything more than a policy argument for Congress to consider when deciding whether to provide interpretive directions of this sort? Is it within the courts' power to disregard interpretive directions that raise this problem, and to refuse to let such directions establish even a rebuttable presumption about the proper interpretation of later-enacted statutes?

NOTE ON THE ADMINISTRATIVE PROCEDURE ACT

Scholars sometimes use the phrase "framework statutes" to refer to statutes that address the *process* for considering and enacting future laws. *See* Elizabeth Garrett, *The Purposes of Framework Legislation*, 14 J. CONTEMP. LEGAL ISSUES 717, 718 (2005) (defining "framework legislation" as "laws establish[ing] internal procedures that will shape legislative deliberation and voting with respect to certain laws or decisions in the future").[55] The Line Item Veto Act, however, might be seen as a different sort of "framework statute"—a statute that attempted to supply a framework into which later statutes would fit.

Given *Clinton v. City of New York*, the Line Item Veto Act did not succeed at doing so. But some other federal statutes are indeed "framework statutes" in the latter sense. A leading example is the Administrative Procedure Act (APA), which Congress originally enacted in 1946. *See* Administrative Procedure Act, ch. 324, 60 Stat. 237 (1946); *see also* Act of Sept. 6, 1966, 80 Stat. 378 (reenacting the APA's provisions in the course of enacting title 5 of the United States Code as such). This Note briefly describes the APA and contrasts it with the Line Item Veto Act.

Before the APA was enacted, Congress had established many administrative agencies and had delegated various powers to them by statute, but Congress had not done much to standardize agency processes, and there were robust political debates about the proper extent of administrative authority. *See generally* George B. Shepherd, *Fierce Compromise: The Administrative Procedure Act Emerges from New*

[55] Under the Constitution, "Each House [of Congress] may determine the Rules of its Proceedings." U.S. CONST. art. I, § 5. As a result, a statute establishing rules of legislative procedure is subject to modification by later rules of either House.

Deal Politics, 90 NW. U. L. REV. 1557 (1996). To this day, different agencies have different structures and proceed in different ways. Still, the APA imposes some common requirements. For instance, 5 U.S.C. § 553 regulates "rule making": to the extent that other statutes empower federal agencies to promulgate substantive rules, § 553 generally requires those agencies to give the public advance notice of the agencies' intention to make rules on a particular subject and the opportunity to participate in the rulemaking process by submitting comments. Likewise, 5 U.S.C. §§ 554 and 556–557 regulate a particular type of "adjudication": to the extent that other statutes empower agencies to issue orders but require those orders "to be determined on the record after opportunity for an agency hearing," § 554 imposes various procedural requirements, and §§ 556–557 specify additional requirements for evidentiary hearings and decisions. The APA also includes some provisions about judicial review of agency action (including both rulemaking and adjudication): 5 U.S.C. § 702 addresses who is entitled to such review, § 704 addresses which actions are reviewable, and § 706 addresses the scope of review.

The Congress that enacted the APA plainly intended it to govern not only agencies that earlier statutes had established and empowered, but also agencies that Congress would establish and empower in the future (unless the later Congress exempted them from the APA). Indeed, Section 12 of the original APA included the following provision: "No subsequent legislation shall be held to supersede or modify the provisions of this Act except to the extent that such legislation shall do so expressly." 60 Stat. at 244 (current version at 5 U.S.C. § 559).

As the material above teaches, though, provisions of this sort do not eliminate the need to interpret later-enacted statutes to determine their relationship to the APA (even if they do not "expressly" address that topic). For instance, take the Indian Gaming Regulatory Act (IGRA), Pub. L. 100–497, 102 Stat. 2467 (1988) (codified as amended at 25 U.S.C. § 2701 *et seq.*). That Act created a new federal agency called the National Indian Gaming Commission. Among other things, IGRA gave the Commission some rulemaking power. *See id.* § 7, 102 Stat. at 2470–71 (codified as amended at 25 U.S.C. § 2706). IGRA did not address whether this power is subject to the procedural requirements set forth in the APA. Should courts conclude that because IGRA grants the Commission rulemaking power without explicitly requiring compliance with the APA, IGRA allows the Commission to promulgate substantive rules without going through the notice-and-comment procedure that the APA described?

Courts would answer this question "no": To the extent that the Commission wants to exercise the rulemaking powers conferred by IGRA, the Commission will need to follow the procedures specified by the APA, just as other agencies do. In theory, though, there might be two different ways to explain that conclusion.

One possibility is that IGRA should be understood to encompass the topic of rulemaking procedure, but IGRA implicitly incorporates the APA's provisions on that topic. On this view, courts would presume that when IGRA granted the Commission rulemaking power, IGRA was implicitly adopting the procedural restrictions on that power previously described in the APA, and IGRA was making those restrictions applicable to the new agency. On that way of thinking, the APA would not apply of its own force to the Commission, but only through incorporation into IGRA.

The other possibility is simpler. We know that in 1946, the APA regulated the topic of administrative procedure for federal administrative agencies in general. If and when Congress enacts later statutes creating new agencies but not addressing the procedures that they should follow, perhaps those statutes need not be interpreted as covering the topic of administrative procedure at all. Instead, a statute like IGRA might be understood to leave the topic of rulemaking procedure to be handled according to the APA, which would operate of its own force to regulate how the National Indian Gaming Commission must proceed.

The second possibility, like the first, does depend on an interpretation of the later-enacted statute (here, IGRA). Specifically, it reflects a conclusion about what is sometimes called the "domain" of that statute—the set of issues that the statute encompasses. *Cf.* Frank H. Easterbrook, *Statutes' Domains*, 50 U. CHI. L. REV. 533 (1983) (introducing this terminology, though for a different purpose). As compared to the first possibility, though, the second possibility rests on a narrower interpretation of the later statute's domain. The second possibility reads statutes like IGRA not to encompass the topic of administrative procedure at all (either by incorporating the APA or by overriding the APA). Instead of itself having any bearing on administrative procedure, IGRA simply leaves room for the APA to apply on its own.

Sometimes, when courts are trying to decide whether two statutes have overlapping "domains," the existence of one of the statutes will affect how courts interpret the other statute. That is a consequence of the presumption against implied repeals, which discourages courts from reading two federal statutes to conflict with each other. If courts interpret two statutes in such a way that the statutes' domains do not overlap at all, then the two statutes can co-exist in all cases, and courts will apply them both (assuming that both are constitutional). That follows from the very definition of a statute's "domain." When two federal statutes have entirely separate "domains," the two statutes cannot come into conflict, because they do not address any of the same questions. Likewise, neither statute will implicitly displace the other as to some field that they both regulate, because there is no such field. As a result, both statutes will simply operate of their own force; courts will apply

Statute #1 to the issues that Statute #1 covers and Statute #2 to the issues that Statute #2 covers.

That is almost certainly what courts would say about the relationship between IGRA and the APA. Given the existence (and prominence) of the APA, courts will not read IGRA as giving the National Indian Gaming Commission rulemaking power free and clear of the APA's restrictions. But courts also will not read IGRA as implicitly incorporating all of the APA's provisions into IGRA itself. Instead, courts will conclude that the topic of rulemaking procedure simply lies beyond IGRA's "domain." They will speak of the APA as applying of its own force to the National Indian Gaming Commission, not via incorporation into IGRA.

With respect to the relationship between the APA and later-enacted statutes creating new administrative agencies, that story usually will be very plausible. Normally, if the later statute neither refers to the APA nor provides contrary directions about administrative procedure, the "domain" of the later statute need not be understood to encompass the topic of administrative procedure at all. On that interpretation, the later statute leaves room for the APA to continue to govern that topic of its own force.

By contrast, courts could not tell a similar story about the relationship between the Line Item Veto Act and later-enacted statutes. The Line Item Veto Act purported to address the legal effect of certain types of line items in later statutes, and to make those line items less binding than they seemed on their face. This topic cannot plausibly be thought to lie beyond the "domain" of the later statutes; the bindingness of those statutes' own provisions is surely a topic that the statutes should be understood to encompass. As a result, the story that courts would use to reconcile the APA and IGRA is unavailable in this context. The only way for courts to preserve the operation of the Line Item Veto Act would be to tell the other story, and to read the later-enacted statutes as implicitly incorporating the Line Item Veto Act into the later-enacted statutes themselves. As noted above, that is a plausible story with respect to the Taxpayer Relief Act of 1997, which explicitly indicated that § 968 and various other limited tax benefits were indeed subject to the Line Item Veto Act. But if a later-enacted statute does not refer to the Line Item Veto Act one way or the other, courts might not be inclined to read the statute as *implicitly* incorporating such a complex set of criteria and procedures.

In any event, the Line Item Veto Act would not operate of its own force with respect to later-enacted statutes. Instead, the provisions in a later-enacted statute would be subject to cancellation by the President only if the later-enacted statute itself says or implies that they are (even if the dissenters in *Clinton v. City of New York* were correct that the Constitution does not prevent the later-enacted statute from giving the President this authority).

What about the relationship between the Dictionary Act and later-enacted statutes? To the extent that 1 U.S.C. § 1 purports to supply definitions for words used in later-enacted statutes, the topic that it addresses surely comes within the "domain" of the later-enacted statutes.[56] What a later-enacted statute means by the words that it uses is a question about the meaning of that statute, not something that lies in a different domain. In this respect, 1 U.S.C. § 1 is like the Line Item Veto Act. Still, the definitions that 1 U.S.C. § 1 suggests are much less complicated than the procedures described in the Line Item Veto Act, and those definitions are not unnatural; the words in question usually can bear the meaning that 1 U.S.C. § 1 suggests. For reasons discussed earlier in this chapter, it might well make sense for courts to presume, absent contrary indications, that later-enacted statutes do indeed use words in the way the Dictionary Act tells us to expect (or that later-enacted statutes "incorporate" the definitions that the Dictionary Act suggests). *See supra* p. 790.

The same analysis might also apply with respect to 1 U.S.C. § 108 ("Whenever an Act is repealed, which repealed a former Act, such former Act shall not thereby be revived, unless it shall be expressly so provided") and 1 U.S.C. § 109 ("The repeal of any statute shall not have the effect to release or extinguish any penalty, forfeiture, or liability incurred under such statute, unless the repealing Act shall so expressly provide . . . ."). Again, those provisions purport to govern the legal effect of later-enacted statutes, and that topic lies within the domain of the later-enacted statutes. For that reason, 1 U.S.C. §§ 108 and 109 cannot fully operate of their own force. As with the definitions supplied by 1 U.S.C. § 1, though, the patterns identified by 1 U.S.C. §§ 108 and 109 probably support a rebuttable presumption that courts can use when they are interpreting later acts of repeal.

NOTE ON *BURWELL V. HOBBY LOBBY STORES, INC.*

The high-profile case of *Burwell v. Hobby Lobby Stores, Inc.*, 573 U.S. 682 (2014), implicated two separate questions that relate to the materials above. First, how does the definition of the word "person" in 1 U.S.C. § 1 affect the proper interpretation of that word in the subsequently enacted Religious Freedom Restoration Act of 1993 (RFRA)? Second, how does RFRA affect the proper interpretation of the even more recently enacted Patient Protection and Affordable Care Act of 2010?

To understand RFRA, you need a little background about the Supreme Court's understanding of the Free Exercise Clause of the Constitution. In the 1960s and 1970s, the Supreme Court interpreted that Clause to prevent some otherwise valid and generally applicable laws from applying to people whose religious practices the laws would

[56] Here, I am simply addressing the *definitions* in 1 U.S.C. § 1—not the instructions that 1 U.S.C. § 1 has been read to provide about the use of legislative history in statutory interpretation. *See supra* pp. 791–793.

substantially burden. For instance, in *Wisconsin v. Yoder*, 406 U.S. 205 (1972), the Court held that although states usually can require parents to send their children to school until age 16, the Free Exercise Clause (as incorporated against the states through the Fourteenth Amendment) prevents states from applying this requirement to members of Old Order Amish communities who have sincere religious objections to sending their children to high school. *Yoder* and other cases from the same era suggested that as a matter of constitutional law, an otherwise generally applicable statute or regulation cannot validly be applied to people whose religious practices it would substantially burden unless the government has a compelling interest in subjecting them to the statute or regulation. *See id.* at 214–15, 221.

In 1990, however, the Supreme Court repudiated this interpretation of the Free Exercise Clause and held that the Constitution does not require most generally applicable laws to include religious exemptions. Justice Scalia's majority opinion in *Employment Division v. Smith*, 494 U.S. 872 (1990), indicated that states can apply their general prohibitions on the use of peyote even to people who use peyote for religious purposes, and states need not show a "compelling interest" in order to justify this application of their laws. More broadly, *Smith* suggested that "the right of free exercise does not relieve an individual of the obligation to comply with a 'valid and neutral law of general applicability . . . ,' " even if the law substantially burdens the individual's religious practices. *Id.* at 879 (quoting United States v. Lee, 455 U.S. 252, 263 n.3 (1982) (Stevens, J., concurring in the judgment)).

In 1993, Congress responded to *Smith* by enacting RFRA, Pub. L. No. 103–141, 107 Stat. 1488 (codified as amended at 42 U.S.C. § 2000bb *et seq.*). As amended in 2000, RFRA's operative provisions include the following:

§ 3. FREE EXERCISE OF RELIGION PROTECTED.

(a) IN GENERAL.—Government shall not substantially burden a person's exercise of religion even if the burden results from a rule of general applicability, except as provided in subsection (b).

(b) EXCEPTION.—Government may substantially burden a person's exercise of religion only if it demonstrates that application of the burden to the person—

(1) is in furtherance of a compelling governmental interest; and

(2) is the least restrictive means of furthering that compelling governmental interest.

(c) JUDICIAL RELIEF.—A person whose religious exercise has been burdened in violation of this section may assert that violation as a claim or defense in a judicial proceeding and obtain appropriate relief against a government. . . .

§ 5. DEFINITIONS.

As used in this Act—

(1) the term "government" includes a branch, department, agency, instrumentality, and official (or other person acting under color of law) of the United States or of a covered entity; [and]

(2) the term "covered entity" means the District of Columbia, the Commonwealth of Puerto Rico, and each territory and possession of the United States . . . .

§ 6. APPLICABILITY.

(a) IN GENERAL.—This Act applies to all Federal law, and the implementation of that law, whether statutory or otherwise, and whether adopted before or after the enactment of this Act.

(b) RULE OF CONSTRUCTION.—Federal statutory law adopted after the date of the enactment of this Act is subject to this Act unless such law explicitly excludes such application by reference to this Act. . . .

As these provisions suggest, RFRA was designed to restore the "compelling interest" test as a limitation on the circumstances in which federal law will impose burdens on religious practices.[57]

Fast forward to 2010, when Congress enacted the Affordable Care Act. Under that Act, employers that have at least fifty full-time employees were supposed to offer their employees a group health plan or group health insurance that provides "minimum essential coverage." *See* 26 U.S.C. §§ 4980H, 5000A(f)(2). The Affordable Care Act imposed significant financial penalties or taxes on employers who did not do so. *See, e.g.*, 26 U.S.C. §§ 4980D, 4980H.

Although "grandfathered health plans" were not subject to many of the Act's requirements, the Affordable Care Act regulated other group health plans and health insurance coverage in various ways. Among other things, the Act specified that "[a] group health plan and a health insurance issuer offering group or individual health insurance coverage shall . . . provide coverage for and shall not impose any cost sharing requirements for" certain categories of preventive health services. 42 U.S.C. § 300gg–13(a). One of those categories read as follows: "with respect to women, such additional preventive care and screenings . . . as provided for in comprehensive guidelines supported by the Health

[57] As enacted in 1993, § 5 of RFRA had defined the term "government" to include *state* governments, and § 6(a) had said that "[t]his Act applies to all Federal *and State* law . . . ." 107 Stat. at 1489 (emphasis added). But in *City of Boerne v. Flores*, 521 U.S. 507 (1997), the Supreme Court held that the Constitution did not give Congress the power to impose RFRA's restrictions on all state laws. In 2000, in recognition of this decision, Congress amended RFRA to delete the references to state law. *See* Religious Land Use and Institutionalized Persons Act of 2000, Pub. L. 106–274, § 7, 114 Stat. 803, 806.

Resources and Services Administration for purposes of this paragraph." *Id.* Thus, the Affordable Care Act delegated authority to the Health Resources and Services Administration (HRSA), which is a component of the federal Department of Health and Human Services (HHS), to identify certain things that group health plans and health insurance would have to cover.

The guidelines that HRSA subsequently issued included "[a]ll . . . contraceptive methods" that had been approved by the Food and Drug Administration (FDA). HHS ultimately authorized HRSA to establish special rules for "religious employers" (such as churches) and other "eligible organizations," but HHS's definition of "eligible organizations" was limited to certain nonprofit entities. By the terms of the regulations, for-profit employers could not escape the so-called "contraceptive mandate" on religious grounds.

The plaintiffs in the *Hobby Lobby* case included three family businesses that were set up as for-profit corporations. The corporations were closely held, meaning that most or all of the stock was owned by just a few individuals. Those individuals—the members of the relevant families—were in charge of running the business, and they sought to do so in accordance with their religious beliefs. They did not have religious objections to contraception per se, but they had sincere religious objections to drugs and devices that may have the effect of preventing a fertilized egg from implanting in the uterus. They believed that four of the FDA-approved "contraceptive methods" fit that description.[58] The plaintiffs in the *Hobby Lobby* case argued that the regulations effectively requiring them to provide insurance coverage for those four methods violated RFRA.

In an opinion by Justice Alito, a majority of the Supreme Court agreed. The majority began by addressing whether a for-profit corporation qualifies as a "person" under RFRA. Here is the majority's analysis of that issue:

> "RFRA itself does not define the term 'person.' We therefore look to the Dictionary Act, which we must consult '[i]n determining the meaning of any Act of Congress, unless the context indicates otherwise.' 1 U.S.C. § 1.
>
> "Under the Dictionary Act, 'the wor[d] "person" . . . include[s] corporations, companies, associations, firms, partnerships, societies, and joint stock companies, as well as individuals.' *Ibid.* . . . Thus, unless there is something about the RFRA context that 'indicates otherwise,' the Dictionary Act provides a quick, clear, and affirmative answer to the question whether the companies involved in these cases may be heard.

---

[58] At the time of the case, this belief was consistent with FDA-approved labeling for all four methods. *See* Brief for the Petitioners, *Sebelius v. Hobby Lobby Stores, Inc.* (No. 13–354), at 9 n.4. In 2022, the FDA announced a change to the labeling for one of the methods.

"We see nothing in RFRA that suggests a congressional intent to depart from the Dictionary Act definition, and HHS makes little effort to argue otherwise. We have entertained RFRA and free-exercise claims brought by nonprofit corporations, [citations omitted], and HHS concedes that a nonprofit corporation can be a 'person' within the meaning of RFRA. . . .

"This concession effectively dispatches any argument that the term 'person' as used in RFRA does not reach the closely held corporations involved in these cases. No known understanding of the term "person" includes *some* but not all corporations. The term 'person' sometimes encompasses artificial persons (as the Dictionary Act instructs), and it sometimes is limited to natural persons. But no conceivable definition of the term includes natural persons and nonprofit corporations, but not for-profit corporations."

Hobby Lobby, 573 U.S. at 707–08.

The majority spent more time on what RFRA means by "exercise of religion,"[59] and whether a for-profit corporation can claim protection under that rubric. The government conceded that *nonprofit* corporations (such as many churches) can indeed invoke RFRA. According to the majority, moreover, the fact that a corporation is operated in order to turn a profit (while still conforming with religious principles) does not always make a dispositive difference. Of course, giant corporations with publicly traded stock probably will not be in a position to invoke RFRA. *See id.* at 717 ("[T]he idea that unrelated shareholders—including institutional investors with their own set of stakeholders—would agree to run a corporation under the same religious beliefs seems improbable."). But the majority concluded that the family businesses that were before the Court could invoke RFRA notwithstanding the fact that the families had chosen to organize their businesses as for-profit corporations. *See id.* at 709–19. In the majority's words, "a federal regulation's restriction on the activities of a for-profit closely held corporation must comply with RFRA." *Id.* at 719.

The majority went on to apply RFRA to the regulation that the plaintiffs were challenging. The majority concluded that as applied to these employers, the contraceptive mandate "substantially burden[ed]" the exercise of religion within the meaning of § 3(a) of RFRA. By the terms of § 3(b) of RFRA, the government therefore had to demonstrate that the challenged application of this burden not only (1) "is in furtherance of a compelling governmental interest" but also (2) "is the least restrictive means of furthering that compelling governmental interest." The majority concluded that the government had not made the

[59] RFRA provides a definition of that term, but it is not very helpful. As amended in 2000, RFRA says that "the term 'exercise of religion' means religious exercise, as defined in section 8 of the Religious Land Use and Institutionalized Persons Act of 2000." *See* 114 Stat. at 806; 107 Stat. at 1489. The cited section, in turn, says that "[t]he term 'religious exercise' includes any exercise of religion, whether or not compelled by, or central to, a system of religious belief." 114 Stat. at 807.

second showing. Thus, "under the standard that RFRA prescribes, the HHS contraceptive mandate is unlawful"; because of RFRA, HHS did not really have the authority "to demand that [these] three closely held corporations provide health-insurance coverage for methods of contraception that violate the sincerely held religious beliefs of the companies' owners." *Id.* at 689–90, 736.

As this summary of the majority opinion suggests, the Court focused almost exclusively on the meaning and application of RFRA. The majority did address the first question identified at the start of this Note: the majority read the word "person" in RFRA in light of the definition previously supplied by the Dictionary Act, because the majority saw nothing to suggest that RFRA was using the word more narrowly. But the Court did not explicitly address the relationship between RFRA and the Affordable Care Act.

In one respect, that is understandable. While we have considered the limits on Congress's ability to bind future Congresses, there are no such limits on Congress's ability to bind future administrative agencies. Once Congress enacted RFRA, federal agencies were bound to comply with RFRA unless and until Congress freed them from that obligation.

But might it be possible to argue that the Affordable Care Act *did* free HHS and its components from RFRA in certain respects? For instance, might one argue that when the Affordable Care Act authorized HRSA to supplement the statute's coverage mandates by specifying "additional preventive care and screenings" for women (*see* 42 U.S.C. § 300gg–13(a)(4)), the Affordable Care Act was granting that authority without regard to RFRA's restrictions?

RFRA itself tries to rule out that sort of argument: § 6(b) of RFRA says that "Federal statutory law adopted after the date of the enactment of this Act is subject to this Act unless such law explicitly excludes such application by reference to this Act." As we have already seen, though, the Congress that enacted RFRA could not really limit future Congresses in this way. *See* Dorsey v. United States, 567 U.S. 260, 274 (2012); *see also* Lockhart v. United States, 546 U.S. 142, 148 (2005) (Scalia, J., concurring) ("We have made clear . . . that an express-reference or express-statement provision cannot nullify the unambiguous import of a subsequent statute."); *id.* at 149–50 (asserting that "such express-reference provisions are ineffective," and citing 42 U.S.C. § 2000bb–3(b)—that is, § 6(b) of RFRA—as an example).

Shortly after the Supreme Court granted certiorari in *Hobby Lobby*, Professor Michael Dorf raised this issue in a blog post. Mike Dorf, *Did the Affordable Care Act Partially Repeal the Religious Freedom Restoration Act?* (Dec. 2, 2013), www.dorfonlaw.org/2013/12/did-affordable-care-act-partially.html. As Professor Dorf noted, "It's conceivable that in delegating . . . implementation authority to HHS, the Congress that enacted the [Affordable Care Act] also delegated authority to HHS to supersede RFRA." What is more, the Affordable Care Act's failure to refer explicitly to RFRA did not end the analysis; "it is possible that a . . . statutory delegation to an agency could *implicitly* confer the power to enact rules that supersede [RFRA's] rules of construction." Still, Professor Dorf himself concluded that the Affordable Care Act should not be interpreted as doing so: "I am aware of nothing in the [Act] that has that implicit effect." Thus, he concluded that the answer to the question in the title of his post—*Did the Affordable Care Act Partially Repeal the Religious Freedom Restoration Act?*—is "no."

Do you agree? If you were trying to decide whether the Affordable Care Act empowered HRSA to promulgate its guidelines without regard to RFRA's restrictions, how would your analysis proceed?

I personally would not be inclined to read the Affordable Care Act as itself incorporating RFRA. But when the agency was promulgating the guidelines about preventive care and screenings to which the Affordable Care Act referred, perhaps RFRA continued to operate of its own force, so that the agency was subject not only to whatever restrictions appeared in the Affordable Care Act but also to the restrictions that appeared in RFRA (and any other applicable laws). On that way of thinking, HRSA's guidelines would need to comply with RFRA as well as with the Affordable Care Act.

Whether that is correct depends on how aggressively one reads the Affordable Care Act. With respect to the guidelines that the Affordable Care Act invited HRSA to issue, perhaps the Affordable Care Act could have been read to "occupy the field," so that the only substantive restrictions on HRSA's authority would be those stated in the Affordable Care Act itself. But the presumption against implied repeals cuts against reading the Affordable Care Act to supersede RFRA in this way. While the Affordable Care Act did impose certain substantive restrictions on the agency, the Act could readily be understood to leave room for other federal statutes (such as RFRA) to impose additional restrictions, even with respect to the tasks that the Affordable Care Act invited HRSA to perform. On that view, *both* the Affordable Care Act *and* RFRA could operate of their own force as HRSA carried out its tasks. Without discussing these issues, that is effectively what the majority opinion in *Hobby Lobby* assumed.

CHAPTER 5

FEDERAL STATUTES AND ADMINISTRATIVE AGENCIES

This book is primarily about the interpretation of statutes in court. Many federal statutory provisions, however, are interpreted in the first instance by administrative agencies rather than by courts. In Professor Eskridge's words, "Most statutory interpretation today is . . . done by agencies and departments, with courts serving merely as 'supervisory institutions,' rather than as 'primary implementation institutions.'" William N. Eskridge, Jr., *Politics Without Romance: Implications of Public Choice Theory for Statutory Interpretation*, 74 VA. L. REV. 275, 297 (1988) (quoting Edward Rubin, Legislation in the Administrative State (Sept. 1987 draft)).

That structure invites two sets of questions. First, because specialist agencies in the executive branch have different capabilities than generalist courts, and because they also play different roles in our system of government, should they use different techniques of statutory interpretation? Second, when Congress has given an agency administrative authority with respect to a particular statute, and when the agency has authoritatively announced an interpretation of one of the provisions that it administers, to what extent should courts defer to that interpretation?

Scholarship on the first set of questions is still underdeveloped, but one leading commentator sees "persuasive grounds for believing that legitimate techniques and standards for agency statutory interpretation diverge sharply from the legitimate techniques and standards for judicial statutory interpretation." Jerry L. Mashaw, *Norms, Practices, and the Paradox of Deference: A Preliminary Inquiry into Agency Statutory Interpretation*, 57 ADMIN. L. REV. 501, 504 (2005) (offering a "highly tentative" discussion of this point). Without saying much about that possibility, though, courts themselves have focused almost exclusively on the second set of questions. This chapter largely follows suit; it is more about interpretation by reviewing courts than about how agencies approach statutes in the first instance.

As you think about the relationship between courts and agencies, it is important to remember that agencies perform many functions with respect to the implementation of statutes. While interpretation is necessary to those functions, Congress has given many agencies additional power to act with the force of law—sometimes by promulgating rules of general applicability to flesh out statutory schemes, sometimes by issuing more particularized orders that again are designed to carry out statutory schemes but that reflect the agencies' discretionary judgments. Agencies that have the authority to act with the force of law in these ways might not need to worry as much as courts about maintaining a distinction between interpretation and policymaking. *See id.* at 513 (observing that "in many situations, agencies have clear lawmaking authority," and referring to "a convergence of interpretation and policymaking"); *id.* at 519 (noting that "agency interpretation is a part of agency policy development"). To be sure, interpretation still matters, both because many statutory provisions have direct legal effect and because agencies cannot legitimately exceed the bounds of the authority that Congress has given them. Within those bounds, though, reviewing courts need to respect the policymaking responsibilities that Congress has delegated to agencies (assuming that the delegation is constitutional).

Section A of this chapter provides a brief introduction to administrative agencies in the federal government—a topic that you will cover in much more detail when you take Administrative Law. Section B addresses current doctrine (which may not be stable) about the deference that courts owe to a federal agency's interpretations of statutory provisions that the agency administers. Section C addresses doctrines about the deference that courts owe to agencies' interpretations of the agencies' own regulations.

A. INTRODUCTION TO FEDERAL ADMINISTRATIVE AGENCIES

Earlier chapters of this book have already alluded to various federal administrative agencies. For instance, you encountered the Bureau of Land Management in *United States v. Locke* (p. 55), the National Marine Fisheries Service in *Yates v. United States* (p. 140), the National Labor Relations Board in *NLRB v. Catholic Bishop of Chicago* (p. 213), the Securities and Exchange Commission in *Morrison v. National Australia Bank Ltd.* (p. 240), and the Bureau of Indian Affairs in *Morton v. Mancari* (p. 706).

To the extent that federal agencies wield governmental power, the power that most agencies wield probably is best regarded as "executive" for constitutional purposes. *See, e.g.*, City of Arlington v. FCC, 569 U.S. 290, 304 n.4 (2013). That classification emerges partly through the process of elimination. *See id.* (observing that the federal government's "legislative" power "is vested exclusively in Congress" and the federal government's "judicial" power is vested in courts staffed by judges with life tenure). Still, characterizing agency actions as "executive" is plausible, because administrative agencies do indeed help to execute the statutes that Congress has enacted. *See id.* (acknowledging that agency rulemaking and adjudication "take 'legislative' and 'judicial' forms," respectively, but insisting that "they are exercises of—indeed, under our constitutional structure they *must be* exercises of—the 'executive

Power' " (quoting U.S. CONST. art. II, § 1, cl. 1)); *accord* Kisor v. Wilkie, 139 S. Ct. 2400, 2422 (2019) (plurality opinion of Kagan, J.).

In keeping with this point, most federal administrative agencies are located squarely within the executive branch of the federal government.[1] A few agencies are simply part of the Executive Office of the President. Many other agencies are located within a particular Cabinet department, like the Department of Agriculture or the Department of Homeland Security. (Those departments themselves are also regarded as agencies, so it is common for one agency to be part of another. *Cf.* 5 U.S.C. § 551(1) (saying that for purposes of the Administrative Procedure Act, " 'agency' means each authority of the Government of the United States, whether or not it is within or subject to review by another agency").[2]) Most agencies that are part of a Cabinet department are headed by a single person who is appointed either by the President (often with the advice and consent of the Senate) or by the Secretary of the relevant department. Typically, these agencies are subject to direction and control by the department's Secretary and ultimately by the President, who has the power to remove the agency head at will.[3]

---

[1] To be sure, there are exceptions. A few entities that could colloquially be called "administrative agencies" are said to be located in the legislative branch. *See, e.g.*, 2 U.S.C. § 1381 (creating the Office of Congressional Workplace Rights as "an independent office within the legislative branch of the Federal Government"); *see also* 31 U.S.C. § 702(a) ("The Government Accountability Office is an instrumentality of the United States Government independent of the executive departments."); *cf.* Fox Television Stations, Inc. v. Aereokiller, LLC, 851 F.3d 1002, 1013 n.4 (9th Cir. 2017) ("[I]t is not clear whether the Library of Congress is part of the executive or legislative branch."). Still, the Constitution imposes strict limits on what legislative-branch agencies can be authorized to do beyond simply supporting Congress's own operations. *Cf.* Immigration & Naturalization Serv. v. Chadha, 462 U.S. 919, 951–52 (1983) (suggesting that Congress cannot authorize entities in the legislative branch to take actions that "ha[ve] the purpose and effect of altering the legal rights, duties and relations of persons . . . outside the Legislative Branch"). Some other entities that could colloquially be called "administrative agencies" are said to be located in the judicial branch. *See, e.g.*, 28 U.S.C. § 991 (establishing the United States Sentencing Commission, which promulgates the United States Sentencing Guidelines, as "an independent commission in the judicial branch of the United States"); *see also* 28 U.S.C. §§ 601–613 (addressing the Administrative Office of the United States Courts). Again, though, that is not the norm. *See* Mistretta v. United States, 488 U.S. 361, 384 (1989) ("The Sentencing Commission unquestionably is a peculiar institution within the framework of our Government.").

[2] The APA's definition of "agency" explicitly excludes both "the Congress" and "the courts of the United States." *Id.* §§ 551(1)(A)–(B), 701(b)(A)–(B). Some courts have interpreted those exclusions broadly, so that the APA does not apply to entities within either the legislative branch or the judicial branch. *See, e.g.*, Muirhead v. Mecham, 427 F.3d 14, 18 (1st Cir. 2005) (concluding that the Administrative Office of the United States Courts is not an "agency" for purposes of the APA because it "is a part of the judicial branch"); *see also* Washington Legal Foundation v. U.S. Sentencing Comm'n, 17 F.3d 1446, 1449–50 (D.C. Cir. 1994) (discussing cases). On the basis of an implied-limitation rule, the Supreme Court has also held that the President himself is not an "agency" for purposes of the APA. *See* Dalton v. Specter, 511 U.S. 462, 470 (1994); Franklin v. Massachusetts, 505 U.S. 788, 800–01 (1992).

[3] Although this is the typical arrangement for agencies that are housed within Cabinet departments, it is not universally true. *See* 38 U.S.C. § 7101(b) (limiting the President's power to remove the chairman of the Board of Veterans' Appeals, which is housed within the Department of Veterans' Affairs); 25 U.S.C. § 2704(b) (same with respect to members of the National Indian Gaming Commission, which is in the Department of the Interior); *see also* MARSHALL J. BREGER & GARY J. EDLES, INDEPENDENT AGENCIES IN THE UNITED STATES 7 (2015) (classifying the Board of Veterans' Appeals and the National Indian Gaming Commission as "independent" despite their location within a Cabinet department).

Apart from agencies that are part of either the Executive Office of the President or particular Cabinet departments, Congress has also set up various agencies that are free-standing entities, some of which enjoy more independence from the President. In particular, a number of agencies that perform "quasi-judicial" or "quasi-legislative" functions are headed by boards or commissions whose members are appointed by the President (with the advice and consent of the Senate) but serve for fixed terms and cannot be removed by the President without cause. *See* Humphrey's Executor v. United States, 295 U.S. 602, 626–32 (1935) (upholding the constitutionality of the Federal Trade Commission Act, which created an agency of this sort); *cf.* Seila Law LLC v. Consumer Fin. Prot. Bur., 140 S. Ct. 2183, 2197–20 (2020) (indicating that Congress usually cannot restrict the President's power to remove executive officials, but taking *Humphrey's Executor* to recognize a limited exception for "multimember bodies with 'quasi-judicial' or 'quasi-legislative' functions"). Agencies that are insulated from the President in this way are often called "independent agencies," but many modern lawyers would still classify them as being in the executive branch. *See, e.g.*, Fed. Maritime Comm'n v. S.C. State Ports Auth., 535 U.S. 743, 773 (2002) (Breyer, J., dissenting) ("Constitutionally speaking, an 'independent' agency belongs neither to the Legislative Branch nor to the Judicial Branch of Government. Although Members of this Court have referred to agencies as a 'fourth branch' of Government, *FTC v. Ruberoid Co.*, 343 U.S. 470, 487 (1952) (Jackson, J., dissenting), the agencies, even 'independent' agencies, are more appropriately considered to be part of the Executive Branch."); In re Aiken County, 645 F.3d 428, 439 (D.C. Cir. 2011) (Kavanaugh, J., concurring) ("As a result of . . . *Humphrey's Executor* . . . , there are two kinds of agencies in the Executive Branch: executive agencies and independent agencies.").

The fact that most administrative agencies are in the executive branch does not mean that the President is in charge of creating them. To the contrary, the Necessary and Proper Clause of the Constitution gives Congress broad power over the structure of the executive branch. Congress is in charge of the creation of offices within the executive branch, and Congress can also decide which functions and powers to assign to which offices. In practice, when Congress vests powers in the Secretary of a department or the head of an agency, the Secretary or head often can delegate some or all of those powers to subordinates within the department or agency. *See* David J. Barron & Elena Kagan, *Chevron's Nondelegation Doctrine*, 2001 SUP. CT. REV. 201, 237 ("[M]ost administrative statutes permit these subdelegations."). But the President normally cannot shift those powers to a different department or agency, nor can the President override agency structures established by statute. *See* Memorandum from Henry B. Hogue & Clinton T. Brass, Coordinators, CONG. RSCH. SERV., *Trump Administration Reform and Reorganization Plan: Discussion of 35 "Government-Wide" Proposals*, at 4 (July 25, 2018).

At various times in the twentieth century, Congress did give the President substantial power to transfer functions within the executive branch. Specifically, Congress periodically delegated authority to the President to propose reorganization plans that would take effect unless one or both houses of Congress passed a disapproval resolution (the sort of "legislative veto" arrangement that the Supreme Court held unconstitutional in *Immigration & Naturalization Service v. Chadha*, 462 U.S. 919 (1983)). *See* HENRY B. HOGUE, CONG. RSCH. SERV., R42852, PRESIDENTIAL REORGANIZATION AUTHORITY: HISTORY, RECENT INITIATIVES, AND OPTIONS FOR CONGRESS 3–34 (2012) (discussing the Economy Act of 1932 and the Reorganization Acts of 1939, 1945, 1949, and 1977). But the last such delegation lapsed in 1981, and current statutes do not give the President any special reorganization authority. *See id.* at 29–33.[4] After *Chadha*, moreover, Congress explicitly ratified by statute all of the reorganization plans that had previously been thought to have taken effect. *See* Act of Oct. 19, 1984, Pub. L. 98–532, 98 Stat. 2705.

In addition to controlling the structure of administrative agencies, federal statutes are also the source of the agencies' powers to act with the force of law with respect to people in the private sector. In general, executive officials (including even the President) lack inherent authority to change the rights, duties, or other legal relations of private individuals or entities. Federal agencies and executive officials can exercise such power only to the extent that a federal statute validly gives it to them. *See, e.g.*, Thomas W. Merrill, *Re-reading* Chevron, 70 DUKE L.J. 1153, 1162 (2021) ("Agencies have uniformly recognized the need to ground their authority to act in some statutory authority conferred on them by Congress.").

To know what powers Congress has conferred upon any particular agency, lawyers and judges must consult the relevant statutes. That can get complicated. If the agency was created as part of a reorganization plan (either enacted by Congress or issued by the President pursuant to statutory authority), lawyers may need to research older statutes defining powers that were then transferred to the new agency. Likewise, even after an agency exists, Congress can enact new statutes giving the agency additional responsibilities and powers. *See, e.g.*, Richard N.L. Andrews, *The EPA at 40: An Historical Perspective*, 21 DUKE ENV'T L. & POL. F. 223, 228–29 (2011) (noting that in the decade after President Nixon created the Environmental Protection Agency via a reorganization plan, "EPA's regulatory authority was . . . created or vastly expanded

[4] Title 5 of the United States Code still contains provisions from the Reorganization Act of 1977, as amended. *See* 5 U.S.C. §§ 901 *et seq.*; *see also* Reorganization Act Amendments of 1984, Pub. L. 98–614, § 3, 98 Stat. 3192, 3192–93 (amending the relevant provisions to replace the legislative veto with a requirement of affirmative approval via bicameralism and presentment). Those provisions contemplated that the President could propose reorganization plans that Congress would consider under special fast-track procedures. *See* 5 U.S.C. §§ 908–12. That arrangement, however, is limited to plans that the President "transmitted to Congress . . . on or before December 31, 1984," *id.* § 905(b), so it lacks continuing force.

piecemeal" by various environmental statutes). For many agencies, though, Congress has enacted a single "organic statute" (sometimes amended by later Congresses) creating the agency and specifying its authority.

The suite of powers that an agency might be given is varied. Start with rulemaking. Congress has given many agencies the power to make substantive rules (sometimes called "legislative" rules) that have the force of law and that can impose enforceable duties on individuals or entities in the private sector. *Cf.* Thomas W. Merrill & Kathryn Tongue Watts, *Agency Rules with the Force of Law: The Original Convention*, 116 HARV. L. REV. 467 (2002) (discussing the delegation of this sort of rulemaking authority, though suggesting that modern courts have found more such delegations than Congress originally intended). Such rules intersect with Congress's statutes in different ways. Some federal statutes themselves give regulated entities various duties, but authorize an administering agency to supplement those provisions by promulgating rules to help promote the statute's purposes. Other statutes have less regulatory content of their own; they focus entirely on empowering an agency, and they rely on the agency to promulgate appropriate requirements for regulated entities. For example, the original version of the Consumer Product Safety Act did not itself establish safety standards for any consumer products, but it authorized the Consumer Product Safety Commission to do so by rule. *See* Pub. L. 92–573, § 7(a), 86 Stat. 1207, 1212–13 (1972) (codified as amended at 15 U.S.C. § 2056).

You might wonder how Congress can authorize agencies to act with the force of law in this way, given the "nondelegation doctrine"—the constitutional principle that "Congress . . . may not transfer to another branch 'powers which are strictly and exclusively legislative.' " *Gundy v. United States*, 139 S. Ct. 2116, 2123 (2019) (plurality opinion of Kagan, J.) (quoting Wayman v. Southard, 23 U.S. (10 Wheat.) 1, 42–43 (1825)). That principle presumably would prevent Congress from giving administrative agencies or executive-branch officials unfettered power to make whatever legal rules they like on whatever topics they choose, without any guidance from Congress. Under longstanding doctrine, however, Congress can authorize executive-branch actors to make various kinds of judgment calls in the course of executing Congress's statutes, and Congress can also provide for those actors to promote statutory policies (and to channel the discretion of implementing officials) by promulgating rules that have the force of law. As long as Congress supplies "intelligible principle[s]" to guide and constrain the exercise of this delegated authority, the Supreme Court has regarded the relevant actors as executing Congress's laws rather than as impermissibly exercising "legislative" power in the constitutional sense.

See J.W. Hampton, Jr., & Co. v. United States, 276 U.S. 394, 409 (1928).[5] As applied by the Court, moreover, the "intelligible principle" test has not been demanding. *See* Mistretta v. United States, 488 U.S. 361, 373–74 (1989) (noting that "we have upheld . . . Congress' ability to delegate power under broad standards," and citing cases). *But cf. Gundy*, 139 S. Ct. at 2133–42 (Gorsuch, J., dissenting) (criticizing the "intelligible principle" language and the cases applying it, and advocating a more restrictive nondelegation doctrine).

Aside from substantive rulemaking power, Congress also has given many agencies the power to conduct particularized adjudications and to render decisions that have some sort of legal effect. Both the nature of those proceedings and the legal effect of the resulting decisions vary widely. Some statutes make agencies the front-line decisionmakers when a private individual or entity wants something from the government—a license to engage in a regulated activity, a visa to enter the country, a patent for an invention, a disability benefit under the Social Security Act, etc. Congress also has given many agencies adjudicatory authority in proceedings that the government itself initiates to enforce either statutory provisions or the agency's own regulations against a person who may have violated them. *See, e.g.*, Consumer Product Safety Act § 15, 86 Stat. at 1221 (codified as amended at 15 U.S.C. § 2064) (describing actions that the Consumer Product Safety Commission can order a manufacturer to take after determining, through a formal adjudicatory process, that a product distributed in commerce fails to comply with an applicable consumer product safety rule in a way that creates a substantial risk of injury). In addition, Congress has authorized some agencies to adjudicate disputes between two private individuals or entities and to issue orders that can affect their legal relations. Again, some of these delegations have raised constitutional questions, but again a great deal of administrative adjudication has been upheld on various theories. *See, e.g.*, Oil States Energy Servs., LLC v. Greene's Energy Group, LLC, 138 S. Ct. 1365 (2018); Commodity Futures Trading Comm'n v. Schor, 478 U.S. 833 (1986); Crowell v. Benson, 285 U.S. 22 (1932); *cf.* Caleb Nelson, *Adjudication in the Political Branches*, 107 COLUM. L. REV. 559 (2007) (discussing when "judicial" rather than "executive" power might be necessary for binding adjudications).

Administrative adjudication can involve pouring some content into the applicable statutes. For instance, Congress has effectively authorized some agencies to flesh out general statutory commands on a case-by-case basis, holding hearings and issuing particularized orders about specific situations. *See, e.g.*, Federal Trade Commission Act, ch. 311, § 5, 38 Stat. 717, 719–20 (1914) (codified as amended at 15 U.S.C. § 45) (prohibiting "unfair methods of competition in commerce" and authorizing the

---

[5] Thus, when an executive-branch agency exercises power delegated by Congress to make so-called "legislative rules," it is not regarded as exercising "legislative Power" in the constitutional sense. Assuming that Congress has provided enough guidance to satisfy the "intelligible principle" test, the agency is instead thought of as exercising "executive" power.

Federal Trade Commission to enforce this prohibition through individualized cease-and-desist orders). Under standard doctrine, moreover, when Congress has authorized an agency both to issue substantive rules of general applicability and to flesh out statutes through case-by-case adjudications, the agency often can choose to make policy through either method. *See* Nat'l Labor Relations Bd. v. Bell Aerospace Co., 416 U.S. 267, 294 (1974) ("[T]he Board is not precluded from announcing new principles in an adjudicative proceeding and . . . the choice between rulemaking and adjudication lies in the first instance within the Board's discretion."); *see also* M. Elizabeth Magill, *Agency Choice of Policymaking Forum*, 71 U. CHI. L. REV. 1383, 1405–10 (2004) (discussing doctrine on this point).

While the statutes that confer power on agencies tend to be specific to a particular agency, Congress has enacted a few overarching statutes that restrict how agencies can use those powers. The most prominent example is the Administrative Procedure Act (APA), which regulates both certain types of rulemaking and certain types of adjudication. When an agency to which Congress has delegated substantive rulemaking power wants to exercise this power, the APA normally requires the agency to publish a "notice of proposed rule making" and to "give interested persons an opportunity to participate in the rule making through submission of written data, views, or arguments," which the agency must consider before promulgating the final version of its rules. *See* 5 U.S.C. § 553; *see also id.* § 553(c) (requiring the agency's final rules to include "a concise general statement of their basis and purpose"); Cigar Ass'n of Am. v. U.S. Food & Drug Admin., 964 F.3d 56, 64 (D.C. Cir. 2020) (noting that this statement "must address significant comments and forms the basis for judicial review"). The APA does not require this notice-and-comment process for "interpretative rules, general statements of policy, or rules of agency organization, procedure, or practice," 5 U.S.C. § 553(b)—terms that the APA does not itself define. In general, though, substantive rules that will have the force of law must go through notice and comment before the agency finalizes them.

The APA also establishes elaborate procedural requirements for certain agency adjudications—those that some other statute requires "to be determined on the record after opportunity for an agency hearing." *Id.* § 554(a). Adjudications of this sort are sometimes called "formal" adjudications, and the APA regulates them in detail. *See id.* §§ 554, 556, 557. The APA has much less to say about other types of adjudication, but such "informal" adjudication might be regulated by an agency's organic statute or by procedural rules made by the agency itself. *Cf.* MICHAEL ASIMOW, FEDERAL ADMINISTRATIVE ADJUDICATION OUTSIDE THE ADMINISTRATIVE PROCEDURE ACT 3–6 (2019) (noting that it is misleading to use the label "informal" for all adjudication that is not covered by the APA's provisions about formal adjudication, and proposing a different taxonomy).

In addition to establishing procedural requirements for the use of certain powers that other statutes give agencies, the APA also addresses judicial review of agency action. The APA contains general provisions about who is entitled to judicial review of agency action, *id.* § 702, which actions are reviewable, *id.* § 704, and the scope of the court's review, *id.* § 706. If a federal statute establishes a special mechanism for judicial review, people who are eligible to use that mechanism can obtain review that way; otherwise, would-be challengers can use "any applicable form of legal action," including suits for injunctive or declaratory relief where appropriate. *Id.* § 703. Alternatively, arguments about the invalidity of an agency's rule or order usually can be raised in defense when the government brings a civil or criminal enforcement proceeding against someone accused of violating the rule or order. *See id.*

B. *CHEVRON* DEFERENCE

Suppose that Congress has given a federal administrative agency the authority to implement a federal statutory program by promulgating substantive rules or issuing particularized orders that supplement and flesh out the statute's requirements. In order to perform those tasks, the agency will need to interpret the relevant statutory provisions. But questions about the meaning of those provisions can also come up in court—sometimes in suits seeking judicial review of the agency's actions, sometimes in other kinds of suits (including suits to which the government is not a party). If the agency has already interpreted the relevant provisions, how much should the agency's interpretation affect the meaning that courts ascribe to the statute? Under what circumstances, if any, should courts defer to an administrative agency's interpretation of statutory provisions that Congress has given the agency authority to administer?

Modern doctrine on that question traces back to the Supreme Court's decision in *Chevron U.S.A. v. Natural Resources Defense Council*, 467 U.S. 837 (1984). As that decision came to be understood, it effectively linked the *administrative* authority that Congress delegated to the agency with a special type of *interpretive* or *gap-filling* authority—the authority to resolve both vagueness and ambiguity in statutory provisions that the agency administers. Specifically, if one of those statutory provisions lends itself to various constructions that the courts consider "permissible," and if the agency authoritatively adopts one of those permissible constructions and offers an adequate explanation of its choice, *Chevron* tells reviewing courts to accept and follow the agency's construction.

This principle is not exactly one of *stare decisis*. The agency itself remains free to change its mind and switch to one of the other permissible constructions, and courts will then be bound to accept the agency's new position (assuming, again, that the agency has offered an adequate explanation both of its new construction and of its reasons for changing).

Instead, so-called "*Chevron* deference" is about the relationship between federal administrative agencies and other actors (including but not limited to state and federal courts) with respect to the implementation and interpretation of federal statutes that the agencies administer.[6]

As we shall see, the Supreme Court is poised to reconsider *Chevron* deference. Before we touch on current controversies, though, you need to understand the scope and evolution of the doctrine.

1. THE BASIS AND SCOPE OF *CHEVRON* DEFERENCE

Chevron U.S.A. Inc. v. Natural Resources Defense Council

467 U.S. 837 (1984)

■ *JUSTICE STEVENS delivered the opinion of the Court:*

In the Clean Air Act Amendments of 1977, Pub. L. 95–95, 91 Stat. 685, Congress enacted certain requirements applicable to States that had not achieved the national air quality standards established by the Environmental Protection Agency (EPA) pursuant to earlier legislation. The amended Clean Air Act required these "nonattainment" States to establish a permit program regulating "new or modified major stationary sources" of air pollution. Generally, a permit may not be issued for a new or modified major stationary source unless several stringent conditions are met. The EPA regulation promulgated to implement this permit requirement allows a State to adopt a plantwide definition of the term "stationary source."[2] Under this definition, an existing plant that contains several pollution-emitting devices may install or modify one piece of equipment without meeting the permit conditions if the alteration will not increase the total emissions from the plant. The question presented . . . is whether EPA's decision to allow States to treat all of the pollution-emitting devices within the same industrial grouping as though they were encased within a single "bubble" is based on a reasonable construction of the statutory term "stationary source."

---

[6] The *Chevron* doctrine is specific to the role of *federal* administrative agencies in interpreting and implementing the *federal* statutes that they administer. Of course, state courts can face parallel questions about whether to defer to a state administrative agency's interpretation of a state statute. But that is a matter of state law, and different states have different doctrines about the relationship between their administrative agencies and their courts in matters of statutory interpretation. *See* Luke Phillips, Comment, Chevron *in the States? Not So Much*, 89 MISS. L.J. 313, 315 (2020) (finding "remarkable variation," but concluding that courts in half of the states use essentially "de novo review," and courts in eleven other states stop well short of "*Chevron*-type review").

[2] "(i) 'Stationary source' means any building, structure, facility, or installation which emits or may emit any air pollutant subject to regulation under the Act.

"(ii) 'Building, structure, facility, or installation' means all of the pollutant-emitting activities which belong to the same industrial grouping, are located on one or more contiguous or adjacent properties, and are under the control of the same person (or persons under common control) except the activities of any vessel." 40 CFR §§ 51.18(j)(1)(i) and (ii) (1983).

I

The EPA regulations containing the plantwide definition of the term stationary source were promulgated on October 14, 1981. [The National Resources Defense Council and two other organizations] filed a timely petition for review in the United States Court of Appeals for the District of Columbia Circuit pursuant to 42 U.S.C. § 7606(b)(1). [Chevron and various industry groups were permitted to intervene as parties supporting the plantwide definition.] The Court of Appeals set aside the regulations. *Natural Resources Defense Council, Inc. v. Gorsuch*, . . . 685 F.2d 718 (1982).[*]

The court observed that the relevant part of the amended Clean Air Act "does not explicitly define what Congress envisioned as a 'stationary source,' to which the permit pro[cess] . . . should apply," and further stated that the precise issue was not "squarely addressed in the legislative history." [*Id.* at 723.] In light of its conclusion that the legislative history bearing on the question was "at best contradictory," it reasoned that "the purposes of the nonattainment program should guide our decision here." [*Id.* at 726 n.39.] Based on two of its precedents concerning the applicability of the bubble concept to certain Clean Air Act programs,[6] the court stated that the bubble concept was "mandatory" in programs designed merely to maintain existing air quality, but held that it was "inappropriate" in programs enacted to improve air quality. [*Id.* at 726.] Since the purpose of the permit program . . . was to improve air quality, the court held that the bubble concept was inapplicable in these cases under its prior precedents. *Ibid.* It therefore set aside the regulations embodying the bubble concept as contrary to law. . . . [W]e now reverse.

The basic legal error of the Court of Appeals was to adopt a static judicial definition of the term "stationary source" when it had decided that Congress itself had not commanded that definition. . . .

II

When a court reviews an agency's construction of the statute which it administers, it is confronted with two questions. First, always, is the question whether Congress has directly spoken to the precise question at issue. If the intent of Congress is clear, that is the end of the matter; for the court, as well as the agency, must give effect to the unambiguously expressed intent of Congress.[9] If, however, the court determines Congress has not directly addressed the precise question at issue, the court does not simply impose its own construction on the statute, as

---

[*] *Editor's note*: Then-Judge Ruth Bader Ginsburg wrote the D.C. Circuit's opinion.

[6] *Alabama Power Co. v. Costle*, . . . 636 F.2d 323 (1979); *ASARCO Inc. v. EPA*, . . . 578 F.2d 319 (1978).

[9] The judiciary is the final authority on issues of statutory construction and must reject administrative constructions which are contrary to clear congressional intent. . . . If a court, employing traditional tools of statutory construction, ascertains that Congress had an intention on the precise question at issue, that intention is the law and must be given effect.

would be necessary in the absence of an administrative interpretation. Rather, if the statute is silent or ambiguous with respect to the specific issue, the question for the court is whether the agency's answer is based on a permissible construction of the statute.[11]

"The power of an administrative agency to administer a congressionally created . . . program necessarily requires the formulation of policy and the making of rules to fill any gap left, implicitly or explicitly, by Congress." *Morton v. Ruiz*, 415 U.S. 199, 231 (1974). If Congress has explicitly left a gap for the agency to fill, there is an express delegation of authority to the agency to elucidate a specific provision of the statute by regulation. Such legislative regulations are given controlling weight unless they are arbitrary, capricious, or manifestly contrary to the statute. Sometimes the legislative delegation to an agency on a particular question is implicit rather than explicit. In such a case, a court may not substitute its own construction of a statutory provision for a reasonable interpretation made by the administrator of an agency.

We have long recognized that considerable weight should be accorded to an executive department's construction of a statutory scheme it is entrusted to administer, and the principle of deference to administrative interpretations

> "has been consistently followed by this Court whenever decision as to the meaning or reach of a statute has involved reconciling conflicting policies, and a full understanding of the force of the statutory policy in the given situation has depended upon more than ordinary knowledge respecting the matters subjected to agency regulations. . . .
>
> ". . . If this choice represents a reasonable accommodation of conflicting policies that were committed to the agency's care by the statute, we should not disturb it unless it appears from the statute or its legislative history that the accommodation is not one that Congress would have sanctioned." *United States v. Shimer*, 367 U.S. 374, 382, 383 (1961).

. . . .

In light of these well-settled principles it is clear that the Court of Appeals misconceived the nature of its role in reviewing the regulations at issue. Once it determined, after its own examination of the legislation, that Congress did not actually have an intent regarding the applicability of the bubble concept to the permit program, the question before it was not whether in its view the concept is "inappropriate" in the general context of a program designed to improve air quality, but whether the Administrator's view that it is appropriate in the context of this particular program is a reasonable one. Based on the examination of the

---

[11] The court need not conclude that the agency construction was the only one it permissibly could have adopted to uphold the construction, or even the reading the court would have reached if the question initially had arisen in a judicial proceeding. . . .

legislation and its history which follows, we agree with the Court of Appeals that Congress did not have a specific intention on the applicability of the bubble concept in these cases, and conclude that the EPA's use of that concept here is a reasonable policy choice for the agency to make.

III

. . . . The Clean Air Amendments of 1970, Pub. L. 91–604, 84 Stat. 1676, "sharply increased federal authority and responsibility in the continuing effort to combat air pollution," [*Train v. Natural Resources Defense Council, Inc.*, 421 U.S. 60, 64 (1975)], but continued to assign "primary responsibility for assuring air quality" to the several States, 84 Stat. 1678. Section 109 of the 1970 Amendments directed the EPA to promulgate National Ambient Air Quality Standards (NAAQS's) and § 110 directed the States to develop plans (SIP's) to implement the standards within specified deadlines. In addition, § 111 provided that major new sources of pollution would be required to conform to technology-based performance standards; the EPA was directed to publish a list of categories of sources of pollution and to establish new source performance standards (NSPS) for each. Section 111(e) prohibited the operation of any new source in violation of a performance standard.

Section 111(a) defined the terms that are to be used in setting and enforcing standards of performance for new stationary sources. It provided:

> "For purposes of this section:
>
> . . . .
>
> "(3) The term 'stationary source' means any building, structure, facility, or installation which emits or may emit any air pollutant." 84 Stat. 1683.

In the 1970 Amendments that definition was not only applicable to the NSPS program required by § 111, but also was made applicable to a requirement of § 110 that each state implementation plan contain a procedure for reviewing the location of any proposed new source and preventing its construction if it would preclude the attainment or maintenance of national air quality standards.

In due course, the EPA promulgated NAAQS's, approved SIP's, and adopted detailed regulations governing NSPS's for various categories of equipment. In one of its programs [relating to the nonferrous smelting industry], the EPA used a plantwide definition of the term "stationary source." . . .[17]

---

[17] The Court of Appeals ultimately held that this plantwide approach was prohibited by the 1970 Act, see *ASARCO Inc.*, . . . 578 F.2d at 325–27. This decision was rendered after enactment of the 1977 Amendments, and hence the [NSPS that used the plantwide approach] was in effect when Congress enacted the 1977 Amendments.

Nonattainment

The 1970 legislation provided for the attainment of primary NAAQS's by 1975. In many areas of the country, particularly the most industrialized States, the statutory goals were not attained. In 1976, the 94th Congress [considered the problem but failed to agree upon a response.] . . .

In light of this situation, the EPA published an Emissions Offset Interpretative Ruling in December 1976, see 41 Fed. Reg. 55524, to "fill the gap," as respondents put it, until Congress acted. The Ruling stated that it was intended to address "the issue of whether and to what extent national air quality standards established under the Clean Air Act may restrict or prohibit growth of major new or expanded stationary air pollution sources." *Id.* at 55524–55525. In general, the Ruling provided that "a major new source may locate in an area with air quality worse than a national standard only if stringent conditions can be met." *Id.* at 55525. The Ruling gave primary emphasis to the rapid attainment of the statute's environmental goals. Consistent with that emphasis, the construction of every new source in nonattainment areas had to meet the "lowest achievable emission rate" under the current state of the art for that type of facility. See *ibid.* The 1976 Ruling did not, however, explicitly adopt or reject the "bubble concept."

IV

The Clean Air Act Amendments of 1977 are a lengthy, detailed, technical, complex, and comprehensive response to a major social issue. A small portion of the statute—91 Stat. 745–751 (Part D of Title I of the amended Act, 42 U.S.C. §§ 7501–7508)—expressly deals with nonattainment areas. The focal point of this controversy is one phrase in that portion of the Amendments.[22]

Basically, the statute required each State in a nonattainment area to prepare and obtain approval of a new SIP by July 1, 1979. In the interim those States were required to comply with the EPA's interpretative Ruling of December 21, 1976. 91 Stat. 745. The deadline for attainment of the primary NAAQS's was extended until December 31, 1982, and in some cases until December 31, 1987, but the SIP's were required to contain a number of provisions designed to achieve the goals as expeditiously as possible.

Most significantly for our purposes, the statute provided that each plan shall

> "(6) require permits for the construction and operation of new or modified major stationary sources in accordance with section 173. . . ." *Id.* at 747.

[22] Specifically, the controversy in these cases involves the meaning of the term "major stationary sources" in § 172(b)(6) of the Act, 42 U.S.C. § 7502(b)(6). . . .

Before issuing a permit, § 173 requires (1) the state agency to determine that there will be sufficient emissions reductions in the region to offset the emissions from the new source and also to allow for reasonable further progress toward attainment, or that the increased emissions will not exceed an allowance for growth established pursuant to § 172(b)(5); (2) the applicant to certify that his other sources in the State are in compliance with the SIP, (3) the agency to determine that the applicable SIP is otherwise being implemented, and (4) the proposed source to comply with the lowest achievable emission rate (LAER).

The 1977 Amendments contain no specific reference to the "bubble concept." Nor do they contain a specific definition of the term "stationary source," though they did not disturb the definition of "stationary source" contained in § 111(a)(3), applicable by the terms of the Act to the NSPS program. Section 302(j), however, defines the term "major stationary source" as follows:

> "(j) Except as otherwise expressly provided, the terms 'major stationary source' and 'major emitting facility' mean any stationary facility or source of air pollutants which directly emits, or has the potential to emit, one hundred tons per year or more of any air pollutant (including any major emitting facility or source of fugitive emissions of any such pollutant, as determined by rule by the Administrator)." 91 Stat. 770.

V

The legislative history of the portion of the 1977 Amendments dealing with nonattainment areas does not contain any specific comment on the "bubble concept" or the question whether a plantwide definition of a stationary source is permissible under the permit program. It does, however, plainly disclose that in the permit program Congress sought to accommodate the conflict between the economic interest in permitting capital improvements to continue and the environmental interest in improving air quality. Indeed, the House Committee Report identified the economic interest as one of the "two main purposes" of this section of the bill. It stated:

> "Section 117 of the bill, adopted during full committee markup[,] establishes a new section 127 of the Clean Air Act. The section has two main purposes: (1) to allow reasonable economic growth to continue in an area while making reasonable further progress to assure attainment of the standards by a fixed date; and (2) to allow States greater flexibility for the former purpose than EPA's present interpretative regulations afford.
>
> "The new provision allows States with nonattainment areas to pursue one of two options. First, the State may proceed under EPA's present 'tradeoff' or 'offset' ruling. The Administrator is authorized, moreover, to modify or amend that ruling in accordance with the intent and purposes of this section.

"The State's second option would be to revise its implementation plan in accordance with this new provision." H.R. Rep. No. 95–294, p. 211 (1977).[25]

. . . .

VI

As previously noted, prior to the 1977 Amendments, the EPA had adhered to a plantwide definition of the term "source" under a NSPS program. After adoption of the 1977 Amendments, proposals for a plantwide definition were considered in at least three formal proceedings.

In January 1979, the EPA considered the question whether the same restriction on new construction in nonattainment areas that had been included in its December 1976 Ruling should be required in the revised SIP's that were scheduled to go into effect in July 1979. After noting that the 1976 Ruling was ambiguous on the question "whether a plant with a number of different processes and emission points would be considered a single source," 44 Fed. Reg. 3276 (1979), the EPA, in effect, provided a bifurcated answer to that question. In those areas that did not have a revised SIP in effect by July 1979, the EPA rejected the plantwide definition; on the other hand, it expressly concluded that the plantwide approach would be permissible in certain circumstances if authorized by an approved SIP. . . .

In April, and again in September 1979, the EPA published additional comments in which it indicated that revised SIP's could adopt the plantwide definition of source in nonattainment areas in certain circumstances. See *id.* at 20372, 20379, 51924, 51951, 51958. On the latter occasion, the EPA made a formal rulemaking proposal that would have permitted the use of the "bubble concept" for new installations within a plant as well as for modifications of existing units. . . . Significantly, the EPA expressly noted that the word "source" might be given a plantwide definition for some purposes and a narrower definition for other purposes. . . .

In August 1980, however, the EPA adopted a regulation that, in essence, applied the basic reasoning of the Court of Appeals in these cases. The EPA took particular note of the two then-recent Court of Appeals decisions, which had created the bright-line rule that the "bubble concept" should be employed in a program designed to maintain air quality but not in one designed to enhance air quality. Relying heavily on those cases, EPA adopted a dual definition of "source" for nonattainment areas that required a permit whenever a change in either the entire plant, or one of its components, would result in a significant

---

[25] . . . . The second "main purpose" of the provision—allowing the States "greater flexibility" than the EPA's interpretative Ruling—as well as the reference to the EPA's authority to amend its Ruling in accordance with the intent of the section, is entirely consistent with the view that Congress did not intend to freeze the definition of "source" contained in the existing regulation into a rigid statutory requirement.

increase in emissions even if the increase was completely offset by reductions elsewhere in the plant. The EPA expressed the opinion that this interpretation was "more consistent with congressional intent" than the plantwide definition because it "would bring in more sources or modifications for review," 45 Fed. Reg. 52697 (1980), but its primary legal analysis was predicated on the two Court of Appeals decisions.

In 1981 a new administration took office and initiated a "Government-wide reexamination of regulatory burdens and complexities." 46 Fed. Reg. 16281. In the context of that review, the EPA reevaluated the various arguments that had been advanced in connection with the proper definition of the term "source" and concluded that the term should be given the same definition in both nonattainment areas and [so-called "PSD areas," which meet the applicable air-quality standards but in which the agency is trying to prevent significant deterioration].

In explaining its conclusion, the EPA first noted that the definitional issue was not squarely addressed in either the statute or its legislative history and therefore that the issue involved an agency "judgment as how to best carry out the Act." *Ibid.* It then set forth several reasons for concluding that the plantwide definition was more appropriate. It pointed out that the dual definition "can act as a disincentive to new investment and modernization by discouraging modifications to existing facilities" and "can actually retard progress in air pollution control by discouraging replacement of older, dirtier processes or pieces of equipment with new, cleaner ones." *Ibid.* Moreover, the new definition "would simplify EPA's rules by using the same definition of 'source' for PSD, nonattainment new source review and the construction moratorium. This reduces confusion and inconsistency." *Ibid.* Finally, the agency explained that additional requirements that remained in place would accomplish the fundamental purposes of achieving attainment with NAAQS's as expeditiously as possible. These conclusions were expressed in a proposed rulemaking in August 1981 that was formally promulgated in October. See *id.* at 50766.

VII

In this Court respondents expressly reject the basic rationale of the Court of Appeals' decision. That court viewed the statutory definition of the term "source" as sufficiently flexible to cover either a plantwide definition, a narrower definition covering each unit within a plant, or a dual definition that could apply to both the entire "bubble" and its components. It interpreted the policies of the statute, however, to mandate the plantwide definition in programs designed to maintain clean air and to forbid it in programs designed to improve air quality. Respondents place a fundamentally different construction on the statute. They contend that the text of the Act requires the EPA to use a dual definition—if either a component of a plant, or the plant as a whole, emits over 100 tons of pollutant, it is a major stationary source. They thus contend that the EPA rules adopted in 1980, insofar as they apply to the maintenance of the quality of clean air, as well as the 1981 rules which apply to nonattainment areas, violate the statute.

Statutory Language

The definition of the term "stationary source" in § 111(a)(3) refers to "any building, structure, facility, or installation" which emits air pollution. This definition is applicable only to the NSPS program by the express terms of the statute; the text of the statute does not make this definition applicable to the permit program. Petitioners therefore maintain that there is no statutory language even relevant to ascertaining the meaning of stationary source in the permit program aside from § 302(j), which defines the term "major stationary source." We disagree with petitioners on this point.

The definition in § 302(j) tells us what the word "major" means—a source must emit at least 100 tons of pollution to qualify—but it sheds virtually no light on the meaning of the term "stationary source." It does equate a source with a facility—a "major emitting facility" and a "major stationary source" are synonymous under § 302(j). The ordinary meaning of the term "facility" is some collection of integrated elements which has been designed and constructed to achieve some purpose. Moreover, it is certainly no affront to common English usage to take a reference to a major facility or a major source to connote an entire plant as opposed to its constituent parts. Basically, however, the language of § 302(j) simply does not compel any given interpretation of the term "source."

Respondents recognize that, and hence point to § 111(a)(3). Although the definition in that section is not literally applicable to the permit program, it sheds as much light on the meaning of the word "source" as anything in the statute. As respondents point out, use of the words "building, structure, facility, or installation," as the definition of source, could be read to impose the permit conditions on an individual building that is a part of a plant. . . . On the other hand, . . . [t]he language may reasonably be interpreted to impose the requirement on any discrete, but integrated, operation which pollutes. This gives meaning to all of the terms—a single building, not part of a larger operation, would be covered if it emits more than 100 tons of pollution, as would any facility, structure, or installation. Indeed, the language itself implies a "bubble concept" of sorts: each enumerated item would seem to be treated as if it were encased in a bubble. . . .

We are not persuaded that parsing of general terms in the text of the statute will reveal an actual intent of Congress. We know full well that this language is not dispositive; the terms are overlapping and the language is not precisely directed to the question of the applicability of a given term in the context of a larger operation. To the extent any congressional "intent" can be discerned from this language, it would appear that the listing of overlapping, illustrative terms was intended to enlarge, rather than to confine, the scope of the agency's power to regulate particular sources in order to effectuate the policies of the Act.

Legislative History

In addition, respondents argue that the legislative history and policies of the Act foreclose the plantwide definition, and that the EPA's interpretation is not entitled to deference because it represents a sharp break with prior interpretations of the Act.

Based on our examination of the legislative history, we agree with the Court of Appeals that it is unilluminating. The general remarks pointed to by respondents "were obviously not made with this narrow issue in mind and they cannot be said to demonstrate a Congressional desire . . . ." *Jewell Ridge Coal Corp. v. Mine Workers*, 325 U.S. 161, 168–169 (1945). Respondents' argument based on the legislative history relies heavily on Senator Muskie's observation that ["a new source is still subject to such requirements as 'lowest achievable emissions rate' even if it is constructed as a replacement for an older facility resulting in a net reduction from previous emission levels." 123 Cong. Rec. 26847 (1977).] But the full statement is ambiguous . . . . We find that the legislative history as a whole is silent on the precise issue before us. It is, however, consistent with the view that the EPA should have broad discretion in implementing the policies of the 1977 Amendments.

More importantly, that history plainly identifies the policy concerns that motivated the enactment; the plantwide definition is fully consistent with one of those concerns—the allowance of reasonable economic growth—and, whether or not we believe it most effectively implements the other, we must recognize that the EPA has advanced a reasonable explanation for its conclusion that the regulations serve the environmental objectives as well. Indeed, its reasoning is supported by the public record developed in the rulemaking process, as well as by certain private studies.

Our review of the EPA's varying interpretations of the word "source"—both before and after the 1977 Amendments—convinces us that the agency primarily responsible for administering this important legislation has consistently interpreted it flexibly—not in a sterile textual vacuum, but in the context of implementing policy decisions in a technical and complex arena. The fact that the agency has from time to time changed its interpretation of the term "source" does not, as respondents argue, lead us to conclude that no deference should be accorded the agency's interpretation of the statute. An initial agency interpretation is not instantly carved in stone. On the contrary, the agency, to engage in informed rulemaking, must consider varying interpretations and the wisdom of its policy on a continuing basis. Moreover, the fact that the agency has adopted different definitions in different contexts adds force to the argument that the definition itself is flexible, particularly since Congress has never indicated any disapproval of a flexible reading of the statute.

Significantly, it was not the agency in 1980, but rather the Court of Appeals that read the statute inflexibly to command a plantwide definition for programs designed to maintain clean air and to forbid such a definition for programs designed to improve air quality. The distinction the court drew may well be a sensible one, but our labored review of the problem has surely disclosed that it is not a distinction that Congress ever articulated itself, or one that the EPA found in the statute before the courts began to review the legislative work product. We conclude that it was the Court of Appeals, rather than Congress or any of the decisionmakers who are authorized by Congress to administer this legislation, that was primarily responsible for the 1980 position taken by the agency.

Policy

The arguments over policy that are advanced in the parties' briefs create the impression that respondents are now waging in a judicial forum a specific policy battle which they ultimately lost in the agency and in the 32 jurisdictions opting for the "bubble concept," but one which was never waged in the Congress. Such policy arguments are more properly addressed to legislators or administrators, not to judges.

In these cases, the Administrator's interpretation represents a reasonable accommodation of manifestly competing interests and is entitled to deference: the regulatory scheme is technical and complex, the agency considered the matter in a detailed and reasoned fashion, and the decision involves reconciling conflicting policies. Congress intended to accommodate both interests, but did not do so itself on the level of specificity presented by these cases. Perhaps that body consciously desired the Administrator to strike the balance at this level, thinking that those with great expertise and charged with responsibility for administering the provision would be in a better position to do so; perhaps it simply did not consider the question at this level; and perhaps Congress was unable to forge a coalition on either side of the question, and those on each side decided to take their chances with the scheme devised by the agency. For judicial purposes, it matters not which of these things occurred.

Judges are not experts in the field, and are not part of either political branch of the Government. Courts must, in some cases, reconcile competing political interests, but not on the basis of the judges' personal policy preferences. In contrast, an agency to which Congress has delegated policy-making responsibilities may, within the limits of that delegation, properly rely upon the incumbent administration's views of wise policy to inform its judgments. While agencies are not directly accountable to the people, the Chief Executive is, and it is entirely appropriate for this political branch of the Government to make such policy choices—resolving the competing interests which Congress itself either inadvertently did not resolve, or intentionally left to be resolved by the agency charged with the administration of the statute in light of everyday realities.

When a challenge to an agency construction of a statutory provision, fairly conceptualized, really centers on the wisdom of the agency's policy, rather than whether it is a reasonable choice within a gap left open by Congress, the challenge must fail. In such a case, federal judges—who have no constituency—have a duty to respect legitimate policy choices made by those who do. The responsibilities for assessing the wisdom of such policy choices and resolving the struggle between competing views of the public interest are not judicial ones: "Our Constitution vests such responsibilities in the political branches." *TVA v. Hill*, 437 U.S. 153, 195 (1978).

We hold that the EPA's definition of the term "source" is a permissible construction of the statute which seeks to accommodate progress in reducing air pollution with economic growth. "The Regulations which the Administrator has adopted provide what the agency could allowably view as . . . [an] effective reconciliation of these twofold ends . . . ." *United States v. Shimer*, 367 U.S. at 383.

The judgment of the Court of Appeals is reversed.

■ *[JUSTICES MARSHALL, REHNQUIST, and O'CONNOR did not participate in this decision.]*

NOTES AND QUESTIONS

1. *Chevron* has become famous for the two-step framework that Justice Stevens articulated in the first paragraph of Part II of the Court's opinion. Where that framework applies, it can cause courts to accept a federal administrative agency's resolution of questions about the proper interpretation or application of a federal statute that the agency administers, even if the courts would otherwise have resolved those questions differently.

As formulated by Justice Stevens, the framework operates as follows.[7] At Step One, the court asks "whether Congress has spoken to the precise question at issue"—that is, whether the statute provides a single determinate answer. *See Chevron*, 467 U.S. at 842. If so, there is no room for deference; the agency does not have leeway to give a different answer than Congress itself has supplied. But if the court concludes that the statute is "silent or ambiguous" on the relevant question (in the nontechnical sense that includes vagueness), then the court proceeds to Step Two: the court will ask "whether the agency's answer is based on a permissible construction of the statute." *Id.* at 843. If the court concludes

[7] In the years since *Chevron*, scholars have discussed different ways of divvying up the analysis. *See, e.g.*, Ronald M. Levin, *The Anatomy of* Chevron*: Step Two Reconsidered*, 72 CHI.-KENT L. REV. 1253 (1997); Matthew C. Stephenson & Adrian Vermeule, Chevron *Has Only One Step*, 95 VA. L. REV. 597 (2009); *cf.* Kenneth A. Bamberger & Peter L. Strauss, Chevron*'s Two Steps*, 95 VA. L. REV. 611 (2009).

that the agency's construction is indeed "permissible," the court will accept and follow it even if it is not the construction that the court would otherwise have chosen. *See id.* at 843 n.11.

Justice Stevens cast Step One as being about whether "the intent of Congress is clear" with respect to the relevant question. *Id.* at 842. Some later cases have spoken instead of whether "the statute is clear and unambiguous." *Bd. of Governors of the Fed. Reserve System v. Dimension Fin. Corp.*, 474 U.S. 361, 368 (1986); *cf.* Thomas W. Merrill, *Textualism and the Future of the* Chevron *Doctrine*, 72 WASH. U. L.Q. 351, 357–58 (1994) (noting that although "[t]he *Chevron* opinion speaks the language of legislative intent," the Court subsequently "reformulate[d]" Step One in more textualist terms); Linda Jellum, Chevron*'s Demise: A Survey of* Chevron *from Infancy to Senescence*, 59 ADMIN. L. REV. 725, 743–71 (2007) (discussing this shift). Either way, though, clarity is itself a vague concept. *See* Antonin Scalia, *Judicial Deference to Administrative Interpretations of Law*, 1989 DUKE L.J. 511, 520–21 ("How clear is clear? It is here, if *Chevron* is not abandoned, that the future battles over acceptance of agency interpretations of law will be fought."); Brett M. Kavanaugh, *Fixing Statutory Interpretation*, 129 HARV. L. REV. 2118, 2141 (2016) (book review) (quoting Justice Scalia's prediction and observing that "the Court has skirmished over exactly this terrain numerous times in the last twenty-five years"); *cf.* Richard M. Re, *Clarity Doctrines*, 86 U. CHI. L. REV. 1497, 1499, 1536–37 (2019) (observing that across a range of doctrines, including *Chevron*, "courts have paradoxically left the nature of legal clarity underspecified"). Suppose that a statute could conceivably be understood in two different ways, but the reviewing court—after applying "traditional tools of statutory construction," *Chevron*, 467 U.S. at 843 n.9—believes that one construction is somewhat better than the other. How *much* better must the one interpretation seem, and how confident must the court be, for the court to say that the statute is "clear"? For purposes of the *Chevron* framework, might the answer depend on *why* the court considers one interpretation better than the other—for instance, on whether the court is using logic that the agency might be in a better position to apply?

Similar questions can arise at Step Two. Even if a statute is "ambiguous" in the sense that matters at Step One, the statute still confines the administering agency's discretion. In effect, the statute can be thought of as giving the agency a menu of options, but the agency needs to stay on the menu; to get reviewing courts to accept its choice, the agency needs to pick one of the constructions that the courts will consider "permissible." That concept too is vague. As a matter of statutory interpretation, how good does a construction need to be in order to be on the menu of options to which courts will defer at Step Two?

In addition to evaluating the permissibility of the agency's bottom line, courts conducting review at Step Two may also evaluate the process by which the agency made its choice and the reasoning on which the agency relied. As Professor Merrill notes, Justice Stevens's opinion in *Chevron* itself observed that the EPA had adopted the bubble concept through notice-and-comment rulemaking and had " 'considered the matter in a detailed and reasoned fashion.' " Thomas W. Merrill, *Re-reading* Chevron, 70 DUKE L.J. 1153, 1182–83 (2021) (emphasis omitted) (quoting *Chevron*, 467 U.S. at 865); *see also id.* at 1193 (arguing that as with judicial review of other agency actions, "[a] critical element in exercising the review of such discretionary agency interpretations . . . is whether the agency developed its position through a process of reasoned decisionmaking"). Ordinarily, when an agency has construed a statute in a manner that triggers the *Chevron* framework, the agency will have gone through either notice-and-comment rulemaking or formal adjudication, and the agency will have offered an explanation of its position. If the agency chose one construction over another for reasons that the statute puts off limits or that do not make sense, or if the agency adopted its position without adequately considering objections or alternatives, reviewing courts might conclude that the agency's construction is not "permissible" at Step Two of the *Chevron* framework even if the agency could end up adopting the same construction for different reasons. *See* 1 KRISTIN E. HICKMAN & RICHARD J. PIERCE, JR., ADMINISTRATIVE LAW TREATISE § 3.5, at 227–33 (6th ed. 2019) (discussing the overlap between analysis under Step Two of the *Chevron* framework and the questions that courts ask when "determining whether an agency policy decision is . . . 'arbitrary and capricious' " within the meaning of the Administrative Procedure Act).

2. Of course, before courts use *Chevron*'s two-step framework to evaluate an agency's interpretation of a statute, the courts have to decide whether the framework is indeed applicable. Professors Merrill and Hickman dubbed that question "Step Zero," and the term has stuck. *See* Thomas W. Merrill & Kristin E. Hickman, Chevron*'s Domain*, 89 GEO. L.J. 833, 836 (2001); *see also, e.g.*, Cass R. Sunstein, Chevron *Step Zero*, 92 VA. L. REV. 187 (2006).[8]

Chevron itself indicated that its framework applies "[w]hen a court reviews an agency's construction of the statute which [the agency] administers," *Chevron*, 467 U.S. at 842, and later cases confirmed that "[a] precondition to deference under *Chevron* is a congressional delegation of administrative authority" with respect to the statutory

[8] Even if the *Chevron* framework does not apply, an agency's views about the proper interpretation or application of a statute might still carry some weight with the courts, but only as persuasive authority. On that topic, modern courts continue to refer to the rubric that the Supreme Court used in *Skidmore v. Swift & Co.*, 323 U.S. 134, 140 (1944) ("We consider that the rulings, interpretations, and opinions of the Administrator under this Act, while not controlling upon the courts by reason of their authority, do constitute a body of experience and informed judgment to which courts and litigants may properly resort for guidance. The weight of such a judgment in a particular case will depend upon the thoroughness evident in its consideration, the validity of its reasoning, its consistency with earlier and later pronouncements, and all those factors which give it power to persuade, if lacking power to control."). So-called "*Skidmore* deference" is regarded as substantially less powerful than *Chevron* deference.

provisions that the agency has interpreted. *Adams Fruit Co. v. Barrett*, 494 U.S. 638, 649 (1990). But what counts as "administrative authority" for this purpose? In keeping with some of the rationales for *Chevron* discussed below, the Supreme Court has indicated that the *Chevron* framework operates only where Congress has given the agency a species of lawmaking power to help implement the provisions in question (or the entire statute containing those provisions). In the Supreme Court's words, "Deference in accordance with *Chevron* . . . is warranted only 'when it appears that Congress delegated authority to the agency generally to make rules carrying the force of law, and that the agency interpretation claiming deference was promulgated in the exercise of that authority.' " *Gonzales v. Oregon*, 546 U.S. 243, 255–56 (2006) (quoting *United States v. Mead Corp.*, 533 U.S. 218, 226–27 (2001)).

In the passage just quoted, the phrase "rules carrying the force of law" does not refer exclusively to regulations of the sort that agencies make through notice-and-comment rulemaking. It can also encompass legal principles that agencies develop via adjudication. In the words of the Supreme Court's opinion in *United States v. Mead Corp.*, a delegation of "authority . . . to make rules carrying the force of law"—that is, a delegation of the sort of administrative authority that potentially makes an agency eligible for *Chevron* deference—"may be shown in a variety of ways, as by an agency's power to engage in adjudication or notice-and-comment rulemaking, or by some other indication of a comparable congressional intent." *Mead*, 533 U.S. at 226–27. But if Congress has not authorized an agency to elaborate upon a statute in a way that has the force of law—for instance, if the agency is empowered merely to investigate alleged violations of the statute and to prosecute or sue alleged violators in court—then the agency's interpretation of the statute will not trigger the *Chevron* framework. *See* Merrill & Hickman, *supra*, 89 GEO. L.J. at 837; *see also, e.g.*, Crandon v. United States, 494 U.S. 152, 177 (1990) (Scalia, J., concurring in the judgment) (noting in this vein that the Department of Justice does not administer federal criminal statutes in the sense necessary for its interpretations of those statutes to receive *Chevron* deference).

Still, exactly what *Mead* meant by "the force of law" is murky. Professors Merrill and Hickman, whose scholarship informed the Court's analysis in *Mead*, had proposed a crisp definition: "Agency action has the force of law when, of its own force and effect, it commands certain behavior and subjects parties to penalties or sanctions if they violate this command." Merrill & Hickman, *supra*, 89 GEO. L.J. at 881. With respect to interpretations announced in agency adjudications, however, that test would have restricted *Chevron* deference to "adjudications that result in binding and self-executing orders"—orders that regulated entities have a duty to obey in the absence of any further proceedings in court. *See id.* at 884. Professor Merrill himself acknowledged that this test is underinclusive, *see* Thomas W. Merrill, *The* Mead *Doctrine: Rules and*

Standards, Meta-Rules and Meta-Standards, 54 ADMIN. L. REV. 807, 832 (2002), and the Supreme Court did not adopt it; under current doctrine, an agency that conducts quasi-judicial adjudications and issues orders that courts are required to treat as presumptively correct might have the authority to act with "the force of law" in the relevant sense even if the agency's orders are not self-executing. But while the Court did not adopt Merrill and Hickman's test, the Court also did not supply a clear alternative of its own. *See id.* at 813 (observing that *Mead* "implicitly treats 'force of law' as an undefined standard that invites consideration of a number of variables of indefinite weight").

Even if an agency does have authority to administer a particular statutory provision in the relevant sense, not everything that is said about the provision in the agency's name automatically triggers the *Chevron* framework. For instance, it is not enough for lawyers representing the agency simply to assert, in a brief submitted to a court, that the agency understands the provision in a certain way. For the agency's interpretation of a statute to qualify for *Chevron* deference, not only must Congress have delegated authority to the agency to implement the statute by "mak[ing] rules carrying the force of law," but the agency must have "promulgated [the interpretation] in the exercise of that authority." *Mead*, 533 U.S. at 226–27; *see also* Merrill & Hickman, *supra*, 89 GEO. L.J. at 887 (agreeing that *Chevron* deference should be limited to "agency interpretations . . . rendered in an agency action that has the force of law"). Usually, then, "[i]nterpretations such as those in opinion letters—like interpretations contained in policy statements, agency manuals, and enforcement guidelines, all of which lack the force of law—do not warrant *Chevron*-style deference." *Christensen v. Harris County*, 529 U.S. 576, 587 (2000); *cf.* Barnhart v. Walton, 535 U.S. 212, 222 (2002) (denying the existence of an "absolute rule" on this point).

3. Even as the Supreme Court has elaborated upon and developed the nuances of the *Chevron* doctrine, the Court often has attributed the essence of the doctrine to Congress. In the Court's words, "*Chevron* is rooted in a background presumption of congressional intent." *City of Arlington v. FCC*, 569 U.S. 290, 296 (2013); *see also* Merrill & Hickman, *supra*, 89 GEO. L.J. at 870–72 (discussing this rationale). At least until recently, the basic idea has been that when Congress gives an agency the type of administrative authority that satisfies Step Zero, Congress normally also intends the agency to have the authority that *Chevron* entails—so that if one of the statutory provisions that the agency administers is "silent or ambiguous" in the relevant sense, the agency gets to choose from among the "permissible" constructions in a way that binds later courts. *See Chevron*, 467 U.S. at 843; *see also, e.g.*, Smiley v. Citibank (S.D.), N.A., 517 U.S. 735, 740–41 (1996) ("We accord deference to agencies under *Chevron* . . . because of a presumption that Congress, when it left ambiguity in a statute meant for implementation by an agency, understood that the ambiguity would be resolved, first and foremost, by the agency, and desired the agency (rather than the courts) to possess whatever degree of discretion the ambiguity allows.").

As this way of talking suggests, Congress is in charge of whether federal administrative agencies have the authority that *Chevron* entails. If Congress so desired, Congress could withhold that authority either from a particular agency or from agencies in general. *See* Laurence H. Silberman, Chevron—*The Intersection of Law & Policy*, 58 GEO. WASH. L. REV. 821, 824 (1990). Conversely, within constitutional limits, Congress could explicitly grant this authority to some or all federal agencies. *See* Cass R. Sunstein, *Interpreting Statutes in the Regulatory State*, 103 HARV. L. REV. 405, 445 (1989) ("If Congress has told courts to defer to agency interpretations, courts must do so."). In practice, explicit grants of this authority are rare; while Congress often expressly gives an agency rulemaking or adjudicative power, Congress usually does not say anything one way or the other about the sort of authority that *Chevron* entails. Still, *Chevron* and its progeny understand Congress to be *implicitly* delegating the latter authority along with the agency's administrative authority. *Chevron* and its progeny can be seen as establishing the following default rule (or canon): a statute that delegates administrative authority to an agency should normally be presumed to be giving the agency the authority described in *Chevron*, too.

According to many commentators, though, the content of this default rule really originated with the courts, not Congress. In the words of two professors who both went on to become distinguished judges, "*Chevron* is a congressional doctrine only in the sense that Congress can overturn it; in all other respects, *Chevron* is a judicial construction, reflecting implicit policy judgments about what interpretive practices make for good government." David J. Barron & Elena Kagan, *Chevron's Nondelegation Doctrine*, 2001 SUP. CT. REV. 201, 212; *see also, e.g.*, Merrill & Hickman, *supra*, 89 GEO. L.J. at 871 ("[T]he evidence supporting the presumption that Congress generally intends agencies to be the primary interpreters of statutory ambiguities is weak."); Antonin Scalia, *Judicial Deference to Administrative Interpretations of Law*, 1989 DUKE L.J. 511, 517 (1989) (suggesting that "any rule adopted in this field represents merely a fictional, presumed intent").

If the *Chevron* doctrine applies to as many statutes as it seemed when commentators made these statements, then the commentators were probably correct. The typical federal statute that delegates administrative authority to an agency does not itself supply much guidance about the respective roles of the agency and the courts in resolving "ambiguities" in the relevant statutory provisions. To the extent that the *Chevron* doctrine reflects a default rule on that topic, the Supreme Court appears to have set the content of the default rule in the way that the Court considered best. *Cf.* Barron & Kagan, *supra*, 2001 SUP. CT. REV. at 212 ("Because Congress so rarely makes its intentions about deference clear, *Chevron* doctrine at most can rely on a fictionalized statement of legislative desire, which in the end must rest on the Court's view of how best to allocate interpretive authority.").[9]

Why might the Court have thought that the default rule reflected in the *Chevron* doctrine is better than other possible default rules? How one evaluates *Chevron*'s allocation of authority depends partly on how one understands the nature of the authority that is being allocated—a topic on which the Supreme Court has vacillated. On one way of talking, *Chevron* is about a presumed delegation of *interpretive* authority. *See, e.g.*, Epic Systems Corp. v. Lewis, 138 S. Ct. 1612, 1629 (2018) ("The *Chevron* Court justified deference on the premise that a statutory ambiguity represents an 'implicit' delegation to an agency to interpret a 'statute which it administers.' " (quoting *Chevron*, 467 U.S. at 841)); *see also Chevron*, 467 U.S. at 844 (discussing "deference to administrative interpretations"). Given Step One of the *Chevron* framework, though, the authority that *Chevron* entails does not come into play unless reviewing courts conclude (after conducting interpretation of their own) that "the statute is silent or ambiguous with respect to the specific issue" that the agency has addressed. *Id.* at 843. The resolution of such issues might still be partly interpretive, but it often is simultaneously creative; rather than simply identifying meanings that Congress already embedded in the statute, it can entail making policy judgments and creating new legal rules or sub-rules. Thus, the Supreme Court often describes *Chevron* as being about the allocation of *gap-filling* authority. *See, e.g.*, FDA v. Brown & Williamson Tobacco Corp., 529 U.S. 120, 159 (2000) ("Deference under *Chevron* to an agency's construction of a statute that it administers is premised on the theory that a statute's ambiguity constitutes an implicit delegation from Congress to the agency to fill in the statutory gaps."); *see also Chevron*, 467 U.S. at 843 (associating administrative authority with " 'the formulation of policy and the making of rules to fill any gap left . . . by Congress' " (quoting *Morton v. Ruiz*, 415 U.S. 199, 231 (1974))); *cf.* Henry P. Monaghan, Marbury *and the Administrative State*, 83 COLUM. L. REV. 1, 6 (1983) ("A statement that judicial deference is mandated to an administrative 'interpretation' of a statute is more appropriately understood as a judicial conclusion that some substantive law-making authority has been conferred upon the agency."). In *Chevron* itself, the Court's phrasing of Step One—whether "the statute is silent or ambiguous with respect to the specific issue" that the agency has addressed, *id.*—reflects uncertainty on this topic; the idea that the statute is "silent" might suggest the possibility of gap-filling, while the idea that the statute is "ambiguous" suggests the need for interpretation.

If one sees *Chevron* as being about the allocation of interpretive authority, and as telling courts when to defer to agencies about the

---

[9] Now that *Chevron* has become a prominent part of administrative law, perhaps it can benefit from feedback effects: when Congress sets up new agencies today and grants them administrative authority without saying anything about *Chevron*, perhaps Congress affirmatively intends to confer the sort of authority that *Chevron* entails. But Judge Barron and Justice Kagan plausibly questioned even that hypothesis. *See id.* at 216.

meaning of the statutes that the agencies administer, one might well question why the doctrine exists. Statutory interpretation is the bread and butter of the federal courts, and it might seem odd to require the United States Supreme Court to accept what executive-branch agencies say on that topic (at least in the absence of statutes clearly establishing this arrangement). To this day, indeed, the Administrative Procedure Act arguably cuts against such a requirement. When courts are conducting judicial review of agency action under the APA (which is the posture of most though not all of the cases in which *Chevron* comes up), 5 U.S.C. § 706 arguably invites courts to exercise independent judgment on questions of statutory interpretation. *See* 5 U.S.C. § 706 ("To the extent necessary to decision and when presented, the reviewing court shall decide all relevant questions of law, interpret constitutional and statutory provisions, and determine the meaning or applicability of the terms of an agency action."); *id.* § 706(2)(C) ("The reviewing court shall . . . hold unlawful and set aside agency action, findings, and conclusions found to be . . . in excess of statutory jurisdiction, authority, or limitations, or short of statutory right.").[10]

Admittedly, agency officials might have some advantages over judges in interpreting the statute that the agency administers. Even if we bracket the creative aspects of interpretation (discussed below) and focus on the search for the meaning intended by Congress, there are some respects in which agency officials might be better able than judges to identify that meaning. As compared to generalist judges, officials in administrative agencies may be more familiar with the complete legislative histories of the statutes that their agencies administer. Because agency officials often work with Congress on legislative proposals, moreover, agency officials probably understand the dynamics of the legislative process better than the typical judge. For both those reasons, agency officials may be better equipped than judges to use the materials of legislative history to reach accurate conclusions about congressional intent.[11] *See generally* Peter L. Strauss, *When the Judge Is*

[10] For competing views about whether § 706 is in tension with *Chevron* deference (understood as a principle about interpretation rather than gap-filling), compare John F. Duffy, *Administrative Common Law in Judicial Review*, 77 TEX. L. REV. 113, 193–97 (1998) (yes), with Ronald M. Levin, *The APA and the Assault on Deference*, 106 MINN. L. REV. 125 (2021) (no). For a suggestion that § 706 is compatible with some forms of deference but not with *Chevron* deference, see Aditya Bamzai, *The Origins of Judicial Deference to Executive Interpretation*, 126 YALE L.J. 908, 985–90 (2017).

[11] Sometimes, indeed, agency officials may have participated in the process of drafting and enacting the very statute that they are subsequently interpreting. Still, that would not necessarily warrant giving them a privileged position as interpreters. For one thing, their extra knowledge of the statute's creation might go along with extra biases: perhaps agency officials will use "interpretation" to achieve goals that they were forced to compromise during the legislative process, or perhaps they will put too much weight on aspects of the legislative process with which they are familiar at the expense of things that happened without their knowledge. Even apart from these concerns, we may not really want interpreters to rely on their personal knowledge of the internal processes that led to a statute's enactment. To the extent that this information is not publicly available, we might prefer interpreters to ignore it—just as courts tend to ignore the after-the-fact testimony of legislators themselves. *Cf.* Smiley v. Citibank

Not the Primary Official with Responsibility to Read: Agency Interpretation and the Problem of Legislative History, 66 CHI.-KENT L. REV. 321 (1990); *accord, e.g.*, ADRIAN VERMEULE, JUDGING UNDER UNCERTAINTY: AN INSTITUTIONAL THEORY OF LEGAL INTERPRETATION 209–10 (2006); Jerry L. Mashaw, *Norms, Practices, and the Paradox of Deference: A Preliminary Inquiry into Agency Statutory Interpretation*, 57 ADMIN. L. REV. 501, 511 (2005). Officials in specialist agencies are also likely to know more than generalist judges about the field that the relevant statute addresses, so they may better understand the nuances of any technical "terms of art," the competing goals that informed the statute, and how the statute fits together with other statutes in the field.

These advantages may mean that if judges and agency officials were both confined to isolation chambers and asked to interpret the statutes that the agency administers, the agency's interpretations would be more accurate in some respects. For purposes of evaluating *Chevron* deference, though, that is not the relevant comparison. When judges review an agency's interpretation of a statute, they will read the agency's explanation of its position before they make up their own minds. The key question, then, is not whether officials in specialist agencies have some advantages over generalist judges, but whether (and to what extent) agency officials have advantages *that they cannot communicate to judges* when they explain their position. Even if an agency's interpretation rests on the agency's detailed knowledge of legislative history or the agency's familiarity with technical terms of art, the agency's explanation of its position may well bring readers up to speed. If reviewing courts find the agency's logic persuasive, *Chevron* deference is beside the point; having been educated by the agency's explanation, the court would embrace the agency's position even without *Chevron*. When *Chevron* matters most is when the agency's logic does *not* persuade reviewing courts—when judges who have read and thought about the agency's explanation nonetheless disagree with the agency's interpretation of the statutory provision in question. It is not obvious that the agency is more likely than the judges to be correct in this subset of cases.

To the extent that interpretation entails a search for the meaning intended by a past Congress, moreover, judges may actually have some advantages over agencies. The structure and norms of the federal courts tend to insulate judges from direct pressure by current political actors; federal judges serve for life (unless they resign or are impeached and convicted), and they normally do not have to answer to anyone for their decisions. By contrast, administrative agencies operate in a more political milieu, facing pressures from both the President and Congress. When agency officials interpret statutes, they may well be trying to advance current policy goals or to please current constituencies, and they may be less interested in identifying the meaning that the enacting

(S.D.), N.A., 517 U.S. 735, 740–41 (1996) (declining to rest *Chevron* deference on the premise that agency officials participated in the legislative process).

Congress intended to embed in the statute. If one values the latter goal, one might think that federal judges are better situated to accomplish it.

Federal judges also have some relevant expertise of their own. They interpret statutes every day, and they may have a more nuanced understanding than agency officials of the general techniques of statutory interpretation.[12] To the extent that generic legal ability helps, moreover, people commonly think of the federal judiciary as having considerable legal talent. All things considered, one might question a doctrine that allocates conventional interpretive authority away from courts and toward executive-branch agencies.

But if *Chevron* instead is about the allocation of *gap-filling* authority, or about the more policy-tinged aspects of interpretation (such as deciding which reading of an otherwise indeterminate provision will work best in practice or will best accomplish the statute's underlying purposes), the case for *Chevron* seems substantially stronger. Where policymaking is concerned, the fact that agencies face more political accountability than federal courts is a good thing, not a bad thing. *See Chevron*, 467 U.S. at 865–66 (emphasizing agencies' accountability to the current President).[13] Sometimes, moreover, the choice of one alternative over another will hinge on the answers to technocratic questions: what are industry practices in this field, or what are the facts on the ground, or what does science tell us? Again, to the extent that the decisionmakers in specialist agencies have more expertise in the relevant field, they may be better positioned to answer those questions than courts would be. *See id.* at 865 (noting that the EPA has "great expertise," while "[j]udges are not experts in the field").

Of course, one should not idealize agencies or exaggerate their prowess in choosing from the array of policies that statutory language makes possible. Scholars have long worried that agencies might be "captured" by the industries that they are supposed to regulate; the people who work for specialist agencies might do their governmental

---

[12] This consideration would be less relevant if one thinks that agencies should use different interpretive techniques than judges, and that reviewing courts should give agencies this leeway. *See* Mashaw, *supra*, 57 ADMIN. L. REV. at 504 (advancing this idea, though noting the difficulty that it would pose for judicial review). *Chevron* deference, however, does not rest on this theory. At Step One, courts are supposed to "employ[ ] traditional tools of statutory construction" (which presumably are the tools used *by courts*) to determine whether a statute leaves room for agency discretion. *See Chevron*, 467 U.S. at 843 n.9.

[13] To the extent that the case for *Chevron* deference depends on agencies' political accountability, one might think that "independent agencies" (typically headed by boards whose members serve for defined terms and are not subject to removal at will) should receive less deference than agencies like the EPA (whose head serves at the President's pleasure). *See* Randolph J. May, *Defining Deference Down: Independent Agencies and* Chevron *Deference*, 58 ADMIN. L. REV. 429 (2006). In practice, though, courts have not drawn this distinction. *See id.* at 442; Kent Barnett & Christopher J. Walker, Chevron *in the Circuit Courts*, 116 MICH. L. REV. 1, 56–57 (2017). Nor is it clear that they should; although the governing boards of independent agencies enjoy some insulation from the President, they still are subject to more political controls than federal judges. *See, e.g.*, Silberman, *supra*, 58 GEO. WASH. L. REV. at 824 ("Congress and the President have a great deal more continuing influence over those agencies than over the judiciary.").

work with an eye toward landing lucrative jobs in the private sector, or they might have other reasons to cater to the industry representatives with whom they regularly interact. The opposite problem is also possible: perhaps agency decisionmakers will be so committed to their agency's mission (such as cleaning up the environment) that they will develop "tunnel vision" and will discount competing goals (such as promoting economic growth). If specialists lack a broad enough perspective to think about the trade-offs associated with their agency's mission, the choices that they make might end up generating more costs than benefits for society as a whole.

Even so, it is certainly conceivable that administering agencies might be better positioned than courts to handle the policy-tinged aspects of interpretation and to fill gaps that lie within the statute's domain. Current doctrine about "Step Zero," moreover, arguably dovetails with this view of the type of authority that *Chevron* entails. Recall that the *Chevron* framework comes into play only if Congress has given an agency a species of lawmaking power with respect to the relevant statutory scheme. *See* United States v. Mead Corp., 533 U.S. 218, 226–27 (2001) (referring to whether "Congress delegated authority to the agency generally to make rules carrying the force of law"). This precondition for *Chevron* deference fits the gap-filling view more naturally than the idea that *Chevron* is about statutory interpretation in a narrow sense.

4. A few years after the Supreme Court issued its opinion in *Chevron*, Professor Peter Strauss suggested that the Court's "otherwise surprising decision" might have been influenced by practical concerns involving the relatively decentralized nature of the federal judiciary. *See* Peter L. Strauss, *One Hundred Fifty Cases Per Year: Some Implications of the Supreme Court's Limited Resources for Judicial Review of Agency Action*, 87 COLUM. L. REV. 1093, 1095 (1987). As Professor Strauss noted, the Supreme Court can review only a small fraction of the cases that courts decide. *See id.* at 1100 (observing that the Supreme Court hears only "about 150 cases annually"—a number that has fallen in half since Professor Strauss wrote). Thus, the Supreme Court has only limited capacity "directly to enforce uniformity upon the courts of appeals in those courts' review of agency decisionmaking." *Id.* at 1121. Without *Chevron*, Professor Strauss suggested, lower federal courts might persistently disagree with each other about the best answer to interpretive questions that Congress had not clearly resolved, with the result that federal statutes would be administered differently in different parts of the country. *See id.* By contrast, Professor Strauss argued, a default rule encouraging each federal court to accept reasonable interpretations adopted by the head or central board of the typical federal administrative agency increases the chances of "national uniformity in the administration of national statutes." *Id.*

Assuming that this sort of national uniformity is desirable, Professors Strauss's argument might seem to supply an additional argument in favor of the *Chevron* doctrine. Still, the force of that argument depends on how agencies react to *Chevron*. If agencies know that courts give them substantial leeway in matters of statutory interpretation, agencies might adopt more aggressive positions that advance the current administration's policy goals but that are only arguably consistent with the relevant statutory constraints. *See* Brett M. Kavanaugh, *Fixing Statutory Interpretation*, 129 HARV. L. REV. 2118, 2150–51 (2016) (book review) (arguing that "*Chevron* encourages the Executive Branch (whichever party controls it) to be extremely aggressive in seeking to squeeze its policy goals into ill-fitting statutory authorizations and restraints," with the result that "agencies in both Republican and Democratic administrations too often pursue policy at the expense of law"). To the extent that agencies push the envelope of "reasonable" interpretation, courts reviewing the agencies' positions under *Chevron* will again face hard questions on which different judges will reach different conclusions. If *Chevron* changes how agencies themselves behave, then, it will not necessarily create greater uniformity in the lower courts' decisions. What is more, the agencies' own positions might swing dramatically from one administration to the next, causing the same statute to be interpreted in very different ways in different four-year periods. *See* Richard J. Pierce, Jr., *The Combination of* Chevron *and Political Polarity Has Awful Effects*, 70 DUKE L.J. ONLINE 91 (2021). This extra instability might have worse consequences than the geographic disuniformity that Professor Strauss discussed. *See id.* at 103.

5. In *INS v. Cardoza-Fonseca*, 480 U.S. 421 (1987), Justice Stevens sought to cabin the principle of deference that he had articulated in *Chevron*. As amended by the Refugee Act of 1980, the Immigration and Nationality Act gave the Attorney General discretion to grant asylum to certain "refugee[s]," defined to include people who were unable or unwilling to return to the country of their nationality "because of . . . a well-founded fear of persecution on account of race, religion, nationality, membership in a particular social group, or political opinion." Refugee Act of 1980, Pub. L. 96–212, sec. 201, §§ 101(a)(42)(A), 208(a), 94 Stat. 102, 102, 105. In an adjudicative proceeding, the responsible agency understood the phrase "well-founded fear" to trigger the same demanding standard of proof as a separate statutory provision that forbade the Attorney General to "deport or return any alien . . . to a country if the Attorney General determines that such alien's life or freedom would be threatened in such country" on account of any of the listed characteristics. *Id.* sec. 203(e), § 243(h)(1), 94 Stat. at 107; *see also* INS v. Stevic, 467 U.S. 407, 429–30 (1984) (holding that under the latter provision, "the governing standard . . . requires . . . evidence establishing that it is more likely than not that the alien would be subject to persecution on one of the specified grounds"). But the Supreme Court disagreed that the two standards were the same. *See, e.g.*, *Cardoza-Fonseca*, 480 U.S. at 431 ("One can certainly have a well-founded fear of an event happening when there is less than a 50% chance of the occurrence taking place.").

In response to the agency's claim of *Chevron* deference, Justice Stevens's majority opinion asserted that "whether Congress intended the two standards to be identical is a pure question of statutory construction for the courts to decide." *Id.* at 446. For purposes of the *Chevron* framework, Justice Stevens suggested, "[t]he narrow legal question whether the two standards are the same is . . . quite different from the question of interpretation that arises in each case in which the agency is required to apply either or both standards to a particular set of facts." The latter sort of question would indeed trigger *Chevron* deference: "There is obviously some ambiguity in a term like 'well-founded fear' which can only be given concrete meaning through a process of case-by-case adjudication," and on such matters *Chevron* required the courts to "respect the interpretation of the agency to which Congress has delegated the responsibility for administering the statutory program." *Id.* at 448. According to Justice Stevens, however, the pure question of law at issue in *Cardoza-Fonseca* was "well within the province of the Judiciary." *Id.*; *see also id.* at 446 ("Employing traditional tools of statutory construction, we have concluded that Congress did not intend the two standards to be identical."). On this view, the *Chevron* framework simply does not reach "pure question[s] of statutory construction" (or at least pure questions of statutory construction that lend themselves to traditional legal analysis).

Notwithstanding the fact that Justice Stevens expressed this idea in a majority opinion, a majority of the Justices may not really have embraced it. Justice Scalia rejected it from the start. *See id.* at 454 (Scalia, J., concurring in the judgment) (protesting what he saw as "an evisceration of *Chevron*").[14] Within less than a year, moreover, another majority opinion seemed to domesticate *Cardoza-Fonseca* by treating it as a "Step One" case. *See* NLRB v. United Food & Commercial Workers Union, 484 U.S. 112, 123 (1987) ("On a pure question of statutory construction, our first job is to try to determine congressional intent, using 'traditional tools of statutory construction.' If we can do that, then that interpretation must be given effect . . . . [*Cardoza-Fonseca*, 480 U.S.] at 446–448. . . . However, where 'the statute is silent or ambiguous with respect to the specific issue, the question for the court is whether the agency's answer is based on a permissible construction of the statute.' [*Chevron*, 467 U.S.] at 843."); *see also* THOMAS W. MERRILL, THE *CHEVRON* DOCTRINE: ITS RISE AND FALL, AND THE FUTURE OF THE ADMINISTRATIVE STATE 93 (2022) ("Over time, *Cardoz[a]-Fonseca* faded from view . . . .").

---

[14] Justice Scalia concurred in the judgment, rather than dissenting, because he thought that the agency's interpretation was contrary to the plain meaning of the statutory language. In other words, Justice Scalia believed that the *Chevron* framework applied with full force to the relevant question, but he concluded that the agency's position failed at Step One.

Still, Justice Stevens himself continued to advocate distinctions along the lines that he had suggested in *Cardoza-Fonseca*. In *Negusie v. Holder*, 555 U.S. 511 (2009), his separate opinion (joined by Justice Breyer) noted that "statutory interpretation is a multifaceted enterprise, ranging from a precise construction of statutory language to a determination of what policy best effectuates statutory objectives." *Id.* at 529 (Stevens, J., concurring in part and dissenting in part). In Justice Stevens's view, courts and agencies should not be presumed to have the same relationship across all these different tasks. Instead, "[c]ertain aspects of statutory interpretation remain within the purview of the courts, even when the statute is not entirely clear, while others are properly understood as delegated by Congress to an expert and accountable administrative body." *Id.* at 531; *see also id.* at 533 ("*Chevron* deference need not be an all-or-nothing venture.").

Justice Stevens acknowledged that his proposed distinctions could be formulated in different ways. "In cases involving agency adjudication," he noted, "we have sometimes described the court's role as deciding pure questions of statutory construction and the agency's role as applying law to fact." *Id.* at 531 (citing *Cardoza-Fonseca*). Similarly, "[i]n the context of agency rulemaking, . . . we might distinguish between pure questions of statutory interpretation and policymaking, or between central legal issues and interstitial questions." *Id.* (citing *Barnhart v. Walton*, 535 U.S. 212, 222 (2002)). In both contexts, though, Justice Stevens was trying to get at the same basic point. In his words, "The *Chevron* framework . . . accounts for the different institutional competencies of agencies and courts: Courts are expert at statutory construction, while agencies are expert at statutory implementation." *Id.* at 530.

That distinction has some intuitive appeal. When Congress authorizes an administrative agency to act with the force of law in implementing a statute, whether through case-by-case adjudication or by promulgating regulations designed to carry out Congress's broad purposes, one might well presume that Congress is authorizing the agency to make certain kinds of judgment calls involving what Justice Stevens called "statutory implementation." By contrast, one might expect courts to have a larger role with respect to at least some pure questions of law—questions of the sort that courts handle every day and that do not implicate the agency's special "institutional competencies." But is it possible to draw this contrast in a way that can be operationalized, or will efforts along these lines just produce a muddle?

What sort of question did *Chevron* itself involve? The case boiled down to the meaning of the phrase "major stationary sources" in § 172(b)(6) of the Clean Air Act (as added by the Clean Air Act Amendments of 1977, Pub. L. 95–95, 91 Stat. 685, 747): could EPA read that phrase to refer to factories as a whole, or did each pollution-emitting device within the factory count as a separate "stationary source"? That seems like a pure question of statutory construction. According to Justice

Stevens's opinion in *Chevron*, though, it is not one that conventional interpretive techniques answered; the statutory text was genuinely indeterminate, and neither the legislative history nor relevant canons resolved the indeterminacy. Under the circumstances, picking one interpretation over the other required policy trade-offs of the sort that the responsible agency might be better positioned than the courts to make. *See, e.g.*, MERRILL, *supra*, at 56–58 (describing the crux of the policy dispute in *Chevron*).

To the extent that the *Chevron* framework does extend to pure questions of statutory construction, should courts apply Step One in such a way that agencies receive deference only in situations like *Chevron* itself—that is, where the traditional tools of interpretation leave courts near equipoise and where picking an answer requires judgment calls that do not play to courts' strengths? If the resolution of a hard question of statutory construction depends on which policies will best promote the statute's purposes, or how far to take one purpose at the expense of another, agencies might deserve deference because of their superior expertise and political accountability. Agencies' expertise may also justify deference when a question involves the meaning of a technical term of art, or the proper way to fit a particular provision into the rest of the statutory scheme. On such questions, if the court agrees that the issue is close, perhaps the agency's answer often is more likely to be correct—even if the court is inclined to think that the agency has adopted the inferior view, and even if the agency's explanation does not change the court's mind.

But what if the dispute boils down to a question about the implications of grammar and syntax, or about how to apply generic principles of statutory interpretation? With respect to many such questions, judges may be more expert than the lawyers who work for a federal administrative agency. And while the agency has an accountability advantage over the courts, its decisionmakers are less directly accountable to the electorate than members of Congress themselves. If the dispute between court and agency boils down to a disagreement about generic principles of interpretation, and if those principles lead the court to believe that Congress probably meant to establish Directive #1, do accountability-based reasons really support giving the agency discretion to enforce Directive #2 instead?

This analysis suggests that when an agency's interpretive authority rests only on *Chevron*'s default rule (rather than more specific indications of congressional intent to make agency interpretations binding on the courts), courts might consider adjusting the trigger for *Chevron* deference according to the nature of the question in dispute. With respect to interpretive questions that do not implicate the agency's special expertise, perhaps the agency's superior accountability justifies deference if, but only if, the court thinks that the competing arguments are close to equipoise. With respect to interpretive questions that do implicate the agency's expertise, but on which the agency might not be able to educate courts enough to appreciate why the agency's answer is better than the alternatives, perhaps courts should have a more forgiving test for indeterminacy, so that the agency will enjoy more interpretive freedom.

Again, though, even if this approach sounds good in theory, could it be put into practice? Would the line-drawing that it requires invite error and confusion? Should courts conclude that trying to make the *Chevron* canon so fine-grained will do more harm than good, and that a blunter canon is preferable notwithstanding its potential overbreadth?

6. Does the *Chevron* framework shed light on what courts do when no agency is in the picture? According to the Supreme Court, *Chevron* reflects the fact that "the resolution of ambiguity in a statutory text is often more a question of policy than of law." *Pauley v. BethEnergy Mines, Inc.*, 501 U.S. 680, 696 (1991). Would the Court emphasize the same point in cases where the Court (rather than an agency) is resolving an ambiguity? If not, is that simply a sign that when judges are resolving ambiguities themselves, they are not so candid or self-conscious about the policymaking dimension of their decision? Or is the decisionmaking process itself more policy-oriented when agencies are in charge than when courts are?

7. Whether courts think of agencies' authority under *Chevron* as primarily interpretive or as primarily creative may have implications for various aspects of *Chevron* deference, including its temporal effect. Imagine the following sequence. At Time 1, Congress enacts a statute that contains various provisions and that also gives an agency administrative authority with respect to those provisions (including the authority to make substantive rules). One of the statute's provisions is "ambiguous" in the *Chevron* sense; it could permissibly be given either Interpretation #1 or Interpretation #2. At Time 2, before the agency has weighed in on the provision's meaning, a private business engages in activity that would be legal under Interpretation #1 but that Interpretation #2 would forbid. At Time 3, the agency authoritatively expresses its support for Interpretation #2 through notice-and-comment rulemaking.[15] At Time 4, a court has to adjudicate a private plaintiff's

[15] The fact that the agency has acted through rulemaking rather than adjudication is an important feature of this hypothetical. When Congress has delegated adjudicative authority to a *Chevron*-qualified agency, and when the agency interprets the relevant statutory provision as part of a formal adjudication, courts conducting direct judicial review of the agency's order are likely to use the *Chevron* framework to test the validity of the agency's interpretation, and they might well allow the agency to apply its interpretation in the matter at hand even though the agency had not announced its interpretation at the time of the underlying events.

To be sure, that approach can be criticized. *See* Abner S. Greene, *Adjudicative Retroactivity in Administrative Law*, 1991 SUP. CT. REV. 261, 278 ("If a question of statutory interpretation is resolvable only at [*Chevron* Step Two], as a matter of agency policy choice, of agency lawmaking, then in keeping with the norm against legislative retroactivity, we should not allow the announced rule to apply retroactively."); *see also* De Niz Robles v. Lynch, 803 F.3d 1165 (10th Cir. 2015) (Gorsuch, J.) (endorsing Greene's view at least when the agency's action departs from judicial precedents that were in place before the agency weighed in); *cf.* Reyes v. Garland,

lawsuit against the business for allegedly violating the statute at Time 2. (Assume that some source of law gives the plaintiff a private cause of action for damages if the business really did violate the statute.) If the interpretation adopted by the agency at Time 3 is permissible, should the court simply accept that interpretation and apply it in the private lawsuit, even though the events relevant to that lawsuit occurred before the agency weighed in? Or should the court instead follow its own best understanding of the law as it stood at Time 2?

When no agency is in the picture, courts routinely apply their own interpretations of ambiguous statutes to events that occurred before the courts announced those interpretations. *Cf.* James B. Beam Distilling Co. v. Georgia, 501 U.S. 529, 549 (1991) (Scalia, J., concurring in the judgment) (acknowledging that "judges in a real sense 'make' law," but emphasizing that "they make it *as judges make it*, which is to say *as though* they were 'finding' it"). If one thinks of agencies as performing the same function as courts, one might think that an agency's authoritative interpretation of a statute should have the same sort of backward-looking effect as a judicial interpretation—and that the court in our hypothetical situation therefore *should* simply follow what the agency now says the statute means. In *Smiley v. Citibank (South Dakota), N.A.*, 517 U.S. 735 (1996), a footnote in Justice Scalia's majority opinion endorsed this view. *See id.* at 744 n.3 (indicating that in situations like our hypothetical, "it would be absurd to ignore the agency's current authoritative pronouncement of what the statute means").

But what if one thinks of the agency's action at Time 3 as being less like interpretation and more like lawmaking? When Congress gives agencies substantive rulemaking authority, the Supreme Court ordinarily presumes that Congress is *not* giving the agencies power to make their rules "retroactive." *See* Bowen v. Georgetown Univ. Hosp., 488 U.S. 204, 208 (1988) ("[A] statutory grant of legislative rulemaking authority will not, as a general matter, be understood to encompass the power to promulgate retroactive rules unless that power is conveyed by Congress in express terms."). On one view, *Chevron* rests on a presumed delegation of a similar sort of policymaking authority: When Congress enacts an ambiguous statutory provision and puts an agency in charge of "administering" the provision in the relevant sense, it is as if Congress has explicitly listed all the directives that the provision might permissibly be understood to establish and has delegated to the agency the substantive authority to choose from that array of directives. If one associates *Chevron* with the delegation of this sort of substantive authority, one might presume that the delegation comes with the same temporal restriction that *Bowen v. Georgetown University Hospital*

11 F.4th 985, 991–92 (9th Cir. 2021) (taking a case-by-case approach to the retroactive application of newly articulated "adjudicatory rules"). But because these issues relate to the circumstances in which agencies can make policy through adjudication rather than through rulemaking, they are best discussed in Administrative Law rather than in this course.

identified. *See* Health Ins. Ass'n of Am. v. Shalala, 23 F.3d 412, 422–25 (D.C. Cir. 1994) (so arguing).

Whether you gravitate toward Justice Scalia's footnote in *Smiley* or toward this competing view may depend on how you characterize the agency's authority. When an agency authoritatively glosses a statute in a manner that qualifies for *Chevron* deference, should judges analogize the agency's gloss to a judicial precedent announced by a court above them in the judicial hierarchy? Or should judges instead think of the agency's gloss in the way that they would think of a supplemental (and nonretroactive) statute—something that applies to events occurring after it comes into force, but that does not attach new legal consequences to prior transactions?

As we shall see later in this chapter (and as *Chevron* itself demonstrates), agencies themselves need not treat their own decisions in the same way that courts treat judicial precedents; the concept of administrative *stare decisis* is weaker than the concept of judicial *stare decisis*, and so agencies have considerable leeway to change their minds about the proper interpretation of a statutory provision. *See infra* p. 926, pp. 993–994. Does that fact bear on the questions raised in this note?[16]

8. For most of his tenure on the Supreme Court (which started two years after the Court decided *Chevron*), Justice Scalia took a broad view of the applicability of the *Chevron* framework. In case after case involving what we would now call "Step Zero," Justice Scalia favored applying the framework even when some of his colleagues did not. Admittedly, he suggested that the *Chevron* framework would result in less deference when applied by textualists like him than when applied by purposivists, because textualists allegedly see more clarity in statutes and hence resolve more cases at Step One. *See* Scalia, *supra* note 16, 1989 DUKE L.J. at 521; *cf.* MERRILL, *supra*, at 117 (calling Justice Scalia "the Court's most enthusiastic proponent of the *Chevron* doctrine but also one of its less deferential Justices"). But where he agreed that a statute's language

[16] In his 1989 essay about *Chevron*, Justice Scalia suggested that when an agency changed its interpretation of an ambiguous statute so as to shift from one permissible construction to another, the agency was not "admitting that it had 'got the law wrong' " the first time. Instead, he wrote, "the agency was simply 'changing the law,' in light of new information or even new social attitudes impressed upon it through the political process—all within the limited range of discretion to 'change the law' conferred by the governing statute." Antonin Scalia, *Judicial Deference to Administrative Interpretations of Law*, 1989 DUKE L.J. 511, 518–19.

Isn't this way of thinking in tension with Justice Scalia's footnote in *Smiley*? To bring out this point, we can modify the hypothetical discussed above. Suppose that immediately after Congress enacts the statute at Time 1, the agency authoritatively endorses Interpretation #1. At Time 2, a business subject to the statute acts in a manner that Interpretation #1 would permit. But at Time 3, the agency changes its mind and authoritatively endorses Interpretation #2. In a separate lawsuit at Time 4, a court must adjudicate a private claim for damages against the business that acted at Time 2. How, if at all, should the court apply the *Chevron* framework in this situation? In trying to identify the legal duties to which the business was subject at Time 2 (when the events relevant to the suit occurred), should the court apply the *Chevron* framework to the administrative interpretation that was then in force (Interpretation #1), or should the court instead apply the *Chevron* framework to what the agency is now authoritatively saying the relevant provision means (Interpretation #2)?

was unclear, Justice Scalia seemed to think that the resulting discretion should be exercised by administering agencies rather than courts.

A number of the cases mentioned above illustrate Justice Scalia's views about Step Zero. For example, in *INS v. Cardoza-Fonseca*, 480 U.S. 421 (1987), Justice Scalia rejected Justice Stevens's distinction between pure questions of statutory construction and questions of statutory implementation; Justice Scalia indicated that the *Chevron* framework applied equally to both. *See id.* at 454–55 (Scalia, J., concurring in the judgment). Likewise, in *United States v. Mead Corp.*, 533 U.S. 218 (2001), Justice Scalia wrote a solo dissent advocating a very loose view of the types of agency pronouncements that can trigger the *Chevron* framework. *See id.* at 257–58 (Scalia, J., dissenting) (arguing that any statement "that represents the official position of the agency" should be enough); *accord* Christensen v. Harris County, 529 U.S. 576, 591 (2000) (Scalia, J., concurring in part and concurring in the judgment).

Soon after his appointment to the Court, Justice Scalia also tangled with Justice Brennan about whether administering agencies should receive *Chevron* deference on questions about the scope of the agencies' own authority. Justice Brennan argued that the *Chevron* framework did not apply to statutory provisions that limited the agency's "jurisdiction." *See* Miss. Power & Light Co. v. Mississippi ex rel. Moore, 487 U.S. 354, 386–87 (1988) (Brennan, J., dissenting). Justice Scalia responded that the Court had already applied *Chevron* to such questions; in his view, "it is settled law that the rule of deference applies even to an agency's interpretation of its own statutory authority or jurisdiction." *Id.* at 381 (Scalia, J., concurring in the judgment). According to Justice Scalia, moreover, the contrary position made little sense; *all* questions about the meaning of statutory provisions that an agency administers can be recast as questions about limits on the agency's authority, so Justice Brennan's proposed distinction would be murky and impractical. *See id.*

The full Court did not resolve this issue for another quarter-century. But in *City of Arlington v. FCC*, 569 U.S. 290 (2013), Justice Scalia assembled a majority for his view. According to his opinion for the Court, "an agency's interpretation of a statutory ambiguity that concerns the scope of its regulatory authority (that is, its jurisdiction)" is entitled to *Chevron* deference to the same extent as the agency's resolution of other statutory ambiguities. *Id.* at 293, 301–05. Of course, courts presumably should exercise independent judgment about whether Congress has indeed given an agency the sort of authority that satisfies Step Zero, just as courts must exercise independent judgment about whether a statutory provision is "ambiguous" for purposes of Step One and the range of interpretations that are "permissible" for purposes of Step Two. But Justice Scalia held that if a statute contains general language empowering the agency to make substantive rules to carry out the statute's provisions, the agency can press those provisions as far as any ambiguities in them "fairly allow," and reviewing courts should not "puzzle over whether the interpretive question presented is 'jurisdictional.'" *See id.* at 301.

By contrast, Chief Justice Roberts's dissent argued that "we do not defer to an agency's interpretation of an ambiguous provision unless Congress wants us to," and a general grant of rulemaking power does not automatically imply that Congress wants the agency to have "interpretive authority" with respect to each and every ambiguity in the statute. *Id.* at 322–24 (Roberts, C.J., dissenting). Instead, courts should determine on an ambiguity-by-ambiguity basis "whether Congress . . . has in fact delegated to the agency lawmaking power over the ambiguity at issue." *Id.* at 317.

Although Chief Justice Roberts cast his position as consistent with the Supreme Court's precedents, he seemed to be asking a more fine-grained question than the Court often had. At least according to the commentators cited in note 3 above, *Chevron* and its progeny articulate a *presumption* that operates in the absence of contrary guidance from Congress, and the content of that presumption reflects the Supreme Court's own ideas about the comparative institutional advantages of judges and administrative agencies. To the extent that Chief Justice Roberts was looking for an *actual* delegation of "interpretive authority" rather than simply a *presumed* delegation, his approach could be seen as a beefed up version of Step Zero, which would have the potential to reduce the applicability of *Chevron* deference pretty dramatically.

9. Toward the end of his life, Justice Scalia may have been rethinking his enthusiasm for *Chevron*. At a minimum, he changed his mind on the related question of whether courts should defer to agencies about the meaning of the agencies' own regulations. *Compare* Auer v. Robbins, 519 U.S. 452 (1997) (Scalia, J.) (granting broad deference), *with* Decker v. Nw. Env't Def. Ctr., 568 U.S. 597, 616–21 (2013) (Scalia, J., concurring in part and dissenting in part) (calling for *Auer* to be overruled, though distinguishing it from *Chevron*); *see also infra* Chapter 5.C (covering *Auer*). In 2015, moreover, he described the Court as having developed the *Chevron* doctrine "[h]eedless of the original design of the [Administrative Procedure Act]" (which, in his view, "contemplates that courts, not agencies, will authoritatively resolve ambiguities in statutes and regulations").[17] *Perez v. Mtge. Bankers Ass'n*, 575 U.S. 92, 109–10 (2015) (Scalia, J., concurring in the judgment); *see also* Brett M. Kavanaugh, *Fixing Statutory Interpretation*, 129 HARV. L. REV. 2118, 2150 n.161 (2016) (book review) ("[I]f anything, *Chevron* seems to flout the language of the Act."); *supra* p. 874 & n.10.

Justice Thomas has agreed that *Chevron* deference "is likely contrary to the APA." *Baldwin v. United States*, 140 S. Ct. 690, 692 (2020) (Thomas, J., dissenting from the denial of certiorari). But even if a federal

[17] Justice Scalia had previously expressed a more muted version of this point. *See Mead*, 533 U.S. at 241 (Scalia, J., dissenting) ("There is some question whether *Chevron* was faithful to the text of the Administrative Procedure Act (APA), which it did not even bother to cite.").

statute explicitly adopted the *Chevron* doctrine, Justice Thomas has suggested that the statute would be unconstitutional. In a separate opinion from 2015, he argued that "*Chevron* deference raises serious separation-of-powers questions." *Michigan v. EPA*, 576 U.S. 743, 761 (2015) (Thomas, J., concurring). On one way of thinking, *Chevron* entails "an allocation of interpretive authority" to agencies—in which case, Justice Thomas argued, it would be "in tension with Article III's Vesting Clause, which vests the judicial power exclusively in Article III courts, not administrative agencies." *Id.* at 761–62; *see also id.* at 761 ("*Chevron* deference wrests from Courts the ultimate interpretative authority to 'say what the law is,' *Marbury v. Madison*, 1 Cranch 137, 177 (1803), and hands it over to the Executive."). On another way of thinking, when agencies resolve statutory "ambiguity," they "typically are not engaged in acts of interpretation at all," but rather "are engaged in the ' "formulation of policy." ' " *Id.* at 762 (quoting *Chevron*, 467 U.S. at 843, in turn quoting *Morton v. Ruiz*, 415 U.S. 199, 231 (1974)). But Justice Thomas suggested that giving agencies this sort of policymaking authority would violate the nondelegation doctrine and the idea that Article I of the Constitution vests all of the federal government's "legislative Powers" in Congress. According to Justice Thomas, "if we give the 'force of law' to agency pronouncements on matters of private conduct as to which ' "Congress did not actually have an intent," ' *Mead*, [533 U.S.] at 229, we permit a body other than Congress to perform a function that requires an exercise of the legislative power." *Id.*

In several opinions both before and after his appointment to the Supreme Court, Justice Gorsuch has elaborated on these arguments. *See, e.g.*, Buffington v. McDonough, 143 S. Ct. 14 (2022) (Gorsuch, J., dissenting from denial of certiorari); Gutierrez-Brizuela v. Lynch, 834 F.3d 1142 (10th Cir. 2016) (Gorsuch, J., concurring). Still, neither argument is airtight. The fact that the federal government's "judicial" power is vested in the federal courts obviously does not mean that no one else can interpret statutes. *See* William N. Eskridge, Jr., *Expanding* Chevron*'s Domain: A Comparative Institutional Analysis of the Relative Competence of Courts and Agencies to Interpret Statutes*, 2013 WIS. L. REV. 411, 416 ("Administrators and agencies interpret statutes all the time . . . ."). Once an administrative agency has announced its interpretation of a statute, moreover, Article III surely does not *always* prevent courts from deferring to that interpretation. At a minimum, Article III presumably does not prevent courts from deferring to agencies as part of the courts' own strategy for arriving at the right answer—as in situations where the courts conclude that deference is warranted based on the agencies' superior expertise. In any event, to the extent that Congress can give agencies the power to make law, one need not speak in terms of "deference" at all; the rules that agencies validly make within their delegated authority would themselves have the force of law, and courts exercising their "judicial" power would need to respect them accordingly. *See* Henry P. Monaghan, Marbury *and the Administrative*

State, 83 COLUM. L. REV. 1, 26 (1983) ("Judicial deference to agency 'interpretation' of law is simply one way of recognizing a delegation of law-making authority to an agency." (emphasis omitted)). On this way of thinking, the key constitutional questions boil down to the nondelegation doctrine, not Article III. Under current understandings of the nondelegation doctrine, moreover, the type of authority that *Chevron* entails usually would not come anywhere close to the constitutional line; the statutes that agencies administer give the agencies "intelligible principle[s]" about how to exercise their authority, and that is all that the nondelegation doctrine is said to require. *See supra* pp. 852–853. One would have to beef up the nondelegation doctrine very substantially before *Chevron* would run afoul of it.

Even if the *Chevron* doctrine is not unconstitutional, though, it might not be a good idea, or at least it might be improvable. *Cf.* MERRILL, *supra*, at 257–73 (sketching one view of "what a better doctrine might look like"). A few months before this book went to press, the Supreme Court granted certiorari on the question of whether to overrule *Chevron*. *See* Loper Bright Enters. v. Raimondo, 143 S. Ct. 2429 (2023). Should the Court do so?

NOTE ON THE "MAJOR QUESTIONS" DOCTRINE

In 1986, then-Judge Stephen Breyer of the U.S. Court of Appeals for the First Circuit published an article that addressed the circumstances in which courts might defer to an administrative agency's interpretation of a statute. Largely on the basis of pre-*Chevron* cases, he observed that courts had made context-specific judgments on this topic, deferring to agencies on some questions but not others. He listed considerations that had mattered to the courts, including "whe[ther] the agency has special expertise that it can bring to bear on the legal question," "whether the words of the statute are phrased so broadly as to invite agency interpretation," and "whether the agency can be trusted to give a properly balanced answer" or instead "suffer[s] from 'tunnel vision.'" Stephen Breyer, *Judicial Review of Questions of Law and Policy*, 38 ADMIN. L. REV. 363, 370–71 (1986). As part of his list, Judge Breyer observed: "A court may also ask whether the legal question is an important one. Congress is more likely to have focused upon, and answered, major questions, while leaving interstitial matters to answer themselves in the course of the statute's daily administration." *Id.* at 370.[18]

[18] Judge Breyer made similar comments in opinions that he wrote for the First Circuit. In several opinions issued soon after *Chevron*, he discussed the circumstances in which courts might defer to an agency on the theory that Congress had implicitly "delegat[ed] . . . a law-declaring function" to the agency with respect to the question at issue. *St. Luke's Hosp. v. Sec'y of Health & Human Servs.*, 810 F.2d 325, 331 (1st Cir. 1987). On the basis of imaginative reconstruction, he asserted that "[t]he less important the question of law, the more interstitial its character, [and] the more closely related to the everyday administration of the statute and to the agency's (rather than the court's) administrative or substantive expertise, the less likely it is that Congress (would have) 'wished' or 'expected' the courts to remain indifferent to the

Judge Breyer went on to discuss the import of the Supreme Court's then-recent opinion in *Chevron*. In his view, that opinion was not necessarily inconsistent with "the complex approach" that courts had previously taken. *Id.* at 373. To be sure, he acknowledged that *Chevron* could be read to embrace "a considerably simpler approach," under which courts would proceed in just two steps: "first decide whether the statute is 'silent or ambiguous with respect to the specific issue' and, if so, accept the agency's interpretation if (in light of statutory purposes) it is 'reasonable.'" *Id.* But while this reading of *Chevron* had already been adopted by the U.S. Court of Appeals for the D.C. Circuit, Judge Breyer asserted that it "seems unlikely in the long run[ ] to replace the complex approach described above." In his view,

> "[T]here are too many different types of circumstances, including different statutes, different kinds of application, different substantive regulatory or administrative problems, and different legal postures in which cases arrive, to allow 'proper' judicial attitudes about questions of law to be reduced to any single simple verbal formula. . . . To read *Chevron* as laying down a blanket rule, applicable to all agency interpretations of law, such as 'always defer to the agency when the statute is silent,' would be seriously overbroad, counterproductive and sometimes senseless."

Id.

Judge Breyer was writing at a time of transition. When *Chevron* was decided, the Supreme Court did not see the case as establishing a new foundation for administrative law. *See* Thomas W. Merrill, *The Story of* Chevron*: The Making of an Accidental Landmark*, 66 ADMIN. L. REV. 253, 275–76 (2014). Within the D.C. Circuit, though, the two-step framework articulated at the start of Part II of Justice Stevens's opinion quickly became "boilerplate doctrine," which could operate without regard to earlier, more contextual approaches. *See id.* at 278. Aided by executive-branch lawyers who saw its usefulness to their positions, this version of *Chevron* eventually "migrat[ed] back to the Supreme Court." *Id.* at 282; *see also* Gary Lawson & Stephen Karn, *Making Law out of Nothing at All: The Origins of the* Chevron *Doctrine*, 65 ADMIN. L. REV. 1, 39 (2013) (noting that the D.C. Circuit is "the leading court in shaping administrative law doctrine" and describing it as "the source of the *Chevron* doctrine").

Thus, Judge Breyer turned out to be wrong that the D.C. Circuit's take on *Chevron* would fade away. In recent years, though, one of the factors that he listed as part of his more complex approach has roared back into focus. This Note traces the development of the so-called "major questions doctrine."

---

agency's views." *Mayburg v. Sec'y of Health & Human Servs.*, 740 F.2d 100, 106 (1st Cir. 1984); *see also id.* ("Conversely, the larger the question, the more its answer is likely to clarify or stabilize a broad area of law, the more likely Congress intended the courts to decide the question themselves.").

We can start with ***FDA v. Brown & Williamson Tobacco Corp.***, 529 U.S. 120 (2000). As enacted in 1906, the federal Pure Food and Drug Act had used the term "drug" to refer to "medicines and preparations recognized in the United States Pharmacopoeia or National Formulary . . . and any substance or mixture of substances intended to be used for the cure, mitigation, or prevention of disease of either man or other animals." Act of June 30, 1906, ch. 3915, § 6, 34 Stat. 768, 769. In 1938, the Food, Drug, and Cosmetic Act broadened this definition to include "articles (other than food) intended to affect the structure or any function of the body of man or other animals." Act of June 25, 1938, ch. 675, § 201(g), 52 Stat. 1040, 1041 (codified at 21 U.S.C. § 321(g)(1)). For many years, the administering agency—the federal Food and Drug Administration (FDA)—maintained that tobacco did not meet the statutory definition of a "drug" unless it was marketed with "therapeutic claims." *See, e.g.*, Letter from FDA Bureau of Enforcement to Directors of Bureaus, Divisions and Districts (May 24, 1963), quoted in *Brown & Williamson*, 529 U.S. at 145. In 1996, however, the agency changed course: it determined that the nicotine in cigarettes and chewing tobacco is a "drug" within the meaning of the 1938 statute and that cigarettes and chewing tobacco are what the statute calls "devices" for the delivery of a drug. Pursuant to this determination, the agency issued an initial set of regulations prohibiting the sale of cigarettes and chewing tobacco to minors, requiring retailers to get photo identification from all purchasers younger than 27, and restricting the kinds of marketing campaigns that manufacturers could use.

In *Brown & Williamson*, the Supreme Court held that the agency did not have the authority to regulate tobacco products as customarily marketed. As we shall see in Chapter 7, the Court's conclusion relied heavily on a series of tobacco-specific statutes that Congress had enacted from 1965 on, at a time when the FDA was disclaiming any role in the regulation of tobacco products. Justice O'Connor's majority opinion took those statutes to occupy the relevant field and to preclude any future regulatory role for the FDA.

But the Court also advanced a separate reason to reject the FDA's claim of regulatory authority. According to the Court, *if* the FDA were correct that cigarettes and chewing tobacco qualified as "devices" within the meaning of the 1938 statute, then the statute would ultimately oblige the FDA to ban them. *See Brown & Williamson*, 529 U.S. at 133, 140 (asserting that "one of the Act's core objectives is to ensure that any product regulated by the FDA is 'safe' . . . for its intended use," in the sense that "the product's probable therapeutic benefits must outweigh its risk of harm"); *id.* at 135 (arguing that the FDA's own findings about the dangers of smoking "logically imply that, if tobacco products were 'devices' under the [Food, Drug, and Cosmetic Act], the FDA would be required to remove them from the market"). As the Court noted, though, it would have been a big deal in 1938 (and remains a big deal today) to authorize the FDA to regulate cigarettes and to direct the FDA to make determinations that could result in the prohibition of tobacco products. For the majority, that fact affected the proper application of the *Chevron* framework, but Justice O'Connor was imprecise about exactly how. Here is what she wrote:

> "[O]ur inquiry into whether Congress has directly spoken to the precise question at issue is shaped, at least in some measure, by the nature of the question presented. Deference under *Chevron* to an agency's construction of a statute that it administers is premised on the theory that a statute's ambiguity constitutes an implicit delegation from Congress to the agency to fill in the statutory gaps. See *Chevron*, [467 U.S.] at 844. In extraordinary cases, however, there may be reason to hesitate before concluding that Congress has intended such an implicit delegation. Cf. Breyer, Judicial Review of Questions of Law and Policy, 38 Admin. L. Rev. 363, 370 (1986) ('A court may also ask whether the legal question is an important one. Congress is more likely to have focused upon, and answered, major questions, while leaving interstitial matters to answer themselves in the course of the statute's daily administration.').
>
> "This is hardly an ordinary case. Contrary to its representations to Congress since 1914, the FDA has now asserted jurisdiction to regulate an industry constituting a significant portion of the American economy. In fact, the FDA contends that, were it to determine that tobacco products provide no 'reasonable assurance of safety,' it would have the authority to ban cigarettes and smokeless tobacco entirely. See Brief for Petitioners 35–36 . . . .
>
> "Our decision in *MCI Telecommunications Corp. v. American Telephone & Telegraph Co.*, 512 U.S. 218 (1994), is instructive. That case involved the proper construction of the term 'modify' in § 203(b) of the Communications Act of 1934. The FCC contended that, because the Act gave it the discretion to 'modify any requirement' imposed under the statute, it therefore possessed the authority to render voluntary the otherwise mandatory requirement that long distance carriers file their rates. *Id.* at 225. We rejected the FCC's construction, finding 'not the slightest doubt' that Congress had directly spoken to the question. *Id.* at 228. In reasoning even more apt here, we concluded that '[i]t is highly unlikely that Congress would leave the determination of whether an industry will be entirely, or even substantially, rate-regulated to agency discretion—and even more unlikely that it would achieve that through such a subtle device as permission to "modify" rate-filing requirements.' *Id.* at 231.
>
> "As in *MCI*, we are confident that Congress could not have intended to delegate a decision of such economic and political significance to an agency in so cryptic a fashion . . . ."

Id. at 159–60;[19] *see also id.* at 133 (indicating that when applying *Chevron*, "we must be guided to a degree by common sense as to the manner in which Congress is likely to delegate a policy decision of such economic and political magnitude to an administrative agency").

As Professor Sunstein has noted, this passage can be interpreted in different ways. *See* Cass R. Sunstein, *There Are Two "Major Questions" Doctrines*, 73 ADMIN. L. REV. 475, 481–82, 484 (2021). The basic problem is that Justice O'Connor did not specify the type of "implicit delegation" that she was discussing.

On the one hand, Justice O'Connor might simply have been talking about the sort of authority that *Chevron* normally allocates between courts and administrative agencies. Under *Chevron*, when statutory language is "ambiguous" for purposes of Step One, Congress ordinarily is presumed to have delegated authority to the administering agency to choose from among the "permissible" constructions in a way that binds courts. In *Brown & Williamson*, Justice O'Connor may have been suggesting that this presumption does not extend to "major" questions of statutory interpretation—with the result that courts do not have to accept an administrative agency's answer to such questions, but instead should exercise independent judgment about the best reading of the relevant statutes. On that view, Justice O'Connor's analysis related to what scholars now call Step Zero. To be sure, that terminology did not exist at the time, so she shoehorned her analysis into Step One instead. But now that we are familiar with Step Zero, her point could be recast in those terms: the predicate for *Chevron* deference does not extend to "major questions," and so courts should answer those questions without deference to the relevant agency's position. *See* Sunstein, *supra*, 73 ADMIN. L. REV. at 477 (calling this the "weak version" of the major-questions doctrine, which "suggests a kind of 'carve-out' from *Chevron* deference when a major question is involved").

Rather than just talking about the allocation of *interpretive* authority, though, Justice O'Connor may have been talking about the delegation of *regulatory* authority to administrative agencies. On this view, she was suggesting that if a federal statute is "cryptic" about whether it gives an administrative agency authority to ban cigarettes, or otherwise to assert sweeping power over "an industry constituting a significant portion of the American economy," courts should conclude that the answer is "no": to delegate such important regulatory power to an executive-branch agency, Congress needs to speak more specifically or clearly than it did in the Food, Drug, and Cosmetic Act. *See id.* at 477, 484 (describing this "strong version" of the major-questions doctrine and noting that *Brown & Williamson* could be read to support it); *see also* Cass R. Sunstein, *Nondelegation Canons*, 67 U. CHI. L. REV. 315, 330–35

[19] Despite the majority's invocation of his law-review article, Justice Breyer dissented in *Brown & Williamson*.

(2000) (describing other canons that likewise put certain decisions off limits to agencies in the absence of clear statutory authorization).

A substantive nondelegation canon of this sort would work differently than the "Step Zero" idea. *See* Cass R. Sunstein, Chevron *Step Zero*, 92 VA. L. REV. 187, 244 (2006) ("On this view, *MCI* and *Brown & Williamson* are not Step Zero decisions at all . . . ."). Instead of simply identifying certain important questions of interpretation that courts should answer for themselves, the canon would tell both courts and agencies what the answer is: under whatever circumstances the canon applies, statutes should not be understood to give an agency "major" policymaking authority unless they do so pretty clearly.

The Supreme Court invoked a limited version of this idea in ***Utility Air Regulatory Group v. EPA***, 573 U.S. 302 (2014). Seven years earlier, in *Massachusetts v. EPA*, 549 U.S. 497 (2007), the Court had held that title II of the Clean Air Act (which addresses mobile sources of air pollution) authorizes the Environmental Protection Agency (EPA) to regulate the emission of carbon dioxide and other greenhouse gases from new motor vehicles if EPA determines that such emissions contribute to climate change.[20] The Court had based this conclusion in part on the Act's general definition of "air pollutant," which appears to apply throughout the Act. *See id.* at 528–29 (citing 42 U.S.C. § 7602(g)). In response, EPA not only regulated tailpipe emissions of greenhouse gases, but also concluded that its determinations had implications for stationary sources of greenhouse gases; in EPA's view, the conclusion that greenhouse gases were covered by title II implied that greenhouse gases were also covered by provisions in titles I and V requiring stationary sources to obtain construction and operating permits if they had the potential to emit more than a specified amount of air pollutants each year. As EPA acknowledged, however, reading those provisions to cover greenhouse gases risked dramatically expanding the need for permits; greenhouse gases are emitted in much greater quantities than the pollutants that had previously been thought to trigger these provisions, and even many hotels and office buildings would meet the statutory thresholds. Ultimately, EPA concluded that the permitting requirements do apply to stationary sources of greenhouse gases, but that the statutory thresholds "cannot be applied literally" to such gases. *See* Prevention of Significant Deterioration and Title V Greenhouse Gas Tailoring Rule, 75 Fed. Reg. 31514, 31547–48 (June 3, 2010). EPA therefore issued what it called a

[20] In reaching this conclusion, the Court did not explicitly refer to either version of the major-questions doctrine. Given the posture of the case, though, the "Step Zero" version might not have been relevant; EPA had concluded that the Clean Air Act did *not* give it the authority in question, so the Court did not have to decide whether the normal *Chevron* framework applies when an agency asserts novel or sweeping authority. *Cf. id.* at 527–28 (citing *Chevron* as usual, but concluding that "[t]he statutory text forecloses EPA's reading"). As for the version that disfavors delegations of major policymaking authority, the majority asserted that mere *regulations* of tailpipe emissions were not "such extreme measures" as banning tobacco products, and "there is nothing counterintuitive" about the idea that the Clean Air Act authorizes EPA to "curtail the emission of substances that are putting the global climate out of kilter." *Id.* at 531.

Tailoring Rule so that the permitting requirements would initially operate only for "the largest emitters of [greenhouse gases]." *See id.* at 31516.

In *Utility Air Regulatory Group*, the Supreme Court reviewed EPA's actions. Justice Scalia's majority opinion concluded that notwithstanding *Massachusetts v. EPA*, the agency could not validly treat greenhouse gases as pollutants for purposes of the relevant provisions in titles I and V of the Act. While the majority[21] acknowledged that the presumption of consistent usage ordinarily would support giving the phrase "air pollutant" the same meaning throughout the Act, the majority emphasized that this presumption can be overcome by context. *Utility Air Regulatory Group*, 573 U.S. at 319–20. As a result, "there is no insuperable textual barrier to EPA's interpreting 'any air pollutant' in the permitting triggers of [the relevant provisions in titles I and V] to encompass only pollutants emitted in quantities that enable them to be sensibly regulated at the statutory thresholds, and to exclude those atypical pollutants that, like greenhouse gases, are emitted in such vast quantities that their inclusion would radically transform those programs and render them unworkable as written." *Id.* at 320. To be sure, EPA had not adopted this position, and the Court reviewed EPA's interpretation under the *Chevron* framework. "Even under *Chevron*'s deferential framework," though, the majority concluded that "EPA's interpretation is not permissible." *Id.* at 321. Justice Scalia offered various reasons for that conclusion, but one of those reasons reflected the version of the major-questions doctrine that disfavors delegations of major regulatory authority. Specifically, the majority opinion made the following argument:

> "EPA's interpretation is also unreasonable because it would bring about an enormous and transformative expansion in EPA's regulatory authority without clear congressional authorization. When an agency claims to discover in a long-extant statute an unheralded power to regulate 'a significant portion of the American economy,' *Brown & Williamson*, 529 U.S. at 159, we typically greet its announcement with a measure of skepticism. We expect Congress to speak clearly if it wishes to assign to an agency decisions of vast 'economic and political significance.' *Id.* at 160; [other citations omitted]. The power to require permits for the construction and modification of tens of thousands, and the operation of millions, of small sources nationwide falls comfortably within the class of authorizations that we have been reluctant to read into ambiguous statutory text. Moreover, in EPA's assertion of that authority, we confront a singular situation: an agency laying claim to extravagant statutory power over the national economy while at the same time

[21] For the portion of *Utility Air Regulatory Group* discussed here, the majority consisted of the four Justices who had dissented in *Massachusetts v. EPA* plus Justice Kennedy—the only Justice who was in the majority in both cases.

> strenuously asserting that the authority claimed would render the statute 'unrecognizable to the Congress that designed' it. Tailoring Rule[, 75 Fed. Reg. at 31555]. Since . . . the statute does not compel EPA's interpretation, it would be patently unreasonable—not to say outrageous—for EPA to insist on seizing expansive power that it admits the statute is not designed to grant."

Id. at 324.

The following year, in ***King v. Burwell***, 576 U.S. 473 (2015), the Supreme Court again invoked the major-questions doctrine. This time, though, the Court used the "Step Zero" version. *See* Sunstein, *There Are Two "Major Questions" Doctrines*, 73 ADMIN. L. REV. at 482–83 (contrasting *King* with *Utility Air Regulatory Group*).

King involved the mechanics of the Patient Protection and Affordable Care Act, Pub. L. 111–148, 124 Stat. 119 (2010). Section 1311 of the Act said that "[e]ach State shall . . . establish an American Health Benefit Exchange . . . for the State," which people within the state could use to shop for health insurance. *See id.* § 1311(b)(1), 124 Stat. at 173 (codified at 42 U.S.C. § 18031(b)(1)). Roughly speaking, section 1321 added that if a particular state did not create an Exchange, the federal Secretary of Health and Human Services "shall . . . establish and operate such Exchange within the State." *Id.* § 1321(c)(1), 124 Stat. at 186 (codified at 42 U.S.C. § 18041(c)(1)). Finally, a separate provision that the Act inserted into the Internal Revenue Code gave tax credits to individuals who enrolled in insurance plans through Exchanges. Under the latter provision, though, taxpayers got credits only with respect to premiums for insurance plans in which they had enrolled through "an Exchange established by the State under [section] 1311 of the Patient Protection and Affordable Care Act." *See id.* § 1401(a), 124 Stat. at 213–19 (enacting I.R.C. § 36B). The IRS promulgated a rule interpreting this language to make tax credits available not only to individuals who had enrolled in Exchanges established by states themselves, but also to individuals who had enrolled in Exchanges established by the Secretary of Health and Human Services in the states that had not created their own Exchanges.

In *King*, the Supreme Court was reviewing the IRS's rule, and hence the interpretation of the statute on which it rested. Not one of the Justices called for applying the *Chevron* framework. Chief Justice Roberts's majority opinion provided the following explanation:

> "When analyzing an agency's interpretation of a statute, we often apply the two-step framework announced in *Chevron*, 467 U.S. 837. Under that framework, we ask whether the statute is ambiguous and, if so, whether the agency's interpretation is reasonable. *Id.* at 842–843. This approach 'is premised on the theory that a statute's ambiguity constitutes an implicit delegation from Congress to the agency to fill in the statutory gaps.' *FDA* v. *Brown & Williamson Tobacco Corp.*, 529 U.S. 120, 159 (2000). 'In

> extraordinary cases, however, there may be reason to hesitate before concluding that Congress has intended such an implicit delegation.' *Ibid.*
>
> "This is one of those cases. The tax credits are among the Act's key reforms, involving billions of dollars in spending each year and affecting the price of health insurance for millions of people. Whether those credits are available on Federal Exchanges is thus a question of deep 'economic and political significance' that is central to this statutory scheme; had Congress wished to assign that question to an agency, it surely would have done so expressly. *Utility Air Regulatory Group* v. *EPA*, 573 U.S. 302, 324 (2014) (quoting *Brown & Williamson*, 529 U.S. at 160). It is especially unlikely that Congress would have delegated this decision to the *IRS*, which has no expertise in crafting health insurance policy of this sort. . . . This is not a case for the IRS.
>
> "It is instead our task to determine the correct reading of [the provision that the Act inserted into the Internal Revenue Code]."

King, 576 U.S. at 485–86.

On the merits, though, the Court reached the same conclusion that the IRS had. Based on other aspects of the statute, the majority decided that "the Act may not always use the phrase 'established by the State' in its most natural sense." *Id.* at 488; *see also id.* at 489 (adding that section 1321 can be read as authorizing the Secretary to establish Exchanges "under [section 1311]"). Thus, the majority thought that the key provision was ambiguous when read in the context of the statute as a whole. According to the majority, moreover, the IRS's interpretation fit the structure and purposes of the Act substantially better than the alternative interpretation.

As commentators have noted, the version of the major-questions doctrine that the Court applied in *King* was purely about Step Zero and the allocation of interpretive authority. *See, e.g.*, Alison Gocke, Chevron*'s Next Chapter: A Fig Leaf for the Nondelegation Doctrine*, 55 U.C. DAVIS L. REV. 955, 978 (2021). Because of the importance of the interpretive question (and because the IRS might not have been the most natural agency to resolve it), the Court did not apply the *Chevron* framework; the major-questions doctrine meant that the Court should identify the best answer for itself. But the major-questions doctrine did not tell the Court what the answer was.

Starting in 2021, however, the Court repeatedly has invoked the more substantive version of the major-questions doctrine, which cuts against reading statutes to delegate major regulatory authority to executive-branch agencies. *See* Mila Sohoni, *The Major Questions Quartet*, 136 HARV. L. REV. 262, 272 (2022) (concluding that the Court has taken the major-questions doctrine "in a new direction"). Three of the relevant cases involved whether agencies had statutory authority for actions that they took during the COVID-19 pandemic. The Supreme Court addressed that issue in the context of motions for emergency relief, and the Court's opinions on those motions may not have full precedential effect. Briefly, though, the three cases were as follows:

- When the epidemic first gripped the United States, Congress enacted economic-relief legislation that included a temporary moratorium on evictions from properties that participated in certain federal housing programs or had federally backed mortgage loans. Congress did not renew this moratorium when it expired, but the Centers for Disease Control and Prevention (CDC) purported to impose a nationwide eviction moratorium of its own, protecting tenants who made certain declarations about their financial status. *See* Temporary Halt in Residential Evictions to Prevent the Further Spread of COVID-19, 85 Fed. Reg. 55292 (Sept. 4, 2020). Congress extended that moratorium for one month when it was about to expire, but Congress did not extend it further. Still, the CDC continued to extend its moratorium on a temporary basis, eventually restricting it to tenants who lived in counties with substantial levels of COVID-19 transmission. *See* Temporary Halt in Residential Evictions in Communities with Substantial or High Transmission of COVID-19 to Prevent the Further Spread of COVID-19, 86 Fed. Reg. 43244 (Aug. 6, 2021). The CDC claimed that a provision in the Public Health Service Act, enacted by Congress in 1944, authorized the CDC to impose this moratorium as a means of preventing the spread of disease,[22] but a majority of the Supreme Court said that this argument was almost certain to lose. *Ala. Ass'n of Realtors v. Dep't of Health & Human Servs.*, 141 S. Ct. 2485, 2488 (2021) (per curiam). According to the majority, the relevant statutory language was not most naturally understood to authorize an eviction moratorium. *See id.* (calling the CDC's position "a stretch"). But "[e]ven if the text were ambiguous," the majority indicated that the major-questions doctrine cut against reading the statute to give the CDC this authority. *Id.* at 2489. In the majority's words, "We expect Congress to speak clearly when authorizing an agency to exercise powers of 'vast "economic and political significance." ' "

---

[22] In particular, the CDC pointed to § 361(a) of the Act, which reads as follows:

> "The Surgeon General, with the approval of the [Secretary of Health and Human Services], is authorized to make and enforce such regulations as in his judgment are necessary to prevent the introduction, transmission, or spread of communicable diseases from foreign countries into the States or possessions, or from one State or possession into any other State or possession. For purposes of carrying out and enforcing such regulations, the Surgeon General may provide for such inspection, fumigation, disinfection, sanitation, pest extermination, destruction of animals or articles found to be so infected or contaminated as to be sources of dangerous infection to human beings, and other measures, as in his judgment may be necessary."

Public Health Service Act, ch. 373, § 361(a), 58 Stat. 682, 703 (1944) (codified as amended at 42 U.S.C. § 264(a)).

Id. (quoting *Utility Air Regulatory Group*, 573 U.S. at 324, in turn quoting *Brown & Williamson*, 529 U.S. at 160). The majority noted that the moratorium reached "[a]t least 80% of the country, including between 6 and 17 million tenants at risk of eviction," and "intrudes into an area that is the particular domain of state law: the landlord-tenant relationship." *Id.* The majority also characterized the CDC's interpretation of the relevant provision of the Public Health Service Act as novel. *See id.* ("This claim of expansive authority under § 361(a) is unprecedented. Since that provision's enactment in 1944, no regulation premised on it has even begun to approach the size or scope of the eviction moratorium.").

- The Supreme Court reached a similar conclusion about a rule promulgated by the Occupational Safety and Health Administration (OSHA) requiring employers with at least 100 employees to mandate that their workers either be vaccinated against COVID-19 or be tested weekly and wear face coverings at work. *See* COVID-19 Vaccination and Testing, 86 Fed. Reg. 61402 (Nov. 5, 2021). The Occupational Safety and Health Act of 1970 authorizes the Secretary of Labor to establish "occupational safety or health standards," which the Act defines as "standard[s] which require[ ] conditions, or the adoption or use of one or more practices, means, methods, operations, or processes, reasonably necessary or appropriate to provide safe or healthful employment and places of employment." Pub. L. 91–596, §§ 3(8), 6(b), 84 Stat. 1590, 1591, 1593 (codified at 29 U.S.C. §§ 652(8), 655(b)). Although the Secretary normally must use notice-and-comment rulemaking, Congress has authorized the Secretary to establish an "emergency temporary standard" without notice and comment "if he determines (A) that employees are exposed to grave danger from exposure to substances or agents determined to be toxic or physically harmful or from new hazards, and (B) that such emergency standard is necessary to protect employees from such danger." *Id.* § 6(c), 84 Stat. at 1593 (codified at 29 U.S.C. § 655(c)). OSHA invoked this provision as the basis for its rule. According to a majority of the Justices, though, the Act should not lightly be read to give OSHA the authority that it was claiming: "This is no 'everyday exercise of federal power,'" but "instead is a significant encroachment into the lives—and health—of a vast number of employees." *Nat'l Fed'n of Indep. Business v. OSHA*, 142 S. Ct. 661, 665 (2022) (per curiam) (quoting *In re MCP No. 165*, 20 F.4th 264, 272 (6th Cir. 2021) (Sutton, C.J., dissenting)); *see also id.* (noting that 84 million employees were covered). In the majority's view, the rule's challengers were likely to succeed on the merits unless the Act "plainly" authorized the rule, which "[i]t does not." *Id.* at 664–65. The majority reasoned that

COVID-19 was not "an *occupational* hazard" per se, and "[p]ermitting OSHA to regulate the hazards of daily life—simply because most Americans have jobs and face those same risks while on the clock—would significantly expand OSHA's regulatory authority without clear congressional mandate." *Id.* at 665. The majority also found it "telling" that "OSHA, in its half century of existence, has never before adopted a broad public health regulation of this kind." *Id.* at 666.

- By contrast, a different majority of the Court held that the Secretary of Health and Human Services, acting through the Centers for Medicare and Medicaid Services, could require health-care providers that participate in Medicare or Medicaid to mandate COVID-19 vaccinations for their staffs. *Biden v. Missouri*, 142 S. Ct. 647, 652–53 (2022) (per curiam) (addressing Omnibus COVID-19 Health Care Staff Vaccination, 86 Fed. Reg. 61555 (Nov. 5, 2021)). Because this requirement applied to many different kinds of providers, it rested on a variety of statutory authorizations, but the majority used hospitals as an example. Congress has provided that for a hospital to participate in Medicare or Medicaid (and hence to receive payment from those programs for care provided to covered patients), the hospital must satisfy various statutory requirements and "such other requirements as the Secretary finds necessary in the interest of the health and safety of individuals who are furnished services in the institution." 42 U.S.C. § 1395x(e)(9). As the majority noted, the agency's vaccine rule "fits neatly within the language" of this provision. *Biden v. Missouri*, 142 S. Ct. at 652. According to the majority, the rule also comported with "the longstanding practice of Health and Human Services in implementing the relevant statutory authorities." *See id.* at 652–53 (explaining that "healthcare facilities that wish to participate in Medicare and Medicaid have always been obligated to satisfy a host of conditions that address the safe and effective provision of healthcare," and "the Secretary routinely imposes conditions of participation that relate to the qualifications and duties of healthcare workers themselves"); *cf. id.* at 653 (acknowledging that "the agency has not previously adopted vaccine mandates as a condition of participation," but suggesting that state laws requiring health-care workers to be vaccinated had previously made such mandates unnecessary, and observing that "[v]accination requirements are a common feature of the provision of healthcare in America"). The majority did not mention the major-questions doctrine, although four dissenters did. *See id.* at 658 (Thomas, J., dissenting).

The next case, decided on the Court's regular docket after full consideration, is the Court's most elaborate statement about the major-questions doctrine.

West Virginia v. EPA

142 S. Ct. 2587 (2022)

■ *CHIEF JUSTICE ROBERTS delivered the opinion of the Court:*

The Clean Air Act authorizes the Environmental Protection Agency to regulate power plants by setting a "standard of performance" for their emission of certain pollutants into the air. 84 Stat. 1683, 42 U.S.C. § 7411(a)(1). That standard may be different for new and existing plants, but in each case it must reflect the "best system of emission reduction" that the Agency has determined to be "adequately demonstrated" for the particular category. §§ 7411(a)(1), (b)(1), (d). For existing plants, the States then implement that requirement by issuing rules restricting emissions from sources within their borders.

Since passage of the Act 50 years ago, EPA has exercised this authority by setting performance standards based on measures that would reduce pollution by causing plants to operate more cleanly. In 2015, however, EPA issued a new rule concluding that the "best system of emission reduction" for existing coal-fired power plants included a requirement that such facilities reduce their own production of electricity, or subsidize increased generation by natural gas, wind, or solar sources. [80 Fed. Reg. 64509 (2015).]

The question before us is whether this broader conception of EPA's authority is within the power granted to it by the Clean Air Act.

I

A

The Clean Air Act establishes three main regulatory programs to control air pollution from stationary sources such as power plants. Clean Air Amendments of 1970, 84 Stat. 1676, 42 U.S.C. § 7401 *et seq.* One program is the New Source Performance Standards program of Section 111, at issue here. The other two are the National Ambient Air Quality Standards (NAAQS) program, set out in Sections 108 through 110 of the Act, 42 U.S.C. §§ 7408–7410, and the Hazardous Air Pollutants (HAP) program, set out in Section 112, § 7412. . . .

. . . . [Section 111] directs EPA to list "categories of stationary sources" that it determines "cause[ ], or contribute[ ] significantly to, air pollution which may reasonably be anticipated to endanger public health or welfare." § 7411(b)(1)(A). Under Section 111(b), the Agency must then promulgate for each category "Federal standards of performance for new sources," § 7411(b)(1)(B). A "standard of performance" is one that

> "reflects the degree of emission limitation achievable through the application of the best system of emission reduction which (taking

into account the cost of achieving such reduction and any nonair quality health and environmental impact and energy requirements) the [EPA] Administrator determines has been adequately demonstrated." § 7411(a)(1).

Thus, the statute directs EPA to (1) "determine[ ]," taking into account various factors, the "best system of emission reduction which . . . has been adequately demonstrated," (2) ascertain the "degree of emission limitation achievable through the application" of that system, and (3) impose an emissions limit on new stationary sources that "reflects" that amount. *Ibid.* . . . Generally speaking, a source may achieve that emissions cap any way it chooses; the key is that its pollution be no more than the amount "achievable through the application of the best system of emission reduction . . . adequately demonstrated," or the BSER. § 7411(a)(1); see § 7411(b)(5). EPA undertakes this analysis on a pollutant-by-pollutant basis, establishing different standards of performance with respect to different pollutants emitted from the same source category. See, *e.g.*, 73 Fed. Reg. 35838 (2008); 42 Fed. Reg. 22510 (1977).

Although the thrust of Section 111 focuses on emissions limits for *new* and *modified* sources—as its title indicates—the statute also authorizes regulation of certain pollutants from *existing* sources. Under Section 111(d), once EPA "has set *new* source standards addressing emissions of a particular pollutant under . . . section 111(b)," 80 Fed. Reg. 64711, it must then address emissions of that same pollutant by existing sources—but only if they are not already regulated under the NAAQS or HAP programs. § 7411(d)(1). Existing power plants, for example, emit many pollutants covered by a NAAQS or HAP standard. Section 111(d) thus "operates as a gap-filler," empowering EPA to regulate harmful emissions not already controlled under the Agency's other authorities. *American Lung Assn. v. EPA*, 985 F.3d 914, 932 (CADC 2021).

Although the States set the actual rules governing existing power plants, EPA itself still retains the primary regulatory role in Section 111(d). The Agency, not the States, decides the amount of pollution reduction that must ultimately be achieved. It does so by again determining, as when setting the new source rules, "the best system of emission reduction . . . that has been adequately demonstrated for [existing covered] facilities." 40 CFR § 60.22(b)(5) (2021); see also 80 Fed. Reg. 64664, and n. 1. The States then submit plans containing the emissions restrictions that they intend to adopt and enforce in order not to exceed the permissible level of pollution established by EPA. See §§ 60.23, 60.24; 42 U.S.C. § 7411(d)(1).

Reflecting the ancillary nature of Section 111(d), EPA has used it only a handful of times since the enactment of the statute in 1970. . . . It was thus only a slight overstatement for one of the architects of the 1990 amendments to the Clean Air Act to refer to Section 111(d) as an "obscure, never-used section of the law." Hearings on S. 300 et al. before the Subcommittee on Environmental Protection of the Senate Committee on Environment and Public Works, 100th Cong., 1st Sess., 13 (1987) (remarks of Sen. Durenberger).

B

Things changed in October 2015, when EPA promulgated two rules addressing carbon dioxide pollution from power plants—one for new plants under Section 111(b), the other for existing plants under Section 111(d). Both were premised on the Agency's earlier finding that carbon dioxide is an "air pollutant" that "may reasonably be anticipated to endanger public health or welfare" by causing climate change. 80 Fed. Reg. 64530. Carbon dioxide is not subject to a NAAQS and has not been listed as a hazardous pollutant.

The first rule announced by EPA established federal carbon emissions limits for new power plants of two varieties: fossil-fuel-fired electric steam generating units (mostly coal fired) and natural-gas-fired stationary combustion turbines. *Id.* at 64512. Following the statutory process set out above, the Agency determined the BSER for the two categories of sources. For steam generating units, for instance, EPA determined that the BSER was a combination of high-efficiency production processes and carbon capture technology. See 80 Fed. Reg. 64512. EPA then set the emissions limit based on the amount of carbon dioxide that a plant would emit with these technologies in place. *Id.* at 64513.

The second rule was triggered by the first: Because EPA was now regulating carbon dioxide from *new* coal and gas plants, Section 111(d) required EPA to also address carbon emissions from *existing* coal and gas plants. See § 7411(d)(1). It did so through what it called the Clean Power Plan rule.

In that rule, EPA established "final emission guidelines for states to follow in developing plans" to regulate existing power plants within their borders. [80 Fed. Reg.] at 64662. To arrive at the guideline limits, EPA did the same thing it does when imposing federal regulations on new sources: It identified the BSER.

The BSER that the Agency selected for existing coal-fired power plants, however, was quite different from the BSER it had chosen for new sources. The BSER for existing plants included three types of measures, which the Agency called "building blocks." *Id.* at 64667. The first building block was "heat rate improvements" at coal-fired plants—essentially practices such plants could undertake to burn coal more efficiently. *Id.* at 64727. But such improvements, EPA stated, would "lead to only small emission reductions," because coal-fired power plants were already operating near optimum efficiency. *Ibid.* On the Agency's view, "much larger emission reductions [were] needed from [coal-fired plants] to address climate change." *Ibid.*

So the Agency included two additional building blocks in its BSER, both of which involve what it called "generation shifting from higher-emitting to lower-emitting" producers of electricity. *Id.* at 64728. Building block two was a shift in electricity production from existing coal-fired power plants to natural-gas-fired plants. *Ibid.* Because natural gas plants produce "typically less than half as much" carbon dioxide per unit of electricity created as coal-fired plants, the Agency explained, "this generation shift [would] reduce[ ] CO_2 emissions." *Ibid.* Building block three worked the same way, except that the shift was from both coal- and gas-fired plants to "new low- or zero-carbon generating capacity," mainly wind and solar. *Id.* at 64729, 64748. "Most of the CO_2 controls" in the rule came from the application of building blocks two and three. *Id.* at 64728.

The Agency identified three ways in which a regulated plant operator could implement a shift in generation to cleaner sources. *Id.* at 64731. First, an operator could simply reduce the regulated plant's own production of electricity. Second, it could build a new natural gas plant, wind farm, or solar installation, or invest in someone else's existing facility and then increase generation there. *Ibid.* Finally, operators could purchase emission allowances or credits as part of a cap-and-trade regime. *Id.* at 64731–64732. Under such a scheme, sources that achieve a reduction in their emissions can sell a credit representing the value of that reduction to others, who are able to count it toward their own applicable emissions caps.

. . . .

Having decided that the "best system of emission reduction . . . adequately demonstrated" was one that would reduce carbon pollution mostly by moving production to cleaner sources, EPA then set about determining "the degree of emission limitation achievable through the application" of that system. 42 U.S.C. § 7411(a)(1). The Agency recognized that—given the nature of generation shifting—it could choose from "a wide range of potential stringencies for the BSER." 80 Fed. Reg. 64730. Put differently, in translating the BSER into an operational emissions limit, EPA could choose whether to require anything from a little generation shifting to a great deal. The Agency settled on what it regarded as a "reasonable" amount of shift, which it based on modeling of how much more electricity both natural gas and renewable sources could supply without causing undue cost increases or reducing the overall power supply. *Id.* at 64797–64811. Based on these changes, EPA projected that by 2030, it would be feasible to have coal provide 27% of national electricity generation, down from 38% in 2014. . . .

From these significant projected reductions in generation, EPA developed a series of complex equations to "determine the emission performance rates" that States would be required to implement. 80 Fed. Reg. 64815. The calculations resulted in numerical emissions ceilings so strict that no existing coal plant would have been able to achieve them without engaging in one of the three means of shifting generation described above. Indeed, the emissions limit the Clean Power Plan established for existing power plants was actually *stricter* than the cap imposed by the simultaneously published standards for *new* plants. Compare *id.* at 64742 with *id.* at 64513.

The point, after all, was to compel the transfer of power generating capacity from existing sources to wind and solar. The White House stated that the Clean Power Plan would "drive a[n] . . . aggressive transformation in the domestic energy industry." White House Fact Sheet, App. in *American Lung Assn. v. EPA*, No. 19–1140 etc. (CADC), p. 2076. EPA's own modeling concluded that the rule would entail billions of dollars in compliance costs (to be paid in the form of higher energy prices), require the retirement of dozens of coal-fired plants, and eliminate tens of thousands of jobs across various sectors. EPA, Regulatory Impact Analysis for the Clean Power Plan Final Rule 3–22, 3–30, 3–33, 6–24, 6–25 (2015). . . .

C

These projections were never tested, because the Clean Power Plan never went into effect. The same day that EPA promulgated the rule, dozens of parties (including 27 States) petitioned for review in the D.C. Circuit. After that court declined to enter a stay of the rule, the challengers sought the same relief from this Court. We granted a stay, preventing the rule from taking effect. *West Virginia v. EPA*, 577 U.S. 1126 (2016). The Court of Appeals later heard argument on the merits en banc. But before it could issue a decision, there was a change in Presidential administrations. The new administration requested that the litigation be held in abeyance so that EPA could reconsider the Clean Power Plan. The D.C. Circuit obliged, and later dismissed the petitions for review as moot.

EPA eventually repealed the rule in 2019, concluding that the Clean Power Plan had been "in excess of its statutory authority" under Section 111(d). 84 Fed. Reg. 32523 (2019). . . .

The Agency determined that "the interpretative question raised" by the Clean Power Plan—"*i.e.*, whether a 'system of emission reduction' can consist of generation-shifting measures"—fell under the "major question doctrine." *Id.* at 32529. . . .

EPA argued that under the major questions doctrine, a clear statement was necessary to conclude that Congress intended to delegate authority "of this breadth to regulate a fundamental sector of the economy." *Ibid.* It found none. "Indeed," it concluded, given the text and structure of the statute, "Congress has directly spoken to this precise question and precluded" the use of measures such as generation shifting. *Ibid.*

In the same rulemaking, the Agency replaced the Clean Power Plan by promulgating a different Section 111(d) regulation, known as the Affordable Clean Energy (ACE) Rule. *Id.* at 32532. Based on its view of what measures may permissibly make up the BSER, EPA determined that the best system would be akin to building block one of the Clean Power Plan . . . . The ACE Rule determined that the application of its BSER measures would result in only small reductions in carbon dioxide emissions. . . .

D

A number of States and private parties immediately filed petitions for review in the D.C. Circuit, challenging EPA's repeal of the Clean Power Plan and its enactment of the replacement ACE Rule. . . .

The Court of Appeals . . . held that . . . the statute could reasonably be read to encompass generation shifting. As part of that analysis, the Court of Appeals concluded that the major questions doctrine did not apply, and thus rejected the need for a clear statement of congressional intent to delegate such power to EPA. [985 F.3d] at 959–968. Having found that EPA misunderstood the scope of its authority under the Clean Air Act, the Court vacated the Agency's repeal of the Clean Power Plan and remanded to the Agency for further consideration. *Id.* at 995. It also vacated and remanded the replacement rule, the ACE Rule, for the same reason. *Ibid.*

[West Virginia and several other parties that had intervened to defend EPA's repeal of the Clean Power Plan filed petitions for certiorari, which the Supreme Court granted.] . . . .

III

A

. . . . The issue here is whether restructuring the Nation's overall mix of electricity generation, to transition from 38% coal to 27% coal by 2030, can be the "best system of emission reduction" within the meaning of Section 111.

"It is a fundamental canon of statutory construction that the words of a statute must be read in their context and with a view to their place in the overall statutory scheme." *Davis v. Michigan Dept. of Treasury*, 489 U.S. 803, 809 (1989). Where the statute at issue is one that confers authority upon an administrative agency, that inquiry must be "shaped, at least in some measure, by the nature of the question presented"—whether Congress in fact meant to confer the power the agency has asserted. *FDA v. Brown & Williamson Tobacco Corp.*, 529 U.S. 120, 159 (2000). In the ordinary case, that context has no great effect on the appropriate analysis. Nonetheless, our precedent teaches that there are "extraordinary cases" . . . in which the "history and the breadth of the authority that [the agency] has asserted," and the "economic and political significance" of that assertion, provide a "reason to hesitate before concluding that Congress" meant to confer such authority. *Id.* at 159–160.

Such cases have arisen from all corners of the administrative state. [The Court summarized the assertions of authority at issue in many of the cases described above: *Brown & Williamson*, *Utility Air Regulatory Group v. EPA*, *Alabama Ass'n of Realtors v. Department of Health & Human Services*, and *National Federation of Independent Business v. OSHA*. The Court also summarized *Gonzales v. Oregon*, 546 U.S. 243 (2006).]

All of these regulatory assertions had a colorable textual basis. And yet, in each case, given the various circumstances, "common sense as to the manner in which Congress [would have been] likely to delegate" such power to the agency at issue, *Brown & Williamson*, 529 U.S. at 133, made it very unlikely that Congress had actually done so. Extraordinary grants of regulatory authority are rarely accomplished through "modest words," "vague terms," or "subtle device[s]." [*Whitman v. American Trucking Ass'ns*, 531 U.S. 457, 468 (2001)]. Nor does Congress typically use oblique or elliptical language to empower an agency to make a "radical or fundamental change" to a statutory scheme. *MCI Telecommunications Corp. v. American Telephone & Telegraph Co.*, 512 U.S. 218, 229 (1994). . . . We presume that "Congress intends to make major policy decisions itself, not leave those decisions to agencies." *United States Telecom Assn. v. FCC*, 855 F.3d 381, 419 (CADC 2017) (Kavanaugh, J., dissenting from denial of rehearing en banc).

Thus, in certain extraordinary cases, both separation of powers principles and a practical understanding of legislative intent make us "reluctant to read into ambiguous statutory text" the delegation claimed to be lurking there. *Utility Air*, 573 U.S. at 324. To convince us otherwise, something more than a merely plausible textual basis for the agency action is necessary. The agency instead must point to "clear congressional authorization" for the power it claims. *Ibid.*

. . . .

B

Under our precedents, this is a major questions case. In arguing that Section 111(d) empowers it to substantially restructure the American energy market, EPA "claim[ed] to discover in a long-extant statute an unheralded power" representing a "transformative expansion in [its] regulatory authority." *Utility Air*, 573 U.S. at 324. It located that newfound power in the vague language of an "ancillary provision[ ]" of the Act, *Whitman*, 531 U.S. at 468, one that was designed to function as a gap filler and had rarely been used in the preceding decades. And the Agency's discovery allowed it to adopt a regulatory program that Congress had conspicuously and repeatedly declined to enact itself. *Brown & Williamson*, 529 U.S. at 159–160; *Gonzales*, 546 U.S. at 267–268; *Alabama Assn.*, [141 S. Ct. at 2486–2487, 2490]. . . .

Prior to 2015, EPA had always set emissions limits under Section 111 based on the application of measures that would reduce pollution by causing the regulated source to operate more cleanly. . . . It had never devised a cap by looking to a "system" that would reduce pollution simply by "shifting" polluting activity "from dirtier to cleaner sources." 80 Fed. Reg. 64726 . . . . And as Justice Frankfurter has noted, "just as established practice may shed light on the extent of power conveyed by general statutory language, so the want of assertion of power by those who presumably would be alert to exercise it, is equally significant in determining whether such power was actually conferred." *FTC v. Bunte Brothers, Inc.*, 312 U.S. 349, 352 (1941).

The Government quibbles with this description of the history of Section 111(d), pointing to one rule that it says relied upon a cap-and-trade mechanism to reduce emissions. See 70 Fed. Reg. 28616 (2005) (Mercury Rule). The legality of that choice was controversial at the time and was never addressed by a court. See *New Jersey v. EPA*, 517 F.3d 574 (CADC 2008) (vacating on other grounds). Even assuming the Rule was valid, though, it still does not help the Government. In that regulation, EPA set the actual "emission cap"—*i.e.*, the limit on emissions that sources would be required to meet—"based on the level of [mercury] emissions reductions that w[ould] be achievable by" the use of "technologies [that could be] installed and operational on a nationwide basis" in the relevant timeframe—namely, wet scrubbers. 70 Fed. Reg. 28620–28621. In other words, EPA set the cap based on the application of particular controls, and regulated sources could have complied by installing them. By contrast, and by design, there is no control a coal plant operator can deploy to attain the emissions limits established by the Clean Power Plan. . . . The Mercury Rule, therefore, is no precedent for the Clean Power Plan. To the contrary, it was one more entry in an unbroken list of prior Section 111 rules that devised the enforceable emissions limit by determining the best control mechanisms available for the source.

This consistent understanding of "system[s] of emission reduction" tracked the seemingly universal view, as stated by EPA in its inaugural Section 111(d) rulemaking, that "Congress intended a technology-based approach" to regulation in that Section. 40 Fed. Reg. 53343 (1975); see *id.* at 53341 ("degree of control to be reflected in EPA's emission guidelines" will be based on "application of best adequately demonstrated control technology"). A technology-based standard . . . is one that focuses on improving the emissions performance of individual sources. . . .

Indeed, EPA nodded to this history in the Clean Power Plan itself, describing the sort of "systems of emission reduction" it had always before selected . . . as "more traditional air pollution control measures." 80 Fed. Reg. 64784. . . .

But, the Agency explained, in order to "control[ ] CO_2 from affected [plants] at levels . . . necessary to mitigate the dangers presented by climate change," it could not base the emissions limit on "measures that improve efficiency at the power plants." *Id.* at 64728. "The quantity of emissions reductions resulting from the application of these measures" would have been "too small." *Id.* at 64727. Instead, to attain the necessary "critical CO_2 reductions," EPA adopted what it called a "broader, forward-thinking approach to the design" of Section 111 regulations. *Id.* at 64703. Rather than focus on improving the performance of individual sources, it would "improve the *overall power system* by lowering the carbon intensity of power generation." *Ibid.* (emphasis added). And it would do that by forcing a shift throughout the power grid from one type of energy source to another. . . .

This view of EPA's authority . . . effected a "fundamental revision of the statute, changing it from [one sort of] scheme of . . . regulation" into an entirely different kind. *MCI*, 512 U.S. at 231. Under the Agency's prior view of Section 111, its role was limited to ensuring the efficient pollution performance of each individual regulated source. Under that paradigm, if a source was already operating at that level, there was nothing more for EPA to do. Under its newly "discover[ed]" authority, *Utility Air*, 573 U.S. at 324, however, EPA can demand much greater reductions in emissions based on a very different kind of policy judgment: that it would be "best" if coal made up a much smaller share of national electricity generation. And on this view of EPA's authority, it could go further, perhaps forcing coal plants to "shift" away virtually all of their generation—*i.e.*, to cease making power altogether.

The Government attempts to downplay the magnitude of this "unprecedented power over American industry." *Industrial Union Dept., AFL-CIO v. American Petroleum Institute*, 448 U.S. 607, 645 (1980) (plurality opinion). The amount of generation shifting ordered, it argues, must be "adequately demonstrated" and "best" in light of the statutory factors of "cost," "nonair quality health and environmental impact," and "energy requirements." 42 U.S.C. § 7411(a)(1). EPA therefore must limit the magnitude of generation shift it demands to a level that will not be "exorbitantly costly" or "threaten the reliability of the grid." Brief for Federal Respondents 42.

But this argument does not so much *limit* the breadth of the Government's claimed authority as *reveal* it. On EPA's view of Section 111(d), Congress implicitly tasked it, and it alone, with balancing the many vital considerations of national policy implicated in deciding how Americans will get their energy. EPA decides, for instance, how much of a switch from coal to natural gas is practically feasible by 2020, 2025, and 2030 before the grid collapses, and how high energy prices can go as a result before they become unreasonably "exorbitant."

There is little reason to think Congress assigned such decisions to the Agency. For one thing, as EPA itself admitted when requesting special funding, "Understand[ing] and project[ing] system-wide . . . trends in areas such as electricity transmission, distribution, and storage" requires "technical and policy expertise *not* traditionally needed in EPA regulatory development." EPA, Fiscal Year 2016: Justification of

Appropriation Estimates for the Committee on Appropriations 213 (2015) (emphasis added). "When [an] agency has no comparative expertise" in making certain policy judgments, we have said, "Congress presumably would not" task it with doing so. *Kisor* v. *Wilkie*, [139 S. Ct. 2400, 2417] (2019); see also *Gonzales*, 546 U.S. at 266–267.

We also find it "highly unlikely that Congress would leave" to "agency discretion" the decision of how much coal-based generation there should be over the coming decades. *MCI*, 512 U.S. at 231 . . . . The basic and consequential tradeoffs involved in such a choice are ones that Congress would likely have intended for itself. See W. Eskridge, Interpreting Law: A Primer on How To Read Statutes and the Constitution 288 (2016) ("Even if Congress has delegated an agency general rulemaking or adjudicatory power, judges presume that Congress does not delegate its authority to settle or amend major social and economic policy decisions."). Congress certainly has not conferred a like authority upon EPA anywhere else in the Clean Air Act. The last place one would expect to find it is in the previously little-used backwater of Section 111(d).

The dissent contends that there is nothing surprising about EPA dictating the optimal mix of energy sources nationwide, since that sort of mandate will reduce air pollution from power plants, which is EPA's bread and butter. *Post* at 2636–2638. But that does not follow. Forbidding evictions may slow the spread of disease, but the CDC's ordering such a measure certainly "raise[s] an eyebrow." *Post* at 2636 . . . .

. . . .

Finally, we cannot ignore that the regulatory writ EPA newly uncovered conveniently enabled it to enact a program that, long after the dangers posed by greenhouse gas emissions "had become well known, Congress considered and rejected" multiple times. *Brown & Williamson*, 529 U.S. at 144 . . . . At bottom, the Clean Power Plan essentially adopted a cap-and-trade scheme, or set of state cap-and-trade schemes, for carbon. See 80 Fed. Reg. 64734 ("Emissions trading is . . . an integral part of our BSER analysis."). Congress, however, has consistently rejected proposals to amend the Clean Air Act to create such a program. See, *e.g.*, American Clean Energy and Security Act of 2009, H. R. 2454, 111th Cong., 1st Sess.; Clean Energy Jobs and American Power Act, S. 1733, 111th Cong., 1st Sess. (2009). . . . "The importance of the issue," along with the fact that the same basic scheme EPA adopted "has been the subject of an earnest and profound debate across the country, . . . makes the oblique form of the claimed delegation all the more suspect." *Gonzales*, 546 U.S. at 267–268 (internal quotation marks omitted).

C

Given these circumstances, our precedent counsels skepticism toward EPA's claim that Section 111 empowers it to devise carbon emissions caps based on a generation shifting approach. To overcome that skepticism, the Government must—under the major questions doctrine—point to "clear congressional authorization" to regulate in that manner. *Utility Air*, 573 U.S. at 324.

All the Government can offer, however, is the Agency's authority to establish emissions caps at a level reflecting "the application of the best system of emission reduction . . . adequately demonstrated." 42 U.S.C. § 7411(a)(1). As a matter of "definitional possibilities," *FCC v. AT&T Inc.*, 562 U.S. 397, 407 (2011), generation shifting can be described as a "system"—"an aggregation or assemblage of objects united by some form of regular interaction," Brief for Federal Respondents 31—capable of reducing emissions. But of course almost anything could constitute such a "system"; shorn of all context, the word is an empty vessel. Such a vague statutory grant is not close to the sort of clear authorization required by our precedents.

The Government, echoed by the other respondents, looks to other provisions of the Clean Air Act for support. It points out that the Act elsewhere uses the word "system" or "similar words" to describe cap-and-trade schemes or other sector-wide mechanisms for reducing pollution. *Ibid.* The Acid Rain program set out in Title IV of the Act establishes a cap-and-trade scheme for reducing sulfur dioxide emissions, which the statute refers to as an "emission allocation and transfer *system*." § 7651(b) (emphasis added). And Section 110 of the NAAQS program specifies that "marketable permits" and "auctions of emissions rights" qualify as "control measures, means, or techniques" that States may adopt in their state implementation plans in order "to meet the applicable requirements of" a NAAQS. § 7410(a)(2)(A). If the word "system" or similar words like "technique" or "means" can encompass cap-and-trade, the Government maintains, why not in Section 111?

But just because a cap-and-trade "system" can be used to reduce emissions does not mean that it is the kind of "system of emission reduction" referred to in Section 111. Indeed, the Government's examples demonstrate why it is not.

. . . [U]nlike Section 111, the Acid Rain and NAAQS programs contemplate trading systems as a means of *complying* with an *already established emissions limit*, set either directly by Congress (as with Acid Rain, see 42 U.S.C. § 7651c) or by reference to the safe concentration of the pollutant in the ambient air (as with the NAAQS). In Section 111, by contrast, it is EPA's job to come up with the cap itself: the "numerical limit on emissions" that States must apply to each source. 80 Fed. Reg. 64768. We doubt that Congress directed the Agency to set an emissions cap at the level "which reflects the degree of emission limitation achievable through the application of [a cap-and-trade] system," § 7411(a)(1), for that degree is indeterminate. It is one thing for Congress to authorize regulated sources to use trading to comply with a preset cap, or a cap that must be based on some scientific, objective criterion, such as the NAAQS. It is quite another to simply authorize EPA to set the cap itself wherever the Agency sees fit.

. . . .

. . . . We have no occasion to decide whether the statutory phrase "system of emission reduction" refers *exclusively* to measures that improve the pollution performance of individual sources, such that all other actions are ineligible to qualify as the BSER. To be sure, it is pertinent to our analysis that EPA has acted consistent with such a limitation for the first four decades of the statute's existence. But the only interpretive question before us, and the only one we answer, is more narrow: whether the "best system of emission reduction" identified by EPA in the Clean Power Plan was within the authority granted to the Agency in Section 111(d) of the Clean Air Act. For the reasons given, the answer is no.

* * *

Capping carbon dioxide emissions at a level that will force a nationwide transition away from the use of coal to generate electricity may be a sensible "solution to the crisis of the day." *New York v. United States*, 505 U.S. 144, 187 (1992). But it is not plausible that Congress gave EPA the authority to adopt on its own such a regulatory scheme in Section 111(d). A decision of such magnitude and consequence rests with Congress itself, or an agency acting pursuant to a clear delegation from that representative body. . . .

■ *JUSTICE GORSUCH, with whom JUSTICE ALITO joins, concurring:*

[*Ed.*: Justice Gorsuch's opinion was wide-ranging. He started by noting that "[o]ne of the Judiciary's most solemn duties is to ensure that acts of Congress are applied in accordance with the Constitution in the cases that come before us," and he asserted that "courts have developed certain 'clear-statement' rules" for this purpose. He characterized the major-questions doctrine as such a rule—a "corollary" of the constitutional principle that the federal government's legislative powers are vested in Congress rather than the executive branch. *See also* NFIB v. OSHA, 142 S. Ct. 661, 668 (2022) (Gorsuch, J., concurring) ("[T]he major questions doctrine is closely related to . . . the nondelegation doctrine."); Gundy v. United States, 139 S. Ct. 2116, 2142 (2019) (Gorsuch, J., dissenting) ("Although it is nominally a canon of statutory construction, we apply the major questions doctrine in service of the constitutional rule that Congress may not divest itself of its legislative power by transferring that power to an executive agency.").

[Justice Gorsuch also tried to provide guidance about when the major-questions doctrine comes into play. Based on both the majority opinion and prior cases, he set out the following "list of triggers" (which "may not be exclusive"):

- "when an agency claims the power to resolve a matter of great 'political significance,' *NFIB* v. *OSHA*, [142 S. Ct. at 665] (internal quotation marks omitted), or end an 'earnest and profound debate across the country,' *Gonzales*, 546 U.S. at 267–268 (internal quotation marks omitted)";
- "when [an agency] seeks to regulate ' "a significant portion of the American economy," ' *ante* at 2608 (quoting *Utility Air*, 573 U.S. at 324), or require 'billions of dollars in spending' by private persons or entities, *King v. Burwell*, 576 U.S. 473, 485 (2015)"; or
- "when an agency seeks to 'intrud[e] into an area that is the particular domain of state law,' " *Ala. Ass'n of Realtors*, 141 S. Ct. at 2486–2487.

[As for "what qualifies as a clear congressional statement authorizing an agency's action," Justice Gorsuch echoed the majority's view that " 'gap filler' provisions" are unlikely sources of major authority. He added that "an agency's attempt to deploy an old statute focused on one problem to solve a new and different problem may also be a warning sign that [the agency] is acting without clear congressional authority." Similarly, he noted that "the agency's past interpretations of the relevant statute" can matter; courts should be skeptical when an agency claims to have found broad authority that it had not previously identified or asserted. Finally, he suggested that skepticism is also warranted "when there is a mismatch between an agency's challenged action and its congressionally assigned mission and expertise."]

■ *JUSTICE KAGAN, with whom JUSTICES BREYER and SOTOMAYOR join, dissenting:*

. . . .

. . . . The majority's decision rests on one claim alone: that generation shifting is just too new and too big a deal for Congress to have authorized it in Section 111's general terms. But that is wrong. A key reason Congress makes broad delegations like Section 111 is so an agency can respond, appropriately and commensurately, to new and big problems. . . . The majority today overrides that legislative choice. In so doing, it deprives EPA of the power needed—and the power granted—to curb the emission of greenhouse gases.

I

The Clean Air Act was major legislation, designed to deal with a major public policy issue. . . . The Act . . . established three major regulatory programs to control air pollution from stationary sources like power plants. . . . The National Ambient Air Quality Standards (NAAQS) and Hazardous Air Pollutants (HAP) programs prescribe standards for specified pollutants, not including carbon dioxide. Section 111's New Source Performance Standards program provides an additional tool for regulating emissions from categories of stationary sources deemed to contribute significantly to pollution. As applied to existing (not new) sources, the program mandates—via Section 111(d)—that EPA set emissions levels for pollutants not covered by the NAAQS or HAP programs, including carbon dioxide.

Section 111(d) thus ensures that EPA regulates existing power plants' emissions of *all* pollutants. When the pollutant at issue falls within the NAAQS or HAP programs, EPA need do no more. But when the pollutant falls outside those programs, Section 111(d) requires EPA to set an emissions level for currently operating power plants (and other stationary sources). That means no pollutant from such a source can go unregulated: As the Senate Report explained, Section 111(d) guarantees that "there should be no gaps in control activities pertaining to stationary source emissions that pose any significant danger to public health or welfare." S. Rep. No. 91–1196, p. 20 (1970). Reflecting that language, the majority calls Section 111(d) a "gap-filler." *Ante* at 2601. It might also be thought of as a backstop or catch-all provision, protecting against pollutants that the NAAQS and HAP programs let go by. But the section is *not*, as the majority further claims, an "ancillary provision" or a statutory "backwater." . . . Even if they are needed only infrequently, . . . backstops can perform a critical function—and this one surely does. Again, Section 111(d) tells EPA that when a pollutant—like carbon dioxide—is not regulated through other programs, EPA must undertake a further regulatory effort to control that substance's emission from existing stationary sources. In that way, Section 111(d) operates to ensure that the Act achieves comprehensive pollution control.

Section 111 describes the prescribed regulatory effort in expansive terms. . . . [T]he provision instructs EPA to decide upon the "best system of emission reduction which . . . has been adequately demonstrated." . . . It imposes . . . meaningful constraints: Take into account costs and nonair impacts, and make sure the best system has a proven track record. But the core command—go find the best system of emission reduction—gives broad authority to EPA.

If that flexibility is not apparent on the provision's face, consider some dictionary definitions—supposedly a staple of this Court's supposedly textualist method of reading statutes. A "system" is "a complex unity formed of many often diverse parts subject to a common plan or serving a common purpose." Webster's Third New International Dictionary 2322 (1971). Or again: a "system" is "[a]n organized and coordinated method; a procedure." American Heritage Dictionary 1768 (5th ed. 2018). The majority complains that a similar definition—cited to the Solicitor General's brief but originally from another dictionary—is just too darn broad. . . . "[A]lmost anything" capable of reducing emissions, the majority says, "could constitute such a 'system' " of emission reduction. *Ante* at 2614. But that is rather the point. Congress used an obviously broad word (though surrounding it with constraints, see *supra* at 2629–2630) to give EPA lots of latitude in deciding how to set emissions limits. And contra the majority, a broad term is not the same thing as a "vague" one. *Ante* at 2609, 2609–2610, 2614. . . .

. . . . [G]eneration shifting fits comfortably within the conventional meaning of a "system of emission reduction." Consider one of the most common mechanisms of generation shifting: the use of a cap-and-trade scheme. Here is how the majority describes cap and trade: "Under such a scheme, sources that receive a reduction in their emissions can sell a credit representing the value of that reduction to others, who are able to count it toward their own applicable emissions caps." *Ante* at 2603–2604. Does that sound like a "system" to you? It does to me too. And it also has to this Court. In the past, we have explained that "[t]his type of 'cap-and-trade' *system* cuts costs while still reducing pollution to target levels." *EPA v. EME Homer City Generation, L.P.*, 572 U.S. 489, 503, n. 10 (2014) (emphasis added). . . .

Other statutory provisions confirm the point. The Clean Air Act's acid rain provision, for example, describes a cap-and-trade program as an "emission allocation and transfer *system*." § 7651(b) (emphasis added). So a "system," according to the statute's own usage, includes the kind of cap-and-trade mechanism that the Clean Power Plan relied on. . . .

There is also a flipside point: Congress declined to include in Section 111 the restrictions on EPA's authority contained in other Clean Air Act provisions. Most relevant here, quite a number of statutory sections confine EPA's emissions-reduction efforts to technological controls—essentially, equipment or processes that can be put into place at a particular facility. . . . So, for example, one provision tells EPA to set standards "reflect[ing] the greatest degree of emission reduction achievable through the application of technology." § 7521(a)(3)(A)(i). Others direct the use of the "best available retrofit technology," or the "best available control technology," or the "maximum achievable control technology." §§ 7491(b)(2)(A), (g)(2), 7475(a)(4), 7479(3), 7412(g)(2). . . . None of those provisions would allow EPA to set emissions limits based on generation shifting, as the Agency acknowledges. See Brief for United States 32–33. But nothing like the language of those provisions is included in Section 111. That matters under normal rules of statutory interpretation. . . .

. . . . [The majority indicates] that today's opinion does not resolve whether EPA can regulate in some non-technological ways; instead, the opinion says only that the Clean Power Plan goes too far. . . . [But] both the nature and the statutory basis of that limit are left a mystery. . . . Section 111 does not impose *any* constraints—technological or otherwise—on EPA's authority to regulate stationary sources (except for those stated, like cost). In somehow (and to some extent) saying otherwise, the majority flouts the statutory text.

. . . . In Section 111, Congress spoke in capacious terms. It knew that "without regulatory flexibility, changing circumstances and scientific developments would soon render the Clean Air Act obsolete."

[*Massachusetts v. EPA*, 549 U.S. 497, 532 (2007)]. So the provision enables EPA to base emissions limits for existing stationary sources on the "best system." That system may be technological in nature; it may be whatever else the majority has in mind; or, most important here, it may be generation shifting. The statute does not care. . . .

II

. . . .

A

"[T]he words of a statute," as the majority states, "must be read in their context and with a view to their place in the overall statutory scheme." *FDA v. Brown & Williamson Tobacco Corp.*, 529 U.S. 120, 133 (2000) . . . .

So too, a court "must be guided to a degree by common sense as to the manner in which Congress is likely to delegate." [*Ibid.*] Assume that a policy decision, like this one, is a matter of significant "economic and political magnitude." *Ibid.* We know that Congress delegates such decisions to agencies all the time—and often via broadly framed provisions like Section 111. . . . But Congress does so in a sensible way. To decide whether an agency action goes beyond what Congress wanted, courts must assess (among other potentially relevant factors) the nature of the regulation, the nature of the agency, and the relationship of the two to each other. . . . In particular, we have understood, Congress does not usually grant agencies the authority to decide significant issues on which they have no particular expertise. So when there is a mismatch between the agency's usual portfolio and a given assertion of power, courts have reason to question whether Congress intended a delegation to go so far.

The majority today goes beyond those sensible principles. It announces the arrival of the "major questions doctrine," which replaces normal text-in-context statutory interpretation with some tougher-to-satisfy set of rules. . . . Apparently, there is now a two-step inquiry. First, a court must decide, by looking at some panoply of factors, whether agency action presents an "extraordinary case[ ]." . . . If it does, the agency "must point to clear congressional authorization for the power it claims," someplace over and above the normal statutory basis we require. *Ante* at 2609 (internal quotation marks omitted) . . . . The result is statutory interpretation of an unusual kind. It is not until page 28 of a 31-page opinion that the majority begins to seriously discuss the meaning of Section 111. And even then, it does not address straight-up what should be the question: Does the text of that provision, when read in context and with a common-sense awareness of how Congress delegates, authorize the agency action here?

The majority claims it is just following precedent, but that is not so. The Court has never even used the term "major questions doctrine" before. And in the relevant cases, the Court has done statutory construction of a familiar sort. It has looked to the text of a delegation. It has addressed how an agency's view of that text works—or fails to do so—in the context of a broader statutory scheme. And it has asked, in a common-sensical (or call it purposive) vein, about what Congress would have made of the agency's view—otherwise said, whether Congress would naturally have delegated authority over some important question to the agency, given its expertise and experience. In short, in assessing the scope of a delegation, the Court has considered—without multiple steps, triggers, or special presumptions—the fit between the power claimed, the agency claiming it, and the broader statutory design.

The key case here is *FDA v. Brown & Williamson*. There, the Food and Drug Administration (FDA) asserted that its power to regulate "drugs" and "devices" extended to tobacco products. The claim had something to it: FDA has broad authority over "drugs" and drug-delivery "devices," and the definitions of those terms could be read to encompass nicotine and cigarettes. But the asserted authority "simply [did] not fit" the overall statutory scheme. 529 U.S. at 143. FDA's governing statute required the agency to ensure that regulated products were "safe" to be marketed—but there was no making tobacco products safe in the usual sense. *Id.* at 133–143. So FDA would have had to reinterpret what it meant to be "safe," or else ban tobacco products altogether. *Ibid.* Both options, the Court thought, were preposterous. Until the agency action at issue, tobacco products hadn't been spoken of in the same breath as pharmaceuticals (FDA's paradigmatic regulated product). And Congress had created in several statutes a "distinct regulatory scheme" for tobacco, not involving FDA. *Id.* at 155–156. So all the evidence was that Congress had never meant for FDA to have any—let alone total—control over the tobacco industry, with its "unique political history." *Id.* at 159. Again, there was "simply" a lack of "fit" between the regulation at issue, the agency in question, and the broader statutory scheme. *Id.* at 143.

. . . . [When *Brown & Williamson* referred to "extraordinary cases" in which "there may be reason to hesitate before concluding that Congress has intended such an implicit delegation," *id.* at 159, the] Court was saying only . . . that there was reason to hesitate before giving FDA's position *Chevron* deference. See *id.* at 132–133, 159–161. And what was that reason? The Court went on to explain that it would not defer to FDA because it read the relevant statutory provisions as negating the agency's claimed authority. See *id.* at 160 ("[W]e are obliged to defer not to the agency's expansive construction of the statute, but to Congress' consistent judgment to deny the FDA this power"); *id.* at 133 (finding at *Chevron*'s first step that "Congress has directly spoken to the issue here and precluded the FDA's" asserted power). In reaching that conclusion, the Court relied . . . not on any special "clear authorization" demand, but on normal principles of statutory interpretation: look at the text, view it in context, and use what the Court called some "common sense" about how Congress delegates. *Ibid.* . . .

The Court has applied the same kind of analysis in subsequent cases—holding in each that an agency exceeded the scope of a broadly framed delegation when it operated outside the sphere of its expertise, in a way that warped the statutory text or structure. [Discussion of *Gonzales v. Oregon*, *Utility Air Regulatory Group v. EPA*, and *Alabama Ass'n of Realtors v. Department of Health and Human Services* is omitted.]

B

The Court today faces no such singular assertion of agency power. As I have already explained, nothing in the Clean Air Act (or, for that matter, any other statute) conflicts with EPA's reading of Section 111. Notably, the majority does not dispute that point. . . . As to the other critical matter in those cases—is the agency operating outside its sphere of expertise?—the majority at least tries to say something. It claims EPA has no "comparative expertise" in "balancing the many vital considerations of national policy" implicated in regulating electricity sources. *Ante* at 2612–2613. But that is wrong.

. . . .

. . . . Consider the Clean Power Plan's component parts—let's call them the what, who, and how—to see the rule's normalcy. The "what" is the subject matter of the Plan: carbon dioxide emissions. This Court has already found that those emissions fall within EPA's domain. We said then: "[T]here is nothing counterintuitive to the notion that EPA can curtail the emission of substances that are putting the global climate out of kilter." *Massachusetts*, 549 U.S. at 531. . . . So too, there is nothing special about the Plan's "who": fossil-fuel-fired power plants. In *Utility Air*, we thought EPA's regulation of churches and schools highly unusual. . . . But fossil-fuel-fired plants? Those plants pollute—a lot—and so they have long lived under the watchful eye of EPA. That was true even before EPA began regulating carbon dioxide. See *Train v. Natural Resources Defense Council, Inc.*, 421 U.S. 60, 78 (1975).

Finally, the "how" of generation shifting creates no mismatch with EPA's expertise. As the Plan noted, generation shifting has a well-established pedigree as a tool for reducing pollution; even putting aside other federal regulation, see *infra* at 2639–2640, both state regulators and power plants themselves have long used it to attain environmental goals. See 80 Fed. Reg. 64664; Brief for Power Company Respondents 47; see also S. Breyer, Regulation and Its Reform 444, n. 1 (1982) (citing literature on the subject from the 1970s). . . . [C]ap and trade and similar mechanisms are an ordinary part of modern environmental regulation. . . .

Why, then, be "skeptic[al]" of EPA's exercise of authority? *Ante* at 2614. . . . Although the majority offers a flurry of complaints, they come down in the end to this: The Clean Power Plan is a big new thing, issued under a minor statutory provision. . . . I have already addressed the back half of that argument: In fact, there is nothing insignificant about Section 111(d), which was intended to ensure that EPA would limit existing stationary sources' emissions of otherwise unregulated pollutants (however few or many there were). . . . And the front half of the argument doesn't work either. The Clean Power Plan was not so big. It was not so new. And to the extent it was either, that should not matter.

As to bigness—well, events have proved the opposite: The Clean Power Plan, we now know, would have had little or no impact. The Trump administration's repeal of the Plan created a kind of controlled experiment . . . . [Even though the Plan was not in effect,] the industry exceeded [the Plan's nationwide emissions] target, all on its own. See App. 265 (declaration of EPA official). And it did so mainly through the generation-shifting techniques that the Plan called for. See *ibid.*; Brief for United States 47. In effect, the Plan predicted market behavior . . . .

. . . .

The majority's claim about the Clean Power Plan's novelty . . . is also exaggerated. As EPA explained when it issued the Clean Power Plan, an earlier Section 111(d) regulation had determined that a cap-and-trade program was the "best system of emission reduction" for mercury. 70 Fed. Reg. 28616–28621 (2005); see 80 Fed. Reg. 64772. In the majority's view, that rule was different because the "actual emission cap" for the contemplated cap-and-trade scheme was based on the use of a plant-specific technology—namely, wet scrubbers. *Ante* at 2610 (internal quotation marks omitted). But the approval of cap and trade allowed EPA to make the emissions limits more stringent than it otherwise could have, because EPA knew that plants unable to cost-effectively install scrubbers could instead meet the limits through generation shifting. See 70 Fed. Reg. 28619. EPA could have designed the Clean Power Plan in the same way—say, by setting emissions limits based on carbon-capture technology, with the expectation that many plants would avail themselves of an approved cap-and-trade program instead. The majority gives no reason to think Section 111(d) allows that approach but disallows the Clean Power Plan. In both, generation shifting is operating to increase the strictness of emissions limits.

And the mercury rule itself was rooted in precedent. . . .

In any event, newness might be perfectly legitimate—even required—from Congress's point of view. I do not dispute that an agency's longstanding practice may inform a court's interpretation of a statute delegating the agency power. . . . But it is equally true, as *Brown & Williamson* recognized, that agency practices are "not carved in stone." 529 U.S. at 156–157 (internal quotation marks omitted). Congress makes broad delegations in part so that agencies can "adapt their rules and policies to the demands of changing circumstances." *Id.* at 157. . . . So it is here. Section 111(d) . . . told EPA to pick the "best system of emission reduction" (taking into account various factors). In selecting those words, Congress understood—it had to—that the "best system" would change over time. Congress wanted and instructed EPA to keep up. . . . EPA followed those statutory directions to the letter when it issued the Clean Power Plan. It selected a system (as the regulated parties agree) that achieved greater emissions reductions at lower cost than any technological alternative could have, while maintaining a reliable electricity market. Even if that system was novel, it was in EPA's view better—actually, "best." So it was the system that accorded with the enacting Congress's choice.

And contra the majority, it is that Congress's choice which counts, not any later one's. The majority says it "cannot ignore" that Congress in recent years has "considered and rejected" cap-and-trade schemes. *Ante* at 2613–2614. But under normal principles of statutory construction, the majority *should* ignore that fact (just as I should ignore that Congress failed to enact bills barring EPA from implementing the Clean Power Plan). As we have explained time and again, failed legislation "offers a particularly dangerous basis on which to rest an interpretation of an existing law a different and earlier Congress" adopted. *Bostock* v. *Clayton County*, [140 S. Ct. 1731, 1747] (2020) (internal quotation marks omitted) . . . . [Thus, in *Massachusetts* v. *EPA*, when the Court recognized EPA's authority to regulate carbon dioxide, the Court said:] "That subsequent Congresses have eschewed enacting binding emissions limitations to combat global warming tells us nothing about what Congress meant" when it enacted the Clean Air Act. 549 U.S. at 529–530. . . .

III

Some years ago, I remarked that "[w]e're all textualists now." Harvard Law School, The Antonin Scalia Lecture Series: A Dialogue with Justice Elena Kagan on the Reading of Statutes (Nov. 25, 2015). It seems I was wrong. The current Court is textualist only when being so suits it. When that method would frustrate broader goals, special canons like the "major questions doctrine" magically appear as get-out-of-text-free cards. Today, one of those broader goals makes itself clear: Prevent agencies from doing important work, even though that is what Congress directed. That anti-administrative-state stance shows up in the majority opinion, and it suffuses the concurrence. . . .

. . . .

It is not surprising that Congress has always delegated, and continues to do so—including on important policy issues. . . . Consider just two reasons why.

First, Members of Congress often don't know enough—and know they don't know enough—to regulate sensibly on an issue. Of course, Members can and do provide overall direction. But then they rely, as all of us rely in our daily lives, on people with greater expertise and experience. Those people are found in agencies. Congress looks to them to make specific judgments about how to achieve its more general objectives. And it does so especially, though by no means exclusively, when an issue has a scientific or technical dimension. Why *wouldn't* Congress instruct EPA to select "the best system of emission reduction," rather than try to choose that system itself? . . . .

Second and relatedly, Members of Congress often can't know enough—and again, know they can't—to keep regulatory schemes working across time. Congress usually . . . can't anticipate changing circumstances and the way they will affect varied regulatory techniques. Nor can Congress (realistically) keep track of and respond to fast-flowing developments as they occur. Once again, that is most obviously true when it comes to scientific and technical matters. The "best system of emission reduction" is not today what it was yesterday, and will surely be something different tomorrow. . . .

Over time, the administrative delegations Congress has made have helped to build a modern Nation. Congress wanted fewer workers killed in industrial accidents. It wanted to prevent plane crashes, and reduce the deadliness of car wrecks. It wanted to ensure that consumer products didn't catch fire. It wanted to stop the routine adulteration of food and improve the safety and efficacy of medications. And it wanted cleaner air and water. If an American could go back in time, she might be astonished by how much progress has occurred in all those areas. It didn't happen through legislation alone. It happened because Congress gave broad-ranging powers to administrative agencies, and those agencies then filled in—rule by rule by rule—Congress's policy outlines.

This Court has historically known enough not to get in the way. . . . Maybe the best explanation of why comes from Justice Scalia. See *Mistretta* [*v. United States*, 488 U.S. 361, 415–16 (1989)] (dissenting opinion). The context was somewhat different. He was responding to an argument that Congress could not constitutionally delegate broad policymaking authority; here, the Court reads a delegation with unwarranted skepticism, and thereby artificially constrains its scope. But Justice Scalia's reasoning remains on point. . . . The scope of delegations, he said,

> "must be fixed according to common sense and the inherent necessities of the governmental co-ordination. Since Congress is no less endowed with common sense than we are, and better equipped to inform itself of the necessities of government; and since the factors bearing upon those necessities are both multifarious and (in the nonpartisan sense) highly political . . . it is small wonder that we have almost never felt qualified to second-guess Congress regarding the permissible degree of policy judgment that can be left to those executing or applying the law." *Id.* at 416 (internal quotation marks omitted).

In short, when it comes to delegations, there are good reasons for Congress (within extremely broad limits) to get to call the shots. . . . Courts should be modest.

Today, the Court is not. Section 111, most naturally read, authorizes EPA to develop the Clean Power Plan—in other words, to decide that generation shifting is the "best system of emission reduction" for power plants churning out carbon dioxide. . . . In rewriting that text, the Court substitutes its own ideas about delegations for Congress's. And that means the Court substitutes its own ideas about policymaking for Congress's. The Court will not allow the Clean Air Act to work as Congress instructed. The Court, rather than Congress, will decide how much regulation is too much.

The subject matter of the regulation here makes the Court's intervention all the more troubling. Whatever else this Court may know about, it does not have a clue about how to address climate change. And let's say the obvious: The stakes here are high. Yet the Court today prevents congressionally authorized agency action to curb power plants' carbon dioxide emissions. The Court appoints itself—instead of Congress or the expert agency—the decision-maker on climate policy. I cannot think of many things more frightening. . . .

NOTES AND QUESTIONS

1. In *Whitman v. American Trucking Ass'ns*, 531 U.S. 457 (2001), Justice Scalia's majority opinion indicated that "vague terms or ancillary provisions" in federal statutes should not be interpreted to "alter the fundamental details of a regulatory scheme," because "Congress . . . does not hide elephants in mouseholes." *Id.* at 468 (attributing this lesson to *MCI Telecommunications Corp. v. AT&T Co.*, 512 U.S. 218, 231 (1994), and *FDA v. Brown & Williamson Tobacco Corp.*, 529 U.S. 120, 159–60 (2000)). The latter words quickly became prominent; as of May 2023, references to elephants in mouseholes have appeared in more than four hundred federal judicial opinions (all since *Whitman*), and the Supreme Court has even referred to "the no-elephants-in-mouseholes canon." *Bostock v. Clayton County*, 140 S. Ct. 1731, 1753 (2020); *see also* Sackett v. EPA, 143 S. Ct. 1322, 1340 (2023) (again invoking this image). The majority in *West Virginia v. EPA* described the major-questions doctrine along these lines: according to the majority, § 111(d) of the Clean Air Act was a minor "backwater" in the overall statutory scheme, and the majority refused to find a grant of major regulatory authority in it.

Justice Kagan's dissent, by contrast, argued that § 111(d) was not a backwater or mousehole at all. While she agreed that it was a "backstop," she argued that it nonetheless played an important role in the overall statutory scheme. According to the dissent, if an air pollutant is not covered by the NAAQS or HAP programs, § 111(d) enables EPA to regulate its emission by existing stationary sources. In Justice Kagan's words, § 111(d) therefore "operates to ensure that the Act achieves comprehensive pollution control." *West Virginia v. EPA*, 142 S. Ct. at 2629 (Kagan, J., dissenting).

Still, how important that role looks might depend on which pollutants trigger it. In retrospect, § 111(d) might seem very important indeed. Carbon dioxide is a major greenhouse gas, and it is emitted in large quantities by many stationary sources in the United States, but it is not currently covered by either the NAAQS or the HAP programs—so the "backstop" function served by § 111(d) seems crucial. But when Congress added § 111 to the Act in 1970, and even when Congress last revised § 111 in 1990, people might well have thought that all of the most troublesome air pollutants would be covered by the NAAQS and HAP programs, and that § 111(d) would have little work to do. Not until *Massachusetts v. EPA*, 549 U.S. 497 (2007), did the Supreme Court make clear that the Clean Air Act's general definition of "air pollutant" encompasses carbon dioxide and other greenhouse gases. At that point, moreover, some people might have thought that EPA would eventually include greenhouse gases in the NAAQS program. But in addition to the political obstacles facing such a move, the Supreme Court's decision in *Utility Air Regulatory Group v. EPA*, 573 U.S. 302 (2014), raised legal obstacles too. This combination of circumstances, which lifted § 111(d) to prominence, would have been difficult for anyone in the enacting Congress to foresee. That does not necessarily defeat Justice Kagan's point; one reason to include a backstop in a statute is to accommodate changes in understandings and needs. Still, the potential significance of § 111(d) became more apparent over time.

2. Even if members of Congress regarded § 111(d) as a minor provision, though, would that tell us anything about what § 111 meant by the word "system" or the phrase "best system of emission reduction"? As a textual matter, the key interpretive question might seem to be something like this: when the states and EPA are developing standards of performance for existing stationary sources under § 111(d), and when they are identifying the "best system of emission reduction" for that purpose, can this "system" include ideas for shifting activity from one type of source to another type of source? Until the very end of the majority opinion, one might have guessed that the majority was going to say "no"; the majority seemed to be leading up to the conclusion that, as relevant to any existing stationary source, a "system of emission reduction" is something that can be put into operation at that particular source, so that the source will generate less pollution per unit of desired output.

If the majority had cast its conclusion that broadly, could it still have drawn support from the major-questions doctrine? Would authorizing EPA to encourage or require generation-shifting *automatically* be a big deal, without regard to the particular pollutant at issue, the number and significance of the sources that emit it, or the potential disruptiveness of shifting to other sources? If not, should the major-questions doctrine still affect how courts interpret the word "system," because generation-shifting requirements would *sometimes* be a big deal?

Ultimately, the majority did not take this route. In the words of the second-to-last paragraph of the majority opinion, "We have no occasion to decide whether the statutory phrase 'system of emission reduction' refers *exclusively* to measures that improve the pollution performance of individual sources . . . ." *West Virginia v. EPA*, 142 S. Ct. at 2615. Instead of providing a general definition of the word "system" or the phrase "system of emission reduction," the majority confined itself to the question that it posed at the start of Part III.A of its opinion: "whether restructuring the Nation's overall mix of electricity generation, to transition from 38% coal to 27% coal by 2030, can be the 'best system of emission reduction' within the meaning of Section 111." *Id.* at 2607. *That* was the issue that the majority used the major-questions doctrine to resolve. As used by the majority, then, the major-questions doctrine was not a way to choose between two possible understandings of the word "system." Instead, the majority used the doctrine more as an implied-limitation rule. In the majority's view, seemingly minor provisions like § 111(d) come with an implicit cap on the uses to which the agency can put them; whatever the surface meaning of its terms, § 111(d) should not be understood to give EPA truly major policymaking authority.[23]

Does it make sense for courts to recognize an implied-limitation rule of this sort? If a statutory provision delegates authority to an agency, but the provision appears designed to play only a minor role in the overall statutory scheme, can courts fairly infer a limitation on the importance of the things that the agency can use the provision to do? Or should the agency be able to assert authority according to the ordinary meaning of the terms that Congress chose, without any such implied limitation?

Especially if the major-questions doctrine operates as an implied-limitation rule, judges will have to draw lines without obvious statutory guideposts. For instance, judges will have to decide which statutory provisions are "mouseholes"—provisions that allow agencies to do run-of-the-mill things but that should not be understood to authorize major initiatives. Likewise, judges will have to decide whether the authority that an agency has asserted is indeed "major," so that clearer-than-usual authorization is necessary. *Cf.* U.S. Telecom Ass'n v. FCC, 855 F.3d 381, 423 (D.C. Cir. 2017) (Kavanaugh, J., dissenting from the denial of rehearing en banc) ("[D]etermining whether a rule constitutes a major rule sometimes has a bit of a 'know it when you see it' quality."). Should

---

[23] Consistent with that idea, Justice Gorsuch's concurring opinion analogized the major-questions doctrine to the presumption against retroactivity (which supports reading implied temporal limitations into seeming general statutory language). *Id.* at 2619 (Gorsuch, J., concurring). In a later footnote, the concurring opinion also indicated that the major-questions doctrine operates as "a clear-statement rule" rather than "an ambiguity canon." *Id.* at 2620 n.3. Still, the import of that footnote is uncertain; Justice Gorsuch did not define what he meant by a "clear-statement rule," and he may have been using the phrase "ambiguity canon" to mean a canon that operates only in cases of equipoise. *See id.* ("Ambiguity canons merely instruct courts on how to 'choos[e] between equally plausible interpretations of ambiguous text,' and are thus weaker than clear-statement rules." (quoting Amy Coney Barrett, *Substantive Canons and Faithful Agency*, 90 B.U. L. REV. 109, 109 (2010))).

we worry that those decisions will end up reflecting the judges' own political and economic views?

Some other implied-limitation rules, like the presumption against retroactivity and the presumption against extraterritoriality, address issues that members of Congress might not have in mind when they enact generally worded statutes. But when Congress delegates even minor authority to an administrative agency, members of Congress presumably think about what they are authorizing the agency to do. To the extent that the major-questions doctrine is supposed to reflect the scope of the authority that Congress intended a particular statutory provision to delegate, why isn't the conventional meaning of the provision's words the best guide to what Congress intended? Does the major-questions doctrine encourage judges to second-guess the language of statutory delegations in ways that textualists usually oppose? If you support the doctrine, how do you respond to Justice Kagan's charge that it amounts to a "get-out-of-text-free card[ ]" for judges who are more concerned about delegations than Congress itself is? *See West Virginia v. EPA*, 142 S. Ct. at 2641 (Kagan, J., dissenting).

This line of questions may seem to suggest that the major-questions doctrine should not operate as an implied-limitation rule, but only as a tool for resolving conventional linguistic indeterminacy in statutory delegations. But does that conclusion go too far? Many federal statutes are structured as follows: they set out some substantive provisions of their own, and they also authorize an administrative agency to make rules and regulations to help carry out those provisions. If the statutory provisions themselves are relatively minor, wouldn't it be natural for courts to infer a corresponding limitation on the scope of the agency's rulemaking authority—so that the agency cannot use that authority to do sweeping things, even if those things would indeed help carry out the statute's provisions? Can courts assume that the agency's rules must remain subsidiary to the statute itself, and that Congress is not authorizing the agency to impose requirements that are out of proportion to the importance of the statute's own provisions? Is that a manageable standard?

3. Rather than casting the major-questions doctrine as a "descriptive" canon (aimed at estimating Congress's intentions with respect to the scope of delegations), some advocates of the doctrine might instead see it as more "normative." For instance, they might cast the nondelegation doctrine as an "underenforced constitutional norm," and they might see the major-questions doctrine as a way to help effectuate constitutional values that courts cannot readily vindicate more directly. *See supra* pp. 211–212 (discussing this type of argument).

That argument, however, raises the same concerns that Chapter 2 suggested with respect to other normative canons. In any event, many scholars disagree that the Constitution establishes a robust rule against congressional delegations of lawmaking power, so they do not accept the premise that the nondelegation doctrine is "underenforced."[24] As Justice Kagan suggested at the end of her dissent in *West Virginia v. EPA*, moreover, if the constitutional nondelegation doctrine is indeed "underenforced," the reason may be that courts are not in a good position to make the judgment calls that a more robust version of the doctrine would require—which, if true, would also counsel against beefing up the doctrine under the guise of statutory interpretation.

4. What should we make of the majority's emphasis on EPA's alleged change of position? According to the majority, between 1970 (when Congress added § 111 to the Clean Air Act) and 2015 (when EPA promulgated the Clean Power Plan rule), "EPA had always set emissions limits under Section 111 based on the application of measures that would reduce pollution by causing the regulated source to operate more cleanly." *West Virginia v. EPA*, 142 S. Ct. at 2610. The majority suggested that this practice had reflected the EPA's "consistent understanding" of the relevant statutory language, *id.* at 2611, and that the Clean Power Plan rule rested on a claim of "newly uncovered" regulatory authority, *id.* at 2614. Quoting a pre-*Chevron* opinion, the majority indicated that EPA's consistent past interpretation was a better guide to the statute's meaning than its new position. *See id.* at 2610 ("[A]s Justice Frankfurter has noted, 'just as established practice may shed light on the extent of power conveyed by general statutory language, so the want of assertion of power by those who presumably would be alert to exercise it, is equally significant in determining whether such power was actually conferred.' " (quoting FTC v. Bunte Bros., Inc., 312 U.S. 349, 352 (1941))). Justice Gorsuch agreed. *See id.* at 2623 (Gorsuch, J., concurring) ("A 'contemporaneous and long-held Executive Branch interpretation of a statute is entitled to some weight as evidence of the statute's original charge to an agency. . . . Conversely, in *NFIB v. OSHA*, the Court found it 'telling that OSHA, in its half century of existence, ha[d] never before adopted a broad public health regulation' under the statute that the agency sought to invoke as authority for a nationwide vaccine mandate." (first quoting United States v. Philbrick, 120 U.S. 52, 59 (1887); then quoting NFIB v. OSHA, 142 S. Ct. 661, 665 (2022) (per curiam))).

As Professor Bamzai has noted, judges had a long tradition of paying some respect both to longstanding understandings of a statute and to understandings that were contemporaneous with the statute's enactment, and this tradition accounts for some of the pre-*Chevron*

---

[24] *Compare* Julian Davis Mortenson & Nicholas Bagley, *Delegation at the Founding*, 121 COLUM. L. REV. 277, 367 (2021) (arguing baldly that "[t]here was no nondelegation doctrine at the Founding"), *and* Nicholas R. Parrillo, *A Critical Assessment of the Originalist Case Against Administrative Regulatory Power: New Evidence from the Federal Tax on Private Real Estate in the 1790s*, 130 YALE L.J. 1288, 1455 (2021) (not going as far as Mortenson and Bagley, but concluding that "[f]oreign or domestic, public or private, [administrative] rulemaking has been with us since the beginning"), *with* Ilan Wurman, *Nondelegation at the Founding*, 130 YALE L.J. 1490, 1498 (2021) (suggesting that Founding-era history supports "a nondelegation doctrine whereby Congress could not delegate to the Executive decisions over 'important subjects' " (quoting Wayman & Southard, 23 U.S. (10 Wheat.) 1, 43 (1825))).

history of judicial deference to executive-branch interpretations. *See generally* Aditya Bamzai, *The Origins of Judicial Deference to Executive Interpretation*, 126 YALE L.J. 908 (2017). Even under *Chevron*, courts may pay attention to customary or contemporaneous understandings of a statute when courts are identifying the range of readings that are available to the administering agency. Where *Chevron* applies, though, the agency ordinarily can switch from one reading to another within the "permissible" range (as long as the agency does not behave arbitrarily and capriciously), and courts will defer to the agency's new reading just as they would have deferred to the agency's initial reading. Indeed, that happened in *Chevron* itself. Likewise, Justice Scalia once wrote that "the capacity of the *Chevron* approach to accept changes in agency interpretation *ungrudgingly* seems to me one of the strongest indications that the *Chevron* approach is correct." Antonin Scalia, *Judicial Deference to Administrative Interpretations of Law*, 1989 DUKE L.J. 511, 518; *see also id.* at 517 (arguing that "when we acknowledge that the agency is free to give the statute whichever of several possible meanings it thinks most conducive to the accomplishment of the statutory purpose," courts should not "hold[ ] the agency to its first answer, or penaliz[e] it for a change of mind").

In *West Virginia v. EPA*, the majority did not mention *Chevron* at all.[25] That is consistent with the idea that the major-questions doctrine is *both* a "Step Zero" doctrine (which makes the *Chevron* framework inapplicable) *and* a substantive nondelegation canon (which guides the courts in their own interpretation of how much authority Congress has given the responsible agency). But how did the alleged novelty of EPA's position intersect with the substantive nondelegation canon? If EPA had interpreted § 111 as giving EPA "major" authority from the start, would the agency's position have fared better in court? To the extent that the major-questions doctrine is a substantive nondelegation canon, does it operate with special force when an agency initially interprets a statutory provision as giving the agency run-of-the-mill authority, and only later re-interprets the provision as conferring "major" authority?

5. In concluding that Congress had not authorized EPA to adopt the Clean Power Plan, the majority observed that the Plan "essentially adopted a cap-and-trade scheme," and "Congress . . . has consistently rejected proposals to amend the Clean Air Act to create such a program." *West Virginia v. EPA*, 142 S. Ct. at 2614. Justice Kagan took the majority to task for attaching legal significance to failed bills. *See id.* at 2641 (Kagan, J., dissenting). Chief Justice Roberts did not respond to this criticism, but Justice Gorsuch did. In his telling, the majority was not using the failed bills "to resolve what a duly enacted statutory text means," but "only to help resolve the antecedent question whether the

[25] *Cf.* Louis J. Capozzi III, *The Past and Future of the Major Questions Doctrine*, 84 OHIO ST. L.J. 191, 224 (2023) (noting that the federal government's brief "didn't even ask for *Chevron* deference").

agency's challenged action implicates a major question." *Id.* at 2621 n.4 (Gorsuch, J., concurring). According to Justice Gorsuch, moreover, that was appropriate: the fact that "Congress has 'considered and rejected' bills authorizing something akin to the agency's proposed course of action" can have evidentiary value as "a sign that an agency is attempting to 'work [a]round' the legislative process to resolve for itself a question of great political significance." *Id.* at 2621 (some internal quotation marks omitted).

Does Justice Gorsuch's distinction work? If the Court uses Congress's consideration and rejection of a bill as evidence in support of applying the major-questions doctrine, and if the major-questions doctrine is a canon of statutory interpretation, isn't there a sense in which the Court is using the failed bill "to resolve what a duly enacted statute means"?

Even if you accept Justice Gorsuch's distinction, what *is* the evidentiary value of the fact that a bill was proposed but that Congress did not enact it? To know what to make of that fact, would a court need to try to identify the reason(s) why the bill failed? For instance, if members of Congress decided not to enact the bill because they thought that existing law authorized the agency to adopt the relevant proposal and that the agency could reach a more expert judgment than Congress about whether the proposal is a good idea, would the fact that the bill failed still support applying the major-questions doctrine? Will courts be able to reach accurate conclusions about the internal legislative dynamics that caused a bill to fail?

6. To decide *West Virginia v. EPA*, the Court had to interpret § 111(d) of the Clean Air Act. But the Supreme Court did not discuss lingering questions about what the text of that provision even is.

Congress added § 111 to the Clean Air Act in 1970. Section 111(b) authorized the Administrator of the EPA to establish "standards of performance" for "new" stationary sources (that is, stationary sources that were constructed or modified after EPA announced the applicable standard of performance). Section 111(d) dealt with "existing" stationary sources. As amended in 1977 and 1978, § 111(d)(1)(A) spoke of "establish[ing] standards of performance for any existing source for any air pollutant (i) for which air quality criteria have not been issued or which is not included on a list published under section 108(a) or 112(b)(1)(A) but (ii) to which a standard of performance under this section would apply if such existing source were a new source." *See* Clean Air Act Amendments of 1970, Pub. L. 91–604, sec. 4(a), § 111(d)(1), 84 Stat. 1676, 1684 (codified as amended at 42 U.S.C. § 7411(d)(1)(A)); Clean Air Act Amendments of 1977, Pub. L. 95–95, § 109(b)(1), 91 Stat. 685, 699; Act of Nov. 9, 1978, Pub. L. 95–623, § 13(a)(2), 92 Stat. 3443, 3458. The language in clause (i) about "air quality criteria" and pollutants "included on a list published under section 108(a)" involved the NAAQS program. Likewise, the reference to "a list published under section . . . 112(b)(1)(A)" involved the Hazardous Air Pollutants (HAP) program; § 112(b)(1)(A) gave the Administrator a duty to publish and periodically revise "a list which includes each hazardous air pollutant for which he intends to establish an emission standard under [§ 112]." Clean Air Act Amendments of 1970, sec. 4(a), § 112(b)(1)(A), 84 Stat. at 1685.

By 1990, EPA had put only eight pollutants on the HAP list, and Congress decided to take action itself. *See* Am. Lung Ass'n v. EPA, 985 F.3d 914, 978 (D.C. Cir. 2021), *rev'd sub nom.* West Virginia v. EPA, 142 S. Ct. 2587 (2022). The 1990 amendments to the Clean Air Act therefore included a new version of § 112. *See* Act of Nov. 15, 1990, Pub. L. 101–549, sec. 301, 104 Stat. 2399, 2531 (codified as amended at 42 U.S.C. § 7412). Instead of relying on EPA to list hazardous pollutants, the new § 112(b)(1) itself listed almost two hundred hazardous pollutants. *Id.* at 2532–35. Still, the new § 112(b)(2) directed the Administrator to "periodically review the list established by this subsection and publish the results thereof, and, where appropriate, revise such list by rule." *Id.* at 2535. Section 112(c) also directed the Administrator to publish and periodically revise "a list of all categories and subcategories of major sources and area sources . . . of the air pollutants listed pursuant to subsection (b)," and then to establish emissions standards for them under § 112(d). *Id.* at 2537.

At the same time that Congress was revising § 112, Congress also had to change the then-existing version of § 111(d)(1)(A), which (as quoted above) had referred to "a list published under section 108(a) or 112(b)(1)(A)." (The new § 112(b)(1) did not include a subparagraph (A).) By mistake, though, the 1990 amendments to the Clean Air Act enacted *two* such changes. One appeared in a section headed "Conforming Amendments," found immediately after the provision enacting the new § 112. It read as follows: "Section 111(d)(1) of the Clean Air Act is amended by striking '112(b)(1)(A)' and inserting in lieu thereof '112(b)'." *Id.* sec. 302(a), 104 Stat. at 2574. The other appeared more than one hundred pages earlier in the same 1990 statute, in a section headed "Miscellaneous Guidance." It said: "Section 111(d)(1)(A)(i) of the Clean Air Act . . . is amended by striking 'or 112(b)(1)(A)' and inserting 'or emitted from a source category which is regulated under section 112'." *Id.* sec. 108(g), 104 Stat. at 2467.

It is not possible to make *both* of these changes to § 111(d)(1). (Once one of the changes is made, the term "112(b)(1)(A)" would no longer appear in § 111(d)(1), so the predicate for the other change would be missing.) The Office of the Law Revision Counsel (OLRC) confronted this issue early on, because it had to figure out how to revise the corresponding section of the *United States Code*. The OLRC made the change that appeared first in the 1990 statute (that is, the one in the "Miscellaneous Guidance" section) and said that the change in the later section "could not be executed, because of the prior amendment." *See* 42 U.S.C. § 7411 note (Amendments) (Supp. II 1991).

Of course, OLRC's action in publishing the *United States Code* did not alter what the law actually is;[26] the question remains what to make of the statute that Congress enacted in 1990, which contains two different amendments to the same language in the pre-existing version of § 111(d)(1). There are various conceivable approaches:

- *Perhaps the amendment that appears earlier in the 1990 statute takes priority.* When a statute contains a series of amendments to an earlier statute, interpreters who are trying to identify the net result might proceed in sequence, starting from the beginning of the new statute. If that is the conventional approach, perhaps it operates even in this unusual situation—with the result that the change contained in the "Miscellaneous Guidance" section would take effect and the other change would not (just as the OLRC concluded).
- *Perhaps "substantive" amendments take priority over mere "conforming" amendments.* The heading of the section that contained the first amendment ("Miscellaneous Guidance") does not sound very important, but it is not purely technical. By contrast, the heading of the section that contained the other amendment was "Conforming Amendments," which *is* purely technical. According to an amicus brief filed on behalf of mostly Republican members of Congress in a related case in the D.C. Circuit, "basic principles of legislative drafting . . . require that substantive amendments be applied first, followed by any remaining conforming amendments that have not been rendered obsolete." Brief for Members of Congress as Amici Curiae in Support of Petitioners at 11, *West Virginia v. EPA*, No. 15–1363 (D.C. Cir. Feb. 23, 2016).
- *Perhaps interpreters should consult the legislative history of the 1990 statute for clues about whether one of the two amendments was included in the final bill by mistake.* A panel of the D.C. Circuit disagreed about how to interpret the legislative history, but one of the judges found modest support for the idea that the conference report that Congress had enacted into law should have included only the "Miscellaneous Guidance" amendment and not the subsequent "Conforming Amendment." *See Am. Lung Ass'n*, 985 F.3d at 1007–08 (Walker, J., concurring and dissenting).
- *Perhaps the 1990 statute should not be understood to make either amendment.* Writing in 2016, a student author proposed this solution on the basis of a purported canon found in Justice Scalia and Bryan Garner's book. *See* Brenden Cline, *Scalia's Swan Song: The Late Justice's "Irreconcilability Canon"*

[26] Even if Congress wanted to delegate a species of lawmaking authority to the OLRC, *Chadha* presumably would prevent Congress from doing so, because the OLRC is a unit within Congress rather than the executive branch.

Resolves the Clean Air Act's Section 111(d) Drafting Error and Promotes Good Lawmaking, 5/19/2016 GEO. ENVTL. L. REV. ONLINE 1 ("The 'irreconcilability canon' says: '[i]f a text contains truly irreconcilable provisions at the same level of generality, and they have been simultaneously adopted, neither provision should be given effect." (quoting ANTONIN SCALIA & BRYAN A. GARNER, READING LAW: THE INTERPRETATION OF LEGAL TEXTS 189 (2012))).[27]

If there are multiple "permissible" resolutions of this problem, should EPA receive *Chevron* deference for its choice among them, or is this not the sort of issue that should trigger the *Chevron* framework?

How one solves this problem matters, because the two amendments contained in the 1990 statute have different imports. Prior to 1990, § 111(d) of the Clean Air Act contemplated establishing standards of performance for existing stationary sources with respect to air pollutants that were not covered by either the NAAQS program or the HAP program. That would remain true if § 111(d)(1) were amended according to the instructions in the "Conforming Amendments" section of the 1990 statute. But if § 111(d)(1) were instead amended according to the instructions in the "Miscellaneous Guidance" section, the situation might be dramatically different. Under those instructions, § 111(d)(1) would now speak of "establish[ing] standards of performance for any existing source for any air pollutant (i) for which air quality criteria have not been issued or which is not included on a list published under section 108(a) or emitted from a source category which is regulated under section 112 but (ii) to which a standard of performance under this section would apply if such existing source were a new source." That syntax is tangled, but it appears to authorize standards of performance for existing sources only for air pollutants that are "not . . . emitted from a source category which is regulated under section 112." In his dissenting opinion in the D.C. Circuit, Judge Justin Walker relied on that language to conclude that § 111(d) no longer authorizes EPA to regulate the emission of *any* air pollutants from existing coal-fired power plants. According to Judge Walker, "[c]oal-fired power plants are a source regulated under § 112," because "[t]heir mercury emissions are regulated under § 112." *Am. Lung Ass'n*, 985 F.3d at 1104 & n.65 (Walker, J., concurring and dissenting).

As one might expect, EPA offered a different interpretation when EPA promulgated the Clean Power Plan rule. As EPA observed, "source categories . . . are not regulated under § 112 with respect to all pollutants, but only with respect to HAP"—the hazardous air pollutants that § 112 covers. *See* Carbon Pollution Emission Guidelines for Existing Stationary Sources: Electric Utility Generating Units, 80 Fed. Reg. 64662, 64714 (Oct. 23, 2015). According to EPA, the phrase "any air

[27] If neither of the 1990 amendments was effective, § 111(d)(1) would continue to refer to "section . . . 112(b)(1)(A)" even though there is no longer any such unit. What should interpreters make of this reference?

pollutant . . . which is not . . . emitted from a source category which is regulated under section 112" should be understood accordingly. In particular, EPA argued that even if § 111(d)(1) incorporated the amendment made by the "Miscellaneous Guidance" provision, the new language would simply prevent EPA from regulating the emission of HAP from coal-fired power plants; EPA could still regulate the emission of non-HAP pollutants, such as carbon dioxide. *Id.*; *see also* Revision of December 2000 Regulatory Finding on the Emissions of Hazardous Air Pollutants from Electric Utility Steam Generating Units, 70 Fed. Reg. 15994, 16030–32 (Mar. 29, 2005) (reaching a similar bottom line, albeit on different grounds, in a prior rulemaking).

Although the Supreme Court did not flag this issue in *West Virginia v. EPA*, Justice Kagan's dissent tacitly rejected the position that Judge Walker had taken below. *See* 142 S. Ct. at 2629 (Kagan, J., dissenting) (indicating that as applied to existing sources, § 111(d) "mandates . . . that EPA set emissions levels for pollutants not covered by the NAAQS or HAP programs," and "thus ensures that EPA regulates existing power plants' emissions of *all* pollutants"). The majority opinion was worded more ambiguously, but it did not pick a fight over this point. *See id.* at 2601 (observing that under § 111(d), once EPA has established a standard of performance for new sources under § 111(b), EPA "must then address emissions of that same pollutant by existing sources—but only if they are not already regulated under the NAAQS or HAP programs").

When interpreters are trying to understand the amendment made by the "Miscellaneous Guidance" section in the 1990 statute, should their reading be influenced by the existence of the other amendment in the "Conforming Amendments" section? In the D.C. Circuit, the panel majority suggested that it was desirable to seek a "harmonizing reading" of the two amendments, so that one did not produce dramatically different results than the other. *Am. Lung Ass'n*, 985 F.3d at 980.

7. The Supreme Court invoked the major-questions doctrine again in *Biden v. Nebraska*, 143 S. Ct. 2355 (2023). In 2022, the Secretary of Education had purported to cancel roughly $430 billion in student-loan debt owed by roughly 43 million borrowers. *See* Federal Student Aid Programs, 87 Fed. Reg. 61512, 61514 (Oct. 12, 2022). As authority, the Secretary pointed to a 2003 statute providing that "the Secretary of Education . . . may waive or modify any statutory or regulatory provision applicable to the student financial assistance programs under title IV of the [Higher Education Act of 1965] as the Secretary deems necessary in connection with a war or other military operation or national emergency." Higher Education Relief Opportunities for Students Act of 2003, Pub. L. 108–76, § 2(a)(1), 117 Stat. 904, 904 (codified at 20 U.S.C. § 1098bb(a)(1)).

At the time of the Secretary's action, the COVID-19 epidemic remained a "national emergency" within the meaning of this statute. *See id.* § 5(4), 117 Stat. at 907 (codified at 20 U.S.C. § 1098ee(4)) (defining "national emergency" to mean "a national emergency declared by the President of the United States"); Presidential Proclamation 9994, 85 Fed. Reg. 15337, 15337 (Mar. 18, 2020) (declaring that "the COVID-19 outbreak in the United States constitutes a national emergency, beginning March 1, 2020"); Notice, 86 Fed. Reg. 11599 (Feb. 24, 2021) (continuing this declaration); Notice, 87 Fed. Reg. 10289 (Feb. 18, 2022) (same). Nonetheless, a majority of the Supreme Court ultimately held that the statute did not give the Secretary the sweeping cancellation authority that the Secretary had asserted. The majority relied partly on its exegesis of the words "modify" and "waive" in the 2003 statute. *See Biden v. Nebraska*, 143 S. Ct. at 2368 ("[S]tatutory permission to 'modify' does not authorize 'basic and fundamental changes in the scheme' designed by Congress." (quoting MCI Telecommunications Corp. v. AT&T Co., 512 U.S. 218, 225 (1994)); *id.* at 2370–71 (indicating that instead of "waiving" any existing provisions, "[w]hat the Secretary has actually done is draft a new section of the Education Act from scratch"). In support of its interpretation, the majority also invoked the major-questions doctrine. *See id.* at 2373 (resisting the idea that Congress has given the Secretary "virtually unlimited power to rewrite the Education Act" and noting that "[t]he ' "economic and political significance" ' of the Secretary's action is staggering by any measure" (quoting *West Virginia*, 142 S. Ct. at 2608, in turn quoting *Brown & Williamson*, 529 U.S. at 160)).

In a thoughtful concurring opinion, Justice Barrett addressed why the major-questions doctrine exists and where it fits in the project of statutory interpretation. She began by discussing what she called "substantive" canons, which correspond to what this book calls "normative" canons. *See id.* at 2376 & n.1 (Barrett, J., concurring) (defining "substantive canons" as "rules of construction that advance values external to a statute," and contrasting them with "linguistic or descriptive canons"). Some normative canons operate simply as tie-breakers. *See id.* at 2376 (using the rule of lenity as an example). But Justice Barrett described other normative canons as being "more aggressive"; they push courts away from "the better interpretation of a statute" if that interpretation "leads to a disfavored result" and if a different interpretation is at least "tenable." *See id.* (calling these canons "strong-form substantive canons" and observing that "[u]nlike a tie-breaking rule, a strong-form canon counsels a court to *strain* statutory text to advance a particular value").

As Justice Barrett acknowledged, canons of the latter sort "are 'in significant tension with textualism' insofar as they instruct a court to adopt something other than the statute's most natural meaning." *Id.* at 2377 (quoting Amy Coney Barrett, *Substantive Canons and Faithful Agency*, 90 B.U. L. REV. 109, 123 (2010)); *see also* Benjamin Eidelson & Matthew C. Stephenson, *The Incompatibility of Substantive Canons and Textualism*, 137 HARV. L. REV. (forthcoming 2024) (persuasively identifying not just "tension" but out-and-out contradiction). Without committing herself to repudiate all strong-form normative canons that currently exist, Justice Barrett said that she was "wary of adopting new ones." *Biden v. Nebraska*, 143 S. Ct. at 2377 n.2 (Barrett, J., concurring).

Critics of the major-questions doctrine have characterized it as just such a canon—one that tries to protect an otherwise underenforced constitutional norm by " 'load[ing] the dice' so that a plausible antidelegation interpretation wins even if the agency's interpretation is better." *Id.* at 2378. Justice Barrett indicated that if this characterization were correct, she would not accept the major-questions doctrine. *See id.* at 2377 n.2. But she argued that the characterization is not correct. When used properly, she suggested, the major-questions doctrine is not a normative canon at all. Instead, "the major questions doctrine is a tool for discerning—not departing from—the text's most natural interpretation." *Id.* at 2376. In Justice Barrett's telling, the major-questions doctrine simply "reflect[s] 'common sense as to the manner in which Congress is likely to delegate a policy decision of such economic and political magnitude to an administrative agency.' " *Id.* at 2378 (quoting *Brown & Williamson*, 529 U.S. at 133).

Justice Barrett's basic point was that all texts must be understood in context, and sometimes the context of a delegation supplies implied limitations. By way of analogy, she offered the following example:

> "Consider a parent who hires a babysitter to watch her young children over the weekend. As she walks out the door, the parent hands the babysitter her credit card and says: 'Make sure the kids have fun.' Emboldened, the babysitter takes the kids on a road trip to an amusement park, where they spend two days on rollercoasters and one night in a hotel. Was the babysitter's trip . . . consistent with a *reasonable* understanding of the parent's instruction? Highly doubtful. In the normal course, permission to spend money on fun authorizes a babysitter to take children to the local ice cream parlor or movie theater, not on a multiday excursion to an out-of-town amusement park. If a parent were willing to greenlight a trip that big, we would expect much more clarity than a general instruction to 'make sure the kids have fun.' "

Id. at 2379–80; *see also id.* at 2382 (similarly noting that "an instruction to 'pick up dessert' is not permission to buy a four-tier wedding cake"). According to Justice Barrett, "[T]he major questions doctrine grows out of these same commonsense principles of communication. Just as we would expect a parent to give more than a general instruction if she intended to authorize a babysitter-led getaway, we also 'expect Congress to speak clearly if it wishes to assign to an agency decisions of vast "economic and political significance." ' " *Id.* at 2380 (quoting *Utility Air*, 573 U.S. at 324, in turn quoting *Brown & Williamson*, 529 U.S. at 160).

Admittedly, Justice Barrett grounded this expectation not just in an estimate of Congress's actual intentions, but also in the context supplied by "the Constitution's structure." *Id.* (emphasizing that Article I vests all of the federal government's legislative powers in Congress); *see also id.* at 2380–81 (claiming that "in a system of separated powers, a reasonably informed interpreter would expect Congress to legislate on 'important subjects' while delegating away only 'the details'" (quoting Wayman v. Southard, 23 U.S. (10 Wheat.) 1, 43 (1825))). Still, she suggested that the major-questions doctrine fits Congress's ordinary practices. *See, e.g., id.* at 2383 ("The shared intuition behind [many of the Court's major-questions cases] is that a reasonable speaker would not understand Congress to confer an unusual form of authority without saying more."); *id.* at 2380 (noting in a parenthetical that "the major questions doctrine rests on 'both separation of powers principles and a practical understanding of legislative intent'" (quoting *West Virginia v. EPA*, 142 S. Ct. at 2609)); *cf. id.* at 2381 (contrasting the major-questions doctrine with "a normative rule that *discourages* Congress from empowering agencies"). She also cautioned against using the major-questions doctrine to distort statutes that, in context, should indeed be understood to delegate major policymaking authority. *See id.* at 2384 ("[T]he doctrine should not be taken for more than it is—the familiar principle that we do not interpret a statute for all that it is worth when a reasonable person would not read it that way.").

---

2. THE RELATIONSHIP BETWEEN *CHEVRON* AND OTHER INTERPRETIVE DOCTRINES

Assuming that the Supreme Court retains *Chevron* in some form, the concept of deference to federal administrative agencies adds another dimension to issues addressed in previous chapters of this book. We have considered how courts should understand the relationship between a statute's apparent purposes and its literal text (Chapter 1), the weight that courts might place on generic canons of construction (Chapter 2), whether and for what purposes courts should pay attention to internal legislative history in determining a statute's meaning (Chapter 3), how much the doctrine of *stare decisis* might constrain the interpretive freedom of later courts (Chapter 4), and a host of related issues. As we have seen, there is room for reasonable disagreement on many of these issues, and different judges take somewhat different positions. Should this diversity of views affect how courts apply the *Chevron* framework—so that even judges who are committed to one position in methodological debates sometimes should accept agency interpretations that are predicated on another position?

Institutional differences between courts and agencies add a further wrinkle. At least to some extent, people's views about the interpretive techniques that courts should use are influenced by beliefs about the courts' capabilities—how well judges can process various categories of information and how reliable their judgments will be. But generalist courts are likely to have different strengths and weaknesses than specialist agencies. As a result, the interpretive techniques that one wants a particular agency to use may be somewhat different than the interpretive techniques that one wants courts to use when no agency is in the picture. *See generally* Cass R. Sunstein & Adrian Vermeule, *Interpretation and Institutions*, 101 MICH. L. REV. 885 (2003) (making this argument and suggesting that theorists have paid too little attention to it). Again, that idea might affect how *Chevron* should work: if proper interpretive methods depend on who is doing the interpreting, then perhaps courts applying the *Chevron* framework should accept some agency interpretations that the courts' own methods would not generate.

These possibilities, however, are predicated on the view that *Chevron* is about the allocation of *interpretive* authority between courts and administering agencies. If *Chevron* is instead about a presumed delegation of *gap-filling* authority to agencies, then one might expect reviewing courts to use their own interpretive methods to identify the location and limits of the relevant gaps. Consistent with this idea, *Chevron* itself indicated that at Step One, when courts are deciding whether a statute leaves room for more than one answer to a particular question, courts should "employ[ ] traditional tools of statutory construction." *Chevron*, 467 U.S. at 843 n.9. Those same tools may also be relevant at Step Two, if a statute is not clear and courts have to decide which interpretations are "permissible."

Admittedly, the Supreme Court's opinion in *Chevron* did not define the phrase "traditional tools of statutory construction," and efforts to do so would be controversial. *See* Abbe R. Gluck, *What 30 Years of* Chevron *Teach Us About the Rest of Statutory Interpretation*, 83 FORDHAM L. REV. 607, 618 (2014) ("The problem . . . is that the Court never sets out what those 'traditional tools' are, likely because it could not agree on them if it wanted to."). Still, the phrase obviously encompassed at least some portion of the tools that judges would use to construe statutes when no agency is in the picture. To the extent that indeterminacies remain after judges use those tools, the *Chevron* framework allows the administering agency to take the lead in choosing among the viable options. But whether an option is viable is something that the judges decide, using the judges' "traditional tools." The rest of this section explores different facets of the interaction between *Chevron* and methodological questions covered in previous chapters of this book.

a. *CHEVRON* AND TEXTUALISM VS. PURPOSIVISM

Start with basic questions about the interplay between text and purpose in statutory interpretation. Although one should not exaggerate debates on that topic, debates do exist: some judges take a hard-line "textualist" approach, others apply a softer version of textualism, and still others incline more toward "purposivism." Imagine an issue as to which these differences matter—for instance, a question of interpretation that textualist judges would answer differently than purposivist judges. If the *Chevron* framework applies, should *all* judges agree that the statute is unclear with respect to this question and that either answer is "permissible"? That is, should textualist judges defer when an agency's interpretation reflects a reasonable application of purposivism, and should purposivist judges defer when an agency's interpretation reflects a reasonable application of textualism?

At first glance, one might not think that the theory behind *Chevron* supports such expansive deference. For its advocates, the *Chevron* framework is meant to give agencies leeway on matters that agencies are better positioned than courts to decide. The choice between textualism and purposivism probably is not one of those matters; agencies have no special expertise in selecting an interpretive philosophy.

As Professors Sunstein and Vermeule have pointed out, though, one of the standard arguments for textualism is that judges are not very good at making the kinds of judgment calls that purposivism requires. Agency decisionmakers might be better; they understand legislative processes, they know the ins and outs of policy within the relevant substantive field, and they also "are likely to be in a better position [than judges] to know whether departures from the text will seriously diminish predictability or otherwise unsettle the statutory scheme." Sunstein & Vermeule, *supra*, 101 MICH. L. REV. at 928. Thus, it is possible to imagine a world in which judges should hew closely to the text when a specialist agency is not in the picture, but should allow agencies to take a more flexible approach in the service of the enacting legislature's goals. *See id.* Conversely, if agencies are not really expert and are vulnerable to capture by special interests, the opposite might be true: "[I]t is not difficult to imagine a legal system in which courts are, and should be, authorized to engage in purposive interpretation, and in which agencies must follow the text unless courts specifically instruct them not to do so." *Id.* at 930–31.

If the choice between textualism and purposivism hinges on institutional capabilities,[28] it is indeed conceivable that the best choice for courts will differ from the best choice for agencies. But that possibility depends on facts that are hard to assess (and that may be different at different times and for different agencies). As a practical matter, judges probably cannot make those assessments with much accuracy. In addition, if agencies are allowed to use interpretive methods that courts are not good at applying, courts might have trouble conducting meaningful judicial review of the agencies' positions. For both of those reasons, it might be better—and would certainly be simpler—for judges

---

[28] Some supporters of textualism might deny that it does; they might favor textualism (absent contrary instructions from Congress) even in a world where interpreters could be trusted to do purposivism well.

to apply the *Chevron* framework in light of the interpretive approach that the judges themselves normally use.

In practice, that is what judges seem to do. When they decide whether a statute is "silent or ambiguous" on some point (at Step One of the *Chevron* framework), and when they identify the range of positions that are "permissible" (at Step Two), they apply what they believe to be the correct interpretive techniques. Judges who themselves embrace purposivism or intentionalism will not necessarily give agencies the leeway to take a more textualist approach. *See, e.g.*, United States v. Locke, 471 U.S. 84 (1985) (Stevens, J., dissenting) (concluding that when Congress required people to file certain papers with the Bureau of Land Management "prior to December 31 of each year," Congress simply meant to require the papers to be filed before the end of the calendar year, and rejecting the agency's more literal reading). Likewise, textualist judges use their own preferred interpretive methods to identify the range of discretion that statutes leave administering agencies. *See, e.g.*, Antonin Scalia, *Judicial Deference to Administrative Interpretations of Law*, 1989 DUKE L.J. 511, 521 ("One who finds *more* often (as I do) that the meaning of a statute is apparent from its text and from its relationship with other laws, thereby finds *less* often that the triggering requirement for *Chevron* deference exists.").

b. *CHEVRON* AND THE CANONS

Judges applying the *Chevron* framework also use many canons of construction in ways that effectively limit deference to administering agencies. Even if a statutory provision could otherwise be read in multiple ways, judges might conclude that canons favor one reading to such an extent that the provision is "unambiguous" at Step One of the *Chevron* framework—and that the administering agency therefore has no discretion to pick a different reading. *See* Arangure v. Whitaker, 911 F.3d 333, 339–40 (6th Cir. 2018) (noting that "[t]he Supreme Court has repeatedly applied canons at step one" and citing many examples); *see also id.* at 342 ("Based on the Court's precedent, most canons are 'traditional tools' of statutory interpretation that should be deployed in *Chevron* step one."). Likewise, even when canons do not eliminate ambiguity entirely, they can at least guide interpreters' reasoning processes, and they can help judges identify boundaries for the readings that judges consider "permissible" at Step Two. In both respects, canons limit the range of readings that agencies can give statutes and that reviewing courts will accept.

The idea that canons can cabin *Chevron* deference is not new. *See, e.g.*, Am. Fed'n of Gov't Employees v. FLRA, 798 F.2d 1525, 1528 (D.C. Cir. 1986). Indeed, the best law-review article on the subject was published just six years after *Chevron* itself. *See* Cass R. Sunstein, *Law and Administration After* Chevron, 90 COLUM. L. REV. 2071, 2105–19 (1990) (categorizing canons and concluding that while most should operate to limit *Chevron* deference, a few should not). Still, some current judges put more stock in canons than their predecessors did, and some current judges are also more skeptical of *Chevron* (or at least take a narrower view of the circumstances in which deference is appropriate). For both those reasons, canons may loom somewhat larger in *Chevron* analysis than they once did.

The Supreme Court's opinion in *Epic Systems Corp. v. Lewis*, 138 S. Ct. 1612 (2018), is a case in point. *See supra* p. 742. On its face, the phrase "other concerted activities" in section 7 of the National Labor Relations Act seems open to various readings. Based largely on the presumption against implied repeals and *ejusdem generis*, though, the Court held that the phrase covers only activities in the real world and does not encompass class-action lawsuits or joint arbitration proceedings. *See Epic Systems*, 138 S. Ct. at 1624–25. According to the Court, moreover, *Chevron* did not require judges to accept the NLRB's contrary position. As one of several reasons for that conclusion, Justice Gorsuch's majority opinion pointed to the canons: "Where, as here, the canons supply an answer, '*Chevron* leaves the stage.'" *Id.* at 1630 (quoting NLRB v. Alternative Entertainment, Inc., 858 F.3d 393, 417 (6th Cir. 2017) (Sutton, J., concurring in part and dissenting in part)).

If this statement was meant to reflect current doctrine, it may be slightly too broad. As we shall see, courts are divided about the interaction between *Chevron* and some purely normative canons that judges would use to break ties if no agency were in the picture. But even if a few canons might not constrain *Chevron* deference, most canons do.

We can start with basic linguistic canons like *noscitur a sociis*, *ejusdem generis*, the presumption of consistent usage, and the presumption against superfluity. *See supra* Chapter 2.B (covering these canons).[29] Of course, these canons are not all-powerful, and they do not always eliminate ambiguity in statutory language. *See, e.g.*, Barton v.

[29] One canon covered in Chapter 2.B that might *not* be of much use in *Chevron* cases is *expressio unius est exclusio alterius*. As we have seen, *expressio unius* might not really be a canon at all. *See supra* p. 133. But be that as it may, the D.C. Circuit has called it "especially feeble" in settings where Congress has authorized an agency to fill gaps left by Congress. *Cheney R.R. Co. v. ICC*, 902 F.2d 66, 69 (D.C. Cir. 1990); *accord* Sunstein, *supra*, 90 COLUM. L. REV. at 2109 n.182. For instance, imagine that a statute establishes a deadline for one type of decision but not another. This structure does not necessarily imply that the second type of decision must remain free from any deadline; if the agency has general rulemaking authority, perhaps the statute simply leaves the agency in charge of whether to establish a deadline. *See* Alliance for Cmty. Media v. FCC, 529 F.3d 763, 779–80 (6th Cir. 2008); Gen. Motors Corp. v. NHTSA, 898 F.2d 165, 170 (D.C. Cir. 1990). More generally, where Congress has empowered an agency to act with the force of law, "the contrast between Congress's mandate in one context with its silence in another" may simply suggest "a decision *not to mandate* any solution in the second context, i.e., to leave the question to agency discretion." *Cheney*, 902 F.2d at 69; *accord, e.g.*, Fisher v. PBGC, 994 F.3d 664, 671 (D.C. Cir. 2021); Catawba Cty. v. EPA, 571 F.3d 20, 36 (D.C. Cir. 2009).

To be sure, some statutory provisions do indeed carry negative implications that agencies are not free to disregard. *See, e.g.*, Nasdaq Stock Mkt. LLC v. SEC, 38 F.4th 1126, 1137–39 (D.C. Cir. 2022); Air Transp. Ass'n v. U.S. Dep't of Agric., 37 F.4th 667, 672–73 (D.C. Cir. 2022). But there cannot be a general presumption in favor of drawing negative inferences, so *expressio unius* is no substitute for more fine-grained interpretation.

Barr, 140 S. Ct. 1442, 1453 (2020) (noting limits on the presumption against superfluity); Am. Hosp. Ass'n v. Azar, 964 F.3d 1230, 1243 (D.C. Cir. 2020) (same). But where courts conclude that these canons do clarify a provision that would otherwise be ambiguous, courts normally will not let the administering agency flout the canons. *See, e.g.*, Nat'l Credit Union Admin. v. First Nat'l Bank & Tr. Co., 522 U.S. 479, 500–03 (1998) (rejecting an agency's interpretation on the basis of the presumption against superfluity and the presumption of consistent usage); Averett v. U.S. Dep't of Health & Human Servs., 943 F.3d 313, 317–18 (6th Cir. 2019) (presumption of consistent usage); Kyocera Wireless Corp. v. Int'l Trade Comm'n, 545 F.3d 1340, 1356–57 (Fed. Cir. 2008) (presumption against superfluity); Cal. Indep. Sys. Operator Corp. v. FERC, 372 F.3d 395, 401 (D.C. Cir. 2004) (*noscitur a sociis* and presumption against superfluity).

The same goes for many other canons. The Supreme Court set the pattern in *Edward J. DeBartolo Corp. v. Florida Gulf Coast Building & Construction Trades Council*, 485 U.S. 568 (1988), when it used the canon that favors avoiding constitutional doubts to reject the NLRB's interpretation of a provision in the National Labor Relations Act. *See id.* at 577 (concluding that in light of the canon, "we must independently inquire whether there is another interpretation, not raising these serious constitutional concerns, that may fairly be ascribed to [the provision]"); *accord* Solid Waste Agency of N. Cook Cty. v. U.S. Army Corps of Eng'rs, 531 U.S. 159, 172–74 (2001) (agreeing that the constitutional-doubts canon qualifies *Chevron* deference). Similarly, in *INS v. St. Cyr*, 533 U.S. 289 (2001), the Supreme Court made clear that the presumption against retroactivity applies at Step One of the *Chevron* framework and thereby limits the range of agency interpretations to which courts will defer. *See id.* at 321 n.45 ("Because a statute that is ambiguous with respect to retroactive application is construed under our precedent to be unambiguously prospective, . . . there is, for *Chevron* purposes, no ambiguity in such a statute for an agency to resolve."); *see also* EEOC v. Arabian Am. Oil Co., 499 U.S. 244, 260 (1991) (Scalia, J., concurring in part and concurring in the judgment) (assuming *arguendo* that the EEOC's guidelines triggered the *Chevron* framework, but invoking the presumption against extraterritoriality to cabin *Chevron* deference).

Lower courts have rejected agency interpretations on the basis of myriad additional canons covered in this book. For instance, just as the Supreme Court relied on the presumption against implied repeals in *Epic Systems*, lower courts have invoked other canons about the interaction between two statutes or statutory provisions. *See, e.g.*, Genus Med. Techs. LLC v. U.S. Food & Drug Admin., 994 F.3d 631, 638–39 (D.C. Cir. 2021) (rejecting the agency's position because of "the 'old and familiar rule' that 'the specific governs the general' "); Hylton v. U.S. Att'y Gen., 992 F.3d 1154, 1157–61 (11th Cir. 2021) (rejecting the agency's position largely on the basis of "the prior-construction canon"—the idea that when the Supreme Court has glossed language in one statute and Congress then uses materially identical language in another statute, the new statute should be presumed to come with the Court's gloss); City of Tacoma v. FERC, 331 F.3d 106, 115 (D.C. Cir. 2003) ("The Commission's failure to interpret consistently two statutory provisions that are *in pari materia* manifests that it has not correctly read 'the language and design of the statute as a whole.' "). Likewise, courts have rejected agency interpretations for violating various federalism canons. *See, e.g.*, Am. Bar Ass'n v. FTC, 430 F.3d 457, 471–72 (D.C. Cir. 2005) (noting that "throughout the history of the country" Congress has left regulation of the practice of law up to the states, and concluding that an agency cannot permissibly interpret "language that is . . . at most ambiguous" as breaking from this established pattern); Cal. State Bd. of Optometry v. FTC, 910 F.2d 976, 980–82 (D.C. Cir. 1990) (making similar use of the presumption that Congress does not intend to regulate the states as sovereigns); *see also infra* Chapter 6 (covering federalism canons).

If one is skeptical of *Chevron* to begin with, one might well think that *all* canons should take priority over it. Conversely, if one is skeptical of the canons, one might think that *Chevron* deference should trump them.[30] But for people who accept both *Chevron* deference and the canons, "[w]hether a canon applies before deferring to an agency likely depends on the character of the canon, measured against the rationales underpinning the *Chevron* . . . framework[ ]." *Kisor v. McDonough*, 995 F.3d 1347, 1358 (Fed. Cir. 2021) (Proust, C.J., concurring in the denial of rehearing en banc); *accord Arangure*, 911 F.3d at 340–42.

At least to my way of thinking, the courts' use of "descriptive" canons to help narrow the range of an agency's interpretive choices is easy to reconcile with the basic rationales for *Chevron* deference. *Chevron* operates only when the meaning of a statutory provision is underspecified, so that either the courts or an administering agency must supply content that cannot confidently be imputed to Congress itself. Advocates of *Chevron* deference argue that for reasons of expertise and

[30] That is Professor Vermeule's position. In his view, the canons are not worth much; because they are "entirely generic," they "provide low-value information" about the meaning of any particular statute or the intentions and purposes behind it. ADRIAN VERMEULE, JUDGING UNDER UNCERTAINTY: AN INSTITUTIONAL THEORY OF LEGAL INTERPRETATION 199–200 (2006). Vermeule concedes that courts may not be able to do any better; most judges are generalists, without specialized knowledge about the particular area of law that a statute addresses. If no agency were in the picture, then, Vermeule would not necessarily object to judicial use of canons. According to Vermeule, though, agencies are far better suited to engage in statute-specific interpretation. *See id.* at 200 (asserting that "agency interpretations . . . are typically the product of deep familiarity with the particular statute at hand and its particular underlying policies"). To the extent that an agency's interpretation conflicts with a canon, Vermeule suggests that what should give way is the canon rather than the agency's interpretation. He takes the extreme position that reviewing courts should not invoke *any* canons or other traditional tools of statutory construction to restrict the range of interpretive options available to an administering agency. *See id.* at 211 (concluding that "courts should defer to agencies whenever the statutory text at issue, viewed on its face and without recourse to the traditional tools, contains a surface-level gap or ambiguity"). *But see* Caleb Nelson, *Statutory Interpretation and Decision Theory*, 74 U. CHI. L. REV. 329, 350–55 (2007) (book review) (explaining why I am not persuaded).

political accountability, the typical administering agency is in a better position than the courts to make the choices that such indeterminacies necessitate. But the standard arguments for deference are limited to questions that Congress has not itself answered—questions as to which the provision is indeed indeterminate. To the extent that Congress has provided a determinate answer to a particular question, nothing in *Chevron* tells courts to presume that Congress has authorized the relevant agency to deviate from that answer.

Admittedly, determinacy exists on a spectrum. At one end of the spectrum, the very terms of a statutory provision sometimes directly address an issue and leave little room for doubt about how people applying the provision should handle it; ordinary conventions of English usage make the statutory language seem clear, and there is no reason to think that members of the enacting Congress were trying to communicate anything else. In such cases, textualists and intentionalists alike might agree that the provision is determinate. Interpretations that emerge only through the application of descriptive canons lie farther along this spectrum; the answers that such canons suggest usually cannot be attributed to Congress with quite as much confidence that members of Congress really had them in mind. Still, assuming that the canons are indeed "descriptive"—i.e., they are reasonably reliable tools for helping courts capture the intended meaning of statutory language—it is natural for courts to use them when trying to separate matters that Congress has authoritatively decided from matters that Congress has left to the responsible agency. With the blessing of many commentators, that is precisely what courts have done: in general, the recognized descriptive canons do restrict the scope of *Chevron* deference. *See, e.g.*, Sunstein, *supra*, 90 COLUM. L. REV. at 2105 (concluding that "*Chevron* is plainly overcome by principles that help to ascertain congressional instructions").

How *Chevron* should interact with "normative" canons is a more complicated question. By definition, normative canons are not tools for identifying the instructions that Congress probably intended to convey. Indeed, many normative canons come into play only if ambiguity remains after interpreters have exhausted such tools. *See, e.g.*, Reno v. Koray, 515 U.S. 50, 65 (1995) ("The rule of lenity applies only if, 'after seizing everything from which aid can be derived,' we can make 'no more than a guess as to what Congress intended.'" (citations omitted)); Brown v. Gardner, 513 U.S. 115, 118 (1994) (referring to "the rule that interpretive doubt [in statutes designed to protect or benefit veterans] is to be resolved in the veteran's favor"); *see also* Montana v. Blackfeet Tribe, 471 U.S. 759, 766 (1985) (invoking the canon that "statutes are to be construed liberally in favor of the Indians, with ambiguous provisions interpreted to their benefit"); Chickasaw Nation v. United States, 534 U.S. 84, 94 (2001) (suggesting that this canon operates only if "the statute is 'fairly capable' of two interpretations"). To the extent that courts use normative canons to guide the courts' choices on matters that Congress has left unclear, those canons might be seen as "rule-ized" versions of the very kinds of discretionary judgments that *Chevron* normally encourages courts to leave to agencies. If one accepts the usual expertise- or accountability-based rationales for *Chevron* deference, one might conclude that courts should not substitute their decisions for those of an administering agency on matters of this sort.

On closer inspection, though, this argument is not a slam dunk. With respect to accountability, some normative canons do not simply reflect the say-so of the courts, but instead reflect ideas built into the Constitution or supported by other aspects of our legal traditions. With respect to expertise, moreover, most normative canons have rationales that go beyond any particular agency's specialty and that agencies may not adequately heed. For reasons of this sort, Professor Sunstein has concluded that certain categories of normative canons should indeed cabin *Chevron* deference. *See, e.g.*, Sunstein, *supra*, 90 COLUM. L. REV. at 2115–16 (observing that some canons, such as "[t]he idea that treaties and statutes should be construed generously to the Indian tribes," reflect "a quite general effort to resolve ambiguities in a way that fairly allocates both burdens and benefits in governmental policies," and concluding that reviewing courts should not let agencies flout these canons); *cf.* Kenneth A. Bamberger, *Normative Canons in the Review of Administrative Policymaking*, 118 YALE L.J. 64, 68–69 (2008) (opposing any categorical approach, but arguing that courts evaluating the permissibility of an agency's interpretation at Step Two "should consider the background values animating the canons" and should ask whether "the agency's expertise, decision process, and substantive outcome point to a satisfactory resolution of norm balancing").

Unfortunately, analysis of these issues quickly gets into difficult trade-offs. On the one hand, *Chevron* presumes that letting a specialist agency take the lead in resolving indeterminacies within the agency's field is likely to yield policy benefits (as well as whatever benefits might flow from the agency's greater political accountability). On the other hand, whenever the interpretations selected by the agency conflict with normative canons that the courts would apply in the agency's absence, requiring courts to accept the agency's interpretations might harm the overarching values that the canons are designed to protect. We might not expect *either* courts *or* agencies to be in a good position to evaluate these trade-offs. After all, if *Chevron* is to be believed, courts will find it hard to assess the policy benefits that particular interpretations will generate within the field of an agency's specialty. Conversely, specialist agencies may have little insight into the harms caused by departures from the normative canons that courts would apply in the agencies' absence. And even if courts knew everything that agencies know and agencies knew everything that courts know, the relevant costs and benefits might still be nearly impossible to compare, because they are of very different types.

It is anyone's guess whether society would be better off if (1) *all* normative canons trumped *Chevron* deference, (2) *no* normative canons trumped *Chevron* deference, (3) *some* normative canons trumped *Chevron* deference while others did not, or (4) courts reviewing agency interpretations handled this question on a case-by-case basis rather than a canon-by-canon basis.

Existing doctrine about the interaction between *Chevron* deference and purely normative canons is correspondingly murky. There is an ongoing circuit split about whether or to what extent the pro-Indian canon cabins *Chevron* deference. *Compare* Rancheria v. Jewell, 776 F.3d 706, 713 (9th Cir. 2015) ("In this circuit, an agency's legal authority to interpret a statute appears to trump any practice of construing ambiguous statutory provisions in favor of Indians."), *with* Cobell v. Norton, 240 F.3d 1081, 1101 (D.C. Cir. 2001) (holding that "*Chevron* deference is not applicable" because the pro-Indian canon controls how ambiguities must be resolved), *and* Cobell v. Salazar, 573 F.3d 808, 812 (D.C. Cir. 2009) (saying that where the pro-Indian canon is relevant, "*Chevron* deference does not disappear" but "applies with muted effect"); *see also* Scott C. Hall, *The Indian Law Canons of Construction v. The* Chevron *Doctrine: Congressional Intent and the Unambiguous Answer to the Ambiguous Problem*, 37 CONN. L. REV. 495, 543–56 (2004) (canvassing the circuit split as it then stood). Likewise, parallel questions about the pro-veteran canon continue to trigger sharp disagreement within the U.S. Court of Appeals for the Federal Circuit. *Compare* Kisor v. McDonough, 995 F.3d 1347, 1360 (Fed. Cir. 2021) (Hughes, J., concurring in the denial of rehearing en banc) (indicating that the pro-veteran canon does not restrict *Chevron* deference to the Department of Veterans Affairs), *with* Procopio v. Wilkie, 913 F.3d 1371, 1382 (Fed. Cir. 2019) (O'Malley, J., concurring) (arguing that "the pro-veteran canon, like every other canon of statutory construction, can and should apply at step one of *Chevron* to help determine whether a statutory ambiguity exists"). The relationship between the rule of lenity and *Chevron* deference is also uncertain: even when the statutory provisions that an agency administers have penal applications, many courts have suggested that *Chevron* deference takes priority over the rule of lenity, but some judges have disagreed. *See infra* pp. 973–976 (noting this debate).[31]

[31] Early on, the D.C. Circuit indicated that two purely normative canons did not limit *Chevron* deference. *See* Wagner Seed Co. v. Bush, 946 F.2d 918, 924–25 (D.C. Cir. 1991) (refusing to hold agencies to the old idea that "remedial" provisions should be "liberally construed," and explaining that "unlike, for example, the rule of *ejusdem generis*," this purported canon "cannot supply the specific congressional intent that *Chevron* requires"); Mich. Citizens for an Indep. Press v. Thornburgh, 868 F.2d 1285, 1292–93 (D.C. Cir.) (reaching the same conclusion about "the interpretative canon that exemptions to the antitrust laws—like all exemptions—should be construed narrowly"), *aff'd by an evenly divided court*, 493 U.S. 38 (1989). Even when no agency is in the picture, though, many modern judges reject at least the first of those canons. *See supra* p. 315 n.55; *see also* ANTONIN SCALIA & BRYAN A. GARNER, READING LAW: THE INTERPRETATION OF LEGAL TEXTS 364–66 (2012) (criticizing "[t]he false notion that remedial statutes should be liberally construed").

What about canons that have *both* normative *and* descriptive justifications? This question can arise in two different contexts, one of which is more difficult to analyze than the other.

First, we can consider situations in which a canon *simultaneously* has descriptive and normative justifications; the canon is a plausible guide to the intended meaning of the statutory provision at issue, but normative considerations give the canon added weight. For example, consider ordinary applications of the presumption against retroactivity. That canon reflects plausible generalizations about Congress's patterns of behavior and likely intent, and it therefore has considerable descriptive force; the premise that members of Congress do not mean their statutes to operate retroactively may well be accurate in most cases. Over and above its descriptive force, though, the canon gets extra weight from our normative distaste for retroactive burdens on private rights. Should courts applying the *Chevron* framework try to estimate how much of the canon's usual weight comes from normative considerations, and should they allow agencies to downplay the canon to that extent?

At least with respect to the presumption against retroactivity, the standard answer is "no." Rather than making any attempt to disaggregate the presumption into descriptive and normative components, the Supreme Court has simply held that the ordinary presumption against retroactivity applies at Step One of the *Chevron* framework and thereby limits the range of agency interpretations to which judges should defer. *See* INS v. St. Cyr, 533 U.S. 289, 320–21 n.45 (2001); *see also* Sunstein, *supra*, 90 COLUM. L. REV. at 2114–15 (anticipating and supporting this conclusion).

That probably makes sense on both theoretical and practical grounds. The normative values that help justify the presumption against retroactivity lie beyond the expertise of any single agency, and it is not obvious that courts should let agencies disregard those values. *See* 1 LAURENCE H. TRIBE, AMERICAN CONSTITUTIONAL LAW 1010–11 (3d ed. 2000) (suggesting that even on purely normative grounds, the presumption against retroactivity should take priority over *Chevron* deference). As a practical matter, moreover, it would be difficult to figure out how much of the presumption's weight is normative, and the answer probably would not affect very many cases anyway (because the descriptive weight of the canon would carry the day at Step One unless there were at least some contrary indications of legislative intent). In any event, current doctrine does not try to get so fine-grained: courts applying the *Chevron* framework use the presumption against retroactivity with all of its ordinary force.

The second set of situations is different. Sometimes, a canon has both descriptive and normative force in some cases, but it has only normative force in others. Should courts applying the *Chevron* framework try to distinguish between cases where the canon has descriptive justifications and cases where it is purely normative, and should they sometimes let agencies disregard the canon in cases of the latter sort?

The Supreme Court has not confronted this question directly, but *Epic Systems* may suggest that the answer again is "no." Although the presumption against implied repeals is a plausible guide to the intended meaning of statutory language in many situations, it probably did not have much descriptive force under the circumstances in *Epic Systems* itself. *See supra* pp. 771–772 (noting that the potential conflict between the National Labor Relations Act and the Federal Arbitration Act depended on constructions that the Supreme Court gave the Federal Arbitration Act well after Congress had enacted the National Labor Relations Act). Even so, the majority opinion in *Epic Systems* still gave the presumption against implied repeals priority over *Chevron* deference. Does that make sense? Are the normative aspects of the presumption against implied repeals strong enough to constrain *Chevron* deference? If not, might there still be reasons for courts to rely on the canon without trying to make case-by-case evaluations of its descriptive force?

The next case involves the interaction between some version of *Chevron* deference and a variety of canons, both descriptive and normative. As you will see, neither the majority nor the dissent devoted much systematic attention to that interaction. But the issues just surveyed lurk beneath the surface of both opinions. As you read the case, consider not only the Justices' specific disagreements about the proper application of particular canons, but also their implicit premises about the relevance of those canons to the *Chevron* framework.

Babbitt v. Sweet Home Chapter of Communities for a Great Oregon

515 U.S. 687 (1995)

■ *JUSTICE STEVENS delivered the opinion of the Court:*

The Endangered Species Act of 1973 (ESA or Act), 87 Stat. 884, 16 U.S.C. § 1531 (1988 ed. and Supp. V), contains a variety of protections designed to save from extinction species that the Secretary of the Interior designates as endangered or threatened. Section 9 of the Act makes it unlawful for any person to "take" any endangered or threatened species. The Secretary has promulgated a regulation that defines the statute's prohibition on takings to include "significant habitat modification or degradation where it actually kills or injures wildlife." This case presents the question whether the Secretary exceeded his authority under the Act by promulgating that regulation.

I

Section 9(a)(1) of the Act provides the following protection for endangered species:

> "Except as provided in sections 1535(g)(2) and 1539 of this title, with respect to any endangered species of fish or wildlife listed pursuant to section 1533 of this title it is unlawful for any person subject to the jurisdiction of the United States to—
>
> . . . .
>
> "(B) take any such species within the United States or the territorial sea of the United States." 16 U.S.C. § 1538(a)(1).

Section 3(19) of the Act defines the statutory term "take":

> "The term 'take' means to harass, harm, pursue, hunt, shoot, wound, kill, trap, capture, or collect, or to attempt to engage in any such conduct." 16 U.S.C. § 1532(19).

The Act does not further define the terms it uses to define "take." The Interior Department regulations that implement the statute, however, define the statutory term "harm":

> "*Harm* in the definition of 'take' in the Act means an act which actually kills or injures wildlife. Such act may include significant habitat modification or degradation where it actually kills or injures wildlife by significantly impairing essential behavioral patterns, including breeding, feeding, or sheltering." 50 CFR § 17.3 (1994).

This regulation has been in place since 1975.

A limitation on the § 9 "take" prohibition appears in § 10(a)(1)(B) of the Act, which Congress added by amendment in 1982. That section authorizes the Secretary to grant a permit for any taking otherwise prohibited by § 9(a)(1)(B) "if such taking is incidental to, and not the purpose of, the carrying out of an otherwise lawful activity." 16 U.S.C. § 1539(a)(1)(B).

In addition to the prohibition on takings, the Act provides several other protections for endangered species. Section 4, 16 U.S.C. § 1533, commands the Secretary to identify species of fish or wildlife that are in danger of extinction and to publish from time to time lists of all species he determines to be endangered or threatened. Section 5, 16 U.S.C. § 1534, authorizes the Secretary, in cooperation with the States, see § 1535, to acquire land to aid in preserving such species. Section 7 requires federal agencies to ensure that none of their activities, including the granting of licenses and permits, will jeopardize the continued existence of endangered species "or result in the destruction or adverse modification of habitat of such species which is determined by the Secretary . . . to be critical." 16 U.S.C. § 1536(a)(2).

Respondents in this action are small landowners, logging companies, and families dependent on the forest products industries in the Pacific Northwest and in the Southeast, and organizations that represent their interests. They brought this declaratory judgment action against petitioners, the Secretary of the Interior and the Director of the Fish and Wildlife Service, in the United States District Court for the District of

Columbia to challenge the statutory validity of the Secretary's regulation defining "harm," particularly the inclusion of habitat modification and degradation in the definition. Respondents challenged the regulation on its face. Their complaint alleged that application of the "harm" regulation to the red-cockaded woodpecker, an endangered species, and the northern spotted owl, a threatened species,[5] had injured them economically.

Respondents advanced three arguments to support their submission that Congress did not intend the word "take" in § 9 to include habitat modification, as the Secretary's "harm" regulation provides. First, they correctly noted that language in the Senate's original version of the ESA would have defined "take" to include "destruction, modification, or curtailment of [the] habitat or range" of fish or wildlife, but the Senate deleted that language from the bill before enacting it. Second, respondents argued that Congress intended the Act's express authorization for the Federal Government to buy private land in order to prevent habitat degradation in § 5 to be the exclusive check against habitat modification on private property. Third, because the Senate added the term "harm" to the definition of "take" in a floor amendment without debate, respondents argued that the court should not interpret the term so expansively as to include habitat modification.

The District Court considered and rejected each of respondents' arguments, finding "that Congress intended an expansive interpretation of the word 'take,' an interpretation that encompasses habitat modification." 806 F. Supp. 279, 285 (1992). The court noted that in 1982, when Congress was aware of a judicial decision that had applied the Secretary's regulation, see *Palila v. Hawaii Dept. of Land and Natural Resources*, 639 F.2d 495 (CA9 1981) (*Palila I*), it amended the Act without using the opportunity to change the definition of "take." 806 F. Supp. at 284. The court stated that, even had it found the ESA " 'silent or ambiguous' " as to the authority for the Secretary's definition of "harm," it would nevertheless have upheld the regulation as a reasonable interpretation of the statute. *Id.* at 285 (quoting *Chevron U.S.A. Inc. v. Natural Resources Defense Council, Inc.*, 467 U.S. 837, 843 (1984)). The District Court therefore entered summary judgment for petitioners . . . .

A divided panel of the Court of Appeals initially affirmed the judgment of the District Court. 1 F.3d 1 (CADC 1993). After granting a petition for rehearing, however, the panel reversed. 17 F.3d 1463 (CADC 1994). Although acknowledging that "[t]he potential breadth of the word 'harm' is indisputable," *id.* at 1464, the majority concluded that the immediate statutory context in which "harm" appeared counseled

[5] . . . . [A] regulation promulgated by the Secretary extends to threatened species, defined in the ESA as "any species which is likely to become an endangered species within the foreseeable future throughout all or a significant portion of its range," 16 U.S.C. § 1532(20), some but not all of the protections endangered species enjoy. See 50 CFR § 17.31(a) (1994). In the District Court respondents unsuccessfully challenged that regulation's extension of § 9 to threatened species, but they do not press the challenge here.

against a broad reading; like the other words in the definition of "take," the word "harm" should be read as applying only to "the perpetrator's direct application of force against the animal taken. . . . The forbidden acts fit, in ordinary language, the basic model 'A hit B.' " *Id.* at 1465. The majority based its reasoning on a canon of statutory construction called *noscitur a sociis*, which holds that a word is known by the company it keeps. . . .

. . . . Our consideration of the text and structure of the Act, its legislative history, and the significance of the 1982 amendment persuades us that the Court of Appeals' judgment should be reversed.

II

Because this case was decided on motions for summary judgment, we may appropriately make certain factual assumptions in order to frame the legal issue. First, we assume respondents have no desire to harm either the red-cockaded woodpecker or the spotted owl; they merely wish to continue logging activities that would be entirely proper if not prohibited by the ESA. On the other hand, we must assume, *arguendo*, that those activities will have the effect, even though unintended, of detrimentally changing the natural habitat of both listed species and that, as a consequence, members of those species will be killed or injured. Under respondents' view of the law, the Secretary's only means of forestalling that grave result—even when the actor knows it is certain to occur[9]—is to use his § 5 authority to purchase the lands on which the survival of the species depends. The Secretary, on the other hand, submits that the § 9 prohibition on takings, which Congress defined to include "harm," places on respondents a duty to avoid harm that habitat alteration will cause the birds unless respondents first obtain a permit pursuant to § 10.

The text of the Act provides three reasons for concluding that the Secretary's interpretation is reasonable. First, an ordinary understanding of the word "harm" supports it. The dictionary definition

---

[9] . . . [I]n order to be subject to the Act's criminal penalties or the more severe of its civil penalties, one must "knowingly violat[e]" the Act or its implementing regulations. 16 U.S.C. §§ 1540(a)(1), (b)(1). Congress added "knowingly" in place of "willfully" in 1978 to make "criminal violations of the act a general rather than a specific intent crime." H.R. Conf. Rep. No. 95–1804, p. 26 (1978). The Act does authorize up to a $500 civil fine for "[a]ny person who otherwise violates" the Act or its implementing regulations. 16 U.S.C. § 1540(a)(1). That provision is potentially sweeping, but it would be so with or without the Secretary's "harm" regulation, making it unhelpful in assessing the reasonableness of the regulation. We have imputed scienter requirements to criminal statutes that impose sanctions without expressly requiring scienter, see, *e.g.*, *Staples v. United States*, 511 U.S. 600 (1994), but the proper case in which we might consider whether to do so in the § 9 provision for a $500 civil penalty would be a challenge to enforcement of that provision itself, not a challenge to a regulation that merely defines a statutory term. We do not agree with the dissent that the regulation covers results that are not "even foreseeable . . . no matter how long the chain of causality between modification and injury." *Post* at 715. Respondents have suggested no reason why either the "knowingly violates" or the "otherwise violates" provision of the statute—or the "harm" regulation itself—should not be read to incorporate ordinary requirements of proximate causation and foreseeability. In any event, neither respondents nor their *amici* have suggested that the Secretary employs the "otherwise violates" provision with any frequency.

of the verb form of "harm" is "to cause hurt or damage to: injure." Webster's Third New International Dictionary 1034 (1966). In the context of the ESA, that definition naturally encompasses habitat modification that results in actual injury or death to members of an endangered or threatened species.

Respondents argue that the Secretary should have limited the purview of "harm" to direct applications of force against protected species, but the dictionary definition does not include the word "directly" or suggest in any way that only direct or willful action that leads to injury constitutes "harm."[10] Moreover, unless the statutory term "harm" encompasses indirect as well as direct injuries, the word has no meaning that does not duplicate the meaning of other words that § 3 uses to define "take." A reluctance to treat statutory terms as surplusage supports the reasonableness of the Secretary's interpretation. See, *e.g.*, *Mackey v. Lanier Collection Agency & Service, Inc.*, 486 U.S. 825, 837, and n. 11 (1988).[11]

Second, the broad purpose of the ESA supports the Secretary's decision to extend protection against activities that cause the precise harms Congress enacted the statute to avoid. In *TVA v. Hill*, 437 U.S. 153 (1978), we described the Act as "the most comprehensive legislation for the preservation of endangered species ever enacted by any nation." *Id.* at 180. Whereas predecessor statutes enacted in 1966 and 1969 had not contained any sweeping prohibition against the taking of endangered species except on federal lands, the 1973 Act applied to all land in the United States and to the Nation's territorial seas. As stated in § 2 of the Act, among its central purposes is "to provide a means whereby the ecosystems upon which endangered species and threatened species depend may be conserved. . . ." 16 U.S.C. § 1531(b).

In *Hill*, we construed § 7 as precluding the completion of the Tellico Dam because of its predicted impact on the survival of the snail darter.

---

[10] Respondents and the dissent emphasize what they portray as the "established meaning" of "take" in the sense of a "wildlife take," a meaning respondents argue extends only to "the effort to exercise dominion over some creature, and the concrete effect o[n] that creature." Brief for Respondents 19. . . . This limitation ill serves the statutory text, which forbids not taking "some creature" but "tak[ing] any [endangered] *species*"—a formidable task for even the most rapacious feudal lord. More importantly, Congress explicitly defined the operative term "take" in the ESA, . . . thereby obviating the need for us to probe its meaning as we must probe the meaning of the undefined subsidiary term "harm." Finally, Congress' definition of "take" includes several words—most obviously "harass," "pursue," and "wound," in addition to "harm" itself—that fit respondents' and the dissent's definition of "take" no better than does "significant habitat modification or degradation."

[11] In contrast, if the statutory term "harm" encompasses such indirect means of killing and injuring wildlife as habitat modification, the other terms listed in § 3—"harass," "pursue," "hunt," "shoot," "wound," "kill," "trap," "capture," and "collect"—generally retain independent meanings. Most of those terms refer to deliberate actions more frequently than does "harm," and they therefore do not duplicate the sense of indirect causation that "harm" adds to the statute. In addition, most of the other words in the definition describe either actions from which habitat modification does not usually result (*e.g.*, "pursue," "harass") or effects to which activities that modify habitat do not usually lead (*e.g.*, "trap," "collect"). To the extent the Secretary's definition of "harm" may have applications that overlap with other words in the definition, that overlap reflects the broad purpose of the Act. See *infra* . . . .

See 437 U.S. at 193. Both our holding and the language in our opinion stressed the importance of the statutory policy. "The plain intent of Congress in enacting this statute," we recognized, "was to halt and reverse the trend toward species extinction, whatever the cost. This is reflected not only in the stated policies of the Act, but in literally every section of the statute." *Id.* at 184. Although the § 9 "take" prohibition was not at issue in *Hill*, we took note of that prohibition, placing particular emphasis on the Secretary's inclusion of habitat modification in his definition of "harm." In light of that provision for habitat protection, we could "not understand how TVA intends to operate Tellico Dam without 'harming' the snail darter." *Id.* at 184, n. 30. Congress' intent to provide comprehensive protection for endangered and threatened species supports the permissibility of the Secretary's "harm" regulation.

Respondents advance strong arguments that activities that cause minimal or unforeseeable harm will not violate the Act as construed in the "harm" regulation. Respondents, however, present a facial challenge to the regulation. Thus, they ask us to invalidate the Secretary's understanding of "harm" in every circumstance, even when an actor knows that an activity, such as draining a pond, would actually result in the extinction of a listed species by destroying its habitat. Given Congress' clear expression of the ESA's broad purpose to protect endangered and threatened wildlife, the Secretary's definition of "harm" is reasonable.[13]

Third, the fact that Congress in 1982 authorized the Secretary to issue permits for takings that § 9(a)(1)(B) would otherwise prohibit, "if such taking is incidental to, and not the purpose of, the carrying out of an otherwise lawful activity," 16 U.S.C. § 1539(a)(1)(B), strongly suggests that Congress understood § 9(a)(1)(B) to prohibit indirect as well as deliberate takings. The permit process requires the applicant to prepare a "conservation plan" that specifies how he intends to "minimize and mitigate" the "impact" of his activity on endangered and threatened species, 16 U.S.C. § 1539(a)(2)(A), making clear that Congress had in mind foreseeable rather than merely accidental effects on listed species. No one could seriously request an "incidental" take permit to avert § 9 liability for direct, deliberate action against a member of an endangered or threatened species, but respondents would read "harm" so narrowly that the permit procedure would have little more than that absurd purpose. "When Congress acts to amend a statute, we presume it intends

[13] The dissent incorrectly asserts that the Secretary's regulation (1) "dispenses with the foreseeability of harm" and (2) "fail[s] to require injury to particular animals," *post* at 731. As to the first assertion, the regulation merely implements the statute, and it is therefore subject to the statute's "knowingly violates" language, see 16 U.S.C. §§ 1540(a)(1), (b)(1), and ordinary requirements of proximate causation and foreseeability. See n. 9, *supra*. . . . Nothing in the regulation purports to weaken those requirements. To the contrary, the word "actually" in the regulation should be construed to limit the liability about which the dissent appears most concerned, liability under the statute's "otherwise violates" provision. The Secretary did not need to include "actually" to connote "but for" causation, which the other words in the definition obviously require. As to the dissent's second assertion, every term in the regulation's definition of "harm" is subservient to the phrase "an act which actually kills or injures wildlife."

its amendment to have real and substantial effect." *Stone v. INS*, 514 U.S. 386, 397 (1995). Congress' addition of the § 10 permit provision supports the Secretary's conclusion that activities not intended to harm an endangered species, such as habitat modification, may constitute unlawful takings under the ESA unless the Secretary permits them.

The Court of Appeals made three errors in asserting that "harm" must refer to a direct application of force because the words around it do.[15] First, the court's premise was flawed. Several of the words that accompany "harm" in the § 3 definition of "take," especially "harass," "pursue," "wound," and "kill," refer to actions or effects that do not require direct applications of force. Second, to the extent the court read a requirement of intent or purpose into the words used to define "take," it ignored § 11's express provision that a "knowin[g]" action is enough to violate the Act. Third, the court employed *noscitur a sociis* to give "harm" essentially the same function as other words in the definition, thereby denying it independent meaning. The canon, to the contrary, counsels that a word "gathers meaning from the words around it." *Jarecki v. G.D. Searle & Co.*, 367 U.S. 303, 307 (1961). The statutory context of "harm" suggests that Congress meant that term to serve a particular function in the ESA, consistent with, but distinct from, the functions of the other verbs used to define "take." The Secretary's interpretation of "harm" to include indirectly injuring endangered animals through habitat modification permissibly interprets "harm" to have "a character of its own not to be submerged by its association." *Russell Motor Car Co. v. United States*, 261 U.S. 514, 519 (1923).

Nor does the Act's inclusion of the § 5 land acquisition authority and the § 7 directive to federal agencies to avoid destruction or adverse modification of critical habitat alter our conclusion. Respondents' argument that the Government lacks any incentive to purchase land under § 5 when it can simply prohibit takings under § 9 ignores the practical considerations that attend enforcement of the ESA. Purchasing habitat lands may well cost the Government less in many circumstances than pursuing civil or criminal penalties. In addition, the § 5 procedure allows for protection of habitat before the seller's activity has harmed any endangered animal, whereas the Government cannot enforce the § 9 prohibition until an animal has actually been killed or injured. The Secretary may also find the § 5 authority useful for preventing modification of land that is not yet but may in the future become habitat

[15] The dissent makes no effort to defend the Court of Appeals' reading of the statutory definition as requiring a direct application of force. Instead, it tries to impose on § 9 a limitation of liability to "affirmative conduct intentionally directed against a particular animal or animals." *Post* at 720. Under the dissent's interpretation of the Act, a developer could drain a pond, knowing that the act would extinguish an endangered species of turtles, without even proposing a conservation plan or applying for a permit under § 10(a)(1)(B); unless the developer was motivated by a desire "to get at a turtle," *post* at 721, no statutory taking could occur. Because such conduct would not constitute a taking at common law, the dissent would shield it from § 9 liability, even though the words "kill" and "harm" in the statutory definition could apply to such deliberate conduct. We cannot accept that limitation. In any event, our reasons for rejecting the Court of Appeals' interpretation apply as well to the dissent's novel construction.

for an endangered or threatened species. The § 7 directive applies only to the Federal Government, whereas the § 9 prohibition applies to "any person." Section 7 imposes a broad, affirmative duty to avoid adverse habitat modifications that § 9 does not replicate, and § 7 does not limit its admonition to habitat modification that "actually kills or injures wildlife." Conversely, § 7 contains limitations that § 9 does not, applying only to actions "likely to jeopardize the continued existence of any endangered species or threatened species," 16 U.S.C. § 1536(a)(2), and to modifications of habitat that has been designated "critical" pursuant to § 4, 16 U.S.C. § 1533(b)(2).[17] Any overlap that § 5 or § 7 may have with § 9 in particular cases is unexceptional, see, *e.g.*, *Russello v. United States*, 464 U.S. 16, 24, and n. 2 (1983), and simply reflects the broad purpose of the Act set out in § 2 and acknowledged in *TVA v. Hill*.

We need not decide whether the statutory definition of "take" compels the Secretary's interpretation of "harm," because our conclusions that Congress did not unambiguously manifest its intent to adopt respondents' view and that the Secretary's interpretation is reasonable suffice to decide this case. See generally *Chevron U.S.A. Inc. v. Natural Resources Defense Council, Inc.*, 467 U.S. 837 (1984). The latitude the ESA gives the Secretary in enforcing the statute, together with the degree of regulatory expertise necessary to its enforcement, establishes that we owe some degree of deference to the Secretary's reasonable interpretation. See Breyer, Judicial Review of Questions of Law and Policy, 38 Admin. L. Rev. 363, 373 (1986).[18]

III

Our conclusion that the Secretary's definition of "harm" rests on a permissible construction of the ESA gains further support from the legislative history of the statute. The Committee Reports accompanying the bills that became the ESA do not specifically discuss the meaning of "harm," but they make clear that Congress intended "take" to apply broadly to cover indirect as well as purposeful actions. The Senate Report

[17] Congress recognized that §§ 7 and 9 are not coextensive as to federal agencies when, in the wake of our decision in *Hill* in 1978, it added § 7(*o*), 16 U.S.C. § 1536(*o*), to the Act. That section provides that any federal project subject to exemption from § 7, 16 U.S.C. § 1536(h), will also be exempt from § 9.

[18] Respondents also argue that the rule of lenity should foreclose any deference to the Secretary's interpretation of the ESA because the statute includes criminal penalties. The rule of lenity is premised on two ideas: First, " 'a fair warning should be given to the world in language that the common world will understand, of what the law intends to do if a certain line is passed' "; second, "legislatures and not courts should define criminal activity." *United States v. Bass*, 404 U.S. 336, 347–350 (1971) (quoting *McBoyle v. United States*, 283 U.S. 25, 27 (1931)). We have applied the rule of lenity in a case raising a narrow question concerning the application of a statute that contains criminal sanctions to a specific factual dispute—whether pistols with short barrels and attachable shoulder stocks are short-barreled rifles—where no regulation was present. See *United States v. Thompson/Center Arms Co.*, 504 U.S. 505, 517–518, and n. 9 (1992). We have never suggested that the rule of lenity should provide the standard for reviewing facial challenges to administrative regulations whenever the governing statute authorizes criminal enforcement. Even if there exist regulations whose interpretations of statutory criminal penalties provide such inadequate notice of potential liability as to offend the rule of lenity, the "harm" regulation, which has existed for two decades and gives a fair warning of its consequences, cannot be one of them.

stressed that " '[t]ake' is defined . . . in the broadest possible manner to include every conceivable way in which a person can 'take' or attempt to 'take' any fish or wildlife." S. Rep. No. 93–307, p. 7 (1973). The House Report stated that "the broadest possible terms" were used to define restrictions on takings. H.R. Rep. No. 93–412, p. 15 (1973). The House Report underscored the breadth of the "take" definition by noting that it included "harassment, *whether intentional or not.*" *Id.* at 11 (emphasis added). The Report explained that the definition "would allow, for example, the Secretary to regulate or prohibit the activities of birdwatchers where the effect of those activities might disturb the birds and make it difficult for them to hatch or raise their young." *Ibid.* These comments, ignored in the dissent's welcome but selective foray into legislative history, see *post* at 726–729, support the Secretary's interpretation that the term "take" in § 9 reached far more than the deliberate actions of hunters and trappers.

Two endangered species bills, S. 1592 and S. 1983, were introduced in the Senate and referred to the Commerce Committee. Neither bill included the word "harm" in its definition of "take," although the definitions otherwise closely resembled the one that appeared in the bill as ultimately enacted. See Hearings on S. 1592 and S. 1983 before the Subcommittee on Environment of the Senate Committee on Commerce, 93d Cong., 1st Sess., pp. 7, 27 (1973) (hereinafter Hearings). Senator Tunney, the floor manager of the bill in the Senate, subsequently introduced a floor amendment that added "harm" to the definition, noting that this and accompanying amendments would "help to achieve the purposes of the bill." 119 Cong. Rec. 25683 (1973). Respondents argue that the lack of debate about the amendment that added "harm" counsels in favor of a narrow interpretation. We disagree. An obviously broad word that the Senate went out of its way to add to an important statutory definition is precisely the sort of provision that deserves a respectful reading.

The definition of "take" that originally appeared in S. 1983 differed from the definition as ultimately enacted in one other significant respect: It included "the destruction, modification, or curtailment of [the] habitat or range" of fish and wildlife. Hearings at 27. Respondents make much of the fact that the Commerce Committee removed this phrase from the "take" definition before S. 1983 went to the floor. See 119 Cong. Rec. 25663 (1973). We do not find that fact especially significant. The legislative materials contain no indication why the habitat protection provision was deleted. That provision differed greatly from the regulation at issue today. Most notably, the habitat protection provision in S. 1983 would have applied far more broadly than the regulation does because it made adverse habitat modification a categorical violation of the "take" prohibition, unbounded by the regulation's limitation to habitat modifications that actually kill or injure wildlife. The S. 1983 language also failed to qualify "modification" with the regulation's limiting adjective "significant." We do not believe the Senate's unelaborated disavowal of the provision in S. 1983 undermines the reasonableness of the more moderate habitat protection in the Secretary's "harm" regulation.[19]

The history of the 1982 amendment that gave the Secretary authority to grant permits for "incidental" takings provides further support for his reading of the Act. The House Report expressly states that "[b]y use of the word 'incidental' the Committee intends to cover situations in which it is known that a taking will occur if the other activity is engaged in but such taking is incidental to, and not the purpose of, the activity." H.R. Rep. No. 97–567, p. 31 (1982). This reference to the foreseeability of incidental takings undermines respondents' argument that the 1982 amendment covered only accidental killings of endangered and threatened animals that might occur in the course of hunting or trapping other animals. Indeed, Congress had habitat modification directly in mind: Both the Senate Report and the House Conference Report identified as the model for the permit process a cooperative state-federal response to a case in California where a development project threatened incidental harm to a species of endangered butterfly by modification of its habitat. See S. Rep. No. 97–418, p. 10 (1982); H.R. Conf. Rep. No. 97–835, pp. 30–32 (1982). Thus, Congress in 1982 focused squarely on the aspect of the "harm" regulation at issue in this litigation. Congress' implementation of a permit program is consistent with the Secretary's interpretation of the term "harm."

IV

When it enacted the ESA, Congress delegated broad administrative and interpretive power to the Secretary. See 16 U.S.C. §§ 1533, 1540(f). The task of defining and listing endangered and threatened species requires an expertise and attention to detail that exceeds the normal province of Congress. Fashioning appropriate standards for issuing permits under § 10 for takings that would otherwise violate § 9 necessarily requires the exercise of broad discretion. The proper interpretation of a term such as "harm" involves a complex policy choice. When Congress has entrusted the Secretary with broad discretion, we are especially reluctant to substitute our views of wise policy for his. See *Chevron*, 467 U.S. at 865–866. In this case, that reluctance accords with our conclusion, based on the text, structure, and legislative history of the ESA, that the Secretary reasonably construed the intent of Congress

---

[19] Respondents place heavy reliance for their argument that Congress intended the § 5 land acquisition provision and not § 9 to be the ESA's remedy for habitat modification on a floor statement by Senator Tunney [and] . . . a floor statement by Representative Sullivan . . . . [Quotations omitted because they also appear in Justice Scalia's dissent.] Each of these statements merely explained features of the bills that Congress eventually enacted in § 5 of the ESA and went on to discuss elements enacted in § 9. Neither statement even suggested that § 5 would be the Act's exclusive remedy for habitat modification by private landowners or that habitat modification by private landowners stood outside the ambit of § 9. Respondents' suggestion that these statements identified § 5 as the ESA's only response to habitat modification contradicts their emphasis elsewhere on the habitat protections in § 7. . . .

when he defined "harm" to include "significant habitat modification or degradation that actually kills or injures wildlife."

In the elaboration and enforcement of the ESA, the Secretary and all persons who must comply with the law will confront difficult questions of proximity and degree; for, as all recognize, the Act encompasses a vast range of economic and social enterprises and endeavors. These questions must be addressed in the usual course of the law, through case-by-case resolution and adjudication. . . .

■ *JUSTICE O'CONNOR, concurring:*

My agreement with the Court is founded on two understandings. First, the challenged regulation is limited to significant habitat modification that causes actual, as opposed to hypothetical or speculative, death or injury to identifiable protected animals. Second, even setting aside difficult questions of scienter, the regulation's application is limited by ordinary principles of proximate causation, which introduce notions of foreseeability. . . .

In my view, the regulation is limited by its terms to actions that actually kill or injure individual animals. Justice Scalia disagrees, arguing that the harm regulation "encompasses injury inflicted, not only upon individual animals, but upon populations of the protected species." *Post* at 716. . . . Building upon the regulation's use of the word "breeding," Justice Scalia suggests that the regulation facially bars significant habitat modification that actually kills or injures *hypothetical* animals (or, perhaps more aptly, causes potential additions to the population not to come into being). Because "[i]mpairment of breeding does not 'injure' living creatures," Justice Scalia reasons, the regulation *must* contemplate application to "*a population* of animals which would otherwise have maintained or increased its numbers." *Post* at 716, 734.

I disagree. As an initial matter, I do not find it as easy as Justice Scalia does to dismiss the notion that significant impairment of breeding injures living creatures. . . . One need not subscribe to theories of "psychic harm," cf. *post* at 734–735, n. 5, to recognize that to make it impossible for an animal to reproduce is to impair its most essential physical functions and to render that animal, and its genetic material, biologically obsolete. This, in my view, is actual injury.

In any event, even if impairing an animal's ability to breed were not, *in and of itself*, an injury to that animal, interference with breeding can cause an animal to suffer other, perhaps more obvious, kinds of injury. The regulation has clear application, for example, to significant habitat modification that kills or physically injures animals which, because they are in a vulnerable breeding state, do not or cannot flee or defend themselves, or to environmental pollutants that cause an animal to suffer physical complications during gestation. Breeding, feeding, and sheltering are what animals do. If significant habitat modification, by interfering with these essential behaviors, actually kills or injures an animal protected by the Act, it causes "harm" within the meaning of the regulation. In contrast to Justice Scalia, I do not read the regulation's "breeding" reference to vitiate or somehow to qualify the clear actual death or injury requirement, or to suggest that the regulation contemplates extension to nonexistent animals. . . .

By the dissent's reckoning, the regulation at issue here, in conjunction with 16 U.S.C. § 1540(a)(1), imposes liability for any habitat-modifying conduct that ultimately results in the death of a protected animal, "regardless of whether that result is intended or even foreseeable, and no matter how long the chain of causality between modification and injury." *Post* at 715 . . . . Even if § 1540(a)(1) does create a strict liability regime (a question we need not decide at this juncture), I see no indication that Congress, in enacting that section, intended to dispense with ordinary principles of proximate causation. Strict liability means liability without regard to fault; it does not normally mean liability for every consequence, however remote, of one's conduct. . . . I would not lightly assume that Congress, in enacting a strict liability statute that is silent on the causation question, has dispensed with this well-entrenched principle. In the absence of congressional abrogation of traditional principles of causation, then, private parties should be held liable under § 1540(a)(1) only if their habitat-modifying actions proximately cause death or injury to protected animals. Cf. *Benefiel v. Exxon Corp.*, 959 F.2d 805, 807–808 (CA9 1992) (in enacting the Trans-Alaska Pipeline Authorization Act, which provides for strict liability for damages that are the result of discharges, Congress did not intend to abrogate common-law principles of proximate cause to reach "remote and derivative" consequences) . . . . The regulation, of course, does not contradict the presumption or notion that ordinary principles of causation apply here. . . .

Proximate causation is not a concept susceptible of precise definition. . . . Proximate causation depends to a great extent on considerations of the fairness of imposing liability for remote consequences. The task of determining whether proximate causation exists in the limitless fact patterns sure to arise is best left to lower courts. But I note, at the least, that proximate cause principles inject a foreseeability element into the statute, and hence, the regulation, that would appear to alleviate some of the problems noted by the dissent. . . .

In my view, then, the "harm" regulation applies where significant habitat modification, by impairing essential behaviors, proximately (foreseeably) causes actual death or injury to identifiable animals that are protected under the Endangered Species Act. Pursuant to my interpretation, *Palila II* [*Palila v. Hawaii Dept. of Land and Natural Resources*, 852 F.2d 1106 (CA9 1988)]—. . . which . . . held that a state agency committed a "taking" by permitting mouflon sheep to eat mamane-naio seedlings that, when full grown, might have fed and sheltered endangered palila [birds]—was wrongly decided according to the regulation's own terms. Destruction of the seedlings did not proximately cause actual death or injury to identifiable birds; it merely prevented the regeneration of forest land not currently sustaining actual birds. . . .

■ *JUSTICE SCALIA, with whom CHIEF JUSTICE REHNQUIST and JUSTICE THOMAS join, dissenting:*

I think it unmistakably clear that the legislation at issue here (1) forbade the hunting and killing of endangered animals, and (2) provided federal lands and federal funds *for the acquisition of private lands*, to preserve the habitat of endangered animals. The Court's holding that the hunting and killing prohibition incidentally preserves habitat on private lands imposes unfairness to the point of financial ruin—not just upon the rich, but upon the simplest farmer who finds his land conscripted to national zoological use. I respectfully dissent.

I

. . . . In my view petitioners must lose—the regulation must fall—even under the test of *Chevron U.S.A. Inc. v. Natural Resources Defense Council, Inc.*, 467 U.S. 837, 843 (1984), so I shall assume that the Court is correct to apply *Chevron*.

The regulation has three features which, for reasons I shall discuss at length below, do not comport with the statute. First, it interprets the statute to prohibit habitat modification that is no more than the cause-in-fact of death or injury to wildlife. *Any* "significant habitat modification" that in fact produces that result by "impairing essential behavioral patterns" is made unlawful, regardless of whether that result is intended or even foreseeable, and no matter how long the chain of causality between modification and injury. See, *e.g., Palila v. Hawaii Dept. of Land and Natural Resources*, 852 F.2d 1106, 1108–1109 (CA9 1988) (*Palila II*) (sheep grazing constituted "taking" of palila birds, since although sheep do not destroy full-grown mamane trees, they do destroy mamane seedlings, which will not grow to full-grown trees, on which the palila feeds and nests). . . .

Second, the regulation does not require an "act": The Secretary's officially stated position is that an *omission* will do. The previous version of the regulation made this explicit. See 40 Fed. Reg. 44412, 44416 (1975) (" 'Harm' in the definition of 'take' in the Act means an act or omission which actually kills or injures wildlife . . . ."). When the regulation was modified in 1981 the phrase "or omission" was taken out, but only because (as the final publication of the rule advised) "the [Fish and Wildlife] Service feels that 'act' is inclusive of either commissions or omissions which would be prohibited by section [1538(a)(1)(B)]." 46 Fed. Reg. 54748, 54750 (1981). In their brief here petitioners agree that the regulation covers omissions, see Brief for Petitioners 47 (although they argue that "[a]n 'omission' constitutes an 'act' . . . only if there is a legal duty to act," *ibid.*).

The third and most important unlawful feature of the regulation is that it encompasses injury inflicted, not only upon individual animals, but upon populations of the protected species. "Injury" in the regulation includes "significantly impairing essential behavioral patterns, including *breeding*," 50 CFR § 17.3 (1994) (emphasis added). Impairment of breeding does not "injure" living creatures; it prevents them from propagating, thus "injuring" *a population* of animals which would otherwise have maintained or increased its numbers. What the face of the regulation shows, the Secretary's official pronouncements confirm. The Final Redefinition of "Harm" accompanying publication of the regulation said that "harm" is not limited to "direct physical injury to an individual member of the wildlife species," 46 Fed. Reg. 54748 (1981), and refers to "injury *to a population*," *id.* at 54749 (emphasis added). . . .[1]

None of these three features of the regulation can be found in the statutory provisions supposed to authorize it. The term "harm" in § 1532(19) has no legal force of its own. An indictment or civil complaint that charged the defendant with "harming" an animal protected under the Act would be dismissed as defective, for the only *operative* term in the statute is to "take." If "take" were not elsewhere defined in the Act, none could dispute what it means, for the term is as old as the law itself. To "take," when applied to wild animals, means to reduce those animals, by killing or capturing, to human control. See, *e.g.*, 11 Oxford English Dictionary (1933) ("Take . . . To catch, capture (a wild beast, bird, fish, etc.)"); Webster's New International Dictionary of the English Language (2d ed. 1949) (take defined as "to catch or capture by trapping, snaring, etc., or as prey"); *Geer v. Connecticut*, 161 U.S. 519, 523 (1896) (" '[A]ll the animals which can be taken upon the earth, in the sea, or in the air, that is to say, wild animals, belong to those who take them' ") (quoting the Digest of Justinian); 2 W. Blackstone, Commentaries 411 (1766) ("Every man . . . has an equal right of pursuing and taking to his own use all such creatures as are *ferae naturae*"). This is just the sense in which "take" is used elsewhere in federal legislation and treaty. See, *e.g.*, Migratory Bird Treaty Act, 16 U.S.C. § 703 (1988 ed., Supp. V) (no person may "pursue, hunt, take, capture, kill, [or] attempt to take, capture, or kill" any migratory bird); Agreement on the Conservation of Polar Bears, Nov. 15, 1973, Art. I, 27 U.S.T. 3918, 3921, T.I.A.S. No. 8409 (defining "taking" as "hunting, killing and capturing"). And that meaning fits neatly with the rest of § 1538(a)(1), which makes it unlawful not only to take protected species, but also to import or export them, § 1538(a)(1)(A); to possess, sell, deliver, carry, transport, or ship any taken species, § 1538(a)(1)(D); and to transport, sell, or offer to sell them in interstate or foreign commerce, §§ 1538(a)(1)(E), (F). The taking prohibition, in other words, is only part of the regulatory plan of § 1538(a)(1), which covers all the stages of the process by which protected wildlife is reduced

[1] The Court and Justice O'Connor deny that the regulation has the first or the third of these features. I respond to their arguments in Part III.

to man's dominion and made the object of profit. It is obvious that "take" in this sense—a term of art deeply embedded in the statutory and common law concerning wildlife—describes a class of acts (not omissions) done directly and intentionally (not indirectly and by accident) to particular animals (not populations of animals).

The Act's definition of "take" does expand the word slightly (and not unusually), so as to make clear that it includes not just a completed taking, but the process of taking, and all of the acts that are customarily identified with or accompany that process ("to harass, harm, pursue, hunt, shoot, wound, kill, trap, capture, or collect"); and so as to include attempts. § 1532(19). The tempting fallacy—which the Court commits with abandon, see *ante* at 697–698, n. 10—is to assume that *once defined*, "take" loses any significance, and it is only the definition that matters. The Court treats the statute as though Congress had directly enacted the § 1532(19) definition as a self-executing prohibition, and had not enacted § 1538(a)(1)(B) at all. But § 1538(a)(1)(B) *is* there, and if the terms contained in the definitional section are susceptible of two readings, one of which comports with the standard meaning of "take" as used in application to wildlife, and one of which does not, an agency regulation that adopts the latter reading is necessarily unreasonable, for it reads the defined term "take"—the only operative term—out of the statute altogether.[2]

That is what has occurred here. The verb "harm" has a *range* of meaning: "to cause injury" at its broadest, "to do hurt or damage" in a narrower and more direct sense. See, *e.g.*, 1 N. Webster, An American Dictionary of the English Language (1828) ("Harm, *v.t.* To hurt; to injure; to damage; *to impair soundness of body, either animal* or vegetable") (emphasis added); American College Dictionary 551 (1970) ("harm . . . *n.* injury; damage; hurt: *to do him bodily harm*"). In fact the more directed sense of "harm" is a somewhat more common and preferred usage; "*harm* has in it a little of the idea of specially focused hurt or injury, as if a personal injury has been anticipated and intended." J. Opdycke, Mark My Words: A Guide to Modern Usage and Expression 330 (1949). See also American Heritage Dictionary 662 (1985) ("*Injure* has the widest range. . . . *Harm* and *hurt* refer principally to what causes physical or mental distress to living things"). To define "harm" as an act or omission that, however remotely, "actually kills or injures" a population of wildlife through habitat modification is to choose a meaning that makes nonsense of the word that "harm" defines—requiring us to accept that a farmer who tills his field and causes erosion that makes silt run into a nearby

---

[2] The Court suggests halfheartedly that "take" cannot refer to the taking of particular animals, because § 538(a)(1)(B) prohibits "tak[ing] any [endangered] *species*." *Ante* at 697, n. 10. The suggestion is halfhearted because that reading obviously contradicts the statutory intent. It would mean no violation in the intentional shooting of a single bald eagle—or, for that matter, the intentional shooting of 1,000 bald eagles out of the extant 1,001. The phrasing of § 1538(a)(1)(B), as the Court recognizes elsewhere, is shorthand for "take any [*member of* an endangered] species."

river which depletes oxygen and thereby "impairs [the] breeding" of protected fish has "taken" or "attempted to take" the fish. It should take the strongest evidence to make us believe that Congress has defined a term in a manner repugnant to its ordinary and traditional sense.

Here the evidence shows the opposite. "Harm" is merely one of 10 prohibitory words in § 1532(19), and the other 9 fit the ordinary meaning of "take" perfectly. To "harass, pursue, hunt, shoot, wound, kill, trap, capture, or collect" are all affirmative acts (the provision itself describes them as "conduct," see § 1532(19)) which are directed immediately and intentionally against a particular animal—not acts or omissions that indirectly and accidentally cause injury to a population of animals. The Court points out that several of the words ("harass," "pursue," "wound," and "kill") "refer to actions or effects that do not require direct *applications of force.*" *Ante* at 701 (emphasis added). That is true enough, but force is not the point. Even "taking" activities in the narrowest sense, activities traditionally engaged in by hunters and trappers, do not all consist of direct applications of force; pursuit and harassment are part of the business of "taking" the prey even before it has been touched. What the nine other words in § 1532(19) have in common—and share with the narrower meaning of "harm" described above, but not with the Secretary's ruthless dilation of the word—is the sense of affirmative conduct intentionally directed against a particular animal or animals.

I am not the first to notice this fact, or to draw the conclusion that it compels. In 1981 the Solicitor of the Fish and Wildlife Service delivered a legal opinion on § 1532(19) that is in complete agreement with my reading:

> "The Act's definition of 'take' contains a list of actions that illustrate the intended scope of the term. . . . With the possible exception of 'harm,' these terms all represent forms of conduct that are directed against and likely to injure or kill *individual* wildlife. Under the principle of statutory construction, *ejusdem generis*, . . . the term 'harm' should be interpreted to include only those actions that are directed against, and likely to injure or kill, individual wildlife." Memorandum of Apr. 17, reprinted in 46 Fed. Reg. 29490, 29491 (1981) (emphasis in original).

I would call it *noscitur a sociis*, but the principle is much the same: The fact that "several items in a list share an attribute counsels in favor of interpreting the other items as possessing that attribute as well," *Beecham v. United States*, 511 U.S. 368, 371 (1994). The Court contends that the canon cannot be applied to deprive a word of all its "independent meaning," *ante* at 702. That proposition is questionable to begin with, especially as applied to long lawyers' listings such as this. If it were true, we ought to give the word "trap" in the definition its rare meaning of "to clothe" (whence "trappings")—since otherwise it adds nothing to the word "capture." . . . In any event, the Court's contention that "harm" in the narrow sense adds nothing to the other words underestimates the ingenuity of our own species in a way that Congress did not. To feed an animal poison, to spray it with mace, to chop down the very tree in which it is nesting, or even to destroy its entire habitat in order to take it (as by draining a pond to get at a turtle), might neither wound nor kill, but would directly and intentionally harm.

The penalty provisions of the Act counsel this interpretation as well. Any person who "knowingly" violates § 1538(a)(1)(B) is subject to criminal penalties under § 1540(b)(1) and civil penalties under § 1540(a)(1); moreover, under the latter section, any person "who otherwise violates" the taking prohibition (*i.e.*, violates it *un*knowingly) may be assessed a civil penalty of $500 for each violation, with the stricture that "[e]ach such violation shall be a separate offense." This last provision should be clear warning that the regulation is in error, for when combined with the regulation it produces a result that no legislature could reasonably be thought to have intended: A large number of routine private activities—for example, farming, ranching, roadbuilding, construction and logging—are subjected to strict-liability penalties when they fortuitously injure protected wildlife, no matter how remote the chain of causation and no matter how difficult to foresee (or to disprove) the "injury" may be (*e.g.*, an "impairment" of breeding). The Court says that "[the strict-liability provision] is potentially sweeping, but it would be so with or without the Secretary's 'harm' regulation." *Ante* at 696, n. 9. That is not correct. Without the regulation, the routine "habitat modifying" activities that people conduct to make a daily living would not carry exposure to strict penalties; only acts directed at animals, like those described by the other words in § 1532(19), would risk liability.

The Court says that "[to] read a requirement of intent or purpose into the words used to define 'take' . . . ignore[s] [§ 1540's] express provision that a 'knowin[g]' action is enough to violate the Act." *Ante* at 701–702. This presumably means that because the reading of § 1532(19) advanced here ascribes an element of purposeful injury to the prohibited acts, it makes superfluous (or inexplicable) the more severe penalties provided for a "knowing" violation. That conclusion does not follow, for it is quite possible to take protected wildlife purposefully without doing so knowingly. A requirement that a violation be "knowing" means that the defendant must "know the facts that make his conduct illegal," *Staples v. United States*, 511 U.S. 600, 606 (1994). The hunter who shoots an elk in the mistaken belief that it is a mule deer has not knowingly violated § 1538(a)(1)(B)—not because he does not know that elk are legally protected (that would be knowledge of the law, which is not a requirement, see *ante* at 696–697, n. 9), but because he does not know what sort of animal he is shooting. The hunter has nonetheless committed a purposeful taking of protected wildlife, and would therefore be subject to the (lower) strict-liability penalties for the violation.

So far I have discussed only the immediate statutory text bearing on the regulation. But the definition of "take" in § 1532(19) . . . governs the meaning of the word *as used everywhere in the Act*. Thus, the Secretary's interpretation of "harm" is wrong if it does not fit with the use of "take" throughout the Act. And it does not. In § 1540(e)(4)(B), for example, Congress provided for the forfeiture of "[a]ll guns, traps, nets, and other equipment . . . used to aid the taking, possessing, selling, [etc.]" of protected animals. This listing plainly relates to "taking" in the ordinary sense. If environmental modification were part (and necessarily a major part) of taking, as the Secretary maintains, one would have expected the list to include "plows, bulldozers, and backhoes." As another example, § 1539(e)(1) exempts "the taking of any endangered species" by Alaskan Indians and Eskimos "if such taking is primarily for subsistence purposes"; and provides that "[n]on-edible byproducts of species taken pursuant to this section may be sold . . . when made into authentic native articles of handicrafts and clothing." Surely these provisions apply to taking only in the ordinary sense, and are meaningless as applied to species injured by environmental modification. The Act is full of like examples. See, *e.g.*, § 1538(a)(1)(D) (prohibiting possession, sale, and transport of "species taken in violation" of the Act). "[I]f the Act is to be interpreted as a symmetrical and coherent regulatory scheme, one in which the operative words have a consistent meaning throughout," *Gustafson v. Alloyd Co.*, 513 U.S. 561, 569 (1995), the regulation must fall.

The broader structure of the Act confirms the unreasonableness of the regulation. Section 1536 provides:

> "Each Federal agency shall . . . insure that any action authorized, funded, or carried out by such agency . . . is not likely to jeopardize the continued existence of any endangered species or threatened species or *result in the destruction or adverse modification of habitat* of such species which is determined by the Secretary . . . to be critical." 16 U.S.C. § 1536(a)(2) (emphasis added).

The Act defines "critical habitat" as habitat that is "essential to the conservation of the species," §§ 1532(5)(A)(i), (A)(ii), with "conservation" in turn defined as the use of methods necessary to bring listed species "to the point at which the measures provided pursuant to this chapter are no longer necessary," § 1532(3).

These provisions have a double significance. Even if §§ 1536(a)(2) and 1538(a)(1)(B) were totally independent prohibitions—the former applying only to federal agencies and their licensees, the latter only to private parties—Congress's explicit prohibition of habitat modification in the one section would bar the inference of an implicit prohibition of habitat modification in the other section. "[W]here Congress includes particular language in one section of a statute but omits it in another . . . , it is generally presumed that Congress acts intentionally and purposely in the disparate inclusion or exclusion." *Keene Corp. v. United States*, 508 U.S. 200, 208 (1993) (internal quotation marks omitted). And that presumption against implicit prohibition would be even stronger where the one section which uses the language carefully defines and limits its application. That is to say, it would be passing strange for Congress carefully to define "critical habitat" as used in § 1536(a)(2), but leave it to the Secretary to evaluate, willy-nilly, impermissible "habitat modification" (under the guise of "harm") in § 1538(a)(1)(B).

In fact, however, §§ 1536(a)(2) and 1538(a)(1)(B) do *not* operate in separate realms; federal agencies are subject to *both*, because the "person[s]" forbidden to take protected species under § 1538 include agencies and departments of the Federal Government. See § 1532(13). This means that the "harm" regulation also contradicts another principle of interpretation: that statutes should be read so far as possible to give independent effect to all their provisions. See *Ratzlaf v. United States*, 510 U.S. 135, 140–141 (1994). By defining "harm" in the definition of "take" in § 1538(a)(1)(B) to include significant habitat modification that injures populations of wildlife, the regulation makes the habitat-modification restriction in § 1536(a)(2) almost wholly superfluous. As "critical habitat" is habitat "essential to the conservation of the species," adverse modification of "critical" habitat by a federal agency would also constitute habitat modification that injures a population of wildlife.

Petitioners try to salvage some independent scope for § 1536(a)(2) by the following contortion: Because the definition of critical habitat includes not only "the specific areas within the geographical area occupied by the species [that are] essential to the conservation of the species," § 1532(5)(A)(i), but also "specific areas outside the geographical area occupied by the species at the time it is listed [as a protected species] . . . [that are] essential to the conservation of the species," § 1532(5)(A)(ii), there may be some agency modifications of critical habitat which do *not* injure a population of wildlife. See Brief for Petitioners 41, and n. 27. This is dubious to begin with. A principal way to injure wildlife under the Secretary's own regulation is to "significantly impai[r] . . . breeding," 50 CFR § 17.3 (1994). To prevent the natural increase of a species by adverse modification of habitat suitable for expansion assuredly impairs breeding. But even if true, the argument only narrows the scope of the superfluity, leaving as so many wasted words the § 1532(5)(A)(i) definition of critical habitat to include currently *occupied* habitat essential to the species' conservation. . . .

II

The Court makes four other arguments. First, "the broad purpose of the [Act] supports the Secretary's decision to extend protection against activities that cause the precise harms Congress enacted the statute to avoid." *Ante* at 698. I thought we had renounced the vice of "simplistically . . . assum[ing] that *whatever* furthers the statute's primary objective must be the law." *Rodriguez v. United States*, 480 U.S. 522, 526 (1987) (*per curiam*) (emphasis in original). Deduction from the "broad purpose" of a statute begs the question if it is used to decide by what *means* (and hence to what *length*) Congress pursued that purpose; to get the right answer to that question there is no substitute for the hard job (or, in this case, the quite simple one) of reading the whole text. "The Act must do everything necessary to achieve its broad purpose" is the slogan of the enthusiast, not the analytical tool of the arbiter.

Second, the Court maintains that the legislative history of the 1973 Act supports the Secretary's definition. *See ante* at 704–706. Even if legislative history were a legitimate and reliable tool of interpretation (which I shall assume in order to rebut the Court's claim); and even if it could appropriately be resorted to when the enacted text is as clear as this, but see *Chicago v. Environmental Defense Fund*, 511 U.S. 328, 337 (1994); here it shows quite the opposite of what the Court says. I shall not pause to discuss the Court's reliance on such statements in the Committee Reports as " '[t]ake' is defined . . . in the broadest possible manner to include every conceivable way in which a person can 'take' or attempt to 'take' any fish or wildlife." S. Rep. No. 93–307, p. 7 (1973) (quoted *ante* at 704). This sort of empty flourish—to the effect that "this statute means what it means all the way"—counts for little even when enacted into the law itself. See *Reves v. Ernst & Young*, 507 U.S. 170, 183–184 (1993).

Much of the Court's discussion of legislative history is devoted to two items: first, the Senate floor manager's introduction of an amendment that added the word "harm" to the definition of "take," with the observation that (along with other amendments) it would " 'help to achieve the purposes of the bill' "; second, the relevant Committee's removal from the definition of a provision stating that "take" includes " 'the destruction, modification or curtailment of [the] habitat or range' " of fish and wildlife. See *ante* at 705. The Court inflates the first and belittles the second, even though the second is on its face far more pertinent. But this elaborate inference from various pre-enactment actions and inactions is quite unnecessary, since we have *direct* evidence of what those who brought the legislation to the floor thought it meant—evidence as solid as any ever to be found in legislative history, but which the Court banishes to a footnote. See *ante* at 706–707, n. 19.

Both the Senate and House floor managers of the bill explained it in terms which leave no doubt that the problem of habitat destruction on private lands was to be solved principally by the land acquisition program of § 1534, while § 1538 solved a different problem altogether—the problem of takings. Senator Tunney stated:

> "*Through [the] land acquisition provisions, we will be able to conserve habitats necessary to protect fish and wildlife from further destruction.*
>
> "Although most endangered species are threatened primarily by the destruction of their natural habitats, a significant portion of these animals are subject to *predation by man for commercial, sport, consumption, or other purposes*. The provisions of [the bill] would prohibit the commerce in or the importation, exportation, or taking

> of endangered species. . . ." 119 Cong. Rec. 25669 (1973) (emphasis added).

The House floor manager, Representative Sullivan, put the same thought in this way:

> "[T]he principal threat to animals stems from destruction of their habitat. . . . [*The bill*] *will meet this problem by providing funds for acquisition of critical habitat*. . . . It will also enable the Department of Agriculture to cooperate with willing landowners who desire to assist in the protection of endangered species, *but who are understandably unwilling to do so at excessive cost to themselves*.
>
> "Another hazard to endangered species arises from those who would *capture or kill them for pleasure or profit*. There is no way that the Congress can make it less pleasurable for a person to take an animal, but we can certainly make it less profitable for them to do so." *Id.* at 30162 (emphasis added).

Habitat modification and takings, in other words, were viewed as different problems, addressed by different provisions of the Act. . . . [These statements] display the clear understanding (1) that habitat modification is separate from "taking," and (2) that habitat destruction on private lands is to be remedied by public acquisition, and *not* by making particular unlucky landowners incur "excessive cost to themselves." The Court points out triumphantly that they do not display the understanding (3) that the land acquisition program is "the [Act's] only response to habitat modification." [*Ante* at 707, n. 19.] Of course not, since that is not so (all *public* lands are subject to habitat-modification restrictions); but (1) and (2) are quite enough to exclude the Court's interpretation. They identify the land acquisition program as the Act's only response to habitat modification *by private landowners* . . . .

Third, the Court seeks support from a provision that was added to the Act in 1982, the year after the Secretary promulgated the current regulation. The provision states:

> "[T]he Secretary may permit, under such terms and conditions as he shall prescribe—
>
> . . . .
>
> "any taking otherwise prohibited by section 1538(a)(1)(B) . . . if such taking is incidental to, and not the purpose of, the carrying out of an otherwise lawful activity." 16 U.S.C. § 1539(a)(1)(B).

This provision does not, of course, implicate our doctrine that reenactment of a statutory provision ratifies an extant judicial or administrative interpretation, for neither the taking prohibition in § 1538(a)(1)(B) nor the definition in § 1532(19) was reenacted. See *Central Bank of Denver, N.A. v. First Interstate Bank of Denver, N.A.*, 511 U.S. 164, 185 (1994). The Court claims, however, that the provision "strongly suggests that Congress understood [§ 1538(a)(1)(B)] to prohibit indirect as well as deliberate takings." *Ante* at 700. That would be a valid inference if habitat modification were the only substantial "otherwise lawful activity" that might incidentally and nonpurposefully cause a prohibited "taking." Of course it is not. This provision applies to the many otherwise lawful takings that incidentally take a protected species—as when fishing for unprotected salmon also takes an endangered species of salmon, see *Pacific Northwest Generating Cooperative v. Brown*, 38 F.3d 1058, 1067 (CA9 1994). Congress has referred to such "incidental takings" in other statutes as well—for example, a statute referring to "the incidental taking of . . . sea turtles in the course of . . . harvesting [shrimp]" . . . , 103 Stat. 1038, § 609(b)(2), . . . and a statute referring to "the incidental taking of marine mammals in the course of commercial fishing operations," 108 Stat. 546, § 118(a). . . .

This is enough to show, in my view, that the 1982 permit provision does not support the regulation. I must acknowledge that the Senate Committee Report on this provision, and the House Conference Committee Report, clearly contemplate that it will enable the Secretary to permit environmental modification. See S. Rep. No. 97–418, p. 10 (1982); H.R. Conf. Rep. No. 97–835, pp. 30–32 (1982). But the *text* of the amendment cannot possibly bear that asserted meaning, when placed within the context of an Act that must be interpreted (as we have seen) not to prohibit private environmental modification. The neutral language of the amendment cannot possibly alter that interpretation, nor can its legislative history be summoned forth to contradict, rather than clarify, what is in its totality an unambiguous statutory text. See *Chicago v. Environmental Defense Fund*, 511 U.S. 328 (1994). There is little fear, of course, that giving no effect to the relevant portions of the Committee Reports will frustrate the real-life expectations of a majority of the Members of Congress. If they read and relied on such tedious detail on such an obscure point (it was not, after all, presented as a revision of the statute's prohibitory scope, but as a discretionary-waiver provision) the Republic would be in grave peril.

Fourth and lastly, the Court seeks to avoid the evident shortcomings of the regulation on the ground that the respondents are challenging it on its face rather than as applied. . . . The Court seems to say that *even if* the regulation dispenses with the foreseeability of harm that it acknowledges the statute to require, that does not matter because this is a facial challenge: So long as habitat modification that *would* foreseeably cause harm is prohibited by the statute, the regulation must be sustained. Presumably it would apply the same reasoning to all the other defects of the regulation: The regulation's failure to require injury to particular animals survives the present challenge, because at least *some* environmental modifications kill particular animals. This evisceration of the facial challenge is unprecedented. It is one thing to say that a facial challenge to a regulation that omits statutory element *x* must be rejected if there is any set of facts on which the statute *does not require x*. It is something quite different—and unlike any doctrine of "facial challenge" I have ever encountered—to say that the challenge must be rejected if the regulation could be applied to a state of facts in which element *x* *happens to be present*. On this analysis, the only regulation susceptible to facial attack is one that *not only* is invalid in all its applications, but also does not sweep up *any* person who *could have been* held liable under a proper application of the statute. That is not the law. . . .

III

In response to the points made in this dissent, the Court's opinion stresses two points, neither of which is supported by the regulation, and so cannot validly be used to uphold it. First, the Court and the concurrence suggest that the regulation should be read to contain a requirement of proximate causation or foreseeability . . . .

The regulation says . . . that "harm" means (1) an act that (2) actually kills or injures wildlife. If that does not dispense with a proximate-cause requirement, I do not know what language would. And changing the regulation by judicial invention, even to achieve compliance with the statute, is not permissible. Perhaps the agency itself would prefer to achieve compliance in some other fashion. We defer to reasonable agency interpretations of ambiguous statutes precisely in order that agencies, rather than courts, may exercise policymaking discretion in the interstices of statutes. See *Chevron*, 467 U.S. at 843–845. . . .

The second point the Court stresses in its response seems to me a belated mending of its holding. It apparently *concedes* that the statute requires injury *to particular animals* rather than merely to populations of animals. See *ante* at 700, n. 13; *ante* at 696 (referring to killing or injuring "*members* of [listed] species" (emphasis added)). The Court then rejects my contention that the regulation ignores this requirement, since, it says, "every term in the regulation's definition of 'harm' is subservient to the phrase 'an act which actually kills or injures wildlife.' " *Ante* at 700, n. 13. As I have pointed out, . . . this reading is incompatible with the regulation's specification of impairment of "breeding" as one of the *modes* of "kill[ing] or injur[ing] wildlife."[5]

[5] Justice O'Connor supposes that an "impairment of breeding" intrinsically injures an animal because "to make it impossible for an animal to reproduce is to impair its most essential physical functions and to render that animal, and its genetic material, biologically obsolete." *Ante* at 710 (concurring opinion). This imaginative construction does achieve the result of extending "impairment of breeding" to individual animals; but only at the expense of also expanding "injury" to include elements beyond *physical harm* to individual animals. For surely the only harm to the individual animal from impairment of that "essential function" is not the failure of issue (which harms only the issue), but the *psychic harm* of perceiving that it will leave this world with no issue (assuming, of course, that the animal in question, perhaps an endangered species of slug, is capable of such painful sentiments). If it includes *that* psychic harm, then why not the psychic harm of not being able to frolic about—so that the draining of a pond used for an endangered animal's recreation, but in no way essential to its survival, would be prohibited by the Act? That the concurrence is driven to such a dubious redoubt is an argument for, not against, the proposition that "injury" in the regulation includes injury to populations of animals. Even more so with the concurrence's alternative explanation: that

But since the Court is reading the regulation and the statute incorrectly in other respects, it may as well introduce this novelty as well—law à la carte. As I understand the regulation that the Court has created and held consistent with the statute that it has also created, habitat modification can constitute a "taking," but only if it results in the killing or harming of *individual animals*, and only if that consequence is the direct result of the modification. This means that the destruction of privately owned habitat that is essential, not for the feeding or nesting, but for the *breeding*, of butterflies, would not violate the Act, since it would not harm or kill any living butterfly. I, too, think it would not violate the Act—not for the utterly unsupported reason that habitat modifications fall outside the regulation if they happen not to kill or injure a living animal, but for the textual reason that only action directed at living animals constitutes a "take."

* * *

The Endangered Species Act is a carefully considered piece of legislation that forbids all persons to hunt or harm endangered animals, but places upon the public at large, rather than upon fortuitously accountable individual landowners, the cost of preserving the habitat of endangered species. There is neither textual support for, nor even evidence of congressional consideration of, the radically different disposition contained in the regulation that the Court sustains. For these reasons, I respectfully dissent.

NOTES AND QUESTIONS

1. Justice Scalia launched his dissent with the argument that in wildlife law, the word "take" has long been a term of art. Both at common law and in federal legislation, he said, to "take" wild animals has meant "to reduce those animals, by killing or capturing, to human control." To be sure, the Endangered Species Act provides its own definition of "take," and that definition includes "harm"—a word that can certainly be read broadly when it appears on its own. According to Justice Scalia, however, the word "harm" has "a *range* of meaning," and it cannot properly be read so broadly when it appears in a wildlife statute's definition of "take." Indeed, Justice Scalia considered that point sufficiently clear that, notwithstanding *Chevron*, the administering agency has no discretion to disagree: "if the terms contained in the definitional section are susceptible of two readings, one of which comports with the standard meaning of 'take' as used in application to wildlife, and one of which does not, an agency regulation that adopts the latter reading is necessarily unreasonable . . . ." In Justice Scalia's view, then, the agency's

---

"impairment of breeding" refers to nothing more than concrete injuries inflicted by the habitat modification on the animal who does the breeding, such as "physical complications [suffered] during gestation," *ibid.* Quite obviously, if "impairment of breeding" meant such physical harm to an individual animal, it would not have had to be mentioned. . . .

understanding of the statutory definition of "take" should have been colored by the fact that "take" was the term being defined.

The majority disagreed. In footnote 10 of its opinion, the majority said that "Congress explicitly defined the operative term 'take' in the ESA, . . . thereby obviating the need for us to probe its meaning as we must probe the meaning of the undefined subsidiary term 'harm.' " According to the majority, then, the term "take" in the Endangered Species Act is simply a placeholder for the definition that Congress supplied, and the label that Congress attached to that definition does not color what the definition itself means.

Exactly four months earlier, the Justices had divided over the same sort of argument. In *Gustafson v. Alloyd Co.*, 513 U.S. 561 (1995), Justice Kennedy's majority opinion had invoked the traditional meaning of the word "prospectus" to help cabin the definition of that term in the Securities Act of 1933. *See id.* at 575–76. The dissenters in *Gustafson*, by contrast, had taken the position suggested by the majority in *Sweet Home*: the meaning of the term "prospectus" in the Securities Act was supplied entirely by the statutory definition, and the Court's interpretation of that definition should not depend on whether Congress used the label "prospectus" or the label "banana." *See id.* at 585 (Thomas, J., dissenting) ("There is no reason to seek the meaning of 'prospectus' outside of the 1933 Act, because Congress has supplied just such a definition in § 2(10). That definition is extraordinarily broad . . . .").

Consistent with the idea that the labels for statutory definitions do not matter, Justices Ginsburg and Breyer joined both the dissent in *Gustafson* and the majority in *Sweet Home*. Consistent with the idea that the labels for statutory definitions *do* matter, Chief Justice Rehnquist did the opposite. But the other six Justices either dissented in both cases (Scalia and Thomas) or joined the majority in both cases (Stevens, O'Connor, Kennedy, and Souter). Aren't those positions inconsistent? The Justices who joined the majority in both cases might have been able to reconcile their positions by invoking *Chevron* deference: perhaps they personally thought that labels *should* color our understanding of statutory definitions (*Gustafson*), but they were willing to defer to an agency's contrary view in *Chevron* cases (*Sweet Home*). But how could Justices Scalia and Thomas explain their positions?

Aside from its possible inconsistency with his position in *Gustafson*, Justice Scalia's argument in *Sweet Home* about the traditional meaning of "take" seems attractive: at least when no agency is in the picture, courts might naturally understand a statutory definition in light of the pre-existing overtones of the word that Congress was trying to define. *See, e.g.*, Bond v. United States, 572 U.S. 844, 861 (2014) (discussing the relevance of "the ordinary meaning of a defined term"); *accord* Sackett v. EPA, 143 S. Ct. 1322, 1337 (2023). But should *Chevron* have dissuaded Justice Scalia from insisting upon that idea in the face of the agency's contrary interpretation? To the extent that Justice Scalia wanted to reject the agency's position on the basis of his understanding of the overtones of a term of art in the agency's own field of specialty, was he giving too little weight to the expertise-based argument for *Chevron* deference?

2. Along the same lines, what do you make of Justice Scalia's invocation of the presumption against absurd results? As he noted, § 11 of the Endangered Species Act authorizes both criminal punishment and relatively stiff civil penalties for any person who "knowingly violates" any provision of the Act. Section 11(a)(1) adds that any person who "otherwise violates" any provision of the Act is subject to a civil penalty of $500 for each separate violation. 16 U.S.C. § 1540(a)(1). Given this latter provision, Justice Scalia asserted, the agency's broad interpretation of the word "harm" in the statutory definition of "take" produces "a result that no legislature could reasonably be thought to have intended." Under the agency's interpretation, people "take" a protected species—in violation of § 9 of the Act—whenever they significantly modify its habitat in a way that significantly impairs essential behavioral patterns and thereby kills or injures some of its members (at least if there is a sufficiently proximate causal link between the people's conduct and the death or injury). According to Justice Scalia, if one accepts this broad interpretation of the statutory definition of "take," then "the routine 'habitat modifying' activities that people conduct to make a daily living"—including "farming, ranching, roadbuilding, construction and logging"—would all "be subjected to strict-liability penalties [under § 11(a)(1)] when they fortuitously injure protected wildlife," even if the people conducting those activities do not know that a protected species is in the area or that they are degrading its habitat. For Justice Scalia, that result was unthinkable.

Footnote 9 of the majority's opinion responded that § 11(a)(1) need not be read as literally as Justice Scalia suggested. According to the majority, § 11(a)(1) should probably be understood to incorporate an implicit foreseeability requirement, and even reading it to incorporate a more demanding scienter requirement is not out of the question. *Cf.* Rehaif v. United States, 139 S. Ct. 2191, 2195 (2019) (discussing the "longstanding presumption, traceable to the common law, that Congress intends to require a defendant to possess a culpable mental state regarding 'each of the statutory elements that criminalize otherwise innocent conduct,'" and adding that "[w]e apply the presumption in favor of scienter even when Congress does not specify any scienter in the statutory text").

Suppose, however, that Justice Scalia was correct that § 11(a)(1) imposes civil penalties on a strict-liability basis. Proceeding from that premise, he argued that the agency's expansive interpretation of the statutory definition of "take" will produce very strange results as a matter of policy. Although those results might be consistent with the stated purposes of the statute, Justice Scalia could not believe that

Congress actually wanted to take those purposes so far. Should that sort of argument be available to a court that is reviewing an agency's interpretation of a statute? When the agency decided to interpret "take" broadly, the agency presumably concluded that the results produced by its interpretation would not be absurd and can sensibly be imputed to the statute. Did *Chevron* permit Justice Scalia to second guess the agency on that policy question? *Cf.* Cass R. Sunstein, *Law and Administration After* Chevron, 90 COLUM. L. REV. 2071, 2116–17 (1990) ("The strongest case for allowing *Chevron* to prevail [over interpretive norms that courts would use in an agency's absence] involve norms that are designed to counteract absurd or unjust results. . . . [A] decision by the court to apply its own judgment in this context would, in effect, substitute a judicial for an administrative determination in circumstances in which Congress has delegated policy-making power to the agency.").

Chevron reflects the intuition that agencies are better suited than courts to make policy judgments, whether because agencies have greater expertise in their field or because agencies are more accountable politically. If you accept that intuition, should courts impose no limits at all on the policy judgments that a *Chevron*-qualified agency can reach in connection with interpreting the statutory provisions that the agency administers? In other words, if the agency's interpretations of those provisions are linguistically permissible, should a reviewing court accept the agency's interpretations without even asking whether, in the court's view, they will produce absurd results? Or does the presumption against absurd results (or, more accurately, results that seem absurd to reviewing courts) still impose an outer bound on the agency's interpretive discretion?

Professor Sunstein suggests that there is some such outer bound, but that reviewing courts should not reject an administering agency's chosen interpretation on the ground of alleged absurdity or irrationality "unless the absurdity or irrationality is so palpable as to be something on which reasonable people could not differ." *Id.* at 2118. In *Sweet Home*, Justice Scalia seemed to take a more aggressive approach. Could Justice Scalia have defended a bifurcated understanding of the relationship between *Chevron* and the presumption against absurd results, under which courts rarely reject an agency's analysis of policies within the agency's specialized field but are not so deferential to the agency's judgments about how those policies trade off against competing policies in other fields? In *Sweet Home*, for instance, might reviewing courts legitimately worry that the Fish and Wildlife Service's interpretive choices were tainted by tunnel vision—that the agency was pursuing its mission of protecting wildlife without adequate heed to the effects of its interpretations on farmers and ranchers? Or does the agency's political accountability—its responsiveness to the President and members of Congress—mitigate this potential problem? Even if the agency's expertise is not directly involved, should the agency's superior political accountability discourage courts from using the presumption against absurd results to restrict the scope of *Chevron* deference?

3. Justice Scalia began Part I of his dissent by saying that he would assume, for the sake of argument, that the majority was correct to apply the *Chevron* framework. Was there any doubt that the *Chevron* framework applied?

As Professor Sunstein has noted, the majority itself did not emphasize *Chevron* as much as one might have expected. *See* Cass R. Sunstein, Chevron *Step Zero*, 92 VA. L. REV. 187, 239–40 (2006). Although the last paragraph of Part II of the majority opinion did invoke *Chevron* and indicate that it applied, the paragraph concluded with the tepid statement that "we owe some degree of deference to the Secretary's reasonable interpretation." *Sweet Home*, 515 U.S. at 703. In support of that statement, moreover, the Court cited then-Judge Breyer's article *Judicial Review of Questions of Law and Policy*, 38 ADMIN. L. REV. 363, 373 (1986), which advocated a complex, multi-factor approach to determining appropriate levels of deference.

It is hard to know what to make of this aspect of the majority opinion. In contrast to Part II, the concluding section of the opinion (Part IV) put *Chevron* front and center. At the start of Part III, moreover, the majority described itself as having concluded that "the Secretary's definition of 'harm' rests on a permissible construction of the ESA"—language that comes from Step Two of *Chevron*. The tone that the Court struck at the end of Part II may simply have reflected the fact that Justice Stevens wrote the Court's opinion in *Sweet Home*, and he tended to think that *Chevron* is more about statutory implementation than statutory interpretation. *See supra* pp. 878–880 (discussing *INS v. Cardoza-Fonseca*, 480 U.S. 421 (1987)).

Still, might Justice Stevens also have been thinking that agencies should receive more deference on "interstitial matters" than on "major questions"? *See* Breyer, *supra*, 38 ADMIN. L. REV. at 370; *see also supra* pp. 888–899 (discussing the major-questions doctrine). The agency's position in *Sweet Home* was both politically controversial and practically important; as interpreted by the agency, the Endangered Species Act had the potential to prohibit or restrict a lot of everyday activities by ordinary people. If you accept the idea of a major-questions exception to *Chevron* deference, should *Sweet Home* have triggered that exception, and how would the case come out then? *Cf.* Sunstein, *supra*, 92 VA. L. REV. at 239 ("*Sweet Home* did not present the sort of minor question, involved in everyday administration, which Judge Breyer treated as the core case for judicial deference to agency interpretation."). What if you accept the version of the major-questions doctrine that operates as a substantive nondelegation or nonregulation canon? *See* Mila Sohoni, *The Major Questions Quartet*, 136 HARV. L. REV. 262, 264 (2022) (casting *Sweet Home* in opposition to recent major-question cases).

4. Should the rule of lenity have affected the Supreme Court's evaluation of the agency's position in *Sweet Home*? Of course, *Sweet Home* was not itself a criminal case. But the Endangered Species Act uses penal as well as nonpenal mechanisms to enforce the duties that it establishes. In particular, § 11(b) makes it a federal crime—punishable by up to a year in prison—for a person knowingly to violate any of the Act's provisions. *See* 16 U.S.C. § 1540(b)(1). Under governing Supreme Court precedent, judges are not likely to say that the statutory definition of "take" has one meaning for administrative purposes and a different meaning in criminal prosecutions. *See, e.g.*, Clark v. Martinez, 543 U.S. 371, 380 (2005) (citing cases). Thus, if the agency adopts a broad reading of the word "harm" in that definition, and if courts defer to the agency's reading, then the Endangered Species Act will criminalize more behavior.

Outside of the *Chevron* framework, the Supreme Court has encouraged judges to keep the rule of lenity in mind as they resolve indeterminacies in the scope of statutory provisions that are subject to penal enforcement, even if the same provisions are also subject to nonpenal enforcement. *See, e.g.*, United States v. Thompson/Center Arms Co., 504 U.S. 505, 517–18 & n.10 (1992) (plurality opinion); *see also supra* pp. 183–185 (discussing the relevance of the rule of lenity to "hybrid civil/criminal statute[s]"); Leocal v. Ashcroft, 543 U.S. 1, 12 n.8 (2004) ("Because we must interpret the statute consistently, whether we encounter its application in a criminal or noncriminal context, the rule of lenity applies."). In *Sweet Home*, though, the agency did not apply the rule of lenity. The agency presumably could have used the common-law heritage of the word "take" to support a relatively narrow interpretation of the statutory definition, along the lines proposed by Justice Scalia. But the agency instead opted for a broader interpretation.

The Supreme Court nonetheless thought that *Chevron* required some deference to the agency's interpretation. Footnote 18 of the majority opinion suggested that courts should not invoke the rule of lenity to restrict the scope of an administering agency's interpretive authority, at least when the court is reviewing an interpretation announced by the agency with sufficient clarity in a prospective regulation.

There are various possible rationales for this position. Perhaps when Congress puts an agency in charge of administering a statutory provision in the sense relevant to *Chevron*, Congress typically wants the agency to have more interpretive freedom than the rule of lenity would allow. If so, then Congress's own likely intentions might support the inference that statutes of this sort effectively turn off the rule of lenity. But even if one does not understand Congress itself to have provided any authoritative instruction on this point, perhaps one could reach the same bottom line on the basis of the justifications for the rule of lenity. Perhaps the rule of lenity is more warranted when courts are interpreting a statute for the purpose of assessing criminal liability after the fact (which is the posture of the ordinary criminal case) than when agencies are interpreting a statute for the purpose of promulgating prospective regulations.

The majority in *Sweet Home* made the latter argument. In footnote 18, the Court noted that the rule of lenity rests partly on the need for people to have "fair warning" of the conduct that will expose them to criminal punishment, and the Court suggested that the agency's regulation adequately addressed this need. After all, even if the Endangered Species Act was initially ambiguous about its application to habitat modification, the agency's regulation resolved that ambiguity and told people what was expected of them going forward.

As the majority acknowledged, however, the rule of lenity also reflects the idea that " 'legislatures and not courts should define criminal activity.' " *Sweet Home*, 515 U.S. at 704 n.18 (quoting *United States v. Bass*, 404 U.S. 336, 348 (1971)). To the extent that resolving genuine indeterminacies in a statutory provision that is subject to penal enforcement amounts to "defin[ing] criminal activity," are agencies in a substantially better position than courts to perform this task? Wouldn't Congress be better than the Fish and Wildlife Service at determining what deserves "the moral condemnation of the community" (*Bass*, 404 U.S. at 348)?[32]

In practice, though, what would it mean to say that courts reviewing agency interpretations in cases like *Sweet Home* should apply the rule of lenity? If a statutory provision that is backed up by the threat of penal enforcement contains some indeterminacy, in the sense that a number of different interpretations would all be "permissible" if not for the rule of lenity, should courts insist that the administering agency select the most lenient of those interpretations? On that view, the rule of lenity would eliminate much of the policy discretion that *Chevron* would otherwise permit the agency to exercise; instead of being able to reach its own judgment about which of the otherwise permissible constructions to choose, the agency would have to adopt the most lenient one. Is the intuition that crimes should be defined by representative legislatures (rather than by either courts or agencies) strong enough to negate the policy rationales for *Chevron*? Is there some reason why the rule of lenity needs to be the *first* of the normative canons that courts apply, so that it entirely displaces the normative arguments behind *Chevron*?

In keeping with footnote 18 in *Sweet Home*, some federal circuit courts have indicated that *Chevron* deference takes priority over the rule of lenity, not just with respect to hybrid civil/criminal statutes but more generally. In the view of these courts, if Congress has given an agency the sort of administrative authority that satisfies Step Zero of the

[32] Suppose you answer this question "yes." Even so, the Endangered Species Act explicitly criminalizes not only knowing violations of the Act, but also knowing violations of any regulation issued under the Act. *See* 16 U.S.C. § 1540(b)(1). Thus, Congress explicitly authorized the relevant administrative agency to use its rulemaking power in ways that would broaden the scope of criminal liability. Does that cut against the idea that when courts review the agency's interpretations of the Act itself, the rule of lenity should cabin *Chevron* deference?

Chevron framework, and if one of the provisions that the agency administers is otherwise "ambiguous" for purposes of Step One, the rule of lenity does not dictate the position that the administering agency must take. *See* Cazun v. Att'y Gen., 856 F.3d 249, 256 n.14 (3d Cir. 2017) (reaching this conclusion with respect to both the rule of lenity and the immigration rule of lenity); Olmos v. Holder, 780 F.3d 1313, 1324 (10th Cir. 2015); Oppedisano v. Holder, 769 F.3d 147, 153 (2d Cir. 2014); Perez-Olivio v. Chavez, 394 F.3d 45, 53 (1st Cir. 2005); *see also* Yi v. Fed. Bur. of Prisons, 412 F.3d 526, 535 (4th Cir. 2005) (taking this view at least where, as in *Sweet Home*, the agency announced its interpretation in a written rule made after notice and comment). By contrast, a plurality of the Fifth Circuit has said that "[w]e must not apply *Chevron* where . . . the Government seeks to define the scope of activities that subject the public to criminal penalties." *Cargill v. Garland*, 57 F.4th 447, 467 (5th Cir. 2023) (en banc) (plurality opinion of Elrod, J.), *cert. granted* (Nov. 3, 2023); *accord* Aposhian v. Wilkinson, 989 F.3d 890, 898–902 (10th Cir. 2021) (en banc) (Tymkovich, J., dissenting from decision to vacate order granting rehearing en banc) (arguing that the rule of lenity is one of the traditional tools of interpretation that should operate before *Chevron* deference comes into play); *see also* Carter v. Welles-Bowen Realty, Inc., 736 F.3d 722, 730–36 (6th Cir. 2013) (Sutton, J., concurring) (addressing a hybrid civil/criminal statute and arguing that "a court should not defer to an agency's anti-defendant interpretation of a law backed by criminal penalties"). At least some current members of the Supreme Court seem to agree that the rule of lenity should trump *Chevron* deference. *See* Guedes v. Bur. of Alcohol, Tobacco, Firearms & Explosives, 140 S. Ct. 789, 790 (2020) (statement of Gorsuch, J., respecting the denial of certiorari) ("[W]hatever else one thinks about *Chevron*, it has no role to play when liberty is at stake. . . . Before courts may send people to prison, we owe them an independent determination that the law actually forbids their conduct."); Whitman v. United States, 574 U.S. 1003, 1004–05 (2014) (statement of Scalia, J., joined by Thomas, J., respecting the denial of certiorari) (doubting that courts should defer to "an executive agency's interpretation of a law that contemplates both criminal and administrative enforcement," and calling footnote 18 in *Sweet Home* a "drive-by ruling" that "deserves little weight").

Recently, a panel of the Sixth Circuit pointed out that "*Chevron* itself involved a statute whose violation could incur criminal penalties." *Hardin v. Bur. of Alcohol, Tobacco, Firearms & Explosives*, 65 F.4th 895, 899 (6th Cir. 2023), *petition for cert. filed* (July 21, 2023). Still, the panel held that *Chevron* deference is inapplicable where a statutory scheme is "predominantly criminal" and addresses an "area[ ] in which the courts are well-equipped to operate." *Id.* at 900–01 (arguing that the administering agency has "no special expertise . . . that the judiciary lacks" with respect to construing the federal statute that prohibits possession of a machinegun, and contrasting "securities, tax, workplace safety, and environmental-law regimes, which include criminal penalties for uniquely regulatory crimes"). This issue is likely to reach the Supreme Court soon.

5. One of the key disputes between the majority and the dissent in *Sweet Home* concerned the proper application of the *noscitur a sociis* canon. Justice Scalia maintained that courts can properly invoke this canon as a basis for rejecting agency interpretations of otherwise ambiguous statutory language. The majority did not necessarily disagree with this point: the *noscitur* canon can indeed operate to limit the scope of *Chevron* deference. But the majority disagreed with Justice Scalia about the force of the canon as applied to the issue in *Sweet Home*.

Recall the key statutory language: as used in the Endangered Species Act, "[t]he term 'take' means to harass, harm, pursue, hunt, shoot, wound, kill, trap, capture, or collect, or to attempt to engage in any such conduct." 16 U.S.C. § 1532(19). The agency's regulation adopted a broad understanding of the word "harm." Justice Scalia conceded that "harm" can be read broadly in other contexts, but he insisted that the agency could not validly read it so broadly in *this* context. One of his principal arguments was that the other nine verbs that appear alongside "harm" in the statute all share "the sense of affirmative conduct intentionally directed against a particular animal or animals."

Is that really true? Suppose you build a target-shooting range right next to the nest of some spotted owls, and you accidentally shoot an owl while aiming for the target. Couldn't the Fish and Wildlife Service legitimately say that you have "take[n]" the owl within the meaning of the Endangered Species Act, because you have "sho[t]" it (and either "wound[ed]" or "kill[ed]" it)? If so, haven't we done away with the idea that in order to "take" a protected animal within the meaning of the Act, an action has to be "intentionally directed against a particular animal or animals"?

If the common theme proposed by Justice Scalia does not quite work, what about the theme proposed by the panel of the D.C. Circuit that heard the case below (and that also invoked *noscitur a sociis* to reject the agency's interpretation of "harm")? According to the panel, the nine verbs that accompany "harm" in the statutory list all "contemplate the perpetrator's direct application of force against the animal taken." *Sweet Home Chapter of Communities for a Great Oregon v. Babbitt*, 17 F.3d 1463, 1465 (D.C. Cir. 1994). To fit "pursue" and "harass" into that mold, though, the panel had to use some force of its own. *See id.* (acknowledging that "one may under some circumstances 'harass' an animal by aiming sound or light in its direction," but noting that "the waves and particles [constituting sound and light] are themselves physical forces launched by the perpetrator"); *see also id.* (admitting that one might "pursue" an animal without any direct application of force against the animal, but arguing that "pursuit would always or almost always be a step toward deliberate capture or destruction" and that the word therefore dovetails with the list's reference to "attempt[s]"). Even "kill" does not necessarily require the direct application of force against the animal. If I drained a pond inhabited by endangered fish, and if I left too little water for the fish to survive, it would be consistent with ordinary usage to say that I "kill[ed]" them.

One might see the problem as follows. Some words in the list—including "pursue," "hunt," and maybe "harass"—arguably are what Justice Scalia called "verbs of purpose"; they apply only when the perpetrator is intentionally directing action against the animal in question. Other words in the list—including "shoot," "trap," "capture," "collect," and maybe "wound"—arguably require application of some sort of direct force either to injure the animal or to imprison it. Aside from "harm" (and possibly "kill"), then, the other words in the list arguably require *either* conduct directed against the animal in question *or* application of some sort of direct force. But these words do not all require *both* of those things. In this context, can one plausibly deploy *noscitur a sociis* to limit the permissible readings of the word "harm" (and, for that matter, "kill")?

Here is one possible idea, which draws upon both the *noscitur* canon and the traditional meaning of "take" in wildlife law. Looking over the list of words in the statutory definition of "take," one might say that some of the words in the list describe traditional takings ("trap," "capture," "collect," and perhaps "kill"), others fall short of traditional takings in the degree of control asserted over the animal but are still along the same lines ("shoot" and "wound"), and still others cover conduct that typically leads up to traditional takings ("pursue" and "hunt"). The word "harass" doesn't fit this model, but at least it connotes deliberate targeting of a particular animal. Could one argue that "harm" should be read in the same way? If so, how exactly should one formulate the proposed reading? Should "harm," like "harass," be understood to require deliberate targeting? (To suggest the viability of such a reading, Justice Scalia quoted an otherwise obscure usage manual for the proposition that "*harm* has in it a little of the idea of specially focused hurt or injury, as if a personal injury has been anticipated and intended.") Alternatively, could "harm" in this context be limited to injuries associated with the assertion of control or partial control over the animal—which might include the physical injury that an exotic bird suffers when someone plucks a feather from it, but not the physical injury that the bird suffers when someone builds a housing development that degrades its habitat?

Of course, even if you yourself might be inclined to read "harm" narrowly, Congress has not delegated administration of the Endangered Species Act to you—or, for that matter, to Justice Scalia. How should *Chevron* interact with the argument just sketched out? As we have seen, canons like *noscitur a sociis* restrict the scope of *Chevron* deference; when such canons dispel ambiguity, courts will not let agencies flout them. *See supra* pp. 938–939; *see also* Dole v. United Steelworkers, 494 U.S. 26, 36, 42–43 (1990) (invoking *noscitur a sociis* along with other arguments at

Step One of the *Chevron* framework). In *Sweet Home*, though, the implications of the *noscitur* canon were contestable; different interpreters might have different ideas about the common themes that link various words in the statutory definition of "take," and different interpreters might also have different ideas about how much weight to give those common themes in limiting the scope of the word "harm." Even if you are sympathetic to Justice Scalia's position on these questions, is the agency's competing view sufficiently close that *Chevron* obliges a reviewing court to accept it?

To the extent that *Chevron* deference reflects ideas about comparative institutional competence, is there reason to think that agencies will be better than courts at applying the traditional canons of statutory interpretation? Often, the answer to that question probably is "no." But might the agency have some advantages over the courts in applying *noscitur a sociis* in this particular case? The argument sketched out above draws on the traditional idea of "take" in wildlife law, which is the agency's field of expertise. If "take" is a term of art in wildlife law, and if this term of art should color our understanding of the common themes linking the words in the statutory definition, might the agency be in a better position than the courts to make the necessary judgment calls?

6. How might Congress's amendment of the Endangered Species Act in 1982 bear on the question that the Court decided in *Sweet Home*? Here is the relevant timeline:

- In 1973, Congress enacted the original version of the Endangered Species Act, which included both § 9(a)(1)(B) (making it unlawful for people to "take" endangered species) and what is now § 3(19) (providing the statutory definition of "take" that the Court considered in *Sweet Home*).
- In 1975, the Interior Department's Fish and Wildlife Service promulgated the precursor of the regulation at issue in *Sweet Home*. *See* Endangered and Threatened Wildlife and Plants: Reclassification of the American Alligator and Other Amendments, 40 Fed. Reg. 44412, 44416 (Sept. 26, 1975) (" 'Harm' in the definition of 'take' in the Act means an act or omission which actually injures or kills wildlife, including acts which annoy it to such an extent as to significantly disrupt essential behavioral patterns, which include, but are not limited to, breeding, feeding or sheltering; significant environmental modification or degradation which has such effects is included within the meaning of 'harm' . . . .").
- In 1979, the federal district court for the District of Hawaii invoked this regulation to hold that the state was "tak[ing]" the endangered Palila bird by maintaining feral sheep and goats on land that overlapped with the bird's critical habitat. *Palila v. Hawaii Dep't of Land & Natural Resources*, 471 F. Supp. 985 (D.

Haw. 1979) (explaining that the sheep and goats ate seedlings that would otherwise grow into mamane trees, an important source of food, shelter, and nest sites for the Palila). In 1981, the United States Court of Appeals for the Ninth Circuit—again invoking the agency's regulation—affirmed the district court's judgment. 639 F.2d 495, 497–98 (9th Cir. 1981).

- Later in 1981, the Fish and Wildlife Service reworded its "harm" regulation to take the form that the Supreme Court ultimately considered in *Sweet Home*. *See* Endangered and Threatened Wildlife and Plants; Final Redefinition of "Harm", 46 Fed. Reg. 54748 (Nov. 4, 1981). As part of its explanation for the change, the agency observed that "[t]he *Palila* decisions can be read to incorrectly imply" that the agency's definition of "harm" encompassed habitat modification "even where there was no injury to the . . . endangered or threatened wildlife." *Id.* at 54748–49. While wanting to reject that position, however, the agency made clear that "where an actual injury occurs, including impairment of essential behavioral patterns," habitat modification "will still be viewed as being subject to section 9 of the Act." *Id.* at 54749.
- In 1982, Congress enacted fairly detailed amendments to various provisions of the Endangered Species Act. The amendments included a new § 10(a)(1)(B), empowering the Secretary of the Interior to issue permits authorizing "any taking otherwise prohibited by section 9(a)(1)(B) if such taking is incidental to, and not the purpose of, the carrying out of an otherwise lawful activity." Endangered Species Act Amendments of 1982, Pub. L. 97–304, sec. 6, 96 Stat. 1411, 1422 (1982) (codified at 16 U.S.C. § 1539(a)(1)(B)).

The 1982 amendment obviously rested on the premise that it is possible for someone to "take" protected wildlife, in the manner that § 9 of the 1973 Act normally prohibits, even though such taking "is incidental to, and not the purpose of, the carrying out of an otherwise lawful activity." As Justice Scalia noted, that premise does not *necessarily* imply that the Act uses the word "take" much more broadly than traditional wildlife law; someone who is fishing for tuna, but whose nets end up catching one member of a protected species of fish, has "take[n]" that fish in the traditional sense even though he was not trying to do so, and a person who plans to cast nets might prudently seek an "incidental taking" permit under § 10. But Justice Scalia conceded that committee reports prepared on this aspect of the 1982 amendment reflected a broader understanding of the word "take" in the original Act. According to Justice Scalia, the reports assumed that in the absence of a permit, § 9 of the 1973 Act would prohibit ordinary development projects that have the effect of destroying or degrading the critical habitat of members of a protected species.

The panel majority below advanced a different interpretation of the committee reports. *See* Sweet Home Chapter of Communities for a Great Oregon v. Babbitt, 17 F.3d 1463, 1468–69 (D.C. Cir. 1994). But suppose that one agrees with Justice Scalia's concession: the committee reports prepared in conjunction with the 1982 amendment reflected a broad understanding of the word "take" in the 1973 Act, and they justified the change to § 10 on that basis. If one puts more stock in legislative history than Justice Scalia did, what should one conclude?

One presumably should not understand the 1982 amendment to § 10 as implicitly amending § 3 of the Endangered Species Act so as to incorporate the then-existing version of the Fish and Wildlife Service's "harm" regulation. The actual text of the 1982 amendment did not purport to change § 3, and it would be very aggressive to read the 1982 amendment as codifying the then-existing version of the regulation (thereby stripping the agency of power to change its mind in the future). Is there a stronger basis for reading the 1982 amendment to § 10 as ratifying at least the permissibility of the "harm" regulation—that is, as confirming the agency's power to read the statutory definition of "take" to encompass habitat modification? Or could one say that the legislative history of the 1982 amendment does not really shed light on the meaning of anything in the 1982 amendment itself, but instead simply explains *why* members of Congress may have enacted that amendment? Even if members of Congress were motivated to enact the 1982 amendment by their assumptions about the meaning of the original Endangered Species Act of 1973, should people trying to interpret the 1973 statute care about this sort of postenactment legislative history?

You might be inclined to answer the latter question "no." Still, doesn't there have to be *some* way in which the combination of the 1982 amendment and its legislative history strengthens the case for the agency's position? Suppose you think that if the Supreme Court had granted certiorari in *Palila* in 1981, the Court should have concluded that the agency's interpretation of "harm" was not a permissible construction of the Endangered Species Act as it then stood. Could you nonetheless conclude that it *is* a permissible construction of the Act as it now stands (after the 1982 amendment), because the concept of "incidental" takings introduced by § 10 provides another set of arguments for understanding the term "take" to include some things like habitat modification?

---

c. *CHEVRON* AND LEGISLATIVE HISTORY

The questions just posed provide a natural segue to our next topic: the interaction between *Chevron* deference and internal legislative history. *Chevron* itself plainly treated internal legislative history as one of the "traditional tools of statutory construction" that courts should consult in determining whether "Congress had an intention on the precise question at issue." *Chevron*, 467 U.S. at 843 n.9; *see also id.* at 851–53, 862–64 (consulting the legislative history of the 1977 amendments to the Clean Air Act in the course of reviewing the agency's understanding of the phrase "stationary source"). But *Chevron* was written in 1984, before Justice Scalia was appointed to the Supreme Court and raised the profile of debates about the use of legislative history in statutory interpretation. With those debates in mind, how should judges on both sides think about the place of legislative history in the *Chevron* framework?

Start with judges who support the use of legislative history in statutory interpretation. Suppose that a statute gives an agency the sort of administrative authority that satisfies Step Zero of the *Chevron* framework, and suppose that one of the statutory provisions the agency administers is ambiguous when read without reference to the publicly available legislative history; someone who did not consult the legislative history would think that the provision could permissibly be read to establish either Directive #1 or Directive #2. As part of notice-and-comment rulemaking or a formal adjudication, the agency picks Directive #1 and cogently explains why, as a matter of policy, Directive #1 is superior to Directive #2. The agency's explanation, however, makes no reference to the legislative history of the provision. In the view of a reviewing court, moreover, the legislative history provides fairly strong evidence that members of the enacting Congress really intended the provision to establish Directive #2. Suppose that if no agency were in the picture, the court would follow the guidance of the legislative history and read the provision to establish Directive #2, without conducting its own analysis of whether Directive #1 or Directive #2 seems better as a matter of policy. Should *Chevron* nonetheless lead the court to accept the agency's contrary interpretation?

If the court favors the use of legislative history as a "descriptive" tool for identifying the directives that Congress as a whole authoritatively intended to establish,[33] then the court might well treat legislative history

[33] In theory, a judge might favor the use of legislative history on "normative" rather than "descriptive" grounds. When the conventional sources of meaning fail to identify a single best interpretation of a statute, and when no agency is in the picture, one might think that " 'a court does pretty well to read the statute to mean what the few legislators having the greatest concern with it said it meant to them' "—not because Congress as a whole has bound the court to adopt that interpretation or because that interpretation is somehow truer to the (indeterminate) directions that Congress has authoritatively given, but simply because this resolution of the indeterminacy is likely to produce better results as a matter of policy than the resolution that the court would come up with on its own. *See supra* p. 441 (quoting HENRY J. FRIENDLY, *Mr. Justice Frankfurter and the Reading of Statutes*, *in* BENCHMARKS 196, 216 (1967)). This normative rationale for the use of legislative history is connected with limitations on the court's own capacities as a policymaker, so it might not have as much force when an agency is in the picture. Even if a generalist court is well advised to choose among the permissible interpretations of ambiguous statutory language by deferring to "what the few legislators having the greatest concern with [the statute] said it meant to them," perhaps a specialist agency can do better than that, and perhaps subsequent courts should defer to the agency's present choices rather than to the choices suggested by some individual members of a now-disbanded Congress.

in the same way that courts treat descriptive canons: if the implications of the legislative history seem sufficiently clear and powerful, the legislative history might restrict the choices that the bare text of the statutory provision would otherwise leave the administering agency. In our hypothetical case, this way of thinking would lead the court to reject the agency's interpretation and to hold that, for purposes of the *Chevron* framework, the provision has to be read as establishing Directive #2. *See, e.g.*, Cuthill v. Blinken, 990 F.3d 272, 278–86 (2d Cir. 2021) (Katzmann, J.) (acknowledging arguments on both sides with respect to the statute's text and structure, but calling legislative history the "clincher" that clarified Congress's intent and left no room for the Board of Immigration Appeals to take a different position); *cf.* Catskill Mountains Chapter of Trout Unlimited, Inc. v. EPA, 846 F.3d 492, 515 (2d Cir. 2017) ("Although we are generally 'reluctant to employ legislative history at step one of *Chevron* analysis,' legislative history is at times helpful in resolving ambiguity; for example, when the ' "interpretive clues [speak] almost unanimously," making Congress's intent clear "beyond reasonable doubt." ' " (quoting Mizrahi v. Gonzales, 492 F.3d 156, 166 (2d Cir. 2007), in turn quoting Gen. Dynamics Land Sys. v. Cline, 540 U.S. 581, 586, 590 (2004))).[34]

Justice Souter's opinion for the Supreme Court in *General Dynamics Land Systems v. Cline*, 540 U.S. 581 (2004), is a case in point. Section

---

Professor Elhauge has made a related argument. As a normative matter, he considers it best for interpreters to try to resolve indeterminacies in statutes in a manner that correlates with what he calls "enactable preferences"—"the set of political preferences that would be enacted into law if the issue were considered and resolved by the legislative process." EINER ELHAUGE, STATUTORY DEFAULT RULES: HOW TO INTERPRET UNCLEAR LEGISLATION 7, 23–38 (2008). Also as a normative matter, he believes that when *judicial* interpreters "have neither clear statutory language nor any reliable basis for inferring current enactable preferences from official actions," they are more likely to produce results that "maximize . . . political satisfaction" in this way if they follow the guidance of legislative history. *Id.* at 115–19. But he believes that when an agency is in the picture, courts are more likely to maximize *current* political preferences (within the range permitted by the statute's range of indeterminacy) if they defer to the agency's interpretation than if they rely upon either outdated legislative history or their own sense of the current political mood. *See id.* at 79–111 (arguing that "agency decisions generally reflect current enactable preferences better than would judicial estimates of those preferences"). For Professor Elhauge, it follows that "*Chevron* deference . . . should be employed before looking at legislative history." *Id.* at 13.

Still, most of the judges who favor the use of legislative history in statutory interpretation probably do so for "descriptive" reasons rather than for these normative reasons. The discussion in the text focuses on the standard "descriptive" rationale for consulting legislative history—the idea that legislative history can help judges identify the intended meaning of otherwise ambiguous statutory language.

[34] Some judges have said flatly that "legislative history should not be considered at *Chevron* step one." *United States v. Geiser*, 527 F.3d 288, 294 (3d Cir. 2008). In context, though, statements of this sort may simply mean that legislative history cannot overcome "unambiguous" statutory text. *Cf. id.* at 298 (concluding that the relevant statute was not ambiguous for purposes of Step One). If a statute seems ambiguous on its face, but the legislative history supplies strong indications of its intended meaning, judges who believe in the use of legislative history may well conclude that the legislative history clarifies the ambiguity and dictates an answer at Step One. *But cf.* In re Gateway Radiology Consultants, P.A., 983 F.3d 1239, 1261 n.9 (11th Cir. 2020) ("The Second Circuit has noted that legislative history will 'rarely speak with sufficient clarity to conclude . . . that Congress has directly spoken to the precise question at issue.' . . . This is not one of those rare—and practically unicornical—times." (quoting Cohen v. JP Morgan Chase & Co., 498 F.3d 111, 122 (2d Cir. 2007))).

4(a)(1) of the Age Discrimination in Employment Act forbids employers "to fail or refuse to hire or to discharge any individual or otherwise discriminate against any individual with respect to his compensation, terms, conditions, or privileges of employment, because of such individual's age." Pub. L. 90–202, § 4(a)(1), 81 Stat. 602, 603 (1967) (codified at 29 U.S.C. § 623(a)(1)); *see also* 29 U.S.C. § 631(a) (limiting this protection to "individuals who are at least 40 years of age"). In 1981, the Equal Employment Opportunity Commission (EEOC) promulgated a regulation interpreting the Act to mean that if a 42-year-old and a 52-year-old apply for the same position in a company, the company "may not lawfully turn down either one on the basis of age," but instead must choose between them "on the basis of some other factor." *See* Final Interpretations: Age Discrimination in Employment Act, 46 Fed. Reg. 47724, 47726 (Sept. 29, 1981). According to the EEOC's interpretation, that was true even if the company wanted to hire the *older* worker; rejecting the 42-year-old simply because he was ten years younger than the other applicant would be discriminating against him "because of [his] age" within the meaning of § 4(a)(1). In *General Dynamics Land Systems*, the Supreme Court conceded that the language of § 4(a)(1) could bear this reading. In the Court's view, however, the phrase "discriminate . . . because of [an] individual's age" could also be understood to refer only to "discrimination preferring young to old"—that is, discrimination because of "relatively old age." *Gen. Dynamics Land Sys.*, 540 U.S. at 592–93 & n.5. What is more, Justice Souter's majority opinion understood the legislative history of the statute to provide strong support for the latter reading. Given the legislative history, the majority concluded that there was no ambiguity for the EEOC to resolve: even if the *Chevron* framework applied (a question on which the Court took no position), the EEOC could not validly read the statutory language to mean something other than what the legislative history indicated that Congress had intended. *See id.* at 600 ("Even for an agency able to claim all the authority possible under *Chevron*, deference to its statutory interpretation is called for only when the devices of judicial construction have been tried and found to yield no clear sense of congressional intent.").

Of course, if an agency tackles the legislative history head on when explaining its interpretation of a statutory provision, and if the agency makes plausible arguments for the proposition that the legislative history does not foreclose its interpretation, the agency might be able to persuade judges that its interpretation is permissible even if the judges themselves would interpret the legislative history differently. To the extent that the agency is more familiar with the relevant legislative processes, the agency may be able to raise points that would not otherwise have occurred to the reviewing judges, and the judges might be convinced that the legislative history is not as clear as they otherwise would have thought. But if the judges persist in thinking that the legislative history is fairly clear, judges who believe in the use of legislative history might well invoke it to restrict the agency's interpretive choices.

In *Chevron* itself, the Supreme Court seemed open to using legislative history to restrict the agency's choices in two different ways. First, the Court checked whether the legislative history "contain[ed] any specific comment on the 'bubble concept' or the question whether a plantwide definition of a stationary source is permissible under the permit program"—the interpretive question that the case presented. *Chevron*, 467 U.S. at 851. If the legislative history had specifically addressed that question and had adequately clarified the intended meaning of the statute, the Court might have concluded (in the words of Step One) that Congress had "directly spoken to the precise question at issue." *See id.* at 842. In fact, however, the legislative history did not help the Court identify a specific intention on this point. Even so, the Court proceeded to make a second use of the legislative history: the Court consulted the legislative history to help identify "the policy concerns that motivated the [statute]," and the Court used this information about the statute's purposes when evaluating the agency's reasoning process. *See id.* at 863. Notwithstanding the silence or ambiguity of the statutory text, if the agency had based its interpretation of the statute on policy goals that the legislative history clearly rejected, then the Court might have found the agency's interpretation "impermissible" at Step Two. Again, though, the agency's position passed this test.

In both of the respects just mentioned, the courts' use of legislative history in *Chevron* analysis can constrain the discretion that statutes would otherwise be understood to leave administering agencies. But it is also possible for the courts' use of legislative history to have the opposite effect. To be sure, the Supreme Court has indicated that "reference to legislative history is inappropriate when the text of the statute is unambiguous." *Dep't of Housing & Urban Dev. v. Rucker*, 535 U.S. 125, 132 (2002). In the view of at least some judges, moreover, legislative history is "irrelevant" to "the threshold question . . . whether the language of the statute is clear or arguably ambiguous." *K Mart Corp. v. Cartier, Inc.*, 486 U.S. 281, 293 n.4 (1988) (opinion of Kennedy, J., joined by White, J.). For other judges, though, a statute's legislative history might sometimes operate to expand the range of interpretations that the judges will accept. For example, suppose that the text of a statutory provision lends itself to two possible readings, but that in the absence of any relevant legislative history, one of those readings would strike the judges as significantly better. (Perhaps a descriptive canon supports it, or perhaps the other reading rests upon a relatively uncommon usage of vocabulary or grammar.) Suppose that if there were no relevant legislative history, the judges would not consider the provision sufficiently ambiguous to let the agency pick the disfavored reading. But suppose that when the judges consult the provision's legislative history, they find some support for that reading—not enough to *compel* the reading, but enough to suggest that it may really have been what Congress meant. To the extent that courts are willing to consult legislative history in statutory interpretation, one can imagine cases in which the legislative history rehabilitates a reading that the courts would otherwise put off limits. In such cases, the courts' willingness to consult legislative history might give the responsible agency more leeway than it otherwise would have.

* * * * *

So far, we have considered the interaction of the *Chevron* framework and legislative history from the perspective of people like Justices Stevens and Souter—judges who think that the use of legislative history can help courts capture the intended meaning of statutory language. But how should people like Justice Scalia approach these questions? As we saw in Chapter 3, Justice Scalia believed that even when a statutory provision is ambiguous on its face, judges should not consult internal legislative history for the purpose of resolving the ambiguity. At least in the absence of an agency construction, Justice Scalia wanted courts to use some other method of selecting among the permissible interpretations of the provision's language. When an agency is in the picture, how should judges of this stripe think about the interaction between legislative history and the *Chevron* framework?

When Justice Scalia was trying to decide whether a statute was "ambiguous" in the sense that matters to the *Chevron* framework, or whether a particular reading was on the menu that he considered "permissible," he did not give any special weight to legislative history. The fact that a reading had some support in the legislative history would not have persuaded Justice Scalia that the reading was "permissible," and the fact that the legislative history cut *against* a reading would not have persuaded Justice Scalia that the reading was *im*permissible. That is what one would expect: Whether a statute is "ambiguous" and which readings are "permissible" are questions that courts have to resolve for themselves, and Justice Scalia's approach to statutory interpretation did not use legislative history.

When agencies are choosing among the readings that Justice Scalia would have considered "permissible," though, should Justice Scalia have insisted that they too must ignore legislative history? Suppose that Congress has authorized an agency to administer a statutory provision (in the sense that satisfies Step Zero of the *Chevron* framework), and suppose that the provision is "ambiguous" (in the sense relevant to Step One). Suppose further that the agency chooses among the possible interpretations on the basis of the provision's legislative history. Even if Justice Scalia would have agreed that the interpretation chosen by the agency is on the menu of permissible options, should he have concluded that the agency's reason for preferring this interpretation is arbitrary and capricious, and that the agency's position therefore fails at Step Two—with the result that the agency would have to go back the drawing board and use a different methodology for choosing among the permissible readings? Or should Justice Scalia have said that it is permissible for *agencies* to consult legislative history even though he did not think that *courts* should?

If the use of legislative history in interpreting federal statutes violates Article I of the Constitution, as Justice Scalia sometimes suggested, then agencies as well as courts presumably should forswear the practice. As we saw in Chapter 3, however, the constitutional argument against the use of legislative history is hardly a slam dunk, and many observers (including me) consider it relatively weak. One might be more sympathetic to Justice Scalia's practical argument that judges are likely to be bad at evaluating legislative history: even if legislative history bears on a particular question of interpretation, judges are insulated from the political process, and they may have too little insight into the dynamics of that process to draw reliable conclusions from the snippets of legislative history that they read. But this argument against *judicial* use of legislative history in statutory interpretation does not necessarily extend to administrative agencies, whose lawyers interact regularly with the legislative process and also have enough technical knowledge to follow discussions about policy details. At least according to Professor Vermeule, "[s]pecialist agencies . . . are far better positioned to comprehend the complex legislative histories of their particular statutes than are generalist judges." ADRIAN VERMEULE, JUDGING UNDER UNCERTAINTY: AN INSTITUTIONAL THEORY OF LEGAL INTERPRETATION 215 (2006); *accord, e.g.*, Peter L. Strauss, *When the Judge Is Not the Primary Official with Responsibility to Read: Agency Interpretation and the Problem of Legislative History*, 66 CHI.-KENT L. REV. 321 (1990). Should that possibility have persuaded Justice Scalia to let agencies consult legislative history even though he would not?

In practice, Justice Scalia did not reject agency interpretations at Step Two of the *Chevron* framework whenever the agency had considered legislative history. Instead, he simply evaluated whether the bottom line reached by the agency fell within the range that he considered permissible (which he determined without invoking legislative history).

---

d. *CHEVRON* AND JUDICIAL *STARE DECISIS*

One might also wonder about the interaction between *Chevron* deference and the courts' doctrines of *stare decisis*. On that topic, the leading case currently is *National Cable & Telecommunications Ass'n v. Brand X Internet Services*, 545 U.S. 967 (2005).

The federal Communications Act of 1934, as amended by the Telecommunications Act of 1996, subjects the providers of "telecommunications services" to regulation as common carriers. 47 U.S.C. § 153(44) (2000 ed.); *see also id.* § 153(46) (defining the term "telecommunications service"). In *AT&T v. City of Portland*, 216 F.3d 871 (9th Cir. 2000), the Ninth Circuit concluded that a cable company's provision of Internet transmission to subscribers through cable broadband is a "telecommunications service[ ]" within the meaning of the Communications Act. *Id.* at 877–78. In 2002, however, the Federal Communications Commission (FCC) promulgated a regulation taking a different view; according to the FCC, broadband Internet services provided by cable companies through cable modems are *not* "telecommunications services" under the Act. When the Ninth Circuit was called upon to review this interpretation, the panel conceded that Congress had put the FCC in charge of administering the relevant provisions of the statute. But the panel nonetheless held that circuit precedent constrained the panel to reject the FCC's interpretation. The panel recognized that when a court simply upholds the permissibility of an agency interpretation (as the Supreme Court had done in *Chevron*), the agency retains the authority to change its mind and adopt a different interpretation later. In *Portland*, however, the Ninth Circuit had not been deferring to an agency interpretation; the FCC had not yet weighed in, and the court had been interpreting the statute on its own. Under these circumstances, the panel asserted, a subsequent panel could not adopt a different interpretation, even out of deference to what the FCC had said in the interim. *Brand X Internet Services v. FCC*, 345 F.3d 1120, 1131 (9th Cir. 2003) ("*Portland*'s construction of the Communications Act remains binding precedent within this circuit, even in light of the FCC's contrary interpretation of the statute.").

When the case reached the Supreme Court, the Court did not really have to discuss how *Chevron* interacts with doctrines of judicial *stare decisis*. Whatever one thinks about whether the interpretation that the Ninth Circuit had adopted in *Portland* remained binding on subsequent panels of the Ninth Circuit, no one could argue that the Ninth Circuit's precedent also bound the Supreme Court. From the perspective of the Supreme Court, then, the case simply called for ordinary application of the *Chevron* framework. But Justice Thomas's majority opinion went out of its way to reject the Ninth Circuit's reasoning. Here is the relevant section of his opinion for the Court:

> "The Court of Appeals declined to apply *Chevron* because it thought the Commission's interpretation of the Communications Act foreclosed by the conflicting construction of the Act it had adopted in *Portland*. See 345 F.3d at 1127–1132. It based that holding on the assumption that *Portland*'s construction overrode the Commission's, regardless of whether *Portland* had held the statute to be unambiguous. 345 F.3d at 1131. That reasoning was incorrect.
>
> "A court's prior judicial construction of a statute trumps an agency construction otherwise entitled to *Chevron* deference only if the prior court decision holds that its construction follows from the unambiguous terms of the statute and thus leaves no room for

agency discretion. This principle follows from *Chevron* itself. *Chevron* established a 'presumption that Congress, when it left ambiguity in a statute meant for implementation by an agency, understood that the ambiguity would be resolved, first and foremost, by the agency, and desired the agency (rather than the courts) to possess whatever degree of discretion the ambiguity allows.' *Smiley* [*v. Citibank (South Dakota), N.A.*, 517 U.S. 735, 740–41 (1996)]. Yet allowing a judicial precedent to foreclose an agency from interpreting an ambiguous statute, as the Court of Appeals assumed it could, would allow a court's interpretation to override an agency's. *Chevron*'s premise is that it is for agencies, not courts, to fill statutory gaps. See [*Chevron*,] 467 U.S. at 843–844 and n. 11. The better rule is to hold judicial interpretations contained in precedents to the same demanding *Chevron* step one standard that applies if the court is reviewing the agency's construction on a blank slate: Only a judicial precedent holding that the statute unambiguously forecloses the agency's interpretation, and therefore contains no gap for the agency to fill, displaces a conflicting agency construction.

"A contrary rule would produce anomalous results. It would mean that whether an agency's interpretation of an ambiguous statute is entitled to *Chevron* deference would turn on the order in which the interpretations issue: If the court's construction came first, its construction would prevail, whereas if the agency's came first, the agency's construction would command *Chevron* deference. Yet whether Congress has delegated to an agency the authority to interpret a statute does not depend on the order in which the judicial and administrative constructions occur. The Court of Appeals' rule, moreover, would 'lead to the ossification of large portions of our statutory law,' [*United States v. Mead Corp.*, 533 U.S. 218, 247 (2001) (Scalia, J., dissenting)], by precluding agencies from revising unwise judicial constructions of ambiguous statutes. Neither *Chevron* nor the doctrine of *stare decisis* requires these haphazard results.

"The dissent answers that allowing an agency to override what a court believes to be the best interpretation of a statute makes 'judicial decisions subject to reversal by executive officers.' *Post* at 1016 (opinion of Scalia, J.). It does not. Since *Chevron* teaches that a court's opinion as to the best reading of an ambiguous statute an agency is charged with administering is not authoritative, the agency's decision to construe that statute differently from a court does not say that the court's holding was legally wrong. Instead, the agency may, consistent with the court's holding, choose a different construction, since the agency remains the authoritative interpreter (within the limits of reason) of such statutes. In all other respects, the court's prior ruling remains binding law (for example, as to agency interpretations to which *Chevron* is inapplicable). The precedent has not been 'reversed' by the agency, any more than a federal court's interpretation of a State's law can be said to have been 'reversed' by a state court that adopts a conflicting (yet authoritative) interpretation of state law.

"The Court of Appeals derived a contrary rule from a mistaken reading of this Court's decisions. It read *Neal v. United States*, 516 U.S. 284 (1996), to establish that a prior judicial construction of a statute categorically controls an agency's contrary construction. 345 F.3d at 1131–1132 . . . . *Neal* established no such proposition. *Neal* declined to defer to a construction adopted by the United States Sentencing Commission that conflicted with one the Court previously had adopted in *Chapman v. United States*, 500 U.S. 453 (1991). . . . *Chapman*, however, had held the relevant statute to be unambiguous. See [*id.*] at 463 (declining to apply the rule of lenity given the statute's clear language). Thus, *Neal* established only that a precedent holding a statute to be unambiguous forecloses a contrary agency construction. . . .

". . . [T]he Court of Appeals erred in refusing to apply *Chevron* to the Commission's interpretation of the definition of 'telecommunications service,' 47 U.S.C. § 153(46). Its prior decision in *Portland* held only that the *best* reading of § 153(46) was that cable modem service was a 'telecommunications service,' not that it was the *only permissible* reading of the statute. See 216 F.3d at 877–880. Nothing in *Portland* held that the Communications Act unambiguously required treating cable Internet providers as telecommunications carriers. Instead, the court noted that it was 'not presented with a case involving potential deference to an administrative agency's statutory construction pursuant to the *Chevron* doctrine,' *id.* at 876, and the court invoked no other rule of construction (such as the rule of lenity) requiring it to conclude that the statute was unambiguous to reach its judgment. Before a judicial construction of a statute, whether contained in a precedent or not, may trump an agency's, the court must hold that the statute unambiguously requires the court's construction. *Portland* did not do so."

Brand X, 545 U.S. at 982–85. The majority went on to conclude that the statutory definition of "telecommunications service" was ambiguous as applied to the cable modem services in question and that the FCC's construction reflected a permissible policy choice that courts were obliged to accept under *Chevron*. *Id.* at 986–1000.

Justice Scalia dissented. With respect to the specific question of the scope of the phrase "telecommunications service," he thought it "perfectly clear" that the statute covers companies that sell cable-modem service to consumers, and he would have held that the FCC's contrary interpretation exceeded the agency's interpretive authority under *Chevron*. *See id.* at 1005–14 (Scalia, J., dissenting). But he also condemned the majority's understanding of the interplay between *Chevron* and judicial doctrines of *stare decisis*. As he noted, the Court's previous statements on this issue had seemed to embrace a very different position. *See* Neal v. United States, 516 U.S. 284, 295 (1996) ("Once we have determined a statute's meaning, we adhere to our ruling under the doctrine of *stare decisis*, and we assess an agency's later interpretation of the statute against that settled law."); *see also* Thomas W. Merrill & Kristin E. Hickman, Chevron*'s* Domain, 89 GEO. L.J. 833, 852 n.96 (2001) (observing, before *Brand X*, that while the interaction between *Chevron* and circuit precedent was an open question, "the Supreme Court has consistently maintained that its own statutory interpretation precedents trump *Chevron*"). In *Brand X*, Justice Scalia expressed particular concern about the combined effect of the majority's new position on this question and the Supreme Court's decision in *United States v. Mead Corp.*, 533 U.S. 218 (2001), from which he had dissented four years earlier:

> "To the extent that it set forth a comprehensible rule, *Mead* drastically limited the categories of agency action that would qualify for deference under *Chevron* . . . . For example, the position taken by an agency before the Supreme Court, with full approval of the agency head, would not qualify. Rather, some unspecified degree of formal process was required—or was at least the only safe harbor. See *Mead, supra*, at 245–246 (Scalia, J., dissenting).
>
> "This meant that many more issues appropriate for agency determination would reach the courts without benefit of an agency position entitled to *Chevron* deference, requiring the courts to rule on these issues *de novo*. As I pointed out in dissent, this in turn meant (under the law as it was understood until today) that many statutory ambiguities that might be resolved in varying fashions by successive agency administrations would be resolved finally, conclusively, and forever, by federal judges—producing an 'ossification of large portions of our statutory law,' 533 U.S. at 247. The Court today moves to solve this problem of its own creation by inventing yet another breathtaking novelty: judicial decisions subject to reversal by executive officers.
>
> "Imagine the following sequence of events: FCC action is challenged as ultra vires under the governing statute; the litigation reaches all the way to the Supreme Court of the United States. The Solicitor General sets forth the FCC's official position (approved by the Commission) regarding interpretation of the statute. Applying *Mead*, however, the Court denies the agency position *Chevron* deference, finds that the *best* interpretation of the statute contradicts the agency's position, and holds the challenged agency action unlawful. The agency promptly conducts a rulemaking, and adopts a rule that comports with its earlier position—in effect disagreeing with the Supreme Court concerning the best

interpretation of the statute. According to today's opinion, the agency is thereupon free to take the action that the Supreme Court found unlawful.

"This is not only bizarre. It is probably unconstitutional. As we held in *Chicago & Southern Air Lines, Inc. v. Waterman S. S. Corp.*, 333 U.S. 103 (1948), Article III courts do not sit to render decisions that can be reversed or ignored by executive officers. . . . 'Judgments within the powers vested in courts by the Judiciary Article of the Constitution may not lawfully be revised, overturned or refused faith and credit by another Department of Government.' [*Id.*] at 113. That is what today's decision effectively allows. Even when the agency itself is party to the case in which the Court construes a statute, the agency will be able to disregard that construction and seek *Chevron* deference for its contrary construction the next time around.

". . . [L]ike *Mead* itself, today's novelty in belated remediation of *Mead* creates many uncertainties to bedevil the lower courts. A court's interpretation is conclusive, the Court says, only if it holds that interpretation to be 'the *only permissible* reading of the statute,' and not if it merely holds it to be 'the *best* reading.' *Ante* at 984. Does this mean that in future statutory-construction cases involving agency-administered statutes courts must specify (presumably in dictum) which of the two they are holding? And what of the many cases decided in the past, before this dictum's requirement was established? Apparently, silence on the point means that the court's decision is subject to agency reversal . . . . How much extra work will it entail for each court confronted with an agency-administered statute to determine whether it has reached, not only the right ('best') result, but 'the only permissible' result? Is the standard for 'unambiguous' under the Court's new agency-reversal rule the same as the standard for 'unambiguous' under step one of *Chevron*? (If so, of course, every case that reaches step two of *Chevron* will be agency-reversible.) Does the 'unambiguous' dictum produce *stare decisis* effect even when a court is *affirming*, rather than *reversing*, agency action—so that in the future the agency *must adhere* to that affirmed interpretation? If so, does the victorious agency have the right to appeal a Court of Appeals judgment in its favor, on the ground that the text in question is in fact *not* (as the Court of Appeals held) unambiguous, so the agency should be able to change its view in the future?

"It is indeed a wonderful new world that the Court creates, one full of promise for administrative-law professors in need of tenure articles and, of course, for litigators. I would adhere to what has been the rule in the past: When a court interprets a statute without *Chevron* deference to agency views, its interpretation (whether or not asserted to rest upon an unambiguous text) is the law."

Brand X, 545 U.S. at 1014–19 (Scalia, J., dissenting).

Justice Stevens joined the majority opinion in full, but he submitted a separate concurrence suggesting that it was limited to precedents established by lower courts. In Justice Stevens's words, the majority opinion "correctly explains why a court of appeals' interpretation of an ambiguous provision in a regulatory statute does not foreclose a contrary reading by the agency," but an interpretation adopted by the Supreme Court might be different; if the Supreme Court were to put a gloss on the provision, there would no longer be any ambiguity for the administering agency to resolve, and the agency would therefore need to follow the precedent established by the Supreme Court's decision. *See id.* at 1003 (Stevens, J., concurring). None of the other members of the six-Justice majority endorsed this idea. In my view, moreover, the idea is inconsistent with the logic of the majority opinion. *See* Hernandez-Carrera v. Carlson, 547 F.3d 1237, 1248 (10th Cir. 2008) ("[T]he holding of *Brand X* applies whether the judicial precedent at issue is that of a lower court or the Supreme Court."). Still, subsequent cases have treated this question as unresolved. *See* Miklin Enters., Inc. v. NLRB, 861 F.3d 812, 823 (8th Cir. 2017) ("[I]t is far from settled that *Brand X* applies to prior decisions of the Supreme Court."); De Niz Robles v. Lynch, 803 F.3d 1165, 1168 n.1 (10th Cir. 2015) (Gorsuch, J.) ("It's a nice question whether *Brand X* permits executive agencies to override not just circuit precedent but Supreme Court decisions too."); *cf.* Sandoz Inc. v. Amgen Inc., 582 U.S. 1, 22 (2017) (Breyer, J., concurring) (suggesting that the agency "may well" be able to depart from Supreme Court decisions under the conditions discussed in *Brand X*, but "we need not now decide any such matter").

* * * * *

The following example may help illuminate how *Brand X* works. Suppose that at Time 1, Congress enacts a statute and authorizes an administrative agency to administer it in the sense that potentially entitles the agency to *Chevron* deference. At Time 2, before the agency has weighed in on a particular question about the meaning of the statute, a case presenting that question reaches a federal appellate court (perhaps a circuit court, perhaps the Supreme Court itself). Because there is no administrative interpretation to which the court might need to defer, the court simply interprets the statute on its own, and the court reads the statute to establish Directive A. At Time 3, however, the agency finally addresses the same question in the course of notice-and-comment rulemaking, and the agency understands the statute to establish Directive B instead. A party who is aggrieved by the agency's action seeks judicial review on the ground that the agency is misinterpreting the statute. If the case winds up before the same court that previously interpreted the statute to establish Directive A (or any other tribunal that is bound by that court's precedents), how should the decision that the court rendered at Time 2 affect the analysis?

Under *Brand X*, the answer depends on exactly what the court said at Time 2. If the opinion that the court issued at Time 2 not only read the statute to establish Directive A but also said or implied that the statute is "unambiguous" for purposes of Step One of the *Chevron* framework, then the court's ordinary doctrines of *stare decisis* might cause the court to take the same position in later cases (and therefore to reject the agency's new position). After all, the opinion that the court issued at Time 2 would be a precedent for the proposition that the agency lacks authority to depart from Directive A. But if the opinion that the court issued at Time 2 simply announced the court's interpretation of the statute without addressing the proper application of the *Chevron* framework or whether other readings would be permissible, then the precedent that the court established at Time 2 does not answer the question that the court is now facing. In that situation, the proper application of the *Chevron* framework will be a question of first impression, which the court should proceed to answer. Despite having previously interpreted the statute to establish Directive A, the court will need to decide whether the statute is "ambiguous" in the sense relevant to *Chevron* and whether Directive B is also on the menu of permissible readings. If it is, and if the agency has provided an adequate explanation of the agency's reasons for preferring it, then the court will accept the agency's position.

To help justify these conclusions, the majority opinion in *Brand X* characterized *Chevron* as being about the delegation of a particular type of lawmaking authority to administrative agencies. *Chevron* and its progeny indicated that when Congress gives an agency the sort of administrative power that satisfies Step Zero, Congress ordinarily should be presumed also to be empowering the agency to make authoritative choices from among the permissible constructions of the provisions that the agency administers—choices that subsequent courts must accept. The majority opinion in *Brand X* described that power as "authority . . . to fill the statutory gap in reasonable fashion." *Brand X*, 545 U.S. at 980. This authority, moreover, is ongoing; the agency can switch from one permissible construction to another, as long as the agency does not behave arbitrarily and capriciously. What is more, Congress is delegating this authority specifically to the agency, not the courts, and the authority does not automatically go away even if the courts interpret the statute first. *See id.* at 982 ("*Chevron*'s premise is that it is for agencies, not courts, to fill statutory gaps.").

This characterization of *Chevron* dovetails with views previously expressed by Justice Scalia. In *Brand X* itself, the majority quoted Justice Scalia's opinion for the Court in *Smiley v. Citibank (South Dakota), N.A.*, 517 U.S. 735 (1996), which associated *Chevron* with "a presumption that Congress, when it left ambiguity in a statute meant for implementation by an agency, . . . desired the agency (rather than the courts) to possess whatever degree of discretion the ambiguity allows." *Id.* at 740–41. Justice Scalia had expressed this understanding of

Chevron as early as 1989. *See* Antonin Scalia, *Judicial Deference to Administrative Interpretations of Law*, 1989 DUKE L.J. 511, 516. In his 1989 essay, moreover, he praised this understanding of *Chevron* for explaining what is really going on when an agency switches from one permissible construction of a statute to another, and why courts should accept the agency's new position just as they would have accepted its old position. In his words,

> "It has always seemed to me utterly unrealistic to believe that when an agency revises one of its interpretative regulations, or one of the legal rules that it applies in its adjudications—when the NLRB, for example, decides that employer action previously held to be an 'unfair labor practice' is no longer so, or when the Federal Trade Commission amends one of its regulations to declare action previously permitted an 'unfair or deceptive trade practice'—the agency was admitting that it had 'got the law wrong.' . . . Rather, the agency was simply 'changing the law,' in light of new information or even new social attitudes impressed upon it through the political process—all within the limited range of discretion to 'change the law' conferred by the governing statute. *Chevron* . . . permits recognition of this reality."

Id. at 518–19; *see also Smiley*, 517 U.S. at 742 (acknowledging that an agency's change of position might sometimes fail judicial review under the arbitrary-and-capricious standard if the agency has not provided an adequate explanation of the change or if the agency failed to consider legitimate reliance interests, but adding that "if these pitfalls are avoided, change is not invalidating, since the whole point of *Chevron* is to leave the discretion provided by the ambiguities of a statute with the implementing agency").

Admittedly, when Justice Scalia made these statements, he was not addressing the interaction between *Chevron* and doctrines of judicial precedent. Still, isn't there some tension between these statements and Justice Scalia's dissent in *Brand X*? If one thinks that Congress has validly delegated power to the typical administering agency to make new law within the range permitted by "ambiguities" in the statutory provisions that the agency administers, and if one thinks that the agency can use this delegated authority to shift from one permissible construction to another, wouldn't one gravitate toward the majority's position in *Brand X*?

Start with Justice Scalia's suggestion that "[i]t is probably unconstitutional" for an agency to be able to override the gloss that an Article III court put upon a statute in a case to which the agency was a party. *Brand X*, 545 U.S. at 1017 (Scalia, J., dissenting). How does that suggestion square with the idea that *Chevron*-qualified agencies are exercising a delegated power to make new law? Suppose that Congress enacts a statute at Time 1 and that a federal court interprets the statute at Time 2. If Congress does not like the policy that the court has imputed to the statute, Congress itself can promptly amend the statute in a way that supersedes the court's interpretation going forward. No one would think that Congress's exercise of this policymaking authority violates the Constitution, even if the decision rendered by the court at Time 2 ends up having no ongoing effect on anyone's legal rights or duties. Why would things be different if an agency, exercising policymaking authority that Congress has validly delegated to it, does essentially the same thing? On Justice Scalia's own understanding of *Chevron*, isn't the agency simply changing the law going forward?

If one rejects Justice Scalia's constitutional argument, is there anything else to be said for the position that he advocated in *Brand X*? The gist of Justice Scalia's position was that notwithstanding *Chevron*, courts should reject an agency's interpretation of a provision that the agency administers if (1) the agency's interpretation deviates from a gloss that the courts themselves had previously put on the provision and (2) in the absence of the agency's interpretation, ordinary doctrines of judicial *stare decisis* would lead the courts to continue to follow the gloss that they had previously adopted. In effect, then, Justice Scalia was arguing that judicial *stare decisis* should trump *Chevron* deference. To defend that position, one might invoke the policy rationales for judicial *stare decisis*, such as the benefit of promoting stability in the law. But stability-based arguments are hard to reconcile with Justice Scalia's view of *Chevron* itself, which downplays any need for administrative *stare decisis*. At least in the absence of any governing judicial precedents, administering agencies have fairly free rein to change their own positions on questions as to which the statutory language is indeterminate, and courts applying the *Chevron* framework will defer to the agencies' new positions on much the same terms that courts would have deferred to the agencies' prior positions. If *Chevron* does not recognize much need for stability within the interstices of the provisions that agencies administer, why should stability become paramount simply because a court happened to address one of those interstices before the agency could get to it?

Of course, the need for stability in legal rules is not the only policy argument for judicial *stare decisis*. There might be other policy reasons for an appellate court to answer legal questions the same way today that it answered those questions last year. Those reasons, though, apply only if the applicable rules of decision have not been changed in the interim by lawmakers who have the authority to do so. If one accepts the implied-delegation theory of *Chevron*, hasn't there been a relevant change in the law when the administering agency exercises the discretion that it has been delegated? Assuming that the court's past opinion did not conclude that the relevant statutory provision has only one permissible reading, is the legal question that the court faced before the agency exercised its delegated authority even the same question as the one that the court faces after the agency has weighed in?

Consider the following hypothetical. At Time 1, Congress enacts a statute and gives an agency the sort of administrative power that triggers the *Chevron* framework. At Time 2, in the course of notice-and-comment rulemaking, the agency adopts a particular reading of one of the provisions that the agency administers. A challenge to that reading goes up to the Supreme Court, but the Court decides that the relevant provision is "ambiguous" (in the sense that matters at Step One) and upholds the agency's authority to adopt the reading that the agency has adopted. Later, at Time 3, the agency wants to switch to a different reading of the same provision. Under *Chevron* as it is commonly understood, the agency would be free to do so, as long as its new reading is also permissible and the agency does not behave arbitrarily and capriciously. But if that is correct, why should the agency have any less power if the Supreme Court got to the statute first? Suppose that at Time 2, before the agency had weighed in, the Supreme Court heard a case about the meaning of the statute, concluded that the relevant provision is ambiguous, and adopted one of the possible readings. If one believes in *Chevron*, wouldn't it be odd to say that the agency cannot switch away from that reading (unless the Supreme Court overrules its precedent under the difficult test for statutory *stare decisis*)?

* * * * *

Under *Brand X*, when an appellate court has issued a published opinion interpreting a statutory provision, and when the same court later reviews an administering agency's decision to put a different gloss on the provision, the precedential effect of the court's earlier opinion will depend on what that opinion held about the proper application of the *Chevron* framework. If the earlier opinion held that the relevant statutory provision is "unambiguous" for purposes of Step One of the *Chevron* framework, or if the earlier opinion identified limits on the range of interpretations that are "permissible" at Step Two, then the precedent established by the earlier opinion might require the court to reject the agency's new position (unless the court decides to overrule the precedent). If the earlier opinion was issued before the *Chevron* doctrine took hold, though, it would not have spoken in those terms; pre-*Chevron* opinions did not explicitly address the proper application of the *Chevron* framework. How should courts applying *Brand X* determine the precedential effect of those pre-*Chevron* opinions?

The Supreme Court faced a version of that question in *United States v. Home Concrete & Supply, LLC*, 566 U.S. 478 (2012). That case involved the statutory deadline for the federal government to assess a deficiency against a taxpayer who files a tax return that underreports the taxpayer's income (and therefore understates the amount of tax owed). If the taxpayer was not acting with the intent of evading taxes, the Internal Revenue Code ordinarily gives the government "3 years after the return was filed" to assess a deficiency. I.R.C. § 6501(a). But if the taxpayer "omits from gross income an amount properly includible therein," and if that amount "is in excess of 25 percent of the amount of gross income stated in the return," then the government has "6 years after the return was filed" to assess a deficiency. *Id.* § 6501(e)(1)(A). In *Home Concrete*, the Court had to decide whether a taxpayer that had overstated its basis in certain property, and therefore had underreported capital gains stemming from the property's sale, had "omit[ted] . . . an amount" from gross income within the meaning of § 6501(e)(1)(A).

In *Colony, Inc. v. Commissioner*, 357 U.S. 28 (1958), the Supreme Court had answered that question "no" under § 275(c) of the Internal Revenue Code of 1939—the statutory predecessor of § 6501(e)(1)(A). Justice Harlan's opinion in *Colony* included the following passages:

> "In determining the correct interpretation of § 275(c) we start with the critical statutory language, 'omits from gross income an amount properly includible therein.' . . .
>
> "Although we are inclined to think that the statute on its face lends itself more plausibly to the taxpayer's interpretation, it cannot be said that the language is unambiguous. In these circumstances we turn to the legislative history of § 275(c). We find in that history persuasive evidence that Congress was addressing itself to the specific situation where a taxpayer actually omitted some income receipt or accrual in his computation of gross income, and not more generally to errors in that computation arising from other causes."

Colony, 357 U.S. at 32–33.

In 2010, however, the Treasury Department promulgated a regulation purporting to reinterpret the key statutory language. According to the regulation, "an understated amount of gross income resulting from an overstatement of unrecovered cost or other basis constitutes an omission from gross income." 26 CFR § 301.6501(e)–1(a)(1)(iii) (2011). The question in *Home Concrete* was whether, given *Chevron*, courts should accept the Treasury Department's interpretation. A majority of the Court answered that question in the negative: "*Colony* has already interpreted the statute, and there is no longer any different construction that is consistent with *Colony* and available for adoption by the agency." *Home Concrete*, 566 U.S. at 487.

In a separate concurrence, Justice Scalia indicated that he was joining this statement because he continued to disagree with *Brand X*. *See id.* at 493–96 (Scalia, J., concurring in part and concurring in the judgment). But the other four members of the majority believed that their conclusion was consistent with *Brand X*. To be sure, Justice Harlan's opinion in *Colony* had conceded that the surface language of what is now § 6501(e)(1)(A) was ambiguous. But the plurality took Harlan's opinion to conclude that this ambiguity was only superficial and that further interpretation identified a single correct answer that could properly be attributed to Congress itself. The plurality explained its reading of Justice Harlan's opinion as follows:

> "For one thing, the Court said that the taxpayer had the better side of the textual argument. *Colony*, 357 U.S. at 33. For another, its examination of legislative history led it to believe that Congress had decided the question definitively, leaving no room for the agency to reach a contrary result. . . . *Id.* at 35–36. Further, it thought that the Commissioner's interpretation (the interpretation once again advanced here) would 'create a patent incongruity in the tax law.' *Id.* at 36–37. And it reached that conclusion despite the fact that, in the years leading up to *Colony*, the Commissioner had consistently advocated the opposite in the circuit courts. . . . Thus, the Court was aware it was rejecting the expert opinion of the Commissioner of Internal Revenue."

Home Concrete, 566 U.S. at 489 (plurality opinion).

The plurality acknowledged that some modern judges might disagree with Justice Harlan's methodology. For instance, modern judges might not use legislative history "to determine whether Congress left a gap to fill." According to the plurality, though, "that is beside the point": *Colony* had held that the statute left no gap of the sort that an administrative agency might fill, and principles of *stare decisis* required future Courts to adhere to that position. *Id.* at 489–90. In other words, the plurality took *Colony* to have held that the statute was not ambiguous in the sense relevant to *Chevron* deference.

Justice Scalia sharply criticized this analysis. His criticisms began with the following line from Justice Harlan's opinion in *Colony*: "it cannot be said that the language is unambiguous." *Colony*, 357 U.S. at 33. Justice Scalia took this line to mean that *Colony* had identified the sort of ambiguity that, after *Chevron*, agencies usually get to resolve.

I am not so sure. When Justice Harlan said that the language of the statute was ambiguous "on its face," *id.*, he was not necessarily saying that the statute was ambiguous in the sense that matters at Step One of the *Chevron* framework. After all, *Chevron* itself allows courts to use "traditional tools of statutory construction" at Step One, and those tools sometimes will dispel ambiguities that appeared on the surface of the text. *See Chevron*, 467 U.S. at 843 n.9.

In the view of the plurality in *Home Concrete*, that was precisely what the Court had concluded in *Colony*. Of course, *Colony* preceded *Chevron* by more than 25 years, so Justice Harlan had not discussed the *Chevron* framework or spoken of Step One and Step Two. Still, the plurality took Justice Harlan effectively to have resolved the case at what would now be considered Step One, with the result that *Colony* stood as a precedent against the agency's authority to adopt a different interpretation.

Is that correct? Although Justice Harlan obviously could not have had *Chevron*'s categories in mind, did his analysis in *Colony* nonetheless bear on the proper application of the *Chevron* framework? More broadly, what clues should modern courts look for when they are applying *Brand X* with respect to pre-*Chevron* precedents? *Cf.* THOMAS W. MERRILL, THE *CHEVRON* DOCTRINE: ITS RISE AND FALL, AND THE FUTURE OF THE ADMINISTRATIVE STATE 155 (2022) (criticizing the idea that courts should re-examine each such precedent and try to "classify it *as if* it had been decided at step 1 or step 2 of the *Chevron* doctrine," and noting that this idea "is open to serious objections on grounds of practicality and judicial economy"); *id.* ("The task of re-examination would have to be undertaken largely by the lower courts, which would undoubtedly lead to conflicts among the circuits about the proper classification of key precedents.").

* * * * *

Justice Thomas, who wrote the majority opinion in *Brand X*, has subsequently reconsidered his position. In a statement dissenting from the denial of certiorari in a case where the petitioner was asking the Court to reconsider *Brand X*, he observed that "[m]y skepticism of *Brand X* begins at its foundation—*Chevron* deference." *Baldwin v. United States*, 140 S. Ct. 690, 691 (2020) (Thomas, J., dissenting from the denial of certiorari). As he had suggested in his separate opinion in *Michigan v. EPA*, 574 U.S. 743 (2015), he argued that *Chevron* conflicts with the Constitution, both because it "compels judges to abdicate the judicial power" and because it "gives federal agencies unconstitutional power." *Baldwin*, 140 S. Ct. at 691 (Thomas, J., dissenting from the denial of certiorari). He added that *Chevron* also probably conflicts with the Administrative Procedure Act. *See id.* at 692. But he wrote that "[e]ven if *Chevron* were sound, I have become increasingly convinced that *Brand X* was still wrongly decided because it is even more inconsistent with the Constitution and traditional tools of statutory interpretation than *Chevron*." *Id.* at 694; *see also id.* at 695 ("*Brand X* takes on the constitutional deficiencies of *Chevron* and exacerbates them.").

Before his appointment to the Supreme Court, Justice Gorsuch had similarly criticized both *Chevron* and *Brand X*. *See* Gutierrez-Brizuela v. Lynch, 834 F.3d 1142 (10th Cir. 2016) (Gorsuch, J., concurring). At least for now, though, both cases remain part of current doctrine. *But cf.* MERRILL, *supra*, at 156 (treating *Home Concrete* as having "rejected" *Brand X*).

C. *AUER* DEFERENCE

Chevron addresses the deference that courts owe to a federal administrative agency's interpretations of statutory provisions that the agency administers. But what about an agency's interpretations of regulations that the agency itself has promulgated?

In *Bowles v. Seminole Rock & Sand Co.*, 325 U.S. 410 (1945), the Supreme Court thought it clear that judges should defer to a federal agency's interpretation of the agency's own regulations. *See id.* at 414 (opining that "a court must necessarily look to the administrative construction of the regulation if the meaning of the words used is in doubt"). According to the Court, the agency's interpretation of the regulation deserves "controlling weight" unless it is "plainly erroneous or inconsistent with the regulation." *Id.*

The Supreme Court took the same position in *Auer v. Robbins*, 519 U.S. 452 (1997). In *Auer*, the Court had to consider not only whether a regulation promulgated by the Secretary of Labor reflected a permissible interpretation of the governing statute (a question that triggered *Chevron* deference), but also what the regulation itself meant. At the certiorari stage, the Court had invited the Solicitor General "to file a brief in this case expressing the views of the United States." 516 U.S. 1109 (1996). The government had duly filed an amicus brief bearing the names of the Solicitor General and other lawyers in the Justice Department plus the Acting Solicitor of Labor and other lawyers in the Labor Department. After the Supreme Court granted certiorari, the government submitted another amicus brief on behalf of much the same cast of people. Ultimately, the Supreme Court treated the government's brief as an authoritative statement of the Secretary of Labor's interpretation of the regulation, and the Court deferred to that interpretation. Writing for a unanimous Court, Justice Scalia explained that under *Seminole Rock*, the Secretary's interpretation of the regulation "is . . . controlling unless 'plainly erroneous or inconsistent with the regulation.'" *Auer*, 519 U.S. at 461. In Justice Scalia's view, "That deferential standard is easily met here." *Id.*

Toward the end of his life, however, Justice Scalia had second thoughts about *Seminole Rock* and *Auer*. Indeed, he expressed concerns about this type of deference even before he started expressing doubts about *Chevron*. In *Talk America, Inc. v. Michigan Bell Telephone Co.*, 564 U.S. 50 (2011), Justice Scalia wrote separately to explain his concerns:

> "[W]hile I have in the past uncritically accepted [the principle of *Seminole Rock* and *Auer*], I have become increasingly doubtful of its validity. On the surface, it seems to be a natural corollary . . . of the rule that we will defer to an agency's interpretation of the statute it is charged with implementing, see *Chevron* . . . . But it is not. When Congress enacts an imprecise statute that it commits to the implementation of an executive agency, it has no control over that implementation (except, of course, through further, more precise, legislation). The legislative and executive functions are not combined. But when an agency promulgates an imprecise rule, it leaves *to itself* the implementation of that rule, and thus the initial determination of the rule's meaning. And though the adoption of a rule is an exercise of the executive rather than the legislative power, a properly adopted rule has fully the effect of law. It seems contrary to fundamental principles of separation of powers to permit the person who promulgates a law to interpret it as well. . . .

> "Deferring to an agency's interpretation of a statute does not encourage Congress, out of a desire to expand its power, to enact vague statutes; the vagueness effectively cedes power to the Executive. By contrast, deferring to an agency's interpretation of its own rule encourages the agency to enact vague rules which give it the power, in future adjudications, to do what it pleases. This frustrates the notice and predictability purposes of rulemaking, and promotes arbitrary government. . . .
>
> "There are undoubted advantages to *Auer* deference. It makes the job of a reviewing court much easier, and since it usually produces affirmance of the agency's view without conflict in the Circuits, it imparts (once the agency has spoken to clarify the regulation) certainty and predictability to the administrative process. The defects of *Auer* deference, and the alternatives to it, are fully explored in [a law-review article by Professor John F. Manning], Constitutional Structure and Judicial Deference to Agency Interpretations of Agency Rules, 96 Colum. L. Rev. 612 (1996). We have not been asked to reconsider *Auer* in the present case. When we are, I will be receptive to doing so."

Talk America, 564 U.S. at 68–69 (Scalia, J., concurring).

Two years later, Justice Scalia wrote another separate opinion calling on his colleagues to overrule *Auer* and to stop deferring to agencies' interpretations of their own regulations. *Decker v. Northwest Environmental Defense Center*, 568 U.S. 597 (2013) (Scalia, J., concurring in part and dissenting in part). According to Justice Scalia, the Court's cases had offered "two principal explanations" for *Auer* deference, but neither was persuasive.

First, the Court sometimes had suggested "that the agency, as the drafter of the rule, will have some special insight into its intent when enacting it." Justice Scalia dismissed this argument as resting on the "false" premise that interpreters are "looking for . . . the agency's *intent* in adopting the rule." According to Justice Scalia, "Whether governing rules are made by [Congress] . . . or an administrative agency, we are bound *by what they say*, not by the unexpressed intention of those who made them." *Id.* at 618.

The second explanation suggested by past cases was that "the agency possesses special expertise in administering its [regulatory program]." Justice Scalia agreed with this premise, but in his view it led only to the conclusion "that agencies and not courts should make regulations." According to Justice Scalia, the expertise argument "has nothing to do with who should interpret regulations." To be sure, the expertise argument might be telling if one believes that "the purpose of interpretation is to make the regulatory program work in a fashion that the current leadership of the agency deems effective." According to Justice Scalia, though, the purpose of interpretation is "[n]ot to make policy, but to determine what policy has been made and promulgated by the agency"—"to determine the fair meaning of the rule." *Id.*[35]

Again, Justice Scalia warned that *Auer* deference improperly combines "the power to prescribe" with "the power to interpret." *Id.* at 620. According to Justice Scalia, *Auer* deference thus "contravenes one of the great rules of separation of powers: He who writes a law must not adjudge its violation." *Id.* at 621; *see also* United Student Aid Funds, Inc. v. Bible, 578 U.S. 989, 990 (2016) (Thomas, J., dissenting from the denial of certiorari) (quoting this passage and criticizing *Auer* deference).

In the following case, a divided Supreme Court declined to overrule *Seminole Rock* and *Auer*, but sought to clarify their limits.

Kisor v. Wilkie

139 S. Ct. 2400 (2019)

■ *JUSTICE KAGAN announced the judgment of the Court and delivered the opinion of the Court with respect to Parts I, II-B, III-B, and IV, and an opinion with respect to Parts II-A and III-A, in which JUSTICES GINSBURG, BREYER, and SOTOMAYOR joined:*

This Court has often deferred to agencies' reasonable readings of genuinely ambiguous regulations. We call that practice *Auer* deference, or sometimes *Seminole Rock* deference, after two cases in which we employed it. See *Auer v. Robbins*, 519 U.S. 452 (1997); *Bowles v. Seminole Rock & Sand Co.*, 325 U.S. 410 (1945). The only question presented here is whether we should overrule those decisions, discarding the deference they give to agencies. We answer that question no. *Auer* deference retains an important role in construing agency regulations. But even as we uphold it, we reinforce its limits. *Auer* deference is sometimes appropriate and sometimes not. Whether to apply it depends on a range of considerations that we have noted now and again, but compile and further develop today. The deference doctrine we describe is potent in its place, but cabined in its scope. On remand, the Court of Appeals should decide whether it applies to the agency interpretation at issue.

. . . .

---

[35] Justice Scalia did not address the interaction between this view of interpretation and common justifications for *Chevron* deference in cases involving the interpretation of statutes. As discussed *supra* pp. 871–877, even if one explains *Chevron* in terms of presumed congressional intent, one might think that the content of *Chevron*'s default rule reflects the premise that administering agencies are better positioned than courts to choose among the various readings that indeterminate statutory language permits. One possible reason to accept this premise, in turn, is that agencies may have comparative advantages in making the kinds of policy judgments that indeterminacies sometimes allow. Thus, Justice Scalia's argument against *Auer* deference in *Decker* might call into question a common rationale for *Chevron* deference as well.

II

. . . .

A

Begin with a familiar problem in administrative law: For various reasons, regulations may be genuinely ambiguous. They may not directly or clearly address every issue; when applied to some fact patterns, they may prove susceptible to more than one reasonable reading. Sometimes, this sort of ambiguity arises from careless drafting—the use of a dangling modifier, an awkward word, an opaque construction. But often, ambiguity reflects the well-known limits of expression or knowledge. The subject matter of a rule "may be so specialized and varying in nature as to be impossible"—or at any rate, impracticable—to capture in its every detail. *SEC v. Chenery Corp.*, 332 U.S. 194, 203 (1947). Or a "problem[ ] may arise" that the agency, when drafting the rule, "could not [have] reasonably foresee[n]." *Id.* at 202. Whichever the case, the result is to create real uncertainties about a regulation's meaning.

Consider these examples:

- In a rule issued to implement the Americans with Disabilities Act (ADA), the Department of Justice requires theaters and stadiums to provide people with disabilities "lines of sight comparable to those for members of the general public." 28 C.F.R. pt. 36, App. A, p. 563 (1996). Must the Washington Wizards construct wheelchair seating to offer lines of sight over spectators when they rise to their feet? Or is it enough that the facility offers comparable views so long as everyone remains seated? See *Paralyzed Veterans of Am. v. D.C. Arena L.P.*, 117 F.3d 579, 581–582 (CADC 1997).
- The Transportation Security Administration (TSA) requires that liquids, gels, and aerosols in carry-on baggage be packed in containers smaller than 3.4 ounces and carried in a clear plastic bag. Does a traveler have to pack his jar of truffle pâté in that way? See *Laba v. Copeland*, 2016 WL 5958241, *1 (WDNC, Oct. 13, 2016).
- The Mine Safety and Health Administration issues a rule requiring employers to report occupational diseases within two weeks after they are "diagnosed." 30 C.F.R. § 50.20(a) (1993). Do chest X-ray results that "scor[e]" above some level of opacity count as a "diagnosis"? What level, exactly? See *American Min. Congress v. Mine Safety and Health Admin.*, 995 F.2d 1106, 1107–1108 (CADC 1993).
- An FDA regulation gives pharmaceutical companies exclusive rights to drug products if they contain "no active moiety that has been approved by FDA in any other" new drug application. 21 C.F.R. § 314.108(a) (2010). Has a company created a new "active moiety" by joining a previously approved moiety to lysine

through a non-ester covalent bond? See *Actavis Elizabeth LLC v. FDA*, 625 F.3d 760, 762–763 (CADC 2010); Tr. of Oral Arg. 12, 35.

- Or take the facts of *Auer* itself. An agency must decide whether police captains are eligible for overtime under the Fair Labor Standards Act. According to the agency's regulations, employees cannot receive overtime if they are paid on a "salary basis." 29 C.F.R. § 541.118(a) (1996). And in deciding whether an employee is salaried, one question is whether his pay is "subject to reduction" based on performance. *Ibid.* A police department's manual informs its officers that their pay might be docked if they commit a disciplinary infraction. Does that fact alone make them "subject to" pay deductions? Or must the department have a practice of docking officer pay, so that the possibility of that happening is more than theoretical? 519 U.S. at 459–462.

In each case, interpreting the regulation involves a choice between (or among) more than one reasonable reading. To apply the rule to some unanticipated or unresolved situation, the court must make a judgment call. How should it do so?

In answering that question, we have often thought that a court should defer to the agency's construction of its own regulation. For the last 20 or so years, we have referred to that doctrine as *Auer* deference, and applied it often. But . . . [b]efore the doctrine was called *Auer* deference, it was called *Seminole Rock* deference—for the 1945 decision in which we declared that when "the meaning of [a regulation] is in doubt," the agency's interpretation "becomes of controlling weight unless it is plainly erroneous or inconsistent with the regulation." 325 U.S. at 414. And *Seminole Rock* itself was not built on sand. Deference to administrative agencies traces back to the late nineteenth century, and perhaps beyond. . . .

We have explained *Auer* deference (as we now call it) as rooted in a presumption about congressional intent—a presumption that Congress would generally want the agency to play the primary role in resolving regulatory ambiguities. See *Martin v. Occupational Safety and Health Review Comm'n*, 499 U.S. 144, 151–153 (1991). Congress, we have pointed out, routinely delegates to agencies the power to implement statutes by issuing rules. See *id.* at 151. In doing so, Congress knows (how could it not?) that regulations will sometimes contain ambiguities. But Congress almost never explicitly assigns responsibility to deal with that problem, either to agencies or to courts. Hence the need to presume, one way or the other, what Congress would want. And as between those two choices, agencies have gotten the nod. We have adopted the presumption—though it is always rebuttable—that "the power authoritatively to interpret its own regulations is a component of the agency's delegated lawmaking powers." *Martin*, 499 U.S. at 151. Or otherwise said, we have thought that when granting rulemaking power to agencies, Congress usually intends to give them, too, considerable latitude to interpret the ambiguous rules they issue.

In part, that is because the agency that promulgated a rule is in the "better position [to] reconstruct" its original meaning. *Id.* at 152. Consider that if you don't know what some text (say, a memo or an e-mail) means, you would probably want to ask the person who wrote it. And for the same reasons, we have thought, Congress would too (though the person is here a collective actor). The agency that "wrote the regulation" will often have direct insight into what that rule was intended to mean. *Mullins Coal Co. of Va. v. Director, Office of Workers' Compensation Programs*, 484 U.S. 135, 159 (1987). The drafters will know what it was supposed to include or exclude or how it was supposed to apply to some problem. To be sure, this justification has its limits. It does not work so well, for example, when the agency failed to anticipate an issue in crafting a rule (*e.g.*, if the agency never thought about whether and when chest X-rays would count as a "diagnosis"). Then, the agency will not be uncovering a specific intention; at most (though this is not nothing), it will be offering insight into the analogous issues the drafters considered and the purposes they designed the regulation to serve. And the defense works yet less well when lots of time has passed between the rule's issuance and its interpretation—especially if the interpretation differs from one that has come before. All that said, the point holds good for a significant category of "contemporaneous" readings. *Lyng v. Payne*, 476 U.S. 926, 939 (1986). Want to know what a rule means? Ask its author.

In still greater measure, the presumption that Congress intended *Auer* deference stems from the awareness that resolving genuine regulatory ambiguities often "entail[s] the exercise of judgment grounded in policy concerns." *Thomas Jefferson Univ. v. Shalala*, 512 U.S. 504, 512 (1994) (internal quotation marks omitted). Return to our TSA example. In most of their applications, terms like "liquids" and "gels" are clear enough. (Traveler checklist: Pretzels OK; water not.) But resolving the uncertain issues—the truffle pâtés or olive tapenades of the world—requires getting in the weeds of the rule's policy: Why does TSA ban liquids and gels in the first instance? What makes them dangerous? Can a potential hijacker use pâté jars in the same way as soda cans? Or take the less specialized-seeming ADA example. It is easy enough to know what "comparable lines of sight" means in a movie theater—but more complicated when, as in sports arenas, spectators sometimes stand up. How costly is it to insist that the stadium owner take that sporadic behavior into account, and is the viewing value received worth the added expense? That cost-benefit calculation, too, sounds more in policy than in law. Or finally, take the more technical "moiety" example. Or maybe, don't. If you are a judge, you probably have no idea of what the FDA's rule means, or whether its policy is implicated when a previously approved moiety is connected to lysine through a non-ester covalent bond.

And Congress, we have thought, knows just that: It is attuned to the comparative advantages of agencies over courts in making such policy judgments. Agencies (unlike courts) have "unique expertise," often of a scientific or technical nature, relevant to applying a regulation "to complex or changing circumstances." *Martin*, 499 U.S. at 151; see *Thomas Jefferson*, 512 U.S. at 512. Agencies (unlike courts) can conduct factual investigations, can consult with affected parties, can consider how their experts have handled similar issues over the long course of administering a regulatory program. See *Long Island Care at Home, Ltd. v. Coke*, 551 U.S. 158, 167–168 (2007). And agencies (again unlike courts) have political accountability, because they are subject to the supervision of the President, who in turn answers to the public. See *Free Enterprise Fund v. Public Company Accounting Oversight Bd.*, 561 U.S. 477, 499 (2010); *Pauley v. BethEnergy Mines, Inc.*, 501 U.S. 680, 696 (1991) (discussing as a matter of democratic accountability the "proper roles of the political and judicial branches" in filling regulatory gaps). It is because of those features that Congress, when first enacting a statute, assigns rulemaking power to an agency and thus authorizes it to fill out the statutory scheme. And so too, when new issues demanding new policy calls come up within that scheme, Congress presumably wants the same agency, rather than any court, to take the laboring oar.

Finally, the presumption we use reflects the well-known benefits of uniformity in interpreting genuinely ambiguous rules. We have noted Congress's frequent "preference for resolving interpretive issues by uniform administrative decision, rather than piecemeal by litigation." *Ford Motor Credit Co. v. Milhollin*, 444 U.S. 555, 568 (1980). That preference may be strongest when the interpretive issue arises in the context of a "complex and highly technical regulatory program." *Thomas Jefferson*, 512 U.S. at 512. After all, judges are most likely to come to divergent conclusions when they are least likely to know what they are doing. . . . But the uniformity justification retains some weight even for more accessible rules, because their language too may give rise to more than one eminently reasonable reading. Consider *Auer* itself. There, four Circuits held that police captains were "subject to" pay deductions for disciplinary infractions if a police manual said they were, even if the department had never docked anyone. Two other Circuits held that captains were "subject to" pay deductions only if the department's actual practice made that punishment a realistic possibility. See *Auer*, 519 U.S. at 460. Had the agency issued an interpretation before all those rulings (rather than, as actually happened, in a brief in this Court), a deference rule would have averted most of that conflict and uncertainty. See *Christopher v. SmithKline Beecham Corp.*, 567 U.S. 142, 158, n. 17 (2012) (noting for this reason that *Auer* deference imparts "predictability to the administrative process" (internal quotation marks omitted)). *Auer* deference thus serves to ensure consistency in federal regulatory law, for everyone who needs to know what it requires.

B

But all that said, *Auer* deference is not the answer to every question of interpreting an agency's rules. Far from it. As we explain in this section, the possibility of deference can arise only if a regulation is genuinely ambiguous. And when we use that term, we mean it—genuinely ambiguous, even after a court has resorted to all the standard tools of interpretation. Still more, not all reasonable agency constructions of those truly ambiguous rules are entitled to deference. As just explained, we presume that Congress intended for courts to defer to agencies when they interpret their own ambiguous rules. But when the reasons for that presumption do not apply, or countervailing reasons outweigh them, courts should not give deference to an agency's reading, except to the extent it has the "power to persuade." *Christopher*, 567 U.S. at 159 (quoting *Skidmore v. Swift & Co.*, 323 U.S. 134, 140 (1944)). We have thus cautioned that *Auer* deference is just a "general rule"; it "does not apply in all cases." *Christopher*, 567 U.S. at 155. And although the limits of *Auer* deference are not susceptible to any rigid test, we have noted various circumstances in which such deference is "unwarranted." *Ibid.* In particular, that will be so when a court concludes that an interpretation does not reflect an agency's authoritative, expertise-based, "fair[, or] considered judgment." *Ibid.* (quoting *Auer*, 519 U.S. at 462); cf. *United States v. Mead Corp.*, 533 U.S. 218, 229–231 (2001) (adopting a similar approach to *Chevron* deference).

We take the opportunity to restate, and somewhat expand on, those principles here to clear up some mixed messages we have sent. At times, this Court has applied *Auer* deference without significant analysis of the underlying regulation. See, *e.g.*, *United States v. Larionoff*, 431 U.S. 864, 872 (1977) (stating that the Court "need not tarry" over the regulation's language given *Seminole Rock*). At other times, the Court has given *Auer* deference without careful attention to the nature and context of the interpretation. See, *e.g.*, *Thorpe v. Housing Authority of Durham*, 393 U.S. 268, 276, and nn. 22–23 (1969) (deferring to an agency's view as expressed in letters to third parties). And in a vacuum, our most classic formulation of the test—whether an agency's construction is "plainly erroneous or inconsistent with the regulation," *Seminole Rock*, 325 U.S. at 414—may suggest a caricature of the doctrine, in which deference is "reflexive." *Pereira v. Sessions*, 138 S. Ct. 2105, 2120–21 (2018) (Kennedy, J., concurring). So we cannot deny that Kisor has a bit of grist for his claim that *Auer* "bestows on agencies expansive, unreviewable" authority. Brief for Petitioner 25. But in fact *Auer* does no such thing: It gives agencies their due, while also allowing—indeed, obligating—courts to perform their reviewing and restraining functions. So before we turn to Kisor's specific grievances, we think it worth reinforcing some of the limits inherent in the *Auer* doctrine.

First and foremost, a court should not afford *Auer* deference unless the regulation is genuinely ambiguous. See *Christensen v. Harris County*, 529 U.S. 576, 588 (2000); *Seminole Rock*, 325 U.S. at 414 (deferring only "if the meaning of the words used is in doubt"). If uncertainty does not exist, there is no plausible reason for deference. The regulation then just means what it means—and the court must give it effect, as the court would any law. Otherwise said, the core theory of *Auer* deference is that sometimes the law runs out, and policy-laden choice is what is left over. But if the law gives an answer—if there is only one reasonable construction of a regulation—then a court has no business deferring to any other reading, no matter how much the agency insists it would make more sense. Deference in that circumstance would "permit the agency, under the guise of interpreting a regulation, to create *de facto* a new regulation." See *Christensen*, 529 U.S. at 588. *Auer* does not, and indeed could not, go that far.

And before concluding that a rule is genuinely ambiguous, a court must exhaust all the "traditional tools" of construction. *Chevron U.S.A. Inc. v. Natural Resources Defense Council, Inc.*, 467 U.S. 837, 843, n. 9 (1984) (adopting the same approach for ambiguous statutes). For again, only when that legal toolkit is empty and the interpretive question still has no single right answer can a judge conclude that it is "more [one] of policy than of law." *Pauley*, 501 U.S. at 696. That means a court cannot wave the ambiguity flag just because it found the regulation impenetrable on first read. Agency regulations can sometimes make the eyes glaze over. But hard interpretive conundrums, even relating to complex rules, can often be solved. See *id.* at 707 (Scalia, J., dissenting) (a regulation is not ambiguous merely because "discerning the only possible interpretation requires a taxing inquiry"). To make that effort, a court must "carefully consider[ ]" the text, structure, history, and purpose of a regulation, in all the ways it would if it had no agency to fall back on. *Ibid.* Doing so will resolve many seeming ambiguities out of the box, without resort to *Auer* deference.

If genuine ambiguity remains, moreover, the agency's reading must still be "reasonable." *Thomas Jefferson*, 512 U.S. at 515. In other words, it must come within the zone of ambiguity the court has identified after employing all its interpretive tools. (Note that serious application of those tools therefore has use even when a regulation turns out to be truly ambiguous. The text, structure, history, and so forth at least establish the outer bounds of permissible interpretation.) Some courts have thought (perhaps because of *Seminole Rock*'s "plainly erroneous" formulation) that at this stage of the analysis, agency constructions of rules receive greater deference than agency constructions of statutes. See, *e.g.*, *Ohio Dept. of Medicaid v. Price*, 864 F.3d 469, 477 (CA6 2017). But that is not so. Under *Auer*, as under *Chevron*, the agency's reading must fall "within the bounds of reasonable interpretation." *Arlington v.*

FCC, 569 U.S. 290, 296 (2013). And let there be no mistake: That is a requirement an agency can fail.

Still, we are not done—for not every reasonable agency reading of a genuinely ambiguous rule should receive *Auer* deference. We have recognized in applying *Auer* that a court must make an independent inquiry into whether the character and context of the agency interpretation entitles it to controlling weight. See *Christopher*, 567 U.S. at 155; see also *Mead*, 533 U.S. at 229–231, 236–237 (requiring an analogous though not identical inquiry for *Chevron* deference). As explained above, we give *Auer* deference because we presume, for a set of reasons relating to the comparative attributes of courts and agencies, that Congress would have wanted us to. But the administrative realm is vast and varied, and we have understood that such a presumption cannot always hold. Cf. *Mead*, 533 U.S. at 236 ("tailor[ing] deference to [the] variety" of administrative action); *Arlington*, 569 U.S. at 309–310 (Breyer, J., concurring in part and concurring in judgment) (noting that "context-specific[ ] factors" may show that "Congress would [not] have intended the agency to resolve [some] ambiguity"). The inquiry on this dimension does not reduce to any exhaustive test. But we have laid out some especially important markers for identifying when *Auer* deference is and is not appropriate.

To begin with, the regulatory interpretation must be one actually made by the agency. In other words, it must be the agency's "authoritative" or "official position," rather than any more ad hoc statement not reflecting the agency's views. *Mead*, 533 U.S. at 257–259, and n. 6 (Scalia, J., dissenting). That constraint follows from the logic of *Auer* deference—because Congress has delegated rulemaking power, and all that typically goes with it, to the agency alone. Of course, the requirement of "authoritative" action must recognize a reality of bureaucratic life: Not everything the agency does comes from, or is even in the name of, the Secretary or his chief advisers. So, for example, we have deferred to "official staff memoranda" that were "published in the Federal Register," even though never approved by the agency head. *Ford Motor Credit*, 444 U.S. at 566, n. 9, 567, n. 10 (declining to "draw a radical distinction between" agency heads and staff for *Auer* deference). But there are limits. The interpretation must at the least emanate from those actors, using those vehicles, understood to make authoritative policy in the relevant context. See, *e.g.*, *Paralyzed Veterans*, 117 F.3d at 587 (refusing to consider a "speech of a mid-level official" as an "authoritative departmental position"); *N.Y. State Dept. of Social Servs. v. Bowen*, 835 F.2d 360, 365–366 (CADC 1987) (rejecting the idea that an "informal memorandum" recounting a telephone conversation between employees could count as an "authoritative pronouncement"); *Exelon Generation Co. v. Local 15, Int'l Brotherhood of Elec. Workers, AFL-CIO*, 676 F.3d 566, 576–578 (CA7 2012) (declining deference when the agency had itself "disclaimed the use of regulatory guides as authoritative"). If the interpretation does not do so, a court may not defer.

Next, the agency's interpretation must in some way implicate its substantive expertise. Administrative knowledge and experience largely "account [for] the presumption that Congress delegates interpretive lawmaking power to the agency." *Martin*, 499 U.S. at 153. So the basis for deference ebbs when "[t]he subject matter of the [dispute is] distan[t] from the agency's ordinary" duties or "fall[s] within the scope of another agency's authority." *Arlington*, 569 U.S. at 309 (opinion of Breyer, J.). This Court indicated as much when it analyzed a "split enforcement" scheme, in which Congress divided regulatory power between two entities. *Martin*, 499 U.S. at 151. To decide "*whose* reasonable interpretation" of a rule controlled, we "presum[ed] Congress intended to invest interpretive power" in whichever actor was "best position[ed] to develop" expertise about the given problem. *Id.* at 149, 153. The same idea holds good as between agencies and courts. "Generally, agencies have a nuanced understanding of the regulations they administer." Brief for Respondent 33. That point is most obvious when a rule is technical; think back to our "moiety" or "diagnosis" examples. But more prosaic-seeming questions also commonly implicate policy expertise; consider the TSA assessing the security risks of pâté or a disabilities office weighing the costs and benefits of an accommodation. Once again, though, there are limits. Some interpretive issues may fall more naturally into a judge's bailiwick. Take one requiring the elucidation of a simple common-law property term, see *Jicarilla Apache Tribe v. FERC*, 578 F.2d 289, 292–293 (CA10 1978), or one concerning the award of an attorney's fee, see *West Va. Highlands Conservancy, Inc. v. Norton*, 343 F.3d 239 (CA4 2003). Cf. *Adams Fruit Co. v. Barrett*, 494 U.S. 638, 649–650 (1990) (declining to award *Chevron* deference when an agency interprets a judicial-review provision). When the agency has no comparative expertise in resolving a regulatory ambiguity, Congress presumably would not grant it that authority.[5]

Finally, an agency's reading of a rule must reflect "fair and considered judgment" to receive *Auer* deference. *Christopher*, 567 U.S. at 155 (quoting *Auer*, 519 U.S. at 462). That means, we have stated, that a court should decline to defer to a merely "convenient litigating position" or "*post hoc* rationalizatio[n] advanced" to "defend past agency action against attack." *Christopher*, 567 U.S. at 155 (quoting *Bowen v. Georgetown Univ. Hospital*, 488 U.S. 204, 213 (1988) and *Auer*, 519 U.S. at 462).[6] And a court may not defer to a new interpretation, whether or

[5] For a similar reason, this Court has denied *Auer* deference when an agency interprets a rule that parrots the statutory text. See *Gonzales v. Oregon*, 546 U.S. 243, 257 (2006). An agency, we explained, gets no "special authority to interpret its own words when, instead of using its expertise and experience to formulate a regulation, it has elected merely to paraphrase the statutory language." *Ibid.*

[6] The general rule, then, is not to give deference to agency interpretations advanced for the first time in legal briefs. See *Bowen*, 488 U.S. at 212–213. But we have not entirely foreclosed that practice. *Auer* itself deferred to a new regulatory interpretation presented in an *amicus*

not introduced in litigation, that creates "unfair surprise" to regulated parties. *Long Island Care*, 551 U.S. at 170. That disruption of expectations may occur when an agency substitutes one view of a rule for another. We have therefore only rarely given *Auer* deference to an agency construction "conflict[ing] with a prior" one. *Thomas Jefferson*, 512 U.S. at 515. Or the upending of reliance may happen without such an explicit interpretive change. This Court, for example, recently refused to defer to an interpretation that would have imposed retroactive liability on parties for longstanding conduct that the agency had never before addressed. See *Christopher*, 567 U.S. at 155–156. Here too the lack of "fair warning" outweighed the reasons to apply *Auer*. *Id.* at 156 (internal quotation marks omitted).

* * *

The upshot of all this goes something as follows. When it applies, *Auer* deference gives an agency significant leeway to say what its own rules mean. In so doing, the doctrine enables the agency to fill out the regulatory scheme Congress has placed under its supervision. But that phrase "when it applies" is important—because it often doesn't. As described above, this Court has cabined *Auer*'s scope in varied and critical ways—and in exactly that measure, has maintained a strong judicial role in interpreting rules. What emerges is a deference doctrine not quite so tame as some might hope, but not nearly so menacing as they might fear.

III

That brings us to the lone question presented here—whether we should abandon the longstanding doctrine just described. In contending that we should, Kisor raises statutory, policy, and constitutional claims . . . . But he faces an uphill climb. He must first convince us that *Auer* deference is wrong. And even then, he must overcome *stare decisis*—the special care we take to preserve our precedents. In the event, Kisor fails at the first step: None of his arguments provide good reason to doubt *Auer* deference. And even if that were not so, Kisor does not offer the kind of special justification needed to overrule *Auer*, and *Seminole Rock*, and all our many other decisions deferring to reasonable agency constructions of ambiguous rules.

A

Kisor first attacks *Auer* as inconsistent with the judicial review provision of the Administrative Procedure Act (APA). . . . Section 706 of the Act, governing judicial review of agency action, states (among other things) that reviewing courts shall "determine the meaning or applicability of the terms of an agency action" (including a regulation).

---

curiae brief in this Court. There, the agency was not a party to the litigation, and had expressed its views only in response to the Court's request. "[I]n the circumstances," the Court explained, "[t]here [was] simply no reason to suspect that the interpretation [did] not reflect the agency's fair and considered judgment on the matter in question." *Auer*, 519 U.S. at 462.

[5 U.S.C. § 706.] According to Kisor, *Auer* violates that edict by thwarting "meaningful judicial review" of agency rules. Brief for Petitioner 29. . . .

To begin with, that argument ignores the many ways, discussed above, that courts exercise independent review over the meaning of agency rules. . . . As we have explained, a court must apply all traditional methods of interpretation to any rule, and must enforce the plain meaning those methods uncover. There can be no thought of deference unless, after performing that thoroughgoing review, the regulation remains genuinely susceptible to multiple reasonable meanings and the agency's interpretation lines up with one of them. And even if that is the case, courts must on their own determine whether the nature or context of the agency's construction reverses the usual presumption of deference. Most notably, a court must consider whether the interpretation is authoritative, expertise-based, considered, and fair to regulated parties. All of that figures as "meaningful judicial review." Brief for Petitioner 29.

And even when a court defers to a regulatory reading, it acts consistently with Section 706. That provision does not specify the standard of review a court should use in "determin[ing] the meaning" of an ambiguous rule. 5 U.S.C. § 706. One possibility, as Kisor says, is to review the issue *de novo*. But another is to review the agency's reading for reasonableness. To see the point, assume that a regulatory (say, an employment) statute expressly instructed courts to apply *Auer* deference when reviewing an agency's interpretations of its ambiguous rules. Nothing in that statute would conflict with Section 706. Instead, the employment law would simply make clear *how* a court is to "determine the meaning" of such a rule—by deferring to an agency's reasonable reading. *Ibid*. Of course, that is not the world we know: Most substantive statutes do not say anything about *Auer* deference, one way or the other. But for all the reasons spelled out above, we have long presumed (subject always to rebuttal) that the Congress delegating regulatory authority to an agency intends as well to give that agency considerable latitude to construe its ambiguous rules. . . . And that presumption operates just like the hypothesized statute above. Because of it, once again, courts do not violate Section 706 by applying *Auer*. To the contrary, they fulfill their duty to "determine the meaning" of a rule precisely by deferring to the agency's reasonable reading. See Sunstein & Vermeule, The Unbearable Rightness of *Auer*, 84 U. Chi. L. Rev. 297, 306 (2017) (If Congress intends "that the meaning of a regulation turns on the agency's interpretation of its meaning," then courts comply with Section 706's command to " 'determine the meaning' [of the regulation] by deferring to that view"); cf. *Arlington*, 569 U.S. at 317 (Roberts, C.J., dissenting) (similarly addressing why *Chevron* deference comports with Section 706). Section 706 and *Auer* thus go hand in hand.

That is especially so given the practice of judicial review at the time of the APA's enactment. Section 706 was understood when enacted to "restate[ ] the present law as to the scope of judicial review." See Dept. of

Justice, Attorney General's Manual on the Administrative Procedure Act 108 (1947); see also *Vermont Yankee Nuclear Power Corp. v. Natural Resources Defense Council, Inc.*, 435 U.S. 519, 546 (1978) (noting that this Court gives some deference to the Manual "because of the role played by the Department of Justice in drafting the legislation"). We have thus interpreted the APA not to "significantly alter the common law of judicial review of agency action." *Heckler v. Chaney*, 470 U.S. 821, 832 (1985) (internal quotation marks omitted). That pre-APA common law included *Seminole Rock* itself (decided the year before) along with prior decisions foretelling that ruling. . . . Even assume that the deference regime laid out in those cases had not yet fully taken hold. At a minimum, nothing in the law of that era required all judicial review of agency interpretations to be *de novo*. Cf. Manning, Constitutional Structure and Judicial Deference to Agency Interpretations of Agency Rules, 96 Colum. L. Rev. 612, 635–636 (1996) (arguing that courts before the APA used "flexible, common law methods to review administrative action"). And so nothing suggests that Section 706 imposes that requirement. Or otherwise said: If Section 706 did not change the law of judicial review (as we have long recognized), then it did not proscribe a deferential standard then known and in use.

. . . .

. . . Kisor turns to policy, leaning on a familiar claim about the incentives *Auer* creates. According to Kisor, *Auer* encourages agencies to issue vague and open-ended regulations, confident that they can later impose whatever interpretation of those rules they prefer. See Brief for Petitioner 37–41. . . .

But the claim has notable weaknesses, empirical and theoretical alike. . . . No real evidence—indeed, scarcely an anecdote—backs up the assertion. As two noted scholars (one of whom reviewed thousands of rules during four years of government service) have written: "[W]e are unaware of, and no one has pointed to, any regulation in American history that, because of *Auer*, was designed vaguely." Sunstein & Vermeule, 84 U. Chi. L. Rev. at 308. And even the argument's theoretical allure dissipates upon reflection. For strong (almost surely stronger) incentives and pressures cut in the opposite direction. "[R]egulators want their regulations to be effective, and clarity promotes compliance." Brief for Administrative Law Scholars as *Amici Curiae* 18–19. Too, regulated parties often push for precision from an agency, so that they know what they can and cannot do. And ambiguities in rules pose risks to the long-run survival of agency policy. Vagueness increases the chance of adverse judicial rulings. And it enables future administrations, with different views, to reinterpret the rules to their own liking. Add all of that up and Kisor's ungrounded theory of incentives contributes nothing to the case against *Auer*.

Finally, Kisor goes big, asserting (though fleetingly) that *Auer* deference violates "separation-of-powers principles." See Brief for

Petitioner 43. In his view, those principles prohibit "vest[ing] in a single branch the law-making and law-interpreting functions." *Id.* at 45. If that objection is to agencies' usurping the interpretive role of courts, this opinion has already met it head-on. Properly understood and applied, *Auer* does no such thing. In all the ways we have described, courts retain a firm grip on the interpretive function. . . . If Kisor's objection is instead to the supposed commingling of functions (that is, the legislative and judicial) within an agency, this Court has answered it often before. See, *e.g.*, *Withrow v. Larkin*, 421 U.S. 35, 54 (1975) (permitting such a combination of functions); *FTC v. Cement Institute*, 333 U.S. 683, 702 (1948) (same). That sort of mixing is endemic in agencies, and has been "since the beginning of the Republic." *Arlington*, 569 U.S. at 304–305, n. 4. It does not violate the separation of powers, we have explained, because even when agency "activities take 'legislative' and 'judicial' forms," they continue to be "exercises of[ ] the 'executive Power' "—or otherwise said, ways of executing a statutory plan. *Ibid.* (quoting U.S. Const., Art. II, § 1, cl. 1). . . .

B

If all that were not enough, *stare decisis* cuts strongly against Kisor's position. . . . To be sure, *stare decisis* is "not an inexorable command." [*Payne v. Tennessee*, 501 U.S. 808, 828 (1991).] But any departure from the doctrine demands "special justification"—something more than "an argument that the precedent was wrongly decided." *Halliburton Co. v. Erica P. John Fund, Inc.*, 573 U.S. 258, 266 (2014).

And that is even more than usually so in the circumstances here. First, Kisor asks us to overrule not a single case, but a "long line of precedents"—each one reaffirming the rest and going back 75 years or more. *Bay Mills*, 572 U.S. at 798 . . . . This Court alone has applied *Auer* or *Seminole Rock* in dozens of cases, and lower courts have done so thousands of times. Deference to reasonable agency interpretations of ambiguous rules pervades the whole corpus of administrative law. Second, because that is so, abandoning *Auer* deference would cast doubt on many settled constructions of rules. As Kisor acknowledged at oral argument, a decision in his favor would allow relitigation of any decision based on *Auer*, forcing courts to "wrestle [with] whether or not *Auer*" had actually made a difference. Tr. of Oral Arg. 30; see *id.* at 47 (Solicitor General agreeing that "every single regulation that's currently on the books whose interpretation has been established under *Seminole Rock* now [would have] to be relitigated anew"). It is the rare overruling that introduces so much instability into so many areas of law, all in one blow.

And third, even if we are wrong about *Auer*, "Congress remains free to alter what we have done." *Patterson v. McLean Credit Union*, 491 U.S. 164, 172–173 (1989) (stating that when that is so, "[c]onsiderations of *stare decisis* have special force"). In a constitutional case, only we can correct our error. But that is not so here. Our deference decisions are "balls tossed into Congress's court, for acceptance or not as that branch elects." [*Kimble v. Marvel Entertainment, LLC*, 576 U.S. 446, 456 (2015).] And so far, at least, Congress has chosen acceptance. It could amend the APA or any specific statute to require the sort of *de novo* review of regulatory interpretations that Kisor favors. Instead, for approaching a century, it has let our deference regime work side-by-side with both the APA and the many statutes delegating rulemaking power to agencies. It has done so even after we made clear that our deference decisions reflect a presumption about congressional intent. See *Martin*, 499 U.S. at 151 . . . . And it has done so even after Members of this Court began to raise questions about the doctrine. See, *e.g.*, *Talk America*, 564 U.S. at 67–69 (Scalia, J., concurring). Given that history—and Congress's continuing ability to take up Kisor's arguments—we would need a particularly "special justification" to now reverse *Auer*.

Kisor offers nothing of that ilk. . . .

IV

[The Court's discussion of Mr. Kisor's particular case is omitted. The U.S. Court of Appeals for the Federal Circuit had upheld an administrative decision on the strength of *Auer* deference. Ultimately, the Supreme Court vacated the Federal Circuit's judgment and remanded so that the Federal Circuit could evaluate (1) whether the regulation in question was indeed ambiguous in the relevant sense and (2) whether the interpretation that Kisor was challenging—which had been articulated by one of the roughly 100 administrative judges who are members of the Board of Veterans' Appeals and who rule on claims for disability benefits—"is of the sort that Congress would want to receive deference."]

■ *CHIEF JUSTICE ROBERTS, concurring in part:*

. . . . We took this case to consider whether to overrule *Auer v. Robbins*, 519 U.S. 452 (1997), and *Bowles v. Seminole Rock & Sand Co.*, 325 U.S. 410 (1945). For the reasons the Court discusses in Part III-B, I agree that overruling those precedents is not warranted. I also agree with the Court's treatment in Part II-B of the bounds of *Auer* deference.

I write separately to suggest that the distance between the majority and Justice Gorsuch is not as great as it may initially appear. The majority catalogs the prerequisites for, and limitations on, *Auer* deference: The underlying regulation must be genuinely ambiguous; the agency's interpretation must be reasonable and must reflect its authoritative, expertise-based, and fair and considered judgment; and the agency must take account of reliance interests and avoid unfair surprise. Justice Gorsuch, meanwhile, lists the reasons that a court might be persuaded to adopt an agency's interpretation of its own regulation: The agency thoroughly considered the problem, offered a valid rationale, brought its expertise to bear, and interpreted the regulation in a manner consistent with earlier and later pronouncements. Accounting for variations in verbal formulation, those lists have much in common.

That is not to say that *Auer* deference is just the same as the power of persuasion discussed in *Skidmore v. Swift & Co.*, 323 U.S. 134 (1944); there is a difference between holding that a court ought to be persuaded by an agency's interpretation and holding that it should defer to that interpretation under certain conditions. But it is to say that the cases in which *Auer* deference is warranted largely overlap with the cases in which it would be unreasonable for a court not to be persuaded by an agency's interpretation of its own regulation.

One further point: Issues surrounding judicial deference to agency interpretations of their own regulations are distinct from those raised in connection with judicial deference to agency interpretations of statutes enacted by Congress. See *Chevron U.S.A. Inc. v. Natural Resources Defense Council, Inc.*, 467 U.S. 837 (1984). I do not regard the Court's decision today to touch upon the latter question.

■ *JUSTICE GORSUCH, with whom JUSTICE THOMAS joined, with whom JUSTICE KAVANAUGH joined as to Parts I, II, III, IV, and V, and with whom JUSTICE ALITO joined as to Parts I, II, and III, concurring in the judgment:*

It should have been easy for the Court to say goodbye to *Auer v. Robbins*. In disputes involving the relationship between the government and the people, *Auer* requires judges to accept an executive agency's interpretation of its own regulations even when that interpretation doesn't represent the best and fairest reading. This rule creates a "systematic judicial bias in favor of the federal government, the most powerful of parties, and against everyone else." [Larkin & Slattery, The World After *Seminole Rock* and *Auer*, 42 Harv. J. L. & Pub. Pol'y 625, 641 (2019) (internal quotation marks omitted).] Nor is *Auer*'s biased rule the product of some congressional mandate we are powerless to correct: This Court invented it, almost by accident and without any meaningful effort to reconcile it with the Administrative Procedure Act or the Constitution. A legion of academics, lower court judges, and Members of this Court—even *Auer*'s author—has called on us to abandon *Auer*. Yet today a bare majority flinches, and *Auer* lives on.

. . . . The Court cannot muster even five votes to say that *Auer* is lawful or wise. Instead, a majority retains *Auer* only because of *stare decisis*. And yet, far from standing by that precedent, the majority proceeds to impose so many new and nebulous qualifications and limitations on *Auer* that the Chief Justice claims to see little practical difference between keeping it on life support in this way and overruling it entirely. . . .

. . . . One can hope that the Chief Justice is right, and that whether we formally overrule *Auer* or merely neuter it, the results in most cases will prove the same. But . . . retaining even this debilitated version of

Auer threatens to force litigants and lower courts to jump through needless and perplexing new hoops and in the process deny the people the independent judicial decisions they deserve. All to what end? So that we may *pretend* to abide *stare decisis*?

.... Respectfully, I would stop this business of making up excuses for judges to abdicate their job of interpreting the law, and simply allow the court of appeals to afford Mr. Kisor its best independent judgment of the law's meaning....

I. How We Got Here

[Part I of Justice Gorsuch's dissent took issue with Justice Kagan's claim that the roots of *Auer* deference stretch back to the nineteenth century. According to Justice Gorsuch, "the seeds of the *Auer* doctrine were first planted only in 1945," when the Court issued its opinion in *Seminole Rock*, and the relevant passage in *Seminole Rock* did not start to become prominent until the mid-1960s.]

II. The Administrative Procedure Act

.... [R]emarkably, until today this Court has never made any serious effort to square the *Auer* doctrine with the APA. Even now, only four Justices make the attempt.... [T]heir arguments are wholly unpersuasive.

A

The first problem lies in § 706. That provision instructs reviewing courts to "decide all relevant questions of law" and "set aside agency action ... found to be ... not in accordance with law." ... [T]he APA further directs courts to "determine the meaning" of any relevant "agency action," including any rule issued by the agency. The APA thus requires a reviewing court to resolve for itself any dispute over the proper interpretation of an agency regulation. A court that, in deference to an agency, adopts something other than the best reading of a regulation isn't "decid[ing]" the relevant "questio[n] of law" or "determin[ing] the meaning" of the regulation. Instead, it's allowing the agency to dictate the answer to that question. In doing so, the court is abdicating the duty Congress assigned to it in the APA.[47]

Justice Kagan seeks to address the glaring inconsistency between our judge-made rule and the controlling statute this way. On her account, the APA tells a reviewing court to "determine the meaning" of regulations, but it does not tell the court "*how*" to do that. Thus, we are told, reading the regulation for itself and deferring to the agency's reading are just two equally valid ways for a court to fulfill its statutory duty to "determine the meaning" of the regulation....

[47] The case before us doesn't arise under the APA, but the statute that governs here is plainly modeled on the APA and contains essentially the same commands. It directs a reviewing court to "decide all relevant questions of law" and to "set aside any regulation or any interpretation thereof" that is "not in accordance with law." 38 U.S.C. § 7292(d)(1).

But the APA isn't as anemic as that. Its unqualified command requires the court to determine legal questions—including questions about a regulation's meaning—by its own lights, not by those of political appointees or bureaucrats who may even be self-interested litigants in the case at hand. Nor can there be any doubt that when Congress wrote the APA, it knew perfectly well how to require judicial deference to an agency when it wished—in fact, Congress repeatedly specified deferential standards for judicial review *elsewhere* in the statute.[48] But when it comes to the business of interpreting regulations, no such command exists; instead, Congress told courts to "determine" those matters for themselves. . . .

. . . .

C

If *Auer* cannot be squared with the text of the APA, Justice Kagan suggests it at least conforms to a reasonable "presumption about congressional intent." *Ante* at 2412. The theory seems to be that whenever Congress grants an agency "rulemaking power," it *also* implicitly gives the agency " 'the power authoritatively to interpret' " whatever rules the agency chooses to adopt. [*Ibid.*] But against the clear statutory commands Congress gave us in the APA, what sense does it make to "presume" that Congress really, secretly, wanted courts to treat agency interpretations as binding? . . . .

. . . .

III. The Constitution

Not only is *Auer* incompatible with the APA; it also sits uneasily with the Constitution. Article III, § 1 provides that the "judicial Power of the United States" is vested exclusively in this Court and the lower federal courts. A core component of that judicial power is " 'the duty of interpreting [the laws] and applying them in cases properly brought before the courts.' " [*Patchak v. Zinke*, 138 S. Ct. 897, 904 (2018) (plurality opinion) (quoting *Massachusetts v. Mellon*, 262 U.S. 447, 488 (1923)).] As Chief Justice Marshall put it, "[i]t is emphatically the province and duty of the judicial department to say what the law is." [*Marbury v. Madison*, 5 U.S. (1 Cranch) 137, 177 (1803).] And never, this Court has warned, should the "judicial power . . . be shared with [the] Executive Branch." [*Miller v. Johnson*, 515 U.S. 900, 922 (1995).] . . . .

. . . . The judicial power has always been understood to provide the people with a neutral arbiter who bears the responsibility and duty to "expound and interpret" the governing law, not just the power to say

48 See, *e.g.*, § 706(2)(A) (arbitrary and capricious, abuse of discretion); § 706(2)(E) (substantial evidence); see also *Universal Camera Corp. v. NLRB*, 340 U.S. 474, 482, n. 14 (1951) (noting that as originally proposed, the APA's judicial review provision would have included an explicit requirement for courts to accord "due weight" to "the experience, technical competence, specialized knowledge, and legislative policy of the agency involved as well as the discretionary authority conferred upon it" (internal quotation marks omitted)).

whether *someone else's* interpretation, let alone the interpretation of a self-interested political actor, is "reasonable."

To be sure, it's conceivable that Congress might seek to limit the ability of judges to remedy an adverse agency action. It might, for example, provide that a court shall have power to set aside agency action pursuant to a regulation only if the action was based on an unreasonable interpretation of the regulation. But even assuming the constitutionality of a hypothetical statute like that, *Auer* is different. It does not *limit* the scope of the judicial power; instead, it seeks to *coopt* the judicial power by requiring an Article III judge to decide a case before him according to principles that he believes do not accurately reflect the law. Under *Auer*, a judge is required to lay aside his independent judgment and declare affirmatively that a regulation *means* what the agency *says* it means—and, thus, that the law *is* what the agency *says* it is. Then the judge is compelled to exercise his judicial authority to adjust private rights and obligations based on the agency's (mis)understanding of the law.

. . . .

IV. Policy Arguments

Lacking support elsewhere, Justice Kagan is forced to resort to policy arguments to defend *Auer*. But even the most sensible policy argument would not empower us to ignore the plain language of the APA or the demands of the Constitution. . . . Besides, the policy arguments offered today are not just unpersuasive, they are troubling.

Take the first and boldest offering. Justice Kagan suggests that determining the meaning of a regulation is largely a matter of figuring out what the "person who wrote it . . . intended." *Ante* at 2412. In this way, we're told, a legally binding regulation isn't all that different from "a memo or an e-mail"—if you "[w]ant to know what [it] means," you'd better "[a]sk its author." *Ante* at 2412–2413. But the federal government's substantive rules are not like memos or e-mails; they are binding edicts that carry the force of law for all citizens. And if the rule of law means anything, it means that we are governed by the public meaning of the words found in statutes and regulations, not by their authors' private intentions. . . . If the best reading of the regulation turns out to be something other than what the agency claims to have intended, the agency is free to rewrite the regulation; but its secret intentions are not the law.

Nor does Justice Kagan's account of the interpretive process even wind up supporting *Auer*. If a court's goal in interpreting a regulation really were to determine what its author "intended," *Auer* would be an almost complete mismatch with the goal. Agency personnel change over time, and an agency's policy priorities may shift dramatically from one presidential administration to another. Yet *Auer* tells courts that they must defer to the agency's *current* view of what the regulation ought to mean, which may or may not correspond to the views of those who actually wrote it. If interpreting a regulation really were just like reading an e-mail, *Auer* would be like seeking guidance about the e-mail's meaning, years or decades later, from the latest user of the computer from which the e-mail was sent. We've repeatedly rejected that approach in the context of statutory interpretation. While Members of this Court sometimes disagree about the usefulness of *pre-enactment* legislative history, we all agree that legislators' statements about the meaning of an already-enacted statute are not "a legitimate tool of statutory interpretation," much less a controlling one. [*United States v. Woods*, 571 U.S. 31, 48 (2013).] So why on earth would we give "controlling weight" to an agency's statements about the meaning of an already-promulgated regulation?

Proceeding farther down this doubtful path, Justice Kagan asserts that resolving ambiguities in a regulation "sounds more in policy than in law" and is thus a task more suited to executive officials than judges. *Ante* at 2413. But this claim, too, contradicts a basic premise of our legal order: that we are governed not by the shifting whims of politicians and bureaucrats, but by written laws whose meaning is fixed and ascertainable . . . . [T]he agency's policy judgment has the force of law *only* insofar as it is embodied in the regulatory text. . . .

To be sure, during the period of *Auer*'s ascendancy some suggested that the meaning of written law is always "radically indeterminate" and that judges expounding it are "for the most part, guided by policy—not text."[98] And in an environment like that it was perhaps thought a small step to conclude that, if legal disputes are going to be resolved on political grounds, then they ought to be resolved by real politicians in the executive branch rather than ersatz politicians on the bench. But . . . [a]rguments like these surrendered the judgment embodied in our Constitution and the APA that courts owe the people they serve their independent legal judgment about the law's meaning. Besides, we've long since come to realize that the real cure doesn't lie in turning judges into rubber stamps for politicians, but in redirecting the judge's interpretive task back to its roots, away from open-ended policy appeals and speculation about legislative intentions and toward the traditional tools of interpretation judges have employed for centuries to elucidate the law's original public meaning. . . .

Pursuing a more modest tack, Justice Kagan next suggests that *Auer* is justified by the respect due agencies' "technical" expertise. *Ante* at 2413–2414. . . . [N]o one doubts that courts should pay close attention to an expert agency's views on technical questions in its field. Just as a court "would want to know what John Henry Wigmore said about an issue of evidence law [or] what Arthur Corbin thought about a matter of contract law," so too should courts carefully consider what the Food and Drug Administration thinks about how its prescription drug safety regulations

[98] O'Scannlain, "We Are All Textualists Now": The Legacy of Justice Antonin Scalia, 91 St. John's L. Rev. 303, 304–305 (2017) (contesting the radical indeterminacy of legal texts).

operate. [Larkin & Slattery, *supra*, 42 Harv. J. L. & Pub. Pol'y at 647.] The fact remains, however, that even agency experts "can be wrong . . . ." [*Ibid.*] *Skidmore* and the traditional approach it embodied recognized both of these facts of life long ago, explaining that, while courts should of course afford respectful consideration to the expert agency's views, they must remain open to competing expert and other evidence supplied in an adversarial setting. Respect for an agency's technical expertise demands no more.

Justice Kagan's final policy argument is that *Auer* promotes "consistency" and "uniformity" in the interpretation of regulations. *Ante* at 2413–2414. If we let courts decide what regulations mean, she warns, they might disagree, and it might take some time for higher courts to resolve those disagreements. But consistency and uniformity are hardly grounds on which *Auer*'s advocates should wish to fight. The judicial process is how we settle disputes about the meaning of written law, and our judicial system is more than capable of producing a single, uniform, and stable interpretation that will last until the regulation is amended or repealed. Meanwhile, under *Auer* courts often disagree about whether deference is warranted, ... and a regulation's "meaning" can be transformed with the stroke of a pen any time there is a new presidential administration. "Consistency," "uniformity," and stability in the law are hardly among *Auer*'s crowning achievements.

V. *Stare Decisis*

[Part V argued that the doctrine of *stare decisis* did not really support the majority's decision (which Justice Gorsuch cast as reshaping *Auer*). Part V also argued that *stare decisis* would not prevent the Court from overruling *Auer* altogether. Characterizing the *Auer* doctrine as being about "interpretive methodology" rather than the meaning of a particular law, Justice Gorsuch began by questioning "whether *stare decisis* should apply here at all." In any event, he argued that "our past expressions of support for *Auer* deference . . . certainly are not entitled . . . to the special, heightened form of *stare decisis* we reserve for narrow statutory decisions." Applying what he called "standard *stare decisis* considerations," Justice Gorsuch argued that the Court could properly overrule *Auer* because it was wrong, had proved unworkable, was "out of step with how courts normally interpret written laws," had greater potential to cause harm because of "the explosive growth of the administrative state over the last half-century," and had not itself generated reliance interests. In response to Justice Kagan's concern that overruling *Auer* would destabilize all precedents that had applied *Auer* deference, Justice Gorsuch observed that past decisions about the meaning of particular regulations "might retain *stare decisis* effect even if the Court announced that it would no longer adhere to *Auer*'s interpretive methodology."]

. . . .

■ [*JUSTICE KAVANAUGH, joined by JUSTICE ALITO, submitted a brief opinion of his own concurring in the judgment. In essence, Justice Kavanaugh's opinion agreed with the two points made by Chief Justice Roberts. Unlike Chief Justice Roberts, though, Justice Kavanaugh did not join any of the majority opinion.*]

NOTES AND QUESTIONS

1. Although *Kisor* was specifically about *Auer* deference, many of the statements in Part II.B of Justice Kagan's opinion seem relevant to *Chevron* as well as to *Auer*. Even if both doctrines continue to survive, the current Supreme Court is unlikely to regard either doctrine as a blank check for agencies to adopt strained readings of either statutes or regulations.

To begin with, Justice Kagan said that courts should not defer to an agency's interpretation of its own regulation unless the regulation is "genuinely ambiguous, even after a court has resorted to all the standard tools of interpretation." *Id.* at 2414. As Justice Kagan noted, this requirement for *Auer* deference mirrors Step One of the *Chevron* framework. *See id.* at 2415 (observing in a parenthetical that *Chevron* had "adopt[ed] the same approach for ambiguous statutes"). In both contexts, moreover, Justice Kagan suggested that courts should not be too quick to "wave the ambiguity flag." In particular, a court should not conclude that a regulation is "genuinely ambiguous" just because it is "impenetrable on first read" and interpreting it requires hard work. *See id.* at 2415. According to Justice Kagan, when courts " 'carefully consider[ ]' the text, structure, history, and purpose of a regulation," they "will resolve many seeming ambiguities . . . without resort to *Auer* deference." *Id.* (quoting Pauley v. BethEnergy Mines, Inc., 501 U.S. 680, 707 (1991) (Scalia, J., dissenting)).

Just as the requirement of "genuine ambiguity" is analogous to Step One of the *Chevron* framework, what Justice Kagan said next is analogous to Step Two. She noted that even if a regulation is "genuinely ambiguous," courts should still use their standard tools of interpretation to identify what she called "the outer bounds of permissible interpretation." *Id.* at 2416. In her words, a court will accept the relevant agency's position about the meaning of a regulation only if the agency's position "come[s] within the zone of ambiguity the court has identified after employing all its interpretive tools." *Id.* Again, she presumably would say the same about Step Two of the *Chevron* framework.

2. While there are obvious parallels between the requirements for *Auer* deference and Steps One and Two of the *Chevron* framework, some differences crept in at Step Zero. Ever since *Mead*, the Supreme Court has indicated that for an agency's interpretation of a statute to trigger the *Chevron* framework, it is not enough that "Congress delegated authority to the agency generally to make rules carrying the force of law"; in addition, the agency must have promulgated its interpretation "in the exercise of that authority." *United States v. Mead Corp.*, 533 U.S. 218, 226–27 (2001). Writing in dissent in *Mead*, Justice Scalia criticized the latter requirement; in his view, any statement by the agency that is "authoritative" (in the sense that it "represents the official position of the agency") should potentially be eligible for *Chevron* deference, even if the agency did not adopt the position in connection with taking action that has the force of law. *Id.* at 257 (Scalia, J., dissenting); *see also id.* at 259 n.6 (indicating that to be "authoritative" in the relevant sense, an interpretation "must represent the judgment of central agency management, approved at the highest levels," so that "it is truly the agency's considered view" rather than "just the opinions of some underlings"). Justice Scalia's position did not prevail for purposes of *Chevron* deference, but it apparently remains relevant to *Auer* deference. Thus, Part II.B of Justice Kagan's opinion in *Kisor* said that for *Auer* to come into play, the interpretation in question "must be the agency's 'authoritative' or 'official position.' " *Kisor*, 139 S. Ct. at 2416 (quoting *Mead*, 533 U.S. at 257–59 & n.6 (Scalia, J., dissenting)). Likewise, in a portion of the opinion not excerpted above, Justice Kagan indicated that courts could properly give *Auer* deference to so-called "interpretive rules" that an agency issued without going through notice and comment, even though such rules "do *not* have the force of law." *Id.* at 2420 (plurality opinion).

What about statements of the sort that had been at issue in *Auer* itself—statements made in an amicus brief filed in the Supreme Court at the Court's invitation? In a footnote, Justice Kagan recognized a "general rule" against deferring to "agency interpretations advanced for the first time in legal briefs." *Id.* at 2417 n.6 (majority opinion). Still, she noted that "we have not entirely foreclosed that practice," and she cited *Auer* as an example. *Id.*

How should one decide whether the amicus brief that the United States submitted in *Auer* was an "authoritative" statement of the relevant agency's "official position"? Most federal agencies are not authorized to conduct litigation in court on their own behalf; instead, the Department of Justice handles the case. *See* 28 U.S.C. § 516 ("Except as otherwise authorized by law, the conduct of litigation in which the United States, an agency, or officer thereof is a party, or is interested, . . . is reserved to officers of the Department of Justice, under the direction of the Attorney General."). That is especially true with respect to cases in the Supreme Court. *See* Anne Joseph O'Connell, *Bureaucracy at the Boundary*, 162 U. PA. L. REV. 841, 920–21 (2014) (noting that even when Congress gives agencies independent litigating authority, the relevant statutes "[u]sually . . . restrict such authority to actions in the lower courts and give power to the Solicitor General at the highest level of litigation"); *see also* Margaret H. Lemos, *The Solicitor General as Mediator Between Court and Agency*, 2009 MICH. ST. L. REV. 185, 187 ("The Solicitor General controls virtually all litigation on behalf of the

United States in the Supreme Court."). In practice, when the Department of Justice files a brief in the Supreme Court in a case involving an agency, the brief often is a joint product of lawyers in the agency and lawyers in the Department of Justice, and the names of both sets of lawyers appear on the brief. If an agency's lawyers vehemently disagreed with a position that the Department of Justice insisted on taking in the brief, then they might not allow their names to be listed on the brief. Still, "an agency's decision to join the [Solicitor General's] brief is at best a rough proxy for agreement with the arguments presented there." *Id.* at 200; *see also id.* at 223 ("My study of the briefs filed in agency cases suggests that the SG tweaks the arguments the Court hears from the government in a substantial percentage of such cases.").

In *Auer*, the government's amicus brief was signed jointly by lawyers from the Department of Justice (including the Solicitor General) and lawyers from the Department of Labor (the agency whose regulation was at issue). To whatever extent an agency's lawyers are on board for a brief's arguments, though, courts are unlikely to know whether the head of the agency is also on board, or what process was used within the agency to sign off on the brief. Should courts assume that the positions taken in such briefs "emanate from those actors . . . [who are] understood to make authoritative policy [for the agency] in the relevant context," and that those positions were adopted through the vehicles that the relevant actors are understood to use for policymaking? *See Kisor*, 139 S. Ct. at 2416.

3. If the House and the Senate were to submit a joint amicus brief about the proper interpretation of a federal statute, courts probably would not give the brief much deference. While courts would consider the arguments in the brief, courts would not think that the brief deserved special weight simply because of its source. Does an agency's interpretation of its regulations deserve more deference than Congress's interpretation of its statutes?

4. In *Kisor*, Justice Kagan treated the interpretation of written laws as being partly law and partly policy. She suggested that courts do not owe deference to agencies with respect to the law part—the application of what she called "the 'traditional tools' of construction." *Kisor*, 139 S. Ct. at 2415 (quoting *Chevron*, 467 U.S. at 843 n.9). To the extent that a legal provision is "genuinely ambiguous"—that is, to the extent that the traditional tools of construction do not yield a single right answer to a particular question—she suggested that policy considerations come into play in choosing among the permissible readings, and that agencies often are better situated than courts to make those kinds of policy choices. In her telling, that is "the core theory of *Auer* deference": in the process of interpretation, "sometimes the law runs out" without identifying a single right answer, "and policy-laden choice is what is left over." *Id.*; *see also id.* ("[O]nly when that legal toolkit is empty and the interpretive question still has no single right answer can a judge conclude that [the question] is 'more [one] of policy than of law.' " (quoting *Pauley*, 501 U.S. at 696)).

This account of *Auer* deference dovetails with at least one understanding of *Chevron* deference. If you think that ascribing a single meaning to a written law is just a matter of normal legal interpretation, then you might well think that it would be strange for courts to defer to agencies about the right answer. But to the extent that choosing among possible interpretations is more a matter of policy than of law, you could plausibly think that courts should defer to agencies, either on the theory that agencies have more relevant expertise or on the theory that agencies are more politically accountable.

Some of Justice Kagan's specific examples got at the same point. Take the first bullet point in Part II.A, involving a regulation that the Department of Justice promulgated to help implement the public-accommodations provisions in the Americans with Disabilities Act. The regulation required theaters and stadiums to have wheelchair areas that provide "lines of sight comparable to those for members of the general public." *Id.* at 2410 (quoting 28 C.F.R. pt. 36, app. A, p. 563 (1996)). That regulation generated the following question: "Must the Washington Wizards construct wheelchair seating to offer lines of sight over spectators when they rise to their feet? Or is it enough that the facility offers comparable views so long as everyone remains seated?" *Id.*

Justice Kagan implied that when an interpreter tried to decide what the regulation required on this point, the interpreter would need to conduct some sort of cost-benefit analysis. In particular, the interpreter would want to know how much it would cost for the stadium owner to provide lines of sight that work even when the spectators in front are standing, "and is the viewing value received worth the added expense?" *Id.* at 2413. As Justice Kagan noted, "That cost-benefit calculation . . . sounds more in policy than in law."

But was Justice Kagan correct that proper interpretation of the regulation requires this sort of policy analysis? The less you think that cost-benefit analysis should inform what interpreters take the word "comparable" to mean, the less space you might see for *Auer* deference.

Justice Kagan acknowledged that *Auer* deference operates only within the bounds identified by the traditional tools of construction. But to the extent that judges disagree about how to apply those tools, they may disagree about how often questions about the meaning of a statute or regulation will require the interpreter to make policy choices (as in Justice Kagan's first example) or to decide how best to promote the purpose behind the statute or regulation (as in Justice Kagan's second example). If you think that interpretation rarely boils down to those kinds of policy judgments, you might think that there are relatively few circumstances in which either *Chevron* deference or *Auer* deference would be desirable. You might go on to argue that the Court's doctrines should not accommodate those unusual circumstances; if the escape hatch of deference is available, perhaps judges will use it more than they should. On the other hand, if you think that policy judgments are necessary more frequently, then you might be inclined to retain *Chevron* and *Auer* for use in the kinds of circumstances that Justice Kagan identified.

CHAPTER 6

FEDERAL STATUTES AND THE FEDERAL STRUCTURE

Many of the questions that we have covered so far can come up whether one is interpreting a federal statute or a state statute. Of course, the answers might not always be the same. The meaning of state statutes is a matter of state law, and the highest court of each state normally gets the last word about the meaning of its own state's statutes. To the extent that other courts are trying to predict what a state's highest court would say on that topic, moreover, they are likely to try to follow the interpretive methods and principles favored by that court, which will not necessarily be identical to the interpretive methods and principles that a majority of the United States Supreme Court would apply when interpreting a federal statute.[1] Still, most of the *issues* that we have considered so far are not specific to the interpretation of federal statutes.

This chapter is different. It canvasses some questions that relate to the structure of American federalism and that therefore are about the interpretation or operation of federal statutes in particular.

A. A SAMPLING OF FEDERALISM CANONS

1. PRESERVING "THE FEDERAL-STATE BALANCE"

The Supreme Court has articulated a set of interrelated canons that address the relationship between federal statutes and state sovereignty and that discourage interpreters from attributing certain directives to Congress. In *United States v. Bass*, 404 U.S. 336 (1971), the Supreme Court expressed the following guiding principle: "[U]nless Congress conveys its purpose clearly, it will not be deemed to have significantly changed the federal-state balance." *Id.* at 349.

In *Bass* itself, the Supreme Court was addressing the scope of a federal statute that made it a federal crime for a convicted felon to "receive[ ], possess[ ], or transport[ ] in commerce or affecting commerce . . . any firearm." *See* Omnibus Crime Control and Safe Streets Act of 1968, Pub. L. 90–351, § 1202(a), 82 Stat. 197, 236; *see also id.* § 1202(c)(1), 82 Stat. at 237 (defining "commerce" in terms that focused on interstate and foreign commerce). As the Court noted (and as we saw in Chapter 2's discussion of the last-antecedent rule), the syntax of this provision was ambiguous: did the phrase "in commerce or affecting

[1] Apart from differences in interpretive methods and principles, there can also be differences in the available resources. For instance, even if the courts of a particular state would be open to the use of legislative history in interpreting state statutes, some state legislatures do not make much legislative history publicly available.

commerce" go only with "transports," or also with "receives" and "possesses"? Nowadays, the Supreme Court probably would say that the Constitution does not give Congress the *power* to forbid simple possession of firearms without any nexus to interstate or foreign commerce. *See* United States v. Lopez, 514 U.S. 549 (1995). Anticipating this issue, the lower court in *Bass* had invoked the canon that favors avoiding constitutional doubts. *See* United States v. Bass, 434 F.2d 1296, 1299–1301 (2d Cir. 1970). When the case reached the Supreme Court, though, Justice Marshall's majority opinion used other tools to resolve the ambiguity. Among other things, Justice Marshall observed that reading the statute to make mere possession of firearms a federal crime (without any connection to interstate commerce) "would mark a major inroad into a domain traditionally left to the States." *Bass*, 404 U.S. at 339. Rather than read the statute "to effect a significant change in the sensitive relation between federal and state criminal jurisdiction," *id.* at 349, the majority assumed that Congress had intended the commerce element to go with all three verbs, thereby "preserv[ing] as an element of all the offenses a requirement suited to federal criminal jurisdiction alone." *Id.* at 350–51.[2]

In the following case, Chief Justice Roberts's majority opinion again invoked "basic principles of federalism" to support reading a federal criminal statute narrowly. As you will see, though, the unusual context of the statute (which Congress enacted to implement a treaty) made the Court's use of those principles questionable.

Bond v. United States

572 U.S. 844 (2014)

■ *CHIEF JUSTICE ROBERTS delivered the opinion of the Court:*

. . . .

I

A

In 1997, the President of the United States, upon the advice and consent of the Senate, ratified the Convention on the Prohibition of the Development, Production, Stockpiling, and Use of Chemical Weapons and on Their Destruction. S. Treaty Doc. No. 103–21, 1974 U.N.T.S. 317. The nations that ratified the Convention (State Parties) had bold

---

[2] Still, the Court did not interpret the commerce element to be particularly demanding (at least in the context of the "receiv[ing]" offense). According to the Court, the prosecution could establish that the receipt of a firearm was "in commerce or affecting commerce" simply by "demonstrat[ing] that the firearm received has previously traveled in interstate commerce." *Id.* at 350; *see also id.* at 350–51 ("This is not the narrowest possible reading of the statute, but canons of clear statement and strict construction do 'not mean that every criminal statute must be given the narrowest possible meaning in complete disregard of the purpose of the legislature.' . . . [G]iven the evils that prompted the statute and the basic legislative purpose of restricting the firearm-related activity of convicted felons, the readings we give to the commerce requirement, although not all narrow, are appropriate." (quoting United States v. Bramblett, 348 U.S. 503, 510 (1955))).

aspirations for it: "general and complete disarmament under strict and effective international control, including the prohibition and elimination of all types of weapons of mass destruction." Convention Preamble, *ibid.* This purpose traces its origin to World War I, when "[o]ver a million casualties, up to 100,000 of them fatal, are estimated to have been caused by chemicals . . . , a large part following the introduction of mustard gas in 1917." Kenyon, Why We Need a Chemical Weapons Convention and an OPCW, in The Creation of the Organisation for the Prohibition of Chemical Weapons 1, 4 (I. Kenyon & D. Feakes eds. 2007) (Kenyon & Feakes). The atrocities of that war led the community of nations to adopt the 1925 Geneva Protocol, which prohibited the use of chemicals as a method of warfare. *Id.* at 5.

Up to the 1990s, however, chemical weapons remained in use both in and out of wartime, with devastating consequences. Iraq's use of nerve agents and mustard gas during its war with Iran in the 1980s contributed to international support for a renewed, more effective chemical weapons ban. *Id.* at 6, 10–11. In 1994 and 1995, long-held fears of the use of chemical weapons by terrorists were realized when Japanese extremists carried out two attacks using sarin gas. *Id.* at 6. The Convention was conceived as an effort to update the Geneva Protocol's protections and to expand the prohibition on chemical weapons beyond state actors in wartime. Convention Preamble, 1974 U.N.T.S. 318 (the State Parties are "[d]etermined for the sake of all mankind, to exclude completely the possibility of the use of chemical weapons, . . . thereby complementing the obligations assumed under the Geneva Protocol of 1925"). The Convention aimed to achieve that objective by prohibiting the development, stockpiling, or use of chemical weapons by any State Party or person within a State Party's jurisdiction. Arts. I, II, VII. It also established an elaborate reporting process requiring State Parties to destroy chemical weapons under their control and submit to inspection and monitoring by an international organization based in The Hague, Netherlands. Arts. VIII, IX.

. . . . [Under the Convention,] "Chemical Weapons" are defined in relevant part as "[t]oxic chemicals and their precursors, except where intended for purposes not prohibited under this Convention, as long as the types and quantities are consistent with such purposes." Art. II(1)(a) . . . . "Toxic Chemical," in turn, is defined as "Any chemical which through its chemical action on life processes can cause death, temporary incapacitation or permanent harm to humans or animals. This includes all such chemicals, regardless of their origin or of their method of production, and regardless of whether they are produced in facilities, in munitions or elsewhere." Art. II(2) . . . . "Purposes Not Prohibited Under this Convention" means "[i]ndustrial, agricultural, research, medical, pharmaceutical or other peaceful purposes," Art. II(9)(a), . . . and other specific purposes not at issue here, Arts. II(9)(b)–(d).

Although the Convention is a binding international agreement, it is "not self-executing." W. Krutzsch & R. Trapp, A Commentary on the Chemical Weapons Convention 109 (1994). That is, the Convention creates obligations only for State Parties and "does not by itself give rise to domestically enforceable federal law" absent "implementing legislation passed by Congress." *Medellín v. Texas*, 552 U.S. 491, 505, n. 2 (2008). It instead provides that "[e]ach State Party shall, in accordance with its constitutional processes, adopt the necessary measures to implement its obligations under this Convention." Art. VII(1), 1974 U.N.T.S. 331. "In particular," each State Party shall "[p]rohibit natural and legal persons anywhere . . . under its jurisdiction . . . from undertaking any activity prohibited to a State Party under this Convention, including enacting penal legislation with respect to such activity." Art. VII(1)(a), *id.* at 331–332.

Congress gave the Convention domestic effect in 1998 when it passed the Chemical Weapons Convention Implementation Act. See 112 Stat. 2681–856. The Act closely tracks the text of the treaty: It forbids any person knowingly "to develop, produce, otherwise acquire, transfer directly or indirectly, receive, stockpile, retain, own, possess, or use, or threaten to use, any chemical weapon." 18 U.S.C. § 229(a)(1). It defines "chemical weapon" in relevant part as "[a] toxic chemical and its precursors, except where intended for a purpose not prohibited under this chapter as long as the type and quantity is consistent with such a purpose." § 229F(1)(A). "Toxic chemical," in turn, is defined in general as "any chemical which through its chemical action on life processes can cause death, temporary incapacitation or permanent harm to humans or animals. The term includes all such chemicals, regardless of their origin or of their method of production, and regardless of whether they are produced in facilities, in munitions or elsewhere." § 229F(8)(A). Finally, "purposes not prohibited by this chapter" is defined as "[a]ny peaceful purpose related to an industrial, agricultural, research, medical, or pharmaceutical activity or other activity," and other specific purposes. § 229F(7). A person who violates section 229 may be subject to severe punishment: imprisonment "for any term of years," or if a victim's death results, the death penalty or imprisonment "for life." § 229A(a).

B

Petitioner Carol Anne Bond is a microbiologist from Lansdale, Pennsylvania. In 2006, Bond's closest friend, Myrlinda Haynes, announced that she was pregnant. When Bond discovered that her husband was the child's father, she sought revenge against Haynes. Bond stole a quantity of 10-chloro-10H-phenoxarsine (an arsenic-based compound) from her employer, a chemical manufacturer. She also ordered a vial of potassium dichromate (a chemical commonly used in printing photographs or cleaning laboratory equipment) on Amazon.com. Both chemicals are toxic to humans and, in high enough doses, potentially lethal. It is undisputed, however, that Bond did not intend to kill Haynes. She instead hoped that Haynes would touch the chemicals and develop an uncomfortable rash.

Between November 2006 and June 2007, Bond went to Haynes's home on at least 24 occasions and spread the chemicals on her car door, mailbox, and door knob. These attempted assaults were almost entirely unsuccessful. The chemicals that Bond used are easy to see, and Haynes was able to avoid them all but once. On that occasion, Haynes suffered a minor chemical burn on her thumb, which she treated by rinsing with water. Haynes repeatedly called the local police to report the suspicious substances, but they took no action. When Haynes found powder on her mailbox, she called the police again, who told her to call the post office. Haynes did so, and postal inspectors placed surveillance cameras around her home. The cameras caught Bond opening Haynes's mailbox, stealing an envelope, and stuffing potassium dichromate inside the muffler of Haynes's car.

Federal prosecutors naturally charged Bond with two counts of mail theft, in violation of 18 U.S.C. § 1708. More surprising, they also charged her with two counts of possessing and using a chemical weapon, in violation of section 229(a). Bond moved to dismiss the chemical weapon counts on the ground that section 229 exceeded Congress's enumerated powers and invaded powers reserved to the States by the Tenth Amendment. The District Court denied Bond's motion. She then entered a conditional guilty plea that reserved her right to appeal. The District Court sentenced Bond to six years in federal prison plus five years of supervised release, and ordered her to pay a $2,000 fine and $9,902.79 in restitution.

Bond appealed, raising a Tenth Amendment challenge to her conviction. The Government contended that Bond lacked standing to bring such a challenge. The Court of Appeals for the Third Circuit agreed. We granted certiorari, the Government confessed error, and we reversed. . . . We "expresse[d] no view on the merits" of Bond's constitutional challenge. [*Bond v. United States*, 564 U.S. 211, 226 (2011) (*Bond I*).]

On remand, Bond renewed her constitutional argument. She also argued that section 229 does not reach her conduct because the statute's exception for the use of chemicals for "peaceful purposes" should be understood in contradistinction to the "warlike" activities that the Convention was primarily designed to prohibit. Bond argued that her conduct, though reprehensible, was not at all "warlike." The Court of Appeals rejected this argument. 681 F.3d 149 (CA3 2012). The court acknowledged that the Government's reading of section 229 would render the statute "striking" in its "breadth" and turn every "kitchen cupboard and cleaning cabinet in America into a potential chemical weapons cache." *Id.* at 154, n. 7. But the court nevertheless held that Bond's use of " 'highly toxic chemicals with the intent of harming Haynes' can hardly be characterized as 'peaceful' under that word's commonly understood meaning." *Id.* at 154 (citation omitted).

The Third Circuit also rejected Bond's constitutional challenge to her conviction, holding that section 229 was "necessary and proper to carry the Convention into effect." *Id.* at 162. The Court of Appeals relied on this Court's opinion in *Missouri v. Holland*, 252 U.S. 416 (1920), which stated that "[i]f the treaty is valid there can be no dispute about the validity of the statute" that implements it "as a necessary and proper means to execute the powers of the Government," *id.* at 432.

We again granted certiorari . . . .

II

In our federal system, the National Government possesses only limited powers; the States and the people retain the remainder. The States have broad authority to enact legislation for the public good—what we have often called a "police power." *United States v. Lopez*, 514 U.S. 549, 567 (1995). The Federal Government, by contrast, has no such authority and "can exercise only the powers granted to it," *McCulloch v. Maryland*, 4 Wheat. 316, 405 (1819), including the power to make "all Laws which shall be necessary and proper for carrying into Execution" the enumerated powers, U.S. Const., Art. I, § 8, cl. 18. . . .

The Government frequently defends federal criminal legislation on the ground that the legislation is authorized pursuant to Congress's power to regulate interstate commerce. In this case, however, the Court of Appeals held that the Government had explicitly disavowed that argument before the District Court. 681 F.3d at 151, n. 1. As a result, in this Court the parties have devoted significant effort to arguing whether section 229, as applied to Bond's offense, is a necessary and proper means of executing the National Government's power to make treaties. U.S. Const., Art. II, § 2, cl. 2. . . .

Notwithstanding this debate, it is "a well-established principle governing the prudent exercise of this Court's jurisdiction that normally the Court will not decide a constitutional question if there is some other ground upon which to dispose of the case." *Escambia County v. McMillan*, 466 U.S. 48, 51 (1984) (*per curiam*); see also *Ashwander v. TVA*, 297 U.S. 288, 347 (1936) (Brandeis, J., concurring). Bond argues that section 229 does not cover her conduct. So we consider that argument first.

III

Section 229 exists to implement the Convention, so we begin with that international agreement. As explained, the Convention's drafters intended for it to be a comprehensive ban on chemical weapons. But even with its broadly worded definitions, we have doubts that a treaty about *chemical weapons* has anything to do with Bond's conduct. The Convention, a product of years of worldwide study, analysis, and multinational negotiation, arose in response to war crimes and acts of terrorism. See Kenyon & Feakes 6. There is no reason to think the sovereign nations that ratified the Convention were interested in anything like Bond's common law assault.

Even if the treaty does reach that far, nothing prevents Congress from implementing the Convention in the same manner it legislates with respect to innumerable other matters—observing the Constitution's division of responsibility between sovereigns and leaving the prosecution of purely local crimes to the States. The Convention, after all, is agnostic between enforcement at the state versus federal level: It provides that "[e]ach State Party shall, *in accordance with its constitutional processes*, adopt the necessary measures to implement its obligations under this Convention." Art. VII(1), 1974 U.N.T.S. 331 (emphasis added) . . . .

Fortunately, we have no need to interpret the scope of the Convention in this case. Bond was prosecuted under section 229, and the statute—unlike the Convention—must be read consistent with principles of federalism inherent in our constitutional structure.

A

In the Government's view, the conclusion that Bond "knowingly" "use[d]" a "chemical weapon" in violation of section 229(a) is simple: The chemicals that Bond placed on Haynes's home and car are "toxic chemical[s]" as defined by the statute, and Bond's attempt to assault Haynes was not a "peaceful purpose." §§ 229F(1), (8), (7). The problem with this interpretation is that it would "dramatically intrude[ ] upon traditional state criminal jurisdiction," and we avoid reading statutes to have such reach in the absence of a clear indication that they do. *United States v. Bass*, 404 U.S. 336, 350 (1971).

Part of a fair reading of statutory text is recognizing that "Congress legislates against the backdrop" of certain unexpressed presumptions. *EEOC v. Arabian American Oil Co.*, 499 U.S. 244, 248 (1991). As Justice Frankfurter put it in his famous essay on statutory interpretation, correctly reading a statute "demands awareness of certain presuppositions." Some Reflections on the Reading of Statutes, 47 Colum. L. Rev. 527, 537 (1947). For example, we presume that a criminal statute derived from the common law carries with it the requirement of a culpable mental state—even if no such limitation appears in the text—unless it is clear that the Legislature intended to impose strict liability. *United States v. United States Gypsum Co.*, 438 U.S. 422, 437 (1978). To take another example, we presume, absent a clear statement from Congress, that federal statutes do not apply outside the United States. *Morrison v. National Australia Bank Ltd.*, 561 U.S. 247, 255 (2010). . . . The notion that some things "go without saying" applies to legislation just as it does to everyday life.

Among the background principles of construction that our cases have recognized are those grounded in the relationship between the Federal Government and the States under our Constitution. It has long been settled, for example, that we presume federal statutes do not abrogate state sovereign immunity, *Atascadero State Hospital v. Scanlon*, 473 U.S. 234, 243 (1985), impose obligations on the States pursuant to section 5 of the Fourteenth Amendment, *Pennhurst State School and Hospital v. Halderman*, 451 U.S. 1, 16–17 (1981), or preempt state law, *Rice v. Santa Fe Elevator Corp.*, 331 U.S. 218, 230 (1947).

Closely related to these is the well-established principle that " 'it is incumbent upon the federal courts to be certain of Congress' intent before finding that federal law overrides' " the "usual constitutional balance of federal and state powers." *Gregory v. Ashcroft*, 501 U.S. 452, 460 (1991) (quoting *Atascadero*, [473 U.S.] at 243). To quote Frankfurter again, if the Federal Government would " 'radically readjust[ ] the balance of state and national authority, those charged with the duty of legislating [must be] reasonably explicit' " about it. *BFP v. Resolution Trust Corporation*, 511 U.S. 531, 544 (1994) (quoting Some Reflections, *supra*, at 539–540; second alteration in original). Or as explained by Justice Marshall, when legislation "affect[s] the federal balance, the requirement of clear statement assures that the legislature has in fact faced, and intended to bring into issue, the critical matters involved in the judicial decision." *Bass*, [404 U.S.] at 349.

We have applied this background principle when construing federal statutes that touched on several areas of traditional state responsibility. See *Gregory*, [501 U.S.] at 460 (qualifications for state officers); *BFP*, [511 U.S.] at 544 (titles to real estate); *Solid Waste Agency of Northern Cook Cty. v. Army Corps of Engineers*, 531 U.S. 159, 174 (2001) (land and water use). Perhaps the clearest example of traditional state authority is the punishment of local criminal activity. *United States v. Morrison*, 529 U.S. 598, 618 (2000). Thus, "we will not be quick to assume that Congress has meant to effect a significant change in the sensitive relation between federal and state criminal jurisdiction." *Bass*, 404 U.S. at 349.

In *Bass*, we interpreted a statute that prohibited any convicted felon from " 'receiv[ing], possess[ing], or transport[ing] in commerce or affecting commerce . . . any firearm.' " *Id.* at 337. The Government argued that the statute barred felons from possessing *all* firearms and that it was not necessary to demonstrate a connection to interstate commerce. We rejected that reading, which would "render[ ] traditionally local criminal conduct a matter for federal enforcement and would also involve a substantial extension of federal police resources." *Id.* at 350. We instead read the statute more narrowly to require proof of a connection to interstate commerce in every case, thereby "preserv[ing] as an element of all the offenses a requirement suited to federal criminal jurisdiction alone." *Id.* at 351.

Similarly, in *Jones v. United States*, 529 U.S. 848, 850 (2000), we confronted the question whether the federal arson statute, which prohibited burning " 'any . . . property used in interstate or foreign commerce or in any activity affecting interstate or foreign commerce,' " reached an owner-occupied private residence. Once again we rejected the

Government's "expansive interpretation," under which "hardly a building in the land would fall outside the federal statute's domain." *Id.* at 857. We instead held that the statute was "most sensibly read" more narrowly to reach only buildings used in "active employment for commercial purposes." *Id.* at 855. We noted that "arson is a paradigmatic common-law state crime," *id.* at 858, and that the Government's proposed broad reading would " 'significantly change[ ] the federal-state balance,' " *ibid.* (quoting *Bass*, 404 U.S. at 349), "mak[ing] virtually every arson in the country a federal offense," 529 U.S. at 859.

These precedents make clear that it is appropriate to refer to basic principles of federalism embodied in the Constitution to resolve ambiguity in a federal statute. In this case, the ambiguity derives from the improbably broad reach of the key statutory definition given the term—"chemical weapon"—being defined; the deeply serious consequences of adopting such a boundless reading; and the lack of any apparent need to do so in light of the context from which the statute arose—a treaty about chemical warfare and terrorism. We conclude that, in this curious case, we can insist on a clear indication that Congress meant to reach purely local crimes, before interpreting the statute's expansive language in a way that intrudes on the police power of the States. See *Bass*, [404 U.S.] at 349.

B

We do not find any such clear indication in section 229. "Chemical weapon" is the key term that defines the statute's reach, and it is defined extremely broadly. But that general definition does not constitute a clear statement that Congress meant the statute to reach local criminal conduct.

In fact, a fair reading of section 229 suggests that it does not have as expansive a scope as might at first appear. To begin, as a matter of natural meaning, an educated user of English would not describe Bond's crime as involving a "chemical weapon." Saying that a person "used a chemical weapon" conveys a very different idea than saying the person "used a chemical in a way that caused some harm." The natural meaning of "chemical weapon" takes account of both the particular chemicals that the defendant used and the circumstances in which she used them.

When used in the manner here, the chemicals in this case are not of the sort that an ordinary person would associate with instruments of chemical warfare. The substances that Bond used bear little resemblance to the deadly toxins that are "of particular danger to the objectives of the Convention." Why We Need a Chemical Weapons Convention and an OPCW, in Kenyon & Feakes 17 (describing the Convention's Annex on Chemicals, a nonexhaustive list of covered substances that are subject to special regulation). More to the point, the use of something as a "weapon" typically connotes "[a]n instrument of offensive or defensive combat," Webster's Third New International Dictionary 2589 (2002), or "[a]n instrument of attack or defense in combat, as a gun, missile, or sword,"

American Heritage Dictionary 2022 (3d ed. 1992). But no speaker in natural parlance would describe Bond's feud-driven act of spreading irritating chemicals on Haynes's door knob and mailbox as "combat." Nor do the other circumstances of Bond's offense—an act of revenge born of romantic jealousy, meant to cause discomfort, that produced nothing more than a minor thumb burn—suggest that a chemical weapon was deployed in Norristown, Pennsylvania. Potassium dichromate and 10-chloro-10H-phenoxarsine might be chemical weapons if used, say, to poison a city's water supply. But Bond's crime is worlds apart from such hypotheticals, and covering it would give the statute a reach exceeding the ordinary meaning of the words Congress wrote.

In settling on a fair reading of a statute, it is not unusual to consider the ordinary meaning of a defined term, particularly when there is dissonance between that ordinary meaning and the reach of the definition. In *Johnson v. United States*, 559 U.S. 133, 136 (2010), for example, we considered the statutory term " 'violent felony,' " which the Armed Career Criminal Act defined in relevant part as an offense that " 'has as an element the use . . . of physical force against the person of another.' " Although "physical force against . . . another" might have meant *any* force, however slight, we thought it "clear that in the context of a statutory definition of '*violent* felony,' the phrase 'physical force' means *violent* force—that is, force capable of causing physical pain or injury to another person." *Id.* at 140. The ordinary meaning of "chemical weapon" plays a similar limiting role here.

The Government would have us brush aside the ordinary meaning and adopt a reading of section 229 that would sweep in everything from the detergent under the kitchen sink to the stain remover in the laundry room. Yet no one would ordinarily describe those substances as "chemical weapons." The Government responds that because Bond used "specialized, highly toxic" (though legal) chemicals, "this case presents no occasion to address whether Congress intended [section 229] to apply to common household substances." Brief for United States 13, n. 3. That the statute *would* apply so broadly, however, is the inescapable conclusion of the Government's position: Any parent would be guilty of a serious federal offense—possession of a chemical weapon—when, exasperated by the children's repeated failure to clean the goldfish tank, he considers poisoning the fish with a few drops of vinegar. We are reluctant to ignore the ordinary meaning of "chemical weapon" when doing so would transform a statute passed to implement the international Convention on Chemical Weapons into one that also makes it a federal offense to poison goldfish. That would not be a "realistic assessment[ ] of congressional intent." *Post* at 872 (Scalia, J., concurring in judgment).

In light of all this, it is fully appropriate to apply the background assumption that Congress normally preserves "the constitutional balance between the National Government and the States." *Bond I*, 564

U.S. at 222. That assumption is grounded in the very structure of the Constitution. . . .

The Government's reading of section 229 would " 'alter sensitive federal-state relationships,' " convert an astonishing amount of "traditionally local criminal conduct" into "a matter for federal enforcement," and "involve a substantial extension of federal police resources." *Bass*, 404 U.S. at 349–350. It would transform the statute from one whose core concerns are acts of war, assassination, and terrorism into a massive federal anti-poisoning regime that reaches the simplest of assaults. As the Government reads section 229, "hardly" a poisoning "in the land would fall outside the federal statute's domain." *Jones*, 529 U.S. at 857. Of course Bond's conduct is serious and unacceptable—and against the laws of Pennsylvania. But the background principle that Congress does not normally intrude upon the police power of the States is critically important. In light of that principle, we are reluctant to conclude that Congress meant to punish Bond's crime with a federal prosecution for a chemical weapons attack.

In fact, with the exception of this unusual case, the Federal Government itself has not looked to section 229 to reach purely local crimes. The Government has identified only a handful of prosecutions that have been brought under this section. Brief in Opposition 27, n. 5. Most of those involved either terrorist plots or the possession of extremely dangerous substances with the potential to cause severe harm to many people. [Citations omitted.] The Federal Government undoubtedly has a substantial interest in enforcing criminal laws against assassination, terrorism, and acts with the potential to cause mass suffering. Those crimes have not traditionally been left predominantly to the States, and nothing we have said here will disrupt the Government's authority to prosecute such offenses.

It is also clear that the laws of the Commonwealth of Pennsylvania (and every other State) are sufficient to prosecute Bond. Pennsylvania has several statutes that would likely cover her assault. See 18 Pa. Cons. Stat. §§ 2701 (2012) (simple assault), 2705 (reckless endangerment), 2709 (harassment). And state authorities regularly enforce these laws in poisoning cases. . . .

The Government objects that Pennsylvania authorities charged Bond with only a minor offense based on her "harassing telephone calls and letters," *Bond I*, 564 U.S. at 214, and declined to prosecute her for assault. But we have traditionally viewed the exercise of state officials' prosecutorial discretion as a valuable feature of our constitutional system. See *Bordenkircher v. Hayes*, 434 U.S. 357, 364 (1978). And nothing in the Convention shows a clear intent to abrogate that feature. . . . Here, in its zeal to prosecute Bond, the Federal Government has "displaced" the "public policy of the Commonwealth of Pennsylvania, enacted in its capacity as sovereign," that Bond does not belong in prison for a chemical weapons offense. *Bond I*, [564 U.S.] at 224; see also *Jones*,

[529 U.S.] at 859 (Stevens, J., concurring) (federal prosecution of a traditionally local crime "illustrates how a criminal law like this may effectively displace a policy choice made by the State").

As we have explained, "Congress has traditionally been reluctant to define as a federal crime conduct readily denounced as criminal by the States." *Bass*, 404 U.S. at 349. There is no clear indication of a contrary approach here. Section 229 implements the Convention, but Bond's crime could hardly be more unlike the uses of mustard gas on the Western Front or nerve agents in the Iran-Iraq war that form the core concerns of that treaty. . . . And there are no apparent interests of the United States Congress or the community of nations in seeing Bond end up in federal prison, rather than dealt with (like virtually all other criminals in Pennsylvania) by the State. The Solicitor General acknowledged as much at oral argument. See Tr. of Oral Arg. 47 ("I don't think anybody would say [that] whether or not Ms. Bond is prosecuted would give rise to an international incident").

This case is unusual, and our analysis is appropriately limited. Our disagreement with our colleagues reduces to whether section 229 is "utterly clear." *Post* at 871 (Scalia, J., concurring in judgment). We think it is not, given that the definition of "chemical weapon" in a particular case can reach beyond any normal notion of such a weapon, that the context from which the statute arose demonstrates a much more limited prohibition was intended, and that the most sweeping reading of the statute would fundamentally upset the Constitution's balance between national and local power. This exceptional convergence of factors gives us serious reason to doubt the Government's expansive reading of section 229, and calls for us to interpret the statute more narrowly.

. . . .

The Convention provides for implementation by each ratifying nation "in accordance with its constitutional processes." Art. VII(1), 1974 U.N.T.S. 331. As James Madison explained, the constitutional process in our "compound republic" keeps power "divided between two distinct governments." The Federalist No. 51, p. 323 (C. Rossiter ed. 1961). If section 229 reached Bond's conduct, it would mark a dramatic departure from that constitutional structure and a serious reallocation of criminal law enforcement authority between the Federal Government and the States. Absent a clear statement of that purpose, we will not presume Congress to have authorized such a stark intrusion into traditional state authority.

The judgment of the Court of Appeals is reversed, and the case is remanded for further proceedings consistent with this opinion.

■ *JUSTICE SCALIA, with whom JUSTICE THOMAS joins, and with whom JUSTICE ALITO joins as to Part I, concurring in the judgment:*

. . . . As sweeping and unsettling as the Chemical Weapons Convention Implementation Act of 1998 may be, it is clear beyond doubt that it covers what Bond did; and we have no authority to amend it. So we are forced to decide—there is no way around it—whether the Act's application to what Bond did was constitutional.

I would hold that it was not, and for that reason would reverse the judgment of the Court of Appeals for the Third Circuit.

I. The Statutory Question

A. Unavoidable Meaning of the Text

.... Applying [the Act's] provisions to this case is hardly complicated. Bond possessed and used "chemical[s] which through [their] chemical action on life processes can cause death, temporary incapacitation or permanent harm." Thus, she possessed "toxic chemicals." [18 U.S.C. § 229F(8)(A).] And, because they were not possessed or used only for a "purpose not prohibited," § 229F(1)(A), they were "chemical weapons." Ergo, Bond violated the Act. . . .

B. The Court's Interpretation

The Court's account of the clear-statement rule reads like a really good lawyer's brief for the wrong side, relying on cases that are *so close* to being on point that someone eager to reach the favored outcome might swallow them. . . . In [*United States v. Bass*, 404 U.S. 336 (1971)], we had to decide whether a statute forbidding " 'receiv[ing], possess[ing], or transport[ing] in commerce or affecting commerce . . . any firearm' " prohibited possessing a gun that lacked any connection to interstate commerce. 404 U.S. at 337–339. Though the Court relied in part on a federalism-inspired interpretive presumption, it did so only *after* it had found, in Part I of the opinion, applying traditional interpretive tools, that the text in question was ambiguous, *id.* at 339–347. Adopting in Part II the narrower of the two possible readings, we said that "*unless Congress conveys its purpose clearly*, it will not be deemed to have significantly changed the federal-state balance." *Id.* at 349 (emphasis added). Had Congress "convey[ed] its purpose clearly" by enacting a clear and even sweeping statute, the presumption would not have applied.

[*Jones v. United States*, 529 U.S. 848 (2000),] is also irrelevant. To determine whether an owner-occupied private residence counted as a " 'property used in interstate or foreign commerce or in any activity affecting interstate or foreign commerce' " under the federal arson statute, [*id.*] at 850–851, our opinion examined *not* the federal-jurisdiction-expanding consequences of answering yes but rather the ordinary meaning of the words—and answered no, *id.* at 855–857. Then, in a separate part of the opinion, we observed that our reading was consistent with the principle that we should adopt a construction that avoids "grave and doubtful constitutional questions," *id.* at 857, and, quoting *Bass*, the principle that Congress must convey its purpose clearly before its laws will be " 'deemed to have significantly changed the federal-state balance,' " 529 U.S. at 858. To say that the best reading of the text conformed to those principles is not to say that those principles can render clear text ambiguous.

The latter is what the Court says today. Inverting *Bass* and *Jones*, it *starts* with the federalism-related consequences of the statute's meaning and reasons backwards, holding that, if the statute has what the Court considers a disruptive effect on the "federal-state balance" of criminal jurisdiction, *ante* at 859, that effect causes the text, even if clear on its face, to be ambiguous. . . . Imagine what future courts can do with that judge-empowering principle: Whatever has improbably broad, deeply serious, and apparently unnecessary consequences . . . *is ambiguous*!

The same skillful use of oh-so-close-to-relevant cases characterizes the Court's *pro forma* attempt to find ambiguity in the text itself, specifically, in the term "[c]hemical weapon." The ordinary meaning of weapon, the Court says, is an instrument of combat, and "no speaker in natural parlance would describe Bond's feud-driven act of spreading irritating chemicals on Haynes's door knob and mailbox as 'combat.'" *Ante* at 861. Undoubtedly so, but undoubtedly beside the point, since the Act supplies its own definition of "chemical weapon," which unquestionably does bring Bond's action within the statutory prohibition. The Court retorts that "it is not unusual to consider the ordinary meaning of a defined term, particularly when there is dissonance between that ordinary meaning and the reach of the definition." *Ibid. So close* to true! What is "not unusual" is using the ordinary meaning of the term being defined for the purpose of resolving *an ambiguity in the definition*. When, for example, "draft," a word of many meanings, is one of the words used in a definition of "breeze," we know it has nothing to do with military conscription or beer. The point is illustrated by the almost-relevant case the Court cites for its novel principle, *Johnson v. United States*, 559 U.S. 133 (2010). There the defined term was "violent felony," which the Act defined as an offense that " 'has as an element the use . . . of physical force against the person of another.' " *Id.* at 135 (quoting § 924(e)(2)(B)(i)). We had to figure out what "physical force" meant, since the statute "*d[id] not define*" *it*. *Id.* at 138 (emphasis added). So we consulted (among other things) the general meaning of the term being defined, "violent felony." *Id.* at 140.

In this case, by contrast, the ordinary meaning of the term being defined is irrelevant, because the statute's own definition—however expansive—is utterly clear: any "chemical which through its chemical action on life processes can cause death, temporary incapacitation or permanent harm to humans or animals," § 229F(8)(A), unless the chemical is possessed or used for a "peaceful purpose," § 229F(1)(A), (7)(A). . . . "When a statute includes an explicit definition, we must follow that definition, *even if it varies from that term's ordinary meaning*." *Stenberg v. Carhart*, 530 U.S. 914, 942 (2000) (emphasis added). . . .

But even text clear on its face, the Court suggests, must be read against the backdrop of established interpretive presumptions. Thus, we presume "that a criminal statute derived from the common law carries with it the requirement of a culpable mental state—even if no such limitation appears in the text." *Ante* at 857. And we presume that "federal statutes do not apply outside the United States." *Ibid.* Both of those are, indeed, established interpretive presumptions that are (1) based upon realistic assessments of congressional intent, and (2) well known to Congress—thus furthering rather than subverting genuine legislative intent. To apply these presumptions, then, is not to rewrite clear text; it is to interpret words fairly, in light of their statutory context. But there is nothing either (1) realistic or (2) well known about the presumption the Court shoves down the throat of a resisting statute today. . . .

C. The Statute as Judicially Amended

I suspect the Act will not survive today's gruesome surgery. A criminal statute must clearly define the conduct it proscribes. If it does not " 'give a person of ordinary intelligence fair notice' " of its scope, *United States v. Batchelder*, 442 U.S. 114, 123 (1979), it denies due process.

The *new* § 229(a)(1) fails that test. Henceforward, a person "shall be fined . . . , imprisoned for any term of years, or both," § 229A(a)(1)—or, if he kills someone, "shall be punished by death or imprisoned for life," § 229A(a)(2)—whenever he "develop[s], produce[s], otherwise acquire[s], transfer[s] directly or indirectly, receive[s], stockpile[s], retain[s], own[s], possess[es], or use[s], or threaten[s] to use," § 229(a)(1), any chemical "*of the sort that an ordinary person would associate with instruments of chemical warfare*," *ante* at 861 (emphasis added). Whether that test is satisfied, the Court unhelpfully (and also illogically) explains, depends not only on the "particular chemicals that the defendant used" but also on "the circumstances in which she used them." *Ibid.* The "detergent under the kitchen sink" and "the stain remover in the laundry room" are apparently out, *ante* at 862—but what if they are deployed to poison a neighborhood water fountain? . . . .

No one should have to ponder the totality of the circumstances in order to determine whether his conduct is a felony. . . .

II. The Constitutional Question

[Justice Scalia concluded that as applied against Ms. Bond, the Act went beyond the powers that the Constitution gives Congress. In response to the idea that the Necessary and Proper Clause combined with the Treaty Clause justified the Act, Justice Scalia argued that "a power to help the President *make* treaties is not a power to *implement* treaties already made." (On that point, he cited Nicholas Quinn Rosenkranz, *Executing the Treaty Power*, 118 HARV. L. REV. 1867 (2005).)]

■ *JUSTICE THOMAS, with whom JUSTICE SCALIA joins, and with whom JUSTICE ALITO joins as to Parts I, II, and III, concurring in the judgment:*

[Although Justice Thomas joined Justice Scalia's opinion in full, he wrote separately to discuss an additional constitutional issue, involving the scope of the federal government's power to make treaties. He suggested that the treaty power enables the United States to reach agreements with other countries on "matters of international intercourse" but does not enable the federal government "to regulate purely domestic affairs." Still, he noted that "the parties have not challenged the constitutionality of the particular treaty at issue here," and he did not analyze that question.]

■ *JUSTICE ALITO, concurring in the judgment:*

[Justice Alito did not join Justice Scalia's constitutional analysis, but he agreed with Justice Thomas about the constitutional limits on the treaty power, and he concurred in the judgment on that basis. Of course, Justice Alito acknowledged that "[t]he control of true chemical weapons, as that term is customarily understood, is a matter of great international concern, and therefore the heart of the Convention clearly represents a valid exercise of the treaty power." But Justice Alito thought that "insofar as the Convention may be read to obligate the United States to enact domestic legislation criminalizing conduct of the sort at issue in this case, . . . the Convention exceeds the scope of the treaty power." For that reason, he concluded that the statute's application to Ms. Bond "cannot be regarded as necessary and proper to carry into execution the treaty power."]

NOTES AND QUESTIONS

1. The constitutional objections raised by Justices Scalia, Thomas, and Alito may not be very persuasive. With respect to Justice Scalia's point about the Necessary and Proper Clause, it would be surprising if the Constitution gave the federal government the power to make treaties but did not give the federal government the power to cause the United States to comply with its obligations under those treaties. As for Justice Thomas's point, it may be true that "the Power . . . to make Treaties" conferred by Article II of the Constitution is limited to matters of legitimate international concern. Such matters, though, surely include the stockpiling and use of chemical weapons—and while Ms. Bond's effort to cause discomfort to a single person obviously is not the paradigm case that motivated the Convention, there is no clear demarcation between hostile uses of toxic chemicals that are matters of legitimate international concern and those that are not. Given that problem, couldn't nations legitimately want to establish a bright-line rule against *all* uses of toxic chemicals to harm other people, so that determining compliance with the treaty would not require a totality-of-the-circumstances analysis?

At least for the sake of argument, then, suppose that the Convention would be a legitimate "Treat[y]" (of the sort that Article II allows the United States to make) even if the Convention is properly interpreted to encompass Ms. Bond's conduct, and hence to require the United States to have domestic laws prohibiting that conduct. Suppose, too, that if the Convention does indeed have this meaning, the Necessary and Proper Clause would give Congress the constitutional power to bring the United States into compliance with the treaty by enacting a federal statute that criminalizes Ms. Bond's conduct. Chief Justice Roberts's majority opinion seemed willing to make both of those assumptions; the majority did not reject the possibility that the Convention did indeed reach Ms. Bond's conduct and that Congress could constitutionally criminalize that conduct as a means of implementing the Convention. As a matter of statutory interpretation, though, the majority held that 18 U.S.C. § 229 did not do so. Thus, the majority indicated that the statute that Congress had enacted to implement the treaty might cover less conduct than the treaty itself—so that the United States would be in compliance with the treaty only if the *states* all have *state* laws that cover the remaining conduct. Given that Congress enacted the statute to implement the treaty, and given that the statute used much the same language as the treaty, isn't the majority's position implausible? *See, e.g.*, David Sloss, Bond v. United States*: Choosing the Lesser of Two Evils*, 90 NOTRE DAME L. REV. 1583, 1589 (2015) (calling the majority's interpretation of the statute "untenable").

2. In defense of its interpretation of the statute, the majority invoked "the background principle that Congress does not normally intrude upon the police power of the States." *Bond II*, 572 U.S. at 863. According to the majority, reading 18 U.S.C. § 229 to encompass all acts of poisoning and other hostile uses of toxic chemicals would federalize "purely local crimes" that traditionally are covered only by state law, and there is a strong presumption against reading federal statutes to encroach upon "traditional state authority" in this way. *Id.* at 858, 860, 863. Indeed, the majority asserted that "the most sweeping reading of the statute would fundamentally upset the Constitution's balance between national and local power." *Id.* at 866. As the majority noted, moreover, "it is appropriate to refer to basic principles of federalism embodied in the Constitution to resolve ambiguity in a federal statute." *Id.* at 859.

Justice Scalia acknowledged these interpretive principles, but he emphasized that they come into play only when a statute is "ambiguous."[3] Because Justice Scalia thought that the text of 18 U.S.C. § 229 clearly covered Ms. Bond's conduct, he saw no room for the majority's narrower reading.

---

[3] In other words, Justice Scalia observed that the "federalism-inspired interpretive presumption" invoked by the majority is not an implied-limitation rule, but instead is simply a tool for resolving conventional indeterminacy in statutory language. *See supra* pp. 230–231 (introducing this terminology).

Even if the statute had been ambiguous, though, would it really have made sense to resolve the ambiguity in light of what the Court called "the 'usual constitutional balance of federal and state powers' "? *See id.* at 858 (quoting Gregory v. Ashcroft, 501 U.S. 452, 460 (1991)). The "usual" balance of federal and state powers reflects the "usual" occasions for federal legislation and the "usual" sources of congressional authority. As the majority acknowledged, though, the statute at issue in *Bond* had been enacted to implement a treaty, not simply to regulate interstate commerce or to do other things that Congress usually does. Maybe that point would not have mattered to Justice Scalia; Part II of his concurring opinion argued that the Constitution does not give Congress any special power to implement treaties. But the majority did not endorse Justice Scalia's constitutional analysis. If the Chemical Weapons Convention is a valid treaty, and if the Constitution does indeed give Congress the power to enact implementing legislation, why would one expect the Chemical Weapons Convention Implementation Act of 1998 to stop short of fully implementing the Chemical Weapons Convention? To the extent that the statute was ambiguous, wouldn't it make more sense to assume that the statute is co-extensive with the treaty than to assume that Congress wanted to follow the patterns that hold true when no treaty is in the picture?

Along the same lines, what do you make of the majority's claim that "the statute—unlike the Convention—must be read consistent with principles of federalism inherent in our constitutional structure"? *See id.* at 856. Isn't Congress's power to implement treaties part of "our constitutional structure," and doesn't that power qualify the relevant "principles of federalism"? Or was the majority silently reflecting Justice Scalia's position that Congress has no special power along these lines? Even if one took that position, couldn't one still assume that Congress wanted to implement the Chemical Weapons Convention to the full extent that Congress could? Or is the existence of a treaty that Congress wants to implement entirely irrelevant to the ordinary relationship between Congress and the states?

3. *Bond* is one of several cases in which the Supreme Court has invoked federalism canons to limit the reach of federal criminal statutes. *See, e.g.*, Jones v. United States, 529 U.S. 848, 858 (2000); United States v. Bass, 404 U.S. 336, 349–50 (1971). That is not surprising; the basic idea of these canons is that federal statutes should not lightly be interpreted to "significantly change[ ] the federal-state balance," *id.* at 349, and "the punishment of local criminal activity" is "[p]erhaps the clearest example of traditional state authority." *Bond II*, 572 U.S. at 858. In the realm of federal criminal law, moreover, both the rule of lenity and normative concerns about overcriminalization reinforce federalism canons.

Still, references to the normal allocation of responsibilities in our federal system are not limited to criminal law. In *U.S. Forest Service v. Cowpasture River Preservation Ass'n*, 140 S. Ct. 1837 (2020), the

Supreme Court stated the relevant principle strongly: "Our precedents require Congress to enact exceedingly clear language if it wishes to significantly alter the balance between federal and state power and the power of the Government over private property." *Id.* at 1849–50; *accord* Sackett v. EPA, 143 S. Ct. 1322, 1341 (2023); *see also, e.g., Gregory*, 501 U.S. at 460 (likewise invoking "the usual constitutional balance of federal and state powers" outside the realm of criminal law).[4] Does the concept of "the balance between federal and state power" have enough content to be helpful?

---

2. WHEN SHOULD FEDERAL STATUTES BE READ TO COVER THE STATES THEMSELVES?

In a number of different contexts, the Supreme Court has wrestled with the obligations that federal statutes should be understood to impose on state governments themselves (as opposed to people and businesses in the private sector). That topic implicates various questions of constitutional law: to what extent does the Constitution give Congress the *power* to impose obligations on states,[5] and what mechanisms can Congress create to enforce such obligations? Within the limits of

---

[4] In a case on its motions docket, the Court has quoted the same principle in support of the version of the major-questions doctrine that discourages reading federal statutes to delegate major regulatory authority to federal administrative agencies. *See* Ala. Ass'n of Realtors v. Dep't of Health & Human Servs., 141 S. Ct. 2485, 2489 (2021) (per curiam); *see also* West Virginia v. EPA, 142 S. Ct. 2587, 2621 (2022) (Gorsuch, J., concurring) ("[T]he major questions doctrine and the federalism canon often travel together. When an agency claims the power to regulate vast swaths of American life, it not only risks intruding on Congress's power, it also risks intruding on powers reserved to the States."); *supra* pp. 888–899 (discussing the major-questions doctrine).

[5] Recently, under the rubric of "anticommandeering" doctrine, the Supreme Court has occasionally spoken as if the Constitution does not allow Congress "to issue orders directly to the States" at all. *Murphy v. NCAA*, 138 S. Ct. 1461, 1475 (2018); *see also* New York v. United States, 505 U.S. 144, 166 (1992) ("[T]he Framers explicitly chose a Constitution that confers upon Congress the power to regulate individuals, not States."). But such statements require qualification.

Certain kinds of direct orders are indeed forbidden. For instance, "Congress may not . . . 'commandee[r] the legislative processes of the States by directly compelling them to enact and enforce a federal regulatory program' "; a federal statute purporting to require state legislatures to enact a particular statute as state law would be unconstitutional. *New York*, 505 U.S. at 161 (quoting Hodel v. Va. Surface Mining & Reclamation Ass'n, 452 U.S. 264, 288 (1981)); *see also Murphy*, 138 S. Ct. at 1478 (indicating more generally that "Congress cannot issue direct orders to state legislatures" requiring them either "to enact or [to] refrain from enacting state law"). Congress also cannot "command the States' officers . . . to administer or enforce a federal regulatory program." *Printz v. United States*, 521 U.S. 898, 935 (1997).

But even if Congress has no authority to "require the States in their sovereign capacity to regulate their own citizens," Congress has substantial authority to enact federal statutes imposing other kinds of duties on states and state officials. *See* Reno v. Condon, 528 U.S. 141, 151 (2000) (upholding the Driver's Privacy Protection Act of 1994, which "regulates the States as the owners of data bases"). At a minimum, Congress can enact its own federal regulations of all actors (public or private) engaged in particular activities. *See Murphy*, 138 S. Ct. at 1478 ("The anticommandeering doctrine does not apply when Congress evenhandedly regulates an activity in which both States and private actors engage."); *see also* Haaland v. Brackeen, 143 S. Ct. 1609, 1634 (2023) ("When a federal statute applies on its face to both private and state actors, a commandeering argument is a heavy lift . . . .").

Congress's constitutional authority, though, courts frequently face questions of statutory interpretation. Even where Congress has the power to impose certain obligations on the states or to expose states to certain types of enforcement mechanisms, when should federal statutes be understood to do so?

a. THE PRESUMPTION AGAINST READING FEDERAL STATUTES TO ABROGATE STATE SOVEREIGN IMMUNITY

We can begin with the sovereign immunity that protects state governments from being haled into court without their consent. Before you can understand the relevant questions of statutory interpretation, you need a thumbnail sketch of the ebb and flow of constitutional doctrine.

Article III of the Constitution extended the federal government's judicial power to various categories of cases and controversies, including "Controversies . . . between a State and Citizens of another State" and "Controversies . . . between a State . . . and foreign States, Citizens or Subjects." U.S. CONST. art. III, § 2; *see also id.* (adding that "the Supreme Court shall have original Jurisdiction" in all of the categories of cases just listed "in which a State shall be Party"). In *Chisholm v. Georgia*, 2 U.S. (2 Dall.) 419 (1793), the Supreme Court interpreted this language to override traditional principles of sovereign immunity and expose even *unconsenting* states to private suits. But this decision was controversial, and it led to the ratification of the Eleventh Amendment: "The judicial power of the United States shall not be construed to extend to any suit in law or equity, commenced or prosecuted against one of the United States by Citizens of another State, or by Citizens or Subjects of any Foreign State." Starting in the late nineteenth century, moreover, the Supreme Court began protecting unconsenting states against being haled into federal court not only in the situations that the Eleventh Amendment described, but in a variety of other situations too. *See, e.g.*, Blatchford v. Native Village of Noatak, 501 U.S. 775, 779–82 (1991) (suit brought by Indian tribe); Principality of Monaco v. Mississippi, 292 U.S. 313, 331–32 (1934) (suit brought by foreign country); Ex parte New York, 256 U.S. 490, 497–503 (1921) (suit in admiralty); Hans v. Louisiana, 134 U.S. 1, 20–21 (1890) (federal-question suit brought against a state by one of its own citizens). The Supreme Court has since made clear that these decisions are more about the original Constitution than about the Eleventh Amendment; they rest on the premise that *Chisholm* was wrong all along and that Article III did not eliminate the states' pre-existing immunities from the suits in question. *See* Alden v. Maine, 527 U.S. 706, 713 (1999); *see also* Caleb Nelson, *Sovereign Immunity as a Doctrine of Personal Jurisdiction*, 115 HARV. L. REV. 1559, 1567–1608 (2002) (discussing the range of original understandings on this point and how one might conclude that *Chisholm* was wrong).

During the public debate over whether to ratify the Constitution, Alexander Hamilton had written that "[i]t is inherent in the nature of sovereignty not to be amenable to the suit of an individual *without its consent*," and each state would retain this attribute of sovereignty after ratification of the Constitution "[u]nless . . . there is a surrender of this immunity in the plan of the convention." THE FEDERALIST NO. 81, at 487–88 (Alexander Hamilton) (Clinton Rossiter ed., 1961). Despite this baseline of immunity, the Supreme Court has held that "the plan of the convention" does expose states to suit by other states and by the federal government itself; states are said to have consented to such suits by ratifying the Constitution and thereby accepting the federal structure. *See, e.g., Monaco*, 292 U.S. at 328–29 (citing cases). More recently (and more randomly), the Court has held that "the plan of the convention" also overrides state sovereign immunity with respect to a few specific types of claims brought by private parties. *See* Central Va. Cmty. Coll. v. Katz, 546 U.S. 356, 377 (2006) (holding that "States agreed in the plan of the Convention not to assert any sovereign immunity defense they might have had in proceedings brought pursuant to 'Laws on the subject of Bankruptcies' " (quoting U.S. CONST. art. I, § 8, cl. 4)); PennEast Pipeline Co. v. New Jersey, 141 S. Ct. 2244, 2259 (2021) (holding that "the States consented in the plan of the Convention to the exercise of federal eminent domain power, including in condemnation proceedings brought by private delegatees" whom Congress has authorized to exercise that power); Torres v. Tex. Dep't of Pub. Safety, 142 S. Ct. 2455, 2466 (2022) (holding that "as part of the plan of the Convention," states have also waived sovereign immunity from suits authorized by federal statutes enacted "under Congress' Article I power '[t]o raise and support Armies' and 'provide and maintain a Navy' " (quoting U.S. CONST. art. I, § 8, cls. 12–13)). Aside from these limited categories of cases, though, each state retains immunity from being sued without its consent unless Congress has validly abrogated that immunity by statute. *See id.* at 2461–62.

From the mid-1990s on, moreover, the Supreme Court has held that the Constitution does not give Congress much power to abrogate state sovereign immunity—that is, to expose states to suit when the "plan of the convention" does not already do so and when the particular state in question has not otherwise consented to suit. Under current doctrine, most of the powers that Article I of the Constitution gives Congress (such as the powers conferred by the combination of the Commerce Clause and the Necessary and Proper Clause) do not enable Congress to expose unconsenting states to lawsuits brought by anyone other than another state or the federal government. *See* Seminole Tribe v. Florida, 517 U.S. 44, 72–73 (1996) (indicating that state sovereign immunity limits the reach of the federal government's judicial power under Article III and holding that "Article I cannot be used to circumvent the constitutional limitations placed upon federal jurisdiction"); Alden v. Maine, 527 U.S. 706, 754 (1999) (holding that Congress also cannot use its Article I powers to abrogate the states' immunity from suit in state court). In keeping with an earlier line of cases, however, the Court has held that § 5 of the Fourteenth Amendment is different. Section 5 says that Congress "shall have power to enforce, by appropriate legislation, the provisions of [the Fourteenth Amendment]," and the Supreme Court has held that this clause enables Congress to abrogate state sovereign immunity; as part of "appropriate legislation" to enforce the Fourteenth Amendment, Congress can expose unconsenting states to private lawsuits. *See, e.g.*, Nevada Dep't of Human Resources v. Hibbs, 538 U.S. 721, 727 (2003) (following *Fitzpatrick v. Bitzer*, 427 U.S. 445 (1976)).

Still, the Supreme Court has established a strong presumption against interpreting federal statutes to *use* this power. In *Atascadero State Hospital v. Scanlon*, 473 U.S. 234 (1985), the Court articulated the relevant principle as follows: "Congress may abrogate the States' constitutionally secured immunity from suit in federal court only by making its intention unmistakably clear in the language of the statute." *Id.* at 242; *cf.* Quern v. Jordan, 440 U.S. 332, 340–45 (1979) (applying a more muted version of this idea).[6]

There are two different ways of understanding the legal basis for *Atascadero*. On one view, the *Atascadero* doctrine is itself a principle of constitutional law—one that requires the federal government to turn especially square corners when it wants to use its legislative powers to expose unconsenting states to private suits. *See* Hilton v. S.C. Pub. Rys. Comm'n, 502 U.S. 197, 204 (1991) (asserting that *Atascadero* and its progeny "establish a rule of constitutional law based on the Eleventh Amendment"). But it is hard to defend *Atascadero* in these terms. In every case where the *Atascadero* principle affects the result, the Constitution does give Congress the power to expose unconsenting states to suit. And while it is theoretically possible that the Framers might have created special procedural hurdles that Congress would have to clear in order to use this power, the Constitution that they actually wrote does not seem to do so.

On the other view, *Atascadero* simply articulates a canon of statutory interpretation (albeit one that, like the rule of lenity, is inspired by constitutional concerns). *See, e.g.*, Raygor v. Regents of the Univ. of Minn., 534 U.S. 533, 541–46 (2002) (discussing *Atascadero* and its progeny in these terms). According to Justice Scalia, indeed, this canon has genuine descriptive appeal: "[S]ince congressional elimination of state sovereign immunity is such an extraordinary act, one would normally expect it to be explicitly decreed rather than offhandedly implied—so something like a 'clear statement' rule is merely normal

---

[6] At the time of *Atascadero*, the Court had not yet recognized robust substantive restrictions on Congress's authority to abrogate state sovereign immunity. One might have thought that once *Seminole Tribe v. Florida* and *Alden v. Maine* recognized such restrictions, the Court would back away from the more process-oriented limitation created by *Atascadero*. But the Court did not do so. *See, e.g.*, Kimel v. Florida Bd. of Regents, 528 U.S. 62, 73 (2000) (continuing to invoke *Atascadero*'s "simple but stringent test," though finding it satisfied in the case at hand (quoting Dellmuth v. Muth, 491 U.S. 223, 228 (1989))).

interpretation." Antonin Scalia, *Common-Law Courts in a Civil-Law System: The Role of United States Federal Courts in Interpreting the Constitution and Laws, in* A MATTER OF INTERPRETATION 3, 29 (Amy Gutmann ed., 1997). To the extent that a federal statute is ambiguous about whether it exposes unconsenting states to suit, some people might also try to defend the canon on normative grounds.

As many observers have suggested, though, the Court probably has given the *Atascadero* principle more force than the statutory-interpretation theory can really support. *See, e.g.*, William N. Eskridge, Jr. & Philip P. Frickey, *Quasi-Constitutional Law: Clear Statement Rules as Constitutional Lawmaking*, 45 VAND. L. REV. 593, 621–23 (1992) (criticizing *Atascadero*'s beefed-up version of "[w]hat had once been a presumption-based approach to resolve federal statutory ambiguity"). The requirement that Congress "mak[e] its intention unmistakably clear," *Atascadero*, 473 U.S. at 242, seems likely to drive a wedge between what Congress intends a statute to communicate and what courts take the statute to mean.[7] That effect might be magnified by *Atascadero*'s special rule against the use of legislative history in this context. *Atascadero* asserted that in order to abrogate state sovereign immunity, Congress must speak with unmistakable clarity "in the language of the statute," *id.*, and subsequent cases have confirmed this idea; if the relevant statutory text is not itself "unmistakably clear" about Congress's intent to expose unconsenting states to suit, no amount of legislative history clarifying the text will be good enough. *See, e.g.*, Dellmuth v. Muth, 491 U.S. 223, 230 (1989) ("Lest *Atascadero* be thought to contain any ambiguity, we reaffirm today that in this area of the law, evidence of congressional intent must be both unequivocal and textual.... Legislative history generally will be irrelevant .... [I]f Congress' intention is not unmistakably clear [in the language of the statute], recourse to legislative history will be futile, because by definition the rule of *Atascadero* will not be met.").

If you oppose the use of legislative history in statutory interpretation more generally, its irrelevance with respect to the abrogation of state sovereign immunity may not trouble you. But what, if anything, justifies the Court's *special* hostility to the use of legislative history to decide

---

[7] According to Justice Stevens, at least, Congress's response to *Atascadero* bears out this point. Shortly after *Atascadero*, Congress amended the statute that had been at issue so as to abrogate the states' immunity from private suits more expressly. *See* Rehabilitation Act Amendments of 1986, Pub. L. 99–506, § 1003(a), 100 Stat. 1807, 1845 (codified at 42 U.S.C. § 2000d–7). Justice Stevens glossed this episode as follows:

> "The prompt congressional reaction to our decision in *Atascadero* illustrates the lack of wisdom of the Court's rigid approach to waivers of sovereign immunity. It was true in that case, as it is in this, that Congress could have drafted a clearer statement of its intent. Our task, however, is not to educate busy legislators in the niceties and details of scholarly draftsmanship, but rather to do our best to determine what message they intended to convey. When judge-made rules require Congress to use its valuable time enacting and reenacting provisions whose original intent was clear to all but the most skeptical and hostile reader, those rules should be discarded."

Lane v. Pena, 518 U.S. 187, 212 (1996) (Stevens, J., dissenting).

whether a federal statute abrogates state sovereign immunity? If § 5 of the Fourteenth Amendment gives Congress the power to expose unconsenting states to certain kinds of private suits, and if the Constitution does not itself qualify that power by establishing any special procedural restrictions for its exercise, does the Court have any basis for ruling out the use of legislative history in this one context? Is the point that because of the special sensitivity of exposing unconsenting states to private suits, the Court can legitimately refuse to attribute that result to a federal statute unless the Court is absolutely positive that Congress intended that result, and legislative history can never produce the requisite certainty? *Cf. Dellmuth*, 491 U.S. at 231 ("[I]t cannot be said with perfect confidence that Congress in fact intended . . . to abrogate sovereign immunity, and imperfect confidence will not suffice given the special constitutional concerns in this area."). If so, shouldn't the Court worry that requiring such a high level of confidence will predictably widen the gap between the directives that the Court understands statutory language to establish and the directives that members of Congress collectively thought they were establishing? Does the Court have the authority to adopt purportedly "interpretive" rules that have this effect?

Or is the point of *Atascadero* that before the Court reads a federal statute to accomplish the sensitive result of exposing unconsenting states to private suits, the Court wants some assurance that members of Congress have focused on this issue and reached a deliberate decision to do so, and the Court thinks that requiring "unmistakably clear" statutory text increases the chances of adequate deliberation? Would this rationale for *Atascadero* be any more legitimate than the rationale considered in the previous paragraph? Doesn't the Constitution put each House of Congress, rather than the Court, in charge of the subconstitutional rules that control the amount of deliberation that occurs during the legislative process? *Cf.* U.S. CONST. art. I, § 5 ("Each House may determine the Rules of its Proceedings . . . .").

In addition to thinking about how much force the presumption articulated in *Atascadero* deserves, one should also think about exactly how to formulate the presumption. To win a judicial judgment against an unconsenting state, a claimant would typically need to establish a constellation of substantive, remedial, and procedural rights: the claimant would need to establish (1) that the law gives the state some substantive duty that the state has breached, (2) that the law also creates a right of action entitling the claimant to a remedy against the state for that breach, and (3) that the law authorizes the court in which the claimant is proceeding to hale the state before it and proceed to judgment even if the state does not voluntarily appear and agree to be bound by the court's decision. A presumption against exposing unconsenting states to suit might focus on any or all of these issues. Thus, one version of such a presumption might say that federal statutes should not lightly be interpreted to impose substantive duties on states. Another version might say that federal statutes should not lightly be interpreted to create rights of action against the states to enforce whatever duties the statutes impose. And a third version might say that federal statutes should not lightly be interpreted to authorize either state or federal courts to assert jurisdiction over unconsenting states and to adjudicate rights of action against them. Are each of these presumptions equally plausible? Should some have more force than others? Should they apply equally to all possible claims against states, or only to certain kinds of claims?

The Court's recent cases about "the plan of the convention" (*Central Virginia Community College v. Katz*, *PennEast Pipeline Co. v. New Jersey*, and *Torres v. Texas Department of Public Safety*, *supra* p. 1047) give rise to an additional question. As a matter of constitutional doctrine, those cases can be seen as end-runs around the Rehnquist Court's suggestion that Article I of the Constitution does not give Congress the power to abrogate the states' immunity from private lawsuits. After all, no statutory abrogation is necessary if the states have already waived their immunity as part of the plan of the convention. *See Central Va. Cmty. Coll.*, 546 U.S. at 379 ("[T]he relevant 'abrogation' is the one effected in the plan of the Convention, not by statute."). By finding a waiver as part of the "plan of the convention," moreover, the Court produces much the same result as if the Court had held that certain provisions in Article I empower Congress to abrogate state sovereign immunity: when Congress is exercising its authority "[t]o establish . . . uniform Laws on the subject of Bankruptcies throughout the United States," U.S. CONST. art. I, § 8, cl. 4, "[t]o raise and support Armies," *id.* cl. 12, "[t]o provide and maintain a Navy," *id.* cl. 13, or to delegate the federal government's eminent-domain power to private parties, Congress is in charge of whether to expose states to claims initiated by private litigants. *See Central Va. Cmty. Coll.*, 546 U.S. at 379 (concluding that because of the waiver in the plan of the convention, "Congress may, at its option, either treat States in the same way as other creditors insofar as concerns 'Laws on the subject of Bankruptcies' or exempt them from operation of such laws"). Should *Atascadero*'s principle of statutory interpretation be limited to the congressional-abrogation theory, or should it also extend to the areas covered by the "plan of the convention" theory—so that even where Congress could expose states to private lawsuits based on the "plan of the convention" theory, courts should apply a strong presumption that Congress has not actually done so? *See PennEast*, 141 S. Ct. at 2262–63 (concluding that "when the Federal Government authorizes a private party to exercise [the government's] eminent domain power," Congress does not have to "speak with unmistakable clarity" in order to enable its delegee to condemn State-owned property).

b. ARE STATES "PERSONS," AND WHEN DO OTHER GENERAL WORDS IN FEDERAL STATUTES REACH STATES?

Even if a suit can proceed against a state, the state normally will not lose on the merits unless the applicable substantive and remedial law gives the state duties to the plaintiff. Over the years, the Supreme Court sometimes has had to decide whether generally worded federal statutes impose duties on state governments as well as on entities in the private sector.

Introducing that question requires some historical background. Before the United States gained its independence, English courts had long wrestled with the circumstances in which generally worded acts of Parliament should be understood to apply to the king. Blackstone articulated a relevant canon, albeit one of uncertain scope:

> "[T]he king is not bound by any act of parliament, unless he be named therein by special and particular words. . . . Yet where an act of parliament is expressly made for the preservation of public rights and the suppression of public wrongs, and does not interfere with the established rights of the crown, it is said to be binding as well upon the king as upon the subject: and, likewise, the king may take the benefit of any particular act, though he be not especially named."

1 WILLIAM BLACKSTONE, COMMENTARIES ON THE LAWS OF ENGLAND 253 (1765). Bacon's Abridgment also recognized a category of generally worded statutes that should be presumed not to cover the king. *See* 5 MATTHEW BACON, A NEW ABRIDGMENT OF THE LAW 559 (6th ed., London 1807) (entry E.5 on "Prerogative") ("[W]here an act of parliament is made for the publick good, the advancement of religion and justice, and to prevent injury and wrong, the king shall be bound by such act, though not particularly named therein. But, where a statute is general, and thereby any prerogative, right, title, or interest is devested or taken from the king, in such case the king shall not be bound; unless the statute is made by express words to extend to him.").

After Independence, of course, the United States did not have a king, and no single individual personified the sovereignty either of the nation as a whole or of any state. Sovereignty was said to reside instead in the people. But the collective people of each state were represented by (and could act only through) their state government. Whether for that reason or because of other considerations, a number of nineteenth-century state courts concluded that the principle stated by Bacon and Blackstone "is applicable to the *state* as well as the crown," with the result that some generally worded provisions of state law were interpreted not to restrict the powers or legal interests of the state government itself. *Whiteacre v. Rector*, 70 Va. 714, 716 (1878); *see also* Dollar Sav. Bank v. United States, 86 U.S. (19 Wall.) 227, 239 (1874) ("The rule thus settled respecting the British Crown is equally applicable to this government, and it has been applied frequently in the different States . . . .").

The federal Supreme Court took a similar position with respect to whether *federal* statutes bound legal interests belonging to the *federal* government. *See, e.g.*, United States v. Herron, 87 U.S. 251, 255 (1874) (invoking and applying "the settled rule of construction that the sovereign authority of the country is not bound by the words of a statute unless named therein, if the statute tends to restrain or diminish the powers, rights, or interests of the sovereign"). In an opinion that he wrote on circuit, Justice Story offered the following formulation and defense of this rule of construction (which, in his view, was "founded upon the legislative intention"):

> "Where the government is not expressly or by necessary implication included, it ought to be clear from the nature of the mischiefs to be redressed, or the language used, that the government itself was in contemplation of the legislature, before a court of law would be authorized to put such an interpretation upon any statute. In general, acts of the legislature are meant to regulate and direct the acts and rights of citizens; and in most cases the reasoning applicable to them applies with very different, and often contrary force to the government itself. It appears to me, therefore, to be a safe rule founded in the principles of the common law, that the general words of a statute ought not to include the government, or affect its rights, unless that construction be clear and indisputable upon the text of the act."

United States v. Hoar, 26 F. Cas. 329, 330 (C.C.D. Mass. 1821) (No. 15,373).

In the mid-twentieth century, the Supreme Court repeatedly invoked this principle as an implied-limitation rule. For instance, in *United States v. United Mine Workers*, 330 U.S. 258 (1947), the United States had seized and was operating most of the bituminous coal mines in the country. At the government's request, a federal district court issued a temporary restraining order to prevent the United Mine Workers from initiating a strike at the mines. Although the Norris-LaGuardia Act and the Clayton Act probably would have prevented the district court from granting this relief at the behest of an ordinary employer, the Supreme Court noted that the United States was operating the mines in its sovereign capacity, *id.* at 289, and the Court refused to read the generally worded Acts to restrict the relief available to the United States. *See id.* at 270, 275–76 (holding that the statutory terms "employer" and "persons" did not include the United States). In support of this holding, the Court noted that "[t]here is an old and well-known rule that statutes which in general terms divest pre-existing rights or privileges will not be applied to the sovereign without express words to that effect." *Id.* at 272.[8] Ten years later, the Court relied on the same

---

[8] *Accord* United States v. Wittek, 337 U.S. 346, 347, 358–59 (1949) (holding that the term "landlord" in the District of Columbia Emergency Rent Act, ch. 553, 55 Stat. 788 (1941), did not include the United States, and invoking the principle that "[a] general statute imposing

principle in interpreting the general Anti-Injunction Act, 28 U.S.C. § 2283. Subject to three explicit exceptions, § 2283 says that a federal court "may not grant an injunction to stay proceedings in a State court," but the Supreme Court held that this restriction does not apply when the injunction is sought by the United States itself. *Leiter Minerals, Inc. v. United States*, 352 U.S. 220, 224–26 (1957).

But no matter how far one takes "the canon of construction that a sovereign is presumptively not intended to be bound by its own statute unless named in it," *United States v. California*, 297 U.S. 175, 186 (1936), the American system of federalism raises additional issues. Whatever the proper doctrines about whether generally worded federal statutes should be understood to reach the *federal* government, to what extent should generally worded federal statutes be understood to reach *state* governments?[9]

In the twentieth century, the Supreme Court faced this question in several different contexts. When state-run enterprises were engaging in the same sort of activity as private companies, the Court frequently understood generally worded federal regulatory statutes to impose duties on them. Thus, the federal Safety Appliance Act—which required "any common carrier engaged in interstate commerce by railroad" to use cars with automatic couplers, ch. 196, § 2, 27 Stat. 531 (1893)—was held to apply to the State of California as owner and operator of the State Belt Railroad along the waterfront at the Port of San Francisco. *United States v. California*, 297 U.S. at 180, 185–87. Later, the Supreme Court held that the same state-owned railroad was also subject to the Railway Labor Act, which imposed duties on "any carrier by railroad, subject to the Interstate Commerce Act." *California v. Taylor*, 353 U.S. 553, 561 (1957) (quoting the definition of "carrier" in the Railway Labor Act, ch. 347, § 1, 44 Stat. 577, 577 (1926)); *see also id.* (noting that "[t]he Interstate Commerce Act . . . applies to all common carriers by railroad engaged in interstate transportation").

In several cases, the Court reached similar conclusions about federal statutes that taxed or regulated every "person" engaged in a particular business. For instance, in *Ohio v. Helvering*, 292 U.S. 360 (1934), the State of Ohio had responded to the end of Prohibition by setting up state ABC stores with a monopoly on liquor sales, and the state argued that its stores were not subject to the taxes that an old federal statute imposed on "[e]very person who sells . . . distilled spirits, wines or malt liquors." *See* Act of Mar. 1, 1879, ch. 125, § 4, 20 Stat. 327, 333–34 (construed as amending Rev. Stat. § 3244); *see also* Act of Feb. 27, 1877, ch. 69, 19 Stat. 240, 248 (amending Rev. Stat. § 3140 to provide that "where not

---

restrictions does not impose them upon the Government itself without a clear expression or implication to that effect").

[9] Under our system of federalism, this question has no precise parallel with respect to the interpretation of state statutes. While it is possible to imagine questions about how far a state statute goes in regulating the conduct of other state governments, relations among sister states differ from relations between the federal government and the states.

otherwise distinctly expressed or manifestly incompatible with the intent thereof, the word 'person,' as used in this title, shall be construed to mean and include a partnership, association, company, or corporation, as well as a natural person"). In an earlier case, the Supreme Court had held that whatever the proper characterization of the state itself, the individual agents who operated state liquor stores were "persons," and the constitutional doctrine of intergovernmental tax immunity did not prevent Congress from taxing their occupation. *See* South Carolina v. United States, 199 U.S. 437, 448, 461 (1905) (indicating that "the [constitutional] exemption of state agencies and instrumentalities from National taxation is limited to those which are of a strictly governmental character, and does not extend to those which are used by the State in the carrying on of an ordinary private business"). In *Ohio v. Helvering*, the Court embraced a more aggressive interpretation of the statute, holding that "when [the state] becomes a dealer in intoxicating liquors," the state itself qualifies as a "person" for purposes of the federal tax statute. 292 U.S. at 371.

A decade later, the Court reached a similar conclusion about the Shipping Act of 1916, ch. 451, 39 Stat. 728, which regulated "any person . . . carrying on the business of forwarding or furnishing wharfage, dock, warehouse, or other terminal facilities in connection with a common carrier by water." *Id.* § 1, 39 Stat. at 728. Although the Shipping Act specified that "[t]he term 'person' includes corporations, partnerships, and associations," it did not mention states in particular. *See id.* at 729. Nonetheless, the Supreme Court held that the Act applied to states and municipalities that operated marine terminals no less than to private companies. *California v. United States*, 320 U.S. 577, 585–86 (1944). The Court based this interpretation on the purposes of the Act and on some legislative history. *See id.* at 585–86 ("[W]ith so large a portion of the nation's dock facilities . . . owned or controlled by public instrumentalities, it would have defeated the very purpose for which Congress framed the scheme for regulating waterfront terminals to exempt those operated by governmental agencies."); *id.* at 586 (citing legislative history in support of the conclusion that the Act reached public terminal operators).[10]

In the same era, the Supreme Court held that states were proper plaintiffs under § 7 of the Sherman Act, which created a right of action in the following terms: "Any person who shall be injured in his business or property by any other person or corporation by reason of anything forbidden or declared to be unlawful by this act, may sue therefor . . . and shall recover three fold the damages by him sustained, and the costs of suit, including a reasonable attorney's fee." *See* Sherman Act, ch. 647,

---

[10] The legislative history that the Court cited referred specifically to "municipal wharves." 53 CONG. REC. 8276 (1916). The Court did not consider the possibility that the Act might reach municipal corporations but not states.

§ 7, 26 Stat. 209, 210 (1890).[11] Again, the Act provided that "the word 'person' . . . shall be deemed to include corporations and associations existing under or authorized by the laws of either the United States, the laws of any of the Territories, the laws of any State, or the laws of any foreign country," but it said nothing specific about other entities. *Id.* § 8, 26 Stat. at 210 (codified at 15 U.S.C. § 7). Still, in *Georgia v. Evans*, 316 U.S. 159 (1942), the Supreme Court held that states were indeed "persons" who could sue under § 7, primarily because "[w]e can perceive no reason for believing that Congress wanted to deprive a State, as purchaser of commodities shipped in interstate commerce, of the civil remedy of treble damages which is available to other purchasers who suffer through violation of the Act." *Id.* at 162;[12] *see also* Pfizer Inc. v. Gov't of India, 434 U.S. 308, 312 n.9, 320 (1978) (noting that the definition of "person" in § 8 "is inclusive rather than exclusive," and concluding that foreign nations are also "persons" who can sue under the successor of § 7).

Georgia v. Evans was about whether federal antitrust laws *benefited* states by giving them the same remedial rights as private entities. A few decades later, though, the Supreme Court relied on this line of cases in concluding that the antitrust laws also impose some *duties* on states, at least when the states are competing in the same market as private companies. In *Jefferson County Pharmaceutical Ass'n v. Abbott Laboratories*, 460 U.S. 150 (1983), a trade association for retail pharmacies sued pharmaceutical manufacturers and the University of Alabama, which operated two pharmacies at its medical center. The suit alleged that the manufacturers were violating the Robinson-Patman Act by selling pharmaceuticals to the University's pharmacies at lower prices than to other pharmacies. *See* Robinson-Patman Act, ch. 592, 49 Stat. 1526, 1526–27 (1936) (amending the Clayton Act to restrict the circumstances in which "any person engaged in commerce" can "discriminate in price between different purchasers of commodities of like grade and quality" or can "knowingly . . . receive a discrimination in price which is prohibited") (codified at 15 U.S.C. § 13). In response, the defendants argued that the general terms "person" and "purchasers" in

[11] Section 4 of the Clayton Act is a slightly modified version of this provision, covering "anything forbidden in the antitrust laws" rather than just anything forbidden under the Sherman Act. *See* Clayton Act, ch. 323, § 4, 38 Stat. 730, 731 (1914) (codified as amended at 15 U.S.C. § 15); *see also* Pfizer Inc. v. Gov't of India, 434 U.S. 308, 311 n.8 (1978) ("Section 7 of the Sherman Act was repealed in 1955 as redundant.").

[12] A year earlier, the Supreme Court had concluded that the United States was *not* a "person" within the meaning of the Sherman Act and could not sue for treble damages under § 7. *United States v. Cooper Corp.*, 312 U.S. 600 (1941). Still, the Court had based that conclusion partly on the fact that other provisions in the Act set out a detailed set of remedies for the United States, including the ability to bring criminal prosecutions and to seek injunctive relief. *See id.* at 607–08 ("It seems evident that the Act envisaged two classes of actions,—those made available only to the Government, which are first provided in detail, and, in addition, a right of action for treble damages granted to redress private injury."). In *Georgia v. Evans*, the Court emphasized that the Sherman Act treated states differently than the United States in this respect. *See Evans*, 316 U.S. at 162 ("If the State is not a 'person' . . . , the Sherman Law leaves it without any redress for injuries resulting from practices outlawed by that Act.").

the Act should not be understood to include state-run pharmacies. But a majority of the Supreme Court disagreed. Without deciding whether the Robinson-Patman Act implicitly exempts "state purchases for consumption in traditional governmental functions," the Court refused to infer an exemption "where a State has chosen to compete in the private retail market." *Jefferson Cty. Pharm. Ass'n*, 460 U.S. at 154; *see also id.* at 171 ("We hold that the sale of pharmaceutical products to state and local government hospitals for resale in competition with private pharmacies is not exempt from the proscriptions of the Robinson-Patman Act.").

Still, these cases coexisted with others in which the Supreme Court articulated a presumption against reading the word "person" in federal statutes to encompass either the United States or individual states. In *United States v. Cooper Corp.*, 312 U.S. 600 (1940), the Court expressed this presumption as follows: "Since, in common usage, the term 'person' does not include the sovereign, statutes employing the phrase are ordinarily construed to exclude it." *Id.* at 604; *accord* United States v. United Mine Workers, 330 U.S. 258, 275 (1947). To be sure, the Court acknowledged that this presumption was not a "hard and fast rule," and that various "aids to construction"—"[t]he purpose, the subject matter, the context, the legislative history, and the executive interpretation of the statute"—"may indicate an intent, by the use of the term, to bring state or nation within the scope of the law." *Cooper Corp.*, 312 U.S. at 604–05. In the absence of such indications, though, the Court suggested that the word "person" in a federal statute ordinarily does not include either "state or nation." *Id.*; *see also* Wilson v. Omaha Indian Tribe, 442 U.S. 653, 667 (1979) ("Particularly is this true where the statute imposes a burden or limitation, as distinguished from conferring a benefit or advantage.").

The Court invoked this latter line of cases in *Will v. Michigan Department of State Police*, 491 U.S. 58 (1989)—an important decision about the statute that modern lawyers know as 42 U.S.C. § 1983 (which dates back to the Civil Rights Act of 1871, ch. 22, 17 Stat. 13, and was reenacted in slightly modified form in the Revised Statutes of 1874). Ever since 1874, the statute has included the following language: "Every person who, under color of any statute, ordinance, regulation, custom, or usage, of any State . . . , subjects, or causes to be subjected, any citizen of the United States or other person within the jurisdiction thereof to the deprivation of any rights, privileges, or immunities secured by the Constitution and laws [of the United States], shall be liable to the party injured in an action at law, suit in equity, or other proper proceeding for redress." Rev. Stat. § 1979, 18 Stat. 348 (1874) (codified at 42 U.S.C. § 1983). In *Will*, the plaintiff asserted that this statute gave him a right of action against the Michigan Department of State Police (a statewide agency that qualified as an arm of the state for purposes of federal concepts of sovereign immunity) for allegedly violating his constitutional rights in connection with an employment decision. But the Supreme Court disagreed on the ground that a state is not a "person" within the meaning of 42 U.S.C. § 1983.[13] The Court relied partly on "the often-expressed understanding" that the word "person" in federal statutes is " ' "ordinarily construed to exclude [the sovereign]." ' " *Will*, 491 U.S. at 64 (quoting *Wilson*, 442 U.S. at 667, in turn quoting *Cooper Corp.*, 312 U.S. at 604). The Court added that "[t]his approach is particularly applicable" when the alternative would entail "subject[ing] the States to liability to which they had not been subject before." *Id.*

Writing in dissent, Justice Brennan acknowledged "[t]he idea that the word 'persons' ordinarily excludes the sovereign," but he argued that "this interpretive principle applies only to 'the enacting sovereign' " (here, the United States rather than the states). *Id.* at 73 (Brennan, J., dissenting) (quoting *United States v. California*, 297 U.S. 175, 186 (1936)). In any event, Justice Brennan thought that the principle was more qualified and context-dependent than the majority suggested. *See id.* at 73–74.

With respect to 42 U.S.C. § 1983 in particular, moreover, Justice Brennan claimed that history supported reading the word "person" to include states. As Justice Brennan noted, the original Dictionary Act—enacted by Congress on February 25, 1871—said that "in all [federal] acts hereafter passed . . . the word 'person' may extend and be applied to bodies politic and corporate . . . unless the context shows that such words were intended to be used in a more limited sense." Act of Feb. 25, 1871, ch. 71, § 2, 16 Stat. 431, 431. Just two months later, Congress enacted the precursor of 42 U.S.C. § 1983 as part of the Civil Rights Act of 1871. *See* Act of Apr. 20, 1871, ch. 22, § 1, 17 Stat. 13, 13. In *Monell v. Department of Social Services*, 436 U.S. 658 (1978), Justice Brennan's opinion for the Court argued that the word "person" in the Civil Rights Act of 1871 should be presumed to have the extended meaning that the Dictionary Act identified, with the result that it encompassed "bodies politic and corporate." *See id.* at 688–89. And while *Monell* had applied

---

[13] In addition to suing the Department, the plaintiff had also sued the Department's director in his official capacity. To the extent that the plaintiff was suing the director in his official capacity for damages payable out of the state treasury, this claim fared no better. The Court reasoned that a claim of this sort "is not a suit against the official but rather is a suit against the official's office," and hence "is no different from a suit against the State itself." *Will*, 491 U.S. at 71; *cf.* Ford Motor Co. v. Dep't of the Treasury, 323 U.S. 459, 464 (1945) (indicating that a state official who is sued for damages in his official capacity is a mere "nominal defendant[ ]" and that "the state is the real, substantial party in interest").

On the other hand, state officials do count as "person[s]" within the meaning of 42 U.S.C. § 1983 when they are being sued for damages in their *individual* capacity (that is, when the plaintiff is seeking a judgment that would run against the officials' own assets unless the state provides indemnification). *See* Hafer v. Melo, 502 U.S. 21 (1991). The same is true when individual state officials are being sued for prospective injunctive relief, even though that relief would restrict what they do on behalf of the state. Under the theory of *Ex parte Young*, 209 U.S. 123 (1908), suits seeking prospective relief against state officials do not qualify as suits against the state for purposes of the federal doctrine of state sovereign immunity, and a footnote in *Will* read the word "person" in 42 U.S.C. § 1983 to draw the same distinction. *See Will*, 491 U.S. at 71 n.10.

this argument to municipal corporations, Justice Brennan's dissent in *Will* claimed that the same argument also supported characterizing states as "person[s]" under 42 U.S.C. § 1983. *See Will*, 491 U.S. at 79 (Brennan, J., dissenting) ("As a 'body politic and corporate,' a State falls squarely within the Dictionary Act's definition of a 'person.' ").

This claim had two potential flaws. First, even if the original Dictionary Act were relevant, it did not necessarily express a presumption in favor of reading the word "person" to include "bodies politic and corporate"; by its terms, it simply said that the word "may" be given this interpretation. *See Monell*, 436 U.S. at 685 n.53 (acknowledging this issue but arguing that "may" meant "shall"); *see also supra* p. 788. Second, the original Dictionary Act probably does not control the meaning of words in 42 U.S.C. § 1983 anyway. In 1874, Congress repealed both the Dictionary Act and the Civil Rights Act of 1871 (along with most other federal statutes then in force) and replaced them with the Revised Statutes of 1874. *See supra* pp. 786–787 (describing the Revised Statutes). The provision that we think of as 42 U.S.C. § 1983 gets its legal force from that act; it is Section 1979 of the Revised Statutes. Section 1 of the Revised Statutes, in turn, was an amended version of the Dictionary Act. *See supra* p. 787 (quoting Rev. Stat. § 1). Section 1 provided principles for use "[i]n determining the meaning of the revised statutes, or of any act or resolution of Congress passed subsequent to [February 25, 1871—the date of the original Dictionary Act]." Rev. Stat. § 1, 18 Stat. 1 (1874). Unlike the original Dictionary Act, though, Section 1 did not say that the word "person" could be interpreted to cover "bodies politic." Instead, Section 1 said simply that "the word 'person' may extend and be applied to partnerships and corporations, . . . unless the context shows that such words were intended to be used in a more limited sense." *Id.*; *see also* 1 REVISION OF THE UNITED STATES STATUTES AS DRAFTED BY THE COMMISSIONERS APPOINTED FOR THAT PURPOSE tit. 1 at 19 (1872, photo. reprint 1981) (indicating that the commissioners who prepared the initial draft of the Revised Statutes deliberately omitted the phrase "bodies politic" lest it be interpreted "to include a government, such as a State").[14] Congress

---

[14] Professor Katherine Mims Crocker called attention to the commissioners' notes in her article *Reconsidering Section 1983's Nonabrogation of State Sovereign Immunity*, 73 FLA. L. REV. 523, 569 (2021), but she argued that "Congress almost certainly enacted the new definition of 'person' by mistake." *Id.* at 570. As she noted, the responsible congressional committee was unhappy about how much the commissioners' overall draft departed from the existing laws, and the committee therefore hired Thomas Jefferson Durant to prepare a revised draft. *Id.* at 568–69. In transmitting that draft to Congress, Durant wrote that "[e]very section reported by the commissioners has been compared with the text of the corresponding act . . . of Congress . . . , and wherever it has been found that a section contained any departure from the meaning of Congress as expressed in the Statutes at Large, such change has been made as was necessary to restore the original signification." *Id.* at 570 (quoting Letter from Thomas J. Durant to the Chairmen and Members of the Committee of the Senate and House of Representatives on the Revision of the Laws, Dec. 10, 1873, at 1). Professor Crocker inferred that Durant and members of Congress must all have missed the commissioners' change to the original Dictionary Act. *See id.* at 570–72.

A contrary inference seems at least equally possible: perhaps Durant noticed the change but believed that the original Dictionary Act had been meant to encompass only entities

has never restored the phrase "bodies politic" to its generic definition of "person." *See* An Act to Codify and Enact into Positive Law, Title 1 of the United States Code, Entitled "General Provisions," ch. 388, 61 Stat. 633 (1947) (retaining the definition of "person" that had appeared in Rev. Stat. § 1 and reenacting it as 1 U.S.C. § 1); Act of June 25, 1948, ch. 645, § 6, 62 Stat. 683, 859 (amending 1 U.S.C. § 1 and giving the definition of "person" its current form, so that it "include[s] corporations, companies, associations, firms, partnerships, societies, and joint stock companies, as well as individuals"). Thus, even if Justice Brennan was correct that the 1871 version of the Dictionary Act illuminated the meaning of the word "person" in the Civil Rights Act of 1871, his argument does not readily apply to the successor of that statute as it has stood from 1874 to the present.[15]

But rather than emphasizing that the definition of "person" applicable to 42 U.S.C. § 1983 does not include the phrase "bodies politic," Justice White's majority opinion in *Will* simply observed that even Justice Brennan acknowledged the ambiguity of that phrase: as used in the original Dictionary Act, the phrase "bodies politic and corporate" could be construed either narrowly (to include only incorporated entities) or more broadly (to include states themselves). At least for purposes of interpreting the word "person" in 42 U.S.C. § 1983, Justice White argued that principles of federalism supported the narrower reading. Thus, the majority's decision to read "person" narrowly relied heavily on "the ordinary rule of statutory construction that if Congress intends to alter the 'usual constitutional balance between the States and the Federal Government,' it must make its intention to do so 'unmistakably clear in the language of the statute.'" *Will*, 491 U.S. at 65 (quoting Atascadero State Hosp. v. Scanlon, 473 U.S. 234, 242 (1985)); *see also id.* at 70 n.9 (asserting that historical sources about the meaning of the phrase "bodies politic and corporate" in the original version of the Dictionary Act "at best suggest that the phrase is ambiguous, which still renders the Dictionary Act incapable of supplying the necessary clear intent").

---

incorporated by the government and that the new language therefore merely clarified "the original signification." Still, whatever Durant was thinking, Congress did drop "bodies politic" from the definition of "person." *Cf. id.* at 573 ("A statutory amendment made inadvertently should still count as a statutory amendment.").

[15] When modern courts interpret the word "person" in Rev. Stat. § 1979 (*i.e.*, 42 U.S.C. § 1983), one can sensibly debate whether they should continue to draw guidance from Rev. Stat. § 1 or instead should consult the current version of 1 U.S.C. § 1. That issue boils down to whether the 1948 statute that amended 1 U.S.C. § 1, and that thereby superseded the language found in Rev. Stat. § 1, should be understood not only as signaling how Congress planned to use the word "person" in future statutes but also as affecting the proper interpretation of statutes that were already on the books, like Rev. Stat. § 1979. Justice Brennan's position, however, assumed that the meaning of the word "person" in Rev. Stat. § 1979 comes *neither* from 1 U.S.C. § 1 *nor* from Rev. Stat. § 1, but instead from the *original* Dictionary Act as adopted by Congress in 1871. Why that would be so is not apparent. Perhaps one could say that Rev. Stat. § 1979 was intended to have exactly the same scope as the corresponding language in the Civil Rights Act of 1871, so courts should use the 1871 definition of "person." But § 1 of the Revised Statutes replaced the 1871 definition, and § 1 explicitly operated "[i]n determining the meaning of the revised statutes" (including Rev. Stat. § 1979). *See* Rev. Stat. § 1, 18 Stat. at 1.

Was the majority correct to apply this "ordinary rule of statutory construction" to 42 U.S.C. § 1983, and to presume that § 1983 was not meant to impose new liabilities on states? Or was Justice Brennan correct to criticize the majority's application of these canons to a statute enacted during Reconstruction by a Congress that was "in the midst of altering the 'balance between the States and the Federal Government' " and "transform[ing] our federal system"? *See Will*, 491 U.S. at 85 (Brennan, J., dissenting).

The Court reprised *Will* in *Vermont Agency of Natural Resources v. United States ex rel. Stevens*, 529 U.S. 765 (2000). That case involved the federal False Claims Act, which authorizes private relators to launch *qui tam* suits in the name of the federal government against "[a]ny person" who "knowingly presents[ ] or causes to be presented" a "false or fraudulent claim for payment" to an officer or employee of the federal government. 31 U.S.C. §§ 3729(a), 3730(b) (2000). In concluding that a state was not a "person" subject to liability under this provision, the Court again invoked "our longstanding interpretive presumption that 'person' does not include the sovereign," *Vermont Agency*, 529 U.S. at 780, and the Court again asserted that this presumption was " 'particularly applicable' " where the federal statute in question would otherwise subject states to new liabilities, *see id.* at 781 (quoting *Will*, 491 U.S. at 64).

More recently, when interpreting the word "person" in a modern federal statute, the Supreme Court has also invoked the generic definition in 1 U.S.C. § 1—the modern version of the Dictionary Act. In *Return Mail, Inc. v. U.S. Postal Service*, 139 S. Ct. 1853 (2019), the Court held that the U.S. Postal Service (which is "an independent establishment of the executive branch of the Government of the United States," 39 U.S.C. § 201) could not initiate administrative proceedings to challenge the validity of someone else's patent, because a federal agency is not a "person" within the meaning of the statutory provisions that authorize such proceedings. Justice Sotomayor's majority opinion began by noting that absent contrary directions, "the Court applies a 'longstanding interpretive presumption that "person" does not include the sovereign,' and thus excludes a federal agency like the Postal Service." *Return Mail*, 139 S. Ct. at 1861–62 (quoting *Vermont Agency*, 529 U.S. at 780–81). According to Justice Sotomayor, this presumption not only "reflects 'common usage,' " *id.* at 1862 (quoting United States v. United Mine Workers, 330 U.S. 258, 275 (1947)), but also "is . . . an express directive from Congress." *Id.* Justice Sotomayor pointed to 1 U.S.C. § 1, which says:

> "In determining the meaning of any Act of Congress, unless the context indicates otherwise—. . .
>
>> "the word[ ] 'person' . . . include[s] corporations, companies, associations, firms, partnerships, societies, and joint stock companies, as well as individuals . . . ."

1 U.S.C. § 1. Although this provision is cast as "includ[ing]" various types of entities, Justice Sotomayor read it as presumptively excluding other types of entities—such as the federal government, which is "[n]otably absent from the list." *Return Mail*, 139 S. Ct. at 1862; *accord United Mine Workers*, 330 U.S. at 275. If valid, the same argument would support a presumption against reading the word "person" in federal statutes to include states.[16]

c. FEDERAL STATUTES AND THE QUALIFICATIONS FOR IMPORTANT STATE OFFICES

In both *Will* and *Vermont Agency*, the Supreme Court was considering whether particular federal statutes created rights of action against states. That issue dovetails with questions about state sovereign immunity, and doctrines about state sovereign immunity may have influenced the Court's analysis. *See, e.g.*, *Will*, 491 U.S. at 65 (citing *Atascadero State Hospital v. Scanlon*, 473 U.S. 234 (1985)); *Vermont Agency*, 529 U.S. at 780 n.9 (distinguishing cases cited by the dissent on the ground that "[n]one of them . . . involved a statutory provision authorizing private suit against a State"). By contrast, the next major case that we will consider—*Gregory v. Ashcroft*, 501 U.S. 452 (1991)—addresses the substantive duties that federal law should be understood to impose upon states, not simply the existence of rights of action to enforce such duties.

As background, you need some information about Congress's constitutional authority to regulate the employment practices of state governments in the same ways that Congress regulates the employment practices of private businesses. The Supreme Court has expressed different views on that topic at different times.

Many of the relevant cases have involved the Fair Labor Standards Act, which requires covered employers to pay non-exempt employees no less than the federally mandated minimum wage (and to pay time-and-a-half for overtime). As originally enacted in 1938, the Act did not purport to impose these duties on state or local governments. *See* Fair Labor Standards Act of 1938, ch. 676, § 3(d), 52 Stat. 1060, 1060 (specifying that the term "employer," as used in the Act, "shall not include . . . any State or political subdivision of a State"). In the 1960s, however, Congress amended the Act to reach workers in hospitals and schools run by states and political subdivisions of states, and the Supreme Court upheld the constitutionality of this amendment in *Maryland v. Wirtz*, 392 U.S. 183 (1968). *See id.* at 195 (indicating that the Constitution does empower Congress to regulate the pay of these state employees, even if the

---

[16] By contrast, municipal corporations might presumptively be included along with other corporations. *Cf.* Cook County v. United States ex rel. Chandler, 538 U.S. 119, 125–29 (2003) (holding that a municipal corporation, like other corporations, is a "person" for purposes of the False Claims Act); *Monell*, 436 U.S. at 690 (holding that "local government units" more generally are "person[s]" for purposes of 42 U.S.C. § 1983).

relevant state interests are characterized as "governmental" rather than "proprietary"). Congress then enacted the Fair Labor Standards Amendments of 1974, Pub. L. 93–259, 88 Stat. 55, which extended the Act to reach state employees more generally. That extension of the Act hit a roadblock in *National League of Cities v. Usery*, 426 U.S. 833 (1976), when a closely divided Supreme Court partially overruled *Maryland v. Wirtz* and held that the Act could not validly be applied to state and local employees who perform "traditional governmental functions." *Nat'l League of Cities*, 426 U.S. at 852; *see also id.* at 840–52 (concluding that the power to determine the wages and hours of those employees is one of the "attributes of sovereignty" that "attach[ ] to every state government" and that the Constitution implicitly prevents Congress from impairing). Nine years later, however, another closely divided opinion changed course again. In *Garcia v. San Antonio Metropolitan Transit Authority*, 469 U.S. 528 (1985), the Court overruled *National League of Cities* and held that the Constitution does *not* prevent Congress from regulating how state and local governments treat public employees who perform traditional governmental functions. According to Justice Blackmun's majority opinion in *Garcia*, the distinction between "governmental" and "proprietary" functions was both unwarranted and unworkable, and courts should not invoke it as a restriction on Congress's power. *See Garcia*, 469 U.S. at 537–47. While Justice Blackmun conceded that states have "sovereign interests" that deserve respect, he argued that those interests "are more properly protected by procedural safeguards inherent in the structure of the federal system than by judicially created limitations on federal power." *Id.* at 552.

In making this argument, Justice Blackmun was alluding to what Professor Herbert Wechsler had called "the political safeguards of federalism." *See* Herbert Wechsler, *The Political Safeguards of Federalism: The Rôle of the States in the Composition and Selection of the National Government*, 54 COLUM. L. REV. 543 (1954). Because members of Congress are chosen state by state and must please constituencies in individual states in order to win re-election, they might have political incentives to be sensitive to state interests when drafting federal statutes. According to Justice Blackmun, the Constitution relies primarily upon those incentives to keep Congress from using its enumerated powers to trample the states. *See Garcia*, 469 U.S. at 554 ("[T]he fundamental limitation that the constitutional scheme imposes on the Commerce Clause to protect the 'States as States' is one of process rather than one of result."). The Court therefore declined to read an implicit federalism-based limitation into the substance of the powers that the Commerce Clause and the Necessary and Proper Clause give Congress. In *Garcia*, the Court held that the Constitution enables Congress to subject a municipal mass-transit system (and, presumably, most other operations of state and local governments) to "the same minimum-wage and overtime obligations" that Congress imposes upon private businesses. *Id.*

As a matter of statutory interpretation, however, at least some Justices are stingy about reading federal statutes to *use* the powers that *Garcia* recognized. The majority opinion in the next case (written by Justice O'Connor, who was one of the four dissenters in *Garcia*) is the leading example.

The case involved another federal statute that imposes duties on employers—the Age Discrimination in Employment Act (ADEA). As originally enacted in 1967, the ADEA had not purported to regulate the employment practices of state governments. *See* Age Discrimination in Employment Act of 1967, Pub. L. 90–202, § 11(b), 81 Stat. 602, 605 (specifying that the term "employer," as used in the Act, "does not include . . . a State or political subdivision thereof"). But in 1974, as part of the same statute that gave rise to *National League of Cities v. Usery*, Congress extended the ADEA to cover most employees of state and local government. Congress accomplished that result in two steps. First, Congress amended the ADEA's definition of "employer" to include "a State or political subdivision of a State and any agency or instrumentality of a State or a political subdivision of a State." Fair Labor Standards Amendments of 1974, Pub. L. 93–259, § 28(a)(2), 88 Stat. 55, 74 (amending § 11(b) of the ADEA, which is codified at 29 U.S.C. § 630(b)). Second, Congress amended the ADEA's definition of "employee" to omit a few categories of government workers whom Congress apparently decided not to protect. *See id.* § 28(a)(4), 88 Stat. at 74 (amending § 11(f) of the ADEA, which is codified at 29 U.S.C. § 630(f), so as to exclude "any person elected to public office in any State or political subdivision of any State by the qualified voters thereof, or any person chosen by such officer to be on such officer's personal staff, or an appointee on the policymaking level or an immediate adviser with respect to the exercise of the constitutional or legal powers of the office"). The next case addressed the scope of the categories that Congress had excluded from the statutory definition of "employee."

Gregory v. Ashcroft

501 U.S. 452 (1991)

■ *JUSTICE O'CONNOR delivered the opinion of the Court:*

Article V, § 26, of the Missouri Constitution provides that "[a]ll judges other than municipal judges shall retire at the age of seventy years." We consider whether this mandatory retirement provision violates the federal Age Discrimination in Employment Act of 1967 (ADEA or Act), 81 Stat. 602, as amended, 29 U.S.C. §§ 621–634, and whether it comports with the federal constitutional prescription of equal protection of the laws.

I

Petitioners are Missouri state judges. Judge Ellis Gregory, Jr., is an associate circuit judge for the Twenty-first Judicial Circuit. Judge

Anthony P. Nugent, Jr., is a judge of the Missouri Court of Appeals, Western District. Both are subject to the § 26 mandatory retirement provision. Petitioners were appointed to office by the Governor of Missouri, pursuant to the Missouri Non-Partisan Court Plan, Mo. Const., Art. V, §§ 25(a)–25(g). Each has, since his appointment, been retained in office by means of a retention election in which the judge ran unopposed, subject only to a "yes or no" vote. See Mo. Const., Art. V, § 25(c)(1).

Petitioners and two other state judges filed suit against John D. Ashcroft, the Governor of Missouri, in the United States District Court for the Eastern District of Missouri, challenging the validity of the mandatory retirement provision. The judges alleged that the provision violated both the ADEA and the Equal Protection Clause of the Fourteenth Amendment to the United States Constitution. The Governor filed a motion to dismiss.

The District Court granted the motion, holding that Missouri's appointed judges are not protected by the ADEA because they are "appointees . . . 'on a policymaking level' " and therefore are excluded from the Act's definition of "employee." . . . The court held also that the mandatory retirement provision does not violate the Equal Protection Clause because there is a rational basis for the distinction between judges and other state officials to whom no mandatory retirement age applies. . . .

The United States Court of Appeals for the Eighth Circuit affirmed the dismissal. 898 F.2d 598 (1990). . . .

We granted certiorari . . . and now affirm.

II

. . . .

A

As every schoolchild learns, our Constitution establishes a system of dual sovereignty between the States and the Federal Government. . . . Over 120 years ago, the Court described the constitutional scheme of dual sovereigns:

> " '[T]he people of each State compose a State, having its own government, and endowed with all the functions essential to separate and independent existence[.]' . . . '[W]ithout the States in union, there could be no such political body as the United States.' Not only, therefore, can there be no loss of separate and independent autonomy to the States, through their union under the Constitution, but it may be not unreasonably said that the preservation of the States, and the maintenance of their governments, are as much within the design and care of the Constitution as the preservation of the Union and the maintenance of the National government. The Constitution, in all its provisions, looks to an indestructible Union,

composed of indestructible States." *Texas v. White*, 7 Wall. 700, 725 (1869), quoting *Lane County v. Oregon*, 7 Wall. 71, 76 (1869).

The Constitution created a Federal Government of limited powers. "The powers not delegated to the United States by the Constitution, nor prohibited by it to the States, are reserved to the States respectively, or to the people." U.S. Const., Amdt. 10. The States thus retain substantial sovereign authority under our constitutional system. . . .

This federalist structure of joint sovereigns preserves to the people numerous advantages. It assures a decentralized government that will be more sensitive to the diverse needs of a heterogenous society; it increases opportunity for citizen involvement in democratic processes; it allows for more innovation and experimentation in government; and it makes government more responsive by putting the States in competition for a mobile citizenry. See generally McConnell, Federalism: Evaluating the Founders' Design, 54 U. Chi. L. Rev. 1484, 1491–1511 (1987); Merritt, The Guarantee Clause and State Autonomy: Federalism for a Third Century, 88 Colum. L. Rev. 1, 3–10 (1988).

Perhaps the principal benefit of the federalist system is a check on abuses of government power. "The 'constitutionally mandated balance of power' between the States and the Federal Government was adopted by the Framers to ensure the protection of 'our fundamental liberties.' " *Atascadero State Hospital v. Scanlon*, 473 U.S. 234, 242 (1985), quoting *Garcia v. San Antonio Metropolitan Transit Authority*, 469 U.S. 528, 572 (1985) (Powell, J., dissenting). Just as the separation and independence of the coordinate branches of the Federal Government serve to prevent the accumulation of excessive power in any one branch, a healthy balance of power between the States and the Federal Government will reduce the risk of tyranny and abuse from either front. Alexander Hamilton explained to the people of New York, perhaps optimistically, that the new federalist system would suppress completely "the attempts of the government to establish a tyranny":

> "[I]n a confederacy the people, without exaggeration, may be said to be entirely the masters of their own fate. Power being almost always the rival of power, the general government will at all times stand ready to check the usurpations of the state governments, and these will have the same disposition towards the general government. The people, by throwing themselves into either scale, will infallibly make it preponderate. If their rights are invaded by either, they can make use of the other as the instrument of redress." The Federalist No. 28, pp. 180–181 (C. Rossiter ed. 1961).

James Madison made much the same point:

> "In a single republic, all the power surrendered by the people is submitted to the administration of a single government; and the usurpations are guarded against by a division of the government into distinct and separate departments. In the compound republic of

America, the power surrendered by the people is first divided between two distinct governments, and then the portion allotted to each subdivided among distinct and separate departments. Hence a double security arises to the rights of the people. The different governments will control each other, at the same time that each will be controlled by itself." *Id.*, No. 51, p. 323.

One fairly can dispute whether our federalist system has been quite as successful in checking government abuse as Hamilton promised, but there is no doubt about the design. If this "double security" is to be effective, there must be a proper balance between the States and the Federal Government. These twin powers will act as mutual restraints only if both are credible. In the tension between federal and state power lies the promise of liberty.

The Federal Government holds a decided advantage in this delicate balance: the Supremacy Clause. U.S. Const., Art. VI, cl. 2. As long as it is acting within the powers granted it under the Constitution, Congress may impose its will on the States. Congress may legislate in areas traditionally regulated by the States. This is an extraordinary power in a federalist system. It is a power that we must assume Congress does not exercise lightly.

The present case concerns a state constitutional provision through which the people of Missouri establish a qualification for those who sit as their judges. This provision goes beyond an area traditionally regulated by the States; it is a decision of the most fundamental sort for a sovereign entity. Through the structure of its government, and the character of those who exercise government authority, a State defines itself as a sovereign. "It is obviously essential to the independence of the States, and to their peace and tranquility, that their power to prescribe the qualifications of their own officers . . . should be exclusive, and free from external interference, except so far as plainly provided by the Constitution of the United States." *Taylor v. Beckham*, 178 U.S. 548, 570–571 (1900). See also *Boyd v. Nebraska ex rel. Thayer*, 143 U.S. 135, 161 (1892) ("Each State has the power to prescribe the qualifications of its officers and the manner in which they shall be chosen").

Congressional interference with this decision of the people of Missouri, defining their constitutional officers, would upset the usual constitutional balance of federal and state powers. For this reason, "it is incumbent upon the federal courts to be certain of Congress' intent before finding that federal law overrides" this balance. *Atascadero*, [473 U.S.] at 243. We explained recently:

> "[I]f Congress intends to alter the 'usual constitutional balance between the States and the Federal Government,' it must make its intention to do so 'unmistakably clear in the language of the statute.' *Atascadero State Hospital v. Scanlon*, 473 U.S. 234, 242 (1985); see also *Pennhurst State School and Hospital v. Halderman*, 465 U.S. 89, 99 (1984). *Atascadero* was an Eleventh Amendment case, but a

> similar approach is applied in other contexts. Congress should make its intention 'clear and manifest' if it intends to pre-empt the historic powers of the States, *Rice v. Santa Fe Elevator Corp.*, 331 U.S. 218, 230 (1947). . . . 'In traditionally sensitive areas, such as legislation affecting the federal balance, the requirement of clear statement assures that the legislature has in fact faced, and intended to bring into issue, the critical matters involved in the judicial decision.' *United States v. Bass*, 404 U.S. 336, 349 (1971)." *Will v. Michigan Dept. of State Police*, 491 U.S. 58, 65 (1989).

This plain statement rule is nothing more than an acknowledgment that the States retain substantial sovereign powers under our constitutional scheme, powers with which Congress does not readily interfere.

. . . .

[Various cases cited by the Court] stand in recognition of the authority of the people of the States to determine the qualifications of their most important government officials. It is an authority that lies at " 'the heart of representative government.' " [*Bernal v. Fainter*, 467 U.S. 216, 221 (1984) (quoting Sugarman v. Dougall, 413 U.S. 634, 647 (1973)).] It is a power reserved to the States under the Tenth Amendment and guaranteed them by that provision of the Constitution under which the United States "guarantee[s] to every State in this Union a Republican Form of Government." U.S. Const., Art. IV, § 4. . . .

The authority of the people of the States to determine the qualifications of their government officials is, of course, not without limit. Other constitutional provisions, most notably the Fourteenth Amendment, proscribe certain qualifications . . . . Here, we must decide what Congress did in extending the ADEA to the States, pursuant to its powers under the Commerce Clause. See *EEOC v. Wyoming*, 460 U.S. 226 (1983) (the extension of the ADEA to employment by state and local governments was a valid exercise of Congress' powers under the Commerce Clause). As against Congress' powers "[t]o regulate Commerce . . . among the several States," U.S. Const., Art. I, § 8, cl. 3, the authority of the people of the States to determine the qualifications of their government officials may be inviolate.

We are constrained in our ability to consider the limits that the state-federal balance places on Congress' powers under the Commerce Clause. See *Garcia v. San Antonio Metropolitan Transit Authority*, 469 U.S. 528 (1985) (declining to review limitations placed on Congress' Commerce Clause powers by our federal system). But there is no need to do so if we hold that the ADEA does not apply to state judges. Application of the plain statement rule thus may avoid a potential constitutional problem. Indeed, inasmuch as this Court in *Garcia* has left primarily to the political process the protection of the States against intrusive exercises of Congress' Commerce Clause powers, we must be absolutely certain that Congress intended such an exercise. "[T]o give the state-displacing weight of federal law to mere congressional *ambiguity* would evade the very procedure for lawmaking on which *Garcia* relied to protect states' interests." L. Tribe, American Constitutional Law § 6-25, p. 480 (2d ed. 1988).

B

In 1974, Congress extended the substantive provisions of the ADEA to include the States as employers. . . . At the same time, Congress amended the definition of "employee" to exclude all elected and most high-ranking government officials. Under the Act, as amended:

> "The term 'employee' means an individual employed by any employer except that the term 'employee' shall not include any person elected to public office in any State or political subdivision of any State by the qualified voters thereof, or any person chosen by such officer to be on such officer's personal staff, or an appointee on the policymaking level or an immediate adviser with respect to the exercise of the constitutional or legal powers of the office." 29 U.S.C. § 630(f).

Governor Ashcroft contends that the § 630(f) exclusion of certain public officials also excludes judges, like petitioners, who are appointed to office by the Governor and are then subject to retention election. The Governor points to two passages in § 630(f). First, he argues, these judges are selected by an elected official and, because they make policy, are "appointee[s] on the policymaking level."

Petitioners counter that judges merely resolve factual disputes and decide questions of law; they do not make policy. Moreover, petitioners point out that the policymaking-level exception is part of a trilogy, tied closely to the elected-official exception. Thus, the Act excepts elected officials and: (1) "any person chosen by such officer to be on such officer's personal staff"; (2) "an appointee on the policymaking level"; and (3) "an immediate advisor with respect to the exercise of the constitutional or legal powers of the office." Applying the maxim of statutory construction *noscitur a sociis*—that a word is known by the company it keeps—petitioners argue that since (1) and (3) refer only to those in close working relationships with elected officials, so too must (2). Even if it can be said that judges may make policy, petitioners contend, they do not do so at the behest of an elected official.

Governor Ashcroft relies on the plain language of the statute: It exempts persons appointed "at the policymaking level." The Governor argues that state judges, in fashioning and applying the common law, make policy. Missouri is a common law state. See Mo. Rev. Stat. § 1.010 (1986) (adopting "[t]he common law of England" consistent with federal and state law). The common law, unlike a constitution or statute, provides no definitive text; it is to be derived from the interstices of prior opinions and a well-considered judgment of what is best for the community. As Justice Holmes put it:

"The very considerations which judges most rarely mention, and always with an apology, are the secret root from which the law draws all the juices of life. I mean, of course, considerations of what is expedient for the community concerned. Every important principle which is developed by litigation is in fact and at bottom the result of more or less definitely understood views of public policy; most generally, to be sure, under our practice and traditions, the unconscious result of instinctive preferences and inarticulate convictions, but nonetheless traceable to views of public policy in the last analysis." O. Holmes, The Common Law 35–36 (1881).

Governor Ashcroft contends that Missouri judges make policy in other ways as well. The Missouri Supreme Court and Courts of Appeals have supervisory authority over inferior courts. Mo. Const., Art. V, § 4. The Missouri Supreme Court has the constitutional duty to establish rules of practice and procedure for the Missouri court system, and inferior courts exercise policy judgment in establishing local rules of practice. See Mo. Const., Art. V, § 5. The state courts have supervisory powers over the state bar, with the Missouri Supreme Court given the authority to develop disciplinary rules. See Mo. Rev. Stat. §§ 484.040, 484.200–484.270 (1986); Rules Governing the Missouri Bar and the Judiciary (1991).

The Governor stresses judges' policymaking responsibilities, but it is far from plain that the statutory exception requires that judges actually make policy. The statute refers to appointees "on the policymaking level," not to appointees "who make policy." It may be sufficient that the appointee is in a position requiring the exercise of discretion concerning issues of public importance. This certainly describes the bench, regardless of whether judges might be considered policymakers in the same sense as the executive or legislature.

Nonetheless, "appointee at the policymaking level," particularly in the context of the other exceptions that surround it, is an odd way for Congress to exclude judges; a plain statement that judges are not "employees" would seem the most efficient phrasing. But in this case we are not looking for a plain statement that judges are excluded. We will not read the ADEA to cover state judges unless Congress has made it clear that judges are *included*. This does not mean that the Act must mention judges explicitly, though it does not. . . . Rather, it must be plain to anyone reading the Act that it covers judges. In the context of a statute that plainly excludes most important state public officials, "appointee on the policymaking level" is sufficiently broad that we cannot conclude that the statute plainly covers appointed state judges. Therefore, it does not.

The ADEA plainly covers all state employees except those excluded by one of the exceptions. Where it is unambiguous that an employee does not fall within one of the exceptions, the Act states plainly and unequivocally that the employee is included. It is at least ambiguous whether a state judge is an "appointee on the policymaking level."

Governor Ashcroft points also to the "person elected to public office" exception. He contends that because petitioners—although appointed to office initially—are subject to retention election, they are "elected to public office" under the ADEA. Because we conclude that petitioners fall presumptively under the policymaking-level exception, we need not answer this question.

C

The extension of the ADEA to employment by state and local governments was a valid exercise of Congress' powers under the Commerce Clause. *EEOC v. Wyoming*, 460 U.S. 226 (1983). In *Wyoming*, we reserved the questions whether Congress might also have passed the ADEA extension pursuant to its powers under § 5 of the Fourteenth Amendment, and whether the extension would have been a valid exercise of that power. We noted, however, that the principles of federalism that constrain Congress' exercise of its Commerce Clause powers are attenuated when Congress acts pursuant to its powers to enforce the Civil War Amendments. *Id.* at 243, and n. 18, citing *City of Rome v. United States*, 446 U.S. 156, 179 (1980). This is because those "Amendments were specifically designed as an expansion of federal power and an intrusion on state sovereignty." *Id.* at 179. One might argue, therefore, that if Congress passed the ADEA extension under its § 5 powers, the concerns about federal intrusion into state government that compel the result in this case might carry less weight.

By its terms, the Fourteenth Amendment contemplates interference with state authority: "No State shall . . . deny to any person within its jurisdiction the equal protection of the laws." U.S. Const., Amdt. 14. But this Court has never held that the Amendment may be applied in complete disregard for a State's constitutional powers. Rather, the Court has recognized that the States' power to define the qualifications of their officeholders has force even as against the proscriptions of the Fourteenth Amendment.

. . . .

Of particular relevance here is *Pennhurst State School and Hospital v. Halderman*, 451 U.S. 1 (1981). The question in that case was whether Congress, in passing a section of the Developmentally Disabled Assistance and Bill of Rights Act, 42 U.S.C. § 6010 (1982 ed.), intended to place an obligation on the States to provide certain kinds of treatment to the disabled. Respondent Halderman argued that Congress passed § 6010 pursuant to § 5 of the Fourteenth Amendment, and therefore that it was mandatory on the States, regardless of whether they received federal funds. Petitioner and the United States, as respondent, argued that, in passing § 6010, Congress acted pursuant to its spending power alone. Consequently, § 6010 applied only to States accepting federal funds under the Act.

The Court was required to consider the "appropriate test for determining when Congress intends to enforce" the guarantees of the Fourteenth Amendment. 451 U.S. at 16. We adopted a rule fully cognizant of the traditional power of the States: "Because such legislation imposes congressional policy on a State involuntarily, and because it often intrudes on traditional state authority, we should not quickly attribute to Congress an unstated intent to act under its authority to enforce the Fourteenth Amendment." *Ibid.* Because Congress nowhere stated its intent to impose mandatory obligations on the States under its § 5 powers, we concluded that Congress did not do so. *Ibid.*

The *Pennhurst* rule looks much like the plain statement rule we apply today. In *EEOC v. Wyoming*, the Court explained that *Pennhurst* established a rule of statutory construction to be applied where statutory intent is ambiguous. 460 U.S. at 244, n. 18. In light of the ADEA's clear exclusion of most important public officials, it is at least ambiguous whether Congress intended that appointed judges nonetheless be included. In the face of such ambiguity, we will not attribute to Congress an intent to intrude on state governmental functions regardless of whether Congress acted pursuant to its Commerce Clause powers or § 5 of the Fourteenth Amendment.

III

Petitioners argue that, even if they are not covered by the ADEA, the Missouri Constitution's mandatory retirement provision for judges violates the Equal Protection Clause of the Fourteenth Amendment to the United States Constitution. Petitioners contend that there is no rational basis for the decision of the people of Missouri to preclude those aged 70 and over from serving as their judges. . . .

. . . .

The Missouri mandatory retirement provision, like all legal classifications, is founded on a generalization. It is far from true that all judges suffer significant deterioration in performance at age 70. It is probably not true that most do. It may not be true at all. But a State " 'does not violate the Equal Protection Clause merely because the classifications made by its laws are imperfect.' " [*Massachusetts Bd. of Retirement v. Murgia*, 427 U.S. 307, 316 (1976)], quoting *Dandridge v. Williams*, 397 U.S. 471, 485 (1970). "In an equal protection case of this type . . . those challenging the . . . judgment [of the people] must convince the court that the . . . facts on which the classification is apparently based could not reasonably be conceived to be true by the . . . decisionmaker." [*Vance v. Bradley*, 440 U.S. 93, 111 (1979).] The people of Missouri rationally could conclude that the threat of deterioration at age 70 is sufficiently great, and the alternatives for removal sufficiently inadequate, that they will require all judges to step aside at age 70. This classification does not violate the Equal Protection Clause. . . .

■ *JUSTICE WHITE, joined by JUSTICE STEVENS, concurring in part, dissenting in part, and concurring in the judgment:*

I agree with the majority that neither the Age Discrimination in Employment Act (ADEA) nor the Equal Protection Clause prohibits Missouri's mandatory retirement provision as applied to petitioners, and I therefore concur in the judgment and in Parts I and III of the majority's opinion. I cannot agree, however, with the majority's reasoning in Part II of its opinion, which ignores several areas of well-established precedent and announces a rule that is likely to prove both unwise and infeasible. That the majority's analysis in Part II is completely unnecessary to the proper resolution of this case makes it all the more remarkable.

I

.... The dispute in this case ... is not whether Congress has outlawed age discrimination by the States. It clearly has. The only question is whether petitioners fall within the definition of "employee" in the Act, § 630(f), which contains exceptions for elected officials and certain appointed officials. If petitioners *are* "employee[s]," Missouri's mandatory retirement provision clearly conflicts with the antidiscrimination provisions of the ADEA. Indeed, we have noted that the "policies and substantive provisions of the [ADEA] apply with especial force in the case of mandatory retirement provisions." *Western Air Lines, Inc. v. Criswell*, 472 U.S. 400, 410 (1985). Pre-emption therefore is automatic, since "state law is pre-empted to the extent that it actually conflicts with federal law." *Pacific Gas & Elec. Co. v. State Energy Resources Conservation and Development Comm'n*, 461 U.S. 190, 204 (1983). The majority's federalism concerns are irrelevant to such "actual conflict" pre-emption. " 'The relative importance to the State of its own law is not material when there is a conflict with a valid federal law, for the Framers of our Constitution provided that the federal law must prevail.' " *Fidelity Federal Sav. & Loan Assn. v. De la Cuesta*, 458 U.S. 141, 153 (1982), quoting *Free v. Bland*, 369 U.S. 663, 666 (1962).

While acknowledging this principle of federal legislative supremacy, ... the majority nevertheless imposes upon Congress a "plain statement" requirement. The majority claims to derive this requirement from the plain statement approach developed in our Eleventh Amendment cases, see, *e.g.*, *Atascadero State Hospital v. Scanlon*, 473 U.S. 234 (1985), and applied two Terms ago in *Will v. Michigan Dept. of State Police*, 491 U.S. 58, 65 (1989). The issue in those cases, however, was whether Congress intended a particular statute to extend to the States *at all*. In *Atascadero*, for example, the issue was whether States could be sued under § 504 of the Rehabilitation Act of 1973, 29 U.S.C. § 794. Similarly, the issue in *Will* was whether States could be sued under 42 U.S.C. § 1983. In the present case, by contrast, Congress has expressly extended the coverage of the ADEA to the States and their employees. Its intention to regulate age discrimination by States is thus "unmistakably clear in the language of the statute." *Atascadero*, 473 U.S. at 242.... The only dispute is over the precise details of the statute's application. We have never extended the plain statement approach that far, and the majority offers no compelling reason for doing so.

. . . .

The majority's plain statement rule is not only unprecedented, it directly contravenes our decisions in *Garcia v. San Antonio Metropolitan Transit Authority*, 469 U.S. 528 (1985), and *South Carolina v. Baker*, 485 U.S. 505 (1988). In those cases we made it clear "that States must find their protection from congressional regulation through the national political process, not through judicially defined spheres of unregulable state activity." *Id.* at 512. We also rejected as "unsound in principle and unworkable in practice" any test for state immunity that requires a judicial determination of which state activities are " 'traditional,' " " 'integral,' " or " 'necessary.' " *Garcia*, 469 U.S. at 546. The majority disregards those decisions in its attempt to carve out areas of state activity that will receive special protection from federal legislation.

The majority's approach is also unsound because it will serve only to confuse the law. First, the majority fails to explain the scope of its rule. Is the rule limited to federal regulation of the qualifications of state officials? . . . Or does it apply more broadly to the regulation of any "state governmental functions"? . . . Second, the majority does not explain its requirement that Congress' intent to regulate a particular state activity be "plain to anyone reading [the federal statute]." See *ante* at 467. Does that mean that it is now improper to look to the purpose or history of a federal statute in determining the scope of the statute's limitations on state activities? If so, the majority's rule is completely inconsistent with our pre-emption jurisprudence. See, *e.g.*, *Hillsborough County v. Automated Medical Laboratories, Inc.*, 471 U.S. 707, 715 (1985) (pre-emption will be found where there is a " 'clear and manifest *purpose*' " to displace state law) (emphasis added). The vagueness of the majority's rule undoubtedly will lead States to assert that various federal statutes no longer apply to a wide variety of state activities if Congress has not expressly referred to those activities in the statute. Congress, in turn, will be forced to draft long and detailed lists of which particular state functions it meant to regulate. . . .

The majority asserts that its plain statement rule is helpful in avoiding a "potential constitutional problem." *Ante* at 464. It is far from clear, however, why there would be a constitutional problem if the ADEA applied to state judges, in light of our decisions in *Garcia* and *Baker*, discussed above. As long as "the national political *process* did not operate in a defective manner, the Tenth Amendment is not implicated." *Baker*, [485 U.S.] at 513. There is no claim in this case that the political process by which the ADEA was extended to state employees was inadequate to protect the States from being "unduly burden[ed]" by the Federal Government. See *Garcia*, [469 U.S.] at 556. In any event, as discussed below, a straightforward analysis of the ADEA's definition of "employee" reveals that the ADEA does not apply here. Thus, even if there were potential constitutional problems in extending the ADEA to state judges, the majority's proposed plain statement rule would not be necessary to avoid them in this case. Indeed, because this case can be decided purely on the basis of statutory interpretation, the majority's announcement of its plain statement rule, which purportedly is derived from constitutional principles, *violates* our general practice of avoiding the unnecessary resolution of constitutional issues.

My disagreement with the majority does not end with its unwarranted announcement of the plain statement rule. Even more disturbing is its treatment of Congress' power under § 5 of the Fourteenth Amendment. . . . Section 5 provides that "[t]he Congress shall have power to enforce, by appropriate legislation, the provisions of this article." Despite that sweeping constitutional delegation of authority to Congress, the majority holds that its plain statement rule will apply with full force to legislation enacted to enforce the Fourteenth Amendment. The majority states: "In the face of . . . ambiguity, we will not attribute to Congress an intent to intrude on state governmental functions *regardless of whether Congress acted pursuant to its Commerce Clause powers or § 5 of the Fourteenth Amendment.*" *Ante* at 470 (emphasis added).

The majority's failure to recognize the special status of legislation enacted pursuant to § 5 ignores that, unlike Congress' Commerce Clause power, "[w]hen Congress acts pursuant to § 5, not only is it exercising legislative authority that is plenary within the terms of the constitutional grant, it is exercising that authority under one section of a constitutional Amendment whose other sections by their own terms embody limitations on state authority." *Fitzpatrick v. Bitzer*, 427 U.S. 445, 456 (1976). Indeed, we have held that "principles of federalism that might otherwise be an obstacle to congressional authority are necessarily overridden by the power to enforce the Civil War Amendments 'by appropriate legislation.' Those Amendments were specifically designed as an expansion of federal power and an intrusion on state sovereignty." *City of Rome v. United States*, 446 U.S. 156, 179 (1980) . . . .

The majority relies upon *Pennhurst State School and Hospital v. Halderman*, 451 U.S. 1 (1981), but that case does not support its approach. There, the Court merely stated that "we should not quickly attribute to Congress an unstated intent to act under its authority to enforce the Fourteenth Amendment." 451 U.S. at 16. In other words, the *Pennhurst* presumption was designed only to answer the question whether a particular piece of legislation was enacted pursuant to § 5. That is very different from the majority's apparent holding that even when Congress *is* acting pursuant to § 5, it nevertheless must specify the precise details of its enactment.

The majority's departures from established precedent are even more disturbing when it is realized, as discussed below, that this case can be affirmed based on simple statutory construction.

II

The statute at issue in this case is the ADEA's definition of "employee" . . . . A parsing of that definition reveals that it excludes from the definition of "employee" (and thus the coverage of the ADEA) four types of (noncivil service) state and local employees: (1) persons elected to public office; (2) the personal staff of elected officials; (3) persons appointed by elected officials to be on the policymaking level; and (4) the immediate advisers of elected officials with respect to the constitutional or legal powers of the officials' offices.

The question before us is whether petitioners fall within the third exception. Like the Court of Appeals, see 898 F.2d 598, 600 (CA8 1990), I assume that petitioners, who were initially appointed to their positions by the Governor of Missouri, are "appointed" rather than "elected" within the meaning of the ADEA. For the reasons below, I also conclude that petitioners are "on the policymaking level."

"Policy" is defined as "a definite course or method of action selected (as by a government, institution, group, or individual) from among alternatives and in the light of given conditions to guide and usu[ally] determine present and future decisions." Webster's Third New International Dictionary 1754 (1976). Applying that definition, it is clear that the decisionmaking engaged in by common-law judges, such as petitioners, places them "on the policymaking level." In resolving disputes, although judges do not operate with unconstrained discretion, they do choose "from among alternatives" and elaborate their choices in order "to guide and . . . determine present and future decisions." The quotation from Justice Holmes in the majority's opinion is an eloquent description of the policymaking nature of the judicial function. . . .

Moreover, it should be remembered that the statutory exception refers to appointees "on the policymaking level," not "policymaking employees." Thus, whether or not judges actually *make* policy, they certainly are on the same *level* as policymaking officials in other branches of government and therefore are covered by the exception. The degree of responsibility vested in judges, for example, is comparable to that of other officials that have been found by the lower courts to be on the policymaking level. See, *e.g.*, *EEOC v. Reno*, 758 F.2d 581 (CA11 1985) (assistant state attorney); *EEOC v. Board of Trustees of Wayne Cty. Community College*, 723 F.2d 509 (CA6 1983) (president of community college).

Petitioners argue that the "appointee[s] on the policymaking level" exception should be construed to apply "only to persons who advise or work closely with the elected official that chose the appointee." Brief for Petitioners 18. In support of that claim, petitioners point out that the exception is "sandwiched" between the "personal staff" and "immediate adviser" exceptions in § 630(f), and thus should be read as covering only similar employees.

Petitioners' premise, however, does not prove their conclusion. It is true that the placement of the "appointee" exception between the "personal staff" and "immediate adviser" exceptions suggests a similarity among the three. But the most obvious similarity is simply that each of the three sets of employees are connected in some way with elected officials: The first and third sets have a certain working relationship with elected officials, while the second is *appointed* by elected officials. There is no textual support for concluding that the second set must *also* have a close working relationship with elected officials. Indeed, such a reading would tend to make the "appointee" exception superfluous since the "personal staff" and "immediate adviser" exceptions would seem to cover most appointees who are in a close working relationship with elected officials. . . .

I join Parts I and III of the Court's opinion and concur in its judgment.

■ *JUSTICE BLACKMUN, joined by JUSTICE MARSHALL, dissenting:*

. . . . Although it may be possible to define an appointed judge as a "policymaker" with only a dictionary as a guide,[1] we have an obligation to construe the exclusion of an "appointee on the policymaking level" with a sensitivity to the context in which Congress placed it. In construing an undefined statutory term, this Court has adhered steadfastly to the rule that "words grouped in a list should be given related meaning," *Dole v. Steelworkers*, 494 U.S. 26, 36 (1990) [internal quotation marks omitted], . . . and that " 'in expounding a statute, we [are] not . . . guided by a single sentence or member of a sentence, but look to the provisions of the whole law, and to its object and policy.' " [*Massachusetts v. Morash*, 490 U.S. 107, 115 (1989)], quoting *Pilot Life Ins. Co. v. Dedeaux*, 481 U.S. 41, 51 (1987). Applying these maxims of statutory construction, I conclude that an appointed state judge is not the kind of "policymaker" whom Congress intended to exclude from the protection of the ADEA.

The policymaker exclusion is placed between the exclusion of "any person chosen by such [elected] officer to be on such officer's personal

[1] Justice White finds the dictionary definition of "policymaker" broad enough to include the Missouri judges involved in this case, because judges resolve disputes by choosing " 'from among alternatives' and elaborate their choices in order 'to guide and . . . determine present and future decisions.' " *Ante* at 482. . . . I hesitate to classify judges as policymakers, even at this level of abstraction. Although some part of a judge's task may be to fill in the interstices of legislative enactments, the *primary* task of a judicial officer is to apply rules reflecting the policy choices made by, or on behalf of, those elected to legislative and executive positions. A judge is first and foremost one who resolves disputes, and not one charged with the duty to fashion broad policies establishing the rights and duties of citizens. That task is reserved primarily for legislators. . . .

Nor am I persuaded that judges should be considered policymakers because they sometimes fashion court rules and are otherwise involved in the administration of the state judiciary. . . . These housekeeping tasks are at most ancillary to a judge's primary function described above.

staff" and the exclusion of "an immediate adviser with respect to the exercise of the constitutional or legal powers of the office." See 29 U.S.C. § 630(f). Reading the policymaker exclusion in light of the other categories of employees listed with it, I conclude that the class of "appointee[s] on the policymaking level" should be limited to those officials who share the characteristics of personal staff members and immediate advisers, *i.e.*, those who work closely with the appointing official and are directly accountable to that official. Additionally, I agree with the reasoning of the Second Circuit in *EEOC v. Vermont*, 904 F.2d 794 (1990):

> "Had Congress intended to except a wide-ranging category of policymaking individuals operating wholly independently of the elected official, it would probably have placed that expansive category at the end of the series, not in the middle." *Id.* at 798.

Because appointed judges are not accountable to the official who appoints them and are precluded from working closely with that official once they have been appointed, they are not "appointee[s] on the policymaking level" for purposes of 29 U.S.C. § 630(f).[2] . . . .

NOTES AND QUESTIONS

1. Article V of the Missouri Constitution spells out the Missouri Non-Partisan Court Plan, to which Judges Gregory and Nugent owed their offices. When a vacancy occurs in a judicial office covered by that plan, a nonpartisan judicial commission sends the governor a list of "three persons possessing the qualifications for such office," and the governor can appoint one of the three. MO. CONST. art. 5, § 25(a). The person whom the governor selects has a relatively short initial term, "ending December thirty-first following the next general election after the expiration of twelve months in the office." *Id.* § 25(c)(1). But if the judge files a timely "declaration of candidacy for election to succeed himself," the judge's name will appear on the ballot at that general election. The judge will not face an opposing candidate; instead, the ballot will simply ask voters whether the judge shall be retained in office. If a majority of those voting on this question say "yes," then the judge shall be retained for a full term. *Id.* As the expiration of that term approaches, the judge can again run in an retention election to succeed himself, and this process can continue until the judge retires at age 70.

With this system in mind, look again at the definition of "employee" provided by § 11(f) of the ADEA, 29 U.S.C. § 630(f). Among other things, the definition excludes "any person elected to public office in any State or

---

[2] I disagree with Justice White's suggestion that this reading of the policymaking exclusion renders it superfluous. *Ante* at 483. There exist policymakers who work closely with an appointing official but who are appropriately classified as neither members of his "personal staff" nor "immediate adviser[s] with respect to the exercise of the constitutional or legal powers of the office." Among others, certain members of the Governor's Cabinet and high level state agency officials well might be covered by the policymaking exclusion, as I construe it.

political subdivision of any State by the qualified voters thereof." Could one argue that this phrase describes Judges Gregory and Nugent, who both had completed their initial terms and were serving full terms that they had won in retention elections? Or is there a difference between being "elected to public office" within the meaning of § 11(f) and simply avoiding the indignity of being thrown out of office in a retention election?

2. Instead of characterizing Judges Gregory and Nugent as having been "elected to public office" by the voters of Missouri, the Supreme Court thought of them as "appointee[s]." The question then became whether they were appointees "on the policymaking level."

To determine the meaning of that phrase in § 11(f), Justice Blackmun's dissent invoked the canon *noscitur a sociis*. In § 11(f), the phrase "an appointee on the policymaking level" is sandwiched between two other phrases: "any person chosen by [a popularly elected] officer to be on such officer's personal staff" and "an immediate adviser with respect to the exercise of the constitutional or legal powers of the office." Both of those phrases, Justice Blackmun observed, refer to people "who work closely with the appointing official and are directly accountable to that official." According to Justice Blackmun, that fact should have colored the Court's understanding of the phrase "appointee on the policymaking level": state judges should not be lumped into that category, because they do not have a close working relationship with the elected official who appointed them (or, for that matter, with other elected officials).

Justice White was not averse to using *noscitur a sociis* here, but he had a different idea about how to apply it. Given the structure of the list, he was willing to infer that the phrase "appointee on the policymaking level" refers to appointees *of an elected official*. In his view, though, that is the only connection with an elected official that the context supports. "There is no textual support for concluding that the [appointee] must *also* have a close working relationship with elected officials."

Who had the better of this argument? As you try to answer that question, imagine that a particular state has some independent regulatory commissions that exercise significant policymaking authority. If an elected official appoints someone to chair such a commission, wouldn't that person be "an appointee on the policymaking level" even if she has nothing further to do with elected officials?

3. Suppose you agree with Justice White: someone can be "an appointee on the policymaking level" within the meaning of § 11(f) despite lacking a close working relationship with any elected officials. Even so, it does not automatically follow that state judges are "appointee[s] on the policymaking level." Figuring out how to apply that phrase to state judges requires us both to interpret the phrase (what does "on the policymaking level" mean?) and to answer some questions of jurisprudence (what exactly do state judges do?). Different people might take different positions about whether state judges are "appointee[s] on the policymaking level."

Justice O'Connor's majority opinion resolved that uncertainty by invoking two principles of statutory interpretation that, in this context, amount to federalism-based canons. The first is the canon about interpreting statutes so as to avoid serious questions about their constitutionality. At the close of Part II.A of her opinion, Justice O'Connor noted that if the Court read the phrase "appointee on the policymaking level" in § 11(f) to include state judges like the plaintiffs, then the ADEA would not purport to protect those judges, and the Court would not have to decide whether the Constitution gives Congress the power to do so—that is, whether Congress can validly prevent states from setting a mandatory retirement age for the state judiciary. Notwithstanding *Garcia,* Justice O'Connor seemed to consider that question sufficiently unsettled to trigger the canon that favors avoiding constitutional doubts.

But even if reading the ADEA to prevent states from setting a mandatory retirement age for the state judiciary would not raise any serious constitutional questions, Justice O'Connor also invoked a second canon—the idea that federal statutes should not lightly be read to "upset the usual constitutional balance of federal and state powers." As applied to the issue in *Gregory*, Justice O'Connor took this principle to mean that the ADEA should not lightly be read to restrict the qualifications that states can establish for important state offices. Indeed, she articulated a very strong version of that idea: the ADEA should not be interpreted to cover state judges unless "anyone reading the Act" would think it "plain" that the Act covers judges. According to Justice O'Connor, it followed that if the phrase "appointee on the policymaking level" in § 11(f) of the ADEA is vague or ambiguous, and if reading that phrase broadly will exclude state judges from the substantive protections of the Act, then the Court should conclude that state judges *are* "appointee[s] on the policymaking level." In other words, the Court should resolve indeterminacies in the ADEA in whichever way will exclude state judges from the ADEA's coverage.

Justice O'Connor offered both a descriptive and a normative justification for that idea. In her view, the canon that she was applying reflects the fact that "Congress does not readily interfere" with various "sovereign powers" retained by each state, including the power of the people of each state "to determine the qualifications of their most important government officials." That formulation suggests that Justice O'Connor saw her federalism-based canon as a window onto congressional intent. But Justice O'Connor also advanced a normative argument. In particular, she suggested that her application of the canon was a way to improve the federal lawmaking process by creating the conditions necessary for the political safeguards of federalism to function. That is the point of her quotation from Professor Tribe's treatise: "[T]o give the state-displacing weight of federal law to mere congressional *ambiguity* would evade the very procedure for lawmaking on which *Garcia* relied to protect states' interests."

To understand this argument, imagine that the Court had resolved the indeterminacy in § 11(f) of the ADEA in the manner that the dissenters favored, so that the ADEA forbade states to establish a mandatory retirement age for state judges. Because the ADEA is not clear about whether it protects state judges, some members of Congress may have voted for the relevant statutory language without realizing that it would have this effect, and hence without taking appropriate account of state interests. According to Justice O'Connor, that would be bad. To increase the chances that the political safeguards of federalism will work as intended, Justice O'Connor urged the Court to resolve indeterminacies in federal statutes in such a way as to minimize incursions upon state sovereignty.

Do the political safeguards of federalism really justify this special interpretive protection? Federalism is not the only thing that the legislative process is designed to protect. To take just one example, the process of bicameralism and presentment is supposed to promote a species of reasoned decisionmaking (albeit with a bias toward inertia). For the process to work as intended, it surely is desirable for members of Congress to understand the ramifications of the bills on which they vote—not just with respect to federalism, but with respect to everything else too. Yet when federal statutes are unclear in ways that do not implicate federalism, courts do not necessarily resolve the indeterminacy in the way that produces the fewest possible changes to our existing legal order. Instead, courts often simply make an *ad hoc* choice among the permissible interpretations—even though some members of Congress may have voted for the statute without realizing what courts would read it to do, and even though the statute might not have been enacted without their votes. Is that a problem? Should courts try to develop canons to guard against other sorts of policy changes that members of Congress may not have specifically contemplated? If not, why is federalism different? *Cf.* John F. Manning, *Clear Statement Rules and the Constitution*, 110 COLUM. L. REV. 399, 432–34, 438 (2010) (denying that the Constitution supports state-protective rules of statutory interpretation, and arguing more generally that "the values enforced by clear statement rules do not properly count as *constitutional* values" once they have been "abstracted from the concrete provisions that define them").

Suppose one thinks that the political safeguards of federalism *do* justify a special canon of the sort that Justice O'Connor applied in *Gregory*. What should trigger that canon? In *Gregory* itself, Justice O'Connor emphasized conventional linguistic indeterminacy in the phrase "appointee on the policymaking level." Suppose, however, that no such phrase had appeared in the ADEA. Instead, suppose that after defining "employer" to include state governments, the ADEA had simply defined "employee" to mean "anyone who is paid to do work for an employer." Would it be appropriate for courts to infer an exception for important state officials (like state judges), on the theory that members of Congress may not have had such officials in mind when they enacted the statute, and hence may not have thought about whether to intrude upon state sovereignty in this way? Does Justice O'Connor's argument about the political safeguards of federalism come into play only when courts are trying to resolve linguistic indeterminacy, or should the canon that she articulated operate as what Chapter 2 calls an "implied-limitation rule"—an interpretive principle that justifies reading implicit exceptions into statutory provisions that are not vague or ambiguous on their face, but that are worded in general terms and that do not necessarily reflect specific attention to the issue that the implied-limitation rule addresses?

4. Although Justice White rejected the federalism-based canon that the majority articulated in *Gregory*, he did not necessarily object to federalism-based implied-limitation rules. For instance, if the ADEA had simply established rules for "employers" without defining that term, Justice White might have concluded that the statute did not reach state governments at all (even though they employ people). Because it is somewhat unusual for Congress to regulate the states as states, one might assume that a general term like "employer" refers only to *private* employers and not to state governments.

As Justice White's separate opinion in *Gregory* emphasized, however, the ADEA clearly *does* regulate the states as states. Ever since 1974, the statutory definition of "employer" has specifically included state governments, and the statute unambiguously forbids state governments to discriminate on the basis of age in many of their employment decisions. The question in *Gregory v. Ashcroft* was much more fine-grained. Congress definitely meant to prohibit age discrimination against some state workers, and Congress apparently meant *not* to prohibit age discrimination against some other state workers—those exempted from the definition of "employee" in § 11(f). But § 11(f) is indeterminate about the proper treatment of state judges: do they fall within the group of state employees who are protected or the group of state employees who are not protected?

To answer that question, the majority in *Gregory* went beyond the canons that Justice White himself had applied in *Will v. Michigan Department of State Police*, 491 U.S. 58 (1989). According to the majority in *Gregory*, even where Congress has provided a clear statement of its intention to regulate the states as states, courts should read the *scope* of the regulation narrowly where possible, at least where the qualifications for important state offices are at stake. In defense of this idea, the majority recited the principle that federal statutes should not lightly be read to upset the usual federal-state balance. According to Justice White, however, that principle has no descriptive force in cases like *Gregory*, where it is clear that Congress did intend to upset the usual federal-state balance to at least some extent.

Was Justice White right about that? Suppose that a federal statute plainly does upset the usual federal-state balance, but that it is indeterminate in some respect that affects its scope. Does Congress's past practice of not upsetting the usual federal-state balance at all have any bearing on the proper resolution of the indeterminacy? For instance, can courts safely assume that Congress probably intended the statute to have the narrowest scope consistent with its language, so that the statute disrupts the federal-state balance as little as possible? Or must the canon used by the majority rest on normative rather than descriptive claims?

The issue flagged by Justice White is not limited to federalism-based canons; it is a recurring issue with respect to implied-limitation rules in general. For instance, Chapter 2 raised similar questions about the presumption against extraterritoriality. *See supra* pp. 273–274. Recall that courts often read implicit territorial limits into seemingly general statutory language, on the premise that Congress normally does not intend statutes to operate "extraterritorially." But what if a statute includes a clause explicitly addressing the statute's territorial reach and calling for the statute to have at least some extraterritorial operation? To the extent that this clause is indeterminate about the scope of that operation, should courts read the clause as narrowly as possible, so as to minimize the statute's extraterritorial reach? Or does the presumption against extraterritoriality drop out once it is clear that Congress did intend the statute to operate extraterritorially and courts are simply trying to determine the precise nature and extent of that operation? To the extent that the presumption against extraterritoriality retains some force in this situation, is that force purely "normative" rather than "descriptive"?

We can ask the same sorts of questions about the presumption against retroactivity. Suppose that a federal statute expressly tells courts to apply the statute in various situations where its application would be retroactive (in the sense described by *Landgraf v. USI Film Products*, 511 U.S. 244 (1994)). To the extent that this retroactivity clause is indeterminate, should courts read it as narrowly as possible, so as to minimize the statute's retroactive operation? Aside from "normative" concerns, does the presumption against retroactivity retain any of its "descriptive" justifications in this context?

The answer to these questions may depend on whether there is any qualitative difference between the kind of extraterritoriality (or retroactivity) that a clause unambiguously contemplates and the kind of extraterritoriality (or retroactivity) about which the clause is indeterminate. For instance, suppose that a federal employment-discrimination statute includes an express extraterritoriality clause that clearly regulates the employment practices of American companies abroad, but is ambiguous about whether it also regulates the employment practices of *foreign* companies outside the United States. The presumption against extraterritoriality probably retains some descriptive force in this situation: it would be much weirder for Congress to regulate what foreign companies do in their home countries than for Congress to regulate the overseas operations of American employers, and interpreters might well presume that Congress did not intend the more unusual type of extraterritoriality. By contrast, if there is no such categorical difference between the things that the clause plainly covers and the things about which the clause is indeterminate, then the presumption against extraterritoriality might have no significant descriptive force—with the result that only the "normative" aspects of the presumption would support interpreting the clause narrowly. In that case, the presumption might be limited to a tie-breaking role, for use when courts have exhausted all of their "descriptive" tools but remain in equipoise about the clause's meaning.

How might one apply this analysis to the question in *Gregory*? As amended in 1974, the ADEA definitely protected many low-level employees of state governments, and in that sense Congress clearly did intend to upset the usual federal-state balance; Congress meant to regulate the states as states. But preventing states from setting mandatory retirement ages for state judges (and other important state officials) is arguably a qualitatively greater intrusion on state sovereignty than preventing states from setting mandatory retirement ages for ordinary state employees. If so, then the "balance" canon invoked by the majority might still have some descriptive force: even though Congress plainly intended to regulate the states' employment practices with respect to *some* employees, it might still be reasonable to presume that Congress did not intend to regulate qualifications for the state judiciary.

5. Justice White's separate opinion also raised another important question: Should the source of Congress's constitutional authority to enact a particular statute affect the canons that courts use to construe the statute? The modern Congress gets many of its regulatory powers from the combination of the Commerce Clause and the Necessary and Proper Clause of Article I. But § 5 of the Fourteenth Amendment gives Congress an additional enumerated power. *See* U.S. CONST. amend. 14, § 5 (specifying that Congress "shall have power to enforce, by appropriate legislation, the provisions of [the Fourteenth Amendment]," including the limitations that the Fourteenth Amendment imposes on the states). In *Gregory*, the majority saw no need to determine which of these powers Congress had been using when it amended the ADEA in 1974: "In the face of . . . ambiguity [about the statute's coverage], we will not attribute to Congress an intent to intrude on state governmental functions regardless of whether Congress acted pursuant to its Commerce Clause powers or § 5 of the Fourteenth Amendment." According to Justice White, however, this statement swept too broadly. In his view, even if the Court was correct about how to interpret statutes that Congress enacted under its commerce powers, the Court should not take the same approach to statutes that Congress enacted under § 5 of the Fourteenth Amendment. Is that right?

The answer might depend on exactly *why* the Court resists reading federal statutes "to intrude on state governmental functions." If that resistance derives from the canon that favors avoiding constitutional doubts, then its trigger might depend on whether a particular federal statute was enacted under Article I or under § 5 of the Fourteenth Amendment. In some respects, § 5 of the Fourteenth Amendment has been understood to give Congress more power to regulate the states as states than the combination of the Commerce Clause and the Necessary and Proper Clause. *See, e.g.*, Fitzpatrick v. Bitzer, 427 U.S. 445, 456 (1976) ("We think that Congress may, in determining what is 'appropriate legislation' for the purpose of enforcing the provisions of the Fourteenth Amendment, provide for private suits against States or state officials which are constitutionally impermissible in other contexts."). To the extent that there are fewer constitutional doubts about Congress's ability to regulate state governments when Congress is acting under § 5 of the Fourteenth Amendment than when Congress is acting under Article I, the canon about avoiding constitutional doubts will apply less frequently in the former context.

On the other hand, if the Court's interpretive rule depends less on the canon about avoiding constitutional doubts than on the Court's desire to create the conditions necessary for the political safeguards of federalism to work, then there might be no relevant distinction between statutes enacted under Article I and statutes enacted under § 5. No matter which of these constitutional provisions is the source of Congress's authority to enact a statute, the legislative process works the same way, and the Court might want the same assurances that members of Congress have considered the state interests at stake.

What if the Court's interpretive rule is a purely descriptive canon, designed to minimize gaps between the meaning that courts ascribe to statutory language and the meaning that members of the enacting Congress collectively intended to convey? Perhaps Congress is more hesitant to "intrude on state governmental functions" for some reasons than for others, and perhaps that distinction correlates with the source of the power that Congress is invoking: Congress might be more likely to want to alter the usual federal-state balance when Congress is acting under § 5 of the Fourteenth Amendment than when Congress is using its powers under Article I. If this empirical premise is true, should the Court fine-tune its interpretive rule so that the rule applies more strongly to statutes enacted under Article I than to statutes enacted under § 5 of the Fourteenth Amendment?

6. Suppose one accepts the federalism-based canons that the Court invoked in *Gregory*, and one also agrees with how the Court applied them: Judges Gregory and Nugent were "appointee[s] on the policymaking level" and hence were not "employees" as § 11(f) of the ADEA defines that term. Does that conclusion end the case?

Before you answer, consider the wording of § 4(a) of the ADEA:

"It shall be unlawful for an employer—

"(1) to fail or refuse to hire or to discharge any individual or otherwise discriminate against any individual with respect to his compensation, terms, conditions, or privileges of employment, because of such individual's age;

"(2) to limit, segregate, or classify his employees in any way which would deprive or tend to deprive any individual of employment opportunities or otherwise adversely affect his status as an employee, because of such individual's age; or

"(3) to reduce the wage rate of any employee in order to comply with this Act."

81 Stat. 602, 603 (1967) (codified at 29 U.S.C. § 623(a)). As amended in 1974, the definition of "employer" in § 11(b) of the ADEA specifically covered states. And while paragraph (2) of § 4(a) arguably protects only "employees" against age discrimination, paragraph (1) does not use that word; it refers instead to "any individual." Even if one agrees with the Court that Judges Gregory and Nugent were not "employees" of the state, and hence that the state's insistence that they retire at age 70 did not violate paragraph (2), might one still say that it violated paragraph (1)?

There are many reasons to resist that conclusion. First, it would dramatically reduce the practical significance of the exclusions that Congress added to the definition of "employee" in 1974. Second, it would create odd results as a matter of policy. (Why would Congress want to protect the people whom it excluded from the definition of "employee" against the sort of age discrimination described in § 4(a)(1) but not against the sort of age discrimination described in § 4(a)(2)?) Third, it would overlook an obvious explanation for the fact that § 4(a)(1) uses the word "individual" rather than "employee": § 4(a)(1) forbids an employer to "refuse to hire" people because of their age, and the victims of such discrimination are not "employee[s]."[17]

Notwithstanding all these arguments, though, the fact remains that the State of Missouri is an "employer" within the meaning of § 4(a)(1). Are the federalism-based canons that the Court deployed in *Gregory*

[17] When Congress enacted the original version of the ADEA in 1967, it was perfectly natural for Congress to use the word "individual" as a substitute for "employee" in § 4(a)(1). Far from drawing artificial distinctions between those words, the original version of the ADEA linked them; § 11(f) defined "employee" to mean "an individual employed by an employer." 81 Stat. at 606. The more complex definition of "employee" at issue in *Gregory* entered the statute only in 1974, when Congress extended the term "employer" to cover state governments and simultaneously exempted certain categories of state workers from the definition of "employee."

strong enough to avoid the conclusion that Judges Nugent and Gregory were "individual[s]"? Or is there some other basis for concluding that § 4(a)(1) did not protect them? For instance, should the 1974 amendment to § 11(f) be understood not only as excluding Judges Nugent and Gregory from the definition of "employee," but also as implicitly removing them from the coverage of the ADEA more generally? If you think of yourself as a textualist, can you take that position?

7. The Government Employee Rights Act of 1991 (GERA), which Congress enacted as a title of the Civil Rights Act of 1991 five months after *Gregory*, extended new antidiscrimination protections to many of the state employees whom § 11(f) of the ADEA exempts. *See* Pub. L. 102–166, § 321, 105 Stat. 1071, 1097–98 (1991), redesignated as § 304 by the Congressional Accountability Act of 1995, Pub. L. 104–1, § 504(a)(3), 109 Stat. 3, 41 (codified as amended at 42 U.S.C. § 2000e–16c). In particular, GERA protects "any individual chosen or appointed, by a person elected to public office in any State or political subdivision of any State by the qualified voters thereof—(1) to be a member of the elected official's personal staff; (2) to serve the elected official on the policymaking level; or (3) to serve the elected official as an immediate advisor with respect to the exercise of the constitutional or legal powers of the office." *Id.* As an exercise, compare this language to § 11(f) of the ADEA and identify the reasons for the following conclusion: even though *Gregory* held that state judges are "on the policymaking level" for purposes of the exceptions in § 11(f) of the ADEA, state judges still are not protected by GERA.

B. FEDERAL STATUTES AND THE PREEMPTION OF STATE LAW

The cases in the previous section spoke about the balance between the federal government and the states. But as a practical matter, the issues that those cases addressed (such as whether particular federal statutes should be interpreted to impose duties on state governments) have less influence on the federal-state balance than the issues that we are about to consider (involving the constraints that federal statutes place on the states' authority to prescribe legal duties applicable to other people). Indeed, the extent to which federal statutes "preempt" state law may well be the most important determinant of the actual balance of power in our system of federalism. To the extent that a federal statute preempts some aspect of state law, that aspect of state law will not have legal effect; even though the state law *purports* to establish a rule of decision for courts or other legal actors, federal law overrides that rule of decision and prevents it from operating (in whole or in part).

Preemption is possible because of the Supremacy Clause of the federal Constitution, which reads as follows:

> "This Constitution, and the Laws of the United States which shall be made in Pursuance thereof; and all Treaties made, or which shall be made, under the Authority of the United States, shall be the supreme Law of the Land; and the Judges in every State shall be bound thereby, any Thing in the Constitution or Laws of any State to the Contrary notwithstanding."

U.S. CONST. art. VI, cl. 2. Because of the Supremacy Clause, federal statutory provisions that are within Congress's power to enact take priority over state law. That is true regardless of the *type* of state law; federal statutes can preempt state common law, state administrative regulations, state statutes, and even provisions in state constitutions.

As we will see, though, figuring out the preemptive effect of a federal statute is largely a matter of statutory interpretation. There are plenty of cases in which federal statutes co-exist harmoniously with state law and courts apply both. In such cases, some of the applicable rules of decision come from federal law and others come from state law (applying of its own force on matters as to which it is not preempted). But there are also cases in which federal law is properly understood to preempt some aspect of state law, either in its entirety or as applied to a particular situation. To the extent that the rules of decision validly supplied by a federal statute conflict with the rules of decision purportedly supplied by state law, or to the extent that federal law has validly restricted the states' power to make law on this topic at all, federal law wins; courts will say that the state law has been preempted, and they will not apply it.

The proper interpretation of a federal statute and the scope of the statute's preemptive effect are questions of federal law. Of course, whether a particular provision of state law is preempted also depends on the meaning of the *state* law: should it be understood to establish a directive of the sort that the federal statute preempts? The proper interpretation of provisions of state law is governed by the law of the relevant state.[18] But while states are in charge of what their own laws

---

[18] This chapter will not delve into those questions of state law. Still, it is worth noting that under state principles of statutory interpretation, the meaning that courts ascribe to a state statute (as a matter of state law) can sometimes be influenced by the conclusions that courts reach (as a matter of federal law) about the meaning and preemptive effect of a federal statute. For instance, suppose that a state statute could plausibly be read in two different ways, but one of those possible interpretations would result in preemption by a federal statute. In some circumstances, the relevant state's canons of interpretation might encourage courts to prefer the other interpretation of the state statute. That preference can be seen as a specific application of the saving canon that we encountered in Chapter 2, which many states have embraced as a guide to the meaning of their state's statutes.

One other aspect of state law is also worth highlighting. Suppose that a state statute does purport to establish a directive of the sort that results in preemption by a federal statute, but the state statute also has other aspects or applications that would not themselves be preempted. Interpreters will then face questions about the "separability" of the state statute. Again, those are questions of state law (subject to any relevant federal constitutional constraints). With near unanimity, though, states recognize a rebuttable presumption in favor of the separability of their state's statutes. *See* Michael C. Dorf, *Facial Challenges to State and Federal Statutes*, 46

mean, they are not in charge of the scope of a federal statute's preemptive effect, any more than they are in charge of the meaning of the federal Constitution.

This section of the book surveys current federal doctrines about the preemptive effect of federal statutes. Cases that raise preemption questions often boil down to close analysis of the particular federal statute in question. Still, the Supreme Court has articulated a taxonomy that recognizes three different categories of preemption: "express" preemption, implied "field" preemption, and "conflict" preemption. We will consider those categories in turn.

One recurring question, which has arisen with respect to all three categories, is whether interpreters should approach federal statutes with a general "presumption against preemption," which would operate as a federalism canon. On occasion, the Supreme Court not only has endorsed such a canon but has formulated it extraordinarily broadly. *See, e.g.*, N.Y. State Conference of Blue Cross & Blue Shield Plans v. Travelers Ins. Co., 514 U.S. 645, 654 (1995) (suggesting that the Court addresses all preemption questions "with the starting presumption that Congress does not intend to supplant state law"); *accord* Maryland v. Louisiana, 451 U.S. 725, 746 (1981). More commonly, though, the Court has described the presumption in somewhat narrower terms, so that it applies chiefly "[i]n areas of traditional state regulation." *Bates v. Dow Agrosciences LLC*, 544 U.S. 431, 449 (2005). According to one classic formulation, when Congress legislates "in a field which the States have traditionally occupied," the Court "start[s] with the assumption that the historic police powers of the States were not to be superseded by the Federal Act unless that was the clear and manifest purpose of Congress." *Rice v. Santa Fe Elevator Corp.*, 331 U.S. 218, 230 (1947); *see also, e.g.*, Egelhoff v. Egelhoff, 532 U.S. 141, 151 (2001) (acknowledging that "[t]here is indeed a presumption against pre-emption in areas of traditional state regulation such as family law," though finding this presumption overcome); Hillsborough County v. Automated Med. Labs., Inc., 471 U.S. 707, 715 (1985) (referring to "the presumption that state or local regulation of matters related to health and safety is not invalidated under the Supremacy Clause"); *cf.* Buckman Co. v. Plaintiffs' Legal Committee, 531 U.S. 341, 347–48 (2001) (asserting that "no presumption against pre-emption obtains in this case" because the topic at issue is not one of traditional state concern).

Even when it is limited to preserving "the historic police powers of the States," however, an across-the-board presumption against preemption may go too far. To be sure, the modern Supreme Court will not lightly infer "field" preemption. With respect to both "express" preemption and "conflict" preemption, though, recent years have witnessed robust debates about whether a general presumption against

STAN. L. REV. 235, 285–86 (1994) (identifying only Virginia and Tennessee as exceptions); *see also* VA. CODE § 1–243 (now establishing a presumption of separability).

preemption is appropriate. The ensuing sections consider that issue as well as others.

1. "EXPRESS" PREEMPTION

Some federal statutes contain provisions that explicitly address preemption and render certain kinds of state laws ineffective. In 2013, for instance, the Drug Supply Chain Security Act added the following provision to the Federal Food, Drug, and Cosmetic Act:

> "Beginning on the date of enactment of the Drug Supply Chain Security Act, no State or political subdivision of a State may establish or continue in effect any requirements for tracing products through the distribution system (including any requirements with respect to statements of distribution history, transaction history, transaction information, or transaction statement of a product as such product changes ownership in the supply chain, or verification, investigation, disposition, notification, or recordkeeping relating to such systems, including paper or electronic pedigree systems or for tracking and tracing drugs throughout the distribution system) which are inconsistent with, more stringent than, or in addition to, any requirements applicable under section 503(e) (as amended by such Act) or this subchapter (or regulations issued thereunder) . . . ."

Pub. L. 113–54, sec. 205, § 585(a), 127 Stat. 587, 638 (2013) (codified at 21 U.S.C. § 360eee–4(a)). Such provisions in federal statutes are not uncommon. *See, e.g.*, Agricultural Risk Protection Act of 2000, Pub. L. 106–224, § 436(a), 114 Stat. 358, 453 ("No State or political subdivision of a State may regulate in foreign commerce any article, means of conveyance, plant, biological control organism, plant pest, noxious weed, or plant product in order—(1) to control a plant pest or noxious weed; (2) to eradicate a plant pest or noxious weed; or (3) [to] prevent the introduction or dissemination of a biological control organism, plant pest, or noxious weed.") (codified at 7 U.S.C. § 7756(a)); Livestock Mandatory Reporting Act of 1999, Pub. L. 106–78, sec. 911(2), § 259, 113 Stat. 1135, 1205 (amending the Agricultural Marketing Act of 1946 to include the following provision: "In order to achieve the goals, purposes, and objectives of this title on a nationwide basis and to avoid potentially conflicting State laws that could impede the goals, purposes, or objectives of this title, no State or political subdivision of a State may impose a requirement that is in addition to, or inconsistent with, any requirement of this subtitle with respect to the submission or reporting of information, or the publication of such information, on the prices and quantities of livestock or livestock products.") (codified at 7 U.S.C. § 1636h).[19] The

[19] Recently, the Supreme Court has criticized the language used by Congress in these and other express preemption clauses. Under the rubric of "anticommandeering" doctrine, the Court has suggested that the Constitution does not give Congress "the power to issue orders directly to the States." *Murphy v. NCAA*, 138 S. Ct. 1461, 1478 (2018); *cf. supra* p. 1045 n.5. Federal statutes purporting to forbid states to enact particular kinds of state laws might appear to violate this principle. *See Murphy*, 138 S. Ct. at 1480. Still, the Court has suggested a work-

Supreme Court refers to such provisions as "express preemption clauses," and it analyzes their preemptive effect under the rubric of "express" preemption.

Within the limits of the enumerated powers that the Constitution gives it, Congress has considerable authority to preempt state law. That authority comes partly from Congress's specific enumerated powers (such as its power to regulate interstate commerce or its power to enact appropriate legislation to enforce the Fourteenth Amendment) and partly from the Necessary and Proper Clause (which enables Congress to preempt state law where necessary and proper for carrying into execution powers vested in the federal government). Express preemption clauses are one way for Congress to exercise this authority. *Cf.* Pac. Gas & Elec. Co. v. State Energy Res. Conservation & Dev. Comm'n, 461 U.S. 190, 203 (1983) ("It is well established that within constitutional limits Congress may pre-empt state authority by so stating in express terms.").

Of course, including an express preemption clause in a federal statute is not the *only* way for Congress to exercise its authority to preempt state law. Most federal statutes do not include an express preemption clause, and they can still have considerable preemptive effect. Whether or not they include an express preemption clause, all federal statutes preempt state laws with which they conflict (as determined according to doctrines of conflict preemption). Still, some federal statutes do include an express preemption clause. Those federal statutes normally have two different types of preemptive effect: the other provisions in the statute will preempt state laws with which they conflict, and the preemption clause will preempt whatever additional state laws it covers. *See, e.g.*, Buckman Co. v. Plaintiffs' Legal Committee, 531 U.S. 341, 352 (2001) (indicating that the typical express preemption clause coexists with " 'the ordinary working of conflict pre-emption principles' " (quoting Geier v. American Honda Motor Co., 529 U.S. 861, 872–73 (2000))).[20]

---

around: regardless of the terms in which it is cast, the typical express preemption clause can be understood to give private actors "a federal right to engage in certain conduct subject only to certain (federal) constraints," and anticommandeering doctrine does not prevent Congress from "regulat[ing] the conduct of private actors." *See id.* at 1480–81.

In my view, a different work-around would be more natural. Even if one thinks that Congress cannot impose any duties at all on state legislatures (which is an aggressive version of "anticommandeering" doctrine), the typical express preemption clause need not be seen as purporting to do so. Instead, preemption clauses are more naturally understood as addressing the legal effect of state law: to the extent that state law purports to supply legal rules of the sort covered by a valid preemption clause, those rules are invalid and ineffective. If a state legislature were to enact a statute of the sort that the preemption clause covers, no one would say that the legislature is liable to anyone for breaching a legal duty. By virtue of the preemption clause, though, the state statute will not have the legal effect that it purports to have; when courts or other legal decisionmakers are trying to identify the rules of decision for a particular case, they will disregard state law to the extent that it is preempted. This analysis does not run afoul of any plausible version of "anticommandeering" doctrine, and it does not require the artificial idea that every preemption clause confers personal "rights" on the private actors who would otherwise be subject to state law.

[20] In *Cipollone v. Liggett Group, Inc.*, 505 U.S. 504 (1992), Justice Stevens's majority opinion suggested that when a federal statute includes an express preemption clause, courts

When a federal statute includes an express preemption clause, courts might occasionally face constitutional questions about whether Congress really has the power to restrict the states' lawmaking authority in the way that the clause says. Usually, though, the preemptive effect of an express preemption clause in a federal statute is a pure question of statutory interpretation: exactly what does the clause mean, and what criteria does it establish for preemption?

The answer to that question obviously depends on the language of the particular clause that the courts are trying to interpret. Still, the rest of this section covers some recurring issues of interpretation that have come up with respect to a variety of preemption clauses.

a. DO SOME PREEMPTION CLAUSES COVER ONLY CERTAIN TYPES OF STATE LAW?

Some preemption clauses are understood to cover all kinds of state law, including the common law that courts apply on questions that come within the reach of the states' lawmaking powers. As worded by Congress, however, some other preemption clauses might focus only on regulations of the sort promulgated by state legislatures or administrative agencies, as opposed to the customary law of torts and contract.

Take the express preemption clause in the Federal Boat Safety Act of 1971, Pub. L. 92–75, § 10, 85 Stat. 213, 217; *see also* Act of Aug. 26, 1983, Pub. L. 98–89, 97 Stat. 500, 531 (slightly rewording the clause in the course of enacting Title 46 of the United States Code as such). The Act confers federal regulatory authority upon the Secretary of the department in which the Coast Guard is operating. *See* 46 U.S.C. §§ 2101(44), 4302. Among other things, 46 U.S.C. § 4302 authorizes the Secretary to prescribe regulations "establishing minimum safety standards for recreational vessels and associated equipment." *Id.* § 4302(a)(1). The Act's preemption clause then sets forth the following general rule:

> "Unless permitted by the Secretary under section 4305 of this title, a State or political subdivision of a State may not establish, continue in effect, or enforce a law or regulation establishing a recreational vessel or associated equipment performance or other safety standard or imposing a requirement for associated equipment . . . that is not identical to a regulation prescribed under section 4302 of this title."

Id. § 4306.

In *Sprietsma v. Mercury Marine*, 537 U.S. 51 (2002), the Supreme Court unanimously held that this clause preempts only "positive

can infer that the statute does not have other pre-emptive effects. *Id.* at 517 (invoking *expressio unius*). In response, Justice Scalia agreed that an express preemption clause would cut against inferring additional *field* preemption, but he denied that it should have any bearing on *conflict* preemption. *See id.* at 547–48 (Scalia, J., concurring in part and dissenting in part). The majority opinions in *Geier* and *Buckman* sided with Justice Scalia on the latter point.

enactments," not duties recognized as a matter of common law. The Court advanced three arguments for this conclusion. First, the Court made an argument about ordinary meaning: in the Court's view, the fact that the preemption clause refers to a law or regulation "implies a discreteness . . . that is not present in the common law." *Id.* at 63. Second, the Court invoked the presumption against superfluity: in the phrase "a law or regulation," if the word "law" encompasses all kinds of law (rather than just statutory law), then the word "regulation" would not have been necessary. *Id.* Third, the Court emphasized that the same Act contained a saving clause[21] saying that compliance with the Act (and federal regulations prescribed under the Act) "does not relieve a person from liability at common law or under State law." 46 U.S.C. § 4311(h). In the Court's view, this provision assumed that there would be a significant number of common-law liability claims to save—meaning that those claims were not already excluded by the preemption clause. *Sprietsma*, 537 U.S. at 63.[22]

In *Medtronic, Inc. v. Lohr*, 518 U.S. 470 (1996), four Justices suggested a similar reading of the preemption clause that the Medical Device Amendments of 1976 added to the Federal Food, Drug, and Cosmetic Act. That clause establishes the following general rule:

> "Except as provided in subsection (b), no State or political subdivision of a State may establish or continue in effect with respect to a device intended for human use any requirement—
>
> "(1) which is different from, or in addition to, any requirement applicable under this Act to the device, and
>
> "(2) which relates to the safety or effectiveness of the device or to any other matter included in a requirement applicable to the device under this Act."

Medical Device Amendments of 1976, Pub. L. 94–295, sec. 2, § 521(a), 90 Stat. 539, 574 (codified at 21 U.S.C. § 360k(a)). Joined by Justices Kennedy, Souter, and Ginsburg, Justice Stevens suggested that the phrase "any requirement" in this provision might not encompass common-law duties. *See Lohr*, 518 U.S. at 489 (opinion of Stevens, J.) (asserting that each time the word "requirements" appears in the relevant section, context suggests that the word refers to "device-specific enactments of positive law by legislative or administrative bodies, not the application of general rules of common law by judges and juries").

In *Lohr*, however, five Justices rejected this potential limitation. Justice O'Connor, joined by Chief Justice Rehnquist and Justices Scalia

---

[21] Saving clauses are the opposite of preemption clauses: they explicitly preserve other sources of law against the possibility of preemption (or at least certain types of preemption).

[22] The Court based this argument on the analysis in *Geier v. American Honda Motor Co.*, 529 U.S. 861 (2000), which is excerpted later in this chapter. As you will see, the preemption and saving clauses in the Federal Boat Safety Act of 1971 resembled those in the National Traffic and Motor Vehicle Safety Act of 1966 (the statute at issue in *Geier*), and the Court interpreted them similarly.

and Thomas, argued that the "ordinary meaning" of the word "requirement" includes common-law duties enforced through damage awards. *Id.* at 510–12 (O'Connor, J., concurring in part and dissenting in part).[23] Justice Breyer "basically agree[d]" with Justice O'Connor, and he added that the contrary interpretation "would have anomalous consequences"; in his view, it would be odd for Congress to strip states of the authority to establish certain duties by statute or written regulation while leaving state courts free to articulate and enforce identical duties as a matter of the common law in force in the state. *Id.* at 503–05 (Breyer, J., concurring in part and concurring in the judgment).

In *Riegel v. Medtronic, Inc.*, 552 U.S. 312 (2008), a solid majority of the Court adhered to the position that Justices O'Connor and Breyer had taken twelve years earlier in *Lohr*. More broadly, the Court indicated that it would adopt the same reading of the word "requirement" in other federal statutes. Justice Scalia's majority opinion asserted that "Congress is entitled to know what meaning this Court will assign to terms regularly used in its enactments." *Id.* at 324. The Court therefore articulated the following presumption: "Absent other indication, reference to a State's 'requirements' includes its common-law duties." *Id.*

In all these cases, the Court seemed to assume that whether the relevant preemption clauses covered only "positive enactments" or also common-law duties was simply a matter of statutory interpretation. But does the Constitution even give Congress the power to distinguish between duties imposed by written state laws and identical duties recognized by courts as a matter of common law, and to preempt the former but not the latter? In other contexts, the Supreme Court has suggested that Congress cannot make the legal effect of state laws depend on which organ of the state government promulgated them. *See* Erie R.R. Co. v. Tompkins, 304 U.S. 64, 78 (1938) ("[W]hether the law of the State shall be declared by its Legislature in a statute or by its highest court in a decision is not a matter of federal concern."); *see also* Highland Farms Dairy, Inc. v. Agnew, 300 U.S. 608, 612 (1937) ("How power shall be distributed by a state among its governmental organs is commonly, if not always, a question for the state itself."). Does the preemption clause in the Federal Boat Safety Act of 1971, as interpreted by the Supreme Court in *Sprietsma*, offend this principle? When that preemption clause refers to "a law or regulation," could it be understood to be focusing less on the organ of government that made the law than on the nature of the law—so that top-down regulations are preempted while customary law is preserved? Would *that* distinction be constitutionally permissible?

---

[23] Four years earlier, Justice Stevens himself had reached the same conclusion about the word "requirement" in a different express preemption clause. *See* Cipollone v. Liggett Group, Inc., 505 U.S. 504, 521 (1992) (plurality opinion of Stevens, J.) ("The phrase '[n]o requirement or prohibition' [in the relevant preemption clause] sweeps broadly and suggests no distinction between positive enactments and common law; to the contrary, those words easily encompass obligations that take the form of common-law rules.").

b. DO COURTS EVER OWE *CHEVRON* DEFERENCE TO AN AGENCY'S INTERPRETATION OF AN EXPRESS PREEMPTION CLAUSE?

Most of the time, when a federal statute contains an express preemption clause, courts will interpret the clause according to their own best lights. But what if Congress has put a federal agency in charge of administering some or all of the statute's other provisions? If the agency promulgates a rule or issues an order that rests on a particular interpretation of the preemption clause, do courts owe *Chevron* deference to the agency's interpretation?

Many scholars have argued that the answer should usually be "no." In a leading article that addresses preemption in general (not just express preemption), Professor Mendelson advanced various normative arguments against *Chevron* deference on preemption questions. *See* Nina A. Mendelson, Chevron *and Preemption*, 102 MICH. L. REV. 737, 779–97 (2004) (questioning "the relative institutional competence of agencies in considering federalism values," and adding that agencies' decisions on questions about the allocation of governmental power may also be tainted by self-interest); *cf. id.* at 797–98 (acknowledging that agencies have advantages over courts on some preemption questions, but arguing that *Skidmore v. Swift* would allow courts to take those advantages into account in appropriate cases without granting across-the-board deference). Professor Merrill has agreed that "courts are as a rule better institutions to resolve preemption questions than agencies." Thomas W. Merrill, *Preemption and Institutional Choice*, 102 NW. U. L. REV. 727, 767 (2008) (emphasis omitted). As a doctrinal matter, moreover, Professor Merrill observes that "*Chevron* is grounded in a delegation of authority from Congress to an agency to determine certain unresolved questions of federal law," and Professor Merrill argues that Congress should not lightly be presumed to have given agencies this authority with respect to a statute's preemptive effect. *Id.* at 771. In his words,

> "If Congress has delegated authority to an agency to make binding determinations of preemption and the agency has invoked that authority in offering its view about the preemptive effect of federal law, then the preconditions for *Chevron* deference have been established. But if these stringent conditions are not satisfied, then courts should not apply the *Chevron* standard to agency views about preemption."

Id. As applied to express preemption, one might cast this point as follows: the typical express preemption clause is not administered by an agency in the sense that satisfies Step Zero of the *Chevron* framework. *Cf.* Adams Fruit Co. v. Barrett, 494 U.S. 638, 649–50 (1990) (concluding that the Department of Labor does not have "administrative authority" with respect to a statutory provision that created a private right of action in court, and judges therefore do not owe *Chevron* deference to the agency's views about the preemptive effect of this provision).

The Supreme Court danced around these issues in *Medtronic, Inc. v. Lohr*, 518 U.S. 470 (1996). The Federal Food, Drug, and Cosmetic Act, as amended, authorizes the Secretary of Health and Human Services to regulate medical devices in various ways. The Secretary, in turn, has delegated this authority to the Commissioner of the Food and Drug Administration (FDA). As noted above, the preemption clause found at 21 U.S.C. § 360k(a) preempts state-law requirements that are not identical to the FDA's requirements but that "relate[ ] to the safety or effectiveness of the device or to any other matter included in a requirement applicable to the device under this Act." At the time of *Lohr*, the FDA had promulgated a regulation interpreting this preemption clause relatively narrowly. *See* 21 C.F.R. § 808.1(d) (1995). In *Lohr*, none of the Justices called for the FDA's interpretation to receive the precise equivalent of *Chevron* deference, nor did any of the Justices provide a general discussion of the significance of agency interpretations of other express preemption clauses. Still, five Justices indicated that the FDA's interpretation of § 360k deserved "substantial weight," because "Congress has given the FDA a unique role in determining the scope of § 360k's pre-emptive effect." *Lohr*, 518 U.S. at 495–96; *cf.* Wyeth v. Levine, 555 U.S. 555, 576 (2009) (glossing § 360k as "authorizing the FDA to determine the scope of the . . . pre-emption clause"). As support for that idea, Justice Stevens's opinion in *Lohr* pointed to two features of the statutory scheme. First, § 360k(b) "explicitly delegated to the FDA the authority to exempt state regulations from the pre-emptive effect of [§ 360k(a)]—an authority that necessarily requires the FDA to assess the pre-emptive effect that the Act and its own regulations will have on state laws." *Lohr*, 518 U.S. at 496. Second, "pre-emption under [§ 360k(a)] does not arise directly as a result of the enactment of the statute; rather, in most cases a state law will be pre-empted only to the extent that the FDA has promulgated a relevant federal 'requirement.' " *Id.*

If the *Lohr* Court gave "substantial weight" to the FDA's interpretation of the express preemption clause only because of these features (which resonate with Professor Merrill's "stringent conditions" for *Chevron* deference), then *Lohr* does not necessarily carry lessons for other cases. In the context of conflict preemption, moreover, more recent opinions have indicated that courts normally do not have to defer to "an agency's *conclusion* that state law is pre-empted," even if courts do pay attention to the agency's "explanation of how state law affects the regulatory scheme." *Wyeth*, 555 U.S. at 576; *see also infra* pp. 1159–1164 (discussing deference in conflict-preemption cases). Whether and under what circumstances agencies deserve deference with respect to express preemption remains an open question. *See, e.g.*, Delaware v. Surface Transp. Bd., 859 F.3d 16, 20–21 (D.C. Cir. 2017); Bell v. Blue Cross & Blue Shield of Okla., 823 F.3d 1198, 1202–03 (8th Cir. 2016). *Compare* Thomas W. Merrill, *Step Zero After* City of Arlington, 83 FORDHAM L. REV. 753, 786 (2014) (arguing that it would be unwise to distinguish express preemption from other types of preemption for purposes of

Chevron deference), *with* Gregory M. Dickinson, *Calibrating* Chevron *for Preemption*, 63 ADMIN. L. REV. 667, 670 (2011) (proposing such a distinction). Given the current Supreme Court's apparent doubts about *Chevron* deference more broadly, though, I would be surprised if the Court extended *Chevron* to agency interpretations of express preemption clauses where Professor Merrill's "stringent conditions" are not satisfied.

c. SHOULD INTERPRETERS APPROACH PREEMPTION CLAUSES WITH A PRESUMPTION AGAINST PREEMPTION?

Another recurring issue involves the Supreme Court's "presumption against preemption." *See supra* p. 1089. In a variety of cases, Justices have disagreed about whether that presumption bears on the proper interpretation of express preemption clauses.

That issue surfaced in *Cipollone v. Liggett Group, Inc.*, 505 U.S. 504 (1992), which involved the preemptive effect of the Federal Cigarette Labeling and Advertising Act, Pub. L. 89–92, 79 Stat. 282 (1965), and its successor, the Public Health Cigarette Smoking Act of 1969, Pub. L. 91–222, 84 Stat. 87 (1970). Section 4 of the 1965 Act required cigarette packages to bear a conspicuous warning ("Caution: Cigarette Smoking May be Hazardous to Your Health."). Pub. L. 89–92, § 4, 79 Stat. at 283 (codified as amended at 15 U.S.C. § 1333). Section 5, which was captioned "Preemption," explicitly restricted the states' authority to require any additional warnings. In particular, § 5(a) of the 1965 Act provided that "[n]o statement relating to smoking and health, other than the statement required by section 4 of this Act, shall be required on any cigarette package." *Id.* § 5(a), 79 Stat. at 283 (codified as amended at 15 U.S.C. § 1334(a)). As amended in 1970, § 5(b) added: "No requirement or prohibition based on smoking and health shall be imposed under State law with respect to the advertising or promotion of any cigarettes the packages of which are labeled in conformity with the provisions of this Act." Pub. L. 91–222, sec. 2, § 5(b), 84 Stat. at 88 (codified at 15 U.S.C. § 1334(b)).

In *Cipollone*, Justice Stevens's majority opinion invoked "the presumption against the pre-emption of state police power regulations" to support a "narrow reading" of these express preemption clauses. 505 U.S. at 518. Justice Scalia, however, disagreed with this aspect of the majority's analysis. "Under the Supremacy Clause," he argued, "our job is to interpret Congress's decrees of pre-emption neither narrowly nor broadly, but in accordance with their apparent meaning." *Id.* at 544 (Scalia, J., concurring in the judgment in part and dissenting in part). Justice Scalia acknowledged that when a federal statute is ambiguous about whether it enters a particular field, the fact that Congress has traditionally left this field to the states might well influence how courts should resolve the ambiguity. In that sense, Justice Scalia was willing to accept "our oft-repeated assumption that, absent convincing evidence of statutory intent to pre-empt, 'the historic police powers of the States [are] not to be superseded.' " But according to Justice Scalia, "that assumption dissolves once there is conclusive evidence of intent to pre-empt in the express words of the statute itself, and the only remaining question is what the *scope* of the pre-emption is meant to be." *Id.* at 545. As a result, Justice Scalia saw little role for the presumption against preemption in express-preemption cases.

One year later, the Court again confronted an express preemption clause in *Morales v. Trans World Airlines, Inc.*, 504 U.S. 374 (1992). This time, however, Justice Scalia wrote the majority opinion, which made no reference to the presumption against preemption. *See, e.g., id.* at 383 ("The ordinary meaning of these words [in the express preemption clause] is a broad one, . . . and the words thus express a broad pre-emptive purpose."). The presumption against preemption cropped up only in Justice Stevens's dissent. *See id.* at 419–21 (Stevens, J., dissenting).

The same pattern repeated itself in subsequent years. Some majority opinions endorsed applying the presumption against preemption to express preemption clauses. *See* Altria Group, Inc. v. Good, 555 U.S. 70, 77 (2008) ("[W]hen the text of a pre-emption clause is susceptible of more than one plausible reading, courts ordinarily 'accept the reading that disfavors pre-emption." (quoting Bates v. Dow Agrosciences LLC, 544 U.S. 431, 449 (2005))); Medtronic, Inc. v. Lohr, 518 U.S. 470, 485 (1996). Other majority opinions conspicuously omitted any reference to the presumption when interpreting express preemption clauses. *See, e.g.*, Riegel v. Medtronic, Inc., 552 U.S. 312 (2008); *see also* Engine Mfrs. Ass'n v. S. Coast Air Quality Mgmt. Dist., 541 U.S. 246, 256 (2004) (explaining this omission on the ground that "not all members of this Court agree" and the issue "makes no difference to resolution of the principal question" in the case at hand).

The Justices again divided over this point in *CTS Corp. v. Waldburger*, 573 U.S. 1 (2014). *Compare id.* at 19 (opinion of Kennedy, J., joined by Sotomayor and Kagan, JJ.) (interpreting an express preemption clause in light of the presumption against preemption) *with id.* at 19–20 (Scalia, J., concurring in part and concurring in the judgment, joined by Roberts, C.J., and Thomas and Alito, JJ.) (reiterating Justice Scalia's position in *Cipollone*). More recently, Justice Thomas's majority opinion in *Puerto Rico v. Franklin California Tax-Free Trust*, 579 U.S. 115 (2016), opposed application of the presumption against preemption to express preemption clauses. *See id.* at 125 ("[B]ecause the statute 'contains an express pre-emption clause,' we do not invoke any presumption against preemption but instead 'focus on the plain wording of the clause, which necessarily contains the best evidence of Congress's preemptive intent.' " (quoting Chamber of Commerce v. Whiting, 563 U.S. 582, 594 (2011) (internal quotation marks omitted))). But three of the five Justices who joined that majority opinion had previously joined opinions taking the opposite position, and the Court may not have uttered its last word on this topic.

The question of whether judges should approach express preemption clauses with a presumption against preemption resembles some questions that have come up earlier in this book. *See* pp. 273–274 (discussing whether the presumption against extraterritoriality favors narrow interpretations of express "extraterritoriality clauses" in federal statutes); pp. 1082–1084 (discussing whether federalism canons favor narrow interpretations of provisions that expressly impose duties on states). As in those other contexts, I do not see much "descriptive" justification for reading all express preemption clauses as narrowly as possible. On this point, then, I agree with Justice Scalia's position in *Cipollone*: when Congress has enacted an express preemption clause, courts cannot safely assume that Congress probably intended whichever reading would preempt the least state law. *See* Caleb Nelson, *Preemption*, 86 VA. L. REV. 225, 301 (2000).

Consider the following hypothetical. Suppose that Congress is about to enact a new federal statute addressing a field that Congress has traditionally left to the states. *Cf. Riegel*, 552 U.S. at 334 (Ginsburg, J., dissenting) (citing cases for the proposition that the presumption against preemption is strongest in "fields of traditional state regulation"). Suppose further that members of Congress are concerned that certain types of state law would get in the way of the new federal statute, and they decide to guard against that problem by enacting an express preemption clause. During the legislative process, they consider three alternative formulations of such a clause. As they understand those formulations, Proposed Clause #1 would displace the most state law, Proposed Clause #2 would displace an intermediate amount of state law, and Proposed Clause #3 would displace the least state law. On the basis of all the considerations that they think relevant (including the states' sovereignty, Congress's own past practices, and the purposes behind the new federal legislation), Congress ultimately picks Proposed Clause #2 and enacts it as part of the federal statute. Would a narrow interpretation of that clause be more likely to capture the clause's intended meaning than a "normal" interpretation? The clause does address a field of traditional state regulation, and Congress might be reluctant to preempt large amounts of state law in such fields. But that reluctance has already played a role in the drafting process; it is why Proposed Clause #2 beat out Proposed Clause #1. Is there any "descriptive" reason for courts to adopt a narrow interpretation of *the words that Congress itself chose*? Wouldn't a "normal" reading of the clause be at least as likely to capture what members of Congress collectively intended?

Admittedly, it is possible to imagine scenarios in which a presumption against preemption could have some "descriptive" force even as applied to express preemption clauses. For instance, suppose that a preemption clause definitely preempts state law in one field but is ambiguous about whether it also reaches a second field. Suppose too that preempting state law in the second field would be a qualitatively greater intrusion on the states, and a more significant departure from Congress's past practices, than preempting state law in the first field. Under those circumstances, courts seeking to resolve the ambiguity in the preemption clause might infer that the clause was intended to address only the first field. Absent particularized arguments of this sort, though, a general presumption against preemption is not a natural tool for identifying the intended meaning of express preemption clauses.

By and large, then, the main arguments for reading express preemption clauses narrowly are "normative" rather than "descriptive." Some such arguments emphasize the substantive values served by certain types of state laws as well as the structural values served by federalism. *See, e.g.*, Betsy J. Grey, *Make Congress Speak Clearly: Federal Preemption of State Tort Remedies*, 77 B.U. L. REV. 559, 606–07 (1997). Other arguments relate to the legislative process. For instance, Professor Grey has invoked the idea that Justice O'Connor embraced in *Gregory v. Ashcroft*: by resolving doubts about the meaning of express preemption clauses in favor of state power, perhaps courts will help create the conditions necessary for the political safeguards of federalism to work. *See id.* at 608 & n.285; *see also supra* pp. 1080–1081. Professor Hills has added that the interest groups that favor preemption are in a better position to put issues on Congress's agenda than people on the other side, so a presumption against preemption will result in more frequent and vigorous debates within Congress. *See* Roderick M. Hills, Jr., *Against Preemption: How Federalism Can Improve the National Legislative Process*, 82 N.Y.U. L. REV. 1, 28 (2007) ("In effect, the anti-preemption rule is a rule in favor of a political donnybrook—a visible and direct confrontation on a hotly contested policy issue.").

d. SHOULD COURTS USE A SPECIAL STYLE OF INTERPRETATION FOR PREEMPTION CLAUSES?

Professor Stabile has advanced a different sort of argument about express preemption clauses. In her view, "it is difficult, if not impossible, for Congress to fashion satisfactory preemption provisions." Susan J. Stabile, *Preemption of State Law by Federal Law: A Task for Congress or the Courts?*, 40 VILL. L. REV. 1, 2 (1995). Doing so would require Congress to "make a comprehensive and accurate determination regarding the appropriate breadth of a statute's preemptive reach," but that is a hard task when the statute covers a lot of ground and has not yet taken effect. *Id.* The problem is compounded by the fact that "any express preemption provision is drafted with a particular set of problems and the then-existing social and legal landscape in mind," and the relevant considerations "change dramatically over time." *Id.* Of course, all legislation faces this difficulty. But the difficulty may loom especially large for preemption clauses, which not only must anticipate appropriate *federal* policy but also should take into account the varying policies that each of the fifty states and innumerable local governments might legitimately want to pursue in the years to come. For better or for worse, moreover, the typical express preemption clause in federal statutes is relatively brief—particularly as compared to the variety of state law that it sometimes is understood to displace—and is often drafted in relatively rule-like terms. *Cf. id.* (noting that express preemption clauses in federal statutes often turn out to be "overinclusive, operating to prevent the attainment of important state interests even when no federal goal is advanced by preemption").

Professor Stabile herself addressed these remarks chiefly to Congress: she concluded that "except in rare circumstances, Congress [should] refrain from including express preemption provisions in the legislation it enacts." *Id.* at 3; *see also id.* at 78–90 (arguing that case-by-case decisionmaking by courts is likely to do a better job). But might her arguments also provide normative support for a canon that encourages courts to read express preemption clauses as narrowly as their words fairly permit, so as to minimize the scope of those clauses? Or is it inappropriate for courts to construe some statutory provisions narrowly simply on the theory that those provisions are ill-advised and that Congress should not have enacted them?

Instead of simply advocating narrow readings, could one argue that because the typical preemption clause is both general and brief, it invites a more flexible and purpose-oriented style of interpretation than more detailed statutory provisions? Would that style of interpretation, which leaves more room for courts to shape the effective content of the clause during the process of application, help address Professor Stabile's concerns?

A leading example of a badly drafted preemption clause is § 514(a) of the Employee Retirement Income Security Act (ERISA), Pub. L. 93–406, 88 Stat. 829 (1974). *See, e.g.*, Catherine L. Fisk & Michael M. Oswalt, *Preemption and Civic Democracy in the Battle Over Wal-Mart*, 92 MINN. L. REV. 1502, 1535 (2008) (calling this preemption clause "ambiguous, hastily considered, and poorly drafted"). Title I of ERISA prescribes various requirements for so-called "employee benefit plan[s]" (including pension plans, health-insurance plans, and various other kinds of plans) that are maintained by private employers or labor unions. Section 514(a) then establishes the following general rule about preemption:

> "Except as provided in subsection (b) of this section, the provisions of this title . . . shall supersede any and all State laws insofar as they may now or hereafter relate to any employee benefit plan described in section 4(a) and not exempt under section 4(b)"[—that is, any employee benefit plan covered by ERISA].

Id. § 514(a), 88 Stat. at 897 (codified at 29 U.S.C. § 1144(a)); *see also id.* § 514(c)(1), 88 Stat. at 897 (defining "State law" to include "all laws, decisions, rules, regulations, or other State action having the effect of law, of any State") (codified at 29 U.S.C. § 1144(c)(1)); *id.* § 514(c)(2), 88 Stat. at 897 ("The term 'State' includes a State, any political subdivisions thereof, or any agency or instrumentality of either, which purports to regulate, directly or indirectly, the terms and conditions of employee benefit plans covered by this title.") (codified at 29 U.S.C. § 1144(c)(2)). Section 514(b) lists some exceptions. For instance, it says that "Subsection (a) shall not apply to any generally applicable criminal law of a State," *id.* § 514(b)(4), 88 Stat. at 897 (codified at 29 U.S.C. § 1144(b)(4)), and it also preserves the operation of "any law of any State which regulates insurance, banking, or securities" (subject to the limitation that most ERISA plans cannot themselves be considered insurance companies, banks, or investment companies for purposes of state laws regulating such entities), *id.* § 514(b)(2), 88 Stat. at 897 (codified at 29 U.S.C. § 1144(b)(2)).

Early on, the Supreme Court noted "[t]he breadth of § 514(a)'s pre-emptive reach." *Shaw v. Delta Air Lines, Inc.*, 463 U.S. 85, 96 (1983). As the Court explained, the fact that § 514(b)(4) exempts "generally applicable criminal law[s]" indicates that § 514(a) would otherwise have preempted some applications of such laws, and hence that state laws can "relate to" employee benefit plans within the meaning of § 514(a) even if the state laws do not single out such plans for special treatment and are not "specifically designed to affect [them]." *Id.* at 98. Likewise, drafting history persuaded the Court that state laws could "relate to" employee benefit plans, and hence could be preempted, even though they addressed different topics than ERISA itself. *See id.*; *accord, e.g.*, FMC Corp. v. Holliday, 498 U.S. 52, 58–59 (1990).[24] As a first stab at defining the scope of preemption, the Court asserted that "[a] law 'relates to' an employee benefit plan, in the normal sense of the phrase, if it has a connection with or reference to such a plan." *Shaw*, 463 U.S. at 96–97; *see also id.* at 98 ("Congress used the words 'relate to' in § 514(a) in their broad sense.").

Starting in the mid-1990s, though, the Court expressed frustration with the "unhelpful text" of the preemption clause. *N.Y. State Conference of Blue Cross & Blue Shield Plans v. Travelers Ins. Co.*, 514 U.S. 645, 656 (1995); *see also, e.g.*, De Buono v. NYSA-ILA Med. & Clinical Servs. Fund, 520 U.S. 806, 809 (1997) (referring to "the opaque language in ERISA's § 514(a)"). Justice Scalia put his finger on the problem: "as many a curbstone philosopher has observed, everything is related to everything else." *Cal. Div. of Labor Standards Enf't v. Dillingham Constr., N.A.*, 519 U.S. 316, 335 (1997) (Scalia, J., concurring). Thus, "unless the Court is willing to decree a degree of pre-emption that no sensible person could

---

[24] *But cf.* Rutledge v. Pharm. Care Mgmt. Ass'n, 141 S. Ct. 474, 483–84 (2020) (Thomas, J., concurring) (suggesting that this conclusion overlooks the implications of the word "supersede" in the preemption clause).

have intended," the Court had to come up with limitations that the phrase "relate to" did not itself make apparent. *See id.* at 335–36.

The Court has tried to do so under the same verbal formulation that its early cases articulated, about whether state law "has a connection with or reference to" an employee benefit plan. *See, e.g.*, Rutledge v. Pharm. Care Mgmt. Ass'n, 141 S. Ct. 474, 479 (2020); *see also* Gobeille v. Liberty Mut. Ins. Co., 577 U.S. 312, 319–20 (2016). In the Court's hands, the "reference" prong is relatively narrow; it picks up state laws that are specific to employee benefit plans. *See Dillingham*, 519 U.S. at 325 ("Where a State's law acts immediately and exclusively upon ERISA plans, . . . or where the existence of ERISA plans is essential to the law's operation, . . . that 'reference' will result in pre-emption."). The "connection" prong is potentially broader. As the Court has acknowledged, however, asking whether state laws have a "connection with" employee benefit plans is not much more helpful than asking whether state laws "relate to" such plans. *See Travelers*, 514 U.S. at 656. The Court has therefore "look[ed] . . . to the objectives of the ERISA statute as a guide to the scope of the state law that Congress understood would survive." *Id.* In a recent case, the Court offered the following summary of the conclusions that it has reached on this point:

> "ERISA is . . . primarily concerned with pre-empting laws that require providers to structure benefit plans in particular ways, such as by requiring payment of specific benefits, *Shaw v. Delta Air Lines, Inc.*, 463 U.S. 85 (1983), or by binding plan administrators to specific rules for determining beneficiary status, *Egelhoff* [*v. Egelhoff*], 532 U.S. 141 [(2001)]. A state law may also be subject to pre-emption if 'acute, albeit indirect, economic effects of the state law force an ERISA plan to adopt a certain scheme of substantive coverage.' *Gobeille*, 577 U.S. at 320 (internal quotation marks omitted). As a shorthand for these considerations, this Court asks whether a state law 'governs a central matter of plan administration or interferes with nationally uniform plan administration.' *Ibid.* (internal quotation marks and ellipsis omitted). If it does, it is pre-empted.
>
> "Crucially, not every state law that affects an ERISA plan or causes some disuniformity in plan administration has an impermissible connection with an ERISA plan. That is especially so if a law merely affects costs. . . .
>
> ". . . ERISA does not pre-empt state rate regulations that merely increase costs or alter incentives for ERISA plans without forcing plans to adopt any particular scheme of substantive coverage. [*Travelers*, 514 U.S.] at 668; cf. *De Buono v. NYSA-ILA Medical and Clinical Services Fund*, 520 U.S. 806, 816 (1997) (concluding that ERISA did not pre-empt a state tax on gross receipts for patient services that simply increased the cost of providing benefits); *Dillingham*, 519 U.S. at 332 (holding that ERISA did not pre-empt a

California statute that incentivized, but did not require, plans to follow certain standards for apprenticeship programs)."

Rutledge, 141 S. Ct. at 480.

Does the text of § 514(a) support these distinctions, or at least allow them? If not, should the Court have taken a different approach? *Cf. id.* at 483–85 (Thomas, J., concurring) (criticizing the Court's doctrine and arguing that "the actual statutory test" has more content than the Court thinks).

NOTE ON THE PREEMPTION CLAUSE IN THE AIRLINE DEREGULATION ACT OF 1978

Under the Civil Aeronautics Act of 1938 and its successor, the Federal Aviation Act of 1958, federal law regulated the economics of the airline industry down to the level of individual air carriers. No carrier could engage in air transportation unless a federal administrative agency called the Civil Aeronautics Board had issued a certificate authorizing the carrier to do so, and the certificates regulated each carrier's business in detail. For instance, the certificate for any particular air carrier would "specify the terminal points and intermediate points, if any, between which the air carrier is authorized to engage in air transportation and the service to be rendered." Federal Aviation Act of 1958, Pub. L. 85–726, § 401(e), 72 Stat. 731, 755; Civil Aeronautics Act of 1938, ch. 601, § 401(f), 52 Stat. 973, 988. Likewise, each carrier had to file a tariff "showing all rates, fares, and charges for air transportation between points served by it"; those rates, fares, and charges had to be "just and reasonable," and they were subject to review by the Board. Federal Aviation Act of 1958 §§ 403–404, 1002, 72 Stat. at 758–60, 788–91; Civil Aeronautics Act of 1938 §§ 403–404, 1002, 52 Stat. at 992–93, 1018–20.

The Airline Deregulation Act of 1978 amended the Federal Aviation Act to phase out much of this federal regulation. At the same time, the Airline Deregulation Act also added an express preemption clause. Subject to a few exceptions that need not concern us, the preemption clause specified that "no State or political subdivision thereof . . . shall enact or enforce any law, rule, regulation, standard, or other provision having the force and effect of law relating to rates, routes, or services of any air carrier having authority under [the relevant title of the Federal Aviation Act] to provide interstate air transportation." Airline Deregulation Act of 1978, Pub. L. No. 95–504, sec. 4, § 105(a)(1), 92 Stat. 1705, 1708. As the Supreme Court observed in *Morales v. Trans World Airlines, Inc.*, 504 U.S. 374 (1992), this clause was meant "[t]o ensure that the States would not undo federal deregulation with regulation of their own." *Id.* at 378.

The phrase "relating to" in the Airline Deregulation Act's preemption clause obviously resembles the parallel language in ERISA's preemption clause, which Congress had enacted four years earlier. At the time of *Morales*, moreover, the Supreme Court had not yet started to express despair about the vapidity of that language. Justice Scalia's majority opinion in *Morales* therefore imported into the Airline Deregulation Act the verbal formulation that the Court had been using in ERISA cases. In his words, "Since the relevant language of the [Airline Deregulation Act] is identical, we think it appropriate to adopt the same standard here: State enforcement actions having a connection with, or reference to, airline 'rates, routes, or services' are pre-empted. . . ." *Id.* at 384.

Morales itself involved efforts by state attorneys general to police airlines' marketing practices. Hoping that the Airline Deregulation Act's preemption clause would not be interpreted to prevent states from applying their general consumer-protection statutes to the airline industry, the National Association of Attorneys General (NAAG) had issued "enforcement guidelines" describing a detailed set of practices that these state statutes allegedly required airlines to follow with respect to fare advertisements and frequent-flyer programs. Various state attorneys general then threatened to file suit against airlines that did not voluntarily follow the prescribed practices with respect to their fare advertisements. Instead of falling into line, however, the airlines sued the attorneys general. On the basis of the express preemption clause in the Airline Deregulation Act, the Supreme Court upheld an injunction against the threatened enforcement actions.

Early in its analysis, the Supreme Court's opinion in *Morales* rejected "the notion that only state laws specifically addressed to the airline industry are pre-empted." *Id.* at 386. As the Court noted, "[w]e have consistently rejected this precise argument in our ERISA cases," and the argument would "creat[e] an utterly irrational loophole"; states would be able to re-regulate the airline industry, contrary to the point of the preemption clause, as long as they did so "by the particular application of a general statute."[25] *Id.* Ultimately, though, the Court focused more on NAAG's enforcement guidelines (which might be seen as a species of regulation that specifically targeted the airline industry) than on the general consumer-protection statutes that the guidelines purported to be implementing. The Court framed the key question as "whether the NAAG guidelines . . . 'relat[e] to' fares," and the Court concluded that "[t]hey quite obviously do"; the very terms of many of the guidelines "bear[ ] a 'reference to' airfares," and the guidelines as a whole purported to "establish binding requirements as to how tickets may be

[25] To appreciate this point, imagine that a state enacts a general price-control statute forbidding sellers to charge more than a "reasonable" price for any goods or services sold in the state (with "reasonableness" being determined according to a list of factors prescribed in the statute). Would you say that the breadth of this state law insulates it from the preemption clause in the Airline Deregulation Act, so that the state can apply its price controls to the rates that airlines charge for flights just as the state can apply its price controls to other services? Or would you say that as applied to the airline industry, either the statute itself or the cap that it is understood to establish for airfares amounts to a "law . . . [or] standard . . . relating to rates, routes or services of any air carrier" within the meaning of the preemption clause?

marketed if they are to be sold at given prices." *Id.* at 387–88; *see also id.* at 388–89 (adding that "beyond the guidelines' express reference to fares, it is clear as an economic matter that state restrictions on fare advertising have the forbidden significant effect upon fares."). The Court added that "[i]n concluding that the NAAG fare advertising guidelines are pre-empted, we do not . . . set out on a road that leads to pre-emption of state laws against gambling and prostitution as applied to airlines." *Id.* at 390. Still, the Court did not articulate a clear test for deciding whether such generally applicable state laws "relat[e] to" an airline's "rates, routes, or services" within the meaning of the preemption clause.

The Court addressed generally applicable laws more directly in *American Airlines, Inc. v. Wolens*, 513 U.S. 219 (1995). American Airlines had changed its frequent-flyer program in a way that allegedly devalued credits previously earned by participants. Proceeding in the Illinois state courts, lawyers initiated plaintiff class actions against the airline. Among other things, the plaintiffs asserted claims under the Illinois Consumer Fraud and Deceptive Business Practices Act, a general consumer-protection statute. Speaking through Justice Ginsburg, however, the Supreme Court held that the Airline Deregulation Act preempted those claims. Insofar as a general consumer-protection statute purported to apply to American's frequent-flyer program in the manner claimed by the plaintiffs, the Court held that it "relat[ed] to" the airline's rates, routes, or services within the meaning of the express preemption clause. *See id.* at 226–28.

On the other hand, the majority held that the Airline Deregulation Act did not prevent the plaintiffs from pursuing some common-law claims seeking monetary relief from the airline for breach of contract. As the majority noted, much of the common law of contracts entails enforcing the parties' "own, self-imposed undertakings," as opposed to "state-imposed obligations." For purposes of the Airline Deregulation Act, the majority thought that this difference mattered. Specifically, the majority suggested that when the preemption clause restricted the states' ability to "enact or enforce any law, rule, regulation, standard, or other provision having the force and effect of law," the clause was most naturally understood to be referring to legal obligations whose substance is dictated by the state. Because "terms and conditions [that] airlines offer and passengers accept are privately ordered obligations" rather than dictates of the government, the majority held that the preemption clause did not prevent states from "hold[ing] parties to their [own] agreements" by granting "[a] remedy confined to a contract's terms." *Id.* at 228–29 & n.5.

To be clear, the majority opinion in *Wolens* was *not* drawing a distinction between written laws (such as statutes or regulations) and unwritten law (such as the common law of contracts). The reason the plaintiffs' breach-of-contract claims could proceed was not that they were based on the common law, but rather that the content of the relevant obligations had been "set by the parties themselves" instead of being prescribed by the state. *See id.* at 222.

Any distinction between written and unwritten law would have been hard to square with the language of the preemption clause, at least as originally enacted. From 1978 until 1994, the preemption clause in the Airline Deregulation Act covered "any law, rule, regulation, standard, or other provision having the force and effect of law." Airline Deregulation Act of 1978, sec. 4, § 105(a)(1), 92 Stat. at 1708. Even if a court might worry about reading the word "law" so broadly as to make the other words in this list superfluous, and even if a court might also hesitate to describe a common-law principle as a "regulation" or a "provision," the words "rule" and "standard" both seem broad enough to encompass common-law duties.

In 1994, though, Congress revised the Airline Deregulation Act's preemption clause and left out the words "rule" and "standard." As part of a broader codification project (bringing many provisions into Title 49 of the United States Code as enacted), Congress replaced the original preemption clause with the following version: "a State [or] political subdivision of a State . . . may not enact or enforce a law, regulation, or other provision having the force and effect of law related to a price, route, or service of an air carrier that may provide air transportation under [the relevant subpart of Title 49]." Act of July 5, 1994, Pub. L. 103–272, § 1(e), 108 Stat. 745, 1143 (enacting 49 U.S.C. § 41713(b)(1)). The 1994 Act indicated that most of its revisions, including the new preemption clause, were made "without substantive change" to the pre-existing law. *See id.* § 1(a), 108 Stat. at 745. But is that really true? Or could one argue that the new language no longer preempts any common-law duties, because the common law is not "a law, regulation, or other provision" within the meaning of the preemption clause?[26]

In the following case, the Supreme Court addressed that question among others. The Court also discussed the lessons of *Wolens*.

---

[26] Although the Supreme Court issued its opinion in *Wolens* in January 1995 (shortly after the new preemption clause took effect), the case did not present this question. By the time the case reached the Court, the plaintiffs were simply seeking monetary relief for the alleged devaluation of frequent-flyer credits that they had earned before 1988. *See Wolens*, 513 U.S. at 224–25. As a result, the new preemption clause may not have been relevant to their claims. In a footnote, the Court did mention that Congress had recently revised the clause. *See id.* at 223 n.1 (adding that "Congress intended the revision to make no substantive change"). The Court's analysis, however, focused on the earlier version.

Northwest, Inc. v. Ginsberg

572 U.S. 273 (2014)

■ *JUSTICE ALITO delivered the opinion of the Court.*

. . . .

I

A

Like many airlines, petitioner Northwest, Inc. (Northwest), established a frequent flyer program, its WorldPerks Airline Partners Program, to attract loyal customers. Under this program, members are able to earn "miles" by taking flights operated by Northwest and other "partner" airlines. Members can then redeem these miles for tickets and service upgrades with Northwest or its airline partners.

Respondent became a member of Northwest's WorldPerks program in 1999, and as a result of extensive travel on Northwest flights, he achieved "Platinum Elite" status (the highest level available) in 2005.

In 2008, however, Northwest terminated respondent's membership, apparently in reliance on a provision of the WorldPerks agreement that provided that "[a]buse of the . . . program (including . . . improper conduct as determined by [Northwest] in its sole judgment[)] . . . may result in cancellation of the member's account." According to respondent, a Northwest representative telephoned him in June 2008 and informed him that his "Platinum Elite" status was being revoked because he had " 'abused' " the program. In a letter sent about two weeks later, Northwest wrote:

> "[Y]ou have contacted our office 24 times since December 3, 2007 regarding travel problems, including 9 incidents of your bag arriving late at the luggage carousel. . . .
>
> ". . . .
>
> "Since December 3, 2007, you have continually asked for compensation over and above our guidelines. We have awarded you $1,925.00 in travel credit vouchers, 78,500 WorldPerks bonus miles, a voucher extension for your son, and $491.00 in cash reimbursements. . . ."

. . . .

B

Alleging that Northwest had ended his membership as a cost-cutting measure tied to Northwest's merger with Delta Air Lines, respondent filed a class action in the United States District Court for the Southern District of California on behalf of himself and all other similarly situated WorldPerks members.[1] Respondent's complaint asserted four separate

---

1 Applying California choice-of-law rules, the District Court held that Minnesota law applies because respondent "was a resident of Minneapolis, appears to fly in and out of

claims. First, his complaint alleged that Northwest had breached its contract by revoking his "Platinum Elite" status without valid cause. Second, the complaint claimed that Northwest violated the duty of good faith and fair dealing because it terminated his membership in a way that contravened his reasonable expectations with respect to the manner in which Northwest would exercise its discretion. Third, the complaint asserted a claim for negligent misrepresentation, and fourth, the complaint alleged intentional misrepresentation. Respondent sought damages in excess of $5 million, as well as injunctive relief requiring Northwest to restore the class members' WorldPerks status and prohibiting Northwest from future revocations of membership.

The District Court held that respondent's claims for breach of the covenant of good faith and fair dealing, negligent misrepresentation, and intentional misrepresentation were pre-empted by the Airline Deregulation Act of 1978 (ADA or Act) as amended, 49 U.S.C. § 41713. These claims, the court concluded, were "relate[d] to" Northwest's rates and services and thus fell within the ADA's express pre-emption clause. Respondent's remaining claim—for breach of contract—was dismissed without prejudice under Federal Rule of Civil Procedure 12(b)(6). The court held that respondent had failed to identify any material breach because the frequent flyer agreement gave Northwest sole discretion to determine whether a participant had abused the program. Respondent appealed the dismissal of his breach of the duty of good faith and fair dealing claim but not the other claims that the court had dismissed.

The Ninth Circuit reversed. 695 F.3d 873 (2012). Relying on pre-*Wolens* Circuit precedent, the Ninth Circuit first held that a breach of implied covenant claim is " 'too tenuously connected to airline regulation to trigger preemption under the ADA.' " 695 F.3d at 879. Such a claim, the Ninth Circuit wrote, "does not interfere with the [Act's] deregulatory mandate" and does not " 'force the Airlines to adopt or change their prices, routes or services—the prerequisite for . . . preemption.' " *Id.* at 880. In addition, the Court held that the covenant of good faith and fair dealing does not fall within the terms of the Act's pre-emption provision because it does not have a "direct effect" on either "prices" or "services." *Id.* at 877, 881.

We granted certiorari. . . .

II

. . . .

B

The first question we address is whether, as respondent now maintains, the ADA's pre-emption provision applies only to legislation enacted by a state legislature and regulations issued by a state administrative agency but not to a common-law rule like the implied

---

Minnesota, and . . . Northwest's principal place of business is Minnesota." That determination was not challenged on appeal.

covenant of good faith and fair dealing. We have little difficulty rejecting this argument.

To begin, state common-law rules fall comfortably within the language of the ADA pre-emption provision. . . . [T]he current version of this provision applies to state "law[s], regulation[s], or other provision[s] having the force and effect of law," 49 U.S.C. § 41713(b)(1). It is routine to call common-law rules "provisions." See, *e.g.*, *Madsen v. Women's Health Center, Inc.*, 512 U.S. 753, 765, n. 3 (1994); *United States v. Barnett*, 376 U.S. 681, 689–700 (1964); *Brown v. United Airlines, Inc.*, 720 F.3d 60, 68 (CA1 2013) ("[W]hen read in context, the word 'provision' in the ADA preemption provision can most appropriately be construed to include common law"). And a common-law rule clearly has "the force and effect of law." In *Wolens*, we noted that this phrase is most naturally read to " 'refe[r] to binding standards of conduct that operate irrespective of any private agreement,' " 513 U.S. at 229, n. 5, and we see no basis for holding that such standards must be based on a statute or regulation as opposed to the common law.

This understanding becomes even clearer when the original wording of the pre-emption provision is taken into account. When first enacted in 1978, this provision also applied to "rule[s]" and "standard[s]," and there surely can be no doubt that this formulation encompassed common-law rules. Indeed, we held in *CSX Transp., Inc. v. Easterwood*, 507 U.S. 658, 664 (1993), that virtually identical language in the Federal Railroad Safety Act of 1970 includes "[l]egal duties imposed . . . by the common law." See also *Riegel v. Medtronic, Inc.*, 552 U.S. 312, 324 (2008) (holding that a State's " 'requirements' " "includ[e] [the state's] common-law duties").

While "rule[s]" and "standard[s]" are not mentioned in the current version of the statute, this omission is the result of a recodification that was not meant to affect the provision's meaning. Those additional terms were deleted as part of a wholesale recodification of Title 49 in 1994, but Congress made it clear that this recodification did not effect any "substantive change." § 1(a), 108 Stat. 745.

In arguing that common-law rules fall outside the scope of the ADA pre-emption provision, respondent relies on our decision in *Sprietsma v. Mercury Marine*, 537 U.S. 51 (2002), which held that the Federal Boat Safety Act of 1971 did not pre-empt a common-law tort claim, but there are critical differences between the pre-emption provisions in the Boat Safety Act and the ADA. The Boat Safety Act provision applies only to "a law or regulation," 46 U.S.C. § 4306, whereas the ADA provision, as just explained, is much more broadly worded.

In addition, . . . [t]he *Sprietsma* decision placed substantial weight on the Boat Safety Act's saving provision, which was enacted at the same time as the pre-emption provision[. Although the Federal Aviation Act of

1958 also included a saving clause,[*] and although the Airline Deregulation Act did not repeal that clause,] we have described the Federal Aviation Act saving clause as "a relic of the pre-ADA/no pre-emption regime." *Morales*, 504 U.S. at 385. That provision applies to the entire, sprawling Federal Aviation Act [which addressed safety regulation as well as economic regulation], . . . and as we held in *Morales*, this "general 'remedies' saving clause cannot be allowed to supersede the specific substantive pre-emption provision [in the ADA]." *Ibid*. . . . For these reasons, respondent's interpretation of the ADA pre-emption provision cannot be squared with the provision's terms.

Exempting common-law claims would also disserve the central purpose of the ADA. The Act eliminated federal regulation of rates, routes, and services in order to allow those aspects of air transportation to be set by market forces, and the pre-emption provision was included to prevent the States from undoing what the Act was meant to accomplish. . . . What is important, therefore, is the effect of a state law, regulation, or provision, not its form, and the ADA's deregulatory aim can be undermined just as surely by a state common-law rule as it can by a state statute or regulation. See *Medtronic, Inc., supra*, at 325 (recognizing that state tort law that imposes certain requirements would "disrup[t] the federal scheme no less than state regulatory law to the same effect"). As the First Circuit has recognized, "[i]t defies logic to think that Congress would disregard real-world consequences and give dispositive effect to the form of a clear intrusion into a federally regulated industry." *Brown*, 720 F.3d at 66–67.

Finally, if *all* state common-law rules fell outside the ambit of the ADA's pre-emption provision, we would have had no need in *Wolens* to single out a subcategory of common-law claims, *i.e.*, those based on the parties' voluntary undertaking, as falling outside that provision's coverage.

Accordingly, we conclude that the phrase "other provision having the force and effect of law" includes common-law claims.

C

We must next determine whether respondent's breach of implied covenant claim "relates to" "rates, routes, or services." A claim satisfies this requirement if it has "a connection with, or reference to, airline" prices, routes, or services, *Morales, supra*, at 384, and the claim at issue here clearly has such a connection. That claim seeks respondent's reinstatement in Northwest's frequent flyer program so that he can access the program's "valuable . . . benefits," including "flight upgrades,

[*] *Editor's note*: Section 1106 of the Federal Aviation Act of 1958 specified that "[n]othing contained in this Act shall in any way abridge or alter the remedies now existing at common law or by statute, but the provisions of this Act are in addition to such remedies." 72 Stat. 731, 798. As revised in 1994, the successor of this provision simply says: "A remedy under this part [of Title 49 of the United States Code] is in addition to any other remedies provided by law." 49 U.S.C. § 40120(c).

accumulated mileage, loyalty program status or benefits on other airlines, and other advantages." App. 49–50.

Like the frequent flyer program in *Wolens*, the Northwest program is connected to the airline's "rates" because the program awards mileage credits that can be redeemed for tickets and upgrades. See 513 U.S. at 226. When miles are used in this way, the rate that a customer pays, *i.e.*, the price of a particular ticket, is either eliminated or reduced. The program is also connected to "services," *i.e.*, access to flights and to higher service categories. *Ibid*.

Respondent argues that his claim differs from the claims in *Wolens* because he "does not challenge access to flights and upgrades or the number of miles needed to obtain air tickets" but instead contests "the termination of his WorldPerks elite membership," Brief for Respondent 12, but this argument ignores respondent's reason for seeking reinstatement of his membership, *i.e.*, to obtain reduced rates and enhanced services. Respondent's proffered distinction has no substance.

Respondent and *amici* suggest that *Wolens* is not controlling because frequent flyer programs have fundamentally changed since the time of that decision. We are told that "most miles [are now] earned without consuming airline services" and are "spent without consuming airline services." Brief for State of California et al. 18 (emphasis deleted). But whether or not this alleged change might have some impact in a future case, it is not implicated here. In this case, respondent did not assert that he earned his miles from any activity other than taking flights or that he attempted to redeem miles for anything other than tickets and upgrades. See Tr. of Oral Arg. 47–48.

III

With these preliminary issues behind us, we turn to the central issue in this case, *i.e.*, whether respondent's implied covenant claim is based on a state-imposed obligation or simply one that the parties voluntarily undertook. Petitioners urge us to hold that implied covenant claims are always pre-empted, and respondent suggests that such claims are generally not pre-empted, but the reasoning of *Wolens* neither dooms nor spares all such claims.

While most States recognize some form of the good faith and fair dealing doctrine, it does not appear that there is any uniform understanding of the doctrine's precise meaning. "[T]he concept of good faith in the performance of contracts 'is a phrase without general meaning (or meanings) of its own.' " *Tymshare, Inc. v. Covell*, 727 F.2d 1145, 1152 (CADC 1984) (Scalia, J.) (quoting Summers, "Good Faith" in General Contract Law and the Sales Provisions of the Uniform Commercial Code, 54 Va. L. Rev. 195, 201 (1968)) . . . . Of particular importance here, while some States are said to use the doctrine "to effectuate the intentions of parties or to protect their reasonable expectations," *ibid.*, other States clearly employ the doctrine to ensure that a party does not " 'violate community standards of decency, fairness, or reasonableness.' " *Universal Drilling Co., LLC v. R & R Rig Service, LLC*, 271 P.3d 987, 999 (Wyo. 2012); [other citations omitted].

Whatever may be the case under the law of other jurisdictions, it seems clear that under Minnesota law, which is controlling here, see n. 1, *supra*, the implied covenant must be regarded as a state-imposed obligation. Respondent concedes that under Minnesota law parties cannot contract out of the covenant. See Tr. of Oral Arg. 33–34; see also *In re Hennepin Cty. 1986 Recycling Bond Litigation*, 540 N.W.2d 494, 502 (Minn. 1995); *Sterling Capital Advisors, Inc. v. Herzog*, 575 N.W.2d 121, 125 (Minn. App. 1998); *Minnwest Bank Central v. Flagship Properties LLC*, 689 N.W.2d 295, 303 (Minn. App. 2004). And as a leading commentator has explained, a State's "unwillingness to allow people to disclaim the obligation of good faith . . . shows that the obligation cannot be implied, but is law imposed." 3A A. Corbin, Corbin on Contracts § 654A, p. 88 (L. Cunningham & A. Jacobsen eds. Supp. 1994). When the law of a State does not authorize parties to free themselves from the covenant, a breach of covenant claim is pre-empted under the reasoning of *Wolens*.

Another feature of Minnesota law provides an additional, independent basis for our conclusion. Minnesota law holds that the implied covenant applies to "every contract," *In re Hennepin Cty., supra*, at 502, with the notable exception of employment contracts. *Hunt v. IBM Mid America Employees Fed. Credit Union*, 384 N.W.2d 853, 857–858 (Minn. 1986). The exception for employment contracts is based, in significant part, on "policy reasons," *id.* at 858, and therefore the decision not to exempt other types of contracts must be based on a policy determination, namely, that the "policy reasons" that support the rule for employment contracts do not apply (at least with the same force) in other contexts. When the application of the implied covenant depends on state policy, a breach of implied covenant claim cannot be viewed as simply an attempt to vindicate the parties' implicit understanding of the contract.

For these reasons, the breach of implied covenant claim in this case cannot stand, but petitioners exhort us to go further and hold that all such claims, no matter the content of the law of the relevant jurisdiction, are pre-empted. If pre-emption depends on state law, petitioners warn, airlines will be faced with a baffling patchwork of rules, and the deregulatory aim of the ADA will be frustrated. But the airlines have means to avoid such a result. A State's implied covenant rules will escape pre-emption only if the law of the relevant State permits an airline to contract around those rules in its frequent flyer program agreement, and if an airline's agreement is governed by the law of such a State, the airline can specify that the agreement does not incorporate the covenant. While the inclusion of such a provision may impose transaction costs and presumably would not enhance the attractiveness of the program, an airline can decide whether the benefits of such a provision are worth the potential costs.

Our holding also does not leave participants in frequent flyer programs without protection. The ADA is based on the view that the best interests of airline passengers are most effectively promoted, in the main, by allowing the free market to operate. If an airline acquires a reputation for mistreating the participants in its frequent flyer program (who are generally the airline's most loyal and valuable customers), customers can avoid that program and may be able to enroll in a more favorable rival program.

Federal law also provides protection for frequent flyer program participants. Congress has given the Department of Transportation (DOT) the general authority to prohibit and punish unfair and deceptive practices in air transportation and in the sale of air transportation, 49 U.S.C. § 41712(a), and Congress has specifically authorized the DOT to investigate complaints relating to frequent flyer programs. See FAA Modernization and Reform Act of 2012, § 408(6), 126 Stat. 87. Pursuant to these provisions, the DOT regularly entertains and acts on such complaints.

....

Because respondent's implied covenant of good faith and fair dealing claim seeks to enlarge his contractual agreement with petitioners, we hold that 49 U.S.C. § 41713(b)(1) pre-empts the claim. The judgment of the Court of Appeals for the Ninth Circuit is reversed, and the case is remanded for further proceedings consistent with this opinion.

NOTES AND QUESTIONS

1. Consistent with the verbal formulation developed in ERISA cases, the Supreme Court said that the "relat[ing] to" language in the Airline Deregulation Act's preemption clause encompasses state laws that have "a connection with, or reference to," an airline's prices, routes, or services. *Ginsberg*, 572 U.S. at 284 (quoting Morales v. Trans World Airlines, Inc., 504 U.S. 374, 384 (1992)). As the Court understands that formulation, the Airline Deregulation Act expressly preempts not only state laws that are specifically designed for the airline industry (and that make "reference to" prices, routes, or services), but also certain applications of more general state laws (which, as applied to airlines, might have an impermissible "connection with" prices, routes, or services). Thus, *Wolens* held that the preemption clause prevented Illinois's general consumer-protection statute from being applied to certain aspects of an airline's frequent-flyer program, and *Ginsberg* reached the same conclusion about Minnesota's version of the implied covenant of good faith and fair dealing.

On the other hand, dicta in *Morales* suggested that the preemption clause would not prevent states from prohibiting gambling and prostitution throughout the state, including on airplanes. *See Morales*, 504 U.S. at 390. The Justices apparently thought that state laws of this sort do not "relat[e] to" an airline's "services" within the meaning of the preemption clause.

How should courts decide which generally applicable state laws are preempted as applied to airlines? Can courts draw the necessary lines just by staring hard at the preemption clause and thinking about the ordinary meaning of its words? Or is it also necessary for courts to think about the purposes behind the Airline Deregulation Act, including the *type* of deregulation that the Act was designed to achieve? *Cf.* Rowe v. N.H. Motor Transp. Ass'n, 552 U.S. 364, 371 (2008) (addressing a preemption clause modeled on the one in the Airline Deregulation Act, and taking *Morales* to have determined that "pre-emption occurs at least where state laws have a 'significant impact' related to Congress' deregulatory and pre-emption-related objectives" (quoting *Morales*, 504 U.S. at 390)).

2. Ever since Congress enacted the Airline Deregulation Act, courts have faced questions about whether and to what extent the Act's preemption clause shields airlines from liability under generally applicable state tort law for personal injuries that passengers suffer on airplanes. By and large, courts have concluded that "Congress did not intend to preempt passengers' run-of-the-mill personal injury claims"—such as the claims of a passenger who "tripped over a piece of luggage allegedly left in the aisle by a flight attendant," or who was struck by a service cart that a flight attendant was pushing, or who was injured by luggage that fell when another passenger opened an overhead bin. *See* Charas v. Trans World Airlines, Inc., 160 F.3d 1259, 1261 (9th Cir. 1998) (en banc).

Another provision in the Airline Deregulation Act supports this conclusion. The Act contemplated that as a condition of operation, each air carrier would maintain insurance to cover "amounts for which . . . such air carrier may become liable for bodily injuries to or the death of any person, or for loss of or damage to property of others, resulting from the operation or maintenance of aircraft . . . ." Airline Deregulation Act, sec. 20(d)(1), § 401(q)(1), 92 Stat. at 1722; *see also* Act of July 5, 1994, 108 Stat. at 1126 (enacting a revised version of this requirement as 49 U.S.C. § 41112(a)). Apparently, then, the enacting Congress did not expect the preemption clause to eliminate all such tort liability. *See* Hodges v. Delta Airlines, Inc., 44 F.3d 334, 338 (5th Cir. 1995) (en banc) (making this point).

To square this conclusion with the language of the preemption clause (which preempts state laws "related to a price, route, or service of an air carrier"), the Ninth Circuit read the word "service" narrowly. In the context of the Airline Deregulation Act's preemption clause, the Ninth Circuit held, " 'service' . . . refers to such things as the frequency and scheduling of transportation, and to the selection of markets to or from which transportation is provided (as in, 'This airline provides service from Tucson to New York twice a day')," but does not encompass things that airlines do for passengers en route. *Charas*, 160 F.3d at 1265–66. In particular, the Ninth Circuit asserted that " 'service' does not refer to the pushing of beverage carts, keeping the aisles clear of stumbling blocks, the safe handling and storage of luggage, assistance to passengers in need, or like functions." *Id.* at 1266; *see also id.* ("Congress used 'service' . . . in the public utility sense—i.e., the provision of air transportation to and from various markets at various times.").

The Ninth Circuit's interpretation of the word "service" has proved too narrow for many other courts to accept. For instance, when the New York legislature enacted a "Passenger Bill of Rights" requiring air carriers to provide electricity, waste-removal services, and refreshments to passengers who are stuck on airplanes during lengthy delays before takeoff, the Second Circuit had "little difficulty" concluding that the requirements "relate[d] to the service of an air carrier" and were therefore preempted. *Air Transport Ass'n of Am., Inc. v. Cuomo*, 520 F.3d 218, 222 (2d Cir. 2008). As the Second Circuit noted, "A majority of the circuits to have construed 'service' have held that the term refers to the provision or anticipated provision of labor from the airline to its passengers and encompasses matters such as boarding procedures, baggage handling, and food and drink—matters incidental to and distinct from the actual transportation of passengers." *Id.* at 223 (citing cases).

Even so, there is fairly widespread agreement that the purposes behind the Airline Deregulation Act do not require preemption of many aspects of ordinary state tort law. *See, e.g.*, Taj Mahal Travel, Inc. v. Delta Airlines, Inc., 164 F.3d 186, 194–95 (3d Cir. 1998) (allowing a travel agency's defamation suit against an airline to proceed); *Hodges*, 44 F.3d at 336–37 (allowing a passenger's personal-injury suit to proceed on the theory that the airline was negligent in letting a case of rum be stowed in an overhead bin).[27] To avoid excessive preemption, some courts have exploited the vagueness of the phrase "related to" in the preemption clause. Drawing upon the modern Supreme Court's cases about the same phrase in ERISA, these courts have observed that the relevant relationship must be determined in light of the purposes of the Airline Deregulation Act.

Day v. SkyWest Airlines, 45 F.4th 1181 (10th Cir. 2022), is a good example. The plaintiff was seeking damages for injuries that she allegedly suffered when a flight attendant accidentally hit her shoulder with a beverage cart. The district court held that the plaintiff's claims were preempted, but the Tenth Circuit reversed. The Tenth Circuit "assume[d] for purposes of this appeal . . . that an airline's 'provision of

[27] *But see* Fawemimo v. American Airlines, Inc., 751 F. App'x 16, 19 (2d Cir. 2018) (distinguishing between personal-injury claims based on "distinct negligent acts" and personal-injury claims challenging airline policies or aircraft design, and concluding that the latter are preempted).

food and drink' constitutes a 'service' " within the meaning of the Airline Deregulation Act's preemption clause. *Id.* at 1184. According to the Tenth Circuit, though, the generally applicable principles of state negligence law that the plaintiff was invoking did not "relate[ ] to" that service in the relevant sense.

As the Tenth Circuit noted, "the [Supreme] Court has said that 'state law relates to an ERISA plan [in the sense prohibited by ERISA's preemption clause] if it has a connection with or reference to such a plan,' . . . and the Court has 'adopt[ed] the same standard' for the [Airline Deregulation Act] . . . ." *Id.* at 1185 (first quoting Rutledge v. Pharm. Care Mgmt. Ass'n, 141 S. Ct. 474, 479 (2020) (quotation omitted); then quoting *Morales*, 504 U.S. at 384). On the basis of ERISA cases, the Tenth Circuit glossed the "connection with or reference to" test as follows:

> "[A] state law has an impermissible 'reference to' airline prices, routes, or services if the law 'acts immediately and exclusively' upon airline prices, routes, or services, or if 'the existence of' airline prices, routes, or services 'is essential to the law's operations.' [*Gobeille v. Liberty Mut. Ins. Co.*, 577 U.S. 312, 319–20 (2016).] A state law that does not 'refer to' airline prices, routes, or services under this test may nevertheless be preempted as impermissibly 'connected with' them if the law (1) governs a central matter of an airline's prices, routes, or services; (2) interferes with uniform national policies regarding airline prices, routes, or services; or (3) will have acute economic effects that effectively limit airlines' choices regarding their prices, routes, and services. *See id.* at 320. In applying this test, a state law is not preempted if it 'has only a "tenuous, remote, or peripheral" connection with [airline prices, routes, or services], as is the case with many laws of general applicability.' [*District of Columbia v. Greater Wash. Bd. of Trade*, 506 U.S. 125, 130 n.1 (1992) (quoting Shaw v. Delta Air Lines, Inc., 463 U.S. 85, 100 n.21 (1983))] . . . . In evaluating a state law for the existence of a 'forbidden connection,' we will consider (1) 'the objectives of the [Airline Deregulation Act] as a guide to the scope of the state law that Congress understood would survive,' and (2) 'the nature of the effect of the state law on' airline prices, routes, and services. [*Cal. Div. of Labor Standards Enf't v. Dillingham Constr. N.A.*, 519 U.S. 316, 325 (1997).]"

Id. at 1186.

Because the principles of state tort law at issue in *Day* were generally applicable, they clearly did not "refer to" airline prices, routes, or services for purposes of the first part of this test. According to the Tenth Circuit, moreover, their application to airlines also did not have an impermissible "connection with" the airlines' services. As the Tenth Circuit explained, "Congress enacted the [Airline Deregulation Act] to achieve 'the *economic* deregulation of the airline industry,' " not to exempt airlines from tort liability for personal injuries caused by a flight attendant's negligence. *Id.* at 1187 (quoting *Charas*, 160 F.3d at 1265); *see also id.* at 1187 (agreeing with the Fifth Circuit that " 'Congress's failure to provide any federal remedy for persons injured by such conduct' " is a sign that Congress did not intend to preempt state tort law (quoting *Hodges*, 44 F.3d at 338, in turn quoting *Silkwood v. Kerr-McGee Corp.*, 464 U.S. 238, 251 (1984))). The practical effect of applying this state tort law to airlines, moreover, would not amount to "the type of 'public utility-style regulation' that Congress intended . . . to preempt." *Id.* at 1188 (quoting *Taj Mahal*, 164 F.3d at 194). In the Tenth Circuit's words, "Although Congress intended to deregulate airlines' economic policies (such as, for instance, the decision not to offer a beverage service or to offer a different range of beverages than other airlines), nothing in the [Airline Deregulation Act] or its legislative history supports the view that Congress also intended to immunize airlines from liability for any violation of generally applicable negligence . . . laws." *Id.* at 1189.

Given the vagueness of the phrase "related to" in the preemption clause, it seems sensible for courts to seek guidance from the purposes of the Airline Deregulation Act and the type of deregulation that Congress wanted to achieve. But is that approach consistent with the analysis that the Supreme Court used in Part II.C of its opinion in *Northwest, Inc. v. Ginsberg*? There, the Court held that if Minnesota's version of the covenant of good faith and fair dealing were applied to Northwest's frequent-flyer program in the manner sought by the plaintiff, the covenant would indeed have a "connection with" both prices and services. Would this application of the covenant have amounted to the type of regulation that the Airline Deregulation Act was intended to prevent? Can you distinguish the principles of tort law that the Tenth Circuit considered in *Day*?

3. In addition to claims about personal injuries caused by negligence, airlines might face many other types of claims under generally applicable state law, including claims about discrimination, intentional torts, labor practices, misappropriation of trade secrets, and more. *See, e.g.*, Bernstein v. Virgin Am., Inc., 3 F.4th 1127, 1141 (9th Cir. 2021) (concluding that the Airline Deregulation Act did not prevent flight attendants from invoking a California law requiring employers to provide employees with rest and meal breaks); DiFiore v. Am. Airlines, Inc., 646 F.3d 81 (1st Cir. 2011) (concluding that the Airline Deregulation Act preempted the Massachusetts Tip Law as applied to an airline's practice of charging a $2 fee for each bag checked with a skycap); Syed v. Frontier Airlines, Inc., 522 F. Supp. 3d 503 (E.D. Mo. 2021) (finding preemption of various claims growing out of a dispute between passengers and a gate agent, but allowing a false-imprisonment claim to proceed); Peterson v. Cont'l Airlines, Inc., 970 F. Supp. 246 (S.D.N.Y. 1997) (allowing various claims to proceed in connection with an incident in which police officers summoned by the airline forcibly removed the plaintiff from an airplane).

In one early case, then-Judge Sonia Sotomayor articulated a framework for deciding whether a plaintiff's claims under generally applicable state tort law are "related to" an airline's "service[s]" within the meaning of the Airline Deregulation Act's preemption clause. Under that framework, courts would ask three questions: (1) "whether the activity at issue in the claim is an airline service"; (2) "whether the claim affects the airline service directly or [only] tenuously, remotely, or peripherally"; and (3) "whether the underlying tortious conduct was reasonably necessary to the provision of the service." *Rombom v. United Air Lines, Inc.*, 867 F. Supp. 214, 221–22 (S.D.N.Y. 1994). In conducting the third inquiry, Judge Sotomayor considered whether "the service was provided in a manner that falls within a spectrum of reasonable conduct" (in which case the tort claim would be preempted) or instead entailed "outrageous conduct that goes beyond the scope of normal aircraft operations." *Id.* at 222. Would this final inquiry effectively require courts to decide whether the airline *should* face liability for the conduct in question, and hence to evaluate the policy of the state law that the plaintiff is invoking? Can the language of the preemption clause, read in the context of the Airline Deregulation Act as a whole, be understood to incorporate these distinctions?

2. IMPLIED "FIELD" PREEMPTION

Most federal statutes do not contain express preemption clauses, but virtually all federal statutes still preempt at least some state law. At a minimum, valid federal statutes preempt state law with which they conflict (in a sense discussed in the next section of this chapter). Apart from this sort of "conflict" preemption, though, courts also discuss the possibility of implied "field" preemption. As a matter of statutory interpretation, certain federal statutes might be understood to occupy a particular field to the exclusion of state law. If courts understand a federal statute to do so, and if the Constitution gives Congress the power to preempt state law throughout the relevant field, then the federal statute will effectively strip the states of lawmaking power in that field—with the result that state law not only cannot validly *conflict with* federal law, but cannot even *supplement* federal law in the defined field.

One can understand why members of Congress might sometimes want to federalize an entire field in this way. For reasons of national policy, members of Congress might decide that a particular industry should be regulated in certain ways but not others. If Congress enacts the regulations that it considers appropriate, it might not want individual states to be able to add further regulations of their own. Even apart from the substance of the regulations, moreover, there sometimes are policy reasons for regulations to be uniform across the country (rather than simply establishing a federal floor that each state can supplement).

Of course, when Congress does indeed make the decision to preempt state law throughout a field, one might expect Congress to say so by enacting an express preemption clause that is worded in such a way as to achieve the desired level of preemption. Even in the absence of an express preemption clause, though, courts have sometimes understood federal statutes as *impliedly* preempting state law on certain topics.

The Supreme Court's doctrines about implied field preemption have changed over time. In the early twentieth century, when Congress enacted a statute regulating some aspect of interstate or foreign commerce, the Court often held that states could no longer act upon the same subject. *See, e.g.*, David E. Engdahl, *Preemptive Capability of Federal Power*, 45 U. COLO. L. REV. 51, 53 (1973). Take the Federal Employers' Liability Act (FELA), ch. 149, 35 Stat. 65 (1908) (codified as amended at 45 U.S.C. § 51 *et seq.*), which gave railroad workers in interstate commerce a federal right of action to collect damages for injuries caused by the negligence of their employer's officers, agents, or other employees. Upon the enactment of this federal statute in 1908, the Supreme Court promptly held that "the laws of the States, in so far as they cover the same field, are superseded." *Second Employers' Liability Cases*, 223 U.S. 1, 55 (1912); *see also* Mich. Cent. R.R. Co. v. Vreeland, 227 U.S. 59, 66 (1913) (taking the FELA to "supersede all legislation over the same subject by the States," and identifying the relevant subject as "the liability of railroad companies to their employés injured while engaged in interstate commerce"); N.Y. Cent. R.R. Co. v. Winfield, 244 U.S. 147, 149–54 (1917) (interpreting the FELA as implicitly preempting the application of state workmen's compensation laws within this field).

As Professor Stephen Gardbaum has explained, many of the Court's cases during this era treated field preemption as "an automatic consequence of congressional action in a given field," without any "systematic reference to congressional intent as the necessary trigger." Stephen A. Gardbaum, *The Nature of Preemption*, 79 CORNELL L. REV. 767, 801 (1994); *see also* Engdahl, *supra*, 45 U. COLO. L. REV. at 53–54 (agreeing with this view, though noting that congressional intent came into play when courts considered whether states could act upon matters that the federal statute did not explicitly address). In the words of one of the cases that Professor Gardbaum emphasizes, "if the State and Congress have a concurrent power, that of the State is superseded when the power of Congress is exercised." *Southern Ry. Co. v. Reid*, 222 U.S. 424, 436 (1912). Professor Gardbaum characterizes this doctrine as one of "latent exclusivity," and he argues that it was "understood more as a doctrine about the constitutional division of interstate commerce powers than as a general, discretionary power of Congress." Gardbaum, *supra*, 79 CORNELL L. REV. at 801–02.

By the 1930s, that doctrine faded: the Court abandoned the "automatic element" in its earlier jurisprudence of field preemption and adopted "a new requirement that a federal statute would be considered to have taken over a given field only if Congress clearly manifested its intent to do so." *Id.* at 806. Still, the Court proved willing to infer the necessary congressional intent from clues that fell considerably short of express preemption clauses.

In *Rice v. Santa Fe Elevator Corp.*, 331 U.S. 218 (1947), the Court summarized its doctrine on this point. The Court began by acknowledging a presumption against preemption: when a federal statute addresses a field that Congress has traditionally left to the states, "we start with the assumption that the historic police powers of the States were not to be superseded by the Federal Act unless that was the clear and manifest purpose of Congress." *Id.* at 230. Nonetheless, the Court asserted that "[s]uch a purpose may be evidenced in several ways." *Id.* The Court proceeded to offer some examples.

First, the *Rice* Court indicated that the very comprehensiveness of a federal statute could sometimes justify inferring field preemption. *See id.* ("The scheme of federal regulation may be so pervasive as to make reasonable the inference that Congress left no room for the States to supplement it."). For instance, in *City of Burbank v. Lockheed Air Terminal*, 411 U.S. 624 (1973), a narrowly divided Court relied on "the pervasive nature of the scheme of federal regulation of aircraft noise" to infer field preemption under the Federal Aviation Act of 1958, Pub. L. 85–726, 72 Stat. 731, as amended by the Noise Control Act of 1972, Pub. L. 92–574, 86 Stat. 1234. *See City of Burbank*, 411 U.S. at 633 (holding that these statutes, together with regulations promulgated under their authority, implicitly stripped states and localities of authority to impose a curfew on jet take-offs).

Later that same Term, though, the Court voiced caution about this idea in *New York State Department of Social Services v. Dublino*, 413 U.S. 405 (1973). There, the Court held that a detailed federal statute incorporating work requirements into the federally funded program of Aid to Families with Dependent Children (AFDC) did not prevent New York from conditioning AFDC benefits on compliance with additional work rules. The Court specifically addressed, and rejected, "the contention that pre-emption is to be inferred merely from the comprehensive character of the federal work incentive provisions." *Id.* at 415. More generally, the Court suggested that contentions of this sort usually deserve little weight (at least absent other considerations):

> "The subjects of modern social and regulatory legislation often by their very nature require intricate and complex responses from the Congress, but without Congress necessarily intending its enactment as the exclusive means of meeting the problem. Given the complexity of the matter addressed by Congress in [the statute at issue], a detailed statutory scheme was both likely and appropriate, completely apart from any questions of pre-emptive intent."

Id.; *accord* De Canas v. Bica, 424 U.S. 351, 359–60 (1976); *see also* Hillsborough County v. Automated Med. Labs., Inc., 471 U.S. 707, 717 (1985) ("We are even more reluctant to infer pre-emption from the comprehensiveness of regulations than from the comprehensiveness of statutes.").

Aside from the comprehensiveness of the federal statutory scheme, *Rice* mentioned two other considerations that allegedly could justify inferring field preemption: (1) "the Act of Congress may touch a field in which the federal interest is so dominant that the federal system will be assumed to preclude enforcement of state laws on the same subject" or (2) "the object sought to be obtained by the federal law and the character of obligations imposed by it may reveal the same purpose." *Rice*, 331 U.S. at 230. As an example of the first consideration, the Court cited *Hines v. Davidowitz*, 312 U.S. 52 (1941), where the Court held that the federal Alien Registration Act of 1940 implicitly prevented states from enforcing their own requirements that noncitizens register with the state. *See id.* at 62–74 (emphasizing not only the comprehensiveness of the federal Act but also its relationship to the federal interests in international relations and national security).

The modern Supreme Court has continued to invoke *Hines*. *See* Arizona v. United States, 567 U.S. 387, 400–03 (2012) (adhering to *Hines*'s view that "the Federal Government has occupied the field of alien registration," and concluding that states cannot supplement federal law in this area by adding extra penalties for conduct that federal law prohibits). Still, the Court will not necessarily infer field preemption simply because of general arguments about the federal interests at stake in the relevant field. *See, e.g.*, Kansas v. Garcia, 140 S. Ct. 791, 804 (2020) (declining to find preemption in another case that touched upon immigration); Va. Uranium, Inc. v. Warren, 139 S. Ct. 1894, 1901 (2019) (plurality opinion of Gorsuch, J.) (refusing to read the federal Atomic Energy Act to preempt a state ban on uranium mining, and noting that "[i]nvoking some brooding federal interest . . . should never be enough to win preemption of a state law"). *Compare* Pac. Gas & Elec. Co. v. State Energy Res. Conservation & Dev. Comm'n, 461 U.S. 190, 205–13 (1983) (finding federal preemption of "the entire field of nuclear safety concerns" regarding the operation of nuclear power plants, but basing this conclusion on the federal government's one-time monopoly over the use of nuclear technology and a variety of other considerations specific to the text and history of the federal statutes in this area), *with* Silkwood v. Kerr-McGee Corp., 464 U.S. 238, 249–56 (1984) (discussing limits on the field recognized in *Pacific Gas & Electric*, and holding that plaintiffs injured in nuclear incidents could seek compensatory and punitive damages under state tort law).

Overall, the Supreme Court has become less willing to infer field preemption than it was a century ago. As a matter of *stare decisis*, the Court does continue to follow some old precedents that understood particular federal statutes to occupy entire fields to the exclusion of state law. *See, e.g.*, Kurns v. R.R. Friction Prods. Corp., 565 U.S. 625 (2012) (following *Napier v. Atlantic Coast Line R.R. Co.*, 272 U.S. 605 (1926), which held that the so-called Locomotive Inspection Act occupied the field of the regulation of locomotive equipment); Norfolk S. Ry. Co. v. Sorrell, 549 U.S. 158, 165 (2007) (citing the *Second Employers' Liability Cases*, 223 U.S. 1 (1912), for the proposition that the FELA "pre-empt[s] state tort remedies"). But there is widespread agreement that in cases of first impression, today's Court is slower to infer field preemption. *See, e.g.*, *Kurns*, 565 U.S. at 638 (Kagan, J., concurring) (observing that "*Napier* is an anachronism" and that "[u]nder our more recent cases, Congress must do much more to oust all of state law from a field"); Camps Newfound/Owatonna, Inc. v. Town of Harrison, 520 U.S. 564, 617 (1997) (Thomas, J., dissenting) ("[O]ur recent cases have frequently rejected field pre-emption in the absence of statutory language expressly requiring it."); *see also Garcia*, 140 S. Ct. at 804 (calling implied field preemption "rare").

Of course, the modern Court does not have a categorical position against the very possibility of implied field preemption, and any such position would be hard to defend. Even if one refuses to infer field preemption on the basis of the general considerations listed in *Rice*, statutory provisions can sometimes convey what the Court has called "a clear, but implicit, pre-emptive intent." *Barnett Bank of Marion County, N.A. v. Nelson*, 517 U.S. 25, 31 (1996). For example, consider the federal Ports and Waterways Safety Act of 1972, Pub. L. 92–340, 86 Stat. 424. Title I of that Act authorized the Secretary of Transportation to promulgate safety standards for both vessel traffic and shore structures. To address the interaction of this authority with state law, § 102(b) specified that "[n]othing contained in this title . . . prevent[s] a State or political subdivision thereof from prescribing *for structures only* higher safety requirements or safety standards than those which may be prescribed pursuant to this title." *Id.* at 426 (emphasis added) (current version at 46 U.S.C. § 70011(c)). Although this provision took the form of a saving clause rather than a preemption clause, it conspicuously protected only state regulation of "structures" in the context of a title that covered vessels too. As a result, the Supreme Court held that the statute "impliedly forbids higher state standards for vessels." *Ray v. Atlantic Richfield Co.*, 435 U.S. 151, 174 (1978). In other words, even though the Ports and Waterways Safety Act did not contain an *express* preemption clause to this effect, the Act authoritatively *implied* that states could not supplement the Secretary's regulations of vessel safety with more demanding requirements of their own.[28]

---

[28] Even in the absence of textual indications of this sort, certain types of federal statutory provisions are normally presumed to federalize various questions of detail that the provisions do not explicitly address. The clearest example involves federal statutes that explicitly create private rights of action, but that do not specify every detail of the remedial rights that they create—who the proper defendants are, or what the measure of damages is, or what substantive defenses can defeat liability, or whether the right of action survives the death of the original parties, or whether the right of action can be assigned from one potential plaintiff to another. Because it would be odd for *state* law to control these details of *federal* rights of action, courts routinely assume that *federal* law governs questions of this sort. *See* Caleb Nelson, *The*

The bottom line is that implied field preemption has waned but is not entirely nonexistent. Sometimes, as in *Ray*, the wording of a federal statutory provision that is not itself cast as a preemption clause will warrant the inference that the federal statute occupies a particular field. Even in the absence of such specific clues, courts might sometimes base the same inference on other considerations of the sort detailed in *Rice*. While *Rice* overstates the modern Supreme Court's willingness to infer field preemption, the category of implied field preemption remains more than a null set.

On the relatively rare occasions when the Court does infer field preemption, the Court must try to define the field that Congress has occupied: exactly what restrictions on state lawmaking power does the relevant federal statute imply?[29] Some federal statutes might be understood as broadly preventing any and all state laws from operating on a particular topic. But the term "field preemption" can also be used to describe somewhat more limited preemptive effects. For instance, a federal regulatory statute might be understood to preempt state laws that were enacted for the purpose of regulating the same topic as the federal statute, but not to prevent the application of state laws that were enacted for other reasons. *Compare* ONEOK, Inc. v. Learjet, Inc., 575 U.S. 373, 376, 385 (2015) (following precedents holding that the Natural Gas Act occupies a particular field, but noting that "[t]hose precedents emphasize the importance of considering the *target* at which the state law *aims*," and concluding that the plaintiffs' claims under generally applicable state antitrust law were not preempted), *with Va. Uranium*, 139 S. Ct. at 1905 (plurality opinion of Gorsuch, J.) (arguing that field-preemption inquiries more commonly "depend[ ] on *what* the State did, not *why* it did it"). Likewise, whether state law is preempted can sometimes depend on its *effects* within the relevant field. *See, e.g.*, English v. General Electric Co., 496 U.S. 72, 84 (1990) (elaborating upon the Court's prior conclusion that federal law occupies the field of nuclear

Persistence of General Law, 106 COLUM. L. REV. 503, 544–45 (2006) (noting that in the absence of statute-specific answers, courts draw the details of federal rights of action from "general" American law rather than from the law of any individual state); *see also* Note on the Details of Federal Rights of Action, *infra* p. 1223.

This effect is not normally described as "field preemption," and using that label might be misleading. After all, the typical federal statute that creates a federal right of action will *not* be presumed to occupy the entire field of liability for the type of conduct that the federal statute addresses; in the absence of an express preemption clause, states normally will remain free to create rights of action of their own in the same field. Still, state law will not govern the details of the federal right of action itself. In a sense, then, a federal statute creating a federal right of action implicitly federalizes a sort of "mini-field" consisting of the details of the remedial right that the statute creates.

There may be other examples of the same phenomenon. In general, it is possible for federal statutes to leave some details unsaid without allowing state law to supply those details.

[29] In theory, the Court also needs to consider the constitutionality of those restrictions: does Congress really have the power to restrict state law in these ways? In practice, though, constitutional considerations are likely to enter the picture when the Court is deciding which restrictions the federal statute implies in the first place. If a particular restriction would be unconstitutional, the Court is unlikely to read the statute as purporting to impose that restriction unless the statute does so fairly clearly.

safety with respect to the operation of nuclear power plants, and concluding that while "part of the pre-empted field is defined by reference to the purpose of the state law in question, . . . another part is defined by the state law's actual effect on nuclear safety"). As with the threshold question of whether to infer field preemption at all, the scope of the relevant field and the criteria for preemption within that field are matters of statutory interpretation, and the answers will be specific to the particular federal statute at issue.

3. CONFLICT PREEMPTION

Suppose that Congress enacts a federal statute, and suppose that the statute is constitutional. Whether or not the statute contains an express preemption clause, and whether or not the statute implicitly occupies a particular field to the exclusion of state law, the statute will preempt any aspects of state law with which it "actually conflicts." *See, e.g.*, California v. ARC America Corp., 490 U.S. 93, 100 (1989). In practice, so-called "conflict preemption" is the most common type of preemption.

As a doctrinal matter, the Supreme Court recognizes two subdivisions of conflict preemption. The first, sometimes called "impossibility" preemption, occurs "where it is impossible for a private party to comply with both state and federal requirements." *English*, 496 U.S. at 79. The second, sometimes called "obstacle" or "purposes and objectives" preemption, occurs "where state law 'stands as an obstacle to the accomplishment and execution of the full purposes and objectives of Congress.' " *Id.* (quoting Hines v. Davidowitz, 312 U.S. 52, 67 (1941)).

This taxonomy, however, is not very illuminating. In practice, relatively few cases involve true "impossibility" preemption,[30] so the

[30] The Supreme Court has suggested that "impossibility" preemption comes into play only when federal law affirmatively *requires* private actors to behave in a way that state law purports to *prohibit*, or vice versa. Other kinds of conflicts between state and federal law—including even out-and-out contradictions—have been said to trigger "obstacle" preemption rather than "impossibility" preemption. *See* Barnett Bank of Marion Cty., N.A. v. Nelson, 517 U.S. 25, 31 (1996) (using the rubric of "obstacle" preemption" rather than "impossibility" preemption where "the Federal Statute authorizes national banks to engage in activities that the State Statute expressly forbids"); Mich. Canners & Freezers Ass'n v. Agric. Mktg. & Bargaining Bd., 467 U.S. 461, 478 & n.21 (1984) (similarly finding "obstacle" preemption where "the Michigan Act authorizes producers' associations to engage in conduct that the federal Act forbids," and explaining that "[b]ecause the Michigan Act is cast in permissive terms[,] . . . this is not a case in which it is impossible for an individual to comply with both state and federal law").

Although "impossibility" preemption is narrow, it does sometimes apply. Take *PLIVA, Inc. v. Mensing*, 564 U.S. 604 (2011), and *Mutual Pharmaceutical Co. v. Bartlett*, 570 U.S. 472 (2013). In both those cases, plaintiffs claimed that state tort law made the manufacturer of a generic drug liable for selling the drug with an inadequate warning label, but the manufacturers responded that federal law had required them to use the label in question. In both cases, a majority of the Justices found "impossibility" preemption. Admittedly, the manufacturers would not have violated either federal law or the duties recognized by state tort law if the manufacturers had simply refrained from selling the relevant drugs at all. According to the Court, though, "impossibility" is the proper rubric when the only way for a regulated entity to comply with both state and federal regulations is to exit the market. *See id.* at 488 (reasoning that "if the option of ceasing to act defeated a claim of impossibility, impossibility pre-emption would be 'all but meaningless' " (quoting *PLIVA*, 564 U.S. at 621)).

Court has ended up discussing most cases of conflict preemption under the rubric of "obstacle" preemption. Those cases, though, are not all the same. Without attempting to be comprehensive, we can identify at least four different types of situations in which the Court has found conflict preemption.

The first and most straightforward type involves clear contradictions between state and federal law—cases in which the rule of decision that state law purports to supply for a particular case or set of cases would contradict a rule of decision explicitly stated or clearly implied by a valid federal statute (or a valid federal regulation promulgated by an agency to which Congress has delegated the power to flesh out federal law in a way that preempts conflicting aspects of state law). Unless the relevant federal law is interpreted to mean something more qualified than what it says on its face, or unless what it says on its face is unconstitutional, the federal law will preempt the conflicting aspects of state law simply by operation of the Supremacy Clause.

A second type of conflict preemption occurs when the combined effect of state and federal law would wholly preclude activity that the Constitution prevents the states from banning. Although this scenario is rare, the Supreme Court offered a hypothetical example in *Florida Lime & Avocado Growers, Inc. v. Paul*, 373 U.S. 132 (1963). There, California law prohibited the sale of avocados with an oil content of less than 8 percent. In the absence of any applicable federal statutes, states might be able to regulate commerce in this way. But if Congress had enacted a valid federal statute prohibiting the sale of avocados with an oil content of more than 7 percent, courts would have held that the state statute was preempted. *See id.* at 143. Purely as a matter of statutory interpretation, of course, the fact that the federal statute bans the sale of some avocados need not mean that it itself confers an affirmative right to sell other avocados. But as a matter of constitutional law, the dormant Commerce Clause might prevent the states from banning the sale of avocados in interstate commerce. With the federal statute in place, applying the state statute would produce that result: people subject to both statutes would not be able to sell any avocados at all. Under these circumstances, the combined effect of the federal statute and the dormant Commerce Clause would produce preemption. *See id.* at 142–43.[31]

[31] In *Florida Lime*, the Supreme Court expressed this conclusion as follows: "A holding of federal exclusion of state law is inescapable and requires no inquiry into congressional design where compliance with both federal and state regulations is a physical impossibility for one engaged in interstate commerce." *Id.* (citing two cases about the dormant Commerce Clause in support of this dictum). This passage is both the source of and the canonical citation for the "impossibility" subdivision of the Supreme Court's taxonomy of conflict preemption. In describing that subdivision, however, the modern Court routinely omits *Florida Lime*'s reference to interstate commerce. *See, e.g.*, Crosby v. Nat'l Foreign Trade Council, 530 U.S. 363, 372 (2000) ("We will find preemption where it is impossible for a private party to comply with both state and federal law, see, *e.g.*, *Florida Lime & Avocado Growers, Inc. v. Paul*, 373 U.S. 132, 142–143 (1963) . . . ."). Because the reference to interstate commerce is what made this type of conflict preemption distinctive, omitting that reference strikes me as a mistake.

In a third type of case, courts might find preemption not because state law contradicts the explicit terms of a valid federal statute, but rather because the rationale for the state law rests on a rejection of the rationale for the federal statute. To be sure, this sort of policy disagreement is not always fatal; the policies that states pursue within their own spheres can sometimes differ dramatically from the policies that lie behind federal statutes. Where state and federal spheres intersect, though, courts have sometimes held that the policy judgments reflected in federal law impose constraints on the rationales that can animate state law. For instance, in *Felder v. Casey*, 487 U.S. 131 (1988), the Supreme Court held that a Wisconsin state law purporting to make plaintiffs provide advance notification before filing suit against government officials cannot validly be applied to suits brought under 42 U.S.C. § 1983, even when those suits are brought in state court. Although the Court did not make the basis for this holding entirely clear, the Court observed that "[t]he question before us . . . is essentially one of pre-emption," *Felder*, 487 U.S. at 138, and the Court emphasized that the Wisconsin statute "is firmly rooted in policies very much related to, and to a large extent directly contrary to, the substantive cause of action provided [by § 1983]," *id.* at 145. Along the same lines, the Court has also held that state law cannot validly deprive state courts of jurisdiction over § 1983 claims against local school boards simply because the state's lawmakers disagree with the policy behind subjecting school boards to such claims. *Howlett v. Rose*, 496 U.S. 356, 380 (1990); *see also* Haywood v. Drown, 556 U.S. 729, 736 (2009) ("[O]ur cases have established that a State cannot employ a jurisdictional rule 'to dissociate [itself] from federal law because of disagreement with its content . . . .' " (quoting *Howlett*, 496 U.S. at 371)).

A fourth type of case focuses less on the state law's *rationale* than on its *effects*. Consider *Jones v. Rath Packing Co.*, 430 U.S. 519 (1977). Under authority purportedly supplied by state law, the director of a local department of weights and measures in California ordered some packages of flour to be removed from sale on the ground that they were mislabeled: the weight of the flour that they contained, as measured by the department, fell short of the weight stated on the packages. According to the Supreme Court, however, the federal Fair Packaging and Labeling Act (FPLA), Pub. L. 89–755, 80 Stat. 1296 (1966) (codified as amended at 15 U.S.C. §§ 1451–1461), preempted this application of state law. As the Court noted, "a major purpose of the FPLA is to facilitate value comparisons [by consumers] among similar products." *Jones*, 430 U.S. at 541. For reasons specific to flour, the Court thought that the challenged application of California state law would hinder achieving that purpose in other parts of the country. The weight of packages of flour depends on both the amount of "flour solids" in the package and the amount of moisture in the flour. The latter factor varies according to the relative humidity of the atmosphere in which the flour is stored. The labeling standard that *federal* regulators applied to flour took account of that fact.[32] But California's own labeling requirements did not tolerate deficiencies in the stated weight of flour packages, even when those deficiencies were caused by loss of moisture during distribution. To be certain of satisfying the California standard, flour manufacturers would have to "ensure that loss of moisture during distribution will not bring the weight of the contents below the stated weight"—which, in turn, would give some national manufacturers an incentive to "overpack" flour packages that might end up in California. *Id.* at 542–43. On the other hand, manufacturers that did not serve the California market (or whose activities were confined to regions with high relative humidity) would not need to include as many flour solids in each package. The Court concluded that "as a result of the application of the California standard, consumers throughout the country who attempted to compare the value of identically labeled packages of flour would not be comparing packages which contained identical amounts of flour solids." *Id.* at 543. Because the effects of applying the state law to flour packages "would prevent 'the accomplishment and execution of the full purposes and objectives of Congress' in passing the FPLA," the Court held that the FPLA preempted this application of state law. *Id.* (quoting Hines v. Davidowitz, 312 U.S. 52, 67 (1941)).

The next case is another example of this same type of conflict preemption.

Geier v. American Honda Motor Co.

529 U.S. 861 (2000)

■ *JUSTICE BREYER delivered the opinion of the Court:*

This case focuses on the 1984 version of a Federal Motor Vehicle Safety Standard promulgated by the Department of Transportation under the authority of the National Traffic and Motor Vehicle Safety Act of 1966, 80 Stat. 718, 15 U.S.C. § 1381 *et seq.* (1988 ed.). The standard, FMVSS 208, required auto manufacturers to equip some but not all of their 1987 vehicles with passive restraints. We ask whether the Act pre-

---

[32] To be sure, when packaged food is distributed in interstate commerce, the FPLA requires the package to bear a label accurately stating the net quantity of its contents, 15 U.S.C. § 1453(a)(2), and "[n]othing in the FPLA explicitly permits any variation between stated weight and actual weight." *Jones*, 430 U.S. at 534. When Congress enacted the FPLA, though, tolerance for "reasonable variations" from the stated weight had long been part of other federal food and drug laws and their implementing regulations. *See, e.g.*, Federal Food, Drug, and Cosmetic Act (FDCA), ch. 675, § 403(e), 52 Stat. 1040, 1047 (1938) (codified as amended at 21 U.S.C. § 343(e)); *see also Jones*, 430 U.S. at 537 ("Since 1914, regulations under the food and drug laws have permitted reasonable variations from stated net weight resulting from packing deviations or loss of moisture occurring despite good commercial practice."). At the time of *Jones*, moreover, regulations promulgated by the federal Food and Drug Administration under the authority of both the FDCA and the FPLA continued to tolerate "[r]easonable variations caused by loss or gain of moisture during the course of good distribution practice." 21 C.F.R. § 1.8b(q) (1976). In the Supreme Court's words, "We can only conclude that under the FPLA, as under the FDCA, a manufacturer of food is not subject to enforcement action for violation of the net-weight labeling requirements if the label accurately states the net weight, with allowance for the specified reasonable variations." *Jones*, 430 U.S. at 537–38.

empts a state common-law tort action in which the plaintiff claims that the defendant auto manufacturer, who was in compliance with the standard, should nonetheless have equipped a 1987 automobile with airbags. We conclude that the Act, taken together with FMVSS 208, pre-empts the lawsuit.

I

In 1992, petitioner Alexis Geier, driving a 1987 Honda Accord, collided with a tree and was seriously injured. The car was equipped with manual shoulder and lap belts which Geier had buckled up at the time. The car was not equipped with airbags or other passive restraint devices.

Geier and her parents, also petitioners, sued the car's manufacturer, American Honda Motor Company, Inc., and its affiliates (hereinafter American Honda), under District of Columbia tort law. They claimed, among other things, that American Honda had designed its car negligently and defectively because it lacked a driver's side airbag. The District Court . . . [granted summary judgment for American Honda on the strength of the federal Act's express preemption clause], 15 U.S.C. § 1392(d) (1988 ed.) . . . . (We . . . refer to the pre-1994 version of the statute throughout the opinion; it has been recodified at 49 U.S.C. § 30101 *et seq.*)

The Court of Appeals agreed with the District Court's conclusion but on somewhat different reasoning. It had doubts . . . that petitioners' lawsuit involved the potential creation of the kind of "safety standard" to which the Safety Act's express pre-emption provision refers. But it declined to resolve that question because it found that petitioner's state-law tort claims posed an obstacle to the accomplishment of FMVSS 208's objectives. For that reason, it found that those claims conflicted with FMVSS 208, and that, under ordinary pre-emption principles, the Act consequently pre-empted the lawsuit . . . .

Several state courts have held to the contrary, namely, that neither the Act's express pre-emption [provision] nor FMVSS 208 pre-empts a "no airbag" tort suit. . . . All of the Federal Circuit Courts that have considered the question, however, have found pre-emption. One rested its conclusion on the Act's express pre-emption provision. . . . Others, such as the Court of Appeals below, have instead found pre-emption under ordinary pre-emption principles by virtue of the conflict such suits pose to FMVSS 208's objectives, and thus to the Act itself. . . . We granted certiorari to resolve these differences. We now hold that this kind of "no airbag" lawsuit conflicts with the objectives of FMVSS 208 . . . and is therefore pre-empted by the Act.

In reaching our conclusion, we consider three subsidiary questions. First, does the Act's express pre-emption provision pre-empt this lawsuit? We think not. Second, do ordinary pre-emption principles nonetheless apply? We hold that they do. Third, does this lawsuit actually conflict with FMVSS 208, hence with the Act itself? We hold that it does.

II

We first ask whether the Safety Act's express pre-emption provision pre-empts this tort action. The provision reads as follows:

> "Whenever a Federal motor vehicle safety standard established under this subchapter is in effect, no State or political subdivision of a State shall have any authority either to establish, or to continue in effect, with respect to any motor vehicle or item of motor vehicle equipment[,] any safety standard applicable to the same aspect of performance of such vehicle or item of equipment which is not identical to the Federal standard." 15 U.S.C. § 1392(d) (1988 ed.).

American Honda points out that a majority of this Court has said that a somewhat similar statutory provision in a different federal statute—a provision that uses the word "requirements"—may well expressly pre-empt similar tort actions. See . . . *Medtronic, Inc. v. Lohr*, 518 U.S. 470, 502–504 (1996) (plurality opinion); *id.* at 503–505 (Breyer, J., concurring in part and concurring in judgment); *id.* at 509–512 (O'Connor, J., concurring in part and dissenting in part). Petitioners reply that this statute speaks of pre-empting a state-law "safety *standard*," not a "requirement," and that a tort action does not involve a safety *standard*. Hence, they conclude, the express pre-emption provision does not apply.

We need not determine the precise significance of the use of the word "standard," rather than "requirement," . . . for the Act contains another provision, which resolves the disagreement. That provision, a "saving" clause, says that "[c]ompliance with" a federal safety standard "does not exempt any person from any liability under common law." 15 U.S.C. § 1397(k) (1988 ed.). The saving clause assumes that there are some significant number of common-law liability cases to save. And a reading of the express pre-emption provision that excludes common-law tort actions gives actual meaning to the saving clause's literal language, while leaving adequate room for state tort law to operate—for example, where federal law creates only a floor, *i.e.*, a minimum safety standard. See, *e.g.*, Brief for United States as *Amicus Curiae* 21 (explaining that common-law claim that a vehicle is defectively designed because it lacks antilock brakes would not be pre-empted by 49 C.F.R. § 571.105 (1999), a safety standard establishing minimum requirements for brake performance). . . . [If] the express pre-emption provision . . . [were interpreted] as applying to standards imposed in common-law tort actions, . . . it would pre-empt all nonidentical state standards established in tort actions covering the same aspect of performance as an applicable federal standard, even if the federal standard merely established a minimum standard. On that broad reading of the pre-emption clause little, if any, potential "liability at common law" would remain. . . . We have found no convincing indication that Congress wanted to pre-empt, not only state statutes and regulations, but also common-law tort actions, in such circumstances. Hence the broad reading cannot be correct. The language of the pre-emption provision permits a narrow reading that excludes common-law actions. Given the presence of the saving clause, we conclude that the pre-emption clause must be so read.

III

We have just said that the saving clause *at least* removes tort actions from the scope of the express pre-emption clause. Does it do more? In particular, does it foreclose or limit the operation of ordinary pre-emption principles insofar as those principles instruct us to read statutes as pre-empting state laws (including common-law rules) that "actually conflict" with the statute or federal standards promulgated thereunder? . . . .

. . . . We now conclude that the saving clause . . . does *not* bar the ordinary working of conflict pre-emption principles.

Nothing in the language of the saving clause suggests an intent to save state-law tort actions that conflict with federal regulations. The words "[c]ompliance" and "does not exempt," 15 U.S.C. § 1397(k) (1988 ed.), sound as if they simply bar a special kind of defense, namely, a defense that compliance with a federal standard automatically exempts a defendant from state law, whether the Federal Government meant that standard to be an absolute requirement or only a minimum one. See Restatement (Third) of Torts: Products Liability § 4(b), Comment *e* (1997) (distinguishing between state-law compliance defense and a federal claim of pre-emption). It is difficult to understand why Congress would have insisted on a compliance-with-federal-regulation precondition to the provision's applicability had it wished the Act to "save" all state-law tort actions, regardless of their potential threat to the objectives of federal safety standards promulgated under that Act. Nor does our interpretation conflict with the purpose of the saving provision, say, by rendering it ineffectual. As we have previously explained, the saving provision still makes clear that the express pre-emption provision does not of its own force pre-empt common-law tort actions. And it thereby preserves those actions that seek to establish greater safety than the minimum safety achieved by a federal regulation intended to provide a floor. . . .

Moreover, this Court has repeatedly "decline[d] to give broad effect to saving clauses where doing so would upset the careful regulatory scheme established by federal law." *United States v. Locke*, [529 U.S. 89, 106–07 (2000)] . . . . We find this concern applicable in the present case. And we conclude that the saving clause foresees—it does not foreclose—the possibility that a federal safety standard will pre-empt a state common-law tort action with which it conflicts. We do not understand the dissent to disagree, for it acknowledges that ordinary pre-emption principles apply, at least sometimes. . . .

Neither do we believe that the pre-emption provision, the saving provision, or both together, create some kind of "special burden" beyond that inherent in ordinary pre-emption principles—which "special burden" would specially disfavor pre-emption here. Cf. *post* at 898–899 [(dissenting opinion)]. The two provisions, read together, reflect a neutral policy, not a specially favorable or unfavorable policy, toward the application of ordinary conflict pre-emption principles. . . .

Why, in any event, would Congress not have wanted ordinary pre-emption principles to apply where an actual conflict with a federal objective is at stake? Some such principle is needed. In its absence, state law could impose legal duties that would conflict directly with federal regulatory mandates, say, by premising liability upon the presence of the very windshield retention requirements that federal law requires. See, *e.g.*, 49 C.F.R. § 571.212 (1999). . . . To the extent that such an interpretation of the saving provision reads into a particular federal law toleration of a conflict that those principles would otherwise forbid, it permits that law to defeat its own objectives . . . . We do not claim that Congress lacks the constitutional power to write a statute that mandates such a complex type of state/federal relationship. . . . But there is no reason to believe Congress has done so here.

. . . .

A "special burden" [of the sort advocated by the dissent] would also promise practical difficulty by further complicating well-established pre-emption principles that already are difficult to apply. The dissent does not contend that this "special burden" would apply in a case in which state law penalizes what federal law requires—*i.e.*, a case of impossibility. See *post* at 892–893 n. 6, 900 n. 16. But if it would not apply in such a case, then how, or when, would it apply? This Court, when describing conflict pre-emption, has spoken of pre-empting state law that "under the circumstances of th[e] particular case . . . stands as an obstacle to the accomplishment and execution of the full purposes and objectives of Congress"—whether that "obstacle" goes by the name of "conflicting; contrary to; . . . repugnance; difference; irreconcilability; inconsistency; violation; curtailment; . . . interference," or the like. *Hines v. Davidowitz*, 312 U.S. 52, 67 (1941); see *Jones v. Rath Packing Co.*, 430 U.S. 519, 526 (1977). The Court has not previously driven a legal wedge—only a terminological one—between "conflicts" that prevent or frustrate the accomplishment of a federal objective and "conflicts" that make it "impossible" for private parties to comply with both state and federal law. Rather, it has said that both forms of conflicting state law are "nullified" by the Supremacy Clause, [*Fidelity Fed. Sav. & Loan Ass'n v.*] *De la Cuesta*, 458 U.S. [141, 152–153 (1982)] . . . , and it has assumed that Congress would not want either kind of conflict. The Court has thus refused to read general "saving" provisions to tolerate actual conflict *both* in cases involving impossibility, see, *e.g.*, *AT&T* [*v. Central Office Telephone, Inc.*], 524 U.S. [214, 228 (1998)], *and* in "frustration-of-purpose" cases, see, *e.g.*, *Locke*, [529 U.S.] at 103–112; *International Paper Co. v. Ouellette*, 479 U.S. 481, 493–494 (1987); see also *Chicago & North Western Transp. Co. v. Kalo Brick & Tile Co.*, 450 U.S. 311, 328–331 (1981). We see no grounds, then, for attempting to distinguish among types of federal-state conflict for purposes of analyzing whether such a conflict warrants pre-emption in a particular case. That kind of analysis, moreover, would engender legal uncertainty with its inevitable systemwide costs (*e.g.*, conflicts, delay, and expense) as courts tried sensibly to distinguish among varieties of "conflict" (which often shade, one into the other) when applying this complicated rule to the many federal statutes that contain some form of an express pre-emption provision, a saving provision, or as here, both. Nothing in the statute suggests Congress wanted to complicate ordinary experience-proved principles of conflict pre-emption with an added "special burden." Indeed, the dissent's willingness to impose a "special burden" here stems ultimately from its view that "frustration-of-purpos[e]" conflict pre-emption is a freewheeling, "inadequately considered" doctrine that might well be "eliminate[d]." *Post* at 907–908, and n. 22. In a word, ordinary pre-emption principles, grounded in longstanding precedent, ... apply. . . . We would not further complicate the law with complex new doctrine.

IV

The basic question, then, is whether a common-law "no airbag" action like the one before us actually conflicts with FMVSS 208. We hold that it does.

In petitioners' and the dissent's view, FMVSS 208 sets a minimum airbag standard. As far as FMVSS 208 is concerned, the more airbags, and the sooner, the better. But that was not the Secretary's view. The Department of Transportation's (DOT's) comments, which accompanied the promulgation of FMVSS 208, make clear that the standard deliberately provided the manufacturer with a range of choices among different passive restraint devices. Those choices would bring about a mix of different devices introduced gradually over time; and FMVSS 208 would thereby lower costs, overcome technical safety problems, encourage technological development, and win widespread consumer acceptance—all of which would promote FMVSS 208's safety objectives. See generally 49 Fed. Reg. 28962 (1984).

A

The history of FMVSS 208 helps explain why and how DOT sought these objectives. See generally *Motor Vehicle Mfrs. Assn. of United States, Inc. v. State Farm Mut. Automobile Ins. Co.*, 463 U.S. 29, 34–38 (1983). In 1967, DOT, understanding that seatbelts would save many lives, required manufacturers to install manual seatbelts in all automobiles. 32 Fed. Reg. 2408, 2415. It became apparent, however, that most occupants simply would not buckle up their belts. See 34 Fed. Reg. 11148 (1969). DOT then began to investigate the feasibility of requiring "passive restraints," such as airbags and automatic seatbelts. *Ibid.* In 1970, it amended FMVSS 208 to include some passive protection requirements, 35 Fed. Reg. 16927, while making clear that airbags were one of several "equally acceptable" devices and that it neither " 'favored' [n]or expected the introduction of airbag systems." *Ibid.* In 1971, it added an express provision permitting compliance through the use of nondetachable passive belts, 36 Fed. Reg. 12858, 12859, and in 1972, it mandated full passive protection for all front seat occupants for vehicles manufactured after August 15, 1975, 37 Fed. Reg. 3911. Although the agency's focus was originally on airbags, 34 Fed. Reg. 11148 (1969) (notice of proposed rulemaking); *State Farm,* 463 U.S. at 35, n. 4; see also *id.* at 46, n. 11 (noting view of commentators that, as of 1970, FMVSS 208 was " 'a de facto airbag mandate' " because of the state of passive restraint technology), at no point did FMVSS 208 formally require the use of airbags. From the start, as in 1984, it permitted passive restraint options.

DOT gave manufacturers a further choice for new vehicles manufactured between 1972 and August 1975. Manufacturers could either install a passive restraint device such as automatic seatbelts or airbags or retain manual belts and add an "ignition interlock" device that in effect forced occupants to buckle up by preventing the ignition otherwise from turning on. 37 Fed. Reg. 3911 (1972). The interlock soon became popular with manufacturers. And in 1974, when the agency approved the use of detachable automatic seatbelts, it conditioned that approval by providing that such systems must include an interlock system *and* a continuous warning buzzer to encourage reattachment of the belt. 39 Fed. Reg. 14593. But the interlock and buzzer devices were most unpopular with the public. And Congress, responding to public pressure, passed a law that forbade DOT from requiring, or permitting compliance by means of, such devices. Motor Vehicle and Schoolbus Safety Amendments of 1974, § 109, 88 Stat. 1482 . . . .

That experience influenced DOT's subsequent passive restraint initiatives. In 1976, DOT Secretary William T. Coleman, Jr., fearing continued public resistance, suspended the passive restraint requirements. He sought to win public acceptance for a variety of passive restraint devices through a demonstration project that would involve about half a million new automobiles. *State Farm,* [463 U.S.] at 37. But his successor, Brock Adams, canceled the project, instead amending FMVSS 208 to require passive restraints, principally either airbags or passive seatbelts. 42 Fed. Reg. 34289 (1977).

Andrew Lewis, a new DOT Secretary in a new administration, rescinded the Adams requirements, primarily because DOT learned that the industry planned to satisfy those requirements almost exclusively through the installation of detachable automatic seatbelts. 46 Fed. Reg. 53419–53420 (1981). This Court held the rescission unlawful. *State Farm,* [463 U.S.] at 34, 46. And the stage was set for [the] then-DOT

Secretary, Elizabeth Dole, to amend FMVSS 208 once again, promulgating the version that is now before us. 49 Fed. Reg. 28962 (1984).

B

Read in light of this history, DOT's own contemporaneous explanation of FMVSS 208 makes clear that the 1984 version of FMVSS 208 reflected the following significant considerations. First, buckled up seatbelts are a vital ingredient of automobile safety. *Id.* at 29003 .... Second, despite the enormous and unnecessary risks that a passenger runs by not buckling up manual lap and shoulder belts, more than 80% of front seat passengers would leave their manual seatbelts unbuckled. [*Id.* at] 28983 .... Third, airbags could make up for the dangers caused by unbuckled manual belts, but they could not make up for them entirely. *Id.* at 28986 (concluding that, although an airbag plus a lap and shoulder belt was the most "effective" system, airbags alone were *less* effective than buckled up manual lap and shoulder belts).

Fourth, passive restraint systems had their own disadvantages, for example, the dangers associated with, intrusiveness of, and corresponding public dislike for, nondetachable automatic belts. *Id.* at 28992–28993. Fifth, airbags brought with them their own special risks to safety, such as the risk of danger to out-of-position occupants (usually children) in small cars. *Id.* at 28992, 29001; see also 65 Fed. Reg. 30680, 30681–30682 (2000) (finding 158 confirmed airbag-induced fatalities as of April 2000, and amending rule to add new requirements, test procedures, and injury criteria to ensure that "future air bags be designed to create less risk of serious airbag-induced injuries than current air bags, particularly for small women and young children"); U.S. Dept. of Transportation, National Highway Traffic Safety Administration, National Accident Sampling System Crashworthiness Data System 1991–1993, p. viii (Aug. 1995) (finding that airbags caused approximately 54,000 injuries between 1991 and 1993).

Sixth, airbags were expected to be significantly more expensive than other passive restraint devices, raising the average cost of a vehicle price $320 for full frontal airbags over the cost of a car with manual lap and shoulder seatbelts (and potentially much more if production volumes were low). 49 Fed. Reg. 28990 (1984). And the agency worried that the high replacement cost—estimated to be $800—could lead car owners to refuse to replace them after deployment. *Id.* at 28990, 29000–29001; see also *id.* at 28990 (estimating total investment costs for mandatory airbag requirement at $1.3 billion compared to $500 million for automatic seatbelts). Seventh, the public, for reasons of cost, fear, or physical intrusiveness, might resist installation or use of any of the then-available passive restraint devices, *id.* at 28987–28989—a particular concern with respect to airbags, *id.* at 29001 (noting that "[a]irbags engendered the largest quantity of, and most vociferously worded, comments").

FMVSS 208 reflected these considerations in several ways. Most importantly, that standard deliberately sought variety—a mix of several different passive restraint systems. It did so by setting a performance requirement for passive restraint devices and allowing manufacturers to choose among different passive restraint mechanisms, such as airbags, automatic belts, or other passive restraint technologies to satisfy that requirement. *Id.* at 28996. And DOT explained why FMVSS 208 sought the mix of devices that it expected its performance standard to produce. *Id.* at 28997. DOT wrote that it had *rejected* a proposed FMVSS 208 "all airbag" standard because of safety concerns (perceived or real) associated with airbags, which concerns threatened a "backlash" more easily overcome "if airbags" were "not the only way of complying." *Id.* at 29001. It added that a mix of devices would help develop data on comparative effectiveness, would allow the industry time to overcome the safety problems and the high production costs associated with airbags, and would facilitate the development of alternative, cheaper, and safer passive restraint systems. *Id.* at 29001–29002. And it would thereby build public confidence, *id.*, necessary to avoid another interlock-type fiasco.

The 1984 FMVSS 208 standard also deliberately sought a *gradual* phase-in of passive restraints. *Id.* at 28999–29000. It required the manufacturers to equip only 10% of their car fleet manufactured after September 1, 1986, with passive restraints. *Id.* at 28999. It then increased the percentage in three annual stages, up to 100% of the new car fleet for cars manufactured after September 1, 1989. *Ibid.* And it explained that the phased-in requirement would allow more time for manufacturers to develop airbags or other, better, safer passive restraint systems. It would help develop information about the comparative effectiveness of different systems, would lead to a mix in which airbags and other nonseatbelt passive restraint systems played a more prominent role than would otherwise result, and would promote public acceptance. *Id.* at 29000–29001.

Of course, as the dissent points out, . . . FMVSS 208 did not guarantee the mix by setting a ceiling for each different passive restraint device. In fact, it provided a form of extra credit for airbag installation (and other nonbelt passive restraint devices) under which each airbag-installed vehicle counted as 1.5 vehicles for purposes of meeting FMVSS 208's passive restraint requirement. 49 C.F.R. § 571.208, S4.1.3.4(a)(1) (1999); 49 Fed. Reg. 29000 (1984). But why should DOT have bothered to impose an airbag ceiling when the practical threat to the mix it desired arose from the likelihood that manufacturers would install, not too many airbags too quickly, but too few or none at all? After all, only a few years earlier, Secretary Dole's predecessor had discovered that manufacturers intended to meet the then-current passive restraint requirement almost entirely (more than 99%) through the installation of more affordable automatic belt systems. 46 Fed. Reg. 53421 (1981); *State Farm*, 463 U.S.

at 38. The extra credit, as DOT explained, was designed to "encourage manufacturers to equip *at least some* of their cars with airbags." 49 Fed. Reg. 29001 (1984) (emphasis added) (responding to comment that failure to mandate airbags might mean the "end of . . . airbag technology") . . . . The credit provision *reinforces* the point that FMVSS 208 sought a gradually developing mix of passive restraint devices . . . .

Finally, FMVSS 208's passive restraint requirement was conditional. DOT believed that ordinary manual lap and shoulder belts would produce about the same amount of safety as passive restraints, and at significantly lower costs—*if only auto occupants would buckle up*. See *id.* at 28997–28998. Thus, FMVSS 208 provided for rescission of its passive restraint requirement if, by September 1, 1989, two-thirds of the States had laws in place that, like those of many other nations, required auto occupants to buckle up (and which met other requirements specified in the standard). *Id.* at 28963, 28993–28994, 28997–28999. The Secretary wrote that "coverage of a large percentage of the American people by seatbelt laws that are enforced would largely negate the incremental increase in safety to be expected from an automatic protection requirement." *Id.* at 28997. In the end, two-thirds of the States did not enact mandatory buckle-up laws, and the passive restraint requirement remained in effect.

In sum, as DOT now tells us through the Solicitor General, the 1984 version of FMVSS 208 "embodies the Secretary's policy judgment that safety would best be promoted if manufacturers installed *alternative* protection systems in their fleets rather than one particular system in every car." Brief for United States as *Amicus Curiae* 25; see 49 Fed. Reg. 28997 (1984). Petitioners' tort suit claims that the manufacturers of the 1987 Honda Accord "had a duty to design, manufacture, distribute and sell a motor vehicle with an effective and safe passive restraint system, including, but not limited to, airbags." App. 3 (Complaint ¶ 11).

In effect, petitioners' tort action depends upon its claim that manufacturers had a duty to install an airbag when they manufactured the 1987 Honda Accord. Such a state law—*i.e.*, a rule of state tort law imposing such a duty—by its terms would have required manufacturers of all similar cars to install airbags rather than other passive restraint systems, such as automatic belts or passive interiors. It thereby would have presented an obstacle to the variety and mix of devices that the federal regulation sought. It would have required all manufacturers to have installed airbags in respect to the entire District-of-Columbia-related portion of their 1987 new car fleet, even though FMVSS 208 at that time required only that 10% of a manufacturer's nationwide fleet be equipped with any passive restraint device at all. It thereby also would have stood as an obstacle to the gradual passive restraint phase-in that the federal regulation deliberately imposed. In addition, it could have made less likely the adoption of a state mandatory buckle-up law. Because the rule of law for which petitioners contend would have stood "as an obstacle to the accomplishment and execution of" the important means-related federal objectives that we have just discussed, it is pre-empted. *Hines*, 312 U.S. at 67 . . . .

Petitioners ask this Court to calculate the precise size of the "obstacle," with the aim of minimizing it, by considering the risk of tort liability and a successful tort action's incentive-related or timing-related compliance effects. See Brief for Petitioners 45–50. The dissent agrees. . . . But this Court's pre-emption cases do not ordinarily turn on such compliance-related considerations as whether a private party in practice would ignore state legal obligations—paying, say, a fine instead—or how likely it is that state law actually would be enforced. Rather, this Court's pre-emption cases ordinarily *assume* compliance with the state-law duty in question. The Court has on occasion suggested that tort law may be somewhat different, and that related considerations—for example, the ability to pay damages instead of modifying one's behavior—may be relevant for pre-emption purposes. See *Goodyear Atomic Corp. v. Miller*, 486 U.S. 174, 185 (1988); . . . see also *English*, 496 U.S. at 86; *Silkwood v. Kerr-McGee Corp.*, 464 U.S. 238, 256 (1984). In other cases, the Court has found tort law to conflict with federal law without engaging in that kind of an analysis. See, *e.g.*, *Ouellette*, [479 U.S.] at 494–497; *Kalo Brick*, 450 U.S. at 324–332. We need not try to resolve these differences here, however, for the incentive or compliance considerations upon which the dissent relies cannot, by themselves, change the legal result. Some of those considerations rest on speculation, see, *e.g.*, *post* at 901 (predicting risk of "no airbag" liability and manufacturers' likely response to such liability); . . . and others, if we understand them correctly, seem less than persuasive, see, *e.g.*, *post* at 902 (suggesting that manufacturers could have complied with a mandatory state airbag duty by installing a *different* kind of passive restraint device). . . .

One final point: We place some weight upon DOT's interpretation of FMVSS 208's objectives and its conclusion, as set forth in the Government's brief, that a tort suit such as this one would " 'stan[d] as an obstacle to the accomplishment and execution' " of those objectives. Brief for United States as *Amicus Curiae* 25–26 (quoting *Hines*, [312 U.S.] at 67). Congress has delegated to DOT authority to implement the statute; the subject matter is technical; and the relevant history and background are complex and extensive. The agency is likely to have a thorough understanding of its own regulation and its objectives and is "uniquely qualified" to comprehend the likely impact of state requirements. *Medtronic*, 518 U.S. at 496; see *id.* at 506 (Breyer, J., concurring in part and concurring in judgment). And DOT has explained FMVSS 208's objectives, and the interference that "no airbag" suits pose thereto, consistently over time. Brief for United States as *Amicus Curiae* in *Freightliner Corp. v. Myrick*, O.T. 1994, No. 94–286, pp. 28–29; Brief for United States as *Amicus Curiae* in *Wood v. General Motors Corp.*, O.T.

1989, No. 89–46, pp. 7, 11–16. In these circumstances, the agency's own views should make a difference. . . .

We have no reason to suspect that the Solicitor General's representation of DOT's views reflects anything other than "the agency's fair and considered judgment on the matter." *Auer v. Robbins*, 519 U.S. 452, 461–462 (1997) . . . . The failure of the Federal Register to address pre-emption explicitly is thus not determinative.

The dissent would require a formal agency statement of pre-emptive intent as a prerequisite to concluding that a conflict exists. It relies on cases, or portions thereof, that did not involve conflict pre-emption. See *post* at 908–909 . . . . And conflict pre-emption is different in that it turns on the identification of "actual conflict," and not on an express statement of pre-emptive intent. . . . While "[p]re-emption fundamentally is a question of congressional intent," *English*, [496 U.S.] at 78, this Court traditionally distinguishes between "express" and "implied" pre-emptive intent, and treats "conflict" pre-emption as an instance of the latter. . . . And though the Court has looked for a specific statement of pre-emptive intent where it is claimed that the mere "volume and complexity" of agency regulations demonstrate an implicit intent to displace *all* state law in a particular area, *Hillsborough*, [471 U.S.] at 717 . . . —so-called "field pre-emption"—the Court has never before required a specific, formal agency statement identifying conflict in order to conclude that such a conflict in fact exists. Indeed, one can assume that Congress or an agency ordinarily would not intend to permit a significant conflict. While we certainly accept the dissent's basic position that a court should not find pre-emption too readily in the absence of clear evidence of a conflict, . . . we find such evidence here. To insist on a specific expression of agency intent to pre-empt, made after notice-and-comment rulemaking, would be in certain cases to tolerate conflicts that an agency, and therefore Congress, is most unlikely to have intended. The dissent . . . apparently welcomes that result, at least where "frustration-of-purpos[e]" pre-emption by agency regulation is at issue. *Post* at 907–908 and n.22. We do not.

. . . . It is possible that some special design-related circumstance concerning a particular kind of car might require airbags, rather than automatic belts, and that a suit seeking to impose that requirement could escape pre-emption—say, because it would affect so few cars that its rule of law would not create a legal "obstacle" to 208's mixed-fleet, gradual objective. But that is not what petitioners claimed. They have argued generally that, to be safe, a car must have an airbag. See App. 4.

Regardless, the language of FMVSS 208 and the contemporaneous 1984 DOT explanation is clear enough—even without giving DOT's own view special weight. FMVSS 208 sought a gradually developing mix of alternative passive restraint devices for safety-related reasons. The rule of state tort law for which petitioners argue would stand as an "obstacle" to the accomplishment of that objective. And the statute foresees the application of ordinary principles of pre-emption in cases of actual conflict. Hence, the tort action is pre-empted. . . .

■ *JUSTICE STEVENS, with whom JUSTICES SOUTER, THOMAS, and GINSBURG join, dissenting:*

Airbag technology has been available to automobile manufacturers for over 30 years. There is now general agreement on the proposition "that, to be safe, a car must have an airbag." *Ante* [(summarizing plaintiffs' theory)]. Indeed, current federal law imposes that requirement on all automobile manufacturers. See 49 U.S.C. § 30127; 49 C.F.R. § 571.208, S4.1.5.3 (1998). The question raised by petitioners' common-law tort action is whether that proposition was sufficiently obvious when Honda's 1987 Accord was manufactured to make the failure to install such a safety feature actionable under theories of negligence or defective design. The Court holds that an interim regulation motivated by the Secretary of Transportation's desire to foster gradual development of a variety of passive restraint devices deprives state courts of [authority] to answer that question. I respectfully dissent . . . .

"This is a case about federalism," *Coleman v. Thompson*, 501 U.S. 722, 726 (1991), that is, about respect for "the constitutional role of the States as sovereign entities." *Alden v. Maine*, 527 U.S. 706, 713 (1999). It raises important questions concerning the way in which the Federal Government may exercise its undoubted power to oust state courts of their traditional jurisdiction over common-law tort actions. The rule the Court enforces today was not enacted by Congress and is not to be found in the text of any Executive Order or regulation. It has a unique origin: It is the product of the Court's interpretation of the final commentary accompanying an interim administrative regulation and the history of airbag regulation generally. Like many other judge-made rules, its contours are not precisely defined. I believe, however, that it is fair to state that if it had been expressly adopted by the Secretary of Transportation, it would have read as follows:

> "No state court shall entertain a common-law tort action based on a claim that an automobile was negligently or defectively designed because it was not equipped with an airbag;
>
> "Provided, however, that this rule shall not apply to cars manufactured before September 1, 1986, or after such time as the Secretary may require the installation of airbags in all new cars; and
>
> "Provided further, that this rule shall not preclude a claim by a driver who was not wearing her seatbelt that an automobile was negligently or defectively designed because it was not equipped with any passive restraint whatsoever, or a claim that an automobile with particular design features was negligently or defectively designed because it was equipped with one type of passive restraint instead of another."

Perhaps such a rule would be a wise component of a legislative reform of our tort system. I express no opinion about that possibility. It is, however, quite clear to me that Congress neither enacted any such rule itself nor authorized the Secretary of Transportation to do so. It is equally clear to me that the objectives that the Secretary intended to achieve through the adoption of Federal Motor Vehicle Safety Standard 208 would not be frustrated one whit by allowing state courts to determine whether in 1987 the lifesaving advantages of airbags had become sufficiently obvious that their omission might constitute a design defect in some new cars. Finally, I submit that the Court is quite wrong to characterize its rejection of the presumption against pre-emption, and its reliance on history and regulatory commentary rather than either statutory or regulatory text, as "ordinary experience-proved principles of conflict pre-emption." *Ante* at 874.

I

.... The purpose of the [Motor Vehicle Safety Act of 1966], as stated by Congress, was "to reduce traffic accidents and deaths and injuries to persons resulting from traffic accidents." 15 U.S.C. § 1381. The Act directed the Secretary of Transportation or his delegate to issue motor vehicle safety standards that "shall be practicable, shall meet the need for motor vehicle safety, and shall be stated in objective terms." § 1392(a). The Act defines the term "safety standard" as a "minimum standard for motor vehicle performance, or motor vehicle equipment performance." § 1391(2).

Standard 208 covers "[o]ccupant crash protection." Its purpose "is to reduce the number of deaths of vehicle occupants, and the severity of injuries, by specifying vehicle crashworthiness requirements ... [and] equipment requirements for active and passive restraint systems." 49 C.F.R. § 571.208, S2 (1998). The first version of that standard, issued in 1967, simply required the installation of manual seatbelts in all automobiles. Two years later the Secretary formally proposed a revision that would require the installation of "passive occupant restraint systems," that is to say, devices that do not depend for their effectiveness on any action by the vehicle occupant. The airbag is one such system. The Secretary's proposal led to a series of amendments to Standard 208 that imposed various passive restraint requirements, culminating in a 1977 regulation that mandated such restraints in all cars by the model year 1984. The two commercially available restraints that could satisfy this mandate were airbags and automatic seatbelts; the regulation allowed each vehicle manufacturer to choose which restraint to install. In 1981, however, following a change of administration, the new Secretary first extended the deadline for compliance and then rescinded the passive restraint requirement altogether. In [*Motor Vehicle Mfrs. Ass'n of United States v. State Farm Mut. Automobile Ins. Co.*, 463 U.S. 29 (1983)], we affirmed a decision by the Court of Appeals holding that this rescission was arbitrary. On remand, Secretary Elizabeth Dole promulgated the version of Standard 208 that is at issue in this case.

The 1984 standard provided for a phase-in of passive restraint requirements beginning with the 1987 model year. In that year, vehicle manufacturers were required to equip a minimum of 10% of their new passenger cars with such restraints. While the 1987 Honda Accord driven by Ms. Geier was not so equipped, it is undisputed that Honda complied with the 10% minimum by installing passive restraints in certain other 1987 models. This minimum passive restraint requirement increased to 25% of 1988 models and 40% of 1989 models; the standard also mandated that "after September 1, 1989, all new cars must have automatic occupant crash protection." 49 Fed. Reg. 28999 (1984); see 49 C.F.R. § 571.208, S4.1.3–S4.1.4 (1998). In response to a 1991 amendment to the Safety Act, the Secretary amended the standard to require that, beginning in the 1998 model year, all new cars have an airbag at both the driver's and right front passenger's positions.[3]

Given that Secretary Dole promulgated the 1984 standard in response to our opinion invalidating her predecessor's rescission of the 1977 passive restraint requirement, she provided a full explanation for her decision not to require airbags in all cars and to phase in the new requirements. The initial 3-year delay was designed to give vehicle manufacturers adequate time for compliance. The decision to give manufacturers a choice between airbags and a different form of passive restraint, such as an automatic seatbelt, was motivated in part by safety concerns and in part by a desire not to retard the development of more effective systems. 49 Fed. Reg. 29000–29001 (1984). An important safety concern was the fear of a "public backlash" to an airbag mandate that consumers might not fully understand. The Secretary believed, however, that the use of airbags would avoid possible public objections to automatic seatbelts and that many of the public concerns regarding airbags were unfounded. *Id.* at 28991.

Although the standard did not require airbags in all cars, it is clear that the Secretary did intend to encourage wider use of airbags. One of her basic conclusions was that "[a]utomatic occupant protection systems that do not totally rely upon belts, such as airbags . . . , offer significant additional potential for preventing fatalities and injuries, at least in part because the American public is likely to find them less intrusive; their development and availability should be encouraged through appropriate incentives." *Id.* at 28963; see also *id.* at 28966, 28986 (noting conclusion of both Secretary and manufacturers that airbags used in conjunction with manual lap and shoulder belts would be "the most effective system of all" for preventing fatalities and injuries). The Secretary therefore

[3] See 49 U.S.C. § 30127; 49 C.F.R. § 571.208, S4.1.5.3 (1998). Congress stated that it did not intend its amendment or the Secretary's consequent alteration of Standard 208 to affect the potential liability of vehicle manufacturers under applicable law related to vehicles with or without airbags. 49 U.S.C. § 30127(f)(2).

included a phase-in period in order to encourage manufacturers to comply with the standard by installing airbags and other (perhaps more effective) nonbelt technologies that they might develop, rather than by installing less expensive automatic seatbelts.[4] As a further incentive for the use of such technologies, the standard provided that a vehicle equipped with an airbag or other nonbelt system would count as 1.5 vehicles for the purpose of determining compliance with the required 10, 25, or 40% minimum passive restraint requirement during the phase-in period. 49 C.F.R. § 571.208, S4.1.3.4(a)(1) (1998). With one oblique exception,[5] there is no mention, either in the text of the final standard or in the accompanying comments, of the possibility that the risk of potential tort liability would provide an incentive for manufacturers to install airbags. Nor is there any other specific evidence of an intent to preclude common-law tort actions.

II

Before discussing the pre-emption issue, it is appropriate to note that there is a vast difference between a rejection of Honda's threshold arguments in favor of federal pre-emption and a conclusion that petitioners ultimately would prevail on their common-law tort claims. I express no opinion on the possible merit, or lack of merit, of those claims. I do observe, however, that even though good-faith compliance with the minimum requirements of Standard 208 would not provide Honda with a complete defense on the merits,[6] I assume that such compliance would be admissible evidence tending to negate charges of negligent and defective design.[7] In addition, if Honda were ultimately found liable, such compliance would presumably weigh against an award of punitive damages. . . .

---

[4] "If the Department had required full compliance by September 1, 1987, it is very likely all of the manufacturers would have had to comply through the use of automatic belts. Thus, by phasing-in the requirement, the Department makes it easier for manufacturers to use other, perhaps better, systems such as airbags and passive interiors." 49 Fed. Reg. 29000 (1984).

[5] In response to a comment that the manufacturers were likely to use the cheapest system to comply with the new standard, the Secretary stated that she believed "that competition, potential liability for any deficient systems[,] and pride in one's product would prevent this." *Ibid.*

[6] *Wood v. General Motors Corp.*, 865 F.2d 395, 417 (CA1 1988) (collecting cases). The result would be different, of course, if petitioners had brought common-law tort claims challenging Honda's compliance with a mandatory minimum federal standard—*e.g.*, claims that a 1999 Honda was negligently and defectively designed *because* it was equipped with airbags as required by the current version of Standard 208. Restatement (Third) of Torts: General Principles § 14(b), and Comment *g* (Discussion Draft, Apr. 5, 1999) ("If the actor's adoption [or rejection] of a precaution would require the actor to violate a statute, the actor cannot be found negligent for failing to adopt [or reject] that precaution"); cf. *ante* at 871–872 (discussing problem of basing state tort liability upon compliance with mandatory federal regulatory requirement as question of pre-emption rather than of liability on the merits); *Florida Lime & Avocado Growers, Inc. v. Paul*, 373 U.S. 132, 142–143 (1963) ("A holding of federal exclusion of state law is inescapable and requires no inquiry into congressional design where compliance with both federal [regulations and state tort law] is a physical impossibility . . . .").

[7] Restatement (Third) of Torts: Products Liability § 4(b), and Comment *e* (1997) . . . .

III

When a state statute, administrative rule, or common-law cause of action conflicts with a federal statute, it is axiomatic that the state law is without effect. U.S. Const., Art. VI, cl. 2; *Cipollone v. Liggett Group, Inc.*, 505 U.S. 504, 516 (1992). On the other hand, it is equally clear that the Supremacy Clause does not give unelected federal judges *carte blanche* to use federal law as a means of imposing their own ideas of tort reform on the States. Because of the role of States as separate sovereigns in our federal system, we have long presumed that state laws—particularly those, such as the provision of tort remedies to compensate for personal injuries, that are within the scope of the States' historic police powers—are not to be pre-empted by a federal statute unless it is the clear and manifest purpose of Congress to do so. *Medtronic, Inc. v. Lohr*, 518 U.S. 470, 485 (1996); *Gade v. National Solid Wastes Management Assn.*, 505 U.S. 88, 116–117 (1992) (Souter, J., dissenting) ("If the [federal] statute's terms can be read sensibly not to have a pre-emptive effect, the presumption controls and no pre-emption may be inferred").

When a federal statute contains an express pre-emption provision, "the task of statutory construction must in the first instance focus on the plain wording of [that provision], which necessarily contains the best evidence of Congress' pre-emptive intent." *CSX Transp., Inc. v. Easterwood*, 507 U.S. 658, 664 (1993). The Safety Act contains both an express pre-emption provision, 15 U.S.C. § 1392(d), and a saving clause that expressly preserves common-law claims, § 1397(k). [Quotations of the same provisions quoted in Part II of the majority opinion are omitted.] . . . .

Relying on § 1392(d) and legislative history discussing Congress' desire for uniform national safety standards, Honda argues that petitioners' common-law no-airbag claims are expressly pre-empted because success on those claims would necessarily establish a state "safety standard" not identical to Standard 208. It is perfectly clear, however, that the term "safety standard" as used in these two sections refers to an objective rule prescribed by a legislature or an administrative agency and does not encompass case-specific decisions by judges and juries that resolve common-law claims. That term is used three times in these sections; presumably it is used consistently. . . . The two references to a federal safety standard are necessarily describing an objective administrative rule. 15 U.S.C. § 1392(a). When the pre-emption provision refers to a safety standard established by a "State or political subdivision of a State," therefore, it is most naturally read to convey a similar meaning. In addition, when the [pre-emption clause and the saving clause] are read together, they provide compelling evidence of an intent to distinguish between legislative and administrative rulemaking, on the one hand, and common-law liability, on the other. This distinction was certainly a rational one for Congress to draw in the Safety Act given that common-law liability—unlike most legislative or administrative rulemaking—necessarily performs an important remedial role in compensating accident victims. Cf. *Silkwood v. Kerr-McGee Corp.*, 464 U.S. 238, 251, 256 (1984).

It is true that in three recent cases we concluded that broadly phrased pre-emptive commands encompassed common-law claims. [See *Cipollone v. Liggett Group, Inc.*, 505 U.S. 504 (1992); *CSX Transp., Inc. v. Easterwood*, 507 U.S. 658 (1993); *Medtronic, Inc. v. Lohr*, 518 U.S. 470 (1996).] . . .

The statutes construed in those cases differed from the Safety Act in two significant respects. First, the language in each of those pre-emption provisions was significantly broader than the text of § 1392(d). [The express preemption clause at issue in *Cipollone* referred to a "requirement or prohibition . . . imposed under State law"; the clause at issue in *CSX* referred to any incompatible state "law, rule, regulation, order, or standard relating to railroad safety"; and the clause at issue in *Medtronic* referred to "any requirement."] Unlike the broader language of those provisions, the ordinary meaning of the term "safety standard" includes positive enactments, but does not include judicial decisions in common-law tort cases.

Second, the statutes at issue in *Cipollone*, *CSX*, and *Medtronic* did not contain a saving clause expressly preserving common-law remedies. The saving clause in the Safety Act unambiguously expresses a decision by Congress that compliance with a federal safety standard does not exempt a manufacturer from *any* common-law liability. In light of this reference to common-law liability in the saving clause, Congress surely would have included a similar reference in § 1392(d) if it had intended to pre-empt such liability. *Chicago v. Environmental Defense Fund*, 511 U.S. 328, 338 (1994) (noting presumption that Congress acts intentionally when it includes particular language in one section of a statute but omits it in another).

The Court does not disagree with this interpretation of the term "safety standard" in § 1392(d). Because the meaning of that term as used by Congress in this statute is clear, the text of § 1392(d) is itself sufficient to establish that the Safety Act does not expressly pre-empt common-law claims. In order to avoid the conclusion that the saving clause is superfluous, therefore, it must follow that it has a different purpose: to limit, or possibly to foreclose entirely, the possible pre-emptive effect of safety standards promulgated by the Secretary. The Court's approach to the case has the practical effect of reading the saving clause out of the statute altogether.[15]

---

[15] The Court surely cannot believe that Congress included that clause in the statute just to avoid the danger that we would otherwise fail to give the term "safety standard" its ordinary meaning.

Given the cumulative force of the fact that § 1392(d) does not expressly pre-empt common-law claims and the fact that § 1397(k) was obviously intended to limit the pre-emptive effect of the Secretary's safety standards, it is quite wrong for the Court to assume that a possible implicit conflict with the purposes to be achieved by such a standard should have the same pre-emptive effect " 'as an obstacle to the accomplishment and execution of the full purposes and objectives of Congress.' " *Ante* at 873. Properly construed, the Safety Act imposes a special burden on a party relying on an arguable, implicit conflict with a temporary regulatory policy—rather than a conflict with congressional policy or with the text of any regulation—to demonstrate that a common-law claim has been pre-empted.

IV

Even though the Safety Act does not expressly pre-empt common-law claims, Honda contends that Standard 208—of its own force—implicitly pre-empts the claims in this case. . . . [That contention, in turn, relies on the idea] that the imposition of common-law liability for failure to install an airbag would frustrate the purposes and objectives of Standard 208.

Both the text of the statute and the text of the standard provide persuasive reasons for rejecting this argument. The saving clause of the Safety Act arguably denies the Secretary the authority to promulgate standards that would pre-empt common-law remedies.[16] Moreover, the text of Standard 208 says nothing about pre-emption, and I am not persuaded that Honda has overcome our traditional presumption that it lacks any implicit pre-emptive effect.

Honda argues, and the Court now agrees, that the risk of liability presented by common-law claims that vehicles without airbags are negligently and defectively designed would frustrate the policy decision that the Secretary made in promulgating Standard 208. This decision, in their view, was that safety—including a desire to encourage "public acceptance of the airbag technology and experimentation with better passive restraint systems," [166 F.3d 1236, 1243 (D.C. Cir. 1999)]—would best be promoted through gradual implementation of a passive restraint requirement making airbags only one of a variety of systems that a manufacturer could install in order to comply, rather than through a requirement mandating the use of one particular system in every vehicle. In its brief supporting Honda, the United States agreed with this submission. It argued that if the manufacturers had known in 1984 that they might later be held liable for failure to install airbags, that risk "would likely have led them to install airbags in all cars," thereby

[16] . . . . I believe the language of this particular saving clause unquestionably limits, and possibly forecloses entirely, the pre-emptive effect that safety standards promulgated by the Secretary have on common-law remedies. . . . [B]ecause there is a textual basis for concluding that Congress intended to preserve the state law at issue, I think it entirely appropriate for the party favoring pre-emption to bear a special burden in attempting to show that valid federal purposes would be frustrated if that state law were not pre-empted.

frustrating the Secretary's safety goals and interfering with the methods designed to achieve them. Brief for United States as *Amicus Curiae* 25.

There are at least three flaws in this argument that provide sufficient grounds for rejecting it. First, the entire argument is based on an unrealistic factual predicate. Whatever the risk of liability on a no-airbag claim may have been prior to the promulgation of the 1984 version of Standard 208, that risk did not lead any manufacturer to install airbags in even a substantial portion of its cars. If there had been a realistic likelihood that the risk of tort liability would have that consequence, there would have been no need for Standard 208. The promulgation of that standard certainly did not *increase* the pre-existing risk of liability. Even if the standard did not create a previously unavailable pre-emption defense, it likely *reduced* the manufacturers' risk of liability by enabling them to point to the regulation and their compliance therewith as evidence tending to negate charges of negligent and defective design. See Part II, *supra*. Given that the pre-1984 risk of liability did not lead to widespread airbag installation, this reduced risk of liability was hardly likely to compel manufacturers to install airbags in all cars—or even to compel them to comply with Standard 208 during the phase-in period by installing airbags exclusively.

Second, even if the manufacturers' assessment of their risk of liability ultimately proved to be wrong, the purposes of Standard 208 would not be frustrated. In light of the inevitable time interval between the eventual filing of a tort action alleging that the failure to install an airbag is a design defect and the possible resolution of such a claim against a manufacturer, as well as the additional interval between such a resolution (if any) and manufacturers' . . . modifying their designs to avoid such liability in the future, it is obvious that the phase-in period would have ended long before its purposes could have been frustrated by the specter of tort liability. Thus, even without pre-emption, the public would have been given the time that the Secretary deemed necessary to gradually adjust to the increasing use of airbag technology and allay their unfounded concerns about it. Moreover, even if any no-airbag suits were ultimately resolved against manufacturers, the resulting incentive to modify their designs would have been quite different from a decision by the Secretary to mandate the use of airbags in every vehicle. For example, if the extra credit provided for the use of nonbelt passive restraint technologies during the phase-in period had (as the Secretary hoped) ultimately encouraged manufacturers to develop a nonbelt system more effective than the airbag, manufacturers held liable for failing to install passive restraints would have been free to respond by modifying their designs to include such a system *instead of* an airbag.[18] It seems

[18] The Court's failure to "understand [this point] correctly," *ante* at 883, is directly attributable to its fundamental misconception of the nature of duties imposed by tort law. A general verdict of liability in a case seeking damages for negligent and defective design of a vehicle that (like Ms. Geier's) lacked any passive restraints does not amount to an immutable, mandatory "rule of state tort law imposing . . . a duty [to install an airbag]." *Ante* at 881 . . . .

clear, therefore, that any potential tort liability would not frustrate the Secretary's desire to encourage both experimentation with better passive restraint systems and public acceptance of airbags.

Third, despite its acknowledgment that the saving clause "preserves those actions that seek to establish greater safety than the minimum safety achieved by a federal regulation intended to provide a floor," *ante* at 870, the Court completely ignores the important fact that by definition all of the standards established under the Safety Act—like the British regulations that governed the number and capacity of lifeboats aboard the *Titanic*[19]—impose minimum, rather than fixed or maximum, requirements. 15 U.S.C. § 1391(2) . . . . The phase-in program authorized by Standard 208 thus set minimum percentage requirements for the installation of passive restraints, increasing in annual stages of 10, 25, 40, and 100%. Those requirements were not ceilings, and it is obvious that the Secretary favored a more rapid increase. The possibility that exposure to potential tort liability might accelerate the rate of increase would actually further the only goal explicitly mentioned in the standard itself: reducing the number of deaths and severity of injuries of vehicle occupants. Had gradualism been independently important as a method of achieving the Secretary's safety goals, presumably the Secretary would have put a ceiling as well as a floor on each annual increase in the required percentage of new passive restraint installations. For similar reasons, it is evident that variety was not a matter of independent importance to the Secretary. . . . The Secretary did not act to ensure the use of a variety of passive restraints by placing ceilings on the number of airbags that could be used in complying with the minimum requirements.[20] Moreover, even if variety and gradualism had been independently important to the Secretary, there is nothing in the standard, the accompanying commentary, or the history of airbag regulation to support the notion that the Secretary intended to advance those purposes at all costs, without regard to the detrimental consequences that pre-emption of tort liability could have for the

---

Rather, that verdict merely reflects the jury's judgment that the manufacturer of a vehicle without any passive restraint system breached its duty of due care by designing a product that was not reasonably safe because a reasonable alternative design—"including, but not limited to, airbags," App. 3—could have reduced the foreseeable risks of harm posed by the product. See Restatement (Third) of Torts: Products Liability § 2(b), and Comment *d* (1997); *id.* § 1, Comment *a* (noting that § 2(b) is rooted in concepts of both negligence and strict liability). Such a verdict obviously does not foreclose the possibility that more than one alternative design exists the use of which would render the vehicle reasonably safe and satisfy the manufacturer's duty of due care. Thus, the Court is quite wrong to suggest that, as a consequence of such a verdict, only the installation of airbags would enable manufacturers to avoid liability in the future.

[19] . . . See Nader & Page, Automobile-Design Liability and Compliance with Federal Standards, 64 Geo. Wash. L. Rev. 415, 459 (1996) (noting that the *Titanic* "complied with British governmental regulations setting minimum requirements for lifeboats when it left port on its final, fateful voyage with boats capable of carrying only about [half] of the people on board") . . . .

[20] Of course, allowing a suit like petitioners' to proceed against a manufacturer that had installed no passive restraint system in a particular vehicle would not even arguably pose an "obstacle" to the auto manufacturers' freedom to choose among several different passive restraint device options. . . .

achievement of her avowed purpose of reducing vehicular injuries. See *Silkwood v. Kerr-McGee Corp.*, 464 U.S. at 257. . . .

V

. . . . [I]t is important to note that the text of Standard 208 (which the Court does not even bother to quote in its opinion) . . . does not contain any expression of an intent to displace state law. Given our repeated emphasis on the importance of the presumption against pre-emption, . . . this silence lends additional support to the conclusion that the continuation of whatever common-law liability may exist in a case like this poses no danger of frustrating any of the Secretary's primary purposes in promulgating Standard 208. See *Hillsborough County v. Automated Medical Laboratories, Inc.*, 471 U.S. 707, 721 (1985); *Silkwood v. Kerr-McGee Corp.*, 464 U.S. at 251 ("It is difficult to believe that [the Secretary] would, without comment, remove all means of judicial recourse for those injured by illegal conduct").

The Court apparently views the question of pre-emption in this case as a close one. *Ante* at 883 (relying on Secretary's interpretation of Standard 208's objectives to bolster its finding of pre-emption). Under "ordinary experience-proved principles of conflict pre-emption," *ante* at 874, therefore, the presumption against pre-emption should control. Instead, the Court simply ignores the presumption . . . .

Our presumption against pre-emption is rooted in the concept of federalism. It recognizes that when Congress legislates "in a field which the States have traditionally occupied . . . [,] we start with the assumption that the historic police powers of the States were not to be superseded by the Federal Act unless that was the clear and manifest purpose of Congress." *Rice v. Santa Fe Elevator Corp.*, 331 U.S. at 230; see *Jones v. Rath Packing Co.*, 430 U.S. 519, 525 (1977). The signal virtues of this presumption are its placement of the power of pre-emption squarely in the hands of Congress, which is far more suited than the Judiciary to strike the appropriate state/federal balance (particularly in areas of traditional state regulation), and its requirement that Congress speak clearly when exercising that power. In this way, the structural safeguards inherent in the normal operation of the legislative process operate to defend state interests from undue infringement. *Garcia v. San Antonio Metropolitan Transit Authority*, 469 U.S. 528, 552 (1985); see . . . *Gregory v. Ashcroft*, 501 U.S. 452, 460–464 (1991). In addition, the presumption serves as a limiting principle that prevents federal judges from running amok with our potentially boundless (and perhaps inadequately considered) doctrine of implied conflict pre-emption based on frustration of purposes—*i.e.*, that state law is pre-empted if it "stands as an obstacle to the accomplishment and execution of the full purposes and objectives of Congress." *Hines v. Davidowitz*, 312 U.S. 52, 67 (1941).[22]

[22] Recently, one commentator has argued that our doctrine of frustration-of-purposes (or "obstacle") pre-emption is not supported by the text or history of the Supremacy Clause, and has suggested that we attempt to bring a measure of rationality to our pre-emption jurisprudence

While the presumption is important in assessing the pre-emptive reach of federal statutes, it becomes crucial when the pre-emptive effect of an administrative regulation is at issue. Unlike Congress, administrative agencies are clearly not designed to represent the interests of States, yet with relative ease they can promulgate comprehensive and detailed regulations that have broad pre-emption ramifications for state law. We have addressed the heightened federalism and nondelegation concerns that agency pre-emption raises by using the presumption to build a procedural bridge across the political accountability gap between States and administrative agencies. Thus, even in cases where implied regulatory pre-emption is at issue, we generally "expect an administrative regulation to declare any intention to pre-empt state law with some specificity."[23] *California Coastal Comm'n v. Granite Rock Co.*, 480 U.S. 572, 583 (1987); see *Hillsborough County v. Automated Medical Laboratories, Inc.*, 471 U.S. at 717–718 (noting that too easily implying pre-emption "would be inconsistent with the federal-state balance embodied in our Supremacy Clause jurisprudence," and stating that "because agencies normally address problems in a detailed manner and can speak through a variety of means, including regulations, preambles, interpretive statements, and responses to comments, we can expect that they will make their intentions clear if they intend for their regulations to be exclusive") . . . . This expectation . . . serves to ensure that States will be able to have a dialog with agencies regarding pre-emption decisions *ex ante* through the normal notice-and-comment procedures of the Administrative Procedure Act (APA), 5 U.S.C. § 553.

When the presumption and its underpinnings are properly understood, it is plain that Honda has not overcome the presumption in this case. Neither Standard 208 nor its accompanying commentary includes the slightest specific indication of an intent to pre-empt common-law no-airbag suits. Indeed, the only mention of such suits in the commentary tends to suggest that they would not be pre-empted. See n. 5, *supra*. In the Court's view, however, "[t]he failure of the Federal

---

by eliminating it. Nelson, Preemption, 86 Va. L. Rev. 225, 231–232 (2000) . . . . Obviously, if we were to do so, there would be much less need for the presumption against pre-emption (which the commentator also criticizes). As matters now stand, however, the presumption reduces the risk that federal judges will draw too deeply on malleable and politically unaccountable sources such as regulatory history in finding pre-emption based on frustration of purposes.

[23] The Court brushes aside our specificity requirement on the ground that the cases in which we relied upon it . . . [addressed] field pre-emption, rather than conflict pre-emption . . . . This distinction, however, does not take the Court as far as it would like. Our cases firmly establish that conflict and field pre-emption are alike in that both are instances of implied pre-emption that by definition do "not [turn] on an express statement of pre-emptive intent." *Ante* at 884; see, *e.g.*, *Freightliner Corp. v. Myrick*, 514 U.S. 280, 287 (1995) . . . ; *English v. General Elec. Co.*, 496 U.S. 72, 79–80, and n. 5 (1990) (noting that field pre-emption rests on an inference of congressional intent to exclude state regulation and that it "may be understood as a species of conflict pre-emption"); *Fidelity Fed. Sav. & Loan Assn. v. de la Cuesta*, 458 U.S. 141, 153 (1982). Given that our specificity requirement was adopted in cases involving implied pre-emption, the Court cannot persuasively claim that the requirement is incompatible with our implied pre-emption jurisprudence in the federal regulatory context.

Register to address pre-emption explicitly is . . . not determinative," *ante* at 884, because the Secretary's consistent litigating position since 1989, the history of airbag regulation, and the commentary accompanying the final version of Standard 208 reveal purposes and objectives of the Secretary that would be frustrated by no-airbag suits. Pre-empting on these three bases blatantly contradicts the presumption against pre-emption. When the 1984 version of Standard 208 was under consideration, the States obviously were not afforded any notice that purposes might someday be discerned in the history of airbag regulation that would support pre-emption. . . . [Likewise,] the States plainly had no opportunity to comment upon either the commentary accompanying the final version of the standard or the Secretary's *ex post* litigating position that the standard had implicit pre-emptive effect.

. . . .

. . . [G]iven the Secretary's contention that he has the authority to promulgate safety standards that pre-empt state law and the fact that he could promulgate a standard such as the one quoted *supra* with relative ease, we should be quite reluctant to find pre-emption based only on the Secretary's informal effort to recast the 1984 version of Standard 208 into a pre-emptive mold. . . . Requiring the Secretary to put his pre-emptive position through formal notice-and-comment rulemaking—whether contemporaneously with the promulgation of the allegedly pre-emptive regulation or at any later time that the need for pre-emption becomes apparent—respects both the federalism and nondelegation principles that underlie the presumption against pre-emption in the regulatory context and the APA's requirement of new rulemaking when an agency substantially modifies its interpretation of a regulation. 5 U.S.C. § 551(5); *Paralyzed Veterans of America v. D.C. Arena L.P.*, 117 F.3d 579, 586 (CADC 1997); *National Family Planning & Reproductive Health Assn. v. Sullivan*, 979 F.2d 227, 240 (CADC 1992).

* * *

Because neither the text of the statute nor the text of the regulation contains any indication of an intent to pre-empt petitioners' cause of action, and because I cannot agree with the Court's unprecedented use of inferences from regulatory history and commentary as a basis for implied pre-emption, I am convinced that Honda has not overcome the presumption against pre-emption in this case. I therefore respectfully dissent.

NOTES AND QUESTIONS

1. In many ways, the version of FMVSS 208 at issue in *Geier* was an unusual sort of safety standard. Not only did it grow out of the enormous political controversy to which the Court alluded, but the aspect of FMVSS 208 that was central to *Geier* established requirements for a manufacturer's fleet rather than for particular cars within that fleet.

Before we consider the inferences that should be drawn from FMVSS 208, let us therefore work through the statutory scheme in a less exotic setting.

Take a relatively simple federal safety standard, such as FMVSS 207 ("Seating systems"). Among other things, FMVSS 207 requires each occupant seat to withstand a specified longitudinal force when tested in accordance with a specified procedure. *See* 49 C.F.R. § 571.207. Imagine that the driver's seat of a particular car satisfies this standard, but only barely. During an accident, the seat is subjected to a slightly higher force and breaks free, causing the driver to sustain serious injuries. The driver brings a product-liability suit against the manufacturer. The suit is premised on the theory that as applied to this situation, the common law of the relevant state gave the manufacturer a duty to design the driver's seat so as to withstand more force. The manufacturer argues that federal law preempts this alleged duty. In light of *Geier*, how should the court analyze that defense?

Geier makes clear that federal law does not *expressly* preempt the common-law duty that the driver is invoking. To be sure, FMVSS 207 (like the other federal safety standards promulgated by the Secretary of Transportation) does trigger the express preemption clause in the federal Safety Act: while FMVSS 207 is in effect, no state has any authority to establish or continue in effect a different "safety standard" of its own with respect to the same aspect of performance.[33] This clause plainly prevents individual states (and the District of Columbia, which the Act includes in its definition of a "State") from establishing a specific statutory or regulatory requirement that driver's seats must be able to withstand higher forces than FMVSS 207 demands. As a policy matter, moreover, it might seem odd to preempt such requirements while preserving common-law duties along the same lines: if Congress did not want states to be able to supplement FMVSS 207 with additional statutory or regulatory requirements about the forces that seats must be able to withstand, why would Congress leave states free to articulate and enforce additional duties on that subject as a matter of common law? *Cf.* Riegel v. Medtronic, Inc., 552 U.S. 312, 323–25 (2008) (refusing to read the express preemption clause in the Medical Device Amendments of 1976 to draw this sort of distinction, partly on the ground that the distinction "would make little sense" and should not lightly be attributed to Congress). But whether odd or not, the Safety Act coupled its preemption clause with the following saving clause: "Compliance with any Federal motor vehicle safety standard issued under this title does

[33] The quoted language comes from the pre-1994 version of the express preemption clause—the version relevant to *Geier*. As the Court noted, when Congress overhauled Title 49 in 1994, Congress reworded the preemption clause too. The relevant part of the new language reads as follows: "When a motor vehicle safety standard is in effect under this chapter, a State or a political subdivision of a State may prescribe or continue in effect a standard applicable to the same aspect of performance of a motor vehicle or motor vehicle equipment only if the standard is identical to the standard prescribed under this chapter." 49 U.S.C. § 30103(b)(1).

not exempt any person from any liability under common law."[34] In *Geier*, all nine Justices agreed that the best way to reconcile this provision with the preemption clause was to take a relatively narrow view of the phrase "safety standard" in the preemption clause. Under that interpretation, the Safety Act's express preemption clause does not itself prevent states from articulating and enforcing common-law standards of care that differ from the standards established by federal regulators. It follows that express preemption will not be a problem for the plaintiff's claim in our hypothetical lawsuit.

What about conflict preemption? At first glance, one might think that the analysis can again stop with the saving clause: perhaps that clause should be understood to preserve *all* common-law liabilities against preemption by whatever federal safety standards the Secretary promulgates. Everyone agrees that states normally can hold manufacturers liable in tort for injuries caused by their *violation* of federal safety standards, and on this view even *compliance* with a federal safety standard would never have the effect of insulating manufacturers from tort liability (unless, perhaps, a particular state's version of the common law so provided).

In *Geier*, though, even Justice Stevens's dissent did not go quite that far. To be sure, the dissent said that "[t]he saving clause . . . arguably denies the Secretary the authority to promulgate standards that would pre-empt common-law remedies." *Geier*, 529 U.S. at 899–900 (Stevens, J., dissenting). But in footnote 6, the dissent seemed to concede that a state cannot validly hold manufacturers liable in damages for doing something that a federal safety standard requires them to do. *See id.* at 892 n.6. In other words, states cannot validly recognize a common-law duty to disobey a federal safety standard established by the Secretary. Thus, when the saving clause said that "[c]ompliance with any Federal motor vehicle safety standard issued under this title does not exempt any person from any liability under common law," even the dissenters seemed willing to read in at least the following limiting phrase: "except liability for complying with the Federal motor vehicle safety standard." In footnote 16, indeed, the dissenters left themselves room to read in a further limitation, applicable when the common-law duty that a particular state wants to recognize would plainly frustrate "valid federal purposes" that lie behind one or more of the safety standards promulgated by the Secretary. *See id.* at 900 n.16.

For its part, the majority read the saving clause to preserve common-law claims only from the express preemption clause and not from "the ordinary working of conflict pre-emption principles." *Id.* at 869 (majority opinion). According to the majority, the saving clause does not even raise any special impediment to the invocation of those principles: "Nothing in the statute suggests Congress wanted to complicate ordinary experience-

[34] Again, the quoted language comes from the pre-1994 version of the Act, but the current version is more or less the same. *See* 49 U.S.C. § 30103(e).

proved principles of conflict preemption with an added 'special burden,' " *id.* at 874, and there is no apparent reason "[w]hy . . . Congress [would] not have wanted ordinary pre-emption principles to apply where an actual conflict with a federal objective is at stake," *id.* at 871. Under ordinary conflict-preemption principles, the majority added, if a particular safety standard promulgated by the Secretary reflects purposes that go beyond simply "creat[ing] a floor, *i.e.*, a minimum safety standard," *id.* at 868, then the Act implicitly preempts aspects of state law (including common-law duties) that would stand as an obstacle to the accomplishment and execution of those purposes.

The majority's analysis makes the scope of conflict preemption depend on careful interpretation of the particular federal safety standard in question, coupled with investigation of the purposes behind it. With respect to the installation of airbags in cars for the 1987 model year, the majority concluded that the relevant version of FMVSS 208 did more than simply "creat[e] a floor"; for reasons considered in the next note, the majority inferred that FMVSS 208 effectively gave manufacturers a federally protected right *not* to install airbags in all of their cars. The majority's arguments on this point, however, were specific to FMVSS 208 and the explanation that the Secretary offered for it. Other safety standards may well be different: if they simply "creat[e] a floor" (rather than giving manufacturers the sort of federally protected discretion that the majority associated with FMVSS 208), individual states can impose tougher duties under the rubric of state common law. Indeed, the majority specifically said that the saving clause in the federal statute "preserves those [common-law tort actions] that seek to establish greater safety than the minimum safety achieved by a federal regulation intended to provide a floor." *Id.* at 870.

To apply *Geier* to our hypothetical case, we therefore would need to ask whether FMVSS 207 was "intended to provide a floor," or whether it also gives manufacturers a federally protected right to do no more than it requires. In the context of some federal safety standards, there might be room for argument on both sides. *See, e.g.*, Lake v. Memphis Landsmen, LLC, 405 S.W.3d 47, 64 (Tenn. 2013) (discussing a split of authority about the preemptive effect of FMVSS 205). But FMVSS 207 does not seem particularly tricky in this respect; it seems quite clearly to be what Justice Breyer called "a minimum safety standard." In our hypothetical case, then, *Geier*'s analysis probably cuts *against* preemption.

2. The crucial difference between our hypothetical case and *Geier* is the difference between FMVSS 207 and the provisions about passive restraints in FMVSS 208. The majority's conclusion in *Geier* hinged on the purposes that the majority attributed to the relevant version of FMVSS 208.

On its face, FMVSS 208 might have seemed simply "to provide a floor." Roughly speaking, it required manufacturers to include a passive-restraint mechanism of some sort in at least 10% of the cars that they built between September 1, 1986, and September 1, 1987, but it said nothing to prevent manufacturers from voluntarily going further. If manufacturers had chosen to install airbags in all of the cars that they made during the 1987 model year, they would have been in full compliance with FMVSS 208.

Still, the majority inferred that FMVSS 208 effectively gave manufacturers a federal right to make this choice for themselves, free from the pressure of state tort law. At least as far as federal law was concerned, FMVSS 208 plainly gave each manufacturer discretion about both (1) the types of passive-restraint mechanisms that the manufacturer would use to satisfy the 10% requirement and (2) whether to install passive restraints in some or all of the remaining 90% of the cars in the manufacturer's fleet. According to the majority, moreover, federal policy hinged on vesting this discretion in manufacturers. For a number of reasons (including the desire to "promote public acceptance" and to give manufacturers more time to improve passive-restraint technology), the Secretary "deliberately sought a *gradual* phase-in of passive restraints"—meaning that the Secretary allegedly did not want every car manufactured in 1987 to include passive restraints. *Geier*, 529 U.S. at 879. In addition, even with respect to the cars that did include passive restraints, the Secretary allegedly wanted manufacturers to use "a mix of several different passive restraint systems" to satisfy FMVSS 208, and not simply to install airbags in each vehicle. *See id.* at 878. Among other things, the Secretary allegedly wanted to facilitate a natural experiment: if different cars were equipped with different sorts of passive-restraint mechanisms, both manufacturers and regulators would be able to gather real-world data about which mechanisms were best. According to the majority, the common-law duty that the Geiers were trying to establish would have interfered with both of these sets of federal goals: to the extent that a manufacturer could have satisfied it only by installing airbags in each relevant car, such a duty "would have stood as an obstacle to the gradual . . . phase-in that the federal regulation deliberately imposed," and it also "would have presented an obstacle to the variety and mix of [passive-restraint] devices that the federal regulation sought." *Id.* at 881. To avoid this interference with the purposes that the majority attributed to FMVSS 208, the majority concluded that the combination of the Safety Act and FMVSS 208 implicitly preempted the common-law duty in question.

To what extent do the federal purposes identified by the majority really support preemption? Take the Secretary's alleged desire to promote experimentation with respect to passive-restraint systems. Suppose that a hypothetical regulator does indeed want manufacturers to have a relatively free hand to experiment. Does it follow that the regulator would necessarily oppose tort compensation for individuals who are harmed during the course of the experiment? Couldn't the regulator's desire to permit experimentation be moderated by a willingness to permit victims of the experiment to recover compensation pursuant to the tort law of individual states? And couldn't a regulator with this mix of purposes have promulgated FMVSS 208 in exactly the form that the Secretary did promulgate it, with exactly the same explanations that the Secretary provided?

To be sure, the very fact that the Secretary wanted to permit experimentation might indicate that as of 1984 (when the Secretary promulgated FMVSS 208), the Secretary considered the existing data insufficient to identify the best type of passive-restraint system. That judgment about the evidence, in turn, might seem inconsistent with letting juries hold manufacturers liable for installing one system (such as automatic seatbelts) rather than another (such as airbags). But is that really true? Does the level of knowledge that will support tort liability have to be the same as the level of knowledge that will make regulators see no need for further experimentation?

Even if you answer those questions in the affirmative, and you therefore think that the Secretary's desire to permit experimentation is flatly inconsistent with holding manufacturers liable in tort for the decisions that they make *at the outset of the experiment*, does this argument automatically apply to all model years covered by the experiment? What if the results of the experiment become clear fairly quickly? Suppose, for instance, that by the end of the 1988 model year, real-world experience had already established quite convincingly that cars with airbags are safer than cars with other passive-restraint systems (such as automatic seatbelts). If a manufacturer nonetheless relied on automatic seatbelts to satisfy its obligations under FMVSS 208, would the Secretary's desire to permit experimentation still justify preemption of tort claims premised on the manufacturer's failure to include an airbag in one of the cars that the manufacturer made in 1989? Couldn't a reasonable regulator who wanted manufacturers to be free to experiment also want manufacturers to face some pressure to take account of the results of the experiment?

Admittedly, the majority in *Geier* did not rely exclusively on the Secretary's alleged desire to facilitate an experiment in which data could be collected about which passive-restraint mechanisms are best. The majority also emphasized the Secretary's alleged desire to phase in passive-restraint systems gradually. Again, though, couldn't a reasonable regulator who favored a gradual phase-in (and who did so for the reasons identified by the majority) still have favored letting the victims of the phase-in recover compensation in tort for their injuries? Take the Secretary's fear of triggering counterproductive forms of public backlash. Even if the Secretary was afraid that a federal *regulatory* requirement mandating passive restraints in all cars for the 1987 model year would trigger such backlash, would the Secretary necessarily have had the same fears about jury determinations in product-liability suits (or seemingly voluntary decisions made by manufacturers in the hope of averting such suits)? Don't prospective mandates in federal regulations provide more of a focal point for public backlash (and also produce more uniformity in practice) than the risk of tort liability down the road?

Overall, did the majority's analysis in *Geier* erroneously equate tort "duties" (which encourage manufacturers to internalize the costs of their design choices but do not otherwise dictate what those choices must be) with the sorts of duties created by command-and-control regulations? While tort law obviously has regulatory as well as compensatory effects, does the manner in which it regulates pose as much of a danger to the purposes behind FMVSS 208 as the majority thought? *Cf.* Catherine M. Sharkey, *Products Liability Preemption: An Institutional Approach*, 76 GEO. WASH. L. REV. 449, 459 (2008) (arguing that in preemption cases, "[t]he Court has oscillated between competing conceptions of tort as either primarily regulatory or compensatory"); *id.* at 461–62, 466 (contrasting *Geier*, where "the majority referred to a verdict in a common-law tort suit as a 'jury-imposed safety standard,' " with cases indicating that "the call for the uniformity of national regulation should not be taken so far as to justify the displacement of state common-law remedies for accident victims").

3. The passive-restraint regulation at issue in *Geier* was unusual, and *Geier*'s logic does not automatically apply to every other federal safety standard that gives manufacturers any sort of choice. The Supreme Court made that clear in *Williamson v. Mazda Motor of America, Inc.*, 562 U.S. 323 (2011).

Williamson involved a different aspect of the same Federal Motor Vehicle Safety Standard that the Court had considered in *Geier*—FMVSS 208. The version of FMVSS 208 at issue in *Williamson* said that as of May 1, 1990, car manufacturers had to install lap/shoulder seatbelt assemblies (rather than just lap belts) at "every forward-facing rear outboard designated seating position." For minivans, this requirement covered most rear seats *except*, in a minivan with three rows of seating, the second-row seat adjacent to the walkway that leads to the back row.[35] As far as the relevant version of FMVSS 208 was concerned, that aisle seat could have *either* a lap/shoulder belt *or* a lap-only belt.

In the *Williamson* case, a Mazda minivan was in a bad accident in California. The passenger who was sitting in the aisle seat in the middle row was wearing her seatbelt, but it was just a lap belt, and she was killed. The other passengers in the minivan were at seating positions with lap/shoulder belts, and they survived.

The Williamsons sued Mazda under California tort law, on the theory that the minivan would have been safer if there had been

[35] Picture a minivan with two captain's chairs in the front, a two-person bench in the middle with an aisle to the back, and a three-person back row. All these seats had to have lap/shoulder belts except for the aisle seat in the middle row.

lap/shoulder belts at *all* seating positions. According to the Williamsons, state common law made Mazda liable in damages for the injuries caused by Mazda's decision to provide only a lap belt for the aisle seat in the middle row. In response, Mazda argued that federal law prevented California from recognizing a duty of the sort that the plaintiffs were alleging—a common-law duty to go beyond the federal requirements and to install lap/shoulder belts at all seating positions in the minivan. Mazda argued that as in *Geier*, the federal safety standard gave the manufacturer a choice with which state tort law could not interfere. On this view, Mazda had a federally protected right to decide for itself, without the threat of tort liability under state law, whether to install a lap/shoulder belt or a lap-only belt for the aisle seat of the minivan's middle row.

Under *Geier*, the first step in evaluating this argument is to identify the purposes behind the federal regulators' decision not to require a lap/shoulder belt at this seating position, but instead to let manufacturers satisfy the federal regulation with *either* a lap/shoulder belt *or* a lap-only belt. When the responsible federal agency had promulgated the regulation at issue in *Williamson*, the agency had provided an account of this decision. During the rulemaking process, General Motors had submitted a comment about "practical difficulties that would be presented if aisleway seating positions were required to be equipped with lap/shoulder belts." *See* Federal Motor Vehicle Safety Standards; Occupant Crash Protection, 54 Fed. Reg. 46257, 46258 (Nov. 2, 1989). The upper part of a lap/shoulder belt would need to be anchored somewhere. One possibility was to anchor it on the side of the vehicle, across the aisle. But that "would stretch the shoulder belt across the aisleway," making it harder for people to get in and out of the back row of seats. *Id.* The other possibility was to anchor the upper end of the shoulder belt to the vehicle's roof. But that would require manufacturers to change the structure of their minivans in ways that allegedly would be costly. *See id.* Ultimately, the agency had agreed with these comments. That is why the final version of the agency's regulation made an exception for "seating positions adjacent to a walkway located between the seat and the side of the vehicle, which walkway is designed to allow access to more rearward seating positions." *Id.* at 46266–67.

In light of this explanation, the Supreme Court concluded that federal law did *not* prevent state common law from making Mazda liable for installing a lap-only belt rather than a lap/shoulder belt. Justice Breyer, who had written the majority opinion in *Geier*, also wrote the Court's opinion in *Williamson*. He acknowledged that "[l]ike the regulation in *Geier*, the regulation here leaves the manufacturer with a choice": as far as the federal safety standard was concerned, the manufacturer could decide to install *either* a lap/shoulder belt *or* a lap-only belt at this seating position. *Williamson*, 562 U.S. at 332. Justice Breyer also acknowledged that holding manufacturers liable under state common law for making the latter decision "would restrict that choice." *Id.* Unlike in *Geier*, though, Justice Breyer concluded that conferring freedom of choice on this point had not been "a significant regulatory objective," and allowing states to impose tort liability therefore would not frustrate the purposes behind the federal regulation. *Id.* In other words, holding Mazda and other manufacturers liable in tort for failing to install lap/shoulder belts would not get in the way of what the agency had been trying to accomplish when it itself decided not to require lap/shoulder belts.

Justice Breyer specifically distinguished the agency's reasons for allowing either lap-only or lap/shoulder belts to satisfy the federal safety standard from the reasons behind the agency decisions that had been at issue in *Geier*. In *Williamson*, he explained, the agency "was not concerned about consumer acceptance" and "had no interest in assuring a mix of devices"; it knew everything that it thought it needed to know to conclude that lap/shoulder belts were safer than lap-only belts. *See id.* at 333. To be sure, the agency did not itself require lap/shoulder belts for this one seating position as of May 1, 1990, because the agency was concerned about the cost of restructuring minivan roofs to accommodate anchors. But according to Justice Breyer, the fact that the agency itself decided that the cost of supplying lap/shoulder belts for this one seating position wasn't worth the benefits does not prove that the agency "sought to forbid common-law tort suits in which a judge or jury might reach a different conclusion." *Id.* at 335.

Justice Breyer explained that "many, perhaps most, federal safety regulations embody some kind of cost-effectiveness judgment" of the sort that lay behind the agency's decision not to require lap/shoulder belts for the seating position in question. *Id.* If that judgment itself implied preemption, then all such regulations would effectively set ceilings as well as floors; state tort law would not be able to supplement the federal regulations with more demanding requirements. According to Justice Breyer, though, routinely reaching that conclusion would flout the saving clause in the federal statute, which indicates that compliance with the federal safety standards does not routinely exempt manufacturers from liability at common law.

4. In *Geier*, the United States had filed an amicus brief that favored preemption. According to the brief, "Standard 208 . . . embodies the Secretary's policy judgment that safety would best be promoted if manufacturers installed *alternative* protection systems in their fleets rather than one particular system in every car," and "[t]hat policy of affirmatively encouraging diversity would be frustrated if manufacturers could be held liable for not installing airbags." Brief for the United States as Amicus Curiae Supporting Affirmance, *Geier v. American Honda Motor Co.*, No. 98–1811, at 25. The brief was signed not only by the Solicitor General and other lawyers in the Department of Justice but also by lawyers in the Department of Transportation (DOT), and the majority in *Geier* took the brief as an authoritative statement of the official position of the Department of Transportation. The majority asserted that this position was entitled to at least some deference. *See Geier*, 529 U.S. at 883 ("We place some weight upon DOT's interpretation of FMVSS 208's objectives and its conclusion, as set forth in the Government's brief, that a tort suit such as this one would ' "stan[d] as an obstacle to the accomplishment and execution" ' of those objections."). *But cf. id.* at 886 (asserting that the majority would have reached the same conclusion "even without giving DOT's own view special weight").

In *Williamson*, by contrast, the United States submitted an amicus brief (again signed by lawyers in the Department of Transportation as well as the acting Solicitor General and other lawyers in the Department of Justice) arguing that the relevant regulation did *not* preempt the Williamsons' tort claims. *See* Brief for the United States as Amicus Curiae Supporting Petitioners, *Williamson*, 562 U.S. 323 (No. 08–1314). Justice Breyer's opinion for the Court again treated this brief as a statement of the agency's position and asserted that "[a]s in *Geier*, 'the agency's own views should make a difference.' " *Williamson*, 562 U.S. at 335 (quoting *Geier*, 529 U.S. at 883).

Justice Breyer seemed to have something like *Auer* deference in mind. *See Geier*, 529 U.S. at 884 (citing *Auer v. Robbins*, 519 U.S. 452, 461–62 (1997)); *see also supra* Chapter 5.C (covering *Auer* deference, which entails deferring to an agency's interpretation of its own regulations). While the Supreme Court has declined to overrule *Auer*, the Court might no longer be so quick to defer to statements that merely appear in a legal brief. *See* Kisor v. Wilkie, 139 S. Ct. 2400, 2417 n.6 (2019). For reasons mentioned in Chapter 5, moreover, one might question Justice Breyer's assumption that a brief signed jointly by the Solicitor General and agency lawyers is equivalent to a statement by the agency itself. *See supra* pp. 1023–1024. Setting those points aside, though, how should a Court that accepts the general concept of *Auer* deference approach an agency's views about whether state law is preempted on the ground that application of the state law would frustrate the purposes behind the agency's regulations?

Speaking generally, such views may be broken down into three components. *Cf.* Nicholas Bagley, Agency Preemption and the Subprime Crisis 37–43 (Oct. 1, 2008), https://ssrn.com/abstract=1729246 (discussing components of conflict-preemption analysis). The first component is the agency's identification of the purposes that lie behind the regulations. The second component is the agency's assessment of whether the practical effects of applying the state law will get in the way of accomplishing those purposes. The third component is the agency's position about the preemptive consequences of the first two components.

Auer may well support deference with respect to the first component (assuming that the agency's position satisfies the criteria discussed in *Kisor*, 139 S. Ct. at 2415–18). To be sure, it might theoretically be possible for courts to defer to an agency's views about the meaning of the agency's regulations without also deferring to the agency's views about the purposes behind those regulations. But the meaning that one attributes to a legal directive and the purposes that one understands the directive to serve are intertwined, and any plausible rationale for deference to the agency's interpretation of its regulations would likely support deference to the agency's understanding of the purposes behind those regulations.

As for the second component, *Auer* is not directly relevant. In some respects, though, agencies may have better sources of information than courts about the practical effects of the challenged aspect of state law, and agencies may also be better able to evaluate information in their fields of expertise. Some type of deference might therefore be appropriate. *Cf.* Thomas W. Merrill, *Preemption and Institutional Choice*, 102 NW. U. L. REV. 727, 775–76 (2008) (suggesting that in preemption cases, courts should "give 'significant weight' to agency views about the practical impact of diverse state rules on the implementation of federal regulatory schemes that they administer or as to which they have significant experience and expertise," but courts should exercise "independent . . . judgment" on "all other issues that bear on the ultimate decision of whether state law is preempted").

What about the third component? Suppose the agency says that the challenged state law would frustrate the purposes behind the agency's regulations to such an extent that the state law is preempted. For a court to agree, the court cannot rely exclusively on the agency's understanding of the purposes behind the agency's regulations or the agency's view that applying state law would get in the way of those purposes. The court also has to reach a conclusion about the meaning of the relevant federal statute. Depending upon how the agency casts its position, the key question of statutory interpretation might take either of two different forms. In some situations, the court will be asking whether the statute itself preempts state laws that would hinder the purposes behind the agency's regulations in the way that the agency has identified. In other situations, the key question might be cast instead in terms of delegation: to what extent (and subject to what procedural safeguards) has Congress given the agency authority to announce the preemption of state laws that the agency deems inconsistent with its regulatory purposes? In either case, though, this third component of the agency's position will implicate a question of statutory interpretation, which lies in the realm of *Chevron* rather than *Auer*. The agency, moreover, might not qualify for *Chevron* deference with respect to this question. *Cf. supra* pp. 1095–1097 (discussing whether courts owe *Chevron* deference to an agency's interpretation of the typical express preemption clause). In *Geier*, for instance, Congress had not necessarily authorized the agency to act with the force of law in determining the scope of conflict preemption, and in any event the agency had not purported to do so; its conclusions about preemption were simply expressed in an amicus brief.

The Supreme Court revisited questions of deference in *Wyeth v. Levine*, 555 U.S. 555 (2009). There, the plaintiff sued a pharmaceutical company under state tort law for allegedly failing to provide an adequate warning about the danger of administering one of the company's drugs via direct intravenous injections. The FDA had approved the labeling that the company was using, and federal regulations restricted the company's ability to make unilateral changes to that labeling. *See id.* at 568–71 (discussing exceptions to those restrictions). As in *Geier*, the United States submitted an amicus brief—signed by lawyers in both the Department of Justice and the Department of Health and Human Services, where the FDA is housed—arguing that federal law preempted the common-law duty that the plaintiff was invoking. *See* Brief for the United States as Amicus Curiae Supporting Petitioner, *Wyeth*, 555 U.S. 555 (No. 06–1249), at 19 (arguing that under the circumstances of the case, "the jury's imposition of liability based on petitioner's use of FDA-approved labeling would interfere with FDA's expert weighing of risks and benefits"); *id.* at 21–22 (arguing that the contrary conclusion reached by the state courts rested on a misinterpretation of the applicable FDA regulations). In *Wyeth*, indeed, the FDA had expressed the same view as part of the process of promulgating a regulation in 2006 (although the FDA had previously taken a different position). *See* Requirements on Content and Format of Labeling for Human Prescription Drug and Biological Products, 71 Fed. Reg. 3922, 3934–35 (Jan. 24, 2006). Nonetheless, a majority of the Supreme Court refused to find preemption. Justice Stevens's opinion for the Court made the following general comments about deference on preemption questions:

> "In prior cases, we have given 'some weight' to an agency's views about the impact of tort law on federal objectives when 'the subject matter is technica[l] and the relevant history and background are complex and extensive.' *Geier*, 529 U.S. at 883. Even in such cases, however, we have not deferred to an agency's *conclusion* that state law is pre-empted. Rather, we have attended to an agency's explanation of how state law affects the regulatory scheme. While agencies have no special authority to pronounce on pre-emption absent delegation by Congress, they do have a unique understanding of the statutes they administer and an attendant ability to make informed determinations about how state requirements may pose an 'obstacle to the accomplishment and execution of the full purposes and objectives of Congress.' *Hines*, 312 U.S. at 67 . . . . The weight we accord the agency's explanation of state law's impact on the federal scheme depends on its thoroughness, consistency, and persuasiveness. Cf. . . . *Skidmore v. Swift & Co.*, 323 U.S. 134, 140 (1944)."

Wyeth, 555 U.S. at 576–77. Applying this analysis, Justice Stevens concluded that neither the FDA's statements in 2006 nor the amicus brief deserved deference. To distinguish *Geier*, he emphasized that (1) the FDA had not given states and other interested parties adequate notice and opportunity to comment before announcing its position in 2006, (2) the FDA had previously opined that plaintiffs *could* bring failure-to-warn claims under state tort law notwithstanding FDA approval of the labels in question, (3) the FDA had not provided a "reasoned explanation" for its change of position, and (4) the FDA's position was not about "the preemptive effect of a specific agency regulation bearing the force of law" (such as FMVSS 208). *See id.* at 577–81.

5. The preceding note addressed the weight that courts should give an agency's positions in cases about alleged conflicts between state law and federal regulations promulgated under the authority of federal statutes. But what role should agencies play in cases about conflicts between state law and federal statutes themselves?

Here, it might be necessary to distinguish between different types of conflict preemption. When state law directly contradicts a federal statutory provision (as interpreted by the administering agency), the analysis is relatively straightforward. Under the *Chevron* framework, if Congress has authorized the agency to act with the force of law in implementing the relevant statutory provision, and if the agency has authoritatively interpreted the provision in a form that satisfies both *Mead* and the two-step *Chevron* framework, then courts are bound to accept that interpretation even if they would have read the provision differently as an original matter. By operation of the Supremacy Clause, moreover, the provision will preempt whatever aspects of state law it contradicts. To the extent that the agency reads the provision broadly (but permissibly), the agency's interpretation will therefore cause the provision to have a more sweeping preemptive effect than the courts might otherwise give it.

In applying the *Chevron* framework, of course, courts will have to consider how *Chevron* interacts with other canons of statutory construction. In some contexts, it might be possible to argue that the presumption against preemption restricts the range of interpretive choices that the responsible agency can permissibly adopt. *See, e.g.*, Ernest A. Young, *Executive Preemption*, 108 NW. U. L. REV. 869, 883–94 (2008) (suggesting that the presumption against preemption should trump *Chevron* deference). Still, few people think that the presumption against preemption obliges either agencies or courts to read every substantive provision in a federal statute as narrowly as possible, simply to minimize its preemptive effect. *See, e.g.*, Smiley v. Citibank (South Dakota), N.A., 517 U.S. 735, 743–44 (1996) (unanimously rejecting this sort of argument); *see also infra* pp. 1175–1178 (discussing the role of the presumption against preemption in conflict-preemption analysis). Under *Chevron*, agencies often will have a range of choices about the proper interpretation of statutory provisions that they administer, and state law that directly contradicts the agency's chosen interpretation will be preempted.

Matters get more complicated when the argument for preemption does not rest on a direct contradiction between state law and the specific terms of a federal statute (as interpreted by the administering agency), but instead rests on a more subtle type of conflict. Suppose that a litigant plausibly argues that the practical effects of the challenged state law would stand as an obstacle to accomplishing some of the purposes that the responsible federal agency associates with the federal statute. Does *Chevron* require courts to give just as much deference to the agency's understanding of those general purposes as courts give to the agency's views about the meaning of a specific statutory provision that Congress has put the agency in charge of administering? And once courts have identified the mix of purposes behind the federal statute (with whatever level of deference to the agency's views is appropriate), does the agency also deserve deference about the extent to which the statute should be understood to strip states of authority to enact laws that would get in the way of accomplishing those purposes? Or is the latter question, at least, one on which courts should usually reach their own judgment without any strong form of deference to the agency? *See supra* p. 1095 (discussing similar issues in the context of express preemption, and citing scholars who argue that courts usually do not owe *Chevron* deference to agencies' views about whether the tension between a federal statute and state law is sufficient to trigger preemption).

6. In conjunction with promulgating the version of FMVSS 208 that was at issue in *Geier*, the Department of Transportation had considered and rejected a proposal to require all cars to have airbags. The agency acknowledged that such a requirement would have "potentially large safety benefits," but it argued that "a number of reasons"—including concerns about cost, environmental hazards, the dangers that airbags posed to "out-of-position occupants" like small children, and the possibility of public backlash—all counseled against imposing such a requirement in the short term. *See* Federal Motor Vehicle Safety Standard; Occupant Crash Protection, 49 Fed. Reg. 28962, 29000–02 (July 17, 1984).[36] Suppose that the agency had made this statement about the undesirability of an all-airbag requirement, but had not promulgated *any* version of FMVSS 208 at all. Would the simple fact that the responsible federal agency had considered and rejected a regulation requiring airbags have justified the conclusion that federal law preempted the common-law duty that the Geiers wanted to invoke? In the absence of any applicable federal safety standard, the express preemption clause in the federal Safety Act obviously would have been

[36] The agency also observed that according to several people who had submitted comments, the agency did not even have the power to impose an airbag requirement; according to these people, such a requirement would be a "design" standard rather than a "performance" standard of the sort that Congress had authorized the agency to promulgate. *Id.* at 29001. For purposes of this note, however, suppose that those commentators were wrong, and that the agency had authority to promulgate a "performance" standard that could be satisfied only by the installation of airbags.

inapplicable, but might Honda still have had a plausible argument for *implied* preemption?

The Court faced something like that question in *Sprietsma v. Mercury Marine*, 537 U.S. 51 (2002). When the motorboat in which she had been riding made a turn, Mrs. Sprietsma fell into the water and was fatally injured by the outboard motor's propeller. Her husband, who was also the administrator of her estate, brought a product-liability suit under state tort law against the company that had made the motor. One of the suit's theories was that the motor should have been protected by a propeller guard and that the lack of this design feature made it unreasonably dangerous. In response, the defendant asserted that the Federal Boat Safety Act of 1971, which was structured much like the statute at issue in *Geier*, preempted this proposed application of state tort law. Although the responsible federal agency had not promulgated any regulations about propeller guards, a special Propeller Guard Subcommittee of the National Boating Safety Advisory Council had studied the matter from 1988 to 1990 and had ultimately recommended against requiring propeller guards—a recommendation that the agency accepted in 1990. According to the defendant, the common-law duty that Mr. Sprietsma was invoking conflicted with the agency's deliberate decision *not* to require propeller guards (at least at the time relevant to the case), and federal law should therefore be understood to prevent state common law from imposing such a duty.

In a unanimous opinion by Justice Stevens, the Supreme Court called this argument a "viable pre-emption theor[y]." *Sprietsma*, 537 U.S. at 64. Ultimately, however, the Court rejected the argument. To explain why the argument failed, the Court relied at least in part on the details of the agency's explanation for its failure to require propeller guards. In particular, the Court reasoned as follows:

> "[The agency's] explanation for its decision . . . reveals only a judgment that the available data did not meet the [Act's] 'stringent' criteria for federal regulation. The [agency] did not take the further step of deciding that, as a matter of policy, the States and their political subdivisions should not impose some version of propeller guard regulation, and it most definitely did not reject propeller guards as unsafe. The [agency's] apparent focus was on the lack of any 'universally acceptable' propeller guard for 'all modes of boat operation.' But nothing in its official explanation would be inconsistent with a tort verdict premised on a jury's finding that some type of propeller guard should have been installed on this particular kind of boat equipped with respondent's particular type of motor. Thus, although the [agency's] decision not to require propeller guards was undoubtedly intentional and carefully considered, it does not convey an 'authoritative' message of a federal policy against propeller guards."

Id. at 66–67. The Court also emphasized that in contrast to *Geier*, the United States had submitted an amicus brief "inform[ing] us that the agency does not view the 1990 refusal to regulate or any subsequent regulatory actions by the [agency] as having any pre-emptive effect." *Id.* at 68.

Suppose that the agency's explanation for its failure to require propeller guards had read differently. In particular, suppose that the agency had asserted that while propeller guards would reduce some types of risks, they would introduce other dangers, and the agency had decided not to require them because the agency wanted each manufacturer to be able to make that decision for itself. Suppose further that the government's amicus brief in *Sprietsma* had supported preemption. Under this revised version of the facts, should the Court have held that the agency's decision not to regulate *did* have the preemptive effect that the defendant claimed? Or should states still have been allowed to recognize the common-law duty that the plaintiff was invoking, because the agency had not in fact promulgated a regulation with which that duty can be said to conflict? *Cf. Sprietsma*, 537 U.S. at 65 ("It is quite wrong to view [the agency's decision not to require propeller guards] as the functional equivalent of a regulation prohibiting all States and their political subdivisions from adopting such a regulation.").

NOTE ON "OBSTACLE" PREEMPTION

1. As *Geier* illustrates, conflict preemption is not limited to cases in which there is an out-and-out contradiction between state law and the terms of a federal statute. But specifying exactly how far conflict preemption reaches has not been easy.

Like many other cases on this topic, *Geier* referred back to Justice Black's opinion for the Supreme Court in *Hines v. Davidowitz*, 312 U.S. 52 (1941). As Justice Black noted, earlier cases about preemption had used various formulations to capture the circumstances in which federal law preempted state law. In some cases, the Court had merely spoken of "difference" between state and federal law, or had described federal law as "occupying the field." In other cases, the Court had found "repugnance," "irreconcilability," "inconsistency," or "interference" between state and federal law, or had described state law as "conflicting" with or "contrary to" federal law. In still other cases, the Court had referred to a "violation" or purported "curtailment" of federal law. According to Justice Black, "there can be no one crystal clear distinctly marked formula." *Id.* at 67. But Justice Black proceeded to offer a formula that judges have repeated ever since: "Our primary function is to determine whether, under the circumstances of this particular case, [state] law stands as an obstacle to the accomplishment and execution of the full purposes and objectives of Congress." *Id.*

What is the legal source of this test? In *Hines*, Justice Black arguably read the test into the Constitution itself. *See id.* (acknowledging the difficulty of supplying "an infallible constitutional test or an exclusive constitutional yardstick," but going on to articulate the obstacle formulation). In *Perez v. Campbell*, 402 U.S. 637 (1971), the Court likewise described the *Hines* formulation as an "articulation of the meaning of the Supremacy Clause." *Id.* at 649. On that view, "any state legislation which frustrates the full effectiveness of federal law is rendered invalid by the Supremacy Clause." *Id.* at 652.

But the text of the Supremacy Clause does not *have* to be read to incorporate the *Hines* formula, and history arguably supports a more modest understanding of the constitutional dimensions of preemption analysis. The Supremacy Clause makes the federal Constitution, federal statutes, and treaties "the supreme Law of the Land," and it declares that "the Judges in every State shall be bound thereby, any Thing in the Constitution or Laws of any State to the Contrary notwithstanding." U.S. CONST. art. VI, cl. 2. Thus, if a federal statute validly establishes a legal directive, state as well as federal courts must follow that directive in cases to which it applies (unless the directive is limited to the federal courts by its own terms). Although the Supremacy Clause focuses more on this point than on preemption *per se*, the courts' obligation to follow directives validly supplied by federal law sometimes will generate a corresponding obligation to disregard directives purportedly supplied by state law. That unquestionably happens when state and federal law each purport to supply a rule of decision for a case, but the two rules contradict each other. In that situation, the court cannot simply apply both rules of decision, so the court will have to choose between them, and the Supremacy Clause tells the court which one to pick; the fact that the court must apply the federal rule means that the court must disregard the state rule. The same is true when federal law itself addresses the authority of state law and validly limits the states' power to legislate on particular topics or in particular ways; in that situation too, giving legal effect to the federal directive (as the Supremacy Clause requires) will entail *not* giving effect to aspects of state law that transgress the limits validly established by federal law. But the Supremacy Clause need not be understood to have further implications for preemption. At least in my view, the mere fact that the practical effects of a particular state law might get in the way of accomplishing some goal associated with a federal statute does not *automatically* generate preemption simply by operation of the Supremacy Clause. *See* Caleb Nelson, *Preemption*, 86 VA. L. REV. 225, 234–76 (2000) (attempting to provide textual and historical support for this view).

That is not to say that courts should never find preemption under these circumstances. My point is simply that preemption under these circumstances does not flow directly from the Supremacy Clause itself. Before finding preemption on the theory that state law "stands as an obstacle to the accomplishment and execution of the full purposes and objectives of Congress," a court that accepted the argument in the previous paragraph would need to think more carefully about the directives that should be read into the particular federal statute in question. Specifically, the court would need to ask whether the relevant federal statute impliedly limits the validity of state laws with certain kinds of effects—state laws that would get in the way of accomplishing the purposes behind the federal statute. If the federal statute is indeed understood to establish such a directive, and if that directive is within Congress's power to establish, then the Supremacy Clause would come into play: the directive that the court has read into the federal statute would be just as binding as any other valid directive established by federal law, and it would preempt whatever state law it covers. But while the Supremacy Clause gives teeth to such directives, it does not itself supply their content.

In keeping with this view, the modern Supreme Court appears to have shifted away from attributing the *Hines* formula to the Supremacy Clause. The Court continues to invoke *Hines* for the proposition that courts should find preemption when state law "stands as an obstacle to the accomplishment and execution of the full purposes and objectives of Congress." Notwithstanding *Perez v. Campbell*, however, the Court now casts that formulation as a matter of statutory interpretation rather than constitutional law. Thus, the Court's unanimous opinion in *Barnett Bank of Marion County, N.A. v. Nelson*, 517 U.S. 25 (1996), observed that the preemptive scope of a federal statute "is basically [a question] of congressional intent" and described the *Hines* formula as a means of identifying "implicit[ ] pre-emptive intent." *Id.* at 30–31.[37] The Court has been speaking in these terms since the 1980s. *See, e.g.*, Nw. Cent. Pipeline Corp. v. State Corp. Comm'n, 489 U.S. 493, 509 (1989) ("In the absence of explicit statutory language signaling an intent to pre-empt [state law], we infer such intent where . . . the state law stands as an obstacle to the accomplishment and execution of congressional objectives . . . ."); *see also* Cal. Fed. Savs. & Loan Ass'n v. Guerra, 479 U.S. 272, 280 (1987) (plurality opinion of Marshall, J.) ("In determining whether a state statute is pre-empted by federal law and therefore invalid under the Supremacy Clause of the Constitution, our sole task is to ascertain the intent of Congress.").

2. Professor Merrill agrees that the Court's current framework for preemption analysis "attempts to assimilate preemption to ordinary statutory interpretation," but he argues that this way of talking

[37] The difference between this account of the *Hines* formulation and the account presented in *Perez v. Campbell* has to do with the nature of the directives that the Court imputes to Congress. If the Supremacy Clause itself incorporates the *Hines* formulation (as *Perez v. Campbell* suggested), then courts need not attribute any sort of "pre-emptive intent" to Congress in order to conclude that a federal statute has broad preemptive effects; the Supremacy Clause itself will nullify all state laws that stand as an obstacle to the accomplishment and execution of the statute's substantive purposes. On the other hand, if the *Hines* formulation is entirely a matter of statutory interpretation (as the modern Court suggests), then its applicability hinges on the courts' willingness to read a directive about preemption into each relevant federal statute. For the modern Court, that has typically entailed attributing some form of "pre-emptive intent" (actual or hypothesized) to the enacting Congress.

misdescribes what judges are actually doing. As he notes, "the key question in most preemption cases entails a discretionary judgment about the permissible degree of tension between federal and state law," and in his view that question "typically cannot be answered using the tools of statutory interpretation." Thomas W. Merrill, *Preemption and Institutional Choice*, 102 NW. U. L. REV. 727, 729 (2008). In particular, Professor Merrill suggests that in most cases of obstacle preemption, talk of Congress's "pre-emptive intent" is a fiction. According to Professor Merrill, when courts pretend that the answers are just a matter of "congressional intent," courts are "attributing to Congress judgments that are in fact grounded in judicial perceptions about the desirability of displacing state law in any given area." *Id.* at 741.

Of course, Professor Merrill acknowledges that courts use "conventional standards of interpretation" to determine the substantive meaning of the relevant federal statute, and in that inquiry "the intent or purpose of Congress is key." *Id.* at 743. In Professor Merrill's telling, though, courts then make their own judgments about whether any tension between state law and the goals that courts have attributed to Congress "is sufficiently severe to warrant the displacement of state law." Those judgments draw on a variety of factors, including both "the pragmatics of the particular issue under consideration" and "larger traditions about the appropriate division of authority between the federal government and the states." *Id.* Ultimately, the courts are trying to carry out the purposes reflected in the federal statute, not the courts' own policy preferences. But the courts are not simply seeking to capture some pre-existing preemptive intent already formulated in the minds of members of Congress.

Professor Merrill suggests that this is as it should be: Congress is not in a position to reach sensible decisions about preemption at the time that it enacts federal statutes, and the courts' framework for preemption analysis should not insist that Congress try to do so. *See id.* at 754 (emphasizing that "Congress cannot predict at the time it legislates every question of federal preemption that will arise in the future," and adding that advance analysis of those questions would also require an "impossible" level of knowledge about the present and future legal rules of "fifty states and thousands of municipalities"); *see also supra* pp. 1100–1101 (noting Professor Stabile's similar arguments against the inclusion of express preemption clauses in federal statutes); Daniel J. Meltzer, *The Supreme Court's Judicial Passivity*, 2002 SUP. CT. REV. 343, 376 ("Preemption issues present a particularly strong case for a robust judicial role."). But even if it might be desirable for courts to make discretionary judgments about preemption, what authorizes the courts to do so? If the types of federal law listed in the Supremacy Clause do not themselves dictate preemption, what makes state law inoperative?

Perhaps one could answer this question by arguing that obstacle preemption is largely a matter of statutory interpretation, but that it (legitimately) entails a different *style* of interpretation than modern courts usually use. For instance, even if some of the preemptive effects currently attributed to federal statutes are hard to attribute to any *actual* "pre-emptive intent" consciously formed by members of the enacting Congress, perhaps those effects could be defended in terms of the sort of *hypothesized* legislative intent that Chapter 1 discussed under the rubric of "imaginative reconstruction." On this way of thinking, obstacle preemption might reflect the courts' judgments about how far reasonable members of the enacting Congress would have wanted the preemptive effects of the relevant federal statute to go if they had specifically addressed preemption, given the purposes that they were trying to achieve and given ordinary patterns in the relations between the federal government and the states.

On many topics, of course, the modern Supreme Court has rejected aggressive forms of imaginative reconstruction. *See, e.g.*, Republic of Argentina v. Weltover, Inc., 504 U.S. 607, 618 (1992) ("The question . . . is not what Congress 'would have wanted' but what Congress enacted . . . ."). But if the barriers to sensible *ex ante* legislation about preemption are higher than the barriers to sensible *ex ante* legislation about other topics, might one argue that courts should be more willing to engage in imaginative reconstruction with respect to the preemptive effects of federal statutes than with respect to other policy questions? After all, if it is true that Congress cannot realistically be expected to specify the preemptive scope of its statutes at the time of enactment, perhaps courts should not insist upon such specification.

In other areas in which advance specification might be especially difficult, the Supreme Court has sometimes been willing to use imaginative reconstruction to help answer questions that Congress was not in a good position to anticipate. At least in the past, for instance, that is how the Court often spoke about the separability of federal statutes—a topic that arises when judges identify potentially unexpected constitutional problems with some aspects or applications of a statute. *See* Chapter 2.D.1; *see also, e.g.*, Miller v. Albright, 523 U.S. 420, 457 (1998) (Scalia, J., concurring in the judgment) (observing that the Court decides separability questions "on the basis of the Court's assessment as to whether Congress would have enacted the remainder of the law without the invalidated provision"). *But see* Barr v. Am. Ass'n of Political Consultants, 140 S. Ct. 2335, 2350 (2020) (plurality opinion of Kavanaugh, J.) (criticizing this approach to separability). Likewise, the Court has used imaginative reconstruction to identify the details of implied rights of action that precedents have read into federal statutes but that members of the enacting Congress probably did not anticipate. *See, e.g.*, Musick, Peeler & Garrett v. Employers Ins. of Wausau, 508 U.S. 286, 294 (1993) ("Our task is . . . to attempt to infer how the 1934 Congress would have addressed the issue had the 10b–5 action been included as an express provision in the 1934 Act."); *see also* Gebser v.

Lago Vista Indep. School Dist., 524 U.S. 274, 284–85 (1998) (undertaking a similar analysis with respect to the private right of action that the Court has read into Title IX of the Education Amendments of 1972).

Should preemption be another realm in which courts deploy imaginative reconstruction more readily than usual? Alternatively, without using the rhetoric of imaginative reconstruction, could one defend an approach that imputes preemptive effects to federal statutes on the basis of a more purposivist analysis than interpreters use in other areas? *Cf.* Note, *Preemption as Purposivism's Last Refuge*, 126 HARV. L. REV. 1056 (2013) (suggesting that the Supreme Court does indeed take a more purposivist approach to preemption than to other questions of statutory interpretation, though arguing that the Court should not do so). Whatever label one uses, a court conducting this sort of analysis would ask what the decisions reflected in the statutory text (and, perhaps, the publicly available legislative history) suggest for the interplay between the federal statute and state law. In the absence of more specific indications of the enacting Congress's preemptive intent, the court would consider the context in which Congress was acting and the policy goals that Congress apparently was trying to advance, as well as more general assumptions about relations between the states and the federal government, and the court would try to decide how far a reasonable legislator in that milieu would have wanted the preemptive effects of the statute to extend. In particular, the court would ask itself whether a reasonable legislator who shared the enacting Congress's mix of policy objectives would have favored preempting state laws of the sort at issue.

This way of describing preemption analysis arguably captures both (1) the influence of Congress's substantive purposes on the courts' decisions about preemption and (2) the type of "discretionary policy judgment" that Professor Merrill sees the courts as making under the rubric of preemption. *See* Merrill, *supra*, 102 NW. U. L. REV. at 741–44. It also reflects how the Supreme Court itself has sometimes talked about preemption. *See, e.g., Felder v. Casey*, 487 U.S. 131, 149 (1988) ("[W]e think it plain that the Congress which enacted § 1983 over 100 years ago would have rejected as utterly inconsistent with the remedial purposes of its broad statute the notion that a State could require civil rights victims to seek compensation from offending state officials before they could assert a federal action in state court.").

If the *Hines* formulation rests on this sort of approach, though, doesn't it go too far (at least if one takes it literally)? Suppose that a bill pending in Congress included an express preemption clause along the lines that *Hines* suggests: "No state may enact or enforce any law or policy—no matter what interests it serves, and whatever form it takes—to the extent that such state law or policy stands as an obstacle to the accomplishment and execution of the full purposes and objectives behind this Act." In many contexts, wouldn't you expect Congress to reject such sweeping language and to replace it with something more muted? Even members of Congress who support the bill's substantive purposes would not necessarily want to displace each and every state law whose practical effects might get in the way of those purposes. *Cf.* Rodriguez v. United States, 480 U.S. 522, 525–26 (1987) (observing, in a different setting, that "no legislation pursues its purposes at all costs" and "it frustrates rather than effectuates legislative intent simplistically to assume that whatever furthers the statute's primary objective must be the law"). Does it follow that the *Hines* formulation should be recast in more cautious language? *See, e.g.*, Crosby v. National Foreign Trade Council, 530 U.S. 363, 373 (2000) ("What is a sufficient obstacle [for purposes of the *Hines* formula] is a matter of judgment, to be informed by examining the federal statute as a whole and identifying its purposes and intended effects."). Or can purposivists and supporters of imaginative reconstruction retain the *Hines* formulation as is, subject to the understanding that "the full purposes and objectives of Congress" often include the purpose of not interfering too much with legitimate state interests?

3. Even if you think that the difficulty of specifying the preemptive effects of federal statutes in advance makes it appropriate for courts to engage in something like imaginative reconstruction on preemption questions, what limits would you put on this approach? Are there circumstances in which courts should not care what preemptive effects Congress might have wanted a particular federal statute to have, because the statute itself does not say enough to provide a foundation for those effects?

Consider *Puerto Rico Department of Consumer Affairs v. Isla Petroleum Corp.*, 485 U.S. 495 (1988). In 1973, in the midst of the oil crisis generated by OPEC's embargo on exports to the United States, Congress directed the President to promulgate regulations about the pricing and allocation of petroleum products within the United States. *See* Emergency Petroleum Allocation Act of 1973, Pub. L. 93–159, 87 Stat. 627. The 1973 statute expressly preempted certain state-law provisions to the extent that they conflicted with the President's regulations. *Id.* § 6(b), 87 Stat. at 633. At first, the President's regulatory authority was set to expire in fifteen months, but Congress ended up extending it on a temporary basis. In 1975, however, Congress provided for the President to lose his regulatory authority as of September 30, 1981. *See* Energy Policy and Conservation Act, Pub. L. 94–163, § 461, 89 Stat. 871, 955 (1975). Pursuant to the 1975 statute, the federal regulatory authority initially conferred by the 1973 statute did indeed expire in 1981. After that date, Puerto Rican authorities promulgated their own regulations of petroleum pricing in Puerto Rico. In response, oil companies filed lawsuits arguing that the 1975 federal statute should be understood to preempt such regulations (whether adopted by state and local governments or by Puerto Rico). According to the oil companies, legislative history established that the purpose behind Congress's elimination of federal regulatory authority had been to secure "a free market in petroleum products," and regulations adopted at the state or local level would stand as an obstacle to the accomplishment of this deregulatory purpose. Without recorded dissent, however, Justice Scalia's opinion for the Supreme Court dismissed that argument as irrelevant:

> "While we have frequently said that pre-emption analysis requires ascertaining congressional intent, . . . we have never meant that to signify congressional intent in a vacuum, unrelated to the giving of meaning to an enacted statutory text. There is no text here . . . to which expressions of pre-emptive intent in legislative history might attach. [The oil companies] have brought to our attention statements that may reflect general congressional approval of a free market in petroleum products, or general congressional belief that such a market would result from enactment of the [1975 statute], or even general congressional desire that it result. But unenacted approvals, beliefs, and desires are not laws. Without a text that can, in light of those statements, plausibly be interpreted as *prescribing* federal pre-emption it is impossible to find that a free market was mandated by federal law."

Isla Petroleum, 485 U.S. at 501. In other words, even assuming that the oil companies were right about the purpose behind the 1975 statute, and even assuming that members of the enacting Congress would have favored preemption under the circumstances of the *Isla Petroleum* case, Justice Scalia was still unwilling to find preemption, because the 1975 statute contained "no text . . . to which expressions of pre-emptive intent in legislative history might attach."

Should we conclude that inferences about conflict preemption work differently when a federal statute manifests a deregulatory purpose than when it manifests a regulatory purpose? Or does *Isla Petroleum* suggest a broader limitation on the relevance of Congress's "pre-emptive intent" (whether actual or hypothesized through imaginative reconstruction)?

Alternatively, might *Isla Petroleum* simply reflect the difference between "unenacted" preemption clauses and the implications of the statutes that Congress really did enact? Even supporters of imaginative reconstruction do not think a statute should be understood to include all provisions that members of the enacting Congress would have favored if those provisions had been proposed. Instead, imaginative reconstruction can be seen as a rhetorical device for use in interpreting the provisions that Congress did indeed enact. In *Isla Petroleum*, those provisions did not lend much support to the oil companies' argument; reasonable legislators could readily have supported both the 1973 statute (which reacted to a crisis by authorizing federal regulation) and the 1975 statute (which set an expiration date for that authority) without favoring the broad preemptive effects that the oil companies later advocated. As a matter of subjective policy preferences, of course, it is possible that some members of Congress in 1975 would have supported a broad preemption clause if one had been proposed. But the legislation that they actually enacted, even if interpreted in a purposivist manner, neither contained nor implied such a clause. Is that all that the Court was saying in *Isla Petroleum*?

4. In his separate opinion in *Wyeth v. Levine*, 555 U.S. 555 (2009), Justice Thomas announced that "I can no longer assent to a doctrine that pre-empts state laws merely because they 'stan[d] as an obstacle to the accomplishment and execution of the full purposes and objectives' of federal law, as perceived by this Court." *Id.* at 604 (Thomas, J., concurring in the judgment) (citation omitted) (quoting *Hines*, 312 U.S. at 67). Justice Thomas harked back to a concern once expressed by Justice Kennedy: "A freewheeling judicial inquiry into whether a state statute is in tension with federal objectives would undercut the principle that it is Congress rather than the courts that pre-empts state law." *Gade v. Nat'l Solid Waste Mgmt. Ass'n*, 505 U.S. 88, 111 (1992) (Kennedy, J., concurring in part and concurring in the judgment).[38] Justice Thomas saw the majority opinion in *Geier* as an example of this problem. In his words, "Applying 'purposes and objectives' pre-emption in *Geier*, as in any case, allowed this Court to vacate a judgment issued by another sovereign based on nothing more than assumptions and goals that were untethered from the constitutionally enacted federal law authorizing the federal regulatory standard that was before the Court." *Wyeth*, 555 U.S. at 600 (Thomas, J., concurring in the judgment); *see also id.* at 587 ("Under the vague and 'potentially boundless' doctrine of 'purposes and objectives' pre-emption, *Geier*[, 529 U.S. at 907] (Stevens, J., dissenting), . . . the Court has pre-empted state law based on its interpretation of broad federal policy objectives, legislative history, or generalized notions of congressional purposes that are not contained within the text of federal law.").

In place of the *Hines* formulation, Justice Thomas argued that "[p]re-emption must turn on whether state law conflicts with the text of the relevant federal statute or with the federal regulations authorized by that text." *Id.* at 588. If a federal statute (or a regulation promulgated under statutory authority) is properly understood to establish a particular legal directive, and if that directive is valid, then aspects of state law that "directly conflict" with it are preempted by operation of the Supremacy Clause. *See id.* at 589. But Justice Thomas suggested that where there is no such "direct conflict" between state law and a legal directive that is properly imputed (through the ordinary techniques of interpretation) to a valid federal statute or regulation, there is nothing to preempt the rules of decision supplied by state law, and those rules remain in force. *See id.* at 593; *see also id.* at 587–88 ("Congressional and agency musings . . . do not satisfy the [constitutional] requirements for enactment of federal law and, therefore, do not pre-empt state law under

[38] To be clear, Justice Kennedy himself did not repudiate the *Hines* formulation.

the Supremacy Clause."); *cf.* Viet D. Dinh, *Reassessing the Law of Preemption*, 88 GEO. L.J. 2085, 2104 (2000) ("The operation of obstacle preemption significantly differs from express or conflict preemption because there is no direct conflict with any federal law precisely on point—for example, either [a] preemption provision or a primary regulatory provision.").

If Justice Thomas had his way, preemption analysis would indeed become what Professor Merrill calls "a routine exercise in statutory interpretation." *See* Merrill, *supra*, 102 NW. U. L. REV. at 742 (arguing that the Court's rhetoric falsely describes preemption in these terms). According to Justice Thomas, courts should use the ordinary tools of statutory interpretation to identify the legal directives that a federal statute establishes, and they should not take it upon themselves to expand the statute's preemptive effects beyond whatever aspects of state law "directly conflict" with those directives.

For a time, Justice Thomas was the only Justice who rejected what he calls " 'purposes and objectives' pre-emption." *Compare* AT&T Mobility LLC v. Concepcion, 563 U.S. 333, 352 (2011) (Scalia, J.) (finding preemption under the *Hines* formulation), *with id.* at 353 (Thomas, J., concurring). More recently, though, Justice Gorsuch has joined Justice Thomas's position. *See* Kansas v. Garcia, 140 S. Ct. 791, 807–08 (2020) (Thomas, J., concurring).

5. When we covered express preemption, we saw that Justices have debated whether to apply a presumption against preemption when interpreting preemption clauses. *See supra* pp. 1097–1099. Similarly, Justices have debated whether the presumption against preemption is relevant in conflict-preemption cases. In *Wyeth v. Levine*, Justice Stevens's majority opinion invoked " 'the assumption that the historic police powers of the States were not to be superseded by the Federal Act unless that was the clear and manifest purpose of Congress,' " *Wyeth*, 555 U.S. at 565 (quoting *Medtronic, Inc. v. Lohr*, 518 U.S. 470, 485 (1996), in turn quoting *Rice v. Santa Fe Elevator Corp.*, 331 U.S. 218, 230 (1947)),[39] and the majority asserted that the Court's analysis of conflict preemption "must be guided by [this] cornerstone[ ] of our pre-emption jurisprudence." *Id.* But Justice Alito's dissent appeared to disagree. *See id.* at 623–24 (Alito, J., dissenting). In warring footnotes, the majority and the dissenters disputed the lessons of precedent on this point.

---

[39] As used in *Rice v. Santa Fe Elevator Corp.*, the passage that Justice Stevens was quoting may simply have expressed the Court's reluctance to infer *field* preemption in fields that states have traditionally occupied. *See Rice*, 331 U.S. at 230 ("Congress legislated here in a field which the States have traditionally occupied. So we start with the assumption that the historic police powers of the States were not to be superseded by the Federal Act unless that was the clear and manifest purpose of Congress." (citations omitted)); *see also id.* (supporting this assumption by citing *Napier v. Atlantic Coast Line R.R. Co.*, 272 U.S. 605, 611 (1926), and *Allen-Bradley Local No. 1111 v. Wisc. Employment Rel. Bd.*, 315 U.S. 740, 749 (1942), both of which were about field preemption). But in *Medtronic, Inc. v. Lohr* (which itself was about express preemption), Justice Stevens's majority opinion indicated that the *Rice* presumption applies "[i]n all pre-emption cases." *Medtronic*, 518 U.S. at 485.

Compare id. at 566 n.3 (majority opinion) ("[T]he dissent argues that the presumption against pre-emption should not apply to claims of implied conflict pre-emption at all, . . . but this Court has long held to the contrary.") *with id.* at 624 n.14 (Alito, J., dissenting) ("[T]he Court has sometimes acknowledged a limited 'presumption against pre-emption,' but it nonetheless remained an open question—before today—whether that presumption applied in conflict pre-emption cases.").

Proper analysis of this question may require courts to draw some distinctions. First, courts might need to distinguish questions about the substantive content of federal law (including questions about whether a federal statute establishes a directive that would contradict some aspect of state law) from questions about the scope of obstacle preemption. Second, with respect to questions about the substantive content of federal law, courts might need to distinguish an across-the-board presumption against preemption (which, in my view, could be defended only on "normative" grounds) from more limited presumptions that are grounded in Congress's actual patterns of legislation and that therefore have "descriptive" justifications.

Start with the first distinction. The scope of conflict preemption obviously depends in part on the substantive meaning that courts attribute to federal statutes; in areas as to which states have concurrent lawmaking power, broader interpretations of federal statutes will potentially contradict more state law (and hence will generate more preemption simply by operation of the Supremacy Clause) than narrower interpretations. But few people think that courts should systematically interpret all substantive directives in federal statutes as narrowly as possible, so that they have the smallest scope and leave the maximum room for state law. In this respect, at least, courts do not apply a presumption against conflict preemption.

Indeed, I have argued that the Supremacy Clause itself cuts against any such artificial canon. The final fourteen words of the Supremacy Clause—specifying that federal law is binding "any Thing in the Constitution or Laws of any State to the Contrary notwithstanding"—are what eighteenth-century lawyers called a *non obstante* provision. At the time, statutory drafters often used such provisions to turn off the presumption against implied repeals, so that interpreters would not adopt artificially narrow readings of the laws covered by the provisions in order to avoid contradicting (and thereby impliedly repealing) other laws. *See* Nelson, *supra,* 86 VA. L. REV. at 235–44. Similarly, the *non obstante* provision in the Supremacy Clause tells interpreters not to read federal statutes artificially narrowly simply to avoid contradicting (and thereby preempting) state laws. *See id.* at 293 ("To the extent permitted by state law, courts are certainly free to alter their construction of *state* law in order to harmonize it with federal law. But the mere fact that a particular interpretation of federal law would contradict . . . a state law is not, in and of itself, reason to seek a different interpretation of the *federal* law.").[40]

Of course, the fact that courts should not read all federal statutes narrowly, simply to minimize their potential for conflict with state law, does not prevent courts from using canons that are grounded in Congress's actual practices and that cut against preemption in particular contexts. (This point relates to the second distinction mentioned above.) If Congress has hitherto left a certain field to the states, and if a new federal statute is ambiguous about whether it says anything in that field, Congress's pattern of staying out of the field can inform how the court resolves the ambiguity. *See* Nelson, *supra*, 86 VA. L. REV. at 294. More generally, if it would be unusual for Congress to establish a particular substantive directive, and if a federal statute can fairly be interpreted to establish a different directive that would better fit Congress's established practices, the latter interpretation might well be best. On the other hand, if a federal statute does indeed enter a field that Congress has traditionally left to the states, the fact that the statute breaks new ground does not necessarily mean that courts should interpret its substantive directives as narrowly as possible. *Cf. supra* pp. 1099–1100 (doubting that there is much "descriptive" justification for applying a presumption against preemption to express preemption clauses).

In my view, a presumption against preemption has more work to do in the context of obstacle preemption—not when the courts are deciding what substantive directives in federal statutes mean, but when courts are deciding whether state law interferes with the purposes behind those directives to such an extent as to justify inferring preemption. As noted above, current doctrine arguably invites courts to make such decisions on the basis of something like imaginative reconstruction; as part of identifying the "pre-emptive intent" that should be imputed to a particular federal statute, judges ask themselves whether a reasonable legislator who accepted the statute's policy objectives would want to preempt the state law in question. In the words of Justice Stevens's dissent in *Geier*, that inquiry is "potentially boundless," and the presumption against preemption "serves as a limiting principle" on it. *Geier*, 529 U.S. at 907 (Stevens, J., dissenting).

Exactly how this limiting principle works is open to debate. But if obstacle preemption amounts to an exercise in imaginative reconstruction, the presumption against preemption could relate to the level of confidence that judges need before they attribute "pre-emptive intent" to Congress on the basis of a federal statute's purposes and objectives. If judges engage in imaginative reconstruction *without* a presumption against preemption, they might infer preemption whenever

[40] In *PLIVA, Inc. v. Mensing*, 564 U.S. 604 (2011), a plurality of the Supreme Court endorsed this argument. *See id.* at 621–23. In Justice Thomas's words (joined on this point by Chief Justice Roberts and Justices Scalia and Alito), "The *non obstante* provision in the Supremacy Clause . . . suggests that courts should not strain to find ways to reconcile federal law with seemingly conflicting state law." *Id.* at 622.

it seems more likely than not that members of the enacting Congress (or, alternatively, reasonable legislators who favored the federal statute's purposes and objectives) would have wanted to preempt the state laws in question. By contrast, if judges apply a presumption against preemption, they might find obstacle preemption only when they are quite confident—or even almost certain—that supporters of the federal statute would indeed have favored preemption notwithstanding the countervailing state interests. That could matter; the judgments that obstacle preemption entails are not cut-and-dried, and the level of confidence that courts demand will affect the frequency with which courts infer such preemption.

Although Justices Thomas and Gorsuch are the only members of the Supreme Court who have categorically opposed obstacle preemption, some other Justices may support approaching obstacle-preemption arguments with a presumption against preemption. In keeping with *Rice v. Santa Fe Elevator Corp.*, that may be particularly true in fields that that the states have traditionally regulated. *See, e.g.*, Egelhoff v. Egelhoff, 532 U.S. 141, 156–57 (2001) (Breyer, J., dissenting) (arguing that to justify finding obstacle preemption with respect to a state statute about family property law, "petitioner has to overcome a strong presumption *against* pre-emption").

C. FEDERAL STATUTES AND "GENERAL" LAW

The final aspect of federalism covered in this chapter concerns the relationship between federal statutes and what has sometimes been called "general common law" or just "general law."[41] In the wake of *Erie Railroad Co. v. Tompkins*, 304 U.S. 64 (1938), that label has fallen into disrepute. But the concept that the label reflects remains relevant to the interpretation of certain terms in federal statutes. The same concept can also come into play when a federal statute prevents state law from governing certain questions but does not itself supply all of the necessary answers. More precisely, unwritten "general" law can potentially supply rules of decision when all three of the following conditions are satisfied: (1) a federal statute preempts state law with respect to some set of questions, (2) the statute does not itself supply substitute rules of decision for each and every one of those questions, and (3) the statute

[41] In modern scholarship, the seminal treatment of the historical conception of the general common law is William A. Fletcher, *The General Common Law and Section 34 of the Judiciary Act of 1789: The Example of Marine Insurance*, 97 HARV. L. REV. 1513 (1984). As Judge Fletcher explains, American lawyers of the early nineteenth century did not routinely use the label "general common law," and indeed would have detected "a redundancy" in that label; in their usage, " 'common law' *was* a general common law shared by the American states rather than a local common law of a particular state." *Id.* at 1515 n.9 (emphasis added). Now that we think of different states as having different common laws, though, the label "general common law" draws a useful contrast with the common law of any particular state.

either implicitly incorporates "general" law or at least does not prevent "general" law from supplementing what the statute says.[42]

To understand this topic, you must first get past some misconceptions. Many modern lawyers associate the concept of "general" law entirely with a particular vision of the relationship between state and federal courts—a vision that prevailed throughout the nineteenth century, but that *Erie* discarded. Under the regime of *Swift v. Tyson*, 41 U.S. (16 Pet.) 1 (1842), federal courts would defer to the settled decisions of a state's highest court about the content of the state's "local" law, including the meaning of provisions in the state's written laws and the content of special local usages that had the force of law. Conversely, state courts would defer to the settled decisions of the United States Supreme Court about the meaning of written federal laws, such as the federal Constitution and federal statutes. But on questions that were not governed by any written enactments (whether state or federal) and that were classified as matters of "general" law (rather than being controlled by special local usages), each set of courts could make its own assessment of the content of the governing legal principles. With respect to such questions, federal courts were not bound by a state supreme court's view of the general law, and state courts were not bound by the United States Supreme Court's view of the general law.[43]

When nineteenth-century courts said that a particular question was one of "general" law, they meant that the governing legal principles were not associated exclusively with a particular sovereign. Unlike special usages adopted by the people of one particular locality, principles of "general" law drew upon sources that crossed jurisdictional lines. In commercial matters, for instance, merchants in different jurisdictions might all follow the same custom, and their respective obligations in connection with a transaction might best be understood in light of that custom. Even when custom did not dictate a rule on some point, reason might; one possible legal rule might be better suited to the needs of commerce, or more consistent with other recognized principles of commercial law, than the possible alternatives. Once the courts of various jurisdictions had started issuing opinions about a particular question of general law, moreover, later courts in other jurisdictions could get some sense of the applicable legal rules simply by amalgamating the past opinions and identifying the common principles or themes in the rules that respected jurists across the world had recognized as law.

---

[42] Apart from areas of *statutory* preemption, the same phenomenon can occur in areas where the Constitution itself displaces state law. *See* Alfred Hill, *The Law-Making Power of the Federal Courts: Constitutional Preemption*, 67 COLUM. L. REV. 1024 (1967); Caleb Nelson, *The Persistence of General Law*, 106 COLUM. L. REV. 503, 507–19 (2006). In theory, indeed, a federal treaty could have the same effect. Given the focus of this course, though, this chapter concentrates on federal statutes.

[43] For a more elaborate description of these arrangements and their perceived basis, see Caleb Nelson, *A Critical Guide to* Erie Railroad Co. v. Tompkins, 54 WM. & MARY L. REV. 921, 924–49 (2013).

Within the United States, of course, the authority of the general law in any particular state depended largely upon the sovereign decisions of that state. On many questions, a state that wanted to deviate from the general law could do so simply by enacting a statute that prescribed a different rule. But to the extent that each of the American states had received the general law into their jurisprudence and had not enacted local statutes deviating from it, the various court systems within the United States could all be thought of as engaging in a common project of trying to articulate the content of that law.

This way of thinking figured prominently in *Swift v. Tyson*. The specific legal question in that case concerned the defenses that Tyson could use to avoid payment on a particular kind of negotiable instrument (called a bill of exchange) that had been endorsed over to Swift. In modern terms, the question was whether Swift qualified as a "holder in due course" of the instrument: had he given up valuable consideration for it, such that he could collect on it without regard to defenses that Tyson could have used against the endorser? At the time of *Swift v. Tyson*, views about what counted as "valuable consideration" for this purpose were in flux. State courts in New York, where Tyson had executed the instrument, arguably took a restrictive view. But as Justice Story emphasized in *Swift v. Tyson*, New York courts had not based that view on anything particular to New York (such as local statutes or usages). Instead, the New York courts had simply been trying to do the same thing that other courts did when faced with this sort of issue—"to ascertain upon general reasoning and legal analogies . . . what is the just rule furnished by the principles of commercial law to govern the case." *Swift*, 41 U.S. (16 Pet.) at 19. To the extent that precedents helped to identify that rule, moreover, the relevant precedents came not just from New York, but from courts throughout the United States and indeed the commercial world more broadly. For Justice Story, it followed that federal courts did not have to accept the potentially idiosyncratic view of the New York state courts about the type of "valuable consideration" that satisfied the holder-in-due-course doctrine. Instead, each court system was free to apply its own best understanding of the principles of the general commercial law on this point.

A century later, the Supreme Court overruled this understanding of the relationship between state and federal courts. Justice Brandeis's majority opinion in *Erie* held that when the federal courts address issues over which the states have lawmaking authority, the federal courts normally must follow the rules declared by a state's supreme court to the same extent that federal courts would follow identical rules declared by the state's legislature. Conversely, when state courts address questions of domestic law that lie beyond the reach of state law (because a federal statute, a treaty, or the Constitution itself preempts state law with respect to these questions) but that written federal law does not answer, state courts are supposed to follow the rules declared by the federal

Supreme Court. *See generally* Henry J. Friendly, *In Praise of* Erie*—and of the New Federal Common Law*, 39 N.Y.U. L. REV. 383, 405–22 (1964) (discussing "the emergence of a federal decisional law in areas of national concern that is truly uniform"). Both of these principles apply without regard to whether the legal questions at issue would previously have been characterized as matters of "general" law.

After *Erie*, when New York's highest court takes a position on a question that would previously have been classified as one of "general" law, we no longer say that the court is simply expressing its understanding of principles of general law. Rather than thinking of each state's highest court as articulating its view of a law that is common to all states, we describe each state's highest court as articulating the law of that particular state. Where past jurists might have spoken simply of "the common law," we speak of "the common law of New York" and "the common law of California." Conversely, on questions that Congress or the Constitution has federalized but that written federal law does not answer, we speak of courts as articulating rules of "*federal* common law."

Notwithstanding the different geographic labels, though, these various bodies of unwritten law still closely resemble each other in content: on a wide variety of issues, the common law of Michigan is not dramatically different than the common law of Illinois. As a result, it remains possible for modern lawyers and judges, drawing upon precedents and practices followed in the various American states, to distill rules that might be regarded as matters of "general" law. To be sure, such rules do not necessarily have the force of law on their own. But even if they do not, we can still coherently speak of common themes and patterns in the principles that diverse jurisdictions recognize as law.

Various modern practices rely on that premise. In cases of first impression, for instance, courts articulating rules of common law for a particular state routinely consult precedents from other jurisdictions, and they usually seem inclined to follow the general current of those precedents. Federal courts do much the same thing when trying to predict how the supreme court of a particular state might handle some issue on which it has not yet taken a position. *See, e.g.*, Hisrich v. Volvo Cars of N. Am., Inc., 226 F.3d 445, 449 n.3 (6th Cir. 2000) (noting the relevance of "restatements of law . . . and the majority rule among other states" in this situation). By statute, indeed, some American legislatures that sit outside any particular state have explicitly adopted something like general American law as their baseline. *See, e.g.*, V.I. Code Ann. tit. 1, § 4 ("The rules of the common law, as expressed in the restatements of the law approved by the American Law Institute, and to the extent not so expressed, as generally understood and applied in the United States, shall be the rules of decision in the courts of the Virgin Islands in cases to which they apply, in the absence of local laws to the contrary."); 7 N. Mar. I. Code § 3401 ("In all proceedings, the rules of the common law, as expressed in the restatements of the law approved by the American Law

Institute and, to the extent not so expressed as generally understood and applied in the United States, shall be the rules of decision in the courts of the Commonwealth, in the absence of written law or local customary law to the contrary . . . .").[44]

If it is indeed still coherent to refer to "general" law, moreover, then modern legislatures might sometimes act against the backdrop that this sort of law supplies. To be sure, modern *state* legislatures probably do not do so very often; if the legislature of New York enacts a state statute that appears to incorporate background doctrines of common law, it is natural to assume that the legislature had New York's particular version of the common law in mind. But *federal* statutes that appear to incorporate background concepts of common law raise a broader range of interpretive possibilities. There are many situations in which Congress might want to refer to some sort of national law on topics that typically are handled at the state level. The concept of "general" law, which reflects common themes and patterns in the doctrines that are now elaborated under the rubric of the law of each American state, fits that bill. On certain kinds of questions that a federal statute puts beyond the reach of state law but does not itself address and answer, courts might sensibly presume that the statute either implicitly incorporates principles of "general" law or leaves room for those principles to operate of their own force.

Although this phenomenon has received little systematic attention, it is not just a theoretical possibility. To the contrary, the modern Supreme Court has repeatedly read federal statutes to incorporate exactly this sort of "general" law. *See, e.g.*, Field v. Mans, 516 U.S. 59, 70 n.9 (1995) (reading the term "fraud" in § 523(a)(2)(A) of the Bankruptcy Code to refer to a concept supplied by "the general common law of torts, the dominant consensus of common-law jurisdictions"); Community for Creative Non-Violence v. Reid, 490 U.S. 730, 740–41 (1989) (taking the term "employee" in the Copyright Act's definition of the phrase "work made for hire" to refer to "the general common law of agency, rather than . . . the law of any particular State"); *see also* Caleb Nelson, *The Persistence of General Law*, 106 COLUM. L. REV. 503 (2006).

This section of the Casebook considers when that conclusion might be appropriate. It begins by canvassing the various approaches that courts might take when a federal statute uses a term that the statute does not usefully define, but that resonates in common-law doctrines usually elaborated under the rubric of state law. The section then

[44] For different views of the legal effect that these statutes give the American Law Institute's Restatements, compare *Estate of Ogumoro v. Ko*, 2011 MP 11, ¶ 64 (N. Mar. I.) ("[W]e hold that the Restatements are the operative rules of decision in the Commonwealth, even when the relevant provision does not accord with United States common law."), with *Banks v. Int'l Rental & Leasing Corp.*, 55 V.I. 967, 973–80 (2011) (denying that 1 V.I.C. § 4 requires the Supreme Court of the Virgin Islands "to treat the Restatements as if they are statutes," and adding that "because our own decisions constitute 'local law' within the meaning of section 4 . . . we therefore possess the discretion to decline to follow the most recent Restatement provision").

considers some other ways in which principles of general American law might operate in conjunction with federal statutes.

1. INTERPRETING FEDERAL STATUTES THAT USE TERMS FAMILIAR TO STATE LAW

Federal statutes often use terms that are familiar to state law (or to the common law more generally). Sometimes Congress specifically defines those terms. But when Congress does not specify how it is using such a term, courts have to answer a series of recurring questions. As the term is used in the federal statute, should it be understood to piggyback upon varying rules of state law, so that the meaning of the term in any particular case comes from the law of the state in which the events relevant to the case occurred? Or should Congress instead be understood to have used the term in a more uniform sense? If the term *is* understood to have a nationally uniform meaning, should courts identify that meaning by reference to the sort of "general" law described above,[45] or should courts instead devise a statute-specific definition of the term that is influenced more by the apparent purposes behind the federal statute than by common themes in state law?

The following materials provide examples of each of these possibilities.

a. THE POSSIBILITY THAT A TERM IN A FEDERAL STATUTE MIGHT BE A MERE PLACEHOLDER FOR DEFINITIONS SUPPLIED BY THE LAW OF INDIVIDUAL STATES

It is unusual for courts to understand a term in a federal statute as being a mere placeholder for varying definitions supplied by the local law of individual states. As the next case shows, though, that approach is not entirely unheard of.

The case concerned the meaning of the phrase "real property" in § 10 of the federal Reconstruction Finance Corporation Act, ch. 8, 47 Stat. 5 (1932). Enacted during the Great Depression, that Act created the Reconstruction Finance Corporation (RFC), a government-owned corporation that Congress authorized to make loans to banks and similar entities. As originally enacted in 1932, the relevant portion of § 10 read as follows:

> "The [Reconstruction Finance Corporation] . . . shall be exempt from all taxation now or hereafter imposed by the United States, by any Territory . . . thereof, or by any State, county, municipality, or local taxing authority; except that any real property of the corporation

[45] To the extent that the "general" law has changed over time, courts that take this route may need to answer some further questions. Should they research how the term was traditionally used at common law, how the term tended to be used in state law at the time that the federal statute was enacted, or how the term tends to be used in state law at the time that they are applying the statute?

shall be subject to State, Territorial, county, municipal, or local taxation to the same extent according to its value as other real property is taxed."

Id. § 10, 47 Stat. at 9–10. In 1941, Congress appended the following language to this provision:

"The exemptions provided for in the preceding sentence with respect to taxation (which shall, for all purposes, be deemed to include sales, use, storage, and purchase taxes) shall be construed to be applicable not only with respect to the Reconstruction Finance Corporation but also with respect to . . . the Defense Plant Corporation . . . and [various other entities affiliated with the Reconstruction Finance Corporation] . . . . Such exemptions shall also be construed to be applicable to the loans made, and personal property owned, by the Reconstruction Finance Corporation or by any [of the covered affiliates, including the Defense Plant Corporation] . . . , but such exemptions shall not be construed to be applicable in any State to any buildings which are considered by the laws of such State to be personal property for taxation purposes."

Act of June 10, 1941, ch. 190, § 3(b), 55 Stat. 248, 248–49.

Reconstruction Finance Corp. v. Beaver County

328 U.S. 204 (1946)

■ *JUSTICE BLACK delivered the opinion of the Court:*

By § 10 of the Reconstruction Finance Corporation Act, as amended, . . . Congress made it clear that it did not permit States and local governments to impose taxes of any kind on the franchise, capital, reserves, surplus, income, loans, and personal property of the Reconstruction Finance Corporation or any of its subsidiary corporations. Congress provided in the same section that "any real property" of these governmental agencies "shall be subject to State, Territorial, county, municipal, or local taxation to the same extent according to its value as other real property is taxed." The Supreme Court of Pennsylvania sustained the imposition of a tax on certain machinery owned and used in Beaver County, Pennsylvania, by the Defense Plant Corporation, an RFC subsidiary. [The state supreme court's holding rested on the view that the machinery was "real property" within the meaning of § 10.] . . .

. . . [The machinery in question was housed in a plant that the Defense Plant Corporation had built on land that it owned in Beaver County. The plant was being used to manufacture aircraft propellers, and the parties stipulated below that the machinery was "necessary and essential" to the plant's operation for that purpose.] Most of the machinery was heavy, not attached to the buildings, and was held in place by its own weight. Other portions of the machinery were attached by easily removable screws and bolts, and some of the equipment and fixtures could be moved from place to place within the plant. The lease contract [under which the government was leasing the plant to a defense contractor] . . . authorized the Government . . . to replace existing equipment, and parts of the machinery appear to have been frequently interchanged and replaced as the convenience of the Government required. The lease contract also provided that the machinery should "remain personalty notwithstanding the fact it may be affixed or attached to realty."

The Government contends that under these circumstances the machinery was not "real" but was "personal" property, and that therefore its taxation was forbidden by Congress. The "real property" which Congress made "subject" to state taxation should in the Government's view be limited to "land and buildings and those fixtures which are so integrated with the buildings as to be uniformly, or, at most, generally, regarded as real property." "Real property," within this definition, would include buildings and "fixtures essential to a building's operations" but would not include fixtures, movable machinery, or equipment, which, though essential to applicant's operations as a plant, are not essential to a building's operation as a building.

The county would, for tax purposes, define real property so as to treat machinery, equipment, fixtures, and the land on which a manufacturing establishment is located as an integral real property unit. This is in accord with the view of the State's Supreme Court which made the following statement in sustaining the tax here involved: "It has long been the rule in Pennsylvania that 'Whether fast or loose, . . . all the machinery of a manufactory which is necessary to constitute it, and without which it would not be a manufactory at all, must pass for a part of the freehold.' . . . Appellant's machinery, being an integrated part of the manufactory, and so, of the freehold, was therefore taxable" under Pennsylvania's definition of real property. [39 A.2d 713, 714 (Pa. 1944).] This interpretation of Pennsylvania's tax law is of course binding on us. But Pennsylvania's definition of "real property" cannot govern if it conflicts with the scope of that term as used in the federal statute. What meaning Congress intended is a federal question which we must determine.

The 1941 Act does not itself define real property. Nor do the legislative reports or other relevant data provide any single decisive piece of evidence as to Congressional intent.[4] Obviously, [Congress] could have intended either, as the Government argues, that content be given to the

---

[4] The 1941 amendments to § 10 added among others the following provision: ". . . such exemptions shall not be construed to be applicable in any State to any buildings which are considered by the laws of such State to be personal property for taxation purposes." The Government contends that this indicates a congressional intent to establish a uniform meaning of the term "real property" regardless of local rules. But the addition also might be taken to indicate that Congress understood that without it under the language of § 10 the local rule would be followed with respect to taxing buildings. In our opinion the addition of the above-quoted language does not tend to lead to one conclusion or the other.

term "real property" as a matter of federal law, under authoritative decisions of this Court, or, as the county contends, that the meaning of the term should be its meaning under local tax laws so long as those tax laws were not designed to discriminate against the Government.

In support of its contention that a federal definition of real property should be applied, the Government relies on the generally accepted principle that Congress normally intends that its laws shall operate uniformly throughout the nation so that the federal program will remain unimpaired. *Jerome v. United States*, 318 U.S. 101, 104; *Commissioner v. Tower*, 327 U.S. 280. But Congress, in permitting local taxation of the real property, made it impossible to apply the law with uniform tax consequences in each state and locality. For the several States, and even the localities within them, have diverse methods of assessment, collection, and refunding. Tax rates vary widely. To all of these variable tax consequences Congress has expressly subjected the "real property" of the Defense Plant Corporation. In view of this express provision, the normal assumption that Congress intends its law to have the same consequences throughout the nation cannot be made. Furthermore, Congress, had it desired complete nationwide uniformity as to tax consequences, could have stipulated for fixed payments in lieu of taxes, as it has done in other statutes. [*See, e.g.*, 42 U.S.C. § 1546 (1946 ed.).] Nor can we see how application of a local rule governing what is "real property" for tax purposes would impair the congressional program for the production of war materials any more than the program would be impaired by the action of Congress in leaving the fixing of rates of taxation to local communities.

We think the congressional purpose can best be accomplished by application of settled state rules as to what constitutes "real property," so long as it is plain, as it is here, that the state rules do not effect a discrimination against the Government, or patently run counter to the terms of the Act. Concepts of real property are deeply rooted in state traditions, customs, habits, and laws. Local tax administration is geared to those concepts. To permit the States to tax, and yet to require them to alter their long-standing practice of assessments and collections, would create the kind of confusion and resultant hampering of local tax machinery which we are certain Congress did not intend. The fact that Congress subjected Defense Plant Corporation's properties to local taxes "to the same extent according to its value as other real property is taxed" indicated an intent to integrate congressional permission to tax with established local tax assessment and collection machinery.

■ *JUSTICE JACKSON took no part in the consideration or decision of this case.*

NOTES AND QUESTIONS

1. Justice Black's opinion understood the phrase "real property" in § 10 of the Reconstruction Finance Corporation Act to refer to whatever the

state or locality where the property was located called "real property" for purposes of its own tax laws. On that view, the scope of the tax exemption that Congress had given the RFC varied from state to state. In states that defined "real property" to include only land, buildings, and things permanently affixed to buildings, machinery of the sort at issue in this case would be exempt from state and local taxation as a matter of federal law. But in Pennsylvania, which defined "real property" to include all machinery that was necessary to constitute a manufacturing plant, the machinery would *not* be exempt from state and local taxation.

As a matter of policy, is there any plausible reason why Congress might have decided to let the size of the RFC's federal exemption from state and local taxation vary from state to state, according to how each state happened to define "real property" for purposes of its own tax laws? Justice Black's opinion emphasized administrative simplicity. If the phrase "real property" in § 10 were *not* understood to piggyback on whatever the relevant state or locality ordinarily meant by that term, taxing authorities might end up having to draw two different lines between "real" and "personal" property—one to classify the RFC's property and another to classify all other property located within the jurisdiction. According to Justice Black, "To permit the States to tax, and yet to require them to alter their long-standing practice of assessments and collections, would create the kind of confusion and resultant hampering of local tax machinery which we are certain Congress did not intend."

To support his intuitions about Congress's intentions, Justice Black pointed to another feature of § 10. As he noted, if something counted as "real property," § 10 subjected it to state and local taxation "to the same extent according to its value as other real property is taxed." Thus, Congress had not tried to ensure that the RFC faced a nationally uniform scheme of taxation with respect to real property; although different states could be expected to apply different tax rates and different mechanisms for assessment, Congress was content to let the RFC's real property be taxed according to varying rules of state law. But does it follow that Congress must also have been content to let varying rules of state law determine what counts as "real property" for this purpose?

What would the latter inference mean for the definition of "personal property" in § 10? Congress apparently was *not* willing to let the RFC's personal property be taxed according to varying rules of state law. Instead, § 10 established a uniform national rule on that topic: it exempted the RFC's personal property from all state and local taxation. If one thinks that Congress's decision to subject the RFC's *real* property to the varying tax regimes of each state and local government implies a decision to let the very definition of "real property" change from state to state, one might draw the contrary inference about Congress's treatment of the RFC's *personal* property: given Congress's insistence that the RFC's personal property be treated the same across the nation, perhaps one can infer that Congress expected the phrase "personal property" in § 10 to have an invariant meaning. But that inference about "personal property" cannot really coexist with the inference that Justice Black drew about "real property." The scope of "personal property" in § 10 is surely linked to the scope of "real property" in § 10; both in common parlance and in the statutory scheme, "personal property" can be thought of as all property that is not "real property." As a result, it is logically impossible for one of those phrases in § 10 to have a uniform national meaning while the other piggybacks upon varying definitions supplied by state or local law. If what counts as "real property" for purposes of § 10 varies from state to state, then so too must what counts as "personal property" for purposes of § 10.

2. Why might § 10 establish a special rule for the RFC's "real property" in the first place? Given Congress's decision to exempt the RFC from most state and local taxation (including taxation of the RFC's "personal property"), what policy concern might have led Congress to let state and local governments tax the RFC's "real property"?

One common way of distinguishing real property from personal property is that real property is immovable. Land, in particular, stays in the same place no matter who owns it. That feature of land may well be relevant to the distinction that Congress drew in § 10. Congress may have thought that if the RFC were exempt from *all* state and local taxation (including even taxes on real property), then the RFC's purchase of land in a particular jurisdiction would cause that jurisdiction to lose part of the tax base that it would otherwise have enjoyed. (After all, if the RFC did not own the land in question, someone else would, and that person probably would be subject to the property taxes of the jurisdiction where the land is located.) Thus, Congress's decision to subject the RFC's real property to state and local taxation on the same terms as other real property may have reflected a desire to protect the tax base that state and local governments would have enjoyed in the absence of the RFC. But that rationale does not necessarily justify exposing the RFC's *personal* property to state and local taxation. Even if the RFC were exempt from state and local taxation on its cars, typewriters, and other forms of movable property that it brought into a particular state, the state government would not necessarily be missing out on tax revenues that it would otherwise have received, because the personal property in question might not have been within the state's borders if the RFC had not brought it there.

Suppose that one accepts this explanation of Congress's decision to draw a distinction between the RFC's "real property" and the RFC's "personal property," and to subject the former but not the latter to state and local taxation. Does this understanding of the policy behind § 10 suggest that Congress was using the phrase "real property" in a nationally uniform sense, to refer to land, buildings, and immovable fixtures? Or might Justice Black's arguments about administrative convenience still justify his conclusion that even readily movable property is subject to state and local taxation *if* the relevant state or locality classifies such property as "real" for purposes of its own tax laws?

3. Is the amendment that Congress enacted in 1941 relevant to the meaning of the phrase "real property" in the original Act? The second sentence that Congress added to § 10 in 1941 made clear that § 10 exempted the RFC's "personal property" from state and local taxation, but added that this exemption "shall not be construed to be applicable in any State to any buildings which are considered by the laws of such State to be personal property for taxation purposes." As the Court observed in footnote 4 of its opinion, that language gave possible arguments to both sides in the *Beaver County* case.

On the one hand, the amendment subjected the RFC's "buildings" to state and local taxation without regard to whether the tax schemes of a particular state or locality classified buildings as "real" or "personal" property. One might infer that Congress saw the RFC's buildings as real property (and therefore as properly subject to state and local taxation under § 10) no matter how a particular state or locality might characterize buildings for purposes of its own tax schemes. The amendment also suggests that Congress did not see a need to piggyback entirely on state and local definitions for the sake of administrative convenience.

On the other hand, if the original Act had been understood to use the phrase "real property" in a uniform way that does not piggyback upon the law of any individual state, then there might have been no need for the 1941 amendment to specify that the RFC's buildings were subject to state and local taxation even if a particular state classified buildings as personal property for purposes of the state's own tax scheme. Wouldn't that have gone without saying?

4. When the *Beaver County* case was litigated in the Supreme Court of Pennsylvania, the county argued that the phrase "real property" in § 10 was a mere placeholder for varying definitions supplied by state and local law. That is the position that Justice Black ended up accepting. But the Defense Plant Corporation had offered a plausible alternative interpretation. In its view, Congress had used the phrase "real property" in § 10 to refer to a species of general law, and to mean the same thing throughout the country. According to the Defense Plant Corporation, whether the corporation's machinery counted as "real property" within the meaning of § 10 depended not upon the local law of Pennsylvania but instead upon "the view prevailing in the majority of the states that have dealt with the subject of chattels made part of the freehold." *Appeal of Defense Plant Corporation*, 39 A.2d 713, 717 (Pa. 1944).

The state supreme court did not choose between these two possible interpretations, because the state supreme court believed that the particular machinery in question qualified as "real property" under *both* approaches. But isn't the interpretation proffered by the Defense Plant

Corporation at least as plausible as the interpretation that Justice Black ended up accepting?

5. By way of counterpoint to *Beaver County*, consider the Supreme Court's interpretation of the federal tax-lien statute, 26 U.S.C. § 6321. That statute reads as follows: "If any person liable to pay any [federal] tax neglects or refuses to pay the same after demand, the amount . . . shall be a lien in favor of the United States upon all property and rights to property, whether real or personal, belonging to such person." In order to apply this provision, courts often have to identify the legal interests that the taxpayer enjoys under the local law of an individual state. But courts do not have to worry about whether the state in question classifies those rights as "property." As the Supreme Court has held, "[s]uch state law labels are irrelevant to the federal question of which bundles of rights constitute property that may be attached by a federal tax lien." *United States v. Craft*, 535 U.S. 274, 279 (2002). Instead, the Supreme Court understands the phrase "property and rights to property" in § 6321 to have a uniform meaning throughout the United States, and to refer to particular sets of legal attributes. *See* Drye v. United States, 528 U.S. 49, 58 (1999) (noting that although state law typically determines "what rights the taxpayer has in the property the Government seeks to reach," courts "look . . . to federal law to determine whether the taxpayer's state-delineated rights qualify as 'property' or 'rights to property' within the compass of the federal tax lien legislation"). Even though § 6321 operates with respect to legal relations created by state law, the Supreme Court has seen no reason to assume that Congress relied upon state law to define the very terms that § 6321 uses.

The approach that the Supreme Court has taken to the terms in § 6321 is more typical than the approach that the Supreme Court took in *Beaver County*. Still, *Beaver County* does not stand completely alone. Consider *De Sylva v. Ballentine*, 351 U.S. 570 (1956). As it stood at the time of *De Sylva*, the federal Copyright Act allowed authors to get a copyright for an initial term of twenty-eight years. Section 24 of the Act added that upon proper application made within one year before the expiration of that initial term, "the author of such work, if still living, or the widow, widower, or children of the author, if the author be not living, or if such author, widow, widower, or children be not living, then the author's executors, or in the absence of a will, his next of kin shall be entitled to a renewal and extension of the copyright in such work for a further term of twenty-eight years . . . ." 17 U.S.C. § 24 (1952 ed.). In *De Sylva*, after first holding that the surviving spouse and children of a deceased author shared equally in the renewal rights conferred by § 24, the Supreme Court addressed "whether an illegitimate child is included within the term 'children' as used in § 24." *De Sylva*, 351 U.S. at 580. Ultimately, the majority held that this question might have different answers in different states. In particular, the majority interpreted the word "children" in § 24 of the federal Copyright Act to refer to people who

(1) had some sort of filial connection to the deceased author (so that describing them as the author's "children" would not be "entirely strange to those familiar with [the word's] ordinary usage") and (2) would inherit from the author on that basis under the law of the relevant state. *De Sylva*, 351 U.S. at 580–82. The majority described itself as "draw[ing] on the ready-made body of state law to define the word 'children' in § 24." *Id.* at 580–81; *cf. id.* at 580 (noting that there is no similar body of federal law because "domestic relations . . . is primarily a matter of state concern"). In support of its conclusion, the majority noted that other terms in § 24 also required reference to state law. *See id.* ("To decide who is the widow or widower of a deceased author, or who are his executors or next of kin, requires a reference to the law of the State which created those legal relationships.").

Similar questions have arisen about the meaning of the word "corporation" in 28 U.S.C. § 1332, the basic statute giving federal district courts jurisdiction on the basis of diversity of citizenship. Congress has provided that for purposes of § 1332, "a corporation shall be deemed to be a citizen of every State and foreign state by which it has been incorporated and of the State or foreign state where it has its principal place of business." 28 U.S.C. § 1332(c)(1); *see also* Hertz Corp. v. Friend, 559 U.S. 77, 84–88 (2010) (summarizing the development of judicial doctrine on this topic and the eventual enactment of § 1332(c) in 1958). In this respect, corporations differ from other entities; the modern Supreme Court regards partnerships and other unincorporated associations as entities that have their own citizenship status for purposes of § 1332, but these unincorporated entities are said to be citizens of every state or foreign country in which any one of their members is a citizen. *See, e.g.*, Grupo Dataflux v. Atlas Global Group, L.P., 541 U.S. 567, 579 (2004). Thus, courts need to know what counts as a "corporation" for purposes of § 1332. For entities created by state law (as opposed to foreign entities), courts have not necessarily tried to identify a list of characteristics that distinguish corporations from other legal entities. At least according to the Seventh Circuit's opinion in *Hoagland v. Sandberg, Phoenix & Von Gontard, P.C.*, 385 F.3d 737 (7th Cir. 2004), § 1332(c)(1) instead has been understood simply to piggyback on the label that state law supplies: an entity created under state law is a "corporation" within the meaning of § 1332(c)(1) if, but only if, the law of the relevant state uses that label. *See id.* at 739–43 (concluding that a firm set up as a "professional corporation" under Missouri law qualifies as a "corporation" for purposes of § 1332(c)(1), while a firm set up as a "limited liability company" under Missouri law would not). The Seventh Circuit acknowledged that this approach would not work well if it "induce[d] states to rename sole proprietorships, mah jongg clubs, or pit bulls 'corporations' in order to make them more . . . suable in federal court," but that does not appear to have happened. *See id.* at 743 ("It is because states are not using the label of 'corporation' to game the diversity statute that the courts are comfortable deferring to the label the state places on a business entity.").[46]

The Seventh Circuit's approach to the word "corporation" in 28 U.S.C. § 1332(c)(1) is not obviously correct. *See id.* at 745–47 (Easterbrook, J., concurring) (raising doubts, though ultimately concluding that Supreme Court precedent blocked other plausible approaches). Neither was *Beaver County*'s approach to the phrase "real property" in § 10 of the Reconstruction Finance Corporation Act. Still, the similarities between *Beaver County* and *Hoagland* might be instructive. Whether those cases are right or wrong, do they help us identify the conditions under which courts might be most willing to read a term in a federal statute as a mere placeholder for definitions supplied by the local law of each individual state? Consider the following tentative list: In both cases, (1) Congress had not itself provided a definition of the term in question, (2) the term was one whose meaning was most commonly elaborated under the rubric of state law, (3) relying upon courts to distill a uniform national definition for purposes of the federal statute would have generated either substantial uncertainty or other administrative problems, (4) reading the term simply to incorporate varying definitions supplied by state law promised to avoid those problems, (5) the context was one in which Congress probably put a premium on administrative ease, (6) reading the term as a mere placeholder for varying definitions supplied by state law would not invite too much manipulation by individual states, and (7) the apparent purposes behind the federal statute did not seem to demand a uniform definition. Should other features be added to this list?

b. THE POSSIBILITY THAT A TERM IN A FEDERAL STATUTE SHOULD BE GIVEN A UNIFORM INTERPRETATION THAT REFLECTS THE STATUTE'S PURPOSES BUT DEVIATES FROM GENERAL LAW

Cases like *Beaver County* and *Hoagland* are exceptional: courts rarely read terms in federal statutes as mere placeholders for varying definitions supplied by state law. To be sure, many federal statutes establish directives that refer in one way or another to legal relations created by state law, and federal statutes can interact with the laws of individual states in many other ways as well. But it is unusual for the very words of a federal statute to have different definitions in different states—so that as used in the federal statute, the words are simply pass-

---

[46] One could make a similar point about the Supreme Court's decision in *Beaver County*, which read the phrase "real property" in § 10 of the Reconstruction Finance Corporation Act to piggyback upon varying definitions supplied by state and local law. In theory, that approach might seem to invite manipulation: if the line between "real property" and "personal property" was otherwise unimportant to a particular state, the state could maximize its tax base by defining "real property" very broadly, so as to expose more of the RFC's property to state and local taxation. In practice, however, there probably was little risk that state and local governments would manipulate their definitions of "real property" with the Reconstruction Finance Corporation Act in mind, both because those definitions served other functions and because manipulating them was unlikely to generate enough extra tax revenues to matter.

throughs for whatever each individual state uses the same labels to cover.

If we think that Congress has used a particular term in a federal statute in the more common way, so that it has a uniform content throughout the nation, we have to figure out what that uniform content is. Suppose that Congress has not provided any explicit definition of how the federal statute is using the term, but the term is one commonly used in *state* law. Should courts usually draw their understanding of the term from a species of general law? That is, should they apply a presumption that Congress was using the term in the same basic way as the majority of states? Or should courts feel free to develop a statute-specific understanding of the term that deviates from how the term is commonly used in American jurisprudence but that the courts see as promoting the purposes behind the particular federal statute in question?

In the next case, the Supreme Court chose the latter route. As we shall see, however, the opinion that follows is not the Court's last word on the subject.

NLRB v. Hearst Publications, Inc.

322 U.S. 111 (1944)

■ *JUSTICE RUTLEDGE delivered the opinion of the Court:*

These cases arise from the refusal of respondents, publishers of four Los Angeles daily newspapers, to bargain collectively with a union representing newsboys who distribute their papers on the streets of that city. . . . [The respondents took the position that] the newsboys are not their "employees" within the meaning of that term in the National Labor Relations Act . . . .[1]

The proceedings before the National Labor Relations Board were begun with the filing of four petitions for investigation and certification by Los Angeles Newsboys Local Industrial Union No. 75. Hearings were held in a consolidated proceeding after which the Board made findings of fact and concluded that the regular full-time newsboys selling each paper were employees within the Act and that questions affecting commerce concerning the representation of employees had arisen. It designated appropriate units and ordered elections. . . . At these the union was selected as their representative by majorities of the eligible newsboys. After the union was appropriately certified, . . . the respondents refused to bargain with it. Thereupon proceedings under § 10 . . . were instituted

---

[1] Section 2(3) of the Act provides that "The term 'employee' shall include any employee, and shall not be limited to the employees of a particular employer, unless the Act explicitly states otherwise, and shall include any individual whose work has ceased as a consequence of, or in connection with, any current labor dispute or because of any unfair labor practice, and who has not obtained any other regular and substantially equivalent employment, but shall not include any individual employed as an agricultural laborer, or in the domestic service of any family or person at his home, or any individual employed by his parent or spouse." [National Labor Relations Act, ch. 372, § 2(3), 49 Stat. 449, 450 (1935) (codified at 29 U.S.C. § 152(3)).]

[before the Board], a hearing was held and respondents were found to have violated §§ 8(1) and 8(5) of the Act . . . . They were ordered to cease and desist from such violations and to bargain collectively with the union upon request. . . .

Upon respondents' petitions for review and the Board's petitions for enforcement, the Circuit Court of Appeals, one judge dissenting, set aside the Board's orders. Rejecting the Board's analysis, the court independently examined the question whether the newsboys are employees within the Act, decided that the statute imports common-law standards to determine that question, and held the newsboys are not employees. 136 F.2d 608.

The findings of the Board disclose that the . . . papers are distributed to the ultimate consumer through a variety of channels, including independent dealers and newsstands often attached to drug, grocery or confectionery stores, carriers who make home deliveries, and newsboys who sell on the streets of the city and its suburbs. Only the last of these are involved in this case.

The newsboys work under varying terms and conditions. They may be "bootjackers," selling to the general public at places other than established corners, or they may sell at fixed "spots." They may sell only casually or part-time, or full-time . . . . The units which the Board determined to be appropriate are composed of those who sell full-time at established spots. Those vendors, misnamed boys, are generally mature men, dependent upon the proceeds of their sales for their sustenance, and frequently supporters of families. Working thus as news vendors on a regular basis often for a number of years, they form a stable group with relatively little turnover, in contrast to schoolboys and others who sell as . . . temporary and casual distributors.

. . . .

I

The principal question is whether the newsboys are "employees." Because Congress did not explicitly define the term, respondents say its meaning must be determined by reference to common-law standards. In their view "common-law standards" are those the courts have applied in distinguishing between "employees" and "independent contractors" when working out various problems unrelated to the [National Labor Relations] Act's purposes and provisions.

The argument assumes that there is some simple, uniform and easily applicable test which the courts have used, in dealing with such problems, to determine whether persons doing work for others fall in one class or the other. Unfortunately this is not true. Only by a long and tortuous history was the simple formulation worked out which has been stated most frequently as "the test" for deciding whether one who hires another is responsible in tort for his wrongdoing.[19] But this formula has been by no means exclusively controlling in the solution of other problems. And its simplicity has been illusory because it is more largely simplicity of formulation than of application. Few problems in the law have given greater variety of application and conflict in results than the cases arising in the borderland between what is clearly an employer-employee relationship and what is clearly one of independent entrepreneurial dealing. This is true within the limited field of determining vicarious liability in tort. It becomes more so when the field is expanded to include all of the possible applications of the distinction.

It is hardly necessary to stress particular instances of these variations . . . . It is enough to point out that . . . results may be contrary . . . depending upon the state or jurisdiction where the determination is made; and that within a single jurisdiction a person who, for instance, is held to be an "independent contractor" for the purpose of imposing vicarious liability in tort may be an "employee" for the purposes of particular legislation, such as unemployment compensation. See, *e.g.*, *Globe Grain & Milling Co. v. Industrial Comm'n*, 98 Utah 36, 91 P.2d 512. In short, the assumed simplicity and uniformity, resulting from application of "common-law standards," does not exist.

. . . .

Two possible consequences could follow. One would be to refer the decision of who are employees to local state law. The alternative would be to make it turn on a sort of pervading general essence distilled from state law. Congress obviously did not intend the former result. It would introduce variations into the statute's operation as wide as the differences the forty-eight states and other local jurisdictions make in applying the distinction for wholly different purposes. Persons who might be "employees" in one state would be "independent contractors" in another. They would be within or without the statute's protection depending not on whether their situation falls factually within the ambit Congress had in mind, but upon the accidents of the location of their work and the attitude of the particular local jurisdiction in casting doubtful cases one way or the other. Persons working across state lines might fall in one class or the other, possibly both, depending on whether the Board and the courts would be required to give effect to the law of one state or of the adjoining one, or to that of each in relation to the portion of the work done within its borders.

Both the terms and the purposes of the statute, as well as the legislative history, show that Congress had in mind no such patchwork plan for securing freedom of employees' organization and of collective

[19] The so-called "control test" with which common-law judges have wrestled to secure precise and ready applications did not escape the difficulties encountered in borderland cases by its reformulation in the Restatement of the Law of Agency § 220. [In addition,] even at the common law the control test and the complex of incidents evolved in applying it to distinguish an "employee" from an "independent contractor," for purposes of vicarious liability in tort, did not necessarily have the same significance in other contexts . . . .

bargaining. The [National Labor Relations] Act is federal legislation, administered by a national agency, intended to solve a national problem on a national scale. . . . It is an Act, therefore, in reference to which it is not only proper, but necessary for us to assume, "in the absence of a plain indication to the contrary, that Congress . . . is not making the application of the federal act dependent on state law." *Jerome v. United States*, 318 U.S. 101, 104. Nothing in the statute's background, history, terms or purposes indicates its scope is to be limited by such varying local conceptions, either statutory or judicial, or that it is to be administered in accordance with whatever different standards the respective states may see fit to adopt for the disposition of unrelated, local problems. Consequently, so far as the meaning of "employee" in this statute is concerned, "the federal law must prevail no matter what name is given to the interest or right by state law." *Morgan v. Commissioner*, 309 U.S. 78, 81, 626 . . . .

II

Whether, given the intended national uniformity, the term "employee" includes such workers as these newsboys must be answered primarily from the history, terms and purposes of the legislation. The word "is not treated by Congress as a word of art having a definite meaning . . . ." Rather "it takes color from its surroundings . . . [in] the statute where it appears," *United States v. American Trucking Associations, Inc.*, 310 U.S. 534, 545, and derives meaning from the context of that statute, which "must be read in the light of the mischief to be corrected and the end to be attained." *South Chicago Coal & Dock Co. v. Bassett*, 309 U.S. 251, 259 . . . .

Congress, on the one hand, was not thinking solely of the immediate technical relation of employer and employee. It had in mind at least some other persons than those standing in the proximate legal relation of employee to the particular employer involved in the labor dispute. It cannot be taken, however, that the purpose was to include all other persons who may perform service for another or was to ignore entirely legal classifications made for other purposes. Congress had in mind a wider field than the narrow technical legal relation of "master and servant," as the common law had worked this out in all its variations, and at the same time a narrower one than the entire area of rendering service to others. The question comes down therefore to how much was included of the intermediate region between what is clearly and unequivocally "employment," by any appropriate test, and what is as clearly entrepreneurial enterprise and not employment.

It will not do, for deciding this question as one of uniform national application, to import wholesale the traditional common-law conceptions or some distilled essence of their local variations as exclusively controlling limitations upon the scope of the statute's effectiveness. To do this would be merely to select some of the local, hairline variations for nation-wide application and thus to reject others for coverage under the

Act. That result hardly would be consistent with the statute's broad terms and purposes.

Congress was not seeking to solve the nationally harassing problems with which the statute deals by solutions only partially effective. It rather sought to find a broad solution, one that would bring industrial peace by substituting, so far as its power could reach, the rights of workers to self-organization and collective bargaining for the industrial strife which prevails where these rights are not effectively established. Yet only partial solutions would be provided if large segments of workers about whose technical legal position such local differences exist should be wholly excluded from coverage by reason of such differences. Yet that result could not be avoided, if choice must be made among them and controlled by them in deciding who are "employees" within the Act's meaning. Enmeshed in such distinctions, the administration of the statute soon might become encumbered by the same sort of technical legal refinement as has characterized the long evolution of the employee-independent contractor dichotomy in the courts for other purposes. The consequences would be ultimately to defeat, in part at least, the achievement of the statute's objectives. Congress no more intended to import this mass of technicality as a controlling "standard" for uniform national application than to refer decision of the question outright to the local law.

The Act, as its first section states, was designed to avert the "substantial obstructions to the free flow of commerce" which result from "strikes and other forms of industrial strife or unrest" by eliminating the causes of that unrest. It is premised on explicit findings that strikes and industrial strife themselves result in large measure from the refusal of employers to bargain collectively and the inability of individual workers to bargain successfully for improvements in their "wages, hours, or other working conditions" with employers who are "organized in the corporate or other forms of ownership association." Hence the avowed and interrelated purposes of the Act are to encourage collective bargaining and to remedy the individual worker's inequality of bargaining power by "protecting the exercise . . . of full freedom of association, self-organization, and designation of representatives of their own choosing, for the purpose of negotiating the terms and conditions of their employment or other mutual aid or protection." 49 Stat. 449, 450.

The mischief at which the Act is aimed and the remedies it offers are not confined exclusively to "employees" within the traditional legal distinctions separating them from "independent contractors." Myriad forms of service relationship, with infinite and subtle variations in the terms of employment, blanket the nation's economy. Some are within this Act, others beyond its coverage. Large numbers will fall clearly on one side or on the other, by whatever test may be applied. But intermediate there will be many, the incidents of whose employment partake in part of the one group, in part of the other, in varying proportions of weight.

And consequently the legal pendulum, for purposes of applying the statute, may swing one way or the other, depending upon the weight of this balance and its relation to the special purpose at hand.

Unless the common-law tests are to be imported and made exclusively controlling, without regard to the statute's purposes, it cannot be irrelevant that the particular workers in these cases are subject, as a matter of economic fact, to the evils the statute was designed to eradicate and that the remedies it affords are appropriate for preventing them or curing their harmful effects in the special situation. Interruption of commerce through strikes and unrest may stem as well from labor disputes between some who, for other purposes, are technically "independent contractors" and their employers as from disputes between persons who, for those purposes, are "employees" and their employers. . . . Inequality of bargaining power in controversies over wages, hours and working conditions may as well characterize the status of the one group as of the other. The former, when acting alone, may be as "helpless in dealing with an employer," as "dependent . . . on his daily wage" and as "unable to leave the employ and to resist arbitrary and unfair treatment" as the latter. For each, "union . . . [may be] essential to give . . . opportunity to deal on equality with their employer." [*American Steel Foundries v. Tri-City Central Trades Council*, 257 U.S. 184, 209 (1921), cited in H.R. Rep. No. 1147, 74th Cong., 1st Sess., 10.] And for each, collective bargaining may be appropriate and effective for the "friendly adjustment of industrial disputes arising out of differences as to wages, hours, or other working conditions."[26] 49 Stat. 449. In short, when the particular situation of employment combines these characteristics, so that the economic facts of the relation make it more nearly one of employment than of independent business enterprise with respect to the ends sought to be accomplished by the legislation, those characteristics may outweigh technical legal classification for purposes unrelated to the statute's objectives and bring the relation within its protections.

To eliminate the causes of labor disputes and industrial strife, Congress thought it necessary to create a balance of forces in certain types of economic relationships. These do not embrace simply employment associations in which controversies could be limited to disputes over proper "physical conduct in the performance of the service."[27] On the contrary, Congress recognized those economic relationships cannot be fitted neatly into the containers designated "employee" and "employer" which an earlier law had shaped for different purposes. Its Reports on the bill disclose clearly the understanding that

---

[26] The practice of self-organization and collective bargaining to resolve labor disputes has for some time been common among such varied types of "independent contractors" as musicians . . . , actors . . . , and writers . . . , and such atypical "employees" as insurance agents, artists, architects and engineers . . . .

[27] Control of "physical conduct in the performance of the service" is the traditional test of the "employee relationship" at common law. Cf., e.g., Restatement of the Law of Agency § 220(1).

"employers and employees not in proximate relationship may be drawn into common controversies by economic forces," and that the very disputes sought to be avoided might involve "employees [who] are at times brought into an economic relationship with employers who are not their employers." [Sen. Rep. No. 573, 74th Cong., 1st Sess. at 6–7.] In this light, the broad language of the Act's definitions, which in terms reject conventional limitations on such conceptions as "employee," "employer," and "labor dispute," leaves no doubt that its applicability is to be determined broadly, in doubtful situations, by underlying economic facts rather than technically and exclusively by previously established legal classifications. . . .

Hence "technical concepts pertinent to an employer's legal responsibility to third persons for the acts of his servants" have been rejected in various applications of this Act both here (*International Association of Machinists v. Labor Board*, 311 U.S. 72, 80, 81; *H. J. Heinz Co. v. Labor Board*, 311 U.S. 514, 520, 521) and in other federal courts . . . . There is no good reason for invoking them to restrict the scope of the term "employee" sought to be done in this case. That term, like other provisions, must be understood with reference to the purpose of the Act and the facts involved in the economic relationship. "Where all the conditions of the relation require protection, protection ought to be given." [*Lehigh Valley Coal Co. v. Yensavage*, 218 F. 547, 552 (2d Cir. 1914).]

It is not necessary in this case to make a completely definitive limitation around the term "employee." That task has been assigned primarily to the agency created by Congress to administer the Act. Determination of "where all the conditions of the relation require protection" involves inquiries for the Board charged with this duty. Everyday experience in the administration of the statute gives it familiarity with the circumstances and backgrounds of employment relationships in various industries, with the abilities and needs of the workers for self organization and collective action, and with the adaptability of collective bargaining for the peaceful settlement of their disputes with their employers. The experience thus acquired must be brought frequently to bear on the question who is an employee under the Act. Resolving that question, like determining whether unfair labor practices have been committed, "belongs to the usual administrative routine" of the Board. *Gray v. Powell*, 314 U.S. 402, 411. . . .

In making that body's determinations as to the facts in these matters conclusive, if supported by evidence, Congress entrusted to it primarily the decision whether the evidence establishes the material facts. Hence in reviewing the Board's ultimate conclusions, it is not the court's function to substitute its own inferences of fact for the Board's, when the latter have support in the record. . . . Undoubtedly questions of statutory interpretation, especially when arising in the first instance in judicial proceedings, are for the courts to resolve, giving appropriate weight to the judgment of those whose special duty is to administer the questioned statute. . . . But where the question is one of specific application of a broad statutory term in a proceeding in which the agency administering the statute must determine it initially, the reviewing court's function is limited. . . . [T]he Board's determination that specified persons are "employees" under this Act is to be accepted if it has "warrant in the record" and a reasonable basis in law.

In this case the Board found that the designated newsboys work continuously and regularly, rely upon their earnings for the support of themselves and their families, and have their total wages influenced in large measure by the publishers who dictate their buying and selling prices, fix their markets and control their supply of papers. Their hours of work and their efforts on the job are supervised and to some extent prescribed by the publishers or their agents. Much of their sales equipment and advertising materials is furnished by the publishers with the intention that it be used for the publisher's benefit. Stating that "the primary consideration in the determination of the applicability of the statutory definition is whether effectuation of the declared policy and purposes of the Act comprehend securing to the individual the rights guaranteed and protection afforded by the Act," the Board concluded that the newsboys are employees. The record sustains the Board's findings and there is ample basis in the law for its conclusion. . . .

■ *[A separate statement of JUSTICE REED's reasons for concurring in the result is omitted.]*

■ *JUSTICE ROBERTS, dissenting:*

. . . . I think it plain that newsboys are not "employees" of the respondents within the meaning and intent of the National Labor Relations Act. When Congress, in § 2(3), said: "The term 'employee' shall include any employee, . . ." it stated as clearly as language could do it that the provisions of the Act were to extend to those who, as a result of decades of tradition which had become part of the common understanding of our people, bear the named relationship. Clearly also Congress did not delegate to the National Labor Relations Board the function of defining the relationship of employment so as to promote what the Board understood to be the underlying purpose of the statute. The question who is an employee, so as to make the statute applicable to him, is a question of the meaning of the Act and, therefore, is a judicial and not an administrative question.

I do not think that the court below suggested that the federal courts sitting in the various states must determine whether a given person is an employee by application of either the local statutes or local state decisions. Quite the contrary. As a result of common law development, many prescriptions of federal statutes take on meaning which is uniformly ascribed to them by the federal courts, irrespective of local variance. *Funk v. United States*, 290 U.S. 371. This court has repeatedly resorted to just such considerations in defining the very term "employee" as used in other federal statutes, as the opinion of the court below shows. There is a general and prevailing rule throughout the Union as to the indicia of employment and the criteria of one's status as employee. Unquestionably it was to this common, general, and prevailing understanding that Congress referred in the statute and, according to that understanding, the facts stated in the opinion below, and in that of this court, in my judgment, demonstrate that the newsboys were not employees of the newspapers.

It is urged that the Act uses the term in some loose and unusual sense such as justifies the Board's decision because Congress added to the definition of employee above quoted these further words: "and shall not be limited to the employees of a particular employer, unless the Act explicitly states otherwise, ..." The suggestion seems to be that Congress intended that the term employee should mean those who were not in fact employees, but it is perfectly evident, not only from the provisions of the Act as a whole but from the Senate Committee's Report, that this phrase was added to prevent any misconception of the provisions whereby employees were to be allowed freely to combine and to be represented in collective bargaining by the representatives of their union. Congress intended to make it clear that employee organizations did not have to be organizations of the employees of any single employer. But that qualifying phrase means no more than this and was never intended to permit the Board to designate as employees those who, in traditional understanding, have no such status.

NOTES AND QUESTIONS

1. The majority probably was correct not to read the word "employee" in the National Labor Relations Act as a mere placeholder for varying definitions supplied by the local law of each individual state. After all, when Congress decided to give collective-bargaining rights to "employees," Congress presumably cared more about real legal and economic relationships than about the potentially idiosyncratic labels that an individual state might have adopted for some other purpose. There is no reason to think that the enacting Congress intended the term "employee" to track local variations in usage—that is, to refer to one set of relationships in one state and another set of relationships in a different state. Instead of being an empty vessel for fifty different definitions, the term "employee" in the National Labor Relations Act presumably was meant to have a single unitary meaning.

But wouldn't it have been natural to think that this single unitary meaning reflects what the majority dismissively called "a sort of pervading general essence distilled from state law"? To say that the term "employee" in the National Labor Relations Act is not simply a placeholder for varying definitions supplied by the local law of each state is not to say that it has no relationship at all to doctrines that have been developed under the rubric of state law. To the contrary, the term "employee" in a federal statute could readily be understood to refer to a species of general American law—the kind of doctrines that one might learn in a course on Agency Law at a national law school trying to prepare students for practice in many different American jurisdictions.

The majority offered two basic reasons for rejecting that possibility. First, the majority suggested that there is too much variety in the laws of the several states for this option to be feasible. Different states draw the line between "employees" and "independent contractors" in different places. Even within a single state, moreover, the line is drawn in different places for different purposes. According to the majority, it would be difficult to distill all these different ideas into a determinate principle of general law even if one wanted to do so.

But the majority went on to suggest that one should not really want to do so, because any definition supplied by general law would be too narrow to serve the purposes of the National Labor Relations Act. According to this second argument, Congress wanted the Act to reduce labor strife, but strikes by some people whom general American law would classify as independent contractors can cause just as much trouble as strikes by people who are true employees. The majority concluded that interpreters should therefore read the term "employee" broadly, so that it covers some people who would be classified as mere independent contractors for other purposes. In the majority's words, "The mischief at which the Act is aimed and the remedies it offers are not confined exclusively to 'employees' within the traditional legal distinctions separating them from 'independent contractors.'"

Leaving aside the possible tension between the majority's first argument (general law is indeterminate about the meaning of "employee") and the majority's second argument (the definition of "employee" suggested by general law is too narrow to serve the purposes of the National Labor Relations Act), what do you make of the second argument? If general American law does indeed suggest some criteria for identifying the boundaries of the term "employee," is it really plausible that the National Labor Relations Act does not use the word in the sense suggested by general law, and that the Act's underlying purposes instead make it necessary to develop special alternative criteria that will cover many more people? If the majority was correct about the Act's underlying purposes, why would Congress have chosen the word "employee" in the first place? Don't the overtones of that word in general American law support a more restrained view of the Act's intended coverage than the view that the Court adopted?

2. Having decided to adopt a statute-specific understanding of the term "employee," informed by the purposes behind the National Labor Relations Act and broad enough to encompass some workers who would be considered independent contractors for other purposes, the majority ultimately deferred to the administering agency's application of the term. *See Hearst Publications*, 322 U.S. at 130–32. In this respect, *Hearst*

Publications is a precursor of *Chevron. See* Chevron U.S.A. Inc. v. Natural Resources Defense Council, 467 U.S. 837, 844 & n.14 (1984) (asserting that "[w]e have long recognized that considerable weight should be accorded to an executive department's construction of a statutory scheme it is entrusted to administer," and citing *Hearst Publications* as an example). In *Hearst Publications*, though, the majority did not speak of deference to the agency until after the majority had decided for itself that the term "employee" did not adopt either general law or the local law of individual states. Arguably, moreover, the Court was not deferring to the NLRB about the answer to a pure question of law, but rather about how to apply the law to the specific working relationships at issue in *Hearst Publications. See* THOMAS W. MERRILL, THE *CHEVRON* DOCTRINE: ITS RISE AND FALL, AND THE FUTURE OF THE ADMINISTRATIVE STATE 37–42 (2022) (discussing different readings of *Hearst Publications*); *see also supra* pp. 878–880 (noting Justice Stevens's later distinction between questions of statutory implementation and pure questions of statutory construction). *But cf. Hearst Publications*, 322 U.S. at 135–36 (Roberts, J., dissenting) (suggesting that either way, "[t]he question who is an employee, so as to make the statute applicable to him, is a question of the meaning of the Act and, therefore, is a judicial and not an administrative question").

3. Three years after *Hearst Publications*, Congress enacted the Labor Management Relations Act of 1947, ch. 120, 61 Stat. 136, which amended the National Labor Relations Act in various ways. Among other things, Congress specifically excluded "any individual having the status of an independent contractor" from the coverage of the term "employee." *Id.* sec. 101, § 2(3), 61 Stat. at 137–38. The legislative history of the 1947 Act indicates that this change was a response to *Hearst Publications* and that "the term ['employee'] is not meant to embrace persons outside that category under the general principles of the law of agency." 93 CONG. REC. 6442 (1947) (statement of Sen. Taft); *see also* H.R. REP. NO. 245, 80th Cong., 1st Sess. 18 (1947) (criticizing *Hearst Publications* along the same lines).

The same basic sequence also took place with respect to the Social Security Act of 1935. That Act too used the term "employee" without providing any special definition; the Supreme Court read the term broadly so as to accomplish what the Court called "the purposes of the legislation" (*United States v. Silk*, 331 U.S. 704, 712 (1947)); and Congress reacted by amending the Act so that the term "employee" was specifically linked to "the usual common-law rules applicable in determining the employer-employee relationship," Act of June 14, 1948, ch. 468, § 2(a), 62 Stat. 438, 438.

As the next case indicates, the modern Supreme Court has understood these episodes to carry a lesson that goes beyond the National Labor Relations Act and the Social Security Act.

C. THE POSSIBILITY THAT A TERM IN A FEDERAL STATUTE MIGHT DRAW ITS MEANING FROM GENERAL LAW

Like *Hearst Publications*, the next case involves the meaning of the word "employee" in a federal statute. In a unanimous opinion, however, the Supreme Court questioned the precedential force of *Hearst Publications* and followed a different line of cases. Instead of coming up with a statute-specific definition, the Court held that the Employee Retirement Income Security Act of 1974 used the term "employee" in the manner suggested by "the general common law of agency"—the sort of doctrines often reflected in the *Restatements of the Law* issued by the American Law Institute,[47] as well as in treatises and other sources that seek to identify common patterns in the principles recognized as law across a host of different American states.

Nationwide Mutual Insurance Co. v. Darden

503 U.S. 318 (1992)

■ *JUSTICE SOUTER delivered the opinion of the Court:*

In this case we construe the term "employee" as it appears in § 3(6) of the Employee Retirement Income Security Act of 1974 (ERISA), 88 Stat. 834, 29 U.S.C. § 1002(6), and read it to incorporate traditional agency law criteria for identifying master-servant relationships.

I

From 1962 through 1980, respondent Robert Darden operated an insurance agency according to the terms of several contracts he signed with petitioners Nationwide Mutual Insurance Co. et al. Darden promised to sell only Nationwide insurance policies, and, in exchange, Nationwide agreed to pay him commissions on his sales and enroll him in a company retirement scheme called the "Agent's Security Compensation Plan" (Plan). . . .

. . . [T]he contractual terms, however, [provided] that Darden would forfeit his entitlement to the Plan's benefits if, within a year of his termination and 25 miles of his prior business location, he sold insurance for Nationwide's competitors. The contracts also disqualified him from receiving those benefits if, after he stopped representing Nationwide, he ever induced a Nationwide policyholder to cancel one of its policies.

---

[47] Admittedly, modern Restatements are not purely compendia of majority rules; to varying degrees, they try to identify the law as their authors think it should be rather than as it is. Nonetheless, there remains a fairly strong correlation between the doctrines expressed in the Restatements and the doctrines that most American jurisdictions have in fact embraced. To the extent that is true, the Restatements still serve the function to which the very first Restatement aspired: courts continue to regard them "as prima facie a correct statement of what may be termed the general common law of the United States." 1 Restatement of Contracts xiv (1932); *see also, e.g.,* Burlington Industries, Inc. v. Ellerth, 524 U.S. 742, 755 (1998) ("[T]he Restatement (Second) of Agency (1957) . . . is a useful beginning point for a discussion of general agency principles."); Field v. Mans, 516 U.S. 59, 70 (1995) (calling the Restatement (Second) of Torts (1976) "the most widely accepted distillation of the common law of torts").

In November 1980, Nationwide exercised its contractual right to end its relationship with Darden. A month later, Darden became an independent insurance agent and, doing business from his old office, sold insurance policies for several of Nationwide's competitors. The company reacted with the charge that his new business activities disqualified him from receiving the Plan benefits to which he would have been entitled otherwise. Darden then sued for the benefits, which he claimed were nonforfeitable because already vested under the terms of ERISA. 29 U.S.C. § 1053(a).

Darden brought his action under 29 U.S.C. § 1132(a), which enables a benefit plan "participant" to enforce the substantive provisions of ERISA. The Act elsewhere defines "participant" as "any employee or former employee of an employer . . . who is or may become eligible to receive a benefit of any type from an employee benefit plan . . . ." § 1002(7). Thus, Darden's ERISA claim can succeed only if he was Nationwide's "employee," a term the Act defines as "any individual employed by an employer." § 1002(6).

It was on this point that the District Court granted summary judgment to Nationwide. After applying common-law agency principles and, to an extent unspecified, our decision in *United States v. Silk*, 331 U.S. 704 (1947), the court found that " 'the total factual context' of Mr. Darden's relationship with Nationwide shows that he was an independent contractor and not an employee." . . .

The United States Court of Appeals for the Fourth Circuit vacated. *Darden v. Nationwide Mutual Ins. Co.*, 796 F.2d 701 (1986). After observing that "Darden most probably would not qualify as an employee" under traditional principles of agency law, *id.* at 705, it found the traditional definition inconsistent with the " 'declared policy and purposes' " of ERISA, . . . and specifically with the congressional statement of purpose found in § 2 of the Act, 29 U.S.C. § 1001.[1] It therefore held that an ERISA plaintiff can qualify as an "employee" simply by showing "(1) that he had a reasonable expectation that he would receive [pension] benefits, (2) that he relied on this expectation, and (3) that he lacked the economic bargaining power to contract out of [benefit plan] forfeiture provisions." 922 F.2d 203, 205 (CA4 1991) (summarizing 796 F.2d 701 (CA4 1986)). The court remanded the case to the District Court, which then found that Darden had been Nationwide's "employee" under the standard set by the Court of Appeals. The Court of Appeals affirmed. 922 F.2d 203 (1991).

---

[1] The Court of Appeals cited Congress's declaration that "many employees with long years of employment are losing anticipated retirement benefits," that employee benefit plans "have become an important factor affecting the stability of employment and the successful development of industrial relations," and that ERISA was necessary to "assur[e] the equitable character of such plans and their financial soundness." None of these passages deals specifically with the scope of ERISA's class of beneficiaries.

II

We have often been asked to construe the meaning of "employee" where the statute containing the term does not helpfully define it. Most recently we confronted this problem in *Community for Creative Non-Violence v. Reid,* 490 U.S. 730 (1989), a case in which a sculptor and a nonprofit group each claimed copyright ownership in a statue the group had commissioned from the artist. The dispute ultimately turned on whether, by the terms of § 101 of the Copyright Act of 1976, 17 U.S.C. § 101, the statue had been "prepared by an employee within the scope of his or her employment." Because the Copyright Act nowhere defined the term "employee," we unanimously applied the "well established" principle that

> "[w]here Congress uses terms that have accumulated settled meaning under . . . the common law, a court must infer, unless the statute otherwise dictates, that Congress means to incorporate the established meaning of these terms. . . . In the past, when Congress has used the term 'employee' without defining it, we have concluded that Congress intended to describe the conventional master-servant relationship as understood by common-law agency doctrine. See, *e.g.*, *Kelley v. Southern Pacific Co.*, 419 U.S. 318, 322–323 (1974); *Baker v. Texas & Pacific R. Co.*, 359 U.S. 227, 228 (1959) (*per curiam*); *Robinson v. Baltimore & Ohio R. Co.*, 237 U.S. 84, 94 (1915)." 490 U.S. at 739–740 (internal quotation marks omitted).

While we supported this reading of the Copyright Act with other observations, the general rule stood as independent authority for the decision.

So too should it stand here. ERISA's nominal definition of "employee" as "any individual employed by an employer," 29 U.S.C. § 1002(6), is completely circular and explains nothing. As for the rest of the Act, Darden does not cite, and we do not find, any provision either giving specific guidance on the term's meaning or suggesting that construing it to incorporate traditional agency law principles would thwart the congressional design or lead to absurd results. Thus, we adopt a common-law test for determining who qualifies as an "employee" under ERISA,[3] a test we most recently summarized in *Reid*:

> "In determining whether a hired party is an employee under the general common law of agency, we consider the hiring party's right to control the manner and means by which the product is accomplished. Among the other factors relevant to this inquiry are the skill required; the source of the instrumentalities and tools; the location of the work; the duration of the relationship between the parties; whether the hiring party has the right to assign additional

[3] As in *Reid,* we construe the term to incorporate "the general common law of agency, rather than . . . the law of any particular State." *Community for Creative Non-Violence v. Reid,* 490 U.S. 730, 740 (1989).

projects to the hired party; the extent of the hired party's discretion over when and how long to work; the method of payment; the hired party's role in hiring and paying assistants; whether the work is part of the regular business of the hiring party; whether the hiring party is in business; the provision of employee benefits; and the tax treatment of the hired party." 490 U.S. at 751–752 (footnotes omitted).

Cf. Restatement (Second) of Agency § 220(2) (1958) (listing nonexhaustive criteria for identifying master-servant relationship); Rev. Rul. 87–41, 1987–1 Cum. Bull. 296, 298–299 (setting forth 20 factors as guides in determining whether an individual qualifies as a common-law "employee" in various tax law contexts). . . .

In taking its different tack, the Court of Appeals cited *NLRB v. Hearst Publications, Inc.*, 322 U.S. at 120–129, and *United States v. Silk*, 331 U.S. at 713, for the proposition that "the content of the term 'employee' in the context of a particular federal statute is 'to be construed "in the light of the mischief to be corrected and the end to be attained." ' " 796 F.2d at 706, quoting *Silk, supra*, at 713, in turn quoting *Hearst, supra*, at 124. But *Hearst* and *Silk*, which interpreted "employee" for purposes of the National Labor Relations Act and Social Security Act, respectively, are feeble precedents for unmooring the term from the common law. In each case, the Court read "employee," which neither statute helpfully defined, to imply something broader than the common-law definition; after each opinion, Congress amended the statute so construed to demonstrate that the usual common-law principles were the keys to meaning. See [*NLRB v. United Ins. Co. of America*, 390 U.S. 254, 256 (1968)] ("Congressional reaction to [*Hearst*] was adverse and Congress passed an amendment . . . [t]he obvious purpose of [which] was to have the . . . courts apply general agency principles in distinguishing between employees and independent contractors under the Act"); Social Security Act of 1948, ch. 468, § 2(a), 62 Stat. 438 (1948) (amending statute to provide that term "employee" "does not include . . . any individual who, under the *usual common-law rules* applicable in determining the employer-employee relationship, has the status of an independent contractor") (emphasis added); see also *United States v. W.M. Webb, Inc.*, 397 U.S. 179, 183–88 (1970) (discussing congressional reaction to *Silk*).

To be sure, Congress did not, strictly speaking, "overrule" our interpretation of those statutes, since the Constitution invests the Judiciary, not the Legislature, with the final power to construe the law. But a principle of statutory construction can endure just so many legislative revisitations, and *Reid*'s presumption that Congress means an agency law definition for "employee" unless it clearly indicates otherwise signaled our abandonment of *Silk*'s emphasis on construing that term " 'in the light of the mischief to be corrected and the end to be attained.' "

. . .

At oral argument, Darden tried to subordinate *Reid* to *Rutherford Food Corp. v. McComb*, 331 U.S. 722 (1947), which adopted a broad reading of "employee" under the Fair Labor Standards Act (FLSA). And *amicus* United States, while rejecting Darden's position, also relied on *Rutherford Food* for the proposition that, when enacting ERISA, Congress must have intended a modified common-law definition of "employee" that would advance, in a way not defined, the Act's "remedial purposes." Brief for United States as *Amicus Curiae* 15–21.[5] But *Rutherford Food* supports neither position. The definition of "employee" in the FLSA evidently derives from the child labor statutes and, on its face, goes beyond its ERISA counterpart. While the FLSA, like ERISA, defines an "employee" to include "any individual employed by an employer," it defines the verb "employ" expansively to mean "suffer or permit to work." 52 Stat. 1060, § 3, codified at 29 U.S.C. §§ 203(e), (g). This latter definition . . . stretches the meaning of "employee" to cover some parties who might not qualify as such under a strict application of traditional agency law principles. ERISA lacks any such provision, however, and the textual asymmetry between the two statutes precludes reliance on FLSA cases when construing ERISA's concept of "employee."

Quite apart from its inconsistency with our precedents, the Fourth Circuit's analysis reveals an approach infected with circularity and unable to furnish predictable results. . . .

. . . . To be sure, the traditional agency law criteria offer no paradigm of determinacy. But their application generally turns on factual variables within an employer's knowledge, thus permitting categorical judgments about the "employee" status of claimants with similar job descriptions. Agency law principles comport, moreover, with our recent precedents and with the common understanding, reflected in those precedents, of the difference between an employee and an independent contractor.

III

While the Court of Appeals noted that "Darden most probably would not qualify as an employee" under traditional agency law principles, . . . it did not actually decide that issue. We therefore reverse the judgment and remand the case to that court . . . .

NOTES AND QUESTIONS

1. *Darden* suggests the following principle: when Congress uses the word "employee" in a federal statute without providing any special definition, interpreters should assume that Congress was using the word in the manner suggested by general law unless Congress has provided specific clues to the contrary. Subsequent cases have therefore extended

---

[5] While both Darden and the United States cite a Department of Labor "Opinion Letter" as support for their separate positions, . . . neither suggests that we owe that letter's legal conclusions any deference under *Chevron U.S.A. Inc. v. Natural Resources Defense Council, Inc.*, 467 U.S. 837, 844 (1984).

Darden to other federal statutes. *See, e.g.*, Clackamas Gastroenterology Assocs., P.C. v. Wells, 538 U.S. 440, 444–51 (2003) (following *Darden*'s approach with respect to the meaning of "employee" in the Americans with Disabilities Act).

The modern Supreme Court has taken a similar approach to many other terms that appear without definitions in federal statutes and that are familiar to the common law. For instance, consider the word "domiciled" in § 101(a) of the Indian Child Welfare Act of 1978 (ICWA), which gives each recognized tribe "jurisdiction exclusive as to any State over any child custody proceeding involving an Indian child who resides or is domiciled within the reservation of such tribe." Pub. L. 95–608, 92 Stat. 3069, 3071 (codified at 25 U.S.C. § 1911(a)). In *Mississippi Band of Choctaw Indians v. Holyfield*, 490 U.S. 30 (1989), the Supreme Court reasoned in two steps. First, the Court held that the word "domiciled" in § 101(a) is not a mere placeholder for varying definitions supplied by the local law of individual states. *Id.* at 43–47 (noting that past cases had established a presumption against this placeholder theory, and calling it "most improbable that Congress would have intended to leave the scope of the statute's key jurisdictional provision subject to definition by state courts as a matter of state law"). Second, the Court tried to identify the content of the word as used in the ICWA. The Court launched its analysis of that question as follows:

> "That we are dealing with a uniform federal rather than a state definition does not, of course, prevent us from drawing on general state-law principles to determine the ordinary meaning of the words used. Well-settled state law can inform our understanding of what Congress had in mind when it employed a term it did not define. Accordingly, we find it helpful to borrow established common-law principles of domicile to the extent that they are not inconsistent with the objectives of the congressional scheme."

Id. at 47–48 (internal quotation marks omitted); *see also id.* at 49 (assuming that Congress had acted against the backdrop of "generally accepted doctrine in this country"). The Court concluded that the relevant general law made it possible for newborn babies to be domiciled within a reservation even though they had never been physically present there.

Field v. Mans, 516 U.S. 59 (1995), is to the same effect. The federal Bankruptcy Code of 1978 permits bankrupt debtors to get most of their debts discharged, but it makes certain debts nondischargeable. In particular, the bankruptcy process normally "does not discharge an individual debtor from any debt . . . for money [or] property . . . to the extent obtained by . . . false pretenses, a false representation, or actual fraud." 11 U.S.C. § 523(a)(2)(A). In *Field*, the Supreme Court noted that the words "false pretenses, a false representation, or actual fraud" are "common-law terms"—and when a federal statute uses such terms "without further specification," the Court's "established practice" is to "find[ ] Congress's meaning in the generally shared common law." *Field*, 516 U.S. at 69, 73–74. Thus, the Court "construe[d] the terms in § 523(a)(2)(A) to incorporate the general common law of torts" as it had stood in 1978. *Id.* at 70 & n.9. As in *Darden*, the Court added that by "the general common law," the Court meant "the dominant consensus of common-law jurisdictions, rather than the law of any particular State." *Id.* at 70 n.9. To identify the content of that general common law, the Court drew upon the Restatement (Second) of Torts, William Prosser's multijurisdictional hornbook on the law of torts, and the Court's own survey of the legal doctrines of each state as they stood on "November 6, 1978 (the day the Act became law)." *Id.* at 70–75. These sources led the Court to conclude that the concept of "fraud" to which Congress had been referring in § 523(a)(2)(A) entailed a notion of "justifiable . . . reliance." *Id.* at 74–75.

2. Is there anything odd about presuming that modern federal statutes, enacted well after the demise of *Swift v. Tyson*, were adopted against the backdrop of "general" common law? Or is the continuing relevance of general law almost inevitable, given the structure of American federalism? Is it really so strange to presume that when Congress uses terms familiar to the common law without providing any special definition, Congress probably has a species of general law in mind? In *Darden* and the other cases just surveyed, was there any plausible alternative to that approach?

---

2. WHEN (AND WHY) MIGHT GENERAL LAW GOVERN OTHER QUESTIONS THAT A STATUTE "FEDERALIZES"?

As we have seen, when a federal statute uses a word that is familiar to the common law, and when the statute does not offer an alternative definition of the word, modern courts frequently understand the word to draw its content from general American law. But federal statutes can also create other occasions for references to general law. In particular, when a federal statute is understood to federalize certain questions (in the sense that state law is preempted as to those questions), but when the statute does not explicitly answer those questions itself, courts sometimes draw the necessary rules of decision from general law, either on the theory that the statute implicitly incorporates those rules or on the theory that the statute creates room for the rules to operate as a matter of "federal common law." *Cf.* Caleb Nelson, *The Legitimacy of (Some) Federal Common Law*, 101 VA. L. REV. 1 (2015).

We have already seen some examples. *See supra* pp. 24–25 (asking whether a federal statute creating a private right of action for damages should be presumed to accommodate the common-law defense of accord and satisfaction, so that claims under the statute can be settled out of court); *supra* pp. 87–91 (discussing whether federal statutes defining crimes should be presumed to accommodate standard common-law defenses). There are many other prominent illustrations too. For instance, the idea that most kinds of federal criminal statutes should be understood to have a scienter requirement of some sort, even if they do not make one explicit, has roots in general law. *See* Morissette v. United States, 342 U.S. 246, 250–63 (1952). So does the principle that "nonjurisdictional limitations periods [established by federal statutes] are presumptively subject to equitable tolling." *Boechler, P.C. v. Comm'r*, 142 S. Ct. 1493, 1500 (2022) ("Equitable tolling is a traditional feature of American jurisprudence and a background principle against which Congress drafts limitations periods.").

The next case is another uncontroversial example.

Meyer v. Holley

537 U.S. 280 (2003)

■ *JUSTICE BREYER delivered the opinion of the Court:*

The Fair Housing Act forbids racial discrimination in respect to the sale or rental of a dwelling. 82 Stat. 81, 42 U.S.C. §§ 3604(b), 3605(a). The question before us is whether the Act imposes personal liability without fault upon an officer or owner of a residential real estate corporation for the unlawful activity of the *corporation's* employee or agent. We conclude that the Act imposes liability without fault upon the employer in accordance with traditional agency principles, *i.e.*, it normally imposes vicarious liability upon the corporation but not upon its officers or owners.

I

For purposes of this decision we simplify the background facts as follows: Respondents Emma Mary Ellen Holley and David Holley, an interracial couple, tried to buy a house in Twenty-Nine Palms, California. A real estate corporation, Triad, Inc., had listed the house for sale. Grove Crank, a Triad salesman, is alleged to have prevented the Holleys from obtaining the house—and for racially discriminatory reasons.

The Holleys brought a lawsuit in federal court against Crank and Triad. They claimed, among other things, that both were responsible for a fair housing law violation. The Holleys later filed a separate suit against David Meyer, the petitioner here. Meyer, they said, was Triad's president, Triad's sole shareholder, and Triad's licensed "officer/broker," see Cal. Code Regs., tit. 10, § 2740 (1996) (requiring that a corporation, in order to engage in acts for which a real estate license is required, designate one of its officers to act as the licensed broker); Cal. Bus. & Prof. Code Ann. §§ 10158, 10159, 10211 (West 1987). They claimed that Meyer was vicariously liable in one or more of these capacities for Crank's unlawful actions.

The District Court consolidated the two lawsuits. It dismissed all claims other than the Fair Housing Act claim on statute of limitations grounds. It dismissed the claims against Meyer in his capacity as officer of Triad because (1) it considered those claims as assertions of *vicarious* liability, and (2) it believed that the Fair Housing Act did not impose personal vicarious liability upon a corporate *officer*. The District Court stated that "any liability against Meyer as an officer of Triad would only attach to Triad," the corporation. The court added that the Holleys had "not urged theories that could justify reaching Meyer individually." It later went on to dismiss for similar reasons claims of vicarious liability against Meyer in his capacity as the "designated officer/broker" in respect to Triad's real estate license.

The District Court certified its judgment as final to permit the Holleys to appeal its vicarious liability determinations. See Fed. Rule Civ. Proc. 54(b). The Ninth Circuit reversed those determinations. 258 F.3d 1127 (2001). The Court of Appeals recognized that "under general principles of tort law corporate shareholders and officers usually are not held vicariously liable for an employee's action," but, in its view, "the criteria for the Fair Housing Act" are "different." *Id.* at 1129. That Act, it said, "specified" liability "for those who direct or control or have the right to direct or control the conduct of another"—even if they were not at all involved in the discrimination itself and even in the absence of any traditional agent/principal or employee/employer relationship, *id.* at 1129, 1131. Meyer, in his capacity as Triad's sole owner, had "the authority to control the acts" of a Triad salesperson. *Id.* at 1133. Meyer, in his capacity as Triad's officer, "did direct or control, or had the right to direct or control, the conduct" of a Triad salesperson. *Ibid.* And even if Meyer neither participated in nor authorized the discrimination in question, that "control" or "authority to control" is "enough . . . to hold Meyer personally liable." *Ibid.* The Ninth Circuit added that, for similar reasons, Meyer, in his capacity as Triad's license-related officer/broker, was vicariously liable for Crank's discriminatory activity. *Id.* at 1134–1135.

Meyer sought certiorari. We granted his petition . . . to review the Ninth Circuit's holding that the Fair Housing Act imposes principles of strict liability beyond those traditionally associated with agent/principal or employee/employer relationships. . . .

II

The Fair Housing Act itself focuses on prohibited acts. In relevant part the Act forbids "any person or other entity whose business includes engaging in residential real estate-related transactions to discriminate," for example, because of "race." 42 U.S.C. § 3605(a). It adds that "[p]erson" includes, for example, individuals, corporations, partnerships, associations, labor unions, and other organizations. § 3602(d). It says nothing about vicarious liability.

Nonetheless, it is well established that the Act provides for vicarious liability. This Court has noted that an action brought for compensation by a victim of housing discrimination is, in effect, a tort action. See *Curtis v. Loether*, 415 U.S. 189, 195–196 (1974). And the Court has assumed that, when Congress creates a tort action, it legislates against a legal background of ordinary tort-related vicarious liability rules and consequently intends its legislation to incorporate those rules. *Monterey v. Del Monte Dunes at Monterey, Ltd.*, 526 U.S. 687, 709 (1999) (listing this Court's precedents that interpret Rev. Stat. § 1979, 42 U.S.C. § 1983, in which Congress created "a species of tort liability," "in light of the background of tort liability" (internal quotation marks omitted)). Cf. *Astoria Fed. Sav. & Loan Assn. v. Solimino*, 501 U.S. 104, 108 (1991) ("Congress is understood to legislate against a background of common-law . . . principles"); *United States v. Texas*, 507 U.S. 529, 534 (1993) ("In order to abrogate a common-law principle, the statute must 'speak directly' to the question addressed by the common law").

It is well established that traditional vicarious liability rules ordinarily make principals or employers vicariously liable for acts of their agents or employees in the scope of their authority or employment. *Burlington Industries, Inc. v. Ellerth*, 524 U.S. 742, 756 (1998) ("An employer may be liable for both negligent and intentional torts committed by an employee within the scope of his or her employment"); *New Orleans, M., & C.R. Co. v. Hanning*, 15 Wall. 649, 657 (1873) ("The principal is liable for the acts and negligence of the agent in the course of his employment, although he did not authorize or did not know of the acts complained of"); . . . Restatement (Second) of Agency § 219(1) (1957) (Restatement). And in the absence of special circumstances it is the corporation, not its owner or officer, who is the principal or employer, and thus subject to vicarious liability for torts committed by its employees or agents. 3A W. Fletcher, Cyclopedia of the Law of Private Corporations § 1137, pp. 300–301 (rev. ed. 1991–1994); 10 *id.* § 4877 (rev. ed. 1997–2001). The Restatement § 1 specifies that the relevant principal/agency relationship demands not only control (or the right to direct or control) but also "the manifestation of consent by one person to another that the other shall act *on his behalf* . . . , and consent by the other so to act." (Emphasis added.) A corporate employee typically acts on behalf of the corporation, not its owner or officer.

The Ninth Circuit held that the Fair Housing Act imposed more extensive vicarious liability—that the Act went well beyond traditional principles. The Court of Appeals held that the Act made corporate owners and officers liable for the unlawful acts of a corporate employee simply on the basis that the owner or officer controlled (or had the right to control) the actions of that employee. We do not agree with the Ninth Circuit that the Act extended traditional vicarious liability rules in this way.

For one thing, Congress said nothing in the statute or in the legislative history about extending vicarious liability in this manner. And Congress' silence, while permitting an inference that Congress intended to apply *ordinary* background tort principles, cannot show that it intended to apply an unusual modification of those rules.

Where Congress, in other civil rights statutes, has not expressed a contrary intent, the Court has drawn the inference that it intended ordinary rules to apply. See, *e.g.*, *Burlington Industries, Inc.*, *supra*, at 754–755 (deciding an employer's vicarious liability under Title VII based on traditional agency principles); *Meritor Savings Bank, FSB v. Vinson*, 477 U.S. 57, 72 (1986) ("Congress wanted courts to look to agency principles for guidance").

This Court has applied unusually strict rules only where Congress has specified that such was its intent. See, *e.g.*, *United States v. Dotterweich*, 320 U.S. 277, 280–281 (1943) (Congress intended that a corporate officer or employee "standing in responsible relation" could be held liable in that capacity for a corporation's violations of the Federal Food, Drug, and Cosmetic Act of 1938 . . .); *United States v. Park*, 421 U.S. 658, 673 (1975) (discussing, with respect to the Federal Food, Drug, and Cosmetic Act, congressional intent to impose a duty on "responsible corporate agents"); *United States v. Wise*, 370 U.S. 405, 411–414 (1962) (discussing 38 Stat. 736, currently 15 U.S.C. § 24, which provides: "[W]henever a corporation shall violate any of the . . . antitrust laws, such violation shall be deemed to be also that of the individual directors, officers, or agents of such corporation who shall have authorized, ordered, or done any of the acts constituting in whole or in part such violation"); see also 46 U.S.C. § 12507(d) ("If a person, not an individual, is involved in a violation [relating to a vessel identification system], the president or chief executive of the person also is subject to any penalty provided under this section").

For another thing, the Department of Housing and Urban Development (HUD), the federal agency primarily charged with the implementation and administration of the statute, 42 U.S.C. § 3608, has specified that ordinary vicarious liability rules apply in this area. And we ordinarily defer to an administering agency's reasonable interpretation of a statute. *Chevron U.S.A. Inc. v. Natural Resources Defense Council, Inc.*, 467 U.S. 837, 842–845 (1984); *Skidmore v. Swift & Co.*, 323 U.S. 134, 140 (1944).

A HUD regulation applicable during the relevant time periods for this suit provided that analogous administrative complaints alleging Fair Housing Act violations may be filed

> "against any person who directs or controls, or has the right to direct or control, the conduct of another person with respect to any aspect of the sale . . . of dwellings . . . *if that other person, acting within the scope of his or her authority as employee or agent of the directing or*

> *controlling person* . . . has engaged . . . in a discriminatory housing practice." 24 CFR § 103.20(b) (1999) (repealed) (emphasis added).

See *Gladstone, Realtors v. Village of Bellwood*, 441 U.S. 91, 107 (1979) (treating administrative actions under 42 U.S.C. § 3610 and civil actions under § 3613 as alternative, but parallel, proceedings).

When it adopted the similar predecessor to this regulation (then codified at 24 CFR § 105.13, see 53 Fed. Reg. 24185 (1988)), HUD explained that it intended to permit a "respondent" (defined at 42 U.S.C. § 3602) to raise in an administrative proceeding any defense "that could be raised in court." 53 Fed. Reg. at 24185. It added that the underscored phrase was designed to make clear that "a complaint may be filed against a directing or controlling person with respect to the discriminatory acts of another only if the other person was acting within the scope of his or her authority as *employee or agent of the directing or controlling person.*" *Ibid.* (emphasis added). HUD also specified that, by adding the words "acting within the scope of his or her authority as employee or agent of the directing or controlling person," it disclaimed any "intent to impose absolute liability" on the basis of the mere right "to direct or control." *Ibid.*; see 54 Fed. Reg. 3232, 3261 (1989).

Finally, we have found no convincing argument in support of the Ninth Circuit's decision to apply nontraditional vicarious liability principles—a decision that respondents do not defend and in fact concede is incorrect. . . .

The Ninth Circuit . . . referred to an owner's or officer's "nondelegable duty" not to discriminate in light of the Act's "overriding societal priority." 258 F.3d at 1131, 1132 . . . .

"[A] nondelegable duty is an affirmative obligation to ensure the protection of the person to whom the duty runs." *General Building Contractors Ass'n, Inc. v. Pennsylvania*, 458 U.S. 375, 396 (1982) (finding no nondelegable duty under 42 U.S.C. § 1981). Such a duty imposed upon a principal would "go further" than the vicarious liability principles we have discussed thus far to create liability "although [the principal] has himself done everything that could reasonably be required of him," W. Prosser, Law of Torts § 71, p. 470 (4th ed. 1971), and irrespective of whether the agent was acting with or without authority. The Ninth Circuit identifies nothing in the language or legislative history of the Act to support the existence of this special kind of liability—the kind of liability that, for example, the law might impose in certain special circumstances upon a principal or employer that hires an independent contractor. Restatement § 214; see 5 F. Harper, F. James, & O. Gray, Law of Torts § 26.11 (2d ed. 1986); Prosser, *supra*, § 71, at 470–471. In the absence of legal support, we cannot conclude that Congress intended, through silence, to impose this kind of special duty of protection upon individual officers or owners of corporations—who are not principals (or contracting parties) in respect to the corporation's unlawfully acting employee.

Neither does it help to characterize the statute's objective as an "overriding societal priority." 258 F.3d at 1132. We agree with the characterization. But we do not agree that the characterization carries with it a legal rule that would hold every corporate supervisor personally liable without fault for the unlawful act of every corporate employee whom he or she has the right to supervise. Rather, which "of two innocent people must suffer," *ibid.*, and just when, is a complex matter. We believe that courts ordinarily should determine that matter in accordance with traditional principles of vicarious liability—unless, of course, Congress, better able than courts to weigh the relevant policy considerations, has instructed the courts differently. Cf., *e.g.*, Sykes, The Economics of Vicarious Liability, 93 Yale L.J. 1231, 1236 (1984) (arguing that the expansion of vicarious liability or shifting of liability, due to insurance, may diminish an agent's incentives to police behavior). We have found no different instruction here.

III

A

Respondents, conceding that traditional vicarious liability rules apply, argue that those principles themselves warrant liability here. For one thing, they say, California law itself creates what amounts, under ordinary common-law principles, to an employer/employee or principal/agent relationship between (a) a corporate officer designated as the broker under a real estate license issued to the corporation, and (b) a corporate employee/salesperson. Brief for Respondents 6–8, 13–36. Insofar as this argument rests *solely* upon the corporate broker/officer's *right to control* the employee/salesperson, the Ninth Circuit considered and accepted it. 258 F.3d at 1134–1135. But we must reject it given our determination in Part II that the "right to control" is insufficient by itself, under traditional agency principles, to establish a principal/agent or employer/employee relationship.

B

The Ninth Circuit did not decide whether *other* aspects of the California broker relationship, when added to the "right to control," would, under traditional legal principles and consistent with "the general common law of agency," *Burlington Industries, Inc. v. Ellerth*, 524 U.S. at 754 (internal quotation marks omitted), establish the necessary relationship. But in the absence of consideration of that matter by the Court of Appeals, we shall not consider it. . . .

The Ninth Circuit nonetheless remains free on remand to determine whether these questions were properly raised and, if so, to consider them.

The judgment of the Court of Appeals is vacated, and the case is remanded for further proceedings consistent with this opinion.

NOTES AND QUESTIONS

1. The Fair Housing Act explicitly creates a federal right of action in favor of plaintiffs who are injured by violations of the Act's substantive provisions. *See* Fair Housing Amendments Act of 1988, Pub. L. 100–430, sec. 8, § 813, 102 Stat. 1619, 1633 (providing that "[a]n aggrieved person may commence a civil action in an appropriate United States district court . . . to obtain appropriate relief with respect to [an alleged] discriminatory housing practice," and addressing the available remedies) (codified at 42 U.S.C. § 3613); *see also* Fair Housing Act, Pub. L. 90–284, § 802(f), 82 Stat. 73, 81 (1968) (defining "discriminatory housing practice" to mean "an act that is unlawful under [specified provisions of the Act]") (codified as amended at 42 U.S.C. § 3602(f)). But the Act does not say much about the proper defendants in these actions. Among other things, the Act does not explicitly address the circumstances in which an individual's actions should be attributed to the entity for which the individual works, or the circumstances in which one person faces vicarious liability because of another person's violation of the Act.

To help answer those questions, the Supreme Court's opinion in *Meyer v. Holley* reasoned that the right of action created by the Act "is, in effect, a tort action." *Meyer*, 537 U.S. at 285. According to the Court, moreover, "when Congress creates a tort action, it legislates against a legal background of ordinary tort-related vicarious liability rules" and should typically be presumed to "intend[ ] its legislation to incorporate those rules." *Id.* When the Court referred to "ordinary tort-related vicarious liability rules," the Court was talking about general American law—the sort of legal principles reflected in the *Restatement (Second) of Agency* and multijurisdictional treatises like Fletcher's *Cyclopedia of the Law of Private Corporations*. Citing those sources, the Court observed that "traditional vicarious liability rules ordinarily make principals or employers vicariously liable for acts of their agents or employees in the scope of their authority or employment." *Meyer*, 537 U.S. at 285.

That made it important to know who was an agent or employee of whom. Under standard principles of agency law, Mr. Crank (the individual whom the Holleys accused of discrimination) was an agent or employee of Triad, Inc. (the real-estate corporation that employed him)—so if he had violated the Fair Housing Act while acting for Triad, then the general principles that the Court read the Act to incorporate would support holding Triad liable. Under general American law, though, liability for what Mr. Crank had done on behalf of Triad would not automatically flow through the corporation to its individual officers or shareholders; although Mr. Crank was an agent or employee of the corporation, he was not thereby an agent or employee of the corporation's individual officers or shareholders. Thus, the mere fact that David Meyer was Triad's president and sole shareholder did not make him vicariously liable too. *See id.* at 282 ("We conclude that the [Fair Housing] Act imposes liability without fault upon the employer in accordance with traditional agency principles, *i.e.*, it normally imposes vicarious liability upon the corporation but not upon its officers or owners.").[48]

2. Did the Supreme Court's reliance on general agency principles make sense? Each of the fifty states may have its own take on the formation of agency relationships and the details of vicarious liability for tort claims. The states' doctrines on these topics will overlap in many ways but will differ from each other in some respects. At least on questions as to which different states have different doctrines, distilling a unitary principle of general American law may require contestable judgments. Would it have been better for the Supreme Court to presume that when a federal statute creates a tort-like right of action but says nothing about vicarious liability, the statute either (a) does not recognize vicarious liability at all or (b) implicitly incorporates varying rules of vicarious liability supplied by the local law of the state in which the relevant acts occurred?

If a state legislature had enacted a state statute worded exactly like the federal Fair Housing Act, the state courts probably would have read the statute to impose vicarious liability along the lines suggested by the state's common law of torts and agency. It is natural to think that the federal statute too should be understood to incorporate some concept of vicarious liability. (For instance, it seems obvious that the Fair Housing Act makes corporations like Triad liable for violations of the Act that their employees commit within the scope of their employment.) Still, to the extent that a federal statute does impose liability in line with common-law principles, we would not necessarily expect the statute to incorporate the common law of any particular state, or to adopt a varying test for liability that changes from one state to the next. Instead of relying on the local law of individual states (in the manner of the *Beaver County* case), the Supreme Court presumed that Congress meant to adopt a species of general American law, which is informed by the vicarious-liability rules of each of the fifty states but which filters out local idiosyncrasies.

3. Note the difference between the Supreme Court's approach and the approach taken by the Ninth Circuit before the case reached the Supreme Court. The Ninth Circuit had held that the Fair Housing Act imposed lots of vicarious liability, because recognizing lots of vicarious liability

[48] Part III of the Supreme Court's opinion did leave room for one theory upon which the general common law of agency might regard Mr. Crank as Mr. Meyer's agent, and hence upon which the Fair Housing Act might make Mr. Meyer vicariously liable. The factual basis for that theory grew out of an aspect of how California regulates real-estate brokers: under California law, a corporation that wants to act as a real-estate broker must be licensed through a designated "broker-officer," who has some responsibilities in that capacity. Triad had designated Mr. Meyer as its "broker-officer," but there apparently was evidence that Mr. Meyer had delegated his responsibilities to Mr. Crank, and the Ninth Circuit thought that Mr. Meyer might have created a personal agency relationship with Mr. Crank. *See* Holley v. Crank, 400 F.3d 667, 673 (9th Cir. 2005) (concluding, on remand from the Supreme Court, that the case could proceed on this theory); *cf.* Sandler v. Sanchez, 206 Cal. App. 4th 1431, 1445 (2012) (speculating that in reaching this conclusion, the Ninth Circuit had relied on evidence of "some form of actual agreement between Meyer and Crank," and suggesting that the two would not otherwise have had an agency relationship).

would promote what the Ninth Circuit took to be the Act's broad remedial purposes. In the service of those purposes, the Ninth Circuit was prepared to craft a statute-specific rule of vicarious liability that went well beyond ordinary tort principles.

Justice Breyer rejected that approach. To the extent that the Fair Housing Act does not specifically address vicarious liability, he read it against the backdrop of general American law, and he was not receptive to arguments that a statute-specific rule of vicarious liability might better serve Congress's purposes. As he put the point, "Congress' silence [about vicarious liability], while permitting an inference that Congress intended to apply *ordinary* background tort principles, cannot show that it intended to apply an unusual modification of those rules." *Meyer*, 537 U.S. at 286.

In sum, Justice Breyer did not treat the statute as containing a gap that courts have broad discretion to fill in whatever way they think will best advance the purposes that they attribute to the statute. Instead, the statute's failure to address vicarious liability meant that ordinary principles applied; even if courts thought that other principles might do a better job of ending housing discrimination, the statute incorporated general American law with respect to vicarious liability, and that is what the courts must use. In this respect, Justice Breyer's opinion in *Meyer* (which was unanimous) dovetails with *Darden* (which was also unanimous) and the Court's movement away from *Hearst Publications*.

4. *Meyer v. Holley* is one of many cases in which the Supreme Court has looked to general American law for principles of vicarious liability in suits under federal antidiscrimination statutes. *See, e.g.*, Burlington Indus., Inc. v. Ellerth, 524 U.S. 742, 754–55 (1998) (using " 'the general common law of agency, rather than . . . the law of any particular State,' " to help determine an employer's liability under Title VII of the Civil Rights Act of 1964 for sexual harassment perpetrated by the plaintiff's supervisor, though observing that " 'common-law principles may not be transferable in all their particulars to Title VII' " (first quoting Community for Creative Non-Violence v. Reid, 490 U.S. 730, 740 (1989), and then quoting Meritor Savings Bank v. Vinson, 477 U.S. 57, 755 (1986))); *see also* Kolstad v. Am. Dental Ass'n, 527 U.S. 526, 542 (1999) (likewise using " 'the general common law of agency, rather than . . . the law of any particular State,' " to help determine when employers are liable for punitive damages in Title VII cases (quoting *Ellerth*, 524 U.S. at 754)).

In several cases of this sort from the late 1990s, the Court said that the American Law Institute's *Restatement (Second) of Agency* (1957)—which was then the latest version—"provides a useful starting point for defining this general common law." *Kolstad*, 527 U.S. at 542; *accord* Faragher v. City of Boca Raton, 524 U.S. 775, 802 (1998); *Ellerth*, 524

U.S. at 755.[49] One reason why the Restatement was just a "starting point" may be that it did not always match current case law; doctrine may have changed to some extent since 1957, and in any event modern Restatements sometimes aim to change legal doctrine rather than simply to distill it. *See* Caleb Nelson, *The Persistence of General Law*, 106 COLUM. L. REV. 503, 510 n.35 (2006) ("[T]he fact that most states have rejected a particular legal rule will not necessarily keep the relevant Restatement from embracing it."). But the Supreme Court also viewed the Restatement as a "starting point" in a different sense. Although the Court treated general agency principles as *presumptively* supplying the rules of vicarious liability for federal statutes like Title VII, the Court asserted authority to adjust those principles in order to promote the purposes of the particular federal statute in question. *See Kolstad*, 527 U.S. at 545 ("In light of the perverse incentives that the Restatement's 'scope of employment' rules create, we are compelled to modify those principles to avoid undermining the objectives underlying Title VII."); *Faragher*, 524 U.S. at 802 n.3 (describing the Court as "adapt[ing] agency concepts to the practical objectives of Title VII"); *see also Ellerth*, 524 U.S. at 764–65 (articulating limits on vicarious liability that reflected not only "agency principles" but also policies that the Court attributed to Title VII, such as "Congress' intention to promote conciliation rather than litigation" and the goal of "encourag[ing] employees to report harassing conduct before it becomes severe or pervasive").

If some aspect of general agency law would get in the way of achieving the purposes behind a particular federal statute, can federal courts legitimately refrain from applying that aspect of agency law in cases under the statute, even if the statute says nothing explicit on this topic and even if courts otherwise understand the statute to incorporate general agency principles? Compare that idea to doctrines of "obstacle preemption," about the circumstances in which a federal statute should be understood to preempt state law. *See supra* pp. 1166–1178. Even if you are skeptical of obstacle preemption where state law is concerned, might the test for whether a federal statute preempts aspects of state law that otherwise would apply of their own force be more demanding than the test for whether a federal statute simply does not incorporate some aspect of general common law? If that aspect of general common law would indeed get in the way of accomplishing the statute's purposes, couldn't courts infer that the statute does not incorporate it? But if courts can do that, what was wrong with the Ninth Circuit's approach in *Meyer v. Holley* (where the Ninth Circuit articulated a special doctrine of vicarious liability so as to promote the purposes that the Ninth Circuit attributed to the Fair Housing Act)?

[49] There is now a *Restatement (Third) of Agency* (2006). The specific section of the *Restatement (Second)* that the Court had invoked in *Ellerth* and *Faragher* does not appear in the *Restatement (Third)*. *See* Vance v. Ball State Univ., 570 U.S. 421, 428 n.2 (2013).

5. In *Meyer v. Holley*, the Supreme Court spoke as if the typical federal statute that creates a tort-like right of action, but that does not say anything one way or the other about vicarious liability, implicitly "incorporate[s]" common-law principles about vicarious liability for torts. On this way of talking, the relevant common-law principles are being read into each individual federal statute. But a different account is also possible: perhaps the general common law could be thought of as operating of its own force within a space created by the statute. That space would consist of issues that are so connected with the federal right of action as to lie beyond the reach of state law, but that the federal statute does not itself address and resolve (either explicitly or even implicitly). If the federal statute preempts state law within this space, but does not occupy the field to the exclusion of unwritten principles of general law, the statute might leave room for those principles to operate as a matter of what modern lawyers call "federal common law"[50] rather than via incorporation into the statute itself.

Each of these ways of talking has advantages and disadvantages. The idea that the general common law can operate of its own force (within the space created by written federal law) avoids the need to handle these issues purely as a matter of statutory interpretation, and hence to pretend that individual federal statutes implicitly adopt elaborate rules on topics that they do not seem to address. But if one does not think of the general common law as being incorporated into individual federal statutes, one needs to explain why it applies at all. Unlike many states, Congress has not enacted a statute explicitly "receiving" the common law and making it applicable at the federal level. *Cf., e.g.*, CAL. CIV. CODE § 22.2 ("The common law of England, so far as it is not repugnant to or inconsistent with the Constitution of the United States, or the Constitution or laws of this State, is the rule of decision in all the courts of this State."). Might the common law nonetheless operate as customary law on issues that Congress has federalized but has not itself resolved?

6. Within the limits of its enumerated powers, Congress obviously can depart from the common law if it wants to. When Congress enacted the Fair Housing Act, for instance, Congress did not have to recognize any vicarious liability at all. When should generally worded federal statutes be interpreted as either incorporating or accommodating common-law ideas that they do not specifically codify, and when should Congress's statutes instead be understood to occupy the fields that the statutes address to the exclusion of those ideas?

The assumption that the Fair Housing Act accommodates or implicitly incorporates standard common-law principles about vicarious liability, even though the Act says nothing explicit on that topic, may

[50] The reason that these principles of common law would be regarded as "federal" common law, rather than being a matter of state law, is that the federal statute preempts state law within the relevant space. Outside of the zone of preemption, state law would operate as usual, and any applicable principles of common law would simply be *state* common law (understandings of which can vary from state to state).

raise echoes of the longstanding canon that statutes in derogation of the common law should be construed strictly. Historically, English courts sometimes applied that canon quite aggressively. Commentators eventually denounced aggressive uses of the canon as a power grab by courts—an attempt to make it very hard for legislatures to change the common-law rules that courts articulated. Courts have taken that criticism to heart, and they do not apply the canon with nearly as much vigor as they once did. At least when it is clear that a statute was intended to deviate from some rule of common law, courts are not stingy about the extent of the deviation.

In *Meyer v. Holley*, though, the Supreme Court saw no reason to think that the Fair Housing Act was intended to deviate from the common law's rules about vicarious liability. Even though the Act did not address vicarious liability, it seems highly unlikely that Congress wanted to overthrow the traditional rules on that subject and to have no vicarious liability at all. (For instance, it would be very strange to say that a real-estate corporation is not vicariously liable for what its agents and employees do on its behalf.) Likewise, the fact that the Act did not say anything about vicarious liability suggests that Congress was not trying to replace the ordinary rules on this topic with a statute-specific substitute.

Sometimes, though, it might not be so clear whether a particular federal statute was or was not meant to depart from common-law principles that could operate within the space that the statute federalizes. For instance, suppose that a federal statute contains a generally worded provision that does not specifically address a discrete issue that the common law ordinarily handles a certain way. Suppose further that unless courts read an implied qualification or embellishment into the statute, the provision's general language would seem to encompass this issue and to depart from the usual common-law rule. Under what circumstances, if any, should courts infer a qualification or embellishment that preserves the common-law rule? When should general statutory language be interpreted as overthrowing common-law ideas that it does not specifically codify, and when should such language instead be presumed to accommodate common-law ideas that it does not specifically reject? Does it matter whether the common-law ideas address issues that are somehow separate from the rules that the statute seems designed to establish (even if readers who have not attended law school would think that the statutory language is broad enough to encompass those issues)?

If you are tempted to say that courts should *never* allow the common law to qualify generally worded statutes in this way, think about federal criminal statutes that do not explicitly contain a scienter requirement, or that do not explicitly address defenses of the sort that the common law supplies. Isn't it appropriate for courts to read generally worded statutes as accommodating our legal traditions? On the other hand, statutes obviously take priority over the common law where they come into conflict. How, exactly, should courts decide whether a conflict exists?

7. In *Meyer v. Holley*, Justice Breyer invoked *Chevron* deference in support of his conclusion: he understood regulations promulgated by the Department of Housing and Urban Development to indicate that "ordinary vicarious liability rules apply" with respect to the Fair Housing Act, and he observed that "we ordinarily defer to an administering agency's reasonable interpretation of a statute." *Meyer*, 537 U.S. at 287–88 (citing both *Chevron* and *Skidmore* without specifying which might apply). If the agency had instead adopted the position later taken by the Ninth Circuit—that is, if the agency had read the statute to depart from general principles of vicarious liability even though the statute said nothing on that topic one way or the other—would the Court have had to accept the agency's position?

What if the agency had agreed that "ordinary" principles of vicarious liability apply, but had weighed in on the content of those principles? Might the answer depend on whether the relevant principles of vicarious liability are thought of as operating through incorporation into aspects of the Fair Housing Act that the agency administers, or whether those principles instead operate of their own force within a space created by the Act? Even if we think of the Act as incorporating the relevant principles of common law, is there any reason for courts to defer to the agency about the content of those principles? Or do the expertise-based arguments for *Chevron* deference, and perhaps even the accountability-based arguments, fall apart in this context? *See* Int'l Longshoremen's Ass'n, AFL-CIO v. NLRB, 56 F.3d 205, 212 (D.C. Cir. 1995) ("[W]hen confronted with a question regarding the meaning of an NLRA provision incorporating common law agency principles, we need not defer to the agency's judgment as we normally might under . . . *Chevron* . . . ."); *accord* Browning-Ferris Indus. of Cal., Inc. v. NLRB, 911 F.3d 1195, 1207 (D.C. Cir. 2018) (explaining that Congress did not empower the NLRB "to recast traditional common-law principles of agency in identifying covered employees and employers," and concluding that "we review *de novo* whether the Board's joint-employer test comports with traditional common-law principles of agency"); *see also* Kisor v. Wilkie, 139 S. Ct. 2400, 2417 (2019) (observing, with respect to *Auer* deference, that "[s]ome interpretive issues may fall more naturally into a judge's bailiwick" than an agency's, and offering as an example "the elucidation of a simple common-law property term"); *cf.* SFPP, L.P. v. FERC, 967 F.3d 788, 795 (D.C. Cir. 2020) ("[T]he Court gives no deference to an agency's interpretation of judicial precedent.").

NOTE ON THE DETAILS OF FEDERAL RIGHTS OF ACTION

Meyer v. Holley is part of a broader phenomenon. For reasons discussed in this note, courts frequently use principles of general American law to answer questions about the details of federal rights of action. To be sure, the general law supplies rules of decision in other enclaves of federal law too; general law is potentially relevant to many questions that Congress or the Constitution has federalized without answering. But the details of federal rights of action are a good example.

A "right of action" is a remedial right—the sort of legal principle that makes a plaintiff eligible to obtain some type of remedy from a court of competent jurisdiction if the plaintiff satisfies all of the elements of the right of action and the defendant does not establish any applicable defense. Many rights of action are created by *state* law, including state common law, and plaintiffs sometimes can use those rights of action to obtain relief for harms that they have suffered because of a defendant's violation of duties created by a federal statute.[51] Separate and apart from whatever rights of action might exist as a matter of state law, though, Congress sometimes creates rights of action as a matter of federal law. For instance, in addition to establishing substantive duties about how people are supposed to behave in the real world, a federal statute might create a private right of action for damages in favor of people who are injured by someone's violation of those duties.

When a federal statute explicitly creates a private right of action, the statute is likely to say something about the parameters of that right of action: who is liable to whom for what? But the statute usually does not address all of the details. To the extent that the right of action makes the plaintiff eligible for an award of damages, what is the proper measure of damages: which harms are compensable, and how should courts calculate the amount of money that will compensate the plaintiff for those harms? Does the measure of damages include prejudgment interest?[52] Is there a requirement of proximate causation, and if so what is the content of that requirement? Can one would-be plaintiff assign the right of action to another? If the plaintiff (or the defendant) dies before judgment, does the right of action survive, so that it becomes a claim by (or against) the

---

[51] For instance, state common law often enables plaintiffs to seek damages for injuries proximately caused by the defendant's negligence, and plaintiffs often can satisfy the element of negligence by proving that the defendant violated a duty imposed by a relevant statute—one that is "designed to protect the class of persons[ ] in which the plaintiff is included[ ] against the risk of the type of harm which has in fact occurred as a result of its violation." W. PAGE KEETON ET AL., PROSSER AND KEETON ON THE LAW OF TORTS 229–30 (5th ed. 1984); *accord* RESTATEMENT (THIRD) OF THE LAW OF TORTS: LIABILITY FOR PHYSICAL AND EMOTIONAL HARM § 14 (AM. L. INST. 2010) (restating this doctrine of "negligence per se"). Under most states' versions of this doctrine, federal statutes can be no less relevant for this purpose than state or local statutes. *See id.* cmt. a. *But see* T&M Jewelry, Inc. v. Hicks, 189 S.W.3d 526, 530 (Ky. 2006) (noting that KY. REV. STAT. § 446.070 "codifies the doctrine of negligence per se in Kentucky," and observing that "'any statute' in KRS 446.070 has been held to be limited to Kentucky statutes and not to [include] federal statutes or local ordinances").

[52] As the Supreme Court has explained, whether prejudgment interest is available as part of a claim is a question about the measure of damages for that claim. *See* Monessen Sw. Ry. Co. v. Morgan, 486 U.S. 330, 335 (1988) ("Prejudgment interest is normally designed to make the plaintiff whole and is part of the actual damages sought to be recovered."). *Post*judgment interest is different; instead of being linked to the underlying right of action, the interest that accumulates on a judgment debt normally is governed by the law of the jurisdiction whose courts rendered the judgment.

deceased party's estate? Is the right of action subject to release, or to out-of-court settlement?

Where *federal* rights of action are concerned, courts usually do not draw the answers to these questions from the local law of individual states. Instead, courts typically presume that when Congress creates a federal right of action, all of the questions just listed are questions of federal law, even if Congress has not explicitly addressed them.[53] That makes sense, because these questions are normally regarded as being part of the same package as the right of action itself. Under standard choice-of-law jurisprudence, for instance, it would be very strange for courts to use one sovereign's law to decide whether a right of action exists but to use a different sovereign's law to identify the measure of damages or to decide whether the right of action is assignable. *See* Nelson, *supra* note 53, 106 COLUM. L. REV. at 544. By the same token, when Congress creates a federal right of action, Congress typically is presumed to be federalizing these questions of detail. *See id.* at 544 & n.203.

That point can be cast in terms of preemption. Of course, the typical federal statute that creates a federal right of action does not necessarily prevent states from creating separate rights of action as a matter of state law. *See, e.g.*, California v. ARC Am. Corp., 490 U.S. 93, 105 (1989). But while each state would be able to define the details of those *state* rights of action, states are not in charge of the details of *federal* rights of action. Normally, states lack lawmaking power to specify the measure of damages for a federal right of action, or to provide that the right of action

---

[53] *See, e.g.*, Uthe Tech. Corp. v. Aetrium, Inc., 808 F.3d 755, 760 n.3 (9th Cir. 2015) ("[I]t stands to reason that the measure of damages corresponding to a federal cause of action such as RICO should be governed by the federal law of damages rather than by state law."); Mallick v. IBEW, 814 F.2d 674, 676 (D.C. Cir. 1987) ("The Supreme Court has repeatedly held that the survivorship of a federal claim is itself an issue of federal law."); In re Nat'l Mtge. Equity Corp. Mtge. Pool Certificates Sec. Litig., 636 F. Supp. 1138, 1152 (C.D. Cal. 1986) ("Where a claim for relief is created by a federal statute, federal law governs the assignability of the claim.").

Recently, some federal district courts have suggested that because the federal Fair Debt Collection Practices Act (FDCPA) does not explicitly address the assignability of the right of action that it creates, state law governs that topic. *See, e.g.*, Cooper v. Nat'l Credit Adjusters, LLC, 2022 WL 17656316 (magistrate judge's report and recommendation) (citing cases), *adopted*, 2022 WL 17631533 (N.D. Tex.). But that strikes me as a mistake: the assignability of a right of action is an aspect of the right of action itself, and it would be odd to conclude that state law controls this aspect of federal rights of action. Of course, if a federal right of action is indeed assignable, courts will sometimes face further questions about whether a particular document amounts to a valid contract of assignment, and the answer to *those* questions might well depend on the contract law of a particular state. *See* Caleb Nelson, *The Persistence of General Law*, 106 COLUM. L. REV. 503, 554–55 (2006) (discussing this distinction). Likewise, state laws against champerty or the like might regulate the assignment of rights of action that are themselves assignable, and federal law will not necessarily prevent states from applying those laws with respect to federal rights of action. *Cf.* Martin v. Morgan Drive Away, Inc., 665 F.2d 598, 604–05 (5th Cir. 1982) (using Louisiana's principles of champerty, albeit via absorption into federal law, to determine the validity of an assignment agreement involving claims under the Sherman Act). Normally, though, the threshold question of whether a federal right of action is subject to assignment at all should be regarded as a question of federal law. *See, e.g.*, Bluebird Partners, L.P. v. First Fid. Bank, N.A. N.J., 85 F.3d 970, 973 (2d Cir. 1996) ("The federal courts have consistently determined that federal law governs the assignability of claims under the federal securities laws."); In re Fine Paper Litig., 632 F.2d 1081, 1090 (3d Cir. 1980) ("[T]he status of assignments under the Sherman and Clayton Acts is a matter of federal law . . . .").

does not survive the plaintiff's death, or to answer other questions that are regarded as part of the federal right of action itself.

If state law is preempted on these questions of detail, but the relevant federal statute does not itself address these questions, where do courts look for answers? Sometimes, judges might come up with statute-specific answers inspired by the purposes that they attribute to the particular federal statute in question. But in the absence of statute-specific guidance, courts routinely draw the necessary rules of decision from general American law, either on the theory that the statute implicitly incorporates principles of general law or on the theory that those principles operate of their own force within the space created by the statute.

For example, suppose that a federal statute explicitly creates a federal right of action for damages but says nothing about ideas of proximate causation. Even though the federal statute does not explicitly address that topic, which harms are compensable under this federal right of action is a matter of federal law. In the absence of statute-specific guidance, moreover, courts are likely to draw the answer from general American law. If the right of action sounds in tort, for instance, courts probably will conclude that the right of action is indeed subject to a proximate-causation limitation, the specifics of which depend on the nature of the right of action. *See, e.g.*, Bank of Am. Corp. v. City of Miami, 581 US. 189, 201–03 (2017) (applying this analysis to the right of action for damages created by the Fair Housing Act).

Admittedly, identifying the content of general American law will not always be easy. On some issues, case law across American jurisdictions will reveal a consensus, which in turn will be reflected in secondary sources like treatises and Restatements. But on other issues, different jurisdictions will fall into different camps, and courts will need to make judgment calls about which camp to pick (or how to reconcile the differences). Even then, though, patterns in the case law will at least limit the plausible alternatives. *Cf.* McDermott, Inc. v. AmClyde, 511 U.S. 202, 208–17 (1994) (approaching a question of maritime law by considering "three principal alternatives" laid out in the *Restatement (Second) of Torts*); *id.* at 209 n.8 ("We are unwilling to consider a rule that has yet to be applied in any jurisdiction.").

The fact that the content of general law can change over time adds another wrinkle. Take the question that the Supreme Court faced in *Monessen Southwestern Railway Co. v. Morgan*, 486 U.S. 330 (1988): when injured railway workers seek damages under the Federal Employers' Liability Act (FELA), are they eligible for prejudgment interest? Because that is a question about the measure of damages, and because "[i]t has long been settled that 'the proper measure of damages [under the FELA] is inseparably connected with the right of action,' " the Court held that "the availability of prejudgment interest under the FELA is a question of federal law." *Id.* at 335 & n.3 (quoting Chesapeake & Ohio

R. Co. v. Kelly, 241 U.S. 485, 491 (1916)). But the FELA did not explicitly address that question. *See id.* at 336. For the Court, the content of the applicable federal rule therefore came from general American law as it stood in 1908, when Congress enacted the FELA. Because the FELA created a right of action for personal injury or wrongful death, and because "[i]n 1908 . . . the common law did not allow prejudgment interest in suits for personal injury or wrongful death," the Court held that the measure of damages in suits under the FELA does not include prejudgment interest. *See id.* at 337–38.

Since 1908, though, general American law has become more hospitable to the award of prejudgment interest. *See* Kansas v. Colorado, 533 U.S. 1, 9–10 (2001) (tracing developments). In *Monessen*, was the Supreme Court correct to assume that the FELA froze in place the principles of general law that existed in 1908, or could the Court instead have held that the availability of prejudgment interest on FELA claims depends upon the principles of general American law that exist when the claims accrue (or, perhaps, when the claims are adjudicated)?

The answer might depend on exactly why general law is relevant. If principles of general law operate of their own force within the space that the FELA federalizes, then courts probably would apply the current version of the general law rather than the version that had existed in 1908. But if general law is relevant only because the FELA is presumed to incorporate it, then courts might presume that the FELA incorporated the principles of general law that existed when Congress enacted the FELA.

Without discussing these possibilities, the Supreme Court's opinion in *Monessen* took the latter approach: the Court presumed that the FELA implicitly incorporated (and froze into place) the common law's rules about prejudgment interest as they stood in 1908. But even if the general law was not operating of its own force, aren't there different ways in which a federal statute like the FELA might implicitly adopt or refer to the general law? Instead of presuming that the FELA incorporated particular principles of general law as they stood in 1908, could the Court instead have presumed that the FELA incorporated something akin to a choice-of-law rule, which would direct courts to apply principles of general law *as they continue to develop*?[54]

[54] Would this sort of "dynamic" reference to general law be constitutional, or might it somehow violate the nondelegation doctrine or the Bicameralism and Presentment Clause? *Compare* United States v. Sharpnack, 355 U.S. 286 (1958) (upholding the constitutionality of the Assimilative Crimes Act of 1948, 18 U.S.C. § 13, which makes the content of federal criminal law in federal enclaves track state criminal law "in force at the time of [the defendant's] act or omission" in the state where the enclave is located), *with* United States v. Paul, 31 U.S. (6 Pet.) 141, 142 (1832) (holding, perhaps simply as a matter of statutory interpretation, that the original 1825 version of the Assimilative Crimes Act "is to be limited to the laws of the several states in force at the time of its enactment"); *see also* RICHARD H. FALLON, JR. ET AL., HART AND WECHSLER'S THE FEDERAL COURTS AND THE FEDERAL SYSTEM 562–64 (7th ed. 2015) (discussing the shift from the original Process Acts, which were interpreted as adopting state procedures on

This issue is not limited to questions about prejudgment interest. Whenever a federal statute is understood to bring certain questions into the domain of federal law without providing specific guidance about how to handle them, and whenever courts therefore draw the content of the applicable federal rules from general American law, courts may eventually have to decide what to do if the content of the general law changes.

There is something to be said for each of the possible approaches mentioned in the preceding paragraphs. On the one hand, when a federal statute implicitly federalizes a question without establishing any special rule about it, members of the enacting Congress can perhaps be presumed to know about and to accept the answer suggested by the then-existing principles of general law. That logic may support the Supreme Court's approach in *Monessen*: Congress enacted the statute against the backdrop of the existing general law, and the statute might be presumed to incorporate those existing rules. On the other hand, the very fact that the relevant federal statute says nothing specific about a particular question of detail may suggest that members of the enacting Congress did not mean to address the substance of that question in any way, and hence did not mean to freeze into place any particular rule to handle it. To the extent members of Congress thought about the question at all, and to the extent they knew that consensus views about the applicable principles might change over time, they might have expected courts to handle the question at all times according to the consensus that prevailed at those times (whether because the general law would operate of its own force or because the statute would be understood to refer to the general law on a dynamic basis).

The Supreme Court has not given this issue any systematic attention, and so the Court has established no overarching doctrine to handle it. *Monessen* points in one direction. But dicta in *Smith v. Wade*, 461 U.S. 30 (1983), point in the opposite direction. *Smith* involved the availability of punitive damages in suits under 42 U.S.C. § 1983, a provision that was enacted as part of the Revised Statutes of 1874 and that dates back to the Civil Rights Act of 1871. In *Smith* as in many other cases, the Supreme Court drew on general tort law to supply details relevant to the federal right of action that § 1983 creates. In a footnote, Justice Brennan's majority opinion observed that past cases had "found useful guidance in the law prevailing at the time when § 1983 was enacted," but the majority suggested that "modern tort decisions" could also be relevant. *Smith*, 461 U.S. at 34 n.2. The majority faulted Justice Rehnquist's dissent for assuming, without analysis, "that Congress necessarily intended to freeze into permanent law whatever principles were current in 1871, rather than to incorporate applicable general legal principles as they evolve." *Id.* According to the majority, "if the prevailing

---

a "static" basis for use in suits at common law in federal courts, to the Conformity Act of 1872, which instead adopted state procedures on a "dynamic" basis); *cf. infra* p. 1305.

view on some point of general tort law had changed substantially in the intervening century (which is not the case here), we might be highly reluctant to assume that Congress intended to perpetuate a now-obsolete doctrine." *Id.*

Apart from these questions of timing, courts also sometimes face questions about the *type* of general law that matters. Suppose that traditional principles of common law established a particular rule, but that all or most state legislatures have now superseded that rule by statute. Suppose further that Congress enacts a federal statute that does not specifically address the relevant issue but that is properly understood to federalize the issue insofar as the statute is concerned. Assuming that courts should draw the content of the applicable federal rule from principles of general law, which principles are relevant? Should courts apply the rule suggested by the traditional common law, on the theory that it governs in the absence of an applicable legislative change? Or should courts instead apply the rule suggested by the modern state statutes, on the theory that it reflects the principles currently recognized as law by most American jurisdictions?

For a well-known example, consider the traditional rule of the common law that claims for personal injury do not survive the claimant's death. State legislatures have abrogated this traditional rule and have established contrary rules by statute. The modern American position, then, is that most claims for personal injury *do* survive the claimant's death and can be litigated on behalf of the claimant's estate by the claimant's personal representative. Against this backdrop, suppose that Congress enacts a statute that creates a federal right of action for damages on behalf of claimants who suffer some personal injury, but that says nothing about the survivability of this right of action. Even though the statute is silent on this point, whether the right of action survives the claimant's death will be treated as an integral detail of the right of action itself, and courts will therefore see it as a matter of federal law. In the absence of statute-specific guidance on this question, moreover, courts are likely to draw the content of the applicable federal rule from principles of general law. But what does that mean? Should the courts be trying to identify the principles of unwritten law that American jurisdictions would recognize in the absence of statutory modification, or should the courts instead take account of the survival statutes by which the states have deviated from the common law on this point?

Again, Supreme Court precedent supplies some support for both answers. *Compare* Mich. Cent. R.R. Co. v. Vreeland, 227 U.S. 59, 67 (1913) (observing that "[n]othing is better settled than that at common law the right of action for an injury to the person is extinguished by the death of the party injured," and holding that because the original version of the FELA did not abrogate this principle, the right of action that it created for personal injury did not survive the injured worker's death—notwithstanding the fact that many states had deviated from the traditional rule as a matter of their own state law),[55] *with* Cox v. Roth, 348 U.S. 207, 210 (1955) (noting that most states have enacted statutes abrogating the parallel common-law rule that claims for personal injury abate upon the death of the tortfeasor, and interpreting the federal Jones Act in a manner consistent with what "has now become the rule in almost every common-law jurisdiction"). In many contexts, though, when federal law is understood to incorporate principles of general American law on some point, modern courts have distilled the content of those principles from patterns established by state statutes as well as state common law. *See, e.g.*, Linear Tech. Corp. v. Micrel, Inc., 275 F.3d 1040, 1048 (Fed. Cir. 2001) (holding that in determining when a particular invention was put "on sale" within the meaning of the federal Patent Act, courts should seek the "common denominator" in "th[e] body of state law" that has developed under each state's version of the Uniform Commercial Code); *see also* Jaffee v. Redmond, 518 U.S. 1, 12–13 (1996) (using "the fact that all 50 States and the District of Columbia have enacted into law some form of psychotherapist privilege" to support recognizing such a privilege under Federal Rule of Evidence 501, a federal statute that explicitly adopts " 'the principles of the common law as they may be interpreted in the courts of the United States in the light of reason and experience,' " and calling it "of no consequence that recognition of the privilege in the vast majority of States is the product of legislative action rather than judicial decision"); *cf.* Moragne v. States Marine Lines, Inc., 398 U.S. 375, 390–93 (1970) (noting that although the traditional common law did not give the relatives of an accident victim any right of action for wrongful death, "the work of the legislatures has made the allowance of recovery for wrongful death the general rule of American law," and recognizing such a right of action as a matter of the unwritten federal maritime law).

* * * * *

As we have seen, when a federal statute creates a right of action, federal law ordinarily is also understood to govern various subsidiary questions that are commonly regarded as being part of the same package as the right of action. In the absence of any statute-specific guidance on those questions, courts routinely draw the content of the applicable federal rules from general American law. Topics that routinely receive this treatment include (1) the principles of vicarious liability that the right of action recognizes; (2) the remedies that the right of action authorizes (including the measure of damages and the availability of prejudgment interest); (3) the generic defenses, if any, that will defeat liability; (4) whether the right of action can be assigned; and (5) whether the right of action survives the death of the original parties.

[55] By the time the Supreme Court decided *Vreeland*, Congress had already amended the FELA to abrogate the common-law rule and provide for survival, but this amendment was enacted after the date of the events in suit. *See* Act of Apr. 5, 1910, ch. 143, § 2, 36 Stat. 291, 291 (codified at 45 U.S.C. § 59).

By contrast, the modern Supreme Court takes a different approach to questions about whether a federal statute creates a right of action in the first place. Under current doctrine, if a federal statute creates substantive duties but does not say anything about private remedial rights for harms caused by violations of those duties, the statute usually will be held not to create such a right of action. In the words of the modern Supreme Court, if the statute does not "display[ ] an intent to create not just a private right but also a private remedy," then "a cause of action does not exist and courts may not create one." *Alexander v. Sandoval*, 532 U.S. 275, 286–87 (2001).

That is a change from prior doctrine. In the mid-twentieth century, if a federal statute established duties that could be said to run to private individuals or entities, courts sometimes held that the statute also authorized courts to recognize a private right of action in favor of plaintiffs who were injured by the violation of those duties, even if the statute did not explicitly address remedial rights. *See, e.g.*, J.I. Case Co. v. Borak, 377 U.S. 426 (1964); *see also* Caleb Nelson, *State and Federal Models of the Interaction Between Statutes and Unwritten Law*, 80 U. CHI. L. REV. 657, 737–41 (2013) (discussing earlier cases). Under current doctrine, though, federal statutes normally do not give rise to federal rights of action unless they say that they do. *See, e.g.*, Ziglar v. Abbasi, 582 U.S. 120, 133 (2017) ("If the statute does not itself so provide, a private cause of action will not be created through judicial mandate.").

Of course, even if a federal statute does not itself create a right of action, private plaintiffs might be able to use generic rights of action established by other sources of law to obtain remedies for harms that they have suffered because of the defendant's violation of the statute. *See, e.g.*, *supra* p. 1224 n.51 (discussing doctrines of "negligence per se"). At least where rights of action for damages are concerned, though, those generic rights of action typically come from state rather than federal law, even when plaintiffs are invoking them in connection with duties created by a federal statute. Although so-called "federal common law" is said to supply rights of action for damages in a few special enclaves (like maritime law), the Supreme Court has indicated that in other areas "a federal court's authority to recognize a damages remedy [as a matter of federal law] must rest at bottom on a statute enacted by Congress." *Hernandez v. Mesa*, 140 S. Ct. 735, 742 (2020).[56]

---

[56] By contrast, the Supreme Court seems open to the idea that principles of federal equity jurisprudence may support recognizing rights to injunctive relief under circumstances not identified by Congress. *See* Armstrong v. Exceptional Child Center, Inc., 575 U.S. 320, 327–31 (2015) (referring to "the equitable relief that is traditionally available to enforce federal law," though concluding that the federal Medicaid Act displaced such relief in the case at hand); *cf. Ziglar*, 582 U.S. at 130–46 (taking for granted that federal detainees can seek injunctive relief to redress unconstitutional conditions of confinement, but declining to recognize a *Bivens* action for damages, and indicating that "whether to provide for a damages remedy" is usually a matter for Congress).

As a matter of terminology, how lawyers refer to remedial rights in equity has changed over time. Historically, rather than referring to "rights of action" in equity, lawyers often used the phrase "equitable jurisdiction" to refer to "situations in which equity would act." *See* Samuel L.

In sum, current doctrine draws a sharp distinction between questions about the *existence* of federal rights of action for damages and questions about the *details* of federal rights of action that do exist. If a federal statute creates substantive duties without saying anything about rights of action for damages, courts typically will conclude both that the statute does not itself create such a right of action and that it does not leave room for courts to recognize a right of action as a matter of federal common law; even if the duties created by the statute could slot readily into a generic right of action supplied by the common law, whether such a right of action exists will be a matter of *state* common law. On the other hand, if a federal statute explicitly creates a right of action without saying anything about details like the measure of damages, those details will be considered questions of federal law, which courts are likely to answer according to principles of general American law (operating either as federal common law or via incorporation into the statute).

There are various possible explanations for this difference. As a doctrinal matter, though, the simplest explanation relates to the "domains" of federal statutes—the set of issues that they encompass. Chapter 4 used that terminology (which comes originally from Judge Easterbrook) to help analyze the interaction between different federal statutes: if the domains of two federal statutes do not overlap, then each statute can have full effect of its own force, but otherwise there may be some respects in which the newer statute impliedly repeals the older one *pro tanto*. *See supra* pp. 838–839. The same concept can also be used with respect to the interaction between a federal statute and state law: the federal statute can preempt state law on issues that come within the federal statute's "domain," but state law will continue to operate of its own force on issues that fall outside that domain.

In the mid-twentieth century, when a federal statute created substantive duties, courts often seemed to assume that questions about the existence of private rights of action came within the statute's domain, even if the statute did not address this topic. *See* Nelson, *supra*, 80 U. CHI. L. REV. at 739–41 (citing cases). But that has changed. To be sure, some federal statutes explicitly create other ways to enforce the duties that they create, and some of those statutory schemes might be understood to preempt private rights of action that state law would

---

Bray & Paul B. Miller, *Getting into Equity*, 97 NOTRE DAME L. REV. 1763, 1775 (2022) (observing that references to "causes of action" in equity are ahistorical). For modern lawyers, though, the historical vocabulary is apt to be confusing, because "jurisdiction" has a different meaning today. *See id.* (acknowledging this point). Nowadays, then, it is not uncommon for lawyers to use the phrase "right of action" to refer to remedial rights of any sort, including rights to remedies that traditionally would have been sought from a court of equity.

Whatever the terminology, there continues to be a general law of equity—unwritten principles that courts use to answer various questions that arise in suits for equitable relief. Both historically and today, moreover, the general law of equity has included principles about the existence of remedial rights—principles that courts use to decide whether a particular plaintiff is asserting the sort of grievance that potentially warrants equitable relief. The hard question, which the modern Supreme Court has not fully answered, is when and why those principles should be understood to have the status of federal law rather than state law.

otherwise supply. Under current doctrine, though, when a federal statute creates substantive duties without saying anything about private rights of action, it is quite common for courts to reach both of the following conclusions. First, the statute does not itself create private rights of action as a matter of federal law, and it also does not create space within which courts can recognize such rights of action as a matter of federal common law. But second, the statute does not preempt generic rights of action that might be supplied by state common law; if a particular state's version of the common law supplies such a right of action, private plaintiffs might be able to use that right of action to obtain remedies for harms that they have suffered because of a defendant's violation of the federal statute. The easiest way to explain both of those conclusions is that the existence of private rights of action simply lies beyond the federal statute's domain; the statute establishes substantive duties, but it leaves the topic of private remedial rights to other sources of law. *See id.* at 741–42.

By contrast, when a federal statute creates not only a duty but also a private right of action, details like the measure of damages for that right of action presumably come within the statute's domain, even if the statute does not explicitly address those details. As explained above, it would be strange to say that the local law of individual states controls the measure of damages for a *federal* right of action. Instead, the federal statute implicitly preempts state law on this topic and leaves room for recognition of a federal rule of decision. The fact that the statute does not specifically address the measure of damages, moreover, does not mean that the measure of damages is zero. As with questions about whether the right of action created by the statute can be assigned and whether it survives the deaths of the original parties, Congress might well leave these details to be handled in the "usual" way without making specific provisions in the statute itself—so the statute's silence on these topics does not prevent courts from handling these details according to principles of general American law. As we have seen, that is what courts tend to do (in the absence of statute-specific guidance). This approach, though, hinges on the assumption that these details do indeed come within the "domain" of the relevant federal statute.

CHAPTER 7

STATUTES OVER TIME*

The conventional view of interpretation treats the meaning of a statute as being largely fixed at the time of enactment. Thus, when courts try to identify the meaning of an old statute that they have not previously interpreted, they often refer back to linguistic conventions from the time of enactment.

Admittedly, modern courts will not always be able to pinpoint the original meaning of an old statute. Sometimes, they will identify two or more possible interpretations, each of which seems about equally plausible. In that case, interpreters will conclude that the original meaning is ambiguous (as far as they can tell), and they probably will go on to choose one of the possible readings. When they do so, they may draw upon considerations that would not have been available at the time of enactment. But conventional accounts of interpretation tend to confine the influence of those sorts of considerations to the zone of ambiguity in the statute's original meaning.

Some modern scholars resist those conventional accounts. Instead, they say, the meaning of a statute can change over time, without any further action by the legislature. Professor William Eskridge has discussed that possibility under the rubric of "dynamic" statutory interpretation. *See* WILLIAM N. ESKRIDGE, JR., DYNAMIC STATUTORY INTERPRETATION (1994).

Different advocates of "dynamic" interpretation may have different ideas about *how* the meaning of a statute might change over time. For many of these scholars, though, the meaning of a statute develops as part of a collaboration between the enacting legislature and successive interpreters.

The metaphors used by advocates of these models provide at least an impressionistic sense of what they have in mind. Alexander Aleinikoff has analogized statutory interpretation to the progress of a ship on a voyage: the enacting legislature builds the ship in a way that "determine[s] where it is capable of going," and the legislature "charts its initial course," but "subsequent navigators play a role" in determining where the ship travels. T. Alexander Aleinikoff, *Updating Statutory Interpretation*, 87 MICH. L. REV. 20, 21 (1988). Ronald Dworkin spoke of a "chain novel" in which the enacting legislature writes one or more early chapters, but hands off the manuscript to subsequent authors who are charged with "mak[ing] the novel being constructed the best it can be." *See* RONALD DWORKIN, LAW'S EMPIRE 229 (1986) (introducing "the chain

* The title of this chapter is also a subheading in RONALD DWORKIN, LAW'S EMPIRE 348–50 (1986).

of law" as a metaphor for the legal enterprise in general); *id.* at 313 (adapting this metaphor to the project of statutory interpretation).

Supporters of dynamic interpretation suggest that their claims are partly about actual practice; as they see things, the meaning that interpreters ascribe to statutes *does* change over time whether or not it should. But their claims are also normative. Academic advocates of dynamic interpretation argue that statutory meanings can legitimately evolve to reflect modern circumstances and values.

In my view, though, the practice of dynamic interpretation is not as wide-ranging as its advocates sometimes suggest. This chapter tries to categorize various phenomena that are sometimes discussed under the rubric of dynamic interpretation, but that are compatible with the conventional emphasis on original meaning. Aside from the categories covered in this chapter, real-world judges may not be very receptive to dynamic interpretation. As a result, practicing lawyers do not normally cast arguments in those terms; they do not concede that the meaning of a statute as enacted contradicts their position, but ask the court to give the statute a different meaning now.

A comment by Judge Guido Calabresi helps to capture that point. In his days as a law professor, Judge Calabresi was interested in the possibility of making statutes work more like common law. *See* GUIDO CALABRESI, A COMMON LAW FOR THE AGE OF STATUTES (1982). After his appointment to the United States Court of Appeals for the Second Circuit, though, he contrasted his academic views with the views that he could take in his role as a judge. In his words, "[S]ome scholars, myself included, have suggested that it might be a good idea if, as a starting point, in certain circumstances, courts were permitted to read the law according to what they perceived to be the will of the current Congress, rather than that of a long-gone-by one. . . . But whatever the merits of such an arrangement in the abstract, it is simply not a part of our legal system." *Hayden v. Pataki*, 449 F.3d 305, 367 (2d Cir. 2006) (en banc) (Calabresi, J., dissenting).

In sum, the project of statutory interpretation remains focused on each statute's *original* meaning. Still, "meaning" is a complicated concept, and this chapter identifies various ways in which the passage of time can matter even on conventional accounts of statutory interpretation.

A. UNEXPECTED APPLICATIONS OF AN INVARIANT DIRECTIVE

We can begin with what Hart and Sacks called "the special problem of new applications of old enactments." HENRY M. HART, JR. & ALBERT M. SACKS, THE LEGAL PROCESS: BASIC PROBLEMS IN THE MAKING AND APPLICATION OF LAW 1172 (tent. ed. 1958) (William N. Eskridge, Jr. & Philip P. Frickey eds., 1994). Certain legal directives are worded in such a way that they have different applications in different circumstances. Such directives might be analogized to mathematical functions: they fix in place a particular relation between inputs and outputs, but changes in the value of an input can produce changes in the value of the output.

To take an artificial example, suppose that a statute enacted in 2015 requires every subsequently constructed factory to incorporate the best technology that exists at the time of construction for the purpose of minimizing the emission of a particular pollutant. From 2015 until 2025, that statute might require new factories to incorporate Technology #1. But if scientific advances in 2025 lead to a new and improved scrubbing system based on Technology #2, the statute will require factories built thereafter to incorporate that technology instead.

In this particular example, few people would say that the "meaning" of the statute itself changed in 2025. Just as a mathematical function will produce a different output when we plug in a different value for a variable that the function makes relevant, so too a change in the circumstances that the statute makes relevant has produced a change in the technology that the statute requires new factories to incorporate. But the statutory directive—the function—remains the same. The change in circumstances has produced a changed *application* but not a changed *meaning.*

In this example, however, the legislature plainly expected technology to continue to change, and it deliberately drafted its directive to produce different results as technology developed. The type of change that has occurred is exactly the type of change that the legislature anticipated. When that is not true—that is, when circumstances have changed in ways that the enacting legislature probably did *not* expect—the line between changes in application and changes in meaning becomes blurrier.

For a sign of that blurriness, consider disagreements about the propriety of "imaginative reconstruction" in statutory interpretation. Suppose that interpreters are trying to decide whether to infer an exception to seemingly general statutory language (or, perhaps, an embellishment to seemingly limited statutory language) on the theory that members of the enacting legislature would have favored such an adjustment if they had foreseen the question that has now arisen. As we have seen in prior chapters, different people have different views about this style of interpretation. But their disagreements may be at least partly about the sort of "meaning" that should matter in statutory interpretation. Some interpreters are more inclined than others to associate the "meaning" of a legal directive with the expected applications of that directive. *See, e.g.*, Lawrence Lessig, *Fidelity in Translation*, 71 TEX. L. REV. 1165, 1174–82 (1993) (appearing to associate meaning with application in a relatively strong sense). To the extent that one associates "meaning" with applications in this way, one will view changes in application as the equivalent of changes in meaning—which, on the traditional view of statutory interpretation, are to be avoided. That logic might lead one to favor a robust version of imaginative reconstruction, under which interpreters try to preserve the original "meaning" of statutory language by inferring adjustments that are necessary to avoid unexpected new applications (or gaps in application). By contrast, people who do *not* link the "meaning" of statutory language quite so closely to the set of expected applications will portray such efforts as affirmatively *distorting* the meaning of the statute that the legislature enacted. *See, e.g.*, Marozsan v. United States, 852 F.2d 1469, 1498–1501 (7th Cir. 1988) (en banc) (Easterbrook, J., dissenting); *cf. supra* Chapter 3.E (discussing the difference between "meaning" and "expected application").

To set the stage for further discussion, we can do no better than to use the issue that Hart and Sacks themselves featured. Until 1890, no American state allowed women to vote. That changed over the course of the next thirty years, but a number of eastern states—including both Pennsylvania and Massachusetts—continued to restrict suffrage to men. In 1920, however, ratification of the Nineteenth Amendment to the federal Constitution took away their power to do so. *See* U.S. CONST. amend. 19 ("The right of citizens of the United States to vote shall not be denied or abridged by the United States or by any State on account of sex."). As a result of the Nineteenth Amendment, women were now eligible to vote in these states. Under pre-existing state law, it seemed to follow that they were also eligible for jury duty. To be sure, that conclusion did not flow inexorably from the federal Constitution itself; the Nineteenth Amendment said nothing about jury service, and nothing else in the federal Constitution was then understood to prevent states from requiring jurors to be men.[1] In both Pennsylvania and Massachusetts, however, the state statutes that were then in effect seemed to say that virtually everyone who could vote was also eligible to serve as a juror. *See* An Act for the Better and More Impartial Selection of Persons to Serve as Jurors, in Each of the Counties of this Commonwealth, No. 41, 1867 Pa. Laws 62 (instructing jury commissioners in each county to pick the requisite number of "sober, intelligent and judicious persons" from "the whole qualified electors of the respective county"); Mass. Rev. Laws, ch. 176, § 1 (1902) (providing that with certain exceptions, "[a] person qualified to vote for representatives to the general court [which, confusingly, is what Massachusetts calls its legislature] shall be liable to serve as a juror"); *see also* Mass. Gen. Laws, ch. 234, § 1 (1920) (reenacting the same words as part of a codification project completed shortly after ratification of the Nineteenth Amendment).

---

[1] Nowadays, a state statute purporting to allow only men to serve on juries would presumably be held to violate the Fourteenth Amendment. But the Fourteenth Amendment was not so understood at the time relevant to the cases featured by Professors Hart and Sacks.

The Supreme Court of Pennsylvania soon concluded that women could now serve on juries in Pennsylvania. As the court noted, the applicable state statute about jury service called for jurors to be drawn from the "qualified electors" in each county. Although that statute had been enacted in 1867, before women could vote in any state or territory of the United States, "the term 'electors' embraces those who may be added to the electorate from time to time," and "the designation 'qualified elector' embraces all electors at the time jurors are selected from the body of electors." *Commonwealth v. Maxwell*, 114 A. 825, 829 (Pa. 1921). Since the Nineteenth Amendment had the effect of "putting women in the body of electors," the 1867 statute "necessarily" made them "eligible to jury service." *Id.*

In the following opinion, however, the Supreme Judicial Court of Massachusetts took a different view of the statutes in effect in Massachusetts.

Commonwealth v. Welosky

177 N.E. 656 (Mass. 1931)

■ *CHIEF JUSTICE RUGG delivered the Court's opinion:*

[During Prohibition, Massachusetts prosecuted the defendant—a woman named Genevieve Welosky—for the crime of keeping liquor with the intention of illegally selling it.] As the jurors were about to be impaneled for the trial . . . , the defendant filed a challenge to the array. . . . The ground on which that challenge rests is that there were no women on the lists from which the jurors were drawn. The contention in support of the challenge raises two inquiries: (1) Whether under the laws of the commonwealth the names of women ought to have been placed upon the jury lists; and (2) whether by such exclusion the constitutional rights of the defendant under the Fourteenth Amendment to the Constitution of the United States have been infringed. . . .

1. The first question to be decided is whether the statutes of this commonwealth require that the names of women otherwise qualified be placed upon jury lists so that they may be drawn for service as jurors.

It is plain that women could not rightly serve as jurors, save in the rare instances where a jury of matrons was called, under the Constitution and laws of this commonwealth prior to the adoption of the Nineteenth Amendment to the Constitution of the United States. The terms of the statute, in the light of the Constitution, express decisions, universal understanding, and unbroken practice, forbid any other view. The trial by jury of the common law and that contemplated by both the Constitution of this commonwealth and that of the United States were by a jury of twelve composed exclusively of men. . . .

The statute to be interpreted is G. L. c. 234, § 1. Its relevant language is: "A person qualified to vote for representatives to the general court[*] shall be liable to serve as a juror," with exceptions not here material.

The words of a statute are the main source for the ascertainment of a legislative purpose. They are to be construed according to their natural import in common and approved usage. The imperfections of language to express intent often render necessary further inquiry. Statutes are to be interpreted, not alone according to their simple, literal or strict verbal meaning, but in connection with their development, their progression through the legislative body, the history of the times, prior legislation, contemporary customs and conditions and the system of positive law of which they are part, and in the light of the constitution and of the common law, to the end that they be held to cover the subjects presumably within the vision of the Legislature and, on the one hand, be not unduly constricted so as to exclude matters fairly within their scope, and, on the other hand, be not stretched by enlargement of signification to comprehend matters not within the principle and purview on which they were founded when originally framed and their words chosen. General expressions may be restrained by relevant circumstances showing a legislative intent that they be narrowed and used in a particular sense. . . .

It is clear beyond peradventure that the words of G. L. c. 234, § 1, when originally enacted could not by any possibility have included or been intended by the general court to include women among those liable to jury duty. The [Massachusetts] Constitution forbade the words, "A person qualified to vote for representatives to the general court," to comprehend women. Women have been qualified to vote in this commonwealth only since the adoption of the Nineteenth Amendment to the Constitution of the United States. It is not argued in behalf of the defendant that the terms of the statutes preceding G. L. c. 234, § 1, that is to say of R. L. c. 176, § 1, and its predecessors in substantially the same words since a time before the adoption of the Constitution, could possibly have imposed jury duty upon women. The argument on this point is two-fold: (A) That the phrase of the statute is general and therefore was intended automatically to include women if their constitutional inhibitions were ever removed; and (B) that, since the General Laws were enacted in December, 1920, after the ratification of the Nineteenth Amendment, the statute was intended to include women. These arguments will be considered in turn.

A. The Nineteenth Amendment was, on August 26, 1920, proclaimed to have been duly ratified. That amendment declared that "The right of citizens of the United States to vote shall not be denied or abridged by the United States or by any State on account of sex." It became forthwith binding upon the people and the several departments of this commonwealth. By its own self-executing force it struck from the

[*] *Editor's note*: The "general court" is what Massachusetts calls its state legislature.

Constitution of this commonwealth the word "male" wherever it occurred as a limitation upon the right to vote. See articles 3 and 32 of Amendments to the Constitution of the commonwealth.[*] . . . The subsequent approval by the people of this commonwealth on November 4, 1924, of article 68 of the Amendments to the Constitution of Massachusetts, whereby the word "male" as a limitation upon the right of citizens to vote was stricken from article 3 of the Amendments as amended, simply manifested the people's adoption of that principle and made our Constitution harmonious in phraseology with that of the United States; but it had no legal effect upon the right of women who were citizens of Massachusetts to vote. That had already been fixed indubitably by the ratification of the Nineteenth Amendment to the Constitution of the United States.

Statutes framed in general terms commonly look to the future and may include conditions as they arise from time to time not even known at the time of enactment, provided they are fairly within the sweep and the meaning of the words and falling within their obvious scope and purpose. But statutes do not govern situations not within the reason of their enactment and giving rise to radically diverse circumstances presumably not within the dominating purpose of those who framed and enacted them. . . .

As [a] matter of strict and abstract verbal interpretation, apart from context, circumstances, and contemporary and antecedent history, the language of G. L. c. 234, § 1, is broad enough to comprise women. The word "person" . . . has been said to be "an ambiguous word" and may refer to those of either or both sexes. *Nairn v. University of St. Andrews*, [1909] A.C. 147, 162. . . . The word "person" may include a national bank, *Central National Bank v. Lynn*, 259 Mass. 1, 14; a corporation, *McDonnell v. Berkshire Street Railway*, 243 Mass. 94, 95; [and] a society, association or partnership, *Commissioner of Corporations & Taxation v. Co-Operative League of America*, 246 Mass. 235, 238; *Commonwealth v. Rozen*, 176 Mass. 129, 131. Yet it was held not to include corporations upon the facts in *Commonwealth v. Phoenix Bank*, 11 Metc. 129, 149. Notwithstanding Pub. St. c. 3, § 3, cl. 16 (G. L. c. 4, § 7, cl. 23), to the effect that the word "person" in construing statutes shall include corporations, it was held not thus inclusive in *Steel Edge Stamping & Retinning Co. v. Manchester Savings Bank*, 163 Mass. 252. It has also been held not to include a woman. *Mashburn v. State*, 65 Fla. 470, 474.

[¶] Several cases have arisen where the question was whether the word "person," when used respecting the right to hold office or to exercise the franchise, included women. In *Nairn v. University of St. Andrews*, [1909] A.C. 147, it appeared that, by Acts of Parliament of 1868 and 1881,

[*] *Editor's note*: With some exceptions, article 3 of the Amendments (adopted in 1821) had conferred a right to vote upon "[e]very male citizen of twenty-one years of age and upwards," but had specified that "no other person shall be entitled to vote" in the elections that it covered. Article 32 of the Amendments (adopted in 1891) had eliminated one of the exceptions in article 3 but had left the rest of the language intact.

the university franchise was conferred upon "every person" whose name was on the register and on whom degrees had been conferred. At that time women were not admitted to graduation and could not receive degrees. In 1889, a further act was passed for the appointment of commissioners with extensive regulatory powers over universities. These commissioners adopted an ordinance enabling the universities to confer degrees on women for satisfactory academic accomplishments. The appellants, having received degrees upon graduation, contended that they had the right to vote. In rejecting that contention, it was said by Lord Loreburn, L.C., at page 161: "It proceeds upon the supposition that the word 'person' in the act of 1868 did include women, though not then giving them the vote, so that at some later date an Act purporting to deal only with education might enable commissioners to admit them to the degree, and thereby also indirectly confer upon them the franchise. It would require a convincing demonstration to satisfy me that Parliament intended to effect a constitutional change so momentous and far-reaching by so furtive a process. It is a dangerous assumption to suppose that the Legislature foresees every possible result that may ensue from the unguarded use of a single word, or that the language used in statutes is so precisely accurate that you can pick out from various Acts this and that expression and, skillfully piecing them together, lay a safe foundation for some remote inference." It was held that the statutory word "person" did not in these circumstances include women. It was held in *Viscountess Rhondda's Claim*, [1922] 2 A.C. 339, that an act of Parliament passed in 1919, providing that "A person shall not be disqualified by sex or marriage from the exercise of any public function," did not entitle a peeress of the United Kingdom in her own right to receive the writ of summons to Parliament. Doubtless, as an abstract conception, it is a public function to sit in the House of Lords and to exercise the prerogatives of a member. But it was held by ten out of twelve law lords sitting in the case, among whom were the most eminent judges of the day, that the word "person" as used in the act could not rightly be interpreted to include women in those entitled to sit in the House of Lords. It was said by Lord Birkenhead in the course of an exhaustive statement reviewing many decisions, at page 369: "A long stream of cases has established that general words are to be construed so as, in an old phrase, 'to pursue the intent of the makers of statutes' . . . and so as to import all those implied exceptions which arise from a close consideration of the mischiefs sought to be remedied and of the state of the law at the moment when the statute was passed." At pages 372, 373, the words of Lord Loreburn in *Nairn v. University of St. Andrews* . . . were quoted with high commendation.

This brief review of authorities demonstrates that "person" by itself is an equivocal word. Its meaning in a statute requires interpretation. The statute here under examination (G. L. c. 234, § 1) is a re-enactment of a long line of statutes of the commonwealth running back to a time shortly after the adoption of the Constitution as well as through all intermediate revisions dealing with qualifications for jury service. Laws of the colony and of the province are in effect the same. In the earlier and later statutes, the same essential and almost the identical words have been employed. The word "person" occurs in them all. The selection of jurors has constantly been required to be from those qualified to vote. Qualifications for voting have been continuously established by the Constitution. By the words of that instrument and its amendments (apart from the effect of the Nineteenth Amendment of the federal Constitution) the right to vote was confined to male inhabitants, male persons, and finally to male citizens, until the word "male" was stricken out in 1924 by Amendment 68. . . . Manifestly, therefore, the intent of the Legislature must have been, in using the word "person" in statutes concerning jurors and jury lists, to confine its meaning to men. That was the only intent constitutionally permissible. There is every presumption that the legislative department of government always intends to act strictly within the bounds of the Constitution. . . .

Possession of property of specified value and payment of taxes as qualifications for voters were required in earlier days and from time to time, but these were gradually eliminated by Amendments to the Constitution until the last of such limitations disappeared with the approval of Amendment 32 in 1891. When the suffrage has been thus widened among male citizens, there has followed, without further legislation and without change in the phrase of the statute, a like extension of citizens liable to service as jurors. These concurring enlargements of those liable to jury service were simply an extension to larger numbers of the same classification of persons. Since the word "person" in the statutes respecting jurors meant men, when there was an extension of the right to vote to other men previously disqualified, the jury statutes by specific definition included them. No amendment to the statute can be conceived which could have made that meaning more clear. This is the force and effect of *Neal v. Delaware*, 103 U.S. 370, at page 389[, where Delaware laws were understood to make Black men eligible for jury duty once the Fifteenth Amendment forbade the state to deny voting rights on the basis of race].

Changes in suffrage and in liability for jury service in the past differ in kind from the change here urged.

The Nineteenth Amendment to the federal Constitution conferred the suffrage upon an entirely new class of human beings. It did not extend the right to vote to members of an existing classification theretofore disqualified, but created a new class. It added to qualified voters those who did not fall within the meaning of the word "person" in the jury statutes. No member of the class thus added to the body of voters had ever theretofore in this commonwealth had the right to vote for candidates for offices created by the Constitution. The change in the legal status of women wrought by the Nineteenth Amendment was radical, drastic and unprecedented. While it is to be given full effect in its field, it is not to be extended by implication. It is unthinkable that those who first framed and selected the words for the statute now embodied in G. L. c. 234, § 1, had any design that it should ever include women within its scope. It is equally inconceivable that those who from time to time had re-enacted that statute had any such design. When they used the word "person" in connection with those qualified to vote for members of the more numerous branch of the general court, to describe those liable to jury service, no one contemplated the possibility of women becoming so qualified. The same is true in general of those who from time to time re-enacted the statute in substantially the same words. No intention to include women can be deduced from the omission of the word "male." That word was imbedded in the Constitution of the commonwealth as a limitation upon those citizens who might become voters and thereby members of a class from which jurors might be drawn. It would have been superfluous also to insert that word in the statute. The words of Chief Justice Gray in *Robinson's Case*, 131 Mass. 376, 380, 381, are equally pertinent to the case at bar: "Whenever the legislature has intended to make a change in the legal rights or capacities of women, it has used words clearly manifesting its intent and the extent of the change intended. . . . In making innovations upon the long-established system of law on this subject, the legislature appears to have proceeded with great caution, one step at a time; and the whole course of legislation precludes the inference that any change in the legal rights or capacities of women is to be implied, which has not been clearly expressed."

The conclusion is irresistible that, according to sound principles of statutory construction, it cannot rightly be held that the scope of R. L. c. 176, § 1, the statute in force on August 26, 1920, now G. L. c. 234, § 1, was extended by the ratification of the Nineteenth Amendment so as to render women liable to jury duty. To reach that result would be directly contrary to every purpose and intent of the general court in enacting that law.

The same reasoning on which rests the conclusion just stated requires without further discussion the holding that the approval in November, 1924, of Amendments, article 68, to the Constitution of this commonwealth, whereby the word "male" was stricken from the Constitution as descriptive of citizens qualified to vote, did not operate to extend the scope of G. L. c. 234, § 1, beyond its previous limits so as to make women liable to jury service without further legislative action. An amendment to the Constitution does not commonly alter the meaning and scope of words in the body of statutory law. The Constitution of this commonwealth contains no reference to the qualifications of jurors. That subject is within the cognizance of the general court.

B. The second argument of the defendant on this branch of the case is that, since the General Laws were enacted on December 22, 1920 (about four months subsequent to the ratification of the Nineteenth Amendment) the Legislature, although using the same essential words theretofore used to describe those liable to service as jurors, namely, "person qualified to vote for representatives to the general court," must have intended to include women.

It is a general principle of statutory construction that the re-enactment of a statute in substantially the same words does not change its meaning or extend its scope. Its words are presumed to continue to have attached to them the same sense as in the preceding enactment. . . .

It is permissible and important to examine proceedings incident to the enactment of the General Laws to determine whether any alteration of meaning in this particular was intended. . . . The report of the commissioners to arrange and consolidate the General Laws, appointed pursuant to Resolves 1916, c. 43, was submitted to the general court on June 1, 1920, almost three months prior to the proclamation of the ratification of the Nineteenth Amendment. The function of the commissioners as indicated by their name was to deal with existing laws and to suggest changes but not to embody them in the draft submitted. That report contained a complete body of the statute laws, but no substantial change in preexisting statutes concerning voting by women, and no change as to jury lists. It was referred to a joint special committee of the general court. On June 2, 1920, St. 1920, c. 579, was approved. It was entitled "An Act to enable women voters to vote at primaries and elections when qualified." It was enacted in anticipation of the ultimate adoption of the Nineteenth Amendment, which had been ratified by resolution of the general court in June, 1919. Gen. Acts 1919, page 483. The joint special committee of the general court submitted their report at a special session held in December, 1920. In that report it is stated that "The subcommittee to which was assigned the legislation of 1920 recommended that the laws relating to intoxicating liquors and woman's suffrage, affected by the Eighteenth and Nineteenth Amendments to the Federal Constitution, be redrawn to conform to these amendments. The Committee voted to correct the laws as to suffrage and to leave the laws as to intoxicating liquors unchanged, which votes were respectively carried out."

The draft of the General Laws reported by the joint special committee shows that they conformed to this paragraph of their report and made changes touching the right of women to vote. See particularly notes appended to chapters 50, 51, 53, 54 and 56 of their report. They made no changes respecting women in any other particular. No change was made touching jury lists. They retained the provision now embodied in G. L. c. 123, § 57, requiring a jury of men to hear and determine the cases there classified.[*] The General Laws were enacted on December 22, 1920, in substantially the form submitted by the joint special committee,

[*] *Editor's note*: The court here was referring to the following provision in a chapter of the Massachusetts General Laws that authorized civil commitment of the insane: "The judge may, in his discretion, issue a warrant to the sheriff or his deputy, directing him to summon a jury of six men to hear and determine whether the alleged insane person is insane."

so far as here material. It is most unlikely that the Legislature should, for the first time, require women to serve as jurors without making provision respecting the exemption of the considerable numbers of women who ought not to be required to serve as jurors and without directing that changes for the convenience of women be made in courthouses, some of which are notoriously overcrowded and unfit for their accommodation as jurors.

Plainly, the joint special committee and the general court in adopting the proposal of that committee had no thought of such a fundamental alteration in making jury lists and conducting jury trials as would be involved in rendering women liable to jury service. No intent of that nature can be imputed to them.

It may be observed in this connection that, pursuant to Resolves 1923, c. 53, a special commission was appointed for an investigation of the subject of making women eligible for jury service. A report of that commission was duly made, but no legislative action has ever been taken in favor of such eligibility.

The conclusion is that, by the true construction of the statutes of this commonwealth, in the light of relevant constitutional provisions, women are not eligible to jury service and that the preparation of the jury lists from which the jury in the case at bar were drawn from men alone was right.

The question of the effect of granting the suffrage to women on statutes providing for the selection of jurors from the members of the electorate has arisen in several states. The conclusion here reached is supported in principle by a respectable body of authority. [Citations omitted.] There are decisions to the contrary. [Citations omitted.]

2. The contention of the defendant is that, by reason of the exclusion of women from the jury list, she has been denied the equal protection of the laws contrary to the guaranty contained in the Fourteenth Amendment to the federal Constitution. [The court rejected this constitutional argument.]

NOTES AND QUESTIONS

1. The phraseology of the key statute at issue in *Welosky* dated back at least to 1835. *See* Mass. Rev. Stat., ch. 95, § 1 (1836) (enacted Nov. 4, 1835) ("All persons, who are qualified to vote in the choice of representatives in the general court, shall be liable to be drawn as jurors, except as is hereinafter provided.").[2] Let us assume, as the Massachusetts court did, that the successive reenactments of this

[2] Earlier statutes similarly referred to "persons" who are "qualified as the Constitution directs, to vote in the choice of Representatives," but they added additional screens. *See, e.g.*, Act of June 26, 1784, § 2, *in* 1 THE LAWS OF THE COMMONWEALTH OF MASSACHUSETTS, FROM NOVEMBER 28, 1780 TO FEBRUARY 28, 1807, at 186, 186–87 (Boston 1807) (limiting the jury pool to "such as the [town] Selectmen shall judge well qualified to serve as Jurors").

language did not change its meaning. Let us also assume that the slight reformulation at the turn of the century (when the legislature recast the provision from plural to singular) also left the meaning unchanged. *See* Mass. Rev. Laws, ch. 176, § 1 (1902) ("A person qualified to vote for representatives to the general court shall be liable to serve as a juror, except that the following persons shall be exempt . . . .").

Those assumptions put the case in the light most favorable to the decision that the court reached in *Welosky*, because they permit us to focus on the meaning of the statute as originally enacted in 1835. As the court acknowledged, of course, that statute was designed to accommodate change: the legislators who formulated and adopted it knew that the qualifications for voting would fluctuate over time, and they enacted the statute to make the qualifications for jury service follow suit. According to the court, however, they never imagined that women would be allowed to vote, and so they expected that the jury statute would cover only men. To avoid unsettling that expectation, the court read the word "person" in the statute to mean "man."

An implicit premise of the court's opinion is that when the jury statute was enacted, legislators would have understood the words "person" and "man" to be synonymous in this context. As a result, the court suggested, interpreters should not ascribe significance to the fact that the legislature used the former word rather than the latter. After all, nothing turned on that choice at the time, and so there was no reason for legislators to focus on which word to use. In the absence of a clearer statement, moreover, the court was reluctant to conclude that because the statute happened to use "person" rather than "man," women could now sit on juries, without the need for any further legislation. Opening juries to women would be a significant step for the state, and the court suggested that members of the legislature should actually think about that step before statutory language is understood to adopt it.

Aren't both of these points plausible? Doesn't it seem unlikely that when legislators adopted the word "person" in 1835, they had women in mind and deliberately intended to cover them (even though the legislature was not then making women eligible either to vote or to serve on juries)? And wasn't the court right that the decision to open juries to women is a significant policy change of the sort that legislation should not be taken to settle by accident?

On the other hand, the statute that the legislature enacted in 1835 (and reenacted repeatedly thereafter) unquestionably reflected a deliberate decision to link eligibility for jury duty with eligibility to vote. Even if members of the enacting legislature assumed that only men would ever be able to vote, how did the court know that this assumption was crucial to the linkage that they established? Is there any reason to presume that *if* members of the enacting legislature had known that women would eventually be allowed to vote, they probably would have wanted to drive a wedge between the requirements for voting and the requirements for jury service, so that only men could serve on juries even after women gained the vote? If the most natural reading of the word "person" in this context covers women as well as men, and if we have no particular reason to read in an unstated limitation preventing women from serving on juries after they become eligible to vote, shouldn't we conclude that the Pennsylvania court was correct in *Maxwell* and the Massachusetts court was wrong in *Welosky*?

2. The Massachusetts statute at issue in *Welosky* contained exemptions for firemen, lighthouse keepers, practicing surgeons, "constant ferrymen," and people in various other occupations that could not readily be interrupted for jury duty. *See* Mass. Gen. Laws, ch. 234, § 1 (1920). In keeping with the fact that the legislature had not drafted these exemptions with women in mind, though, the statute did not contain any exemption for, say, nursing mothers. The Massachusetts court saw the absence of any women-specific exemptions as an additional argument in support of its conclusion. According to the court, if and when the Massachusetts legislature made a deliberate policy decision to include women as well as men in the jury pool, it could be expected to enact appropriate exemptions for "the considerable numbers of women who ought not to be required to serve as jurors." *Welosky*, 177 N.E. at 662.

Whatever one might think of the attitudes that this prediction reflected, the Massachusetts legislature arguably shared those attitudes. Thus, when the Massachusetts legislature finally did extend jury duty to women in 1949, it added exemptions for "women trained nurses; women assistants in hospitals; women attendant nurses; mothers of children under sixteen years of age or women having custody of such children[;] and women members of religious orders." An Act Regulating the Preparation of Jury Lists and Making Women, with Certain Exceptions, Liable to Serve as Jurors in Certain Cases, ch. 347, § 1, 1949 Mass. Acts 306, 306. It also added that "[n]o woman shall be required to serve in the trial of any prosecutions under [statutory provisions about rape, other sex crimes, obscenity, and the like] if, upon her representation[,] it appears to the presiding justice that she would be likely to be embarrassed by hearing the testimony or by discussing the same in the jury room." *Id.* § 2, 1949 Mass. Acts at 306–07. Assume for the sake of argument that as a policy matter, most legislators at the time of *Welosky* would have opposed subjecting women to jury duty without providing exemptions of this sort. Does that assumption have any bearing on the proper application of the statutes that were at issue in *Welosky*?

3. If you think that the Massachusetts court was wrong in *Welosky*, how would you have handled *State v. Kelley*, 229 P. 659 (Idaho 1924)? Idaho was one of the first states to give women full voting rights; in 1896, it amended its state constitution to make women qualified electors. As in Pennsylvania and Massachusetts, moreover, a statute dating back to the 1880s linked voting rights to eligibility for jury service. *See* Idaho Terr. Rev. Stat. § 3941 (1887) ("A person is competent to act as a juror if he be:

1. A citizen of the United States and an elector of the county; 2. In possession of his natural faculties and not decrepit; 3. Possessed of sufficient knowledge of the language in which the proceedings of the courts are held."). In Idaho, however, other pre-existing state statutes specifically defined each type of jury used in the state as "a body of men." *See* Idaho Terr. Rev. Stat. § 3935 (1887) (general definition of jury); *id.* §§ 3937, 3938, 3940 (definitions of trial juries, grand juries, and juries of inquest); *see also id.* § 3939 ("A trial jury in the district consists of twelve, and in the Probate and Justices' Courts, of six men, unless the parties to the action or proceeding agree upon a less number.").[3] In *Kelley*, the Supreme Court of Idaho interpreted these provisions to "limit jury duty to men" even after women became eligible to vote. *Kelley*, 229 P. at 660. Courts facing similar questions in other states reached the same conclusion. *See, e.g.*, People v. Lensen, 167 P. 406 (Cal. 1917) (interpreting pre-1917 California statutes that resembled the Idaho statutes at issue in *Kelley*); State v. Mittle, 113 S.E. 335 (S.C. 1922) (reaching a similar conclusion about a provision in the South Carolina Constitution of 1896 specifying that "[t]he petit jury of the Circuit Court shall consist of 12 men").

Was the *Kelley* court correct, because one reading of the word "men" covers only males and we have no basis for concluding that members of the enacting legislature wanted to link jury service to voting rights without regard to sex? Or does that logic put too much weight on the fact that the legislature happened to use the word "men" rather than "people" back in the 1880s, at a time when nothing seemed to turn on that choice?

4. How would you have understood the statutory scheme that was in force in Ohio when women gained the right to vote?[4] The state's basic statutes about jury service were not cast in sex-specific terms. *See* Ohio Gen. Code § 11423 (1910) (directing the jury commissioners for each county to select a number of "judicious and discreet persons" who meet "the qualifications of electors of such county" and whom all the jury commissioners consider "competent in every respect to serve as a juror"); *id.* § 11424 (directing the county clerk to put pieces of paper with "the names of the persons so selected" into the county's "jury wheel"); *id.* § 11426 (providing for the names of "persons" to be summoned to serve as grand or petit jurors to be drawn from the jury wheel as necessary). But a more specialized provision, allowing the court to cause a new grand jury to be summoned after the discharge of an existing grand jury, spoke of convening "fifteen good and lawful men." *See id.* § 13568 ("After the discharge of the grand jury, the court, when necessary, may order the sheriff to call together a new grand jury, from the by-standers or

[3] By the time of *Kelley*, these provisions had been recodified as Idaho Comp. Stat. §§ 6512–6518 (1919).

[4] In Ohio, that was a two-step process. A state statute enacted in 1919 permitted women to vote in presidential elections, and the ratification of the Nineteenth Amendment to the federal Constitution in 1920 had the effect of enabling them to vote in other elections too. In 1923, the state constitution was amended to conform with the Nineteenth Amendment.

neighboring citizens, of fifteen good and lawful men having the qualifications of grand jurors . . . ."). Should the latter statute have colored the Ohio courts' understanding of the more basic provisions about jury service, leading the courts to conclude that further legislative action was necessary to make women eligible for any sort of jury duty in Ohio? Or should the Ohio courts have concluded that the basic statutes did make women who enjoyed "the qualifications of electors" eligible for jury duty? If you take the latter position, would you say that new grand juries summoned pursuant to § 13568 should still have been limited to men even after women became eligible to vote (and therefore became eligible for other forms of jury service)? Or would you say, as the Supreme Court of Ohio ultimately did, that § 13568 "did not use the word 'men' in a specific sense, differentiating between men and women, but in a generic sense"—so that it refers to everyone eligible for jury service under the other relevant statutes, including women? *See* Browning v. State, 165 N.E. 566, 567 (Ohio 1929).

5. In *Welosky*, the Massachusetts court ascribed no significance to the fact that in November 1924, the state constitution was amended to conform to the Nineteenth Amendment. But didn't that amendment to the state constitution eliminate a plausible argument for the court's conclusion? Before November 1924, the Massachusetts constitution purported to restrict voting rights to "male citizen[s]," MASS. CONST., Articles of Amendment, art. 3, and the statute about jury duty established the general rule that "[a] person qualified to vote for representatives to the general court shall be liable to serve as a juror," Mass. Gen. Laws, ch. 234, § 1 (1920). If not for the federal Constitution, then, Massachusetts law (as it stood before 1924) would have restricted both voting rights and jury service to men. The Nineteenth Amendment made the first restriction unconstitutional, but the Nineteenth Amendment did not itself invalidate the second restriction. Before 1924, couldn't one have argued that notwithstanding the Nineteenth Amendment, the state constitution's purported restriction on voting rights remained relevant to the proper application of the statute about jury duty? Would you describe that argument as being about principles of separability, or instead as being about the meaning of the phrase "[a] person qualified to vote for representatives to the general court" in the statute about jury duty?

6. In the course of discussing the problem raised in *Welosky*, Hart and Sacks spoke as if the key questions were (1) whether the statute's purpose would be "better served by an interpretation that attributes to the language a fixed or a changed meaning over time" and (2) if the latter, whether the statute's purpose would be served by "an interpretation that attributes to the language the particular change here in issue." *See* HART & SACKS, *supra*, at 1183. In what sense was Ms. Welosky asking the court to attribute a "changed meaning" to the statute, and in what sense was she simply advocating a particular view of the meaning that the statute had had all along?

B. "OPEN-TEXTURED" TERMS AND PHRASES

However you would have handled *Welosky*, many statutes establish rules that lend themselves to different applications under the different circumstances that exist at different times. Some of those applications, moreover, might well have surprised members of the enacting legislature. At least in that sense, the idea that statutes take on a life of their own after enactment is uncontroversial. *See, e.g.*, Union Bank v. Wolas, 502 U.S. 151, 158 (1991) (unanimous opinion by Stevens, J.) ("The fact that Congress may not have foreseen all of the consequences of a statutory enactment is not a sufficient reason for refusing to give effect to its plain meaning.").

A related and equally uncontroversial phenomenon grows out of what the philosopher Friedrich Waismann called the "open-textured" nature of many words. Waismann coined that term to call attention to the fact that at any given time in the development of language, the members of a particular linguistic community use words without agreeing upon "rules . . . for all imaginable possibilities." Friedrich Waismann, *Verifiability*, 19 PROCEEDINGS OF THE ARISTOTELIAN SOCIETY, SUPPLEMENTARY VOLUMES 119, 122 (1945). As a result, changes in circumstances can expose latent indeterminacies in the way that a particular word was previously used—indeterminacies that have been lurking in the word all along, but that do not become apparent until circumstances change in such a way as to make them salient.[5]

Waismann himself offered a fanciful illustration of this point. Suppose we see a creature that looks exactly like a cat, but that then "gr[ows] to a gigantic size" or proves capable of being "revived from death" under certain conditions. *Id.* at 121–22. Should we refer to such a creature as a "cat" notwithstanding the way in which it differs from other cats of our acquaintance? Our existing linguistic conventions do not tell us one way or the other; whatever criteria we have commonly used for applying the word "cat" are not sufficiently well specified either to include or to exclude this creature. In this respect, our prior usage of the word "cat" has contained a time-released indeterminacy—one that has been present each time we have used the word to refer to feline creatures, but that we have never before had occasion to notice.

It is important to understand the subtlety of Waismann's example. The point is not that all words in current use are indeterminate in their application to any phenomena that we have not yet encountered. Our

---

[5] Modern law professors often use the term "open-textured" in a less useful way, to refer to ordinary vagueness. *See* Frederick Schauer, *A Critical Guide to Vehicles in the Park*, 83 N.Y.U. L. REV. 1109, 1126 n.62 (2008) (noting and lamenting this departure from Waismann's coinage). Because Waismann used the term to describe a distinct phenomenon for which we lack any other word, I will adhere to his usage.

current usage of the word "dog," for instance, unambiguously excludes Waismann's quasi-cat, even though we have never encountered that creature. (Admittedly, conventional usages of words do change over time, and perhaps we will come to call Waismann's quasi-cat a "dog" when we encounter such a creature in the year 2510. But that usage would be inconsistent with specifications that we currently associate with the word "dog.") Conversely, the word "creature" in current usage unambiguously *includes* Waismann's creature, at least as Waismann described it.[6] Waismann's point is not that our current vocabulary has application only to the precise phenomena that we have experienced so far, but simply that our current vocabulary is likely to be better specified with respect to known phenomena than with respect to phenomena that mankind has not yet encountered. In particular, many words in current usage contain latent indeterminacies that changing circumstances might expose.

Waismann's point is about language, not law. But because law works through language, the point has implications for theories of statutory interpretation. Suppose one accepts the conventional idea that interpreters should try to identify and enforce the original meaning of statutory language. If a statute enacted in 2023 requires "dogs" to be licensed, and if I am right that the conventional meaning of the word "dog" at the time of enactment unambiguously excludes Waismann's quasi-cat, then one will most likely refrain from applying the statute to that creature.[7] That is so even if, by the time Waismann's creature is discovered in the year 2510, members of society have come to use the word "dog" to cover any four-footed creature, and even if members of society in 2510 therefore refer to Waismann's quasi-cat as a "dog" in their own conversations. Under traditional approaches to statutory interpretation, the key question will not be what the word "dog" means in ordinary usage *at the time of interpretation*, but rather what it meant in ordinary usage *at the time the legislature used it* (when, on our assumptions, it would not naturally have been applied to Waismann's creature). On the other hand, if a separate statute enacted in 2023 also required "cats" to be licensed, then the discovery of Waismann's creature will expose a latent indeterminacy in the original meaning of that statute: the ordinary meaning of the word "cat" in 2023 contained the latent indeterminacy described above, and so the cat-licensing statute might or might not be understood to apply to Waismann's creature.

---

[6] By the same token, if I were to use the phrase "all red things (whether past, present, or future)," I would be referring unambiguously to red spaceships, red ray guns, and other red items whose characteristics (other than color) are currently unimaginable to me.

[7] Interpreters who use imaginative reconstruction aggressively might extend the statute to Waismann's quasi-cat if they believe that doing so will serve the enacting legislature's purposes and that members of the enacting legislature would have wanted to cover the quasi-cat if they had known about it. But most current interpreters probably would not use imaginative reconstruction so aggressively.

Before you conclude that this discussion of time-released indeterminacies in statutory language is of purely academic interest (if that), consider the following case.

In re Erickson

815 F.2d 1090 (7th Cir. 1987)

■ *JUDGE EASTERBROOK delivered the opinion for the panel:*

Wis. Stat. § 815.18(6), which makes certain property unavailable to satisfy a civil judgment, allows the judgment debtor to exempt 8 cows, 10 pigs, 50 chickens, 2 horses or 2 mules, 10 sheep, one year's feed for the livestock, and some farm equipment, including: "one wagon, cart or dray, one sleigh, one plow, one drag, one binder, one tractor not to exceed in value the sum of $1,500, one corn binder, one mower, one springtooth harrow, one disc harrow, one seeder, one hay loader, one corn planter," and miscellaneous tools worth as much as $300. Debtors in federal bankruptcy cases sometimes may exempt the property that states protect from civil execution. See 11 U.S.C. § 522(b)(2)(A). They may use this exemption for "implements, professional books, or tools, of the trade of the debtor", see § 522(f)(2)(B), even though they have given their creditors security interests in the items. In this bankruptcy case, where the parties have agreed that the debtor may keep as an "implement" or "tool of the trade" any asset mentioned in Wis. Stat. § 815.18(6), we must decide whether a baler is a "hay loader" and whether a haybine is a "mower". (We need not and do not decide whether the agreement was provident.)

A baler not only loads hay on a wagon but also ties it in bales; a haybine not only mows hay but also conditions it. Both the bankruptcy judge and the district judge concluded that the extra functions of the machines did not prevent their exemption under § 815.18(6).... Dorchester State Bank, which had security interests in the baler (worth $400) and the haybine (worth $1,500), . . . appeal[s] . . . .

The problem in this case comes from the fact that technology has done more to change farm implements than the Wisconsin legislature has done to change § 815.18(6). The "mower" and "hay loader" were added to the list in 1935, and § 815.18(6) has been unchanged (with an immaterial exception) since then. The statutory list comprises the equipment that in 1935 would have kept a small farm in operation. But small farms now use a different set of equipment. We concentrate on the haybine, because the same principles influence the treatment of both haybine and baler. The mower, which cuts hay, has been succeeded by the haybine (also called a "mower-conditioner"), which cuts and crushes hay in a single operation so that the hay dries faster. If the statute applies only to farm implements customary in 1935, and therefore omits the haybine, it does not achieve its purpose today; yet if the statute exempts all successors of the listed equipment, technological change may dramatically enlarge the exemption without legislative consideration. One need only think of the technological successor of the statutory "binder"—the self-propelled combine, which may be worth $1 million. Asked at oral argument if a combine would be exempt under § 815.18(6), Erickson's counsel replied that it would. That cannot be right, yet neither is it appropriate to say that the statute covers only machines called "mowers".

This is so in part because language evolves. Janitors have become custodians; garbage collectors have become sanitary engineers; hearing examiners turned into administrative law judges; referees in bankruptcy are now bankruptcy judges; employees are terminated rather than fired, and spies are "terminated with extreme prejudice" rather than assassinated. The longer the time, the more the language changes. Hamlet says to Guildenstern in Act II, scene 2: "I am but mad north-north-west: when the wind is southerly I know a hawk from a handsaw." He means that he is feigning madness, shown because he can tell one bird from another when he wants. (To Shakespeare, a "handsaw" was a heron—or so some scholars believe. We stand clear of the debate about what exactly this line means.) If § 815.18(6) said that a farmer may exempt "8 cows, 10 pigs, 50 chickens, 2 horses or 2 mules, 10 sheep, 1 hawk, and 1 handsaw", that we now think of a handsaw as a tool would not subject the handsaw's value to the $300 limit the statute places on "miscellaneous tools".

There is a more compelling reason, however, why "mower" is not limited to the thing called a mower today, or even the thing called a mower in 1935. A statutory word of description does not designate a particular item (e.g., "a Massey-Ferguson Mower, Model GY-2589, manufactured in 1935, serial number 3875808") but a class of things that share some important feature. Which feature is important depends on the function of the designation and how it will be interpreted by the audience to whom the word is addressed. Cf. Saul Kripke, *Wittgenstein on Rules and Private Language* 19, 28, 98–109 (1982). If someone at a dinner party says: "Pull up a chair to the table", he means a table chair and not an overstuffed easy chair, even though both are called chairs. The word "chair" in an exemption statute, however, might include easy chairs but not Chippendale chairs—because the function of the statute is to leave the person a place to sit rather than to protect an antique valued (and valuable) for its beauty and age rather than its comfort. (There is a standing injunction not to sit on Chippendale chairs because that might destroy their value.) And if a change in language or function should cause a new name to be applied to a place to sit—say, if reclining chairs with stereo speakers built in should come to be called "stereoloungers"—it would be necessary to examine the function of the denotation yet again rather than say that a "stereolounger" is not a "chair" and that is that.

When asked at oral argument whether a mower with a built-in stereo cassette deck would still be a "mower", the Bank's lawyer answered yes, because it would still cut the hay. Yet it would have a second function, entertainment, just as the haybine has a second function, crushing the hay. The Bank's counsel balked at this extension because the crushing function makes the haybine more valuable as a farm implement and thus enlarges the shelter provided by the statutory exemption. Erickson's haybine is worth $1,500, considerably more than a mower. (Erickson also actually owns an old mower, valued at $25.) Yet the tape deck, too, would increase the market value of the mower.

There cannot be an "equal value" principle in § 815.18(6). The "mower" has changed through time. When brought to market in the mid-nineteenth century, the mower was a simple, horse-drawn successor to the reaper. See Michael Partridge, *Farm Tools Through the Ages* 145–46 (1973). When in 1935 Wisconsin first created an exemption for a mower, many implements called "mowers" were horse drawn. Most mowers designed to be pulled by tractors drew power for the blades from the friction of wheel against ground. See Harris P. Smith & Lambert H. Wilkes, *Farm Machinery and Equipment* 286–87 (6th ed. 1976). The tractor-mounted mower, which drew power direct from the drive shaft of the tractor, was not introduced until 1930. After 1935 mowers grew in size, complexity, and efficiency. In 1952 the pitman drive for the blades was replaced by pitmanless cams, which reduced vibration and increased operating speed. *Id.* at 289. Later machines, still called "mowers", grew larger and more sophisticated; some had hydraulic lifts so that they could be maneuvered more accurately. *Id.* at 294–96. The "mower" that could be found on a farm in 1975 probably had no more parts in common with a horse-drawn 1935-vintage mower than a 1975 haybine had in common with a 1975 mower. The Bank does not deny that a mower made in 1975 would qualify as a "mower", which dooms the argument that an increase in value eliminates the exemption.

Changes in value also cut both ways. The exemption for a tractor is limited to $1,500, for example; in 1935 this might have exempted a small tractor, but now it does not. A true "equal value" principle would interpret "$1,500" as denoting real (inflation-adjusted) rather than nominal dollars, or perhaps it would adjust the exemption to, say, the percentage of the value of the debtor's tractor that $1,500 would have represented in 1935. The Bank does not ask us to increase the value of the exemption for Erickson's tractor; it is no more appropriate to ensure that the exemption for the "mower" is worth now what it was worth in 1935. A legislature can write an exemption with a dollar limit (as it did for tractors and tools) or without; when it chooses the latter course a court may not treat the statute as if it had the missing valuation rule. The exemption for a mower does not depend on value, just as an exemption for an "automobile" would not. A 1986 Audi 5000CS Turbo Quattro and a 1976 Volkswagen Rabbit probably have less in common (and surely have a greater difference in value) than a 1975 mower and a 1975 haybine, yet both are cars; so too with farm equipment.

This does not necessarily require a decision in Erickson's favor. Our inability to apply either a "plain meaning" or "same value" approach does not identify with any confidence what a mower *is*, although it forecloses some ways of identifying what a mower is not. The bankruptcy and district judges concluded that a haybine is a "mower" because it is the "technological successor" to the mower. But the self-propelled combine is the technological successor to the binder, and if you allow enough leeway the Boeing 747 is the technological successor of the chariot. The ability to trace a line of descent is not sufficient—not unless the scope of the statute is entirely liberated from its history and function. A statute designed to allow family farmers to keep the minimum equipment necessary to work the land cannot readily exempt a self-propelled combine, "technological successor" or not. (We needn't consider the possibility that the self-propelled combine is the "successor" to the tractor and so is limited by the $1,500 maximum for tractors.) The role of an exemption in the statutory structure, not the march of technology, is the centerpiece in identifying the meaning of the language.

Alas, § 815.18(6) has no legislative history, and apparently not a single Wisconsin court has construed its language. We are on our own. We cannot determine the meaning of "mower" by using the principle Erickson presses on us: that exemptions are "remedial" statutes and therefore to be "liberally" construed. *Julius v. Druckrey*, 254 N.W. 358 (Wis. 1934). This tells us the direction to move but does not help us figure out how far to go. "Liberality" may answer the question whether both a direct-drive mower and a friction-drive mower are statutory "mowers"; it does not answer any more complex problem. Finding the meaning of a statute is more like calculating a vector (with direction and length) than it is like identifying which way the underlying "values" or "purposes" point (which has direction alone).... Too much "liberality" will undermine the statute as surely as too literal an interpretation would. The statute is designed to give farmers a fresh start. See generally Thomas H. Jackson, *The Fresh-Start Policy in Bankruptcy Law*, 98 Harv. L. Rev. 1393 (1985). Any fresh-start policy must balance the gains from new beginnings against the costs of making it harder for lenders to collect. The more difficult collection becomes, the fewer assets are available to secure loans, the costlier is credit. Every expansion of the Wisconsin exemption statute makes loans riskier for banks and so raises the interest rate (or makes banks unwilling to lend at all to some people). This effect, which burdens the frugal and the spendthrift alike, can swamp the gains of fresh starts. Identifying the "liberal" function of exemptions does not assist us to determine when the increased cost of credit hurts farmers more than the fresh start helps them.

We must turn to the statute's structure and function. If the function of § 815.18(6) is to enable farmers to keep a minimal set of equipment to work the fields, then a haybine is a "mower". It performs the mowing function of the mower, and its additional drying function used to be performed by rakes and other tools. The haybine and the mower have many features in common; the haybine is a close rather than a distant descendant of the mower. The Bank does not dispute the district court's conclusion that the mower is obsolete, and that farmers use mower-conditioner combinations. Nothing in the case suggests that Erickson's haybine is gold-plated or otherwise designed to evade the bankruptcy laws.

No implement could be a mower without having a lot in common with the thing known as a mower in 1935, but the haybine meets this test. It contains the kind of mowing gear that used to be sold as a "mower", plus a bar to bend the hay (so that the butt end flips up when the stalk is cut) and rollers to crush it. Perhaps the change in terminology is itself evidence that a haybine is "enough" separated from the old mower to be a "different" tool, but we hesitate to rely too much on that. The manufacturers' invention of a new name, as opposed to using "enhanced mower" as a handle, may have been a marketing device rather than an attempt to describe the technical differences between the implements. And the alternative name ("mower-conditioner") suggests the close link.

To the extent there is doubt—and there is still substantial doubt, for the age of this statute prevents "literal" application to today's farm equipment, even a piece of equipment called a "mower"—we accept the decision of the bankruptcy and district judges. The views here of judges skilled in the law of the state in which they sit are entitled to respect. [Citations omitted.[*]] The law has need of tie-breakers, and if this case be a tie (it comes close), the nod goes to the district court's construction. . . .

NOTES AND QUESTIONS

1. *Erickson* exposes what Friedrich Waismann would call the open texture of the term "mower" that the Wisconsin legislature added to the exemption statute in 1935. Mower-conditioners of the sort at issue in *Erickson* did not exist at that time, and the word "mower" was not sufficiently well specified either to encompass or to exclude them unambiguously.

To be sure, the mere fact that a particular machine did not exist in 1935 does not automatically prevent the statutory term "mower" from covering it (and from doing so unambiguously). That is one implication of Judge Easterbrook's observation that the term "mower" should not be understood to "designate a particular item (e.g., a Massey-Ferguson Mower, Model GY-2589, manufactured in 1935, serial number 3875808)." If the Massey-Ferguson company were to make another machine of the

[*] *Editor's note*: At the time of *Erickson*, Seventh Circuit precedent told circuit judges to give some deference to federal district judges about the meaning of state laws in the district judges' state. Later, though, the Supreme Court rejected this practice. *See* Salve Regina Coll. v. Russell, 499 U.S. 225, 231 (1991) ("We conclude that a court of appeals should review *de novo* a district court's determination of state law.").

same model in 1936, that machine plainly would be a "mower" within the meaning of the 1935 amendment. Indeed, if the Massey-Ferguson company were to start manufacturing a new and improved model in 1937 that was simply a somewhat better version of the mowers available in 1935, it too would surely qualify as a "mower" within the meaning of the statute.

Marie Erickson's mower-conditioner,[8] however, was neither so similar to the mowers of 1935 as to make clear that the statutory term "mower" covered it nor so different as to make clear that the statutory term did *not* cover it. If people in 1935 had been asked what the word "mower" meant in the context in which the Wisconsin statute used that word, they presumably would have talked about various features; they would have identified a "mower" as a piece of farm machinery, and they would have talked about its ability to cut tall herbage. But their definition probably would not have been so finely specified as to permit us to conclude that the word (as used in 1935) either unambiguously applies or unambiguously does not apply to the modern mower-conditioner.

Admittedly, that conclusion is not inevitable. If the term "mower" as used in 1935 was commonly understood to mean "any machine that mows, no matter what else it does," then the original meaning of the statutory language would unambiguously have encompassed modern mower-conditioners. (Indeed, that would be true even if people later stopped using the word "mower" so broadly, so that mower-conditioners were not called "mower[s]" when they finally were invented. For purposes of interpreting the 1935 statute, Judge Easterbrook was not interested in the subsequent evolution of the word "mower," except to the extent that it sheds light on the criteria that governed people's application of that word in 1935.) Conversely, if the term "mower" as used in 1935 was commonly understood to refer exclusively to "a machine whose sole function is to mow," then the original meaning of the statutory language would unambiguously have excluded modern mower-conditioners. (Again, that would be true even if the meaning of the word "mower" later expanded, so that people ultimately came to call mower-conditioners "mowers.") But Judge Easterbrook did not think that either of these possible closure rules was built into the term "mower" as the Wisconsin legislature used it in 1935. Nor did he identify other criteria associated with the word "mower" in 1935 that would unambiguously cause the word either to cover or to exclude mower-conditioners. In his view, then, the invention of the mower-conditioner exposed a latent indeterminacy in the word that the Wisconsin legislature used in 1935.

---

[8] Just as some people refer to all photocopiers as "xerox machines" and all facial tissues as "kleenexes," so too Judge Easterbrook's opinion referred to all mower-conditioners as "haybines." In fact, however, Haybine® is the registered trademark of a particular manufacturer (New Holland). The generic term is mower-conditioner.

2. If you are with Judge Easterbrook that far, how would you proceed to handle this indeterminacy? What considerations should interpreters take into account when trying to decide whether a modern mower-conditioner qualifies for exemption as a "mower" within the meaning of the 1935 statute?

Judge Easterbrook himself seemed to be asking whether the mower-conditioner (1) has enough of the characteristics that people associated with the word "mower" in 1935 and (2) does not have so many other characteristics as to swamp the ones that it shares with the paradigmatic "mower[s]" of 1935. He made this evaluation, moreover, in the context of the particular statute in which the word "mower" appears, and in light of the purposes that he ascribed to that statute—allowing farmers in financial distress to keep equipment that they need to work their land, but not otherwise giving them free rein to hide assets from their creditors. This approach still left him with "substantial doubt" about whether the statutory term "mower" should be interpreted to encompass Ms. Erickson's mower-conditioner, but he ultimately resolved the indeterminacy in favor of inclusion. Regardless of your ultimate bottom line, do you agree with how he structured the inquiry?

In the course of his discussion, Judge Easterbrook alluded to some hypothetical examples that did not strike him as so difficult. For instance, he suggested that the word "mower" in the exemption statute *would* cover a mower that was equipped with a tape deck and *would not* cover a "gold-plated" machine that performed the function of mowing but that really existed for the purpose of sheltering assets from creditors. Is the latter conclusion consistent with Judge Easterbrook's usual willingness to read statutes to be just as rule-like as they seem on their face?

3. Should the sort of interpretation that Judge Easterbrook undertook in *Erickson* be classified as "dynamic"? To the extent that the term "mower" in the 1935 statute included a time-released indeterminacy, and to the extent that Judge Easterbrook resolved that indeterminacy by reading the term to encompass Ms. Erickson's modern mower-conditioner, there is a sense in which he imported into the statute something that was not there at the outset. But is that process any different than the resolution of less exotic types of indeterminacy in statutory language—indeterminacy that is apparent from the start?

To the extent that the application of statutory language to some particular case requires the resolution of any sort of indeterminacy in the statutory language, there is a sense in which interpretation is *always* "dynamic." But there is also a sense in which the court is simply doing the best it can to identify and apply the (original) meaning of the statute. When the court resolves an indeterminacy as part of that process, would you say that the court has changed the statute's meaning? Does your answer to that question depend on the precedential force of the court's opinion—so that an opinion by a district court (or a federal circuit court interpreting state law) does not change the statute's meaning, but an opinion that will bind interpreters in future cases does? If so, could one fairly say that the "dynamic" aspect of a judicial decision resolving an indeterminacy in statutory language is primarily a consequence of the doctrine of *stare decisis*?

4. In *Erickson,* the passage of time exposed a latent indeterminacy in a particular term: in the vocabulary of 1935, the meaning of "mower" was not sufficiently well specified to make clear whether it included or excluded a modern mower-conditioner. To help resolve this time-released indeterminacy in the statutory text, Judge Easterbrook considered the fit between the various possible interpretations of the statutory language and the purposes that he attributed to the statute.

Even though Judge Easterbrook is a prominent "textualist," so-called "purposivists" would presumably have no objection to the general approach that he used in *Erickson.* But the more one inclines toward "purposivism" rather than "textualism," the more one will want to use the same approach to identify the meaning of statutory language as a whole (rather than simply the meaning of an individual word or phrase within the statute). Purposivists are more likely than textualists to expect the passage of time to expose indeterminacies that are not keyed to particular words, but that interpreters are nonetheless authorized to resolve. The existence of that sort of time-released indeterminacy is more controversial than the existence of "open-textured" terms, so the next section gives it separate treatment.

C. AGING STATUTES AND IMAGINATIVE RECONSTRUCTION

Everyone agrees that legislatures enact statutes on the basis of various premises and assumptions, including premises that the statutes do not (explicitly) codify. Everyone also agrees that the passage of time can undermine the premises behind a particular statute in ways that the enacting legislature did not expect. Over the years, though, different interpreters have expressed different ideas about how to proceed in the face of such change.

On one way of thinking, the key question is whether the typical statute should be understood to imply a time-released delegation of authority to subsequent interpreters. When Congress enacts a statute, it might be understood to be setting a particular formulation in stone and instructing interpreters to apply that formulation unless and until Congress changes it. In the alternative, though, Congress might be assumed to be telling interpreters something along the following lines: "Here is a verbal formula that we expect you to follow fairly closely now, while circumstances are much like those that we ourselves confronted during the drafting process. But if and when the premises that underlie our formulation cease to apply, you are authorized to adjust the formula appropriately. More generally, to the extent that relevant circumstances change in ways that we have not foreseen, you should infer appropriate exceptions or embellishments as you think best to continue serving the mix of purposes that we are trying to advance."

Admittedly, reading this instruction into each individual statute seems artificial. But purposivists might say that something like this instruction is implicit in ordinary communication, or at least in the kind of communication that entails establishing general directives for future action. Alternatively, purposivists might say that in our system of government, the authority just described is part of the judicial power unless the legislature turns it off.

In any event, when a statute does not explicitly speak to these issues, purposivists are more likely than textualists to infer exceptions or embellishments that (in their view) will help the statute continue to serve its intended purposes in the face of changed circumstances. As time goes by, moreover, they will have increasing opportunities to do so. After all, the passage of time will present interpreters with more and more situations that members of the enacting legislature could not have foreseen (or at least probably did not foresee), and purposivists may sometimes react by making their own judgments about how the statute's underlying purposes bear on those situations.

Should we think of this phenomenon as a form of "dynamic" interpretation? From the purposivists' perspective, the authority to adjust a statute's verbal formulas (by inferring appropriate exceptions or embellishments where necessary to continue serving the statute's original purposes) has been implicit from the moment that the statute was enacted. The necessary adjustments, moreover, are driven by the mix of purposes that the statute was designed to serve—which the statute again has reflected from the outset. In both those respects, this form of purposivist interpretation is linked to the original meaning that purposivists would attribute to the statute. But after circumstances have changed in such a way as to trigger the latent exceptions or embellishments that purposivists recognize, outside observers who are asked to restate the statute's upshot probably would use a different formulation than they would have used before circumstances changed. In that sense, at least, purposivist adjustments to statutory language might be described as changing the statute's meaning.

From the 1930s to the 1970s, many distinguished federal judges seemed receptive to a fairly strong form of purposivism. In one 1952 opinion, for instance, Judge Learned Hand addressed "the baffling question which comes up so often in the interpretation of all kinds of writings: how far is it proper to read the words out of their literal meaning in order to realize their overriding purpose?" Judge Hand's answer entailed imaginative reconstruction: "Flinch as we may, what we do, and must do, is to project ourselves, as best we can, into the position of those who uttered the words, and to impute to them how they would have dealt with the concrete occasion." *United States v. Klinger*, 199 F.2d 645, 648 (2d Cir. 1952), *aff'd by an evenly divided court*, 345 U.S. 979 (1953).[9] This approach is obviously originalist in one sense; Judge Hand was trying to reconstruct the purpose and presumed judgments of the *enacting* legislature. *See, e.g.*, Fishgold v. Sullivan Drydock & Repair Corp., 154 F.2d 785, 788–89 (2d Cir.) (L. Hand, J.) (observing that "we are to reconstruct, as best we may, what was the purpose of Congress when it used the words," and conducting this project in light of "the situation at the time that the Act was passed" rather than "what has happened [since then]"), *aff'd*, 328 U.S. 275 (1946). Especially as applied to matters that the enacting legislature might not have understood itself to be resolving, though, the approach left open the possibility of reading statutes to have some content that would not have been apparent at the time of enactment.

Justice Felix Frankfurter expressed similar views. To be sure, he was willing to apply broadly worded statutes to situations that the enacting Congress had not specifically contemplated if those situations were part of the general problem that Congress had considered and addressed. *See* Barr v. United States, 324 U.S. 83, 99–100 (1945) (Frankfurter, J., dissenting) (indicating that when a statute "appropriately describ[es] a general problem," courts should not "excise a particular situation" from the statutory language simply because the situation was " 'unforeseen' by Congress"); *see also* Felix Frankfurter, *Some Reflections on the Reading of Statutes*, 47 COLUM. L. REV. 527, 539 (1947) (observing that "often the very reason for casting a statute in very general terms" is to guard against the possibility that "a specific manifestation was not thought of"). But according to Justice Frankfurter, the fact that statutes could apply to "an unforeseen situation" did not mean that they applied to "an unforeseen problem." In his words, "[i]f the problem itself was not in the contemplation of Congress, . . . how can it be said that Congress legislated concerning that problem?" *Barr*, 324 U.S. at 100 (Frankfurter, J., dissenting).

Since the 1980s, though, the Supreme Court has been more reluctant to make *ad hoc* purposivist adjustments to statutory language. *Cf.* Frank H. Easterbrook, *Judges as Honest Agents*, 33 HARV. J. L. & PUB. POL'Y 915, 923 (2010) (referring to the current Supreme Court's "reluctance to engage in the imaginative-reconstruction exercise"). Take *United States v. Lorenzetti*, 467 U.S. 167 (1984). Paul Lorenzetti was a federal employee

---

[9] *See also* Cabell v. Markham, 148 F.2d 737, 739 (2d Cir.) (L. Hand, J.) ("Of course it is true that the words used, even in their literal sense, are the primary, and ordinarily the most reliable, source of interpreting the meaning of any writing: be it a statute, a contract, or anything else. But it is one of the surest indexes of a mature and developed jurisprudence not to make a fortress out of the dictionary; but to remember that statutes always have some purpose or object to accomplish, whose sympathetic and imaginative discovery is the surest guide to their meaning."), *aff'd*, 326 U.S. 404 (1945); *cf.* Thomas W. Merrill, *Learned Hand on Statutory Interpretation: Theory and Practice*, 87 FORDHAM L. REV. 1, 3–5, 9–12 (2018) (noting that Learned Hand consistently endorsed imaginative reconstruction in extrajudicial statements from 1935 through the end of his career, but observing that his opinions about the federal Copyright Act did not actually rely on that approach).

who was injured in a car accident while on the job. He obtained compensation from the United States under the Federal Employees' Compensation Act (FECA), a workers' compensation statute that dates back to 1916. He also sued the other driver, eventually reaching a settlement that paid him for noneconomic losses such as pain and suffering (the only form of damages available to him under the relevant state's No-Fault Act, but not something that his FECA award covered). The United States argued that in light of this outside recovery, a provision of FECA now found at 5 U.S.C. § 8132 gave him an obligation to reimburse the United States. Because "§ 8132 was passed prior to the enactment of no-fault statutes," a panel of the Third Circuit thought that "the problem is one that Congress could not have considered." *Lorenzetti v. United States*, 710 F.2d 982, 985 (3d Cir. 1983). For the panel, it followed that interpreters should not simply parse the language of § 8132, but instead should "analyze the purposes underlying the statute in order to determine its proper scope." *Id.* But the Supreme Court unanimously disagreed. According to the Court, the language of § 8132 did require reimbursement, and "the fact that changing state tort laws may have led to unforeseen consequences does not mean that the federal statutory scheme may be judicially expanded to take those changes into account." *Lorenzetti*, 467 U.S. at 179. In Justice Blackmun's words, "It is for Congress, not the courts, to revise longstanding legislation in order to accommodate the effects of changing social conditions." *Id.*

Of these two contrasting approaches, which would you expect members of Congress themselves to want courts to use? As you ponder that question, keep in mind the contrast between rules and standards. The more rule-like a directive is understood to be, the more closely those applying it will hew to judgment calls that are built into the directive itself—judgment calls made by members of the enacting legislature. Conversely, the more standard-like a directive is understood to be, the more leeway future judges or other implementing officials will have to reach their own conclusions about how the directive's underlying purposes play out in different circumstances. Relatively rule-like directives therefore play a substantial role in what Professor Schauer calls the "intertemporal allocation of power." FREDERICK SCHAUER, PLAYING BY THE RULES: A PHILOSOPHICAL EXAMINATION OF RULE-BASED DECISION-MAKING IN LAW AND IN LIFE 160 (1991). From a legislator's perspective, that role has both advantages and disadvantages. By establishing a relatively rule-like directive, today's legislator can exert more control over future decisionmakers (whose policy analysis may not otherwise coincide with the legislator's), but at the cost of locking those decisionmakers into results that even the legislator would not really consider desirable under the circumstances.

As with other aspects of the choice between rules and standards, how to weigh those advantages and disadvantages when drafting legislation is itself a difficult policy question. It is hard to predict how any particular legislator would resolve that question in any particular situation. Simply recognizing that the question exists, though, helps us identify an important feature of the different possible approaches to cases like *Lorenzetti*. Even on the Supreme Court's approach, the typical statutory directive becomes somewhat more standard-like as it ages; most statutes contain some time-released indeterminacies, and courts are likely to choose among the permissible interpretations by making their own assessments of which choice will better serve the enacting legislature's purposes. But the approach taken by the Third Circuit panel in *Lorenzetti* would increase that effect. If changing circumstances allow courts to adjust even seemingly determinate statutory language in the service of the enacting legislature's perceived purposes, provisions that appear relatively rule-like when enacted will become more and more standard-like over time.

Whichever approach one favors in the abstract, one must also think about the relationship between the courts' interpretive practices and the meaning of Congress's statutes. One might put the question this way: Assuming that the federal judiciary has become less receptive to imaginative reconstruction than it was in the 1950s, how should modern courts interpret statutes that were enacted in the 1950s? Suppose that in the 1950s, interpreters were relatively willing to read exceptions or embellishments into old statutes so that the statutes would continue to serve what the interpreters took to be the statutes' underlying purposes. Suppose further that when legislators drafted and enacted statutes in the 1950s, they expected courts to take that approach as the statutes aged. If future courts do not in fact do so, but rather hew closely to the statutory text after circumstances have changed, might one say that these courts are themselves engaging in a species of "dynamic" interpretation? Or is the mix between purposivism and textualism that prevails when a statute is enacted not part of the background that informs the "original meaning" of that statute?

Coda: A Problem from the Copyright Act of 1909

So far we have considered three different phenomena that are commonly discussed in connection with "dynamic" interpretation: (1) the courts' application of seemingly determinate statutory language to situations that people could not have foreseen at the time of enactment, (2) the courts' resolution of time-released indeterminacies in statutory language, and (3) the courts' occasional embellishment of the surface meaning of statutory language to help statutes continue to serve their intended purposes in the face of new conditions. Although these phenomena are distinct, they do overlap. Here is a brief summary of an old but accessible case that puts pressure on our taxonomy.

The Copyright Act of 1909 enabled people to get federal copyrights in various works, including musical compositions. The Act specified that such a copyright conferred "the exclusive right . . . to perform the copyrighted work publicly for profit if it be a musical composition and for the purpose of public performance for profit." Act of March 4, 1909, ch. 320, § 1(e), 35 Stat. 1075, 1075. When Congress enacted this language, scientists had made the discoveries that eventually led to radio broadcasts, but the technology had not yet been commercialized; there were no broadcasting stations in the United States. Once such stations arose, though, courts had to decide whether someone who performed a musical composition in a studio, but whose performance was broadcast over the airwaves, was "perform[ing] the . . . work publicly for profit" within the meaning of the Copyright Act. If so, what about the broadcasting company: was it too "perform[ing] the . . . work publicly for profit" within the meaning of the Copyright Act (or, alternatively, could it be held liable for contributing to any infringement by the performer)?

Consider the allegations of the complaint in *Jerome H. Remick & Co. v. American Automobile Accessories Co.*, 298 F. 628 (S.D. Ohio 1924). The defendant was a commercial business that manufactured radios and parts for radios. For the purpose of advertising its products and creating more demand for them, it established radio station WLW in Cincinnati, securing a commercial license from the appropriate unit within the federal Department of Commerce. On October 22, 1923, the defendant's radio station allegedly broadcast a rendition of a song called "Dreamy Melody." The plaintiff, who owned the copyright in that song, sued the defendant for infringement on the theory that the defendant's behavior amounted to a "public performance for profit" within the meaning of the Act. In keeping with the remedies that the Act authorized, the plaintiff sought an injunction against further infringement as well as "statutory damages" in the amount of $250. *See* Copyright Act of 1909 § 25, 35 Stat. at 1081 (making infringers liable to injunctive relief, disgorgement of profits, and compensatory damages, but adding that "in lieu of actual damages and profits" the copyright owner could recover "such damages as to the court shall appear to be just," and establishing a floor of $250 for such damages); *see also* Act of Aug. 24, 1912, ch. 356, 37 Stat. 488 (amending some details of this provision).

The defendant moved to dismiss the plaintiff's complaint. The district court granted this motion, but the Sixth Circuit reversed and remanded. Excerpts from both opinions follow.

Jerome H. Remick & Co. v. American Automobile Accessories Co.

298 F. 628 (S.D. Ohio 1924)

■ *JUDGE HICKENLOOPER:*

. . . .

Plaintiff's rights being entirely dependent upon the statute, and the recovery sought being an arbitrary penal sum, not in any sense dependent upon proof of actual profits or damages to an equivalent amount, we are inclined to the opinion that the statute should be subjected to strict construction, notwithstanding the provision of the section covering infringement that such arbitrary minimum recovery "shall not be regarded as a penalty." [35 Stat. at 1081; 37 Stat. at 489.]

. . . .

. . . . While these statutes "should be given a fair and reasonable construction," with a view to protecting the author in such manner that he may have the benefit of the property right conferred for a limited term of years . . . , it is clear that this protection should not be extended beyond the express language of the statute, nor a property right created which was clearly not within the mind of Congress when the act was passed.

And in determining the intent of Congress, as expressed in the act, it is the duty of the courts to read the enactment "according to the natural import of the words used," and, if the language used by Congress is unambiguous, there is no room for construction, nor can we speculate as to what Congress might have done, or might have intended, had the matter been specifically brought to its attention . . . .

. . . .

The question, therefore, resolves itself into a determination whether the broadcasting of a rendition of complainant's musical composition was a performance of it publicly for profit in the common, ordinary, and reasonable acceptation of this phrase. We are familiar with the holding of the United States District Court for the District of New Jersey in the case of *M. Witmark & Sons v. L. Bamberger & Co.*, 291 F. 776, in which the court concluded that the rendition of a song for broadcasting purposes was a public performance of the musical composition, and that such performance was unquestionably for profit within the decision of *Herbert v. Shanley Co.*, 242 U.S. 591 [(1917)]. While, considered seriatim, this opinion might be said to arrive at a logical conclusion, viz. that the singing was a performance, that it was public in the sense that those could listen who cared to and were equipped with receiving instruments, and that it was for profit because of its advertising value, and therefore every element of a public performance for profit had been disclosed, we have been unable to bring ourselves to the conclusion that such broadcasting was within what Congress had in mind when using the language "publicly perform for profit."

Funk & Wagnalls' Standard Dictionary (1911) defines a performance:

"(2) Specifically a representation on the stage or before an audience or spectators; an exhibition of feats; any entertainment at a place of amusement; as two performances daily."

While not found in other standard dictionaries, it is just this idea which we think Congress had in mind in passing the enactment in its present form. In order to constitute a public performance in the sense in which we think Congress intended the words, it is absolutely essential that there be an assemblage of persons—an audience congregated for the purpose of hearing that which transpires at the place of amusement. This is in no wise contrary to the case of *Herbert v. Shanley Co., supra,* for there was there such audience congregated in a popular restaurant in New York, and it could make little difference whether the patrons paid for their entertainment in the form of an admission fee, a cover charge, or as an addition to the menu prices.

. . . . We simply feel that the rendition of a copyrighted piece of music in the studio of a broadcasting station, where the public are not admitted and cannot come, but where the sound waves are converted into radio frequency waves and thus transmitted over thousands of miles of space, to be at last reconverted into sound waves in the homes of the owners of receiving sets, . . . is not a public performance within the intendment of Congress in enacting the Copyright Law. The auditor, "listening in" at Indianapolis, Cleveland, or Chicago, would be surprised to learn that he had, that evening, attended a public performance in Cincinnati. . . .

[In 1897, when Congress first prohibited the public performance of copyrighted musical compositions without a license from the owner,] "[t]he purpose of the amendment evidently was to put musical compositions on the footing of dramatic compositions . . . ." *White-Smith Music Co. v. Apollo Co.,* [209 U.S. 1, 16 (1908)]. . . . [T]he close association in the act of provisions relating to the drama and to public performance of musical compositions would seem to demonstrate conclusively that Congress had in mind a place of such performance to which the public was admitted for the entertainment there of the senses, a congregating together for this purpose, and the payment, in one way or another, of compensation for the entertainment provided. This would seem to be the whole extent of the exclusive privilege or property right granted, and the effect of the act should not be extended beyond such clear and unambiguous import of the words used. . . .

Jerome H. Remick & Co. v. American Automobile Accessories Co.

5 F.2d 411 (6th Cir. 1925)

■ *JUDGE MACK delivered the opinion for the panel:*

. . . .

While the fact that radio was not developed at the time the Copyright Act was enacted may raise some question as to whether it properly comes within the purview of the statute, it is not by that fact alone excluded from the statute. In other words, the statute may be applied to new situations not anticipated by Congress, if, fairly construed, such situations come within its intent and meaning. Thus it has been held both in this country and England that a photograph was a copy or infringement of a copyrighted engraving under statutes passed before the photographic process had been developed. . . . While statutes should not be stretched to apply to new situations not fairly within their scope, they should not be so narrowly construed as to permit their evasion because of changing habits due to new inventions and discoveries.

Bills have been introduced in both House and Senate to permit broadcasting without infringing copyrights. The rights of composer, producer, performer, and the public under this new method of reproduction are eminently matters for considered legislation; but, until Congress shall have specifically determined the relative rights of the parties, we can but decide whether and to what extent statutes covering the subject-matter generally, but enacted without anticipation of such radical changes in the method of reproduction, are, fairly construed, applicable to the new situation.

A performance, in our judgment, is no less public because the listeners are unable to communicate with one another, or are not assembled within an inclosure, or gathered together in some open stadium or park or other public place. Nor can a performance, in our judgment, be deemed private because each listener may enjoy it alone in the privacy of his home. Radio broadcasting is intended to, and in fact does, reach a very much larger number of the public at the moment of the rendition than any other medium of performance. The artist is consciously addressing a great, though unseen and widely scattered, audience, and is therefore participating in a public performance.

That, under the Copyright Act, a public performance may be for profit, though no admission fee is exacted or no profit actually made, is settled by *Herbert v. Shanley*, 242 U.S. 591. It suffices, as there held, that the purpose of the performance be for profit, and not eleemosynary; . . . [the statute is directed] against a commercial, as distinguished from a purely philanthropic, public use of another's composition . . . . It is immaterial, in our judgment, whether that commercial use be such as to secure direct payment for the performance by each listener, or indirect payment, as by a hat-checking charge, when no admission fee is required, or a general commercial advantage, as by advertising one's name in the expectation and hope of making profits through the sale of one's products, be they radio or other goods. . . .

Reversed and remanded.

NOTES AND QUESTIONS

1. Was the surface meaning of the Copyright Act determinate as applied to the situation in *Remick*? If you think it was, which side do you think it favored? Would you say that the plaintiff's victory in the Sixth Circuit simply reflected a new application of the original meaning of the Act's language? Or would you say that the Sixth Circuit was embellishing upon the surface meaning of the Act's language so that the Act would continue to serve its intended purposes under circumstances that the enacting Congress had not foreseen?

In the alternative, would you say that *Remick* is another illustration of an open-textured term in statutory language, along the same lines as *Erickson*? On that view, the surface meaning of one or more of the words in the Copyright Act ("perform"? "publicly"?) contained a time-released indeterminacy that the subsequent development of broadcasting stations exposed.

Does your opinion about which court reached the right decision depend on which of these characterizations you accept?

2. Most courts that considered these issues in the 1920s agreed with the Sixth Circuit, not the district court. In keeping with the Sixth Circuit's view, moreover, the Supreme Court soon held that a hotel was "perform[ing]" copyrighted musical works by maintaining a master radio receiver and wiring it so that the broadcasts received by the master set were transmitted to each hotel room. *Buck v. Jewell-LaSalle Realty Co.*, 283 U.S. 191, 198 (1931) ("While this may not have been possible before the development of radio broadcasting, the novelty of the means used does not lessen the duty of the courts to give full protection to the monopoly of public performance for profit which Congress has secured to the composer."). *But cf.* Twentieth-Century Music Corp. v. Aiken, 422 U.S. 151 (1975) (endorsing the Sixth Circuit's decision in *Remick* but limiting *Buck*). Do you agree with *Buck*'s interpretation of the statutory term "perform"? If so, do you think that the hotel's performance is "public[ ]" in the necessary sense? How about "for profit"? Does your answer depend on other facts, like the number of rooms in the hotel and whether the hotel advertised its radio service as a way to attract patrons?

3. Although the Copyright Act of 1909 restricted "public performance[s] for profit" of copyrighted musical compositions, the statute added the following qualification: "The reproduction or rendition of a musical composition by or upon coin-operated machines shall not be deemed a public performance for profit unless a fee is charged for admission to the place where such reproduction or rendition occurs." Copyright Act of 1909

§ 1(e), 35 Stat. at 1076. This exception became known as the "jukebox exemption." But it did not start out with that label, because jukeboxes did not exist in 1909 (at least in anything like their later form). The jukebox exemption thus provides another opportunity to consider how statutory language applies to matters that were not within the contemplation of members of the enacting legislature.

Professor Litman reports that when Congress enacted this exemption in 1909, "what everyone had in mind" was the coin-operated phonograph. Jessica Litman, *War Stories*, 20 CARDOZO ARTS & ENT. L.J. 337, 352 (2002). As introduced in 1889, each coin-operated phonograph could play only one song, which could be heard only through a "listening tube" that a patron would put to his ear. KERRY SEGRAVE, JUKEBOXES: AN AMERICAN SOCIAL HISTORY 5 (2002). Some advances had been made by 1909, but the coin-operated phonographs of that day still offered customers little choice of songs and could not play those songs loudly enough to be heard in a bar or restaurant. *Id.* at 8–12, 14. One of their principal uses, indeed, apparently was simply to advertise the song that they played so that more people would buy the sheet music for it. *See* Litman, *supra*, 20 CARDOZO ARTS & ENT. L.J. at 352. Because this use redounded to the benefit of copyright owners, the exemption for coin-operated machines in the Copyright Act of 1909 was thought to be consistent with the interests of composers and music publishers. *See* Jessica Litman, *Copyright Legislation and Technological Change*, 68 OR. L. REV. 275, 287–88 (1989) (noting that the treatment of musical compositions in the Act "apparently embodied the agreement of the affected parties"); *see also* H.R. REP. NO. 2222, 60th Cong., 2d Sess. 9 (1909) (reporting that the exception for coin-operated machines "is understood to be satisfactory to the composers and proprietors of musical copyrights," and adding that "[a] representative of one of the largest musical publishing houses in the country stated that the publisher finds [arcades featuring coin-operated phonographs] of first assistance as an advertising medium"), *cited in* Litman, *supra*, 68 OR. L. REV. at 287 n.62.

In the 1920s, however, new electrical recording and amplification methods permitted the development of the modern jukebox. *See* Eugene Mooney, *The Jukebox Exemption*, 10 COPYRIGHT L. SYMP. 194 (1959). With the end of Prohibition in 1933, bars became a natural home for the new machines, and the jukebox industry boomed. SEGRAVE, *supra*, at 45. By the 1950s, according to one estimate, Americans were using jukeboxes for more than 9 billion "plays" each year, and the nation's jukeboxes were grossing $500 million annually. *See* Mooney, *supra*, 10 COPYRIGHT L. SYMP. at 205–06 nn. 48 & 50. But because of the exemption for "coin-operated machines" in the Copyright Act of 1909, jukebox operators did not have to pay any performance royalties to the composers or music publishers who owned the copyrights in the songs that the jukeboxes played. *Id.* at 194.

Suppose that Professor Litman is correct that when Congress enacted the exemption for coin-operated machines, members of Congress were thinking of "un-amplified, one-play, novelty machines" that were often used "to promote the sale of sheet music" and that did not generate substantial revenue anyway. Litman, *supra*, 20 CARDOZO ARTS & ENT. L.J. at 352. The subsequent development of jukeboxes put considerable pressure on the purpose behind the exemption. Should courts have held that jukeboxes were not "coin-operated machines" within the meaning of the Copyright Act of 1909? *Cf.* Irving Berlin, Inc. v. Anziano, 4 F.R.D. 33, 34 (S.D.N.Y. 1944) (reporting that in the 1940s, music publishers filed three test cases advancing the theory "that the coin-operated machines in use when the statute was passed are entirely different from 'juke-boxes' ").

When courts confront a new situation that members of Congress probably did not foresee at the time of enactment, and when the surface meaning of the statutory language is ambiguous as applied to this unforeseen situation, courts naturally tend to resolve the ambiguity in light of the underlying substantive purposes that they impute to the enacting legislature. The Sixth Circuit's decision in *Remick*, which interpreted the phrase "public performance" in the Copyright Act of 1909 to include radio broadcasts, is a good example. But when the surface meaning of the statutory language seems *un*ambiguous, courts are often very reluctant to infer purpose-based exceptions or embellishments for unanticipated situations. The jukebox exemption is a case in point. Notwithstanding the fact that modern jukeboxes did not exist in 1909, the category of "coin-operated machines" defined by the 1909 statute seems unambiguously to encompass them, and courts were unlikely to reach a different conclusion just because members of the enacting legislature might have worded the statute differently if they had known about the industry that would develop.

In a sense, the fact that jukeboxes fit into the exemption for coin-operated machines depended on a "fortuity": without necessarily meaning to establish a policy that would encompass machines like jukeboxes, members of Congress happened to cast the exemption in terms that *did* encompass those machines. *See* Litman, *supra*, 68 OR. L. REV. at 302–03 (arguing that the jukebox exemption was not unique in this respect, and that "[a]s case law developed [under the Copyright Act of 1909], the application of copyright law to new technology depended more on linguistic fortuity than anything else"). Does this experience carry any lessons for statutory interpretation? Or are the lessons more relevant for the people who *draft* statutory language than for the people who subsequently interpret it? *Cf. id.* at 277–78 (criticizing Congress and the Copyright Office for "settl[ing] on a scheme for statutory drafting that features meetings and negotiations among representatives of industries with interests in copyright," and blaming this process for generating excessively "fact-specific language" that has not accommodated technological change well).

D. THE IMPORTANCE OF *WHEN* COURTS RESOLVE INDETERMINACIES

Suppose that a legislature enacted a statute at Time 1. When interpreters construe the statute at Time 2, though, they detect an intractable ambiguity: the statutory language could equally well be understood to establish either Directive *A* or Directive *B*, and the permissible sources of information available to interpreters do not shed light on which directive members of the enacting legislature were trying to establish. For purposes of this hypothetical, it does not matter whether the ambiguity is time-released or instead has been apparent from Time 1 on. All that matters is that the statute is genuinely ambiguous about whether it establishes Directive *A* and Directive *B*—with the result that interpreters will have to choose between those two readings on some basis that was not set in stone at the moment of enactment. As the materials that follow explain, the reading that interpreters choose will often depend to some extent on exactly when they are making the choice.

1. THE RELEVANCE OF CURRENT POLICY CONSIDERATIONS

One simple reason why the choices that interpreters make within a statute's zone of indeterminacy might depend on when those choices are being made is that ideas of sound policy can change over time. In the situation that we are hypothesizing, if interpreters have no other basis for choosing between Directives *A* and *B*, interpreters might think about which reading would produce better results in practice. In making that assessment, they are likely to draw upon current understandings of economics, current societal values, current institutional arrangements, and other considerations that are salient at the time of interpretation.

To be sure, conventional accounts of interpretation confine such considerations to the zone of indeterminacy. In many situations, moreover, interpreters trying to identify that zone will already have taken account of the policy landscape that prevailed at the time the statute was enacted. After all, evidence about the policies that would have been considered sensible at the time of enactment will sometimes help clarify what members of the enacting legislature probably meant—which, on conventional accounts, will in turn be relevant to what modern-day courts should read the statute to mean. For a stylized example, imagine that the language of a statute might plausibly be understood to establish either Directive *A* or Directive *B*, but that Directive *A* would have struck people at the time of enactment as silly or unnecessary while Directive *B* would have seemed quite sensible. On the conventional account of interpretation, this information about the policy preferences that prevailed at the time of enactment may well support reading the statute to establish Directive *B*—even if modern-day policymakers would consider Directive *A* sensible too.

On occasion, though, whatever information courts can permissibly consult about the policy preferences that prevailed at the time of enactment will not shed light on the choice between Directive *A* and Directive *B*. Imagine a case of that sort: the statutory text is genuinely ambiguous, and the information that courts can permissibly consult about legislative intent does nothing to break the tie. Even on conventional accounts of interpretation, courts facing this situation will have to pick between the two possible interpretations on some basis other than either the determinate original meaning of the text or the likely intentions of the enacting legislature.[10] In this situation, at least, contemporary normative considerations play a relatively uncontroversial role in the courts' choices. *Cf.* Antonin Scalia, *Judicial Deference to Administrative Interpretations of Law*, 1989 DUKE L.J. 511, 515 (noting that in matters of statutory interpretation, "[p]olicy evaluation . . . is part of the traditional judicial tool-kit").

To the extent that current normative considerations drive the resolution of a particular indeterminacy, the meaning that interpreters will attribute to the statute if the question is first presented to them at Time 2 may differ from the meaning that interpreters would attribute to the statute if the question were first presented to them at Time 1 or Time 3. This effect can readily be described as a species of "dynamic" interpretation. Of course, as with the other phenomena that we have considered, this form of dynamic interpretation is limited: it operates only within the zone of indeterminacy left by the (original) meaning of the statute in question. But in choosing among permissible interpretations within that zone, interpreters are likely to draw upon the normative principles of their own time—which, in some cases, might lead to a different choice than their predecessors or successors would have made if responsibility for responding to the indeterminacy had fallen to them.

2. THE RELEVANCE OF MODERN CONSTITUTIONAL DOCTRINE

Some of the canons that we studied earlier in the course can have the same sort of "dynamic" effects: within a statute's zone of indeterminacy, the interpretations that certain canons favor may depend on when interpreters are applying those canons. Consider, for instance, the canon that favors avoiding constitutional doubts. As we saw in Chapter 2, that canon discourages courts from reading a statute in a way that would raise serious questions about the statute's constitutionality. To the extent that this canon is "normative" rather than "descriptive," it

[10] This formulation assumes that courts will not simply hold the statute void for vagueness. But that assumption is warranted; absolute determinacy in statutes is impossible, and modern constitutional doctrine does not come anywhere close to demanding it.

is triggered by constitutional questions that would be considered serious at the time that the courts are interpreting the statute. According to that version of the canon, if a statute enacted at Time 1 is genuinely ambiguous about whether it establishes Directive *A* or Directive *B*, and if a court interpreting the statute at Time 2 thinks that the constitutionality of Directive *B* is open to serious question, the canon will favor reading the statute to establish Directive *A* instead—even if no one at the time of enactment would have doubted the constitutionality of *either* directive.

To be sure, the Supreme Court has cautioned against invoking this canon when the statute is *not* genuinely ambiguous. If the ordinary descriptive tools of statutory interpretation otherwise favor Directive *B* over Directive *A*, the doubts raised by post-enactment developments in constitutional doctrine are not supposed to affect the courts' reading of the statute. That is one way of understanding Justice Kennedy's opinion in *Harris v. United States*, 536 U.S. 545 (2002). *See supra* pp. 227–228. There, the Court refused to embrace "a strained reading" of the relevant statute simply to avoid a constitutional question that members of the enacting legislature would not have perceived. *Harris*, 536 U.S. at 556. The Court specifically rejected the idea that the canon about avoiding constitutional doubts "embrace[s] a dynamic view of statutory interpretation, under which the text might mean one thing when enacted yet another if the prevailing view of the Constitution later changed." *Id.*

But the Court's aversion to that idea was premised on the view that the statutory text did indeed "mean one thing when enacted"; according to the Court, the statute was most naturally read in the way that implicated the constitutional question, and adopting the other reading would require "stretch[ing] the text." *Id.* When a statute is less determinate, courts sometimes do invoke the constitutional-doubts canon to help resolve the indeterminacy even when the constitutional question that they are avoiding would not have occurred to anyone at the time of enactment. As a tool for responding to indeterminacy in statutory language, then, the constitutional-doubts canon can have some "dynamic" effects: within the range of a statute's indeterminacy, the interpretation(s) that courts take the canon to support will depend to some extent on exactly when courts are applying the canon.

3. THE RELEVANCE OF OTHER STATUTES

The same is true of canons that tell interpreters to read one statute in light of other statutes. Despite his commitment to trying to detect and enforce the original meaning of statutory language, Justice Scalia had no objection to this form of dynamic interpretation on questions as to which the original meaning is indeterminate. In his opinion for the Court in *West Virginia University Hospitals v. Casey*, 499 U.S. 83 (1991), he put the point this way:

> "Where a statutory term presented to us for the first time is ambiguous, we construe it to contain that permissible meaning which fits most logically and comfortably into the body of both previously and subsequently enacted law. . . . We do so not because that precise accommodative meaning is what the lawmakers must have had in mind (how could an earlier Congress know what a later Congress would enact?), but because it is our role to make sense rather than nonsense out of the *corpus juris.*"

Id. at 100–01; *see also* United States v. Fausto, 484 U.S. 439, 453 (1988) (Scalia, J.) (noting that it is common for courts to "interpret a statutory text in light of surrounding texts that happen to have been subsequently enacted"). On this view, if a statute enacted at Time 1 is genuinely ambiguous about whether it establishes Directive *A* or Directive *B*, but a statute enacted some years later at Time 2 would mesh better with Directive *B*, courts interpreting the first statute at Time 3 (in a case of first impression) should tend to favor that resolution of the ambiguity.

Justice O'Connor's majority opinion in *FDA v. Brown & Williamson Tobacco Corp.*, 529 U.S. 120, 143 (2000), expanded on this point as follows:

> "At the time a statute is enacted, it may have a range of plausible meanings. Over time, however, subsequent acts can shape or focus those meanings. The 'classic judicial task of reconciling many laws enacted over time, and getting them to "make sense" in combination, necessarily assumes that the implications of a statute may be altered by the implications of a later statute.' *United States v. Fausto*, 484 U.S. at 453. This is particularly so where the scope of the earlier statute is broad but the subsequent statutes more specifically address the topic at hand. As we recognized recently in *United States v. Estate of Romani*, [523 U.S. 517 (1998),] 'a specific policy embodied in a later federal statute should control our construction of the [earlier] statute, even though it ha[s] not been expressly amended.' [*Id.*] at 530–31."

The Court relied heavily on this principle in *Brown & Williamson* itself. As we saw in Chapter 5, the case concerned the meaning of the term "drug" in federal statutes administered by the Food and Drug Administration (FDA). *See supra* pp. 890–893 (discussing *Brown & Williamson* in the context of *Chevron* deference and the major-questions doctrine). The key language dated back to the Food, Drug, and Cosmetic Act of 1938 (FDCA), which defined the term to include "articles (other than food) intended to affect the structure or any function of the body of man or other animals." Act of June 25, 1938, ch. 675, § 201(g), 52 Stat. 1040, 1041 (codified at 21 U.S.C. § 321(g)(1)). After many years of maintaining that this definition did not reach the nicotine in cigarettes and chewing tobacco as those products are customarily marketed, the FDA adopted a different position in 1996: it asserted that the nicotine in tobacco products is a "drug" within the meaning of the statute that

Congress enacted in 1938, that the products themselves are "devices" for the delivery of that drug, and that the statute empowered the FDA to regulate them on that basis. In *Brown & Williamson*, however, the Supreme Court held that the law as it stood in 1996 did not permit the FDA to take this position. Even if the language that Congress had adopted in 1938, considered in isolation, could be read as the FDA was now reading it, that reading did not fit well with statutes that Congress had enacted from 1965 on, and the existence of those later statutes effectively limited the range of interpretations that the FDA could give the earlier language.

The majority referred, in particular, to six federal statutes that Congress had enacted since 1965 and that "directly addressed the problem of tobacco and health": the Federal Cigarette Labeling and Advertising Act, Pub. L. 89–92, 79 Stat. 282 (1965) (specifying a health warning that must appear on cigarette packages); the Public Health Cigarette Smoking Act of 1969, Pub. L. 91–222, 84 Stat. 87 (1970) (strengthening the language of the required warning and prohibiting radio and television advertisements of cigarettes); the Alcohol and Drug Abuse Amendments of 1983, Pub. L. 98–24, 97 Stat. 175, 178 (1983) (requiring the Secretary of Health and Human Services to give Congress a triennial report that describes "current findings on . . . the addictive property of tobacco"); the Comprehensive Smoking Education Act, Pub. L. 98–474, 98 Stat. 2200 (1984) (changing the labeling requirements for cigarette packages, requiring warnings to appear in print advertisements and on billboards, obliging manufacturers to provide the Secretary with "a list of the ingredients added to tobacco in the manufacture of cigarettes," and instructing the Secretary to make reports to Congress as appropriate on the basis of this information); the Comprehensive Smokeless Tobacco Health Education Act of 1986, Pub. L. 99–252, 100 Stat. 30 (1986) (establishing a similar regulatory regime for chewing tobacco); and the ADAMHA Reorganization Act, Pub. L. 102–321, 106 Stat. 323, 394–95 (1992) (making states ineligible for certain federal block grants unless state law forbids "any manufacturer, retailer, or distributor of tobacco products to sell or distribute any such product to any individual under the age of 18"). *See Brown & Williamson*, 529 U.S. at 137–38. The majority made two different uses of these statutes.

First, the majority took these statutes to "foreclose[ ] the removal of tobacco products from the market." *Id.* at 137. The majority reasoned as follows:

> "When Congress enacted these statutes, the adverse health consequences of tobacco use were well known, as were nicotine's pharmacological effects. . . . Nonetheless, Congress stopped well short of ordering a ban. Instead, it has generally regulated the labeling and advertisement of tobacco products, expressly providing that it is the policy of Congress that 'commerce and the national economy may be . . . protected to the maximum extent consistent

> with' consumers 'be[ing] adequately informed about any adverse health effects.' 15 U.S.C. § 1331. Congress' decisions to regulate labeling and advertising and to adopt the express policy of protecting 'commerce and the national economy . . . to the maximum extent' reveal its intent that tobacco products remain on the market. Indeed, the collective premise of these statutes is that cigarettes and smokeless tobacco will continue to be sold in the United States."

Id. at 138–39; *see also id.* at 137 (noting the prefatory language of an old agricultural statute, enacted in 1938 and still in force at the time of *Brown & Williamson*, declaring that "[t]he marketing of tobacco constitutes one of the great basic industries of the United States with ramifying activities which directly affect interstate and foreign commerce at every point, and stable conditions therein are necessary to the general welfare"). For the majority, it followed that "[a] ban of tobacco products by the FDA would . . . plainly contradict congressional policy." *Id.* at 139. According to the majority, however, by reading the definition of "drug" in the Food, Drug, and Cosmetic Act to reach the nicotine in tobacco, the FDA was setting itself on a course that would ultimately require it to ban cigarettes and chewing tobacco: if those products were indeed subject to the regulatory regime that the Act establishes for "devices" used to deliver "drugs," then the FDA—given its findings about the adverse health effects of tobacco use—would have a statutory duty "to remove them from the market entirely." *Id.* at 143; *see also id.* at 142 (arguing that if something qualifies as a "drug" or "device" within the meaning of the Food, Drug, and Cosmetic Act, and if the FDA concludes that it "cannot be used safely for any therapeutic purpose," then the Act obliges the FDA to order its removal from the market). To avoid putting the commands of the Food, Drug, and Cosmetic Act at loggerheads with the policy reflected in Congress's post-1964 statutes, the majority argued that the agency could not validly read the FDCA's definition of "drug" to reach the nicotine in cigarettes and chewing tobacco. *See id.* at 143 ("The inescapable conclusion is that there is no room for tobacco products within the FDCA's regulatory scheme. If they cannot be used safely for any therapeutic purpose, and yet they cannot be banned, they simply do not fit.").

Writing in dissent, Justice Breyer denied that interpreting the FDCA's definition of "drug" to reach the nicotine in tobacco products would necessarily force the FDA to ban those products. *See id.* at 174–81 (Breyer, J., dissenting) (suggesting that if the agency reasonably concluded that a ban would drive a substantial number of smokers to even more dangerous products available on the black market, the statute would permit the agency to stop short of a ban). But suppose one accepts the majority's view that if the definition of "drug" that Congress included in the FDCA in 1938 is interpreted to reach the nicotine in cigarettes and chewing tobacco, the statute would ultimately leave the FDA with no choice but to ban those products. Suppose one also accepts the majority's view that such a ban would contradict the policy authoritatively reflected in the tobacco-specific statutes that Congress enacted from 1965 on. What should follow? Might one simply conclude that the later statutes impliedly repeal certain aspects of the FDCA as applied to tobacco products—so that the FDA cannot ban tobacco products but still enjoys regulatory authority over them? Or should one conclude (as the majority did) that the existence of the later statutes should prevent the agency from reading the FDCA to reach cigarettes and chewing tobacco in the first place? Is the idea behind the latter argument that when an agency is choosing between two possible readings of a statute, one of which would cause the statute to conflict with later legislation in such a way as to produce an implied repeal of some aspect of the statute that the agency is interpreting, the agency sometimes will be obliged to adopt the other reading instead? Does the presumption against implied repeals support that conclusion, or does the fact that the *earlier* statute is the one whose meaning is at issue complicate references to that presumption? (Re-read note 3 on pp. 732–733 above.)

Even if one otherwise would accept the majority's argument, it is not obvious that the post-1964 statutes really prevented agencies from making determinations, pursuant to authority granted by earlier statutes, that would result in the prohibition of cigarettes. Suppose that there is doubt about the proper interpretation of *both* sets of statutes: the definition of "drug" that Congress adopted as part of the FDCA in 1938 might or might not be understood to reach the nicotine in cigarettes and chewing tobacco, and the post-1964 statutes might or might not be understood to prevent agencies from forbidding the sale of those products. The majority opted to adjust its reading of the earlier statute to fit its reading of the later statutes. But couldn't the majority instead have adjusted its reading of the later statutes to fit the FDA's reading of the earlier statute? Is one way of reconciling the two sets of statutes clearly preferable to the other?

In addition to maintaining that the post-1964 statutes "foreclosed the removal of tobacco products from the market," the majority also advanced a second argument about those statutes. Throughout the period during which Congress enacted them, the FDA was taking the position that existing law did not give it regulatory jurisdiction over tobacco products as customarily marketed. Although bills that would have explicitly given the FDA such jurisdiction were proposed, those bills consistently failed to pass.[11] Instead, Congress itself regulated tobacco products in the manner that it considered appropriate. In the majority's words, the statutes that Congress enacted from 1965 on "created a

---

[11] In keeping with the modern trend, the majority specifically declined to treat the failure of these bills as the equivalent of a statute establishing the opposite, or as otherwise having legal effect. *See Brown & Williamson*, 529 U.S. at 155 ("We do not rely on Congress' failure to act—its consideration and rejection of bills that would have given the FDA this authority . . . ."). Nonetheless, the majority did see fit to mention the bills' existence, apparently as relevant "background" for understanding the statutes that Congress did enact. *See id.* at 147.

distinct regulatory scheme to address the problem of tobacco and health." *Brown & Williamson*, 529 U.S. at 144; *see also id.* at 148–49 & 157 (inferring from the exclusivity of Congress's labeling requirements that the statutory scheme is an alternative to, rather than a complement of, regulation by the FDA pursuant to the FDCA). When agencies other than the FDA took steps to regulate cigarettes, moreover, Congress acted in various ways to strip them of authority to do so. *See id.* at 144–49 (chronicling Congress's enactment of the Federal Cigarette Labeling and Advertising Act of 1965, which came "in reaction to the [Federal Trade Commission's] attempt to regulate cigarette labeling and advertising" and by which Congress "reserved exclusive control over both subjects to itself"); *id.* at 149–50 (noting that Congress's subsequent ban on radio and television advertisements of cigarettes superseded a rule that the Federal Communications Commission had proposed on that topic); *id.* at 150–51 (observing that in the mid-1970s, when a federal district court held that the Consumer Products Safety Commission had authority to regulate cigarettes, Congress immediately and explicitly eliminated that authority by statute). According to the majority, the post-1964 statutes reflect a general policy of reserving the relevant field to Congress: "in addressing the subject, Congress consistently evidenced its intent to preclude any federal agency from exercising significant policymaking authority in the area." *Id.* at 157; *see also id.* at 144 (asserting in particular that "Congress's tobacco-specific statutes have effectively ratified the FDA's long-held position that it lacks jurisdiction under the FDCA to regulate tobacco products").

Of course, as Justice Breyer noted in dissent, the post-1964 statutes did not actually *say* anything so sweeping. *See id.* at 182 (Breyer, J., dissenting) ("[W]hatever individual Members of Congress after 1964 may have assumed about the FDA's jurisdiction, the laws they enacted did not embody any such 'no jurisdiction' assumption."). According to Justice Breyer, moreover, the overall legislative record was equally consistent with the idea that the enacting Congresses wanted to "leav[e] the jurisdictional question just where [they] found it"—so that the post-1964 statutes established some requirements that Congress wanted to establish but did not otherwise disturb whatever authority prior statutes might give the FDA. *Id.*

Justice Breyer surely was correct that the post-1964 statutes did not themselves establish a legal directive to the effect that the FDA lacks regulatory jurisdiction over tobacco products. Once they exist, though, might they nonetheless shed some light on how interpreters should handle unresolved indeterminacies in the FDCA about that point? Consider, in particular, the possible relevance of the labeling provisions in the tobacco-specific statutes that Congress enacted after 1964. As they stood at the time of *Brown & Williamson*, the post-1964 statutes not only specified a warning that manufacturers had to include on every cigarette package, but also forbade both states and federal administrative agencies to require cigarette packages to bear any other "statement relating to smoking and health." *See* 15 U.S.C. § 1334(a) (2000 ed.) ("No statement relating to smoking and health, other than the statement required by [the post-1964 statutes], shall be required on any cigarette package."). Justice Breyer himself conceded that this provision "plainly" prohibited the FDA from requiring the labels of cigarette packages to include "any other 'statement relating to smoking and health.' " *Brown & Williamson*, 529 U.S. at 184 (Breyer, J., dissenting). But authority over product labels is a substantial part of the regulatory power that the FDCA ordinarily gives the FDA. Because that authority cannot coexist with the tobacco-specific statutes that Congress enacted after 1964, the post-1964 statutes would have superseded at least this aspect of the FDCA if the FDCA had been construed to let the FDA regulate tobacco products. *See id.* at 181 (Breyer, J., dissenting) (conceding that in this one respect, the post-1964 statutes are indeed "inconsistent with the FDA's exercise of jurisdiction" over tobacco products under the FDCA). Was Justice Breyer correct to discount this conflict? Or was the majority correct to see the conflict as an important sign that the post-1964 statutes did not simply *supplement* whatever regulatory authority the FDCA might give the FDA over tobacco products, but instead established an *alternative* to that authority?

As you think about that question, assume that the definition of "drug" that Congress enacted as part of the FDCA in 1938 could plausibly be read either broadly (so as to bring tobacco products within the FDA's reach) or more narrowly (so as to exclude them from that reach). Assume further that neither reading was set in stone before 1965: although the FDA had disclaimed authority to regulate tobacco products under the FDCA, it could legitimately have changed its mind. Was that still true after 1965? Or did Congress's enactment of a separate regulatory scheme, which conflicted with the authority that the FDCA would have given the FDA over labels if the FDCA was interpreted to reach tobacco products, alter the force of the arguments that could thereafter be advanced about the proper resolution of the ambiguity in the FDCA? If you agree with the majority that the post-1964 statutes *did* affect the force of the arguments that could thereafter be advanced about the meaning of the FDCA, how would you describe that effect? Would you say that the post-1964 statutes effectively amended the FDCA? Or would you say instead that their existence simply affected the proper resolution of the lingering ambiguity in the FDCA? Given that the post-1964 statutes did not directly address the FDA's authority over tobacco products, and given that they shed little light on what Congress had in mind in 1938, can you articulate the way in which you think they matter?

In the specific context of tobacco regulation, the relevant legal landscape has changed since *Brown & Williamson*. In 2009, Congress enacted legislation giving the FDA regulatory authority over tobacco products. *See* Family Smoking Prevention and Tobacco Control Act, Pub.

L. 111–31, § 101, 123 Stat. 1776, 1783–1830 (2009) (establishing a new chapter of the FDCA that gives the FDA a special and very detailed set of powers to regulate, but not ban, tobacco products); *see also id.* §§ 201–206, 123 Stat. at 1842–50 (overhauling the warnings that must appear on packages of cigarettes and smokeless tobacco, giving the FDA authority to change those warnings, and otherwise modifying the Federal Cigarette Labeling and Advertising Act). Does Congress's ability to enact such tailored solutions to important problems favor one side or the other in *Brown & Williamson*? Or is it simply a neutral fact—an important aspect of our separation of powers, but not one that affects how courts should understand the statutes that Congress has already enacted?

E. THE EFFECT OF *STARE DECISIS*

The doctrine of *stare decisis* might seem antithetical to the idea of "dynamic" statutory interpretation. After all, *stare decisis* operates to freeze a particular interpretation of a statute in place. Over time, though, the accumulation of precedent can itself affect the meaning that future courts are supposed to ascribe to a statute. Thus, what might appear to be "dynamic" interpretation of a statute is sometimes simply an artifact of *stare decisis*.

For a simple example, suppose that the original meaning of a statute is indeterminate on some question: understood in its appropriate context, the statute fixes the range of choices that future interpreters will have on that question, but it does not pinpoint the precise answer that interpreters should adopt. If the relevant court of last resort chooses from among the permissible interpretations of the statute, and if the doctrine of *stare decisis* tells future interpreters to respect that decision even if they would have made a different choice as a matter of first impression, there is a sense in which the meaning that our legal system attributes to the statute has changed. From the perspective of lawyers advising clients, for instance, what started off uncertain is now more definite.

Stare decisis can also produce other sorts of "dynamic" effects. Suppose that as enacted, a federal statute could permissibly be read to establish Directive *A* or Directive *B*, but not Directive *Z*. Nonetheless, the federal Supreme Court reads the statute to establish Directive *Z*. Outside commentators might well criticize this interpretation as mistaken; the Court has read the statute to mean something that the acceptable techniques of statutory interpretation do not really support. Indeed, the Court itself might come to agree that its past decision departed from the range of permissible choices. But the doctrine of *stare decisis* may cause the Court to adhere to its past interpretation of the statute even after the Court recognizes its error. What is more, the fact that the Court has understood the statute to establish Directive *Z* may radiate outward to affect how the Court reads other provisions of the same statute (or related statutes). If Directive *Z* would interact poorly with the original meaning of those provisions, then the Court might seek to avoid practical problems by adjusting the meaning that it ascribes to those provisions too. In a variety of ways, the fact that the Court has understood the statute to establish Directive *Z* might affect how the Court resolves other interpretive questions.

One of Professor Eskridge's most prominent examples of dynamic interpretation—the Supreme Court's performance in *United Steelworkers v. Weber*, 443 U.S. 193 (1979)—arguably illustrates this phenomenon. As Professor Eskridge notes, and as you saw when we studied *Weber* in Chapter 3, *Weber* arguably grew out of the Court's prior decision in *Griggs v. Duke Power Co.*, 401 U.S. 424 (1971). *See supra* pp. 390–392.

The basic statutory provisions are excerpted on pp. 360–362 above, but here is a quick refresher. Section 703(a)(1) of the Civil Rights Act of 1964 forbade employers "to discriminate against any individual" with respect to the terms or conditions of employment "because of such individual's race," and § 703(a)(2) also forbade employers "to limit, segregate, or classify" their employees[12] in any way that "would . . . tend to deprive any individual of employment opportunities . . . because of such individual's race." Section 703(d) specifically forbade employers and unions to "discriminate against any individual because of his race . . . in admission to . . . any program established to provide . . . training," including on-the-job training. Brian Weber, a white employee of Kaiser Aluminum & Chemical Corp., alleged that Kaiser was violating these provisions by operating an affirmative-action plan that made white employees ineligible for half of the openings in an on-the-job training program to which Weber wanted access. As a matter of original meaning, §§ 703(a) and 703(d) might have been thought to support his position. In *Griggs*, however, the Supreme Court had interpreted § 703(a)(2) to prohibit employers from using criteria for hiring or promotion that had a disparate impact on Black workers unless some sort of "business necessity" required those criteria. The practical result of *Griggs* was that if a company made training and promotion decisions without taking race into account, but those decisions had the effect of producing racial imbalances because white workers satisfied the criteria for training and promotion at a higher rate than Black workers, then the company might be liable to Black workers. To eliminate the racial imbalances that triggered this risk, the company might want to engage in race-based affirmative action. But if that response would itself make the company liable to *white* workers, then the company would face a serious practical problem: it might be exposed to liability under Title VII whatever it did. Assuming that the Court was not prepared to overrule *Griggs*, the practical realities of the situation generated some pressure to read §§ 703(a) and 703(d) as permitting race-conscious affirmative action—as

[12] In 1972, Congress amended this provision to refer to "applicants for employment" as well as "employees." *See* Equal Employment Opportunity Act of 1972, Pub. L. 92–261, § 8(a), 86 Stat. 103, 109.

the Court did in *Weber*. *See, e.g.*, William N. Eskridge, Jr., *Spinning Legislative Supremacy*, 78 GEO. L.J. 319, 337 (1989) (presenting this argument in a light sympathetic to *Weber* and neutral as to *Griggs*); Michael Evan Gold, Griggs' *Folly: An Essay on the Theory, Problems, and Origin of the Adverse Impact Definition of Employment Discrimination and a Recommendation for Reform*, 7 INDUS. REL. L.J. 429, 509 (1985) (presenting this argument in a light hostile to both decisions).

Professor Eskridge does not himself think that the majority's position in *Weber* conflicts with the original meaning of the statute that Congress enacted in 1964. *See* Eskridge, *supra*, 78 GEO. L.J. at 335 ("[O]n the whole I consider the text of title VII to be ambiguous on the issue of voluntary affirmative action in training programs."). But if you think that Justice Rehnquist's dissent had the better of the arguments about original meaning, then *Weber* reflects a type of dynamic interpretation that differs from the ones we have already encountered: instead of simply resolving an indeterminacy built into the original statute, the Court arguably departed from the statute's original meaning. *See, e.g.*, Daniel A. Farber, *Statutory Interpretation and Legislative Supremacy*, 78 GEO. L.J. 281, 303 (1989) (agreeing with Justice Rehnquist's dissent that from the perspective of original meaning, "the *Weber* holding . . . contradicts both the plain language and the legislative history of title VII"). As Professor Eskridge notes, moreover, the reading of § 703(a)(2) that the Court had adopted in *Griggs* may have helped Justice Brennan build a majority for the position that the Court took in *Weber*. In Professor Eskridge's estimation, "if [the question presented in *Weber*] had come before the Court in 1971 and not 1979, the Court might well have decided the issue differently." WILLIAM N. ESKRIDGE, JR., DYNAMIC STATUTORY INTERPRETATION 37 (1994).

Does it follow, as Professor Eskridge says, that "[t]his simple thought experiment vitiates all the originalist theories of statutory interpretation"? *Id.* Or does this thought experiment simply illustrate the effects of *stare decisis*? Couldn't one recognize a "*stare decisis* exception" to the proposition that interpreters should adhere to the (original) meaning of a statute, but still consider that proposition valid where the exception is inapplicable? On that view, if no relevant precedents bear on a particular question of interpretation, or if relevant precedents do exist but meet the criteria for being overruled, interpreters should adhere to the statute's original meaning—even if they think that some other position would better fit current values, or would reflect the likely preferences of members of the current legislature, or would accomplish policy goals that the interpreters themselves consider desirable.

Even on that view, of course, there would still be disputes about how to identify the statute's "original meaning." Some of those disputes, moreover, would become more salient with the passage of time. For instance, different interpreters would still have different views about whether and to what extent the typical statute allows interpreters to infer exceptions and embellishments to help serve the enacting legislature's goals in circumstances that members of the enacting legislature did not foresee. Likewise, different interpreters might have different views about the normative principles or other considerations that should influence the resolution of conceded indeterminacies in the statute. Different interpreters would also have different understandings of the principles of *stare decisis*, which do "inject an evolutionary or dynamic element into statutory construction." Thomas W. Merrill, *Pluralism, the Prisoner's Dilemma, and the Behavior of the Independent Judiciary*, 88 NW. U. L. REV. 396, 400 (1993); *see also* William N. Eskridge, Jr., *Interpreting Legislative Inaction*, 87 MICH. L. REV. 67, 108–13 (1988) (discussing what Professor Eskridge calls "building block interpretations" of statutes, which might not comport with the original meaning but which the legislature does not override and which shape subsequent interpretations). To the extent that you disagree with some of your classmates about dynamic interpretation, how much of the disagreement boils down to one or another of these more familiar disputes?

F. STATIC AND DYNAMIC REFERENCES

Some statutes establish rules by referring to another source of law. As time passes, interpreters might face the following question: should they understand the reference to be "static" (so that the statute effectively adopts the other source of law as it stood when the statute was enacted), or is the reference instead "dynamic" (so that at any given moment, the statute refers to the other source of law as it stands at that moment)?

Often, referential statutes are ambiguous on this point. In the case that follows, the Supreme Court understood the relevant reference to be dynamic. Note, however, that this conclusion concerns the *original* meaning of the referential statute—the content of the directive that it established from the start.

Jam v. International Finance Corp.

139 S. Ct. 759 (2019)

■ *CHIEF JUSTICE ROBERTS delivered the opinion of the Court [joined by JUSTICES THOMAS, GINSBURG, ALITO, SOTOMAYOR, KAGAN, and GORSUCH]:*

The International Organizations Immunities Act of 1945 grants international organizations such as the World Bank and the World Health Organization the "same immunity from suit . . . as is enjoyed by foreign governments." 22 U.S.C. § 288a(b). At the time the IOIA was enacted, foreign governments enjoyed virtually absolute immunity from suit. Today that immunity is more limited. Most significantly, foreign governments are not immune from actions based upon certain kinds of commercial activity in which they engage. This case requires us to determine whether the IOIA grants international organizations the virtually absolute immunity foreign governments enjoyed when the IOIA was enacted, or the more limited immunity they enjoy today.

. . . .

I

A

In the wake of World War II, the United States and many of its allies joined together to establish a host of new international organizations. Those organizations, which included the United Nations, the International Monetary Fund, and the World Bank, were designed to allow member countries to collectively pursue goals such as stabilizing the international economy, rebuilding war-torn nations, and maintaining international peace and security.

Anticipating that those and other international organizations would locate their headquarters in the United States, Congress passed the International Organizations Immunities Act of 1945, 59 Stat. 669. The Act grants international organizations a set of privileges and immunities, such as immunity from search and exemption from property taxes. 22 U.S.C. §§ 288a(c), 288c.

The IOIA defines certain privileges and immunities by reference to comparable privileges and immunities enjoyed by foreign governments. For example, with respect to customs duties and the treatment of official communications, the Act grants international organizations the privileges and immunities that are "accorded under similar circumstances to foreign governments." § 288a(d). The provision at issue in this case provides that international organizations "shall enjoy the same immunity from suit and every form of judicial process as is enjoyed by foreign governments." § 288a(b).

The IOIA authorizes the President to withhold, withdraw, condition, or limit the privileges and immunities it grants in light of the functions performed by any given international organization. § 288. Those privileges and immunities can also be expanded or restricted by a particular organization's founding charter.

B

When the IOIA was enacted in 1945, courts looked to the views of the Department of State in deciding whether a given foreign government should be granted immunity from a particular suit. If the Department submitted a recommendation on immunity, courts deferred to the recommendation. If the Department did not make a recommendation, courts decided for themselves whether to grant immunity, although they did so by reference to State Department policy. *Samantar v. Yousuf*, 560 U.S. 305, 311–312 (2010).

Until 1952, the State Department adhered to the classical theory of foreign sovereign immunity. According to that theory, foreign governments are entitled to "virtually absolute" immunity as a matter of international grace and comity. At the time the IOIA was enacted, therefore, the Department ordinarily requested, and courts ordinarily granted, immunity in suits against foreign governments. . . .[1]

In 1952, however, the State Department announced that it would adopt the newer "restrictive" theory of foreign sovereign immunity. Under that theory, foreign governments are entitled to immunity only with respect to their sovereign acts, not with respect to commercial acts. The State Department explained that it was adopting the restrictive theory because the "widespread and increasing practice on the part of governments of engaging in commercial activities" made it "necessary" to "enable persons doing business with them to have their rights determined in the courts." Letter from Jack B. Tate, Acting Legal Adviser, Dept. of State, to Acting Attorney General Philip B. Perlman (May 19, 1952), reprinted in 26 Dept. State Bull. 984–985 (1952).

In 1976, Congress passed the Foreign Sovereign Immunities Act. The FSIA codified the restrictive theory of foreign sovereign immunity but transferred "primary responsibility for immunity determinations from the Executive to the Judicial Branch." *Republic of Austria v. Altmann*, 541 U.S. 677, 691 (2004); see 28 U.S.C. § 1602. Under the FSIA, foreign governments are presumptively immune from suit. § 1604. But a foreign government may be subject to suit under one of several statutory exceptions. Most pertinent here, a foreign government may be subject to suit in connection with its commercial activity that has a sufficient nexus with the United States. § 1605(a)(2).

C

The International Finance Corporation is an international development bank headquartered in Washington, D.C. The IFC is designated as an international organization under the IOIA. Exec. Order No. 10680, 3 C.F.R. 86 (1957); see 22 U.S.C. §§ 282, 288. One hundred eighty-four countries, including the United States, are members of the IFC.

The IFC is charged with furthering economic development "by encouraging the growth of productive private enterprise in member countries, particularly in the less developed areas, thus supplementing the activities of" the World Bank. Articles of Agreement of the International Finance Corporation, Art. I, Dec. 5, 1955, 7 U.S.T. 2193, T.I.A.S. No. 3620. Whereas the World Bank primarily provides loans and grants to developing countries for public-sector projects, the IFC finances

[1] The immunity was "virtually" absolute because it was subject to occasional exceptions for specific situations. In *Republic of Mexico v. Hoffman*, 324 U.S. 30 (1945), for example, the State Department declined to recommend, and the Court did not grant, immunity from suit with respect to a ship that Mexico owned but did not possess.

private-sector development projects that cannot otherwise attract capital on reasonable terms. See Art. I(i), *ibid*. . . .

The IFC expects its loan recipients to adhere to a set of performance standards designed to "avoid, mitigate, and manage risks and impacts" associated with development projects. IFC Performance Standards on Environmental and Social Sustainability, Jan. 1, 2012, p. 2, ¶ 1. Those standards are usually more stringent than any established by local law. The IFC includes the standards in its loan agreements and enforces them through an internal review process. . . .

In 2008, the IFC loaned $450 million to Coastal Gujarat Power Limited, a company located in India. The loan helped finance the construction of a coal-fired power plant in the state of Gujarat. Under the terms of the loan agreement, Coastal Gujarat was required to comply with an environmental and social action plan designed to protect areas around the plant from damage. The agreement allowed the IFC to revoke financial support for the project if Coastal Gujarat failed to abide by the terms of the agreement.

The project did not go smoothly. According to the IFC's internal audit, Coastal Gujarat did not comply with the environmental and social action plan in constructing and operating the plant. The audit report criticized the IFC for inadequately supervising the project.

In 2015, a group of farmers and fishermen who live near the plant, as well as a local village, sued the IFC in the United States District Court for the District of Columbia. They claimed that pollution from the plant, such as coal dust, ash, and water from the plant's cooling system, had destroyed or contaminated much of the surrounding air, land, and water. Relying on the audit report, they asserted several causes of action against the IFC, including negligence, nuisance, trespass, and breach of contract. The IFC maintained that it was immune from suit under the IOIA and moved to dismiss for lack of subject matter jurisdiction.

The District Court, applying D.C. Circuit precedent, concluded that the IFC was immune from suit because the IOIA grants international organizations the virtually absolute immunity that foreign governments enjoyed when the IOIA was enacted. 172 F. Supp. 3d 104, 108–109 (DDC 2016) (citing *Atkinson v. Inter-American Development Bank*, 156 F.3d 1335 (CADC 1998)). The D.C. Circuit affirmed in light of its precedent. 860 F.3d 703 (2017). Judge Pillard wrote separately to say that she would have decided the question differently were she writing on a clean slate. *Id.* at 708 (concurring opinion). Judge Pillard explained that she thought the D.C. Circuit "took a wrong turn" when it "read the IOIA to grant international organizations a static, absolute immunity that is, by now, not at all the same 'as is enjoyed by foreign governments,' but substantially broader." *Ibid.* . . .

We granted certiorari. . . .

II

The IFC contends that the IOIA grants international organizations the "same immunity" from suit that foreign governments enjoyed in 1945. Petitioners argue that it instead grants international organizations the "same immunity" from suit that foreign governments enjoy today. We think petitioners have the better reading of the statute.

A

The language of the IOIA more naturally lends itself to petitioners' reading. In granting international organizations the "same immunity" from suit "as is enjoyed by foreign governments," the Act seems to continuously link the immunity of international organizations to that of foreign governments, so as to ensure ongoing parity between the two. The statute could otherwise have simply stated that international organizations "shall enjoy absolute immunity from suit," or specified some other fixed level of immunity. Other provisions of the IOIA, such as the one making the property and assets of international organizations "immune from search," use such noncomparative language to define immunities in a static way. 22 U.S.C. § 288a(c). Or the statute could have specified that it was incorporating the law of foreign sovereign immunity as it existed on a particular date. See, *e.g.*, Energy Policy Act of 1992, 30 U.S.C. § 242(c)(1) (certain land patents "shall provide for surface use to the same extent as is provided under applicable law prior to October 24, 1992"). Because the IOIA does neither of those things, we think the "same as" formulation is best understood to make international organization immunity and foreign sovereign immunity continuously equivalent.

That reading finds support in other statutes that use similar or identical language to place two groups on equal footing. In the Civil Rights Act of 1866, for instance, Congress established a rule of equal treatment for newly freed slaves by giving them the "same right" to make and enforce contracts and to buy and sell property "as is enjoyed by white citizens." 42 U.S.C. §§ 1981(a), 1982. That provision is of course understood to guarantee continuous equality between white and nonwhite citizens with respect to the rights in question. . . . Similarly, the Federal Tort Claims Act states that the "United States shall be liable" in tort "in the same manner and to the same extent as a private individual under like circumstances." 28 U.S.C. § 2674. That provision is most naturally understood to make the United States liable in the same way as a private individual at any given time. See *Richards v. United States*, 369 U.S. 1, 6–7 (1962). Such "same as" provisions dot the statute books, and federal and state courts commonly read them to mandate ongoing equal treatment of two groups or objects. See, *e.g.*, *Adamson v. Bowen*, 855 F.2d 668, 671–672 (CA10 1988) (statute making United States liable for fees and expenses "to the same extent that any other party would be liable under the common law or under the terms of any statute" interpreted to continuously tie liability of United States to that of any other party); *Kugler's Appeal*, 55 Pa. 123, 124–125 (1867) (statute making the procedure for dividing election districts "the same as" the procedure for dividing townships interpreted to continuously tie the former procedure to the latter).

The IFC objects that the IOIA is different because the purpose of international organization immunity is entirely different from the purpose of foreign sovereign immunity. Foreign sovereign immunity, the IFC argues, is grounded in the mutual respect of sovereigns and serves the ends of international comity and reciprocity. The purpose of international organization immunity, on the other hand, is to allow such organizations to freely pursue the collective goals of member countries without undue interference from the courts of any one member country. The IFC therefore urges that the IOIA should not be read to tether international organization immunity to changing foreign sovereign immunity.

But that gets the inquiry backward. We ordinarily assume, "absent a clearly expressed legislative intention to the contrary," that "the legislative purpose is expressed by the ordinary meaning of the words used." *American Tobacco Co. v. Patterson*, 456 U.S. 63, 68 (1982) (alterations omitted). Whatever the ultimate purpose of international organization immunity may be—the IOIA does not address that question—the immediate purpose of the immunity provision is expressed in language that Congress typically uses to make one thing continuously equivalent to another.

B

The more natural reading of the IOIA is confirmed by a canon of statutory interpretation that was well established when the IOIA was drafted. According to the "reference" canon, when a statute refers to a general subject, the statute adopts the law on that subject as it exists whenever a question under the statute arises. 2 J. Sutherland, Statutory Construction §§ 5207–5208 (3d ed. 1943). For example, a statute allowing a company to "collect the same tolls and enjoy the same privileges" as other companies incorporates the law governing tolls and privileges as it exists at any given moment. *Snell v. Chicago*, 133 Ill. 413, 437–439, 24 N.E. 532, 537 (1890). In contrast, a statute that refers to another statute by specific title or section number in effect cuts and pastes the referenced statute as it existed when the referring statute was enacted, without any subsequent amendments. See, *e.g.*, *Culver v. People ex rel. Kochersperger*, 161 Ill. 89, 95–99, 43 N.E. 812, 814–815 (1896) (tax-assessment statute referring to specific article of another statute does not adopt subsequent amendments to that article).

Federal courts have often relied on the reference canon, explicitly or implicitly, to harmonize a statute with an external body of law that the statute refers to generally. Thus, for instance, a statute that exempts from disclosure agency documents that "would not be *available by law* to a party . . . in litigation with the agency" incorporates the . . . law governing attorney work-product privilege as it exists when the statute is applied. *FTC v. Grolier Inc.*, 462 U.S. 19, 20, 26–27 (1983) (emphasis added); *id.* at 34 n. 6 (Brennan, J., concurring in part and concurring in judgment). Likewise, a general reference to federal discovery rules incorporates those rules "as they are found on any given day, today included," *El Encanto, Inc. v. Hatch Chile Co.*, 825 F.3d 1161, 1164 (CA10 2016), and a general reference to "the crime of piracy as defined by the law of nations" incorporates a definition of piracy "that changes with advancements in the law of nations," *United States v. Dire*, 680 F.3d 446, 451, 467–469 (CA4 2012).

The same logic applies here. The IOIA's reference to the immunity enjoyed by foreign governments is a general rather than specific reference. The reference is to an external body of potentially evolving law—the law of foreign sovereign immunity—not to a specific provision of another statute. The IOIA should therefore be understood to link the law of international organization immunity to the law of foreign sovereign immunity, so that the one develops in tandem with the other.

The IFC contends that the IOIA's reference to the immunity enjoyed by foreign governments is not a general reference to an external body of law, but is instead a specific reference to a common law concept that had a fixed meaning when the IOIA was enacted in 1945. And because we ordinarily presume that "Congress intends to incorporate the well-settled meaning of the common-law terms it uses," *Neder v. United States*, 527 U.S. 1, 23 (1999), the IFC argues that we should read the IOIA to incorporate what the IFC maintains was the then-settled meaning of the "immunity enjoyed by foreign governments": virtually absolute immunity.

But in 1945, the "immunity enjoyed by foreign governments" did not *mean* "virtually absolute immunity." The phrase is not a term of art with substantive content, such as "fraud" or "forgery." See *id.* at 22; *Gilbert v. United States*, 370 U.S. 650, 655 (1962). It is rather a concept that can be given scope and content only by reference to the rules governing foreign sovereign immunity. It is true that under the rules applicable in 1945, the *extent* of immunity from suit was virtually absolute, while under the rules applicable today, it is more limited. But in 1945, as today, the IOIA's instruction to grant international organizations the immunity "enjoyed by foreign governments" is an instruction to look up the applicable rules of foreign sovereign immunity, wherever those rules may be found—the common law, the law of nations, or a statute. In other words, it is a general reference to an external body of (potentially evolving) law.

C

In ruling for the IFC, the D.C. Circuit relied upon its prior decision in *Atkinson*, 156 F.3d 1335. *Atkinson* acknowledged the reference canon, but concluded that the canon's probative force was "outweighed" by a structural inference the court derived from the larger context of the IOIA. *Id.* at 1341. The *Atkinson* court focused on the provision of the IOIA that gives the President the authority to withhold, withdraw, condition, or limit the otherwise applicable privileges and immunities of an international organization, "in the light of the functions performed by any such international organization." 22 U.S.C. § 288. The court understood that provision to "delegate to the President the responsibility for updating the immunities of international organizations in the face of changing circumstances." *Atkinson*, 156 F.3d at 1341. That delegation, the court reasoned, "undermine[d]" the view that Congress intended the IOIA to in effect update itself by incorporating changes in the law governing foreign sovereign immunity. *Ibid.*

We do not agree. The delegation provision is most naturally read to allow the President to modify, on a case-by-case basis, the immunity rules that would otherwise apply to a particular international organization. The statute authorizes the President to take action with respect to a single organization—"any such organization"—in light of the functions performed by "such organization." 28 U.S.C. § 288. The text suggests retail rather than wholesale action, and that is in fact how authority under § 288 has been exercised in the past. . . . In any event, the fact that the President has power to modify otherwise applicable immunity rules is perfectly compatible with the notion that those rules might themselves change over time in light of developments in the law governing foreign sovereign immunity.

The D.C. Circuit in *Atkinson* also gave no consideration to the opinion of the State Department, whose views in this area ordinarily receive "special attention." *Bolivarian Republic of Venezuela* v. *Helmerich & Payne Int'l Drilling Co.*, 581 U.S. 170, 181 (2017). Shortly after the FSIA was enacted, the State Department took the position that the immunity rules of the IOIA and the FSIA were now "link[ed]." Letter from Detlev F. Vagts, Office of the Legal Adviser, to Robert M. Carswell, Jr., Senior Legal Advisor, OAS, p. 2 (Mar. 24, 1977). The Department reaffirmed that view during subsequent administrations, and it has reaffirmed it again here.[ ] That longstanding view further bolsters our understanding of the IOIA's immunity provision.

D

The IFC argues that interpreting the IOIA's immunity provision to grant anything less than absolute immunity would lead to a number of undesirable results.

The IFC first contends that affording international organizations only restrictive immunity would defeat the purpose of granting them immunity in the first place. Allowing international organizations to be sued in one member country's courts would in effect allow that member to second-guess the collective decisions of the others. It would also expose international organizations to money damages, which would in turn make it more difficult and expensive for them to fulfill their missions. The IFC argues that this problem is especially acute for international development banks. Because those banks use the tools of commerce to achieve their objectives, they may be subject to suit under the FSIA's commercial activity exception for most or all of their core activities, unlike foreign sovereigns. According to the IFC, allowing such suits would bring a flood of foreign-plaintiff litigation into U.S. courts, raising many of the same foreign-relations concerns that we identified when considering similar litigation under the Alien Tort Statute. See *Jesner v. Arab Bank, PLC*, 584 U.S. ___, 138 S. Ct. 1386 (2018); *Kiobel v. Royal Dutch Petroleum Co.*, 569 U.S. 108, 116–117 (2013).

The IFC's concerns are inflated. To begin, the privileges and immunities accorded by the IOIA are only default rules. If the work of a given international organization would be impaired by restrictive immunity, the organization's charter can always specify a different level of immunity. The charters of many international organizations do just that. See, *e.g.*, Convention on Privileges and Immunities of the United Nations, Art. II, § 2, Feb. 13, 1946, 21 U.S.T. 1422, T.I.A.S. No. 6900 ("The United Nations . . . shall enjoy immunity from every form of legal process except insofar as in any particular case it has expressly waived its immunity"); Articles of Agreement of the International Monetary Fund, Art. IX, § 3, Dec. 27, 1945, 60 Stat. 1413, T.I.A.S. No. 1501 (IMF enjoys "immunity from every form of judicial process except to the extent that it expressly waives its immunity"). Notably, the IFC's own charter does not state that the IFC is absolutely immune from suit.

Nor is there good reason to think that restrictive immunity would expose international development banks to excessive liability. As an initial matter, it is not clear that the lending activity of all development banks qualifies as commercial activity within the meaning of the FSIA. To be considered "commercial," an activity must be "the *type*" of activity "by which a private party engages in" trade or commerce. *Republic of Argentina v. Weltover, Inc.*, 504 U.S. 607, 614 (1992); see 28 U.S.C. § 1603(d). As the Government suggested at oral argument, the lending activity of at least some development banks, such as those that make conditional loans to governments, may not qualify as "commercial" under the FSIA. See Tr. of Oral Arg. 27–30.

And even if an international development bank's lending activity does qualify as commercial, that does not mean the organization is automatically subject to suit. The FSIA includes other requirements that must also be met. For one thing, the commercial activity must have a sufficient nexus to the United States. See 28 U.S.C. §§ 1603, 1605(a)(2). For another, a lawsuit must be "based upon" either the commercial activity itself or acts performed in connection with the commercial activity. See § 1605(a)(2). Thus, if the "gravamen" of a lawsuit is tortious activity abroad, the suit is not "based upon" commercial activity within the meaning of the FSIA's commercial activity exception. See *OBB Personenverkehr AG v. Sachs*, 577 U.S. 27, [33–36] (2015); *Saudi Arabia v. Nelson*, 507 U.S. 349, 356–359 (1993). At oral argument in this case, the Government stated that it has "serious doubts" whether petitioners' suit, which largely concerns allegedly tortious conduct in India, would satisfy the "based upon" requirement. Tr. of Oral Arg. 25–26. In short, restrictive immunity hardly means unlimited exposure to suit for international organizations.

. . . .

The judgment of the United States Court of Appeals for the D.C. Circuit is reversed, and the case is remanded for further proceedings consistent with this opinion.

■ *JUSTICE KAVANAUGH took no part in the consideration or decision of this case.*

■ *JUSTICE BREYER, dissenting:*

The International Organizations Immunities Act of 1945 extends to international organizations "the same immunity from suit and every form of judicial process as is enjoyed by foreign governments." 22 U.S.C. § 288a(b). The majority, resting primarily upon the statute's language and canons of interpretation, holds that the statute's reference to "immunity" moves with the times. As a consequence, the statute no longer allows international organizations immunity from lawsuits arising from their commercial activities. In my view, the statute grants international organizations that immunity—just as foreign governments possessed that immunity when Congress enacted the statute in 1945. In reaching this conclusion, I rest more heavily than does the majority upon the statute's history, its context, its purposes, and its consequences. And I write in part to show that, in difficult cases like this one, purpose-based methods of interpretation can often shine a useful light upon opaque statutory language, leading to a result that reflects greater legal coherence and is, as a practical matter, more likely to prove sound.

I

The general question before us is familiar: Do the words of a statute refer to their subject matter "statically," as it was when the statute was written? Or is their reference to that subject matter "dynamic," changing in scope as the subject matter changes over time? It is hardly surprising, given the thousands of different statutes containing an untold number of different words, that there is no single, universally applicable answer to this question.

. . . .

The Court, like petitioners, believes that the language of the statute itself helps significantly to answer the static/dynamic question. See *ante* at 767–769. I doubt that the language itself helps in this case. Petitioners point to the words "as is" in the phrase that grants the international organizations the "same immunity from suit . . . *as is* enjoyed by foreign governments." Brief for Petitioners 23–24. They invoke the Dictionary Act, which states that "words used in the present tense include the future" "unless the context indicates otherwise." 1 U.S.C. § 1. But that provision creates only a presumption. And it did not even appear in the statute until 1948, *after* Congress had passed the Immunities Act. Compare § 1, 61 Stat. 633, with § 6, 62 Stat. 859.

More fundamentally, the words "as is enjoyed" do not conclusively tell us *when* enjoyed. Do they mean "as is enjoyed" at the time of the statute's enactment? Or "as is enjoyed" at the time a plaintiff brings a lawsuit? . . . .

Linguistics does not answer the temporal question. . . . It is *purpose*, not linguistics, that can help us here.

The words "same . . . as," in the phrase "same immunity . . . as," provide no greater help. The majority finds support for its dynamic interpretation in the Civil Rights Act of 1866, which gives all citizens the "*same* right" to make and enforce contracts and to buy and sell property "*as* is enjoyed by white citizens." 42 U.S.C. §§ 1981(a), 1982 (emphasis added). But it is *purpose*, not words, that readily resolves any temporal linguistic ambiguity in that statute. The Act's objective, like that of the Fourteenth Amendment itself, was a Nation that treated its citizens equally. Its purpose—revealed by its title, historical context, and other language in the statute—was "to guarantee the then newly freed slaves the same legal rights that other citizens enjoy." *CBOCS West, Inc. v. Humphries*, 553 U.S. 442, 448 (2008). Given this purpose, its dynamic nature is obvious.

. . . .

The majority wrongly believes that it can solve the temporal problem by bringing statutory canons into play. It relies on what it calls the "reference canon." That canon, as it appeared more than 75 years ago in Sutherland's book on statutory construction, says that "when a statute refers to a general subject, the statute adopts the law on that subject as it exists *whenever a question under the statute arises.*" *Ante* at 769 (citing 2 J. Sutherland, Statutory Construction §§ 5207–5208 (3d ed. 1943); emphasis added).

But a canon is at most a rule of thumb. Indeed, Sutherland himself says that "[n]o single canon of interpretation can purport to give a certain and unerring answer." 2 Sutherland, *supra*, § 4501, p. 316. And hornbooks, summarizing case law, have long explained that whether a reference statute adopts the law as it stands on the date of enactment or includes subsequent changes in the law to which it refers is "fundamentally a question of legislative intent and purpose." Fox, Effect of Modification or Repeal of Constitutional or Statutory Provision Adopted by Reference in Another Provision, 168 A.L.R. 627, 628 (1947); see also 82 C.J.S., Statutes § 485, p. 637 (2009) ("The question of whether a statute which has adopted another statute by reference will be affected by amendments made to the adopted statute is one of legislative intent and purpose"); *id.* at 638 (statute that refers generally to another body of law will ordinarily include subsequent changes in the adopted law only "as far as the changes are consistent with the purpose of the adopting statute").

. . . .

II

. . . . We are "free to consider statutory language in light of a statute's basic purposes," [*Dole Food Co.*, 538 U.S. at 484 (Breyer, J., concurring in part and dissenting in part)], as well as " 'the history of the times when it was passed,' " *Leo Sheep Co. v. United States*, 440 U.S. 668, 669 (1979) (quoting *United States v. Union Pacific R. Co.*, 91 U.S. 72, 79 (1875)). In this case, historical context, purpose, and related consequences tell us a great deal about the proper interpretation of the Immunities Act.

Congressional reports explain that Congress, acting in the immediate aftermath of World War II, intended the Immunities Act to serve two related purposes. First, [the Act] would "enabl[e] this country to fulfill its commitments in connection with its membership in international organizations." S. Rep. No. 861, 79th Cong., 1st Sess., 3 (1945); see also *id.* at 2–3 (explaining that the Immunities Act was "basic legislation" expected to "satisfy in full the requirements of . . . international organizations conducting activities in the United States"); H.R. Rep. No. 1203, 79th Cong., 1st Sess., 3 (1945) (similar). And second, it would "facilitate fully the functioning of international organizations in this country." S. Rep. No. 861, at 3.

A

I first examine the international commitments that Congress sought to fulfill. By 1945, the United States had entered into agreements creating several important multilateral organizations, including the United Nations (UN), the International Monetary Fund (IMF), the World Bank, the UN Relief and Rehabilitation Administration (UNRRA), and the Food and Agriculture Organization (FAO). See *id.* at 2.

The founding agreements for several of these organizations required member states to grant them broad immunity from suit. The Bretton Woods Agreements, for example, provided that the IMF "shall enjoy immunity from every form of judicial process except to the extent that it expressly waives its immunity." Articles of Agreement of the International Monetary Fund, Art. IX, § 3, Dec. 27, 1945, 60 Stat. 1413, T.I.A.S. No. 1501. UNRRA required members, absent waiver, to accord the organization "the facilities, privileges, immunities, and exemptions which they accord to each other, including . . . [i]mmunity from suit and legal process." 2 UNRRA, A Compilation of the Resolutions on Policy: First and Second Sessions of the UNRRA Council, Res. No. 32, p. 51 (1944). And the UN Charter required member states to accord the UN "such privileges and immunities as are necessary for the fulfillment of its purposes." Charter of the United Nations, Art. 105, 59 Stat. 1053, June 26, 1945, T. S. No. 993.

These international organizations expected the United States to provide them with essentially full immunity. And at the time the treaties were written, Congress understood that foreign governments normally enjoyed immunity with respect to their commercial, as well as their noncommercial, activities. Thus, by granting international organizations "the same immunity from suit" that foreign governments enjoyed, Congress expected that international organizations would similarly have immunity in both commercial and noncommercial suits.

More than that, Congress likely recognized that immunity in the commercial area was even more important for many international organizations than it was for most foreign governments. Unlike foreign governments, international organizations are *not* sovereign entities engaged in a host of different activities. See R. Higgins, Problems & Process: International Law and How We Use It 93 (1994) (organizations do not act with " 'sovereign authority,' " and "to assimilate them to states . . . is not correct"). Rather, many organizations (including four of the five I mentioned above) have specific missions that often require them to engage in what U.S. law may well consider to be commercial activities. See *infra* at 778.

Nonetheless, under the majority's view, the immunity of many organizations contracted in scope in 1952, when the State Department modified foreign government immunity to exclude commercial activities. Most organizations could not rely on the treaty provisions quoted above to supply the necessary immunity. That is because, unless the treaty provision granting immunity is "self-executing," *i.e.*, automatically applicable, the immunity will not be effective in U.S. courts until Congress enacts additional legislation to implement it. See *Medellin v. Texas*, 552 U.S. 491, 504–505 (2008); but see *id.* at 546–547 (Breyer, J., dissenting). And many treaties are not self-executing. Thus, in the ordinary case, not even a treaty can guarantee immunity in cases arising from commercial activities.

The UN provides a good example. As noted, the UN Charter required the United States to grant the UN all "necessary" immunities, but it was not self-executing. In 1946, the UN made clear that it needed absolute immunity from suit, including in lawsuits based upon its commercial activities. See Convention on Privileges and Immunities of the United Nations, Art. II, § 2, Feb. 13, 1946, 21 U.S.T. 1422, T.I.A.S. No. 6900 (entered into force Apr. 29, 1970); see also App. to S. Exec. Rep. No. 9117, p. 14 (1970) ("The U. N.'s immunity from legal process extends to matters arising out [of] its commercial dealings . . ."). But, until Congress ratified that comprehensive immunity provision in 1970, no U.S. law provided that immunity *but for* the Immunities Act. *Id.* at 1. Both the UN and the United States found this circumstance satisfactory because they apparently assumed the Immunities Act extended immunity in cases involving both commercial and noncommercial activities: When Congress eventually (in 1970) ratified the UN's comprehensive immunity provision, the Senate reported that the long delay in ratification "appears to have been the result of the executive branch being content to operate under the provisions of the" Immunities Act. *Id.* at 2.

In light of this history, how likely is it that Congress, seeking to "satisfy *in full* the requirements of ... international organizations conducting activities in the United States," S. Rep. No. 861, at 2–3 (emphasis added), would have understood the statute to take from many international organizations with one hand the immunity it had given them with the other? If Congress wished the Act to carry out one of its core purposes—fulfilling the country's international commitments—Congress would not have wanted the statute to change over time, taking on a meaning that would fail to grant not only full, but even partial, immunity to many of those organizations.

B

Congress also intended to facilitate international organizations' ability to pursue their missions in the United States. To illustrate why that purpose is better served by a static interpretation, consider in greater detail the work of the organizations to which Congress wished to provide broad immunity. Put the IMF to the side, for Congress enacted a separate statute providing it with immunity (absent waiver) in all cases. See 22 U.S.C. § 286h. But UNRRA, the World Bank, the FAO, and the UN itself all originally depended upon the Immunities Act for the immunity they sought.

Consider, for example, the mission of UNRRA. The United States and other nations created that organization in 1943, as the end of World War II seemed in sight. Its objective was, in the words of President Roosevelt, to " 'assure a fair distribution of available supplies among' " those liberated in World War II, and " 'to ward off death by starvation or exposure among these peoples.' " 1 G. Woodbridge, UNRRA: The History of the United Nations Relief and Rehabilitation Administration 3 (1950). By the time Congress passed the Immunities Act in 1945, UNRRA had obtained and shipped billions of pounds of food, clothing, and other relief supplies to children freed from Nazi concentration camps and to others in serious need. 3 *id.* at 429; see generally L. Nicholas, Cruel World: The Children of Europe in the Nazi Web 442–513 (2005).

These activities involved contracts, often made in the United States, for transportation and for numerous commercial goods. See B. Shephard, The Long Road Home: The Aftermath of the Second World War 54, 57–58 (2012). Indeed, the United States conditioned its participation on UNRRA's spending what amounted to 67% of its budget on purchases of goods and services in the United States. *Id.* at 57–58 .... Would Congress, believing that it had provided the absolute immunity that UNRRA sought and expected, also have intended that the statute be interpreted "dynamically," thereby removing most of the immunity that it had then provided—not only potentially from UNRRA itself but also from other future international organizations with UNRRA-like objectives and tasks?

C

This history makes clear that Congress enacted the Immunities Act as part of an effort to encourage international organizations to locate their headquarters and carry on their missions in the United States. It also makes clear that Congress intended to enact "basic legislation" that would fulfill its broad immunity-based commitments to the UN, UNRRA, and other nascent organizations. S. Rep. No. 861, at 2. And those commitments, of necessity, included immunity from suit in commercial areas, since organizations were buying goods and making contracts in the United States.

To achieve these purposes, Congress enacted legislation that granted necessarily broad immunity. And that fact strongly suggests that Congress would not have wanted the statute to reduce significantly the scope of immunity that international organizations enjoyed, particularly organizations engaged in development finance, refugee assistance, or other tasks that U.S. law could well decide were "commercial" in nature. See *infra* at 778.

To that extent, an examination of the statute's purpose supports a static, not a dynamic, interpretation of its cross-reference to the immunity of foreign governments. Unlike the purpose of the Civil Rights Act, the purpose here was not to ensure parity of treatment for international organizations and foreign governments. Instead, as the Court of Appeals for the D.C. Circuit pointed out years ago, the statute's reference to the immunities of "foreign governments" was a "shorthand" for the immunities those foreign governments enjoyed at the time the Act was passed. *Atkinson v. Inter-American Development Bank*, 156 F.3d 1335, 1340, 1341 (1998).

III

Now consider the consequences that the majority's reading of the statute will likely produce—consequences that run counter to the statute's basic purposes. Although the UN itself is no longer dependent upon the Immunities Act, many other organizations, such as the FAO and several multilateral development banks, continue to rely upon that Act to secure immunity, for the United States has never ratified treaties nor enacted statutes that might extend the necessary immunity, commercial and noncommercial alike.

A

The "commercial activity" exception to the sovereign immunity of foreign nations is broad. We have said that a foreign state engages in "commercial activity" when it exercises " 'powers that can also be exercised by private citizens.' " *Republic of Argentina*, 504 U.S. at 614. Thus, "a contract to buy army boots or even bullets is a 'commercial' activity," even if the government enters into the contract to "fulfil[l] uniquely sovereign objectives." *Ibid.*; see also H. R. Rep. No. 94–1487, p. 16 (1976) ("[A] transaction to obtain goods or services from private parties would not lose its otherwise commercial character because it was entered into in connection with an [Agency for International Development] program").

As a result of the majority's interpretation, many of the international organizations to which the United States belongs will discover that they are now exposed to civil lawsuits based on their (U.S.-law-defined) commercial activity. And because "commercial activity" may well have a broad definition, today's holding will at the very least create uncertainty for organizations involved in finance, such as the World Bank, the Inter-American Development Bank, and the Multilateral Investment Guarantee Agency. The core functions of these organizations are at least arguably "commercial" in nature; the organizations exist to promote international development by investing in foreign companies and projects across the world. See Brief for International Bank for Reconstruction and Development et al. as *Amici Curiae* 1–4; Brief for Member Countries and the Multilateral Investment Guarantee Agency as *Amici Curiae* 13–15. The World Bank, for example, encourages development either by guaranteeing private loans or by providing financing from its own funds if private capital is not available. See Articles of Agreement of the International Bank for Reconstruction and Development, Art. I, Dec. 27, 1945, 60 Stat. 1440, T.I.A.S. No. 1502.

Some of these organizations, including the International Finance Corporation (IFC), themselves believe they do not need broad immunity in commercial areas, and they have waived it. See, *e.g.*, Articles of Agreement of the International Finance Corporation, Art. 6, § 3, Dec. 5, 1955, 7 U.S.T. 2214, 264 U. N. T. S. 118 (implemented by 22 U.S.C. § 282g); see also 860 F.3d 703, 706 (CADC 2017). But today's decision will affect them nonetheless. That is because courts have long interpreted their waivers in a manner that protects their core objectives. See, *e.g.*, *Mendaro v. World Bank*, 717 F.2d 610, 614–615 (CADC 1983). (This very case provides a good example. The D.C. Circuit held below that the IFC's waiver provision does not cover petitioners' claims because they "threaten the [IFC's] policy discretion." See 860 F.3d at 708.) But today's decision exposes these organizations to potential liability in *all* cases arising from their commercial activities, without regard to the scope of their waivers.

Under the majority's interpretation, that broad exposure to liability is at least a reasonable possibility. And that being so, the interpretation undercuts Congress' original objectives and the expectations that it had when it enacted the Immunities Act in 1945.

B

The majority's opinion will have a further important consequence—one that more clearly contradicts the statute's objectives and overall scheme. It concerns the important goal of weeding out lawsuits that are likely bad or harmful—those likely to produce rules of law that interfere with an international organization's public interest tasks.

To understand its importance, consider again that international organizations, unlike foreign nations, are multilateral, with members from many different nations. See H. R. Rep. No. 1203, at 1. That multilateralism is threatened if one nation alone, through application of its own liability rules (by nonexpert judges), can shape the policy choices or actions that an international organization believes it must take or refrain from taking. Yet that is the effect of the majority's interpretation. By restricting the immunity that international organizations enjoy, it "opens the door to divided decisions of the courts of different member states," including U.S. courts, "passing judgment on the rules, regulations, and decisions of the international bodies." *Broadbent v. Organization of Am. States*, 628 F.2d 27, 35 (CADC 1980); cf. Singer, Jurisdictional Immunity of International Organizations: Human Rights and Functional Necessity Concerns, 36 Va. J. Int'l L. 53, 63–64 (1995) (recognizing that "[i]t would be inappropriate for municipal courts to cut deep into the region of autonomous decision-making authority of institutions such as the World Bank").

Many international organizations, fully aware of their moral (if not legal) obligations to prevent harm to others and to compensate individuals when they do cause harm, have sought to fulfill those obligations without compromising their ability to operate effectively. Some, as I have said, waive their immunity in U.S. courts at least in part. . . .

Other organizations have attempted to solve the liability/immunity problem by turning to multilateral, not single-nation, solutions. The UN, for instance, has agreed to "make provisions for appropriate modes of settlement of . . . [d]isputes arising out of contracts or other disputes of a private law character." Convention on Privileges and Immunities of the United Nations, Art. VIII, § 29, 21 U.S.T. 1438, T.I.A.S. No. 6900. It generally does so by agreeing to submit commercial disputes to arbitration. See Restatement (Third) of Foreign Relations Law of the United States § 467, Reporters' Note 7 (1987). Other organizations, including the IFC, have set up alternative accountability schemes . . . .

These alternatives may sometimes prove inadequate. And, if so, the Immunities Act itself offers a way for America's Executive Branch to set aside an organization's immunity and to allow a lawsuit to proceed in U.S. courts. The Act grants to the President the authority to "withhold," to "withdraw," to "condition," or to "limit" any of the Act's "immunities" in "light of the functions performed by any such international organization." 22 U.S.C. § 288.

Were we to interpret the statute statically, then, the default rule would be immunity in suits arising from an organization's commercial activities. But the Executive Branch would have the power to withdraw immunity where immunity is not warranted, as the Act itself provides.

And in making that determination, it could consider whether allowing the lawsuit would jeopardize the organization's ability to carry out its public interest tasks. In a word, the Executive Branch, under a static interpretation, would have the authority needed to separate lawsuit sheep from lawsuit goats.

Under the majority's interpretation, by contrast, there is no such flexibility. The Executive does not have the power to tailor immunity by taking into account the risk of a lawsuit's unjustified interference with institutional objectives or other institutional needs. Rather, the majority's holding takes away an international organization's immunity (in cases arising from "commercial" activities) across the board. And without a new statute, there is no way to restore it, in whole or in part. Nothing in the present statute gives the Executive, the courts, or the organization the power to restore immunity, or to tailor any resulting potential liability, where a lawsuit threatens seriously to interfere with an organization's legitimate needs and goals.

Thus, the static interpretation comes equipped with flexibility. It comes equipped with a means to withdraw immunity where justified. But the dynamic interpretation freezes potential liability into law. It withdraws immunity automatically and irretrievably, irrespective of institutional harm. It seems highly unlikely that Congress would have wanted this result.

* * *

. . . . My decision rests primarily not upon linguistic analysis, but upon basic statutory purposes. Linguistic methods alone, however artfully employed, too often can be used to justify opposite conclusions. Purposes, derived from context, informed by history, and tested by recognition of related consequences, will more often lead us to legally sound, workable interpretations—as they have consistently done in the past. These methods of interpretation can help voters hold officials accountable for their decisions and permit citizens of our diverse democracy to live together productively and in peace—basic objectives in America of the rule of law itself. . . .

NOTES AND QUESTIONS

1. Section 1 of the International Organizations Immunities Act defined what the Act means by an "international organization." *See* Act of Dec. 29, 1945, ch. 652, § 1, 59 Stat. 669, 669 (defining the term to mean "a public international organization in which the United States participates pursuant to any treaty or under the authority of any Act of Congress authorizing such participation or making an appropriation for such participation, and which shall have been designated by the President through appropriate Executive order as being entitled to enjoy the privileges, exemptions, and immunities herein provided") (codified at 22 U.S.C. § 288). Section 2(b) then set forth the language at issue in *Jam*:

"International organizations, their property and their assets, wherever located, and by whomsoever held, shall enjoy the same immunity from suit and every form of judicial process as is enjoyed by foreign governments, except to the extent that such organizations may expressly waive their immunity for the purpose of any proceedings or by the terms of any contract." *Id.* § 2(b), 59 Stat. at 669 (codified at 22 U.S.C. § 288a).

As a purely textual matter, the temporal reference point of the phrase "the same immunity from suit . . . as is enjoyed by foreign governments" is ambiguous. One can certainly read that phrase as the majority did in *Jam*, to mean the immunity that foreign governments enjoy at whatever time the statute is being applied. Alternatively, though, one could read the phrase as Justice Breyer did, to mean "the same immunity . . . as is [now] enjoyed by foreign governments"—that is, the immunity that foreign governments enjoyed in 1945, when the statute was enacted (and hence when Congress uttered the phrase).

The majority thought that its reading was "more natural" than Justice Breyer's, but the majority also invoked a canon about statutes that adopt rules from other sources of law by reference. That canon was not used frequently enough to have a well-established name, but the majority called it "the 'reference' canon." *Jam*, 139 S. Ct. at 769. As described by the majority (and also by the Sutherland treatise on statutory interpretation), the canon draws a sharp distinction between "specific" and "general" references. In the treatise's jargon, a "statute of specific reference" is a statute that adopts rules from another statute by "refer[ring] specifically to [that] particular statute by its title or section number." 2B NORMAN J. SINGER & J.D. SHAMBIE SINGER, SUTHERLAND STATUTES AND STATUTORY CONSTRUCTION § 51:7 (7th ed. 2012). According to the treatise (and the majority), courts ordinarily treat this sort of "specific reference" as a *static* reference to the other statute as it stood when the referring statute was enacted, not as it might be amended later. *See id.* § 51:8 ("A statute of specific reference incorporates provisions as they exist at the time of adoption, without subsequent amendments, unless a legislature has expressly or by strong implication shown its intention to incorporate subsequent amendments . . . ." (footnote omitted)). By contrast, a "general reference" statute (that is, a statute that "refers to the law on a subject generally," *id.* § 51:7) is said to trigger the opposite presumption. In the treatise's words, "A statute which refers to a subject generally . . . adopts the law on the subject at the time the law is invoked, which includes all amendments and modifications subject to the reference statute's enactment." *Id.* § 51:8 (footnotes omitted). Because the statute at issue in *Jam* made "a general rather than specific reference" to the immunity that foreign governments enjoy, Chief Justice Roberts's majority opinion presumed that the reference kept pace with changes in that body of law. *Jam*, 139 S. Ct. at 769.

This distinction between "specific" and "general" references dates far back. *See, e.g.*, Jones v. Dexter, 8 Fla. 276, 281–83 (1859), *partially overruled on other grounds by* Bushnell v. Dennison, 13 Fla. 77 (1869); Culver v. People ex rel. Kochersperger, 43 N.E. 812, 814 (Ill. 1896); 2 J.G. SUTHERLAND & JOHN LEWIS, STATUTES AND STATUTORY CONSTRUCTION § 405 (2d ed. 1904). But does it make sense? Suppose that a new federal statute says that international organizations have "the same immunity that the Foreign Sovereign Immunities Act (FSIA) gives foreign governments." That is a "specific" reference to a named statute, so Chief Justice Roberts apparently would presume that the reference is static; even if Congress subsequently amends the FSIA, international organizations would continue to have the immunity that the FSIA gave foreign governments when the referring statute was enacted. By contrast, if the referring statute had said that international organizations have "the same immunity as is enjoyed by foreign governments in American courts," that would be a "general" reference, which keeps pace with changes in the body of law to which it refers. Should there really be a stark difference between the presumed meaning of these two formulations? The FSIA *is* the law that identifies the immunity enjoyed by foreign governments in American courts, so the differing presumptions seem artificial.

2. If "general" references to a body of law are presumed to be dynamic, is there a good reason to presume that "specific" references to a particular statute should be presumed to be static? When the legislature establishes rules on one topic by incorporating rules that another named statute or statutory provision establishes for a different topic, members of the legislature have that particular statute or statutory provision in mind, and they presumably know the content of the rules that it states at the time that the legislature is referring to it. Perhaps members of the legislature intend to adopt that version without regard to any subsequent changes (which legislators are not yet in a position to evaluate). Still, that story invites a question: if legislators are indeed trying to adopt a fixed set of rules, why would they do so by referring to the other statute rather than just by writing out the content of the rules that they want to adopt? *Cf. Jam*, 139 S. Ct. at 768 (observing that if Congress had intended to give international organizations a static version of immunity, "[t]he statute could . . . have simply stated that international organizations 'shall enjoy absolute immunity from suit,' or specified some other fixed level of immunity").

In some situations, there are plausible answers to this question. Perhaps the relevant rules are long and complex, and it is easier for the legislature to incorporate them by reference than to write them all out again. Or perhaps the rules that the legislature wants to incorporate are a mix of statutory language and uncodified gloss, and members of the legislature are not sure that simply repeating the words of the other statute will bring in the then-existing doctrines that courts have developed in the context of the other statute.

But when one statute adopts rules by referring to another statute, it is also possible that members of the legislature are not really trying to *incorporate* the other statute. Perhaps they are simply *pointing at* the other statute—that is, telling courts where to look for certain rules, without freezing the content of those rules in place. Sometimes, a legislature might want the rules on one topic to be whatever the rules on another topic are, so that there is an ongoing linkage between the law in these two areas. That seems especially likely when the two topics have some logical or historical relationship—like, say, the connection between eligibility to serve on a jury and eligibility to vote. But even in other contexts, it is not obvious that "specific" references should be presumed to be static.

3. Historically, the presumption that some references to other sources of law are static may have begun in the special context of statutes that adopt rules for one jurisdiction by referring to the law of a different jurisdiction. After Independence, many states enacted provisions adopting (and thereby continuing in force) not only the common law of England but also British statutes, sometimes without any explicit date restriction. *See* ELIZABETH GASPAR BROWN, BRITISH STATUTES IN AMERICAN LAW, 1776–1836, at 24–26 (1964). For different reasons, federal statutes sometimes adopted state law. *See, e.g.*, Act of Mar. 3, 1825, ch. 65, § 3, 4 Stat. 115, 115 (effectively adopting state criminal law within some federal enclaves); Process Act of 1789, ch. 21, § 2, 1 Stat. 93, 93 (establishing the general rule that "the forms of writs and executions . . . and modes of process . . . in the [federal] circuit and district courts, in suits at common law, shall be the same in each state respectively as are now used or allowed in the supreme courts of the same"); *see also* Process Act of 1792, ch. 36, § 2, 1 Stat. 275, 276. According to the Supreme Court, "such adoption has always been considered as referring to the law existing at the time of adoption," not as subsequently amended. *Kendall v. United States ex rel. Stokes*, 37 U.S. (12 Pet.) 524, 625 (1838); *see also* Wayman v. Southard, 23 U.S. (10 Wheat.) 1, 41 (1825) ("So far as the Process Act adopts the State laws, as regulating the modes of proceeding in suits at common law, the adoption is expressly confined to those in force in . . . 1789."); Bank of the U.S. v. Halstead, 23 U.S. (10 Wheat.) 51, 57 (1825) (emphasizing the word "now" in the Process Act of 1789, which referred to the time of enactment); *cf.* United States v. Paul, 31 U.S. (6 Pet.) 141, 142 (1832) (reaching the same conclusion about the reference to state criminal laws in § 3 of the Act of March 3, 1825, even though that statute did not make its temporal reference point explicit).

A presumption of static incorporation made perfect sense as applied to the states' reception of British statutes; while the state legislatures naturally wanted to retain much of the legal system that had been in force before Independence, their reasons for adopting British law did not extend to *new* British statutes. The presumption that federal statutes likewise adopt state law on a static basis is not as obviously correct, but it arguably reflected constitutional concerns. Under antebellum understandings of the nondelegation doctrine, Congress could choose to incorporate pre-existing rules into federal law, but it was not clear that Congress could validly give the force of federal law to whatever rules a state legislature might enact in the future. *See, e.g.*, United States v. Knight, 26 F. Cas. 793, 797 (C.C.D. Me. 1838) (No. 15,539) (Story, J.) ("I must confess, that I entertain very serious doubts, whether congress does possess a constitutional authority to adopt prospectively state legislation on any given subject; for that, it seems to me, would amount to a delegation of its own legislative power. . . . At all events, I should not be disposed to give such a construction to any act of congress, unless it was positively required by its words and its intent . . . ."), *aff'd*, 39 U.S. (14 Pet.) 301 (1840).

To this day, as a matter of state constitutional law, some state courts say that their state's legislature cannot validly adopt legal rules from other jurisdictions on a dynamic basis. *See, e.g.*, Abbott Labs. v. Mylan Pharm., 15 So. 3d 642, 654–55 (Fla. App. 2009); State v. Dougall, 570 P.2d 135, 138 (1977); *see also* Michael C. Dorf, *Dynamic Incorporation of Foreign Law*, 157 U. PA. L. REV. 103, 108 & n.13 (2008) (citing cases from additional states and providing detail); *cf.* Jim Rossi, *Dynamic Incorporation of Federal Law*, 77 OHIO ST. L.J. 457 (2016) (criticizing this aspect of state nondelegation doctrine). That doctrine has faded at the federal level. *See, e.g.*, United States v. Sharpnack, 355 U.S. 286 (1958) (upholding Congress's dynamic incorporation of state law into the Assimilative Crimes Act of 1948, 18 U.S.C. § 13); *see also* Conformity Act, ch. 255, § 5, 17 Stat. 196, 197 (1872) (abandoning the static conformity of the Process Acts and providing instead that "the practice, pleadings, and forms and modes of proceeding in other than equity and admiralty causes in the circuit and district courts of the United States shall conform, as near as may be, to the practice, pleadings, and forms and modes of proceeding existing at the time in like causes in the courts of record of the State within which such circuit or district courts are held . . . ."). Even so, there may still be a presumption that "[w]hen lawmaking bodies incorporate by reference laws from other jurisdictions," the reference "is usually static." Dorf, *supra*, 157 U. PA. L. REV. at 104 (emphasis omitted).

To the extent that this presumption reflects nondelegation concerns, though, is there any reason for it to apply when a federal statute simply refers to another federal statute (as opposed to laws from other jurisdictions)? Even if such a reference were dynamic, any future changes to the incorporated statute will themselves go through the process of bicameralism and presentment, so giving them the force of federal law would not seem to violate the constitutional requirements for exercises of the federal government's legislative powers. *Cf.* Edward R. Hayes, *Effect of Changes in Legislation Incorporated by Reference*, 43 MINN. L.

REV. 89, 103 (1958) ("The objection most strongly asserted against incorporation of future legislation . . . or materials, *at least from bodies other than the legislature purposing to act by reference*, is that an unconstitutional delegation of legislative power will occur." (emphasis added)). In the absence of constitutional concerns, should courts simply use their ordinary tools of interpretation to decide whether a particular reference is "static" or "dynamic," without applying an artificial canon (such as the idea that "specific" references should be presumed to be static)?

4. The Sutherland treatise that Chief Justice Roberts invoked in *Jam* has gone through many editions; Jabez Sutherland published the first edition in 1891, but the treatise remains in print and is periodically updated. The majority opinion in *Jam* cited the third edition of the treatise, which was published in 1943 and hence might be thought to identify the canons that were in vogue when Congress enacted the International Organizations Immunities Act in 1945. In *Jam* itself, this nuance did not matter; the current edition of the treatise recites the same ideas, and those ideas have been in the treatise ever since the second edition (published in 1904). *Compare* 2 J.G. SUTHERLAND & JOHN LEWIS, STATUTES AND STATUTORY CONSTRUCTION § 405 (2d ed. 1904), *with* 2B NORMAN J. SINGER & J.D. SHAMBIE SINGER, SUTHERLAND STATUTES AND STATUTORY CONSTRUCTION §§ 51:7–51:8 (7th ed. 2012). On some issues, though, the content of the canons that courts recognize might change over time.

Imagine that Congress enacted a statute in 1945, at a time when judicial doctrine supported applying a particular canon. But suppose that courts do not interpret the statute for many years—and by the time the courts have to decide what the statute means, judicial doctrine about the content of the canon has changed. Should courts continue to apply the version of the canon that courts would have applied in 1945, on the theory that the "original meaning" of the statute reflects the principles of interpretation that courts would have used when the statute was enacted? Or should courts apply their current canons?

To answer that question, do you need to know *why* judicial doctrine about the content of the canon has changed? For instance, if courts have concluded that the old version of the canon was a bad guide to the intended meaning of statutes, and if the new version is thought to be better in that respect, would you want courts to apply the new version even to old statutes? Do you also need to make assumptions about whether members of Congress are responsive to the courts' canons? For instance, if you believe that canons are likely to have "feedback effects," so that legislators draft and evaluate bills in light of the canons that are then in use, will you be more likely to think that courts should continue applying the old version of the canon to statutes that were enacted before courts articulated the new version? *Cf.* Abbe R. Gluck & Lisa Schultz Bressman, *Statutory Interpretation from the Inside—An Empirical Study of Congressional Drafting, Delegation, and the Canons: Part I*, 65 STAN. L. REV. 901, 929 (2013) (concluding on the basis of surveys that congressional staffers with drafting responsibilities know more about some canons than others).

INDEX

References are to Pages